DICTIONARY OF AMERICAN BIOGRAPHY

AMERICAN
COUNCIL
* OF *
LEARNED
SOCIETIES
*

D1418383

DICTIONARY

OF AMERICAN BIOGRAPHY

The *Dictionary of American Biography* was published originally in twenty volumes. Supplementary volumes were added in 1944 and 1958. This edition of the work combines all twenty-two volumes.

The present Volume I (Abbe–Brazer) contains Volumes I and II of the original edition, but these are now denominated "Part 1" and "Part 2" of the Volume. Volumes II through XI are arranged similarly, the Second Part in each instance representing a volume of the original series. For ease in reference, although the articles follow one another in strict alphabetical order, each Second Part is preceded by a half-title page which relates that Part to its place in the original numbering of the volumes.

The Errata list at the head of Volume I contains corrections of fact and additional data which have come to the attention of the Editors from the first publication of the work up to the present. Minor typographical corrections have been made in many instances directly on the plates.

PUBLISHED UNDER THE AUSPICES OF
THE AMERICAN COUNCIL OF LEARNED SOCIETIES

The American Council of Learned Societies, organized in 1919 for the purpose of advancing the study of the humanities and of the humanistic aspects of the social sciences, is a nonprofit federation comprising forty-five national scholarly groups. The Council represents the humanities in the United States in the International Union of Academies, provides fellowships and grants-in-aid, supports research-and-planning conferences and symposia, and sponsors special projects and scholarly publications.

DICTIONARY

OF

American Biography

VOLUME X

TROYE - ZUNSER

Edited by

DUMAS MALONE

Charles Scribner's Sons *New York*

Prompted solely by a desire for public service the New York Times Company and its President, Mr. Adolph S. Ochs, have made possible the preparation of the manuscript of the Dictionary of American Biography through a subvention of more than $500,000 and with the understanding that the entire responsibility for the contents of the volumes rests with the American Council of Learned Societies.

VOLUME X, PART 1
TROYE - WENTWORTH

(VOLUME XIX OF THE ORIGINAL EDITION)

CROSS REFERENCES FROM THIS VOL-
UME ARE MADE TO THE VOLUME
NUMBERS OF THE ORIGINAL EDITION.

CONTRIBUTORS
VOLUME X, PART 1

Thomas P. Abernethy	T. P. A.	Charles E. Clark	C. E. C.
Adeline Adams	A. A.	Eliot Clark	E. C.
James Truslow Adams	J. T. A.	Walter E. Clark	W. E. C.
Nelson F. Adkins	N. F. A.	Rufus E. Clement	R. E. C.
Robert Greenhalgh Albion	R. G. A.	Frederick W. Coburn	F. W. C.
Horace Newton Allen	H. N. A.	Wesley R. Coe	W. R. C.
George M. Anderson	G. M. A.	Arthur C. Cole	A. C. C.
Russell H. Anderson	R. H. A.	Rossetter G. Cole	R. G. C.
Gertrude L. Annan	G. L. A.	Theodore Collier	T. C.
Marguerite Appleton	M. A.	R. D. W. Connor	R. D. W. C.
John Clark Archer	J. C. A.	Mary Roberts Coolidge	M. R. C.
Raymond Clare Archibald	R. C. A.	Greta A. Cornell	G. A. C.
Frederick W. Ashley	F. W. A.	Robert Spencer Cotterill	R. S. C.
Roland H. Bainton	R. H. B.	E. Merton Coulter	E. M. C.
Carlos H. Baker	C. H. B.	Alexander Cowie	A. C.
Frank Collins Baker	F. C. B.	Katharine Elizabeth Crane	K. E. C.
Henry G. Barbour	H. G. B.	Arthur Lyon Cross	A. L. C.
Gilbert H. Barnes	G. H. B.	Whitman Cross	W. C.
Claribel R. Barnett	C. R. B.	William J. Cunningham	W. J. C.
Harold K. Barrows	H. K. B—s.	Merle E. Curti	M. E. C.
Clarence Bartlett	C. B—t.	Edward E. Curtis	E. E. C.
George A. Barton	G. A. B.	Carl C. Cutler	C. C. C.
Ernest Sutherland Bates	E. S. B—s.	Charles William Dabney	C. W. D.
G. Philip Bauer	G. P. B.	Virginius Dabney	V. D.
Howard K. Beale	H. K. B—e.	Edward E. Dale	E. E. D.
William G. Bean	W. G. B.	Tenney L. Davis	T. L. D.
Elbert J. Benton	E. J. B.	Richard E. Day	R. E. D.
William C. Binkley	W. C. B.	James Quayle Dealey	J. Q. D.
Edith R. Blanchard	E. R. B.	D. Bryson Delavan	D. B. D.
Louise Pearson Blodget	L. P. B.	William H. S. Demarest	W. H. S. D.
Helen C. Boatfield	H. C. B.	Edward H. Dewey	E. H. D.
Louis H. Bolander	L. H. B.	Everett N. Dick	E. N. D.
Charles K. Bolton	C. K. B.	Hobert Cutler Dickinson	H. C. D.
Ethel Stanwood Bolton	E. S. B—n.	Theodore Diller	T. D.
Henry E. Bourne	H. E. B.	Irving Dilliard	I. D.
Witt Bowden	W. B.	Charles A. Dinsmore	C. A. D.
J. Bartlet Brebner	J. B. B.	Armistead M. Dobie	A. M. D.
Carl Bridenbaugh	C. B—h.	John J. Dolan	J. J. D.
John E. Briggs	J. E. B.	Elizabeth Donnan	E. D.
Robert C. Brooks	R. C. B.	Randolph C. Downes	R. C. D.
Lawrason Brown	L. B.	William Howe Downes	W. H. D.
C. A. Browne	C. A. B.	Stella M. Drumm	S. M. D.
Waldo R. Browne	W. R. B.	Edward A. Duddy	E. A. D.
Robert Bruce	R. B.	Andrew G. Du Mez	A. G. D-M.
Isabel M. Calder	I. M. C.	Edward Dwight Eaton	E. D. E.
Lester J. Cappon	L. J. C.	Walter Prichard Eaton	W. P. E.
Zechariah Chafee, Jr.	Z. C., Jr.	Edwin Francis Edgett	E. F. E.
O. P. Chitwood	O. P. C.	Everett E. Edwards	E. E. E.
E. Clowes Chorley	E. C. C.	L. Ethan Ellis	L. E. E.

Contributors

Contributors

Lester B. Mason . . . . L. B. M
Frank Jewett Mather, Jr. . . F. J. M., Jr.
William R. Maxon . . . . . W. R. M.
Robert Douthat Meade . . R. D. M.
John C. Mendenhall . . . . . J. C. M.
A. Howard Meneely . . . . A. H. M.
Newton D. Mereness . . . N. D. M.
George P. Merrill . . . . . . G. P. M.
Perry Miller . . . . P. M.
C. Bowie Millican . . . . . C. B. M.
Broadus Mitchell . . . . . B. M.
Carl W. Mitman . . . . . C. W. M.
Frank Monaghan . . . . . F. M.
Robert E. Moody . . . . . R. E. M.
Richard B. Morris . . . . . R. B. M.
Jarvis M. Morse . . . . . . J. M. M.
Frank Luther Mott . . . . F. L. M.
H. Edward Nettles . . . . H. E. N.
A. R. Newsome . . . . . . A. R. N.
Jeannette P. Nichols . . . J. P. N.
Robert Hastings Nichols . . R. H. N.
Roy F. Nichols . . . . . . R. F. N.
Herman C. Nixon . . . . . H. C. N.
A. B. Noble . . . . A. B. N.
Alexander D. Noyes . . . . A. D. N.
Francis R. Packard . . . . F. R. P.
Stanley M. Pargellis. . . . . S. M. P.
Edd Winfield Parks . . . . E. W. P.
William Patten . . . . . . W. P.
Charles O. Paullin . . . . C. O. P.
Frederic Logan Paxson . . F. L. P.
C. C. Pearson . . . . C. C. P.
Edmund L. Pearson . . . . E. L. P.
Henry G. Pearson . . . . H. G. P.
James H. Peeling . . . . . J. H. P.
Hobart S. Perry . . . . . H. S. P.
Henry J. Peterson . . . . H. J. P.
James M. Phalen . . . . . J. M. P—n.
Francis S. Philbrick . . . . F. S. P.
Paul Chrisler Phillips . . . P. C. P.
John A. Pollard . . . . . . J. A. P.
David deSola Pool . . . . . D. deS. P.
John M. Poor . . . . . . J. M. P—r.
Jennie Barnes Pope . . . . J. B. P.
Dorothy B. Porter . . . . D. B. P.
Louise Pound . . . . L. P.
Julius W. Pratt . . . . . . J. W. P.
Richard J. Purcell . . . . . R. J. P.
Arthur Hobson Quinn . . . A. H. Q.
Lowell Joseph Ragatz . . . L. J. R.
P. L. Rainwater . . . . . . P. L. R.
P. O. Ray . . . . P. O. R.
Thomas T. Read . . . . . . T. T. R.
Herbert S. Reichle . . . . H. S. R—e.
Elizabeth M. Richards . . . E. M. R.
Leon B. Richardson . . . . L. B. R.
Robert E. Riegel . . . . . R. E. R.

Donald A. Roberts . . . . D. A. R.
Benjamin L. Robinson . . . . B. L. R.
Herbert Spencer Robinson . . H. S. R—n.
William A. Robinson . . . W. A. R.
William M. Robinson, Jr. . . W. M. R., Jr
L. Harding Rogers, Jr. . . . . L. H. R., Jr.
Flora Rose . . . . F. R.
Harold E. Ross . . . . . . H. E. R.
Frederick D. Rossini . . . . F. D. R.
Peyton Rous . . . . P. R.
W. Carl Rufus . . . . . . W. C. R.
William Sener Rusk . . . . W. S. R.
Verne Lockwood Samson . . . V. L. S.
Carl Sandburg . . . . . . C. S.
Louis Bernard Schmidt . . . . L. B. S—t.
William O. Scroggs . . . . W. O. S.
Elias Howard Sellards . . . E. H. S.
James Lee Sellers . . . . . J. L. S.
Thorsten Sellin . . . . . . T. S—n.
Joseph J. Senturia . . . . . J. J. S.
Henry Sewall . . . . H. S—l.
Robert Francis Seybolt . . . R. F. S.
William E. Shea . . . . . W. E. S—a.
Augustus H. Shearer . . . A. H. S.
Lester B. Shippee . . . . . L. B. S—e.
Richard H. Shryock . . . . R. H. S.
George N. Shuster . . . . G. N. S.
Eleanor M. Sickels . . . . E. M. S.
Wilbur H. Siebert . . . . W. H. S.
Kenneth C. M. Sills . . . . K. C. M. S.
Marian Silveus . . . . . . M. S.
Lesley Byrd Simpson . . . L. B. S—n.
Theodore Sizer . . . . . . T. S—r.
Emily E. F. Skeel . . . . . E. E. F. S.
David Eugene Smith . . . . D. E. S.
Harry Worcester Smith . . . H. W. S.
William E. Smith . . . . . W. E. S—h
Herbert Solow . . . . . . H. S—w.
Raymond J. Sontag . . . . R. J. S—g.
George A. Soper . . . . . G. A. S.
J. Duncan Spaeth . . . . . J. D. S.
E. Wilder Spaulding . . . . E. W. S.
Oliver L. Spaulding, Jr. . . . O. L. S., Jr.
Thomas M. Spaulding . . . T. M. S.
Robert Elliott Speer . . . . R. El. S.
Robert Ernest Spiller . . . . R. Er. S.
Richard J. Stanley . . . . . R. J. S—y.
Harris Elwood Starr . . . . H. E. S.
Bertha Monica Stearns . . . B. M. S.
Raymond P. Stearns . . . . R. P. S.
Wayne E. Stevens . . . . W. E. S—s
De Lisle Stewart . . . . . D-L. S.
Edgar I. Stewart . . . . . E. I. S.
George R. Stewart, Jr. . . . . G. R. S., Jr.
Randall Stewart . . . . . R. S.
Anson Phelps Stokes . . . . A. P. S.
Richard G. Stone . . . . . R. G. S.

Contributors

Lionel M. Summers	L. M. S.	Luther Allan Weigle	L. A. W.
Charles S. Sydnor	C. S. S.	Elizabeth Howard West	E. H. W.
Thomas E. Tallmadge	T. E. T.	Allan Westcott	A. W—t.
William A. Taylor	W. A. T.	Alexander Wetmore	A. W—e.
David Y. Thomas	D. Y. T.	George F. Whicher	G. F. W.
Milton Halsey Thomas	M. H. T.	Arthur P. Whitaker	A. P. W—r.
Herbert Thoms	H. T.	Isabel M. S. Whittier	I. M. S. W.
Irving L. Thomson	I. L. T.	Robert H. Wienefeld	R. H. W.
Edward Larocque Tinker	E. L. T.	Jerome K. Wilcox	J. K. W.
Bruce R. Trimble	B. R. T.	Vernon L. Wilkinson	V. L. W.
Alonzo H. Tuttle	A. H. T.	Mary Wilhelmine Williams	M. W. W.
Edward M. Van Cleve	E. M. V-C.	Samuel C. Williams	S. C. W.
Lewis G. Vander Velde	L. G. V-V.	Tyrrell Williams	T. W.
Arnold J. F. van Laer	A. J. F. v-L.	Albert Potter Wills	A. P. W—s.
George Van Santvoord	G. V-S.	Maude H. Woodfin	M. H. W.
Henry R. Viets	H. R. V.	Vann Woodward	V. W.
Harold G. Villard	H. G. V.	Walter L. Wright, Jr.	W. L. W., Jr.
Edna Vosper	E. V.	James Ingersoll Wyer	J. I. W.
Rufus W. Weaver	R. W. W.		

DICTIONARY OF
AMERICAN BIOGRAPHY

Troye—Wentworth

TROYE, EDWARD (1808–July 25, 1874), painter of American blood horses, was born near Geneva, Switzerland, and died in Georgetown, Ky. He was of French descent, his grandfather, a nobleman, having been exiled from France for political reasons. Jean Baptiste de Troy, Edward's father, was an artist of note, and one of his paintings, "The Plague of Marseilles," now hangs in the Louvre. All his children were educated in the arts, and several of them gained distinction in their several fields. For some years Edward lived with his father in England, but at the age of twenty emigrated to the New World, changing his name to Troye.

In the West Indies, where he first resided, he was connected with a sugar plantation and employed his leisure time in sketching and painting. Ill health compelling him to seek a different climate, he went to Philadelphia, Pa., and soon found employment with the art department of *Sartain's Magazine*. In July 1839 he was married, in Kentucky, to Cornelia Ann Van der Graff, a grand-daughter of one of the Dutch governors of Ceylon.

Troye's best work, which was done between 1835 and 1874, is to be seen in his paintings of blood horses. Since photography did not become commercial until after the seventies, Troye's portraits are the truest delineations of the forebears of the great racers of the American turf, and so have much historical as well as artistic value. Before the Civil War he painted for the plantation owners of the South, where the leading thoroughbred studs of the United States were to be found. His chief patrons were A. Keene Richards of Georgetown, Ky., and the Alexander family of Lexington, and with them he spent the middle and latter part of his life. With Richards

he made a trip in the fifties to Arabia and the Holy Land, where Richards selected and purchased a number of Arab horses, while Troye painted horses, Damascus cattle, the Dead Sea, the bazaar of Damascus, and other scenes and objects. Copies of some of these paintings are preserved at Bethany College, Bethany, W. Va.

Troye's most notable paintings are those of American Eclipse and Sir Henry, heroes of the memorable North-South match in 1823; the mighty Boston and his son Lexington, the leading sire in America for sixteen years; Lecomte, Lexington's valiant foe in the four-mile heat match at the Metairie course in New Orleans; Reel, a great brood mare, dam of Lecomte; Glencoe, sire of Reel; Revenue, Bertrand, Richard Singleton, Reality, Black Maria, Leviathan, Wagner, Ophelia—dam of Gray Eagle, and numerous others. Hanging in the Capitol at Washington is Troye's great painting of Gen. Winfield Scott, mounted on a son of Glencoe, a charger given by A. Keene Richards to John Hunt Morgan [*q.v.*], the daring leader of Morgan's cavalry, and painted from life.

Up to 1912 not more than twenty of Troye's paintings were known in the East, but since that time over three hundred of them have been located and three-quarters of them photographed. The chief collections in America are in the hands of the Jockey Club, New York; the Alexander family in Kentucky; Walter Jeffords, Pennsylvania; Harry Worcester Smith, Massachusetts; A. Kenneth Alexander, New York; Louis Lee Haggin, Kentucky; David Wagstaff, and Harry T. Peters of New York; Robert Gilmor, Long Island; and the Francis P. Garvan collection given to Yale University in memory of Harry Payne and Payne Whitney. Troye was the author of *The Race Horses of America* (1867), of which only the first number was published. At his death he was survived by a daughter.

[Information from Troye's daughter, the late Anna V. T. Christian; Mrs. John C. Pack, of Singleton, Ky., and Mrs. E. K. Schwartz, of New Orleans, daughters of A. Keene Richards; W. S. Vosburgh, "Horse Portraiture in America," in *Daily Racing Form* (Chicago), Mar. 18, 1919; C. E. Fairman, *Art and Artists of the Capitol of the U. S. A.* (1927); Harry Worcester Smith, "Edward Troye (1808–1874), The Painter of American Blood Horses," *The Field* (London), Jan. 21, 1926.]

H. W. S.

TRUDE, ALFRED SAMUEL (Apr. 21, 1847–Dec. 12, 1933), lawyer, was born on shipboard in New York harbor. His parents, Samuel and Sallie (Downs) Trude, were immigrants from England, who shortly settled at Lockport, N. Y. Here Alfred spent his boyhood, attending the public schools. At seventeen he set out to seek his fortune in Chicago, which was his home thereafter. On Apr. 7, 1868, he married Algenia Pearson of Lockport, by whom he had three sons and two daughters.

Shortly after his marriage, he enrolled in the Union College of Law (now the Northwestern University Law School) at Chicago, at the same time pursuing office study under A. B. Jenks. Admitted to the bar in 1871, he soon attracted the attention of Joseph Medill [*q.v.*], editor and proprietor of the *Chicago Tribune* and mayor of the city, who in 1872 appointed the young man city prosecutor. After their official relation had ceased, Trude long remained the *Tribune's* attorney. His success in that connection brought him another valuable client in Wilbur F. Storey [*q.v.*] of the *Chicago Times*, whose attorney he became in 1876, when he prevented, on the ground that Storey was not a fugitive from justice, the latter's extradition to Wisconsin on the charge of libeling Milwaukee's chief of police. In one decade, it is said, Trude appeared for Storey and the *Times* in about five hundred cases, and the wide publicity given to the first of these led to retainers in many other extradition cases, notably the "Newburg Poker Case," in which he prevented the discharge on *habeas corpus* of two gamblers who had taken $150,000 from a client. Another early case which enhanced his reputation was the divorce suit of *Linden* vs. *Linden*, in which the plaintiff, the daughter of a wealthy packer, had married a coachman in the belief that he was a British peer. Trude appeared for the defendant, and a decree was denied. After successfully prosecuting actions against various railway companies, Trude was retained by such important corporations as the Chicago & Alton Railroad and the Chicago City Railway Company. He also appeared in famous testamentary litigation, such as contests of the wills of Wilbur F. Storey and Henrietta Snell.

Although his success in civil practice was phenomenal, it was his frequent appearance in criminal causes which brought his name into the headlines of the daily newspapers. Almost a half century before his death, he had already appeared in thirty-four murder cases and had been successful in all but three. Among his successful defenses was that of the Reno brothers who, however, were lynched after their acquittal. In some famous cases he was the prosecutor—notably in *State* vs. *Prendergast*, in which the defendant was convicted and hanged for murdering Mayor Carter Henry Harrison [*q.v.*] on the last night of the World's Columbian Exposition (1893). One of the most successful trial lawyers of his time—before the age of excessive specialism—Trude was a product of the jury system and his forte lay in resourcefulness, adroitness, and persuasive address rather than in profound legal learning. In the latter, nevertheless, he was by no means deficient and his wide range of practice gave him a technical knowledge of many diverse branches of the law.

In the midst of his professional activities, he found time for public and party service. During the last eight years of the century, he was a member of the Chicago School Board. For a long period he was active in local politics, and in 1896 and again in 1900 he was a delegate to the National Democratic Convention. His last years were spent in retirement.

[*The Bench and Bar of Chicago* (n.d.), published before 1886; John Moses and Joseph Kirkland, *Hist. of Chicago* (1895), vol. II; J. W. Leonard, *The Book of Chicagoans*, 1905 and 1926; *Who's Who in America*, 1918–19; *Chicago Daily Tribune*, Dec. 14, 1933; *N. Y. Times*, Dec. 13, 1933.]

C. S. L.

TRUDEAU, EDWARD LIVINGSTON (Oct. 5, 1848–Nov. 15, 1915), physician, pioneer scientific student of tuberculosis in America, was born in New York City, the third child of James and Céphise (Berger) Trudeau. His father, the grandson of Zenon Trudeau, lieutenant governor of upper Louisiana from 1792 to 1799, was a Confederate officer, a friend and companion of John J. Audubon [*q.v.*], a sculptor of some ability, and a physician. Soon after the boy's birth his parents separated. His mother returned to Paris, with her father, François Eloi Berger, the son of a long line of physicians and a successful practising physician of New York. There young Trudeau lived until his eighteenth year, studying at the Lycée Bonaparte. Returning to New York, he prepared to enter the United States Naval Academy, but, when his brother developed tuberculosis, he resigned in order to nurse him until he died. Tiring of the work in the School of Mines of Columbia College, now part of the School of Engineering of Columbia University, and caring little for the life of a stock broker, he began in 1868 the study of medicine and was graduated from the College of Physicians and Surgeons, now a part of Columbia University. He was steadied in his cetermination for a career by his desire to win the confidence, approbation, and love of Charlotte G. Beare of Douglaston, Long Island. He was married to her on June 29, 1871, and in his autobiography he repeatedly acknowledged her influence throughout his life. After a short hospital experience he began practice on Long Island but soon, in 1872, removed to New York, associated himself with Fessenden Nott Otis [q.v.], and engaged in teaching and dispensary work. Infected no doubt by his brother, he developed in 1873 rather extensive pulmonary tuberculosis, which led him to the Adirondacks, where he continued to live, considering himself always an exile from New York. Having inherited a modest income, he fished and hunted until 1880, when he began to devote more time to medical practice, at Paul Smiths in the summer and in Saranac Lake during the winter.

He was interested chiefly in two phases of tuberculosis, early diagnosis and the discovery of a cure, both closely related to his consuming passion, aiding in recovery from tuberculosis. The cure he sought in the laboratory; early diagnosis and treatment he pursued in the sanatorium. He was a keen diagnostician, his grasp of prognosis was as excellent as it was cautious. He published little upon clinical tuberculosis, much from the laboratory. He spoke optimistically, he wrote guardedly, with the result he had little to retract. Impressed with the need of caring for patients with pulmonary tuberculosis and small means, stimulated by an article by Herman Brehmer, in 1884 he established on sixteen acres, bought and presented to him by Adirondack guides, lifelong friends, the Adirondack Cottage Sanitarium, now the Trudeau Sanatorium, the first in America. For thirty years, practically unaided, he met the yearly deficit, ultimately $30,-000, by soliciting contributions and by donations from his own modest income, and he left an endowment fund of $600,000. At his death the sanatorium accommodated 150 patients and consisted of 36 buildings on 60 acres. He was already familiar with the work of Pasteur and Tyndall, when a translation of Robert Koch's paper on the etiology of tuberculosis came into his hands. This led to the establishment of a small, very primitive laboratory in his home, eventually causing a fire that destroyed his house in 1893 and prompted George C. Cooper to build the present Saranac Laboratory in 1894. There the first immunity experiments in tuberculosis in America were performed, various substances tested on animals, and in a hole nearby the beneficial influence of fresh air on tuberculous rabbits was controlled. Among his earlier publications were "An Experimental Study of Preventive Inoculation in Tuberculosis" (*Medical Record,* Nov. 22, 1890) and "The Treatment of Experimental Tuberculosis by Koch's Tuberculin, Hunter's Modification and Other Products of the Tubercle-Bacillus" (*Medical News,* Sept. 3, 1892, and also in *Transactions of the Association of American Physicians,* vol. VII, 1892, pp. 99-101). Two of his later studies were reported as "Artificial Immunity in Experimental Tuberculosis" (*Ibid.,* vol. XVIII, 1903, p. 97 and in *New York Medical Journal,* July 18, 1903) and "Two Experiments in Artificial Immunity against Tuberculosis" (*Medical News,* Sept. 30, 1905, and *Transactions of the National Association for Study and Prevention of Tuberculosis ... 1905,* 1906) . In 1915 *An Autobiography* was published posthumously (title page 1916). He became in 1904 the president of the National Association for the Study and Prevention of Tuberculosis, later the National Tuberculosis Association; in 1905 president of the Association of American Physicians; in 1910 president of the Congress of American Physicians and Surgeons, where, too weak to be heard, he spoke on "Optimism in Medicine" (for extensive quotation see Chalmers, *post,* introduction).

His most striking characteristics were his personal charm, his optimism, his wonderful never flagging enthusiasm, his wide sympathies, his choice of forceful picturesque diction in speech and writing, his ability to interest others, to make and keep friends, his love of people. Such characteristics made him a keen scientist and a great physician. Strongly influenced after the death of his brother by broad and tolerant religious views, he led in the organizations of the churches at Paul Smiths and in Saranac Lake, in the affairs of which he took deep interest until his death. Of his four children, one, a physician, survived him, another boy died in infancy, a daughter was claimed by the disease he was struggling to control, and in 1906 his eldest son died suddenly while convalescing from pneumonia. Trudeau never recovered from this blow, and gradually his disease, long quiescent, becoming more active, required collapse therapy that for a time relieved him. He died in Saranac

Lake and was buried at St. Johns-in-the-Wilderness, at Paul Smiths.

[*Autobiog., ante*; Stephen Chalmers, *The Beloved Physician* (1916), and in *Atlantic Monthly,* Jan. 1916; *Jour. of Outdoor Life*, Jan. 1925; *N. Y. Times*, Nov. 16–18, 21, 23, 1915; personal association.]   L. B.

TRUDEAU, JEAN BAPTISTE [See Truteau, Jean Baptiste, 1748–1827].

TRUE, ALFRED CHARLES (June 5, 1853–Apr. 23, 1929), leader in agricultural education, was born at Middletown, Conn., the son of Charles Kittredge and Elizabeth Bassett (Hyde) True. Frederick William True [*q.v.*] was his younger brother. Their father, a Methodist minister, was then a professor at Wesleyan University. Following a boyhood spent in rural communities of Connecticut, Massachusetts, and New York, True prepared for college at the Boston Latin School and graduated from Wesleyan University in 1873. After two years as principal of the high school at Essex, N. Y., he taught in the state normal school at Westfield, Mass., for seven years. On Nov. 23, 1875, he married Emma Fortune of Essex, N. Y., by whom he had a daughter and a son. Following graduate work at Harvard from 1882 to 1884 he returned to Wesleyan University, where during the next four years he gave instruction in Latin and Greek.

At Wesleyan he formed an acquaintance with Wilbur O. Atwater [*q.v.*], who in 1888 founded the office of experiment stations in the United States Department of Agriculture. The following year True was induced to join the staff of the department and remained connected with it until his death. As editor in the office of experiment stations, one of his first duties was the preparation of an article on the experiment-station movement and the history of agricultural education and research in the United States for use in connection with the Paris Exposition of 1889. This task enabled him to approach the problems of agricultural education and research from a national point of view and to visualize agricultural colleges and stations as permanent agencies for the general welfare. During the early nineties when the office functioned largely as a clearing house of information, True prepared publications and encouraged the dissemination of accurate information on agricultural matters. After his appointment to the directorship (1893) the functions of the office expanded greatly. Investigations in human nutrition resulted in his assuming leadership in research and education in the field of home economics. He also aided in making farmers' institutes a vital means of popular education. The irrigation and drainage investigations of the department and the agricultural experiment stations in the territories likewise came under his supervision. Owing largely to confidence in True's breadth of view and liberality and his sound and unbiased judgment, the office of experiment stations became "an unique example of national administration" in which "influence rather than coercion is the policy" (Conover, *post*, p. 104). In 1915 the office became part of the states relations service, of which True was director until 1923; in this capacity he was spokesman for the department in programs of cooperation in the research and education carried on pursuant to the Smith-Lever Act of 1914.

True's influence as an official was supplemented by his leadership in the Association of American Colleges and Experiment Stations, finally known as the Association of Land Grant Colleges and Universities. He contributed frequently to its programs; served on its committees, notably that on agricultural instruction, was its editor and bibliographer for many years, its president in 1913, and dean of the seven successive graduate schools of agriculture which it sponsored between 1902 and 1916. In 1913 he was chairman of the official delegation of the United States at the General Assembly of the International Institute of Agriculture at Rome. During the World War he was a leader in the efforts to increase food production and conservation. After 1923 he was engaged mainly in the preparation of three monographs, *A History of Agricultural Extension Work in the United States, 1785–1923* (1928), *A History of Agricultural Education in the United States, 1785–1925* (1929), and "A History of Agricultural Experimentation and Research in the United States" (unpublished)—a trilogy such as no other person could have produced, for no one else was privileged to study more intensively from a national point of view the growth of the entire movement for agricultural education over a period of forty years.

[*Am. Men of Sci.* (4th ed., 1927); H. P. Sheldon, "Uncle Sam's Hired Men Who Serve You," *Hoard's Dairyman*, Aug. 27, 1920; *Wis. Country Mag.*, Nov. 1929; *Proceedings* of the Asso. of Am. Agric. Colls. and Experiment Stations and its successors, especially vols. XXVII (1914), XXXVII (1924), XLIII (1930); *Experiment Station Record*, Mar., July 1923, Apr., July, Oct. 1929; *Jour. of Home Economics*, July 1929; *U. S. Dept. Agric. Official Record*, May 2, 1929; U. S. Dept. of Agric., press release, Apr. 24, 1929; L. S. Ivins and A. E. Winship, *Fifty Famous Farmers* (1924); *Rus*, 1925; *Who's Who in America*, 1928–29; Milton Conover, *The Office of Experiment Stations* (1924); *Evening Star* (Washington, D. C.), Apr. 24, 25, 1929; *Washington Post*, Apr. 25, 1929; manuscript letters in U. S. Dept. of Agric. Lib.; manuscript bibliog. of True's writings in Office of Experiment Stations Lib., U. S. Dept. of Agric.]   E. E. E.

TRUE, FREDERICK WILLIAM (July 8, 1858–June 25, 1914), zoölogist, born in Middletown, Conn., brother of Alfred Charles True [*q.v.*], was a son of the Rev. Charles Kittredge and Elizabeth Bassett (Hyde) True, and a descendant of Henry Trew of England who settled at Salem, Mass., about 1636. He received his collegiate education at the University of the City of New York, where he was graduated with the degree of bachelor of science in 1878. In November of that year he entered the service of the federal government as a clerk with the fish commission and in 1879 was expert special agent in the fisheries branch of the Tenth Census. In 1880 he was custodian of the exhibits of the United States fish commission at the Berlin Fisheries Exhibition.

In July of the following year he went to the Smithsonian Institution as a clerk in the National Museum. His service under the Smithsonian continued with steady advancement until his death and covered difficult scientific and administrative labors. From 1881 to 1883 he was librarian for the National Museum, serving also for the first two years as acting curator of the division of mammals. In 1883 he became curator and retained direct supervision of the division until 1909. In the early eighties he was designated curator-in-charge and had administrative supervision of the entire museum at such times as the assistant secretary was absent; this designation was changed in 1894 to executive curator, which title carried with it additional duties.

When the National Museum was reorganized in 1897 True was made head curator of the department of biology, with direction of all of the biological work of the organization, a position in which his duties were largely administrative. During the absence of Samuel P. Langley [*q.v.*] that year, True served for a period as acting secretary of the Smithsonian Institution, and until 1901 he bore the major burden of administration in the National Museum. On June 1, 1911, he became assistant secretary of the Smithsonian in charge of the library and of the international exchange service, a position that he occupied until his death. In the exposition work that was an important feature of the activities of the Institution during this period True had a prominent part. He directed the preparation of exhibitions shown at Nashville, Tenn., in 1897; at Omaha, Nebr., in 1898; at Buffalo, N. Y., in 1901; at Charleston, S. C., in 1902; at St. Louis, Mo., in 1904; and at Portland, Ore., in 1905. He was, also, an official representative of the United States government at the Seventh International Zoölogical Congress in 1907.

True was profound as a student, and exact and punctilious as an administrative officer. He cared little for sports or pastimes, finding his recreation in music, literature, and art. Of a retiring disposition, he was not interested in social activities beyond association with friends and colleagues and when not at the museum was usually engaged in studies at home. His early scientific interests were directed toward the lower groups of animals, but, finding that his eyesight would not permit continued use of the microscope, he turned to the mammals and in research on this group made his outstanding scientific contributions. He published many papers, and was known especially for his studies of the whales and their allies. A collection of these which he began for the National Museum is one of the most extensive in the world. His memoirs on the family *Delphinidae,* on the whalebone whales, and on the beaked whales were of much significance, and in later years he was occupied with studies of fossil cetaceans, a subject to which he made noteworthy contributions. In his investigations he went to many other museums and visited whaling stations in Newfoundland. At the time of his death he was recognized as the foremost living authority on the *Cetacea.* On Feb. 16, 1887, he married Louise Elvina Prentiss of Washington, D. C.; two of their children survived him.

[*Ann. Report of the Board of Regents of the Smithsonian Institution, 1914* (1915); J. M. Cattell, *Am. Men of Sci.* (2nd ed., 1910); *Who's Who in America,* 1914–15; *Evening Star* (Washington), June 25, 1914; records in the Smithsonian Institution; family sources.]

A. W—e.

TRUEBLOOD, BENJAMIN FRANKLIN (Nov. 25, 1847–Oct. 26, 1916), educator, publicist, and professional worker for international peace, was born in Salem, Ind., and adhered throughout his life to the Quaker principles of his parents, Joshua and Esther (Parker) Trueblood. After graduating from Earlham College in 1869, he began his educational work as professor of classics at Penn College, Iowa. From 1874 to 1890 he served as president of Wilmington College, Ohio, and of Penn College. His thorough scholarship, his virility, and his high moral principles won the respect of his colleagues and students; his faculty for using homely and terse words, his humane and charming strain of humor, and his rare combination of modesty and heartiness won their love and devotion. On July 17, 1872, he married Sarah H. Terrell of New Vienna, Ohio. In 1890 he broadened his educational activity by becoming a professional worker for international peace. A year abroad as agent for the Christian Arbitration and Peace

Society provided an opportunity for studying European conditions and for becoming acquainted with leaders in the peace movement. From that time until his death he was important in its councils, both in England and on the Continent, and the more influential because of his mastery of several modern languages. From 1892 until 1915 he served as secretary of the American Peace Society and as editor of its periodical, the *Advocate of Peace*. The fortunes of the peace movement in the United States were at a low ebb, and much of the organizing work of his predecessors, William Ladd and Elihu Burritt [*qq.v.*], had to be done over again. The first western man to assume the leadership of organized pacifism in the United States, he made the movement a truly national one. As a result of his tireless activity in organizing branch peace societies, of writing not only for peace periodicals but for other magazines, and of lecturing on innumerable occasions, he played a responsible part in the rapid expansion of the peace movement. A repeated visitor at the state department and at the White House, he was treated at the national capital with greater respect than most pacifists. His influence was extended by his active participation in the Lake Mohonk arbitration conferences, the International Law Association, and the American Society of International Law.

As editor of the *Advocate of Peace* he set a new standard for pacifist journalism. Without sacrificing the moral, ethical, and religious elements that had given so much impetus to pacifism, he interpreted the peace movement and the forces promoting war with realism as well as vision. His analyses of contemporary events were characterized by shrewdness, insight, and literary merit. Himself an uncompromising foe of all wars, militarism, and violence, he believed it was necessary to enlist the support of every shade of opinion if pacifism and internationalism were to be translated into actualities. An intelligent advocate of arbitration and the limitation of armaments, he believed that, as a result of the solidarity of humanity and the principle of progress that governed history, the groping steps and strivings toward world organization must inevitably, and in the relatively immediate future, lead to a true world federation. He gave to the peace movement an historical sense, a more substantial ground for its optimism, and a sense of realism that did much to mitigate the sentimentalism of many of its friends. In spite of the catholic character of his philosophy and program of peace, he only partly understood the relationships between industrial and financial capitalism and war; and his appreciation of the importance of socialism and the labor movement for eliminating war did not lead him to make an effective alliance with those forces. Among his numerous publications perhaps the most important were *The Federation of the World* (1899) and *The Development of the Peace Idea and Other Essays* (1932), with an introduction by Edwin D. Mead.

[Letters of Trueblood in the Roosevelt Papers in the Lib. of Cong., in the Frederick Bayer Papers in the Kongelig Bibliothek in Copenhagen, and in the files of the International Peace Bureau in Geneva; C. E. Beals, *Benj. Franklin Trueblood* (1916); E. L. Whitney, *The Amer. Peace Soc.* (1928); *Who's Who in America*, 1916–17; *N. Y. Times*, Oct. 27, 1916.]

M. E. C.

TRUMAN, BENJAMIN CUMMINGS (Oct. 25, 1835–July 18, 1916), journalist, author, eldest son of Henry Hammond Truman and his first wife, Susan (Cummings), and a descendant of Joseph Truman who settled in New London (Conn.) about 1666, was born in Providence, R. I. He attended public school there and a Shaker school in Canterbury, N. H., and at seventeen took charge for a year of a district school in Merrimack County, N. H. Returning to Providence, he learned typesetting, and from 1855 until late in 1859 was a compositor and proofreader on the *New York Times*. In the latter year he entered the employ of John W. Forney [*q.v.*] of Philadelphia, publisher of the *Press*, and in 1861 went to Washington to work on Forney's *Sunday Morning Chronicle*. Upon the outbreak of the Civil War he was sent to the front as a correspondent and in March 1862, declining a commission in a regiment of volunteers, became an aide on the staff of Andrew Johnson, military governor of Tennessee. Nominally he so remained until near the end of the war, though his talent for doing many things at the same time enabled him to render distinguished service as a correspondent and to serve from time to time on the staffs of Generals J. S. Negley, John H. King, and Kenner Garrard.

In the late summer of 1865 Truman was sent by President Johnson as a confidential agent to investigate opinion and conditions in the far South, and from the first of September 1865 to the middle of March 1866 he traveled in Alabama, Georgia, Florida, Tennessee, Arkansas, Mississippi, Louisiana, and Texas, sending frequent illuminating letters to the *New York Times* and making observations which he submitted to the President in the form of a report, dated Apr. 9, 1866 (*Senate Executive Document No. 43, 39 Cong., 1 Sess.*). He testified before the congressional Committee on Reconstruction on Apr. 5 (*House Report No. 30*, pt. IV, pp. 136–40, 39

Cong., 1 Sess.) and shortly thereafter was sent as a special treasury agent to South Carolina and Florida. Declining appointment as paymaster with the rank of major in the Regular Army, he served from December 1866 until late in 1869 as special agent of the Post Office Department on the Pacific Coast, in this capacity visiting China, Japan, and Hawaii. On Dec. 8, 1869, at Los Angeles, he married Augusta Mallard and soon afterward went to Washington as a correspondent of the *New York Times* and the San Francisco *Bulletin*. He was again in California in 1870, became interested in the *San Diego Bulletin*, and in February 1872 assumed the editorship of the *Evening Express* of Los Angeles. In the following year he bought the *Los Angeles Star*, but four years later sold it and again became a special agent of the Post Office Department. For eleven years (1879–90) he was chief of the literary bureau of the Southern Pacific Railway; for the next two years the manager of a Southern California exhibit in Chicago; and subsequently for a time assistant chief of floriculture at the World's Columbian Exposition there. Returning to Los Angeles, he edited for some years the weekly *Western Graphic*. In 1900 he was one of the California commissioners to the Paris exposition and toured the Near East as a correspondent.

Besides his newspaper articles and sketches, Truman produced a number of books and pamphlets, including: *Life, Adventures, and Capture of Tiburcio Vasquez, the Great California Bandit and Murderer* (1874); *Semi-Tropical California* (1874); *Occidental Sketches* (1881); *The Field of Honor* (London, 1883; New York, 1884), a history of dueling; and a *History of the World's Fair* (copr. 1893). He also produced two plays, one of them a dramatization of Tennyson's *Enoch Arden*. He died in Los Angeles, survived by his wife and one of their two children.

Truman was jovial and expansive in manner, had amazing energy, and wrote voluminously. He has been called one of the most brilliant and successful of the Civil War correspondents, since by ingenuity or luck he was often enabled to get important news to the press ahead of his rivals, and in at least one notable instance ahead of the War Department (Elmer Davis, *History of the New York Times*, 1921, p. 57). His letters to the *Times* and his report and testimony on conditions in the South during the early period of Reconstruction are among the valuable sources of information covering that field.

[Autobiog. letter and other data in E. M. Treman and M. E. Poole, *The Hist. of the Treman, Tremaine, Truman Family in America* (1901), I, 193–98; *Who's Who in America*, 1916–17; *Printers and Printing in Providence, 1762–1907* (n.d.), p. lxxxv; *The New Internat. Year Book*, 1916 (1917); *Mil. Order of the Loyal Legion . . . Commandery of Cal., Circular No. 24, Ser. of 1916* (1916); *Sixty Years in Southern Cal. . . . Reminiscences of Harris Newmark* (3rd ed., 1930), ed. by M. H. and M. R. Newmark; *N. Y. Times*, July 30, 1916, pt. III, p. 4; *Los Angeles Times*, July 19, 1916.]
W. J. G.

TRUMBULL, BENJAMIN (Dec. 19, 1735– Feb. 2, 1820), Congregational clergyman, historian, was born in Hebron, Conn., the eldest child of Benjamin and Mary (Brown) Trumble and a descendant of John Trumble who came to Roxbury, Mass., in 1639 and was made a freeman of Rowley in 1640. The spelling of the family name was changed to Trumbull about 1768. After preliminary study with the Rev. Elijah Lathrop, Benjamin entered Yale College and was graduated in 1759. Having completed his theological studies with the Rev. Eleazar Wheelock, he was licensed to preach on May 21, 1760, by the Windham Association of Ministers, and in August of the same year was called to the Congregational Church in North Haven, Conn. There on Dec. 24, 1760, he began services as pastor which were to continue until his death sixty years later, interrupted only by a period of six months during the Revolution when he served as chaplain of General Wadsworth's brigade (June 24 to Dec. 25, 1776). Upon his return to North Haven, he was chosen captain of a company of sixty volunteers.

Trumbull was a man of great energy and character. Though he never neglected his duty to his parish, he felt obligated to serve the state. This sentiment, combined with the repeated pleas of his friends, among whom were his father's first cousin, Gov. Jonathan Trumbull [*q.v.*], and Secretary of State George Wyllys, induced him to undertake the writings of a history of Connecticut. He worked under great difficulties, his pastoral activities often necessitating the suspension of his writing for months at a time. In 1797, more than twenty years after he had undertaken the task, he published the first volume—*A Complete History of Connecticut, Civil and Ecclesiastical from the Emigration of Its First Planters, from England, in MDCXXX, to MDCCXIII*. This was followed by a two-volume edition in 1818—*A Complete History of Connecticut . . . to the Year 1764*. A reprint of the 1818 edition, limited to one thousand copies, was published in 1898 by H. D. Utley of New London. From the date of its appearance until the present time, Trumbull's work has proved invaluable to the student of Connecticut history. Though more a chronicle than a history, it faithfully records the events which took place during the period covered. In recent years, a certain amount of new material has been discovered which makes necessary some corrections and modification in Trumbull's statements; but the book yet remains one of the most important single pieces of writing devoted to the history of Connecticut. After its completion he set to work on his *A General History of the United States of America . . . 1492–1792*. It was to have been a three-volume work, but he lived to complete only the first volume, covering the period to 1765, which appeared in 1810. Although Trumbull's lasting fame rests on his historical writing, he published sixteen other books and pamphlets, thirteen of which were either sermons or theological treatises, and the remaining three discussions of current political problems. Worthy of special mention perhaps are *A Plea, in Vindication of the Connecticut Title to the Contested Lands, Lying West of New York* (1774) and *An Appeal to the Public . . . with Respect to the Unlawfulness of Divorces* (1788). From material he had collected was published in 1924 *A Compendium of the Indian Wars in New England*, edited by F. B. Hartranft.

A portrait of Trumbull, painted by George Munger in 1818, was reproduced as the frontispiece to the 1818 edition of the history of Connecticut. From this portrait one gathers the impression that Trumbull was a man of great melancholy. The statement of his contemporaries is to the effect that such he was. So keenly did he feel the weight of the sins of the world upon his shoulders that the fact was manifest not only in his sermons but also in his general demeanor. Those who listened to his preaching felt that he was about to weep at any moment. This lugubriousness was not conducive to inspiring sermons, and the large attendance at his church services was due rather to his reputation as a patriot and historian than to any personal magnetism.

He was married on Dec. 4, 1760, to Martha, daughter of Ichabod and Martha Tillotson Phelps of Hebron, Conn., by whom he had seven children, two of whom were sons; Lyman Trumbull [*q.v.*] was his grandson.

[Introduction to Trumbull's *Complete Hist. of Conn.* (edition of 1898) ; F. B. Dexter, *Biog. Sketches Grads. Yale Coll.*, vol. II (1896) ; *Christian Spectator*, Mar. 1820 ; H. P. Johnston, *Yale and Her Honor-Roll in the Am. Revolution* (1888) ; *Proc. Mass. Hist. Soc.*, vol. XVII (1880) ; W. B. Sprague, *Annals of the Am. Pulpit*, vol. I (1857) ; S. B. Thorpe, *North Haven Annals* (1892) ; J. H. Lea, *Contributions to a Trumbull Geneal.* (1895) ; *A Geneal. Chart of Some of the Descendants of John Trumbull* (n.d.) ; *Columbian Reg.* (New Haven, Conn.), Feb. 12, 19, 1820.]   R. M. H.

TRUMBULL, HENRY CLAY (June 8, 1830–Dec. 8, 1903), Sunday-school missionary, editor, and author, was born in Stonington, Conn., the sixth child of Gurdon and Sarah Ann

(Swan) Trumbull, and a younger brother of James Hammond Trumbull [*q.v.*]. He was of Puritan stock, a descendant of John Trumbull, mariner, who settled in Charlestown, Mass., about 1636, and of William Cheseborough and Walter Palmer, earliest settlers of Stonington. The boy's father was a man of varied business interests—whaling and sealing, the New York and Stonington Railroad, and the local banks—who served at different times as postmaster, representative and senator in the General Assembly of Connecticut, and commissioner of the state school fund. Henry attended Stonington Academy and Williston Seminary, but because of ill health had little formal education after the age of fourteen, being employed in later youth as a clerk in the Stonington bank. Beset by lung trouble, he gave up thought of a college education and at twenty-one removed to Hartford, where he became a clerk in the offices of the Hartford, Providence & Fishkill Railroad.

Under the influence of revival meetings conducted by Charles G. Finney [*q.v.*], he became superintendent of a mission Sunday-school in April 1852, and on June 1 united with the historic First (Center) Church in Hartford. Common interest in the revival and the Sunday-school brought him into intimacy with the family of Dr. Thomas Hopkins Gallaudet [*q.v.*], whose daughter Alice Cogswell he married on May 23, 1854. From 1856 to 1858 he was an apothecary, an editor, and a cotton and wool broker successively; he was also prominent in the state campaigns of the newly organized Republican party. As secretary of the first Connecticut Sunday-school Convention, 1857, he prepared so thorough and pointed a report that plans were made, with the cooperation of the American Sunday School Union, to employ a state Sunday-school missionary, and he was offered and accepted the post, giving full time to its duties after Sept. 1, 1858. On Sept. 10, 1862, he was ordained in order that he might qualify for the chaplaincy of the 10th Connecticut Regiment, then stationed at New Bern, N. C., where he joined it. He was captured by Confederates while ministering to the wounded after the assault on Fort Wagner in July 1863, and was held prisoner, suspected as a spy, for four months. After exchange, he was in active service on the Virginia front until the end of the war, being mustered out with his regiment, Aug. 25, 1865.

Refusing attractive offers in various editorial, educational, and business relationships, he resumed his work for the Sunday-schools, becoming secretary for New England of the American Sunday School Union. As chairman of the executive committee of the National Sunday School Convention, he issued the call for the meeting of 1872 which initiated the International Uniform Sunday School Lessons. In 1875 he became editor and part owner of the *Sunday School Times,* and removed with his family to Philadelphia, which was henceforth his home. Through this periodical, he contributed powerfully to the development of the Sunday-school movement in the United States and throughout the world, and gave stimulus and guidance to the spread of Bible study under the regimentation of the uniform lesson system. In 1888 he delivered the Lyman Beecher Lectures at Yale, which were published under the title *The Sunday School, Its Origin, Mission, Methods and Auxiliaries* (1888). Visiting Palestine in 1881, he succeeded in identifying the site of Kadesh-Barnea, and his book entitled *Kadesh-Barnea,* published in 1884 after two years of further study and research, remains the most important work on this subject. From 1886 to 1897, he served as chaplain-in-chief of the Loyal Legion.

Trumbull was an effective speaker and a stimulating and resourceful writer. He was, in the best sense of the term, a nineteenth-century Puritan. He wrote thirty-three books, notable among which, besides the two already mentioned, are: *Teaching and Teachers* (1884), *The Blood Covenant* (1885), *Hints on Child-Training* (1891), *Friendship the Master-Passion* (1892), *A Lie Never Justifiable* (1893), *War Memories of an Army Chaplain* (1898), *Border Lines in the Field of Doubtful Practices* (1899), *Illustrative Answers to Prayer* (1900), *Individual Work for Individuals* (1901), *How to Deal with Doubts and Doubters* (1903). At his death he was survived by six of his eight children.

[J. H. Lea, *Contributions to a Trumbull Geneal.* (1895); P. E. Howard, *The Life Story of Henry Clay Trumbull* (1905); *Congregationalist,* Nov. 7, Dec. 19, 1903; *Sunday School Times,* Dec. 12, 19, 1903; *The Congregational Year-Book, 1904* (1904); *Pub. Ledger* (Phila.) and *Phila. Inquirer,* Dec. 9, 1903.]
L. A. W.

TRUMBULL, JAMES HAMMOND (Dec. 20, 1821–Aug. 5, 1897), historian, philologist, and bibliographer, was the son of Gurdon and Sarah Ann (Swan) Trumbull of Stonington, Conn., and a brother of Henry Clay Trumbull [*q.v.*]. Prepared at Tracy's Academy, Norwich, he entered Yale College in 1838 but withdrew two years later because of poor health. After assisting James Harvey Linsley in cataloging the mammalia, birds, reptiles, fish, and shells of Connecticut, he was appointed assistant secretary of state in Connecticut in 1847. He received the nomination of the Whig party for the office of

secretary of state in 1852, but failed to win the election and declined similar nominations in 1853 and 1854. Following service as state librarian and registrar, he was again appointed assistant secretary of state in 1858. Three years later he was elected secretary of state on the Republican ticket and held the office until 1866. Upon the establishment of the Watkinson Library of Reference at Hartford, he was appointed trustee and librarian, and after 1866 devoted his full time to the duties of librarian. In 1890 he was appointed librarian emeritus.

While serving as assistant secretary of state Trumbull transcribed, edited, and published *The Public Records of the Colony of Connecticut, Prior to the Union with New Haven Colony, May, 1665* (1850). This was followed in 1852 by a second volume, covering the period from 1665 to 1677; and in 1859 by a third, covering the period from 1678 to 1689. In the appendix of the third volume was printed "Extracts from the Records of the United Colonies of New England," comprising such portions of the records as were not published in the second volume (1794) of Ebenezer Hazard's *Historical Collections*; these "Extracts" appeared as a separate publication in 1859. He contributed "A Sketch of the Life of Thomas Lechford" to Lechford's *Plain Dealing* (1867), and to the *Note-Book Kept by Thomas Lechford* (1885). The caustic criticism of Connecticut by Samuel Andrew Peters [*q.v.*] evoked from Trumbull's pen *The True-Blue Laws of Connecticut and New Haven and the False-Blue Laws Invented by the Rev. Samuel Peters* (1876), and *The Rev. Samuel Peters, His Defenders and Apologists* (1877), reprinted from the *Hartford Courant*. He also edited *The Memorial History of Hartford County, Connecticut, 1633–1884* (2 vols., 1886).

Trumbull made his most noteworthy contributions as the historian and philologist of the Indians. He published in 1865 a translation of John Eliot's Catechism for the Indians, and edited Roger Williams' "A Key into the Language of America" (*Publications of the Narragansett Club,* vol. I, 1866). Between 1869 and 1876 he contributed seven papers on the language of the Indians to the *Transactions* of the American Philological Association. He prepared "The Composition of Indian Geographical Names, Illustrated from the Algonkin Languages," for the *Collections of the Connecticut Historical Society* (vol. II, 1870); "On Some Alleged Specimens of Indian Onomatopœia," for the *Transactions of the Connecticut Academy of the Arts and Sciences* (vol. II, 1871–73); and an introduction for Abraham Pierson, *Some Helps for the Indians,* published at Hartford in 1873 and included in *Collections of the Connecticut Historical Society* (vol. III, 1895). His "Origin and Early Progress of Indian Missions in New England, with a List of Books in the Indian Language" appears in the *Proceedings of the American Antiquarian Society* (1874), and his *Indian Names of Places, Etc., in and on the Borders of Connecticut: with Interpretations of Some of Them* was published at Hartford in 1881. To *The Memorial History of Hartford County* he contributed "Indians of the Connecticut Valley." Upon Trumbull's death, a "Natick Dictionary" in manuscript was deposited in the library of the American Antiquarian Society; it was published by the Smithsonian Institution in 1903 (*Bureau of American Ethnology, Bulletin 25,* 1903). Trumbull was also a bibliographer of note. His *Catalogue of the American Library of the Late Mr. George Brinley of Hartford, Conn.* (5 vols., 1878–97) still serves as a guide to Americana. At the time of his death a "List of Books Printed in Connecticut, 1709–1800," existed in manuscript and it was subsequently edited by his daughter and published in 1904 by the Acorn Club.

Trumbull's work brought him several honorary degrees, the complimentary appointment as lecturer on Indian languages at Yale, and membership in many historical, philological, and scientific societies. After a brief illness he died at Hartford. He was survived by his widow, Sarah A. (Robinson) Trumbull, whom he had married in 1855, and a daughter, Annie Eliot Trumbull.

[A. W. Wright, "Biog. Memoir of James Hammond Trumbull, 1821–1897," *Nat. Acad. of Sciences, Biog. Memoirs,* vol. VII (1913), separately printed in 1911; *Proc. Am. Antiquarian Soc.,* n.s., vol. XII (1899); *Cat. of the Officers and Grads. of Yale Univ. in New Haven, Conn., 1701–1924* (1924); *Hartford Courant,* Aug. 6, 1897.]   I. M. C.

TRUMBULL, JOHN (Apr. 13, 1750 o.s.–May 11, 1831), poet and jurist, was a member of an illustrious Connecticut family whose first American representative, John Trumble, was in Roxbury, Mass., in 1639, and the following year was made a freeman of Rowley. John Trumbull the poet was born at Westbury (now a part of Watertown), Conn. His father, John, a Congregational minister and a fellow of Yale College, was known as a man of sound judgment in practical affairs; he was a first cousin of Jonathan Trumbull, 1710–1785 [*q.v.*], Revolutionary governor of Connecticut. The poet's mother, Sarah (Whitman), a grand-daughter of Solomon Stoddard [*q.v.*], instructed and encouraged the boy while he made an almost incredible but well authenticated record of precocity, which culminated in a successful examination for entrance into Yale College at the age of seven. Being over-young for college life, Trumbull was honorably rusticated to Westbury until he was thirteen. He matriculated at Yale in 1763.

Although a faithful student, he disapproved of the Yale curriculum because of its concentration on "solid learning," *i.e.,* theology, mathematics, and linguistics, to the neglect of English composition and the interpretation of literature. Accordingly, with the cooperation of friends, including Timothy Dwight and David Humphreys [*qq.v.*], he satirized the course of study and attempted by example to create among the students a love of belles-lettres. The poetry which he wrote as a student was chiefly of two kinds: "correct" but undistinguished elegies written under the aegis of the neo-classical school, and brilliant, if fragmentary, comic verses with an occasional admixture of mild bawdry. From the former type he hoped ultimately for fame; the latter, which exhibited his true talents, he circulated privately among friends. His burlesque "Epithalamium," written in 1769, artfully combined wit and scholarship. In prose he produced a series of polished Addisonian essays, which were published in *The Boston Chronicle* (Sept. 4–7, 1769–Jan. 18–22, 1770). His valedictory oration, *An Essay on the Uses and Advantages of the Fine Arts,* which was promptly printed in 1770, was distinguished by its early plea for the abandonment of neo-classical rules in poetry; but the verses which concluded the oration were an egregious example of the very practices its thesis had condemned. Graduated and awarded a Berkeley fellowship in 1767, he continued his studies at Yale for three years more.

After receiving his master's degree in 1770, he spent a year in Wethersfield, Conn., studying law, writing verse, and (probably) teaching school. Upon returning to Yale in 1772 as a tutor, he soon commenced the composition of his comic satire on the abuses of collegiate instruction, *The Progress of Dulness,* a poem of seventeen hundred lines in octosyllabic couplets. Published in three parts during 1772 and 1773, it provoked local storms of criticism; but it pleased impartial judges and was reprinted in 1794, 1797, and 1801. During the second year of his tutorship Trumbull also brought to completion a series of thirty-eight essays, begun in 1770 under the pen-name, "The Correspondent," which he published in *The Connecticut Journal* (Feb. 23–July 6, 1770; Feb. 12–Sept. 3, 1773).

Having passed his bar examination in 1773, Trumbull moved to Boston, there to continue his legal studies under John Adams, whose confidential friend he remained for many years. In

Boston, Trumbull gained some of the political background for his comic epic, *M'Fingal*; but the poems that he wrote at the time showed him to be still dominated by the duller vices of the age of Pope. His first poem reflecting national affairs, *An Elegy on the Times* (1774), a glittering, bombastic piece, bore a patriotic message that was vitiated by the poet's untimely note of caution against violence. When Adams left Boston in August 1774, Trumbull retired to the relative security of New Haven, where he commenced the practice of law. He remained at New Haven until the menace of a British invasion in 1777 influenced him to withdraw to his native hamlet, Westbury. In 1781 he established himself at Hartford.

In the fall of 1775, at the suggestion of "some leading members of the first Congress," Trumbull wrote the initial canto of *M'Fingal*. This was published early in 1776 with a 1775 imprint. After the war, he divided this part into two cantos and wrote two additional ones. The whole work, containing approximately three thousand lines, was first published at Hartford in 1782. The framework of the poem is a loosely unified narrative of the misfortunes of the Tory squire, M'Fingal; but the poem virtually constitutes a comprehensive review of the blunders and cowardice of the British leaders throughout the Revolution. Despite its pro-Whig bias, the efficacy of *M'Fingal* as an agent of anti-Tory propaganda has been exaggerated. It had but three editions during the war, whereas Paine's *Common Sense*, published at the same time, had a sale of more than one hundred thousand copies within a few months. Though a patriot, Trumbull was not a fiery revolutionist of the stripe of Paine or Freneau. His principal powers were intellectual and critical rather than emotional. Consequently he invested his poem with literary qualities which received their fullest recognition after the war, when, despite Puritan prejudice against satirical poetry, *M'Fingal* was accepted as an important contribution to belles-lettres. Its inexhaustible wit, its air of learning without pedantry, and its buoyant Hudibrastic couplets that fitted snugly in the memory made it a cherished possession of the American people in an era when good native poets were not plentiful. Reprinted more than thirty times between 1782 and 1840, it was the most popular American poem of its length before Longfellow's *Evangeline*.

The merits of *M'Fingal* gave Trumbull the position of literary leader of the "Hartford Wits" during the eighties and nineties. Notwithstanding the grave competition of Dwight and Bar-

low, however, he did little to sustain his reputation. After 1782 he commenced no poetry of major importance; his small part in "The Anarchiad," which appeared in *The New Haven Gazette and the Connecticut Magazine* (1786–87), and in *The Echo* (1807), first published in the *American Mercury*, his miscellaneous newspaper verses and critical essays, and his lexicographical assistance to Noah Webster merely called attention to his declining creative powers. His literary defection, however, was balanced by his increasing interest in law and politics. After the Revolution, like most of the "Hartford Wits," he became a strong Federalist. He first held office in 1789, when he became state's attorney for the county of Hartford. In 1792 and 1800 he was elected to the state legislature. He was appointed judge of the superior court of Connecticut in 1801 and judge of the supreme court of errors in 1808. Both of these positions he held until he was removed from office by politics in 1819. Although the jurist thus survived the poet, the latter was not forgotten. In 1820 *The Poetical Works of John Trumbull* was issued in two volumes. The last six years of his life Trumbull spent at Detroit, Mich., where he died at two in the morning on May 11, 1831. On Nov. 21, 1776, he married Sarah Hubbard, by whom he had two sons and two daughters.

[The two principal collections of Trumbull MSS. are in the possession of Cornell Univ. Lib. and the Burton Hist. Coll. (Detroit). Yale Univ. possesses indispensable biog. material; the best collection of editions of *M'Fingal* is in the Watkinson Library (Hartford); the "Memoir of the Author" prefixed to Trumbull's *Poetical Works* is autobiographical but not infallible as to fact; the only full-length work on Trumbull is Alexander Cowie, *John Trumbull: Connecticut Wit* (1936); useful articles and books include Henry Bronson, *The Hist. of Waterbury, Conn.* (1858); Alexander Cowie, "John Trumbull as Revolutionist," in *Am. Lit.*, Nov. 1931; F. B. Dexter, *Biog. Sketches of the Grads. of Yale Coll.*, vol. III (1903); S. G. Goodrich, *Recollections of a Lifetime* (1857); Annie Marble, *Heralds of Am. Literature* (1907); V. L. Parrington, *The Connecticut Wits* (1926), and *The Colonial Mind* (1927); A. P. Stokes, *Memorials of Eminent Yale Men* (1914); J. H. Trumbull, *The Origin of M'Fingal* (1868); M. C. Tyler, *The Lit. Hist. of the Am. Revolution* (1897); R. J. Purcell, *Conn. in Transition* (1918); *A Geneal. Chart of Some of the Descendants of John Trumbull* (n.d.); J. H. Lea, *Contributions to a Trumbull Geneal.* (1895); *Detroit Courier*, May 12, 1831; *Proc. Am. Antiquarian Soc.*, Oct. 17, 1934.]   A. C.

TRUMBULL, JOHN (June 6, 1756–Nov. 10, 1843), the painter of the Revolution, was born in Lebanon, New London County, Conn. The youngest of six children of Gov. Jonathan Trumbull [*q.v.*] and Faith (Robinson) Trumbull, he was "emphatically well born." Soon after his birth he was subject to convulsions caused by the overlapping of the bones of the cranium, but the natural form of his head was restored at the age of three. A year or so later he severely injured his left eye. Gilbert Stuart, once puzzling over one of Trumbull's drawings, remarked, "This looks as if it was drawn by a man with but one eye" (Dunlap, *post,* I, 217). The sickly child attended the local school, learning to read Greek at the age of six, and was ready for college at twelve. His predilection for drawing began at an early age. He begged his father to allow him to study under John Singleton Copley [*q.v.*], but the governor packed him off to Harvard at the age of fifteen in the middle of his junior year. He graduated in 1773, the youngest boy in his class. On the side he learned French and copied engravings. Returning to Lebanon, he taught school temporarily, copied more engravings, and made his first essays at historical composition.

Shortly after the outbreak of the Revolution the governor secured his son's appointment as adjutant, and a "sort of aid-du-camp" to Gen. Joseph Spencer of the 1st Connecticut Regiment. Brought to Washington's attention by the accurate drawings he had made of the British gun emplacements, Trumbull was appointed second aide-de-camp to the new commanding general (General Order, July 27, 1775, *Proceedings of the Massachusetts Historical Society,* vol. XV, 1878, p. 132), but he felt himself unequal to the "elegant duties" of this post and was thankful when commissioned major of brigade (August 1775). He participated in the action at Dorchester Heights the following March and witnessed the British evacuation of Boston, proceeding afterwards to New York. On June 28, 1776, he became deputy adjutant-general with the rank of colonel under Gen. Horatio Gates, going with him to Crown Point and Ticonderoga, and later into Pennsylvania; he afterwards accompanied Gen. Benedict Arnold to Rhode Island, wintering in Providence. When in February he finally received his signed commission from Congress, he returned it "within an hour" because it was dated three months late.

His military career suddenly terminating, Trumbull, now twenty-one, went to Boston to take up art. For a time he rented the famous painting rooms occupied by John Smibert [*q.v.*], but in the summer of 1778 he offered his services to Gen. John Sullivan as a volunteer aide-de-camp in the Rhode Island campaign, during which he conducted himself gallantly. The following year Trumbull was in Boston once more, pursuing his study of painting. In the fall of 1779, however, he undertook a speculation for the supply of military stores to the American army. Foreseeing the possible failure of the project, the rebel officer secured through his father's friend John Temple, afterwards British consul-general,

permission to study painting in London and in May 1780 sailed for France. He obtained a letter to Benjamin West [*q.v.*] from Franklin in Paris, proceeded to London, and was received with the usual kindness by West, who accepted him as a pupil. The pleasant life of making twice-removed copies after the old masters at West's studio on Newman Street was rudely interrupted by Trumbull's arrest on Nov. 19, 1780, on "suspicion of treason" under suspension of the *habeas corpus* act. His imprisonment in Tothill Fields Bridewell was said to have been a reprisal for the tragic hanging of Major André. Both Charles James Fox and Edmund Burke interested themselves in the case and ultimately secured his release (see Lewis Einstein, *Divided Loyalties,* 1933, p. 374). Trumbull immediately crossed to the Continent, where he attempted to negotiate a loan for Connecticut through his father's Amsterdam bankers, M. de Neufville & Son, for whom he painted a full-length portrait of Washington (1780). This was engraved by Valentine Green and published the following year, the first authentic portrait of Washington issued in Europe. After a vexatious delay in Spain he returned to Boston. During the winter of 1782 and the fall of 1783 he acted as confidential agent for his brother Joseph [*q.v.*], then engaged in a contract for army supplies, at New Windsor, N. Y. At the end of the war he again considered entering "regular commerce." His practical father urged law. When the painter "dwelt upon the honors paid to artists" in antiquity, his father rejoined in the oft-quoted phrase, "You appear to forget, sir, that Connecticut is not Athens" (*Autobiography,* p. 89).

In December 1783 Trumbull embarked for London. When hoped-for commercial connections did not develop he went to the benevolent Mr. West and was again accepted as a pupil, working in the studio by day and attending the Royal Academy school evenings. In 1785, after copying West's celebrated "Battle of La Hogue" for his master, and composing his "Priam and the Dead Body of Hector," he fortunately abandoned the Greeks and the Romans for contemporary history. His first subjects, the "Battle of Bunker's Hill" and the "Death of General Montgomery in the Attack of Quebec," were painted in West's studio and under his direction, and were completed in the spring of 1786. Inspired by Boydell's publications and encouraged by his master, he embarked on a plan of publishing engravings after the paintings and associated himself in this undertaking with Antonio C. de Poggi, an Italian artist and publisher of Bond Street, London, by whom six plates were issued.

Armed with letters from John Adams, the minister to Great Britain, Trumbull proceeded to Paris in the summer of 1785 in search of suitable engravers, and there was encouraged by Thomas Jefferson to continue the scheme. After traveling in France and in Germany, where he left his paintings with his agent Poggi, he returned to London in November 1786. "Bunker's Hill" was ultimately engraved by John G. von Müller of Stuttgart, and "Quebec" by J. F. Clemens of Denmark, both dated 1798, twelve years after the completion of the paintings.

The next three years in London, stimulated by travel, broadened by study, and encouraged by praise, were the most creative in the artist's life. The small painting of the "Declaration of Independence," which occupied eight years, was begun. This brilliant and dignified achievement remains the most important visual record of the heroic period of American history, although not historically accurate in every detail. Thirty-six of the forty-eight portraits were from life, the rest from portraits by others and from memory; thirteen signers were not represented; and four non-signers were included. The "Surrender of Lord Cornwallis at Yorktown," the "Death of General Mercer at the Battle of Princeton," and the "Capture of the Hessians at Trenton" followed, all painted in West's studio. Finding his American Revolutionary subjects none too popular in England, Trumbull expediently undertook to celebrate a feat of British arms, selecting the "Sortie Made by the Garrison of Gibraltar" and producing a little masterpiece (Jean L. Brockway, "Trumbull's Sortie," *Art Bulletin*, March 1934, with checklist of replicas. In 1787 and again in 1789 Trumbull was in Paris, painting French and British officers, staying with Jefferson, who tentatively offered him a post of private secretary in the American legation in Paris at £300 a year (letter, May 21, 1789, *Autobiography*, p. 155). Trumbull declined this offer, however, and returned to America to further his "national work."

Congress was then meeting in New York, whither Trumbull repaired in December 1789 to obtain portraits for the four historical compositions already undertaken and to secure subscriptions for the engravings of the first two. Washington headed the list with four sets and, as his *Diary* records, obligingly sat a number of times for his former aide. Later in the same city Trumbull solicited commissions from the city council and painted twelve portraits in all. "Heads" and subscribers were collected in New England, Pennsylvania, Virginia, and South Carolina. Yorktown was visited and the terrain

for the "Surrender of Cornwallis" studied. In 1792 Trumbull was again in Philadelphia, where he painted the large portrait of "Washington before the Battle of Princeton" (engraved in stipple by Thomas Cheesman) for Charleston, S. C. The picture was rejected, and another had to be painted. Subscriptions languished, and Trumbull, the best portrait-painter in America, Stuart excepted, again abandoned painting, never to resume it on the same plane or with so little competition.

In 1793 at the particular request of John Jay, envoy extraordinary to Great Britain, Trumbull became his private secretary, prompted perhaps by the realization of an earlier ambition (he had solicited a foreign secretaryship from Congress after his resignation from the army) or by the opportunity to supervise the engraving of his paintings. The mission set out from New York in May 1794, and the complicated negotiations were concluded in November. After committing Jay's Treaty to memory, Trumbull proceeded to Paris to repeat it to Monroe, visited Stuttgart to ascertain what progress had been made with his "Bunker's Hill," and then returned to Paris, where he undertook a series of unsuccessful commercial ventures. Paintings from broken-up noble collections were purchased with funds supplied by West and auctioned at Christie's in London in 1797 (W. Buchanan, *Memoirs of Painting*, 1824, I, 257). The second speculation, the purchase of brandy in France, a business involving eight months' time, ended disastrously. In August 1796 Trumbull was appointed the fifth member of the commission to oversee the execution of the seventh article of the Jay Treaty, a post which he accepted with some hesitancy, but in which he acquitted himself with distinction. In the summer of 1797 he revisited Stuttgart to get his picture and the engraved plate. Returning via Paris, he found himself listed among the suspect and was denied permission to proceed to Calais, but his friend, the painter David, got him out of his uncomfortable predicament (see C. L. Lokke, in *New England Quarterly*, March 1934). In London once more (November 1797) the work of the commission was resumed, terminating in May 1804.

The years between 1799 and 1804 are passed over without comment in Trumbull's *Autobiography*. He resided in Bath in 1801 and 1802. He married, without consulting or advising his family, a pretty Englishwoman, Sarah (Hope) Harvey, Oct. 1, 1800, about whom there has been much mystery (see *Diary of William Dunlap*, 1930, III, 738–39, 800–01, for gossip). Whoever she was, her social position was inferior to that of her husband, who devoted only six lines to her in the *Autobiography,* on the occasion of her death in 1824. Two pleasing portraits exist of her at Yale, one by Samuel L. Waldo and the other by her husband (1800), who also painted her on her death bed. There were no children. As a young man in Connecticut, Trumbull, with a number of others, was involved with a country girl. A child was born, and Trumbull, the most affluent of the group, was claimed as father. He contributed towards the support of the child, John Trumbull Ray, as he was later named, apprenticing him to a gentleman farmer in England and finally purchasing him a lieutenant's commission in the British army. (A miniature portrait of Ray in a scarlet uniform is in the possession of Maria Trumbull Dana of New Haven.)

Wearying of Europe, Trumbull decided to settle in Boston, sailing with his wife in April 1804, but he found Gilbert Stuart [*q.v.*] so well established there that he wisely decided to go to New York. Trumbull was a rapid painter, averaging five sittings to a head, for which he charged one hundred dollars, and correspondingly more for half and full lengths. The Timothy Dwight and the Stephen van Rensselaer at Yale are in the new and less fortunate style of the erstwhile diplomat and merchant, to whose art the constant interruptions in his work proved fatal. A large collection of pictures purchased in Paris was hung in the Park Theatre, the "first public exhibition of original pictures by the old masters of Europe . . . in America" (Dunlap, *post,* II, 49), did not pay the costs, and was returned to London. In December 1808, thoroughly soured by lack of patronage, Trumbull sailed for London for the fourth and last time, but neither portrait painting, a projected panorama of Niagara Falls, nor his "large pictures" proved successful. Hope of a speedy return to America was destroyed by the declaration of war in 1812.

As soon as hostilities ceased, Trumbull embarked for New York, arriving in September 1815. There, because of his own waning talents and competition from such men as S. F. B. Morse, Thomas Sully, John Wesley Jarvis, John Vanderlyn [*qq.v.*], and others, he met with little success. In Washington, however, where Congress was in session, Timothy Pitkin championed the aging painter's "long suspended" plan for the painting of his Revolutionary subjects in the Capitol. The subjects already executed (in miniature for the engraver) were exhibited in the House in 1816; and at length Trumbull was commissioned by Congress (Feb. 6, 1817) to paint four pictures in the Rotunda. A contract was eventually drawn up (March 1817) for the

execution of the "Surrender of General Burgoyne at Saratoga," the "Surrender of Lord Cornwallis at Yorktown," the "Declaration of Independence," and the "Resignation of Washington," the price being settled at $8,000 each.

President Madison unhappily insisted that the figures be "as large as life," which the monocular Trumbull rarely painted well even in his best period. Other painters, especially Vanderlyn, resented the award to the combative and overbearing ex-Revolutionary soldier. The last of the four twelve-by-eighteen-foot canvases—all painted in New York—, replicas of the miniature paintings now at Yale, was finished in April 1824 after seven years of effort, twenty-five years or more after their conception. The heavy-handed, chalky-colored replicas (see Trumbull's *Description of the Four Pictures . . . in the Rotunda of the Capitol,* 1827) were not successful. John Quincy Adams records his disappointment in seeing the enlarged "Declaration" (*Diary,* Sept. 1, 1818), which Trumbull exhibited commercially before its installation, in New York, Philadelphia, and Baltimore. The other enlargements were exhibited in like manner and with considerable profit. The pictures were installed under the supervision of the artist in 1824. Four years later it was found necessary to remove and repair them on account of dampness and wanton injury (*Autobiography,* p. 281).

In the meantime other troubles beset the aging painter. His wife died in 1824, and the apartments at Park Place and Church Street were given up. Negotiations were undertaken for the engraving of the "Declaration," subscriptions for which were solicited in advance, the work finally being entrusted (contract December 1820) to the young Asher Brown Durand [*q.v.*]. Although the print established the reputation of the engraver it was another financial disappointment to Trumbull. In 1817 Trumbull had become president of the American Academy of Fine Arts; but lack of public interest, the opposition of cliques, and finally the secession of most of the artists resulted in the founding of the National Academy of Design (1826) under the presidency of Morse, leaving the dictatorial and cantankerous Trumbull the captain of a sinking ship. For years he had been in debt to his bankers, and at length, pressed for settlement, he liquidated his New York State land holdings. In 1832 a military pension was secured. Replicas of earlier work and large religious paintings, "nearly all of which should have been destroyed" (Weir, *post,* p. 42), were unhappily completed by the artist.

At this juncture Prof. Benjamin Silliman of Yale, Trumbull's nephew by marriage, suggested the establishing of a gallery at New Haven to contain Trumbull's unsalable pictures. He induced friends to finance an annuity of one thousand dollars on condition that Trumbull's collection be turned over to Yale College, which agreed to erect a gallery after the artist's design for the reception of the pictures. The Trumbull Gallery, the earliest art museum connected with an educational institution in America, was opened to the public in October 1832. The artist wrote a carefully prepared catalogue (1832), and Silliman became curator. Silliman was also somewhat responsible for the publication of Trumbull's *Autobiography*. When William Dunlap [*q.v.*] wrote his history of American painting in 1834 he used the manuscript biography that Trumbull had dictated to James Herring [*q.v.*], adding his own emotional observations and gossip. Trumbull justly attacked the *Arts of Design* (*New York American*, Dec. 13, 1834), Dunlap replying. Silliman urged the aged artist to elaborate and publish his early notes, and in 1841 the defensive *Autobiography, Letters, and Reminiscences of John Trumbull, from 1756 to 1841* appeared. It has remained the chief source for all later writers. In 1841 the old man returned from New Haven to New York, where he died two years later at the age of eighty-seven. According to his instructions he was buried beside his wife beneath the Trumbull Gallery. The bodies were removed, along with the pictures, in 1866 to a new and larger building, and again, April 1928, to the new Yale Gallery of Fine Arts.

Trumbull was a handsome man, as can be seen from Stuart's early portrait, his two self-portraits, the small full-length by George W. Twibill, and especially the Waldo and Jewett at Yale. Ball Hughes's marble bust of Trumbull is at Yale. In 1849 the American Art-Union issued a portrait medal. Trumbull was dignified and courtly in bearing, punctilious, frank and abstemious, high-strung, excitable, impetuous, exceedingly sensitive and ready to take offense. As an old and disappointed man he was irritable, uncompromising, and haughty. He was, however, a gentleman by birth, education, and instinct.

Some notice should be paid to Trumbull, the amateur architect. He drew up plans for a series of dormitory buildings for Yale in 1792 and designed the Barclay Street quarters of the American Academy (1831), the Trumbull Gallery, and the Congregational church in Lebanon (1804). He might have become a better architect than he was painter; the opportunity, as Edmund Burke had once told him, was far greater. Yet it is impossible not to be grateful for Trumbull's determined devotion to historical painting. Far

as he is from being America's greatest painter, he is nevertheless inextricably a part of America's past; no schoolboy but sees the Revolution through his eyes. His 250 to 300 faithful representations, drawn from life, of the principal actors and actions of the Revolution make him at once the chief, the most prolific, and the most competent visual recorder of that heroic period.

[For biog. materials, in addition to the incomplete and stuffy *Autobiog., Reminiscences, and Letters of John Trumbull* (1841), and William Dunlap, *The Hist. of the Rise and Progress of the Arts of Design in the U. S.* (3 vols., 1918), ed. by F. W. Bayley and C. E. Goodspeed, see *A Geneal. Chart of Some of the Descendants of John Trumbull of Newcastle-on-Tyne* (n.d.); J. H. Lea, *A Geneal. of the Ancestors . . . of George Augustus and Louisa* (*Clap*) *Trumbull* (1886); Trumbull's *Letters Proposing a Plan for the Permanent Encouragement of the Fine Arts by the Nat. Government* (1827), *Address Read before the Am. Acad. of Fine Arts* (1833), and a series of cats. and explanations of his pictures prepared by Trumbull; *Cat. of Paintings by Col. Trumbull . . . Am. Acad. of the Fine Arts* (1831); S. F. B. Morse, *Examination of Col. Trumbull's Address* (1833); Benjamin Silliman, in *Am. Jour. of Science and Arts*, vol. I, no. 2 (1819), vol. VIII, no. 1 (1824), July–Sept. 1840, and Oct.–Dec. 1843; *Am. Acad. of Fine Arts, Charter and By-Laws* (1817); T. S. Cummings, *Hist. Annals of the Nat. Acad. of Design* (1865); and obituaries in *N. Y. American*, Nov. 10, *N. Y. Spectator, Columbian Reg.* (New Haven), Nov. 11, and *Daily Morning Courier* (New Haven), Nov. 11, 13, 1843. See also John Durand, *John Trumbull* (1881); J. F. Weir, *John Trumbull* (1901), with an excellent appraisal of the paintings; Theodore Bolton, *Early Am. Portrait Painters in Miniature* (1921), with a checklist; J. H. Morgan, *Paintings by John Trumbull at Yale Univ.* (1926); with good illustrations and keys to the eight hist. pictures; B. L. Belden, *Indian Peace Medals Issued in the U. S.* (1927), pp. 23–24; Theodore Sizer, "The Trumbull Gallery, 1832–1932," *Yale Alumni Weekly*, Oct. 28, Nov. 4, 1932; *Conn. Tercentenary . . . John Trumbull and Trumbull Memorabilia . . . Yale Univ.* (1935), a convenient checklist; Theodore Bolton and H. L. Binsse, in *Antiquarian*, July 1931. The Trumbull and Silliman papers at Yale, which include Trumbull's marriage certificate, are the largest manuscript source. Important material is in the possession of the Robert Fridenberg Gallery, New York; the N. Y. Pub. Lib.; the N. Y. Hist. Soc.; the Conn. Hist. Soc.; the Mass. Hist. Soc.; the Boston Athenaeum; M. B. Brainard of Hartford, Conn.; and in the records of the First Ecclesiastical Soc., Lebanon, Aug. 13, 1804. Many references to Trumbull occur in the writings of Jefferson, Rufus King, J. Q. Adams, and others. Trumbull's paintings and drawings, and engravings after his designs are scattered in pub. and private colls., among them those at Yale : the Wadsworth Athenaeum, Hartford; the City Hall and Chamber of Commerce, New York, and the coll. of Mrs. I. Sheldon Tilney, N. Y. City. His painting cabinet, etc., is at Yale. Forgeries abound, particularly of his pencil and sepia portrait studies; the largest group appears in the Ed. Frossard sale of 1894. The most important of many auction sales were those of Dec. 1806 and Feb. 1807 (the "Silliman Sale"), Jan. 1926, and Mar. 1931 (Trumbull-Silliman correspondence), Am. Art Asso., N. Y.]   T. S—r.

TRUMBULL, JONATHAN (Oct. 12, 1710– Aug. 17, 1785), governor of Connecticut, was born at Lebanon, Conn., the second son of Joseph and Hannah (Higley) Trumble. He did not adopt the present spelling of the name until 1766. His great-grandfather, John Trumble, had emigrated from England to Roxbury, Mass., in 1639 and the following year was made a freeman of Rowley; his father was an early settler in Lebanon, where he developed a considerable mercantile business. In 1727 Jonathan graduated from Harvard and returned to Lebanon to prepare for the ministry. He was licensed to preach by the Windham Association and in 1731 was considering a call to the church of nearby Colchester when his elder brother Joseph, their father's business associate, died. Recognizing a call to duty, Jonathan abandoned his own plans and took his brother's place. On Dec. 9, 1735, he married Faith Robinson, daughter of Rev. John Robinson of Duxbury, Mass., a union which raised his social standing considerably. To them were born four sons and two daughters. Joseph [q.v.], the eldest son, was the first commissary-general of the Continental Army; Jonathan [q.v.], after a military and political career, also became governor of Connecticut; and John, 1756–1843 [q.v.], acquired fame as a painter. John Trumbull, 1750–1831 [q.v.], the poet and wit, was a second cousin of these three.

Trumbull soon disclosed an exceptional aptitude for commerce. With various partners he developed an extensive trade, establishing direct commercial connections with Great Britain instead of dealing only indirectly through Boston and New York as did most Connecticut merchants. By the 1760's Trumbull was one of the outstanding figures of Connecticut commerce; but in 1766 came a change. For reasons not entirely clear, his business suffered a reversal from which it never recovered. He was forced into virtual—though not legal—bankruptcy, and at the outbreak of the Revolution still owed large sums to his British creditors.

While Trumbull was still in his early twenties he entered politics. First sent to the General Assembly in 1733, he was returned frequently and in 1739 served as speaker. His abilities soon attracted attention and he was chosen assistant in 1740, the first time his name appeared in nomination—an unusual achievement for a man of thirty. For the next ten years he was regularly reëlected until a political reversal in 1750–51 led to his loss of the assistantship. Elected again to the Assembly, he served twice more as speaker. He was restored to the Council in 1754 in his previous order of seniority. In 1766 Gov. Thomas Fitch [q.v.], who had taken the oath required of all governors by the Stamp Act, was defeated for reëlection. Trumbull, now second councilor, had sided with the majority in this dispute and was in consequence advanced to the deputy governorship. In this capacity he served

for three and a half years. As deputy governor he was also regularly named chief justice of the superior court. Though not trained in the law, he had judicial experience. In 1744 he had become a justice of the quorum and two years later was named judge of the Windham county court, a position which he had held, with one three-year interruption, ever since. He had also served continuously as judge of the Windham probate court since 1747. His most conspicuous action as chief justice was in successfully turning aside the application of the royal customs officers for writs of assistance (1768–69).

Upon the death of Gov. William Pitkin, 1694–1769 [q.v.] in October 1769, the Assembly named Trumbull to the governorship, a position which he continued to fill until his voluntary retirement in 1784. In the period of increasing tension between the colonies and the mother country Trumbull stood as a stanch supporter of colonial rights. As early as 1770 he foresaw the possibility of independence, distressing as the thought still seemed to him ("The Trumbull Papers," post, I, 403). When hostilities actually began he was the only colonial governor to take the radical side. He threw himself at once into active support of the Continental Army, and when independence was proclaimed, welcomed its declaration. The scene of little actual fighting, but close to several major fields of operation, Connecticut became a principal source of supply for the American troops. In supervising this work, for which his previous business experience well fitted him, Trumbull made his chief contribution to the cause. His relations with Washington became close, the commander writing him on an average of every ten days until 1778, letters appearing less frequently thereafter except in times of emergency. The General counted heavily upon the Governor's supplying him with food, clothing, and munitions. To a large extent Trumbull was able to meet Washington's expectations —if not his hopes—but at times the General expressed bitter disappointment at what seemed indifference to his most pressing needs. Neither man could always comprehend the other's situation. Trumbull sometimes failed to appreciate the inevitable waste of *matériel* incident to military operations and felt that Washington's demands exceeded what Connecticut could reasonably be expected to provide. The General similarly failed to understand the difficulty of Trumbull's position as head of a community that had always been freer from outside control than any other colony and was now living in terror of occasional British raids. At one time Trumbull seemed to show a greater admiration for Gates than for Washington, but there is at present no available evidence that he was involved in the "Conway cabal." In spite of difficulties, Trumbull and Washington cooperated loyally. Without the former's help as a civilian leader the army's sufferings would have been immeasurably increased, and on his death Washington acknowledged that his services "justly entitled him to the first place among patriots" (*Colonial Society of Massachusetts Publications*, vol. VII, 1905, p. 183). In 1846 a newspaper story appeared telling how Washington's reliance upon Trumbull's advice and help had led the General to remark at a moment of perplexity, "We must consult Brother Jonathan." The expression was said to have spread throughout the army and the people until "Brother Jonathan" became a generic term to describe America and Americans. The historical accuracy of the legend must be doubted, however. The British, indeed, used the term "Brother Jonathan" to designate the Americans as early as March 1776, but there is no contemporary evidence to connect Jonathan Trumbull with the origin of the phrase (Albert Matthews, "Brother Jonathan," *Ibid.*, pp. 95–125).

While Trumbull was devoting his energies to the prosecution of the war, he was also facing political difficulties at home. He became the victim of a whispering campaign to the effect that he was secretly trading with the enemy. The rumor helped reduce his popular majority to a mere plurality in the elections of 1780 and 1781, although in both years the Assembly returned him to office over his rivals. In January 1782 he demanded a legislative investigation, which led to his complete vindication, the committee expressing the belief that the rumors were circulated by the British in an effort to discredit a leading patriot. The committee's report quieted the opposition but a year later political storms broke once more. Trumbull's firm belief in the necessity of a stronger central government and his support of the unpopular plan for half pay for disbanded officers brought renewed opposition in May 1783. Again he was chosen only by the Assembly. Wearied by his years of strenuous service and disliking the prospect of further opposition, the old man, just passing his seventy-third birthday, informed the October Assembly that he would not again be a candidate. His *Address . . . Declining Any Further Election to Public Office* (1783), which pled for a federal union stronger politically and financially than the existing government, marks him as a John the Baptist of Federalism. In May 1784 he retired from office and devoted the remaining fifteen months of his life to his long-neglected personal affairs and to the subject of his youthful interest, the study of theology.

Trumbull, as described by a contemporary, was "about five feet, seven inches high, has dark eyes, a Roman nose, sallow countenance, long chin, prominent forehead, high and broad cheek bones, hollow cheeks and short neck. In person of a handsome figure and very active" (Peters, *post*, p. 10). He had little interest in what seemed the lighter things of life. His son John's artistic ambitions gained no sympathy from him and his own election to the American Academy of Arts and Sciences in 1782 would have remained unacknowledged but for the prompting of Ezra Stiles ("Trumbull Papers," IV, 404, 412). For Hebrew, Greek, and Latin, however, he retained a lasting affection. Yale and the University of Edinburgh conferred the degree of LL.D. upon him. A strong sense of duty and of divine leadership was part of his Puritan heritage. Throughout the war, in times of deepest gloom as well as in the hour of final triumph, his letters repeat the thought "the Lord reigneth," which conviction was the unshakable foundation of his faith.

[Sources include Trumbull MSS., Conn. State Lib. and Conn. Hist. Soc., Hartford; "The Trumbull Papers," 4 vols., in *Colls. Mass. Hist. Soc.*, 5 ser. IX and X (1885), 7 ser. II and III (1902); Peter Force, *Am. Archives* (9 vols., 1837–53); Jared Sparks, *The Writings of George Washington* (12 vols., 1834–37); W. C. Ford, *The Writings of George Washington* (14 vols., 1889–93), J. C. Fitzpatrick, *The Writings of George Washington*, vols. I–XI (1931–34); C. J. Hoadly, *The Public Records of the Colony of Conn.*, vols. VII–XV (1873–90), and *The Public Records of the State of Conn., 1776–81* (3 vols., 1894–1922); Zebulon Ely, *The Death of Moses the Servant of the Lord; a Sermon Preached at the Funeral Solemnity of His Excellency Jonathan Trumbull* (1786). I. W. Stuart, *Life of Jonathan Trumbull, Sen., Gov. of Conn.* (1849); Jonathan Trumbull, *Jonathan Trumbull Gov. of Conn., 1769–1784* (1919); Samuel Peters, "Hist. of Jonathan Trumbull, the Present Rebel Governor of Conn.," *Political Mag.*, Jan. 1781. For family connections see J. H. Lea, *Contributions to a Trumbull Geneal.* (1895); *A Geneal. Chart of Some of the Descendants of John Trumbull* (n.d.). Portraits of Trumbull by his son John are in the Gallery of Fine Arts and Trumbull College, Yale University, and in the Wadsworth Athenaeum, Hartford, Conn.]   L. W. L.

TRUMBULL, JONATHAN (Mar. 26, 1740–Aug. 7, 1809), Revolutionary soldier, governor of Connecticut, congressman, and senator, was born in Lebanon, Conn., the son of Jonathan Trumbull [*q.v.*] and his wife Faith (Robinson) Trumbull. At the age of fifteen he entered Harvard College and was graduated in 1759 as salutatorian of his class. Three years later he was awarded the degree of M.A. and delivered the valedictory oration at the commencement exercises. In March 1767 he married Eunice Backus of Norwich, Conn., by whom he had a son and four daughters.

His political career began with his election in 1770 as selectman of Lebanon, an office which he held during the succeeding five years. He also represented Lebanon in the state legislature at various times—in 1774, 1775, 1779, 1780, 1788. In May of the last-mentioned year he was elected speaker of the House. On July 28, 1775, the Continental Congress unanimously chose him "Pay master of the forces for the New York department," an office which he occupied, in the face of grave difficulties arising from an impoverished treasury, until July 29, 1778, when he retired in order to undertake the task of settling the accounts of his brother Joseph [q.v.], commissary-general of the army, who had recently died. He was the first person to serve as comptroller of the treasury, a position to which he was unanimously elected by Congress on Nov. 3, 1778. He resigned in April 1779, and on Nov. 9 was chosen commissioner of the board of treasury but declined the office. On June 8, 1781, he was appointed secretary to Washington and remained a member of the latter's military family until the close of the war, when he retired for a period from public life in order to look after his private affairs.

Upon the erection of the new government under the Constitution, he was elected to the First, Second, and Third congresses. The esteem in which he was held by his fellow legislators is attested by the fact that in October 1791 he was chosen speaker of the House. In October 1794 he was elected to succeed Stephen Mix Mitchell [q.v.] in the Senate of the United States. After serving from Mar. 4, 1795, to June 10, 1796, he resigned in order to become deputy governor of Connecticut. Upon the death of Oliver Wolcott [q.v.] in December 1797, he succeeded to the governorship, an office which he held by annual election during the remainder of his life. Ever a stanch Federalist, he viewed the policies of Jefferson and his followers with repugnance. When Henry Dearborn [q.v.], the secretary of war, requested the use of the militia in conformity with the act passed by Congress on Jan. 9, 1809, for the enforcement of the Embargo, Trumbull refused on the ground that the measure in question was an unconstitutional invasion of the rights of the states. On Feb. 23, in an address (published in the *Connecticut Courant*, Mar. 1, 1809) to the legislature which had been called into special session to consider the situation, he justified the opposition of Connecticut to the Embargo by ironically employing the language of the Virginia Resolves of 1798, of which James Madison, president-elect and heir to Jefferson's

policies, was the author (Henry Adams, *History of the United States*, vol. IV, 1890).

Trumbull died of dropsy of the heart and was buried at Lebanon. While his successes in public life may be ascribed in part to family influence, they were mainly due to his natural capacity for the management of large affairs. In the transaction of business he was orderly and unhurried. A man of cheerful spirit and affable manners, he possessed the gift of easy intercourse with all ranks of society.

[Manuscript correspondence of Trumbull in the Conn. Hist. Soc.; Zebulon Ely, *The Peaceful End of the Perfect Man . . .* (1809); Timothy Dwight, *A Discourse Occasioned by the Death of His Excellency Jonathan Trumbull* (1809); O. D. Hine, *Early Lebanon* (1880); W. C. Ford, *The Writings of George Washington* (14 vols., 1889–93); J. C. Fitzpatrick, *The Writings of George Washington*, vols. I–XI (1931–34); "The Trumbull Papers," *Mass. Hist. Soc. Colls.*, 7 ser. II, III (1902); W. C. Ford and J. C. Fitzpatrick, *Jours. of the Continental Congress*, vols. I–XXXI (1904–34); Jonathan Trumbull, *Jonathan Trumbull, Gov. of Conn., 1764–1784* (1919); E. C. Burnett, *Letters of Members of the Continental Congress*, vols. I–VI (1921–33); R. J. Purcell, *Conn. in Transition* (1918); *Conn. Courant* (Hartford), Aug. 16, 1809.]   E. E. C.

TRUMBULL, JOSEPH (Mar. 11, 1737–July 23, 1778), commissary-general of the Continental Army, was born at Lebanon, Conn., the eldest son of Jonathan Trumbull [q.v.] and his wife, Faith Robinson; the younger Jonathan and the painter John Trumbull [qq.v.] were his brothers. After graduating from Harvard in 1756, he was engaged for eleven years in his father's firm, making two trips to England in behalf of its interests. In 1767 he was elected to the General Assembly of Connecticut and served therein almost continuously for six years. In May 1773 he was chosen a member of the state committee of correspondence, and in August 1774 was selected to represent Connecticut in the Continental Congress as alternate to Roger Sherman [q.v.]. He had in the meantime joined to his knowledge of business affairs some acquaintance with military matters by serving as captain of a trainband. Hence in April 1775 he was appointed by the Assembly commissary-general of the Connecticut troops, concentrated near Boston. His efficiency in provisioning them so favorably impressed Washington that on July 10, 1775, he urged Congress to entrust Trumbull with the task of victualing all the patriot forces, and on July 19 Congress appointed him commissary-general of the army with the rank and pay of colonel.

His problem was to produce order out of the chaos which characterized the business of feeding the army. It was a task fraught with numerous difficulties. Transportation was slow and laborious. Purchasing was hampered by currency depreciation, lack of funds, and state embargoes. Both Congress and the states appointed numerous commissaries who disputed his authority. Such disputes were often intensified by personal and sectional animosities. A court of inquiry appointed by Washington in December 1775 to examine complaints against him found fault with the prices fixed by him for provisions but acquitted him of any fraudulent intent. In 1776 he was drawn into controversy with General Schuyler regarding the right of the commissary-general to exercise plenary control over the provisioning of the northern army. While Trumbull's conduct in the matter was not without blemish, his claim of authority was sustained by both Washington and Congress (J. C. Fitzpatrick, *The Writings of George Washington,* vol. V, 1932, pp. 257, 357-58).

In the spring of 1777 Congress voted to reorganize the commissary department by creating two commissary-generals, one of purchases and the other of issues. Trumbull was offered the former post, but declined it on the ground that the new scheme was unworkable since the deputy commissaries were to be appointed by and made responsible to Congress. Subsequent events seemed to justify his contention, for in the following year Congress reestablished the previous system. In the meantime Trumbull had been elected to membership on the board of war, but after brief service (November 1777-April 1778) was compelled to resign by reason of poor health. Retiring to Lebanon, he succumbed to illness induced by his exhausting labors as commissary-general. While his services to the Continental Army were undramatic, they were indispensable. "Few armies, if any," wrote Washington, "have been better and more plentifully supplied than the troops under Mr. Trumbull's care" (*Ibid.,* V, 192). In March 1777 Trumbull was married to Amelia Dyer.

[Papers of Joseph Trumbull in possession of the Conn. Hist. Soc.; Jonathan Trumbull, "Joseph Trumbull," in *Records and Papers of the New London County Hist. Soc.,* Pt. III, vol. II (1897); C. J. Hoadly, *The Pub. Records of the Colony of Conn.,* vols. XII-XIV (1881-87), and *The Pub. Records of the State of Conn.* (3 vols., 1894-1922); "The Trumbull Papers," in *Mass. Hist. Soc. Colls.,* 7 ser. II (1902); Jonathan Trumbull, *Life of Jonathan Trumbull, Gov. of Conn.* (1919); E. C. Burnett, *Letters of Members of the Continental Cong.,* vols. I-IV (1921-28), and "The Continental Cong. and Agric. Supplies," in *Agric. Hist.,* July 1928.]   E. E. C.

TRUMBULL, LYMAN (Oct. 12, 1813-June 25, 1896), jurist, United States senator, was born in Colchester, Conn., the son of Benjamin and Elizabeth (Mather) Trumbull, and a grandson of Benjamin Trumbull [*q.v.*]. He attended Bacon Academy in his native town, and when twenty years old went to Greenville, Ga., where

he taught school for three years. In the meantime he read law and in 1836 was admitted to the bar. The following year he began practice in Belleville, Ill., and soon entered politics. He was elected to the state legislature as a Democrat in 1840, but resigned in 1841 to accept appointment as secretary of state, in which capacity he served until removed by the governor in 1843. He then practised law and was a candidate for various offices until 1848, when he was elected justice of the state supreme court; in 1852 he was reëlected for a term of nine years.

He had served but two years of this term, however, when he was elected to the United States House of Representatives as an anti-Nebraska Democrat, but before taking his seat a three-cornered legislative contest, in which Lincoln, in order to elect a free-soiler, threw his Whig support to Trumbull, resulted in his being sent to the Senate. The three terms that he served (1855-73) were marked by the bitter struggle over slavery and reconstruction, during which he was first a Democrat, next a leading Republican, and ultimately a supporter of the ill-starred Liberal Republican movement. The failure of this movement left him no haven but the long-deserted Democratic fold. This pilgrimage appears opportunistic, but it was fundamentally dictated by convictions determined by considerations of law as well as of politics.

In the Kansas controversy Trumbull and his colleague, Stephen A. Douglas [*q.v.*], were diametrically opposed in matters of principle. Countering Douglas' proposal to admit Kansas (1856), Trumbull presented a bill uniting Kansas and Nebraska (*Congressional Globe,* 34 Cong., 1 Sess., p. 1369). Both senators opposed the Lecompton constitution, but on differing grounds. Douglas would have the people settle the question of slavery by vote; Trumbull, now a full-fledged Republican, asserted plenary congressional jurisdiction. When secession became an issue, he opposed the Crittenden compromise and supported a resolution declaring that the Constitution was ample in its scope and needed to be obeyed rather than amended—an earnest of his later war-time defense of that much transgressed document.

During the war he was at once Lincoln's able helper and stanch opponent, his attitude being determined by that of the executive toward the Constitution. An authoritative spokesman of the administration, he often tried to school his master in matters of executive propriety. He opposed legalizing Lincoln's extraordinary acts performed while Congress was in recess, saying: "I am disposed to give the necessary power to the

Administration to suppress this rebellion; but I am not disposed to say that the Administration has unlimited power and can do what it pleases, after Congress meets" (*Congressional Globe,* 37 Cong., 1 Sess., p. 392). In introducing his radical confiscation bill (December 1861) he declared that he wanted "no other authority for putting down even this gigantic rebellion than such as may be derived from the Constitution properly interpreted." He would suppress the "monstrous rebellion according to law, and in no other way" (*Ibid.,* 2 Sess., p. 18). He censured the method, but not the motive, of Lincoln's arbitrary arrests and led the movement which, while indemnifying the President for previous suspensions of the writ of *habeas corpus,* regulated further suspensions. In 1864, as chairman of the judiciary committee, he introduced the resolution which became the basis of the thirteenth amendment to the Constitution. When the first state sought admission under Lincolnian reconstruction he was the President's agent, but was foiled by Sumner and the Democrats.

Trumbull's powerful personal and committee influence aided the Radicals in the early stages of the fight with Johnson. His bill to enlarge the powers of the Freedmen's Bureau failed to pass over the veto. The veto of his civil rights bill, designed to give effect to the thirteenth amendment, alienated him from the Administration after a period of patient tolerance and dignified expostulation. He urged its repassage to offset the actions of the executive, and spoke of "the spirit of this message, of the dangerous doctrines it promulgates, of the inconsistencies and contradictions of its author, of his encroachments upon the constitutional rights of Congress, of his assumption of unwarranted powers, which, if persevered in and not checked by the people, must eventually lead to a subversion of the Government and the destruction of liberty" (*Ibid.,* 39 Cong., 1 Sess., p. 1760). These episodes mark an opposition which lasted until the impeachment furor. They also presage his departure from the leadership of radicalism. His decreasing activity in the Stevens-Sumner program was followed, as this group insisted on more and more humble submission of the rebel states, by participation with the moderates who attempted rather ineffectually to check the Radicals. Again, his was a legal criterion; he was one who was "willing to be radical lawfully" rather than one "who would rather be radical than right" (*Chicago Tribune,* May 26, 1870). This viewpoint drove him to oppose the impeachment proceedings and he was one of the famous seven who saved Johnson from conviction. This heresy,

together with his reconstruction attitude, lost him Republican leadership. The excesses of the Grant administration drove him into the Liberal Republican movement. He was among those suggested for the presidential nomination, but loyally stumped several states for Greeley. After the movement collapsed he finished his senatorial term and then retired to Chicago, where he practised law.

His appearance as counsel for the Tilden side in the disputed election of 1876 marked his return to the Democratic fold and he was that party's unsuccessful candidate for the governorship of Illinois in 1880. His last political excursion found him skirting the edges of Populism; in 1894 he drafted a platform which Chicago Populists took to a national conference in St. Louis. His death removed one of the ablest statesmen of his generation, an unpretentious, scholarly constitutionalist, who failed to scale political heights because of a conscience and a lack of popular appeal. The conscience drove him from party to party seeking a place where he could abide, and his colorless public personality denied him the kind of support on which spectacular careers are built. He was twice married: first, June 21, 1843, to Julia Maria Jayne, who died in August 1868; and second, Nov. 3, 1877, to Mary Ingraham; three sons by his first wife survived him.

[Trumbull Papers, Lib. of Cong.; Horace White, *The Life of Lyman Trumbull* (1913); A. H. Robertson, "The Political Career of Lyman Trumbull" (1910), M. A. thesis, Univ. of Chicago; L. E. Ellis, "A Hist. of the Chicago Delegation in Cong., 1843–1925," *Trans. Ill. State Hist. Soc.,* 1930; E. D. Ross, *The Liberal Republican Movement* (1919); *Chicago Tribune,* June 26, 1896.]
         L. E. E.

TRUTEAU, JEAN BAPTISTE (Dec. 11, 1748–Jan. 30?, 1827), Indian trader, explorer, school-master, was born in Montreal, Canada, the son of Joseph and Catherine (Menard) Truteau. He always spelled the name Truteau but was generally referred to as Trudeau. His own children adopted this corrupt spelling. He established himself as school-master of the village of St. Louis in 1774 and continued to teach for more than forty years. In June 1794 he was engaged by the Missouri Trading Company for a term of three years to take charge of an exploring expedition under the direction of Jacques Clamorgan and Antoine Reihle. This company was organized in that year by some St. Louis merchants under the advice of Zenon Trudeau, the Spanish lieutenant-governor, who took a great interest in the exploration of the Upper Missouri country and the expansion of the fur trade. The avowed object was to exploit the fur trade of the Upper Missouri and to penetrate the sources of the Missouri River, and "beyond to the Southern Ocean," a term applied in that day to the Pacific Ocean. The instructions given to Truteau, approved by the governor, directed him to keep a record of all that should come under his observation. Accordingly, Truteau began his journal June 7, 1794, the day of his departure. It was in two parts, the first to Mar. 26, 1795 (in *American Historical Review*, Jan. 1914), and the second from May 24, 1795, to July 20, 1795 (in *Missouri Historical Society Collections*, vol. IV, 1912, with biographical sketch). This journal came to the attention of Thomas Jefferson, who sent extracts from it to Capt. Meriwether Lewis on Nov. 16, 1803, and on Jan. 22, 1804, a translation of the whole journal. Truteau's journal proved a valuable contribution to the knowledge of the Upper Missouri and its tribes of Indians, especially applicable to the years 1794 and 1795. The expedition, however, was not a profitable venture on account of desertions, jealousies, and lack of confidence in Jacques Clamorgan, who was one of the most active among the organizers.

He was at home in 1798, and the following year Governor Trudeau made a gift of a mortgage debt on Truteau's dwelling, amounting to four hundred dollars, to the school-master's two sons, "under grateful acknowledgments . . . for having educated my numerous family and for many favors." This dwelling was a stone house known as 18 and 20 North Main Street in St. Louis. Governor Trudeau described the schoolmaster as his kinsman. Jean Baptiste Truteau was a man of importance in the village of St. Louis, and his name appeared in public documents of the time with many of the principal citizens. A subscription list of "well-to-do people," making patriotic gifts to aid Spain in war, mentions his name. He was married on May 1, 1781, to Madeleine Le Roy, the widow of François Herbert dit Bellhomme and the daughter of Julien and Marie (Saucier) Le Roy. They had five children. He died in the neighboring village of St. Louis and was buried in Carondelet.

[Cyprien Tanguay, *Dictionnaire Généalogique des Familles Canadiennes,* vol. VII (1890), p. 377; St. Louis Cathedral marriage and burial registers; Trudeau letters in possession of Mo. Hist. Soc.; journals, *ante*; Louis Houck, *A Hist. of Mo.* (1908), vol. II and *Spanish Regime in Mo.* (1909), vols. I–II; "Trudeau's Journ.," in *S. D. Hist. Colls.,* vol. VII (1914); "Trudeau's Description of the Upper Missouri," in *Miss. Valley Hist. Rev.,* July, Sept. 1921; *Original Journals of the Lewis and Clark Expedition,* vol. VII (1905), ed. by R. G. Thwaites.]   S.M.D.

TRUXTUN, THOMAS (Feb. 17, 1755–May 5, 1822), naval officer, was born near Hemp-stead, Long Island, the son of Thomas **and Sarah** (Axtell or Axtill) Truxtun. His father was an English barrister practising in New York, and an incorporator of Grace Church, Jamaica, L. I. The son in 1761 attended the Rev. Samuel Seabury's school at Hempstead. After his father's death about 1765, he came under the guardianship of his father's executor, John Troup of Jamaica, and at twelve went to sea, sailing under Capt. Joseph Holmes and later Capt. James Chambers in the London trade. At fifteen he was impressed and served briefly in H.M.S. *Prudent,* attracting the attention of the commander, who noted his abilities and offered him aid in advancement. He obtained his release, however, and, reëntering the merchant service, was at twenty a ship commander. In 1775 he brought a powder shipment to the colonies, and later that year he was captured with his vessel and cargo in the West Indies.

Subsequently, in the Revolution, he became an ardent privateersman, serving as lieutenant in the *Congress,* and then in command successively of the *Independence,* 10, which in 1777 captured a sugar ship of sixteen guns and other prizes; of the *Mars,* 24, which aroused British protests by sending into French ports prizes taken in the Channel; of the *Independence* again in 1780, in which at L'Orient he was reprimanded by John Paul Jones for flying "a kind of broad pennant"; and of the *St. James,* 20, which in 1781–82 sailed for France after beating off a 32-gun British blockader. The *St. James* brought back the most valuable cargo entered at Philadelphia during the Revolution, and Washington, at a dinner in Truxtun's honor, declared his services worth a regiment. He was master or part owner of other privateers (Naval Records of the American Revolution, MSS., Library of Congress), and in 1780 paid taxes in Philadelphia on $15,200 (*Pennsylvania Archives,* 3 ser. XV, 1897, p. 210).

After the war he returned to commerce, making many voyages and taking out the first Philadelphia ship to China, the *Canton,* in 1786. In June 1794 he was made a captain in the new American navy, ranking fifth among the six captains then appointed. In this year he published *Remarks, Instructions, and Examples Relating to Latitude and Longitude,* together with a chart of his voyages showing favorable routes, a treatise on winds and currents, and appendices on the masting of warships and the duties of naval officers. Three years later he published *Instructions, Signals, and Explanations Offered for the U. S. Fleet* (1797), and in 1806, *A Few Extracts from the Best Authors on Naval Tac-*

tics; all of these evidence a keen mind and high professional attainments. In June 1798 at the outbreak of naval warfare with France, he sailed in the frigate *Constellation,* whose construction he had supervised in Baltimore, and after two short cruises commanded a squadron consisting of the *Constellation* and four smaller vessels stationed between St. Christopher and Puerto Rico. In these waters, Feb. 9, 1799, he won the first of his two celebrated victories, capturing after an hour's fighting the French frigate *Insurgente.* His return home in May was greeted with general acclamation. "I wish," wrote President Adams (*Works,* VIII, 636), "all the other officers had as much zeal." Though in August the restoration of two former captains, Silas Talbot and Richard Dale [*qq.v.*], with senior rank, angered Truxtun to the point of resignation, he was persuaded to continue in the service, and in December sailed in the *Constellation* for his former station, with his command increased to ten vessels. On the night of Feb. 1–2, 1800, after an all-day chase, occurred his battle with *La Vengeance,* lasting from 8 P.M. to 1 A.M. Reversing the odds of the *Insurgente* action, the *Vengeance* had a broadside of 555 pounds to the *Constellation's* 372. After "one of the warmest combats between frigates that is on record" (Cooper, *post,* I, 354), the guns of the *Vengeance* were completely silenced, but as Truxtun was about to board his mainmast was carried away and the enemy escaped in the darkness. The *Constellation,* after repairs at Jamaica, returned late in March to Norfolk. For his hard-fought action Truxtun received the thanks of Congress and a gold medal, and in popular regard he became unquestionably the hero of the war.

After commanding the *President* during the last months of hostilities, he retired to his home at Perth Amboy, N. J., opposite the governor's mansion. A visitor at this time described him as suffering from gout: "Hercules at his distaff and Achilles in female attire were not stranger figures, than the brave commodore, sitting at his desk, penning his instructions for the American Navy, arrayed in his uniform coat, cocked hat and cockade, a flannel petticoat in place of breeches, and his feet rolled up in pieces of the same texture." The visitor added: "But he is now about to leave us, perhaps forever, and as he rises in his wrath, let the Bey [*sic*] of Algiers and all perfidious pirates tremble" ("A Colonial Capital," *Proceedings of the New Jersey Historical Society,* 4 ser. III, 1918, p. 15). The new assignment to which the visitor referred, in the spring of 1801, was to the *Chesapeake* at Norfolk, to command the second squadron

against Tripoli. But the new Jefferson administration, hostile politically, refused Truxtun a captain for his flagship, and construed his consequent withdrawal from the command as resignation from the navy. The loss to the country was serious, for Truxtun was only forty-seven, and his positive, energetic character would have animated the Tripolitan campaign. His fighting spirit and rigid discipline, however, had already set excellent standards for the young navy. He lived for four or five years after his retirement at Perth Amboy, and later in Philadelphia. In 1806 he was approached by Aaron Burr [*q.v.*] with offers of a naval command in connection with Burr's projected western state, but he declined on discovering Burr's schemes to be unsanctioned by the President. He was prominent in Philadelphia politics, a leader in the agitation of 1809 against the Embargo, unsuccessful Federalist candidate for Congress in 1810, and sheriff of Philadelphia, 1816–19. He was married, May 27, 1775, to Mary Fundran (probably anglicized from Vaudreuil or Von Drieull) of Perth Amboy, and had two sons and eleven daughters. He was buried in Christ Church yard, Philadelphia. William Talbot Truxtun [*q.v.*] was his grandson.

[For parentage, etc., see "Records of St. George's Church, Hempstead, L. I.," *N. Y. Geneal. and Biog. Record,* July 1881, p. 145; Henry Onderdonk, *Antiquities of the Parish Church, Jamaica, L. I.* (1880); "Abstract of Wills, N. Y., 1760–66," *N. Y. Hist. Soc. Colls., 1897* (1898), p. 421. Truxtun's biography appeared first in Isaac Bailey, *Am. Naval Biog.* (1815), and was included with slight additions in the later compilations of Frost and Peterson; see also J. F. Cooper, *Hist. of the Navy of the U. S.* (1839), esp. I, 354; G. W. Allen, *Our Naval War with France* (1909), containing references to manuscript sources; S. S. Robison, "Commodore Thomas Truxtun, U. S. Navy," *Proc. U. S. Naval Inst.,* Apr. 1932; Truxtun Papers (1798–1800) in Hist. Soc. of Pa., Phila.; Letters to Officers, vols. I–V (1794–98) and other papers in Navy Dept. Lib.; *The Works of John Adams,* vols. VIII (1853), IX (1854); *The Works of Alexander Hamilton* (1851), vols. V, VI; S. H. Wandell and Meade Minnigerode, *Aaron Burr* (2 vols., 1925); James Parton, *The Life and Times of Aaron Burr* (1886), II, 141; J. T. Scharf and Thompson Westcott, *Hist. of Phila.* (1884), vol. I: *Poulson's Am. Daily Advertiser* (Phila.), May 7, 1822.]
                                                    A. W—t.

TRUXTUN, WILLIAM TALBOT (Mar. 11, 1824–Feb. 25, 1887), naval officer, was born in Philadelphia, Pa., grandson of Commodore Thomas Truxtun [*q.v.*], and only son of William Truxtun by his marriage to Isabelle Shute Martin of South Carolina. His father was a naval lieutenant who died at Key West in 1830. The son became a midshipman on Feb. 9, 1841, and his early service at sea was in the *Dolphin* and *Falmouth* of the Home Squadron. He next cruised in the brig *Truxtun* on the African coast, in the suppression of the slave trade, and after six months at the newly established Naval Academy was made passed midshipman, Aug. 10, 1847. In 1847–48 he was on the Brazil station, and came home as prize-master of the former slaveship *Independence,* captured off Rio. After three years in the Pacific, he served on board the *Dolphin* in 1853 in soundings for the first Atlantic cable, and in 1854 in the Strain expedition, surveying the Isthmus of Darien for a canal route. Only his iron constitution carried him through the hardships of this latter duty in the tropics, which is believed to have caused some permanent injury to his health.

After the outbreak of the Civil War, he was assigned in June 1861 as executive of the sailing sloop-of-war *Dale* in the North Atlantic Blockading Squadron, and subsequently commanded her on the southeast coast blockade, being senior officer during the summer of 1862 in St. Helena Sound, S. C. Made lieutenant commander July 16, 1862, he commanded the *Chocura* from October 1862 to November 1863, chiefly on the Wilmington blockade, and thereafter the gunboat *Tacony* until the close of the war. The *Tacony* operated in the North Carolina sounds during the summer of 1864, took part in an hour's sharp action with batteries at Plymouth, N. C., Oct. 31, 1864, before its occupation, and was engaged in Admiral Porter's squadron in both attacks on Fort Fisher, December 1864 and January 1865. Porter in a letter to Truxtun (Feb. 18, 1865) remarked: "There has been no other officer in this squadron in whom I have more confidence or for whom I have a higher respect" (*Official Records, post,* XI, 473).

His post-bellum service included duty as superintendent of naval coal shipments, 1866–67; in command of the *Jamestown,* North Pacific Squadron, 1868–70; in command of the *Brooklyn* in the North and South Atlantic, 1873–75; and at the Boston and Norfolk navy yards, 1876–80. Thereafter he had special duty on the Norfolk harbor commission, and from 1885 until his retirement he commanded the Norfolk yard. He was commissioned commodore May 1, 1882, and was nominated for rear admiral in February 1886, but he had aroused some political opposition during his navy-yard administration, and his promotion was delayed until prevented by his retirement for age Mar. 11, 1886. Truxtun was popular at Norfolk, where he had made his home for a considerable period and identified himself with commercial and social interests, and his funeral in Christ Church was described as the most imposing and largely attended in that city since the war. He was twice married: first, Oct. 15, 1856, to Annie Elizabeth, daughter of John E. Scott of Philadelphia, who died in 1873; and second, Sept. 2, 1875, to Mary Calvert Walke of Norfolk. There were three children of the first marriage, and five of the second; one of the sons, William, became a lieutenant commander in the navy and died in 1905.

[L. R. Hamersly, *The Records of Living Officers of the U. S. Navy and Marine Corps* (4th ed., 1890); *War of the Rebellion: Official Records* (*Navy*), see Index; W. H. Powell and Edward Shippen, *Officers of the Army and Navy Who Served in the Civil War* (1892); *The Virginian* (Norfolk), and the *Norfolk Landmark,* Feb. 26, 1887; *Army and Navy Journal,* Mar. 12, 1887; other material from family sources.]   A. W—t.

TRYON, DWIGHT WILLIAM (Aug. 13, 1849–July 1, 1925), landscape painter, was born at Hartford, Conn. His mother was Delia O. (Roberts) Tryon. His father, Anson Tryon, the descendant of New England artisan stock, died in Dwight's infancy, and the boy came up in narrow circumstances with only a common-school education. From early childhood he drew and drew well. At fifteen he became clerk and bookkeeper for Brown & Gross, booksellers, at Hartford. The work brought before him handsomely illustrated books, among them some with illustrations after Turner, for whom he conceived an admiration that was to be life long. To the shop came such notables as Horace Bushnell, Samuel L. Clemens (Mark Twain), Harriet Beecher Stowe [*qq.v.*], all of whom Tryon came to know. Meanwhile he began to paint in such spare moments as his work in the book store permitted. Thus he had to cultivate the useful habit of working much from memory. His mother was custodian of the Wadsworth Athenaeum, where hung impressive landscapes by Thomas Cole and Frederick Edwin Church [*qq.v.*]. At twenty-one Tryon sold his first picture. About this time he considered studying medicine, and his reading to this end grounded him in anatomy. In 1872 he exhibited, at the National Academy of Design in New York, a picture that was bought by the dealer Samuel Putnam Avery [*q.v.*]. In 1873 he married Alice H. Belden and, against the advice of "Mark Twain" and others of his notable acquaintances, set up a studio at Hartford. His support was giving lessons—as was to be the case all his life—but he soon began to sell his pictures. His first really notable picture, "Clay Cliffs, Block Island," painted for the Centennial Exhibition of 1876 in Philadelphia, is a stately affair executed rather tightly in the manner of such older contemporaries as John Frederick Kensett or William Trost Richards [*qq.v.*], but in every way a remarkable performance for a self-trained artist of twenty-seven.

Feeling the defects of such training, at the

end of 1876, having auctioned off his pictures and effects for $2,000, he sailed for Paris. Living with his young wife, he escaped the usual Bohemian contacts. Nothing better showed his ever stoical perception of what concerned himself than his disregard of the new Impressionism and his avoidance of the big popular ateliers in favor of the small private class of that austere disciple of Ingres, Jacquesson de la Chevreuse. From him Tryon learned a sound but unassertive construction, methods always thoughtful, restrained and highly selective, much dependence on delicately modulated edges—precision and refinement in all things. Among French landscapists he knew Daubigny well, and Harpignies slightly, while he deeply valued the advice of J. B. A. Guillemet. There were summers in Brittany and Normandy, excursions to Holland and Venice, all productive of pictures in his new mature manner—notable among these "The River Maas," at Smith College and three pictures he showed at the Salon of 1881. The $2,-000 ran out in five years; so at thirty-two, in 1881, he returned to America, took a studio in New York, and after a couple of years settled for good on the harbor of South Dartmouth, often called Padanaram, near New Bedford. He was soon successful as a teacher in New York, and in 1885 he was appointed visiting professor of art at Smith College. This position he held for thirty-eight years. Honors followed him. In 1882 he was elected to the Society of American Artists; in 1890 made an associate of the National Academy and next year a member. In America and Europe he received no less than eighteen medals or awards.

Secure financially through his teaching, he painted rather few pictures, took infinite pains with them, always sold them well, and through saving and prudent investment gradually built up a handsome fortune. In 1889 Charles Lang Freer [q.v.], the collector, bought from Tryon that exquisite and eventually much medaled picture, "The Rising Moon." It was the harbinger of some forty Tryons that are preserved in the Freer Gallery at Washington. The relation between artist and patron soon ripened into friendship. Tryon did four big landscape decorations, "The Seasons," for Freer's house at Detroit, and in a modest way he followed Freer's example as a fastidious and enthusiastic collector. The preciousness that characterized Tryon's taste and art was reflected neither in his manner of life nor yet in his personal appearance. The months from April to November he spent at Padanaram, fishing and sailing on the lumpy waters of Buzzards Bay, in admirable little boats of his own

design. The remaining six months, at New York, were passed in teaching and a carefully restricted output of painting. Never quite a recluse, he was always most at ease in rustic company, avoiding general social relations, and disregarding freely the conventions of speech and dress. His aspect was that of a Yankee sailor—bronzed and wrinkled by the sun and wind, with steady blue eyes shading to brown, and an undersized but stocky and powerful frame that tipped the scales at 140 pounds.

His art is on the whole crepuscular. He loved the moments at dusk when infinitesimal differences of tone retain and assert pensively the almost lost definition of objects about to disappear. The foreground is generally deep, the interest lies in a few well chosen and placed forms—trees or farm houses in far middle distance—with skies thinly veiled and saturated with faint light. His exquisiteness carries with it a certain thinness and monotony, yet one cannot comprise with such words a performance that won the admiration of Homer D. Martin and Whistler. In technique Tryon was highly experimental and ingenious. For greater durability he preferred to canvas a carefully made ply board; in his latter years he painted on a white ground; his underpainting was generally bold and highly colorful. After scraping down and over-painting, something of the underlying richness qualified the apparent monochrome. He made curious and successful ventures in heavily loaded and permanently fixed pastels. Practising an art rather of taste and reflection than of vigorous imagination, his place is not with our greater landscapists. Among those of second order he is surely one of the most accomplished.

His powerful frame broke rather suddenly. He had tramped the woods, sailed a canoe from New York to New Bedford, shipped on fishing smacks. In his early seventies he still took the *Skat,* the little catboat that he had designed himself, single-handed about Buzzards Bay. At seventy-five cancer of the stomach developed, and the next year he died. Two years earlier he had provided for the art museum at Smith College. It was completed only after his death, and after that of his wife, four years later, it received a handsome endowment.

[C. H. Caffin, *The Art of Dwight W. Tryon. An Appreciation,* privately printed (1909), with excellent illustrations; H. C. White, *The Life and Art of Dwight William Tryon* (1930); F. F. Sherman, *Am. Painters of Yesterday and Today* (1919); *Smith Alumnae Quart.,* Nov. 1925; *Who's Who in America,* 1924–25; *N. Y. Times,* July 2, 12, 19, 22, 1925.]   F. J. M., Jr.

TRYON, GEORGE WASHINGTON (May 20, 1838–Feb. 5, 1888), conchologist, was born in Philadelphia, the eldest son of Edward K. and Adeline (Savidt) Tryon. He was named for his grandfather, a gunsmith. After passing through several private schools, he entered the Friends' Central School in 1850, completing a three years' course in June 1853. Soon afterward he studied French, German, and music with private tutors, thus completing his formal education. Edward K. Tryon had carried on successfully the well-established business of manufacturing and selling firearms and sportsman's accoutrements which he had inherited from his father, and in due course his son succeeded him. The younger George Washington Tryon, however, retired from business about 1868 with a modest sum, sufficient in his estimation to justify unrestrained pursuit of science and letters.

Tryon began when he was seven years old to collect natural history specimens, especially shells of mollusks, which were favorites from the start. Orderliness was one of the child's notable mental qualities and even before his undeveloped mind could grasp the meaning of taxonomy he arranged his specimens according to an original system. In 1859, at the age of twenty-one, he was elected a member of the Academy of Natural Sciences of Philadelphia, and from that time until his death in 1888 he was active in promoting its welfare. Largely through his efforts a new building was erected. In 1866 the conchological section of the Academy was formed and under its auspices large collections were gathered, including Tryon's own private collection which numbered more than 10,000 species. At the time of his death, the section had one of the largest and most complete collections of Mollusca in the world. Tryon was a curator of the Academy from 1869 to 1876 and conservator of the conchological section from 1875 until his death.

His first paper on conchology, "On the Mollusca of Harper's Ferry, Virginia," was presented in 1861 (*Proceedings of the Academy of Natural Sciences of Philadelphia*, 2 ser. V, 1862), and subsequently more than seventy papers on land, freshwater, and marine mollusks came from his pen. Among his contributions were *A Monograph of the Terrestrial Mollusca Inhabiting the United States* (1866); *A Monograph of the Freshwater Univalve Mollusca of the United States* (*In Continuation of Prof. S. S. Haldeman's Work . . .*), with a preface dated 1870; Part IV, "Strepomatidae" (1873), of W. G. Binney's *Land and Fresh Water Shells of North America* (4 vols., 1865–73); and *Structural and Systematic Conchology* (3 vols., 1882–84). He also edited and published the *American Journal of Conchology* from 1865 to 1872. His

chief work, however, was his *Manual of Conchology, Structural and Systematic, with Illustrations of the Species,* in which it was designed to describe and figure all of the living species of the Mollusca known to science. The first volume appeared in 1879. Of the first series on the marine shells, nine volumes had been completed and of the second series, the land shells, three volumes had been issued at the time of his death. Fortunately for the science of malacology, the work was continued under Dr. Henry A. Pilsbry.

Tryon was very fond of music and made an effort to spread a love of music among the people and to elevate popular taste. To this end he arranged a series of songs for amateur singers. He also edited and published librettos of more than fifty standard operas and himself wrote an unsuccessful comic opera, *Amy Cassonet or the Elopement,* published in 1875. Interested likewise in art, he occasionally painted for his own pleasure. He twice visited Europe, in 1874 and 1877, publishing an account of the earlier trip in *The Amateur Abroad* (1875). Tryon was a bachelor, of a quiet, frank, and unpretentious disposition. He was a member of the Society of Friends for a number of years and later attended the services of the Unitarian Church of Philadelphia.

[*Conchologists' Exchange,* Mar.–Apr. 1888, reprinting article from *Public Ledger* (Phila.), Feb. 7, 1888; *Am. Naturalist,* Mar. 1888; W. S. W. Ruschenberger, "A Biog. Notice of George W. Tryon, Jr.," in *Proc. Acad. Nat. Sci. of Phila.,* 3 ser. XVIII (1889), and separately reprinted.]   F. C. B.

TRYON, WILLIAM (1729–Jan. 27, 1788), colonial governor, was born at "Norbury Park," Surrey, England, the son of Charles Tryon of "Bulwick," Northamptonshire, and Lady Mary Tryon, the daughter of Robert Shirley, the first Earl Ferrers. He was commissioned lieutenant in the 1st Regiment of Foot Guards in 1751 and promoted to be captain with army rank of lieutenant-colonel seven years later. Marriage with Margaret Wake of London in 1757 brought him control of an estate of £30,000 and, in 1764, probably through her connection with Lord Hillsborough, appointment as lieutenant-governor of North Carolina. Upon the death of the governor, Arthur Dobbs, in March 1765, Tryon took command of the province and a few months later was commissioned governor. In his long service in America he was faced with one difficulty after another which his military background hardly prepared him to handle in a pacific spirit. During the Stamp Act controversy he actively supported the customs and naval officers in their refusal to permit the entrance and clearance of vessels whose papers lacked the required stamps. Commerce in the Cape Fear region came to a standstill. When the inhabitants intimidated the officers into abandoning their policy, he was helpless and hinted at the need of British troops.

Disturbances of a different origin soon gave him an opportunity for more forceful action. The movement known as the Regulation developed in the frontier counties largely because of inadequate currency, inequitable taxation, and the greed of officials. The governor was not altogether deaf to the grievances of the Regulators and urged a few reforms. But some of the accused officials, especially Edmund Fanning [q.v.], the register of Orange County, were his personal friends, and he answered the riotous demonstrations of the Hillsboro mob in 1768 by leading a force of militia into the disaffected region to restore order. Conditions grew no better, and in September 1770 the Regulators broke up the superior court at Hillsboro and severely mishandled several officials and lawyers. Under a drastic riot act the ringleaders were indicted and outlawed, and in the following March the governor again organized an armed force. His column, consisting of about 1,100 militia, met some 2,000 Regulators at the Alamance on May 16, 1771, and inflicted a crushing defeat upon them. While still on this campaign, he received word of his transfer to New York to replace Lord Dunmore, who was going to Virginia. Tryon, who had long sought the change, left his troops still engaged in the work of pacification and sailed to New York in July. Although marred by the violence of its close, his administration had been on the whole successful. He was responsible for establishing the provincial capital at New Bern and the erection there of an executive residence, "Tryon's Palace," one of the finest buildings in colonial America. His negotiations with the Cherokee had led to the establishment of a satisfactory boundary. Personally he was popular in the eastern counties, and his departure was witnessed with regret.

In New York he was again beset with frontier disturbances, the result of conflicting grants by New York and New Hampshire, within the present state of Vermont. The violent actions of Ethan Allen and his followers led the governor to seek the use of British regulars, but his request was denied by General Haldimand. Difficulties also arose over the purchase of large tracts of lands from the Indians in the Mohawk Valley, an operation in which the governor was personally interested to the extent of 40,000 acres. To consult on these problems, he was finally summoned to England. Leaving New York in April 1774 he did not return until fourteen months later, after the commencement of the Revolution. In October 1775, fearing for his personal safety, he took refuge on board ship in New York harbor, where he remained until the landing of Lord Howe's troops in August 1776. Wartime conditions prevented the restoration of his civil functions, although he busied himself in administering the oath of allegiance to all available Loyalists. Yet he was essentially a military man and longed for a more active part in the war. He had been advanced to the rank of colonel in 1772 and in 1777 obtained permission to command a force of Loyalists. He was promoted to the rank of major-general in America in 1778 and made colonel of the 70th Foot. His chief military activities consisted in a series of raids upon Connecticut, which succeeded well in their purpose of destroying supplies and diverting some of Connecticut's energies from support of Washington's army to home defense. As the war continued, Tryon's vindictive spirit mounted. He frankly expressed a wish to "burn every Committee Man's house within my reach" (O'Callaghan, post, VIII, 736), and Sir Henry Clinton was said to have privately disapproved the extremes to which he carried his acts of retaliation (Dartmouth MSS., post, Eleventh Report, p. 423). In 1780 illness, which had frequently incapacitated him throughout his American career, compelled his return to England. Although promoted lieutenant-general in 1782 and made colonel of the 29th Foot the next year, his active career was over. He died at his London home and was buried in the family tomb at Twickenham.

Against Tryon's proneness to settle disputes with force must be set the fact that he achieved a very real popularity with most of those with whom he came in personal contact. He was a stanch supporter of the established church and gave active encouragement to education. His inquiring mind led him to make extensive tours through both his provinces. He was intensely loyal to the crown but always expected rewards for his faithful services—the suppression of the Regulators was, he thought, worth at least a baronetcy. The conflicting qualities of his nature were well summed up by an unfriendly Loyalist in New York who wrote of him as "the pink of politeness, and the quintessence of vanity. . . . The man is generous, perfectly good-natured, and no doubt brave, but weak and vain to an extreme degree. You should keep such people at home; they are excellent for a Court parade" (Colonial Records of North Carolina, post, vol. VIII, p. xxxix).

[*The Colonial Records of N. C.,* vols. VII, VIII (1890); *Documents Relative to the Colonial Hist. of the State of New-York,* VIII (1857), ed. by E. B. O'Callaghan; "The MSS. of the Earl of Dartmouth," *Great Britain. Hist. MSS. Commission Eleventh Report,* app. pt. 5 (1887), *Fourteenth Report,* app. pt. 10 (1895); *Gentleman's Mag.,* Dec. 1757, p. 577, Feb. 1788, p. 179; *Army Lists, 1755–1783;* R. D. W. Connor, *Hist. of N. C.,* vol. I (1919); J. S. Bassett, "The Regulators of North Carolina," *Amer. Hist. Assn. Report . . . 1894* (1895); M. D. Haywood, *Gov. William Tryon and his Administration of the Province of N. C.* (1903); Lorenzo Sabine, *Biog. Sketches of Loyalists of the Amer. Rev.,* new ed. (1864), vol. II. The date for birth given in this sketch is taken from copy of epitaph in Haywood, *ante,* and for death *Ibid.,* and from *Gentleman's Mag., ante,* although the *D. N. B.* gives birth-date as 1725 and death-date as Dec. 27, 1788.]
L. W. L.

TSCHERINOFF, MARIE VAN ZANDT [See VAN ZANDT, MARIE, 1858–1919].

TUBMAN, HARRIET (*c.* 1821–Mar. 10, 1913), fugitive slave, abolitionist, was born in Dorchester County on the Eastern Shore of Maryland, the daughter of Benjamin Ross and Harriet Greene, both slaves. She was first named Araminta, but early assumed the name Harriet. In childhood she received a head injury to which have been attributed spells of somnolence which overtook her without warning at intervals during the rest of her life. From her early teens she worked as a field hand—plowing, loading and unloading wood—an activity which developed in her great strength and remarkable powers of endurance. In 1844, her master forced her to marry a man named John Tubman who was unfaithful to her. Much later she married a man named Nelson Davis. About 1849 she made her escape from slavery, guided in her flight only by the north star. It was not long afterwards that she became one of the most conspicuous figures in the work of the "Underground Railroad," winning the appellation "Moses" by leading, in all, more than three hundred slaves from bondage to freedom in the North and Canada.

From the time of her escape until the beginning of the Civil War she was busy making journeys into the South to lead out slaves. An important "station" on one of her routes was the home of the Quaker Thomas Garrett [*q.v.*] of Wilmington, Del., who gave her all the help within his power. Between her journeys she worked as a cook in order to raise the money she needed to aid the fugitives. In 1857 she rescued her own parents, who were very old, and settled them in Auburn, N. Y., on a little tract of land purchased from William H. Seward. Although she could neither read nor write, her shrewdness in planning hazardous enterprises and skill in avoiding arrest were phenomenal. When rescu-

ing a group of slaves, she enforced a rule which she herself had laid down, threatening with death any passenger who thought of surrender or attempted to return. She seemed absolutely fearless and was willing to endure any hardship. To a remarkable degree she was guided in her work by visions and sustained by her faith in God. John Brown, who met her in Canada and subsequently referred to her as "General" Tubman, confided in her and relied on her for assistance in his campaign against slavery in Virginia. She was well known in the office of the *National Anti-Slavery Standard* in New York and in abolition circles in Boston and from time to time was presented as a speaker at anti-slavery meetings. After the outbreak of the Civil War she was sent to Gen. David Hunter in South Carolina with a letter from Governor Andrew of Massachusetts and attached herself to the Union army, working as cook, laundress, and nurse; frequently acting as guide in scouting parties and raids; and rendering noteworthy service as a spy within the Confederate lines.

After the war Harriet continued to labor for her people. For a time she was concerned with an attempt to establish schools for freedmen in North Carolina. She was able to finish paying for her home in Auburn with the proceeds of a little book, *Scenes in the Life of Harriet Tubman* (1869), written for her benefit by Mrs. Sarah Hopkins Bradford and published through the generosity of Gerrit Smith, Wendell Phillips [*qq.v.*], and certain Auburn neighbors. Here in her own home she supported several children and penniless old people, being further aided by the proceeds of a revised edition of Mrs. Bradford's book, *Harriet the Moses of Her People* (1886). The Harriet Tubman Home for indigent aged negroes continued to exist for a number of years after her death, and the citizens of Auburn erected a shaft in her memory.

[S. H. Bradford, *Harriet the Moses of Her People,* which was reprinted in 1901, contains reminiscences and testimonials from all the prominent Abolitionists mentioned above, a number of the Union officers under whom Harriet served, and others. See also P. E. Hopkins, "Harriet Tubman (Moses)," *Colored American Mag.,* Jan.–Feb. 1902; *Freedmen's Record,* Mar. 1865; Lillie B. C. Wyman, "Harriet Tubman," *New England Mag.,* Mar. 1896; *American Mag.,* Aug. 1912; W. H. Siebert, *The Underground Railroad* (1898); H. H. Swift, *The Railroad to Freedom* (1932); *Albany Evening Jour.,* Mar. 11, 1913; *N. Y. Times,* Mar. 14, 1913.]
D. B. P.

TUCK, AMOS (Aug. 2, 1810–Dec. 11, 1879), congressman, was born at Parsonsfield, Me., fourth of six children of John and Betsey (Towle) Tuck, and a descendant of Robert Tuck who settled on the New Hampshire coast in 1638. His parents were people of strong character, intelligent, industrious, ambitious for their children, but handicapped by the grinding struggle for a livelihood on a New England farm. The boy farmed at home until he was seventeen, then, with intermittent attendance at various schools, worked as a common laborer, taught district school, and in time accumulated resources financial and scholastic for admission to Dartmouth College.

After his graduation in 1835 he taught school, studying law in the meantime, and upon his admission to the bar in 1838 began practice in Exeter where within a few months he was admitted to partnership with James Bell, his former preceptor. In 1842, as a Democrat, he served a term in the New Hampshire legislature, but in 1844 definitely broke with the Democratic party on the Texas question and three years later, after an exciting and embittered contest, was elected to the Thirtieth Congress by a fusion of independent Democrats and Whigs. The contest conducted in New Hampshire by Amos Tuck and John P. Hale [q.v.], who was elected to the Senate as a result of the same campaign, was in many respects a forerunner of the great party upheavals of the next decade and attracted national attention. Tuck served three terms in Congress (1847–53). His independent position in the House, where with Joshua R. Giddings [q.v.] of Ohio and John G. Palfrey [q.v.] of Massachusetts he constituted a nucleus of anti-slavery sentiment, was prominent rather than influential. His views, however, well expressed in his speech of Jan. 19, 1848, against the Mexican War and extension of slavery, were eventually to become predominant in the Northern states.

Defeated for a fourth term because of a temporary waning of anti-slavery fervor in his state together with an effective gerrymander by the legislature, he continued active in the movement against slavery, but his essential sanity and political acumen kept him out of its more extravagant manifestations and his activity was therefore vastly more effective—so effective, indeed, that his admirers have often claimed that the Republican party was really a New Hampshire creation. At all events, he was instrumental in 1853 and 1854 in bringing about a merger of the dissatisfied into a new party alignment. At the Republican convention of 1856 he was a vice-president and in 1860 he was a member of the platform committee; in 1861 he attended the unsuccessful conference at Washington which endeavored to avert the final break between North and South. He was a loyal adherent of President Lincoln, with whom he had

formed a personal friendship in Congress and from whom in 1861 he accepted the post of naval officer for the district of Boston and Charlestown. He served in this capacity until removed by President Johnson in 1865.

From the professional standpoint the most successful period of Tuck's career followed the Civil War. Although he retained his residence at Exeter, his clients were now of national importance and their affairs took him into courtrooms and business offices in the financial centers of the country. He was interested in the Western railroad development and his shrewd sense of investment values enabled him to accumulate a large estate. He was a trustee of Phillips Exeter Academy from 1853 to 1879, and from 1857 to 1866 of Dartmouth College, where in 1900 his son Edward Tuck established the Amos Tuck School of Administration and Finance. Tuck's fine appearance, personal charm, and public spirit gave him a prominent place in that group of lawyers and party leaders which made Exeter one of the influential centers of New England life of the nineteenth century. He was twice married, first to Sarah Ann Nudd, who bore him eight children, and after her death early in 1847, on Oct. 10 of the same year to Mrs. Catharine (Townsend) Shepard, daughter of John Townsend of Salisbury. Three of his children survived him.

[*Autobiog. Memoir of A. Tuck* (privately printed, 1902); C. R. Corning, *Amos Tuck* (1902); J. W. Dearborn, *Sketch of the Life and Character of Hon. Amos Tuck* (n.d., 1889); Joseph Dow, *Tuck Geneal.: Robert Tuck of Hampton, N. H. and His Descendants* (1877); C. H. Bell, *The Bench and Bar of N. H.* (1894) and *Hist. of the Town of Exeter, N. H.* (1888); L. M. Crosbie, *The Phillips Exeter Acad.* (1923); J. K. Lord, *A Hist. of Dartmouth Coll.* (1913); *Biog. Dir. Am. Cong.* (1928); J. O. Lyford, *Life of Edward H. Rollins* (copr. 1906); *Concord Daily Monitor*, Dec. 12, 1879; MSS. in Dartmouth Coll. archives.]   W. A. R.

TUCKER, GEORGE (Aug. 20, 1775–Apr. 10, 1861), political economist, author, was born in Bermuda, the son of Daniel Tucker, mayor of Hamilton, and his first wife, Elizabeth (Tucker) Tucker, a distant relative. George was sent to Virginia at the age of twelve, and placed in the charge of his distant kinsman, St. George Tucker [q.v.], also a native of Bermuda, who had succeeded George Wythe as professor of law in the College of William and Mary. Here George graduated in 1797; he afterwards practised law in Richmond, then in Pittsylvania Court House (now Chatham), and Lynchburg. After serving in the Virginia legislature he was elected to Congress for three successive terms, obtaining there (1819–25) a reputation as debater and constitutional lawyer. Having attracted the attention of James Madison, whom he came to know intimately—as he also knew Jefferson, he was appointed professor of moral philosophy in the University of Virginia when it opened in 1825, and as the oldest member of the staff was elected the first chairman of the faculty. He had already published *Essays on Subjects of Taste, Morals, and National Policy, by a Citizen of Virginia* (1822), *The Valley of Shenandoah* (2 vols., 1824), and other works. He now issued, under the name "Joseph Atterley," *A Voyage to the Moon* (1827), a satirical romance, not very diverting or pointed, with occasional unimportant references to political economy and a good deal of bastard astronomy and botany. He worked hard for six months in 1829 as contributing editor of an ill-starred weekly inaugurated at the University, *The Virginia Literary Museum*. His humor was not appreciated in the academically self-conscious atmosphere of the new institution.

He must have labored for a long period on *The Life of Thomas Jefferson* (2 vols., 1837), in which he supplemented extensive research, often in out-of-the-way journals, by many conferences with Madison. He tried honestly to hold even justice between Republicans and Federalists, and on the whole succeeded. The advantages which he enjoyed of personal association with the chief Republican actors had, of course, their corresponding embarrassments. Tucker's sins are sometimes of commission, but oftener of omission. It must be remembered, however, that his own sympathies were on the side of Jefferson's opinions. He frequently does not understand, or does not admit, the degree to which Jefferson controlled the actions of such men as Madison and Giles. However, Tucker's exposition of the national problems that arose, and of the conflict over them, is a genuine contribution to history, for he often was able to see what was involved better than did many of the actors themselves. This same year he published *The Laws of Wages, Profits, and Rent Investigated* (1837), and in 1839 *The Theory of Money and Banks Investigated*. Apart from his own wisdom, Tucker had sufficient reason, in the recent panic and current depression, for upholding the policy of a national bank, or rather of several national banks, in order to prevent the excesses of local banks of issue. His *Progress of the United States in Population and Wealth in Fifty Years* (1843, appendix 1855), while noticing the tendency of the rate of population growth to decrease, calculated that the population three generations from the time he wrote would be just twice what it actually turned out to be.

In 1845, at the age of seventy, he retired from the University of Virginia, and thereafter lived in Philadelphia. When seventy-five, he commenced *The History of the United States* (4 vols., 1856–57), much of which embraced an account of his own times. When eighty-four he was his own publisher of *Political Economy for the People* (1859), and the next year issued *Essays, Moral and Metaphysical*. His mental activity was matched by surprising bodily stamina; in 1860 he traveled throughout Virginia and to Chicago, and the next year visited Southern cities as far down as Mobile. At the last place, in disembarking from a steamboat, he was struck by a bale of cotton and rendered unconscious for days. He survived long enough to be brought back to the home of his son-in-law, "Sherwood," in Albemarle County, Va. Tucker married, in 1801, Maria Ball Carter, grand-daughter of Elizabeth Lewis, Washington's sister; before her death in 1823, she bore him four daughters and a son, of whom two daughters and possibly the son survived him. His second marriage to Mary (Byrd) Farley, daughter of Mary Byrd of "Westover," was childless. His third wife, Louisa (Bowdoin) Thompson of the Eastern Shore of Virginia, died in 1859 without issue.

Tucker's principal formal works on economic theory belong to periods separated by twenty years. The two first, *The Laws of Wages, Profits, and Rent Investigated* (1837) and *The Theory of Money and Banks Investigated* (1839), published while he was teaching these subjects in the University of Virginia, are detailed and vivid, with frequent spirited criticism of other writers. The last, *Political Economy for the People* (1859), was prepared a decade and a half after his retirement; much detail has dropped out, there is little or no controversial matter, and the whole subject is treated as a summary of his wisdom and experience. His essential views, however, did not change. Tucker was always the political economist in the proper meaning of that term, that is, he cultivated the science because it could "exert a great influence on the public prosperity, in teaching governments how best they may improve the sources of national wealth, whether by regulation or forbearance, may least injuriously raise the public revenue, and most beneficially expend it" (*Wages, Profits, and Rent*, p. v). He followed his investigations of theory, therefore, with positive recommendations as to public policy. In general he was an adherent of the English and French classical school; his American environment, exhibiting in his lifetime prodigious economic progress, never dissuaded him, as it did Henry Charles Carey and Mathew Carey, Daniel Raymond, John Rae, and Georg Friedrich List [*qq.v.*], from the apprehensions and pessimism born of older civilizations. He sometimes approached the more optimistic position, but these inklings never formed themselves into anything like a system which should overset the old preoccupation with diminishing returns. This was in spite of the fact that he knew H. C. Carey's work from an early period, and certainly must have been thrown with him in Philadelphia, especially as they were both members of the American Philosophical Society. Tucker's mentor was Adam Smith, and his chief theoretical differences were with David Ricardo. This in itself indicates the narrow dimension of his contribution. He declared that Ricardo, though "entitled to all his reputation for a thorough knowledge of the subjects of money and finance, is mistaken in his elementary principles of the science; that the origin and progress of rents admits of a more simple and natural explanation than he has given; that his theory of wages is inconsistent with itself, and that of profits [is] contradicted by the whole history of capital in the civilized world" (*Wages, Profits, and Rent*, p. iv). Yet his criticism of Ricardo is mainly textual; it is in part based upon misapprehension, due perhaps to Ricardo's elliptical style; in fact, he virtually argues himself around to Ricardo's position of ascribing prime importance in the origin of rent to the differences in qualities of soils (*Ibid.*, p. 113). Tucker, while introducing judicious refinements of the doctrine, was permanently impressed with Malthus' principle of population, and applied it consistently throughout his thinking; it had much to do, doubtless, with leading him to his elaborate studies of the census, and bore immediately upon his insistence that American negro slavery would extinguish itself (about the year 1925 he thought) by becoming unprofitable to the masters. This would be in consequence of the progressive lessening of the value of labor, to the point where the earnings of a slave would not repay the cost of rearing him. "This," he said, "may be called the euthanasia of the institution, as it will be abolished with the consent of the master no less than the wishes of the slave" (*Progress of the United States*, p. 110). Tucker gave an early indication of the propriety of separating, in economic analysis, the functions of capitalist and enterpriser (*Wages, Profits, and Rent*, p. 91 and note). He condemned usury laws in unmeasured terms, not only as violating his general principle of governmental non-interference in commercial transactions, but as positively injurious to debtors by circumventions of the laws.

Of all the great economic and social questions of Tucker's time—tariff protection, internal improvements, banking regulation, and slavery—the last was the most portentous for the welfare of the country and especially of the South. As a resident on Virginia plantations, as a member of Congress at the time of the Missouri Compromise, as a teacher of the social sciences within the South, and as a witness of the preliminaries of the Civil War, he saw the political and economic situation of his section become increasingly critical. Though his opposition to slavery was unmistakable, and he steadily looked forward to the attenuation of the institution—earlier through deportation and manumission, and later as a consequence of the increase of population—his utterances were discreetly academic. Though, except upon specific minor points, he was never seduced into becoming its advocate, refusing to indulge in the imbecilities of his colleague Albert Taylor Bledsoe [q.v.], he was far removed from the fiery and effective opposition of such a man as Hinton Rowan Helper [q.v.]. The *Letters from Virginia* (1816), giving every appearance of Tucker's authorship, though also attributed to William Maxwell and James Kirke Paulding [qq.v.], condemned slavery in unmeasured terms, and ridiculed the planters, all under the cover of anonymity; the *Speech of Mr. Tucker, of Virginia, on the Restriction of Slavery in Missouri . . . February 25, 1820* (1820) discovered insuperable constitutional objections to preventing the extension of slavery; and the criticism of slavery, sufficiently explicit in his books of the 'thirties and 'forties, was reduced to a pallid mention in his *Political Economy for the People* published almost on the eve of the Civil War.

[Robley Dunglison, "Obituary Notice of Professor George Tucker," in *Proc. Am. Philosophical Soc.*, IX (1865), 64–70; T. A. Emmet, *An Account of the Tucker Family of Bermuda* (1898); Albert Welles, *The Pedigree and Hist. of the Washington Family* (1879); P. A. Bruce, *Hist. of the Univ. of Va., 1819–1919*, II (1920), III (1921); J. S. Patton, *Jefferson, Cabell and the Univ. of Va.* (1906), pp. 101–02; *Daily Richmond Enquirer*, Apr. 13, 1861.]   B. M.

TUCKER, GILBERT MILLIGAN (Aug. 26, 1847–Jan. 13, 1932), editor, author, publicist, was the son of Luther Tucker [q.v.] and his third wife, Margaret Lucinda (Smith) Burr Tucker. He was born at Albany, N. Y., where his father was conspicuous in the field of agricultural journalism. After preparation at the Albany Academy, he entered Williams College in 1864 and completed the four-year course in three years, earning the degree of A.B. with honors in 1867. He at once became associated with his father and elder brother in the publication of the *Cultivator and Country Gentleman*. In 1897 when the first part of the title was dropped, he became editor-in-chief, so continuing until the *Country Gentleman* was sold to the Curtis Publishing Company in 1911, when he retired from active business.

Tucker's editorial policy was vigorous and forthright. He had strong opinions and limitless courage in their support, yet was open-minded and tolerant withal. He opposed strongly, and believed detrimental to agricultural interests, such policies as the expansion of the state canal system and the development of western farm lands—particularly by irrigation—at public expense, foreseeing the danger of over-production and consequently injury to agriculture. He also disapproved of the Eighteenth Amendment to the Constitution, calling it "an absurd and dangerous anomaly." He spoke and wrote frequently on these and kindred subjects. During his connection with the *Country Gentleman,* he served on various federal and state commissions dealing with agricultural affairs. He was deeply interested in, and at one time president of, the old New York State Agricultural Society. He was a trustee of Cornell University, 1905–06; a member, elder, and trustee of the Reformed Church; a Mason; a member of the Order of Founders and Patriots; and in politics a Republican, although in later life he came to disbelieve in the policy of tariff protection.

Deeply interested in philological subjects, he was a student of New Testament Greek and a frequent writer on the English language, with special reference to the differences in its usage in England and America. He maintained that the purity of English has been better preserved on the West side of the Atlantic, and held that most of the so-called "Americanisms" originated many years ago in the mother country. He was the author of *Our Common Speech* (1895); *American English* (1921); *A Layman's Apology* (1913), a volume of essays on religious subjects; *American Agricultural Periodicals* (an historical sketch, privately printed, 1909); and contributions to the daily press, *North American Review, New Englander, Presbyterian Review,* and other journals.

On June 7, 1877, Tucker married Sara Edwards Miller, daughter of the Rev. William Augustus Miller of Albany. She died in 1930. They had one son, who survived his father, and one daughter who died unmarried in 1926. Tucker died at Albany in his eighty-fifth year.

[Ephraim Tucker, *Geneal. of the Tucker Family* (1895); *Who's Who in America,* 1930–31; *N. Y. Times,* Jan. 14, 1932; *Knickerbocker Press* (Albany), Jan. 14, 1932; family material; personal acquaintance.]

J. I. W.

TUCKER, HENRY HOLCOMBE (May 10, 1819–Sept. 9, 1889), Baptist clergyman, was born near Camak, Warren County, Ga., the son of Germain Tucker and Frances Henrietta, daughter of Henry Holcombe [*q.v.*]. Both his parents were of Virginia ancestry; his paternal grandfather, Isaiah Tucker, was a wealthy planter. After the death of his father at the age of twenty-seven, Henry's mother married again and the family removed to Philadelphia. The boy was prepared for college in the academic department of the University of Pennsylvania, and in 1834 he entered the freshman class of the University. In his senior year he transferred to Columbian College (now George Washington University), Washington, D. C., where he was graduated with the degree of A.B. in 1838.

Returning to the South, he entered business in Charleston, S. C. In 1842 he decided to study law and repaired to Forsyth, Ga., where he was admitted to the bar in 1846. Two years later he married Mary Catherine West, who lived but a few months after their marriage. Her death seems to have turned his mind toward the ministry, for he soon gave up the practice of law, sold his library, was licensed to preach, and removed to Penfield in order to take private instruction in theology under John L. Dagg [*q.v.*], then president of Mercer University. Although he preferred to enter the pastorate, he was persuaded to undertake educational work and accepted a position with the Southern Female College at Lagrange, Ga., where he was ordained to the Baptist ministry in 1851. For a short time subsequently he was professor in the Richmond Female Institute, Richmond, Va. In 1853 he was offered the presidency of Wake Forest College, Wake Forest, N. C., but since he had just accepted the pastorate of a church at Alexandria, Va., he declined. While in Alexandria, he married Sarah O. Stevens. In 1856 he became professor of belles-lettres and metaphysics in Mercer University, a position which he held until the institution was closed by the Civil War in 1862.

He was opposed to secession and used his utmost influence against it, but when Georgia seceded he remained loyal to the South. Foreseeing a salt famine, he organized a company for the manufacture of salt, which was extremely helpful in the dark days of the war. He also organized the Georgia Relief and Hospital Association, a voluntary organization for the care of sick and wounded soldiers. After the war he was elected editor of the *Christian Index,* Jan. 1, 1866, but resigned in July to accept the presidency of Mercer University, in which office he served until 1871. The period was one of extreme difficulty for all educational institutions of the South, but Mercer made progress. In 1870 the institution was moved from Penfield to Macon. This removal, which was favored by Tucker, caused much resentment and friction, which probably was in part the cause of his resignation in 1871. The following fourteen months he spent in Europe, chiefly at Rome and Paris. In Rome he assisted in establishing a Baptist Church and himself baptized in the Tiber the first candidate for membership. In Paris he preached for the American Church most of the winter. On returning to America he became chancellor of the University of Georgia, at Athens, and served as such from 1874 to 1878. In the latter year he became proprietor and editor of the *Christian Index,* which he conducted until his death in 1889. Under his control the paper attained a position of wide and commanding influence not only in Georgia but far beyond its borders.

Tucker was not a great scholar, but he was a logical and consistent thinker and an excellent teacher. As a speaker and writer he was master of a clear style characterized by conciseness and finish. In his preaching he was ardent and earnest, and his discourses were enlivened by flashes of wit and humor. Though he held but one pastorate, he did much preaching throughout his life. He published a volume of sermons in 1884 under the title *The Old Theology Re-stated in Sermons,* and in 1869, a small volume entitled *The Gospel in Enoch,* which occasioned much favorable comment. After his death, *Select Writings by the Late Henry Holcombe Tucker* (copr. 1902), edited by B. J. W. Graham, was issued. He died at Atlanta, Ga., survived by his wife and two children.

[William Cathcart, *The Baptist Encyc.* (1881); *Hist. of the Baptist Denomination in Ga.* (1881); R. L. Robinson, *Hist. of the Ga. Baptist Asso.* (1928); B. D. Ragsdale, *Story of Ga. Baptists* (copr. 1932); T. H. Martin, *Atlanta and Its Builders* (1902), vol. II; W. J. Northen, *Men of Mark in Ga.,* vol. III (1911); *Atlanta Constitution,* Sept. 10, 1889.]　　W.J.M.

TUCKER, HENRY ST. GEORGE (Dec. 29, 1780–Aug. 28, 1848), jurist, was born at "Matoax," in Chesterfield County, Va., the son of St. George Tucker [q.v.] and Frances (Bland) Randolph Tucker. John Randolph of Roanoke, 1773–1833 [q.v.] was his half-brother and Nathaniel Beverley Tucker, 1784–1851 [q.v.] was his brother. In 1799 he graduated from the College of William and Mary, where he studied law under his father. Shortly after he attained his majority he went to Winchester, Va., where he began the general practice of law. In spite of his youth, his outstanding talents were swiftly

recognized, and his practice grew rapidly in volume and in importance. He appears to have gained no little reputation by his handling of litigation involving the estates of Lord Fairfax. On Sept. 23, 1806, he married Anne Evelina Hunter. John Randolph Tucker, 1823–1897 and Nathaniel Beverley Tucker, 1820–1890, were their sons and Henry St. George Tucker, 1853–1932 [qq.v.] their grandson. He served for the session of 1807–08 in the Virginia House of Delegates. Upon the outbreak of the War of 1812 he enlisted as a volunteer. From 1815 to 1819 he sat in the federal House of Representatives. Though the House then included among its members such men as Clay, Calhoun, and Webster, he took a prominent part in its activities. In 1816 he opposed the act to increase the salaries of members of Congress and refused to accept the increase in his own salary. From 1819 to 1823 he served in the state Senate.

His judicial career, which absorbed seventeen years of his life and in which he added no little to his renown, began in 1824, when he was elected judge of the superior courts of chancery for the Winchester and Clarksburg districts. An indefatigable worker, he gave unstintedly of his time and labor to his judicial duties. Yet he organized and taught with signal success during the seven years of his chancellorship a private law school at Winchester. In this period he wrote his *Commentaries on the Laws of Virginia* (2 vols., 1836–37). This work, with such other publications as *A Few Lectures on Natural Law* (1844) and *Lectures on Constitutional Law* (1843) firmly established his reputation in the field of legal authorship. In 1831 he was elected president of the supreme court of appeals of Virginia. For a decade he presided with dignity and distinction over that high court, winning the acclaim of his colleagues on the bench, the members of the Virginia bar, and the people of the State. So highly did he consider his office that he declined an appointment as federal attorney-general at the hands of President Jackson. In 1841 he resigned from the court to accept the professorship of law in the University of Virginia. Though handicapped by lack of health, he yet taught with such vigor and enthusiasm as to win the warm plaudits of his students. In 1842, when he was chairman of the faculty, upon his motion, the "Honor System" was adopted at the University of Virginia, which has operated there for more than ninety years as a spiritual asset of the institution. His failing health compelled him, in 1845, to retire, and he returned to Winchester, where he died.

Glowing tributes were paid to him after his

death. His varied activities had brought him into contact with most of the distinguished Virginians of his day. Though his restless energy had been scattered over many fields, he literally touched nothing that he did not adorn. It is quite remarkable how closely his career paralleled that of his father. Each was a lawyer, a legislator, a judge, a teacher of law, and a judicial writer. Each was a soldier in his country's service, and each ventured into the field of light poetry. Yet Henry St. George Tucker need shine in no reflected glory.

[S. N. Hurst and R. M. Brown, *A Complete Alphabetical, Chronological Annotated Digest of All the Reported Decisions of . . . Va.,* vol. I (1897), p. 35 ; J. R. Tucker, "The Judges Tucker of the Court of Appeals of Va.," *Va. Law Register,* Mar. 1896; S. S. P. Patteson, "The Supreme Court of Appeals of Va.," *Green Bag,* July 1893 ; S. E. M. Hardy, "Some Va. Lawyers," *Ibid.,* Jan. 1898; P. A. Bruce, *Hist. of the Univ. of Va.,* vols. I–IV (1920–21) ; faculty minutes of the Univ. of Va.] A. M. D.

TUCKER, HENRY ST. GEORGE (Apr. 5, 1853–July 23, 1932), congressman from Virginia and lawyer, was born at Winchester, Va., the great-grandson of the emigrant, St. George Tucker, the grandson of Henry St. George Tucker, 1780–1848, and the son of John Randolph Tucker, 1823–1897 [*qq.v.*]. His mother was Laura (Powell) Tucker. After attending private schools in Loudoun County and at Richmond, he entered Washington and Lee University, where he received the degrees of master of arts in 1875 and bachelor of laws in 1876. On Oct. 25, 1877, he was married to Henrietta Preston Johnston, the daughter of William Preston Johnston [*q.v.*]. She died in 1900 leaving six children. He practised law at Staunton, Va., from 1876 to 1889, when he succeeded his father as Democratic representative in Congress. He served there until 1897. His advocacy of the popular election of federal senators and his attitude toward silver stand out in his congressional career of this period. Denouncing the control of legislative bodies by corporate wealth, he declared that "an aptness for percentages and the successful manipulation of railroads and stock boards are often regarded as the most essential of Senatorial equipments" (*Cong. Record,* 52 Cong., 1 Sess., p. 6063). A bi-metallist, he voted for the repeal of the Sherman Silver Act and, thereafter, consistently opposed the remonetization of silver except at the ratio of 20 to 1. At the Democratic State convention at Staunton, Va., in June 1896 he alone defended Cleveland. "I am not going," he said, "to stand before a crowd of Virginia Democrats and blackguard a man that you elected" (*Rockbridge County News,* June 11, 1896). His refusal to indorse the plat-

form of 16 to 1 in that campaign, although he supported Bryan, cost him the political support of his district.

From 1897 to 1902 he was associated with Washington and Lee University as professor of law, as dean of the law school, and, after the death of William L. Wilson [*q.v.*], as acting president, 1900–01. On Jan. 13, 1903, he was married to Martha Sharpe of Wilkes Barre, Pa., who died in 1928. He was dean of the department of law and jurisprudence at Columbian University (George Washington University) from 1903 to 1905, president of the American Bar Association, 1904-05, and president of the Jamestown Tercentennial Exposition, 1905-07. An anti-machine Democrat, he was an unsuccessful candidate for the governorship of Virginia in 1909 and in 1921. He was the author of *Limitations on the Treaty-Making Power Under the Constitution of the United States* (1915) and *Woman's Suffrage by Constitutional Amendment* (1916), and he edited *The Constitution of the United States* by John Randolph Tucker, 1823–1897 [*q.v.*], in two volumes (1899).

Reëlected to Congress in March 1922, he served continuously until his death. In that postwar era he was regarded as one of the most ardent exponents of state rights and as one of the zealous defenders of the *laissez-faire* interpretation of the Constitution in Congress ; and he was opposed generally to the social and economic legislation of that period, the proposed child labor amendment, woman's suffrage, the Eighteenth Amendment, and similar legislative proposals. "When the powers of the Government can be used to settle the question of competition in commercial life, the act becomes tryanny," is an apposite expression of his political philosophy (*Cong. Record,* 67 Cong., 2 Sess., p. 7596). He attracted nation-wide attention in 1925 by refusing to accept an increase in salary for that session, citing as a precedent for his action his grandfather's refusal in Congress in 1816 in similar circumstances. He died in Lexington, survived by his third wife, Mary Jane (Williams) Tucker, to whom he had been married on June 26, 1929.

[Letters in possession of the family ; L. G. Tyler, *Men of Mark in Va.,* V (1909) ; *Memorial Services Held in the House of Representatives* (1933) ; Allan Nevins, *Grover Cleveland* (1932) ; *Who's Who in America,* 1930–31 ; *Colonial Families of the U. S.,* V (1915), ed. by G. N. Mackenzie ; *Rockbridge County News* (Lexington), July 28, 1932 ; *N. Y. Times,* July 24, 1932 ; dates for degrees from contemporary catalogs of the university and *Lexington Gazette* and *Citizen* (Lexington), June 25, 1875, and June 23, 1876.] W. G. B.

TUCKER, JOHN RANDOLPH (Jan. 31, 1812–June 12, 1883), naval officer, the son of

Susan (Douglas) and John Tucker, lately of Bermuda, was born at Alexandria, Va., then within the limits of the District of Columbia. He received his early education in local schools, and on June 1, 1826, he was appointed to the United States Navy as a midshipman. He became passed midshipman on June 10, 1833. He was commissioned lieutenant from Dec. 20, 1837. On June 7, 1838, he was married at Norfolk, to Virginia Webb. They had three children. Tall, with imposing presence, he was known to the sailors as "Handsome Jack." He had the reputation of being a resolute fighter, a strict disciplinarian, and a splendid seaman. Alternating with duty at the Norfolk yard, he served in the Home Squadron, in the East Indies, during the Mexican War on the *Stromboli*, first as executive officer, then as commander, in the Home Squadron, and in the Mediterranean Squadron. He was promoted to be commander from Sept. 14, 1855. He commanded the receiving ship at Norfolk for three years, was on "waiting orders" for nearly two years, broken by a short tour on a board of inspection, and was rounding out a year as ordnance officer at the Norfolk yard when Virginia seceded. He resigned on Apr. 18, 1861, but under the policy of the Lincoln administration his separation from the service was recorded as a dismissal.

He was immediately appointed in the short-lived Virginia state navy and in the Confederate States Navy on June 8, 1861, to rank as commander from Mar. 26, 1861. He was placed in charge of the naval defenses of the James River and was ordered to command the steamer *Yorktown*, which under his superintendency was converted into the protected cruiser *Patrick Henry*. His vessel was stationed at Mulberry Island to protect the right flank of the Confederate Army of the Peninsula. He participated in the battle of Hampton Roads on Mar. 8–9, 1862, in the demonstration against the enemy's fleet below Fort Monroe in April 1862, and after the evacuation of Norfolk commanded the fleet in its retirement up the James River to Drewry's Bluff, where the pursuing ships were severely repulsed on May 15, 1862. He left the *Patrick Henry* in August 1862 for Charleston, S. C., where he assumed command of the ironclad ram *Chicora*. He took part in the night attack upon the blockading squadron off Charleston on Jan. 31, 1863, and was shortly afterward given command of the Charleston Squadron. He was promoted to captain of the Provisional Navy of the Confederate States from May 13, 1863. When Charleston was evacuated in February 1865, he destroyed his vessels and formed his crews into a naval brigade,

which was assigned to duty at Drewry's Bluff, where he commanded ashore and Rear Admiral Raphael Semmes afloat. Upon the evacuation of Richmond, his command was assigned to the rear guard of Lee's army and distinguished itself at the battle of Sailor's Creek on Apr. 6, only to be surrendered by the corps commander in consequence of losses elsewhere on the field. He was imprisoned at Fort Warren, from where he was released on July 24, 1865, upon taking the oath of allegiance to the United States.

After much difficulty he obtained employment as agent of the Southern Express Company at Raleigh, N. C., where he remained until he received a commission as rear admiral in the Peruvian navy. He commanded the combined fleets of Peru and Chile in the war with Spain, but the war was concluded in 1869 without an opportunity to engage the Spanish fleet. He was then appointed president of an hydrographical commission to survey the upper waters of the Amazon, which he accomplished in the face of hostile Indians. He was sent to New York to prepare the charts for publication but the financial difficulties of Peru caused the termination of the commission in 1877. He retired to Petersburg, Va., where he died from heart failure.

[*War of the Rebellion: Official Records* (*Navy*) and (*Army*) indexed as John R. Tucker and not to be confused with John Randolph Tucker, the attorney-general of Va.; records of the Naval Lib. and of the Navy Dept.; J. H. Rochelle, *Life of Rear Admiral John Randolph Tucker* (1903); L. G. Tyler, *Encyc. of Va. Biog.* (1915), vol. III; W. H. Parker, *Recollections of a Naval Officer* (1883), pp. 253–322; J. T. Scharf, *Hist. of the Confederate States Navy* (1887); *Richmond Dispatch*, June 14, 1883.]
W. M. R., Jr.

TUCKER, JOHN RANDOLPH (Dec. 24, 1823–Feb. 13, 1897), lawyer, teacher, and congressman from Virginia, was born at Winchester, Va., the son of Anne Evelina (Hunter) and Henry St. George Tucker, 1780–1848 [*q.v.*], the nephew of Nathaniel Beverley Tucker, 1784–1851, and the grandson of St. George Tucker [*qq.v.*]. His brother was Nathaniel Beverley Tucker, 1820–1890 [*q.v.*]. He attended private schools at Winchester and Richmond, and in 1839 he entered the University of Virginia, where he studied moral and political philosophy under his kinsman, George Tucker [*q.v.*], and also mathematics and physical science, the teaching of which he was urged by his preceptors to follow. However, he studied law under his father at the university and received the law degree there in 1843. On Oct. 5, 1848, he married Laura Holmes Powell of Loudoun County, Va. Henry St. George Tucker, 1853–1932 [*q.v.*], was their son. From 1845 until 1857 he practised law at Winchester. An ardent believer in state-rights principles he took an active part in politics, serving as Democratic elector in 1852 and 1856, participating in the gubernatorial campaign in 1855 against the Know-Nothing party, and supporting Breckinridge in 1860. As attorney-general of Virginia from 1857 to 1865, he represented the state in important civil and criminal cases before the state courts. From 1865 to his death, though he was during most of this time either teaching law at Washington and Lee University (1870–74; 1889–97) or serving in Congress (1875–87), he still engaged in the practice of law. It is said he appeared before the federal Supreme Court oftener, with one exception, than any other Virginian during this period. He represented the Chicago anarchists before this body, and, when surprise was expressed by some friends, he replied, "I do not defend anarchy; I defend the Constitution" (Hamilton, *post*, pp. 152, 153). Other notable cases with which he was associated were the trial of Jefferson Davis and the Florida case before the electoral commission.

Upon entering Congress in 1875, he immediately became a leader on the Democratic side of the House and showed himself to be "an old-fashioned, strict-constructionist, state-rights logician" (Smith, *post*, I, 589), resisting every tendency toward centralization and applying the yard stick of constitutionality to every measure before Congress. "It is unfashionable, I know," he once remarked, "to stickle for the Constitution" (*Cong. Record*, 49 Cong., 1 Sess., App. p. 59). He championed tariff reform, characterizing the perversion of the taxing power "from the purpose of revenue to the grant of a bounty or special privilege . . . if . . . directly . . . a robbery; if indirectly . . . a fraud" (*Cong. Record*, 47 Cong., 1 Sess., App. p. 275). He advocated the repeal of the internal revenue system—"nests of Federal patronage which have infested the States for twenty years, and have been the source of more petty tyranny and of more interference with the freedom of elections . . . than has ever been known before in the history of the country" (*Ibid.*, p. 475); favored the Chinese exclusion bill in order to protect "the young Hercules of the Pacific" (*Ibid.*, App. p. 56); aided in the defeat of the Blair education bill; supported a sound money policy; and in 1880 introduced a quorum-counting rule that was subsequently adopted by the House under the speakership of Thomas B. Reed.

After his retirement from Congress, he returned to Washington and Lee University as professor of constitutional and international law and in 1893 was made dean of the law school.

In 1892–93 he was president of the American Bar Association. He was the author of *The Constitution of the United States* (2 vols., 1899, published posthumously). Among his published public addresses were *The Southern Church Justified in its Support of the South* (1863), *Paper Read Before Social Science Association . . . at Saratoga Springs, N. Y., on the Relations of the United States to Each Other as Modified by the War and the Constitutional Amendments* (1877), and *The History of the Federal Convention of 1787* (1887) read before the graduating class of the Yale Law School. His speeches were polished, and he was known for his witticism, oratory, and ability as a story teller.

[Alexander Hamilton, *Memorial of John Randolph Tucker* (1897) and in *Report of . . . Va. State Bar Asso. . . . 1897* (1897); *Report of . . . the Am. Bar Asso. 1897* (1897); R. T. Barton, "John Randolph Tucker," *Va. Law Register*, May 1897; T. C. Smith, *The Life and Letters of James Abram Garfield* (2 vols., 1925); O. F. Morton, *A Hist. of Rockbridge County, Va.* (1920); Philip Slaughter, *A Hist. of Bristol Parish, Va.* (2nd ed., 1897); *Rockbridge County News* (Lexington), Feb. 18, 1897.]   W. G. B.

TUCKER, LUTHER (May 7, 1802–Jan. 26, 1873), agricultural journalist, was born in Brandon, Vt., the youngest of six children of Stephen and Olive (Green) Tucker and a descendant of Robert Tucker who settled in Weymouth, Mass., about 1635. His mother died soon after his birth, and the family scattered, leaving Luther in the care of a neighbor. His formal schooling was meager, but through his own efforts he acquired a good education and became adept as a writer. At the age of fourteen he was apprenticed to a printer of Middlebury, Vt., and in 1817 moved with his master to Palmyra, N. Y. During his journeyman years he worked in New York, Philadelphia, Baltimore, and Washington. In the spring of 1825 he entered into a partnership with Henry C. Sleight of Jamaica, Long Island, printer of standard works for New York houses; some of these bear the imprint of Sleight & Tucker.

A little more than a year later, under the firm name of Luther Tucker & Company, Sleight and Tucker established the *Rochester Daily Advertiser* in Rochester, N. Y., where Tucker took up his residence. With Henry O'Reilly [*q.v.*] as its editor, the *Advertiser* began publication in October 1826; two years later Tucker bought his partner's interest. The success of the *Advertiser*, together with his interest in agriculture, led him to establish the *Genesee Farmer*, Jan. 1, 1831, which despite strong prejudice against "newspaper farming," soon gained a large following. The *Genesee Farmer* was published weekly, but from January 1836 to December 1839

Tucker published also the *Monthly Genesee Farmer and Horticulturist*, made up of selections from the weekly.

In 1839 he sold the *Advertiser* to devote his full time to farming and his agricultural journal. In October of that year, however, the death of Jesse Buel [*q.v.*] left the Albany *Cultivator* without a head, and at the solicitation of his friends and Buel's family Tucker purchased it, merging with it his *Genesee Farmer*, and early in 1840 moved to Albany to carry on the *Cultivator* at that place. Here he became an outstanding member of the New York State Agricultural Society and held various offices. At the annual meeting in 1841 a new constitution which he had prepared was adopted by the Society. This document provided for the holding of state fairs, and thus to Tucker much credit is due for the long series of New York fairs, held annually without a break since 1841, which have contributed largely to the progress of New York agriculture.

In July 1846 Tucker established the *Horticulturist,* under the editorship of his friend Andrew J. Downing [*q.v.*]. It at once assumed a position of influence and is still considered America's most notable contribution to the periodical literature of horticulture. Tucker sold it in 1852, however, the year of Downing's death, and in 1853 began to issue a weekly edition of the *Cultivator* which he called the *Country Gentleman*. Since this gradually took the place of the monthly in the interest and preference of the public, he consolidated the two papers in January 1866 under the title of *Cultivator and Country Gentleman*. At the time Tucker established the *Country Gentleman* his eldest son, Luther H. Tucker, became associated with him as business manager, the firm name being changed to Luther Tucker & Son. Another son, Gilbert Milligan Tucker [*q.v.*], entered the firm in 1867. The senior Tucker continued as editor until his death, when his sons took over the conduct of the paper.

In disposition Tucker was unassuming, kindly, and generous. He exerted for many years an important influence on agricultural matters, and did perhaps more than any other American of his time to promote the literature of agriculture. He was regarded by his contemporaries as the leader and model of agricultural journalists of the country and no fewer than ten other agricultural editors received their training under him. He was remarkably successful in enlisting large numbers of the best farmers of the country as contributors to his publications. With Willis Gaylord [*q.v.*] he compiled in 1840 a work in two volumes entitled *American Husbandry,*

being a series of essays on agriculture first published principally in the *Cultivator* or the *Genesee Farmer*.

Tucker was married three times: first, Nov. 19, 1827, to Naomi Sparhawk, who died Aug. 4, 1832, at Rochester, a victim of the cholera; second, Oct. 4, 1833, to her sister, Mary Sparhawk, who died Mar. 8, 1844, of consumption; and third, June 1, 1846, to Mrs. Margaret Lucinda (Smith) Burr, who survived him. A son and a daughter were born of the first marriage, a son and three daughters of the second, and two sons of the third. Tucker died in Albany after a few weeks' illness and was buried in the Albany Rural Cemetery.

[*Cultivator and Country Gentleman*, Jan. 30, Feb. 6, 13, 20, Mar. 6, 13, Apr. 10, 1873; *Country Gentleman*, Jan. 4, 1906; Ephraim Tucker, *Geneal. of the Tucker Family* (1895); W. E. Ogilvie, *Pioneer Agricultural Journalists* (1927); *N. Y. Tribune*, Jan. 28, 1873; *Horticulturist*, Mar. 1873; *Moore's Rural New Yorker*, Feb. 8, 1873; *Gardener's Monthly*, Mar. 1873; *Rochester Hist. Soc. Pub. Fund Ser.*, VI (1927), 263–64, 270–71, 279–90.]
C. R. B.

TUCKER, NATHANIEL BEVERLEY (Sept. 6, 1784–Aug. 26, 1851), author, professor of law, was born at "Matoax," Chesterfield County, Va. He was usually referred to as Beverley Tucker. He was the son of St. George Tucker [*q.v.*] and Frances (Bland) Randolph Tucker. Along with his brother, Henry St. George Tucker, 1780–1848, and his half-brother, John Randolph, 1773–1833 [*qq.v.*], he was privately tutored, and he graduated from the College of William and Mary in 1801. He began the practice of law in Charlotte County, Va., but with little success. There he married Mary Coalter and devoted his ample leisure to the study of history and politics. In 1809 he removed to "Roanoke," where he struggled with the law and lived largely on the bounty of John Randolph, who exercised an important influence over his political views. In the War of 1812 he served as a lieutenant and later was promoted to a staff appointment. In 1815, although his practice was improving, he removed with his family to Missouri. There his wife died, and he married Eliza Taylor. After her death he was married a third time, on Apr. 13, 1830, to Lucy Anne Smith. He was instrumental in the organization of Jefferson County and served as a judge in the circuit courts of the territory and later of the state. He resisted unsuccessfully the admission of "Yankeys" to the new state and was a violent opponent of the Missouri Compromise.

In the winter of 1833–34 he returned to Virginia and shortly afterward was appointed professor of law at William and Mary, a post he held until his death. From his academic retreat he poured forth letters, books, and speeches in defense of the rights of the South. As a lecturer and letter writer he had his greatest influence. During his fifteen years as professor he gave his political views wide currency among his students. He published books on political economy that are permeated with his doctrine of state sovereignty and reflect the theories of his colleague, Thomas R. Dew. Probably his greatest political influence was effected by his extensive letter writing. Among his correspondents were Calhoun, Tyler, Jefferson Davis, Hammond, Wise, and William G. Simms. His ideas were important in the development of President Tyler's "exchequer plan" (Tyler, *post*, II, 29–30). His last public appearance was as a delegate from Virginia to the Nashville Convention of 1850, and he died in the following year at Winchester, Va.

His principal works include three novels: *George Balcombe* (1836), published anonymously; *The Partisan Leader* (2 vols., 1836); and *Gertrude,* published as a serial in the *Southern Literary Messenger,* September 1844 to December 1845 as well as numerous writings on political economy and law, of which *A Discourse on the Importance of the Study of Political Science as a Branch of Academic Education in the United States* (1840) and *The Principles of Pleading* (1846) are the most significant. *George Balcombe,* the most thoroughly literary in purpose, received high praise at the time. Edgar Allan Poe wrote, "George Balcombe, we are induced to regard, upon the whole, as *the best* American novel . . . its interest is intense from beginning to end . . . its most distinguishing features are invention, vigor, almost audacity, of thought" ("Marginalia," ccxxv). Tucker's books were nearly all devoted to an exposition of extreme state rights. As early as 1820 he expressed himself boldly in favor of secession and for thirty years maintained this view with inflexible consistency. His philosophy was firmly rooted in eighteenth-century agrarianism; he believed in aristocratic government and had no patience with Jacksonian Democracy—especially as it began to invade his own beloved state. The Nullification Proclamation and the Force Bill outraged his doctrine of state sovereignty and led to the writing of his best known novel, *The Partisan Leader.* At the request of friends in South Carolina, the book was secretly printed before its completion in the hope of swaying the election of 1836—though Tucker believed Van Buren's triumph assured. The title page bore the fictitious date of 1856, and the situation described is almost prophetic in its exactness. The modern reader marvels at the clearness with which he

foresaw the approach of civil war, and that as early as 1835 some in the South felt that secession was inevitable. The novel was suppressed but was reprinted as propaganda by both sides in the later struggle. Today it cannot claim a high place in literature; the language seems stilted, the seriousness unrelieved by humor, and the outlook limited. His position in literary history rests on the fact that he was one of the earliest American disciples of Scott, though his execution, praised in 1836, is now (1936) outmoded and unnatural. Tucker represented the survival of eighteenth century thought in pre-war Virginia. Hatred of centralization in government, "shirtsleeve democracy," and "Yankee industrialism," along with his intense love for Virginia, agrarianism, and the idealized slave characterize his thought. He was among the last of Virginia's political thinkers and is perhaps excluded from the fame of his predecessors because his philosophy belonged to a time that was past and was based upon a dying economy.

[Letters in possession of his grandson, George P. Coleman, Williamsburg, Va.; M. H. Woodfin, "Nathaniel Beverley Tucker," *Richmond College Hist. Papers,* vol. II, no. 1 (1917); W. C. Bruce, *John Randolph of Roanoke* (2 vols., 1922); *Hist. Mag.,* June 1859; L. G. Tyler, *Letters and Times of the Tylers* (2 vols., 1884–85); Carl Bridenbaugh, "Introduction," *Partisan Leader* (1933); V. L. Parrington, *The Romantic Rev. in America* (1927); a more favorable view by Poe, *ante,* and lxv as well as Carl Van Doren in *Cambridge Hist. Am. Lit.* (1917), vol. I, and H. Findlay in *Lib. of Southern Literature,* vol. XII (1907); a biog. with letters in preparation by P. W. Torrentine, Cambridge, Mass.; *International Mag.,* Oct. 1851.]   C. B—h.

TUCKER, NATHANIEL BEVERLEY (June 8, 1820–July 4, 1890), Confederate agent, was born in Winchester, Va., the grandson of St. George Tucker [*q.v.*], an emigrant from Bermuda, the nephew of Nathaniel Beverley Tucker, 1784–1851, and the son of Henry St. George Tucker, 1780–1848 [*qq.v.*]. His mother was Anne Evelina (Hunter) Tucker, and John Randolph Tucker, 1823–1897 [*q.v.*], was his brother. In 1831 the family removed to Richmond. The boy was prepared for college at the Richmond Academy and in 1837 went to the University of Virginia. For a year he worked under Charles Ellet [*q.v.*] on the building of the James River & Kanawha Canal and then undertook the management of one of the family plantations. On Jan. 21, 1841, he was married to Jane Shelton Ellis and shortly afterward established himself at "Hazelfield" in Jefferson County. They had eight children. Leaving "Hazelfield" after a few years, he occupied himself with various undertakings, lost his capital and acquired debts in a business in Richmond, manufactured munitions for a time during the Mexican War, built up a practice in representing claims before Congress and before the federal departments, and was active in politics. From 1853 to 1856 he edited the *Washington Sentinel*. In 1857 he succeeded Nathaniel Hawthorne as consul at Liverpool. He enjoyed his personal and family connections in Europe, the friends and family of his late cousin, Henry St. George Tucker, who had been director and treasurer of the East India Company, as well as such Americans as George M. Dallas and John Y. Mason [*qq.v.*], the ministers to Great Britain and France and both friends and relatives by marriage. More than six feet tall and fine-featured, he possessed a manner and personality that made him many friends. In 1861 in a notice seeking his recognition and arrest, Seward described him as "a large man, upwards of fifty, florid complexion" with "plausible and boisterous manners" (*Official Records, post,* 2 ser., vol. II, p. 176).

Upon the secession of Virginia he returned home and joined the Confederate army. Soon he entered into a contract to provide supplies for the army, and in 1862 he was in New Orleans seeking passage abroad. He reached Paris and for a time entertained high hopes, but, thwarted on every hand, he returned home unsuccessful. In 1864 he was sent to Canada on a delicate mission to arrange for an exchange of cotton for bacon and, apparently, to make some kind of secret diplomatic representations to Northern men of influence. He was successful in making a contract for the exchange of the two commodities, pound for pound, but in the confusion at the end of the war the terms were never carried out.

After the war he was harassed by the unfounded suspicions and animosities of the period. Accused of complicity in the plot to murder Lincoln, a reward of $25,000 was offered for him until November 1865, when the offer was revoked. In spite of the entire lack of evidence against him and in spite of his own knowledge of the partisan reasons for such persecution, this charge continued to be a source of distress to him (see his *Address ... to the People of the United States,* 1865, and Rowland, *post*). He spent a series of unprofitable years in England, Mexico, and Canada and in 1872 returned to the United States. He lived the remaining years of his life at Washington and, in the summer, at Berkeley Springs, W. Va., advocating the claims of various interests to Congress, to the federal departments, and to the public, writing for newspapers, and valiantly struggling with the difficulties of poverty and illness. Such stanch Republicans as James G. Blaine and Hamilton Fish professed to be his friends, and at his death the

Washington Post (*post*) said of him that "he was perhaps as well known personally to leading politicians throughout the country as any man of his time."

[J. E. Tucker, *Beverley Tucker. A Memoir by his Wife* (n.d.), in possession of Beverley Tucker of Richmond, Va.; *War of the Rebellion: Official Records* (*Army*), 1 ser., XLVI, pt. 3, XLIX, pt. 2, LII, pt. 2, LIII, 2 ser., II, VIII, 4 ser., II, III; J. B. Jones, *A Rebel War Clerk's Diary* (1935), ed. by Howard Swiggett, vol. II, p. 319; *Jefferson Davis* (1923), ed. by Dunbar Rowland, vols. II, VII; *Richmond Dispatch* and *Washington Post,* July 5, 1890.]   K. E. C.

TUCKER, ST. GEORGE (June 29, 1752 o.s.– Nov. 10, 1827), jurist, was born at Port Royal, Bermuda, the son of Henry and Anne (Butterfield) Tucker. He was distantly related to George Tucker [*q.v.*]. In his late teens he emigrated to Virginia. He enrolled as a student in the College of William and Mary and graduated in 1772. He was admitted to the bar and began the practice of his chosen profession in Williamsburg. His career as a lawyer was interrupted by the outbreak of the Revolutionary War, into which he threw himself on behalf of the struggling colonies. At the battle of Guilford Court House he distinguished himself by his bravery and military skill as a colonel of the Chesterfield County militia. Later he became lieutenant-colonel of a troop of horse and took part in the siege of Yorktown, where he was wounded. On Sept. 23, 1778, he married Frances (Bland) Randolph, the widow of John Randolph of "Matoax," Chesterfield County, and mother of John Randolph of Roanoke, 1773–1833 [*q.v.*]. Nathaniel Beverley Tucker, 1784–1851, and Henry St. George Tucker, 1780–1848, were their sons, John Randolph Tucker, 1823–1897 and Nathaniel Beverley Tucker, 1820–1890, grandsons, and Henry St. George Tucker, 1853–1932 [*qq.v.*], a great-grandson. She died in 1788. His letters to her while he was in the Revolutionary Army bear testimony of his devotion as a husband. They are, at the same time, historical documents of no mean importance ("Southern Campaign, 1781," in *Magazine of American History,* July, Sept. 1881). On Oct. 8, 1791, he married Lelia (Skipwith) Carter, the daughter of Sir Peyton Skipwith.

In public office he spent virtually the whole remainder of his life. In 1786 he became one of the commissioners at the Annapolis convention. His judicial career, in which he was to attain distinguished eminence, began when he became judge of the general court of Virginia in 1788. In 1800 he became professor of law in the College of William and Mary. In 1803 he was elected to the supreme court of appeals of Virginia as the successor of Edmund Pendleton [*q.v.*].

He sat for eight years, adding no little to his own growing fame and enhancing the reputation of the court. He resigned from this court in 1811, but in 1813 he was appointed by President Madison judge of the district court for the district of Virginia. For nearly fifteen years he continued as a federal judge before failure in health prompted his resignation. He then retired to the home of Joseph C. Cabell [q.v.] in Nelson County, Va., where he died. His grandson, John Randolph Tucker, 1823–1897 [q.v.], many years later cited his opinion in *Kamper* vs. *Hawkins* (1 *Va. Reports,* 20), in the general court, that the state constitution of 1776 was a sovereign act of the people of Virginia and therefore the supreme law, and that any act of the legislature or the government in conflict with it was null and void. Among his other important opinions are his dissenting opinion in *Woodson* vs. *Randolph,* also in the general court, holding that it was a violation of the federal Constitution for Congress to undertake to change the rules of evidence with reference to a state contract sued upon in a state court (1 *Brockenbrough and Holmes Reports,* 128) and his opinion, in the supreme court of appeals of Virginia, in *Turpin* vs. *Locket* (6 *Call Reports,* 113) sustaining the constitutionality of the act of 1802 by which the glebes of the Episcopal Church were to be applied to the relief of poor of each parish (for discussion see Call, *post,* and Hardy, *post,* p. 58).

His reputation rests in no small part on his juridical writings. His pamphlet *Dissertation on Slavery: with a Proposal for its Gradual Abolition in Virginia* (1796 and reprinted in Philadelphia 1861), advocating the emancipation of children born to slave mothers, was widely read and acclaimed. His annotated edition of *Blackstone's Commentaries* (5 vols., 1803) was one of the most important law books of its day. In an appendix he discussed the principles of government as related to the nature and interpretation of the federal Constitution. He also wrote minor poetry of some charm, as *Liberty, a Poem on the Independence of America* (1788) and *The Probationary Odes of Jonathan Pindar* (2 pts. 1796), originally published in the *National Gazette* and often erroneously attributed to Philip M. Freneau.

[Daniel Call, "Memoir," 4 *Call Report* (Va.), p. xxvi; J. R. Tucker, "The Judges Tucker of the Court of Appeals of Va.," *Va. Law Register,* Mar. 1896; S. S. P. Patteson, "The Supreme Court of Appeals of Va.," *Green Bag,* July 1893; S. E. M. Hardy, "Some Va. Lawyers," *Ibid.,* Jan. 1898; H. St. George Tucker, "Patrick Henry and St. George Tucker," *Univ. of Pa. Law Rev.,* Jan. 1919; W. C. Bruce, *Life of John Randolph of Roanoke* (2 vols., 1922); S. N. Hurst and R. M. Brown, *A Complete Alphabetical, Chronological Annotated Digest of All the Reported Decisions of . . . Va.,* vol. I

(1897); *Colonial Families of the U. S.,* vol. V (1915), ed. by G. N. Mackenzie; T. A. Emmett, *An Account of the Tucker Family of Bermuda* (1898); *Gentleman's Mag.,* Nov. 1828.]   A. M. D.

TUCKER, SAMUEL (Nov. 1, 1747–Mar. 10, 1833), naval officer, was born in Marblehead, Mass., third of the eight children of Andrew and Mary (Belcher) Tucker. His father was a prosperous ship captain, said to have come from Dundee, Scotland, and his mother was of English extraction. At the age of eleven the boy ran away from home and went to sea, enlisting on board the *Royal George* bound for Louisbourg. At seventeen he was a second mate. Rising to first mate, he later became a master and on the eve of the Revolution was in command of the *Young Phoenix,* trading with Spain and England and importing salt. In the meantime, on Dec. 21, 1768, he had married Mary Gatchell of Marblehead, who bore him several children.

It is said that Tucker saw his first Revolutionary service in 1775 as lieutenant of a company of soldiers. On Jan. 20, 1776, Washington commissioned him captain of the *Franklin,* an army warship, and directed him to cruise against British vessels. A few months later he was transferred to the *Hancock,* a superior command. During 1776, alone or in company with another ship of the army, he captured several valuable prizes, including two transports carrying Scottish troops and two ships laden with beef, pork, and other supplies. Congress on Mar. 15, 1777, recognized his services by appointing him a captain in the navy, but several months elapsed before he received a command, the frigate *Boston.* On Feb. 17, 1778, he weighed anchor at Marblehead and sailed for France, carrying as passengers John Adams, recently appointed commissioner to France, and his son John Quincy Adams. The elder Adams, who characterized Tucker as an able seaman, and a brave, vigilant officer, though of no great erudition, has left a description of this eventful voyage (*The Works of John Adams,* vol. III, 1851, esp. p. 97). Noteworthy were the rough weather that shattered the mainmast, the escape of the *Boston* from the watchful enemy, the chasing of prospective prizes, the capture of the valuable privateer *Martha,* whose captain had served twenty years in the Royal Navy, and the anxieties of all as the ship neared her destination. On Aug. 22, after a successful cruise in French waters in which he captured four small prizes, Tucker sailed for America, accompanied by the *Providence,* Commodore Abraham Whipple [q.v.], and the *Ranger,* Capt. John Paul Jones [q.v.]. The little fleet captured three prizes before arriving at its destination, Portsmouth, N. H.

In the spring of 1779 Tucker sailed southward

to Chesapeake Bay and on July 29, accompanied by the *Deane,* Commodore Samuel Nicholson [*q.v.*], two ships of the Virginia navy, and a convoy of merchantmen, sailed out of the bay. The two frigates made a successful cruise of about five weeks, capturing eight prizes, including four New York privateers, and the packet *Sandwich* and the sloop of war *Thorn,* each of sixteen guns. On Sept. 6 they arrived at Boston, with 250 prisoners, among whom were several officers. In November the *Boston* with several other naval ships sailed on important service. After a brief cruise, during which a privateer of twelve guns was captured, the fleet arrived at Charleston, S. C., where Tucker participated in the siege of Charleston, with the *Boston* anchored in the Cooper River. On the surrender of the city he and his vessel fell into the hands of the enemy. He was almost immediately paroled and his vessel was taken into the Royal Navy and renamed the *Charleston.* Exchanged for the captain of the *Thorn,* Tucker obtained leave of absence from the navy and in 1781 made several cruises in that vessel, now a privateer, and captured among other ships the packet *Lord Hyde.* About Aug. 1 near the mouth of the St. Lawrence the *Thorn* was captured by the frigate *Hind* and Tucker and his officers were landed on the island of St. John's (now Prince Edward Island). Furnished with an open boat to carry them to Halifax, they laid a course for Boston, where in due time they arrived. This ended Tucker's active service in the navy.

In comfortable circumstances by reason of prize money, Tucker lived for several years in a house on Fleet Street, Boston. Returning to the merchant service, in 1783–85 he commanded several vessels trading with West India and European ports. In 1786 the *Cato,* a ship in which he had a large pecuniary interest, sank in the harbor of Lisbon. Giving up the sea, he moved to Marblehead and purchased there an interest in two grist mills and a granary. Failing in this enterprise, in 1792 he purchased a farm in Bristol, Me., on which he spent the rest of his life. From 1814 to 1818 he was a member of the Massachusetts house and later he was twice elected to the Maine house. In 1820 he carried to Washington the electoral vote of Maine, making the journey of 600 miles in less than five days. A statement made at this time (*Daily National Intelligencer,* Washington, Dec. 16, 1820) that he had taken sixty-two prizes, more than 600 cannon, and 3,000 prisoners probably exaggerated his Revolutionary services. In 1821 a private act of Congress pensioned him at the rate of twenty dollars a month and ten years later a general act

increased his pension to $600 a year. His wife died Dec. 30, 1831, and Tucker some fifteen months later, at Bremen, Me.

[J. H. Sheppard, *The Life of Samuel Tucker* (1868), is not free from legendary materials. See also Sheppard's briefer sketch in *New-Eng. Hist. and Geneal. Reg.,* Apr. 1872; G. W. Allen, *A Naval Hist. of the Am. Rev.* (2 vols., 1913); C. O. Paullin, *Out-Letters of Continental Marine Committee and Board of Admiralty* (1914); Ephraim Tucker, *Geneal. of the Tucker Family* (1895); Samuel Roads, *Hist. and Traditions of Marblehead* (1880); *Niles' Weekly Register,* Apr. 6, 27, 1833. W. P. Chipman, *In Ship and Prison* (copr. 1908) is a fictional account of Tucker.]   C. O. P.

TUCKER, STEPHEN DAVIS (Jan. 28, 1818–Oct. 9, 1902), inventor and manufacturer, was born at Bloomfield, N. J. His parents were Benjamin and Jane (Davis) Tucker; his first American ancestor, grandfather of Benjamin, was Timothy Tucker, who came to America prior to 1732. On June 3, 1834, young Tucker was apprenticed to a member of the firm of R. Hoe & Company of New York, manufacturers of printing presses, to learn "the art, trade and mystery of finisher or whitesmith," and with the same firm he remained for fifty-nine years, until his retirement as senior partner. In 1842 he was set to work in the experiment room which had just been established. At first his work there consisted merely in the fabrication and testing of models, but his inventive genius soon manifested itself. He proved to be "one of the most brilliant mechanics that this country ever produced" (*Scientific American,* June 5, 1915), and in the course of his long service with the company took out nearly one hundred patents for improvements in printing, some in his own name alone and some in conjunction with Richard M. Hoe [*q.v.*]. Among his most important inventions were those which made (or helped to make) practicable the printing of both sides of a paper at once, the printing of a continuous web of paper instead of individual sheets, and the folding of newspapers by machinery as they come off the press. In 1846 he became foreman of his department, and in 1848 was sent to Paris to set up new Hoe presses for *La Patrie* and start their operation. Further business of the firm kept him in France for two years. He was admitted as a partner May 28, 1860, and finally retired on Aug. 31, 1893, transferring his share to Robert Hoe, 1839–1909 [*q.v.*].

Tucker continued to live in New York, but traveled abroad extensively. He devoted much of his leisure to the study of sundials and assembled a collection of more than sixty specimens in ivory, bone, silver, and wood, illustrating both artistic and scientific aspects; this he left to the Metropolitan Museum of Art in New York.

He also wrote a "History of R. Hoe & Company," which is of great value for the study of the printing art in the nineteenth century. It was not intended for publication and was never printed, but there are copies in the Library of Congress, the Newberry Library (Chicago), and the Stephen Spaulding Collection at the University of Michigan, besides three or four in private possession. He died in London. He was twice married: first, about 1852, to Aimée Désirée, daughter of Jean Cherouvrier of Le Mans, who died Sept. 12, 1860; and second, Nov. 4, 1862, to Sarah Ann, daughter of William Conquest of London, who survived him.

[This account is based mainly on information supplied by Tucker's daughters; only scattered references to him or to his work are to be found in print. Something can be gleaned from his own "History of R. Hoe & Company," but it is quite impersonal and deals mostly in "we," not in "I."]　　　　　　　T. M. S.

TUCKER, WILLIAM JEWETT (July 13, 1839–Sept. 29, 1926), clergyman, educator, was born at Griswold, Conn., the son of Henry and Sarah White (Lester) Tucker, and a descendant of Robert Tucker, who settled in Weymouth, Mass., in 1635. His mother died when he was a child and he spent the greater part of his youth in the home of his maternal uncle, the Rev. William R. Jewett, at Plymouth, N. H. He was educated at Plymouth, at Kimball Union Academy, and at Dartmouth College, where he graduated in 1861. After teaching for a period at Columbus, Ohio, he entered the Andover Theological Seminary and was graduated from that institution in 1866. During his course in the Seminary he served for a time as agent of the United States Christian Commission with the Army of the Cumberland in the campaign before Atlanta. After a period spent as representative of the American Home Missionary Society in Kansas and Missouri, he was ordained, Jan. 24, 1867, and assumed the pastorate of the Franklin Street (Congregational) Church in Manchester, N. H., transferring his activities to the Madison Square (Presbyterian) Church in New York in 1875. In 1880 he became professor of sacred rhetoric in the Andover Theological Seminary.

At Andover, in addition to the usual duties of his professorship, Tucker was specially concerned with the social responsibilities of the church. In connection with his lectureship in pastoral theology he developed courses in sociology, then a novelty in divinity schools. In 1891 he founded a social settlement in Boston called Andover House (afterwards South End House) modeled after Toynbee Hall in London, which, under the immediate supervision of Robert A. Woods, soon achieved a distinguished success. His Andover period was far from peaceful, however. In 1884 five professors in the Seminary, including Tucker, founded a periodical called the *Andover Review*. The articles in this journal, some of them republished in book form under the title *Progressive Orthodoxy* (1886), soon attracted the unfavorable attention of the conservative wing of Congregationalism. While numerous utterances of the editors were considered to be heterodox, particular objection was raised to their refusal to admit that infants and members of races which had never enjoyed the advantage of Christian teaching are necessarily doomed to eternal perdition. This doctrine of a "second probation" was especially objectionable to the missionary organizations of the church. Charges were filed against the five professors in 1886, at the end of that year they were tried before the board of visitors of the seminary, and Prof. Egbert C. Smyth [q.v.] was found guilty, while the other four (against whom the evidence was practically the same as against Professor Smyth) were acquitted by a tie vote. Upon appeal, the supreme court of Massachusetts in 1890 pronounced the proceedings faulty, and in 1892, at a second trial, Smyth was acquitted. The "Andover controversy" thus ended in a complete victory for the faculty.

In 1893 Tucker became president of Dartmouth College. Serious problems confronted him upon his accession. The institution had long been a stronghold of conservatism—dominated by a reactionary theology, averse to educational experimentation, and working in large part with the material facilities of the eighteenth century. To the solution of these problems Tucker brought educational vision and insight of a rare order, acumen and resource in business management, adroitness in matters of finance, and powers of leadership which ensured harmonious cooperation of all the branches of the college. As a result of his efforts student attendance rose from three hundred to eleven hundred, the teaching body was increased in like proportion, material facilities were modernized, finance reorganized and placed upon a sounder basis. The spirit of contention which had marked much of the previous history of the institution disappeared, theological dictation vanished, and, most of all, the spirit of the college became such as to enable it more intelligently to meet the educational demands of the age.

Tucker's moral leadership was also impressive. Exerted under the advantage of direct personal contact at Andover, it was no less effective at Dartmouth where his opportunities, for the most part, were limited to chapel services and other public exercises. His personality awakened veneration, respect, and sincere affection, and through the strength of his appeal he became an influence for good in generations of college graduates. He retired from the presidency of Dartmouth in 1909. The remainder of his life, so far as his health permitted, was devoted to literary activity. In addition to numerous articles in the magazines and to his contributions to books issued by the Andover faculty, he had already published *The Making and the Unmaking of the Preacher* (1898). In 1910 appeared two volumes, *Personal Power* and *Public Mindedness*; in 1911, *The Function of the Church in Modern Society*; in 1916, *The New Reservation of Time,* and in 1919 an autobiography, *My Generation.*

Tucker was twice married: on June 22, 1870, to Charlotte Henry Rogers of Plymouth, N. H., who died in 1882, and in June 1887 to Charlotte Barrell Cheever of Worcester, Mass. Two daughters were born of the first marriage and one of the second; all three survived their father.

[In addition to Tucker's autobiography, see J. K. Lord, *A Hist. of Dartmouth Coll.* (1913); L. B. Richardson, *Hist. of Dartmouth Coll.,* vol. II (1932); J. W. Buckham, *Progressive Religious Thought in America* (1919); *Granite Monthly,* June 1903; E. M. Hopkins, *William Jewett Tucker, a Tribute* (1926); *Who's Who in America,* 1926–27; Ephraim Tucker, *Geneal. of the Tucker Family* (1895); *Manchester Union* (Manchester, N. H.), Sept. 30, 1926.]   L. B. R.

TUCKERMAN, BAYARD (July 2, 1855– Oct. 20, 1923), author, the son of Lucius and Elizabeth Wolcott (Gibbs) Tuckerman, was born in New York City. Through his father, an iron manufacturer, son of the Rev. Joseph Tuckerman [q.v.], he was descended from John Tuckerman who came to Massachusetts Bay about 1649; his mother, daughter of the elder George Gibbs [q.v.] and sister of the younger George and of Oliver Wolcott Gibbs [qq.v.], was a granddaughter of Oliver Wolcott [q.v.], signer of the Declaration of Independence. Having studied with private tutors, Bayard Tuckerman spent two years at the Pension Roulet at Neuchâtel, Switzerland, before entering Harvard College, where he graduated with the class of 1878. Returning to Paris the year of his graduation, he soon undertook a serious study of English literature, producing after four years *A History of English Prose Fiction from Sir Thomas Malory to George Eliot,* published in New York in 1882. While this volume has long since been superseded, it was much esteemed by the author's contemporaries. In September 1882, at Ipswich, Mass., Tuckerman married Annie Osgood Smith, daughter of the Rev. John Cotton Smith [q.v.], and settled down to a life of domestic felicity and

the joys of authorship; a son and three daughters were born to them.

His *Life of General Lafayette* (2 vols., 1889), a thorough, careful, and interesting biography, written in a clear and unpretentious style, was the first account of Lafayette based upon an adequate, modern critical apparatus. The same year was marked by his publication of *The Diary of Philip Hone, 1828–1851* in two volumes; this was a satisfactory collection of excerpts from Hone's voluminous diary, but otherwise the editing was slight, for Tuckerman's edition contains almost no notes. In 1893 he published, in the Makers of America Series, a biography, *Peter Stuyvesant,* which was useful and well-written, but hardly an important contribution to American historiography. His *William Jay and the Constitutional Movement for the Abolition of Slavery* (1894) was a significant addition to the literature of the anti-slavery movement, for it was based upon voluminous manuscript materials that have never been utilized by any other historian. His *Life of General Philip Schuyler, 1733–1804* (1903), although still standard in its field, is not marked by any great biographical skill, but it was based upon valuable manuscript materials which have since been scattered and probably lost. Although Tuckerman later compiled two small genealogies —*Notes on the Tuckerman Family of Massachusetts* (privately printed, 1914) and *A Sketch of the Cotton Smith Family of Sharon, Connecticut* (privately printed, 1915)—his book on Schuyler was his last important literary production. Increasing ill health prevented the completion of a history of chivalry, upon which he had spent several years of research.

From 1898 to 1907 Tuckerman lectured on English literature at Princeton University, but while he enjoyed academic life his first choice was for the quiet and severe life of the country, and a private income made him independent and permitted him to indulge his inclinations. He never became a great scholar, but he fully deserved the old-fashioned title of "scholar and gentleman" which his intimate friends bestowed upon him.

[Sources include *Harvard College, Class of 1878, Fiftieth Anniversary Report, 1878–1928* (n.d.); *Harvard Graduates' Magazine,* Dec. 1923; *Who's Who in America,* 1922–23; Tuckerman's genealogical books, mentioned above; George Gibbs, *The Gibbs Family of Rhode Island and Some Related Families* (1933); death notice in *Boston Transcript,* Oct. 22, 1923; information from a daughter, Mrs. Wm. M. Elkins. Tuckerman's MSS. are in the possession of Mrs. Bayard Tuckerman, Ipswich, Mass., and Bayard Tuckerman, Jr., Hamilton, Mass.]   F. M.

TUCKERMAN, EDWARD (Dec. 7, 1817– Mar. 15, 1886), botanist, distinguished authority upon lichens, was born in Boston, Mass., the eldest son of a merchant of the same name and Sophia (May) Tuckerman. He was a brother of Frederick Goddard Tuckerman and a nephew of the Rev. Joseph Tuckerman [*qq.v.*]. Prepared for college at Boston Latin School, he graduated (B.A.) from Union College in 1837 and from Harvard Law School in 1839. Two years later he visited Europe, to pursue special studies in philosophy, history, and botany, an important influence in his later work being his studies at Upsala, Sweden, under the famous lichenologist Elias Fries. Returning in 1842, he reëntered Union College and received the degree of M.A. the next year. Desiring then to obtain an academic degree from Harvard, he matriculated as a senior in 1846, graduating (B.A.) in 1847. Subsequently he entered Harvard Divinity School, and completed the courses of study in 1852. He married Sarah Eliza Sigourney Cushing, in Boston, May 17, 1854, and shortly thereafter removed to Amherst, Mass., to lecture in history at Amherst College. He was appointed professor of botany in 1858, and held this position the rest of his life, which was passed at Amherst. During his later years he became almost totally deaf; he died from complications of Bright's disease, without issue.

Tuckerman was a man of uncommonly broad scholarly culture, whose life was devoted unreservedly to study. He was early attracted to lichens, and his botanical publications up to 1841 dealt with New England plants of this group, largely of his own collecting in the White Mountains. By that time, however, he had also contributed to the New York *Churchman* no less than fifty-four articles upon biographical, historical, and theological topics. In 1842 he described *Oakesia*, a new genus of flowering plants from New England. While a student at Union he was appointed curator of the college museum, and here also he issued privately, *Enumeratio Methodica Caricum Quarundam* (1843), an erudite revision of the sedges (*Carex*), which Asa Gray (*post*, p. 541) mentions as early displaying Tuckerman's genius as a systematizer. This was followed by three other papers on New England flowering plants, including (1849) an elaboration of the American pondweeds (*Potamogeton*). But otherwise, aside from his *Catalogue of Plants Growing without Cultivation within Thirty Miles of Amherst College* (1875), summarizing twenty years' study, his published botanical work is chiefly upon lichens.

In the field of American lichenology Tuckerman is outstanding. Lichens had been studied scarcely at all by American students, and he himself was the first to explore for them in the mountains of New England. This he did with notable success and thoroughness, in the most difficult regions. In 1845 there appeared his *Enumeration of North American Lichenes*; then his "Synopsis of the Lichenes of New England, the other Northern States, and British America" (*Proceedings of the American Academy of Arts and Sciences*, vol. I, 1848, pp. 195–285). The latter was the first attempt to describe and classify all the lichens known from temperate North America, and it proved a great stimulus to the study of this group. From 1848 to 1872 Tuckerman published numerous other papers, of which the more important are a supplement to his *Enumeration* describing many new species from California and the southern United States (*American Journal of Science*, 1858, 1859); four parts of a continued series of critical notes in *Proceedings of the American Academy* (vols. IV–VII, 1860–68, vol. XII, 1877), relating largely to the Cuban lichens collected by Charles Wright; an illustrated brochure (1862) upon the lichens of the United States Exploring Expedition under Wilkes; *Lichens of California, Oregon, and the Rocky Mountains* (1866); besides accounts of species from many foreign regions, as well as of material collected on several governmental surveys. These studies were definitely contributory to *Genera Lichenum: An Arrangement of North American Lichens* (1872), regarded as Tuckerman's greatest work. He planned also a comprehensive treatise containing descriptions of all the lichens known from the United States, and the first volume appeared in 1882 as *A Synopsis of the North American Lichens: Part I*; the second, completed by Henry Willey, was published two years after Tuckerman's death.

Though never robust, Tuckerman was in early life an intrepid explorer; Tuckerman Ravine on Mount Washington was named in his honor. He is commemorated also by a genus of Compositæ, *Tuckermania*. He was elected a member of the National Academy of Sciences in 1868. Of gentle, sensitive disposition and retiring temperament, he was noted for his amiability, helpfulness, and exquisite taste, and equally for his keen independent criticism, his fondness for antiquarian and genealogical research, and his studious attention to philosophy, divinity, and law. In the words of his friend Asa Gray (*post*, p. 544), he was "much more than an excellent specialist."

[Asa Gray, "Edward Tuckerman," *Proc. Am. Acad. Arts and Sci.*, XXI (1886), 539–47, with bibliog., repr. in *Am. Jour. Sci.*, July 1886 (3 ser. XXXII, 1–7); H. H. Goodell, "Edward Tuckerman: Biog. Sketch," and Henry Willey, "Bibliog. Sketch," *Bot. Gaz.*, Apr. 1886

(XI, 73-74 and 74-78); W. G. Farlow, "Memoir of Edward Tuckerman," with bibliog., *Nat. Acad. Sci. Biog. Memoirs*, vol. III (1895), preprint, 1887; Bruce Fink, in *Proc. Iowa Acad. Sci.*, XI (1904), 25-29, portr.; *Am. Naturalist*, June 1886 (XX, 578-79); Bayard Tuckerman, *Notes on the Tuckerman Family* (priv. printed, 1914).]

W. R. M.

TUCKERMAN, FREDERICK (May 7, 1857–Nov. 8, 1929), comparative anatomist and naturalist, was born in Greenfield, Mass., the son of Frederick Goddard Tuckerman [*q.v.*] and Hannah Lucinda (Jones), and a nephew of the botanist Edward Tuckerman [*q.v.*]. He received the degree of B.S. from both the Massachusetts Agricultural College and Boston University in 1878 and that of M.D. from the Harvard Medical School in 1882. After a period of study in London and Berlin, 1882–83, he lectured on anatomy and physiology at the Massachusetts Agricultural College until 1886. Subsequently he was a fellow of Clark University, 1889–90, and again went abroad to study in London, Berlin, and Heidelberg; from the University of Heidelberg he received the degrees of A.M. and Ph.D. in 1894. After his return to America, he made his home at Amherst, Mass. Having adequate means, he sought no university position, but gave his time to independent research in comparative anatomy and natural history and to genealogical studies. He also took an active interest in local church and town affairs.

Tuckerman's best genealogical work concerned his wife's family, the Coopers of Boston. He published "Thomas Cooper of Boston and His Descendants" and "Notes from the Rev. Samuel Cooper's Interleaved Almanacs of 1764 and 1769" in the *New-England Historical and Genealogical Register* (January 1890, April 1901) and "Diary of Samuel Cooper, 1775–1776" and "Letters of Samuel Cooper to Thomas Pownall, 1769–77," in the *American Historical Review* (January 1901, January 1903). An excellent biography of Charles Anthony Goessmann [*q.v.*], professor of chemistry in the Massachusetts Agricultural College, was written by him in 1911 (*United States Catholic Historical Society, Historical Records and Studies*, vol. VI, pt. 1, 1911) and, in 1929, his *Amherst Academy: A New England School of the Past* was published posthumously. He was also a contributor to the *Dictionary of American Biography*. He supported the Appalachian Mountain Club, contributing to their publication *Appalachia* in 1918, 1921, and 1926, and was considered an authority on the history of the White Mountains. His researches in comparative anatomy, especially on the gustatory and taste organs, were sound (*Journal of Anatomy and Physiology*, vols. XXIII, XXIV, XXV, 1889–91, and *Journal of Morphology*, vols. II,

IV, VII, 1889–92). He held membership in the American Society of Naturalists, the Boston Society of Natural History, Anatomische Gesellschaft (Jena), and the American Association of Anatomists. On Sept. 6, 1881, he married Alice Girdler Cooper, daughter of James Sullivan Cooper; she and two daughters survived him.

[Bayard Tuckerman, *Notes on the Tuckerman Family* (privately printed, 1914); *Who's Who in America*, 1928–29; *Boston Transcript*, Nov. 8, 1929; *Amherst Record*, Nov. 13, 1929; reports from Tuckerman's family.]

H. R. V.

TUCKERMAN, FREDERICK GODDARD (Feb. 4, 1821–May 9, 1873), poet, son of Edward and Sophia (May) Tuckerman, was born in Boston, Mass. He came from a distinguished family; his elder brother, Edward Tuckerman [*q.v.*], became professor of botany at Amherst College; his cousin, Henry Theodore Tuckerman [*q.v.*], was a critic and essayist of some repute; his uncle, Joseph Tuckerman [*q.v.*], was a noted philanthropist and Unitarian clergyman. Tuckerman entered Harvard College with the class of 1841, but left at the end of his first year on account of serious eye trouble. After a year of rest, however, he persisted in his education and was graduated from the Harvard Law School in 1842. He was admitted to the bar in 1844, but practised only a few years, since private means enabled him to devote himself to his chief interests—literature, botany, and astronomy. Retiring to Greenfield, Mass., in 1847, he lived there, except for two holidays in Europe, until his death in 1873. He published some of his observations on eclipses and won a reputation as an authority on the local flora, but for the most part his life was passed in seclusion from the world. He married Hannah Lucinda Jones, June 17, 1847; she died at the birth of her third child, Frederick [*q.v.*], in 1857.

A number of Tuckerman's poems—several of which had first appeared in the *Living Age, Putnam's*, or the *Atlantic Monthly*—were collected and privately printed at Boston under the title *Poems* in 1860, and published in England in 1863 and in Boston in 1864 and 1869. Some of them won favorable comment from Emerson and Longfellow, but Tuckerman was overlooked by Stedman in compiling his *American Anthology* and as a poet had virtually slipped from memory when he was rediscovered by Walter Prichard Eaton in 1909 ("A Forgotten American Poet," *Forum*, January 1909). In 1931, Witter Bynner edited and published, with a critical introduction, *The Sonnets of Frederick Goddard Tuckerman*, containing in addition to some which had appeared in the *Poems*, three previously unpublished sequences. Although Tuckerman's sonnets were unnoticed by his contemporaries—even by Emerson and Longfellow—Bynner ranks them "with the noblest in the language" (Introduction, *post*, p. 36), finding in them "not only ... the fine thoughts of a devout stoic," but "the subtly fine craft of a devout poet." Not bound by conventional sonnet forms, Tuckerman "shuffled the rhyme-scheme to suit the rise and fall of his meaning" and revealed "an anachronistic fondness for the juxtaposition of fine and homely phrases and images," together with "an ... emotional use of words that Edgar Allan Poe might have envied" (*Ibid.*, pp. 18–19). He died at Greenfield, in his fifty-third year.

[Bayard Tuckerman, *Notes on the Tuckerman Family* (privately printed, 1914) ; Witter Bynner, Introduction, in *Sonnets of Frederick Goddard Tuckerman* (1931), portr. ; *Bookman*, Apr. 1931 ; death notice in *Boston Daily Globe*, May 12, 1873.]   H. R. V.

TUCKERMAN, HENRY THEODORE (Apr. 20, 1813–Dec. 17, 1871), critic, essayist, and poet, was born in Boston, Mass., a nephew of Joseph Tuckerman [*q.v.*] and the son of Henry Harris and Ruth (Keating) Tuckerman. His sister Ruth became the mother of Henry Cuyler Bunner [*q.v.*]. The elder Tuckerman, a prosperous merchant, sent his son to the Latin School and thence to Harvard, where, however, the young man remained for only two years. Ill health caused him to seek relaxation in foreign travel, and he spent the years 1833–34 mostly in Italy, where he began his lifelong, romantic devotion to literature and art. Upon his return he published *The Italian Sketch Book* (1835). The years 1836–38, passed again in Italy and Sicily, resulted in a travel romance, *Isabel, or Sicily, a Pilgrimage* (1839). Tuckerman now determined upon a literary career, and with his return to Boston started contributing poems and essays to periodicals. For a time in 1843 he edited the *Boston Miscellany of Literature and Fashion*, but in 1845 he removed to New York City, where he settled down to a quiet literary and social life. A brief visit to England in 1852–53 was the basis of a small volume, *A Month in England* (1853), which embodied reflections on English life and art.

A man of independent financial means, Tuckerman had ample opportunity to indulge his love of meditation and study. In his essay "New England Philosophy" (*The Optimist*), he decries the national spirit of commercialism, which carries with it "want of serenity" and of poetic feeling. His works of travel, in their emphasis on the picturesque and on the historic and literary associations of European life, as well as in their quiet, leisurely style, show the influence of Irving and sometimes of Sterne. As a literary critic, Tuckerman is best understood in the light of his essay on Hazlitt (*Characteristics of Literature,* second series), where he finds the function of the critic that of feeler and sympathizer, as well as that of analyst. Following more or less Hazlitt's critical manner are his *Thoughts on the Poets* (1846) and the two series of *Characteristics of Literature* (1849, 1851). Always fascinated by pictorial art and sculpture, Tuckerman produced in 1847 *Artist-Life, or Sketches of American Painters,* which twenty years later he expanded into a significant volume, *Book of the Artists: American Artist Life* (1867). His interest in biography found expression in *The Life of Silas Talbot* (1850), *Mental Portraits* (1853), *Essays, Biographical and Critical* (1857), and *The Life of John Pendleton Kennedy* (1871). Characteristic familiar essays are collected in *The Optimist* (1850) and *The Criterion* (1866), and a series of Irvingesque sketches in *Leaves from the Diary of a Dreamer* (1853). A volume of *Poems* (1851) shows many of the traits discernible in his prose—love of retirement, interest in art, fascination with the historic and literary associations of Italy, and indulgence in sentiment that sometimes passed into sentimentality. Perhaps his work of greatest lasting importance is *America and Her Commentators: with a Critical Sketch of Travel in the United States* (1864).

Although of a quiet, retiring nature, Tuckerman entered freely into the social life of New York, having as friends such men as Washington Irving, Dr. John W. Francis, and Fitz-Greene Halleck [*qq.v.*]. His love of the city of his adoption is evinced in his edition (1865) of Dr. Francis' *Old New York.* Representing with Rufus W. Griswold and Evert A. Duyckinck [*qq.v.*] the easy, romantic scholarship of the forties and fifties in America, he readily passed in his day for a man of genius, having even a small English audience. Harvard in 1850 gave him the honorary degree of M.A.; and the king of Italy conferred upon him an order "in recognition of his labors on behalf of Italian exiles in the United States." Tuckerman never married. He died in New York City and was buried in Mount Auburn Cemetery, Cambridge, Mass.

[See Bayard Tuckerman, *Notes on the Tuckerman Family of Mass.* (priv. printed, 1914) ; *N. Y. Tribune*, Dec. 18, 1871 ; *Evening Post* (N. Y.), Dec. 18, 20, 1871 ; R. W. Griswold, *Poets and Poetry of America* (1842), and *The Prose Writers of America* (1847) ; E. A. and G. L. Duyckinck, *Cyc. of Am. Lit.* (1875), vol. II ; E. A. Duyckinck, *A Memorial of Henry T. Tuckerman* (1872) ; N. F. Adkins, *Fitz-Greene Halleck* (1930), *passim* ; F. L. Mott, *A Hist. of Am. Mags.* (1930). For a full list of Tuckerman's works, as well as for many critical articles, see S. A. Allibone, *A Critical Dict. of Eng. Lit.*, vol. III (1871). Some information has been furnished by Miss Sydney R. McLean, who is preparing a biography of Tuckerman.]   N. F. A.

TUCKERMAN, JOSEPH (Jan. 18, 1778–Apr. 20, 1840), Unitarian clergyman, the son of Edward and Elizabeth (Harris) Tuckerman and a descendant of John Tuckerman who came from England to Massachusetts Bay about 1649, was born in Boston, Mass. He was educated at the Boston Latin School and Harvard College, graduating in 1798. William Ellery Channing and Joseph Story were his classmates, the latter his roommate. Tuckerman studied for the Unitarian ministry with Rev. Thomas Thacher and must have been an outstanding pupil, for he was invited by the Boston Mechanic Association to preach for them on Feb. 22, 1800, and was generously thanked for his "pathetic Elegant and Judicious Oration, commemorative of the Sublime virtues and preëminent services of the late General Washington," which was then printed, under the title, *A Funeral Oration: Occasioned by the Death of General George Washington.* In 1801, on Nov. 4, he was ordained to his first and only pastorate, in Chelsea, to receive the munificent sum of five hundred dollars a year. He was now settled, with a salary, and on July 5, 1803, he married Abigail Parkman of Boston. She died July 28, 1807, leaving him with three young children, and on Nov. 3, 1808, he married Sarah Cary, of a family prominent socially in Chelsea, who bore him seven children. Bayard Tuckerman [q.v.] was his grandson.

In 1805, Tuckerman became one of the original members of the Anthology Society, publishers of the *Monthly Anthology and Boston Review.*

During his ministry in Chelsea, he started (1812) the Boston Society for the Religious and Moral Improvement of Seamen ("Report," *Christian Disciple,* July 1813), said to have been the first of its kind in the United States. He wrote a number of tracts for the benefit of this movement. His interest in seamen was duplicated by his interest in those he called "the neglected poor in our cities," and when he removed from Chelsea to Boston in 1826, on account of ill health, he began a "ministry-at-large," which was in effect a city mission for the poor. His work in this field was described in his book, *The Principles and Results of the Ministry at Large, in Boston* (1838). Many of his sermons and tracts dealing with charitable subjects were also printed. The idea of the ministry-at-large took him to England in 1833–34; he established missions in London and Liverpool and stimulated those already established in other places, and his influence extended into France. He continued his work in Boston on his return, but his health broke down in 1836. Seeking its restoration, he went to Santa Cruz and in 1838 to Cuba; he died in Havana.

Tuckerman had "a thin, aquiline face, and hair combed back from the brow" (Sprague, *post,* p. 350), and both dress and manner proclaimed his profession. He cared little for doctrines, and criticized Channing as well as those not of his communion. Devoted to his calling, he labored throughout his life for the good of others. The power of his personality is indicated by the fact that a society of ladies calling themselves the "Tuckerman Sewing Circle" were still sewing and selling what they made for the "Poor's Purse" as late as 1888; while in *A Memorial of Joseph Tuckerman* printed that year the statement is made that "the impetus which he gave to intelligent philanthropy has not yet passed away either in this country or in England."

[W. B. Sprague, *Annals Am. Pulpit,* vol. VIII (1865); *A Memorial of Joseph Tuckerman* (Worcester, 1888); *Proc. Mass. Hist. Soc.,* 1 ser. II (1880); Mellen Chamberlain, *A Doc. Hist. of Chelsea, Mass.* (1908), vol. II; *Vital Records of Chelsea, Mass.* (1916); *Seventy-fifth Anniv. of the Founding of the Ministry-at-Large in Boston, 1826–1901* (1901); W. E. Channing, *A Discourse on the Life and Character of the Rev. Joseph Tuckerman* (1841); Bayard Tuckerman, *Notes on the Tuckerman Family* (privately printed, 1914); *Boston Transcript,* May 8, 1840.]

E. S. B—n.

TUCKEY, WILLIAM (*c.* 1708–Sept. 14, 1781), organist, choirmaster, composer, was born in Somersetshire, England. The date of his birth is established only through the statement on his tombstone that he died in his seventy-third year. From an advertisement in the *New-York Mercury* (Mar. 11, 1754) it is known that he was for a time vicar choral and parish clerk of the Bristol Cathedral.

On Jan. 31, 1753, he was appointed parish clerk of Trinity Church, New York, at a salary of twenty-five pounds per annum (Dix, *post,* p. 262). That he had a wife and several children is disclosed by the fact that the vestry made provision for their transportation to America (*Ibid.*). He was also given charge of the music at the church, and he soon convinced the vestry of the necessity of teaching vocal music to the pupils of the Charity School. Through such teaching he developed the Trinity Church choir, which became noted both in and outside the city. In 1756 he was summarily dismissed from the office of parish clerk because of his "refusal to officiate in time of Divine Service" (*Ibid.,* p. 300), but he evidently continued to act as musical director of the church. It is certain that he continued his career as chorus master, for in 1762 he advertised for volunteers for a chorus to sing the *Te Deum* (*New York Weekly Post Boy,* Sept. 4), and four years later he announced a "Rehearsal of Church-Musick," and a forthcoming concert (*New-York Mercury,* Oct. 6, 1766). On Oct. 30, 1766, he was paid fifteen pounds for playing the organ at the dedication of the "new Episcopal chapel . . . called St. Paul's," assisted by a "suitable Band of Music, vocal and instrumental" (*Ibid.,* Nov. 3, 1766). On Jan. 16, 1770, he conducted a performance of the overture and sixteen numbers from Handel's *Messiah,* the first American rendering from this oratorio. The performance was held in "Mr. Burns's Room," New York.

During these years Tuckey had also been offering concerts of secular music. The earliest of these was announced in the *Post Boy* (Dec. 15, 1755) as a "Concert of Vocal and Instrumental musick," "for the benefit of Messrs. Cobham and Tuckey." At a benefit concert, "followed by a ball" (Apr. 21, 1769), Tuckey announced that "by particular desire" the concert would end with "God Save the King." It is possible that this was the first appearance of the British national hymn on an American concert program (Sonneck, *post,* p. 179).

After the *Messiah* performance in 1770 Tuckey's name does not appear in connection with concerts in New York. In 1771 he advertised for subscriptions to the publication of a number of his compositions—"an Hymn . . . together with a Psalm Tune; . . . a performance adapted for a FUNERAL, consisting of three Dirges . . . together with an anthem . . ." (*New-York Mercury,* Mar. 11), and he was probably the anonymous author of a collection of church music proposed in an advertisement in the *New-York Journal,* July 1, 1773. He died in Philadelphia, and was buried in the burial grounds of Christ Church. As a choir master, Tuckey takes rank with William Selby of Boston and Andrew Adgate [*qq.v.*] of Philadelphia. He labored hard to establish regular choral singing, but the time was not ripe for his efforts, though he achieved some remarkable results. As a composer he contributed to the literature of early American choral music, even though solicitations for subscriptions to his works were apparently not successful enough to warrant their publication. There is record of a "Thanksgiving Anthem," performed in Trinity Church, Boston, "before his excellency, General Amherst" (*Boston Evening Post,* Dec. 15, 1760); and an "Ode on Masonry," performed at the Cobham-Tuckey concert, was no doubt of Tuckey's composition. The only work by him now extant is an "Anthem Taken Out of the 97th Psalm," subsequently called "Liverpool," and as

such included in James Lyon's collection, *Urania* (*c.* 1761).

[O. G. Sonneck, *Early Concert-Life in America* (1907); H. E. Krehbiel, "Music in Trinity Church," *N. Y. Tribune,* July 26, 1903; Morgan Dix, *A Hist. of the Parish of Trinity Church in the City of N. Y.,* vol. I (1898); A. H. Messiter, *A Hist. of the Choir and Music of Trinity Church, N. Y.* (1906); *Grove's Dict. of Music and Musicians, Am. Supplement* (1931); J. T. Howard, *Our Am. Music* (1931); E. L. Clark, *A Record of the Inscriptions on the Tablets and Grave-Stones in the Burial-Grounds of Christ Church, Phila.* (1864).]   J.T.H.

TUDOR, FREDERIC (Sept. 4, 1783–Feb. 6, 1864), known as the "Ice King" from his success in building up the business of shipping ice from Boston to cities in tropical latitudes, was born in Boston, Mass. Son of a family that was prominent in Boston in the years following the Revolution (his father was William Tudor, who married Delia Jarvis), he did not, like his brothers, attend Harvard College, but went into business at the age of thirteen. When he was twenty-one he and his brother William [*q.v.*] conceived the idea of sending a cargo of ice to Martinique, and, in spite of the ridicule of their friends, with the aid of their cousin, James Savage [*q.v.*], they put their plan into effect, the vessel arriving at Saint-Pierre in March 1806. For the next fifteen years, alone, in debt and sometimes in jail for it, Tudor persisted in his scheme. By 1821 he had established himself in Havana and Charleston, and had undertaken a venture in New Orleans. His assistant, Nathaniel J. Wyeth [*q.v.*], had mastered the technique of ice-cutting on the ponds around Boston; Tudor himself, through much experiment, had learned how to ship his ice with the least possible loss, had devised a structure that would keep his commodity in warm climates, and had succeeded in making the use of ice an accepted thing in cities there. In the next ten or a dozen years he had to meet a good deal of competition; but his vigorous, not to say ruthless methods, his fanatical belief in his business, and his determination to become rich and enjoy the "delicious essence" of flattery overcame all obstacles. In May 1833 he sent his first cargo to Calcutta, and the success of this long-dreamed-of project made possible a worldwide expansion of his business. The number of tons of ice shipped from Boston, beginning with 130 in 1806, rose to 1,200 in 1816; to 4,000 in 1826; to 12,000 in 1836; to 65,000 in 1846; to 146,000 in 1856 (*Boston Board of Trade, Third Annual Report,* 1857, p. 80). In this last year 363 cargoes were sent to fifty-three different places in the United States, the West Indies, the East Indies, China, the Philippines, and Australia (*Ibid.,* pp. 79–82, and Justin Winsor, *The*

Memorial History of Boston, vol. IV, 1883, p. 221). To Boston the trade was invaluable. "Mr. Tudor and his ice came just in time to preserve Boston's East-India commerce from ruin. Our carrying trade between Calcutta and Europe had declined almost to extinction. . . . For a generation after the Civil War, until cheap artificial ice was invented, this export trade increased and prospered. Not Boston alone, but every New England village with a pond near tidewater was able to turn this Yankee liability into an asset, through the genius of Frederic Tudor" (S. E. Morison, *The Maritime History of Massachusetts,* 1921, pp. 282–83). Notwithstanding the growth of his enterprise, Tudor's embarrassments continued: the loss of over $200,000 in an unlucky coffee speculation kept him dependent on his creditors; for years he carried on a fierce fight with his agent in Havana for the control of the business there. It was not until he had reached the age of sixty-five that, with his debts extinguished and his lawsuit won, he was a free man. Characteristic of him was the sentence he printed on the cover of his "Ice House Diary"—"He who gives back at the first repulse and without striking the second blow despairs of success, has never been, is not, and never will be a hero in war, love, or business . . ."

Masterful in all his dealings and not without a power of fascination which compelled men to obey him ("I have so willed it"), Frederic Tudor was an extreme example of militant, despotic, and punitive individualism. With his quick and originating mind, he initiated many undertakings: he brought to Boston the first steam locomotive, a toy affair of one horse-power, which ran on the sidewalk; he designed a new type of hull for sailing vessels; he developed a graphite mine in Sturbridge, Mass.; he created the Maolis Gardens at Nahant, probably the first amusement park in the United States. Living at the age of eighty, he was in his last years a marked man in the life of Boston, already, as "Ice King," the hero of a legend in the "romance" of American business—a legend that only grows with the passage of time. On Jan. 2, 1834, at the age of fifty, he married Euphemia Fenno, aged nineteen, of Mount Upton, N. Y.; by her he had six children. He died in Boston.

[See *Deacon Tudor's Diary* (1896), ed. by William Tudor; memoir to be published in *Proc. Mass. Hist. Soc.,* vol. LXV (in preparation); Tudor's letter on the ice trade, *Proc. Mass. Hist. Soc., 1855–58,* vol. III (1859); *Bull. of the Business Hist. Soc.,* Sept. 1932, which contains three of Tudor's business letters taken from the Tudor papers in the lib. of the Grad. School of Business Administration, Harvard Univ.; F. A. Wilson, *Some Annals of Nahant, Mass.* (1928); and obituary in *Boston Transcript,* Feb. 8, 1864. The bulk of his papers, including the "Ice House Diary," is in the possession of Frederic Tudor of Sandwich, Mass.]

H. G. P.

TUDOR, WILLIAM (Jan. 28, 1779–Mar. 9, 1830), author, the son of Col. William and Delia (Jarvis) Tudor, was born in Boston, Mass. His father was a prominent merchant and scholar, the son of Deacon John Tudor who was taken from England to Boston about 1714 at the age of six. After graduation from Harvard in 1796, young Tudor entered John Codman's counting-room and was sent to Paris on business. A year later he sailed for Leghorn on another mission. Both ventures were disappointing, but Tudor made many friendships and strengthened his love of letters. He next went to the West Indies at the request of his brother Frederic [*q.v.*] to develop a trade in ice. On his return he was elected to the Massachusetts legislature, where he served a number of times, and in 1809 he delivered the annual Fourth of July oration in Boston, which went through two editions. At this period he was employed by Stephen Higginson [*q.v.*] in a none-too-successful attempt to force quantities of English manufactures into Europe against the hostile decrees of Bonaparte. He also aided a group of Americans in a futile attempt to establish at Birmingham the manufacture of cut nails.

Turning at last to other activities, he became the founder and first editor (1815–17) of the *North American Review,* and was the largest contributor to the first four volumes. An original member of the Anthology Society (1805), he frequently contributed to the pages of its magazine, the *Monthly Anthology and Boston Review.* He helped to found the Boston Athenaeum, a library and art museum; suggested a plan for the purchase of land on Bunker Hill in Charlestown on which the American redoubt had been raised and where Warren fell; and was active in the affairs of the Massachusetts Historical Society, to which he had been elected in 1816. Tudor was a keen critic of contemporary manners, and his *Letters on the Eastern States* (1820), now forgotten, contains much that is of permanent value. In this book he fell foul of Mathew Carey [*q.v.*], an excitable Irishman then living in Philadelphia, whose *The Olive Branch* (1814) had been intended to soften political asperities caused by the war with England. He received little epistolary comfort from Tudor, and his pamphlet on the encounter (1821) ran to almost seventy pages. In 1821 Tudor gathered into a small book under the title *Miscellanies* various essays, some from the *Anthology,* others from the *North American Review.* They have a human touch and interest that make them readable today. They range from "Secret Causes of the American and French Revolutions" to essays on cranberry sauce, purring cats, and the miseries of human life. Two years later Tudor published *The Life of James Otis, of Massachusetts,* which is said to be his best effort. The same year he was appointed United States consul at Lima and for the ports of Peru (appointment confirmed, Dec. 9, 1823), and was of service during the feud between Peru and Colombia. In 1827 he was advanced to be chargé d'affaires at Rio de Janeiro (appointment confirmed, Dec. 27). While in Brazil he wrote an allegory on current international politics which was published anonymously under the title *Gebel Teir* (1829). His health was affected by the climate at Rio de Janeiro, and he died there of fever. He was buried at Rio. He never married.

[See *Deacon Tudor's Diary* (1896), ed. by William Tudor; C. C. Smith, in *Proc. Mass. Hist. Soc.,* vol. I (1879), p. 429; Josiah Quincy, *The Hist. of the Boston Athenaeum* (1851); J. S. Loring, *The Hundred Boston Orators* (1853); *Jour. of the Proc. of the Soc. Which Conducts the Monthly Anthology* (1910), with intro. by M. A. De Wolfe Howe; death notice in *Boston Daily Advertiser,* May 3, and letter, May 8, 1830. Stuart's portrait of Tudor is reproduced in Lawrence Park, *Gilbert Stuart, an Illustrated Descriptive List of His Works* (4 vols., 1926).]

C.K.B.

TUFTS, CHARLES (July 17, 1781–Dec. 24, 1876), a founder of Tufts College, son of Daniel and Abigail (Tufts) Tufts, was born in a part of Medford later incorporated in Somerville, Mass. He was a lineal descendant of an early English colonist, Peter Tufts, who settled in Charlestown, Mass., about 1638. It is believed that he was long associated with his father in farming and brickmaking, pursuits which he followed in later years. On Apr. 8, 1821, he married Hannah, daughter of Jacob and Hannah Robinson, of Lexington, Mass., an earnest and liberal-minded young woman fourteen years his junior, who exerted a strong guiding influence upon her husband.

Tufts received very little formal education but contrived, nevertheless, to acquire a considerable fund of knowledge. A strongly religious man in adult life, he became deeply interested in the work of the Universalist Church, first in Charlestown and later in Somerville, and it was to a considerable extent his proselyting interest in Universalist doctrines that impelled him to set aside a portion of his extensive farm properties for educational purposes. When in 1840 the Massachusetts Convention of Universalists proposed the establishment of a theological seminary, Tufts offered a building site. Before the plan could materialize, however, it became identified with attempts to bolster up the Clinton Liberal

Institute (1845) and resulted finally in a project for a Universalist college (May 1847). As the movement progressed, Tufts offered approximately twenty acres of land on the Medford-Somerville line. Although some of the conditions attached to the grant caused hesitation, the site, known as Walnut Tree Hill, was formally approved by the trustees of the nascent institution on Jan. 8, 1852, and a charter of incorporation was presently obtained for Tufts College. In 1856 and 1864 Tufts deeded other properties to the college under various conditions, one of which was that its name should never be changed. He also served as a trustee of the college from 1856 until his death. His gifts, amounting altogether to more than one hundred acres of land, together with lesser adjacent tracts from other sources, established the college in a physical sense and placed it in a unique position within the Boston metropolitan area.

Tufts was a man of medium stature, with small, mild features and a gentle manner which gave little hint of his decided opinions and inflexible will. He was shrewd in his calculations, but "without a particle of deceit." Both natural inclination and extreme deafness caused him to live somewhat as a recluse, and it was only through his benefactions that he came into public notice.

[Records of the Trustees of Tufts Coll., 1852–78, vol. I; Trustees of Tufts Coll., Fund File: original Tufts papers; C. D. Elliot, in *Tufts Coll. Grad.,* Jan. 1910; H. S. Ballou, *Hosea Ballou, 2d, D.D., First President of Tufts Coll.* (1896); Charles Brooks, *Hist. of the Town of Medford, 1630–1855* (1886), revised by J. M. Usher; L. T. Tufts and E. C. Booth, "Tufts Geneal.: Descendants of Peter" (1925) New-Eng. Hist. Geneal. Soc.; *Universalist Reg.,* 1842, 1844; *Hist. of Tufts Coll., 1854–1896* (1896), ed. by A. B. Start; *Universalist,* Jan. 6, 1877; *Christian Leader,* Apr. 28, 1928; obituary in *Boston Transcript,* Dec. 27, 1876.]

H.L.H.

TUFTS, COTTON (May 30, 1732–Dec. 8, 1815), physician, was born in Medford, Mass., the fourth child of Simon and Abigail (Smith) Tufts, and a nephew of John Tufts [*q.v.*]. His great-grandfather, Peter Tufts, emigrated from England to Charlestown about 1638. His father, who was a graduate of Harvard College, was the first physician to practise in Medford. Young Cotton, a serious student, entered Harvard at fourteen and, having received three scholarships, the last one of fifteen pounds, was graduated with the degree of A.M. in 1749. After a short period of teaching school, he studied medicine with his elder brother Simon, a graduate of Harvard College, who had followed in his father's footsteps in Medford, and began practice in Weymouth, April 1752. It appears, however, that he spent part of the preceding year in Weymouth, for during an epidemic of diphtheria he took an active part in assisting the older physicians; as a result he settled there and spent the rest of his life in that community.

Tufts not only became the leading practitioner of Weymouth but was also an important figure in medical, scientific, and political affairs of Massachusetts. In 1765 he planned a state medical society, a project which fell through for lack of adequate support, and in 1781 it was he who was most forceful in organizing the Massachusetts Medical Society. He was elected president in 1787. It is said that he missed attending only two out of forty meetings in Boston during a period of thirteen years, although he lived twelve miles away and travel was often difficult in winter. In 1780 he became one of the charter members of the American Academy of Arts and Sciences. He represented the town of Weymouth in the meetings against the Stamp Act, and after the Revolution, although he had not entered the army, he voted affirmatively in the Massachusetts convention to ratify the new United States Constitution in 1788. Locally, he was a deacon of his church, a trustee of Derby Academy in Hingham, and president of the society for the Reformation of Morals. Harvard College granted him an honorary degree of M.D. in 1785. He was a friend of John Adams [q.v.], whose private affairs he administered while Adams was at his London post (*The Works of John Adams*, vol. IX, 1854, pp. 548–49). He was twice married, first (Dec. 2, 1755) to Lucy Quincy, daughter of John Quincy of Braintree, by whom he had one son, Cotton, graduate of Harvard College in 1777; second (Oct. 22, 1789) to Mrs. Susanna Warner of Gloucester, who survived him.

[The date of birth is from *Vital Records of Medford, Mass.* (1907); the marriage dates from *Vital Records of Weymouth* (1910), vol. II. The principal biog. source is Jacob Norton, *Sermon Delivered . . . at the Interment of the Hon. Cotton Tufts* (1816), a somewhat rare pamphlet. See also *New-Eng. Hist. and Geneal. Reg.*, Apr. 1847, Apr. 1855, Jan. 1857; *Proc. Mass. Hist. Soc.*, 3 ser., vol. II (1909), which contains Tuft's diaries for 1772 and 1784; W. L. Burrage, *A Hist. of the Mass. Medic. Soc.* (1923); *Pubs. Colonial Soc. of Mass.*, vol. XVI (1925); James Thacher, *Am. Medic. Biog.* (1828); obituary in *New-England Palladium and Commercial Advertiser*, Dec. 15, 1815; letters and memorabilia in the Boston Medic. Lib.]

H. R. V.

TUFTS, JOHN (May 5, 1689–Aug. 17, 1752), pioneer compiler of church music, Congregational minister, was born in Medford, Mass., the third of twelve children of Capt. Peter Tufts and his second wife, Mercy (Cotton) Tufts. His father was a son of Peter Tufts who emigrated from England to America about 1638; his mother was a daughter of the Rev. Seaborn Cotton

and Dorothy, daughter of Gov. Simon Bradstreet [q.v.]. He was graduated from Harvard College in 1708 and was ordained as minister of the Second Church of Christ in West Newbury, June 30, 1714. A few references to Tuft's ministerial activities may be noted in town histories of Essex County, but his career as a country minister was notable mainly by reason of the influence exerted upon American music by the publication, probably in 1714 or 1715, of his *A Very Plain and Easy Introduction to the Art of Singing Psalm Tunes: with the Cantus or Trebles of Twenty-eight Psalm Tunes, Contrived in Such a Manner, As That the Learner May Attain the Skill of Singing Them, with the Greatest Ease and Speed Imaginable* (Hood, *post*, p. 65). No copy of the first edition is known. This book, in which letters were used on the staff instead of notes, was considered "a daring and unjustifiable innovation," and Tufts's carefully chosen selection of tunes met with caustic criticism. One writer said: "Truly, I have a great jealousy that if we once begin to sing by rule the next thing will be to pray by rule and preach by rule, and then comes popery" (quoted in Coffin, *post*, p. 186). Another critic objected to the book as "Quakerish and Popish, and introductive of instrumental musick; the names given to the notes are blasphemous; it is a needless way since the good Fathers are gone to heaven without it; its admirers are a company of young upstarts; they spend too much time about learning, and tarry out a-nights disorderly" (quoted in Fisher, *post*, pp. 6–7). Despite such objections Tufts's book achieved wide popularity. The music was simple, but for its purpose very effective. Under varying titles the book went through at least eleven editions, some of them prepared to be bound up in the Bay Psalm Book, the last one printed in 1774. In its defense the Rev. Thomas Symmes wrote his tract on the *Reasonableness of Regular Singing* (1720), Tufts's name appearing in it as one of "the subscribers willing to countenance and promote *Regular Singing*, or Singing by Note." Other publications of Tufts's were *Anti-Ministerial Objections Considered* (1725) and *A Humble Call to Archippus, Or the Pastor Exhorted, To Take Heed That He Fulfill His Ministry* (1729).

Apart from his activity as an innovator in the field of church music Tufts appears to have led for many years the uneventful life of a rural minister. He married, Nov. 9, 1714, Sarah Bradstreet, daughter of Dr. Humphrey Bradstreet, by whom he had four children. On Feb. 26, 1738, a council of ten ministers and twenty delegates was called to consider " 'the distressed, state and condition of ye second church of Christ in Newbury by reason of their reverend pastor Mr. John Tufts being charged by a woman or women of his indecent carriage and also of his abusive and unchristian behavior towards them'" (Coffin, *post*, p. 207–08). Tufts vehemently opposed the investigation and demanded his dismission, which was granted Mar. 2, his church refusing to recommend him for employment as a Christian minister. He thereupon retired to the adjoining town of Amesbury, where he died (*Vital Records of Amesbury, Mass.*, 1913).

[For a discussion of the bibliog. problems, see Joseph Sabin, *A Dict. of Books Relating to America*, pt. CLI (1935), continued by R. W. G. Vail. In addition to Charles Brooks, *Hist. of the Town of Medford* (1886), and T. B. Wyman, *The Geneals. and Estates of Charlestown* (1879), vol. II, see F. J. Metcalf, *Am. Writers and Compilers of Sacred Music* (copr. 1925); George Hood, *A Hist. of Music in New England* (1846); N. D. Gould, *Church Music in America* (1853); W. A. Fisher, *Notes on Music in Old Boston* (1918); *New-Eng. Hist. and Geneal. Reg.*, Apr. 1847, Apr. 1855, Jan. 1856, July 1875; E. H. Pierce, in *Musical Quart.*, Apr. 1930; J. J. Currier, *Hist. of Newbury, Mass.* (1902); and Joshua Coffin, *A Sketch of the Hist. of Newbury* (1845).]

F. W. C.

TULANE, PAUL (May 10, 1801–Mar. 27, 1887), merchant and philanthropist, was the son of French parents. His father, Louis Tulane, born in 1767 at Rillé, near Tours, France, of a line of local judges, removed to Santo Domingo in young manhood, with his wife and a brother-in-law, to engage in commercial pursuits. In a slave insurrection the brother-in-law's family perished, but Louis and his wife escaped to the United States and settled in 1792 near Princeton, N. J., and here Paul was born. He attended a private school and Somerville Academy and at fifteen, after the death of his mother, became a clerk for about a year in the store of Thomas White at Princeton. This experience was followed by a tour of the South and West with a cousin of means visiting from France.

In 1822 Paul Tulane established himself in business in New Orleans with a strong faith in the future of the region. As head of the house of Paul Tulane & Company of New Orleans, and of Tulane, Baldwin & Company of New York, he built up a retail and wholesale trade in dry goods and clothing, with a large clientele in the Mississippi Valley, and by 1840 had acquired a fortune estimated at a quarter of a million dollars. About 1858 he busied himself chiefly with real-estate transactions and acquisitions, dividing his time and his investments between New Orleans and New Jersey in anticipation of a Southern backset from the slavery controversy. After a residence of fifty-one years in New Orleans. he removed permanently to an elegant

stone mansion in Princeton, where he died. A bachelor, of reserved disposition, he survived all members of his immediate family.

Tulane's was a rugged personality. Physically, he was short and heavily built; as a business man he was frugal, industrious, and tenacious, exacting to the last penny. He was liberal in his philanthropy, however, spending thousands of dollars on individuals and local organizations in the interest of religion, charity, and education. The First Presbyterian Church of Princeton was a special recipient of his donations, but his most significant gifts were those by which the University of Louisiana, a state institution founded in 1834 at New Orleans, was converted in 1884 into the independent Tulane University of Louisiana in the same city. Tulane's first donation was made in 1882, through his own initiative and without solicitation. It consisted of all his New Orleans real estate and was valued at $363,000. Other gifts from him followed making a total estimated at more than a million dollars. He expressed the intention to make still further contributions, but his death without a will intervened and his property was divided among his nieces and nephews. At the time of his first donation he chose with care the first members of a board of administrators for his fund, headed by Randall L. Gibson [*q.v.*], and gave them general instructions to provide for the higher education of the white youth of New Orleans. This group arranged with the state to absorb the existing University of Louisiana, with "Tulane" prefixed to the name, instead of starting a rival university in the city.

[W. P. Johnston, "Tulane University of Louisiana," in E. W. Fay, *The Hist. of Educ. in La.* (Bur. of Educ., Circular of Information No. 1, 1898, ch. viii); Alcée Fortier, *Louisiana* (1909), vol. II; *Princeton Press*, Apr. 2, 1887; *Times-Democrat* (New Orleans), Mar. 29, Apr. 2, 1887.]

H. C. N.

TULLY, WILLIAM (Nov. 18, 1785–Feb. 28, 1859), physician, was born at Saybrook Point, Conn., the only child of Col. William Tully, an officer of the Revolution, who married Eunice (Tully), his cousin. He was a descendant of John Tully of Horley, Surrey County, England, whose widow came with her son and daughter to Saybrook about 1647. As a boy Tully attended the district school and was later prepared for college by the Rev. Frederick W. Hotchkiss, of Saybrook. Entering Yale in 1802, he graduated in 1806, and then taught school for a short time in his native town. In the spring of 1807 he began the study of medicine with Dr. Mason F. Cogswell of Hartford and in the fall of the following year attended the medical school of Dartmouth under Dr. Nathan Smith, 1762–1829 [*q.v.*]. Returning to Saybrook in 1810, he studied for a time with Dr. Samuel Carter. In March of this year he entered the office of Dr. Eli Ives [*q.v.*] of New Haven, professor of materia medica at Yale. In October 1810 Tully was licensed by the Connecticut Medical Society, and in May 1811 he began to practise in Enfield, Conn.

For the next few years he changed his location so rapidly that a biographer refers to him as "The Peregrinating Dr. William Tully" (Ferris, *post*). On Jan. 5, 1813, he married Mary, daughter of the Rev. Elam Potter, and in March of that year removed to Milford, Conn. Two years later he went to Cromwell, Conn., and in September 1818, to Middletown. In the latter place he became an intimate friend of Dr. Thomas Miner, a physician and scholar of considerable repute, who is said to have had a noteworthy influence on Tully's subsequent literary career. In 1807 Yale conferred the degree of A.M. on him and in 1819 the honorary degree of M.D. The following year he published an article, "On the Ergot of Rye," in the *American Journal of Science* (April 1820) and another, "Scutellaria Laterifolia," in the *Middlesex Gazette* (Nov. 30, 1820). An article by him entitled "Diversity of the Two Sorts of Datura Found in the United States" appeared in the former journal in 1823, and in this same year, with Dr. Thomas Miner, he published *Essays on Fevers*. In June 1822 Tully removed to East Hartford and in July 1824 was appointed president and professor of theory and practice and medical jurisprudence in the Vermont Academy of Medicine, at Castleton. When this school was reorganized in 1830 he retired as president but continued for eight years as professor of materia medica and therapeutics.

In January 1826 he removed to Albany, N. Y., where he practised as a colleague of Dr. Alden March [*q.v.*], but continued his lectures at Castleton. In 1828 he wrote "An Essay, Pharmacological and Therapeutical, on Sanguinaria-Canadensis," which appeared in the *American Medical Recorder* (January, April 1828), and won him a prize. Appointed professor of materia medica and therapeutics at Yale in 1829, he removed to New Haven and taught there as well as at Castleton. In collaboration with Ives and M. C. Leavenworth, he published *Catalogue of the Phenogamous Plants and the Ferns Growing without Cultivation, within Five Miles of Yale College* (1831). Other papers, on sanguinaria, chlorite of potassa, congestion, narcotine and sulphate of morphine, were prepared by him during this period. He is said to have made the first

half ounce of quinine sulphate from cinchona bark produced in the United States (Ferris, p. 24). In August 1842, as a result of strained relations with his colleagues, he resigned his chair at Yale and in 1851 removed to Springfield, Mass. Here was published his compendious work of more than 1,500 pages, *Materia Medica, or, Pharmacology and Therapeutics* (2 vols., 1857–58). In this work appears his modification of the well-known Dover's powder which later became known as Tully's powder.

Tully died in Springfield and was buried in the Grove Street Cemetery, New Haven. He had eleven children, but of these only a son and two daughters survived him. According to his successor at Yale, he was "doubtless the most learned and thoroughly scientific physician of New England" (Bronson, *post*, p. 5). "As a teacher he stimulated scientific zeal in his students, as a physician he studied his patients carefully and was a good diagnostician" (Ferris, p. 35). In appearance he was tall and square-shouldered, with large head and prominent eyes. As a lecturer "he spoke distinctly and without gesticulation, reading from his manuscript in a loud, almost stentorian voice, with an uniform and slightly nasal tone, and assured air" (Bronson, p. 5). His eminence in his day is attested by the large number of medical and scientific societies to which he belonged.

[H. B. Ferris, in *Yale Jour. of Biology and Medicine*, Oct. 1932; Henry Bronson, in *Proc. and Medic. Communications of the Conn. State Medic. Soc.*, 2 ser. vol. I (1863); Kate C. Mead, in *Bull. of the Johns Hopkins Hospital*, Mar. 1916, and in H. L. Kelly and W. L. Burrage, *Am. Medic. Biogs.* (1920); S. H. Parsons, "The Tully Family of Saybrook, Conn.," *New-England Hist. and Geneal. Reg.*, Apr. 1849; F. B. Dexter, *Biog. Sketches, Grads. Yale Coll.*, vol. VI (1912); G. C. Gates, *Saybrook at the Mouth of the Conn.* (1935); *Springfield Republican*, Mar. 1, 1859; diary and letters in Yale Univ. Lib.]   H. T.

TUPPER, BENJAMIN (Mar. 11, 1738–June 7, 1792), Revolutionary soldier, pioneer, was born in Stoughton, Mass., the son of Thomas and Remember (Perry) Tupper. Since his father died early, Benjamin had but a common-school education, and was apprenticed to a tanner in Dorchester until he was sixteen. Subsequently he worked as a farm hand until the outbreak of the French and Indian War, when he enlisted in the company of his uncle, Capt. Nathaniel Perry. At the close of the war he left the army with the rank of sergeant. After teaching school for a few years in Easton, he married, Nov. 18, 1762, Huldah White of Bridgewater, and migrated to Chesterfield, Hampshire County, in western Massachusetts.

In 1774, Tupper joined the Revolutionary

cause, serving as militia lieutenant in purging western Massachusetts of Loyalist sentiment. In 1775 he took a heroic part in the siege of Boston and in the destruction of the British lighthouse on Castle Island. From 1776 to the end of the war he served as lieutenant-colonel and then colonel of Massachusetts troops, participating in the battle of Long Island, the Saratoga campaign, and the battle of Monmouth, and constructing defenses at West Point and on the Mohawk–Lake George Indian frontier. He retired from the army in 1783 with the brevet rank of brigadier-general and on his return to Chesterfield was elected representative in the state legislature. In 1786 he returned to the field and took an active part in defending Springfield against the insurgent, Daniel Shays [q.v.].

The last ten years of Tupper's life were identified with the westward movement. He was one of the 288 Continental officers to sign the Newburgh Petition in 1783, seeking the creation of a new territory in the Northwest for occupation by soldiers. With the settlement of the Indian and land problems by ordinances and treaties between 1783 and 1785, Tupper represented Massachusetts on the corps of state surveyors sent west by Congress under Thomas Hutchins. He personally conducted in 1785 preliminary surveying in numbers three and four of the Seven Ranges. On his return to the East, he joined with Gen. Rufus Putnam [q.v.] in inaugurating the movement that led to the formation of the Ohio Company. In an "Information" that appeared in Boston and Worcester papers early in 1786, the Ohio country was described and Revolutionary officers and soldiers were invited to form a settlement association. Tupper was elected delegate to represent Hampshire County at the appointed organization meeting in March in Boston. By this body the Ohio Company was formed and a petition was sent to Congress for a purchase which resulted in the grant and settlement of Marietta at the mouth of the Muskingum and in the creation of the Northwest Territory.

Tupper took an active part in the affairs of the Company and of his adopted home. He accompanied the original settlers to Marietta in 1788, and served on committees for determining the place and value of sites for settlement, for receiving applications for mills, for devising donation methods to attract settlers, for the location of roads and the leasing of city lots. With Putnam he was made judge of common pleas and quarter sessions and held the first civil court in the Territory on Sept. 9, 1788. Subsequently, as Putnam was occupied with other duties, Tupper

was practically sole administrator of local justice on the Muskingum until his death.

Tupper had seven children. His daughter Rowena was the first wife of Winthrop Sargent, 1753–1820 [q.v.], secretary of the Northwest Territory.

[A. B. Hulbert, *The Records of the Original Proceedings of the Ohio Company* (2 vols., 1917) and *Ohio in the Time of the Confederation* (1918); *Life, Journals and Correspondence of Rev. Manasseh Cutler* (1888), vol. I; A. T. Nye, "Gen. Benjamin Tupper," in S. P. Hildreth, *Biog. and Hist. Memoirs of the Early Pioneer Settlers of Ohio* (1852); W. L. Chaffin, *Hist. of the Town of Easton, Mass.* (1886), F. B. Heitman, *Hist. Reg. of Officers of the Continental Army* (1914).]

R. C. D.

TUPPER, HENRY ALLEN (Feb. 29, 1828–Mar. 27, 1902), Baptist clergyman, denominational leader in foreign missionary enterprises, was born in Charleston, S. C., the son of Tristram—a native of Dresden, Me.—and Eliza (Yoer) Tupper. His first American ancestor was Thomas Tupper, a descendant of exiles from Hesse Cassel to England, who emigrated to New England in 1635, and in 1637 was one of the founders of Sandwich, Mass. Tristram settled in Charleston in 1810 and thereafter conducted a commission house. For more than fifty years the Tupper family was prominent in the business, social, and religious affairs of the city. Henry attended local schools and from 1844 to 1846 was a student in the College of Charleston. He then enrolled at Madison University (now Colgate University), Hamilton, N. Y., where he was graduated with the degree of A.B. in 1849. The following year he spent at the theological seminary connected with the University, and was much influenced by the prevailing missionary zeal. On Nov. 1, 1849, he married Nancy Johnstone Boyce, by whom he had twelve children, six of whom survived him.

In 1850 he was ordained to the Baptist ministry and became pastor of the church in Graniteville, S. C. Three years later he accepted a call to the church at Washington, Ga., where he served until 1872. He was active in local temperance work, preached to the colored people twice a week, and gave the community a varied leadership. He traveled abroad and dreamed of active mission work in foreign fields, even going so far as to plan a self-sustaining colony in Japan. With the advent of the Civil War, however, he took part in that struggle as chaplain of a Georgia regiment in the Confederate army.

His real life work began when he accepted, in 1872, the office of corresponding secretary of the Board of Foreign Missions of the Southern Baptist Convenion, with headquarters in Richmond. To the missionary enterprises of his denomination he now gave tirelessly of his strength, thought, and means. In 1883–84 he went to Mexico and consummated plans for establishing mission schools for girls in Coahuila. His liberality was proverbial. In 1883 he recorded that he had received "from the Lord" since 1854 in income $279,500.98, and of that sum had donated $124,-541.39 for religious work. In his vacations he wrote several books for young people of a type considered suitable for Sunday school libraries. They included *The Truth in Romance* (1887), published under the pseudonym Tföffer, the old German spelling of his family name; and *The Carpenter's Son* (1889), an interpretation of the life of Christ. His major works, however, were a lengthy history and survey of the mission enterprise, under the title *The Foreign Missions of the Southern Baptist Convention* (1880) and *A Decade of Foreign Missions, 1880–90* (1891). He retired from the secretaryship of the mission board in 1893. For a time he was president of the board of trustees of the Woman's College of Richmond, and he served, also, as a trustee of Hollins College and of Richmond College. In his closing years, 1896–1902, he was instructor in Bible in Richmond College.

[Tupper's surviving children have many of his letters and other papers, including a manuscript diary kept over a long period of years; the files of the Foreign Mission Board of the Southern Baptist Convention, in Richmond, Va., contain much of his correspondence; for printed sources, see *Am. Ancestry*, vol. V (1890); G. B. Taylor, *Va. Baptist Ministers, Fifth Series, 1902–14* (1915); H. A. Tupper, *The First Century of the First Baptist Church of Richmond* (1880); *The Religious Herald*, Apr. 3, 1902; *Foreign Mission Jour.*, May 1902; *Who's Who in America*, 1901–02; *Times* (Richmond), Mar. 28, 1902.]   M. H. W.

TURELL, JANE (Feb. 25, 1708–Mar. 26, 1735), poet, daughter of the Rev. Benjamin Colman [*q.v.*] and his first wife, Jane Clark, was born in Boston, Mass., where her father was pastor of the Brattle Street Church. As the only girl in the family until her seventh year and as a child afflicted with a constitution "wonderful weak and tender," she received an uncommon share of attention from her father and responded by developing a precocious memory for Scripture texts, Biblical stories, and passages from the catechism. Gov. Joseph Dudley and other gentlemen who frequented Mr. Colman's house used to place little Jane on the table to hear her talk and "owned themselves diverted" by her recitations. At a very early age she learned to read and rapidly went through her father's library. A hymn written in her eleventh year was followed a few years later by verse-paraphrases of the Psalms, which Mr. Colman criticized and returned to her with edifying poems of his own. He made it clear to her, however, that "a Poeti-

cal Flight now and then" was not to be allowed to interrupt her daily hours of reading and devotion. Jane Colman's marriage to the Rev. Ebenezer Turell, graduate of Harvard College in the class of 1721 and minister at Medford, took place on Aug. 11, 1726. Her husband cultivated her literary gifts by reading aloud to her books of "Divinity, History, Physick, Controversy, as well as Poetry," as they sat together during the long winter evenings. Mrs. Turell continued her writing, both in verse and in prose. Besides keeping a religious diary, she composed a poetic eulogy on Sir Richard Blackmore, whom she admired "not as the first of Poets, but as one of the best; consecrating his Muse to the cause of Virtue and Religion"; an appreciative tribute to Edmund Waller "for the Purity of his Style and delicacy of Language"; and "An Invitation into the Country, in Imitation of Horace." She died, with all the pious expressions that the occasion demanded, at Medford, aged twenty-seven. The only one of her four children who survived her died a year later.

Immediately after her death Mrs. Turell was immortalized in a volume entitled *Reliquiae Turellae, et Lachrymae Paternae* (Boston, 1735), published in London under the title of *Memoirs of the Life and Death of the Pious and Ingenious Mrs. Jane Turell . . . Collected Chiefly from Her Own Manuscripts* (1741). This contains a poetic epistle by the Rev. John Adams, two funeral sermons preached in her honor by her father, and a memoir by her husband. It is the only source of first-hand information about Mrs. Turell's life and character, and the only form in which her poems were published. It also contains selections from her religious meditations and specimens of her letters to her father and his replies. The image presented to the world by the joint efforts of husband and father was that of a devout woman according to the strict Puritan pattern. Piety was her grace, poetry merely a grace note. Her verse has no importance except as an indication of the literary taste of Boston during the first quarter of the eighteenth century.

[The date of birth is given in *A Report of the Record Commissioners of the City of Boston . . . Births* (1894) as Feb. 25, 1707; in *Records of the Church in Brattle Square, Boston* (1902), however, the date of baptism is given as Feb. 29, 1708. In addition to *Reliquiae Turellae* (1735), see Ebenezer Turell, *The Life and Character of the Rev. Benjamin Colman, D.D.* (1849); E. A. and G. L. Duyckinck, *Cyc. of Am. Lit.*, vol. I (1855), for specimens of Mrs. Turell's verse; and *Vital Records of Medford, Mass.* (1907) for the date of her death.]   G. F. W.

TURNBULL, ANDREW (*c.* 1718–Mar. 13, 1792), was a Scotch physician and colonizer, who, after visting Mediterranean lands and marrying Maria Gracia Dura Bin, a Grecian lady of Smyrna, undertook to cultivate sub-tropical products in the new British province of East Florida. In June 1766 he was granted by *mandamus* 20,000 acres of land therein, and five months later, with his wife and four children, he landed at St. Augustine. He located his land at Mosquito (now Ponce de Leon) Inlet, hired a manager, and ordered cattle. Returning alone to England in the spring of 1767, he allied himself with Sir William Duncan and Lord George Grenville—the latter represented by Sir Richard Temple—in a project for colonizing 500 indentured Greeks, who, after seven or eight years of service, were to receive fifty acres each and five for each child. His partners added 81,400 acres and promised £6,000 for expenses. The government provided a vessel and a bounty of forty shillings a head for the adult Greeks.

In the summer of 1768 Turnbull brought back in eight vessels 200 Peloponnesian Greeks, 110 south Italians, and nearly 1,100 Minorcans, who found buildings and provisions awaiting them. In August, during his temporary absence, a sizable band of Italians and Greeks mortally wounded his manager and carried stores on board the schooner *Balmar* for flight to Havana. Gov. James Grant dispatched two vessels with troops in time to halt the *Balmar,* although some thirty insurgents escaped in her boat. These were subsequently taken at the Florida Keys and two were hanged for piracy. During these first months about 300 colonists died of scurvy and gangrene. Malaria carried off hundreds more while they were clearing seven miles of low land along the Halifax and Hillsboro rivers, constructing walled canals, planting maize, making gardens, and producing indigo for export. The cost of the enterprise for the first year had been about £28,000 and provisions were nearly exhausted when the Lords of the Treasury granted £2,000 for relief.

Early appointed to the Provincial Council and secretaryship by Grant, Turnbull resigned the former office under Lieut.-Gov. John Moultrie [*q.v.*] on account of differences of opinion. He also quickly antagonized Gov. Patrick Tonyn by participating in a scheme to lease lands from the Indians and by opposing, with Chief Justice William Drayton [*q.v.*] and others, Tonyn's measures as the Revolution approached. When the governor denounced them as disloyal, they adopted a loyal address, which Drayton and Turnbull carried to England early in 1776. Tonyn then broke up the latter's colony of New Smyrna by drafting many recruits therefrom for his

militia and galleys and by welcoming the other colonists to St. Augustine.

In August 1778 Turnbull removed thither with his family, and was soon sued for debt by his partners' heirs. Tonyn heard the case and had the debtor detained two years for want of the bond he imposed. Released in May 1781 by surrendering all but a fraction of New Smyrna, Turnbull and his family sailed for Charleston. There he practised medicine until his death. On his and his children's joint claims of over £15,-000 for their losses in Florida, they received £916 13s d4; on his individual claim of over £6,400 he got nothing. He had three daughters and four sons; one of the sons being Robert J. Turnbull [*q.v.*].

[Carita Doggett, *Dr. Andrew Turnbull and the New Smyrna Colony of Florida* (1919); W. H. Siebert, *Loyalists in East Florida, 1774 to 1785* (2 vols., 1929); *Acts of the Privy Council of England, Colonial Series,* IV (1911), 815, V (1912), 564–65, 591; A. J. Morrison, *Travels in the Confederation* (1911), translated from the German of J. D. Schöpf; *S. C. and Am. Gen. Gazette,* Oct. 31–Nov. 7, 1766, Jan. 30–Feb. 6, 1767; *S. C. Gazette,* Aug. 3–10, 1767, July 4, 11, 1768, Feb. 28, Dec. 19, 1771, Oct. 11, 1773; *Ga. Gazette,* June 29, July 6, Oct. 19, 1768.]   W. H. S.

TURNBULL, ROBERT JAMES (Jan. 1775–June 15, 1833), publicist, was born in New Smyrna, Fla., the third son of Andrew [*q.v.*] and Maria Gracia (Dura Bin) Turnbull, the latter a native of Smyrna. His father was a Scotch physician who had obtained a British grant in 1766 and soon thereafter had led to Florida several thousand colonists from the region of the Mediterranean. The project failed, Dr. Turnbull embraced the colonial cause in the Revolution, thereby forfeiting his grant, and he moved to South Carolina in 1782. The son was educated at an academy at Kensington (London), and studied law in Philadelphia, and under John Julius Pringle [*q.v.*] in Charleston. Admitted to the bar in 1794, Turnbull began practice in Charleston, but in 1810 he gave up his profession and retired to a large plantation, maintaining, however, a residence in Charleston. Though widely popular and distinctly politically-minded, he took no part in public affairs, except to serve on the special court in 1822 for the trial of the Denmark Vesey conspirators. His influence was largely developed during the last decade of his life, and by his writings rather than by the spoken word, though he was no mean public speaker.

He wrote *A Visit to the Philadelphia Prison* (1796), which was published in French in 1800 and attracted considerable attention. He contributed a communication on plantation manage ment and the treatment of slaves in South Carolina to the anonymous work of Edwin Clifford Holland [q.v.], entitled *Refutation of the Calumnies Circulated Against the Southern and Western States, Respecting the Institution and Existence of Slavery among Them* (1822). There is no record of any other product of his pen for several years, but his later writings indicate that he was an interested observer of prevailing tendencies in American life and government. An ardent Jeffersonian, he became haunted by the spectre of national consolidation under the doctrine of implied power, angered by the sectional aspects of the protective tariff—a scheme "for rendering the South *tributary* to the North," and convinced that the growth of anti-slavery agitation imperiled the South. The South, he felt, must resist. "Let us say *distinctly to Congress, 'Hands off*—mind your *own* business.' ... If this fails, let us separate. It is not a case for reasoning or for negotiation" (*The Crisis,* no. 27, p. 137).

In 1827 he published his most important work, *The Crisis: or, Essays on the Usurpations of the Federal Government,* which appeared after two-thirds of the essays had been published in the *Charleston Mercury* over the pen name, "Brutus." It is doubtful if the thinking of the people of any other state has ever been so impressed and influenced by a single publication as was that of South Carolina by this work. It is often said incorrectly that in it Turnbull originated the doctrine of nullification in its South Carolina form, but it cannot be denied that it was "the first bugle-call to the South to rally" (Hamilton, *post,* p. 15), and it prepared the ground admirably for the seed others were soon to sow. Frankly confessing his feelings to be more sectional than national, he "struck at every evil in sight in such a bold, fearless, direct manner as to win the unbounded admiration of the masses" (Houston, *post,* p. 50). Seeking to show that Congress and the Supreme Court had transformed the Constitution into a "dead letter" which might mean anything or nothing, he attacked the nationalism of Monroe and Calhoun. He declared that since the chief interest of the North and West was in usurpation, while that of the South lay in the preservation of the compact, the interest of the former demanded that the government become more national, and that of the latter that it become more federal. The remedy lay in resistance to implied power, to the tariff, and to the anti-slavery movement, in insistence upon the compact theory, and in reliance upon the sovereignty of the states, even to the point of separation. The essays are effectively written,

well-reasoned, and, admitting their premises, unanswerable.

Having tasted blood, Turnbull was in the thick of the fight for the rest of his life. The legislature in 1828 passed a series of resolutions written by him affirming the compact theory with each state as judge. In 1828 Hamilton and Calhoun proclaimed the nullification doctrine. Turnbull had supported Jackson in 1824 and 1828, but in 1830 he became his caustic critic. In that year he wrote *The Tribunal of Dernier Ressort,* and in a notable public address, declaring that he had "trodden no path which has not been hallowed by the footsteps of Jefferson" (*Proceedings of the State Rights Celebration at Charleston, S. C., July 1, 1830,* p. 38), he again passionately proclaimed his principles and his adherence to the "Carolina doctrine." Just a year later, he addressed the State Rights and Free Trade party, defending nullification as the "Rock of Safety for the Union," and declaring his readiness to oppose secession with his last breath, except as a last resort from tyranny (*Proceedings of the Celebration of the 4th of July, 1831, ... by the State Rights and Free Trade Party,* p. 55). He was in the same year a member of the Free Trade convention at Columbia and wrote its report. In February 1832 he attended and addressed a similar convention in Charleston, and on July 4 he delivered an oration in which he characterized nullification as the "inherent, unmodified, all preserving principle of American liberty," as "the ground-work of Mr. Jefferson's faith," and, as "a medium course between those unspeakably dreadful evils *Submission* and *Secession,*" the rightful remedy for usurpation. He pleaded for the preservation of a federal Union of sovereign states, arguing that the state governments could not enslave the people because they could impose none but direct taxes. "As long as these republics remain free, sovereign, and independent, it is impossible that tyranny can ever advance a single step in our country." (*An Oration ... Before the State Rights & Free Trade Party, ... on the 4th of July, 1832,* 1832, pp. 7, 8, 17, 20.)

In the nullification convention he took a leading part, writing its *Address.* Upon Jackson's proclamation, he volunteered for military service. He refused to believe the experiment a failure. "Is it little to have put a bit in the teeth of the Tariff-Mongers?" He thought it no little victory to have "foiled the barbarian fury" of Jackson. "With but our one-gun battery of Nullification, we have driven the enemy from his moorings, compelled him to slip his cable, and put to sea." But, he added, the contest was only well begun, and at the second session of the convention he made an elaborate speech in advocacy of the ordinance which he wrote and proposed requiring a test oath and nullifying the "Bloody Bill" of Congress. (*Speeches Delivered in the Convention, of the State of South-Carolina . . . March, 1833,* 1833, pp. 35, 52–62.)

He died suddenly in the summer and his funeral was the occasion of a tremendous demonstration by the State Rights party. Great as was his influence in life, it was perhaps greater afterwards, since with James Hamilton he largely determined the pattern of the thinking of Robert Barnwell Rhett [*q.v.*]. Turnbull was three times married: first, on Jan. 10, 1797, to Claudia Butler Gervais of Charleston; second, to Valeria, the daughter of John Lightwood of Charleston; and, third, to Anna Beresford McCall of Charleston.

[C. S. Boucher, *The Nullification Controversy in South Carolina* (1916); D. F. Houston, *A Critical Study of Nullification in South Carolina* (1896); *Proc. of the Convention of the State of S. C. upon the Subject of Nullification* (1832); *Speeches Delivered in the Convention of the State of S. C. in March, 1833* (1833); Dumas Malone, *The Public Life of Thomas Cooper* (1926); James Hamilton, *An Eulogium on the Public Services and Character of Robert J. Turnbull, Esq.* (1834); Gaillard Hunt, *John C. Calhoun* (1907); Laura A. White, *Robert Barnwell Rhett: Father of Secession* (1931); *Charleston Mercury,* June 17, 18, 19, 1833; *Southern Patriot* (Charleston), June 15, 1833; *Charleston Courier,* June 17, 1833; Carita Doggett, *Dr. Andrew Turnbull and the New Smyrna Colony of Florida* (1919).]   J. G. deR. H.

TURNBULL, WILLIAM (1800–Dec. 9, 1857), soldier, engineer, was born in Philadelphia, Pa., the son of William Turnbull by his second wife, Mary, daughter of Charles Nisbet [*q.v.*]. The elder Turnbull emigrated to Philadelphia from Scotland about 1770. He was a shipping merchant and later an ironmaster with a blast furnace near Pittsburgh. In 1798 he returned to Philadelphia. Young William entered the United States Military Academy Sept. 30, 1814, and graduated July 1, 1819. He was assigned as second lieutenant in the Corps of Artillery and served in this arm, principally engaged on topographic duty, until Aug. 20, 1831, being promoted to first lieutenant Jan. 15, 1823. Transferred with the rank of captain to the topographical engineers, he was engaged in 1831–32 on the survey of a railroad route in the state of Mississippi and then assigned to the construction of the Potomac Aqueduct across the Potomac River at Georgetown. This was his most important work and engaged his time for eleven years, during which he was promoted to the grade of major. The masonry piers of this aqueduct were founded on bed rock which lay thirty to forty feet below the water surface and was covered with

about twenty feet of mud. The river itself was subject to floods and, in winter, to floating ice. The method of construction was by coffer dams, which Turnbull designed. This aqueduct was one of the first important works of American engineering and gave Turnbull a wide reputation. Two reports by him were published (*House Document 261,* 24 Cong., 1 Sess., 1836, and *House Document 459,* 25 Cong., 2 Sess., 1838). After his death, both of these being out of print, the demand for them by engineers called forth the publication of *Reports on the Construction of the Piers of the Aqueduct of the Alexandria Canal across the Potomac River at Georgetown, District of Columbia* (1873). After the aqueduct was completed Turnbull was engaged in the improvement of harbors on some of the Great Lakes and on Lake Champlain until the Mexican War.

In this conflict he served as chief topographical engineer on the staff of Gen. Winfield Scott and took an active part in all operations from the siege of Vera Cruz to the capture of the city of Mexico. For his services he was awarded the brevet of lieutenant-colonel for gallant and meritorious services in the battles of Contreras and Churubusco, and that of colonel for similar services in the battle of Chapultepec. After the war, he was superintending engineer of the construction of the custom house at New Orleans (1848–49); he surveyed Whale's Back Rock, Portsmouth, N. H., for a lighthouse site and examined into the practicability of bridging the Susquehanna River at Havre de Grace (1850–52); he served on a board to examine into the feasibility of an additional canal around the Falls of the Ohio (1852–53); and as engineer in charge of harbor improvements on Lake Erie and Lake Ontario (1853–56) and of lighthouse construction at Oswego, N. Y. (1853–55).

Early in 1826 he married Jane Graham Ramsay, sister of George Douglas Ramsay [*q.v.*], and established a home in Washington. Of six sons and four daughters, five sons and three daughters survived him. One son, Charles N. Turnbull (1832–1874), was also a graduate of the Military Academy and an officer of the topographical engineers, serving with distinction in the Civil War.

[A. D. Turnbull, *William Turnbull 1751–1822, with Some Account of Those Coming After* (privately printed, 1933); G. W. Cullum, *Biog. Reg. Officers and Grads. U. S. Mil. Acad.* (1st ed., 1879), vol. I; *Daily Jour.* (Wilmington, N. C.), Dec. 11, 1857; *Daily Nat. Intelligencer* (Washington), Dec. 11, 12, 1857.]   G. J. F.

TURNER, ASA (June 11, 1799–Dec. 13, 1885), Congregational clergyman, educator, brother of Jonathan Baldwin Turner [*q.v.*], was born in Templeton, Mass., the son of Asa and Abigail

(Baldwin) Turner, and a descendant of John Turner who emigrated from England in 1635 and settled in Roxbury, Mass., through his son John who was admitted freeman of Medfield, Mass., in 1649. Asa attended a district school and later worked on his father's farm, teaching during the winter months. In the fall of 1821, having decided to become a minister, he entered Amherst Academy in order to prepare for college, and within two years was able to meet the requirements for admission to Yale. Graduating in 1827, he enrolled at the Yale Divinity School, where he was soon recognized as a student of unusual ability. On Sept. 6, 1830, he was ordained at New Haven by the New Haven West Association.

That same year he became one of a group of seven theological students, known as the "Yale Band." Formally organized as the "Illinois Association," these students signed a pledge, Feb. 21, 1829, indorsed by the president of Yale College, expressing their willingness to go to Illinois for the purpose of establishing a seminary of learning, where some of them would teach, while the others occupied preaching stations in the surrounding country. Elected a trustee of the proposed educational institution Dec. 18, 1829, a position in which he served until 1844, Turner took an active part in the campaign for endowment, soliciting funds in Andover, Boston, Troy, Albany, and New York City. The money was secured within a few months, and on Jan. 4, 1830, Illinois College, at Jacksonville, was opened for instruction. On Aug. 31, 1830, Turner married Martha Bull, daughter of Dr. Isaac Dickerman and Mary (Watson) Bull, of Hartford, Conn.

Having decided to establish himself in Quincy, Ill., he set out on the westward journey, Sept. 14, 1830. The spot which he had chosen for his labors was sadly in need of spiritual and intellectual cultivation; there were no schools or churches. Working against indifference and actual opposition, he established a Presbyterian Church in December 1830. Early in the following year he persuaded a schoolmaster to settle in the town and open a school. Turner soon became the leading spirit in the development of the civic and intellectual life of Quincy. In the summer of 1832, at the request of Illinois College, he went East to solicit additional funds and to assist in securing instructors. His mission for the college successfully fulfilled, he returned late in the spring of 1833 accompanied by twenty people pledged to help in the work of "colonizing and civilizing." Many others had been persuaded to follow as settlers. Once more he entered vigorously into his work as missionary and preacher.

A Presbyterian when he first arrived in Quincy, he decided to become a Congregationalist, and on Oct. 10, 1833, by unanimous vote, his church adopted the Congregational form of government, becoming the first of this order in Illinois. Turner traveled throughout the northern part of the state—visiting Iowa, also, in 1834 and 1836—promoting camp meetings and urging the erection of churches. Late in 1837, after having organized thirteen churches, he went again to New England.

After his return the following spring, he and the Rev. J. A. Reed, of Warsaw, Ill., established at Denmark, Iowa, May 5, 1838, the first Congregationalist Church west of the Mississippi, and three months later Turner became its pastor. His ministry in Denmark, which began Aug. 3, 1838, continued for thirty years. In July 1839 the American Home Missionary Society appointed him first missionary agent for Iowa. Within a few months he was exploring northern Iowa, which was then uninhabited. His letters to Eastern friends and societies induced many families to move thither. He pleaded with Eastern churches for missionaries, and by 1842 had persuaded twelve young ministers to join him in developing the frontier country. Before his active missionary work ceased, he had inspired more than one hundred others to follow their example. He was also responsible for the organization of the "Iowa Association," formed by seven Yale theological students in 1837, for the purpose of establishing an educational institution in Iowa. After much effort, he obtained from the territorial Assembly, Feb. 3, 1843, a charter for Denmark Academy, and later in the year he went East to raise money for its support. Instruction at the academy was begun in September 1845, and three years later, Nov. 1, 1848, Iowa College was opened at Davenport. For the establishment of these pioneer institutions, Turner's labors were chiefly responsible, and he served as trustee of both until his death. He was also an active participant in the movement for the organization of a system of public schools. In the anti-slavery campaign in Iowa he took a vigorous part, expressing his views courageously at various political conventions. During the Civil War he supported the cause of abolition in his sermons and in articles published in Eastern religious journals. Failing in health in 1868, he withdrew from his pastorate and retired to Oskaloosa, where he died.

[Obit. Record Grads. Yale Coll. (1886); T. O. Douglass, The Pilgrims of Iowa (1911); C. F. Magoun, Asa Turner, a Home Missionary Patriarch, and His Times (1889); Manual of the First Congregational Church of Quincy, Ill. (1865); C. H. Rammelkamp, Ill. Coll.: A

Centennial Hist., 1829–1928 (1928); Iowa State Reg. (Des Moines), Dec. 16, 1885.]　　　　　R. F. S.

TURNER, CHARLES YARDLEY (Nov. 25, 1850–Dec. 31, 1918), mural painter, was born in Baltimore, Md., the son of John C. and Hannah (Bartlett) Turner. The Turners were Friends, and years later the quiet interior of the meeting-house often inspired the painter. The boy's home was one of culture, but his father's three marriages left little for his maintenance after preparatory schooling at the public and Friends' schools. He soon began to support himself as photographic finisher, attending at night the art classes of the Maryland Institute for the Promotion of the Mechanic Arts. After his graduation from the Maryland Institute in 1870, he spent several days as apprentice in the architectural office of Frank E. Davis and then set out for New York (1872). He studied for the next six years at the National Academy and at the Art Students' League, which he helped to organize, and continued to earn his living by photographic work. In 1878 he began study in Paris under Jean Paul Laurens, the mural decorator, Munkácsy, the Hungarian colorist, and Léon Bonnat, the figure painter. On his return to America he became an instructor in drawing and painting at the Art Students' League (1881–84) and a director of the Maryland Institute.

His earliest popular success was his "Grand Canal at Dordrecht" (1882), but he struck his stride as figure painter in the literary and historical field, a Miles Standish series being much in demand. The "Bridal Procession" (1886), now in the Metropolitan Museum of Art, "Days That Are No More," suggested by Tennyson's lines, and the etching of Hannah Thurston, Bayard Taylor's heroine, are further examples. His water colors were also frequently successful, especially his "Dordrecht Milkmaid" (1882), while "Chrysanthemums," a decorative oil in the Brooklyn Institute of Arts and Sciences, illustrates his versatility in color. In 1886 he became an Academician. He was assistant director of decoration at the Chicago World's Fair (1893) and director of color at the Pan-American Exposition (1901) at Buffalo. Increasingly, however, his interests turned to mural painting, reaching their fullest development in the Baltimore Court House panels, "The Burning of the Peggy Stewart" (1905). The fact that the decorations by John La Farge, E. H. Blashfield, and J. P. Laurens in the same building do not subordinate the Turners indicates at least their admirable adaptation to their position. Other Turner murals are to be seen in the DeWitt Clinton High School, the Appellate Courts Building, the

National Bank of Commerce, the Manhattan, Martinique, and Waldorf-Astoria hotels, all in New York; the Hotel Raleigh in Washington, court houses in Jersey City, Newark, Baltimore, Youngstown, and Cleveland, and the state Capitol, Madison, Wis.

In 1912 Turner became the director of the Maryland Institute School of Art and Design, and in the same year received the medal of honor for painting given by the Architectural League of New York. He was engaged in painting a poster-picture, "The Madonna of the War," in the plaza outside the Baltimore Court House in connection with the United War Work drive when he contracted the influenza which resulted in his death. He died in New York and was buried in the Friends Burial Grounds, Baltimore. He never married. In his later years he was affiliated with a firm of interior decorators. Turner is recalled as a man of unusual kindliness, charm, and simplicity. His later pictures show well-formed features, a Vandyke beard, and brilliant eyes.

[Who's Who in America, 1918–19; Addresses Delivered on the Occasion of the Unveiling of . . . "The Burning of the Peggy Stewart" (copr. 1905), Municipal Art Soc. of Baltimore; Pauline King, Am. Mural Painting (1902), ch. xiii; The Brochure of the Mural Painters (copr. 1916); Am. Art Ann., 1919, Am. Art News, Jan. 4, 1919; obituaries in Sun (Baltimore) and N. Y. Times, which also contains a death notice, Jan. 2, 1919.]　　　　　W. S. R.

TURNER, DANIEL (1794–Feb. 4, 1850), naval officer, was born probably at Richmond, Staten Island, N. Y., although there is a possibility that he was born in Rhode Island, where at Newport he made his home for many years, and one obituary notice gives New Jersey as his birthplace. On Jan. 1, 1808, he was appointed to the navy as a midshipman. After a period of service at the New York naval station he cruised on board the *Constitution,* 1809–11. On June 8, 1812, he was ordered to take command of the gunboats at Norwich, Conn. He was commissioned lieutenant on Mar. 12, 1813, and two days thereafter received orders to proceed to Sacketts Harbor, N. Y. For a time he commanded the *Niagara,* the second vessel in the squadron of Commodore O. H. Perry [*q.v.*], but previous to the battle of Lake Erie he was succeeded by Capt. J. D. Elliott [*q.v.*] and was given the command of the *Caledonia,* thus being the third officer in rank during the battle. His conduct on that occasion was highly commended by Perry, who described him as "an officer that in all situations may be relied on" (*American State Papers, Naval Affairs,* vol. I, 1834, p. 295). He was one of those who received the thanks of Congress and was awarded a silver medal. In the summer of 1814 he commanded the *Scorpion* of the fleet of Commodore Arthur Sinclair and participated in the capture of several British vessels on Lake Huron, the burning of the fort and barracks at St. Joseph, and the attack on Mackinac. On Sept. 5 the *Scorpion* was surprised and captured by the enemy under circumstances that were regarded as not discreditable to Turner. A court of inquiry decided that his conduct on this occasion was that of a discreet and vigilant officer. After a period of imprisonment he was exchanged.

In 1815–17 he was with the frigate *Java* and in 1819–24 with the cruiser *Nonsuch,* cruising part of the time in the Mediterranean. On Mar. 3, 1825, he was promoted master commandant. After a tour of duty at the naval rendezvous at Boston he cruised in the West Indies, 1827–30, as commander of the *Erie.* For three years he was stationed at the Portsmouth (N. H.) navy yard. On Mar. 3, 1835, he was promoted captain. After a long period on waiting orders he commanded the *Constitution* of the Pacific Squadron, 1839–41. From 1843 to 1846 he was in command of the Brazil Squadron. His last duty was performed at the Portsmouth navy yard as its commandant. He died suddenly at Philadelphia of a heart affection, leaving a wife and daughter. On May 23, 1837, he had married in that city Catharine M. Bryan.

[Bureau of Navigation, Records of Officers, 1804–58; Navy Register, 1815–50; Usher Parsons, *Brief Sketches of the Officers Who Were in the Battle of Lake Erie* (1862); *Daily National Intelligencer* (Washington, D. C.), Feb. 7, 1850; *Newport Mercury,* Feb. 9, 1850; *Public Ledger* (Phila.), Feb. 6, 7, 1850; Veterans Administration, Pension Files, War of 1812; Theodore Roosevelt, *The Naval War of 1812* (1889).]

C. O. P.

TURNER, EDWARD (Nov. 25, 1778–May 23, 1860), jurist, was born in Fairfax County, Va., the son of Lewis Ellzey and Theodosia (Payne) Turner, and a grandson of William Payne who, according to "Parson" Weems, once knocked George Washington down (M. L. Weems, *A History of the Life . . . of . . . George Washington,* 2nd ed., 1800, p. 49). In 1786 the Turners moved to Kentucky. Becoming a student in Transylvania University, Edward attended at intervals, as time and means permitted, and studied law while serving as clerk in the office of George Nicholas [*q.v.*]. About this time Nicholas was championing Jefferson's Kentucky resolutions (1798). With a Democratic background, therefore, and with letters of introduction from Gen. Green Clay [*q.v.*] of Kentucky, late in 1801 Turner went to Natchez, Miss., where the Democrats were just coming into power.

The young lawyer was well received, for within a few months he was made aide-de-camp and private secretary to the governor and clerk of the lower house of the territorial legislature. On Sept. 5, 1802, he was married to Mary, daughter of Cato West, a prominent Democrat of Jefferson County, and about the same time became clerk of the court of that county. In the summer of 1803 he was appointed by the federal government register of the newly established land office at Washington, Miss. Losing this place in December 1804, he returned to Jefferson County, where he practised law until 1810 and then moved to a plantation he had acquired in Warren County. He was elected to the legislature in 1811. In February of that year his wife died, and on Dec. 27, 1812, he married Eliza Baker, daughter of a wealthy planter from New Jersey. Returning to Natchez in 1813, he became city magistrate and president of the board of selectmen. Two years later, he was again elected to the legislature and was chosen to prepare a digest of the laws of the territory. This was published in 1816—*Statutes of the Mississippi Territory . . . Digested by Authority of the General Assembly.* As a representative of Adams County in the convention of 1817 he was a member of the committee that drafted the first constitution of Mississippi, and he continued to shape the affairs of the new state as chairman of the judiciary committee in the first state legislature (1817–18), and as speaker of the house in 1819 and 1820. For a short time in 1820–21 he was attorney-general.

In 1822 he was appointed judge of the criminal court of Adams County and in 1824 was advanced to the supreme court of Mississippi. Five years later he became chief justice and remained in this office until the adoption of the constitution of 1832, which provided for the popular election of judges. In 1834 he was elected chancellor, serving until 1839, in which year he was an unsuccessful candidate for governor on the Whig ticket. In 1840 he was again elected to the supreme court to fill a term which expired in 1843. He was not a candidate for reëlection, but in 1844 he was sent to the state Senate and served one term.

The last twelve years of his life he held no political office, but continued for several years to serve as president of the trustees of Jefferson College at Washington, Miss. By his marriages and by the practice of law he had become comparatively wealthy and he lived in comfort in his home near Natchez. He was survived by his wife and two daughters. Although Turner is remembered chiefly as a jurist, "his warmest friends," according to Henry S. Foote (*post,* p. 19), "did not claim for him any very extraordinary knowledge of law as a science." His success in public and private life was due to the fact that his "intellect was of a sound and practical cast, and his industry most remarkable." He was also "of unsurpassed integrity" and he had "exceedingly kind and conciliatory manners."

[9 *Miss. Reports,* 10–12; H. S. Foote, *The Bench and Bar of the South and Southwest* (1876); J. D. Lynch, *The Bench and Bar of Miss.* (1881); Dunbar Rowland, *Official Letter Books of W. C. C. Claiborne, 1801–1816* (1917), vols. I, II, and *Mississippi* (1907), vol. II; *Biog. and Hist. Memoirs of Miss.* (1891), vol. II; *Frank Leslie's Illustrated Newspaper,* Nov. 6, 1858; J. F. Claiborne, *Miss., as a Province, Territory and State* (1880); manuscript diary of B. L. C. Wailes [*q.v.*]; information supplied by L. P. Conner of Natchez, from family records.]   C. S. S.

TURNER, EDWARD RAYMOND (May 28, 1881–Dec. 31, 1929), historian, was born in Baltimore, Md., the son of Charles and Rosalind (Flynn) Turner. After attending the public schools of Baltimore he matriculated at St. John's College, Annapolis, receiving the degree of B.A. in 1904. Shortly thereafter he entered the graduate school of the Johns Hopkins University, where he devoted himself to the study of history. The American Historical Association awarded him the Justin Winsor Prize in 1910 for his dissertation, published the following year with the title *The Negro in Pennsylvania.* In the same year that he received the degree of Ph.D. (1910), he was called to Bryn Mawr College as associate in history; and, after remaining there one year, he accepted a professorship of European history at the University of Michigan. While occupying that chair, from 1911 to 1924, Turner established himself as an able and attractive lecturer.

In the field of historical research he devoted himself to English constitutional history. At first he planned to study the development of the cabinet during the reign of the early Hanoverians, but he eventually extended his research through the seventeenth and eighteenth centuries. His early contributions to the *English Historical Review* (such as the one published in April 1915) and the *American Historical Review* brought him into prominence both in England and the United States, and during the remainder of his life he continued his study of conciliar development. By reason of his abundant learning and energy Turner was also able, during the same time, to produce numerous manuals that enjoyed wide popularity. Thus there appeared: *Ireland and England* (1919); *Europe, 1789–1920* (1920); *Europe since 1870* (1921); *Europe,* 1450–1789 (1923); and *Europe since 1789* (1924).

In 1924 Turner accepted the professorship of English history at Yale University. The following year he was selected to succeed his former teacher, John Martin Vincent, as professor of European history at the Johns Hopkins University, and he returned to his native city. On Sept. 1, 1917, he had married Eleanor Howard Bowie of Baltimore. There were three children, of whom two survived him. At the Johns Hopkins he entered upon his new duties with great enthusiasm, invigorating the department of history and injecting new interest in the study of recent European diplomatic history. Strenuous academic duties, however, did not prevent him from progressing toward the completion of his *magnum opus,* for in 1927–28 appeared two volumes on *The Privy Council of England in the Seventeenth and Eighteenth Centuries.* Unfortunately, the premature death of Turner prevented him from completing his work, but two more volumes, left by him in type, were published in 1930–32 under the title, *The Cabinet Council of England in the Seventeenth and Eighteenth Centuries,* while materials for another were left with his widow. It was his desire "to make these four volumes a repository of all the available information on his subject" (Adair, *post,* p. xvi). Final conclusions, "flowing from the evidence," were to follow.

During almost his entire professional life, Turner spent his summers and sabbatical years in England, carrying on his research. During his last years he devoted much attention to the origins of the World War, being a frequent contributor to the *American Historical Review, Current History,* and other journals. Occasionally he became involved in controversies with certain "revisionists," but he defended his position with learning and conviction. His wide research, his mastery of numerous languages, and his love of literature are constantly reflected in his works.

[Information from Mrs. Eleanor Bowie Turner; personal recollection of the author; E. R. Adair, sketch of Turner and discussion of his work in introduction of *The Cabinet Council,* vol. II (1932); *The Johns Hopkins Alumni Mag.,* Mar. 1930, in "Necrology"; "Edward Raymond Turner, 1881–1929," in *Jour. of Modern Hist.,* Mar. 1930; editorial note in *Current Hist.,* Feb. 1930; *Am. Hist. Rev.,* Apr. 1930, p. 689, and reviews, *Ibid.,* Jan., Oct. 1928; *Sun* (Baltimore), Jan. 1, 1930; *Times* (London), Jan. 2, 1930.]   R. H. W.

TURNER, FENNELL PARRISH (Feb. 25, 1867–Feb. 10, 1932), missionary executive, was born in Danielsville, Dickson County, Tenn., the son of William Allen and Mary Jane (Pickett) Turner. Reared in the family of a Methodist minister and descended from a long line of ministers, he was naturally predisposed to the profession of his father and began preaching when in his teens. The oldest of the family, he shared the responsibility of helping to educate the younger children. He himself attended the common schools, then the Wall School at Chapel Hill, Tenn., and in 1891 graduated from Vanderbilt University. He interrupted his college course for two years, 1888–1890, to be principal of Dixon Academy, at Shelbyville, Tenn. For a year, 1891–92, he was a student in the Biblical department of Vanderbilt University but left to give full time to the *Tennessee Methodist,* of which he became assistant editor and business manager in 1891.

In 1895 he became state secretary of the Young Men's Christian Association for North Carolina. From this position he passed in 1897 to that of general secretary of the Student Volunteer Movement for Foreign Missions, then closely associated with the student department of the international committee of the Young Men's Christian Association; that same year, Nov. 3, he was married to Rose Vaughan of Nashville, Tenn. The Student Volunteer Movement, at the time Turner took charge of it, was scarcely ten years old. As a recruiting and educating agency for Protestant foreign missions, it had a large part in the religious life of the colleges and universities of the United States and Canada and in the growth of American foreign missions. The quadrennial conventions held by the Movement drew more students from more of the colleges and universities of North America than any other gatherings, secular or religious. Turner's twenty-two years (1897–1919) as its secretary spanned the Movement's most prosperous years, and for its development he was to no small degree responsible. In 1911 he brought about the organization of the Board of Missionary Preparation and was chiefly responsible for it until 1916. In 1918 he became the secretary of the Committee of Reference and Counsel of the Foreign Missions Conference of North America—the body coördinating the Protestant foreign mission boards of the Continent—and the following year he resigned from the secretaryship of the Student Volunteer Movement to give his entire time to the new post. From 1919 to 1928 he was also recording secretary of the Foreign Missions Conference. During these years in New York, he found time to serve with several other organizations whose work was closely related to that in which he was chiefly engaged: from 1912 to 1919 he was a member of the general committee of the World's Student Christian Federation; in 1910 he attended the World Missionary Conference at Edinburgh; from 1920 to 1928 he was a member of the committee of the newly formed International Missionary Council, and was present at four of the meetings of that body, including the memorable one at Jerusalem in 1928; he was a member of the executive committee of the World Alliance for Promoting International Friendship through the Churches, and of the administrative committee of the Federal Council of the Churches of Christ in America; and he was a delegate to international gatherings which planned for Protestant activities in Latin America—at Panama in 1916, at Montevideo in 1925, and in Havana in 1929. In these and many other connections he had a share in the formulation of the policies for the international outreach of Protestant Christianity.

In 1928, when the strain of the years of heavy administrative duties had at last become insupportable, he severed most of his major New York connections and became secretary for missionary education and foreign extension of the General Sunday-school Board of the denomination of his youth, the Methodist Episcopal Church, South, and served until 1930. In 1930–31 he traveled in Asia as a member of the research staff of the Laymen's Foreign Missions Inquiry. His report, "Missionary Personnel in India, Burma, China, and Japan," was published in *Laymen's Foreign Missions Inquiry: Fact-Finders' Reports,* vol. VII (1933). Shortly after his return from the East, increasing ill health forced him to retire to Southern California and a few months later he died at Santa Cruz. Not especially gifted in public address, and never writing much under his own name, Turner gave most of his energy to administration, to personal counsel, to service on boards and committees, and to editing papers and reports. A prodigious and not a quick worker, he willingly and patiently bore burdens which, as the years passed, broke his health. Kindly, companionable, unassuming, and unselfish, he won and held a wide circle of friends.

[*Who's Who in America,* 1932–33; *Missionary Rev. of the World,* May 1932, and *Christian Advocate* (Nashville), Feb. 19, 1932, both giving Feb. 9 as day of death; *N. Y. Times,* Feb. 11, 1932, which gives day of death as Feb. 10; material furnished by family and friends.]   K. S. L.

TURNER, FREDERICK JACKSON (Nov. 14, 1861–Mar. 14, 1932), historian, was born at Portage, on the northern fringe of agricultural Wisconsin, and passed his boyhood near the route over which explorers and missionaries had made their way from the St. Lawrence Valley to that of the Mississippi. He had local schooling, reënforced from a background of New England culture by his parents Andrew Jackson and Mary (Hanford) Turner, who were able to give him the best in education that the state afforded. His father, from Plattsburg, N. Y., a journalist and a politician, was a local historian as well. While Turner was at the University of Wisconsin, Prof. William Francis Allen [q.v.] taught him to examine sources and to weigh the inferences they suggested. Between 1884, when he was graduated, and 1888, when he took the degree of M.A., Turner gave up youthful ideas of journalism and elocution and determined to venture upon the new career of professor of history. Allen had already set him to work on the manuscripts of Lyman C. Draper [q.v.] in the State Historical Society, where his young friend Reuben Gold Thwaites [q.v.] had now been installed as Draper's successor. Out of these initial studies came material for "The Character and Influence of the Indian Trade in Wisconsin," which Turner offered as his dissertation for the doctorate at the Johns Hopkins in 1890 (*Johns Hopkins University Studies in Historical and Political Science,* 9 ser., 1891). At the University of Wisconsin, where he was assistant professor of history, 1889–91, professor of history, 1891–92, and professor of American history, 1892–1910, he took part in a deliberate attempt to erect a distinguished school of social studies.

Turner was a teacher with unusual power to inspire devotion, and an appearance of youth and simplicity that never quite deserted him. He became a useful professor, with a practical political instinct that made him a central figure in his university and threatened to divert him from paths of quiet scholarship. But he was aware of the nearness of unique archives in which American life could be investigated at its beginnings, and he never strayed far from the themes of his early studies. Invited to present a brief paper at the special meeting of the American Historical Association to be held at the World's Fair in Chicago, he assembled data for an essay on "The Significance of the Frontier in American History," which he read July 12, 1893 (first printed in 1894 in *Proceedings of the State Historical Society of Wisconsin . . . 1893,* and reprinted that year in *Annual Report of the American Historical Association . . . 1893*). Without warning he set forth a new hypothesis, and then and there opened a new period in the interpretation of the history of the United States. At the age of thirty-two he found himself treated as one of the significant figures in historical writing. Returning to his teaching work, where his distinctive course soon became the "History of the West," he adjusted himself slowly to the idea of his own importance.

He wrote little. His relatively small output may be attributed in part to a caution inspired by early success, in part to his endless patience with his students, and largely to the painstaking procedure by which he assembled and verified his facts. He was not working in a field already standardized, or yielding to easy narration, but in one in which small fragments, each of slight importance, needed to be brought together for impressive aggregates. Brief essays came from his study; but there were only a dozen which he cared to reprint, along with "The Significance of the Frontier," in *The Frontier in American History* (1920); and only a dozen more for *The Significance of Sections in American History* (1932), a posthumous recipient of the Pulitzer Prize. He edited "Correspondence of the French Ministers to the United States, 1791–1797" (*Annual Report of the American Historical Association . . . 1903,* vol. II, 1904). He was persuaded by A. B. Hart to prepare the *Rise of the New West* (1906), as a volume in the cooperative work, *The American Nation.* In this he disclosed the various sectional unities in the period 1819–29. He left incomplete at death a continuation of this; it was later published as *The United States, 1830–1850: The Nation and Its Sections* (1935), with an introduction by Avery Craven.

It was neither the bulk of his writing that brought Turner international recognition, nor the number of advanced students whom he trained at Wisconsin, for these were relatively few. It was rather the penetrating influence of his hypothesis, which incited investigation by his co-workers and led to a change in the trend of historical writing upon the United States. Trained historical craftsmen came into American historiography only in the decade at the close of which Turner took his doctorate; they told the American story with increasing accuracy, but without developing any convincing formula to account for the obvious fact that emigrants from western Europe and their descendants had brought into being a nation as variant from any of those from which they came as though it were of a different breed. Earlier historians had written in terms of religious liberty and revolt against the tyranny of England, or in admiration of the triumph of the principle of democracy. Where their writings were not antiquarian in character they were often nationalist or party tracts. Turner made necessary a new synthesis.

Seeking an explanation for that quality that appeared not to derive from the European sources of American culture, Turner looked for elements in the American environment that were novel in it. He observed that for three centuries the immigrants had found lodgment in an open continent where there was little to impede their free access to good land. He observed as well that for many centuries the peoples of Europe had lived in an environment of owned land, where the individual not born to estate had little chance to acquire it. The "hither edge of free land" became the magic element in the Turner hypothesis. Once recognized, it led him to see in the American frontier an influence unusual in history and perhaps formative in shaping American culture. He stated the formula with modesty, often asking his students whether they could "prove an inference." Some of his followers were prompted to state it dogmatically, and to go far beyond the master in applying it; but Turner was content to point out the possibility that human nature in a free environment might behave differently from the same nature under social and economic pressure, that equality of opportunity might have something to do with democracy in politics, that isolation on a new frontier might encourage the survival of the robust and the opinionated, that the necessity of repeatedly setting up social and governmental institutions brought about a laboratory process in which nonessentials dropped out while tested principles survived, that the relationship between frontiersmen and government led naturally to a nationalism more intense than that of the older communities. He traced in his famous essay the spread over the continent of a series of frontiers: of the discoverer and explorer, the missionary, the soldier, the trapper, and the farmer. But his hypothesis was derived largely from the experiences of the frontier farmers who first changed the face of nature, and who added new units of social and economic life to the United States. He pointed out, as well, that whatever the influence of the frontier had been, it was now in 1893 about to terminate. Free land had gone, after three centuries of access to its "hither edge"; and he foretold a future different from the past in so far at least as the open frontier had been a positive force.

For the rest of his creative life Turner tested his hypothesis, applying it at times to microscopic examination of limited regions and periods, and trying at other moments to reconcile it with larger views of American development. He regarded the frontier less as a place than as a continuous process sweeping the continent, and regarded the region where it was temporarily operating as a section with aspects and interests deriving from its cultural state. This led him easily to a consideration of other varieties of sections, owing their identity to topography, natural resources, or the racial components of their people. He observed in these the American equivalents of the distracted nationalities of Europe. On this note he ended.

From the day that he read his essay Turner was a marked man, but, declining all calls to other institutions, he continued until 1910 to serve his university. Soon welcomed to the inner councils of the American Historical Association, he served as its president in 1909–10. During the period 1910–15, he was a member of the board of editors of the *American Historical Review*. In 1910 he accepted a professorship at Harvard. Here, in an atmosphere less hospitable to his trend of thought than that of Wisconsin, he continued until retirement in 1924. He planned thereafter to reside in Madison, but poor health intervened and winters in California gave way to residence in Pasadena, where the Huntington Library welcomed him as research associate. He died at the age of seventy-one. He was married on Nov. 25, 1889, to Carolina Mae Sherwood of Chicago, who, with one of their children, survived him.

[Turner's reference books and notes were presented by him to the Huntington Lib., and the bulk of his correspondence is deposited there. See Max Farrand, in the *Huntington Lib. Bulletin*, no. 3, Feb. 1933, pp. 157–64. Carl Becker, in H. W. Odum, ed., *American Masters of Social Science* (1927), gives an appraisal of Turner's work and a careful bibliography of his writings. Other friendly appreciations are: E. E. Robinson, in *N. D. Hist. Quart.*, July 1932; Joseph Schafer, in *Wis. Mag. of Hist.*, Sept. 1931, June 1932, June 1933, June 1934; Constance L. Skinner, *Ibid.*, Sept. 1935; M. E. Curti, "The Section and the Frontier in American History: The Methodological Concepts of Frederick Jackson Turner," in S. A. Rice, ed., *Methods in Social Science* (1931); F. L. Paxson, "A Generation of the Frontier Hypothesis," in *Pacific Hist. Rev.*, Mar. 1933. Destructive criticism is offered in J. C. Almack, "The Shibboleth of the Frontier," in *Historical Outlook*, May 1925; B. F. Wright, Jr., "American Democracy and the Frontier," in *Yale Rev.*, Winter, 1931; L. M. Hacker, "Sections—or Classes," in *The Nation*, July 26, 1933, with reply by Benjamin Stolberg, *Ibid.*, Sept. 13, 1933. A valuable aid is E. E. Edwards, "References on the Significance of the Frontier in American History," *Bibliographical Contributions*, No. 25, Oct. 1935, U. S. Dept. of Agriculture Lib. See also R. G. Thwaites, *The Univ. of Wisconsin* (1900); *Am. Hist. Rev.*, July 1932, pp. 823–24; review of Turner's last book by J. D. Hicks, in *Am. Hist. Rev.*, Jan. 1936; obituary and editorial, *N. Y. Times*, Mar. 16, 17, 1932.] F. L. P.

TURNER, GEORGE (Feb. 25, 1850–Jan. 26, 1932), lawyer, United States senator, was born in Edina, Mo., the son of Granville Davenport and Maria (Taylor) Turner. His father, a cabinet maker, was of English and Dutch ancestry; his mother, of Scotch-Irish. They had moved from Kentucky to Missouri in 1825. The boy's schooling was meager, and at the age of thirteen, the Civil War then being in progress, he became a military telegrapher in the Union service. After the war, he studied law in the office of a brother in Mobile, where he was admitted to the bar in 1870. President Grant in 1876 appointed him United States marshal for the middle and southern districts of Alabama, and he served until 1880. During this period he was the acknowledged Republican leader of the state. He was chairman of the Alabama delegation at the Republican National Convention of 1880, and held his negroes in line for Grant through the six days' battle between the Grant and Blaine forces.

In 1885 President Arthur appointed him associate justice of the supreme court of Washington Territory. Resigning in 1888, he entered upon the practice of law in Spokane. He was a member of the state constitutional convention of 1889 and chairman of its judiciary committee. He is credited with the authorship of the bill of rights, regarded by jurists as exceedingly comprehensive. The Puget Sound tidelands were coveted by railway interests, and his successful campaign in the convention to save them for the state created an opposition to him which repeatedly prevented his election to public office later. Working with scanty capital in the panic years of the nineties, Turner and some Spokane friends developed the Le Roi mine, at Rossland, B. C. It became a rich producer and was sold to a British syndicate for $4,000,000. Turner's sagacity and his skill in bending insurgent stockholders to his purpose were largely responsible for this success. He was president of the Le Roi and, later, of the Constitution mine and the Sullivan group, near Cranbrook, B. C. With profits from the Le Roi, he joined Frank Graves of Spokane in the purchase of the *Seattle Post-Intelligencer.* They paid $50,000 for the paper in September 1897 and some two years later sold it for $350,000 to Senator John L. Wilson backed by James J. Hill [*qq.v.*]. This paper was the principal Republican organ of the state; Turner made no effort to change its policy while he was an owner, and it continued to attack his acts as United States senator.

Turner was elected to the Senate on a fusion ticket of Silver Republicans, Democrats, and Populists, and served from Mar. 4, 1897, to Mar. 3, 1903. At the expiration of his term, the legislature was under Republican control, and there was no possibility of his reëlection. He had won high regard as a constitutional lawyer, and on the day following his retirement President Theodore Roosevelt notified him of his appointment, with Secretary of War Elihu Root and Senator Henry Cabot Lodge [*q.v.*], as a member of the Alaska Boundary Tribunal. In 1910 President Taft appointed him as counsel for the United States in the Northeastern fisheries dispute with Great Britain, which was arbitrated at The Hague. President Taft also appointed Turner to the International Joint Boundary Commission, on which he served in 1913 and 1914, resigning because of the demand for his legal services in Spokane. From 1918 to 1924, however, by President Wilson's appointment, he acted as counsel for the United States before this commission.

Turner was always a dramatic figure. He belonged to the pioneer tradition, with its vision, independence, and fighting spirit. He was most happy in the stress of the old party conventions, which released his vivid eloquence. His rise to eminence in the face of educational disadvantages was due to an orderly mind, phenomenal memory, and untiring will. On June 4, 1878, he married Bertha C. Dreher, daughter of George and Catherine Dreher of Montgomery, Ala. He died at his home in Spokane, survived by his widow.

[N. W. Durham, *Hist. of the City of Spokane* (1912), I, 421, 481, 488, II, 116; *Who's Who in America*, 1930–31; *Biog. Dir. Am. Cong.* (1928); Jonathan Edwards, *An Illustrated Hist. of Spokane County* (1900); *Spokesman-Review* (Spokane), Jan. 27, 1932; information as to certain facts from relatives and associates.]
G. W. F.

TURNER, HENRY McNEAL (Feb. 1, 1834– May 8, 1915), bishop of the African Methodist Episcopal Church, editor, author, was born near Abbeville, S. C. He was the son of Hardy Turner and Sarah (Greer) and came of mixed blood. Losing his father when still young, Turner worked for a time in the cotton fields and was then apprenticed to a blacksmith. He was fifteen before he was taught to read. He was next employed by a law firm, learned to write, and mastered arithmetic. He joined the Methodist Episcopal Church, South, and in 1853 was licensed to preach. He became a successful revivalist among the negroes and held meetings in most of the Southern states until 1857, when he settled in St. Louis. In the following year he was admitted to the Missouri Conference of the African Methodist Episcopal Church, to which he thereafter adhered.

Placed in charge of a mission in Baltimore and criticized locally for his imperfect command of English, he studied grammar, Latin, Greek, and Hebrew. He was ordained deacon in 1860 and elder in 1862. In the latter year he was installed as pastor of Israel Church, Washington, where he came into contact with many prominent men. In 1863 he was made an army chaplain by President Lincoln—the first colored man to be appointed to such a position—and was attached to the 1st Regiment, United States Colored Troops. Mustered out in 1865, he was appointed chaplain in the regular army by President Johnson and assigned to the Georgia office of the Freedmen's Bureau. He soon resigned in order to build up the African Methodist Episcopal Church in Georgia. Under his vigorous proselyting a large number of churches were established, which became rallying points for the freed negroes. One of the founders of the Republican party in Georgia, Turner was elected a delegate to the Georgia Constitutional convention in 1867, and a member of the state legislature for Bibb County in 1868. Here he aroused the jealousy of the white Republicans, while his outspoken and provocative language made him bitterly hated by the Democrats. In 1869 he was appointed postmaster at Macon by President Grant at the request of Senator Charles Sumner, which office he relinquished because of the opposition of the white patrons. He subsequently served as a United States customs inspector and as a government detective.

In 1876 he was made manager of the African Methodist Episcopal Book Concern in Philadelphia, and from 1880 until 1892 he was bishop of his Church for Georgia. For twelve years he was chancellor of Morris Brown College (now Morris Brown University) in Atlanta. He visited South and West Africa, introduced African Methodism there, and advocated the return of the negroes to Africa. He founded several periodicals, including the *Southern Christian Recorder* (1889) and the *Voice of Missions* (1892) and was the author of *The Genius and Theory of Methodist Polity* (copr. 1885) and the compiler of a catechism and a hymn book.

Turner was very tall, with an elephantine frame and massive head. He possessed a coarse nature, his manners and movements were crude, and he cared nothing about his dress or personal appearance. He was an eloquent speaker, had a guttural voice, and was given to angry tirades and bitter sarcasm against both negroes and whites. He was married four times and had numerous children, of whom only two survived him. His first marriage, to Eliza Ann Peacher, occurred on Aug. 31, 1856, in Columbia, S. C.; his second, to Mrs. Martha De Witt of Bristol, Pa., in August 1893; his third, to Harriet A. Wayman of Baltimore, Md., widow of Bishop Alexander Wayman [q.v.], on Aug. 16, 1900; and his last to Laura Pearl Lemon of Atlanta, Ga., divorced wife of a minister named Powell. Turner died in Windsor, Ontario, and was buried in Atlanta.

[M. M. Ponton, *Life and Times of Henry M. Turner* (1917); R. R. Wright, *Centennial Encyc. of the Afri-* can *Methodist Episcopal Church* (1916); *Who's Who in America,* 1914–15; *Atlanta Constitution,* Aug. 17, 1900, Dec. 4, 1907, May 9, 1915; *Atlanta Jour.,* May 9, 1915.]
H. G. V.

TURNER, JAMES MILTON (May 16, 1840–Nov. 1, 1915), negro leader, minister to Liberia, was born a slave in St. Louis County, Mo., on the St. Charles Road plantation of Charles A. Loring. His father, John Turner, also known as John Colburn after a master, had been removed from Virginia by one Benjamin Tillman, following the 1831 slave insurrection led by Nat Turner [q.v.]. Taught veterinary medicine by Tillman, Turner subsequently bought his freedom and in 1843 purchased his wife Hannah and their son, then in his fourth year. The boy's aptitude displayed at a clandestine school so pleased his parents that they sent him to Oberlin College, where he spent his fourteenth year in the preparatory department under the tutelage of James Harris Fairchild [q.v.].

In the Civil War he served as a Northern officer's servant, and is said to have received at Shiloh an injury that caused a lifelong limp. After the war he directed his attention to negro public education as required by the Missouri constitution of 1865. In April 1866 he was appointed by the Kansas City school board to conduct a school for negroes during the winter; no earlier negro public school in Missouri is recorded. In June 1868 he was reappointed. Meanwhile, he had become interested in plans for a negro institute in Jefferson City, Mo. For this undertaking, now Lincoln University, he gave and collected money and served as trustee. Oratorical ability soon made him the acknowledged leader of Missouri negroes and as such a figure in Republican politics. The Columbia (Mo.) *Statesman* in 1870 pictured him as "possessed of a fine flow of language and never wanting an idea" (quoted in Dilliard, *post,* p. 379).

On nomination of President Grant, confirmed by the Senate, Mar. 1, 1871, Turner became minister resident and consul general to Liberia, the first negro, it is said, to serve in the diplomatic corps. He presented his credentials at Monrovia on July 25 of that year and served until May 20, 1878. Liberia's frequent governmental changes and native uprisings kept him busy writing long, apologetic dispatches to the Department of State. Thorough observation of conditions led him to oppose settlement by American negroes on the ground that they were unfitted for equatorial life. Colonization activities of philanthropists he described as "well-meaning" but "absolutely injurious in results" (see *Papers Relating to the Foreign Relations of the United States,* 1877, pp. 370–75); he urged instead help for native tribes. After European receptions, Turner returned to the United States to be fêted widely; admiring negroes hauled his carriage through the streets of St. Louis. Later he married Ella De Burton of St. Joseph's Parish, La., who died Mar. 2, 1908; they had no children. On Apr. 18, 1882, he appeared before the Missouri Historical Society, St. Louis, to eulogize Dred Scott [q.v.] and to present an oil painting of him to the society in behalf of the widow of Theron Barnum, to whose family Scott had been attached. In 1886 he presented to President Cleveland the claim that negro members of the Cherokee nation were entitled to a proportionate share of $300,-000 allotted that nation by Congress, and as their attorney was instrumental in securing an appropriation of $75,000 for them in 1889. He also interested himself in claims for Choctaw and Chickasaw freedmen.

Caught in the débris of an explosion in Ardmore, Okla., Turner died there. His funeral, conducted by Missouri negro Masons, was the largest ever held in St. Louis for a member of his race. Crowds thronged to the service, where tribute was paid to his leadership and generosity. He was buried in Father Dickson Cemetery, near his birthplace. A "citizen's memorial service" was held two weeks later.

[The fullest source of information is Irving Dilliard, "James Milton Turner, a Little Known Benefactor of His People," *The Jour. of Negro Hist.*, Oct. 1934; it cites newspaper articles, letters, memoranda, and quotes at length from Turner's dispatches to the Department of State.]   I. D.

TURNER, JOHN WESLEY (July 19, 1833–Apr. 8, 1899), soldier, son of John Bice and Martha (Voluntine) Turner, was born near Saratoga, N. Y. His father was a prominent railroad and canal constructor, and in 1843 the family removed to Chicago, where the elder Turner helped build the Galena & Chicago Union Railroad. John Wesley was appointed to the United States Military Academy from Illinois, graduated in 1855, and was commissioned lieutenant of artillery. As a subaltern he served in Oregon and in hostilities against the Seminoles in Florida.

In August 1861 he was commissioned captain in the commissary department and served as chief commissary under Gen. David Hunter [q.v.] in Kansas from December 1861 to March 1862, and in the same capacity under General Hunter when the latter was in command of the Department of the South in April 1862. During this tour of duty he was employed as an artillery officer in the attack on Fort Pulaski, Apr. 10–11, 1862. In May of the same year he was assigned as chief commissary on the staff of Gen. Ben-

jamin F. Butler [q.v.] at New Orleans and remained with him to the end of the year. In the spring of 1863 he returned to General Hunter in the Department of the South, and when Hunter was relieved by Gen. Quincy A. Gillmore [q.v.], Turner was made chief of staff and chief of artillery, June 13, 1863, and as such took part in the siege of Fort Wagner and the attack on Fort Sumter. For his services he received the brevet of major, United States Army, and was commissioned brigadier-general of volunteers. In the operations of 1864 Turner commanded a division in the Army of the James under General Butler on Bermuda Hundred and in front of Petersburg, and received the brevet of lieutenant-colonel, United States Army, for gallant services in action at the Petersburg mine, and the brevet of major-general of volunteers for gallant services in the campaign of 1864. From Nov. 20, 1864, to Jan. 12, 1865, he was chief of staff of the Army of the James. In the campaign of 1865 he commanded a division of the XXIV Army Corps and took an active part in the operations leading to the surrender of Lee at Appomattox. For his services at the capture of Fort Gregg he received the brevet of colonel, United States Army, and later those of brigadier and major-general. At the end of active operations he was appointed to the command of the District of Henrico, which included the city of Richmond; this position he held from June 1865 to April 1866. His administration was both efficient and tactful. On being mustered out of the volunteer service in 1866 he became purchasing and depot commissary at St. Louis. In September 1871 he resigned from the army.

Being accustomed to command and to assume great responsibilities, and having a pleasing personality and great tact, he was as successful in civil life as he had been in his military career. From 1872 to 1877 he was president of the Bogy Lead Mining Company, and for eleven years (1877–88), street commissioner of St. Louis. He served, also, as president of the St. Joseph Gas and Manufacturing Company (1888–97), and as a director of the American Exchange Bank and of the St. Louis Savings and Safe Deposit Company (1893–99). On Sept. 18, 1869, he married Blanche Soulard of St. Louis, by whom he had seven children. His death occurred in St. Louis and his wife and children survived him.

[G. W. Cullum, *Biog. Reg. . . . Grads. U. S. Mil. Acad.* (3rd ed., 1891); *Thirteenth Ann. Reunion, Asso. Grads. U. S. Mil. Acad.* (1899); *War of the Rebellion: Official Records (Army)*; William Hyde and H. L. Conard, *Encyc. of the Hist. of St. Louis* (1899, vol. IV); *St. Louis Globe-Democrat*, Apr. 8, 9, 1899.]

            G.J.F.

TURNER, JONATHAN BALDWIN (Dec. 7, 1805–Jan. 10, 1899), educator, agriculturist, was born in Templeton, Mass., the son of Asa and Abigail (Baldwin) Turner, and a brother of Asa Turner [*q.v.*]. He obtained his early education in local district schools, in which he later became a teacher. When his brother Asa graduated from college in 1827, he persuaded his father to let Jonathan go to New Haven to prepare for Yale, and at the end of two years he was admitted to the college. Early in the spring of his senior year a call came to Yale from Illinois College, at Jacksonville, for an instructor in Latin and Greek. The president of Yale recommended Turner and offered to excuse him from final examinations and to forward his diploma if he would accept. As a result, in May 1833 he became a member of the Illinois faculty. The following year he was appointed professor of rhetoric and belles-lettres. He returned to the East in 1835 to marry, on Oct. 22, Rhodolphia S. Kibbe of Somers, Conn. He early became a leader in the movement for public schools in Illinois, lecturing in its behalf throughout the central part of the state. One of the organizers of the Illinois State Teachers' Association in 1836, he enlisted the aid of teachers and parents in his campaign. He was successful as an instructor, but in 1843–44 he edited the *Statesman,* a local paper, and by his vigorous condemnation of slavery alienated the Southern students in the college and the slavery advocates in Jacksonville. In 1847 he resigned his professorship because of ill health and disagreement with the college officials over slavery and denominational questions.

He now devoted himself primarily to his gardens and orchards, which he had been developing since 1834, and to agricultural experiments. He made the Osage orange popular for farm hedges, and invented various implements for planting and cultivating crops. The preservation of game life and of national resources also engaged his attention. When the Illinois State Natural History Society was organized, June 30, 1858, he was elected president. In spite of these activities he found time to further various educational projects. The free school law of 1855 was largely the result of his untiring efforts, and his influence had much to do with the establishment of the first normal school in Illinois in 1857. His most notable contribution to education, however, was in connection with the campaign for land grant colleges. At a county institute of teachers held at Griggsville, May 13, 1850, he presented a plan for a state university for the industrial classes in each of the states of the Union. This he presented, also, to a convention of farmers which convened in Granville on Nov. 18, 1851. The plan was approved by this convention, which also adopted certain resolutions including one which pledged the members to "take immediate steps for the establishment of a university in the State of Illinois." These resolutions and Turner's plan were printed and widely circulated. Other conventions were held later, and at one which met at Springfield, Jan. 4, 1853, a petition was drawn up requesting the legislature to ask Congress to appropriate lands to each state for the establishment of industrial universities. Such a request, the first probably from any state, was made by the Illinois legislature in 1853 (*Journal of the House of Representatives of . . . Illinois,* 1853). Through the Industrial League, organized to carry on propaganda in behalf of industrial education, of which he became principal director, Turner gave time and strength to the movement for years. Meanwhile, it was gathering strength in other parts of the country, and in 1857 Justin Morrill [*q.v.*], then a representative from Vermont, introduced a bill in Congress providing that public lands be donated to the states and territories to provide colleges of agriculture and the mechanic arts. This failed to pass over a presidential veto, but a similar bill became a law in 1862. Shortly after its passage, the small colleges of Illinois united to secure the advantages of the land grant, but chiefly through Turner's activities the legislature of 1867 decided to establish "a single new industrial university" (now the University of Illinois), which was located at Urbana, Champaign County. After the university was incorporated, Feb. 28, 1867, he devoted the remainder of his life to a study of the Bible and its teachings. His published works included *Mormonism in All Ages* (1842); *The Three Great Races of Men* (1861); *Universal Law and Its Opposites* (1892); and *The Christ Word Versus the Church Word* (1895). He died in Jacksonville, Ill., survived by four of his seven children.

[*Obit. Record Grads. Yale Univ. . . . 1890–1900* (1900); M. T. Carriel, *The Life of Jonathan Baldwin Turner* (1911); J. W. Cook, *Educational Hist. of Ill.* (1912); E. J. James, *The Origin of the Land Grant Act of 1862* (1910); I. L. Kandel, *Federal Aid for Vocational Education* (1917); C. H. Rammelkamp, *Ill. Coll., A Centennial Hist., 1829–1929* (1928); *Chicago Tribune,* Jan. 12, 1899.]   R. F. S.

TURNER, JOSIAH (Dec. 27, 1821–Oct. 26, 1901), editor, the eldest son of Josiah and Eliza (Evans) Turner, was born in Hillsboro, N. C. He was educated at Caldwell Institute and at the University of North Carolina. Admitted to the bar about 1845, he built up a considerable practice, more by native cleverness than by legal learning and ability. In 1856 he married Sophia Devereux of Raleigh, by whom he had four sons and a daughter. His public life began with his election to the House of Commons in 1852 as a Whig. Reëlected for the succeeding term, he was defeated for the state Senate in 1856, but was elected in 1858 and again in 1860. At the session of 1861 he contested every move of the secessionists and voted against calling the secession convention, but upon the passage of the ordinance, he enlisted immediately in the state forces and became a captain of cavalry. He participated in the battle of New Bern and was soon afterwards wounded and disabled. In November 1862 he resigned his commission and in 1863 was elected as a peace candidate to the Confederate Congress, where he was actively hostile to the administration and frankly urgent for making terms with the United States.

When the war ended he was no less eager for the restoration of the state but, distrusting William W. Holden [q.v.], the provisional governor, as a former Democrat and a secession leader, he was active in the movement which led in November 1865 to Holden's defeat. In the same campaign Turner won election to Congress, but he was denied his seat. He was subsequently for two years president of the North Carolina Railroad. In 1868, when Holden was elected governor, Turner was elected to the state Senate, but was denied his seat because of disabilities. In this same year he purchased the Raleigh *Sentinel,* in the editorial conduct of which he made his chief reputation. Bitterly hostile to congressional reconstruction, he threw himself into the task of discrediting and defeating the "Carpet-bag" government. With a positive genius for political polemics, sparing little nor caring where he struck, quick-witted, ingenious in keeping political opponents on the defensive, he now, by ridicule and telling nicknames, brought the Republican leaders into contempt, and again, with a lash of scorpions held them up to public condemnation. No man was so bitterly hated and feared by them. He never overlooked a vital point, never lost his temper, and never forgot or forgave. To him more than to any one man belongs the credit for the overthrow of reconstruction in North Carolina. When in 1870 Governor Holden sought to sustain his administration and carry the election by armed force, Turner roused the state to effective opposition. His own illegal arrest and imprisonment under the Governor's orders was the great event in his life and furnished one of the charges upon which Holden was later impeached.

Turner's later career was pathetic. Essentially destructive, when the crisis was past he could not find peace but continued to fight. He expected high office, but his party regarded him as too erratic and too violent, and he soon turned on his late associates. He declined a nomination to Congress in 1872 and was denied one in 1874. He was a delegate to the convention of 1875, where he loudly clamored for the repudiation of the "Carpet-bag" bonds before his party was ready for such drastic action. He lost his newspaper, which was sold in 1876 under mortgage. Defeated for the state Senate in that year, he ran for Congress as an independent in 1878 and was defeated. He had already been elected to the lower house of the legislature for the term of 1879, but was so persistently disorderly that he was finally expelled. After another defeat for Congress in 1884, he retired and ended his life a partisan Republican. He died at his home near Hillsboro.

[S. A. Ashe, *Biog. Hist. of N. C.,* vol. III (1905); J. G. deR. Hamilton, *Reconstruction in N. C.* (1914); *Alumni Hist. of the Univ. of N. C.* (1924); R. D. W. Connor, *North Carolina,* vol. II (1929); *News and Observer* (Raleigh, N. C.), Oct. 27, 1901; files of the *Sentinel.*]   J. G. deR. H.

TURNER, NAT (Oct. 2, 1800–Nov. 11, 1831), leader of slave insurrection, the son of Nancy, a slave woman and native of Africa, was born on the plantation of her owner, Benjamin Turner, in Southampton County, Va. He successively became the property of Samuel Turner, Thomas Moore, and Putnam Moore, and in 1830 he was hired to Joseph Travis, whom Mrs. Thomas Moore had married. His mother was little removed from savagery at the time of his birth, and his father, whose name has not survived, ran away while Nat was a child. Nat, who was precocious, was given the rudiments of an education by one of his master's sons, and, early developing a religious fanaticism, under his mother's encouragement came to believe himself inspired. A fiery preacher, he soon acquired leadership among the negroes on the plantation and in the neighborhood. According to his sworn confession, he deliberately set about convincing them of his divine inspiration, and presently believed himself chosen to lead them from bondage. He began to see signs in the heavens and on the leaves, and to hear voices directing him. An eclipse of the sun in 1831 convinced him that the time was near and caused him to enlist four other slaves, to whom he communicated his plans. They plotted an uprising for July 4, but abandoned it. After a new sign was seen in a peculiar solar phenomenon on Aug. 13, they settled upon Aug. 21 as the day of deliverance.

With seven others Nat attacked the Travis family and murdered them all. Securing arms and horses, and enlisting other slaves, they ravaged the neighborhood. In one day and one night they butchered horribly and mangled the bodies of fifty-one white persons—thirteen men, eighteen women, and twenty-four children. With the blood of the victims Nat sprinkled his followers. At the first armed resistance the revolt collapsed and on Aug. 25 Nat went into hiding in a dugout, less than two miles from the Travis farm, where he remained, successfully concealed in the daytime, for six weeks. Discovered by accident, he was at once tried, and after conviction was hanged at Jerusalem, the county seat. He faced his fate with calmness. Thomas R. Gray, who was assigned to defend him, said: "He is a complete fanatic, or plays his part most admirably" (Gray, *post*, p. 19). Of his sixty or seventy followers, twenty-eight were convicted and condemned; sixteen, including the one woman involved, were executed, and twelve were transported. The number that were killed in the suppression of the uprising has never been ascertained.

The revolt, following closely upon slave insurrections in Martinique, Antigua, Santiago, Carácas, and the Tortugas, caused a profound shock in the slaveholding states. Exaggeration magnified both the real and the false, and for weeks there was widespread terror. As a result almost every Southern state enacted new laws which greatly increased the severity of the slave codes, though, after a brief time, most of them were more honored in the breach than in the observance. The insurrection dealt a death blow to the manumission societies which had flourished in the South, and put an end there to the organized emancipation movement. Further, the blame for the uprising was placed upon the Garrisonian abolitionists, though not a scintilla of evidence ever connected them with it, and intensified the detestation and dread with which the South regarded them. Perhaps the most important result of all was that never again was the slaveholding South free from the fear, lurking most of the time, of a wholesale and successful slave uprising, a fact potent in the history of the republic during the next thirty years.

[W. S. Drewry, *The Southampton Insurrection* (1900), S. B. Weeks, "The Slave Insurrection in Virginia, 1831," in *Mag. of Am. Hist.*, June 1891 ; R. R. Howison, *A Hist. of Virginia*, vol. II (1848), pp. 439–41 ; W. S. Forrest, *Hist. and Descriptive Sketches of Norfolk and Vicinity* (1853) ; T. R. Gray, *The Confession, Trial, and Execution of Nat. Turner* (1881), published earlier as *The Confessions of Nat Turner . . . to Thomas R. Gray* (1832) ; *Richmond Enquirer*, Aug. 26, 30 ; Sept. 2, 6 ; Nov. 15, 18, 1831.]   J. G. deR. H.

TURNER, ROSS STERLING (June 29, 1847–Feb. 12, 1915), painter, teacher of art, was born at Westport, N. Y. His parents, David and Eliza Jane (Cameron) Turner, moved in his boyhood to Williamsport, Pa., where Ross attended the local academy, showing special aptitude for freehand and mechanical drawing. He was for several years a draftsman at the Patent Office, Washington, doing work which has been deplored as too mechanical and irksome for a man with Turner's "delicate touch and freedom of brush stroke" (Walker, *post*), but which in reality may have been good training toward his spontaneous water colors and exquisite illuminations, his chief contributions to the art of his period. In 1876 Turner went to Munich, where as an art student he was associated with Frank Duveneck, Joseph Rodefer DeCamp, Julius Rolshoven [*qq.v.*], and other young Americans. He was at Venice when Whistler was there, and he gave, shortly before his death, a talk at the Whistler House, Lowell, Mass., on his recollections of Whistler. Turner settled in 1882 in Boston where, two years later, he married Louise Blaney, sister of Dwight Blaney, a fellow artist. They made their home at Salem. Turner soon became one of the most popular teachers of water color in New England, instructing literally thousands of young people at his Boston studio, at the Massachusetts Institute of Technology (1884–1914), and for a time at the Massachusetts Normal Art School. Among his publications the most important is a manual, *On the Use of Water Colors for Beginners* (1886). He made many illustrations, and he exhibited frequently at the American Water Color Society, New York. He was a pioneer in the movement for decoration of school rooms.

Commuting for many years between Salem and Boston, with a summer studio at Wilton, N. H., Turner had an uneventful though busy and useful career. He was modest, friendly, and possessed of a wide range of interests. His chief recreation was outdoor painting in water color, in which he was facile and proficient. In his later life he discovered the charm of the Bahamas as a sketching ground, and there, at Nassau, he died. He was survived by his wife and two sons. He had previously developed a form of art of which he was one of the few modern exponents, that of the illuminated manuscript, where he used the materials and followed the manner of the medieval craftsmen. His illuminations were exhibited from time to time at the Society of Arts and Crafts, Boston. He was a charter member of the Guild of Boston Artists (formed in 1913), which in March 1915 held a memorial exhibition of his works. According to a friend, he was a "charming companion, simple as a child with the broader wisdom that declines to see evil" (Walker, *post*, p. 299).

[*Who's Who in America*, 1914–15; C. H. Walker, in *Technology Rev.*, Apr. 1915; F. T. Robinson, *Living New England Artists* (1888), with reproductions of several early water colors; cat. of the memorial exhibition, Guild of Boston Artists, Mar. 22, 1915; *Artists Year Book*, 1905; *Am. Art Ann.*, 1915; *Am. Art News*, Feb. 20, 1915; obituary in *Boston Globe*, Feb. 13, 1915.]   F. W. C.

TURNER, SAMUEL HULBEART (Jan. 23, 1790–Dec. 21, 1861), Protestant Episcopal clergyman, educator, was born in Philadelphia, Pa., the son of the Rev. Joseph Turner, a native of England, and Elizabeth (Mason), the daughter of a physician of Devonshire, England. He received his early education under private tutors and at the Quaker Academy on Fourth Street, near Chestnut, and in January 1806 entered the University of Pennsylvania. Graduating in 1807, he prepared for the ministry under the personal direction of Bishop William White [*q.v.*]. Looking back on this course of study in later years, he acknowledged his great indebtedness to the learned bishop, but confessed that "a good deal of reading without much thought . . . left my mind poorly disciplined" (*Autobiography, post*, p. 33). His awareness of this defect led him to seek the remedy, and he early developed habits of exact scholarship and sustained thinking. He was ordained deacon Jan. 27, 1811, and priest in 1814. His first charge was that of the church at Chestertown, Md. The parish was a small one and the young minister was free to devote much of his time to the further pursuit of his studies without neglecting his pastoral duties. His reputation for scholarship grew and he was offered a Latin professorship in St. John's College at Annapolis, which he declined. Removing to Philadelphia in 1817, he was appointed, early the following year, superintendent of theological students in the diocese of Pennsylvania. The duties were not onerous, for only two young men were in his care; but one of these was Alonzo Potter [*q.v.*], who was later to attain eminence as bishop of Pennsylvania.

At this time the Protestant Episcopal Church was formulating plans for a theological school, and on the establishment of the General Theological Seminary in New York, Turner was made professor in historic theology, his appointment dating from Oct. 8, 1818. When the institution was moved to New Haven in 1820, Turner went with it. On its reorganization in New York in 1822 he became professor of Biblical learning and interpretation, a position which he held for forty years. He had, therefore, a large part in shaping the traditions of the seminary, and since theological education in the United States was then in its formative stage, his influence was not inconsiderable in wider circles.

Along with his chair at the seminary he held for some years, beginning in 1830, the professorship of the Hebrew language and literature in Columbia College. His earlier writings, all of them on Biblical subjects, were for the most part translations of the more conservative German books of the day; but in 1841 he published an original work entitled *A Companion to the Book of Genesis,* and this was followed by a series of commentaries dealing with other parts of the Bible. They were all characterized by solid learning and sober judgment. A reviewer remarked that his books showed an "intimate acquaintance with German theology" but were "in no respects tainted by its neology" (Johnson, *post,* p. 29). At the same time, his sturdy, matter-of-fact exegesis with its resolute rejection of forced and fantastic interpretation of Holy Scripture played its part in paving the way for a just appreciation of that Biblical criticism which was later to revolutionize the study of the Bible, and would have sadly disturbed him.

During the latter half of his ministry the effects of the Oxford Movement were making themselves felt in the Episcopal Church in the United States, and the seminary was necessarily involved in the long controversy which followed. Turner, who opposed the movement but would have classed himself among the "moderates," defended his position throughout with a becoming sobriety of argument. His appeal was always to learning, "without which," in his own words, "piety is the more likely to degenerate into fanaticism and the suggestions of fancy to be taken for illapses of inspiration." He was married on May 23, 1826, to Mary Esther Beach of Cheshire, Conn., who died Sept. 2, 1839. At his death in New York City, he was survived by two sons and a daughter. His own account of his life, *Autobiography of the Rev. Samuel H. Turner, D.D.,* appeared in 1863.

[In addition to the *Autobiog.*, see S. R. Johnson, *Sermon Commemorative of the Life and Services of Rev. Samuel H. Turner* (1863); *N. Y. Times* and *N. Y. Tribune*, Dec. 23, 1861.]   H. E. W. F.

TURNER, WALTER VICTOR (Apr. 3, 1866–Jan. 9, 1919), engineer, inventor, son of George and Beatrice (Brandon) Turner, was born in Epping Forest, Essex, England. After completing his education in the Textile Technical School at Wakefield, Yorkshire, he engaged in the woolen textile business in that country. In 1888 he was sent by his employer to the United

States to investigate wool growing. In 1893 he became secretary and manager of the Lake Ranch Cattle Company, Raton, N. Mex., and a year or two later, with a partner, started a similar business of his own, which, however, was not successful.

One day he happened to pick up parts of an airbrake triple valve from a wrecked freight train, which so fascinated him that he spent days studying it until he had mastered its intricacies. Ideas for improvements came to him and in 1897, to gain mechanical experience, he obtained a job as a car repairer for the Atchison, Topeka & Santa Fé Railway. During the succeeding six years he rose to be mechanical instructor for the entire system and gained a wide reputation as a mechanical genius, particularly in the airbrake field. Meanwhile, he devised and patented several airbrake improvements. In 1903 he entered the employ of the Westinghouse Air Brake Company at Wilmerding, Pa., as mechanical expert and applied himself to the betterment of the existing braking equipment. His advancement was rapid; in 1910 he was made chief engineer and in 1916, manager of engineering, which position he held at the time of his death. During his career Turner acquired over 400 patents and gained the reputation of being the foremost pneumatic engineer in the world. One of his greatest inventions was the "K" triple valve, first patented Oct. 25, 1904, of which at the time of his death there were more than 2,000,000 in use. This valve solved many difficulties connected with the operation of long freight trains, making it possible to handle a train of 100 or more cars, whereas previously the maximum had been fifty; this gain led in its turn to the building of heavier locomotives and larger capacity cars. By the use of this valve, also, passenger trains could be brought to a stop in half the distance formerly required. Another invention, the electro-pneumatic brake, permitted a vast increase in traffic in subways and elevated railways without any increase in rolling stock. One of his last achievements was the system for automatically increasing or decreasing the braking power of a car as the number of passengers increased or decreased.

Turner was a frequent contributor to technical publications and often lectured before engineering societies of which he was a member. He was also the author of books regarded as classics in their field. Among these are *Development in Air Brakes for Railroads* (1909), and *Collection of Air Brake Papers* (n.d.). In 1911, for his paper "The Air Brake as Related to Progress in Locomotion" (*Journal of the Franklin Institute*, December 1910, January 1911), he was awarded the Edward Longstreth medal of merit by the Franklin Institute, Philadelphia, which organization likewise awarded him the Elliott Cresson gold medal in 1912 for his airbrake inventions and developments. On Dec. 9, 1887, he married Beatrice Woolford at Wakefield, England, and at the time of his death at Wilkinsburg, Pa., he was survived by his widow and three children.

[*Jour. of the Franklin Institute*, Mar. 1919; *Mechanical Engineering*, Apr. 1919; *Railway Rev.*, Jan. 11, 1919; *Railway Age*, Jan. 10, 1919; *Railway and Engineering Rev.*, Mar. 24, 1906; *Pittsburgh Post* and *Pittsburg Dispatch*, Jan. 10, 1919; *Who's Who in America*, 1918–19; Patent Office records.] C. W. M.

TURNEY, PETER (Sept. 22, 1827–Oct. 19, 1903), jurist, governor of Tennessee, Confederate soldier, the son of Hopkins Lacy and Teresa (Francis) Turney, was born at Jasper, Marion County, Tenn. His father, the son of a German immigrant, was a prominent figure in Tennessee politics, serving as a member of the state legislature (1828–37), representative in Congress (1837–43), and United States senator (1845–51). His mother's family was of prominent Virginia stock which emigrated to Tennessee late in the eighteenth century. Peter was educated in the public schools at Winchester, Franklin County, and at a private school in Nashville. At the age of seventeen he became surveyor but soon abandoned this work to read law in his father's office. Following his admission to the bar in 1848, he practised in partnership with his father until the latter's death in 1857. He was twice married: first, in 1851, to Cassandra Garner of Winchester, who died in 1857; and second, in 1858, to Hannah F. Graham of Marion County; by his first wife he had three children, and by his second, nine.

Following the election of Lincoln in 1860, Turney became an active advocate of secession, and was one of the leaders in the attempt to secure a convention to take Tennessee out of the Union. When this proposal was rejected by popular vote in February 1861, he led the citizens of Franklin County in the adoption of an ordinance withdrawing their county from Tennessee and attaching it to Alabama. He at once raised a volunteer regiment and marched it to Virginia, where it was mustered into the Confederate service as the 1st Tennessee, with himself as colonel. He was attached to the Army of Northern Virginia, and served under "Stonewall" Jackson until the battle of Fredericksburg, Dec. 13, 1862, when Turney was wounded. On his recovery he was transferred to Florida, where he surrendered in May 1865.

At the close of the war he resumed his law practice at Winchester, and soon gained political prominence through his opposition to the reconstruction program of Gov. William G. Brownlow [*q.v.*]. When the Democrats gained control of the state in 1870, he was elected a member of the supreme court and was reëlected in 1878 and 1886, serving as chief justice from 1886 to 1893. In his work as a judge he was described by a contemporary as "one who refuses to conform to custom and defies classification" (Pitts, *post*, p. 72). He impressed his associates as a man of strong common sense with a clear perception of practical justice, who framed his opinions by going at once to the heart of a case and deciding it and then giving briefly his reasons with little citation of authorities.

Although he had taken little active part in politics, he was known to be a Democrat of the conservative school, and therefore was selected by that element of his party to become its candidate for governor in 1892, with the hope that the party might be saved from the threatened domination of the agrarian movement. He won the election and during his first term was able to preserve nominal harmony in the party, although he failed to appeal to the younger and rural element. As a result his candidacy for reëlection in 1894 was a close contest in which H. Clay Evans [*q.v.*], his Republican opponent, received a bare majority of the votes on the face of election returns. The Democratic leaders at once raised a charge of fraud and demanded a recount by the legislature. A legislative investigating committee finally reported that an "honest count" gave the victory to Turney by a majority of over 2,000 votes. As a result of the antipathy thus aroused, he was not considered again for public office and at the close of his term, in 1897, he returned to his home at Winchester, where he died.

[Sources include John Allison, *Notable Men of Tenn.* (1905) ; J. T. Moore and A. P. Foster, *Tenn. the Volunteer State* (4 vols., 1923) ; D. M. Robison, *Bob Taylor and the Agrarian Revolt in Tenn.* (1935) ; J. A. Pitts, *Personal and Professional Reminiscences of an Old Lawyer* (1930) ; O. R. Temple, *East. Tenn. and the Civil War* (1899) ; *Biog. Dir. Am. Cong.* (1928) ; *Who's Who in America*, 1903–05 ; *Nashville Banner*, Oct. 19, 1903. Turney's supreme court opinions are in 47–92 *Tenn. Reports* ; official records of his terms as governor are in House and Senate Jours. of the 48th and 49th Tenn. Gen. Assemblies ; the legislative report on the election of 1894 was published with the title, *Contest for Gov. of Tenn., Complete Proceedings of the Joint Convention and the Investigating Committee* (2 vols., 1895).]   W. C. B.

TUTHILL, WILLIAM BURNET (Feb. 11, 1855–Aug. 25, 1929), architect, was born in New York City, the son of George F. and Jane (Price) Tuthill. On his father's side he was descended from Henry Tuthill who came to America about 1637 and about 1644 settled in Southold, L. I. After graduating from the College of the City of New York in 1875, Tuthill entered the office of Richard Morris Hunt [*q.v.*], where he carried on his architectural studies for two years. In 1877 he opened his own office. He had an extensive practice for over fifty years. His most important work was Carnegie Hall in New York City (1891), with Dankmar Adler and Louis H. Sullivan of Chicago as associate architects. Adler and Sullivan were engaged because of the Auditorium in Chicago, which they had just completed, but there is little evidence that they exercised more than a general supervision of practical matters. Carnegie Hall was acoustically a tremendous success. In its design Tuthill studied the acoustics of all the more important European concert halls, and as a result developed an unusual empirical command of the subject that led him to be called in as consultant for many churches and concert halls. A valuable manuscript monograph on the subject still exists (1936) in the possession of his son. Among Tuthill's other buildings were the Harlem Young Women's Christian Association (1888), the Jekyl Island Club, Jekyl Island, Ga. (1888), the Princeton Inn, Princeton, N. J. (1893), a Carnegie library, Pittsburgh (1894) ; and the Post Graduate Medical School and Hospital (1892), the Women's Medical College of the New York Infirmary (1900), the Columbia Yacht Club (1900), the Home for the Friendless (1902), and the white marble Schinasi residence (1909), all in New York City. He also had charge of the alteration of the Church of the Messiah, New York City (1918). Tuthill's architecture is on a broadly eclectic basis ; often, as the taste of the time decreed, over-lavish in surface decoration. But beneath its peculiarities of detail the basic creative planning is sound and practical ; after over forty years Carnegie Hall is still the musical center of New York, and the wide-spreading, low-pitched roofs of the Columbia Yacht Club are inviting and excellent in mass.

In addition to being an able architect, Tuthill was one of those born musicians who seem to develop naturally into the art, without much training. Possessed of an excellent tenor voice, he joined the Oratorio Society of New York in 1878 and for many years served as its secretary (1881–1917). He was also an accomplished 'cellist and was a member of an amateur quartet, which, with changing membership, played weekly for over thirty-six years. He was an intimate friend of most of the musical world of New York of his time. In 1891 he was a member of the board of directors of the concerts given in Carnegie Hall under Walter Damrosch. In 1919 he and his son were the founders of the Society for the Publication of American Music, and served as executive officers. His exuberant vitality can be seen in the fact that in addition to his architecture and his music, he found time to write several once-popular architectural books: *Practical Lessons in Architectural Drawing* (copyright 1881), which passed through many editions; *Interiors and Interior Details* (1882); *The City Residence, Its Design and Construction* (1890); *The Suburban Cottage, Its Design and Construction* (2nd ed., 1891); and *The Cathedral Church of England* (1923). In 1881 he married Henrietta Elizabeth Corwin of Newburgh, N. Y., who died Mar. 11, 1917. She was an organist and pianist. They had two children, a daughter who died as an infant, and a son who became a musician.

[For information on Henry Tuthill, see G. F. Tuttle, *The Descendants of William and Elizabeth Tuttle* (1883). See *Music Festival . . . for the Inauguration of the Music Hall Founded by Andrew Carnegie* (1891) and *Festival of Music: the Oratorio Soc. of N. Y.*, 1920 for Tuthill's musical activities, and obituary in *N. Y. Times,* Aug. 27, 1929. Family information has been supplied by Burnet C. Tuthill, Tuthill's son.]

T. F. H.

TUTTLE, CHARLES WESLEY (Nov. 1, 1829–July 17, 1881), astronomer, writer on historical and antiquarian subjects, lawyer, was born at Newfield, Me., the eldest of the seven children of Moses and Mary (Merrow) Tuttle. His father was descended from John Tuttle (or Tuthill) who by 1640 had settled at Dover, N. H., and his mother from Dr. Samuel Merrow (or Merry) who as early as 1720 was living at Dover. At Newfield he became especially interested in natural history and astronomy, and in his teens he constructed a small telescope. Following his mother's death in 1845, he lived with relatives at Dover. Under the influence of an uncle, he became a carpenter's apprentice, devoting his spare time to astronomy, mathematics, and history. In 1849 he went to Cambridge, Mass., and began work as a carpenter. With the aid of Truman Henry Safford [*q.v.*], whom he met there, he gained admission to the Harvard Observatory, where he so impressed the director, William Cranch Bond [*q.v.*], by his knowledge of astronomy that in October 1850 he was appointed an assistant. He immediately began taking part in the program set for the great equatorial. On Nov. 15, 1850, he made his most important contribution to astronomy by explaining Saturn's "dusky" ring (see W. C. Bond, "Observations on the Planet Saturn," *Annals of the Astronomical Observatory of Harvard College,* vol. II, 1857). Outside the routine of the Observatory he compared "the lustre of the stars" at sea level (the Isles of Shoals) and on the summit of Mount Washington (1852), independently discovered Comet 1853 I (*Astronomical Journal,* Mar. 15, p. 47, Apr. 25, 1853, p. 72), computed cometary orbits and ephemerides, and took part in the eclipse expedition to the summit of Mount Washington in May 1854. By this time the effects of observation on his eyes made it clear that he must give over his ambitions in practical astronomy, and he resigned as observer to begin the study of law at the Harvard Law School in September 1854. In August 1855 he visited England on an expedition for the United States Coast Survey. He was admitted to the bar in March 1856 at Boston, where he began practice. In 1857 he opened an office in Newburyport, Mass., but returned to Boston about 1858. He was admitted to practice in the United States circuit courts (1858) and before the United States Supreme Court (1861). In 1860 he was appointed a United States commissioner and in 1874 took testimony for use before the Court of Alabama Claims.

As a result of historical and antiquarian studies connected with Maine and New Hampshire, he contributed many articles, often brief but of rich content, to such publications as the *New-England Historical and Genealogical Register,* the *Proceedings of the Massachusetts Historical Society, Notes and Queries,* and to newspapers of Dover and Boston. After his death appeared his *Capt. John Mason* (1887), edited by J. W. Dean, and *Capt. Francis Champernowne . . . and Other Historical Papers* (1889), edited by A. H. Hoyt. He was always the discriminating, accurate scholar, the master of clear, concise expression, interested only in bringing the facts to light. From time to time he addressed historical societies, and showed his continued interest in astronomy by occasional lectures as well as by observations and computations. He was a member of many historical and antiquarian societies. He received the honorary degree of A.M. from Harvard in 1854 and of Ph.D. from Dartmouth in 1880. He married, Jan. 31, 1872, Mary Louisa Park, daughter of John C. Park of Boston, who survived him.

[See C. W. Tuttle, "The Tuttle Family of New Hampshire," *New-Eng. Hist. and Geneal. Reg.,* Apr. 1867; John Wentworth, *The Wentworth Geneal.* (2nd ed., 1878), vol. I, p. 260, vol. II, p. 284; J. W. Dean, in C. W. Tuttle, *Capt. Francis Champernowne* (1889), the most complete account, and in *New-Eng. Hist. and Geneal. Reg.,* Jan. 1888; E. F. Slafter, in *Proc. Mass. Hist. Soc.,* 2 ser., vol. I (1885); *Annals of the Astronomical Observatory of Harvard Coll.,* vol. I (1856), p. clxxix; S. I. Bailey, *The Hist. and Work of Harvard Observatory* (1931); obituary in *Boston Daily Advertiser,* July 18, 1881. In the lib. of the New-Eng. Hist.-Geneal. Soc., Boston, is galley proof of an article on Tuttle written during his lifetime.]   J. M. P—r.

TUTTLE, DANIEL SYLVESTER (Jan. 26, 1837–Apr. 17, 1923), bishop of the Protestant Episcopal Church, was a descendant of William Tuttle, or Tothill as the name was spelled in Devonshire, who settled in New Haven (Conn.) in 1639. His great-grandfather, Jehiel Tuttle, was an officer in the French and Indian War, his grandfather, Charles, a soldier of the Revolution. Second son among four children of Daniel Bliss Tuttle and Abigail Clark (Stimson), Daniel Sylvester was born in Windham, N. Y., where his father was the village blacksmith. Family devotions were regularly held in his parents' Methodist home, but it was Thomas S. Judd, Windham's Episcopal rector, whose kindly interest in the boy inclined him toward the ministry. Following such education as the district school afforded and three years under Judd's tutelage, he entered the academy in Delhi, N. Y., in 1850, paying part of his way by milking cows and by assistant teaching. In 1853 he was baptized in the Episcopal Church and confirmed by Bishop Wainwright. Using money he earned by teaching for a year in Scarsdale, N. Y., he enrolled in Columbia College as a sophomore in 1854 and graduated in 1857, second in his class. After two years as a tutor in New York, he entered the General Theological Seminary, from which he was graduated in 1862. On June 29 of that year he was ordered deacon and on July 19, 1863, he was elevated to the priesthood having gone meanwhile to Morris, N. Y., to assist Rev. George L. Foote, whom he succeeded, and whose daughter, Harriet Minerva, he married on Sept. 12, 1865.

While ministering diligently among his rural parishioners, he was surprised, Oct. 5, 1866, by election as missionary bishop of Montana with jurisdiction in Utah and Idaho. Not yet thirty, he remained in Morris till he reached the required age and then after consecration in Trinity Chapel, New York, May 1, 1867, left his wife and infant son behind and went to his new field. For the next nineteen years he labored in the rocky vineyard of the Northwest. Of powerful frame and democratic, "Bishop Dan" was well fitted for frontier life. His letters to his wife (*Reminiscences, post*) present a vivid picture of the region and its hindrances to the advancement of the gospel. In 1868 he was elected bishop of Missouri, but because he felt that his part in the winning of the West had just begun, did not accept. The following year he established his family in Salt Lake City, where he and the Mormons grew to respect each other, despite their religious differences (*Ibid.,* ch. xii). A second call to Missouri he accepted in 1886, and thereafter St. Louis was his home.

On Sept. 7, 1903, through seniority, he became presiding bishop of his church. A harmonizer whose utterances were marked by liberality and courtesy, he took virtually no part in church controversy, although he vigorously opposed the movement toward the election of presiding bishops, on the ground that God should designate the church's head (*Churchman,* Aug. 23, 1913). His humility, kindly wit, sagacity, and long years of service endeared him to all groups. A deep, resonant voice made the more impressive his carefully prepared sermons, while his long snow-white beard, high bald head, and dignified bearing gave him a striking presence. From middle life he was quite deaf and presided over meetings only with the aid of an informer. He was physically strong, however, made a practice of walking the two miles from his St. Louis home to the downtown cathedral, and at his summer place at Wequetonsing, Mich., he was swimming and cutting wood after he was eighty. From its founding he was a trustee of the Missouri Botanical Garden.

He died at the age of eighty-six, of grippe contracted while conducting a funeral. He had been a bishop for fifty-six years, and had helped consecrate eighty-nine bishops. Predeceased by his wife (1899) and four children, he was survived by two sons. St. Louis mourned him as its most distinguished citizen, and a $500,000 building was reared in his memory, adjoining his beloved Christ Church cathedral. Wholly expressive of the man was the inscription placed by his desire on his gravestone in Bellefontaine Cemetery: "God be merciful to me a sinner."

[Tuttle's own *Reminiscences of a Missionary Bishop* (1906) chronicle his life until his removal to the Missouri diocese. See also: G. F. Tuttle, *The Descendants of William and Elizabeth Tuttle* (1883); *Who's Who in America,* 1922–23; Wm. Hyde and H. L. Conard, *Encyc. of the Hist. of St. Louis* (1899), vol. IV; *Church News* (St. Louis), May 1923, and Sept.-Oct. 1924; *The Living Church Annual, 1924* (1923); *St. Louis Post-Dispatch,* Oct. 23, 1921, Apr. 17, 18, 20, 1923; *Living Church,* Oct. 11, Dec. 6, 1924; *Churchman,* Apr. 28, 1923; information from Mrs. George M. Tuttle of St. Louis. A life-size portrait by Charles F. Galt hangs in the Tuttle Memorial.]   I. D.

TUTTLE, HERBERT (Nov. 29, 1846–June 21, 1894), historian, college professor, was born in Bennington, Vt., the son of Charles J. Tuttle and Evaline (Boynton) Tuttle. In 1853 the family moved to Hoosick Falls, N. Y. As a student in the University of Vermont, from which he was graduated in 1869, Tuttle attracted the attention of President James B. Angell [*q.v.*], his first teacher of history, who noted the orderliness of his mind and his keen interest in the growth of political institutions. Tuttle desired to make journalism his profession, and President Angell aided him in securing a position on the *Boston Daily Advertiser,* which he held nearly two years, for a time acting as Washington correspondent. Still richer opportunities for observation came in October 1871, when he began a long residence in Europe, at first as special correspondent of the *Advertiser* in Paris, and from 1873 to 1879 as Berlin correspondent of the London *Daily News.* In 1872 he reported the proceedings of the Court of Alabama Claims at Geneva for the *New York Tribune,* and it was probably upon the recommendation of George W. Smalley [*q.v.*], London correspondent of the *Tribune,* that the great London daily offered this young American of twenty-six so important a post as Berlin.

Tuttle had not been in Berlin long before he conceived the idea of writing a history which should show the relation of the earlier Prussia, and especially the work of Frederick the Great, to the triumphant Prussia and Germany of the seventies. He had discovered "how inadequate was Carlyle's account . . . of the working system of the Prussian government" (*History of Prussia,* 1888, vol. II, p. vi). When Andrew D. White [*q.v.*] went to Berlin in 1879 as American minister, he encouraged Tuttle's project and suggested an academic career. President Angell, now at the University of Michigan, gave him his first appointment, inviting him to lecture on international law (1880–81) during his own absence in China. In the fall of 1881 White, as president of Cornell University, gave him a similar appointment, and until 1883 he divided his time between Michigan and Cornell. In 1883 he was made associate professor at Cornell. In 1887 he was promoted to a full professorship, with the history of political institutions added to his title. In 1890 he was made professor in his chosen field, Modern European history. While he was still in Berlin he had published a volume of essays on *German Political Leaders* (New York, 1876). The first volume of his *History of Prussia* (dated 1884) appeared late in 1883, an introduction covering the period from 1134 to 1740. Of the five planned (an introduction and four volumes on Frederick the Great), Tuttle lived to complete only the introduction, two volumes on Frederick (1888), and part of a third (1896). His health broke down in 1893, and he died in Ithaca on June 21, 1894. His *History of Prussia* is based upon documentary collections, edited mainly by German scholars, and upon monographs published since Carlyle wrote. His career as a teacher was equally significant. His

students remembered him as incisive and judicial, with a horror of exaggeration or inaccuracy. His comments were occasionally touched by a sub-acid wit. He had little sympathy with the more radical plans of departmental organization, and when, upon the recommendation of President Charles Kendall Adams [*q.v.*], the trustees of the university created "The President White School of History and Political Science," in recognition of White's gift of his noble library, Tuttle so vigorously opposed the appointment of a dean of the School that the plan was not fully carried through. Tuttle was one of the original members of the American Historical Association, and was a frequent contributor to learned and critical journals. On July 6, 1875, he married Mary McArthur Thompson of Hillsboro, Ohio, who survived him.

[Tuttle's full name was Charles Herbert Tuttle, but he dropped the first name before 1876. Sources include J. F. and C. H. Boynton, *The Boynton Family* (1897); H. B. Adams, in Tuttle's *Hist. of Prussia,* vol. IV (1896), pp. xi–xlvi, an amplification of an article in *Ann. Report Am. Hist. Asso. . . . 1894* (1895); W. T. Hewett, *Cornell Univ.: A Hist.* (1905), vol. II; H. M. Jones, *The Life of Moses Coit Tyler* (1933), based on an unpublished dissertation by T. E. Casady; Mary M. T. Tuttle, *Memorial to Herbert Tuttle* (priv. printed, 1910); obituaries in *Evening Post* (N. Y.) and *N. Y. Tribune,* June 22, 1894; recollections of Tuttle's colleagues. A bibliog. of Tuttle's writings appears in his *Hist. of Prussia,* vol. IV (1896).]   H. E. B.

TUTWILER, HENRY (Nov. 16, 1807–Sept. 22, 1884), Alabama educator, was born in Harrisonburg, Va., the son of Henry and Margaret (Lorchbaugh) Tutwiler. He was of German descent, and there was a family tradition that his ancestors came from the German section of Switzerland, settling first in Pennsylvania and moving later into the Valley of Virginia. The boy was for the most part self-taught, although for a short time he attended a school kept by a Presbyterian minister, the Rev. Daniel Baker [*q.v.*]. When the University of Virginia opened its doors in 1825, Tutwiler was one of the first students to enroll. He devoted himself to mathematics and the classics and completed his course in 1829, but spent another year in the University studying law. More than fifty years later he delivered an address before the alumni of the University published under the title *Early Years of the University of Virginia* (1882). In 1831, when the newly established University of Alabama was seeking a faculty, the trustees turned to the University of Virginia to find professors, and Henry Tutwiler was highly recommended for the chair of ancient languages. He moved to Alabama in that same year and made his home there for the remainder of his life.

It was said of Tutwiler that although he held

the professorship of ancient languages he was really a whole faculty, for he had a knowledge of law and was a student of science as well, showing special interest in chemistry and astronomy. The early years of the University of Alabama were not happy, and in 1837 the entire faculty resigned. For the next ten years Tutwiler held professorships in various small colleges in Alabama and at the end of that time turned to the fulfilment of a life-long ambition, the education of boys. Near the village of Havana, in the present Hale (then part of Greene) County, he opened in 1847 Greene Springs School for Boys, which soon attained wide recognition for the advanced ideas of education it embodied. Called the "Rugby of the South," it gave training primarily in the classics and mathematics, but laid an emphasis on the sciences which was unusual. Even more unusual in the equipment of a preparatory school of that time were its chemical laboratory, telescope, and library of 1,500 volumes.

Tutwiler insisted that trained teachers were as important for his boys as for college students, and the faculty of the Greene Springs School compared very favorably with those of the colleges of the day. Respect for the individual student was an important tenet of his educational creed: corporal punishment was forbidden, and students were not divided into classes, but in each study the student was placed in the class which he was prepared to enter. Tutwiler remained at the head of the Greene Springs School until his death in 1884, twice declining the presidency of the University of Alabama with the statement that he was determined never again to put himself in any position where he could not be his own master. His scholarly interests filled his life and left small place for other things. He was a Whig and opposed secession, but he took no active part in the political events of his day. Nevertheless, though indirect, his influence in the life of the South through the students who went out from the Greene Springs School was very great. Tutwiler was married in Tuscaloosa, Dec. 24, 1835, to Julia Ashe, of a distinguished North Carolina family. He died at Greene Springs, survived by eleven children, one of whom, Julia Strudwick Tutwiler [q.v.], was also a noted educator.

[T. M. Owen, Hist. of Ala. and Dict. of Ala. Biog. (1921), vol. IV; Willis Brewer, Alabama (1872); W. G. Clark, Hist. of Educ. in Ala. (1889); A. B. Moore, Hist. of Ala. (1927), vol. I; T. C. McCorvey, "Henry Tutwiler and the Influence of the University of Virginia on Education in Alabama," Trans. Ala. Hist. Soc. (1904), vol. V; P. A. Bruce, Hist. of the Univ. of Va., vols. II, III (1920–21); Montgomery Advertiser, Sept. 26, 1884; Daily Register (Mobile), Sept. 27, 1884.]
H. F.

TUTWILER, JULIA STRUDWICK (Aug. 15, 1841–Mar. 24, 1916), educator, social reformer, was born in Greene Springs, Ala., the daughter of Henry Tutwiler [q.v.] and Julia (Ashe). Her father had views of education far in advance of the practices of his day and in 1847 established at Greene Springs a boys' school in which to carry out his ideas. One of his convictions was that his daughters should be as well educated as his sons. Julia, who was the third girl in the family, responded eagerly to the teaching offered her and after receiving her early training from her father, was sent for two years of study in Philadelphia. In January 1866 she enrolled in Vassar College, where she remained for half a school year. She showed unusual ability in languages, and was subsequently permitted to spend a year in Lexington, Va., studying Greek and Latin under the tuition of professors in Washington and Lee University. Still later, after teaching for a time in the Tuscaloosa Female Seminary, she spent three years in advanced study in Germany and France at a time when such study was most unusual for a woman. At the end of this period she passed the government examinations required of teachers in the Prussian schools and received a teacher's certificate.

She returned to Alabama in 1876 and devoted the rest of her life to education and social service there. She introduced kindergarten methods which she had learned in Germany and taught for a time in her father's school at Greene Springs, but her primary interest was in the education of women. In 1882, while she was co-principal of the Livingston Female Academy at Livingston, Ala., she persuaded the state legislature to appropriate $2,500 to establish a normal department in the school—the first gift, according to her own statement (Bennett, post, p. 13), which the women of Alabama had ever received from the state. As a result, the Alabama Normal College was incorporated Feb. 22, 1883, with Julia Tutwiler as co-principal. In 1888 she became sole principal, and later her title was changed to president.

The creation of a normal school was only the first step in her long struggle to secure vocational training for women in Alabama. Her paper, "The Technical Education of Women" (Education, Boston, November 1882), attracted wide attention and had considerable influence. In 1893 with the support of the women of the state and the agricultural interests, she secured a grant from the legislature for the Alabama Girls Industrial School, which was opened in October 1896 at Montevallo, Shelby County. She was offered the presidency of this school but declined. In 1896 she persuaded officials of the University of Alabama to permit several young women prepared at the Alabama Normal College to enter the junior year in the University and to reside in a cottage on the campus. In this first year these women captured sixty per cent. of the honors awarded to the junior class, and in 1900, when the first women received degrees from the University, four of the six honors awarded to graduates went to "Miss Julia's" students. After that experiment the doors of the University were thrown open to women on equal terms with men.

Active also in prison reform in Alabama, she was for many years the superintendent of prison and jail work for the Woman's Christian Temperance Union. Her efforts were instrumental in securing the classification of prisoners and the separation of the sexes, the first juvenile reform school, and the first law providing for the inspection of jails and prisons. She labored to secure the establishment of night schools and vocational education in prisons, and fought the convict leasing system, although she never succeeded in driving it from the state. She wrote many magazine articles on subjects relating to prison reform and the education of women, and composed poems for her own pleasure. One of these, "Alabama," has become the state song. In 1910 she became president emeritus of the Alabama Normal College, and six years later died in Birmingham.

[T. M. Owen, *Hist. of Ala. and Dict. of Ala. Biog.* vol. IV (1921); *A Woman of the Century* (1893), ed. by F. E. Willard and M. A. Livermore; *Who's Who in America*, 1916–17; I. H. Weed, in *Am. Mag.*, Sept. 1911; Helen C. Bennett, "Julia Tutwiler, First Citizen of Alabama," *Pictorial Rev.*, Apr. 1913; Edna Kroman, "Julia S. Tutwiler, Pioneer in Education of Women in Alabama," *Birmingham News*, July 22, 1923; H. L. Hargrove, *Julia S. Tutwiler of Alabama* (n.d.); *Montgomery Advertiser* (Montgomery, Ala.), Mar. 25, 1916.]
H. F.

TWACHTMAN, JOHN HENRY (Aug. 4, 1853–Aug. 8, 1902), painter, was born in Cincinnati, Ohio, the son of Frederick Christian and Sophia (Droege) Twachtman. Both his parents came from the province of Hanover, Germany. His father, born in Erichshagen, where his forebears had been for several generations prosperous farmers, came to America at an early age and settled in Cincinnati. As a boy John helped his father in making decorated window shades. Later he studied drawing at the night school of the Ohio Mechanics' Institute, and at the University of Cincinnati School of Design. In 1875, with Frank Duveneck [q.v.], the son of family friends, Twachtman went to Munich. After working there two years under Ludwig Löfftz, he

joined Duveneck and William Merritt Chase [q.v.] at Venice for a year. Returning to America in 1878, he painted in New York (1879) and at Avondale, near Cincinnati. He spent the winter of 1880 in Florence, where Duveneck had settled the year before. After his marriage in the spring of 1881 to Marthe Scudder, daughter of Jane (Hannah) and John Milton Scudder [q.v.], he traveled abroad, visiting London and spending a short time in Holland. At Schleissheim, near Munich, he painted a number of large canvases directly from nature and, after a short stay in Venice, returned to New York. In 1883 he was again in Europe, this time studying in Paris at the Julian Atelier under Jules Joseph Lefebvre and Gustave Boulanger. In the summer he painted at Honfleur and at Arques-la-Battaille, near Dieppe, where he produced many of the most characteristic examples of this period. After wintering in Venice (1884), he returned to the United States. He had sent many of his pictures in advance, but unhappily the ship was lost at sea and with it much of the best work of Twachtman's continental experience.

After unsuccessfully endeavoring to combine farming and painting, Twachtman worked in Chicago on one of the great war cycloramas, then popular, picturing the battle of Gettysburg. In 1888 he joined his friend, Julian Alden Weir [q.v.], at Branchville, Conn. In the fall of 1889 he acquired a place near Greenwich, Conn., and there during the following ten years many of his finest pictures were painted. At this time he became an instructor of the antique class at the Art Students' League, a position he held until his death. From his anchorage at Round Hill he made several more distant excursions in order to paint Niagara Falls and Yellowstone Park. Later he spent the summers at Gloucester, Mass., in company with Duveneck, J. R. De Camp, C. A. Corwin, and E. H. Potthast, whom he had known in Florence. Separated from his family, he lived much alone. Never robust in physique, he was somewhat indifferent and careless about his health. He died at Gloucester, still comparatively young, survived by his wife and five children. Prizes awarded him included a medal at the World's Columbian Exposition, Chicago (1893); the Webb Prize, Society of American Artists (1888); the Temple gold medal, Pennsylvania Academy of the Fine Arts (1895); and a silver medal, Pan-American Exposition, Buffalo (1901). He was a member of the Society of American Artists, from which he later resigned, the Ten American Painters, the New York Etching Club, and the Pastel Club, New York.

The art of John Twachtman falls into three distinct periods. The work of the first period (1875–81) is characterized by strong contrast of values, in subdued variations of brown and black; vigorous brushwork, the pigment heavily applied; and direct rendering from nature. The small decorative panels of buildings, shipping, and waterways painted at Venice are more spirited and personal than the larger and more ambitious landscapes of the same time. Among the pictures of the early period are the highly original "Brooklyn Bridge"; the "Italian Landscape," dated 1878, in the Museum of Fine Arts, Boston; the graphic and powerfully realistic "Oyster Boats," dated New York, 1879, and the "Venice" with the dogana in the background.

The second period is marked by a reaction against the heavy impasto and dark tones of the Munich tradition. The color is in variations of silvery greys and greens, showing a close study of relative values and atmospheric perspective; the pigment is applied thinly with a delicate but precise technique over a fine French linen; the composition is restricted to very simple themes. There is seldom an attempt at sunlight or full color. Most characteristic of Twachtman's style at this time are the pictures painted in France and Holland, notably the "Arques-la-Battaille" dated 1885; "Windmills," with striking silhouette and effective spatial arrangements; "Canal Boats"; "Winding Path"; the "Sketch" in the Museum of Fine Arts, Boston; and "L'Étang."

The final period belongs to America. It was not until Twachtman settled at Greenwich in 1889 that he seems definitely to have found himself. Impressionism had in the meantime an obvious influence on his development. From subdued hues of neutral greys the color changes to the higher key of sunlight, the delicately attuned relations of gold, blue, and violet, or the ethereal and pallid harmony of winter landscape. The painter's artistic nature is revealed in delicacy rather than strength, in the sensitive rather than the striking, in the subtle rather than the obvious. He was a master of nuance; his mood is one of intimacy and charm. He was not a realist in the literal sense of the term and openly declared the decorative intention of his work. Particularly worthy of note in the final period are the series of waterfalls painted on Twachtman's own place at Greenwich and the pictures of winter—"Falls in January," the ice and snow patterned against the turbulent brook; "The Cascade"; and similar motives in the Metropolitan Museum and the Worcester Art Museum, Worcester, Mass.; "Snow," in the Worcester Art Museum; "Old Mill in Winter"; "Round Hill Road," in the National Gallery of Art, Washington; "February," in the Museum of Fine Arts, Boston; "Snowbound" and "Hemlock Pool," which Twachtman himself considered one of the best of his pictures. The figure subjects are less widely known, but they remain among the most personal and distinguished examples of Twachtman's brush. Most of the subjects are his own family, painted in the intimate environment of his home.

Twachtman occupies a unique position in American painting. Not following the earlier tradition, which portrayed the scenic aspects of nature or its romantic associations, he found his interest in the expressive organization of form, and the harmonic relation of line and color. His intention was more truly esthetic than pictorial. His art is therefore related to the doctrine of Whistler and the cult of "art for art's sake" so prevalent in the nineties. He had a militant dislike of conventional composition, banalities, and sentimentality. He took a purely sensuous delight in the beauty of the visible world, and a keen enjoyment in esthetic adventure. But if Whistler quickened Twachtman's artistic sensibility and stimulated the search for new discoveries in line and form, Monet awakened his appreciation of light and color. He thus responds to the two dominant influences of his generation. Dependent upon optical stimulation and the exhilaration of the moment, Twachtman's art lacks something of the intellectual and universal; finely attuned to the fleeting, it misses the eternal. Both his expression and presentation were nevertheless very personal and original. The distinction of his art rests upon beauty of design, harmonic tonal relations, and the sensitive interpretation of evanescent effect.

[*Who's Who in America*, 1901–02; Samuel Isham, *The Hist. of Am. Painting* (1927 ed.); Eliot Clark, in *Art in America*, Apr. 1919, *Internat. Studio*, Jan. 1921, *Scribner's Mag.*, Dec. 1922, and *John Twachtman* (1924); Allen Tucker, *John Twachtman* (copr. 1931); R. J. Wickeden, "The Art and Etchings of John Henry Twachtman," booklet published by Frederick Keppel & Co., New York; Carolyn C. Mase, in *Internat. Studio*, Jan. 1921; Margery A. Ryerson, in *Art in America*, Feb. 1920; Royal Cortissoz, in *N. Y. Tribune*, Jan. 12, 1919, reprinted in *American Artists* (1923); Charles De Kay, in *Arts and Decoration*, June 1918; C. C. Curran, in *Lit. Miscellany*, Winter 1910; J. Alden Weir and others, in *North Am. Rev.*, Apr. 1903; obituary in *N. Y. Times* and editorial in *N. Y. Daily Tribune*, Aug. 9, 1902; information from Mrs. Twachtman.]   E. C.

TWAIN, MARK [See Clemens, Samuel Langhorne, 1835–1910].

TWEED, WILLIAM MARCY (Apr. 3, 1823–Apr. 12, 1878), political boss, was born in New York City, the son of Richard and Eliza Tweed. His great-grandfather, a blacksmith, emigrated from Kelso, Scotland, in the middle of the eighteenth century. His father was a chairmaker, and young William was taken from the public school to begin learning the same trade at the age of eleven. At thirteen, however, he was apprenticed to a saddler and worked with him nearly two years. He then attended a private school at Elizabeth, N. J., for one winter, learned bookkeeping, and became a junior clerk in a mercantile office in New York. Meanwhile, his father had bought an interest in a small brush factory, and William at seventeen became its bookkeeper. He was made a member of the firm at nineteen. At twenty-one he married the daughter of the principal owner of the factory, Mary Jane Skaden. She bore him eight children and died in 1880. Tweed was a sober, steady young man, but big-bodied and powerful, and on occasion he could use his fists effectively. He became a volunteer fireman, and in 1848 helped to organize a new engine company, Americus No. 6. At the age of twenty-seven he was elected its foreman. The head of a tiger which was painted on the engine became in time the symbol of Tweed's political organization, Tammany Hall.

Volunteer fire companies were often stepping stones to political power, and Tweed's capacity for leadership, which began to display itself at an early age, inevitably led him into politics and alliance with Tammany. In 1850, the year he became foreman of "Big 6," he ran for assistant alderman in his home ward, but was defeated by a small margin. In 1851 he was nominated by the Democrats for alderman. There seemed small chance for him to win, but he persuaded a friend, a prominent educator, to run as an independent Whig, which split the Whig vote sufficiently to insure Tweed's election—his first venture in political strategy. The common council to which he was elected came to be known in New York as "The Forty Thieves." Tweed's capacity as an aldermanic grafter soon rendered further honest toil unnecessary. In 1852 he was elected to Congress, but served only two years (1853–55), continuing to sit as alderman. He preferred municipal politics. A wave of Know-Nothingism, however, caused his defeat for alderman in 1855. He and two other men, Peter B. Sweeny [q.v.] and Richard B. Connolly, later his chief partners in the "Tweed ring," had now begun to be drawn together in the faction of Tammany Hall opposing Mayor Fernando Wood [q.v.], who was finally forced out of the Hall. In 1856 Tweed was chosen as a member of the newly created, bi-partisan, popularly elected board of supervisors, intended to check corruption at elections, but which itself became an agency for graft.

Tweed was also appointed school commissioner. In 1857 he succeeded in having his friend Sweeny nominated for district attorney, and another ally, George G. Barnard, for recorder, and both were elected. Connolly was elected county clerk. Thus was the foundation laid for the Tweed machine.

He was now a sachem of Tammany, and by 1859 was considered one of the most powerful men in the organization. He well-nigh dominated the state Democratic convention of 1860 and sent his friend Barnard to the state supreme court bench. In 1861 he ran for sheriff, but lost. Nevertheless, he succeeded in bringing about the defeat of Wood for mayor, and one of his dearest aims was accomplished. But the campaign had cost him his entire fortune of about $100,000. He made the office of supervisor pay, however, and within two years, it is said, he had recovered practically half his loss. He was made chairman of the Democratic central committee of New York County in 1860. Another cog in his machine, A. Oakey Hall [q.v.], was now district attorney. Tweed had become chairman of Tammany's general committee, and thereafter was supreme dictator of nominations for mayor and other positions. He opened a law office in the autumn of 1860. His knowledge of law was small, but he collected some huge fees for "legal services," the Erie Railroad alone paying him more than $100,000. In 1864 he bought a controlling interest in a printing concern, which thereafter did all the city's printing and which all railroads, ferries, and insurance companies must patronize if they wished to stay in business. He also organized a marble company and bought a quarry in Massachusetts from which the stone for the new county court house—for that gigantic swindle was now under way—was bought at extortionate prices. By 1867 Tweed was doubtless a millionaire, and had moved his family from the lower East Side up to a Murray Hill residence just off Fifth Avenue. He assisted in launching the Brooklyn Bridge project in 1866, and received a $40,000 block of stock as his perquisite.

He practically secured control of the State in 1868, when he placed in the governor's chair John T. Hoffman [q.v.], who had been Tammany mayor of the city for two years. In Hoffman's stead as mayor the Tweed henchman, A. Oakey Hall, was elected. Another puppet was made speaker of the Assembly. Tweed had been elected state senator in 1867, and his luxurious, seven-room hotel suite in Albany was virtually state Democratic headquarters. He was still New York County Democratic chairman, and for New York City was school commissioner, assistant street commissioner, and president of the Board of Supervisors. In 1868 he realized a life-long ambition when he was made grand sachem of Tammany. In 1869 the "ring," convened in Albany, decided that all bills thereafter rendered against the city and county must be one-half fraudulent. Later the proportion was raised to 85 per cent. ("Report of the Special Committee of the Board of Aldermen," pp. 74–76, 397, 403). The money thus gained was to be divided into five parts, of which Tweed, City Chamberlain Sweeny, Comptroller Connolly, and Mayor Hall received one share each, while the fifth was used to bribe smaller politicians. Bogus naturalization of immigrants and repeating at elections were now carried to hitherto unknown lengths. Tweed was a partner with Jay Gould and James Fisk [qq.v.] in the plundering of the Erie Railroad, and was a director (often without investment) in banks, gas, and street railroad companies.

By this time *Harper's Weekly*, with Thomas Nast [q.v.] as its cartoonist, was beginning its long campaign against Tweed and his group (especially Jan. 22, 1870, and thereafter). But many leading citizens, Peter Cooper and Horace Greeley among the rest, were so deceived that they gave approval to the new city charter in 1870, which riveted the rule of the "ring" more firmly on the city. Samuel J. Tilden [q.v.] asserted that it cost Tweed more than a million dollars to put the charter through the legislature, and Tweed himself testified that he paid about $600,000 ("Report . . . of the Board of Aldermen," p. 73). The *New York Times*, under the ownership of George Jones [q.v.], began its attacks on Tweed late in 1870 (editorial, Sept. 20, 1870). The uncompleted county courthouse (its final cost was $12,000,000, of which two-thirds was fraudulent) had begun to arouse suspicion, but most of the newspapers and leading citizens were still servile in loyalty to the "ring" (see report of a committee of business men, Nov. 1, 1870, in N. Y. *World*, Nov. 6, N. Y. *Times*, Nov. 7). When Tweed's daughter was married in May 1871, gifts to her from prominent citizens were valued at $700,000. That spring Sheriff O'Brien and another discontented official turned over to the *Times* proofs of enormous swindling by the "ring." Learning that the *Times* had these figures, the boodlers offered Jones $5,000,000 not to publish them. Nast was offered $500,000 to cease his attacks. Both offers were rejected, and the *Times* published the evidence (especially July 8, July 20–29, 1871). On Sept. 4, 1871, at a mass meeting in Cooper Union, a committee of seventy was formed to

take action. An injunction was obtained against further taxation or payment of money. On Oct. 26, on Tilden's affidavit, a civil suit was brought to recover stolen money (*N. Y. Times*, Oct. 26, 27, 1871). Tweed's $2,000,000 bail was quickly raised, Jay Gould supplying $1,000,000. By fraud at the polls he was reëlected to the state Senate that autumn. On Dec. 16 he was arrested in a criminal action. Connolly, Sweeny, and others implicated had fled to Canada and Europe.

At Tweed's first criminal trial, the jury disagreed; but at the second, in November 1873, he was convicted and sentenced to twelve years in prison and a fine of $12,750. The court of appeals reduced the sentence to a year and a $250 fine, and in January 1875 Tweed left the prison on Blackwell's Island. He was at once rearrested on a civil action brought by the state to recover $6,000,000 of the "ring's" stealings. Failing to procure $3,000,000 bail, he was sent to prison. Here he was treated leniently, taking a carriage ride almost every afternoon, and frequently visiting his home, accompanied by two turnkeys. On Dec. 4, while visiting his home, he escaped by the back door while the turnkeys sat in the parlor. Aided by friends, he lay in hiding near New York for several weeks, then got away to Cuba, and from there went to Spain disguised as a common seaman. Identified by Spanish officials through a Nast cartoon (in *Harper's Weekly*, July 1, 1876), he was arrested and returned to America in November 1876. Judgment in the civil suit had been obtained against him in his absence, and in default of payment he was again committed to Ludlow Street Jail, this time in strict confinement. He was now failing steadily in health. Hoping that he might secure release from jail in return for his testimony, he supplied considerable information to the state, and before an aldermanic investigating committee in the winter of 1877–78 he testified frankly about many of his crooked transactions. He died in his room at the jail at the age of fifty-five. At his request, his wife and a married daughter had gone abroad to escape humiliation, and they were in Paris at the time of his death.

Tweed was genial and generous in disposition, and not vindictive toward his enemies. Nast's cartoons were not bad portraits of him, though his facial expression was milder and his photographs show that he might easily have been mistaken for a thoroughly respectable man. He was crafty, but even more remarkable for boldness and plausibility. The amount which his "ring" filched from the city has been variously estimated at from $30,000,000 to $200,000,000.

[D. T. Lynch, "Boss" Tweed (1927); M. R. Werner, Tammany Hall (1928); R. H. Fuller, Jubilee Jim: The Life of Colonel James Fisk, Jr. (1928); obituaries and articles in Evening Post (N. Y.), N. Y. Times, Sun (N. Y.), N. Y. Herald, N. Y. Tribune, World (N. Y.), Apr. 12–14, 1878; "Report of the Special Committee of the Board of Aldermen Appointed to Investigate the 'Ring' Frauds," Documents of the Board of Aldermen of the City of N. Y. . . . Part II—1877, Doc. No. 8 (1878); C. F. Wingate, "An Episode in Municipal Government," North American Review, Oct. 1874, Jan., July 1875, Oct. 1876; W. C. Gover, The Tammany Hall Democracy of the City of New York and the General Committee for 1875 (1875); A. P. Genung, The Frauds of the New York City Government Exposed (1871); S. J. Tilden, The New York City "Ring" (1873); Charles O'Conor, comp., Peculation Triumphant (1875), a collection of documents on the trials; J. D. Townsend, New York in Bondage (1895), by Tweed's counsel, 1876–78; H. L. Clinton, Celebrated Trials (1897); Harold Zink, City Bosses in the United States (1930), with good chapter on Tweed and definite references; scrapbooks of newspaper clippings relating to N. Y. City politics, N. Y. Pub. Lib.]

A. F. H.

TWICHELL, JOSEPH HOPKINS (May 27, 1838–Dec. 20, 1918), Congregational clergyman, was a native of Connecticut and spent practically his entire life there, becoming one of its best known and most beloved citizens. Born in the nearby town of Southington, he was called to Hartford in 1865 to take charge of the newly organized Asylum Hill Congregational Church and remained as pastor and pastor emeritus until his death more than fifty years later. He was the son of Edward Twichell, a tanner and manufacturer, by his first wife, Selina Delight Carter, his ancestry running back to Benjamin Twichell, born in Chesham Parish, Buckinghamshire, England, who emigrated to Massachusetts about 1630. Prepared for college in the schools of Southington, Joseph graduated from Yale with the class of 1859. He began his theological studies at Union Seminary, New York, but they were interrupted by the outbreak of the Civil War. From 1861 to 1864 he saw active service as chaplain of the 71st New York Volunteers, in the meantime, Jan. 30, 1863, being ordained in his native town. When mustered out, he entered Andover Theological Seminary, from which he graduated in 1865. That same year, recommended to the Asylum Hill Church by Horace Bushnell [q.v.], he began his Hartford pastorate, and on Nov. 1, married Julia Harmony Cushman of Orange, N. J., by whom he had nine children. For thirty-nine years (1874–1913) he was an active member of the Board of Fellows of Yale University.

During his half century in Hartford he exerted much influence in the religious and civic affairs of his city and state. He was handsome, athletic, abounding in good humor, and had a sympathetic understanding of all sorts and conditions of men, derived in part from his army experiences. His humanness is indicated by the fact that he was invariably alluded to as "Joe" Twichell. Although not a scholar in the academic use of the term, he had a well stocked and well disciplined mind, keen discernment, sound judgment, and a fine literary taste. His influence was exerted not only directly, but indirectly through his close association with newspaper editors, writers, and public officials, who held him in high esteem. He was so often introduced into Charles Dudley Warner's conversation "that many persons felt they had a certain acquaintance and wished they knew him better" (Mrs. J. T. Fields, Charles Dudley Warner, 1904, p. 41). Upon taking up his residence in Hartford, he at once became a member of the circle that included Warner, Calvin and Harriet Beecher Stowe [qq.v.], and other notable people. When Samuel L. Clemens [q.v.] came to the city in 1868 to supervise the publication of a book, he met Twichell and a most intimate friendship began. Twichell was one of the officiating clergymen at Clemens' wedding in Elmira; later the two were neighbors in Hartford; they tramped together, and traveled together. They were companions on the trip described in A Tramp Abroad, in which Twichell figures as "Harris" (Paine, post, II, 629, 666), and it was Twichell who made the suggestion that prompted the writing of the sketches which formed the basis of Life on the Mississippi (Ibid., I, p. 531). In his description of the pastor's appearance in the pulpit with "green hair," the humorist affectionately immortalized his friend in a most amusing skit (Mark Twain's Autobiography, post, I, 342–43). They stood together, in a Republican stronghold, in support of Cleveland rather than Blaine for the presidency, a stand which almost cost Twichell his pastorate (Ibid., II, 20–26). When apart, the two corresponded at length, their letters disclosing that there was no one to whom Clemens revealed his soul more fully than to Twichell. The latter's own literary output was not great. He made contributions to periodicals, among them "Mark Twain" (Harper's Monthly, May 1896), and "Qualities of Warner's Humor" (The Century, January 1903); and he published two more substantial works, John Winthrop (copr. 1891), in the Makers of America Series, and Some Old Puritan Love-Letters (1893), being the correspondence of John and Margaret Winthrop.

[R. E. Twitchell, Geneal. of the Twitchell Family (1929); Yale Univ. Obit. Record . . . 1919 (1920); A. B. Paine, Mark Twain (3 vols., 1912); Mark Twain's Autobiog. (2 vols., 1924); and Mark Twain's Letters (2 vols., 1917); Who's Who in America, 1918–19; Congregationalist, Jan. 2, 1919; Hartford Daily

Times, Dec. 20, 1918; *Hartford Daily Courant*, Dec. 21, 1918.]   H. E. S.

TWIGGS, DAVID EMANUEL (1790–July 15, 1862), soldier, the son of Brigadier- General John Twiggs, who was called the "Savior of Georgia" in the Revolution, and his wife, Ruth Emanuel, was born in Richmond County, Ga. He was appointed a captain in the 8th United States Infantry in March 1812, and served in minor capacities during the war with Great Britain. He became a major of the 28th Infantry in September 1814, but his regiment was disbanded the following June, and he was without a commission. When interest in military affairs revived, he was commissioned a major of the 1st Infantry on May 14, 1825, lieutenant-colonel of the 4th Infantry, July 15, 1831, and colonel of the 2nd Dragoons, June 8, 1836. It was in the last capacity that he joined Zachary Taylor's forces at the beginning of the War with Mexico. Shortly thereafter arose the unfortunate dispute between himself and Brevet Brigadier-General William J. Worth [*q.v.*], whose regular rank was that of colonel, junior to Twiggs. Through the awkward handling of this controversy over prestige and rank by Taylor, the troops lost confidence in all three of their superiors. Twiggs, however, gave a good account of himself at Palo-Alto and Resaca de la Palma, so that, on June 30, 1846, he was promoted to the grade of regular brigadier-general. After the capture of Monterey, Taylor asked for another promotion for him, although Twiggs had ostensibly been ill and had taken no part in the fight. Singularly enough, he was brevetted a major-general for gallantry at Monterey.

Throughout the northern campaign he had commanded the 1st Division, but when Scott's southern campaign began he was withdrawn to the south. He served at Vera Cruz and commanded the vanguard of that army in its progress toward Mexico city. Although his leadership at Cerro Gordo was more intrepid than intelligent and his feint before Mexico city lacked vigor, his work mainly showed dogged perseverance and bravery. He was a stanch and loyal supporter of his commander when too many of the other commanders about him were insubordinate and conniving. On Mar. 2, 1847, Congress voted him a sword, with a jeweled hilt and a gold scabbard, in testimony of his gallantry at Monterey, and he was subsequently presented two others by the legislature of Georgia and by the city of Augusta. He was a member of the court of inquiry on Worth's defiant conduct, and was military governor of Vera Cruz from December 1847 to March 1848. Twiggs was a robust, powerfully built man, nearly six feet tall, with thick red face, heavy white hair, and an abundant beard. To his soldiers he was the embodiment of dynamic physical energy. They called him variously "Old Davy," "The Horse," and "Bengal Tiger."

After the war his peace-time duties of departmental commander, mostly in the South, simmered into the routine of the decade preceding the Civil War. In February 1861, he was in command of the Department of Texas. It was then, because of his Southern affiliations, that he surrendered all of the Union forces and stores under his control to the Confederate general, Ben McCulloch [*q.v.*]. He was, accordingly, promptly dismissed from the United States Army. On May 22, 1861, he was made a major-general of the Confederate army and assigned to the command of the district of Louisiana. At this time he was the ranking general of the Confederate forces, but he was too old to take the field. He died and was buried near his birthplace in the old Twiggs Cemetery, about ten miles from Augusta. He was survived by his second wife and two children. His first wife was Elizabeth Hunter, of Virginia; and his second was a Mrs. Hunt, of New Orleans, La. His daughter became the wife of Abraham C. Myers [*q.v.*], of the Confederate army.

[*Georgia's Roster of the Revolution* (1920); F. B. Heitman, *Hist. Reg. and Dict. of the U. S. Army* (1903); W. A. Ganoe, *The Hist. of the U. S. Army* (1924); *Men of Mark in Ga.*, vol. II (1910); J. H. Smith, *The War with Mexico* (2 vols., 1919); *Battles and Leaders of the Civil War* (1887–88), vol. I; *Confed. Mil. Hist.* (1899), vol. VI; records in the Old Files Section, Adjutant-General's Office, Washington, D. C.; information from the family.]
                                    W. A. G.

TWINING, ALEXANDER CATLIN (July 5, 1801–Nov. 22, 1884), inventor, engineer, astronomer, was the son of Stephen and Almira (Catlin) Twining, and was born in New Haven, Conn., where his father for many years was steward and treasurer of Yale College. He was a descendant of William Twining who was in Yarmouth in 1643. Upon completing his preparatory school work at Hopkins, N. H., Twining entered Yale and graduated in 1820 with the degree of A.B. He then took two years of post-graduate work for his master's degree and entered Andover Theological Seminary to study for the ministry. He did not complete the course, however, for the reason that he had meanwhile become intensely interested in mathematics and engineering. Subsequently he returned to Yale, where for two years he served as a tutor (1823–24), and engaged in further study in natural philosophy and mathematics. Later he entered the United States Military Academy at West Point, and took a course in civil engineering, specializing at the same time in mathematics and astronomy. While there Twining observed the remarkable star shower of November 1833. As a result he formulated independently a theory of the cosmic origin of meteors, which was also propounded at the time by Denison Olmsted [*q.v.*]; that is, that shooting stars are bodies coming into the air from external space, and that their discussion belongs to astronomy and not to terrestrial physics (*American Journal of Science and Arts,* vol. XXVI, no. 2, 1834). Between 1834 and 1839 Twining engaged in railroad engineering, chiefly for the Hartford & New Haven Railroad Company, locating most of its northern routes out of New Haven. He later served for many years as a railroad consultant not only in New England but in the Middle West. In 1839 he accepted the chair of mathematics and natural philosophy at Middlebury College, Middlebury, Vt. Ten years later he resigned, and returned to New Haven in order to resume his engineering practice and the inventive work which he had undertaken in the meantime.

His most important invention was a method of manufacturing ice, the initial patent for which was granted on Nov. 8, 1853 (patent no. 10,221), although he filed a caveat of the invention in 1849. Because this was one of the earliest applications of the absorption process for the manufacture of ice on a commercial scale, Twining was granted extensions of his patent in 1864 and 1871. Although he devoted all his time to it after 1849, he never succeeded in having his process introduced commercially. He wrote a number of papers on mathematical problems. He married Harriet Amelia Kinsley of West Point on Mar. 2, 1829, and at the time of his death in New Haven was survived by six children.

[T. J. Twining, *Geneal. of the Twining Family* (1890); *Obit. Record Grads. Yale Coll.* (1885); *Cat. of the Officers and Grads. of Yale Univ.* (1895); E. H. Knight, *Knight's Am. Mechanical Dict.,* vol. II (1875); A. C. Twining, *The Rights of Am. Inventors: A Petition in the 45th Cong., Jan. 28, 1879* (1879); obituaries in *New Haven Evening Reg.,* Nov. 22, and *New Haven Morning Courier,* Nov. 24, 1884.]   C. W. M.

TWITCHELL, AMOS (Apr. 11, 1781–May 26, 1850), pioneer New Hampshire surgeon, was born in Dublin, N. H., the son of Samuel and Alice (Willson) Twitchell, and a descendant of Benjamin Twitchell who emigrated from England to Dorchester about 1630. He was the seventh of nine children. His father, a patriot-farmer of 1775, served in the state legislature and established a library in Dublin as early as 1793.

Following a preliminary education in the New Ipswich Academy, Twitchell entered Dartmouth College and, after a struggle against poverty and poor health, was graduated with the degree of A.B. in 1802. While in college he formed warm friendships with Daniel Webster and the elder George Cheyne Shattuck [*qq.v.*]. Stimulated to study medicine by the energetic Nathan Smith, 1762–1829 [*q.v.*], then forming the medical school at Dartmouth, he became one of Smith's most ardent pupils, and later his life-long admirer and friend. Receiving the degrees of A.M. and B.M. in 1805, Twitchell first practised medicine in Norwich, Vt., then in Marlborough, N. H., and finally in Keene, N. H., where he settled in 1810 and remained until his death. He married Elizabeth, daughter of Dr. Josiah Goodhue, one of his teachers, in 1815; there were no children. Honors came to him, and he was offered many teaching positions in medicine, all of which he refused in order to continue his arduous practice. He became an overseer of Dartmouth College in 1816, having received the degree of M.D. there in 1811, served as president of the New Hampshire Medical Society (1829–30), and held membership in the American Medical Association, the College of Physicians of Philadelphia, and the National Institution for the Promotion of Science (1841). He died in Keene, May 26, 1850, after a period of over forty years as the leading surgeon of northern New England.

Twitchell became an outstanding figure in his time at an early age, owing to a bold and dramatic operation. At the age of twenty-six, on Oct. 18, 1807, while in practice at Marlborough, he saved the life of a man severely injured by a gun-shot wound in the neck, by tying the carotid artery, an operation not previously thought possible without fatal results. The scene in the farmhouse, with the mother holding open the wound and the young surgeon acting under great pressure in the dire emergency, was modestly but effectively described by Twitchell many years later (*New England Quarterly Journal of Medicine and Surgery,* October 1842). Only once had this operation been performed before, by a surgeon in the British navy, unknown to Twitchell.

In Keene, Twitchell led the life of a country practitioner, performing many operations with exceptional skill. He was one of the first in the United States to perform extensive amputations for malignant disease, operations for stone in the bladder and ovarian tumors, tracheotomy, and trephining of the long bones for suppuration. He traveled by chaise, with frequent changes of horses; known throughout the countryside, "the doctor" got the best and fastest horse, and he often covered a hundred miles or more a day. His health, never very good, was carefully guarded by a rigorous diet, total abstinence from tobacco and alcohol, and frequent short rest periods. He was a stanch upholder of the best of American medical traditions, although a frequent advocate of conservative reforms in the American Medical Association during its period of formation. Honest, intellectual, with both surgical acumen and originality, Twitchell should be regarded as one of the outstanding early American physicians.

[The date of Twitchell's birth, given by Bowditch as Apr. 14, is from Dartmouth Coll. records. The chief source is H. I. Bowditch, *Memoir of Amos Twitchell* (1851), with portrait. See also R. E. Twitchell, *Geneal. of the Twitchell Family* (1929); Albert Smith, in *N. H. Jour. of Medicine*, June 1851; *Am. Jour. of the Medic. Sciences*, July 1850; H. J. Bowditch, in *Charleston Medic. Jour.*, Nov. 1849; *Medic. Communications, Mass. Medic. Soc.* (1854); L. W. Leonard and J. L. Seward, *The Hist. of Dublin, N. H.* (1920); obituary in *N. H. Statesman* (Concord), June 7, 1850; Twitchell MSS. in the Boston Medic. Lib.]   H. R. V.

TYLER, BENNET (July 10, 1783–May 14, 1858), theologian and educator, was born in Middlebury, Conn., the son of James and Anne (Hungerford) Tyler. An accident when he was fifteen years of age incapacitated him for a life of manual labor and his family determined out of their meager resources to send him to college. He prepared under his pastor, the Rev. Ira Hart, and entered Yale in 1800, graduating four years later. After teaching a year in the academy at Weston, Conn., he studied theology with the Rev. Asahel Hooker of Goshen. In 1807 he was invited to the church in South Britain, Conn., and on Nov. 12 of that year was married to Esther Stone of Middlebury. Ordained and installed over the church June 1, 1808, he continued a highly successful ministry for fourteen years, then to his surprise, Mar. 6, 1822, he was called to the presidency of Dartmouth College. This institution he served acceptably for six years, his most outstanding service being the raising of a fund of ten thousand dollars to aid students fitting for the ministry. His inclinations, however, turned strongly towards the pastorate and he accepted an urgent call to the Second Church of Portland, Me., being installed in September 1828.

In this same year a sermon preached by Dr. Nathaniel W. Taylor [*q.v.*] at the Yale Commencement let loose a flood of theological controversy among the New England churches, especially in Connecticut, between the "Old School" Calvinists and the "New Divinity" as promulgated from New Haven. Being an ardent conservative and one of the ablest interpreters of the old theology, Tyler was drawn into the debate and became a recognized leader of the

conservatively orthodox. On Sept. 10, 1833, forty ministers met in East Windsor, Conn., and resolved to establish a theological seminary—if twenty thousand dollars could be raised—to counteract, as far as possible, the harmful effects of the "New Divinity" as taught in New Haven. The money was raised in a few weeks, the corner-stone of the Theological Institute of Connecticut, now the Hartford Theological Seminary, was laid May 13, 1834, and Tyler was inducted into office as president and professor of Christian theology on the same day. This position he held for twenty-three years, resigning on account of the infirmities of age July 16, 1857.

In closing his services with the Theological Institute he delivered an address in which he set forth with great clarity and force the convictions that had governed his thinking and actions—the absolute sovereignty of a perfect God, the total depravity of human nature, the federal headship of Adam, the substitutionary death of Christ, man's natural ability but moral inability to repent, the elective grace of the Almighty, regeneration effected by the direct agency of the Holy Spirit, the endless punishment of the wicked. These doctrines he had held consistently and unchanged during all his years of public service. After his retirement he lived less than a year, dying some two months after Nathaniel W. Taylor, his chief opponent. Not an original or speculative thinker, Tyler dwelt contentedly in the Calvinistic system as modified by Jonathan Edwards and tempered by Timothy Dwight [*qq.v.*]. To him it was real Christianity, the complete and final revelation of the divine plan; whosoever sought to mitigate its severities or deny its logical implications, him he conscientiously opposed. Although a fearless controversialist, he was a man of amiable disposition, genial temper, and genuine humility. He had six sons and six daughters; one of the daughters became the first wife of Calvin E. Stowe [*q.v.*]. In addition to numerous sermons and tracts he published *Letters on the Origin and Progress of the New Haven Theology* (1837), *A Review of President Day's Treatise on the Will* (1838), *A Treatise on the Sufferings of Christ* (1845), *New England Revivals* (1846), *Letters to the Rev. Horace Bushnell Containing Strictures on His Book Entitled "Views of Christian Nurture"* (two series, 1847, 1848). After his death, *Lectures on Theology with a Memoir by Rev. Nahum Gale* (1859) was issued.

[In addition to the memoir by Gale, his son-in-law, see F. B. Dexter, *Biog. Sketches Grads. Yale Coll.*, vol. V (1911); C. M. Geer, *The Hartford Theological Sem.* (1934); J. K. Lord, *A Hist. of Dartmouth Coll.*, vol. II (1913); William Cothren, *Hist. of Ancient Wood-*

bury (2 vols., 1854–72); *Am. Congregational Year Book* (1859).]

C. A. D.

TYLER, CHARLES MELLEN (Jan. 8, 1832–May 15, 1918), Congregational clergyman, college professor, was born in Limington, Me., the son of Daniel and Lavinia (Small) Tyler. He was a descendant of Job Tyler who emigrated from England to Newport, R. I., as early as 1638, and later settled in Andover, Mass. He received his early education from his father, a lawyer by profession, in the common schools, and at Lewiston Academy. Financial reverses interrupted his schooling, and for a time he worked in a ship-chandler's shop at Belfast and later for the wholesale grocery house of D. L. Gibbons, Boston. Subsequently, after taking the senior year at Phillips Academy, Andover, he entered Yale and graduated with the class of 1855. He distinguished himself as a scholar and won prizes in Latin, English composition, and oratory. Having spent a year in Union Theological Seminary, New York, he accepted a call to the First Congregational Church, Galesburg, Ill., and was ordained and installed in June 1857. A year later he became pastor of the Congregational Church in Natick, Mass., which position he held until 1867. During this period he took an active interest in civic affairs and in 1861–62 was a member of the Massachusetts legislature. He came of fighting stock, both his grandfather and his great-grandfather having been soldiers in the Revolution, and he and his father served in the Civil War, the latter as a paymaster under General McClellan, and Charles as chaplain of the 22nd Massachusetts Volunteers, with rank of captain. He was with the army in the Wilderness Campaign and about Petersburg. An outcome of his war experiences was the publication of a little book, *Memorials of Lieut. George H. Walcott, Late of the 30th U. S. Colored Troops* (1865). From 1867 to 1872 he was pastor of the South Church, Chicago.

In the latter year he took charge of the Reformed Dutch Church, Ithaca, N. Y., which later became the First Congregational Church. Thereafter until his death he was intimately connected with the affairs of Ithaca and Cornell University. He became a trustee of the University in 1886 and was active in this position until 1892, at which time he had assumed a professorship there. Two years before, Henry W. Sage [*q.v.*], a friend of Tyler, had endowed the Susan Linn Sage School of Philosophy, the organization of which included a chair of history and philosophy of religion and Christian ethics. Tyler was chosen in 1891 to be its first occupant and served in this capacity for twelve years, becoming professor

emeritus in 1903. In addition to contributions to periodicals, he published a substantial work, entitled *Bases of Religious Belief, Historic and Ideal* (1897). A résumé of modern thought on the subject with some critical comment, rather than an original treatise, it was valuable in its day to students as an introduction and guide. In 1907 he was again elected a trustee of the University, and served until his death. He was twice married: first, in New Haven, Conn., Dec. 10, 1856, to Ellen A., daughter of Thomas and Harriet N. (Rich) Davis, who died Jan. 14, 1891; second, June 1892, to Kate E. Stark, professor of music at Syracuse University. By his first wife he had two daughters; he died at the home of one of them, in Scranton, Pa.

[W. I. T. Brigham, *The Tyler Geneal.* (1912); *Obit. Record Grads. Yale Univ. . . . 1918* (1919); W. T. Hewett, *Cornell Univ., A Hist.* (1905); *Who's Who in America*, 1918–19; *Cornell Alumni News*, May 23, 1918.]

H. E. S.

TYLER, DANIEL (Jan. 7, 1799–Nov. 30, 1882), soldier, industrialist, was born in Brooklyn, Windham County, Conn. His parents were Daniel Tyler, III, a Revolutionary officer, descended from Job Tyler, one of the early settlers of Andover, Mass., and Sarah (Edwards) Chaplin Tyler, a grand-daughter of Jonathan Edwards [*q.v.*]. After attending the public schools, the boy was sent in 1812 to Plainfield Academy to prepare for Yale, but secured instead an appointment to the United States Military Academy in 1816. Three years later, as a lieutenant of light artillery, he began service in New England, and in 1824 he was ordered to the Artillery School of Practice at Fortress Monroe, Va. His own need for professional knowledge led him to import the best books on the subject and then to translate from the French a work on drill and maneuvers originally published in Paris in 1824. This translation was used by a commission appointed in 1826 to prepare a light artillery system for the American army, and in 1828 Tyler was sent to France to make further study of the French system. Admitted to the artillery school at Metz, he found it so far superior to that at Fortress Monroe that he proceeded at great expense to obtain copies of every drawing and treatise on the French system and to translate their latest manual of exercise and instruction for field artillery (1829). His detailed inspection of French armories and construction of small arms he turned to good advantage in 1830 when he investigated the armory at Springfield, Mass., exposing the inferior quality of the arms produced there and pointing to political influence as the cause. Likewise, as superintendent of inspectors of contract arms in 1832, he rejected as defective most of the muskets delivered by manufacturers. When the Ordnance Corps was reorganized, he was recommended for the commission of captain, but President Jackson, doubtless owing to political pressure, refused to appoint him. Tyler then resigned from the army, May 31, 1834. On May 28, 1832, in Norwich, Conn., he married Emily Lee.

After an unsuccessful venture in iron-making in Lycoming County, Pa., he turned to the financing and engineering of a series of transportation projects. In the early 1840's, as president of the Norwich & Worcester Railroad and the Morris Canal & Banking Company, he rescued both from bankruptcy. During 1844–45 he was asked to complete the construction of a railroad from Macon, Ga., to Atlanta, then for sale at $150,000, scarcely one-tenth of the capital already expended. Through Tyler's financial aid and the backing of a group of Macon men, the rechartered Macon & Western Railroad was opened for traffic in ten months and was soon paying a dividend of eight per cent. Anticipating disunion, Tyler resigned in 1849 from the presidency of the road and returned to Connecticut. During the 1850's he reorganized and improved a number of railroads in Pennsylvania, New Jersey, and Kentucky.

With the outbreak of the Civil War, in April 1861 Tyler was chosen to command the 1st Connecticut Regiment; in May he was commissioned brigadier-general, and shortly before the Bull Run campaign he was given a division command. Whether or not this campaign "was gotten up," as Tyler said, "by Gen. McDowell . . . to make him the hero of a short war" ("Autobiography," Mitchell, *post*, p. 49), Tyler disobeyed orders by failing to go to Centreville to intercept the Confederates' communication with Fairfax Court House and by bringing on a premature engagement, July 18, at Blackburn's Ford, where he was repulsed by Beauregard (*War of the Rebellion: Official Records, Army*, 1 ser., II, 311–12; Fry, *post*, pp. 17–25). His opponent failed to follow up the advantage, but during the main battle of Bull Run, July 21, Tyler did not press the attack when he could have, and he must bear some of the blame for the disastrous outcome of that battle. He was in action at Corinth in 1862 and in command of Maryland Heights and Harpers Ferry during the summer of 1863, and he also aided in recruiting, prison-camp administration, and army investigations.

After the death of his wife in 1864 he moved to New Jersey and traveled extensively year after year in Europe and in the South. In Charleston, S. C., in 1872, he met Samuel Noble [*q.v.*],

who induced him to examine the iron deposits of Eastern Alabama. They explored the country on horseback, and the upshot of the visit was the organization of the Woodstock Iron Company by Tyler, his son Alfred, and Noble in 1872. Furnace No. 1 was erected immediately at a cash investment of $200,000, and gave rise to the town of Anniston, named for Tyler's daughter-in-law. The company and the town enjoyed a steady growth despite the depression years immediately following: a second furnace was added in 1879; a cotton mill with 10,000 spindles, a water works, and a car factory were built; improvements in agriculture were introduced. During his last years he served as president of the Mobile & Montgomery Railroad with his residence in Montgomery and spent his winters in Guadalupe County, Tex., where he had invested in railroad lands, but he visited Anniston frequently. He died in New York City, but was buried in Anniston. Three sons and two daughters survived him.

[W. I. T. Brigham, *The Tyler Geneal.* (1912), vol. I; D. G. Mitchell, *Daniel Tyler: A Memorial Vol. Containing His Autobiog. and War Record* (1883); J. B. Fry, *McDowell and Tyler in the Campaign of Bull Run, 1861* (1884); T. M. Vincent, "The Battle of Bull Run," *Military Order of the Loyal Legion of the U. S., Commandery of D. C., War Papers*, no. 58 (1905); G. W. Cullum, *Biog. Reg. . . . U. S. Mil. Acad.* (3rd ed., 1891), vol. I; *Fourteenth Ann. Reunion, Asso. Grads. U. S. Mil. Acad.* (1883); Ethel Armes, *The Story of Coal and Iron in Ala.* (1910); U. B. Phillips, *A Hist. of Transportation in the Eastern Cotton Belt* (1908); *N. Y. Times*, Dec. 1, 1882; *Army and Navy Journal*, Dec. 2, 1882.]   L.J.C.

TYLER, JOHN (Feb. 28, 1747–Jan. 6, 1813), Revolutionary patriot, judge, governor of Virginia, and father of President John Tyler [*q.v.*], was the son of John Tyler, marshal of the colonial vice-admiralty court of Virginia, and his wife Anne Contesse. He was descended from Henry Tyler who had emigrated from England before the middle of the seventeenth century and settled in York County. Here at the ancestral home the fourth John Tyler was born, and hence he went at an early age to the College of William and Mary. Versifying and fiddling broke the monotony of his student days, and upon completion of his collegiate course he devoted five years to the reading of law under direction of Robert Carter Nicholas [*q.v.*]. During this impressionable period he became a friend of Thomas Jefferson and an admirer of Patrick Henry, whose speech against the Stamp Act he heard in 1765; the famous comparison with which it closed was repeated by him to William Wirt for the benefit of future generations (Wirt, *Sketches of the Life and Character of Patrick Henry*, 1817, p. 65). Having completed his legal training, he removed to Charles City County and took up the practice of his profession.

As the Revolutionary movement was already under way, a young man of ability had many opportunities to distinguish himself. The first of these came in the form of an appointment to the committee of safety of Charles City County in 1774. The following year Tyler raised a company of volunteers and accompanied Patrick Henry on his march against Lord Dunmore to recapture the powder which His Lordship had removed from Williamsburg. In 1776 the young lawyer married Mary Marot Armistead, daughter of Robert Armistead of York County, and established his home at "Greenway," near the court house of Charles City County. During the same year Tyler was appointed one of the judges of the newly organized high court of admiralty for Virginia. In 1777 he, along with Benjamin Harrison "the Signer" [q.v.], was elected to represent Charles City County in the House of Delegates. During 1780 he was appointed a member of the Council of State, but finding it impossible to execute the functions of this office in addition to other duties, he resigned it in 1781. This year Benjamin Harrison was elected governor of Virginia, and Tyler succeeded him as speaker of the House of Delegates. After Harrison retired from the governorship in 1784, he again sought a seat in the House, but was defeated by Tyler (W. C. Ford, ed., *Letters of Joseph Jones of Virginia,* 1889, p. 145). Harrison, however, secured an election from another county and then defeated Tyler for the speakership by a narrow margin (Breckinridge papers, Library of Congress, Archibald Stuart to John Breckinridge, Oct. 24, 1785). During all these years in the Assembly, Tyler maintained his friendship for Patrick Henry. They worked together in their support of congressional authority and strenuous opposition to Great Britain. Tyler favored a congressional impost on imports, and opposed the negotiation of a separate peace with Great Britain. At the end of the war he refused to support Henry in his lenient policy toward the Loyalists, but worked with him to defeat Madison's attempt to provide for the payment of British debts until Great Britain should comply with the terms of the treaty of peace (I. S. Harrell, *Loyalism in Virginia,* 1926, pp. 128, 132, 193; L. G. Tyler, *Judge John Tyler, Sr., and His Times,* pp. 14–16). His most important act as a member of the House was to present in 1785 a resolution calling a federal convention to meet at Annapolis in 1786 (J. B. McMaster, *A History of the People of the United States,* I, 1883, p. 279).

In the Virginia convention of 1788, Tyler was elected vice-president, and stood with Henry against the adoption of the federal Constitution. When the point was carried against them, the public life of the Admiralty Judge was seriously affected. The new government now took over the duties of his court, and he was transferred to the general court of Virginia. In this position he was one of the first judges to assert the overruling power of the judiciary. The relative aloofness of this position was not disturbed for some years, but Tyler retained his interest in politics. When national parties began to develop, he became an ardent Republican and kept in touch with his old friend Thomas Jefferson (Lipscomb and Bergh, *The Writings of Thomas Jefferson,* XI, 1904, pp. 32–35, 69–70; XIII, 1904, pp. 165–68). In 1808 he was elected governor of Virginia and held that post until 1811, when he accepted an appointment as judge of the federal court for the district of Virginia. As governor he opposed submission to the maritime policy of Great Britain and advocated a progressive policy in regard to public education and improved communications. The state Literary Fund sprang from one of his urgent messages.

His life was lived in troubled times, but despite his vehemence there was an air of benevolence in his manner and a touch of humor in his blue eyes. His facial features were much like those of his distinguished son, with a large Roman nose. He was an aristocrat by nature, but a democrat by choice. In politics he was a liberal, but an unruffled conservative in his private life. While war was still raging in the country, he died and was buried beneath the quiet shades of "Greenway."

[The most extensive account of the life of Judge Tyler is given by his grandson Lyon G. Tyler, in *The Letters and Times of the Tylers,* vols. I, II (1884–85). Another account by the same author is *Judge John Tyler, Sr., and His Times* (1927). Briefer sketches appear in Margaret V. Smith, *Virginia, 1492–1892 . . . A Hist. of the Executives* (1893), pp. 313–14; H. B. Grigsby, *The Hist. of the Va. Federal Convention of 1788,* vol. I (1890), 247–54; and Charles Campbell, *Hist. of the Colony and Ancient Dominion of Va.* (1860), pp. 723–24. For an obituary, see *Enquirer* (Richmond), Jan. 12, 1813.]   T. P. A.

TYLER, JOHN (Mar. 29, 1790–Jan. 18, 1862), tenth president of the United States, was the second son of Judge John Tyler [q.v.] and Mary (Armistead) Tyler. There was something classical in the simple dignity of Virginia's aristocratic republicans of that day, and the life of the Tyler homestead, "Greenway," in Charles City County, where young John was born, represented these qualities in full measure. There was a certain delicacy in the boy's manner, but he had his share of sterner stuff and was, on one occasion at least, a ringleader in a rebellion against his schoolmaster. *"Sic Semper Tyrannis"* was his father's only comment upon the incident. Completing his career at the local school, at the age of twelve he was bundled off to the College of William and Mary. Here he followed in the footsteps of his father, finding relaxation from studies in fiddling and poetry. He was also deeply interested in political subjects, and often sought his father's advice concerning them. Finishing his collegiate course at the age of seventeen, he read law under the direction of his father for two years and then entered upon the practice of his profession in his native county. It was only two more years before he was elected to the House of Delegates, and on Mar. 29, 1813, he married Letitia Christian, daughter of Robert Christian of New Kent County.

The War of 1812 was in progress. Tyler served for a month around Richmond as captain of a company of volunteers, but the enemy did not appear and he returned to civil life. In the Assembly he supported President Madison and the war and gave early notice that he was a strict constructionist of the school to which his father belonged. The Assembly had passed resolutions instructing Virginia's senators to vote against a bill proposing to recharter the Bank of the United States. One senator refused to comply, and the other complied under protest. Tyler introduced resolutions to censure them for their conduct. With a gracious manner and a definite gift for public speaking, the young member from Charles City became increasingly popular with his constituents and in the House of Delegates. He was elected to that body for five successive years, and finally, during the session of 1815–16, was chosen to sit on the executive council of the state. This service, however, was cut short by his election in 1816 to the federal House of Representatives. His membership in this body continued until 1821, when ill health forced him to resign. During these five years he put himself still further on record as a strict constructionist. As a member of a committee to report on the operation of the Bank of the United States, he favored the revocation of its charter (*House Document No. 92*, 15 Cong., 2 Sess., 1816). He voted against Calhoun's "bonus" bill for the aid of internal improvements, against a protective tariff, for the censure of Andrew Jackson's conduct in the Florida campaign, and against the adoption of the Missouri Compromise measure of 1820. His Virginia colleagues in Congress, with few exceptions, and the powerful *Richmond Enquirer*, supported him in his denial that the federal government had the right to control the question of slavery in the territories. The Tylers, both fa-

ther and son, were consistent in their opposition to the slave trade, and wished to see slavery pass away, but they trusted to time and climate for its ultimate abolition. They held that good faith to the Southern states required that while slavery existed, it should have all the protection of any other property (Tyler, *post,* I, 313).

On his retirement from Congress, Tyler bought "Greenway," which on the death of his father in 1813 had descended to an older brother, Dr. Wat Henry Tyler; and there for two years he lived the life of a private citizen. In 1823 he was again elected to the House of Delegates and from this post took a leading part in the exciting events connected with the presidential campaign of 1824. Along with the majority of the Jeffersonian Republicans of Virginia, he supported William H. Crawford in that contest. Andrew Jackson he considered a mere military hero, and of little value as a civilian. After the election of Adams and the appointment of Clay as secretary of state, Tyler refused to believe the "bargain and corruption" story, and wrote to Clay stating his opinion (Calvin Colton, ed., *The Private Correspondence of Henry Clay,* 1856, pp. 119–20). In 1825 and again in 1826 Tyler was elected governor of Virginia, and in this capacity worked for the development of roads and schools, as his father had done before him. While not a supporter of the Adams administration, Tyler did not at once follow John Randolph and the *Enquirer* into the Jackson camp (C. H. Ambler, *Thomas Ritchie,* 1913, p. 111; Tyler, *post,* I, 375–76). In 1827 he was elected to the United States Senate by the anti-Jackson element in the Assembly. In 1828 he voted against the "tariff of abominations" and supported Jackson for the presidency as a "choice of evils." However, Tyler soon flew in the face of the President by opposing his appointment of several newspaper editors to high federal posts (C. G. Bowers, *The Party Battles of the Jackson Period,* 1922, p. 82). There were apparently some phases of Jackson's democracy with which he did not sympathize. This fact is further illustrated by his stand, as a member of the Virginia constitutional convention of 1829–30, in favor of the "federal ratio" of apportionment for the upper house of the Assembly (Tyler, I, 397–404). Jackson's veto of the Maysville road bill was an action after Tyler's own heart, and so was the President's opposition to the rechartering of the Bank of the United States, but the removal of the deposits was another matter. In the Senate he supported the resolutions which condemned the President for this act. While not a believer in nullification, Tyler considered Jackson's nullification proclamation as subversive of the Constitution and he cast the only vote record-ed in the Senate against the Force Bill. But his state-rights views did not lead him into merely obstructionist tactics. It was he who first formu-lated a plan of conciliation and brought Calhoun and Clay together to agree upon the compromise tariff of 1833 (Tyler, I, 455–60; A. C. Cole, *The Whig Party in the South,* 1913, pp. 24–25).

It cannot be said that Tyler was ever a Jack-son man in the strict sense of the term. He sup-ported him in 1828 and again in 1832, but not without reservations, and considered him dis-tinctly unsound on constitutional principles. Coming finally to a definite break with the ad-ministration, he became a member of the South-ern state-rights group in Congress which co-operated and acted with the National Republicans within the newly forming Whig party. Neither Tyler nor any of his group pretended to accept the nationalistic doctrines of Clay and his fol-lowing.

In 1833 Tyler was reëlected to the Senate. Virginia supported him without reservation in his stand on the Force Bill (C. H. Ambler, *Thomas Ritchie,* p. 152). But times were chang-ing. The Jacksonians, under the lead of John Randolph and Thomas Ritchie of the *Enquirer,* got control of the state, and Tyler became a member of the opposition. In 1836 the legislature instructed him to vote for the expunging of reso-lutions censuring Jackson for removal of the deposits, and he resigned his senatorship rather than comply (*Letter of John Tyler . . . to the . . . General Assembly of Virginia,* 1836). In this year the Virginia Whigs supported him as their vice-presidential candidate on a ticket which was split between Harrison and White as to the first place. William C. Rives [*q.v.*] was elected to the seat in the Senate vacated by Tyler, but by 1839 the Whigs had ousted the Democrats from the control of the Assembly and Tyler was again a member of that body. In this year Rives came up for reëlection. Meanwhile, he had broken with the Democrats on the sub-treasury issue, and the Whigs were anxious to win him over. In the election, John Y. Mason was the regular Demo-cratic candidate and Tyler the regular Whig. A number of Whigs, however, deserted Tyler and voted for Rives with the result that none of the candidates was able to secure a majority. It ap-pears that Henry Clay was cognizant of this scheme to desert Tyler in order to win Rives, and that he had held out hopes of the vice-presi-dential nomination for Tyler in case his friends would cooperate. But Tyler had no part in any of these schemes (Henry A. Wise, *Seven De-cades of the Union,* p. 158; Tyler, I, 588–93).

It did, nevertheless, come about that Tyler was nominated for the second place on the Harrison ticket of 1840; that he was elected in the boister-ous campaign of that year; and that, Harrison dying within a month of his inauguration, he be-came president of the United States by right of succession. No vice-president had ever thus be-come president, and there were those who would have withheld from him the full title, but Tyler maintained his claim. Henry Clay certainly in-tended to withhold from him the leadership of the Whig party, and in this he was successful. Tyler's constitutional views were well known when he was nominated and elected, but the ma-jority of the Whigs were nationalists, with Clay as their leader, and they could not refrain from bringing forward the old measures of the Na-tional Republican party, which they had mini-mized in the recent canvass. Tyler regarded this as an act of bad faith, but, hoping to avoid a break, he held a conference with Clay and tried to reach an agreement with him on the bank question (Tyler, II, 127–28; *Speech of Mr. Cush-ing . . . on the Post Office Bill,* 1841). Clay, how-ever, wished no agreement. This was the last meeting between the two men. Clay said, "I'll drive him before me," but Tyler still hoped for conciliation. His retention of Harrison's cabi-net could have had no other meaning, but he found that Harrison's plans as to the use of the patronage were a bit too strong for him (Tyler, II, 310). He signed an act abolishing the sub-treasury system, but insisted that the "distribu-tion" measure be dropped from the tariff bill of 1842 before he would sign it (Thomas H. Ben-ton, *Thirty Years' View,* 1856, II, 413–17). Furthermore, his policy on the question of in-ternal improvements was far more conservative than had been that of Jackson or Adams.

It was the bank question that brought on the crisis between the President and the party. Tyler had made it clear from the beginning that he would not sanction a measure which permitted a National Bank to establish branches in the states without their previous consent. He devised a plan, known as the "exchequer system," which would have avoided this difficulty, and recom-mended it to Congress, but Clay did not wish to satisfy Tyler on that point (Wise, *Seven Decades,* pp. 204–05; Tyler, II, 15–16, 131, 134). A bill was passed chartering a bank along the lines de-sired by Clay, and Tyler promptly vetoed it. Conferences were thereupon held. Three mem-bers of the cabinet, followers of Clay, later averred that the President had agreed to a re-vised plan for a bank, and a second bill was pre-sented to Congress, but Tyler had never seen it

(A. C. Gordon, *John Tyler*, pp. 30–31; Wise, pp. 185–90). Feeling that it did not properly safeguard the rights of the states, he vetoed it when it was passed (J. F. Jameson, ed., "Correspondence of John C. Calhoun," *Annual Report of the American Historical Association for the Year 1899*, vol. II, 1900, pp. 487–89). At the behest of Clay, the cabinet members then resigned, with the exception of Webster who saw no reason for such action. Thus Tyler became a president without a party.

It was not believed that his administration would result in much constructive work, but this did not prove to be the case even on the legislative side, while as an administrator and negotiator Tyler made a remarkable record. His hand was seen in many constructive acts of Congress, prominent among which was the entire reorganization of the Navy, the establishment of a depot for nautical charts and instruments, which developed into the National Observatory; and the act to test the practicability of establishing a system of magnetic telegraphs for the use of the United States, which has had a many-sided development, especially in the Weather Bureau. The government was conducted with a minimum of waste and extravagance despite the fact that Congress had provided no system for the keeping of public funds. The Seminole War was brought to an end. Dorr's Rebellion was quieted without Federal interference (Edward Everett, ed., *The Works of Daniel Webster*, 1851, vol. VI, 237–38), a treaty was negotiated with China opening the doors of the Orient for the first time, and the Monroe Doctrine was enforced in the case of Texas and the Hawaiian Islands.

The greatest achievements were the negotiation of the Webster-Ashburton treaty and the annexation of Texas. Webster has usually been given all the credit for the settlement of the northeastern boundary dispute with Great Britain, but many of the provisions were Tyler's own, and it was Tyler who oiled the wheels of the negotiation which not only settled the question of the boundary, but dealt with several other difficult though lesser causes of friction between the two countries (J. H. Latané, *A History of American Foreign Policy*, 1927, pp. 210–22; *William and Mary College Quarterly Historical Magazine*, July 1916, pp. 1–8; *Tyler's Quarterly Historical and Genealogical Magazine*, III, 255–57; Tyler, II, 216–18). Early in his administration Tyler broached the Texas question to Webster, but he hesitated to press it on account of the slavery issue (Tyler, II, 126–27). After Webster's resignation, Upshur negotiated the treaty of annexation, but the latter's untimely death left the matter still unsettled. The appointment of a new secretary of state to finish the work was a delicate matter. In this crisis, Henry A. Wise [*q.v.*] committed the President to the appointment of Calhoun (Wise, *Seven Decades*, pp. 221–25). On the score of friendship and policy, the President accepted the situation and Calhoun took over the Texas negotiation. His partisans hoped to capitalize the appointment and make the South Carolinian the Texas candidate for the succession (C. H. Ambler, ed., "Correspondence of R. M. T. Hunter," *Annual Report of the American Historical Association for the Year 1916*, vol. II, 1918, pp. 51–55; Ambler, *Thomas Ritchie*, pp. 227, 232). But Tyler's reluctance to appoint Calhoun received ample justification when Clay and Van Buren came out against immediate annexation and the Senate rejected the treaty. Tyler was then supported for the presidency by a strong element in many states, but when the Democrats selected Polk as their candidate on an annexationist platform Tyler withdrew in his favor (U. B. Phillips, ed., "The Correspondence of Robert Toombs, Alexander H. Stephens, and Howell Cobb," *Annual Report of the American Historical Association for the Year 1911*, vol. II, 1913, p. 59; *The Madisonian Pamphlet*, Letter of John Tyler "To my Friends throughout the Union," 1844; Tyler, II, 341, III, 139–43, 147, 153, 169; *Tyler's Quarterly Historical and Genealogical Magazine*, Oct. 1924, pp. 81–97). Polk was elected, but Texas was annexed by joint resolution while Tyler was still president. He could retire with the satisfaction of knowing that he had accomplished much for his country.

One who saw him at the time he occupied the White House said: "In his official intercourse with all men, high or low, he was all that could be asked: approachable, courteous, always willing to do a kindly action, or to speak a kindly word. . . . He was above the middle height, somewhat slender, clean-shaven, with light hair. His light blue eyes were penetrating, and had a humorous twinkle which aided the notable faculty he possessed for telling a good story, and for making keen conversational hits" (W. O. Stoddard, *William Henry Harrison, John Tyler, and James Knox Polk*, 1888, p. 55). It was this amiability and efficiency which enabled him to accomplish so much as an administrator.

The ex-President retired to "Sherwood Forest." His first wife, who bore him seven children, died in 1842. Two years later he himself had narrowly escaped death when a large gun exploded during trials on board the warship *Princeton*. One of the victims of that accident was David Gardiner of New York; and his daughter, Julia, being thrown with Tyler under these tragic circumstances, became his bride within a few months (June 26, 1844). She presided as mistress of the White House during the closing scenes of the administration, and now became mistress of "Sherwood Forest." She had seven children. The family lived the quiet life of rural Virginia until the outbreak of the Civil War called Tyler again into public activity. Believing in the desirability of conciliation, he proposed a convention of the border states to meet and consider compromises which might save the Union. The Virginia Assembly proposed a convention of all the states for this purpose, and when it met in Washington in February 1861 Tyler acted as its chairman. These efforts failing, Tyler in March was a member of the Virginia convention which met to consider the question of secession. As soon as all compromise measures had failed, he declared for separation. When Virginia seceded he urged that Southern troops occupy Washington and that the South appropriate the name and the flag of the old Union. He believed an offensive to be better than a defensive policy (Tyler, II, 658–62). These proposals were rejected, but Tyler served in the provisional Congress of the Confederacy and was elected to a seat in the Confederate House of Representatives. He died before he was able to take his place, and lies buried in Hollywood Cemetery, Richmond. His memory has been dimmed by the writings of historians who find a record of courageous consistency bewildering.

[The most complete account of the life of President Tyler is in *The Letters and Times of the Tylers* (3 vols., 1884, 1885, 1896), by his son Lyon G. Tyler. Other accounts are in H. A. Wise, *Seven Decades of the Union* (1872); *Observations on the Political Character and Services of President Tyler and His Cabinet* (1841), by "A Native of Maryland" (John L. Dorsey); anonymous, *Life of John Tyler* (1843); J. R. Irelan, "History of the Life, Administration and Times of John Tyler," *The Republic*, vol. X (1888); *John Tyler* (1932), address of C. G. Bowers; A. C. Gordon, *John Tyler* (1915), an address, reprinted in substance in *Virginian Portraits* (1924). Special phases of his administration are discussed by J. H. Smith, *The Annexation of Texas* (1911); J. S. Reeves, *American Diplomacy under Tyler and Polk* (1907); and C. M. Fuess, *The Life of Caleb Cushing* (1923). Some of Tyler's later papers are published in "An Echo from the Civil War," by Stephen F. Peckham, in *Journal of Am. History*, Oct. 1911, pp. 611–63, and Mar. 1912, pp. 73–86. There is a collection of Tyler papers (8 vols.) in the Lib. of Cong. and another in the library of Duke Univ. *The William and Mary College Quart. Hist. Mag.* and *Tyler's Quart. Hist. and Geneal. Mag.* contain many letters and other articles bearing on his administration. For an obituary see *Daily Richmond Enquirer*, Jan. 20, 1862.]

T. P. A.

TYLER, MOSES COIT (Aug. 2, 1835–Dec. 28, 1900), historian and educator, son of Elisha and Mary (Greene) Tyler and a descendant of Job Tyler, an early settler of Andover, Mass.,

was born in Griswold, Conn. After various wanderings the family settled in Detroit, where Moses attended the public schools, and whence he entered the University of Michigan. In Detroit he came strongly under the influence of the Rev. Harvey D. Kitchel, who strengthened his lifelong tendency to religious preoccupation. In 1853 Tyler withdrew from the institution at Ann Arbor to enter Yale, where he was graduated in 1857. After attending the theological seminaries at New Haven and Andover, but without a degree from either, he was ordained to the Congregationalist ministry at Owego, N. Y., in August 1859, and after a year there became pastor of a Congregational Church in Poughkeepsie, where he was formally installed in February 1861. During this period he was an ardent disciple of Henry Ward Beecher [*q.v.*]. On Oct. 26, 1859, he had married Jeannette Hull Gilbert, by whom he had a daughter and a son. Failing health and dissatisfaction with orthodox theology led him to resign his pulpit in October 1862.

At one time or another Tyler took up various reforms, including the temperance movement, abolition, and the cause of women's rights, but the one to which he gave most time was the advocacy of "musical gymnastics," a system of calisthenics invented by Dio Lewis [*q.v.*], under whose influence the future historian fell after leaving Poughkeepsie for Boston. At Lewis' suggestion, Tyler went to England in April 1863 to crusade for physical education. He was extraordinarily successful as a lecturer on calisthenics, and gradually extended the range of his topics to include literary addresses and a defense of the Union cause. He was gradually drawn into journalism, and thought for a time of making it his career. The best of Tyler's essays from this period, reprinted in *Glimpses of England* (1898), reveal him as an ardent liberal.

After returning to the United States, in December 1866, Tyler was for a time at a loss, but in 1867 received appointment as professor of rhetoric and English literature at the University of Michigan. He did much to modernize instruction in literature at Ann Arbor, for he was an extraordinarily effective teacher. In the meantime his own interests were increasingly directed to the interpretation of American colonial history, the reading of H. T. Buckle's *History of Civilization* helping to arouse his enthusiasm and his curiosity. Finding no way to carry forward effective investigation at Michigan, Tyler resigned his professorship in 1873 and secured an appointment to the staff of the *Christian Union*, then under Beecher's control, believing that it would give him leisure and access to

Eastern libraries. The association proved unhappy, however, owing to the Tilton-Beecher scandal and to Tyler's moral disgust with "the gilded age," and he returned thankfully to Michigan in 1874. Here he remained as professor of English literature until 1881, when Andrew D. White [q.v.], a lifelong friend, called him to Cornell as the first professor of American history in the country. In both institutions Tyler helped to introduce German methodology into graduate instruction. Except for a personal controversy with President Charles Kendall Adams over the organization and control of the Cornell department of history, Tyler's years in Ithaca were uneventful, though he was occasionally troubled by a mild religious melancholia. In 1881 he was ordered deacon and in 1883 ordained priest in the Protestant Episcopal Church. The last fifteen years of his life were in many ways the most effective, for he labored happily at American history, helped to found the American Historical Association (1884), gained wide recognition as an authority on the colonial literature of the country, and was generally recognized as a leader in the cause of "critical" as opposed to "patriotic" history. He died at Ithaca, survived by his wife and both children. Personally, he was a genial, humorous, quick-tempered, ever-active man.

Tyler produced a mass of more or less ephemeral essays and reviews, a group of scholarly articles, one or two minor volumes, and a few textbooks, but his permanent reputation is due to his historical and biographical researches. During his second period at Michigan he wrote *A History of American Literature during the Colonial Time, 1607–1765* (2 vols., 1878). This he followed by *Patrick Henry* (1887), the first modern biography of the Virginia leader, and by *The Literary History of the American Revolution 1763–1783* (2 vols., 1897), written at Cornell. With the last-named work should be associated his *Three Men of Letters* (1895), critical biographies of George Berkeley, Timothy Dwight, and Joel Barlow, characterized by great charm and insight; these he planned to follow by a book to be called *"Vivi Memorabiles,"* which was not completed. Because of Tyler's thorough preparation, clearness of style, and sanity of judgment, his four volumes of literary history have become by common consent the standard account of the first two centuries of American literary development.

[The Tyler papers in the library of Cornell Univ. were used in H. M. Jones, *The Life of Moses Coit Tyler* (1933), based on an unpublished dissertation from original sources by T. E. Casady. Tyler's daughter, Jessica Tyler Austen, published *Moses Coit Tyler:*

Selections from His Letters and Diaries (1911). See also W. I. T. Brigham, *The Tyler Geneal.* (2 vols., 1912); W. P. Trent, in *Forum*, Aug. 1901; G. L. Burr, in *New Eng. Hist. and Geneal. Reg.*, Apr. 1901, supp.; *Who's Who in America*, 1899–1900; *Yale Univ. Obit. Record*, 5 ser. (1910); *N. Y. Times*, Dec. 29, 1900.]

H. M. J.

TYLER, RANSOM HUBERT (Nov. 18, 1815–Nov. 21, 1881), legal writer, son of Peter and Eunice Tyler, was born in Franklin County, Mass., whence, when he was three, his family moved to Oswego County, N. Y. During his boyhood he worked on his father's farm and in the winter attended public school. Having shown an eagerness for an education, he was sent to Mexico Academy, where he acquired a good classical schooling. In 1836 he began the study of law, at the same time taking charge of the principal school of Fulton village, and in 1840 he was admitted to practice. Four years later he was appointed master in chancery, keeping this office until its termination, as the result of constitutional changes, in 1846. After serving as district attorney for three years, he was elected county judge for a term running from Jan. 1, 1852, to Dec. 31, 1855, and again for a similar term beginning Jan. 1, 1864.

Between his judgeships Tyler edited gratuitously for one year the *Oswego County Gazette* and in 1858 ran unsuccessfully for Congress on the Democratic ticket. In 1861, however, he changed his political allegiance to support Lincoln. During this same period his strong religious tendencies led him to publish a book entitled *The Bible and Social Reform or, the Scriptures as a Means of Civilization* (1860). The hold that theology had on him was further demonstrated by his first legal textbook, *American Ecclesiastical Law* (1866), in which he not only discussed the laws of the several states bearing on ecclesiastical organizations, but also dissected the dogmas of the various creeds with a skill that won contemporary praise.

Closely following this publication came texts and treatises on various aspects of civil law, namely *Commentaries on the Law of Infancy, including Guardianship and Custody of Infants, and the Law of Coverture, embracing Dower, Marriage and Divorce, and the Statutory Policy of the Several States in Respect to Husband and Wife* (1868, 2nd ed., 1882); *A Treatise on the Law of Boundaries and Fences* (1874); *A Treatise on the Remedy by Ejectment and the Law of Adverse Enjoyment in the United States* (1870, 1874, 1876); *A Treatise on the Law of Usury, Pawns or Pledges, and Maritime Loans* (1873); and *A Treatise on the Law of Fixtures* (1877). In addition, he contributed to periodical literature. All his books were the products of considerable research and valuable for their wealth of material, but they were subject, as a whole, to the criticism of prolixity, poor arrangement, and, ofttimes, lack of clarity.

Apart from his legal interests, Tyler was at one time a bank president and for a period was an officer in the New York militia, attaining the rank of brigadier-general before resigning. He took an abiding interest in religious and social activities and traveled extensively, through Europe, Asia, and Africa. Friendly and generous by nature, he was liked and respected by his community. He was married twice, first to Nancy D. Cadwell, and after her death, to Mary E. Douglas. He died at his home in Fulton, N. Y., survived by his second wife and one child.

[Sources include *Landmarks of Oswego County, N. Y.* (1895), ed. by J. C. Churchill; Crisfield Johnson, *Hist. of Oswego County, N. Y.* (1877); clippings from an unidentified newspaper preserved by the Am. Antiquarian Soc. in "Roe Contemporary Biography," vol. II, p. 42. Tyler's middle name is given as Hebbard in some accounts, but appears as Hubert in the Alumni Register of Hamilton College, which in 1853 awarded him the honorary degree of A.M. (*The Hamilton Coll. Bull.*, Nov. 1922).]　　L. M. S.

TYLER, ROBERT (Sept. 9, 1816–Dec. 3, 1877), lawyer, politician, and editor, son of President John Tyler [*q.v.*] and Letitia (Christian), was born in Charles City County, Va. Like his father and grandfather, he was educated at the College of William and Mary, graduating in 1835. He then studied law under Prof. Beverley Tucker and began practice in Williamsburg. On Sept. 12, 1839, he married Elizabeth Priscilla, daughter of Thomas Abthorpe Cooper, the famous Irish tragedian and protégé of William Godwin (John Bernard, *Retrospections of America*, 1887, p. 164). When John Tyler became president in 1841, Robert took up his residence in Washington, acting as private secretary to his father, while his wife presided as mistress of the White House during the first year of the administration. The young man found time while thus engaged to write two serious poems of a religious nature; *Ahasuerus*, and *Death: or Medorus' Dream*, published in 1842 and 1843 respectively.

Toward the close of President Tyler's term of office, Robert moved to Philadelphia and at once began to take a leading part in the politics of that city. In 1844 he was elected president of the Irish Repeal Association. In 1847 he became solicitor to the sheriff of Philadelphia, and a little later was made prothonotary to the supreme court of Pennsylvania. During the Mexican War he recruited a regiment in Philadelphia, but its services were declined (L. G.

Tyler, *post*, II, 456). Meanwhile, he had become a political friend of James Buchanan, secretary of state under President Polk. Buchanan had not been friendly to the Tyler administration, and the ex-president seems to have had no part in making this alliance nor in shaping the career of his son at this time (*Ibid.*, II, 494). In 1852 Robert Tyler supported Buchanan for the Democratic nomination for the presidency. In 1854 he became one of the earliest advocates of a Pacific railway. In 1856 Henry A. Wise, a close friend of the Tylers, was elected governor of Virginia, and he and Robert Tyler were able to bring Virginia to the support of the Pennsylvanian in the Cincinnati convention of 1856. This service was followed by Tyler's appointment in 1858 to the chairmanship of the Democratic executive committee of Pennsylvania (C. H. Ambler, "Correspondence of Robert M. T. Hunter," *Annual Report of the American Historical Asso. . . . 1916*, 1918, II, 299–300).

When the Civil War broke out, a Philadelphia mob attacked the home of the Virginian because of his well-known Southern sympathies, and he was forced to flee to Richmond. It was not long before President Davis appointed him to be register of the Confederate Treasury. In this capacity he published valuable reports on Confederate shipping and finance. At the end of the war, he removed his family to Montgomery, Ala., and in 1867 became editor of the Montgomery *Mail and Advertiser*. This position enabled him to take a leading part in the expulsion of Carpet-bag rule from Alabama, and his work was recognized by his appointment as chairman of the Democratic state central committee, in which capacity he served for several years. Thus, in very different scenes and circumstances, he twice became the leader of his party in the state of his residence. Strong convictions, fervor of temperament, and ability as a political speaker and writer enabled him to attain his position quite independently of any aid from his more famous father. When he died, at the age of sixty-one, his remains were interred in Montgomery.

[The most complete sketch of Tyler's career is in T. M. Owen, *Hist. of Ala. and Dict. of Ala. Biog.* (1921), vol. IV; see also L. G. Tyler, *The Letters and Times of the Tylers*, vol. II (1885); William Brewer, *Ala., Her Hist., Resources, War Record, and Public Men* (1872); P. G. Auchampaugh, *Robert Tyler, Southern Rights Champion* (1934) and "John W. Forney, Robert Tyler, and James Buchanan," in *Tyler's Quart. Hist. and Geneal. Mag.*, Oct. 1933; *Mobile Daily Reg.*, Dec. 5, 6, 1877. The Confederate treasury reports are in the Lib. of Cong., in pamphlet form.]　　T. P. A.

TYLER, ROBERT OGDEN (Dec. 22, 1831–Dec. 1, 1874), soldier, was born at Hunter,

Greene County, N. Y., the son of Frederick and Sophia (Sharp) Tyler and a nephew of Daniel Tyler [*q.v.*]. He was descended from Job Tyler who was in Newport, R. I., in 1638 and later went to Massachusetts. Robert's grandfather, Daniel Tyler, was adjutant to Gen. Israel Putnam during the Revolution, and three uncles were army officers. Given an excellent preparatory education, he entered the United States Military Academy in 1849, graduated in 1853, and became a second lieutenant of the 3rd Artillery. He soon participated in a movement of troops from the Missouri River to Salt Lake and San Francisco (1854–55). In 1856—he was promoted first lieutenant on Sept. 1 of that year—he was engaged in Indian wars in what is now the state of Washington. In 1859, he went to the Sioux country in Minnesota.

At the opening of the Civil War he was in garrison at the Fort Columbus Recruiting Station, N. Y. He accompanied the relief expedition to Fort Sumter, S. C., in April 1861, and then went to Baltimore to assist in the opening of that city to Federal forces. In May 1861 he transferred as a captain to the quartermaster's department and opened a supply depot at Alexandria, Va. In September he became colonel of the 1st Connecticut Heavy Artillery. He found this regiment, considerably demoralized, within the defenses of Washington, but soon brought it to a state of high efficiency. The following spring he participated in the Peninsular campaign. He prepared his batteries to bombard Yorktown, but owing to the fact that the Confederates withdrew just before the batteries were ready to fire, there was no engagement. With great effort the batteries were moved up for an attack on Richmond, which also never occurred. At Gaines's Mill, June 27, 1862, the batteries did good work in assisting the Federals north of the Chickahominy. In the retreat to Malvern Hill, Tyler brought off all his guns but one and used them in repulsing the Confederate attack on July 1. For these services he was appointed a brigadier-general of volunteers on Nov. 29, 1862. The following month he had charge of the Federal batteries which fired upon Fredericksburg. In the Gettysburg campaign he commanded the artillery reserve of 130 guns and, under direction of Gen. Henry J. Hunt [*q.v.*], chief of artillery, disposed these guns to maximum advantage, especially in stopping Pickett's charging infantry. In 1864 Tyler's artillery served as infantry throughout the Wilderness campaign. It distinguished itself at Spotsylvania, May 17–24, driving back the Confederate forces under Gen. Richard Ewell

[*q.v.*]. At Cold Harbor, on June 1, it was one of the brigades selected for the famous bloody assault. Early in this action Tyler was shot through the ankle, a wound from the effects of which he never recovered.

Returning to duty in December, he was assigned to board duties, and to the command of districts outside of the theatre of active operations. On Mar. 13, 1865, he was brevetted major-general for gallant conduct and meritorious services. He was mustered out of the volunteer service Jan. 15, 1866, and on July 29 was appointed to the Regular Army as a lieutenant-colonel in the quartermaster's department. In this capacity he served at many important military headquarters, with constantly declining health. In an effort to recuperate he took a year's leave in 1872, visiting the Far East. A diary relating to part of this trip was published in *Memoir of Brevet Major-General Robert Ogden Tyler* (1878). Failing to find the relief he had sought, Tyler died at Boston in the year after his return from the East, and was buried in Hartford, Conn. He never married. He was noted for strictness and justice, but was of kindly disposition.

[W. I. T. Brigham, *The Tyler Geneal.* (1912, vol. I); G. W. Cullum, *Biog. Reg. Officers and Grads. U. S. Mil. Acad.* (3rd ed., 1891), vol. II; *War of the Rebellion: Official Records (Army)*; F. B. Heitman, *Hist. Reg. and Dict. U. S. Army* (1903), *Sixth Ann. Reunion Asso. Grads. U. S. Mil. Acad.* (1875); *N. Y. Tribune,* Dec. 2, 1874.]   C. H. L—a.

TYLER, ROYALL (July 18, 1757–Aug. 26, 1826), playwright, novelist, jurist, was born in Boston, Mass., the son of Royall and Mary (Steele) Tyler. His father, grandson of Thomas Tyler who settled in Boston about 1680, was a graduate of Harvard, a merchant, and a member of the King's Council from 1765 to 1771. Royall, junior, was christened William Clark, but his name was afterwards changed to Royall by action of the General Court. Entering Harvard College July 15, 1772, he attracted attention by his ability, his wit, and his lively nature. Upon his graduation in 1776, Yale College bestowed the degree of B.A. upon him, in early recognition of those intellectual qualities of which he had already given evidence. While engaged in the study of law with Francis Dana [*q.v.*] in Cambridge, he was one of the leaders of a group of young men who were interested in writing, painting, and politics.

He joined the Independent Company of Boston and in 1778 served as aide to General Sullivan, with the rank of major, in the attack on Newport, but owing to his mother's widowhood, his military service was not continuous. On

Aug. 19, 1780, he was admitted to the bar, practising first in Falmouth, now Portland, Me., then in Braintree, Mass., where he became engaged to be married to Abigail Adams, daughter of John Adams [*q.v.*], then in France. Adams, however, insisted that his wife and daughter join him at Auteuil in the summer of 1784, and in 1785 Tyler received word that the engagement was cancelled. No reason was given, but the subsequent marriage of Abigail Adams to her father's secretary of legation, Col. William Stephens Smith [*q.v.*], makes it unnecessary to lay too much stress on the persistent tradition that John Adams distrusted the stability of Tyler. The latter was of an extremely sensitive nature, however, and retired for some months to his mother's home at Jamaica Plain; but before the close of the year he resumed active practice, this time in Boston, where he resided with Joseph Pearce Palmer and renewed his friendship with little Mary Palmer, who was afterward to be his wife.

Early in 1787 he joined the staff of Gen. Benjamin Lincoln [*q.v.*], again with the rank of major, and assisted in the suppression of Shays's Rebellion, partly by his eloquence in addressing the rioters. He was less successful in his diplomatic journey into Vermont to secure Shays, but it was on a mission connected with the fugitives that he was sent by Governor Bowdoin to New York City. He arrived on Mar. 12, 1787.

In New York, inspired by the production of *The School for Scandal* and other plays he undoubtedly saw at the old John Street Theatre, and by his acquaintance with the well-known low comedian, Thomas Wignell [*q.v.*], he wrote *The Contrast,* produced Apr. 16, 1787, by the American Company, the second play and the first comedy written by a native American and produced by a professional company. It was instantly successful, being repeated five times in New York and soon played in Baltimore, Philadelphia, Boston, and Charleston. Tyler gave the copyright to Wignell, who published it in Philadelphia in 1790 as by "a citizen of the United States," with a list of subscribers headed by Washington. The play is a sterling social comedy, comparing the American officer and gentleman, in Colonel Manly, with Dimple, the imitator of British affectations. Charlotte, the flirt of that day, is as real today as she was then, and Jonathan was the prototype of a long succession of stage Yankees. The scene in which Jonathan goes to the play without knowing it has become a classic. During recent years *The Contrast* has been produced at many of the leading American universities and little theatres, and always with effect; and its influence upon playwrights like William Dunlap [*q.v.*], who were inspired by its success in its own day, can hardly be estimated.

Tyler followed *The Contrast* with a comic opera in two acts, *May Day in Town; or, New York in an Uproar,* performed at the John Street Theatre, May 19, 1787. It probably reflected the confusion occasioned by the custom of moving households on May 1 in New York, but it has not survived, even in manuscript. Neither has *The Georgia Spec; or, Land in the Moon,* a comedy in three acts which ridiculed the land speculations in the Yazoo country in Georgia. It was first played in Boston, at the Haymarket Theatre, Oct. 30, 1797, and in New York, Dec. 20 and later. According to the memoir of Tyler, prefaced by his son, he also wrote a farce, *The Farm House; or, The Female Duellists,* which, according to the son (T. P. Tyler, *post*), "was performed and was especially popular." It has not survived, and the cast as given at the Boston Theatre is identical with that of Kemble's farce of the same name. Tyler may have adapted the English play. The same authority attributes to Tyler *The Doctor in Spite of Himself,* evidently an adaptation of Molière.

Tyler's ability as a playwright must be judged by *The Contrast* and by four unpublished manuscripts. The first, bearing two titles, *The Island of Barrataria* [*sic*] and *Tantalization or The Governor of a Day,* is an amusing farce in three acts based upon the second part of *Don Quixote.* Through Sancho Panza, who is made governor of the island for one day and decides the cases brought before him with a shrewd common sense which contrasts sharply with the verbiage of the lawyers, Tyler satirizes cleverly the methods of his own profession. It would act well, though no sure record exists of its production. Three sacred dramas, *The Origin of the Feast of Purim, or The Destinies of Haman and Mordecai; Joseph and His Brethren;* and *The Judgment of Solomon,* are written in blank verse of a flexible and even distinguished character, but could hardly have been placed upon the stage. They represent Tyler as a writer of verse, in which he had a facility that resulted in a large quantity of satiric and occasional poems contributed to periodicals. Practically all of these were printed anonymously and it is not now possible to identify them with surety.

In 1794, Tyler entered into a literary partnership with his friend Joseph Dennie [*q.v.*] under the name of "Colon and Spondee," which proposed to furnish verse and prose of a familiar and satiric nature. Tyler was "Spondee," and the pieces so signed in the *Eagle; or Dartmouth Centinel,* and later in *The New Hampshire Journal; or The Farmers' Weekly Museum,* and probably in the *Portfolio,* are Tyler's. They are clever and to the historian are of value in their description of customs and in their representation of Federalist opinion. The best are probably contained in a collection, *The Spirit of the Farmers' Museum* (1801). In more serious vein his long reflective poem, *The Chestnut Tree,* written in 1824 but not published until 1931, is of importance not only for its picture of the village life of his time, but also for its prophecies of the results of the machine age.

More important than Tyler's fugitive verse was his novel *The Algerine Captive,* published in 1797 and republished in London in 1802. Through the career of the hero of this picaresque story, Dr. Updike Underhill, Tyler satirizes college education and medical quackery in the North, and slavery in the South; then, through the capture of Underhill by the Algerines, he paints the miseries of prisoners in that country. One of his uncles had indeed been lost in that manner, and, though Tyler's picture is imaginary, it is vivid. In fact, his fancy was so fertile that his *Yankey in London* (1809), a series of letters supposed to be written by an American living there, deceived some of the English critics.

Tyler's literary work did not interrupt his professional career. It was disturbed, however, by that curious melancholy which had visited him earlier and which apparently caused him to retire from Boston in 1791 and begin his career again in Guildford, Vt. Perhaps some explanation may be found in the charming diary of Mary Palmer, who, against his mother's opposition, became his wife in 1794. He held many professional positions of distinction, being state's attorney for Windham County, 1794–1801; side or assistant judge, 1801–07; and chief justice of the supreme court of Vermont, 1807–13. He was also professor of jurisprudence at the University of Vermont from 1811 to 1814, and trustee from 1802 to 1813. Indeed the only publication in book form in which his name is printed is his two-volume *Reports of Cases Argued and Determined in the Supreme Court of Judicature of Vermont 1800 to 1803* (1809–10). In his most important decision, rendered in 1802, he stated that since according to the constitution of Vermont no inhabitant could own a slave, the bill of sale could not operate in favor of any master who brought a slave within Vermont territory, and that the question was not affected by the laws of the United States.

Undaunted by suffering during his last few years through cancer of the face, which caused blindness and finally ended fatally, Royall Tyler died in Brattleboro, Vt., where he had been living since 1801. He left a tradition there of charm and high spirit, of energy and versatility. Up to two weeks before his death he had been writing a semi-autobiographical story, "The Bay Boy." His ultimate fame will rest upon *The Contrast* and *The Algerine Captive,* pioneer achievements in drama and fiction, to neither of which did he permit his name to be attached.

[Biographical details are based on an unpublished manuscript memoir by Rev. Thomas P. Tyler, son of Royall Tyler, in the Vt. Hist. Soc.; and on *Grandmother Tyler's Book* (1925), the autobiography of Mary Palmer Tyler, ed. by Frederick Tupper and Helen Tyler Brown. The Tyler papers have been deposited in the Vt. Hist. Soc. by Miss Brown, great-granddaughter of Tyler, who has in preparation a biography with A. W. Peach and H. S. Wardner, to all of whom the present writer is indebted. A brief account by Miss Brown is given as an introduction to the limited edition of *The Contrast* (1920). See also B. H. Hall, *Hist. of Eastern Vt.* (1858); M. R. Cabot, *Annals of Brattleboro* (2 vols., 1921); Henry Burnham, *Brattleboro, Vt.* (1880); Frederick Tupper, "Royall Tyler, Man of Law and Man of Letters," *Proc. Vt. Hist. Soc.* (1928); H. M. Ellis, *Joseph Dennie and His Circle* (1915); A. H. Quinn, *A Hist. of the Am. Drama from the Beginning to the Civil War* (1923).]

A. H. Q.

TYLER, SAMUEL (Oct. 22, 1809–Dec. 15, 1877), lawyer, writer, the elder son of Grafton and Anne (Plummer) Tyler, was born in the Forest of Prince Georges County, Md., on the Patuxent River tobacco plantation which had been owned by his paternal ancestors since 1660. After a classical education in the academy of Dr. James Carnahan [*q.v.*] at Georgetown, D. C., he attended Middlebury College, Vt. (1826–28) and studied law in the office of John Nelson in Frederick, Md., where he was admitted to the bar in 1831 and practised for thirty-five years. Though often in court in this period, he was more an office lawyer than an advocate. To the quiet of the office and the seclusion of the library his scholarly temperament inclined him, and from the boundless book-learning he acquired therein his principal achievements in the legal field resulted. On the ancient refinements of the adjective law he became an especial authority, and in 1852 the Maryland legislature appointed him one of three commissioners to simplify the practice and pleading in the various courts of the state. In the allotment of work among the commissioners his particular task was the reform of preliminary procedure; when his recommendations therefor were accepted he drew up a statute incorporating them (*Laws Made and Passed by the General Assembly of . . . Maryland,* 1856, ch. 112) and subsequently published *A Treatise on the Mary-land Simplified Preliminary Procedure and Pleading* (1857), thus rendering invaluable service to the administration of justice and to the legal profession in the state.

Meanwhile, through articles on logic and metaphysics which he contributed to the *Princeton Review* he gained the approval of Europe and the esteem and correspondence of Sir William Hamilton, celebrated philosopher of the Scottish school of Realism. Several of these papers were collected under the titles *A Discourse of the Baconian Philosophy* (1844) and *The Progress of Philosophy in the Past and in the Future* (1858), and brought him certain academic honors, yet he contributed nothing original to the history of thought and his works on the subject have been long since consigned to the philosophic potter's field.

Abandoning active practice, he lectured from 1867 until his death as professor of law in Columbian (now George Washington) University in Washington, D. C., and during these years published the works that more than any others have caused the survival of his name. His American edition (1871) of H. J. Stephen's *Treatise on the Principles of Pleading* and his *Commentary on the Law of Partnership* (1877), both elementary works for students, are still in frequent use. His authorized *Memoir of Roger Brooke Taney, LL.D.* (1872), notwithstanding the fact that it is an undiluted panegyric of his most intimate friend and a partisan defense of the cause of the Confederacy, long remained the standard biography of the Chief Justice. Indeed, the fragment of Taney autobiography and the anecdotes contained therein would seem to assure its permanence as a source book. Other minor works from his pen were *Robert Burns as a Poet and as a Man* (1848) and *The Theory of the Beautiful* (1873). Tyler was tall, lean, dark, bookish, something of a recluse, but jovial. He died at Georgetown, D. C., and was buried there in Oak Hill Cemetery. His wife, Catherine M. Bayly, whom he married at Frederick, Apr. 16, 1833, and two of their four children survived him.

[Sources include records in the possession of a descendant, Miss Dorothy F. Williams, Chicago, Ill.; Frederick County Marriage Record, 1778–1865, Clerk's office, Frederick, Md.; *Washington Post*, Dec. 17, 18, 19, 1877; *The Sun* (Baltimore), Dec. 17, 19, 1877; E. A. and G. L. Duyckinck, *Cyc. of Am. Lit.* (1875), II, 382; *The Biblical Repertory and Princeton Rev. Index Vol.* (1871); list of other periodical contributions in S. A. Allibone, *A Critical Dict. of Eng. Lit. and British and Am. Authors* (1871); review by Moorfield Storey of *Memoir of Roger Brooke Taney* in *North Am. Rev.*, Jan. 1873. The date of Tyler's death is often given erroneously as Dec. 15, 1878.]
J. J. D.

TYLER, WILLIAM (June 5, 1806–June 18, 1849), Roman Catholic prelate, son of Noah and Abigail (Barber) Tyler, was born at Derby, Vt., from which his parents soon removed to a small farm near Claremont, N. H. The family of the Rev. Daniel Barber (brother of Abigail Tyler) became famous in Catholic circles as the first family of Puritan stock to be converted to Catholicism, the Rev. Daniel and his wife entering the church, their two sons becoming Jesuits, their four daughters Ursuline nuns, and their daughter-in-law a Visitation nun. About 1821 the Tylers were also converted. William was educated in the classical school at Claremont conducted by his cousin, the Rev. Virgil H. Barber. As a convert, and a promising youth of sound training and musical ability, Tyler challenged the attention of Bishop Benedict J. Fenwick [*q.v.*], who took him into his household and instructed him in theology (1826), and apparently sent him to a seminary in Montreal for a brief sojourn. Ordained a priest by Fenwick (June 3, 1829), Father Tyler rejoiced in seeing four sisters join the Sisters of Charity, though his three brothers continued in the world. As perverts, the Tylers aroused some Protestant hostility, but, on the whole, Tyler found no unusual difficulties as a curate at the cathedral in Boston or as a missionary at Canton and Sandwich, Mass., and at Aroostook and Benedicta, Fenwick's Catholic colony, in Maine. A tall, slender, delicate man, his quiet meekness, saintly zeal, methodical life, and humility disarmed criticism, and won the affection of Irish immigrants who were ordinarily suspicious of Yankee priests. As a priest at the cathedral, he made missionary tours of the countryside and visits to the shanty-chapels on public works, and served as vicar-general of the diocese.

At the Fifth Provincial Council of Baltimore, the bishops petitioned Rome to erect a new see at Hartford, Conn., with Tyler as bishop. Consecrated by Fenwick (Mar. 17, 1844), Tyler found that southern New England was even less fertile soil for Catholicism than Massachusetts. As Hartford was a small town with only a wooden church, he moved his headquarters to Providence, with a Catholic population of 2,000. There he lived in a wretched cottage, but, aided by gifts from the Leopoldine Society of Vienna and the Society for the Propagation of the Faith of Lyons, he managed to enlarge his Cathedral of SS. Peter and Paul into one of the best churches in New England (1847). With assistance from All Hallows Seminary, Dublin, and with the beginning of Irish immigration on a large scale, the little diocese of 10,000 doubled its population and increased the number of its priests from six to fourteen. Constant crusading against liquor sellers and intemperance resulted in a reformation of conduct, but made Tyler rather unpopular among wealthy Catholics of Providence (*American Catholic Historical Researches,* Jan. 1895). While he built only four primitive churches and made a contribution that seems intangible and undramatic, he quietly laid the foundations of the church in an unfriendly region with a minimum of nativist friction. In summary of his character, Bishop John Bernard Fitzpatrick [*q.v.*] of Boston confided to his diary that though Tyler was neither learned nor brilliant, he was a model for young priests because he was a firm, diligent man of sound prudence, who squandered no time from his duty.

[L. M. Wilson, *Barber Geneal.* (1909); R. H. Clarke, *Lives of the Deceased Bishops of the Cath. Church in the U. S.,* vol. II (1888); William Byrne, *The Hist. of the Cath. Church in the New Eng. States* (1899), vol. II, p. 122; *Cath. Encyc.,* vol. VII (1910), p. 144; Louis de Goesbriand, *Cath. Memoirs of Vt. and N. H.* (1891); T. S. Duggan, *The Cath. Church in Conn.* (1930); *Metropolitan Cath. Directory* (1850), p. 216; *Cath. Observer* (Boston) and *Pilot* (Boston), June 1849; obituary in *Republican Herald* (Providence, R. I.), June 20, 1849.] R.J.P.

TYLER, WILLIAM SEYMOUR (Sept. 2, 1810–Nov. 19, 1897), college professor, was the eldest of three sons of Joab and Nabby (Seymour) Tyler, and a descendant of Job Tyler, an early settler of Andover, Mass. He was born in Harford, Pa., a pioneer village in the beechwood forests along the Susquehanna, where his father and grandfather, natives of Attleboro, Mass., had been among the earliest settlers. As a boy he learned the frugal, industrious habits, the sturdy self-reliance, and the intense aspirations of a New England community transplanted into the wilderness. His education, begun in the schoolroom under his father's roof, was intermittently continued at various local academies and under the tutelage of neighboring ministers. He entered the junior class at Hamilton College in September 1827, but left to teach school after completing one term. In February 1829 he joined the junior class at Amherst College, where he graduated as valedictorian in 1830. There followed one year of teaching at Amherst Academy, two years of theological study at Andover interrupted by two years as a tutor in Amherst College, and a final year of divinity under the Rev. Thomas H. Skinner of New York. Tyler was then ready to become a home missionary in the West, but was recalled to Amherst unexpectedly to fill a tutorship vacated by his brother. At the end of his term (August 1836) he was appointed professor of Latin and Greek, and remained in the active service of the college—as Williston Professor of Greek from 1847—for fifty-six years. In 1893 he became professor emeritus.

Within this exceptionally long term of active service, which was only twice interrupted by periods of travel in Europe and the Holy Land, Tyler taught every member of fifty-one successive classes, until in 1888 Greek was made an optional study. His conception of Greek civilization as a dramatic moment in the unfolding of human nature's highest possibilities so vitalized his treatment of ancient literature that his students often felt that they were hearing the authentic voice of Demosthenes or Plato. Besides performing countless services for the college outside the range of his classroom duties, Tyler was ceaselessly interested in the religious and educational affairs of western Massachusetts. He was ordained to the Congregational ministry at North Amherst on Oct. 16, 1859, and frequently supplied pulpits in nearby towns. His activity at convocations was so great that he was playfully called the bishop of Hampshire County. His sermons from the college pulpit were remembered by generations of undergraduates because of their pointed applications and robust fervor. Tyler was chiefly responsible for framing the constitution and policy of Williston Seminary, and was president of its board of trustees from its foundation. He was also a trustee of Mount Holyoke Seminary (later College) from 1862, and of Smith College from 1871, and president of the board of trustees of both institutions. He was a founder of the Amherst chapter of Phi Beta Kappa and its first president, and a member of many national societies concerned with the study of classical philology and archeology.

Tyler was married on Sept. 4, 1839, to Amelia O. Whiting of Binghamton, N. Y. They had four sons, all graduates of Amherst; one became a professor of Greek in Smith College and one returned to Amherst as professor of biology. The Tyler home inevitably became a center of pilgrimage for visiting dignitaries and alumni. In spite of the many calls upon his time, however, Tyler worked untiringly as a scholar, editing numerous Latin and Greek authors for classroom use, writing popular or learned articles for magazines and encyclopedias, and composing the sermons, occasional discourses, and memorial addresses that were constantly demanded of him. His finest book was a labor of love, the *History of Amherst College during its First Half Century* (1873), later abridged and continued as *A History of Amherst College during the Administrations of its First Five Presidents* (1895), to the writing of which the author brought both an intimate knowledge of personalities and events and the deep feeling of consecration characteristic of the founders of the college. More than any other one man Tyler had given himself to the making of Amherst College, and his history of its achievement is his best monument.

[*Autobiog. of William Seymour Tyler* (1912), ed. by C. B. Tyler; W. I. T. Brigham, *The Tyler Geneal.* (2 vols., 1912); *Obit. Record Grads. Amherst Coll.*, vol. IV (1898); *Amherst Coll. Biog. Record* (1927); *Springfield Republican*, Nov. 20, 1897.]   G. F. W.

TYNDALE, HECTOR (Mar. 24, 1821–Mar. 19, 1880), merchant, Union soldier, was the son of Robinson and Sarah (Thorn) Tyndale. His father, who was reputed to be a lineal descendant of William Tyndale the Bible translator and martyr, had emigrated from Ireland to Philadelphia early in the nineteenth century and become a dealer in china and glass; his mother was a Philadelphian by birth and a member of the Society of Friends. Young Tyndale was educated at a Philadelphia school, upon leaving which he was offered an appointment to the United States Military Academy. Yielding to the wishes of his mother he declined the appointment, and went into business with his father. In August 1842 he married Julia Nowlen, and, at the death of his father in 1845, he and his brother-in-law, Edward P. Mitchell, formed a partnership in the business of importing glass. He subsequently made numerous trips to Europe, visiting the leading factories there, collecting many specimens of pottery, and becoming an authority in the field of ceramics.

A Free-soiler in politics, he affiliated himself with the rising Republican party, and served as a member of the first Republican committee in Philadelphia. In 1859 the wife of John Brown stopped at Philadelphia on her way to Charles Town, Va. (now W. Va.), to visit her imprisoned husband, and, after his execution, to bring his body North for burial. Tyndale believed her to be in such personal danger at that time that he voluntarily served as her escort. He was never an abolitionist, but years after this incident occurred his political enemies accused him of disloyalty to the Union because of his gallant gesture in behalf of a defenseless woman.

Tyndale was in Paris at the outbreak of the Civil War. He immediately hastened home, and in June 1861 was commissioned major of the 28th Regiment, Pennsylvania Volunteers. This regiment participated in a total of forty-three engagements during the war, Tyndale taking part in practically all of them. He commanded the forces near Harpers Ferry in August 1861, and at that time received several wounds. In April 1862 he was promoted lieutenant-colonel. He

next served in Banks's Corps in the Shenandoah Valley campaign, and under Pope in the battles of Chantilly and second Bull Run. At Antietam, where three horses were shot from under him, he was twice wounded and left on the field for dead. Because of his conspicuous bravery at that battle he was promoted brigadier-general, Nov. 29, 1862. He subsequently went to the support of Thomas at Chattanooga; led a bayonet charge to relieve Geary at Wauhatchie, Tenn.; distinguished himself at Missionary Ridge; and, with Sherman, participated in the campaign to relieve Knoxville. With health seriously impaired by disease and strenuous campaigning, he resigned from the service in August 1864. He was brevetted major-general the following March for gallant and meritorious service during the war.

As a civilian, Tyndale was highly esteemed. He was a successful merchant; a member of many patriotic and scientific societies; and, as the Republican candidate for mayor of Philadelphia in 1868, was defeated by a narrow margin. He was trustee of a fund which provided a number of university scholarships in physics, and one of these, at the University of Pennsylvania, bears his name. He died in Philadelphia; his wife, but no children, survived him.

[John McLaughlin, *A Memoir of Hector Tyndale* (1882); *Re-union of the 28th and 147th Regiments, Pa. Volunteers* (1872); F. B. Heitman, *Hist. Reg. and Dict. U. S. Army* (1903); *Public Ledger* (Phila.) and *Phila. Press*, Mar. 20, 1880; *Phila. Record*, Mar. 22, 1880; *N. Y. Tribune*, Mar. 21, 1880; *Pa. Mag. of Hist. and Biog.*, Jan. 1916, pp. 1–3; *Univ. of Pa. Cat.*, *1931–32* (1931), p. 163.]   R. W. I.

TYNG, EDWARD (1683–Sept. 8, 1755), naval officer, was born in Boston, Mass., the grandson of Edward Tyng who came to Massachusetts from England about 1630 and died in Dunstable in 1681, and the son of Col. Edward Tyng, whose wife was a daughter of Ensign Thaddeus Clarke of Portland, Me. The father was appointed governor of Annapolis Royal, Nova Scotia, and on his way to the colony was captured by the French and taken to France, where he died in prison. In 1736 in consideration of the sufferings and great expense of the father the Massachusetts General Court granted the son a tract of land (*The Acts and Resolves of the Province of the Massachusetts Bay*, vol. XII, 1904, pp. 325, 462). As a youth Edward followed the sea and later was a merchant in Boston. His first wife, whom he married Jan. 8, 1725, was Elizabeth, daughter of Capt. Cyprian Southack [*q.v.*] and widow of Francis Parnel; his second, a sister of Gen. Samuel Waldo [*q.v.*], Ann Waldo, to whom he was married Jan. 27, 1731, and by whom he had seven children.

On Apr. 16, 1740, Governor Belcher appointed Tyng captain of the batteries and fortifications in Boston and a few months later made him commander of the province snow *Prince of Orange*, recently built for the protection of the navigation and trade of the colony. During 1741–43 Tyng cruised after Spanish privateers chiefly off the New England coast, but on one cruise he went as far southward as St. Augustine, Fla. On the outbreak of King George's War in 1744, after a chase off Cape Cod of some twelve hours, he overtook a French privateer commanded by Captain Delabroitz and forced her to strike her colors. Out of gratitude Boston voted him its thanks and the merchants of the town presented him with a silver cup. In July he was sent to Annapolis Royal with reinforcements. His arrival there proved most opportune, for the place was besieged by the Indians and French, who fled on his approach, to the great relief of the besieged. For the rest of the year he was employed in convoy duty off the New England coast and to the eastward as far as the Grand Banks. Early in 1745 he was promoted to the command of the frigate *Massachusetts*, in which vessel, alone or in company with provincial or Royal vessels, he cruised after French ships. He was also employed in blockade and transport duties. As senior officer of the Massachusetts navy, he participated in the taking of the *Vigilante*, of 64 guns, the capture of Louisbourg, and the destruction of St. Ann. He was one of the leading American naval officers of the colonial period. His death occurred at Boston, after a stroke of paralysis. His residence was on Milk Street and he also owned property on Fleet Street and near Windmill Point.

[*Mass. Hist. Soc. Colls.*, 1 ser. X (1809), 180–83; Timothy Alden, *A Coll. of Am. Epitaphs* (1814), II, 97–101; Elias Nason, *A Hist. of the Town of Dunstable* (1877); Waldo Lincoln, *The Province Snow "Prince of Orange"* (1901); S. G. Drake, *A Particular Hist. of the Five Years' French and Indian War* (1870); L. E. de Forest, *Louisbourg Journals, 1745* (1932); H. M. Chapin, *Privateering in King George's War* (1928); *A Report of the Record Commissioners of the City of Boston* (1898), containing Boston marriages, 1700–1751; Justin Winsor, *The Memorial Hist. of Boston*, vol. II (1882).]   C.O.P.

TYNG, STEPHEN HIGGINSON (Mar. 1, 1800–Sept. 3, 1885), Episcopal clergyman, born at Newburyport, Mass., was the fourth child of Dudley Atkins, who adopted the name of Tyng on inheriting the estate of his kinswoman, Sarah (Tyng) Winslow. He was a descendant of Joseph Atkins, who came to Newbury, Mass., in 1728, and also of Edward Tyng, who died in Dunstable, Mass., in 1681. Stephen's mother, Sarah, was the eldest daughter of the Hon. Stephen Higginson of Salem, Mass., a descendant

of Francis Higginson [*q.v.*], one of the founders of Salem in 1629. After attending private schools young Tyng entered Harvard College, where he was graduated at the age of seventeen. Two years later he abandoned an unusually promising business career to prepare for the ministry of the Episcopal Church and studied theology under the direction of the Rt. Rev. Alexander V. Griswold [*q.v.*]. He was ordered deacon on Mar. 4, 1821, by Bishop Griswold, whose daughter, Anne, he married on Aug. 5 of that year; he was ordained priest in 1824 by Bishop Kemp of Maryland. His fifty-seven years of active ministry were spent at St. John's Church, Georgetown, D. C. (1821–23); Queen Anne's Parish, Prince Georges County, Md. (1823–29); St. Paul's Church, Philadelphia (1829–34); Church of the Epiphany, Philadelphia (1834–45) and St. George's Church, New York (1845–78).

Tyng was one of the outstanding figures in religious circles. He was a man of imperious temper—which he did not always control—and of commanding personality; he did not take kindly to opposition and was at times autocratic. He was described as "the prince of platform orators" and Henry Ward Beecher said of him, "He is the one man that I am afraid of. When he speaks first I do not care to follow him" (T. L. Cuyler, *Recollections of a Long Life*, 1902, p. 200). He shared with the Rev. Dr. Francis Lister Hawks [*q.v.*] the distinction of being the greatest preacher in the Episcopal Church. Noted for his fearlessness in the pulpit, at times he rose to great heights of eloquence and moved his hearers like a wind-swept sea. Vast congregations flocked to hear him; St. Paul's Church in Philadelphia, when he was rector, was popularly known as "Tyng's Theatre." He was one of the first to recognize the importance of Sunday schools and his own school in Philadelphia had more than two thousand children. This work in religious education he continued in New York, and under his direction St. George's parish was the first to establish mission chapels for the poor on the East Side of the city.

Tyng's ministry covered a period of great importance in the development of the Episcopal Church in the United States. At the outset the Evangelicals were dominant. That dominance was challenged by the high churchmen who were profoundly influenced by the Tractarian movement. The development of ritual in the services of the church followed. A few years after he went to St. George's, broad churchmanship became dominant under the leadership of men like Phillips Brooks and David H. Greer [*qq.v.*]. Against all these developments Tyng set his face like steel; he was a typical low churchman. Trained in the straitest school of the Evangelicals, he never faltered in his allegiance; broad churchman was just as obnoxious to him as high churchman, and both he fought tooth and nail. He was content to walk in the old paths. In his early ministry in Maryland he crossed swords with Bishop James Kemp and in his later years in New York he entered the lists against Bishop Horatio Potter. Like Bishop Manton Eastburn of Massachusetts, Tyng never changed a theological opinion, with the unhappy result that he never rose above the position of being the leader of a party in the church.

Among his publications were *Lectures on the Law and the Gospel* (3rd ed., 1844), *Recollections of England* (1847), *The Israel of God* (1849), *Christ Is All* (1849), *Christian Titles* (1853), *Fellowship with Christ* (1854), *The Rich Kinsman; the History of Ruth the Moabitess* (1855), *The Captive Orphan; Esther, Queen of Persia* (1860); *Forty Years Experience in Sunday Schools* (1860); *The Spencers, a Story of Home Influence* (1869). He also served as an editor of the *Episcopal Recorder* (Philadelphia), and of the *Protestant Churchman* (New York). He resigned the rectorship of St. George's, New York, in 1878 and was made rector emeritus. The closing years of his life were marked by mental decline, and he died at Irvington-on-Hudson, N. Y. His first wife died in 1832, and in July 1833 he married Susan Mitchell. He had four children by his first wife, and five by his second.

[F. H. Atkins, *Joseph Atkins, the Story of a Family* (1891); C. R. Tyng, *Record of the Life and Work of the Rev. Stephen Higginson Tyng, D.D., and Hist. of St. George's Church, N. Y., to the Close of His Rectorship* (1890); Henry Anstice, *Hist. of St. George's Church in the City of N. Y.* (1911); *Churchman*, Sept. 12, 1885; *N. Y. Tribune*, Sept. 5, 1885.]   E. C. C.

TYSON, GEORGE EMORY (Dec. 15, 1829–Oct. 18, 1906), whaler, Arctic explorer, was born at Red Bank, N. J., son of Peter and Clarica Tyson. In his infancy his parents moved to New York City, where he attended the public schools and afterwards worked in an iron foundry. An early interest in Arctic adventure led him in February 1850 to ship from New London in the whaler *M'Clellan*, and he was one of twelve volunteers from the ship who wintered in 1851–52 in Cumberland Sound. He rose to mate and master, and in 1860–70 was steadily engaged in command of Arctic whalers, taking the *Antelope* in 1864 to Repulse Bay, furthest north for whaleships of the time. He had frequently met the explorer Charles Francis Hall [*q.v.*], and in 1870 was invited by Hall to be sailing-master and ice-

pilot in his projected Arctic expedition in the *Polaris*. Though at first prevented by other engagements, he finally joined in a specially created post as assistant navigator. With seven officers, three scientists, and fifteen seamen, the *Polaris* left Brooklyn, June 29, 1871, and after making a furthest north record (82° 11') wintered in Hall Basin, North Greenland. Hall died in November. In the ensuing period, marked by much friction and indiscipline, Tyson, now second in command, was apparently a neutral and stabilizing influence. In subsequent investigations his honesty and modesty were recognized, as well as his stamina and temperamental fitness for Arctic hardships. Capt. Edwin White, a fellow whaler, described him as "the best man to consult with that I have ever met . . . his power of endurance ahead of anyone I ever traveled with" (*Arctic Experiences, post*, p. 423). In the autumn of 1872, on Oct. 15, the *Polaris,* endeavoring to work southward and leaking badly, was nearly crushed by ice. Having built a storehouse on the ice, Tyson and others were shifting supplies to it when the ship broke loose in the darkness, leaving nineteen of them—Tyson, the meteorologist Meyers, eight seamen, and two Eskimos with their wives and five children—adrift on the floe. Their ensuing experience is among the most extraordinary in Arctic annals. For six and a half months they drifted southward through winter darkness, dependent for food chiefly on the desperate efforts of the Eskimo hunters, and forced toward the last to shift from floe to floe and cling to their boat to prevent its being washed away by stormy seas. Without a life lost, they were picked up, Apr. 30, 1873, by the sealer *Tigress* off Labrador.

Later that year Tyson was made temporary lieutenant and ice-master in the *Tigress,* purchased by the United States Navy, and sent north to seek the remaining *Polaris* party, who, it was learned later, had left her and been rescued by a whaler. In 1877–78 he also commanded the *Florence,* sent to the Arctic to establish a preliminary base for the Howgate expedition, subsequently abandoned. During his later years he lived in Washington, D. C., where he had a position as captain of the guard in the Navy Department. He was married, probably about 1870, to Helen (McElroy) Myers, a widow with three sons.

[*Arctic Experiences: Containing Capt. George E. Tyson's Wonderful Drift on the Ice-Floe, A History of the Polaris Expedition* (1874), ed. by E. V. Blake; C. H. Davis, *Narrative of the North Polar Expedition: U. S. Ship Polaris* (1876); J. E. Nourse, *Narrative of the Second Polar Expedition Made by Charles F. Hall* (1879), being *Sen. Exec. Doc. 27, 45 Cong., 3 Sess.*; *The Cruise of the Florence* (1879) ed. by H. W. Howgate; *Who's Who in America*, 1903–05; obituary articles in *Washington Post*, Oct. 20, 21, 1906.]

A. W—t.

TYSON, JAMES (Oct. 26, 1841–Feb. 21, 1919), physician and teacher, was born in Philadelphia, Pa., the son of Dr. Henry Tyson and Gertrude (Haviland) Caswell Tyson. His father, who practised medicine in Reading, Pa., was a direct descendant of Cornelius Teisen of Germantown (born in Crefeld), one of the many Germans who emigrated to America from the Palatinate about the beginning of the eighteenth century. After getting his schooling at the Friends' Central School in Philadelphia, Tyson entered Haverford College, from which he received the degrees of A.B. (1861) and A.M. (1864). He studied medicine in the medical department of the University of Pennsylvania and was graduated in 1863. During his last year in the medical school he was a medical cadet in the United States army hospital at Broad and Cherry Streets, Philadelphia. After his graduation he served as an acting assistant surgeon in the United States Army until July 1863, when he resigned to become resident physician in the Pennsylvania Hospital. Later he again became an acting assistant surgeon in the army, serving in that capacity until the close of the Civil War. He then entered into private practice in Philadelphia. In 1868 began his long association with the University of Pennsylvania. He was lecturer on microscopy (1868), on urinary chemistry (1870), and on pathological anatomy and histology (1874), professor of general pathology and morbid anatomy (1876), and professor of clinical medicine (1889). In 1899 he succeeded the younger William Pepper [*q.v.*] in the chair of medicine, which he held until 1910, when he was retired as emeritus professor of medicine. From 1888 to 1892 he was dean of the medical faculty. He was on the staffs of many hospitals, including the Pennsylvania and the Philadelphia, and was one of the incorporators and very active in the affairs of the Rush Hospital for Consumptives. He was consulting physician to St. Mary's Hospital, the Kensington Hospital for Women, and the Jewish Hospital.

He was a frequent contributor to periodical medical literature and the author of a number of successful books: *The Cell Doctrine, Its History and Present State* (1870), *A Guide to the Practical Examination of Urine* (1875), *A Treatise on Bright's Disease and Diabetes* (1881), *Manual of Physical Diagnosis* (1891), and *The Practice of Medicine* (1896), all of which went through several editions. For some years he was an assistant editor of the *Philadelphia Medical*

Times and a member of the editorial board of the *Philadelphia Medical News*; from 1871 to 1877 he edited the *Transactions* of the Pathological Society of Philadelphia. Tyson served as president of the Philadelphia County Medical Society (1897), the Pathological Society of Philadelphia (1882–84), the College of Physicians of Philadelphia (1907–10), and the Pennsylvania State Medical Society (1911). He was one of the founders of the Association of American Physicians (1886), its first secretary, and in 1907 its president. In 1887 he was elected a member of the American Philosophical Society. For some years he was recorder of the biological and microscopical section of the Academy of Natural Sciences of Philadelphia. In 1894 an undergraduate society, named in his honor the James Tyson Medical Society, was founded among the medical classes at the University of Pennsylvania. On Dec. 5, 1865, Tyson married Frances Bosdevex, of Belgian descent. They had a son, who became a physician, and a daughter. There are excellent oil paintings of Tyson at the University of Pennsylvania and in the College of Physicians of Philadelphia.

[J. W. Jordan, *Colonial and Revolutionary Families of Pa.* (1911), vol. I; *Who's Who in America*, 1918–19; M. H. Fussell, in *Trans. Coll. of Physicians of Phila.*, 3 ser., vol. XLIII (1921); *Jour. Am. Medic. Asso.*, Mar. 3, 1919; *Medic. Record* (N. Y.), and *N. Y. Medic. Jour.*, Mar. 1, 1919; obituary in *Pub. Ledger* (Phila.), Feb. 22, 1919; personal acquaintance; autobiog. notes in MS. in the possession of Mrs. H. W. Stokes of Phila., Tyson's daughter; information from Mrs. Stokes.]   F. R. P.

TYSON, JOB ROBERTS (Feb. 8, 1803–June 27, 1858), lawyer, congressman, historical writer, was born in or near Philadelphia, the son of Joseph and Ann (Trump) Tyson and a descendant of Reynier Tyson who settled in what is now Germantown, Pa., in 1683. Joseph Tyson, a Philadelphia merchant, started his son on a business career, but the youth turned to school teaching and the study of law, and in 1827 was admitted to the bar. On Oct. 4, 1832, he married Eleanor, daughter of Thomas P. Cope [*q.v.*], a prominent Philadelphia merchant and philanthropist. He was vice-provost of the Philadelphia Law Academy, 1833–58; a solicitor of the Pennsylvania Railroad, 1847–55; an early director of the Philadelphia public schools; a member of the Select Council of Philadelphia, 1846–49; and a Whig congressman for one inconspicuous term, 1855–57. He was an effective writer and an excellent speaker; a score or more of his speeches were printed. Participating actively in the reforms of the thirties, he was a friend of temperance and a foe of lotteries. He hoped to solve the slavery problem by colonization, served in the ranks of the Society for Alleviating the Miseries of Public Prisons, and drafted a report on the impropriety of capital punishment. He was a manager of the Apprentices' Library in Philadelphia, and a trustee of Girard College and of the Pennsylvania Female College. On Jan. 15, 1836, he was elected a member of the American Philosophical Society.

His greatest interest was history. One of the early members of the Historical Society of Pennsylvania and an officer from 1829 to 1848, he was among the first to grasp the importance of intensive study of Pennsylvania history. The Indians, the Revolution, the social and intellectual state of Penn's colony, the life of William Penn, the history of art in America, were objects of his study. In his *Discourse . . . on the Colonial History of the Eastern and Some of the Southern States* (1842), also published in *Memoirs of the Historical Society of Pennsylvania* (vol. IV, pt. 2, 1850), he attacked New England historians for their claims, denying that enlarged social freedom owed its existence to the Puritans and maintaining rather that it triumphed in spite of their hostility, and that Penn's contribution to liberty was more significant. This paper marks him as a pioneer in readjusting the balance of historical interpretation. The most tangible results of his historical interest are the first volumes of the printed archives of Pennsylvania. As a member of a joint committee of the Philosophical and Historical societies he was instrumental in petitioning the legislature (1836) to provide for the printing of the archives, and his brother, J. Washington Tyson, as chairman of a committee of the legislature, reported favorably upon the project. Thus a beginning was made with three volumes (1838–40) containing the minutes of the Provincial Council, and the series has been continued intermittently ever since. Tyson planned to write a history of the state, but died before he could make systematic use of his collected material.

[F. W. Leach, "Old Philadelphia Families—The Tyson Family," *North American* (Phila.), July 21, 1912; H. L. Carson, "A History of the Historical Society of Pennsylvania" (MSS. in Hist. Soc. of Pa. and Free Library of Phila.) ; *Biog. Dir. Am. Cong.* (1928) ; *Dollar Newspaper* (Phila.), June 30, 1858; *North American and United States Gazette* (Phila.), June 28, 1858.]
R. F. N.

TYSON, LAWRENCE DAVIS (July 4, 1861–Aug. 24, 1929), soldier, newspaper publisher, and senator from Tennessee, was born near Greenville, N. C., the son of Richard Lawrence and Margaret Louise (Turnage) Tyson. His ancestors had settled in Pitt County, N. C., about 1720; his father served with the Confederate forces throughout the Civil War. Tyson graduated from the United States Military Academy in 1883, was commissioned lieutenant of the 9th Infantry, and took part in the campaign against the Apache Indians. On Feb. 10, 1886, he married Bettie Humes McGhee, daughter of Charles M. McGhee [*q.v.*], a leading railroad financier of the South. From 1891 to 1895, by appointment of the War Department, he was professor of military science in the University of Tennessee at Knoxville. While here he studied law, receiving the degree of LL.B. in 1894; in April 1896 he resigned his commission in the army and entered on the practice of law in Knoxville. Two years later, during the war with Spain, he was appointed colonel of the 6th United States Volunteer Infantry and served in Puerto Rico; in 1899, after peace was declared, he was for some months military governor of the north-central portion of that island. He was mustered out of the service, May 15, 1899.

Resuming practice in Knoxville, he was elected to the House of Representatives of the Tennessee General Assembly of 1903, and was chosen speaker; he was delegate-at-large to the Democratic National Convention of 1908; and in 1913 was an unsuccessful candidate for the United States senatorship. He served for a number of years as brigadier-general and inspector-general of the Tennessee National Guard. When the United States entered the World War, he was placed by the governor in command of the Tennessee National Guard but in August 1917 was appointed by President Wilson brigadier-general, National Army, and assigned to the 59th Brigade of the 30th Division, at Camp Sevier, S. C. His brigade of 8,000 men, made up in large part of soldiers from Tennessee, embarked for France on May 10, 1918, and in July was sent to join the British forces in Belgium. It was in almost continuous action from July 5 to Oct. 20, 1918, suffering losses of some 3,000 in killed and wounded. Its signal achievement was its participation in the breaking of the Hindenburg line: "The 59th brigade went through the line at St. Quentin tunnel, advancing further to Bellicourt and neighboring towns. This was accomplished in three days of terrific fighting" (Official Records, quoted by Hamer, *post*, p. 23). Tyson subsequently received the Distinguished Service Medal.

Returning to his home in Knoxville, he purchased and became publisher of the Knoxville *Sentinel*. In 1920 he was indorsed by the state Democratic convention for the vice-presidential nomination, but in the Democratic National Convention he withdrew his name and seconded the nomination of Franklin D. Roosevelt. Nominated by a primary election in 1924, he won election as United States senator for the term beginning in 1925. In the Senate he advocated adherence to the World Court and was joint author of the Tyson-Fitzgerald bill which gave full retirement compensation to disabled emergency officers of the United States in the World War. In 1927 he was a delegate to the conference of the Interparliamentary Union held in Paris. He was interested in the larger industrial concerns of his city and region, was president of coal companies and textile mills, and in 1923 was president of the American Cotton Manufacturers' Association. With his wife he gave Tyson Park to the city of Knoxville. He died in Philadelphia, survived by his wife and a daughter; his only son died in the World War.

[P. M. Hamer, *Tenn., A Hist.* (1933), vol. III; W. T. Hale and D. L. Merritt, *A Hist. of Tenn.* (1913), vol. VII; G. W. Cullum, *Biog. Reg. Officers and Grads. U. S. Mil. Acad.*, vols. III (1891), VI (1920), VII (1930); *Who's Who in America*, 1928–29; *Biog. Dir. Am. Cong.* (1928); *Lawrence D. Tyson: Memorial Addresses in the Senate and House of Representatives* (1930); *News-Sentinel* (Knoxville), Aug. 25, 1929; *Knoxville Jour.*, Aug. 24, 25, 1929.]   S. C. W.

TYSON, STUART LAWRENCE (Nov. 12, 1873–Sept. 16, 1932), Protestant Episcopal clergyman, was born in Pennllyn, Pa., the son of Herbert Benezet and Mary (Stuart) Tyson. His father was a nephew of Job Roberts Tyson [*q.v.*] and a descendant of Reynier Tyson who emigrated to Pennsylvania from Crefeld, Prussia, in 1683. Reynier was probably a brother of Cornelius, ancestor of James Tyson [*q.v.*]. After routine schooling, Stuart went to Nashota House, Wisconsin, the Anglo-Catholic seminary of the Episcopal Church, to prepare for the ministry. He was graduated in 1895, and in this same year, Apr. 25, he married Katharine Emily Rosengarten of Philadelphia, who was killed in an accident in 1915. In 1895, also, he was ordained deacon, and two years later, priest. After a brief pastorate in Milwaukee, Wis., he went to Oxford, England, in 1899, where he remained eight years as student at St. John's College, special preacher at the University (1899–1903), assistant at St. Paul's Church (1904–07), and tutor (1903–05). He received three degrees from Oxford—M.A., B.D., and D.D., the last awarded in 1923 "in course."

Tyson returned to America in 1907 to become professor of New Testament at the Western Theological Seminary, Chicago. From here he went in 1908 to the University of the South, where he served five years as professor of New Testament and liturgics. He resigned in 1913 to give his chief time and labor to lecturing under the auspices of the Tyson Lectureship Foundation for the Promotion of Christian Knowledge, an organization of Episcopalian clergymen, laymen, and laywomen which he was instrumental in establishing for the popular interpretation of the Scriptures in the light of scientific truth. In 1919 he accepted appointment as lecturer, special preacher, and honorary vicar at the Cathedral of St. John the Divine, New York. In 1924 he was transferred to the staff of St. George's Church.

This last appointment may be said to mark the climax in the long process of his theological development. Educated in a conservative school, Tyson was led by his Biblical studies, continued through many years, into the liberal wing of contemporary religious thought. His preaching became a vigorous advocacy of liberalism. His lecturing, which long absorbed his best attention, was devoted to expounding the modern significance of the Bible. In the controversies which broke out in the Episcopal Church in the decades before and after the World War, he was a consistent modernist. He sprang quickly to the defense of priests who fell under attack of their bishops for heresy. Thus, in 1914, he was chairman of the Heaton Defense Committee, when the Rev. Lee W. Heaton, a Texas rector, was cited by Bishop Harry T. Moore for trial on charges that he "had denied the supernatural and the divinity of Jesus." Tyson also figured prominently in the cases of Bishop-elect Herbert Shipman and of the Rev. Percy Stickney Grant [*q.v.*]. It was his steadfast contention that clergymen should have full right to "think freely, and to use present-day knowledge in religion as well as in all other relations of life." As the New York diocese fell more and more into the hands of conservatives, it was natural that he should move from the Cathedral to St. George's. A year later (1925) his divorce of his second wife, Anna Gertrude W. Mullins—whom he married Mar. 17, 1917—on grounds of cruelty, created a situation which led to his retirement from the Episcopal ministry. Tyson declared that the resignation, thus precipitated by unhappy outward events, was in reality "the final result of a process" within himself which had begun long before. In 1925 he entered the Congregational ministry, and in his last years was pastor of the Community Church, Summit, N. J., a society composed predominantly of Unitarians and Universalists.

Tyson died in New York after a week's illness from pneumonia. He was survived by his third wife, Margaretta Wentz, whom he married Apr. 18, 1927, and by twelve of thirteen children by

Udden

Uhler

his first wife. He was the author of *The Eucharist in St. Paul* (1923), and numerous lectures, sermons, and articles.

[*Who's Who in America*, 1918–19, 1932–33; *N. Y. Times*, Sept. 17, 1932; *N. Y. Herald Tribune*, Sept. 17, 1932; *Churchman*, Sept. 24, 1932; F. W. Leach, "Old Philadelphia Families—The Tyson Family," *North American* (Phila.), July 21, 1912.] J. H. H.

UDDEN, JOHAN AUGUST (Mar. 19, 1859–Jan. 5, 1932), geologist, was born in Uddabo, Lekasa parish, Vestergötland, Sweden, the son of Andrew Larsen and Inga Lena (Andersdotter) Udden. Two years after his birth his parents emigrated to America, and settled in Minnesota, where Udden spent his early youth. He was graduated with the B.A. degree from Augustana College, Rock Island, Ill., in 1881, studied at the University of Minnesota in 1886, and received the M.A. degree from Augustana in 1889. From 1881 to 1888 he taught natural science, German, and civics at Bethany College, Lindsborg, Kan., and from 1888 to 1911 was professor of geology and natural history at Augustana College. He held membership in several scientific societies, and was a fellow of the American Association for the Advancement of Science. His fields of investigation included stratigraphic and areal geology, work of the atmosphere, till in the upper Mississippi Valley, clastic sediments, and related subjects. His published papers on these subjects number about one hundred titles.

The geologic activities of Udden had far-reaching effects upon the development of both theoretical and economic geology. The qualities of his mind and the circumstances of his early scientific training combined to give him preeminent characteristics as a research geologist. Because of the slight development of specialized geological training in his early school days, he received relatively little professional guidance in the subject. He early determined to rely upon his own powers of observation and reasoning. The richness and originality of his work and the independence of his geological thought are attested by all his principal papers. His study on the "Mechanical Composition of Clastic Sediments," published in the *Bulletin of the Geological Society of America*, Dec. 14, 1914, established an adequate quantitative method of treating the material, and outlined the major features of this early branch of sedimentology.

His active mind was ever alert for the development of new geological methods. He was one of the first in America to point out and stress the value of seismograph observations for locating geologic structure. His work on the technique of examining subsurface material, now universally followed, was purely pioneer research. In Texas he worked on a virgin field with an observant, open, and critical mind, and his labors found their rich reward in the contributions made to the science of geology and to the economic development of the state. In grateful recognition of services that he gave, his many friends joined in establishing in his honor the Johan August Udden Publication and Research Fund of The University of Texas.

Udden was geologist of the Bureau of Economic Geology and Technology of The University of Texas from 1911 to 1915, and director of the Bureau from that time until his death. He was a special assistant with the Iowa Geological Survey, 1897–1903, geologist for the University of Texas Mineral Survey, 1903–04, geologist for the Illinois Geological Survey, 1906–11, and special agent of the United States Geological Survey, 1908–14. His distinguished services were recognized by his native country in 1911, when he was decorated with the Order of the North Star by the king of Sweden. At his death he was survived by his widow, Johanna Kristina Davis, to whom he had been married in 1882, and one of their four children.

[*Who's Who in America*, 1930–31; C. L. Baker, "Memorial of Johan August Udden," *Bull. Geological Soc. of America*, Apr. 30, 1933 (includes a bibliography of Udden's publications); E. H. Sellards, *Bull. Am. Asso. Petroleum Geologists*, Mar. 1932; *Memorial to Dr. Johan August Udden: The Univ. of Tex. Bull.*, No. 3201, Nov. 1932; *Alcalde* (Univ. of Tex.), Mar. 1932; *Dallas Morning News*, Jan. 6, 1932.] E. H. S.

UHLER, PHILIP REESE (June 3, 1835–Oct. 21, 1913), entomologist, librarian, was born in Baltimore, Md., the son of George Washington Uhler, a merchant of that city, and Anna Maria (Reese) Uhler. His great-grandfather, Erasmus Uhler, emigrated to America from England and served as a private in the Revolutionary War. Uhler was educated at the Latin School conducted by Daniel Jones and at Baltimore College. He began to collect insects after his father had bought a farm near Baltimore, and in this he was encouraged by the Rev. John Gottlieb Morris [*q.v.*], a well-known entomologist. One of Uhler's earliest published papers was his "Descriptions of a Few Species of *Coleoptera* Supposed to be New" (*Proceedings of the Academy of Natural Sciences of Philadelphia*, vol. VII, 1856). In 1860 he wrote his first paper on *Hemiptera* (*Ibid.*, vol. XII, 1861), and from that time on for the rest of his life his entomological papers related almost entirely to this group. He described many new forms and had a broad, comprehensive view of the whole complex. In 1861 his *Synopsis of the Neuroptera of North Amer-*

ica, translated from the Latin of Hermann August Hagen, was published by the Smithsonian Institution. In 1863 he was appointed librarian of the Peabody Institute in Baltimore, and early in 1864 was called to Cambridge by J. L. R. Agassiz [*q.v.*], for whom he worked as an assistant and as librarian in the Museum of Comparative Zoology. He taught entomology to some of the Harvard undergraduates and gave a series of lectures in the museum. At the same time he attended lectures at Harvard by Asa Gray, Jeffries Wyman, Agassiz and his son, and Nathaniel Southgate Shaler. He returned to Baltimore in 1867 to become assistant librarian of the Peabody Institute, and in 1870 was made librarian, a position he held for the rest of his life. In addition to his entomological work he wrote several geological papers, and with N. H. Morison he prepared an elaborate catalogue of the Peabody library (5 vols., 1883–92), which was a model of its kind. He was of much assistance in the early days of the Johns Hopkins University and was associate in natural history from 1876 until the last year of his life. He was married in 1869 to Sophia Werdebaugh, who died in 1883; on Apr. 29, 1886, he married Pearl Daniels of Baltimore. He had a son by his first wife and a daughter by his second.

His last entomological paper, "Recognition of Two North American Species of Cicada," published in *Entomological News* in March 1905, completed practically fifty years of active publishing life. He built up a very large collection, which he presented before his death to the United States National Museum. He was a modest man but an excellent speaker, and, like nearly all great naturalists, he was always ready to help younger workers. Probably his last work was done on a monograph of the *Capsidae*, which, although an enormous manuscript accumulated, was never published as a whole. His eyesight failed him almost completely in 1907, and at that time he virtually stopped work. His entomological writings in 1903 covered fifty-two titles. This is not a large number; but his work was careful and sound and broad. For many years he was the leading American worker in a very important group and a world authority on entomology.

[Uhler's middle name appears in the Johns Hopkins official publications as Rhees. For biog. materials, see *Who's Who in America,* 1912–13; L. O. Howard, in *Entomological News,* Dec. 1913; *Proc. Entomological Soc. of Washington,* vol. XVI (1914); obituary in *Sun* (Baltimore), Oct. 22, 1913. A list of his writings appeared in *Psyche,* Feb., Apr. 1903.]   L. O. H.

ULLOA, ANTONIO DE (Jan. 12, 1716–July 5, 1795), first Spanish governor of Louisiana, was born in Seville, Spain, the second son of Bernardo de Ulloa y Sousa, the economist, and his wife, Josefa de la Torre Guiral. He had a long and varied career in the service of the crown —in the navy, in the colonial administration, and on special missions. Several conspicuous failures marred his record, but later investigations always showed that he was the victim either of circumstances beyond his control or of influential officials whose misconduct he tried to correct. Moreover, his failures as an administrator were outweighed by the success of his writings. His two most important works were the result of an expedition to South America (1735–44) which he and Jorge Juan y Santacilia made in company with La Condamine and other French scientists. One of these works, *Relación histórica del viage a la América meridional* (Madrid, 1748), published in English as *A Voyage to South America* (1758), was translated into several other languages and won him an enviable reputation both at home and abroad. The other, a confidential report on conditions in the viceroyalty of Peru written about 1749 in collaboration with Jorge Juan, revealed grave abuses in the Spanish régime and probably stimulated the reform movement already in progress at court. Published with some alterations at London under the title *Noticias Secretas de America* (1826), it is one of the best-known accounts of Spanish America.

At the close of a disastrous administration as governor of Huancavélica (Peru) and superintendent of its important quicksilver mine (1758–64), Ulloa was appointed governor of Louisiana, which had just been ceded to Spain by France. Arriving at New Orleans in March 1766, he found that the resources at his command were utterly inadequate to his needs and throughout the period of his residence there he had to let the last French governor, Aubry, continue to govern the province in the name of the king of Spain. The situation was not only anomalous: it was impossible. In October 1768, the publication of a Spanish order altering the commercial regulations provoked a Creole uprising, and Ulloa was expelled from the province. Though again he appears to have been not wholly responsible for his failure—his government had not supported him properly, and Aubry wrote that the trouble had been brewing for a decade and that a storm was necessary to clear the air—the task of pacifying Louisiana was entrusted to another man, Alejandro O'Reilly [*q.v.*], and Ulloa returned to Spain. His conduct as commander of a squadron in the war with Great Britain (1779) resulted in his being court-martialed (1779–81), but he was vindicated, and during the last years of his life he held high office in the Spanish navy. By his wife, Francisca Ramírez de Laredo, daughter of the Conde de San Javier, he had nine children, one of whom—Francisco Javier de Ulloa—rose to the rank of admiral and secretary of the navy.

[A. P. Whitaker, "Antonio de Ulloa," *Hispanic American Hist. Rev.*, May 1935, with bibliographical references, particularly to Spanish sources; J. W. Caughey, *Bernardo de Gálvez in La.* (1934); J. E. Winston, "The Cause and Results of the Revolution of 1768 in Louisiana," *La. Hist. Quart.*, Apr. 1932; E. W. Lyon, *Louisiana in French Diplomacy* (1934).]

A. P. W—r.

UNANGST, ERIAS (Aug. 8, 1824–Oct. 12, 1903), Lutheran missionary, was born in Easton, Pa., the son of Jacob and Eleanora Unangst. He attended the local schools for several years and in 1847 registered in the academy of Pennsylvania (now Gettysburg) College. In 1854 he received the B.A. degree from the college. He studied at the Lutheran Theological Seminary at Gettysburg thereafter and was ordained to the ministry by the Allegheny Synod in 1857. He then read medicine for several months in preparation for his work as a foreign missionary. On Sept. 24, 1857, he was married to Phebe Ann Miliken, of Lewistown, Pa., and a month later they sailed from Boston for India, where they arrived in April 1858, during the Sepoy rebellion. After thirteen years in India he returned to America on a furlough in 1871, but was called back to the Guntur mission in less than a year. In 1882 he was again in America on a furlough, and again returned to India earlier than he had planned because of the death of a fellow missionary. In 1895, at the age of seventy-one, Unangst returned to America, after having labored in India as a missionary more than thirty-five years. He spent the remainder of his life in Hollidaysburg, Pa., at the home of one of his eight children. His wife had died while engaged in active service in India in 1888.

When Unangst arrived in the Guntur mission field of the General Synod of the Lutheran Church, it had scarcely emerged from the period of its beginnings. He was the connecting link between its founder, John C. F. Heyer [q.v.], and a later generation of missionaries. Accordingly, he had many of the hardships and perplexing responsibilities of the pioneer. At times he worked under great difficulties; once for a period of four years, 1866–70, he was the only missionary in the field. But his patience and zeal, his tact and devotion triumphed, and under his leadership the Guntur mission prospered in spite of obstacles. He had the restless spirit of a creator of new enterprises. He planned and urged

the development of special work among the women of the middle and upper classes, and a similar program for work among the men of these classes. He saw the need of a trained native ministry, and assisted in establishing an institution for that purpose. He excelled as a linguist, both in the original languages of the Bible and in Telugu. For a quarter of a century he was associated with other missionaries of the Telugu country in preparing for the revision of the Telugu translation of the Bible, and in completing the revision. This was done under the Madras Auxiliary Bible Society and the British and Foreign Bible Society. He made several trips to London to meet with the group who were engaged in this enterprise. He published *Historical Sketch of India Missions* in 1879. He also translated hymns into Telugu and wrote several original hymns.

[L. B. Wolf, *After Fifty Years; or, an Hist. Sketch of the Guntur Mission* (1896); A. R. Wentz, *Hist. of the Gettysburg Theological Seminary* (1927); *The Alumni Record of Gettysburg Coll.* (1932); *Luth. Missionary Jour.*, Dec. 1903; *Pittsburg Dispatch*, Oct. 13, 1903.]

S. G. H.

UNCAS (*c.* 1588–*c.* 1683), sachem of the Mohegan Indians, was the son of Oweneco, a Pequot sachem, and of Meekunump, daughter of another Pequot sachem. In 1626 he married a daughter of Sassacus [q.v.], chief sachem of the Pequots, and later a daughter of Sebequanash, a Hammonassett sachem. Rebelling against Sassacus, Uncas was defeated and banished. He fled to the Narragansetts, but later made his peace with his kinsmen and returned to the Pequots. It is said that he rebelled thus more than once. On his final revolt the Pequot territory was divided, and Uncas became ruler of the western part, called Moheag, his tribe becoming known as the Mohegans. He courted the favor of the English and in May 1637, with Miantonomo [q.v.], chief sachem of the Narragansetts, joined them in war on the Pequots. He was not wholly trusted, however, and was accused of harboring the enemy. In June 1638 he went to Boston with an escort of thirty-seven men and offered the Governor a present of wampum, which was refused until he had satisfied the government of his loyalty; he was then given "a fair, red coat" and food for his homeward journey, and "departed very joyful" (*Winthrop's Journal, post,* I, 271). Later that year he signed a treaty of peace with Miantonomo and with the English at Hartford.

In 1643 he complained to the Commissioners of the United Colonies that Miantonomo had hired a Pequot to kill him, and that some of the followers of Sequasson, an undersachem of the Narragansetts, had shot at him as he was going down the Connecticut. An attempt by John

Haynes [*q.v.*], governor at Hartford, to make peace between Uncas and Sequasson failed, and in the war which followed, through treachery, Uncas captured Miantonomo and delivered him to the English at Hartford. The Commissioners of the United Colonies at Boston now gave Uncas permission to kill the Narragansett chief, and agreed to assist him should the Narragansetts make war on him. Accordingly, Miantonomo was killed by a brother of Uncas, and when the Narragansetts demanded satisfaction the English intervened. The peace agreement made in September 1644 was of short duration, however, and in the spring of 1645 Uncas was besieged in his stronghold on the Connecticut by the Narragansett sachem Pessacus and almost forced to surrender, but was saved by the English under Thomas Leffingwell, to whom he gave a grant of the lands forming the site of the present Norwich. Another agreement between the hostile tribes was reached but soon Uncas undertook to chastise a Narragansett sachem for an alleged offense, and thus created further trouble. Ordered to appear before the English at New Haven to answer for his conduct, he acknowledged himself guilty on some points and was released. In July 1647 many Indians brought complaints against him to the United Colonies; one complained that Uncas had captured his wife, and the Commissioners made him give her up; but in answer to the Pequot complaint that he was unjust and had many times over collected the fines due the English, they merely reproved Uncas. In 1661, however, when he made war without cause on Ousamequin or Massasoit [*q.v.*], the good friend of the Massachusetts colony, the English forced him to give up his captives and stolen goods, and in 1675 he was ordered to appear in Boston to surrender his arms and to leave two of his younger sons as hostages to secure his neutrality or cooperation in King Philip's War.

Uncas was tricky, untrustworthy, and dissolute. Daniel Gookin [*q.v.*], governor of the "praying Indians," described him in his late years as "an old and wicked, wilful man, a drunkard, and otherwise very vicious; who has always been an opposer and underminer of praying to God" (*Collections of the Massachusetts Historical Society*, 1 ser. I, 1792, p. 208). The apparent forbearance toward him displayed by the English of Connecticut and Massachusetts was probably owing to the fact that Uncas was neighbor to Connecticut whereas his enemies, the Narragansetts, lived in the much detested colony of Roger Williams.

[*Winthrop's Journal* (2 vols., 1908), ed. by J. K. Hosmer; "Acts of the Commissioners of the United Colonies of New England," *Records of the Colony of New Plymouth*, vols. IX–X (1859), ed. by David Pulsifer; F. M. Caulkins, *Hist. of Norwich, Conn.* (1866); S. G. Drake, *The Book of the Indians* (8th ed., 1841); F. W. Hodge, *Handbook of Am. Indians* (1910).]
J. T. A.

UNDERHILL, FRANK PELL (Dec. 21, 1877–June 28, 1932), pharmacologist, toxicologist, was born in Brooklyn, N. Y., the son of David Bonnett and Emma (Housie) Underhill, and a descendant of the ninth generation from John Underhill [*q.v.*]. After attending the public high school of Norwalk, Conn., his entire academic career was devoted to Yale University, where he received the degrees of Ph.B. in 1900, and Ph.D. in 1903. Until 1918 he was on the staff of the Sheffield Scientific School, where he was associated with Russell H. Chittenden and Lafayette B. Mendel. He was professor of pathological chemistry from 1912 to 1918, held the chair of experimental medicine from 1918 to 1921, and that of pharmacology and toxicology from 1921 until his death. The most significant of his earlier researches pertained to the physiologic action of proteins and tartrates, and to the effects of chemical substances upon the behavior of sugars, salts, and water within the body. With H. Gideon Wells, he was the co-discoverer of tartrate nephritis.

Closely identified with the beginnings of the Chemical Warfare Service, Underhill attained therein the rank of lieutenant-colonel. He was appointed the United States representative to the Interallied Gas Warfare Conference at Paris, in October 1918, and became vice-president of the conference. With a staff of experts he investigated chlorine, phosgene, and chlorpicrin, and detailed their effects upon the animal body in his book, *The Lethal War Gases: Physiology and Experimental Treatment* (1920). These investigations laid bare in striking fashion the significance of bodily water exchange in lethal gas poisoning. A method of treatment for war-gas victims was evolved, based upon blood-letting in the period of blood dilution, and the introduction of fluid during the period of blood concentration. The value of such treatment was fully demonstrated in animals, and Underhill arranged for extensive application on the western front just as the World War closed.

Returning to the Yale University School of Medicine after the war, he next traced a close relationship between war-gas poisoning and the acute devastating form of influenza. In both he regarded water as of prime significance. Still another condition, that of extensive superficial burns, he attacked intensively from a like viewpoint, and discovered the effects of fluid administration to be very beneficial. He described the successful treatment of twenty-one patients seriously burned in a New Haven theatre fire. During his last years, he was deeply interested in pellagra. He investigated this disease in its possible relationships to vitamin deficiencies as well as to a canine condition known as "black tongue."

In person, Underhill was of the scholarly type, reserved and quiet; in action and speech, he was unhurried and certain. He was single in purpose; no compelling hobby distracted him. Throughout his career, he exhibited remarkable and careful industry, a discriminating intellect, and unquestionable scientific honesty. Many research associates and a still greater number of medical and chemical pupils profited by his guidance. The influence of his research contributions, numbering nearly two hundred, has extended throughout the world to benefit workers in widely varying fields, both theoretical and clinical. Among his major works are: *The Physiology of Amino Acids* (1915), *A Manual of Selected Biochemical Methods* (1921), and *Toxicology; Or the Effects of Poisons* (1924, second edition, 1928). He was frequently consulted on commercial questions, and was likewise a very effective medico-legal expert. He was chairman of the committee on biological chemistry of the National Research Council, and an associate editor of *Chemical Abstracts*. His many memberships in medical and other scientific societies included Die Kaiserlich Leopoldinisch-Carolinisch Deutsche Akademie der Naturforscher zu Halle. At his death in New Haven, he was survived by his widow, Lavina Reed Chasmar, of Norwalk, Conn., to whom he had been married on Sept. 2, 1903. Their two children died in infancy.

[*Who's Who in America*, 1932–33; J. C. Frost, *Underhill Genealogy* (1932), vol. III; H. G. Barbour, "The Scientific Activities of Frank Pell Underhill," *Yale Jour. of Biology and Med.*, Mar. 1933 (contains complete bibliography); *Bull. of Yale Univ.*, Oct. 15, 1933; *New Haven Jour.-Courier*, June 29, 1932.] H. G. B.

UNDERHILL, JOHN (c. 1597–Sept. 21, 1672), colonial military leader and magistrate, was a son of John and Honor (Pawley) Underhill originally of Kenilworth, Warwickshire. His father was a military adventurer in the Dutch service, and John, "bred to arms" in the Netherlands, evidently received little education. Influenced by English refugees, he adopted the outward forms of Puritanism, but he displayed little of the moral stamina which characterized the Puritan fathers. When, on Dec. 12, 1628, he married Helena de Hooch he was "a Cadet in the guard" of the Prince of Orange. He was an apt pupil in a great military school.

In 1630 he moved to Boston to help organize the militia of the Massachusetts Bay. The Boston church accepted him (Aug. 27, 1630); the colony appointed him, with Daniel Patrick, captain of the militia, voted him supplies and money, and allotted him land; and, in 1634, the town chose him one of its first selectmen. In colonial military affairs he encountered popular apathy and insufficient supplies, and in an effort to enlarge the military stores he went to England in the winter of 1634–35.

When Indian troubles arose, Underhill helped in avenging Oldham's death at Block Island (August 1636). Lent to Saybrook Plantation in April 1637, he cooperated with Mason's Connecticut forces in destroying Mystic Fort and scattering the Pequots. He might have returned to Massachusetts a hero, had it not been for the bitter theological controversy going on there. Underhill had allied himself with the Antinomians and signed the petition in behalf of the Rev. John Wheelwright [*q.v.*]; the orthodox party was now in control, and Underhill was received as a seditious person. He made the situation worse for himself by imprudent words (*Massachusetts Historical Society Collections,* 4 ser., vol. VII, 1865, pp. 170–74), and was disfranchised, discharged from military service (Nov. 15, 1637), and disarmed (Nov. 20, 1637). Humiliated, he spent the winter of 1637–38 in England and published in 1638 *Newes from America* (reprinted *Ibid.,* 3 ser., vol. VI, 1837), now a classical account of the Pequot troubles. Returning to Boston, he was accused of making contemptuous speeches and was brought before the General Court which, for "his gross & palpable dissimulation & equivocation," banished him (Sept. 6, 1638). He fled to Dover (N. H.) just in time to escape a church trial for adultery.

At Dover, he organized a church of which Hanserd Knollys became pastor, secured the governorship, and scorned Massachusetts' claims upon the region and Boston's summons for a church trial. By publishing their accusations, however, Massachusetts officials so reduced Underhill's Dover adherents that, by October 1639, he begged forgiveness and thereafter, in expiation, supported Massachusetts claims to New Hampshire (*Ibid.,* 4 ser., VII, 178–79). Before the Boston church (Mar. 5, 1640), he confessed to adultery (Records of the First Church of Boston, *post,* p. 13); but his repentance was judged insincere, and he was excommunicated. Subsequently, however, he satisfied the church and on Sept. 3, 1640, he was reinstated (*Ibid.,* p. 15); shortly afterwards (Oct. 7, 1640) the General

Court suspended his sentence of banishment and on June 2, 1641, repealed it.

Offers from New Amsterdam tempted him, but he yielded temporarily to pleas to move to Stamford, Conn., which in 1643 he represented in the New Haven Court. Soon afterwards, being employed by the Dutch to fight Indians, he acquitted himself well, moved to Long Island, and later became member of the Council for New Amsterdam and schout of Flushing. After the Anglo-Dutch war began, he narrowly escaped imprisonment for sedition, because in May 1653 he denounced Stuyvesant's "iniquitous government" for its dealings with the Indians, unjust taxation, and other oppressive measures toward the English. He offered his services to the United Colonies, was refused, secured commission as a privateer at Providence (May 19, 1653), and endangered the United Colonies' unpatriotic neutrality by seizing the Dutch West Indies Company's property at Hartford (June 27, 1653), precipitating a ten-year dispute with the Hartford government. After his wife's death in 1658, he married Elizabeth Feake, probably became a Quaker, and moved to Oyster Bay, establishing an estate (Killingworth) on land given by the Indians. He helped reduce the New Amsterdam Dutch to English control (1664–65), was a member of the Hempstead Convention (Mar. 1, 1664/5), surveyor of customs for Long Island (Apr. 22, 1665), and, later, high constable and under sheriff of North Riding, Yorkshire, Long Island. Retiring from public life, Mar. 14, 1666/7, he died at Killingworth, survived by at least two daughters and one son by his first wife and three daughters and two sons by the second.

[The Underhill Soc. of America, sponsored by M. C. Taylor, has pub. valuable material concerning Underhill in J. C. Frost, *Underhill Geneal.* (4 vols., 1932) and H. C. Shelley, *John Underhill* (1932); these are decidedly favorable to Underhill and should be read in connection with J. K. Hosmer, *Winthrop's Jour.* (2 vols., 1908), "Records of the First Church of Boston" (manuscript in Mass. Hist. Soc. Lib.), Nathaniel Shurtleff, *Records of the Gov. and Company of the Mass. Bay*, vol. I (1853), and L. E. and A. L. de Forest, *Capt. John Underhill* (1934). See also *Docs. Rel. to the Colonial Hist. of . . . N. Y.*, vols. II (1858), XIV (1883).]
R. P. S.

UNDERWOOD, BENJAMIN FRANKLIN (July 6, 1839–Nov. 10, 1914), freethinker, lecturer, editor, the son of Raymond C. and Harriet (Booth) Underwood, was born in the city of New York. He received a slender education in the common schools and at Westerly Academy in Westerly, R. I., which he supplemented by wide reading in philosophy, science, and literature. Having enlisted at the outbreak of the Civil War in the 15th Massachusetts Volunteer Infantry, he was wounded and captured at the battle of Ball's Bluff, Oct. 21, 1861, and was confined for some months in Libby Prison. Released through an exchange of prisoners, he returned to Massachusetts, where he married Sara A. Francis, a young suffragist leader, on Sept. 6, 1862. Reënlisting, in the 5th Rhode Island Heavy Artillery, he served with it for the duration of the war, being promoted to first lieutenant and commended for bravery in action.

After the war he took up platform work as a freethinker. Unlike Robert Green Ingersoll [*q.v.*], he possessed a logical rather than rhetorical type of mind and had considerable philosophic acumen. During the seventies and eighties he terrorized the churches of the East by his custom of issuing a public challenge to the clergy of the large cities to meet him in a series of debates, these series running from three to as many as thirty meetings. It was an unusual clergyman who was able to rival him in forensic ability, and gradually ministers became so wary of accepting his challenges that only the boldest ventured to enter the lists against him. The issue usually turned upon the acceptance or interpretation of the theory of evolution, of which he was one of the earliest and most zealous American supporters. The most notable of these intellectual combats was one in which Prof. Asa Gray [*q.v.*] of Harvard participated, in a symposium organized by Underwood in Boston (1873). Although influenced by the deism of Thomas Paine as well as by the agnosticism of Herbert Spencer, Underwood's own position approached that of orthodox materialism. During his earlier, more aggressive years he published a number of lectures and pamphlets on such topics as *Darwinism* (1875), *The Crimes and Cruelties of Christianity* (1877), *Christianity and Materialism, Will the Coming Man Worship God?, Modern Scientific Materialism, Naturalism vs: Supernaturalism, Spiritualism from a Materialistic Standpoint, Paine, the Religious and Political Reformer, Woman: Her Past and Present, Her Rights and Wrongs*—little materialistic tracts containing much trenchant argument. From 1880 to 1886 he edited the Boston *Index*; then, moving to Chicago, he edited the *Open Court* in 1887 and the *Illustrated Graphic News* in 1888; from 1893 to 1895 he was editorial writer for the *Philosophical Journal*; in 1893 he acted as chairman of the Congress of Evolution held in connection with the World's Columbian Exposition. He moved to Quincy, Ill., in 1897 to assume the editorship of the *Quincy Journal*, a position which he held until within a year of his death. In spite of his penchant for debate, he was of a genial, kindly disposition, and during his later life he became much more reserved in the expression of his anti-religious views and seems to have modified them to a considerable extent. In 1913 he retired from active work and returned to his boyhood's home in Westerly, R. I., where he died.

[L. M. Underwood, *The Underwood Families of America* (2 vols., 1913); *Who's Who in America*, 1914–15; editorial by H. N. Wheeler and obituary in *Quincy Jour.*, Nov. 12, 1914; manuscript copy of debate with the Rev. C. S. Bates of Cleveland, Mar. 21, 22, 23, 1889.]   E. S. B—s.

UNDERWOOD, FRANCIS HENRY (Jan. 12, 1825–Aug. 7, 1894), author, lawyer, and United States consul, was the son of Roswell Underwood, a farmer of Enfield, Mass., and Phoebe (Hall) Underwood. He was probably a descendant of Joseph Underwood who emigrated from England to Massachusetts in 1637. In spite of extreme poverty he managed to prepare himself for college and entered Amherst with the class of 1847. After one year, however, he left college to teach school in Kentucky, declining the offer of an uncle to pay the expenses of his education on condition that he become a minister. In the South he studied law, was admitted to the bar (1847), and married, in Taylorsville, Ky., May 18, 1848, Louisa Maria Wood. His original antipathy to slavery was increased by what he saw of the institution, and he returned to Massachusetts in 1850 an ardent advocate of Free Soil principles. After twelve months of private law practice in Webster, Mass., he was appointed clerk of the state Senate for the session of 1852. Political feeling in the North had been roused by the passage of the Fugitive Slave Law, but had not yet taken form. Underwood succeeded in interesting John Punchard Jewett [*q.v.*], the publisher of *Uncle Tom's Cabin,* in a scheme for establishing a magazine which should enlist the literary forces of New England in a crusade against slavery. He secured the cooperation of a distinguished list of contributors and was ready to launch the new venture in December 1853. But at the last moment the publishers declined to proceed and the whole scheme had to be temporarily abandoned.

Underwood next entered the publishing house of Phillips, Sampson & Company, Boston, as literary editor, and for some time devoted himself to extending his acquaintance among Boston and Cambridge authors. He then revived the project of a magazine. The cautious Phillips was slow to accept the proposal, but Underwood's efforts were warmly seconded by William Lee, a junior member of the firm, and by Harriet Beecher Stowe. Their united persuasions at length overcame the publisher's reluctance. On May 5, 1857, occurred the memorable dinner at the Parker House when Emerson, Lowell, Holmes, Longfellow, John Lothrop Motley, and James E. Cabot joined Phillips and Underwood in discussing plans for the yet unnamed magazine. In consequence of this and several succeeding dinners Underwood, who naturally expected to act as editor, was sent abroad to solicit contributions from British authors. He returned in midsummer to find the success of the project imperiled by the financial panic of 1857. Realizing at once that the prestige of James Russell Lowell [*q.v.*] as editor would strengthen the undertaking, Underwood, "without a suggestion from any person," nominated his friend for the position, and Lowell accepted. At the same time Holmes christened the new publication the *Atlantic Monthly.* The first number appeared under the date of November 1857, and almost at once the magazine assumed the lead among American periodicals. Underwood's connection with the enterprise that he had projected and brought into being lasted only two years, during which time he loyally performed the routine work of assistant editor, sifting all contributions and making up numbers subject to Lowell's approval. In 1859 both Phillips and Sampson died, their firm was dissolved, and the *Atlantic* became the property of Ticknor & Fields. Underwood, to his deep regret, was not retained by the new proprietors.

After leaving the *Atlantic* he was elected (1859) clerk of the Superior Criminal Court of Boston. Social, literary, and civic affairs occupied much of his time. He was an original member and second president of the Papyrus Club, and for ten years served on the Boston school committee. To secure leisure for more sustained literary work he resigned his clerkship in 1866 and engaged in private business ventures, some of which proved to be unfortunate. Meanwhile he wrote manuals of English and American literature; *Cloud-Pictures* (1872), a volume of short stories; *Lord of Himself* (1874), *Man Proposes* (1885), and *Doctor Gray's Quest* (1895), novels; and biographies of Longfellow, Lowell, and Whittier. His wife, by whom he had had five children, died in 1882. By appointment of President Cleveland (confirmed, Apr. 28, 1886) Underwood succeeded Francis Brett Harte [*q.v.*] as United States consul at Glasgow. He was recalled when the Democrats went out of office, but returned to Scotland (appointment confirmed, Sept. 2, 1893) at the beginning of Cleveland's second term, this time to be consul at Leith. He died in Edinburgh. Underwood's life abroad brought him many friendships and new distinctions, including an honorary LL.D. from the University of Glasgow. He also found consolation in a young Scotch wife, Frances

Findlay of Callendar, near Glasgow. In the interval between his consulships he wrote his best book, *Quabbin, the Story of a Small Town* (1893), a pleasantly discursive account of Enfield as he remembered it from his boyhood. Nevertheless, his last years were not entirely happy. He was painfully conscious that he had not won the recognition that his industry, talent, and genial nature deserved. Always it had been his fate to play a secondary rôle, contributing much to the fame of others but gaining little credit for himself. As Francis Parkman lucidly pointed out to him, he was "neither a Harvard man nor a humbug" and so, being both unassuming and unsupported, a victim of his own merit.

[L. M. Underwood, *The Underwood Families of America* (2 vols., 1913); *Amherst Coll. Biog. Record* (1927); J. T. Trowbridge, "The Author of Quabbin," *Atlantic Monthly*, Jan. 1895; Bliss Perry, "The Editor Who Was Never the Editor," *Park-Street Papers* (1908); M. A. DeW. Howe, *The Atlantic Monthly and Its Makers* (1919); obituary in *Times* (London), Aug. 9, 1894; scrapbook of newspaper clippings relating to Underwood's years in Scotland in the Jones Lib., Amherst.]   G. F. W.

UNDERWOOD, HORACE GRANT (July 19, 1859–Oct. 12, 1916), missionary, was born in London, England, the fourth of six children of John and Elizabeth Grant (Maire) Underwood. His father, whose inventive work as a manufacturing chemist had won him recognition from the Royal Society of Arts, emigrated to New Durham, N. J., in 1872, and engaged in the manufacture of inks and special papers, a business which developed into the Underwood Typewriter Company. At ten Horace was sent to a Catholic school in France; he continued his studies in America at Hasbrouck Institute, Jersey City; at the University of the City of New York (later New York University), from which he graduated in 1881; and at the New Brunswick Theological Seminary, where he completed his course in 1884.

Having had a missionary career in view from childhood, he was ordained in November 1884 to the Dutch Reformed ministry and commissioned missionary to Korea by the Presbyterian Board. He arrived at Chemulpo, Apr. 5, 1885, and, though missionaries were not welcomed in that newly opened land, he was given duties at the government hospital just established. He soon acquired the language, and in 1890 published *A Concise Dictionary of the Korean Language*. He began the translation of the Scriptures into Korean, and was chairman of the board of translators until his death. In 1886 he opened an orphanage at Seoul, which became the John D. Wells Academy. In 1889 he organized the Sai Mun An Church, of which he was still the pastor when he died. At Seoul he married, Mar. 13, 1889, Dr. Lillias Stirling Horton, then serving as physician to the queen. On their wedding trip to the northern border, Underwood crossed over into Manchuria with thirty Koreans, whom he there baptized, thus conforming with the letter of his promise not to engage in such work while traveling in Korea. This promise was exacted because of a proselyting trip he had made with the Rev. Henry Gerhard Appenzeller [*q.v.*] in 1888, which resulted in the issuance of a decree, later recalled, forbidding the teaching of Christianity in Korea. Underwood's work, with that of his associate missionaries, raised Korea to the foremost place among mission fields. From 1897 to 1901 he published at his own expense a native paper, the *Christian News*. He was instrumental in organizing the Seoul branch of the Young Men's Christian Association, and aided in establishing the Severance Hospital and the Chosen Union Christian College (Presbyterian-Methodist). After the assassination of the queen in 1895, he became the trusted intermediary of the king, even conveying his food from his own table to avoid the danger of poisoning. This activity was criticised, certain publications calling him "Underwood the schemer" (*Underwood of Korea, post,* p. 154). He died at Atlantic City and was buried at New Durham, N. J. He was the author of *An Introduction to the Korean Spoken Language* (1890), *The Call of Korea* (1908), and *The Religions of Eastern Asia* (1910). He was a member of the Royal Asiatic Society and the British Foreign Bible Society. He lectured on missions at Princeton in 1908 and at New York University in 1909. His wife died in Seoul, Oct. 20, 1921. She was the author of *Fifteen Years among the Topknots* (1904), *Tommy Tompkins in Korea* (1905), and *Underwood of Korea* (1918). Their only son became an author and a missionary in Korea.

[L. M. Underwood, *The Underwood Families of America* (1913), vol. II; *Who's Who in America,* 1916–17; *Biog. Record, Theological Seminary, New Brunswick* (1912); Lillias H. Underwood, *Underwood of Korea* (1918); W. E. Griffis, *A Modern Pioneer in Korea* (1912); H. H. Underwood, *Modern Educ. in Korea* (1926); H. N. Allen, *A Chronological Index of Korea* (1901), and *Things Korean* (1908); J. S. Gale, *The Vanguard* (1904); Lillias H. Underwood, and A. J. Brown, in *Missionary Review of the World,* Dec. 1916; obituary in *N. Y. Times,* Oct. 13, 1916; personal recollections; information from Underwood's family.]   H. N. A.

UNDERWOOD, JOHN CURTISS (Mar. 14, 1809–Dec. 7, 1873), jurist, was the son of John and Mary (Curtiss) Underwood of Litchfield, Herkimer County, N. Y. On his father's side he was a direct descendant of William Underwood, who came from England to Concord, Mass., probably prior to 1640, and in 1652 moved to Chelmsford. One of William's descendants, Parker Underwood, removed from Chelmsford to Litchfield, where his grandson, John Curtiss Underwood, was subsequently born and reared. He was graduated from Hamilton College in 1832. While there he became one of the founders of the Alpha Delta Phi fraternity. After his graduation he went to Virginia; obtained employment as a tutor; began the study of law; and later returned to Herkimer County to begin practice. On Oct. 24, 1839, he married Maria Gloria Jackson of Clarksburg, Va. (now W. Va.)—a double cousin of "Stonewall" Jackson, and a member of the family in which Underwood had formerly served as tutor. The couple soon acquired about eight hundred acres of land in Clarke County, established their home there, and sought to introduce dairying into that portion of Virginia (*Underwood Families, post,* I, 364–77). Three children were born to them.

A Free-soiler in politics, Underwood was a delegate to the Republican National Convention of 1856, and during the ensuing campaign incurred such unpopularity by his utterances on the subject of slavery that he removed from Virginia. In 1860 he was a delegate to the convention which nominated Lincoln, in behalf of whose candidacy he stumped New England and the Middle States. After the election he was nominated as United States consul to Callao, Peru, the nomination being confirmed July 26, 1861. On July 25, however, Lincoln nominated him fifth auditor of the Treasury and the appointment was confirmed on Aug. 1. On Jan. 25, 1864, he was appointed judge of the district court of Virginia, in which capacity he asserted the right of the United States to confiscate property of "persons in rebellion," and advocated extension and protection of negro civic rights. The most noteworthy case with which he was connected was that of Jefferson Davis. At the session of the grand jury held at Norfolk in May 1866, at which Davis was indicted for treason, Underwood delivered a charge of some length and severity. The session adjourned to meet in Richmond on June 5, and local feeling was running so high that there was speculation as to whether Underwood would risk assassination by appearing. He was present at the appointed time, however, and in another charge to the grand jury scathingly denounced the press and many residents of Richmond. Later, he refused to admit Davis to bail, on the ground that he was a military prisoner, and not, in consequence, within

the power of the civil authorities (*New York Herald,* May 12, June 6, 7, 12, 1866).

When the drastic Reconstruction acts of March 1867 were applied to Virginia, Underwood was chosen delegate to, and president of, the constitutional convention which assembled at Richmond, Dec. 3, 1867. This convention drew up what came to be known as the "Underwood Constitution" (*Underwood Families,* I, 376). Certain of its provisions, subsequently eliminated by popular vote on ratification in 1869, would have placed the government "based on such a constitution, in the hands of negroes, 'scalawags' and 'carpet-bag' adventurers" (Burgess, *post,* p. 227). With its proscriptive features removed, however, the constitution proved to be satisfactory, and remained the organic law of Virginia from 1869 until 1902.

Underwood eventually acquired several thousand acres of land. To a portion of this he obtained title at the close of the war by methods which evoked widespread criticism, involved him in litigation, and even caused him to be subjected to physical assault. His death from apoplexy occurred at his residence in Washington, D. C.

[L. M. Underwood, *The Underwood Families of America* (1913); *N. Y. Herald,* May 12, June 6, 7, 12, 1866, Dec. 9, 1873; *N. Y. Times,* May 12, June 6, 8, 1866, Nov. 12, Dec. 9, 1873; *The Debates and Proceedings of the Constitutional Convention of the State of Va.* (1868); J. W. Burgess, *Reconstruction and the Constitution* (1902); H. J. Eckenrode, *The Pol. Hist. of Va. During the Reconstruction* (1904); R. F. Nichols, "U. S. vs. Jefferson Davis," *Am. Hist. Rev.,* Jan. 1926.]
       R. W. I.

UNDERWOOD, JOSEPH ROGERS (Oct. 24, 1791–Aug. 23, 1876), jurist, representative and senator from Kentucky, was born in Goochland County, Va., the eldest of eight children of John and Frances (Rogers) Underwood. He was a descendant of Thomas William (or William Thomas) Underwood, who was born about 1675 and came to Virginia from England as a boy. Joseph's father was a person of standing in his community and often represented the county in the legislature. His resources were so meager, however, that he found it impossible properly to educate all his children. Hence, when twelve years old, Joseph was sent to his uncle, Edmund Rogers, in Barren County, Ky., who gave him the attention of a parent. He was instructed for a year by Rev. John Howe, near Glasgow, spent a term under Samuel Findley at Danville, and later attended a school at Lancaster. He entered Transylvania University and was graduated in 1811. He immediately began the study of law in Lexington under the instruction of Robert Wickliffe, but before he had secured a license to practise he volunteered in a

regiment recruited to avenge the massacre at
the River Raisin. Elected lieutenant in the 13th
Kentucky Regiment, he became a part of the
army commanded by Gen. William Henry Harrison [q.v.]. On May 5, 1813, his company was
defeated and captured at Fort Meigs, and he
was imprisoned at Fort Wayne.

In July he returned to Kentucky, received his
license to practise law, and before the end of
the year settled at Glasgow. He was town trustee and county auditor until 1823, when he removed to Bowling Green, where he maintained
a residence for the rest of his life. In 1816, when
everybody in the state was a Jeffersonian Democrat, he entered politics and secured membership in the lower house of the legislature, representing Barren County. After serving four
years, he decided to retire from politics; but in
1825, during the excitement of the "Old Court,
New Court" parties, he returned to the legislature as a representative of the former. He was
reëlected the next year, and in 1828 he ran for
lieutenant-governor as an anti-Jackson man, but
was defeated. The same year Gov. Thomas Metcalfe appointed him associate justice of the
court of appeals, in which capacity he served
until his resignation in 1835.

Immediately thereafter he was elected to the
lower house of Congress as a Whig, where he
served four successive terms (Mar. 4, 1835–
Mar. 3, 1843). He declined another term, and
in 1845 was elected to the state legislature and
chosen speaker. In 1847 he was elected to the
United States Senate, of which he was a member until Mar. 3, 1853. As a national legislator
he favored the distribution of the surplus revenues among the states, and in 1837, even when
the panic was upon the country, demanded of
Congress the completion of the payments promised. He opposed the famous rule of the House
excluding slavery petitions, on the ground that
the abolitionists would wax strong as the result
of the agitation which would be raised if it
were passed. He took the Whig position of
opposition to the Mexican War and the acquisition of territory. Being a strong believer in
liberty for all, he applauded the revolutionary
movement in Europe in 1848, though he opposed the reception of Kossuth by Congress as
meddling. In the troubles of 1850 he took a calm
attitude and supported the compromise measures. Though he strongly supported the South
on slavery, he never mentioned secession. He
thoroughly believed in the colonization movement, and sought federal aid in returning free
negroes to Africa. He was a consistent advocate
of national economy, opposing large armies and

navies, the extension of pensions, the padding of
mileage accounts, and various petty expenditures
by public officials. A great admirer of Henry
Clay, he served as a presidential elector on his
ticket in 1824 and in 1844.

Underwood remained a Unionist throughout
the Civil War, though he had a son in the Confederate army. In 1860 he again entered the Kentucky legislature and served until 1863, when he
finally relinquished public office for the practice
of law and agriculture. The war made him a
Democrat; he attended the national convention
in Chicago in 1864, and the next year he was instrumental in reorganizing the party in Kentucky. He was a large man physically, benevolent, public-spirited, and truly a man of the people. He accumulated a considerable fortune.
On Mar. 26, 1817, he married Eliza M. Trotter;
she died in 1835, and on Feb. 27, 1839, he married Elizabeth Cox, a daughter of the mayor of
Georgetown, D. C.; by each marriage he had
eight children. A son by his second wife, John
C. Underwood, became lieutenant-governor of
Kentucky, and a grandson, Oscar W. Underwood [q.v.], became a senator from Alabama;
a brother, Warner Lewis Underwood, was a
Kentucky congressman and United States consul at Glasgow, Scotland.

[For sources, see L. M. Underwood, *The Underwood Families of America* (1913); Lewis and R. H. Collins, *Hist. of Ky.* (1882); *The Biog. Encyc. of Ky.* (1878); *Biog. Dir. Am. Cong.* (1928); *Am. Rev.*, June 1848; *Louisville Commercial*, Aug. 25, 1876. A few letters from Underwood to J. J. Crittenden are in the Crittenden MSS. in the Lib. of Cong.]   E.M.C.

UNDERWOOD, LORING (Feb. 15, 1874–
Jan. 13, 1930), landscape architect, was born at
Belmont, Mass., the youngest of three children
of William James and Esther Crafts (Mead)
Underwood. His grandfather, William Underwood, emigrated to Boston from England in
1817. Having completed his preparatory work
at the Noble & Greenough School, Boston, Underwood entered Harvard College, from which
he received the degree of A.B. in 1897. On Oct.
14, 1897, he married Emily Walton of Newark,
N. J., who with three daughters survived him.
The year 1898–99 he spent in study at the Bussey Institution at Harvard, and the following
year he spent in travel and study abroad. In
Paris he attended the École d'Horticulture,
studying under Edouard André, the celebrated
French landscape architect. Thus was laid the
educational foundation which, coupled with his
sensitiveness to beauty and his intense love of
nature, made him one of the outstanding landscape architects of his day. On his return from
abroad in 1900 he established his home in Bel-

mont and soon afterwards began the practice of his profession in Boston, where he maintained an office until his death. During the World War he rendered notable service as landscape architect of the housing development at Bath, Me., one of the United States Housing Corporation's villages for war workers. He was also a member of the Fuel Administration. In 1919 Laurence S. Caldwell joined him as partner.

Although he was landscape architect for the Mother Church, the First Church of Christ, Scientist, Boston, and other New England institutions, designed several subdivisions, and was for many years consulting landscape architect for Vassar College, it is not so much for these as for the many smaller home gardens which he designed that he will be long remembered. His field was largely New England. He was much sought after as a lecturer upon old New England gardens, and upon village and landscape improvement. His lectures were illustrated by lantern slides made by a direct color process, in the use of which he was a pioneer. For the display of these lantern slides he invented an ingeniously devised five-sided standard with interior illumination. His book, *The Garden and Its Accessories* (1906), remains after thirty years the outstanding American work on the subject. He was also the author of *A Garden Diary and Country Home Guide* (copyright 1908). Of a generous nature and keenly interested in all that pertained to his chosen profession, he gave freely of his time and abilities in many positions of responsibility. He was at one time president of the Boston Society of Landscape Architects; at the time of his death he was a member of the visiting committee of the School of Landscape Architecture of Harvard University, a director of the Massachusetts Horticultural Society, and a trustee of the Lowthorpe School.

[See L. M. Underwood, *The Underwood Families of America* (1913), vol. II; *Who's Who in America*, 1930–31; *Harvard Coll. Class of 1897, Twenty-fifth Anniversary Report* (n.d.); *Harvard Grads.' Mag.*, Mar. 1930; obituary notice in *Landscape Architecture*, Apr. 1930; obituaries in *Boston Transcript*, Jan. 13, and *Boston Herald*, Jan. 14, 1930; unpublished data in the possession of L. S. Caldwell, Boston. A large part of Underwood's collection of lantern slides is in the lib. of the School of Landscape Architecture, Harvard Univ.]   K. McN.

UNDERWOOD, LUCIEN MARCUS (Oct. 26, 1853–Nov. 16, 1907), botanist, was born in New Woodstock, N. Y., the son of John Lincklaen and Hannah Jane (Smith) Underwood. He was descended probably from Joseph Underwood (1614–1677) of Hingham and later of Watertown, Mass. Farm duties greatly ham-

pered Underwood's early education. Having prepared for college intermittently at near-by Cazenovia Seminary, he entered Syracuse University (1873), where he became greatly interested in geology and entomology, and, self-instructed, began his lifelong study of ferns. Upon graduation (1877) he taught school for a year and obtained the degree Ph.M. from Syracuse. In July 1878 he published in *L. B. Case's Botanical Index* an enumeration of the ferns growing near Syracuse, his first paper. During the following school year he taught natural sciences at Cazenovia and completed graduate studies in geology at Syracuse, receiving the degree Ph.D. (1879). He taught in Hedding College, Abingdon, Ill., the next year, and in 1880 became professor of geology and botany at Illinois Wesleyan University, where he remained three years. Here he published his first book, *Our Native Ferns and How to Study Them* (1881), a synoptical work which (under a slightly changed title) passed through six editions in twenty years, serving more than any other agency to stimulate the study of ferns in the United States. Here began also his special interest in the *Hepaticae*, a group upon which he published subsequently more than a score of important papers, the most widely known being his *Descriptive Catalogue of the North American Hepaticae North of Mexico* (1884). His keen zoölogical interest at this time is shown by several papers, mainly bibliographical, on spiders, myriapods, and crustaceans. The organization of the Indiana Academy of Sciences (1885) resulted largely through his efforts.

In 1883 Underwood was called to Syracuse University as instructor in geology, zoölogy, and botany, and in 1886 became professor. He taught here seven years, meanwhile gradually giving up zoölogy for cryptogamic botany and contributing the text on the *Hepaticae* to the sixth edition (1890) of Asa Gray's *Manual of the Botany of the Northern United States*. There followed a year given to study as Morgan Fellow at Harvard and to botanical work in Florida. In 1891 he accepted the professorship of botany at De Pauw University, transferring after four years to the Alabama Polytechnic Institute as professor of biology. He became professor of botany at Columbia University in July 1896, and remained in this position until his death. In 1899 he published *Moulds, Mildews, and Mushrooms,* an introduction to the study of fungi. This and the two synoptical works on ferns and hepatics afford the clew to much of Underwood's effort—an impelling desire to popularize botanical knowledge. From early boyhood he exhibited genius in classifying not only objects of natural history but historical data of all sorts. He compiled an elaborate genealogy, *The Underwood Families of America* (2 vols., 1913), which appeared posthumously.

Underwood's eleven years at Columbia University, the botanical department of which is affiliated with the New York Botanical Garden, left a notable impress. They were given not only to botanical exploration in the West Indies, the examination of fern "types" in European herbaria, and the publication of numerous papers on ferns (chiefly American), but also to the trenchant advocacy of sounder methods in taxonomy and of radical reform in botanical nomenclature. From 1901 he served as chairman of the board of scientific directors of the Botanical Garden, and in this capacity took a leading part in initiating, in 1905, publication of the *North American Flora,* a project he had long cherished. Temporarily deranged by overwork and worry, he died by his own hand at his home in Redding, Conn. He was married, Aug. 10, 1881, to Marie Annette Spurr, of Oakland, Cal., descended in the seventh generation from Jan Wybesse Spoor of Albany, N. Y.

In personality Underwood was uncommonly genial and forthright, keen, sympathetic, and imbued with a spirit of unselfish helpfulness. His professional accomplishment was essentially that of an inspiring pioneer and exceptionally energetic organizer.

[Biographical and memorial sketches by C. C. Curtis, M. A. Howe, J. H. Barnhart, and N. L. Britton, in *Bull. Torrey Botanical Club,* vol. XXXV, pp. 1–40 (Jan. 1908); N. L. Britton, in *Columbia Univ. Quart.,* Dec. 1907; H. H. Rusby, in *Jour. N. Y. Botanical Garden,* vol. VIII, pp. 263–69, portr. (Dec. 1907); obituary in *Hartford Times,* Nov. 18, 1907; private information.]   W. R. M.

UNDERWOOD, OSCAR WILDER (May 6, 1862–Jan. 25, 1929), representative and senator from Alabama, was born in Louisville, Ky., the son of Eugene Underwood and the latter's second wife, Frederica Virginia (Smith) Wilder Underwood. His earliest paternal ancestor in America, Thomas William (or William Thomas) Underwood, born *c.* 1675 near Norfolk, England, came to Virginia as a boy; and his grandfather, Joseph Rogers Underwood [*q.v.*], a native of Virginia, was representative and senator from Kentucky. When Oscar was three years old, his parents took him with them to St. Paul, Minn., and he spent the next decade at that frontier outpost. In 1875 his father and mother returned to Louisville, and he attended the common schools and the Rugby School there. He was a student at the University of Virginia from 1881 to 1884, and was elected to

the presidency of the Jefferson Society, one of the highest honors within the gift of the student body. In 1884 he was admitted to the bar. After a brief period of practice in Minnesota, he removed to Birmingham, Ala., then a small but growing town. In 1894 he announced his candidacy for the House of Representatives from the Birmingham district. He took his seat in March of the following year and served until June 1896, when he was succeeded by Truman H. Aldrich, who had contested his election. He was then elected to the nine succeeding Congresses, and served continuously from Mar. 4, 1897, until Mar. 3, 1915. The following day he took his seat in the Senate, where he remained for two terms (1915–27).

Early in his career as a congressman Underwood proclaimed his belief in the principle of a tariff for revenue only enunciated by President Grover Cleveland. The fact that he stood on this platform was evidence of his independence of mind, for Birmingham was already a center of the iron and steel industry, an industry which believed in protection. In no sense a spectacular figure, Underwood forged to the front by virtue of his high character, his winning personality, and his unflagging industry. Those who knew him best respected him most, and after the Democrats captured control of the House in the elections of 1910, he was chosen by his party as floor leader (1911–15). At the same time he became chairman of the powerful ways and means committee. In the years immediately preceding, the Democrats had given little evidence of a coherent policy, and there was some uneasiness in the country as to whether Underwood, who was without great experience as a party helmsman, could mold them into a compact fighting force. Not only was he able to convince his party and the public of his ability to lead, but at the same time his detailed knowledge of the tariff, gained through years of close study, was an invaluable asset. The tariff was the issue of the hour.

President Taft called Congress in special session in 1911 to act on his Canadian reciprocity program. Putting aside narrow partisanship, Underwood gave unstinted support to reciprocity, since he felt it to be to a considerable degree compatible with the principles and purposes of the Democratic party. But at the same time he took the lead in revising many of the tariff schedules downward. This tariff legislation was all vetoed by President Taft. Thus was created an outstanding issue of the presidential campaign of 1912. Underwood's leadership at the special session of 1911 met and overcame a serious challenge from the powerful William Jennings Bryan. Bryan charged him publicly with protecting certain interests in his tariff schedules. Underwood abandoned his usual suavity as he lashed back at the Commoner in denial of the accusation (*Congressional Record, 62* Cong., 1 Sess., pp. 3510–12), and his colleagues of the ways and means committee came to the floor of the House and supported him. The episode was a boomerang for Bryan, for the applause that greeted the Underwood statement left no doubt as to the attitude of the House.

Underwood conducted himself with such conspicuous ability in Congress that by the time the Democrats convened at Baltimore in 1912 to nominate a candidate for the presidency, he was among the leading contenders. In fact William F. McCombs, manager for Woodrow Wilson, felt when the convention opened that Underwood had the greatest potential strength of any of the aspirants (McCombs, *post,* p. 138). He polled 117½ votes on the first ballot, but his candidacy was opposed bitterly by Bryan, and his potential strength was never realized. He declined to be considered for the nomination for vice-president after Wilson had been named to head the ticket. Following Wilson's election, Underwood cooperated to the fullest in carrying out the new President's legislative program. His work in framing the important tariff bill which bears his name and in holding the Democratic majority in line behind the Federal Reserve act was especially noteworthy.

Taking his seat in the Senate in 1915, he was recognized as one of its most influential members. As a member of the appropriations committee during the World War, he had charge of some highly important appropriation bills during the illness of Senator Thomas S. Martin [*q.v.*]. In the Senate fight over the League of Nations, Underwood stood with Wilson, although he personally was of the opinion that the President ought to have agreed to certain mild reservations. He was strongly dissatisfied with the Senate rules, and in 1923, after two years as floor leader, he declined to offer for that position again. His acceptance of President Harding's appointment as one of the four representatives of the United States at the conference on limitation of armament in 1921–22, and his work in securing the ratification of the treaties drafted there, was looked at askance by his more partisan colleagues. He would probably have had opposition if he had sought the post of floor leader again.

In 1923 he announced that he was going to give the South a chance to select a Southerner to carry the banner of Democracy in the presidential election of the following year. The Ku Klux Klan was sweeping the country, and was in control in many states, especially in the South, where much of Underwood's strength lay. He was strongly advised to say nothing to offend the Klan, but that organization seemed to him fundamentally un-American, and he felt in duty bound to denounce it in no uncertain terms. On the eve of the Democratic National Convention in New York City, he declared that the Klan would be the paramount issue, and when the convention met he and others failed by a margin of only one vote to have an anti-Klan plank included in the platform. After the prolonged deadlock between the forces of William G. McAdoo and Alfred E. Smith had continued for fifty ballots, it is said that Smith offered to throw all his strength to Underwood if he could get the support of two Southern states, in addition to Alabama (Kent, *post,* p. 494). However, Underwood's uncompromising hostility to the Klan and national prohibition had alienated the South, so there was slight chance of his becoming a real contender.

Before the expiration of his second senatorial term in 1927, he announced that he would not be a candidate for reëlection, and at the close of the term he retired to his handsome estate, "Woodlawn," near "Mount Vernon" in Virginia. He was nearly sixty-five years of age and anxious to spend his remaining years in literary and other congenial pursuits. During his retirement he wrote *Drifting Sands of Party Politics* (1928), in which he discussed governmental principles. In the pages of this book he revealed himself as a devout follower of Thomas Jefferson, an advocate of a minimum of government and a maximum of personal liberty. He elaborated upon his oft-expressed opposition to sumptuary legislation, particularly the Eighteenth Amendment, as well as his objections to federal regulation of child labor. His strong aversion to all extensions of the federal authority caused him to be regarded by many as an ultra-conservative. While in the Senate he had taken a leading part in the fight against government operation of a power plant at Muscle Shoals, his position being that it should be used for the manufacture of nitrates, the purpose for which it was erected. He also opposed the woman's suffrage amendment.

Underwood was offered an appointment to the United States Supreme Court by President Harding (*New York Times,* Jan. 26, 1929; information from family), but such a position was not congenial to his temperament. He accepted two appointments from President Coolidge, one in 1927 as a member of the international commission between the United States and France, under the treaty of Sept. 15, 1914, and the other in 1928 as a delegate to the sixth international conference of American states held in Havana, Cuba, in that year. He attended this conference, but his health was beginning to fail, and in December he suffered a cerebral hemorrhage. This was followed by a paralytic stroke which proved fatal. Word of his death was received with unaffected and sincere expressions of sorrow in official Washington. His body was taken to Birmingham for burial, and the demonstrations which marked the obsequies there had seldom been equaled in the history of the state. He was married on Oct. 8, 1885, to Eugenia Massie of Charlottesville, Va., who died in 1900. On Sept. 10, 1904, he married Bertha Woodward of Birmingham. She and two sons by his first marriage survived him.

[O. W. Underwood, *Drifting Sands of Party Politics* (2 ed., 1931), with sketch of Underwood by C. G. Bowers; F. R. Kent, *The Democratic Party* (1928); W. F. McCombs, *Making Woodrow Wilson President* (1921); *Biog. Directory of the Am. Congress: 1774–1927* (1928); *Who's Who in America,* 1928–29; T. M. Owen, *Hist. of Alabama and Dictionary of Alabama Biography* (1921), vol. IV; obituary compiled by the Associated Press and published in afternoon papers, such as *Evening Star* (Washington), Jan. 25, 1929; obituary and editorial, *N. Y. Times,* Jan. 26, 1929; funeral notice, Jan. 29, 1929; L. M. Underwood, *The Underwood Families of America* (1913), vol. II; newspaper clippings in possession of his widow relative to his fight against the Ku Klux Klan; letters from his former colleagues in Congress; correspondence with his family.]　　　　　　　　　　　　V. D.

UPCHURCH, JOHN JORDAN (Mar. 26, 1820–Jan. 18, 1887), founder of the Ancient Order of United Workmen, was born on a farm in Franklin County, N. C., one of four children of Ambrose and Elizabeth (Hill) Upchurch. After 1824, when the father was shot dead by his wife's brother-in-law, the family was extremely poor. In 1837 Upchurch left the farm to learn the trade of millwright. Four years later, June 1, 1841, he married Angelina Green, a Pennsylvanian, who became the mother of his fifteen children. Soon afterward, with his wife's uncle, John Zeigenfuss, he opened a hotel in Raleigh, said to have been the first temperance house south of the Mason and Dixon line. When this venture failed, he worked briefly for the Raleigh & Gaston Railroad, attempted horse taming for a time, and in 1846 moved to Pennsylvania, where he entered the employ of the Mine Hill & Schuylkill Haven Railroad, in 1851 becoming master mechanic.

In June 1864, train hands, seeking a raise, went on strike, and for two weeks, according to

his own account, Upchurch operated the road in the interest of the government with men provided by the War Department. The strike was broken, and Upchurch determined to unite employers and employees "in one grand organization" opposed to trade unions (*Life, post,* pp. 22, 24). On Jan. 1, 1865, he resigned from the railroad to engage in oil speculation, but with its collapse at the end of the Civil War, returned, off and on, to railroading. In 1868 he settled in Meadville, Pa., where he joined the League of Friendship, Supreme Mechanical Order of the Sun, one of the many secret workers' orders then springing up. The Meadville lodge soon split, and on Upchurch's initiative a section reorganized, Oct. 27, 1868, as Jefferson Lodge No. 1 of the Ancient Order of United Workmen. One of the main objects of the new order was "To discountenance strikes" (*Ibid.,* p. 57), but since the organization had the character of a lodge rather than a trade union, it proved impotent to affect strike movements seriously one way or the other. When, a year after its inception, it levied a dollar per capita assessment to pay substantial death benefits, it began to transform itself into a fraternal benefit society, and became the model for a movement characteristic of the period in America.

The demand of a rising but propertyless working class for a bulwark against sickness, old age, and funeral expenses underlay the rapid expansion of mutual-benefit societies. Impetus was given by the policies of the oldline commercial insurance houses, whose rates were very high. Indirectly, the societies were influenced by the English friendly societies of the sixteenth century and directly, although subordinately, by the secrecy, ritualism, and sociability of Freemasonry. Dozens of them went bankrupt until, late in the eighties, actuarial calculations were adopted and reserves built up. The Ancient Order of United Workmen pioneered in this field under the direction of Upchurch, who in 1873 had been made Past Supreme Master Workman, and today he is generally regarded as the founder of the mutual-benefit system, which in 1919 numbered two hundred fraternal societies in the United States and Canada, with more than 120,000 subordinate lodges and some 9,000,000 members.

Upchurch continued to work as master mechanic for various railroads until about 1881, after which time he had no regular employment. In 1885, at the solicitation of the Order he visited California, where he was fêted by many lodges, and the next year visited Boston and Philadelphia. He wrote an autobiography, *The Life, Labors, and Travels of Father J. J. Up-*

church (1887), which was edited and published posthumously by his fraternal brother, Sam Booth. He died in Steelville, Mo., where he had settled, and was buried in Bellefontaine Cemetery, St. Louis.

[Sources include M. W. Sackett, *Early Hist. of Fraternal Beneficiary Societies in America* (1914); Walter Basye, *Hist. and Operation of Fraternal Insurance* (copr. 1919); F. H. Hankins, "Fraternal Orders," *Encyc. of the Social Sciences*, VI (1931), 423; Arthur Preuss, *A Dict. of Secret and Other Societies* (1924); A. C. Stevens, *The Cyc. of Fraternities* (1899); *St. Louis Globe-Democrat*, Jan. 19, 1887. In Upchurch's autobiog. (*Life*, p. 13), the year of his birth is given as 1822, but all other references to year of birth in the *Life*, including description of coffin plate (p. 228), give 1820.] H. S—w.

UPDEGRAFF, DAVID BRAINARD (Aug. 23, 1830–May 23, 1894), Quaker preacher, evangelist, editor, was descended from the family of Op den Graeff, German Mennonites with Dutch names who settled in Germantown, Pa., with Pastorius in 1683. He was born in Mount Pleasant, Ohio, the youngest son of David and Rebecca (Taylor) Updegraff. His mother was a preacher, and on both sides of his line of ancestry there were prominent Quaker preachers, the most noted of whom was his maternal grandmother, Ann Taylor. He was prepared for college in the local schools of Ohio and in 1851 entered Haverford College, where he remained for only one academic year. Returning to Mount Pleasant, he entered business. He was twice married, first, on Sept. 23, 1852, to Rebecca B. Price and, second, on Sept. 4, 1866, to Eliza J. C. Mitchell. There were four children by each marriage.

Updegraff's main interest lay in religious interpretation, and he had marked gifts as an evangelist of the type which flourished in America in the seventies and eighties of the nineteenth century. His successful career in this field dates from 1869, when he began to have meetings for prayer in his own home. In the early stages of his public ministry he worked for the most part among his own Quaker fellowship in the Middle West, especially in Ohio. He soon, however, widened his range of service and became a noted leader in the popular summer gatherings at Mountain Lake Park, Garrett County, Md., at Pitman Grove, N. J., and in the great interdenominational camp-meetings then being held both in the East and the West. As his views took final shape in his preaching he became noted as the fervid exponent of a special type of religious thought, which may fitly be called "Pentecostal Christianity." He advocated two stages of religious experience, which he called justification and sanctification. Justification for him meant the divine act by which a sinner is ab-

solved from the guilt and penalty of his sin; sanctification was represented as a state of baptism by the Holy Spirit, perfect peace, joy, love, and freedom from the power of sin.

Within the Society of Friends itself to which he belonged, he was widely known as an innovator and as a leader of a transformed Quakerism. He represented an intense form of evangelical thought and a dramatic style of preaching. He advocated the introduction of singing and set pastoral leadership, believed in conversion at a definite moment, and had a critical attitude toward silence in worship and toward the Quaker doctrine of the inward light. Midway in his career he was baptized with water in the Berean Baptist Church of Philadelphia. This brought him into sharp conflict with the leaders of the Society of Friends in America, which throughout its history had been opposed to the practice of outward baptism on the part of its members. He carried many Ohio Friends with him, and many other Friends elsewhere, influenced by his powerful personality, remained loyal to him through the controversies which followed. From 1887 to 1893 he edited a periodical entitled the *Friends' Expositor*, in which he vigorously interpreted his views and defended his position. In 1892 he published a volume of sermons and addresses with the title, *Old Corn*, which contains the substance of his teaching. He defended his position on baptism in two printed booklets. The more important one was printed in Columbus, Ohio, in 1885, as *An Address to the Ohio Yearly Meeting on the Ordinances*; the other was *The Ordinances: an Interview* (Richmond, Ind., 1886). He died at his home in Mount Pleasant, May 23, 1894.

[Dougan Clark and J. H. Smith, *David B. Updegraff and His Work* (1895); *Biog. Cat. of the Matriculates of Haverford Coll., 1833–1922* (1922); files of *Friends' Expositor, Christian Worker,* and *Friends' Review*; obituary in *Wheeling Reg.* (Wheeling, W. Va.), May 25, 1894.] R. M. J.

UPDIKE, DANIEL (*c.* 1693–May 15, 1757), attorney-general of Rhode Island, son of Ludowick and Catherine (Newton) Updike, was born in North Kingstown, R. I. His grandfather was Gilbert Updike (Gysbert Opdyck), who came to New Amsterdam from Wesel sometime before 1638. When New Amsterdam was taken over by the English, in 1664, he emigrated to Rhode Island, and there married the daughter of Richard Smith, who had purchased a very large tract of land from the Narragansett Indians. Daniel was instructed at home by a private tutor and supplemented his education by a period of travel. He then took up the study of law, and after his admission to the bar established himself at Newport. Natural ability and an attractive personality quickly brought him to the front in the affairs of the colony. In 1722 he was elected attorney-general, which office he held continuously for the next ten years. One of his most important cases was the trial in 1723 of thirty-six pirates captured by an English vessel off the coast of Long Island. In 1724 he was appointed one of the commissioners who, with representatives from Connecticut, sought to locate definitely the boundary line between that colony and Rhode Island. The settlement of this controversy was protracted until 1726 when, since no agreement could be reached, the final decision was made by the King in Council.

Updike declined election as attorney-general in 1732 to accept nomination for governor; he was defeated, however, by his opponent, William Wanton. In 1740 he again represented his colony in a boundary line debate, this time with Massachusetts. The case was discussed before commissioners appointed by the King, Updike's speeches being described by a contemporary, Judge Lightfoot, as a brilliant performance (Wilkins Updike, *Memoirs, post*, p. 49). The decision reached by the commissioners proved unsatisfactory to the Massachusetts delegation, and the location of this boundary also was eventually settled by the King in Council.

Since Updike's retirement from the attorney-generalship, a law had been passed providing that each county of Rhode Island Colony should have its own attorney-general, and in 1741 Updike was elected to the office for Kings County, and held it until 1743 when the law was repealed. He was then again elected attorney-general for the whole colony, remaining as such until his death. In 1749, when the supreme court of Rhode Island ruled that no English statutes could be considered in force unless definitely adopted by the colony, Updike was one of the group of lawyers who selected the statutes to be proposed for adoption.

Not only was he an outstanding leader in the political life of Rhode Island, he was active, also, in its literary and social interests. He was a charter member of the society for the promotion of knowledge and science which was founded in Newport in 1730, and out of which grew the Redwood Library. Dean Berkeley, during his stay in Newport, was the friendly counselor of this society, and Updike became intimately associated with him. Updike was married first, Dec. 20, 1716, to Sarah, daughter of Gov. Benedict Arnold: she died in 1718, and on Dec. 22, 1722, he married Anstis Jenkins, whose inheritance added considerably to his own ample patrimony;

his third wife was Mary (Godfrey) Wanton, whom he married Mar. 14, 1745. In appearance he was a man slightly above the average height, with a dignified bearing, and a clear, pleasing voice, which contributed to his success as a speaker.

[C. W. Opdyke, *The Op Dyck Geneal.* (1889); J. O. Austin, *The Geneal. Dict. of R. I.* (1887), p. 397; Wilkins Updike, *Memoirs of the R. I. Bar* (1842); J. R. Cole, *Hist. of Washington and Kent Counties, R. I.* (1889); *The Biog. Cyc. of Representative Men of R. I.* (1881); J. R. Bartlett, *Records of the Colony of R. I.*, vols. IV, V (1859–60); Wilkins Updike, *A Hist. of the Episcopal Church in Narragansett, R. I.* (2nd ed., 3 vols., 1907), ed. by Daniel Goodwin.]   E. R. B.

UPHAM, CHARLES WENTWORTH(May 4, 1802–June 15, 1875), Unitarian clergyman, congressman, and historian of the Salem witchcraft delusion, was born in St. John, New Brunswick, the son of Joshua and Mary (Chandler) Upham. He was a descendant of John Upham who emigrated from England to Weymouth, Mass., in 1635. Joshua Upham, a native of Brookfield, Mass., a graduate of Harvard, and a Loyalist during the American Revolution, had served in the British army during the war, and at its close had emigrated to New Brunswick, where he held the office of judge of the supreme court until his death in 1808. Charles attended school in St. John, and at the age of twelve he was apprenticed to an apothecary. In 1816 he went to Boston to work for his cousin, Phineas Upham, a merchant; but this benevolent kinsman, soon perceiving that the boy's inclination was for study rather than business, placed him under the tutelage of Deacon Samuel Greele, and in 1817 sent him to Harvard College. Upham amply justified his kinsman's aid by graduating in 1821, second in his class. He next spent three years in the Cambridge Divinity School, and on Dec. 8, 1824, was ordained as associate pastor of the First Church (Unitarian) of Salem. Here he served until 1844—twelve years as the colleague of the Rev. John Prince—when, suffering from a bronchial ailment, he resigned.

During his career as clergyman, he distinguished himself as a learned champion of Unitarianism. In his discourse *Principles of the Reformation* (1826), he urged the necessity of advancing beyond the religious beliefs of the Pilgrim fathers. In 1833–34 he engaged in an extended controversy with the Rev. George B. Cheever [*q.v.*] in the columns of the *Salem Gazette* on the subject of Unitarian versus Trinitarian principles. Upham's chief proposition, in the support of which he displayed a formidable knowledge of the history and literature of the Reformation, was that Ralph Cudworth, who had been quoted by Cheever in defense of the Trinitarian doctrine, was in reality a Unitarian. By 1840, in *The Scripture Doctrine of Regeneration*, he could rejoice in the "abandonment of Calvinism" and the "general diffusion of rational Christianity."

Having partially recovered his health, in 1848 Upham turned to politics, aligning himself with the Whig party. In 1849–50 he was a member of the state House of Representatives and in 1850–51, of the state Senate. He warmly supported the presidential candidacy of Zachary Taylor, and at the request of the city authorities of Salem he delivered a eulogy, July 18, 1850, on the late President's life and character. He was a delegate to the state constitutional convention of 1853, and was a member of the Thirty-third Congress (1853–55). As a congressman he opposed the Kansas-Nebraska Act, approaching the subject not as an abolitionist or moral reformer, but as a historian, insisting upon the validity of the principles involved in the ordinance of 1787 and the Missouri Compromise. An active supporter in 1856 of the newly organized Republican party, he wrote a campaign biography of John C. Frémont. He was a member of the state Senate from 1857 to 1859 and served as its presiding officer. From 1859 to 1861 he was again a member of the state House of Representatives.

Retiring from political life in 1860, Upham devoted his energies to historical research. He is remembered chiefly as the author of *Salem Witchcraft* (2 vols., 1867). To furnish a background for the events of 1692, he reconstructed in admirable detail the local family history of Salem Village. His account of the witch trials is still of use to historians. A controversy arose as to the part taken by Cotton Mather [*q.v.*] in the persecution of the witches: Upham had argued that Mather fomented the delusion to increase his power in the community; William F. Poole [*q.v.*] defended Mather in the *North American Review* (April 1869); Upham, with characteristic love of debate, replied in a spirited brochure of ninety finely printed pages (*Salem Witchcraft and Cotton Mather*, 1869). Although the question is still a disputed one, recent scholarly opinion seems inclined to exculpate Mather (K. B. Murdock, *Selections from Cotton Mather*, 1926, p. xv).

It seems likely that Upham's reputation as a man will suffer as a result of his having incurred the ill will of Nathaniel Hawthorne. Because of Upham's activity in securing the removal of Hawthorne as surveyor of customs at Salem, the novelist is believed to have drawn, in the character of Judge Pyncheon, a satirical portrait of his political opponent (see W. S. Nevins,

"Nathaniel Hawthorne's Removal from the Salem Custom House," *Historical Collections of the Essex Institute*, April 1917; Julian Hawthorne, *Nathaniel Hawthorne and His Wife*, 1885, I, 339, 438). Pyncheon, in the words of Henry James, is "a superb, full-blown hypocrite, a large-based, full-nurtured Pharisee" (*Hawthorne*, 1879, p. 124). This portrait, however, contains elements of caricature, and, like many other famous satirical sketches, it is doubtless unfair to its prototype. Upham was apparently held in high esteem by many of his contemporaries. He numbered Edward Everett among his friends, and Emerson, his classmate at Harvard, referred to his "frank and attractive" manners, and his large "repertory of men and events" (Ellis, *Memoir, post*, p. 12). He died in Salem. On Mar. 29, 1826, he married Ann Susan, daughter of the Rev. Abiel Holmes [*q.v.*] of Cambridge, and sister of Oliver Wendell Holmes; they had fourteen children, all but three of whom died either in infancy or in early life.

[F. K. Upham, *The Descendants of John Upham of Mass.* (1892); G. E. Ellis, *An Address . . . at the Funeral Services of Charles W. Upham* (1875), and *Memoir of Charles Wentworth Upham* (1877); *Biog. Dir. Am. Cong.* (1928); S. A. Eliot, *Heralds of a Liberal Faith* (1910), vols. I, II; *Salem Gazette*, June 18, 1875; *Boston Transcript*, June 15, 1875.]   R. S.

UPHAM, SAMUEL FOSTER (May 19, 1834–Oct. 5, 1904), Methodist Episcopal clergyman, for many years professor in Drew Theological Seminary, was born in Duxbury, Mass. His father, Frederick Upham, also a Methodist minister, was descended from John Upham who emigrated from England to Weymouth, Mass., in 1635; his mother, Deborah Bourne of Sandwich, Mass., was a descendant of Richard Bourne, missionary to the Indians, who died in Sandwich in 1682. Samuel prepared for college at East Greenwich (R. I.) Academy, and graduated from Wesleyan University in 1856. He was immediately admitted to the Providence Conference of the Methodist Episcopal Church on trial, was ordained deacon in 1858, and elder in 1860. From the beginning of his ministry he was a popular preacher, and his advancement was rapid. From 1856 to 1864 he served churches in Taunton, Mass., Pawtucket, R. I., New Bedford, Mass., and Bristol, R. I. In 1864 he transferred to the New England Conference, where at different times he was pastor of three Boston churches, and also of churches in Lowell, Lynn, and Springfield, Mass. In 1865 he was chaplain of the Massachusetts House of Representatives. Appointed professor of practical theology at Drew Theological Seminary, Madison, N. J., in 1880, he began his duties there on Mar. 13, 1881, and continued in the performance of them until his death some twenty-three years later.

Samuel, or "Sammy" Upham, as he was affectionately called, was one of the best known and most highly esteemed of the Methodist ministers of his day. If some excelled him in learning and scholarly productivity, not many surpassed him in personal attractiveness, shrewd wisdom and sound judgment, ability and disposition to be helpful to individuals, and power to interest and influence an audience. He was a kindly, companionable, sagacious person with whom young and old felt at home, and at Drew he was the friend, counsellor, and prophet of many. He was blessed with wit and humor, was fond of his cronies, and "loved a joke no matter what its age" (Tipple, *post*, p. 108). He was an adept in the use of ridicule and could be merciless in exposing error. His preaching was trenchant, practical, and arousing, and few were called upon more often for sermons and addresses on special occasions. In the councils of the Church and in the management of its institutions his influence was strong and lasting. From 1871 until his death he was a trustee of Wesleyan University and from 1880 till his death, of the Methodist preparatory school, Wilbraham Academy, Wilbraham, Mass. He was a member of all the General Conferences from 1880 to 1904 inclusive; one of the board of managers of the Missionary Society and for sixteen years its representative on the General Missionary Committee; member and secretary of the committee on constitutional law; and chairman of the hymnal commission, which prepared the official Methodist hymnal. As a member of the committee on itinerancy in the General Conference of 1900, he was instrumental in having the time limit to pastorates removed. On several occasions he received votes for the office of bishop. He was married, Apr. 15, 1857, to Lucy Graves Smith of Middletown, Conn.; they had five sons.

[F. K. Upham, *The Descendants of John Upham of Mass.* (1892); *Alumni Record of Wesleyan Univ.* (4th ed., 1911); *Official Minutes of the ... New Eng. Conf. of the M. E. Ch., 1905* (n.d.); E. S. Tipple, *Drew Theological Sem., 1867–1917* (copr. 1917); *Who's Who in America*, 1903–05; *Christian Advocate* (N. Y.), Oct. 13, 1904; *Zion's Herald* (Boston), Oct. 12, 1904.]
H. E. S.

UPHAM, THOMAS COGSWELL (Jan. 30, 1799–Apr. 2, 1872), teacher, metaphysician, and author, was born at Deerfield, N. H., a member of a distinguished family descended from John Upham who settled in Weymouth, Mass., in 1635. His father, Nathaniel Upham, served in Congress; one brother, Nathaniel, was a judge of the supreme court of New Hampshire; another,

Francis, a well-known professor of mental philosophy at Rutgers Female College, New York. His mother was Judith Cogswell, daughter of Thomas Cogswell, of Gilmanton, N. H. Upham graduated from Dartmouth College in 1818, and from Andover Theological Seminary in 1821. He made there such an outstanding record for indefatigable study and scholarship that he became tutor in Hebrew under Prof. Moses Stuart [*q.v.*]; and in 1823 he published an excellent translation, *Jahn's Biblical Archaeology,* from the Latin of Johann Jahn, with additions and corrections. From 1823 to 1824 he served as associate pastor of the Congregational Church at Rochester, N. H. In 1824 he was chosen professor of mental and moral philosophy at Bowdoin College, which chair he held until his retirement in 1867. His remaining years were spent in study and writing at Kennebunkport, Me., and later in New York City, where he died.

At Bowdoin he was one of the best known teachers in a rather distinguished faculty. Although he came to his professorship from a pastorate, he soon gave up preaching and public speaking, and made his strong religious influence felt in the classroom, in small groups of students, and with individuals. He was actively interested in the social reforms of the day, was an earnest and liberal patron of the colonization of negroes, a strong supporter of the temperance movement, and one of the earliest American advocates of international peace, collaborating with William Ladd [*q.v.*] and writing one of the essays published in *Prize Essays on a Congress of Nations* (1840). In 1852 he spent a year in European and Eastern travel, publishing in 1855 *Letters Aesthetic, Social, and Moral, Written from Europe, Egypt, and Palestine.* He also served Bowdoin well in practical affairs, at one time raising by his own efforts the then surprisingly large sum of nearly $70,000. Yet it is as an author in his chosen field of mental philosophy that Upham was best known. Brought to Bowdoin to oppose the doctrines of Kant and his school, he found himself after long effort unable to refute the teachings of the German metaphysician, and was on the point of resigning his professorship when suddenly he conceived a distinction between the intellect, the sensibilities, and the will which he embodied in his *A Philosophical and Practical Treatise on the Will* (1834), his outstanding work. This has been called "one of the first original and comprehensive contributions of American scholarship to modern psychology" (Foster, *post*, p. 249). This work and a succeeding volume, *Outlines of Imperfect and Disordered Mental Action* (1840), made him to be regarded more as a psychologist than a theologian, and did much to liberate American philosophy and theology from the thraldom of the elder Jonathan Edwards [*q.v.*]. A bibliography of Upham's works contains more than sixty items, and includes, in addition to philosophical treatises, a religious classic, *Principles of the Interior or Hidden Life* (1843), and some books of verse, notably *American Cottage Life* (1851), first published anonymously about 1828 as *Domestic and Religious Offering.*

In character and appearance, Upham was distinctly of the academic type of the early nineteenth century. Modest, retiring, very reserved, almost secretive, absent-minded, kindly, with remarkable self-control, he was "in the best sense a quietest [*sic*], and seemed . . . to have attained to a high state of repose in God" (Packard, *post,* p. 21). Having no children, he and his wife, Phebe Lord, whom he married on May 18, 1825, and whose portrait by Gilbert Stuart in the Bowdoin Art Museum reveals an unusual loveliness of person and character, adopted several children, and made their home, in the words of Harriet Beecher Stowe, who was received there on her arrival in Brunswick, "delightful . . . a beautiful pattern of a Christian family, a beautiful exemplification of religion" (Hatch, *post,* p. 60).

[F. K. Upham, *The Descendants of John Upham* (1892); A. S. Packard, *Address on the Life and Character of Thomas C. Upham, D.D.* (1873); L. C. Hatch, *The Hist. of Bowdoin Coll.* (1927); F. H. Foster, *A Genetic Hist. of New England Theology* (1907); death notice in *N. Y. Times,* Apr. 3, 1872; letters and newspaper articles in Bowdoin Coll. lib.]   K. C. M. S.

UPHAM, WARREN (Mar. 8, 1850–Jan. 29, 1934), geologist, archeologist, writer on historical subjects, was born at Amherst, N. H., the son of Jacob and Sarah (Hayward) Upham, and a descendant of John Upham who emigrated from England to Weymouth, Mass., in 1635. After his graduation from Dartmouth College in 1871, he was engaged on the geological survey of New Hampshire (1874–78), and on the geological survey of Minnesota and the United States Geological Survey (1879–95). He went to Minnesota in 1879. On Oct. 22, 1885, he married Addie M. Bixby of Aurora, Minn.; there was one child, who died at birth. From 1895 to 1914 he was secretary and librarian of the Minnesota Historical Society, and from 1914 to 1933 archeologist of the society.

Upham's life affords the unusual example of a diligent scholar at the height of his career in one science changing his major field after the age of fifty. Before 1905 most of his work was in geology; after 1905, in archeology and history. An indefatigable and patient worker, he

published almost two hundred papers on geology. Of these all but about twenty are on glacial geology and nearly related subjects, which were his principal fields of work. His greatest contribution to geology probably is contained in the fine series of county reports issued by the Minnesota Geological Survey, but his best known paper is "The Glacial Lake Agassiz," *United States Geological Survey Monographs,* vol. XXV (1896), which includes many of the principal results of his studies in Minnesota, North Dakota, and Manitoba. This monograph, a classic on the subject of post-glacial physiography, describes an ancient lake vastly greater than the present Lake Superior, its beaches, deltas, and other shore features that became wonderfully well exposed when the lake shrank to become the present Lake Winnipeg. In 1896 Upham issued, jointly with G. F. Wright, a volume entitled *Greenland Ice Fields and Life in the North Atlantic.*

His most important historical publications appeared in the *Collections of the Minnesota Historical Society,* among them "Groseilliers and Radisson, the First White Men in Minnesota" (vol. X, pt. 2, 1905), "Minnesota Biographies" (vol. XIV, 1912), which he compiled with Rose B. Dunlap, and "Minnesota Geographic Names" (vol. XVII, 1920). He was one of the editors of *Minnesota in Three Centuries* (1908). He was particularly interested in the history of man before the period of the graphic arts, and published two noteworthy contributions on the subject: "Man in the Ice Age at Lansing, Kan., and Little Falls, Minn." (*American Geologist,* Sept. 1902), and "Valley Loess and the Fossil Man of Lansing, Kan." (*Ibid.,* Jan. 1903). Although the conclusions of these discourses were not generally accepted as indisputable proof of the presence of man in North America during the Ice Age, Upham died with the conviction that man inhabited the region beyond the ice edge during at least a part of that period, and recent discoveries in Minnesota lend strong support to that theory. Upham was courtly, modest, unobtrusive, almost retiring until his own field was mentioned; he then became alert, authoritative, and entertaining. He was endeared to all his associates by his modesty regarding his own attainments, his thoughtfulness for others, and his willingness to give without stint both his time and his knowledge. He died at St. Paul, Minn., where he had lived for many years.

[See F. K. Upham, *The Descendants of John Upham* (1892); Mary U. Kelly and Warren Upham, *Upham and Amherst, N. H.* (1897); *Who's Who in America,* 1932–33; *Am. Men of Sci.* (5th ed., 1933), ed. by J. M. and Jaques Cattell; "Minn. Biogs.," *Minn. Hist. Soc.*

Colls., vol. XIV (1912); obituary in *Minneapolis Jour.*, Jan. 30, 1934. A bibliog. of Upham's articles on geology appears in *U. S. Geological Survey Bull. 746* (1923).]

W. H. E.

UPJOHN, RICHARD (Jan. 22, 1802–Aug. 17, 1878), architect, born in Shaftesbury, Dorsetshire, England, was the son of James Upjohn, surveyor and master in the grammar school, and of Elizabeth Plantagenet Dryden Michell, daughter of the rector of Holy Trinity Church, Shaftesbury. His parents had planned that he should enter one of the learned professions, but he insisted on becoming a draftsman and was accordingly apprenticed to a cabinetmaker. A master craftsman at twenty-two, he established his own business in Shaftesbury, and on Nov. 14, 1826, he married in London Elizabeth Parry, daughter of the Rev. John Parry of Denbigh, North Wales. He prospered, but, ambitious, headstrong, and incautious, he became entangled in grandiose schemes and was soon hopelessly in debt. During his early childhood, the Upjohn family had spent some time in St. John's, Newfoundland, where James Upjohn had established a business. Now, refusing to let an uncle shoulder his debts, Richard set out for America with his wife and young son, Richard Michell [*q.v.*], and landed in New York on June 1, 1829 (diary in the possession of his grandson, Hobart Upjohn). In the fall of 1830 he finally settled in New Bedford, Mass., became a draftsman for Samuel Leonard, builder and sperm-oil merchant, and opened an evening school of drawing. Upon seeing some drawings for the Boston Custom House, he exclaimed, according to a family story, "If that is architecture, I am an architect," and forthwith opened his office and advertised for work.

In February 1834 he moved to Boston, and for four years worked spasmodically for Alexander Parris [*q.v.*]. He also did considerable work of his own, including numerous Greek villas, and a Gothic iron fence for Boston Common. In 1837 he completed St. John's Church, Bangor, Me., his first Gothic Church, and the first of much Maine work, which culminated in the large stone mansion for R. H. Gardiner at Gardiner, Me. In the spring of 1839 he was chosen draftsman for repairs and alterations in Trinity Church, New York, and when a new building was decided upon he was retained officially as architect. In August he moved to New York. The new Trinity Church, begun in 1841 and consecrated in 1846, of unprecedented richness and purity of style, won immediate fame, equalling, if not surpassing, that of Grace Church, New York, by the younger James Renwick [*q.v.*]. From that time

on, work flowed into Upjohn's office faster than he could handle it. He designed not only Gothic churches, but houses and civil buildings as well. Many of his houses were in the Italian or "bracketed" styles, and the Trinity Building (1852)—at the time New York's finest office building—was called Italian Renaissance.

The long list of Upjohn's important work includes an "Italian villa" for Edward King, Newport (see A. J. Downing, *The Architecture of Country Houses*, 1850, pp. 317–21); the alterations of the Van Rensselaer Manor-house, Albany, N. Y., in a kind of pseudo-Colonial; of the Van Buren house, Kinderhook, N. Y.; of the Pierrepont house, Brooklyn, N. Y., all done between 1840 and 1850. Other buildings, designed between 1840 and 1855, include the city hall and Taunton Academy, Taunton, Mass., and the much praised Corn Exchange Bank Building, New York; the Church of the Ascension, New York; Bowdoin College Chapel; the Church of the Pilgrims, Brooklyn, a building of marked originality; Grace Church, Newark, N. J.; St. James', New London, Conn.; the Church of the Holy Communion, Twentieth Street and Sixth Avenue, New York; St. Paul's Church, Buffalo, N. Y.; St. Mark's, Augusta, Me.; St. Paul's, Brookline, Mass.; and Grace Church, Utica, N. Y. During the period of the growing influence of Richard Michell Upjohn upon the office work, the best works were the Central Congregational Church, Boston, Mass., and St. Thomas's, New York. Upjohn's favorite work, and in many ways his best, is Trinity Chapel, West Twenty-fifth Street, New York (1853), with unusual direct simplicity of design and unusual height. The delicate detail of the monument to unknown Revolutionary soldiers, Trinity Churchyard, is also an achievement rare for the time. Upjohn's careful and sensitive use of the precedent of English Gothic was widely imitated but rarely equalled; his influence in the United States was in many ways similar to the influence in England of A. W. N. Pugin. Like most early Gothic Revival architects, Upjohn was more interested in effect than in structure and used lath-and-plaster vaults frequently, apparently without compunction. Yet in Trinity Chapel there is an honest use of materials everywhere, and in *Upjohn's Rural Architecture* (1852) the designs show a simple and functional use of wood.

Upjohn is important as the chief instrumentality in the founding of the American Institute of Architects, of which he was president from its beginning (1857) until his resignation in 1876. At the first meeting, in his office and at his invitation, the group took the name "New York Society of Architects," but soon adopted the present name, and the new society became the successor to the short-lived American Institution of Architects, founded in 1837. As president Upjohn supported the highest possible professional standards. The foundations of the present competition code and the present standards of professional ethics were laid during his administration, and largely at his instigation. The same high ethical standards controlled his personal life. He refused to design the Arlington Street Unitarian Church, Boston, since it seemed to him an anti-Christian, because Unitarian, enterprise; his attitude in this probably caused the loss to him of the Harvard College Chapel, designs for which he had prepared the same year. He made it a practice to do at least one mission church a year free. His influence was spread indirectly by many architects who were trained in his office or worked for him, among them Leopold Eidlitz [q.v.], Alpheus Morse, Charles Babcock (later professor of architecture at Cornell), Joseph C. Wells, and Charles Clinton, of Clinton and Russell. His great hobby was painting, and he brought back from a European trip in 1850 many landscapes of high merit. He was an honorary member of both the Royal Institute of British Architects and the Institute of Portuguese Architects. He died at Garrison, N. Y., survived by his wife and five children.

[I. N. P. Stokes, *The Iconography of Manhattan Island*, vols. III (1918), V–VI (1926–28); Glenn Brown, *The Am. Institute of Architects, 1857–1907* (n.d.); obituaries in *Am. Architect and Building News*, Aug. 24, *N. Y. Times*, Aug. 18, and *N. Y. Tribune*, Aug. 19, 1878; biog. in MS. by Upjohn's grandson, Hobart B. Upjohn; office records and drawings in the possession of H. B. Upjohn of New York.]   T. F. H.

UPJOHN, RICHARD MICHELL (Mar. 7, 1828–Mar. 3, 1903), architect, the son of Richard Upjohn [q.v.] and Elizabeth (Parry) Upjohn, was born in Shaftesbury, England, and was brought to America in his second year. He received a good education in private schools, and in 1846 entered his father's office, where during his father's extended European trip in 1850 he had full charge. In 1851–52 he studied in Europe. On his return he opened his own office but soon returned to his father's as a full partner (1853) and exercised a growing influence on the design. During the sixties and seventies, it is sometimes difficult to determine which was the controlling mind. St. Thomas's Church, New York, is typical of the work of this period; its towers probably indicate the son's taste.

Upjohn's work was less dominantly ecclesiastical than his father's. He was the architect of the Mechanics' Bank, New York (1858), one of the early buildings to use rolled-iron beams and brick floor arches; the building of the Newark Banking and Insurance Company, Newark, N. J.; a large school in Hartford, Conn., and the first building for Trinity School, New York. Among his noteworthy churches were the old Madison Square Presbyterian Church, New York; Park Church, Hartford, Conn.; the Presbyterian Church and manse, Rye, N. Y.; the De Lancey Memorial, Geneva, N. Y.; St. Mark's Pro-Cathedral, San Antonio, Tex.; and St. Paul's Cathedral at Fond du Lac, Wis. One of his best churches was the American church, St. John's, in Dresden, Germany. The main entrance gateway of Greenwood Cemetery, Brooklyn, is his design (1861); and it is probable that the Central Congregational Church, Boston, with its simple and exquisite 235-foot stone tower and spire is his also. His most famous work was the state capitol at Hartford, Conn. (1885), for which drawings were begun in 1872. The only such building in America to combine a dome with wings in a Gothic style, it presented problems of exceptional difficulty. Upjohn had intended to use a square tower, but the state authorities were unable to conceive of a capitol without a dome and forced him to design one; the resulting dome is, nevertheless, a brilliant adaptation. Under the influence of Ruskin, Upjohn's work is often full of such "Victorian Gothic" mannerisms as polychromy and the dominance of the horizontal line. The Trinity school building, with its erratic detail and its rich plate tracery over flat-headed windows, is typical, and the lavish color and carving of the Hartford capitol, in which the modern eye often sees only the bizarre, is an excellent example of Ruskinian principles conscientiously applied.

Upjohn was a fellow of the American Institute of Architects from its beginning, and for two years a president of its New York chapter; he was also a member of the Institute's important committee for examining unsafe buildings. He lived in Brooklyn for most of his later life. Much interested in local history, he was one of the founders of the Long Island Historical Society. In character he was reserved, in his later years almost a recluse. Strong-willed, impulsive, at times hot-tempered, he was an indomitable worker, making many of the office drawings himself. He retired gradually from the practice of architecture during the nineties, his interests becoming more and more financial; by 1895 his architectural career had ceased. On Oct. 1, 1856, he married Emma Degen Tyng, daughter of the Rev. James H. Tyng, in Morristown, N. J. There were nine children, of whom the youngest became an architect. Upjohn died in Brooklyn, survived by five sons and three daughters.

[*Who's Who in America*, 1901–02; *Proc. . . . Am. Institute of Architects . . . 1903*, vol. XXXVII (1904); *Am. Architect and Building News*, Mar. 14, 1903; *Am. Art Ann.*, 1903; R. M. Upjohn, *The State Capitol, Hartford, Conn.* (1886); obituaries in *Brooklyn Daily Eagle*, Mar. 3, and *Evening Post* (N. Y.), Mar. 4, 1903; family records, office drawings and records in the possession of Upjohn's son, Hobart B. Upjohn of New York.]   T. F. H.

UPSHUR, ABEL PARKER (June 17, 1791– Feb. 28, 1844), jurist, cabinet officer, publicist, one of twelve children of Littleton Upshur and Ann (Parker) Upshur, and a descendant of Arthur Upshur who settled on the Eastern Shore of Virginia in the seventeenth century, was born in Northampton County, Va. His father, a Federalist member of the Virginia legislature of 1809, voted against the resolutions thanking Jefferson for his services to the country and later served as a captain in the War of 1812. Abel Upshur studied at the College of New Jersey (Princeton) until his expulsion as a participant in a student rebellion in 1807 and then continued his studies at Yale, but did not graduate. After reading law in the office of William Wirt of Richmond, he began practice in that city. In 1812–13 he was a member of the House of Delegates from his native county, and served again in that capacity, 1825–27. He was also a member of the Virginia constitutional convention of 1829–30, in which he was an opponent of the proposed democratic changes in the constitution. He denied the existence of any original principles of government, insisting instead that the interests and necessities of the people determined the principles of government (*Proceedings and Debates, post*, p. 69). He rejected the theory of "natural law," maintaining that the only natural law was "the law of force . . . the only rule of right" (*Ibid.*, p. 67). From 1826 to 1841, he was a member of the supreme court of Virginia, and in politics he was associated with the extreme state-rights, proslavery group.

In September 1841, Upshur was appointed secretary of the navy by President Tyler, and in 1843 he succeeded Webster as secretary of state. An ardent advocate of the annexation of Texas as vital to the security of the South, he reopened negotiations with that republic, but they were interrupted by his death in the explosion of a gun on board the battleship *Princeton*, and were completed by his successor, Calhoun.

A particularistic jurist and planter-philosopher of Tidewater Virginia, Upshur often ex-

pressed his views upon slavery, government, and banks. The South constituted, in his opinion, the only bulwark of conservatism in America against the rising tide of agrarianism, leveling democracy, and all the *isms* of the free North. "It is clear," he wrote pessimistically, "that in this country Liberty is destined to perish a suicide. . . . And perish when she may, I am much deceived if her last entrenchment, her latest abiding place, will not be found in the slave holding states" ("Domestic Slavery," *Southern Literary Messenger*, October 1839). Law, and not the principle of numerical majority, he held to be the basis of liberty—a juridical conception. In a letter to his intimate friend, Judge Beverley Tucker, commenting upon Dorr's Rebellion, Upshur wrote: "This is the very madness of democracy, and a fine illustration of the workings of the majority principle" (Tyler, *post*, II, 198). His pamphlet, *A Brief Enquiry into the True Nature and Character of our Federal Government* (1840), a review of Story's *Commentaries*, was regarded by his friends as a complete refutation of the nationalistic theory of the Constitution. It was reprinted in 1863 by Northern Democrats as a means of setting forth the political philosophy of the Confederacy (Adams, *post*, p. 77). In an address (1841) before the literary societies of the College of William and Mary upon "The True Theory of Government," Upshur rejected almost *in toto* the natural rights philosophy, characterizing it as one that "overlooks all social obligations, denies the inheritable quality of property, unfrocks the priest, and laughs at the marriage tie" (*Southern Literary Messenger*, June 1856, p. 410). A supporter of banks, he opposed the requirement of specie as the basis of credit and also opposed laws which declared banks insolvent when unable to redeem their notes in specie. "A bank," he wrote, "without a single dollar in specie, yet having good notes of others, equal to its own notes outstanding, and its other indebtedness, is perfectly solvent, and entitled to credit" (*A Brief Enquiry into the True Basis of the Credit System*, 1840, p. 11). He furthermore urged the minimum regulation of banks, believing that the "general law of the land, the common law . . . affords ample means . . . of keeping them within proper limits" (*Ibid.*, p. 20).

Upshur was married twice: first, to Elizabeth Dennis, and second, in 1826, to his cousin, Elizabeth Upshur; she, with their daughter, survived him.

[C. H. Ambler, *Thomas Ritchie, A Study in Virginia Politics* (1913); T. H. Benton, *Thirty Years' View*, vol. II (1856), J. P. Kennedy, *Memoirs of the Life of William Wirt* (1849), I, 399; *Niles' National*

Register, Sept. 18, 1841, Feb. 12, 26, 1842, Mar. 2, 1844; L. G. Tyler, *The Letters and Times of the Tylers* (2 vols., 1884–85); *Proc. and Debates of the Va. State Convention of 1829–30* (1830); *Wm. and Mary Coll. Quart.,* Apr. 1895, Oct. 1907, Jan. 1928, Jan. 1931; H. A. Wise, *Seven Decades of the Union* (1872), pp. 197–200; Mary Upshur Sturges, "Abel Parker Upshur," *Mag. of Am. Hist.,* Sept. 1877; R. G. Adams, "Abel Parker Upshur," in S. F. Bemis, *The Am. Secretaries of State,* vol. V (1928); *Daily Nat. Intelligencer* (Washington), Feb. 29, 1844.]   W. G. B.

UPSHUR, JOHN HENRY (Dec. 5, 1823–May 30, 1917), naval officer, was born at Eastville, Northampton County, Va., and had originally the surname Nottingham, being the son of Elizabeth Parker (Upshur) and John Evans Nottingham. He was a nephew of Abel Parker Upshur [*q.v.*] and of Capt. George P. Upshur, U. S. N., and perhaps because of these relationships both he and his brother, Dr. George L. Upshur, were given in childhood their mother's family name, upon authorization of the Virginia legislature. After attending the grammar school connected with the College of William and Mary (1834–41), he entered the navy, Nov. 4, 1841, as a midshipman. A Mediterranean cruise in the *Congress* (1842–43) was followed by service throughout the Mexican War in the sloop *St. Mary's,* including duty ashore, Mar. 10–25, 1847, with the naval battery at the siege of Vera Cruz. During the next year he attended the United States Naval Academy, then under the superintendency of his uncle, George P. Upshur, and graduated as passed midshipman, Aug. 10, 1848, ranking 17 in his class of 235 members. During the next decade his chief assignments were in the Mediterranean Squadron (1849–50), in the storeship *Supply* with Perry's mission to Japan (1852–55), as flag lieutenant in the *Cumberland,* African Squadron (1857–59), and as an instructor at the Naval Academy (1859–61). In the Civil War he served in the *Wabash* at the capture of Hatteras Inlet, in subsequent operations in the North Carolina sounds, and at the capture of Port Royal, Nov. 7, 1861. As senior lieutenant of the *Wabash* and one of the officers commanding gundeck divisions, he could share considerably in Commander C. R. P. Rodgers' praise of these officers for handling their divisions at Port Royal "in a manner which illustrated the highest power both of men and guns" (*War of the Rebellion: Official Records, Navy,* vol. XII, p. 267). Made lieutenant commander, July 16, 1862, he subsequently commanded the side-wheeler *Flambeau* in the Charleston blockade. In November 1863 Rear Admiral Samuel Phillips Lee selected him as chief of staff and commander of the flagship *Minnesota,* North Atlantic Blockading Squadron, a position he held until September 1864. He was then assigned to the fast side-wheeler *A. D. Vance,* and commanded her in both attacks on Fort Fisher, Dec. 23–25, 1864, and Jan. 13–15, 1865. After the second action, in which he had charge of the reserve division, Admiral David Dixon Porter recommended his advancement, stating that he "was employed night and day in landing army stores and guns, and covering the troops" (*Ibid.,* vol. XI, p. 455). He was made commander, July 25, 1866; captain, Jan. 31, 1872; commodore, July 11, 1880; and rear admiral, Oct. 1, 1884. In 1870 he incurred a court martial and reprimand for having paid money to an appointee to the Naval Academy to induce the latter's withdrawal in favor of his son. There were, however, many extenuating circumstances, and it was testified at his trial that he was "in all matters of duty even fastidiously particular" (*House Executive Document, post,* p. 15). His later sea commands included the *Frolic* in the Mediterranean (1865–67), the *Pensacola* and afterwards the *Brooklyn* in South American waters (1873–76), and the Pacific Squadron (1884–85). He was a member of the Board of Inspectors (1877–80) and, after a year's leave in Europe, commandant of the Brooklyn navy yard (1882–84).

On June 1, 1885, he retired, and made his subsequent home in Washington, D. C. Here he lived until his ninety-fourth year, a well-known figure at the Metropolitan Club, in full possession of his faculties to the last, and highly respected not only for his long and notable service but for his southern charm of manner (he was called "the Chesterfield of the Navy"), his keen mind, and his strict standards of conduct. His burial was in Arlington. By his first marriage in 1851 to Kate, daughter of Capt. William G. and America (Peter) Williams, and great-grand-daughter of Martha Washington, he had two sons and two daughters. He was married, second, to Agnes (Maxwell), widow of Philip Kearny [*q.v.*], who died July 2, 1917.

[L. G. Tyler, in *William and Mary Coll. Quart.*; Apr. 1895; *Who's Who in America,* 1916–17; L. R. Hamersly, *The Records of Living Officers of the U. S. Navy and Marine Corps* (1902 ed.); *Memoir and Correspondence of Charles Steedman* (1912), ed. by A. L. Mason; *War of the Rebellion: Official Records* (*Navy*); *House Exec. Doc. 308,* 41 Cong., 2 Sess., which contains the proceedings at Upshur's court martial; Personnel Files, Navy Dept. Lib.; *Sea Power,* July 1917; *Army and Navy Jour.,* June 2, 1917; obituary in *Evening Star* (Washington, D. C.), May 31, 1917.]   A. W—t.

UPTON, EMORY (Aug. 27, 1839–Mar. 15, 1881), soldier, tactician, author, was born on a farm west of Batavia, N. Y., the tenth child and sixth son of Daniel and Electra (Randall) Upton. He was a descendant of John Upton, who seems to have been in Massachusetts as early as 1639, bought land in Salem in 1658, and later moved to North Reading. During the winter of 1855–56, Emory Upton was a student at Oberlin College. Interested from early youth in military history, he secured appointment to the United States Military Academy, which he entered on July 1, 1856. He was an excellent student, and was notably outspoken on controversial subjects. As personal feelings grew tense over the issues that provoked the Civil War, he had the most celebrated physical encounter—with Wade Hampton Gibbes of South Carolina—in the history of West Point (Schaff, *post,* pp. 143–48). Graduating number eight on the list of forty-five with the first (May 6) class of 1861, he was at once appointed second lieutenant, 4th Artillery, and sent to help drill Federal volunteers then assembling about Washington. On May 14 he was advanced to first lieutenant in the newly organized 5th Artillery (field batteries), and continued to drill volunteers until assigned to active field service under Gen. Daniel Tyler [*q.v.*] in the 1st Division of McDowell's army in northern Virginia. From that time to the close of the Civil War, Upton's career was one of the most notable in the annals of the army, comprising as it did varied service (artillery, infantry, and cavalry) and participation in a large number of engagements; it also brought him by successive promotions to the rank of brevet major-general, United States Army.

Four of the many actions in which he commanded troops brought advanced rank "for gallant and meritorious services": at Rappahannock Station, Va., Nov. 7, 1863; at Spotsylvania, Va., May 10, 1864, where Upton, wounded in the charge, was promoted to brigadier-general on the spot by Grant; at the Opequon (or Winchester, Va.), Sept. 19, 1864, where after the death of Gen. D. A. Russell, Upton succeeded to command of the 1st Division, VI Army Corps, and though soon dangerously wounded, continued in active command while being carried about the field on a stretcher until the battle had been won (Wilson, *post,* I, 554); and at Selma, Ala., Apr. 2, 1865, where dismounted Federal cavalry, of which he led a detachment, broke through and surmounted stockaded fortifications defended by sheltered infantry and superior artillery, capturing the city and arsenal. For nearly three months after the Opequon engagement, Upton was disabled and on sick leave; meanwhile, J. H. Wilson [*q.v.*], assigned to command the cavalry in the farther South, requested and

secured his services for the latter part of the Tennessee-Alabama-Georgia campaign. Upton also participated in the Antietam and Fredericksburg campaigns, the thirty-five-mile march by the VI Corps from Manchester, Md., to Gettysburg, Pa., mostly through the night of July 1–2, 1863, and in the battles of the Wilderness and Cold Harbor, and about Petersburg. The timeliness, good judgment, and precision with which he executed orders were frequently commended in the reports of his superiors.

After the Civil War, Upton continued in the Regular Army, with much lower rank because of the reduction of the military establishment. For short periods he was stationed in Tennessee and Colorado; then transferred to West Point as a member of the board of officers appointed to consider the system of infantry tactics which he had prepared. That system, with which his name has since been associated, was adopted in 1867. After a short station in Kentucky, he secured leave of absence and with his wife spent several months in Europe. Returning in the late summer of 1868, he was again assigned to regular duties for short periods. From July 1, 1870, to June 30, 1875, he was commandant of cadets and instructor in artillery, infantry, and cavalry tactics at West Point. Those five years were the height of Upton's career in time of peace, and his influence upon the corps of cadets was particularly marked; meanwhile, he served on the board appointed to assimilate the tactics adopted in 1873. In the summer of 1875 he was relieved at the Military Academy and assigned to professional duty on a trip around the world via San Francisco and the Orient, and for the greater part of two years studied the army organizations of Asia and Europe. At Shanghai, October 1876, he wrote out an elaborate plan for a military academy in China on the model of West Point. Returning, he was appointed superintendent of theoretical instruction in the Artillery School, Fort Monroe, Va., where he was stationed nearly three years and during two periods commanded the post. After service as member of the board to codify army regulations, he was assigned to command the 4th Artillery and the Presidio of San Francisco.

There, before reaching the age of forty-two, he died by a shot from his own hand, an act explained in brief by "an incurable malady of the head and its passages that ultimately became unbearable" (Wilson, II, 368; Michie, *post,* pp. 474–97). His resignation as colonel of the 4th Artillery was written out and signed on the day before. Upton's tragic death was a shock to the nation, and particularly to the army, which had looked to him as a model of life and conduct as well as its leading tactician. Known always as a strict disciplinarian who drilled his men in all weathers and occasionally put them through new evolutions, he won and held their confidence and loyalty to a remarkable degree. His face, somewhat "pointed," was habitually in an attitude of concentration, "with force and determination in every line." In the field he took nothing for granted; was enterprising, resourceful, and energetic; acted upon personally ascertained or well-assimilated facts; and carried military books on campaigns which he studied in connection with situations developing from day to day. He was of strong religious nature and was in the habit of saying his prayers every night. On occasions he was excitable and angry, and after the great sacrifices at Cold Harbor, Va., in June 1864, he severely criticized the chief command (Michie, pp. 108–09). He rose to his greatest heights in the excitement and turmoil of battle. On Feb. 19, 1868, he married Emily Norwood Martin, who died Mar. 30, 1870, after much illness. His funeral was at Auburn, N. Y., Mar. 29, 1881, and he was buried in Fort Hill Cemetery there.

Upton wrote more on tactics and critical military history than any other officer of his day. Two books were published in his lifetime—*A New System of Infantry Tactics, Double and Single Rank, Adapted to American Topography and Improved Firearms* (1867, rev. ed., 1874); and *The Armies of Asia and Europe* (1878). A monumental work, "The Military Policy of the United States from 1775," upon which he had been engaged for several years, he was able to complete only down to the second year of the Civil War. In 1903–04 the manuscript was re-examined by Elihu Root, who was then secretary of war, and in 1904 *The Military Policy of the United States* was published, under the editorship of J. P. Sanger; in 1914 a separate reprint of the Mexican War section was made. Some of the recommendations contained in Upton's treatise have been adopted; others no longer apply to changed conditions of warfare; yet it remains the most important work on a subject nowhere else treated on the same scale and in equal detail. Its outstanding features are searching analyses of the American national military policy and fearless comments upon its results. Intense application to those engrossing subjects, usually in connection with the full discharge of routine military duties, may have been a contributing factor to Upton's breakdown in the prime of life.

[G. W. Cullum, *Biog. Reg. Officers and Grads., U. S. Mil. Acad.* (1891), vol. II; *Twelfth Ann. Reunion, Asso. Grads., U. S. Mil. Acad.* (1881); Morris Schaff, *The Spirit of Old West Point, 1858–1862* (1907); *War of the Rebellion: Official Records (Army)*; U. S. Grant, *Personal Memoirs*, II (1886), 223–25, 234–36; J. H. Wilson, *Under the Old Flag* (1912); W. F. Scott, *The Story of a Cavalry Regiment* (1893); I. O. Best, *Hist. of the 121st N. Y. State Infantry* (1921); E. N. Gilpin, "The Last Campaign," *Jour. U. S. Cavalry Asso.*, Apr. 1908; *Army and Navy Jour.*, Mar. 19 and 26, 1881; *Harper's Weekly*, Apr. 9, 1881; *Morning Call* (San Francisco), Mar. 16, 1881; P. S. Michie, *The Life and Letters of Emory Upton* (1885); W. H. Upton, *Geneal. Colls. for an Upton Family Hist.* (1893); J. A. Vinton, *The Upton Memorial* (1874); information from various army officers, from E. S. Martin, New York, and from the Seymour Library, Auburn, N. Y.]   R. B.

UPTON, GEORGE BRUCE (Oct. 11, 1804– July 1, 1874), merchant, capitalist, was born in Eastport, in the District of Maine, the second of the two sons of Daniel Putnam and Hannah (Bruce) Upton. He was descended from John Upton who seems to have been in Salisbury, Mass., as early as 1639, and later owned land in Salem. George's father died in 1805, and his mother moved to Billerica, Mass., where she lived with her brother. Her sons were prepared for college in the local school, but the elder elected to go to sea, and the younger to enter business. After an apprenticeship of about three years with several retail merchants in Boston, George, in 1821, became confidential clerk in the dry goods firm of Baker & Barrett on Nantucket Island. When the senior member retired in 1825, Upton formed a partnership with Barrett. In addition to retail business, the firm engaged in sperm whaling, shipbuilding, and the manufacture of candles on a large scale. Upton became active, also, in public affairs, serving as representative in the Massachusetts legislature in 1837 and 1841, and as senator from Nantucket and Dukes County in the state Senate in 1839, 1840, and 1843. In 1844 he was a delegate to the Whig convention that nominated Henry Clay for the presidency.

Foreseeing the decline of business in Nantucket, in 1845 Upton moved to Manchester, N. H., where he acted as agent for a print works then being established. In 1846, however, he went to Boston, where he became a merchant and capitalist. From 1846 to 1854 he was treasurer of the Michigan Central Railroad, and was associated with other important business and financial organizations. On his own account, he engaged in shipping, and managed some famous clippers. Again he became active in public affairs, serving as a member of the executive council in 1853 and in the state constitutional convention of the same year. He was best known for the position he took on the question of commerce in time of war, and for his interest in the welfare of seamen. In protest against the ratification of the Clarendon-Johnson treaty in connection with the *Alabama* claims, he made representations to the United States government relative to the capture of his vessel *Nora*. Regarding these Lord John Russell made disparaging remarks (see *Selections from Speeches of Earl Russell,* 1870, II, 244–45). Whereupon Upton in a public letter, dated Mar. 23, 1870, charged the British people with being responsible for Confederate commerce raiders, and with having operated them. Through these charges, he attracted international attention. In the interest of seamen he promoted the Sailors' Snug Harbor, at Quincy, Mass., and in an article, "Shipwreck and Life-Saving," published in *Old and New,* a Boston periodical, in May 1874, he made some radical suggestions about life-saving equipment on ships. On May 2, 1826, he married Ann Coffin Hussey in Nantucket, by whom he had eight children; his widow, one son, and three daughters survived him. He died in Boston.

[*Vital Records of Nantucket, Mass., to the Year 1850,* vol. IV (1927); W. H. Upton, *Upton Family Records* (1893); J. A. Vinton, *The Upton Memorial* (1874); *New England Hist. and Geneal. Reg.,* Jan. 1875; *Boston Past and Present* (1874); *Boston Transcript* and *Boston Post,* July 2, 1874.]   S. G.

UPTON, GEORGE PUTNAM (Oct. 25, 1834–May 19, 1919), journalist, music critic, and author, was born at Roxbury, Mass., the eldest of three children of Daniel Putnam and Lydia (Noyes) Upton. His father, a first cousin of George Bruce Upton [*q.v.*], was a descendant of John Upton who purchased land in Salem in 1658. George Putnam Upton was educated at the Roxbury Latin School and at Brown University, from which he was graduated in 1854 with the A.M. degree. During the following winter he taught school at Plymouth, Mass. In October 1855, he went to Chicago where he immediately secured a position on the staff of the *Native Citizen.* Six months later he became city editor of the *Chicago Evening Journal.* The meager musical life of the young growing city soon drew his attention, and he started the first musical column to appear in a Chicago newspaper, reviewing all the earliest important musical events in the history of the city. In 1862 he joined the staff of the *Chicago Daily Tribune* and continued to serve this paper for fifty-seven years in various capacities—first as city editor and war-correspondent at the front (1862–63), then as music critic (1863–81), associate editor (1872–1905), and editorial writer from 1870 until his death. After 1909 he compiled the *Tribune's* annual review. He was one of the

founders of the Chicago Apollo Musical Club in September 1872 and served as its first president. The first concert of the Club, on Jan. 21, 1873, aroused much enthusiasm and lent new impetus to the musical life of Chicago after the great fire. Starting as a male chorus, it expanded into a mixed chorus, and later developed into one of the leading choral organizations in the West.

Upton's local reputation was established by his writings as a music critic, usually under the *nom de plume* "Peregrine Pickle." In the earlier years of his journalistic experience he was frequently called upon to combine the duties of literary, art, dramatic, and music critic. His work as such coincided with the formative period of Chicago's civic and art life. As he was for some time the only local critic able to speak with authority, his influence was very great. His position as a music critic was unusual. He had no real background of musical education, played no instrument well, and did not sing, but his natural fondness for music, his literary training, his clear judgment and keen analytical and critical abilities well fitted him for his task. His attitude towards performing artists was a singularly kindly one; he took pains to understand what he was called upon to write about and was unusually free from harshness when he could not praise. His autobiographic *Musical Memories* (1908) is a valuable and entertaining record of musical events and personalities, principally in Chicago, extending over a period of a half-century. From the beginning he was a warm friend and enthusiastic supporter of Theodore Thomas [*q.v.*], and after the great conductor's death he edited *Theodore Thomas. A Musical Autobiography* (2 volumes, 1905).

Upton's first published work as an author was *Letters of Peregrine Pickle* (1869). Soon thereafter he began a notable series of works in the field of musicology, all marked by accuracy of statement and a genial style of expression. It includes *Woman in Music* (1880, revised editions, 1886, 1909), *Standard Operas* (1886, and five later revised editions), *Standard Oratorios* (1887), *Standard Cantatas* (1888), *Standard Symphonies* (1889), *Standard Light Operas* (1902), *Musical Pastels* (1902), *Standard Concert Guide* (1908, three later revisions), *Standard Concert Repertory* (1909), *Standard Musical Biographies* (1910), *In Music Land* (1913), and *The Song, Its Birth, Evolution, and Functions* (1915). In collaboration with Mrs. G. K. Hack, he published *Edouard Remenyi* (1906). He also found time to translate for American music-lovers Max Muller's *Deutsche Liebe* with the English title *Memories,* Theodor Storm's

Immensee, and Ludwig Nohl's biographies of Haydn, Liszt, and Wagner. In *Life Stories for Young People* (1904–12), a series of thirty-six small volumes, he published translations of German studies of great historical characters. He was twice married. His first wife, Sarah E. Bliss, of Worcester, Mass., to whom he was married on Nov. 15, 1862, died on May 2, 1876. Of their two children one died at birth, the other in 1917. His second wife, Georgiana S. Wood, of Adrian, Mich., to whom he was married on Sept. 22, 1880, died on Oct. 1, 1927. In his personal contacts he was affable, modest, and possessed of a quiet humor. He died in Chicago. His remains were cremated and his ashes buried at Danvers, Mass.

[Information from Upton's personal friends and from the family records; *Who's Who in America,* 1918–19; J. A. Vinton, *The Upton Memorial* (1874); *Grove's Dict. of Music and Musicians, Am. Supp.* (1930); *A Hundred Years of Music in America* (1889), G. L. Howe, publisher, W. S. B. Mathews, associate ed.; Florence French, *Music and Musicians in Chicago* (copr. 1899); L. C. Elson, *The Hist. of Am. Music* (rev. edition, 1925); *Chicago Daily Tribune,* May 20, 1919.]
R. G. C.

UPTON, WINSLOW (Oct. 12, 1853–Jan. 8, 1914), astronomer and meteorologist, was born at Salem, Mass., and was the third son and fifth child of James Upton and his second wife, Sarah Sophia (Ropes) Upton. His father was a business man with musical talent, whose *Musical Miscellanea,* a collection of original musical compositions, was printed for private circulation in 1872. He was descended from John Upton who purchased land in Salem in 1658 and later moved to North Reading. Winslow Upton entered Brown University and graduated as valedictorian of his class in 1875. While he attained to equal excellence in his studies of ancient classics and of science, he felt that his forte lay rather in scientific investigation. He went to the University of Cincinnati for graduate work in astronomy, and was there awarded the degree of A.M. in 1877. After two years as assistant at the Harvard Observatory, a year as assistant in the United States Lake Survey at Detroit, a year as computer in the United States Naval Observatory at Washington, and two years as computer and assistant in the United States Signal Office, he was appointed professor of astronomy at Brown University in 1883, and he held this position until his death. He was secretary of the faculty (1884–91), director of the Ladd Observatory (1890–1914), and dean of the university (1900–01). He was a member of the American Philosophical Society, of the Deutsche Meteorologische Gesellschaft, and of the United States astronomical expeditions to

observe the total eclipses at Denver, Colo., in 1878 and at the Caroline Islands in 1883. He also observed solar eclipses in Russia (1887), in California (1889), in Virginia (1900), and in Manitoba, Canada (1905). During a sabbatical year (1896–97) he was a research assistant at the observatory of Harvard University in Arequipa, Peru; and during part of a later sabbatical leave (1904–05) he was connected with the observatory on Mount Wilson.

Shortly after his advent at Brown University Upton taught classes in mathematics, meteorology, and logic, as well as astronomy. At the Ladd Observatory for many years he conducted meteorological and other observations, in part for the federal government. His published papers included a number on meteorological topics in the *Annals of the Astronomical Observatory of Harvard College, Zeitschrift für Meteorologie,* and the *American Meteorological Journal.* Other notes and articles were published in the *Bulletin of the Essex Institute,* the *Memoirs of the National Academy of Science, Astronomische Nachrichten,* the *Sidereal Messenger,* and the *Astronomical Journal.* His small *Star Atlas* was published at Boston in 1896. For over twenty years (1893–1914) he wrote monthly letters on astronomical topics for the *Providence Journal,* and he was editor of the astronomical parts of the *Providence Journal Almanac* (1894–1910). He had unusual scientific ability coupled with rare clarity of thought and power of lucid exposition. In the class room he aroused enthusiasm, and he was in constant demand as a lecturer. He was an active church worker, and endowed with great kindliness of spirit and charm of personality. At different times he was glee-club and choir leader, and church organist. On Feb. 8, 1882, he married Cornelia Augusta, daughter of William H. Babcock of Lebanon Springs, N. Y., who with two daughters survived him.

[Sources include J. A. Vinton, *The Upton Memorial* (1874); W. H. Upton, *Upton Family Records* (1893); *Who's Who in America,* 1912–13; *Hist. Cat. of Brown Univ., 1764–1914* (1914); R. C. Archibald, in *Sci.,* Feb. 1914, with bibliog.; *Brown Alumni Monthly,* June 1900, p. 2, July 1901, p. 22, Feb. 1914, pp. 169–71, with portraits; resolutions adopted by faculty and Sigma Xi, Brown Univ., in *Popular Astronomy,* Apr. 1914, with portrait; obituary in *Providence Jour.,* Jan. 9, 1914; personal reminiscences. A poem on Upton's death by H. L. Koopman appeared in *Brown Alumni Monthly,* Feb. 1914; another, by V. E. Atwell, in *Popular Astronomy,* May 1915.]
R. C. A.

URBAN, JOSEPH (May 26, 1872–July 10, 1933), architect and stage designer, was born in Vienna, Austria, son of Joseph and Helen (Weber) Urban. His father, a supervising official in the Viennese school system, intended him for the law, but his artistic bent was too strong. He studied at the Staatsgewerbeschule and the art academy in Vienna, became a pupil of Baron Karl von Hasenauer, and was well grounded in architecture, at the same time practising illustration and studying interior decoration. One of his earliest commissions was to decorate the Abdin palace in Cairo. He also did the interior of the new town hall in Vienna and designed the "Tzar's Bridge" in St. Petersburg. He was prominent in the Secessionist movement and arranged its exhibition in Vienna. In 1900 he won the grand prize for decoration at the Paris exposition, and in 1901 came to America to decorate the Austrian building at the Louisiana Purchase Exposition (St. Louis), for which he won the grand prize in 1904. Returning to Vienna, he became interested in stage sets for the Hofburg Theatre, and in 1911–12, when the Boston Opera Company was started, he was invited to that city as art director. For the Boston company he made several sets, notably one for *Pelleas and Melisande,* which were revelations in America of the new stage art. He was introduced to New York by his set for *The Garden of Paradise* (1914), and in that year he left Boston for New York to design first the Ziegfeld *Follies* of 1915 (which owed much of their fame to him), and then sets for the Metropolitan Opera and for James K. Hackett's productions of *Macbeth* and *The Merry Wives of Windsor.* By this time "Urban blue" had become famous, and he was in great demand for all sorts of decorative projects. In addition to his office in New York he established a large studio and shop near his residence in Yonkers, and worked day and night on his various projects, even returning to architecture in the 1920's. He designed furniture, motor cars, modernistic interiors, stage sets, theatres, clubs, houses, and public buildings. Among his buildings and interiors are the Ziegfeld Theatre on Sixth Avenue, New York, with an interior shaped like an egg; the New School for Social Research, New York; the Tennis and Oasis clubs at Palm Beach, and certain residences there; the interior of the Central Park Casino; the St. Regis roof garden (gilt flowers on sapphire walls); and a vast design, never carried out, for a new opera house in New York. Urban had always advocated the use of clear colors in exterior as well as interior architecture, and had popularized tints of his own. He was, accordingly, chosen to devise the color chart for the Century of Progress exposition at Chicago in 1933.

A man so prodigiously fecund and versatile as Urban is often looked upon with some suspicion by his fellow craftsmen. It is perhaps true that Urban was not, as artist, an originator. His decorative style owed much to the Secessionists and *l'art nouveau* of the late nineties. In stage design he was not a great pioneer like Adolphe Appia or Gordon Craig. In architecture his name cannot be written large. But all modern decorators, scene designers, and architects in America none the less owe him a debt of gratitude, because by popularizing the new styles he made their task so much the easier. Urban's sets for the Boston Opera House, for example, were the first large-scale examples of the new stagecraft in America, and their popularity was important. Subsequently, his use of broad masses of color, his employment of broken pigmentation in scene painting to take various light effects, his pervasive beauty of costume under the play of light, in the Ziegfeld *Follies,* spread the gospel to thousands of people ordinarily little affected by new art movements. It is perhaps not far-fetched to say that Urban's sets for the *Follies* made possible the public acceptance of the architectural scheme of the Century of Progress. In architecture, the egg-shaped interior of the Ziegfeld Theatre, purely functional, may be destined to influence American theatre building in the future. In the decorative arts, his frequent use of metal had an almost immediate influence, as did his use of large spaces of clear color. How far that influence will extend to exterior architecture remains to be seen. But, at any rate, as a popularizer of artistic innovations Urban was an important figure.

He was a large, florid, genial, witty man, with a cascade of chins and an enormous capacity for work. He often worked from 9 A.M. till 2 the next morning, designing sets (built in his studios) for five operas and ten or twelve plays and musical comedies a year, in addition to his decorative jobs and architectural projects. This work entailed reading scripts, attendance at rehearsals, the supervision of lighting and of practical construction. He smoked a hundred Turkish cigarettes a day, and had a pot of coffee always on his desk. His one recreation was attending prize fights. He died in New York, from a not surprising heart ailment, July 10, 1933, after an illness which had to his bitter disappointment prevented him from going to Chicago to see his colors applied on the exposition buildings. He was admitted to American citizenship in 1917. In 1918 he divorced his first wife, Mizzi Lefler, and on Jan. 23, 1919, married Mary Porter Beegle of New York. He was survived by his wife and a daughter of his first marriage, an artist.

[*Who's Who in America*, 1932–33; "Urban, the Ambidextrous," in *N. Y. Times*, June 17, 1917; F. E. W. Freund, in *Internat. Studio*, Jan. 1923; Shepard Vogelgesang, in *Arch. Record,* Feb. 1931; *Theatre Arts Mag.,* Dec. 1932, p. 950, picture of an Urban stage set; *Outlook,* June 18, 1930; obituaries in *N. Y. Times* and *N. Y. Herald Tribune,* July 11, 1933; information from Gretl Urban, Urban's daughter.]   W. P. E.

URSO, CAMILLA (June 13, 1842–Jan. 20, 1902), violinist, was born in Nantes, France, the daughter of Salvator Urso, an organ and flute player born in Sicily, and his wife, Emilie (Girouard) Urso, a native of Portugal. Camilla began to play the violin at the time she was six years of age; at the age of seven she gave her first recital in the town of her birth. Her father took her to Paris, where, after many difficulties, she was admitted to the Paris Conservatory of Music and became a pupil of Lambert-Joseph Massart. She studied and practised for eight, and sometimes ten, hours a day. In 1852 she came to America as a child prodigy, and played in concerts with such famous stars as Henriette Sontag and Marietta Alboni. She had been engaged under a very favorable contract to make a tour of the South, but the agent proved unreliable and the child violinist was stranded for a time until the Germania Society asked her to appear as soloist at several of its concerts. She later made tours with Sontag. About 1855 Urso's parents settled in Nashville, Tenn., and for seven years she made no more public appearances, but devoted all her time to practising. In 1862 she again resumed her concert work, playing first in New York as soloist with the New York Philharmonic Society. For the next thirty years she played continually both in America and in Europe. She made two trips to Australia, in 1879 and 1894, and one to South Africa, in 1895. After this she settled permanently in New York City, where she devoted her later years to teaching. Except for a tour in vaudeville houses, she thereafter seldom appeared in concert.

According to those who knew her, and heard her play, Urso was a true artist, without affectation or conscious showmanship. George P. Upton [*q.v.*] described her in the early days as "a most serious child, with large dark eyes and with a manner and dignity that seemed strange in one so young. . . . Her face was so solemn and unchanging in its expression that it seemed as if a smile had never visited it" (Upton, *post,* p. 70). When she was about twenty-four years of age the same author said that she "still had that same pale, serious, inscrutable face, the same dark, lustrous melancholy eyes, and the same calm but gracious dignity of manner; but with the advancing years she had gained a more finished style, great individuality, and exquisitely grace-

ful motions of the arm in bowing" (*Ibid.,* p. 71). In 1862 she was married in Paris to Frédéric Luères. She died in New York City almost in obscurity.

[*Grove's Dict. of Music and Musicians, Am. Supp.* (1930); Charles Barnard, *Camilla Urso, A Tribute* (1885); G. P. Upton, *Musical Memories* (1908); *Musical Courier,* Jan. 22, 29, 1902; *N. Y. Times,* Jan. 22, 1902.]   J. T. H.

USHER, JOHN PALMER (Jan. 9, 1816–Apr. 13, 1889), lawyer, secretary of the interior in Lincoln's cabinet, was descended from a young English Puritan, Hezekiah Usher, who settled in Boston, Mass., about the middle of the seventeenth century, becoming a bookseller and later a selectman. Among his descendants were John Usher who became lieutenant-governor of New Hampshire in 1692 and Dr. Nathaniel Usher, who with his wife, Lucy (Palmer), lived in Brookfield, Madison County, N. Y., when their son, John Palmer, was born. After receiving a common-school education Usher studied law in the office of Henry Bennett of New Berlin, N. Y., and was admitted to the bar in 1839. A year later he moved to Terre Haute, Ind., and began the practice of his profession. He rode the circuit, and was sometimes engaged with Abraham Lincoln in the argument of cases. In 1850–51 he served in the Indiana legislature.

When the Republican party was organized in 1854, Usher became an active supporter of its principles and in 1856 was an unsuccessful candidate for Congress. He was appointed attorney-general of Indiana in November 1861, but four months later resigned to accept the position of assistant secretary of the interior at Washington. In January 1863 he was appointed head of that department, following the resignation of Caleb B. Smith [*q.v.*]. In his first report he called special attention to the benefits of the new homestead law, remarking that in less than a year after it went into operation almost a million and a half acres had been taken up. He recommended a small tax on the net profits of gold and silver mines, larger Indian reservations, also larger appropriations—with a policy guided by justice and humanity—for these wards of the nation. His last report contained a comprehensive statement concerning public lands, which, he said, had included about one fifth of the entire country and had been the cause of about one fourth of all the laws passed by Congress to that date.

When the Civil War closed Usher decided to retire from political life and resume the practice of law in one of the growing Western states. He accordingly resigned as secretary of the interior on May 15, 1865, and removed with his family to Lawrence, Kan., where he accepted appointment as chief counsel for the Union Pacific Railroad—a position which he held to the end of his life. He represented the company in much important litigation in both state and federal courts. Usher's only writings were his two reports (1863, 1864) as secretary of the interior (*Executive Document No. 1*, vol. III, 38 Cong., 1 Sess.; and *House Executive Document No. 1*, pt. 5, 38 Cong., 2 Sess.) and a chapter in *Reminiscences of Abraham Lincoln* (1886), edited by A. T. Rice; but in 1925 Nelson H. Loomis published *President Lincoln's Cabinet, by Honorable John P. Usher,* a pamphlet containing the substance of an after-dinner speech delivered in 1887 together with a newspaper interview. On Jan. 26, 1844, Usher married Margaret Patterson; they had four sons. He died in a hospital in Philadelphia.

[Usher kept no diary and preserved no papers. *President Lincoln's Cabinet* (1925) contains an authoritative biog. by N. H. Loomis. See also *Kan. State Hist. Soc. Colls.,* vol. XII (1912); C. W. Taylor, *The Bench and Bar of Ind.* (1895); E. P. Usher, *A Memorial Sketch of Roland Greene Usher* (1895), containing a genealogy; *Lawrence Daily Jour.,* Apr. 14, 1889; *Lawrence Evening Tribune,* Apr. 15, 1889; *Topeka Capital-Commonwealth,* Apr. 16, 1889. Important facts have also been obtained from a son, the late Samuel C. Usher.]   T. L. H.

USHER, NATHANIEL REILLY (Apr. 7, 1855–Jan. 9, 1931), naval officer, son of Nathaniel and Pamela (Woolverton) Usher and nephew of John Palmer Usher [*q.v.*], was born in Vincennes, Ind. He entered the Naval Academy in 1871 and was graduated in 1875. After two years duty on the Asiatic Station, he was sent to the Paris Exposition of 1878 as a member of the American naval delegation. During the early gold rush days in Alaska, as an officer of the *Jamestown,* he assisted in maintaining law and order in the Territory. In 1884 he was sent with Winfield Scott Schley [*q.v.*] to the Arctic on the Greely Relief Expedition, sailing as watch officer of the *Bear* but being transferred to the *Alert,* a ship donated by the British government. In the years 1886–89 he made a cruise around the world in the *Juniata.*

During the Spanish-American War Usher commanded the torpedo boat *Ericsson* and was at Key West with her when the *Maine* was blown up in Havana Harbor. He is credited with capturing the first Spanish prize taken in the war. While Cervera's fleet lay in Santiago Harbor, Usher volunteered to run in with the *Ericsson* and torpedo the hostile vessels, but his offer was not accepted. In the battle of Santiago his vessel took a prominent part and his report of the engagement is a model of concise, vivid narrative ("Naval Operations of the War with Spain," *House Document No. 3,* 55 Cong., 3 Sess., pp.

547–48). After the war he held a succession of important posts, including service on the General Board and in the Bureau of Navigation, and the commands of the cruiser *St. Louis* and the battleship *Michigan.* He rose rapidly in the service, attaining the rank of rear admiral in 1911.

Usher commanded successively three different divisions of the Atlantic Fleet, and soon after the outbreak of the World War was made commandant of the Brooklyn Navy Yard. Recognizing the fact that the United States would very likely be drawn into the war, he did his utmost to build up and modernize the ships under his command. When war was finally declared he was obliged to commandeer docks, outfit ships, and prepare convoys for the men, munitions, and food that must be rushed to France. Under his direction a secret service was organized known as the Commandant's Aide for Information, a mine-sweeping force was developed, and the scout-patrol system was instituted. It was chiefly because of his monumental energy and organizing ability that the Port of New York was able to ship the major part of all the supplies and eighty per cent. of all the men that America sent to the aid of her Allies. In 1918 Usher was given command of the Third Naval District.

When he retired on Apr. 7, 1919, he was the guest of honor at a dinner at the Waldorf in New York, which was attended by 1,500 persons. Franklin D. Roosevelt, then assistant secretary of the navy, said of him: "No officer stands higher in his appreciation of the broad needs of this great democratic country in the matter of defence, and no one more tactfully, more forcefully, and more skillfully welded the naval reserve, the civilian, into the trained machine of the regular Navy" (*Sun,* New York, Apr. 8, 1919). France, in recognition of his services to the cause of the Allies, bestowed upon him the ribbon of the French Legion of Honor, and he was awarded the Navy Cross by his own government. He was a man of commanding presence, the idol of his men, and held in high esteem in the service. After his retirement he lived on his farm at Potsdam, N. Y. He married Anne Usher of Potsdam in 1891; he left no children.

[*Army and Navy Journal,* Jan. 17, 1931; *N. Y. Times,* Jan. 10, 1931; U. S. Navy Dept. Registers and Annual Reports; *Who's Who in America,* 1928–29; Service Record in Bureau of Navigation, Navy Dept.; L. R. Hamersly, *The Records of Living Officers of the U. S. Navy* (7th ed., 1902); E. P. Usher, *A Memorial Sketch of Roland Greene Usher, to Which is Added a Geneal. of the Usher Family in New England* (1895).]   L. H. B.

VACA, ALVAR NÚÑEZ CABEZA de [See NÚÑEZ CABEZA DE VACA, ALVAR *c.* 1490–*c.* 1557].

VAIL, AARON (Oct. 24, 1796–Nov. 4, 1878), diplomat, was born in Lorient (Morbihan), France, the son of a New York merchant, Aaron Vail, and his wife, Elizabeth Dubois, who was born in Saint Servan (Ille et Vilaine), France. The father, who seems to have come of a Quaker family of Dutchess County, N. Y., was appointed American commercial agent at Lorient in 1803 and served there usefully during the Napoleonic era, rearing a large family on a meager income. After his death in 1815 his family came to the United States. Aaron obtained a clerkship in the American legation at Paris, traveled considerably in Europe, and served as clerk in the Department of State. On Aug. 1, 1831, he was appointed secretary of legation at London. After the refusal of the Senate to confirm Van Buren's appointment as minister to Great Britain, Vail was appointed chargé d'affaires at London and filled this important position from July 13, 1832, until April 1836; he then became secretary of legation once more, and remained in London until December 1836 in that capacity. Completely at home in London society and on excellent terms with such British statesmen as Palmerston and Wellington, the bachelor chargé received the approval of President Jackson, with whom he corresponded directly, as well as that of the Department of State, for his conduct of the business of the legation. Perhaps his most difficult task was handling the American protest and claims for compensation arising out of the release of slaves from American ships forced by circumstances to put in at British West Indian ports. Vail finally persuaded the British government to refer the cases to the judicial committee of the Privy Council, but no further satisfaction was obtained during his term as chargé.

After the Canadian rebellion of 1837 it was believed that many Americans imprisoned in Canada on suspicion of having been involved were being held arbitrarily and without the prospect of a trial. On Apr. 3, 1838, Vail was appointed special agent to go to Canada to investigate. In his reports to the secretary of state, Apr. 21 and May 5, he stated his belief that Americans implicated in the revolt were being treated "in the mildest manner consistent with the demands of justice" (*House Executive Document No. 39*, 27 Cong., 1 Sess., p. 5). Appointed chief clerk of the Department of State June 26, 1838, he served until July 15, 1840. During this period he acted on numerous occasions as secretary of state. In the latter capacity he received notice from the Republic of Texas of the withdrawal of its offer of annexation to the United States; he protested vigorously the seizure by British authorities of American fishing craft on the coast of Nova Scotia, and he attempted to prevent the outbreak of the "Aroostook war" on the border between Maine and Canada. From May 20, 1840, to Aug. 1, 1842, when Washington Irving assumed the duties of minister, Vail served as chargé d'affaires at Madrid. During the periods of his life when he was not in public service he seems to have lived in New York or in Europe. He died at Pau (Basses-Pyrénées), France.

[*Reg. of the Dept. of State*, July 1, 1933; *The Works of James Buchanan* (12 vols., 1908–11), ed. by J. B. Moore; H. M. Wriston, *Exec. Agents in Am. Foreign Relations* (1929); *Sen. Doc. 174*, 24 Cong., 2 Sess.; *Sen. Doc. 1*, 25 Cong., 3 Sess.; *Sen. Doc. 107, House Ex. Doc. 186*, 26 Cong., 1 Sess.; *House Ex. Doc. 39*, 27 Cong., 1 Sess.; MSS. in Dept. of State; birth register of Lorient, France; municipal records of Pau; Beckles Willson, *America's Ambassadors to England* (1929), extensive but in part unreliable.]   E. W. S.

VAIL, ALFRED (Sept. 25, 1807–Jan. 18, 1859), telegraph pioneer, the son of Stephen and Bethiah (Young) Vail, was born at Morristown, N. J., where his father was the owner and operator of the Speedwell Iron Works. The records of the Presbyterian Church in Morristown show that he was given a middle name, Lewis, which he apparently never used. Upon completing a common-school education in his native town he entered his father's establishment. Possessed of a considerable amount of native mechanical skill, he soon became an expert mechanician and by the time he was twenty he had complete charge of the machine shop, where he continued for a number of years. About 1830 he decided to become a Presbyterian minister, and after taking some college preparatory work entered the University of the City of New York in 1832, graduating in 1836. Although his health was poor, he immediately began his theological studies.

On Sept. 2, 1837, however, at the University, he saw Prof. Samuel F. B. Morse [*q.v.*] give one of his first exhibitions of the telegraph. Vail at once perceived the significance of Morse's invention and expressed a desire to become associated with him in perfecting and exploiting it. Morse, being greatly in need of mechanical as well as financial assistance, grasped this unexpected opportunity, and on Sept. 23, 1837, a contract was drawn up between Vail and Morse, Vail binding himself to construct a complete set of instruments and to secure both United States and foreign patents at his own expense, while in return he received a fourth interest in the American rights and a half interest in patents which might be secured abroad. He had no money of his own but quickly induced his father to finance the undertaking, and thereupon Vail, Morse, and a third associate, Leonard D. Gale, went to work on the telegraph in the shops of the Speedwell Iron Works. On Jan. 6, 1838, a successful demonstration was made of the improved electric telegraph through three miles of wire stretched around one of the shops. Vail's father furnished the message for this occasion: "A patient waiter is no loser." Within the month Vail and Morse held their first public exhibition of the telegraph in New York City, when "Attention, the Universe, by kingdoms right wheel," was the terse message successfully transmitted. The mechanical perfection of practically all the instruments used was the result of Vail's skill, and he worked enthusiastically with Morse in demonstrating the telegraph before the Franklin Institute, Philadelphia, on Feb. 8, 1838, and before members of Congress on Feb. 21 of that year. The partners felt that the telegraph ought to be owned by the government and hoped that as a result of this latter demonstration Congress would purchase the invention. This hope was disappointed, but the demonstration in Washington aroused the interest of one congressman, Francis O. J. Smith, who within a month became a financial partner and received a four-sixteenths interest in the invention, brought about by the reduction of Vail's interest from four to two sixteenths.

The new capital thus acquired enabled Morse to proceed to Europe to secure his foreign patents, and with his departure Vail's interest in the telegraph waned. He did very little work on it in 1838, and in 1839 he went to Philadelphia to represent his father's interests. Here he remained until 1843; but when in March of that year Congress passed the act providing for an experimental telegraph line between Washington and Baltimore, Vail became Morse's chief assistant and received the test message "What hath God wrought!" at Baltimore on May 24, 1844. He remained with Morse for the next four years, publishing in 1845 *The American Electro Magnetic Telegraph,* but again lost interest in the work, and in 1848 resigned his position as superintendent at Philadelphia. Returning to Morristown, he lived there in retirement until his death, giving much of his time in later years to compiling material for a genealogy of the Vail family. Vail profited little from the telegraph, for he did not improve the opportunities it afforded, failing to take up the manufacture of telegraph instruments, and he died poor and unhappy. He was twice married: first, July 23, 1839, to Jane Elizabeth Cummings, who died in 1852; and second, Dec. 17, 1855, to Amanda O.

Eno, who with three sons by his first marriage survived him. He died in Morristown, in his fifty-second year.

[H. H. Vail, *Geneal. of Some of the Vail Family* (1902); F. B. Read, *Up the Heights of Fame and Fortune* (1873); *Gen. Alumni Cat., N. Y. Univ.,* vol. I (1906); *Hist. of the First Presbyt. Ch., Morristown, N. J.,* pt. II (n.d.), containing "The Combined Registers, from 1742 to 1885"; death notice in *N. Y. Times,* Jan. 20, 1859; E. L. Morse, *Samuel F. B. Morse: His Letters and Journals* (1914, vol. II); J. D. Reid, *The Telegraph in America* (1879); "The Invention of the Electro-Telegraph," *Electrical World,* July 20–Dec. 21, 1895; U. S. National Museum records.]   C. W. M.

VAIL, STEPHEN MONTFORT (Jan. 15, 1816–Nov. 26, 1880), Methodist Episcopal clergyman, educator, was born in Union Vale, Dutchess County, N. Y., the son of James Vail, a farmer, and Anna (Montfort) Vail. When he was fourteen years old he entered Cazenovia Seminary, Cazenovia, N. Y., and in 1834, Bowdoin College, from which he was graduated with honors in 1838. For his professional education he went to Union Theological Seminary, New York City, completing the course there in 1842. That same year he was admitted on trial to the New York Conference of the Methodist Episcopal Church, and in September was married to Louisa R. Cushman. He was ordained deacon in 1844, and elder in 1846. His pastoral appointments were to Fishkill, N. Y. (1842–44), Sharon, Conn. (1844–46), and Pine Plains, N. Y. (1846–47). In 1847 he became principal of Pennington Seminary, Pennington, N. J., leaving there two years later to accept the chair of Hebrew in the Methodist General Biblical Institute, Concord, N. H., which, opened in 1847, was the first distinctively theological institution established by American Methodists. In this position he served until 1869.

Two interests which Vail furthered brought him prominence. At a time when Methodists in general opposed education as a requirement for the ministerial office on the ground that the call of God and a vital personal experience were the essential requisites, Vail was a vigorous advocate of theological training. Because of articles in support of his views on this subject, published while he was at Pennington, which were deemed by some contrary to Methodist principles, he was placed on trial before the New Jersey Conference. The charges were so trivial, however, that he was speedily acquitted. During the many years he was connected with the General Biblical Institute he was indefatigable in his efforts to build up the school and also to raise the educational standards of his denomination. In 1853 he published *Ministerial Education in the Methodist Episcopal Church.* A second interest, and one that made him more widely known, was in the abolition of slavery. It led him to cross swords with prominent men of his own calling who defended the institution on Biblical grounds. In 1860 he published a sermon entitled *The Church and the Slave Power,* and in 1864, *The Bible Against Slavery.* The latter was a reply to Bishop John Henry Hopkins [*q.v.*] of the Protestant Episcopal Church who had advanced arguments to the effect that slavery is not a sin because it is not forbidden in the Scripture, and to Nathan Lord [*q.v.*], president of Dartmouth College, who contended that slavery was divinely ordained, and therefore not to be questioned.

A Methodist and a stanch Republican and supporter of the Union, he was regarded as worthy of recognition by President Grant, who in 1869 appointed him consul at Ludwigshafen, Bavaria, in which position he served until 1874. Returning to the United States, he retired to his farm at Pleasant Plains, Staten Island. He died at the home of a son-in-law in Jersey City, survived by his wife and six children. In addition to the writings already mentioned he published *Life in Earnest; or Memoirs and Remains of the Rev. Zenas Caldwell,* which appeared in 1855.

[*Commemorative Biog. Record of Dutchess County, N. Y.* (1897); H. W. Cushman, *A Hist. and Biog. Geneal. of the Cushmans: The Descendants of Robert Cushman* (1855); *Gen. Biog. Cat. of Bowdoin Coll.* (1912); sketch in *Minutes of the Ann. Conferences of the M. E. Church, Spring Conferences of 1881* (1881), reprinted in Stephen Allen and W. H. Pilsbury, *Hist. of Methodism in Me.* (1887); *Christian Advocate* (N. Y.), Dec. 2, 1880; *Zion's Herald,* Jan. 6, 1881; death notice in *N. Y. Times,* Nov. 27, 1880.]   H. E. S.

VAIL, THEODORE NEWTON (July 16, 1845–Apr. 16, 1920), telephone and utilities executive, was born near Minerva, Carroll County, Ohio, the son of Davis Vail, a Quaker farmer and iron worker, and Phebe (Quinby) his wife. There were ten children, of whom seven survived childhood, and of these Theodore was the third. In 1847 Davis Vail took his family back to his former home in New Jersey, and went to work again in the Speedwell Iron Works near Morristown, well known through its association with his cousin, Alfred Vail [*q.v.*], and the electric telegraph.

Theodore went to the public schools and to the Morristown Academy until he had finished the high school grade. By this time he had become interested in reading, especially along the lines of geography and human achievement; but his real education was mainly a casual one in the school of versatile experience. At seventeen he went to work in a drugstore where there was a telegraph office; he learned to use the instrument, and by the time he was nineteen he was at work in New York as an operator for the Western Union Telegraph Company. This career was interrupted by the decision of his father to go West. The family moved in 1866 to Waterloo, Iowa, and Theodore went with them. Here he learned what it was to be a pioneer, breaking the loam and harvesting rich crops. Baseball was the recreation of the region, and in Iowa Vail conceived his lifelong enthusiasm for the game.

In 1868 he went back into the telegraph service and was soon night operator at Pine Bluffs, in the Indian country among the Black Hills on the Union Pacific Railway. From this telegraph service he went into the mail service, and on Aug. 3, 1869, at Newark, N. J., he married Emma Louise Righter, a cousin on his mother's side. They settled in Omaha, whence he went on his mail trips across the continent. On July 18, 1870, a son was born to them. Vail was soon devising improvements in the operation and routings of the railway mail service. This initiative brought him advancement and in 1873 transfer to the office of the railway mail service at Washington; in 1874 he became assistant general superintendent. Under Postmaster-General Marshall Jewell [*q.v.*], on Sept. 16, 1875, he inaugurated the Fast Mail between New York and Chicago, over the New York Central and Hudson River Railroad; the first train, carrying only mail, started from New York at a speed of more than forty-one miles an hour, faster than any passenger train had ever traveled (Paine, *post,* p. 77). With the beginning of 1876 Theodore Vail became general superintendent of the railway mail service.

Meantime Alexander Graham Bell [*q.v.*] had invented the telephone and Gardiner Greene Hubbard [*q.v.*] had begun to organize the business. Hubbard recognized the need for a young man of vision, ability, and force to carry on the development of the telephone industry. Knowing Vail through his active interest in the postal service, Hubbard singled him out and persuaded him to undertake the work under the title of general manager of the Bell Telephone Company. Between May 1878 and September 1887, Vail organized the expanding telephone system; he merged the rapidly multiplying local exchanges into more efficient companies; he put into effect a practical system of financing the telephone industry; he provided for anticipatory technical development and for improved and more economical manufacture of telephone apparatus, with the Western Electric Company as the manufacturing unit, so as to improve the quality and extend the distance of telephone transmission. His culminating contribution in this period was to unify the industry by connecting all the operating companies and exchanges by a long-distance telephone system. For this purpose, with Edward J. Hall, Jr., as the active man, he incorporated in 1885 a special subsidiary company, the American Telephone & Telegraph Company, of which he was the first president.

By 1887 his vitality was depleted, for no plan had been too great for his quick mind to undertake, and no detail too small to receive his personal attention. He resigned from the telephone company and from all other responsibilities, and retired in 1889 to a farm he had bought at Lyndonville, Vt. There, some years before, his interest in scientific agriculture and in practical education had led him to give the funds necessary to rehabilitate and reopen (in 1884) an industrial school, Lyndon Institute.

Soon, however, a visitor from South America interested him in the industrial development of the Argentine Republic; and after several years, during which he spent much time in Europe without losing touch with the telephone company, he turned his interest and energy into utility projects in Argentina. This was his chief occupation from 1894 to 1907. He financed and developed a great water-power plant at Córdoba and electrified and made profitable a street railway system in Buenos Aires. After the death of his wife in February 1905, and of his only child, Davis, in December 1906, he sold out his South American interests and returned to Vermont. Marrying on July 27, 1907, Mabel R. Sanderson of Boston, and making his niece, Katherine Vail, his adopted daughter, he again turned his attention to agriculture and education for country life. In 1910, at Lyndonville, he was instrumental in establishing the Lyndon School of Agriculture.

Meantime the telephone had been spreading throughout the United States. The Bell Companies had grown from 180,680 telephones (Dec. 31, 1887) to 2,773,547 telephones (Dec. 31, 1906). In 1900 the American Telephone & Telegraph Company had taken over from the American Bell Telephone Company its function as the chief corporation of the telephone system, retaining its former long-distance functions in a special long-line department. With the expiration of the Bell telephone patents in 1893 and 1894, hundreds of independent telephone companies sprang up and entered into local competition with the Bell organizations. It was not yet generally realized that the telephone was a natural monopoly and that the existence of a multiplicity of telephone companies would prevent nation-wide telephone efficiency. The directors of the Bell company now urged Vail to take hold of the industry again, and on May 1, 1907, his election as president of the American Telephone & Telegraph Company was announced.

His first step was to move the headquarters of the company from Boston to New York. With the purpose of fostering and increasing public understanding and confidence he made the annual reports a medium for the frank discussion of telephone problems. He hastened the unification of the telephone industry by personally making the acquaintance of all the chief officers of the Bell companies throughout the country and by a policy of cooperation with the independent telephone companies. Under this policy, companies that preferred to remain independent could secure long distance service by contract from the adjacent Bell company; these were called Bell-connected. By such steps the Bell System came more and more to realize its natural ideal—"One Policy, One System, Universal Service." Vail went further, toward a unification of all electric communications, affiliating the Western Union Telegraph Company with the American Telephone & Telegraph Company in 1909, with himself as president of both companies, and inaugurating improvements of service such as the night letter and telephone reception of telegrams. The federal government claimed, however, that this association was in violation of the anti-trust laws, and in 1913, the two companies were separated without formal legal action in court (*Annual Report of the American Telephone & Telegraph Company*, 1913).

Meanwhile, by selecting the right men and properly supporting them in their work, Vail pushed forward the progress of telephony: scientific research resulted in new inventions and technical improvement, as well as in efficient construction; popular education increased the field of the telephone; able commercial management brought profits; and world telephony was rendered certain. The first long stride in this direction was the telephone conquest of the desert and the mountains. On Jan. 25, 1915, during the Panama-Pacific Exposition at San Francisco, the first transcontinental telephone line was opened with conversations between President Woodrow Wilson at Washington, Alexander Graham Bell at New York, Thomas A. Watson at San Francisco, and Theodore N. Vail at Jekyl Island, off the coast of Georgia. The same year telephone engineers under John J. Carty developed radio telephony so that on Oct. 21, communications sent out from Arlington, Va., were simultaneously received in Paris and at Honolulu. In 1917 a collection of Vail's papers and addresses was privately printed under the title, *Views on Public Questions.*

After the United States went into the World War, telephone battalions were organized, in accordance with plans suggested by Carty and approved by Vail, and they built an American telephone system in France. On July 31, 1918, the government took over control of all the wire communication systems, and Vail was requested to continue with his own organization the conduct of the telephone business for the government, reporting to the Postmaster General. The wires were returned to the owning companies on July 31, 1919. Just previously, June 18, Vail had resigned the presidency of the American Telephone & Telegraph Company, and become chairman of the Board of Directors. He had always lived unsparingly; in April 1920 he went to the Johns Hopkins Hospital, Baltimore, where he died on Apr. 16. He was buried in the old cemetery at Parsippany, N. J. The chief organizer of the telephone business, in little more than forty years he had "made neighbors of a hundred million people."

[A. B. Paine, *In One Man's Life* (1921), repr. as *Theodore N. Vail: A Biog.* (1929); J. W. Stehman, *The Financial Hist. of the Am. Telephone and Telegraph Company* (1925); *Ann. Reports of the Directors of the Am. Telephone and Telegraph Company, 1907–19*; *Boston Transcript*, Apr. 16, 1920; *Evening Post* (N. Y.), Apr. 17, 1920; *Evening Caledonian* (St. Johnsbury, Vt.), Apr. 16, 1920; *Wall Street Journal*, Apr. 17, 23, 1920; *Western Electric News*, May, Aug. 1920; papers in the Theodore N. Vail Collection of the Am. Telephone Hist. Lib., New York City.]

W. C. L.

VALENTINE, DAVID THOMAS (Sept. 15, 1801–Feb. 25, 1869), compiler of historical materials, was born in East Chester, Westchester County, N. Y., the second son of Daniel and Miriam (Fisher) Valentine, and a descendant of Benjamin Valentine of Holland, who settled near the town of Yonkers in 1679. On his mother's side he was descended from English stock which became established in America as early as 1611. He received his principal schooling in the Westchester Academy at White Plains, and in 1815 removed to New York City, where he found employment as a grocer's clerk. A few years later he became a member of the national guard, and after passing through the lower ranks he declined to become major of the regiment in 1826, and definitely retired from military life. Meanwhile he had acquired the friendship of persons prominent in municipal political affairs, and through their influence he became clerk of the marine court. He held his position from 1826 until 1830, when he was appointed deputy-clerk of the common council. In 1842 he became

clerk of the council and chief of the legislative department and held the position without interruption until 1868, despite numerous political changes. In January 1868, however, he was superseded in office—a circumstance which probably hastened his death.

Pursuant to a legislative resolution, Valentine published in 1841 his first *Manual of the Corporation of the City of New York,* and thereafter he added a volume annually until 1867. These volumes, copiously illustrated, and containing a jumbled mass of historical and miscellaneous matter, became so popular that they were said to have become by 1869 "almost a necessity among New-Yorkers" (*New York Times, post*). Now adequately indexed, these manuals constitute an extremely useful, if uneven, source of information relative to New York life. Other literary activities of Valentine include a *History of the City of New-York* (1853), chiefly the work of W. I. Paulding, a member of Valentine's corps of scholarly assistants, informative but badly organized, and extending only to the year 1756; *A Compilation of the Laws of the State of New York, Relating Particularly to the City of New York* (1862); *Compilation of Existing Ferry Leases and Railroad Grants Made by the Corporation of the City of New York* (1866); and *Ordinances of the Mayor, Aldermen, and Commonalty* (1859).

Popularly and affectionately referred to as "Old Uncle David" during his declining years, Valentine was one of the most respected and beloved residents of New York City. Had he not remained so absorbed in uncovering, compiling, and preserving local historical and antiquarian materials, he could probably have risen with ease to high official position. He became a member of the New-England Historic and Genealogical Society in 1855. He was twice married, first to Martha Carnell, on June 24, 1821. They had three sons and two daughters. After her death, he was married to Caroline M. Spicer, who, with the children of his first wife, survived him.

[T. W. Valentine, *The Valentines in America, 1644–1874* (1874); *New-Eng. Hist. and Geneal. Register,* Oct. 1869; Otto Hufeland, compiler, *Hist. Index to the Manuals of the Corp. of the City of N. Y.* (1900); *An Index to the Illustrations in the Manuals of the Corp. of the City of N. Y.* (1906); William Cushing, *Initials and Pseudonyms* (1885); *N. Y. Times, N. Y. Herald*, Feb. 26, 1869.]

R. W. I.

VALENTINE, EDWARD VIRGINIUS (Nov. 12, 1838–Oct. 19, 1930), sculptor, the youngest of nine children of Mann Satterwhite and Elizabeth (Mosby) Valentine, was born at Richmond, Va., where his father was a prosperous merchant, a member of a family that had been in Virginia since the middle of the seventeenth century. He received his early education from tutors and in private schools. His wish to become a sculptor led him to the study of anatomy, and in 1856 he began to attend lectures at the Medical College of Virginia, Richmond. By 1857 he had made several portrait busts, and in the fall of 1859 he went to Paris, where he studied drawing from the nude under Thomas Couture, and modeling under François Jouffroy. He then traveled to Italy, visited numerous galleries, and studied in Florence. In 1861 he was accepted as a pupil in the Berlin studio of August Kiss, where his charm and goodness completely won the old sculptor's heart. While he was in Berlin he received from the South photographs of Gen. Robert E. Lee, and made from them a portrait statuette, which he sold for the benefit of the Southern cause. In the fall of 1865 he studied for a time at the Royal Academy, Berlin.

Toward the end of 1865 he returned to Richmond, where he opened a studio. He had won praise in Berlin for a bust from life of Dr. Franz von Holtzendorff, and in London for the Lee statuette. But in Richmond, in the tragic circumstances of the Reconstruction, he at first received no orders. Undaunted, he continued to work diligently, producing the heads entitled "The Penitent Thief" and "The Woman of Samaria," and a number of portrait and genre studies of the American negro. Among the latter are "Uncle Henry," a character study of the old-time plantation negro; "The Nation's Ward," a happy-go-lucky African; and a mildly satirical statuette, "Knowledge Is Power," which suggests the "Rogers groups" and shows a darky boy sound asleep over his tattered book. A much-admired bust of General Lee, done from life, was followed by portraits of J. E. B. Stuart, Albert Sidney Johnston, Joseph E. Johnston, Col. John S. Mosby, Commodore Matthew F. Maury, and other Southern leaders, most of them done from life. At last, in 1870, came a really inspiring commission, resulting in Valentine's finest work, the marble recumbent figure of Lee for the Lee Mausoleum at Washington and Lee University, Lexington, Va. In 1908 Valentine's bronze standing figure of Lee was unveiled in Statuary Hall, Washington, D. C., as the gift of the State of Virginia. Many examples of Valentine's work are to be seen in Richmond—at the Jefferson Hotel, which has his marble statue of Thomas Jefferson, in Monroe Park, where his bronze figure of Gen. W. T. Wickham stands, and in the Valentine Museum, former home of his brother Mann. His other works include the stat-

ues of Jefferson Davis in Richmond, of which there is a replica in New Orleans, John C. Breckinridge in Lexington, Ky., Gen. "Stonewall" Jackson in Lexington, Va., and John J. Audubon in New Orleans. His classical group representing Andromache and Astyanax after their farewell to Hector was shown at the World's Columbian Exposition, Chicago, in 1893. It is said that he refused to commemorate by his work any Northern hero. Though many of his statues are historically interesting as likenesses, artistically they leave something to be desired; they are on the whole rather wooden and lifeless. Valentine served as president of the Valentine Museum, the Richmond Art Club, and the Virginia Historical Society. He was married on Nov. 12, 1872, in Baltimore to Alice Churchill Robinson (d. Aug. 23, 1883), and on Jan. 5, 1892, to Katherine Cole (Friend) Mayo (d. Feb. 5, 1927). There were no children. He died in Richmond.

[*Who's Who in America*, 1930–31; Elizabeth G. Valentine, *Dawn to Twilight; Work of Edward V. Valentine* (1929); Lorado Taft, *The Hist. of Am. Sculpture* (1924 ed.); C. E. Fairman, *Art and Artists of the Capitol of the U. S.* (1927); Margaret J. Preston, in *Am. Art Review*, May 1880, an uncritical article; obituary in *Richmond Times-Dispatch*, Oct. 20, 1930.]   A. A.

VALENTINE, MILTON (Jan. 1, 1825–Feb. 7, 1906), Lutheran theologian, educator, was born near Uniontown, Carroll County, Md., the son of Jacob and Rebecca (Picking) Valentine, and a descendant of George Valentine who emigrated from Germany in the early part of the eighteenth century and settled in Frederick County, Md., in 1740. Milton worked on the farm until he was twenty-one, meanwhile preparing for college at the Taneytown Academy. In 1846 he enrolled at Pennsylvania College, Gettysburg, and was graduated in 1850; he then entered the Lutheran Theological Seminary in the same town, where he was graduated in 1852, and was licensed as a minister. He served for a year as supply pastor at Winchester, Va., a year as missionary in Pittsburgh, a year as regular pastor at Greensburg, Pa., and four years as principal of Emmaus Institute at Middletown, Pa. In 1859 he became pastor of St. Matthew's Lutheran Church at Reading, where he ministered with conspicuous success for seven years. In 1866 he accepted the professorship of Biblical and ecclesiastical history in the Lutheran Theological Seminary at Gettysburg.

The seminary was passing through a crisis. It had been founded in 1826, and Pennsylvania College in 1832, by Samuel S. Schmucker [*q.v.*], moving spirit in the early history of the General Synod of the Lutheran Church in the United

States. Schmucker's position was that of a liberally conservative Lutheranism, based upon the Scriptures as "the inspired Word of God and the only perfect rule of faith and practice" and upon the Augsburg Confession as "a summary and just exhibition of the fundamental doctrines of the Word of God." Diverging from this central position, there began in the 1850's a movement towards the left on the part of certain zealous advocates of "American Lutheranism," impatient of liturgies and interested in revivals and other "new measures"; and toward the right, partly owing to immigration, a strong swing toward "Old Lutheranism" or "Symbolism," the supporters of which proposed as a confessional basis not only the Augsburg Confession but the whole body of Lutheran symbolical books as contained in the Book of Concord. The growing strength of the second of these movements seriously threatened the seminary at Gettysburg. Though Schmucker resigned in 1864, the Pennsylvania Ministerium withdrew to found its own seminary in Philadelphia, and led in the organization of another general body of Lutherans, the General Council, in 1867. The directors of the seminary had faced this crisis with courage and vigor, securing funds for two new professorships and calling Valentine to one of them. After two years of teaching in this post he was elected president of the college, to which he gave for sixteen years a scholarly, effective administration. In 1884 he returned to the service of the seminary, becoming professor of theology and chairman of the faculty. He retired because of increasing age and impaired hearing in 1903, with the title of professor emeritus.

Valentine was an accurate scholar, a penetrating thinker, and a stimulating teacher. He was a vigorous defender of the position of General Synod Lutheranism, which he described as "standing for the principle of union in generic and Catholic Lutheranism on the great historic Confession of Augsburg, which has always been recognized as the one decisive determining standard of our Church, apart from any of the developed specialties of explanation which have been asserted by some, and into which they have been pleased to restrict themselves" (*Lutheran Observer*, March 6, 1891). From 1871 to 1906 he was an editor of the *Quarterly Review of the Evangelical Lutheran Church* (later the *Lutheran Quarterly*). He was a member of the joint committee which, laboring from 1885 to 1888, prepared the Common Service which is now used in public worship by most English-speaking Lutheran churches. His textbooks, *Natural Theology* (1885) and *Theoretical Ethics* (1897),

were widely used. In 1898 he published *Christian Truth and Life,* a volume of sermons. His greatest work, *Christian Theology,* in two volumes, edited by his son, M. H. Valentine, appeared in 1907. On Dec. 18, 1855, he married Margaret G. Galt of Taneytown, Md., by whom he had four children.

[T. W. Valentine, *The Valentines in America* (1874); A. R. Wentz, *Hist. of the Gettysburg Theological Seminary* (1926); S. G. Hefelbower, *The Hist. of Gettysburg Coll.* (1932); *Lutheran Quart.,* Jan. 1907; *Pub. Ledger* (Phila.), Feb. 9, 1906.]   L. A. W.

VALENTINE, ROBERT GROSVENOR (Nov. 29, 1872–Nov. 14, 1916), administrator and industrial counselor, was born at West Newton, Mass., the only child of Charles Theodore and Charlotte Grosvenor (Light) Valentine. He was a descendant of John Valentine who was made a freeman of Boston, Mass., in 1675. Robert prepared for college at Hopkinson's School, Boston, and was graduated at Harvard in 1896. From 1896 to 1899 and from 1901 to 1903 he taught English at the Massachusetts Institute of Technology, the intervening period being spent in the National City Bank, New York. Beginning in 1903, through the interest of James Stillman [*q.v.*], he had a miscellaneous business experience with railroads and financial institutions in New York and Omaha until ill health from overwork forced him to retire from business in 1904. That same year, Dec. 31, he married Sophia French of South Braintree, Mass. During the administration of Theodore Roosevelt he became private secretary to Francis E. Leupp [*q.v.*], commissioner of Indian affairs, whose assistant he became in 1908. Upon Leupp's retirement in 1909, President Taft appointed Valentine to the head of the Indian Office.

His administration of that office was a notable one. He was resourceful in the protection of the enormous Indian properties against the many attempts at encroachments upon them, and was eager for the development of the best of the Indian cultures. One of his acts as commissioner created considerable political difficulties because of the religious susceptibilities that it awakened. By an Indian Office circular (Number 601), he prohibited the wearing of religious garb and the display of religious insignia in what had formerly been religious schools for Indians but had been taken over as government institutions. In the spring of 1912 the Indian Office under his administration was under political fire and a Congressional investigation followed. The committee in its report divided on political lines, the four Democratic members finding against him, and the three Republican members supporting him (*House Report No. 1279,* 62 Cong., 3

Sess.). That same year he threw in his lot with Theodore Roosevelt in the Bull Moose campaign, and resigned from the Taft administration.

The range of Valentine's experience thus far —educational, financial, administrative, sociological—was all useful though unconscious preparation for his real life work, short as that was; for his significance, apart from his enduring work at the Indian Office, is that of founder of the new profession of industrial counselor. For four years he specialized as adviser on industrial relations, and the impact of his example and achievements led to the recognition of the need of a body of specialists like himself. Others before him had diagnosed the so-called labor problem as essentially a human problem—the problem of men and women, with their impulses and desires, behind the mechanism of industry. Valentine was the first, however, to draw profound conclusions from this discernment. Just because the terms of this human equation, he argued, were subtle and excessively complicated, there was the greater necessity for making these elusive aspects of the relation of capital and labor the subject of organized study. Instead of ignoring the human problem, or leaving it to caprice, Valentine maintained that personal relations must be studied with the same scientific spirit as are the processes of production and the fiscal side of business. Such knowledge, he was convinced, could be achieved only by professionals, that is, by men who devoted their entire time to it, with a function as well-defined as that of the lawyer or the financial expert. With this insight and with astonishing courage—for he had neither funds nor backers—in the winter of 1912, Valentine advertised himself in Boston as an industrial counselor, thus inaugurating, so far as history records, the beginning of this profession.

Basic to this profession was the need of what Valentine called "an industrial audit" which would bear the same relation to the social health of an industry that a periodic financial audit bears to the solvency of a business. Such an industrial audit called for the invention of a technique adapted, by appropriate adjustments, to every variety of business. Valentine helped to install such an audit in diverse types of industrial organizations, just as he served as adviser on labor problems for diverse clients. Like an old-fashioned lawyer, he served labor unions, employees, and public officials. Notable among the services rendered the last-named was his work for Mayor John Purroy Mitchel [q.v.] in the very difficult transit strike in New York City, during the summer of 1916.

Essentially Valentine was an educator. He disseminated ideas and imparted ferment—in his work for his clients, as chairman of the first wage board under the Massachusetts minimum wage law (1913), as lecturer at Wellesley College (1915–16), in formal addresses, and through the mere contagion of casual contact. He was a poet by temperament who was dominated by scientific ardor to institutionalize sound human relations. The astonishing aspect of his career is that he succeeded in establishing recognition of his idea of scientific order in the human aspects of industry although he had so brief a period for accomplishment. He died from a sudden heart attack, survived by his widow and a daughter.

[T. W. Valentine, *The Valentines in America* (1874); *Harvard Coll. Class of 1896: Twenty-fifth Anniversary Report* (1921); *Reports of the Commissioner of Indian Affairs to the Secretary of the Interior*, 1909–12; *Bull. of the Taylor Society*, Jan. 1916; *Modern Hospital*, Apr. 1916; *Survey*, Nov. 25, 1916; *Who's Who in America*, 1916–17; *Boston Herald* and *Boston Globe*, Jan. 8, 1917; *N. Y. Times*, Nov. 15, 1916.]
F.F.

VALLANDIGHAM, CLEMENT LAIRD (July 29, 1820–June 17, 1871), politician, was born in New Lisbon, Ohio, the fifth of seven children of Clement Vallandigham, a Presbyterian minister, and his wife, Rebecca Laird. On his mother's side he was of Scotch-Irish stock; on his father's, he was descended from Michael Van Landegham, a Flemish Huguenot, who was in Stafford County, Va., as early as 1690. Vallandigham attended the New Lisbon Academy founded by his father and in 1837 entered Jefferson College, Canonsburg, Pa., as a junior. The following year he left to teach at Snow Hill, Md., but returned to the college in 1840 only to leave without graduating after a heated argument with the president over a question of constitutional law. He then read law for two years and was admitted to the Ohio bar. Though case law and argument bored him, both his practice and his reputation as a political speaker grew rapidly. In 1845 he went to Columbus as the youngest member of the Ohio legislature; he was reëlected in 1846 and chosen speaker of the House by his Democratic colleagues. The following year he formed a partnership with Thomas J. S. Smith at Dayton, Ohio. Here he soon became part owner and editor of the Dayton *Empire,* but the extent of his law practice caused him to relinquish his editorship in 1849.

Handsome, high-spirited, and self-willed, Vallandigham was devoted to the South as the home of his ancestors, and idealized Southern character. He served as an officer in the Ohio militia and became a brigadier-general in 1857, although he objected to the maintenance of a strong national army and ardently opposed centralization of government. He earnestly supported the Mexican War and although he disapproved of slavery as a moral and political evil, he advocated a policy of non-interference where it existed, opposed the Wilmot Proviso and the repeal of the Ohio "Black Laws," and supported the compromise measures of 1850. Long before the Civil War he was demanding the suppression of abolitionist fanatics and a return to Jeffersonian state rights, the Constitution as the fathers wrote it, and the Union as it had been.

He was defeated for Congress in 1852 by the abolitionists and the Liberty party, and in 1854 by the Know-Nothings. Two years later, denouncing the Republicans as dangerous sectionalists headed for civil war, he ran again for Congress. Successfully contesting the official count, which gave his opponent a majority of nineteen, he was seated by the House in May 1858, and later that year was reëlected by a scant margin. On the floor of the House, Feb. 24, 1859, he vigorously attacked the tariff of 1857 as a manufacturer's tariff. In the fall of 1859, changing trains at Harpers Ferry, Va., (now W. Va.), he interrogated the wounded John Brown and subsequently stated his conviction that Brown had been the instrument of a widespread conspiracy. For this interview he was condemned by many Republican journals which charged him with "pumping" their martyr. In the excited Thirty-sixth Congress he pleaded for freedom of speech and of the press, denounced sectionalism and ultraism on either side, and declared that the West would not allow disunion. As secretary of the National Democratic Committee in 1860 and a delegate at the Charleston convention he opposed the views of Stephen A. Douglas [q.v.] on popular sovereignty, but supported Douglas as the only "Union" candidate fit for the presidency. He vehemently denounced the radical utterances of Lincoln and Seward and declared that the Southern "fire-eaters" would vanish if the Republican party were destroyed. In a speech at Cooper Union, New York City, Nov. 2, 1860, he said he would never, "as a Representative in the Congress of the United States, vote one dollar of money whereby one drop of American blood should be shed in a civil war" (J. L. Vallandigham, *post*, p. 141). In Congress he supported the Crittenden Resolutions and other attempts at compromise, going to the extent of proposing (Feb. 20, 1861) a division of the Senate and of the electoral college into four sections, each to have the power of veto. His able opposition to every defense measure proposed in the

House soon incurred for him the intense hatred of the Republicans.

By the time of his return to Ohio he was suspected of treasonable intent and had become one of the most unpopular and most bitterly abused men in the North. Standing for freedom of expression, for compromise, and for the restoration of peace on any terms, he called the congressmen who condemned him radicals, rebels, and liars. In May 1862, attempting to give the Democrats a policy by which to save their party, he declared their purpose: "To maintain the Constitution as it is, and to restore the Union as it was" (*Speeches, post*, p. 365). His eloquent and impassioned oratory in a war-weary and uncertain North gained support among thousands of people who thought him the true apostle of liberty. His party convention enthusiastically renominated him for Congress in 1862, but he was defeated. Thenceforth he was regarded as the leader of the Peace Democrats or "Copperheads" in the Northwest. Believing that the Democratic victories in 1862 vindicated his policy, he delivered a speech in the House, Jan. 14, 1863, in which he said that the time had come to negotiate a peace, and that prolonging the war would mean that the Northwest would join the South, and the Union be permanently broken. His thrusts at the Republicans encouraged the pro-Southern element and the disloyalists in the order of the Sons of Liberty, of which he was commander; they pleased President Davis, and made the Federal administration wince.

When in the spring of 1863 Gen. Ambrose E. Burnside [q.v.] issued General Order Number 38, warning the peace party that the "habit of declaring sympathies for the enemy" would not be allowed in the Military District of Ohio, and that expressed or implied treason would not be tolerated, Vallandigham, who had promoted resistance to conscription, defied the military in speeches at Columbus and Mount Vernon, calling the "wicked and cruel" war a diabolical attempt to destroy slavery and to set up a Republican despotism. On May 5, 1863, he was arrested in Dayton and the next day was tried by a military commission in Cincinnati for expressing treasonable sympathy. He was condemned to confinement in Fort Warren, but President Lincoln shrewdly banished him (May 19) to the Confederacy. Treated kindly by the Confederates, he ran the blockade to Bermuda, thence sailed to Halifax, and in August settled at Windsor, Ont., across the river from Detroit. An appeal was taken to the federal courts in an attempt to get a decision on the validity of his trial before the military body, but in February

Vallandigham

1864 the Supreme Court decided that it had no power to issue a writ of *habeas corpus* to a military commission (*Ex parte Vallandigham*, 1 *Wallace*, 243).

Meanwhile the Peace Democrats of Ohio, choosing him as the symbol of their principles, in July 1863 made him their candidate for governor. Mobs rioted in his behalf and committees of Democrats importuned Lincoln to return him to Ohio, but were refused on grounds of military necessity. After carrying on his campaign through friends and through correspondence, he polled a large vote, but was defeated decisively by John Brough [*q.v.*], a War Democrat running on the Republican ticket. On June 15, 1864, he suddenly appeared to deliver a speech before a Democratic convention at Hamilton, Ohio, and was afterwards escorted in triumph to Dayton. Allowed to go unnoticed by the President, he denounced "King Lincoln" and spat upon General Order Number 38. He ended his extensive pre-campaign speaking tour in Chicago, where he talked to crowds in the streets and in August irreparably damaged his party's cause by forcing into the national Democratic platform a resolution (written by himself and John McElwee) declaring the war a failure and demanding an immediate cessation of hostilities.

The Vallandigham influence and Northern victories defeated the Democracy in 1864. On Jan. 23, 1865, Vallandigham begged Horace Greeley [*q.v.*] to bring about peace, but the failure of the conference at Hampton Roads in February ended his peace efforts. He regretted the assassination of Lincoln because he feared that in retaliation the radicals would bring greater evils upon the country. In 1866 he went to Philadelphia to attend the "National Union Convention" of supporters of President Johnson, but though hundreds of people called at the Girard House to see him, he was forced to withdraw from the convention to make harmony possible in the party ranks. He entered the state elections in 1867 with his accustomed vigor and invective, and was deeply grieved when the Democratic leaders refused to choose him senator. As a member of the Ohio delegation to the National Democratic Convention of the following year, though Salmon P. Chase [*q.v.*] was his personal preference for the presidential nomination, he supported George H. Pendleton [*q.v.*] until the latter withdrew from the contest; then, after the movement toward Chase had failed, he turned to Horatio Seymour [*q.v.*]; in the subsequent campaign the Republican incumbent, Gen. Robert C. Schenk [*q.v.*], defeated Vallandigham for Congress.

In succeeding months Vallandigham reached

Vallejo

the conclusion that it was time to accept the results of the Civil War and to drop the old issues; early in 1871 he won the Ohio Democracy to this view and invited dissatisfied Republicans to join the Democrats in turning to living issues of a new day, but he died before the movement he thus helped to start took shape in the Liberal Republican party of 1872. Whatever his policy at any time, Vallandigham advocated it with the ardor and sincerity of a fanatic. In 1871 he was retained as counsel for the defendant in a murder case and while demonstrating to a friend the way in which the victim had been shot he mortally wounded himself. On Aug. 27, 1846, he had married Louisa A. McMahon by whom he had two sons, one of whom lived to maturity.

[Sources include Vallandigham letters in Western Reserve Hist. Soc.; *Speeches, Arguments, Addresses and Letters of Clement L. Vallandigham* (1864); McClellan MSS., Blair MSS., William Allen MSS. in Lib. of Cong.; *Cong. Globe*, 36 and 37 Cong.; *War of the Rebellion: Official Records (Army)*, 2 ser. V, VII. For accounts of Vallandigham's career see J. L. Vallandigham, *A Life of Clement L. Vallandigham* (1872), by a brother; E. N. Vallandigham, in *Putnam's Mag.*, Aug. 1907; W. H. Van Fossan, in *Ohio Archæol. and Hist. Quart.*, July 1914; Henry Howe, *Hist. Colls. of Ohio* (2 vols., 1902); S. D. Cone, *Biog. and Hist. Sketches: A Narrative of Hamilton and Its Residents* (n.d.; preface dated 1896). See also J. G. Nicolay and John Hay, *Abraham Lincoln* (1890), VII, 328–60; E. J. Benton, "The Movement for Peace without a Victory during the Civil War," *Western Reserve Hist. Soc. Colls.*, pub. no. 99 (1918); J. G. Randall, *Constitutional Problems under Lincoln* (1926); E. C. Kirkland, *The Peacemakers of 1864* (1927); H. C. Hubbart, "'Pro-Southern' Influences in the Free West, 1840–1865," *Miss. Valley Hist. Rev.*, June 1933; C. H. Coleman, *The Election of 1868* (1933); *The Am. Ann. Cyc.*, *1863* (1864), *1871* (1872); *Cincinnati Daily Enquirer*, June 19, 1871.]
W. E. S—h.

VALLEJO, MARIANO GUADALUPE (July 7, 1808–Jan. 18, 1890), prominent early California citizen and military leader, was born in Monterey, Cal., son of Ignacio Vallejo and María Antonia Lugo. At fifteen he was attached as cadet to the Monterey garrison; by 1827 he was ensign in the company at the Presidio (now San Francisco). On the occasion of the formidable Estanislao Indian rebellion of 1829, when the neophytes of the San José mission rose against the missionaries, young Vallejo was sent against the Indians with a hundred men and a number of Indian auxiliaries. He defeated and scattered the rebels, but his victory was marred by his failing to prevent the murder of some of the prisoners by his Indian allies. Elected a deputy to the territorial congress in 1830 (illegally, it seems, since he was an officer in the army), he supported the rebellion of the Californians against their Mexican governor, Manuel Victoria, in 1832. That same year, on Mar. 6, he married María Francisca Felipa Benicia Carrillo of San Diego, by whom in the course of time he had between thirteen and seventeen children. The new governor, the able and humane José Figueroa, a close friend of Vallejo's, had Vallejo removed as deputy but made him commander of an expedition to reconnoitre the northern frontier, where the activities of the Russians at Fort Ross were causing uneasiness among the Californians. Vallejo found the Russians to be peacefully engaged in the fur trade and no menace to California, but his report on the danger from the warlike Indians of that region and the encroachment of American immigrants decided Governor Figueroa to establish a military post there. The commandant of the new garrison at Sonoma was Vallejo, and his organization of the frontier defenses and his control of the Indians were, perhaps, his most valuable contributions to the state. The secularization of the mission properties carried on by Figueroa led naturally to the appointment of Vallejo as administrator of the Solano mission, a duty which he performed efficiently and humanely, befriending the Indians and settling them on the mission lands, although in so doing he ran afoul of the belligerent Father Mercado of Solano.

With the death of Figueroa in 1835 Vallejo was again forced into politics, this time against the bombastic centralist governor Mariano Chico and his lieutenant Gutiérrez. He supported his nephew, Juan Bautista Alvarado [q.v.], in the rebellion that led to the proclamation of the "free state" of California in 1836, and in 1838, under Alvarado's governorship, was named commander of the state forces. A petty quarrel over military etiquette estranged the two, and Vallejo retired to his post at Sonoma, where, with an imposing force of Indian allies and his own troops, he made himself a semi-independent chieftain, a *cacique* on the Spanish-American pattern, and the most powerful figure in the north. Alvarado's appointment of William Hartnell as administrator of the missions widened the gap between the two. When Hartnell invaded the Sonoma country in the discharge of his duties, he was promptly arrested and deported by Vallejo, and thereafter Vallejo was left to himself until the end of the Mexican régime in 1846. Vallejo had protected and encouraged the immigration of American families into his territory, being, as he said, powerless to prevent it. The presence of the Frémont expedition of 1846 encouraged an enemy of the Vallejos, one Merritt, and a number of idle Americans at Fort Sutter to undertake their headless and planless "Bear Flag Republic." Their single exploit was the capture and imprisonment of Vallejo and his

brother Salvador, and the theft of their cattle. The two brothers were kept prisoners for two months by the unaccountable Frémont.

A powerful agent in securing the submission of California to the United States, Vallejo was elected to the constitutional convention of 1849, and to the first state Senate of California, where he staged a long fight to have the state capital fixed at Vallejo in his own territory. Thereafter he devoted his energies largely to clearing the titles of his princely holdings, some of which he retained. In his latter years he was no longer the great *cacique* of the Mexican days, but he kept up his magnificent hospitality at the great house at Sonoma to the end of his life. He died in Sonoma in comparative poverty, a well loved and respected country gentleman. His unpublished "Historia de California" is a somewhat colored, but charming and valuable account of early California.

[See H. H. Bancroft, *Hist. of Cal.* (7 vols., 1884–90) ; T. H. Hittell, *Hist. of Cal.* (4 vols., 1885–97) ; Zephyrin Engelhardt, *The Missions and Missionaries of Cal.* (6 vols., 1908–30) ; C. E. Chapman, *Hist. of Cal., the Spanish Period* (1921) ; Eugène Duflot de Mofras, *Exploration du Territoire de l'Orégon, des Californies* (2 vols., Paris, 1844), valuable for its description of Spanish Cal.; Alfred Robinson, *Life in Cal. before the Conquest* (1846) ; P. M. G. Vallejo, "Memoirs of the Vallejos," in *Bulletin* (San Francisco), Jan. 27–Feb. 16, 1914; M. L. Lothrop, "Mariano Guadalupe Vallejo, Defender of the Northern Frontier," unpublished dissertation in the Univ. of Cal. lib., 1927; M. G. Vallejo, "Historia de California," MS. in the Bancroft Lib., Berkeley, Cal.; and obituary in *Morning Call* (San Francisco), Jan. 19, 1890. There are thirty-seven vols. of manuscript material from the archives of the Vallejo family in the Bancroft Lib.]   L. B. S—n.

VALLENTINE, BENJAMIN BENNATON (Sept. 7, 1843–Mar. 30, 1926), journalist, playwright, was born in London, the son of Benjamin Vallentine, a toy merchant, and Rosa (Nathan) Vallentine. He always gave King Edward VI's School, Birmingham, as the place of his education, but the truth seems to be that most of his education was not obtained at any school. As a youth, he spent several years in Australia, where he was clerk in a shipping firm at Sydney. He studied for the English bar, and contributed to Sydney newspapers. In 1870 he returned to England, and the next year came to New York City, where he lived until his death.

In New York he became partner in a shipping house, but after the panic of 1873 turned to journalism. He was one of the founders of *Puck* in 1877, and served as managing editor from 1877 to 1884. For *Puck* he wrote the series of papers beginning in the March 1877 issue, which constitute his chief claim to remembrance. They purport to be the letters of one Lord Fitznoodle, a musical-comedy Britisher, concerning his adventures among the Americans. The satire, which frequently cuts both ways, is always good-natured and urbane. After leaving *Puck,* Vallentine served as managing editor of Irving Bacheller's newspaper syndicate (1886–88). He did much editorial writing and dramatic criticism for New York newspapers, and held other editorial positions. Always interested in the theatre, he became a familiar figure on Broadway and had a wide circle of theatrical acquaintance. He wrote, collaborated on, or adapted, a good many plays, most of them having no pretension to depth. None of the plays seems to have been published, except a one-act version of *In Paradise,* but some, including *Fadette* (a comic opera), *A Southern Romance,* and *In Paradise,* were produced in New York, the first in 1892, the second in 1897, and the third in 1899.

In his later years Vallentine fell upon hard times. He was registered at New York University Law School in 1907–08. In 1908 he took a civil service position as audit-inspector with the municipal finance department, but the salary was low and had to be pieced out by donations from his family and "loans" from his friends. He had never married, and lived in a furnished room, spending much of his time at his old haunt, the Lotos Club. About two years before the end his health failed, and he underwent several operations. Then one day in his eighty-third year he fell unconscious in a restaurant and was taken to Bellevue Hospital. Annoyed at finding himself in a public hospital ward, he tried to get up —and fell dead.

Vallentine's friends remember him as a tiny man, with great flashing black eyes and quick, nervous gestures. He never lost his British accent nor all of his British way of looking at things. He was a good conversationalist, and had an amazing memory and wide information. Every one testifies to the essential fineness of his character. He was a lively and interesting person rather than a man of genius; yet his connection with *Puck* and his creation of the comic character which gave him his nickname of "Fitznoodle" entitle him to be remembered.

[Sources include files of *Puck*; *Who's Who in America,* 1924–25; *Who's Who in New York* (1911); *Phila. Sunday Mirror,* July 30, 1880; *N. Y. Times,* Sept. 5, 1899, Mar. 31, 1926, Apr. 4, 1926; *World* (N. Y.), Mar. 31, 1926; *Dramatic Compositions Copyrighted in the United States, 1870 to 1916* (1918); records of the Gen. Reg. Office, London, of N. Y. Univ. Law School, and of Newspaper Club, N. Y.; personal recollections of Walter R. Benjamin, Stephen L. Newman, Eva Ingersoll Wakefield, and Anna Fisch, all of New York, and of members and employees of the Lotos Club, N. Y. In his latter years Vallentine seems to have used Benton instead of Bennaton for a middle name.]

E. M. S.

VALLIANT, LEROY BRANCH (June 14, 1838–Mar. 3, 1913), jurist, was born at Moulton, Ala. His father, Denton Hurlock Valliant, a native of Tennessee, was descended from John Valliant (or Vaillant), a Londoner of French parentage, who settled on the Eastern Shore of Maryland in the seventeenth century (1658, according to family tradition), and from Jonathan Hurlock who came to the same section of Maryland from England in the first half of the eighteenth century. His mother, before marriage Narcissa Kilpatrick, a native of Tennessee, was of Irish and Scottish ancestry. An orphan at six, Valliant, helped by relatives, received a good education, first at private schools, then at the University of Mississippi, where he was graduated in 1856, and later at the Cumberland University Law School in Tennessee, where he was graduated in 1858. That same year, when the fascinating William Walker [*q.v.*] was starting one of his Nicaraguan expeditions, Valliant joined a band of Walker's "emigrants" and embarked by river for New Orleans, but because of lack of funds was put off the boat with his companions at Memphis. In later years Valliant expressed religious thankfulness for the abortive outcome of this youthful adventure.

After settling at the prosperous river town of Greenville, Miss., he was admitted to the bar in 1859, and practised law until the Civil War. In 1861 he entered the Confederate military service. At the battle of Shiloh, as captain of Company I, 22nd Mississippi Regiment, he was for a while in command of that regiment because all his ranking officers had been killed or wounded. Shortly afterwards, shattered in health and with sight permanently impaired, he returned to Greenville where eventually, with restored health, he resumed his career as a lawyer, serving for a term as chancellor of his district. In 1874, partly because of dissatisfaction with the progress of reconstruction, he left Mississippi, went to St. Louis, and there in the course of twelve years acquired considerable reputation as a lawyer and as a public speaker. Appointed by the governor in 1886 to a temporary judgeship on the circuit court of St. Louis, in the fall of that year he was elected judge of the same court for a constitutional term of six years, and reëlected in 1892. In 1898, while still a circuit judge, he was elected for a four-year term to fill a vacancy in the supreme court of Missouri, and in 1902 was reëlected for another term of ten years. After twenty-six years of useful public service in Missouri, he finally retired Dec. 31, 1912, broken in health, but still alert mentally and beloved by the legal profession. He died at Greenville; his body was taken to St. Louis and buried in Bellefontaine Cemetery. In October 1862 he had married Theodosia Taylor Worthington of Leota Landing, Miss., who with their three sons survived him.

Valliant's judicial activities on the Missouri supreme court are set forth in 147–247 *Missouri Reports*. As a judge he was sound rather than brilliant. He wrote the majority opinion of the court in *Morgan* vs. *Wabash Railroad Company* (1900), 159 *Mo.*, 262, which after years of controversy finally established the so-called humanitarian doctrine as a Missouri exception to the rather harsh English common-law rule of contributory negligence. Another of his important opinions was in the case of *State ex rel. Koeln* vs. *Lesser* (1911), 237 *Mo.*, 310, holding that under the taxation statutes of Missouri the stocks in non-Missouri corporations even if owned by Missouri residents are not subject to taxation as personal property in Missouri.

[James Cox, *Old and New St. Louis* (1894); A. J. D. Stewart, *The Hist. of the Bench and Bar of Mo.* (1898); William Hyde and H. L. Conard, *Encyc. of the Hist. of St. Louis* (1899), vol. IV; *Who's Who in America*, 1912–13; "In Memoriam," 248 *Mo. Reports* (1913); Henry Lamm, "Address in Memory of Judge Leroy B. Valliant," *Proc. 31st Ann. Meeting Mo. Bar Asso.* (1913); *St. Louis Globe-Democrat*, Mar. 5, 6, 1913; newspaper clippings at Mo. Hist. Soc., St. Louis.]
T. W.

VAN ALLEN, FRANK (Jan. 10, 1860–Aug. 28, 1923), missionary physician, the son of Martin and Martha (Bowen) Van Allen, was born in Dubuque, Iowa, to which place his parents had removed from New York State. He was a descendant of Pieter van Allen who came to New Netherland in 1658. The boy's preparatory education was obtained in Lake View High School, Chicago, Ill., where he distinguished himself as a student. Entering Yale in 1881, he received from that institution the degrees of B.A. in 1885, M.D. in 1887, and B.D. in 1888. He was ordained to the Congregational ministry at West Haven, Conn., on May 21, 1888, and in September was married in Chicago to Harriet Adelia Gurnee. Sailing with his wife from New York Oct. 13, under commission of the American Board of Commissioners for Foreign Missions, he arrived in Dindigul, Madura, South India, on Nov. 28. Except for several furloughs, he spent the remainder of his life in Madura, engaged in medical missionary service.

After a brief time in Dindigul he moved to Madura City, where he took charge of a mission dispensary which had been in operation since 1834. Under his direction it rendered a continually increasing service. In 1890 he reported the treatment of 13,000 cases; six years later the

number had doubled; and in 1897 it reached 47,200. The following year a new men's hospital, the Albert Victoria Memorial, was completed, and on Oct. 29 it was opened by the governor of Madras. On this occasion an address was delivered by the Raja of Ramnad, one of the chief donors. The cost was $14,000, provided almost entirely by non-Christians of India, and the expense of maintenance was borne largely by "native" subscriptions. Van Allen never charged specific fees for any service, but received "thank-offerings," which, even before 1896, approximated $7,000. In 1902 the gifts amounted to 6,300 rupees, including a donation of 1,800 from a *Zamindar* (land-owner) for the cure of his wife, who had not walked for four years previously. In 1905, another *Zamindar* gave 5,000 rupees. That year, the in-patients of the hospital numbered 346, the out-patients, 20,800, and 1,100 operations were performed, including many leg amputations. These figures indicate the extent of service rendered, and its generous support by Indians. The doctor came to hold a place of highest esteem throughout the district. Branches of the hospital were opened at Aruppukottai and Manamadura, in the latter place in connection with a leper colony. On the death of his wife in 1911 Van Allen founded for the needy the Harriet Gurnee Fund. They had four children.

His work was recognized by the government of India, which bestowed on him in 1914 the *Kaiser-i-Hind* medal. He had rendered especially conspicuous service during times of plague and cholera. Ultimately, he fell victim to the risks of his own service. Unknown to others until the last year of his affliction, he suffered for a decade from an incurable disease, contracted while he operated on a patient. Shortly before his death he resigned the headship of the hospital and retired to the nearby village of Melur to live his remaining days among the Christians there.

[*Quarter-Centenary Record of the Class of 1885, Yale Univ.* (1913); *Yale '85 Forty-five Years After* (1932); *Yale Univ. Obit. Record*, 1925; *The Congregational Year-Book*, 1923; *Missionary Herald*, 1888–1923, especially Oct. 1923; *Harvest Field*, vol. XLIII (1923); *Yale Divinity News*, Mar. 1924.]   J. C. A.

VAN ALSTYNE, FANNY CROSBY [See CROSBY, FANNY, 1820–1915].

VAN AMRINGE, JOHN HOWARD (Apr. 3, 1835–Sept. 10, 1915), professor of mathematics and dean of Columbia College, was born in Philadelphia, Pa., the son of William Frederick Van Amringe (1791–1873), the author of two scientific works, and Susan Budd Sterling, daughter of James Sterling of Burlington, N. J.

His grandfather, Leon Van Amringe, was born in Rotterdam, South Holland; married Elizabeth Oborne, a Hampshire woman, in London; and emigrated to America in 1791 (M. H. Thomas, "Van Amringe ... Family Records," *New-England Historical and Genealogical Register,* Oct. 1935, pp. 392–95). The family moved to New York City about 1840. Van Amringe was educated by his father and at the Montgomery Academy in Orange County, N. Y., whence he entered Yale in 1854. He remained there two years, and after a two-year interlude of teaching entered Columbia College, graduating in 1860 with second honors. The same year he was appointed tutor in mathematics; in 1863 he became adjunct professor. On June 20, 1865, he married Cornelia, daughter of William Goelet Bucknor of New York City; they had three sons and one daughter. Van Amringe became professor of mathematics in the School of Mines, Columbia University, in 1865 and in the School of Arts in 1873. In 1894 he succeeded Henry Drisler [*q.v.*] as dean of the School of Arts (renamed Columbia College in 1896). For a short time in 1899 he was acting president of Columbia University. He resigned his offices, June 30, 1910, and was made emeritus professor of mathematics. After the death of his former teacher and colleague, Prof. Charles Davies, he became editor of the Davies Series of mathematical textbooks. He wrote various professional papers, two pamphlets on life insurance (1872 and 1874), and many articles on Columbia and its alumni. He was one of the founders of the New York Mathematical Society (later the American Mathematical Society), and its first president (1888–90). He was one of the most popular members of the Century Association, and was vice-president at the time of his death. Long active in Episcopal organizations in New York, he served as vestryman of Trinity Church and trustee of the General Theological Seminary. He was a tall man, with a military bearing, and wore a great drooping mustache. His death occurred in Morristown, N. J.

"Van Am," as he was universally called, is a unique figure in the history of Columbia. "As a teacher he was clear, quick and incisive; having a perfect mastery of his subject, he expected and demanded hard work of his students, and was intolerant of inattention or neglect. Keen to detect a fault and sharp to reprimand, he was equally ready to recognize good work and anxious to do strict justice" (Pine, *post,* p. 192). Probably no other teacher in Columbia's history influenced the lives and ideals of his students as did Van Amringe. Probably no other teacher of

his day was so loved and revered, and "his boys" have delighted to perpetuate his memory at Columbia in song and stone and bronze and oils. Scarcely had he become an alumnus when he began to arouse an interest in the college among the alumni, and to restore the semi-moribund alumni association; imbuing others slowly with his own enthusiasm, he made the association a vital and vivifying influence in the whole university. He was at first secretary, then president of the association, and later president of the alumni of the federated schools of the university. He was unanimously elected president of the Columbia University Club in New York City on its foundation in 1901 and held office until his death. For decades no alumni gathering was complete without him. He was a fluent orator, speaking in "exquisitely phrased sentences, rich in thought and suggestion, often imbued with deep feeling and genial humor" (*Ibid.,* p. 194). He prepared the alumni necrology for many years, and used this material as a basis for nine new editions of the *General Catalogue,* which he edited from 1865 to 1906. His interest in history, originally stimulated by his courses with Francis Lieber [*q.v.*], was life-long. He compiled *An Historical Sketch of Columbia College* (1876), and wrote the section on Columbia for *Universities and Their Sons* (5 vols., 1898–1900), revising this for *A History of Columbia University, 1754–1904* (1904).

[The *Columbia Alumni News,* Nov. 5, 1915, sec. 2, is devoted to Van Amringe; it contains a biog. by J. B. Pine and memorial addresses by N. M. Butler and Seth Low; a somewhat cynical estimate by a colleague appears in J. W. Burgess, *Reminiscences of an Am. Scholar* (1934). See also *Who's Who in America,* 1914–15; *N. Y. Times* and *N. Y. Herald,* Sept. 11, 1915; J. J. Chapman, in *Evening Post* (N. Y.), Sept. 24, 1915; *Outlook,* Sept. 22, 1915; N. M. Butler, in *Columbia Spectator,* Apr. 20, 1931. The date of Van Amringe's birth, sometimes given as 1836, is from the family Bible.]   M.H.T.

VAN BEUREN, JOHANNES (*c.* 1680–July 27, 1755), physician, founder of a family of well-known physicians of New York City and vicinity, was born in Amsterdam and came to New York at the age of twenty-two. He had been a student of the renowned Dutch physician Hermannus Boerhaave, who had made the medical department of the University of Leyden famous throughout Europe. With this training he soon established a large practice in New York, where few of the so-called physicians had ever seen the inside of a medical school. In the words of a local historian, "few physicians amongst us are eminent for their skill. Quacks abound like locusts in Egypt, and too many have recommended themselves to a full practice and profitable subsistence" (William Smith, *History of New-York,* 1814, p. 325).

After practising in New York for more than twenty years, he removed about 1724 to Flatbush, Long Island, and lived there until 1728, when he returned to New York. In 1736, an almshouse, known as the "Publick Workhouse and House of Correction," was built on the site of the present City Hall. The hospital department was a room about twenty-five feet square on the second floor, containing six beds, and Van Beuren, through the influence of the governor of the colony it is said, was appointed its first medical director. He held the position until his death. His salary was £100 a year, out of which he was expected to provide his own medicines. This was the beginning of Bellevue Hospital, which may lay claim to being the oldest hospital in the United States. As Boerhaave in Holland was among the first to teach that pure air, cleanliness, and simple buildings are the first requirements for a hospital, it may be presumed that these principles were established by his former pupil in the new hospital in New York.

Van Beuren was married at New York, on June 15, 1707, to Maria Meyer, the daughter of Pieter Meyer and his wife, Batje Jans, of New York. They had fifteen children. His marriage and the baptisms of all but two of the children are recorded in the register of the Dutch Church. Five of his sons were physicians, and one of them, Beekman Van Beuren, who was the physician at the almshouse from 1765 to 1776, is credited with the introduction of inoculation for smallpox in the public institutions of the city. William Holme Van Buren [*q.v.*] was a descendant.

[*An Account of Bellevue Hospital* (1893), R. J. Carlisle, ed.; William Jones, "The Van Beuren Family of New York and New Jersey," *N. Y. Geneal. and Biog. Record,* Jan. 1932.]   W. J.

VAN BRUNT, HENRY (Sept. 5, 1832–Apr. 8, 1903), architect and writer, was born in Boston, Mass., the son of Commodore Gershom Jaques Van Brunt, of the United States Navy, and Elizabeth Price (Bradlee) Van Brunt. On his father's side he was descended from Rutger Joesten van Brunt, who emigrated from the Netherlands in 1653 and in 1657 settled in New Utrecht, Long Island (now part of Brooklyn). One of his mother's ancestors is said to have been Nathaniel Bradlee, a participant in the Boston Tea Party. Van Brunt was educated at the Boston Latin School and at Harvard University. During his freshman year, he had a serious accident to his hip, which left him at least a partial invalid for the rest of his life. He graduated in 1854. He

then entered the Boston office of George Snell, architect, as a student; in 1856 he went to New York and became a student in the famous office-atelier of Richard Morris Hunt [*q.v.*], where he remained for several years. During the Civil War he was for two years clerk to Commodore L. M. Goldsborough of the North Atlantic Squadron and saw service in Virginia and North Carolina. In 1863 he formed a partnership, Ware and Van Brunt, with William Robert Ware [*q.v.*], whom he had met in Hunt's office. The work done with Ware included the First Church, Boston, Memorial Hall, Weld Hall, and the east wing of the college library at Harvard, and the library of the University of Michigan. Ware retired completely from the partnership in 1881; it was not formally dissolved, however, till 1883. Van Brunt thereupon took into partnership Frank M. Howe, who had been an employee of the firm since 1868, and the remainder of his architectural work was done under the firm name of Van Brunt and Howe. Commissioned by his friend Charles Francis Adams [*q.v.*], president of the Union Pacific Railway (1884–90), to design a large number of railroad stations in the West, Van Brunt sent Howe to Kansas City to open an office in 1885 and followed him soon after. Few architects of their training were then settled in the Middle West, and a large amount of work came to them. It included the railroad stations at Ogden, Utah; Sioux City, Iowa; Portland, Ore.; and Omaha, Nebr.; the store of the Emery, Bird, Thayer Dry Goods Company at Kansas City, large houses for the Armour and Griffiths families and for August R. Meyer, and other work largely residential and commercial. They were associated with McKim, Mead and White in the New York Life Insurance Building at Kansas City and, as the most important architectural firm west of Chicago, were commissioned to design the Electricity Building at the World's Columbian Exposition of 1893 at Chicago. Van Brunt had been one of the earliest members of the American Institute of Architects, and a fellow since 1864; he was secretary in 1861 and president in 1899. He declined to run for the office a second time because he was planning a long tour in Europe for study and rest, his first trip out of the United States. It signalled his practical retirement from active practice.

Van Brunt's architectural work is characteristic of the eclecticism of his time. He started with a strong bias towards Ruskin-inspired Gothic, but later worked in the popular Romanesque and in various types of classic as well; the work which seems best today, however, is characterized by a strong personal search for original and honest expression. His most important contribution was in his writings; many magazine articles on architectural subjects are distinguished for their keen analysis, and their graceful and persuasive style. Some of these were republished (with other material) in *Greek Lines and Other Architectural Essays* (1893). Van Brunt was also the translator of Viollet-le-Duc's *Entretiens sur l'Architecture* (2 vols., 1863–72) as *Discourses on Architecture* (1875). The courtliness, dignity, and gentleness which so characterized his manner are well expressed in his writing. His accomplishments are all the more remarkable in view of the physical disability against which he labored. He married Alice Sterritt Osborn at Salem, Mass., Oct. 6, 1869. He died in Milton, Mass., survived by his wife and their seven children.

[T. G. Bergen, *Geneal. of the Van Brunt Family* (1867); *Who's Who in America,* 1901–02, with an error in the mother's name; *Harvard Coll. . . . Class of 1854* (1894); Élie Brault, *Les Architectes par Leurs Oeuvres* (3 vols., 1892–93); *Proc. Thirty-seventh Ann. Convention Am. Inst. of Architects* (1904); G. C. Mitchell, *There Is No Limit: Architecture and Sculpture in Kansas City* (1934); *Am. Architect and Building News,* Apr. 11, 1903; obituaries in *N. Y. Tribune* and *Kansas City Jour.,* Apr. 9, 1903; information from Van Brunt's son, Courtlandt Van Brunt.]   T. F. H.

VAN BUREN, JOHN (Feb. 10, 1810–Oct. 13, 1866), lawyer, politician, was born in Kinderhook, N. Y., the son of Martin Van Buren [*q.v.*] and Hannah (Hoes) Van Buren. He was sent first to the Albany public schools, then to Albany Academy whence he went to Yale. In college he drank and gambled freely, studied little, worried the faculty and president of Yale, and cost his father unnecessary expense and sleepless nights. Upon graduation he read law with Benjamin F. Butler and later with Aaron Vanderpoel, whose niece Elizabeth he afterward married (June 22, 1841). In July 1831 he was admitted to the Albany bar, and one month later he sailed with his father to London to become an attaché of the American legation. His fine physique, ready wit and good humor, and aristocratic and gracious bearing made him a favorite at the English court. The Whig press of America dubbed him "Prince John." Before returning home he traveled on the Continent, and in 1838 he again visited England and Ireland.

His activities in politics were so like his father's that he soon won another title, "Young Fox." By 1834 he was a member of the "Albany regency." For a time he was a law examiner in Albany and a law partner of James McKnown (1837–45), later taking as a partner Hamilton W. Robinson. In 1845 he joined the radical wing

of the New York Democracy and won the office of attorney general (1845). He prosecuted the anti-rent cases and after his resumption of private practice took part in the notorious Forrest divorce suit, in which he lost prestige. Although he was popular with the New York bar and powerful with juries, his political activities during the forties rather obscured his legal career (McAdam, *post,* I, 505).

Much of his time was consumed in lobbying in the state legislature. His power was felt in nearly every Democratic state convention from 1836 to 1848, and especially in campaigns for his father. He published a pamphlet, *The Syracuse Convention,* in 1847. He was influential in organizing the "Barnburners," and in behalf of them and the Free-soil groups he persuaded his father to accept the nomination for president at Buffalo in 1848. His zeal and oratory stirred the Free-soilers deeply. Some of their leaders wanted him for their standard bearer, but he chose to fight for his father, who had lost the Democratic presidential nomination to Polk at Baltimore (1844). John as a delegate to the convention led the enraged "Barnburners" in their withdrawal. He stumped the state, denouncing the Fugitive-slave Law and everywhere electrifying his audiences with his Free-soil evangelism. Had he grasped the full significance of the Free-soil movement he could have been one of the chief leaders of the forthcoming Republican party, but he was unhappy outside the Democracy and returned to it in 1849. He supported the compromise measures of 1850. In 1853 he threatened to denounce Pierce (R. F. Nichols, *The Democratic Machine, 1850–1854,* 1923, p. 212), but was kept quiet by Marcy and Tilden, and finally came out strongly for popular sovereignty in Kansas. He wanted a convention of states (1860) to arrange for guarantees to the slavery interests and to prevent war. He denounced Lincoln for calling for troops so soon after the firing on Fort Sumter. In many speeches he defended General McClellan, bitterly assailed the draft, the suspension of the writ of *habeas corpus,* and the use of colored troops. He supported Seymour for governor in 1862 and McClellan for president in 1864, and was himself defeated in his candidacy for the attorney generalship of the state in 1865. He threw his waning influence to Andrew Johnson (1866), but his failing health caused him to seek its improvement in England. He died of a kidney disease while on the *Scotia* en route to New York, leaving his only child, Anna, and was buried in Albany beside his wife, who had died in 1844.

Van Buren

Van Buren

[Van Buren MSS. and Marcy MSS. in Lib. of Cong.;
the private collection of Blair MSS.; Van Buren let-
ters in N. Y. State Lib., Albany; D. S. Alexander, *A
Political History of the State of N. Y.*, vol. II (1906);
D. T. Lynch, *An Epoch and a Man: Martin Van Buren
and His Times* (1929); W. L. Mackenzie, *The Life and
Times of Martin Van Buren* (1846); E. M. Shepard,
Martin Van Buren (1888); H. D. A. Donovan, *The
Barnburners* (1925); John Bigelow, *Retrospections of
an Active Life*, vol. I (1909), pp. 86–90; David Mc-
Adam and others, *Hist. of the Bench and Bar of New
York*, vol. I (1897); Harriet C. W. Van Buren Peck-
ham, *Hist. of Cornelius Maessen Van Buren . . . and
His Descendants* (1913); G. B. Vanderpoel, *Genealogy
of the Vanderpoel Family* (1912); obituaries in *Eve-
ning Post* (N. Y.), Oct. 16, 19, 1866; *N. Y. Tribune*,
Oct. 17, 20, 1866.]   W. E. S—h.

VAN BUREN, MARTIN (Dec. 5, 1782–July
24, 1862), eighth president of the United States,
was born in Kinderhook, near Albany, N. Y.,
the third of five children of Abraham and Maria
(Hoes) Van Buren, both of whom were of
Dutch descent. Abraham was descended from
Cornelis, who was the son of Maes of Buurmal-
sen and came to New Netherland in 1631 as a
leaseholder of Van Rensselaer. Maria Hoes was
the widow Van Alen and mother of two children
when she married the bachelor Abraham. Martin's parents were frugal truck farmers and keepers of an inherited tavern who became respectable slave-owning citizens in the village. In the
inadequate village schools the boy gained a fair
knowledge of English and a smattering of Latin.
After graduation at the age of fourteen, he became a clerk in the law office of Francis Silvester, a Federalist. He read little from law books,
but devoured every Republican pamphlet, journal, or periodical that he could find. Obstinately,
but good-naturedly, he refused from the beginning to adopt Silvester's Federalism. By 1800 the
yellow-haired law clerk had won a local reputation for his clear thinking, clever presentation
and summaries of his petty cases, extemporaneous debating, and stanch Republicanism. As a
reward for his campaign for Jefferson (1800)
he was sent as a delegate to the congressional
caucus in Troy. In 1801 he entered as a clerk the
almost clientless office in New York City of the
young William Peter Van Ness [*q.v.*], a devotee
of Aaron Burr.

Upon his return to Kinderhook (1803) he was
licensed to practice law and became the partner
of his half-brother, James I. Van Alen. He flung
himself immediately into Republican politics as
the champion of the Clinton-Livingston factions,
in opposition to Burr, thereby annoying the Van
Nesses. His income came from the pockets of
Jeffersonian-Republican small landholders in
whose cases in court he had often to oppose the
eloquent Elisha Williams. By 1807 he was affluent enough to marry, on Feb. 21, the sweetheart

of his youth, his kinswoman Hannah Hoes. She
bore him four sons: Abraham, John [*q.v.*], Martin, and Smith Thompson. Soon he moved to
Hudson, where as the newly appointed surrogate
(1808–13), he launched himself on an ambitious
political career. Already his enemies had pronounced him a hypocrite, a heartless, selfish, intriguing politician. He was a manipulator in
politics, but he was honest and generous in his
private and public relations. In taverns as well
as court rooms his ready wit, friendly smile, and
cheerful disposition won voters and juries to his
side. He was only five feet six and was slender
but stood erect like a soldier. He dressed immaculately, as his preceptor Silvester had taught
him. Rarely was he incensed at even his worst
enemies. He could see no reason why political
opponents could not be personal friends.

Until 1821 he was enmeshed in state politics.
In his fight for state leadership he moved in a
maze of political intrigue and bitterness, but always remained a partisan Republican. In 1807
he was admitted as counselor to practise before
the state supreme court. In a race against Edward P. Livingston he was elected state senator
in April 1812 on an anti-Bank platform. In August he was deeply chagrined at his failure to
receive the appointment as attorney general of
the state, which went to Thomas Addis Emmet,
and at first blamed DeWitt Clinton. In November, in the legislative session to select presidential
electors, he supported Clinton, as the nominee of
the Republican caucus, though the rivalry of the
two men was becoming intense. He helped to
secure the election of Daniel D. Tompkins [*q.v.*]
as vice-president in 1816 and annoyed Clinton
that year by opposing certain details of the canal
bill. The next year, however, he supported the
canal project against the wishes of his group,
defending his course by saying that he could not
sacrifice a popular blessing to humiliate Clinton.
Van Buren was soon chosen regent of the University of the State of New York (1815), a recognition of his importance. In 1816 he was re-
elected senator (1816–20) and chosen attorney
general of New York (1816–19). He then moved
his family to Albany. His wife died in 1819. He
never attempted to marry again until late in life
when he was rejected by the spinster, Margaret
Silvester, who was the daughter of his old preceptor. In the state Senate he was establishing
himself as a leader. In 1817, however, Clinton
was elected governor, and in 1819, gaining control of the Council of Appointment, he removed
Van Buren from the attorney generalship. While
bitterly attacking Clinton for cooperating with
Federalists, Van Buren acted secretly to reëlect

Rufus King [q.v.] to the United States Senate (1820) and to gain Federalist aid in defeating Clinton. He asked for a state constitutional convention, which convened in 1821, largely because he opposed the arbitrary power of Chief Justice Ambrose Spencer [q.v.] and favored a reorganization of the judicial system. His chief work in the convention was in securing an agreement between extreme radicals and conservatives that could be accepted by all. As chairman of the committee on appointments, he advocated the decentralization of the power held by the old Council of Appointment, by the distribution of the appointing power among local authorities, the legislature, and the governor. He was unsuccessful in his opposition, probably for the sake of patronage, to the popular election of all judicial officers. (N. H. Carter and W. L. Stone, *Reports of the Proceedings and Debates of the Convention of 1821 Assembled for the Purpose of Amending the Constitution of New York*, 1821.)

Clinton had been reëlected governor in 1820, largely because of his canal policy, but the "Bucktails" won control of the legislature and in February 1821 elected Van Buren to the United States Senate. In August 1820 his brother-in-law, Moses I. Cantine, and Isaac J. Leake bought the *Albany Argus*. The paper was given the contract for the state printing. In 1823, when Edwin Croswell [q.v.] became editor, Van Buren wrote that without a paper edited by "a sound, practicable and above all discreet republican . . . we may hang our harps on the willows" (quoted in Mackenzie, *post*, p. 190). Croswell made the *Argus* a highly influential organ. Van Buren was chief of a group of leaders, soon nicknamed the "Albany regency," which included William L. Marcy, Azariah C. Flagg, Benjamin F. Butler (1795–1858), Edwin Croswell, Michael Hoffman, and later Silas Wright and John A. Dix [qq.v.]. "They were formidable in solidarity," and achieved extraordinary success (Fox, *post*, pp. 281–86). Van Buren's primacy among them was not owing merely to his amiability and caution, but to his shrewd judgment of measures and men, to his power of analysis and exposition. His political philosophy was practical and sincere. Reckless opposition to public sentiment seemed to him inconsistent with good statesmanship, and he thought that those who dispensed the public bounty would, to a greater or less degree, influence and control the public mind. However, in attacking Clinton he said that a good administration would rally around "the governmental standard the good the virtuous and the capable" (Lynch, p. 175), and he and the other members of the "regency" faithfully performed the duties of the important offices they obtained.

As United States senator he was still preoccupied with factional fights from which he hoped to emerge as the leader of a unified national party. Not until 1823 did he avow his intention openly to support William H. Crawford for president, hoping that by delay he could avoid party strife in New York and give his state a chance finally to choose between opposing candidates. In Washington he was considered the leader of the Crawford faction and he was active in the last and well-known congressional caucus, called to nominate his candidate (*Daily National Intelligencer*, Feb. 16, 1824). He considered Jackson unpromising and tried to persuade either Clay or Gallatin to run with Crawford. In New York in 1824, Clinton, who was a Jacksonian, was again elected governor, routing the "regency" (C. H. Rammelkamp, "The Campaign of 1824 in New York," *Annual Report of the American Historical Association . . . 1904*, 1905, pp. 175–201). Van Buren tried to produce a deadlock in the House of Representatives while it was voting for presidential candidates, in order that the Clay-Adams men would have to appeal to New York for a decision, but the prayerful Stephen Van Rensselaer [q.v.] blocked that plan by voting for Adams. Van Buren's early bitterness towards Adams was probably caused by the latter's offer of the ministerial post in London to Clinton. In the Senate he voted yea on the tariff bills of 1824 and 1828, guided partisan opposition, served on the finance committee and as chairman of the judiciary committee. He opposed the sending of envoys to the Panama conference, offering the explanation that he was opposed to all forms of international alliances. In his speeches on internal improvements (*Register of Debates in Congress*, vol. II, 1826, 19 Cong., 1 Sess., cols. 20–21, 619, 717–18), he laid down a policy of opposition to which he steadfastly adhered. Congress, he said, had no constitutional right to construct commercial roads and canals within states. His practical objections to the program of his political rivals were strengthened by the consideration that most of the projects would deflect trade from the Erie Canal and New York. So adept was he in politics that he was reëlected senator (1827) with the aid of Clinton's friends. By this time, however, he was turning to Jackson, and took the liberty of telling Jackson to refrain from answering defamatory pamphlets. He read such pamphlets and planned the answers, advising editors here and there what to say about campaign issues. After pronouncing a touching eulogium upon Clinton, who died in 1828, he ran for governor of New York in order that a "Bucktail" state administration would be in control after he should become Jackson's secretary of state. He resigned the governorship to enter the cabinet after making to the legislature several recommendations, one of which—the enactment of a safety-fund banking law, as suggested by Joshua Forman [*q.v.*]—was adopted. He returned to Washington society, of which he was enamoured, and became at once the most influential member of the Jackson cabinet.

As secretary of state he favored the introduction of his New York political spoils system into the federal administration. Approached on the subject, he replied: "We give no reasons for our removals" (Lynch, p. 325). Being a widower, he pleased the President by his friendly course towards Peggy Eaton (see sketch of Margaret O'Neale). He helped Jackson write his famous toast, "Our Federal Union—It must be preserved" (*Autobiography*, p. 414). So completely did he win the President's confidence that Jackson said that Van Buren was "one of the most frank men" he had known, "a *true man* with no guile" (*Jackson Correspondence*, IV, 260). Before the end of 1830 Jackson proposed to Van Buren that they run on the same ticket, he to resign after a year and leave Van Buren to carry on his policies (*Autobiography*, pp. 506–07). This Van Buren refused to do and persuaded the President that it was best for him to resign as secretary of state so that the cabinet could be reorganized. His resignation (Apr. 11, 1831) brought about that of other members and enabled Jackson to eliminate Calhoun's supporters, while his prompt appointment as minister to Great Britain, ostensibly taking him out of politics, showed that he was still in Jackson's confidence (*Ibid.*, pp. 403–08; Bassett, *Life of Jackson*, II, 522–25, 532). Although Van Buren seems deliberately to have kept himself ignorant of the Jackson-Calhoun quarrel (Bassett, II, 514–15), he was accused of causing it, and had heaped upon his head such opprobrious terms as "Flying Dutchman," "Red Fox of Kinderhook," and "Little Magician."

His unusual tact stood him in good stead as secretary of state. He maneuvered Jackson into appointing young energetic ministers, soon established order and confidence in his department, and quieted the fears of the foreign diplomatic corps, who expected trouble with the frontier President. He settled the old dispute over the West Indian trade between Great Britain and the United States, secured an agreement with France by which that country ultimately and reluctantly paid claims for compensation for injuries inflicted upon American commerce during the Napoleonic wars, negotiated a treaty with Turkey providing for free access to the Black Sea and a most favored nations clause, and tried to buy Texas from Mexico, arguing that it was a necessity for the development of the Mississippi Valley and that Mexico would finally lose it through revolution if she did not sell to the United States. Jackson's Maysville Road veto was largely the work of Van Buren, who drafted the message (*Autobiography*, pp. 315–22; Bassett, *Life of Jackson*, II, pp. 484–96), and he supported Jackson in his other important domestic policies. In August 1831 he was on his way to London as minister to Great Britain, but in January 1832 his appointment was rejected by the deciding vote of Vice-President Calhoun. He then took his son John with him to travel in France and in Holland.

His return, purposely timed to follow his nomination for vice-president in May 1832, was celebrated extensively in New York City. His graciousness, his courtesy toward even his bitterest foes, and his charming conversation made him a favored guest at such celebrations as the New York Democrats could provide. In the course of the presidential campaign he aided Jackson in defeating a bill to recharter the Bank of the United States and opposed the theories of nullification, as he did internal improvements at national expense, but he intentionally remained vague on the tariff. Contrary to some opinions, he did not disagree with Jackson over the removal of the government's deposits in the Bank, but he did hesitate about the time of their removal (*Jackson Correspondence*, V, 179–82, 183–84). When Jackson appealed to him to have the New York Assembly issue a public defense of his message on nullification, Van Buren wrote the report of the joint committee, endeavoring to show the soundness of the party on the state-rights question, while supporting the President against the nullifiers (*Documents of the Senate of . . . New York . . . 1833*, 1833, no. 34; *Autobiography*, pp. 548–53; *Jackson Correspondence*, IV, 504–08).

Elected vice-president in 1832 as Jackson's running mate, he proved to be an able and fair presiding officer of the Senate. Not once did he lose the confidence of Jackson. It has been remarked that toward his chief he had a "perfect bedside manner" (J. F. Jameson, Preface to *Jackson Correspondence*, Vol. IV, p. v). Accepted by his party as Jackson's protégé, he was nominated for the presidency by a convention held in Baltimore in May 1835, Richard M. Johnson [*q.v.*] being nominated for vice-president.

His platform was enunciated in the letters he wrote during the campaign, especially in the able letter of Aug. 8, 1836, to Sherrod Williams (*Niles' Weekly Register,* Sept. 10, 1836, pp. 26–30). It was clear that he opposed the distribution of the surplus in the treasury and the improvement of rivers above ports of entry, and that he would not recharter the Bank under any consideration. He had supported Tallmadge's resolution on the Missouri Compromise calling for the non-extension of slavery and had signed a call for a meeting in Albany to protest against the extension of slavery (1820), but in 1831 he had announced himself as a stanch advocate of the right of slave-owning states to control slavery within their respective boundaries. He had advised Governor Marcy in 1835 to condemn the activities of the Garrison abolitionists (message of Jan. 5, 1836), and in 1836, in the Senate, he had given a casting vote in favor of the bill barring abolitionist propaganda from the mails (*Register of Debates,* 24 Cong., 1 Sess., Col. 1675; see also T. H. Benton, *Thirty Years' View,* I, 587–88).

In the election of 1836 there were Democratic defections in the South to Hugh L. White [*q.v.*] and to Willie P. Mangum [*q.v.*], who received the vote of South Carolina; and votes were cast for two Whig candidates, William Henry Harrison and Daniel Webster [*qq.v.*]; but Van Buren had a large electoral majority over the field. As president, he filled the vacancy in the Department of War by appointing Joel R. Poinsett [*q.v.*], and retained all the other members of Jackson's cabinet. In his optimistic inaugural address (Richardson, *post,* III, 313–20), which concluded with a tribute to his predecessor, he urged the preservation of American democracy as a world experiment. His desire to hold together the northern and southern wings of his party was manifested in his avowed opposition to the abolition of slavery in the District of Columbia against the wishes of the slave states, and to any interference with slavery in the states where it existed. Throughout his administration he was plagued by abolitionist agitators and those who would silence them, but his chief problems were economic. The panic of 1837 soon burst upon him. In spite of the fury of clamor against it, he held steadfastly to Jackson's specie circular, and in his message to the special session of Congress (Sept. 4, 1837, Richardson, III, 324–46) he properly said that the panic was the result of over-action in business and over-expansion of credit. Adamant in his determination to divorce the "money power" from the federal government, and distrustful of the "pet banks"

as well as of a central institution, he urged that an independent treasury be established. His recommendations that the installment of the surplus scheduled for distribution to the states in October be withheld, and that treasury notes be temporarily issued to meet the pressing needs of the government, were adopted, but the first independent treasury bill failed of passage. Not until 1840 was Van Buren able to secure the necessary legislation, with some compromise in regard to specie payments, and this was repealed by the Whigs in 1841. The independent treasury was not effectually established until 1846. It has generally been regarded as distinctly creditable to Van Buren's foresight, but at the time of his official advocacy of it he alienated conservative, or bank, Democrats, especially in New York and Virginia, while he was denounced by the Whigs for his "heartlessness" in not undertaking measures of relief and particularly for his failure to resort to paper money. He followed his lifelong policy of refusing to answer villifiers, believing always that "the sober second thought of the people" would uphold him.

Though he was embarrassed by American sympathy with the Canadian rebellion of 1837, and the seizure by Canadian authorities in American waters of the insurgent vessel *Caroline,* his successful effort to preserve peace between Great Britain and the United States was patriotic and commendable, notwithstanding the accusations of the opposing factions that his officials were "the tools of Victoria." His wise policy of conciliation, however, cost him political support along the northern border, as it did also in Maine, in connection with the continued controversy over the northeastern boundary. He refused to annex independent Texas because he wanted no war with Mexico and at heart was opposed to the further extension of slavery. Throughout his administration he and his able cabinet were plagued with the terrible depression, to which crop failures contributed. Calhoun's cooperation, Blair's influential *Globe,* and Jackson's fidelity could not overcome such obstacles. As president, Van Buren had been far more than a wily politician, but perhaps no amount of courage, patriotism, and ability would have availed to carry through an effective program or to gain popular approval in such troublous times. "Little Van" was a "used up man" in the "hard-cider" campaign of 1840. The Whigs, evading issues and appealing to emotions, triumphantly elected William Henry Harrison [*q.v.*] over the decorous President, with an electoral vote of 234 to 60, and a popular plurality of nearly 150,000. Van Buren even lost New York.

He greeted Whigs and Democrats alike at the White House and shattered precedent by calling on President-elect Harrison at Gadsby's. After the inauguration, he retired to the old William Van Ness farm at Kinderhook which he had bought; he now repaired it extensively and called it "Lindenwald." He presently found occasion to deny a statement that he would not again run for the presidency, but he also informed the public that he would take no step to secure another nomination. He made a tour of the West and Southwest, stopping at "Ashland" to see Clay, and at "The Hermitage" to pay his respects to Jackson (1842). Many Democrats throughout the North and West rallied to his support. He answered quite frankly, against the advice of informed friends, many inquiries as to his views on political issues. In the well-known "Hammet letter" (Washington *Globe*, Apr. 27, 1844), published on the same day as Clay's "Raleigh letter," he courageously said that the annexation of Texas would mean war with Mexico and that he saw no need for immediate action, but that he would yield to the popular decision at the polls. This stand probably lost him the Democratic nomination (McCormac, *Polk*, pp. 224–30). His opponents published a year-old letter of Jackson favoring annexation, and succeeded in getting the two-thirds rule adopted by the Democratic convention at Baltimore (1844). Van Buren withdrew his name for the sake of party harmony and James K. Polk [*q.v.*] was nominated. His principles, except on annexation, were adopted in the platform. His followers expected recognition, but President Polk soon let it be known that they were not in favor. He offered Van Buren the London mission purposely to exile him, but Van Buren could not be shelved so easily.

The discontent engendered by his defeat at Baltimore, accentuated by bitter factional strife within the party in New York, turned half the Democrats of the state against the administration. The introduction of the Wilmot Proviso in 1846 provided a rallying point for this discontent and the latent anti-slavery feeling that had been steadily increasing. The next year the "Barnburners" seceded from the state convention, and, meeting at Herkimer, adopted a platform, drafted by Van Buren's son John [*q.v.*], opposing the extension of slavery to the territories to be acquired from Mexico. Van Buren himself drew up a similar address, which, after revision by his son and Samuel J. Tilden, was issued in February 1848 as the address of "Barnburner" Democrats in the legislature. Both "Barnburners" and "Hunkers" sent delegates to the National Democratic Convention of 1848, but the former at length withdrew. At a convention at Utica in June they nominated Van Buren for the presidency, paving the way for a general convention later. At Buffalo, in August, a gathering of anti-slavery men from all parties, organized the Free-soil party, on a platform of opposition to the extension of slavery into the territories. Van Buren, already nominated by the best organized group in the convention, was chosen to head the ticket. He had become convinced, perhaps at the convention of 1844, that northern Democrats had yielded to the "slavocracy" long enough, but accepted the nomination reluctantly, preferring to remain a farmer and to write his memoirs. The Free-soilers helped to defeat Cass by splitting the ticket. For a while Van Buren was popular with the New York Free-soilers, but he alienated them when he supported the compromise measures of 1850. He returned to the Democratic fold in 1852, assured by the elder Blair that he could trust Pierce, but he soon found that his trust was misplaced. He was indignant at the "half baked politicians" who repealed the Missouri Compromise (1854). He hoped the Union would be saved by the election of Buchanan, who promised a peaceful settlement of the Kansas question. Shocked deeply by the Civil War, he found his only solace in his confidence in Abraham Lincoln and refused to be associated with Buchanan, whom he now despised, in holding an ex-president's meeting (suggested by Franklin Pierce) to decide on some course relative to the cause of the Union. After months of suffering with asthma, he died in the summer, despondent over the situation of the Union armies. Funeral services were held in the Dutch Reformed Church of which he had been a faithful member. He left a manuscript, published by his sons under the title, *Inquiry into the Origin and Course of Political Parties in the United States* (1867). His uncompleted autobiography was edited by J. C. Fitzpatrick and published as "The Autobiography of Martin Van Buren" (*Annual Report of the American Historical Association for the Year 1918*, Vol. II, 1920).

[Elizabeth H. West, *Calendar of the Papers of Martin Van Buren* (1910), is an excellent guide to the voluminous Van Buren MSS. in the lib. of Cong., acquired to the time of its compilation; there is valuable material about him in that repository in the papers of various persons who were associated with him; and there is a collection of his letters in the N. Y. State Lib., at Albany. Valuable printed collections are C. Z. Lincoln, *State of N. Y. Messages from the Governors* (1909), vol. III, pp. 230–59; J. D. Richardson, *A Compilation of the Messages and Papers of the Presidents*, vol. III (1896); William McDonald, "The Jackson and Van Buren Papers," in *Proc. Am. Antiquarian Soc.*,

vol. XVIII (1908) ; Van Buren—Bancroft correspond-
ence, in *Mass. Hist. Soc. Proc.*, vol. XLII (1909) ; J.
S. Bassett, ed., *Correspondence of Andrew Jackson* (6
vols., 1926–33). Among biographies may be cited W.
M. Holland, *The Life and Political Opinions of Martin
Van Buren* (1835) ; W. L. Mackenzie, *The Life and
Times of Martin Van Buren* (1846), a bitter attack but
contains letters ; W. A. Butler, *Martin Van Buren:
Lawyer, Statesman and Man* (1862) ; George Bancroft,
Martin Van Buren to the End of His Public Career
(1889), to 1841, written for the campaign of 1844 ; E.
M. Shepard, *Martin Van Buren* (1888) ; D. T. Lynch,
An Epoch and a Man: Martin Van Buren (1929). For
particular phases see J. S. Bassett, "Martin Van Buren,"
in S. F. Bemis, ed., *The American Secretaries of State
and Their Diplomacy*, vol. IV (1928) ; J. D. Hammond,
The History of Political Parties in the State of N. Y.
(2 vols., 1842) ; D. S. Alexander, *A Political History
of the State of N. Y.*, vols. I, II (1906) ; D. R. Fox,
The Decline of Aristocracy in the Politics of N. Y.
(1919) ; William Trimble, "Diverging Tendencies in
N. Y. Democracy in the Period of the Locofocos," in
Am. Hist. Rev., Apr. 1919 ; H. D. A. Donovan, *The
Barnburners* (1925) ; T. H. Benton, *Thirty Years' View*
(2 vols., 1856) ; R. H. Gillet, *The Life and Times of
Silas Wright* (2 vols., 1874) ; J. S. Bassett, *The Life of
Andrew Jackson* (1911) ; E. I. McCormac, *James K.
Polk* (1922) ; C. G. Bowers, *The Party Battles of the
Jackson Period* (1922) ; R. C. McGrane, *The Panic of
1837* (1924) ; W. E. Smith, *The Francis Preston Blair
Family in Politics* (2 vols., 1933) ; F. J. Turner, *The
United States: 1830–1850* (1935). For genealogy and
local materials, see Harriet C. W. Van Buren Peckham,
*History of Cornelis Maessen Van Buren . . . and His
Descendants* (1913) ; E. A. Collier, *A History of Old
Kinderhook* (1914). For obituaries see *Evening Post*
(N. Y.), July 24, 1862 ; *N. Y. Times, N. Y. Tribune,*
July 25, 1862.]   W. E. S—h.

VAN BUREN, WILLIAM HOLME (Apr.
4, 1819–Mar. 25, 1883), physician, surgeon, and
teacher of medicine and surgery, was born at
Philadelphia, Pa., the son of Abraham Van
Beuren, a merchant of Philadelphia, and his second wife, Sarah Holme. He dropped the "e"
from the first syllable of his name, although his
father used the longer form. His grandfather,
Abraham Van Beuren, and his great-grandfather,
John Van Beuren, were both physicians, and his
great-great-grandfather was Johannes Van Beuren [*q.v.*]. He entered Yale College as a sophomore in the class of 1838, but was required to
leave during his junior year because of a student
prank. He subsequently entered the medical
school of the University of Pennsylvania, from
which he was graduated with the degree of M.D.
in 1840. Yale later recognized his work by giving him honorary degrees. Immediately after his
graduation he entered the army as an assistant
surgeon, ranking first in the competitive examination which gave him admission, and served in
Florida and on the Canadian frontier. He resigned from the army in 1845, and settled in New
York City, where he soon built up a large practice, and became a member of the surgical staff
of Bellevue Hospital. From 1851 to 1852 he was
professor of genito-urinary organs and venereal
diseases in the Medical Department of the Uni-

versity of the City of New York. From 1852 to
1866 he was professor of anatomy. He was appointed professor of surgery in Bellevue Hospital Medical College in 1866 and retained this
position until his death. This hospital was originally the medical department of the New York
City almshouse, of which Johannes Van Beuren,
was the first director. He was one of the visiting
surgeons of the New York Hospital from 1852
to 1865, afterwards one of its consulting surgeons, and in 1876 was made president of its
medical board. He was also for many years on
the consulting staff of the Bellevue, Women's,
Presbyterian, and other hospitals. In 1859 he
was elected vice-president of the New York
Academy of Medicine.

During the Civil War he was a member of the
standing Executive Committee of the United
States Sanitary Commission, which received and
distributed during the war $5,000,000 in money
and $15,000,000 in supplies. He declined an ap-
pointment as surgeon-general of the United
States Army. At the close of the war he suffered
a serious illness from which he finally recovered.
He traveled for some time in Europe, and upon
his return gave up most of his visiting practice
and devoted himself to consultations, literary
work, and to the preparation of his lectures. In
collaboration with C. E. Isaacs, he translated
Bernard and Huette's *Illustrated Manual of Operative Surgery and Surgical Anatomy* (1852)
and C. B. Morel's *Compendium of Human Histology* (1861). He also published *Contributions
to Practical Surgery* (1865), *Lectures Upon
Diseases of the Rectum* (1870), which went
through many editions, and, with E. L. Keyes,
published *A Practical Treatise on the Surgical
Diseases of the Genito-Urinary Organs, Including Syphilis* (1874). A bibliography of his works
is included in the *Index-Catalogue of the Library
of the Surgeon-General's Office, United States
Army*, volume XV (1894). He was married on
Nov. 8, 1842, to Louisa Dunmore Mott, eldest
daughter of the well-known surgeon, Valentine
Mott [*q.v.*]. They had three children, of whom
two daughters survived him.

[H. A. Kelly, W. L. Burrage, *Am. Medic. Biogs.*
(1920) ; William Jones, "The Van Beuren Family of
New York and New Jersey," *N. Y. Geneal. and Biog.
Record*, Jan. 1932 ; a memorial address by E. L. Keyes,
printed in the *N. Y. Medic. Jour.*, Apr. 14, 1883 ; R. J.
Carlisle, *An Account of Bellevue Hospital* (1893) ;
Obit. Records of Grads. of Yale Univ., 1880–90 (1890) ;
N. Y. Times, N. Y. Evening Post, Mar. 26, 1883.]
                                                   W. J.

VANCE, AP MORGAN (May 24, 1854–Dec.
9, 1915), orthopedic surgeon, was born in Nashville, Tenn., the son of Morgan Brown and Su-

san Preston (Thompson) Vance. He attended rural schools in Tennessee and the public schools and Moss Academy at New Albany, Ind., to which place the family moved in 1868. Entering the medical department of the University of Louisville in 1876, he was graduated in 1878. Through association with Dr. David W. Yandell [q.v.], one of the foremost surgeons of the city, he was influenced to undertake a thorough study of anatomy and a career in surgery. After graduation he obtained a resident internship in the Hospital for Ruptured and Crippled Children in New York City. Having a natural mechanical bent, he devised and improved apparatus for crippled limbs and diseased spines, which with little change are in current use; this work he continued throughout his career.

Returning to Louisville in 1881, he elected to confine his practice to surgery and became the first exclusive practitioner of this specialty in Kentucky. This departure from established custom caused criticism, which, however, soon died out. While his chief interest was in orthopedic surgery, this branch was too limited a specialty for the Louisville of that period, and he accepted whatever surgery came his way. For years he had the largest operating practice in Louisville. His greatest contribution to surgery was his improvement of the operation of osteotomy for the correction of deformity of long bones of the extremities. He advocated and perfected a bloodless subcutaneous operation by means of a small chisel inserted through a minute incision of the skin ("Femoral Osteotomy," *New York Medical Journal*, Dec. 1, 1888). He also improved the procedure of tenotomy for the treatment of congenital clubfoot. The ingenuity and manual dexterity that enabled him to produce orthopedic apparatus made him an outstanding surgical technician. His skill, together with accurate judgment of indications for operation, brought unusual success to his surgical practice. He adopted asepsis from its inception and was an early advocate of operative treatment for appendicitis. Though frequently offered teaching positions, he refused them in order to devote his time to clinical practice. He did, however, exert a powerful influence upon the surgical thought of the city through the internes of the hospital with which he was connected. He was the medical representative upon the commission which built the Louisville City Hospital and was responsible for its plans and scope; he was the prime mover in the organization and construction of the Children's Free Hospital; and served them both as attending surgeon, as he did, also, the hospital of SS. Mary and Elizabeth. For

thirty-five years he was surgeon to the Masonic Widows and Orphans Home.

He was active in every movement which involved the local profession and a constant attendant upon the meetings of the county and state societies, both of which he served as president. He was a member of the Southern Surgical and Gynecological Association, the American Association of Gynecology and Obstetrics, and the American Orthopedic Association, and was a fellow of the American College of Surgeons. His writings were confined to journal articles, mainly on the subject of orthopedic surgery. An invalidism from nephritis limited his activities for two years before his death, which occurred at his home in Louisville. His memory is kept alive by a ward bearing his name, endowed by popular subscription, in the Children's Free Hospital, for which he had done so much in his lifetime. He was married in 1885 to Mary Josephine Huntoon of Louisville, daughter of Dr. B. B. Huntoon, superintendent of the Kentucky Institute for the Blind; they had eight children.

[*Am. Jour. of Obstetrics*, Mar. 1917; *Jour. Am. Medic. Asso.*, Dec. 18, 1915; *Ky. Medic. Jour.*, Apr. 1, 1916; *Courier-Journal* (Louisville), Dec. 10, 1915; *Evening Post* (Louisville), Dec. 9, 1915; H. A. Kelly and W. L. Burrage, *Am. Medic. Biogs.* (1920).]

J. M. P—n.

VANCE, ZEBULON BAIRD (May 13, 1830–Apr. 14, 1894), governor of North Carolina, senator, son of David Vance, a farmer and country merchant, and Mira Margaret Baird, was born in Buncombe County, N. C. After attending the neighborhood schools, he went to Washington College, Tenn. (1843–44), but withdrew upon the death of his father, who left a widow and eight children. Later, he studied law at the University of North Carolina (1851–52). He received his county-court license in 1852, settled at Asheville, and was immediately elected county solicitor. In 1853 he was admitted to practice in the superior court. He was never a close student of the law and such success as he won at the bar was as an advocate. With the crude, unlettered farmers of his mountain circuit from whom the jurors were drawn, ready wit, broad humor, quick repartee, and boisterous eloquence were indispensable to success, and in the use of these weapons Vance was unsurpassed.

Politics, not the law, was his major interest. Having been reared in "devotion to the Federal Union" (application for pardon, June 3, 1865), he began his political career as a Henry Clay Whig. Upon the dissolution of the Whig party, he declined to follow some of his fellow Whigs into the Democratic party, which he believed to be saturated with a "bitter spirit of disunion," and aligned himself with the newly organized American party. He served one term (1854) in the North Carolina House of Commons. Elected to the 35th and 36th congresses, he served from Dec. 7, 1858, to Mar. 3, 1861. His congressional career was characterized by support of Union measures and opposition to the disunion sentiment then arising in the South. He was elected to the 37th Congress but was prevented from taking his seat by the secession of North Carolina.

In the presidential election of 1860, Vance supported the Bell and Everett ticket. He came out of the campaign with a reputation as a masterly stump speaker. Though upholding the constitutional right of secession, before April 1861 he opposed the exercise of the right for any cause then existing but favored calling a state convention as a means of "demanding terms of the Northern people" and of making "our voices heard among the Southern states whose course is rapidly inoculating the people with dogmas which we cannot approve" (letter of Jan. 9, 1861, in *Raleigh Register,* Jan. 16, 1861). The convention was defeated by popular vote but Vance continued his campaign against secession until Lincoln's call for troops. Thereupon he promptly reversed his position and urged North Carolina to support the other Southern states. On May 20, a state convention, called by the legislature, adopted an ordinance of secession. In the meantime, Vance had organized at Asheville (May 4) a company of "Rough and Ready Guards" of which he was elected captain. During the summer of 1861 he was on active duty with his company along the North Carolina coast. In August, he was elected colonel of the 26th North Carolina Regiment and led it with conspicuous gallantry in the New Bern campaign and in the Seven Days' battle near Richmond.

In the state election of 1862, the Confederate administration, which had become unpopular in North Carolina, furnished the chief issues. For governor, the Confederate party, as the Democrats then called themselves, nominated William Johnston, an "original secessionist"; the Conservatives, composed chiefly of old-line Union Whigs, led by W. W. Holden [*q.v.*], editor of the *North Carolina Standard* and a caustic critic of the Davis administration, selected Vance. Accepting the nomination, Vance pledged himself to "the prosecution of the war at all hazards and to the utmost extremity" (letter of acceptance, June 16, 1862, Dowd, *post,* p. 67). Despite this positive statement, the *Raleigh Register,* organ of the Confederate party, denounced his action as disloyal, dubbed him "the Yankee candidate,"

and warned the people that the North would accept his election as "an indisputable sign that the Union sentiment is in the ascendancy in the heart of the Southern Confederacy" (quoted in S. A. Ashe, *History of North Carolina,* II, 1925, p. 738). He won by an unprecedented majority, was inaugurated Sept. 8, and in his inaugural address committed his administration to a vigorous war policy. Unfortunately the Richmond government chose to accept the Confederate party's misrepresentation of Vance's position and thus laid the basis for most of the controversies it had with him during his two administrations.

In his efforts to keep the North Carolina regiments recruited to their full strength, to equip and provision them, and to sustain the morale of the civilian population, Vance was handicapped by the critical, if not hostile, attitude of the Confederate administration. Its officials charged him with deliberately obstructing the enforcement of the conscription acts. Vance certainly thought them "harsh and odious," and probably unconstitutional, and insisted that it was for the courts, not the conscription officers, to determine that question. He refused to permit the conscription of state officials and demanded that military officers respect the writ of *habeas corpus* when issued by a proper court. Afterwards he made it his "proudest boast" that during his administration no man in North Carolina was denied the privilege of the great writ, the right of trial by jury, or the equal protection of the law. He tried in vain to explain to President Davis that his policy was designed to mitigate as far as possible the severities of the law that it might be enforced among an "unwilling people" (Dowd, p. 92). Though critical of their administration of the law, Vance gave the conscription officers his full support in every effort to enforce it that he thought legal. In 1864 he wrote to the President that its enforcement in the state had been "ruthless and unrelenting" (*Ibid.,* pp. 91–93), and the fact that 18,585 North Carolina conscripts were enrolled in the Confederate armies by September 1864 seems to justify his statement (Ashe, *History of North Carolina,* II, 776).

By 1863 the North Carolina mountains were filled with evaders of conscription and soldiers from practically every Confederate state. To the Confederate authorities these men were "deserters" and deserved no consideration; to Vance, they were "absentees" who should be "persuaded" to return to their duty. Accordingly, in January by proclamation he offered a pardon to all North Carolina soldiers who should return to their regiments by a stated date. His proclamation, reported a colonel, "has brought in a great many stragglers, deserters, or other absentees that never would have otherwise come in" (*Ibid.*, II, 807). Vance himself wrote in a private letter: "Deserters are pouring thro' [Raleigh] in hundreds, really, to their colors" (To E. J. Hale, Oct. 26, 1863, Hale Papers).

To supplement the inadequate resources of the state, Vance procured from the legislature of 1862–63 an appropriation of $2,324,000 for the purchase of cotton and naval stores to be exchanged for supplies abroad, sent agents to England to make purchases, and organized a fleet of swift steamers to run the blockade into the port of Wilmington. They were distributed chiefly to North Carolina soldiers and civilians, but "large quantities were [also] turned over to the Confederate Government for the troops for other states." In a single shipment in 1863, for instance, Vance sent 14,000 uniforms to Longstreet's army in Tennessee (Vance, *The Last Days of the War in North Carolina*, 1885, pp. 28–29. For the best account of these operations see D. H. Hill, *North Carolina in the War Between the States*, 1926, vol. I, ch. x). The Confederate government disapproved of Vance's blockade-running operations and offered "downright opposition" to them (Vance to Seddon, Jan. 7, 1864, in Dowd, *post*, pp. 89–90). Nevertheless, these operations not only supplied the soldiers but also caught the imagination of the people and greatly strengthened their morale.

By 1863, Holden had become convinced that the struggle for Southern independence was hopeless and inaugurated a campaign for peace and the restoration of the Union. At first he advocated peace through negotiations by the Confederate government with the United States government, but failing to move President Davis, he shifted his position to a demand for peace by separate state action. The movement received widespread support and Holden counted on its popularity to force Vance to take the leadership. But Vance proved unexpectedly independent, declared his inflexible opposition to the scheme, and on it broke with Holden. Thereupon Holden announced his candidacy for governor in 1864. The issue, he declared, was simply peace or war. Accepting the issue as thus defined, Vance threw himself into the campaign with all his vigor. Hitherto Holden's pen had been the most effective political weapon in the state; it was now matched by one which proved even more powerful—the oratory of Vance. Vance was elected by an overwhelming majority, and thus held the great mass of North Carolinians to the support of a cause which most of them felt to be contrary to their real interests. In 1865, certain Confederate congressmen and senators, unable to persuade President Davis to open peace negotiations with the United States government, agreed upon a plan of peace by separate state action and selected North Carolina to lead the way. At their request, William A. Graham [*q.v.*] laid their plan before Vance, but Vance flatly refused to have anything to do with it. If other states were whipped, he said, let them say so; as for himself, he declined to have his state "lead the roll of infamy" (Vance to Mrs. Spencer, Apr. 27, 1866, in Cornelia P. Spencer Papers).

When Sherman approached Raleigh in April 1865, Vance attempted to negotiate with him with a view to procuring his recognition of the state government. Failing, and being erroneously informed that Sherman intended to arrest him as a political prisoner, Vance left Raleigh, Apr. 12, for Charlotte to consult with President Davis as to his future course. After an unsatisfactory conference, he determined to proceed without further regard for the Confederate authorities (Dowd, p. 486). Accordingly, on May 2 at Greensboro, he surrendered to General Schofield, who directed him to join his family at Statesville and there await further orders. Arrested by order of President Johnson on his thirty-fifth birthday, he was sent to Washington, and imprisoned in the Old Capitol Prison. He was held there until July 6, when he was released on parole. No reason was ever officially assigned for his arrest or his release.

Returning to North Carolina, Vance formed a law partnership in Charlotte. On June 3, 1865, while in prison, in compliance with the President's amnesty proclamation of May 29, he filed his application for a pardon, which was finally granted Mar. 11, 1867. Again free to enter politics, he was elected in 1870 to the United States Senate, but after two years of vain effort to have his disabilities under the Fourteenth Amendment removed, he surrendered his certificate of election to the legislature on Jan. 20, 1872. Soon thereafter Congress removed his disabilities. At the next session of the legislature (1872–73), he was the Democratic nominee for the Senate but was defeated by another Democrat through a combination of bolting Democrats and the Republican members.

In 1876 the Democrats girded themselves to overthrow the Republican régime and undo the work of Reconstruction, and selected Vance as their candidate for governor. The Republicans nominated Judge Thomas Settle (1831–1888), who challenged Vance to a joint debate. In Settle, Vance found the ablest opponent he had ever met on the stump; but in all that makes up a great popular orator Vance was much his superior. He was elected and inaugurated Jan. 1, 1877. His administration was distinguished by a revival of railroad enterprises; the stimulus it gave to agriculture and industry; the enlargement and improvement of public schools and charitable institutions for both races; the repudiation of the fraudulent Reconstruction state bonds and the adjustment of the state's legal debt on a basis acceptable to its creditors. It marked the beginning of a new era in North Carolina.

Vance served only two of the four years of his term. In 1879 he was again elected to the United States Senate and took his seat on Mar. 18. Reelected in 1885 and in 1891, he served in the Senate until his death. His senatorial career added both to his fame and to his hold on his constituents. He was a prodigious worker, a diligent student of public problems, and an able debater. An important function of Southern senators in those years was to serve as mediators between the victorious North and the defeated South. In this work few senators were so effective as Vance. His colleagues, with whom he was very popular, soon learned that while devoted to the interests of the South, he nursed no bitterness toward the North. To the North, he was a defender and interpreter of, but never an apologist for, the South; upon the South, he urged the duty of genuine acceptance of the verdict of the war and unfeigned loyalty to the restored Union.

It was Vance's misfortune throughout most of his senatorial career to be cast in the rôle of a minority senator, whether the Republicans or the Democrats were in power. He was a tariff-for-revenue man and for many years was the minority leader on the finance committee. Upon him, in 1890, fell the chief burden of opposition in the Senate to the McKinley Tariff Bill. He was a determined opponent of the internal revenue system, not only because it adversely affected the whiskey and tobacco industries of his state but also because it was notoriously a source of frauds and political corruption. During Cleveland's two administrations, he broke with the President on civil service reform and the money question. He thought the civil service act unconstitutional and as an ardent party man was indignant that the President treated his recommendations as to federal appointments in North Carolina with but scant respect. His last speech in the Senate was in opposition to the repeal of the Sherman Silver Act. He was a great opposition senator, but his name is not connected with any piece of constructive legislation.

Vance's close application to his work undermined his health and impaired one of his eyes. An operation for its removal in 1891 left him almost a nervous wreck. He vainly sought rest and health in foreign travel. In 1894 his physician ordered a complete rest in Florida. Two weeks after his return to Washington he died at his home in that city. He was buried in Asheville. By his first wife, Harriet N. Espy, of North Carolina, to whom he was married on Aug. 3, 1853, Vance had four sons. She died in 1878 and in 1880 he married Mrs. Florence Steele Martin, of Kentucky, who survived him. They had no children.

Vance was fond of books and read widely in history and biography. His most important addresses and essays are: *The Duties of Defeat* (1866); "Address . . . before the Southern Historical Society" in 1875 (*Our Living and Our Dead*, vol. III, no. 5, Nov. 1875; also *Southern Historical Society*, vol. XIV, 1886); *The Last Days of the War in North Carolina* (1885, reprinted in Dowd, *post*); the chapter, "Reconstruction in North Carolina," in H. A. Herbert, ed., *Why the Solid South* (1890). Many of his addresses were autobiographical in their character. His most popular lecture, "The Scattered Nation," dealing with the history of the Jews, was delivered in almost every important city in the United States. Besides its reprint in Dowd (*post*) and in Shurter, *Oratory of the South* (1908), it has been published in separate editions (1904, 1916).

[None of the numerous biographical sketches of Vance is adequate. The best is contained in *The Ceremonies Attending the Unveiling of the Bronze Statue of Zebulon B. Vance . . . and the Address of Richard H. Battle . . . 1900* (n.d.), the address being reprinted in abridged form in S. A. Ashe, ed., *Biog. Hist. of North Carolina*, vol. VI (1907), pp. 477–95. The most pretentious biography, Clement Dowd, *Life of Zebulon B. Vance* (1897), is valuable primarily for the letters and speeches of Vance reprinted therein. Important unpublished sources are: Vance Letterbook, 1862–65 (2 vols.); Executive Papers: Zebulon B. Vance, 1862–65 (36 boxes); Vance Letterbook, 1877–79; Zebulon B. Vance Papers, 1827–1902 (18 vols.); Cornelia P. Spencer Papers, 1859–1903 (2 vols.); and E. J. Hale Papers, 1850–67 (3 vols.), all in possession of the N. C. Hist. Commission at Raleigh. For a different interpretation of Vance's war policies see A. B. Moore, *Conscription and Conflict in the Confederacy* (1924), and F. L. Owsley, *State Rights in the Confederacy* (1925).]   R. D. W. C.

VAN CORTLANDT, OLOFF STEVENSZEN (1600–Apr. 5, 1684), prominent merchant in New Amsterdam and New York City, was born probably in the Netherlands, and apparently spent his youth entirely in the Dutch Republic. No special significance need be attached to the Scandinavian origin of his name and that of his father, Steven, or Stevens. Oloff

Stevenszen seems to have lived near Wijk bij Duurstede, in the province of Utrecht (see *Records of the Reformed Dutch Church, post*). Since he afterwards adopted the surname "Van Cortlandt" (1643), it has been plausibly surmised that he hailed from a very small village called Cortlandt, which existed at that time near Wijk bij Duurstede. He emigrated in the *Haering* (*Herring*), serving in the capacity of a soldier employed by the Dutch West India Company, and arrived in New Amsterdam in March 1638. On July 1, 1640, he was appointed commissioner of cargoes. In 1641 he began the purchase of real estate; in 1643 he is mentioned as a public storekeeper; in 1645 he was one of the Eight Men, and in 1650 he presided over the Nine Men. He held the office of city treasurer in 1657, 1659, 1660, 1661, and 1664; and he was burgomaster (mayor) from 1655 to 1660, and again in 1662 and 1663. In 1663 he was one of the commissioners sent to Hartford to treat on the Connecticut boundary. He served as deacon in the Reformed Church as early as 1646, while the more honorable office of elder was conferred upon him in or before 1670. He was a member of various committees in the city and the colony from 1647 to 1664, and, when in 1664 New Amsterdam became New York, he was chosen to negotiate with the English. Under the new government he acted as alderman in 1665, 1667, 1670, and 1672. In 1667 he was deputy mayor.

During the last ten years of his life he was rated as the fourth richest person in the colony (O'Callaghan, *Documents, post*, II, 699–700). Part of his wealth he owed to his wife, Anneken Loockermans, a native of Turnhout in the Spanish Netherlands (now Belgium), whom he married on Feb. 26, 1642. Van Cortlandt dealt in miscellaneous merchandise, owned a brewery on Brewer (or Brouwer) Street, and helped finance various commercial ventures. He was a hard-headed business man. When he saw fit, he did not hesitate to oppose such personages as the Rev. Evarardus Bogardus and Governor Stuyvesant [*qq.v.*]; and on one occasion at least he refused to permit the tax collector, Paulus van der Beeck, to visit his wine cellar (*The Records of New Amsterdam, post*, II, 234). The progenitor of one of the most prominent families in the American colonies, he was the father of seven children, of whom the eldest, Stephanus [*q.v.*], and the youngest, Jacobus, achieved especial distinction. His daughter Maria, who married Jeremias Van Rensselaer, was present at his death; he still appeared in good health and died "while in his prayers" (*Correspondence of Maria Van Rensselaer, post*, p. 173). In addition to his interesting coat of arms, there are two memorials which attest his opulence and sagacity. One is Van Cortlandt Manor, near Croton, built by his son Stephanus; the other, Van Cortlandt Park, at the northern extremity of New York City, is a symbol of the wealth in real estate amassed by him and his son Jacobus.

[L. E. De Forest, *The Van Cortlandt Family* (1930), with excellent bibliog.; *Records of the Reformed Dutch Church in New Amsterdam and New York, Marriages* (1890), ed. by S. S. Purple; *The Records of New Amsterdam from 1653 to 1674* (7 vols., 1897), ed. by Berthold Fernow; E. B. O'Callaghan, ed., *Calendar of Hist. MSS.*, vols. I–II (1865–66), and *Docs. Rel. to the Col. Hist. of N. Y.*, vols. I–II (1856–58); A. J. F. van Laer, ed., *N. Y. State Lib., Van Rensselaer Bowier MSS.* (1908), *Correspondence of Jeremias Van Rensselaer* (1932), *Correspondence of Maria Van Rensselaer, 1669–1689* (1935).]

A. H.

VAN CORTLANDT, PHILIP (Aug. 21, 1749–Nov. 5, 1831), Revolutionary officer, member of Congress, was the eldest son of Pierre [*q.v.*] and Joanna (Livingston) Van Cortlandt. He was born in New York City a few months before his parents established their residence at the manor-house near Croton. As a boy he attended a small school which his father maintained on the estate. At the age of fifteen he was sent to Coldenham Academy, where he spent a term of nine months studying mathematics, surveying, and bookkeeping. This concluded his formal schooling, but he gained practical experience in surveying by working with Nathaniel Merritt, one of his father's employees. Until the outbreak of the Revolutionary War he was engaged in surveying and disposing of tracts of land which had once been part of the manor of Cortlandt, and in operating several gristmills for his father.

During the year 1775 he made the transition from the position of the moderate Whigs to that of the revolutionary radicals. He was a member of the Provincial Convention, which met at the Exchange in New York City on Apr. 20, 1775, and the following month was chosen as one of Westchester County's representatives in the First Provincial Congress. On June 18 he accepted a commission as lieutenant-colonel of the 4th New York Regiment, but severe illness prevented him from participating in Montgomery's expedition against Montreal. After serving on Washington's staff for a short time, he received a commission as colonel of the reorganized 2nd New York and joined his regiment at Trenton on the day following the battle. He was assigned to duty at Peekskill, started a march to the relief of Fort Stanwix (August 1777), but was ordered back east to assist Gates's army at Saratoga. Rejoining Washington's forces, he was at

Valley Forge, was detached temporarily from his command to supervise the encampment in the spring of 1778, and then returned to his regiment in Ulster County, where he was stationed until April 1779. His effective cooperation with the Sullivan-Clinton expedition won him high praise. He was a member of the court martial which heard charges preferred by Pennsylvania authorities against Benedict Arnold, and he felt that Arnold should have been dismissed from the service. In the spring of 1780 he was sent to Fort Edward and later in the year was transferred to the post at Schenectady, where the 2nd, 4th, and 5th New York regiments were consolidated under his command. In June 1781 Washington ordered him to join the Continental forces on the lower Hudson in time to take an active part in the campaign which culminated in the surrender of Cornwallis. He was brevetted brigadier-general in 1783 for his conspicuous bravery and resourcefulness at Yorktown.

He was elected a delegate to the Poughkeepsie convention in 1788 and joined with the Federalists in voting to ratify the Federal Constitution. His subsequent political activity, however, reflected his conversion to Anti-Federalist principles. He served twice in the state Assembly (1788, 1790) and in the state Senate from 1791 to 1793. In December of the latter year he took his seat in the House of Representatives, beginning a period of service in Congress which continued for sixteen years. During his legislative career he seldom spoke on any measure before the House, but he was punctilious in the performance of his committee and other duties. The record of his votes indicates that he soon joined the Jeffersonian faction and that, when the Republican party came into power, he proved to be a reliable partisan who voted for party measures as a matter of course. In his sixtieth year he withdrew from politics and spent the remainder of his life managing his extensive real-estate holdings. The manor-house became his residence after his father's death in 1814. Although he had never married, he carried on the tradition of generous hospitality which had been established at Croton by his grandfather, Philip. Public affairs took little of his time, but he emerged from his retirement in 1824 to honor Lafayette, accompanying his friend on a large part of the country-wide tour. He died at the manor-house on Nov. 5, 1831, and was buried in Hillside Cemetery, Peekskill.

[An autobiog. fragment found in Van Cortlandt's papers was printed in *Mag. of Am. Hist.*, May 1878. See also L. E. De Forest, *The Van Cortlandt Family* (1930); Helen L. B. Parmelee, in *N. Y. Geneal. and Biog. Record*, July 1874; J. T. Scharf, *Hist. of West-*chester County, vol. II (1886), pp. 423–36; E. A. Werner, *Civil List . . . of N. Y.* (1889); T. H. Benton, *Abridgement of the Debates of Cong.*, vols. I–IV (1857); John Schuyler, *Institution of the Order of the Cincinnati* (1886), pp. 319–21, on Van Cortlandt's death. A portrait by A. U. Wertmuller, painted in 1795, is in the coll. of Thomas B. Clarke of New York.]
J. A. K.

VAN CORTLANDT, PIERRE (Jan. 10, 1721–May 1, 1814), first lieutenant-governor of the State of New York, born at New York City, was the youngest son of Philip and Catharine (De Peyster) Van Cortlandt, and a grandson of Stephanus Van Cortlandt [q.v.]. Little is known concerning his youth beyond the fact that he spent considerable time with his brothers at the manor-house near Croton. On May 28, 1748, he married his second cousin, Joanna Livingston, whose father, Gilbert, had been heir to a large part of the property of Robert Livingston [q.v.], first lord of Livingston manor. He established his new home on Stone Street, New York City, where his first son, Philip [q.v.], was born, but he moved in September 1749 to Croton and occupied the remodelled manor-house which he had just inherited under the terms of his father's will. There he became deeply interested in the management of his farms and mills, and found great enjoyment in hunting and fishing. His home was famous even beyond the borders of the province for its generous hospitality.

Although he accepted a commission in the provincial militia, and marched to the relief of Albany during the French and Indian War, his public career did not begin until 1768, when he was elected to the seat in the Assembly which had originally been assigned to the manor of Cortlandt. In the Assembly he was inclined to follow the leadership of the Livingstons. He was no defender of the royal prerogative and the "court party" of the De Lanceys received scant support from him, but the intensification of the quarrel with Great Britain caused him, like many other moderate Whigs, to hesitate. The Loyalists sent Governor Tryon in the autumn of 1774 to urge upon him the honors and emoluments which would be his if he refused to join the "rebels"; he declined, however, to give the governor any assurances. On Oct. 19, 1775, he accepted a commission from the provincial congress as colonel of the 3rd Regiment of Westchester militia. He was a member of the second, third, and fourth provincial congresses, became an energetic leader of the Committee of Safety in 1776, and served as president of the Council of Safety during its brief existence in 1777. He presided over the sessions of the convention which drafted New York's first constitution and, with the establishment of the new state government (1777), became lieutenant-governor, a position to which he was periodically reëlected for eighteen years. Although he was a loyal follower of George Clinton, 1739–1812 [q.v.], in politics, his partisanship was never offensive, and he was universally praised for the dignity and impartiality with which he conducted the sessions of the state Senate. His continuous and vigorous service in public office was an important factor in enabling New York to play an effective part in the struggle for independence.

Pleading illness in 1795, Van Cortlandt withdrew from public life. His retirement ended his service on the board of regents of the University of the State of New York, to which he had been named in 1784. The remaining nineteen years of his life were devoted to the affairs of his Croton estate. The many visitors to the manor-house found him a tall, patriarchal gentleman, affable and courteous in the manner of the old school of landed aristocrats. He was deeply religious. Although a member of the Dutch Reformed Church, he manifested an increasing interest in the work of the Methodists. Bishop Francis Asbury, Freeborn Garrettson, Woolman Hickson, and other Methodist leaders were frequently guests in his home. He gave the land and subscribed to the building fund for the local Methodist meeting-house, and set aside each year after 1805 a certain grove on his estate for Methodist camp-meetings which he was eager to attend. He died at the manor-house in his ninety-fourth year and was buried in the family cemetery on the estate.

[See L. E. De Forest, *The Van Cortlandt Family* (1930); J. B. Wakeley, in *Ladies' Repository*, Dec. 1866, pp. 705–10; *Journals of the Provincial Cong. . . . of N. Y.* (1842); E. A. Werner, *Civil List . . . of N. Y.* (1889); Robert Bolton, *A Hist. of the County of Westchester* (2 vols., 1848); J. T. Scharf, *Hist. of Westchester County* (1886), vol. II, pp. 423–36; death notice in *N. Y. Gazette & General Advertiser*, May 12, 1814. There is an excellent portrait by John Wesley Jarvis in the possession of Miss Anne S. Van Cortlandt at the manor-house.]   J. A. K.

VAN CORTLANDT, STEPHANUS (May 7, 1643–Nov. 25, 1700), merchant and colonial official, eldest son of Oloff Stevenszen Van Cortlandt [q.v.] and Annetje (or Anneken) Loockermans, was born in his father's substantial house on Brouwer Street, New Amsterdam. His formal education was acquired in the school established by the Dutch Church. Under his father's astute guidance, however, he quickly became proficient in commercial affairs. Before he was twenty-one, he was executing commissions for Jan Baptist Van Rensselaer of Amsterdam and exchanging wine, duffels, and blankets for the beaver skins which his brother-in-law, Jeremias Van Rensselaer, sent down the Hudson from Albany. These mercantile ventures were not interrupted by the English conquest of New Netherland, for Stephanus soon found favor with the new officials, who were not above conniving with him in importing goods contrary to the Acts of Trade (O'Callaghan, *Documents, post*, III, 307–08). He had already acquired a considerable estate when he married (Sept. 10, 1671) Gertrude, daughter of Philip P. Schuyler of Albany.

Van Cortlandt's public career was long and notable. Commissioned an ensign of militia in Kings County in 1668, he was regularly promoted until he reached the rank of colonel. Sir Edmund Andros [q.v.] summoned him (1674) to membership in the governor's council, and the instructions of every governor from Dongan to Bellomont contained his name as a councilor. In 1677 he became, by appointment from Governor Andros, the first native-born mayor of the city of New York, a position to which he was again appointed in 1686 and 1687. When the Dominion of New England was created he was named as one of the forty-two councilors to serve under Andros. This close association with the scheme of James II to establish centralized royal control in the northern colonies placed him in an embarrassing position when news reached New York that the "glorious revolution" had driven the king from his throne. As a ranking provincial councilor and mayor of the city of New York, Van Cortlandt endeavored for a time to restrain the rebellious groups which accepted the leadership of Capt. Jacob Leisler [q.v.], but he was not sufficiently resourceful to maintain public confidence in the integrity of the provincial government. Leisler maliciously accused him of being "papist," defied his authority as a councilor, and finally compelled him to flee for his life. During his enforced absence from his home he wrote plaintively to Andros, then in England, concerning his many misfortunes. With an eye to the future he urged his friend to present his case to Auditor General Blathwayt in order that he might "get here the Collectors place or at least that commission off auditor with a certaine sallary may bee confirmed unto me" (*Ibid.*, III, 650). His opportunity for revenge came when he was designated a member of the council under the new governor, Henry Sloughter. Supported by Frederick Philipse and Nicholas Bayard [qq.v.], he vigorously pushed the prosecution of Leisler on charges of treason and persuaded the governor, who was inclined to hesitate, that the condemned man should be executed at once. However timorous he had been in dealing with Leisler, the rebel, he did not lack assurance in disposing of Leisler, the condemned.

Throughout his career Van Cortlandt was closely associated with the amorphous jurisprudence of the provincial courts. After 1677 he presided at intervals over the mayor's court in the city of New York. Occasionally he was a member of the admiralty courts *ad hoc,* which antedated the creation by the British government in 1697 of the vice admiralty for the dominions. For several years (1688–91) he was a judge of the court of oyer and terminer which sat in Kings County, and he served as councilor during the period when the governor's council constituted a court of chancery. When the supreme court of the province was established by the judiciary act of 1691, he was named an associate justice, serving until his elevation to the post of chief justice, which occurred less than a month before his death.

The royal governors constantly summoned him to administrative as well as judicial posts. Under Gov. Benjamin Fletcher he became an important adviser on Indian relations, accompanying the governor in 1693 to the conference at Albany with sachems of the Five Nations which was designed to preserve the Iroquois alliance during King William's War. In 1698 he was appointed commissioner of customs and collector of revenues in recognition of the services which he had rendered a decade earlier in handling the provincial revenues for Gov. Thomas Dongan [*q.v.*]. But he failed to satisfy Lord Bellomont [*q.v.*], who wrote in 1700 to the Board of Trade that the new collector "gives a just account of all the money that comes to his hands, but he is grown very crazy and infirm, and is a very timorous man. In a word he has never yet made any seizure since his being Collector and I believe never would if he were 50 years to come, in that post" (*Ibid.,* IV, 721). The governor might have softened these harsh words had he been aware that at the very moment he sent off the report his receiver of revenues had been stricken by a fatal illness.

Like most of the provincial councilors of his generation, Stephanus Van Cortlandt used his official position to secure large grants of land. In 1677 Governor Andros issued a general license authorizing him to purchase from the Indians such tracts as he might desire. Apparently the first purchase under the license was made in 1683 and included the region on the east bank of the Hudson "at the entering of the highlands just over against Haverstraw." Several years

later he received from Governor Dongan a patent for the lands immediately north of his original purchase. These two tracts, somewhat extended by additional negotiations with the Indians in 1695, were erected into the manor of Cortlandt by a royal patent, dated June 17, 1697, which endowed the manor lord with the usual legal rights and emoluments and the special privilege, included in only two other grants, of sending a representative to the provincial assembly. Van Cortlandt never resided upon his manor. He used the manor-house, which was a fort-like structure, as a hunting-lodge, trading-post, and office for the transaction of such manorial business as concerned the Indians who remained within its borders. He was the last as well as the first lord of his manor, for in disposing of his property he followed the Dutch rather than the English custom. By the terms of his will his eldest son, John, was to receive the region of Verplanck's Point, while the remainder of his real estate was to be divided equally, after the death of his widow, among his eleven children. The manor lands, which according to the survey of 1732 included 87,713 acres, were not finally divided among the legal heirs until 1753.

[L. E. De Forest, *The Van Cortlandt Family* (1930); *A Jour. Kept by Coll. Stephen Courtland & Coll. Nich. Beyard* (1693); *Correspondence of Jeremias Van Rensselaer, 1651–1674* (1932), ed. by A. J. F. van Laer; E. B. O'Callaghan, ed., *Docs. Rel. to the Col. Hist. of . . . N. Y.,* vols. III–IV (1853–54), *Calendar of Hist. MSS.,* vol. II (1866), and *Documentary Hist. of the State of N. Y.,* vols. I, II (1849); *N. Y. Hist. Soc. Colls., Publication Fund Ser.,* vol. I (1868); J. R. Brodhead, *Hist. of the State of N. Y.,* vol. II (1871); G. W. Schuyler, *Colonial New York* (2 vols., 1885); Mariana G. Van Rensselaer, *Hist. of the City of N. Y. in the Seventeenth Century* (2 vols., 1909); E. F. De Lancey, *Origin and Hist. of Manors in the Province of N. Y.* (1886), reprinted from J. T. Scharf, *Hist. of Westchester County, N. Y.* (1886), vol. I, pp. 31–160.]   J. A. K.

VAN CURLER, ARENT (1620–July 1667), colonist, was born at Nykerk, in the Netherlands, and was baptized Feb. 6, 1620. According to one account he was the son of Hendrik, and according to another, of Joachim van Curler (*Van Rensselaer Bowier Manuscripts, post,* p. 78, note 34); he was a grand-nephew of Kiliaen van Rensselaer, the first patroon of Rensselaerswyck on the upper Hudson in New Netherland. In his eighteenth year he came to New Netherland as assistant to the commissary of Rensselaerswyck; later he was secretary and bookkeeper. In 1641 he received the title of *commis* and assumed full representative authority in government and trade, with some judicial powers. The tenant farmers of Rensselaerswyck, unskilled in New World agriculture, were supplied by the patroon with houses, capital and all the facilities of production. In addition to duties connected with these allotments, the *commis* had responsibilities relating to the breeding of horses and cattle, the care of a growing fur trade, and the fostering of an export trade along the Atlantic coast.

Exact accounts of all transactions were to be sent to the patroons. A sharp reminder from Amsterdam that reports were deficient and in arrears (*Van Rensselaer Bowier Manuscripts*, pp. 658–68) brought from Van Curler the letter of June 16, 1643 (O'Callaghan, *History, post*, I, 456–65), in which some of the difficulties attending the experiment of absentee farming in the wilds of New Netherland were pointed out. Van Curler complained that Adriaen van der Donck [*q.v.*], officer of justice and *schout*, labored to undermine him, and betrayed the patroon's interests. Relief came when Van der Donck removed to his estate by the Harlem River. In 1644 Van Curler married Anthonia Slachboom, widow of Jonas Bronck; the next year he visited Holland. From the second patroon, Johannes van Rensselaer, he obtained the lease of a farm four miles north of the present Albany. Desiring a more congenial field for his ambitions, Van Curler in 1661 procured from Director Petrus Stuyvesant [*q.v.*] a license to purchase the Indian flat, Schonowe, on the Mohawk, to which in the following year he removed. The settlement planted there became Schenectady.

Van Curler gained an enduring influence over the neighboring Indian tribes. He interposed with success to save Father Isaac Jogues [*q.v.*] and his companions from death at the hands of the Mohawks. In 1660 he took part in the treaty which terminated the first Esopus war. At this period the relations of the French in Canada with their southern neighbors did not forbid exchanges of good will. In the winter of 1666, when Governor De Courcelle, in an ill-considered expedition into the Mohawk country, faced starvation with his force, Van Curler headed a movement to supply them with provisions. A year later De Tracy, the Canadian lieutenant-general, sent Van Curler an invitation to visit him in Canada. Accompanied by several Indians, Van Curler set forth by the way of Lake Champlain. Embarking in a small boat, he was overtaken by a sudden gale and was drowned. Perou Bay, the scene of the disaster, was long known as Corlaer's Bay. A more impressive memorial was the name, Corlaer, which the Indians thereafter bestowed on the English governors of New York in commemoration of Van Curler's courage and human understanding. A

memorial tablet was dedicated in Schenectady in 1909.

[For sources, see A. J. F. van Laer, in *Yearbook of the Dutch Settlers Soc. of Albany*, vol. III (1928) ; *N. Y. State Lib.: Van Rensselaer Bowier MSS.* (1908), translated and ed. by A. J. F. van Laer ; E. B. O'Callaghan, *Docs. Rel. to the Colonial Hist. . . . of N. Y.*, vol. III (1853), and *Hist. of New Netherland* (2nd ed., 1855) ; Jonathan Pearson, *A Hist. of the Schenectady Patent* (1883) ; *Minutes of the Court of Rensselaerswyck, 1648–1652* (1922), translated and ed. by A. J. F. van Laer. A journal ascribed to Van Curler is printed in *Ann. Report Am. Hist. Asso. . . . 1895* (1896), but according to A. J. F. van Laer (*Van Rensselaer Bowier MSS.*, p. 271) it cannot be Van Curler's.]

R. E. D.

VAN DAM, RIP (*c.* 1660–June 10, 1749), merchant, colonial politician, was born in Fort Orange (Albany, N. Y.), of a Dutch family living in New Netherland before the English conquest. His parents were Claas Ripse van Dam, a carpenter, and Maria Bords. Early in life Rip voyaged to Jamaica in command of the sloop *Catharine*. He subsequently embarked in trade, and at the age of thirty was listed among the merchants of New York City. He was also concerned in ship building on the North River. In 1693 he was elected a member of the board of aldermen, a station which he filled for three successive years, but he was not conspicuously active in politics until 1702. In that year the seizure and condemnation of some of the vessels in which he had investments, under Acting Governor Nanfan, head of the Leisler party, aroused his antagonism to the popular element of his day as well as to the unpopular navigation acts. Van Dam's resentment embraced the lieutenant-governor, the collector who seized the ships, and the chief justice who condemned them, and he sent petitions attacking these officers to the King, but the trouble subsided later the same year with the accession of Queen Anne to the throne, the arrival of Lord Cornbury [*q.v.*] as Nanfan's successor, and the elevation of Van Dam to the Council.

Van Dam was a councilor for more than thirty years. During most of this time he took no prominent part in controversy, though in 1713 there was friction between Gov. Robert Hunter [*q.v.*] and the Council; two years later the legislature approved an act for appointing a London agent to take notice of measures in Parliament injurious to the colony; and Hunter's successor, Gov. William Burnet [*q.v.*], had trouble with the Assembly. Meanwhile Van Dam built houses, supplied provisions for the troops, furnished money for the colonial treasury, and filled contracts for repairs and improvements to the royal fort. He also invested in forest land, being interested in large patents in the Hudson River region and the Mohawk region.

In 1731, by the death of Gov. John Montgomerie, Van Dam as senior member and president of the Council became the executive head of the province. For thirteen months he exercised the powers of the office and received the salary. Then Gov. William Cosby [q.v.] arrived, and demanded an equal division of the emoluments, by virtue of an order from the King. When Van Dam refused, inasmuch as Cosby's receipts from the governorship while still in England had been three times as great as the disputed salary (Smith, post, II, 4-7), the Governor sued in "the Equity side of the Exchequer." Cosby's report of his grievances to the home government (Documents, post, VI, 8) described Van Dam as pleading that no such court as the Equity side of the Exchequer existed, that the judges' commissions were void, and that "no Supream or other Court . . . had any being, Jurisdiction, or authority by prescription" (Ibid., p. 11). Van Dam's plea was overruled; but he continued the war with formal charges, alleging that Cosby had failed to fortify the port against the designs of the French. Cosby complained to London, and the Lords of Trade recommended Van Dam's dismissal from the Council. He was suspended by Cosby on Nov. 24, 1735. He failed to recognize this action as removal, however, or George Clarke [q.v.] as the new president of the Council, and appointed municipal officers for New York City after Cosby's death in March 1736, whereupon Clarke issued a proclamation of warning against these appointments. The threat of civil war was dispersed when dispatches from England brought recognition of Clarke as president; his appointment as lieutenant-governor soon followed, and Van Dam's public career came to an end.

In the struggle for popular rights and against prerogative, Rip Van Dam won leadership with William Smith and James Alexander [qq.v.], two of the ablest men in the colony. Prolonging the fight into the later years of his life, he heard complaints of his senility issuing from quarters where there was more reason to complain of his vigor. As a councilor, he was often called upon to settle the disputes of the Reformed churches and other religious societies, a difficult task in view of the unsettled state of those congregations at that period. A disposition to conciliate and tranquillize marked his efforts in this field.

Van Dam married Sara van der Spiegel in September 1684 and had a number of children, of whom two sons and three daughters reached maturity. One of his grand-daughters became the wife of Robert Livingston, third proprietor of the Manor of Livingston.

[Frederic De Peyster, Memoir of Rip Van Dam (1865); E. B. O'Callaghan, Docs. Rel. to the Col. Hist. of . . . N. Y., vols. IV-VI (1853-55); N. Y. State Lib. . . . Calendar of Council Minutes, 1668-1783 (1902); Jour. of the Legislative Council of the Colony of N. Y. (1861); J. G. Wilson, The Memorial Hist. of the City of N. Y., vols. II, IV (1892, 1893), passim; Ecclesiastical Records: State of N. Y. (7 vols., 1901-16), ed. by E. T. Corwin; William Smith, The Hist. of the Late Province of N. Y. (2 vols., 1829-30); "The Letters and Papers of Cadwallader Colden," N. Y. Hist. Soc. Colls., Pub. Fund Ser., vols. L, LI (1918-19); H. L. Osgood, The Am. Colonies in the Eighteenth Century (1924), vol. II; D. T. Valentine, Manual of the Corporation of the City of N. Y., 1864, 1865, the latter containing a reprint of De Peyster's Memoir and portraits of Van Dam and his wife; Calendar of N. Y. Colonial MSS.—Land Papers (1864); S. S. Purple, Records of the Reformed Dutch Church in New Amsterdam and N. Y.: Marriages (1890); Jonathan Pearson, Contributions to the Geneals. of the First Settlers of Albany (1872); Van Dam's will in Colls. N. Y. Hist. Soc., Pub. Fund Ser., vol. XXVIII (1896).] R. E. D.

VANDENHOFF, GEORGE (1813–June 16, 1885), actor, lawyer, was born in Liverpool, England, the son of John Vandenhoff, a well-known actor (see The Dictionary of National Biography). The family, a few generations back, had come to England from the Netherlands. Vandenhoff was educated at Stonyhurst College and later studied for the law. For a time he was solicitor to the trustees of the Liverpool docks. On Oct. 14, 1839, he made his stage début as Leon in Beaumont and Fletcher's Rule a Wife and Have a Wife at Covent Garden, where he also acted in new plays by Leigh Hunt and Sheridan Knowles, and as Mercutio in Madame Vestris' famous revival of Romeo and Juliet. In 1842, on Sept. 21, he made his American début at the Park Theatre, New York, as Hamlet, with Henry Placide [q.v.] as Polonius. Of his Hamlet, Porter's Spirit of the Times, Sept. 24, 1842, recorded, "Taken as a whole, the character has not been more ably performed in this city for the past six years." Vandenhoff followed Hamlet with Virginius, Macbeth, Benedick, and Claude Melnotte, and then began a tour which included the chief cities of the East and took him as far south as New Orleans. At the Walnut Street Theatre, Philadelphia, he played Rolla to the Elvira of Charlotte Cushman [q.v.]; in Boston, where he acted for five weeks, he added Coriolanus and Hotspur to his list of rôles. He acted in New Orleans in February 1843, visited Richmond (where he acted one night with Hackett), Baltimore, and Philadelphia once more, where he played Mercutio to Charlotte Cushman's Romeo. In May he was back at the Park, and then finished his season in Boston. He had made little money, but many friends, and decided to remain in America indefinitely.

From 1843 to 1853 he lived in New York, acted frequently in most American cities, taught elocution, and gave many public readings of "Shakespeare, Sheridan and the Poets." In October 1843 he was leading man for William C. Macready at the Chestnut Street Theatre, Philadelphia, and he has left interesting records of that actor and his methods. At the Park, in 1844, he supported the elder Booth, and in 1846 he played Faulconbridge in the revival of *King John* made by Mr. and Mrs. Charles Kean. One of his most interesting ventures, however, was at Palmo's Opera House, New York, in the spring of 1845, where he staged an English version of Sophocles' *Antigone,* with Mendelssohn's music and an attempt to reproduce a Greek stage. In January 1853 he returned to England, where he acted first in Liverpool in repertory. On Oct. 25, 1853, he reappeared in London, at the Haymarket, as Hamlet, highly praised by the leading papers. He made his great success, however, in what was for him a new style of part—Captain Cozens in Planché's *Knights of the Round Table,* a racy adventure comedy which ran fifty-four nights.

At the end of the season he resolved to retire as soon as he could. He sailed for Boston, and on Aug. 20, 1855, was married in Trinity Church to Mary MaKeath, an American actress. They acted jointly in the English provinces for a year, and then returned to the United States. Shortly thereafter Vandenhoff carried out his plan to retire. The truth seems to be that he never really cared for stage life. In 1858 he was admitted to the New York bar and resumed the practice of law, but continued his popular public readings. His interesting volume of reminiscences, *Leaves from an Actor's Note Book,* was published in 1860. He had already written (1858) a social satire in verse, and in 1861 published *The Art of Elocution* and *Life,* a poem. In 1874 he reappeared in support of Genevieve Ward [*q.v.*] as Wolsey and as Gloster in *Jane Shore.* This was his last stage appearance. He died in Brighton, England, June 16, 1885. Vandenhoff was tall, graceful, scholarly, and somewhat aloof. In his earlier years his acting was of the "new school" of ease and naturalness, but in later years he declared Irving to be "an intellectual machine with the pronunciation and gait of a barbarian." Junius Booth he praised highly, but Lawrence Barrett and John McCullough he considered to have all the faults of the conventional "tragedian." His own book shows him a man of breeding, taste, and good sense.

[The date of birth is from the Cat. of Dramatic Portraits, Harvard Theatre Coll. Other sources include George Vandenhoff, *Leaves from an Actor's Note Book* (1860); G. C. D. Odell, *Annals of the N. Y. Stage,* vols. IV–VII (1928–31); *N. Y. Dramatic Mirror,* Aug. 14, 1886.]

W. P. E.

VAN DEPOELE, CHARLES JOSEPH (Apr. 27, 1846–Mar. 18, 1892), scientist, inventor, pioneer in electric light and traction, was born in Lichtervelde, Belgium, the fourth child of Peter John and Marie Thérèse Coleta (Algoed) van de Poele. Precocious—he fashioned an electric light when he was fifteen years old, in 1861—and inspired in part by his father's work in the East Flanders railway shops, Van Depoele devoted himself early to scientific experiment. After attending a higher school in Poperinghe, he was apprenticed in 1865 to the wood-carving firm of Buisine-Rigot at its shops in Lille and Paris. In Lille he studied at the Imperial Lyceum and continued his preoccupation with electricity. In 1869 he emigrated to America and settled in Detroit, Mich.

In Detroit, Van Depoele became a successful manufacturer of church furniture, but he soon began to concentrate his efforts in the field of electricity. As early as 1870 he exhibited arc lights and as early as 1874 was demonstrating the feasibility of electric traction by both overhead and underground conductors. By 1878, when he was visited by Edison, the old church in which he had finally established his shop, at 28 Pine Street, had become famous. Styled "Detroit's Edison" by the *Detroit Free Press* on Nov. 13, 1878, he proceeded to work towards vibratory regulation for arc lights, and by July 1879, he had demonstrated his improved lights publicly. Early in 1880 the Van Depoele Electric Light Company was formed, and later in the year Van Depoele transferred his experiments in electric traction to the factory of the Detroit Novelty Works at Hamtramck, Mich., where he made tests on a half-mile track. In 1881 the Van Depoele Electric Light Company of Chicago was incorporated; and in 1884, the Van Depoele Electric Manufacturing Company. Meanwhile, in Chicago, Jan. 18, 1883, Van Depoele gave a public demonstration of electric traction, the current being furnished from two wires laid along the track. At the Chicago Inter-State Industrial Exposition early the following September he continued with the first practical demonstration in the world of a spring-pressed under-running trolley. In 1884 and 1885 he was successful in Toronto with both the underground conduit and the overhead systems. On Nov. 14, 1885, his overhead system was put into operation in South Bend, Ind. The *South Bend Tribune* of Nov. 16 ran a proud headline: "South Bend the First

City in the Union to Secure Practical Electric Traction"—and a reporter announced: "The bray of the festive mule must go." In the winter of 1885–86 Van Depoele's system was adopted in Minneapolis, Minn., Montgomery, Ala., and other cities, and by the end of 1886 eight lines had been installed in the United States and Canada. In this year he contributed an article, "Electric Transmission of Power," to the *Telegraphic Journal and Electrical Review* of London (Mar. 5, 1886). Two years later, in March 1888, the Van Depoele system was operating in ten cities, with three other lines under construction—claiming a greater number of lines than all other companies combined (*Senate Miscellaneous Document No. 84*, 50 Cong., 1 Sess.).

In 1888 Van Depoele's electric railway patents were sold to the Thomson-Houston Electric Company of Lynn, Mass., and Van Depoele himself was engaged by that concern as electrician, with American and foreign royalties for his patented railway systems. The sale of the Van Depoele Electric Manufacturing Company followed in 1889, and in this year Van Depoele's telpher and reciprocating patents were assigned to the Thomson-Houston International Company. In November 1891, while planning an electrical exhibit for the World's Columbian Exposition in Chicago, Van Depoele contracted a severe cold, which with resulting complications caused his death after an illness of over four months.

Van Depoele filed in all some 444 applications for patents, of which at least 249 were granted to him under his own name. After his death seventy-two further applications were made, and of these some forty-six were allowed and assigned to the Thomson-Houston Electric Company. Van Depoele's achievements covered a wide variety of electrical inventions and improvements, especially in the field of traction. His little "Giant" generator, patented Sept. 21, 1880, with its smooth regulation of power, was considered one of the best on the market. His first patent on electric railways was granted Oct. 2, 1883; his first on an overhead conductor, Aug. 11, 1885. The patent for his carbon contact or commutator-brush, which he first used in 1882 and which revolutionized motor construction, was taken up Oct. 9, 1888. Other basic patents of prime importance were his alternating-current electric reciprocating engine (1889); his multiple-current pulsating generator (1890); his telpher system (1890), first used in the mines at Streator, Ill., in 1885; his multiple rock-drill (1891); his coal-mining machine (1891); and his gearless electric locomotive (1894). He was experimenting with electric refrigeration before

June 16, 1886, and in the winter of 1889–90 at his residence at 502 Essex Street in Lynn he made several photographs in color. The two most distinctively original of his achievements, however, were the pivoted spring-pressed under-running trolley and the carbon commutator-brush. Of this latter epochal invention alone it has been justly said that the traction industry "would have been indefinitely postponed"—even "impossible" —"without the discovery of the carbon brush" (Rice and Crowther, *post*, p. 600).

Van Depoele was a man of broad culture. Bilingual from the beginning in French and Flemish, he became proficient as well in Dutch, Latin, Greek, English, and other languages. On Nov. 23, 1870, he married Ada Mina, daughter of Cornelius and Cornelia (Weavers) van Hoogstraten of Detroit, and by her he had three sons and four daughters. He became a naturalized American citizen on Apr. 23, 1878. He died in Lynn, Mass., and was buried in St. Mary's Cemetery there. A portrait bust of him, in bronze, by Robert Kraus of Boston, is in the Lynn Public Library.

[Notes, drawings, letters, etc., assembled by Van Depoele's daughter, Romanie Adeline (Van Depoele) Phelan, of Lynn, Mass.; catalogues of the Van Depoele Electric Light and Manufacturing Company, Chicago, Ill.; *The Official Gazette of the U. S. Patent Office*, 1878–98; *The Canadian Patent Office Record*, vol. XVII (1889); *Selected U. S. Patents Relating to Electric Railways Owned or Controlled by the Thomson-Houston Electric Co., Brush Electric Co., and Allied Corporations* (1891); T. C. Martin and J. Wetzler, *The Electric Motor and Its Applications* (1892); *U. S. Circuit Court for the District of Conn.: In Equity, No. 753, Thomson-Houston Electric Co. vs. The Winchester Ave. Railroad Co., et al., Complainant's Proofs* (4 vols., 1895), and report of case in 71 *Federal Reporter*, 192; "The Work of Van Depoele," *Electrical Rev.* (London), June 5, 1896; D. McKillop, "The Father of the Trolley," *Electrical Age*, Dec. 1905; B. G. Lamme, "The Development of the Street Railway Motor in America," *Electric Jour.* (Pittsburgh, Pa.), Oct. 1918; E. W. Rice, Jr., and S. Crowther, "Trials of the Early Electric Trail," *Magazine of Business*, Nov. 1928; *Detroit Free Press*, Mar. 20, 1892.]   C. B. M.

VANDERBILT, CORNELIUS (May 27, 1794–Jan. 4, 1877), steamship and railroad promoter, financier, born at Port Richmond, Staten Island, N. Y. (now part of New York City), was the fourth child and second son of Cornelius and Phebe (Hand) Vander Bilt. His paternal ancestors, who came from Holland and settled on Long Island in the latter half of the seventeenth century, wrote the family name in three words, van der Bilt. The subject of the present sketch preferred to write it Van Derbilt, but during his lifetime other members of the family consolidated the name into one word. His father, a poor man with a large family, did a bit of farming on Staten Island, and some boating and lightering around New York harbor. The blue-eyed, flaxen-haired, boisterous boy Cornelius had no inclination and little opportunity for education, and did not spend a day in school after he was eleven. Already big in body and strong, he became at that age his father's helper. At about thirteen he is said to have superintended the job of lightering a vessel, his father being engaged elsewhere. He had barely reached his sixteenth birthday when, with $100 advanced by his parents, he bought a small sailing vessel called a piragua and began a freight and passenger ferrying business between Staten Island and New York City. On Dec. 19, 1813, when he was only nineteen years old, he married his cousin and neighbor, Sophia Johnson, daughter of his father's sister Eleanor, and set up a home of his own near his birthplace.

The War of 1812 had opened new opportunities for him, and he was busy day and night. Among other important jobs, he had a three months' contract from the government for provisioning the forts in and around New York harbor. Before the war was over, he had several boats under his command. He built a schooner in 1814 for service to Long Island Sound, and, in the following two years, two larger schooners for the coastwise trade. These he sent out—he himself being in command of the largest—not only as cargo boats, but also as traders up the Hudson River and along the coast from New England to Charleston. In 1818 he startled his friends by selling all his sailing vessels and going to work as a captain for Thomas Gibbons [q.v.], owner of a ferry between New Brunswick, on the Raritan estuary, and New York City—an important link in the New York-Philadelphia freight, mail, and passenger route. Gibbons was fighting for life against the steam-navigation monopoly in New York waters which had been granted to Robert Fulton by the New York legislature several years before. Vanderbilt loved a fight; he took Gibbons' one small vessel, put her in better condition, selected a hard-bitten crew and drove them to the limit of endurance, and within a year had turned a losing venture into a profitable one. When he entered Gibbons' service, he removed his family to New Brunswick, took over a rundown tavern by the river-side there, and installed his wife as hotel keeper. She renovated the house and made it famous for good food and service. "Bellona Hall," as it was called, became a favorite stopping place for travelers between New York and Philadelphia. In addition to her duties as chief factotum of the hotel, Mrs. Vanderbilt gave birth to a child about every two years while living in New Brunswick; she had thirteen in all.

Vanderbilt soon induced Gibbons to build a larger and finer steamer, the *Bellona* (1818). Meanwhile, the New York monopoly had brought suit against Gibbons, and for several years there was legal, and sometimes physical, warfare. Only Vanderbilt's lusty, dynamic spirit and resourcefulness kept his employer's line in operation. For months on end New York deputy sheriffs tried to arrest him whenever his boat entered New York waters, but he foiled them in one way or another. He is said to have built a secret compartment on the vessel in which he would hide at such times. Finally, in 1824, the United States Supreme Court ruled that a monopoly such as that granted by the New York legislature was unconstitutional (*Gibbons* vs. *Ogden, 9 Wheaton*, 1). During the eleven years of his service with Gibbons, young Vanderbilt increased and broadened the business enormously. He had built seven more steamers for his employer, some for the New York-New Brunswick-Elizabeth ferries, others to ply a new line on the Delaware.

Vanderbilt had ambitions of his own; and in 1829, having accumulated a considerable nest-egg through his own and his wife's exertions, he resigned from Gibbons' employ in order to enter the steamboat business on his own. Much against the will of his wife, he disposed of "Bellona Hall" and moved her and the eight or nine children to New York City. His first ventures were on the Hudson River, where other concerns were already operating; he inaugurated rate wars with a characteristic zest for conflict. Here, in a competition for the trade between New York and Peekskill, he came into collision, in 1834, with Daniel Drew [q.v.]. The fare between the two points was finally cut to twelve and a half cents, and then Drew sold out to Vanderbilt. The latter now entered the Albany trade, where a more powerful corporation, the Hudson River Association, was functioning. He put two boats on the Albany run and began cutting rates again. In the end his opponents paid him a goodly sum for his agreement to withdraw from competition for ten years. He next established lines on Long Island Sound and on to Providence and Boston. Later he returned to the Hudson River. He is given credit for bringing about a great and rapid advance in the size, comfort, and elegance of steamboats. The "floating palaces" of the 1840's and 1850's would not suffer greatly by comparison with the boats of today in such waters; in many cases they were more luxurious, even if they lacked electric appliances and some other modern conveniences. Vanderbilt found pleasure in making his vessels stanch, fast, handsome, and comfortable. About 1846 he launched on the

Hudson perhaps the finest boat yet seen by New Yorkers; it was named for himself.

Before this time he was undoubtedly a millionaire. He was supposed to have passed the half million mark at the age of forty. But he and his family had so far failed to make any impression upon the exclusive New York society of that day. Cornelius himself was not a figure for the drawing-room or for a luncheon table of fastidious gentlemen. He was apt to be loud, rustic, and coarse in speech, his talk interlarded with profanity and slang of the wharves. He was a big, bumptious, ruthless, tobacco-chewing, hard-headed, hard-swearing, hard-fighting man, yet constructive, courageous, clear-sighted in business matters, broad-visioned for his day, and graced by a certain alluring frankness and faithfulness to a bargain. It is believed that a certain smoldering resentment because of the social cold shoulder turned to him, together with the persuasion of his wife, caused him to build a fine mansion on Staten Island and take his family back there in 1840. But he still wanted to pry open those closed doors on Manhattan, and in 1846, despite his wife's protests, he began building a town house on Washington Place. Scarcely was it ready when Mrs. Vanderbilt was committed to a private sanitarium for insanity, upon his delation, and perhaps because of her tearful yet stubborn refusal to move back to New York. She was released in the spring of 1847, after a few months' confinement, and went obediently to the new home in the city.

The gold rush opened new vistas to Vanderbilt, whom men were now calling "Commodore." Before the end of 1849, traffic to California was beginning to go via Panama, freight and passengers crossing the Isthmus on muleback. Vanderbilt conceived the idea of starting a line of his own via Nicaragua—through the San Juan River to Lake Nicaragua and perhaps thence by canal to the Pacific. At first he called this the American Atlantic & Pacific Ship Canal Company. A trip to England in 1850 in search of capital to finance the venture was fruitless, and he proceeded to develop the route himself. He procured from the Nicaraguan government a charter for himself in the name of the Accessory Transit Company (see *Senate Executive Document No. 68,* 34 Cong., 1 Sess., 1856). He then improved to some extent the channel of the San Juan River, built docks on the east and west coasts of Nicaragua and at Virgin Bay on Lake Nicaragua, and made a fine twelve-mile macadam road from the latter place to his west-coast port. Meanwhile, he was beginning the construction of a fleet of eight new steamers with which he ran lines from New York, and later from New Orleans. His route was two days shorter than that via Panama; he greatly reduced the New York-San Francisco passenger fare and garnered most of the traffic.

He made money so rapidly that in 1853 he announced that he was going to take the first vacation of his life. He built a steam yacht, the *North Star,* sumptuously appointed, and with his entire family, even to sons-in-law and grandchildren, and with several invited guests, including the Rev. Dr. John Overton Choules as chaplain and chronicler, he embarked for a triumphal tour of Europe. Dr. Choules wrote a fulsome history of the voyage, full of unconscious humor, which was published as *The Cruise of the Steam Yacht North Star* (1854). Before going abroad, Vanderbilt resigned the presidency of the Accessory Transit Company, and committed its management to Charles Morgan and Cornelius K. Garrison [*qq.v.*] who, during his absence, manipulated the stock and secured control of the company; but by shrewd buying he won it back in a few months. However, William Walker [*q.v.*], the American filibuster who had seized control of the Nicaraguan government, allied himself with Morgan and Garrison, rescinded the Transit Company's charter on the ground that its terms had been disregarded, and issued a new charter to the rival group. Vanderbilt thereupon aided in bringing about Walker's downfall early in 1857. The doughty "Commodore," now sixty-three, but a harder fighter than ever, had to battle his way through other enemies in Wall Street and Central America, but he triumphed, and the Transit Company was his own again. Scarcely had he brushed aside the last opposition, however, when he approached the Pacific Mail Steamship Company, and the United States Mail Steamship Company, the great carriers via Panama, and offered to abandon the Nicaragua line if they would buy the *North Star* for some $400,000 and pay him $40,000 a month indemnity. They came to his figures reluctantly, but a year later, when he threatened to open the Transit line again, they increased his monthly stipend to $56,000 (*Congressional Globe,* June 9, 1858, 35 Cong., 1 Sess., pp. 2843–44). In the middle fifties he built three vessels, one of which, the *Vanderbilt,* was the largest and finest he had yet constructed, and entered into competition for the Atlantic trade with the Cunard Line and the Collins Line (see sketch of E. K. Collins), even offering to carry the mails to Havre for nothing. He found this an unprofitable venture, however, and at the beginning of the Civil War was glad to sell his Atlantic line for $3,000,000, retaining only the *Vanderbilt*, which he fitted up as a warship and turned over to the government. It has been claimed that he intended only to make a loan of this vessel, but it was interpreted as a gift (Smith, *post*, p. 237). His connection with the expedition of Nathaniel P. Banks [*q.v.*] to New Orleans was less happy, for many of the vessels chartered by him under commission of the government proved unseaworthy. However, his name was expunged from the Senate resolution of censure (*Congressional Globe*, 37 Cong., 3 Sess., Jan. 29, 1863, and *Senate Report 75*, 1863, 37 Cong., 3 Sess.; Myers, *post*, II, 132–37).

Of Vanderbilt's thirteen children, one boy had died young and all of the nine daughters were living. His youngest and favorite child, George, born in 1839, was a soldier in the Civil War and died in 1866 from effects of exposure in the Corinth campaign. His second son, Cornelius Jeremiah, an epileptic, gambler, and ne'er-do-well, had been a great disappointment. The eldest son, William Henry [*q.v.*], he had regarded as being of little force, and had exiled to a farm on Staten Island, though later he became aware of his ability and at last gave him opportunity to use it. This was in connection with railroad enterprises, to which Vanderbilt turned from shipping as he neared seventy. He had begun buying New York & Harlem Railroad stock in 1862 when it was selling at a very low figure. In 1863 he induced the city council to give him permission to extend the line by street-car tracks to the Battery. The stock, which he had already driven up, rose greatly upon public announcement of the ordinance, and even more when Vanderbilt was elected president. Daniel Drew now plotted with members of the council to sell Harlem stock "short," rescind the ordinance, and buy the shares for delivery after the price had dropped to a certain figure. The plot was carried out, but the price dropped much less than was expected, for Vanderbilt bought every share that was offered, and presently it was discovered that the "short" traders had sold more shares than were in existence. The price rapidly rose, and when Vanderbilt forced a settlement, many of the plotters were ruined. He made William vice-president of the Harlem road, and thereafter his son was his first lieutenant.

He next turned his attention to the Harlem's competitor, the Hudson River Railroad, another rundown property. While buying control of the railroad, he sought authority from the legislature to combine the two. Undeterred by his former experience, Drew again plotted, this time with some of the legislators, to sell the stock "short,"

defeat the consolidation bill, hammer down the price, and make a "killing." The former story was repeated: the bill was lost; the price declined considerably but not enough; Vanderbilt, aided by other operators, bought every share offered; the "shorts" discovered that they had agreed to deliver far more shares than were in existence; the price rose greatly; and again Cornelius had revenge on those who had tried to break him. He bided his time on the consolidation of the roads, improving their equipment and service, as he did that of every property he owned, and presently had them on a paying basis. He next sought control of the New York Central Railroad, running from Albany to Buffalo. Its directors countered by forming an alliance with Drew's Hudson River boat line and sending through freight and passengers from Albany to New York by that route. But when the river froze in early winter and the steamboats were stopped, they sought to transfer traffic to the Hudson River road, only to discover that Vanderbilt was halting its trains on the east side of the river, a mile from Albany. Stock in the New York Central declined and Vanderbilt bought quantities of it, finally securing control in 1867. He promptly spent $2,000,000 of his own money in improving the line and buying new rolling stock. He united these two railroads by legislative act in 1869, as the New York Central & Hudson River Railroad, and in 1872 leased the Harlem Railroad to it. He increased the capital stock by $42,000,000 (which was a stock-watering operation of magnitude), but out of three inefficient roads he created a single line, giving uninterrupted service.

In 1868 he sought control of the Erie Railway, a rival line to Buffalo and Chicago. He pursued the same tactics as before, buying every share of stock offered. But this time Drew, Jay Gould, and James Fisk, Jr. [*qq.v.*], who were in control of Erie, outmaneuvered him, throwing 50,000 shares of fraudulent stock into the market, then fleeing to New Jersey to avoid prosecution and bribing the New Jersey legislature to legalize the stock issue. Vanderbilt lost millions by this *coup*, but the plotters had to compromise with him in order to return to New York with impunity, and his loss was greatly reduced. Upon the insistence of his son William that extension of their rail system to Chicago was advisable, in 1873 he bought control of the Lake Shore & Michigan Southern Railway, and two years before his death the Michigan Central Railroad and the Canada Southern Railway. Thus did he create one of the great American systems of transportation. In the last years of his life, his influence on national finance was stabilizing. When the panic of 1873 was at its worst, he announced that the New York Central was paying its millions of dividends as usual, and let contracts for the building of the Grand Central Terminal in New York City, with four tracks leading from it, giving employment to thousands of men. He saw to it, however, that the city paid half the cost of the viaduct and open-cut approaches to the station.

His first wife died in 1868, and on Aug. 21, 1869, he married Frank Armstrong Crawford, a young lady from Mobile, Ala., who survived him when he died on Jan. 4, 1877, after an illness of about eight months. His fortune was estimated at more than $100,000,000, of which he left about $90,000,000 to William and about $7,-500,000 to the latter's four sons; he expressed his contempt for womankind by leaving less than $4,000,000 to be distributed among his own eight daughters (*New York Tribune*, Jan. 9, 1877). His wife received a half million in cash, the New York home, and 2,000 shares of New York Central stock. Vanderbilt bestowed no money philanthropically until late in life, when he gave $1,-000,000 to Vanderbilt University (previously Central University) at Nashville, Tenn., of which he is regarded as the founder, and $50,000 to the Church of the Strangers in New York, of which his friend, the Rev. Charles F. Deems [q.v.], was pastor.

[W. A. Croffut, *The Vanderbilts and the Story of Their Fortune* (1886), apparently the source of most of the legends; A. D. H. Smith, *Commodore Vanderbilt. An Epic of American Achievement* (1927), an undocumented popularization; James Parton, *Famous Americans of Recent Times* (1867); Meade Minnigerode, *Certain Rich Men* (1927); "Cornelius Vanderbilt," in *Hunt's Merchants' Mag. and Commercial Rev.*, Jan. 1865; "The Vanderbilt Memorial," in *Nation*, Nov. 18, 1869, a critical contemporary appraisal; B. J. Hendrick, "The Vanderbilt Fortune," in *McClure's Mag.*, Nov. 1908, a good article; E. H. Mott, *Between the Ocean and the Lakes. The Story of Erie* (1899); Gustavus Myers, *Hist. of the Great American Fortunes* (1910), vol. II, biased but documented and valuable; W. O. Scroggs, *Filibusters and Financiers* (1916); John Moody, *The Railroad Builders* (1919); Allan Nevins, *The Emergence of Modern America* (1927); F. C. Hicks, *High Finance in the Sixties* (1929); Matthew Josephson, *The Robber Barons* (1934); J. J. Clute, *Annals of Staten Island* (1877); records of the Moravian Church at New Dorp, Staten Island; scrapbook of clippings on the Cornelius Vanderbilt will, 1877–78, N. Y. Pub. Lib.; Frank Armstrong (Crawford) Vanderbilt and R. L. Crawford, *Laurus Crawfurdiana. Memorials of the Crawford Family* (privately printed, 1833), valuable for second marriage; obituaries in *N. Y. Tribune*, *N. Y. Times*, Jan. 5, 1877.]   A. F. H.

VANDERBILT, CORNELIUS (Nov. 27, 1843–Sept. 12, 1899), financier, philanthropist, son of William Henry [q.v.] and Maria Louisa (Kissam) Vanderbilt, and grandson of Cornelius Vanderbilt [q.v.], the founder of the for-tune, was born on a farm near New Dorp, Staten Island, N. Y. William Kissam and George Washington Vanderbilt [qq.v.] were younger brothers. He first attended the village common school near his home and later private schools in New York City. At the age of sixteen he took a clerkship in the Shoe and Leather Bank. When he left that place four years later to go into the banking house of Kissam Brothers, it is said that he was receiving $50 a month and was living within his income (*New York Times*, Sept. 13, 1899). He had by this time become a favorite of his grandfather, who insisted, however, that he must work his way upward. When he was about twenty-four he was taken by the elder Cornelius into the service of the New York & Harlem Railroad as assistant treasurer. A little later he became treasurer and held that place until 1880, when he was elected vice-president; from 1886 until his death he was president of the road. He was frequently praised by his grandfather for his thoroughness and reliability, and received from him a special legacy of $5,000,000. In 1883 his father resigned his presidencies of the several Vanderbilt railroads, and, under the new arrangement specified by him, Cornelius was elected chairman of the board of directors of the New York Central & Hudson River and Michigan Central Railroads, and president of the Canada Southern Railway. Upon the death of his father in 1885, Cornelius became the head of the Vanderbilt family, and—although the fortune was not held in common—the chief director of its investments. These were profitable, though conservative.

He was the hardest worker of the family. He built a palatial home on Fifth Avenue, and a mansion, "The Breakers," at Newport, R. I., but he had little or no time for society. He was often at his desk in the Grand Central Station Building before any clerk arrived in the morning. A director in many corporations, he took his duties seriously, attending meetings and scanning reports from every corporation minutely. His philanthropic and other activities outside his business were enormous. He was a trustee of the College of Physicians and Surgeons, which his father so greatly aided, and he and his three brothers united in adding the Vanderbilt Clinic to it, while their sister, Mrs. William D. Sloane, gave it a maternity hospital. Vanderbilt was trustee or executive chairman of several other hospitals in New York, a trustee of Columbia University (1891–99), of the General Theological Seminary, and of the new Cathedral of St. John the Divine, one of the board of managers of the Domestic and Foreign Missionary Society of the Protestant Episcopal Church, and for the last twelve years of his life chairman of the executive committee of the Metropolitan Museum of Art. Among his gifts to the Metropolitan was Rosa Bonheur's famous painting, "The Horse Fair," in 1887. He founded the Railroad Branch of the Y. M. C. A. and gave it a handsome clubhouse in New York. He was a warden of St. Bartholomew's Church and contributed generously for ground and buildings for a new parish house. In a single day he often attended meetings at three or four of these institutions. Such strenuous activity undoubtedly shortened his life. His four sons were all students at Yale, and in memory of William Henry, the eldest, who died while a junior there, he presented to the University in 1893 a dormitory then regarded as large and costly. His gifts to Yale are said to have reached a total of $1,500,000. Vanderbilt suffered a slight stroke of paralysis in 1896, and thereupon resigned many of his official posts. He died in New York City of cerebral hemorrhage in 1899. On Feb. 4, 1867, he had married Alice Claypoole Gwynne, daughter of the late Abram E. Gwynne of Cincinnati (*New York Tribune,* Feb. 7, 1867). She survived him, as did three sons, Cornelius, Alfred Gwynne, (lost on the *Lusitania,* 1915), and Reginald; and two daughters, Gertrude, who married Harry Payne Whitney and became a well-known sculptress, and Gladys, who married Count Laszio Szechenyi.

[Seth Low, "Cornelius Vanderbilt," *Columbia Univ. Quart.,* Dec. 1899, pp. 39–43; J. G. Wilson, in *N. Y. Geneal. & Biog. Record,* Oct. 1899, pp. 197–99; F. L. Ford, "The Vanderbilts and the Vanderbilt Millions," *Munsey's Magazine,* Jan. 1900; *Who's Who in America,* 1899–1900; obituaries in *N. Y. Tribune, N. Y. Times,* Sept. 13, 1899. See also bibliographies of the other Vanderbilts.]   A. F. H.

VANDERBILT, GEORGE WASHINGTON (Nov. 14, 1862–Mar. 6, 1914), capitalist, agriculturist, pioneer in forestry, the youngest son of William Henry [*q.v.*] and Maria Louisa (Kissam) Vanderbilt, was born near New Dorp, Staten Island, N. Y. He was educated mostly by private tutors, and spent much of his youth in touring the world with them. He was shy and studious, caring little for finance, though he succeeded in increasing his own fortune materially during his lifetime. He fell in love with the mountains of western North Carolina, and in 1889 began buying land south and southwest of Asheville, eventually acquiring 130,000 acres, it is said, including Mount Pisgah (5,749 feet), one of the most beautiful peaks in the Appalachians. Here he planned the finest country home in America. He had studied architecture, forestry, and landscape gardening in preparation

for it. He worked with the architect, Richard Morris Hunt [*q.v.*], on the plans, and superintended the construction of the building, the final cost of which was reported as $3,000,000. He spent millions more in improving the estate, which he named "Biltmore." Frederick Law Olmsted [*q.v.*] was the landscape gardener. Until the death of his widowed mother in 1896, he lived with her in her New York home. That mansion then reverted to him, but he promptly went to live in his North Carolina château. He married on June 2, 1898, Edith Stuyvesant Dresser of Newport, R. I., who proved a congenial helpmate in all his plans.

He became a scientific farmer and stockbreeder, as well as one of the pioneers in scientific forestry in America. His sales of pedigreed hogs came to be events of importance. One of his Jersey cows broke all records for milk production, and the milk and ice cream from his dairies, sold over a wide area of country, were the finest obtainable. It was said after his death: "The stimulus afforded by his example towards improved agricultural methods in the South is beyond all estimate" (*American Forestry,* June 1914, p. 425). He founded and conducted the Biltmore Nursery, which specialized in trees and plants of the Appalachian region, and at the time of his death was doing a handsome business. He built many miles of roads and trails through his great forest area, making it almost as accessible as a park. Gifford Pinchot was his first superintendent of forests, passing from that place to the head of the United States Division of Forestry in 1898. Vanderbilt founded the Biltmore School of Forestry on his estate, where large numbers of young men received training. He planned and built the model village of Biltmore as a center for the employees on his property. He bought another home in Washington, but spent most of his time in his Carolina mountains, overseeing his numerous operations, studying trees, birds, and animals, or doing research in his large library, which was especially rich in works on nature. He spoke eight languages and had a reading acquaintance with others. Among other benefactions, he built in 1888 and presented to the New York Free Circulating Library (later New York Public Library) its Jackson Square Branch, and gave to Columbia University the ground on which the Teachers College was built. He also built a private museum in New York City, filled it with objects of art which he had collected all over the world, and presented it to the American Fine Arts Society. He offered to sell the major portion of his forest land to the United States for a forest reserve, but the offer was not accepted until after his death, when the government bought a large tract from Mrs. Vanderbilt. He died in Washington, D. C., after an operation for appendicitis. Besides his widow, he left a daughter, Cornelia Stuyvesant.

[O. W. Price, "George W. Vanderbilt, Pioneer in Forestry," *American Forestry,* June 1914; D. A. Willey, "Forest Conservation at Biltmore," *American Homes and Gardens,* July 1909; B. M. Trebor, "Into the Azure of the Blue Ridge," *Travel,* Apr. 1911; Gifford Pinchot, *Biltmore Forest . . . An Account of its Treatment, and the Results of the First Year's Work* (1893); "Biltmore Forest," *Harper's Weekly,* July 28, 1900; *Who's Who in America,* 1912–13; obituaries in *N. Y. Times, N. Y. Tribune, Sun* (N. Y.), Mar. 7, 1914.] A. F. H.

VANDERBILT, WILLIAM HENRY (May 8, 1821–Dec. 8, 1885), financier, railroad operator, son of Cornelius Vanderbilt, 1794–1877 [*q.v.*] and Sophia (Johnson) Vanderbilt, was born at New Brunswick, N. J., where his mother operated a hotel while his father was master of a ferry-boat running thence to New York City. When he was eight years old, his parents removed to New York, and he attended grammar school. He was not physically strong during boyhood and adolescence, a weakness with which his able-bodied and dynamic father could not sympathize. At seventeen he was put to work in a ship-chandler's shop, but about a year later he became a clerk in the banking house of Drew, Robinson & Company, of which one of the partners was Daniel Drew [*q.v.*]. At the age of nineteen William offended his father, now well-nigh a millionaire, by marrying Maria Louisa Kissam, a young woman of refinement and good family, but the daughter of an impecunious Brooklyn clergyman. Cornelius himself had married at nineteen, but he thought it folly for one so weak and footless as William to do the same. William's health declined within a year after his marriage, and, believing that he would never amount to much in business or finance, the father bought a seventy-acre farm for him at New Dorp, Staten Island, and sent him and his wife to it to make their own way. William quietly accepted the situation, and proceeded to make the farm a paying venture. There were born his eight children, four sons and four daughters, all of whom later lived in Fifth Avenue mansions. He increased the size of his farm to 350 acres and handled it so well that its profits rose.

During the depression of 1857 the Staten Island Railroad, a line thirteen miles long, became insolvent, and William soon afterward asked his father's influence in having him appointed receiver. The father, though still doubtful of William's ability, acquiesced, and to his surprise the latter succeeded in rehabilitating the road. He was therefore a railroad executive before his fa-

ther went into that business. When Cornelius acquired control of the New York & Harlem Railroad, he made William vice-president (1864) and gave him a home on Fifth Avenue; and thus, when he was forty-three years old, the son's ability belatedly received parental recognition. The contemptuous ignoring and suppression of it for two-thirds of his lifetime, however, was a bitter drop in his cup; it gave him a somewhat dour exterior, and instilled cynicism into his nature. Soon after receiving the Harlem office, he was also made vice-president of the Hudson River Railroad, the second line acquired by his father. Even though he began to take an efficient hand in railroad affairs, showing great ability in management, in improving track and equipment, in regulating rates and conciliating labor, he was never permitted to become a full executive until his father's failing hand relinquished the reins in the last few months of his life. Then, with less than nine years of life left to him, he rapidly began to expand his activities.

One of his first problems was a contest over his father's will, brought jointly by a scapegrace brother, Cornelius Jeremiah, who had been cut off with $200,000, and two of his eight sisters, who had received only from $300,000 to $500,000 apiece. The bulk of the estate was left to William. The decision of the surrogate in his favor in March 1879 was followed by a secret compromise (*New York Tribune,* Apr. 8, 9, 1879). It was reported that William in settlement had given each of the eight sisters another half million in bonds, and had pacified Cornelius Jeremiah by guaranteeing to him the income from a million dollars.

It was at his insistence that his father had bought control of the Lake Shore & Michigan Southern Railway and the Michigan Central Railroad, and acquired considerable stock in the Canada Southern Railway. William now welded the last-named line into the New York Central network, combining it with the Michigan Central, and became president of all the affiliated corporations. Within three years he had bought control of the Chicago & North-Western Railway and a large interest in the Cleveland, Columbus, Cincinnati & Indianapolis Railway, which paved the way for the later entry of the Vanderbilt lines into Cincinnati and St. Louis. Controlling interest in the rival New York, Chicago & St. Louis Railway (Nickel Plate), opened in 1882, was acquired after that date by the Lake Shore & Michigan Southern. The former road was forced into the hands of receivers in 1885, sold at foreclosure in 1887, and reorganized by the Vanderbilt interests. In 1885 the New York,

West Shore & Buffalo Railway (West Shore), paralleling the line of the New York Central & Hudson River, was leased by Vanderbilt at the instance of J. Pierpont Morgan [q.v.]. When the New York Central trainmen and laborers refused to take part in the great railroad strike of 1877, despite a cut in their wages, Vanderbilt distributed $100,000 among them as reward for their loyalty (New York Tribune, Aug. 1, 1877). Like his father, he was constructive. He not only greatly improved the railroad lines under his domination, but enormously increased his own fortune.

Following the report on rate discrimination made in 1879 by the committee headed by A. Barton Hepburn [q.v.], Vanderbilt, recognizing the unpopularity of unified control, turned over to J. Pierpont Morgan 250,000 shares of his railroad stock for sale in Europe, in order to avoid depressing the American market (New York Tribune, Nov. 21, 27, 1879). The sale, which greatly increased the prestige of Morgan and relieved Vanderbilt, also brought much foreign capital into American business. For several years Vanderbilt was a large shareholder and a director of the Western Union Telegraph Company; but in March 1881 he resigned his directorate and sold most of his holdings in the company (Ibid., Mar. 27, 1881). Probably warned by failing health, he resigned all his railroad presidencies in May 1883. Thereafter, he ordered, Vanderbilts should be chairmen of the boards of directors, and the presidents be practical, working executives of somewhat less power. His two older sons, Cornelius and William Kissam [qq.v.] were thereupon elected board chairmen of the various Vanderbilt lines.

Soon after his father's death, Vanderbilt erected a mansion on Fifth Avenue which was the talk of the nation, and acquired a gallery of paintings, not to mention sculpture and other items, which was declared to be the finest private collection then in existence. Nevertheless, he remained temperate and simple in personal habits to the end. His sons and daughters were all brought up in the same tradition. He was fond of horses and driving, as his father had been, and was often seen on suburban roads handling the reins of a pair of fast trotters. He was the owner of several racing horses. He made many benefactions during his lifetime. He gave $450,-000 all told to Vanderbilt University, Nashville, Tenn., $50,000 to St. Bartholomew's Episcopal Church, and, in 1884, $500,000 for new buildings to the College of Physicians and Surgeons. When the Khedive of Egypt presented an ancient obelisk to the United States, Vanderbilt paid the expense of c. $100,000 for removing it from Egypt and setting it in Central Park, New York (New York Tribune, July 21, 1880). In 1884 he insisted upon returning to Mrs. Ulysses S. Grant the deeds to certain real-estate parcels, her husband's swords, medals, works of art, and gifts from foreign governments, all forced by the General upon Vanderbilt in pledge for a loan of $150,000 which he was unable to repay.

It was believed that during the less than nine years of his sole power, William Henry Vanderbilt had nearly or quite doubled the fortune left him by his father. When he died suddenly of cerebral hemorrhage in New York in 1885, it was found that he had bequeathed $10,000,000, half outright and half in trust, to each of his eight children, Cornelius, William K., Frederick W., George W., Mrs. Elliott F. Shepherd, Mrs. William D. Sloane, Mrs. W. Seward Webb, and Mrs. H. McK. Twombly; most of them had already been given mansions. To his eldest son, Cornelius, he gave $2,000,000 more, and $1,-000,000 conditionally to the latter's eldest son, also named Cornelius. More than a million was distributed among various missions, churches, hospitals, the Y. M. C. A., the Metropolitan Museum of Art, and Vanderbilt University. The residue of the fortune was divided between the two eldest sons, Cornelius and William K., subject to the payment of a $200,000 annuity to his widow. To her also he left his home and objects of art; after her death these were to pass to the son George. He had provided elsewhere for the rebuilding of the little Moravian Church at New Dorp, Staten Island, where his father and mother had been parishioners and where he and all his brothers and sisters were christened; and in the cemetery adjoining he had erected a magnificent family mausoleum.

[W. A. Croffut, The Vanderbilts and the Story of Their Fortune (1886), with reprint of will; Earl Shinn (Edward Strahan), Mr. Vanderbilt's House and Collection (4 vols., 1883–84); also article on the house in American Architect and Building News, May 21, 1881; I. K. Morris, Morris's Memorial History of Staten Island New York (1898), vol. II; "The Vanderbilt Family of New York," a scrapbook of clippings from the N. Y. Evening Post, N. Y. Pub. Lib.; scrapbook of clippings on the Cornelius Vanderbilt will, 1877–78, N. Y. Pub. Lib.; obituaries in N. Y. Herald, N. Y. Tribune (two pages), Dec. 9, 1885; N. Y. Herald, Dec. 9, 1900, long article with family tree. See also Gustavus Myers, History of the Great American Fortunes (1910), vol. II; John Moody, The Railroad Builders (1919); Matthew Josephson, The Robber Barons (1934); A. D. H. Smith, Cornelius Vanderbilt (1927); and other works cited in the bibliography of his father.]
A. F. H.

VANDERBILT, WILLIAM KISSAM (Dec. 12, 1849–July 22, 1920), capitalist, sportsman, second son of William Henry [q.v.] and Maria Louisa (Kissam) Vanderbilt and grandson of "Commodore" Cornelius Vanderbilt [*q.v.*], was born on his father's farm on Staten Island, N. Y. He was a brother of Cornelius (1843–1899) and George Washington Vanderbilt [*qq.v.*]. He studied under private tutors for several years, and then was sent for a time to school in Geneva, Switzerland. At nineteen, however, he was set to work in the office of the Hudson River Railroad, of which his grandfather was president and principal owner. He worked his way upward in the railroad offices until in 1877 he was made second vice-president of the New York Central & Hudson River Railroad, in which place he served for six years. In 1883 his father resigned his railroad presidencies, and William Kissam was elected chairman of the board of directors of the Lake Shore & Michigan Southern Railway; he was president (1882–87) of the New York, Chicago & St. Louis Railway, and became chairman of the board in 1887. After the death of his father in 1885, he and his brother Cornelius were the chief managers of the family fortune and investments. As a director in the Vanderbilt railroads and other corporations he served diligently and efficiently, though he was never as fond of business as his brother Cornelius. The latter's partial disablement in 1896 and death in 1899 brought William more actively into the executive work of the Vanderbilt railroads. But the management of such vast properties was irksome to him, and in 1903 he voluntarily permitted the direction of the New York Central system (now comprising nearly 12,000 miles of track) to pass to what was described as the Rockefeller-Morgan-Pennsylvania combination (*New York Tribune,* Mar. 25, 1903). The Vanderbilts were large owners of Pennsylvania Railroad stock, and continued to be dominant in the ownership of the New York Central lines, but thereafter the executive direction was in other hands. Vanderbilt continued, however, as a board member of many railroads until his death, and materially aided in increasing the size of the Vanderbilt fortune.

An enthusiastic yachtsman, he was one of the syndicate which built and sailed the *Defender,* the successful holder of the *America's* cup against a British challenge in 1895 (H. L. Stone, *The America's Cup Races,* 1930). He owned many race horses, being a particularly important figure on the turf in France. He was active in the affairs of the Metropolitan Opera Company and in theatrical matters. He joined with his brothers in founding the Vanderbilt Clinic, and made gifts to the Y. M. C. A. and to Columbia University. During the World War he took an active interest in hospital work and aviation, and contributed towards the relief of war sufferers in Italy. His interest in and benefactions to the Lafayette Escadrille resulted in his being elected honorary president of that organization, and being decorated with the Cross of the Legion of Honor by the French government (*New York Times,* July 23, 1920). He collected a large gallery of fine paintings, which he bequeathed to the Metropolitan Museum of Art. He died in Paris. He married Alva Murray Smith of Mobile, Ala., on Apr. 20, 1875. It is said that in the eighties she fully established the social position of the family, who had hitherto been frowned on by the Astors and Ward McAllister. She divorced Vanderbilt on Mar. 5, 1895, and later married Oliver H. P. Belmont (*New York Tribune,* Mar. 6, 1895, Jan. 12, 1896). Vanderbilt on Apr. 25, 1903, married Mrs. Anna (Harriman) Sands Rutherfurd, daughter of Oliver Harriman (*Ibid.,* Apr. 23, 26, 30, 1903). He left three children, all by his first wife: William K., Jr., Harold S., and Consuelo, who married the Duke of Marlborough.

[R. N. Burnett, "William Kissam Vanderbilt," *Cosmopolitan,* Mar. 1904; B. J. Hendrick, "The Vanderbilt Fortune," in *McClure's Magazine,* Nov. 1908; J. V. Van Pelt, *A Monograph of the William K. Vanderbilt House* (1925); *Who's Who in America,* 1920–21; certificate of first marriage, Dept. of Health, City of N. Y., Borough of Manhattan; obituaries in *N. Y. Times, N. Y. Tribune,* July 23, 1920. See also bibliographies of the other Vanderbilts.]   A. F. H.

VANDERBURGH, WILLIAM HENRY (*c.* 1798–Oct. 14, 1832), fur trader, was born in Vincennes, Ind., one of the nine children of Henry and Frances (Cornoyer) Vanderburgh. His father, who was a captain in the 5th New York Regiment during the Revolution, moved after the war to Vincennes, where he married and was appointed a judge of the supreme court of Indiana Territory in 1800. William Henry entered the United States Military Academy in 1813, but did not graduate. He soon went West, and in a few years established a reputation as a fur trader with the Missouri Fur Company. During the Leavenworth expedition to the upper Missouri in 1823, as captain of the Missouri Fur Company's volunteers he participated on Aug. 10 in the demonstration against the villages of the Arikaras (*South Dakota Historical Collections,* vol. I, 1902, pp. 196 ff.), made in retaliation for the earlier attack of these Indians upon the trading party led by Gen. William H. Ashley [*q.v.*]. Sometime afterward he left the Missouri Fur Company and became a partner in the powerful American Fur Company, a concern ambitious to gain complete control of the Northwestern fur business.

Vanderburgh soon won the confidence of the company's management, particularly that of Kenneth MacKenzie [q.v.], the autocratic factor of the field headquarters at Fort Union, at the mouth of the Yellowstone. MacKenzie put him in charge of the Rocky Mountain trappers, and his subsequent operations greatly aided the company in eventually achieving its coveted monopoly. Entering the bitter competition for the mountain trade, Vanderburgh proved an indefatigable leader against the partisans of the Rocky Mountain Fur Company, headed by such experienced frontiersmen as James Bridger and Thomas Fitzpatrick [qq.v.]. With his parties he penetrated to the heart of the mountains in 1829–30, suffering great hardships, and on one occasion (1830) fighting a battle with the Blackfoot Indians.

In 1832 he went with his followers to the summer rendezvous of the mountain men at Pierre's Hole, where the employees of companies and the free trappers alike congregated. So successful had he already been in trailing them to some of their best trapping grounds, that Bridger and Fitzpatrick here proposed to him to divide the territory, but Vanderburgh refused. On leaving Pierre's Hole they therefore led him a wild-goose chase. He followed them toward the Three Forks of the Missouri, thus coming unaware into the territory of the hostile Blackfoot. On Oct. 14, 1832, with an advance party of six of his men, he was ambushed by about a hundred Blackfoot warriors on an affluent of the Jefferson River. He and one of his followers, Alexis Pillon, were killed. The remainder of the party retreated, but encountered a company of friendly Flathead and Pend d'Oreille Indians with whom they returned to bury the mutilated body of their unfortunate chief. Able, chivalrous, and energetic, "bearing himself always with the air and quality of a leader" (Chittenden, *post*, II, 665), Vanderburgh was one of the outstanding figures in that group of hardy adventurers who made the fur-trading epoch of the early Northwest one of the most colorful in American history.

[H. M. Chittenden, *The Am. Fur Trade of the Far West* (2 vols., 1902); Doane Robinson, "Official Correspondence of the Leavenworth Expedition into South Dakota in 1823," *S. Dak. Hist. Colls.*, vol. I (1902); geneal. data from Hazel Whiteleather, Ind. State Lib., Indianapolis.]   J. M. H.

VAN DER DONCK, ADRIAEN (May 7, 1620–c. 1655), colonist, lawyer, was born in the city of Breda in the province of North Brabant. His parents were Cornelis van der Donck and Agatha, daughter of Adriaen van Bergen, a member of a party of Dutch patriots which recovered the castle of Breda from the Spanish in 1590. Van der Donck received his early education in his native city, and about 1638 entered the University of Leyden, where he studied law. Seeking employment, he was brought to the attention of Kiliaen van Rensselaer, patroon of Rensselaerswyck in New Netherland, who was looking for a *schout,* or officer of justice, for his manor. Satisfied of the young man's fitness, Van Rensselaer engaged him; he was commissioned *schout,* May 13, 1641, and arrived at his new post in August of that year. He was given the lease of the farm called "Welys Burg" on Castle Island.

As *schout* he served as sheriff or officer of justice and was in charge of the collection of debts due the patroon from the tenants. Though aristocratic by birth and training, he showed considerable sympathy with the farmers of Rensselaerswyck, declining to press them when they had difficulty in meeting their obligations. In consequence he was accused of laxity in caring for his employer's interests. Van Rensselaer seems also to have expected Van der Donck to exercise a guiding influence over young Arent van Curler [q.v.], the Patroon's grand-nephew, who was *commis* or business agent of the manor. Since the two young men were almost of an age, this situation bred ill feeling which soon grew into enmity. Van Curler complained to the Patroon; the Patroon forbade Van der Donck to carry out a scheme for establishing a colony at Katskill; and during the confused state of affairs following the death of Van Rensselaer in 1643 or 1644, Van der Donck's service as *schout* came to an end. He remained upon his farm at Castle Island, however, until his buildings were destroyed by fire in 1646. Meanwhile, in the summer of 1645 he successfully negotiated a treaty between the Dutch and the Mohawk Indians, and for this service, he was given permission to establish a colony, "Colen Donck," at Nepperhaen on the left bank of the Hudson, opposite the Palisades. Van der Donck was known as the "Jonker" (about the equivalent of esquire), and from this title the settlement on his land derived its present name of Yonkers.

In February 1649, Van der Donck was made secretary of the Board of Nine Men under Petrus Stuyvesant [q.v.]. In this capacity he wrote the famous "Remonstrance" (*Vertoogh van Nieu-Neder-Land,* 1650), setting forth the people's grievances, and he was one of the three sent to The Hague to present it to the States-General. His connection with this act gained him the enmity of Stuyvesant and his secretary Van Tienhoven, who tried in various ways to embarrass him at The Hague. While detained in the Netherlands by the government he finished his legal course at Leyden, received a degree, *Supremus in jure*, Apr. 10, 1653, and was admitted to practice as an advocate before the supreme court of the Netherlands.

During this time he was engaged in writing an account of New Netherland, which was officially recommended to the States-General in May 1653, and in July he was granted a fifteen-year copyright on his work. He had been authorized to prepare a history, but Stuyvesant had refused him access to the official records. Thus his book, *Beschrijvinge van Nieuvv Nederlant*, is, as its title indicates, a description rather than a narrative. It was first published in 1655 at Amsterdam and reprinted in 1656. Van der Donck returned to America late in 1653 with permission to give legal advice, but not to appear before the courts of New Netherland, since there was no lawyer in the colony able to meet him. He died before the end of 1655. In 1645 he had married Mary Doughty, daughter of Francis Doughty, an English minister of New Amsterdam. After his death, his widow married Hugh O'Neale of Maryland.

[E. B. O'Callaghan, *Docs. Rel. to the Col. Hist. . . . of N. Y.*, vols. I, II (1856, 1858); A. J. F. van Laer, *Minutes of the Court of Rensselaerswyck, 1648–1652* (1922), and *N. Y. State Lib.: Van Rensselaer Bowier MSS.* (1908); P. C. Molhuysen, *Bronnen Tot de Geschiedenis der Leidsche Univ.*, III (1918), 70; E. B. O'Callaghan, *Hist. of New Netherland* (2 vols., 1846); J. R. Brodhead, *Hist. of the State of N. Y.* (2 vols., 1846); J. T. Scharf, *Hist. of Westchester County, N. Y.* (1886), I, 66–71.]   E. L. W. H.

VANDERGRIFT, JACOB JAY (Apr. 10, 1827–Dec. 26, 1899), river captain, pioneer oil producer, was born in Allegheny, Pa., the son of William and Sophia (Sarver) Vandergrift. He attended private and public schools in Pittsburgh but was thrown on his own resources at an early age and became a cabin boy successively on the river steamboats *Bridgewater* and *Pinta*. Employed subsequently on boats plying the Allegheny River, he attracted the attention of his employers because of his industry and energy, and advanced rapidly. He was the first captain with sufficient courage and determination to utilize the space in front of his boat as well as on the sides in towing barges. Prior to 1853 he was in command of the *Hail Columbia,* one of the finest steamboats on the Wabash River. By 1858 he had purchased part interest in the *Red Fox* and in the *Conestoga*.

Just before the Civil War he went to what is now West Virginia, attracted by newspaper accounts of the oil wells there. The outbreak of the war forced him to sacrifice his investments and leave the state. Going to Oil City, Pa., then little more than a wilderness, he became a shipper of oil, and later a dealer, making much money through his transactions. About 1868 he formed a partnership with George V. Forman, under the firm name of Vandergrift, Forman & Company, and entered upon extensive operations, laying miles of pipes for facilitating oil transportation from wells to shipping depots. In 1872 John Pitcairn [*q.v.*] joined the firm, which about that time established the Imperial Refinery, having a daily capacity of two thousand barrels. Although not the builder of the first pipe line, Vandergrift is said to have been the first to make a pipe line profitable. In 1877 the "United Pipe Lines of Vandergrift, Forman & Company" were consolidated with others as "United Pipe Lines," which, in turn, in 1884 was merged into the National Transit Company. Vandergrift and his partner Pitcairn also laid what was probably the first natural gas line of any importance and demonstrated to the manufacturing world the value of gas. Vandergrift subsequently formed gas companies in neighboring West Virginia. In addition to founding the Pittsburgh Petroleum Exchange and the Seaboard National Bank of New York, he was interested in iron and steel production and built the town of Vandergrift, Pa., as a model dwelling place for the employees of his Apollo Iron and Steel Company. He was also a large investor in Pittsburgh real estate, and made his home in that city after 1881.

From his ample fortune he built an orphan home there and aided churches and hospitals. He was twice married: first, Dec. 29, 1853, to Henrietta Morrow of Pittsburgh, who bore him four daughters and five sons; she died in 1881, and on Dec. 4, 1883, he married Frances G. (Anshutz) Hartley. On the morning of the day of his death he went to his office and worked until noon as was his custom. He was buried in Allegheny Cemetery, Pittsburgh.

[Erasmus Wilson, *Standard Hist. of Pittsburgh* (1898); *The Biog. Encyc. of Pa.* (1874); *Encyc. of Contemporary Biog. of Pa.*, vol. I (1889); G. I. Reed and others, *Century Cyc. of Hist. and Biog. of Pa.* (1904, vol. II); *Pittsburg Dispatch*, Dec. 27, 1899.]   A. I.

VANDERGRIFT, MARGARET [See Janvier, Margaret Thomson, 1844–1913].

VAN DER KEMP, FRANCIS ADRIAN (May 4, 1752–Sept. 7, 1829), scholar, author, was born in Kampen, Overyssel, in the Netherlands, the son of John Van der Kemp, an army captain, and his wife, Anna Catharina (Leydekker). For several years he was a cadet in an infantry regiment and at the same time cultivated the classical languages. In September 1770 he entered Groningen University, where he devoted himself to linguistic and philosophical studies. At the end of three years he left the institution because his deistical ideas (*Autobiography*, p. 13) and his attachment to a celebrated teacher who was charged with Arminianism made his presence intolerable. He next became a student in a Baptist seminary at Amsterdam, where he engaged in an examination of the Christian religion (*Ibid.*, pp. 18–20), giving his attention to the New Testament apart from dogmatic theology. Satisfied of the truth of the Gospel, he was admitted as candidate for the ministry on Dec. 18, 1775. The following year, Nov. 13, he was installed pastor at Leyden. Disputes with his consistory, principally over a demand for his subscription to a creed, ended in victories for the young preacher.

A burning interest in political agitation earned for Van der Kemp the friendship of the leaders in the Patriot movement, which sought to reduce the power of the Stadtholder and to restrain the House of Orange within constitutional limits. In behalf of this movement he wrote books and pamphlets, often anonymously. When, to shield the printer, he announced his responsibility for a certain publication, he was involved in criminal procedures, which dragged along a year or two and ceased in 1782 with his acquittal. In 1775 the Patriot party found itself in natural sympathy with the American colonies in the uprisings which led to independence, and Van der Kemp publicly advocated the principles which were the foundation of the American cause. With John Adams, who appeared in Amsterdam as American commissioner in the summer of 1780, he formed a friendship to which a correspondence of many years bears witness.

As the political struggle in Holland verged on civil war, the Mennonist pastor became captain of a militia company, withdrawing from the charge of his peaceful congregation. In the first clash of opposing forces, the court party was victor and Van der Kemp was taken prisoner. When, in 1787, the wife of the Stadtholder, a Prussian princess, maneuvered successfully to bring a Prussian army to Amsterdam, only banishment remained for prominent Patriots. Accordingly, the following year Van der Kemp sailed with his family for New York, arriving May 4. The exile's reception by eminent Americans included an invitation to the hospitality of Mount Vernon (Jared Sparks, *The Writings of George Washington*, vol. IX, 1847, pp. 368–69). After six years devoted to experimental agriculture near Kingston, N. Y., he established a home by Oneida Lake on a tract which he named Kempwyk, near Bernhard's Bay. Here he entered on a life which, if not idyllic, had consolations for ill fortune. He was appointed a justice of the peace, and he organized a society of agriculture and natural history. His impaired fortunes, however, compelled him to seek a new home, and his final residence was in Olden Barneveld (the present Barneveld). Farming, correspondence, discursive studies, and literary work filled up his remaining years. At the solicitation of Gov. DeWitt Clinton, he translated the Dutch colonial records of New York. The resulting twenty-four manuscript volumes were burned in the fire that destroyed the capitol in 1911. Some examples of his miscellaneous writings in Dutch are in American libraries. He was married, May 20, 1782, to Reinira Engelberta Johanna Vos; three children were born to them. In 1903 *Francis Adrian Van der Kemp, 1752–1829: An Autobiography*, with a historical sketch, was published by Helen L. Fairchild.

[The *Autobiog.* contains lists of Van der Kemp's writings in Dutch and English; see also DeWitt Clinton, *Letters on the Natural Hist. and Internal Resources of ... N. Y.* (1822), pp. 216–19; C. F. Adams, *The Works of John Adams* (10 vols., 1850–56); Crisfield Johnson, *Hist. of Oswego County, N. Y.* (1877); J. C. Churchill, *Landmarks of Oswego County, N. Y.* (1895); *Hist. of Oneida County, N. Y.* (1878).]

R. E. D.

VANDERLYN, JOHN (Oct. 15, 1775–Sept. 23, 1852), historical and portrait painter, was born in Kingston, N. Y., the son of Nicholas and Sarah (Tappen) Vanderlyn, and the grandson of Pieter Vander Lyn (1687–1778), a New York painter of the descendants of early Dutch families in Manhattan (see C. X. Harris, "Pieter Vanderlyn," *New York Historical Society Quarterly Bulletin*, Oct. 1921). John was sent to the Kingston Academy, where he remained until he was sixteen. When not busy at school he worked in the shop of a blacksmith and wagon painter, and, according to Tuckerman's picturesque but uncertain account, it was there that he was met by Aaron Burr [*q.v.*], who became his chief patron. In 1792 John was taken to New York by his brother Nicholas and introduced to Thomas Barrow, a print-seller, in whose shop he worked for about two years. His first lessons in drawing were taken under Archibald Robertson [*q.v.*], with whom he studied three years. He painted a few portraits in Kingston, where he returned for a winter, and a few more in New York, and was allowed to copy some of the portraits of Gilbert Stuart [*q.v.*]. His copy of Stuart's portrait of Aaron Burr was so well done that Burr sent him to Philadelphia to study under Stuart for eight or nine months, employed him on his return to paint his portrait and that of his daughter, Theodosia, and in the autumn of 1796 supplied him with means for a five years' stay in Paris. There he studied under "Mr. Vincent, an eminent painter" (possibly Antoine Paul Vincent). In 1801 he returned to America, and in 1802 painted two pictures of Niagara Falls which were engraved and published in London in 1804.

In the spring of 1803 he returned to Europe. He spent two years in Paris (1803–05), two in Rome (1805–07), where he met and became an intimate friend of Washington Allston [q.v.], and then seven more in Paris (1808–15), traveling widely at intervals. In the second year at Rome he painted his "Marius amid the Ruins of Carthage," which made a great stir. In 1808, at the Paris Salon, it received a gold medal conferred at the behest of Napoleon. It was this success that led the artist to make a stay of seven years in Paris, where he prospered. He made copies after the masterpieces of Raphael, Titian, and Correggio in the Louvre; in 1812 his nude figure, "Ariadne," made a still greater sensation than the "Marius." It was the last of his notable achievements. It was bought and engraved by Asher B. Durand [q.v.], and finally came into the possession of the Pennsylvania Academy of the Fine Arts.

After his return to New York in 1815 Vanderlyn's popularity gradually waned. He painted a number of portraits of eminent men, including four presidents (Monroe, Madison, Jackson, and Taylor), John C. Calhoun, Burr, George Clinton, and Robert R. Livingston. The portrait of Zachary Taylor belongs to the Corcoran Gallery of Art, Washington; those of John A. Sidell, Francis L. Waddell, and a self-portrait are in the Metropolitan Museum, New York; several others are owned by the New York Historical Society. An enmity grew up between Vanderlyn and John Trumbull [q.v.] over the paintings for the rotunda of the Capitol (see Isham, post, p. 130), but in 1832 the House of Representatives commissioned Vanderlyn to make a full-length copy of Stuart's Washington. In 1837 he was one of four painters invited to undertake paintings in the rotunda. Going to Paris to paint his "The Landing of Columbus" under this commission, he employed a French artist to assist him, a procedure in which there was nothing unusual. Hostile critics made the most of it, however, and charged him with fraud.

His last years were tragic and embittered. For some twelve years his large panoramas of Paris, Versailles, Athens, and Mexico were exhibited in the New York Rotunda, built for this purpose, in the City Hall Park, New York, but

they were costly failures. His affairs went from bad to worse. Worry and poverty crushed his spirit. Finally, in 1852, he reappeared in his native town and borrowed a shilling from an old friend to pay for the transportation of his baggage to the hotel. The following morning he was found dead in his room. He was unmarried. An imposing funeral was given him by the townspeople. His early work is his best, but the "Marius" was vastly overrated and the "Ariadne" is not much more than an accomplished academic study of the nude. Later he leaned too much upon the old Italian masters and thus lost touch with nature; the big historical panel in the Capitol is a typically meretricious example of the so-called grand style. His portraits were somewhat uneven, and only a few of them have any distinction aside from their merits as likenesses.

[There are many references to Vanderlyn in the letters and journals of Aaron Burr. See also Marius Schoonmaker, *The Hist. of Kingston, N. Y.* (1888); William Dunlap, *The Hist. of the Rise and Progress of the Arts of Design in the U. S.* (1918), ed. by F. W. Bayley and C. E. Goodspeed; H. T. Tuckerman, *Book of the Artists* (1867); W. J. Kip, in *Atlantic Monthly*, Feb. 1867; *Putnam's Monthly*, June 1854; C. H. Caffin, *The Story of Am. Painting* (1907); Samuel Isham, *The Hist. of Am. Painting* (1905); Suzanne La Follette, *Art in America* (1929); J. E. Stillwell, *The Hist. of the Burr Portraits* (1928); *Description of the Panorama of the Palace and Gardens of Versailles* (1820); obituaries in *Ulster Republican* (Kingston, N. Y.), and *Rondout Courier* (Kingston), Oct. 1, 1852; inscription on monument in Wiltwyck Cemetery, Kingston, N. Y.]   W. H. D.

VAN DER STUCKEN, FRANK VALENTIN (Oct. 15, 1858–Aug. 16, 1929), composer, conductor, was born in Fredericksburg, Gillespie County, Tex. He was the son of Jan Frank and Sophia (Schoenewolf) Van der Stucken. His father was of Belgian and his mother of German birth, and after the Civil War the family went to Belgium to live. The lad's musical education was started as soon as he reached Europe, and he was first entered at the Conservatory of Music in Antwerp, where he became a pupil of Pierre Benoît. From 1866 to 1876 he studied violin with Émile Wambach in Brussels, and for the following two years he was a pupil of Reinecke, Grieg, and Langer in Leipzig. By the time he was twenty years of age, he had shown much promise as a composer, and had produced his "Gloria," for chorus and orchestra; his "Te Deum," for solo, chorus and orchestra; and a "Festmarsch" for orchestra. In the season 1881–82, he was *Kapellmeister* for the Stadt Theatre in Breslau. At Breslau he composed his suite on Shakespeare's "Tempest" (1885), "Festzug" (1891), "Pagina d'Amore" (copyright 1891), and a lyric drama, "Vlasda" (copyright 1891). Franz Liszt invited him to Weimar in 1883 to give a concert of his own works under Liszt's patronage. This event occurred in November, and the program included a symphonic prologue to Heine's tragedy, "William Ratcliff."

Van der Stucken's reputation had already extended to the land of his birth, and in 1884 he was invited to succeed Leopold Damrosch [q.v.] as the conductor of the Arion Society, a male chorus in New York City. He held this position until 1895, and in 1892 took the organization on a European tour. Meanwhile, he appeared frequently as an orchestral conductor. During the season 1885–86, he presented a series of "novelty concerts" at Steinway Hall, where he gave the American premiere of Brahm's Third Symphony. Two years later, 1887–88, he gave a series of "symphonic concerts" at Chickering Hall in New York. It was in these concerts that he adopted a policy for which he is perhaps most remembered, the inclusion of a number of "all-American" programs, presenting exclusively the works of American musicians. He was certainly one of the first to offer such programs, and for this he won the undying gratitude of those who urged the cause of American music. In 1889 he gave a program of American compositions at the French International Exhibition. Throughout his whole life he fought for the recognition of American talent at home and abroad.

He was much in demand as a conductor of music festivals. In 1887 he directed a festival in Indianapolis; in 1891, one in Newark; in 1894, another in New York. He left New York in 1895 to live in Cincinnati, Ohio, where he had been offered the conductorship of the Cincinnati Symphony Orchestra and a position as director of the Cincinnati Conservatory of Music. He retained the directorship of the College until 1903, and was conductor of the Cincinnati orchestra until 1907. After the death of Theodore Thomas [q.v.], Van der Stucken was appointed conductor of the Cincinnati May Music Festivals, which he directed regularly from 1906 until 1912. From 1908 he lived mostly in Europe, returning to America for the Cincinnati Festivals (1923, 1925, 1927), and for other events that demanded his attention. He appeared frequently abroad as conductor of the Wagner festival at Antwerp in 1913; in a concert of orchestral works at Copenhagen, 1919; as conductor of a series of Wagner and Gluck concerts in Antwerp during the season 1920–21; and as director of the Ysaye concerts in Brussels, 1921 and 1923. He was decorated with the Order of Leopold and made an Officier de l'Ordre de la Couronne by the king of Belgium. He died in Hamburg, Germany, following a surgical operation, and was survived by his wife, Mary

Vollmer, to whom he had been married in June 1880, and four children. As a composer, Van der Stucken had a fine talent for orchestration; his scores sparkle with subtle effects. His music is seldom heard today, but in his own time it was highly praised. Rupert Hughes said of his songs: "It is always the unexpected that happens, though this unexpected thing almost always proves to be a right thing. Without any sense of strain or bombast he reaches superb climaxes; without eccentricity he is individual . . ." (*American Composers, post,* p. 193). In addition to the works already mentioned, his compositions included "Pax Triumphans" (1902), a symphonic prologue first presented at the Brooklyn, N. Y., Festival in 1900; a festival march, "Louisiana"; a "Festival Hymn" for men's chorus and orchestra; and many shorter works for orchestra, chorus and for solo voice.

[*Who's Who in America,* 1928–29; Henry Hadley, commemorative address on Van der Stucken, published by the American Academy of Arts and Letters, *Acad. Publication,* no. 77 (1932); *Grove's Dict. of Music and Musicians,* 3rd ed., vol. V (1928), and the *Am. Supp.* (1930); *Baker's Biog. Dict. of Musicians* (3rd ed., 1919); Rupert Hughes and Arthur Nelson, *Am. Composers* (revised ed., 1914); J. T. Howard, *Our Am. Music* (1931); *Musical Courier,* Aug. 24, 1929; Olin Downes, "An American Pioneer," *N. Y. Times,* Aug. 25, 1929; *N. Y. Times,* Aug. 20, 21, 1929.]   J.T.H.

VANDER VEER, ALBERT (July 10, 1841– Dec. 19, 1929), surgeon, was born in Root, Montgomery County, N. Y., the son of Abram Harris and Sarah (Martin) Vander Veer. His parents were both descendants of early Dutch settlers, the Vander Veers going back to Cornelis Janse Vander Veer who settled in Long Island in 1659. Vander Veer attended the union schools of Palatine, N. Y., and Canojoharie Academy. At the age of eighteen he began his medical studies under Dr. Simeon Snow. In 1861–62 he studied in Albany under Dr. John Swinburne, a surgeon, and attended lectures at the Albany Medical College (later part of Union University). Leaving Albany in 1862 to enlist in the army, he had the distinction of being one of the original hundred commissioned as United States medical cadets. When he was mustered out of service in 1865, he was a surgeon with the rank of major. During the Civil War he was stationed in Washington, D. C., at the hospital of Columbian College (later George Washington University), and there in 1863 he received the degree of M.D. After the war he spent a short time studying at the College of Physicians and Surgeons, New York City.

He returned to Albany in 1866 and on June 5, 1867, married Margaret E. Snow, the daughter of his former teacher, by whom he had six children. His long association with Albany Medical

College began in 1869. He taught anatomy (1869–74), surgery (1876–1914), and served as dean (1897–1904). In 1914 he became professor emeritus of surgery, and in 1915 resigned. In 1874–76 he studied in London, Paris, and Berlin. He was for many years attending surgeon of Albany Hospital (1869–1904) and in 1904 became surgeon in chief. In Albany he was the first to take up the practice of abdominal surgery, and was considered one of the city's most eminent surgeons. He received honorary degrees from several institutions of learning and held office in many societies. He was president of the American Medical Association (1916), the American Surgical Association (1905), the American Association of Obstetricians and Gynecologists, the Medical Society of the State of New York (1885), and the Holland Society of New York (1904). He was decorated with the order of Orange-Nassau by the queen of Holland. He was vice-president of the Albany Institute of Art for thirty years and regent of the University of the State of New York from 1895 to 1927, serving also as vice chancellor (1915–21) and chancellor (1921–22). Forceful and energetic, he devoted himself earnestly to his hospital work, to his practice, and to the societies of which he was a member. Yet he seemed to find time to read extensively and to contribute widely to medical periodicals. In the later years of his life he spent much of his time at his Adirondacks camp, where he farmed on a small scale. A religious man, he was elder of the First Presbyterian Church, Albany, for over forty years. He was survived by three sons, all physicians.

[L. P. De Boer, *The Van der Veer Family* (1913); J. J. Vander Veer, *A Geneal. of . . . the Vander Veer Family in America* (1912); *Who's Who in America*, 1928–29; J. J. Walsh, *Hist. of Medicine in N. Y.* (1919); A. V. Raymond, *Union Univ., Its Hist.* (1907); *Annals of Surgery*, Dec. 1930; F. C. Curtis, in *Albany Medic. Annals*, "Alumni Meeting Number," vol. XL (1930); *Jour. Am. Medic. Asso.*, Dec. 28, 1929; *Trans. Am. Surgical Asso.*, vol. XLVIII (1930); *Surgery, Gynecology, and Obstetrics*, Jan. 1932; obituary in *Knickerbocker Press* (Albany), Dec. 20, 1929; bibliog. of Vander Veer's publications, in *Index-Cat. of the Lib. of the Surgeon-General's Office*, 1 ser., vol. XV (1894), 2 ser., vol. XX (1915).]   G. L. A.

VANDER WEE, JOHN BAPTIST (Feb. 20, 1824–Feb. 24, 1900), known in religion as Brother Alexius, provincial of the Xaverian Brothers, was born in Antwerp, Belgium. Having received considerable schooling in his native city, in 1845 he joined the Congregation of the Brothers of St. Francis Xavier (Xaverian Brothers), the impoverished and somewhat unstable foundation for which Theodore Ryken (Brother Francis Xavier) had obtained a rule only four years previously. Two years later, Oct.

3, 1847, he was professed in the little community of seventeen members. Trained under Ryken in a martyr-like spirit of sacrifice, he became an ideal religious and one of a colony sent in 1848 to establish the first foreign foundation at Bury, England. On the verge of actual starvation, he was forced to remove the colony to Manchester in 1850, where he re-introduced into England May processions and the scapular of Mount Carmel. From this mother-house, the congregation later developed a number of thriving schools in the British Isles. Ill health forced Brother Alexius to return to Bruges, where in 1854 he reorganized St. Francis Xavier's Institute into a popular school for English youths. In 1863 he was in Manchester in charge of the Catholic Collegiate Institute, and in that city assisted in the establishment of an orphange at Mayfield founded by the Duchess of Leeds (the former Louisa Caton of Baltimore, Md.). Apparently his association with her turned his mind toward America, where the Xaverian Brothers had established themselves in Louisville, Ky., in 1854, and in Baltimore in 1866.

In 1872 he left for America, and three years later was named provincial of the Xaverian Brothers in the United States. The Society was desperately poor, its brothers receiving salaries of only $130 a year. It had a small community in Louisville; a few parochial schools; and in Baltimore, St. Mary's Industrial School, an orphanage and home for needy and often wayward boys. With indomitable will and the practice of the severest economies, Brother Alexius labored with remarkable success during twenty-five years of command, though never did he ascribe any credit to himself. With little episcopal assistance and few donations of any consequence, he managed to build, without leaving any indebtedness, Mount St. Joseph's College and Provincial House in Baltimore, St. Xavier's College in Louisville, St. John's Preparatory School in Danvers, Mass.—one of the largest Catholic institutions of its kind—and a college novitiate at Old Point Comfort, Va. He also answered episcopal or pastoral invitations to take over parochial schools or high schools in Lowell, Lawrence, Somerville, and Worcester, Mass.; in Norfolk and Portsmouth, Va.; and in Wheeling, W. Va. Under his régime, St. Mary's Industrial School in Baltimore became one of the largest protectories for boys in the United States and served as a model for Catholic and state institutions for boy training. A humble man, severe in self-discipline yet affable, Brother Alexius was notably successful as an administrator and business man, retaining full control of the community until his rather sudden death from pneumonia. At the end, there was no public funeral or eulogy, but his devoted counselor, Cardinal Gibbons, presided over his funeral before his remains were interred in the Bonnie Brae Cemetery of Baltimore.

[Brother Julian, C.F.X., *Men and Deeds, The Xaverian Brothers in America* (1930); *Mount St. Joseph Collegian*, 5 no. 10; MSS. and chronicles in the archives of Mount St. Joseph Coll.; *Sun* (Baltimore), Feb. 26, 1900; information from an associate, Brother Isidore, C.F.X.]   R. J. P.

VAN DE VELDE, JAMES OLIVER (Apr. 3, 1795–Nov. 13, 1855), Roman Catholic prelate, was born near Termonde, Belgium, of a family of some social and political importance. Schooled in the home of an aunt in Saint-Armand who sheltered a proscribed priest-tutor, the boy was later enrolled in a boarding school at Ghent. Thereafter he taught French and Flemish at Puers and at a college in Mechlin, where he also studied theology in the seminary. Aroused by a patriotic disgust at Belgium's domination by Holland in the forced union decreed by the Congress of Vienna, Van de Velde was studying English and Italian with the object of going either to England or to Italy, when Charles Nerinckx [*q.v.*], in quest of Belgian priests, induced him to accompany him back to America in 1817. At Georgetown College, the young Belgian entered the Society of Jesus, and both taught in the college and followed courses in theology. Ordained by Archbishop Ambrose Maréchal [*q.v.*] on Sept. 25, 1827, he served about four years as chaplain at the Visitation Convent and attended missions in Montgomery County, Md.

In 1831 he was ordered to St. Louis University, where he became vice-president (1833) and president (1840–43). Four years after taking his solemn vows, he represented the vice-province of Missouri in the congregation of procurators of the Society assembled at Rome (1841) and came to know Pope Gregory XVI. As vice-provincial of Missouri (1843–48), he erected several churches, fostered the Jesuit missions of the far West, built an enlarged novitiate for the growing Society, and represented the province at the Sixth Council of Baltimore (1846). In 1848, when he was procurator and socius to the vice-provincial, he was named successor to Bishop William Quarter [*q.v.*] of Chicago, with the command to accept the undesired honor. Consecrated by Archbishop Peter Richard Kenrick at St. Louis (Feb. 11, 1849), Van de Velde undertook the burden, which was aggravated by the apparent hostility of some Irish priests who wanted neither a Jesuit nor a Belgian ordinary, regardless of his decided merits and recognized character as a scholar and self-sacrificing priest. At Chicago his tenure was brief and unhappy, yet he succeeded in reviving religion in the old French settlements as an Irishman could not have done, dedicated several churches, and began seventy, several of which were for the recent German immigrants. His first petition to resign and return to his Society was refused by Rome. In 1852 the Council of Baltimore urged him to retain his see and honored him as its emissary to Rome with the decrees of the Council. Apparently Rome heard his plea, for a year later (July 29, 1853) he was transferred to the quiet diocese of Natchez, although for a time he carried the burden of the dioceses of Chicago and Quincy in addition to his own charge. At Natchez he founded two schools and had started a college when he died suddenly of yellow fever, which he incurred in attending the stricken.

[R. H. Clarke, *Lives of the Deceased Bishops of the Cath. Church in the U. S.*, vol. II (1888), pp. 372–90; J. G. Shea, *Hist. of the Cath. Church in the U. S.*, vol. IV (1892); Francis Janssens, *Sketch of the Cath. Church in Natchez, Miss.* (1886); G. J. Garraghan, *The Catholic Church in Chicago* (1921); J. E. Rothensteiner, *Hist. of the Archdiocese of St. Louis* (1928); *Metropolitan Cath. Almanac* (1856), p. 301; *Cath. Almanac* (1856); Woodstock Letters, vol. X, 1880, p. 121; *N. Y. Freeman's Journal*, Sept. 15, 1849, Nov. 24, Dec. 8, 1855; obituary in *Daily Democratic Press* (Chicago), Nov. 17, 1855.]   R. J. P.

VAN DE WARKER, EDWARD ELY (Nov. 27, 1841–Sept. 5, 1910), gynecologist, was born in West Troy (later Watervliet), N. Y., the son of Martin P. and Lydia Myra (Ely) Van de Warker. His great-grandfather was Martin Van de Warker, who served as a private in the Revolutionary War. His mother was the daughter of John Burgoyne Ely, a descendant of a family of Loyalist sympathies in the Revolution. Van de Warker was first sent to a private school; he later attended Rensselaer Polytechnic Institute, and in 1859 began the study of medicine at Albany Medical College (later part of Union University), where in 1863 he received the degree of M.D. In the same year he became assistant surgeon in the 162nd Regiment, New York Volunteers; later he was surgeon-in-chief, 3rd Brigade, 1st Division, XIX Army Corps, and post surgeon, Winchester, Va., on the staff of Gen. Francis Fessenden. At the close of the Civil War he had attained the rank of major. In 1865 he entered upon the practice of his profession in Troy, N. Y., and on Dec. 23 married Louisa Margaret Gardner of Hancock, Mass., who died in 1868. They had one daughter. Van de Warker moved to Syracuse in 1870 and was married a second time on Nov. 6, 1872, to Helen Augusta Adams of that city. Van de Warker became one of the leading physicians of Syracuse, attained eminence as a surgeon, and was a pioneer in gynecology. As an operator he had few peers. He won immediate recognition for his plastic surgery at the pelvic outlet; he was known to have performed 2,000 laparotomies with relatively few mortalities. He was considered expert in diagnosis as well. He founded and was for many years surgeon-in-chief of the Syracuse Hospital for Women and Children, and served as surgeon to the Central New York Hospital and as consulting surgeon to St. Anne's Maternity Hospital. A founder of the American Gynecological Society, he belonged to many other medical organizations. He acted as president of the Onondaga Medical Society (1878), of the Central New York Medical Association (1885), and of the Syracuse Academy of Medicine; he was chairman of the section of obstetrics, American Medical Association (1887).

A man of wide culture and varied knowledge, his genial temperament made him a delightful companion. He contributed numerous articles to the medical journals of his time, of which the most important were "Mechanical Therapeutics of Versions and Flexions of the Uterus" (*Transactions of the American Gynecological Society,* vol. VII, 1883); "A Gynecological Study of the Oneida Community" (*American Journal of Obstetrics,* Aug. 1884), and "Extra-Uterine Pregnancy and Its Treatment by Electricity" (*Transactions of the American Gynecological Society,* vol. XII, 1888). His interests were not entirely confined to medicine. He was also the author of *Woman's Unfitness for Higher Co-Education* (1903), "Abandoned Canals of the State of New York" (*Popular Science Monthly,* Sept. 1909), and "A Winter Vacation to the Windward Islands" (*Medical News,* Aug. 10, 17, Sept. 17, 1889). Van de Warker retired from active service in 1908 because of failing health and died two years later, survived by the daughter of his second marriage.

[Heman Ely, *Records of the Descendants of Nathaniel Ely* (1885); *Album of the Fellows of the Am. Gynecological Soc., 1876–1900* (1901); H. A. Kelly and W. L. Burrage, *Am. Medic. Biogs.* (1920); *Albany Medic. Annals,* Oct. 1910; *Trans. Am. Gynecological Soc.,* vol. XXXVI (1911); date of death and information concerning Van de Warker's parents from his daughter, Mrs. A. M. Wose; date of birth and information on ancestry from the Empire State Soc. of the Sons of the Am. Revolution.]   G. L. A.

VAN DORN, EARL (Sept. 17, 1820–May 8, 1863), Confederate general, was born near Port Gibson, Miss., the descendant of Pieter van Dorn who in the seventeenth century emigrated from Holland to the colony that is now New York.

He was the son of Sophia Donelson (Caffery) and Peter Aaron Van Dorn. His father was a graduate of the College of New Jersey (Princeton) in 1795 and removed from New Jersey to Virginia and then to Mississippi, where he was a lawyer and judge of the probate court. His mother was the niece of Mrs. Andrew Jackson. The boy was appointed a cadet of the United States Military Academy at West Point in 1838, was graduated in 1842, and was commissioned in the infantry. In 1843 he married Caroline Godbold of Mt. Vernon, Ala. He was in garrison at Fort Brown, Tex., at the outbreak of the war with Mexico and served in the field with distinction through the war. He was wounded at the city of Mexico. As a first lieutenant, promoted in 1847, he took part in the Seminole hostilities in Florida in 1849–50. In 1855 he was appointed captain in the 2nd (now 5th) Cavalry and until the beginning of the Civil War served with his regiment in Texas and the Indian Territory. In an action with the Comanches near Washita Village he received four wounds, two of them from arrows. He was promoted major in 1860.

He resigned from the army on Jan. 31, 1861, was appointed brigadier-general of Mississippi state troops, and was made major-general to succeed Jefferson Davis. Appointed as colonel of cavalry in the Confederate regular army and assigned to duty in Texas, he received the surrender of most of the Union troops there in April. His appointment as brigadier-general in the provisional army followed, and in September he was appointed major-general. In January 1862 he became commander of the transmississippi district. With a heterogeneous force, partially organized and trained, and hampered rather than helped by a body of wild Indians, he fought and lost the decisive battle of Pea Ridge, Ark., in March. Transferred east of the Mississippi, he operated to thwart the early movements against Vicksburg and in October was defeated by Rosecrans in a severe battle at Corinth, Miss. He was criticized for his conduct, but a court of inquiry found the charges disproved. Upon the arrival of General Pemberton, his senior, to take command, he was put in charge of the cavalry. In a brilliant raid on the Union depots at Holly Springs, Miss., in December, he captured the garrison and destroyed stores of great value, effectively crippling Grant's projected campaign. As he sat at his desk in his headquarters at Spring Hill, Tenn., he was shot and killed by a personal enemy. His death was a serious loss to the service, for he was an excellent cavalry commander. As he was defeated in both the important battles in which he was in chief command, his real merits have been generally overlooked.

[Some letters and papers in Lib. of Cong.; *A Soldier's Honor with Reminiscences of Major-Gen. Earl Van Dorn by his Comrades* (1902), ed. by E. V. D. Miller; G. W. Cullum, *Biog. Register of the Officers and Grads. of the U. S. Military Acad.*, 3rd ed., vol. II (1891); *War of the Rebellion: Official Records* (*Army*); R. U. Johnson and C. C. Buel, *Battles and Leaders of the Civil War*, vols. I–II (1887–88); *Confederate Military Hist.* (1899), vol. VII, ed. by C. A. Evans; A. V. D. Honeyman, *The Van Doorn Family* (1909).]   T. M. S.

VAN DYCK, CORNELIUS VAN ALEN (Aug. 13, 1818–Nov. 13, 1895), Arabic scholar, medical missionary, was born at Kinderhook, N. Y., the son of Henry L. and Catherine (Van Alen) Van Dyck. After preparation at Kinderhook Academy, he attended Jefferson Medical College in Philadelphia, graduating in 1839. Appointed a missionary of the American Board of Commissioners for Foreign Missions, he sailed from Boston for Syria in January 1840, and in April reached Beirut. After accompanying William McClure Thomson [*q.v.*] on an extensive tour through northern Syria, he went in July to Jerusalem. In January 1841 he was transferred to Beirut, where he studied Arabic intensively under his lifelong friend Butrus al-Bustāni, the lexicographer, Nasif al-Yaziji, a poet of distinction, and Yusuf al-Asir, a Moslem mufti. A tenacious memory and natural linguistic ability enabled him to acquire rapidly a thorough knowledge of both speech and literature. On Dec. 23, 1842, he married Julia, daughter of Peter Abbott, formerly British consul general in Beirut, and in June of the following year moved to 'Abeih in the Lebanon, where he and Dr. Thomson conducted a high school for boys. During the succeeding six years he prepared Arabic textbooks on geography, navigation, natural history, algebra, geometry, and plane and spherical trigonometry. These books, later revised, long continued in general use. His geography of Syria and neighboring regions, full of apt quotations from classical Arabic travelers and geographers, had an especially wide popularity. Meanwhile he was studying theology, and on Jan. 14, 1846, was ordained by the mission.

Three years later he was transferred to Sidon, his headquarters for extensive medical and preaching tours until November 1857, when he moved to Beirut to continue the translation of the Bible into Arabic which had been begun in 1848 by Eli Smith [*q.v.*]. Working in close cooperation with the ablest native and European scholars, he completed the work in 1865 and at once proceeded to America to supervise the preparation of electrotype plates. During his two

years in New York he also taught Hebrew in Union Theological Seminary. Returning to Beirut in September 1867 he became editor of the mission press of its weekly journal *al-Nashrah*, and, at the same time, professor of pathology in the medical department of the Syrian Protestant College, professor of astronomy in the department of arts and sciences, and director of the astronomical and meteorological observatory. He found time also to carry on medical practice and to write Arabic texts on pathology, chemistry, internal medicine, physical diagnosis, and astronomy. After resigning his professorship in 1883, he practised in the Hospital of St. George until 1893, meanwhile publishing in Arabic eight volumes of science primers, a popular volume on astronomy, and a translation of Mrs. E. R. Charles's *Chronicles of the Schönberg-Cotta Family* (1864). His last work was a translation of Lew Wallace's *Ben Hur*. He was survived by his wife, two sons, and two daughters.

Van Dyck played an important part in the modern renaissance of Arabic literature by showing that it was possible to write correct and idiomatic Arabic in a style so simple as to be readily understood even by the unlearned. Although one of the great pioneer missionary physicians, he is remembered chiefly for his extraordinary mastery of Arabic, and his intimate understanding of the people among whom he worked with so complete a lack of offensive condescension that Lebanese and Syrians adopted him as one of themselves.

[Sources include H. H. Jessup, *Fifty-three Years in Syria* (1910); H. A. Kelly, *A Cyc. of Am. Medic. Biog.* (2 vols., 1912); E. T. Corwin, *A Manual of the Reformed Church in America* (1902); obituary in *Times* (London), Nov. 28, 1895; information furnished by W. T. Van Dyck, of Beirut, Syria, a son. Van Dyck's Arabic publications are listed in Edward Van Dyck, *Iktifā' al-Qanū' bima Huwa Matbū'* (Cairo, 1897), and in J. E. Sarkis, *Mu 'jam al-Matbū' āt al 'Arabīyah w-al-Mu 'arrabah* (Cairo, 1928).]   W. L. W., Jr.

VAN DYKE, HENRY (Nov. 10, 1852–Apr. 10, 1933), poet, preacher, author, university teacher, diplomat, was born in Germantown, Pa., where his father, Henry Jackson van Dyke, was pastor of the First Presbyterian Church. His ancestry in the direct male line was derived from Jan Thomasse van Dyke, the first magistrate of New Utrecht, Long Island, who emigrated to America in 1652. His grandfather was a well-known physician and a graduate of Princeton. His mother, Henrietta Ashmead, belonged to an old and distinguished Germantown family. The elder Van Dyke having accepted a call to Brooklyn the year after his son's birth, most of Henry's boyhood was spent in Brooklyn and New York, where his father was prominent in the councils of the Presbyterian Church. Preparing at the Brooklyn Polytechnic Institute, he took the degree of A.B. at Princeton in 1873 and graduated from the Princeton Theological Seminary in 1877. The following year was spent in study at Berlin and travel abroad. His first pastorate was at the United Congregational Church, Newport, R. I. (1879–83). On Dec. 13, 1881, he was married to Ellen Reid of Baltimore, Md. From 1883 to 1899 he was minister of the Brick Presbyterian Church in New York, returning for brief periods in 1902 and 1911. In 1884 appeared his first book, *The Reality of Religion*; in 1889, *The Poetry of Tennyson*, revised and enlarged in later editions; in 1896, *The Gospel for an Age of Doubt,* being the Lyman Beecher lectures at Yale. Two of his most popular books of outdoor essays belong to this period, *Little Rivers* (1895), *Fisherman's Luck* (1899). His *The Story of the Other Wise Man* (1896) and *The First Christmas Tree* (1897) were first read at the Brick Church as Christmas sermons. In 1899 he accepted a call to Princeton University as Murray Professor of English Literature, the chair having been endowed for him in memory of Dr. James O. Murray [*q.v.*], his predecessor at the Brick Church and at Princeton. In 1900 he moved to Avalon, his Princeton home for the remainder of his life. In the foreword to his collected works (17 vols., 1920–22), he wrote: "This edition is named after the old house where I live. . . . It is a pleasant camp,—this Avalon, with big friendly trees around it, and an ancient garden behind it, and memories of the American Revolution built into its walls and the gray towers of Princeton University just beyond the treetops." The period 1900–1914 was one of abundant literary productivity. In volumes of poems, essays, stories, travel-sketches, and literary criticism, he shared with an ever-widening circle of readers the delights of his fishing-trips to Canada during vacations, his travels abroad, his human interest in people of all sorts and conditions, as well as the fruits of study and meditation in his library among companionable books. Among his stories and romances are *The Ruling Passion* (1901), *The Blue Flower* (1902), *The Unknown Quantity* (1912); among his essays, *Days Off* (1907) and *Out of Doors in the Holy Land* (1908). In 1908–09 he was lecturer at the Sorbonne, the lectures appearing as *The Spirit of America* (1910) and in French as *Le Génie de l'Amérique* (1909).

In 1912 he was elected president of the National Institute of Arts and Letters, and in the following year President Wilson appointed him minister to the Netherlands and Luxembourg (appointment confirmed, June 27, 1913). Finding it impossible to reconcile his ardent conviction of the right of the allied cause with his duties as minister in a neutral country, he resigned on Sept. 6, 1916. On his way home in 1917 he visited the battle fronts in France, received the degree of D.C.L. at Oxford, and, having volunteered for active service in the United States Navy, he was appointed lieutenant commander in the Chaplain Corps. He was active in arousing public opinion in favor of a vigorous prosecution of the war and in the formation of a league to enforce peace, of which he was one of the original advocates. In 1919 the cross of a commander of the Legion of Honor was conferred on him by the French government. He returned in 1919 to his Princeton professorship, retiring in 1923. He was professor emeritus until his death, and until 1929 he delivered annually a series of university literary lectures to crowded audiences. In 1931 he celebrated his golden wedding. After a brief illness he died Apr. 10, at dawn, in his home at Avalon in his eighty-first year. He was survived by his wife and five of their nine children.

A religious leader whose influence extended far beyond the pale of his own church, an inspiring teacher of college youth, a writer of outdoor essays and short stories in prose of classic purity, of musical verse in the Victorian tradition, a sympathetic interpreter of Tennyson, an influential moulder of public opinion, a fervent patriot, he crowded into a single life an achievement astonishing for its versatility and competence of execution. He was not only an eloquent preacher but an organizer of institutional activities, making the Brick Church a center of civic consciousness and a power in the fight against political corruption. In the doctrinal controversies that shook the Presbyterian Church he was a valiant champion of a positive evangelical Christianity, defending it against a materialistic and rationalistic philosophy on the left and a hard and dogmatic Calvinism on the right. In an address before the New York Presbytery (1890), "Is This Calvinism or Christianity," he repudiated the doctrine of reprobation as "measuring the mind of God by the logic of the seventeenth century"; "The Bible as It Is," in *Historic Presbyterianism* (1893), is a plea for liberty of investigation. His "A Plea for Peace and Work" (1893) was signed by about 235 Presbyterian ministers, and he was a member of the original committee appointed by the moderator of the General Assembly, 1900, to consider the restatement of doctrine. The "Brief Statement of the Reformed Faith" was adopted by an overwhelming vote by the General Assembly of 1902 (see *Outlook*, May 31, 1902, p. 299), and his election as moderator was a recognition of his leadership in the movement for revision. Perhaps his most lasting contribution to his church was his work as chairman of the committee on *The Book of Common Worship*, completed only two years before his death, in which his own deeply devout spirit, his sense of form, his loyalty to the faith of his fathers, and his literary taste contributed to produce a devotional manual rich with the treasures of Christian experience.

Versatility marks the work of Henry van Dyke in the field of letters. His outdoor essays are in the main stream of the American tradition of Thoreau, Burroughs, Muir, though his interest in human character and his deep religious faith, always part of his delight in nature, give them a quality of their own. Of his poem, "God of the Open Air," he said: "It best expresses me." He was an ardent angler, and his skill as a fisherman was excelled only by his skill as a narrator of his fisherman's luck. He was as particular in the choice of the right word as in the choice of the right fly, and he could cast as unerringly in the pools of fancy as in the pools where the brook-trout lurked. The sketches and stories of his French-Canadian guides and friends are among his best. In them he avoids the sentimentality and tendency to preach into which the warmth of his heart and the fervor of his convictions sometimes led him. His *The Story of the Other Wise Man* has been translated into all European and several Oriental languages, and remains his best-known tale. The two volumes of verse in the Avalon edition contain nature lyrics, patriotic songs, hymns, odes, narrative verse, and a Biblical drama. He is always clear and melodious, and, though facile, he had the conscientious craftsman's contempt for slipshod work. Changing standards of taste, the reaction against the Victorians, the rise of a critical realism that challenged the "genteel tradition" have diminished the literary prestige of most of Van Dyke's contemporaries, and from this diminution his own work has not escaped, but when all reservations are made, his place in American letters is secure as master of a lucid style exquisitely adapted to its end.

At the root of his nature was a love of the genuine and simple. The academician in his robes of office, the diplomat in silk hat and black cape, the Oxford D.C.L. in his gown of crimson, he was most at home in his flannel shirt, felt hat, and wading boots, and declared: "The good word of a plain fisherman or hunter is worth more than a D.D. from a learned University." He was devoted to his father, to his brother Paul [*q.v.*], and to his own family, of whose life his daughter Brooke has given a charming picture. In politics a Democrat, he was on intimate terms of friendship with Grover Cleveland and Woodrow Wilson, and he always enjoyed the good fellowship of meetings with literary friends like Mark Twain, James Whitcomb Riley, and Hamilton Mabie. To younger aspirants for literary honors, especially his Princeton students, he gave generous encouragement. The vivid character portrait by Maxwell Struthers Burt in *The Van Dyke Book* (1920 ed.) reveals the impression he made on a discriminating novelist and poet of a younger generation. He called himself an adventurous conservative, and this sums up his essential quality as man and writer.

[*Who's Who in America*, 1932–33; Tertius van Dyke, *Henry Van Dyke, a Biog.* (1935); *The Van Dyke Book* (1905; rev. ed., 1920), ed. by Edwin Mims, with a biog. sketch by Brooke van Dyke; Shepherd Knapp, *A Hist. of the Brick Presbyt. Church in the City of N. Y.* (1909); F. H. Law, *Modern Great Americans* (1926); M. J. Gilley, "Lit. Works of Henry van Dyke," 1923, master's thesis, Columbia Univ.; *Outlook*, May 1, 1897; *Suburban Life*, May 1908; "Book-News," May 1906, pub. by Wanamaker's, Phila.; *Princeton Alumni Weekly*, May 5, 19, July 3, 1933; obituary in *N. Y. Times*, Apr. 11, 1933; personal reminiscences.]

J. D. S.

VAN DYKE, JOHN CHARLES (Apr. 21, 1856–Dec. 5, 1932), art critic and librarian, was born at New Brunswick, N. J., a descendant of Jan Thomasse van Dyke who emigrated from the Netherlands to New Amsterdam in 1652. His father, John Van Dyke, served in Congress and as justice of the supreme court of New Jersey. His mother, Mary Dix Strong, was the daughter of Prof. Theodore Strong [*q.v.*]. The family moved to Minnesota in 1868, and John added to the conventional education which he received from tutors that of a hard-riding and straight-shooting plainsman. After study in the Columbia Law School, he was in 1877 admitted to the bar, but never practised. Returning in 1878 to his native New Brunswick, he served first as assistant librarian of the Gardner A. Sage Library, New Brunswick Theological Seminary, and then (1886) as librarian, a position which he held until his death. From the vantage point of his librarianship, with its relatively easy duties and long vacations, he pursued personal studies in art which bore fruit in numerous books, mostly of a popular and interpretative sort, which were widely read and influential. His criticism was urbane, sensitive, free from eccentricity. In a perhaps excessive avoidance of overstatement it recalls the contemporary literary criticism of William Dean Howells. In

1889 he became a lecturer upon modern art at Rutgers College and from 1891 to 1929 was professor of the history of art. From about 1884 till about 1904 he was the favorite contributor of the *Century Magazine* on artistic subjects, supplying, for example, the brief and excellent comment on Timothy Cole's masterpieces of reproductive wood-engraving, which were later published in book form as *Old English Masters, with Cole's Engravings* (1902). For his special studies he traveled widely. In the literature of art criticism, he intentionally read little, preferring to stand on his own vivid impressions before the work of art itself. His artistic pilgrimages he varied by travels for the study of natural beauty, and every three or four years produced a book on natural appearances. In his later years the books on nature predominate. Such books as *The Desert* (1901), *The Opal Sea* (1906), *The Mountain* (1916) were hailed by English critics, perhaps because they represented the sober, elegant, and faithful tradition of Gilbert White of Selborne, but in America their quietness obscured their distinguished merits. They are likely, nevertheless, to outlast the art books, which were more nearly attuned to the times.

Perhaps the best of Van Dyke's writing on art is in the twelve little volumes of *New Guides to Old Masters* (1914), in which he resolutely eschewed the merely perfunctory and informational, and set down briefly the personal impressions of the ideal spectator that he was before the pictures. Coming out in 1914, the little books hardly had a reading; they remain a mine of discerning appreciation. His most sensational book, *Rembrandt and His School* (1923), was shaped by his exaggerated faculty of visual discrimination. Possessed of an extraordinary acuteness of vision that tended to be microscopic, he saw immediately, in pictures, features that are generally unnoticed, small repaints, subtle differences of style or handling. Finding many differences in style in the eight hundred or more pictures officially ascribed to Rembrandt, he brought these pictures into stylistic groups most of which seemed to correspond to the score of known pupils and imitators of Rembrandt, thus leaving a residuum of only fifty pictures for the master himself. This invoked a great and unwelcome publicity, and virtually he was scoffed out of court. He stood by his guns, however, and in 1927, in *The Rembrandt Drawings and Etchings,* tried to reduce the list to about a tenth of its traditional proportions. No critic has accepted these puristic views, but many believe that the books brought about a useful ventilation of the mephitic atmosphere of commercial *expertise.*

Van Dyke was president of the National Institute of Arts and Letters, and a member of the American Academy of Arts and Letters. He was a man of magnificent stature, easily carried, with large gray-blue eyes that belied the habitual fixity of his fine olive mask. He wore his clothes well, said the right word and never too much, and exhibited a native dignity and kindliness. He had the gift of companionship, a perfect rectitude, an elevation of character entirely without pretentiousness. In any group of gentlemen he was a moral and physical ornament. He died in New York City. He was unmarried.

[*Who's Who in America*, 1930–31; W. B. Aitken, *Distinguished Families in America Descended from . . . Jan Thomasse Van Dyke* (1912); J. C. Van Dyke, *The Raritan, Notes on . . . a Family* (1915); *New Brunswick Seminary Bull.,* Mar. 1933; obituary in *N. Y. Times,* Dec. 6, 1932; personal acquaintance.]

F. J. M., Jr.

VAN DYKE, NICHOLAS (Sept. 25, 1738–Feb. 19, 1789), member of the Continental Congress, president of the State of Delaware, was born at New Castle, Del., the son of Nicholas Van Dyke and his wife, Lytie Dirks. He was of the fourth generation in descent from Jan Thomasse Van Dyke who came to New Amsterdam in 1652 from Amsterdam, Holland, and was the third of the family in America to bear the name of Nicholas. The Van Dkyes were a prominent burgher family in Holland and Jan Thomasse was one of the founders of New Utrecht in New Amsterdam. Early in the eighteenth century the family moved to St. George's Hundred in Delaware, where it soon became one of the largest landholders in the province. Of Nicholas' education there seems to be little information available. He was trained for the law, was admitted to practice before the supreme court in Philadelphia in 1765, at the age of twenty-seven, and probably received his training in that city. Soon thereafter he returned to New Castle, in the Lower Counties, where he was a practising lawyer until his death.

Like many of the young lawyers of his day he threw in his lot with the Whigs in 1774, although he remained steadfastly one of the moderate faction. He served on the provincial committee of correspondence, on the committee appointed to solicit funds for the relief of the people of Boston in 1774, and was a member of the New Castle Council of Safety in 1776. In the Delaware constitutional convention of 1776 he was one of the more active delegates, participated in formulating rules for the convention, sat on committees charged with the function of provisioning the state's troops, and assisted in preparing a declaration of rights and in writing the preliminary draft of a constitution. In the first election under the new government he was elected to the Council, the upper legislative house, and, during 1779 served as the speaker of the house. Throughout the war period he held the rank of major in the New Castle County militia, but saw no active service.

On Feb. 22, 1777, during the period in which the moderates controlled the state legislature, Van Dyke was elected to the Continental Congress, and he was returned annually until 1782. The post, however, held few attractions for him, for he was interested primarily in state politics and was ill much of the time. Moreover, he was dissatisfied with the scant provision made by his state for its delegates. Aside from his service on a few minor committees and his signature to the Articles of Confederation, the *Journals* reveal scant participation in the deliberations of Congress, and infrequent attendance. To repeated pleas from his colleagues for more adequate representation from Delaware he paid little heed.

For more than three and a half years during the critical post-war years, from Feb. 1, 1783, until Oct. 27, 1786, he was president of Delaware, having been elected by joint vote of the two legislative houses. His administration witnessed the passage of numerous measures designed to improve commerce and to place the finances of the state on a sound basis. He also dealt with continued agitation on the part of Delaware statesmen to have title to the lands northwest of the Ohio given to the states in common. Following his presidency he again sat in the Council for part of one term. Van Dyke was twice married, first to Elizabeth Nixon and, after her death, to Charlotte Standley. He died in New Castle County, Del., and is buried in the Immanuel Churchyard at New Castle. Nicholas Van Dyke [*q.v.*] was his son.

[W. B. Aitken, *Distinguished Families in America Descended from Wilhelmus Beekman and Jan Thomasse Van Dyke* (1912) ; H. C. Conrad, *Hist. of the State of Del.* (1908), vols. I, III ; J. T. Scharf, *Hist. of Del.* (1888), vol. I ; E. C. Burnett, *Letters of Members of the Cont. Cong.*, vols. II–V (1923–31) ; *Minutes of the Council of the Del. State from 1776 to 1792, Papers of the Hist. Soc. of Del.*, vol. VI (1887) ; *Proc. of the Convention of the Del. State Held at New-Castle . . . 1776* (reprint, 1927) ; G. H. Ryden, *Letters To and From Cæsar Rodney* (1933) ; J. L. Martin, *Martin's Bench and Bar of Phila.* (1883) ; *Biog. Dir. Am. Cong.* (1928) ; one volume of Van Dyke's letters and papers, and four volumes of Delaware State papers containing some of his official papers, Library of Congress ; *Independent Gazetteer; or, the Chronicle of Freedom* (Philadelphia), Mar. 2, 1789.] J. H. P.

VAN DYKE, NICHOLAS (Dec. 20, 1770–May 21, 1826), lawyer, United States senator, the son of Nicholas Van Dyke [*q.v.*] and Eliza-

beth Nixon, was born in New Castle, Del. He attended the College of New Jersey and was graduated in the class of 1788. He then read law under the direction of Kensey Johns, a New Castle attorney, and was admitted to the bar in 1792. He established himself in practice in New Castle, and was married to Mary, the daughter of Kensey Johns, his tutor, and his wife, Susannah Galloway. Kensey Johns, 1759–1848 [*q.v.*], was his brother-in-law. Like his father, young Van Dyke's sympathies were from the beginning with the more moderate group in Delaware politics; like him, too, he entered political life, first as a member of the Delaware House of Representatives in 1799 for one term. From 1801 until 1806 he was attorney-general of Delaware. Elected to Congress in 1807 to fill a vacancy, he remained a member of that body until Mar. 3, 1811. Although recognized as a Federalist, he was moderate in his views, and on questions of legislation was invariably guided by his own judgment. Thus he was quite willing to support Jefferson's embargo measure in 1808 but, convinced of the futility of the administration's policy by the beginning of 1809, he demanded a change: "the Emperor of France applauds our magnanimity in abandoning the ocean, and Great Britain laughs at the imbecility of the measure" (*Annals of Congress*, 10 Cong., 2 Sess., 1290). He criticised those who spoke of war with England, but attacked the failure of the President to make specific recommendations for improving the military and naval establishments.

During 1816 Van Dyke was a member of the state Senate, but in the same year he was elected to the United States Senate where he continued in service from March 1817 until his death. As a senator he frequently gave voice to the traditional state-rights sentiments of his father and other Delaware politicians of the Revolutionary and post-Revolutionary period. Although personally opposed to slavery he refused to vote against the admission of Missouri on the ground that Congress had no authority to impose restrictions on slavery, and that slaves had not been freed by the Declaration of Independence. Wherever emancipation had been effected, he asserted, it was by the authority of state laws, and every state had assumed and invariably exercised at its discretion the right of legislation on this class of people (*Annals of Congress*, 16 Cong., 1 Sess., 302). When the Delaware Assembly sent up to Congress a resolution urging the passage of legislation which would prohibit the introduction of slavery into the territory of the United States or into any newly organized states, Van Dyke joined with Representative

Louis McLane [*q.v.*] in an open letter express-ing his objections to the sentiments of the reso-lution. During his senatorship he demonstrated ability as a debater and sat on the committees of claims, pensions, public lands, and military ap-propriations.

Van Dyke's daughter, Dorcas Montgomery, was married to Charles Irénée, the son of Vic-tor Marie Du Pont [*q.v.*], on Oct. 6, 1824. Gen-eral Lafayette, a personal friend of Senator Van Dyke, attended the wedding, an outstanding so-cial event, and gave the bride away. Early in the spring of 1826 Van Dyke's health showed signs of rapid decline and he reached his home with difficulty but a short while before his death. He was buried on his farm at St. George's Hun-dred, but was later reinterred in the Immanuel Churchyard in New Castle. He was widely known for the remarkable ease and elegance of his manner, and the fluency of his speech; he was fond of literature and his taste for archi-tecture was reflected in the construction of sev-eral fine houses in New Castle.

[W. B. Aitken, *Distinguished Families in America Descended from Wilhelmus Beekman and Jan Thomasse Van Dyke* (1912) ; *Biog. and Geneal. Hist. of the State of Del.* (1889) ; H. C. Conrad, *Hist. of the State of Del.* (1908), vols. I, III ; W. T. Read, *Life and Corres. of George Read* (1870) ; and J. T. Scharf, *Hist. of Del.* (1888), vol. I ; Thomas Holcombe, *Hist. of Immanuel Ch.,* New Castle, Del. (1890) ; *Am. Watchman and Del. Advertiser* (Wilmington), May 23, 1826.] J. H. P.

VAN DYKE, PAUL (Mar. 25, 1859–Aug. 30, 1933), historian, was born in Brooklyn, N. Y., the son of the Rev. Henry Jackson and Henrietta (Ashmead) van Dyke, and the brother of Henry van Dyke [*q.v.*]. He was graduated from the College of New Jersey (Princeton) in 1881, and from the Princeton Theological Seminary in 1884. He studied at the University of Berlin during 1884–85. After his ordination in 1887 as a Presbyterian minister, he spent ten years in religious work, as pastor at Geneva, N. Y. (1887–89), and at Northampton, Mass. (1892–98), and as instructor in church history at the Princeton Theological Seminary (1889–92). From 1898 until his retirement in 1928 he was professor of modern history in Princeton University. His theological training was reflected in the vigor-ous moral judgments which marked his teaching and his first books, *The Age of the Renascence* (1897), and *Renascence Portraits* (1905). Af-ter the completion of the latter work, he began an exhaustive search in the archives and libraries of Europe for material on the life of Catherine de Medicis. This task was interrupted from July 1917 to July 1919 by war work as secretary of the American University Union at Paris, where his sympathetic help revived many whose lives

and hopes had been shattered. He himself be-lieved this work the most useful of his life, and in his letters from Paris the conviction that the war was a moral crusade finds vehement ex-pression. After the war he continued his interest in the American University Union, serving as director of the continental division at Paris from 1921 to 1923, and again during 1928–29.

His most important work, *Catherine de Medicis* (2 vols., 1922), immediately won international recognition as a definitive history of the religious wars in France. As a biography the work was less successful, in part because of Van Dyke's unwillingness to impose his views on the reader and in part because, although all the elements of the portrait were assembled, the figure of Catherine never clearly emerged. His later bio-graphical studies, *Ignatius Loyola, the Founder of the Jesuits* (1926), and *George Washington, the Son of His Country, 1732–1775* (1931), were less important as scholarly works but more suc-cessful as portraits. In 1928 he published *The Story of France from Julius Cæsar to Napoleon III,* which was noteworthy for the vivid descrip-tions of cultural life in France during the Mid-dle Ages and Renaissance. Among his honorary degrees was that of *Docteur ès Lettres,* granted by the University of Toulouse. He was twice Harvard lecturer at the provincial universities of France, and Louis Liard lecturer at the Sor-bonne, Paris. He was an officer of the Legion of Honor.

His slight, delicate figure and gentle manner gave little indication of the vigor of his per-sonality. Although the dogmatism of his earlier years gradually gave place to tolerance, he re-mained to the end inflexible in devotion to honor and duty. In political and social life he was a Jeffersonian Democrat, and his love both of his own country and of France was intimately con-nected with his faith in democracy. He died at his summer home at Washington, Conn. He was unmarried.

[*Who's Who in America,* 1930–31 ; *After Fifty Years, the Record of the Class of 1881, Princeton* (1931) ; *Biog. Cat. of Princeton Theological Seminary, 1815–1932* (1933) ; obituary in *N. Y. Times,* Aug. 31, 1933 ; file in the office of the secretary, Princeton Univ. ; papers in the possession of Tertius van Dyke, Prince-ton ; personal acquaintance.] R. J. S—g.

VANE, Sir HENRY (1613–June 14, 1662), Puritan statesman, for one year governor of Massachusetts Bay, was the eldest of twelve chil-dren born to Sir Henry Vane, Knight, and Fran-ces Darcy his wife. A recent biographer claims that his mother was a grand-daughter of Vincent Guicciardini, a descendant of the Florentine his-torian (Willcock, *post,* p. 351). He was baptized May 26, 1613, at Debden, Essex, which was probably his birthplace, rather than Hadlow, Kent, as is sometimes stated (*Ibid.*, p. 7). He was educated at Westminster School and at sixteen entered Oxford at Magdalen Hall. Since his principles prevented his taking the required oaths, he remained only a brief time and then went to the Continent to study, probably at Leyden, and visited Vienna and Nürnberg. He early became a Puritan and his position in England became uncomfortable. In 1635 he sailed for Massachusetts in the *Abigail,* arriving at Boston on Oct. 6.

He was admitted as a member of the church on Nov. 1 and as a freeman of the colony on Mar. 3 following, and the same day was chosen to serve on the commission for military discipline. Previously, however, he had been made one of three arbiters to whom citizens of Boston had to submit their cases before they could proceed to law (Hosmer, *Vane*, p. 32), and with the Rev. Hugh Peter [*q.v.*] had secured the calling of a meeting at which the two endeavored to reconcile the factions of the former governors John Winthrop and Thomas Dudley [*qq.v.*]. On May 25, 1636, Vane was elected governor of Massachusetts, when he had been in the colony less than eight months and was but twenty-three years old. His first task, carried through successfully, was to establish a series of regulations governing the entrance of ships into the port, and to soothe the feelings and close the mouths of a group of sea captains resentful of the fact that the king's colors were not displayed by the colony—John Endecott [*q.v.*], not long before, having cut the cross from the ensign as idolatrous.

Vane had arrived in Massachusetts just in time to hear the trial of Roger Williams [*q.v.*], with whose views he was in sympathy. On July 26, 1636, as governor, he received word from Williams that the Pequots and Narragansetts were threatening war. In August a punitive expedition under Endecott was sent against the Pequots—a move which was one of the causes of the Pequot War of 1637; but through the magnanimous intercession of the banished Williams the Narragansetts were kept from taking a hostile part, and in October 1636 a treaty was effected at Boston between the English and Miantonomo [*q.v.*], the Narragansett sachem. Shortly afterward a theological storm broke which wrecked Vane's career in America. The arguments of Mrs. Anne Hutchinson [*q.v.*], who laid stress on inner illumination of the spirit, had divided the local clergy into those who preached a "covenant of works" and those who preached a "covenant of grace." Her opponents, claiming that she was teaching a religion which absolved those adhering to it from obedience to law, thus undermining the foundations of the colony, demanded her suppression. Former Gov. John Winthrop [*q.v.*], the Rev. John Wilson [*q.v.*], and most of the other leaders were opposed to her. The Rev. John Cotton [*q.v.*], with whom Vane lived, was at first her supporter, but he eventually joined the majority. Vane, with her brother-in-law, the Rev. John Wheelwright [*q.v.*], stood by her and was bitterly reviled. Disheartened, in December he tendered his resignation as governor, pleading that letters from home necessitated his return to England; but he was persuaded to reconsider and retained the governorship until the end of his term.

The controversy was carried into the election of 1637. Since Vane was strong in Boston, his opponents secured the holding of the election at Newtown, and he was defeated by Winthrop. The next day Boston chose Vane as one of its deputies to the General Court, which promptly quashed the election on the ground of a technical irregularity, but when he was chosen again at a new election he was allowed to take his seat. The struggle was not yet over, however. The General Court on May 17 passed an act prohibiting, under penalties, any newcomer from remaining in the colony more than three weeks without the consent of the magistrates; this move was designed to prevent any addition to the ranks of the Hutchinson party and to allow the incumbent authorities to remain in control. Winthrop circulated an argument in manuscript defending the act and Vane answered him in another, defending civil liberty and religious toleration; both were published, more than a century later, by Thomas Hutchinson [*q.v.*] in *A Collection of Original Papers Relative to the History of the Colony of Massachusetts Bay* (1769) and reprinted in *The Publications of the Prince Society,* vol. II (1865).

Vane sailed for England Aug. 3, 1637. He had not been always wise in his acts as governor, but he was always honest and generous-minded, and his later and more important career in England probably owed much to the lessons in toleration which his experience among the sectarians of New England afforded him. Although he left Massachusetts under the disapproval of the leaders of the colony, he harbored no resentment, and later gladly served the cause of his one-time fellow citizens. When in 1645 he befriended two Massachusetts men in difficulties Winthrop commented: "Sir Henry Vane, . . . though he might have taken occasion against us for some dishonor which he apprehended to have been unjustly put upon him here, yet both now, and at other times he showed himself a true friend to New England, and a man of a noble and generous mind" (*Winthrop's Journal, post*, II, 256). To Roger Williams he was a loyal and a valuable friend. In 1644 he helped Williams to secure the Rhode Island charter, which bore Vane's signature as one of the commissioners for plantations; in 1652 he was instrumental in having rescinded the commission granted the year before to William Coddington [*q.v.*] as proprietary governor of the schismatic colony of Aquidneck; two years later he wrote an affectionate letter to the citizens of Rhode Island upbraiding them for the dissensions within the colony.

From the time of his return to England, however, the story of his life belongs in the main to English history (see *Dictionary of National Biography*). In 1639 he was appointed joint treasurer of the navy and in 1640 was knighted by Charles I. On July 1 of that year, at St. Mary's, Lambeth, he married Frances, daughter of Sir Christopher Wray of Ashby in Lincolnshire; they had thirteen children. Vane was elected to both Short and Long parliaments and was instrumental in securing the condemnation of Strafford and Laud, but had no part in the trial and condemnation of the King. He was a member of all Councils of State. Not in sympathy with the Protectorate, after the dissolution of the Long Parliament he retired from public life. Under Richard Cromwell he was once more a member of Parliament, but when the Long Parliament reassembled, he was expelled. Following the Restoration, he was excepted from the act of indemnity, and, after two years in prison was tried for treason, found guilty, and executed on Tower Hill.

[J. K. Hosmer, *The Life of Young Sir Henry Vane* (1888); C. H. Firth, in *Dict. Nat. Biog.*; W. W. Ireland, *The Life of Sir Henry Vane the Younger* (1905); John Willcock, *Life of Sir Henry Vane the Younger* (1913); H. M. King, *Sir Henry Vane, Jr., Gov. of Mass. and Friend of Roger Williams and R. I.* (1909), uncritical; *Winthrop's Jour.* (2 vols., 1908), ed. by J. K. Hosmer; N. B. Shurtleff, *Records of the Gov. and Company of the Mass. Bay*, vol. I (1853); C. F. Adams, *Three Episodes of Mass. Hist.* (2 vols., 1892).]

J. T. A.

VAN FLEET, WALTER (June 18, 1857–Jan. 26, 1922), horticulturist, physician, was born of Dutch ancestry at Piermont, Rockland County, N. Y., son of Solomon Van Reusselean and Elvira (Du Bois) Van Fleet. His childhood was spent on a small farm in the vicinity of Watsontown, Pa., where his father was principal of Watsontown Academy. He developed in boyhood a keen interest in the growing of plants and at twelve began work in hybridization. Becoming interested in birds, he published a number of articles on birds in technical and popular periodicals (1876–88), as well as a popular bird book for children. In 1878, under contract as wood chopper with the Collins Railroad Construction Company, he visited the upper tributaries of the Amazon, where an attack of tropical fever nearly cost him his life. Returning home in the summer of that year, he entered Hahnemann Medical College in Philadelphia, from which he was graduated with the degree of M.D. in 1880, later taking post-graduate work in Jefferson Medical College (1886–87). From 1880 to 1891 he was actively engaged in the practice of medicine at Watsontown, Duboistown, and Renovo, Pa., though he made a bird-collecting trip of five months to Nicaragua and the Isthmus of Panama.

While practising medicine he began the systematic breeding of the gladiolus and the canna, and in 1891 definitely took up plant-breeding as a vocation. In 1894 he settled at Little Silver, N. J., where for a short time he was managing editor of *Orchard and Garden*. Aside from two years (1897–99) during which he acted as colony physician in the Ruskin Colony at Dickson, Tenn., he devoted the rest of his life to the production of improved varieties of plants. For a number of years he was associate editor of the *Rural New Yorker* (Oct. 1899–Nov. 1909). In 1909 he became an expert plant-breeder in the federal bureau of plant industry at Chico, Cal., and Washington, D. C. His work in the Department of Agriculture covered a wide range and included extensive experimentation on the production of chestnuts resistant to the Asiatic bark blight. Noteworthy new varieties of plants as diverse as azalea, canna, freesia, geranium, gladiolus, Lonicera, rose, pepper, sweet corn, tomato, chestnut, gooseberry, pear, and strawberry resulted from his work; of these some fifty have been named and commercially disseminated. Van Fleet's outstanding achievements, however, were with the rose. He early recognized the need in America for roses of vigorous growth, disease-resistant foliage, and large flowers, sufficiently hardy for garden culture through a wide climatic range. He was keenly perceptive of plant characters, indefatigably industrious, and exactingly critical of his productions. A large number of his roses have succeeded under varying climatic conditions; this is notably true of the climbing and pillar varieties, American Pillar, Dr. W. Van Fleet, Philadelphia, Silver Moon, Alida Lovett, Bess Lovett, Mary Lovett, Mary Wallace, Heart of Gold, Breeze

Hill, and Glenn Dale. The American Pillar and Dr. W. Van Fleet have for some years been recognized as the most generally successful and widely planted climbers in America. Their general good behavior has been an important factor in the recent widespread development of popular interest in rose growing. Among his publications, in addition to his numerous papers on ornithology and horticulture in technical and popular journals and in the *American Rose Annual,* were a series of contributions, "Ruralisms," to the *Rural New Yorker, The Gladiolus* (1911), with Matthew Crawford, *The Cultivation of American Ginseng* (1913), *Golden Seal under Cultivation* (1914), *The Cultivation of Peppermint and Spearmint* (1915), and a brochure on the growing of hardy roses.

Modest and retiring to the point of diffidence, Van Fleet was a most kindly and considerate worker with his associates. At the same time he was outspokenly and incisively critical of the overpraise and misrepresentation of plant novelties indulged in at times by commercial plantsmen. In his editorial work this sometimes led to intense controversy and even to litigation. In 1918 he was awarded the George Robert White medal for eminent services in horticulture by the Massachusetts Horticultural Society; in 1921 he received gold medals from the American Rose Society and the city of Portland, Ore., and a silver medal from the Portland Rose Society, all in recognition of the merit of the Mary Wallace rose. On Aug. 7, 1883, he married Sarah C. Heilman of Watsontown, Pa., who survived him. He died at Miami, Fla.

[*Who's Who in America,* 1920–21; *Official Record, U. S. Dept. of Agriculture,* Feb. 1, 1922; Peter Bisset, in *Am. Florist,* Feb. 18, 1922; C. L. Linz, in *Florists' Exchange,* Feb. 4, 1922; F. L. Mulford, in *Nat. Horticultural Mag.,* Apr. 1929; *Am. Rose Ann.,* 1922; obituary in *Evening Star* (Washington, D. C.), Jan. 28, 1922; records of U. S. Dept. of Agriculture; personal recollections.]   W. A. T.

VAN HISE, CHARLES RICHARD (May 29, 1857–Nov. 19, 1918), geologist, university president, publicist, was born in Fulton, Rock County, Wis., the son of pioneer parents, William Henry and Mary (Goodrich) Van Hise. Prepared at Evansville Academy, he entered the University of Wisconsin in 1874, and after a year's absence in 1877–78, was graduated with the degree of bachelor of metallurgical engineering in 1879. Subsequently he received in course the degrees of B.S. (1880), M.S. (1882), and Ph.D. (1892). He was employed as instructor in metallurgy, 1879–83, assistant professor, 1883–86, and professor, 1886–88; professor of mineralogy, 1888–90; professor of Archaean and ap-

plied geology, 1890–92, and professor of geology, 1892–1903. He was also non-resident professor of structural geology in the University of Chicago from 1892 to 1903, and from 1883 a member of the United States Geological Survey. In April 1903 he was chosen president of the University of Wisconsin; he assumed office in the fall, and was formally inaugurated in June 1904. This position he filled until his death.

Van Hise received his training in geology under Roland Duer Irving [*q.v.*] at a time when the modern science of microscopic petrology was just developing. His first research work of importance was undertaken in collaboration with his instructor and resulted in a paper by the two, "Crystalline Rocks of the Wisconsin Valley," published in *Geology of Wisconsin: Survey of 1873–1879* (vol. IV, 1882). With the termination of the state survey, Irving and Van Hise continued under the United States Geological Survey, and in 1892 Van Hise saw through the press the last product of their joint work, *The Penokee Iron-Bearing Series of Michigan and Wisconsin,* published as Monograph XIX of the federal survey. As planned by Irving this report was to be the first of a series treating each of the important iron-producing districts of the Lake Superior region; after Irving's death the project was carried on by Van Hise as geologist in charge of the Lake Superior division from 1888 to 1900. He was joint author of Survey monographs dealing with the Marquette and Crystal Falls districts and of the special folio of the *Geologic Atlas* dealing with the Menominee iron-bearing district of Michigan; he also supervised the preparation of Survey monographs on four other districts of the region. Meanwhile he published in 1892 a notable series, *Correlation Papers; Archean and Algonkian* (Bulletin 86, United States Geological Survey), and in 1896 "Principles of North American Pre-Cambrian Geology," in the *Sixteenth Annual Report* of the United States Geological Survey. His constant effort to ascertain the fundamental laws governing observed phenomena led him further to *A Treatise on Metamorphism* (Monograph XLVII, United States Geological Survey, 1904), in which he endeavored to show that the changes in rock characteristics take place in accordance with recognized physical and chemical laws. When he accepted the presidency of his University, he necessarily abandoned much of his geological work, but a revision and enlargement of his *Correlation Papers* of 1892, prepared in collaboration with C. K. Leith, appeared in 1909 under the title, *Pre-Cambrian Geology of North America* (Bulletin 360, United States Geological

Survey) and with the same associate in 1911 he brought out *The Geology of the Lake Superior Region* (Monograph LII), the first general treatise on the subject.

As president of the University of Wisconsin, Van Hise exhibited the same breadth of outlook that characterized him as a scientist. Believing that as a state institution its primary duty was to serve the citizens of the commonwealth, he proceeded to develop not only the research activities of the University, but an extension department exceeding in scope any then existing, with numerous means of placing "accumulated knowledge" at the service of Wisconsin citizens. His conviction that it was the duty of the University to give state leadership led him to enter aggressively upon debatable ground, and frequently brought severe, perhaps just, criticism. Nevertheless, under his administration the University increased enormously in material equipment, nearly trebled in enrollment, and excited favorable attention throughout the United States and abroad. Moreover, his conception of the peculiar functions of a state university gained wide recognition and influenced the policies of other institutions.

He served in the capacity of consulting geologist on the Wisconsin Geological and Natural History Survey from 1897 to 1903 and for several years as chairman of the Wisconsin State Conservation Commission appointed in 1908. Late in that year he was called into wider public service as a member of the National Conservation Commission and subsequently contributed to the conservation movement what has been called its most valuable book, *The Conservation of Natural Resources in the United States* (1910). From 1909 he was a trustee of the Carnegie Foundation for the Advancement of Teaching; in 1912 he was a member, and for part of the time chairman, of the board appointed to arbitrate a dispute between the eastern railroads and the Brotherhood of Locomotive Engineers. His contact with problems of the social order set him seeking again for fundamental principles, and in 1912 he published *Concentration and Control; A Solution of the Trust Problem in the United States*. During the World War he gave much time and energy to the work of conservation and allocation of the food supply, preparing for the Food Administration an outline of a series of lectures to be given in colleges and universities, under the title *Conservation and Regulation in the United States during the World War* (2 parts, 1917–18). He was frequently called to Washington for consultation and during August and September 1918 visited France and England

with a party of observers who were guests of the British government. He was an enthusiastic believer in a league of free nations to enforce peace and on Nov. 8, 1918, in Madison, delivered the opening address before a convention of supporters of the project. At the time of his death he was working on a synthesis of his geological and social studies, a treatise on the influence of mineral resources upon the history of civilization, foreshadowed in his address, "The Influence of Applied Geology and the Mining Industry upon the Economic Development of the World," delivered in 1910 before the International Geological Congress at Stockholm (*Compte Rendu,* 1912, pp. 259–61).

Van Hise was the recipient of many academic honors. He was a member of the National Academy of Sciences and other scientific bodies both in the United States and abroad, and in several held office. He was married on Dec. 22, 1881, to Alice Bushnell Ring, who bore him three daughters. He died in Milwaukee, Wis., from meningitis following a nasal operation.

[Biog. sketch (inaccurate in certain details) and addresses by E. A. Birge, T. C. Chamberlin, and Albert Shaw, in *Memorial Service in Honor of Charles Richard Van Hise at the Univ. of Wis.* (1919); J. F. A. Pyre, *Wisconsin* (1920); *Who's Who in America,* 1918–19; C. K. Leith, in *Bull. Geol. Soc. of America,* Mar. 1920, with bibliog.; T. C. Chamberlin, in *Jour. of Geology,* Nov.–Dec., 1918, and in *Memoirs Nat. Acad. Sci.,* vol. XVII (1924), with bibliog.; *Engineering and Mining Jour.,* Dec. 7, 1918; *Science,* Dec. 20, 1918; *School and Society,* Dec. 28, 1918; *Wisconsin State Jour.* (Madison), Nov. 19, 20, 21, 1918; *Milwaukee Sentinel,* Nov. 20, 1918.]   G. P. M.

VAN HOOK, WELLER (May 16, 1862–July 1, 1933), surgeon was born at Greenville, Floyd County, Ind., the son of William Russell and Matilda (Weller) Van Hook. He was graduated from the Louisville, Ky., high school in 1881, from the University of Michigan in 1884, and from the College of Physicians and Surgeons of Chicago (later the medical department of the University of Illinois) in 1885. Following an internship at the Cook County Hospital he took up general practice near Chicago's west side medical center. In 1894 he went abroad and for a year did graduate work in Berlin and Vienna. Upon his return to Chicago he announced the limitation of his practice to surgery.

In 1892 he was appointed professor of principles of surgery at the College of Physicians and Surgeons, and at about the same time he became associated with the Chicago Post-Graduate Medical School as an instructor in clinical surgery. Four years later he transferred to the chair of surgery at Northwestern University Medical School, where he remained until 1908. He was an able teacher and had exceptional operative skill. While he had a general surgical practice he devoted himself especially to the surgery of the genito-urinary tract, in which field he was a pioneer in experimental work. He devised the generally employed method of repair of wounds of the ureter by lateral implantation of the upper segment of the divided tube into the lower; also, a method of implanting the severed ureter directly into the bladder. In April 1896 he published in *Annals of Surgery* his newly devised method of operation for the correction of hypospadias. This method, generally known as the Van Hook-Mayo operation, is equally applicable to the repair of epispadias. In addition to numerous articles in journals, he wrote the chapter "Constitutional Reactions to Wounds and Their Infections" for J. C. Warren and A. P. Gould, *The International Text-Book of Surgery* (1900), and, in collaboration with Dr. A. B. Kanavel, the chapter "Surgery of the Intestines" for W. W. Keen, *Surgery, Its Principles and Practice* (1906–13).

When or how he became a devotee of Theosophy is not recorded. From 1908 until his death he was a constant contributor of essays to *The Theosophist, The Messenger,* and *Reincarnation.* These essays are collected into two volumes, *The Cultural System* (1925) and *The Future Way* (1928). He speaks of them as "a group of essays upon various topics of the divine wisdom." In 1925 he published *Voyages,* a volume of essays concerning which in the "Foreword" he says: "The musings joined together here were written down, for the most part, on a pilgrimage in nineteen hundred and thirteen, to shrines and holy spots in Europe and Asia." His writings are graceful in style, poetic, deeply religious, widely tolerant. Coincident with the growth of his interest in Theosophy and probably as a result thereof, his enthusiasm for professional work and his prestige in the field of surgery waned. Though he continued his surgical practice, the younger generation of the city's medical profession knew him only as a name and his later years were passed in comparative obscurity. He died of a cerebral hemorrhage at his summer home at Coopersville, Mich. On June 16, 1892, he was married at Sweet Springs, Mo., to Anna C. Whaley of St. Louis, Mo.

[*Alumni Record of the Univ. of Ill., Chicago Departments* (1921); *Who's Who in America,* 1912–13, which is authority for dates of birth and marriage; *The Plexus,* June 1899; *Jour. Am. Medic. Asso.,* July 22, 1933; *Hist. of Medicine and Surgery and Physicians and Surgeons of Chicago* (1922); *Chicago Tribune,* July 2, 1933.] J. M. P—n.

VAN HORN, ROBERT THOMPSON (May 19, 1824–Jan. 3, 1916), representative from

Missouri, journalist, was born in East Mahoning, Indiana County, Pa., the son of Henry and Elizabeth (Thompson) Van Horn. He seems to have been descended from Christian Barentsen Van Horn who emigrated from Holland to New Netherland before 1653. As a boy he attended a subscription school near his birthplace, and by the age of nineteen he had largely mastered the printer's trade. From 1843 to 1855 he worked at his trade in Pennsylvania, New York, and Ohio, and he also studied law. He married Adela H. Cooley of Pomeroy, Ohio, on Dec. 2, 1848. They had four children. In 1855 he removed to Kansas City, Mo., which was his home the rest of his life. He bought the *Kansas City Enterprise,* a weekly, changed its name to the *Western Journal of Commerce,* later the *Kansas City Journal,* and in 1858 he began publishing it as a daily. It was a conservative (Douglas) Democratic paper until 1860, but upon the outbreak of the Civil War it became Unionist and Republican. With certain temporary exceptions he owned and controlled the *Journal* until 1897. Even while in Congress he wrote many of its editorials. His editorials were optimistic, stimulating, and logical. Though his style was a modernized sledge-hammer type, he was, nevertheless, a lucid and vigorous writer. Until the unique journalistic caliber of William Rockhill Nelson [*q.v.*] became manifest in the 1890's, if not thereafter, Van Horn was Kansas City's greatest press agent.

In 1861 he was elected mayor on the Union ticket and took control of the defense of the city. In September he was attached to the 13th Regiment of the Missouri Infantry for the defense of Lexington, Mo., was wounded, surrendered, and exchanged, and then placed as lieutenant-colonel with the 25th Missouri Infantry. His regiment was soon assigned to the Army of the Tennessee, and he took part in the battles of Shiloh and Corinth. In 1863 he returned to Missouri on recruiting assignment but because of his political duties resigned from the service in 1864. From 1863 to 1865 he was a state senator, and he again served as mayor before his senatorship expired. He was a delegate to every Republican national convention from 1864 to 1884 inclusive and was one of the "Immortal 306," who stood by Grant for a third term in 1880. In 1864 he was elected representative to Congress, served three consecutive terms, and later filled that office two more terms, 1881 to 1883 and 1895 to 1897. Because of his ability and whole-hearted work for the development of Kansas City, as well as the influence of the *Journal,* he was usually successful in winning office in a normally Democratic district. His work in Congress was marked by his stanch adherence to conservative Republican policies and by his effective efforts to aid Kansas City in becoming an industrial and railway metropolis.

Through his newspaper editorials and policies, his personal contacts with capitalists, and his state legislative and congressional activities he was able to achieve extraordinary results in making Kansas City the leading railroad center west of Chicago. When Leavenworth and St. Joseph were much larger towns and rivals for bridges and railroads across the Missouri River, he was successful in obtaining the Hannibal Bridge in 1869, and instrumental in bringing a half dozen trunk lines into Kansas City to aid her in outstripping them. He died in Kansas City.

[J. M. Greenwood, *Col. Robert Van Horn* (1905) and in *Mo. Hist. Rev.*, Jan. 1910–Apr. 1910; C. W. Whitney, *Kansas City, Mo.* (1908), vols. I–II; Roy Ellis, *A Civic Hist. of Kansas City* (1930); T. S. Case, *Hist. of Kansas City* (1888); H. C. McDougal, *Recollections* (1910); C. S. Williams, "Christian Barentsen Van Horn and his Descendants" (1911) a typescript in the Lib. of Cong.; *Kansas City Jour.*, Jan. 4, 1916.]

H. E. N.

VAN HORNE, WILLIAM CORNELIUS (Feb. 3, 1843–Sept. 11, 1915), railroad executive, the first of five children of Cornelius Covenhoven Van Horne and his second wife, Mary Minier (Richards), was born in Will County, Ill. On the paternal side, his ancestors were Dutch. His grandfather, Abraham Van Horne, was an officer in the Revolutionary forces and later a minister in the Dutch Reformed Church. On the maternal side, William was of German and French descent. His father, Cornelius, received his education at Union College, Schenectady, studied law, and became active in politics as a Democrat. He moved to Illinois in 1832, and, partly by farming and milling and partly by practising his profession as a lawyer, managed to earn a meager living and to rear his family. It was in these surroundings that William spent the first eight years of his life. There was no school or church in the vicinity and the boy's only schooling, until 1851 when the family moved to Joliet, was that furnished by his mother. When he was three years old he began to make sketches and early showed evidence of ability to draw. In Joliet his father was soon well established and within a year was elected the first mayor of the city. William made the most of his opportunity to attend the public school, to read every book that came his way, and to develop a hobby in collecting rock specimens and studying geology.

The auspicious beginning of the family's life in Joliet was changed when in 1854 the father died. The mother was left practically penniless but managed somehow to keep the family supplied with bread and the children at school. William, who was not an industrious student but had a quick intelligence and a retentive memory, was employed intermittently to deliver telegraph messages and learned to send and receive in the Morse code. At the age of fourteen he was given his first full-time job as telegraph operator, with the Illinois Central Railroad. Later he was engaged in similar capacity by the Michigan Central Railroad. He was the first operator in his district, and one of the earliest in the country, to receive by sound alone and dispense with the use of the recording tape. When the Civil War began he promptly enlisted, but his superintendent secured his release because his services as telegraph operator and general assistant were important to the railroad and because he was the main support of his mother.

In 1862 Van Horne transferred his service to the Chicago & Alton Railroad as ticket agent and operator in Joliet; in 1864, he became train dispatcher for the same railroad in Bloomington; four years later he was appointed superintendent of telegraph and two years afterward superintendent of transportation; in 1872, he became general superintendent of a subsidiary line, the St. Louis, Kansas City & Northern Railway. His success in that position led in 1874 to his appointment as general manager and subsequently as president of the Southern Minnesota Railroad, with offices in La Crosse, Wis. This road, then in its second receivership, was in wretched physical condition and the morale of employees was notoriously low, but under Van Horne the property was soon rehabilitated and the receivership terminated in 1877. He was so successful in this connection that when the road was acquired by another system he was asked in 1879 to return to the Chicago & Alton as its general superintendent. After brief service with his old employers, however, he became general superintendent of the Chicago, Milwaukee & St. Paul.

The size of that system, and its many problems of operation and development of traffic, afforded Van Horne new opportunities for the exercise of his abilities. During his two years as general superintendent he accomplished much in increasing the efficiency of train operation and in reducing operating costs. He had also to assume leadership in competitive struggles with rivals and in connection with one of those encounters (in 1880) he crossed swords with James J. Hill [q.v.], when the Chicago, Milwaukee & St. Paul threatened to invade the territory occupied by the nucleus of the present Great Northern. Hill had known of Van Horne's earlier success and was so strongly impressed by the qualities he exhibited in their encounter that he gave Van Horne the great opportunity of his life by recommending him to the directors of the Canadian Pacific Railway as the man most highly qualified to carry out the tremendous task of creating and giving the breath of life to the proposed transcontinental line from Montreal to a terminus on the Pacific Ocean. Van Horne took charge of the work of construction at Winnipeg on Dec. 31, 1881.

The story of the building of the Canadian Pacific is mainly a history of his achievements in overcoming stupendous difficulties. The physical problems and those concerning the relations of the company with its employees were peculiarly his; the problems of finance and relations with the government rested mainly on the shoulders of the directors, but they shared their burdens with him. The project was carried to completion in 1886 and Van Horne, who had served from 1881 to 1884 as general manager, and from 1884 to 1888 as vice-president, was elected president in August 1888. The eleven years of his presidency were marked by further growth in mileage, earning power, and ramification of auxiliary services. Failing health led him to resign on June 12, 1899, and accept election as chairman of the board of directors and member of the executive committee. In these positions, however, he was never active, and in 1910 he withdrew from all official connection with the Canadian Pacific.

The relief from heavy responsibilities in 1899 had quick and beneficial effect upon his health. Leisure he had found distasteful, so he turned to new and distant fields for additional creative work. A visit to Cuba in 1900 fired his imagination with the possibilities of a 350-mile railroad through the eastern provinces of the island. Because of legal complications incident to American occupation, it was not possible to obtain a charter until Cuba had established its own republican government, but, impatient of delay and firm in his faith in the soundness of the project, Van Horne did the unprecedented, accepting temporarily a revocable license in lieu of a charter and proceeding to purchase property for right of way and terminals. By this evidence of confidence in the honor of the Cuban people, by his skill as a diplomat in surmounting obstacles, and by his courteous and aboveboard dealings with the public authorities, he succeeded in winning public approval, and the needed charter was granted very soon after the Republic was organized. On Dec. 1, 1902, the Cuba Railroad was opened for traffic, less than two years from the date of Van Horne's first visit to the island.

His next railroad activity was in Guatemala, where in 1903 he undertook to direct the construction of the last sixty-five miles of a railroad from Puerto Barrios to the city of Guatemala. The completion of the line was delayed by insurrections and the depression of 1907, but the last spike was driven in January 1908. This relatively small enterprise gave Van Horne more trouble per mile of railroad than any other he had undertaken. Coincident with his activities in Cuba and Guatemala, he was a director or officer in several large industrial enterprises, such as the Laurentide Pulp Company, Grand Mère, Quebec; a salt company at Windsor, Ontario; tramway systems in several Canadian cities, as well as in Mexico and Brazil; and the Dominion Coal Company and the Dominion Iron and Steel Company of Cape Breton. He was also a member of the board of the Equitable Life Assurance Society, but knew little of its finance and was horrified by the scandals of 1905 and 1906. With advancing years and impairment of health his activities began to diminish, but in a few things he maintained continued interest. Returning from his last trip to Cuba in June 1915, he was stricken with fever and died in Montreal on Sept. 11 of that year.

In addition to his imposing graystone house in Montreal, Van Horne had a beautiful summer home in St. Andrews, N. B., and a pretentious winter home in Camagüey, Cuba. He took intense interest in designing and supervising the construction of the buildings and grounds, and himself painted some of the mural decorations. His early talent for drawing and painting had been developed as a means of diverting his mind from business cares and his later paintings had artistic merit. For many years he followed his early bent toward paleontology and treasured a large collection of fossils. Other hobbies of his were the collection of paintings and of rare Japanese pottery.

With Van Horne's ability to deal with men, either in directing work or in business transactions, was coupled a strange shyness in formal social gatherings. He declined more than once to accept an invitation from McGill University, of which he was a trustee, to receive an honorary degree. When he retired from the presidency of the Canadian Pacific, his colleagues among railroad executives had made plans for a testimonial dinner in New York as a tribute to him personally and to his substantial contributions to transportation, but Van Horne's dislike of publicity and his aversion to speechmaking blocked their efforts to do him public honor. When knighthood was offered to him, both in 1890 and at the end of 1891, he asked that it be deferred, but finally, in 1894, he accepted royal appointment as an Honorary Knight Commander of the Order of St. Michael and St. George. Prior to 1890 he had become naturalized under the Canadian laws.

In personal characteristics Sir William was of imposing and handsome appearance—tall, massively built, and bearded. Officially he was cold and austere, a leader of the driving type; personally, with friends, he was genial and companionable. He was entertaining as a story-teller, with a tendency in his late years to exaggerate. From those who worked under him he demanded first of all complete loyalty; to them he too was loyal and generous, but he was not noted for his contributions to charity, public institutions, and the like. His wealth was devoted in the main to his family, to his three homes, and to his hobbies.

In March 1867, while a train dispatcher at Bloomington, Ill., he married Lucy Adaline Hurd of Galesburg, Ill., who in 1858, because of her beauty and personal distinction, had been chosen to read the address of welcome when Abraham Lincoln visited Galesburg. Three children were born to them: a son who died in his fifth year and a son and a daughter who with their mother were living when Sir William died.

[The writer, as a youth, was employed by the Canadian Pacific Railway, and occasionally came in contact with Van Horne. The chief source is Walter Vaughan, *The Life and Work of Sir William Van Horne* (1920). See also O. D. Skelton, *The Railway Builders* (1916); J. M. Gibbon, *Steel of Empire* (1935); H. A. Innis, *A Hist. of the Canadian Pacific Railway* (1923); Beckles Willson, *The Life of Lord Strathcona and Mount Royal* (1915), vol. II; J. G. Pyle, *The Life of James J. Hill* (1917), vol. I; *Who's Who in America*, 1914–15; *Montreal Daily Star*, Sept. 13, 1915; *N. Y. Times*, Sept. 12, 1915.] W. J. C.

VAN ILPENDAM, JAN JANSEN (*c.* 1595–1647), commissary at Fort Nassau on the Delaware, apparently belonged to a well-to-do family of Haarlem, whose name appears on the records of that city as early as 1444. He himself, however, came from Leyden and was probably the Jan Jansen van Ilpendam who in 1616, at Delft, married Judick Hame. In May 1633 he sailed as supercargo on the yacht *Pernambuco* for Brazil, where, in 1635, at the taking of Porto Calvo, he was captured by the Portuguese. Returning to Amsterdam in the summer of 1636 he was appointed on Sept. 4 by the West India Company supercargo on the ship *Rensselaerswyck,* a privately owned vessel, which arrived at Manhattan on Mar. 4 of the following year. He was still at Manhattan on Aug. 5, 1637, when the ship made ready to return to Holland, but seems shortly afterwards to have been appointed commissary at Fort Nassau. In the spring of 1638, Willem

Kieft [*q.v.*], the newly arrived director general of New Netherland, sent Jan Jansen to the South River to protest in due form against the action of Peter Minuit [*q.v.*] in erecting there the arms of the Queen of Sweden; two years later, Van Ilpendam made a similar protest to Peter Ridder, the new Swedish commissioner, but in spite of these protests, his relations with the Swedish remained friendly. He assumed a more aggressive attitude toward the English, however, when, in 1641, some Englishmen of New Haven formed a Delaware Company and through their agents bought lands on both sides of the river, at the Varkens kill and on the Schuylkill. Acting under instructions from Kieft, Van Ilpendam promptly expelled the English from the Schuylkill, and two years later sat as one of the commissioners in a Swedish court of inquiry ordered by Governor Printz to examine the English who continued to trade on the Varkens kill. In 1644, some Boston merchants obtained a charter to trade on the Delaware River and Kieft once more ordered Van Ilpendam to protest against them, instructing him "rather to sink the English ship than to let it pass the fort" (quoted by Johnson, *post*, I, 396). On all these occasions Van Ilpendam seems to have acted with diligence and discretion. In 1645, however, he was accused of fraud and summoned to appear at Manhattan. The case against him was investigated by Cornelis van der Hoykens, the public prosecutor, from whose findings it appeared that Van Ilpendam had "grossly wronged the Company, both in giving more to the Indians than the ordinary rate and in other instances specified in the complaint, affidavits and in his accounts" (*Documents, post*, XII, 26). The Council, thereupon, on Feb. 8, 1646, ordered him with his papers and the fiscal's complaint to be sent to Amsterdam by the first ship, to defend himself before the directors of the Company. He died, apparently, not long after his departure from New Netherland, since on Aug. 16, 1647, his second wife, Catalyntje van Strassel, gave a power of attorney to Jan de Laet for a settlement of his accounts.

["Minutes of the Amsterdam Chamber of the Dutch West India Company, 1635–1636," *N. Y. Geneal. and Biog. Record*, July 1918; *N. Y. Colonial MSS. in N. Y. State Lib.*, see E. B. O'Callaghan, *Calendar of Hist. MSS*. . . . pt. I (1865); *Docs. Rel. to the Col. Hist. of . . . N. Y.*, vols. I (1856), XII (1877); J. R. Brodhead, *Hist. of the State of N. Y* (1853). vol. I; and Amandus Johnson, *The Swedish Settlements on the Delaware* (1911), vol. I.] A. J. F. v–L.

VAN LENNEP, HENRY JOHN (Mar. 18, 1815–Jan. 11, 1889), missionary and educator, was born at Smyrna in Asiatic Turkey, the son of Adèle Marie (de Heidenstam) and Richard

Van Lennep, both members of European families long resident in the Levant. His parents, acting on the advice of American missionaries, sent him at the age of fifteen to be educated in the United States, where he prepared for college in the Mount Pleasant Institute of Amherst, Mass., and in the Hartford (Conn.) Grammar School. In 1837 he graduated from Amherst College. Since he had decided while in college to become a missionary, he next spent a year at Andover Theological Seminary, then completed his religious training under the direction of Dr. Joel Hawes at Hartford, Conn. On Aug. 27, 1839, he was ordained as a Congregational minister at Amherst. On Nov. 3, he married Emma L., the daughter of Henry Bliss of Springfield, Mass., and later in the same year sailed for Turkey as a missionary of the American Board of Commissioners for Foreign Missions. He was at first stationed at Smyrna, where his wife died on Sept. 7, 1840. After extensive preaching tours through western Turkey and Greece, he visited the United States in 1843 to marry, on Sept. 4, Mary Elizabeth Hawes, the daughter of his former teacher. She died on Sept. 27 of the next year. On his return to Turkey in 1844 he was transferred to Constantinople. During the next ten years he not only carried on regular missionary duties but also taught in the seminary, later Robert College, at Bebek, a suburb of Constantinople, and traveled widely. A visit to Syria and Palestine in 1847 provided the material for his *Bible Lands, Their Modern Customs and Manners Illustrative of Scripture* (1875). Late in 1849 he was in the United States and on Apr. 18, 1850, married Emily Ann Bird, whose father, Isaac Bird, had been a missionary in Syria but had retired to live in Hartford, Conn. William Bird Van Lennep [*q.v.*] was their son. In 1854 he was transferred from Constantinople to Tokat, a city in north central Anatolia, to establish a mission station and theological seminary. His valuable *Travels in Little-Known Parts of Asia Minor* (2 vols., 1870), illustrated with his own sketches, is based on careful notes taken on journeys during which he visited and described many important archeological remains of the Hittite period. In 1861 he left Tokat and until 1863 was in the United States, but he returned to preach and teach in Smyrna until 1869, when failing eyesight and disagreement with mission policy led to his permanent settlement in the United States.

For three years he taught natural science, Greek, and modern languages in Ingham University at LeRoy, N. Y. He then retired to Great Barrington, Mass., and devoted himself to writing. His familiarity with local customs, mentalities, and languages, together with his lack of condescension toward the people of Turkey, made him an effective preacher and teacher. He used French, Armenian, Greek, and Turkish in addition to English, and he found his recreation in music, archeology, and painting. His *Oriental Album* (1862), a volume of colored representations of near eastern types and costumes, provides evidence of his proficiency as an artist. He died at Great Barrington.

[*The Encyc. of Missions* (1891), vol. II, ed. by E. M. Bliss; *Biog. Record of the Alumni of Amherst College* (1883), ed. by W. L. Montague; *Appletons' Ann. Cyc. . . . 1889* (1890); *N. Y. Tribune*, Jan. 12, 1889; a few letters in L. F. Hawes, *Memoir of Mrs. Mary E. Van Lennep* (1847); MS. "Footsteps of Homer: Niobe of Mt. Sipylus," in Princeton Univ. Lib.; information from son, E. J. Van Lennep, Great Barrington, Mass.]

W. L. W., Jr.

VAN LENNEP, WILLIAM BIRD (Dec. 5, 1853–Jan. 9, 1919), surgeon, was born at Constantinople, Turkey, the son of Emily (Bird) and Henry John Van Lennep [*q.v.*]. His early education, while living abroad, was entirely under the supervision of his parents. In 1869 the family returned to the United States. Between 1869 and 1872 he attended the Sedgwick School in Great Barrington, Mass. He graduated from Princeton College in 1876. In 1876 and 1877 he studied medicine in a doctor's office in LeRoy, N. Y. In 1880 he graduated from the Hahnemann Medical College of Philadelphia and received the gold medal of the faculty. Following graduation he served an internship of six months at the New York Homeopathic Charity Hospital, Ward's Island. He then returned to Philadelphia for a short time assisting Dr. Bushrod W. James in practice. From 1882 to 1884 he attended post graduate courses in London, Paris, and Vienna. He settled in Philadelphia upon his return from Europe and devoted himself to the practice of surgery exclusively. On Apr. 28, 1886, he was married to Clara Reeves Hart, the daughter of Thomas Hart of Philadelphia. He taught in the Hahnemann Medical College faculty from 1886 to his death, as professor of surgery after 1895. He was surgeon to the Pennsylvania Homoeopathic Hospital for Children and the Children's Homoeopathic Hospital of Philadelphia, senior surgeon of Hahnemann Hospital of Philadelphia, consulting surgeon of the Camden Homoeopathic Hospital, Woman's Homoeopathic Hospital of Philadelphia, Trenton Homeopathic Hospital, and the Harper Memorial Hospital. In 1888 he purchased the *Hahnemannian Monthly* from Pemberton Dudley and associated with himself as editor Clarence Bartlett. In 1910 he was elected dean of Hahnemann College. In that office he was instrumental in raising the standards required by modern medicine. He established new laboratories, obtained the Elkins Amphitheatre in the hospital, the amphitheatre in the maternity building, the library and reading room, and many other advancements.

Physically a giant, he was a man of remarkable personality and multiplicity of talents. He was whole-heartedly devoted to Hahnemann, sacrificing all efforts and interests in its behalf. As a teacher he is well remembered by all who sat before him. In all matters pertaining to medical and homeopathic affairs he was consulted frequently by men important in political and medical movements for advancement. He was a member of several medical societies and an active member of the Union League of Philadelphia. During the latter part of 1918, his health broke, and although not regarded as seriously ill, he died suddenly, survived by his wife and daughter.

[T. L. Bradford, *Homoeopathic Bibliog. of the U. S.* (1892) and *Index of the Homoeopathic Medical College of Pa. and the Hahnemann Medical College and Hospital* (1918); W. H. King, *Hist. of Homoeopathy* (1905), vol. IV; *Hahnemannian Monthly*, Jan. 1919; *Philadelphia Inquirer*, Jan. 10, 1919; personal acquaintance.]   C. B—t.

VAN METER, JOHN BLACKFORD (Sept. 6, 1842–Apr. 8, 1930), clergyman and educator, was born in Philadelphia, Pa., his father being Thomas Hurley Van Meter, of Dutch descent, and his mother, Johnetta (Blackford) Van Meter, whose ancestors were English and French. When the boy was about four years old, his father died, and some years later the family removed to Baltimore, Md. Van Meter was graduated in 1859 from the Male Central High School (later Baltimore City College). In recognition of his scholarly and other achievements, several institutions later granted him honorary degrees. On Dec. 19, 1866, he married Lucinda Cassell of Westminster, Md., by whom he had two daughters. For several years he taught in the public schools of Baltimore, and during 1868–69 was principal of the Male Academic and Female Collegiate Institute at Westminster, a Methodist institution. He began preaching in the Methodist Episcopal Church in 1864, and was ordained deacon in 1866 and elder in 1868. He had charge of circuits in Maryland and Pennsylvania (1864–68), and later held pastorates in Washington, D. C., Plainfield, N. J., and Baltimore. For ten years (1872–81) he was chaplain in the United States Navy, being for a time stationed at the naval academy at Annapolis. He resigned the position to take charge of the Huntington Avenue Methodist Episcopal Church in Baltimore.

There he was closely associated with John Franklin Goucher [*q.v.*], pastor of the First Methodist Church, in the founding of the Woman's College of Baltimore (later Goucher College). Though the institution came into existence under the auspices of the Baltimore Conference of the Methodist Episcopal Church, the success of the undertaking was largely due to the efforts of these two men. From 1882 to 1885 Van Meter was a member of the publishing committee of the *Baltimore Methodist,* through which was carried on the campaign for funds for the college. He was a member of all important committees of the Conference connected with its founding and of the board of trustees (1885–88, 1914–30). In 1888, when the college was opened, he was appointed professor of psychology, ethics, and the Bible, the first member of the faculty to be named. In 1914 he was retired with the rank of professor emeritus. He was dean of the college from 1892 to 1910 and acting president from 1911 to 1913. But, as President Goucher was frequently absent for long periods, Van Meter was the real administrator of the institution during much of his connection with it. It was he who largely shaped and maintained the educational policy of the college, a pioneer in the modern educational movement for women in the South, and who placed it among the best colleges of the country. It is a tribute to his zeal and ability that, though the college was practically bankrupt in 1911 when he became acting head, its high scholastic standards were intact. On the intellectual and spiritual ideals of its students he also exerted much influence. He was kindly, delightfully humorous, and so broadly tolerant as to be subjected to criticism for religious heresy. He died in Baltimore.

[*Who's Who in America,* 1918–19; J. T. Ensor, in *Minutes of the Baltimore Conference of the M. E. Church* (1930); pubs. of Goucher Coll.; T. P. Thomas, "Hist. of Goucher Coll." (in preparation); *Sun* (Baltimore), June 2, 1914, and Apr. 9, 1930 (obituary); private information.]   M. W. W.

VAN NAME, ADDISON (Nov. 15, 1835–Sept. 29, 1922), librarian and philologist, was born in Chenango, a few miles from Binghamton, N. Y. His father owned a sawmill and was interested in the shipping on the canal. Prepared for college at the Binghamton Academy and the Phillips Academy at Andover, he graduated from Yale College in 1858 at the head of his class, having won distinction also in various other ways. During one school year, probably in 1858–59 he taught in Perth Amboy, N. J. From July 1859 to January 1861 he was in Europe, spending the first year at the universities of Halle and Tübingen, and the last six months in travel. He passed the year following his return in Binghamton. In July 1861 he was appointed instructor in Hebrew in the theological department. He held this position until 1866. On May 2, 1865, he was licensed to preach by the (Congregational) New Haven West Association but never made any use of the license. In 1865 he was appointed librarian of Yale. He married in Berlin, Prussia, on Aug. 19, 1867, Julia Gibbs, the daughter of Josiah Willard Gibbs, 1790–1861, and the sister of his classmate, Josiah Willard Gibbs, 1839–1903 [qq.v.]. She died Jan. 4, 1916, leaving two sons and a daughter. An article, "Contributions on Creole Grammar," was published in the *American Philological Association Transactions, 1867–70* (1871); in 1873 the *Congrès International des Orientalistes: compte rendu de la première session* (vol. I) published his review of a book on the early history of Japan; in the same year the *American Cyclopaedia* published his article on the Arabic language and literature; and in 1875 *Johnson's New Universal Cyclopaedia* had an article from his pen on the Chinese language and literature. He built up the Yale collection of oriental literature until it became one of the best in the United States and gave his own books on the Far East to Yale in 1920. He was librarian of the American Oriental Society from 1873 to 1905, and of the Connecticut Academy of Arts and Sciences from 1865 to 1905. He attended the meeting in 1876 at which the American Library Association was formed, and he was a member of many other bibliothecal, bibliophilic, and bibliographic societies both in this country and abroad. His *Catalogue of the William Loring Andrews Collections of Early Books* (1913) is an excellent description of a number of books gathered to illustrate the first century of printing.

His chief work, however, was as librarian of Yale for forty years. He had an unusual range of interests, a remarkable memory for books, and extraordinarily good judgment in buying. When he took charge of the library it had about 44,500 volumes; when he resigned it had 300,000. This was a marvellous growth at a time when little money was available for books or service, but the most striking thing about this quarter of a million books is not their number but their quality. Becoming librarian emeritus in 1905, he spent some of his leisure years in Europe and his winters usually in Florida. He died in New Haven after a brief illness. On his eightieth birthday the Yale Corporation gave to the library his portrait, painted by W. Sergeant Kendall, the dean of the school of fine arts.

[*Second Biog. Record of the Class of Fifty-Eight, Yale College* (1869), *Fourth* . . . (1897), *Fifth* . . . (1908); *Yale Univ. Obituary Record, 1923* (1923); *Yale Weekly,* Oct. 6, 1922; votes of Yale Corporation; *New Haven Journal-Courier,* Sept. 30, and Oct. 3, 1922; information from family; personal acquaintance; statements of appointments at Yale from official records.]

A. K—h.

VAN NESS, WILLIAM PETER (*c.* 1778–Sept. 6, 1826), politician, jurist, was one of the sons of Peter and Elbertie (Hogeboom) Van Ness. The father was a Revolutionary patriot and county judge; two other sons gained some distinction—John P. became a member of Congress, and Cornelius P., governor of Vermont and minister to Spain. William was born at Claverack (later Ghent), Columbia County, N. Y.; he lived for a time in Kinderhook and for a time in Hudson, but for most of his life in New York City. His education was as thorough as the Kinderhook Academy, Columbia College, where he graduated in 1797, and private study in the law office of Edward Livingston [q.v.] could make it. In 1800 he began the practice of law in New York City as the admirer and protégé of Aaron Burr [q.v.]. In February 1801 he went with Burr to Albany, and wrote back to Livingston, his former preceptor, that the Republicans wanted Burr instead of Jefferson for president (*An Examination,* p. 61).

From that day until he became a judge, his political record was as devious as that of any of the New York politicians of the early years of the century when parties were still wavering and undeveloped. Burr admired and trusted him and was in turn worshipped by Van Ness, who became his defender in Peter Irving's *Morning Chronicle,* in politics, and on the dueling field. Van Ness entered with alacrity into the political broils of the Clintons, the Livingstons, and Burr. When James Cheetham [q.v.] published a vicious attack on Burr for his activities in state politics and in the presidential election of 1801, Van Ness replied in a pamphlet entitled *An Examination of the Various Charges Exhibited against Aaron Burr* (1803), signed Aristides—a specimen of invective justifiably compared to the *Letters of Junius.* At the time, no one but Van Buren and Burr, who supplied information on several local and national politicians, seems to have known the identity of the author. Van Ness wrote with such peculiar ferocity and venom that Cheetham's pamphlets appeared almost tame in comparison; Burr was so ably defended that newspapers rang with the unknown author's story of confused truth and fiction.

Breaking, in March 1804, with Van Buren, who, having come of age, chose to enter politics as a Clintonian, Van Ness threw himself more zealously into the political arena to the detriment of his law practice. Believing in duels as a gentlemanly method of ridding the party of its enemies, he played the rôle of second to Burr in the Burr-Hamilton duel (1804), a tragedy which he might have prevented. When the coroner's jury indicted him as accessory in the murder of Hamilton, he fled to Kinderhook and sent pleas for help to Van Buren, with whom he had become reconciled. Through the influence of the latter in the courts and with Governor Daniel D. Tompkins [q.v.], Van Ness procured the restoration of his civil rights. He was subsequently associated with Van Buren in several enterprises, including the Bank of Hudson in which they were both directors, but in 1812 clashed with him over a state senatorship, to which Van Buren was elected. In that year President Madison appointed Van Ness a judge in the federal court for the Southern District of New York, a position which he held until his death. In 1811 the New York legislature had requested him, aided by John Woodworth, to codify the laws for public information. The result, *Laws of the State of New York*, with notes, was published in 1813; it was notably successful in method and arrangement. His other works were *Reports of Two Cases in the Prize Court for the New York District* (1814) and *A Concise Narrative of General Jackson's First Invasion of Florida* (1826), published the year of his death. His careless supervision permitted the clerk of his court to embezzle more than $100,000, but the episode had no permanent effect upon his own reputation for business integrity. He was highly respected by his friends for his ability and party loyalty. Apparently he never married.

[J. G. Wilson, *The Memorial Hist. of the City of N. Y.*, vol. III (1893); *Names of Persons for Whom Marriage Licenses Were Issued . . . New York* (1860), p. 422; E. A. Collier, *A Hist. of Old Kinderhook* (1914); P. F. Miller, *A Group of Great Lawyers of Columbia County, N. Y.* (1904); D. S. Alexander, *A Pol. Hist. of . . . N. Y.*, vol. I (1906); D. T. Lynch, *An Epoch and A Man: Martin Van Buren and His Times* (1929); W. L. Mackenzie, *The Life and Times of Martin Van Buren* (1846); "Autobiography of Martin Van Buren," ed. by J. C. Fitzpatrick, in *Ann. Report Am. Hist. Asso., 1918*, vol. II (1920); Van Buren MSS., in Lib. of Cong.; *Niles' Weekly Register*, Sept. 16, 1826; *N. Y. Evening Post*, Sept. 7, 1826.]   W. E. S—h.

VAN NEST, ABRAHAM RYNIER (Feb. 16, 1823–June 1, 1892), clergyman of the Reformed Church in America, was born in New York City. He was the son of George Van Nest and Phoebe, daughter of Abraham Van Nest. His first American ancestor was Peter Van Nest who emigrated from the Netherlands in 1647 and settled in Brooklyn. Abraham Rynier graduated from Rutgers College in 1841, and from the New

Brunswick Theological Seminary in 1847. After serving briefly a mission at Greenpoint, Long Island, and the Associate Reformed Church of Newburgh, N. Y., he was from 1848 to 1862 pastor of the Twenty-first Street Reformed Church of New York City.

He then went abroad and for some fifteen years ministered to American residents there. During the year 1863–64 he was in charge of the American Chapel in Paris, and the year following, of the American Chapel at Rome. His most notable service, however, was in Florence (1866–75), where he established a church into which he drew people of diverse religious traditions and modes of life. For it he compiled a liturgical service, which became a model for other churches of a similar character. His sympathies were broad and his evangelical zeal intense; he became affiliated with the Waldenses and later with the Free Church of Italy. His fine personal and intellectual qualities, and his unfailing devotion to good causes, sustained by financial resources of his own, enabled him to accomplish much. Among his other activities, he had a principal part in the founding of the Protestant Orphanage at Florence. After leaving that city he established the American Union Church at Geneva.

Returning to the United States in 1878, he became pastor of the Third Reformed Church of Philadelphia, continuing in this pastorate until impaired health caused his retirement in 1883. For nine years thereafter until his death he was without charge. In 1879 he was president of the General Synod of the Reformed Church in America. He was zealous in furthering the welfare of New Brunswick Theological Seminary, and was a trustee of Rutgers College from 1878 until his death. His publications included occasional sermons and many articles in the religious press. He helped prepare for the press *Lectures on Pastoral Theology* (1853), by James Spencer Cannon, and *Expository Sermons on the Heidelberg Catechism* (2 vols., 1864), by George W. Bethune [q.v.], and wrote *Memoir of Rev. Geo. W. Bethune, D.D.* (1867). He died in New York City.

[E. T. Corwin, *Manual of the Reformed Church in America* (1902); *Biog. Notices of Grads. of Rutgers Coll.* (1892); *Acts and Proc. of the Gen. Synod of the Reformed Church in America*, vol. XVIII (1893); *Christian Intelligencer*, June 8, July 6, 1892.]   W. H. S. D.

VAN NOSTRAND, DAVID (Dec. 5, 1811–June 14, 1886), publisher, was born in New York City, fifth child of Jacob and Harriet (Rhodes) Van Nostrand. The founder of his family in America was Jacob Jansen, who emigrated from the Netherlands to settle on Long Island in 1638. To avoid confusion with other Jansens, Jacob's children added "van Noorstrandt" to the name, referring to the district of their father's origin, and as generations passed, this became transmuted into Van Nostrand. David's father, a successful merchant in New York City, died leaving eight children when David was only ten years old; but their mother was able to care for them and give them the beginnings of an education. David studied at Union Hall, Jamaica, Long Island, until he was fifteen, when he entered the employ of John P. Haven, a New York publisher and bookseller. Four years later, having saved a little money, he contemplated taking up his studies again; but he had become so valuable to Haven that the latter persuaded him to remain by promising him a partnership upon his coming of age. Van Nostrand accordingly continued with Haven until 1834, when he formed a partnership in a similar enterprise with William Dwight. The panic of 1837 drove the young men out of business, and Van Nostrand accepted the offer of a position from a friend, Lieut. John G. Barnard [q.v.], an army engineer, stationed at New Orleans in charge of the construction of fortifications in Louisiana and Texas.

While he was serving as clerk of accounts and disbursements in Barnard's office, Van Nostrand eagerly studied military engineering and kindred sciences and improved his acquaintance with engineers, scientists, and military men. Returning to New York about 1848, he opened a bookstore at Broadway and John Street. His acquaintance with military and technical men and writings now stood him in good stead; he was solicited by army and navy officers to import foreign books on military and naval science, and soon had built up an excellent trade. The United States Military Academy and other institutions were among his customers. He also ventured into publishing, issuing trade editions, usually enlarged and augmented, of various works, some of which had first been published for the government. In 1864 he took over from George Palmer Putnam [q.v.] the publication of The Rebellion Record, edited by Frank Moore [q.v.]; Van Nostrand issued volumes VII–XI (1864–68). In 1869 he installed his own printing plant, moving to more spacious quarters at 23 Murray Street, and established Van Nostrand's Eclectic Engineering Magazine. Devoting himself to the publishing of scientific, technical, and military works, he made his concern the largest specialized publishing house in America; and built up an extensive business abroad. He is credited with giving a distinct impulse to scientific investigation in the United States by his importation of foreign treatises, and with en-

couraging American technical men to write by publishing their work. Among the notable works he sponsored were Egbert L. Viele's Hand-book for Active Service (1861); Brig. Gen. Silas Casey's Infantry Tactics (1862); Henry Jomini's Life of Napoleon (2 vols., 1864), translated from the French by Gen. H. W. Halleck; Jomini's Treatise on Grand Military Operations (2 vols., 1865); Albert J. Myer's Manual of Signals (2nd ed., 1866); James B. Francis' Lowell Hydraulic Experiments (2nd ed., 1868); Julius Weisbach's Manual of Mechanics (1870); Charles B. Stuart's Lives and Works of Civil and Military Engineers (1871); and Squire Whipple's Elementary and Practical Treatise on Bridge Building (1872). He continued until his death to publish Van Nostrand's Engineering Magazine (the shorter title was adopted in 1878); six months after he died it was merged with the American Railroad Journal in the Railroad and Engineering Journal.

Van Nostrand was a member of the Union League Club and the St. Nicholas Society, and was one of the founders of the Holland Society of New York. He was twice married: his first wife, a daughter of Rev. Isaac Lewis of New York, died within eighteen months of their marriage; his second, Sarah A. Nichols of New York, survived him. He left no children.

[H. A. Stoutenburgh, A Doc. Hist. of the Dutch Congregation of Oyster Bay (1902); B. J. Lossing, Hist. of N. Y. City (1884), II, 705; J. C. Derby, Fifty Years among Authors, Books, and Publishers (1884); A Classified Cat. of Am. and Foreign Scientific Books for Sale by David Van Nostrand, Publisher and Importer (1871); Van Nostrand's Engineering Mag., July, Dec. 1886; Year Book of the Holland Soc. of N. Y., 1886–87; Union League Club Report, 1887; Publisher's Weekly, June 19, 1886; N. Y. Times and N. Y. Tribune, June 15, 1886.]
A. F. H.

VAN OSDEL, JOHN MILLS (July 31, 1811–Dec. 21, 1891), architect, was born in Baltimore, Md., the eldest of eight children of James H. Van Osdel, said to have been a descendant of Lyman Van Arsdale who emigrated to New York in 1653. Leaving his wife and family in Baltimore, the elder Van Osdel, a carpenter, cabinet maker, and building contractor, went to establish himself in New York. At fourteen, temporarily deprived, through an accident, of the father's support, John undertook to provide for the family by making benches and stools, on an original investment of one board. In New York, where the family soon went, Van Osdel entered into apprenticeship with his father and studied architectural books at the Apprentice Library. At eighteen he embarked in business for himself. In 1831 he married Caroline Gailer of Hudson, N. Y. Returning to Baltimore, he worked at his trade and found time to write one of the numerous carpentry handbooks of the time. In New York, to which he returned in 1836, he reached a turning point in his career—his meeting with William Butler Ogden [*q.v.*], the most prominent citizen of Chicago. Employed by Ogden to plan and erect a large mansion, he established his family in Chicago in 1837, the year of its incorporation as a city. The Ogden house on Ontario and Rush streets, which was burned in the fire of 1871, had a cupola and classic porticoes, occupied with its grounds a full city block, and was perhaps the most imposing dwelling in Illinois at the time. After one more excursion to New York in 1840, where for a short time he is said to have been associate editor of the *American Mechanic,* Van Osdel returned to Chicago and lived there until his death.

When Van Osdel went to Chicago the city contained only thirteen brick buildings; of the remainder more than half were one-story cottages, many of log construction. There were no architects. In 1844, after Van Osdel had spent a year or two in the machinery business and in shipbuilding (he finished two of the first steamboats built in the city), the building-contractors of the town promised to give him their support if he would open an architectural office. In that year six hundred new buildings were put up. In the three years ending in 1859, it is said, Van Osdel earned $32,000 and had to his credit most of the buildings of importance in the rapidly growing city, including the very large Second Presbyterian Church in Gothic, unusual in 1851. During the great fire of 1871, with characteristic resourcefulness, he dug a great pit in which he buried all his plans and records. While the embers were still red he opened a new office and in eighteen months erected 8,000 lineal feet of new buildings. Among them were the Palmer House, the Tremont House, the Oriental and Kendal buildings, and the McCormick and Reaper Blocks. He also designed what were regarded as the three finest residences in Illinois—those of Peter Schuttler in Chicago, Joel A. Matteson in Springfield, and John Wood in Quincy, Ill. His health, not unnaturally, showed signs of strain; in 1873 he spent some time in the Yosemite and the far West and for a year following was in Europe. In 1883 his recollections were published in the *Inland Architect and Builder* (Mar., Apr. 1883). He was trustee of Illinois Industrial University (later the University of Illinois) and was early actively interested in the development of technical training. In politics he was a Garrisonian Abolitionist. He was an active participant in the campaign of 1860, and

published a pamphlet and even wrote a poem on the subject. After the death of his first wife, in 1846 he married Martha McClellan of Kendall County, Ill.; since he had no children by either marriage, he adopted a boy, who died in youth, and three girls.

Van Osdel lived to see the development of skeleton construction, and the passing of his methods of design and construction. His first buildings (notably the second court house, begun in 1851) were in the style of the Greek Revival, as was the Rush Medical College (1844); of his later buildings none rises much above the low level of the taste of the time. A gentleman of the old school, with a charming dignity, wearing by custom a dress coat with brass buttons, he carried gracefully and modestly the honor of being Chicago's first architect.

[A. T. Andreas, *Hist. of Chicago* (3 vols., 1884–86); *Biog. Sketches of the Leading Men of Chicago* (1868), pp. 91–95; *Industrial Chicago* (3 vols., 1891); D. W. Wood, *Chicago and Its Distinguished Citizens* (1881); *Chicago* (1881); obituary in *Chicago Tribune*, Dec. 22, 1891; scrapbook made by Van Osdel's nephew, in the Art Institute of Chicago.]   T. E. T.

VAN QUICKENBORNE, CHARLES FELIX (Jan. 21, 1788–Aug. 17, 1837), Jesuit missionary and educator, was born at Peteghem in East Flanders, where he received his preliminary education. Later he attended a school at Denyze and the seminary at Ghent. After ordination as a Catholic priest in 1812, he taught in a preparatory seminary at Roulers and held a curacy at St. Genoix, near Courtrai. The negotiations between the United States and Great Britain which led to the Treaty of Ghent aroused interest in the former country, and among those who were attracted to the American mission field was Van Quickenborne. On Apr. 14, 1815, he entered the Jesuit novitiate at Rumbeke, and two years later he was assigned to the Maryland mission of the Society of Jesus.

After his arrival in the United States he taught the Scriptures at Georgetown College, conducted religious services in Alexandria, Va., and served as master of novices at Whitemarsh, where he built a stone chapel. He also attended the Catholic congregation at Annapolis, in which place, with the financial aid of the Carrolls, he erected a brick chapel. His religious and charitable services among the poor, and especially among the neglected negroes, challenged such attention that Archbishop Ambrose Maréchal [*q.v.*] described him as a saint. An enthusiastic priest of unbounded zeal and dynamic energy, he was named, in 1823, superior to conduct a Jesuit band of priests, novices, and lay brothers to Missouri.

In a log-cabin at Florissant Van Quickenborne as superior of the Jesuits and as the bishop's vicar general of Upper Louisiana founded the Missouri province of his Society. Soon a church, St. Regis Seminary for Indian boys, a school for Indian girls under the Ladies of the Sacred Heart, and a school at St. Charles gave evidence of his successful labors. In 1828 he established St. Louis College, which in 1832 was incorporated as St. Louis University. A born missionary, as early as 1827 he journeyed into the Osage Indian country, and later visited the Potawatomi, Kickapoo, and other western tribes. In 1836 the first Jesuit mission with a resident priest was founded among the Kickapoo tribesmen, and soon after St. Mary's Mission was established among the Potawatomi Indians near what is now Leavenworth. In the meantime he undertook a series of missionary excursions through Missouri, Illinois, and Iowa, becoming the pioneer of the Catholic faith in Edwardsville, Galena, and Springfield, Ill., and in Keokuk and Dubuque, Iowa. On these excursions he not only preached to the Indians but ministered to the scattered Catholic settlers and laborers in the lead mines. In 1835 and in the year following he was on the site of future Kansas City performing the first recorded baptisms and marriages in that region. He also rendered no small service to the missions of the West by training such Jesuits as Christian Hoecken, Pierre De Smet, and Peter Verhaegen [qq.v.]. In order to finance his work and to popularize Jesuit enterprises he gave lectures and collected money in the East. Accounts of the missions which he wrote to his superiors were published in the *Annales de la Propagation de la Foi* from 1826 to 1836. Worn out by his strenuous labors, Van Quickenborne died before he was fifty, while stationed in the missionary parish of Portage des Sioux.

[Scattered information, sometimes conflicting, is supplied by *Catholic Encyc.*; *Records of the Am. Catholic Hist. Soc.*, vol. II (1889), p. 198, vol. XXII (1911), p. 265, vol. XXVII (1916), pp. 99 f.; *Am. Catholic Hist. Researches*, Apr. 1895; J. G. Shea, *Hist. of the Cath. Missions among the Indian Tribes of the U. S.* (1855); *Metropolitan Cath. Almanac* (1838); John Rothensteiner, *Hist. of the Archdiocese of St. Louis* (1928); G. J. Garraghan, *Catholic Beginnings in Kansas City, Mo.* (1920) and *Saint Ferdinand de Florissant* (1923); J. A. Griffin, *The Contribution of Belgium to the Catholic Church in America* (1932).]   R.J.P.

VAN RAALTE, ALBERTUS CHRISTIAAN (Oct. 17, 1811–Nov. 7, 1876), founder of a Dutch settlement in Holland, Mich., was born at Wanneperveen near Zwartsluis, in the Netherlands. His father, the Rev. Albertus van Raalte, and his mother, Christina Caterina Harking, were the parents of sixteen other children. Christiaan was a favored son, and in June 1829 he

matriculated at the University of Leyden, where he studied medicine and then theology. At the University he met Anthony Brummelkamp, who profoundly affected his whole career by inspiring him to religious fervor. When he had completed the theological course, he received a license to preach in the Reformed Church, but he was not formally admitted to the ministry because he refused to subscribe to all the regulations of the Dutch Reformed Church. On Nov. 1, 1834, a new church had been founded, which was named the *Gereformeerde,* instead of the *Hervormde,* Church, and Van Raalte's sympathies were strongly with the seceders because he thought that the established church needed a second reformation. For a time he served as minister in the new church, and in 1844 he removed to Arnhem in order to assist Brummelkamp in training candidates for the ministry in the newly formed denomination. The next year, owing to unfavorable economic conditions prevailing in the Netherlands, a small number of Van Raalte's acquaintances made preparations to emigrate to North America. During a severe illness in the summer of 1846 the thought occurred to him that he should, like a modern Moses, lead his comrades through the wilderness in a foreign country (A. Brummelkamp, Jr., *Levensbeschryving van wijlen Prof. A. Brummelkamp,* Kampen, 1910). Prompt action followed this thought.

In November 1846 he arrived in New York, and about one week later he was cordially received in Albany by Dr. I. N. Wyckoff, who gave him great encouragement. In December he arrived at Detroit, and in the following month he and his companions formulated a plan to found a settlement in western Michigan. On Feb. 9, 1847, accompanied by his wife, Christina Johanna De Moen, to whom he had been married on Mar. 11, 1836, and several men, he arrived at a place that he decided to name Holland, in honor of his native country. Two years later the settlement was visited by Wyckoff, who published a description in *The Christian Intelligencer,* Sept. 20, 1849. Rapidly the number of Dutch settlers increased. Van Raalte was their preacher as well as their physician. In 1867, however, he resigned his position as minister, claiming that, since he had never been ordained, the congregation needed a real minister. He strongly favored the cause of education, and he may be regarded as one of the founders of Hope College and the theological seminary situated at Holland, Mich. He founded *De Hope,* a religious periodical in the Dutch language. He was a born leader, ambitious, industrious, aggressive, broad-minded, patient, undaunted by danger and hardship. but he was afflicted after 1855 by financial worries and bodily disease. At his death he was survived by two sons and five daughters.

[*Album Studiosorum Academiae Luqduno Batavae* (1875); J. A. Wormser, *Een Schat in aarden Vaten*, I, *Het Leven van Albertus Christiaan van Raalte* (1915); H. E. Dosker, *Levensschets van Rev. A. C. v. Raalte* (1893); Anthony Brummelkamp, *Holland in Amerika* (1847); *Zalsmans Jaarboekje* contains numerous articles on Van Raalte; A. J. Pieters, *A Dutch Settlement in Michigan* (1923); J. Van Hinte, *Nederlanders in Amerika* (1928), 2 vols.]   A. H.

VAN RENSSELAER, CORTLANDT (May 26, 1808–July 25, 1860), Presbyterian clergyman, was born in Albany, N. Y., the son of Stephen Van Rensselaer [*q.v.*] by his second wife, Cornelia, daughter of the distinguished jurist William Paterson [*q.v.*]. He grew up with all the advantages that wealth and the high social position of his family afforded. Having received his preliminary education in a boarding school at Hyde Park, conducted by Dr. Benjamin Allen, he entered Yale College in 1823 and was graduated four years later. He then studied law and in 1830 was admitted to the New York bar. Believing, however, that a man of property "is under peculiar obligation to make himself useful," and doubting that it was possible for him to retain proper religious feelings and be "occupied with the ordinary vanities and pursuits of the world" (*Memorial, post,* p. 24), he abandoned law and prepared for the ministry. After spending two years at Princeton Theological Seminary, he completed his course at Union Seminary, Hampden-Sidney, Va., and was ordained to the ministry on Apr. 18, 1835, by the Presbytery of Hanover.

For a time he devoted himself to giving religious instruction to the slaves on Virginia plantations, but increasing opposition to such work soon compelled him to abandon it. On Aug. 2, 1836, he was called by a few Presbyterians in Burlington, N. J., to become their pastor and establish a church. He at once began work and on June 29, 1837, was formally installed. During his comparatively short pastorate, lasting only to May 19, 1840, he developed a vigorous organization and superintended the building of a church edifice. Never again a regular pastor, he maintained a lively interest in the welfare of this congregation for the remainder of his life.

Following his resignation, he ministered to a feeble church in Washington, D. C., for a time and in 1843 was drafted by Princeton Theological Seminary to raise much needed funds. As a result of his solicitations in various parts of the country, he presented the institution with an endowment of $100,000. In February 1846 he was called to the work in which he rendered his most conspicuous service—that of corresponding secretary and chief executive officer of the Presbyterian Board of Education. During the fourteen years he occupied this position he greatly widened the scope of the board's activities. When he assumed office these activities were confined chiefly to furnishing support to candidates for the ministry; under his direction the board furthered the organization of parochial schools, a project in which he was much interested, and the establishment of Presbyterian academies and synodical colleges. He wrote and lectured extensively, originated and edited the *Presbyterian Magazine* (1851–59), and published each year from 1850 until his death a volume of articles, *The Home, the School, and the Church,* on the subject of education. Shortly after his death there was issued, 1861, a collection of his writings, *Essays and Discourses,* which includes a considerable work entitled, "Historical Contributions Relative to the Founders, Principles, and Acts of the Presbyterian Church, with Special Reference to the Division of 1837–8." In 1857 he was elected moderator of the General Assembly (Old School).

He was a man of large frame and everything about him suggested strength and endurance. Seemingly never at rest, he studied and wrote through long hours of travel, and even at business meetings, when his attention was not required, he composed letters or made notes for future use. During his last illness he continued to dictate almost to the end. He was well informed, but not a scholar; an instructive preacher, rather than an effective one. His administrative gifts were marked, and what he lacked in other respects he made up for in perseverance and industry. His devotion to his calling was complete and his services were rendered gratuitously; of his wealth he gave freely to many causes. His death occurred in his fifty-third year at his residence on the Delaware River, Burlington, N. J., and he was buried in the family vault at Albany. On Sept. 13, 1836, he had married Catharine Ledyard Cogswell, by whom he had seven children.

[*Memorial of Cortlandt Van Rensselaer* (1860), containing addresses and articles from the *N. Y. Commercial Advertiser,* July 27, 1860, *World* (N. Y.), Aug. 10, 1860, *N. Y. Observer,* Aug. 2, 1860, and other papers; W. W. Spooner, *Hist. Families of America* (n.d.); Alfred Nevin, *Encyc. of the Presbyterian Church in the U. S. A.* (1884); *Princeton Theological Sem. Biog. Cat.* (1909).]   H. E. S.

VAN RENSSELAER, MARIANA GRISWOLD (Feb. 25, 1851–Jan. 20, 1934), author and art critic, was born in New York City, the daughter of George and Lydia (Alley) Griswold.

She is said to have been a descendant of Matthew Griswold who emigrated to New England in 1639 and settled first in Windsor, Conn., later at Lyme. She was educated chiefly by private tutors at home and by foreign travel, especially in Germany. On Apr. 14, 1873, in Dresden, she married Schuyler Van Rensselaer, an engineer, a descendant of Kiliaen van Rensselaer who was the original holder of the great Van Rensselaer land patent of 1635. They lived in New Brunswick, N. J., her husband's home, until his death in 1884; they had one son, George Griswold, who died tragically in 1892. Going back to New York after her husband's death, Mrs. Van Rensselaer turned to writing and produced a long series of books and articles, chiefly on art and architecture. Her *Book of American Figure Painters* appeared in 1886. In the same year she published a series of reviews, "Art in Phoenicia and Cyprus," in the *American Architect and Building News* (Mar. 20–May 22, 1886), which revealed her surprising scholarship as well as her charm of style. Her other books include *American Etchers* (1886); *Henry Hobson Richardson and His Works* (1888), her most important work on architecture, noteworthy as the first significant monograph on a "modern" American architect; *Six Portraits* (1889), on Italian Renaissance artists; *English Cathedrals* (1892), with illustrations by Joseph Pennell [*q.v.*]; and *Art Out of Doors* (1893), on gardens and landscape architecture. She also produced *Should We Ask for the Suffrage?* (1894), a pamphlet vigorously opposing woman's suffrage; *One Man Who Was Content* (1897), a collection of short stories; *Poems* (1910); and *Many Children* (1921). Her best-known work is her monumental and authoritative *History of the City of New York in the Seventeenth Century* (2 vols., 1909), the research for which had occupied her for years. Largely as a result of its publication she received the honorary degree of Litt.D. from Columbia University in 1910. In 1923 she was awarded the gold medal of the American Academy of Arts and Letters for distinction in literature. Her other activities included serving as an inspector of New York City schools for two years and as president of the Public Education Association of New York (1899–1906). For many years she lived in a fine old house at 9 West Tenth Street, where she died.

Her work is important as the almost perfect expression of a cultural breadth, a cultivated tolerance, and an artistic sensitivity which, united, were characteristic of the finest flowering of nineteenth-century American life. Though not profound, her books are in general sound and, what

is more, delightful reading. Except in the New York *History,* her scholarship lies rather in the tasteful synthesis of existing learning than in any deep research of her own, and therein is its greatest value. She not only expressed the new interest in art that was current in the educated America of the eighties and nineties, but she became one of its chief leaders. Such a book as her *English Cathedrals,* for example, did a great deal to rewaken the public to the beauty of Gothic architecture, as well as to pave the way for many less sound and less well written popularizations to follow. She popularized taste and knowledge in the only true way, by honesty of approach and beauty of style. Her *Richardson* remains a model of appreciative biography, a charming monument to a great man. She was an honorary member of the American Institute of Architects, the American Society of Landscape Architects, and the American Historical Association, and in 1933 was elected a fellow of the New York State Historical Association.

[E. E. Salisbury, *The Griswold Family of Conn.* (1884); *Who's Who in America,* 1934–35; *Who's Who in N. Y.,* 1914; Catherine M. C. Hardie, "Treating More Esp. of Helena Van Rensselaer and Jacob Wendell," MS. in N. Y. Pub. Lib.; obituaries in *N. Y. Herald Tribune* and *N. Y. Times,* Jan. 21, 1934.]

T. F. H.

VAN RENSSELAER, MARTHA (June 21, 1864–May 26, 1932), home economist, was born in Randolph, N. Y. Her father, Henry Killian Van Rensselaer, was a direct descendant of Kiliaen van Rensselaer, first patroon of the manor of Rensselaerswyck. Her mother, Arvilla Owen, was of Welsh ancestry and is said to have been related to Robert Dale Owen [*q.v.*]; she was a remarkable woman who, in spite of the cares of a large family, still found time to reach outside the narrow intellectual boundaries imposed by a restricted income in a little village. In 1884 Martha Van Rensselaer graduated from Chamberlain Institute in Randolph. When she returned there as its preceptress after some years of rich and varied adventure in teaching, she realized one of her childhood dreams. For six years (1894–1900) she served as school commissioner of Cattaraugus County. It was while pursuing this task, which gave her wide and intimate contacts with rural people, that she began to picture the possibilities for the education of country women to which she later devoted herself. In 1900 she was called to Cornell University to organize a service for farm women similar to the extension courses offered farmers. This began with a reading course, centered on the problems of the farm home, in which six thousand readers were enrolled the first year.

Under her direction in 1903 the first credit course in home economics was offered at Cornell; in 1904 the course for farm women was included in the newly created New York State College of Agriculture, and in 1907 a department of home economics was organized at Cornell with Martha Van Rensselaer as lecturer. In 1911 she became professor of home economics, in 1924 director of the School of Home Economics established in 1919 as part of the New York State College of Agriculture, and in 1925 director of the New York State College of Home Economics.

During these years, in which a reading-course for farm homes developed under her direction into a vast extension service available to all the homes of the state and led to the establishment of a college, Martha Van Rensselaer served in many other capacities. She was a member of the executive staff of the United States Food Administration during the World War, home-making editor of the *Delineator* (1920–26), assistant director of the White House conference on child health and protection (1929–32), and chairman of the committee on home-making, housing, and family life of President Hoover's conference on home-building and ownership. She was sent to Belgium on special service for the American Relief Commission and was made chevalier of the Order of the Crown. She received the degree of A.B. at Cornell in 1909. She was president of the American Home Economics Association (1915–16). In 1923 she was chosen as one of the twelve most distinguished women of the United States by a committee appointed by the National League of Women Voters. With Flora Rose and Helen Canon, she published *A Manual of Home-Making* (1919). She lived to see the foundations rise of a magnificent new building that to her characterized the ideal for which she had spent her years at Cornell. She died in 1932 after a long and serious illness which had not been allowed to interfere with her program of living.

[*Who's Who in America*, 1930–31; *Cornell Univ., Twenty-Eighth Ann. Report by President Schurman, 1919–20*; Cornell Univ. Cats.; *Jour. of Home Economics*, Sept. 1932; obituaries in *Ithaca Jour. News*, May 26, *N. Y. Times* and *N. Y. Herald Tribune*, May 27, 1932.]   F. R.

VAN RENSSELAER, NICHOLAS (*c.* Sept. 25, 1636–1678), clergyman, was born in Amsterdam, North Holland, the eighth child of Kiliaen and Anna (van Wely) van Rensselaer. Kiliaen, a wealthy merchant and a director of the West India Company, was the first patroon of the Manor of Rensselaer on the Hudson River in New Netherland. Of Nicholas' early life little is known; while visiting Brussels, he met Charles

Stuart, later Charles II, King of England, then an exile on the Continent. Young Van Rensselaer, with fortunate prevision, assured the prince that the Stuarts would be restored to power in England, and that he would ascend the throne of his father. Because of this incident Charles remembered Van Rensselaer when he had forgotten greater Dutch benefactors.

On Oct. 2, 1662, Van Rensselaer was received in the Classis of Amsterdam, and not long after he accompanied Michiel van Gogh, Dutch ambassador, to London as chaplain of the embassy. Charles II in 1664 launched his first war against the Dutch, but when van Gogh returned home the following year, the chaplain remained, and the King gave him a license to preach to the Dutch congregation at Westminster. In addition, Van Rensselaer was ordained a deacon of the Church of England by the Bishop of Salisbury, and was appointed lecturer at St. Margaret's, Lothbury. As a personal mark of regard, Charles gave him a gold snuffbox, which is preserved by the Van Rensselaer family. In 1670 Van Rensselaer was in the Netherlands again, matriculating as a V. D. M.—minister of God's word—at the University of Leyden. He gave his residence as Amsterdam and his age as thirty-three. Two years later he was accepted by the Classis of Amsterdam as an "Expectant for Foreign Churches." These ordinations and appointments were the basis of his claim and preferment in the province of New York.

When Sir Edmund Andros [*q.v.*] came to New York as governor, he was accompanied by Nicholas van Rensselaer, who was recommended to him by the Duke of York for a Dutch pulpit. Andros took great interest in the provincial churches, but, though he had much regard for English orders, he did not look upon Dutch orders with the same respect. One of his first acts was an attempt to induct Van Rensselaer into the church of Albany as colleague of Gideon van Schaats. The Albany consistory resisted, holding that if Van Rensselaer was an Anglican clergyman, then he was not a minister of the Church of Holland. A temporary adjustment of the difficulty was obtained when William Van Nieuwenhuysen, pastor of the Reformed Church of New York, came to Albany as Van Schaats' assistant. Undefeated, Van Rensselaer went to New York with the understood purpose of administering baptism to children. Opposed by Van Nieuwenhuysen, he complained to the governor, and the dispute came before the Council. The proceedings, lasting from Sept. 25 to Oct. 2, 1675, opened with the introduction of Nieuwenhuysen's declaration that he did not look upon

Van Rensselaer as a lawful minister, or his admittance to the Albany pastorate as lawful. After Van Rensselaer's submission of his papers, Van Nieuwenhuysen still insisted that in order to administer the sacraments of the Dutch Church, a minister should have promised "to conduct himself in his services conformably to their Confession, Catechism and Mode of Government." Van Rensselaer accepted these requirements, and was installed in the Albany pastorate. A year later Jacob Leisler [q.v.] and Jacob Milborne declared that Van Rensselaer was not orthodox and Van Rensselaer sued the two for slander. The case finally reached the Governor's Council, and the parties were ordered to be reconciled "by the friendly shaking of hands" (*Minutes of the Court, post*, II, 146–50, 153–55, 162–67).

In 1677 Van Rensselaer was deposed by the governor on the charge of leading a bad life. The authorities to whom reference was made for support of the accusation were Van Nieuwenhuysen and Schaats. It was not unnatural that Van Rensselaer should have been the victim of religious animosity. He had come to America from the most liberal school of learning in Europe, established in memory of the siege of Leyden, and there he may easily have learned to reconcile doctrinal distinctions. Conditions, however, were unpropitious for so broad a mission. Then, too, Charles II, his patron, had lately waged a second war against the Netherlands; moreover, Charles's court, where the young preacher began his ministry, was not esteemed as a school for piety. On Feb. 10, 1675, Van Rensselaer married Alida Schuyler, sister of Peter Schuyler [q.v.]; he had no children. After his death his widow married Robert Livingston [q.v.].

[E. T. Corwin, *Ecclesiastical Records: State of N. Y.* (7 vols., 1901–16); E. B. O'Callaghan, *The Doc. Hist. of the State of N. Y.* (quarto ed.), III (1850), 526–30; E. T. Corwin, *A Manual of the Reformed Church in America . . . 1628–1902* (1902); M. K. Van Rensselaer, *The Van Rensselaers of the Manor of Rensselaerswyck* (copr. 1888); Maunsell Van Rensselaer, *Annals of the Van Rensselaers in the U. S.* (1888); N. Y. State Lib. *Van Rensselaer Bowier Manuscripts* (1908) and *Minutes of the Court of Albany, Rensselaerswyck and Schenectady*, vols. II–III (1928–32), tr. and ed. by A. J. F. van Laer; W. W. Spooner, *Historic Families of America* (n.d.).]   R. E. D.

VAN RENSSELAER, SOLOMON (Aug. 6, 1774–Apr. 23, 1852), soldier, congressman, was born in Rensselaer County, N. Y., the son of Henry Kiliaen van Rensselaer, a general in the Revolution, and his wife, Alida (Bradt). He was fifth in descent from Kiliaen van Rensselaer, the first patroon (J. B. Holgate, *American Genealogy*, 1848). In 1792 Solomon entered the United States Army as a cornet of cavalry, and in 1794 served as a captain under Gen. Anthony

Wayne [q.v.] in his campaign against the Indians. He was seriously wounded in the battle of Fallen Timbers, Aug. 20, 1794; was commissioned major in 1799; and was honorably discharged June 15, 1800. He was adjutant general of New York, 1801–09, 1810–11, and 1813–21.

At the opening of the War of 1812 he was assigned to the post of aide-de-camp to his relative, Maj.-Gen. Stephen Van Rensselaer [q.v.], and went with him to the Niagara River. In August 1812, upon receipt of news that Henry Dearborn [q.v.] and Sir George Prevost had arranged an armistice, he negotiated with General Sheaffe a supplementary agreement by which either party might, during the armistice, bring forward troops and supplies on Lake Ontario—an arrangement very advantageous to the United States. When the elder Van Rensselaer resolved to throw his army across the river and seize the British position at Queenstown (Queenston), Solomon was detailed to command the advance party of militia. His part in the attack of Oct. 13, 1812, was successfully carried out. With a force of some three hundred, he gained a foothold on the Canadian shore, and though he suffered several wounds, the troops under his direction scaled the heights above Queenstown and captured a British battery near the summit. Van Rensselaer's wounds necessitated removing him to the American side, and in later years he ascribed the ensuing disaster to his enforced absence from the battlefield— a view of the matter hardly sustained by the facts. In February 1813 the Council of Appointment restored him to the position of adjutant general of the state, and although he campaigned actively for Stephen Van Rensselaer, Federalist candidate for governor against Daniel D. Tompkins [q.v.] in the spring of 1813, he continued in his position and was apparently on excellent terms with Tompkins.

Elected to Congress in 1818 and reëlected in 1820, he opposed the Missouri Compromise. In January 1822 he resigned his seat to accept the postmastership at Albany, to which he had been named over the protest of Vice-President Tompkins, Senator Van Buren, and Senator Rufus King [qq.v.], the first two objecting to having this office assigned to a former Federalist (C. F. Adams, *Memoirs of John Quincy Adams*, vol. V, 1875, pp. 479–82; J. C. Fitzpatrick, "The Autobiography of Martin Van Buren," *Annual Report of the American Historical Association . . . 1918*, vol. II, 1920, pp. 125–26). Upon Jackson's election to the Presidency, Van Rensselaer's New York opponents sought to bring about his removal, but Van Rensselaer went to Washington and by calling attention to his honorable wounds in a dramatic interview with Jackson, saved his position (J. W. Forney, *Anecdotes of Public Men*, 1873, 281–83). He was removed, however, by Van Buren in 1839. In the Whig convention at Harrisburg in December 1839, he was a delegate from New York and claimed credit for swinging the delegation from that state to Harrison and thus bringing about his nomination. He was rewarded with restoration to the Albany postmastership in 1841, only to be again removed by Tyler two years later. He sought the same office again from Taylor in 1849, but without success.

As a young man, a penchant for sharp criticism of opponents involved him in a number of personal quarrels, among them an affray with Lieutenant-Governor Tayler of New York in 1807 (see D. R. Fox, *The Decline of Aristocracy in the Politics of New York*, 1919, pp. 104–07) and a near-duel with Peter B. Porter in 1812. In later life he was on cordial terms with some of his former enemies. It is evident that he thought of himself as an ill-rewarded military hero—a rôle for which the chief bases were the gallant but futile assault at Queenstown and the wounds he received there and at Fallen Timbers. In 1836 he published *A Narrative of the Affair of Queenstown in the War of 1812*. He was married, Jan. 17, 1797, to his cousin, Harriet Van Rensselaer, by whom he had several children.

[In addition to sources cited above, see C. Van R. Bonney, *A Legacy of Hist. Gleanings* (2 vols., 1875); *Albany Evening Jour.*, Apr. 24, 1852.] J. W. P.

VAN RENSSELAER, STEPHEN (Nov. 1, 1764–Jan. 26, 1839), eighth patroon, soldier, congressman, was born in New York, the son of Stephen and Catherine (Livingston) Van Rensselaer, and fifth in direct descent from Kiliaen van Rensselaer, the first patroon. Upon his father's death in 1769, which left the five-year-old child heir to a vast landed estate in Rensselaer and Albany counties, his grandfather, Philip Livingston [*q.v.*], took charge of his education which was begun at Albany and after numerous changes due to the disturbances of wartime was completed at Harvard, where he was graduated in 1782. On June 6, 1783, he married Margaret Schuyler, daughter of Gen. Philip Schuyler [*q.v.*], and in 1785 went to occupy the manor house near Albany. By granting perpetual leases at moderate rentals in kind, he brought more of his estate under cultivation than had any of his predecessors, but he refused to sell any part of his lands outright. He was elected as a Federalist to the New York Assembly in 1789 and 1790, served in the state Senate from 1791 to 1795, and as lieutenant-governor from 1795 to 1801. In

1801 he was the unsuccessful Federalist candidate for governor against George Clinton [*q.v.*]. He sat in the Assembly in several subsequent sessions and in the constitutional conventions of 1801 and 1821.

Meanwhile he had become a major-general in the state militia, and although without active military experience, was called upon by Gov. Daniel D. Tompkins [*q.v.*] in 1812 to take command of the entire northern frontier of the state. He set up his headquarters at Lewiston and by October 1812 had assembled some six thousand troops on the Niagara frontier, but the men lacked discipline and equipment, and their efficiency was further impaired by the refusal of Brig.-Gen. Alexander Smyth [*q.v.*] of the regular army to take orders from or cooperate with Van Rensselaer. Without the support of Smyth, who held his brigade at Buffalo, Van Rensselaer ventured to attack Queenstown (Queenston), Oct. 13, 1812. The advance column secured a foothold on the Canadian shore, but when the remainder of the militia refused to cross the river to their support, they were compelled to surrender, with an aggregate loss of nearly a thousand men. Modern critics hold that the possible advantages to be gained by a successful attack at this point were not sufficient to justify the risk, and that Van Rensselaer was culpable for not having better ascertained the temper of his army (Babcock, *post*, pp. 55–56). Van Rensselaer's correspondence shows that he believed an aggressive stroke was expected by his superiors and that he was both stung and alarmed by criticism of his inaction in the army itself (Solomon Van Rensselaer, *post*). After the defeat he resigned his command and returned to Albany. In the spring of 1813 he again received the Federalist nomination for governor but was defeated by Tompkins.

In 1822 he was elected to Congress to succeed his kinsman Solomon Van Rensselaer [*q.v.*], and retained his seat until 1829. In the choice of the president by the House of Representatives in 1825, he cast the deciding vote in the New York delegation and therefore in the election. He was thought to have pledged his vote to William H. Crawford [*q.v.*], but cast it, on the first ballot, for John Quincy Adams. Van Rensselaer explained to Van Buren that upon taking his seat, being still in doubt how to vote, he had bowed his head in prayer and upon opening his eyes had seen at his feet a ballot bearing Adams' name.

The Patroon's chief services to his state were neither military nor political but economic and educational. An early advocate of a canal to connect the Hudson with the Great Lakes, he was a

Van Rensselaer

member of the first canal commission in 1810 and of the second, instituted in 1816, of which from 1825 to his death he was president. In 1820 he was chosen president of the state's first board of agriculture, which he had been instrumental in creating. He bore the expense of a geological survey by Amos Eaton [q.v.] of a belt of land following the Erie Canal across New York and thence across New England, with special reference to soil and agricultural possibilities (*A Geological and Agricultural Survey of the District Adjoining the Erie Canal . . . Taken under the Direction of the Hon. Stephen Van Rensselaer*, 1824). In 1824 he established at Troy a school primarily for the training of teachers "for instructing the sons and daughters of farmers and mechanics" in "the application of science to the common purposes of life" (letter of Van Rensselaer's, quoted by Ricketts, *post*, p. 64). The school was incorporated in 1826 as Rensselaer Institute and later became Rensselaer Polytechnic Institute, a pioneer among schools of its kind. He also gave liberally to other educational causes. In 1819 he was elected to the Board of Regents of the University of the State of New York, of which he was chancellor from 1835 to his death. He was president of the Albany Lyceum of Natural History and of the Albany Institute.

Probably the foremost man in the state in point of wealth and social prominence, Van Rensselaer was loved for his simple tastes, democratic behavior, and genial manners. As a landlord he was lenient to a fault (Cheyney, *post*, p. 25) and he refused to subject his tenants to political pressure (Hammond, *post*, I, 161). A genuine aristocrat, he was yet ready to meet the new democracy half way. His integrity was unchallenged, and political opponents held no rancor against him. Van Buren, a member of the opposite party, wrote of him as "that good and true gentleman Patroon Van Rensselaer" ("Autobiography," *post*, p. 514). After the death of his first wife, Margaret Schuyler, who had born him three children, Van Rensselaer married, May 17, 1802, Cornelia, daughter of William Paterson [q.v.]. Cortlandt Van Rensselaer [q.v.] was one of nine children of this second marriage.

[D. D. Barnard, *A Discourse on the Life, Services and Character of Stephen Van Rensselaer; Delivered before the Albany Inst., Apr. 15, 1839* (1839); J. B. Holgate, *Am. Geneal.* (1848); Cuyler Reynolds, *Geneal. and Family Hist. of Southern N. Y. and the Hudson River Valley* (1914), vol. I; L. L. Babcock, *The War of 1812 on the Niagara Frontier* (1927); Solomon Van Rensselaer, *A Narrative of the Affair of Queenstown in the War of 1812* (1836); "Autobiog. of Martin Van Buren," ed. by J. C. Fitzpatrick, *Ann. Report Am. Hist. Asso. . . . 1918*, vol. II (1920); Margaret Bayard Smith, *The First Forty Years of Washington Society* (1906), ed. by Gaillard Hunt; P. C. Ricketts, *The Centennial Celebration of Rensselaer Poly. Inst.* (1925); E. P.

Van Santvoord

Cheney, *The Anti-Rent Agitation in . . . N. Y.* (1887); J. D. Hammond, *The Hist. of Pol. Parties in . . . N. Y.* (2 vols., 1842); D. R. Fox, *The Decline of Aristocracy in the Politics of N. Y.* (1919); *Albany Argus*, Jan. 28, 1839.]
                                                            J.W.P.

VAN SANTVOORD, GEORGE (Dec. 8, 1819–Mar. 6, 1863), jurist, was born in Belleville, N. J., the great-great-grandson of Cornelis Van Santvoord, a Dutch clergyman who emigrated probably from Leyden to Schenectady in 1740, and the son of Staats Van Santvoord, a Dutch Reformed pastor at Belleville who later removed to Schodack, N. Y. A brief and uncongenial experience as a clerk in dry goods stores in Albany and New York preceded the boy's entrance upon advanced studies. He went to the academy at Kinderhook, in 1841 was graduated from Union College in Schenectady, studied law in Kinderhook, and was admitted to the bar in 1844. Shortly thereafter he married Elizabeth, the daughter of Peter Van Schaack and granddaughter of Peter Van Schaak [q.v.]. They removed to Lafayette, Ind. In 1845 he delivered a *Eulogy of Andrew Jackson* (1914) at Lafayette, Ind., and in the same year published *Indiana Justice* (1845), a comprehensive manual for justices of the peace in the state. Owing to sickness in his family, he returned to Kinderhook in the autumn of 1846, where he practised law for five years. Again, after a year in New York City, he removed to Troy in 1852 and entered into law partnership with David L. Seymour. Seven years later he formed another partnership with Benjamin H. Hall of the same city, in which he remained until his death. He was twice elected to the New York Assembly, in 1852 from Columbia County (*Albany Argus*, Jan. 29, Mar. 8, 31, 1852) and four years later from Rensselaer, and from 1860 to 1863 he was district attorney of the latter county.

Although widely respected as a member of the bar, his chief contribution was as a writer on legal topics. In an address to the graduating class of the law school of Albany University in 1856, *The Study of the Law as a Science* (1856), he expressed some of his fundamental convictions. He considered law as a science, "laid broad and deep upon those universal principles," and found inspiration in the systematic exposition of the civil law, the introduction of whose liberal principles he felt was necessary to break "the churlish and exclusive spirit of the common law." Thus, a study of the codes appealed to him for their close approximation to the civil law and for the reëvaluation of the classic doctrine of *stare decisis* that they necessitated (pp. 236, 237). In *A Treatise on the Principles of Pleading in Civil Actions under the New-York*

Code of Procedure, first published in 1852, he attempted to provide a systematic body of knowledge of the rules of pleading under the code. His volume was a lucid and valuable contribution, which, for New York lawyers, supplanted to some extent the works of Chitty and other English writers. Along this line also was his *Treatise on the Practice in the Supreme Court of the State of New York in Equity Actions* (2 vols., 1860–62). Perhaps his most widely read volume was his *Sketches of the Lives and Judicial Services of the Chief Justices of the United States* (1854), which stressed the biographical treatment of the occupants of the bench from Jay to Taney and gave comparatively less emphasis to constitutional decisions. Other ventures in the field of biographical writing included a series of articles on the leaders of the French Revolution, which appeared in the *United States Magazine and Democratic Review* (Feb., Apr.–July 1849 and Apr. 1851), and his *Life of Algernon Sidney* (1851), a highly laudatory but useful study, based upon documentary sources and written from the anti-monarchical point of view. He was killed in a railroad accident at East Albany.

[Jonathan Pearson, *Contributions for the Genealogies of the First Settlers of . . . Schenectady* (1873), pp. 236, 237; *Memorial of George Van Santvoord* (1863); *Albany Evening Jour.,* Mar. 6, 1863; copies of *Eulogy, ante,* and *Indiana Justice, ante,* and family information from his son, Seymour Van Santvoord, Troy, N. Y.]

               R. B. M.

VAN SCHAACK, HENRY CRUGER (Apr. 2, 1802–Dec. 16, 1887), author, antiquarian, was born in Kinderhook, N. Y., a son of Peter Van Schaack [*q.v.*] by his second wife, Elizabeth Van Alen. His mother was of Dutch stock, tracing descent to Lourens Lourensen, in 1630 a resident of Beverwyck (Albany). Van Schaack's academic education was carefully supervised by his father, who trained him for the practice of law. At twenty-one he was admitted to the bar. After a brief stay at Black Rock, near Buffalo, he moved to Manlius, N. Y., married Adaline Ives (1827), opened a law office, and settled down to the quiet life of a country lawyer.

But the practice of law, though nominally his profession for half a century, soon yielded place to his keen interest in antiquarian pursuits. In 1823 he fell heir to the papers of his uncle Henry Van Schaack, an officer in the French and Indian Wars, an officer of the Crown in Albany, and a Loyalist in the Revolution. In 1832 his father's manuscripts were added to his collection; and there followed in 1833 the papers of his brother-in-law, Maj. John Frey of Palatine Bridge, and those of Matthew Vischer of Albany. Later he acquired many items from the papers of

John Jay. The most interesting of these materials, as well as manuscripts acquired from other sources, by gift as well as by exchange (for he characteristically notes that he never bought an autograph), he arranged in three great folio volumes which he entitled "An Autographic History of the American Revolution: Consisting of Letters and Other Writings of Revolutionary Characters, Illustrated by Engravings and Elucidated by Historic and Biographic Notices in Print." Among the materials thus preserved are letters and other documents written by, or relating to, colonial governors of New York, officers of the Crown, the first officers of the State of New York, and members of the Continental Congress. There are also autographs of forty-four of the signers of the Declaration of Independence, as well as those of the framers of the Constitution, of the presidents and vice-presidents through Andrew Jackson's administration, and of all of the members of the successive cabinets of Washington and John Adams. With these he arranged letters and documents written by lesser figures, as well as quantities of clippings from newspapers and magazines.

From his rich collections Van Schaack drew the material for a biography of his father, *The Life of Peter Van Schaack, LL.D.* (1842)—"the first attempt," wrote C. F. Adams, "to present to the public of the United States a justificatory memoir of one of the Tories in the Revolution" (*North American Review,* July 1842, p. 97). His other publications include *Henry Cruger, the Colleague of Edmund Burke* (1859), *A History of Manlius Village* (1873), *An Old Kinderhook Mansion* (1878), *Captain Thomas Morris in the Country of the Illinois* (1882), and a biography of his uncle, *Memoirs of the Life of Henry Van Schaack* (1892), published posthumously. At Van Schaack's death his manuscript collections were left to three of his fourteen children.

[Sources include E. A. Collier, *A Hist. of Old Kinderhook* (1914); A. J. Vanderpoel, "A Law Library's Treasures," *Chicago Legal News,* Mar. 4, 1882; personal recollections of Robert H. Van Schaack of Evanston, Ill., a grandson; obituary in *Evening Post* (N. Y.), Dec. 19, 1887; prefatory notes in Van Schaack's "Autographic Hist.," now in the possession of the Chicago Hist. Soc. (vol. I), R. H. Van Schaack (vol. II), and Pierrepont Prentice of N. Y. City (vol. III).]

               G. V.–S.

VAN SCHAACK, PETER (March 1747–Sept. 17, 1832), lawyer, was of Dutch origin, a descendant of Elias (or Claas) van Schaack, three of whose four sons took oath of allegiance to King William III in Albany in 1699. Emanuel, the youngest of these four, was the father of Cornelius Van Schaack, fur-trader, owner of a sloop and of extensive lands near Kinderhook, N. Y., who on Oct. 6, 1728, married Lydia Van Dyck, daughter of Dr. Hendrik Van Dyck and Lydia (Schuyler) of Albany. Their seventh child and fourth son, Peter, was baptized in the Reformed Dutch Protestant Church at Kinderhook, Apr. 24, 1747. Prepared for King's College by the Rev. Richard Charlton, a graduate of Trinity College, Dublin, he became an accomplished Latin scholar and was noted for the purity and elegance of his English, both written and oral. Entering college in 1762, he there became intimately acquainted with Gouverneur Morris, Robert R. Livingston, Egbert Benson, and John Jay [qq.v.]. His friendship with Benson and Jay continued throughout his life. In 1765, while still an undergraduate, he eloped with Elizabeth Cruger, daughter of a wealthy New York merchant, who soon became reconciled with his son-in-law. On graduation in 1766 he ranked at the head of his class and proceeded to study law, first in Albany with his brother-in-law, Peter Silvester, an agent of Sir William Johnson [q.v.], and later in New York with William Smith, 1728–1793 [q.v.], the historian.

In 1769 he was admitted to the bar, and in 1773 was appointed reviser of the statutes of the Colony of New York, in the work of which office he injured his eyesight seriously. The result of his labors, *Laws . . . from the Year 1691 to 1773 Inclusive,* was published in 1774. In May 1774 he became a member of the New York Committee of Fifty-one to correspond with the sister colonies, in November of the Committee of Sixty for executing the association entered into by the Continental Congress, and in the following May, of the Committee of One Hundred. About this time his wife's precarious health and his own failing eyesight led him to return to Kinderhook, where he was promptly elected to the local Committee of Safety. Though he strongly disapproved of the British government's treatment of the colonies and supported such American measures as non-importation and non-consumption, prolonged meditation and consultation of Locke, Grotius, and other writers failed to convince him that it was right to offer armed resistance to the royal government. At the meeting of the Committee of Safety in Albany on May 29, 1776, he therefore refused to pledge himself to take up arms against Great Britain and was expelled from the Committee. Thereupon he attempted to maintain neutrality. (Memoranda outlining his position are printed in Van Schaack, *post,* pp. 54–59 and 71–76.) When summoned to take oath of allegiance to the State of New York at Albany, Jan. 9, 1777, he refused and on Jan. 25 was ordered to Boston, but was called back

by order of the Convention, Feb. 3, and permitted to remain on parole at Kinderhook until after his wife's death in April 1778. In June of that year he obtained permission from Gov. George Clinton to go to England for an operation by an oculist, but his further refusal to take oath of allegiance (July 18) subjected him to the penalties of the Banishment Act of June 13, 1778, and in October he sailed for seven years of exile in England.

His voluminous letters, published by his son (H. C. Van Schaack, *post*), give an excellent picture of his life during this period. Through his brother-in-law, Henry Cruger, M.P. for Bristol, he became acquainted with Lord Eldon and other prominent lawyers and consulted with them on professional matters. He attended debates in Parliament to hear Fox, Burke, Sheridan, Pitt, and Mansfield, and traveled fairly extensively in England. In London he renewed his friendship with John Jay. In 1784 the legislature of New York restored him to citizenship and in 1785 he returned to take the oath of allegiance, settling at Kinderhook and building a house there. He was readmitted to the bar (April 1786), is said to have edited a work called *Conductor Generalis* (1786) for use of local magistrates, and engaged extensively in the practice of law until his eyesight failed entirely. Between 1786 and 1828 he gave, it is said, legal instruction to about a hundred young men who came to him as resident pupils. Though he took no active part in politics, he was keenly interested in the adoption of the federal Constitution and sympathized with the Federalist party. On Apr. 27, 1789, he married Elizabeth Van Alen of Kinderhook. Her seven children, besides three children by his first wife, survived when he died at Kinderhook.

[B. F. Butler, in the *Sentinel* (Kinderhook), Sept. 20, 1832; H. C. Van Schaack, *The Life of Peter Van Schaack, LL.D.* (1842), and "An Old Kinderhook Mansion," in *Mag. of Am. Hist.*, Sept. 1878; P. F. Miller, *A Group of Great Lawyers of Columbia County, N. Y.* (1904); E. A. Collier, *A Hist. of Old Kinderhook* (1914); "A Law Library's Treasures," in *Chicago Legal News*, Mar. 4, 1882.]   G. V.–S.

VAN SCHAICK, GOOSE (Sept. 5, 1736–July 4, 1789), soldier, was the son of Sybrant Van Schaick, mayor of Albany, N. Y., from 1756 to 1761, and Alida (Roseboom) Van Schaick. He was the descendant of Goosen Gerritse Van Schaick, who was a brewer in Albany in 1649. His own name was often spelled Gosen or Goosen. It is said that he entered upon the campaigns of the French and Indian War at the age of twenty. He served as captain in the New York provincial levies that accompanied Colonel Bradstreet in his successful and decisive campaign of 1758 against Fort Frontenac, and from 1760 to 1762 he served as lieutenant-colonel, first of the 2nd Regiment of New York Provincials and later of the 1st New York Regiment. A patriot at the outbreak of the Revolution, he became a colonel and saw constant service during the war in the defense of the northern and western frontiers of New York.

Soon after being commissioned he was campaigning in Cherry Valley against Joseph Brant; he was sent in 1776 into Tryon County and stationed at Johnstown; he was at Albany to muster the Continental troops at that place to hear the Declaration of Independence read to the populace on July 19, 1776; he was wounded at Ticonderoga on July 6, 1777; and he served at Monmouth under Stirling (see sketch of William Alexander). His most famous exploit, however, was his expedition against the Onondaga in April 1779, when he was serving under Gen. James Clinton. With about 500 men he left Fort Schuyler, invaded the country of the Onondaga, burned their principal settlement together with provisions and stores, slaughtered their cattle, took 32 prisoners and killed a number of the Indians, in six days without the loss of a man. The Continental Congress on May 10, 1779, resolved "that the thanks of Congress be presented to Colonel Van Schaick, and the officers and soldiers under his command" (Heitman, *post*). The 1st Regiment under Van Schaick seems to have been famed for its excellent discipline. Even Van Schaick's vigorous punitive expedition was a preliminary to the better-known campaign of Gen. John Sullivan in the Indian country in the summer of 1779. Gen. James Clinton, who joined Sullivan on this expedition, left Van Schaick in command at Albany. In recognition of his services Van Schaick was made a brevet brigadier-general on Oct. 10, 1783, and he remained in service until November of that year. He had married on Nov. 15, 1770, Maria Ten Broeck, by whom he had six children. He died at Albany.

[N. Y. Sec. of State, *Marriage Licenses* (1860); *N. Y. State Historian, Annual Report . . . 1897*, "Colonial Series," vol. II (1898); *N. Y. Hist. Soc. Colls. . . . 1915*, "Muster and Pay Rolls of . . . the Revolution" (1916); *Public Papers of George Clinton*, vols. I–VII (1899–1904) ed. by Hugh Hastings; F. B. Heitman, *Hist. Register of Officers of the Continental Army* (1914); A. J. Parker, *Landmarks of Albany County* (1897); Jonathan Pearson, *Contributions for the Genealogies of . . . Albany* (1872) and in *Colls. on the Hist. of Albany*, vol. IV (1871), ed. by Joel Munsell; W. W. Campbell, *Annals of Tryon County* (4th ed., 1924); records of the War Department, Washington, D. C.; service in French and Indian War from Peter Nelson, Albany, N. Y.; although date of death often said to be July 4, 1787, he was apparently alive on Sept. 9, 1787, when, according to Munsell, *ante*, II (1867), p. 299, he received title to land in Albany; the date given here is in accord with various authorities.]   E. W. S.

VAN SLYKE, LUCIUS LINCOLN (Jan. 6, 1859–Sept. 30, 1931), agricultural chemist, was born at Centerville, N. Y., the son of William J. and Katherine (Keller) Van Slyke. After preliminary education in the local schools, Van Slyke entered the University of Michigan, where he received the degree of A.B. in 1879, that of A.M. in 1881, and that of Ph.D. in 1882. He was assistant in the chemical laboratory at Michigan (1882–85), professor of chemistry at Oahu College and government chemist of the Hawaiian Islands (1885–88), lecturer in chemistry at the University of Michigan (1888–89), chief chemist at the New York state agricultural experiment station at Geneva, N. Y. (1890–1929), a position which he filled with great distinction, and professor of dairy chemistry in the New York State Agricultural College, Cornell University (1920–29).

As chief chemist it was the duty of Van Slyke to carry on and supervise research in all phases of chemistry connected with agriculture, and to examine feeds, fertilizers, and insecticides in connection with the enforcement of the New York state agricultural laws. He also directed the enactment of helpful legislation for the control of agricultural products, and gave valuable advice in regard to the enforcement of regulations. He will be remembered best, however, for his valuable pioneer work in the field of dairy chemistry. At the time of his appointment to the position at Geneva, the butter and cheese factory system of handling milk, which was firmly established, had given rise to many dairy problems of a purely chemical nature. In connection with these Van Slyke began work on the chemical composition of the constituents of milk and their relation to one another, a subject on which there was very little definite knowledge. The results of his work are classic. Special mention should be made of his researches on milk casein, which had a practical value in the improvement of the art of cheese making and an immense scientific value in contributing to an understanding of the nature and behavior of colloids. Van Slyke wrote easily and forcefully. During his long career he was the author or joint author of more than a hundred and thirty experiment station bulletins and reports, and he was a constant contributor to scientific journals. He was the author of four textbooks: *Modern Methods of Testing Milk and Milk Products* (1906); *The Science and Practice of Cheese Making* (1909), with C. A. Publow; *Fertilizers and Crops* (1912); and *Cheese* (1927), with W. V. Price. He was also a contributor to A. H. Allen's *Commercial Organic Analysis*. In 1897 he was president of the New

York State Dairymen's Association, and in 1901 president of the Association of Official Agricultural Chemists.

Van Slyke was a man of pleasing personality, with a keen interest in civic, social, and religious life. He was for many years elder of the Presbyterian Church of Geneva. He was a tireless and exacting worker, under whom many able chemists received their early training. He was married three times—first to Lucy W. Dexter (June 15, 1882), by whom he had two sons; second to Julia Hanford Upson of Honolulu, H. I. (Apr. 5, 1888), by whom he had one son; and third to Mrs. Hedwig Shaul of Geneva, N. Y. (June 2, 1926), who survived him.

[*Who's Who in America*, 1930–31; R. W. Thatcher, in *Jour. of Industrial and Engineering Chemistry*, Nov. 1925; L. H. and E. Z. Bailey, *Rus* (1925), p. 681; *Experiment Station Record*, Dec. 1931; *Jour. Asso. Official Agricultural Chemists*, May 15, 1932; obituary in *N. Y. Times*, Oct. 1, 1931; information from members of the experiment station staff, Geneva, N. Y., including the spelling of Mrs. Shaul's name.]   H. E. R.

VAN TWILLER, WOUTER (*c.* 1580–*c.* 1656), governor of New Netherland, was born in Gelderland, now a part of the Netherlands, the eldest son of Rijckert and Maria (Van Rensselaer) Van Twiller, the sister of Kiliaen Van Rensselaer, the first patroon, and the aunt of Nicholas Van Rensselaer [*q.v.*]. Wouter Van Twiller was a clerk in the service of the Dutch West India Company at the time he was appointed director-general, or governor, of New Netherland. In 1633 he arrived at New Amsterdam with a company of soldiers from Holland. David Pietersen De Vries [*q.v.*] told interesting anecdotes about this "unfit" person "whom they had made out of a clerk into a governor, who was the sport of the people" (Jameson, *post,* p. 187). Nevertheless, Van Twiller prudently dealt with the English who in 1633 sailed up the Hudson in the *William,* and he permitted them to return peaceably to England. With firm hand he aided the Dutch settlements on the banks of the Connecticut, but he obviously lacked adequate numbers of colonists with which to stem the rapidly rising tide of English immigration.

The animosity of De Vries resulted in a lengthy letter from Van Twiller's uncle in Amsterdam, whose eminence had no doubt played a part in the promotion of the nephew, although Van Rensselaer himself denied it. He had heard, so he said, that Wouter had too often got drunk, was too proud, and not sufficiently interested in religion. More serious was his negligence in keeping books properly and sending reports to Amsterdam. However, he was permitted to retain his position a little longer. One point in his favor had been his aim to imitate his father and his uncle, who had transferred barren wastes in the province of Gelderland into fertile fields and had fattened ill-fed cattle. Unfortunately, the West India Company, influenced by its more wealthy counter-part, the East India Company, misunderstood the potentialities of colonization in North America. What the merchants of Amsterdam wanted was trade in furs and quick profits for themselves, instead of a slower gain through the development of agriculture.

However, Van Twiller strengthened Fort Amsterdam and built a church and a bridge across the creek in the busiest part of town. His uncle's farms on Manhattan were carefully tilled under his care, and he himself developed a tobacco plantation. In 1636 a settlement on Long Island was started, and in 1637 he bought for himself Pagganck, now Governor's Island, and two islands in the East River, now Ward's and Blackwell's. Yet the company in Holland remained ill-pleased, for, in spite of the uncle's warnings, the governor still neglected his books and failed to report regularly. Everardus Bogardus [*q.v.*], moreover, frankly called him "a child of the devil; a consummate villain" (O'Callaghan, *Hist., post,* p. 167). In 1637 Willem Kieft [*q.v.*] was appointed to succeed him. Only the Indians had fully appreciated his good qualities. He had been kind to them and had treated them as equals. For years after his departure, according to the board of accounts (*Documents, post,* I, 151), the Indians were daily calling for the return of Wouter. He was in no hurry to leave either, and he actually bought more land before he departed and obtained from Kieft a lease on Bouwerie No. 1, belonging to the company. Early in 1639 he arrived in the Netherlands, and he immediately proceeded to the headquarters of the company, showing the officials all his books and papers. His uncle reported that the latter were now fully satisfied. Kieft remained his agent in the colony, and after the death of Van Rensselaer, Van Twiller managed his patroonship. In 1649 and 1650 his name appears in various records in New Netherland. He died in 1656 or 1657, survived by his widow, Maria (Momma) Van Twiller.

[E. B. O'Callaghan, *Hist. of New Netherland,* vol. I (1846) and *Calendar of Hist. MSS. in the office of the Sec. of State,* vol. I (1865); *Documents Relative to the Colonial Hist. of . . . N. Y.,* esp. vol. I (1856), procured and ed. by J. R. Brodhead and E. B. O'Callaghan; G. Beernink in *Gelre Vereeniging . . . Werken,* no. 12 (1916) esp. pp. 116, 143, 145 and in *Gelre Vereeniging . . Bijdragen,* XV (1912), esp. pp. 91, 124; A. J. F. van Laer, *The Correspondence of Jeremias Van Rensselaer* (1932) and *Van Rensselaer Bowier MSS.* (1908), esp. p. 36; *Narratives of New Netherland, 1609–1664* (1909), ed. by J. F. Jameson; M. G. Van Rensselaer,

Hist. of . . . N. Y. (1909), vol. I; Hist. of . . . N. Y., vol. I (1933), ed. by A. C. Flick.]   A. H.

VAN TYNE, CLAUDE HALSTEAD (Oct. 16, 1869–Mar. 21, 1930), historian, the son of Lawrence M. and Helen (Rosacrans) Van Tyne, was born at Tecumseh, Mich. Starting as a youth in the banking business he rose, while in his early twenties, to the position of cashier in the Iosco County Savings Bank, in northern Michigan. Well launched on a promising career he nevertheless aspired to pursue the profession of a scholar. Accordingly he entered the University of Michigan whence he was graduated in 1896. On June 19 of that year he married Belle Joslyn of Chesaning, Mich. During vacations he had made adventurous bicycle tours, across the Rocky Mountains and in Europe, and later he made a rowing trip down the Danube with his wife. He pursued graduate studies at Heidelberg, Leipzig, and Paris (1897–98), and in 1900 took his Ph.D. degree at the University of Pennsylvania, where he remained as senior fellow in history until January 1903. Then, after six months' work of investigation in Washington in connection with the Carnegie Institution, he came in the autumn of 1903 to the University of Michigan as assistant professor. Three years later, when Prof. A. C. McLaughlin went to the University of Chicago, Van Tyne was promoted to the rank of professor and was made head of the department of American history. In 1911 he became head of the department of history, with which the American group was reunited. Thanks to his consideration for young men, his high standards, and his eye for breeding and culture as well as technical proficiency he succeeded in developing a loyal and scholarly staff.

In spite of his devotion to his research Van Tyne had a strong sense of his academic duties and served on many important committees. A dominating figure in the University, he was also active outside it. During the period 1916–21 he was a member of the board of editors of the *American Historical Review*. Meantime, in 1913–14, he was lecturer in the French provincial universities on the Fondation Harvard pour les relations avec les universitiés Françaises. Some years later he went to India, on the invitation of Sir Frederick Whyte, the first president of the legislative assembly, to estimate the experiments that were being carried on there under the Act of 1919. The resulting observations he embodied in two articles in the *Atlantic Monthly* (July, September 1922) and in a book, *India in Ferment* (1923), which subjected him to some criticism from those who disapproved of British rule. In 1927 he occupied the Sir George Watson chair of American history, literature, and institutions in the British universities, an annual lectureship. The lectures, which were marked by both maturity and charm, were printed under the title, *England and America, Rivals in the American Revolution* (1927).

Van Tyne's scholarly publications were reasonably numerous and of increasingly high quality. Among the earlier ones may be mentioned an edition of *The Letters of Daniel Webster* (1902); a *Guide to the Archives of the Government of the United States in Washington* (1904), compiled for the Carnegie Institution in collaboration with Waldo G. Leland; and *A History of the United States for Schools* (1911), written in collaboration with Prof. A. C. McLaughlin. Within his special field of interest he published several important works. The earliest of these was his dissertation, *The Loyalists in the American Revolution* (1902), an over-ambitious but promising book. Next to appear was *The American Revolution, 1776–1783* (1905), in the American Nation series. At length, after years of research, he published *The Causes of the War of Independence* (1922), the first volume of *A History of the Founding of the American Republic* which he designed as the main work of his life but only half of which he finished. The first volume was valued by his co-workers chiefly as a synthesis of the specialized studies of many investigators, to whom Van Tyne made conscientious acknowledgment. The succeeding volume, *The War of Independence, American Phase* (1929), was widely hailed as a fresh, illuminating, and distinctly readable treatment. The acquisition by William L. Clements of the Shelburne, the Clinton, the Greene, and the Germain papers brought within his reach rich treasures, of which he availed himself. Unhappily his work was cut short by a serious illness in the spring of 1929 and he died Mar. 21, 1930. He was survived by his wife, a daughter, and three sons. In 1930 he received the Henry Russel Award for the most scholarly work produced that year by a member of the University of Michigan faculty, and for his last book he was posthumously awarded a Pulitzer Prize (*New York Times,* May 13, 1930).

Van Tyne was a stimulating though exacting teacher. He was distinguished in appearance, gifted with a whimsical humor, and possessed of a power of apt allusion drawn from rich stores of extensive reading. Very individual in speech and writing, he was vehement in pressing his own opinions and rather inclined to be intolerant of those whose standards differed from his.

Vanuxem

Van Vechten

[A. L. Cross, in *Michigan Alumnus*, Mar. 29, 1930; memoir prepared by W. G. Leland for publication in *Proc. Am. Academy of Arts and Sciences*; *Who's Who in America*, 1928–29; obituary in *N. Y. Times*, Mar. 22, 1930; *Am. Hist. Review*, July 1930, p. 941; critical reviews of chief works, *Am. Hist. Review*, July 1903, Jan. 1923, Apr. 1930.] A. L. C.

VANUXEM, LARDNER (July 23, 1792–Jan. 25, 1848), geologist, the son of James and Rebecca (Clarke) Vanuxem, was born in Philadelphia. His father, a native of Dunkirk, France, was a prosperous shipping merchant; his mother was a daughter of Elijah Clarke of New Jersey. Since the son's tastes inclined more to science than to business, he early eschewed the commercial opportunities his father afforded him and, with his parents' approval, went to Paris and entered the École des Mines, where he was graduated in 1819. Returning to the United States, he became professor of chemistry and mineralogy in South Carolina College. During his incumbency he made a geological survey of North Carolina and participated in similar work in South Carolina, publishing his reports in various newspapers and in Robert Mills's *Statistics of South Carolina* (1826).

In November 1827 he resigned his professorship in order to devote himself to geological studies. He examined certain mines in Mexico and a little later was engaged in geologic reconnaissance surveys in New York, Ohio, Kentucky, Tennessee, and Virginia. About 1830 he purchased a farm near Bristol, Pa., and soon afterward married Elizabeth, daughter of John Newbold of Bloomsdale. When the Geological Survey of New York was instituted in 1836, he was assigned to the investigation of the Fourth District, but was soon transferred to the Third. His duties included studies of the extent and limits of the iron and salt bearing formations, and of the relation of the rocks of New York to the "Coal Measures" of Pennsylvania. The results of his work appeared in *Geology of New-York, Part III, Comprising the Survey of the Third Geological District* (1842), upon which his reputation as a scientist largely rests. Prior to this survey no uniform system of nomenclature had been adopted for American geology. The need being imperative, Vanuxem suggested that the geologists of Pennsylvania and Virginia collaborate with those of New York in establishing a common system of names. Out of this cooperation grew the Association of American Geologists and Naturalists, formed in 1840, which in 1847 became the American Association for the Advancement of Science. Later, Vanuxem collaborated with James Hall [*q.v.*] in arranging the state geological collections in Albany. Having ample means, apparently, he then retired to private life and died in his home at Bristol, Pa.

Vanuxem's investigation of the sedimentaries was excellent work for that period, but his treatment of what he termed the "Primary Class" of crystalline rocks was scant, as was to be expected at a time when petrography had not been developed into an exact science. In some respects he seems to have been in advance of his time, for he showed in the *Geology of New York* a leaning toward views not in harmony with the Mosaic account of the creation, which in his day was considered sacrosanct. Moreover, he appears, perhaps faintly, to have postulated the theory of evolution (p. 27). His intellectual pursuits were varied. He spent much time in the investigation of the Scriptures and left many manuscripts recording his findings and views; he took much interest in new forms of religion, such as Mormonism and Millerism; he made a study of phrenology. He was an early advocate of the emancipation of women from the restrictions then prevailing. The views and actions which his independent thinking led him to adopt caused many to regard him as "a very peculiar man."

[Maximilian La Borde, *Hist. of the S. C. Coll* (1874); E. L. Green, *A Hist. of the Univ. of S. C.* (1916); H. V. Cubberly, *Bloomsdale: Sketches of the Old-Time Home of the John Newbold Family* (1930); *Jour. of the Elisha Mitchell Scientific Soc.*, July–Dec. 1890; W. J. Youmans, *Pioneers of Sci. in America* (1896); *Am. Jour. of Sci. and Arts*, May 1848; *North Am. and U. S. Gazette* (Phila.), Jan. 28, 1848.] F. L. G.

VAN VECHTEN, ABRAHAM (Dec. 5, 1762–Jan. 6, 1837), lawyer, was born in Catskill, N. Y., where his great-grandfather had purchased land and settled about 1681. His parents, Teunis Van Vechten and Judikje, daughter of Jacob Ten Broeck, were of Dutch colonial stock. On his paternal side he was a direct descendant of Teunis Dircksen van Vechten, who emigrated with his family from Holland in 1638, settling first at Beaverwyck and later at Greenbush, N. Y. Abraham Van Vechten received his early education at Esopus, attended King's College for a time, and pursued the study of law at Albany in the office of John Lansing [*q.v.*], an intimate friend. As the first lawyer admitted to practice under the state constitution at the October term of the supreme court in 1785, when new rules were adopted, Van Vechten has frequently been called "the father of the New York bar," although such a title would seem to slight the claims of distinguished colonial predecessors. He opened a law office at Johnstown, N. Y., but, after a brief sojourn, established his permanent practice in Albany.

He soon entered Federalist politics, but at the

start his political career was jeopardized by a remark, attributed to him, to the effect "that the Yankees had already obtain't too much influence in our Government and that it was high time the Dutch people should rally against them." In 1796 he was appointed by Gov. John Jay [*q.v.*] district attorney for the fifth district of the state. Two years later he declined an appointment as associate justice of the state supreme court. He was elected to the state Senate in 1798 and served until 1805, performing valuable services as chairman of the judiciary committee and as a member of the court for the correction of errors. He went on record as opposed to the methods of the Republican promoters of the state bank, fearing competition with the Federalist bank in Albany (D. S. Alexander, *A Political History of the State of New York*, vol. I, 1906, p. 188). During the years 1798–1805 he served, also, as recorder of Albany. In 1805 he was elected to the Assembly from Albany County and remained a member until 1813, ably advocating the Federalist position in opposition to the Embargo (*Ibid.*, pp. 168, 169). In the Federalist victory of 1809 he became attorney-general, only to be turned out by the Clintonians two years later. Again, in 1813, he was made attorney-general, succeeding his friend Thomas Addis Emmet [*q.v.*], and was succeeded in office in 1815 by Martin Van Buren [*q.v.*].

Van Vechten occupied a position of commanding influence at the constitutional convention 1821, which he attended as a delegate from Albany. He vigorously defended the judiciary from attack, asserting that the convention had been assembled to amend the constitution and that "no man had ever dreamed of its being for the purpose of dismissing officers from our government" (C. Z. Lincoln, *The Constitutional History of New York*, 1906, I, 682–83). He likewise opposed the proposition to vest the impeachment power in a majority of the Assembly as against the two-thirds required under the first constitution (*Ibid.*, IV, 601). Such topics as the freehold qualification for voters, the extension of the elective franchise, and the power and jurisdiction of the court of chancery were also the subjects of addresses which he made.

After the convention he retired from political life and devoted himself intensively to his legal career, where his solid learning, his powers of clear and logical analysis and argument, his unusual gift of eloquence, and his distinguished bearing established him among the leaders of the bar. One biographer claims that Van Vechten served as defense counsel in the celebrated trial of David D. How for the murder of Othello

Church, held at Angelica, N. Y., in 1825 (Proctor, *post*, p. 73), although the record does not substantiate this claim (*cf.* J. D. Lawson, *American State Trials*, vol. VI, 1916, pp. 865–79; Joseph Badger, *Life and Confession of David D. How*, n.d.). The most notable case with which he was associated was that of *Gibbons* vs. *Ogden* (9 *Wheaton*, 1), where he prepared an opinion denying the power of the state legislature to grant a license giving Livingston and Fulton the sole right to navigate the waters of the state. In this position he was fully sustained by Chief Justice Marshall. Owing to illness, Van Vechten took no part in the proceedings before the Supreme Court. In May 1784 he married Catharine, daughter of Philip Pieterse and Anna (Wendell) Schuyler of Albany; they had fifteen children, of whom ten survived infancy.

[Peter Van Vechten, *The Geneal. Records of the Van Vechtens from 1638 to 1896* (1896); Joel Munsell, *The Annals of Albany*, vol. X (1859); S. V. Talcott, *Geneal. Notes of N. Y. and New England Families* (1883); L. B. Proctor, "Abraham Van Vechten, the Father of the Bar of the State of N. Y.," *Albany Law Journal*, July 30, 1898; N. H. Carter and W. L. Stone, *Rec. of the Proc. and Debates of the Convention of 1821 . . . N. Y.* (1921); D. R. Fox, *The Decline of Aristocracy in the Politics of N. Y.* (1919); *Albany Argus*, Jan. 9, 1837; Van Vechten's Letterbook (MS.), N. Y. Hist. Soc.]

R. B. M.

VAN WINKLE, PETER GODWIN (Sept. 7, 1808–Apr. 15, 1872), lawyer, United States senator, was the second son of Peter and Phoebe (Godwin) Van Winkle. He was born in New York City, and came from an old Knickerbocker family, the American progenitor of which, Jacob Van Winkle, settled in New Netherland about 1634. What formal education he received was obtained in the primary and secondary schools of his native city. In early manhood he moved to Parkersburg, Va. (now W. Va.), where he began the study of law and in 1835 was admitted to the bar. Although actively engaged in his profession, he was at one time or another recorder of the town, a member of its governing board of trustees, and president of this board— a position equivalent to that of mayor. Beginning in 1852 he served as treasurer and later as president of the Northwestern Virginia Railroad Company, which, in connection with the Baltimore & Ohio Railroad, built and operated a line from Grafton to the Ohio River. He was also for a number of years an attorney and lobbyist for the Baltimore & Ohio.

He was a member of the Virginia constitutional convention of 1850–51, though he seems not to have played a conspicuous rôle in its proceedings. He did, however, take a prominent part in the convention held at Wheeling in June 1861, in which sat representatives from northwestern Virginia. This convention passed an ordinance providing for the reorganization of the government of Virginia on a basis of loyalty to the Union. The government thus created was to supersede that centering at Richmond. Francis H. Pierpont [*q.v.*] was chosen governor, and Van Winkle was selected as a member of his advisory council. This convention at an adjourned session (in August) also passed an ordinance which provided for the division of Virginia and the creation of what became the state of West Virginia.

A constitutional convention was assembled at Wheeling on Nov. 26, 1861. Van Winkle was one of the leading members of this body, and had much to do with the framing of the constitution. He urged the inclusion in West Virginia of the counties in the extreme eastern section, mainly in order that the Baltimore & Ohio Railroad should be entirely on West Virginia and Maryland soil. When the government of West Virginia was organized, he was a member of the first legislature and had an important part in the legislation enacted by it. In August 1863 he was one of the two chosen United States senators; he drew the long term and so served for six years.

In the Senate his record on routine policies must have impressed the leadership of the Republican party favorably, for he became a member of the important finance committee and chairman of the committee on pensions. His career as a whole, while not a brilliant one, was characterized by exceptional courage and independence of spirit. Though he went along with his party in voting for the Thirteenth and Fifteenth amendments, he refused to follow its leaders on some measures of prime importance. In a rather lengthy speech (Apr. 21, 1864) in opposition to the repeal of the Fugitive Slave Law, he declared himself in favor of turning over the government of the Southern states to the loyal local citizens, though they might formerly have been disloyal, and of withdrawing from that section all federal soldiers as soon as safety should permit. He also opposed the granting of citizenship to the freedmen, believing that the majority of them were not equal to this responsibility. Consistently with this view, he voted against the Fourteenth Amendment in opposition to the wishes of a large majority of his party. His greatest offense against party regularity, however, was his refusal to vote for conviction in the impeachment proceedings against President Johnson. This defiance of the leadership of his party was loudly condemned in West Virginia; the Wheeling *Intelligencer* referred to him as "West Virginia's Betrayer," and de-

clared that there was not a loyal citizen in the state who had not been misrepresented by that vote. With feeling so strong against him, there was no prospect of his being returned to the Senate, and so he did not become a candidate for reelection. Leaving Washington at the end of his term, he spent the three remaining years of his life at Parkersburg. In 1831 he married Juliette, daughter of William P. and Martha Rathbun, of Paramus, Bergen County, N. J., by whom he had several children.

[Daniel Van Winkle, *A Geneal. of the Van Winkle Family* (copr. 1913) ; *Biog. Dir. Am. Cong.* (1928) ; G. W. Atkinson and A. F. Gibbens, *Prominent Men of W. Va.* (1890) ; V. A. Lewis, *How West Va. Was Made* (1909) ; J. C. McGregor, *The Disruption of Va.* (1922) ; *The Jour. of the House of Delegates of the State of W. Va.*, 1 Sess. (1863) ; *Wheeling Daily Intelligencer,* June, Aug. 1861, Nov. 1861–Feb. 1862, May 18, 1868, Apr. 16, 1872 ; *State Journal* (Parkersburg), Apr. 18, 1872; T. C. Miller and Hu Maxwell, *W. Va. and Its People* (1913), vol. III.]   O. P. C.

VAN WYCK, CHARLES HENRY (May 10, 1824–Oct. 24, 1895), lawyer, soldier, legislator, the second son of Dr. Theodorus C. and Elizabeth (Mason) Van Wyck, was born at Poughkeepsie, N. Y. He was descended from Cornelius Barentse van Wyck who emigrated to Long Island in 1660. Charles spent his youth at Bloomingburg, Sullivan County, N. Y., at which place his father was a practising physician. He was graduated from Rutgers College, the ranking student of the class of 1843. After graduation he turned to the study of law and was admitted to the bar in 1847. Three years later he was elected district attorney of Sullivan County, and was reëlected to this position for three successive terms (1850–56).

He began politics as a member of the Barnburner wing of the Democratic party, but joined the new Republican movement and represented his district in Congress from Mar. 4, 1859, to Mar. 3, 1863. He recruited the 56th New York Volunteers and commanded the regiment from Sept. 4, 1861, until he was promoted to the rank of brigadier-general, Sept. 27, 1865. He served in the Peninsular and South Carolina campaigns and remained in the army of occupation in South Carolina until August 1865. On Jan. 15, 1866, he was mustered out of the service. He was reëlected to Congress in 1866 and 1868. On the last occasion his election was contested, but he was seated, after a congressional investigation, on Feb. 17, 1870. As congressman he took a leading part in investigations of the New York custom house service and of contracts of the War Department.

In 1857 he acquired lands near Nebraska City, Nebr., and in 1874 removed to that place. He was an active member of the Nebraska constitutional convention of 1875, and was elected to the state Senate for three successive terms (1877, 1879, 1881). In the legislature he was an active advocate of railroad rate legislation and tax relief. As United States senator from 1881 to 1887 he was a strong supporter of tariff reform, railroad regulation, protection of the public lands, and direct popular election of senators. To make possible the last named, he proposed an amendment to the federal Constitution. In the senatorial preferential ballot (provided in the Nebraska constitution) he received an overwhelming plurality for reëlection, but was rejected by the state legislature. He was an active leader of the Farmers' Alliance and of the Populist movement in Nebraska. He would probably have been the Populists' candidate for governor in 1890 but for a peculiar composition of their first convention, for which a personal foe of Van Wyck was responsible. In 1892 he received the nomination but failed of election. In 1894 he was a candidate on the Populist ticket for the state Senate; he was physically unable to make an active campaign, however, and in the election the Republicans were victorious. He was a man of strong and positive personality, an entertaining and eloquent speaker, a genial and generous host, a friend of the masses. He died in Washington and was buried at Milford, Pa., the early home of his wife, Kate Brodhead, whom he married Sept. 15, 1869; she and a daughter survived him.

[Anne Van Wyck, *Descendants of Cornelius Barentse Van Wyck and Anna Polhemus* (1912); J. C. Fisk and W. H. D. Blake, *A Condensed Hist. of the 56th Regiment of N. Y.* (n.d.); M. U. Harmer and J. L. Sellers, "Charles Henry Van Wyck," *Nebr. Hist. Mag.*, Apr.–Dec. 1929; *Omaha Daily Bee*, Oct. 25, 1895; *Nebr. City News*, Oct. 25, 1895; J. S. Morton and Albert Watkins, *Hist. of Nebr.*, vol. III (1913); *Biog. Dir. Am. Cong.* (1928).]   J. L. S.

VANZETTI, BARTOLOMEO (1888–1927) [See SACCO, NICOLA, 1891–1927].

VARDAMAN, JAMES KIMBLE (July 26, 1861–June 25, 1930), governor of Mississippi, senator, was born near Edna, Jackson County, Tex., to which his parents, William Sylvester and Mary (Fox) Vardaman, had removed from Mississippi in 1858. After the Civil War, in which the father was a Confederate soldier, the family returned from Texas and settled on a farm in Yalobusha County, Miss. James, the fourth of the six children, after attending the public schools in that county and reading law at Carrollton, was admitted to the bar at the age of twenty-one. He began to practise at Winona, Miss., and there edited in 1883 the Winona *Ad-*

vance. On May 31 of the same year he was married to Anna E. (Burleson) Robinson, a native of Alabama. From 1890 to 1896 he edited the Greenwood *Enterprise,* and in the latter year he established the Greenwood *Commonwealth,* which he edited until 1903. While editing the *Enterprise* he served three terms in the state legislature and in 1894 was speaker of the House. During the Spanish-American War he was captain and later major in the 5th United States Volunteer Infantry, serving in Santiago, Cuba, from August 1898 to May 1899.

In 1895 and 1899 he sought in vain to obtain the nomination for the governorship in the state conventions, which at that time either partially concealed or avoided rifts in the all-powerful Democratic party in Mississippi. When a law was passed in 1902 providing for nominations by party primaries, factionalism within the party became more probable; and it became more necessary for the officeseeker to know the technique of swaying the masses. It was Vardaman's good fortune that a split could be made in the party with more ease than formerly; it was due to his own skill that the party was fractured on class lines. In the next campaign he brought into play his extraordinary power as a political speechmaker. By riding on great eight-wheeled lumber wagons drawn by many yokes of white oxen and by making such declarations as that his first audiences had been "barnyard inhabitants and jackasses," he established his brotherhood with the farmers. He further appealed to the poor white man by asserting that the political dominance of his race was being endangered by the education of the negro. While he doubtless believed this, raising the negro issue may have saved him from being branded as a Populist, even though he was appealing to the economically discontented, many of whom had recently voted the Populist ticket. His interest in the common man seems to have been sincere. With a keen eye for dramatic values in his campaigns, he accentuated his striking appearance by wearing his black hair down to his shoulders and by dressing in immaculate white. He became the idol of the masses, was nominated in the Democratic primary, and was inaugurated governor in January 1904. Though he was charged with extending the spoils system, he made a praiseworthy attack on the system of leasing state convicts to private persons and corporations.

In the summer of 1907, a few months before the close of his administration, he was a candidate for the federal Senate but was defeated in the Democratic primary. To keep from being forgotten while out of office, he began to publish

221

the *Issue*, a weekly political newspaper, at Jackson in 1908. Early in 1910 he again sought a senatorship. The legislature had not been bound by a primary nomination, and after a prolonged, bitter, and corrupt fight, it elected Le Roy Percy. Vardaman charged that the will of the people had been disregarded, and to them he appealed in the 1911 primary and was elected. He entered the Senate on Mar. 4, 1913. There he became conspicuous by strenuously opposing the President's war policies. He was one of the "little group of willful men" who aroused Wilson's indignation by their successful filibuster against the Armed Neutrality Bill, and he was one of the six who voted against the resolution declaring war against Germany. He maintained that the war was injurious to the common people who had put him in office, and for a time many of his constituents agreed with this view. Also, he resented Wilson's refusal to follow his advice on several occasions early in the administration. By the time an enthusiastic support of the war had become the prevailing sentiment in his state, it was too late for Vardaman to withdraw from the opposition with any consistency. He was defeated in 1918 by Pat Harrison, who was aided by a direct appeal from Wilson to the voters of Mississippi. That Vardaman still had a large following was shown when he again ran for the Senate in 1922. Though he was defeated in the second primary, he had received a plurality in the first. Yet he was already so broken in body and mind that most of his speeches had to be made by his friends. Realizing that this was the end, he soon removed to Birmingham, Ala., and there spent his remaining years with his two daughters, who with one of their two brothers and their mother survived him.

[A. S. Coody, *Biog. Sketches of James Kimble Vardaman* (1922); *Vardaman's Attitude toward President Wilson, the Democratic Administration and the American Government* (1918), an opposition pamphlet; *Who's Who in America*, 1930–31; *Biog. Directory Am. Cong.* (1928); *Daily News* (Jackson, Miss.), June 26, 27, 1930; *Commercial-Appeal* and *Evening Appeal* (Memphis, Tenn.), June 26, 1930.]   C. S. S.

VARDILL, JOHN (1749–Jan. 16, 1811), clergyman and British spy, the son of Capt. Thomas and Hannah (Tiebout) Vardill, was baptized on July 5, 1749 (T. A. Wright, *Records of the Reformed Dutch Church . . . New York: Baptisms*, 1902, p. 152). He was born in New York City, where his father, a native of Bermuda, was a ship-owner, and at one time port warden. John graduated from King's College in 1766, and, later, while studying theology, was attached unofficially to the college as a tutor. One of his students was John Parke Custis, stepson of

Washington (W. C. Ford, *Letters of Jonathan Boucher to George Washington*, 1889, p. 45). Vardill was an assistant to Dr. Samuel Clossy, the professor of anatomy; he taught "Languages and other Branches of Science," and was a great favorite of the president, Myles Cooper [*q.v.*]. At the commencement of 1769 he received a master's degree. When he was about to go to England for ordination, the governors of the college voted him a hundred pounds for his services (Minutes, Nov. 11, 1773), and elected him a fellow and professor of natural law (*Ibid.*, Dec. 28, 1773).

In the meantime he had brought himself into public notice as a controversialist, having had a part in writing "A Whip for the American Whig" (Hugh Gaines' *New York Gazette*, Apr. 4, 1768–July 10, 1769), and other essays in connection with the controversy between William Livingston and Thomas Bradbury Chandler [*qq.v.*] over an American episcopate. On Dec. 7, 1772, in the *New York Gazette and the Weekly Mercury* over the signature "Causidicus" he attacked the Rev. John Witherspoon's *Address to the Inhabitants of Jamaica and Other West-India Islands, in Behalf of the College of New-Jersey* (reprinted with Causidicus' attack in William Nelson, *Archives of New Jersey*, 1 ser., vol. XXVIII, 1916, pp. 289–308, 345–59), through which, Vardill claimed, "the Youth of North-America were to be lured by the Charmer's Voice in to the Bosom of Nassau-Hall." He was also the author in 1773, over the signature "Poplicola," of broadcasts against the non-importation agreement and in favor of receiving the tea shipments (see Charles Evans, *American Bibliography*, vol. IV, 1907, p. 385). These appeared in *Rivington's New York Gazetteer*.

He was ordained deacon, Apr. 4, 1774, and priest the following day in the Chapel Royal, St. James's Palace, by Richard Terrick, Bishop of London (Records in the Bishop of London's Registry), and was made M.A. at Oxford, June 28, 1774. On Dec. 6, 1774, following the death of the Rev. John Ogilvie [*q.v.*], he was unanimously elected assistant minister of Trinity Church, New York, although on Dec. 1, he had been attacked anonymously in the *New York Journal* as "a poetaster, the tool of a party, a newswriter, a pamphleteer, a paltry politician, who will forever . . . keep a spirit of dissension among you" (quoted in *Archives of the General Convention, post*, IV, 135). Such of his verses as have survived (manuscripts in New York Historical Society) bear out these accusations, although a rejoinder praising his "universally known and acknowledged" abilities and his "most engaging sweetness of disposition" appeared in the same paper for Dec. 22, 1774. Vardill remained in England, however, to promote the granting of a charter making King's College a university, a project which the Revolution prevented. He continued writing for periodicals in defense of the government, under the name of "Corrolænus," for which he received thanks and promises of patronage. By correspondence he nearly won over to the Crown with promises of judgeships two members of Congress, "but the negotiation was quashed by the unexpected fray at Lexington in April 1775" (Einstein, *post*, p. 412). "In consequence of these and such like services and to give the Loyalists at New York a Proof of the Attention and Rewards which would follow their Zeal and Loyalty" (*Ibid.*, p. 412), he was appointed Regius Professor of Divinity in King's College, with a salary of £200, and the appointment was announced in *Rivington's New York Gazetteer*, Dec. 8, 1774, although the royal warrant was not granted until some time later.

Vardill never returned to America, but spent the years 1775 to 1781 as a spy in the service of the Crown. In a memorial which he addressed to the commissioners on Loyalists claims, Nov. 16, 1783, he recited the precise nature of his services and, while admitting that he had been paid for his services in England, claimed compensation for the salary he had never received from King's College and Trinity Church, New York; the claim was not allowed (Coke, *post*, p. 255). He was given an office at 17 Downing Street, close to that of the Prime Minister, and spent his time mainly in spying on American sympathizers in England. When the Abbé Raynal visited London bearing letters from Franklin in Paris, and when Jonathan Austin came over as Franklin's confidential agent, Vardill found the means to examine their correspondence without their knowledge; on another occasion he induced a New Yorker named Van Zandt, who had come over on business of Congress, with letters from Franklin, to become a British spy. Vardill's greatest feat, however, was in securing the theft, by Joseph Hynson, a seaman in the confidence of Silas Deane [*q.v.*], of the entire confidential correspondence that passed between the American commissioners and the French court from March to October 1777, which corroborated reports of the imminence of French intervention. Within three months of the theft of these papers, Vardill was rewarded by the granting of the royal warrant (Jan. 8, 1778) for his appointment as Regius Professor in New York.

Vardill was in Dublin in 1785 and 1786, but little is known of him until 1791, when he was given the living of Skirbeck, Lincolnshire (*Gentleman's Magazine*, July 1791). He was married and had a daughter.

[Arthur Lowndes, ed., *Archives of the Gen. Convention*, vol. IV (1912); *N. Y. Geneal. and Biog. Record*, Oct. 1894; Lewis Einstein, *Divided Loyalties* (1933); B. F. Stevens's *Facsimiles of Manuscripts in European Archives Relating to America, 1773 to 1783*; D. P. Coke, *The Royal Commission on the Losses and Services of American Loyalists* (1915), ed. by H. E. Egerton; *Gentleman's Mag.*, Jan. 1811.]   M. H. T.

VARE, WILLIAM SCOTT (Dec. 24, 1867–Aug. 7, 1934), contractor, politician, was born on a farm in South Philadelphia, the son of Augustus and Abigail (Stites) Vare. His father was a native of the Isle of Jersey; his mother was of Puritan New England stock. As a boy "he milked the cow, he followed the plow"—according to a campaign ditty current years afterward. The elementary schooling which he received ended when he was twelve, and he went to work in John Wanamaker's store as a cash boy. Later he was employed by his brother George, then a produce merchant, as a huckster, and acquired an intimate acquaintance with the South Philadelphia district and its people which was of much political value to him subsequently. From the time he reached his majority he was closely associated with his brothers George and Edwin. George was recognized as the leader until his death in 1908, then Edwin was in control until he died in 1922, after which time William was sole master of the powerful machine, which, as ward leaders, they had established. They had become contractors and they used their political influence to secure fat commissions from the city, by means of which they acquired considerable private fortunes. On July 29, 1897, William married Ida Morris of Philadelphia.

Apart from this direct connection between business and politics, which often led to denunciation of the brothers as "contractor-bosses," there was nothing to distinguish their earlier course from that of other minor machine leaders. After innumerable factional fights, however, first as allies of Boies Penrose [*q.v.*], and later as opposed to him, they extended their influence from their own wards into neighboring ones, and became known as the "Dukes of South Philadelphia." In 1917 Edwin and William gained control of the Republican organization of the city. Already their support had been a prime factor in the election of Martin G. Brumbaugh to the governorship of Pennsylvania in 1914. At this time Edwin was generally considered a much abler man than William, but the former never attained national prominence, the highest office that he held being that of state senator. Beginning as ward committeeman, William was a member of the Select Council, 1898–1901; recorder of deeds, 1902–12; representative in Congress, Apr. 24, 1912–Jan. 2, 1923, and Mar. 4, 1923–Mar. 3, 1927; state senator, January–November 1923. His only defeat in a popular election, and that by a small majority although Penrose opposed him, occurred in 1911, when he ran for the Philadelphia mayoralty. He was district delegate to each of the national conventions of the Republican party from 1908 to 1920; delegate-at-large in 1924 and 1928, and national committeeman in 1934.

The climax of Vare's career came in the primaries of 1926, when on a light wine and beer platform he defeated George Wharton Pepper and Gifford Pinchot for the Republican nomination to the United States Senate. In the ensuing election he was successful over William B. Wilson, Democratic candidate, by approximately 170,000 votes. Before the election had taken place, however, in accordance with a resolution of May 17, 1926, a special senatorial committee, headed by James A. Reed of Missouri, began a probe into the Pennsylvania primary fight. After a prolonged controversy the Senate, by a vote of 58 to 22, Dec. 6, 1929, rejected Vare on the ground that his primary expenditures were excessive, and that fraud and corruption had been practised. As a matter of fact the expenditures had been less than half those of the faction headed by Pepper, his principal competitor. At the Republican National Convention of 1928, Vare stampeded the Pennsylvania delegation to Hoover (*New York Times*, June 12, 13, 1928), thus contributing largely to the nomination of the latter. No *quid pro quo* came from the White House after the inauguration, much to the disgust of the Philadelphia organization; nevertheless Vare supported Hoover in the campaign of 1932. In 1930, however, he had bolted Pinchot, Republican nominee for governor, in favor of John M. Hemphill, Democratic-Liberal and wet candidate.

In 1928 Vare's health failed but he continued his leadership until ousted by a factional combination two months before his death, which occurred at his summer home in Atlantic City. A member of the Methodist Church, his personal conduct was above reproach. Avowedly a machine leader, he maintained his organization largely by spoils and political charity, gaining popular support by "giving the people something they can see," *i.e.*, lavish expenditure of the city's money on public improvements in South Philadelphia. Throughout his career, however, he opposed child labor and vigorously supported workmen's compensation, mothers' assistance, and other social reform bills.

[Files of Phila. newspapers from 1900 are replete with articles and editorials, mostly hostile, on the Vares; their activities are defended by the *Sunday Dispatch*, a machine organ. Edwin Vare's career and character are admirably discussed in Harold Zink, *City Bosses in the U. S.* (1930); for a similar discussion of William Vare, see W. L. Whittlesey, "Vare of Philadelphia," in the *Outlook*, Dec. 28, 1927. William Vare's autobiog., *My Forty Years in Politics* (1933), deals with his public record but throws little light on the source of campaign funds or the inside manipulation of the organization; for facts regarding the senatorial investigation, see *Senate Report 1197*, 69 Cong., 2 Sess., pt. 2, *Senate Report 1858*, 70 Cong., 2 Sess., and *Senate Report 47*, 71 Cong., 2 Sess.; other sources include *Biog. Dir. Am. Cong.* (1928); *Who's Who in America*, 1932–33; *Evening Pub. Ledger* (Phila.), Aug. 7, 1934; *N. Y. Times*, Aug. 8, 1934.]

R. C. B.

VARELA Y MORALES, FÉLIX FRANCISCO JOSÉ MARÍA DE LA CONCEPCIÓN (Nov. 20, 1788–Feb. 18, 1853), patriot, educator, and priest, son of Francisco Varela, a Spanish military officer, and Josepha de Morales, was born in Habana, Cuba. After his father's early death, he was trained by a maternal uncle, Bartolomé Morales, governor of Saint Augustine, Fla., who soon sent him to the ancient College and Seminary of San Carlos in Habana. A boy of marked piety with a genius for languages and philosophy, he was ordained a priest (1811) and despite his youth given the chair of philosophy in the college, where he also taught physics and chemistry, Latin, and rhetoric. An educational reformer who would modernize the curriculum, change methods of teaching, and make philosophy a part of common life, Father Varela was not only an inspiring teacher but the author of numerous philosophical brochures and books: *Propositiones Variae ad Tyronum Exercitationem* (1811); *Elenco de las Doctrinas que Enseñaba en Filosofía el P. Varela* (1812); *Institutiones Philosophiae Eclecticae ad Usum Studiosae Juventutis Editae* (1812–14), two parts published in Latin, two in Spanish; *Lección Preliminar del Curso de 1818* (1818): *Apuntes Filosoficos, sobre la Dirección del Espiritu Humano* (Habana, 1818); and *Las Lecciónes de Filosofía* (4 vols., Habana, 1818–20), his most important work. An eclectic in philosophy, he opposed the scholasticism which had dominated Spanish thought for centuries, and followed the eighteenth-century philosophers in substituting for it theories that rested on experience and the use of the reason. In the natural sciences, he depended largely on the laboratory. No pedant, he taught in simple language. As a recreation, he studied music and played the violin or took part in the proceedings of the Royal Patriotic Society of Habana. His oratory, which was notable, was characterized by simplicity, clarity, brevity, and good taste. Upon the establishment of a constitutional monarchy in Spain, Varela gave a course on the new constitution in the college. His lectures drew a large attendance of students and patriots, and his published *Observaciones sobre la Constitución Política de la Monarquía Española* (Habana, 1821) won favor with his liberal countrymen. The following year he was sent to Spain as a delegate to the Cortes in Madrid, where he served on various commissions and drew up a plan of provincial government which would give the Spanish colonies a high degree of local autonomy. Perhaps the first Cuban abolitionist, he also suggested a plan for the gradual abolition of slavery in Cuba.

With the establishment of an absolute monarchy in Spain in 1823, Varela fled to New York (Dec. 17, 1823). Going to Philadelphia, he established *El Habanero,* a literary and political paper, its circulation forbidden in Cuba, to which he contributed articles violent enough to bring danger of assassination (1824–26). About this time he translated into Spanish Thomas Jefferson's *A Manual of Parliamentary Practice* and Humphrey Davy's *Elements of Agricultural Chemistry.* In 1825 he went to New York, where as an assistant at St. Peter's Church he ministered to the Latin peoples. With the aid of Spanish merchants, he bought Christ Church from the Episcopalians (St. James) and served as pastor until 1835, when he was transferred to his final rectorship of the Church of the Transfiguration. He republished in 1827 his *Miscelánea Filosófica* (Habana, 1819), edited the poems of the Cuban, Manuel de Zequeira (1829), and published in two volumes his *Cartas á Elpidio sobre la Impiedad, la Superstición y el Fanatismo* (New York, 1835–38), a defense of Christianity against impiety and false liberalism, a third volume remaining in manuscript. Aroused by nativism, he wrote for the *Truth Teller* (1825) and the *New York Weekly Register and Catholic Diary* (1833), and contributed to *El Mensagero Semanal* (1828–31) of New York and occasionally to the *Revista Bimestre Cubana* (1831) of Habana. For a time he was editor of the *Young Catholics' Magazine,* and in 1841 he joined with Charles C. Pise [*q.v.*] in editing the short-lived *Catholic Expositor and Literary Magazine* (1841–44), for which he wrote a number of apologetic essays marked by learning and fluency.

More than a litterateur and a defender of the faith, Varela was an active priest of boundless zeal for souls and sympathy for the poor and the immigrants. He established one of the first total abstinence societies (*Freeman's Journal,* Mar.

20, 1841), several parochial schools, and a day nursery for the children of laboring women. He did not spare himself in the cholera epidemic. As early as 1829 he was named joint-administrator of the diocese with John Power [*q.v.*], when Bishop John Dubois was in Europe. Ten years later Bishop John Hughes left the same two priests in charge. In 1837 and in 1846 Varela attended the councils of Baltimore as a theologian; from 1839 to his death, he was one of Hughes's vicar-generals. Although he was honored by St. Mary's Seminary with a doctorate in sacred theology (1841), most of his honors came after his death in a living tradition in New York as a worthy priest (*Ibid.,* Feb. 4, 1865) and a growing renown among Cubans as a philosopher and patriot. In 1851 he retired to Saint Augustine, where he died. His old students built a chapel to his memory in the cemetery in Saint Augustine.

[For a discussion of the date of death, often given as Feb. 25, see A. L. Valverde y Maruri, *La Muerte del Padre Varela* (Habana, 1924). See also J. I. Rodriguez, *Vida del Presbítero Don Félix Varela* (1878); and art. in *Am. Cath. Quart. Rev.,* July 1883; Sergio Cuevas Zequeira, *El Padre Varela* (1923); W. F. Blakeslee, *Records Am. Cath. Hist. Soc. of Phila.,* Mar. 1927; J. M. Mestre, *De la Filosofía en la Habana* (1862); J. M. Guardia, in *Revue Philosophique,* Jan. 1892, pp. 51–164; J. T. Smith, *The Cath. Church in N. Y.* (1905), vol. I; J. G. Shea, *A Hist. of the Cath. Church within ... the U. S.* (1890); *Hunt's Merchants' Mag.,* Sept. 1842; *Truth Teller,* Jan. 23, 1847; *N. Y. Freeman's Jour.,* Mar. 12, 19, 1853; U. S. Cath. Hist. Soc., *Hist. Records and Studies,* vol. II (1900), pp. 47–48; *Ceremonies at the Laying of the Cornerstone of a Chapel ... St. Augustine, Fla., Dedicated to ... Félix Varela* (1853). For bibliog. materials, see C. M. Trelles, *Bibliografía Cubana del Siglo XIX* (3 vols., 1911–12).]
R. J. P.

VARICK, JAMES (fl. 1796–1828), one of the founders of the African Methodist Episcopal Zion Church and its first bishop, was born near Newburgh, N. Y., probably about 1750 (see Hood, *post,* p. 162), though a considerably later date has been given (Flood and Hamilton, *post,* p. 687). He first came into notice in 1796 when certain colored members of the Methodist Episcopal Church living in New York secured permission from Bishop Francis Asbury to hold meetings by themselves in the intervals between the services held for them by the white ministers. With several others he hired a house on Cross Street, between Mulberry and Orange streets, and fitted it up as a place of worship. Three years later the congregation organized a church under the laws of the state of New York, which was to be subject to Methodist government and known as the African Methodist Episcopal Zion Church; in 1800 a frame building for its meetings was completed and dedicated. A white minister was regularly appointed to have charge of it, but colored preachers also conducted services.

As a result of a number of causes, in 1820 the church declared its independence. Preliminary action was taken at a meeting of official members, held in Varick's house in July of that year, at which Varick and others were appointed a committee to consider the matter. Subsequently, July 26, 1820, the church adopted resolutions severing the existing connection with the Methodist Episcopal organization. Varick was later appointed chairman of a committee to draw up a Discipline based on that of the Methodists. On Oct. 1, 1820, the church elected Abraham Thompson and Varick, both of whom had long been preachers, elders with the power of performing all the functions of that office until ordained by regularly constituted authorities. Several other churches, including one in Philadelphia, one in New Haven, Conn., and one on Long Island, soon affiliated themselves with Zion Church and on June 21, 1821, a Conference was formed with Varick as district chairman, or presiding elder. Patient efforts to secure ordination from Methodist Episcopal bishops having failed, on July 17, 1822, he and two others, all of whom had previously been made deacons, were ordained elders by three former ministers of the Methodist Church who had withdrawn from the connection. That same year Varick was elected bishop of the African Methodist Episcopal Zion Church and served as such until his death.

Through all the years leading up to the establishment of this denomination, he had been a wise and patient leader. His character was never questioned; he had the confidence of prominent Methodists, and is said to have been an able debater and a forceful preacher. He was married and had three sons and four daughters. After his death, which occurred shortly before the Conference that convened May 15, 1828, Christopher Rush (1777–July 16, 1873), born a North Carolina slave, who had also been influential in Zion Church, succeeded him as bishop.

[Christopher Rush, *A Short Account of the Rise and Progress of the African Methodist Episcopal Church in America* (1843); J. W. Hood, *One Hundred Years of the African Methodist Episcopal Zion Church* (1895); T. L. Flood and J. W. Hamilton, *Lives of Methodist Bishops* (1882); J. M. Buckley, *A Hist. of Methodists in the U. S.* (1896), Am. Church Hist. Ser., vol. V.]
H. E. S.

VARICK, RICHARD (Mar. 25, 1753–July 30, 1831), soldier, was the son of Johannis and Jane (Dey) Varick and a great-grandson of Jan van Varick who came to New York from the Netherlands prior to June 1, 1687, and removed to Hackensack, N. J., about 1712. Richard removed to New York City in 1775 and became a captain in the first New York regiment in June of that year. Subsequently he became military secretary to Gen. Philip John Schuyler [*q.v.*], and lieutenant-colonel and deputy mustermaster-general of the Northern department. Under the reorganized muster department he was deputy commissary-general of musters until June 1780. In August of that year Benedict Arnold [*q.v.*], commanding at West Point, appointed him his aide. Varick was prostrated on the discovery of Arnold's treason and petitioned Washington for a court of inquiry, which acquitted him with honor.

Despite the verdict, however, Varick found that he was an object of suspicion. He wrote to Washington (Nov. 12, 1780) that he wished to remain in the army but the abolition of the muster department and Arnold's treason had left him stranded, and he petitioned that Washington express to Congress his opinion of Varick. This letter is indorsed "No answer necessary" (Washington Papers, Library of Congress). Not quite half a year later, having obtained the approval of Congress to appoint a confidential secretary and staff of writers to record his letters in books to "preserve them from damage and loss," Washington selected Varick as his recording secretary and turned over to him to arrange, classify, and copy, all the correspondence and records of the headquarters of the Continental Army. In the face of such a display of confidence the whispered slanders against Varick were forever silenced. Varick took quarters in Poughkeepsie and the actual copying began early in 1781; the task was completed in 1783, and the forty-odd volumes of transcripts resulting are a monument to secretarial ability and finished skill. Washington expressed his approbation of the manner in which the work was performed and begged Varick to accept his thanks "for the care and attention" which he had given to the task. "I am fully convinced," he wrote, "that neither the present age or posterity will consider the time and labour which have been employed in accomplishing it, unprofitably spent" (Washington to Varick, Jan. 1, 1784; Washington Papers).

In 1784 Varick became recorder of New York City; in 1786, with Samuel Jones [*q.v.*], he was entrusted with the codification of the New York statutes (*Laws of the State of New-York, Comprising the Constitution and the Acts of the Legislature Since the Revolution*, 2 vols., 1789). Speaker of the New York Assembly in 1787 and 1788, and attorney-general in 1788–89, he became mayor of New York in the latter year and held office until the triumphant Republicans swept out all Federalists in 1801. In 1790 he was appointed with two others to provide new buildings for the state government, which were to be used, temporarily, by the government of the United States. With Alexander Hamilton [*q.v.*], he attempted, unsuccessfully, to stem the tide of popular disapproval against the Jay treaty in an hysterical public meeting at the city hall in the summer of 1795. In 1817 he was one of the appraisers for the Erie Canal. He was a founder of the American Bible Society and its president from 1828 to 1831, and president of the New York Society of the Cincinnati from 1806 until his death. He died in Jersey City and was buried in the Dutch Reformed Church at Hackensack. On May 8, 1786, he had married Maria, daughter of Isaac and Cornelia (Hoffman) Roosevelt; she survived him by a decade, but they left no children.

[*N. Y. Geneal. and Biog. Record*, Jan. 1877; *Journals of the Continental Congress*; Washington MSS. in Lib. of Cong.; J. G. Wilson, *The Memorial Hist. of the City of N. Y.*, vols. II, III (1892, 1893); F. B. Lee, *N. J. as a Colony and as a State* (1902), vols. III, IV; Martha J. Lamb, *Hist. of the City of N. Y.*, vol. II (1880); E. A. Werner, *Civil List . . . of N. Y.* (1899); C. B. Whittelsey, *The Roosevelt Geneal.* (1902); H. P. Johnston, "Colonel Varick and Arnold's Treason," *Mag. of Am. Hist.*, Nov. 1882; John Schuyler, *Institution of the Soc. of the Cincinnati* (1886); F. B. Heitman, *Hist. Reg. of Officers of the Continental Army* (1893); *N. Y. Evening Post for the Country*, Aug. 5, 1831.]

J. C. F—k.

VARNUM, JAMES MITCHELL (Dec. 17, 1748–Jan. 10, 1789), lawyer, Revolutionary soldier, was born at Dracut, Mass., the eldest son of Maj. Samuel Varnum, a prosperous farmer, and his second wife, Hannah Mitchell. He was a descendant of George Varnum, who came to America about 1635, and a brother of Joseph Bradley Varnum [*q.v.*]. James was sent to Harvard College, but, probably on account of participation in the student disorders of April 1768, he was expelled. He then entered Rhode Island College (now Brown University), and was graduated with honors in its first class, 1769, defending in his commencement forensic the thesis that America should not become independent. After teaching school for a short time, he decided to study law and entered the office of Oliver Arnold, attorney-general of Rhode Island. He was married on Feb. 8, 1770, to Martha Child, the daughter of Cromwell Child, of Warren, R. I. Varnum made rapid professional advancement after his admission to the bar in 1771, due to his extraordinary mental alertness and powers of concentration. His acquaintance with literary masterpieces from which he quoted fluently and copiously helped him to take advantage of the current mode of courtroom oratory.

His powerful physique led him to become a sturdy advocate of gymnastic exhibitions and military drill. In October 1774 he became a colonel of the Kentish Guards, a troop which later sent thirty-two commissioned officers into the Continental Army; among them was Varnum's close friend Nathanael Greene [*q.v.*]. In May 1775 Varnum was commissioned colonel of the 1st Regiment, Rhode Island Infantry, which became in 1776 the 9th Continental Infantry. This command served in the siege of Boston and held important positions in the battles of Long Island and White Plains. In December the Rhode Island Assembly appointed Varnum brigadier-general of state militia on the continental establishment. He was commissioned brigadier-general in the Continental Army by General Washington on Feb. 21, 1777, and became active in recruitments and reënlistments. His brigade saw complicated service in 1777; Washington ordered him in November to command Forts Mercer and Mifflin on the Delaware. His gallant, though unsuccessful, defense of these key posts, won him commendation, and during the following winter at Valley Forge the commander-in-chief referred to him as "the light of the camp" (Varnum, *post*, p. 158).

After the evacuation of Philadelphia he was ordered to Rhode Island where he took part in the campaign around Newport. He was then made commander of the department of Rhode Island, Jan. 27, 1779. In order to resume his neglected law practice he resigned from the service in the Continental Army in March 1779, but accepted, the following month, a commission as major-general of Rhode Island militia, a rank that he held until May 1788. He was elected in May 1780 to the Continental Congress and served at intervals until 1787. A contemporary, Thomas Rodney [*q.v.*], characterized him at this time as "a man about thirty, of florid habit, he has read some little of books, is fond of Speaking and Spouting out everything that his reading has furnished him . . . his temper and councils are very precip[it]ate and but little calculated to be useful in such an Assembly, he is very desirous of enlarging its powers" (*Letters of Members, post*, vol. VI, 1933, p. 19). Varnum's law cases were many and notable. He was an original member of the Society of the Cincinnati, and later succeeded General Greene as president of the Rhode Island branch.

An interest in the Northwest Territory and the Ohio Company of Associates, of which he became a director in August 1787, led to Varnum's acceptance of an appointment as United States judge for the Territory at a time when his health was in a very precarious state. He journeyed on horseback to Marietta, Ohio, arriving on June 5, 1788, and a month later delivered a Fourth of July address that was published by the Ohio

Company in 1788 and is still prized by collectors. He energetically assisted in framing a code of territorial laws—his last official act. He died at Marietta and was buried with great ceremony at the Campus Martius. Later his remains were reinterred in Oak Grove Cemetery. His wife remained in the East and survived him forty-eight years. There were no children.

[J. M. Varnum, *The Varnums of Dracutt in Mass.* (1907); A. B. Gardiner and J. M. Varnum, biographical sketch in *Mag. of Am. Hist.*, Sept. 1887; Wilkins Updike, *Memoirs of the R.-I. Bar* (1842); S. R. Coburn, *Hist. of Dracut, Mass.* (1922); F. B. Heitman, *Hist. Reg. of Officers of the Cont. Army* (1893); *Biog. Dir. Am. Cong.* (1928); *Letters of Members of the Cont. Cong.*, vol. VI (1933) ed. by E. C. Burnett; *Providence Gazette and Country Jour.*, Mar. 7, 1789.]

F. W. C.

VARNUM, JOSEPH BRADLEY (Jan. 29, 1750/51–Sept. 11, 1821), Revolutionary soldier, speaker of the federal House of Representatives, senator from Massachusetts, was born at Dracut, Mass., a son of Samuel and Hannah (Mitchell) Varnum and a brother of James Mitchell Varnum [q.v.]. Later assertions by Federalists of Varnum's illiteracy were malicious, but he was largely self-taught and sometimes betrayed a lack of early educational advantages. He was married, on Jan. 26, 1773, to Molly Butler, the daughter of Jacob Butler, of Pelham, N. H., a woman of strong character and marked domesticity, who bore her husband twelve children. They received as a gift from his father 160 acres of land with half a dwelling-house and a barn. Farming remained Varnum's primary and preferred occupation throughout his career, and he was proud, in 1818, of owning 500 acres with "more than ten miles of good stone fence upon it" (*Magazine of American History, post,* p. 408). Observance of the British troops in Boston in 1767 interested Varnum in military tactics, and in 1770 one of two militia companies at Dracut elected him captain. He was replaced in 1774 by an older man though still employed as instructor, and in this capacity he was present at the Battle of Lexington. From January 1776 to April 1787, he was captain of the Dracut Minute-men, and he served in the campaigns against Burgoyne in 1777, at Rhode Island in 1778, and later in suppressing Shays's Rebellion.

He represented Dracut in the Massachusetts lower house, 1780–85, and northern Middlesex County, in the Senate, 1786–95. A mild anti-Federalist, he was sent to the Massachusetts convention to ratify the national Constitution (see his speech on the bill of rights, *Massachusetts Centinel,* Feb. 6, 1788). He was a somewhat irregular candidate for the Second and Third congresses but was nominated regularly in 1794 for the Fourth Congress against Samuel Dexter [q.v.], a Federalist. He was elected by a majority of eleven votes, most of his support coming from Dracut and the adjoining towns. The election was protested, because the local board of selectmen, of which Varnum was a member, returned sixty more votes than Dracut was entitled to, but, in accordance with the lax rules of the period, he was exonerated in a Republican Congress of charges of political corruption.

In Congress he favored national defense through the militia as against a standing army, opposed building the *Constitution* and other naval vessels, denounced President John Adams' personal extravagance, and was an early opponent of slavery and the slave trade. He was several times called upon to preside during executive sessions. He benefited from the Jefferson-Randolph dispute when the speaker of the House sided with the latter, and the power of the administration was put behind Varnum in his election to the speakership in the Tenth Congress by one vote. His speakership occurred "in an epoch of commanding mediocrity" (Fuller, *post,* p. 30), and he was reëlected in the Eleventh Congress. A very important adjustment made in his term of office was that of limitation of debate in the House. The speaker, unfortunately for his own standing at home, attached his signature to the Embargo act and brought down upon his head accusations of subserviency to the administration and the South by the New England Federalists (*Salem Gazette,* Jan. 12, 1810). In 1809 he was nominated by the Republicans for lieutenant-governor of Massachusetts, but was defeated.

In 1810, the Massachusetts legislature, deadlocked for several days, finally chose Varnum senator to succeed Timothy Pickering [q.v.]. He took his seat in March 1811 and before long was accused by his opponents, and probably justly, of conspiring with the southwestern "war hawks" to bring on the war of 1812. After the declaration of war he and several Democratic representatives were mobbed in Boston (*Boston Gazette,* July 12, 1812). He remained the stanchest New England supporter of "Mr. Madison's war." In 1813 he was president *pro tempore* of the Senate and acting vice-president of the United States. He ran for governor of Massachusetts on a "win the war" platform in 1813, but was badly defeated by Caleb Strong [q.v.]. In 1814 he spoke at length in the Senate against Giles's bill for an army of 80,000 men. "The justice of Varnum's criticism could not fairly be questioned," says Henry Adams (*History of the United States,* vol. VIII, 1891, p. 109). At that date he was the only New England war man in Congress.

Still a useful legislator, Varnum served in the Senate until 1817, when he was succeeded by Harrison Gray Otis, 1765–1848 [q.v.]. He re-entered the Massachusetts Senate where he opposed the separation of Maine from Massachusetts. He was a delegate to the state convention to amend the constitution in 1820. Despite his record as a militarist he became a pioneer member of the Massachusetts Peace Society, the predecessor of the American Peace Society. Late in life he revolted from the established Congregational Church and joined the Baptists. He was buried without pomp or ceremony in the Varnum Cemetery at Dracut. He was the author of *An Address Delivered to the Third Division of Massachusetts Militia, at a Revue, in the Plains of Concord ...*, printed by William Hilliard in 1800.

[Biography compiled by F. W. Coburn, *Courier-Citizen* (Lowell, Mass.), Aug. 1–Oct. 31, 1933; manuscript "Book of Third Division of the Militia of Mass.," owned by the Town of Dracut; J. M. Varnum, *The Varnums of Dracutt in Mass.* (1907); "Autobiography of General Joseph B. Varnum," *Mag. of Am. Hist.,* Nov. 1888; *Biog. Dir. Am. Cong.* (1928); H. B. Fuller, *The Speakers of the House* (1909); D. S. Alexander, *Hist. and Procedure of the House of Rep.* (1916); Henry Wilson, *Hist. of the Rise and Fall of the Slave Power in America* (1872), vol. I; *Columbian Centinel* (Boston, Mass.), Sept. 15, 1821.]   F. W. C.

VASEY, GEORGE (Feb. 28, 1822–Mar. 4, 1893), botanist, was born near Scarborough, England, of English parents, who removed the year following to Central New York, settling at Oriskany. He was the fourth of ten children and, the family being in humble circumstances, had to quit school at twelve to work in a village store. Already deeply interested in plants, he devoted his spare time to their analysis and was fortunate in making the acquaintance of Dr. P. D. Knieskern, under whose stimulating guidance he became familiar with the rich local flora and was put in touch with John Torrey [q.v.], Asa Gray [q.v.], and other botanists. After graduation from the Oneida Institute he began the study of medicine at the age of twenty-one, attending the Berkshire Medical Institute, Pittsfield, Mass. Toward the last of the year 1846 he married a Miss Scott, of Oriskany, and began the practice of medicine at Dexter, N. Y. In 1848 he removed to northern Illinois, where, at Elgin and Ringwood, he spent eighteen years in professional practice. During this period he continued his botanical studies, collected extensively the unspoiled prairie flora of the region, and extended widely his botanical contacts through correspondence. He helped organize the Illinois Natural History Society and was its first president. Early in 1866 his wife's failing health led him to remove to the southern part of the state, where, however, she soon died. Late in 1867 he married Mrs. John W. Cameron, daughter of Dr. Isaac Barber, of New York.

Fortunately there now came to Vasey the opportunity of devoting himself wholly to botanical pursuits. In the latter half of 1868 he accompanied his friend Maj. John Wesley Powell [q.v.] on an exploring expedition to Colorado, as botanist. Shortly after his return he was made curator of the natural history museum of the State Normal University of Illinois, and in 1870 was associated with Prof. Charles V. Riley [q.v.] in the editorship of the *American Entomologist and Botanist*. On Apr. 1, 1872, he was appointed botanist of the United States Department of Agriculture, in Washington, D. C., and put in charge of the United States National Herbarium, which had been transferred from the Smithsonian Institution in 1868. Up to this time Vasey had published little, and that of a popular nature. The task of organizing thoroughly the National Herbarium, of identifying and arranging the material that had long accumulated, largely from voyages and transcontinental railroad surveys under government auspices, was a difficult undertaking which occupied him closely for several years and was carried through with notable success. His next work of general interest was the preparation of an exhibit of the woods of American forest trees, accompanied by herbarium specimens, for the Centennial Exhibition in Philadelphia. As a guide to this exhibit he published *A Catalogue of the Forest Trees of the United States Which Usually Attain a Height of Sixteen Feet or More* (1876). But grasses now claimed his attention and upon this difficult group, in which he became a distinguished specialist, he published voluminously to the end of his life. Besides papers describing new genera and species from all parts of the United States, his more important publications are: *Agricultural Grasses of the United States* (1884); *A Descriptive Catalogue of the Grasses of the United States* (1885); *Grasses of the Southwest* (2 vols. in 1, 1890–91) and *Grasses of the Pacific Slope* (2 vols. in 1, 1892–93), published also under the title: *Illustrations of North American Grasses* (2 vols., 1891–93); and *Monograph of the Grasses of the United States and British America* (1892). Under his direction, also, experimental studies of grasses and other forage plants suited to arid regions of the West were initiated.

Of gentle dignity and kindly disposition, Vasey was beloved by a wide circle of friends. He died at his home in Washington from acute peritonitis, survived by his wife and six children.

[F. V. Coville, in *Bull. Torrey Bot. Club*, XX, 218–20 (May 10, 1893); W. M. Canby and J. N. Rose, in *Bot. Gaz.*, XVIII, 170–83, with portr. (May 1893); William Frear, in *Agric. Science*, VII, 249–52, with portr. (June 1893); B. L. Robinson, in *Proc. Am. Acad. Arts and Sci.*, XXVIII, 401–03 (1893); *Evening Star* (Washington, D. C.), Mar. 6, 1893; also official sources.]   W. R. M.

VASSALL, JOHN (1625–July ? 1688), colonial entrepreneur, was born in Stepney, Middlesex County, England, the son of William and Anne (King) Vassall and the grandson of John Vassall. His grandfather, probably a religious refugee from France, attained position and security in England, fitted out and commanded two ships against the Spanish Armada, and was later a member of the Virginia Company. His uncle and his father, Samuel and William, were both interested in American colonization, Samuel as a merchant trading extensively with the colonies and as an incorporator of the first Massachusetts company and patentee of large tracts of land, and William as an assistant in the company and an actual settler. In June 1635, at the age of ten, John sailed from England with his father and mother and his five sisters. The family settled first at Roxbury in Massachusetts and the next year at Scituate in the colony of New Plymouth. His father, by reason of his wealth and ability, became influential in both colonies and was involved in the effort to obtain more liberal qualifications for the electorate. In 1646 he returned to England. Two years later he went to Barbados, acquired extensive land holdings, and died there in 1655.

John Vassall remained in Scituate, where he was a member of the militia in 1633 and lieutenant under Cudworth in 1652. He became a captain and later, in Jamaica, was spoken of as "colonel." When Charles II granted Carolina to the Lords Proprietors he, with Henry Vassall, a cousin in London, and some other adventurers proposed to the Lords Proprietors to found a colony. Early in the summer of 1664 the settlers arrived at Cape Fear in what is now the state of North Carolina, and on Nov. 24, 1664, he was appointed surveyor general. He was the leading promoter of the enterprise in the colony, and Henry Vassall was the London agent. Holding out as inducements the promise of land, freedom of religion, and the right to vote, they encouraged settlers from New England, the West Indies, and Europe to join them, but the colony was unsuccessful. In these circumstances he wrote to John Leverett, 1616–1679 [*q.v.*], asking for aid; and in May 1667 the colony of Massachusetts Bay voted to send relief to Cape Fear. On Oct. 6 of that year he was at Nansemond in Virginia and wrote to Sir John Colleton of the breaking up of this Clarendon County settlement. He seems to have remained there some time trying to obtain redress of grievances against the Lords Proprietors. On Mar. 2, 1672, he was reported as having arrived in Jamaica, where he settled in St. Elizabeth's Parish with his wife, Anne (Lewis) Vassall. He maintained his connections with the mainland colonies throughout his life, interested in the carrying trade among them, the West Indies, and Europe. By his will, proved in Jamaica on July 6, 1688, he provided for the education of his son Samuel at Harvard College. Another son, Leonard, lived most of his life in Boston and died there. His great-grandson, John Vassall, built the "Craigie-Longfellow" house in Cambridge and was living there when the Revolution broke out. He, a Loyalist like many others of the family, went to England.

The vast family estates in the United States were confiscated, and the family name has left no mark on later republican history. Some of John Vassall's fortune, however, was inherited by Elizabeth Vassall Fox, a great-great-granddaughter, the wife of the third Lord Holland, who became a political hostess in London and made "Holland House" the center for the Whig party that was to revolutionize England's own political and social system.

[Samuel Deane, *Hist. Scituate, Mass.* (1831), pp. 366–70; James Sprunt, *Chronicles of the Cape Fear River* (1914); *Mass. Hist. Soc. Colls.*, 2 ser., vol. IV (1816) and 3 ser., vol. VIII (1843), p. 267; *New England Hist. and Geneal. Register*, Jan. 1863; *The Colonial Records of N. C.*, I (1886); *Records of the . . . Mass. Bay*, vol. IV, pt. 2 (1854), ed. by N. B. Shurtleff; *Great Britain Public Record Office. Calendar of State Papers, Colonial Series. Am. and West Ind., 1661–1668* (1880); *Ibid. . . . 1669–1674* (1889); *Ibid. . . . 1675–1676* with addenda (1893); *Ibid. . . . 1677–1680* (1896); Lib. of Cong. Transcripts of Public Record Office Papers, and British Museum Additional MSS.; C. M. Calder, *John Vassall and His Descendants* (1921); F. A. Crisp, *Visitation of England and Wales*, "Notes," vol. XIII (1919); C. K. Shipton, *Biog. Sketches of those who Attended Harvard College in the Classes 1690–1700* (1933); for members of family *Dict. Nat. Biog.* and Thomas Bridgman, *Memorials of . . . King's Chapel Burial Ground* (1853), with text of inscription on monument to Samuel Vassall (1586–1667), which implies incorrectly that the later Vassalls in America were descended from Samuel rather than from his brother William.]   K. E. C.

VASSAR, MATTHEW (Apr. 29, 1792–June 23, 1868), brewer and merchant, founder of Vassar College, was born at East Tuddingham, County of Norfolk, England. According to family tradition, the name was originally spelled Vasseur and the great-grandfather was a French refugee. James Vassar, Matthew Vassar's father, and his wife, Anne (Bennett) Vassar, and his brother Thomas, emigrated to America and settled in Dutchess County, N. Y., in 1796. Finding the local barley did not brew good ale, the brother Thomas returned to Norfolk and obtained English barley-corn for American planting. From this time, the brewing improved, and soon the family moved in from the countryside to the brewery in Poughkeepsie. The boy Matthew ran away from home at the age of thirteen and earned his own way for three years at a farm and country store, and then returned to Poughkeepsie in 1808. On Mar. 7, 1813, he was married to Catherine Valentine, who died in 1863, leaving no children. In 1811 the brewery was burned, and Matthew began an independent brewing business. In addition to his brewery, he engaged in other enterprises, and financed his nephew in the colonization of land in central Michigan. This resulted in the founding of the town of Vassar, named after him. Another venture was a whaling industry. He owned a whaling dock in Poughkeepsie and was part-owner of a whaling fleet. In 1845 he went to Europe, and, in his autobiography, he stated that he visited Guy's Hospital in London, "the founder of which a family relative," and "seeing this Institution first suggested the idea of devoting a portion of my Estate to some Charitable purpose" (*post*, p. 33). His niece, Lydia Booth, was the proprietress of a school for girls in Poughkeepsie, which was later sold to Milo P. Jewett [*q.v.*]. The business of the purchase brought Jewett in contact with Vassar; and the plan of a college for women was the result. Vassar's earlier intention had been the founding of a hospital, later realized by the gift of his two nephews in 1882 to Vassar Brothers Hospital.

His native prudence and sagacity stood him in good stead in the founding of his college, but it is curious to observe that his plans for the intellectual program of his college were better laid than those for its material welfare. The enormous building that he erected in 1861–65 was ill-suited to a woman's college; but the program of studies under the first active president, John Howard Raymond [*q.v.*], was fully abreast of the times and challenged comparison with the best colleges for men. Throughout the four years, 1861–65, Vassar advertised his venture extensively; and the result was an enrollment that crowded his building to capacity from the start and produced a worldwide interest in the venture. A number of women's colleges had been founded before 1865, and several coeducational institutions were open, but Vassar's advertising first brought the idea of higher education for women forcibly to the attention of the modern world, and within ten years the battle had been fought and won. It was proved that mental activity in the abstruse branches of learning did not injure

woman's health, and that there were many women eager for intellectual life. The English colleges for women and many other colleges in America were the result of this demonstration. Coeducation soon became the practice from coast to coast in state-supported institutions. The opening of universities on the European continent followed not long afterward.

Vassar's early board of trustees included Samuel F. B. Morse and Henry Ward Beecher, and his correspondence on education with such men as Henry Barnard was voluminous. His private library shows that he also owned works by Herbert Spencer and John Stuart Mill. Indeed, his thought ran ahead of his day; and he was less interested in demonstrating that woman's mind was equal to man's than he was in developing a curriculum suited to the needs of women in the modern world. His hopes in this direction were frustrated by the apparent necessity of the demonstration of mental equality; and the curricula of the early women's colleges therefore closely resembled those for men. His belief in woman's suffrage and his faith in woman's capacity, however, strongly affected the life of the early students. The development of the social sciences and the application of studies to American life led many early graduates into fields of social work. He never had any formal schooling. His turns of speech and poor spelling, together with his occupation as a brewer, developed a misunderstanding of the real genius of the man. This has since been corrected by the publication of his autobiography and letters, and by other records continually coming to light showing his broad vision and steady faith in his enterprise. Many of his sayings stamp him as one of the genuinely original Americans in the second half-century of the republic. He died of a heart seizure, while reading his letter of resignation from the board of trustees at the college. His gifts during his life to the institution amounted to over $800,000. His two nephews, whom he had interested in the venture, increased this to a million and a quarter by their gifts.

[*The Autobiog. and Letters of Matthew Vassar* (1916), ed. by E. H. Haight; J. M. Taylor and E. H. Haight, *Vassar* (1915); MSS., records, maps, etc., in the possession of Vassar College.]   H. N. M.

VATTEMARE, NICOLAS MARIE ALEXANDRE (Nov. 8, 1796–Apr. 7, 1864), founder of a system of international exchanges, ventriloquist, and impersonator, was born in Paris, the son of an advocate. He spent brief periods in a seminary and in a hospital as a student. In Germany, where he had been sent in 1814 with a group of Prussian prisoners, he began the use of his natural gift of ventriloquism and as "Monsieur Alexandre" soon became one of the popular entertainers of the day. He appeared in London in 1822 under the management of W. T. Moncrieff, in whose *Rogueries of Nicholas* he was a great success. His brief appearance in the United States began at the Park Theatre in New York City, Oct. 28, 1839.

Impressed by the number of duplicate books and art objects in libraries and museums which he visited, he had evolved the idea of a system of exchange and had won some support for it in Europe. Early in 1840 he sent Congress a memorial on the subject which received favorable action (*House Doc. 50, 26* Cong., 1 Sess.). Traveling extensively in the United States and Canada, he enlisted the sympathy and aid of prominent people, and returned to France in 1841 with many items for exchange. The expansion of his system and the development of an agency for handling exchanges occupied him until his return to America in 1847. His second memorial to Congress (*Sen. Miscellaneous Doc. 46, 30* Cong., 1 Sess.) and various appeals to state legislatures resulted in his appointment as agent by Congress and a few states to handle their exchanges, and in the granting of some financial aid. After his return to France in 1850, his system continued to flourish for a few years, but it gradually declined in popularity, support was withdrawn, and Vattemare's hope of its permanent establishment failed. Whatever success he attained was due largely to the cooperation given him in America. He seems to have been temperamentally unsuited to carrying out some of his own ideas, which, indeed, were better suited to be the work of an institution than of one man. Some of his suggestions seem impracticable and naïve (see *Proceedings of a Meeting of Citizens of the City of Albany Held Nov. 27, 1847*, 1849, p. 12), but he was interested in moral and social effects as well as in the exchange of material things. In his *Report on the Subject of International Exchanges* (1848), one of his numerous publications, he points out the value of such exchanges in lessening national prejudices and developing good will. He lost no opportunity to urge the establishment of free libraries and museums. It is generally conceded that he was largely instrumental in the founding of the Boston Public Library (H. G. Wadlin, *The Public Library of the City of Boston*, 1911, pp. 1–8, 17–19). He was also responsible for what was known as the American Library in Paris, a collection of American books and documents housed in the Hôtel de Ville, which has since been lost. Evidence that Vattemare count-

ed among his friends many prominent people is to be found in his *Album Cosmopolite* (1837), a collection of letters, miscellaneous autographs, and reproductions. He was a chevalier of the *Légion d'honneur*. The elder of his two sons, Hippolyte, and his son-in-law, C. Moreau, were associated with him in the work of his agency. He died in Paris.

[Vattemare's first name sometimes appears as Nicholas. The chief biog. sources are Hippolyte Vattemare, "Notices of the Life of Alexander Vattemare," *Hist. Mag.*, Dec. 1868; *Memoirs and Anecdotes of Monsieur Alexandre* (1822); J. P. Quincy, in *Proc. Mass. Hist. Soc.*, 2 ser., vol. I (1885); "Strange Career of an Artist," in *Hours at Home*, Oct. 1868; Alphonse Passier, *Les Échanges Internationaux Littéraires et Scientifiques, Leur Histoire . . . 1832–1880* (1880); W. B. Trask, in *New-Eng. Hist. and Geneal. Reg.*, Oct. 1865, pp. 367–69; Elizabeth M. Richards, "Alexandre Vattemare and His System of International Exchanges," 1934, thesis, Columbia Univ.; obituaries in *La Siècle* (Paris), Apr. 11, and *Le Constitutionnel* (Paris), Apr. 12, 1864. Vattemare's papers and records of his agency are in the N. Y. Pub. Lib.; other MSS. are in the Boston Pub. Lib.]   E. M. R.

VAUDREUIL-CAVAGNAL, PIERRE DE RIGAUD, Marquis de (1704–Aug. 4, 1778), the last French governor of Canada, was a native of that colony, third son of Philippe Rigaud, Marquis de Vaudreuil, likewise governor (1703–25), and of Louise Elisabeth de Joybert. As governor's son Pierre was brought up in mild luxury and early entered the army, rising in 1726 to the rank of major. Two years later he accompanied the expedition of the Sieur de Lignery against the Fox Indians in what is now Wisconsin. Then known as the Sieur de Cavagnal, he appears to have acted as commissary and was sent to announce the news of the failure of the expedition to the governor (*Collections of the State Historical Society of Wisconsin*, vol. XVII, 1906, p. 31). In 1730 young Vaudreuil was awarded the cross of the order of St. Louis, the most coveted honor in the army, and in 1733 was appointed governor of Trois Rivières, the third largest settlement in New France. Ten years later he was chosen for the governorship of the colony of Louisiana, succeeding Jean Baptiste Le Moyne, Sieur de Bienville [*q.v.*], and arriving at New Orleans early in 1743. His appointment pleased the colonists, for he had a hereditary reputation for liberality and kindness. His administration did not belie his name; he held a small court, noted for its brilliancy; his good breeding and geniality pleased the populace, and his administration of ten years was so successful that it was long remembered. He carried through one Indian expedition against the Chickasaw, but he had no large problems to meet and left New Orleans in May 1753 on receipt of the news of his promotion to the governorship of Canada. The annals and official papers of Vaudreuil's administration of Louisiana were captured by the British somewhere on the high seas during the transport between Louisiana and France.

After a sojourn at Paris and the court of Versailles, Vaudreuil was commissioned governor of New France, where he arrived on June 23, 1755, to take up the duties of his office. He found the colony on the brink of war with England. On his arrival he was received with pleasure both by the colonists, the tribesmen, and the French officers. He was a native Canadian, had had a successful experience as governor of Louisiana, and it was anticipated that his defense of Canada would prove notable. Notable it was, but not in the expected ways. Vaudreuil had an exaggerated opinion of his military prowess; he was weak and vacillating, and allowed himself to be drawn into the corrupt ring that surrounded the intendant Bigot. He refused to support the plans of Montcalm, who was sent to conduct the war for France; he is even held responsible for the defeat on the Plains of Abraham, Sept. 13, 1759, since he countermanded Montcalm's order for a guard to prevent the English approach. After the death of Montcalm, Vaudreuil retreated to Montreal, where the following summer he was besieged and on Sept. 8, 1760, capitulated. By this last act as governor Vaudreuil ruined the French cause in Canada. He withdrew to France, arriving in December 1760, and soon after was arrested and thrown into the Bastille. At his trial the next year he was acquitted of dishonesty, although his reputation for intelligence suffered. He was granted a pension and continued to live in Paris, a lonely, discredited figure, until his death. The marquise, older than he, died in 1764; they had no children, but collateral descendants preserved his memory and his portraits. His papers were burned in 1870 to keep them from falling into the hands of the invading Germans.

The almost unanimous testimony of historians of the time is that Vaudreuil was contributory to the fall of New France; that he was jealous of better soldiers than himself; that he talked more than was prudent; and that, while not actually dishonest, he granted monopolies to his relatives and failed to check the corruption that went on around him. His officers said, "The Marquis de Vaudreuil has sold the country" (Doughty, post, III, 306). His chief virtue was his patriotic devotion to his native land, and his championship of Canadians and Indian allies in the last days of the rule of France in America.

[For the date of death, see *Report Concerning Canadian Archives . . . 1905* (1906), vol. I, p. 434. See also Charles Gayarré, *Hist. of La.* (1903), vol. II, pp. 17–35; G. M. Wrong, *The Rise and Fall of New France* (1928), vol. II; A. G. Doughty, *The Siege of Quebec* (6 vols., Quebec, 1901), which contains a number of Vaudreuil's letters; Francis Parkman, *Montcalm and Wolfe* (1884), vol. I, p. 366; Adam Shortt, ed., *Docs. Relating to Canadian Currency . . . during the French Period* (1925), vol. II, pp. 831–35, n. Vaudreuil's Louisiana papers are among the Loudoun papers in the Huntington Lib., San Marino, Cal.]   L. P. K.

VAUGHAN, BENJAMIN (Apr. 30, 1751–Dec. 8, 1835), diplomat, political economist, and agriculturist, was born in Jamaica, the eldest of eleven children of Samuel Vaughan, a London merchant, and Sarah, daughter of Benjamin Hallowell of Boston. He was sent to Newcome's school at Hackney, and then, with his brother William, was placed under the care of Joseph Priestley [*q.v.*] in the Dissenters' Academy at Warrington. He next studied at Cambridge, though his Unitarian principles disqualified him for formal matriculation and a degree, and then proceeded to study law in the Inner Temple.

During the period of the American Revolution, Vaughan engaged in propagandist activities for the Americans. Politically he was drawn to the Earl of Shelburne, who frequently employed him in confidential matters. From 1776 to 1779 he collected and edited, with Franklin's assistance, the *Political, Miscellaneous and Philosophical Pieces . . . Written by Benj. Franklin* (London, 1779). Vaughan's edition is particularly valuable; not only are his notes prime source material, but it "is the only edition of Franklin's writings (other than his scientific) which was printed during his lifetime . . . and contains an 'errata' made by him for it" (P. L. Ford, *Franklin Bibliography*, 1889, p. 161). In 1780–81 Vaughan studied medicine in Edinburgh, where he made friends with Adam Smith and Dugald Stewart. Family tradition states that he turned to medicine to win his wife, Sarah Manning, whom he married June 30, 1781, for her father, William Manning, a prominent London merchant, refused his consent until Vaughan could earn a living. Instead of practising medicine, however, Vaughan became a partner in his father-in-law's business.

Vaughan's most important work was done in connection with the Anglo-American peace negotiations of 1782. In March, when the Whigs came into power, he suggested Richard Oswald to Shelburne as a fitter person to negotiate with the Americans for "a permanent and affectionate peace" than the "bargaining" diplomats and in July was himself sent to Paris to counteract Charles James Fox's false declaration that the government was insincere. Vaughan was uniquely fitted for this mission; he knew Shelburne intimately, was a close friend of Franklin, and was connected with Henry Laurens [q.v.] by marriage. In September John Jay [q.v.] prevailed upon him to return to London as a counteragent to Rayneval, whom Jay believed to be sacrificing American to French and Spanish interests. Vaughan's services in promoting confidence between the American commissioners and Shelburne and in reconciling conflicting opinions were valuable, but the unofficial nature and the delicacy of these services precluded any answer to Fox's charges of "a secret agent" and double dealing.

During the next decade Vaughan was busily occupied with political matters and the doctrine of free trade. In 1789 he published *A Treatise on International Trade*. He was ardently sympathetic with the French Revolution and contributed to the *Morning Chronicle,* under the *nom-de-plume* of "A Calm Observer," a series of letters on the dangers of the Russo-Prusso-Austrian alliance. These appeared in book form as *Letters on the Subject of the Concert of Princes and the Dismemberment of Poland and France* (London, 1793). In 1792 he entered Parliament for Calne, but apparently spoke only on Wilberforce's annual bills for the abolition of the slave trade. His English career was abruptly terminated by his flight to France in consequence of an investigation by the Cabinet of the activities of Revolutionary enthusiasts in England (May 8, 1794). In Paris he was imprisoned at the Carmelite Monastery, but owing, probably, to the good offices of Robespierre, he was released after a month and retired to Switzerland.

In 1796 he followed his family and brothers, one of whom was Charles Vaughan [q.v.], to America and settled on the family lands at Hallowell, Me. He retired from active politics, but corresponded with the first six Presidents and in 1828 forwarded to John Quincy Adams copies of his papers relative to the definition of the Maine boundary in 1782–83. He did much quietly for his adopted country. He belonged to many scientific and literary societies, was one of the founders of the Maine Historical Society, and carried on numerous experiments in agriculture, reports on some of which he communicated to the Massachusetts Agricultural Society under the signature of "A Kennebec Farmer." Harvard bestowed the degree of LL.D. on him in 1807 and Bowdoin in 1812. His library, said to have been the largest in New England with the exception of Harvard's, was divided, portions going to Harvard, Bowdoin, and the Augusta Insane Hospital. Besides the above-mentioned

books, Vaughan published a second collection of Franklin's works in London, 1793, and assisted Marshall in the 1806 edition. In 1800 he produced *The Rural Socrates or an Account of a Celebrated Philosophical Farmer Lately Living in Switzerland and Known by the Name of Kliyogg,* an enlarged and emended edition of Arthur Young's translation of the work of Hans Kaspar Hirzel. Letters to his brother, John Vaughan, were read before the American Philosophical Society in 1825, and published under the title "On the Grous of North America," in *Early Proceedings of the American Philosophical Society . . . 1744 to 1838* (1884). The copy in the Huntington Library of *An Abridgement of the Second Edition of a Work, Written by Dr. Currie, of Liverpool in England, on the Use of Water in Diseases of the Human Frame . . . with Occasional Remarks* (Augusta, 1799), bears a manuscript note on the title-page, "By Benjamin Vaughan." Vaughan was extraordinarily modest. He never published anything under his own name and consequently much of his work remains unidentified.

One of his striking traits was his genius for friendship. He knew and corresponded with most of the eminent liberal thinkers of his time. Franklin undertook his autobiography at Vaughan's and Abel James's solicitation. Vaughan was a loved member of the group of radicals associated with Priestley, John Horne Tooke, Bentham, Romilly, and Dumont. John Adams even confided to him in 1783 his suspicions of Franklin's Gallophilism. He corresponded with Talleyrand and Robespierre, and was invited to attend the First Constitutional Assembly. Though a Federalist, he maintained a cordial correspondence with Jefferson. Vaughan's wife died in 1834, and his own death occurred in Hallowell the year following; they had three sons and four daughters.

[Vaughan requested that no biography of him be written. The most comprehensive account of his career is G. S. Rowell, "Benjamin Vaughan," *Mag. of Hist.,* Mar. 1916; see also William Vaughan, *Tracts on Docks and Commerce* (London, 1839); R. H. Gardiner, "Memoir of Benjamin Vaughan, M.D. and LL.D.," *Maine Hist. Soc. Colls.,* 1 ser., VI (1859); J. H. Sheppard, "Reminiscences and Geneal. of the Vaughan Family," *New England Hist. and Geneal. Reg.,* Oct. 1865; Wm. W. Vaughan, *Hallowell Memories* (1931); E. H. Nason, *Old Hallowell on the Kennebec* (1909); Nehemiah Cleaveland, *Hist. of Bowdoin Coll.* (1882); Lord Fitzmaurice, *Life of William, Earl of Shelburne,* vol. III (1876); *Papiers de Barthélemy* (6 vols., 1886–1910), vols. IV and V; H. C. Bolton, *Scientific Correspondence of Joseph Priestley* (1892); *Kennebec Journal* (Augusta, Me.), Dec. 16, 1835. Most of Vaughan's private letters to Shelburne are in the possession of the present Marquis of Lansdowne; some letters and many papers are in the Shelburne Papers in the William L. Clements Lib., Univ. of Mich.; of the MSS. left by Vaughan at his death many were destroyed by a fire in the house of his son-in-law; some are in the Pa. Hist. Soc., and others are in possession of the family. The Adams copies of Vaughan's papers on the peace negotiation of 1782–83 are still among the Adams Papers; nine of the letters in this lot were published in *Proc. Mass. Hist. Soc.*, 2 ser. XVII (1903).]

E. V.

VAUGHAN, CHARLES (June 30, 1759–May 15, 1839), merchant, promoter of attempts to develop the Kennebec Valley in Maine, was born in London, England. His father, Samuel Vaughan, was a prosperous London merchant interested in colonial trade; he owned a plantation in Jamaica and had dealings with Boston, where he met Sarah Hallowell, who became his wife. Charles, their son, was brought up on the Jamaican plantation, where his more celebrated brother Benjamin [*q.v.*] was born. Moving to New England in 1785, Charles spent the rest of his life there, marrying about 1790 in Boston, Frances Western Apthorp, whose sister had recently married Charles Bulfinch [*q.v.*]. The Vaughans had two sons and two daughters who survived childhood.

Soon after his arrival in New England Vaughan entered upon a long and prominent connection with the "Kennebec Purchase" in Maine. His maternal grandfather, Benjamin Hallowell, had been one of the "Proprietors of the Kennebec Purchase," popularly known as the "Plymouth Company," incorporated in 1753 to take over a region some thirty-one miles wide along the Kennebec, originally a grant to some of the Plymouth settlers. With over-optimistic zeal, Vaughan plunged into two costly developments. At Hallowell, just below Augusta, with a view to establishing a great center at the head of navigation of the Kennebec, he constructed houses, stores, and mills, set up a printing press, built one of the most up-to-date gristmills in the region and a brewery which, it is said, turned out a greater amount of malt liquor than any other in New England. More visionary was his effort to establish a seaport at Jones Eddy near the mouth of the Kennebec, four miles below Bath. He built wharves, warehouses, and a wet dock for masts, which were an important export; he also maintained an agent there to chart the port and transact the expected business. In 1790 he visited England to develop trade connections for his new enterprises. The Jones Eddy project was a complete failure, however. It had an excellent location, being much more accessible than Wiscasset on the Sheepscott, to which exports from the Kennebec had to be carried through a narrow river; but tradition proved stronger than geographical advantage. Wiscasset remained the chief port of the region until after 1812, and, in spite of Vaughan's efforts,

Bath rather than Jones Eddy became the official port of entry. Long before Vaughan's death, only the rotting wharves remained as relics of his venture.

Returning from England in 1791, he established himself as a merchant in Boston, sending Kennebec products on the first leg of the old triangle which included the West Indies and England. He was an incorporator of the Boston Library Society, the Massachusetts Society for Promoting Agriculture, the Massachusetts Society for the Aid of Immigrants, and of Hallowell Academy. In 1793, with Bulfinch and William Scollay, he was a promoter of Boston's first block of brick houses, the Franklin or Tontine Crescent. A year later he withdrew from the venture, and when it led to Bulfinch's bankruptcy in 1796 Bulfinch conveyed his equity to Vaughan (Bulfinch, *post*, p. 98; Place, *post*, pp. 56–59, 72). Two years later Vaughan himself was drawn into bankruptcy by his numerous ventures. His brother Benjamin, who had settled at Hallowell, bought in the ancestral lands on the Kennebec and Charles retained only his Hallowell house, to which he retired for the remainder of his life. He continued as agent for the non-resident owners in the Purchase, prosecuting squatters with a vigor that occasionally involved shooting. With his characteristic energy and enthusiasm he devoted himself to the development of Maine agriculture, and is credited with important developments in farming and stock-raising, through the importation and improvement of animals, seeds, and fruit trees. "Spared the pain of protracted weakness and infirmity," Vaughan died at eighty at Hallowell.

[*Me. Hist. Soc. Colls.*, 1 ser. II (1847), 291, IV (1856), 43–48, V (1857), 331, VI (1859), 89, VII (1876), 278–81, 286; 2 ser. IV (1893), 210; *New England Hist. and Geneal. Reg.*, Oct. 1865; James Sullivan, *The Hist. of the District of Me.* (1795); E. S. Bulfinch, *The Life and Letters of Charles Bulfinch* (1896); C. A. Place, *Charles Bulfinch, Architect and Citizen* (1925); W. W. Vaughan, *Hallowell Memories* (1931); William Vaughan, *Memoir of William Vaughan* (1839); *Boston Transcript*, May 20, 1839; *The Age* (Augusta, Me.), May 21, 1839.]

R. G. A.

VAUGHAN, DANIEL (c. 1818–Apr. 6, 1879), astronomer, mathematician, chemist, physiologist, was born at Glenomara, near Killaloe, County Clare, Ireland, one of several children of John Vaughan (or Vaughn). He was first taught by a private tutor and later attended Killaloe Classical Academy, under the care of his uncle Daniel, a priest. It was intended that he should study for the priesthood, but in 1840 he set out for the United States, where he looked for greater freedom in pursuit of studies involving the higher mathematics. He traveled in Virginia and other southern states, and in 1842 was engaged as tutor by a Colonel Stamp in Bourbon County, Ky. Soon a neighborhood school was arranged where the classics, physical geography, astronomy, geology, and advanced mathematics were taught. Stamp's large library was a great attraction to Vaughan, who later walked to Cincinnati, one hundred miles and back again, to obtain the newest scientific books. His own library, gathered from 1842 on, contained the works of Tycho Brahe, Kepler, Laplace, Humboldt, and other European scientists. He had decided linguistic ability, and, after tutoring for two or three years, he accepted the chair of Greek in a college at Bardstown, Ky., which gave him more time for his strictly scientific studies. In 1850 he removed to Cincinnati. There he lectured on chemistry at the Eclectic Medical Institute, and published an article on "Chemical Researches in Animal and Vegetable Physiology" in the *Eclectic Medical Journal* (December 1850). For a number of years he was much in demand as a lecturer on astronomy and other scientific subjects before teachers' institutes, schools, academies, and colleges in the surrounding region. He became a member of the American Association for the Advancement of Science in 1851, and prepared for it an article on "Chemical Action of Feeble Currents of Electricity" (*Proceedings,* vol. V, 1851) and one on "Solar Light" (*Ibid.,* vol. VI, 1852). His work in experimental physiology later brought him a fellowship in the Association.

In 1852, after seven months' study of the problem of the rings of Saturn, he wrote a paper on "The Stability of Satellites Revolving in Small Orbits" (*Ibid.,* vol. X, 1857); in discussing the disintegration of any near satellites by the tremendous tidal action of Saturn he anticipated by many years the demonstration made by J. E. Keeler [*q.v.*] of the nature of the rings of Saturn. In 1854 he published *The Destiny of the Solar System,* lectures delivered in Cincinnati, and wrote on "Researches in Meteoric Astronomy" (*Report . . . of the British Association for the Advancement of Science,* 1855). Six other papers, which led to much correspondence with European scientists, were published in the *London, Edinburgh, and Dublin Philosophical Magazine* between May 1858 and December 1861. In 1858 appeared *Popular Physical Astronomy,* a collection of his lectures, which reveals the high quality of his astronomical researches. From 1860 to 1872 he held the chair of chemistry at the Cincinnati College of Medicine and Surgery, reading a notable valedictory address at the time of his resignation. After this, for a time, he continued to lecture in Kentucky. When he returned to Cincinnati, his meager income gave his friends anxiety, for he would not ask help. His writing brought him very little, and his lectures became less frequent. At last he disappeared and was forgotten. In April 1879 he was found prostrated by pulmonary hemorrhages and near death from starvation in a wretched tenement room. On Apr. 6, after receiving the last rites of the Roman Catholic Church, he died.

Vaughan was tall, slender, and fine-featured, and wore a long chin beard. Timid and never self-assertive, he was very gentle and patient in his scientific explanations. He never married. His room at the medical college was his laboratory, study, and living-room. A constant reader, he was a familiar figure at the public library on Vine Street, where he quietly sat and read, often with his woolen shawl about him. Since his death he has been almost forgotten, yet, without connection with observatories or astronomers, without a telescope, so far as is known, he grasped many of the profoundest problems of physical astronomy and through sheer mathematical genius was able to offer remarkably brilliant solutions.

[See Otto Juettner, *Daniel Drake and His Followers* (1909), with portrait; J. U. Lloyd, *Etidorpha* (7th ed., 1897), with portrait; *Pop. Sci. Monthly,* May, Aug., Nov. 1879; and obituary in *Cincinnati Commercial,* Apr. 7, 1879. There is a bronze bust of Vaughan in the Cincinnati Pub. Lib. on Vine St.]   D-L. S.

VAUGHAN, VICTOR CLARENCE (Oct. 27, 1851–Nov. 21, 1929), biochemist, hygienist, medical teacher and administrator, investigator of disease, was born near Mount Airy, Randolph County, Mo., the eldest of five children of John and Adeline (Dameron) Vaughan. His paternal grandfather, Sampson Vaughan, emigrated from Wales to North Carolina about 1810; his maternal forebears were of the Du Puy and Dameron families of Virginia. In 1872 Vaughan received the degree of B.S. from Mount Pleasant College, Huntsville, Mo., where he was student-instructor in Latin and chemistry. After two more years of teaching at Mount Pleasant, he went to the University of Michigan. There in 1875 he received the degree of M.S.; in 1876, that of Ph.D.; and in 1878, that of M.D. In the meantime he lectured to medical students on physiological chemistry (1875–83). On Aug. 16, 1877, he married a childhood friend, Dora Catherine Taylor; he and his wife had five sons, four of whom became physicians. His positions at Michigan included those of professor of physiological chemistry, and associate professor of therapeutics and materia medica (1883–87), director of the hygienic laboratory (1887–1909), professor of hygiene and physiological chemistry (1887–1921), and dean of the medical school (1891–1921). As a junior member of the faculty of the medical school he initiated a policy of strengthening its personnel through additions determined solely by merit; later he was largely responsible for increases in the length of the medical course and in requirements for entrance; when he became dean in 1891 he not only built up what was perhaps the ablest faculty in the country but secured increased clinical facilities, developed the medical library, and gave vigorous encouragement to graduate work. As a result of his efforts the medical school at Michigan had a prominent place in the national movement to elevate and standardize American medical education about the beginning of the twentieth century.

As late as 1880 Vaughan discredited the ubiquity of bacterial agents as causes of infectious disease. In 1888, however, he and F. G. Novy went to Berlin to study bacteriology and hygiene in the laboratory of Robert Koch. They returned within the year to preside over the first laboratory in the United States for the systematic teaching of bacteriology to students and physicians. There Vaughan and successive groups of carefully chosen assistants investigated the bacteriology and treatment of tuberculosis, typhoid fever, and summer diarrhoea. Vaughan published much on disease that was provocative of thought, but even more important than his own discoveries was the stimulus his teaching and example provided many younger workers. His work upon ptomaines with Novy led to biochemical investigations of food poisons and had a beneficial effect upon the development of methods of food preservation. Their *Cellular Toxins* (1902) was preceded by three expanding editions of a book on ptomaines, leucomaines, and bacterial proteins. Vaughan's *Protein Split Products* (1913), written with two of his sons, contains valuable ideas upon protein fever; it was followed by *Infection and Immunity* (1915) and *Protein Poisons* (1917), the Herter lectures for 1916. Vaughan early developed the interest in public health and in popular education in preventive medicine for which he is best known. For many years he was an active member of the Michigan state board of health (1883–95, 1901–18); in 1885 he received one of the Lomb prizes for his *Healthy Homes and Foods for the Working Classes* (1886); and under the supervision of George Miller Sternberg [*q.v.*] of the American Public Health Association he carried on experimental work on disinfectants. In 1898, when he served as a major in the Spanish-American War, he was appointed a member of the com-

mission headed by Walter Reed [*q.v.*] to study the cause and prevention of typhoid fever, then epidemic in military camps. After the death of the two other members of the commission, it fell to Vaughan to complete the classic *Report on the Origin and Spread of Typhoid Fever in the U. S. Military Camps* (2 vols., 1904). Some years later, with H. F. Vaughan and G. T. Palmer, he published *Epidemiology and Public Health* (2 vols., 1922–23).

He published several other books and upwards of two hundred articles, carried on private practice for many years, became a medico-legal expert in toxicology with a national reputation, and was the founder of *Physician and Surgeon* (1879), of which he was managing editor for some time, and the *Journal of Laboratory and Clinical Medicine* (1915). He was president of the American Medical Association (1914–15) and of the American Tuberculosis Association (1920), and a member of numerous scientific and other learned societies in the United States and abroad. In 1921–22 and 1925–26 he was chairman of the division of medical sciences of the National Research Council. Throughout the World War he served in the office of the surgeon-general and on the executive committee of the general medical board of the Council of National Defense, rising to the rank of colonel. He later received a Distinguished Service Medal for his work in epidemiology and was made knight of the Legion of Honor by the French government. He was a tireless worker, placid, genial, and unhurried, but capable of an incisive and indomitable opposition when obstruction threatened what seemed the true road of progress. With students his popularity was great and his influence immense. His informal autobiography, *A Doctor's Memories* (1926), gives a vivid and pleasing picture of a man whose honesty and sincerity won confidence and friendship wherever he went. He died in Richmond, Va., where he had been living for two years.

[In addition to Vaughan's *A Doctor's Memories* (1926), see *Who's Who in America*, 1928–29; *Cat. of Grads. . . . Univ. of Mich.* (1923); *Jour. of Laboratory and Clinical Medicine*, June 1930, a memorial number with a full bibliog.; *Am. Men of Sci.* (4th ed., 1927), ed. by J. M. and Jaques Cattell; C. H. McIntyre, in *Builders of Am. Medicine* (1932); obituary in *Richmond Times-Dispatch*, Nov. 22, 1929.]   H. S—l.

VAUX, CALVERT (Dec. 20, 1824–Nov. 19, 1895), landscape architect, was born in London, England, the son of Dr. Calvert Bowyer and Emily (Brickwood) Vaux. Having received his early education at the Merchant Taylors' School in London, to which he was admitted in December 1833, he entered the office of Lewis N. Cottingham, a well-known architect of the time, as an articled pupil. In the summer of 1850 Andrew Jackson Downing [*q.v.*] visited England for the purpose of securing the services of a trained architect to assist him in his growing practice and chose Vaux (see A. J. Downing, *Rural Essays,* 1853, p. xlvi). Until Downing's untimely death in 1852 Vaux worked with him at their joint office at Newburgh on the Hudson, and assisted in the design of the grounds about the Capitol and the Smithsonian Institution at Washington. About 1857 he removed to New York City, where he lived for the rest of his life. In the same year he published his only book, *Villas and Cottages: a Series of Designs Prepared for Execution in the United States,* which contains a record of his early architectural work. It was revised in 1864 and reprinted in 1867.

In 1857, in collaboration with Frederick Law Olmsted [*q.v.*], Vaux submitted a design for Central Park, New York. Upon the acceptance of their plan, submitted under the signature of "Greensward," the two were put in charge of its execution, Olmsted as architect in chief, and Vaux as consulting architect. (A full account of their difficulties is to be found in Olmsted and Kimball, *post,* vol. II). For a number of years the two were associated in private practice, Vaux supplying the knowledge of architecture which Olmsted lacked. Their work includes Prospect Park in Brooklyn, Morningside Park and Riverside Park in New York City, the South Park in Chicago, the state reservation at Niagara Falls, and a suburban village at Riverside, near Chicago. For many years Vaux was landscape architect to the department of public parks of New York City (1881–83, 1888–95). It has been said of him that nothing "could have induced him to degrade his art or misuse the reputation which secured his employment, by consenting to modify his criticism, or give the sanction of his name to a plan he could not approve. He was a modest and unassuming gentleman, a most genial companion, a loyal and incorruptible public servant . . ." (Howland, *post,* p. 19). On Nov. 19, 1895, he was drowned in Gravesend Bay. He was survived by two sons and two daughters. His wife, Mary Swan McEntee, daughter of James S. McEntee of Rondout, N. Y., whom he married on May 4, 1854, died in 1892.

[C. J. Robinson, ed., *A Reg. of the Scholars . . . Merchant Taylors' School . . . 1562 to 1874,* vol. II (1883), p. 256; F. L. Olmsted, Jr., and Theodora Kimball, eds., *Frederick Law Olmsted* (2 vols., 1922–28); *Memories of Samuel Parsons,* ed. by Mabel Parsons; Samuel Parsons, Jr., in *Trans. Am. Soc. Landscape Architects . . . 1908* (n.d.); E. H. Hall, in *Sixteenth Ann. Report . . . Am. Scenic and Hist. Preservation Soc.* (1911); "Calvert Vaux, Designer of Parks," *Park International,* Sept. 1920. H. E. Howland, in *Reports . . . of the Century Asso. for the Year 1895* (1896);

obituaries in *Garden and Forest,* Nov. 27, *Evening Post* (N. Y.), Nov. 21, and *N. Y. Tribune,* Nov. 22, 1895; unpub. data in the possession of Vaux's daughter, Mrs. G. L. Hendrickson.]   K. McN.

VAUX, RICHARD (Dec. 19, 1816–Mar. 22, 1895), lawyer, public official, penologist, was born in Philadelphia, Pa., the son of Roberts [*q.v.*] and Margaret (Wistar) Vaux. He received his early education at the Friends' Select School and under private tutors. After studying in the office of William Morris Meredith [*q.v.*], secretary of the treasury under Zachary Taylor, he was admitted to the bar, Apr. 15, 1837, at the age of twenty. Shortly thereafter he went abroad and carried with him dispatches from the American minister in London, Andrew Stevenson [*q.v.*]. Vaux remained in London for a year, serving meanwhile as secretary of the legation *ad interim,* and later as private secretary to the minister. He was not inclined to enter upon a diplomatic career, however, although the opportunity presented itself.

Returning to Philadelphia in 1839, he found that he had been nominated by the Democrats for a seat in the Pennsylvania House of Representatives. Although he failed of election, this event marked the beginning of a long political career, during which he held both local and federal offices. In 1840 he was a delegate to the Democratic state convention and in 1842 he lost the election for mayor of Philadelphia by a few hundred votes. He was appointed an inspector of the Eastern Penitentiary and a member of the board of controllers of the city public schools. From 1841 to 1847 he served as Recorder, a judicial office, and during his incumbency none of his decisions was reversed on appeal. After two more defeats as a candidate for mayor, 1845 and 1854, he was finally elected in 1856. He immediately undertook administrative reorganization and helped to make the changes necessitated by the consolidation of the city in 1854. In 1859 he became a member of the board of directors of Girard College and from 1862 to 1865 served as president of the board. During this period he was instrumental in introducing vocational and technological training into the college curriculum. In 1872 he was defeated for congressman-at-large. Years later, however, he served out the unexpired term of Congressman Samuel J. Randall, May 20, 1890–Mar. 3, 1891, but he was defeated as candidate to succeed himself, in the next election. He rose to the position of Grand Master of the Pennsylvania Grand Lodge of Masons; was president of the Philadelphia Club (1888–94); and was identified with the Historical Society of Pennsylvania and the American Philosophical Society. On Mar. 12, 1840, he married Mary, daughter of Jacob Shoemaker and Sarah (Morris) Waln; a son and four daughters, with his wife, survived him.

His chief interest undoubtedly lay in the field of penology. He served for fifty-three years (1839–92), as one of the governing board of the Eastern Penitentiary, which his father had helped to plan and manage, and for forty years (1852–92) as president of the board. There was no wavering in his complete faith in the system of separate confinement, the defense of which he undertook on all suitable occasions. He published *Short Talks on Crime-Cause and Convict Punishment* (1882) and *Brief Sketch of the Origin and History of the State Penitentiary for the Eastern District of Pennsylvania, at Philadelphia* (1872). He was an orator of ability, whose somewhat archaic and dignified language harmonized well with his physical appearance and made him especially acceptable on commemorative occasions. He brought about the wearing of gowns by the judiciary of Philadelphia, and it is said that the Law Association finally adopted the custom "with no enthusiasm, and mainly to secure relief from Mr. Vaux's importunity" (R. D. Coxe, *Legal Philadelphia*, 1908, p. 183).

[R. W. Davids, *The Wistar Family* (1896); G. P. Donehoo, *Pennsylvania: A Hist.* (1926), vol. IX; *U. S. Mag. and Democratic Rev.*, Aug. 1847; J. W. Jordan, *Colonial Families of Phila.* (1911), vol. I; J. H. Martin, *Martin's Bench and Bar of Phila.* (1883); E. P. Oberholtzer, *Phila.: A Hist. of the City and Its People* (n.d.), vol. IV; *Biog. Dir. Am. Cong.* (1928); H. E. Barnes, *The Evolution of Penology in Pa.* (1927); *Abstract of the Proc. of the Grand Lodge . . . of Free and Accepted Masons of Pa.* (1896); *Press* (Phila.), Mar. 23, 1895; *Pennsylvanian* (Phila.), Mar. 14, 1840, for marriage notice.]   T. S—n.

VAUX, ROBERTS (Jan. 21, 1786–Jan. 7, 1836), philanthropist, was a descendant of a French family the members of which left their homeland in the seventeenth century and settled in Sussex, England. His father, Richard, son of George Vaux, a London physician, emigrated to Philadelphia in his early youth and died there in 1790 at the age of thirty-nine, leaving two children, Roberts and Susannah, and his wife, Ann (Roberts), who was a descendant of one of William Penn's friends and companions, Hugh Roberts. Both the parents were Quakers. Roberts Vaux received his schooling at the Friends' Academy in Philadelphia, and at eighteen entered the employ of a highly respected merchant, John Cooke. Upon reaching his majority he set up a business of his own, which he carried on for a few years. The death of his sister in 1814 created in him an emotional crisis which resulted in his resolving to retire from active business and devote his life to the service of his fellow

men. The same year, Nov. 30, he married Margaret Wistar, daughter of Thomas Wistar; she bore him two sons, one of whom was Richard [*q.v.*].

In a short time Vaux became associated with almost every worthy public and private activity for social welfare in his community. He took a leading part in the creation of a free public school system and was the first president of the board of controllers of the public schools of Philadelphia, serving in that capacity from 1818 to 1831. Profoundly interested in prison problems, he was one of the officers of the Philadelphia Society for Alleviating the Miseries of Public Prisons, which his father-in-law had helped to found. He prepared most of its memorials to the legislature and stanchly defended the system of separate confinement of prisoners. In 1821 he was appointed to the commission which planned the Eastern Penitentiary, and it was he who drafted the legislation for its administration. Until his death he took an active interest in the work of this institution. Out of an address which he delivered before the Prison Society grew the movement for the establishment, in 1826, of a house of refuge for juvenile delinquents. His most eloquent and persuasive writing was in exposition and defense of penal reforms; among them may be mentioned *Notices of the Original, and Successive Efforts, to Improve the Discipline of the Prison at Philadelphia, and to Reform the Criminal Code of Pennsylvania: with a Few Observations on the Penitentiary System* (1826); and *Reply to Two Letters of William Roscoe, Esquire, of Liverpool, on the Penitentiary System of Pennsylvania* (1827).

Penology was but one of his many interests, however: he was a manager of the Pennsylvania Hospital; as a member of the building committee and later as a manager, he had an active part in the creation of the Frankford Asylum for the Insane; he assisted in the founding of an institution for the instruction of the blind and another for the deaf and dumb. An ardent advocate of temperance, he served as president of the Pennsylvania State Temperance Society, and as vice-president of the United States Temperance Convention. The Philadelphia Saving Fund Society, the Philadelphia Hose Company, and the Apprentices' Library Company numbered him among their founders. He assisted in the organization of the Academy of Natural Sciences, the Linnaean Society, the Franklin Institute, the Athenaeum, and the Historical Society of Pennsylvania; published papers on the locality of Penn's treaty (*Memoirs of the Historical Society of Pennsylvania*, vol. I, pt. I, 1826); and wrote *Memoirs of the Lives of Benjamin Lay and Ralph*

Sandiford (1815), and *Memoirs of the Life of Anthony Benezet* (1817). Political life apparently attracted him little. He served as a member of the Philadelphia common council (1814–16), but he declined in 1834 a presidential appointment as director of the Bank of the United States, to which he was violently opposed, and had earlier, 1832, declined an appointment as commissioner to treat with the "emigrating Indians west of the Mississippi River." It was only at the insistence of his friends that he accepted, in the fall of 1835, the position of justice of the court of common pleas. He died in Philadelphia less than three months later.

[R. W. Davids, *The Wistar Family* (1896); T. Mc-Kean Pettit, "Memoir of Roberts Vaux," *Memoirs of the Hist. Soc. of Pa.*, vol. IV, pt. 1 (1840); Henry Simpson, *The Lives of Eminent Philadelphians Now Deceased* (1859); G. P. Donehoo, *Pennsylvania: A Hist.* (1926), vol. IX; H. E. Barnes, *The Evolution of Penology in Pa.* (1927); J. F. Lewis, *Hist. of the Apprentices' Library of Phila.* (1924); J. M. Willcox, *A Hist. of the Phila. Saving Fund Soc.* (1916); J. J. McCadden, "Educ. in Pa.," manuscript thesis, Teachers Coll., Columbia Univ., and "Roberts Vaux and His Associates in the Pa. Soc. for the Promotion of Public Schools," *Pa. Hist.*, Jan. 1936; death notice in *Poulson's Am. Daily Advertiser* (Phila.), Jan. 8, 1836.]

T. S—n.

VAWTER, CHARLES ERASTUS (June 9, 1841–Oct. 27, 1905), educator, son of John Henderson and Clara (Peck) Vawter, was born in Monroe County, Va. (now W. Va.). His father, a farmer and civil engineer, at the age of sixty joined the Confederate army with his four sons, and all five in time became captains. Charles, who had entered Emory and Henry College in 1858, left upon the outbreak of the war to enlist in the Monroe County Guards, a part of the "Stonewall Brigade." He soon proved himself a leader; he was appointed a captain of sharpshooters in 1862 and served in the field until March 1865, when he was captured and imprisoned in Fort Delaware. Released in June, he returned to Emory and Henry, where he graduated in 1866 and in July of that year married Virginia Longley, daughter of Prof. Edmund Longley. Seven children were born of this union, all of whom survived their father. After teaching for a year, he entered the University of Virginia, graduated in mathematics with distinction, and was elected professor of mathematics and teacher of Hebrew at Emory and Henry. Taking office in 1868, he served this institution for ten years. In 1878 Vawter was selected to build and organize the Miller Manual Labor School of Albemarle County, Va.; the trustees of the school appointed by the county judge, were Col. Charles Scott Venable [*q.v.*] and Prof. Francis Henney Smith, of the University of Virginia, his old friends. This school was founded by a bequest

of Samuel Miller of $1,250,000 in Virginia state certificates; Vawter persuaded the legislature to pass an act which preserved its endowment to the school and aided many other schools in Virginia holding similar certificates.

Vawter came to his task with enthusiasm, rich experience, and clear views on education. He was greatly interested in the development of public schools in Virginia and the South and had very definite views of the kind of education the Southern people needed. The Miller School, an institution for orphan boys and girls, established on a farm, with buildings and shops especially erected and equipped, offered him a rare opportunity to realize his ideal of a school that would train the mind and hand together. He made it his life work to build here an industrial school which became a model for all the South and caused him to be recognized as a leader in the new education. He had great influence in promoting the development of industrial education in the public schools throughout the country. He was a member of the state board of education and rendered valuable service in organizing the public schools of Virginia under the constitution of 1902; he served as chairman of the board of trustees of the Normal and Industrial School for girls at Farmville, Va., which became a State Teachers' College; he was also chairman of the board of the Normal and Industrial Institute for Negroes at Petersburg and of the state board of charities and corrections. For a number of years he was rector of the board of trustees of the Virginia Polytechnic Institute, and aided President J. M. McBryde [*q.v.*] in shaping the policies of that institution. He took great interest in the work of the Conference for Education in the South, which he helped to organize in 1898, taking a part in all of their meetings and speaking wherever he could help. He had also a large part in the educational work of the Methodist Episcopal Church (South); he was a trustee of Emory and Henry College, and president for many years of the Virginia Sunday School Association.

[O. F. Morton, *A Hist. of Monroe County, W. Va.* (1916); G. V. Bicknell, *The Vawter Family in America* (1905); *Who's Who in America*, 1903–05; *The Miller Manual Labor School of Albemarle, Crozet, Va.* (1892); reports of the Miller School, 1880–1904; *The Outlook*, Nov. 11, 1905; *Times-Dispatch* (Richmond, Va.), Oct. 28, 1905.]

C. W. D.

VEAZEY, THOMAS WARD (Jan. 31, 1774–July 1, 1842), governor of Maryland, was descended from John Veazey who emigrated from England to Maryland in the latter half of the seventeenth century. In what became Cecil County he acquired a plantation, "Cherry Grove," which remained in the family for many generations. Here was born Thomas Ward, the son of Edward Veazey, a planter who was also high sheriff of Cecil County from 1751 to 1753, and of Elizabeth (De Coursey) of Queen Anne County. After graduating from Washington College, Chestertown, Md., in 1795, Veazey became a planter at "Cherry Grove." He was interested in politics, however, and in 1808 and 1812 was chosen presidential elector, voting for James Madison. In 1811 and again in 1812 he was elected to the Maryland House of Delegates; but he left it to become a lieutenant-colonel of Maryland troops in the War of 1812. From 1833 to 1835 he served on the council of Gov. James Thomas. In January 1836, he was elected on the Whig ticket to succeed Thomas, and was reelected in the two years following.

His first term was troubled by strife over the state constitution. At that time Maryland was a mere federation of counties and cities in which the majority of the population could be dominated in the legislature by the minority. The state Senate was chosen by an electoral college. In the voting of 1836 for these electors, nineteen Democrats were chosen to represent districts totaling more than 200,000 population, whereas twenty-one Whigs represented less than half that number. Bent upon remedying this state of affairs, the Democratic electors asked the Whigs to agree in advance to choose a majority of men who favored constitutional reform; when the Whig electors refused, the Democrats left for home instead of going into session to elect senators. Veazey met the situation courageously, announcing that the old Senate would continue to function until a new one was legally elected; and he called upon the existing senators to assemble for duty. Public opinion supported the Governor, and the recusant electors returned to Annapolis and cooperated in electing a new Senate. Following up this moral victory, Veazey recommended constitutional reform in his message of Nov. 25, 1836, and the episode resulted in the adoption of a series of amendments amounting practically to a new instrument of government.

His other policies were also, in general, wise and progressive. He urged a registration law to prevent fraud in elections; he stood for sound financial methods; he encouraged internal improvements, especially the completion of the Chesapeake & Ohio Canal and the Baltimore & Ohio Railroad; and he recommended repeatedly the reorganization and expansion of the educational system with the aim of making it general and public. Owner of many slaves, he was hostile

to abolitionist meddling from outside the state, but he favored the work of the American Colonization Society. He was three times married: on Nov. 18, 1794, to Sarah Worrell of Kent County, Md., who died in 1795 leaving an infant daughter who did not survive childhood; on Mar. 29, 1798, to Mary Veazey, a cousin, who bore him five children; and on Sept. 24, 1812, to Mary Wallace of Elkton, Md., who also bore him five children. He spent his last years at "Cherry Grove."

[H. E. Buchholz, *Govs. of Md.* (1908); *Tercentenary Hist. of Md.*, vol. IV (1925); J. T. Scharf, *Hist. of Md.* (3 vols., 1879); G. N. Mackenzie, *Colonial Families of the U. S. A.*, vol. I (1907); G. A. Hanson, *Old Kent, the Eastern Shore of Md.* (1876); George Johnston, *Hist. of Cecil County, Md.* (1881); E. S. Riley, *A Hist. of the Gen. Assembly of Md.* (copr. 1905); legislative journals and documents, 1835–38; *Baltimore Clipper*, July 7, 1842; *Am. and Commercial Daily Advertiser* (Baltimore), July 9, 1842.]   M. W. W.

VEBLEN, THORSTEIN BUNDE (July 30, 1857–Aug. 3, 1929), economist and social theorist, was born in Cato township, Manitowoc County, Wis., the sixth of twelve children of Thomas Anderson and Kari (Bunde) Veblen. His parents had emigrated from Norway in 1847 and had settled on the Wisconsin frontier under conditions of enormous hardship. When Veblen was eight the family moved to Wheeling township in Minnesota, where his father took up a 290-acre farm tract. The boy grew up in a clannish Norwegian community, well insulated against the more mobile life of the Americans around. He learned more of Norwegian speech than of English. At seventeen, because of his father's zeal for education, he was packed into a buggy and deposited at Carleton College, Northfield, Minn., where he spent three years in the preparatory department, and finished the college course in three more, graduating in 1880. He suffered a good deal—a strange "Norskie" boy among Americans, lacking money and social standing, uneasy in the theological atmosphere in which the college was drenched. He had a lazy manner and a biting tongue that infuriated students and faculty alike; the only teacher who saw his promise and whom Veblen liked was John Bates Clark, at whose theory of distribution he was to aim his sharpest shafts years afterward. He read English literature, dabbled in poetry, delivered ironical orations, studied philosophy and economics, trifled with some of the radical doctrines then current, fell in love. After graduation he taught for a year (1880–81) at Monona Academy, Madison, Wis., then, lured by the growing reputation of the Johns Hopkins University, he left for Baltimore to do graduate work. When he failed to get a fellowship he left before the end of the term to study philosophy at Yale with President Noah Porter [*q.v.*] and social theory with William Graham Sumner [*q.v.*]. Both men were impressed with him, and both his essay, "Kant's Critique of Judgment" (*Journal of Speculative Philosophy,* July 1884) and his history of the surplus revenue of 1837 (awarded the John Addison Porter prize in 1884) marked him as a distinctive mind. Yet he had to struggle along, lonely, always in debt, earning his board by teaching in a military academy, regarded as a foreigner and an agnostic. When he took his Ph.D. degree, in philosophy, in 1884, he found that no teaching post was available. Disheartened he went back to his Minnesota farm.

The next seven years were probably the most miserable in Veblen's life. His education among Americans had unfitted him for the narrow life of a Norwegian farmer, yet it had not placed any other way of life within his grasp. He seemed to disintegrate. While he read aimlessly and without stint he kept complaining of his health, railing at the parasitism of business men, mocking the sanctities of a conventional Lutheran community. He tried repeatedly for a teaching position but always without success. On Apr. 10, 1888, he married Ellen May Rolfe, with whom he had had a college romance, and whose connections with a prominent business family held out some hope of employment. But an untoward turn of events shattered even that hope, and Veblen and his wife settled down on a farm in Stacyville, Iowa, waiting for something to turn up. Nothing did. He finally decided to get back to some institution of learning as a graduate student and use that as a fresh point of departure.

In 1891, at the age of thirty-four, he turned up at Cornell University, rustic, anaemic, strange-looking in his corduroys and coonskin cap. J. Laurence Laughlin, who was worlds apart from Veblen and yet saw some of his quality, managed to obtain a special fellowship for him. Veblen's first essay, "Some Neglected Points in the Theory of Socialism" (*Annals of the American Academy of Political and Social Science,* Nov. 1891), contained many of the germs of his later theories. He seemed to spring into sudden maturity. And when Laughlin, called to be the head of the economics department at the new University of Chicago, secured him a teaching fellowship there (1892–93) at $520 a year, Veblen's long quest for some niche in the academic world seemed at last realized. Although he was never regarded with favor by the ruling powers, the next year he became a reader in political economy, then an associate,

in 1896 an instructor, and in 1900 an assistant professor. He dug down into anthropology and psychology and used them to focus a sharp new light upon economic theory. The titles of his essays, generally published in learned journals, reveal the turn of his mind: "The Economic Theory of Woman's Dress," "The Instinct of Workmanship and the Irksomeness of Labor," "The Beginnings of Ownership," "The Barbarian Status of Women," "Why is Economics not an Evolutionary Science?," "The Preconceptions of Economic Science," "Industrial and Pecuniary Employments." His work as managing editor of the university's *Journal of Political Economy* (1896–1905, and in effect earlier) gave his thinking further range and depth. He met, either in the university or nearby, a group of mature minds with which he could match his own: Jacques Loeb [*q.v.*], Franz Boas, James H. Tufts, John Dewey, William I. Thomas, Lester F. Ward [*q.v.*], Albion W. Small [*q.v.*].

His first book, *The Theory of the Leisure Class,* published in 1899 when Veblen was forty-two, gave him prominence overnight. Into it he poured all the acidulous ideas and fantastic terminology that had been simmering in his mind for years. It was a savage attack upon the business class and their pecuniary values, half concealed behind an elaborate screenwork of irony, mystification, and polysyllabic learning. The academic world received it with hostility. The literary men, led by William Dean Howells, were delighted with its merciless exposure of aristocratic attitudes but missed its attack on the business men and the middle class. Veblen now proceeded to a more direct analysis of business, and in 1904 he published *The Theory of Business Enterprise,* based on the material turned up in the *Reports of the Industrial Commission* (19 vols., 1900–02). It contains Veblen's basic economic theory—dealing with the effects of the machine process, the nature of corporate promoting, the use of credit, the distinction between industry and business, and the influence of business ideas and pressures upon law and politics.

It was a decade before Veblen published another book. In the interim he wrote essays on the methodology of economics for the professional journals. In them, in a manner that was exasperating because it was at once summary and elegiac, he rejected not only the prevailing economic doctrines but also the unconscious premises behind them. His life was disturbed by marital difficulties, and when, in 1904, his wife reported one of his relationships to the university authorities it became impossible to remain at Chicago. In 1906 he went as an associate professor to Leland Stanford Junior University at the invitation of President David Starr Jordan. For a time he was reunited with his wife at Palo Alto, but soon the difficulties between them began again, and the two were finally separated. They had no children. Veblen was relatively happy at Stanford. He spent part of his time in a mountain cabin, with a little farm around him. He made friends, had the esteem of the faculty, went his own way. But once more an unconventional relationship with a woman violated the academic mores, and in December 1909 he was forced to leave. He sought a Carnegie grant for an archeological expedition to the Baltic and Cretan regions, and dug deep into the literature of the subject. But the grant was not forthcoming. Finally through the efforts of Herbert J. Davenport he was invited to the University of Missouri, as lecturer, and began his teaching there in 1911. About that time he secured a divorce, and on June 17, 1914, he was married to Anne Fessenden (Bradley); she also had been divorced, and had two daughters. Veblen stayed at Missouri for seven years. It was there that his most famous course, which he had already begun to teach at Chicago—Economic Factors in Civilization—reached its classic form. It was rambling, erudite, omniscient; it swept all history and all cultures. His classroom manner was casual and inarticulate to the point of despair. He cared little about teaching itself, and had no talent for it. But while he was never popular with the run of students he had many disciples and won their unstinted affection. The book which most nearly approximates the content of his principal course is *The Instinct of Workmanship* (1914). It is at once the most searching and most perplexing of all his books, an ambitious book, full of provocative blind alleys. While Veblen himself later called it his only important book (Dorfman, *post*, p. 324) it must be finally set down as a splendid failure. Plunging morass-deep into instinct psychology it emerges with the thesis that the instinct of workmanship, deeply ingrained in man since savage times, has been thwarted throughout history by the piling up of predatory and pecuniary institutions.

After 1914 Veblen's interests turned from topics of professional concern to current issues, and his writing took on a faster tempo and a more strident tone. His tenure at Missouri also became precarious, and finally in 1918 he burned his academic bridges and moved to New York, where he became first an editor of the *Dial* (issue of Oct. 5, 1918) and then, in 1919, a member of the faculty of the New School for Social Research. To this period belong his more revolu-

tionary writings. Much of Veblen's appeal up to that time had lain in the fact that his most savage attacks on the social system had been in the blandest manner. He had combined his uncompromising idol-smashing with all the intellectual qualities of the liberal mind—detachment, subtlety, complexity, understatement, irony. His *Imperial Germany and the Industrial Revolution* (1915), has a bareness of structure not found in his earlier books, although it was still ambiguous enough to suffer the supreme irony of having George Creel's Committee on Public Information use it as grist for the propaganda mills, while the Post Office Department held it up as subversive doctrine. Its thesis was that Germany's strength lay in the fact that she borrowed the industrial techniques from England but instead of borrowing the English democratic procedure she combined them with the unqualified feudal-militaristic institutions congenial to business. In *An Inquiry into the Nature of Peace* (1917) Veblen made his meaning clearer by describing patriotism and business enterprise as useless to the community at large, and analyzing them as the principal obstructions to a lasting peace. In *The Higher Learning in America* (1918) he levelled so bitter and direct an attack on the "conduct of universities by business men" that on reading an earlier draft friends had advised him to withhold it from publication. Every one of Veblen's books was in reality directed to an analysis of business enterprise. In *The Vested Interests and the State of the Industrial Arts* (1919) he came closer to his subject with a savageness of tone that repelled many of his disciples who had been accustomed to his subtler manner. He defined a vested interest as "a marketable right to get something for nothing," pointed out that the aim of business was to maximize profits by restricting or "sabotaging" production, and sharpened his now familiar antithesis between business and industry. During the "red hysteria" of 1919–20 Veblen, writing editorials for the *Dial*, described the passions aroused by the concern for the safety of capitalist institutions as a form of *dementia praecox*, contrasted the aims of Bolshevism with those of the guardians of the "vested interests," and wrote openly of the possibilities of a revolutionary overturn. In his papers collected in *The Engineers and the Price System* (1921) he sketched out a technique of revolution through the organization of a soviet of technicians who would be in a position to take over and carry on the productive processes of the nation. Veblen was no longer hiding his meaning behind elaborate anthropological analogies. His irony was still there, but it was soaked in vitriol.

Veblen's last years were lonely and his life tapered off. For a while he had plans, as the head of a group of technicians, for pushing further the investigation of the revolutionary rôle of engineers. But as with his other plans, nothing came of it: he had no talent for promotion or organization. His investigations for the Food Administration among the I. W. W. for five months in 1918 had met with no official response. His attempts to become part of Wilson's peace conference mission had come to nothing (Dorfman, p. 374). No one would furnish money for a projected trip (1924–25) to England to study British imperialism. On Oct. 7, 1920, his second wife died. He felt tired, ill, rootless. Finally some admiring ladies, solicitous for his health, took him into their home and watched over him. He had reached the stage of being greatly lionized and little understood, and he moved about like a ghost among groups of liberal intellectuals, with his pale sick face, his sharp Van Dyke, his loose-fitting clothes, his shambly gait, his weak voice so infrequently used, his desperate shyness. His last book, *Absentee Ownership and Business Enterprise in Recent Times* (1923), while the best summary of his doctrine, shows some signs of failing powers. In 1925 an offer of the presidency of the American Economic Association, made after considerable opposition from within the organization, was rejected by Veblen because, as he said, "They didn't offer it to me when I needed it" (Dorfman, p. 492). In May 1926 Ellen Rolfe died, and Veblen returned to his cabin near Palo Alto. Here he lived with his step-daughter until his death in 1929, reading aimlessly, worrying incessantly about his losses through investment, watching the movement of events with a dull ache of bitterness and resignation. Six months before the end he said "Naturally there will be other developments right along, but just now communism offers the best course that I can see" (*Ibid.*, p. 500). He died, of heart disease, in Palo Alto, leaving instructions to have his body cremated and the ashes thrown into the sea, and that no memorial of any kind should be raised for him and no biography written.

Veblen's was perhaps the most considerable and creative body of social thought that America has produced. While his thinking does not fall easily into the accepted categories of liberalism and radicalism, he has affected both traditions powerfully. His intellectual attitudes and methods are those of liberalism, especially in his apparatus of disinterestedness and his lack of a program or of real direction; but his criticism of capitalist society is drastic and, at least in its implications, revolutionary. Nor is it easy to judge of the claim that he represents a strain of thought indigenous to America. He seems to have been relatively unaffected by other American writers. But while his intellectual material was largely European, the deepest sources of his impulses and attitudes lay in the transplanted European stock of the American Northwest and Middle-West, rugged, hard-bitten, agrarian, suspicious of urban finance, vigorously populist. In economic theory his influence was crucial in weakening the hold of neo-classical theory and introducing a more realistic "institutional school." But his most powerful effect was not on academic theory but on economic opinion and policy. He was in no small measure responsible for the trend toward social control in an age dominated by business enterprise.

[Joseph Dorfman, *Thorstein Veblen and His America* (1934), a very full account, supersedes all previous treatments of Veblen and must be drawn upon for all later treatments. Shorter and more interpretive studies are: W. C. Mitchell, introduction to *What Veblen Taught* (1936), a book of selections from Veblen; Lewis Mumford, "Thorstein Veblen," *New Republic*, Aug. 5, 1931; E. S. Bates, "Thorstein Veblen," *Scribner's Mag.*, Dec. 1933; Max Lerner, "Veblen and the Waste Land," *New Freeman*, Feb. 25, 1931; "What is Usable in Veblen?," *New Republic*, May 15, 1935; and "Gateway to Veblen's World," *Nation*, Mar. 11, 1936; John Chamberlain, in *Farewell to Reform* (1932). A complete bibliography of Veblen's writings, arranged chronologically is in Dorfman. For certain personal details see *Bulletin of Yale Univ. Obit. Record of Grads. Deceased during the Year Ending July 1, 1930*; A. A. Veblen, *Veblen Genealogy* (1925), in Lib. of Cong., "autographed from the typed copy"; obituaries in *N. Y. Times, San Francisco Chronicle*, Aug. 6, 1929.]

M. L.

VEDDER, ELIHU (Feb. 26, 1836–Jan. 29, 1923), figure and mural painter, illustrator, born in New York, was the son of Elihu and Elizabeth Vedder, and a descendant of Harmon Albertse Vedder (*c.* 1637–*c.* 1715), an early Dutch settler in Schenectady, N. Y. He spent much of his boyhood in Schenectady, with several trips to Cuba, where his father was engaged in business. For a time he attended the Brinkerhoff School in Jamaica, L. I. His artistic talent asserted itself early, and as a boy of twelve he began to study art by himself. For a time he worked under Tompkins H. Matteson [*q.v.*] in Sherburne, N. Y. In 1856 he went to Europe, where he studied under François Edouard Picot in Paris for eight months and then went to Florence to live. Returning to America, he arrived penniless in New York at the outbreak of the Civil War. Serious work met with no success, and he resorted to such pot-boilers as comic valentines, sketches for *Vanity Fair*, and diagrams for dumb-bell exercises for a teacher of calisthenics. During these difficult times, living in a bare room in Beekman Street, he conceived the ideas for his early pictures, "The Fisherman and the Genii," "The Roc's Egg," "The Questioner of the Sphinx," "The Lost Mind," and "The Lair of the Sea-Serpent," but it was not until 1865 that he succeeded in finishing them. In that year he was admitted into the National Academy, became a member of the Society of American Artists, and for a second time went abroad. After spending some time in France, he went early in 1867 to Rome, where he made his home for the rest of his life, though he also had a villa on the island of Capri. He made frequent visits to America, where he held periodical exhibitions of his work, now received with increasing admiration.

The distinctive merit of Vedder's work is its rare imaginative power and thoughtfulness. His workmanship is heavy; his color is not remarkable. He is essentially a painter of abstract ideas rather than visible realities, and he penetrated farther into that realm than any other American painter except Albert Pinkham Ryder [q.v.]. It was in 1884 that he published his series of more than fifty illustrations to the *Rubáiyát of Omar Kháyyám*, his *magnum opus*. The character of these drawings, which he called accompaniments, was ponderously beautiful. They had the charm of sweeping rhythmic line that is the preëminent technical merit of his designs, and supplemented the text with genuine insight and deep sympathy. When they were exhibited in Boston in the spring of 1887, they were accompanied by a group of sixteen paintings, the "Cup of Death," the "Soul between Doubt and Faith," the "Fates Gathering in the Stars," and the "Last Man." The originality and solemnity of these motives, in which Vedder gave thrilling hints of an unknown world and intangible realities, made a deep impression. In the last phase of his life as an artist he turned to mural decoration. On the wall of the staircase landing in the Library of Congress, Washington, is his large mosaic "Minerva" (1897), with five wall paintings (1896) which symbolize "Government," "Corrupt Legislation," "Anarchy," "Good Administration," "Peace and Prosperity." In conception they show but little invention, and in imaginative force they fall below the standard set by the easel paintings. They have the dignity befitting their place in a great public building, but they are devoid of charm. The tympanum (1894) which decorates the west wall of the Walker Art Building, Bowdoin College, Brunswick, Me., is a more satisfactory example of Vedder's weighty style. He also

decorated a ceiling (1893) in the C. P. Huntington mansion in New York, the subject being "The Sun with the Four Seasons." Examples of his painting may be seen in the Metropolitan Museum of Art ("The Lost Mind," 1864–65, and "African Sentinel"), the Museum of Fine Arts in Boston ("The Lair of the Sea-Serpent," 1864, "The Questioner of the Sphinx," 1863, "The Fisherman and the Genii," "Lazarus," an Italian landscape, and the portrait of Kate Field), at Wellesley College, and the Carnegie Institute, Pittsburgh, Pa.

Vedder was married to Caroline Beach Rosekrans of Glens Falls, N. Y., July 13, 1869. He died in Rome, survived by one of his three children, a daughter. He published three books: *Miscellaneous Moods in Verse* (1914), *Doubt and Other Things* (1922), and *The Digressions of V* (1910), a rambling and entertaining memoir, without continuity of narrative but full of whimsical and ironic comments on men and things, which gives a faithful portrait of the man himself.

[In addition to *The Digressions of V*, see *Who's Who in America, 1922–23*; Samuel Isham, *The Hist. of Am. Painting* (1905); Suzanne La Follette, in *Art in America* (1929); Pauline King, *Am. Mural Painting* (1902); Herbert Small, *Handbook of the New Lib. of Cong.* (1901); W. H. Bishop, in *Am. Art Rev.*, June, July 1880; W. H. Downes, in *Atlantic Monthly*, June 1887; W. C. Brownell, in *Scribner's Mag.*, Feb. 1895; Elisabeth L. Cary, in *Internat. Studio*, Sept. 1908; Ferris Greenslet, in *Outlook*, Nov. 26, 1910; H. T. Carpenter, in *Bookman*, Apr. 1912; F. J. Mather, Jr., in *Scribner's Mag.*, July 1923; Cat. of the Doll and Richards Gallery, Boston, 1887; obituaries in *Nation*, Feb. 21, 1923, p. 207, and *N. Y. Times*, Jan. 30, 1923.]   W. H. D.

VENABLE, CHARLES SCOTT (Apr. 19, 1827–Aug. 11, 1900), mathematician, soldier, and educator, was born at "Longwood," Prince Edward County, Va. A descendant of Abraham Venables, who emigrated from England to Virginia by 1687, he came of a line of country gentlemen, members of the House of Burgesses and the General Assembly, officers in the armies of the Revolution and the War of 1812, builders of Virginia institutions. His father, Nathaniel E. Venable (1791–1846), graduated at Hampden-Sidney College in 1808 and served in the War of 1812; his mother, Mary Embra Scott, was the daughter of Capt. Charles Scott, a Revolutionary officer. Reared in the atmosphere of a cultured home and taught by private tutors, the boy entered Hampden-Sidney at twelve and graduated at fifteen in 1842. From 1843 to 1845 he was a tutor in mathematics in the College, then, after spending a year at the University of Virginia, he became professor in 1846. The year 1847–48 also he spent at the University of Virginia, where altogether he completed the courses in six schools, and in 1852–53 he studied mathematics and astronomy at Berlin and Bonn. He remained at Hampden-Sidney until 1856, when he became professor of natural philosophy at the University of Georgia. In November 1857 he was elected professor of mathematics at South Carolina College (later University of South Carolina). In 1860 he was appointed on a commission to make observations in Labrador on the eclipse of that year.

Entering with spirit into the conflict of 1861 he took part as a lieutenant in the Congaree Rifles in the reduction of Fort Sumter. He then joined the Governor's Guards and fought as a private in the first battle of Manassas. He assisted in the defense of New Orleans and helped in building the fortifications at Vicksburg. When in 1862 Gen. Robert E. Lee was made military adviser to the President of the Confederacy, he selected Venable as one of his aides, with the rank of major; later he became lieutenant-colonel. Venable continued with General Lee to the end at Appomattox and then, following the example of his great leader, took up the work of training young men. He was elected professor of mathematics at the University of Virginia in 1865 and taught there continuously until his retirement.

A dignified and forceful gentleman, with marked talents and wide learning, Venable inspired the admiration and devotion of all. He was affectionate as a father with his students, though stern when necessary. From the beginning he did much for the development of the University. Owing to his initiative, in 1867 new schools were organized for applied chemistry and engineering. As chairman of the faculty (1870–73, 1886–88), he was chiefly responsible for the establishment and endowment of the School of Astronomy, and for the addition of the Schools of Biology and Agriculture, and of Natural History and Geology (Bruce, *post*, IV, 27). He induced the legislature to increase the small annuity of the University from $15,000 to $40,000.

Venable was chairman of the trustees of the Miller Manual Labor School of Albemarle County, Va., and helped to make it one of the foremost industrial schools in the South. Compelled by ill health to retire from active service at the University of Virginia in 1896, he was made emeritus professor. He was married, first, on Jan. 16, 1856, to Margaret Cantey McDowell, daughter of Gov. James McDowell [*q.v.*]; and second, on July 5, 1876, to Mrs. Mary (Southall) Brown, widow of Col. J. Thompson Brown. There were five children by the first marriage

and one child by the second. Francis Preston Venable [*q.v.*] was his son, and one of his daughters married Raleigh Colston Minor [*q.v.*].

Besides a long series of mathematical textbooks for schools and colleges, his only publications were *An Address Delivered before the Society of Alumni of the University of Virginia ... July 26, 1858* (1859); *The Campaign from the Wilderness to Petersburg. Address ... before the Virginia Division of the Army of Northern Virginia ... Oct. 30, 1873* (1879); and "Report of Prof. C. S. Venable on the Total Eclipse of July 18, 1860," in *Report of the Superintendent of the Coast Survey ... 1860* (1861).

[Elizabeth M. Venable, *Venables of Virginia* (privately printed, 1925); Richard McIlwaine, *Addresses and Papers* (1908), pp. 60–61; W. M. Thornton, *Charles Scott Venable, A Memorial Address* (1901); P. A. Bruce, *Hist. of the Univ. of Va.* (5 vols., 1920–22); A. L. Long, *Memoirs of Robert E. Lee* (1886); obituary in *Times* (Richmond), Aug. 12, 1900.] C. W. D.

VENABLE, FRANCIS PRESTON (Nov. 17, 1856–Mar. 17, 1934), professor of chemistry, university president, was born in Prince Edward County, Va. The son of Charles Scott Venable [*q.v.*] and Margaret Cantey (McDowell) Venable, he was reared in the cultural atmosphere of a university community, since his father, after service on the staff of Gen. Robert E. Lee during the Civil War, accepted the chair of mathematics in the University of Virginia. Here Venable was graduated in 1879, having been inspired by the able teaching of Prof. James W. Mallet [*q.v.*] to specialize in chemistry. He taught for a while in the high schools of New Orleans, but ambition was stirred in him and within a year he went to Germany to study at Bonn and Göttingen under such eminent leaders in chemistry as Kekulé, Clausius, and Wallach, receiving the degree of Ph.D. from the University of Göttingen in 1881.

While studying in Germany he was called in 1880 to the chair of chemistry in the University of North Carolina. When he arrived at Chapel Hill he found only a dingy basement, with no equipment, in which to begin his life's work. Undaunted, he utilized to the best advantage the meager funds available in the days of penury which followed the Reconstruction period. Laboratory equipment was improvised and improvements on standard equipment were made. Modest researches were undertaken with the students collaborating, and there developed the healthy combination of teaching and research which characterized the whole of Venable's career. The success of his early efforts led in time to the setting apart of a special building for his work; a fund to purchase a department library was begun; and original researches, chiefly on the atomic weight of zirconium, were accomplished.

In 1883, feeling the need of organized scientific effort on the part of the University faculty and of a medium of publication, Venable joined with Joseph A. Holmes [q.v.], professor of geology, in the organization of the Elisha Mitchell Scientific Society. He was its first president and made frequent contributions to its *Journal* embodying the results of the researches he carried out in cooperation with his students.

In 1900 Venable's qualities of leadership and his grasp of University affairs made him a logical choice for the presidency of the University of North Carolina. During his administration the financial affairs of the University were set in order, athletics were encouraged in the student body, and creative scholarship on the part of the faculty was demanded. The strain of his activities finally proved too great for his health and in 1914 he was persuaded by friends to resign the presidency and resume his professorship. In this decision he was influenced largely by the prospect of returning to the laboratory, to close contact with students, and to his own research. Convinced that his investigation of the atomic weight of zirconium had resulted in too low a number, he now attacked this problem again in cooperation with Prof. J. M. Bell, and found that the atomic weight should be at least a unit higher. The variable results obtained, unexplainable at the time but faithfully recorded in the literature, were shown later by George de Hevesy to be due to the presence of considerable proportions of the element hafnium, then unknown.

In addition to a long list of papers, Venable published a number of books on chemical subjects: *A Course in Qualitative Chemical Analysis* (1883); *A Short History of Chemistry* (1894); *The Development of the Periodic Law* (1896); *Inorganic Chemistry* (1898), in collaboration with J. L. Howe; *The Study of the Atom* (1904); *A Brief Account of Radio-activity* (copr. 1917); *Zirconium and Its Compounds* (1922). He served in 1899 as vice-president of Section C (Chemistry) of the American Association for the Advancement of Science, and in 1905 as president of the American Chemical Society; he was the recipient of honorary degrees from various institutions; but perhaps the honor that touched him most deeply was the designation during his last years of the new laboratory erected on the University campus as Venable Hall.

Venable married Sallie Charlton Manning on Nov. 3, 1884. Toward the close of his life, as the failure of his bodily powers gradually compelled him to retire from classroom and research laboratory, he found consolation in the affectionate regard of his fellows, in the happiness of his home, and in his garden. He was survived by his wife, three daughters, and two sons.

[E. M. Venable, *Venables of Va.* (copr. 1925); *Who's Who in America*, 1932–33; K. P. Battle, *Hist. of the Univ. of N. C.* (2 vols., 1907–12); J. M. Bell, "Francis Preston Venable," *Industrial and Engineering Chemistry*, July 1924, and "Dr. F. P. Venable's Contributions to Chemistry," *Jour. of Chemical Educ.*, June 1930; *Ibid.*, Aug. 1926; *Jour. of the Elisha Mitchell Sci. Soc.*, Dec. 1934; *News and Observer* (Raleigh), Mar. 18, 1934; personal acquaintance.]
                                                    C. H. H.

VENABLE, WILLIAM HENRY (Apr. 29, 1836–July 6, 1920), teacher, writer, author of *Beginnings of Literary Culture in the Ohio Valley*, was descended from William Venable who settled near the Delaware River about 1680 and became a Quaker preacher. The third of five children of Quaker parents, William and Hannah (Baird) Venable, William Henry was born in a log cabin on a farm near Waynesville, Ohio. In 1843 the family moved to Ridgeville, a hamlet near Cincinnati, where the boy attended a district school and through the influence of his father began to read Josephus, Plutarch, Shakespeare, *Don Quixote*, and *Lewis and Clark's Journal*. In his late adolescence he began to teach at Sugar Grove; he attended a teachers' institute held at Miami University, and studied for three years, teaching to support himself, at the South-western Normal School, Lebanon, Ohio. In 1860 he went for one year to Vernon, Ind., as principal of the Jennings Academy. He helped to edit the *Indiana School Journal*, and on Dec. 30, 1861, married Mary Ann Vater of Indianapolis, who bore him seven children.

Returning to Cincinnati in 1862, he taught natural science in Chickering Institute for twenty-five years, being proprietor of the school from 1881 to 1886. In 1889 he became teacher of English literature in the Hughes High School; subsequently he taught in the Walnut Hills High School and served as head of the department of English. He helped to develop the educational system of Cincinnati and had some influence in a wider sphere through the textbooks in literature and expression which he compiled, his *School History of the United States* (1872), and his activities in connection with teachers' institutes and associations. Some of his thoughts on education were set forth in a volume of short papers, *Let Him First be a Man, and Other Essays* (1893). He also enjoyed a local reputation as a poet, dealing for the most part with homely themes: "My Catbird," "The School Girl," "Tunes Dan Harrison used to Play." Several volumes of his verse were published during his lifetime, and after his death his son, Emerson Venable, edited *The Poems of William Henry Venable* (1925).

Venable is chiefly remembered, however, for his *Beginnings of Literary Culture in the Ohio Valley* (1891), the result of more than twenty years of interest in the intellectual life of his native region. During that time, in preparing numerous papers for local journals and historical societies, he had assembled through research in libraries and conversations with members of an elder generation a store of information which he was urged to publish. Encouraged by several friends interested in local antiquities, including the publisher Robert Clarke [*q.v.*], he assembled a volume of more than five hundred pages—which he modestly described as "discursive, even desultory . . . a repository of accumulated notes" —and equipped it with an excellent index. Though in no sense a finished treatise, the book is a valuable compilation, and Venable's appreciation of the significance of the material and his scrupulous work in gathering and preserving it entitle him to the gratitude of later students of the field.

[*William Henry Venable: An Appreciation Read before the Cincinnati Schoolmasters Club, Oct. 9, 1920* (1921); *Who's Who in America,* 1918–19; *The Biog. Cyc. and Portrait Gallery . . . of Ohio* (6 vols., 1883–95), vol. IV; *Ohio Centennial Anniv. Celebration at Chillicothe* (1903), ed., by E. O. Randall; *Hist. of Cincinnati and Hamilton County, Ohio* (1894); Emerson Venable, *Poets of Ohio* (1909); *Cincinnati Enquirer,* July 7, 1920; *Commercial Tribune* (Cincinnati), July 7, 1920.]　　　　　　　　W. E. S—h.

VERBECK, GUIDO HERMAN FRIDOLIN (Jan. 23, 1830–Mar. 10, 1898), missionary to Japan, was born in the town of Zeist, in the Netherlands, the son of Carl Heinrich Willem and Ann Maria Jacobmina (Kellerman) Verbeek; Guido changed the spelling of the family name. His parents were deeply religious and he was reared under Moravian influence, attending the Moravian Church and school in his native town. At Zeist he learned not only Dutch, but German, English, and French. Later he was a student in the Polytechnic Institute of Utrecht. From his mother he derived a love for poetry and music; he played a number of instruments and sang. In 1852 he emigrated to the United States, going first to Wisconsin, then, in 1853, to Brooklyn, and, soon after—to put into practical use his knowledge of engineering—to Arkansas. Apparently he had thought from time to time of being a missionary, and during a serious illness while in Arkansas he made a definite decision to follow that calling.

Accordingly, in 1855 he entered the Presby-

terian theological seminary at Auburn, N. Y., and was there until 1859. Toward the close of this period he learned that the foreign board of the Dutch Reformed Church was looking for a Dutch-American to send as a missionary to the newly opened Japan, where for centuries the only direct contact with Europe had been through Dutch merchants. He offered himself and was accepted. On Mar. 22, 1859, he was ordained, and on Apr. 18, he married Maria Manion of Philadelphia. They sailed for Japan with the party which initiated the work of his board in that country, and established a home in Nagasaki. The long-standing edicts against Christianity were still prominently displayed throughout Japan and such little missionary work as was possible had to be done inconspicuously, largely through the distribution of literature and through teaching English. Not until 1866 did he baptize the first two converts—men who had come in contact with Christianity through a volume found floating on the water at Nagasaki. In Nagasaki he established a small school, where English was taught by means of the Bible. Before many years, at the request of the government, he took charge of a school for interpreters in Nagasaki, using chiefly the New Testament and the Constitution of the United States as his texts. Students of his, among them Okuma and Soyeshima, later rose to prominence in national affairs. With the overthrow of the Shogunate and the restoration of the Emperor some of his former pupils became influential at Yedo (Tokyo). In 1869, at the invitation of the new administration, he went to Yedo and headed a school which laid the foundations for the Imperial University. His advice was sought by some of the most powerful ministers of state as they endeavored to reorganize Japan. It was partly as the result of his suggestion that the Iwakura mission (1871–73) was sent to America and Europe.

In 1873, after a vacation in Europe and America, Verbeck became attached to the government in a more advisory capacity, and either translated or supervised the translation into Japanese of the Code Napoléon, the constitutions of many of the states of Europe and America, and numerous western laws, legal documents, and treatises on law. At the same time, now that Christianity was officially (1873) tolerated, he taught Bible classes, preached on Sundays, and later taught in a theological seminary. His health being threatened under the pressure of his many duties, he resigned from the government, was decorated by the Emperor, spent some months in the United States resting, and on his return to Japan in

1879 gave himself almost entirely to his missionary duties. For longer or shorter periods he preached, taught in the theological school (later a part of the Meiji Gauin), lectured at the government school for nobles, helped prepare a hymn book and other religious literature in Japanese, and assisted in the translation of the Bible. Modest and unassuming, he was courageous in upholding what he believed to be right. Never robust, he was able by self-discipline and a carefully ordered life to perform an immense amount of work and to conserve his mental powers to the end of his life. He died in Tokyo, survived by five sons and two daughters; one of his sons was William Verbeck [q.v.].

[W. E. Griffis, *Verbeck of Japan* (1900) ; R. E. Speer, *Servants of the King* (1909) ; annual reports of the Board of Foreign Missions of the Reformed Protestant Dutch Church (after 1868 the Board of Foreign Missions of the Reformed Church in America) ; *Gen. Biog. Cat. of Auburn Theological Sem.* (1918) ; Mrs. W. I. Chamberlain, *Fifty Years in Foreign Fields* (1925) ; *N. Y. Times*, Mar. 13, 1898, which gives date of death incorrectly.] K. S. L.

VERBECK, WILLIAM (Jan. 18, 1861–Aug. 24, 1930), educator, inventor, was born in Nagasaki, Japan, son of the Rev. Guido Herman Fridolin Verbeck [q.v.] and Maria (Manion). Until he was seventeen, except for a brief visit to America, he lived in the Orient, receiving his early education from his father. Later he attended the high school in Oakland, Cal., and the California Military Academy. He enlisted in the California National Guard, in which he rose to the rank of major. For a time he was commandant at St. Matthews Hall, San Mateo, Cal. In June 1885, however, he went to New York to market certain inventions which he had perfected, but litigation soon exhausted his resources, and in October of the same year he joined the faculty of the Peekskill Military Academy, Peekskill, N. Y. The following summer, July 28, he married Katharine Jordan of San Mateo, and in the fall became co-principal at Cayuga Lake Military Academy, Aurora, N. Y.

His work at Aurora attracted the attention of the Rt. Rev. Frederick D. Huntington [q.v.], bishop of Central New York, and two years later Verbeck became head of St. Johns School, Manlius, N. Y., now the Manlius School, a diocesan preparatory school founded in 1869. Only twelve students greeted him in the fall of 1888, but, within a year, the number had increased to sixty, and within five years, to double that number. He reorganized the institution, combining the stereotyped military system with English public school methods, following somewhat, particularly with respect to self-government, the methods employed by Henry A. Coit [q.v.] of St. Paul's School. Discarding both the autocratic English prefect system and cold, austere military authority, he secured his ends by developing *esprit de corps* and school loyalty. Successful in an extraordinary degree, notwithstanding financial difficulties and fires that all but destroyed the plant, he built up a school which at the time of his death numbered about three hundred boys. His ability was widely recognized. He was elected a member of the National Institute of Social Sciences in 1914, was president of the Association of Military Colleges and Schools of the United States, 1918–20, and was created a Commander of the Order of the Crown of Italy in 1926.

In New York, also, he served as an officer of the National Guard, and in June 1910, Gov. Charles E. Hughes appointed him adjutant-general. In the federalization of the National Guards of the states thereafter undertaken by the government, it became necessary to reorganize the New York troops into a modern division. Verbeck performed the duty with vigor and ability. His appointment expired Dec. 31, 1912, and he retired from the Guard with rank of brigadier-general. A pioneer in the scout movement, he was one of the first three national scout commissioners of the Boy Scouts of America, 1910–11, a member of the National Council, 1911–16 and, except for a brief interval, an honorary member until his death.

He was endowed with no little mechanical ingenuity, and between Sept. 25, 1883, and June 5, 1917, he was granted six patents; the most of these covered photographic camera mechanisms, and included a folding stereoscope and a panoramic photographic apparatus. He was a capable writer and a ready speaker. Personally magnetic, he had great appeal, especially for boys. He participated in field and track sports, was an expert fencer and swordsman in French and Japanese styles, and was an adept in oriental sword tricks. Versed in jiu jitsu, he could wrestle and box. He was a good horseman, an expert marksman, and an inspiring drill master. His funeral was held in a Japanese garden of his own creation at the school, and he was buried on the site of a proposed new chapel under the inscription: "He rests here where he lived, among the boys he loved." His wife and three sons survived him.

[For Verbeck's educational ideas, see his article, "The Ideal Military School," *The Manlius Bull.*, Dec. 1916 ; other sources of information include *Who's Who in America*, 1930–31 ; *N. Y. Herald Tribune*, Aug. 25, 1930 ; *Manlius Bull.*, Nov. 1930 ; *Gen. Orders No. 13, Aug. 25, 1930, Adjutant General's Office, N. Y.*; Patent

Office reports; minutes and correspondence of the executive board, Boy Scouts of America; personal acquaintance.]   J. F., Jr.

VERBRUGGHEN, HENRI (Aug. 1, 1873–Nov. 12, 1934), violinist, conductor, was born in Brussels, the son of Henri and Elisa (Derode) Verbrugghen. The father was a well-to-do manufacturer, and he intended that his only son should become a surgeon. From early childhood the lad was musical, and after studying under Jeno Hubay at the Brussels Conservatoire he made a public appearance at the age of eight. He then studied with Eugène Ysaye and a year later made such a success when he played before the Cercle Littéraire et Musicale that Ysaye persuaded the boy's parents that he should follow a musical career. In 1888 Verbrugghen went to London with Ysaye, where he played in orchestras under Sir George Henschel, Sir Frederic Cowen, and Sir Henry Wood. Three years later he went to Glasgow to become concertmaster in the Scottish Orchestra recently founded by Henschel. In 1894 he spent a year in Paris as concert-master of the Lamoureux Orchestra, but in 1895 he resumed his position in Glasgow, with the added appointment of assistant conductor. During the next few years he acted successively as teacher of violin at the Royal Irish Academy of Music in Dublin, and as an orchestral conductor in Colwyn and Llandudno, Wales. In 1902 he organized the Verbrugghen String Quartet, and from 1902 to 1905 he conducted the Promenade Concerts in Queens Hall, London. After this engagement he returned once more to Glasgow, where he had been appointed head of the departments of orchestra, opera, and chamber-music at the Athenaeum. In 1911 he succeeded Henry Coward as conductor of the Glasgow Choral Union.

In 1915 an official committee from New South Wales visited Europe in search of a musician to become head of the state conservatory at Sydney, Australia. Verbrugghen was chosen from 400 applicants, and he held the position for seven years, acting also as conductor of a symphony orchestra in Sydney. During the season of 1922–23 he came to America. When he appeared as one of five guest conductors with the Minneapolis Symphony Orchestra, his conducting made such an impression on the audiences and the sponsors of the orchestra that he was offered a three-year contract as permanent conductor. Verbrugghen remained as director until the season of 1931–32, but after the first concert of that season he collapsed at rehearsal, and ill health prevented his resuming his duties. After a period of rest and convalescence he was able to ac-cept (1933) the chairmanship of the music department at Carleton College, Northfield, Minn., a position he held at the time of his death in Northfield. In April 1930 Verbrugghen was made an officer of the Belgian Crown by King Albert, and the order was formally bestowed at one of his concerts. He was married, Sept. 21, 1898, to Alice Gordon Beaumont of London. He was survived by his wife and four of their six children.

[*Who's Who in America*, 1934–35; *Baker's Biog. Dict. of Musicians* (3rd ed., 1919), ed. by Alfred Remy; obituaries in *Minneapolis Tribune*, *N. Y. Times*, and *N. Y. Herald Tribune*, Nov. 13, 1934; *Musical Courier*, Nov. 17, 1934; *Musical America*, Nov. 25, 1934.]
                                                            J. T. H.

VERENDRYE, PIERRE GAULTIER DE VARENNES, Sieur de la [See LA VERENDRYE, PIERRE GAULTIER DE VARENNES, SIEUR DE, 1685–1749.]

VERHAEGEN, PETER JOSEPH (June 21, 1800–July 21, 1868), Jesuit educator and provincial, was born at Haecht in Flanders of a family of some prominence. In 1821 he came to Philadelphia with a number of Belgian youths, all of whom were inclined to the priesthood, and in October entered the novitiate of the Jesuits at Whitemarsh, Md. Two years later he accompanied the band of Jesuits led by Charles Van Quickenborne [q.v.] to Florissant in Missouri. Early in 1825 he was raised to the priesthood at the Seminary of the Barrens, in Perry County, Mo. After the Jesuits had taken over the academy opened by Bishop Louis G. du Bourg [q.v.] in St. Louis and had erected new buildings, Van Quickenborne, in 1829, named Verhaegen rector. Within a short time the institution had 150 students. The faculty came to include Pierre De Smet [q.v.], J. A. Elet, James Oliver Van de Velde [q.v.], and other enthusiastic Belgian priests and scholars, and the prestige of the college increased rapidly. In 1832 Verhaegen obtained an act incorporating it as St. Louis University. Four years later he became superior of the Indian missions, which he described in a significant article, "The Indian Missions of the United States under the Care of the Missouri Province of the Society of Jesus" (*Annals of the Propagation of the Faith*, London, 1841); this article did much to stimulate interest in western missions in the East and in Europe.

In 1844 Father Verhaegen became provincial of the Maryland Province of the Society of Jesus. When the Jesuits assumed control of St. Joseph's College at Bardstown, Ky., in 1847, Verhaegen became its president, inspiring new life into what had been a declining institution. Three years later he became pastor at St. Charles, Mo., where he served until his death except for occasional intervals when he served as professor of moral and dogmatic theology at St. Louis University or was absent on lecture and missionary tours.

Verhaegen was considered one of the best-educated Jesuits in the whole province, and he was an able linguist, a sound philosopher, an inspiring teacher, and a preacher whose learned discourses evidenced wide reading. A man of dynamic energy, he proved a capable organizer and administrator of men, schools, and missions. There were few in his day who better understood the management of Indians and the spirit of the pioneer West.

[*Catholic Encyc.*, XIII, 363; John Rothensteiner, *Hist. of the Archdiocese of St. Louis* (2 vols., 1928); J. J. Conway, *Hist. Sketch of the Church and Parish of St. Charles Borromeo* (1892); B. J. Webb, *The Centenary of Catholicity in Ky.* (1884), *Records of the Am. Cath. Hist. Soc. of Phila.*, Sept. 1908, June 1909; W. H. Hill, *Hist. Sketch of the St. Louis Univ.* (1879); *Memorial Vol. of the Diamond Jubilee of St. Louis University* (1904); J. A. Griffin, *The Contribution of Belgium to the Catholic Church in America* (1932).]
R. J. P.

VERMILYE, KATE JORDAN [See JORDAN, KATE, 1862–1926].

VERNON, SAMUEL (Dec. 6, 1683–Dec. 5, 1737), silversmith, was born at Narragansett, R. I., the son of Daniel Vernon who had been born in London of a wealthy merchant's family. Heavy losses in the great London fire of 1666 may have been the cause of his coming to America about that time. Daniel was a man of good cultural background and that he was a man of standing in his community is witnessed by his marriage at Narragansett, on Sept. 22, 1679, to Ann Dyre, the widowed daughter of Edward Hutchinson, the younger, and grand-daughter of the famous Anne Hutchinson [q.v.]. Further witness to his standing is the list of local public offices he filled.

Nothing is known of the early years of Samuel Vernon and of his professional training, but the high quality of his work is evidence of a good apprenticeship. As he was second cousin to Edward Winslow, 1669–1753 [q.v.], of Boston, one of the most able of colonial silversmiths, there is a possibility that he served his apprenticeship in the Winslow workshop. Whatever his training, Samuel Vernon stands at the head of the list of producers of beautiful silver in early Rhode Island. This silver is notable not only for its craftsmanship but also for the variety of design and the novelty of many of the pieces. Several of his productions are found in the Victoria and Albert Museum in London. His mark was his initials in Roman capitals over a *fleur-*

de-lis, the whole within a heart. His shop was in Newport. In 1715 he engraved the plates for the first indented bills of credit of the first bank established by the Colony of Rhode Island and Providence Plantations. He received two hundred pounds for the work and the plates were used for various issues up to the year 1737.

He served as assistant in the Rhode Island General Court from 1729 until his death, and also as a judge of the superior court of judicature. In 1730 he became a member of a committee "to have a care and oversight of the people and goods that should be suspected to come from Boston" where some smallpox had appeared. He was married, on Apr. 10, 1707, to Elizabeth Fleet of Long Island who bore him eight children and who preceded him in death. William Vernon [q.v.] was his son.

[See Harrison Ellery, "The Vernon Family and Arms," *New-Eng. Hist. and Geneal. Reg.*, July 1879; the Ellery genealogy and *The Diary of Thomas Vernon, a Loyalist, R. I. Hist. Tracts*, no. 13 (1881); C. L. Avery, *Early Am. Silver* (1930); E. R. Potter, S. S. Rider, *Some Account of the Bills of Credit or Paper Money of R. I., R. I. Hist, Tracts*, no. 8 (1880); *Records of the Colony of R. I. and Providence Plantations*, vol. IV (1859). William Davis Miller of Kingston, R. I., has made the most thorough study of Vernon and his silver, but the results of his study have not yet been published.]
K. A. K.

VERNON, WILLIAM (Jan. 17, 1719–Dec. 22, 1806), merchant, member of the Continental Navy Board, was born in Newport, R. I., the youngest of the eight children of Samuel Vernon [q.v.] and Elizabeth (Fleet) Vernon. He was married to Judith, the daughter of Philip Harwood. She bore him three sons before her death in 1762. He built up a considerable fortune during the "golden age" of Newport commerce, the four decades preceding the Revolution. In partnership with his brother Samuel he was active in trading along all three sides of the old Newport commercial triangle—rum to Africa, slaves to the West Indies, and molasses back to Newport. The firm's letter books throw considerable light on this trade. In 1756, for instance, William and the Redwoods (Abraham Redwood [q.v.]), accepted a note from two Guinea Coast traders for 4,353 gallons of rum, payable in good slaves at the rate of 115 gallons each for man-slaves and ninety-five gallons for women. The firm also engaged in privateering, and in King George's War owned the very successful *Duke of Marlborough* as well as having an interest in others (see Chapin, *post*). William owned a splendid mansion that became British and French headquarters during the Revolution, and in 1774 had five negroes in his household.

The Vernon family divided during the Revolution, Thomas becoming one of the most active of the many Newport Loyalists while William and his other brothers were active on the side of the patriots. In 1773 the Assembly had named William and two others to petition the king about the cod fisheries; in 1774 he was one of the local Committee of Correspondence; and in 1775 he was one of a committee appointed to collect facts concerning British depredations, his own brig, the *Royal Charlotte,* having been seized by Capt. James Wallace of H.M.S. *Rose* and condemned in Boston. By 1776 the British occupation caused Vernon to leave Newport for the remainder of the war.

On Apr. 19, 1777, the Continental Congress appointed James Warren [*q.v.*], of Plymouth, John Deshon, of New London, and Vernon to serve as the "Navy Board of the Eastern Department" or "Eastern Navy Board." This group, which sat at Boston with Vernon as chairman, was authorized "to have the Superintendence of all Naval and Marine Affairs of the United States of America within the four Eastern States under the direction of the Marine Committee . . .," —later under the Board of Admiralty (*Rhode Island Historical Society Publications,* VIII, 208–10; Paullin, *post,* pp. xxvii, 148). They were to have charge of the building, manning, and fitting for sea of all naval vessels, providing the necessary materials and stores, to keep registers of personnel, and order courts martial. A similar group for the "Middle Department" sat at Philadelphia. Vernon did invaluable work for the infant American navy in this capacity, and his correspondence reveals the extreme difficulties common to all those who were involved with money and supplies for the American cause. He advanced large sums from his own fortune for the purpose and wrote in 1778 that although the enemy had at least £12,000 sterling of his property in addition to his Newport real estate, it "never broke my rest a moment" (*Rhode Island Historical Tracts,* no. 13, p. 136).

Returning to Newport after the Revolution, he resumed his local importance. He was a wide reader, spoke several languages and corresponded with many of the notable men of his day. Always public spirited, he was an incorporator and second president of the Redwood Library, an overseer of the poor, and a benefactor of the College of New Jersey, now Princeton University.

[Two volumes of papers of the business firm of Varnum, in Newport Historical Society; *The Diary of Thomas Vernon, A Loyalist, R. I. Hist. Tracts,* no. 13 (1881); H. W. Preston, *R. I. and the Sea* (1932); H. M. Chapin, *R. I. Privateers in King George's War* (1926); G. C. Mason, *Newport Illustrated* (1875); "Papers of William Vernon and the Navy Board," *R. I. Hist. Soc. Pubs.,* n.s., vol. VIII (1900); C. O. Paullin, *Out-Letters of the Continental Marine Committee*

and Board of Admiralty (1914), vol. I; *Records of the Colony of R. I. and Providence Plantations,* vol. VII (1862); *Providence Gazette* (Providence, R. I.), Jan. 3, 1807.]

R. G. A.

VEROT, JEAN MARCEL PIERRE AUGUSTE (May 23, 1805–June 10, 1876), Roman Catholic prelate, was born in Le Puy, France, where he received a classical education before going to Saint-Sulpice in Paris for philosophy and theology. As a Sulpician, he was ordained by Archbishop de Quelen of Paris (Sept. 20, 1828) and sent to Baltimore, Md. (1830), where he taught for a number of years in St. Mary's College and Seminary. A catechism which was widely used, several manuscripts on philosophy, theology, and scripture, a few articles in Abram Ryan's *Pacificator,* and pastorals in his later years comprised his total literary output. As pastor at Ellicott's Mills, Sykesville, Clarksville, and Doughoregan manor (1854–58), he took a personal interest in the poor and in the slave population. In 1857 Archbishop John Joseph Hughes [*q.v.*] sought his services as superior of his provincial seminary at Troy, N. Y., but about this time he was named vicar-apostolic of Florida, and on Apr. 25, 1858, he was consecrated as titular bishop of Danaba by Archbishop F. P. Kenrick in the Baltimore cathedral.

At that time Florida had only three or four priests and as many dilapidated churches, established in the Spanish régime. Verot was virtually a missionary who faced torturous visitations in which he revived the faith of Spaniards and half-breeds, preached to the Indians, and built chapels and stations in outlying settlements. He enlarged churches at Fernandina, replaced a church at Tallahassee, established schools for boys and girls in Saint Augustine, brought the Sisters of Mercy from Hartford, Conn., and introduced a number of priests and nuns, as well as a colony of Brothers of the Christian Schools, from Europe. In his pastoral letters and in northern visits he encouraged Catholic colonists to come to Florida, and was one of the first to make known the opportunities there for emigrants from the North and from Europe. Deeply impressed with the Spanish tradition, he repaired the ancient cathedral of Saint Augustine with the native cochina shell, excavated the foundations of the ruined Nuestra Señora de la Leche and restored the Spanish chapel, and enlarged the church at Key West. In 1861, in a sermon on slavery, *A Tract for the Times: Slavery and Abolition,* he outlined the attitude of the Church, which condemned the slave trade, imposed a code of rights and duties of masters and slaves, and sustained the property rights of masters in their negroes. The publication of this sermon, widely quoted in the press, was suppressed in Baltimore by Secretary Seward. The first year of the Civil War saw Verot transferred to the see at Savannah, with Florida continued under his care. The war brought ruin and devastation. Churches and religious institutions were pillaged and destroyed, sometimes wantonly, by Federal troops, as at Jacksonville, Dalton, and Saint John's Bar. Verot was especially disliked as a rebel-bishop, yet he attended Andersonville, did all that was possible for northern prisoners, and furnished nuns as nurses in the military hospitals. With peace came the labors of physical and social reconstruction. Verot made begging journeys throughout the North. Churches were rebuilt and restored; colored benevolent societies were established at Saint Augustine; schools were fostered; the Ursulines burned out at Columbia established an academy at Macon, while the Sisters of Mercy erected a school at Columbus; and the Sisters of Charity at Savannah welcomed Jefferson Davis' penniless children.

At the Vatican Council in 1870 Verot was the *enfant terrible* who spoke frequently in the negative on the question of papal infallibility, urged corrections in the breviary, suggested that for propriety's sake clerics be forbidden to hunt and kill game, and advised that instead of condemning obscure errors of German idealists it would be better to condemn any theory that negroes have no souls. On July 13, he was one of the eighty-eight who voted *non placet* on the question of papal infallibility. He was one of fifty-five bishops who signed a letter to the pope explaining their policy of remaining away from the final ballot (July 18) rather than scandalize by openly and publicly voting *non placet* on the definition of the dogma. On its passage, as a loyal Catholic, Verot gave his formal adherence to the doctrine. During the sessions, Saint Augustine was made a see. Verot disinterestedly accepted Florida, and on his return installed Bishop Ignatius Persico in the superior diocese of Savannah. To the end, he labored courageously and successfully in his impoverished state.

[R. H. Clarke, *Lives of the Deceased Bishops of the Cath. Church in the U. S.,* vol. III (1888), pp. 94–107; J. G. Shea, *Hist. of the Cath. Church in the U. S.,* vol. IV (1892); Cuthbert Butler, *The Vatican Council* (1930); F. J. Zwierlein, *The Life . . . of Bishop McQuaid* (1926), vol. II; *Sadliers' Cath. Directory* (1877); *Records Am. Cath. Hist. Soc.,* June 1900; *N. Y. Freeman's Jour.,* May 22, July 10, Nov. 27, 1858, June 24, July 8, 1876; obituary in *Daily Fla. Union* (Jacksonville), June 13, 1876.]   R. J. P.

VERPLANCK, GULIAN CROMMELIN (Aug. 6, 1786–Mar. 18, 1870), author, congressman, was born in New York City, the son of

Daniel Crommelin and Elizabeth (Johnson) Verplanck. He was a descendant of Abraham Verplanck who settled in New Amsterdam about 1635; his uncle, for whom he was named, his father, a judge and congressman, and his grandfather, William Samuel Johnson [*q.v.*], were all Federalists of note in New York. His mother died when he was three years old and his grandmothers directed his early education. He was graduated at Columbia in 1801 and then read law under Josiah Ogden Hoffman [*q.v.*]; in 1807 he was admitted to the bar. On Oct. 2, 1811, he married Mary Elizabeth Fenno, a sister of Hoffman's wife and the grand-daughter of John Fenno [*q.v.*]; two sons were born to them.

Verplanck was a Federalist, but by 1808 Federalism in New York was at a low ebb. Imitating the Democratic-Republicans, who had sometime before organized their Tammany Society, Verplanck, with Isaac Sebring and Richard Varick, founded in New York the Washington Benevolent Society to perpetuate Federalism, and this society became the model of others formed elsewhere. It was of service in restoring the prestige of the Federalists in 1809, but it was soon deprived of Verplanck's presence and aid. While defending a student threatened with loss of his diploma, Verplanck became a principal with Hugh Maxwell [*q.v.*] in the Columbia College commencement riot of 1811. De Witt Clinton presided over the resulting trial and, seeking Federalist support, he fined Verplanck $200 (see *The Trial of Gulian C. Verplanck, Hugh Maxwell and Others . . .,* 1821). This event resulted in a pamphlet and press war that lasted nearly a decade. Among the pamphlets was one by Verplanck, *A Fable for Statesmen and Politicians* (1815), to which Clinton replied in *An Account of Abimelech Coody* (1815), which was bitterly personal. In 1815 Verplanck went to Europe and spent two years in travel, vainly trying to save his wife's life. During the trip he acutely observed political matters and the English judicial system. On his return he and Charles King [*q.v.*] founded the *New York American,* in which appeared seven poetical satires by Verplanck aimed at Clinton and his administration. These have a caustic erudition that class them among the best ever written in English; later they were published as *The State Triumvirate, A Political Tale, and the Epistles of Brevet-Major Pindar Puff* (1819). From 1821 to 1824 he was a professor in the General Theological Seminary of the Episcopal Church, in New York, and published *Essays on the Nature and Uses of the Various Evidences of Revealed Religion* (1824), a work comprised chiefly of philosophical considerations and only secondarily of textual criticism. It condemns the *a priori* method and is based upon inductive reasoning and legal principles of evidence, which Verplanck, the lawyer, applied to revelation. It is one of the earliest works in America influenced by the Scottish school of common-sense philosophy and it represents a conservative deistic approach.

Verplanck was elected to the New York Assembly in 1820, 1821, and 1822, where educational measures were his chief interest. In 1824 he was elected, largely because of his opposition to the high tariff, to the House of Representatives, of which he remained a member. He was placed upon the Ways and Means Committee and was its chairman from 1831 to 1833. It was the Verplanck tariff bill that was under consideration when Clay introduced his famous tariff compromise. Verplanck was chiefly instrumental in 1831 in obtaining a law improving the copyrights of authors; for this achievement he was tendered a dinner by the *literati* of New York, at which he delivered an address on "The Law of Literary Property" (published in *Discourses and Addresses*). He supported Jackson in 1828, but would not follow him in his opposition to the Bank, and he was not renominated. Now estranged from the Democrats, he headed the assembly nominations and though defeated, he ran as Whig candidate for mayor of New York in 1834. He lost in a close contest, but it was New York's first direct mayoralty election and the earliest in which the name Whig was prominent. The same year he refused to consider the nomination for governor because he was opposed to any association with the anti-Masonic group. He passed most of his remaining life on the family estate in Fishkill, though he served in the New York Senate from 1838 to 1841. The Senate was then the court for the correction of errors, which reviewed the decisions of the court of chancery, and Verplanck wrote many elaborate opinions, frequently carrying the court with him when he differed with the Chancellor. Some of the most valuable changes in the state constitution made by the conventions of 1846 and 1868 are said to have been suggested by Verplanck's speech in the Senate in 1839 (*Speech . . . in the Senate of New York on the Several Bills and Resolutions for the Amendment of the Law and the Reform of the Judiciary System,* 1839).

In 1847 he published *Shakespeare's Plays: with His Life,* in three volumes, with woodcuts by H. W. Hewet, an edition important as an illustration of the development of wood engraving, and as the second serious attempt of American Shakespearean scholarship to use the latest Eng-

lish researches, especially those of J. P. Collier, in connection with the original editions. With Robert C. Sands and William Cullen Bryant [*q.v.*] he edited the *Talisman,* an annual, 1828–30. Some of his essays are collected in *Discourses and Addresses on Subjects of American History, Arts, and Literature* (1833). He belonged to many societies and was a member of the board of regents of the University of the State of New York, 1826–1870, and president of the Board of the Commissioners of Emigration, 1848–70.

[W. E. Ver Planck, *The Hist. of Abraham Isaacse Ver Planck and His Male Descendants in America* (1892); C. H. Hart, *A Discourse on the Life and Services of the Late Gulian Crommelin Verplanck* (1870), pub. also in *N. Y. Geneal. and Biog. Record,* Oct. 1870; *Gulian C. Verplanck* (1870), pub. also in *Proc. Century Asso. in Honor of the Memory of Gulian C. Verplanck* (1870); W. C. Bryant, *A Discourse on the Life, Character, and Writings of Gulian Crommelin Verplanck* (1870); D. R. Fox, *The Decline of Aristocracy in the Politics of N. Y.* (1919); L. B. Mason, "The Political Career of Gulian Crommelin Verplanck," MS. in the Columbia Univ. Lib.; *N. Y. Times,* Mar. 19, 1870.]

L. B. M.

VERRILL, ADDISON EMERY (Feb. 9, 1839–Dec. 10, 1926), zoölogist, was born at Greenwood, Me., the second son of George Washington and Lucy (Hillborn) Verrill. On his father's side he was a descendant of Samuel Verrill who was in Gloucester, Mass., in 1727; on his mother's, of early Pennsylvania Quakers. He was prepared for college at the Norway Liberal Institute in Norway, Me., where his family lived after 1853, and in 1859 entered Harvard College. There he was Agassiz's assistant in the Museum of Comparative Zoölogy from 1860 to 1864, two years after his graduation from the Lawrence Scientific School with the degree of B.S. As an undergraduate he spent several summers with Alpheus Hyatt and Nathaniel S. Shaler [*qq.v.*] in field work in Maine, Labrador, and on the islands of Anticosti and Grand Manan. In 1864 he was called to Yale University as professor of zoölogy; in 1907 he retired as professor emeritus. For a number of years (1870–94) he also taught geology in the Sheffield Scientific School, and for two years (1868–70) acted as professor of entomology and comparative anatomy at the University of Wisconsin. On June 15, 1865, he was married to Flora Louisa Smith of Norway, Me., sister of his associate, Prof. Sidney I. Smith. In 1873 appeared his *Report upon the Invertebrate Animals of Vineyard Sound and Adjacent Waters,* the first extensive ecological study of the marine invertebrates of the southern New England coast, for many years a standard reference work. For sixteen years (1871–87) he was in charge of the scientific work of the United States Commission of Fish and Fisheries in southern New England. In connection with this he devised a cradle sieve, a rake dredge, and a rope tangle for collecting starfishes in oyster beds, the latter of which has great value in commercial oyster-growing (see C. D. Sigsbee, *Deep-Sea Sounding and Dredging,* 1880, pp. 163–68). His scientific studies were interrupted for several years by his work in preparing zoölogical definitions for the revised edition of *Webster's International Dictionary* (1890). During the ensuing years he investigated the invertebrate life of the northern New England coast, the Gulf Stream, the Pacific coast of Central America, the Bermudas, and the West Indies. Everywhere he turned, his discerning eyes found new types of animal life which others had overlooked; he once estimated that he had discovered a thousand undescribed forms. Much of his most important work appeared after his retirement in 1907 at the age of sixty-eight; at eighty-five, still sturdy and vigorous, he extended his studies to the Hawaiian Islands and during the next two years discovered many new species. At last, however, his remarkable vitality was exhausted, and toward the end of his eighty-eighth year he died at Santa Barbara, Cal., survived by four of his six children.

His publications over a period of sixty-four years covered a wide range, but the majority deal with marine invertebrates, among them sponges, corals, sea-stars, worms, mollusks, *Crustacea,* and representatives of other groups. Some of these were comprehensive monographs which are still standards of reference. His most successful work was probably that on corals and coelenterates (including studies of the *Actinaria* and *Alcyonaria* of the Canadian Arctic expeditions, 1922), where he not only described new species and worked out a sound system of classification but made careful observations on mode of life. Other notable work includes his *Monograph of the Shallow-Water Starfishes of the North Pacific Coast* (1914), *Report on the Starfishes of the West Indies, Florida, and Brazil* (1915), and several valuable unpublished reports, among them one on the higher *Crustacea* of Connecticut, and another on the deep-sea *Alcyonaria* of the Blake expedition, which Verrill considered in many respects his most important work. His *Bermuda Islands* (2 vols., 1901–07), which deals with the history, geology, botany, and zoölogy of Bermuda, attests the breadth of his knowledge in diverse fields. In addition to his notable achievements in the classification of marine invertebrates, he built up a large zoölogical collection in the Peabody Museum at Yale, of which he was curator for forty-

three years (1867–1910), and served as associate editor of the *American Journal of Science* for fifty years (1869–1920). He was an early member of the National Academy of Sciences and of many other American and foreign learned societies, and for some years was president of the Connecticut Academy of Arts and Sciences.

Tall, with thick, wavy hair, and piercing blue eyes, he is remembered as a man with a marvelous memory, an encyclopedic mind, and an uncanny aptitude for close discrimination. He had great skill in drawing, producing with little effort vivid sketches of even the most intricate structures. In contrast with Hyatt, whose bent was philosophical, and Shaler, with a gift for generalization and popularization, Verrill was the patient, painstaking investigator, capable of giving a vast accumulation of details clarity and order, and of making the most minute distinctions salient. Standing a little aside from the main course of biological investigation as it developed in his lifetime, Verrill held firmly to a belief in the value of taxonomical work as a basis for other scientific investigations. He himself would never have been satisfied with a knowledge of animals under laboratory conditions alone. It is perhaps partly as a consequence of this that his true position as one of the greatest systematic zoölogists of America has not yet been fully recognized.

[*Geneal. and Family Hist. . . . of Conn.* (1911), vol. I, ed. by W. R. Cutter, etc.; *Who's Who in America,* 1926–27; W. R. Coe, in *Nat. Acad. of Sci. . . . Biog. Memoirs,* vol. XIV (1932), with full bibliog., in *Am. Jour. of Sci.,* May 1927, in *Sci.,* July 8, 1927, and in *Yale Alumni Weekly,* June 10, 1927; G. D. Smith, in *Yale Sci. Monthly,* Mar. 1907; Edwin Linton, in *Sci.,* May 21, 1915; obituary in *New Haven Jour.-Courier,* Dec. 11, 1926.]

W. R. C.

VERWYST, CHRYSOSTOM ADRIAN (Nov. 23, 1841–June 23, 1925), missionary and Indian linguist, was a native of the town of Uden, North Brabant, the Netherlands. His family was induced to emigrate to the United States by the representations of the Rev. Theodore J. Van den Broek, a Dominican missionary who had worked in the West with Samuel Charles Mazzuchelli [*q.v.*]. In 1848, after Van den Broek's visit, a considerable group removed from the Netherlands and formed a settlement in Brown County, Wis. The Verwyst family, consisting of father, mother, and four sons, landed at Boston after a voyage of fifty-five days in a sailing vessel and remained there several years. By 1855 they had earned enough money to make the journey to Wisconsin and join their kinsmen in the settlement called "Franciscus Bosch," where they bought sixty acres of land and built a log cabin. It took the combined efforts of father and sons four years to clear thirty of the sixty acres.

In 1859 Verwyst decided to enter the priesthood and began his studies with the local priest; the next year he was admitted to St. Francis Seminary, near Milwaukee, where he remained as a student five years. He was drafted for the Union army in 1863 and, though he was not a citizen, was obliged to buy his exemption. After this experience he did not take out his citizen's papers for about fifteen years. Ordained on Nov. 5, 1865, he was first stationed for three years in Waupaca County, with headquarters at New London; in 1868 he was transferred to Hudson, and officiated in Saint Croix and Pierce counties for four years; in 1872 he became resident priest for six years at Seneca, Crawford County, where he built a church and parsonage. He was sent next to minister to the Indians and whatever white groups might be found in the Lake Superior region. After four years of a wandering ministry he determined to enter the Franciscan order. Following his novitiate, when he took the name Chrysostom, he was sent in 1883 to Bayfield, Wis., where a Franciscan monastery was established. There Verwyst spent the remainder of a long and useful life, except for a short sojourn in Missouri and California (1897–1900) for the improvement of his health, and a period of twelve years (1900–12) at Ashland, Wis.

A specialist in the Chippewa language, in 1901 he published at Harbor Springs, Mich., *Chippewa Exercises: Being a Practical Introduction into the Study of the Chippewa Language*. He also prepared two articles for the State Historical Society of Wisconsin: "Geographical Names in Wisconsin, Minnesota, and Michigan Having a Chippewa Origin" (*Collections,* vol. XII, 1892, pp. 390–98) and "Historic Sites on Chequamegon Bay" (*Collections,* vol. XIII, 1895, pp. 426–40). His study of the *Missionary Labors of Fathers Marquette, Ménard and Allouez in the Lake Superior Region* was published in Chicago in 1886 and his *Life and Labors of Rt. Rev. Father Frederic Baraga* at Milwaukee in 1900. He published for a time a monthly Chippewa magazine entitled *Anishinable Enamaid,* and in 1907 put out *Katolik gagikwemasinaigan mi sa Katolik enamiad gegikimind.* In 1915 the fiftieth anniversary of his ordination was celebrated at Bayfield. A stalwart figure, with soft brown eyes, and a scholar's habit, he was a man without guile, open and aboveboard, cheerful and gentle, beloved alike of white men and Indians.

[Sources include Verwyst's own account of his life, "Reminiscences of a Pioneer Missionary," *Proc. Wis.* State Hist. Soc. . . . *1916* (:917), pp. 148–85; necrology in *Official Cath. Directory, 1926*; personal acquaintance.]

L. P. K.

VERY, JONES (Aug. 28, 1813–May 8, 1880), mystic sonneteer and transcendentalist, was born in Salem, Mass., eldest of six children of a union of cousins, Jones and Lydia (Very) Very. His earliest American ancestor, the widow Bridget Very, settled in Salem about 1634, and her descendants, several of whom fought in the Revolution, farmed and followed the sea for six generations. The elder Jones privateered in the War of 1812, was briefly imprisoned in Halifax, N. S., and returned to be master until his death (Dec. 22, 1824) of the Boston barque *Aurelia.* On this ship young Jones accompanied his father in 1823 to Kronstadt, Russia, and in 1824 to New Orleans, where he attended grammar school while the ship was lading. After his father's death the youth continued his education until 1827, when he began work as errand boy for a Salem auctioneer. The normal child now became a grave adolescent, turned by circumstances from the family sea-going tradition. Sporadically tutored for four years by a friendly Salem pundit, J. F. Worcester, Very in 1832 became assistant in the Fisk Latin School of Henry Kemble Oliver [*q.v.*]. There he fulfilled three semesters of collegiate requirements, and earned future tuition expenses. He entered Harvard in February 1834 as a second-term sophomore. His unusual maturity and studious habits brought him few friends, but he was regularly a speaker at college "exhibitions," won both junior and senior Bowdoin Prizes, and was graduated in 1836 with second honors. That autumn his undergraduate record netted him an appointment as Greek tutor to the freshmen, enabling him to study simultaneously at the Harvard Divinity School.

This marked the beginning of Very's two most important years. Hitherto mildly Unitarian, he was soon overtaken by a species of religious exaltation. By September 1837, convinced that he must set down allegedly audible pronouncements of the Holy Ghost, he began to compose religious sonnets with remarkable celerity, and was even moved to tears when the Rev. Henry Ware questioned the veracity of his visions. All his work, he constantly insisted, was "communicated" to him. In Salem that December, Elizabeth Palmer Peabody [*q.v.*] heard him read his Bowdoin Prize essay, "Epic Poetry." Knowing the Verys well, she helpfully suggested to Emerson that Jones lecture at the Lyceum in Concord. When Very met him in early April 1838 Emerson was enthusiastic, and

Jones, inspired, returned to Cambridge to write another essay, this time on Shakespeare, which he sent to Emerson in August. Among his colleagues, however, Very's spiritual intoxication had brought his sanity in question. Requested to withdraw, he attended his last faculty meeting, Sept. 10, 1838, and a week later entered McLean Asylum, Somerville, remaining until Oct. 17. Having successfully preached his doctrine of "willess existence" to the inmates, Jones devoted the remainder of the autumn to the attempted conversion of Emerson. Among the transcendentalists he enjoyed some popularity; and men who talked earnestly with him doubted rumors of his insanity. James Freeman Clarke's pronouncement, "Monomania? ... Monosania!," was bolstered by Emerson's "Profoundly sane!" Very believed in complete, unquestioning submission to the will of God, and seemed the answer to Emerson's recent plea for a "newborn bard of the Holy Ghost." When Clarke in March and April 1839 published twenty-seven of Very's sonnets in his *Western Messenger,* impetus was given to the preparation, under Emerson's aegis, of a book of Very's prose and verse, *Essays and Poems.* Published in September 1839, the verses were called by W. H. Channing "an oracle of God"; by William Cullen Bryant, "among the finest in the language"; and Emerson, who planned to send copies to Carlyle and Wordsworth, thought they bore "an unquestionable stamp of grandeur." Hawthorne, who disliked Very, none the less called him "a poet whose voice is scarcely heard . . . by reason of its depth." Less notice was given Very's prose essays, "Epic Poetry," "Hamlet," and "Shakespeare," though the latter, partly a result of conversations with his friend Edward Tyrrell Channing [*q.v.*], reveals the core of Very's belief. Through some of the poems runs a vague undercurrent of human warmth, but their philosophy contains the worst elements of Asiatic quietism. Emerson rightly regarded Very's doctrine as too other-worldly, utterly lacking in the Yankee vigor which would have stiffened and saved it. The poems are characterized by clarity and simplicity; but color is inordinately subdued, ideas few, and humor absent. They are distinguished only by sincere religious emotion.

By April 1840 this fervor had faded sufficiently for Emerson to recognize its underlying philosophic negativity. The friendship waned. Very returned to Salem to write increasingly mediocre verse. Lacking a degree in divinity, he was licensed to preach (1843) by the Cambridge Association, and held temporary pastorates in Eastport, Maine, and North Beverly, Mass. But he was too shy to preach well, and at forty-five had virtually retired. He was tall, slender, and hollow-cheeked. He lived with his sisters, doing occasional genealogical research for the Essex Institute, contributing to newspapers. He called himself a "failure," and lived out forty years of anticlimax in his provincial haven, with his mind and hopes directed toward that other world to which he had formerly enjoyed at least a visionary access.

[Two editions of Very's work were posthumously published: *Poems* (1883), with a valuable intro. memoir by Wm. P. Andrews; and *Poems and Essays* (1886), containing some six hundred poems, ed. by J. F. Clarke. Biog. material is best set forth in Emerson's journals and letters; *Essex Inst. Hist. Colls.,* vols. I–II (1859–60); *Bull. Essex Inst.,* Jan., Feb., Mar. 1881; G. W. Cooke, *An Hist. and Biog. Intro. to Accompany the Dial* (2 vols., 1902); Rose H. Lathrop, *Memories of Hawthorne* (1897); F. B. Sanborn and W. T. Harris, *A. Bronson Alcott* (2 vols., 1893); Records of the Harvard College Faculty, vol. XI, 1829–40; obituary in *Salem Observer,* May 15, 1880. Critical estimates are to be found in the *Dial,* vol. II, no. 1, vol. III, no. 1; Albert Ritter, *Jones Very, der Dichter des Christentums* (Leipzig, 1903); Gamaliel Bradford, *Biog. and the Human Heart* (1932); and P. P. Burns, "Jones Very," *Howard Coll. Studies,* June 1922.] C. H. B.

VERY, LYDIA LOUISA ANN (Nov. 2, 1823–Sept. 10, 1901), author, was born in Salem, Mass., the youngest child of Capt. Jones and Lydia (Very) Very, and a sister of Jones Very [*q.v.*]. Shortly after Captain Very's death in 1824, the family moved from Lydia's birthplace, at Boston and Essex Streets, to 154 Federal St., where Lydia remained throughout her life. Educated in the Salem public schools and at the classical school conducted by Henry Kemble Oliver [*q.v.*], she began in 1846 a period of about thirty years of primary teaching. When her brother Washington opened his private school in 1847, she relinquished her initial charge in order to join him. But he died in 1853; the school lapsed; and until her retirement in 1878, she taught the lower grades at Bowditch Grammar School. Never married, she lived with her mother, her sister Frances, and her brothers, Jones and Washington. Short, plump, brownhaired, energetic, she was the hardest worker of her Unitarian family, and its most ardent humanitarian.

This uneventful career was punctuated in 1856 by the appearance of *Poems,* a small volume of verse, printed at Andover, Mass. More deeply influenced by her friend Elizabeth Palmer Peabody [*q.v.*] than by her brother Jones's mysticism, she centered her interest in children, animals, and flowers. Her poetry shows no transcendentalism, though she must certainly have been exposed to it; and her view of nature, if fresh and hearty, is entirely orthodox. Except for occasional contributions to the *Salem Gazette* and the *Boston Transcript,* she published nothing more for thirty years. After the death of Jones in 1880, however, lacking another vocation, she returned to literature. First fruit of this regeneration was *Poems and Prose Writings* (1890), a copiously augmented reprint of her earlier volume, together with some essays on Salem scenery which show her less skilful in prose than in verse. Receiving a copy of this, the aged Whittier wrote in 1891, "I heartily thank thee for sending me the volume, and am truly thy friend." Her sister died in 1895. Lonely but undaunted, she persuaded a Boston publisher to bring out three books in 1898. Some skill in drawing enabled her to illustrate them herself. Her *Sayings and Doings among the Insects and Flowers,* first published at Salem in 1897, tells sixteen nature-stories with charming simplicity, and one of them, "The Town Pump," contains gentle satire on Salem selectmen. The novels are unfortunately third-rate; *The Better Path, or Sylph, the Organ-grinder's Daughter* (1898) moralizes sentimentally, *A Strange Disclosure* (1898) is an undistinguished tale of New England small-town life, and *A Strange Recluse* (Salem, 1899) tells of a wealthy London clubman who casts bread upon the waters and gets it back sodden with romance. Her last work, *An Old-fashioned Garden, and Walks and Musings Therein* (1900), far surpasses the novels. An anecdotal review, in simplest language, of her quiet life, it tells of the garden, childhood sports, pets; of her "Thoreau Field Club," formed to seek arbutus along Salem turnpike; of the evil effects on nature of advancing industry. The book ends with a salute to earth, the last lyrical expression of optimism from a sane, industrious spinster, who died in the early morning of Sept. 10, 1901.

[Jones Very, "The Very Family," *Essex Inst. Hist. Colls.*, vols. I–II (1859–60); *Vital Records of Salem, Mass.*, vol. II (1918); Salem town records for 1901; *Who's Who in America*, 1899–1900; Sidney Perley, *The Poets of Essex County* (1889); *Salem Gazette,* Feb. 22, 1889; *Boston Transcript,* Feb. 21, 1890, and Sept. 10, 1901 (obituary); obituary in *Salem News,* Sept. 10, 1901; letter from J. G. Whittier on Lydia Very's poems, 1891, in colls. of the Essex Inst.]

C. H. B.

VESEY, DENMARK (c. 1767–July 2, 1822), mulatto rebel, because of his intelligence and beauty became at the age of fourteen the protégé of one Captain Vesey, a slaver of Charleston, S. C., trading from St. Thomas to Santo Domingo. The name "Télémaque" that his owner gave him was corrupted to "Denmark." At Cap Français (now Cape Haytien) the boy was sold to another, but later was returned as subject to epi-

lepsy and for the next twenty years sailed with his master as a faithful slave. In 1800, having drawn $1,500 in the East Bay Street Lottery, Charleston, he purchased his freedom for $600 and set up for himself as a carpenter. Active and powerful, he accumulated a considerable estate, and was the reputed autocrat of several wives and a numerous progeny. Without particular grievances on his own account, he resented his children's inheritance of slavery from their mothers, and, stimulated by events in Santo Domingo, he laid the foundation, 1818–22, for his uprising. Admitted to the Second Presbyterian Church in 1817, he joined the African Methodist congregation when they built their church, and acquired great influence through classes organized ostensibly for religious instruction. He was literate and quoted Scripture with powerful effect, identifying the negroes with the Israelites; and he interpreted the debate on the Missouri Compromise to mean that negroes were held by their masters in defiance of law. Exempt from slave restrictions, he carried his message to the plantations from the Santee to the Euhaws, a belt of more than a hundred miles. Meetings were held at Vesey's house, 20 Bull Street, where contributions were taken for arms; a blacksmith was set to making daggers, pikes, and bayonets, and a white barber to fashioning wigs and whiskers of European hair. The plans of the conspirators are not clear, but probably after taking the city they would have been guided by circumstances. Betrayed by a negro, they advanced the date for the uprising to Sunday night, June 16, but such effective precautions had been taken that the conspiracy collapsed.

Next day a court of two magistrates and five freeholders, customary in South Carolina since colonial times in cases involving slaves or persons of color, convened as both judge and jury, and, having laid down the customary rule of evidence that testimony of two should establish guilt, proceeded to the trial of the suspects. Carefully chosen men of integrity comprised the court, but when the *Charleston Courier* (June 21, 1822) published a communication on the "Melancholy Effect of Popular Excitement," citing the death of an innocent negro some years earlier as the result of a joke, the court protested against the insinuation of disrespect and drew a rebuke from Judge William Johnson [*q.v.*], apparently the author of the original communication (*Charleston Courier,* June 29, 1822). After a three days' search Vesey was taken on the night of June 22 at the house of one of his wives. He had counsel and ably defended himself, cross-examining witnesses with skill, but on the testimony of informers, some of whom thus saved themselves, he was condemned to be hanged (notice of execution, *Ibid.*, July 3, 1822). Of the negroes brought to trial, thirty-five were hanged, thirty-four were sent out of the state, and sixty-one were acquitted. Four whites, at least three of whom were foreign-born, were tried in the court of sessions for misdemeanor, and fined and imprisoned.

The true extent of the conspiracy will never be known, for Vesey and his aides died without making revelations. In the face of the intense excitement that prevailed, it was considered remarkable that the customary machinery of the law functioned and that no unusual punishments were inflicted. The local newspapers kept quiet about the insurrection and referred only briefly to the trials.

[A summary is in W. G. Simms, *The Hist. of S. C.* (1840), appendix; a sketch of Vesey is in *An Account of the Late Intended Insurrection among a Portion of the Blacks of this City. Published by the Authority of the Corporation of Charleston* (1822); the same sketch is repeated in *An Official Report of the Trials of Sundry Negroes Charged with an Attempt to Raise an Insurrection in the State of South Carolina* (1822), by L. H. Kennedy and Thomas Parker; see also Achates (Thomas Pinckney?), *Reflections, Occasioned by the Late Disturbances in Charleston* (1822); T. W. Higginson, "Denmark Vesey," *Atlantic Monthly*, June 1861; A. H. Grimké, *Right on the Scaffold, or, The Martyrs of 1822* (1901).] A. K. G.

VESEY, TÉLÉMAQUE [See VESEY, DENMARK, *c.* 1767–1822].

VESEY, WILLIAM (Aug. 10, 1674–July 11, 1746), Anglican clergyman, rector of Trinity Church in New York City, was born in Braintree, Mass., the son of William and Mary Vesey. His father was evidently a farmer and a Jacobite, for in 1699 Governor Bellomont wrote that he had been sentenced to stand in the pillory for "desperate words" against the king (O'Callaghan, *Documents, post*, IV, 534–35). Vesey was graduated at Harvard College in 1693, the year the New York Assembly passed the Ministerial Act, which Gov. Benjamin Fletcher interpreted as establishing the Church of England in the colony. Following graduation, Vesey preached on Long Island for about two years and then went to Boston to assist at King's Chapel. On Nov. 2, 1696, he was called to New York on condition that he go to London for ordination according to the liturgy of the Church of England. With a loan of £95 from the wardens and vestrymen he departed in November 1696; received an honorary degree of M.A. from Merton College, Oxford; was ordained priest, Aug. 2, 1697, by the Bishop of London; and on Dec. 25, having returned to New York, was inducted

by Fletcher into the parish of Trinity Church, which had meanwhile been granted a charter of incorporation.

Fletcher's successful efforts to have the law interpreted in favor of the Church of England brought Vesey into many controversies with the royal governors, who held widely divergent views concerning the rights vested in Trinity and its rector. Disagreements, beginning under Richard, Lord Bellomont [*q.v.*], over the King's (later Queen's) Farm and other land grants; struggles over the payment of the rector's salary; differences with Gov. Robert Hunter [*q.v.*] concerning the rights of the Presbyterians in Jamaica and the use of the fort chapel for services, brought stormy times for Vesey, whose extreme conservatism and positive ideas about the church made him resist determinedly and often none too tactfully any attempt to infringe on what he regarded as his prerogatives. So bitter did feeling become between Vesey and Hunter, who accused the former of being a Jacobite, that Vesey left for England in 1714 to lay his case before the Bishop of London. His exoneration appears to have been complete, for he not only remained rector of Trinity but became the Bishop's commissary in New York and New Jersey, in both of which capacities he served until his death. His last years were more peaceful, though he was violently opposed to Whitefield's preaching in New York.

Vesey enjoyed the respect and confidence of his parishioners, among whom were many of the most prominent citizens politically, financially, and socially. He cooperated with the Society for the Propagation of the Gospel in Foreign Parts in providing missionaries and teachers for the poor, and in establishing a charity school in connection with Trinity; he was also the trustee of many bequests for the city's poor, and in his own will left £50 for that purpose. He preached at various missions throughout his district and at his death had twenty-two congregations in his charge. Vesey and Rector streets in New York City were named for him. His widow, Mary, daughter of Lawrence Reade, whom he married in 1698, became the wife of Judge Daniel Horsmanden [*q.v.*].

[Morgan Dix, *A Hist. of the Parish of Trinity Church in the City of N. Y.*, vol. I (1898); J. G. Wilson, *Centennial Hist. of the Protestant Episcopal Church in the Diocese of N. Y.* (1886); E. B. O'Callaghan, *Documents Relative to the Colonial Hist. of the State of N. Y.*, vols. IV (1854), V (1855), and *The Documentary Hist. of the State of N. Y.*, vol. III (1850); E. T. Corwin, *Ecclesiastical Records: State of N. Y.*, vols. II–IV (1901–02); C. K. Shipton, *Sibley's Harvard Grads., Vol. IV, 1690–1700* (1933); "The Case of William Atwood," in *N. Y. Hist. Soc. Colls.*, Pub. Fund Ser., vol. XIII (1881).] E. L. J.

VEST, GEORGE GRAHAM (Dec. 6, 1830–Aug. 9, 1904), representative and senator in the Confederate Congress and United States senator from Missouri, was born at Frankfort, Ky., the son of John Jay and Harriet (Graham) Vest. He graduated from Centre College in 1848, and from the law department of Transylvania University in 1853. The following year he went to Pettis County, Mo., and began the practice of law at Georgetown; in 1856 he moved to Boonville, Cooper County.

In 1860 he was presidential elector on the Douglas ticket, and that year was elected to the Missouri House of Representatives, where he was made chairman of the committee on federal relations. He was the author of the "Vest Resolutions" denouncing coercion of the South, and in large part formulated the stinging legislative report condemning the seizure of Camp Jackson by the Federal forces under Nathaniel Lyon [q.v.]. Probably he was the author also of the "Ordinance of Secession" adopted by the Southern wing of the Missouri legislature at Neosho in the fall of 1861. This assembly chose him as a representative in the Confederate Congress, where he served from February 1862 until January 1865, resigning to accept a seat in the Confederate Senate.

After the fall of the Confederacy Vest returned to Missouri, where he resumed the practice of law, first at Sedalia, and later at Boonville. In 1877 he moved to Kansas City, and two years later was elected as a Democrat to the United States Senate, of which he was a member until Mar. 3, 1903. As a delegate to the Democratic convention held at Baltimore in 1872, he worked for the temporary Democratic-Liberal Republican coalition and for the nomination of Horace Greeley [q.v.]. His senatorial career, in the main, was characterized by a disinclination to recognize new developments and new issues in American life; he adhered largely to bygone principles and precedents. Credit must be accorded to him, however, for his outstanding opposition to the high protective tariff measures of his day. He steered the Wilson Tariff Bill through the Senate, and, although the Gorman amendments added a greater degree of protection than he wished, he nevertheless made the leading speech in its defense. When Spain was ceding Puerto Rico and the Philippines to the United States, Vest was one of the leading exponents of the theory that it was unconstitutional to "acquire territory to be held and governed permanently as colonies." In 1900 the *Chicago Journal* pronounced Vest "that great big little fellow . . . with a tremendous intellect in a body

so small and emaciated," and went on to assert that he was "still half the brains of the Democratic side of the Senate" (quoted in the *Boonville Weekly Advertiser,* Feb. 24, 1900).

He was a lawyer of the highest ability, and was at his best in pleading before a jury. His jury oration entitled "Tribute to a Dog" not only won him the case in which it was used, but has ever since been accounted a masterpiece of its kind. As a stump speaker few could equal him in wit or in power to sway the emotions of an audience. In 1854 he married Sallie E. Sneed of Danville, Ky. He died in Sweet Springs, Mo., and was buried in St. Louis; his wife and two children survived him.

[*Pictorial and Geneal. Record of Greene County (Mo.,* 1893); H. L. Conard, *Encyc. of the Hist. of Mo.* (1901), vol. VI; A. J. D. Stewart, *The Hist. of the Bench and Bar of Mo.* (1898); A. E. Trabue, *A Corner in Celebrities* (1923); J. P. Boyd, *Vital Questions of the Day* (1894); E. M. C. French, *Senator Vest, Champion of the Dog* (1930); *Biog. Dir. Am. Cong.* (1928); *Who's Who in America,* 1903–05; *Kansas City Jour.,* Aug. 10, 1904; *St. Louis Globe-Democrat,* Aug. 10, 11, 1904.]
H. E. N.

VETCH, SAMUEL (Dec. 9, 1668–Apr. 30, 1732), soldier, trader, who formulated the first adequate plan for the expulsion of the French from North America, was born at Edinburgh, Scotland. The second son of William Veitch (*sic*) and Marion Fairly, he spent his boyhood uneasily in northern England while his hunted, proscribed father preached for Presbyterianism and conspired against Episcopacy and Toryism on both sides of the Border. In his teens he received some higher education in the Netherlands. After the accession of William and Mary, his Whig connection and his own ability gained him a commission in a Scottish regiment. In 1698, as a captain in the forces of William Paterson's "Company of Scotland Trading to Africa and the Indies," he went out to Darien (Central America) and was made a member of the colonial council. He came to disapprove of Paterson and his ill-calculated venture, however, and when the colonists fled to New York in 1699, he accompanied them and remained in that province.

His handsome, commanding presence, his wide experience, and his natural gifts soon commended him to the Scots of his own generation and clannish spirit. Robert Livingston [q.v.] of Albany, secretary of Indian affairs, whose daughter Margaret Vetch married on Dec. 20, 1700, was a son of the Rev. John Livingston who had persuaded William Veitch to abandon the study of medicine for the Presbyterian ministry. Vetch was soon deep in the Albany Indian trade, which by extension included illegal trade overland with the French at Montreal. About 1702 he moved to Boston, where he engaged in maritime commerce with Acadia and Canada. This commerce was contrary to the British trade laws, and was resented by the colonists, especially settlers on the border, who were suffering from French and Indian attacks. In 1701 Vetch's sloop *Mary* was condemned for illicit trading, but it was subsequently restored to him. In 1705 Gov. Joseph Dudley [*q.v.*], whose confidence he had gained, sent him with others to Quebec to negotiate a truce with the Governor of Canada and arrange for an exchange of prisoners, but the terms proposed by the Canadian authorities were not accepted by Massachusetts. Vetch, however, who claimed that certain concessions had been granted him as a reward for his services, improved the opportunity to trade profitably with the French and Indians of Acadia, to whom he furnished arms and ammunition. Public opinion in Massachusetts became aroused, and in 1706 Vetch with five others was tried by the General Court and fined. The next year he carried his case to England, where the Privy Council, ruling that the General Court of Massachusetts, being a legislative body, had no power to try cases and impose sentences, ordered a retrial by the Suffolk County Court. Vetch, safe in England, escaped retrial, and only one of the other defendants was convicted.

Meanwhile, Vetch had won favor and made his most distinctive contribution to colonial history by proposing a plan for conquering the French in America which included the Albany scheme of 1690 and New England's designs on Acadia and Newfoundland ("Canada Survey'd," *Calendar of State Papers, Colonial Series, America and West Indies, 1708–09*, pp. 41–51). His proposals for an attack on Montreal by way of Lake Champlain and a complete investment of Quebec by land and sea were well calculated to succeed. Thereafter Acadia, Newfoundland, and even the Spanish colonies could be attended to. An acquiescent, optimistic Whig ministry in March 1709 dispatched Vetch to carry out the enterprise, empowering him to enlist colonial assistance from Pennsylvania northward. A fleet, bearing a commander-in-chief, munitions, and five regiments, was to follow in April. Col. Francis Nicholson [*q.v.*] accompanied Vetch as a volunteer.

Bad weather delayed their arrival at Boston until Apr. 30, but colonial enthusiasm vied with Vetch's impatient energy, and although Quaker Pennsylvania and New Jersey failed him, within two months he had three well-trained New England regiments and their transports waiting at Boston, while the land expedition commanded by Nicholson was ready with its boats at Wood Creek on Lake Champlain. Vetch had engineered the best cooperative colonial efforts up to that time, only to have it wasted when his expected British auxiliary was diverted to Portugal. Even then the colonial leaders decided to attack Port Royal, in Acadia, but the naval commanders at the northern ports refused to assist and the scheme was dropped. Deeply discouraged, the colonies sent Nicholson, Col. Peter Schuyler [*q.v.*], and five Iroquois chiefs to implore Queen Anne for remuneration and for aid the next year. With British aid arriving late in 1710, the easy conquest of Port Royal and Acadia (called thereafter Annapolis Royal and Nova Scotia) was effected and Vetch, although Nicholson had commanded, received the promised military governorship. In 1711, at the insistence of Massachusetts, he took part in the expedition against Canada which a Tory ministry entrusted to Rear Admiral Sir Hovenden Walker and General "Jack" Hill. He generously did his best to help by piloting and advice, but Walker's ludicrous fears and ineptitude brought the expedition to disastrous failure at the mouth of the St. Lawrence.

Vetch's subsequent career was unhappy. Completely ignored in England, he spent his own and his friends' resources in maintaining Annapolis for the British Crown. His former protégé, Nicholson, who secured the civil governorship of Nova Scotia, harried him unmercifully at Annapolis and Boston and would have utterly ruined him but for the death of Queen Anne and the return of the Whigs to power. Vetch fled to England in 1714, and secured the civil governorship in January 1715, only to lose it in 1717 while still engaged in a vain effort to clear up his affairs. Tempted by several unfulfilled ministerial promises of remunerative employment, he remained in England and died in 1732 a prisoner in king's bench for debt.

[*Sloane MS. 3607* (letter-book, 1711–13), British Museum; MSS. of the Canada Expedition, Huntington Lib., San Marino, Cal.; papers in the possession of Mrs. R. W. Kelley, Mrs. J. L. Redmond, and J. R. Speyers, Esq., of New York, and of Dr. J. C. Webster, Shediac, N. B.; H. L. Osgood, *The Am. Colonies in the Eighteenth Century* (1924), vols. I, II; *Hist. of the State of N. Y.* (1933), ed. by A. C. Flick, vol. II; *Calendar of State Papers, Colonial Ser., America and West Indies, 1706–15* (6 vols., 1916–28); Thomas M'Crie, *Memoirs of Mr. William Veitch and George Brysson* (1825); Everett Kimball, *The Public Life of Joseph Dudley* (1911); George Patterson, "Hon. Samuel Vetch, First English Governor of Nova Scotia," *Nova Scotia Hist. Soc. Coll.*, vol. IV (1885); J. C. Webster, *Samuel Vetch* (privately printed, Shediac, N. B., 1929); sketch by R. H. Vetch, in *Dict. Nat. Biog.*; E. B. O'Callaghan, *Docs. Rel. to the Col. Hist. of ... N. Y.*, vols. IV, IX (1854–55). Portraits of

Vetch, his wife and daughter, are in the possession of Mrs. R. W. Kelley and J. R. Speyers.]   J. B. B.

VETHAKE, HENRY (1792–Dec. 16, 1866), teacher, economist, was born in Essequibo County, British Guiana, and was brought to the United States by his parents at the age of four. Graduating at Columbia College in 1808, he subsequently taught mathematics and geography there; he also studied law. In 1813 he became professor of mathematics and natural philosophy at Queen's College (now Rutgers University). He moved rapidly from one institution to another, going to the College of New Jersey in 1817, to Dickinson College in 1821, and returning to the College of New Jersey in 1829 as professor of natural philosophy. In 1832 he became professor in the University of the City of New York, which he left in about three years to become president—for eighteen months—of Washington College, Lexington, Va. Here he also occupied the chair of intellectual and moral philosophy. His longest period of academic service was at the University of Pennsylvania, where he was professor of mathematics and philosophy (1836–55) and of philosophy (1855–59), vice-provost (1845–55), and provost (1855–59). He was not successful in administrative work. In 1859 he was appointed professor of mathematics in the Polytechnic College, Philadelphia, where he remained until his death. On Apr. 15, 1831, he was elected a member of the American Philosophical Society.

Vethake's political economy was thoroughly orthodox. Despite his hopeful American environment, where rapid progress was being made in all departments of economic life, and notwithstanding his residence in Philadelphia, which was the home of the budding nationalist school, he was obsessed with the notion of diminishing returns. He was opposed to practically every form of governmental interference in economic life, and constantly betrayed the current European fear that the capitalist would be inconvenienced for humanitarian objects. He affords a good illustration of the transfer of classical economic inhibitions to the new continent. His *Introductory Lecture on Political Economy* (1831), devoted mainly to a defense of the science, then unfamiliar in this country, may be read today with profit. One of the earliest in a long line of scholars proficient in the mathematical and natural sciences who expounded political economy, he appreciated the limitations and at the same time the difficulties of social studies. By the time he published *The Principles of Political Economy* (1838, 1844), he had broadened his concept of wealth to include services, and

that of capital to embrace knowledge and skills, but this natural introduction to a liberal treatment of the whole subject was denied in the subsequent chapters. His acceptance of the wage-fund theory, *i.e.*, that wages were paid out of a predetermined allocation by capitalist employers, led him to declare, in the way so familiar in British economic writing of the period, that "no advantage can be derived, by the receivers of wages, from the trades' unions" (p. 327), and that: "Although . . . the action of the trades' unions can hardly be stigmatized as of a *dishonest* character, . . . such action is, nevertheless, a violation to a certain extent of the rights of property. And if these rights may be once violated by the trades' unions, they may be again and again violated by them; and the apprehension of this taking place would constitute a check to the accumulation of capital with its usual rapidity; inducing, in consequence, a fall of wages below the usual rate" (p. 330). He was opposed to the statutory shortening of hours for all but children, and held that the leisure time provided the worker might tend to "deteriorate instead of improving his condition, by being spent . . . in dissipation and vice . . ." (p. 335). He refused to condemn the production of commodities by convicts, was wary of even private charity, and could tolerate public works to relieve the unemployed only if wages on them were below the going rate. However, he came close to approving the absorption of economic rent in taxes. He edited, and published in 1840, J. R. McCulloch's *A Dictionary, Practical, Theoretical, and Historical, of Commerce and Commercial Navigation*, with additional articles, mostly embracing American material, and was the editor, and in large part the author, of *Encyclopædia Americana, Supplementary Volume* (1848); this last named, while in the main prepared from secondary sources, showed his wide range of knowledge and ability to cull essential data. He contributed to a number of periodicals, writing always with great taste and clarity. He was married in 1836.

[S. A. Allibone, *A Critical Dict. of English Lit.*, vol. III (1871); J. L. Chamberlain, *Universities and Their Sons: Univ. of Pa.*, vol. I (1901); H. M. Lippincott, *The Univ. of Pa.* (1919); *Washington and Lee Univ. . . . Hist. Papers*, no. 6 (1904); *Pub. Ledger* (Phila.), Dec. 18, 1866.]   B. M.

VEZIN, HERMANN (Mar. 2, 1829–June 12, 1910), actor, was born in Philadelphia, Pa., the son of Emilie (Kalinsky) and Charles Henri Vezin, a merchant of French ancestry. He was graduated from the University of Pennsylvania in 1847 with the degree of A.B., and in 1850 received the degree of M.A. In the same year he went to England, bent upon becoming an actor in spite of the traditional parental opposition, and made his first appearance in that country at the Theatre Royal in York. After various provincial engagements, during which he rose from the playing of minor rôles to the acting of such leading characters as Richelieu, Sir Edward Mortimer, Claude Melnotte, and Young Norval, he made his London début in 1852. Except for a brief professional tour of the United States in 1857–58, he remained on the British stage for the rest of his long life, sometimes in support of stars, sometimes at the head of his own companies, and sometimes in the direction of theatres. He acted with Fechter, Samuel Phelps, Henry Irving, and in 1878 played Dr. Primrose in support of Ellen Terry in W. G. Wills's successful play, *Olivia,* dramatized from *The Vicar of Wakefield.* In 1863 he married Jane Elizabeth Thompson, who as Mrs. Charles Young had made a reputation as an actress both in Australia and in England, and he acted in many plays with her between their marriage and her death in 1902. In 1889 he was called upon by Irving to appear as Macbeth at the Lyceum Theatre in his stead in an emergency, receiving high praise from him and substantial acknowledgment in the form of a diamond ring and a check for £120.

Not imposing in stature, Vezin was described by Sir J. Forbes-Robertson as a "bright and dapper little man, then (1874) at the height of his popularity," and as "learned and dictatorial on the art of acting" (*A Player, post,* pp. 226 and 116). He was scholarly and intellectual in his impersonations rather than thrilling and inspiring, and had a somewhat hard and formal delivery. Yet so excellent an authority as Henry Morley declares in his *Journal of a London Playgoer* (1866, p. 326) that he was "a quietly good actor, who can rightly speak blank verse and give true but enforced expression to a poet's thought." During his long career he acted many hundred characters in every type of play, among the most important being Sir Giles Overreach in *A New Way to Pay Old Debts,* Hamlet, Ford in *The Merry Wives of Windsor* (with Phelps as Falstaff), Jaques in *As You Like It* (with Mr. and Mrs. Kendal), Dan'l Druce, James Harebell in *The Man o'Airlie,* and Lesurques and Dubosc in *The Courier of Lyons.* His appearances on the stage during his later years were only occasional, his time being occupied in giving lessons to stage aspirants, and in appearing at recitals and readings. His last acting was as Old Rowley in Sir Herbert Tree's production of *The School for Scandal* at His Majesty's Theatre in April 1909. He had been active on

the British stage for nearly sixty years, and had been a resident of London, where he died, for the greater part of that period. He had a son who also became an actor.

[C. E. Pascoe, *The Dramatic List* (1879); Dutton Cook, *Nights at the Play* (2 vols., 1883); W. M. Phelps and John Forbes-Robertson, *The Life and Life-Work of Samuel Phelps* (1886); H. B. Baker, *The London Stage . . . from 1576 to 1888* (2 vols., 1889); Clement Scott and Cecil Howard, *The Life and Reminiscences of E. L. Blanchard* (2 vols., 1891); Erskine Reid and Herbert Compton, *The Dramatic Peerage* (1892); John Hollingshead, *Gaiety Chronicles* (1898); Bampton Hunt, ed., *The Green Room Book* (1906); Johnston Forbes-Robertson, *A Player under Three Reigns* (1925); *Stage* (London), June 16, 1910; *Athenaeum* (London), June 18, 1910; *N. Y. Dramatic Mirror,* Jan. 1, June 18, 1910; obituary in *Times* (London), June 14, 1910.]   E. F. E.

VIBBARD, CHAUNCEY (Nov. 11, 1811– June 5, 1891), railroad executive, congressman, capitalist, was born in Galway, N. Y. His father, Timothy Vibbard, Jr., was a descendant of a French family of the island of Jersey; his mother, Abigail (Nash), was of pioneer English stock. Chauncey attended the common schools of Galway and Mott's Academy for Boys in Albany, completing his course at fifteen. He became a clerk in a wholesale grocery store in Albany, and later clerk in a wholesale dry-goods house in New York City, then for some two years was a book-keeper in Montgomery, Ala. Late in 1836 he returned to his native state and was appointed chief clerk of the Utica & Schenectady Railroad, opened to traffic in that year. Here at last was work to his taste. He quickly mastered a maze of details, and made himself so necessary to the company that by 1849 he was general superintendent of the road; he had also become a stockholder.

An able organizer with considerable vision, Vibbard drew up with his own hand the first railroad time-table followed in the state and pledged his word to the public that, barring extraordinary difficulties, the trains should run as scheduled—an almost unheard-of thing at that time. He increased the comfort of passenger travel, and sought every appliance that would make for speed, safety, and efficiency. He saw that railroad conditions between Buffalo and Albany were essentially absurd: no less than ten little railroads functioned over portions of the distance; delays, inconvenience, and unnecessary costs were inevitable. He urged over a long period that these roads be consolidated, and at length the idea was taken up by Erastus Corning [*q.v.*], president of the Utica & Schenectady, with the result that in 1853 all the roads were welded into one line known as the New York Central, with a capital of $23,085,600. From

1853 to 1865 Vibbard was general superintendent of the consolidated line; he reorganized the system and made it a smoothly working machine. Meanwhile, by wise investments, he built up a considerable private fortune. He was for several years the principal owner of a large liquor concern in New York (dealing mostly with the South), which went out of business because of the Civil War.

In 1861 he was sent as a Democrat to Congress. In 1862 he was appointed director and superintendent of military railroads. He refused a renomination to Congress, although he could easily have been reëlected. In 1864 he supported McClellan's candidacy for the Presidency. In 1865 he resigned his position with the New York Central to devote his time to private business interests, though he continued as a large holder of railroad stocks. He was a partner in Vibbard & Foote, extensive dealers in railroad supplies, and was one of the owners of the Day Line of steamboats between New York and Albany. He served three years as president of the Family Fund Insurance Company, was one of the original stockholders in New York's first elevated railway, and was a director of the Central Branch Union Pacific Railroad. In his later years he was interested in developing railways in the southern United States and in Central and South America. His wife, Mary A. (Vedder) of Milton, N. Y., died in 1884, and Vibbard himself died in Macon, Ga., in 1891, leaving a daughter and two sons.

[Obituaries in *World* (N. Y.), *N. Y. Herald, N. Y. Times,* June 6, 1891; *N. Y. Tribune,* June 7, 1891; F. W. Stevens, *The Beginnings of the New York Central Railroad* (1926); annual reports of the N. Y. Central R.R., 1854–65; *Biog. Dir. Am. Cong.* (1928).]

A. F. H.

VICK, JAMES (Nov. 23, 1818–May 16, 1882), seedsman, florist, and publisher, was born at Chichester, near Portsmouth, England, son of James and Elizabeth (Prime) Vick. In his boyhood he was a friend of Charles Dickens and their friendship continued in after years. In 1833 he came to the United States with his parents, settling first in New York City. Here he learned the printer's trade and worked for a time on the *Knickerbocker Magazine.* His case in the composing room adjoined that of Horace Greeley, who remained his lifelong friend. In 1837 he removed to Rochester, N. Y., and worked as a compositor in several newspaper offices. During a printer's strike the leading journeymen started a paper called the *Workingman's Advocate,* which in a few months passed into the hands of Vick and one or two others, who soon sold it to Henry O'Reilly [*q.v.*]. About this time Vick published Frederick Douglass' paper, the *North Star.*

Being passionately fond of flowers, in his leisure time he cultivated a garden and developed a taste for agriculture and horticulture. In 1848 he began to import seeds from abroad. Over the signature of "Young Digger" he contributed articles to the *Genesee Farmer,* published in Rochester. These brought him into contact with the management of the paper and in 1850 he was made one of the editors, the others being Daniel Lee and Patrick Barry [*q.v.*]. After the death of Andrew J. Downing [*q.v.*], editor of the *Horticulturist,* Vick purchased that magazine from Luther Tucker [*q.v.*] and published it in Rochester from 1853 to 1855 with Barry as editor. From 1857 to 1862 he was editor of the *Rural New Yorker,* also published in Rochester. It was while connected with this journal that he began the seed business which was destined to bring him a world-wide reputation.

The seeds which he had imported from abroad he planted in a little garden on Union Street, and gradually increased his stock; later he had gardens elsewhere. Soon he was sending out so many seeds that he had to begin to charge for them. They were sent by mail in answer to mail orders accompanied by cash. By 1862 his business had so increased that for the remainder of his life he gave it his whole attention. He employed a force of 150, and often the firm received 3,000 letters a day; in some seasons he spent $30,000 for postage. The circulation of his *Floral Guide,* or annual catalogue, reached 200,000 copies. In 1878 he founded *Vick's Monthly Magazine,* later known as *Vick's Illustrated Monthly Magazine* and under other titles, which he himself edited.

With the establishment of his business, seeds were placed within easy reach and a new era in the culture of flowers began in the United States. For about twenty years his name was a household word and he was more widely known than any other seed merchant at home or abroad. In various ways he exercised great influence on the horticulture of the country. He made some notable advances in the cross breeding of garden flowers, among his creations being the white double phlox, fringed petunia, white gladiolus, "the sunrise" amaranthus, and the Japan cockscomb. Vick's gardens in the blooming season were a great attraction to visitors and did much to beautify Rochester. His name is commemorated there in Vick Park, and Portsmouth Terrace was named after his birthplace. In all his dealings he maintained the highest character for honesty, integrity, and liberality, and he was always ready to help in any good work. He served as secretary of the American Pomological Society (1862–64), and was a corresponding member of the Royal Horticultural Society. For twenty-five years he was superintendent of the Sunday school connected with the First Methodist Episcopal Church. He died of pneumonia and was buried in Mount Hope Cemetery, Rochester. On July 5, 1842, he married Mary Elizabeth, daughter of John and Susan Seelye, of Rochester, who with four sons and three daughters survived him.

[*Rochester Democrat and Chronicle* and *Rochester Morning Herald*, May 17, 1882; *Vick's Monthly Magazine*, June 1882; *Rural New Yorker*, May 27, 1882; *Thirteenth Ann. Report of the Secretary of the State Hort. Soc. of Mich.* (1884); *Proc. Western N. Y. Horticultural Soc.*, 1883; J. M. Parker, *Rochester: A Story Historical* (1884); *Rochester Hist. Soc. Pubs.*, vol. VI (1927); J. F. Hart, *The Industries of the City of Rochester* (1888).]   C. R. B.

VICTOR, FRANCES FULLER (May 23, 1826–Nov. 14, 1902), author, historian, was born in Rome Township, Oneida County, N. Y., of New England stock, the eldest of the five daughters of Lucy (Williams) Fuller and her husband, whose name is said to have been Adonijah. When she was thirteen years old her family moved to Ohio. Frances and her sister Metta Victoria wrote verse for newspapers while still in their teens and, having attended a girls' school at Wooster, went to New York to seek literary careers. Friends of Alice and Phoebe Cary, they belonged to the coterie that buzzed around that impresario of "female poets," Rufus Wilmot Griswold [*q.v.*]. He is said to have edited their joint volume, *Poems of Sentiment and Imagination, with Dramatic and Descriptive Pieces* (1851). Frances returned home to assist her sick parents, is said to have married a Jackson Barritt of Pontiac, Mich., in 1853, and forgot her literary aspirations. In 1862 she married a naval engineer, Henry Clay Victor, whose brother, Orville James Victor [*q.v.*], had married Metta Victoria. The next year her husband was ordered to duty at San Francisco, and she followed him. Stimulated by a new environment and by the necessity, in that greenback era, of supplementing her husband's salary, she began again to write and contributed to various San Francisco and Sacramento newspapers. In 1865 the Victors moved to Oregon. Mrs. Victor conceived a strong enthusiasm for the Pacific Northwest and, by systematic travel and study, collection of documentary material, and interviews with old inhabitants, became the most competent authority on the region and its history. Her first books on it were *The River of the West* (1870) and *All Over Oregon and Washington* (1872). The first is chiefly an account, largely autobi-

ographical, of Joseph L. Meek, the second a handbook of the region. After her husband perished in the wreck of the *Pacific*, Nov. 4, 1875, Mrs. Victor lived by her writing. She was a member for eleven years of Hubert Howe Bancroft's staff and wrote part of the *History of the Northwest Coast* (2 vols., 1884) and the whole of the *History of Oregon* (2 vols., 1886–88), the *History of Washington, Idaho, and Montana* (1890), the *History of Nevada, Colorado, and Wyoming* (1890), and volumes VI and VII of the *History of California* (1890), besides contributing biographical sketches to other portions of the work. She had a pleasing style, strove for accuracy and fairness, and usually attained them. Her historical work is still regarded with respect. After her work with Bancroft was completed she was for a time in narrow circumstances and sold toilet articles from door to door in Salem, Ore. Later a small pension and her earnings kept her in modest comfort. Among her other separate publications are: *The New Penelope* (1877), a volume of short stories and verse; *Atlantis Arisen: or, Talks of a Tourist about Oregon and Washington* (1891); *The Early Indian Wars of Oregon* (1894); and *Poems* (1900). She was able to work cheerfully to the last. She died unexpectedly in a Portland boarding house in her seventy-sixth year.

[H. H. Bancroft, *Literary Industries* (1890); Alfred Powers, *Hist. of Oregon Lit.* (1935); Joseph Gaston, *The Centennial Hist. of Ore.* (4 vols., 1912); W. A. Morris, "The Origin and Authorship of the Bancroft Pacific States Pubs.," *Quart. Ore. Hist. Soc.*, Dec. 1903; *Morning Oregonian* (Portland), Nov. 15, 1902 (obituary), Nov. 16 (editorial and article).] G. H. G.

VICTOR, ORVILLE JAMES (Oct. 23, 1827–Mar. 14, 1910), author, publisher, was born at Sandusky, Ohio, of German and English stock, the son, it is said, of Henry and Gertrude (Nash) Victor. After completing a four-year course in the Norwalk Academy, he read law in the office of Charles B. Squire of Sandusky, contributed verse and prose to several magazines, and in 1852 became assistant editor, under Henry David Cooke [*q.v.*], of the *Daily Register*. In July 1856 he married Metta Victoria Fuller (Mar. 2, 1831–June 26, 1885), who was at that time a more important literary personage than he was.

From his marriage almost to the close of his long life Victor was associated with various New York publishing houses that specialized in the production of cheap, popular books and magazines. For a number of years he was the chief editor of Erastus F. Beadle's enterprises. He was the editor, at various times, of such magazines as the *Cosmopolitan Art Journal*, the *United States Journal, Beadle's Magazine of To-day*, the

Western World, the *Saturday Journal,* and the *Banner Weekly.* His own works include: *The History, Civil, Political, and Military, of the Southern Rebellion* . . . (4 vols., 1861–68); issued originally in monthly parts; *The American Rebellion: Some Facts and Reflections for the Consideration of the English People* (London, 1861); *Incidents and Anecdotes of the War* (1862); *History of American Conspiracies* (1863); and paper-backed biographies of Winfield Scott, Anthony Wayne, John Paul Jones, Ethan Allen, Israel Putnam, Giuseppe Garibaldi, and Abraham Lincoln. These biographies were part of the Dime Biographical Library, one of the many "Libraries" that Victor edited. His work, in general, is that of a competent, industrious, and undistinguished publisher's drudge.

In 1860, however, he made history and conferred a memorable boon on his compatriots by inventing the American dime novel. He himself signed none of the hundreds of such novels published by the firms of Beadle & Company and Beadle & Adams, but he first conceived the idea, worked out the details, and taught a corps of writers to produce the kind of story he wanted. Among the authors that he engaged and trained were Augustine Joseph Hickey Duganne [*q.v.*], Mary A. Denison, Edward Sylvester Ellis [*q.v.*], Ann Sophia Stephens [*q.v.*], and his own wife. She produced at least one masterpiece of the kind, *Maum Guinea and Her Plantation Children,* published during the early part of the Civil War. The Beadle dime novels were simple, brisk, wholesome stories of adventure, usually in a Western or Southwestern setting, and were sold by the million to Northern soldiers. Their success provoked competition, and competition brought with it sensationalism. Victor lived to see the *genre* that he had devised fall into disrepute and dwindle to insignificance. His home for many years was at Hohokus, N. J., where, during his wife's lifetime, he liked to entertain his literary friends. He died there in his eighty-third year.

[*Who's Who in America,* 1901–02; C. M. Harvey, "The Dime Novel in Am. Life," *Atlantic Monthly,* July 1907; *N. Y. Tribune,* Mar. 17, 1910; E. L. Pearson, *Dime Novels* (1929).]   G. H. G.

VIEL, FRANÇOIS ÉTIENNE BERNARD ALEXANDRE (Oct. 31, 1736–Dec. 16, 1821), priest and Latin scholar, was born in New Orleans, La. His father, Dr. Bernard Alexandre Viel, a native of France, emigrated to Louisiana and was among the first surgeons to practise in the colony. His mother was Marie Macarthy, part Irish and part Creole. In 1747 Dr. Viel took his eleven-year-old son to France and placed him in the Royal Academy of Juilly conducted by the Oratorian brotherhood. He proved a splendid student and soon led his classes. For nine years he never left the institution even for holidays. Exposed to such continuous religious influence it was almost inevitable that, after his graduation, he should join the Oratorians. He was the first native-born Louisianian to take holy orders. He was sent as an instructor to Soissons, then to Mans, and finally in 1760 returned to his alma mater, the Academy of Juilly, where he taught the humanities and rhetoric until in 1776 he was appointed *grand préfct* of the college. When the French Revolution destroyed all the Oratorian institutions of learning and scattered the order in 1792, Abbé Viel returned to Louisiana and became the parish priest of the Attakapas, where for twenty years he served his simple agricultural flock, earning their love and affection. In 1812 he was recalled to France to aid in the reestablishment of his order, and for five years taught at Juilly until he suffered a slight stroke. When he recovered he was permitted to devote the rest of his life to the useless but learned avocation to which he was fanatically attached—the translation into Latin verse of the works of great French authors. He was a Latin scholar of the utmost distinction.

When he fled from Paris in 1792 he left with a friend a manuscript he had just completed, a rhymed version in Latin of Fénelon's *Télémaque* (1797). Six of his former pupils discovered it and, to do him honor, paid for its publication in 1808. Four years later when Viel returned to Paris he corrected this edition and in 1814 brought out a second one. He called it *Telemachiada* and dedicated it to his six ex-students who had made the first edition possible. Altogether he did five volumes of translations of the works of various authors, one of which, *Le Voyage de la Grande Chartreuse* (1782), ran into seven editions. His rendering of these French masterpieces into Latin verse was so beautiful in its accuracy and richness that the poet Barthélemy, who had been his pupil, wrote a poem in which he spoke of

"Viel qui de Fénelon virgilisa la prose."

The abbé died on Dec. 16, 1821, at the College of Juilly, where he had spent the best part of his life, first in acquiring and then in disseminating learning.

[E. L. Tinker, *Les Écrits de Langue Française au XIXe Siècle* (1932); Alfred Mercier, in *Comptes-Rendus de l'Athénée Louisianais,* July 1890; Gustave Devron, *Ibid.,* July 1899, with a portrait; Charles Hamel, *Histoire de l'Abbaye et du Collège de Juilly* (Paris, 1868); Charles Richomme, *Histoire de l'Université de Paris* (Paris, 1840); obituary in *Journal des Débats* (Paris), Dec. 20, 1821.]   E. L. T.

VIELE, AERNOUT CORNELISSEN
(1640–c. 1704), interpreter and negotiator with
the Indians, was born in New Amsterdam, probably the son of Cornelis Volkertszen and Maria
(du Trieux) Viele. His father was an emigrant
from Holland, an inn-keeper and trader, and apparently prosperous. The boy was baptized on
May 27, 1640. He was a resident of Albany as
early as 1659, and the year following he joined
in a petition to forbid white men trading within
the Indian country. He married Gerritje Gerritse Vermeulen, the step-daughter of Arent
Janse Timmerman, probably in 1663. Twelve
years later he was a recognized interpreter between the red men and the white, and this service he performed in 1682 at Albany at a conference between the Five Nations and commissioners from Maryland. At this period he had
acquired command of the Iroquois dialects, with
a degree of skill in the studied features of Indian
oratory. Public speaking among the Indians was
a formal art, which the envoys of the Canadian
governors, and some at least of the French missionaries, cultivated and which their rivals for
the affections of the Indians could not afford to
neglect. Viele had need of every resource when
as the deputy of Gov. Thomas Dongan [q.v.] he
harangued an Onondaga audience, in opposition
to Charles Le Moyne and the eloquent Jesuit,
Father Lamberville, and planted the arms of the
Duke of York in the Onondaga Castle. A few
years later he led a large party of men, advance
agents of New York trade, into the Ottawa country north of the Great Lakes. They were captured by the vigilant French, and he was taken
to Quebec, from which he returned home, escaping apparently, after an imprisonment of four
months.

From 1688 to 1690 he was living for considerable periods with the Onondaga, who were in
those years enjoying their ascendancy among
the Iroquois. While he was on one of these missions, it would seem, the Schenectady massacre
occurred. Five of his family, his eldest daughter,
her two children, a daughter-in-law, and a grandson, perished. His son, Aernout, was carried
away, but escaped after three years of captivity.
These events gave an added motive to his efforts
to protect the New York border. In 1691 he was
enrolled as a fusilier. He supported Lieut.-Gov.
Jacob Leisler [q.v.] in the civil strife that rent
the colony and was appointed resident general
agent by him. Governor Fletcher kept him employed at the Onondaga outpost, from which he
reported danger signals when Frontenac was
stirring. Governor Bellomont (see sketch of
Richard Coote, Earl of Bellomont) continued

the settled Indian policy after the peace between
France and England at Ryswick; and Viele, who
was then living on Long Island, was soon on
guard again at Onondaga Castle. His journal,
from Apr. 14 to May 7, 1699, gives the details of
his journey and transactions (*Documents, post*,
vol. IV, pp. 560–62).

A second trading adventure is recorded. For
two years he was journeying in the country of
the Shawnee to the southward of the province.
In regions nearer home he acquired property.
From Indians on the Hudson he received land in
the region soon to be comprised by Dutchess
County. Later, the Mohawk gave him title to a
tract on the river near Schenectady. He was
prominently connected with the Reformed Dutch
Church in Albany. After 1704 his name falls out
of the records, which seems a fair indication that
he was dead.

[*Documents Relative to the Colonial Hist. of . . . N.
Y.*, vols. III (1853), IV (1854), IX (1855), procured
and ed. by J. R. Brodhead and E. B. O'Callaghan;
Calendar of Hist. MSS. in the office of the Sec. of State,
vol. I (1865), ed. by E. B. O'Callaghan; *Minutes of the
Court of Albany, Rensselaerswyck, and Schenectady*,
vol. III (1932), trans. and ed. by A. J. F. van Laer;
Jonathan Pearson, *A Hist. of the Schenectady Patent*
(1883) and *Contributions for the Geneal. of the First
Settlers of Albany* (1872); *Viele Records* (1913) and
Sketches of . . . Knickerbacker-Viele (1916), ed. by
K. K. Viele.]　　　　　　　　　　　　　R. E. D.

VIELE, EGBERT LUDOVICUS (June 17,
1825–Apr. 22, 1902), engineer, was born at Waterford, N. Y., the son of John Ludovicus and
Kathlyne Knickerbacker Viele. The founder of
his family in America, Cornelis Volkertszen, father of Aernout Cornelissen Viele [q.v.], was a
tavern keeper in New Amsterdam as early as
1639. John Ludovicus Viele was a state senator,
a judge of the court of errors, and a regent of the
University of the State of New York. Egbert
attended the common schools of Lansingburg,
graduated with honors at the Albany Academy,
and began the study of law. In 1843, however,
he secured appointment to the United States Military Academy, where he graduated in 1847. He
was sent at once to join an infantry regiment
fighting in the Mexican War, and after the peace
he saw service on the southwestern frontier. On
June 3, 1850, he married Teresa Griffin, who
bore him eight children.

In 1853 he resigned his commission, returned
to New York, and opened an office as a civil engineer. From 1854 to 1856 he was employed by
the state of New Jersey, and in the latter year
became chief engineer of the projected Central
Park in New York City. He made preliminary
surveys and submitted a plan for the development of the park, but after a reorganization of

the park commission in the following year his design was superseded by that of Frederick Law Olmsted and Calvert Vaux [qq.v.], and his services were discontinued. In 1860 he was engineer of Prospect Park, Brooklyn.

While engineer of Central Park Viele began a study of the original topography of Manhattan Island, and later repeatedly called attention to the necessity for recognizing the natural drainage system of the island in planning streets and sewers. In 1865 he published a pamphlet, *The Topography and Hydrology of New York,* urging sanitation from the point of view of the engineer. He thus had a part in the movement which resulted in the Metropolitan Health Law of 1866. His *Topographical Atlas of the City of New York,* published by Julius Bien [q.v.] in 1874, "showing the original water courses and made land," was of much value to the erectors of large buildings.

Meanwhile, in the first year of the Civil War, Viele's *Hand-book for Active Service* (1861) was published in New York and also (in two parts) in Richmond, Va. Viele became a captain of engineers in the 7th New York Militia, served in the defenses of Washington, and on Aug. 17, 1861, was made a brigadier-general of volunteers. He was second in command of the Port Royal expedition, participated in the capture of Fort Pulaski and the taking of Norfolk, Va., was military governor of Norfolk from May to October 1862, and was then put in charge of the draft in northern Ohio. In 1863 he resigned and resumed his engineering practice in New York. About 1868 he promulgated a plan for the "Arcade" underground railway, a presage of the subways which came much later. He served as a commissioner of parks for New York City in 1883–84, and in 1885–87 as a Democratic representative in Congress. In that body he did much to further the building of the Harlem Ship Canal. He then returned to private life and to his practice. About 1895, while visiting England, he spoke before a committee of the House of Lords upon American municipal administration. As a member of the International Congress of History, he gave the closing address at The Hague Congress in 1898. He was an early member and a vice-president of the American Geographical Society, president of the Aztec Society, and a trustee of the Holland Society of New York. His first marriage was terminated by divorce in 1872 and shortly afterward he married Juliette H. Dana. Two sons and two daughters survived him; the elder son, Herman Knickerbacker Vielé, studied civil engineering with his father and later became an artist; the young-

er, Egbert Ludovicus, Jr., was taken by his mother to France and there attained distinction as a poet, under the name Francis Vielé-Griffin.

[Viele apparently used no accent in his signature; his son H. K. Vielé, in "Gen. Egbert L. Vielé," *N. Y. Geneal. and Biog. Record,* Jan. 1903, uses the accent and spells the middle name Lodovickus, while Viele's daughter, Kathlyne Knickerbacker Viele, in *Viele 1659–1909* (1909) and *Viele Records* (1913), uses the forms adopted in this sketch. See also *Who's Who in America,* 1901–02; G. W. Cullum, *Biog. Reg. Officers and Grads. U. S. Mil. Acad.* (3rd ed., 1891), vol. II; *Thirty-third Ann. Reunion Asso. Grads. U. S. Mil. Acad.* (1902); *Year Book of the Holland Soc. of N. Y.* (1903); *Biog. Dir. Am. Cong.* (1928); *Bull. Am. Geog. Soc.,* Apr. 1902; C. C. Cook, *A Description of the N. Y. Central Park* (1869); *Army and Navy Jour.,* Apr. 26, 1902; *N. Y. Tribune,* Apr. 23, 1902.]   A. F. H.

VIGNAUD, HENRY (Nov. 27, 1830–Sept. 16, 1922), journalist, diplomat, historian, christened Jean Hélidore, was born in New Orleans, La., the eldest of the six children of Jean Lucien and Clémence (Godefroy) Vignaud. His paternal grandparents, born in Provence, came with their parents to Louisiana in the eighteenth century. He was educated in the schools of New Orleans, in which, 1852–56, he was also a teacher. His career as a journalist commenced with articles for the newspapers of New Orleans; from 1857 to 1860 he edited a weekly paper at Thibodaux, La., *L'Union de LaFourche,* and in 1860–61 he was editor of a weekly review devoted to French culture, *La Renaissance Louisianaise.* He also tried his hand at drama and is said (Cordier, *post*) to have had two plays produced at the French theatre of New Orleans.

With the outbreak of the Civil War he became a captain in the 6th Louisiana Regiment but was made prisoner in 1862, when New Orleans was captured. Escaping, he reached Paris and never returned to the United States. In Paris he entered the service of the Confederate mission under John Slidell [q.v.]. His duties seem to have been chiefly journalistic and he wrote for the *Index,* the Confederate organ published in London, and for the *Mémorial Diplomatique,* a Paris weekly, winning the praise of Henry Hotze, in charge of Confederate propaganda (*Official Records of the Union and Confederate Navies, 2* ser. III, 1178). Of the latter paper he became the regular musical and dramatic critic, and also, 1867–75, the *administrateur.*

Vignaud's diplomatic career in the Confederate mission was brief, but in 1869 he was appointed to a secretaryship in the Roumanian legation at Paris, and in 1872 he served as translator for the United States in the presentation of the *Alabama* claims for the Geneva arbitration (F. W. Hackett, *Reminiscences of the Geneva Tribunal,* 1911, pp. 106, 125 n.). On Dec. 14, 1875, recommended by Elihu B. Washburne (E. B. Washburne, *Recollections of a Minister to France*, 1887, II, 324), he was appointed second secretary of the United States legation in Paris, and on Apr. 11, 1885, was promoted to be first secretary. For thirty-four years he was the indispensable member of the Paris mission, frequently acting as chargé d'affaires, and serving always with distinction. His dispatches, *e.g.*, those of October 1884, relating to the good offices of the United States in the Franco-Chinese War, display a very high degree of understanding and diplomatic skill. He enjoyed the complete confidence of his own as well as of the French government and was often called upon for special services, as, for example, to be umpire in the arbitration, 1905, of French claims against Haiti. On Mar. 31, 1909, at the age of seventy-eight, he resigned his position as secretary of the embassy, but was appointed honorary counselor. Public recognition of his long service came from the American colony in Paris and from the Department of State (*New York Herald*, Paris, May 9, 1909), from the French government, which promoted him to the rank of Grand Officier in the Legion of Honor, and from Tulane University, which conferred upon him the degree of LL.D.

Vignaud's distinction as a historian was achieved after the age of seventy. He had earlier worked at histories of America, which he left in manuscript as *"ouvrages sans valeur"* (Cordier, *post*), but his special interest in Columbus grew out of his close association with Henry Harrisse and with the Peruvian scholar Manuel Gonzalez de la Rosa, and the publications of the Columbian anniversary of 1892. Convinced by De la Rosa that the famous letter of Toscanelli of 1474 was not genuine, he presented a paper on the subject, as also did De la Rosa, at the Congress of Americanists of 1900 (*Congrès International des Américanistes, XIIe Session*, 1902, pp. 11–62). Two volumes followed: *La Lettre et la Carte de Toscanelli* (1901) and, somewhat revised and enlarged, *Toscanelli and Columbus* (1902), after which Vignaud brought out three volumes on Columbus and one on Amerigo Vespucci: *Études critiques sur la vie de Colomb avant ses découvertes* (1905); *Histoire critique de la grande entreprise de Christophe Colomb* (2 vols., 1911); and *Améric Vespuce, 1451–1512* (1917). At the age of ninety-one he summarized his views on Columbus in a small book, *Le vrai Christophe Colomb et la Légende* (1921).

Vignaud's conclusions respecting Columbus may be briefly stated as follows: Columbus was born in 1451, of humble origins; he did not go to

sea as a boy, but was a weaver, like his father; he did not go to Portugal until 1476, never made a voyage to Iceland, had no letter from Toscanelli suggesting that the Indies could be reached by the west, and did not set out in 1492 to find the Indies, but to discover islands and lands to the west, which in fact he found. These views, contradicting many points of the accepted Columbus tradition, aroused a controversy that is not yet ended. It is probably fair to say that, while his findings have deserved and received the most careful attention, they have not been generally accepted.

Vignaud also displayed a broad interest in the whole range of studies of aboriginal America and of the earliest European contacts with the new world. His address of Nov. 4, 1913, as president of the Société des Américanistes de Paris (*Journal . . . des Américanistes de Paris*, n.s. XI, 1 ff.) is a masterly analysis of the problems of this field of research, and his numerous contributions, for the most part published in the *Journal . . . des Américanistes* (n.s., vols. I–XIV, 1903–22), indicate the scope of his scholarship. His work was recognized by the award of numerous honors and prizes, and by election as a foreign corresponding member of the Institut de France.

Vignaud was married in 1879 to Louise Compte of Paris, who survived him a few years. They had no children, and made their home in Bagneux, a southern suburb of Paris, where their ancient and comfortable house was the scene of Vignaud's historical labors and of a hospitality freely extended, especially to American scholars. His library of many thousand books, pamphlets, and maps, is now the property of the University of Michigan. Among his papers was an unfinished history of cartography in approximately 650,000 words. He was of medium height and build, wiry and energetic. His kindly and keen features, with roughly trimmed beard, his animation, and his personal characteristics were French. He was perfectly bilingual, speaking and writing both French and English with distinction. He combined versatility of interest with powers of intense application and mastery of details, and possessed a boundless capacity for work.

[*Who's Who in America*, 1922–23; short sketches of Vignaud by Henri Cordier, one of his most intimate friends, in *Jour. . . . des Américanistes de Paris*, n.s. XV (1923), 1–17, with excellent portrait, geneal. table, and bibliog.; by E. A. Parsons, *La. Hist. Quart.*, Jan. 1922; and by Stoddard Dewey, in *Ex Libris* (Am. Lib. in Paris), June 1924, with photographs of Vignaud in his library and in his garden; *Le Mémorial Diplomatique* (Paris), 1863–75, containing many signed articles by Vignaud and his musical and dramatic criticisms; Vignaud's correspondence in U. S. Dept. of State, Diplomatic Archives, Despatches, France, 1875–1909; review of Vignaud's historical work by Henri Froidevaux in *France-Amérique*, Oct. 1921; dates of appointments from Dept. of State; obituary in *N. Y. Times*, Sept. 19, 1922, and editorial, Sept. 20; personal recollections of conversations and visits, 1907–14.]   W. G. Le—d.

VIGO, JOSEPH MARIA FRANCESCO (Dec. 3, 1747–Mar. 22, 1836), soldier, merchant, was born in Mondovì, Piedmont, now a part of Italy, the son of Matheo and Maria Magdalena (Iugalibus) Vigo. While a youthful member of a Spanish regiment, he was sent to New Orleans and there became interested in the fur trade. He soon received his discharge, became a very successful trader, and gained at the same time great influence with the French settlers and with the Indians. In 1772 he had reached out as far as the new post at St. Louis, where he established his headquarters and ultimately formed a secret partnership with Fernando de Leyba, the Spanish lieutenant governor at St. Louis.

When George Rogers Clark [*q.v.*] made an expedition, on behalf of Virginia, for the protection of the early American settlers in the northwest country, Vigo became interested in the American cause. Twice he journeyed to Kaskaskia from St. Louis to give assistance to Clark. The last time, on Jan. 29, 1779, was after his return from Vincennes, where he had gone at the instance of Clark to aid the American commandant. Imprisoned by the British, he was later released as a Spanish citizen, and he very promptly carried information and financial aid to Clark. There at Kaskaskia was inaugurated that memorable campaign which ended the British influence in the northwest territory and fixed the claims of the Americans to the northwest country. Clark was sadly in need of assistance, having only Virginia colonial money that was of no value with the French inhabitants. Francis Vigo, as he was usually called in America, threw his fortune into the balance and rendered assistance so valuable that he shares with Clark the responsibility for this conquest. When Virginia later ceded all this territory to the confederation of American states, she made the condition that the United States should assume and pay all expenses and indebtedness incurred by her in maintaining defense of the same; but Vigo was not repaid in his lifetime. He gave freely of his time, influence, and fortune, to the American cause, but he spent his declining years in comparative want. When an old man he sold his family silver to buy food. Nearly one hundred years passed before the federal Supreme Court ordered his claims to be paid, and his heirs received about $50,000.

Vigo removed from St. Louis to Vincennes before 1783 and soon became a naturalized citizen of the United States. After the Revolution he rendered conspicuous service, both civil and military. He was executor in the will of Governor De Leyba, dated at St. Louis on June 10, 1780. Sometime before 1783 he married Elizabeth Shannon, the daughter of Clark's quartermaster. She died on Mar. 20, 1818, leaving no descendants. Vigo lived during his last years on a farm near Vincennes, but spent much of his time at the home of his old friend William Henry Harrison [*q.v.*]. For many years he was a practising member of the Roman Catholic Church but in his later days he fell away from that faith. He died without receiving the last rites of the Church and was buried in the Protestant Cemetery. In the city of Vincennes, where he died and was buried, a street bears his name. There are a county and township in Indiana named for him, and great tribute was paid to him at the dedication of the memorial to George Rogers Clark.

[Bruno Roselli, *Vigo: A Forgotten Builder of the American Republic* (1933); J. J. Thompson, "Penalties of Patriotism, Vigo," in *Jour. of the Ill. State Hist. Soc.*, Jan. 1917; Dorothy Riker, "Francis Vigo," in *Ind. Mag. of Hist.*, Mar. 1930; "Governors Messages and Letters. Messages and Letters of Wm. H. Harrison," *Ind. Hist. Coll.* (1922), vol. I, ed. by Logan Esarey; B. J. Griswold, *Fort Wayne* (1927); W. H. English, *Conquest of the Country Northwest of the River Ohio* (2 vols., 1896); C. C. Baldwin, "A Centennial Law Suit," in *Western Reserve and Northern Hist. Soc., Tract 35*, Dec. 1876; 91 *U. S. Reports*, 326; *House Reports 13, 25 Cong., 3 Sess.* (1838); *House Report 525, 27 Cong., 2 Sess.* (1842); *House Report 216, 30 Cong., 1 Sess.* (1848); Voorhis Memorial Coll., George Rogers Clark Papers, Mo. Hist. Soc. Lib. Mo.; Burton Coll. Public Lib., Detroit, Mich.; Draper Coll., Wis. State Hist. Soc. Lib., Madison, Wis.; Vigo Papers, D. A. R. Chapter, Vincennes. For law suit of heir see sketch of John Law.]   S. M. D.

VILAS, WILLIAM FREEMAN (July 9, 1840–Aug. 27, 1908), lawyer, cabinet member, senator from Wisconsin, was the son of Judge Levi Baker Vilas and Esther Green (Smilie) Vilas, and a descendant of Peter Vilas (1704–1756), an emigrant from England. Brought by his parents from his birthplace, Chelsea, Orange County, Vt., to Madison, Wis., in 1851, he was graduated at the University of Wisconsin in 1858, and at the Law School of the University of Albany (N. Y.), in 1860. He was admitted to the bar in Madison in 1860, but before he became heavily involved in legal practice he went to war with the 23rd Wisconsin volunteer regiment, rising to the rank of lieutenant-colonel. Mustered out, he returned to Madison and gained immediate distinction in his profession. He served the state, 1875–78, as reviser of statutes (*Revised Statutes of the State of Wisconsin*, 1878) and assisted in reëditing the first twenty volumes of *Wisconsin Reports* (published 1875–76). He became a professor of law (1868–85, 1889–92) and a regent (1881–85, 1898–1905) of the University of Wisconsin, a worker on many non-political bodies and commissions, and in 1885 a member of the Wisconsin legislature.

At the home-coming banquet for General Grant given by the Society of the Army of the Tennessee in the old Palmer House in Chicago, Nov. 13, 1879, Vilas made the successful speech of an evening too full of oratory (*Milwaukee Sentinel*, Nov. 14, 1879). He was established by this as the most prominent Democratic orator in Wisconsin, and he contested thereafter with General Edward S. Bragg [*q.v.*] for the reality of party leadership. In 1884 he was permanent chairman of the convention that nominated Cleveland for the presidency, and served as chairman of the committee that notified the nominee. Cleveland appointed him postmaster-general and relied upon him as a counselor and friend. In 1887 the President and his young wife were entertained at the handsome Vilas mansion in Madison (*Wisconsin State Journal*, Oct. 7, 1887; *New York Herald*, Oct. 8, 1887). As postmaster-general (Mar. 6, 1885–Jan. 16, 1888), Vilas was useful because of an intimate knowledge of the West and an unusual degree of executive ability; but he issued a circular warning postal employees against "offensive partisanship" that evoked a scolding from civil service reformers (*Wisconsin Magazine of History*, Sept. 1932, p. 5). In 1888, when L. Q. C. Lamar [*q.v.*] was elevated to the Supreme Court, Vilas was shifted to the Department of the Interior. Here his special abilities had even greater value since the business of the department was largely in the West and since the arbitrary accumulation of unrelated bureaus in the department gave skill in administration a chance to show itself He knew, perhaps, too much for his comfort. Part of his fortune was based upon speculations in land and lumber, and these aroused intermittent attacks from his political opponents in Wisconsin (*Wisconsin State Journal*, Jan. 18, 1893; *Milwaukee Sentinel*, Oct. 22, 1894). Upon the termination of the Democratic administration in 1889 he returned to Madison. In 1891 he was elected by the Democratic legislature to succeed John C. Spooner [*q.v.*] in the United States Senate. He was defeated by Spooner six years later and retired to private life. A trusted friend of Cleveland, Vilas adhered to the gold standard, fought Bryan in the convention at Chicago, and was chairman of the committee that drafted the platform of the "Gold Democrats" at Indianapolis in September 1896.

For the rest of his life he was an onlooker in politics, with Republicans dominating his state, and a new order rising to power in the LaFollette group. He was the first citizen of Madison, after the death of General Lucius Fairchild [*q.v.*], and was active in the rebuilding of the University of Wisconsin under Presidents Thomas C. Chamberlin, Charles Kendall Adams, and Charles R. Van Hise [*qq.v.*]. Under the influence of Van Hise he provided, by a carefully drafted will, that his large estate should go to the University after the death of his wife and the one daughter who survived him. He was married on Jan. 3, 1866, to Anna Matilda Fox.

[Vilas' papers, as yet sealed, are in the custody of the State Hist. Soc. of Wis., and may be expected to provide abundant materials for the history of business in the Northwest. His widow procured the private printing of *Selected Addresses and Orations of William F. Vilas* (1912), with a brief biographical sketch. There are sketches of his life in 137 *Wisconsin Reports*, xxxi-liii; and in *Proc. State Hist. Soc. of Wis.* (1909), pp. 155–64, by B. W. Jones; and there are excellent obituaries in *Milwaukee Journal*, Aug. 27, 1908; and *Milwaukee Sentinel*, Aug. 28, 1908. See also C. H. Vilas, *A Genealogy of the Descendants of Peter Vilas* (1875); R. G. Thwaites, *The University of Wisconsin* (1900).]
F. L. P.

VILLAGRÁ, GASPAR PÉREZ de (c. 1555–c. 1620), officer of the expedition of Juan de Oñate [*q.v.*] to New Mexico in 1598, author of an epic poem on New Mexico, was born probably between 1551 and 1555 in Puebla de los Angeles, Spain, the son of Hernán Pérez de Villagrá and a descendant of the illustrious Pérez family of the town of Villagrá. Apparently he was graduated from the University of Salamanca with the degree of bachelor of letters, but it is unknown when and why he traveled to America. He is first heard of when he enlisted in and lent his services to the Oñate expedition in 1596. Over his own protests he was appointed *procurador general,* captain of cavalry, and member of the council of war. Of his services on that undertaking it has been said: "As a faithful vassal of his king he . . . did not spare himself but contributed money and risked his life. Frequently in a single year he traveled more than 1,500 leagues; at other times he fought heroically, as at the siege of the *peñol* of Ácoma . . . But he was indefatigable: hunger. thirst, long journeys, countless dangers, downpours, scorching heat, and cold snows he experienced with resignation" (from the Spanish of González Obregón, *post,* I, vi). These experiences earned for him appointments as *juez asesor* in ecclesiastical affairs (1598) and *factor* of the royal treasury in New Mexico. In 1599 he went back to Mexico for a year to report on New Mexico and enlist more soldiers. In 1603 he received for himself and his descendants the title of *hijos dalgo del solar*; between 1603 and 1605 he was made captain of the Tepehaunes Indians and given charge of the *alcaldía mayor* of Guaneceví, Durango.

In 1608 or 1609 Villagrá returned to Spain. In 1610 his *Historia de la Nueva Mexico,* an epic poem of thirty-four cantos, was published at Alcalá de Henares. The poem summarizes the earlier expedition to New Mexico and gives in detail the events of the Oñate expedition until the suppression of the revolt at Ácoma in 1599. Although it has little to recommend it as a literary composition, it has "the distinction of being the first published history of any American commonwealth" (Hodge, *post,* p. 17). In 1613 Villagrá asked permission to return to New Spain to meet charges of cruelty in punishing deserters; he was sentenced to banishment from New Mexico for six years and from Mexico city for two, and was ordered to pay the costs of the trial. He went back to Spain in the same year. In 1620 he was appointed by the king *alcalde mayor* of Zapotitlan, Guatemala, and was on his way to America to assume his new duties when he died suddenly at sea. He was survived by his wife, Catalina de Soto, a son, and a daughter who married a grandnephew of Montezuma. He is described by companions as heavy-set and of small stature, bald but with a heavy gray beard tinged with red.

[The best sources for information on Villagrá's life are "*Documentos Relativos á Gaspar Villagrá,*" in *Historia de la Nueva Mexico por el Gaspar de Villagrá* (2 vols., 1900), ed. by Luis González Obregón, and *Hist. of N. Mex.* (1933), a translation of Villagrá's hist. by Gilberto Espinosa, with intro. and notes by F. W. Hodge. See also J. G. Shea, "The First Epic of Our Country," *U. S. Cath. Hist. Mag.,* Apr. 1887; and H. R. Wagner, *The Spanish Southwest* (1924).]

C. W. H.

VILLARD, FANNY GARRISON [See Villard, Helen Frances Garrison, 1844–1928].

VILLARD, HELEN FRANCES GARRISON (Dec. 16, 1844–July 5, 1928), reformer, was born in Boston, Mass., the fourth child of the abolitionist William Lloyd Garrison [*q.v.*] and Helen Eliza (Benson) Garrison. "We shall demand for her the rights of a human being, though she be a female," wrote her militant father some weeks later. Named for her mother and paternal grandmother, Fanny (as she was always called) grew up a healthy, beautiful child, in a home surcharged with the exciting atmosphere of the greatest reform movement in American history. Educated in the Winthrop School, Boston, she spent her early years in close contact with the abolition struggle. After the Civil War, on Jan. 3, 1866, she married Henry Villard [*q.v.*], Washington correspondent of the *Chicago Daily Tribune.* After an extended visit to Europe (July 1866–June 1, 1868), the young couple settled in Boston, where a daughter was born to them in 1868, and a son in 1870. During another visit to Germany in 1872 a second son was born. In 1876 the Villards established their home in New York, and in 1879 acquired a summer estate at Dobbs Ferry, N. Y., where their fourth child, a son, was born and died. During all these years Mrs. Villard's life was centered in her family and in the career of her husband, which involved much travel in the United States and abroad and another prolonged visit to Germany (1883–86).

The death of her husband in November 1900 marked the beginning of her public career. Possessed of wealth and leisure and her father's crusading spirit, she found she could make an excellent platform appearance and command a loyal following. With intense and widely extended activity, she now gave herself to philanthropy and social reform. In the great tradition of her father, she participated in the militant work of the National Association for the Advancement of Colored People, serving as a member of its advisory committee. Always a woman suffragist, she labored indefatigably until victory came with the passage of the Nineteenth Amendment in 1920. For many years (1897–1922) she headed the Diet Kitchen Association, which under her leadership first established public milk stations for infants and children in New York City. In her last years she devoted her best energies to the cause of peace, which she interpreted, as did her father, in terms of absolute non-resistance. At the close of the World War she gathered about her a determined group of pacifists and in October 1919 founded the Women's Peace Society, which she led as president until her death. In 1921, at the Conference of the Women's International League for Peace and Freedom, in Vienna, she presented resolutions calling for "non-resistance under all circumstances . . . immediate, universal, and complete disarmament, . . . absolute freedom of trade the world over" (*Report of the 3rd International Congress of Women,* 1921, p. 150). She died in her eighty-fourth year and was buried at her home at Dobbs Ferry.

Fanny Garrison Villard was a woman of infinite charm and grace. Her inward serenity of mind and sweetness of temper matched the outward beauty of her person. Her exquisite refinement was salted by a high sense of humor and an intense absorption in current affairs. Her gentleness and culture as wife and mother revealed themselves in later years as the adornments of a courage and rock-like resolution which were the central elements of her character. Her father lived in her again. No one who saw the spectacle will forget her marching up Fifth Avenue in her old age at the head of the women's peace parade, her white head, crowned with its little black bonnet, nodding its defiance at the hostile but admiring crowds. A lady in personal bearing and social caste, she was democratic to the core, an ardent lover of mankind, and a passionate and valiant idealist.

[W. P. and F. J. Garrison, *William Lloyd Garrison* (4 vols., 1885–89); *Memoirs of Henry Villard* (2 vols., 1904); *Luncheon Given by Women's Peace Society in Celebration of Mrs. Henry Villard's 80th Birthday* (1924), pamphlet, with addresses; personal statement, with data, by Oswald Garrison Villard, *N. Y. Times,* July 6, 1928.]   J. H. H.

VILLARD, HENRY (Apr. 10, 1835–Nov. 12, 1900), journalist, railway promoter, financier, whose name was originally Ferdinand Heinrich Gustav Hilgard, was born in Speyer, Rhenish Bavaria, the son of Gustav Leonhard Hilgard and Katharina Antonia Elisabeth (Pfeiffer) Hilgard. He came from an important family, his father being a jurist who rose to the supreme court of Bavaria, while two of his uncles were leaders in the revolution of 1848 in Rhenish Bavaria. Young Heinrich's sympathy with their republican sentiments estranged him from his father and the boy was sent for a time to a military school at Phalsbourg in Lorraine. He graduated from the Gymnasium in Speyer, and attended the universities of Munich and Würzburg for a time, but disagreed again with his father and emigrated to America. Fearing that his father would have him returned to Germany and placed in the army, he adopted the name Villard, which had been borne by one of his schoolmates at Phalsbourg. Upon landing at New York in October 1853, he proceeded to the West by easy stages, spent some time in Cincinnati and Chicago, and eventually arrived at the home of relatives in Belleville, Ill. During the year 1855–56 he successively read law, peddled books, sold real estate, and edited a small-town newspaper, but made little progress along any line except the mastery of the English language.

Increasing facility in the use of his adopted tongue served to equip him for the field of journalism which was to occupy his attention largely for the next decade. In 1858 he served as a special correspondent for the *Staats-Zeitung* of New York, observed and reported the Lincoln-Douglas debates for that paper, began a personal friendship with Lincoln, and collected his Lincoln stories, which have since been widely quoted.

Service with this German-American paper, however, he regarded merely as preliminary to his real objective—a regular berth with the English-language press. Late in 1858 reports of the discovery of gold in the Pike's Peak country so aroused his adventurous spirit that he conceived a plan for a journey to the Rocky Mountains in the rôle of a correspondent, made a connection with the *Cincinnati Commercial,* and in the spring of 1859 set out across the Plains. His sojourn of some months in the mining camps not only enabled him to make the acquaintance of several noteworthy men, including Horace Greeley, but provided him with the materials for a guidebook for immigrants which he published in 1860 under the title *The Past and Present of the Pike's Peak Gold Regions,* a very accurate account of the natural resources of Colorado and a rather extraordinary achievement for a young man of twenty-five who seven years before had not known a word of English.

As correspondent for the *Commercial* he covered the Republican National Convention at Chicago in 1860, and he served in a similar capacity for that paper, as well as for the *Daily Missouri Democrat* of St. Louis and the *New York Tribune* during the ensuing campaign. With the election of Lincoln, he was selected by the *New York Herald* as its correspondent at Springfield, Ill. Here he remained until the departure of Lincoln for Washington, supplying his paper with regular dispatches, which the *Herald* was forced to share with other members of the New York Associated Press. Since at the same time Villard corresponded freely with Western papers, a considerable portion of the political news which the country read during those memorable weeks was supplied by the young immigrant who had not yet turned his twenty-sixth birthday.

With the outbreak of the Civil War, he supported the Union cause and became a war correspondent, first for the *New York Herald,* and later for the *New York Tribune,* accompanying the Union armies in Virginia and the West until late in November 1863, when ill health forced him to abandon field work for a time. The following year, in conjunction with the Washington representative of the *Chicago Daily Tribune,* he organized a news agency to compete with the New York Associated Press, and represented his agency with the Army of the Potomac in the campaign of 1864 in Virginia. Upon the conclusion of the war, he served as a correspondent in the United States and Europe until the autumn of 1868, when he became secretary of the American Social Science Association, with headquarters in Boston. This work, in addition to bringing him into the movement for civil service reform, enabled him to study and investigate public and corporate financing, including that of railways and banks, and thus indirectly prepared him for the most notable phase of his career—that of railway promoter and financier.

In 1871, to restore his failing health, he went to Germany and then to Switzerland. In Germany again, in the winter of 1873, he was brought into contact with a protective committee for the bondholders of the Oregon & California Railroad Company. He became a member of the committee, and the following year was sent to Oregon as their representative, to investigate and recommend as to the future policy to be employed by the bondholders. He perfected a plan for the harmonious operation of the Oregon & California Railroad, the Oregon Central Railroad, and the Oregon Steamship Company, which owned a fleet of steamers plying between Portland and San Francisco; in 1876 he became president of the first and last named companies. Meanwhile he had joined a committee for the protection of the bondholders of the Kansas Pacific Railway, and when in 1876 this company became financially embarrassed he was named a receiver for the road, a position which forced him to match his wits with such redoubtable foes as Jay Gould and Sidney Dillon [qq.v.] of the Union Pacific. It was in connection with this company that he achieved his first important financial success and laid the foundation of his later fortune.

Villard's real love, however, was the Oregon country. On his first visit to the region he had been very favorably impressed with its possibilities and there gradually developed in his mind the idea of building a railway empire in the Far Northwest. Perceiving the great strategic value of the south bank of the Columbia River as a railway route, he purchased the Oregon Steam Navigation Company from Simeon Gannett Reed [q.v.] and his associates in 1879, organized the Oregon Railway & Navigation Company, and proceeded to construct a railway eastward from Portland along that route. His plan was to make this line the Pacific Coast outlet for any northern transcontinental railway which might be built, and to concentrate the trade of the Northwest in Portland. As he progressed with his plans, however, he clashed with the Northern Pacific, then recovering from the financial disasters of the seventies, whose objective was Puget Sound. Appreciating the great advantage which the superior harbor of the Sound would give the Northern Pacific over his own road with terminus at Portland, Villard re-

solved to prevent the completion of the rival road. When his offer of running rights over his line to tidewater was refused, he decided to purchase a controlling interest in the Northern Pacific. After quietly buying the stock of the Company to the limit of his resources (December 1880–January 1881), he appealed to his friends and supporters for assistance. Issuing a confidential circular to about fifty persons, he asked them to subscribe toward a fund of eight million dollars, the precise purpose of which was not then revealed. It is eloquent testimony to the confidence which he inspired in men that, besides the sum first requested, an additional twelve million dollars was eventually subscribed. This transaction, commonly known as the "Blind Pool," remains one of the notable achievements in the annals of railway finance.

With the means thus secured he established his control of the Northern Pacific; he organized a holding company—the Oregon & Transcontinental—to harmonize the interests of his various railway properties; on Sept. 15, 1881, he became president of the Northern Pacific, and completed the line in 1883. Since he also controlled the Oregon & California Railroad, and had recently organized the Oregon Improvement Company for the development of the natural resources of the region, he now dominated every important agency of transportation in that part of the country. His triumph, however, was of short duration. Because of a combination of circumstances, including faulty estimates of construction costs, the Northern Pacific, upon its completion, was confronted with a huge deficit which forced the resignation of Villard from the presidency early in 1884. From 1884 to 1886 he was in Germany, recovering from a nervous breakdown; in the latter year he returned to New York as agent of the Deutsche Bank. With the aid of German capital he saved the Oregon & Transcontinental in September 1887, and reëntered the board of the Northern Pacific in 1888, where, for the next two years, he strove earnestly, but unsuccessfully, to effect an adjustment of the clashing interests of the various cities and transportation companies of the Pacific Northwest. His failure in this effort was attended by his retirement from the Oregon Railway & Navigation Company, though after a brief interval he continued as chairman of the board of the Northern Pacific until 1893, when his railway career came to an end.

Meanwhile Villard was displaying his versatility by activities along other lines. His early realization of the possibilities of the electrical industry prompted him to extend financial assistance to Thomas A. Edison and to found the

Edison General Electric Company in 1889. In 1881 he inaugurated, under the direction of Raphael Pumpelly [q.v.], the Northern Transcontinental Survey, an examination of the Northern Pacific land grant of genuine scientific value. Nor had his activity as a financier dulled his earlier interest in journalism. When, through his financial successes with the Kansas Pacific and the Oregon Railway & Navigation Company, he became a man of wealth, his thoughts quickly turned to the possibility of controlling a journal of independence and fearlessness, and of such high editorial standards as to compel attention from the entire country. Accordingly, in 1881, he acquired a controlling interest in the New York *Evening Post,* placed Horace White, E. L. Godkin, and Carl Schurz [qq.v.] in charge of the editorial department, and, as a guarantee of independence on the part of the paper, promptly abdicated the right of influencing its editorial policy.

During the years 1879 to 1883 Villard was probably the most important railway promoter in the United States. In those years he was frankly aiming at a monopoly of transportation facilities in the Pacific Northwest; yet he showed no disposition to take unfair advantage of such a position, or to victimize the people of the region. Although alert to the protection of his interests against rival companies, he displayed fairness, moderation, and breadth of view in dealing with the cities on the Coast. On Jan. 3, 1866, Villard married the only daughter of William Lloyd Garrison [q.v.]. In 1879 he established a home at Dobbs Ferry, N. Y., where in his sixty-sixth year he died. He was survived by his wife, Helen Frances Garrison Villard [q.v.], with a daughter and two sons.

[Villard MSS., Widener Library, Harvard Univ.; *Heinrich Hilgard Villard: Jugend Erinnerungen, 1835–1853* (1902); *Memoirs of Henry Villard* (2 vols., 1904); Villard's *The Past and Present of the Pike's Peak Gold Regions* (1860), repr. (1932) with introduction and notes by Le Roy R. Hafen; E. V. Smalley, *Hist. of the Northern Pacific R.R.* (1883); Allan Nevins, *The Evening Post* (1922); J. B. Hedges, *Henry Villard and the Railways of the Northwest* (1930); *N. Y. Times,* Nov. 13, 1900.] J. B. H.

VILLERÉ, JACQUES PHILIPPE (Apr. 28, 1761–Mar. 7, 1830), first Creole governor of the state of Louisiana, was born in the parish of St. John the Baptist, near New Orleans, La., the son of Joseph Roy Villeré, naval secretary of Louisiana under Louis XV, and of Louise Marguerite de la Chaise, grand-daughter of one of the treasurers of the colony. His father was executed by the Spanish authorities under Alexander O'Reilly [q.v.] in 1769, after the revolt of the French inhabitants against the Spanish

governor, Antonio de Ulloa [q.v.], and the boy was educated in France at royal expense as reparation for the death of his father. He served for a time as lieutenant of artillery in Santo Domingo, resigning to return to Louisiana where in 1784 he married Jeanne Henriette Fazende. In time he became one of the leading sugar planters of the vicinity of New Orleans. In his plantation residence the British established headquarters in 1815 just prior to the battle of New Orleans, while Villeré was serving as a major-general of Louisiana militia.

Meanwhile he had been a member of the convention which in 1812 framed the first constitution for the state of Louisiana, and unsuccessful candidate for the governorship in the election of that year. He was elected governor in 1816, and served four years. The second governor of the state and the first Creole to hold that position, he used his office to diminish the friction between the French element of the population and the United States authorities, but was criticized for neglecting his fellow Creoles in matters of patronage. In opposition to certain views of the contemporary medical fraternity, he advanced the opinion that yellow fever was not due directly to climate, observing that Louisiana prisoners, segregated from the city, did not become victims of the disease (*Journal of the House . . . Fifth Legislature of . . . Louisiana,* 1820, pp. 6–7). He exerted an administrative influence for better educational facilities, but his term in the governorship was on the whole uneventful— "quiet, prosperous and healing." In the last year of his administration he announced the entire extinguishment of the state debt and the existence of a current surplus of $40,000 in the treasury. He was honored in death with a military funeral. He was a man of vigor with an interest in practical and public affairs, and direct descendants bearing his name have continued to play important rôles in the affairs of New Orleans.

[Alcée Fortier, *Louisiana* (1914), vol. II, and *A Hist. of La.* (1904), vols. II, III; H. E. Chambers, *A Hist. of La.* (1925); Arthur Meynier, Jr., *Meynier's Louisiana Biogs.* (1882); *L'Abeille* (New Orleans), Mar. 9, 1830; records of St. Louis Cathedral, New Orleans, Book X, p. 113.] H. C. N.

VINCENNES, FRANÇOIS MARIE BISSOT, Sieur de (June 17, 1700–Mar. 25, 1736), founder of the Indiana city bearing his name, was born at Montreal, the headquarters for western traders, the son of Jean Baptiste Bissot, Sieur de Vincennes [q.v.] and Marguerite Forestier) Bissot. His godfather was François Margane, Sieur de la Valterie. Hence he frequently signed himself Margane, which confused early writers with the belief that he was not a son of Jean Baptiste Bissot, Sieur de Vincennes. While merely a lad the younger Vincennes accompanied his father to his western post, and after his death remained for several years in command at Ke-ki-onga, the Miami village on the site of Fort Wayne. In 1722 he was commissioned ensign in the colonial army. Meanwhile, the several tribes of the Miami began moving down the Wabash River, and Vincennes accompanied the Ouiatenon and built a fort near Lafayette, Ind., where he commanded for about four years. The Piankashaw Miami passed still farther down the Wabash, building villages on the White River, then within the jurisdiction of Louisiana, rather than of Canada. For some time the authorities of the former colony had been attempting to establish a post on the lower Wabash, and now persuaded Vincennes to ally himself with French Louisiana. Some time in 1731 or 1732 Vincennes complied with the request of the governor of Louisiana and built a fort on the site that now bears his name. In two letters written by him from that post in 1733 (Roy, *post*, pp. 92–93) he described his fort, the Indians he controlled, and the commerce for which his post was well situated. He also mentioned the war with the Chickasaw, which was to bring about his tragic death.

Louisiana was at this time engaged in a desperate struggle with the Indians on the Mississippi, especially with the Chickasaw, who harbored the refugee Natchez and traded with the English of Carolina. The governor of Louisiana, Jean Baptiste le Moyne, Sieur de Bienville [*q.v.*], in the spring of 1736 gathered all his resources; from Illinois and the Wabash he summoned the French officers and traders to a rendezvous somewhere near the site of Memphis. Vincennes from his post joined Pierre D'Artaguiette of Illinois, and together they advanced down the Mississippi to the designated place. But Bienville was detained, and the Indians from the upper posts grew impatient and hastened their officers into a premature attack. They were seriously defeated; and Vincennes, a Jesuit priest, and seventeen other young Frenchmen were dragged to the Chickasaw village on the headwaters of Tombigbee River in the present state of Mississippi and there tortured and burned at the stake. The day of the defeat was Palm Sunday of 1736, although dated two months later by many authorities. Vincennes not only built a post on the Wabash, but he assisted Louisiana in its struggle to maintain the Mississippi Valley for France. His fort was an outpost, and of him it is said "his name will be perpetuated as

long as the Wabash flows by the dwellings of civilized man" (Bancroft, *post,* p. 368).

[P. G. Roy, "Sieur de Vincennes Identified," in *Ind. Hist. Soc. Pub.,* VII (1918), no. 1; George Bancroft, *Hist. of the U. S.,* vol. III (1840); C. W. Alvord, *The Illinois Country* (1920); P. C. Phillips, "Vincennes in its Relation to French Colonial Policy," in *Ind. Mag. of Hist.,* Dec. 1921; G. J. Garraghan, *Chapters of Frontier Hist.* (1934).]
L. P. K.

VINCENNES, JEAN BAPTISTE BISSOT, Sieur de (Jan. 19, 1668–1719), explorer and French officer in the Mississippi Valley, was the son of François and Marie (Couillard) Bissot, the former a Norman from Pont-Audemer, who emigrated to New France before 1639. In 1672 François was granted the seigniory of Vincennes, on the southern bank of the St. Lawrence River, opposite Quebec, where he had already established a mill and a tannery. The seigniory was to pass to his sons (*Bulletin, post,* Mar. 1919, p. 65). At his death in 1673 his son-in-law, Louis Jolliet, became the guardian of the boys. He placed Jean Baptiste in the seminary at Quebec, where Jolliet himself had been educated. The lad, now Sieur de Vincennes, remained at school for four years, 1676 to 1680, then, as "he was not fit for the ecclesiastical estate," he was dismissed and in 1687 went to France. There, through the patronage of his godfather, the former intendant, Jean Talon, Vincennes obtained a commission as ensign in the marine, the branch of the army that was stationed in New France. In 1696 he married Marguerite Forestier, the daughter of the chief surgeon of New France. François Marie Bissot, Sieur de Vincennes [*q.v.*], was their son.

Just when Vincennes first visited the West does not appear, for when Governor Frontenac in 1696 sent him to command among the Miami Indians he was already well known to them and much beloved. In 1698 he accompanied Henry de Tonty to the West, leaving the party during its voyage on Lake Michigan to proceed to St. Joseph River, where the Miami dwelt (*Early Narratives of the Northwest,* 1917, ed. by L. P. Kellogg, pp. 342, 345). From this time until his death Vincennes continued to live among these Indians and to carry on trade with them. In 1705 he was suspended from his position in the army, because he exported brandy for trade; but later he was pardoned, because he had rescued Iroquois prisoners and assisted in maintaining the peace of 1701. Meanwhile the Miami tribe had removed from St. Joseph River to the present Maumee, where a great village called Ke-ki-onga was built on the site of Fort Wayne, Ind. This was Vincennes' headquarters, and there he lived and died. In 1712 he went to the aid of

Dubuisson of Detroit, who was involved in a contest with the Fox Indians at that post. After their defeat Vincennes was sent to carry the news to Quebec, but he returned to his command the same autumn. His services in preventing the Miami from going over to the British were so important that thirty years after his death his name and influence were invoked to bring the Miami back to the French alliance. For twenty years he was the principal personage among the Miami and cooperated with other officers in maintaining French power in the West.

[P. G. Roy, "Sieur de Vincennes Identified," in *Ind. Hist. Soc. Pub.*, VII (1918); J. D. Dunn, "Who was our Sieur de Vincennes," in *Ind. Mag. of Hist.*, June 1916; B. J. Griswold, *The Pictorial Hist. of Fort Wayne* (1917), vol. I; *Bulletin des Recherches Historiques*, Mar. 1919, Apr. 1900.]   L. P. K.

VINCENT, FRANK (Apr. 2, 1848–June 19, 1916), traveler, author, and collector, was born in Brooklyn, N. Y., the son of Harriet (Barns) and Frank Vincent, a member of the drygoods firm of Vincent, Clark & Company, in New York City. His father had an estate at Tarrytown-on-the-Hudson and sent his son to the Peekskill Military Academy and, in 1866, to Yale College. Lack of health caused him to leave college at the end of his second term and another attempt in 1867 proved equally abortive; but Yale conferred upon him, in 1875, an honorary degree of M.A., and he was later, in 1905, enrolled with his old class, 1870, as a graduate member.

Undiscouraged by the apparent failure of his formal education, he resolved (*Biographical Record, post*, pp. 352–53) to "survey the entire field of literature, science, and art . . . in famous standard and epoch-making books"; and to make a systematic tour of the most interesting parts of the world" and to write of the less frequented and less known countries. These ambitions he later considered fulfilled. He claimed, in the fifteen years from 1871 to 1886, to have traveled 355,000 miles "over the entire world" and alone to have crossed Lapland and to have penetrated 1,000 miles into Brazil, where he discovered the double cataract of the Iguaçú. In those days, few Americans ventured beyond the usual European tour, and Vincent was acclaimed a Marco Polo, while his lucid and lively, though careless, style was admired by Longfellow and others of the New England school. Probably it is the first of his books that has remained the most readable, *The Land of the White Elephant* (1874), describing his adventures in 1871–72 in Cambodia, Siam, and Burma, entertainingly illustrated with numerous maps, plans, and engravings. With sketchbook in hand, camera and diary also, armed with letters to the influential, he wandered Hero-

dotus-like, ceaselessly asking questions, setting down wonders and facts, hobnobbing with kings, premiers, high priests, or exploring fearlessly and with good-natured acceptance of hardship. It was not only the culinary arts and more obvious customs that he recorded; native ideas and emotions found in him a sympathetic, though superficial, interpreter. If there is absence of the scientific spirit in sifting his information, the impression left on the reader is all the more vivid.

From these lands, chiefly from Cambodia, he brought home a collection of antiquities and more recent art objects in bronze, lacquer, stone, and painted wood, including fragments of Buddha statues, about 1,000 years old, from the great temple of Nagkon Wat. These he gave, in 1885, to the Metropolitan Museum of Art in New York, and thus became a patron (now known as fellow-in-perpetuity). For over twenty years, he wrote successfully for publication. Among his books were *Norsk, Lapp, and Finn* (1881); *Around and About South America* (1890); *In and Out of Central America* (1890); and *Actual Africa* (1895). He edited *The Plant World* (1897) and *The Animal World* (1898) for Appletons' Home Reading Books Series.

His personality was eager, almost aggressive. On June 3, 1909, when sixty-one, he married a distant cousin, Harriet Stillman Vincent of Brooklyn. They had no children. They made their home in New York City, but he died in Woodstock, N. Y., and was buried in Sleepy Hollow Cemetery at Tarrytown. He had become an honorary member of some twenty-six scientific and literary societies and the recipient of nine decorations from sovereigns and foreign governments on four continents.

[*Obituary Record of Yale University . . . 1916* (1916); *The Biog. Record of the Class of 1870 Yale College* (1911); *Metropolitan Museum of Art, Annual Reports . . . 1871 to 1894* (reprint 1895); files of the museum; *Who's Who in America*, 1912–13; Vincent's own books, esp. the prefaces; date of death from *N. Y. Times*, June 21, 1916.]   F. B. H.

VINCENT, JOHN HEYL (Feb. 23, 1832–May 9, 1920), bishop of the Methodist Episcopal Church, educational leader, was born in Tuscaloosa, Ala. His father, John Himrod Vincent, a Pennsylvanian, was of Huguenot ancestry, a descendant of Levi Vincent, born in France, who died in New Jersey in 1763; his mother, Mary Raser, was the daughter of a Philadelphia sea-captain. In 1837 the Vincents returned to the vicinity of Lewisburg, Pa. The father was farmer, trader, miller, postmaster, and Methodist Sunday School superintendent. Young Vincent attended local schools, worked in a store, and was principal of an academy. He had early determined to be a minister, however, and in 1850 was licensed as an exhorter and local preacher. As such he traveled Luzerne Circuit, carrying a translation of Dante among the pious books in his saddle-bags. At his mother's death in 1852 he went to relatives in Newark, N. J., where he studied briefly in the Wesleyan Institute. The next year he joined the New Jersey Conference of the Methodist Episcopal Church on trial, was ordained deacon in 1855, and elder in 1857.

Transferring to the Rock River Conference, in Illinois, he held pastorates in Joliet, Mount Morris, Galena, and Rockford. At Galena, U. S. Grant, then undistinguished, was an inconspicuous member of his congregation, and the two became life-long friends. Vincent's progressive ideas in religious education early began to attract attention. To fit himself for better teaching service he visited the Holy Land in 1862–63. His promotion to Trinity Church, Chicago, in 1864 gave him his opportunity for leadership. The work of the American Sunday School in those days was confined to one hour a week, in which Scripture verses were memorized and dull lessons recited from "Question Books." Vincent and his progressive associates saw that there could be little improvement without better trained teachers, and no effective training until there was uniformity of subject and teaching material. Accordingly he advocated and was largely instrumental in introducing uniform lessons into the Chicago schools. This innovation made possible, in 1864, a Union Sunday School Institute for the Northwest, with a regular publication, the *Northwestern Sunday School Teachers' Quarterly*, which, he said later, "met a want and kindled a fire." The next year this journal became a monthly, the *Sunday School Teacher* (Chicago), and in 1866 its pages contained a specimen of a new system of study in leaflet form, a revolutionary departure, which led within a few years to uniform lessons for all Protestant denominations in the United States and ultimately, for the entire Protestant world. In 1866 the Methodist Episcopal Church plucked Vincent out of the pastorate and his local leadership and placed him in New York as general agent of its Sunday School Union, and in 1868 elected him editor of Sunday School literature and corresponding secretary of the Sunday School Union. In that office he served for twenty years. He soon became the recognized leader of the American Sunday School movement. He edited the *Sunday School Journal* and the *Berean Lessons*, which won enormous popularity, and he directed the teacher-training activities which his energy had set up all over the country.

His idea of holding a protracted national training institute bore fruit in 1874 in a Sunday School teachers' assembly, which met for two weeks in August at Fair Point on Lake Chautauqua in western New York. The location of this summer school he discussed with his friend Lewis Miller [q.v.] of Akron, Ohio, a Methodist Sunday School superintendent, an enthusiastic promoter of religious education. On Miller's advice it was located in the camp-meeting grove. The two men admirably supplemented each other, Miller functioning as president and Vincent as superintendent of instruction. From this small beginning developed the so-called Chautauqua movement, a system of popular education. Beginning as a summer tent-school for Sunday School teachers, the assembly developed rapidly into a summer resort, for study and lectures. In 1878 Vincent presented a plan for a course of prescribed reading, extending through four years, with examinations and a diploma, designed to afford multitudes of belated students what he called "the college outlook"—a glimpse of literature, science, and religion. This "Chautauqua Literary and Scientific Circle" (C. L. S. C.) was immediately and immensely popular, local "circles" springing up in hundreds of places. It marked the beginning of directed home study and correspondence schools in America, and the summer classes at Chautauqua were the forerunner of summer schools under college auspices. The Chautauqua platform presented to immense audiences the most eminent scholars, lecturers, reformers, and publicists, and found an extension in similar "daughter assemblies" and later in thousands of local "Chautauquas," in which popular programs, entertaining, instructive, and "uplifting," were given for brief periods in halls or tents.

From 1878 to 1888 Vincent's career was crowded with activity: he planned the Chautauqua summer programs and directed them; edited the Sunday School literature for his Church, which attained a circulation of millions of copies; founded in 1885 the Oxford League for Methodist young people; and filled countless speaking engagements, traveling with an expert stenographer, making Pullman sections his workshops, and employing every labor-saving device available. In 1888, however, the General Conference elected him bishop. He could no longer give his major attention to Chautauqua and the Sunday School, but the old fire burned in him, and in his contacts with the younger ministers he continually gave expression to his cherished ideals. The religious views of his early days had been modified by his reading of Horace Bushnell and Robertson of Brighton, and he became the advocate of intellectual and spiritual culture, for education rather than emotion, for a more sane evangelism, and for a type of religion which should pervade the whole of life. The Itinerants' Club, which he fathered, was the Sunday School Institute idea applied to the Methodist ministry. It introduced the young minister to helpful books, suggested improved methods of parish work and saner types of evangelism. His official residences were at Buffalo, N. Y. (1888–92), Topeka, Kan. (1892–1900), and after 1900, when he was placed in charge of Methodist work in Europe, at Zurich, Switzerland. In 1904, at the age of seventy-two, he was retired. His last years, spent in Indianapolis and Chicago, were devoted to reading, writing, and lecturing along the lines in which he had won eminence. He married, Nov. 10, 1858, Elizabeth Dusenbury of Portville, N. Y., by whom he had one son, George Edgar Vincent.

Bishop Vincent was above medium height, gracious in manner, with a rich and flexible voice. As a lecturer on education, morals, and the training of children, he excelled. He was tolerant in temper, liberal for his time in his theology, giving the hospitality of the Chautauqua platform to such leaders as Edward Everett Hale, Charles William Eliot, and Lyman Abbott [qq.v.]. He was the first Methodist to be invited to Harvard as University preacher. His influence was always exerted in behalf of moderate denominational self-assertion and interdenominational comity. His books included: *Sunday School Institutes and Normal Classes* (1872); *The Modern Sunday School* (1887); *The Chautauqua Movement* (1886); *Our Own Church* (1890); *The Revival and After the Revival* (1883); *A Study in Pedagogy* (1890).

[Autobiog. in *Northwestern Christian Advocate*, Apr. 6–Nov. 2, 1910; L. H. Vincent, *John Heyl Vincent* (1925); J. L. Hurlbut, *The Story of Chautauqua* (1921); Ellwood Hendrick, *Lewis Miller* (1925); H. M. Hamill, "Hist. of the Teacher-Training Movement," *World-Wide Sunday-School Work* (1910); Boyd Vincent, *Our Family of Vincents* (1924); *Chicago Daily Tribune*, May 10, 1920.]   J. R. J.

VINCENT, MARVIN RICHARDSON (Sept. 11, 1834–Aug. 18, 1922), clergyman and theological professor, was born in Poughkeepsie, N. Y., the son of Leonard M. and Nancy M. (Richardson) Vincent; his father and his maternal grandfather, Marvin Richardson, were Methodist ministers. Admitted to Columbia College in 1850, he became a pupil of Charles Anthon and Henry Drisler [qq.v.], whose instruction in the classics laid the foundation for his life-long interest in the study of words. Graduating with the degree of A.B. in 1854, he taught

for eight years, first in the Columbia Grammar School (1854–58) and next, as professor of Latin, in the Troy Methodist University (1858–62).

For a year, 1862–63, he served as acting pastor of the Pacific Street Methodist Episcopal Church, Brooklyn, but, changing his denominational convictions, he was ordained by the Presbytery of Troy on June 18, 1863. For the next ten years he was pastor of the First Presbyterian Church of Troy, during which period he became widely known as a scholarly preacher. From 1873 to 1887 he was pastor of the Church of the Covenant, New York. In the latter year he was called by the board of directors of the Union Theological Seminary, New York—of which he had been a member since 1873—to the chair of Sacred Literature in succession to Edward Robinson, W. G. T. Shedd, and Philip Schaff [qq.v.]. This call he accepted with a "goodly amount of diffidence," and for twenty-nine years gave instruction in the literature of the New Testament. During most of these years he was also a trustee of Columbia (1889–1913). When failing health compelled him in 1916 to become professor emeritus, he retired to Forest Hills, L. I., where six years later death came to him as a not unwelcome visitor. In 1858, he married Hulda F. Seagrave of Providence, R. I.

By the time he came to Union Seminary, Vincent had reached the conviction that the Bible portrays "the historical development of God in man"; that its value centers in "the Incarnate Word [who] is the final interpreter of the written word"; and that its authority "as a rule of faith and practice must be tested by His spirit, example and teaching." Disinclined to controversy but believing in the "right to prosecute the free investigation of the Scriptures within the church," he supported the cause of his colleague, Charles A. Briggs [q.v.], when the latter was tried for heresy before the Presbytery of New York.

Vincent's pen was active and versatile. Apart from numerous sermons, addresses and pamphlets, he published *In the Shadow of the Pyrenees* (1883), a travel book; *The Age of Hildebrand* (1896), in Ten Epochs of Church History; and in 1904 a metrical version of Dante's *Inferno*. To the study of the New Testament he contributed *A History of the Textual Criticism of the New Testament* (1899), *A Critical and Exegetical Commentary on the Epistles to the Philippians and to Philemon* (1897), which is marked by sound judgment and clarity of presentation; and *Word Studies in the New Testament* (4 vols., 1887–1900). The last-named substantial work is not a commentary but a study of the vocabulary of the Greek New Testament, designed to serve the needs of students of the English Bible. The impulse to the *Studies* was received when, as professor at Troy University, he collaborated with his colleague Charlton T. Lewis [*q.v.*] in translating in two volumes (1860–62) John Albert Bengel's *Gnomon Novi Testamenti*. Accomplished as a New Testament scholar, competent in theology, and endowed with the gifts of charming manners, humor, and good fellowship, Vincent was an admirable example of a culture at once Christian and Greek.

[*Union Theol. Sem. Bull.*, Jan. 1923; obituary of Leonard M. Vincent, in *Minutes of the Ann. Conferences of the Methodist Episcopal Church*, 1893; *Gen. Cat. Union Theol. Sem.* (1926); *Who's Who in America*, 1922–23; *N. Y. Times*, Aug. 19, 1922; personal acquaintance.]   J. E. F.

VINCENT, MARY ANN (Sept. 18, 1818– Sept. 4, 1887), actress, followed her profession continuously from the age of sixteen until within four days of her death. She was born in Portsmouth, England, the daughter of an attaché of the Royal Navy named John Farlow, who died when she was only two years old. After the death of her mother two years later, she was brought up by her grandmother. Acquaintance with members of a theatrical troupe aroused her interest in the stage at an early age, and in April 1835 she made her début at a theatre in Cowes, Isle of Wight, as a chambermaid in *The Review, or the Wags of Windsor*. Her second rôle was a much more important one, that of Volante in John Tobin's then popular comedy, *The Honeymoon*. She remained at the theatre in Cowes until the end of the season. In August of the same year she was married to James R. Vincent, an actor nine years her senior, and thereafter, throughout her entire career, she was known both on and off the stage as Mrs. J. R. Vincent. After acting here and there in the provincial theatres of Great Britain, she and her husband accepted an engagement at the National Theatre in Boston, arriving in that city on Nov. 7, 1846, and making their first appearance on Nov. 11 in *Popping the Question*, as Miss Biffin and Mr. Primrose. Mrs. Vincent remained at the National Theatre for two years after the death of her husband on June 11, 1850. Her marriage in 1854 to John Wilson, an actor, was unhappy, and after a separation it ended in divorce twelve years later.

Going to the Boston Museum on May 10, 1852, as Mrs. Pontifex in *Naval Engagements*, she was uninterruptedly, with the exception of the season of 1861–62, a member of its stock company for more than thirty-five years. A list of the characters she acted there is virtually the repertory of that theatre from season to season. She became its leading comedienne, and later its leading old lady, playing a range of parts as varied as those of Nancy Sikes in *Oliver Twist*, Mrs. Malaprop in *The Rivals*, Mrs. Candour in *The School for Scandal*, Maria in *Twelfth Night*, Goneril in *King Lear*, and Queen Gertrude in *Hamlet*, as well as many parts in the ephemeral plays of the day. The total number of these characters acted by her was well over four hundred, and the number of her performances on the stage of the Boston Museum extends far into the thousands. On Thursday, Sept. 1, 1887, she suffered a stroke of apoplexy at her home after having acted Mrs. Keziah Beekman in *The Dominie's Daughter* the previous evening, and died early Sunday morning. She was buried from St. Paul's Church, Boston, of which she was a communicant, and her remains were interred in Mount Auburn Cemetery in Cambridge.

In the eyes of Boston Mrs. Vincent was more than an actress. Her name was a household word, even among the many who never went to a theatre. With William Warren [*q.v.*], the leading comedian of the Boston Museum for many years, she was a Boston institution. An associate recalls "the jolly, chubby, little figure, the bobbing curls, the inimitable, tripping walk, and the gasping pleasant voice, all suggestive of mirth and merriment" (Ryan, *post*, p. 44). She was hospitable and charitable, fond of animals, and but for the solicitude of her friends she would have spent almost every cent she earned in helping the poor and friendless. Her fiftieth year on the stage was commemorated at the Museum on Apr. 25, 1885, with afternoon and evening performances in which she appeared as Mrs. Hardcastle in *She Stoops to Conquer* and as Mrs. Malaprop in *The Rivals*. The Vincent Memorial Hospital in Boston was founded in her memory, being opened in 1891 with ceremonies presided over by Bishop Phillips Brooks [*q.v.*]; the Vincent Club of young society women, named in her honor, adds to the funds for its support by the giving of annual amateur theatricals.

[J. B. Richardson, *Mrs. James R. Vincent, A Memorial Address* (1911); Catherine M. Reignolds-Winslow, *Yesterday with Actors* (1887); G. P. Baker, in *Famous American Actors of Today* (1896), ed. by F. E. McKay and C. E. L. Wingate; E. H. Sothern, *The Melancholy Tale of "Me"* (1916); Kate Ryan, *Old Boston Museum Days* (1915); *Boston Herald*, Apr. 19, 26, and *Boston Daily Globe*, Apr. 26, 1885; *Boston Transcript*, Apr. 27, 1885, and Sept. 6, 1887; *Boston Times*, Sept. 11, 1887; *Theatre*, Nov. 7, 1887.]
                                    E. F. E.

VINTON, ALEXANDER HAMILTON (May 2, 1807–Apr. 26, 1881), clergyman of the Protestant Episcopal Church, was born in Prov-

Boston schools, Jonathan and a brother were sent to London in 1770, to complete their training and make contacts under Franklin's tutelage. Jonathan's understanding of accounts and his single-minded devotion to business made a favorable impression on Franklin. To the young man's mother he wrote: "It has been wonderful to me to see a young Man from America in a Place so full of various Amusements as London is, as attentive to Business, as diligent in it, and keeping as close at home till it was finished" (A. H. Smyth, *The Writings of Benjamin Franklin,* vol. V, 1906, p. 312).

When Franklin became a commissioner of the Continental Congress to France in 1776, Williams gave up the promising business connections he had made in London and joined his kinsman. He was immediately employed by the commissioners as their agent at Nantes to inspect the arms and other supplies they were having shipped from that port. Congress had already appointed a commercial agent there, Thomas Morris, whose constant drunkenness made him totally unfit for work. Morris, a half-brother of Robert [*q.v.*], was jealous of Williams and would not cooperate with him. Affairs at Nantes got into such a tangle that Franklin and Silas Deane [*q.v.*] in desperation sent John Ross, a Philadelphia merchant temporarily in France, to make an investigation. Ross, assured that reports of Morris' debauchery were not exaggerated, advised Williams to assume control until William Lee [*q.v.*], who had been asked by Congress to join Morris, should arrive. Through this attempt to carry on temporarily the vital work of making shipments, selling prizes, etc., Williams became involved in the controversy which arose between Deane and Arthur Lee [*q.v.*], and was charged by Lee with plotting to supersede all other officials at Nantes and with appropriating for private purposes 100,-000 livres of public money. The charges were found false by a committee of merchants at Nantes and were never considered by Congress, but Franklin was so incensed at the Lees' unjustified denunciations that he made no further attempt to place Williams in public service, though he was several times employed to purchase supplies.

He remained in Europe engaged in various business ventures until Franklin returned home in 1785. On Sept. 12, 1779, he married Mariamne, daughter of William Alexander of Edinburgh, Scotland. Williams accompanied Franklin to America, and a few years later established a home at Philadelphia, where his rating as a well-to-do merchant, joined with his relationship to Franklin, found him ready acceptance. He became in 1796 associate judge in the court of common pleas, and acquired reputation, also, as a scientist. He had worked with Franklin in some of his later experiments and published in 1799 a treatise entitled *Thermometrical Navigation.* Other results of his experimentation appeared in the *Transactions* of the American Philosophical Society, of which he was at various times secretary, councillor, and vice-president.

His scientific interests brought him into contact with Thomas Jefferson, who, impressed by Williams' theoretical knowledge of fortifications, acquired while he was in France, appointed him in 1801 inspector of fortifications and superintendent at West Point, with the rank of major. Shortly afterward, Congress established the military academy, and Williams, as the ranking engineer at West Point, became automatically its first superintendent. His interest in military education, as in all questions of national defense, was deep, but in his attempts to make a first-rate school he labored under so many handicaps that the academy cannot be said to have prospered. The number of instructors, fixed by Congress, was too small, and there were frequent changes; many subjects considered by Williams to be essential for military education were not included; the buildings and equipment were inadequate; a library hardly existed and the war department refused to purchase scientific books on the plea that so many changes in scientific thought were occurring that textbooks could not be sufficiently up to date to be useful. Dissatisfied with his rank and limited control over cadets who were not in the engineering corps, Williams resigned in 1803, but at Jefferson's insistence accepted reappointment in 1805, with the rank of lieutenant-colonel of engineers and with complete authority over all cadets.

His work at West Point was additionally impeded by the fact that his duties as the ranking engineer of the army called him frequently away on long trips of inspection. He also had charge of some construction work, notably the defenses of New York harbor, which he personally planned and supervised. In his absences the academy barely continued to exist. With the retirement of Jefferson, Williams suffered another blow. A Federalist, he had always been distrusted by the secretary of war, Henry Dearborn [*q.v.*]; under Madison's secretary of war, William Eustis [*q.v.*], the antagonism of the war department toward the Military Academy increased. Supplies and funds were withheld; new cadets were not appointed when vacancies occurred. Williams specifically recommended to both Jefferson and Madison two things—removal of the academy to Washington, where it would

Wakefield, R. I., where he built a church with funds collected largely in Providence and New York. He then went to St. Stephen's, Providence, where again he built a church. At Easter, 1841, he became rector of Trinity Church, Newport, R. I. Called to Emmanuel Church, Brooklyn, in 1844, he began a pastorate of eleven years, during which he rose to prominence in his denomination. Facing discouraging conditions in his parish, by unwearied labors and the influence of his own character and spirit he built up a strong church, which was merged with Grace Church and established in a new edifice on Brooklyn Heights. In 1846 he was called to All Saints, New York, and in 1847 he was asked to become associate rector of Trinity Church, New Haven, Conn., with right of succession; on June 3, 1848, he was elected bishop of Indiana; but all these positions he declined. In the memorable contests over the bishopric of New York in 1852 and 1854 Vinton both times came within a few votes of election as provisional bishop. Becoming assistant minister of Trinity Parish, New York, in 1855, he was assigned to Saint Paul's Chapel, and four years later transferred to Trinity Church, where the eloquence of his preaching attracted large congregations. In 1869 he became first professor of ecclesiastical polity and canon law in the General Theological Seminary, which position he held until his death.

Vinton's fluency of utterance, his exceptional command of language, and his grace of manner brought him an enviable reputation as a public speaker; he was also a clear thinker and a logical debater, conspicuous in the councils of the Church. An ardent evangelical, he carried on his ministry with fervor and enthusiasm. An extreme low churchman in the beginning, he made in practice, if not in dogma, a considerable advance toward the high church position. His military and legal training were an aid to him. He had a high estimate of authority, was well disciplined, prompt, and direct, with, however, a tendency to peremptoriness which sometimes offended. His preparation for the bar was an excellent background for his work in canon law. A number of his sermons and addresses were printed, but his chief publication was *A Manual Commentary of the General Canon Law and the Constitution of the Protestant Episcopal Church in the United States* (1870). After ten months of failing health, he died at his home in Brooklyn.

[J. A. Vinton, *The Vinton Memorial* (1858); G. W. Cullum, *Biog. Reg. Officers and Grads. U. S. Mil. Acad.* (3rd ed., 1891), vol. I; G. C. Mason, *Annals of Trinity Church, Newport, R. I.*, 2 ser. (1894); *Fourth Ann. Reunion Asso. Grads. U. S. Mil. Acad.* (1873); *Francis Vinton; Priest and Doctor* (1873); *Sun* (N. Y.), Sept. 30, 1872.]   H. E. S.

VINTON, FRANCIS LAURENS (June 1, 1835–Oct. 6, 1879), Union soldier, mining engineer, was born at Fort Preble, Portland Harbor, Me., the son of an army officer, John Rogers Vinton, and Lucretia Dutton (Parker). His mother died in 1838, and his father was killed at the siege of Vera Cruz in 1847. Thereafter, until 1851, when he was appointed to the United States Military Academy by President Fillmore, the boy was cared for by his uncle, Francis Vinton [q.v.], who had left the army for the Protestant Episcopal ministry.

Vinton graduated at West Point tenth in his class in 1856 but resigned within a few months and proceeded to France, where he entered the École des Mines. After four years of study he returned to the United States, where he at once obtained a position as instructor in mechanical drawing at Cooper Union, New York City. In February 1861, he left to head an expedition to explore the mineral resources of Honduras, but had barely started before the news of the outbreak of the Civil War caused him to return to the United States. He was commissioned captain in the 16th United States Infantry on Aug. 5, 1861, and was soon given permission to raise a regiment, of which he was made colonel on Oct. 31, 1861. He commanded this regiment, the 43rd New York, with skill and distinction in the various battles of the Virginia peninsular campaign (March–August 1862). After September 1862 he commanded a brigade in the VI Corps (Army of the Potomac) until he was wounded in the battle of Fredericksburg, Dec. 13, 1862, so severely that he was never able to rejoin his command. Appointed a brigadier-general of volunteers on Mar. 13, 1863, he resigned less than two months later.

In the following year, when the School of Mines of Columbia College opened its doors, Vinton was selected by Thomas Egleston [q.v.], whom he had known at the École des Mines, to fill the chair of civil and mining engineering. A man of great personal charm and extremely popular with his students, he taught such subjects as mechanical drawing and elementary civil engineering with great skill, but his presentation of mining was necessarily confined to European practice, since he had had no contact with mining in America. To a man who had successfully commanded a brigade of soldiers in combat this must have seemed a task which offered but little scope for his real capacity. After thirteen years in the chair he resigned and went to Denver, Colo., where he established himself as a consulting mining engineer. Here, in addition to engineering employment, he found congenial work as Colorado correspondent of the *Engineering and Mining Journal* of New York, to which, during the next two years, he contributed well written and beautifully illustrated articles. On a professional trip to Leadville, Col., then coming to the height of its glory, he became infected with erysipelas and died within a few days, at the age of forty-four. His impressive funeral services were chiefly a recognition of the distinction of his military career, but were attended by the most prominent mining men of the state.

[*N. Y. Herald*, Oct. 7, 1879; G.W. Cullum, *Biog. Reg. Officers and Grads. U. S. Mil. Acad.* (3rd ed., 1891), vol. II; *Engineering and Mining Jour.*, Oct. 11, 25, 1879; *Eleventh Ann. Reunion Asso. Grads U. S. Mil. Acad.* (1880); J. A. Vinton, *The Vinton Memorial* (1858); *Army and Navy Jour.*, Oct. 11, 1879.]
T.T.R.

VINTON, FREDERIC (Oct. 9, 1817–Jan. 1, 1890), librarian, was born in Boston, Mass., the son of Josiah and Betsey S. (Giles) Vinton and a descendant of John Vinton, of Huguenot stock, who was a resident of Lynn, Mass., as early as 1648. Prepared for college at the academies of Weymouth and Braintree, Frederic was graduated at Amherst in the class of 1837. Intending to enter the ministry, he studied at the Andover Theological Seminary and at Yale, 1840–42. Although he was never ordained, he was in charge of a church in St. Louis from 1843 to 1845. His health failing, he returned to the East and taught at Nantucket and at Eastport, Me., from 1845 to 1851. In the latter year he was engaged by his brother, Alfred Vinton, a prominent citizen of St. Louis, to catalogue his large private library, and Frederic's studies in connection with this catalogue determined his future career. This manuscript catalogue, now in the Library of Princeton University, contains, in an extensive preface, a discussion of the principles of classification which antedates any other printed in America.

After another year of teaching in South Boston, Vinton was appointed, in 1856, assistant librarian of the Boston Public Library, under its first librarian, Edward Capen, whom he aided in the preparation of the printed catalogues issued in 1858, 1861, and 1865. He was largely responsible for the classification of the Bates Hall collection. In 1865 he became first assistant librarian of the Library of Congress, under Ainsworth Rand Spofford [*q.v.*], where he was engaged in the preparation of the *Catalogue of the Library of Congress: Index of Subjects* published in 1869, and the annual volumes of the alphabetical catalogue from 1867 to 1872. In

1873 he became the first full-time librarian of the College of New Jersey (now Princeton University). The Chancellor Green Library Building had just been completed, and his first task was the classification and the arrangement of the collection of about 18,000 volumes. Under his intelligent and forceful management, the library grew rapidly and at the time of his death in 1890 numbered 70,000 volumes. The years from 1877 to 1884 he spent in the preparation of the *Subject-Catalogue of the Library of the College of New Jersey at Princeton* (1884), one of the most scholarly and useful publications of the sort up to that time. Despite his infirm health, he was a man of great energy and devotion to his profession and he was one of the small group who founded the American Library Association in 1876. To the *Princeton Review* and other journals he contributed articles dealing with books, libraries, and missions.

Vinton married, Sept. 13, 1843, Phoebe Clisby, daughter of Seth and Elizabeth Clisby of Nantucket; she died Feb. 23, 1855, and on June 1, 1857, he married Mary B. Curry, daughter of Cadwallader Curry of Eastport, Me., who survived him. The four children of his first marriage died in infancy; two children were born to his second wife, who survived him.

[S. R. Winans in *Princeton Coll. Bull.*, Apr. 1890, with a list of Vinton's writings; J. A. Vinton, *The Vinton Memorial* (1858); manuscript records of Amherst Coll. Alumni Council, of the Boston Pub. Lib., and of the Lib. of Cong.; Vinton's annual reports (MSS.) in Princeton Univ. Lib.; *Amherst Coll. Biog. Record* (1927); *Obit. Record Grads. Amherst Coll.*, 1883; *Library Jour.*, June 1890; *N. Y. Times*, Jan. 2, 1890.]
J. T. C.

VINTON, FREDERIC PORTER (Jan. 29, 1846–May 20, 1911), portrait painter, was the son of William Henry and Sarah Ward (Goodhue) Vinton. He was born at Bangor, Me., but was taken by his parents to Chicago when he was ten, and his education was begun in the public schools of that city. After five years the family returned to New England, and the boy obtained a place as clerk for the Boston firm of Gardner Brewer & Company, and was later employed by C. F. Hovey & Company until about 1864. By this time he had fully determined to be a painter, his choice being confirmed by the sympathy and advice of William Morris Hunt [*q.v.*]. He entered the drawing class of the Lowell Institute, took anatomy lessons from Dr. William Rimmer [*q.v.*], and drew from casts in the Athenæum gallery. In order to raise funds for European study he then worked for ten years in two Boston banks, in the meanwhile contributing art criticisms to the *Boston Advertiser*. In 1875, having laid up $1000, he went to Paris and entered the atelier of Léon Bonnat. The following year he went to Munich with Frank Duveneck [q.v.] and studied for a year in the Academy there, but he did not care for Munich methods and returned to Paris to study for a time under Jean Paul Laurens. He was the only American in Laurens' studio. Here he painted his first Salon picture, "A Gypsy Girl," now owned by the city of Lowell, Mass.

In 1878 Vinton returned to Boston, took a studio in Winter Street, and painted the vigorous portrait of Thomas G. Appleton which was his first great success. Many sitters came to him and he was soon ranked among the foremost American portrait painters. For thirty-three years he was busily occupied in Boston, producing some three hundred portraits. He had for sitters such men as Charles Francis Adams, Wendell Phillips, Francis Parkman, Gen. Charles Devens, Senator George F. Hoar, William D. Howells, and others equally prominent. Few portraits of men made by Americans are as fine as his best examples, such, for instance, as his "Dr. Samuel A. Green," in the Groton (Mass.) Library. In 1882 he went to Spain with William M. Chase [q.v.] and made ten fine copies of the masterpieces of Velasquez in Madrid, which were exhibited in Boston and elsewhere on his return. In June 1883 he married Annie M. Pierce of Newport, R. I. He was at that time occupying Hunt's old studio in Park Square, Boston, but in 1892 he bought a house in Newbury Street and constructed a pair of handsome and well lighted studios on the top floor. There he lived and worked until his death. He had no children.

In November 1911 a memorial exhibition of his work was opened in the Museum of Fine Arts, Boston. It contained 124 paintings, of which one half were portraits and the rest landscapes, genre pieces, and copies after Velasquez. Vinton was a confirmed realist who ennobled his prose by his breadth of style and dignity. He believed that nothing but truth will endure, and in his practice he endeavored to live up to that difficult standard. He was a National Academician and a member of the National Institute of Arts and Letters.

[Biog. and appreciation by Arlo Bates, in *Memorial Exhibition of the Works of F. P. Vinton* (Museum of Fine Arts, Boston, 1911); *Who's Who in America*, 1910–11; *Boston Transcript*, May 20, 24, 1911; *Boston Daily Advertiser*, Nov. 12, 1878; *Atlantic Monthly*, June 1875; F. T. Robinson, *Living New England Artists* (1888); *Am. Art News*, June 17, 1911; *Cat. of Paintings* (Museum of Fine Arts, Boston, 1921).]

W. H. D.

VINTON, SAMUEL FINLEY (Sept. 25, 1792–May 11, 1862), lawyer and congressman, a descendant of John Vinton whose name appears in the records of Lynn, Mass., in 1648, and the eldest of seven children of Abiathar and Sarah (Day) Vinton, was born in South Hadley, Mass. His father was a farmer; his grandfather, also named Abiathar, was a soldier in the Revolutionary War. Young Vinton prepared for college with the aid of his local pastor, entered Williams in 1808, taught school at intervals to meet expenses, and graduated with the class of 1814. He read law under the direction of Stephen Titus Hosmer, subsequently chief justice of the supreme court of Connecticut, was admitted to the Connecticut bar in 1816, and a few months later commenced practice in Gallipolis, Ohio, a village of French *émigrés*. Here, in 1824, he married Romaine Madeleine Bureau, who died in 1831, having borne him two children. He rose rapidly in public esteem as an advocate. In 1822 he was elected to Congress and continued to serve until Mar. 3, 1837. At this time he had declined to be a candidate for reëlection, but in 1842 he yielded to the demands of the Whigs, and served again as congressman from 1843 to 1851. He was at various times a member of the committees on public lands, roads and canals, and the judiciary; he was made chairman of the Committee of Ways and Means during the war with Mexico, after he had declined the nomination for speaker of the House.

Vinton's first speech in Congress, in May 1824, was on a resolution which he offered with a view to the protection of the lives of passengers on steamboats navigating the Ohio and Mississippi rivers. As a remedy for the unprofitable management of the school lands in Ohio, he introduced and successfully promoted the passage of a bill to authorize that state to sell those lands and invest the proceeds in a trust fund, a precedent which was subsequently followed in other states. When in February 1828 a bill for the appropriation of funds for the Indian service, and particularly for the removal of Indians from lands east of the Mississippi to a reservation west of that river, was before Congress, Vinton, for the purpose of preventing any disadvantage to either slave states or free states, moved and made a memorable speech in support of an amendment which provided that no Indians living north of 36° 30' should be aided in removing south of that line, nor any Indians living south of it be aided in removing north of it. Vinton spoke frequently, but usually briefly and effectively, on such subjects as the survey and sale of public lands so as to prevent speculation, the Cumberland Road and other internal improvements, the tariff (favoring protection), and the apportionment of representatives. He opposed the annexation of Texas, and opposed a direct tax for the prosecution of the war with Mexico. On Feb. 12, 1849, he reported from the Committee of Ways and Means the bill providing for the establishment of the Department of the Interior, which became a law nineteen days later. Vinton was the unsuccessful Whig candidate for election as governor of Ohio in 1851. He served for one year, 1853–54, as president of the Cleveland & Toledo Railroad, and then returned permanently to Washington, D. C. In April 1862 he was appointed by President Lincoln as one of three commissioners to appraise emancipated slaves within the District, but he died less than a month later. Sarah Madeleine Vinton Dahlgren [q.v.] was his daughter.

[J. A. Vinton, *The Vinton Memorial* (1858); (S.) M. V. Dahlgren, "Samuel Finley Vinton, a Biog. Sketch," *Ohio Archæol. and Hist. Soc. Pubs.*, vol. IV (1895); "Memoir of the Hon. Samuel F. Vinton," *Am. Rev.*, Sept. 1848; Calvin Durfee, *Williams Biog. Annals* (1871); *Biog. Dir. Am. Cong.* (1928); *Daily Nat. Intelligencer* (Washington, D. C.), May 12, 1862.]

N. D. M.

VISSCHER, WILLIAM LIGHTFOOT (Nov. 25, 1842–Feb. 10, 1924), journalist, actor, was born in Owingsville, Ky., the son of Frederick and Elizabeth Walker (Lightfoot) Visscher. He was a descendant of Harmen Visscher, who emigrated from Hoorn in the Netherlands before 1644 and settled in Beverwyck (later Albany). He was educated at Bath Seminary, Owingsville, and Stevenson's Academy, Danville, Ky., and left his studies to enlist in the Union forces as a member of the 24th Kentucky Volunteers. He was mustered out at Covington, Ky., after serving about three years as hospital steward. In 1865 he became private secretary and amanuensis to George Dennison Prentice [q.v.], editor of the *Louisville Daily Journal,* and in 1868 received the degree of LL.B. from the University of Louisville. In the seventies he went west and for most of the rest of his life was occupied in newspaper work, first in Saint Joseph and Kansas City, Mo., later as editorial writer for some of the most important journals in the West, including the San Francisco *Daily Mail* in the late seventies, the *Cheyenne Daily Sun* (1883–85), the Denver *Great West* (1885–86), the Portland *Morning Oregonian* (1889), and the Tacoma *Globe* in the nineties. After about 1895 he lived in Chicago, where he was a special contributor to the *Herald* and other papers.

He wrote much journalistic verse (*Black Mammy*, 1886; *Blue Grass Ballads,* 1900; *Poems of the South,* 1911) and some plays, sketches, and indifferent novels (*Fetch Over the Canoe,* 1908; *Amos Hudson's Motto,* 1905), and had consid-

erable success on the lecture platform and on the stage. Early in the century he played leading parts in New York in Opie Read's *The Jucklins* and *The Starbucks.* In *Ten Wise Men and Some More* (1909) he recorded reminiscences of his pioneer and journalistic friends, among whom were such well-known figures as Col. W. F. Cody ("Buffalo Bill"), Eugene Field, Bill Nye, and Franklin K. Lane. His best-remembered work, *A Thrilling and Truthful History of the Pony Express* (1908), is a vivid account of the system of swift communication between East and West before the coming of the transcontinental railroads. He also wrote the last chapter of the 1917 edition of Cody's *Buffalo Bill's Own Story.* He married on Mar. 16, 1876, Emma Mason (d. 1896) of Pittsfield, Ill., by whom he had one child, a daughter. He died in Chicago of a heart attack. He is described as short of stature, broad-shouldered and vigorous, with bright, twinkling eyes and a carefree manner.

[S. V. Talcott, *Visscher* (1883); *Who's Who in America,* 1922–23; Opie Read, *I Remember* (1930), pp. 204–13; publisher's note, in *Poems of the South,* pp. ii–iii; obituary in *Chicago Daily Tribune,* Feb. 11, 1924; unpublished memoir by Viva G. V. Weber, Visscher's daughter.]

J. C. F–h.

VITALE, FERRUCCIO (Feb. 5, 1875–Feb. 26, 1933), landscape architect, was born at Florence, Italy, the son of Lazzaro and the Countess Giuseppina (Barbaro) Vitale. He was educated at the Classical School of Florence, and at the Royal Military Academy of Modena from which he was graduated in 1893. As a commissioned officer in the Italian army he was sent to Washington in 1898 and made military attaché to the Italian embassy. Later that same year he was sent to the Philippines as a military observer. Not long afterward he resigned his commission in the Italian army and devoted himself to landscape architecture. For generations many of his ancestors on his mother's side had been students of the fine arts at the University of Padua and patrons of art in Venice; his father was an architect of distinction and brilliance. With this background, after several years of practice in his father's architectural office and further study in Florence, Turin, and Paris, Ferruccio Vitale entered upon his profession.

In 1904 he returned to the United States and in association with George F. Pentecost, Jr., established an office in New York for the practice of landscape architecture. That same year he was admitted to membership in the American Society of Landscape Architects, and four years later he was elected to fellowship in the society. His practice was extensive, embracing not only the design of many private estates but also the planning of towns and suburbs. For Washington, D. C., he designed Meridian Hill Park. Although he did not become a naturalized American citizen until 1921, he contributed notable service during the World War as a member of the town planning division of the United States Housing Corporation, working at Dayton, Ohio, and at Watertown, N. Y. On Sept. 24, 1927, President Coolidge named him a member of the National Commission of Fine Arts to succeed James L. Greenleaf of New York whose term had expired. He served on this Commission until 1931, when because of ill health he was forced to resign. At the time of his death he was a member of the architectural commission of the Century of Progress exposition at Chicago.

Throughout his whole professional life Vitale worked unceasingly to bring about a closer collaboration among the arts and to strengthen the position of landscape architecture as one of the fine arts. As a member of the board of trustees of the American Academy in Rome and as a member of its executive committee he rendered valuable service to this end. It was in great measure through his efforts that there was established in 1915 the first fellowship in landscape architecture at the American Academy in Rome. He was also instrumental in the founding of the second and third Academy fellowships. He was one of the founders and a trustee of the Foundation for Architecture and Landscape Architecture at Lake Forest, Ill. He was a member of the Architectural League of New York and winner of its gold medal in 1920. He was a past president of the New York Chapter of the American Society of Landscape Architects and was elected an honorary member of the American Institute of Architects in 1927. On May 29, 1910, he married Rosamond Flower Rothery of Wellesley, Mass., who with two daughters survived him.

[Unpublished data in possession of Mrs. Ferruccio Vitale; "Ferruccio Vitale: a Minute on His Life and Service Prepared for the New York Chapter of the American Society of Landscape Architects," in *Landscape Architecture*, July 1933; *Who's Who in America*, 1930–31; *N. Y. Times*, Feb. 27, 1933.]   K. McN.

VIZCAÍNO, SEBASTIÁN (c. 1550–c. 1628), merchant-explorer, was born in Spain, probably the son of Antonio Vizcaíno of the town of Corcho, a commoner. Vizcaíno is said to have served in the royal army in Portugal in 1567. He went to Mexico about 1585 and, becoming interested in the very profitable China trade, made at least one voyage to Manila between 1586 and 1589. He was a passenger on the unlucky galleon *Santa Ana* when it was taken off Lower California and burned by Thomas Cavendish in November 1587, and lost a good part of his fortune. In

1593 a company which he had organized for the exploration of the Gulf of California, reputedly rich in pearls, received a commission from the viceroy of New Spain, and in 1594 an expedition was sent out under the command of one Pérez del Castillo, who bungled it badly and returned to face criminal action. Apparently no blame was attached to Vizcaíno, for the following year his company was given a new contract, and in June 1596 he sailed from Acapulco with three ships and 230 men. The expedition was entirely fruitless, though Vizcaíno asserted that he had reached latitude 29° 30′, and by the following December he was back at Acapulco. After many delays and long negotiations, a new voyage was undertaken in 1602 to explore the outer coast of California as far as Cape Mendocino, locate good harbors that might be used as refuges for the Manila galleons, and find the supposed Strait of Anian, through which the English and French were rumored to have reached the Pacific.

A full complement of men, experienced navigators to advise the *general,* Vizcaíno, two cosmographers, and a company of missionaries left Acapulco in three good vessels on May 5, 1602. Vizcaíno explored the difficult coast of Lower California in the teeth of the heavy northwest gale that prevails on that coast almost the year round and reached San Diego Bay in November. After resting and refitting he sailed northward again and on Dec. 15 discovered Monterey Bay, which he called "the best harbor that could be desired." Vizcaíno had encountered all the hardships of the northern passage—head winds, fog, thirst, hunger, and scurvy—and had so many disabled men that he sent one of his vessels back with them. With the two remaining vessels he pushed on up the coast to Cape Mendocino, which he reached on Jan. 12, 1603, missing San Francisco Bay in the bad weather. At Cape Mendocino his expedition was found to be so badly battered that there were not enough hands to man the sails, and he decided to return. On Feb. 18, 1603, he reached Mazatlán. This expedition, the first to make a scientific exploration of the west coast, furnished the first maps of that dangerous coast, did much to explode the myth of the Northwest Passage, and discovered Monterey Bay.

Vizcaíno strongly recommended the establishment of a port at Monterey for the protection and refitting of the Manila galleons. Winning some support, he went to Spain to plead his case before the Council of the Indies and received a royal decree establishing the port of Monterey with him in charge (1607). Meanwhile, however, a new viceroy in New Spain, the marquis of Montesclaros, opposed the plan on the grounds of expense and expediency, and the undertaking was abandoned for a hundred and sixty years. By way of compensation Vizcaíno was put in command of an expedition to discover the fabulous islands, "Rica de Oro" and "Rica de Plata," which were supposed to lie in the neighborhood of Japan. The expedition sailed in 1611, established the non-existence of the islands, made an ineffectual attempt to promote relations with Japan, and returned to Mexico in January 1614. In 1615 Vizcaíno was in the New Spanish province of Avalos, where he enlisted a force to defend the coast against Dutch attack. Beyond that date nothing is known of him. He had married, sometime before 1589, a woman of some property and in 1596 had one son.

[*Colección de Documentos Inéditos,* vol. VIII (Madrid, 1867), ed. by Louis Torres de Mendoza; Francisco Garrasco y Guisasola, *Documentos Referentes al Reconocimiento de las Costas de las Californias* (Madrid, 1882); *Hist. Soc. of Southern Cal. Pubs.,* vol. II, pt. 1 (1891); H. R. Wagner, *Spanish Voyages to the Northwest Coast of America in the Sixteenth Cent.* (1929); George Davidson, *The Discovery of San Francisco Bay* (1907); H. E. Bolton, *Spanish Exploration in the Southwest* (1916); C. E. Chapman, in *Southwestern Hist. Quart.,* Apr. 1920; Juan de Torquemada, *The Voyage of Sebastian Vizcaino to the Coast of Cal.* (1933), translated from Torquemada's *Monarquía Indiana* (Madrid, 1615); Martín Fernández de Navarrete, *Colección de los Viages . . . que Hicieron los Españoles desde Fines del Siglo XV* (Madrid, 5 vols., 1825–37).]
L. B. S—n.

VOGRICH, MAX WILHELM KARL (Jan. 24, 1852–June 10, 1916), pianist, composer, editor, was born in Hermannstadt (Nagy-Szeben), Transylvania, the son of Tobias Wogritsch and Therese (Schäffer) Wogritsch. He started his career as a musical prodigy, and at the age of five began to study piano. At the age of seven he made his first public appearance. From 1866 to 1869 he was a pupil at the Leipzig Conservatory, studied piano with Ignaz Moscheles, Ernst Wenzel, and Carl Reinecke, and theory and composition with Moritz Hauptmann, Ernst Richter, and Reinecke, and then started in earnest on his career as a pianist. He toured Europe, Mexico, and South America from 1870 to 1878, and then came to the United States for the first time. He gave several recitals in New York, and toured the country as accompanist to the celebrated violinist August Wilhelmj. He was also associated with Eduard Reményi, for George P. Upton [*q.v.*], in his *Musical Memories* (1908, p. 63), mentions Vogrich as Reményi's "*protégé,* a young musician of extraordinary talent, who has since become a lost Pleiad." The young Vogrich was, however, not entirely lost, for, although he did not continue to appear publicly as a pianist, and left America to live in Australia from 1882 to 1886, he returned to New York in 1886 and

stayed there for sixteen years, busying himself with composition and music editing. From 1902 to 1908 he lived in Weimar, and in 1908 moved to London, where he stayed until the outbreak of the World War in 1914. He spent the last two years of his life in New York City, acting during this time as adviser to the music publishing firm of G. Schirmer.

Vogrich was a prolific composer, and many of his works were widely used in their day. He composed three operas, all to his own librettos: "Vanda," produced in Florence, 1875; König Arthur," Leipzig, 1893; and "Der Buddha," Weimar, 1904. He was the composer of incidental music to Ernst von Wildenbruch's "Die Lieder des Euripides" (copyright, 1905), and of a dramatic scene, "The Highland Widow." His oratorio, "The Captivity" (copyright, 1890), was performed at the Metropolitan Opera House, New York, in 1891, and his "Memento Mori" (1910), for violin and orchestra, was played in Berlin in 1912 and in New York the season preceding his death. His violin concerto, "E pur si muove" (1913), was dedicated to Mischa Elman, who performed it in Berlin in 1913 and in New York in 1917. Others of his works were: two cantatas, "The Diver" (copyright, 1888), and "Der junge König und die Schäferin" (copyright, 1890); a "Missa Solemnis"; two symphonies, in E minor and A minor; an Andante and Intermezzo for violin and orchestra; a concerto in E minor for piano; as well as many pieces for piano, and for violin and piano, songs, and shorter choruses.

A year before his death Vogrich came into newspaper prominence when he sued the estate of the widow of Theodore Havemeyer, the sugar magnate, for thirty thousand dollars. Vogrich claimed that Mrs. Havemeyer had promised to bequeath him this sum, and when the will was published he was the beneficiary of only ten thousand dollars. It was currently understood in musical circles that Vogrich had been Havemeyer's protégé. When Havemeyer was living, Vogrich had charge of the music in his household, and had benefited so largely from Havemeyer's generosity that he was enabled to give up his routine work in New York and settle in Europe where he could devote himself entirely to composition. He died following a surgical operation, and was survived by his wife, Alice Rees, formerly an English singer, whom he had met in Australia.

[Books on American music give scanty recognition to Vogrich. L. C. Elson omits him entirely in *The Hist. of Am. Music* (revised ed., 1915); in Rupert Hughes and Arthur Elson, *Am. Composers* (revised ed., 1914), his name is included in a list; and J. T. Howard, in *Our American Music* (1913), gives him only a brief paragraph. The articles in *Grove's Dict. of Music and Musicians, Am. Supp.* (1930), and in *Baker's Biog. Dict. of Musicians* (1919) are more detailed. For information about the suit against the Havemeyer estate see the *N. Y. Times*, Oct. 12, 1915. An extensive obituary notice appeared in the *Musical Courier*, June 15, 1916, and a shorter one in the *N. Y. Times*, June 11, 1916.]   J. T. H.

VOLCK, ADALBERT JOHN (Apr. 14, 1828–Mar. 26, 1912), caricaturist, dentist, was born in Augsburg, Bavaria, one of two sons of Andrew von Volzeck, a prominent manufacturer and land owner. He studied at the Polytechnic Institute, Nürnberg, and perhaps at the University of Munich, participated in the march on Berlin in 1848, and was forced to flee because of his revolutionary sympathies. In 1849, penniless and without friends, he landed in America, where he lived first in St. Louis, Mo., and then joined the gold rush. In 1851 he was recommended to Dr. Chapin A. Harris [q.v.], one of the founders of the Baltimore College of Dental Surgery, for appointment as an instructor. In 1852, having studied as well as taught, he received the degree of D.D.S. He was married on July 6, 1852, to Letitia Roberta Alleyn of Baltimore, Md., by whom he had two sons and three daughters. He was a charter member of the Maryland State Dental Association, one of the first users of porcelain in the filling of teeth, and a founder of the Association of Dental Surgeons. He was instrumental during the Civil War in getting medicine into the South.

During the war, in an effort to combat the activities of Thomas Nast [q.v.], Northern caricaturist, Volck made a series of caricatures favorable to the South under the pseudonym of V. Blada. Notable among these are drawings of Lincoln and Gen. Benjamin F. Butler as "Don Quixote and Sancho Panza," of Lincoln passing through Baltimore on his way to his inauguration, and of Gov. Thomas Hicks of Maryland as "Judas." The most important and best known collection of his work is *Confederate War Etchings* (n.d.), which contains twenty-nine plates; a volume of *Sketches from the Civil War in North America* (1863) bears a London imprint, possibly false. Volck was responsible for the illustrations in *Bombastes Furioso Buncombe* (1862) and the *American Cyclops* (1868) of James Fairfax McLaughlin. He also illustrated *A Popular Life of General Robert E. Lee* (1872), by Emily V. Mason. He is said to have drawn the head of Jefferson Davis for the ten-cent stamp of the Confederacy, but it is probably the work of his brother, Frederick Volck, a sculptor. His caricatures of General Butler, by whose orders he had been incarcerated in Fort McHenry in 1861, were used to defeat Butler when

he was a candidate for the governorship of Massachusetts. After the war his interest in political satire, for which he had a marked natural gift, seems to have died. His portrait in oils of Robert E. Lee (1870) is in the Valentine Museum, Richmond, Va. About 1880 he became interested in working in bronze and silver. His most interesting achievements are a bas-relief of Basil L. Gildersleeve [q.v.], a shield in memory of the Confederate women in the Confederate Museum in Richmond, and a large bowl presented in 1897 to Mayor Alcaeus Hooper of Baltimore. In the seventies he was one of the founders of the famous Wednesday Club of Baltimore, and he made many illustrations for its theatrical productions and musical soirées, besides carving for the main lounge of the clubhouse a tremendous wooden mantel. Later he was the founder of the Charcoal Club. He died in Baltimore, survived by two daughters and a son.

[Sources include Meredith Janvier, *Baltimore in the Eighties and Nineties* (1933); G. C. Keidel, in *Argus* (Catonsville, Md.), Oct. 2–Nov. 20, 1915; Murat Halstead, in *Cosmopolitan*, Aug. 1890; *Mag. of Hist.*, extra number 60, 1917, which reprints much of Volck's work; Albert Shaw, *Abraham Lincoln, His Path to the Presidency* (1929) and *Abraham Lincoln, the Year of His Election* (1929); Frank Weitenkampf, *Am. Graphic Art* (1912); C. W. Drepperd, *Early Am. Prints* (1930); August Dietz, *The Postal Service of the Confederate States of America* (1929); A. H. Starke, *Sidney Lanier* (1933); *Sun* (Baltimore), Mar. 27 (obituary) and Mar. 31, 1912, Feb. 4, 1917; minute books of Md. State Dental Asso. and Asso. of Dental Surgeons; information from Henrietta Volck Falkinburg, Volck's daughter. Many of Volck's caricatures are in the possession of the Peabody and Pratt libraries, Baltimore, Md.]

G. M. A.

VOLK, LEONARD WELLS (Nov. 7, 1828–Aug. 19, 1895), sculptor, son of Garret and Elizabeth (Gesner) Volk, was born at Wellstown (later Wells), N. Y., one of a family of twelve. On his mother's side he was a direct descendant of Anneke Jans Bogardus. He spent his boyhood on a farm and attended district schools in Avon and Palmyra, N. Y., and in Berkshire County, Mass. At sixteen he began to learn marble carving in his father's shop at Pittsfield, Mass. He practised his craft at Bethany, Batavia, and Buffalo, N. Y., and in the autumn of 1848 went to St. Louis, Mo., where a year later he began his self-taught studies in drawing and modeling. Early works were a copy in marble of Joel T. Hart's bust of Henry Clay, and a portrait of Father Theobald Mathew (1850). Archbishop Kenrick of St. Louis gave him his first order, high-relief portraits for a mausoleum. On April 22, 1852, he married Emily Clarissa, daughter of Dr. Jonathan King Barlow of Bethany, and settled for a year in Galena, Ill. There he met his wife's cousin, Stephen A. Douglas [q.v.], who became deeply interested in his career. Volk returned to St. Louis and thence went to Rock Island, Ill., and engaged in business. In 1855, supplied with funds by Douglas, Volk left his wife and child in Pittsfield, and went to Rome. When he returned to the United States in 1857, he opened a studio in Chicago and at once became a leader in art movements there. He organized the first art exhibition held there (1859); he was one of the founders of the Chicago Academy of Design (1867) and its president for some time. Taking advantage of the Lincoln-Douglas debates (1858), he made close studies from life of both contestants. Direct results of these are the colossal Douglas monument at Chicago, statues of Lincoln and Douglas in the Illinois State Capitol, Springfield (1876), a marble statue and a marble bust of Lincoln (1860). The bust, exhibited in Paris in 1867, was placed in the building of the Chicago Historical Society, where it was destroyed in the great fire of 1871; the original model was preserved. Other important works are the statuary for the soldiers' monument at Girard, Pa., said to be the first of its kind in the country; the soldiers' monument at Rock Island, Ill.; a bronze statue of Gen. James Shields, in Statuary Hall, Washington, D. C. (1893); and a statue of Lincoln at Rochester, N. Y. In 1880 Volk published a small book, *History of the Douglas Monument at Chicago.*

Although Volk attempted ideal figures (such as his Faith and Ione), his talent lay rather in faithful portraiture. Among his many authentic studies of his contemporaries are those of Elihu B. Washburne, Zachariah Chandler, James H. McVicker, J. Young Scammon, and David Davis. He was probably the only sculptor to study Lincoln closely and advantageously from life, and his life-mask and casts of Lincoln's hands are invaluable historic mementos. He approached his art by the avenue of the marble carver's craft, and it is to his credit that he was untouched by the pseudo-classicism he saw in Italy during his three visits there. Shortly after his wife's death in the spring of 1895, he died at Osceola, Wis., where he was accustomed to spend the summers. He was survived by a son, who became eminent as a painter, and a daughter.

[*Biog. Sketches of the Leading Men of Chicago* (1868); Lorado Taft, *The Hist. of Am. Sculpture* (1903); C. E. Fairman, *Art and Artists of the Capitol of the U. S.* (1927); obituary in *Chicago Tribune,* Aug. 20, 1895; biog. statement, signed by Volk, in N. Y. Pub. Lib.; information from Volk's grandson, Jerome D. Volk of Lovell, Me.] A. A.

VON HOLST, HERMANN EDUARD [See HOLST, HERMANN EDUARD VON, 1841–1904].

VONNOH, ROBERT WILLIAM (Sept. 17, 1858–Dec. 28, 1933), painter, born at Hartford, Conn., was the son of William and Frederika (Haug) Vonnoh. The family moved in Robert's boyhood to Boston, where he attended the public schools. At the age of fourteen, admiring another boy's drawings, he decided to be an artist, and his mother permitted him to enter a lithographer's shop. In 1877 he entered the recently established Massachusetts Normal Art School (later the Massachusetts School of Art), from which he was graduated in 1879. Meanwhile he taught in the Boston Free Evening Drawing School in Roxbury and at Thayer Academy, South Braintree. With money he had saved he went to Paris in 1881 and became a pupil of Boulanger and Lefebvre at the Académie Julian, but an unfortunate investment of his fund brought him home after two years. During 1883–85 he was principal of the East Boston Evening Drawing School; during 1884–85 he taught at the Cowles Art School, and in 1886–87 at the school of drawing and painting in the Boston Museum of Fine Arts. He married, July 7, 1886, Grace D. Farrell. Four years of study at Paris followed. In 1891 Vonnoh took an instructorship at the Pennsylvania Academy of the Fine Arts, Philadelphia, which he held through 1894, and entered upon a professional career in which he painted upwards of 500 portraits, many of them of great distinction. Many of his pupils, among them W. J. Glackens and Maxfield Parrish, became well-known artists. He later returned to the Pennsylvania Academy for two more years as instructor (1918–20).

Vonnoh's point of view as a creative painter was succinctly set forth in his article, "The Relation of Art to Existence" (*Arts and Decoration,* Sept. 1922). Pleading vigorously for vocational training, this amounted to a well-written diatribe against the forms of literary education prevalent in colleges and schools. The author asserted that "it is not so important to know how to read and write if one must know it at the expense of genuinely productive work. . . . Literary education teaches children how to tell others to do things that they themselves cannot do" (p. 329). Vonnoh himself was a man of great personal charm and cultivation, with marked linguistic ability. He maintained studios at New York and Los Angeles, and he was one of the founders of the summer art colony at Lyme, Conn. His second marriage, Sept. 17, 1899, was to Bessie O. Potter, American sculptor. The two had the distinction of being the only man and wife who were members of the National Academy of Design.

Winning as painter many prizes and honorable mentions, Vonnoh was represented in his lifetime at the Metropolitan Museum, New York, by "La Mère Adèle"; by portraits of S. Weir Mitchell at the College of Physicians, Philadelphia; the "Family of Woodrow Wilson," at the White House; Col. Lucius Hudson Holt, at the United States Military Academy, West Point; Gov. Hiram Bingham, in the Connecticut State House; Charles Francis Adams, in the Massachusetts Historical Society, and many others. One of his latest works, painted *con amore* at the request of the alumni association, was the likeness of Walter Smith, English-born founder of the Normal Art School. At the presentation of this work, during the semi-centennial celebration of the school in December 1925, the artist gave personal reminiscences of his days as an art student in Boston. A published list of his honors then showed that as early as 1884 he won the gold medal of the Massachusetts Charitable Mechanics' Association, and that he was awarded bronze medals at the Paris expositions of 1889 and 1900, a gold medal at the Panama-Pacific Exposition (1915), and the Proctor portrait prize of the National Academy of Design (1904). Vonnoh's portraits were strong and serious, never daring or experimental. He painted many landscapes, some of them of great charm. Always interested in problems of craftsmanship, he made his own frames, which were thoroughly consistent with the tonality of his pictures. Failing eye-sight from 1925 onward brought to a rather somber close a career that had been remarkably productive and fortunate. Vonnoh's last years were spent at Gréz-sur-Loing, France; he died at Nice from a heart attack. He was survived by his wife.

[*Who's Who in America*, 1928–29; *Am. Art News*, Dec. 30, 1905; "Vonnoh's Half Century," *Internat. Studio*, June 1923; *Bull. Mass. School of Art*, Jan.–Feb., Apr.–May 1926; Cat. of La. Purchase Exposition, 1904; obituaries in *Art News*, Jan. 6, 1934, and *N. Y. Times*, Dec. 29, 1933; information from Bessie Potter Vonnoh.]   **F.W.C.**

VON RUCK, KARL (July 10, 1849–Nov. 5, 1922), physician, the son of George and Clara von Ruck, was born in Constantinople, Turkey, where his father, a native of Stuttgart, was stationed in the German diplomatic service. He attended the University of Stuttgart, where he obtained the degree of B.S. in 1867. Then studying medicine at the University of Tübingen, he was graduated M.D. there in 1877. After further study in England and at the University of Michigan he received the degree of M.D. from the University of Michigan in 1879. He practised his profession at Norwalk, Ohio, first as a general practitioner, then developing a surgical practice, and later settling upon the specialty of tuberculosis. From the beginning of his medical studies he was interested in this disease from contact at Tübingen with Felix von Niemeyer, an important clinician of the time. Also during a period of study in Berlin in 1882 he was present at the meeting there when Robert Koch announced the discovery of the tubercle bacillus.

To further his specialized work he removed to North Carolina and took over a sanitorium at Sulphur Springs near Asheville. Its destruction by fire shortly thereafter caused his removal to Asheville and the founding of Winyah Sanitorium at that place in 1888. This was one of the earliest private sanatoria for tubercular patients and made for him a comfortable fortune. In 1895 he organized the Von Ruck Research Laboratory for Tuberculosis, where after two years of immunological investigation he produced a modification of Koch's first tuberculin, a watery extract of the tubercle bacillus. He was an early advocate of the complement-fixation test for the diagnosis of tuberculosis and for its use in the quantitative estimate of immunity to the disease. Application of his laboratory research to the clinical material of the sanitorium resulted in 1912 in his anti-tuberculosis vaccine. This vaccine was used widely in the treatment of tuberculous patients, although designed primarily for the protective immunization of children and others exposed to tuberculous infection. This pioneer work in tuberculosis subjected him to much criticism and ridicule, which, to a man of his strong convictions and intolerance of opposition, was doubly galling. Though he was throughout his career in constant controversy with his fellow-workers in the tuberculosis field, his work and many of his ideas have been generally accepted. About 1913 he turned over the management of Winyah Sanitorium to his son, in order to concentrate on research. In collaboration with his son, Silvio Von Ruck, he published *Studies in Immunization against Tuberculosis* in 1916. He married Delia Moore of Ottawa County, Ohio, on Dec. 25, 1872. The death of his only son, Silvio, and of his only grandchild, Silvia, almost simultaneously of pneumonia in 1918 was a crushing blow, followed by the death of his wife in 1921. He died of nephritis the next year.

[H. J. Achard, "Karl von Ruck," *Am. Rev. of Tuberculosis*, Jan. 1923; *Am. Jour. of Clinical Med.*, Dec. 1922; *Jour. of the Am. Med. Assn.*, Nov. 11, 1922; *N. Y. Times*, Nov. 7, 1922; Stuttgart given as birthplace in *Who's Who in America*, 1922–23, but Achard, *ante*, gives Constantinople on authority of Von Ruck's verbal statement to him.]   **J.M.P—n.**

VON TEUFFEL, BLANCHE WILLIS HOWARD [See HOWARD, BLANCHE WILLIS, 1847–1898].

VOORHEES, DANIEL WOLSEY (Sept. 26, 1827–Apr. 10, 1897), senator from Indiana, was born in Butler County, Ohio, the descendant of Steven Coerte Van Voorhees, an emigrant from Holland about 1660, and the son of Stephen and Rachel (Elliott) Voorhees. Taken to Indiana when two months old, he was brought up on a farm in Fountain County, and, though he early evinced more of a taste for books than for manual labor, he always considered himself as belonging to the farming class. In 1849 he was graduated from Indiana Asbury (now De Pauw) University and then read law. On July 18, 1850, he was married to Anna Hardesty of Greencastle, Ind. They had four children. Admitted to the bar in 1851, in 1853 he became prosecuting attorney for the circuit court. In 1857 he removed to Terre Haute, which became his permanent home. After his defeat for Congress in 1856, President Buchanan appointed him federal district attorney for Indiana. Elected to Congress, he served in the House of Representatives from Mar. 4, 1861, to Feb. 26, 1866, when his election was successfully contested by Henry D. Washburn. He was one of the most virulent of those Democrats whose criticisms were heard throughout the war period. To him abolitionism and secession were equally hateful; and he bewailed the breaches of the Constitution and the tyranny of the war government in terms of unmeasured opprobrium. He was, however, by no means an irreconcilable partisan. He voted for the bill to make Grant a lieutenant-general and was one of eight Democratic absentees when the Thirteenth Amendment passed the House. He introduced the resolution—which so alarmed the extreme Republicans—unqualifiedly indorsing President Johnson's Reconstruction policy.

From 1869 to 1873 he was again in the House of Representatives, in 1877 was appointed to the Senate and served from Nov. 6, 1877, to Mar. 3, 1897. In his twenty years as senator he attained the eminence attached to long service and oratorical ability (for his speeches see *Speeches*, 1875, comp. by C. S. Voorhees, and *Forty Years of Oratory*, 2 vols., 1898). His views on financial questions were typical of his party and state and rested on the desire for a large and freely circulating currency, on the belief that protection bore hardly on the farmers, and on a distrust of New England and the "money power." With the passage of time, however, his attitude became less strictly agrarian, and he supported President Cleveland in the various questions that divided the Democratic party. As chairman of the committee on finance, he led the fight for the repeal of the Sherman silver purchase act during the extra session of 1893, and in the following year he was the nominal manager in the Senate for the Wilson tariff bill.

Large and tall, with fair hair and "dark-grey hazel" eyes, he won the sobriquet of "Tall Sycamore of the Wabash" and was unrivalled in the middle West as a stump speaker and forensic orator. Two of his best known achievements as a lawyer were his defense of John E. Cook, one of John Brown's associates in the Harpers Ferry tragedy, and his defense of Mary Harris of Washington, D. C., for murder. He was generous and sympathetic to a fault. Though too ready to lend his aid to those seeking money from the government, yet he did not, himself, profit by his government positions and was also generous with his own money. He died poor in spite of a lucrative practice. He was influential in the building of the present Library of Congress. He died in Washington, and his funeral services were in St. John's Episcopal Church. He was buried in Terre Haute.

[Biog. sketches by A. B. Carlton, in *Speeches, ante*; and by T. B. Long, in *Forty Years of Oratory, ante*; W. W. Thornton, in *Green Bag*, Aug. 1902; H. D. Jordan, in *Miss. Valley Hist. Rev.*, Mar. 1920; J. G. Blaine, *Twenty Years of Congress* (2 vols., 1884–86); Hugh McCulloch, *Men and Measures of Half a Century* (1888); the inconclusive evidence for his connection with the Knights of the Golden Circle during the Civil War in F. G. Stidger, *Treason Hist. of the Order of Sons of Liberty* . . . (1903); E. W. Van Voorhis, *A Geneal. of the Van Voorhees Family* (1888); *Evening Star* (Washington, D. C.), Apr. 10, 1897.]   H. D. J.

VOORHEES, EDWARD BURNETT (June 22, 1856–June 6, 1911), agriculturist, was born at Minebrook, Somerset County, N. J., the son of John and Sarah (Dilley) Voorhees. He was a descendant of Steven Coerte Van Voorhees who emigrated from the Netherlands and settled on Long Island in 1660. At twenty-one Edward entered Rutgers College, where he was graduated with the degree of A.B. in 1881. The following year he spent as assistant to Prof. Wilbur O. Atwater [q.v.] at Wesleyan University, Middletown, Conn. In 1883 George H. Cook [q.v.], then director of the New Jersey State Experiment Station, offered him the position of assistant chemist, which he accepted. On Oct. 18 of the same year he married Anna E. Amerman, by whom he had two daughters and five sons. In 1888 he was promoted to chief chemist, and in 1890 he became, also, professor of agriculture at Rutgers, in which position he served until his death. Consciously or unconsciously Dr. Cook had prepared his assistant to fill the place which by Cook's death in 1889 was suddenly left vacant, but it was not until 1893 that Voorhees was appointed thereto. In 1896 he was made director of the College Station as well, and for some fifteen years he arranged the work of the two stations so that the College Station pursued fundamental research while the State Station set into practical application and made available to the farmers of New Jersey the scientific findings.

Voorhees was president of the Association of Official Agricultural Chemists (1893–94), secretary-treasurer of the Association of American Agricultural Colleges and Experiment Stations (1897–1903), and president in 1904, vice-president of the State Board of Agriculture (1893 to 1901), and its president (1901–11). He lent his influence to the fight against tuberculosis in cattle, was president for a short time of the state tuberculosis commission, and for a year was head of the New Jersey Microscopical Society. In the summer of 1904 he visited the experiment stations of England, Scotland, Ireland, Belgium, France, and Italy and brought home much valuable information. In 1898 he published *Fertilizers,* which was immediately accepted as a standard college textbook and went through thirteen editions; for use in secondary schools, he wrote *First Principles of Agriculture* (1896). He collaborated with Herbert Myrick in preparing *The Book of Corn* (1903); in 1907 he published *Forage Crops for Soiling, Silage, Hay and Pasture.* Besides these books, he wrote numerous articles for scientific journals.

Perhaps the founding of short agricultural courses for farmers was Voorhees' most useful work. He had rare ability as a teacher, not only of students, but of the thousands of farmers with whom he spent much of his time, lecturing to them, listening to their problems, and advising them. He always emphasized his one great precept, "improve the land." Under his management the experiment farm carried out extensive field tests with respect to top-dressing of meadows, special crop fertilizers, spraying of orchards, control of strawberry weevil, egg production, milk sanitation, and many other problems. Lectures and demonstrations explained to the farmers of the state the principles underlying the failure or success of these experiments. As a result of such leadership there came a more intensive specialization of agriculture, improved farming practice, and larger returns for the effort expended. His skill in choosing able men to collaborate with him insured continuation of the work when his own labor was finished.

[E. W. Van Voorhis, *A Geneal. of the Van Voorhees Family in America* (1888); J. McK. Cattell, *Am. Men of Sci.* (2nd ed., 1910); *Who's Who in America,* 1910–11; *U. S. Dept. of Agric., Experiment Station Record,* Aug. 1911; *Proc. of the Thirty-second Ann. Meeting of the Soc. for the Promotion of Agricultural Sci.* (1912); C. R. Woodward and I. N. Waller, *New Jersey's Agricultural Experiment Station* (1932); *Thirty-ninth Ann. Report of the State Board of Agriculture* (Trenton, 1912); *Trenton True American,* June 8, 1911.]
L. G.

VOORHEES, PHILIP FALKERSON (1792–Feb. 23, 1862), naval officer, was born in New Brunswick, N. J. He entered the navy as a midshipman, Nov. 15, 1809, and fought through the War of 1812, participating in the capture of the *Macedonian* by the *United States,* and of the *Epervier* by the *Peacock.* For his services in the latter engagement he was awarded a silver medal by Congress (J. F. Loubat, *The Medallic History of the United States,* vol. I, 1878, p. 198). His life was uneventful for many years except for a Mediterranean cruise in the *North Carolina* (1825–27). In 1831 he sailed again for the Mediterranean commanding the *John Adams* bearing dispatches for David Porter [q.v.], chargé d'affaires at Constantinople. He returned to the United States in 1834, and for the next seven years resided at Annapolis, Md., where he married Anne Randall, May 12, 1835; by this marriage he had two children.

On July 15, 1842, Voorhees, who by this time had risen to the rank of captain, again sailed for the Mediterranean commanding the frigate *Congress,* and the next year was ordered to join the Brazil squadron under Commodore Daniel Turner [q.v.]. On Sept. 28, 1844, he assisted in rescuing H.M.S. *Gorgon* which was stranded in the Rio de la Plata. The following day while off Montevideo, a schooner from Buenos Aires, the *Sancala,* fired on an American brig, the *Rosalba,* lying near the *Congress.* For this action Voorhees captured the *Sancala* and the whole Argentine squadron which was blockading Montevideo. The squadron was released after an apology but the *Sancala* was retained. Voorhees also refused to allow the blockade to be enforced against American vessels. Commodore Turner finally released the *Sancala,* though he considered Voorhees' action justifiable. The following spring Voorhees returned home, reaching Annapolis, Mar. 12, 1845.

On June 2 he was court-martialed for his action against the Argentine squadron and sentenced to reprimand and suspension for three years. Again, on June 24, he was court-martialed on a series of trivial charges, chief of which was disobedience to an order of Commodore Turner. He was found guilty on two specifications and suspended for eighteen months. George Bancroft [q.v.], secretary of the navy, dissatisfied with the findings of the court, ordered it to review its proceedings. The court re-convened, Aug. 5–8, 1845, and ordered Voorhees "To be dismissed from the service of the United States"; but President Polk mitigated his sentence to suspension from duty for five years. On Jan. 7, 1847, the President removed the suspension, and in 1849 Voorhees was ordered to take command of the East India squadron "in manifestation of his complete rehabilitation in honor as well as in rank" (*Official Opinions of the Attorneys General of the United States,* vol. VI, 1856, p. 202).

In 1855 he was placed by the naval retiring board on the reserved list on furlough pay. Voorhees appealed from the decision of the board, but the decision was sustained. Voorhees applied for a review of his case and President Buchanan referred the matter to the attorney-general who rendered a decision highly favorable to Voorhees, deeming him to be the victim of many blunders and misunderstandings. He was then placed on the reserve list with leave pay. He presented a memorial to Congress in December 1860 asking for restoration to active service, but nothing came of it. Though Voorhees was guilty of an error in judgment in capturing the Argentine squadron, his motives were admirable. Even the court that sentenced him to dismissal praised his "Uniform character, previous to these occurrences, for integrity, his gallant services as an officer, and his long continuance in the naval service, without reproach or dereliction of duty" (*Ibid.,* p. 202). His remaining years were passed quietly in Annapolis.

[*American and Commercial Advertiser* (Baltimore), Feb. 26, 1862; *Sun* (Baltimore), Feb. 25, 1862; J. B. Moore, *The Works of James Buchanan,* vol. VI (1909); *Defence of Philip F. Voorhees . . . before a Gen. Naval Court Martial* (1845); *Defence of Philip F. Voorhees before the Court of Inquiry* (1857); *Memorial of Capt. Philip F. Voorhees to the Senate and House* (1860); J. B. Moore, *A Digest of International Law,* vol. I (1906), pp. 178–82; *Niles' National Reg.,* Dec. 14, 1844, Feb. 22, Mar. 22, June 14, 1845; M. M. Quaife, *The Diary of James K. Polk,* vol. I (1910), pp. 41–43; log of U.S.S. *Congress,* Sept. 28–29, 1844 (MS.), Navy Dept.; letters to and from Voorhees, and transcript of service, Navy Dept.; information from Randall family, Annapolis, and from records of births and marriages, St. Anne's Episcopal Church, Annapolis.]   L. H. B.

VOORSANGER, JACOB (Nov. 13, 1852–Apr. 27, 1908), rabbi, was born in the Netherlands, at Amsterdam, the son of Wolf and Alicia (Pekel) Voorsanger. He was educated at the Jewish theological seminary of his native city, receiving the degree of rabbi in 1872. After spending a time in London, he came to the United States in 1873, and on Aug. 24 married, at Cincinnati, Eva Corper, by whom he had eight children. He occupied pulpits in Philadelphia (1873–76), Washington, D. C. (1876–77),

Providence, R. I. (1877–78), and Houston, Tex. (1878–86). In 1886 he became assistant to Elkan Cohn at the Temple Emanu-El, San Francisco, and from 1889 to his death served as its rabbi. Largely through his efforts, the University of California created a Semitic department in 1894, and from that time on he was professor of Semitic languages and literature, giving generously of his time and efforts, and collecting funds for the library. He also officiated as chaplain and special lecturer at the Leland Stanford Junior University.

In his day, Voorsanger was the foremost rabbi of the Pacific Coast. He spoke English fluently and without foreign accent, and commanded a direct and terse style. He belonged to the reform school of Judaism, but he had an inherent love of Jewish tradition which held him back from the radical reform tendencies in vogue in America in the last quarter of the nineteenth century. Though with the reform Judaism of his day he opposed the ideology of Zionism, he was interested in Palestine, visiting the country a few years before his death, and on his return writing a sympathetic series of articles appealing for the support of Jewish Palestinian institutions.

Voorsanger was a gifted journalist. He was editor of *The Jewish South,* of Houston, Tex., from 1881 to 1883, and *The Sabbath Visitor,* of Cincinnati, from 1883 to 1886. In 1895 he founded the weekly magazine *Emanu-El,* which he developed into the leading Jewish paper on the Pacific Coast, continuing as its editor till his death. He was the author of *The Chronicles of Emanu-El* (1900), a valuable contribution to the history of San Francisco Jewry, and was a contributing editor of *The Jewish Encyclopedia.* In 1913 Rabbi Martin A. Meyer edited a volume of Voorsanger's sermons, under the title *Sermons and Addresses by Jacob Voorsanger.*

Communal activities occupied a prominent place in his many-sided interests. He was a governor of the Hebrew Union College, a founder and vice-president of the California Red Cross Society, the first president of the Manila Library Association, and a member of the Hebrew Veterans of the Spanish-American War. It is claimed that in the San Francisco earthquake and conflagration of 1906, he was the first public man to organize immediate relief measures. Within one hour after the shock, while buildings were still tottering and flames were raging, he began to marshal men and food, and within four hours the mayor made him chairman of relief. He was a man of imposing stature and a born organizer and leader. Of broad sympathies and forceful personality, he worked with voice and pen for humanitarian causes. His companionable, democratic ways won him friendship and respect. His erudition, eloquence, ready pen, and public spirit made him a strong civic and religious force.

[*The Jewish Encyc.*, XII (1912), 451; *The Am. Jewish Year Book*, 5664 (1903); *Year Book of the Central Conference of Am. Rabbis*, vol. XVIII (1908); *Who's Who in America*, 1906–07; *Hebrew Union Coll. Jubilee Volume* (1925); *The Am. Hebrew* (N. Y.), May 1, 1908; *Emanu-El* (San Francisco), May 1–June 26, 1908; *Jewish Tribune* (Portland, Ore.), May 1, 1908; *Am. Israelite* (Cincinnati, Ohio), Apr. 30, May 4, 1908; *Bulletin* (San Francisco), Apr. 28 and 30, 1908; name of wife from Voorsanger's son, Dr. Elkan Voorsanger.]   D. deS. P.

VOSE, GEORGE LEONARD (Apr. 19, 1831–Mar. 30, 1910), engineer, educator, born at Augusta, Me., was the son of Hon. Richard Hampton Vose, prominent in the legal and political life of that state, and of Harriet Green (Chandler) of Boston. He was a descendant of Robert Vose of Lancashire, England, who emigrated to Dorchester, Mass., some time prior to 1654. In 1848, after high-school training at Augusta and at Salem, Mass., Vose entered the office of Samuel Nott, a prominent civil engineer of Boston. Subsequently he studied for a time in the Lawrence Scientific School at Harvard. In 1850 he began his professional work in the field of railroad engineering, and for some ten years was widely engaged upon railroad location and construction in various parts of the United States and Canada.

In the mean time he published *Handbook of Railroad Construction* (1857), one of the earliest works on the subject to appear in the United States. Three years later he withdrew from the practical activities in which he had been engaged and gave his attention chiefly to writing and teaching. From 1860 to 1864 he was associate editor of the *American Railway Times,* Boston. In 1866 he removed from Salem, Mass., where he was then living, to Paris, Me. Here he concerned himself with various professional matters and prepared his *Manual for Railroad Engineers and Engineering Students* (2 vols., 1873), which went through several editions. In 1872 he was appointed professor of civil engineering at Bowdoin College, Brunswick, Me. His students included a considerable number who later became prominent in the engineering profession, among them Robert E. Peary and George E. Waring [*qq.v.*]. In 1881 Vose was called to the Massachusetts Institute of Technology as professor of civil engineering, where he remained for five years. The active interest which he took in the Boston Society of Civil Engineers led to his election as its president in 1884, in which capacity he served until 1887. His later years were passed at his home in Maine, ill health preventing him from engaging in much professional work. He died at Brunswick, in the seventy-ninth year of his age.

His years of practical experience, together with a rare gift of awakening the keen interest of his students in the subject he taught, made him an exceptionally successful instructor. His books gave him a wide reputation. In addition to the works already mentioned and various articles in periodicals, he was the author of *Orographic Geology* (1866); *A Graphic Method for Solving Certain Algebraic Problems* (1875); *An Elementary Course of Geometrical Drawing* (1878); *A Sketch of the Life and Works of Loammi Baldwin* (1885); *Bridge Disasters in America* (1887). On Nov. 9, 1854, in Bethel, Me., he married Abba Valentine Thompson, daughter of Rev. Zenas Thompson; she died in 1870 and on Apr. 16, 1872, he married Charlotte Buxton Andrews. He had four daughters and a son.

[*Jour. of the Asso. of Engineering Societies*, Feb. 1911; E. F. Vose, *Robert Vose and His Descendants* (1932); W. B. Lapham and S. P. Maxim, *Hist. of Paris, Me.* (1884); *Daily Kennebec Jour.*, Mar. 31, 1910.]   H. K. B—s.

VOUGHT, CHANCE MILTON (Feb. 26, 1890–July 25, 1930), aircraft designer and manufacturer, was born in New York City, the son of George Washington and Annie Eliza (Colley) Vought. He attended the public schools of New York City, the Pratt Institute, Brooklyn, and New York University, where he specialized in the study of internal combustion engines. Subsequently he enrolled at the University of Pennsylvania, but left in 1910 without graduating and became consulting engineer for Harold F. McCormick of Chicago. For three years he was associated with McCormick in experimental developments. Ambitious, daring, and of strong mechanical bent, Vought learned to fly at the age of twenty, under the instruction of the Wright brothers. He became a finished and skilful, though not a professional, pilot, and continued to fly actively until 1917.

From 1912 onwards his career was exclusively devoted to aeronautics. His first aviation appointment was that of consulting engineer for the Aero Club of Illinois. In 1914 he became editor of the pioneer aviation weekly, *Aero & Hydro*. Later in that year, in association with the Mayo Radiator Works in New Haven, Conn., he designed and constructed an advanced training plane, used by the British during the World War. This airplane laid the foundation of his reputation as a designer. In 1916, as chief engineer of the Wright Company, Dayton, Ohio, he produced the famous Vought-Wright Model V military biplane. In 1917, soon after the Wright-Martin Aircraft Company merger, Vought launched out for himself in the Lewis & Vought Corporation, which was financed by Birdseye B. Lewis. During the war he served as consulting engineer to the bureau of aircraft production in Washington, and to the Engineering Division of the Army Air Corps at McCook Field, Dayton.

The early days of the Lewis & Vought Corporation in Long Island City were perhaps the most interesting, as they were the most critical of Chance Vought's career. Possessing a remarkable charm of manner and at home in any society, he was idolized by his small group of a dozen workmen. Neither by education nor instinct was he a plodding, finished calculator. He had, however, an intuitive, artistic sense for clean, streamlined airplanes, combined with practical ability and a thorough knowledge of the structure and uses of aircraft, particularly as regards naval requirements. An indefatigable worker, he developed new designs practically alone, and knew how to realize his drawings in the shop, working at times with his own hands. He had a keen business sense, and could hasten a government payment when necessary to meet the payroll of his small concern. The Lewis & Vought Corporation and its successor, the Chance Vought Corporation, rapidly became the outstanding constructors of the two-place advanced training plane known as the Vought VE-7 (1919). Even in the period of the box-like aircraft, Vought designs had been singularly attractive in appearance, and as design improved, Vought airplanes continued in the forefront. The Vought UO-1 (1922–25) convertible observation airplane, specially designed for use from battleships and cruisers and for operations on aircraft carriers, solved the difficult problem of catapulting a heavy and fully equipped plane. The FU-1 single-seat high-altitude supercharged fighter (1925) was but little less noteworthy. The Vought O2U Corsair was a famous single-float seaplane, convertible into a landplane for catapulting and deck landing. This type, as a stock naval seaplane, set four world's records for speed and altitude. Vought worked above all for tactical flexibility in naval aircraft, developed his types by wise evolution, and maintained unsurpassable standards of workmanship. The operations of the Chance Vought Corporation were highly successful and in 1930 it employed 700 men as compared with the initial dozen.

In February 1929 Vought joined with the Pratt & Whitney Aircraft Company of Hartford and the Boeing Airplane Company in forming the vast United Aircraft & Transport Corporation, securing thereby an excellent return for his interests. He was very active on the directorate of the United, and continued as president and consulting engineer of the Chance Vought unit until his death. During his busy career he found time to write many papers and articles for technical journals on aircraft design, construction, and performance, and to be active in the Aircraft Committee of the Society of Automotive Engineers. He was a member of many clubs, loved New York, the theatre, and American life. He died in the Southampton Hospital, Southampton, Long Island, of septicemia, leaving his large personal fortune to his wife, Ena (Lewis) Vought, daughter of Birdseye B. Lewis, whom he married Dec. 4, 1920, and to their two children. His wife had been closely associated with him in his work, and had personally assisted him in the shop in the earlier stages of his career.

[E. E. Wilson, "Chance Milton Vought," lecture before Am. Soc. of Mechanical Engineers, Jan. 22, 1931; "Chance M. Vought Dies at Southampton," *U. S. Air Services*, Sept. 1930; "America's Aircraft Builders and Their Products," *Sportsman Pilot*, Oct. 1929; *N. Y. Times*, July 26, 1930.]   A. K—n.

VROOM, PETER DUMONT (Dec. 12, 1791–Nov. 18, 1873), lawyer, congressman, governor and chancellor of New Jersey, was born in Hillsboro Township, Somerset County, N. J., the son of Col. Peter Dumont and Elsie (Bogert) Vroom. The male line was Dutch, the first Vroom to come to America being Cornelius Petersen Coursen of Langeraer, the Netherlands, who arrived on Long Island about 1638, but the original stock is said to have been French Huguenot. The name Vroom (or de Vroom) was first taken by Hendrick, son of Cornelius Petersen; otherwise the family retained the name of Coursen (or Corsen). The elder Peter Vroom (1745–1831) rose by successive degrees from the rank of lieutenant to that of lieutenant-colonel in the 2nd Battalion of the Somerset, N. J., militia in the Revolutionary War. Subsequently he was sheriff of Somerset County, county clerk, member of the General Assembly (1790–98, and 1813) and of the Legislative Council (1798–1804); he was also a justice of the peace and judge of the court of common pleas.

Vroom received his preparatory education at the Somerville Academy, Somerville, N. J., and was graduated from Columbia College, New York City, in 1808. He read law under George McDonald at Somerville and was admitted to the New Jersey bar as attorney in 1813 and as counsellor in 1816 and became sergeant-at-law in 1828. He practised successively at Schooleys Mountain (1813), Hackettstown (1814–16),

Flemington (1817–21), and Somerville, where he remained about twenty years. While at Flemington he married, May 21, 1817, Ann V. D. Dumont of Somerset County. Although he had been a Federalist, in 1824 he became a strong supporter of Andrew Jackson. He served as a member of the New Jersey Assembly in 1826, 1827, and 1829. In 1829 he was elected to the combined office of governor and chancellor of the state. He served until 1832 (when he was defeated by Samuel L. Southard, a Whig) and again from 1833 to 1836. The equity opinions he rendered as chancellor were so sound that "for the most part, they stood unquestioned" for many years after (Whitehead, *post*, p. 382). In 1837 he was appointed by President Van Buren one of three commissioners to adjust land-reserve claims in Mississippi under a treaty with the Choctaw Indians (appointment confirmed, Mar. 8, 1837). He was elected to Congress in 1838 but, owing to irregularities in some of the returns, was not commissioned. After what is known as the "Broad Seal War," the courts established that he was elected by a clear majority, and he was seated, serving in the House of Representatives from Mar. 4, 1839, to Mar. 3, 1841.

At the end of his term he removed permanently to Trenton. After the death of his first wife he married, Nov. 4, 1840, Maria Matilda Wall, daughter of Gen. Garret D. and Maria (Rhea) Wall of Burlington, N. J. In 1844 he was a delegate to the convention that framed the constitution of New Jersey. In 1848 he was associated with Henry Woodhull Green, William Lewis Dayton [*qq.v.*] and Stacy G. Potts in framing statutes to comply with the new constitution. He declined an appointment as chief justice of the state supreme court, but in 1854 accepted appointment (confirmed Feb. 9, 1854) by President Pierce as minister to the court of Prussia. He was in Berlin until 1857, when he was recalled at his own request. In Prussia he handled well the difficult question of the right of Germans, naturalized as American citizens but living in Prussia, to claim exemption from the compulsory military law of their native country.

In 1860 Vroom was placed upon the Breckinridge and Lane Democratic electoral ticket. He was opposed, however, to the secession movement and was a member of the futile peace conference which met at Washington, Feb. 4, 1861. He supported George Brinton McClellan for president in 1864, and in 1868 was an elector on the Seymour and Blair presidential ticket. In 1865 he took the place of his son, John P. Vroom, who died that year, as law reporter of the New Jersey supreme court and served until 1873. He

was one of the commissioners of the sinking fund of the state from 1864 until his death. He was vice-president of the American Colonization Society and the American Bible Society, and was long a ruling elder of the Reformed Dutch Church at Somerville. Of vigorous constitution, a hard worker at all times, he practised his profession with undiminished powers until a short time before his death, which occurred in Trenton.

[*Biog. Dir. Am. Cong.* (1928); L. Q. C. Elmer, in *N. J. Hist. Soc. Colls.*, vol. VII (1872); J. P. Snell and Franklin Ellis, *Hist. of Hunterdon and Somerset Counties* (1881); Abraham Messler, *Centennial Hist. of Somerset County* (1878), and *Sermons . . . on the . . . Death of the Hon. Peter D. Vroom* (1874); John Whitehead, *Judicial and Civil Hist. of N. J.* (1897); *Biog. Encyc. of N. J.* (1877); *Our Home*, Dec. 1873; obituary in *Daily State Gazette* (Trenton, N. J.), Nov. 19, 1873.]   A. V—D. H.

WABASHA (*c.* 1773—*c.* 1855), chief of the Mdewakanton Sioux occupying the region south of the Minnesota River, was born probably in the vicinity of the present Winona, Minn. The name, also spelled Wapasha, was borne by a succession of chiefs, of whom this one was perhaps the best known. His father, the first historical bearer of the name, was born about 1718, was closely allied to the British before and during the Revolution, and died about 1799. The second Wabasha, known also as La Feuille and The Leaf, first came into prominence through his conferences with Zebulon M. Pike, on the upper Mississippi, in the fall of 1805. He sided with the Americans in their difficulties with the Winnebagos, Menominees, and Sauks. During the War of 1812, though he never openly broke with the British, he seems to have favored the Americans. At any rate the British suspected him and actually tried his son-in-law, Rolette, by court-martial for collusion with the Americans. He was a conspicuous and forceful figure in the great council of Aug. 5–19, 1825, at Prairie du Chien, between representatives of the federal government and the tribes of the central north. In the Sauk War of 1832 (see sketch of Black Hawk) he supported the Americans, and it was probably a band of his warriors who fell upon the remnants of Black Hawk's band on the Iowa side of the Mississippi. On his death he was succeeded by his nephew, perhaps his son, Wabasha, often known as Joseph Wabasha, under whom his people were removed to the upper Minnesota. The latter, at his death on Apr. 23, 1876, was succeeded by his son, the fourth Wabasha, also known as Joseph Wabasha, who for many years was chief of the Santee Sioux on the Niobrara reservation in Nebraska, and was a citizen of the United States.

The second Wabasha, in spite of John Shaw's statement that he was exceptionally tall (*post*, p.

214), appears to have been of less than medium stature. That he was impressive in bearing was, however, the common testimony of all who met him; and there is equal agreement that he had notable abilities and high character. Pike wrote of him with great respect, and Stephen H. Long, who visited him in 1817, noted that he was considered one of the most honest and honorable of any of the Indians, and endeavored to inculcate into the minds of his people the sentiments and principles adopted by himself (*post,* p. 17). Keating (*post,* I, 258) recorded his reputation for wisdom, prudence, and skill in oratory, and Beltrami, the Italian traveler (*post,* II, 181), asserted that he needed only "an embroidered coat, a large portfolio . . . and spectacles" to have all the appearance of a great statesman.

[*Handbook of Am. Indians,* pt. 2 (1910), ed. by F. W. Hodge; "Jour. of Stephen W. Kearny," *Mo. Hist. Soc. Colls.,* vol. III (1908); S. H. Long, "Voyage in a Six-oared Skiff . . . in 1817," *Minn. Hist. Soc. Colls.,* vol. II (1860), esp. pp. 17, 21; W. H. Keating, *Narrative of an Expedition . . . Under Stephen H. Long* (1825), I, 257–58; J. C. Beltrami, *A Pilgrimage in Europe and America* (1828), II, 181; John Shaw, "Sketches of Indian Chiefs and Pioneers of the North-West," *Wis. Hist. Soc. Colls.,* X (1888), 214; C. C. Willson, "The Successive Chiefs Named Wabasha," *Minn. Hist. Soc. Colls.,* vols. II (1860) and XII (1908).]
W. J. G.

WACHSMUTH, CHARLES (Sept. 13, 1829–Feb. 7, 1896), paleontologist, was born in the city of Hanover, Germany, the only son of Christian Wachsmuth, a lawyer and member of the Frankfurt Parliament of 1848. Although the boy was in feeble health almost from the hour of his birth, his father decided to prepare him for the law, but he was obliged to give up his studies, and, upon advice of his physician, entered a mercantile house in Hamburg. In 1852 he was sent to New York as an agent of the company, and about two years later he went west, and settled in Burlington, Iowa, where he entered the grocery business. In the meanwhile, in an effort to regain his health in the out-of-doors, he devoted his leisure to the collecting of fossils.

In 1865 the business prospered so that he was able to retire and to devote all of his time to collecting and studying—a pursuit that he enjoyed with signal success to his very last day. He acquired large collections of the rare crinoids and a special library on the subject which attracted the attention of scientists the world over. Louis Agassiz [*q.v.*], on one of his western lecturing tours, visited him, became very enthusiastic over the acquirements, and in 1873 purchased the material for the Museum of Comparative Zoölogy at Cambridge. He induced Wachsmuth to go to Cambridge with him, where he could continue his studies to greater advantage, and

Wachsmuth worked with Agassiz until the latter's death in December of that year. Returning once more to Burlington he began to make a new collection, but with very different and much enlarged ideas from those that he had previously held. He soon made the acquaintance of a young lawyer, Frank Springer [*q.v.*], who had a strong interest in crinoids, and the friendship of the two men developed into a partnership that lasted through life.

The joint plan of Springer and Wachsmuth was a pretentious one. It involved the personal critical examination of all the collections of crinoids throughout the world, and a complete revision of everything ever described. This stupendous undertaking occupied fifty years, the work being carried on by Springer alone for twenty years after Wachsmuth's death. The resulting monumental monograph, *North American Crinoidea Camerata,* superbly illustrated, was dedicated to Agassiz and appeared in 1897 as volumes XX and XXI of the *Memoirs of the Museum of Comparative Zoölogy.* Usually associated with Springer, Wachsmuth published numerous other memoirs on the morphology of the crinoids. Some of the most important appeared in the *Proceedings of the American Academy of Natural Sciences* in Philadelphia: "Transition Forms in Crinoids" (3 ser., vol. VIII, 1879), "Revision of the Palæocrinoidea" (3 ser., vols., IX, XI, XV, XVI, 1880–87), "The Summit Plates in Blastoids, Crinoids, and Cystids" (3 ser., vol. XVII, 1888), "Discovery of the Ventral Structure of Taxocrinus and Haplocrinus" (3 ser., vol. XVIII, 1889), and "The Perisomic Plates of Crinoids" (3 ser., vol. XX, 1891). His "Notes on the Internal and External Structure of Paleozoic Crinoids" appeared in the *American Journal of Science and Art,* August 1877. A complete bibliography of his publications is to be found in the *American Geologist, post.* After Wachsmuth's death, several monographs left unfinished were completed by Springer.

Widely honored by his fellow scientists, Wachsmuth was elected member of many learned societies both at home and abroad, and throughout life carried on an extensive correspondence with most of the savants in his field the world over. His wife, Bernandina Lorenz, also of Hanover, to whom he had been married in 1855, survived him. He was interred at Aspen Grove Cemetery, Burlington.

[Personal acquaintance of the author; C. R. Keyes, "Biographical Sketch of Charles Wachsmuth," *Am. Geologist,* Mar. 1896, and "Memorial of Charles Wachsmuth," *Proc. Iowa Acad. Sci.,* vol. IV (1897); Samuel Calvin, "Memoir of Charles Wachsmuth," *Bull. Geo-*

logical Soc. of America, vol. VIII (1897), Apr. 30, 1897.]   C. R. K.

WACKER, CHARLES HENRY (Aug. 29, 1856–Oct. 31, 1929), brewer, executive, city planner, was the only child of Frederick Wacker, a German emigrant who settled in Chicago in 1854, and his wife, Catharine Hummel. He was educated in the schools of Chicago and studied one year at Lake Forest Academy. He started in business as an office boy, 1872–76, in the firm of Carl C. Moeller & Company, grain commissioners, and then toured Europe and Africa for three years, spending some time studying in Stuttgart and Geneva. Returning to his position in 1879, he remained there until the following year when his father took him into partnership in the malting business to form the firm of F. Wacker & Son which in 1882 became Wacker & Birk Brewing and Malting Company. From 1884 until 1901 he was president of this firm, and, from 1895 to 1901, he was also president of the McAvoy Brewing Company, with which it was consolidated in 1889. In 1901 he turned his attention to real estate and, from 1902 to 1928, he was president of the Chicago Heights Land Association.

His interest in civic affairs was given an impetus by his connection with the World's Columbian Exposition in Chicago in 1893 as a member of the board of directors and of various committees. He became an enthusiastic supporter and eventually the leader of a movement, started by the Merchants and Commercial Clubs, to beautify the city of Chicago. He was vice-chairman of the Merchants Club's Committee from 1907 to 1909, and its chairman for a short time in 1909. In 1909 Mayor Busse and the City Council created the Chicago Plan Commission to improve and beautify Chicago's "loop" and lake front, and appointed Wacker chairman. He held this position until Nov. 4, 1926, when he resigned because of illness. In appreciation of his remarkable work and untiring efforts in sponsoring and developing the Chicago Plan, the City Council renamed South Water Street, the double-decked drive along the river, which Wacker had been most influential in securing as a part of the Plan, Wacker Drive.

He was made secretary of the Chicago Zoning Commission in 1920, was president of the Chicago Relief and Aid Society, and, when it merged with the Chicago Bureau of Charities to form the United Charities of Chicago, became (1909–12) the first president of that body. He was a director of many important companies, and a member of a great many social clubs, German clubs, and singing societies. In 1921 he was awarded a medal of honor by the Société des Architectes Français. Some of his articles and addresses on the Chicago Plan were published; among them are An S-O-S to the Public Spirited Citizens of Chicago (1924), and articles in the American City, October 1909, and in Art and Archæology, September-October 1921. He was twice married, first to Ottilie Marie Glade on May 10, 1887, and, after her death, to Ella G. Todtmann, Mar. 19, 1919. By the first marriage there were two sons and a daughter, who, with his second wife, survived him.

[Who's Who in America, 1928–29; Who's Who in Chicago, 1926; A. T. Andreas, Hist. of Chicago, vol. III (1886); A Biog. Hist. with Portraits of Prominent Men of the Great West (1894); One Hundred Years of Brewing (1903); W. D. Moody, Wacker's Manual of the Plan of Chicago (1911); D. H. Burnham and E. H. Bennett, Plan of Chicago Prepared Under the Direction of the Commercial Club (1909); Chicago Daily Tribune, Nov. 1, 1929.]   J. K. W.

WADDEL, JAMES (July 1739–Sept. 17, 1805), clergyman, was born in Newry, Ireland, the son of Thomas Waddel. His parents emigrated in the fall of 1739 and settled on White Clay Creek in south-eastern Pennsylvania. He was educated in the "log college" of Samuel Finley [q.v.] at Nottingham, Pa., and served as a tutor there. Later, while preparing himself for the ministry, he taught in the academy of Robert Smith at Pequea in Lancaster County, Pa., and in the classical school of John Todd of Louisa, Va. As a young man in Virginia he was much influenced by the charm and evangelical zeal of Samuel Davies [q.v.]. Licensed to preach by the Presbytery of Hanover on Apr. 2, 1761, and ordained at a meeting of the presbytery held in Prince Edward County on June 16 and 17, 1762, he received calls from congregations both in Virginia and in Pennsylvania. On Oct. 7, 1762, he accepted a call from a congregation in Northumberland and Lancaster counties of the Northern Neck of Virginia. During the first year there he was assisted in reviving the fervor of his congregation by the forceful preaching of George Whitefield [q.v.]. As a nonconformist preacher he was naturally subject to attack by the Anglican clergy. In all such encounters he seems to have borne himself well. The magistrate had become very lax in the enforcement of the laws in regard to dissenters, and they permitted him to take the qualifying oaths six months after his acceptance of his first charge in Virginia. There is no record of his ever being oppressed by the law. In 1768 he married Mary, the daughter of James Gordon of Lancaster County, Va. One of their ten children married Archibald Alexander [q.v.] and became the mother of Joseph A. and Samuel D. Alexander [*qq.v.*]. In 1776 or 1777 he accepted a call from the Tinkling Spring congregation in Augusta County and in 1778 removed with his family to the Shenandoah Valley. Later he was pastor of the two congregations of Tinkling Spring and Staunton. In 1785 he removed east of the Blue Ridge to a plantation he called "Belle Grove," not far from the town of Gordonsville and lived there for the rest of his life. He established a group of churches in Orange, Louisa, and Albemarle counties and preached regularly in the Hopewell church near Gordonsville, in the Brick church near Orange Court House, and in the old meeting house on the Rockfish Gap road about five miles from Charlottesville.

In person he was tall and very thin. His eyes were light blue, his complexion fair, his face and forehead long and narrow. His manner was gentle. He spoke with animation but never ranted. His voice was low, sweet, and very distinct. Although he permitted his daughters to learn the minuet, he was a stanch defender of the Calvinistic theology and a determined opponent of the philosophical deism then dominant in the South. His ministry helped to establish the cordial understanding between the Virginia squirearchy and the Presbyterian Church. His eyesight had never been good and in 1787 he became blind. In 1798 he underwent an operation for cataract, as a result of which he recovered his sight for a time. During the eleven years of his blindness he continued to preach as before, or perhaps with increased effectiveness. He died at his home.

[W. B. Sprague, *Annals of the Am. Pulpit*, vol. III (1858) ; W. H. Foote, *Sketches of Virginia* (1 Ser., 1850) ; William Wirt, *The Letters of the British Spy* (1803), letter VII ; J. W. Alexander, *Memoir of the Rev. James Waddel* (1880), reprinted from *Watchman of the South* in 1844 ; J. R. Graham, *The Planting of the Presbyterian Church in Northern Virginia* (1904) ; Arista Hoge, *The First Presbyterian Church, Staunton, Va.* (1908). He spelled his name with one l and pronounced it "waddle." Many of his descendants spell it with two ll's and pronounce it with accent on last syllable.]   T. C. J., Jr.

WADDEL, JOHN NEWTON (Apr. 2, 1812–Jan. 9, 1895), clergyman and educator, was born at Willington, S. C., the son of Elizabeth Woodson (Pleasants) and Moses Waddel [*q.v.*]. He pronounced his surname as did his father. He is reputed to have said that he had "waddeled" through life thus far and could "waddle" on to the end. He received his early education in a neighborhood school and in a grammar school at Athens, Ga. He graduated from Franklin College (the University of Georgia) in 1829. Upon graduation he taught for several years in his father's old academy at Willington. On Nov. 27, 1832, he was married to Martha A. Robertson. They had eight children. In 1837 he removed to

Alabama and from there to Mississippi, where, in 1842, he established the Montrose Academy which became an educational center of that part of Mississippi. Being made a charter member of the board of trustees, he took a leading part in the founding of the University of Mississippi at Oxford. On Oct. 23, 1843, he was ordained to the Presbyterian ministry and supplied a group of churches in and around Montrose. From 1848 to 1857 he taught ancient languages in the University of Mississippi and during this period also supplied the Presbyterian Church at Oxford. There his wife died in 1851, and on Aug. 24, 1854, he was married to Mary A. Werden of Berkshire County, Mass., who died in 1862 after some years of invalidism. In 1857 he resigned to go to the Presbyterian Synodical College at La Grange, Tenn., to teach ancient languages and in 1860 became president of that institution. When the Federal army occupied La Grange in December 1862 he received official orders to discontinue his labors as a minister in that place. Thereupon he slipped through the Federal lines and later became a chaplain in the Confederate army. Later still he was placed in charge of all the chaplains connected with the army of Joseph E. Johnston. In the meantime he had taken a leading part in the organization of the first General Assembly of the Southern Presbyterian Church at Augusta, Ga., in December 1861 and was stated clerk of that body from 1861 to 1865. In 1868 he was elected moderator of the General Assembly, the highest office in the gift of his church. At the close of the Civil War he became chancellor of the University of Mississippi and shortly afterward, on Jan. 31, 1866, was married to his third wife, Harriet (Godden) Snedecor. As chancellor he made a tour of the leading colleges and universities of America, seeking for his own university the best thing that could be found in the leading institutions of this country. In 1874 he resigned the chancellorship. From 1874 to 1879 he was secretary of education for the Southern Presbyterian Church, with headquarters in Memphis. From 1879 to 1888 he was chancellor of the Southwestern Presbyterian University at Clarksville, Tenn.

He wrote numerous articles for the religious papers and reviews, a short history of the University of Mississippi, *Historical Discourse . . . on the . . . University of Mississippi* (1873), and *Memorials of Academic Life: Being an Historical Sketch of the Waddel Family* (1891). He was a faithful minister of the Gospel, but he was preëminently an educator whether in the academy, in the university, or in the pulpit. There must be assigned to him an honorable place among the leading educators in the entire South during the time in which he lived. He died in Birmingham, Ala.

[Diary in Lib. of Cong.; Memorial in Minutes of Nashville Presbytery, Apr. 1895, pp. 12–15, Hist. Foundation of Presbyterian and Reformed Churches, Montreat, N. C.; Memorials of Acad. Life, ante; Hist. Cat. of the Univ. of Miss. (1910); H. A. White, Southern Presbyterian Leaders (1911), with picture incorrectly labelled as of James Waddell; Birmingham Age-Herald, Jan. 10, 1895; information from great-granddaughter, Elizabeth H. West, Lubbock, Texas.]

W. L. L.

WADDEL, MOSES (July 29, 1770–July 21, 1840), teacher and clergyman, was born in Rowan, now Iredell County, N. C., the son of William and Sarah (Morrow) Waddel, who emigrated from County Down, Ireland, and settled in Rowan County, N. C., in 1767. His surname was accented on the first syllable. He got his elementary schooling in a neighborhood school and received advanced instruction at Clio's Nursery, established by James Hall [q.v.] in 1778. Completing his school education there in 1784, he began to teach pupils in the neighborhood of his home. In 1788 he removed with his parents to Greene County, Ga., and there opened a school. He graduated from Hampton-Sydney College in 1791 and later studied theology under Virginia clergymen. After receiving his license in May 1792, he preached for a time in the vicinity of Charleston, S. C., but soon removed to Columbia County, Ga., and established a school near Appling. While living there, he preached at the Calhoun settlement across the Savannah River, some fifty miles away, in Abbeville District, S. C. There he met and in 1795 married Catherine, the sister of his most distinguished pupil, John C. Calhoun [q.v.]. She lived slightly more than a year after their marriage. In 1800 he married Elizabeth Woodson Pleasants of Halifax County, Va., and in 1801 removed to Vienna, a town on the South Carolina side of the Savannah, and opened another school. John Newton Waddel [q.v.] was their son.

In 1804 he removed to Willington, a community about six miles south of Vienna, and there opened the school that gained and maintained a widespread reputation. The first school house was a two-room log cabin. In 1809 four recitation rooms and a chapel were built. The students studied in log and brick huts about the school house and boarded with neighboring farmers. A monitorial form of student government, which was headed by the master, made for strict discipline. Although some of his pupils thought him cruel and severe, he had an unusual capacity for stimulating in boys a desire to learn. A. B. Longstreet, in his Master William Mitten, described

his Willington teacher as a man of "about five feet nine inches; of stout muscular frame, and a little inclined to corpulency. . . . His head was uncommonly large, and covered with a thick coat of dark hair. . . . His eyes were gray, and overshadowed by thick, heavy eye-brows, . . . [and] his tout ensemble was . . . extremely austere" (post, p. 108). At Willington, between 1804 and 1819, Waddel taught most of those four thousand students that in various places received instruction from him. In addition to large numbers of clergymen, he trained many senators, governors, congressmen, judges, and lawyers. His most distinguished pupils were John C. Calhoun, William H. Crawford, Hugh S. Legaré, George McDuffie, A. B. Longstreet, and James L. Petigru [qq.v.].

In 1818 he published a most tedious religious tract, Memoirs of the Life of Miss Caroline Elizabeth Smelt, which, however, went through several editions. In 1819 he became president of Franklin College (the University of Georgia). He is usually given the credit for building up the student body there and stimulating its religious life. Retiring in 1829, he lived in Willington until 1836, when he returned to Athens following a paralytic stroke.

[Notes, letters, diary, and memoir in Lib. of Cong.; J. N. Waddel, Memorials of Academic Life (1891); A. B. Longstreet, Master William Mitten (1864), esp. chap. VIII and Eulogy on the Life and Services of the Late Rev. Moses Waddel, D.D. (1841); Colyer Meriwether, "History of Higher Education in South Carolina," United States Bureau of Education, Circular of Information, no. 3 (1888), pp. 211–35; George Howe, Hist. of the Presbyterian Church in S. C., vol. II (1883); W. B. Sprague, Annals of the American Pulpit, vol. IV (1858); Writings of Hugh S. Legaré, vol. I (1846), ed. by M. S. Legaré Buffen; W. J. Grayson, James Louis Petigru, A Biog. Sketch (1866); R. M. Lyon, "Moses Waddel and the Willington Academy," N. C. Hist. Rev., July 1931; Abbeville Press and Banner (S. C.), July 7, 28, 1887; information from grand-daughter, Elizabeth H. West, Lubbock, Texas.]

R. M. L.

WADDELL, ALFRED MOORE (Sept. 16, 1834–Mar. 17, 1912), congressman and author, was born at Hillsboro, N. C., the son of Hugh and Susan (Moore) Waddell and the great-grandson of Hugh Waddell, Francis Nash, and Alfred Moore [qq.v.]. He was educated at the Bingham School and Caldwell Institute in Hillsboro and at the University of North Carolina, 1851–53. After studying law with Frederick Nash [q.v.], John L. Bailey, William H. Battle [q.v.], and Samuel F. Phillips, he was admitted to the bar in 1855 and in the following spring settled in Wilmington, his permanent residence, excepting a year, 1882–83, as a newspaper editor in Charlotte. His chief joy and distinction, however, were in public service, oratory, and historical authorship rather than in the practice of law.

He was clerk and master in equity of New Hanover County, 1858–61. Stanchly conservative and unionist, he supported the American presidential ticket in 1856, opposed the growing secession movement, purchased and edited a unionist newspaper, the *Wilmington Herald,* in 1860–61, and went with the North Carolina delegation to the Constitutional Union National Convention in 1860 as an alternate. During the Civil War he served first as adjutant and in 1863–64 as lieutenant-colonel of the 41st North Carolina regiment (3rd Cavalry), from which he resigned on account of impaired health.

He accepted the results of the war and favored a conservative readjustment of the Southern régime, advocating limited negro suffrage in an address to negroes in Wilmington in the summer of 1865 (*Sentinel,* Raleigh, Aug. 8, 1865). After three years of radical Reconstruction and the outrages of the Kirk-Holden war in 1870 the Conservative party attacked the Republican-negro régime in the campaign of 1870. First elected to Congress that year, he served by re-election until 1879. In Congress he spoke eloquently and with wide acclaim in temperate defense of the South, in deprecation of partisanship and sectionalism, and for the honor, character, and solidarity of the American union. He opposed the Ku Klux Act of 1871 as unnecessary, unconstitutional, and partisan, though he voted for congressional investigations of alleged Southern outrages, served reluctantly on the joint select investigating committee of 1871, and signed the minority report. As chairman of the House committee on the postoffice and post-roads, 1877–79, he sought improvements in the postal service and the establishment of postal savings banks. Democratic overconfidence and inactivity and a wide distribution of his limited negro suffrage speech caused his defeat in 1878. He was a delegate to the Democratic national conventions of 1880 and 1896, and an elector-at-large in 1888.

His fine stage presence, genial personality, and polished eloquence placed him in great demand in North Carolina and other states for commencement, patriotic, historical, and political addresses. For five months in 1880 he canvassed Vermont, Maine, and New York for the Democratic ticket. Pride in his state and his distinguished lineage stimulated him to historical authorship. *A Colonial Officer and His Times, 1754–1773. A Biographical Sketch of Gen. Hugh Waddell of North Carolina* (1890), *Some Memories of My Life* (1908), *A History of New Hanover County and the Lower Cape Fear Region, 1723–1800,* vol. I (1909), and several addresses possess descriptive strength and substantial worth, if not the highest scholarship. Ordinarily dignified and reserved, he was in critical times a bold, courageous leader. He made fervent speeches in the bitter "White Supremacy" campaign of 1898, redeemed the state from the abuses of Republican-Populist-negro rule, and he was the chief leader of the white citizenship in Wilmington that on Nov. 9–10 forcibly rid the city of a negro newspaper, offending whites and negroes, and a corrupt and unpopular government, and precipitated a bloody race riot. Elected mayor, he quickly restored peace and order and until 1905 gave to the city a dignified, clean, and peaceful government. He was an Episcopalian and a Mason. He was married three times: to Julia Savage in 1857, to Ellen Savage, her sister, in 1878, and in 1896 to Gabrielle deRosset, who with two children of his first wife survived him.

[*Some Memories of My Life, ante; Who's Who in America,* 1912–13; James Sprunt, *Chronicles of the Cape Fear River* (1914); J. G. deR. Hamilton, *N. C. since 1860* (1919) and *Reconstruction in N. C.* (1906); *Morning Star* (Wilmington), Mar. 19, 1912.]

A. R. N.

WADDELL, HUGH (1734?–Apr. 9, 1773), soldier, was born in Lisburn, County Down, Ireland, the son of Hugh and Isabella (Brown) Waddell. He spent several years of his boyhood in Boston, Mass., whither his father had fled after a fatal duel. After the death of his father, who had returned to Ireland and found himself propertyless there, young Waddell emigrated to North Carolina. In 1754, soon after his arrival, he went as a lieutenant with the regiment of James Innes to help Virginia drive the French from the Ohio and was promoted to be a captain, although mismanagement caused the troops to be disbanded in the summer without active service. In the winter of 1754–55, he was clerk of the council of the new governor, Arthur Dobbs [*q.v.*], who had been a friend of his father in Ireland. In 1755 Dobbs ordered him to protect the frontier from the Cherokee and Catawba. In Rowan County near present-day Statesville, he built Fort Dobbs, authorized by the Assembly of 1755, a substantial three-story blockhouse of oak logs, and commanded its garrison until late in 1757. With Virginia commissioners he negotiated an offensive-defensive alliance with the Cherokee and Catawba in 1756. "Finding him in his person and character every way qualified ... as he was young, active and resolute," Governor Dobbs sent him as major in command of three companies to aid the expedition of John Forbes [*q.v.*] against Fort Duquesne in 1758; and in this successful campaign he "had great honour done him being employed on all reconnoitring parties, and dressed and acted as an Indian . . ." (*Colonial Records, post,* VI, 282). Indian outrages on the frontier in 1759 caused Dobbs to send him as colonel in command of two companies, with authority to summon the militia of the frontier counties and cooperate with South Carolina or Virginia; and in February 1760 with great gallantry, he defended Fort Dobbs against an Indian night attack. In 1762 he married Mary, the daughter of Roger Haynes of "Castle Haynes" near Wilmington, and settled at "Bellefont," Bladen County.

His military renown as the foremost soldier in the colony before the Revolution, his marriage, and his character and ability brought wealth, social prestige, and political influence. He owned land in Rowan, Anson, Bladen, and New Hanover counties and had mercantile interests with his brother-in-law, John Burgwin, at Wilmington and in the back country. He was a justice of the peace in Rowan and Bladen and intermittently represented each in the colonial assembly— the former in 1757, 1758, 1759, and 1760; the latter in 1762, 1766, 1767, and 1771. He visited England and Ireland in 1768. He was one of the chief leaders of the "inhabitants in arms" who at Brunswick on Feb. 19-21, 1766, defied the new royal governor, William Tryon, and offered successful armed resistance to the enforcement of the Stamp Act. Nevertheless, his relations with Tryon were close. He commanded the armed escort of the governor on his visit to the Cherokee in 1767 and in 1771 volunteered his services for the military suppression of the Regulators in the back country, who were violently resisting excessive taxes, exorbitant fees, and dishonest local government. As general and commander in chief under the governor, he was ordered to raise troops in the west and join the eastern forces headed by the governor. Intercepted by armed Regulators near Salisbury, he was unable to take part in the battle of Alamance on May 16, but soon thereafter he marched with troops to pacify the western counties. Dobbs in 1762 and Tryon in 1771 recommended him for appointment to the council. He died from an illness of several months' duration and was buried at "Castle Haynes."

[*The Colonial Records of N. C.,* vols. V–IX (1887–90); *The State Records of N. C.,* vol. XXII (1907); A. M. Waddell, *A Colonial Officer and his Times . . . A Biog. Sketch of Gen. Hugh Waddell* (1890).]
A. R. N.

WADDELL, JAMES IREDELL (July 13, 1824–Mar. 15, 1886), Confederate naval officer, was born at Pittsboro, Chatham County, N. C., the son of Francis Nash and Elizabeth Davis (Moore) Waddell, and the great-grandson of Hugh Waddell [*q.v.*]. He was reared by his pa-

ternal grandparents and became a midshipman of the United States Navy on Sept. 10, 1841. On May 27, 1842, he was seriously wounded in a duel with Midshipman Archibald H. Waring. The episode gave him a limp for life and cost him eleven months of active duty. Until the outbreak of the Civil War his most vigorous service afloat was his Mexican War tour of duty from Feb. 21 to Oct. 6, 1846, aboard the *Somers,* active off Vera Cruz. At the end of the Mexican War he was married to Ann S. Iglehart, of Annapolis, Md., in 1848. Promotion to the rank of passed midshipman became effective on Aug. 10, 1847, in the middle of a two-year assignment for instruction at the naval school at Annapolis, later the Naval Academy. His promotion to the rank of lieutenant on Sept. 15, 1855, came in the course of a three-year cruise to Brazil aboard the *Germantown.* A short voyage in 1857 to Central America aboard the storeship *Release* brought him some favorable mention for courage in connection with an epidemic of yellow fever that appeared just after leaving Aspinwall. Afterward, until July 11, 1859, he taught navigation in the Naval Academy. During this period one of his students described him as a handsome, well proportioned man, slightly over six feet tall and weighing about two hundred pounds—a "splendid specimen of manhood" of "noble bearing . . . gracious . . . courtly . . . radiant with kindness" (*North Carolina Booklet, post,* p. 128).

When he returned from duty in the Orient in 1862 he resigned, and his name was stricken from the rolls Jan. 18. Secretly entering the Confederacy by way of Baltimore, he was commissioned a lieutenant in the Confederate States Navy on Mar. 27, 1862. He saw Farragut's fleet capture New Orleans. Hardly a month later he served with the Drewry's Bluff batteries in the repulse of the James River flotilla supporting McClellan's Peninsular campaign. Similar battery duty at Charleston, until March 1863, ended his services within the Confederacy. He went to Paris for duty aboard some vessel acquired by James D. Bulloch [*q.v.*]. On Oct. 19, 1864, near Funchal, Madeira, he took command of the new fast Indiaman, *Sea King,* and transformed her into the Confederate *Shenandoah.* Under orders to concentrate upon the untouched New England whaling fleets in the Pacific, he reached Melbourne on Jan. 25, 1865. Several prizes were burned and bonded on this initial leg of the cruise. A defective propeller shaft and bearing demanded that the *Shenandoah* be dry-docked. After a general overhauling of the ship and some brief legal difficulties over alleged recruiting among neutrals the ship left Melbourne on Feb. 18. In extricating himself from these charges, Waddell made good use of the international law he had read while teaching at Annapolis. Though Confederate officers claimed then, and with apparent sincerity long afterward, that the charges were groundless, forty-two welcome "stowaways" appeared on deck just out from Melbourne. More surprising to this generation is that Waddell, always short-handed, procured American recruits from the crews of nearly all his prizes—even from those that carried newspapers telling of Lee's surrender at Appomattox. His course from Melbourne is best traced by his prizes. Four whalers at Ascension Island were captured on Apr. 1; the Sea of Okhotsk yielded one in May—over a month after Appomattox. The Bering Sea in a week, June 21–28, afforded twenty-four or twenty-five. Three were used as cartels; the remainder burned. A newspaper aboard one of the first Bering Sea prizes told of Lee's defeat, but it also carried Davis' Danville Proclamation declaring that the war would be continued with renewed vigor. Seamen from the prizes continued to enlist in the Confederate navy; and Waddell continued his search. No additional sails were sighted until Aug. 2, when the *Shenandoah* fell in with the British merchantman *Barracouta,* roughly a thousand miles west of Acapulco, Mexico, and thirteen days from San Francisco. She reported the complete collapse of the Confederacy.

In such circumstances the *Shenandoah* had no standing in maritime law to protect her against Seward's claim that such Confederate ships were pirates. The dangers of landing in the nearest port of the United States were obvious. Waddell disregarded all advice to beach his ship and let each man shift for himself or seek the nearest British colonial port. With fine courage and magnificent seamanship he laid a course for England by the way of Cape Horn. On Nov. 6, flying the only Confederate flag that ever went around the world, the *Shenandoah* stood in to Liverpool—some 17,000 miles without speaking a ship. The "piratical" officers remained in England until after amnesty was offered. In 1875 Waddell became a captain for the Pacific Mail Company. Two years later he wrecked the *San Francisco* on an uncharted reef, but no passengers were lost. He died in Annapolis while commanding the Maryland state flotilla for policing the oyster beds. He was survived by his widow but no children.

[*War of the Rebellion: Official Records* (*Navy*); personnel records, Naval Records Office, Washington, D. C.; S. A. Ashe, "Capt. J. I. Waddell, *N. C. Booklet,* vol. XIII (1913); J. T. Mason, "The Last of the Confederate Cruisers," *Century Mag.,* Aug. 1898; J. D. Bulloch, *The Secret Service of the Confederate States in Europe* (1883), vol. II; W. C. Whittle, "The Cruise

of the Shenandoah," *Southern Hist. Soc. Papers,* vol. XXXV (1907), reprinted from *Portsmouth Star,* Mar. 13–Apr. 3, 1907; John Grimball, "Career of the Shenandoah," *Ibid.,* vol. XXV (1897), reprinted from the *News* (Charleston, S. C.), Feb. 3, 1895; C. E. Hunt, "The Shenandoah," *Mag. of Hist. with Notes and Queries,* extra no. 12 (1910) for charges against the integrity of Waddell; *Sun* (Baltimore), Mar. 16, 17, 1886.]

J. D. H—l.

WADE, BENJAMIN FRANKLIN (Oct. 27, 1800–Mar. 2, 1878), senator from Ohio, the tenth of eleven children of James and Mary (Upham) Wade, was a native of Feeding Hills, a hamlet near Springfield, Mass. His father traced his descent from Jonathan Wade of County Norfolk, England, who emigrated in 1632 and became an honored citizen of Medford, Massachusetts Bay Colony. His mother was the daughter of a Baptist clergyman of West Springfield. Decius S. Wade [*q.v.*] was his nephew. Reared amidst the poverty and hardships of a New England farm, Wade received little education in childhood, save that acquired from his mother and at a local school in the winter months. With his parents he moved in 1821 to the frontier community of Andover, Ohio, where two of his brothers had gone a year earlier. For the next few years he was by turns a farmer, drover, laborer, medical student, and school teacher in Ohio and New York state, but about 1825 he settled down to the study of law in Canfield, Ohio, and in 1827 or 1828 was admitted to the bar. Diffidence in public speaking threatened his ambitions at the outset, but perseverance gradually made him a vigorous advocate, and partnerships with Joshua R. Giddings [*q.v.*] in 1831 and Rufus P. Ranney [*q.v.*] in 1838 brought him a wide and successful practice in northeastern Ohio. On May 19, 1841, he was married to Caroline M. Rosekrans of Ashtabula and they took up their residence in Jefferson, Ohio, his place of practice. She bore him two sons, James F. and Henry P. Wade, and with them survived him.

Once established in the law, Wade turned his attention to politics and public office. After a term (1835–37) as prosecuting attorney of Ashtabula County he was elected to the state Senate in 1837. There he identified himself with the anti-slavery element; his outspoken opposition to a more stringent fugitive-slave law in Ohio is said to have been responsible for his failure to be reëlected in 1839. But he was returned to the Senate for a second term in 1841 and was chosen by the legislature in 1847 to sit as president-judge of the third judicial circuit. His forceful and business-like methods on the bench, together with his rising popularity, commended him to the Whigs in the legislature and in 1851, apparently without effort on his part, he was elected to the United States Senate. Twice re-elected as a Republican, he served until Mar. 3, 1869.

Wade's entrance into the Senate in the early fifties was eventful in the history of slavery and the Union. Rough in manner, coarse and vituperative in speech, yet intensely patriotic, he speedily became a leader of the anti-slavery group in Congress. At heart an abolitionist, he supported a move in 1852 to repeal the Fugitive-slave Law (*Congressional Globe*, 32 Cong., 1 Sess., p. 2371) and denounced the Kansas-Nebraska Bill (*Ibid.*, 33 Cong., 1 Sess., pp. 337–40). He also opposed the several efforts to win Kansas for slavery and almost every other measure or device for the promotion or protection of the system. When the controversy in the Senate became intensely personal and Wade was much involved, he entered into a secret compact (1858) with Simon Cameron and Zachariah Chandler [*qq.v.*] whereby they pledged themselves to make their own the cause of any Republican senator receiving gross personal abuse, and to "carry the quarrel into a coffin" (Riddle, *post*, pp. 215–16). He was an ardent supporter of the proposed homestead legislation of the period, saying in 1859 that it was "a question of land to the landless," while the bill to buy Cuba was "a question of niggers to the niggerless" (*Congressional Globe*, 35 Cong., 2 Sess., p. 1354). During the secession crisis of 1860–61 he took his stand on the Republican platform of 1860, and as a member of the Senate Committee of Thirteen voted against the Crittenden proposals (*Senate Report No. 288*, 36 Cong., 2 Sess.), holding that the time for compromise had passed.

With the outbreak of war, Wade became one of the most belligerent men in Congress, demanding swift and decisive military action. Personally a fearless man, he played a dramatic part in momentarily stemming a portion of the Union retreat from Bull Run (July 21, 1861). When the army was reorganized he pressed vigorously for another forward movement, and when McClellan delayed, Wade became one of his sharpest critics. With Senators Chandler and J. W. Grimes he was instrumental in setting up the Committee on the Conduct of the War. From the moment of its creation the Committee, under Wade's chairmanship, became a violently partisan machine, suspicious of the loyalty of those who ventured to dissent from its wishes and bent upon an unrelenting prosecution of the war. Its members worked in close cooperation with Secretary of War Stanton, a kindred spirit whom Wade had urged for that office, but they were generally critical of the President. Like other Radical Republicans in Congress, Wade seemed temperamentally incapable of understanding Lincoln and deplored his cautious and conservative policies. He himself favored drastic punitive measures against the South, including legislation for the confiscation of the property of the Confederate leaders and the emancipation of their slaves (*Congressional Globe*, 37 Cong., 2 Sess., p. 3375; Edward McPherson, *The Political History of the United States . . . during the Great Rebellion* (1864, pp. 196 ff.). He was not overburdened with constitutional scruples where measures that he favored were concerned. At the same time he decried the President's "dictatorship" and found Lincoln's clement reconstruction policy, announced on Dec. 8, 1863, particularly obnoxious. When he and Henry Winter Davis [*q.v.*] attempted to counteract it by a severe congressional plan, embodied in the Wade-Davis bill, and Lincoln checked this by a "pocket-veto," announcing his reasons in a proclamation (July 8, 1864), their indignation was unbounded. The resultant Wade-Davis Manifesto (Aug. 5), a fierce blast, condemned the President's "executive usurpation" as a "studied outrage on the legislative authority" and insisted that in matters of reconstruction Congress was "paramount and must be respected" (Appletons' *American Annual Cyclopaedia . . . 1864*, 1865, pp. 307–10). Previously Wade had joined with others in indorsing the Pomeroy circular, designed to replace Lincoln with Salmon P. Chase (G. F. Milton, *The Age of Hate*, 1930, p. 28), but when that project collapsed and the Manifesto aroused a storm of disapproval in Ohio, he gave his support to Lincoln in the closing weeks of the election contest in 1864. But he continued to resist the President's reconstruction policy, characterizing it as "absurd, monarchical, and anti-American" (*Congressional Globe*, 38 Cong., 2 Sess., p. 1128).

The accession of Johnson to the presidency in April 1865 was hailed by Wade and his faction as a godsend, and they hastened to make overtures to him in behalf of their own measures. When to their surprise he took over Lincoln's policy, Wade dubbed him either "a knave or a fool," and contended that to admit the Southern states on the presidential plan was "nothing less than political suicide" (H. K. Beale, *The Critical Year*, 1930, pp. 49, 314). From December 1865 onward, along with Charles Sumner, Thaddeus Stevens, and other vindictive leaders, he waged a persistent campaign against Johnson, pressing for the enactment of the congressional program, including the Civil Rights, Military Reconstruction, and Tenure of Office bills. At the opening of the session in December 1865 Wade promptly introduced a bill for the enfranchisement of negroes in the District of Columbia (*Congressional Globe*, 39 Cong., 1 Sess., p. 1), and supported negro suffrage in the campaign of 1866, although he was willing to readmit the Southern states if they ratified the fourteenth amendment within a reasonable time (*Ibid.*, 39 Cong., 2 Sess., p. 124). His methods during the period leave the impression that he, like Stevens, was ready to resort to almost any extremity in order to carry through the congressional policies or gain a point.

The Radicals succeeded in having Wade elected president *pro tempore* of the Senate when that office became vacant (Mar. 2, 1867). According to the statute then in force, he would have succeeded to the presidency in the event of Johnson's removal. But it appears that the prospect of Wade's succession really became an embarrassment to them, for many of the conservatives felt that he would be no improvement and might prove less satisfactory than Johnson (*Diary of Gideon Welles*, 1911, vol. III, 293; Oberholtzer, *post*, II, 134n.). Wade himself voted for Johnson's conviction despite the fact that he was an interested party. So expectant was he of success that he began the selection of his cabinet before the impeachment trial was concluded (Adam Badeau, *Grant in Peace*, 1887, pp. 136–37; C. G. Bowers, *The Tragic Era*, 1929, pp. 188–89). Thwarted in his presidential ambitions by Johnson's acquittal, and having failed of reëlection to the Senate, Wade sought the second place on the ticket with Grant in 1868. However, after leading on the first four ballots in the Republican convention, he lost the nomination to Schuyler Colfax.

Upon his retirement from the Senate in 1869 Wade resumed the practice of law in Ohio. He became general counsel for the Northern Pacific Railroad and served for a time as one of the government directors of the Union Pacific. In 1871 Grant appointed him a member of the commission of investigation which visited Santo Domingo and recommended its annexation (*Report of the Commission of Inquiry to Santo Domingo*, 1871). Seven years later he died in Jefferson, Ohio.

[The chief documentary sources for Wade's public career are the *Cong. Globe* and the "Report of the Joint Committee on the Conduct of the War," *Senate Report No. 108*, 37 Cong., 3 Sess., (3 vols., 1863); *Senate Report No. 142*, 38 Cong., 2 Sess., (3 vols., 1865). A. G. Riddle, *The Life of Benjamin F. Wade* (1886), is too brief and uncritical to be of much historical value. Short sketches of Wade's life are to be found in L. P. Brockett, *Men of Our Day* (1872), pp. 240–62, a contemporary eulogistic account; *The Biog. Cyclopædia and Portrait Gallery . . . of . . . Ohio*, vol. I (1883), 293–94; *Biog. Dir. Am. Cong.* (1928); *N. Y. Herald* and *N. Y. Times*, Mar. 3, 1878. J. F. Rhodes, *Hist. of the U. S.* (9 vols., 1893–1922); and E. P. Oberholtzer,

A Hist. of the U. S. since the Civil War (4 vols., 1917–31) contain numerous references to Wade, as do the biographies of his political contemporaries. D. M. DeWitt, *The Impeachment and Trial of Andrew Johnson* (1903) is useful for the post-war period. This work, like the more recent studies of the war and reconstruction eras, is hostile to Wade and his faction.]

A. H. M.

WADE, DECIUS SPEAR (Jan. 23, 1835–Aug. 3, 1905), Montana jurist, was born near Andover, Ashtabula County, Ohio, the son of Charles H. and Juliet (Spear) Wade. Charles Wade was a farmer, and the son worked on the farm with but little schooling until he was sixteen years old. Then he began to teach school in winter and to attend the academy at Kingsville, Ohio, in summer. He also studied law in the office of his uncle, Benjamin F. Wade [*q.v.*]. In 1857 he was admitted to practice and established himself in Jefferson, Ohio. He was elected probate judge of Ashtabula County in 1860. The next year he volunteered for three months' service in the Federal army and was made lieutenant, but apparently he soon left the army to resume his duties as judge. On June 3, 1863, he married an English girl named Bernice Galpin, by whom he had one daughter. He served as probate judge till 1867 and then practised law for two years. In 1871 he was appointed chief justice of Montana by President Grant; he was reappointed every four years until the expiration of his fourth term in 1887.

When Wade went to Montana the supreme court judges also acted as district judges, and each of them traveled extensively by stagecoach and on horseback. No decisions of the supreme court were published before 1868, and few precedents had been established. The statutes were vague, and the customs of the miners' courts were the generally accepted law. Litigation, which was extensive, for the most part involved mining claims and water rights in an arid country where the English common law did not seem to apply. Decisions had to be reached by the formation of new principles or by the application of old rules to new conditions. In the case of *Robertson* vs. *Smith* (1 *Montana Reports*, 410) Wade's decision in the district court, based on the miners' law, was affirmed by Knowles in the supreme court. In 1872 Congress passed a law opening mineral deposits in public lands and defining in a general way the rights to quartz claims but leaving much to be determined by the courts. Terms had to be defined and rules made governing ambiguous situations. In a long series of cases Wade and Associate Justice Hiram Knowles formulated the mining and irrigation law for Montana. In the first six volumes of the *Montana Reports* almost half of the decisions were Wade's,

and few of them were reversed on appeal. **In**
fourteen out of seventeen cases taken to the
United States Supreme Court, his opinions were
affirmed. When Wade retired from the bench in
1887 he entered into partnership with Edwin
Warren Toole [q.v.] and William Wallace. In
1889 he was appointed a member of a commission
to draft a code supplanting the conflicting and
confusing laws of the territory. It was adopted
by the legislature in 1895, and *The Codes and
Statutes of Montana* (2 vols.) was published in
the same year. Wade wrote the four chapters on
the bench and bar in Montana which appear in
Joaquin Miller's *An Illustrated History of Montana* (2 vols., 1894) and a number of newspaper
articles on Montana history. He was also the
author of a novel, *Clare Lincoln* (1876). He
lived and practised in Helena until 1895, when he
returned to Ohio. He died in Ohio near Andover.

[See Joaquin Miller, *An Illustrated History of Montana* (2 vols., 1894), which contains a biog. sketch
and summaries of important cases; C. P. Connelly, in
Mag. of Western Hist., May 1891; Theodore Brantley,
in *Contributions to the Hist. Soc. of Mont.,* vol. IV
(1903); *Ohio Law Bull.,* Oct. 9, 1905; *Proc. Mont. Bar
Asso. . . . 1914* (n.d.), pp. 316–21; obituaries in *Anaconda Standard,* from which the date of death is taken,
and *Helena Independent,* Aug. 5, 1905.]   P. C. P.

WADE, JEPTHA HOMER (Aug. 11, 1811–
Aug. 9, 1890), financier, was one of the founders
of the American commercial telegraph system.
He was born in Romulus, Seneca County, N. Y.,
the son of Jeptha and Sarah (Allen) Wade and a
descendant of Benjamin Wade, a clothier, who
was living in Elizabeth, N. J., in 1675. The elder
Jeptha Wade, a surveyor and civil engineer, died
in 1813, and about this time or later the family
moved to Seneca Falls. The boy learned the carpenter's trade, and as a young man operated a
small sash and blind factory. Interest in art, however, led him to study painting with Randall
Palmer, a local portrait painter, and for five or
six years after 1837 he traveled through New
York, Louisiana, and Michigan as an itinerant
painter of portraits. While at Adrian, Mich., he
learned of the invention of the daguerreotype and
purchased a camera to widen his field of portraiture.

The news of the success of the telegraph in
1844 led him to study the possibilities of the invention of Morse and in 1847 he contracted to
build a telegraph line from Detroit to Jackson—
"a frail, one-wire affair." Other lines, which
came to be known as the Wade Lines, followed in
rapid succession—from Detroit to Milwaukee,
from Detroit to Buffalo by way of Cleveland,
from Cleveland to Cincinnati and St. Louis.
Meanwhile Royal E. House, Henry O'Reilly,

Ezra Cornell [qq.v.], and other men were building up individual systems and in the early fifties
competition became furious. In 1854 the lines of
Wade and House were consolidated, with Wade
as the general agent, controlling a network over
the Old Northwest. Similar consolidations of
other systems were taking place at the same time,
and in 1856 most of the western lines were combined in the Western Union Telegraph Company,
with Anson Stager [q.v.], formerly of the
O'Reilly lines, as general superintendent and
Wade as general agent. Within a few years
Wade pushed on into the Far West, organizing
the California State Telegraph Company and the
Pacific Telegraph Company to connect St. Louis
with San Francisco. A line to Salt Lake City
from the West was completed in October 1861,
putting out of business the firm operating the
pony express and preparing the way for the
transcontinental railroad and the daily mail.
Wade was promoted from the position of general
agent to that of managing director, and in 1866
became president of the enlarged Western Union,
but illness in 1867 caused him to give up the responsibilities of that office.

About 1856 he had established his residence in
Cleveland, and thenceforth was closely identified
with Cleveland business. In 1867 he took a leading part in the organization of the Citizens' Savings & Loan Association and became its president, and later he held the same office with the
National Bank of Commerce. He was also actively interested in railroad building and management and served on the boards of directors of
most of the lines entering Cleveland. He was
sinking-fund commissioner, a member of the
public park commission, and a director of the
Cleveland workhouse board, and also a member
of the National Garfield Monument Association.
In 1882 he gave Wade Park, a tract of seventy-
five acres of land, to the city of Cleveland, and
other philanthropies evidenced his generous public spirit. A part of the site of the Western Reserve University was one of his gifts.

Wade was twice married: on Oct. 15, 1832, to
Rebecca Loueza Facer, who died Nov. 30, 1836,
and on Sept. 5, 1837 to Susan M. Fleming, who
died in August 1890. In physique Wade was
slightly over six feet tall and powerfully built.
In his personal characteristics he was modest and
easily approached, genial and an interesting conversationalist. He never lost his interest in
painting and music.

[S. C. Wade, *The Wade Geneal.* (1900); J. H. Ken-
nedy, in *Mag. of Western Hist.,* Oct. 1885; H. F. Big-
gar, *Loiterings in Europe* (Cleveland, 1908); J. D.
Reid, *The Telegraph in America* (1879); *Cleveland
Past and Present* (1869); *A Hist. of Cleveland and Its
Environs,* vols. I, II (1918); *Cleveland Weekly Leader*

and Herald, Aug. 16, 1890, reprinting article from the *Sunday Leader,* Aug. 10, 1890.]   E. J. B.

WADE, MARTIN JOSEPH (Oct. 20, 1861–Apr. 16, 1931), Iowa jurist, was the son of Irish immigrant parents, Michael and Mary (Breen) Wade, who, soon after their marriage at Worcester, Mass., settled at Burlington, Vt., where Martin was born. Having spent his later boyhood in Butler County, Iowa, he attended St. Joseph's College at Dubuque. In 1886 he received the degree of LL.B. from the University of Iowa and began to practise law in partnership with C. S. Ranck at Iowa City. His marriage to Mary Gertrude McGovern of Iowa City on Apr. 4, 1888, was the culmination of a college romance. Having a penchant for teaching, Wade began lecturing on torts in the law college of the University of Iowa in 1890; during the following year he was an instructor in law; and from 1892 to 1894 served as professor of law, giving courses in as many as five subjects. An unexpected appointment to fill a vacancy on the bench of the local district court in December 1893 changed the course of his career, though he remained on the faculty of the university as professor of medical jurisprudence from 1894 to 1903. As a result of that experience he published in 1909 *A Selection of Cases on Malpractice of Physicians, Surgeons and Dentists.* In 1894 he was elected to his position as judge in the eighth district without opposition, and in 1898 was reëlected for four years. If the selection of Wade as president of the Iowa State Bar Association in 1897 was an indication of his professional standing, his election to Congress in 1902, the only Democrat in the Iowa delegation, was probably due to his political sagacity. Though he served only one term as United States representative (1903–05), this sojourn in Washington introduced him to national politics. From 1907 to 1914 he was a member of the Democratic National Committee, and during the campaign of 1908 he was on the executive committee.

In March 1915 he left a thriving law practice in the firm of Wade, Dutcher, and Davis, which he had organized in 1905, to become United States district judge for the southern district of Iowa (appointment confirmed, Mar. 3, 1915). Admirably qualified for the position by temperament, legal training, courage, and a deep sense of justice, he conducted his court with impressive dignity and in strict adherence to his conception of righteousness. Always intensely patriotic, he brought to the bench an aggressive loyalty to the American system of government. The Constitution, he thought, was inspired. Good citizenship was his principal obsession. He was tireless in explaining the government to aliens and declared that his naturalization work was of prime importance. His remarks upon sentencing Kate Richards O'Hare for obstructing enlistment during the World War (*O'Hare* vs. *United States, 253 Federal Reporter,* 538) were typical of his patriotic fervor. He regarded militant pacifists and socialists as public enemies. In hundreds of prohibition enforcement cases he lectured bootleggers about respect for law. Wade fathered the Iowa statute of 1921 requiring that the principles of republican government and the meaning of the Constitution must be taught in the public schools. With W. F. Russell he published *The Short Constitution* (copyright 1920), which purported to be "talks" by a judge on constitutional rights and was intended to be the first in a series of volumes on "elementary Americanism." He also conceived of teaching good citizenship by the "case method" and prepared some brief *Lessons in Americanism* (copyright 1920) that were to be syndicated to newspapers, and, with W. H. Bateson, *The Constitution through Problems* (copyright 1931). Though none of these projects attained popularity, he never lost his enthusiasm for patriotic uplift. He spent the last four years of his life in California and died in Los Angeles, survived by his wife and his two daughters.

[*Who's Who in America,* 1930–31; *Biog. Dir. Am. Cong.* (1928); C. R. Aurner, *Leading Events in Johnson County, Iowa, Hist.,* vol. II (1913); Cats. of the Univ. of Iowa; *Iowa Official Registers; Proc. Iowa State Bar Asso.,* vol. XXXVII (1931); obituaries in *Iowa Jour. of Hist. and Politics,* July 1931, *Iowa City Press-Citizen,* Apr. 16, and *Des Moines Reg.,* Apr. 17, 1931.]   J. E. B.

WADSWORTH, JAMES (Apr. 20, 1768–June 7, 1844), community builder, pioneer in public school education, was born in Durham, Conn., the youngest of the three sons of John Noyes and Esther (Parsons) Wadsworth, and a descendant of William Wadsworth, who settled in Cambridge, Mass., about 1632 and accompanied Thomas Hooker to Hartford, Conn., in 1636. James graduated from Yale College in 1787 and spent the winter of that and the following year in teaching at Montreal, Canada. His father had died while the son was in college, leaving a fair estate to his children. At the suggestion of a relative, Jeremiah Wadsworth [*q.v.*] of Hartford, Conn., who had secured holdings in the Phelps and Gorham Purchase in western New York, James and his brother William bought a portion of his land there and became agents for the remainder.

The property acquired by them was on the east bank of the Genesee River, in what are now the townships of Geneseo and Avon. In the summer of 1790 they started on their journey from Durham to their wilderness possessions, William with an oxcart, a few men, and a slave woman, traveling overland; James, in charge of household effects and provisions, taking the water route to Canandaigua. They established themselves a little below the present town of Geneseo, and as time went on prospered remarkably. They constantly extended their cultivated land, raised corn, hemp, which they manufactured into rope, and some tobacco; maintained herds of cattle, bred mules, and in later years prosecuted wool-growing on a large scale. Their operations both as agriculturists and land agents ultimately brought them substantial returns, with which they increased their own holdings until they were among the largest land owners of cultivated areas.

Their influence in developing the Genesee country was unparalleled. William was the practical man of affairs, James the thinker, planner, and counselor. Most of the agency work fell to him. From February 1796 to November 1798 he was in Europe, with the cooperation of Robert Morris, Aaron Burr, DeWitt Clinton, and others, interesting foreign capitalists in American investments. He was a student of political economy and the physical sciences, and sought through the application of the latter to improve agricultural methods. With a view to instructing others along these lines, he frequently arranged for the insertion of articles in newspapers and agricultural periodicals, and for the preparation of pamphlets on scientific subjects. These he was in the habit of distributing gratuitously. His chief interest, in fact, outside his business affairs, was in public education. No one in the state was more energetic in efforts to improve the common-school system. He urged the establishment of county academies for the better training of schoolmasters; was instrumental in securing the enactment of legislation authorizing the sending of Lectures on School-Keeping by Samuel Read Hall [q.v.] to the trustees of each school district; and sought to interest persons in preparing suitable textbooks, setting aside $30,000 for that purpose, a part of which was to be offered in premiums for the best treatises on prescribed subjects, and the remainder to be expended in stereotyping the works selected. Through his tireless efforts the school district library system was finally established in New York State. When certain educational papers were started he contributed liberally to their support, and frequently bore the entire expense of large editions containing special articles. He gave freely toward the erection of schoolhouses and churches, and toward the maintenance of lecture courses on scientific subjects. For the town of Geneseo he built and endowed a public library, and it is reputed to have been in part through his influence that his friend John Jacob Astor, 1763–1848 [q.v.], provided for the founding of the Astor Library in New York City.

On Oct. 1, 1804, he married Naomi, daughter of Samuel and Jerusha (Wolcott) Wolcott of East Windsor, Conn. At his death, in Geneseo, he left two sons and two daughters. One of the sons was James S. Wadsworth [q.v.].

[F. B. Dexter, *Biog. Sketches Grads. Yale Coll.*, vol. IV (1907); H. R. Stiles, *The Hist. and Geneals. of Ancient Windsor, Conn.* (2nd ed., vol. II, 1892); Samuel Wolcott, *Memorial of Henry Wolcott . . . and Some of His Descendants* (1881); Orsamus Turner, *Hist. of the Pioneer Settlement of Phelps and Gorham's Purchase* (1851); L. L. Doty, *A Hist. of Livingston County, N. Y.* (1876); Henry Barnard, *Am. Jour. of Education*, Sept. 1858; H. G. Pearson, *James S. Wadsworth of Geneseo* (1913); James Renwick, in *Monthly Journal of Agriculture*, Oct. 1846; *Albany Evening Journal*, June 10, 1844.]   H. E. S.

WADSWORTH, JAMES SAMUEL (Oct. 30, 1807–May 8, 1864), Union soldier, was the son of James Wadsworth [q.v.] and his wife, Naomi, daughter of Samuel Wolcott of East Windsor, Conn. Born at Geneseo, N. Y., at a time when the hardships of the first settlement there were over, Wadsworth grew up among pioneer surroundings, but as the prospective heir to a great landed estate. He spent two years at Harvard, without graduating, studied law, and was admitted to the bar, but did not practise, his legal education having been intended only to prepare him for the management of his properties. On May 11, 1834, he married Mary Craig Wharton, daughter of John Wharton, a Quaker merchant of Philadelphia. His position in the community and his own sense of public duty made him active in politics throughout his life, although he had no ambition for office. At first a Democrat, his strong anti-slavery sentiments made him join in organizing the Free-Soil party, which merged with the Republican party in 1856. He was a delegate to the unofficial "peace conference" in Washington in February 1861.

From the outbreak of the Civil War his life and fortune were unreservedly at the service of the country. "It always seemed to me," wrote his friend John Lothrop Motley, "that he was the truest and the most thoroughly loyal American I ever knew" (Pearson, *post*, p. 34). But he was no candidate for high military rank. The governor of New York, on the understanding that he could name two major generals of volunteers, offered an appointment to Wadsworth, who advised the selection of a regular army officer instead, and accepted only when this was found impossible. "I am better than a worse man," was his sagacious comment, and he was frankly gratified when the grant of power to the governor was refused. He went to the front, however, and offered his services as an aide to Gen. Irvin McDowell, a gift accepted with hesitation, for a middle-aged gentleman of national reputation would not seem to be either physically or mentally suitable for an orderly officer. But he proved at the battle of Bull Run that both in hard riding and in intelligent obedience he could match the youngest of the staff. On Aug. 9, 1861, he was commissioned brigadier-general of volunteers. The appointment, which was partly political, was intended to conciliate Republicans of Democratic antecedents. Wadsworth accepted it after considering in his usual detached fashion what the effect on the public service might be. He was, indeed, much better qualified than most of the non-professional general officers. Though destitute of military training like the rest, he had the habit of command, rarer among Union than among Confederate volunteers, and his civil occupations had fitted him peculiarly well for the care of his men in the field. A military education would not have shown him how to organize a system of supply by ox team, as he did when his brigade was camped in the Virginia mud near Arlington during the first winter of the war and mule-drawn wagons could not get through. He was fortunate in not being required to command a large force in action until he had been nearly two years in service and the men under him were seasoned veterans. When the Army of the Potomac moved to the peninsula in the spring of 1862, he was left in command of the defenses of Washington. Doubtful of getting service in the field, he accepted the Republican nomination for governor of New York but was defeated at the election. In December 1862, after the battle of Fredericksburg, he took command of the 1st Division, I Corps. It had a small part in the battle of Chancellorsville and a very great one at Gettysburg. On the first day of the battle, in spite of terrific loss, it held the Confederates in check while the rest of the army was hastening to the battlefield. On the second and third days it held Culp's Hill, on the right of the Union line. In the reorganization of the army for the 1864 campaign, Wadsworth received the 4th Division of the V Corps, made up largely of regiments from his old command. After nearly succeeding in breaking through the Confederate center on the second day (May 6) of the battle of the Wilderness, it was outflanked and driven back. Wadsworth had already had two horses shot under him; his third was unmanageable, and the Confederate line was close upon him before he could

turn. He was shot in the head, and the enemy's advance passed over his body. He died two days later in a Confederate field hospital. He was survived by his wife and their six children.

[C. C. Baldwin, *Wadsworth* (copr. 1882); H. G. Pearson, *James S. Wadsworth of Geneseo* (1913), an adequate biog., with ample citations of authorities; L. F. Allen, *Memorial of the Late Gen. James S. Wadsworth* (1865); *Proc. Century Asso. in Honor of . . . Brig. Gen. James S. Wadsworth* (1865); *War of the Rebellion: Official Records* (Army); *Battles and Leaders of the Civil War* (4 vols., 1887–88); N. Y. Monuments Commission, *In Memoriam, James Samuel Wadsworth* (1916); Morris Schaff, *The Battle of the Wilderness* (1910); obituary in *N. Y. Times,* May 11, 1864.]   T. M. S.

WADSWORTH, JEREMIAH (July 12, 1743–Apr. 30, 1804), Revolutionary soldier and congressman, was born in Hartford, Conn., the son of the Rev. Daniel Wadsworth, pastor of the First Church of Christ, and Abigail Talcott, the daughter of Gov. Joseph Talcott [*q.v.*]. William Wadsworth, the first American ancestor of the family, came to America from England about 1632. Jeremiah was four years of age when his father died and he was placed in charge of his uncle, Matthew Talcott, a ship-owner of Middletown. At the age of eighteen, in the hope of improving his health, he embarked as a common sailor aboard one of his uncle's vessels, followed the sea for about ten years and rose to the rank of captain. On Sept. 29, 1767, he was married to Mehitable Russell, the daughter of the Rev. William Russell, of Middletown; they had three children.

His early championship of colonial rights combined with his knowledge of mercantile affairs induced the legislature, in April 1775, to appoint him commissary to the Revolutionary forces raised in Connecticut. On June 18, 1777, the Continental Congress elected him deputy commissary-general of purchases, and he served until his resignation the following August. Upon the retirement of Joseph Trumbull [*q.v.*] as commissary-general, he was appointed, in April 1778, to fill the post and remained until he resigned on Dec. 4, 1779. Despite scarcity of funds and lack of cooperation on the part of state authorities, he kept the Continental Army so well provisioned that Washington wrote, "since his appointment our supplies of provision have been good and ample" (W. C. Ford, *The Writings of George Washington,* VII, 1890, p. 141). At the request of Rochambeau he served as commissary also to the French troops in America until the close of the war, and in the summer of 1783 he went to Paris in order to submit a report of his transactions. Proceeding to England and Ireland in March 1784, he invested the considerable balance remaining to his credit in merchandise that he disposed of profitably upon his return to America.

He was a member of the state convention called in 1788 to consider the ratification of the federal Constitution, and voted in its favor, possibly for financial as well as political reasons since he held public paper that was bound to appreciate in value upon adoption of a new frame of government. He was elected a Federalist to Congress in 1787 and 1788, but attended only in 1788. He was a strong advocate of assumption, a policy in which he appears to have had a large speculative interest (*The Journal of William Maclay,* new edition, 1927, pp. 174, 231, 323). In 1795 he was elected to the state legislature and to the executive council, remaining a member of the latter body by annual election until 1801.

His business interests were varied and important. He was a founder of the Bank of North America in Philadelphia and of the Hartford Bank, a director of the United States Bank, president of the Bank of New York, and one of the promoters of the Hartford Manufacturing Company, established in 1788, "the first purely wool-manufacturing concern founded on a strictly business basis, and the first in which power machinery was employed" (A. H. Cole, *The American Wool Manufacture,* 1926, I, 64). He established in 1794 the first partnership for insurance in Connecticut. He introduced fine breeds of cattle from abroad and engaged in experiments with a view to improving agriculture. Honorary degrees were awarded to him by Yale and Dartmouth colleges for his interest in the promotion of literary institutions. He died at Hartford and was laid to rest in the Ancient Burying Ground.

[Manuscript letters and papers in the Conn. Hist. Soc., Hartford, and the N. Y. Hist. Soc., New York City; R. R. Hinman, *A Hist. Coll. from Official Records . . . of the Part Sustained by Conn. during . . . the Revolution* (1842); H. A. Wadsworth, *Two Hundred and Fifty Years of the Wadsworth Family in America* (1883); *Diary of Rev. Daniel Wadsworth* (1894); S. V. Talcott, *Talcott Pedigree in England and America* (1876); C. J. Hoadly, *The Pub. Records of the Colony of Conn.,* vols. XIV (1887), XV (1890); *Record of Conn. Men . . . During the . . . Revolution* (1889), ed. by H. P. Johnston; W. B. Weeden, *Econ. and Social Hist. of New England* (1890), vol. II; C. J. Hoadly, *The Pub. Records of the State of Conn.,* vols. I (1894), II (1895), III (1922); W. C. Ford, *Jours. of the Cont. Cong.,* vols. VIII–XXIV (1904–34); *Conn. as a Colony and as a State* (4 vols., 1904), ed. by Forrest Morgan; G. L. Clark, *A Hist. of Conn.* (1914); E. C. Burnett, *Letters of Members of the Cont. Cong.* (7 vols., 1921–34); *Conn. Courant* (Hartford), May 2, 1804.]
E. E. C.

WADSWORTH, PELEG (May 6, 1748–Nov. 12, 1829), Revolutionary general and member of Congress, was born in Duxbury, Mass., the son of Deacon Peleg Wadsworth and his wife, Lusanna Sampson. He was descended from an Englishman, Christopher Wadsworth, who set-

tled in Duxbury in 1632. After graduating from Harvard College in 1769, he kept a private school in Plymouth and prepared pupils for college and for the army. In 1774 he was elected captain of a company of minute-men and member of the committee of correspondence for Plymouth County. When the news of the battle of Lexington arrived, he marched, Apr. 20, 1775, to Marshfield to stand off a British regiment, but before any fighting occurred the red-coats retired. Shortly afterwards he accompanied Col. Theophilus Cotton's regiment to Roxbury, and as engineer under the orders of John Thomas [q.v.] laid out the American lines at that place and at Dorchester Heights. He also investigated the problem of erecting defenses at Cape Cod.

On Feb. 13, 1776, he was appointed aide-de-camp to Artemas Ward [q.v.] and served in that capacity until Apr. 23, 1776, when Ward was forced to resign because of failing health. The same year he saw service under Washington in New York and on Long Island, and in 1778 under Sullivan in Rhode Island. On Aug. 25, 1778, he was appointed adjutant-general, and on July 7, 1779, brigadier-general of the Massachusetts militia. Amid these activities he found time to serve on the board of war of Massachusetts and, for a term (May 28, 1777–May 1, 1778), as representative from Duxbury in the legislature. In 1779 he was second in command of an expedition dispatched by the authorities of Massachusetts under Solomon Lovell and Dudley Saltonstall [q.v.] to expel the British from Fort George (Castine, Me.). The attempt failed and the Americans retreated after sustaining serious losses in men and matériel. A committee of inquiry appointed by the legislature of Massachusetts honorably acquitted Wadsworth of responsibility for the disaster. In March 1780 he was placed in command of the eastern department with headquarters at Thomaston, Me. On the night of Feb. 18, 1781, a party of British raided his dwelling and carried him off to Fort George where he remained captive until June 18, when he managed to effect his escape with a companion by cutting a hole in the roof of his prison by means of a gimlet obtained from a barber at the fort.

After the war he removed to Falmouth (Portland), Me., where for several years he was engaged in trade and politics. He served as selectman, as representative in Congress from 1793 to 1807, and as chairman of a committee to consider the separation of the district of Maine from Massachusetts. In 1806 he removed to Oxford County where he had purchased 7800 acres of land and where he procured the incorporation of the town of Hiram. Here he spent the remainder of his days, living like a patriarch in a commodious frame house, "Wadsworth Hall," which served as church, court, school, and drilling place for the community. Lumbering, farming, and civic affairs engaged his attention. He lies buried in the family graveyard on his estate. On June 18, 1772, he was married to Elizabeth Bartlett, of Plymouth, by whom he had eleven children. A daughter, Zilpah, became the wife of Stephen Longfellow, and was the mother of Henry Wadsworth Longfellow and Samuel Longfellow [qq.v.]. Henry Wadsworth Longfellow, during his youth, lived in a brick house (the first in Portland), built by the General in 1785 and 1786, and known today as the "Wadsworth-Longfellow House." Peleg's son, Henry, became a naval officer and lost his life in the Tripolitan War. After him the poet was named.

[Papers and personal belongings of Wadsworth are in "Wadsworth Hall" and the "Wadsworth-Longfellow House." He wrote a series of autobiographical letters to his children which were edited by H. L. Bradley and published in 1903 under the title, *A Story About a Little Good Boy.* Consult also: W. D. Williamson, *The Hist. of the State of Me.* (1832), vol. II; F. H. Underwood, *The Life of Henry Wadsworth Longfellow* (1882); H. A. Wadsworth, *Two Hundred and Fifty Years of the Wadsworth Family in America* (1883); Levi Bartlett, *Geneal. . . . of the Bartlett Family* (1876); *Coll. and Proc. of the Me. Hist. Soc.,* 2 ser., vols. I (1890), II (1891), V (1894), VI (1895), X (1899), XVI (1910), XVII (1913), XVIII (1914), XIX (1914); *Mass. Soldiers and Sailors of the Revolutionary War,* vol. XVI (1907); Nathan Goold, *The Wadsworth-Longfellow House* (1908); E. K. Gould, *Storming the Heights* (1932); *Biog. Dir. Am. Cong.* (1928); *Portland Advertiser,* Dec. 1, 1829.]   E. E. C.

WAGGAMAN, MARY TERESA McKEE (Sept. 21, 1846–July 30, 1931), writer, was born in Baltimore, Md., the daughter of John and Esther (Cottrell) McKee. Her father, a native of Ireland, joined the gold rush to California in 1849, acquired a fortune, and became a shipbroker in New York. Her mother, the daughter of an Anglican clergyman, died when Mary was six years of age. The child was brought up in Mount de Sales Convent, Catonsville, Md. At the outbreak of the Civil War her father took her to New York to live in the home of friends, in whose well-filled library she spent much of the next two years attempting to supplement her education. In the autumn of 1863, when her father, a Southern sympathizer, was seized and imprisoned for several months at Fort Lafayette, New York, she became one of a group of ardent Southern sympathizers in the Northern city. In the spring of 1864 she returned to the convent to be valedictorian of her graduating class. After her father was released from prison upon Lincoln's orders, she accompanied him to Liverpool, where they joined other exiles who were attempt-

ing to send supplies through the blockade to the depleted South. At the close of the Civil War they returned, broken in fortune, and took up their residence in Baltimore. There in 1870 she married Dr. Samuel J. Waggaman (d. 1913), who later became a professor in the National College of Pharmacy, Washington, D. C., where shortly after their marriage they established their home. They had eleven children, six of whom survived their mother.

She began writing during her school days. When twenty-five years of age she published a poem, "The Legend of the Mistletoe," in *Harper's New Monthly Magazine* (January 1872). When her eldest son became a communicant and she could find no story which would properly inculcate lessons of piety, she wrote *Little Comrades, A First Communion Story* (1894) for her own children. Its enthusiastic reception by Catholic children led her to write others, and for thirty-five years she contributed short stories and serials, and infrequently poems, to Catholic periodicals. Among her earlier serials subsequently published in book form were *Tom's Luck-Pot* (1897), *Little Missy* (1900), and *Corinne's Vow* (1902); and among the later ones, *The Secret of Pocomoke* (1914), *Grapes of Thorns* (1917), and *The Finding of Tony* (1919). At the age of seventy-seven she wrote a winning story (published in *The Columbiad,* 1923) in a contest of over 3,000 contestants. Shortly before her death, at the age of eighty-five, she completed a final serial story. In 1903 she published *Carroll Dare,* a novel of colonial Maryland and revolutionary France, and the next year *Strong-Arm of Avalon* (1904), her only other venture into historical fiction. After her death an autobiographical article, "An American Bastile," describing her Civil War experiences, was published in the *Ave Maria* (May 28, June 4, 1932). In her later writing she was primarily concerned that her stories should strengthen the religious faith and loyalty of young Catholic readers. To this aim she sacrificed realism, variety, and literary distinction. Her characters, however, never become priggish or pretentious; her plots are inventive; and her style easy, natural, and straightforward.

[*N. Y. Times,* Aug. 1, 1931; *Evening Star* (Washington, D. C.), July 31, 1931; *Baltimore Catholic Review,* Aug. 7, 1931; *Catholic World,* Sept. 1931; *Commonweal,* Aug. 26, 1931; communications from Mrs. Waggaman's daughter, Mrs. Charles P. Neill, Washington, D. C.]   V. L. S.

WAGNER, CLINTON (Oct. 28, 1837–Nov. 25, 1914), laryngologist, was born in Baltimore, Md., of a German-American family whose ancestor, Basil Wagner, was said to have received, in 1667, a grant of land from the Crown in the province of Frederick, afterwards Carroll County, Md. His mother, of Welsh descent, *née* Peters, was born in Baltimore in 1806. He attended St. James College, Hagerstown, Md., then entered upon the study of medicine in Baltimore, and received the degree of M.D., at the University of Maryland in 1859. He entered the Medical Corps of the United States army, the first of twenty-eight applicants, served at Fort Leavenworth, Kan., and later at San Antonio Arsenal, Tex., where his command was surrendered to the Confederates by David E. Twiggs [*q.v.*] at the opening of the Civil War. Wagner, loyal to the Union, was given a position of much responsibility by the Surgeon-General Hammond of the army and after several promotions became medical director of the regular, or Second Division, V Corps, of the Army of the Potomac, ranking as brevet lieutenant-colonel. He established numerous field hospitals and organized on the Mississippi River the first floating hospital in Western waters. He was many times at the front during severe engagements and risked great personal perils. One of the most notable was at Gettysburg, where he established a field hospital near Little Round Top, the site of which is now marked by a monument bearing his name. He continued in the Medical Corps of the army after the war, but resigned in 1869 and went abroad to study laryngology in London, Vienna, Berlin, and Paris. After two years he returned to New York City and established himself as a specialist. His brilliant qualities as a teacher and as a practitioner soon attracted attention; he established the Metropolitan Throat Hospital and Dispensary, modeled after the London Throat Hospital of Golden Square, and rivaling the best institutions of its kind abroad. It soon became famous among students in the United States as the first special hospital and school of instruction of graduates in laryngology and rhinology.

Wagner devised many new instruments and surgical methods, and his long experience as a general surgeon and his extraordinary technical skill enabled him to perform with success major operations upon the throat and neck that few specialists were in the habit of undertaking. He was the best master of thyrotomy of his time. In a pioneer thesis, *Habitual Mouth-Breathing* (1881), he called attention to mouth-breathing in its relation to medicine. Many of his most valuable contributions were published in the *Transactions of the American Laryngological Association* from 1879 to 1893. In 1882 he was among the first to enter upon the organization of the New York Post-Graduate Medical School

and Hospital, where he became its first professor of laryngology and rhinology. An important achievement of his career was the founding of the New York Laryngological Society in 1873, nearly fifteen years before a similar organization was founded in Europe and five years before the organization of the American Laryngological Association, which grew out of the New York society. In 1914 Wagner became an honorary fellow of the national Association.

In the midst of a brilliant and prosperous professional career, he retired from active practice in New York. For several years he resided at Colorado Springs and other well-known health resorts of the Southwest. Later he spent much time abroad, published practical studies of many popular sanitaria, and acquired an unusually wide and accurate knowledge of climatology. He was a man of untiring energy and indomitable courage; no difficulty seemed to him unsurmountable, and no danger too great. As a pioneer in American laryngology he stands in the foremost rank. He was married on Aug. 28, 1882, to Elizabeth Vaughan of London, who survived him. They were detained abroad at the outbreak of the World War and made their residence at Geneva, Switzerland, where he died.

[Personal acquaintance; *Who's Who in America*, 1901–02; F. J. Stockman, biographical article in H. A. Kelly, W. L. Burrage, *Am. Medic. Biog.* (1920); memoir by D. B. Delavan, *Trans. Am. Laryngological Asso.*, vol. XXXV (1915); and obituary notice in *Medic. Record*, Dec. 5, 1914; *N. Y. Times*, Nov. 26, 1914.]
                                             D. B. D.

WAGNER, WEBSTER (Oct. 2, 1817–Jan. 13, 1882), manufacturer of sleeping-cars, was born at Palatine Bridge, N. Y., the son of John and Elizabeth (Strayer) Wagner, both of German descent, whose families had settled in the Mohawk Valley at an early date. After obtaining an ordinary education and working on his father's farm, Wagner learned the wagon-making trade from an older brother and engaged in that business with him. Since the venture was not successful, in 1843 Wagner became station master of the New York Central Railroad in Palatine Bridge, holding the position for upwards of fifteen years and adding to his duties those of freight agent. Struck with the possibilities in special cars for the use of the night-travelling public and being a skilled craftsman in wood, he undertook the design of a sleeping-car. By 1858, with the financial help of Commodore Vanderbilt, he had completed four sleeping-cars and put them into operation on the New York Central Railroad. These cars had a single tier of berths, and the bedding was packed away by day in a closet at the end of the car. While they were crude affairs, they immediately became popular. Wagner thereupon organized the New York Central Sleeping Car Company at Palatine Bridge to manufacture his cars, which were used exclusively on the New York Central Railroad and its various branches. By 1865 he had evolved a more comfortable coach or drawing-room car, and in that year the New York Central Sleeping Car Company was reorganized as the Wagner Palace Car Company to manufacture both sleeping and drawing-room cars. The drawing-room car, which was put into service in the late summer of 1867, became as popular as the sleeping-car; both yielded fortunes to Wagner and his associates. About 1870 Wagner contracted with George M. Pullman [q.v.] to use the latter's newly patented folding upper berth, and hinged back and seat cushions for the lower berth, with the distinct understanding that the Wagner Company would use cars containing the Pullman inventions only on the lines of the New York Central Railroad. In 1875, however, when the Pullman Company's contract with the Michigan Central Railroad expired, Wagner secured the contract to run his cars over that road, thus making a through connection for the Vanderbilt lines between New York and Chicago. As a result of this breach of contract, the Pullman Company brought an infringement suit against Wagner's company for a million dollars' damages; the suit was still in process at the time of Wagner's death.

Wagner was also very active in New York state politics. He was elected assemblyman by the Republicans of Montgomery County in 1870, and in the following year was elected senator from the eighteenth district. Thereafter he continued in the state Senate until his death, having been reëlected without opposition at the end of each two-year term. As a delegate to the Republican National Convention in Chicago in 1880, he was extremely active in securing the nomination of President Garfield, being strongly opposed to the third-term aspirations of General Grant. He was married to Susan Davis of Palatine Bridge, and at the time of his death, which occurred in a train collision on the New York Central Railroad at Spuyten Duyvil, N. Y., he was survived by his widow and five children.

[Joseph Husband, *The Story of the Pullman Car* (1917); *Proc. of the Senate and Assembly of the State of New York in Relation to the Death of the Hon. Webster Wagner* (1882); *N. Y. Tribune, N. Y. Times,* Jan. 15, 17, 1882; *Sun* (N. Y.), Jan. 16, 1882.]
C. W. M.

WAGNER, WILLIAM (Jan. 15, 1796–Jan. 17, 1885), merchant, philanthropist, was born in Philadelphia, Pa., the youngest child of John Wagner, a cloth merchant and importer, and his wife Mary (Ritz) Baker Wagner, a daughter of Christian Ritz. William graduated from the Philadelphia Academy in 1808. Four years later he was placed in the counting house of a relative, but soon afterward was entered as an apprentice to Stephen Girard [q.v.]. He continued his studies in Latin, French, and mathematics, attracting the favorable attention of his master, and in 1814 Girard placed the youth in charge of a convoy of goods to be stored in Reading, Pa., in the fear that the British might reach Philadelphia. Two years later, Wagner was made assistant supercargo of Girard's ship, *Helvetius,* sailing on a two-year voyage to the Far East. As a boy he had begun to collect specimens of ores and minerals, and during this voyage he managed to gather a large collection of minerals, shells, plants, and organic remains, the nucleus of a museum which became the foundation of the Wagner Free Institute of Science.

Upon his return to Philadelphia in 1818 he retired from Girard's employ and engaged in business on his own account. He married Caroline M. Say, daughter of Dr. Benjamin Say [q.v.], on Jan. 1, 1824. In 1833 he attempted to mine anthracite coal in Schuylkill County, with heavy financial loss, but seven years more of successful commercial pursuits permitted him to retire from business, in 1840, to devote himself to studies in geology and mineralogy. His first wife having died, he married Louisa Binney in March 1841, and after a two-year tour of Europe bought a large property known as "Elm Grove," in the suburbs of Philadelphia, where he lived until his death.

In the residence he built on this land Wagner arranged a museum for his collections, and in 1847 began to give free lectures on geology, mineralogy, and conchology. After a few seasons his house was found to be too small to accommodate the audiences that desired admittance, but in 1852 he obtained permission to use part of Commissioners Hall, in the District of Spring Garden; and in 1854, when that district was absorbed into the city of Philadelphia, he received permission from the city government for continued use of the building, which was then unoccupied.

The opportunity thus offered he seized upon to establish his cherished project—a free institute of science. He gathered around him a distinguished faculty, all of whom served gratuitously. Wagner himself occupied the chair of geology, mineralogy, and mining. The legislature of Pennsylvania granted a charter for the Wagner Free Institute of Science, and its first season was inaugurated May 21, 1855. The lecture room was always filled to overflowing. When in 1859 the Philadelphia city government desired possession of the building, a new building was at once projected, and on June 2, 1860, on property owned by Wagner, the cornerstone was laid. The structure was completed in 1864, but was not occupied for lectures until the end of the Civil War. Dedicated May 11, 1865, the Wagner Free Institute of Science, together with an ample endowment for the continuance of the work, was turned over by its founder to a board of trustees. It had been incorporated Mar. 30, 1864, and by the act of incorporation was empowered to confer degrees.

Wagner died in Philadelphia some twenty years later, and was buried in a tomb in the institution he had founded. He had "struggled for more than three-score years to found his Free Institute of Science, and not only worked and waited . . . but denied himself many of the luxuries, if not what many persons would deem the necessaries, of life" (Westbrook, *post,* pp. 19–20). His wife also gave her encouragement and even her private patrimony to the establishment of the Institute. Wagner's greatest interest in science lay in the field of paleontology, and his best-known contribution to the subject was a paper he read before the Academy of Natural Sciences, Philadelphia, in January 1838 (*Journal,* vol. VIII, 1839). In H. G. Bronn's *Handbuch einer Geschichte der Natur* (Stuttgart, 1848), Wagner's name was applied to several fossil specimens which he seems to have described for the first time.

[R. B. Westbrook, *In Memoriam: William Wagner* (1885); Henry Leffman, Joseph Willcox, and Sydney Skidmore, in *Founder's Week Memorial Volume* (Phila,. 1909); W. H. Dall, "Notes on the Paleontological Publications of Prof. William Wagner," *Trans. Wagner Free Inst. of Sci.,* vol. V (1898); J. T. Scharf and Thompson Westcott, *Hist. of Phila.* (1884), vol. II; J. W. Jordan, *Colonial Families of Phila.* (1911), vol. II; *Phila. Press,* Jan. 19, 1885; *Public Ledger* (Phila.), Jan. 19, 1885.]   J. J.

WAHL, WILLIAM HENRY (Dec. 14, 1848–Mar. 23, 1909), scientific journalist, metallurgist, the son of John H. and Caroline R. Wahl, was born in Philadelphia, Pa. After graduating from Dickinson College, Carlisle, Pa., in 1867 with the degree of A.B., he entered the University of Heidelberg, Germany, where in 1869 he received the degree of Ph.D. In 1870 he was employed upon the *Journal of the Franklin Institute,* and in 1871, when he became secretary of the Institute, he also became editor of the *Journal.* He held both positions until 1874. He collaborated with Prof. Spencer F. Baird [*q.v.*] of the Smithsonian Institution in compiling the *Annual Record of Science and Industry* for the

years 1873–78, was an instructor in the physical sciences at the Academy of the Protestant Episcopal Church, Philadelphia (1871–73), and later taught physics and physical geography at the Philadelphia Central High School (1873–74). From 1875 to 1876 he acted as editor of the department of arts, sciences, and patents of the *American Exchange and Review.* In 1876 he became editor of the *Polytechnic Review,* which in 1879 was merged with the *Engineering and Mining Journal.* From 1880 to 1895 he was a member of the staff of the *Manufacturer and Builder of New York.* It was, however, as secretary of the Franklin Institute and editor of its *Journal* from 1882 to the time of his death that Wahl achieved distinction. During a critical period of several years in which the existence of the Institute was seriously jeopardized, he maintained the normal work of the organization, himself receiving a compensation so small as to be wholly incommensurate with his labors. Under his editorship the *Journal,* which had been for the most part a reprint of current scientific material, became a valuable source of original information. Nor were his literary activities confined to the congenial task of editing the *Journal.* He translated and edited a number of books relating to chemistry, metallurgy, and general science, and wrote a *Report on the Light Petroleum Oils Considered as to their Safety or Danger* (1873), and with W. H. Greene, "A New Process for the Manufacture of Manganese on the Commercial Scale" (*Journal of the Franklin Institute,* March 1893), and "A New Method of Reducing Metallic Oxides" (*Ibid.,* June 1893).

Among his contributions to practical and applied science, the most important was the discovery and application of aluminum as an energetic oxidizing agent for the creation of high temperatures in metallurgical operations, the basis of what is known as the "thermit process." This was the outgrowth of an attempt to smelt or produce metallic manganese and chromium free from carbon. In order to make a receptacle or crucible containing no carbon and sufficiently refractory to withstand very high temperatures, graphite crucibles were lined with magnesite, a highly refractory magnesium mineral. Since the temperatures obtained with ordinary coke or coal fires were insufficient to produce the reducing temperature and reaction desired, powdered or granulated metallic aluminum was mixed with the charge. The aluminum was capable of removing and appropriating the oxygen of the manganese monoxide, thus setting free the manganese, and the heat liberated by the reaction was sufficient to bring to an intense heat and liquefy the contents of the crucible. Similar results were obtained with chromite or chromic oxide, one of the most refractory minerals known. Though these processes were subsequently patented, Wahl never obtained any monetary benefit from them.

On Sept. 9, 1874, he married Julia Lowther of Seafield, County Mayo, Ireland, and after her death made her sister, Mary B. Lowther, his wife. He resigned his office as secretary of the Franklin Institute on Jan. 13, 1909. On the following Mar. 23 he died, survived by his wife. He devised his entire fortune of about eighty thousand dollars to the Franklin Institute.

[*Who's Who in America*, 1908–09; *Jour. of the Franklin Inst.*, June 1909; F. L. Garrison, in *Trans. Am. Inst. Mining Engineers*, vol. XXI (1893), p. 887; *Am. Men of Sci.* (1906), ed. by J. M. Cattell; obituary in *Pub. Ledger*, Mar. 24, 1909.]   F. L. G.

WAIDNER, CHARLES WILLIAM (Mar. 6, 1873–Mar. 10, 1922), physicist, was born in the suburbs of Baltimore, Md., the son of Charles W. Waidner of Baltimore and Sophia (List) Waidner, born in Germany, who was brought to America at the age of one year, her father having left the year previous on account of participation in the Revolution of 1848. Waidner's education was obtained in the public schools and Friends High School, Baltimore, and at the Johns Hopkins University, where he secured "Proficiency in Electrical Engineering" in 1892 and the degrees of A.B. (1896) and Ph.D. (1898). Here he came under the influence of Prof. Henry A. Rowland [*q.v.*] and the inspiration of Rowland's immediate associates at a time of exceptional progress in the field of physics. In 1897–98 he held a fellowship, and in the following year an assistantship in physics. In 1899 he was appointed to the faculty of Williams College, Williamstown, Mass.

After two academic years at Williams College, Waidner was appointed, Aug. 1, 1901, to the staff of the National Bureau of Standards, newly organized under Samuel Wesley Stratton [*q.v.*], becoming the first chief of the Section, later the Division, of Heat and Thermometry. The immediate problem confronting his section was the establishment of a standard scale of temperature, and his work to this end, in collaboration with Dr. George K. Burgess, led eventually to the adoption of the International Temperature Scale. The quality and scope of their studies soon brought the Bureau of Standards recognition as one of the leaders in pyrometric research. After the temperature scale had been established, attention could be given to problems involving the application of temperature measurements, such

as precise calorimetry, the thermodynamic properties of refrigerants, physical constants and properties of materials. During the World War, the division was in charge of work on engines for aviation. All these and other subjects are treated in the publications of the Division of Heat and Thermometry (since 1923 the Division of Heat and Power).

Waidner's outstanding characteristics were his clear views and accurate thinking on scientific matters, and his devotion to the welfare and progress of those with whom he was associated. The creative thought and sympathetic inspiration of the chief contributed largely to many important pieces of work of his division which do not bear his name, and perhaps his greatest contribution to science is to be found in the work of the men whom he trained and inspired. During the entire period of his active service to the government, he was a member of the editorial committee which passed on all scientific papers prepared by the staff of the National Bureau of Standards. To him this meant much more than a perfunctory reading of all papers. It meant a critical study of every one of them to make sure that the institution which was to such an extent his scientific offspring should not publish any statement or opinion which was open to either doubt or misunderstanding. He was also for some time chairman of the personnel committee of the Bureau. Completely absorbed in his work he seldom rested and never took a vacation unless his immediate health required it. He was appointed chief physicist of the Bureau of Standards in 1921 but died early in the following year, leaving no near relatives.

[Sources include *Who's Who in America*, 1920–21; *Am. Men of Sci.* (3rd ed., 1921); *Jour. Washington Acad. of Sci.*, Apr. 19, 1922; *Science*, Apr. 14, 1922; G. A. Weber, *The Bureau of Standards: Its Hist., Activities, and Organization* (1925); *Evening Star* (Washington), Mar. 11, 1922; *Washington Post* and *Sun* (Baltimore), Mar. 12, 1922; records of the National Bureau of Standards; personal acquaintance. A bound collection of Waidner's papers, many of which were published in the *Jour. of Research* of the Bureau of Standards, is deposited in the library of that institution.]   H. C. D.

WAILES, BENJAMIN LEONARD COVINGTON (Aug. 1, 1797–Nov. 16, 1862), scientist and planter, was born in Columbia County, Ga. He was the eldest of the nine children of Levin and Eleanor (Davis) Wailes, who were both natives of Prince George's County, Md. In 1807 the family moved to the Mississippi Territory where Wailes received his education in Jefferson College at Washington, Mississippi Territory, and in the field, surveying with his father. From 1814 to 1820 he was engaged in surveying and in clerical work at land offices in the old southwest; for a time, he was also assistant to the Choctaw agent and attended the treaty conferences of 1818 and 1820 with the Choctaws. He became locally known as an authority on the geography of their country. On Mar. 30, 1820, he was married to his distant cousin, Rebecca Susanna Magruder Covington, daughter of Brigadier-General Leonard Covington. They lived first near and then in the village of Washington, and ten children were born to them. Though Wailes was register of the land office at Washington from 1826 to 1835, his chief vocation was cotton planting. Eventually he managed, in addition to a small establishment at Washington, two plantations in Warren County which belonged in the family, and in all controlled about 150 slaves.

He is chiefly remembered, however, for his interest in the natural phenomena of the region in which he lived, its soil, rocks, fossils and shells, and the plant and animal life. For many years he collected specimens in all these fields and, in addition to stocking his own cabinet, helped build collections at Jefferson College, at the University of Mississippi, and at the state capitol. His interests brought him in contact with John J. Audubon, Joseph Henry, Joseph Leidy, J. Louis Agassiz, and Benjamin Silliman, 1779–1864 [qq.v.]. To most of these, as well as to other scientists and to the Smithsonian Institution, he supplied information and specimens of the natural history of his region. In 1852 he was appointed assistant professor of agriculture and geological sciences in the University of Mississippi, and in this capacity performed the field work for a projected survey of the state. He entered with zeal upon this task. Later, the writing of the report unexpectedly devolved upon him. His *Report on the Agriculture and Geology of Mississippi* (1854) was written under too much pressure and covered too many fields of knowledge to remain a distinguished contribution to any one of them; nevertheless, judged as a pioneer work, it was well done. Today it is chiefly valuable to the student of agricultural history.

After the completion of this work, the history of his region became an increasingly absorbing interest to Wailes, and in November 1858 he organized a state historical society of which he was the first and only president. Though this died at the end of a year, a number of valuable documents were collected and preserved, and several worth-while studies were made. Wailes wrote a short life of General Covington, which was privately printed in 1928 under the title *Memoir of Leonard Covington*. In history as in

natural science he was more interested in collecting information than in interpreting it and he was generous in furnishing information about the history of his locality to such men as James Parton, Charles Lanman, and Peter Force [qq.v.]. He served for nearly forty years as a trustee of Jefferson College and was president of the board at the time of his death. Except for serving in the state legislature in 1825 and 1826 he eschewed politics, but as a Whig he chafed at the rising power of the Democrats and he watched with apprehension their movement toward secession.

[The chief sources are a thirty-six volume manuscript diary kept by Wailes during the last ten years of his life, and numerous loose manuscript papers divided between The Mississippi Department of Archives and History and a grand-daughter, Mrs. Charles B. Brandon, of Natchez. Volumes I–IV and X–XIII of the diary are in the Archives; volumes V–IX and XIV–XXXVI, in the possession of Mrs. Brandon. See also, B. L. C. Wailes, *Memoir of Leonard Covington* (1928); *Miss. Hist. Soc. Pubs.*, vol. V (1902); James Parton, *Life of Andrew Jackson* (1860), vols. I, II.]

C. S. S.

WAINWRIGHT, JONATHAN MAYHEW (Feb. 24, 1792–Sept. 21, 1854), bishop of the Protestant Episcopal Church, was born at Liverpool, England, the son of Peter Wainwright, an English merchant, and Elizabeth, daughter of the Rev. Jonathan Mayhew [q.v.] of Boston. His father had come to Boston, Mass., shortly after the American Revolution, but prior to Jonathan's birth had returned to England, where he remained until the boy was about eleven years old. Jonathan spent several years at a Church of England school, and after the return of his parents to the United States, he attended an academy in Sandwich, Mass., where he prepared for Harvard. He was graduated at that institution in 1812, and from 1815 to 1817 was instructor there in rhetoric and oratory.

Meanwhile he studied theology, under the care of the rector of Trinity Church, Boston, and on Apr. 13, 1817, was ordained deacon in St. John's Church, Providence, R. I. Having been called to Christ Church, Hartford, Conn., he was admitted to the priesthood there on Aug. 16, 1817. In 1819 he became assistant minister at Trinity Church, New York, but in January 1821 assumed the rectorship of Grace Church, where he served for thirteen years. In 1834 he reluctantly left New York to assume the rectorship of Trinity Church, Boston, to which position he was called partly because his pacific character and Massachusetts background made his presence in the diocese peculiarly desirable at a time when it was sadly divided. Early in 1838, however, he welcomed the opportunity to return to New York as assistant minister at Trinity, in charge of the congregation of St. John's Chapel. During the temporary absence of the rector, Dr. William Berrian, Wainwright was placed in charge of Trinity Parish as assistant rector.

Although not inclined to controversy and considerate of the opinions of others, he nevertheless became involved with the Rev. Dr. George Potts, a Presbyterian divine, in what proved to be one of the celebrated disputations of the day. Rufus Choate had made the assertion that the Pilgrim Fathers had founded a "state without a king and a church without a bishop." Wainwright retorted that "there cannot be a church, without a bishop." The newspaper letters through which the controversy was conducted were later published under the title: *Can There Be a Church Without a Bishop? Controversy Between Rev. Drs. Wainwright and Potts . . . Letters Originally Published in the Commercial Advertiser* (1844). In 1852 he was a delegate to the third jubilee anniversary of the Society for the Propagation of the Gospel in Foreign Parts, held in Westminster Abbey, London. Oxford honored him with the degree of D.C.L.

Upon his return to the United States, he was chosen provisional bishop of New York. His consecration service, Nov. 10, 1852, marks the first time a bishop of the English Church participated in consecrating a prelate on American soil. Wainwright's election terminated a protracted controversy within the diocese caused by doctrinal differences and the suspension of Bishop Benjamin T. Onderdonk [*q.v.*]. Uniting firmness with conciliation and impartiality, Wainwright soon brought harmony into the long-distracted diocese. He was a man whose intellectual, moral, and physical qualities were well balanced. In person he was of striking appearance, well proportioned, and of benevolent countenance. A dignified courtesy, ripeness of learning, a sanguine temperament, and strong social inclinations gained him much popularity.

A devoted advocate of higher education, he was one of the founders in 1829 and a member of the original council of the University of the City of New York (later New York University), incorporated to afford a liberal and non-sectarian school of higher learning. At first active in the enterprise, he withdrew his name as a candidate for chancellor, and later became inactive, probably because of a growing conviction that the university would not be entirely non-sectarian, and would prove a rival to Columbia College, of which he was long a trustee. He was one of the first members of the examining board of Trinity College, Hartford, Conn., and was for several years secretary to the board of trustees of the General Theological Seminary in New York. As a writer he was indefatigable, publishing sermons, addresses, and a number of books. He was the chief working member of the committee which prepared the standard edition of the *Book of Common Prayer,* and he supervised the American edition of the *Illustrated Prayer Book* (1843). His publications include: *A Collection of Psalm, Hymn, and Chant Tunes, Adapted to the Service of the Episcopal Church* (1823); *The Pathways and Abiding-Places of Our Lord Illustrated in the Journal of a Tour Through the Land of Promise* (1851); *The Land of Bondage, its Ancient Monuments and Present Condition; Being the Journal of a Tour in Egypt* (1852). Worn out by untiring labors and ceaseless devotion to his office, he died in New York City in his sixty-third year. On Aug. 10, 1818, he married Amelia Maria, daughter of Timothy Phelps, of New Haven, Conn. She and eight of their fourteen children survived him, one of whom was Jonathan Mayhew Wainwright, 1821–1863 [*q.v.*]. In 1856 *A Memorial Volume: Thirty-four Sermons by the Rt. Rev. Jonathan Mayhew Wainwright, D.D., D.C.L.,* was published under the editorship of his widow, with a biographical memoir by the Rt. Rev. George W. Doane.

[J. N. Norton, *Life of Bishop Wainwright* (1858); J. G. Wilson, *The Centennial Hist. of the Protestant Episcopal Church in the Diocese of N. Y., 1785–1885* (1886); W. B. Sprague, *Annals of the Am. Pulpit,* vol. V (1859); Morgan Dix, *A Hist. of the Parish of Trinity Church in the City of N. Y.,* vols. III, IV (1905–06); *Contributions to the Hist. of Christ Church, Hartford,* vol. I (1895); W. R. Stewart, *Grace Church and Old N. Y.* (copr. 1924); T. F. Jones, *N. Y. Univ.* (1933); *N. Y. Daily Times,* Oct. 2, Nov. 11, 1852, Sept. 22, 25, 1854; information from Hon. J. Mayhew Wainwright of New York City.]   L. C. M. H.

WAINWRIGHT, JONATHAN MAYHEW (July 21, 1821-Jan. 1, 1863), naval officer, was born in New York City, the son of Jonathan Mayhew Wainwright [*q.v.*] and Amelia Maria (Phelps) Wainwright. On June 13, 1837, he was appointed midshipman and soon thereafter was ordered to the sloop *Porpoise* employed in the survey of harbors south of the Chesapeake. After a cruise in the East Indies on board the *John Adams* (1838–40), he was attached to the *Macedonian* and made a voyage to the West Indies. He next spent several months at the naval school at Philadelphia preliminary to an examination for passed midshipman, to which grade he was promoted from June 29, 1843. A period of duty with the depot of charts and instruments in Washington was followed by a cruise in the East Indies on board the *Columbia* (1845–46). After promotion to a lieutenancy from Sept. 17, 1850, he served in the Mediterranean on board the *San Jacinto* (1851–

53). Duties at several receiving ships were interrupted in 1856–57 when he was with the *Merrimack* on special service and in 1858–59 when he was with the *Saratoga* of the Home Squadron. At the outbreak of the Civil War he was on waiting orders.

His first active duty in the war was that of a lieutenant on board the *Minnesota* of the Atlantic Blockading Squadron, April–July 1861. On Jan. 18, 1862, he was given command of the *Harriet Lane,* the flagship of the mortar flotilla of the West Gulf Blockading Squadron, and a month later he seized, off the coast of Florida, the Confederate vessel *Joanna Ward* and sent her as a prize to New York. When on Apr. 24 Farragut ran past Forts Jackson and St. Philip on the lower Mississippi, the mortar flotilla supported the movement. Wainwright took a position within five hundred yards of Fort Jackson and kept up a continuous fire. As commander of the flagship of the flotilla he had a prominent part in the operations of Commander David Dixon Porter [*q.v.*] that culminated in the surrender of the forts and the Confederate naval forces. He was commended by Porter for his coolness and bravery. In October with the *Harriet Lane* he participated in the capture of Galveston. On Jan. 1, 1863, when the Confederates recaptured this port his ship was attacked by the *Bayou City* and the *Neptune,* and was carried by boarding. Bravely fighting a superior force, Wainwright was killed instantly by a musket ball through the head after receiving three wounds in the head and three in the left thigh. He was buried at Galveston. After the war his body was sent to New York and was interred near that of his father in the cemetery of Trinity Church.

In December 1844 he was married to Maria Page of Clarke County, Va., who died on Dec. 22, 1854. Jonathan Mayhew Wainwright, the eldest of the four children that survived him, entered the navy and was killed in 1870 in an engagement with pirates; a second son rose to be a major in the army, and a daughter, Marie, became a well-known actress.

[See O. S. Phelps and A. T. Servin, *The Phelps Family of America* (2 vols., 1899), which gives the date of birth as July 27; R. C. M. Page, *Geneal. of the Page Family in Va.* (1883); Record of Officers, Bureau of Navigation, 1832–63; *Navy Reg.,* 1838–63; *War of the Rebellion: Official Records* (Navy), 1 ser., vols. XVIII–XIX, XXIV; D. D. Porter, *The Naval Hist. of the Civil War* (1886); *Am. Ann. Cyc.,* 1864; Veterans' Administration, Civil War Records; obituary in *N. Y. Tribune,* Jan. 12, 1863. Some information has been supplied by a grandson of Wainwright.]   C. O. P.

WAINWRIGHT, RICHARD (Jan. 5, 1817–Aug. 10, 1862), naval officer, was born in Charlestown, Mass., the son of Lieutenant-Colonel Robert Dewar and Maria Montresor (Auchmuty) Wainwright, and a descendant of Richard Wainwright who was a planter in South Carolina in the early eighteenth century. His father (1781–1841), an officer of the United States Marine Corps, is noted for his suppression of a mutiny in the Massachusetts state prison in 1824, an authentic record of which for many years formed one of the standard selections in school readers. Wainwright entered the navy as a midshipman on May 11, 1831, and after some preliminary training in his profession at Norfolk made a cruise in the Mediterranean (1833–36). He prepared at the Norfolk naval school for his examination for the grade of passed midshipman, a rank to which he was promoted from June 15, 1837. After a period of service at the Washington navy yard he was ordered to duty with the United States Coast Survey. In September 1841 he was promoted lieutenant. From 1842 to 1845 he was with the *Vincennes* of the Home Squadron, and from 1846 to 1847 with the *Columbia* of the Brazil Squadron. In 1848 he returned to the Coast Survey, serving there until 1856, part of the time as commander of the *J. Y. Mason.* After a period of service with the *Merrimack* of the Pacific Squadron (1857–60), he was assigned to ordnance duty at the Washington navy yard, where he was stationed in 1861. He was promoted commander from Apr. 24 of that year. In October he commanded the sailors at Fort Ellsworth near Alexandria, and in November he conveyed a detachment of seamen to Cairo, Ill. On the last day of the year he was detached from the navy yard and ordered to command the *Hartford,* the flagship of Flag Officer D. G. Farragut [*q.v.*], preparing for service on the lower Mississippi. On Apr. 24, 1862, when the fleet passed Forts St. Philip and Jackson, the flagship was subjected to a galling fire from the forts and was set on fire by a fire raft, being with difficulty saved from the flames. On the following day, when it was steaming up the river, shots were exchanged with the batteries on shore. The flagship arrived off New Orleans much riddled, with a loss of thirteen men. Later when she passed and repassed the batteries at Vicksburg she gave a good account of herself. On July 15 below Vicksburg she engaged the enemy's ram *Arkansas* and suffered a loss of nine men. In all of the operations of the squadron Wainwright until the last days of July had a distinguished part. He then suffered an attack of remittent fever which proved fatal within two weeks. His death occurred on board his vessel at Donaldsville, La.

On Mar. 1, 1849, he was married to Sally

Franklin Bache, a great-grand-daughter of Benjamin Franklin and a grand-daughter of Richard Bache and Alexander J. Dallas [qq.v.]. Richard Wainwright [q.v.] was the eldest of his four surviving children.

[Annette Townsend, *The Auchmuty Family in Scotland and America* (1932); Record of Officers, Bureau of Navigation, 1832–63; *Navy Reg.*, 1817–62; Pension Records, Veterans' Administration; *War of the Rebellion: Official Records (Navy)*, vols. IV, XVIII–XIX, XXII; R. S. Collum, *Hist. of the U. S. Marine Corps* (1890); obituary in *Evening Star* (Washington, D. C.), Aug. 19, 1862; letter from Richard Wainwright, Jr., Sept. 22, 1933.]   C. O. P.

WAINWRIGHT, RICHARD (Dec. 17, 1849–Mar. 6, 1926), naval officer, was born in Washington, D. C., the son of Richard Wainwright [q.v.] and Sally Franklin (Bache) Wainwright. As a youth he attended private schools in Washington. In 1864 he received from President Lincoln on the recommendation of Admiral Farragut an appointment at large to the United States Naval Academy, then at Newport, R. I. On his graduation in 1868 he joined the *Jamestown* of the Pacific Fleet, and two years later was promoted master. From 1870 to 1873 he was with the *Colorado*, the flagship of the Asiatic Fleet. His marriage to Evelyn Wotherspoon of New York City, Sept. 11, 1873, occurred a few days before he received his lieutenancy. After periods of service with the bureau of equipment, the hydrographic office, and the United States Coast Survey, he was with the Asiatic Fleet (1877–80). While he was absent from the United States, the U.S.S. *Huron* was wrecked off Hatteras, and a naval court of inquiry headed by Admiral David Dixon Porter placed the blame on the dead officers, among whom were several of Wainwright's friends. On his return home Wainwright made an intensive study of the case and proved that the wreck was caused by erroneous data furnished to the officers by an expert in Washington. As a result of his findings the court was reconvened, its verdict reversed, and the officers exculpated.

From 1880 to 1884 Wainwright was on special duty with the bureau of navigation. From 1884 to 1887 he was with the *Tennessee* and *Galena* of the North Atlantic station, part of the time as secretary to the commander-in-chief. He was steel inspector (1887–88), instructor at the United States Naval Academy (1888–90), on special duty with the *Alert* (1890–93), on duty at the hydrographic office (1893–96), and chief of the intelligence office (1896–97). When in November 1897 he left the last-named position to go to the battleship *Maine*, his services were commended by Theodore Roosevelt, then assistant secretary of the navy. In the meantime,

September 1894, he had been commissioned lieutenant commander. As executive officer of the *Maine* he was next in command to Admiral C. D. Sigsbee [q.v.] when that vessel was sunk in Havana harbor, Feb. 15, 1898. Soon thereafter he was attached to the tender *Fern* as the navy's representative in the recovery of the bodies and in the examination of the hull for evidence of the cause of the disaster. On his return to Washington he applied for sea duty and was chosen to command the *Gloucester,* formerly the pleasure yacht *Corsair* of J. Pierpont Morgan, a small frail naval vessel, without armor and with an inferior battery. It was intended to protect her with armor, but on Wainwright's protest this was not done, and he was able to sail without delay and arrive in Cuban waters in time to participate in the battle of Santiago Bay, July 3, 1898. When the Spaniards steamed out of the harbor, he fearlessly attacked at close range the destroyers *Furor* and *Pluton,* each the superior of the *Gloucester,* and after a brief engagement sank one and beached the other, killing or wounding two-thirds of their officers and men. He next turned his attention to the burning Spanish flagship *Infanta Maria Teresa* and rescued some two hundred officers and men, including Cervera, the Spanish admiral. He also rescued part of the crew of the *Almirante Oquendo.* Later in July he participated in the naval operation off Puerto Rico, entering the harbor of Guanica under circumstances that added to his reputation for courage and initiative. For his eminent and conspicuous conduct in the battle of Santiago he was advanced by Congress ten numbers in rank. A loving cup was presented to him by the citizens of Gloucester, Mass., and a sword by the people of Washington, D. C. John Davis Long [q.v.], secretary of the navy, wrote that his action with the two Spanish destroyers was "one of the most intrepid and brilliant heroisms in all naval history" (Long, *post,* II, 34).

Wainwright was made a commander from Mar. 3, 1899; a captain from Aug. 10, 1903; and a rear-admiral from July 11, 1908. From 1899 until 1902 he was at the Naval Academy, during the latter part of the period as its superintendent. He commanded the *Newark* (1902–04), the *Louisiana* (1907–08), the second division of the Atlantic Fleet (1908–09), and the third division of the same (1909–10). His last duty was as aid for operations to the secretary of the navy. He was retired as rear-admiral on Dec. 17, 1911. Both before and after his retirement he contributed articles to naval periodicals, chiefly to the *Proceedings of the United States Naval Institute.* These include "Fleet Tactics"

(*Proceedings of the United States Naval Institute*, vol. XVI, 1890), "The Battle of the Sea of Japan" (*Ibid.*, vol. XXXI, 1905), and "The General Board" (*Ibid.*, vol. XLVIII, 1922). He was joint editor with R. M. Thompson of *Confidential Correspondence of Gustavus Vasa Fox* (2 vols., 1918–20). Wainwright made his home in Washington, D. C. He left two children, one of whom was a naval officer. He was of average height, slender and erect.

[Annette Townsend, *The Auchmuty Family* (1932); Record of Officers, Bureau of Navigation, 1864–93; *Navy Register*, 1865–1926; *Who's Who in America*, 1924–25; J. D. Long, *The New Am. Navy* (2 vols., 1903); R. W. Neeser, *Statistical and Chron. Hist. of the U. S. Navy* (1909); E. S. Maclay, *Hist. of the U. S. Navy*, vol. III (1902); *Army and Navy Reg.*, Mar. 20, 1926; *Army and Navy Jour.*, Mar. 13, 1926; *Proc. U. S. Naval Inst.*, vol. LII (1926); obituary in *Evening Star* (Washington, D. C.), Mar. 7, 1926.]
C. O. P.

WAIT, SAMUEL (Dec. 19, 1789–July 28, 1867), college president, was born in White Creek, Washington County, N. Y., the son of Joseph and Martha Wait, farmers, and the grandson of Elder William Wait. Schoolmates in the neighborhood remembered him as physically well developed, persevering in his studies, companionable. In 1809 he joined the Baptist Church at Middletown, Vt., where his family had moved after residing in nearby Granville, N. Y., and Tinmouth, Vt. He became pastor at Sharon, Mass., in 1816, and was ordained there in 1818. On June 17, 1818, at Sharon, he was married to Sarah, the daughter of Deacon Jonathan Merriam. While studying, in 1813, at Salem Academy, Washington County, N. Y., he had become convinced that a preacher must have "strength to meet the infidel on his own ground, and this strength at this day must be derived from study" (Brewer, *post*, p. 4). Accordingly he became a theological student in Philadelphia and then a student and tutor, 1822–26, in Columbian College (now George Washington University, Washington, D. C.), which the organized Baptists were endeavoring to establish. Columbian College probably could not award degrees at that early date but because of his work he received the A.M. degree from Waterville College, Me., in 1825.

A trip southward with President William Staughton [*q.v.*] in search of funds for Columbian College in 1826–27 resulted in his acceptance of a pastorate at New Bern, N. C., in 1827. Deeply impressed with the sad condition of the Baptists, he participated actively in the organization of the North Carolina Baptist state convention in 1830, and when no other acceptable person would serve, he became its general agent.

He toured the state in a covered wagon for two years, 1830–32, at a salary of about a dollar a day, out of which he supported the wife and child who accompanied him, and effectively educated the Baptists in cooperation. When the state convention determined to establish an institution for educating ministers Wait was again called into service, and he toured the state for one more year, spreading the news and collecting funds and serviceable articles. In February 1834, Wake Forest Manual Labour Institute was opened, and Wait, as the principal, accepted a varied assortment of boys as pupils. A farm house served for classrooms; former slave cabins as dormitories; a tent as dining-hall. He also directed them in working the community farm that was to help support the school and the pupils. A competent faculty was gradually assembled, the manual labor aspect abandoned, and a new building erected. In 1838 the Institute became Wake Forest College, and Wait was its president until 1846; thereafter he was president of the board of trustees. Without reputation for eloquence or great scholarship, he laid well the foundations of the school among a very plain but aspiring people. Between 1850 and 1860 he wrote "Origin and Early History of Wake Forest College," published in the *Wake Forest Student*. After a happy pastorate at Yanceyville he was president of Oxford Female College from 1851 to 1856. His last years were spent in Wake Forest at the home of his only child.

[Manuscript diary, 1826–27, letters, 1829–60, and scrapbook, in Wake Forest College Library; J. B. Brewer, "Life and Labors of Elder Samuel Wait, D.D.," *N. C. Bapt. Hist. Soc. Papers*, vol. I, no. 1, Oct. 1906; W. L. Wait, "The Early Life of Doctor Samuel Wait," *Wake Forest Student*, Apr. 1885; William Cathcart, *The Bapt. Encyc.* (1881); G. W. Paschal, "History of Wake Forest College," *Wake Forest Bull.*, Nov. 1924–July 1927, and *Hist. of Wake Forest Coll.* (1935); *Biblical Recorder*, July 31, 1867.]
C. C. P.

WAIT, WILLIAM (Feb. 2, 1821–Dec. 29, 1880), lawyer and writer on law, was born at Ephratah, N. Y., the son of William and Polly (Vail) Wait, both members of the Society of Friends. After the death of his father in 1825, he was reared at the home of his mother's parents at Vail Mills, near Broadalbin, N. Y. He was educated at the district school and apprenticed to a local shoemaker. He began the study of law while engaged in his trade, by which he supported his mother and three sisters, but finally finished his legal education in the office of Daniel Cady [*q.v.*], who had become interested in him. In 1846 he was admitted to the bar and in 1848 was elected prosecuting attorney of Fulton County, N. Y. A subsequent fifteen years of practice in Johnstown, the county seat of Fulton County, failed to earn for him more than a local reputation as a lawyer of average ability. In 1865, however, after several years of arduous labor, he published in two large volumes his first treatise, *The Law and Practice in Civil Actions*. Written to discharge what Blackstone had termed a lawyer's duty to his profession, this work on practice, pleading, and evidence in civil actions and proceedings brought in the lower New York courts became a *vade mecum* for the local magistrates and legal practitioners. Code procedure in New York was then in a confused stage of transition from the common-law forms, and a well-indexed manual on actions and defenses with practical forms and precedents was gratefully received by the legal profession. By this treatise, which was subsequently expanded and passed through eight editions, Wait's reputation was made. He abandoned active practice and zealously devoted himself to his legal writings.

His topical *Digest of New York Reports* (5 vols., 1869–77), though not a great work, was extremely useful to contemporary lawyers, especially those who lacked access to original reports. His next publication, *The Code of Civil Procedure of the State of New York* (1870), which embodied recent statutory provisions, was republished five times between 1871 and 1877. In 1872 he produced one of the earliest manuals for quick search, *A Table of Cases Affirmed, Reversed, or Cited,* for the state of New York. Its usefulness in saving lawyers many hours of search and in enabling them to avoid the citation of decisions subsequently reversed or restricted was instantly acclaimed. A contemporary's assertion that "every State in the Union ought to have a similar work executed" (*American Law Review,* Jan. 1873, p. 336) has found fruition in *Shepard's Citations,* a growing refinement and elaboration on Wait's first effort in this field. About the same time Wait prepared a thorough and reliable work on New York practice, *The Practice at Law, in Equity, and in Special Proceedings in All the Courts of Record in the State of New York* (7 vols., 1872–80). Revised by later writers to include subsequent statutes and decisions, *Wait's Practice at Law* continues to be a standard authority on New York adjective law. It was followed in 1875 by his edition of Herbert Broom's *Commentaries on the Laws of England,* a work based largely on Blackstone's *Commentaries.* Wait's last important work was *A Treatise upon Some of the General Principles of the Law . . . Including . . . Actions and Defenses* (7 vols., 1877–79), a topical digest of the general principles of law. Beginning with such topics as "Actions" and "Agency" and continu-

ing through "Wills," every legal subject was concisely digested. Each point represented the actual holding of an American or English decision. These volumes were in reality a *corpus juris* for lawyers and students of that day. The painstaking care with which he conducted his legal research resulted in overwork and physical exhaustion, and after an illness of only a few months he died of consumption at his home in Johnstown. In 1850 he married Margaret E. Stewart (d. 1853), by whom he had one daughter. In 1858 he married Caroline Van Alen of Kinderhook, N. Y. They had three daughters and two sons. Wait's books had brought him a fortune of $100,000, which he left to his wife and the four children who survived him.

[Information on Wait's parentage, early life, and marriages has been supplied by his son, William Wait of Peekskill, N. Y. Other information is from Fulton County records; obituaries in *N. Y. Times* and *Albany Evening Jour.,* Dec. 30, 1880, the latter reprinted in *Albany Law Jour.,* Jan. 8, 1881; and book reviews in *Central Law Jour.,* Feb. 16, 1877, and *Albany Law Jour.,* Aug. 20, 1870, Mar. 4 and Oct. 21, 1871, May 4 and Oct. 5, 1872, Jan. 15, 1876, Mar. 17, 1877, and Jan. 11, 1879.]   V. L. W.

WAIT, WILLIAM BELL (Mar. 25, 1839–Oct. 25, 1916), educator of the blind, inventor, was born at Amsterdam, N. Y., the son of Christopher Brown and Betsey Grinnell (Bell) Wait and a descendant of Thomas Wait who came to America from England in 1634. He was graduated from Albany Normal College in 1859 and became a teacher in the New-York Institution for the Blind, where he remained two years, with the exception of three months when he was in the army during the Civil War. Reënlistment was refused because of nearsightedness, so he studied law and was admitted to the bar in 1862. The field of teaching attracted him, however, and he became superintendent of the public schools in Kingston, N. Y. He had barely entered upon his duties when he was called, in October 1863, to become the superintendent of the New-York Institution for the Blind in New York City and from this time until his death, a period of more than fifty-three years, he was continuously employed in its service. From 1905 on he was emeritus principal.

Programs and aims for the education of the blind were in the 1860's strongly influenced by sentiment, and for many years the Institution for the Blind had been designated a charity; its inmates included children and some adults, former pupils who stayed on in the shelter of the Institution, occupied as teachers of the oncoming children or as workers in the mechanical department. An air of dependency permeated the group. Wait began quickly to dispel this pall, and the

Institution gradually took on a strictly educational aspect. Wait conceived it his duty to exalt the pedagogical purpose of the Institution and to subordinate or altogether abandon the eleemosynary. In 1912 he was instrumental in having the name of the school changed to The New York Institute for the Education of the Blind. In his annual report for 1866, he first published the results of his studies concerning improved methods for printing literature in tangible form. Two years later, in his report, he presented a horizontal point system, a variant of that set up in 1829 by Louis Braille of Paris. He gave increasingly greater attention to the perfecting of this punctographic means of publishing, which came to be known as the New York Point System, and was successful in promoting its adoption until it was used by a large majority of readers in America. To him belongs greatest credit for increasing the opportunities of the blind to study textbooks and to read the classics in literature in a form adapted to their needs and without the intermediary of a reader. In 1878 another system, known as American Braille, was promoted and there ensued a war of the "points" that ended in a compromise—a system quite different from either—which became effective after Wait's death.

For the printing of books in the New York Point System he invented the stereograph, a plate embossing machine, and for the use of blind writers a smaller apparatus called the kleidograph simulating the typewriter. These inventions and his other services to the blind in the production of literature won for him in 1900 the John Scott Medal of the Franklin Institute of Philadelphia. He also devised a musical notation in the horizontal point system. In 1871 he was one of the founders of the American Association of Instructors of the Blind and for forty years a dominant power in the organization. Through its agency he bore a large part in determining the character of the training for young blind people of the United States. His most important articles appeared in its *Proceedings* (see *Index, 1922*). Among his published works are: *Elements of Harmonic Notation* (1888); *The New York Point System* (1893); *Phases of Punctography* (1913); *The Uniform Type Question* (1915); *New Aspects of the Uniform Type Folly* (1916). He was an indomitable leader in advancing education of the blind to the status of a profession, a promoter of pedagogical ideals and practices, a foe of sentimentalism in dealing with the blind, and a doughty champion of their right to intellectual development. On Oct. 27, 1863, he was married to Phebe Jane Babcock,

who became one of the pioneers among women physicians in New York City. She died in 1904, and two of their four children survived him.

[*Who's Who in America*, 1916–17; J. C. Wait, *Family Records of the Descendants of Thomas Wait* (1904); *New England Hist. and Geneal. Reg.*, Oct. 1919; *Outlook for the Blind*, Oct. 1916; *Am. Asso. of Instructors of the Blind, Twenty-Fourth Biennial Convention* (1918); *N. Y. Times*, Oct. 26, 1916.]

E. M. V—C.

WAITE, MORRISON REMICK (Nov. 29, 1816–Mar. 23, 1888), chief justice of the United States, was born in Lyme, Conn., whither his great-great-grandfather, Thomas Wait, had moved from Sudbury, Mass., about the beginning of the eighteenth century. It is said that his family was connected with Thomas Wayte, one of the signers of the death warrant of Charles I (*Harper's New Monthly Magazine*, February 1876, p. 315). Waite's father, Henry Matson Waite, was chief justice of Connecticut and his grandfather, Remick Waite, served for many years as justice of the peace. His mother was Maria (Selden) Waite, grand-daughter of Col. Samuel Selden, the story of whose distinguished services in the Revolution became a family heritage. Waite was graduated at Yale College in 1837 in the class with William M. Evarts. In October 1838 he entered the law office of Samuel M. Young, Maumee City, Ohio, and in 1839 he was admitted to practice. In 1850 the firm moved to Toledo. Young soon retired and Waite was joined by his younger brother, Richard. By this time Waite's law practice had assumed large proportions, and in the ten years from 1851 to 1861 he argued thirty-one cases before the Ohio supreme court. His legal work, at first, was largely confined to financial adjustments, foreclosures of mortgages, untangling of titles, and such matters. In the law of real estate and the status of legal titles he became a recognized authority. It was this training which made him indispensable to the railroad interests.

Waite took an active part locally in the campaign which resulted in the election of William Henry Harrison to the presidency. At twenty-nine he was an unsuccessful candidate for Congress. In 1849 he was elected to the state legislature where he served one term. In 1862 he ran as an independent Republican candidate for Congress and was again defeated. During the Civil War, he was the leader in practically every meeting and movement in his locality whose aim was the promotion of the Union cause (Waggoner, *post*). In 1863 he was offered by the governor of Ohio an appointment to the state supreme court, but he refused it. He did, however, become a close and trusted adviser of the governor.

In 1871 Waite was appointed by President Grant to serve with Caleb Cushing and William M. Evarts [*qq.v.*] as American counsel in the Geneva Arbitration. He contributed five of the thirteen chapters of the American *Argument,* in which he set forth clearly and simply the facts regarding the building, escape, and depredations of the Southern cruisers, the use of British ports as bases of operations for Confederate officers, and lack of "due diligence" on the part of the British government (Hackett, *post,* p. 124). Waite also replied "in excellent tone and temper" (*Ibid.,* p. 306) to Sir Roundell Palmer's argument upon the special question of the supply of coal in British ports to Confederate cruisers. "Sir Roundell Palmer was overwhelmed" (Jones, *post,* p. 259).

On his return from Geneva he was elected to the Ohio constitutional convention of 1873, and became its president. He contributed considerably to the work of the convention, especially to the debates on the judiciary. On Jan. 20, 1874, during a session of the convention, a messenger brought news that, on the previous day, Waite had been nominated chief justice of the United States. The appointment came as a general surprise. He had had no previous judicial experience and had never practised before the court over which he was called to preside. Beyond his service in the Geneva Arbitration, his reputation was not extensive. These facts and the character of Grant's other nominations caused some apprehension. The nomination, however, was well received by the bar of the country. Waite was confirmed unanimously by the Senate on Jan. 21.

He immediately assumed a large share of the work of the Court, writing the opinion in the first case to be argued after he went on the bench (*Tappan* vs. *Merchants' National Bank,* 86 *United States,* 490). In the fourteen years of his chief justiceship he gave the opinion of the Court in more than a thousand cases. His opinions covered a wide range. There were problems growing out of the war yet to be decided. Much of the radical reconstruction legislation was still on the statute books. The war amendments were yet to be construed. The development of the Western states, transcontinental railroads, the agrarian movements, the control of public utilities and rates, the relation of states to the liquor traffic brought new and grave problems before the Court. In all these matters Waite contributed substantially.

The doctrine of the Slaughterhouse Cases was soon reaffirmed by Waite in *Minor* vs. *Happersett* (88 *United States,* 162). Upholding the right of a state to deny the vote to women, he held that suffrage was not a privilege of United States citizenship and that the Fourteenth Amendment did not add to the privileges and immunities of citizens. In *McCready* vs. *Virginia* (94 *United States,* 391) he held that the right to plant or take oysters in the waters of a state was not a right pertaining to United States citizenship, and that it might be denied persons not citizens of the state. In *United States* vs. *Reese* (92 *United States,* 214) Waite demolished the Radical Reconstruction plan of protecting the negro by direct federal action, holding sections three and four of the Civil Rights Act of May 31, 1870, unconstitutional. In *United States* vs. *Cruikshank* (92 *United States,* 542) he held that the Fourteenth Amendment did not authorize Congress to legislate affirmatively for the protection of civil rights and did not add to the rights of one citizen against another.

In the famous case of *Munn* vs. *Illinois* (94 *United States,* 113) he upheld the power of a state to regulate the charges of grain elevators and public warehouses—businesses that were "clothed with a public interest." In other Granger cases the Court upheld state laws fixing maximum rates for passengers and freight on all railroads operating within the state. By its action in these cases the Court profoundly affected the course of American social and economic development (Warren, *post,* II, 581). The due process clause was narrowly interpreted, while the power of the states was necessarily enlarged. In *Peik* vs. *Chicago & Northwestern Railway Company* (94 *United States,* 164), Waite held that until Congress acted, a state regulation of railroads was valid, "even though it may indirectly affect those without," but this position was reversed in the case of *Wabash, St. Louis & Pacific Railway Company* vs. *Illinois* (118 *United States,* 557), with Waite dissenting.

The wide scope of authority left the states, together with the dictum that "for protection against abuses by the legislatures, the people must resort to the polls, not to the court" (94 *United States,* 113), has created the impression that Waite recognized practically no limits to the police power under the due process or any other clause. However, it was Waite himself who laid the foundation for the modern interpretation of due process, as a limitation on state power. His statements in *Railroad Company* vs. *Richmond* (96 *United States,* 521) that "appropriate regulation of . . . property is not 'taking' property," and in *Spring Valley Water Works* vs. *Schottler* (110 *United States,* 347) that reasonable "regulations do not deprive a person of his property without due process of law," were followed by a dictum in the Sinking Fund Cases: "The United States . . . equally with the States . . . are prohibited from depriving persons or corporations of property without due process of law" (99 *United States,* 718–19). Then came his famous dictum in *Stone* vs. *Farmers' Loan and Trust Company:* "From what has been said it is not to be inferred that this power . . . of regulation is itself without limit. . . . [It] is not a power to destroy. . . . The State cannot . . . do that which . . . amounts to a taking of private property . . . without due process of law" (116 *United States,* 331). Upon these dicta rested the decision of the rate cases, in 1890 after Waite's death (134 *United States,* 418), which made the Court the final judge in matters of rates.

Waite's interpretation of the contract clause constitutes another major contribution to constitutional development. Under the reserved power to alter or amend charters, the states were permitted wide discretion in interfering with rates of charge (*Ruggles* vs. *Illinois,* 108 *United States,* 526; *Spring Valley Water Works* vs. *Schottler,* 110 *United States,* 347). In *Stone* vs. *Farmers' Loan and Trust Company* (116 *United States,* 307) the chief justice held that although a charter had specifically provided that the company 'might fix charges, this fact did not imply that a railroad commission could not also fix rates. In 1879, in *Stone* vs. *Mississippi* he held that certain police powers, over lotteries in this case, could not be contracted away. "No legislature can bargain away the public health or the public morals" (101 *United States,* 819).

These decisions not only modified profoundly the decision of doctrine of vested rights as established in the Dartmouth College case but they also indicated Waite's willingness to allow the states to exercise wide regulatory power over corporate enterprises in matters pertaining to the "public interest." The authority of the state was always presumed. This principle of wide state power is seen in a number of cases involving suability of states. In *Louisiana* vs. *Jumel* (107 *United States,* 711) he held that a suit against a state officer was a suit against the state itself when the result was to compel the state specifically to perform a contract. In *New Hampshire* vs. *Louisiana* (108 *United States,* 76) he held that a suit by a state on behalf of its citizens against another state was in violation of the Eleventh Amendment. When the Court finally found a way to break down this harsh rule of non-suability, Waite did not lend his support. He was on the side of the minority in the case of *United States* vs. *Lee* (106 *United States,*

196) when the Court held that a suit in ejectment against federal officers in control of the "Arlington" estate of the Lee family was not a suit against the United States but against agents of the government acting unconstitutionally.

In the interpretation of the commerce clause he held in *Hall* vs. *De Cuir* (95 *United States,* 485) that a state provision against race discriminations in interstate conveyances was an undue interference with the power of Congress. In *Pensacola Telegraph Company* vs. *Western Union* (96 *United States,* 1) he held an act of Florida, which attempted to confer an exclusive franchise upon a corporation, unconstitutional as an interference with an act passed by Congress, under its power to regulate commerce. Commerce was broadened to include the transfer of intangibles, such as telegraphic communications. In *Western Union Telegraph Company* vs. *Texas* (105 *United States,* 460) he held invalid a Texas act which placed a specific tax on each message sent out of the state.

Waite scanned closely the claims of individuals as against the state, even interpreting the bill of rights strictly. In *Reynolds* vs. *United States* (98 *United States,* 145) he upheld an act of Congress forbidding polygamy in the territories, interpreting freedom of religion as pertaining to belief not action contrary to law. In *Boyd* vs. *United States* (116 *United States,* 616) he concurred in the decision that a federal act requiring defendants in revenue cases to produce private papers or else the allegations of the government attorney would be taken as confessed, was unconstitutional because it forced one to testify against himself. But he disagreed that this act amounted to an unreasonable search and seizure. He dissented in *Kring* vs. *Missouri* (107 *United States,* 221), interpreting the *ex post facto* clause narrowly.

In the application of international law several important cases were decided by Waite. In *Wildenhus's Case* (120 *United States,* 1), he upheld the authority of the State of New Jersey in taking jurisdiction over the crew of a Belgian merchant vessel in a New Jersey port when a murder was committed aboard the vessel. In doing so he upheld the doctrine that local authorities have jurisdiction over matters which are of such a nature as to disturb the peace of the port. In *United States* vs. *Arjona* (120 *United States,* 479) he upheld the power of Congress to punish for the counterfeiting of foreign securities on the basis of the "necessary and proper" clause. The commerce clause was also suggested as authority for this power. In *United States* vs. *Rauscher* (119 *United States,* 407) he dissented from the decision that a fugitive extradited from England could be tried only for the crime for which he was extradited.

As Justice Miller said, Waite's "style was eminently judicial, terse, vigorous, and clear," and his administrative duties were discharged "with eminent skill, courtesy, and tact" (126 *United States,* 610–11). In 1875 he refused to allow his name to be considered for the presidential nomination the following year, believing it very improper to make the Supreme Court bench a stepping stone to political office. In civic affairs, however, he was active throughout his life. He was a trustee of the Peabody Education Fund for the fourteen years preceding his death, and was one of the members of the Yale Corporation from 1882 until his death. He was a vestryman in the Protestant Episcopal Church and a constant attendant at services. He was married on Sept. 21, 1840, to his second cousin, Amelia C. Warner of Lyme. They had five children, one of whom died in infancy. Waite was impressive in appearance. He was of medium height and heavy-set, but gave the appearance of a much taller man. He was in good health until five days before his death, when he caught cold, which developed into pneumonia. He was survived by his widow, two sons, and a daughter.

[Sketches of Waite appear in 126 *U. S. Reports,* 585–612; *Ohio State Bar Asso. Proc. . . . 1888* (1888), pp. 173–88; F. R. Jones, in *Green Bag,* June 1902, pp. 257–62; H. L. Carson, *The Hist. of the Supreme Court of the U. S.* (1902), vol. II; B. R. Cowen, in W. D. Lewis, ed., *Great American Lawyers,* vol. VII (1909); A. P. Stokes, *Memorials of Eminent Yale Men* (2 vols., 1914); Charles Warren, *The Supreme Court in U. S. History* (1928), vol. II. His opinions are in 86–126 *U. S.* See also J. T. Wait, "Henry Matson Waite," in *New-Eng. Hist. and Geneal. Register,* Apr. 1870, pp. 101–05, containing genealogy; Clark Waggoner, ed., *Hist. of the City of Toledo* (1888); F. W. Hackett, *Reminiscences of the Geneva Tribunal of Arbitration* (1911); J. B. Uhle, "The Opinions of Chief Justice Waite," *Current Comment,* May 15, 1890; obituaries in *Chicago Legal News, N. Y. Times,* Mar. 24, 1888. Through the courtesy of members of the family, the author has had access to private letters of Waite, his wife, and his father, scrapbooks of newspaper clippings, his personal expense book, and other records.]   B. R. T.

WAKELEY, JOSEPH BURTON (Feb. 18, 1809–Apr. 27, 1875), Methodist Episcopal clergyman and author, was born in Danbury, Conn., the son of James and Rebecca (Cooke) Wakeley. Although some secondary sources give Beaumont as his middle name, the entry recording his birth in the Danbury vital records gives Burton; on the title pages of his books his name commonly appears as J. B. Wakeley. He attended the district school of his native town and early showed eagerness to learn and an exceptional memory. His father, a hatter by trade and a man of excellent sense and wide reading, determined,

if possible, to give the boy a college education. He also encouraged him to practise oratory and to attend courts and other places where speakers of ability might be heard. Business reverses prevented Joseph from going to college, and except for his district school training his formal education was limited to a term in an academy at Fairfield, Conn., and another at Seabury Academy, Stamford. Fascinated by tales of the sea, he shipped as a cabin boy on a vessel bound to Liverpool from New York, but finding that he must serve grog he left the vessel before it sailed. A brig upon which he next secured a position was nearly wrecked when a few days out of port, and put back into Chesapeake Bay for repairs. Cured of his desire to be a sailor, he returned to Danbury, learned the hatter's trade, and finally went into business for himself. In July 1831 he married Jane McCord of Sing Sing (Ossining), N. Y. His parents were Congregationalists, but Joseph joined the Methodist Church.

His talents were such that he felt he could devote his life to some higher service than that of making hats, and his friends were of the same opinion. Methodist officials saw in him the possibilities of an effective preacher, and in May 1833 he joined the New York Conference of the Methodist Episcopal Church on trial; in 1835 he was ordained deacon, and in May 1837, elder. During his ministry of forty-two years he held many appointments, serving, among others, churches in New York, Trenton, Newark, Jersey City, Poughkeepsie, and Yonkers. From 1866 to 1868 he was presiding elder of the Poughkeepsie district, and from 1868 to 1872, of the Newbury district. He overcame many of the defects in his early education by hard study, and the oratorical training of his youth stood him in good stead, so that he did not suffer greatly by comparison when speaking on the same platform with Henry Ward Beecher, John B. Gough, and Horace Greeley. He was a large-hearted, humane person, of exuberant spirits, with a keen sense of humor and a copious stock of anecdotes at his command, interested in people and in the practical problems of life. To the temperance movement and later to the prohibition movement he gave vigorous support, publishing in 1875 *The American Temperance Cyclopædia of History, Biography, Anecdote, and Illustration.*

Outside of his regular duties, his chief interest was in antiquarian research, and it is for his contributions to the history of early Methodism that he is chiefly remembered. Among his published works were *The Heroes of Methodism* (1856); *Lost Chapters Recovered from the Early*

History of American Methodism (1858); *Anecdotes of the Wesleys: Illustrative of Their Character and Personal History* (1869); *The Bold Frontier Preacher: A Portraiture of Rev. William Cravens, of Virginia* (1869); *The Prince of Pulpit Orators: A Portraiture of Rev. George Whitefield* (1871). He was also the editor of Henry Boehm's *Reminiscences, Historical and Biographical, of Sixty-four Years in the Ministry* (1865). Wakeley died at the home of a friend in New York City after a few days' illness and was buried at Sing Sing.

[W. E. Ketcham, "Memoir of J. B. Wakeley, D.D.," in Wakeley's *Lost Chapters Recovered from the Early Hist. of Am. Methodism* (ed. copr. 1889); *Minutes of the New York Conference of the M. E. Church* (1876); John M'Clintock and James Strong, *Cyc. of Biblical, Theological, and Ecclesiastical Literature*, vol. X (1881); *Christian Advocate*, May 6, 1875; *N. Y. Times*, Apr. 29, 1875; vital records of Danbury, Conn., in Conn. State Lib.]   H. E. S.

WALCOT, CHARLES MELTON (c. 1816–May 15, 1868), actor and dramatist, was born in London, England, received a public school education, and was then trained as an architect. He is said to have emigrated to Charleston, S. C., probably in 1837, and to have become treasurer of the Charleston Theatre. Natural inclination and a singing voice carried him to the stage. He married about this time Miss Powell, an actress, and evidently went touring, for his son Charles Melton [q.v.], was born in Boston in 1840. The first record of Walcot in New York is at the Military Garden, June 28, 1842, when he played Wormwood in *The Lottery Ticket* and later other rôles. The next season found him at Mitchell's famous Olympic, where he remained, with few interruptions, for the next seven years, and built up a substantial reputation both as an eccentric comedian and a dramatic actor. Those were busy days for any actor, especially in a stock company where the bills were changed sometimes almost every night and each bill numbered more than one play or skit. For the first two or three years Walcot was seldom off the program. He was the first to play Don César de Bazan in America, at the Olympic, Dec. 9, 1844. More interesting to a later age, no doubt, would be Walcot's own farces, or burlesques, in the composition of which he seems to have been adept. On Jan. 1, 1844, at the Olympic, was produced *The Imp of the Elements, or The Lake of the Dismal Swamp*. Much more successful were his *Don Giovanni in Gotham* and its successor, *The Don Not Done, or Giovanni from Texas* (Olympic, Mar. 25, 1844), described as "an original musical, fantastical, local extravaganza." On Mar. 27 came his *Old Friends and New Faces*, in which Mrs. Walcot played four

rôles. On Apr. 8 Mitchell had the temerity to produce *The Marriage of Figaro*, "with the overture and music selected chiefly from Mozart's operas." Walcot sang Figaro, but how much of Mozart's music he selected to render we do not know. There are many evidences that he fancied himself as a vocalist. To finish that season, he had a brief try at summer management at Vauxhall Gardens. He appeared at the Arch Street Theatre, Philadelphia, Oct. 29, 1847, as Sir Harcourt Courtly in Dion Boucicault's *London Assurance*, and at various times acted other rôles in standard comedy, including those of Charles Surface and Bob Acres. Among the rôles, other than burlesque, in which he was esteemed seem to have been those of Bert Lavater in Planché's drama of that name, and Redlaw in an adaptation of Dickens' *The Haunted Man*. In 1852 he was engaged by J. W. Wallack, and except for a brief excursion abroad and a briefer experiment in stage management in Baltimore (1853) he played chiefly at Wallack's until 1859.

Ireland (*post*, p. 400) says he was "one of the very best light and eccentric comedians who ever trod our stage." Earlier criticisms found fault sometimes with his exaggerated methods and facial contortions. It was generally conceded that he was an "honest, upright and kind-hearted man." Existing portraits show a sensitive face beneath an unusually high, bald, and domelike forehead, with side hair combed forward and slight side whiskers, almost the portrait of a pleasant clergyman rather than an actor. Many of his burlesques were topical, and hence were a part of the mid-century movement, both in England and America, to free the stage of "classical" shackles and bring it closer to contemporary life. Though his plays are quite forgotten, Walcot evidently had no inconsiderable share in this movement. After leaving Wallack's, he acted less and less, chiefly because his voice was failing him, and he died at a son's home in Philadelphia in May 1868.

[The date of Walcot's birth is given sometimes as Sept. 20, 1815. He is said to have been the son of Thomas B. Melton and to have been named Charles Walcot Melton. His wife's name is given by some writers as Anne. Sources include J. N. Ireland, *Records of the N. Y. Stage* (2 vols., 1867); T. A. Brown, *Hist. of the Am. Stage* (1870); G. C. D. Odell, *Annals of the N. Y. Stage* (7 vols., 1927–31); Frederic Boase, *Modern Eng. Biog.* (3 vols., 1892–1901); Theatre Coll., Harvard College Lib.; obituary in *Am. Ann. Cyc.*, 1868.]   W. P. E.

WALCOT, CHARLES MELTON (July 1, 1840–Jan. 1, 1921), actor, was born in Boston, Mass., the son of Charles Melton Walcot [q.v.] and his wife. He made his first appearance on the stage in Charleston, S. C., in 1858 under the name of Brown but soon resumed his own name. Like many youthful stock actors, he began with old men's parts. In 1859 he played at the National Theatre, Cincinnati, in 1860–61 at Richmond, Va., and in 1861–62 at the Winter Garden, New York, where he had character parts. He then appeared (1862–63) with Laura Keene [q.v.] at her theatre in *Old Heads and Young Hearts* and other plays. On May 31, 1863, he married Isabella Nickinson, a young actress of sixteen, and thereafter until her death they always appeared together. In 1864 Walcot played Horatio during the famous hundred-night run of Booth's *Hamlet* in New York. Three years later the Walcots moved to Philadelphia, where they remained, chiefly at the Walnut Street Theatre, for a number of years. In 1872, however, Walcot supported Charlotte Cushman [q.v.] and played Fagin to Lucille Western's Nancy Sikes. He later played at McVicker's, Chicago, and at the Madison Square and Palmer's in New York, and toured the entire country in Bronson Howard's *The Banker's Daughter* (1879). In 1887 the Walcots joined Daniel Frohman's famous Lyceum Stock Company in New York. There they enjoyed a period of long runs, with light work, great public favor, and the opportunity for domestic stability and social life. In an interview published in the *New York Dramatic Mirror*, Apr. 18, 1896, Walcot contrasted conditions in the nineties with those of his youth, when he had to be able to support visiting stars in their repertoires, alternating, for example, Iago and Othello with Booth on successive nights, and getting up new plays constantly. His rôles at the Lyceum included those of dignified or comic middle-aged or elderly men in plays like *The Wife,* by H. C. de Mille and David Belasco (1887), and *The Princess and the Butterfly* (1897) and *Trelawney of the Wells* (1898) by Pinero; he also appeared in Pinero's *Lady Bountiful,* in a revival of *Old Heads and Young Hearts,* and many of the other Lyceum plays.

After the turn of the century his parts grew fewer, for the last of the stock companies had vanished. Early in the century he supported Otis Skinner for two years in *The Duel.* In 1908 he acted with John Barrymore, in 1909–10 with Henrietta Crosman. In the Empire Theatre revival of *Trelawney of the Wells,* January 1911, he again took his rôle of Sir William Gower. He was then seventy-one. His wife had died (June 2, 1906), and he sorely missed the companionship which had characterized both their domestic and artistic life. He spent his last years

inactively in his home in New York, where he died. In appearance he somewhat resembled his father, though his forehead was less doming and his face and aspect ruddier. In his Lyceum days he often wore a moustache, and offstage could have passed for a genial though dignified British squire. His dramatic schooling under such players as Laura Keene, Edwin Booth, and Charlotte Cushman had been thorough, and he had profited by it, adding to natural gifts as a comedian the skill to touch any required stop. In method he bridged a gap between the older, broad romantic acting and the new realistic method, and in his best years, at the Lyceum, he brought to the nascent new drama, with intelligent adaptability, the authority of the "old school." Much the same could be said of Mrs. Walcot. They were both greatly loved by the public.

[G. C. D. Odell, *Annals of the N. Y. Stage,* vol. VII (1931); Daniel Frohman, *Memories of a Manager* (1911); Harvard Theatre Coll., which contains letters from Walcot; death notices in *N. Y. Times, N. Y. Herald,* Jan. 4, 1921.]   W. P. E.

WALCOTT, CHARLES DOOLITTLE (Mar. 31, 1850–Feb. 9, 1927), paleontologist and administrator, youngest of four children of Charles Doolittle and Mary (Lane) Walcott, was born at New York Mills, Oneida County, N. Y. He was a descendant of William Walcott who emigrated from England to Salem, Mass., in 1637. Since his father died when Charles was a child, he was early thrown upon his own resources, and his education was limited to that provided by the public schools and the Utica Academy. His systematic training ceased altogether in 1868. He worked for two years as a clerk in a hardware store, meanwhile showing a growing interest in natural history, which manifested itself mainly in the collection of fossils and minerals. In 1871 he turned definitely toward a geological career. Going to Trenton Falls, N. Y., he associated himself with W. P. Rust, a farmer, under an arrangement that gave him his board and lodgings with a certain part of his time for study. There he formed a collection of Trenton fossils sufficient to attract the attention of Prof. J. L. R. Agassiz [q.v.] of Harvard. It was arranged that he should enter upon a course of study under Agassiz's supervision, but Agassiz's death prevented the carrying out of the plan. In 1876 Walcott entered the employ of James Hall, 1811–1898 [q.v.], state geologist of New York, at Albany. In July 1879 he was appointed a field assistant with the newly organized United States Geological Survey under the direction of Clarence King [q.v.]. He remained with the survey under the régime of King and

J. W. Powell [*q.v.*], gradually advancing in position. Until 1879 his work had been mainly directed to a study of the Cambrian formations of the New England states and areas east of the Mississippi. His first assignment under King was in the Grand Canyon region of Colorado and Utah. In 1882 he collaborated with Arnold Hague [*q.v.*] in a survey of the Eureka mining district of Nevada, gradually assuming administrative duties as well, until in 1893 he was promoted to the position of geologist in charge. On the retirement of Powell in 1894 he was selected as his successor and remained in that position until 1907. As director of the survey, Walcott simply became head of a body of scientific men already organized, of whom he had, through association, a thorough working knowledge. It remained for him to develop and strengthen the organization on lines already laid down, and this he did most effectively through affiliation with state organizations and professors in the various universities. He also took up the work of reclamation begun by Powell and had a very active part in the work which led eventually to the establishment of the Forest Service and the Bureau of Mines. At the time of his resignation in 1907 the annual appropriations for the support of the survey had more than tripled, while the personnel, both in number and efficiency, exceeded that of any similar existing organization.

But Walcott was not more interested in administration than in paleontology, and the demands of so large and growing an organization he found irksome. When in 1907 he was offered the secretaryship of the Smithsonian Institution he welcomed it as a possible relief from some of his most wearisome administrative burdens. That his hopes in this direction were not to be fully realized was early apparent. The growing activities of the National Museum, the Zoölogical Park, and other governmental bureaus administered by the institution, together with those of the Smithsonian proper, all demanded time and attention. Further, owing to his official position and proved executive ability, he was involved in many other projects. He exerted great influence in the founding of the Freer Gallery, and was active in the founding and organization of the Carnegie Institution, the National Research Council, and the National Advisory Committee for Aeronautics, over which he presided until his death. He was secretary and chairman of the executive committee of the board of trustees of the Carnegie Institution, and treasurer (1899–1902), vice-president (1907–17), and president (1917–23) of the National Academy of Sciences. The World War brought other duties. Later he

took an active part in inaugurating the air-mail service, in organizing work in surveying and mapping by aerial photography, and in drafting the air commerce act of 1926. In the meantime the institution over which he presided was threatened with decline to secondary rank through the shrinking value of its endowment and the vastly larger endowments of institutions newly organized. Plans to check this decline were set in motion a short time before Walcott's death.

The demands made upon him were certainly sufficient to warrant a complete abandonment of all personal scientific work. Yet season after season he found time for field work, mainly in the Canadian Rockies, returning each year enthusiastic over new materials and discoveries, but in later years lacking in stamina for his manifold duties. He did extensive work on the Cambrian field of geology and wrote some notable papers on the organization of the trilobite. His first paleontological paper, "Description of a New Species of Trilobite," appeared in the *Cincinnati Quarterly Journal of Science* in July 1875; his last, *Pre-Devonian Paleozoic Formations of the Cordilleran Province of Canada* (1928), some time after his death. Of the upwards of 222 titles in his bibliography, 110 dealt with the Cambrian formations. Of his faunal studies, the most comprehensive is said to be "The Fauna of the Lower Cambrian or *Olenellus* Zone" (*Tenth Annual Report of the United States Geological Survey*, pt. I, 1890) ; his most monumental work is his *Cambrian Brachiopoda* (2 vols., 1912), Monograph 51 of the United States Geological Survey. The most striking of his field discoveries was that of the Middle Cambrian Burgess shale of British Columbia, with its undreamed-of wealth of fossil invertebrate remains still retaining recognizable impressions of their softer parts. From these beds alone he had at the time of his death described seventy genera of fossil forms, and a hundred and thirty species (Schuchert, *post*, p. 457).

Walcott was a man of large frame, tall, erect, and impressive in appearance; in his younger days he wore a full reddish beard. He was reserved, dignified, and calm, with a slight stiffness of manner that at first gave an impression of coldness. In the midst of the most distracting administrative duties he could always find immediate relief in scientific research. He was a member of the leading scientific societies in Europe and America and received a number of honorary degrees, among them that of Sc.D. from Cambridge University in 1909 and that of Ph.D. from Kongelige Frederiks Universitet, Norway, in 1911. He was awarded the Bigsby Medal of the Geological Society of London in 1895, and its Wollaston Medal in 1918; the Hayden Medal of the Academy of Natural Sciences of Philadelphia in 1905; the Gaudry Medal of the Société Géologique de France in 1917, and the Mary Clark Thompson Medal of the National Academy of Sciences in 1921. On June 22, 1888, he married Helena Burrows Stevens, by whom he had three sons and a daughter. After the death of his first wife in a railroad accident in 1911, he married Mary Morris Vaux (June 30, 1914), who survived him.

[The best material on Walcott is contained in N. H. Darton, "Memorial of Charles Doolittle Walcott," *Bull. Geological Soc. of America*, Mar. 1928, with bibliog. See also F. A. Virkus, *The Abridged Compendium of Am. Geneal.*, vol. II (1926); *Who's Who in America*, 1926–27; "Charles Doolittle Walcott . . . Memorial Meeting," *Smithsonian. Miscellaneous Colls.*, vol. LXXX, no. 12 (1928); G. O. Smith, *Charles Doolittle Walcott* (1927), reprinted from *Am. Jour. of Sci.*, July 1927; Charles Schuchert, in *Report of the Nat. Acad. of Sci.* (1928), reprinted from *Sci.*, May 13, 1927; T. C. Chamberlain, in *Jour. of Geology*, Oct.–Nov. 1927; "Eminent Living Geologists," *Geological Mag.* (London), Jan. 1919; obituary in *Evening Star* (Washington, D. C.), Feb. 9, 1927.]   G. P. M.

WALCOTT, HENRY PICKERING (Dec. 23, 1838–Nov. 11, 1932), physician and public health administrator, was born in Hopkinton, Mass., the son of Samuel Baker and Martha (Pickman) Walcott. Following his graduation at Harvard College in 1858, Walcott studied medicine under Morrill and Jeffries Wyman [*qq.v.*] and took his degree of M.D. in 1861 at Bowdoin College, Brunswick, Me. He went to Europe in June 1861 to further his medical studies in Vienna and Berlin, returning to America in November 1862. Subsequently he began to practise in Cambridge, Mass., at first as assistant to his former teacher, Dr. Morrill Wyman. After service on the Cambridge school committee and as city physician, he was appointed in 1882 a member of the State Board of Health, Lunacy, and Charity. The public health movement was vaguely coming into being and the pioneer efforts of Lemuel Shattuck [*q.v.*] were bearing fruit. Four years of membership were followed by twenty-nine years as chairman.

Walcott's first task was the reorganization of the badly maintained Tewksbury State Almshouse. This accomplished, he next, in 1886, widened the influence of the Board of Health by giving it advisory power regarding public water supplies, drainage, sewerage, and the protection of the purity of inland waters. By assuming only advisory capacity and never mandatory powers, he upheld the town and local authorities and never usurped any of their jealously-guarded rights. That he succeeded well is evident, for

the decisions of the Board were almost invariably accepted without question by the towns. Subsequently the Board of Health of which he was chairman recommended and planned the Metropolitan Sewerage Commission to coördinate the work of many communities near Boston. A special commission of which he was chairman in 1893 recommended the building of the Charles River Basin in Boston, a public health measure of first importance. Finally, he planned and saw executed in 1895 the metropolitan water supply system for Boston. He also established an antitoxin laboratory, under the direction of Theobald Smith, for the manufacture of diphtheria antitoxin for free distribution in the state.

In addition to his chairmanship of the Board of Health, Walcott was chairman of the Metropolitan Water and Sewerage Board and was president of the American Public Health Association, of the Massachusetts Medical Society, the Massachusetts Horticultural Society and the American Academy of Arts and Sciences. For many years he was a trustee of the Carnegie Institution of Washington, chairman of the trustees of the Massachusetts General Hospital and, in 1912, he served as president of the Fifteenth International Congress on Hygiene and Demography in Washington. He was an honorary fellow of the Royal Sanitary Institute of Great Britain. He was one of the incorporators of the Cambridge Hospital in 1872 and served as its president for twenty-five years. In 1890, while serving as Overseer, he was made a member of the Board of President and Fellows of Harvard College, and acting president in 1900 and again in 1905.

Besides tributes to Charles W. Eliot and Reginald H. Fitz [*qq.v.*] in *Proceedings of the Massachusetts Historical Society,* vols. LII and LX (1919, 1927), and a memoir of Morrill Wyman [*q.v.*], printed in *Sons of the Puritans* (1908), Walcott wrote an essay on Alexander Agassiz [*q.v.*] which he delivered before the American Academy of Arts and Sciences (*Proceedings,* vol. XLVIII, 1913). Otherwise his writing was practically confined to the annual reports of the Board of Health. In them one finds the germinal ideas of most of the public health movement in America. Building on the sound foundations laid by Lemuel Shattuck, Walcott erected a structure of wide usefulness to his local community, and helped to make public health the concern of all civilized peoples. He was the most important man in the field in his day. On May 31, 1865, he was married to Charlotte Elizabeth, daughter of Reuben Richards of Boston. His wife died in 1879. Of the three children, one died as a baby, one became a cotton merchant and the other a judge, lawyer, and bank president. He was intimate with the leading Bostonians in science and in literature; among them were William James, Charles W. Eliot, Alexander Agassiz, Nathaniel S. Shaler, and Charles Sprague Sargent [qq.v.]. He was one of the most beloved and honored figures in Boston during his many years of service to the commonwealth. He retired, except for his connections with Harvard University, fifteen years before his death. He died in his ninety-fourth year in Cambridge, Mass., partially deaf, wholly blind for the previous five years but with intellect, wit, and good spirits unimpaired.

[His chief contributions to public health are contained in George C. Whipple, *State Sanitation* (2 vols., 1917), dedicated to Walcott. See also: A. S. Walcott, *The Walcott Book* (1925); *New England Jour. Med.*, Nov. 17 and Dec. 1, 1932; X. Henry Goodnough, *Ibid.*, Nov. 9, 1933; M. J. Rosenau, in *Summarized Proc. Am. Acad. of Arts and Sci.*, vols. LXXXII–LXXXVI (1934); *Who's Who in America,* 1932–33; *Report of the Class of 1858, Harvard Coll.,* 1868, 1888, 1898; *Boston Evening Transcript,* Nov. 11, 1932; *Boston Herald, N. Y. Times,* Nov. 12, 1932.]   H. R. V.

WALDEN, JACOB TREADWELL (Apr. 25, 1830–May 21, 1918), Protestant Episcopal clergyman and author, the son of Jacob Treadwell and Beulah Hoffman (Willett) Walden, was born at Walden, Orange County, N. Y., a town founded by his father. During most of his life the son was known simply as Treadwell Walden. After studying at St. James' College, Maryland, and at St. Paul's College, Long Island, in 1850 he entered the General Theological Seminary, New York. Graduating in 1853, he was ordained deacon by Bishop J. M. Wainwright, July 2, 1854, in Trinity Church, New York. In January 1855 he became assistant at Trinity Church, Newark, in February 1856 was put in charge of it, and there was ordained priest by Bishop G. W. Doane on May 19 of that year. In September 1857 he became rector of Christ Church, Norwich, Conn. While here he published *The Sunday School Prayer Book* (copr. 1862), a collection marked by more attention to the nature of children and by less rigorous theology than was common in most similar books of the period. In March 1863 he went to St. Clement's Church, Philadelphia, for which he secured the erection of a parish house and other improvements. He served on the committee appointed by the United States Sanitary Commission to investigate the treatment of Union prisoners, and is said to have drafted its report (*Narrative of Privations and Sufferings of U. S. Officers and Soldiers while Prisoners of War,* 1864). St. Clement's was involved in financial difficulties, how-

ever, and in 1868, conscious of his vestry's lack of confidence, Walden resigned.

In February 1870 he was called to St. Paul's Church, Indianapolis. He at once took a prominent part in the church life of the city and the affairs of the diocese of Indiana. In 1871 he published *Our English Bible and Its Ancestors,* a series of parish lectures on the history of the English version and the need for a revision. In the appendix he argued that the New Testament word *metanoia* means "change of attitude" rather than "repentance for sin," a subject to which he was to return in future publications. Although his work in Indianapolis seems to have been successful, he left in 1872, and in the next year became rector of St. Paul's, Boston. Compelled by ill health to resign in May 1876, for some years he lived and occasionally officiated in or near New York. Meanwhile, the essay on *metanoia* had appeared as an article in the *American Church Review* (July 1881), and in his *An Undeveloped Chapter in the Life of Christ* (1882). In 1882 he was called to St. Paul's, Minneapolis.

Three years later he retired from the active ministry and subsequently spent several years in England. After his return in 1889 he divided his time between Boston, Mass., and Wonalancet, N. H. In 1896 an enlarged treatment of his favorite subject was published as *The Great Meaning of Metanoia.* Walden's place in the development of the Episcopal Church lies in the part he played in the humanizing and liberalizing movement by which the broad church group grew out of the older evangelical. He was twice married: first, in 1858, to Elizabeth Leighton Law, of Norwich, Conn., who died in 1883; and second, in 1885, to Grace Gordon of Boston. He was survived by two sons by his first wife. Walden died in Boston.

[*Who's Who in America,* 1916–17; *Living Church,* June 1, 1918; *The Living Church Annual and Churchman's Almanac* (1919); *Boston Transcript,* May 21, 1918; records of the dioceses with which Walden was connected, and of St. Clement's, Phila.]   E. R. H., Jr.

WALDEN, JOHN MORGAN (Feb. 11, 1831–Jan. 21, 1914), bishop of the Methodist Episcopal Church, was born near Lebanon, Ohio, the son of Jesse and Matilda (Morgan) Walden, who moved to Hamilton County in 1832. He was of Virginian ancestry, his great-grandfather Walden having moved from Culpeper County to Kentucky in 1770, and his grandfather, Benjamin, to Ohio in 1802. After the death of his mother in 1833 John went to live with relatives near Cincinnati. He attended a local school until 1844, when he went to work. Becoming a wanderer, he found employment as a carpenter, in a country store and postoffice, and in connection with theatrical performances. A carpenter for whom he worked interested him in Thomas Paine's writings, and he became a skeptic. He read extensively in Scott and Goldsmith and wrote romantic stories over the name of Ned Law for the Hamilton, Ohio, *Telegraph* (1849-53). After attending Farmers' College, College Hill, Ohio, in 1849, he taught for a year in Miami County, where he was converted by a Methodist circuit rider. Returning to Farmers' College he was graduated in 1852 and for two years was a teacher there.

In 1854 he went to Fairfield, Ill., where he published the *Independent Press,* opposing in his editorials the liquor traffic and "squatter sovereignty." The Illinoisans starved him out by refusing to support his paper, and in 1855 he returned to Ohio, where he reported for the *Cincinnati Commercial.* So deeply interested in the Kansas troubles did he become while reporting the National Democratic Convention of 1856 that he went to Kansas, where he established the Quindaro *Chindowan,* a free-soil organ. He was a delegate to five free-state conventions, including the Leavenworth constitutional convention (1858). That same year he campaigned over half the Territory, opposing the Lecompton constitution.

On Sept. 8, 1858, he was admitted on trial to the Cincinnati Conference of the Methodist Episcopal Church. The first two years of his ministry were spent on circuits, and on July 3, 1859, he married Martha Young of Cheviot, Ohio. In 1860 he was admitted to the Conference in full connection and sent to the York Street Church, Cincinnati. While he was here the Civil War began, and he became very active and raised two regiments to defend the city against threatening attack. After service in connection with the Ladies' Home Mission in Cincinnati (1862-64) and as corresponding secretary of the Western Freedmen's Aid Commission and of the Methodist Freedmen's Aid Society, he became in 1867 presiding elder of the East Cincinnati District. The following year he was chosen an assistant agent of the Western Methodist Book Concern. His penchant for statistics and organization, his business ability, and his sympathetic cooperation with preachers made the Concern a financial success.

At the General Conference of 1884 he was elected bishop. In his official capacity he presided at some time over every Conference in the United States and inspected Methodist missionary work in Mexico, South America, Europe, China, and Japan, doing much to shape the mis-

sionary policy of his Church. He was a delegate to the Ecumenical Conferences in London, 1881, Washington, 1891, and Toronto, 1911. With respect to church organization he insisted upon strict adherence to the written law, but otherwise he was liberal in his views. He was noted for his wit and for his optimistic spirit. He was happiest when, attired in a white slouch hat and linen duster, he started out for a day's recreation with fish bait in his pocket. His wife and three of his five children survived him. In recognition of his work for the colored race the name of Central Tennessee College, in Nashville, was changed in 1900 to Walden University.

[D. H. Moore, *John Morgan Walden* (1915); *Biog. Cyc. and Portrait Gallery . . . of the State of Ohio,* vol. V (n.d.); *The Biog. Encyc. of Ohio of the Nineteenth Century* (1876); H. C. Jennings, "Bishop John Morgan Walden," *Jour. of the Twenty-seventh Delegated Gen. Conference of the Methodist Episcopal Church* (1916); C. T. Greve, *Centennial Hist. of Cincinnati and Representative Citizens* (1904), vol. II; *Who's Who in America,* 1912-13; *Cincinnati Enquirer,* Jan. 22, and *Cincinnati Times-Star,* Jan. 28, 1914; Walden Papers, in possession of Mrs. S. O. Royal.]   W. E. S—h.

WALDERNE, RICHARD (*c.* 1615-June 1689), pioneer, soldier, was born at Alchester in Warwickshire, England, the eighth child and seventh son of William and Catharine (Raven) Walderne. He was baptized on Jan. 6, 1615 (*New England Historical and Genealogical Register,* January 1854, p. 78). After a preliminary visit "to see the country" (1635-37), he emigrated to New England about 1640, settling at Dover, N. H. With him he brought a wife, of whom nothing is known beyond the tradition (Bodge, *post,* p. 293) that she was "a Gentlewoman of a very good family (whose parents were very unwilling She Should come away)." Having acquired large tracts of land at Cochecho (part of the present Dover) and Penacook (now Concord), Walderne became principally engaged in lumbering and trade with the Indians. He filled at various times practically all of the important local offices, both administrative and judicial, and served almost without interruption from 1654 to 1674 and again in 1677 as a representative to the General Court at Boston, in which body he was several times chosen speaker (Scales, *post,* pp. 202f.).

Especially delegated in 1662 to deal with the Quaker "menace" at Dover, Walderne zealously discharged his duty by sentencing three "vagabond" women of the sect to be whipped at the cart's tail through thirteen towns to the end of the Bay Colony's jurisdiction (Bouton, *post,* I, 243). His achievements as major of the Norfolk County militia were inconspicuous except on one occasion when, by a "contrivement" akin to treachery, he managed to take without bloodshed some two hundred hostile Indians, who had sought refuge by mingling with the pacified tribes of New Hampshire. Some six or seven of these captives were later hanged and most of the remainder sold into slavery (Belknap, *post,* I, 142f.; Bouton, I, 357–60; Bodge, p. 306). The incident was remembered bitterly by the local tribes, and when with the resumption of general hostilities Cochecho was raided on the night of June 27–28, 1689, the Major was singled out by them for special torture before being put to death (Scales, pp. 219f.).

Upon the establishment of a separate provincial government for New Hampshire in 1680, Walderne was appointed one of the President's Council; and after the death of President Cutt in 1681 he became acting president until the arrival of Cranfield. His extensive land holdings and prominent position in the colony marked him naturally as the one first to be sued by Robert Mason in the attempt of the latter to make good his hereditary claims. Walderne refused to defend himself at the trial or produce evidence of his title, for he declared that the jury were personally interested and hence incapable of doing justice. Judgment was given against him and a fine imposed for the "mutinous and seditious words" with which he had addressed the court (Bouton, p. 514, note). Walderne was twice married; the second time, to Anne Scammon, sister of Richard Scammon of local fame (*New England Historical and Genealogical Register,* January 1854, p. 65, note; January 1855, pp. 55f.). His descendants continued for generations to occupy a distinguished place in New Hampshire political affairs.

[For sources see John Scales, *Hist. Memoranda Concerning Persons and Places in Old Dover, N. H., Collected by Rev. Dr. Alonzo Hall Quint, and Others* (1900); S. D. Bell, in *N. H. Hist. Soc. Colls.,* vol. VIII (1866); G. M. Bodge, *Soldiers in King Philip's War* (3rd ed., 1906); Nathaniel Bouton, *Provincial Papers, Documents and Records Relating to the Province of N. H.,* vol. I (1867), vol. II (1868). The account of the seizure of the Indians at Cochecho was first given in Jeremy Belknap, *The Hist. of N. H.* (3 vols., 1784–92) and was based upon tradition; but some corroborative evidence appears in the *Provincial Papers* and a critical discussion of the incident is to be found in Bodge.] G. P. B.

WALDO, DAVID (Apr. 30, 1802–May 20, 1878), physician, Santa Fé trader, banker, was the son of Jedediah and Polly (Porter) Waldo and a descendant of Cornelius Waldo who settled in Ipswich, Mass., as early as 1647. He was born in Clarksburg, Harrison County, Va. (now W. Va.), and in his early youth engaged in rafting logs down the Ohio River. In 1820 he moved to Gasconade County, Mo., where he prospered, and served in various county offices. He was also major of the militia. Determining to attend medical college, he set about cutting pine logs in order to finance his education. Binding his logs into a large raft he floated them down the Gasconade, Missouri, and Mississippi rivers, and delivered them to Laveille and Morton at St. Louis for the sum of $500. He pursued his medical studies at Transylvania University, Lexington, Ky.

Waldo began to practise medicine in Gasconade County, but soon moved to Osceola, then to Independence, Mo., and finally to Taos, in what is now the state of New Mexico. On May 5, 1829, he received his third degree in Masonry from Missouri Lodge No. 1, but he subsequently returned to Taos; he became a citizen of Mexico in 1830, and an *ayuntamiento* of Taos. He is supposed to have become interested in commerce as early as 1827 and he finally gave up his practice to enter the Santa Fé trade, in which he continued for over thirty years. He amassed a great fortune before the Mexican War, and returned to Missouri, where he subsequently became captain of Company A in the regiment commanded by Alexander William Doniphan [*q.v.*]. One of his brothers was killed at Mora in 1847. After the war, Waldo returned to Independence, Mo., and on Mar. 27, 1849, married Eliza Jane Norris, born June 25, 1822, at Mount Sterling, Ky. They had five children.

Of several fortunes acquired in the overland trade, Waldo lost two—one by a storm when trading in Chihuahua, and the other by reason of a fire which destroyed his large train of merchandise intended for trade with Fort Laramie. It is said that his sustained energy, perseverance, and indomitable will gave him a force quite irresistible. He had quick perception and sound judgment, was honest and fair in all his dealings, and was generally liked and respected. He owned and enjoyed a large and valuable library and spoke French and Spanish with facility. During the Mexican War he rendered useful service in translating documents captured from the Mexicans by American troops. An ardent Mason, he gave a valuable lot in Taos to Bent Lodge No. 204, on June 15, 1860. After his retirement from the overland trade he made contracts with the United States government for carrying provisions to the army at distant points and carrying mail to Santa Fé. The latter part of his life was devoted largely to banking. He died in Independence, Mo.

[Waldo MSS., Mo. Hist. Soc., St. Louis; Waldo Lincoln, *Geneal. of the Waldo Family* (1902), vol. I; *Missouri Grand Lodge Bull.* (St. Louis), Apr. 1925; W. E. Connelley, *Doniphan's Expedition* (1907); *Hist. of Franklin, Jefferson, Washington, Crawford and Gasconade Counties, Mo.* (1888); *House Report No. 284,*

34 Cong., 1 Sess.; *Down the Santa Fé Trail and into Mexico: The Diary of Susan Shelby Magoffin* (1926), ed. by Stella M. Drumm; R. E. Twitchell, *The Leading Facts of New Mexican Hist.* (5 vols., 1911–17), vols. II, V.]   S. M. D.

WALDO, SAMUEL (1695–May 23, 1759), Boston merchant, capitalist, and politician, was a grandson of Cornelius Waldo who was living in Ipswich, Mass., as early as 1647, and the eldest surviving child among the twelve born to Jonathan and Hannah (Mason) Waldo of Boston. He was baptized in the First Church of that city on Dec. 22, 1695. According to tradition, he went to the Boston Latin School, which his sons later attended. He began business as a merchant on capital advanced by his father; and in 1722 married Lucy, daughter of Major Francis and Sarah (Whipple) Wainwright of Ipswich. Their children were Samuel, Jr., Lucy, Hannah, Francis, Sarah, and Ralph. Waldo imported miscellaneous merchandise such as "choice Irish duck, fine Florence wine, negro slaves, and Irish butter" which he sold from his home on Queen Street. He also dealt in rum, fish, and lumber. As an official mast-agent, he collaborated with Thomas Westbrook of Falmouth (Portland, Me.) in getting out white pines for the British navy. One product of his activities in this line was the famous colonial lawsuit of *Frost* vs. *Leighton* (see *American Historical Review,* January 1897). It was Waldo who employed Leighton to cut timber on Frost's farm, and Waldo's lawyer who defended him.

Land speculation on a great scale was Waldo's chief interest, and his career is significant mainly for his unwearied efforts to develop his wild lands on the coast of Maine between the Muscongus and Penobscot rivers. In 1729, when Col. David Dunbar established himself at Pemaquid on the Maine coast and began to bring in settlers, the Muscongus proprietors chose Waldo to go to England and press their claims against Dunbar. Waldo remained abroad two years, until the Privy Council handed down a verdict which gave him victory. He now became the chief proprietor of the Muscongus grant, henceforth called the Waldo patent, and started to settle the region and to manufacture lime and iron. At the same time he entered on large plans with Thomas Westbrook for industries on the Stroudwater River in Falmouth. Strong opposition to his settlement projects arose, however, and doubts as to validity of his title to the eastern lands were circulated. To meet this attack Waldo published in 1736 a pamphlet entitled *A Defence of the Title . . . to a Tract of Land . . . Commonly Called Muscongus Lands,* setting forth proofs of his legal ownership. Blaming Gov. Jonathan

Belcher [*q.v.*] for his difficulties, he returned to England in 1738 and for three years was a leader in the conspiracy to oust the governor. Belcher's successor, commissioned in 1741, was Waldo's permanent attorney, William Shirley [*q.v.*].

About this time financial difficulties beset Waldo. One of the means he adopted for extricating himself was to bring about in 1743 a foreclosure against his former partner, Thomas Westbrook, as a result of which he acquired all of Westbrook's properties. With a friend in the governor's chair, he also resumed operations in Maine, only to have them blocked by King George's War. In the Louisburg campaign of 1745 he served as a brigadier-general, second in command of the Massachusetts forces. An unsigned portrait of Waldo with the harbor and fort of Louisburg in the background, now in the Walker Art Gallery at Bowdoin College, was painted at this period, presumably in 1749 and probably by the artist Robert Feke [*q.v.*], rather than by John Smibert, to whom it has sometimes been attributed (H. W. Foote, *Robert Feke, Colonial Painter,* 1930, pp. 72–73, 198–200). The picture shows Waldo as an elegant military officer, tall and portly. In the 1750's he again renewed his land schemes and advertised abroad for settlers, chiefly in Scotland, Ireland, and Germany. By this time he and Governor Shirley had become bitter enemies as the result of a dispute over certain military fees which Waldo claimed and the Governor refused to sanction. In 1757 Shirley was replaced by Thomas Pownall [*q.v.*], and in the spring of 1759 the new governor conducted an expedition down to the Penobscot River and there built a fort. Waldo, now sixty-three years old, accompanied the party; on May 23, while walking about near the present city of Bangor, he fell dead of apoplexy. He was buried at the new fort, but in 1760 his body was removed to King's Chapel Burial Ground, Boston. Today his association with Maine is perpetuated in several names such as Waldoboro, Waldo County, Brigadier's Island, and Mount Waldo.

[Knox MSS., Mass. Hist. Soc., vol. L; "The Belcher Papers," *Mass. Hist. Soc. Colls.,* 6 ser., VI–VII (1893–94); *Correspondence of William Shirley* (2 vols., 1912), ed. by C. H. Lincoln; G. A. Wood, *William Shirley, Gov. of Mass.,* vol. I (1920); Court Files (Suffolk) of the Supreme Judicial Court, Boston, 1737–1740/41; Thomas Hutchinson, *Hist. of the Province of Mass. Bay,* vol. II (1765); Waldo Lincoln, *Geneal. of the Waldo Family* (1902), vol. I; *New-Eng. Hist. and Geneal. Reg.,* July 1874; Jennison Papers, Am. Antiquarian Soc.; *Me. Hist. Soc. Colls.,* 1 ser. IX (1887), 2 ser. XI (1908).]   A. C. F.

WALDO, SAMUEL LOVETT (Apr. 6, 1783–Feb. 16, 1861), portrait painter, was born at Windham, Conn., one of eight children of Zacheus Waldo and Esther (Stevens) Waldo. His father, a farmer, was a descendant of Cornelius Waldo who emigrated to New England about 1647. Waldo was educated in the country schools and at the age of sixteen was allowed to go to Hartford to take drawing lessons of an obscure portrait painter named Stewart, who was an indifferent instructor. Having sold a picture for fifteen dollars, the young student presently (1803) took a studio in Hartford, but he met with scant success and was obliged to supplement his slender income by painting signs. In Litchfield, Conn., where he painted several portraits he met the Hon. John Rutledge of South Carolina, who invited him to go to Charleston. There he met with pronounced success and remained about three years. By 1806 he had laid aside enough money to go to England, with letters to Benjamin West and John Singleton Copley [qq.v.] in London. According to Dunlap, he painted a few portraits in London at five guineas each, "but had not employment enough to pay expenses" (post, II, 357). He was married at Liverpool or Chester on Apr. 8, 1808, to Josephine Elza Wood, who died in 1825.

Returning to America in January 1809, he settled in New York. There for more than fifty years he worked diligently as a portrait painter, after 1820 in partnership with William Jewett [q.v.], one of his pupils. In 1826 he was one of the thirty founders of the National Academy of Design and in 1847 became an associate. The firm of Waldo and Jewett prospered, and numerous excellent if somewhat literal likenesses were executed by the two painters in collaboration. It is probable that Waldo painted the heads and hands, while his assistant painted the backgrounds and costumes. Examples of their work in public collections include the portrait of G. W. Parke Custis of Arlington, Va., in the Corcoran Gallery, Washington; a sketch from life of Gen. Andrew Jackson (1817), and "Old Pat, the Independent Beggar," with several other canvases, including a self-portrait and a portrait of his second wife, in the Metropolitan Museum, New York; the portrait of Mrs. William Steele, in the City Art Museum of St. Louis, Mo.; the likeness of Peter Remsen owned by the New York Historical Society; several portraits of former mayors of New York in the City Hall; the portrait of President James Madison in the possession of the Century Association, New York; and two portraits of John Trumbull. Thomas B. Clarke acquired his portrait of R. G. Livingston de Peyster (1828), a prominent New York merchant, that of Rebecca Sanford

Barlow (1810), and a portrait of a lady which has been warmly praised for its freshness of color and admirable modeling. Isham aptly describes the work of Waldo and Jewett as "scores of heads . . . of dignified, benevolent gentlemen, with white hair and white chokers, or of ladies in wonderful caps and shawls" (post, p. 141) and praises their "quiet and unaggressive" painting for its technical merit. Other critics were not so indulgent; one of them calls Waldo "really a commercial face maker," who was "competent but never inspired" (Mather, post, p. 26). After the death of his first wife, Waldo married Deliverance Mapes on May 8, 1826, in New York City. He died in New York in 1861, at the age of seventy-seven.

[Waldo Lincoln, Geneal. of the Waldo Family (1902); vital records, Windham, Conn.; William Dunlap, A Hist. . . . of the Arts of Design in the U. S. A. (3 vols., 1918), ed. by F. W. Bayley and C. E. Goodspeed; Samuel Isham, The Hist. of Am. Painting (1905); F. F. Sherman, in Art in America, Feb. 1930; F. J. Mather, C. R. Morey, and W. J. Henderson, The Am. Spirit in Art (1927); H. W. French, Art and Artists in Conn. (1879); Art News, Jan. 24, 1931; cats. of T. B. Clark Coll., 1899 and 1928, and of Corcoran Gall. of Art, 1908; death notice in N. Y. Herald, Feb. 18, 1861.]

W. H. D.

WALDO, SAMUEL PUTNAM (Mar. 12, 1779–Feb. 23, 1826), author, was born at Pomfret, Conn., the third child of Samuel and Mary (Putnam) Waldo, a grandson of Gen. Israel Putnam [q.v.], and a descendant of Cornelius Waldo who was living in Ipswich, Mass., as early as 1647. Of his boyhood the records are meager. His writings give evidence of his early reading and taste for literature, and according to his own statement (Biographical Sketches . . . of Naval Heroes, p. 283), he was in Boston in 1797 at the launching of the U.S.S. Constitution. There is no record of his attendance at college or service in the War of 1812, but he speaks of travel in the South and of having visited Jefferson at Monticello in 1813 (Ibid., p. 388). He studied law and practised at East Windsor, Conn., from about 1805 to 1816. In the next year he began his literary career by writing out and publishing at Hartford Capt. Archibald Robbins' oral narrative of his shipwreck and slavery in Africa in 1815–17. This work went through eleven editions in one year. Though the title, Journal Comprising an Account of the Loss of the Brig Commerce . . . by Archibald Robbins, gives no hint of Waldo's part in its composition, he identified himself in later works as its "compiler."

Of the popular writings he published in the next five years, the first was The Tour of James Monroe, President of the United States, through the Northern and Eastern States in 1817 (1818), later editions of which included also an account of President Monroe's summer travel in 1818 and a sketch of his life. Waldo's *Memoirs of Andrew Jackson, Major General ... and Commander in Chief of the Division of the South* (1818) passed quickly through five editions, and at least two reprints appeared in 1828, one as "by a citizen of Massachusetts" and another as "by a citizen of Hagerstown, Md." Like his other books, it met a contemporary interest but has slight historical value, leaning heavily on *The Life of Andrew Jackson* published by John H. Eaton [*q.v.*] in 1817. Waldo had, however, some acquaintance with naval officers, had access to General Putnam's books and papers, and, according to his own statement (Preface to *Biographical Sketches ... of Naval Heroes*), had collected "records, pamphlets, newspapers, and even hand-bills" of the Revolutionary period. Hence somewhat more value is attached to the *Life and Character of Stephen Decatur* (1821) and to his last book, *Biographical Sketches of Distinguished American Naval Heroes in the War of the Revolution* (1823). In the preface to the latter volume he remarked that he had sold 80,000 copies of his works in the preceding four years but "added nothing to his pecuniary means." In 1819 he established at Hartford the *Rural Magazine and Farmers' Monthly Museum,* but published only five numbers, February–July (file in the Library of Congress). In a postscript to the last number he stated that "the work has been solely furnished by the Editor, except a few original poems." He also wrote "A Brief Sketch of the Indictment, Trial, and Conviction of Stephen and Jesse Boorn for the Murder of Russell Colvin" which appeared as the third part of a book on this sensational trial—*Mystery Developed, or Russell Colvin (Supposed to be Murdered) in Full Life ...* (1820). Though his writings show some reading and range of interests, they have otherwise little distinction. His biographical formula was a pound of rhetoric to an ounce of fact, and he was much inclined to dilate on the blessings of his country, free from the "poverty, crime, or social disorders" of other lands. He was unmarried. His death at Hartford in early middle age is said to have been hastened by the death of his betrothed.

[Waldo Lincoln, *Geneal. of the Waldo Family* (1902), vol. I; J. D. Hall, *Geneal. and Biog. of the Waldos in America* (1883); J. H. Trumbull, *Memorial Hist. of Hartford County, Conn.* (1886), vol. I; Pomfret (Conn.) Vital Records, Conn. State Lib.; *Connecticut Observer* (Hartford), Mar. 6, 1826.]   A. W—t.

WALDRON, RICHARD [See WALDERNE, RICHARD, 1615–1689].

WALES, JAMES ALBERT (Aug. 30, 1852–Dec. 6, 1886), cartoonist, was born in Clyde,

Ohio, the son of William Washington and Martha (Dimm) Wales. After attending school in Sandusky he went to Toledo to study wood engraving. Later he went to the engraving shop of Bogart & Stillman in Cincinnati, where he found another Ohio boy, William Allen Rogers [*q.v.*], also trying to learn to draw. He drew political cartoons on the presidential campaign of 1872 for the *Cleveland Leader* and in 1873 went to New York, where some of his early work was done for *Wild Oats* and *Frank Leslie's Illustrated Newspaper.* In the fall of 1875, with Frank Hegger, the portrait photographer, he went to London. He drew for *Judy,* the *Illustrated Sporting and Dramatic News,* and the *London Illustrated News,* tried for a position on the staff of *Vanity Fair,* and made a trip to Paris, where he spent most of his time studying the best drawings in the Louvre. On his return to New York he worked for *Frank Leslie's* for a time. In 1877 he joined the staff of the English edition of *Puck,* established by Joseph Keppler [*q.v.*] and Adolph Schwarzmann. On Mar. 25, 1878, he married Claudia Marshall Cooper, a first cousin of Richard Harding Davis [*q.v.*].

Beginning with Feb. 12, 1879, Wales started in *Puck* a series of full-page political portraits under the general title of "Puck's Pantheon." Incisive, sardonic, they were well drawn and quite comparable to the best work being done. These drawings definitely established his reputation. Soon afterwards he was doing front and back covers and double-page spreads for *Puck* on social and political subjects. Characteristic examples are those on the Chinese question (Mar. 12, 1879), "A Suggestion for the Next St. Paddy's Day Parade" (Mar. 19, 1879), and "The Irish Idea of a 'Christian Burial'" (May 7, 1879). Less dramatically vindictive in political satire than Thomas Nast [*q.v.*], but more of a realist than Keppler, he had a decided and recognized gift for portraiture. Rogers spoke enthusiastically of his work. When the *Judge* was started by W. J. Arkell, Oct. 29, 1881, as a political rival to *Puck,* Wales took a prominent part in it, but in June 1885, becoming dissatisfied with the paper's policy, he returned to *Puck.* He died suddenly in his thirty-fifth year from a heart attack and was buried at Clyde. He was survived by his wife and two sons. He was tall and ruddy-faced, with a silky turned-up moustache and wore pince-nez. There is little question that if he had lived he would have been recognized as one of the foremost American caricaturists.

[Frank Weitenkampf, *Am. Graphic Art* (1924); W. A. Rogers, *A World Worth While* (1922); obituaries in *N. Y. Times, N. Y. Tribune, World* (N. Y.), Dec. 7,

1886, *New Yorker Staats-Zeitung*, Dec. 8, and *Mail and Express* (N. Y.), Dec. 9; *Journalist*, Dec. 18, 1886; information from J. A. Wales, Jr., E. P. Allen, and S. H. Horgan.]   W. P.

WALES, LEONARD EUGENE (Nov. 26, 1823–Feb. 8, 1897), judge, was born at Wilmington, Del., the son of John and Ann (Patten) Wales, and a descendant of Nathaniel Wales who came with his father, Nathaniel, from Yorkshire, England, to Boston in 1635. John Wales was prominent in public life in Delaware, and from 1849 to 1851 served as United States senator. Leonard completed his preparatory studies at the Hopkins Grammar School, New Haven, Conn., and then entered Yale, where he was graduated in 1845. Having studied law in his father's office in Wilmington, he was admitted to the bar on May 8, 1848. For the ensuing two years he gave much of his time to editorial work on the *Delaware State Journal*, organ of the Whig party, to which the Wales family adhered. In May 1849 he was appointed clerk of the United States circuit and district courts for Delaware and served as such until 1864. In 1853 and 1854 he was city solicitor of Wilmington, and in 1856 he took an active part in organizing the Republican party in Delaware. Upon President Lincoln's call for volunteers in 1861, Wales was among the first in the state to respond. He was commissioned a second lieutenant in Company E, 1st Delaware Volunteers, which was stationed along the line of the Philadelphia, Wilmington & Baltimore Railroad, south of the Susquehanna River. After the expiration of his three months' term of enlistment, he returned to civil life, but in May 1863 he was appointed a member of the Delaware board of enrollment, which administered the national draft law.

In September 1864 Gov. William Cannon appointed him as associate justice (for New Castle County) of the Delaware superior court. Entering upon his duties Oct. 1, 1864, he held the office for nearly a score of years, functioning not only as a *nisi prius* judge and in the orphans' court but also, in accordance with the Delaware system, sitting *en banc* as a member of the court of general sessions of the peace and jail delivery, of the court of oyer and terminer, and of the court of errors and appeals. Upon assuming judicial station he ceased to participate in partisan politics but continued certain quasi-public activities. He was especially interested in the work of the Historical Society of Delaware and served for a number of years as its president. True to ancestral traditions, he promoted various educational enterprises, being a founder of the West End Reading-Room in Wilmington and of the Ferris Reform School.

On Mar. 10, 1884, upon nomination of President Arthur, Wales was confirmed as United States judge for the district of Delaware, and was sworn in four days later. Subsequently, for about three years, he took over the work of the judge of the New Jersey district, who had become incapacitated. It is said that only in a single instance were any of his decisions reversed upon appeal to a higher tribunal (*Report of the . . . American Bar Association, post,* p. 532). His reported opinions indicate learning, logical reasoning, and clarity of expression. After the establishment of the circuit courts of appeal in 1891, he was regularly called to sit with its judges when they held sessions in his circuit. He continued performing his duties almost to the last, dying in his native city after less than a week's illness. He was never married.

[C. M. R. Carter, *John Redington . . . with Notes on the Wales Family* (1909); *Obit. Record Grads. Yale Univ., 1890–1900* (1900); *Hist. and Biog. Encyc. of Del.* (1882); *3–6 Houston's Del. Reports*; *Report of the . . . Am. Bar Asso.* (1897); "Leonard Eugene Wales" (1898), in *Hist. and Biog. Papers of the Hist. Soc. of Del.,* vol. III; *Every Evening: Wilmington Daily Commercial,* Feb. 9, 1897.]   C. S. L.

WALKE, HENRY (Dec. 24, 1808–Mar. 8, 1896), naval officer, was born on his father's plantation, "The Ferry," in Princess Anne County, Va., the son of Anthony and Susan (Carmichael) Walke, and a descendant of Thomas Walke who came from Barbados to Virginia in 1662. His father, a graduate of Yale College and former diplomatic agent to Algiers, settled with his family at Chillicothe, Ohio, in 1811. Henry attended the local academy, and on Feb. 1, 1827, entered the navy as a midshipman. During his early cruising he was at sea in two hurricanes, one in the *Natchez* in 1827, and another in the *Ontario* in 1829 in which he showed characteristic courage by leading men aloft to furl a topsail. He was made a lieutenant in 1839, sailed around the world in the *Boston,* 1840–43, and in the Mexican War was executive of the bomb-brig *Vesuvius,* participating in operations against Vera Cruz, Alvarado, Tuxpan, and Tabasco. Just before the Civil War he commanded the storeship *Supply* at Pensacola, and after the seizure of the Pensacola Navy Yard by the South, on Jan. 12, 1861, he entered under a flag of truce and took its garrison and non-combatants to New York. Though obviously justifiable, this action involved leaving his station and violation of orders. He was court-martialed, but the sentence "to be admonished" was very lightly imposed.

In September 1861, he joined Commodore

Foote's flotilla on the upper Mississippi, and served during the next two years with great energy and distinction. Commanding the gunboat *Tyler* in the autumn of 1861, he was frequently under fire in reconnaissance work, and on Nov. 7 with the *Tyler* and *Lexington* effectively covered transport and troop movements in Grant's operation against Belmont. He was shifted to the *Carondelet* in January 1862 and participated in the attack on Fort Henry, Tennessee River, on Feb. 6. Without returning to the base at Cairo, he then proceeded in advance to the next point of attack, Fort Donelson, Cumberland River, and on Feb. 13 carried on alone a six-hour bombardment that, in his opinion, did more damage than the attack of the four ironclads, including his own, next day. His most celebrated exploit was the subsequent running of the batteries at Island No. 10, an operation which he alone favored in the preliminary council, eagerly volunteered for, and, after thorough preparation, executed successfully on the stormy night of Apr. 4. This was "one of the most daring and dramatic events of the war" (A. T. Mahan, *The Gulf and Inland Waters*, 1883, p. 34). The *Carondelet*, with the *Pittsburg* under Egbert Thompson [*q.v.*], rendered invaluable service in covering the army's passage of the river below. The personnel of both vessels received official thanks, and General Pope wrote warmly of Walke's "thorough and brilliant" cooperation (*War of the Rebellion: Official Records, Navy*, XXII, 724). The *Carondelet* was also conspicuous in engagements with the Confederate flotilla above Fort Pillow, May 10, at Memphis, June 6, and in the hard running fight with the ram *Arkansas* in the Yazoo River, July 15.

Walke became a captain, though only after reconsidered action, on July 16, 1862. In command of the new ironclad *Lafayette*, February–August 1863, he fought under Porter in the passing of the Vicksburg batteries on Apr. 16, the five-hour action at Grand Gulf, Apr. 29, and subsequent operations until the fall of Vicksburg. From September 1863 to August 1865 he commanded the *Sacramento* in the Atlantic in pursuit of Confederate raiders, and held the *Rappahannock* blockaded at Calais for fifteen months. He was made commodore in 1866; commanded the Mound City Naval Station, 1868–69; became rear admiral in 1870; and retired in 1871. His home thereafter was in Brooklyn, N. Y. He was thrice married, to Sara J. Aim, Jane Ellen Burges, and Julia Reed, the last of whom with two sons and two daughters survived him. His skill in painting, which he cultivated in later years, is evidenced by a number of pictures, in-cluding the sketches that illustrate his *Naval Scenes and Reminiscences of the Civil War* (1877). This book, while historically valuable, is contentious in tone, emphasizing his war service, which he felt was inadequately recognized in his post-war assignments. He asserted in an appeal to President Grant that he had "fought more for his country than any other officer in the navy" (Personnel Files, Navy Library). The statement seems almost justified by his gunboat record and his eager exploitation of every opportunity for fighting.

[Sources cited in the text; *Officers of the Army and Navy (Regular) Who Served in the Civil War* (1892), ed. by W. H. Powell, Edward Shippen; L. R. Hamersly, *The Records of Living Officers of the U. S. Navy* . . . (4th ed., 1890); "The Walke Family of Lower Norfolk County," *Va. Mag. of Hist. and Biog.*, Oct. 1897; *Court Martial of Commander Henry Walke, U. S. N.* (1861); obits. in *Mil. Order of Loyal Legion of U. S., Commandery . . . of N. Y., Circular no. 2*, series of 1896–99; *N. Y. Herald*, Mar. 7, 9, 1896.]   A. W—t.

WALKER, ALEXANDER (Oct. 13, 1818–Jan. 24, 1893), journalist and author, was born in Fredericksburg, Va., the son of Alexander and Susan Walker. His father was a merchant. The boy attended Fredericksburg Academy, and, after a brief experience teaching school, entered the University of Virginia in 1836. Here he studied ancient languages, mathematics, and natural philosophy. He was out the next year, but returned to study law during the session of 1838–39. In 1840 he opened a law office in New Orleans, during the heat of the Harrison-Van Buren campaign. He at once offered his services to the Democratic leaders and made many speeches in the campaign. He was later a member of nearly all the ante-bellum Democratic conventions. Indeed, his interest in politics and journalism prevented his law practice from becoming extensive. He became one of the managers of the *Jeffersonian* of New Orleans, the chief Democratic organ of the state. In 1842 he married Mary Elizabeth McFarlane, daughter of Dr. James S. McFarlane, head of the Marine Hospital in New Orleans. By appointment of Governor Johnson, he was judge of the city court in New Orleans from 1846 to 1850.

Walker was a firm believer in "manifest destiny" and heartily sympathized with those who were seeking to unite all the countries of the continent into one nation. In 1845 he urged the annexation of Texas; he was one of the supporters of the noted filibuster, William Walker [*q.v.*], and in 1851 he was a backer of the disastrous expedition of Gen. Narciso Lopez to Cuba. During the Mexican War he was connected with the *New Orleans Daily Delta*. In 1852 the *Delta* office published his *City Digest*.

His unsigned account of the yellow fever epidemic in New Orleans appeared in *Harper's Magazine* in November 1853. From 1855 to 1857 he edited the *Cincinnati Enquirer,* then the leading Democratic paper in the West. In 1856 he published *Jackson and New Orleans,* a very full account of the achievements of Jackson and the American army in 1814–15. Four years later he added a chapter to this book and changed its title to *The Life of Andrew Jackson* (1860); in this form it was reissued in 1866 and again in 1890. From Cincinnati he went to Washington, D. C., but after a short stay returned in 1858 to New Orleans and the *Daily Delta.*

He was a member of the Louisiana secession convention in 1861 and was subsequently with Gen. Albert Sidney Johnston's army in Tennessee; he wrote a graphic account of the battle of Shiloh, which appeared in the *Delta* and in H. C. Clarke's *Diary of the War for Separation* (1862). When New Orleans was captured he was sent for a short time as a prisoner to Ship Island. After the surrender of Lee at Appomattox he returned to New Orleans. With Henry J. Labatt he compiled a work called *The Bankrupt Law* (1867). He edited the *New Orleans Times* until its suspension by Judge E. H. Durell [*q.v.*] during the controversy between Henry Clay Warmoth and P. B. S. Pinchback [*qq.v.*] over the governorship in 1872; he then helped establish the *Herald,* which was merged with the *Daily Picayune* in 1874. He continued to edit the *Picayune* until 1875. Thereafter, although not again an editor, he was a frequent contributor to the daily press. He wrote on New Orleans duels, on the Myra Clark Gaines case, and on other matters of local history and tradition. In 1884 he contributed to the *Times-Democrat* a series of articles on General Butler in New Orleans. He wrote zestfully, with a fluent style. Journalism was his chief interest, his social inclinations enabling him to get a peculiarly rich satisfaction out of newspaper experiences. He died, survived by two sons, at the home of the younger, in Fort Smith, Ark.

[Univ. of Va. alumni records; *Univ. of Va. . . . with Biog. Sketches* (1904); obituaries in the *Daily Picayune* and *Times-Democrat,* both of New Orleans, Jan. 25, 1893; information from the librarian of the Wallace Library, Fredericksburg, Va.]   R. P. M.

WALKER, AMASA (May 4, 1799–Oct. 29, 1875), business man, economist, congressman, was born in Woodstock, Conn., the son of Walter and Priscilla (Carpenter) Walker, and a descendant of Samuel Walker of Lynn, Mass., who came to New England about 1630. His childhood was spent in Brookfield, Mass., to which place his parents moved not long after his birth.

Here he attended the district school and worked on the farm—or for the card manufacturers of Leicester at seventy-five cents a week—until he was fifteen years old, when he became a clerk in a country store. During the next six years he varied this employment by farm work, by teaching, and by an attempt to prepare for Amherst College which failed because of his frail health. At twenty-one, with a partner, he purchased a store in West Brookfield, but three years later sold his share in the small business and became an agent for the Methuen Manufacturing Company. His next move carried him to Boston, where in 1825 he established a boot-and-shoe store with Charles G. Carleton, whose sister Emeline he married on July 6, 1826. Her death occurred two years later, and on June 23, 1834, he married Hannah Ambrose of Concord, N. H. To this marriage three children were born.

While he was extending his business southward and westward from Boston, Walker's attention was drawn to the railroad as the coming means of transportation. In a series of articles published in the *Boston Daily Advertiser and Patriot* in 1835, under the signature "South Market Street," he urged the building of a railroad to connect Boston and Albany; he was also one of a committee to visit Albany in order to induce the citizens of that city to build their end of such a road. Four years later, on a trip to the West, he presented to audiences in St. Louis and Alton, Ill., the desirability of a railroad connecting Boston with the Mississippi River, but his suggestion that the time would come when a man might travel from Boston to St. Louis eating and sleeping on the train provoked only mirth.

In 1840, being now provided with a modest livelihood despite heavy losses in the panic of 1837, he retired from business, partly because of ill health but also because he wished to devote his time to study and to public service. The first months after his retirement were spent in Florida in search of health, but for the most part the years which followed were crowded with activities. In 1842 he visited Oberlin College, which he had helped to found, and for seven years thereafter, at irregular intervals and without remuneration, he lectured at Oberlin on political economy. From 1853 to 1860 he was an examiner in political economy at Harvard, and from 1860 to 1869 he lectured at Amherst College.

Walker's special interest in the field of economics was the monetary system, to which he had turned his attention after the panic of 1837. In 1857 he published in *Hunt's Merchants' Maga-*

zine and Commercial Review a series of articles on the subject, which also appeared in pamphlet form as *The Nature and Uses of Money and Mixed Currency* (1857). The panic of 1857 gave him an opportunity to put his opinions to practical test. When the business men of Boston agreed to maintain specie payment in that city Walker argued that it could not be done for more than two weeks and that the tightening of credit necessitated by the effort would result in the ruin of many business houses. His proposal that the suspension should take place at once met with shocked opposition; but twelve days later, after a number of failures, suspension was forced upon the Boston banks. The publicity which this episode gained brought him much into demand as a speaker on currency problems. His most considerable publication, *The Science of Wealth: A Manual of Political Economy* (1866), was widely read and in 1876 was quoted by Walker's son, Francis Amasa Walker [*q.v.*], in his better-known work, *The Wages Question* (pp. 141, 231). Amasa Walker's qualifications for the authorship of his treatise he described as "a practical knowledge of business and banking affairs generally, and a most earnest and persistent search for the truth in all matters appertaining to my favorite science" (*Science of Wealth*), p. ix).

In politics, Walker was successively a Clay protectionist, a member of the Anti-Masonic party, a Democrat, a Free-Soiler, and a Republican. In 1848 he was elected to the Massachusetts House of Representatives and was the candidate of Free-Soilers and Democrats for speaker. The next autumn he entered the state Senate. In 1851 and 1852 he was secretary of state of Massachusetts, and the following year he served as chairman of the committee on suffrage of the constitutional convention of the state. In 1859 he was chosen for a second term in the state House of Representatives, where he assisted in revising the Massachusetts banking laws. Elected as a Republican to fill a vacancy in Congress (Dec. 1, 1862–Mar. 3, 1863), he joined in the monetary debates of that body and throughout the remainder of his life, both in his private correspondence and in articles in periodicals, he frequently expressed his views on monetary questions, especially his belief in the need for contraction of the currency.

During the years after his retirement from business Walker lived in the Brookfield residence which had belonged to his father. He was president of the Boston Temperance Society in 1839; ten years earlier he had been a founder and the first secretary of the Boston Lyceum. Though warmly attached to the anti-slavery cause, he insisted that reform must be accomplished by constitutional means. His heart was also enlisted in the cause of world peace and as vice-president he attended the International Peace Congress held in England in 1844 and the Paris Congress of 1849.

[Holmes Ammidown, *Hist. Colls.* (1874), vol. II; F. A. Walker, *Memoir of Hon. Amasa Walker, LL.D.* (1888), repr. from *New-Eng. Hist. and Geneal. Reg.*, Apr. 1888; *New-Eng. Hist. and Geneal. Reg.*, Jan. 1898; J. P. Munroe, *A Life of Francis Amasa Walker* (1923); D. H. Hurd, *Hist. of Worcester County, Mass.* (1889); *Biog. Dir. Am. Cong.* (1928); *Boston Transcript*, Oct. 29, 1875; Hugh McCulloch Papers, vol. III, Lib. of Cong.]   E. D.

WALKER, ASA (Nov. 13, 1845–Mar. 7, 1916), naval officer, son of Asa T. and Louisa (Morrell) Walker, was born in Portsmouth, N. H. He entered the United States Naval Academy, then temporarily located at Newport, R. I., Nov. 27, 1862. The following summer as a midshipman on the *Macedonian* he cruised for four months off the coast of Spain and northern Africa in vain pursuit of the Confederate cruiser *Alabama*, which was never sighted. In 1866 he was graduated and was sent on a voyage to the East Indies on the *Sacramento*, which was wrecked in the Bay of Bengal, June 19, 1867, at the mouth of the Sambalding River but without loss of life. Walker's subsequent service included a number of long voyages in Asiatic waters, where he acquired a wide reputation for his skill as a navigator. In 1883 he sailed as navigating officer of the *Trenton*, which had just been fitted out with a complete installation of electric lights, probably the first warship in the world to be so equipped. He spent four tours of duty at the Naval Academy, as assistant in mathematics (1873–74, 1879–83), head of the department of astronomy, navigation, and surveying (1886–90), and head of the department of mathematics (1893–97). His *Navigation* (1888) was used as a textbook at the Naval Academy for many years.

On May 23, 1897, Walker, then a commander, was given command of the *Concord*. On this vessel he transported a heavy load of ammunition from Mare Island to Dewey's squadron off Yokohama, joining him on Feb. 9, 1898, and participating in all the further movements of the fleet. When Commodore Dewey arrived off the coast of Luzon, Philippine Islands, Walker in the *Concord*, supported by the *Boston*, proceeded at full speed and reconnoitered Subig Bay. On Apr. 30 Walker reported that there were no Spanish ships in the vicinity, and on the morning of May 1 Dewey in his flagship, the *Olympia*, steamed into Manila Bay with his fleet. The *Concord* was the fifth in line. In the battle which followed, the *Concord* shelled and destroyed the Spanish transport, *Mindanao*. Walker also assisted in the later operations leading up to the capture of the city of Manila. Throughout the campaign Dewey reposed the fullest confidence in Walker's skill and judgment. On June 10, 1898, he was advanced nine numbers in grade "for eminent and conspicuous conduct" in the battle of Manila Bay.

Walker was promoted to the rank of captain in 1899, and was given duty at the Naval War College (1899–1900) and on the naval examining board (1900–05), as a member of the naval general board. Finally he was made superintendent of the Naval Observatory (1906–07), his last service. He was commissioned rear admiral in 1906, and was retired for age, Nov. 13, 1907. His remaining years were passed quietly at his home at Annapolis, Md. He lived to become the last surviving commander who fought under Dewey at Manila Bay. Walker married Ruth Leavitt Brooks of Portsmouth, N. H., on Dec. 16, 1867. By her he had a daughter who died in childhood and a son. His wife died, Jan. 31, 1877, and on June 11, 1890, he married Arabella W. Grant of Frankfort, Ky., who died in 1927.

[*Who's Who in America*, 1914–15; *Autobiog. of George Dewey* (1913); "The Battle of Manila Bay," *Century Mag.*, Aug. 1898; *Army and Navy Jour.*, Aug. 24, 1867, Mar. 11, 1916; ann. registers, and materials in the superintendent's office, U. S. Naval Acad.; archives in office of naval records, U. S. Navy Dept.; obituaries in *Evening Capital* (Annapolis, Md.), and *Sun* (Baltimore), Mar. 8, 1916; information concerning the family from Dr. W. D. Walker, Walker's son.]

L. H. B.

WALKER, MADAME C. J. [See WALKER, SARAH BREEDLOVE, 1865–1919].

WALKER, DAVID (Sept. 28, 1785–June 28, 1830), negro leader, was born in Wilmington, N. C., of a free mother and a slave father. His status was that of a free man and in his youth he traveled widely in the South. At an early age he acquired a deep and bitter sympathy with the enslaved members of his race and in his wide reading, particularly in historical works, he sought parallels to the American negro's situation in the enslavement and oppression of ancient peoples. Some time before 1827 he went to Boston where he established a second-hand clothing business on Brattle Street. In 1829 there appeared the work for which he is best known, an octavo pamphlet of seventy-six pages entitled *Walker's Appeal in four articles together with a Preamble to the Colored Citizens of the World, but in particular and very expressly to those of the United States of America*. The text of the appeal was a closely reasoned, eloquent and occasionally rhetorical argument against slavery.

The author called upon the colored people to rise against their oppressors and to resort to whatever violence might be necessary, but, at the same time, he counseled forgiveness of the past if the slaveholders would let their victims go.

The *Appeal* was calculated to stir up the suppressed race to mob and race violence by its forceful, primitive, emotional tone, but, on the other hand it contained a religious and prophetic vein that pled with the slaveholders to repent of their sins while there was still time, since the wrath of God must surely overwhelm them otherwise. Many anti-slavery leaders and free negroes rejected Walker's policy of violence and he circulated his pamphlets at his own expense. His courage and sincerity could possibly have served his cause more effectively had he adopted other tactics, but his course at least testifies to the strength of these two characteristics. A second edition of the pamphlet appeared in 1830 and penetrated the South to spread consternation there among the slaveholders, especially in the seaboard slave states, where incoming ships were searched for it. In a single day after a copy was discovered in Georgia the legislature rushed through a law that made "the circulation of pamphlets of evil tendency among our domestics" a capital offense. A price was set on Walker's head in the South, and the mayor of Savannah wrote with reference to the possible punishment of the author to the mayor of Boston, Harrison Gray Otis [*q.v.*]. The latter replied in a letter (Feb. 10, 1830), a copy of which he sent also to William B. Giles [*q.v.*], governor of Virginia, in which he condemned the tendency of the pamphlet but stated that the author had not made himself amenable to the laws of Massachusetts. True to his expressed intention Walker published a third, revised, and still more militant edition of the pamphlet in March 1830. Three months later he died. It was rumored and widely believed that his death was due to poisoning, but this has never been proved.

In 1828 he was married in Boston to a woman referred to simply as "Miss Eliza ———" in H. H. Garnet's *Walker's Appeal, With a Brief Sketch of His Life* (1848). The only child of the marriage, Edwin G. Walker, born posthumously, was elected in 1866 to the House of Repesentatives of the Massachusetts legislature.

[John Daniels, *In Freedom's Birthplace* (1914); *William Lloyd Garrison, 1805–1879, The Story of His Life*, vol. I (1885); G. W. Williams, *Hist. of the Negro Race in America* (1883), vol. II; S. J. May, *Some Recollections of Our Antislavery Conflict* (1869); *Richmond Enquirer* (Richmond, Va.), Feb. 18, 1830.]   M. G.

WALKER, DAVID (Feb. 19, 1806–Sept. 30, 1879), jurist, son of Jacob Wythe and Nancy

(Hawkins) Walker, was born in what is now Todd County, Ky. His father's ancestors are said to have come to Virginia from Staffordshire, England, about 1650. David was an apt pupil; he began the study of Latin when he was seven, and soon thereafter was reading the classics.

Admitted to the bar in Kentucky in 1829, he went to Little Rock, Ark., in 1830, and shortly afterward settled in Fayetteville. From 1833 to 1835 he served as prosecuting attorney. He was a member of the convention of 1836 which drew up the first state constitution, and there worked to prevent unfair apportionment, advocating that the number of free white males be adopted as the basis of apportionment in order that the slaveholding counties might not dominate the state. In 1840 he was elected to the state Senate as a Whig. Four years later he was nominated for Congress, but was defeated by the matchless campaigner, Archibald Yell [q.v.]. In November 1848, much to his surprise, while on a visit to Kentucky, Walker was elected associate justice of the supreme court of Arkansas by a Democratic legislature over so prominent a Democrat as Elbert H. English [q.v.]. In the presidential election of 1860 he canvassed the state for the Bell and Everett ticket. The following year he was elected to the state convention called to consider the matter of secession. He was made president of the convention and was largely instrumental in preventing secession at that time. When, however, following the bombardment of Fort Sumter, the convention reassembled and voted for secession, Walker appealed to the five opponents to make the vote unanimous. Some raiding Federal soldiers arrested him in 1862, but he was released on taking the oath of allegiance. He served as chief justice of the Arkansas supreme court from 1866 until the state government was reorganized under the Reconstruction Act. Upon the overthrow of the Carpet-bag régime (1874) he was elected associate justice of the supreme court and served until 1878, when he resigned on account of failing health.

He was interested in the economic development of the state and went to Boston in 1870 in an effort to secure a railroad for northern Arkansas. Gov. Augustus H. Garland [q.v.] appointed him delegate to the Centennial Exposition in Philadelphia, where he delivered an address setting forth the natural resources and attractions of his state. His bearing was so dignified and reserved that many thought him unapproachable; yet he had numerous intimate friends. He started fourteen young men on their professional careers by boarding them and teaching them law. He was charitable, giving freely of his store to those

in want, particularly in the short harvest year of 1874. In 1833 he married Jane Lewis Washington of Kentucky, who bore him six sons, two of whom died in infancy, and two daughters. David Shelby Walker [q.v.] was his cousin.

[*Jour. of the Proc. of the Convention Met to Form a Constitution . . . for the People of Ark.* (1836); *Jour. of Both Sessions of the Convention of the State of Ark.* (1861); *Jour. of the House of Representatives . . . of Ark.* (1848); *Ark. Reports,* 1848–54, 1866–68, 1874–78; John Hallum, *Biog. and Pictorial Hist. of Ark.* (1887); Fay Hempstead, *A Pictorial Hist. of Ark.* (1890) and *Hist. Rev. of Ark.* (1911); *Va. Mag. of Hist. and Biog.,* Apr. 1897; D. Y. Thomas, *Ark. in War and Reconstruction, 1861–1874* (1926); *Ark. Gazette* (Little Rock), Oct. 3, 1879; information from Miss Sue Walker, a grand-daughter.]   D. Y. T.

WALKER, DAVID SHELBY (May 2, 1815– July 20, 1891), jurist, governor of Florida, was born near Russellville, Logan County, Ky., the son of David and Mary (Barbour) Walker. His forebears had come to Kentucky from Virginia and had soon risen to prominence in public life. His father represented Fayette County in the Kentucky legislature (1793–96), fought in the War of 1812, and was a member of the federal House of Representatives from 1817 until his death in 1820. David's mother died when he was about six years of age, after which time he lived with his sister at La Grange, Oldham County, Ky., and was educated in private schools. In 1837 he removed to Tallahassee, Fla., where his brother George was living and also his kinsman, Gov. Richard K. Call [q.v.]. Here he studied law in his brother's office, was admitted to the bar, and began the practice of his profession.

With the powerful support of Governor Call, Walker began his political career by representing the seventh district in the first state Senate in 1845, resigning before the completion of his term. In 1848 he was elected mayor of Tallahassee; in 1848–49 he was a representative of Leon County in the state House of Representatives; and in 1850 he was appointed register of public lands and as such became *ex-officio* superintendent of schools, which positions he held until 1859 (Rerick, *post,* I, 221). He was an able and energetic superintendent and is considered the founder of the public-school system of Florida because of his influence in securing the passage of the basic law of 1853 (*Ibid.,* I, 226). Upon the collapse of the Whig party he affiliated with the American party and was its candidate for governor in 1856 (*Ibid.,* II, 230). Although defeated he polled a large vote because of his record as superintendent, and because he advocated lowering the price of public lands. In 1859 he was chosen associate justice of the Florida supreme court (*Ibid.,* II, 89).

Walker opposed the secession of Florida and

during the Civil War devoted himself to his judicial duties. In November 1865 he was elected governor without opposition under the Johnson reconstruction régime, and was inaugurated Dec. 20. He was in ill health and his administration was a troubled one because of numerous conflicts with the commander of the Federal forces in the state. He opposed the bringing of immigrants to Florida on the ground that the negroes had the right to furnish the labor supply, and he advised against the ratification of the Fourteenth Amendment (*Journal of the Senate of the Fourteenth General Assembly of . . . Florida, 1865*). The initiation of the congressional plan of reconstruction in 1867 brought his administration to an end. He was nominated for Congress by the Democrats in August 1868, but declined (Davis, *post*, p. 538). Resuming the practice of law in Tallahassee, he continued in private life until 1879 when, with the end of the Carpet-bag government, he was chosen a judge of the second judicial circuit, which position he held until his death. Throughout his public career he enjoyed a very great measure of popularity, and, notwithstanding the brevity of his term, he is classed as one of the best of the Florida governors. During the last years of his life he made a reputation as an able jurist. Though successful as a lawyer, he died comparatively poor because of his lavish charity. He was twice married: first, May 22, 1842, to Philoclea, daughter of Col. Robert W. Alston, who died May 7, 1868, and second, to Elizabeth Duncan. Of his first marriage there were born three sons and one daughter; of his second, one daughter, all of whom survived him. He was buried in the Episcopal cemetery at Tallahassee. David Walker [*q.v.*] was a cousin.

[Sources include J. A. Groves, *The Alstons and Allstons of North and South Carolina* (1901), incorrect as to date of marriage; R. H. Rerick, *Memoirs of Fla.* (2 vols., 1902); W. W. Davis, *The Civil War and Reconstruction in Fla.* (1913); *Florida Times-Union* (Jacksonville), July 21, 22, 1891; information as to certain facts from Walker's grand-daughter, Evelyn Cockrell, Thomasville, Ga., and from a grand-nephew, C. B. Gwynn, Tallahassee, Fla.; Register of marriages, St. John's Church, Tallahassee; Walker's reports as superintendent of schools, in the journals of the legislature, 1854–58.]   R. S. C.

WALKER, FRANCIS AMASA (July 2, 1840–Jan. 5, 1897), educator, economist, statistician, the son of Amasa Walker [*q.v.*] and Hannah (Ambrose) Walker, was born in Boston. His father's activities as a political economist, patron of education, and persistent advocate of social reforms insured the boy a stimulating home environment and a social direction of thought. Francis matriculated at Amherst College at fifteen, but lost one year because of weak eyes. After obtaining the A.B. degree in 1860,

he spent nine years in such varied activities as studying law (1860–61) in the Worcester office of Charles Devens and George F. Hoar [*qq.v.*], fighting in the Civil War (August 1861–January 1865), teaching Latin and Greek at Williston Seminary in Easthampton (1865–68), and writing editorials for Samuel Bowles's *Springfield Daily Republican* (January 1868–January 1869). He married, on Aug. 16, 1865, Exene Stoughton of Gill, Mass. They had seven children, five sons and two daughters.

The war brought opportunity to shoulder responsibilities beyond his years as an assistant adjutant-general. He rose from private to brevet brigadier-general (Mar. 13, 1865), and despite wounds, imprisonment at Libby, and permanent impairment of health, he closed his military career with an idealized concept of human relationships in warfare. His own *History of the Second Army Corps in the Army of the Potomac* (1886) scarcely mentions him; but his subsequent career showed that his experiences as a young officer had made him, by the age of twenty-four, a mature man possessed of poise and judgment, with a strong sense of the importance of discipline and keen insight into human nature. At the same time he emerged with a fun-loving temperament, although he was capable of truly Jovian wrath, and a personal charm which amounted to genuine magnetism.

In 1866 David A. Wells [*q.v.*] became special commissioner of the revenue and in January 1869 Walker was appointed, first, a special deputy under Wells and, next, chief of the Bureau of Statistics. He reorganized the Bureau along scientific lines, introducing some foreign improvements, and established his reputation as a statistician. He struggled to free the Bureau from dependence upon politics and special interests. In superintending the census of 1870 Walker had to work under the act of 1850, which gave him inadequate authority and in practice substituted party patronage for intelligence as the guiding principle of census-taking. The effect upon the figures, for the South particularly, was disastrous, as Walker was the first to admit. But a decade later, as superintendent of the tenth census (1879–81), working under a new law (1879), he appointed his own staff of enumerators. The scope of this inquiry extended to twenty-two quarto volumes—almost an encyclopedia of population, products, and resources. The work was enthusiastically praised, also bitterly criticized. However, it "immediately established in Europe the reputation of General Walker as a statistician of the highest order" (Dewey, *post*, p. 168). Walker strongly urged that the census bureau be given a permanent organization allowing uninterrupted maintenance of needed services and more skilled enumeration. When funds for Walker's retention as superintendent of the census of 1870 had failed, Grant had made him commissioner of Indian affairs (November 1871–December 1872) in order that he might continue his supervision of the census without pay. He prosecuted his labors on the census, contributing to a *Statistical Atlas of the United States* (1874), and injected common sense and honesty into the administration of Indian affairs (Wright, *post*, pp. 267–68). In 1874 he published *The Indian Question.*

Walker's thorough statistical investigations, together with service as chief of the bureau of awards at the Centennial Exposition in Philadelphia (1876), gave him a tremendous fund of information on the economic and social situation in the United States. The political situation he knew all too well from his necessary contacts with politicians. This equipment, added to his training and natural endowments, helped to make him notable as an economist, educator, and public administrator. As professor of political economy and history in the Sheffield Scientific School of Yale (1873–81) and as president of Massachusetts Institute of Technology (November 1881–January 1897) Walker dared to be a pioneer, abandoning old ideas for new, and stoutly defending his innovations in the comparatively fresh fields of economics and education.

His unceasing demand for a fresh consideration of principles powerfully stimulated the development of economics, and, because of his special combination of humanitarian sympathy with practical realism, he laid significant emphasis on human factors in industry. He became a foremost figure in a new inductive and historical school of economics. Of first importance was his attack upon the wages-fund theory; he showed that wages were not wholly dependent upon the amount of pre-existing capital, but also and more particularly upon the current productivity of labor. Thereafter, economists who did not abandon the theory materially modified it. According to his theory of distribution, which aroused sharp controversy, interest was regulated by a general principle of supply and demand, the profits of the entrepreneur were like rent, and the laborer was left "as the residual claimant to the remaining portion of the product" (J. L. Laughlin, in *Journal of Political Economy,* March 1897, p. 30; see diagram in Walker, *Political Economy,* 1888, p. 254; and critical discussion of his treatment of the entrepreneur in L. H. Haney, *History of Economic Thought,* 1920, p.

613). Competition he firmly believed in as the fundamental basis of economic life. However, he recognized that perfect competition is not attained in practice.

In his fight for the independence of economic thought, Walker's bitterest battle concerned money. He defined money to include banknotes, and everything serving as a medium of exchange. He asserted that the government had the right to declare irredeemable paper legal tender, adding however that governments were not yet wise enough to avoid over-issue, and effectively exposing the inflation fallacy. His adherence to international bimetallism Walker proclaimed when a delegate to the International Monetary Conference of 1878 and he held to the doctrine ever afterward. He declined to go as a delegate to the abortive Brussels Conference of 1892, and as a member of a commission to Europe in 1897, but he remained unflagging in his zeal, preaching everywhere the necessity for broadening the base of the world's money by international agreement for the use of silver with gold. Bryan's claim that the United States could do this alone, Walker strongly denied. He sensed early the sectional animosity which was to rage over the election of 1896, pleaded for tolerance and understanding between creditors and debtors, and tried desperately to offset the free-coinage movement by organizing business men behind international bimetallism. He failed, and suffered denunciation and misrepresentation for his pains.

In his discussion of economic conditions Walker showed to what ridiculous pass the blind acceptance of *laissez-faire* led its worshippers. He advocated a limited reduction of hours of labor from fourteen to ten or eleven for increased efficiency, but he doubted whether an eight-hour law could be applied safely throughout industry and he thought unemployment due chiefly to the effects of world-wide division of labor. Immigration gave him great concern, as causing recourse to such violent laborers' weapons as the boycott, picketing, and sabotage, which he supposed native workmen would not employ. The decreasing native birthrate he ascribed to the "competitive shock" of immigration. Relations between labor and capital seemed to him, in 1888, to have reached an equilibrium which could not be disturbed without threatening public welfare. A classic example of his controversies on economic principles was that with Prof. S. M. MacVane of Harvard, over the wages-fund theory (*Quarterly Journal of Economics,* April 1887, pp. 265–88; April 1888, pp. 263–96).

Walker is said to have become "unquestionably the most prominent and the best known of American writers" in the economic field (F. W. Taussig, quoted in *Springfield Daily Republican*, Jan. 6, 1897, p. 7). His influence extended into England (markedly), Italy, and France, but not far into Germany. As a theoretic economist perhaps he stood higher abroad than at home, where in his lifetime he was considered greater as a statistician and administrator. This was due to three main facts: his public duties deprived him of time for deep study of the economic writings that appeared in his later years; he espoused currency doctrines distasteful to his section and profession in the United States; and he had an innate sense of fairness in controversy which, in spite of his exuberance of speech, made men say they were luckier to have him to disagree with than some men to agree with. This last characteristic was well illustrated in his position on protection. He was a free-trader, partly because he realized that protectionism was incompatible with internationalism; yet the free-traders attacked him because he conceded that the protectionists had established a claim to a hearing. Similarly, cotton, woolen, worsted, and silk manufacturers urged him for membership upon the tariff commission of 1882, while lumber protectionists objected.

Walker's crowning work was in the field of education. He shouldered the burden of technical education at a difficult time and won for it public recognition. He increased the enrollment of Massachusetts Institute of Technology from 302 to 1198, and its buildings from one to four, adding much expensive laboratory equipment and five new departmental courses. Most important, "he knew young men, he rejoiced in young men, and his knowledge was power over them and power in them" (Tyler, *post*, p. 64). He had vigor and enthusiasm left over for the advancing of strenuous educational reforms. College subjects should be pursued seriously, he thought, as a valued occupation rather than as an excuse for prolongation of childhood. From the first, the laboratory method should be employed as much as possible, in order to maintain interest and a sense of responsibility in pupils of mechanical trend as well as in those of retentive memory. Technical schools should give grounding in history and political science to broaden pupils' understanding beyond their special fields; and these schools should maintain separate identities in order to free them from arrogant attitudes on the part of classical associates. He stood out against absorption of the Institute by Harvard. So loyal was he that he declined several more lucrative openings in other institutions. By his ardent advocacy of educational reforms he spread

democratic doctrines of learning and teaching far beyond the walls of Massachusetts Institute of Technology, serving on school committees, on boards of education, and as college trustee. He set the Institute on a solid basis of permanent usefulness.

Upon his death the *Springfield Daily Republican* (Jan. 6, 1897) said that "in him the sense of life abounded." This vitality, coupled with unselfishness and loyalty, gave him special usefulness as an active public citizen. He continually served his community upon time-taking committees and commissions, and he served many groups and causes removed from Boston; a partial list of his affiliations fills nearly five pages in his biography. Such service is too pervasive to be measured accurately.

Walker lectured widely at colleges and universities, and before special groups such as the National Academy of Science (vice-president, 1891–97), the American Economic Association (president, 1885–92), and the American Statistical Association (president, 1882–97). Leading periodicals published these lectures or comments upon them if they were controversial. His most significant conclusions appeared in book form, the chief being *The Wages Question* (1876); *Money* (1878); *Money in Its Relation to Trade and Industry* (1879); *Land and its Rent* (1883); *Political Economy* (1883), a textbook of many editions and revisions; and *International Bimetallism* (1896). To this output were added his reports as president of M.I.T. and in other official capacities and a continuous stream of magazine and newspaper articles, letters, and rejoinders, covering a wide field of public affairs. His *Discussions in Economics and Statistics* (2 vols., 1899), were edited by D. R. Dewey; and his *Discussions in Education* (1899) by J. P. Munroe.

[J. P. Munroe, *A Life of Francis Amasa Walker* (1923), contains a bibliography of his writings and reported addresses. See also D. R. Dewey, "Francis A. Walker as a Public Man," *Rev. of Reviews*, Feb. 1897; J. L. Laughlin, "Francis Amasa Walker," *Jour. of Pol. Economy*, Mar. 1897; H. W. Tyler, "The Educational Work of Francis A. Walker," *Educational Review*, June 1897; C. D. Wright, "Francis Amasa Walker," *Quart. Pubs. Am. Statistical Asso.*, June 1897; *Mass. Inst. of Technology. Meetings Held in Commemoration of . . . Francis Amasa Walker* (1897); Silvanus Hayward, "Gen. Francis A. Walker," *New-Eng. Hist. and Geneal. Register*, Jan. 1898. A few letters have been salvaged by the family and occasional items may be found in the MSS. of W. B. Allison, E. Atkinson, W. E. Chandler, Manton Marble, and John Sherman. Perhaps the best newspaper obituaries appeared in the *Boston Herald* and *Springfield Daily Republican*, Jan. 6, 1897.]

J. P. N.

WALKER, GILBERT CARLTON (Aug. 1, 1832–May 11, 1885), congressman, governor of Virginia, was born in Cuba, Allegany County,

N. Y. (*Binghamton Daily Republican*, May 12, 1885). Self-confident and well prepared in a Binghamton school, he entered Williams College in 1851 but soon withdrew and entered Hamilton College, Clinton, N. Y., where he graduated in 1854. After studying law privately he settled to its practice in 1855, in Owego, Tioga County, N. Y. Two years later he married Olive Evans of Binghamton. From 1859 to 1864 he practised in Chicago. He participated actively in politics but failed of election as district attorney in Tioga County and as corporation counsel in Chicago, for both of which offices the Democrats had nominated him. Like many others, during the Civil War he changed from Douglas Democrat to Unionist.

Early in 1865 he moved to Norfolk, Va., hoping that the climate of that region would be helpful in his fight against tuberculosis, the disease which eventually caused his death. In Norfolk business enterprises engaged him, notably the Exchange National Bank of which he was organizer and president. Soon, however, natural inclination and the advantage of being a Carpet-bagger took him into Reconstruction politics. Though defeated for the Virginia constitutional convention of 1867, he was of great service to the state—through influential friendships in Washington—in having the new constitution adopted without its most radical and most objectionable provision, that disfranchising all who having held office under the United States had aided the "rebellion." Important native business men and politicians, including William Mahone [*q.v.*], arranged for his nomination for the governorship by the "True Republican" faction and for the retirement of the "Bourbon," or Democratic, candidate in favor of him as a "Conservative." In 1869, accordingly, he canvassed the state against Gen. H. H. Wells, the candidate of the "Radicals," or Republicans, and of certain important railroad interests. Men noted that Walker was handsome, dignified in public, affable in private, a ready and pleasing speaker though not an orator, and "not a Yanky; he don't look like one" (letter cited in Blake, *post*, p. 107 n.). The immediate outcome was the restoration of Virginia to the Union under "Conservative" auspices, for which he was long acclaimed "savior of the state." As governor for somewhat over four years (1869–74), Walker advocated strict enforcement of law and order and scrupulous compliance with the spirit of the new national enactments with respect to the civil and political equality of the freedmen. This stand brought him further credit and applause. He proposed also the funding of the state's huge debt upon

terms very hard for the state and the transfer of the state's very large interests in transportation companies to private hands for what they would bring; and both policies became law through his management of the negro vote in the legislature (Pearson, *post*, ch. 3). It was currently believed that in both these transactions he profited personally (Blake, p. 136 n.), and his fiscal schemes almost immediately proved unworkable. Moreover, Capitol gossip long had it that he was given to reckless dissipation. Nevertheless, he was representative in Congress from the Richmond district for two terms (1875–79). He then returned to his native state, where he was once more lawyer, politician, and promoter, first in Binghamton, and after 1881 in New York City, where he died. He was buried in the lot owned by his father-in-law in Spring Forest Cemetery, Binghamton.

[H. J. Eckenrode, *The Political Hist. of Va. during the Reconstruction* (1904); C. C. Pearson, *The Readjuster Movement in Va.* (1917); N. M. Blake, *William Mahone* (1935); *Biog. Dir. Am. Cong.* (1928); *Messages and Official Papers of Hon. G. C. Walker, Gov. of Va.* (1871), copy in Va. State Lib.; obituaries in *The State* (Richmond), *Richmond Dispatch, Binghamton Daily Republican*, and *N. Y. Times*, May 12, 1885; memoranda from Binghamton Public Library.]

C. C. P.

WALKER, HENRY OLIVER (May 14, 1843–Jan. 14, 1929), portrait, figure, and mural painter, son of Thomas Oliver and Sarah Lucy Walker, was born in Boston, Mass. After a common-school education he engaged in commercial pursuits until 1879, when he made the inevitable flight to Paris. He studied for three years as a pupil of Léon Bonnat, and then returned to Boston and opened a studio. A successful exhibition in 1883 served to make his work known; thereafter he was busily employed in portrait painting. Soon he turned his attention to ideal figure subjects, and made his first essays in decorative work. About 1889 he moved to New York. On Apr. 19, 1888, he was married to Laura Margaret, daughter of John P. Marquand. They established their home at Lakewood, N. J.; in later years they had summer homes at Cornish, N. H., and Belmont, Mass. In New York Walker continued to paint portraits, but he also produced some excellent ideal pictures, and he now had opportunities to make mural decorations, a specialty in which he soon made his mark. Among his ideal paintings are "Boy and Muse," in the William T. Evans collection; "Narcissus," in the Boston Museum of Fine Arts; "Girl and Kitten," in the Thomas B. Clarke collection; and "A Morning Vision," in the Metropolitan Museum, New York. The "Portrait of Mrs. Evans and Son," which came to the National Gallery of Art with the other works from the Evans collection, is noteworthy.

His mural decorations for public buildings must be placed first among his achievements. His Library of Congress paintings, "Joy and Memory" and "Lyric Poetry" (one large tympanum and six small tympani in one of the corridors), are among the most decorative and poetic of the many mural works in the library. The two historical paintings in the Massachusetts State House, the "Pilgrims on the Mayflower" and "John Eliot Preaching to the Indians," in the nature of the case are less interesting from a decorative point of view, and less personal and spontaneous than the Washington work. The large square panel in the Appellate Court House, New York, is a handsome allegory entitled "The Wisdom of the Law," with eleven figures, well composed and pleasing in color, but the symbolism is somewhat far-fetched. The motive of the lunette in the Minnesota Capitol is "Yesterday, Today and Tomorrow." Other murals by Walker are in the Essex County Court House, Newark, N. J. Walker was a member of the National Academy (1902), the National Society of Mural Painters, and of numerous other societies. He won many prizes and medals. He died in Belmont, Mass., in his eighty-sixth year.

[*Who's Who in America*, 1910–11; Pauline King, *Am. Mural Painting* (1902); Herbert Small, *Handbook of the New Lib. of Cong.* (1901); *Am. Art Ann.*, 1923–24; cats. of the Thomas B. Clarke coll., 1899, and the W. T. Evans coll., 1901; obituaries in *Am. Art Ann.*, 1929, and *N. Y. Times*, Jan. 15, 1929.]   W. H. D.

WALKER, JAMES (Aug. 16, 1794–Dec. 23, 1874), clergyman and college president, was born in what was a part of Woburn, now Burlington, Mass., the son of James Walker, commissioned major-general by President Adams in 1798, and of Lucy (Johnson) Walker, a descendant of Edward Johnson, 1598–1672 [*q.v.*]. Prepared for college at the school at Groton, Mass., afterward Lawrence Academy, he graduated from Harvard College in 1814. After assisting Benjamin Abbot at Phillips Exeter Academy for a year, he studied divinity at Cambridge under Henry Ware and received his license to preach on May 15, 1817. He accepted the call of the Harvard Church in Charlestown and was ordained on Apr. 15, 1818. In the controversy between the Trinitarians and Unitarians he immediately became a leader among the "liberals." He was an organizer of the American Unitarian Association in 1825, and he contributed to the *American Unitarian Tracts* and to *The Christian Examiner*, which he edited from 1831 to 1839. On Dec. 21, 1829, he married Catherine Bartlett, the daughter of George Bartlett of Charlestown. They had no children. In July 1839 he resigned his pulpit to become Alford Professor of Natural Religion, Moral Philosophy and Civil Polity at Harvard. In 1853 he became president of the university. His administration was competent but uneventful; when he intended to retire in 1858 the faculty unanimously requested that he remain, on the grounds of public duty. In 1860 he resigned on the plea of advancing years.

Though a theological liberal in the 1820's, he was temperamentally conservative and cautious. He kept clear of all reform agitations, regarded Theodore Parker as a "phenomenon," and made it a rule never to preach about anything until people in the omnibus had stopped talking about it. He was an erudite but not original mind. His pamphlet, "Philosophy of Man's Spiritual Nature in Regard to the Foundations of Faith," in the *American Unitarian Tracts* (1 Ser., No. 87, 1834) was eagerly seized upon by young Transcendentalists for its assertion "that, to a rightly constituted and fully developed soul, moral and spiritual truth will be revealed with a degree of intuitive clearness, and certainty, equal at least to that of the objects of sense" (p. 19). However, in such a passage he was simply repelling scepticism by the argument that innate faculties exist in the soul for the apprehension of spiritual truth; he was following implicitly the lead of the Scotch Realists, from whom he derived almost his entire thought. In 1849 he edited Dugald Stewart's *Philosophy of the Active and Moral Powers* and in 1850 Thomas Reid's *Essays on the Intellectual Powers of Man.* Drawing upon these sources, he became the preeminent expounder of the metaphysics of early nineteenth century Unitarianism, of a commonsense rationalism combined with a simple piety and a lofty ethical tone. Thoroughly provincial, he traveled out of New England only twice, to deliver ordination sermons in Baltimore and in Cincinnati. He was devoid of esthetic interests, his sermons are closely knit but sententious. His contemporaries sometimes complained that he lacked decision, which they attributed to his faculty for seeing all sides of all questions; but he won their affection and respect by his apparent sincerity, his dialectical powers, his great physical vitality, above all by his handsome and commanding presence, which they thought similar to Webster's. His last years he spent in Cambridge, an honored and dignified figure. He published *Sermons Preached in the Chapel of Harvard College* in 1861, and another collection was issued after his death, *Reason, Faith, and*

Duty (1876). He left his library and $15,000 to Harvard.

[*Addresses at the Inauguration of the Rev. James Walker* (1853); W. O. White, "Introduction," to *Reason, Faith, and Duty, ante*; Joseph Lovering, "Memoir," *Amer. Acad. of Arts and Sciences Proc.*, vol. X (1875), pp. 485–95; H. W. Foote, *The Wisdom from Above, Sermon Preached at King's Chapel, Sunday, Jan. 3, 1875* (1875); *Mass. Hist. Soc. Proc.*, 1 Ser., vol. XIII (1875), 2 Ser., vol. VI (1891); C. A. Bartol, "The Great Man and the Little Child," *Unitarian Review*, Feb. 1875; *Hist. of the Harvard Church in Charlestown, 1815–1879* (1879), pp. 164–207 for bibliography of Walker's publications; *Services at the Dedication of a Mural Monument to James Walker* (1884); *Boston Evening Transcript*, Dec. 28, 1874; *Boston Daily Advertiser*, Dec. 26, 1874; the manuscript catalogue of Walker's library, Widener Lib., Harvard University.]   P.M.

WALKER, JAMES BARR (July 29, 1805–Mar. 6, 1887), clergyman, editor, and author of theological works, was born in Philadelphia, the son of James and Margaret (Barr) Walker; his father died before the child's birth. In his infancy his mother moved with her family to a frontier farm near Pittsburgh, and, after a little schooling, James was apprenticed to learn printing. Subsequently, finding no employment in Pittsburgh, he walked to Philadelphia and obtained work in printing-shops there; later he was similarly employed in New York City, and for a time he taught school at New Durham, N. J. On business for an uncle he went to Ravenna, Ohio, where he bought a half-interest in the *Western Courier* and began the practice of law. In the late twenties, apparently, he entered Western Reserve College, then at Hudson, Ohio, where he had an intense religious experience and was fired by Theodore D. Weld [*q.v.*] with abolitionist enthusiasm. Leaving college after about a year to become an agent for the American Bible Society, he traveled over western Ohio, which was then just being settled. On June 6, 1833, he married Rebecca, daughter of Thomas Randall of Bridgewater, Mass. For the two years following he conducted a religious paper at Hudson, but opposition to his anti-slavery views caused him to sell it. After a little theological study he was ordained, Sept. 21, 1837, by the Presbytery of Portage, and became pastor of the Presbyterian Church at Akron, Ohio, which he served for two years.

In 1839 he moved to Cincinnati, to publish the book which gave him fame, *The Philosophy of the Plan of Salvation*. It was issued in 1841, anonymously, and by 1855, when it appeared in a fifth enlarged edition, still anonymously, it had sold over twenty thousand copies, was being extensively used as a textbook in the United States, and had been published in England and Scotland and translated into French, German, Italian, Welsh, and Hindustani. The book held its position until the 1870's, the later printings bearing Walker's name. The appeal of this treatise on Christian apologetics lay in its original method and in its clear, untechnical language.

In 1840 Walker established in Cincinnati a religious paper, *The Watchman of the Valley*. His anti-slavery views and his Oberlin theology aroused hostility, but despite advice to leave the city he continued the paper until 1842. He then became pastor of the Congregational Church in Mansfield, Ohio, which, composed chiefly of abolitionists and temperance reformers, flourished under his leadership. In 1846 he organized in Chicago another religious paper, *The Herald of the Prairies*. After managing this for four years he was recalled to the Mansfield Church and served it until 1857, leaving to take charge of the Congregational Church of Sandusky, Ohio.

Having accumulated independent means, in 1863 he left Sandusky to live at Mansfield. From 1859 to 1865 he was a lecturer in Chicago Theological Seminary. For a Christian college in a Christian community, on the Oberlin model, he bought a large tract in Benzie County, Mich., and after two years spent in preparation for the enterprise, he took up his residence at Benzonia, where for five years he lived in frontier conditions. He was a member of the Michigan Senate in the session of 1865. Because of financial mismanagement he left the community, giving his lands for educational purposes. In 1870 he became professor of intellectual and moral philosophy and belles-lettres in Wheaton College, Wheaton, Ill., and in 1871, pastor of the Congregational Church there. At Wheaton he lived until his death, serving the church until 1880 and teaching until 1884. His first wife died in 1875 and on Apr. 3, 1876, he married Mary A. (Myrtle) Weamer, widow of Capt. George Weamer of Norwalk, Ohio. He had no children, but reared in his home thirteen orphans. He published several other theological books, which sold largely but were not as popular as his first, and in 1881, *Experiences of Pioneer Life in the Early Settlements and Cities of the West*, an autobiography.

[In addition to the *Experiences*, see W. L. Chaffin, *A Biog. Hist. of Robert Randall and His Descendants* (1919); *Congregational Year-Book* (1888); *Advance* (Chicago), Mar. 17, 1887; *Congregationalist* (Boston), Mar. 17, 1887; *Chicago Tribune*, Mar. 9, 1887.]
                                    R. H. N.

WALKER, JOHN BRISBEN (Sept. 10, 1847–July 7, 1931), publisher, was born at the country home of his parents, John and Anna (Krepps) Walker, on the Monongahela River near Pittsburgh, Pa. After attending Gonzaga

College in Washington, D. C., he entered Georgetown College, but left after two years to accept in 1865 an appointment to the United States Military Academy at West Point. In 1868, having resigned from the Military Academy, he accompanied the new minister, John Ross Browne [q.v.], to China, where he served as a military adviser during the reorganization of the Chinese military service. Returning to America in 1870, he engaged in the manufacture of iron in the Kanawha Valley in West Virginia, and in four or five years estimated his holdings at half a million dollars. He was engaged in the construction of a large blast furnace when he lost all his property in the financial panic of the seventies. Turning to journalism, he wrote a series of articles on the mineral industries for Murat Halstead's *Cincinnati Commercial* which led to his appointment as the managing editor of the *Pittsburgh Telegraph* in 1876 and three months later to a similar position on the *Washington Chronicle*. In 1879, the *Chronicle* having been discontinued, Walker purchased sixteen hundred acres of land near Denver, Colo., and developed a highly successful alfalfa ranch. He also bought and reclaimed over five hundred lots of bottom land in Denver. Selling both the ranch and the Denver lots at a large profit, he returned to the East and in 1889 bought the expiring *Cosmopolitan Magazine* from Joseph N. Hallock. In five years he had increased the circulation from 16,000 to 400,000 and had made the *Cosmopolitan* one of a great triumvirate of inexpensive but good American illustrated magazines. He quickly followed the example of McClure in going to fifteen cents in 1893, and two years later joined Frank A. Munsey and McClure at the ten-cent level. The *Cosmopolitan* was one of the pioneers in bringing the popular magazine into close touch with current affairs. Walker was both publisher and editor, though he was aided for varying periods by such distinguished associates as W. D. Howells, H. H. Boyesen, A. S. Hardy [q.v.], and others. He was the first president of the American Periodical Publishers' Association. In 1905 he sold the *Cosmopolitan* to W. R. Hearst.

Walker's was a restless and adventurous mind, continually entertaining new projects. In December 1895 he sent Hobart C. Chatfield-Taylor to Spain to feel out officials on the possibility of the United States buying the independence of Cuba for $100,000,000. In 1897 he founded and for several years maintained Cosmopolitan University, a free correspondence school with a nominal matriculation fee. He urged a credit system based on convertible bonds to prevent panics

(1897), a national clearing house (1899), and a parcels post (1903). He was an enthusiast in regard to aviation, automobiles, and good roads, and in 1896 he offered a prize for the automobile showing the greatest speed, simplicity and ease of operation, and safety, and the lowest cost on a run from City Hall Park, New York, to Irvington, the contest being won by a Duryea Motor Wagon which made the 16½ miles in 65 minutes. Two years later he bought out the Stanley Automobile Company and began the manufacture of Locomobile steam cars at a factory he built at Philipse Manor, on the Hudson. He was the first president of the Automobile Manufacturers' Association, organized a national highway commission, and invented and manufactured the automatic road crowner, a machine for removing moisture from clay and thus preventing winter freezing.

After the outbreak of the World War, he became active in the Friends of Peace and Justice, which was interested in preventing the entrance of the United States into the conflict, and he was chairman of their national convention in Chicago in 1915. Besides the *Cosmopolitan*, he was for several years publisher of the *Twentieth Century Home* (later the *Twentieth Century*), a women's monthly, and *Your Affairs*, a pacifist monthly. He was the author of many articles and pamphlets on political and economic questions, and of "A Modern Swiss Family Robinson," published serially in the *Cosmopolitan* (October 1904–May 1905). He was married three times: to Emily Strother, daughter of D. H. Strother [q.v.], by whom he had eight children and from whom he was divorced; to Ethel Richmond, by whom he had four children; and to Iris Calderhead, who with nine of his children survived him. Walker was a man of versatile talents, dynamic energy, both mental and physical, and a disinterested passion for social justice.

[See *Who's Who in America, 1920–21*; "Notes on Some American Mag. Editors," *Bookman*, Dec. 1900; "The Napoleon of the Mags.," *N. Y. Herald*, Sept. 3, 1893; C. H. Towne, *Adventures in Editing* (1926); files of *Cosmopolitan Mag.*, 1889–1905, which throws much light on Walker's activities; obituaries in *N. Y. Times* and *N. Y. Herald Tribune*, July 8, 1931. Information has been supplied by Iris Calderhead Walker.]

F. L. M.

WALKER, JOHN GRIMES (Mar. 20, 1835– Sept. 15, 1907), naval officer, was born at Hillsboro, N. H., son of Alden Walker, a merchant and cotton manufacturer, and Susan (Grimes) Walker. He was a descendant of Philip Walker who was brought to Rehoboth, Mass., by his mother previous to 1643. After his mother's death in 1846 he lived with his uncle Gov. James W. Grimes [q.v.] of Iowa, and by his aid secured an appointment as midshipman, Oct. 5, 1850. Through his uncle's subsequent service as United States senator, 1859–69, and chairman of the Senate naval committee, 1864–69, Walker also gained political contacts and influence of value in his later years. Following a long Pacific cruise in the *Falmouth* he attended the Naval Academy for a year, graduating in June 1856, at the head of his class. He then cruised in the Brazil Squadron and in 1859–60 was an instructor in mathematics at the Naval Academy.

In the Civil War, after serving briefly in the *Connecticut,* he became first lieutenant, Nov. 2, 1861, of the steamer *Winona,* West Gulf Squadron, was wounded slightly in the passage of the forts below New Orleans, and participated in Farragut's advance to Vicksburg. He was made lieutenant commander July 16, 1862, and given command of the small ironclad *Baron De Kalb* of Admiral D. D. Porter's Mississippi Squadron. In the *De Kalb* he led the brilliant gunboat attack on Arkansas Post, Jan. 10–11, 1863, for which he received special mention (*Official Records of the Union and Confederate Navies,* 1 ser., XXIV, 118). He was afterward greatly relied upon by Porter as one of his ablest younger officers. He took part in four subsequent expeditions up the Yazoo River, during the last of which, in June, he commanded five vessels which destroyed shipping and stores valued at $2,000,-000. He temporarily commanded a naval battery ashore in the siege of Vicksburg, and after its fall he had charge of the naval units in a joint expedition against Yazoo City, during which the *De Kalb* was sunk, July 13, 1863, by a torpedo. After leave in the North he commanded the *Saco,* January 1864–January 1865, and subsequently the *Shawmut,* under Porter on the Atlantic coast blockade. He was advanced five numbers for distinguished war service and was promoted, July 25, 1866, to commander.

Notable in his later career were his three years on the staff of Admiral Porter at the Naval Academy, 1866–69; his secretaryship of the lighthouse board, 1873–78; a period of two years' leave, 1879–81, during which he gained valuable experience through administrative work with the Chicago, Burlington, & Quincy Railway; and his long duty, 1881–89, as chief of the Bureau of Navigation. In this position, and up to his retirement, he was generally recognized as the most influential officer in the navy, simple in manners, with Yankee humor and nasal twang, but of excellent judgment, progressive ideas, and keen knowledge of human nature. Admiral Albert Gleaves (*Life and Letters of Rear Admiral Stephen B. Luce . . .,* 1925, p. 172) speaks of

him as "politically the most powerful man in the service" and "one of the ablest administrators and executives the Department has ever had." He was made commodore Feb. 12, 1889, and given command of the Squadron of Evolution, which, late in 1891, during strained relations with Chile, was sent to the South Atlantic. Here he commanded the station till September 1892, and then till June 1893 the North Atlantic station. From April to August 1894, during the establishment of the Hawaiian Republic and agitation for its annexation, he was entrusted with the North Pacific command, and his reports, favorable to recognition of the republic and emphasizing the need of American naval vessels in the Islands, had considerable influence on congressional and public opinion.

He retired for age on Mar. 20, 1897, but in July following President McKinley appointed him to the Nicaragua Canal Commission, and in June 1899 he became president of the new Isthmian Canal Commission to study both the Nicaragua and Panama routes. The commission's report in November 1902 favored the Nicaragua route, but after negotiations with the French Panama Company, in which Walker took a prominent part, and a reduction of the company's price on its rights and property from $109,000,000 to $40,000,000, the commission shifted in favor of Panama. He remained head of the commission until the final transfer of the French rights in May 1904, and was again head of the reorganized commission which administered the Canal Zone and operations till Apr. 1, 1905, when the whole commission resigned to permit more unified control. After his final retirement Walker made his home in Washington. He died from heart failure near Ogunquit, Me., during a summer visit to that vicinity. His body was cremated and the ashes interred at Arlington. He was married, Sept. 12, 1866, to Rebecca, daughter of Henry G. Pickering of Boston, and had two sons and four daughters.

[J. B. R. Walker, *Memorial of the Walkers of the Old Plymouth Colony* (1861); William Salter, *The Life of James W. Grimes* (1876); James Barnes, "Rear Admiral John G. Walker," *Review of Reviews* (N. Y.), Sept. 1897; J. G. Walker, "The Engineer in Naval Warfare," *North Am. Rev.,* Dec. 1890; Report and Letters to the Navy Department relating to the Sandwich Islands, *Sen. Ex. Doc. 16,* 53 Cong., 3 Sess.; statement before the committee on interoceanic canals, *Sen. Doc. 253,* 57 Cong., 1 Sess.; *Report of the Isthmian Canal Commission 1899–1901, Rear Admiral John G. Walker . . . President* (2 vols., 1901–02); *Army and Navy Jour.,* Sept. 21, 28, 1907; *Washington Post,* Sept. 17, 1907; official papers, letters, etc., in the Navy Department and in the possession of the Walker family.]   A. W—t.

WALKER, JONATHAN HOGE (July 20, 1754–Jan. 1824), jurist, was born near Hoges-

Walker   Walker

town, Cumberland County, Pa., the son of William and Elizabeth (Hoge) Walker and the grandson of William Walker who fought under the Duke of Marlborough and emigrated to Pennsylvania about 1710. His maternal grandfather, John Hoge, a large landholder, was the founder of Hogestown and the uncle of Moses Hoge [q.v.]. His father was a prosperous farmer and during the French and Indian War saw service as a subaltern. During the Revolution Jonathan accompanied several expeditions against the Indians in western Pennsylvania, from which experiences he developed an interest in the transmontane section of the state and a desire to live there. In his late twenties he entered Dickinson College and graduated there with the first class in 1787. Then he read law in the office of Stephen Duncan, at Carlisle, whose daughter Lucretia (or Lucy) he married. In the spring of 1790 he was admitted to the bar of Northumberland County. Shortly thereafter he set himself up in practice at Northumberland, one of the first resident attorneys in that frontier village. In his political affiliations he was a Jeffersonian, though surprisingly mild in temper for one who lived in the democratic hotbeds of Carlisle and Northumberland and fraternized with such radical souls as Robert Whitehill and Thomas Cooper [qq.v.]. His Republicanism won him, on Mar. 1, 1806, an appointment from Gov. Thomas McKean as president judge of the 4th Pennsylvania district, comprising the counties of Center, Mifflin, Huntingdon, and Bedford. During the same year he removed to Bellefonte, where he lived until 1810, when he established himself in Bedford. When in 1818 Congress created western Pennsylvania as a separate judicial district, President Monroe appointed him federal judge for the district. He held his first court at Pittsburgh in December 1818, and he removed to Pittsburgh the following year. In 1818 he made an address to the people of the district, which was characteristic of him in its expressions of feeling and sense of his duties and responsibilities as a judge.

He was a very large man, more than six feet tall and of heavy build. As a judge he commanded the confidence of the people for impartial decisions. He was an excellent scholar and carried with him through life the taste and appreciation for the classics that he acquired in college. He died in Natchez, Miss., while visiting his eldest son. His second son was Robert J. Walker [q.v.]

[Hist. of that Part of the Susquehanna and Juniata Valleys Embraced in . . . Mifflin, Juniata . . . Snyder (1886), esp. vol. I, p. 463; H. C. Bell, Hist. of Northumberland County, Pa. (1891); J. W. F. White,

"The Judiciary of Allegheny County," in Pa. Mag. of Hist. and Biog., July 1883; W. H. Egle, Pa. Genealogies; Scotch-Irish and German (1886); J. H. Tyler, The Family of Hoge (1927), ed. by J. F. Hoge.]
J. H. P.

WALKER, JOSEPH REDDEFORD (Dec. 13, 1798–Oct. 27, 1876), trapper-explorer, guide, was born probably in Virginia, shortly before his parents moved to Roane County, Tenn. In 1819 he moved to the neighborhood of Independence, Mo., and in the following year was with a party of trappers that entered New Mexico only to be expelled by the Spanish authorities. For the greater part of the next twelve years he operated from Independence as a trader and trapper, serving for a time as sheriff of Jackson County. He was one of the imposing company led by Benjamin Bonneville [q.v.] which on May 1, 1832, left Fort Osage for the mountains. In July of the following year, at the Green River rendezvous, Bonneville sent him, with about fifty men, on an exploration westward. Walker led his men to Great Salt Lake, then to the Humboldt River, and on to what has since been known as Walker Lake. From there they scaled the Sierra Nevada and after a long and difficult passage in which they narrowly escaped with their lives descended the western slope, reaching Monterey in November. So far as it is known, they were the first whites to cross the Sierra from the east and were also, it is generally maintained, the first to see the Yosemite Valley. Starting on his return in February 1834, Walker crossed the Sierra farther to the south by the gap since known as Walkers Pass and reached the Great Basin, rejoining Bonneville on Bear River, in the present Utah, in the early summer. Henceforth he was "Captain" Walker.

For the next nine years he seems to have remained in the mountains, living from time to time among the Shoshones, though he is recorded as having reached Los Angeles on a horse-buying venture in 1841. In August 1843, at Fort Bridger, he joined Joseph B. Chiles's company of emigrants, and later led a part of it, by way of Walkers Pass, to the coast. Returning with a cavalcade of horses, he overtook J. C. Frémont's second expedition, homeward bound, at Las Vegas de Santa Clara and accompanied it to Bent's Fort. He guided Frémont's third expedition (1845–46) to California, but returned to the Rockies before the beginning of the conquest. In April 1847 he was again in Jackson County, where he remained for nearly two years, but contrived to reach California among the first of the Forty-niners. For a time he sold cattle at the mines, and was later the leader of various prospecting parties. In 1861 he led a company to

350

Arizona and in the following year discovered a number of rich placers on the future site of Prescott. At the age of sixty-nine, though still vigorous, he brought his wanderings to a close and made his home with his nephew, James T. Walker, in Ignacio Valley, Contra Costa County, Cal., where he remained until his death.

Walker was more than six feet tall and of large frame. According to Washington Irving he was "brave in spirit, though mild in manners" (*The Adventures of Captain Bonneville,* 1850, p. 30). He was truthful, honest, and exceptionally modest regarding his exploits. His restless energy and insatiable curiosity carried him over vast stretches of territory, and none of the "mountain men" had a better knowledge of the geography of the West. He came of an adventurous family. Of his brothers, Joel P. has the distinction of having headed the first family of avowed emigrants to reach Oregon (1840), Samuel S. died on his way to California in 1849, Isaac appears to have been killed by Mormons in Arizona, and John to have fallen at the Alamo in 1836.

[D. S. Watson, *West Wind, the Life Story of Joseph Reddeford Walker* (1934) ; H. H. Bancroft, *Hist. of Cal.,* vol. III (1885), pp. 389–92, vol. V (1886), pp. 765–66; R. G. Thwaites, *Early Western Travels,* vols. XXVIII (1906), XXX (1906) ; H. M. Chittenden, *The Am. Fur Trade of the Far West* (1902), vol. I ; F. N. Fletcher, *Early Nev., the Period of Exploration* (1929) ; *Hist. of Contra Costa County, Cal.* (1882) ; *Adventures of Zenas Leonard* (1904), ed. by W. F. Wagner ; information from Francis P. Farquhar, San Francisco.]   W. J. G.

WALKER, LEROY POPE (Feb. 7, 1817–Aug. 22, 1884), Confederate secretary of war, was born and died in Huntsville, Ala. His father, John Williams Walker, a native of Virginia, was president of the first constitutional convention of Alabama (1819), and one of the first two United States senators from that state ; his mother was Maria, daughter of Leroy Pope. Walker entered the University of Alabama in the class of 1835 but left college in his junior year ; later he studied law at the University of Virginia and under Arthur F. Hopkins [*q.v.*] at Huntsville, Ala. Admitted to the bar in 1837, he began practice in Mississippi but after a year returned to Alabama, settling first at Bellefonte and later at Moulton. He served as state solicitor and in 1843 was elected to the lower house of the legislature from Lawrence County. From 1847 to 1850 he represented Lauderdale County and served as speaker. In the latter year he was a delegate to the Nashville Convention, and in the fall, having been elected a judge of the circuit court, he moved back to Huntsville. Three years later he resigned and returned to the legislature. Active in Democratic politics and effective on the stump, he was chosen presidential elector for the state at large in 1848, 1852, and 1856.

By 1860 Walker was definitely identified with the secessionist wing of his party. He was chairman of the Alabama delegation to the Democratic convention at Charleston, and as such announced the withdrawal of the delegation; he was also a delegate to the Richmond convention, and supported John C. Breckinridge [*q.v.*] in his campaign. The Alabama secession convention sent Walker as special commissioner to Tennessee in an effort to induce that state to secede, and he was received by the legislature, which he addressed. On Feb. 21, 1861, President Jefferson Davis made him secretary of war in his first cabinet. The appointment was determined by political expediency rather than by Walker's fitness for that office, since Davis wished to unite all the states and leading interests of the South in support of his administration, and Walker had been recommended by William L. Yancey [*q.v.*]. Walker was utterly inexperienced in administration, and the tremendous and, in many cases, impossible tasks that confronted him as secretary weighed upon him heavily. Criticism in Congress convinced both Walker and Davis that the former should resign, and he was offered a foreign mission which he declined. He planned to run for the Senate if Clement C. Clay [*q.v.*] retired, and in the meantime desired a military appointment. On Sept. 16, 1861, he resigned with his health seriously impaired, and the following day Davis appointed him brigadier-general. He served in the Department of Alabama and West Florida, and was in command, first at Mobile, and later at Montgomery. His efforts to secure an assignment to active duty failing, he resigned Mar. 31, 1862. He was appointed the following year judge of a military court and served in that capacity until 1865.

After the war Walker resumed the practice of his profession in Huntsville. He served as president of the constitutional convention of 1875 and was delegate at large to the Democratic national conventions of 1876 and 1884. Widely known and popular in the state, respected for his learning, wisdom, and character, an able lawyer with a large, important, and profitable practice, he exerted an influence in Alabama out of all proportion to his activity in public affairs. He was twice married: first, to a Miss Hopkins of Mississippi; second, in July 1850, to Eliza Dickson Pickett, daughter of Judge William Dickson Pickett and Eliza Goddard (Whitman) Pickett of Montgomery.

[Sources include C. A. Evans, *Confederate Mil. Hist.* (1899), vol. I ; *Jour. of the Cong. of the Confederate*

States of America, vol. I (1904); J. B. Jones, A Rebel War Clerk's Diary (1866), I, 37–39; T. W. Palmer, A Reg. of the Officers and Students of the Univ. of Ala. (1901); "The Cabinet at Montgomery," Harper's Weekly, June 1, 1861; Daily Reg. (Mobile), Aug. 23, 1884; information as to certain facts from members of the family. Walker's official letter-book (Feb. 21–Sept. 15, 1861) is in the Confederate States of America material in MSS. Div., Lib. of Cong.]

J. G. deR. H.

WALKER, MARY EDWARDS (Nov. 26, 1832–Feb. 21, 1919), physician, woman's rights advocate, was born in Oswego, N. Y., the daughter of Alvah and Vesta (Whitcomb) Walker. Among her ancestors was the "Widow Walker," one of the early settlers of Plymouth Colony, who came to America before 1643. Her early education was obtained in the school conducted by her father, mother, and sisters on the family farm near Oswego. From her father, who in addition to teaching was a farmer and physician, she acquired an ambition to study medicine, in disregard of the prejudices which in the 1840's and 1850's looked with scandalized disapproval on attempts by women to invade any of the professions except teaching. Overcoming all the many obstacles in her path she succeeded in completing her studies and in 1855 received her physician's certificate from the Syracuse Medical College. She began to practise at Columbus, Ohio, but soon removed to Rome, N. Y. In neither place did she find the services of a woman doctor in great demand.

While teaching school in New York City at the age of sixteen, she began to pursue those objectives known as "woman's rights." She discarded skirts for full trousers, partly concealed by long flapping coats. For the first three years of the Civil War she was a nurse in the Union army. Between March and August 1864, she appears to have served as a spy while nominally attached to the 52nd Ohio Infantry in the capacity of contract surgeon. On Oct. 5, 1864, she was commissioned and assigned to duty as an assistant surgeon. In the army she dressed like her brother officers, trousers with gold stripes, felt hat encircled with a gold cord, and an officer's greatcoat. Her jacket was cut like a blouse and fitted loosely at the neck.

Following her resignation from the army in June 1865, she worked for a short time on a New York newspaper—one of the first women in America to be so employed—and then set herself up as a practising physician in Washington, D. C. She continued wearing men's attire, a frock coat and striped trousers by day, and full evening dress when on the lecture platform or at evening social gatherings. She wore her hair in curls, in order, so she said, that "everybody

would know that I was a woman." Her wearing of trousers brought her many vexations. Not only did boys rotten-egg her and men make her the butt for sardonic or ribald humor—"Bill" Nye (Edgar W. Nye [q.v.]) called her a "self-made man"—but her own sex also disapproved of her. Women made faces at her in the streets and in a myriad other ways manifested their dislike for her labors in their behalf. Several times she was arrested for "masquerading in men's clothes"—occasions which she welcomed because of the opportunities they provided for displaying the permission said to have been given her by Congress to wear trousers. That Congress ever gave such permission is open to question. The Congressional Records do not yield any information on this point.

While in Washington she took part in the agitation for the popular election of United States senators and other similar reforms, and gave play to her genuine talent as an inventor. She is credited with devising the inside neckband on men's shirts which protects the skin from the collar button, and the return post-card sent out with registered mail. Most of her zeal, however, went into the improvement of woman's lot. In 1897 she founded a colony for women only called "Adamless Eden." She was a believer in spiritualism and possessed a highly individualistic literary style for which she found outlet in two books: Hit (1871), and Unmasked, or the Science of Immorality (1878). Her genuinely fine and kindly soul took great pride in the bronze medal given her by Congress for her war service, although the medal was stricken from the list by the Board of Medal Awards, on Feb. 15, 1917, because the occasion for its giving was not of record in the War Department archives. A fall on the Capitol steps at Washington in 1917 was the indirect cause of her death near Oswego two years later. She was never married.

[A biography of Dr. Walker by Mrs. C. M. Poynter of Omaha, Nebr., is in preparation. See records in the War Dept., Washington, D. C.; Who's Who in America, 1918–19; J. B. R. Walker, Memorial of the Walkers of the Old Plymouth Colony (1861); Lineage Book, Nat. Soc., D.A.R., vol. CIX (1929); Personal Recollections of the War of the Rebellion, ed. by A. N. Blakeman, vol. IV (1912); Literary Digest, Mar. 15, 1919; Washington Post, N. Y. Times, Feb. 23, 1919.]

W. E. S—a.

WALKER, PINKNEY HOUSTON (June 18, 1815–Feb. 7, 1885), jurist, son of Joseph G. Walker, a Kentucky lawyer, and Martha (Scott), was born on a farm in Adair County, Ky. He was of Scotch-Irish descent, his first American ancestor, John Walker, having come to America from Ireland between 1726 and 1730. Attending country school in winter, helping his father on the farm in summer, and working in a village store occupied most of Pinkney's time as a youth until he was nineteen years of age, when he went to live in Rushville, Ill. After four years in a store there, he attended an academy at Macomb for several months and then entered upon the study of law in the office of his uncle, Cyrus Walker. Admitted to the bar in 1839, he practised in Macomb, at first in partnership with Thomas Morrison and later with his uncle. In 1848 he returned to Rushville where, after practising five years, most of the time in partnership with Robert S. Blackwell, he was elected to the circuit bench to fill a vacancy. He was reëlected in 1855, but resigned early in 1858 to accept an appointment tendered by Gov. William H. Bissell [q.v.], as justice of the supreme court of Illinois. In June of that year he was elected to that position and also in 1867 and 1876, serving continuously until his death. From 1864 to 1867 and in 1874–75 he was chief justice.

Among Walker's most important opinions may be mentioned *Carroll* vs. *East St. Louis,* 67 *Ill.,* 568 (1873) and *Starkweather* vs. *American Bible Society,* 72 *Ill.,* 50 (1874), in which he pointed out the danger involved in the use of a corporation as a legal device for holding land in perpetuity; and *Ruggles* vs. *People,* 91 *Ill.,* 256 (1878), in which he held that a grant by the state to a railroad company of a power to fix rates did not bar subsequent legislative regulation of rates under the police power. He concurred in the opinion in *Munn* vs. *Illinois,* 69 *Ill.,* 80, upholding the power of the state to regulate and fix maximum rates of charge in grain elevators. Walker's opinions were neither brilliant nor scholarly, but were characterized by practicality, cogency of reasoning, and clarity of expression. He was a prodigious worker. Especially was he incessant in his endeavors to keep the supreme court docket clear, a no small undertaking during his first twelve years as a judge when there were but three justices on the bench. On one occasion, between the second week in November (the close of the September term) and the first of the following January, he wrote sixty-two opinions, and during his judicial career, approximately 3,000—said to be the largest number ever written by a judge in the United States. His integrity and fairness were uniformly recognized by associates on the bench and by lawyers who practised before him. Though a Democrat in politics, his appointment to the supreme bench was at the hands of a Republican governor, and his three elections came from a normally Republican district.

Physically, Walker was of a large and powerful frame and until the last years of his life possessed such rugged health that during all his years as judge he never missed a session of the court. He was a lover of books, and read much in the field of science and philosophy. He was known for his many acts of generosity and kindness, and as a judge was patient and considerate, especially with young and inexperienced members of the bar. On June 2, 1840, he married Susan McCroskey, a native of Adair County, Ky. To them nine children were born, five of whom, two sons and three daughters, survived their father.

[E. S. White, *Geneal. of the Descendants of John Walker* (1902); *The Biog. Encyc. of Ill. of the Nineteenth Century* (1875); ... M. Palmer, *The Bench and Bar of Ill.* (1899), vol. I; *Chicago Legal News,* Feb. 14, 21, 1885, May 11, 1889; "In Memoriam, Pinkney H. Walker," 113 *Ill. Reports,* 13–28; J. E. Babb, "The Supreme Court of Ill.," *The Green Bag,* May 1891; *Proc. Ill. State Bar Asso.* (1886); *Chicago Tribune,* Feb. 9, 1885.]   G. W. G.

WALKER, REUBEN LINDSAY (May 29, 1827–June 7, 1890), Confederate soldier, civil engineer, was born in Logan, Albemarle County, Va., the son of Meriwether Lewis and Maria (Lindsay) Walker and a great-grandson of Thomas Walker [q.v.]. After graduating from the Virginia Military Institute in 1845, Reuben practised his profession of civil engineering and later engaged in farming in New Kent County, Va. He was married in 1848 to Maria Eskridge of Staunton, Va., and after her death, in 1857 to Sally Elam, daughter of Dr. Albert Elam of Chesterfield County and grand-daughter of Gov. James Pleasants [q.v.] of Virginia.

At the beginning of the Civil War Walker was made captain of the Purcell Battery and was hurried off to Aquia Creek, Va. During the following four years he served without a day's leave of absence. He arrived at Manassas in time to shell the retreating enemy and during the remainder of 1861 was with his battery in Virginia. In March 1862 he was promoted major and served as chief of artillery for A. P. Hill's division. Though ill in Richmond during the Seven Days' Battle, he was connected with Hill's command until the end of the war. At Fredericksburg, Hill reported that Lieutenant-Colonel Walker directed the fire from his guns "with admirable coolness and precision," and he was cited in numerous other battle reports. Shortly after Fredericksburg he was promoted colonel, and became chief of artillery when Hill was made commander of the III Army Corps. He commanded sixty-three guns at Gettysburg and was in the remaining hard-fought campaigns in Virginia. In February 1865 he was appointed briga-dier-general of artillery.

Walker was not a dashing artilleryman like Alexander, Chew, and Pegram, nor was he as intellectual as Long or Alexander; but he showed an engineer's knowledge and appreciation of topography and was unexcelled in the Confederate artillery as an organizer. He was also outstanding for his courage and dogged devotion to duty, his physical hardihood, and his noble appearance. Six feet four inches in height and of massive frame, with long dark hair, sweeping moustache and imperial beard, and a superb horseman, he was one of the most striking figures in Lee's army.

After the war he engaged in farming. In 1872 he moved to Selma, Ala., and until 1874 was superintendent of the Marine & Selma Railroad Returning to Virginia in 1876, he was employed by the Richmond & Danville Railroad until 1877. Later he was superintendent of the Richmond street railways and served as construction engineer for the Richmond & Alleghany Railroad. He superintended the building of the women's department of the Virginia State Penitentiary and in 1884 was appointed superintendent of construction of the Texas State Capitol, residing in Austin until 1888. Before his appointment there had been much scandal in connection with the management of this project, and Walker was put in charge because of his integrity, faithfulness, and efficiency. He died on his Virginia farm at the confluence of the Rivanna and the James. While a Confederate soldier he had fought in sixty-three battles and engagements and in his later years he grew sensitive to the query, "Why General, not wounded in the war?" Drawing himself up to his giant's height and squaring his great shoulders he would reply, "No, sir, and it was not my fault" (Wise, *post*, pp. 753-54). His wife and eight children survived him.

[*War of the Rebellion: Official Records (Army)*; J. C. Wise, *The Long Arm of Lee* (2 vols., 1915); C. A. Evans, *Confed. Mil. Hist.* (1899), vol. III; R. C. M. Page, *Geneal. of the Page Family in Virginia* (1893); C. G. Chamberlayne, *Ham Chamberlayne—Virginian* (1932); *Richmond Dispatch*, June 8, 1890; information from the Walker family.]   R. D. M.

WALKER, ROBERT FRANKLIN (Nov. 29, 1850–Nov. 19, 1930), Missouri jurist, was born at Florence, Morgan County, Mo., of Scottish and Virginian ancestry through his father, Belford Stephenson Walker, and of Welsh ancestry through his mother, Abigail (Evans) Walker. His parents, both natives of Delaware County, Ohio, moved to Morgan County, Mo., at an early age. Walker graduated from the University of Missouri with the degree of B.S. in 1873, and from the same institution received that of M.S. in 1877. After teaching school and studying law in Missouri and in Texas, he was admitted to the Missouri bar in 1876, and at Versailles, the county seat of Morgan County, began a distinguished professional career of fifty-four years, thirty-five of which were in public service.

As prosecuting attorney of Morgan County (1877–85), assistant attorney-general of Missouri (1885–89), and attorney-general (1893–97), Walker became thoroughly familiar with the substantive and procedural law of crimes. A Cleveland Democrat in 1896, he publicly supported the Palmer and Buckner national ticket, thus bringing to an end, seemingly, his political career. In 1897 he gave up his residence in Versailles and moved his law office to St. Louis, where he soon became known as a safe, industrious, and successful lawyer in private practice. In 1912, when the animosities of 1896 were forgotten, Walker was elected as a regular Democrat to the supreme court of Missouri for a term of ten years, and reëlected in 1922. His death occurred at Jefferson City thirteen months before the expiration of his second term.

Walker's judicial actions and opinions are recorded in 247–326 *Missouri Reports*. The opinions exhibit adequate learning, a realistic grasp of modern social conditions, a desire to make law fit in with those conditions, jealousy in guarding the individual right from encroachment by the police power, and a rhetorical grace above the average in American legal literature. His most important work was in criminal appeals. Without trying to overrule earlier cases, he intentionally and tactfully accomplished much in the gradual mitigation of the older Missouri doctrine that all error presumes prejudice against the defendant in criminal appeals. Toward the end of his life he was able to say: "Where it is disclosed by the record that the accused had a fair trial there is an increasing and commendable tendency on the part of appellate courts, not to disturb a verdict of guilty for mere technicalities" (*State vs. Cutter*, 318 *Mo.*, 687).

Although it was not generally known in his lifetime, Walker was a writer of poetry, always simple in style and generally humorous or satiric in tone. Some of his shorter and lighter verses, written while he was a member of the supreme court, were published anonymously in the "Just-a-Minute" column of the *St. Louis Post-Dispatch* (oral statement from Clark McAdams, editor, September 1933). In 1927 Walker caused to be printed an uncopyrighted book of 180 pages, entitled *Random Rhymes by R. E. Klawfera*. When reversed the pseudonym becomes Ar Ef Walker. This book is now valuable because much of it relates to the personal, gossipy, or seamy side of Missouri political history. One of the poems, "Bill and John," is a bitter and merited denunciation of two eminent and successful corporation lobbyists. Walker was twice married; first, Sept. 20, 1877, to Nannie A. Wright of Fayette, Mo., who died in 1892; second, Sept. 28, 1896, to Mrs. Geneva C. Percy of Brooklyn, New York. A daughter and a son, children of the first wife, survived him.

[A. J. D. Stewart, *The Hist. of the Bench and Bar of Mo.* (1898); *The Book of St. Louisans* (2nd ed., 1912); *Who's Who in America*, 1930–31; *Mo. Bar Jour.*, Dec. 1930; 326 *Mo. Reports* (1931); *A Sheaf of Memories* (n.d.), addresses by Walker before the Old Settlers Asso. of Morgan County; *St. Louis Post-Dispatch*, Nov. 20, 1930; letters from daughter and from registrar, Univ. of Mo.; newspaper clippings and other data in Mo. Hist. Soc., St. Louis.]   T. W.

WALKER, ROBERT JOHN (July 19, 1801–Nov. 11, 1869), whose name is sometimes given as Robert James and most often as Robert J. Walker, United States senator, secretary of the treasury, governor of Kansas Territory, was born in Northumberland, Pa., the son of Jonathan Hoge Walker [*q.v.*] and his wife Lucretia (or Lucy) Duncan. Prepared for college at town schools and by private tutors, Robert attended the University of Pennsylvania, where he graduated first in his class in 1819. Money had to be borrowed for his board and tuition from his landlord, the Rev. Samuel B. Wylie; it was repaid in a few years by young Walker himself. He was admitted to the bar in Pittsburgh in 1821. Walker at once plunged into politics. In the fall of 1823 he was one of the sponsors of a meeting of the Republicans of Allegheny County to nominate Andrew Jackson for the presidency, and wrote the address which called on the party in Pennsylvania to support him at a state convention. The Harrisburg convention of 1824 marked the success of this movement, and Walker's speech was adopted as the address of the convention. Subsequently, a laudatory biographer said: "Thus at the early age of twenty-two, we find Mr. Walker the acknowledged leader of the democracy of . . . Pennsylvania." (*United States Magazine and Democratic Review*, Feb. 1845, p. 157).

None the less, in 1826 he moved to Natchez, Miss. Thither he had been preceded by his brother Duncan, with whom he entered into a lucrative law practice. But Walker's associations were mainly with the more eager and speculative spirits of those flush times. His speculations in plantations, slave, and wild lands were magnificent, involving a debt of several hundred thousand dollars. At the same time he always posed as the friend of the squatter and small farmer. Though known as a Jackson man, Walker did not at first take conspicuous part in politics. In 1834, however, he was taken up by the Democratic managers of the state as almost the only available man able to cope in debate with the redoubtable and eccentric Senator George Poindexter [*q.v.*]. Walker's successful campaign for the Senate was carefully managed by an inner ring of which William M. Gwin was the most important member. It was marked by the introduction of a type of stump speaking and sectional appeal which was new in Mississippi. The great stroke of this campaign of 1835, however, was the procurement of an "original letter" from Andrew Jackson, expressing confidence in the candidate. Some have questioned the authenticity of this letter (Claiborne, *post*, p. 416), but it was conspicuously useful to Walker for some years, serving as a sort of certificate of respectability when he was accused of being too intimate with banks and bankers.

Walker took his seat in the Senate on Feb. 22, 1836. He was one of the most ardent of the southwestern group, and rarely missed an opportunity to speak in favor of the claims of new states to public lands, in favor of preëmption and lower prices, and against distribution of the surplus, the protective tariff, and abolitionism. He won an early notoriety by seeking a quarrel with Clay; and, being an eager and indefatigable worker, he soon won a place for himself. He was conspicuous in the debates on the complicated matters connected with the surplus revenues and the "American system"; and his friends gave him credit for the permanent preëmption law of 1841. He was a powerful supporter of the independent treasury plan. He was reëlected to the Senate for the term beginning Mar. 4, 1841, over Seargent S. Prentiss [*q.v.*]. He was definitely identified with the anti-bank and repudiating party in Mississippi.

Walker's service as a senator is chiefly memorable for his activities in connection with the annexation of Texas. By temper, by conviction, and by interest he was an expansionist. His resolution of Jan. 11, 1837, calling for recognition of the independence of Texas was with difficulty put through the Senate, but his efforts won great applause in Texas. His opportunity came only with the presidency of John Tyler. It is doubtful whether he inspired Tyler's bank vetoes, but it is certain that he was one of the President's foremost allies in the efforts of 1843–45 to add Texas to the Union. In January 1844 he wrote to Andrew Jackson that the Senate would ratify a treaty of annexation, and urged him to put pressure on Houston to secure one. A published letter of his, dated Jan. 8, 1844 (*Letter of Mr. Walker of Mississippi, Relative to the Annexation of Texas,* 1844), was very widely circulated and served as the major weapon in the campaign to prepare public opinion for the expected treaty. It contained an elaborate argument that annexation would help toward the ultimate extinction of slavery, but the claim has been made that this was omitted from the version of the letter circulated in the South (G. L. Prentiss, *A Memoir of S. S. Prentiss,* 1855, II, 336). When Tyler's treaty of annexation came to the Senate, Walker was the leader in defending it; many factors, however, combined to bring about its decisive defeat.

Meanwhile, the Democratic party was engaged in the difficult task of selecting a presidential candidate. Walker appears to have been at the center of the manipulations which resulted in the rejection of Martin Van Buren and the nomination of James K. Polk [*qq.v.*]. There is some indication that it was on his initiative that Van Buren's letter (published Apr. 27, 1844), which declared against immediate annexation, was solicited. Walker, long the leader of the annexationists, was too shrewd a politician to play the game of Tyler or Calhoun; his rôle, then, was that of leader of an insurgent group, working to defeat Van Buren and secure an annexationist candidate who would divide the embittered factions as little as possible. This group, potently aided by Thomas Ritchie of Virginia, was successful at the Baltimore convention. In the campaign of 1844 Walker also served as head of the Democratic campaign committee in Washington. In this capacity he was betrayed by over-eagerness, for he circulated a pamphlet, *The South in Danger* (1844), which was so violent in its attempts to identify the Whigs with abolitionism that the Whigs reprinted it for use in the North.

Walker's last service to Texas was in February 1845, when he drafted the compromise resolutions which finally resolved the deadlock in the Senate over annexation. Meanwhile, Polk was being subjected to pressure to give him an important place in the cabinet. Dallas and the westerners favored him for the state department, but Polk finally made him secretary of the treasury. The appointment was clearly a concession to Lewis Cass and the western Democrats, though Andrew Jackson wrote to Polk on May 2, 1845, that Walker, because of his financial associations. was the only one of the cabinet of whom

he disapproved (J. S. Bassett, ed., *Correspondence of Andrew Jackson,* VI, 1933, p. 405).

During his four years as secretary, Walker, despite bad health, was indefatigable. His first concern was to secure the establishment of the independent or "constitutional" treasury system for the handling of public monies; until this was obtained he felt that the country had its "hand in the Lions mouth." Far more of his energy, however, was devoted to the revision of the tariff, a matter in which he saw eye to eye with the President. His well-known report of 1845 on the state of the finances, which at once became a classic of free-trade literature, set forth with emphasis the constitutional, economic, and social arguments in favor of a tariff for revenue only (*House Document No. 6, 29* Cong., 1 Sess.). It smells a little of the study but remains a very able state paper; and at the time it was utilized in the current controversy in England as well as in the United States. The tariff bill of 1846, largely framed by Walker, was put through as an administration measure with difficulty and with the aid of personal lobbying by him. It was, however, a moderate protective rather than a free-trade measure, and from Walker's point of view it was mutilated by the omission of duties on tea and coffee.

The financing of the Mexican War was carried out simply and successfully. Walker had close personal relations with the powerful Washington firm of Corcoran and Riggs, and although it is possible that certain financiers enjoyed the use of government funds longer than was proper, the public borrowings were made on favorable terms and without scandal (*Diary of Polk,* III, 140 ff.). Walker initiated two administrative changes of importance. On his urgent recommendation, provision was made for the establishment of a warehousing system for the handling of imports (9 *United States Statutes at Large,* 53), such as has remained in use ever since. His last public report was a study of this system, based especially on the data obtained by commissioners whom he had sent to England (*Report of the Secretary of the Treasury on the Warehousing System (Senate Executive Document No. 32, 30* Cong., 2 Sess.). He was also mainly responsible for the creation of the Department of the Interior in 1849. The bill for its organization was drawn by him as a direct result of his administrative experience, and was carried through the Senate by Jefferson Davis assisted by Daniel Webster. Polk signed the bill though he did not approve of it.

Walker constantly urged in the cabinet the acquisition of all the territory the United States could get—which, by the autumn of 1847, meant all of Mexico. His views were well known, and when he was joined by Buchanan and Vice-President Dallas, anti-slavery northerners expressed great alarm. Polk was not to be stampeded by any pressure from official advisers, and had at least the tacit support of all his cabinet save Walker and Buchanan in his final decision to submit the Trist treaty to the Senate (February 1848). It was said, but cannot be proved, that Walker lobbyed behind Polk's back for the rejection of the treaty. At any rate, a few months later Walker and the President were talking cordially about the possible annexation of Yucatan, while it was the Secretary of the Treasury who suggested $100,000,000 as the sum which might be, and was, offered for Cuba.

When he went out of office in 1849, Walker made no attempt to resume participation in state politics. Until 1857 he lived as a private citizen in Washington, attending to his extensive speculative interests—lands in Mississippi, Louisiana, and Wisconsin, projects for a Pacific railroad, a quicksilver mine in California; practising in the Supreme Court; and, in 1851–52, making a long stay in England to sell the securities of the Illinois Central Railroad. In 1853 he was offered and accepted the mission to China, but there was disagreement or misunderstanding about it and he resigned, feeling that President Pierce had abused him badly. Walker's influence was rated highly by politicians behind the scenes, and in 1856 he was again brought into active politics as a supporter of Buchanan's presidential ambitions. After the election he was regarded as a strong candidate for the State Department; but there was strong objection from the South. His appointment as governor of Kansas Territory (March 1857) was made with the concurrence of all Democratic factions, and both Buchanan and Douglas had to urge him to accept the position. But Kansas, though the grave of governors, offered a great opportunity to a man confident in his own powers, and it seems likely that Walker saw the governorship as a stepping-stone to the Senate and the presidency (F. W. Seward, *Seward at Washington*, 1891, II, 299).

Walker's understanding with Buchanan was explicit that the *bona fide* residents of Kansas should choose their "social institutions" by fair voting, and he stood steadily by the implications of this pledge. His inaugural address, however, was not read or approved by the cabinet. Designed as an appeal to the patriotism and self-interest of the Kansans, and containing the "isothermal" thesis that climatic conditions would be the ultimate determinant of the location of slavery, it aroused a storm of protest in the South. *"We are betrayed,"* wrote a fire-eater at once (Harmon, *post*, p. 9). Walker suddenly became a liability to the administration. This was because of his attempts to conciliate the free-state party in Kansas by promising with reiterated emphasis that he would do his utmost, with the support of the administration at Washington, to enable a majority of the people in Kansas to rule. Walker's ambition was to bring a pacified and Democratic state into the Union, and he was convinced that it would be a free state. He failed to accomplish this, less because of certain blunders he made than because of the failure of the administration to support him. But he did prevent recurrence of civil war. Finally, when he failed to persuade the President that the so-called ratification of the Lecompton Constitution was unacceptable, in December 1857 he resigned in a letter which was a pamphlet. He subsequently took some part in the agitation against the Lecompton Constitution.

Walker was at heart a Free-Soiler as early as 1849 and is said to have freed his slaves in 1838. The outbreak of the Civil War, accordingly, found him an eager Unionist, though still very much a Democrat, and in the spring of 1861 he was speaking at Union meetings. In 1862 he and F. P. Stanton became proprietors of and frequent contributors to the very loyal *Continental Monthly*, which lasted until the end of 1864. From April 1863 to the latter part of 1864 he undertook a financial mission in Europe which he himself later summarized by saying that while abroad he had "caused to be taken and bought" 250 millions of Federal bonds (*National Intelligencer*, Nov. 12, 1869). His prestige in England, both because of his treasury report of 1845 and his governorship of Kansas, was considerable, and he made use of it not only in favor of the Union bonds but also in the publication of a series of pamphlets showing, not very candidly, how slavery, Jefferson Davis, and the repudiation of debts were almost synonymous terms.

Walker's subsequent activities were obscure but characteristic. His law business had long been concerned chiefly with the prosecution of claims. He seems to have been concerned with a minor phase of the peace parleys at Montreal in 1864–65 (Dunbar Rowland, ed., *Jefferson Davis . . . His Letters, Papers and Speeches*, 1923, VII, 327, n. 1); he acted as lobbyist of the Russian minister and Seward in putting the Alaska purchase bill through Congress; and during his last illness he penned an article urging the advantages which would come to Nova Scotia were it to submit to annexation to the

United States (*Washington Chronicle*, Apr. 23, 1869). He died in Washington on Nov. 11, 1869.

Walker was "a mere whiffet of a man, stooping and diminutive, with a wheezy voice and expressionless face" (Claiborne, p. 415); he weighed less than a hundred pounds. Though his health was bad and he may have been epileptic (McCormac, *post,* p. 529, n. 88), he was a particularly energetic and busy person who greatly impressed his associates by his encyclopedic knowledge. At one of the busiest periods of his life he was engaged, as a labor of love, on a "history of republics." His marriage on Apr. 4, 1825, to Mary Blechynden Bache, a great-granddaughter of Benjamin Franklin, grand-daughter of A. J. Dallas, and daughter of Richard Bache of Texas, seems to have been happy; there were eight children of whom five survived him.

[Materials concerning Walker are widely scattered. Among accounts of his life are W. E. Dodd, *Robert J. Walker, Imperialist* (1914), a short sketch; H. D. Jordan, "A Politician of Expansion: Robert J. Walker," *Miss. Valley Hist. Rev.,* Dec. 1932; G. J. Leftwich, articles in *Green Bag,* Mar. 1903; and *Pubs. Miss. Hist. Soc.,* VI, 1902, pp. 359–71; *U. S. Mag. and Democratic Rev.,* Feb. 1845, pp. 157–64; J. F. H. Claiborne, *Mississippi,* vol. I (1880); H. S. Foote, *Casket of Reminiscences* (1874); J. W. Forney, *Anecdotes of Public Men* (1873), pp. 117–30; obituary in *National Republican* (Washington, D. C.), Nov. 12, 1869; and, in particular, death notice and article in Washington *Daily Morning Chronicle,* Nov. 12, 1869. For important aspects of his career, see G. W. Brown, *Reminiscences of Gov. R. J. Walker* (1902); W. A. Dunning, "Paying for Alaska," *Pol. Science Quart.,* Sept. 1912; H. B. Learned, "The Establishment of the Secretaryship of the Interior," *Am. Hist. Rev.,* July 1911; and "The Sequence of Appointments to Polk's original Cabinet," *Ibid.,* Oct. 1924; E. I. McCormac, *James K. Polk* (1922); A. B. Morris, "Robert J. Walker in the Kansas Struggle" (MS.), 1916; M. M. Quaife, ed., *The Diary of James K. Polk* (4 vols., 1910); J. E. Winston, "Robert J. Walker, Annexationist," *Texas Rev.,* Apr. 1917; "Mississippi and the Independence of Texas," *Southwestern Hist. Quart.,* July 1917; and "The Lost Commission," *Miss. Valley Hist. Rev.,* Sept. 1918; *Trans. Kan. State Hist. Soc., 1889–96* (1896), containing documents of Walker's administration as governor; G. D. Harmon, "President James Buchanan's Betrayal of Governor Robert J. Walker of Kansas," *Pa. Mag. Hist. and Biography,* Jan. 1929; A. E. Taylor, "Walker's Financial Mission to London," *Jour. of Economic and Business Hist.,* Feb. 1931. Various MS. collections of his contemporaries in the Lib. of Cong. and the Hist. Soc. of Pa. are important.]

H. D. J.

WALKER, SARAH BREEDLOVE (Dec. 23, 1867–May 25, 1919), pioneer negro business woman, known throughout her later life as Madam C. J. Walker, was born in Delta, La. Her parents were Owen and Minerva Breedlove, poor negro farmers, and her childhood was evidently one of great poverty and hardship, for at the age of six she was orphaned and placed in the care of an older sister. She was married in Vicksburg at the age of fourteen to C. J. Walker and at twenty she was left a widow with a small

daughter to support. She removed to St. Louis, Mo., where she worked as a washerwoman, and reared and educated her daughter. She herself studied in the public night schools of that city. In 1905 she hit upon the formula of a preparation for improving the appearance of the hair of the negro. She experimented on herself and her family with such success that she became convinced of the commercial possibilities of her product, and after a year spent in preliminary work in Denver, Colo., she traveled for two years to promote the preparation. In that time her mail-order business grew to such dimensions that an office was necessary and she settled in Pittsburgh in 1908, staying just long enough to establish a branch there in charge of her daughter. She then resumed her traveling. In 1910 she settled in Indianapolis, Ind., where she founded the Madam C. J. Walker laboratories for the manufacture of various cosmetics and a training school for her agents and beauty culturists. At the height of her career she had about two thousand agents selling her preparations and did a business of more than $50,000 annually. One of her most original ideas was to organize these agents into clubs for business, social, and philanthropic purposes and to bring delegates together in three-day conventions at regular intervals. She stimulated their activities and gave them prestige in their respective communities by offering cash prizes to the clubs that did the largest amount of philanthropic or educational work among colored people.

When she died in May 1919 she was the sole owner and the president of the Madam C. J. Walker Manufacturing Company; she also owned town houses in New York and Indianapolis, and a conventionally handsome and luxurious country estate, "Villa Lewaro," at Irvington-on-the-Hudson. By the terms of her will one-third of her fortune of more than a million dollars went to her daughter and the remaining two-thirds to educational institutions and charities. Throughout her life too she retained a great simplicity and kindliness of character, was always easily approachable and genuinely interested in all movements for the education or uplifting of her race. The methods she taught and the use of her application were popularized by the "straightening" feature on which she capitalized to create a nationwide and even international market. Healthy by-products were the diffusing of the knowledge and practice of personal hygiene among all classes of colored people and the opening up of business careers as agents and beauty culturists for negro women. It is probably true, as an editorial in the *Crisis* of July

1919 stated, that in her lifetime Madam Walker "revolutionized the personal habits and appearance of millions of human beings." She died at her home in Irvington.

[Personal letter from F. B. Ransom, attorney for Madam Walker during her life and for the Sarah B. Walker estate; conversations with Dr. W. E. B. Du Bois, W. E. Pickens, and other personal friends; *Who's Who of the Colored Race*, 1915; *The Madam C. J. Walker Beauty Manual* (1928); *Crisis*, July 1919; *Indianapolis News*, and *N. Y. Times*, May 26, 1919.]
                                                    M. G.

WALKER, SEARS COOK (Mar. 23, 1805–Jan. 30, 1853), mathematician and astronomer, was born in Wilmington, Mass., the son of Benjamin Walker and Susanna (Cook) Walker, and a brother of Timothy Walker [*q.v.*]. The devotion of his mother guarded his childhood after the death of his father in 1811, and directed his education in preparation for entrance into Harvard College. For a decade after his graduation in 1825, he taught school near Boston and in Philadelphia, whither he removed in 1827. During this period he acquired an astronomical clock, a twenty-inch transit instrument, and a small Dollond telescope; and from about 1836, when he gave up his school to become actuary to the Pennsylvania Company for Insurance on Lives and Granting Annuities, his leisure hours were devoted to astronomical observation and study. In 1837 he founded one of the first astronomical observatories in the United States in connection with the Philadelphia High School and imported from Munich superior instruments of observation.

He then began to make extensive contributions to the *Proceedings and Transactions of the American Philosophical Society* and to astronomical journals, concerning the observations made at his observatory and including a large body of observations of occultations of stars by the moon; as early as 1834 he had prepared parallactic tables which greatly reduced the time required to compute the phases of an occultation. But he made his recognized entrance into the ranks of scientific investigators, on Jan. 15, 1841, when he read a brilliant memoir on "Researches Concerning the Periodical Meteors of August and November," before the American Philosophical Society (*Transactions*, new series, vol. VIII, 1843). In 1845 he accepted a position in the astronomical staff of the United States Naval Observatory in Washington, D. C., and in 1847 advanced the prestige of this newly founded institution by his announcement, on Feb. 2, 1847, that the planet Neptune, which had been discovered on Sept. 23, 1846, was identical with a star seen twice by Lalande in May 1795, and which had been referred to as fixed star No. 26266 in Lalande's catalogue. His researches in this relation enabled him to determine the orbit of Neptune thus early after its discovery.

From 1847 until his death, Walker was in charge of the computations of geographical longitude in the United States Coast Survey. His discussion of the largest collection of observations of moon culminations and occultations ever made in America, undertaken with the object of determining the longitude of a central datum point for American surveys, led to the conclusion that longitudes deduced from moon culminations could not be reconciled with those from occultations. His examination of the theory of these observations, in the course of seeking for an explanation of the discrepancies which his discussion had revealed, led him to break sharply with traditions of long standing and gave weight and finality to his conclusion that the new electric telegraph furnished the best means for determining the difference of longitude from place to place, and hence the longitude of any certain place from a prime meridian. The telegraphing of transits of stars was original with him, as was also the application of the graphic registration of time-results to the registry of time-observations for general astronomical purposes. This system came to be known as the American method. On Oct. 10, 1846, the transit of a star was telegraphed by the Naval Observatory to Philadelphia. As Walker stated before the American Association for the Advancement of Science, "this was the first practical application of the method of star-signals, which is [destined] sooner or later to perfect the geography of the globe" (*Proceedings*, vol. II, 1850, p. 184). This was the last of those researches, justly regarded as models of practical application of some of the most refined processes of analysis, which have afforded him a place of prominence among American astronomers.

Impaired mental health soon caused him to cease his labors, and, under the care of his sister, Susan, who had been the center of his home in Washington, he traveled to Cincinnati, Ohio, to pass his last days in the family circle of his elder brother. He was buried near Cincinnati. His "Researches Relative to the Planet Neptune" is to be found in the *Smithsonian Contributions to Knowledge*, vol. II (1851); his "Ephemeris of the Planet Neptune," in the same, vol. II, Appendices 1 to 3, and in vol. III (1852), Appendix 1. Occasional writings appeared in the *Proceedings of the American Philosophical Society*, and the *Astronomical Journal*, Apr. 20, 1850, to Apr. 11, 1851.

[*Wilmington Records of Births, Marriages, and Deaths* (1898) ; B. A. Gould, Jr., "An Address in Commemoration of Sears Cook Walker," *Trans. Am. Asso. Advancement of Sci.*, vol. VIII (1855) ; *Ann. Report, Superintendent of the Coast Survey*, 1846, 1848, 1850, 1851, 1853 (1846–54) ; *Astronom. Jour.*, Mar. 15, 1853; *Cincinnati Daily Enquirer*, Feb. 1, 1853.]

G. W. L.

WALKER, THOMAS (Jan. 25, 1715–Nov. 9, 1794), physician, soldier, and explorer, the second son of Thomas and Susanna (Peachy) Walker, was born in King and Queen County, Va. His ancestors are supposed to have emigrated from Staffordshire, England, to tidewater Virginia in the middle of the seventeenth century; and he is believed to have received his education at the College of William and Mary, but there is uncertainty in both cases. Certain it is that his father died in his youth and that he went to live in Williamsburg with his sister, Mary Peachy, who had married the senior Dr. George Gilmer. Here he acquired a knowledge of medicine and later removed to Fredericksburg where he practised for some years, acquiring eminence in the field of surgery. His pupil, William Baynham [*q.v.*], bore witness to the excellence of his training. He also kept a general store and carried on importing and exporting operations. In 1741 he was married to Mildred Thornton, the widow of Nicholas Meriwether and a relative of George Washington. Through this union he acquired about 11,000 acres of land in the present Albemarle County, known as the "Castle Hill" estate. This was the foundation of his fortune. His trading operations probably carried him to the valley of Virginia, for soon he had valuable connections in that section.

In 1748 he made one of a company of prominent western land speculators who explored the southern end of the Virginia valley and staked out rich claims for themselves under a grant made to one of the associates. A large tract surrounding the present town of Abingdon came into Walker's possession in this manner. In 1749 the Loyal Land Company was organized on the basis of a grant of 800,000 acres from the Council of Virginia, and Walker became its chief agent. In 1750 he led a party of explorers westward to spy out their lands. The journal he kept on this occasion is well known and marks him as the first white man to have made a recorded expedition to the Kentucky country. Unfortunately for his associates, he failed to reach the green meadows of the blue grass country. In 1752 he made his first appearance in the Virginia House of Burgesses, but during the same year he was commissioned deputy surveyor of Augusta County and relinquished his seat (*Jour-

nals of the House of Burgesses of Virginia, 1752–1758*, H. R. McIlwaine, ed., 1909, pp. vii–ix). In 1755 he became commissary-general to the Virginia troops serving under George Washington in the French war, and was present at the memorable defeat of Braddock. Charges were brought against him in the House of Burgesses in 1759 by Thomas Johnson of Louisa County that his commissary accounts were irregular. He was absolved from the charges of fraud, but it appears that he had contracted a secret partnership in the supply business with Andrew Lewis [*q.v.*], an associate in land speculations and a commander of the troops Walker supplied (*Journals of the House of Burgesses of Virginia, 1758–61*, 1908, pp. 88–90).

In 1756 Walker was back in the House of Burgesses, this time as a member from the frontier county of Hampshire, which he continued to represent until 1761. The place of his residence during the years since 1748 is something of a mystery. It is certain that he carried on business operations in Louisa as early as 1754, and it is likely that the commissary business took him to Hampshire, which lies across the Potomac from the strategic point of Cumberland, Md. Though not necessarily the case, it is probably true that he resided in these respective counties during the years he represented them in the legislature. In 1761 he sat for the first time for Albemarle County; in 1763 he was a commissioner to sell lots in Charlottesville, the new county seat (Edgar Woods, *Albemarle County in Virginia*, 1932), and in 1765 he built the homestead on the "Castle Hill" estate. From this time forward he made his home at "Castle Hill," where he was a neighbor of Peter Jefferson, and later acted as guardian for his son Thomas. In 1768 Walker represented Virginia at the important Indian treaty at Fort Stanwix. The next year he signed the non-importation agreement and thereafter took an important part in the revolutionary movement. In 1775 he was named one of a commission to negotiate with the Ohio Indians at Pittsburgh, and in 1776 was a member of the Virginia Committee of Safety. When the state government was organized in that year, he became a member of the executive council (*Journals of the Council of the State of Virginia*, H. R. McIlwaine, ed., vol. I, 1932). In 1779 he headed the Virginia commission which extended the North Carolina-Virginia boundary to the westward. Daniel Smith [*q.v.*] was also a member of the commission. Having completed this service, he was again a member of the Council but declined reappointment in 1781 (*Official Letters of the Governors of the State of Virginia*,

H. R. McIlwaine, ed., 3 vols., 1926–29). The following year he ended his public career by representing Albemarle in the House of Delegates. Here he served on a committee appointed to vindicate Virginia's claim to western lands. His first wife died on Nov. 16, 1778, and some time thereafter he married her cousin, Elizabeth Thornton. By his first wife he had twelve children, most of whom married into prominent Virginian families and two of whom, John and Francis, attained distinction, the former serving as United States senator and the latter as a member of the federal House of Representatives. Francis W. Gilmer [q.v.] was his grandson; Reuben L. Walker [q.v.] was a great-grandson; and a grand-daughter, Judith P. Walker, married William C. Rives [q.v.].

Thomas Walker is typical of that company of bold spirits who explored and exploited the early frontier, being a man of action rather than of ideas. He died at the age of seventy-nine and was buried at "Castle Hill."

[*Jour. of an Exploration in the Spring of the Year 1750*, by *Dr. Thomas Walker* (1888), with a sketch of the life of Walker by a descendant, Dr. William C. Rives, of Washington, D. C., who possesses Walker's correspondence and papers; *First Explorations of Ky.* (1898), edited by J. S. Johnston, The Filson Club Publications, no. 13; Archibald Henderson, "Dr. Thomas Walker and the Loyal Company of Virginia," *Proc. Am. Antiquarian Soc.*, n.s., vol. XLI (1932); A. W. Burns, "Daniel Boone's Predecessor in Kentucky" (mimeograph copy in Lib. of Cong.); *Christopher Gist's Jours.* (1893), edited by W. M. Darlington; Philip Slaughter, *Memoir of Col. Joshua Fry* (1880?); T. P. Abernethy, *Western Lands and the Revolution* (to be published); W. B. Blanton, *Med. in Va. in the Eighteenth Century* (1931); *Va. Gazette and Gen. Advertiser* (Richmond), Nov. 12, 1794.]   T. P. A.

WALKER, THOMAS BARLOW (Feb. 1, 1840–July 28, 1928), lumber magnate and art collector, was born in Xenia, Ohio, the son of Platt Bayliss and Anstis (Barlow) Walker. His father died in Missouri on his way to the California gold fields in 1849 and six years later the widowed mother and her children moved to Berea, Ohio, where Walker supplemented his early schooling with an occasional term at Baldwin University. Working to help support the family and to finance his education, he sold grindstones for Fletcher Hulet, traveling for the purpose all over the Northwest. On Dec. 9, 1863, he married Hulet's daughter, Harriet, and with her took up his permanent residence in Minneapolis.

Until the late sixties Walker was employed as surveyor, an occupation which revealed to him the value of the pine stands of northern Minnesota. His knowledge, together with money furnished by Minneapolis men, made possible the firm of Butler, Mills & Walker, which invested heavily in pine lands, especially through the purchase of Chippewa Half-Breed Scrip, which was supposedly non-transferable. A federal investigation of these purchases exonerated Walker and other purchasers from blame on the specific point designated by Congress, but the report stated that the "testimony reveals a reckless carelessness in making large purchases, and we think, on the part of many of the claimants, guilty participation in an ingenious device to evade the orders of the Government" (Report of the Jones Commission, *post*, p. 12). Walker escaped disaster in the panic of 1873 by disposing of most of his holdings before the crash, but subsequently, with new partners from time to time, he extended his timber holdings until he was the largest operator in Minnesota. Eventually the Walker lumber interests were concentrated in the family, largely through the Red River Lumber Company. In the late eighties Walker and his sons began to invest in California lands, seeking "enough timber to enable the mills to run permanently with the timber supply always growing" (*Minneapolis Times*, May 3, 1905). Lumbering, sale of cut-over ore lands, real-estate deals in and about Minneapolis, and various other ventures made Walker a millionaire many times over. By the early years of the twentieth century he had practically withdrawn from active business, to devote most of his time to civic and philanthropic enterprises and especially to his growing art collection.

Walker's interest in art started with the purchase of a portrait of Washington by Rembrandt Peale [q.v.], and by 1880 he had to build a special room to house his acquisitions. Subsequently additions were made to his home to form the Walker Art Gallery, which was opened to the public. He was one of the founders of the Minneapolis Society of Fine Arts and was its president from 1888 to 1893, but was unwilling to merge his treasures with those of the Society and finally built an edifice to house his paintings, jewelry, stones, pottery, jade, and glass. This collection was of uneven merit, many trivial and bizarre objects being mingled with those of unquestioned significance. In 1925 he organized the Walker Foundation, a corporation to administer the gallery and collections, and two years later gave the Foundation a permanent endowment. In 1915 he contributed "Memories of the Early Life and Development of Minnesota," to the *Collections of the Minnesota Historical Society* (vol. XV).

He was a conservative Republican, impatient of the vagaries of "reformers" (see letter to *Min-*

neapolis Tribune, Sept. 13, 1907). In 1895 he published *A Review of Our Tariff Rates from 1821 to 1895.* He supported actively the Young Men's Christian Association, the Methodist Episcopal Church, of which he was a member, the Minneapolis Public Libary, which he had helped to found, and many other philanthropic enterprises. At his death he was survived by five sons and a daughter.

[*Who's Who in America,* 1926–27; *Sketches of the Life of the Honorable T. B. Walker* (1907), comp. by P. B. Walker; Report of the Jones Commission, *Sen. Ex. Doc. 33,* 43 Cong., 1 Sess.; M. N. Orfield, *Federal Land Grants to the States with Special Reference to Minnesota* (1915); W. W. Folwell, *A Hist. of Minn.,* esp. IV (1930), 465 ff.; *Minneapolis Daily Times,* July 30, 1903; R. I. Holcombe and W. H. Bingham, *Compendium of Hist. and Biog. of Minneapolis and Hennepin County* (1914); M. D. Shutter, *Hist. of Minneapolis* (1923); *Minneapolis Journal,* July 28, 1928, and *passim.*] L. B. S—e.

WALKER, TIMOTHY (July 27, 1705–Sept. 1, 1782), Congregational clergyman, was born in Woburn, Mass., one of the twelve children of Capt. Samuel Walker and his wife, Judith Howard. Nine of these children died within two months in 1738, victims of diphtheria. Timothy was graduated from Harvard College in 1725. In March 1730, before he was twenty-five, he was called to the first parish to be established in Penacook (later Rumford and still later Concord), N. H. Before he was installed, he made an agreement that if through extreme old age he should be unable to carry on the whole work of the ministry his salary should be reduced; but as sole minister of Concord he continued till the day of his death.

The township of Penacook had been granted in 1726 by Massachusetts to one hundred selected settlers from Andover and Haverhill. It lay within the district designated as the shire of Bow by New Hampshire, and its boundary lines were not clearly established. In 1727 the entire Bow district was granted by New Hampshire to a group of absentee proprietors. Thirteen years later the Crown made a settlement whereby the township was thrown into New Hampshire, and the Massachusetts pioneers were threatened with dispossession. Walker, as agent for the Rumford proprietors, made three trips to England in 1753, 1755, and 1762, in order to appeal directly to the King in Council, and finally, in behalf of the settlers and original landholders, won a favorable decision from the Crown. This judgment, that a change of provincial boundaries did not affect titles to private property, is important in the history of Colonial land tenure.

Walker's house was the town's chief mansion during the first half-century of its development. His diaries, of which only fragments remain, were kept from the time of his ordination in 1730 until his death in 1782 and are valuable in recreating the picture of life in a pioneer village. Edited by J. B. Walker, they were published in 1889 under the title, *Diaries of Rev. Timothy Walker.* In the fifty-two years of his ministry Walker preached every Sabbath but one. Often he took his gun into the pulpit with him. In theology he was a moderate Calvinist, accepting the Half-way Covenant. While the town had no legal government, it was necessary for him to depend on voluntary contributions from his parishioners; in 1750 his salary had become so meager that the people, through Walker's son-in-law, petitioned the governor for a permanent subsidy, stating that the loss of "a gentleman of unspotted character and universally beloved by us" would be irreparable (Lyford, *post,* I, 189–90). His will shows that he had accumulated very little property; he preferred to labor along with his flock for the necessities of life. He may best be styled as a farmer-preacher, insisting upon the duties of practical religion, and rarely entering into the religious controversies of his century. Two controversial sermons of his were published, however. The first, *The Way to Try All Pretended Apostles* (1743). The former was preached in January 1742. George Whitefield's "pretended" evangelical powers had stirred Walker, with many others, to protest. In this sermon he gave a vivid characterization of the evangelists: "by their Gesture, their Tone, their Delivery, of avowing so much of transport they endeavour what they can to depress and darken the Understanding, and to warm the Imagination, and to alarm the Affections, and when once these are set up to tyrannize over the Understanding, the Mind is thereby rendered susceptible of any Impressions, and so men become moulded into any Form which their enthusiastic or designing Leaders would have them." Later, in 1771, when Hezekiah Smith [*q.v.*], a Baptist evangelist from Haverhill, came to preach at Concord, Walker attacked him in a sermon entitled *Those Who Have the Form of Godliness* (1772), so vehement that two men left the meeting house and turned Baptist. Testimony to the strength of his influence is furnished by the fact that the peripatetic Whitefield let Concord severely alone.

During his active career Walker was able to keep up an interest in the classics and maintain general admiration from family and friends. On Nov. 12, 1730, he had married Sarah Burbeen of Woburn, who bore him five children. His daughter, Sarah, became the wife of Benjamin Rolfe, second in distinction among the Concord inhabitants, and after Rolfe's death, married Benjamin Thompson [*q.v.*], later Count Rumford.

[Samuel Sewall, *The Hist. of Woburn* (1868) ; *Woburn Records*, pts. I, III (1890, 1891) ; Nathaniel Bouton, *The Hist. of Concord* (1856) ; J. O. Lyford, *Hist. of Concord, N. H.* (2 vols., 1896) ; *Concord Town Records, 1732–1820* (1894) ; *N. H. State Papers*, vol. XXIV (1894), ed. by A. S. Batchellor.]   E. H. D.

WALKER, TIMOTHY (Dec. 1, 1802–Jan. 15, 1856), writer on legal subjects, jurist, teacher, was born in Wilmington, Middlesex County, Mass., the son of Benjamin Walker, a farmer, and Susanna (Cook) Walker, and a brother of Sears Cook Walker [*q.v.*]. He was sixth in direct descent from Elder William Brewster [*q.v.*] of the *Mayflower*. Until he was sixteen he worked on his father's farm with scarcely any schooling, but in 1822, having succeeded in preparing himself for college, he entered Harvard. In 1826 he was graduated as first scholar. The following three years he taught mathematics in the Round Hill School, Northampton, Mass., conducted by George Bancroft [*q.v.*]. During this time he contributed to the *North American Review*, delivered lectures on natural science, published *Elements of Geometry* (1829), and attended law lectures given by Judge Samuel Howe [*q.v.*]. In the fall of 1829 he entered the Harvard Law School, where he remained one year, coming under the instruction of Justice Joseph Story [*q.v.*] and his colleagues. Early in August 1830 he arrived in Cincinnati, Ohio, and entered the law office of Storer and Fox as a student.

After being admitted to the bar in 1831 he began the practice of law. Two years later with Judge John C. Wright, who had been a judge of the supreme court of Ohio and a member of Congress, he organized what was a private law school, with a few students and without the power to confer degrees. In 1835 it became a part of Cincinnati College, founded in 1818, and until 1867 was known as the Law School of Cincinnati College; in 1896 it became a part of the University of Cincinnati. In 1842 he accepted an appointment as judge of the court of common pleas of Hamilton County to fill a vacancy, and in 1843 became the editor of the *Western Law Journal*. When in 1855 Ohio was divided into two federal judicial districts he was appointed to draw up rules of practice for the circuit and district courts of the southern district. He had published an argument in favor of codification as early as 1835 and continued for the rest of his life to work for simplification of the rules of pleading and practice, and for changes in the laws having to do with crime and with the status of married women. Most of the reforms he ad-

vocated he saw before his death incorporated into the laws of Ohio. His most important contribution to the law, however, and his greatest achievement, was a series of lectures delivered in the law school he founded, published as *Introduction to American Law* (1837). "While pursuing my legal studies," he writes, "I found myself much in the condition of a mariner without chart or compass. I experienced at every step the want of a first book upon the law of this country. . . . In a word, I came to the conclusion that fewer facilities have been provided for studying the elementary principles of American Jurisprudence, than perhaps for any other branch of useful knowledge" (*Introduction*, p. v). The book received instant recognition by the legal profession and went through eleven editions, the last published in 1905.

On Aug. 1, 1855, Walker was thrown violently from his carriage. Returning to his office before complete recovery, he contracted a heavy cold which settled on his lungs and in the following January caused his death at his home in Walnut Hills, Cincinnati. A contemporary legal magazine commented on "the vigor and clearness of his mind, the absolute precision of his ideas, his quickness and his conciseness . . ." and on the fact that he "never did a discourteous or an unfair thing" (*Monthly Law Reporter*, Apr. 1856, pp. 708–09). He was married on Mar. 11, 1840, to Ella Page Wood, by whom he had three sons and two daughters.

[See A. G. W. Carter, *The Old Court House* (1880), pp. 122–24 ; C. T. Marshall, *A Hist. of the Courts and Lawyers of Ohio* (1934), vols. I, III ; H. P. Farnham, ed., *Ohio Jurisprudence*, vol. I (1928), p. cvi ; Clara L. de Chambrun, *The Making of Nicholas Longworth* (1933), which contains part of Walker's diary ; and obituaries in *Cincinnati Gazette* and *Cincinnati Daily Enquirer*, Jan. 16, 1856.]   A. H. T.

WALKER, WILLIAM (May 8, 1824–Sept. 12, 1860), adventurer, was born in Nashville, Tenn. His father, James Walker, was a native of Scotland who settled in Nashville in 1820 and married Mary Norvell of Kentucky. William, the eldest of four children, enjoyed unusual educational advantages for a young man of his time and environment. After graduating from the University of Nashville in 1838, he studied medicine at the University of Pennsylvania, where he received the degree of M.D. in 1843. He continued his medical studies in Paris for a year and then spent a year in European travel. Finding the practice of medicine distasteful, he next studied law and in due course was admitted to the bar in New Orleans. As his clients were few, Walker soon turned to journalism, and in 1848 became one of the editors and proprietors of the New Orleans *Daily Crescent*. His newspaper did not prosper, and in 1850 he joined the great migration then under way to California.

After another brief experience in journalism in San Francisco, Walker removed to Marysville, Cal., where he devoted his energies to law and politics. His three years as editor and lawyer among the pioneers of California involved him in several duels and once brought him a jail sentence for contempt of court. In 1853 he became interested in "colonizing" the Mexican states of Sonora and Lower California with American settlers. After failing to obtain the sanction of the Mexican authorities for his plans, he organized an armed expedition on his own account, and in October of that year sailed from San Francisco on the pretext that certain Mexicans had urged him to come and protect them from the Apache Indians, who were then committing depredations in Northwestern Mexico. After landing, Nov. 3, at La Paz, Walker proclaimed Lower California an independent republic, with himself as president. On Jan. 18 following he annexed—on paper—the neighboring state of Sonora. Meantime, since the federal authorities in San Francisco prevented the departure of supplies and reinforcements, Walker and his followers were threatened with starvation. Constantly beset by hostile Mexicans, they retreated northward into the United States and surrendered to a military force stationed at the border. Walker and his chief associates were brought to trial in San Francisco for violating the neutrality laws, but Walker was acquitted by a sympathetic jury, and the fines imposed on his associates were never paid.

In 1855 Walker fitted out an expedition of "emigrants" to Nicaragua, whither he had been invited by the leader of a revolutionary faction then badly in need of outside aid. He landed in Nicaragua with fifty-seven followers and at once joined in the fighting. With the help of the Accessory Transit Company, an American transportation concern operating between Atlantic ports and San Francisco by way of Nicaragua, he captured Granada, then the capital, and brought the revolution to an end. Under the peace agreement he became commander-in-chief of the army, which he proceeded to recruit with Americans brought to Nicaragua free of charge by the Transit Company. He was now virtually master of the state. In May 1856, the new régime was recognized by the United States, and in July Walker had himself inaugurated as president.

Walker cherished grandiose schemes of uniting the small Central American republics into a military empire. He planned an interoceanic canal which would bind his government to the European powers by the strong ties of commerce, and he proposed to develop the agricultural resources of Central America by reintroducing African slavery. He did not contemplate annexation to the United States, as many American historians have assumed, but repeatedly disavowed such a purpose. All these plans came to nothing, however, for he made the two-fold mistake of taking sides in a struggle between two groups of capitalists in New York for control of the Accessory Transit Company and joining forces with what proved to be the weaker of the two. Claiming that the Company's derelictions had voided its charter, Walker seized its ships and other property in Nicaragua and turned them over to the favored group, to whom he issued a new charter. The opposition was headed by Cornelius Vanderbilt [q.v.], a relentless and none too scrupulous fighter, who resolved upon Walker's destruction. Vanderbilt dispatched agents to Central America to aid a recently formed coalition of neighboring republics in expelling Walker from Nicaragua. Through their operations Walker was soon cut off from reinforcements from the United States and was closely besieged by allied forces from Honduras, El Salvador, Guatemala, and Costa Rica. On May 1, 1857, he surrendered to Commander Charles Henry Davis [q.v.], of the United States Navy, who had intervened to prevent further bloodshed.

After returning to the United States, Walker was soon busy with preparations for a second expedition to Nicaragua, of which he claimed still to be the lawful president. In November he eluded the federal authorities and sailed from Mobile, but shortly after landing near Grey Town he and his followers were arrested by Commodore Hiram Paulding [q.v.] of the United States Navy and sent back to the United States. Nearly three years passed before Walker again succeeded in reaching Central America. In August 1860 he landed in Honduras, evading American and British naval forces stationed off the coast of Nicaragua to prevent his landing there. He planned to proceed into Nicaragua by land, but while on his way along the coast he was arrested, Sept. 3, by Capt. Norvell Salmon of the British navy and turned over to the Honduran authorities. He was condemned to death by a court martial and died by the fusillade at Trujillo on Sept. 12.

Walker's personal appearance revealed none of the characteristics which have caused him to be designated as the greatest of American filibusters. Below medium height, weighing but little over a hundred pounds, homely and extremely shy and reticent, he evoked wonder and incredulity from those who first saw him after hearing of his exploits. But from all accounts, when once aroused he seemed a wholly different man, and this may explain his ability to maintain iron discipline and something like personal devotion among his heterogeneous and often wild and desperate followers. His legal and journalistic experience made him a fluent and lucid writer, and his story of his career, *The War in Nicaragua* (1860), published a few months before his last expedition, is a remarkably accurate and impersonal narrative.

[Walker's own story is the best source. Other works include: W. O. Scroggs, *Filibusters and Financiers* (1916); Lorenzo Montúfar y Rivera Maestre, *Walker en Centro-América* (Guatemala, 1887); J. J. Roche, *By-ways of War* (1901); M. P. Allen, *William Walker, Filibuster* (1932); *Evening Post* (N. Y.), Sept. 21, 24, 28, 1860.]   W. O. S.

WALKER, WILLIAM HENRY TALBOT (Nov. 26, 1816–July 22, 1864), soldier, was born in Augusta, Ga., a descendant of a family which had moved to that state from Charles City County, Va., in the late eighteenth century. His father, Freeman Walker, was the first mayor of Augusta and a senator from Georgia; his mother was Mary Washington (Creswell) of Wilkes County, Ga., a niece of Gov. Matthew Talbot of Georgia. After attending school in Augusta, William entered the United States Military Academy and was graduated in 1837, number forty-six in a class of fifty. He was commissioned second lieutenant of the 6th Infantry and before the end of the year saw active service in the Florida Indian War. At the battle of Okeechobee, Dec. 25, 1837, he was thrice severely wounded and was brevetted first lieutenant for gallant conduct. On Oct. 31, 1838, he resigned from the army, but was reappointed Nov. 18, 1840, and rejoined his regiment, serving through the Florida war On Nov. 7, 1845, he was promoted captain. He then served in the Mexican War and was brevetted major, Aug. 20, 1847, for heroic conduct at Contreras, and lieutenant-colonel, Sept. 8, 1847, for similar gallantry at Molino del Rey. In the latter battle he was desperately wounded and for a long time it was feared that he would die. The state of Georgia presented him with a sword of honor in 1849. After the Mexican War, he was on sick leave and recruiting service from 1847 to 1852, and deputy governor of the military asylum at East Pascagoula, Miss., from 1852 to 1854. In the latter year he became commandant of cadets and instructor in military tactics at West Point, serving as such until 1856, and being promoted in 1855 to major. For a brief time he was on fron-

tier duty in Minnesota, and then on sick leave until 1860.

Though Walker sincerely regretted the conflict between the North and the South, he resigned his commission in the United States Army Dec. 20, 1860. One of the most experienced officers who entered the Confederate service, he would probably have attained greater fame had he not been in such poor physical condition. He was appointed major-general of Georgia volunteers on Apr. 25, 1861, and on May 25 was made brigadier-general in the Confederate army. During the next five months he served at Pensacola, Fla., and as a brigade commander in northern Virginia. On Oct. 29, 1861, he resigned his commission, ostensibly because of ill-health, and unquestionably he had been reported as sick in Richmond two months before. Nevertheless, in November he was appointed major-general of Georgia state troops and Gen. Alexander R. Lawton [*q.v.*], Confederate commander at Savannah, wrote Secretary of War Benjamin, "that the feelings with which he [Walker] has now left the Confederate service, fomented by the temper which Governor Brown has (in the past at least) exhibited toward the War Department, might cause great embarrassment here, if he is permitted to assume command under state authority" (*War of the Rebellion: Official Records, Army*, 1 ser. VI, 307).

Walker reëntered the Confederate service on Mar. 2, 1863, as a brigadier-general. On May 18, Gen. J. E. Johnston [*q.v.*] reported to Jefferson Davis that Walker was the only officer in his western command competent to head a division, and obtained his appointment, Jan. 25, 1864, as major-general. He commanded a division in Mississippi, and after the fall of Vicksburg was ordered to Georgia in time for the battle of Chickamauga. In this battle he was in command of the reserves. Later, in his official report, he criticized Gen. D. H. Hill [*q.v.*] for disintegrating the reserves in their attack and declared that if he could have made his own dispositions he felt "satisfied that the enemy's left would have been carried much easier than it was, and many a gallant man been saved, and his retreat intercepted" (*Ibid.*, 1 ser. XXX, pt. 2, p. 242). Walker served with the Army of Tennessee during the campaign in northern Georgia. He was killed in a sortie from Atlanta while in front of his division and his body left in the Union lines. It was later recovered, however, and interred in the old family burial ground at Summerville, Ga., now a part of Augusta. He married Mary Townsend of Albany, N. Y., and had two sons and two daughters.

[*War of the Rebellion: Official Records (Army)*; C. A. Evans, *Confederate Mil. Hist.* (1899), esp. vol. VI; G. W. Cullum, *Biog. Reg. Officers and Grads. U. S. Mil. Acad.*, vol. I (1879); M. J. Wright, *Gen. Officers of the Confederate Army* (1911); W. A. Clark, *A Lost Arcadia or the Story of My Old Community* (1909); W. J. Northen, *Men of Mark in Ga.*, vol. III (1911); information as to certain facts from William Robinson and W. H. T. Walker, Jr., Augusta.]   R. D. M.

WALKER, WILLIAM JOHNSON (Mar. 15, 1790–Apr. 2, 1865), physician, financier, and philanthropist, was born in Charlestown, Mass., the son of Maj. Timonthy Walker, merchant and shrewd investor in real estate, and of Abigail (Johnson) Walker, lineal descendant of Edward Johnson [*q.v.*], author of the *Wonderworking Providence of Sion's Savior in New England*. From Phillips Academy at Andover, Walker went to Harvard, zealously studied Latin and geometry, and graduated in 1810. Immediately he began to study medicine and received the degree of M.D. from Harvard College in 1813. His subsequent training abroad, under Laennec, Corvisart, and Sir Astley Cooper, taught him to use the percussion method in diagnosing chest and abdominal ailments. In 1816 he returned to Charlestown, where on Apr. 16 he married Eliza Hurd, and began to practise medicine. Despite his imperious will and extreme independence, fundamental kindliness made his professional career eminently successful. He was appointed physician and surgeon to the State Prison and consulting surgeon to the Massachusetts General Hospital. Not the least of his accomplishments was the inspiring instruction of several young men who became famous doctors, among others, Morrill Wyman [*q.v.*]. As orator before the Massachusetts Medical Society in 1845 he presented *An Essay on the Treatment of Compound and Complicated Fractures*, published that same year, based on detailed records of his cases and on wide reading. Advocating extremely high professional standards, he emphasized the necessity of cleanliness in all operations and dressings. Shortly thereafter he retired from his practice to accumulate a large fortune in railroad and manufacturing stocks in order, as he later wrote to President Stearns of Amherst, "that I may contribute to education."

In 1861, Walker left his family for a boarding house in Newport, R. I., to devote the remainder of his life to well-planned philanthropy. In 1860 he had offered Harvard a sum of approximately $130,000, for reforming the Medical School. His plan called for more laboratory and clinical work, at the expense of the prevalent deadening lecture system. The Harvard Corporation refused the gift because he demanded an entirely new faculty acceptable to himself.

Thereupon Walker changed his will, originally in favor of Harvard exclusively, so as to divide his wealth, after leaving $260,000 to his family and forty women friends, among Amherst, Tufts, the Massachusetts Institute of Technology, and the Boston Society of Natural History. During the year 1861, Walker endowed at Amherst and Tufts professorships in mathematics, to be filled by young men of proved ability. At Amherst he provided for tutorial instruction in mathematics for classes chosen according to their ability and interest in the subject. The pedagogical theories of the Rev. Thomas Hill [*q.v.*], added to his own medical experience, led him to urge that all students in geometry make their own figures and scales, teaching themselves by eye and hand, before the logical demonstrations. His practical and experimental aims in education were again emphasized in his ideas for field trips in connection with his gift to Williams College of a building for the study of natural history. The scientific and industrial outlook of the projected Massachusetts Institute of Technology, and his regard for William Barton Rogers [*q.v.*], its chief founder, caused him to provide, in 1863, about two-thirds of the fund of $100,000 demanded in the charter before the Institute could begin operations.

In the midst of his planning, Walker died suddenly of a self-diagnosed heart disease. His will brought his total contributions to American education to about $1,250,000.

[A sketch of Walker by President W. A. Stearns of Amherst in a speech delivered at the laying of the cornerstone of Walker Hall on June 10, 1868 (pamphlet, Amherst), and a letter of Walker to the Trustees of Tufts College (MS., at Tufts) present valuable information. Other bits appear in T. F. Harrington, *The Harvard Medic. School* (1905), vol. III; W. S. Tyler, *Hist. of Amherst Coll.* (1873); J. P. Munroe, "The Mass. Inst. of Technology," *New England Mag.*, Oct. 1902; E. S. Rogers, *Life and Letters of Wm. Barton Rogers* (1896), vol. II; *Medic. Communications of the Mass. Medic. Soc.*, vol. X, no. 5 (1865); T. B. Wyman, *Geneals. and Estates of Charlestown* (1879); *Boston Transcript*, Apr. 7, 1865.]   A. A. L.

WALKER, WILLISTON (July 1, 1860–Mar. 9, 1922), church historian, born in Portland, Me., came of clerical New England stock. His father, George Leon Walker, was a distinguished Congregational minister. His Christian name was the family name of his mother, Maria Williston. He received the degree of A.B. from Amherst College in 1883, and graduated from the Hartford Theological Seminary in 1886. On June 1 of that year he married Alice Mather, by whom he had two daughters. With his bride he went to Europe for further study and received the degree of Ph.D. at Leipzig in 1888.

Appointed associate professor of history in

Byrn Mawr College, as successor to Woodrow Wilson, he served in that capacity until 1889. From the latter year until 1892 he was associate professor of church history at the Hartford Theological Seminary and from 1892 to 1901 professor of Germanic and Western Church history in the same institution. In 1901 Yale University called him to succeed George Park Fisher [*q.v.*], as Titus Street Professor of Ecclesiastical History, which position he held for the remainder of his life. From 1896 on he acted as a trustee of Amherst College, and beginning in 1901, as secretary of the corporation. For the school year 1916–17 he served as acting dean of the Yale Graduate School, and as provost of the University from 1919 until his death. As first incumbent of this office he contributed to the efficiency of the administration of the university by the coördination of departments. He was president of the American Society of Church History and of the New Haven Colony Historical Society, and was a member of several other organizations, particularly those concerned with the history of the colonial period.

His interest was ever unflagging in the work of the Church and especially in that of the Congregational body. In 1913 he served on the committee of nineteen which drafted a new constitution for the denomination, and in 1919 he was a member of the commission on Christian unity between the Congregational and Episcopalian bodies. His concern for Christian unity and for Christian missions is evidenced by the following publications: *The Validity of Congregational Ordination* (1898), Dudleian Lecture at Harvard University; "The War and Church Unity" in *Religion and the War* (1918), by members of the faculty of the School of Religion, Yale University; *Approaches Towards Church Unity* (1919), edited in collaboration with Newman Smyth [*q.v.*]; *Twenty Years of Work, a Paper Presented on the 20th Annual Meeting of the Woman's Congregational Home Missionary Union of Connecticut* (1905).

As a lecturer on church history Walker was possessed of singular charm. The story of the Church in his hands unrolled as a colorful panorama of stirring deeds. His writing was characterized by sobriety, balance of arrangement, and judgment, thoroughness, and accuracy. His major contributions to historical scholarships lay in the field of Congregational history in New England, on which he published three books: *The Creeds and Platforms of Congregationalism* (1893); *A History of the Congregational Churches in the United States* (1894), in the American Church History series; *Ten New*

England Leaders (1901); and several articles. Outside of the colonial period his best two works from the scholarly standpoint are his doctoral dissertation, *On the Increase of Royal Power in France under Philip Augustus* (Leipzig, 1888) and *John Calvin* (1906, French translation, Geneva, 1909). On the order of textbooks are: *The Reformation* (1900), and *A History of the Christian Church* (1918). His *Great Men of the Christian Church* (1908) contains a series of popular brief biographies.

[*Yale Alumni Weekly*, Mar. 17, 1922; *Yale Divinity News*, Mar. 1922; R. S. Fletcher and M. O. Young, *Amherst Coll.: Biog. Record* (1927); C. M. Geer, *The Hartford Theological Sem.* (1934); *Congregationalist*, Mar. 23, 1922; *Proc. Am. Antiquarian Soc.*, Apr. 1922; *Who's Who in America*, 1920–21; *New Haven Jour.- Courier*, Mar. 10, 1922.]   R. H. B.

WALLACE, CHARLES WILLIAM (Feb. 6, 1865–Aug. 7, 1932), educator and Shakespearean investigator, was born at Hopkins, Mo., the son of Thomas Dickey and Olive (McEwen) Wallace. His father, a farmer and county judge, was a descendant of Thomas Wallace, who emigrated from Ireland in 1726 and settled in New Hampshire. Wallace was educated in public schools, took the degree of B.S. at Western Normal College, Shenandoah, Iowa, in 1885, and received the degree of A.B. at the University of Nebraska in 1898. He had graduate work at Nebraska (1900–02), at the University of Chicago, and at various German universities (1904–06). He received the degree of Ph.D. from the University of Freiburg in Breisgau in 1906. His pedagogical experience included teaching in country schools, in normal schools in Iowa and Nebraska, and the principalship of a preparatory school to the University of Nebraska (1897–1900) which he founded. He was assistant instructor in English at the University of Nebraska (1901–03), instructor, adjunct professor, and assistant professor in successive years, associate professor (1907–12), and professor of English dramatic literature (1912), a title he retained until his death. He is best known for his researches in Shakespeare and the Tudor drama, which he carried on from 1907 to 1916. He and his wife examined in England, they reported, over five million original records, finding many documents of interest and importance, several groups of which Wallace published. During 1916 and 1917 he lectured on Shakespeare before learned societies and universities throughout the United States.

In 1918 he went to Wichita Falls, Tex., on an extended leave of absence. He had long interested himself in oil geology, and he entered the venturesome oil industry late in life as an inde pendent operator with the object of obtaining funds for the scholarly investigations to which he was devoted. His first successful developments were in Wichita County; in 1922 he bought rights in Archer County and later made further purchases, obtaining large holdings in a region previously thought dry. He personally directed drilling operations, and his ventures brought large returns. He died of cancer in Wichita Falls in 1932. At the time of his death he was working on a collection of records pertaining to Shakespeare and the English stage which he had planned for years to publish. His wife, Hulda Alfreda (Berggren) Wallace of Wahoo, Neb., whom he married on June 14, 1893, was associated with him in study at the University of Nebraska, in his London researches, and even in his management of his oil fields. She lacked his advanced academic training but was a rapid and accurate worker, much the quicker worker, indeed, of the two. They were a remarkably devoted married pair, and Wallace never failed to pay tribute to her assistance.

Wallace's publications include *Spider-Webs in Verse* (1892), *Globe Theatre Apparel* (1909) and *Keysar vs. Burbage and Others* (1910), both printed privately in London, *The Evolution of the English Drama up to Shakespeare* (Berlin, 1912), and a series of articles in *University Studies of the University of Nebraska:* "The Newly-Discovered Shakespeare Documents" (vol. V, 1905), "The Children of the Chapel at Blackfriars, 1597–1603" (vol. VIII, 1908), "Three London Theatres of Shakespeare's Time" (vol. IX, 1909), "Shakespeare and His London Associates" (vol. X, 1910), and "The First London Theatre" (vol. XIII, 1913). He also wrote "Gervase Markham, Dramatist" (*Jahrbuch der Deutschen Shakespeare-Gesellschaft*, 1910), "New Shakespeare Discoveries" (*Harper's Magazine*, Mar. 1910), "Shakspere's Money Interest in the Globe Theatre" (*Century Magazine*, Aug. 1910), "Shakspere and the Blackfriars" (*Ibid.*, Sept. 1910), "The Swan Theatre and the Earl of Pembroke's Servants" (*Englische Studien*, vol. XLIII, pt. III, 1911), and a series of important articles in the London *Times*, Sept. 12, 1906 (letter), Oct. 2 and 4, 1909, Mar. 28, 1913, Apr. 30 and May 1, 1914, and May 8 and 15, 1915. His discoveries were of undoubted value, but, since all were not published and since other scholars have now worked in his field, it is hard justly to estimate their importance. He was the finder of a new signature of Shakespeare and of much new material that threw light on the intricate history of the Tudor

stage. He himself felt that because of this material the entire dramatic literature of the period needed reëditing and the history of the drama rewriting. The zeal, industry, and the surprising success of the Wallace quests were unmistakable, but Wallace's absorption in his work seems to have destroyed his perspective, for he anticipated results disproportionate even to what he had already accomplished.

[Sources include *Who's Who in America*, 1932–33; obituary in *Nebr. State Jour.*, Aug. 8, 1932; personal acquaintance; and information from Mrs. Wallace. See also G. G. Greenwood, *The Vindication of Shakespeare* (London, 1911), which contains criticism of Wallace's work.]   L. P.

WALLACE, DAVID (Apr. 24, 1799–Sept. 4, 1859), governor of Indiana, congressman, a great-grandson of Andrew Wallace who emigrated from Scotland with his widowed mother in 1724, was born in Pennsylvania, the son of Andrew and Eleanor (Jones) Wallace, the latter believed to be a niece of John Paul Jones. While David was still a child the family moved to Ohio, first to Troy and then to Cincinnati. After having been engaged in mercantile pursuits, Andrew Wallace acquired the *Liberty Hall Gazette and Cincinnati Mercury*, which he published for some two years, and then moved to Brookville, Ind., where he kept a tavern. During the War of 1812 he served as a quartermaster to Gen. William Henry Harrison.

David, the eldest of seven brothers, thus grew up on what was then the Western frontier. When about fifteen, he was sent to New Orleans to enter business and stayed there for perhaps a year. He then obtained an appointment to the United States Military Academy, largely through the interest of General Harrison. After graduating in his class of 1821, he remained at West Point for a time as a teacher of mathematics. On June 1, 1822 he resigned his commission, returned to Brookville, and entered the office of an attorney to study law. He was admitted to the bar in 1824 and soon had a lucrative business, being reputed one of the most brilliant young men in the state. Before long he was equally prominent in politics. A devoted admirer of Henry Clay, he ultimately became one of the Whig leaders of Indiana. Meanwhile, 1828–30, he represented Franklin County in the lower house of the legislature; in 1831 and again in 1834, he was elected lieutenant-governor. An ardent advocate of state banking, he did much to bring about the adoption of the charter of the State Bank of Indiana.

In the early summer of 1832 he moved to Covington, Ind., and when elected governor in 1837, to Indianapolis, where he made his home for the rest of his life. He ran for governor on a platform of public improvements, which he enthusiastically sponsored; unfortunately, however, the state lost millions through procuring loans from Eastern speculators. This loss, together with the effects of the financial depression of the time, left the state burdened with debt and unfinished improvements. The resentment of the public was so great that Wallace's friends decided it was unwise to renominate him for governor in 1840. He was elected to Congress in that year, however, and served on the ways and means committee during the sessions of 1841 and 1842. Though the Whig party was somewhat weak at the time, Wallace would probably have been reëlected to Congress in 1842 had his Democratic rival not succeeded in discrediting him for his really enlightened support of a measure that was unpopular because of its supposed extravagance, namely, the appropriation of $30,-000 to Samuel F. B. Morse [q.v.] to enable him to perfect the telegraph.

Wallace resumed the practice of law in Indianapolis. He was a member of the state constitutional convention of 1850, and in 1856 was elected judge of the court of common pleas, on which he served with distinction until his death. He was married twice: first, to Esther French Test, by whom he had four sons, one of whom was Gen. Lewis Wallace [q.v.]; second, to Zerelda G. Sanders, by whom he had two daughters and a son. At the time of his death, the Indianapolis bar paid him marked tribute for his high character as a courteous and urbane gentleman, a talented and eloquent advocate, especially in criminal cases, and a judge with wide legal knowledge, who was ever kindly but possessed an inflexible sense of justice.

[G. S. Wallace, *Wallace: Geneal. Data* (1927); *Lew Wallace, An Autobiog.* (2 vols., 1906); *Proc. of the Indianapolis Bar upon the Occasion of the Death of Hon. David Wallace* (1859); N. M. Woods, *The Woods-McAfee Memorial* (1905); J. P. Dunn, *Greater Indianapolis* (1910), vol. II; *A Biog. Hist. of Eminent and Self-Made Men of the State of Ind.* (1880), vol. II; W. W. Woollen, *Biog. and Hist. Sketches of Early Ind.* (1883); G. W. Cullum, *Biog. Reg. Officers and Grads. U. S. Mil. Acad.* (3rd ed., 1891), vol. I; C. W. Taylor, *Biog. Sketches and Review of the Bench and Bar of Ind.* (1895); *Biog. Dir. Am. Cong.* (1928); R. L. Rusk, *The Lit. of the Middle Western Frontier* (1926), I, 137, n.]   A. L. L.

WALLACE, HENRY (Mar. 19, 1836–Feb. 22, 1916), editor and writer on agricultural subjects, was born near West Newton, Pa., the son of Martha (Ross) and John Wallace, a farmer who had emigrated from Ireland in 1832. From 1855 to 1857 he attended Geneva Hall, a preparatory school in Logan County, Ohio, and in 1859 graduated from Jefferson College, now Washington and Jefferson College, in Pennsylvania. From 1860 to 1861 he studied at the theological seminary at Allegheny, now Pittsburgh Theological Seminary, and from 1861 to 1863 at the theological seminary at Monmouth, Ill. Meanwhile he taught for a year, 1859–60, in Columbia College in Kentucky and in an academy at West Newton during the summer of 1861. He was licensed to preach by the United Presbyterian presbytery of Monmouth on Apr. 9, 1862, and was ordained on Apr. 1, of the next year. On Sept. 10, 1863, he married Nannie Cantwell, of Kenton, Ohio, who died in 1909. They had five children.

He was pastor of the United Presbyterian Church in Rock Island, Ill., and Davenport, Iowa, from 1863 to 1871 and in Morning Sun, Iowa, from 1871 to 1876. Failing health compelled him to give up the ministry in 1877, when he removed to Winterset, Iowa, to take up farming and recover his health. Tuberculosis had taken the other members of his family, and he was the sole survivor. He was the agricultural editor of the *Madisonian* for a year, and he was then dismissed by the editor for his reflections on "the unwillingness of politicians to forward the agricultural interests" (*Own Story, post*, III, p. 20). Then buying a half interest in the *Winterset Chronicle*, he increased the number of its subscribers from 400 to 1400. He became the contributing editor of the *Iowa Homestead* at ten dollars a week, and served in this capacity for twelve years, becoming part owner of this journal. In 1895, with his two sons, Henry Cantwell Wallace [q.v.] and John P. Wallace, he bought *Wallaces' Farm and Dairy*, later *Wallaces' Farmer*, and was the editor of this journal until his death.

A man of strong physique, tall, well-proportioned, and commanding, he possessed a keen intellect and stood high in the estimation of his fellowmen, whether farmers, churchmen, or politicians. He combined agricultural journalism and religion so successfully that *Wallaces' Farmer* became one of the leading agricultural periodicals. It was read not only for its treatment of farm problems but also for its sermons. In 1908 he was appointed by President Theodore Roosevelt as a member of the Country Life Commission; in 1910 he was elected president of the National Conservation Congress; in 1911 he was chairman of the national committee on the men and religion movement; and in 1913 he was appointed with James Wilson to investigate agricultural conditions in Great Britain (see report, *Agricultural Conditions in Great Britain and Ireland*, n. d.). He was an able public speaker and an influential leader in political and religious movements, a champion of railroad regulation and of agricultural education. He was a prolific writer on agricultural subjects and was the author of *The Doctrines of the Plymouth Brethren* (1878), *Clover Culture* (1892), *Uncle Henry's Letters to the Farm Boy* (1897), *Clover Farming* (1898), *Trusts and How to Deal with Them* (1899), *The Skim Milk Calf* (1900), and *Letters to the Farm Folks* (1915). After his death three small volumes of his *Uncle Henry's Own Story of his Life* (1917–19) were published.

[*Uncle Henry's Own Story, ante*; *Tributes to Henry Wallace* (1919); *Who's Who in America*, 1916–17; *Annals of Iowa*, Oct. 1921; *Biog. and Hist. Cat. of Washington and Jefferson College* (1902); *Iowa State Register* (Des Moines), Feb. 23, 24, 1916; *N. Y. Times*, Feb. 23, 1916; information from Henry Agard Wallace, his grandson.]　　　　　　　　　　　　　　L. B. S—t.

WALLACE, HENRY CANTWELL (May 11, 1866–Oct. 25, 1924), agricultural journalist and secretary of agriculture, was born in Rock Island, Ill., the son of Nannie (Cantwell) and Henry Wallace [*q.v.*]. He attended the city schools and helped his father on the farm, at the same time learning the printer's trade in the newspaper offices in Winterset. From 1885 to 1887 he attended the Iowa State Agricultural College, now the Iowa State College of Agriculture. He then rented one of his father's farms and was married, on Nov. 24, 1885, to Carrie May Broadhead of Muscatine, Iowa. They had six children, among them Henry Agard Wallace. Returning to the Iowa State Agricultural College in 1891, he graduated in 1892. James Wilson [*q.v.*], recognizing the importance of dairying, obtained the appointment of Wallace as assistant professor of agriculture in dairying. In 1894 he became part owner and publisher, with Charles F. Curtiss, of the *Farm and Dairy,* published at Ames, Iowa. In a few months he, his father, and his brother, John P. Wallace, became the owners and decided to move it to Des Moines. The name was changed to *Wallaces' Farm and Dairy* and later to *Wallaces' Farmer.* Henry C. Wallace became associate editor and, on the death of his father, editor. He held to the policies of his father in editing this journal, one of the leading agricultural periodicals in the United States. The editorial columns dealt with a variety of agricultural topics and the leading problems of the time, both domestic and foreign. He exerted a large influence through various farm organizations, among which may be mentioned especially the Cornbelt Meat Producers Association, of which he was the secretary for fourteen years. He labored for the equalization of railroad rates for farm products and became

a recognized leader of national movements for the advancement of agricultural interests. During the World War he bitterly opposed the food administration policy of Herbert Hoover.

When the Republicans returned to power in 1921 on a platform promising farm relief, Harding appointed him as secretary of agriculture and, reappointed by Coolidge, he served in this capacity until his death. He opposed the transfer of all marketing functions to the Department of Commerce. He urged that the Department of Agriculture should not only assist the farmer in increasing the efficiency of production but that it should also develop improved systems of marketing. The adjustment of production to the needs of consumption was emphasized as a proper function of the department. A champion of conservation, he fought for the retention of the forest service, which Secretary Fall attempted to have transferred to the Department of the Interior. He had an important part in framing agricultural legislation. He supported the principles of the McNary-Haugen Bill. He reorganized the department into more unified and effectively correlated bureaus, established the bureau of agricultural economics and the bureau of home economics, and inaugurated the radio service for market reports. He was a zealous advocate of education, being concerned primarily with the improvement of the rural schools, the establishment of courses in agriculture in the high schools, and the advancement of the agricultural colleges along scientific and practical lines. After his death, *Our Debt and Duty to the Farmer* (1925) was published with a last chapter written jointly by Nils A. Olsen and Henry A. Wallace. A United Presbyterian by training and profession, he was an active churchman and a loyal supporter of Y. M. C. A. work, with which he was officially connected in various capacities. His funeral services were held at the White House, and he was buried at Des Moines.

[L. H. Pammel, *Henry Cantwell Wallace* (n.d.) in Prominent Men I Have Met Series; L. S. Ivins and A. E. Winship, *Fifty Famous Farmers* (1924), pp. 401–07; E. R. Harlan, *A Narrative Hist. of the People of Iowa* (1931), vol. III; *Who's Who in America*, 1924–25; Herman Steen, "H. C. Wallace," *Prairie Farmer*, Mar. 5, 1921; *N. Y. Times*, Oct. 26, 28, 30, 1924; *Des Moines Register*, Oct. 26, 1924.]　　　　　　　L. B. S—t.

WALLACE, HORACE BINNEY (Feb. 26, 1817–Dec. 16, 1852), literary, art, and legal critic, brother of John William Wallace [*q.v.*], was born in Philadelphia, Pa., the son of John Bradford and Susan (Binney) Wallace, and a lineal descendant of John Wallace, who came to Newport, R. I., from Scotland in 1742. His father was a lawyer and a member of the state legislature, and his mother was prominent in Philadelphia society. His schooling began under a "venerable woman" in Burlington, N. J., the home of his paternal grandparents and the summer home of his parents. In 1822, his father's land interests took the family to Meadville, on the fringe of the wilderness, where his training was continued by his father and the Rev. William Lucas. Before his fifteenth year, he had revealed an unusual gift for higher mathematics, and when he entered the University of Pennsylvania in 1830, he soon placed himself at the head of his class. After two years, he transferred to the College of New Jersey at Princeton, where he took the degree of A.B. in 1835. His interest in science led him to enter the office of Thomas Harris, M.D., and to study for one term in the Medical School of the University of Pennsylvania, but surgery had no attraction for him and he undertook instead a special course in chemistry under Dr. Robert Hare [q.v.]. He then entered his father's office to study law until the death of the latter in 1837, when he transferred to the office of Charles Chauncey, and was admitted to the bar of Philadelphia in the spring of 1840. He never practised, but devoted his attention to legal and literary commentary. When his mother died on July 9, 1849, he went to Europe for twelve months to study the arts, particularly church architecture. Failing health prompted him to go abroad again on Nov. 13, 1852, and he died suddenly, presumably a suicide, in Paris, where he had gone for medical treatment. He was buried in the cemetery at Montmartre, but was reinterred in St. Peter's churchyard, Philadelphia, on Mar. 4, 1853. He never married.

While still in college, Wallace began to write anonymously for the periodicals, and presumably published a number of stories and essays which even his contemporaries failed to identify. His modesty led him to withhold his name from his only novel, *Stanley, or the Recollections of a Man of the World* (2 vols., 1838). After his return from his first trip abroad, he came to the attention of Rufus W. Griswold [q.v.], editor of *Graham's Magazine*, who dedicated his *Prose Writers of America* (1847) to him as the most promising young writer of his acquaintance. Various works attributed to Griswold have been, in part, credited also to Wallace, among which are *Napoleon and the Marshals of the Empire* (2 vols., 1848) and a pamphlet, *The Military and Civil Life of George Washington* (1849).

His legal writings, the only ones which he published under his own name, consist of detailed and critical commentaries on *A Selection of Leading Cases in Various Branches of the Law*, by John William Smith (2 vols., 1844), and on *A Selection of Leading Cases in Equity*, by Frederick Thomas White and Owen Davies Tudor (2 vols. in 3, 1849–51). He and his collaborator, J. I. Clark Hare [q.v.], supplied numerous examples and extended comment on American cases paralleling the English ones cited by the original authors. Together they also published *Select Decisions of American Courts* (2 vols., 1847), a purely American compilation on the same plan, which was revised in 1857 under the title *American Leading Cases*. In all this work, Wallace demonstrated an analytical legal mind and a clear style.

After his death, his literary miscellanies, most of them unfinished essays of philosophical nature, were collected in two volumes, *Art, Scenery, and Philosophy in Europe* (1855), and *Literary Criticisms and Other Papers* (1856), containing some of his best writing. Auguste Comte recognized him as his leading American disciple and compared his mind to that of Jefferson (Preface to *Système de Politique Positive*, Paris, 1853, III, xvii), and Wallace, in an essay in *Art, Scenery, and Philosophy* (p. 332), acknowledges his master's discovery that "mental and moral subjects are capable of being embraced and analyzed by science." His essays on Michael Angelo, Leonardo, and Raphael show esthetic as well as scientific perception, two faculties which he clearly distinguished in his own thought. Those on his contemporaries, G. P. Morris [q.v.], later abridged as a preface to Morris' *Poems* (1860), and R. W. Griswold [q.v.], have not the same philosophical detachment. His early grasp of positivism places him as a promising figure in the transition stages of nineteenth-century thought, but his modesty in publication and his premature death make it difficult to estimate his true weight.

["Memoir," and "Obituary" by Horace Binney, in Wallace's *Art, Scenery, and Philosophy in Europe* (1855) ; J. A. Phelps, *The Wallace Family in America* (1914).]   R. Er. S.

WALLACE, HUGH CAMPBELL (Feb. 10, 1863–Jan. 1, 1931), financier, politician, diplomat, was the son of Thomas Bates Wallace, a merchant of Lexington, Mo., and his second wife, Lucy (*née* Briscoe), widow of Frank P. Gaines. His ancestor William Wallace emigrated as a child with relatives from Northern Ireland in 1724 to Pennsylvania and later moved to Virginia. Hugh Wallace's success in business and politics was foreshadowed by his energy, shrewdness, and business acumen as a schoolboy in Lexington. He was a born trader ; he always seemed to have a job ; he was hardly grown when he made a business trip to Texas and New Mexico. At twenty-two he was appointed receiver of public moneys in Salt Lake City by President Cleveland, and held office from 1885 to 1887, when he resigned to join his older brother in Tacoma, Wash. They organized a bank, and Hugh also engaged in extensive real estate and commercial activities. He was closely identified with the development of Tacoma and throughout his life retained an important interest in the city's financial affairs. He organized a steamship line to Alaska during the Klondike gold rush, and acquired an interest in Alaskan gold mines. He became one of the most influential financiers of the Northwest.

While visiting President Cleveland in Washington, D. C., he met Mildred Fuller, daughter of Chief Justice Melville W. Fuller, and married her on Jan. 5, 1891. Two of their three children died in infancy. He never ran for public office, though he was offered nominations for governor and United States senator in the state of Washington, and he held only two political appointments in his life. Friendly, eloquent, keen-witted and clear-headed, convincing in his sincerity, of unquestioned integrity, he was early in the councils of the Democratic leaders of the Northwest. He was elected to the Democratic National Committee in 1892 and 1896, resigned in 1896, and was elected again for a four-year term in 1916. He was a delegate-at-large from Washington to Democratic national conventions from 1896 to 1912, and took a prominent part in the presidential campaigns of 1892, 1912, and 1916. Following Wilson's election Wallace refused the secretaryship of war but became an intimate member of the President's unofficial family, a trusted adviser, particularly in regard to Western politics. After the United States entered the World War he made unofficial confidential visits to England, France, and Italy for President Wilson.

On Feb. 27, 1919, the President appointed him ambassador to France. During the difficult postwar days Wallace worked tirelessly to keep French friendship for the United States unbroken, so wholeheartedly and so ably that among the many harsh things said in the press of both countries, little or no criticism of Wallace appeared. Following the withdrawal of the American delegation to the Peace Conference he was appointed American representative on the Supreme Council and the Conference of Ambassadors at Paris, and although empowered to act only as observer and not as active participant, his influence was considerable. He signed for the United States the treaty concerning the Ar-

chipelago of Spitzbergen (Feb. 9, 1920), and the Treaty of Trianon (June 4, 1920). He resigned on Mar. 4, 1921, but at President Harding's request remained at his post until the arrival of his successor in July. The French government bestowed on him the Grand Cross of the Legion of Honor, and during the rest of his life he spent much of his time in France, where he had established many warm friendships. In 1927 he was named American representative in the International Academy of Diplomacy, organized under French auspices. In 1930 he became president of the Foch National Memorial, Incorporated. During and following his term as ambassador he assembled a valuable library of works dealing with the history of the Franco-American relations, which he presented to the United States government for the American embassy in Paris shortly before his death. He died of heart disease at his home in Washington, D. C., after a long illness.

[F. W. Dawson, *The Speeches of the Hon. Hugh C. Wallace . . . 1919–21* (copr. 1921); Beckles Willson, *America's Ambassadors to France* (1928); *Who's Who in America*, 1930–31; W. H. Miller, *Hist. and Geneals. of the Families of Miller, Woods, Harris, Wallace . . . and Brown*, pt. V (1907); G. S. Wallace, *Wallace: Geneal. Data* (1927); *N. Y. Times*, Jan. 2, 1931 (see also *N. Y. Times Index* for preceding years); *Tacoma Daily Ledger*, Jan. 2, 3, 1931; *Washington Post*, Feb. 16, 1919; *Lit. Digest*, Mar. 29, 1919; *Current Opinion*, Apr. 1919.]   I. L. T.

WALLACE, JOHN FINDLEY (Sept. 10, 1852–July 3, 1921), civil engineer and railroad executive, was born at Fall River, Mass., the son of the Rev. David Alexander and Martha (Findley) Wallace. His family moved to Boston in 1854 and subsequently to Monmouth, Ill., where on Jan. 1, 1857, his father took office as the first president of Monmouth College. Here the son was enrolled as a student during the years 1865–71, but he refused to take certain subjects required for a degree and consequently did not graduate. He married Sarah E. Ulmer on Sept. 11, 1871. To help pay his college expenses he worked as a rodman on the Carthage & Burlington Railroad in 1869, and as a draftsman for the Rockford, Rock Island & St. Louis in 1870. His first permanent position was that of assistant engineer in the employ of the United States (1871–76), working on improvements in the upper Mississippi, particularly on surveys of the Rock Island rapids and for a ship canal at Keokuk, Iowa. During the next few years he engaged in private practice at Monmouth, but served also as city engineer and county surveyor.

From 1878 to 1881 he was chief engineer and superintendent of the Peoria & Farmington Railroad and from 1881 to 1883, of the Central

Iowa Railway in Illinois; these five years were spent largely in supervising construction between Peoria and Keithsburg. He was chief engineer and master of transportation of the Central Iowa between Oskaloosa and Peoria from 1883 to 1886; in 1886–87 he was engaged in surveys and construction for the Northern Pacific in Wyoming, and in 1887–89 was bridge engineer for the Atchison, Topeka & Santa Fé. He then re-entered consulting practice in association with E. L. Corthell [*q.v.*] and during the next two years was concerned with bridges over the Mississippi River at St. Louis and New Orleans, and the entrance of the Santa Fé, the Chicago & Alton, and the Illinois Central railroads into Chicago. He was also for a time resident manager of the Chicago, Madison & Northern. In 1891 he began a thirteen-year connection with the Illinois Central, rising through various offices to that of general manager in 1901. His work included the elevation of the Chicago tracks, the provision of facilities to handle the crowds visiting the World's Columbian Exposition, and the construction of terminals at Chicago, New Orleans, and Memphis.

Wallace became interested in Panama through a visit to the Isthmus in December 1896. He was suggested for membership on the first Canal Commission, but failed to receive an appointment. In June 1904, however, he was made the first chief engineer of the Canal, in which position he served for about a year. He favored the sea-level plan, but the type had not yet been determined by Congress; most of his work, therefore, was of a preliminary nature, although some actual excavation was begun. When the Canal Commission was reorganized in April 1905, with Theodore P. Shonts [*q.v.*] as chairman, Wallace was made a member, retaining also the position of chief engineer; he continued, however, to feel hampered by the lack of authority and by conflicting instructions and in June 1905, attracted by an offer from a private concern, he resigned. The Secretary of War, William H. Taft [*q.v.*], objected strongly to his resignation, and a bitter controversy, involving a senatorial investigation, ensued (*Senate Document 401*, 59 Cong., 2 Sess.). Wallace defended his administration in a series of articles in the *Engineering Magazine* (September-November 1905, March 1906), and subsequently contributed an article, "Panama and the Canal Zone," to *America Across the Seas* (1909), by Hamilton Wright and others.

After his withdrawal from the Canal project, he was connected with a large variety of enterprises. He was president and chairman of the board of Westinghouse, Church, Kerr & Company (1916–18), member of the executive committee of the Taylor-Wharton Iron & Steel Company (1915–21), and chairman of the board of the Southern Oil & Transport Corporation (1917–21), and was employed as a consultant by many other concerns. He became chairman of the Chicago Railway Terminal Commission in 1914. Professional honors accorded him included election as first president of the Western Society of Engineers in 1896, as first president of the American Railway Engineering and Maintenance-of-Way Association in 1899, and as president of the American Society of Civil Engineers in 1900. He died in Washington, D. C., whither he had been called to testify before the Senate Committee on interstate commerce.

[Printed sources include: *Who's Who in America, 1920–21* ; James Wallace, *Wallace-Bruce and Closely Related Families* (1930) ; *Railway Age*, July 9, 1921; W. F. Johnson, *Four Centuries of the Panama Canal* (1906), pp. 286–315 ; brief autobiog. in *Sen. Doc. 401*, 59 Cong., 2 Sess., I, 543 ff. ; "First Ann. Report of the Isthmian Canal Commission," *House Doc. 226*, 58 Cong., 3 Sess. ; "Ann. Report of the Isthmian Canal Commission . . . Dec. 1, 1905," *Sen. Doc. 127*, 59 Cong., 1 Sess. ; *Outlook*, May 6, July 8, 1905, June 24, 1911; *World's Work*, Apr. 1907 ; *Chicago Tribune* and *Evening Star* (Washington, D. C.), July 4, 1921. The Wallace collection in the N. Y. Pub. Lib. includes many of his professional reports and a number of volumes of "Personal Memoranda."] R. E. R.

WALLACE, JOHN HANKINS (Aug. 16, 1822–May 2, 1903), originator of the *American Trotting Register*, was born on a farm in Allegheny County, Pa., the son of Robert and Elizabeth (Hankins) Wallace. His father was descended from Scotch-Irish ancestors who emigrated to Pennsylvania early in the eighteenth century; his maternal grandmother, from Edward Riggs who emigrated to Boston in 1633. As a boy John Wallace was more interested in books than in farming, and excessive application to his studies when attending Frankfort Springs Academy resulted in impaired health. Urged to live in the open, he went to Iowa in 1845 and on a farm at Muscatine, speedily regained his health.

Here he began studies in the breeding and pedigrees of cattle. The region, however, was one in which the breeding of horses, especially light-harness horses, was carried on extensively, and he soon transferred his attention to equine genealogies. There then existed no reliable stud book devoted to the American thoroughbred, and none whatever of trotting horses. Accordingly, Wallace spent several years in compiling such a work, and in 1867 published in New York the first volume of *Wallace's American Stud Book*. It was not a financial success, but as an appendix he had included pedigrees of trotting horses. The interest which these aroused led him to abandon all other pursuits and make trotting horses and their pedigrees his life-study. In 1871 he brought out the first volume of *Wallace's American Trotting Register,* and in 1874 the second volume. In the meantime he had returned to Pennsylvania and in 1875 he removed to New York City, which was thereafter his home. In that year he began publishing *Wallace's Monthly,* a magazine devoted to the interests of the trotting horse. In 1886 he brought out the first volume of *Wallace's Year-Book of Trotting and Pacing,* an annual compendium of statistics. After publishing nine volumes of the *Trotting Register* and six of the *Year Book,* he sold his publications in 1891 for the sum of $130,000 and retired to private life. Six years later he published *The Horse of America* (1897), in which he presented the result of much valuable investigation together with a defense of his career and his theories of horse breeding. Interested also in his own ancestry, he published *Genealogy of the Riggs Family* (1901) and *Genealogy of the Wallace Family* (1902). He was twice married: first, on October 2, 1845, to Ellen Ewing of Uniontown, Pa.; she died in 1891, and on May 3, 1893, he married Ellen Wallace Veech, his first wife's niece.

When Wallace began his studies there was no recognized trotting breed of American horses. In 1876 he organized in New York the National Association of Trotting Horse Breeders, and two years later, under his auspices, the Trotting Standard was devised and in 1879 adopted to govern all registration in the *Trotting Register.* The enormous stimulation of light-harness horse breeding in America and the world-wide fame of the American trotter were direct outcomes of these achievements. When in 1891 he sold out his publications over 16,000 different trotting stallions had been registered as standard and more than twice that many mares. In 1933 over 70,000 stallions and at least 150,000 mares had been registered. Single specimens of the breed have sold as high as $125,000, and American standard blood has become dominant in all parts of the world. To Wallace more than to any other one person these results are attributable.

[Biog. sketch appended to Wallace's *The Horse of America* (1897); *Wallace's Mo.,* Aug. 1878; *Horse Rev.,* May 11, 18, 1903; B. F. Gue, *Hist. of Iowa* (1903), vol. IV; *N. Y. Herald,* May 3, 1903; *Sun* (N. Y.), May 4, 1903; personal acquaintance.]   J. L. H.

WALLACE, JOHN WILLIAM (Feb. 17, 1815–Jan. 12, 1884), legal scholar and author, was born in Philadelphia, which was his home for the most of his life. His father, John Bradford Wallace, grandson of William Bradford, 1721/22–1791 [*q.v.*], the "patriot printer," stood

high as a lawyer among the members of a very distinguished bar; his mother, Susan (Binney) Wallace, according to her brother Horace Binney [*q.v.*] possessed "the most uniformly . . . bright and vivid mind" that he had ever known (Flanders, *post,* p. xviii). Wallace was educated by his parents and at the University of Pennsylvania, where he graduated in 1833. He studied law with his father and John Sergeant [*q.v.*], and was admitted to the bar on Oct. 27, 1836. With his abilities and distinguished connections he would have found easy the way to professional honors, but he never engaged in active legal practice. In 1841 he became librarian and treasurer of the Law Association of Philadelphia. He contributed the American notes to the third volume of *Cases, Chiefly Relating to the Criminal and Presentment Law, Reserved for Consideration,* known as "British Crown Cases Reserved" (6 vols., Philadelphia, 1839–53). Pursuing his duties as librarian in his enthusiastic and scholarly way, he published anonymously in the *American Law Magazine* (January 1844) a contribution which was republished as *The Reporters, Chronologically Arranged: with Occasional Remarks upon Their Respective Merits* (1844). By this book, with revised and enlarged editions (1845, 1855, and 1882), full of professional learning lightly carried, his memory lives among legal scholars.

In 1844 he became a standing master in chancery of the supreme court of Pennsylvania. The first of three volumes of his reports of *Cases in the Circuit Court of the United States for the Third Circuit,* covering the years 1842–62, appeared in 1849, the others in 1854 and 1871. In 1850 he visited England and Scotland and met great barristers and judges of the day. After the death of his brother Horace Binney Wallace [*q.v.*], he took the latter's place as coeditor with J. I. Clark Hare [*q.v.*] of J. W. Smith's *Selection of Leading Cases on Various Branches of the Law* and *American Leading Cases,* collaborating in the preparation of three editions of the first and two of the second. From 1857 to 1860 he was again abroad, mainly in Italy, and upon his return resigned his librarianship, Nov. 26, 1860, though he continued until Dec. 3, 1864, to serve as treasurer of the Law Association. On Mar. 21, 1863, he had become the reporter of the Supreme Court of the United States, from which office he resigned on Oct. 9, 1875. The twenty-three volumes of *Wallace's Reports* cover a period of great importance in the Court's history (December 1863–October 1874) and are of the highest quality.

After being for twenty-four years a member of

the Historical Society of Pennsylvania, Wallace became its president, Apr. 13, 1868, and served as such until his death. Among his publications, in addition to those mentioned above, were: *The Want of Uniformity in the Commercial Law between the Different States of Our Union* (1851); *Pennsylvania as a Borrower . . . Her Ancient Credit: Her Subsequent Disgrace: Her . . . Future* (1863); *An Address Delivered at the Celebration by the New York Historical Society, May 20, 1863, of the Two Hundredth Birth Day of Mr. William Bradford* (1863); *A Discourse Pronounced on the Inauguration of the New Hall, March 11, 1872, of the Historical Society of Pennsylvania* (1872); *An Address of Welcome, from the Librarians of Philadelphia, to the Congress of Librarians of the United States* (1876); "Early Printing in Philadelphia" (*Pennsylvania Magazine of History and Biography*, vol. IV, 1880, pp. 432–44); *An Old Philadelphian, Colonel William Bradford, the Patriot Printer of 1776: Sketches of His Life* (privately printed, 1882; published, 1884).

Wallace was a devout Roman Catholic. He was a man of positive opinions, likes, and dislikes, but reserved in expression. His manners were marked by a courtesy that had become old-fashioned. His attainments were both wide and profound in law, history, and belles-lettres, and also in other unusual fields such as the art of printing, and all his publications were characterized by literary quality. He married (June 15, 1853) Dorothea Francis Willing, who survived him, as did his only child, a daughter.

[Prefaces to 1 *Wallace* and *The Reporters*; Henry Flanders, in *Pa. Mag. of Hist. and Biog.*, VIII (1884), v–xliv; C. J. F. Binney, *Geneal. of the Binney Family* (1886); *Univ. of Pa. Biog. Cat.* (1894); *Phila. Press*, Jan. 14, 1884; *Legal Intelligencer* (Phila.), Jan. 18, 1884.]   F. S. P.

WALLACE, LEWIS (Apr. 10, 1827–Feb. 15, 1905), lawyer, soldier, diplomat, author, commonly known as "Lew" Wallace, was born at Brookville, Ind., the son of David [*q.v.*] and Esther French (Test) Wallace. His mother, to whom he was deeply attached, died during his boyhood. He early displayed a love of adventure; his father tried to keep him in school, but the boy was irked by ordinary tasks and preferred to draw caricatures or to play truant. As he grew older, however, he carried his books to the woods as often as his gun and rod. When his father was elected governor of Indiana in 1837 and the family moved to Indianapolis, Lew's zest for reading was stimulated by the advantages of the state library. Before he was sixteen he began to support himself by copying records in the county clerk's office. About the same time,

Prescott's *Conquest of Mexico* made such a deep impression upon him that he determined to write upon the theme. Thus *The Fair God* of later years had its inception. In 1844–45 he reported the proceedings of the Indiana House of Representatives for the *Indianapolis Daily Journal*, and soon afterwards began the study of law in his father's office. When the Mexican War began, he raised a company of which he became second lieutenant and which was assigned to the 1st Indiana Infantry. His services in Mexico gave him experience without involving him in the dangers of any serious engagement.

He campaigned against Taylor in 1848 and edited a Free-Soil paper, chiefly because of resentment against Taylor's treatment of the Indiana regiments. Following the campaign he became a Democrat. Admitted to the bar in 1849 he began practice in Indianapolis. Soon he moved to Covington, and in 1850 and 1852 was elected prosecuting attorney. In 1853 he changed his residence to Crawfordsville, and in 1856 was elected to the state Senate. There he advocated a reform in divorce laws and in 1859 proposed the popular election of United States senators. In the summer of 1856 he had organized a military company at Crawfordsville which he drilled so efficiently that most of its members became officers in the Civil War.

After Fort Sumter was fired upon, Gov. O. P. Morton [*q.v.*] made him adjutant-general of the state. Within a week he had 130 companies in camp, seventy more than the state quota, and was made colonel of the 11th Regiment. Soon at the front, he helped to capture Romney, on the South Branch of the Potomac, and to evict the enemy from Harpers Ferry. An excellent disciplinarian and popular with his men, he was promoted rapidly. On Sept. 3, 1861, he was made a brigadier-general and on Mar. 21, 1862, after his service at the capture of Fort Donelson, Tenn., a major-general. Unfortunately, he incurred the ill will of General Halleck, who twice removed him from command; the first time he was restored by President Lincoln, the second time, by General Grant. In November 1862, he was president of the military commission that investigated the operations of the army under Maj.-Gen. D. C. Buell [*q.v.*]. The following year he saved Cincinnati from capture by Gen. E. Kirby-Smith [*q.v.*], after which event the President gave him command of the Middle Division and VIII Army Corps, with headquarters at Baltimore. With 5,800 men, part of them inexperienced, he held a force of 28,000 under Gen. Jubal A. Early [*q.v.*] at the Monocacy, July 9, 1864. Though defeated, he probably saved Washington from capture, and was highly commended by Grant in his *Memoirs* (*post*, II, 306). He served on the court martial which tried the assassins of Lincoln, and was president of the court that tried and convicted Henry Wirz [*q.v.*], commandant of Andersonville Prison.

At the close of the war he undertook to procure munitions and to raise a corps of veterans for the Mexican liberals, and spent some time in Mexico. Returning to Crawfordsville, he practised law, and in 1870 was an unsuccessful candidate for Congress on the Republican ticket. In 1878 he was appointed governor of New Mexico, serving until 1881, when President Garfield appointed him minister to Turkey. There he lived for four years, 1881–85, winning the confidence of the Sultan to an unusual degree. In 1890 he declined an offer of the mission to Brazil tendered by President Harrison.

Wallace is best known, however, as a man of letters. In 1873 he published *The Fair God*, a story of the conquest of Mexico, which won him wide recognition. The fame thus attained was greatly enhanced by *Ben Hur; A Tale of the Christ* (1880), of which 300,000 copies were sold within ten years. It was translated into a number of foreign languages, including Arabic and Chinese, and was successfully dramatized. The extraordinary success of this work was largely due to the fact that the greatest figure in history was with the deepest reverence brought into a strong story dramatically told. Among his other publications were *The Life of Benjamin Harrison* (1888), written for campaign purposes; *The Boyhood of Christ* (1888); *The Prince of India* (1893), inspired by his stay in Constantinople; and *The Wooing of Malkatoon* (1898), a poem, with which was included *Commodus*, a tragedy, written many years earlier. In 1906 appeared *Lew Wallace, An Autobiography*, which Wallace had brought down only to 1864, but which was sketchily completed by his wife and Mary H. Krout.

On May 6, 1852, he married Susan Arnold (Dec. 25, 1830–Oct. 1, 1907), born in Crawfordsville, the daughter of Col. Isaac C. and Maria Aken Elston. Fifty years later he called her "a composite of genius, common-sense, and all best womanly qualities" (*Autobiography*, I, 209). She was a frequent contributor to newspapers and periodicals, and one of her poems, "The Patter of Little Feet," had wide popularity. Other publications by her include *The Storied Sea* (1883); *Ginèvra: or The Old Oak Chest* (1887); *The Land of the Pueblos* (1888); and *The Repose in Egypt* (1888).

Wallace's poise and urbanity marked him as a man of the world, yet he was simple in taste and democratic in ideals. For politics he had no aptitude; the law he did not like; the military life challenged his adventurous spirit but could not hold him after his country had no special use for his services; art, music, and literature were his most vital and permanent interests. Many a young person had reason to remember the gracious hospitality of his study, built as "a pleasure-house for my soul." Never a church member, he believed in the divinity of Christ. His last years were serene. He lectured frequently and received unstinted praise. He died at Crawfordsville, and five years after his death his statue was unveiled in the Capitol at Washington as representative of the state of Indiana.

[In addition to the *Autobiog.*, see *Commemorative Biog. Record of Prominent and Representative Men of Indianapolis and Vicinity* (1908); J. P. Dunn, *Greater Indianapolis* (1910), vol. II; M. H. Krout, "Personal Record of Lew Wallace," *Harper's Weekly*, Mar. 18, 1905; Meredith Nicholson, in *Review of Reviews*, Apr. 1905; *N. Y. Tribune, Indianapolis Star, Indianapolis News* and *Daily Sentinel* (Indianapolis), Feb. 16, 1905; *Senate Doc. 503*, 61 Cong., 2 Sess.; *War of the Rebellion: Official Records (Army)*; *Personal Memoirs of U. S. Grant* (2 vols., 1885–86).]   A. L. L.

WALLACE, WILLIAM (Mar. 16, 1825–May 20, 1904), inventor, manufacturer, was born in Manchester, England, the second son of Thomas and Agnes Wallace. At the age of seven he emigrated with his parents to the United States, and for nine years the family moved about from place to place, stopping wherever the father could find work at his trade of wire drawing. Meanwhile, Wallace obtained a little common-school education. In 1841 his parents finally settled in Derby, Conn., and with his father and two brothers he went to work for the Howe Manufacturing Company. Here he remained until 1848, when he and his brothers went into the wire-drawing business with their father under the firm name of Wallace & Sons; two years later they established their plant at the newly founded industrial town of Ansonia, Conn.

In 1853 the business was incorporated, and from that time until his retirement in 1896, Wallace was active in the organization, becoming president on the death of his father. He built up a large business, rolling copper and brass and drawing wire, and by 1880 Wallace & Sons was the largest establishment of its kind in the Connecticut Valley. Throughout this long period Wallace personally supervised most of the mechanical affairs, mapping out work, laying out new buildings, installing equipment, and devising many of the special tools and machines used in the factory.

Becoming interested in electricity, he installed

a well-equipped laboratory in his home, and established personal contacts with the electrical pioneers of the United States. The results of his studies and experiments became manifest about 1874, when he constructed dynamo-electric machinery at his plant. In this enterprise he had the cooperation of the well-known electrician Moses G. Farmer [q.v.]. In 1875 and 1876 a number of dynamos employing armatures of the Siemens, Gramme, Pacinotti, and multi-polar types were constructed. One of these, the Wallace-Farmer dynamo, based on Farmer's patent of 1872, was used at the Centennial Exhibition at Philadelphia in 1876, and was the only one employed for illuminating the exposition buildings and grounds. Wallace's company began the manufacture of this type of machine for the market early in 1875, adapting it later for arc lighting in connection with Wallace's plate-carbon arc lamp, patented Dec. 18, 1877, and believed to be the first commercial arc light made in the United States. Wallace was the first to demonstrate the operation of arc lights in series. In 1876 he developed a low-tension dynamo for the Western Union Telegraph Company to take the place of batteries. In conjunction with his brother Thomas, he constructed also an enormous electro-disposition plant at Ansonia for the purpose of copper-plating the steel wire used by the Postal Telegraph Company in the installation of the harmonic telegraph system developed by Elisha Gray [q.v.]. In this plant thirty-one huge Wallace plating dynamos were used and over one hundred miles of steel wire at a time were copper plated. Wallace spent large sums of money in public exhibitions, with a view to bringing the possibilities of the dynamo to public attention; but with the beginning of the establishment of the electrical industry in the United States in the 1880's, he retired from the field and confined his attention to rolling copper and brass.

Wallace was a lovable man, genial and agreeable in manner and always willing to assist others in every possible way. After the purchase of his organization by the Coe Brass Company in 1896, he took up his residence in Washington, D. C. On Sept. 15, 1849, he married Sarah Mills at Birmingham, Conn.; he was survived by a son and a daughter.

[Trans. Am. Soc. of Mechanical Engineers, vol. XXV (1904); W. J. Hammer, "William Wallace and His Contributions to the Electrical Industry," Electrical Engineer, Feb. 1–22, 1893; Electrical World and Engineer, June 4, 1904; W. G. Lathrop, The Brass Industry in the U. S. (1926); Samuel Orcutt and Ambrose Beardsley, The Hist. of the Old Town of Derby, Conn. (1880); Washington Post, May 21, 1904.]
C. W. M.

WALLACE, WILLIAM ALEXANDER ANDERSON (Apr. 3, 1817–Jan. 7, 1899), frontiersman, Texas ranger, popularly known as "Bigfoot" Wallace, was born near Lexington, Va., the son of Andrew and Jane (Blair) Wallace. His family were of colonial stock and Scottish origin. Wallace went to Texas in 1837 to avenge the massacre of a brother and a cousin at Goliad in March of the previous year, drifted inland from Galveston, and settled down to the life of a farmer. In 1840 he enlisted as a private in a company of rangers under John Coffee Hays [q.v.] whose duty it was to protect the frontier country around San Antonio from hostile Indians and lawless whites. In the course of this service he fought in the battle on the Salado—an incident in Woll's invasion of Texas in 1842—and later in that year, after Woll's retreat to Mexico, in the futile Mier expedition which ended for Wallace with nearly two years in Mexican prisons. On Sept. 28, 1845, about a year after his release, he enlisted as first sergeant in Capt. R. A. Gillespie's Texas Mounted Rangers and on June 29, 1846, one day after the company was mustered out, he reënlisted in Gillespie's company, then a part of Hays's 1st Regiment, Texas Mounted Rifle Volunteers. With this organization he served in the Mexican War, being honorably discharged as first lieutenant in September 1846. In 1850 he was himself designated by Governor Bell to raise a company of volunteers for frontier service.

The recital of his more formal military service is by no means the whole story of his Indian warfare. Time and time again in the course of his fifty active years he had to leave his Medina River farm with a hastily gathered band of neighbors to protect life and property from Indian raiders. In particular, a contract he entered into in 1850 to carry the mail between San Antonio and El Paso brought its share of Indian conflict. Five hundred of the six hundred miles to be traversed lay in entirely unsettled country, much of which was infested with hostile Indians; the trip took a month. On only one occasion, however, when careless camp guards let the Comanches steal his mules, did he fail to deliver the mail in El Paso on schedule time. He had no sympathy with the Civil War and took no part in it, save to protect the noncombatants on the frontier whose men were away in the army.

In his prime Wallace stood six feet two inches in his moccasins and weighed 240 pounds. He never lost a tooth; he never wore glasses. His outdoor life, especially his Indian warfare, developed exceptional quickness of eye and hand. Despite his limited schooling he was for a frontiersman well read. He was greatly admired and beloved for his prowess, his generosity, his geniality, and his story-telling ability and although he was not so able a leader as Hays, Ben McCulloch, or Lawrence S. Ross [*qq.v.*], he became a folk-hero of Texas. Never married, he lived alone for the most part until his early seventies, when the palsy which he attributed to his Mexican prison experience forced him to live with friends who could give him needed physical care. He died, near Devine, Tex., of pneumonia. Texas rewarded his public service with a gift of 1280 acres of public land, and honored him after death by removing his body from its first burial place at Devine to the State Cemetery at Austin.

[Record book of P. H. Bell, no. 77, Tex. State Lib.; Tex. Land Office records; Laws of Tex. (Special, Mar. 30, 1888, General, Feb. 20, 1899); records of Adj.-General's Office, War Dept., Washington; two letters of Wallace privately owned (photostats, Univ. of Tex. Lib.); *Frontier Times*, May and July 1926, April 1928, June 1931; *Dallas Morning News*, Oct. 5, 1898, Sept. 15, 1929; *Daily Express* (San Antonio), Jan. 8, 1899; sundry narratives to be used with caution, the most popular being J. C. Duval, *The Adventures of Big-Foot Wallace* (1870) and the most convincing, A. J. Sowell, *Rangers and Pioneers of Texas* (1884) and *Early Settlers and Indian Fighters of Southwest Texas* (1900), containing a sketch which is practically the same as Sowell's *Life of Bigfoot Wallace* (1899), with an additional paragraph on the last illness, death, and burial of Wallace; G. S. Wallace, *Wallace: Geneal. Data* (1927).]   E. H. W.

WALLACE, WILLIAM JAMES (Apr. 14, 1837–Mar. 11, 1917), jurist, was born in Syracuse, N. Y., the son of Elisha Fuller and Lydia (Wheelwright) Wallace. He obtained his secondary education in the private schools of Syracuse and his academic legal training in Hamilton College, obtaining the degree of LL.B. from that institution in 1857. He was admitted to the bar of the state of New York, and began practice in Canastota, but he soon moved to Syracuse, where sometime later he became a member of the firm of Ruger, Wallace & Jenney.

In 1873 Wallace was elected mayor of Syracuse. In the succeeding year he was appointed, by President Grant, United States district judge for the northern district of New York. When, in 1882, the position of judge of the second circuit court fell vacant, Wallace was promoted to that bench. At that time there was but one judge for the whole circuit, which was, in the magnitude of its business, the most important in the United States. Wallace himself stated that "the business of the Federal Courts in this city [New York] alone which devolved upon the circuit judge was, in my deliberate judgment, as extensive, as important, and as various as was allotted to any single judge in this country or in

England to undertake" (*Dinner in Honor of Judge . . . Wallace, post,* pp. 18–19). The pressure was somewhat relieved by Act of Congress on Mar. 3, 1887, curtailing the jurisdiction of the circuit courts and providing for an additional circuit judge. That act was, in turn, followed by the act creating the circuit courts of appeal. On the establishment of these latter courts, Wallace was appointed presiding judge for the circuit, in which office he remained until his retirement in 1907 when he resumed active practice with the firm of Wallace, Butler & Brown.

During his long tenure Wallace earned for himself the respect of the legal world by the caliber of his decisions, which were characterized by Mr. Justice Lurton as having "enriched for all time the judicial literature of his country" (*Ibid.,* p. 29). Further evidence of the respect in which he was held is furnished by his nomination in 1897 by the Republican party for the important position of chief judge of the court of appeals of New York (though he was not elected). While to a later day his views may seem ultra-conservative, they were probably not more so than those held in general by a federal bench not noted for its liberalism.

Wallace was twice married: first to Josephine Robbins of Brooklyn, N. Y., who died in 1874, and second, in April 1878, to Alice Wheelwright. The latter also predeceased him so that on his death, which occurred in Jacksonville, Fla., he was survived only by an adopted daughter.

[*The Dinner in Honor of Judge William J. Wallace on His Retirement from the Bench given by Members of the Bar of the State of N. Y.* (1907); J. L. Bishop, in *N. Y. County Lawyers' Asso., Year Book,* 1917; *Who's Who in America,* 1916–17; C. E. Fitch, *Encyc. of Biog. of N. Y.* (1916), IV, 345; *N. Y. Times,* Mar. 13, 1917; *Albany Evening Journal,* Mar. 12, 1917.]
L. M. S.

WALLACE, WILLIAM ROSS (1819–May 5, 1881), poet, was born probably in Lexington or in Paris, Ky. He is said to have been the son of a Presbyterian minister and was presumably of the Highland Scotch stock of the Pennsylvania and Virginia frontier. It is probable that he is the William Wallace of Paris, Ky., and later of Hanover, Ind., who appears as a student at Hanover College in 1833–35. He is said also to have lived in Bloomington, Ind. His first printed poem was *The Battle of Tippecanoe* (Cincinnati, 1837). He returned to Lexington to study law, and practised his profession in New York City from 1841 until his death. He was twice married and had three children, a daughter by his first wife, and a son and daughter by his second. His second wife was a Miss Riker, whom he is said to have married in October 1856 (*New York Times, post*).

During the first two decades of his residence in New York Wallace seems to have been more occupied with literature than with legal affairs. He became a frequent contributor to *Harper's Magazine* and *Harper's Weekly, Godey's Lady's Book,* the *New York Ledger,* the *Celtic Monthly,* the *Journal of Commerce,* and the *Louisville Daily Journal,* and his best known lyrics, odes, and love songs were collected as *Meditations in America, and Other Poems* (1851). A longer work, *Alban the Pirate* (1848), a poetical romance "intended to illustrate the influence of certain prejudices of society and principles of law upon individual character and destiny" (Griswold, *post,* p. 551), met with little success. The outbreak of the Civil War stirred Wallace to write a number of fervently patriotic songs, among them "The Sword of Bunker Hill" and "Keep Step with the Music of the Union" (1861) and "The Liberty Bell" (1862), which were set to music and became widely popular. After the war he seems to have published little or nothing. He moved on terms of easy intimacy with such local "literati" as Samuel Woodworth, George P. Morris, and Thomas Dunn English [*qq.v.*], and was a close friend of Edgar Allan Poe after the latter's return to New York in 1844. He was responsible for inducing Poe to have his daguerreotype taken by M. B. Brady in 1848. After Poe's death he defended his memory against the aspersions of John Neal [*q.v.*]. He is said to have been "not unlike Poe in both temperament and habits. He was not a little like him in physique—in brightness of the eye, and in a superb courtliness of manner. He had the same, or a similar, irresolute will; but he was a delightful companion to meet if you met him at the right time" (Benton, *post,* pp. 732-33).

William Cullen Bryant commended Wallace for his "splendor of imagination" and "affluence of poetic diction," George D. Prentice [*q.v.*] pronounced him "the greatest lyrical poet of the country," and Poe, taking Wallace as his text, vigorously belabored the New England group for their failure to recognize any merit but their own (*The Works of Edgar Allan Poe, post*). Nevertheless only a few of Wallace's poems, and those chiefly his militant patriotic songs, have survived as anthology pieces. Though every one knows

> "And the hand that rocks the cradle
> Is the hand that rules the world,"

the name of the writer is seldom connected with the familiar quotation. The lyrics that were praised by contemporaries for their general resemblance to the poetry of Shelley and Keats have been forgotten by posterity for the same reason.

["Wallace's Poèms," *U. S. Democratic Rev.,* Dec. 1857; R. W. Griswold, *The Poets and Poetry of America* (1873); Joel Benton, in *Forum,* Feb. 1897; E. C. Stedman and G. E. Woodberry, eds., *The Works of Edgar Allan Poe,* vol. VIII, p. 280; Mary E. Phillips, *Edgar Allan Poe* (2 vols., 1926); Hervey Allen, *Israfel* (2 vols., 1926); H. S. Mott, *The New York of Yesterday* (1908); G. E. Woodberry, *The Life of Edgar Allan Poe* (2 vols., 1909); records of Hanover Coll., Hanover, Ind.; obituaries in *N. Y. Times* and *N. Y. Herald,* May 7, 1881.]

G. F. W.

WALLACK, HENRY JOHN (1790–Aug. 30, 1870), actor, was born in London, England, and was the eldest child of William H. and Elizabeth (Field) Granger Wallack. His father was of Jewish ancestry. The family were all theatrical; Mrs. Wallack had for a time been David Garrick's leading woman, and the best traditions of the eighteenth-century English stage were bred into her descendants. Her four children by Wallack—Henry John, James Willliam [*q.v.*], Mary, and Elizabeth—all became actors, and all save Elizabeth spent some time in the United States. After an uneventful early training, Henry Wallack had by his twenty-eighth year become so noted an actor in England that he was engaged for a long American contract, and made his début in Baltimore in 1819. He brought with him his wife, the former Fanny Jones, a dancer of great beauty and charm, who appeared whenever opportunity offered for her talent. After long stays in Baltimore, Philadelphia, and Washington, Wallack first played in New York in May 1821 at the Anthony Street Theatre. Notices of this first engagement show that he appeared in such rôles as those of Brutus, Octavian, Rob Roy, Coriolanus, Captain Bertram in *Fraternal Discord,* and Gambia in the opera, *The Slave.* The *New York Mirror* (June 5, 1824) said of him, "Few men . . . possess so noble a person or a more intelligent and beautiful countenance; the expression of his eye is quick and full of meaning—his movements are easy and correct—his voice mellow and musical." After the birth of her daughter Fanny in 1822, Mrs. Wallack became a dramatic actress and was attached to the Park Theatre for ten years. She was the mother of Wallack's three children—James William [*q.v.*], Julia (Mrs. Hoskins), and Fanny (Mrs. Charles Moorhouse), all well-known actors.

After an extended tour of the country, Wallack became leading man of the Chatham Garden Theatre in 1824. He returned to England in 1828–32 and 1834–36, acting in the latter period as stage manager and leading actor at Covent Garden. His wife obtained a divorce about 1833, and about a year later Wallack married Miss

Turpin, a singer. When his brother James opened the National Theatre in New York in September 1837, Henry was his stage manager, and acted important rôles. In the autumn of 1839 he appeared opposite Edwin Forrest [q.v.] in several parts, such as Iago to Forrest's Othello. On Nov. 25 of that year he and his second wife began a long engagement at the New Chatham Theatre. On Dec. 23 Wallack's two daughters made their débuts there with their father in *The Hunchback.* Fanny was an actress of unusual talent; Julia spent most of her time thereafter in opera. In the summer of 1840 Wallack returned to England, where in 1843 he rented Covent Garden for a short and disastrous season. He appeared again in America, as Sir Peter Teazle in *The School for Scandal,* in September 1847 when the Wallacks opened the Broadway Theatre, and throughout that season his daughter Fanny was leading lady there. Wallack spent most of his latter years in the United States, dying in New York at the age of eighty. One of his last appearances was as Falstaff in 1858. His second wife died in 1879. He played a tremendous and varied repertoire during his lifetime, his parts ranging from the chief Shakespearean heroes to Rolla in *Pizarro,* Fagin in *Oliver Twist,* and Anthony Absolute in *The Rivals.*

[G. C. D. Odell, *Annals of the N. Y. Stage* (6 vols., 1927–31); J. N. Ireland, *Records of the N. Y. Stage* (2 vols., 1866–67); M. J. Moses, in *Theatre,* May 1905; C. H. Haswell, *Reminiscences of an Octogenarian* (1896); article on J. W. Wallack, in *Dict. of Nat. Biog.*; Robinson Locke Dramatic Coll., and coll. of newspaper clippings on the Wallacks, N. Y. Pub. Lib.]

A. F. H.

WALLACK, JAMES WILLIAM (c. 1795–Dec. 25, 1864), actor, son of William H. and Elizabeth (Field) Granger Wallack, and brother of Henry John Wallack [q.v.], was born in London, England. He made his first appearance at the age of four at the Royal Circus in a fairyland pantomime. His father wished him to follow a naval career, but young Wallack was so unhappy at the prospect, so eager to be an actor that the father relented. At twelve the boy appeared with the troupe of the Academic Theatre in London, where plays were given with casts of children. His vigorous and capable performance attracted the notice, it is said, of Richard Brinsley Sheridan, the dramatist, who obtained for him a place in the company of the Drury Lane Theatre. There Master Wallack rose in favor, and when the house was burned in February 1809, he went to the Royal Hibernian Theatre, Dublin. In October 1812 he returned to the rebuilt Theatre Royal, Drury Lane, and at about seventeen played Laertes to the Hamlet of Robert William

Elliston. During the next six years he scored in such parts as Benedick, Petruchio, and Mercutio. Lord Byron, one of the governing board of the theatre in 1815–16, is said to have been his close friend. In 1817 he married Susan Johnstone, daughter of John Johnstone, a popular singer.

On Sept. 7, 1818, he made his American début before an enthusiastic audience at the Park Street Theatre, New York, as Macbeth. James H. Hackett [q.v.], a contemporary, describes him as of distinguished figure and bearing, with abundant dark hair, sparkling eyes, and finely cut features (*Notes and Comments, post,* p. 120). His acting was of the school of Kemble. All accounts mention his rich and sonorous voice, clear articulation, quick and vigorous movement, revealing a nervous, exuberant vitality. He played in Boston and other American cities, even as far south as Savannah, in Shakespearean rôles and as Don César de Bazan, Captain Bertram in *Fraternal Discord,* Massaroni in *The Brigand,* and Don Felix in *The Wonder.* After a season in England (1820) he returned to America and in New York played Hamlet, Rolla, Macbeth, Richard III, and Romeo. An injury to his leg in a stage-coach accident made him slightly lame for the rest of his life. He returned to England in 1823 to become stage manager at Drury Lane under Elliston. In 1827 he played Iago there to the Othello of Edmund Kean, with whom he acted also as Edgar, Malcolm, Macduff, Faulconbridge, and Richmond.

The autumn of 1828 brought him again to America. When he played at the Arch Street Theatre in Philadelphia, the competition of Edwin Forrest at the Walnut and Thomas Abthorpe Cooper [qq.v.] at the Chestnut resulted in his being paid $200 nightly, a very high salary for the period. From 1834 to 1836 he was again in England, but his American engagements were becoming more and more important, and in 1836 he offered $1,000 for a satisfactory play by an American writer. Nathaniel P. Willis' *Tortesa the Usurer,* first produced in April 1839, is believed to have been the one accepted. On Sept. 1, 1837, he assumed the management of the National Theatre in New York, the first of four Wallack theatres, with his brother Henry as stage manager. When the house was burned Sept. 23, 1839, he took over Niblo's Garden for a time. After tours in America, England, and Ireland, he appeared in London in 1843 as leading actor and stage manager of the Princess Theatre, where he achieved one of his greatest successes as Don César de Bazan. In 1844 was again at the Park, New York. He is said to have crossed the Atlantic thirty-five times.

Early in 1851 he appeared at the Haymarket, London, as actor and stage manager. But his wife's death that year brought on an illness and greatly saddened him. Upon his recovery, he appeared for the last time in England at St. Pierre in J. S. Knowles's *The Wife*. Back in New York in 1852, he took over Brougham's Lyceum at Broadway and Broome Streets, and, with his sons John Lester [*q.v.*] as stage manager and Charles as treasurer, opened it in September with *The Way to Get Married*. There for nine years the second of the Wallack theatres flourished, with the manager himself playing many and varied parts—his implacable Shylock, his gentle Sir Edward Mortimer in Colman's *The Iron Chest*, his whimsical Jaques of *As You Like It*, his Martin Heywood in Jerrold's *The Rent Day*, his Petruchio, Mortimer, Erasmus Bookworm, Dick Dashall, and many others. To Wallack's thoroughness as stage manager Edward A. Sothern [*q.v.*] attributed much of his success (*Birds of a Feather, post*, p. 57). A grand benefit was given him on the afternoon and evening of May 29, 1855, at the Academy of Music, Forrest, E. L. Davenport [*q.v.*], and others of America's foremost actors taking part. In 1861 he and Lester opened the new Wallack's Theatre at Broadway and Thirteenth Street. Wallack had ceased acting by this time, but at the close of the season in 1862 he spoke a few words, his last public appearance. His health declined rapidly thereafter until his death on Christmas Day, 1864. Though the admirable versatility of Wallack's acting is considered by one critic to have been in a sense a hindrance to him (Odell, *post*, II, 529), he remains the most distinguished member of a notable family whose history for over fifty years was inseparably linked with that of the New York stage.

[See *A Sketch of the Life of James William Wallack (Senior)* (1865); M. J. Moses, *Famous Actor-Families in America* (1906), which has a discussion of the date of birth, and article in *Theatre*, May 1905; William Oxberry, *Oxberry's Dramatic Biog.*, vol. V (1826); John Genest, *Some Account of the English Stage* (1832); T. A. Brown, *A Hist. of the N. Y. Stage* (3 vols., 1903); G. C. D. Odell, *Annals of the N. Y. Stage*, vol. II (1927); Lester Wallack, *Memories of Fifty Years* (1889); A. C. Dayton, *Last Days of Knickerbocker Life in N. Y.* (1897 ed.); W. C. Russell, *Representative Actors* (1872); F. G. De Fontaine, *Birds of a Feather . . . Talks with Sothern* (1878); J. H. Hackett, *Notes and Comments* (1863); *Wilkes' Spirit of the Times*, Mar. 8, 1862; Robinson Locke Dramatic Coll. and other clippings, N. Y. Pub. Lib.; obituaries in *N. Y. Tribune*, Dec. 26, and *N. Y. Herald*, Dec 27, 1864.]
                                        A. F. H.

WALLACK, JAMES WILLIAM (Feb. 24, 1818–May 24, 1873), actor, son of Henry John [*q.v.*] and Fanny (Jones) Wallack, was born in London, England, but was brought to America

in 1819 for a stay of several years. At the age of four he made his first stage appearance in Philadelphia, playing the part of Cora's child with his uncle, James William Wallack [*q.v.*], in *Pizarro*. When the latter seized him with well-simulated anger, he spoiled the scene by screaming and begging "Uncle Jim" not to hurt him, while the house rocked with laughter. He attended private schools in New York and in England. At fourteen he became call boy at the Bowery Theatre, New York, where he also played small parts. At seventeen, after several seasons with provincial touring companies in England, he joined his father, then stage manager at Covent Garden Theatre, London. Two years later he was engaged for the National Theatre, New York, and there in three years rose from "walking gentleman" to leading juvenile. When his uncle, the elder James William, opened there in 1837 in *The Rivals*, young James played Fag. Later he was engaged for the Bowery Theatre, and soon began playing leads in tragedy and comedy. Sometime before 1844 he was married at New Orleans to Mrs. Ann Duff (Waring) Sefton, a notable tragic actress, who thereafter appeared with him in many plays. His two children by her both died young. He played Othello at the Haymarket, London (1851), Macbeth in Philadelphia (1852), and later toured America with great success. In 1853 and 1855 he made two losing ventures as a manager in London and Paris. Thereafter he remained in the United States, where his earnings were large.

He was at his best in tragedy or romantic and somber drama, especially in parts where a rugged physique and a deep, powerful, but flexible voice could be displayed to advantage. Macbeth, Othello, Hotspur, Iago, Richard III, and Leon de Bourbon in *The Man in the Iron Mask* were favorite parts with his public, and he is declared to have been the only American who made a success with Byron's *Werner*. In 1861 he and Mrs. Wallack for a few weeks played with Edwin L. Davenport [*q.v.*], and then for three years divided honors in a Shakespearean repertoire. In 1865 he joined the stock company of his cousin Lester Wallack [*q.v.*] at the latter's theatre in New York. On Dec. 27, 1867, he appeared for the first time in the rôle of Fagin in *Oliver Twist*. He was not anxious to play the part, studied it carelessly, did little rehearsing, and went to the theatre with only a vague notion of what he was going to do. But once into the part, his natural genius inspired him, and the character became the talk of New York. Here also he scored heavily in the eccentric character of Johnson in

The Lancashire Lass, one of his phrases, "a party by the name of Johnson," becoming a catchword of the day. At Booth's Theatre in the winter of 1872–73 he made a deep impression as Matthias in *The Bells* and displayed his old versatile genius as Mercutio, Jaques, and other classic characters. But he had contracted tuberculosis and was compelled to retire in mid-season. He died a few months later on a train near Aiken, S. C., whither he had gone in search of health.

[G. C. D. Odell, *Annals of the N. Y. Stage,* vols. V–VII (1927–31); M. J. Moses, *Famous Actor-Families in America* (1906); *The Autobiog. of Joseph Jefferson* (1897); Alfred Ayres, in *Theatre,* May 1902; Robinson Locke Dramatic Coll. and other clippings, N. Y. Pub. Lib.; obituary in *N. Y. Times,* May 25, 1873.]

A. F. H.

WALLACK, JOHN LESTER [See WALLACK, LESTER, 1820–1888].

WALLACK, LESTER (Jan. 1, 1820–Sept. 6, 1888), actor, dramatist, son of James William [*q.v.*] and Susan (Johnstone) Wallack, was born in New York City so near midnight on Dec. 31, 1819, that the exact date was in question. He was christened John Johnstone Wallack. His early education was obtained in private schools in England. At fifteen, at a school at Brighton, he played his first dramatic part, that of Rolla in *Pizarro,* and did well until he spoiled the evening by making his death-fall so close to the footlights that the curtain came down across him, whereupon his fellow-actors dragged him under it by the legs, while the audience roared with laughter. "I hesitated long," says he, "before I made up my mind to become an actor" (*Memories of Fifty Years,* p. 24). His first professional appearance was therefore delayed until he was nearly twenty, when he played Angelo in Willis' play, *Tortesa the Usurer,* with his father in the English provinces. Resolved not to lean on his father's name, he was billed as "Allan Field." A year later he played with his uncle Henry [*q.v.*] at Rochester, near London, under the name of John Lester. For a time he was a member of the Theatre Royal company, Dublin, and in 1844 stage manager and actor at the Theatre Royal, Southampton. In 1845 at the Queen's Theatre, Manchester, he played Benedick to the Beatrice of the beautiful Helen Faucit, and Mercutio to the Romeo of Charlotte Cushman. On the latter's high recommendation he was engaged for the Haymarket, London, but through unfortunate circumstances did not make a very good impression.

An offer of £8 a week in 1847 took him to America, where he made his first appearance at the Broadway Theatre, New York, on Sept. 27 as Sir Charles Coldstream in *Used Up,* a farce.

During that season (under the name of John Wallack Lester) he handled such parts as Captain Absolute, Mercutio, Sir Frederick Blount in Bulwer-Lytton's *Money,* and Osric in *Hamlet.* At the Chatham Theatre in July 1848 he made a sensation as Don César de Bazan; at the Broadway in August he played Cassio to Edwin Forrest's Othello, and in December won another success as Edmond Dantès in *The Count of Monte Cristo.* That year he was secretly married to Emily Mary Millais, sister of Sir John Millais, the artist. During 1849 Wallack presented two of his own plays, *The Three Guardsmen,* with himself as d'Artagnan and his cousin James William [*q.v.*] as Athos, and *The Four Musketeers, or Ten Years After,* both winning great popular acclaim. In September 1850 he entered Burton's company at the Chambers Street Theatre, where he was noted for his Sir Andrew Aguecheek and Charles Surface. When his father took over Brougham's Lyceum in September 1852, Lester was stage manager. Here his numerous parts, mostly comic or romantic, included those of Claude Melnotte, Wildrake, Bassanio, Don Pedro, Orlando, Sir Benjamin Backbite, and Captain Absolute. He also appeared in his own plays, as De Rameau in *Two to One* (1854), Peveril in *First Impressions* (1856), Leon Delmar in *The Veteran* (when, as C. H. Haswell says in his *Reminiscences of an Octogenarian,* 1896, the sacrifice of Lester's beautiful whiskers for this part "excited general lamentation among the young womanhood of the city"), Manuel in *The Romance of a Poor Young Man,* and Wyndham Otis in *Central Park* (1861). The Wallack company included among other famous actors Laura Keene, John Brougham, E. A. Sothern, Henry Placide, and George Holland [*qq.v.*].

When the new Wallack's Theatre was opened at Broadway and Thirteenth Street in 1861, it was Lester who was the real manager. There he appeared for the first time as Lester Wallack and played many new parts: Elliott Grey in his own play, *Rosedale* (1863), Hugh Chalcote in *Ours,* Henry Beauclerc in *Diplomacy* (1878), and Prosper Couramont in *A Scrap of Paper* (1879). Many famous names are found in the company from time to time—the younger James W. Wallack, John Gibbs Gilbert, Edwin L. Davenport [*qq.v.*], Charles Fisher, and Charles J. Mathews, for examples. This house closed in April 1881, and the new Wallack Theatre at Broadway and Thirtieth Street was opened on Jan. 4, 1882. Wallack managed it until 1887, when he retired. On May 21, 1888, one of the most famous of all theatrical benefits was given for him; *Hamlet* was played with Edwin Booth in the lead, Lawrence Barrett as the Ghost, Joseph Jefferson and William J. Florence as the grave-diggers, Helena Modjeska as Ophelia, Gertrude Kellogg as the Queen, Rose Coghlan as the Player Queen, and other well-known players in the supporting parts. Wallack died less than four months later at his home near Stamford, Conn. He was survived by his wife and four children. His reminiscences, *Memories of Fifty Years,* was published in 1889.

[In addition to Wallack's *Memories of Fifty Years* (1889), see M. J. Moses, *Famous Actor-Families in America* (1906); Edward Robins, *Twelve Great Actors* (1900); *Wilkes' Spirit of the Times,* Apr. 26, 1862; William Stuart, in *Galaxy,* Oct. 1868; W. J. Florence, in *North Am. Rev.,* Oct. 1888; *Critic,* May 26, Sept. 15, 1888; Arthur Wallack, in *Evening Post* (N. Y.), July 23, Dec. 17, 1910; Robinson Locke Dramatic Coll. and other newspaper clippings, N. Y. Pub. Lib.; obituary and editorial in *N. Y. Times,* Sept. 7, 1888.]

A. F. H.

WALLER, EMMA (*c.* 1820–Feb. 28, 1899), actress, was born in England, and after a brief stage career in the provincial theatres of that country traveled to the United States in 1851 with Daniel Wilmarth Waller, to whom she had been married in 1849. Her husband was an actor and is said to have been a native of New York, the son of a merchant named Wilmarth, the transposed name by which he and his wife were known being assumed for professional purposes at the outset of their joint stage career. Although Mr. Waller acted Hamlet and other tragic rôles in New York soon after their arrival, there is no authentic record of his wife's appearance in that city at this time. Going to San Francisco in 1853, they sailed thence for Australia, where at Melbourne Mrs. Waller acted Lady Macbeth. Returning to London, Mrs. Waller made her début at the Drury Lane on Sept. 15, 1856, as Pauline in Bulwer-Lytton's *The Lady of Lyons.* In the diaries of E. L. Blanchard he notes that "as Pauline—she lacked vigour, but was gentle and graceful" (Scott and Howard, *post,* I, 164). If his judgment is correct, she must have grown appreciably in physical and intellectual intensity, for she became one of the leading emotional actresses on the American stage.

Towards the end of 1857 the Wallers returned to the United States, where they thereafter remained. Mrs. Waller made her début at the Walnut Street Theatre in Philadelphia on Oct. 19, 1857, as Ophelia to the Hamlet of Mr. Waller. On the second and third nights of that engagement she acted successively Pauline and Lady Macbeth. She was described as "of stately presence, neither slender nor stout in person, and had an interesting and expressive face" (*New York Dramatic Mirror, post,* p. 17); the same spectator adds that she acted Lady Macbeth with an "intensity of . . . passion" that was "almost painful." Her first appearance in New York was on Apr. 5, 1858, as Marina to her husband's Ferdinand in a new version of John Webster's tragedy, *The Duchess of Malfi.* Thereafter she starred for some twenty years throughout the country, often with Mr. Waller as her principal associate, among her most conspicuous characters being Queen Margaret in *Richard III* and Queen Katharine in *Henry VIII* (both in support of Edwin Booth), Meg Merrilies in *Guy Mannering,* Nelly Brady in Edmund Falconer's *The Peep o'Day,* and Julia in Sheridan Knowles's *The Hunchback.* Though Mrs. Waller was accused of imitating the Meg Merrilies of Charlotte Cushman, she had never seen her in the part, and her Meg was an original assumption of that character. "The weird dignity of her bearing," wrote William Winter, "was impressive beyond words; there were moments, indeed, when she seemed to be a soul inspired by communion with beings of another world" (*post,* p. 196). She was also one of a number of actresses who seemed to take pleasure in impersonating male Shakespearean characters, among the most noteworthy of these being her interpretations of Hamlet and Iago. She closed her career as an actress in 1878 as Hester Stanhope in a modern play entitled *An Open Verdict.* Afterwards, like many other actors and actresses, she gave public readings from Shakespeare and other dramatists, her last noteworthy public appearance being made at Chickering Hall in New York on Dec. 1, 1881. Mr. Waller died in 1882, and for some years thereafter she taught elocution in New York. Ill health finally compelled her to abandon all active professional work, and she lived in complete retirement at the home of her son in New York, where she died.

[J. N. Ireland, *Records of the N. Y. Stage,* vol. II (1867); T. A. Brown, *Hist. of the Am. Stage* (1870) and *A Hist. of the N. Y. Stage* (3 vols., 1903); G. C. D. Odell, *Annals of the N. Y. Stage,* vols. VI–VII (1931); Clement Scott and Cecil Howard, *The Life and Reminiscences of E. L. Blanchard* (2 vols., 1891); William Winter, *The Wallet of Time,* vol. I (1913); obituaries in *N. Y. Tribune,* Mar. 2, 1899, *Boston Transcript,* Mar. 11, and *N. Y. Dramatic Mirror,* Mar. 11.]

E. F. E.

WALLER, JOHN LIGHTFOOT (Nov. 23, 1809–Oct. 10, 1854), Baptist clergyman, editor, and denominational leader, was born in Woodford County, Ky., the son of Edmund and Elizabeth (Lightfoot) Waller, and a descendant of Col. John Waller who emigrated to Virginia about 1635. He came of a line of pioneer Baptist preachers: his great-uncle John Waller was incarcerated repeatedly by the Virginia colonial authorities for preaching the Gospel "contrary to law"; his grandfather, William E. Waller, was a useful minister in both Virginia and Kentucky; his father was renowned for his evangelistic zeal and is reported to have baptized 1,500 persons. Scantily rewarded for his ministerial labors, Edmund Waller nevertheless assembled a good library and sent his older sons to school. Upon their return he placed his younger children under their instruction and from his brothers John Lightfoot Waller received his early education. Later he spent fifteen months at the Nicholasville Academy, where he completed the requirements in Latin and Greek for admission to Transylvania University. Unable to attend college, he purchased the textbooks used in Transylvania and, studying at home, finished the required college course. So retentive was his memory and so thorough his knowledge of whatever he read that his father called him his "Theological Encyclopaedia." He taught a select school in Jessamine County from 1828 to 1834; joined the Glen's Creek Baptist Church in 1833; and in August of the following year married Amanda M. Beatty.

The Baptists at this time were numerically the leading religious body in Kentucky. In 1830, however, Alexander Campbell [q.v.] and others caused a division by seeking to restore "original Christianity." Waller ably defended the faith of his fathers in a pamphlet entitled *Letters to a Reformer, Alias Campbellite* (1835), in which he reviewed the history of the so-called "Current Reformation." This won for him the reputation of being a courageous and vigorous writer. Strongly urged by his admirers, he accepted in 1835 the editorship of the *Baptist Banner*, Shelbyville, Ky., then the only Baptist paper in Kentucky. By 1841 the influence of this periodical had been greatly extended through its absorption of the *Pioneer* of Illinois and the *Baptist* of Tennessee. Thereafter it was known as the *Baptist Banner and Western Pioneer*. The Baptist ministry soon recognized in their young lay editor an able champion of their faith and a wise counselor in all their plans. In 1840 Waller was ordained at Louisville, and for a brief period was a country pastor. For two years, 1841–43, he was the general agent of the General Association of Kentucky Baptists, the acceptance of which office occasioned his retirement as editor.

From 1842 to his death, he participated in many public religious debates, vigorously defending the Baptist position against the chosen representatives of the Presbyterians, the Methodists, the Disciples, and the Universalists. Due largely to his capable and militant leadership,

Kentucky Baptists made notable advancement; the college at Georgetown was reorganized, the General Association of Kentucky Baptists was established for missionary ends, the widespread opposition to an educated ministry waned, and Sunday Schools, Bible, missionary, and benevolent societies multiplied. He founded in 1845 the *Western Baptist Review*, a monthly publication, later called the *Christian Repository*, a periodical which was for many years a potent factor in moulding the religious thought of Southern Baptists. In 1849 he was chosen by popular vote as a delegate to the Kentucky constitutional convention. The next year he resumed editorship of the *Baptist Banner and Western Pioneer*. In 1852 he was elected president of the Bible Revision Association, serving in that capacity until his death. His writings include "The History of Kentucky Baptists," in Lewis Collins' *Historical Sketches of Kentucky* (1847) and *Open Communion Shown to be Unscriptural and Deleterious . . . to Which is Added A History of Infant Baptism* (1859). He died in Louisville, and was buried in Frankfort, Ky.

[J. H. Spencer, *A Hist. of Ky. Baptists* (1886), vol. I; W. B. Sprague, *Annals of the Am. Pulpit*, vol. VI (1860); William Cathcart, *The Baptist Encyc.* (1881); *Western Rev.*, 1845–49; *Christian Repository*, 1849–54; *Va. Mag. of Hist. and Biog.*, Jan. 1914; *Tri-Weekly Ky. Yeoman* (Frankfort), Oct. 12, 1854.]

R. W. W.

WALLER, THOMAS MACDONALD (c. 1840–Jan. 25, 1924), lawyer, governor of Connecticut, was born in New York, the son of Thomas Christopher Armstrong and Mary his wife, emigrants from Ireland. His parents and a brother died before he was nine years old. For a summer he sold papers in New York and then shipped as a cabin boy on a fishing vessel. In 1849 he was aboard the schooner *Mount Vernon*, which was to sail for California from New London, Conn., but through the interest of a New London merchant, Thomas K. Waller, he elected to remain in the East. Waller adopted him, and upon reaching his majority Armstrong took his benefactor's name. He attended the Bartlett High School in New London, studied law, and in 1861 was admitted to the New London County bar. On Apr. 22 of that year he enlisted in Company E, 2nd Connecticut Volunteers, but on account of trouble with his eyes was discharged the following June. In partnership with a schoolmate, Samuel H. Davis, he then entered upon the practice of law in New London.

His career in Democratic politics began in 1867–68, when he served as representative from New London in the General Assembly. His maiden speech was in advocacy of bridging the

Connecticut River at Saybrook and was based on what was for him a characteristic argument: "You cannot resist the 19th Century." In 1870 and 1871 he was secretary of state, and in 1872 and 1876 was returned to the General Assembly, serving as speaker during his last term. From 1876 to 1883 he was the state's attorney for New London County. In 1883 he was elected governor by a majority of 2,390 in a normally Republican state. In the election of 1885 he received a plurality, but not the constitutional majority required at that time, and his opponent was therefore chosen by a Republican legislature. From 1885 to 1889 he was consul-general at London, England.

After his return he removed his law practice to New York but retained his residence in New London. In New York he formed the firm of Waller, Cook & Wagner, which became identified with public service corporations in the West. As the leader of Connecticut Democrats he seconded the nomination of Grover Cleveland at the Chicago convention in 1884. At the convention of 1896 he uncompromisingly attacked Bryan's free-silver policy and as a protest against his nomination led the Connecticut delegation from the hall. It was in this campaign that Waller rose to his greatest heights. The New York *Sun* had already conferred on him the title of "The Little Giant from Connecticut," for he resembled Stephen Douglas in size, physical vigor, eloquence, and power on the platform. As leader of the "Gold Democrats" in Connecticut he spoke before a hissing gallery at the Grand Opera House in New Haven, and in ten minutes had the crowd in sympathy with him personally, if not with his faction of the party. Although he reconciled the opposing factions after the campaign, his influence in the party was diminishing. After 1900 he took little part in politics, although he was one of the two vice-presidents of the Connecticut constitutional convention of 1902. Thenceforward he was the "Grand Old Man" of Connecticut Democrats.

In New London "Tom" Waller was known as a rough and ready, breezy, democratic individual who had intense personal magnetism and unusual ability as a public speaker. He was mayor of the city from 1873 to 1879. Against considerable opposition he discouraged small-town ways of doing things, and thus laid the foundation for municipal growth. He was also active in real-estate developments, notably that of Ocean Beach, and was an incorporator of the street railway and of the Mechanics Savings Bank. His wife was Charlotte Bishop of New London,

by whom he had one daughter and five sons. Waller died at Ocean Beach.

[F. C. Norton, *The Governors of Conn.* (1905); *Encyc. of Conn. Biog.* (1917), vol. IV; W. F. Moore, *Representative Men of Conn.* (1894); Dwight Loomis and J. G. Calhoun, *The Judicial and Civil Hist. of Conn.* (1895); *Who's Who in America,* 1918–19; *New London Day,* Jan. 25, 1924, and following days; *New Haven Journal-Courier,* Jan. 26, 1924.]

W. G. La—d.

WALLIS, SEVERN TEACKLE (Sept. 8, 1816–Apr. 11, 1894), lawyer, author, was born in Baltimore, Md., the second son of Philip and Elizabeth Custis (Teackle) Wallis, both descended from families long settled upon the Eastern Shore of Chesapeake Bay. After attending private schools and St. Mary's College, Baltimore, where he graduated in 1832, he studied law in the office of William Wirt [*q.v.*] and of Judge John Glenn, and in 1837 was admitted to the bar. He was one of the founders of the Maryland Historical Society in 1844, and that same year became a corresponding member of the Royal Academy of History, Madrid; two years later he was admitted a fellow of the Royal Society of Northern Antiquities, Copenhagen. In 1847 he made his first visit to Spain, and in 1849, commissioned by the government to report upon the titles to public lands in Florida, he embarked upon his second visit. Both inspired literary productions. He proved a prolific writer, leaving addresses, verses, and criticisms which, when collected for publication by admiring friends, filled four volumes (*Writings of Severn Teackle Wallis,* Memorial Edition, 1896). He was a frequent contributor to the daily press, and his anonymous articles on current topics were often recognizable from their terseness, pungency, wit, and wealth of illustration.

A Whig in early life, Wallis became a Democrat upon the disintegration of his party, but he was preëminently the reformer, never surrendering his personal independence of opinion. His first appearance as a candidate was in 1847, when he was defeated for the legislature. In 1851 he made an unsuccessful bid for the office of state's attorney, but in 1857 refused the post of district attorney proffered him by President Buchanan. He joined in the reform movement of 1858 in Baltimore, writing an influential address, and the following year was a member of the committee which drew up a series of reform bills adopted by the legislature in 1860; one of these measures was an election law which made possible a reform government for Baltimore. In 1861, after the struggle between the sections had brought open rupture, his sympathies were with the Confederacy, although he did not advocate secession. He was elected against his wishes a delegate to the special Assembly held at Frederick in April 1861, and as chairman of the Committee on Federal Relations of the House of Delegates, he expressed his views in several reports, arguing vigorously against the doctrine of military necessity. This action made him obnoxious to the Washington government, and along with other prominent Marylanders he was arrested in September and suffered imprisonment for fourteen months. His letters to the press in the heated campaign of 1875, when he supported the Reform ticket, are among the choicest of Maryland polemics. Subsequently, despite frail health, he participated actively in the campaigns of 1882 to 1887, in which his thoughtful eloquence was a powerful weapon.

For almost half a century Wallis was regarded as the leader of the Maryland bar. He argued thousands of cases before the state courts and appeared before the United States Supreme Court in many important cases. His eloquence brought him into frequent demand as an occasional speaker. For twenty years he served as provost of the University of Maryland. He was one of the original trustees of Peabody Institute and president of the board during the last year of his life. From 1892 until his death he was president of the Maryland Historical Society. He also served as president of the Civil Service Reform Association of Maryland and the Reform League of Baltimore. Though domestic in his tastes—loving his home, his books, and his friends—he never married.

[C. Sems and E. S. Riley, *The Bench and Bar of Md.* (1901) ; J. T. Scharf, *Hist. of Baltimore City and County* (1881) ; *The Biog. Cyc. of Representative Men of Md. and the D. C.* (1879) ; R. H. Spencer, *Geneal. and Memorial Encyc. of the State of Md.* (1919), vol. II ; W. H. Browne, Introduction to Wallis' *Works*, vol. I ; Bernard Steiner, "Severn Teackle Wallis," *Sewanee Rev.*, Jan.–Apr. 1907 ; *Hist. of Baltimore, Md.* (1898) ; S. C. Chew, *Addresses on Several Occasions* (1906) ; W. C. Bruce, *Seven Great Baltimore Lawyers* (1931) ; and J. U. Dennis, "Some Personal Recollections of a Quartet of the Baltimore Bar," *Report of the . . . Md. State Bar Asso.*, 1905 ; *Proc. Md. Hist. Soc. in Commemoration of . . . Severn Teackle Wallis* (1896) : *Sun* (Baltimore), and *Baltimore American*, Apr. 11, 1894 ; several letters preserved at the Maryland Hist. Soc.]   E. L.

WALN, NICHOLAS (Sept. 19, 1742–Sept. 29, 1813), lawyer, Quaker preacher, was born at Fair Hill, near Philadelphia, Pa., the son of Nicholas and Mary (Shoemaker) Waln and a cousin of Robert Waln, 1765–1836 [*q.v.*]. His great-grandfather, Nicholas Waln, born in the West Riding of Yorkshire, emigrated in the *Welcome* and arrived at New Castle, Del., in 1682. Waln was educated in the William Penn Charter School, and became both a good Latin and German scholar. He was admitted to the bar, Oct. 8,

1762, and had eight cases as a minor in a single term of court. He quickly became a successful lawyer. In 1763–64 he spent a year as a student in the Inns of Court in London. On his return to Philadelphia his fees for a year, on his own testimony, reached the mark of £2000. In February 1772 he experienced a remarkable religious conversion which culminated in a unique public prayer (reported in Joseph Oxley's *Journal of His Life*, 1838, p. 474). He immediately withdrew from the practice of law and gave himself completely to the service of the Society of Friends, of which he was a lifelong member. He was married, May 22, 1771, to Sarah Richardson. They had seven children, only three of whom reached maturity.

In 1783 Waln went on an extensive religious visit of two years to England, visiting the families of the members of the Society of Friends as well as the public meetings in that country. His preaching was marked by unusual power, and he was recognized at home and abroad as one of the most impressive Quaker preachers of that period. In 1795 he paid a similar visit to the Quaker meetings and families in Ireland. He possessed an almost uncanny gift for feeling out the states of mind and conditions of life of persons in his audiences, and acquired, especially during the visit in Ireland, the reputation of being a "prophet." During the period between 1772 and 1813 he exercised a notable influence upon the Society of Friends in Philadelphia, and in his travels he reached most of the centers of Quaker life and thought in America. In 1789 he was appointed clerk (chief official) of the Philadelphia Yearly Meeting, which included the Friends of Pennsylvania and New Jersey. From the year 1777 until 1789 he was clerk of meeting of ministers and elders. He took an important part in the proceedings of the meeting at the critical time of the Revolutionary War in its dealing with the "Free Quakers," who supported the patriotic cause with arms. In this connection he appears as one of the characters in Dr. S. Weir Mitchell's novel, *Hugh Wynne*. Notwithstanding the weight and solemnity of Waln's preaching, he was inclined to humor and was noted for his wit and repartee.

[Mary I. Harrison, *Annals of the Ancestry of Charles Custis Harrison and Ellen Waln Harrison* (1932) ; R. C. Moon, *The Morris Family of Phila.*, vol. II (1898) ; J. W. Jordan, *Colonial Families of Phila.* (1911), vol. I ; *Quaker Biogs.*, vol. IV (1914) ; James Bowden, *The Hist. of the Soc. of Friends in America*, vol. II (1854) ; Isaac Sharpless, *A Hist. of Quaker Government in Pa.* (1898), vol. II ; H. D. Eberlein and H. M. Lippincott, *The Colonial Homes of Phila.* (1912) ; minutes of the Phila. Yearly Meeting, 1789–1813, unpublished ; John Smith, "MS. Memorials," vol. III, 1722–77, in Haverford Coll. Lib. ; *Friend*, 1848, pp.

53–54, 1904, p. 140; obituary in *Poulson's Am. Daily Advertiser*, Oct. 1, 1813.]   R. M. J.

WALN, ROBERT (Feb. 22, 1765–Jan. 24, 1836), merchant, manufacturer, politician, was born in Philadelphia, Pa., the youngest son of Robert and Rebecca (Coffin) Waln and a great-grandson of Nicholas Waln who settled in Pennsylvania in 1682. He entered his father's counting-house at an early age. Upon his father's death in 1791 he entered into a joint partnership at 57 South Wharves with Jesse Waln, his cousin, who had also been trading in foreign merchandise. Together they built up a thriving business in the West India and English trades, and later concentrated upon the East India and Chinese trades. Their enterprises were on a large scale, Stephen Girard [*q.v.*] being the only one who exceeded them in their business ventures. On Oct. 10, 1787, Waln married Phebe Lewis, by whom he had nine children. One of his sons was Robert Waln [*q.v.*].

He was very active in civic and national affairs, especially during the exciting period between the adoption of the Constitution and the War of 1812. He was a member of the Pennsylvania state legislature (1794–98) and of the House of Representatives, where he first filled a vacancy and then served a term from Dec. 3, 1798, to Mar. 3, 1801. Like all substantial ship-owners at that time, he was a Federalist and therefore opposed to the ruling party because of the restrictions placed upon shipping. He was one of the Federal leaders who engaged a thousand sailors to protect their political meeting in January 1809 from being interrupted by the Republicans, the result of which was an extensive riot. He also entered into a violent debate with John Rutledge of South Carolina and John Randolph of Virginia, when he presented a petition in the Sixth Congress regarding the slave trade and the Fugitive Slave Law (Simpson, *post*, p. 929). During the War of 1812 he constructed one of the first cotton textile mills at Trenton, N. J. He also had an extensive interest in the Phoenixville iron-works. Because of these two connections, he became an ardent protectionist and became strongly identified with the high tariff acts of 1816, 1824, and 1828. When the famous Boston Report was published exerting a strong influence for free trade, Waln was selected by the Pennsylvania Society for the Encouragement of Manufactures and Arts as best fitted to reply. His report of over one hundred pages, *An Examination of the Boston Report* (1828), was considered as having successfully countered all the assertions made by the free traders. Waln's other offices included those of

vice-president of the Philadelphia chamber of commerce (1809), director of the Philadelphia Insurance Company (1804–13), first president of the Mercantile Library (1821–24), and trustee of the University of Pennsylvania (1829). He was a member of the common council of the city of Philadelphia (1794, 1796) and of the select council (1807, 1809, 1811). He was an orthodox Quaker and actively entered into the controversy against Elias Hicks [*q.v.*], who was advocating the liberalization of the Quaker rules and regulations. His *Seven Letters to Elias Hicks* (1825) attracted a great deal of attention.

[J. K. Simon, *Biog. of Successful Phila. Merchants* (1864), pp. 129–32; Henry Simpson, *Lives of Eminent Philadelphians* (1859); J. T. Scharf and Thompson Westcott, *Hist. of Phila.* (1884), vol. III, p. 2213; H. M. Lippincott, *Early Phila.* (1917); E. P. Oberholtzer, *Phila., a Hist. of the City*, vol. II (1912); H. D. Eberlein and H. M. Lippincott, *The Colonial Homes of Phila.* (1912); Abraham Ritter, *Phila. and Her Merchants* (1860); letter from James Canby to David Lewis, May 22, 1819, in Ridgway Branch of the Lib. Company of Phila.; *Biog. Dir. Am. Cong.* (1928); J. F. Watson, *Annals of Phila.*, vol. I (1856), vol. III (1879); J. W. Jordan, *Colonial and Revolutionary Families of Pa.* (1911), vol. III, and *Colonial Families of Phila.* (1911), vol. I; obituary in *Poulson's Am. Daily Advertiser*, Jan. 25, 1836.]   H. S. P.

WALN, ROBERT (Oct. 20, 1794–July 4, 1825), author, known as Robert Waln, Jr., son of Robert [*q.v.*] and Phebe (Lewis) Waln, was born in Philadelphia, Pa., and died unmarried at Providence, R. I., in his thirty-first year. The wealth and social position of his family made it unnecessary for him to earn his living. On the other hand, the traditions of the Society of Friends with whom they had long been affiliated forbade idleness. The young man showed an active interest in the great importing business conducted by Jesse and Robert Waln, his father and father's cousin, with Canton and the East. But literature was his chosen pursuit. His education, obviously liberal, was broadened by extensive and purposeful reading, for which Philadelphia afforded rich opportunities, while at the stately country seat of his father, Waln-Grove, at Frankford, five miles from Philadelphia, was an unusually large and well-equipped library. He maintained an eager interest in current American literary activity, contributed to the periodicals of the times and was conversant with their editors, and developed a special aptitude for criticism and biography. He exemplifies very well a Philadelphia tradition of aristocratic scholarship and belles-lettres.

His first independently published work (February 1819) was a vivid satire on manners in the wealthy inner circle of Philadelphia society: *The Hermit in America on a Visit to Philadelphia. . . . Edited by Peter Atall, Esq.* In March of the same year this had a second edition, in which considerable alterations were made. Early in 1821 appeared a second series of the Hermit's observations. These works are both in prose. In November 1820 Waln had published *Sisyphi Opus, or Touches at the Times,* written in classical couplets, touching on some of the same themes. Another satire, purely literary in subject, also written in couplets, *American Bards,* had been published in August 1820. Part of this, the author said, had been written during a voyage "beyond the Cape of Good Hope." It should not be confused with a contemporary piece of the same title.

During 1823 he published, in quarto numbers, an elaborate work on China, its geography, history, customs, and trade relations. His interest in this subject was definitely related to the family business. Intensive research during many years was supplemented by a four months' residence in Canton from September 1819 to January 1820. The first draft of the manuscript was largely written during the long voyage home. About the same time he took over the editorship of the *Biography of the Signers to the Declaration of Independence* (vols. III–VI, 1823–24), which had been begun by John and James Sanderson. Altogether he edited or wrote some fourteen of the lives. From Waln-Grove in the summer of 1824 he issued proposals for publishing by subscription a *Life of the Marquis de La Fayette,* completing it at the same place in June 1825. His sudden death occurred scarcely three weeks later. In August was published posthumously his *Account of the Asylum for the Insane Established by the Society of Friends, near Frankford, in the Vicinity of Philadelphia.* All these works show a remarkable ability for compiling and verifying facts. His talent is further shown by his lyric poems, which, though few in number, bring the more intimate side of his personality attractively to view. They are to be found chiefly in the little volume containing "Sisyphi Opus." A few remain uncollected from current publications, like the *Atlantic Souvenir.* So also does some of his prose.

[Sources include records of the Phila. Monthly Meeting, Southern District, of the Soc. of Friends, from which the date of birth is taken; colls. of the Geneal. Soc. of Pa., the Hist. Soc. of Pa., and the Ridgway Branch of the Lib. Company of Phila.; Samuel Kettell, *Specimens of Am. Poetry* (1829), vol. III, p. 213; obituary in *Poulson's Am. Daily Advertiser,* July 9, 1825.]   J. C. M.

WALSH, BENJAMIN DANN (Sept. 21, 1808–Nov. 18, 1869), entomologist, was born in Clapton, London, England, the son of Benjamin Walsh. He was of a well-to-do family; one of his brothers became a clergyman and another, editor of the *Field,* London, and author of a standard treatise on the horse. Benjamin was intended for the church, and was educated at Trinity College, Cambridge, where he received the degree of B.A. in 1831, became a fellow in 1833, and in 1834 was awarded the degree of M.A. He resigned the fellowship, however, and declined to follow the study of divinity. For some years he led a literary life, writing for *Blackwood's Magazine,* and in 1837 publishing *The Comedies of Aristophanes, Translated into Corresponding English Metres.* About this time he married Rebecca Finn, and at the age of thirty emigrated to the United States, expecting to settle in Chicago. He finally made his home in Henry County, Ill., near the town of Cambridge, where for thirteen years he engaged in farming. He then moved to the town of Rock Island, where he carried on a successful lumber business for seven years more.

In England he had known and worked with Charles Darwin, who had aroused his interest in natural history. Retiring from business about 1858, he devoted the rest of his life to entomology. He wrote many articles for the agricultural newspapers and published a number of admirable articles in the *Proceedings of the Boston Society of Natural History* and in the *Transactions of the American Entomological Society.* These papers were of very high rank and attracted the attention of scientific men both in America and in Europe. He became, also, one of the editors of a journal started in Philadelphia known as the *Practical Entomologist.* His ability as an incisive writer, his breadth of knowledge, and his power to prophesy accurately the future of economic entomology were extraordinary. He often pointed out what the states and the federal government should do against the certainty that insect ravages would increase. He was the first to show that American farmers were planting their crops in such a way as to facilitate the multiplication of insects, and was one of the first to suggest the introduction of foreign parasites and natural enemies of imported pests. His witty and vigorous invective against charlatanistic suggestions as to remedies attracted great attention. In 1868, with Charles V. Riley [*q.v.*], he founded and edited the *American Entomologist.* His death occurred in the following year as the result of a railway accident near Rock Island.

Walsh's bibliography shows 385 titles of individual record and 478 in co-authorship with Riley. The latter titles, however, are mainly those of short notes and answers to correspondents in the columns of the *American Entomolo-*

gist. His longer scientific papers were sound and in many respects ahead of his time. He was an early adherent of the doctrine of evolution, and in 1864 published a long paper, "On Certain Entomological Speculations of the New England School of Naturalists" (*Proceedings of the Entomological Society of Philadelphia,* vol. III), in which he attacked the anti-evolutionary views of Agassiz and Dana. In 1867 he was appointed state entomologist of Illinois, and assumed the duties of that position, although his appointment was not confirmed until the next biennial session of the legislature. He was the second state entomologist to be appointed, Asa Fitch [*q.v.*] of New York being the first. Walsh's sole report was published in the *Transactions of the Illinois State Horticultural Society* for 1867. His work in entomology made a great impression both on scientific men and on the leading agriculturists, and undoubtedly the influence of this mature, cultivated, and far-seeing man accounts in part for Riley's brilliant career. Walsh's collections and many of his notes were destroyed in the Chicago fire of 1871.

[For sources, see W. W. R. Ball and J. A. Venn, *Admissions to Trinity Coll., Cambridge,* vol. IV (1911); Samuel Henshaw, *Bibliog. of the More Important Contributions to Am. Economic Entomology* (1890); E. A. Tucker, in *Trans. Ill. State Hist. Soc. for 1920* (1921); C. V. Riley, in *Am. Entomologist,* Dec. 1869, Jan. 1870; *Ill. State Jour.* (Springfield), Nov. 23, 1869. The date of birth is that given by Riley; E. A. Tucker gives July 1808; the birthplace is from Ball and Venn.]

L. O. H.

WALSH, BLANCHE (Jan. 4, 1873–Oct. 31, 1915), actress, daughter of Thomas P. and Armenia (Savorie) Walsh, was born on the lower East Side of New York, where her father, popularly known as "Fatty" Walsh, was a well-to-do saloonkeeper and Tammany politician. She spent fifteen months of her girlhood in the living quarters of the Tombs, New York's famous prison, where her father then held the position of warden. She received a common-school education. Her parents (her mother in particular) were inveterate theatre-goers, and Blanche, even when a girl, began to take much interest in amateur acting. In 1888, at the age of fifteen, she made her first professional appearance in a small part in Bartley Campbell's melodrama, *Siberia.* Marie Wainwright, then a famous star, became interested in her and took her into her company in 1889, her first appearance in New York being at the Fifth Avenue Theatre in December, as Olivia in *Twelfth Night.* She was nearly a month short of her seventeenth birthday, but was tall and womanly enough in appearance to play mature parts. She remained with that company three years, playing also Grace Harkaway

in Dion Boucicault's *London Assurance* and Queen Elizabeth in *Amy Robsart.* She often spoke of Miss Wainwright as her chief mentor in dramatic art. In 1892 she "created"—as the profession has it—the rôle of Diana Stockton in Bronson Howard's popular society drama, *Aristocracy,* following this with another success, *The Girl I Left Behind Me.* In January 1895 she went with Nat Goodwin as leading woman, playing in *A Gilded Fool, In Mizzoura, David Garrick, The Nominee, The Gold Mine,* and *Lend Me Five Shillings.* A dramatization of Du Maurier's novel, *Trilby,* was one of the hits of the autumn of 1895. When Virginia Harned, the star in it, was taken ill in 1896, Blanche Walsh assumed her place and completed the season amid much acclaim. She then returned to Goodwin's company and spent the summer with him in Australia, playing her former parts and adding *Gringoire* and Lydia Languish in *The Rivals* to the list.

Returning to New York in the autumn of 1896, she joined A. M. Palmer's stock company, first appearing in *Heartsease.* In January 1897, in *Straight from the Heart,* she played two parts, those of a brother and sister. She was tall and had strongly handsome features which lent themselves fairly well to a not too heavy type of masculine characterization. She once essayed briefly even the part of Romeo. In William Gillette's *Secret Service,* she went with the company to England. After a brief stay as leading woman with Sol Smith Russell in *A Bachelor's Romance,* she appeared with the Empire Theatre Stock Company in the winter of 1898–99. In 1899 she joined Melbourne McDowell, and for two years played the Sardou repertoire in which the late Fanny Davenport [*q.v.*] had long starred—*La Tosca, Fédora, Théodora,* and *Cleopatra.* In 1901–03 there followed *Marcelle, More Than Queen, Joan of the Sword Hand,* and *La Madeleine.* In 1903 she was cast in the greatest success of her career, and did probably her finest piece of acting in the rôle of the unfortunate servant girl, Maslova, in a dramatization of Tolstoy's novel, *Resurrection.* Next came another Tolstoy story, *The Kreutzer Sonata,* which she revived in later years. Among her later plays were *The Woman in the Case, The Straight Road, The Test,* and *The Other Woman.* During the last three years of her life, she appeared in one-act plays in vaudeville. She married Alfred Hickman, actor, when he was playing the part of Little Billee with her in *Trilby* in 1896, divorced him in 1903, and on Nov. 15, 1906, married William M. Travers, also an actor. She died in Cleveland, Ohio, survived by her husband.

[*Who's Who in America*, 1914–15; *The Green Room Book*, 1908, ed. by John Parker; T. A. Brown, *A Hist. of the N. Y. Stage*, vol. III (1903); *Munsey's Mag.*, Jan., Oct. 1900; obituaries in *N. Y. Times, Sun* (N. Y.), *N. Y. Herald*, Nov. 1, 1915; reminiscences by Blanche Walsh in *Theatre*, July 1905; three vols. on Blanche Walsh in the Robinson Locke Dramatic Collection, N. Y. Pub. Lib.]   A. F. H.

WALSH, HENRY COLLINS (Nov. 23, 1863–Apr. 29, 1927), explorer, author, and editor, was born in Florence, Italy, of American parents, and was brought to America at the age of nine. His father, Robert M. Walsh, was the son of Robert Walsh [*q.v.*]; his mother was Margaret Blount Mullen, who came of a prominent Southern family. Walsh attended Georgetown College, Washington, D. C., and in 1888 was awarded the degree of M.A. The following year he published *By the Potomac, and Other Verses,* proceeds from the sale of which were dedicated to the Georgetown building fund. Meanwhile he had begun a journalistic career as a reporter for the *Times* of Philadelphia, going thence to Mansfield, Pa., and subsequently to New York City.

In 1894 he read an advertisement which stated that for $500 a person passengers could join an expedition being organized for Arctic exploration by Dr. Frederick A. Cook. Walsh secured a reduced rate by promising to serve as historian of the voyage, and in 1896 published *The Last Cruise of the Miranda,* an account of a venture which had led to "little discovery and many hardships." Thereafter he traveled extensively through Central America, sojourned in Copán in 1896, and the following year made a trip by caravan through Morocco and sections of the Atlas Mountains. His interest in travel revived in 1911, when he cruised through the West Indies. In 1925 he penetrated farther into Endless Cavern, Newmarket, Va., than any man before him had gone. His experiences were described partly in magazine articles and partly in *The White World* (1902), written in collaboration with other members of the Arctic Club, of which he was one of the organizers, and edited by Rudolf Kersting.

Walsh had a wide editorial and journalistic experience. In 1888 he and his brother, W. S. Walsh, started a literary magazine, *American Notes and Queries,* which they edited from May to October of that year. During the Spanish-American War, he was a correspondent in the field for the *New York Herald* and *Harper's Weekly.* After a period of service on the editorial staff of the *Catholic World,* he became successively co-editor (1902–06) of the *Smart Set,* editor of the *Travel Magazine* (1907–10), mem-

ber of the staff of the American Press Association (1911–18), and associate editor of the *National Marine* (1919–21). After 1924 he served as vice-president of the Nomad Publishing Company. Walsh helped to organize the Explorers' Club of New York, and served as president of the Nomad Club and of the Adventurers' Club, also of New York. He was known as a fascinating raconteur. Though born a Catholic, he did not continue in that faith and was buried in Westminster Cemetery, Philadelphia, in which city he died, while absent from his home in New York on a visit to his sister. He was unmarried.

[*Who's Who in America*, 1926–27; *Am. Catholic Who's Who*, 1911; *N. Y. Herald Tribune*, Apr. 30, 1927; W. H. Brewer, *The Arctic Club* (1906); records of Georgetown Univ.; information from Katherine Walsh, sister, and F. S. Dellenbaugh.]
                                        G. N. S.

WALSH, MICHAEL (*c.* 1815–Mar. 17, 1859), politician and editor, was born near Cork, Ireland, and was brought to America in his childhood. His father, Michael Welsh [*sic*], owned a mahogany yard in New York City, and young Mike, as he always called himself, in a turbulent boyhood on the city streets and as a runaway apprentice acquired a realistic knowledge of life among the poor. Learning the printer's trade, he traveled to New Orleans, but in 1839 returned to New York to set up in business for himself. He worked for a time as reporter and Washington correspondent for the *Aurora,* and tried unsuccessfully to found a paper of his own. Proclaiming himself the champion of the "subterranean" democrats ignored by political leaders, he organized young laborers of the city into the Spartan Association, with a view to exemplifying democratic principles by destroying Tammany control of the local Democratic organization. This aim was reached most simply by forcibly removing the enemy from ward meetings, and as the method was soon copied, the organized gang became a new feature in political practice.

In 1843 Walsh founded his own paper, the *Subterranean,* as a means of rousing the working class against the capitalists and politicians who exploited them. His vigorous and denunciatory editorials, for which he sacrificed advertising, pictured vividly the darker side of city life, and at least twice caused his imprisonment for libel. Agreeing with George Henry Evans [*q.v.*] on the ills of society, he accepted the National Reform program, in 1844 merged the *Subterranean* with Evans' *Working Man's Advocate,* and became a frequent speaker at National Reform Conventions; but his bitter and direct attacks on individuals were an embarrassment to

Evans, and the partnership lasted only three months. Walsh then revived the *Subterranean,* conducting it for two years more, and renewed his activity in local politics.

Social reform, however, was losing ground before the anti-slavery issue. As the New York Democrats split over the free-soil controversy, Walsh joined the Hunkers, and denounced the abolitionists who neglected the wage slaves of the North for the cause of the remote negro. He served three uneventful terms in the state Assembly (1846, 1847, 1852), and in 1852 was elected to Congress. There he won some reputation as a ready debater, supported President Pierce's territorial policy, and urged higher pay for enlisted men in the army. He was defeated by John Kelly [*q.v.*] in 1854, in an extremely close election. When Walsh charged fraud in the count, Kelly made the counter accusation that Walsh was the son of an unnaturalized alien and consequently ineligible.

Walsh then visited Europe, reputedly to get contracts from the Russian government for George Steers [*q.v.*], whose shipbuilding skill he had praised in Congress. He returned penniless, and next visited Mexico on a similar mission. Back in New York, discredited by growing intemperance, he made another unsuccessful venture into journalism. After a convivial night, he was found dead in an area-way, with some suspicion of foul play. He was survived by his widow, Catherine Riley or Wiley, and two children.

[*Sketches of the Speeches and Writings of Mike Walsh . . . Compiled by a Committee of the Spartan Association* (1843); M. P. Breen, *Thirty Years of N. Y. Politics* (1899); J. R. Commons, *Hist. of Labour in the U. S.* (1921), I, 527–30; J. F. McLaughlin, *The Life and Times of John Kelly* (1885); M. R. Werner, *Tammany Hall* (1928); *Working Man's Advocate,* 1844–45; *Congressional Globe,* 33 Cong., 1 and 2 Sess.; *N. Y. Herald, N. Y. Times, N. Y. Tribune,* Mar. 18, 19, 1859.]   H. C. B.

WALSH, ROBERT (Aug. 30, 1784–Feb. 7, 1859), journalist and litterateur, son of Robert and Elizabeth (Steel) Walsh, was born in Baltimore, where his father, since his arrival about 1770, had become a substantial merchant. The elder Walsh may have been born in County Longford, Ireland, or in France, and according to tradition, he succeeded to the title of Count Walsh and Baron Shannon. The Steel family was of Pennsylvania Quaker stock. The younger Robert was prepared by the French Sulpicians of St. Mary's Seminary, Baltimore, for Georgetown College, where he delivered an address on the occasion of Washington's visit to the college. In 1806, as soon as St. Mary's Seminary was empowered by the legislature to grant academic de-

grees, both the bachelor's and master's degrees were conferred upon him. In the meantime, he had read law under Robert Goodloe Harper [*q.v.*] and had become an ardent Federalist. A youth of means, he traveled and studied in France and the British Isles for three years, gaining a wide acquaintance in France through his family connections and in London through William Pinkney [*q.v.*], whom for a time he served as a secretary. He contributed to the Parisian press, became an intimate of Canning, some of whose speeches he later edited, and is said to have written the article on military conscription in France which appeared in the *Edinburgh Review* of January 1809.

On his return to America, Walsh settled in Philadelphia, and edited during its last years (1809–10) the *American Register.* On May 8, 1810, he was married by Bishop Michael Egan to Anna Maria, daughter of Jasper Moylan and a niece of Stephen Moylan and of Bishop Moylan of Cork. They had twelve children. For a brief period, Walsh practised law in a cursory way, but his interest was in books, in journalism, and in conducting a salon, which attracted local and visiting scholars and writers. In 1810, he published a brochure entitled *A Letter on the Genius and Dispositions of the French Government,* which was republished in England and favorably noticed in the *Edinburgh Review* and in the *Quarterly Review* (London). When illness compelled Joseph Dennie [*q.v.*] to relinquish in 1811 the active editorship of the *Port Folio,* to which Walsh had contributed, the latter founded the first American quarterly, *The American Review of History and Politics,* which survived only through eight issues because of its Federalist tone and the War of 1812. In 1813 he published *Essay on the Future State of Europe* and *Correspondence Respecting Russia Between Robert Goodloe Harper, Esq., and Robert Walsh, Jun.* In 1817 he founded another *American Register,* which survived for about a year. He wrote biographical sketches for the *Encyclopædia Americana* (1829–33), edited by Francis Lieber, and a life of Franklin for *Delaplaine's Repository of the Lives and Portraits of Distinguished American Characters* (1815). In 1819 he published *An Appeal from the Judgments of Great Britain Respecting the United States of America,* which brought congratulatory notes from Jefferson, John Adams, and John Quincy Adams and a vote of thanks from the Pennsylvania legislature, but occasioned denunciatory notices in British publications. In 1820, Walsh in association with William **Fry** founded the *National Gazette and Literary Register,* with which he maintained his connection for fifteen years. A successful liberal tri-weekly, it soon became a daily despite its unpopular support of abolition. In the meantime, Walsh edited (1822–23) the *Museum of Foreign Literature and Science*, founded by Eliakim Littell [*q.v.*], and in 1827 established the *American Quarterly Review*, which he conducted for ten years. He also edited with introductory material many volumes of *The Works of the British Poets*, issued first by Mitchell, Ames & White and later by S. F. Bradford of Philadelphia, contributed an article on Madame de Stael to the *Philadelphia Year Book* (1836), and published *Didactics: Social, Literary and Political* (2 vols., 1836), in which he expressed his views on a multiplicity of subjects. Edgar Allan Poe described him as "one of the finest writers, one of the most accomplished scholars, and when not in too great a hurry, one of the most accurate thinkers in the country" (*Southern Literary Messenger*, May 1836, p. 399).

Aside from his literary activity, Walsh won some reputation as an educator, serving as professor of English in the University of Pennsylvania (1818–28), as a trustee (1828–33), and as a manager of Rumford's Military Academy at Mount Airy, Pa. On Jan. 17, 1812, he was elected to membership in the American Philosophical Society. Ill health finally forced his retirement from many of his activities and in 1837 he settled permanently in Paris, where he founded what was probably the first American salon. He contributed some studies to French magazines and was a correspondent of the *National Intelligencer* (Washington) and of the *Journal of Commerce* (New York). For both financial and social reasons, he welcomed an appointment as consul-general in 1844, in which position he served until 1851. He died in Paris and was buried at Versailles. He married as his second wife (J. C. Walsh, *post*, p. 224) a Mrs. Stocker of Philadelphia.

[After the death of Walsh his papers were accidentally destroyed. There are biog. sketches by two descendants, J. C. Walsh, in *Jour. Am. Irish Hist. Soc.*, XXVI (1927), and H. C. Walsh, in *U. S. Cath. Hist. Mag.*, vol. II, no. 7 (1889); and by J. R. Dunne, in a master's essay (MS.), submitted at Cath. Univ. (1933). See also J. G. Shea, *Memorial of the First Centenary of Georgetown Coll., D. C.* (1891); J. S. Easby-Smith, *Georgetown Univ.* (1907), vol. I; M. J. Riordan, *Cathedral Records from the Beginning of Catholicity in Baltimore* (1906); E. A. and G. L. Duyckinck, *Cyc. of Am. Lit.* (2 vols., 1875); R. W. Griswold, *The Prose Writers of America* (1847); F. L. Mott, *A Hist. of Am. Mags.* (1930); *Memorial Vol. of the Centenary of St. Mary's Seminary . . . Baltimore, Md.* (1891); Consular Letters (State Dept.), vol. IX; *Hist. Mag.*, May 1859; *N. Y. Tribune*, Mar. 1, 1859.]   R. J. P.

WALSH, THOMAS (Oct. 14, 1871–Oct. 29, 1928), poet, critic, and editor, was born in Brook-

lyn, N. Y., eldest of the seven children of Michael Kavanagh and Catherine (Farrell) Walsh. He seems to have inherited some of the traits of his maternal grandfather, John Farrell, who belonged to the gentry of County Longford, Ireland, and, after having been educated for the Catholic priesthood, married, emigrated to the United States in 1848, and achieved a considerable measure of success. Thomas attended St. Francis Xavier College, New York, and then entered Georgetown University, Washington, D. C., where he received the degree of Ph.B. in 1892, and that of Ph.D. in 1899. He also studied at the Columbia law school, New York (1892–95). In 1904 he made the first of seven journeys to Europe and South America, through which he acquired a lasting interest in Spanish and Hispanic civilization. His connection with the literature, art, and scholarship of Spain resulted, as his correspondence shows, in his forming innumerable friendships. He was elected to the Royal Academy of Letters of Seville (1911), to the Hispanic Society of America (1916), and to the Academia Columbiana of Bogota (1920). In 1925 Spain conferred on him the Cross of Isabella the Catholic.

Some of Walsh's early verse was printed at Georgetown in 1892. Later volumes of his poetry appeared under the titles: *The Prison Ships and Other Poems* (1909), *The Pilgrim Kings* (1915), *Gardens Overseas and Other Poems* (1918), *Don Folquet and Other Poems* (1920). Dramatic blank verse and satire in various forms were the media through which his best gifts found expression. Seldom genuinely lyrical, he was often able to weave together subtle thought with unmistakable emotional passion in a manner reminiscent of ancient Celtic art. His achievements as a translator and anthologist are represented in the following: *Eleven Poems of Rubén Darío* (1916), *Hispanic Anthology* (1920), and *The Catholic Anthology* (1927, 1932). In 1930 *Selected Poems of Thomas Walsh*, a memorial volume edited by John Bunker, appeared; besides a selection from the published volumes, it contains a few original poems and translations not otherwise issued. Among his manuscripts as yet unpublished are: "The Life, Letters and Idylls of Fray Luis de Leon," "The Life of Juana Inez," "The Wives of the Prophets," and "Modern Poets of Spain and South America." Walsh wrote and read several occasional poems, the most notable probably being "Antietam," read before the Society of the Army of the Potomac on the battlefield of Antietam, 1910. He served temporarily as a member of the editorial staff of the *Catholic Encyclopedia*, contributed to Charles

Dudley Warner's *Library of the World's Best Literature* (1896–97) and from 1924 to 1928 was assistant editor of the *Commonweal,* New York. During 1919 he was placed in charge of relief work done by the National Catholic Welfare Conference in Lithuania, Poland, and the Ukraine. He took an active part in the general social life of Brooklyn, to which city he was devoted, and was an ardent supporter of Catholic cultural and philanthropic efforts. During the last years of his life, he was in chronic poor health, an affliction which did not dampen his spirits or curtail his literary output. The scholar, however, gradually supplanted the poet. He contributed literary criticism to the *Saturday Review of Literature* (New York), the *Poetry Review* (London), *Books,* the literary supplement of the *New York Herald Tribune,* the *Catholic World* (New York), and other periodicals. He died suddenly in Brooklyn and was buried in the same city.

His personal influence was remarkable. Until stricken by disease he was an exceptionally handsome man, whose black hair and mobile mouth set off expressive and winning eyes. A resonant voice, doubtless in part responsible for his success as a lecturer, likewise helped to make him "the perfect dinner guest." He was an admirable raconteur, who relied upon wide experience and a mastery of paradoxical speech. During his early years he had given promise of becoming an excellent pianist, and though he never exercised a native talent for painting, he became a discriminating critic of that art. He had a wide circle of friends both at home and abroad, particularly among young artists and literary men, whom he befriended and encouraged. The service he rendered indirectly to Catholic culture will remain of genuine historical importance, and his awareness of Hispanic civilization was virtually unrivalled in his time. He never married.

[Memoirs by John Bunker and appreciations by E. L. Keyes and Michael Williams, in *Selected Poems of Thomas Walsh* (1930); a memoir by L. Walsh, sister, privately distributed; B. R. C. Low, *Brooklyn Bridge* (1933); G. N. Shuster, *The Catholic Spirit in Modern English Lit.* (1922); *Alumni Reg. of Georgetown Univ.* (1924); *The Am. Catholic Who's Who,* 1911; *Who's Who in America,* 1928–29, where date of birth is given incorrectly; *Commonweal,* Nov. 7, 1928; *N. Y. Times,* Oct. 30, 1928.]   G. N. S.

WALSH, THOMAS JAMES (June 12, 1859–Mar. 2, 1933), senator from Montana, was born in Two Rivers, Wis., the son of Felix and Bridget (Comer) Walsh. His parents met and were married after migrating from Ireland to the United States. After obtaining a public-school education, Walsh began to teach at the age of sixteen, and finally became principal of the high

school at Sturgeon Bay, Wis. Teaching provided the funds for a law course at the University of Wisconsin, from which in 1884 he received the degree of LL.B. He was largely self-educated; recognizing the gaps in his formal education, he filled them in by his own efforts.

For six years he practised law with his brother, Henry C. Walsh, in Dakota Territory at Redfield (now S. Dak.). On Aug. 15, 1889, he married Elinor C. McClements of Chicago, a school teacher; she died on Aug. 30, 1917. In 1890 he moved to Helena, Mont. In Montana, still in the frontier stage of development, he rapidly attained prominence. His reputation was made chiefly in copper litigation, but he became widely known also as a constitutional lawyer. He refused an offer to become general counsel for the Anaconda Copper Company, which he at times represented and at other times opposed in the courts. In 1906 he was an unsuccessful Democratic candidate for election to the federal House of Representatives, and in 1910 he was defeated for the Senate. Nevertheless he persisted, and in 1912 was elected to the Senate, in which he served from March 1913 until his death.

For nearly ten years after his entrance into public life, Walsh's career in the Senate was one of single-minded although unspectacular devotion to the public welfare, and he was invariably found on the progressive side in debates. He could be depended on to expound lucidly constitutional points at issue, but he was not yet a figure of national importance in the popular mind. He advocated such advanced proposals as woman's suffrage and the child-labor amendment, and was identified with the section of the Clayton Act of 1914 which protected farm organizations and trade unions from suit under the Sherman Anti-Trust Act. A devoted follower of Woodrow Wilson, Walsh upheld the League of Nations, the Treaty of Versailles, and the World Court, and advocated the limitation of armaments. He was a leader in the prolonged fight in 1916 to confirm the nomination of Louis D. Brandeis to the Supreme Court. He denounced the "anti-Red" raids of Attorney-General A. Mitchell Palmer after the war, saying, "I do not think it is any answer at all to the charge that illegal things have been done to say that there are Bolshevists and anarchists in this country. If there are, they are entitled to whatever protection the law affords" (*Congressional Record,* 66 Cong., 3 Sess., p. 150).

On Apr. 29, 1922, the Senate passed a resolution introduced by Robert M. LaFollette [*q.v.*], directing the committee on public lands to investigate the leasing of naval oil reserves in

Wyoming and California, and calling on the secretary of the interior for all pertinent information. Walsh was asked by LaFollette and Senator Kendrick of Wyoming to take charge of the investigation, because they believed that the chairman and other majority members of the committee were unsympathetic with the inquiry. Considerable publicity had attended the LaFollette resolution, but public interest quickly died down and Walsh was left to examine the evidence undisturbed. Eighteen months were spent in a preliminary digest of the material; in October 1923 the first public hearing was called, and the scandal of Teapot Dome and Elk Hills was slowly disclosed to an incredulous public. Walsh considered his rôle in the investigation a routine part of his public duty, but one commentator remarked that "no more magnificent display of a legal drive through a thwarting jungle of facts to incredible but proved conclusions has ever been witnessed in Washington" (William Hard, *Collier's,* Mar. 15, 1924, p. 7). Calm precision of language, unemotional clarity of mind, and definiteness of purpose characterized his conduct of the investigation. Through his efforts all the sordid details of the transactions were uncovered, and the leases were subsequently voided. It is a commentary on the contemporary attitude toward political morality that the most vigorous condemnation by much of the press and the public was reserved for the public servants responsible for bringing the facts to light (Allen, *post,* p. 154). The perspective of time, however, shows that the oil inquiry was Walsh's most valuable public service.

A delegate to every Democratic National Convention from 1908 to 1932, Walsh was chosen permanent chairman in 1924 and again in 1932. His name was presented for the presidential nomination at the convention of 1924, but his maximum strength was 123 votes, on the 102nd ballot. After the long battle between the Smith and the McAdoo forces had ended in the compromise nomination of John W. Davis on the 103rd ballot, Walsh was offered the vice-presidential nomination but declined it. His suave but firm direction of the convention was universally applauded. In 1928 he allowed himself to be mentioned as a pre-convention candidate for the presidential nomination, and unsuccessfully contested the California primary with Smith, but he abandoned his candidacy before the convention opened.

Walsh's activities in the Senate after the Teapot Dome disclosures were consistent with his earlier career. He voted against the McNary-Haugen bill to provide an equalization fee for farm products on the ground that the plan was unconstitutional, despite popular pressure for it in the West. He voted to submit repeal of the Eighteenth Amendment to the states, although he had been a consistent prohibitionist for many years. He opposed confirmation of the appointment of Judge John J. Parker to the Supreme Court because of the nominee's judicial record on sustaining drastic injunctions to uphold "yellow-dog" contracts. A lifelong interest in Irish independence was reflected in Walsh's proposal that the United States bring the problem of Ireland to the attention of the League of Nations in the latter's capacity as an international public forum. He believed that Anglo-American friendship was endangered by the recurrence of trouble in Ireland.

The outstanding physical feature of Walsh during his early years in Washington was a remarkably long, drooping moustache, which later he clipped short. (For a discussion of his physical appearance in his latter years, see *New Republic,* July 2, 1924.) As a boy he had been an enthusiastic baseball player, and he organized the centennial baseball team in Two Rivers in 1876. Later in life he turned for recreation to golf, fishing, and horseback riding. He was a devout member of the Roman Catholic Church, and his private life was characterized by personal dignity and great kindliness.

In 1933, when Walsh was seventy-three, President-elect Roosevelt selected him to be attorney-general. The press praised the choice as one of the most satisfactory for the new cabinet, and one newspaper said "no wise Democratic politician is likely to go to him in his new job looking for special favors. It would be like asking the statue of Civic Virtue for a chew of tobacco" (New York *Sun,* ed., Mar. 1, 1933). On Feb. 25, 1933, Walsh was married in Habana to Señora Maria Nieves Perez Chaumont de Truffin, the widow of a Cuban banker and sugar grower. Starting for Washington for the inauguration, Walsh was ill for several days in Florida, and he died suddenly on a northbound train early on the morning of Mar. 2, 1933. In addition to his widow, he was survived by a daughter of his first marriage. His death unquestionably weakened the incoming administration.

[Among sketches of Walsh the following may be cited: William Hard, in *Collier's,* Mar. 15, 1924; and *Am. Monthly Rev. of Reviews,* Apr. 1928; J. W. Owens, in *New Republic,* July 2, 1924; Charles Michelson, in *N. American Review,* Feb. 1928; "Wherefore Walsh," *Independent,* Apr. 21, 1928; *N. Y. Times,* Feb. 10, 1924; Oct. 13, 1929; Mar. 3, 7, 10, 1933; *N. Y. Herald-Tribune,* Mar. 3, 1933; *News-Week,* Mar. 4, 11, 1933; *Nation,* Mar. 15, 1933. He himself published "The True History of Teapot Dome" in the *Forum,* July 1924. Important official sources are "Leases upon

Naval Oil Reserves," 68 Cong., 1 Sess., *Senate Report No. 794* (3 pts., 1924–25); *Official Report of the Proc. of the Democratic Nat. Convention* (1924, 1928, 1932). More general accounts of value are M. E. Ravage, *The Story of Teapot Dome* (1924); F. L. Allen, *Only Yesterday* (1931); M. R. Werner, *Privileged Characters* (1935); Mark Sullivan, "The Twenties," *Our Times*, vol. VI (1935). Supplementary details of personal information have been given by John Walsh, brother of the Senator.]   L. P. B.

WALTER, ALBERT G. (June 21, 1811–Oct. 14, 1876), surgeon, was born in Germany. He received the degree of doctor of medicine from Königsberg University, and then took a year's graduate work in Berlin, where he was the pupil and assistant of the celebrated Johann Friedrich Dieffenbach, who suggested that he emigrate to America. The ship which carried him was wrecked off the coast of Norway and he lost all his belongings. Making his way to London, he worked for a year to earn sufficient money to continue his passage to America. Meanwhile, he pursued his studies and made the acquaintance of the distinguished English surgeon Sir Astley Cooper, who always remained his firm friend. Upon reaching the United States, he went to Nashville, Tenn., where he remained two years and then, in 1837, removed to Pittsburgh, in which city he lived until his death.

Walter's versatility as a surgeon is revealed by the fact that he was one of the earliest American pioneers in the field of orthopedic surgery, a skilled oculist, and a most resourceful general surgeon. He is reputed to have cut more tendons in one patient than had any other surgeon; his fame as an accident surgeon, also, was nationwide. His chief claim to distinction, however, is based on his performance of an epoch-making laparotomy for the relief of ruptured bladder, Jan. 12, 1859, the patient making a good recovery. A partial bibliography of his writings records more than forty, the most of which were articles which appeared in various periodicals. Particular mention should be made, however, of his *Conservative Surgery in Its General and Successful Adaptation in Cases of Severe Traumatic Injuries of the Limbs* (1867). He was impressed with the work of Lister and early practised antisepsis, although he argued against the value of carbolic acid and with great enthusiasm set forth the value of pure air. This, he said, "is not only harmless but priceless to man and to the rest of creation whether in a healthy or an afflicted condition. Poison mingled with the air and not pure air is the enemy the surgeon has to contend with . . . and the only method of averting injurious effects is the prompt removal of the patient to a place free from all contaminating influences" (*Conservative Surgery*).

His faults were open and glaring: he was intolerant, greatly lacking in consideration for his colleagues, and highly egotistical. On the other hand he was a man of remarkable talent and marvelous industry. He was fond of animals and was the first president, 1874, of the Humane Society of Pittsburgh. It was his love of surgery and his ability to do it well, combined with his driving energy, that made him impatient, blinded him to the rights of his colleagues, and led him to fail to conform to professional etiquette. His criticisms were generally well founded, for surgery in Walter's day was for the most part badly done; but unfortunately they were not tactfully expressed. Had he possessed leadership with tact he might have had the profession solidly behind him, for he is easily the outstanding figure in the medical annals of Pittsburgh, and holds an important place in the surgical history of the United States. In 1846 he married Frances Anne Butler, daughter of Maj. John J. Butler and niece of Dr. Joseph Gazzam, a well-known local practitioner. He left a son and daughter.

[Theodore Diller, *Pioneer Medicine in Western Pa.* (1927); H. A. Kelly, and W. L. Burrage, *Am. Medic. Biogs.* (1920); *Pittsburg Daily Dispatch*, Oct. 16, 1876.]   T. D.

WALTER, THOMAS (Dec. 13, 1696–Jan. 10, 1725), clergyman, defender of "the new way" of singing, was born in Roxbury, Mass., a son of the Rev. Nehemiah Walter, who emigrated with his father to America from Ireland about 1679, and Sarah Mather, a daughter of Increase Mather [*q.v.*]. As a boy he early displayed a retentive memory and quick perceptions. When he entered Harvard College his uncle, the Rev. Cotton Mather [*q.v.*], wrote in his diary (*post*, p. 128): "I have a Nephew now a Student at Cambridge. I would use various Means, both to preserve him from Temptations and prepare him for Services. I would send for him, talk with him, and bestow agreeable Books of Piety upon him." In 1713 Thomas was graduated with the A.M. degree and a reputation for brilliance and conviviality. He was unsuccessfully recommended on Nov. 7, 1716, by Cotton Mather for the chaplaincy of the Castle. His association with young theological radicals of the day, especially his intimate friendship with John Checkley [*q.v.*], gave his orthodox father and uncle many anxious moments, but on Oct. 29, 1718, he was safely ordained as his father's assistant pastor at Roxbury, and his grandfather, Increase Mather, preached the ordination sermon. He was married, on Dec. 25, 1718, to Rebeckah, the daughter of the Rev. Joseph Belcher, of Dedham. Their only daughter survived him.

In 1719 he engaged in public controversy with Checkley. The young Puritan had help in this literary enterprise, out of which grew his *A Choice Dialogue Between John Faustus, a Conjurer, and Jack Tory His Friend* (1720). His uncle recorded (*Diary*, p. 703): "My kinsman at Roxbury, intending an Answer, to a vile, horrid, monstrous Book, newly published among us, I assist him with Materials." The "monstrous book" was Checkley's *A Modest Proof of the Order and Government . . . in the Church*, published in 1723. Walter, meantime, was compiling another work which followed closely upon the work of John Tufts [*q.v.*] and which appeared in 1721 with the title: *The Grounds and Rules of Musick Explained; or, an Introduction to the Art of Singing by Note; Fitted to the meanest capacity*. The preface was signed by approving ministers. The tunes were in three parts. Simple as was the musical technique involved, this book stood for an effort, scientifically and artistically conceived, to correct in the New England churches what Walter called "an horrid medley of confused and disorderly sounds." It ran through successive editions, the latest being that of 1764. Another book, *The Sweet Psalmist of Israel*, appeared in 1722. Walter's participation in his uncle's introduction of inoculation for smallpox nearly cost both men their lives. The incident of the throwing of a heavily-loaded bomb into the chamber in which Walter, who had submitted himself to the experiment, was sleeping, is told at length in Cotton Mather's *Diary* (p. 657). The diarist also gives many of the gruesome details of his nephew's consumption which appeared not long after the grenado episode. He died after a lingering illness and was buried in the Roxbury Cemetery in the tomb that contained the remains of the Rev. John Eliot, and later, those of his father.

[The best connected account of Thomas Walter is C. F. Adams, Jr., "Notices of the Walter Family," in *New-England Hist. and Geneal. Reg.*, July 1854. The many references to him in *The Diary of Cotton Mather*, *Mass. Hist. Soc. Coll.*, 7 ser., vols. VII–VIII (1911–12), are poignantly interesting. For a contemporary account of the grenado incident see *Boston News-Letter*, Nov. 20, 1721. Other data are in *A Report of the Record Commissioners, Containing the Roxbury . . . Ch. Records* (1881), and F. S. Drake, *Town of Roxbury* (1905). L. C. Elson, *Hist. of Am. Music* (rev. ed., 1925), briefly evaluates Walter's contribution to musical technique. See also George Hood, *A Hist. of Music in New England* (1846); M. B. Jones, "Bibliographical Notes on Thomas Walter's 'Grounds and Rules of Musick Explained,'" *Proc. Am. Antiquarian Soc.*, vol. XLII (1933); E. H. Pierce, "The Rise and Fall of the 'Fugue-Tune' in America," *Musical Quart.*, Apr. 1930; F. J. Metcalf, "Thomas Walter, the Second Native Compiler," *Choir Herald*, Sept. 1913.]   F. W. C.

WALTER, THOMAS (*c.* 1740–Jan. 17, 1789), is an outstanding figure in early American botany, concerning whose life comparatively little is known. A native of Hampshire, England, he emigrated to eastern South Carolina as a young man, acquired a plantation on the banks of the Santee River, and there passed the remainder of his life. Presumably he devoted much of his time to agriculture, though certainly also, as an avocation, to a laborious study of the vegetation of that then little-known region, a task for which he appears to have been exceedingly well equipped by temperament and liberal education. Here, completely isolated from the scientific world, he prepared in Latin a succinct descriptive treatise summarizing his studies of the flowering plants found within a radius of fifty miles of his home. The manuscript, dated Dec. 30, 1787, was taken to England early in 1788 by his intimate friend John Fraser, on the latter's return from a long botanical tour in Georgia and the Carolinas, and was published in London that year at Fraser's expense. This book, *Flora Caroliniana*, is the sole record of Walter's work. It is classical not only in text but in importance, and is the first tolerably complete account of the flora of any definite portion of eastern North America in which an author used the so-called binomial system of nomenclature. In it Walter described upward of one thousand species of flowering plants from specimens collected by Fraser and himself, these representing some 435 genera. Of the former more than two hundred are described as new; of the genera thirty-two are so indicated, though only four of these are given distinctive names. Walter's herbarium, which is said to have contained originally all the species treated in the *Flora*, was taken to England with the manuscript and remained in the possession of the Fraser family until 1849, when it was presented to the Linnean Society of London. During the interval it had suffered serious injury and loss. It was acquired by the British Museum (Natural History) in 1863 and has since been studied by many American botanists as an aid in interpreting Walter's brief descriptions. Walter is known otherwise chiefly from his joint effort with Fraser to introduce into general cultivation in England a native Carolina grass, *Agrostis perennans*, from which extraordinary results were expected. This venture, interestingly set forth in a rare folio by Fraser (*A Short History of the Agrostis Cornucopiæ: or the New American Grass*, 1789), ended in dismal failure.

Walter was married three times: on Mar. 26, 1769, to Anne Lesesne, of Daniels Island, who died Sept. 11, 1769; on Mar. 20, 1777, to Ann Peyre, who died in December 1780; and later, to

Dorothy Cooper. Two of three daughters by his second marriage and one by his third married and left numerous descendants. He was buried, at his own request, in a small botanical garden which he had established on his plantation. The much-quoted inscription upon his tombstone gives the year of his death erroneously as 1788. Concerning Walter's extraction, early life, and education, and his motive in emigrating to South Carolina, nothing is known, though a good deal may be inferred. He was unquestionably a sound, conservative scholar, indefatigable, modest, and of discriminating judgment, who, though living in the very midst of a singularly bitter local warfare during the Revolutionary period, was able nevertheless to produce a remarkable work of lasting scientific importance.

[For additional data, with numerous source references as to Walter's plantation, marriages, and descendants, *Flora Caroliniana* and herbarium, the visits of botanists to Walter's grave, and the curious long-standing error as to the date of his death, see W. R. Maxon, "Thomas Walter, Botanist," *Smithsonian Misc. Colls.*, vol. XCV, no. 8 (Apr. 1936), pp. 1–6; *The State* (Columbia, S. C.), Apr. 28, 1935; W. C. Coker, "A Visit to the Grave of Thomas Walter," *Jour. of the Elisha Mitchell Sci. Soc.*, Apr. 1910.]				W. R. M.

WALTER, THOMAS USTICK (Sept. 4, 1804–Oct. 30, 1887), architect, was born in Philadelphia, Pa., the son of Deborah (Wood) and Joseph Saunders Walter. His grandfather, Frederick Jacob Walter, born in Germany, spent his boyhood in Philadelphia as a "redemptioner," and became a prosperous bricklayer. Walter's youth was marked by his apprenticeship to his father, a bricklayer and stone mason, and by his studies under William Strickland [q.v.] and others at the Franklin Institute. He became a master bricklayer in 1825. In 1828 he reëntered Strickland's office for over two years of intensive training in architecture and engineering, and in 1830 began his own practice. His first important commission was for the Philadelphia County Prison, usually called Moyamensing, built in the "castellated" manner. The commission for Girard College followed in 1833. Through the influence of Nicholas Biddle the premiated design was abandoned for one of classical derivation. The white marble building was peripteral in plan, with the Corinthian order of the monument of Lysicrates, Athens, as its chief ornamental feature. The interior, following the requirements of the Girard will, was divided into four groined rooms, each fifty feet square, on each of two floors, rising to an attic floor with four domes on pendentives. A roof of marble slabs, basement areas for the control of the temperature of the vestibules, and an arched treatment whereby the entablature could be replaced, block by block,

were additional features of an archeological triumph. Four pendant buildings were placed axially to either side. The echoes in the vaulted rooms made recitations difficult, and the limited number of windows permitted by the style indicated the weakness inherent in the temple form for a modern school. Girard College marked the climax, and at the same time sounded the death knell, of the Greek Revival in America. A trip to Europe in 1838 afforded Walter the opportunity to study the practical arrangements of English and Continental schools, many of which he was able to use at Girard. Between 1843 and 1845 he was concerned with the construction of a breakwater at La Guaira, Venezuela, said to be still in use. He had the misfortune to lose his eldest son and assistant, Joseph S. Walter, from fever during this undertaking.

From 1851 to 1865 Walter was in Washington in charge of the extension of the United States Capitol, adding the wings of the present structure, the dome, and projecting a center extension, revised as late as 1904 by Carrère and Hastings, and still pending (1936). The cornerstone of the wings was laid July 4, 1851, with Daniel Webster as the orator. Walter had been one of four to win premiums for competitive designs for the extension and had been appointed by President Fillmore to prepare plans, which the latter subsequently approved. Charles F. Anderson, who also designed one of the premiated designs, long claimed credit for the wings and may have influenced the placing of the legislative chambers in the wings instead of at the north and south sides as Walter had intended. He also seems to have had influence, through Capt. Montgomery C. Meigs [q.v.], who knew his plans, in details of ventilation, acoustics, and heating. Anderson's drawings, however, are now lost, and only in the unlikely event that a drawing among the Walter papers, signed by the Corps of Topographical Engineers (Brown, *post*, plate 140), was designed by Anderson does there appear to be any need of a revision of the generally accepted belief that Walter is chiefly responsible for the wings as built, admirably adapted to their purpose, to the older parts of the building, and to the significance of the structure. The interior details are certainly his. The cast-iron dome designed by Walter extends nearly thirteen feet beyond its base and, despite its magnificent silhouette, needs the proposed center extension to satisfy the eye of the spectator. Walter also urged that the rotunda be rebuilt and the pilasters replaced by columns, in order to give a more apparent support to the dome. Other works of Walter's in Washington include the completion of the Treasury, begun by Robert Mills [*q.v.*], by the addition of the west and south façades, and, after the removal of the State Department, the north façade; the addition of two great wings to Mills's noble reminiscence of the Parthenon, long the Patent Office; the extension of the old Post Office, later the Land Office, from Mills's designs; St. Elizabeth's Hospital; and designs for the State, War, and Navy Building. In the last instance Walter's conception is seen only in the interior, the numerous colonnettes which now adorn the exterior having been added after his retirement. Walter also designed the naval barracks at Brooklyn and at Pensacola while in the government employ.

Walter's work in Philadelphia, done largely before his departure for Washington, includes such admirable adaptations of classical modes to city architecture as the Matthew Newkirk House, long known as St. George's Hall, and the Dundas House, both with Ionic porticoes. He also assisted Nicholas Biddle in his construction of a peripteral design for his home on the Delaware, "Andalusia." He designed the Preston Retreat and Wills Eye Hospital, various churches, banks, and private houses in Philadelphia, court houses at Reading and at West Chester (based on classic temples with Wren towers added), the beautiful Hibernian Hall, Charleston, S. C., and churches and banks at West Chester, Baltimore, and Richmond. After his virtual retirement in 1865 Walter consulted with John McArthur, 1823–1900 [*q.v.*], regarding the tower of the City Hall, Philadelphia, then rising, and was associated with him in the decorative work the building called for.

Throughout his life Walter was an active leader in the Baptist Church. He wrote *A Guide to Workers in Metals and Stone* (1846), and in collaboration with J. Jay Smith contributed to and compiled *Two Hundred Designs for Cottages and Villas* (1846). He helped to organize the American Institute of Architects in 1857, and became its second president in 1876, holding that office until his death. He was long associated with the Franklin Institute in various official positions. His first wife was Mary Ann E. Hancocks, who died during her eleventh confinement; his second wife was Amanda Gardiner, who bore him two children. He was urbane and cultivated, a conscientious worker, an expansive conversationalist, the firm ruler of his home. Universal deference was paid him in his later years in Germantown. He was handsome and of courtly bearing, with a ruddy complexion and leonine white hair in his later years. His portrait as a young man was painted by John Neagle.

[In addition to "Geneal. Sketches," MS. in the Hist. Soc. of Pa., prepared by Walter in 1871, see G. C. Mason, Jr., in *Proc. Am. Inst. of Architects . . . 1888*, vol. XXII (n.d.); "Mr. Nicholas Biddle and the Architecture of Girard Coll.," *Pa. Mag. of Hist. and Biog.*, no. III, vol. XVIII (1894); R. A. Smith, *Phila. As It Is* (1852), Louisa C. Tuthill, *Hist. of Architecture* (1848), pp. 264–66; *Documentary Hist. . . . of the U. S. Capitol* (1904); Glenn Brown, *Hist. of the U. S. Capitol*, vol. II (1903); "Who Was the Architect of the U. S. Capitol Extension?" *Architecture*, July 1917; H. P. Caemmerer, *Washington, The National Capitol* (1932); W. S. Rusk, "Thornton, Latrobe, and Walter and the Classical Influence in Their Works" (in MS.); *Phila. Press*, Oct. 31 (death notice) and Nov. 1, 1887. Many of Walter's letters, notebooks, sketchbooks, drawings, and account books, and the Neagle portrait are owned by Mrs. C. H. Wegemann of Baltimore, Md. Other sketches and drawings are in the possession of Glenn Cook and Walter Cook of Baltimore; the Coll. of Architecture, Cornell Univ.; the Lib. of Cong.; the office of the architect of the Capitol; the office of public buildings and parks, Navy Building; and the office of the supervising architect, Treasury Dept.]

W. S. R.

WALTERS, ALEXANDER (Aug. 1, 1858– Feb. 2, 1917), bishop of the African Methodist Episcopal Zion Church, was born in a room behind the kitchen of the Donohue Hotel in Bardstown, Nelson County, Ky., the sixth of the eight children of Henry Walters and Harriet (Mathers). His mother, a tall, commanding, light-brown woman of more than two hundred and fifty pounds, was a native of Virginia; his father, born in Larue County, Ky., was the son of his white master. Alexander received the little formal education he was fortunate enough to secure in private schools conducted by the colored churches of Bardstown during the period of the Civil War and Reconstruction. Because of his intelligence and piety he was chosen by the local African Methodist Episcopal Zion Church to be educated for the ministry. His school career lasted for a period of approximately ten years, ending about 1875.

In 1876 he joined a crew of waiters and was sent to work in the Bates House in Indianapolis, Ind. In March of the following year he was licensed to preach and was appointed pastor of the newly organized African Methodist Episcopal Zion Church of that city. On Aug. 28, 1877, he married Katie Knox, by whom he had five children. His rise was meteoric; successive pastorates took him to Corydon Circuit, Cloverport Circuit, and Louisville, Ky.; to San Francisco, Cal.; to Chattanooga and Knoxville, Tenn.; and to New York City. In 1888, at the early age of thirty, he assumed the pastorate of one of the largest and most influential of all the churches of his connection, the historic "Mother Zion" of New York. In 1889 he was sent to London, England, as a delegate to the World's Sunday School Convention; later in the year he was appointed general agent of the Book Concern of his denomination. At the General Conference which met at Pittsburgh in May 1892, he was elected to the bishopric of his Church, one of the youngest persons ever chosen for this high office.

Closely akin to Alexander Walters' interest in his Church was his zeal for the welfare of his race. In 1890 he joined with T. Thomas Fortune and others in issuing a call for a meeting to consider an organization for race protection. This meeting, held in Chicago, established the Afro-American League, which in 1898, at Rochester, N. Y., was reorganized as the National Afro-American Council, with Walters as its president. Convinced that the Republican party of his day did not merit the undivided support of his race, he became a Democrat and was chosen president of the National Colored Democratic League. As such he enjoyed a cordial relationship with Woodrow Wilson, who, in a letter to Walters in 1912, promised "to assure my colored fellow-citizens of my earnest wish to see justice done them in every matter, and not mere grudging justice, but justice executed with liberality and cordial good feeling" (Walters, *My Life and Work*, p. 195).

At the time of his death he was a trustee of the United Society of Christian Endeavor, a member of the administrative council of the Federal Council of Churches of Christ in America, a former president of the Pan African Conference, a vice-president of the World Alliance for Promoting International Friendship through the Churches, and a trustee of Livingstone College and of Howard University. His first wife died in 1896, and he was survived by his second wife, Lelia Coleman of Bardstown, Ky., and six children. Tall, light brown, of commanding presence, he undoubtedly owed some of his success to his personal appearance; but he was endowed as well with the gift of fluent speech, and with exceptional organizing ability. A man of deep piety and evangelical fervor, he possessed also a liberal and progressive mind. An autobiography, *My Life and Work* (1917), appeared the year of his death.

[*Minutes of the Gen. Conference of the African Methodist Episcopal Zion Church, 1892–1916*; J. W. Hood, *One Hundred Years of the African Methodist Episcopal Zion Church* (1895); J. T. Haley, *Afro-American Encyc.* (1895); G. C. Clement, *Boards for Life's Buildings* (1924); *Who's Who in America, 1916–17*; *N. Y. Times*, Feb. 3, 1917.]   R. E. C.

WALTERS, HENRY (Sept. 26, 1848–Nov. 30, 1931), capitalist, art collector, was born in Baltimore, Md., the son of William Thompson Walters [*q.v.*] and Ellen (Harper). After attending Loyola College in Baltimore he entered Georgetown University, Washington, where he

was graduated in 1869 and in 1871 received the degree of M.A. He then spent two years in the Lawrence Scientific School of Harvard University, where in 1873 he was awarded the degree of B.S., and two years in study at Paris. His father having already engaged in the linking of Southern railroads, Henry was destined for the same career. He had much more technical knowledge than the elder Walters, however, and carried on much more extensive operations. He had his first experience in the engineering corps of the Valley Railroad in Virginia, then being extended by the Baltimore & Ohio to Lexington; later he was in the operating superintendent's office of the Pittsburgh & Connellsville Railroad.

Joining the staff of the Atlantic Coast Line Railroad, of which his father was the chief organizer, he became in 1889 vice-president and general manager. He participated in the formation of the Atlantic Improvement & Construction Company (later the Atlantic Coast Line Company), a holding company incorporated in 1889 which enabled the Walters, Michael Jenkins, B. F. Newcomer, and other Baltimore men to build up and retain control of the Atlantic Coast Line Railroad and greatly to expand the system. The Petersburg Railroad was purchased by the Richmond & Petersburg Railroad, and in 1900 the Atlantic Coast Line Railroad Company of Virginia was incorporated and became the parent company in consolidations which by the time of his death gave Walters—as chief stockholder, and chairman of the board—control of 10,000 miles of railway. In many of the transactions leading to this result the Safe Deposit & Trust Company, of Baltimore, of the board of directors of which Walters was chairman, took a leading part. Important acquisitions were the Plant system of railroads in Georgia and Florida in 1902, which brought in over 1600 miles of line, and the Louisville & Nashville Railroad, a controlling interest in which was purchased in 1903 for $50,000,000 from J. P. Morgan & Company; Walters became chairman of the board of the Louisville & Nashville. Besides holding directorships in many railroads and several financial institutions, he represented the railroad owners on the staff of the director-general of railroads from 1918 to 1920. At the height of his career he was said to be the richest man in the South.

Art collecting, which with his father had been an avocation, became with Henry Walters a serious study and a ruling passion. From the time that he first went abroad with his father, during the Civil War, he knew painters and sculptors in their studios. Later he returned to Europe annually, usually spending about three months in acquiring objects of art. Besides many paintings and prints, he purchased oriental and occidental ceramics, sculptures in marble, stone, alabaster, metal and wood, jades and jewelry, textiles of all sorts, lacquer, miniatures, watches, illuminated manuscripts, and incunabula; he also acquired a large art library. For L. S. Olschki, *Incunabula Typographica* (1906) he wrote the preface. His largest single purchase was the collection of Don Marcello Massarenti, containing 900 pieces, in 1902. His collections were housed in a new gallery in Baltimore, opened in 1909. In his will he left his galleries with all of their contents to the city of Baltimore, together with one quarter of his estate for an endowment. They were opened under public ownership in 1934. Walters had earlier made other benefactions to Baltimore, among them four public baths. He spent most of his time in New York and had several other homes besides that in Baltimore.

An enthusiastic yachtsman, he owned the steam yacht *Narada,* and was regularly a member of the syndicate which built defenders of the *America's* cup. He was a close friend of Sir Thomas Lipton, the English yachtsman. At the age of seventy-three, Apr. 11, 1922, he married Sarah Wharton (Green) Jones, of Wilmington, N. C., whom he had known since his youth. He was of small stature, though stout in his later years, with rather thin face and high-bridged nose. A quiet, modest man, he was always fending off photographers and avoiding every kind of publicity. Like his father, he was fond of finger rings, which he changed daily. He was an officer of the Legion of Honor of France. Continuing work almost to the end, he died in New York City and was buried in Baltimore.

[*N. Y. Times,* Dec. 1, 8, 1931; *Sun* (Baltimore), Dec. 1, 1931; *Who's Who in America,* 1932–33; *The Walters Coll.* (1927); *First Ann. Report of Trustees of Walters Gallery* (1933).]   B. M.

WALTERS, WILLIAM THOMPSON (May 23, 1820–Nov. 22, 1894), merchant, railroad president, art collector, was born in Liverpool, Pa., the son of Henry and Jane (Thompson) Walters, both of Scotch-Irish descent. The father, a country merchant in comfortable circumstances, impressed by the unexploited mineral resources of western Pennsylvania, sent his son to Philadelphia to be trained as a civil and mining engineer. Returning to his native district, young Walters explored it on foot and horseback. He was first employed at an iron furnace at Farrandsville, then in Lycoming County, where about this time the first iron was made on a commercial scale with coke. Soon afterwards he entered the employ of Burd Patterson at the Pioneer Furnace, Pottsville, where the practicability of smelting iron with anthracite was demonstrated. In 1841, when the canal along the Susquehanna River from Columbia, Pa., to Havre de Grace, Md., was opened, Walters removed to Baltimore and entered the produce commission business, trading particularly with Pennsylvania. As a result of this business interest, he later became the controlling director in the Baltimore & Susquehanna Railroad (afterwards the Northern Central), connecting Baltimore with the canal. In 1847 he formed a partnership with Charles Harvey in the foreign and domestic liquor trade, in which he continued until 1883, when his expanding interest in railroads absorbed his time.

Walters' commission business, which early shifted from Pennsylvania to Virginia and the Carolinas, was responsible for his important participation in the railroad development of the South. He became intimately acquainted with Southern merchants and planters, making interest on loans to them as well as receiving commissions on the sale of their produce. An investor in a steamship line between Baltimore and Savannah, and in other water routes, he was quick to recognize that the many railroads being built in the South between 1840 and 1860, unconnected though they were, would prove the successful rivals of steamboat transport. Often these little railroads, joining the cities on the fall line and spreading westward from the Southern ports, fell into financial difficulties from lack of coördination and from over-expansion, and before the Civil War, Walters, with a few Baltimore associates, began buying up these "ribbons of rust," and was about to commence their consolidation, centering upon Wilmington and Norfolk, when the war compelled abandonment of such plans. Walters had opportunity to employ his organizing ability two decades later, however, when the Southern roads, physically ruined by the war, were financially wrecked by the depression following 1873. A primary reason for coöperation between the roads was the development of truck farming in eastern North Carolina and Virginia, which required efficient through service. Walters led the cooperative movement through the successive stages of informal agreements, physical connection and formal contracts for handling through traffic, and the holding company, and was ready at the time of his death to begin with outright absorption and consolidation. His first notable achievement was an agreement with Northern roads for the carriage of perishable produce from the Carolinas and Virginia to Philadelphia, New York, and Boston. This was followed by the incorporation in Connecticut, in 1889, of the Atlantic Improvement & Construction Company, a holding company, the name of which was changed a year before Walters' death to the Atlantic Coast Line Company, which under his son Henry Walters [q.v.] was the means of effecting consolidation of roads reaching from Washington to Florida and Gulf ports, and to Memphis and St. Louis.

Walters began buying pictures when a young man, and while resident in Paris from 1861 to 1865—because his active Southern sympathies made him unpopular in Baltimore—he became intimately acquainted with many painters. He attended the Paris expositions of 1867, 1878, and 1889, and that of Vienna in 1873, buying many canvases of contemporary painters, such as Corot, Munkacsy, Millet, Millais, Delacroix, Detaille, Fortuny, Gerôme, and Alma-Tadema. He compiled *Antoine-Louis Barye, from the French of Various Critics* (1885), for which he wrote a preface. His paintings, in addition to an important collection of Eastern ceramics, crowded his Baltimore home and were placed later in two galleries added to his house, which were occasionally opened to the public. These collections were enormously enlarged by his son, who at death bequeathed them, with a new gallery, to the city of Baltimore. Walters was the patron of poor artists, the chief of whom was the sculptor William Henry Rinehart [q.v.], who began life as a stone-cutter in Maryland. Walters was a trustee of the Corcoran Gallery, Washington, and chairman of the art gallery committee of the Peabody Institute, Baltimore. In 1845 he married Ellen Harper of Philadelphia, who died in London in 1862. Walters bred fine stock on his farm near Baltimore, and brought the Percheron horse to America. For Du Huÿs' *The Percheron Horse* (1868) he wrote the preface. He was a small man, with a thin, straight nose, walrus mustache, stubbly beard and hair, and keen eyes. A trait noticeable to his friends was a fondness for trinkets of gold and enamel, of which he gathered a large number.

[F. A. Richardson and W. A. Bennett, *Baltimore Past and Present* (1871); *Biog. Cyc. of Representative Men of Md. and the D. C.* (1879); G. W. Howard, *The Monumental City* (1889); *Sun* (Baltimore), Nov. 23, 1894; *Baltimore American*, Nov. 23, 1894; H. D. Dozier, *A Hist. of the Atlantic Coast Line Railroad* (1920); S. W. Bushnell, *Oriental Ceramic Art; Illustrated by Examples from the Collections of W. T. Walters* (1897); M. J. Lamb, "The Walters Collection of Art Treasures," *Mag. of Am. Hist.*, Apr. 1892; M. Reizenstein, "The Walters Art Gallery," *New England Mag.*, July 1895; R. B. Gruelle, *Notes: Critical and Biog.: Collection of W. T. Walters* (1895).]
B. M.

WALTHALL, EDWARD CARY (Apr. 4, 1831–Apr. 21, 1898), Confederate general, United States senator, was born in Richmond, Va. His parents, Barrett White and Sally (Wilkinson) Walthall, moved to Holly Springs, Miss., when he was ten years of age, and there he was educated in St. Thomas Hall, at that time a well-known classical school. After reading law for a year with a brother-in-law at Pontotoc, he returned to Holly Springs and continued this study while serving as deputy clerk of the circuit court. In 1852 he was admitted to the bar and began to practise at Coffeeville. In 1856 he was elected attorney for the tenth judicial district of Mississippi and was reëlected three years later.

Upon the outbreak of the Civil War a volunteer company known as the Yalobusha Rifles was organized in Coffeeville and Walthall was elected first lieutenant. In the summer of 1861 he was elected lieutenant-colonel of the 15th Mississippi Infantry to which his company had been attached. When the Confederates were disastrously defeated at Mill Springs, or Fishing Creek, Ky., in January 1862, Walthall was commanding his regiment and displayed unusual bravery and steadiness. Thereafter he was usually placed where these qualities were especially needed and he became noted for his dependability and resourcefulness when outnumbered or when his army was being forced to retreat. On Apr. 11, 1862, he was made colonel of the 29th Mississippi Infantry, which he commanded at Corinth. He served through the campaign in Tennessee and Kentucky preparatory to the fighting about Chattanooga, and he was commissioned brigadier-general on Apr. 23, 1863, to take rank from Dec. 13, 1862. At Chickamauga nearly one-third of his men were killed or wounded in a severe engagement with a force under George H. Thomas [q.v.] against whom Walthall was several times matched. In mid-November 1863, with his brigade reduced to 1,500 men, he was on the defensive in the famous fight on Lookout Mountain which has sometimes been called the "battle above the clouds." The following day the 600 men left in his brigade participated in the battle of Missionary Ridge, and to them fell the task of covering the retreat of the Confederate army. Though Walthall was painfully wounded in the foot, he would not leave his saddle until his men were withdrawn from the field. After participating in the fighting about Atlanta, he was sent with Hood into Tennessee and at Franklin had two horses shot under him. On the retreat from Nashville he was chosen to command the infantry of the rear-guard, cooperating with Forrest's cavalry. On June 10, 1864, he was commissioned major-general, and won a reputation as one of the ablest of the Confederate division commanders.

On his way home at the end of the war he met Lucius Q. C. Lamar [q.v.]; this was the beginning of a lifelong and intimate friendship and of a brief law partnership at Coffeeville. In 1871 Walthall moved to Grenada. He was one of the leaders in the overthrow of the Carpet-bag government in the state, and a delegate to all except one of the National Democratic Conventions from 1868 to 1884. When Lamar was made secretary of the interior, Walthall was appointed to succeed him in the Senate, and by election and reëlection he remained in that body from March 1885 until his death except for a period from January 1894 to March 1895 when ill health caused him to resign. Before he resigned he had already been elected for the term beginning in March 1895, and he then reëntered the Senate. He served as chairman of the committee on military affairs and was a member of the committees on public lands and on the improvement of the Mississippi River. Declining physical strength limited his activities during most of the time he was in the Senate and he seldom participated in debate. Yet he was respected by the members of both parties and wielded a great deal of influence in his own. As a leader of the minority at a time when some sectional animosity remained he displayed the same strength and resourcefulness as when fighting against odds on the battlefield. His influence rested chiefly upon his strong character and his conciliatory manners. The olive branch that had been put forward so dramatically by Lamar in his eulogy of Charles Sumner was carried more quietly but probably with equal effectiveness by Walthall.

He was twice married, first to Sophie Bridges, who died within a year of their marriage in 1856, and then, in 1859, to Mary Lecky Jones, of Mecklenburg County, Va., whose death followed shortly after his. He had no children, but left an adopted daughter. Though his death occurred in Washington, D. C., he was buried at Holly Springs, Miss.

[*Biog. Dir. Am. Cong.* (1928); *Appleton's Ann. Cyc. 1898* (1899); *Biog. and Hist. Memoirs of Miss.* (1891), vol. II; Dunbar Rowland, *Mississippi* (1907), vol. II; Edward Mayes, *Lucius Q. C. Lamar* (1896); *Confed. Mil. Hist.* (1899), vol. VII; E. T. Sykes, "Walthall's Brigade," in *Miss. Hist. Soc. Pubs.*, centenary series, vol. I (1916); *Ibid.*, first series, vols. IV (1901), and XI (1910); Memphis *Commercial Appeal*, Apr. 22–26, 1898; *Washington Post*, Apr. 22, 1898.]   C. S. S.

WALTHER, CARL FERDINAND WILHELM (Oct. 25, 1811–May 7, 1887), Lutheran clergyman, theologian, was born at Langenschursdorf, near Waldenburg, Kingdom of Saxony, the eighth of the twelve children of the local pastor, Gottlob Heinrich Wilhelm Walther, and his wife, Johanna Wilhelmina Zschenderlein. He attended the Gymnasium at Schneeberg, 1821–29, and at the age of eighteen felt himself "born for nothing but music," but under pressure from his father matriculated at the University of Leipzig as a student of theology. During his university years he suffered poverty, illness, and doubts about his salvation, consorted with a group of pietistically inclined students, read deeply in Luther's writings, and sought advice successfully from Martin Stephan, of St. Johannes Church, near Dresden. Stephan, of lowly origin and irregular education, was a popular, orthodox, erratic, widely influential preacher. After Walther completed his studies at Leipzig in 1833, he became a private tutor at Kahla and was ordained in January 1837 as pastor at Bräunsdorf, but in the easy-going, mildly rationalistic atmosphere of the Saxon State Church he was thoroughly unhappy. In September 1838 Stephan, who was in trouble with both the civil and the ecclesiastical authorities, decided to emigrate to the United States and found an independent Christian community. Upwards of 700 people rallied to him, including six clergymen and various candidates for ordination. Among them were Walther, his older brother, Otto Hermann Walther, and several of their friends. The emigrants sailed from Bremerhaven in five ships, one of which was lost at sea. Walther himself landed at New Orleans on Jan. 5, 1839, and proceeded to St. Louis, Mo. Some of the company settled there, but the greater number occupied a tract of 4,440 acres in Perry County, Mo., where Walther became pastor of the settlements called Dresden and Johannesburg.

Shortly after their arrival in Perry County, the emigrants made the belated discovery that Stephan was a libertine and a rascal, deposed him from office, and expelled him from their domain. Out of the confusion following the discovery Walther emerged as the leader of the community. In December 1839 he and three associates—Ottomar Fuerbringer, T. J. Brohm, J. F. Bünger—opened a school in a log cabin at Altenburg. This school was moved to St. Louis in 1850 and named Concordia Theological Seminary. Long before Walther's death it had become the largest Protestant theological seminary in the United States. In 1841 Walther removed to St. Louis to succeed his deceased brother as pastor of the Trinity congregation. On Sept. 21 of that year, at Dresden, Perry County, he married Christiane Emilie Bünger, by whom he had six children. On Sept. 7, 1844, he issued the first number of *Der Lutheraner* as the exponent of strict confessional Lutheranism. This journal was welcomed throughout the Middle West by scattered Lutheran clergymen holding similar convictions and led directly to the organization at Chicago Apr. 26, 1847, of the German Evangelical Lutheran Synod of Missouri, Ohio, and Other States, which is commonly known as the Missouri Synod. Walther was its president, 1847–50 and 1864–78. In 1850 he became professor of theology in Concordia Seminary without relinquishing his position as chief pastor of the four Saxon Lutheran congregations in St. Louis. In 1855 he established a second periodical, *Lehre und Wehre,* more technically theological than *Der Lutheraner* and animated by the same militant orthodoxy. In 1872 the Missouri Synod entered into a loose confederation with several other Middle Western synods that agreed with it in doctrine. Walther was the first president of this Synodical Conference. The Missouri Synod was now the largest body of Lutherans in the United States and was organized and directed with an efficiency comparable to that of the Prussian Army. Walther dominated its every activity.

He did not look the masterful man that he was. He was of medium height, uncommonly slender, and never in robust health. By middle life he was toothless, and hairless above the temples, and as he refused to wear false teeth his goatee was in grotesque proximity to the end of his nose. But his magnetic personality exercised its spell over individuals and crowds alike. He was a winning speaker and a powerful debater; his memory was a veritable concordance to the whole corpus of early Lutheran theology; and his capacity for work was astounding. He took no thought for himself: the sale of his books enriched the synodical treasury; he did not take a penny in royalties, supporting his family on a meager salary. He had a genius for friendship, conducted an extensive correspondence, and was almost immeasurably hospitable. His one interest outside his work was music: he was an excellent organist and had a fine baritone voice. He displayed his greatest power, though not the most admirable side of his character, in theological controversy. Throughout a good part of his career he was engaged in a series of controversies with other theologians on the nature of the church and the ministerial office and on other matters, and in these controversies he evinced not only immense learning and acumen but bitter feeling, intolerance, and an over-weening belief in his own inerrancy. The climax of his career as a polemical theologian was a contro-

versy over the nature of predestination that began as early as 1868, almost disrupted the Synodical Conference, and did not subside till after his death. As a theologian he was not consciously, it would seem, an innovator; he regarded himself as a pupil of Luther and the Lutheran scholastics, reproducing their thought for the use of his own generation. Actually, his was too vigorous a mind to be a mere receptacle for others' thought. His greatness, however, lay in his genius for organization and leadership. His influence has been greater than that of any other American Lutheran clergyman of the nineteenth century.

Of his many publications the most important are: *Die Stimme unserer Kirche in der Frage von Kirche und Amt* (1852); *Die rechte Gestalt einer vom Staate unabhängigen evangelisch-lutherischen Ortsgemeinde* (1863); *Die evangelisch-lutherische Kirche die wahre sichtbare Kirche Gottes auf Erden* (1867); *Amerikanisch-Lutherische Evangelien-Postille* (1871); *Americanisch-Lutherische Pastoraltheologie* (1872); *Lutherische Brosamen* (1876); an edition of J. G. Baier's *Compendium Theologiae Positivae* (1879); *Amerikanisch-Lutherische Epistel-Postille* (1882). Since his death many of his prayers, sermons, lectures, occasional addresses, and letters have been published, and some of them have been translated into English.

After the death of his wife, Aug. 23, 1885, he felt his own end approaching, divested himself of many of his duties, but continued to teach and preach until compelled to take to his bed. He died at St. Louis after a long illness and was buried in Concordia Cemetery.

[No bibliography and no adequate biography exist. Of manuscript material the principal depository is Concordia Seminary. Printed works include: Martin Günther, *Dr. C. F. W. Walther: Lebensbild* (1890), from which several other biographies derive; J. F. Köstering, *Auswanderung der sächsischen Lutheraner* (1866); G. A. Schieferdecker, *Geschichte der ersten deutschen lutherischen Ansiedelung in Altenburg, Perry Co., Mo.* (1865); J. Hochstetter, *Geschichte der Ev.-Luth. Missouri Synod* (Dresden, 1885); C. F. W. Walther, *Kurzer Lebenslauf des weiland ehrw. Pastors Joh. Friedr. Bünger* (1882); Wm. Sihler, *Lebenslauf* (2 vols., 1880); Anton Baumstark, *Unsere Wege nach Rom* (Freiburg, 1870); G. J. Fritschel, ed., *Geschichte der Lutherischen Kirche in Amerika,* vol. II (Gütersloh, 1897); *Briefe von C. F. W. Walther* (2 vols., 1915–16, cover period 1841–71); J. L. Gruber, *Erinnerungen an Professor C. F. W. Walther und seine Zeit* (1930); G. Mezger, ed., *Denkstein zum 75en Jubiläum der Missourisynode* (1922); W. H. T. Dau, ed., *Ebenezer: Reviews of the Work of the Missouri Synod* (1922); D. H. Steffens, *Doctor Carl F. W. Walther* (1917); W. G. Polack, *The Story of C. F. W. Walther* (1935). For an obituary, see *St. Louis Globe-Democrat,* May 8, 1887.]

G. H. G.

WALTON, GEORGE (1741–Feb. 2, 1804), signer of the Declaration of Independence, United States senator, the son of Robert Walton and Sally or Mary (Hughes) Walton, was born near

Farmville, Prince Edward County, Va. His grandfather had emigrated to America from England in 1682. He was left an orphan at an early age and grew up in the household of an uncle. He was apprenticed to a carpenter, who, impressed with Walton's character, intelligence, and ambition, gave him a portion of his wages and released him from his apprenticeship so that he could attend a local school. He was, however, largely self-taught. He removed to Savannah, Ga., in 1769 where he studied and was admitted to the bar in 1774. There he became an ardent patriot and joined with others to call a meeting of the patriot party in July 1774. He was a member of the committee on resolutions and also of the committee of correspondence. At a second meeting in August, he played an important part in condemning the British colonial measures and in allying the Georgia group with the Continental patriot party. He was also a member of the group that called and organized the Provincial Congress at the Liberty Pole in 1775. Unanimously chosen secretary of the Provincial Congress, he served on the committees of intelligence, helped to draw up the articles of association, and wrote addresses to the people and to the king. When the Council of Safety was organized he was elected its president.

The Provincial Congress, on Feb. 2, 1776, elected Walton a delegate to the Continental Congress and, with the exception of 1778, when other interests prevented his attending the sessions, and 1779, when he was governor of the state, he served continuously until Sept. 27, 1781. As a member of the important committees on Western Lands, the Treasury Board, Indian Affairs, and the Executive Committee in charge of Federal Affairs in Philadelphia, he evinced zeal, intelligence and ability. He was a strong advocate of independence and a signer of the Declaration. In the debate on the Confederation he urged that Indian trade be made a monopoly and that its control be vested in Congress. He also advocated equal vote for the states. In January 1777, Walton and George Taylor [q.v.] represented the government at Easton, Pa., and negotiated a treaty with the Six Nations. In Georgia he led the conservative Whigs who favored the union of the civil and military authority and opposed the radical Whigs led by Button Gwinnett [q.v.]. His ardent defense of Lachlan McIntosh [q.v.], who killed Gwinnett in a duel in 1777, led him into difficulties, when, as governor of the state in 1779, he forwarded a forged letter to Congress which brought about the transfer of McIntosh from Georgia. For this conduct, the legislature in 1783 censured Walton and or-

dered the attorney-general to bring suit against him, yet on the preceding day it had elected him chief justice of the state. He was commissioned colonel of the 1st Regiment of Georgia Militia on Jan. 9, 1778, and served gallantly at the siege of Savannah, where his leg was broken by a ball. He fell from his horse and was captured by the British who considered their prize so valuable that they asked for a brigadier-general, at least, in exchange. He was finally exchanged for a captain of the navy in September 1779.

When the British overran Georgia in 1779 the patriot government was torn by dissension. One faction chose John Wereat as governor but a more influential group elected Walton, who held office from November 1779 to January 1780. He was returned to Congress in 1780 and protested against the idea of peace on the principle of *uti possidetis*. He was one of the signers of the *Observations upon the Effects of Certain Late Political Suggestions* (1781) in which he favored extending liberal commercial privileges to Spain. The Loyalist assembly of 1780 disqualified Walton from holding any office in the state, but the patriot legislature immediately appointed him commissioner of Augusta and authorized him to lay out the city of Washington, Ga.

In 1783 he was commissioned by the Confederation to go on to Tennessee and negotiate a treaty with the Cherokee Indians. Thereafter he served for six years as chief justice of Georgia. In 1786 he served on a commission to locate the boundary line between Georgia and South Carolina. He was appointed a delegate to the Philadelphia Convention of 1787 but did not attend because of pressing judicial engagements. He attended, however, the Georgia Constitutional convention of 1788, served as a presidential elector in 1789, and was elected governor a second time in 1789. This administration was marked by the establishment of a new constitution, the location of the capital at Augusta, by frontier difficulties, and the pacification of the Creek Indians. He retired to his estate "Meadow Garden" in 1790, but was shortly elected a judge of the superior court of Georgia and served from 1790 to 1792, from 1793 to 1795, and from 1799 until his death. He was appointed in 1795 to fill out the unexpired term of James Jackson in the United States Senate. His term was uneventful but served to ally him with the Federalist Party.

In 1775, Walton was married to Dorothy Camber, who, although she was the daughter of a loyal British subject, was noted for her wholehearted support of the patriot cause. Walton was one of the founders and a trustee of Richmond

Academy, and a member of the committee to locate Franklin College. As a trustee of the University of Georgia he formulated plans to promote higher education in the state. Small of
stature, comely in appearance, Walton was
haughty, dignified and stern of manner; he was
warm in his attachments and bitter in his enmities. His violent temper would brook not the
slightest deviation from what he thought his due,
but in spite of this characteristic he was respected by the people and honored by election to many
public offices. In 1795 he built a new home "College Hill"; here he died, survived by his wife
and one of their two sons. He was buried in the
Rosney Cemetery but was removed, July 4,
1848, to the monument erected in Augusta to
the Georgia signers of the Declaration of Independence.

[L. B. Andrus, "1933 Memoranda . . . in Re Walton
Families," 1934, mimeograph copy in the Library of
Congress; *Biog. Dir. Am. Cong.* (1928); *Letters of
Members of the Cont. Cong.*, vols. I–IV (1921–33), ed-
ited by E. C. Burnett; *The Rev. Records of the State of
Ga.* (3 vols., 1908), edited by A. D. Candler; *Hist.
Colls. of the Ga. Chapters, D. A. R.*, vol. II (1929);
Hist. Colls. Joseph Habersham Chapter, D. A. R. (2
vols., 1902); C. C. Jones, *Biog. Sketches of the Dele-
gates from Ga. to the Cont. Cong.* (1891), and *Hist.
of Ga.* (1883), vol. II; L. L. Knight, *Ga. Roster of the
Rev.* (1920); *Men of Mark in Ga.*, vol. I (1907), edited
by W. J. Northen; John Sanderson, *Biog. of the Signers to the Declaration of Independence*, vol. IV (1823);
Warren Grice, *The Ga. Bench and Bar*, vol. I (1931);
Columbian Museum and Savannah Advertiser, Feb. 11,
1804.]   F. M. G.

WALWORTH, CLARENCE AUGUSTUS
(May 30, 1820–Sept. 19, 1900), Roman Catholic missionary, was born in Plattsburg, N. Y.,
the fourth of five children of Reuben Hyde Walworth [*q.v.*], for many years chancellor of New
York, and his first wife, Maria Ketchum (Averill). At the Albany Academy and at the Sloan
School at Williamstown, Clarence prepared for
Union College, Schenectady, from which he was
graduated in 1838. For three years he read
law under capable practitioners of Canandaigua
and Albany, and in 1841 was admitted to the
bar. As a member of the firm of Chapin & Walworth, he practised law in Rochester for a year,
then, somewhat unsettled in mind and soul, he
began to study for the ministry of the Protestant Episcopal Church, in which he had been
recently confirmed.

For three years he attended the General Theological Seminary, New York City, which was
then torn with dissension over Puseyism, Trac-
tarianism, and High-Church thought. After an
unsuccessful attempt to establish a monastic
foundation in the Adirondacks on the model of
the Nashotah Mission in Wisconsin, he joined
the Roman Catholic Church in 1845, taking the

names Alban Alphonsus at his confirmation. Despite the grief of his parents, he soon determined
to become a priest of the Order of the Most Holy
Redeemer (Redemptorists), and with two other
young converts, Isaac T. Hecker and James Alphonsus McMaster [*qq.v.*], went to the Redemptorist College of St. Trond in Belgium to continue his theological studies. Here he made his
vows, Oct. 15, 1846, and subsequently proceeded
for further study to Witten in Holland, where
he was known as "Brother *Pourquoi*" because
of his inquisitive and critical mind. Ordained a
priest, Aug. 27, 1848, by Bishop Paredis of Rure-
monde in Dutch Limbourg, he was ordered to
the Redemptorist houses at Clapham near London and at Hanley in Worcestershire. For two
years he preached on the English missions, relieved the sufferings of Irish famine refugees,
and witnessed the crisis associated with the reestablishment of the Catholic hierarchy in England. After the establishment of the Redemptorist province in the United States, he was assigned to the American mission band. Returning to America in 1851, he preached missions
throughout the East for seven years and then,
with Hecker and three other converts, he was
released from his vows by Pius IX and assisted
in the foundation of the Congregation of St. Paul
the Apostle (Paulists), in 1858. Again he
preached missions, with notable effect. Cardinal
Gibbons assigned responsibility for his vocation
to a mission conducted by Walworth in New Orleans in 1854.

Broken in health by this arduous life, Father
Walworth served temporarily as a chaplain to
soldiers on Staten Island, then joined the Albany diocese. For thirty-four years, from 1866
until the year of his death, he was pastor at St.
Mary's Church, Albany. As a charity worker, a
temperance advocate, a crusader against corruption in politics, and an outspoken critic of
industrial evils, he challenged attention. Noteworthy among his publications were: *The
Gentle Skeptic* (1863); *The Doctrine of Hell*
(1873); *Ghosts* (1878), a brochure; *Andiato-
rocté* (1888); *Reminiscences of Edgar P. Wadhams* (1893); *The Oxford Movement in America* (1895); *The Walworths of America* (1897);
and "Reminiscences of a Catholic Crisis in England Fifty Years Ago" (*Catholic World*, June
1899–January 1900). Despite failing sight and
hearing, he managed with an amanuensis to contribute articles to periodicals until his last
months, when paralysis left him speechless and
helpless. At the end, he was buried with religious and civic honors in the family cemetery at
Saratoga Springs.

[There is autobiographical material in Walworth's
writings mentioned above. See also Ellen H. Walworth,
Life Sketches of Father Walworth (1907); Walter Elliott, in *Cath. World*, June 1901; *Albany Evening Journal*, Sept. 19, 1900.]   R. J. P.

**WALWORTH, JEANNETTE RITCHIE
HADERMANN** (Feb. 22, 1837–Feb. 4, 1918),
writer, was born in Philadelphia, Pa., the fourth
daughter of Matilda Norman, a native of Baltimore, and Charles Julius Hadermann von Win-
singen, a German political exile. When Jeannette was a child the family moved to Mississippi,
where for a time her father taught modern languages at Jefferson College, Washington, Miss.,
near Natchez. Her education was informal but
effective, her father being her chief instructor.
At the age of sixteen she became a governess on
a Louisiana plantation, and she seems to have
remained so occupied until the Civil War.

At the close of the war she went to New Orleans to enter journalism. She wrote a few articles signed "Ann Atom," for the Sunday edition
of the *New Orleans Times,* but although they
attracted attention they paid nothing. She entrusted her first novel to a New York firm which
failed before the book appeared. In 1870, however, her *Forgiven at Last* was published by
Lippincott, and it was followed shortly by *Dead
Men's Shoes* (1872). These books were written
on a plantation in Tensas Parish, La. Encouraged
by Samuel R. Crocker of the Boston *Literary
World,* she was able to have her next novel,
Against the World, published in Boston by Shepard & Gill in 1873. In that year she married
Major Douglas Walworth, of Natchez, Miss., a
widower. The marriage was childless. For the
next five years she lived on her husband's plantation in Arkansas, and here wrote *Heavy Yokes*
(1876) and *Nobody's Business* (1878). After a
stay in Memphis, where she contributed to the
Memphis Appeal over the name "Mother Goose,"
she moved with her husband to New York. Here
the Major planned to establish a law practice,
and Mrs. Walworth hoped to find a more ready
market for her books.

For the next sixteen years she was a very pro-
ductive writer. In April 1884 she contributed
"The Natchez Indians—A Lost Tribe" to the
Magazine of American History. Judge Albion
W. Tourgée [*q.v.*] published one of her novels
in *The Continent* (June 6–27, 1883), recommend-
ing it as a picture of Southern life. Some of her
tales appeared in Frank Leslie's periodicals;
Scruples (1886) came out in the Boston *Beacon*
before appearing as a book in Cassell's Rainbow
Series; *Lippincott's Magazine* and the *Overland
Monthly* also printed her work. A Mormon study,
The Bar Sinister (1885), was reprinted with

several variations in title; *Southern Silhouettes,*
after serial publication in the New York *Evening Post,* appeared as a book in 1887 and was
well received. In 1889 she published *History of
New York in Words of One Syllable.* About
1888 the Walworths returned to Natchez, where
Major Walworth became editor of the *Democrat.*
Books by Mrs. Walworth continued to appear
until 1898, several being reprinted two or more
times. After the death of her husband in 1915,
she lived with relatives in New Orleans.

Much of her writing was, in her own opinion,
on a sub-literary level. She utilized familiar
scenes and conditions as the background for
stories which, in plot and character, rarely rose
above melodrama. Her style was clear but unimpressive. Her best work, however, *Southern
Silhouettes,* a series of post-war sketches, was
notably effective. In some of her stories, such as
The New Man at Rossmere (1886) and *A Little
Radical* (1889), she displayed an unusual penetration into the changing social and industrial
conditions in the South. She was a shrewd observer and a witty and interesting companion.

[*Literary World* (Boston), Sept. 18, 1886; *Times-
Picayune* (New Orleans), Feb. 5, 1918; C. A. Walworth, *The Walworths of America* (1897); information
from relatives.]   R. P. M.

WALWORTH, REUBEN HYDE (Oct. 26,
1788–Nov. 28, 1867), jurist, last chancellor of
New York, a descendant of William Walworth
who came to Connecticut in 1689, was born in
Bozrah, Conn., the third son of Benjamin Walworth, a veteran of the Revolution, and Apphia
(Hyde) Walworth. When still a child, he went
with his family to Hoosick, Rensselaer County,
N. Y., where he worked on his father's farm until he was seventeen. He acquired the rudiments
of Latin from a half-brother, supplemented his
farm work with work in a country store, and
then entered the law office of John Russell in
Troy. Admitted to the bar in 1809, he removed
the following year to Plattsburgh, where he took
up practice. Two years later he accepted an appointment as master in chancery and also served
as justice of the peace for Clinton County. During the War of 1812 he served as adjutant-general of the state militia, distinguishing himself
in the land battles at Plattsburgh, Sept. 6 and 11,
1814. From 1821 to 1823 he represented his district in Congress as a Democrat. He defended
Jackson's conduct as governor of Florida and
advocated recognition of the Spanish-American
states, but in the main his activities in Congress
were unimportant (*Annals of Congress,* 17
Cong., 1 Sess., cols. 570, 1141; 2 Sess., cols. 648,
1060). In 1823 he accepted an appointment as

circuit judge of the supreme court for the fourth judicial district of New York, which he held until his appointment in 1828 as chancellor.

Coming into office five years after the enforced retirement of James Kent [q.v.], and occupying the chancellorship for twenty years, Walworth contributed significantly to the system of New York equity jurisprudence which had been erected by Chancellor Kent. His achievements as a jurist are recorded in the eleven volumes of Paige's and the three volumes of Barbour's *Chancery Reports,* and in the decisions of the court of errors reported by Wendell, Hill, and Denio. In the law of evidence and in equity pleading and practice, Walworth's decisions filled numerous gaps in the New York law (see especially 1–3 *Paige, passim*), and he added materially to the law relating to injunctions (see, for example, 2 *Paige,* 26, 116, 316), to arbitration in equity matters, and the adoption of statutes in the Northwest Territory (7 *Wendell,* 539, 544). Both Kent and Joseph Story [q.v.] valued his judicial labors very highly. A large number of appeals were taken from his decisions to the court of errors and in about one-third of these cases his decisions were reversed. In *Gable et al.* vs. *Miller et al.* (10 *Paige,* 627) the court of errors criticized his learned exposition of theological doctrines to determine whether church trustees were diverting property from the purposes for which it was originally intended, holding that his discussion of such matters would lead to controversies throughout the state (2 *Denio,* 548, 549, 553). Walworth did not appear to be especially sensitive about appeals from his decisions, declaring that they "should be allowed in every case not manifestly frivolous," since only thus could the court of chancery be preserved (26 *Wendell,* 155).

Though in private life Walworth was courteous and refined, on the bench he was highly unconventional and frequently harassed counsel with pointed interrogations and biting sarcasm. This habit won him a host of enemies, and when President Tyler sent his name to the Senate in 1844 to fill a Supreme Court vacancy, Thurlow Weed, writing with Whig animus to Senator Crittenden, said: "He is recommended by many distinguished Members of the Bar of the State *merely because they are anxious to get rid of a querulous, disagreeable, unpopular Chancellor.* Indeed so odious is he that our Senate, when a majority of his own political friends were members, voted to abolish the office of Chancellor. Those who recommended him admit and avow that they did so to get him out of his present office" (quoted in Charles Warren, *The Supreme*

Court in United States History, vol. II, 1922, p. 389). Weed's suggestion that the matter be tabled in order that a better selection be made was actually followed. The abolition of the court of chancery under the New York constitution of 1846 has been attributed in large measure to the desire of the bar to retire Walworth to private life. Thus, ironically enough, he contributed to one of the most important reforms in nineteenth-century law, the merger of the courts of law and equity.

Upon his retirement from office in 1848 he was the candidate of the Democratic party for governor, but ran third in the election in which Hamilton Fish [q.v.] was victorious, his defeat being due in large measure to the defection of the Free-Soilers. He then retired from political life, later declining a place in the cabinet of President Buchanan. At the outbreak of the Civil War he advocated conciliation and was a prominent delegate to the peace convention. Unlike Kent, who made use of his forced retirement to write the *Commentaries,* Walworth turned from judicial labors to write an extensive genealogy of his mother's family, the Hydes, who traced their descent from Mary Chilton, a passenger on the *Mayflower.* This work, *Hyde Genealogy* (2 vols., 1864), he completed at his Saratoga residence, "Pine Grove," the rendezvous of many celebrities, which had been an informal court during his term as chancellor. By his first wife, Maria Ketchum (Averill), whom he married Jan. 6, 1812, Walworth had six children, one of whom was Clarence A. Walworth [q.v.]. By his second marriage, Apr. 16, 1851, to Sarah Ellen (Smith) Hardin of Kentucky, widow of John J. Hardin [q.v.], he had one son, who died in infancy. He was an active Presbyterian, an incorporator of the American Board of Foreign Missions, a vice-president of the American Bible Society and of the American Tract Society, and president of the American Temperance Union.

[In addition to Walworth's *Hyde Geneal.* (1864), consult C. A. Walworth, *The Walworths of America* (1897), and E. H. Walworth, in *N. Y. Geneal. and Biog. Record,* July 1895. Sharply conflicting estimates of the Chancellor will be found in Irving Browne's sketch, in *Green Bag,* June 1895, and in W. L. Stone's *Reminiscences of Saratoga* (1875). See also John Livingston, *Portraits of Eminent Americans Now Living,* vol. II (1853); D. S. Alexander, *A Political Hist. of the State of N. Y.,* vols. I, II (1906); 49 *Barbour's N. Y. Reports,* 651–58; campaign circular of 1848 (N. Y. Public Lib.); *Albany Law Journal,* Sept. 30, 1876.]

R. B. M.

WANAMAKER, JOHN (July 11, 1838–Dec. 12, 1922), merchant, born in a small frame house on the outskirts of Philadelphia, was the eldest of the seven children of Nelson and Elizabeth Deshong (Kochersperger) Wanamaker. He was descended on both sides from early settlers, his father being of German and Scotch ancestry and his mother of French Huguenot. His paternal grandfather, John Wanamaker, and his father operated a brickyard until the competition of larger brickyards caused the former in 1849 to move to a farm near Leesburg, Ind., where Nelson and his family joined him in 1850. After a hard year during which the elder John died, the family returned to Philadelphia. Nelson Wanamaker went back to brickmaking, and John at thirteen became an errand boy for a publishing house at $1.25 a week. He soon shifted to the men's clothing business, gradually advancing to the position of salesman. But in 1857 a breakdown in his health forced him to take an extended trip west. Wanamaker returned, towards the end of the year, to become secretary of the Young Men's Christian Association in Philadelphia at a salary of $1,000 a year. He thus became the first paid Y. M. C. A. secretary in the country (Gibbons, *post,* I, 41) ; his success in the face of widespread opposition established the value of such an officer. His marriage to Mary Erringer Brown in 1860 crystallized the problem of his future and led him to break finally with paid religious work.

In 1861 Wanamaker and his brother-in-law, Nathan Brown, invested their modest combined capital in a men's clothing business. In ten years Wanamaker and Brown's "Oak Hall" had become the largest retail men's clothing store in the country (*Ibid.,* I, 113). Brown died in 1868, but the store continued under the original name. The following year Wanamaker opened a more fashionable men's store, known as John Wanamaker & Company, at 818–22 Chestnut Street. In 1876 with characteristic showmanship he converted the rambling old freight depot of the Pennsylvania Railroad at Thirteenth and Chestnut Streets into a huge dry goods and men's clothing store, the "Grand Depot," which attracted considerable attention from visitors to the Centennial Exposition. After the fair, Wanamaker tried to get merchants in other lines to lease space in the "Grand Depot," as it was called until 1885. Failing this, he inaugurated on Mar. 12, 1877, his "new kind of store," a collection of specialty shops under one roof (Gibbons, I, 153). This venture precipitated the first serious crisis in his meteoric career, but after a year of uncertainty, success was evident and the store soon became one of the largest department stores in America.

Wanamaker was always master in his establishments, but he knew how to utilize the skill of close associates. The lower Chestnut Street store he delegated to his brothers. He induced Robert C. Ogden [*q.v.*] to take charge of "Oak Hall" in 1879. Wanamaker's sons, Thomas B. and Lewis Rodman [*q.v.*], entered the business after completing their college work at the College of New Jersey (Princeton) in 1883 and 1886 respectively. In 1885 Wanamaker promoted Ogden and Thomas B. Wanamaker to a partnership in profits in the "Grand Depot." During Wanamaker's term as postmaster-general Ogden successfully managed the department store. In 1896 Wanamaker bought from the receivers the old store of Alexander T. Stewart [*q.v.*] in New York City and placed Ogden in charge. Continued growth encouraged Wanamaker in 1902 to begin enlarging both department stores. The panic of 1907 broke when he was in the midst of this building program ; again he was almost ruined. The burden on the aging merchant was increased through the retirement of Ogden in 1907 and the illness of his son Thomas, who died in 1908. But again the storm was weathered. In the development of the modern department store, Wanamaker moved consistently with the vanguard and was often a pioneer. He was an inveterate innovator and even a gambler, and his stores were in an eternal flux of change and reconstruction. He did not create the one-price system, but, beginning in 1865, he implemented it by guaranteeing their money back to dissatisfied customers. He was a master of the art of publicity, notably newspaper advertising. His paternalistic attitude towards his employees led him to set up an employee's mutual-benefit association (1881), training classes for clerks, continuation classes for boys and girls which in 1896 became the John Wanamaker Commercial Institute, and other educational and recreational features.

Wanamaker's apparently inexhaustible energy led him into a wide variety of undertakings, to each of which he managed somehow or other to give effective attention. Next to his mercantile activity, the most characteristic feature of his career was his religious work, especially in connection with the Bethany Sunday School (Presbyterian) which he founded in 1858. He was an outstanding lay leader and derived genuine pleasure and relaxation from his religious activities. An early temperance worker, he hailed the passage of the prohibition amendment and fought the relaxation of the Sunday blue laws in Pennsylvania. His vigorous Christianity saw no inconsistency in requiring military drill of the young men in his store or in offering the government trained complements of men from his employ in 1898 and 1917. A consistent Republican,

Wanamaker in 1886 was considered for the nomination for mayor. In 1888 he raised a large campaign fund to aid the election of Benjamin Harrison. For this he was rewarded with the postmaster-generalship (Mar. 5, 1889). The circumstances surrounding his appointment and his use of the spoils system brought down on his head the severe condemnation of the civil-service reformers. As postmaster-general, he instituted several technical improvements, experimented with rural free delivery, and advocated parcels post and postal savings, both of which were adopted much later; he favored government ownership of the telegraph and the newly perfected telephone services. For several years in the nineties, he waged a vigorous but unsuccessful fight against the Quay machine in Pennsylvania. He sought the Republican nomination for the United States Senate in 1896–97, and for the governorship in 1898. On the outbreak of the World War, he at first urged neutrality, but with the sinking of American ships by German submarines he used his widely read store editorials to increase the clamor for American entry on the side of the Allies.

Wanamaker remained active in his business and religious undertakings to the end of his long life. He died at his home at "Lindenhurst," near Philadelphia, on Dec. 12, 1922, after an illness of about three months. His son, Rodman, succeeded him as sole owner and director of the two department stores. Two daughters also survived him. His wife had died in 1920.

[H. A. Gibbons, *John Wanamaker* (2 vols., 1926), laudatory but not uncritical; J. H. Appel, *The Business Biography of John Wanamaker, Founder and Builder* (1930), and *Golden Book of the Wanamaker Stores* (2 vols., 1911–13); obituaries in *Public Ledger* (Philadelphia), *N. Y. Times*, Dec. 13, 1922. For the civil-service reformers' case against Wanamaker, see W. D. Foulke, *Fighting the Spoilsmen* (1919), ch. 4; *Selections from the Correspondence of Theodore Roosevelt and Henry Cabot Lodge, 1884–1918* (1925), vol. I.]
J.J.S.

WANAMAKER, LEWIS RODMAN (Feb. 13, 1863–Mar. 9, 1928), merchant, the second son of John Wanamaker [*q.v.*] and Mary Erringer (Brown), was born in Philadelphia. His father, whose formal education ended before the completion of grade school, believed strongly in the value of a college training for his children. Rodman, like his elder brother Thomas B., was sent to the College of New Jersey (Princeton). He received his A.B. degree in 1886 and after spending a few months in Europe married, on Nov. 4, Fernande Antonia Henry of Philadelphia and entered his father's "Grand Depot" store. In 1888 he was put in charge of the buying office in Paris, where he remained for ten years. He returned in 1898 to assist his father, whose sphere of activity had been increased in 1896 by the acquisition of the old store of A. T. Stewart in New York City. In 1902 Rodman was made a member of the firm. His rôle in the management of the huge Wanamaker enterprises was expanded considerably with the retirement of Robert C. Ogden [*q.v.*] from the business in 1907 and the death of his brother Thomas in 1908. John Wanamaker's diary and letters reveal the extent to which he relied upon Rodman in the trying financial crisis of 1907, as well as the close personal bond which existed between father and son. The latter became resident manager of the New York store in 1911. On the death of his father in 1922, he became sole owner and director of both the Philadelphia and the New York corporations.

To his father's emphasis on goods of sturdy quality and the satisfaction of customers, Rodman added an emphasis on "art in trade." From his headquarters in Paris he shipped to America a stream of gowns, paintings, antiques, house furnishings, and other *objets d'art* which at first bewildered the members of the firm at home, but soon became an integral part of the business of Wanamaker's, as of other leading department stores. Wanamaker was an important art patron. He was for a long time president of the American Art Association in Paris. For his services in encouraging French art, he was decorated by the French government in 1897 and again in 1907. He gave a collection of works of art to his alma mater. He also made a notable collection of rare musical instruments, which were used in a series of public concerts given in the New York and Philadelphia stores by outstanding artists. He conceived the idea of installing in the grand court of the Philadelphia store the organ which had been used at the Louisiana Purchase Exposition in St. Louis and of constructing for the New York store a magnificent organ which was completed in 1921.

Wanamaker was an early aviation enthusiast, and was particularly interested in demonstrating the feasibility of commercial transatlantic flights. As early as 1914 he financed the construction of two planes for a transatlantic flight. The war interrupted further activity along this line. On July 1, 1927, however, about a month after Lindbergh made his successful flight, Wanamaker's *America,* commanded by Commander Richard Byrd, successfully completed a flight to France, being the first tri-motored plane to make the crossing. Wanamaker financed three expeditions among the Indian tribes of the West. These were led by Dr. Joseph K. Dixon, who in *The Vanish-*

ing Race (1913) recorded the proceedings at the last Council of the Chiefs, witnessed by the second expedition in 1909. The collection of Indian articles gathered by the expeditions was turned over to the United States government. Although he devoted considerable time to public affairs, Rodman Wanamaker never attained the position in public life which his father held. During the World War, he served without pay as special deputy police commissioner in New York City in charge of police reserves. He was also chairman of the mayor's committee to welcome foreign guests and the homecoming troops. In 1923 he gave to the city the perpetually burning light in Madison Square as a memorial to the city's war dead. He served at various times as consular representative in Philadelphia for Paraguay, Uruguay, and the Dominican Republic. In addition to his French decorations, he was honored by the governments of Great Britain, Italy, Belgium, Serbia, and Venezuela.

Wanamaker's first wife died in 1900, having borne him three children, Fernande, John, and Marie Louise. A second marriage, to Violet Cruger on July 27, 1909, ended in a divorce on Nov. 5, 1923. Wanamaker remained in active charge of both stores until his death at Atlantic City on Mar. 9, 1928. His holdings in the stores were placed in charge of a group of trustees to be administered in the interest of his children, all of whom survived him. With his death, the Wanamaker name disappeared from the list of active directors of the stores.

[H. A. Gibbons, *John Wanamaker* (2 vols., 1926); J. H. Appel, *The Business Biography of John Wanamaker, Founder and Builder* (1930); Princeton University, *After Twenty-Five Years. Class Record of 1886. 1886–1911* (n.d.); *Who's Who in America*, 1926–27; obituaries in *N. Y. Times, Public Ledger* (Philadelphia), Mar. 10, 1928.]   J. J. S.

WANAMAKER, REUBEN MELVILLE (Aug. 2, 1866–June 18, 1924), jurist, was born in North Jackson, Mahoning County, Ohio. His parents, Daniel and Laura (Schoenberger) Wanamaker, were of Pennsylvania Dutch extraction. He attended the local schools and Ohio Northern University, Ada, Ohio, where his studies were interrupted from time to time by periods of teaching. On Apr. 7, 1890, he married Fannie Jane Snow, daughter of Prof. Freeman Snow. His legal training was received at Ohio Northern and in the offices of Ridenour & Halfhill in Lima. In 1893 he began practice in Akron, in partnership with W. E. Young. Elected prosecuting attorney of Summit County in 1895 and 1897, he became widely known through his successful prosecution of the leaders of an attempted lynching in August 1900. In May 1906 he be-

came a judge of the common-pleas court of Ohio; in 1912 he was elected as a Progressive to the supreme court of Ohio for the term beginning Jan. 1, 1913, and in 1918, as a Republican, was reëlected. Two years later he was defeated by Frank B. Willis for the Republican nomination to the United States Senate. Before the completion of his second term on the supreme bench, as a result of a long-continued nervous breakdown, he took his own life by jumping from a window at Mount Carmel Hospital, Columbus. His wife, a son, and a daughter survived him.

Wanamaker was a unique figure. According to general opinion an extreme radical, he was in fact less radical in thought than in manner of expression and in disregard of the conventional attitudes of a judge. He had little respect for judicial precedent and often supported his opinions by quoting from Lincoln and the Bible rather than by citing decided cases. "My experience upon the bench has taught me that precedents are followed when they square with the judgment desired to be rendered," he declared in a dissenting opinion. "They can with equal fidelity be ignored when they do not square with the judgment desired to be rendered" (102 *Ohio State,* 547). "Case law," he said in an earlier opinion (89 *O. S.,* 388–89), "is fast becoming the great bane of bench and bar. Our old time great thinkers . . . have been succeeded very largely by an industrious . . . army of sleuths, of the type of Sherlock Holmes, hunting some precedent in some case, confidently assured that if the search be long enough . . . some apparently parallel case may be found to justify even the most absurd and ridiculous contention."

At times almost vitriolic in his condemnation of the opinions of his judicial colleagues, he accused them of usurpation of power, juggling of words, sophistry. In spite of his habit of extravagant expression, however, Wanamaker made a real contribution to the jurisprudence of Ohio. At a time when most judicial thinking was somewhat stereotyped and concerned chiefly with the protection of property rights, he struck out boldly for a liberal construction of constitutions and laws in favor of the rights and needs of the common man. "Written constitutions," he said, "were adopted not as a sword against public interest but as a shield to protect the public interest" (93 *O. S.,* 227). Coming to the supreme bench shortly after the adoption (1912) of the constitutional amendment providing for municipal home rule, he fought long and hard in lengthy dissenting opinions for a liberal interpretation of the amendment which would give to the cities complete power of local self-government, including the right, free from any review by the state public utilities commission, to fix rates to be charged by all public utilities.

Never particularly sound in his thinking in regard to constitutional law, he made his greatest contribution in the field of criminal jurisprudence. Here he became the voice of the court in eradicating from the law of Ohio many outworn technicalities. In his opinions the doctrines of included offenses, double jeopardy, *corpus delicti,* and variance between indictment and proof received a new and modern meaning. One of his opinions in this field was to the effect that it is not necessary for the trial court in an indictment for murder to charge assault and battery as an included offense, and in another he declared that there is no material variance between an indictment which charges the stealing of several "rungs" and proof of the stealing of several "rugs." In addition to his work on the bench he did some occasional writing, contributing a number of articles to the *Saturday Evening Post* and in 1918 publishing a book, *The Voice of Lincoln.*

[Wanamaker's opinions, in 87–100 *Ohio State Reports*; "Memorial," 112 *Ohio State Reports*, lxv; C. T. Marshall, *A Hist. of the Courts and Lawyers of Ohio* (1934), vols. III, IV; *Ohio Law Reporter,* June 23, 1924, July 13, 1925; *Columbus Citizen* and *Akron Beacon Journal,* June 18, 1924; *Ohio State Journal* (Columbus), June 19, 1924.]   A. H. T.

WANLESS, WILLIAM JAMES (May 1, 1865–Mar. 3, 1933), medical missionary in India, was born in Charleston, Ontario, Canada, the son of John and Elizabeth Wanless. After education in the schools at Charleston, Mount Forest, and Guelph he engaged in business, but a religious awakening led him to determine to devote his life to medical missionary service. Accordingly he entered the University Medical College, New York City, where he was graduated in 1889. During his student days as one of the early members of the Student Volunteer Movement for Foreign Missions he was active in awakening missionary interest by addresses and by a unique pamphlet, *The Medical Mission, Its Place, Power and Appeal* (1911), which was the forerunner of missionary literature of its type. On Apr. 1, 1889, he was appointed a missionary of the Presbyterian Board of Foreign Missions, and was enabled to sail for India the following fall by special contributions from the Bryn Mawr (Pa.) Presbyterian Church, which supported him during his entire missionary career.

He began work at Sangli with a small dispensary, his equipment being improvised from packing boxes. In 1892, however, he moved to Miraj, where the prime minister of the state, who had been one of his patients, gave land for a hospital, which was erected by gifts from John H. Converse [*q.v.*], president of the Baldwin Locomotive Works. The Maharajah of Kolhapur, also a patient, became a devoted friend and munificent benefactor and was deeply influenced in his anti-caste attitude by the democracy and brotherhood which he saw in the hospital. From the beginning Wanless' skill and ability drew ever increasing patronage and support, and with funds received from his patients and other friends he developed the most extensive and effective medical missionary plant in India. He established, also, in 1897, the first missionary medical school in India and, in 1900, a leper asylum. A tuberculosis sanitarium, which now bears his name, was projected by him and opened for patients in 1931. From all over southern Asia patients came to Miraj, attracted by his fame, and his medical students were to be found throughout India and far up into Mesopotamia. During his superintendency approximately a million patients passed through the hospitals, and he himself performed annually some 6,000 operations. He was as earnest and thorough an evangelist as he was a skilful and efficient physician and surgeon.

Wanless was thrice decorated by the government of India. In 1910 he received the Kaiser-i-Hind Medal, Second Class; in 1920 he was awarded the Kaiser-i-Hind Medal, First Class; and in 1928 he was knighted for his extraordinary service. The only American to receive this last honor previously was J. C. R. Ewing [*q.v.*], who was for forty-three years a missionary in India. In 1928 ill health compelled Wanless to retire to America, but he was called back to India in 1930, where he remained some months, aiding in the establishment of the tuberculosis sanitarium. He was a vigorous personality, overflowing with energy and good cheer. A remarkable testimony to his place in public esteem was a great meeting of representatives of all communities, held in Poona in January 1928, under the chairmanship of the Aga Khan, for the presentation of a farewell address enclosed in a silver casket. Wanless was married twice: on Sept. 5, 1889, to Mary Elizabeth Marshall, who died Aug. 12, 1906; and on Dec. 5, 1907, to Lillian Emery Havens, who survived him. He died in Glendale, Cal. Some account of his activities is given in his book, *An American Doctor at Work in India,* which appeared in 1932.

[In addition to the above mentioned book, see *Who's Who* (British), 1932; *Presbyt. Advance,* Sept. 23, 1915, Mar. 16, 1933; *Presbyt. Mag.,* Sept. 1928; *Missionary*

Rev. of the World, Apr. 1933; *Los Angeles Times,* Mar. 4, 1933.]   R. El. S.

WANTON, JOSEPH (Aug. 15, 1705–July 19, 1780), governor of Rhode Island, son of William and Ruth (Bryant) Wanton, and descended from Edward Wanton who was in Boston, Mass., as early as 1658, was born into a family prominent in Rhode Island affairs. His father was governor of Rhode Island from 1732 to 1734, his father's brother John was governor from 1734 to 1741, while a first cousin, Gideon Wanton, was governor in 1745–46 and 1747–48. Joseph received no formal education, but acquired from his father and other residents of Newport a practical knowledge of ship-building, privateering, and other occupations associated with the sea. Admitted a freeman of the colony in 1728, he became in 1738 a deputy collector of customs at Newport, which position he held for over ten years. From about 1759 until the collapse of the family fortunes in 1780, he engaged, with two of his sons, in general merchandising under the firm name of Joseph & William Wanton. They dealt extensively with the Browns of Providence, from whom they bought quantities of spermaceti candles for resale in America and the West Indies. To the latter islands the firm also exported fish, cheese, lumber, pork, and mutton, and from thence imported molasses and loaf sugar. Business between the Browns and the Wantons declined in 1774, probably because of the royalist leanings of the latter.

Joseph Wanton was first elected governor in April 1769. Since he was both the elected executive of a charter colony and an officer bound to enforce British colonial regulations, he had a difficult time during his six-year tenure. In 1769 he had to deal with the case of the *Liberty,* a British sloop scuttled by a group of Newporters (*Records, post,* VI, 593–94); and in 1772, with Daniel Horsmanden [*q.v.*], Frederick Smythe, and Peter Oliver [*q.v.*], the chief justices of New York, New Jersey, and Massachusetts, and Robert Auchmuty [*q.v.*], judge of the vice-admiralty court at Boston, he was appointed to inquire into the affair of the *Gaspee* (*Ibid.,* VII, 57–192). Throughout these and other disturbances the governor succeeded reasonably well in appearing to enforce order without unduly restraining the patriot cause, with which he partially sympathized. He believed, however, that for the good of all concerned, America should remain a part of the British empire, and consequently, with the outbreak of hostilities at Lexington, he opposed further revolutionary measures. Although reelected May 3, 1775, for another term, he declined to appear, May 4, to take the oath of office

and the following day declined to sign the commissions of the troops that had been raised. The General Assembly in June suspended him from acting as governor, and on Oct. 31 deposed him (*Records,* VII, 311–99).

Although Wanton lost the confidence of the patriots, he retained their respect and was not personally molested. He remained in Newport until his death in the summer of 1780, taking no further part in public affairs. A man of large build and impressive appearance, he liked expensive clothes and a bountiful table. On Aug. 21, 1729, he had married Mary, daughter of John Winthrop, F.R.S. They had five daughters and three sons. Although he was often spoken of as a wealthy man, little of Wanton's estate survived the Revolution. His liquid assets were invested in the mercantile firm, which suffered reverses during the war, especially after 1779 when the state confiscated the property of his sons Joseph, Jr., and William, who had openly espoused the British cause; a loan of £500 to his son-in-law, William Browne [*q.v.*] of Salem, Mass., later governor of Bermuda, was never repaid. His father had left the Quakers and his mother the Presbyterians at the time of their marriage; their son was an Episcopalian, a member of Trinity Church in Newport. His gubernatorial career resembled that of Thomas Hutchinson of Massachusetts, but the two men differed widely in personal characteristics. Wanton was less intellectual and less ambitious than his renowned contemporary, but he suffered adversity with greater fortitude.

[J. R. Bartlett, *Hist. of the Wanton Family of Newport, R. I.* (1878); *Records of the Colony of Rhode Island,* vols. VI–VII (1861–62), ed. by J. R. Bartlett; Wilkins Updike, *A Hist. of the Episc. Church in Narragansett, R. I.* (3 vols., 1907); G. C. Mason, *Annals of Trinity Church, Newport, R. I.,* 1 ser. (1890); *New Eng. Hist. and Geneal. Reg.,* July 1926; letters and other MSS. in the R. I. state archives, the R. I. Hist. Soc., and the John Carter Brown Library.]   J. M. M.

WARBURG, PAUL MORITZ (Aug. 10, 1868–Jan. 24, 1932), banker, born in Hamburg, was one of the sons of Moritz and Charlotte (Oppenheim) Warburg. His father was a member of the Hamburg banking house of M. M. Warburg & Company, founded in 1798 by his great-grandfather and conducted thereafter by the family. Paul Warburg, after graduating in 1886 from the Gymnasium at Hamburg, began work with a Hamburg exporting firm, afterwards serving in shipping and banking houses, first at London, then at Paris. In 1895 he was admitted as partner in the Warburg firm at Hamburg. In the same year he married Nina J. Loeb, daughter of Solomon Loeb, of Kuhn Loeb & Company, and in 1902, coming to New York, he became a member of that firm. He became an American citizen in 1911.

Warburg had made special study of the central banking organism in the principal European countries, notably Germany, France, and England. In the United States, after the panic of 1907, he joined publicly with those bankers and public men who were urging fundamental reform in the American banking system. His recognized knowledge of the subject brought him in contact with Senator Nelson W. Aldrich [*q.v.*], under whose auspices, in 1908, Congress was induced to create a national monetary commission, to investigate the question and report on a feasible plan. The tentative plan of legislation submitted by Senator Aldrich in 1911, if not virtually drawn up by Warburg, undoubtedly reflected many of his ideas (Laughlin, *post,* pp. 15, 16). With its provision for a national reserve association (like a central bank) with branches, the majority of whose managing officers should be chosen by the private banks in the system, Warburg was in entire sympathy.

Congress refused to adopt the proposal and when, in 1913, it enacted the Federal Reserve law, providing for separate regional reserve banks under the supervision of a reserve board appointed by the president, the banking community generally opposed the change. It has been claimed, and denied, that certain fundamental principles that were incorporated in the Aldrich bill through the influence of Warburg were accepted in the new act (E. R. A. Seligman, in Warburg, *The Federal Reserve System,* II, 8; Willis, *post,* pp. 523 ff.). At any rate, he accepted the altered administrative provisions. The result of this cordial acquiescence and of Warburg's recognized knowledge of the problem was that he was nominated by President Wilson on June 15, 1914, as one of the five appointed members of the first Federal Reserve Board. The Senate finally approved his nomination on Aug. 7, 1914. Warburg was an exceedingly useful member of the Reserve Board during his four-year term, which covered practically the period of the World War and involved operations of a previously unimagined magnitude by the Reserve System. When his term was about to expire in 1918, the United States was at war with Germany. President Wilson was admittedly disposed to renominate him, but Warburg wrote frankly to the President that insistence on the renomination of a citizen of German birth would expose both the President and the Reserve Board to attack, at a crucial moment. Warburg therefore retired to private life, devoting himself thereafter chiefly to the organization and operation of the International Acceptance Bank.

In his capacity as private banker, Warburg came into nation-wide notice in March 1929 because of his plain warning, in his annual report to his shareholders, of the disaster threatened by the wild stock speculation then raging throughout the country. Almost without exception, responsible bankers had refrained from public warnings of the kind. Warburg declared the spectacular rise in market values of company stocks to be "in the majority of cases, quite unrelated to respective increases in plant, property, or earning powers" (Mar. 8, 1929; quoted in *The Federal Reserve System,* I, 824). He described the great speculation as sustained only "by a colossal volume of loans carrying unabsorbed securities," and predicted that, "if orgies of unrestrained speculation" were not brought under control, "the ultimate collapse is certain not only to affect the speculators themselves, but also to bring about a general depression involving the entire country." When his warning was abundantly fulfilled by the panic of October 1929 on the Stock Exchange, and by the swiftly succeeding aftermath of extreme commercial depression, he condemned emotional predictions of irretrievable ruin as vigorously as he had warned against the delusions of the period of speculation. With the idea that the gold standard was responsible for the entire collapse he had no sympathy whatever. In his analysis of the causes of the depression, he stressed the bad effects of efforts to maintain high prices by "tariff barriers and other artificial expedients, in the face of constantly accelerated mass production" (*New York Times,* Jan. 25, 1932, p. 5).

Besides being chairman of the International Acceptance Bank, Warburg was chairman of the Manhattan Company, a director of important railroads and corporations, and a trustee or director of several institutions of educational character. From 1921 to 1926 he was a member of the advisory council of the Federal Reserve Board, and he served as chairman of the economic policy commission of the American Bankers' Association. In 1930 he published *The Federal Reserve System. Its Origin and Growth* (2 vols.). He died at his home in New York City, leaving a son and a daughter.

[Warburg Papers, in private hands; *Annual Reports* Fed. Reserve Board, 1914–18; *Reports* of annual meetings of Am. Acceptance Council, 1929–31; *Annual Reports* of chairman to shareholders of International Acceptance Bank, 1921–29; H. P. Willis, *The Federal Reserve System* (1923); J. L. Laughlin, *The Federal Reserve Act. Its Origin and Problems* (1933); "Two Bankers on the Depression," *New Republic,* Jan. 21, 1931; "Paul M. Warburg," *Nation,* Feb. 3, 1932; *Who's Who in America,* 1930–31; obituaries in *N. Y.*

Times Jan. 25, 1932; *American Banker*, Jan. 26, 1932; information from Warburg's son, James P. Warburg.]

A. D. N.

WARD, AARON MONTGOMERY

WARD, AARON MONTGOMERY (Feb. 17, 1843–Dec. 7, 1913), merchant, was born at Chatham, N. J., the son of Sylvester A. and Julia Laura Mary (Green) Ward. During his childhood his parents migrated to Niles, Mich., where he attended public school until he was fourteen. He was then apprenticed to a trade, but left his master to work in a barrel-stave factory at twenty-five cents a day and later became a day laborer in a brickyard. When he was nineteen years old he went to St. Joseph, Mich., to work in a general store for five dollars a month and his board; at the end of three years he was put in charge of the store with a salary of $100 a month. Going to Chicago about 1865, he was employed by Field, Palmer & Leiter for two years and then worked for a short time for the wholesale dry-goods house of Willis, Gregg & Brown. When this firm failed, he became a traveling salesman for Walter M. Smith & Company, dry-goods wholesalers in St. Louis.

It was while he was traveling out of St. Louis that Ward obtained an intimate knowledge of rural conditions which enabled him to make a distinctive contribution to American life. A source of chronic complaint by people living in the country was the small price received for farm produce compared with the high cost of goods bought at retail. Ward conceived the idea of buying in large quantities for cash direct from the manufacturer and selling for cash direct to the farmer. Back in Chicago, working for C. W. Pardridge, a State Street dry-goods firm, he awaited his chance to go into business for himself. He was ready to start when the Chicago fire of 1871 intervened to wipe out practically all his savings. In the spring of 1872, however, he resigned his position and invested all he had saved, $1,600, in the new business. This, with $800 contributed by George R. Thorne, his partner, constituted the total capital.

The partners began their operations in the loft of a livery stable on Kinzie Street between Rush and State streets. Their first stock was a small selection of dry goods, the first catalogue a single price sheet. Ward was a keen judge of merchandise and he bought at prices which enabled him to sell to the consumer in the country at prices he could pay. From the beginning he followed the policy of satisfying the customer or allowing the return of goods. In 1873–74 purchasing agencies of the National Grange bought through him to stock their cooperative retail stores and he thus earned the good will of farmers in Illi-

nois and Iowa. Making accessible to people in rural sections throughout the country a variety of goods which they could not otherwise have enjoyed with their limited purchasing power, his enterprise succeeded from the beginning, and was forced repeatedly to move to larger quarters as sales increased. Since the business was conducted on a cash basis, it survived the panic of 1873. New lines were added after 1874 and an eight-page catalogue replaced the single price sheet. By 1876 the catalogue had 150 pages, with illustrations; by 1888, annual sales had reached one million dollars. With the building of the Ward Tower at Michigan Boulevard and Madison Street in 1900, the successful business and its founder attracted national attention. At the time of his death, annual sales amounted to some $40,000,000, customers were served in all parts of the world, and the staff of employees numbered 6000.

Ward's public spirit was demonstrated by the protracted legal battle he carried on in the Illinois courts to maintain free from all obstruction the park between Michigan Boulevard and the lake shore, now Grant Park, and it is largely owing to his foresight and tenacity that Chicago has a lake frontage which is the heritage, not of a privileged few, but of the mass of the people, for whom Ward seems really to have cared. He retired from active management of the company in 1901, although he still retained the title of president. Since he had no sons, the management of the business passed into the hands of the five sons of his partner, Thorne. Ward spent much time at his large estate, "La Belle Knoll," at Oconomowoc, Wis., where he raised fine horses. He died at Highland Park, Ill.

On Feb. 22, 1872, in the same year in which he started his mail-order business, Ward married Elizabeth J. Cobb of Kalamazoo, whose sister had married his partner. Mrs. Ward was left the large fortune which her husband had received from the earnings of his mail-order business. During her lifetime, and through her will, she dispensed considerable sums to charitable institutions. Her principal benefactions, however, were to Northwestern University, to which institution in 1923 she gave $4,223,000 for a medical and dental school as a memorial to her husband, adding in 1926 $4,300,000 for the enlargement and maintenance of the school. She died July 26, 1926. The Wards had no children, although it was generally believed until after Mrs. Ward's will was probated that Marjorie Ward, an adopted daughter, was their own.

[P. T. Gilbert and C. L. Bryson, *Chicago and Its Makers* (1929); *Who's Who in America*, 1912–13;

Dedication of the Montgomery Ward Memorial Building, Northwestern Univ. (1927); The Hist. and Progress of Montgomery Ward & Company (1925), published by the company; Northwestern Alumni News, Nov. 1926; Inter-Ocean (Chicago), Chicago Daily News, Dec. 8, 1913; Chicago Daily Tribune, Dec. 8, 1913, July 27, 29, 30, 1926; information and corroboration from officials of Northwestern Univ. and of Montgomery Ward & Company, and from George Merrick, Esq., Ward's personal attorney].   E. A. D.

WARD, ARTEMAS (Nov. 26, 1727–Oct. 28, 1800), Revolutionary general, was descended from William Ward, a Puritan, one of the original settlers of Sudbury and Marlborough, Mass. His father, Nahum Ward, was a founder of Shrewsbury, where Artemas was born, and his mother was Martha How, the daughter of Capt. Daniel How and Elizabeth Kerley. He attended school in Shrewsbury and was graduated at Harvard College in 1748. After teaching for a brief period in Groton, he established, in 1750, a general store in Shrewsbury, which he continued to run until the burden of his official duties forced him to abandon it. On July 31, 1750, he was married to Sarah Trowbridge of Groton, a descendant of John Cotton [q.v.], and she became the mother of his eight children. He was elected to many town offices including those of assessor, clerk, selectman, moderator, and treasurer. On Jan. 21, 1762, he was appointed a justice of the Worcester county court of common pleas, and later, in 1775, he became its chief justice.

During the French and Indian War he took part in Abercromby's ill-starred attack upon Ticonderoga in 1758 and was promoted from the rank of major to that of colonel in the provincial militia. The hardships of the campaign impaired his health and thereafter he was never robust. For many years he represented Shrewsbury in the General Court, distinguishing himself by his opposition to royal authority. In 1768 he was one of the "Glorious Ninety-two" who refused to vote for the rescinding of Samuel Adams' famous "Circular Letter." So obnoxious to Governor Bernard was his conduct that the latter deprived him of his military commission in 1766, and in 1768 and 1769 vetoed his election to the council. Hutchinson, succeeding Bernard, reluctantly approved his election in 1770, and Ward remained a member of the board until 1774. In the organization of resistance to General Gage as governor, during the autumn and winter of 1774–75, he played an important rôle, serving as a member of the conventions held in Worcester County to champion colonial rights and of the First and Second Provincial congresses. When the news of the battle of Lexington reached Shrewsbury, he lay ill, but at dawn on the following day, Apr. 20, he mounted his horse and rode to Cambridge, where he assumed command of the patriot forces under authority granted to him by the Second Provincial Congress. On May 19 he was formally commissioned general and commander-in-in chief of the Massachusetts troops. During the following weeks he directed the siege of Boston and began the conversion of the undisciplined bands of militia-men into an army. He was not present at the battle of Bunker Hill because he believed it to be his duty to remain at his headquarters in Cambridge, but he designated the detachments participating in it and issued the orders he considered necessary.

On June 17 the Continental Congress, which had chosen Washington for the supreme command of the American forces, selected Ward as second in command with the rank of major-general. Upon arriving at Cambridge, Washington assigned to Ward the command of the right wing. On Mar. 4, 1776, Ward ordered General Thomas to seize Dorchester Heights, thus forcing the British to evacuate Boston. Shortly thereafter, on Mar. 22, he tendered his resignation on the ground of failing health. It was accepted by Congress on Apr. 23, but at Washington's request, he remained temporarily in command of the forces left in Massachusetts after the withdrawal of the main body to New York. Until relieved by William Heath [q.v.], on Mar. 20, 1777, he devoted his attention chiefly to strengthening the defenses of Boston.

During the next three years he served on the Executive Council. From 1780 to 1781 he was a member of the Continental Congress, and from 1782 to 1787, barring one year, a member of the state legislature. He appeared on many committees of the latter body and was elected speaker. During Shays's Rebellion he defended the judiciary in a speech before a mob which had assembled about the steps of the court house in Worcester. He served as a Federalist in the First and Second congresses (1791–93, 1793–95), and was assigned to many committees dealing with military affairs. In 1798 illness compelled him to resign his position on the bench. He died of paralysis and was buried in Mountain View Cemetery in Shrewsbury. His homestead, now the property of Harvard University, is kept as a memorial.

Whatever his official position, Ward was conscientious, hard-working, and inflexible in his opinions. Deeply devoted to the interests of Massachusetts, he believed that Providence had set a seal of especial favor upon the state and that its citizens were the chosen people. His relations with Washington lacked cordiality. He resented the strictures which Washington passed upon the men of Massachusetts at the outbreak of the Revolution. When Washington visited the state in 1789, he passed Ward's house but the general was not present to greet him.

[Manuscript letters, diaries, and papers of Ward are widely held. Among the principal collections are those of the Massachusetts Historical Society, the Massachusetts State Archives, Boston, and the American Antiquarian Society, Worcester, Mass. Consult also: Peter Force, *Am. Archives*, 4 ser., vols. I–VI (1837–46), 5 ser. (3 vols., 1848–53) ; A. H. Ward, *Hist. of the Town of Shrewsbury* (1847), and *Ward Family* (1851) ; Elizabeth Ward, *Old Times in Shrewsbury* (1892) ; W. T. Davis, *Hist. of the Judiciary of Mass.* (1900) ; R. Frothingham, *Hist. of the Siege of Boston* (1903) ; P. H. Epler, *Master Minds at the Commonwealth's Heart* (1909) ; Charles Martyn, *The Life of Artemas Ward* (1921), and *The William Ward Geneal.* (1925).]   E. E. C.

WARD, ARTEMUS [See BROWNE, CHARLES FARRAR, 1834–1867].

WARD, CYRENUS OSBORNE (Oct. 28, 1831–Mar. 19, 1902), author, editor, labor leader, was the seventh of the ten children born to Justus and Silence (Rolph) Ward; Lester Frank Ward [*q.v.*] was a brother. They were descendants of Andrew Warde who emigrated to Massachusetts and died in Fairfield, Conn., in 1659. Three years after Cyrenus' birth, in western New York, his parents moved to St. Charles, Kane County, Ill., where until 1848 he aided his father in various frontier activities connected with farming, milling, and construction work, becoming meanwhile a skilled mechanic. He traveled extensively in the Middle West, touring as a violinist with a concert company. His leisure was largely devoted to the study of botany, geology, and ancient and modern languages. On Oct. 25, 1857, he married Stella A. Owen of Wysox, Pa., and the following year, in partnership with his wife's brother, built a hub factory at Myersburg, Pa.; later he was connected with other manufacturing enterprises.

He enlisted for the Civil War, but was rejected. In 1864, however, he was appointed machinist in the Brooklyn Navy Yard, and while employed there became deeply interested in labor problems. His pamphlets and speeches attracted the notice of such journalists as Charles A. Dana and Horace Greeley [*qq.v.*] and led in the late sixties to connections with the *Sun* and the *New York Tribune*. He traveled extensively abroad during the years when the international labor movement was being organized, attended several labor conferences, met Karl Marx and other noted labor leaders, and contributed to the *Sun* a series of articles entitled "A Mechanic Abroad" and "Cooperation Abroad." On his return to America he resumed work as a mechanic and engaged actively in the labor movement as lecturer, writer, and organizer. His ardent support of social reforms and of the political organization of workers made it difficult for him to retain employment, and he finally devoted himself completely to the cause of labor. Establishing his own printing office, in 1878 he published his first book, *A Labor Catechism of Political Economy*. The extensive sale of this work enabled him to extend his activities as lecturer and writer. He also published numerous pamphlets and labor journals, including *The Voice of the People,* a newspaper. In 1878 he became associate editor of *Man,* a journal devoted to progress and reform.

In 1884 he was appointed to a position with the Geological Survey at Washington, and soon thereafter was transferred to the Bureau of Labor, as translator and librarian. He had long been collecting information about the working classes of ancient times, and in 1887 completed the text of the first volume of his most noted work, *A History of the Ancient Working People*—later entitled *The Ancient Lowly*. Failing to secure a publisher, he set up a print shop in his own house, and in 1889, after two years of arduous labor, the first edition appeared. It immediately attracted wide attention both as a work of learning and also as an ardent and sympathetic interpretation of working-class history. Scholars were inclined to question the validity of many of his conclusions regarding the meaning of ancient records, but his use of inscriptions and casual sources and his emphasis on neglected phases of ancient life were recognized as contributing significantly to the study of antiquity. In 1892 and again in 1896 he traveled widely in Europe, studying current conditions and newly discovered inscriptions and sources in preparation for a second volume of the *History*, which he published in 1900. The next year he died in Yuma, Ariz., whither he had gone in quest of health.

In addition to those already mentioned his writings include a drama based on Abraham Lincoln and the Civil War, *The Equilibration of Human Aptitudes and Powers of Adaptation* (1895), and numerous pamphlets, bulletins of the Bureau of Labor, and articles in periodicals. His distinctive traits were versatility combined with great energy and intensity of purpose, idealism, and sympathy for the working people, whom he urged to refrain from violence and to achieve a socialistic state by political methods. He exerted significant influence on the organization of labor, the movement for social reform, and the interpretation and utilization of history for the advancement of working-class aims.

[Manuscript sketch, "Cyrenus Osborne Ward, A Sketch," by F. E. Ward, a son; G. K. Ward, *Andrew Warde and His Descendants, 1597–1910* (1910); L. F. Ward, *Glimpses of the Cosmos* (1913); E. P. Cape, *Lester F. Ward, A Personal Sketch* (1922); preface to 1892 ed. of *A Labor Catechism of Political Economy*: *N. Y. Times*, Mar. 21, 1902; *Evening Star* (Washington), Mar. 21, 1902..   W. B.

WARD, ELIZABETH STUART PHELPS (Aug. 31, 1844–Jan. 28, 1911), writer, was born in Boston, Mass., the eldest child of Elizabeth (Stuart) and Austin Phelps [*q.v.*] and the descendant of Nathaniel Phelps who emigrated from England with his father in 1630 and died in Northampton, Mass. She was baptized as Mary Gray, but after her mother's death she changed her name. Her father was the son of a Congregational minister whose eminently orthodox career was interrupted by a remarkable case of "house possession," in consequence of which for about seven months strange phenomena were manifested in his parsonage. Turnips thumping from the ceiling to the study table were among the crasser forms. A man of complete veracity, he wrote a record of this peculiar experience; but many years later the manuscript was destroyed by his grandchildren, for reasons now difficult to appreciate. Of the actuality of the manifestations, it should be added, they had no doubts; nor did they offer any explanation. This event in the Phelps family cannot be overlooked; it can hardly be overemphasized in dealing with the work of the grand-daughter, always interested in psychic phenomena. In 1848 Austin Phelps accepted a professorship at the Theological Seminary at Andover, the youthful home of his wife, the fifth child of Moses Stuart [*q.v.*], one of the most redoubtable theologians that even New England has produced. With all the prestige of the most scholarly academic background, with a brilliant mind, nervous temperament, intense susceptibility to artistic and spiritual impressions, Elizabeth (Stuart) Phelps was attuned to exquisite pleasure and exquisite pain. Under the name of "H. Trusta" she published extraordinarily popular religious tales, written in an easy, natural style, lightened by many glints of humor. *A Peep at Number Five* (1851) is a really charming record of a clergyman's home. *The Sunny Side* (1851) reached the astonishing circulation of some 100,000 copies. *The Angel Over the Right Shoulder* (1851), under the thinnest veil of fiction, shows "the difficult reconciliation between genius and domestic life" (*Chapters, post,* p. 12). "The struggle killed her, but she fought till she fell," her daughter recorded years later

(*Ibid.,* p. 15). It was over when that daughter was eight years old, but one of the strongest influences in her life was the memory of her mother; and many of her own tales, especially *The Story of Avis* (1877), deal with similar struggles.

The death of their gifted mother left the care of three small children to their father, already beginning the nervous invalidism that tortured the remainder of his life. Of his devotion to his children, of his ideal fatherhood, of the atmosphere of his home his daughter wrote glowingly in *Austin Phelps* (1891) and *Chapters from a Life* (1896). It was he who influenced her reading, cultivating a taste severe and catholic; it was from him that she received her real education, although she was a day pupil at schools in Andover, where she had sound training in mathematics and sciences, as well as in languages and literatures. Philosophy and theology were inevitable elements in the very fiber of one bred on Andover Hill. In *Chapters from a Life* (Chap. ii) she wrote some pages about the Andover of her youth that deserve to rank among American classics. Although a resident of the academic center of New England theology and the daughter of one of its most fervent exponents, she was trained in a religion of love and hope, "natural, easy, pleasant." "The fear of an ungodlike God never haunted us," she wrote; "in Creeds we were not over-much instructed" (*Austin Phelps, ante,* p. 154). That the religion thus early acquired was satisfying and sustaining her whole later life testified. Although a motherless and often a lonely child, she seems to have grown through a normal girlhood, enlivened by the usual social and intellectual pleasures, plus a superfluity of young men, mostly of the class known as "theologues," whom in her fiction she alternately pitied and patronized, but rarely escaped.

Crashing into all normal life, destroying its balance and its beauty, came the Civil War; and to her it brought personal tragedy. The shock caused by the death of the boy whom she loved proved almost too much for her physical and mental poise, and for several years she was very nearly a recluse. From the grief of that period and the long brooding emerged *The Gates Ajar,* begun in 1864 and published in 1868 (but title page dated 1869). From childhood she had written, and at thirteen she had begun to publish; now she concentrated the technique and facility thus acquired to "comfort some few . . . of the women whose misery crowded the land" (*Chapters, ante,* p. 97). The result was amazing to the author, as, for different reasons, it is to readers today. In a tale almost devoid of incident, by means of conversations loaded with Biblical quotations and their literal interpretations, this orthodox daughter of an ultra-orthodox theological professor swept away the then current conceptions of heaven, substituting a place of light and love, where the dear dead retained their familiar characteristics and all the things that they had loved worthily here. It reads strangely now, because of its subject and its method; but it brought solace to many thousands and became one of the most influential works of fiction ever written by an American. The circulation in this country fell somewhat below 100,000 but was greater in England; and the book was translated into many European languages. Its success made the author "the most astonished girl in North America," she wrote (*Ibid.*, p. 110); she received letters from all over the world; she was extolled, and she was vituperated. Incredible it all seems now; nevertheless it is true. That the time had come for some such revolution in thought in no way detracts from the originality and daring of the author. One result is easily understood. Thereafter whatever she wrote was published and read; but the overwhelming success was never repeated. She wrote better books, but none that touched the popular imagination so vividly or met the popular need so directly. In *Beyond the Gates* (1883), *The Gates Between* (1887), *Within the Gates* (1901), and in several short stories she again attempted eschatology. Both by inheritance and by temperament she was attuned to the psychic; but her deep spiritual reverence, her Yankee common sense, probably also her keen humor kept her from swinging far from her moorings in orthodox religion.

She wrote voluminously, mainly fiction; also she essayed verse, *Poetic Studies* (1875), *Songs of the Silent World* (1884, but title page dated 1885), but never with the success of prose. As few but the greatest have done she understood and expressed the sufferings of gifted and sensitive women, the depths of loneliness, the torture of jangled nerves. This last experience was hers by birthright. Like her father she was a victim of insomnia in some of its most excruciating forms. These nervous disorders made her at times almost a recluse and deprived her of many coveted forms of service. While still young she had written one of her most intense tales, "The Tenth of January," in the *Atlantic Monthly* (March 1868), dealing with the collapse of a factory building. *The Silent Partner* (1871) and many short stories testify to her sympathy with the narrow lives of women in industry. *Doctor Zay* (1882) is one of the first American novels to deal with women in medicine. Indeed the

problem of the adjustment of women to the complications of modern life was never far from her thought. It reached its highest expression in *The Story of Avis* (*ante*), "a woman's book, hoping for small hospitality at the hands of men" (*Chapters, ante*, p. 157).

For many years her summer home was at East Gloucester, Mass., and here she came to know the pathos and the tragedy of the fisher folk. Here too were seared upon her imagination the horrors of intemperance. For three years she was connected with a mission for temperance reform, and in it she had experiences she counted among the richest in her life. The relinquishment of this work on account of illness was to her a great trial; but she passed on her sympathetic understanding of her neighbors in two tales that rank high in American fiction, *The Madonna of the Tubs* (1886) and *Jack, the Fisherman* (1887). Gloucester also furnished the background for *A Singular Life* (1894), although the first chapters deal with Andover and its theological seminary. Andover repudiated her interpretation of its theology, and Gloucester resented her treatment of its morals; but the reading public of New England took the book to its heart as it had done none of hers since *The Gates Ajar*. It is an impassioned, utterly sincere plea for practical religion in the story of a young minister who tried to live like a "Christ-man" in a liquor-drenched town, among hard-working people. The dominant motive in this book is the dominant motive in all the best of her writing, as it was in her life. Outgrowing much of her early creed, losing interest in theology, she centered her thought on the central figure of Christianity and found solution for life's problems in the teaching and example of Jesus Christ. As a result of lifelong familiarity with the Gospels she wrote *The Story of Jesus Christ: an Interpretation* (1897). Into this she put her whole heart, but she had neither the critical acumen nor the scholarship to treat the great subject in an original manner. She valued the book far more highly than did even her most admiring readers.

She was married to Herbert Dickinson Ward [*q.v.*] on Oct. 20, 1888. They had no children. At their new home in Newton Center, Mass., they wrote several books in collaboration. In *The Master of the Magicians* (1890) and *Come Forth* (1890, but title page dated 1891) they worked on Biblical romances, but without marked success. Throughout the remainder of her life she continued to write prolifically. *Austin Phelps* (*ante*), the biography of her father, and *Chapters from a Life* (*ante*), which she refused to term an autobiography, are especially delightful: indeed they may be considered essential for the understanding of academic New England and its intellectual aristocracy. It was hardly possible that so intense a personality as hers should be at all times balanced and tolerant. Frequently in both her style and her treatment one is aware of the excess to which the nervous temperament is prone. Often even her best writing is marred by redundance and exaggeration; but that she was a master of lucid, fluent, poignant English there is no doubt. "Provincial" is a word easy to apply to her, hard to defend. It is true that she usually wrote about the intellectual, oversensitive people of New England; but also it is true that she saw them as human beings, occasionally had glimpses of their naked souls, perceived for herself and helped her reader to perceive the tragedy and the glory of the will to do "the painful right."

[*Austin Phelps* and *Chapters from a Life, ante*; "Memorial of the Author," by Austin Phelps in Elizabeth Stuart Phelps, under pseud. H. Trusta, *The Last Leaf from Sunny Side* (1853); O. S. Phelps and A. T. Servin, *The Phelps Family of America* (1899), vol. II; *Boston Evening Transcript*, Jan. 30, Feb. 4, 1911.]

E. D. H.

WARD, FREDERICK TOWNSEND (Nov. 29, 1831–Sept. 21, 1862), adventurer, was born and reared in Salem, Mass., the son of Elizabeth Colburn (Spencer) and Frederick Gamaliel Ward, a ship's master and later a ship-broker and merchant. He was the descendant of Miles Ward who emigrated from England to Salem about 1639. In boyish games at school his capacity for leadership emerged, and he showed coolness and daring in sailing small boats in the bay. He went to school at home and from 1846 to 1848 at Norwich University in Norwich, Vt., where he acquired the foundations of a good military training. For the next twelve years he roamed far and wide on sea voyages or commercial ventures, interspersed with military service in Tehuantepec, with William Walker in Nicaragua, and with the French in the Crimea. In 1859 he appeared in Shanghai, China, where he took service on a Yangtse River steamer. No remarkable exterior appearance suggested the pent-up energies, the forceful leadership, or the daring that characterized his actions. In the thickest battle he went unarmed, but invariably carried a riding-whip or cane—a custom followed later by Gordon.

The year 1860 marked a crisis in the Taiping Rebellion, when the rebels, barred from Central China, were trying to obtain the rich coast provinces about Shanghai. Anglo-French resistance protected that international port, but officials and merchants outside were frantic. Just at this time

he was introduced to Takee, a Chinese merchant, who became a broker between him and the officials and later his paymaster. Ward married Chang Mei, Takee's daughter. They had no children. For a cash payment Ward agreed to recapture Sungkiang. His first following of foreign adventurers failed, but a second expedition of Filipinos with white officers proved successful. Encouraged by this victory, he tried in the same manner to capture Tsingpu; but, unfortunately for him, it was defended by a strong body of Taipings reinforced by a company of adventurers under Savage, an Englishman. In one of the attacks on this city he was wounded, and his force thereupon rested for several months at Sungkiang. Meanwhile he sought for a larger army. Since an adequate foreign legion would be both politically objectionable and costly, he thought that a sufficient army of well-drilled Chinese under foreign officers would be effective and comparatively inexpensive. Official support was gained; but the foreign consuls, particularly the British, opposed his whole project, and he was arrested in May 1861. Asserting Chinese naturalization, he avoided a trial, and he escaped from a British warship on which he was detained. Early in 1862 his new army was ready. Meanwhile a change had taken place in the Franco-British policy: they were combining with the Chinese to clear a thirty mile radius about Shanghai. His command, now called the "Ever Victorious Army," was enthusiastically acclaimed and cooperated effectively in several campaigns with the Anglo-French forces near Shanghai and Ning-po. During the summer more than 4,000 men served under his banner, and Ward himself, with brevet rank as brigadier-general, was cited for bravery in the capture of Tsingpu early in August. His enterprise had justified itself in the teeth of foreign opposition in its beginnings, and of Chinese jealousy of its present successes. Other Chinese armies resented the superior airs of Ward's men; officials worried over the cost of the force; and widespread gossip credited Ward with untoward ambitions, though none of his actions ever revealed such. His loyalty to the United States was shown in his offer, just before his death, of 10,000 taels to the Federal government for carrying on its Civil War. While directing the attack on Tzeki, he received a mortal wound and died the following day. A magnificent state funeral was accorded him at Sungkiang, his headquarters, and a memorial temple was there erected in his honor in which, until recently, regular sacrifices were offered to his spirit.

Henry Andrea Burgevine [*q.v.*], who succeeded to the command, soon lost his position. Charles

George Gordon ("Chinese" Gordon), after an interval, succeeded; and his success was achieved with the instrument forged by Ward, a fact sometimes—unjustly—forgotten.

[Holger Cahill, *A Yankee Adventurer; the Story of Ward and the Taiping Rebellion* (1930); R. S. Rantoul, "Frederick Townsend Ward," *Essex Institute Hist. Colls.,* vol. XLIV (1908); E. A. Powell, *Gentlemen Rovers* (1913); H. B. Morse, *In the Days of the Taipings* (1927); J. W. Foster, *Diplomatic Memoirs* (1909), vol. II; F. W. Williams, *Anson Burlingame* (1912); *Norwich University* (1911), vol. II, ed. by W. A. Ellis; clippings and papers in the Essex Institute, Salem, Mass.]
W. J. H—1.

WARD, GENEVIEVE (Mar. 27, 1838–Aug. 18, 1922), actress, was born in New York City, daughter of Samuel and Lucy (Leigh) Ward, and grand-daughter of Gideon Lee, mayor of the city in 1833, and through her grandmother a descendant of Jonathan Edwards [*q.v.*]. Named Lucy Geneviève Teresa, she later dropped all but the middle name, which she herself wrote with the accent. She was taken abroad by her mother to be educated and at fifteen elected to become a singer. Rossini sent her to a teacher in Florence. but at eighteen her career was interrupted by her unfortunate marriage (Nov. 10, 1856) to a Russian count, Constantine de Guerbel, whom she met in Italy. A civil contract was performed by the American consul at Nice, which the count appeared to regard as sufficient, but the bride and her mother did not, and they set the time for a church ceremony in Paris. The count failed to appear, and Genevieve found herself, like the heroine of the melodrama, "wedded but no wife." Her father was summoned to Europe, and the family pursued the reluctant bridegroom to Warsaw, where they caught him and by the aid of diplomatic intervention compelled a ceremony. Immediately thereafter the three Wards departed, and never saw him again. Genevieve resumed her studies, and made her French début in April 1859, at Paris, as Elvira in *Don Giovanni.* Her English début was at a Philharmonic concert in London in 1861. Her New York début was at the Academy of Music, Nov. 10, 1862, as Violetta in *La Traviata,* under the name of Mme. Guerrabella. Shortly thereafter, during a Cuban tour (where she was hissed for wearing boots and cloak in the rôle of the page in *Ballo in Maschera*), her singing voice failed her, and for the next decade she had no public record. But she was studying for the dramatic stage, and on Oct. 1, 1873, in Manchester, England, she appeared as Lady Macbeth. The *Manchester Guardian* (Oct. 3) was mildly favorable. She continued to practise and play, and in 1875 reached Drury Lane. In 1877 she went to France to study at the Comédie-Française (she was a gifted lin-

guist), and on Feb. 11, in that year, she played Lady Macbeth in French. She returned to England with a considerable "classic" repertoire, and Sept. 2, 1878, made her dramatic début in America, at Booth's Theatre, New York, as Jane Shore. She acted throughout the country the following winter. A Boston critic, writing of her in the *Boston Daily Advertiser,* Apr. 7, 1879, said, "She is of the school of Ristori, and is not so very far behind that admirable performer." The *New York Post* had previously said her acting was "good, but traditional." On her return to England she secured a play which was new, and effective—*Forget-Me-Not,* by Herman Merivale, a play in the school of Dumas *fils* and Sardou, which gave her talents exact scope. She produced this at the Lyceum, London, August 1879, with a young leading man named Johnson Forbes-Robertson, and so great was its success that she subsequently acted it over two thousand times, and in most countries around the globe which possessed an English-language theatre. It boasted the once-famous line, "There would be no place in creation for such women as I, if it were not for such men as you." (For an account of her performance, see Winter, *post,* II, 405 ff.)

For the next two decades she was professionally active in England, America, and Australia. On Mar. 3, 1883, after a second American tour, she produced Legouvé's *Medea,* and also revived *Forget-Me-Not.* Her last American tour was made in 1887. In 1891 she toured to South Africa. She joined Henry Irving's company at the Lyceum in 1893, playing Eleanor in *Becket* (1893), Morgan le Fay in *King Arthur* (1895), Margaret in *Richard III* (1896). In 1897 she ventured out of her traditional repertoire to play Mrs. Borkman in Ibsen's *John Gabriel Borkman* at the Strand. She never visited America again, but lived quietly in England, teaching younger players, with a record of having acted in seventy-seven plays behind her. She reappeared in 1918, with George Alexander at the St. James, because, she said, "of the war strain." That year, with Richard Whiteing, she published *Both Sides of the Curtain,* which contains personal reminiscences. She celebrated her eighty-fourth birthday by appearing as the Queen in *Richard III.* She died the same year in London. She was, in her prime, said to have "broad, ample shoulders and a waist that typifies good health." She was above average height, with a Roman nose, firm chin, dark eyes, heavy brows—a commanding female, in brief, and though graceful, with a well-trained, flexible voice, born for parts of emotional amplitude and intellectual dominance rather than "sex appeal." Her pictures show a strong resemblance to Ristori. In later years her face grew thin, long, and intellectual, like that of Irving. After her early adventure, she never married again.

[*Who's Who in America*, 1912–13; Zadel B. Gustafson, *Genevieve Ward, A Biog. Sketch from Original Material* (1882); Genevieve Ward and Richard Whiteing, *Both Sides of the Curtain* (1918); William Winter, *The Wallet of Time* (2 vols., 1913); obituaries in *Times* (London), and *N. Y. Times*, Aug. 19, 1922; Harvard College Theatre Coll.]   W. P. E.

WARD, GEORGE GRAY (Dec. 30, 1844– June 15, 1922), engineer, was born at Great Hadham, Hertfordshire, England, the eldest of seven children of Benjamin and Esther (Gray) Ward. His early education was obtained in a private school at Cambridge, to which his parents had removed. Fascinated by the telegraph instrument, he obtained permission, when but six years of age, to visit the local telegraph office at the railroad station, and within a year he had become a proficient telegrapher. At eleven he left school, entered the service of the Electric Telegraph Company, and quickly mastered what knowledge was then available of theoretical telegraphy. Eager for wider experience, he joined in 1865 the Egyptian telegraphic service and was stationed at Alexandria for three years. In a cholera epidemic that visited the city, he and two or three others were the only telegraphers to stay on duty in order to maintain communication with the outside world. His services were especially acknowledged by the Viceroy, Ishmael Pasha. In 1867 he married at Cambridge, England, Marianne, the daughter of William Smith. She died in 1918, leaving three children. In 1869 he joined the French Atlantic cable company and was appointed chief operator at St. Pierre and Miquelon. During the laying of the cable to St. Pierre, he was one of six telegraphers selected for the electrical staff on board the steamship *Great Eastern*. At St. Pierre he remained until 1875, when failing health forced a return to England.

The year 1875 marked the end of his active career as a telegrapher; from that time his services were essentially those of an engineer, promoter, and executive. Within a few years he assumed a leading position among cable executives and maintained it for almost forty years. Shortly after his return to England, he accepted the position of general superintendent in the United States of the Direct United States Cable Company then being organized under the direction of Lawrence Oliphant. In cooperation with Oliphant, he built stations and cable lines and made arrangements for an interchange of traffic with other lines. So efficient was his work that he not only broke the existing monopoly of the Anglo-American Telegraph Company but also reduced the charges for cable services and cut by two-thirds the time necessary to receive a reply. The efficiency of the new company was so evident that the Anglo-American proposed a pool in which the Western Union Telegraph Company later joined. When the pool broke up in 1883 he assumed charge of the interests of both the Direct and of the French companies.

When James Gordon Bennett and John William Mackay [*qq.v.*] decided to break the power of the Western Union by establishing a new cable company, in 1884, they offered Ward the general managership of the newly organized Commercial Cable Company. In 1890 he became vice-president and held both positions until his death, as well as gradually assuming directorships in subordinate and affiliated companies. Under his direction at least five cables were thrown across the Atlantic, while he was primarily responsible for the diplomatic and engineering aspects of the work that resulted in the first cable across the Pacific,—laid to Honolulu in 1902, Manila in 1903, and to China and Japan in 1906. He also laid the cable between the United States and Cuba. In laying the Pacific cable, he planted colonists on the Midway Islands. International recognition for his services came in decorations presented by both the German and Japanese emperors. The Commercial Cable Company was largely his creation, made possible by his aggressive leadership, practical experience, and tactful personality. He died in New York City and was buried from the Episcopal Church of the Heavenly Rest, of which he had been vestryman and warden.

[*Telegraph Age*, Jan. 1, 1908; *Telegraph and Telephone Age*, Jan. 16, 1910, July 1, 1922; *Telegraphist*, Jan. 1, 1885; *Who's Who in America*, 1922–23; *N. Y. Times*, June 16, 25, 1922; information from his son, George Gray Ward, New York City.]   H. U. F.

WARD, HENRY AUGUSTUS (Mar. 9, 1834– July 4, 1906), naturalist, was the son of Henry Meigs and Elizabeth (Chapin) Ward, and a descendant of Andrew Warde who died in Connecticut in 1659. In 1807 Levi Ward, Henry's grandfather, moved westward to the Genesee Valley, the final settlement being made at "The Grove," a large farm in present-day Rochester, N. Y. His father's love for books caused him to neglect the farm and drew violent remonstrances from his wife; this domestic atmosphere, resulting from a state of continual impecunity, and an overemphasis on religious matters, made his youth a strenuous and unhappy one. His interest in natural history seems to have first made itself evident when, although too young for formal classes, he succeeded in joining the geological excursions of Dr. Chester Dewey. When his father fled to the West in 1846, the boy was placed with a farmer, who, fortunately, encouraged him to read. In 1849, with some assistance from an uncle, he entered Middlebury Academy, at Wyoming, N. Y. With a rather vague idea of entering the ministry, he then attended Williams College, 1851–52, and exhibited great interest in science and modern languages. At Williams, James Orton [q.v.] became an intimate friend. Insufficiently prepared to meet college requirements he returned to Rochester and through the intervention of another uncle entered Temple Hill Academy in Geneseo where he made the friendship of the family of James S. Wadsworth [q.v.], and it was through their help and his own exertions that he was enabled to begin his life's career—collecting scientific materials.

When Agassiz was to lecture in Rochester in 1854 James Hall, 1811–1898 [q.v.], commended him to the care of Henry Ward. So thoughtful was that care that Agassiz persuaded the Ward family to let Henry continue his studies at Cambridge, Mass., where he studied and worked in Agassiz's museum. In 1854 he was offered an opportunity of studying in the School of Mines in Paris with one of the young Wadsworths who was commended to his care. Until 1859 the two studied and traveled together. When the elder Wadsworth was no longer able to render financial aid, Ward began his collecting trips. He financed himself for several years by selling specimens of fossils to European museums, but he was at last forced to return to America. Obsessed by the idea of a "cabinet of natural history" both as a source of information to students and income for himself, he managed to stimulate an interest in his project on the part of his family and returned to Europe to make additions to his collection. In 1861 he returned to Rochester, was married, on Nov. 8, to Phoebe A. Howell, and accepted the professorship of natural sciences in the University of Rochester where he remained for almost fifteen years.

In 1862 he contracted to supply Vassar College with a "cabinet," and completed the project in two years. He then developed his own collection, expanded into a second building, and began systematically to prepare material for order and sale. This was the beginning of Ward's Natural Science Establishment. He gathered around him a group of men to be trained in science, and in later years many of them (among them Carl E. Akeley, Frederic A. Lucas [qq.v.], William M. Wheeler and William T. Hornaday) occupied high scientific posts. He also continued his trips,

sometimes as appointed officer on some commission, sometimes merely to add to his own materials. He crossed the Atlantic fifty times in these pursuits. Lewis Brooks commissioned him to prepare a collection of natural history for the University of Virginia, and he exhibited at the Centennial Exposition in Philadelphia. In 1887 he discovered an unusual meteorite in Durango, Mexico, and from that time his chief interest centered on meteorites. His general natural history collection shown at the World's Columbian Exposition in 1893, was bought by Marshall Field to become the nucleus of the Field Museum of Natural History.

A second marriage, on Mar. 18, 1897, six years after the death of his first wife, to Mrs. Lydia (Avery) Coonley [see Lydia Arms Avery Coonley Ward], gave him financial backing to further his interest, and the meteorite collection grew. Notable exploits in the assembling of this collection were the securing of a specimen from the Shah of Persia and one from the government of Colombia. All his life a brilliant and pleasing conversationalist he was his own best agent. But Ward not only collected, he studied, and his catalogues of meteorites contain most valuable information as to exact localities—a knowledge necessary in determining whether or not a group is a single fall. His last great collection of meteorites (also in the Field Museum) contains representatives of more falls than any other collection ever made. He had just finished preparations for another expedition across South America, when he was killed by an automobile in Buffalo, N. Y. His death cut short a valuable work of three volumes describing his meteorite collection and dealing with the subject in general. He was cremated and his ashes rest in Mount Hope Cemetery, Rochester, N. Y. He was survived by his widow and the four children of his first wife.

[Who's Who in America, 1906–07; G. K. Ward, Andrew Warde and His Descendants (rev. ed., 1910); G. W. Chapin, The Chapin Book (1924), vol. I; A. H. Strong, Henry A. Ward, Reminiscences and Appreciation, Rochester Hist. Soc. Pubs. (1922); W. T. Hornaday, "The King of Museum Builders," Commercial Travelers Mag., Feb. 1896, and "A Great Museum Builder," Nation, July 12, 1906; O. C. Farrington, obit. article in Science, Aug. 3, 1906; R. H. Ward, "Mammoths and Meteors," Rochester Democrat and Chronicle (Sunday ed.), Sept. 17–Oct. 29, 1933; Ibid., July 5, 1906.]
W. G.

WARD, HENRY DANA (Jan. 13, 1797–Feb. 29, 1884), reformer, Adventist, Episcopal clergyman, seventh of ten children of Thomas Walter and Elizabeth (Denny) Ward, was born at Shrewsbury, Mass. His father, the third son of Gen. Artemas Ward [q.v.], served in the Revolutionary War and later was sheriff of Worcester

County, Mass. Henry Dana Ward was graduated (B.A.) from Harvard in 1816 and received the degree of M.A. in 1819. He married as his first wife Abigail Porter Jones, daughter of Samuel Jones of Lebanon Springs, N. Y. She died Dec. 23, 1837.

Ward's first reform activity to bring him out of obscurity was in the Anti-Masonic movement. In the year 1828 he wrote an appeal to his brother Masons, a kindly yet deadly attack on the order, entitled *Free Masonry: Its Pretensions Exposed in Faithful Extracts of Its Standard Authors; with A Review of Town's Speculative Masonry . . . by a Master Mason.* In the same year he began to publish a monthly, the *Anti-Masonic Review and Magazine,* in New York. He traveled from state to state with religious zeal stirring up opposition to Masonry; he was one of the outstanding agitators present when the Anti-Masonic party was organized in Vermont, Aug. 5, 1829; and he was present at the Massachusetts and New York conventions the same year. The following year he was among the leaders in the Rhode Island convention and associated with such men as Thurlow Weed and William H. Seward in the national organization of the party.

After the recession of the Anti-Masonic movement, Ward became much interested in the Adventist movement led by William Miller [*q.v.*], and in October 1840 was elected chairman of the General Conference of Christians Expecting the Advent of the Lord Jesus Christ, held in Boston. His published address on this occasion shows him to have been a student of both history and theology (*The First Report of the General Conference of Christians . . . 1841*). He did not accept Miller's reckoning as to the date of Christ's expected return to earth—Oct. 22, 1844—and was opposed to the attempt to fix a definite date, but contented himself with the belief that Christ's return in person would be the next event in the fulfillment of prophecy. As time passed he became inactive in the movement, although he apparently remained an Adventist in belief all his life.

In 1844 he was ordained to the Protestant Episcopal ministry by the bishop of Rhode Island, and soon afterward became rector of a small parish in Kanawha County, Va. (now W. Va.), where he ministered for two or three years. In Virginia he married his second wife, Charlotte Galbraith, daughter of Richard and Rebecca (Allen) Galbraith and a member of a Scotch-Irish family from Dublin. Struggling to support a growing family, he moved to New York City about 1848 and established a girls' school. For

about two years in the early fifties he was rector of St. Jude's Church, New York, but most of his time was given to teaching, in New York or Flushing, L. I., until about 1868, when he retired and moved to Philadelphia. Here he lived in a modest fashion until his death. His later days were occupied in religious studies and writing. Among his works were: *The Gospel of the Kingdom* (1870), *The History of the Cross* (1871), and *The Faith of Abraham and of Christ* (1872). Stricken with paralysis while walking on the streets of Philadelphia, he died the same day. He was buried in Shrewsbury, Mass.

Ward had three sons and one daughter; one son died in infancy, the others attained some distinction—Artemas as an advertising man and the publisher of *The Grocer's Encyclopedia* (1911) and Henry Galbraith as a federal judge.

[I. C. Wellcome, *Hist. of the Second Advent Message and Mission* (1874); M. E. Olsen, *A Hist. of the Origin and Progress of Seventh-day Adventists* (1925); Charles McCarthy, "The Antimasonic Party," *Ann. Report of the Am. Hist. Asso. . . . 1902* (1903), vol. I; Charles Martyn, *The William Ward Geneal.* (1925); *Jour. of the Proc. of the One-Hundredth Conv. of the Protestant Episcopal Church in the Diocese of Pa.* (1884); *Phila. Press,* Mar. 1, 1884.]   E. N. D.

WARD, HERBERT DICKINSON (June 30, 1861–June 18, 1932), author and publicist, was born in Waltham, Mass., the only child of Ellen Maria (Dickinson) and William Hayes Ward [*q.v.*], and the descendant of William Ward who emigrated from England about 1638 and settled in Sudbury, Mass. The boy's earliest memories were of Utica, N. Y., and Ripon, Wis., where his father was teaching. About 1868 the family settled in Newark, N. J. His mother, whose health had long been frail, died in 1873, and his father's two unmarried sisters continued to live with the family and direct the household. Under the watchful eyes of parents and aunts the boy was brought up in what he later called the "Spartan Puritan" tradition. Gray's *Elegy,* repeated by his father until the child knew it by heart, was his Mother Goose. At the age of seven he was encouraged to begin the study of Hebrew, while for modern languages he was sent abroad twice for periods of schooling in Germany and Switzerland. A final year at Phillips Academy at Andover prepared him to enter Amherst College, his father's college, where he graduated with the class of 1884. Though he had become a more ardent collector of minerals than candidate for the ministry, he agreed, at his father's insistence, to complete a theological course before deciding on a profession. Accordingly, after a year of teaching at Catawba College, Newton, N. C., he spent two years at Union Theological Seminary and a year at the Theological Seminary at Andover, supporting himself in part by writing Sunday-school lessons and conducting the Biblical research department for the *Independent*. He was licensed to preach but never ordained.

Though a man of unusual cultivation and markedly original views, he never overcame the handicap of being the son of a notable father and the husband of a famous wife. The decisive event of his year at Andover was his meeting there with Elizabeth Stuart Phelps (see sketch of Elizabeth Stuart Phelps Ward), whom he married, despite her seventeen years' advantage in age, on Oct. 20, 1888. The couple lived in Newton Center, Mass., and Ward became active in the literary and social life of Boston. In collaboration with his wife he wrote three novels, *A Lost Hero* (1891), *Come Forth* (1891), and the *Master of the Magicians* (1890), of which the last, an historical romance of ancient Babylon, was chiefly his own work. He also wrote independently several novels and collections of short stories, of which the most important were *A Republic without a President* (1891), *The White Crown* (1894), *The Burglar Who Moved Paradise* (1897), and *The Light of the World* (1901). His friendship with Daniel S. Ford, owner and editor of the *Youth's Companion,* and with Edwin A. Grozier of the *Boston Post* led him to contribute religious articles and editorials to both publications. He joined the staff of the *Post* for a year about 1899; with the *Youth's Companion* he had no official connection. He served as a member of the Massachusetts prison commission from 1891 to 1901. After his wife's death, he made his home chiefly in South Berwick, Me., in a house inherited from his paternal grandmother. He married, on Dec. 27, 1916, Edna J. Jeffress of Edwardsville, Ill., by whom he had one daughter. The last years of his life were occupied with publicity writing and social work. During the "Liberty Loan" drives he was a publicity agent for the federal treasury department, and later he was attached to the Italian embassy at Washington in a similar capacity. After some ten years of virtual retirement he died in the hospital at Portsmouth, N. H.

[Autobiog. material in his article "My Father," *Independent,* Dec. 28, 1918; *Amherst College Biog. Record* (1929); *Amherst Grads. Quart.,* Aug. 1932; *Who's Who in America,* 1924–25; Charles Martyn, *The Wm. Ward Geneal.* (1925), esp. pp. 271, 394; *N. Y. Times,* June 20, 1932.]
G. F. W.

WARD, JAMES EDWARD (Feb. 25, 1836–July 23, 1894), shipowner, was born in New York City, the son of James Otis and Martha T. (Dame) Ward, and a descendant of William Ward who settled in Sudbury, Mass., about 1638. James Otis Ward had moved from his father's

farm near Roxbury, Mass., to New York City, where he became a ship chandler on South Street and soon acquired an interest in numerous sailing vessels, thus beginning the long association of the family name with the Cuban trade. He died in 1855, and the following year the business was reorganized in his son's name, as James E. Ward & Company, with Henry P. Booth and Samuel C. Shepherd as silent partners. Ward soon turned over the chandlery business to his younger brother, George Edgar Ward, and the firm, with its offices and piers at the foot of Wall Street on East River, devoted itself to shipping. By 1875, it owned some forty sailing vessels and occasionally also chartered steamers for the Cuban trade. Some of the Ward vessels ran with sufficient regularity to be termed packets, but the principal business was general freighting to Cuba similar to that later developed by Walter D. Munson [q.v.]. The chief freight from New York consisted of flour, potatoes, pork products, papers, hardware, and machinery, while the return cargoes, in addition to the all-important sugar, included tobacco and fruit.

The celebrated Ward Line really dates from 1877, when the firm instituted direct passenger and mail service to Havana. Their chief competitors at this time were the lines of Francis Alexandre & Sons and William P. Clyde & Sons, but the latter group soon restricted its activity to the coastal trade. Ward and his associates, in beginning the new enterprise, sold their sailing vessels to pay for the *Niagara* and the *Saratoga,* iron steamships of about 2,300 tons, built for them by John Roach [q.v.] at Chester, Pa., and rated as the finest then under the American flag. The *Saratoga* was subsequently sold to Russia for use as a cruiser and Roach built a second vessel of that name in 1878. Continued additions gave the Ward Line the heaviest tonnage among American lines in foreign service. In 1881 it was incorporated, with a capital of $2,300,000, as the New York & Cuba Mail Steam-ship Company; this has remained its official name. Booth was president, W. H. T. Hughes secretary-treasurer, and Ward apparently chairman of the board and guiding spirit.

Serious competition developed in the later eighties. Henry B. Plant [q.v.] in 1886 connected Havana with the new railroad to Tampa by a small, fast steamer which secured a mail contract worth $58,000 a year, leaving the Ward Line barely $1,300. Shortly afterwards, the Compañía Transatlantica Española, backed by a heavy Spanish subsidy, entered the New York-Havana run. This was apparently too much for the Alexandre line, which went out of business in 1888, selling a number of steamships to the Ward Line, which also took over its Mexican service to Progreso, Tampico, and Vera Cruz. The new competition resulted in the reduction of freight rates from $5 to $1.60 a ton and first-class passenger rates from $60 to as little as $35, and forced the Ward Line to omit dividends for two years. Ward claimed and gained considerable credit for keeping the American flag afloat in the merchant marine when he could have operated more cheaply with foreign bottoms. He was a strong supporter of the American Shipping and Industrial League, formed to lobby for merchant-marine relief, and the Ward Line, represented by Hughes, was prominent in the hearings which led to the Postal Aid Act, approved Mar. 3, 1891. Under this act the Ward Line received a subsidy of one dollar a mile, or about $200,000 a year.

At Ward's death in 1894 his line had ten iron or steel ships with a total tonnage of about 30,-000. In 1907, it was the largest of the six companies combined in the short-lived holding company of Charles W. Morse [*q.v.*], and upon Morse's failure, it was combined in 1908 with the Mallory, Clyde and Porto Rico lines in another holding company headed by Henry R. Mallory, but it retained its autonomous identity. Ward had married, Oct. 1, 1857, Harriet A. Morrill, who died in 1885. Of their three children only one daughter reached maturity. Ward died of Bright's disease, at his summer home at Great Neck, L. I., after an illness of several months. His portrait indicates a certain resemblance to Grover Cleveland, with a solid build, black moustache, and a frank, keen expression of the eyes behind rimmed spectacles.

[Charles Martyn, *The William Ward Geneal.* (1925); *Sen. Ex. Doc. 54*, 51 Cong., 1 Sess.; *House Report 1210*, 51 Cong., 1 Sess.; J. H. Morrison, *The Hist. of Am. Steam Navigation* (1903); W. L. Marvin, *The Am. Merchant Marine* (1902); G. M. Jones, *Govt. Aid to Merchant Shipping* (1925); *Wilson's N. Y. City Co-partnership Directory,* 1856–84; *The Trow Copartnership and Corporation Directory . . . of N. Y.,* 1885 ff.; obituaries in *N. Y. Daily Tribune, Evening Post* (N. Y.), and *N. Y. Times,* July 24, 1894.] R. G. A.

WARD, JAMES HARMON (Sept. 25, 1806– June 27, 1861), naval officer and author, was born in Hartford, Conn., the son of James and Ruth (Butler) Ward and the descendant of Andrew Warde, an English emigrant who died in Fairfield, Conn., about 1659. In 1823 he was graduated from the American Literary Scientific and Military Academy at Norwich, Vt., later Norwich University, and on Mar. 4, 1823, was appointed a midshipman in the navy. The following year he sailed on the *Constitution* for the Mediterranean, where he remained for four years.

On his return he entered Washington College (now Trinity) at Hartford, where he spent a year in scientific study. On Apr. 11, 1833, he married Sarah Whittemore. They had three sons. His subsequent service took him to the Mediterranean again, the coast of Africa, and the West Indies. He was one of the most scholarly officers in his service and was a recognized authority on ordnance and naval tactics. In 1844–45 he delivered a popular course of lectures on ordnance at the naval school at Philadelphia, which he published as *An Elementary Course of Instruction on Ordnance and Gunnery* (1845). This book became widely known and exerted a real influence on the improvement of naval science. In 1852 it was officially adopted as a textbook at the Naval Academy at Annapolis. He urged upon the government the necessity of establishing a naval school, and when the naval school, later the Naval Academy, was opened at Annapolis in October 1845 he was appointed to be executive officer, a post soon designated as commandant of midshipmen. He also acted as head of the department of ordnance and gunnery. Detached in 1847, he commanded the *Cumberland,* Matthew C. Perry's flagship on the Mexican coast, during the remainder of the war. In 1856 and 1857, while cruising in the *Jamestown* off the African coast, he wrote *A Manual of Naval Tactics* (1859), a scholarly work that ran into four editions. In 1860 he published a popular treatise on steam, called *Steam for the Million.*

When the Civil War broke out, he, then a commander, was stationed at the Brooklyn Navy Yard. Gideon Welles summoned him to Washington to plan for the rescue of Sumter. He volunteered to command a relief expedition but was finally convinced by General Scott that such an expedition would be futile. He proposed a "flying flotilla" for use on Chesapeake Bay and the Potomac River. His idea was accepted and in May he was given command of a small fleet called the Potomac Flotilla, consisting of three steamers, the *Thomas Freeborn,* the *Reliance,* and the *Resolute,* and three coast survey schooners. On June 1 he silenced the Confederate batteries at Aquia Creek. On June 27, in an attempt to dislodge another battery at Matthias Point, he sent a working party ashore to throw up breastworks. As it was returning to the boats it was attacked by a large hostile force. Covering the embarkation with the guns of his fleet, he was shot in the abdomen as he was in the act of sighting the bowgun of the *Thomas Freeborn.* He died within an hour. His body was taken to Hartford, where it was buried with the rites of the Roman Catholic Church.

[Archives of the Office of Naval Records and Lib.,
Navy Department; *War of Rebellion: Official Records
(Navy)*, 1 ser., vols. IV–VI; *Battles and Leaders of the
Civil War*, vol. II (1888); *Diary of Gideon Welles*
(1911), vols. I, II; *Norwich Univ.* (1911), vol. II, ed.
by W. A. Ellis; J. R. Soley, *Hist. Sketch of the U. S.
Naval Acad.* (1876), pp. 62–63; *U. S. Naval Inst.
Proc.*, vol. LXI (1935); G. K. Ward, *Andrew Warde
and His Descendants* (1910); *N. Y. Tribune*, July 1–3,
1861; *Daily Morning Jour. and Courier* (New Haven),
June 29, July 1, 2, 1861; spelling of middle name from
grandson, James H. Ward, Berrien Springs, Mich.]

L. H. B.

WARD, JAMES WARNER (June 5, 1816–
June 28, 1897), author, librarian, was born at
Newark, N. J., son of William and Sara (Warner) Ward. He attended the Boston public
schools until he was fourteen, when he began
business as a freight checker in a shipping house
in Salem, Mass. In 1834 he went to Columbus,
Ohio, and opened a school. At nineteen he married Roxanna Wyman Blake, who bore him a
son and a daughter. After the death of his wife
in 1844, he moved to Cincinnati, where he became a pupil of and later assistant to Prof. John
Locke [*q.v.*] of the Medical College of Ohio. In
1851 he was elected professor of general literature and botany in the Ohio Female College, situated in College Hill, seven miles north of Cincinnati. On June 29, 1848, he married Catherine
McClyment Lea, daughter of John and Catherine
(McClyment) Lea of Cincinnati, and a niece of
Henry Charles Lea [*q.v.*], the historian. Ward
left the Ohio Female College in 1854 and for a
year, in association with Dr. John A. Warder
[*q.v.*], edited the *Horticultural Review and Botanical Magazine* in Cincinnati. In 1859 he moved
to New York City, where he spent the next fifteen years first as clerk, later as deputy auditor
in the customs house. In July 1874 he began a
card catalogue of the Grosvenor Library in Buffalo. The library had been given its charter in
1859, was opened in 1870, and by 1874 had a
book collection of 17,900; the staff consisted of
two, the librarian and his assistant. Ward became librarian on Oct. 1, 1874, and began twenty-one years of efficient service in which he
brought the library from its infancy to a position
of real eminence. The first modern inventory
was taken in 1876, and the gaps in the collections
were filled out. Ward was one of the first members of the American Library Association, organized in 1876, and took part in technical discussions as reported in the *Library Journal*. He
had active supervision, together with the architect, of the details of construction of the present
building of the Grosvenor Library, which in 1895
superseded the rented quarters. At that time the
book collection numbered 38,000, a large collection for the day. Ward retired, Jan. 15, 1896,

and spent the winter in Worcester, Mass., and
in the South, returning to Buffalo, where he died
at his home, June 28, 1897, aged eighty-one years.
He was survived by his wife.

Ward took an active interest in music, art,
and the natural sciences, especially astronomy,
botany, and microscopy. He contributed papers
on these subjects to the journals of the day, composed for the voice and organ, and was the author of much poetry. In 1852 he wrote a poem
entitled *Woman*, originally prepared for the
Young Men's Mercantile Library Association of
Cincinnati, which was revised and read for the
graduating exercises of the Ohio Female College, July 17, 1852, and published by the college.
In 1857 was published a volume of poems, *Home
Made Verses and Stories in Rhyme*, which were
usually signed "Yorick," and in 1868 *Higher
Water*, a parody on *Hiawatha* describing a
stream of the Ohio River. Ward is perhaps best
known in the world of books as editor of A. W.
Sangster's *Niagara River and Falls from Lake
Erie to Lake Ontario* (1886), a series of etchings
with an accompanying text which includes a
poem, "To Niagara," by Ward. He was a member of several microscopical societies and of the
Torrey Botanical Club.

[Sources include J. H. and G. H. Lea, *The Ancestry
. . . of John Lea* (1906), from which the date of birth
is taken; Grosvenor Lib. records; correspondence with
Ward's family; early Buffalo and N. Y. directories;
surrogate's records, Erie County, N. Y.; *Bull. Torrey
Botanical Club*, Nov. 1873; preface to *Woman* (1852);
obituaries in *Buffalo Express, Buffalo Evening News*,
and *Buffalo Commercial*, June 30, 1897; interviews
with friends of Ward.]

A. H. S.

WARD, JOHN ELLIOTT (Oct. 2, 1814–
Nov. 29, 1902), lawyer, politician, diplomat, was
born at Sunbury, Liberty County, Ga. His father, William Ward, was a member of the Midway colony of Puritans from Massachusetts
which settled in Liberty County before the Revolutionary War. Through his mother, Anne
(McIntosh) Ward, he was a descendant of John
McIntosh Mohr, who led a clan of Scottish
Highlanders to Georgia in General Oglethorpe's
time. Ward entered Amherst College in 1831,
but left because of a prejudice against Georgians
existing at that time. He attended law lectures
at Harvard, studied under Dr. Matthew Hall
McAllister [*q.v.*] in Savannah, and was admitted
to the bar by special act of legislature in 1835
before he was twenty-one.

Early in the following year he was appointed
solicitor-general for the eastern district of
Georgia, and served until 1838 when he became
United States district attorney for Georgia. He
resigned in 1839 to enter the Georgia legislature, to which he was again elected in 1845 and

1853, serving as speaker in 1853–54. In 1857 he was made president of the state Senate and acting lieutenant-governor. He is credited with being more responsible than any other person for the final breaking down of the traditional prejudices between up-country Georgians and Savannah representatives in the legislature, even though he led the opposition against the popular bank-control measures of Gov. Joseph E. Brown [q.v.]. Meanwhile, in 1852, reluctant to leave an extensive law practice in Savannah, he had declined the offer of appointment to the United States Senate tendered him by Gov. Howell Cobb [q.v.]. In 1854 he was elected mayor of Savannah, and during his term was so successful in dealing with the great yellow-fever epidemic on the one hand, and in carrying out thorough political and police reforms on the other, that he was offered the renomination without opposition; this, however, he declined.

At Cincinnati in 1856 he was president of the National Democratic Convention which nominated Buchanan. In December 1858 President Buchanan appointed him envoy extraordinary and minister plenipotentiary to China, his particular mission being to exchange ratifications of the new American treaty with China and to settle outstanding American claims. Because of his determined refusal to kotow he was unable to effect a direct exchange of ratifications with the emperor. "I kneel only to God and woman," he declared (Martin, *post*, p. 200). He accomplished his mission, however, in a manner entirely satisfactory to President Buchanan. He also won the hearty appreciation of his European colleagues in China by his intelligent and friendly cooperation, but he was not blind to certain high-handed tactics on the part of some of them, and he denounced the infamous coolie trade which was carried on for foreign firms by American ships.

He left China on Dec. 15, 1860, arriving home in the opening days of the Civil War. Bitterly disappointed at the secession of Georgia, he took no part in the hostilities, and in January 1866 removed to New York City, where he engaged in the private practice of law. In 1902, a few weeks before his death, he returned to Liberty County, where he died at Dorchester in his eighty-ninth year. He married in 1839 Olivia Buckminster Sullivan, daughter of William Sullivan of Boston; eight children were born to them.

[For sources see I. W. Avery, *The Hist. of the State of Ga. from 1850 to 1881* (1881); W. J. Northen, *Men of Mark in Ga.*, vol. II (1910); W. A. P. Martin, *A Cycle of Cathay* (1896); *Who's Who in America*, 1901–02; *Savannah Morning News*, Dec. 1, 1902;

Ward's official correspondence is in archives of the U. S. Dept. of State, Washington, D. C., parts of it having been published in "Correspondence and Dispatches of the Ministers to China," *Sen. Ex. Doc. 30,* 36 Cong., 1 Sess. (1860), and in "Chinese Coolie Trade," *House Ex. Doc. 88,* 36 Cong., 1 Sess. (1860); President Buchanan's third annual message, giving account of Ward's mission to China is in *A Compilation of the Messages and Papers of the Presidents,* vol. VII (1897).]　　　　　　　　　　　I. L. T.

WARD, JOHN QUINCY ADAMS (June 29, 1830–May 1, 1910), sculptor, born on the Ward homestead near Urbana, Ohio, was one of the seven children of John Anderson and Eleanor (Macbeth) Ward, and a grandson of Col. William Ward, who in 1805 laid out and named the town of Urbana. His earliest ancestor of American record is said to have been John Ward of Norfolk, England, who landed at Jamestown, Va., in the first half of the seventeenth century. For two centuries thereafter, the Ward family took an important part in conquering the wilderness. As a boy Ward delighted not only in fishing and hunting, but also in making clay images of men on horseback and of the farm animals, often working in the shop of the village potter. The meager education then obtainable in Ohio schools was at times eked out by lessons from private tutors. At the age of sixteen he was put at work on the farm, in tasks he disliked. He milked cows, but he wanted to model horses. Seeing his unfitness for farming, his Presbyterian parents vaguely hoped that he might become a doctor or a minister, and let him study medicine a while. His health suffered. A fortunate visit to his sister in Brooklyn, N. Y., proved the turning-point in his life. In Brooklyn, at nineteen, Ward realized his dearest hope and began work in the studio of Henry Kirke Brown [q.v.]. No better training could have been devised. Student, helper, companion, he remained seven years under a genial, broad-minded master, who in 1854 carved "J. Q. A. Ward, Asst." on the base of an equestrian statue of Washington, a work still deemed one of the best in the country. While with Brown, Ward practised every craft used in sculpture; he worked in clay, plaster, marble, and even in bronze. He helped in the chasing and riveting of the Washington equestrian. "I spent more days inside that horse," he said, "than Jonah did inside the whale." He passed two winters (c. 1857–59) in Washington, D. C., where he made busts of Alexander H. Stephens, Joshua Giddings, Senator John Parker Hale, Hannibal Hamlin. His success in creating small objects to be cast in precious metal was such that in 1861 the Ames Company, founders of Brown's equestrian, engaged him to design and model the costly hilts for the presentation swords then in demand, as well as cane tops, table bells, pistol mountings. That year he opened a studio in New York, the city where he was to live and work for half a century.

Among the first statues to be placed in New York's Central Park, and one of the best to be found there today, was Ward's "Indian Hunter," a lithe figure striding forward with bow and arrows, and holding back an eager dog (1868). This work had been conceived as a statuette in 1857. For further study, Ward spent months among the Indians of the Northwest. In 1861 he modeled his popular statuette, "The Freedman," cast in bronze in 1865, an authentic figure of a negro, seated, looking very quietly at the shackles from which he had been released. From childhood Ward well knew both Indian and negro types. His "Reminiscent Sketch of a Boyhood Friend," printed in the *Times-Citizen* of Urbana, Ohio, in 1908, is a beautifully written tribute to "Uncle Cæsar," a negro. Both "Indian Hunter" and "Freedman" were shown in the Paris Exposition of 1867. When exhibited in New York, the "Hunter" met the approving eye of August Belmont, who at once gave the artist a commission for a bronze statue of his father-in-law, Matthew Calbraith Perry [*q.v.*], unveiled at Newport, R. I., in 1868. Thereafter Ward never lacked commissions. For Boston's Public Gardens he had already made a granite group called the "Good Samaritan," commemorating the first use of ether as anesthetic. The 7th Regiment Memorial, a heroic bronze figure of a Civil War soldier on a high granite pedestal, was signed by Ward in 1869, and was placed in Central Park four years afterward. In 1872 his statue of Gen. John F. Reynolds was unveiled at Gettysburg, Pa. Two years later, at Hartford, Conn., appeared his statue of the Revolutionary hero, Gen. Israel Putnam. In 1870 he made for Central Park a bronze figure of Shakespeare in doublet, hose, and short cloak, a book in his hand, his attitude pensive. All these works showed the sculptor's solidity of structure and his technical mastery; but the finer flowering of his genius was yet to come.

His equestrian monument to Gen. George H. Thomas, "the Rock of Chickamauga," aroused great enthusiasm when unveiled at Washington, D. C., in 1878. There were those who criticized the easy pose, the loose rein, but Ward had made deliberate choice of both as characteristic of Thomas. In 1879 came his statue of William Gilmore Simms, for Charleston, S. C., and two years later, at Spartanburg, S. C., his Gen. Daniel Morgan, picturesque Revolutionary fighter. With two other figures of Revolutionary heroes,

Ward reached the midmost of his career and almost attained the zenith of his art. His statue of the elderly Lafayette, represented as at the period of his historic visit to the United States in 1824–25, was unveiled at Burlington, Vt., in the summer of 1883. In the autumn of the same year, his "Washington" was erected on the steps of the sub-Treasury in Wall Street, near the scene of the first inauguration. It is a quiet, commanding figure, clad in the civilian costume of 1789, enhanced by a cloak which, together with the upright fasces, solidifies a nobly simple composition. Many critics consider this not only the finest work by Ward but also the consummate monumental representation of Washington—this even when bearing in mind Houdon's famous statue.

Ward's "Pilgrim," placed in Central Park by the New England Society (1885), appeared two years before the Saint-Gaudens "Puritan" was unveiled at Springfield, Mass. Contrasts and comparisons naturally occur to mind yet without discredit to either sculptor. If the Bible-clasping Puritan is the more dramatic performance, Ward's well-armed and well-booted Pilgrim in stout buff-leather has its own austere authenticity, unemphasized by melodrama. Again, comparisons are often drawn between Ward's "Horace Greeley," vivid and active in his fringed arm-chair in front of the old Tribune Building, New York (1890), and Saint-Gaudens' equally whiskered "Peter Cooper," enthroned like a Renaissance prince in front of Cooper Union. Each artist created an admirable characterization of his sitter. Ward, both from circumstance and by choice, gave his subject no delightful adventitious architectural adornments.

A more elaborate production is the Gen. James A. Garfield monument in Washington (1887). The bronze figure of Garfield surmounts a stone pedestal adorned by three vigorous male figures in bronze, "Student," "Warrior," "Statesman," symbolizing three phases of Garfield's life. A decade earlier Ward had encircled the cupola of the capitol at Hartford, Conn., with emblematic figures; a decade later he was to contribute a colossal figure of "Poetry" for the rotunda of the Library of Congress. His forte, however, lay in realistic rather than in idealized representation. He preferred masculine themes. Of special importance is his Henry Ward Beecher monument, erected in front of Borough Hall, Brooklyn, N. Y. (1891). The commanding solidity of the preacher's figure in the well-known Inverness overcoat is at once stressed and humanized by a lyric quality, unusual with Ward, seen in the two pedestal compositions; one shows a negro girl placing a palm at Beecher's feet, the other, two children bringing a garland of oak leaves. Other prominent personages in New York life commemorated in bronze statues by Ward were W. E. Dodge, W. H. Fogg, Roscoe Conkling, August Belmont. Among his many portrait busts in bronze or marble are those of Dr. Valentine Mott, Orville H. Dewey, James T. Brady, Col. E. F. Shepard, W. H. Vanderbilt, Abraham Coles, Joseph Drexel, Gov. Horace Fairbanks, George W. Curtis, Alexander Lyman Holley, and William W. Corcoran.

Noted productions of Ward's final decade include the Stock Exchange pediment, New York (1903), the Soldiers and Sailors monument, Syracuse, N. Y. (1907), the General Sheridan equestrian, Albany, N. Y., and the Major General Hancock equestrian, placed in Fairmount Park, Philadelphia, two years after the sculptor's death. In the first and last of these works he had the able collaboration of Paul Bartlett. A lifetime of study, skill, and experience is garnered up in the vast pediment of the Stock Exchange; Ward's design, beautifully in harmony with his own outlook on life, makes Integrity the central motive, irradiating a sculptured world of the various activities dear and necessary to man. As to the details of the Hancock equestrian, Ward and Bartlett were sometimes at friendly variance, but Ward, the better horseman, was usually right. This work filled his mind during his last days: after a colleague chosen to inspect it had brought back a good report, he said, "Now I can go in peace."

In American art he was a unique figure, of a kind that will not occur again. He brought primitive Ohio vigor to sophisticated New York and set it to work there. He was a born leader and organizer, with the true pathfinder's instinct. Made a member of the National Academy of Design in 1863, he became its president in 1874, whereupon, undaunted by an honor never before given to a sculptor, he warned that body against "dropping into a conceited security." "Give the younger man a chance" was a well-known saying of his. No worthy enterprise in art ever lacked his support. On the formation of the National Sculpture Society, he was acclaimed its president. In 1899, when the society and the city in collaboration erected New York's sculptured arch of welcome to Admiral Dewey, he was the head and front of the actual work, spurring the sculptors to their highest endeavor. His own contribution was the so-called quadriga crowning the arch, "Naval Victory" in her sea chariot drawn by six sea horses, a group of brilliant distinction.

Ward's art was peculiarly American. He was the first native sculptor to create, without benefit of foreign training, an impressive body of good work. In youth he had stood awestruck before Powers' "Greek Slave"; arrived at man's estate, he found himself wholly out of sympathy with the mid-Victorian pseudo-classic ideals fostered in Florence and Rome. "Emasculate!" he cried. He traveled in Europe but never lived or worked there. He nevertheless admired the strength and sincerity of the French school of sculpture dominant in the latter part of the nineteenth century. Strength and sincerity were among his own gifts. Every one who met him was impressed by his virility, his integrity, his devotion to art. Numerous organizations, from academies to zoölogical societies, claimed his membership, sought his counsel, and gave him honors. He belonged to the American Academy of Arts and Letters; he was a trustee of the American Academy in Rome and one of the founders of the Metropolitan Museum of Art. His speeches and writings had style. He had his convictions, his prejudices. He was a good friend and, if need arose, a great fighter, one who well knew when, where, and how to show wrath. "Quincy Ward wasn't redheaded for nothing." His strong bodily frame matched his mind. His friends often said that he looked like a less gnarled, less saddened Michelangelo. About 1858 he married Anna, daughter of John and Rebecca (Noyes) Bannan. She died in 1870. His second wife, Julia, daughter of Charles and Julia (Devens) Valentine, lived but a year after their marriage in 1878. In 1906 Ward married Rachel Smith, a widow, daughter of Simon and Jane (Lefevre) Ostrander of Newburg, N. Y. He died at his home in New York, leaving a widow but no children, and is buried at Urbana, where a replica of the Indian Hunter marks his grave.

[Sources are *Who's Who in America*, 1908–09; *Who's Who in N. Y.*, 1909; Lorado Taft, *The Hist. of Am. Sculpture* (1903); C. H. Caffin, *Am. Masters of Sculpture* (1903); G. W. Sheldon, in *Harper's New Monthly Mag.*, June 1878; Russell Sturgis, in *Scribner's Mag.*, Oct. 1902; Edna M. Clark, *Ohio Art and Artists* (1932); Montgomery Schuyler, in *Putnam's Mag.*, Sept. 1909; William Walton, in *International Studio*, June 1910; Adeline Adams, *John Quincy Adams Ward, an Appreciation* (1912); obituaries in *N. Y. Times*, *N. Y. Tribune*, May 2, 1910, editorial in *Times*, May 3; information from Mrs. Ward; personal acquaintance. The name of Ward's first wife is sometimes given as Bauman or Bamman.]   A. A.

WARD, JOSEPH (May 5, 1838–Dec. 11, 1889), pioneer Congregational clergyman and educator of South Dakota, was born at Perry Centre, N. Y., the son of Dr. Jabez and Aurilla (Tufts) Ward, and a descendant of William

Ward who settled at Sudbury, Mass., about 1638. Joseph grew up in a community dominated by New England traditions, and in a home strongly influenced by religion. After attending the public schools of his locality, he tried his hand at teaching and at farming for a time, and then entered Phillips Academy, Andover, where he was graduated in 1861. That same year he matriculated at Brown University. His college course was interrupted by service in the Union army but sickness intervened and sent him back to his studies, although his summer vacations were spent with the United States Christian Commission. He graduated from Brown in 1865 and then spent three years at Andover Theological Seminary, an institution marked by a missionary spirit which did much to determine Ward's subsequent career. On Aug. 12, 1868, he married Sarah Frances Wood.

Accepting a missionary appointment at Yankton, then the capital of Dakota Territory, he was ordained there on Mar. 17, 1869. His activities in behalf of the religious and educational interests of the region were numerous and varied. Under his leadership the Congregational Association of Dakota was formed, and his influence over the Dakota missions was such that he may be regarded as the father of Congregationalism in Dakota. Owing to the fact that Yankton was not then a separate school district and there was no adequate provision for securing funds by taxation, it was practically impossible to maintain common schools. A few years before Ward's arrival, a public school supported by the enterprise of the Yankton women had been started, and to supplement its work Ward opened a private school. It had a larger growth than had been expected and in 1872 was formally converted into the Yankton Academy. Ward continued in charge of it until he began to promote the establishment of a college, at which time the academy was given over to public control and transformed into the Yankton high school, the earliest public high school in Dakota. Yankton College, the first institution of collegiate rank in the upper Mississippi Valley, the founding of which was largely the result of Ward's activities, was chartered Aug. 30, 1881, and the corner stone of its first building laid June 15, 1882. This institution he served as president and professor of mental and moral philosophy until his death.

He played a very conspicuous part in keeping the school lands of the Territory out of the hands of Eastern speculators, and the education law of South Dakota was almost wholly his work. Interested in every humanitarian enterprise, he was largely instrumental in securing the establishment in 1879 of the Dakota Hospital for the Insane. In the struggle for statehood, also, he played a large part, especially in the formation of the Citizen's Constitutional Association, which brought about the constitutional convention at Sioux Falls in 1883. This convention, formed by direct authority of the people without authorization from the legislature or enabling act of Congress, framed a worthy organic law for the future state.

Spurning all chances for political advancement, Ward in his last years devoted himself to the service of Yankton College. In 1886 he became involved in a theological dispute over the possibility of future probation for those who died ignorant of Christ's teachings. Scornful of "institutional cowardice," he fought on what he considered the side of liberty, despite the fact that it threatened for a time to wreck the college. The storm soon passed and in 1887 Yankton College graduated its first class. A little more than two years later Ward died, the immediate cause of his death being blood poisoning occasioned by diabetes. He was survived by his wife and five children.

[G. H. Durand, *Joseph Ward of Dakota* (1913); W. J. McMurtry, *Yankton Coll.* (1907); Doane Robinson, *Hist. of S. Dak.* (2 vols., 1904); *Eighth Ann. Cat. of Yankton Coll.* (1890); *State of S. Dak.: First Ann. Report of the Supt. of Public Instruction* (1890); *Congregational Year-Book* (1890); *Andover Rev.*, Jan. 1890; *Advance*, Dec. 19, 1889; *Press and Dakotan* (Yankton), Dec. 19, 1889; Charles Martyn, *The William Ward Geneal.* (1925).]   E. I. S.

WARD, LESTER FRANK (June 18, 1841– Apr. 18, 1913), sociologist, was born in Joliet, Ill. His father, Justus Ward, was a mechanic of an inventive turn of mind; his mother, Silence (Rolph), daughter of a clergyman, is said to have been a woman of scholarly tendencies and versatile accomplishments. Frank was the youngest of ten children. During his early years, spent in Illinois and in Buchanan County, Iowa, to which place his parents moved in his boyhood, he lived in close contact with nature under frontier conditions. At the age of seventeen he went to Pennsylvania, where, at Myersburg, his brother, Cyrenus Osborne Ward [*q.v.*], later a labor leader, was then manufacturing wagon hubs. Beginning in 1861, he spent four terms at the Susquehanna Collegiate Institute at Towanda. In August 1862 he enlisted in the Union army and served until November 1864, when he was discharged on account of wounds received at Chancellorsville. On Aug. 13, 1862, just before his enlistment, he had married Elisabeth Carolyn Vought, by whom he had a son who lived less than a year; his wife died in 1872, and on Mar.

6, 1873, he married Rosamond Asenath Simons.

In 1865 he secured a position in the United States Treasury Department at Washington, with which he remained connected until 1881. Meanwhile, he studied at Columbian College (now George Washington University), from which he received the degree of A.B. in 1869, that of LL.B. in 1871, and that of A.M. in 1872. After leaving the Treasury Department he became assistant geologist in the United States Geological Survey. He was appointed geologist in 1883, and paleontologist in 1892. His chief contributions to the natural sciences include "Types of the Laramie Flora" (*Bulletin No. 37,* 1887, United States Geological Survey), *Status of the Mesozoic Floras of the United States* (1905), a monograph of the Survey, and various articles in its *Annual Reports*. The range of his interests was broad and included biology, anthropology, psychology, and sociology. He was an ardent advocate of the evolutionary hypothesis, and enlisted with enthusiasm in the conflict then waging between science and theology.

Valuable as are Ward's studies in the natural sciences, he is best known because of his leadership in the field of American sociology. Though others had written in this field in earlier years, he became the great pioneer of modern and evolutionary sociology in the United States, through the publication in 1883 of *Dynamic Sociology*. This was followed by *The Psychic Factors of Civilization* (1893); *Outlines of Sociology* (1898); *Pure Sociology* (1903); and *Applied Sociology* (copr. 1906). The last two are a restatement of his general teachings. The *Textbook of Sociology* (1905), by J. Q. Dealey and Ward, is mainly a condensation of the *Pure Sociology*.

Ward sought to give a strongly monistic and evolutionary interpretation to social development. Utilizing his broad background in the modern sciences, he vigorously argued that the human mind is a great factor in evolution. Its emotional, willing aspects have produced ambitious aspirations for individual and social improvement, and the intellect, when rightly informed with scientific truth, enables the individual or the social group to plan intelligently for future development. The mind, in other words, becomes "telic," thus enabling mankind to pass from passive to active evolutionary processes, and from natural to human or social evolution. This ability will usher in an age of systematic planning for human progress, an age in which government will stress social welfare and democracy will pass into "sociocracy."

Ward's point of view throughout is strongly democratic and humanitarian. He assumes wide differences in human heredity and racial aptitudes, yet argues that whatever talent or genius may be latent can be called forth by a stimulating social environment and a general education in the sciences, physical and social, with their applications. Even the mediocre, he taught, might be enabled to double or treble their attainments, if given an education suited to their mentality. Education and freedom from economic strain, he argued, are the essential bases for human progress. Governments, therefore, should aim gradually to abolish harsh poverty and to develop wise national systems of general education, suited in one aspect for genius, in another, for ordinary minds.

In 1906, desirous of greater leisure to prepare *Glimpses of the Cosmos* (6 vols., 1913-18), his "mental autobiography," Ward sought and obtained a call to the chair of sociology in Brown University. This chair he held for the remainder of his life. In *Glimpses of the Cosmos* he republished his minor writings in their biographical and historical background. It also contains a summary of what he considered to be his chief contribution to social philosophy.

In maturity Ward was six feet in height, blonde but sunburned from much outdoor life, athletic in build but slightly stoop-shouldered in old age. He enjoyed excellent health almost to the end of his life and even in his later years he was a tireless walker, geologizing and botanizing for his avocation. He lived simply. In manner he was unassuming, somewhat modest and retiring in disposition, but dignified in bearing. Even in his 'teens he was fond of languages. He studied Greek, Latin, and French with little outside help, and, in later years, German. For reading purposes he acquired some acquaintance with other languages, including Russian, Hebrew, and Japanese. He traveled widely over the United States and Europe and in 1903, as president of the Institut International de Sociologie, he presided over the deliberations of that learned body at the Sorbonne, Paris. He died in Washington, D. C.

[In addition to *Glimpses of the Cosmos,* see E. P. Cape, *Lester F. Ward, A Personal Sketch* (1922); H. W. Odum, *Am. Masters of Social Sci.* (copr. 1927); E. P. Kimball, *Sociology and Education: An Analysis of the Theories of Spencer and Ward* (1932); *Who's Who in America,* 1912–13; *The Cyc. of Am. Biogs.,* vol. VII (1903); *Brown Alumni Mo.,* Apr. 1906; *Am. Jour. of Sociology,* July, Sept. 1919; G. K. Ward, *Andrew Warde and His Descendants* (1910); *Evening Tribune* (Providence), Apr. 19, 1913. Ward's manuscript material, books, and letters are in the lib. of Brown University and the Lib. of Cong.; his diary, covering a period of over forty years, was destroyed by his heirs for personal reasons, but an earlier portion was preserved and, edited by B. J. Stern, was published as *Young Ward's Diary* (copr. 1935).]   J. Q. D.

WARD, LYDIA ARMS AVERY COONLEY (Jan. 31, 1845–Feb. 26, 1924), author, was born at Lynchburg, Va., the daughter of Benjamin Franklin and Susan Howes (Look) Avery. She was a descendant of Christopher Avery who emigrated from England and settled in Salem, Mass., about 1630. Until her marriage in 1867 to John Clark Coonley and for a few years thereafter, her life was spent chiefly in Louisville, Ky. Removing to Chicago in 1873, she soon won a prominent place in the social and cultural life of that city. For nearly a quarter-century her home was a center of "light and leading" for all who were in any way identified with Chicago's higher interests, and for many distinguished visitors to the city as well. "In that home," wrote Jane Addams, "I first unfolded plans for founding a settlement in Chicago, and met with that ready sympathy and understanding which her adventuring and facile mind was always ready to extend to a new cause she believed to be righteous."

Her first husband died in 1882, and on Mar. 18, 1897, she was married to the scientist, Henry Augustus Ward [*q.v.*]. After about 1909, save for rather frequent periods of travel, she lived at Wyoming, N. Y., in which village the Avery family had maintained an ancestral summer residence for many decades. Here, as previously in Chicago, she kept a kind of "open house" for the world at large and, in particular, for young and struggling workers in the arts. Here, also, she organized an elaborate summer school, liberally attended sessions of which were held in 1914, 1916, and 1917. A beautiful community hall, dedicated in 1902, stands today in the village of Wyoming as a tangible expression of her generosity and public spirit.

Although she was a frequent contributor to various periodicals from about 1878 onward, her first book, *Under the Pines and Other Verses,* did not appear until 1895. This was followed by *Singing Verses for Children* (1897), *Love Songs* (1898), and in 1921 by a collected edition of her poems in three volumes entitled *The Melody of Life, The Melody of Love,* and *The Melody of Childhood.* She also wrote the words for Dr. George F. Root's cantata *Our Flag with the Stars and Stripes* (1896), and for several other musical compositions.

While a few of her poems are reprinted in some of the standard anthologies and have become widely known, her literary work was more of a recreational and ephemeral by-product than the chief concern of a life spent in untiring human service. She was one of those whose peculiar genius finds its most congenial expression in the exercise of direct inspirational influence through personal contact, and in this sphere she made a notable contribution to American life— a contribution which was vicariously reflected in the work of many men and women who became prominent in various cultural activities. She died in Chicago, survived by four of six children by her first husband.

[E. McK. and C. H. J. Avery, *The Groton Avery Clan* (1912); *Chronicles of an American Home* (1930), ed. by W. R. Browne; *Who's Who in America, 1922–23*; *Chicago Tribune,* Feb. 27, 1924.]   W. R. B.

WARD, MARCUS LAWRENCE (Nov. 9, 1812–Apr. 25, 1884), governor of New Jersey, congressman, philanthropist, was the son of Moses and Fanny (Brown) Ward. His paternal ancestor, John Ward, came with his widowed mother from England and settled in 1635 at Wethersfield, Conn.; in 1666 he became one of the founders of Newark, N. J. Here his descendant, Moses Ward, was for many years a successful manufacturer of candles, and here Moses' son Marcus was born. Educated in local private schools, he became a clerk in a variety store in Newark and later entered his father's establishment, becoming in time a partner in the firm of M. Ward & Son. In this connection he became widely known throughout the state and made a private fortune.

From his early years Ward took an interest in everything concerning his native city. He became a director in the National State Bank in Newark in 1846, was long chairman of the executive committee of the New Jersey Historical Society, and aided in the formation of the Newark Library Association and the New Jersey Art Union. In 1856 he first took an active part in politics, embracing with vigor the cause of the newly formed Republican party. Because of his intense anti-slavery convictions, he went to Kansas in 1858 to take part in the struggle against the admission of slavery there, but found too much mob violence for his taste, and soon returned to Newark and his business. In 1860 he was a delegate to the Republican convention at Chicago which nominated Abraham Lincoln for the presidency.

Soon after the outbreak of the Civil War he began to devise means to ameliorate the condition of the families of those New Jersey soldiers who by death or illness had left their wives and children destitute, and also the condition of such soldiers themselves as needed better hospital accommodations than the Government had prepared. With his own funds, and assuming direct oversight of the project, he took possession of a whole floor in the Newark Custom House, employed eight clerks, and there laid plans for carrying out his patriotic and benevolent ideas. He established a kind of free pension bureau, through which he secured soldiers' pay and transmitted it to their families. He founded a soldiers' hospital in his city—The Ward U. S. Hospital, the foundation of the later Soldiers' Home. In 1862 he consented to run as a Republican candidate for governor, but was defeated by the Democrat Joel Parker [q.v.]. He was a delegate in 1864 to the convention at Baltimore that renominated Lincoln; in the same year he became a member of the Republican National Committee, and continued as such until the nomination of General Grant for the presidency. In 1865 he was elected governor of New Jersey by a large majority. During his administration of three years (Jan. 16, 1866–Jan. 18, 1869) he secured the passage of a public-school law, an act eliminating partisanship in the control of the state prison, and other measures of reform. After a few years of retirement he was elected in 1872 representative in Congress from the sixth New Jersey district and served from Mar. 4, 1873, to Mar. 3, 1875. He was renominated in 1874, but was defeated in a Democratic tidal wave. Declining the federal office of commissioner of Indian affairs, he now retired to private life. After two trips to Europe he visited Florida, where he contracted the malarial fever which brought his death.

On June 30, 1840, Ward married Susan, daughter of John and Elizabeth (Longworth) Morris, by whom he had eight children; two sons, with their mother, survived him. The younger son, Marcus L. Ward, Jr., who outlived his brother, put the family fortune to a unique use by establishing at Maplewood, N. J., in memory of his father, the Ward Homestead, with accommodations for 120 bachelors and widowers who have been prominent in the business or social life of New Jersey and are over sixty-five years of age. The Homestead is like a large country club in appearance, and has a large endowment fund.

[M. D. Ogden, *Memorial Cyc. of N. J.*, vol. I (1915); W. H. Shaw, *Hist. of Essex and Hudson Counties, N. J.* (1884), vol. I; *The Biog. Encyc. of N. J. of the Nineteenth Century* (1877); *Proc. N. J. Hist. Soc.*, 2 ser. VIII (1885), IX (1887); John Livingston, *Portraits of Eminent Americans Now Living* (1854), vol. IV; *Harper's Weekly*, Dec. 9, 1865; *Biog. Dir. Am. Cong.* (1928); *N. Y. Times*, Apr. 26, 1884.]   A. V–D. H.

WARD, MONTGOMERY [See Ward, Aaron Montgomery, 1843–1913].

WARD, NANCY (fl. 1776–1781), Indian leader, was born among the Cherokee Indians and lived at the Overhill town of Great Echota in what is now Monroe County, Tenn. Her father is believed to have been a British officer and her mother a sister of the Cherokee chief Attakulla-culla. Distinguished among the Cherokee by the title of "Beloved Woman" or "Pretty Woman," she enjoyed the right to sit in council and, especially, the right to revoke by her single will any tribal sentence of punishment or death. It is said that she was one of the first to introduce negro slavery and the use of cattle among the Cherokee. An advocate of peace within the tribe and beyond the tribe, she helped the white frontiersmen again and again. At the outbreak of the Revolution it was she who warned the Watauga and Holston settlers in time to save themselves from destruction at the hands of the Indians. She also exercised her right to spare the prisoners captured in the raids and to pardon them even though already condemned and bound to the stake. Later in the war she again reported early news of Indian attack and supplied the Americans with beef cattle from her own large herd. When the Indians were repulsed she sought to intercede for her people, but, although she seems to have been kindly treated, her mission was unsuccessful.

Her part in the unsettled years after the Revolution is obscure, and, although her name was mentioned by Nuttall (*post*, p. 130) as late as 1819, it is not clear that she was still living at that time.

[James Mooney, "Myths of the Cherokee," *Nineteenth Annual Report of the Bureau of Am. Ethnology*, pt. 1 (1900); *Calendar of Va. State Papers*, vol. I (1875); "Southern Frontier Life in Revolutionary Days," *Southern Hist. Asso. Pubs.*, vol. IV (1900), pp. 457–58; Thomas Nuttall, *A Jour. of Travels into the Arkansa Territory . . . 1819* (1821); J. G. M. Ramsey, *The Annals of Tenn.* (1853), reprint with index (1926).]   K. E. C.

WARD, NATHANIEL (c. 1578–October 1652), author, clergyman, was born in Haverhill, England, the son of John and Susan Ward. His father was a Puritan minister. In 1596 Nathaniel entered Emmanuel College, Cambridge, where he received the degree of A.B. in 1599 and that of A.M. in 1603. Educated to be a barrister, he practised law for some time in England. A visit to Heidelberg in 1618 and a chance meeting with the great theologian David Pareus changed the course of his career. Pareus persuaded him to enter the ministry and helped him to obtain the post of chaplain to the British merchants at Elbing, Prussia. In 1624 he returned to England, where he was curate of St. James's, Piccadilly, London, 1626–28. In the latter year he was presented by Sir Nathaniel Rich to the rectory of Stondon Massey, where he preached Puritan doctrine unhindered until 1631. Laud then called him to answer charges of non-conformity, but did not attempt to remove him. In 1633, however, he was dismissed summarily from office, and the following year emigrated to Massachusetts Bay. Going directly to Agawam (Ipswich), he was installed in the church there as a colleague of the Rev. Thomas Parker [q.v.].

Poor health interrupted his work in the pastorate. After his resignation, he was appointed in 1638 by the General Court to assist in the preparation of a legal code for Massachusetts, "the first code of laws to be established in New England." According to John Winthrop these laws, which were enacted in 1641, were "composed by Mr. Nathaniel Ward" (*Winthrop's Journal*, 1908, ed. by J. K. Hosmer, II, 49). Known as the "Body of Liberties," this code was in effect a bill of rights, setting one of the cornerstones in American constitutional history. That the laws were in advance of English common law is attested by the eightieth, which in contrast to the English provision that a man might punish his wife with a "reasonable instrument," explicitly stated: "Everie married woeman shall be free from bodilie correction or stripes by her husbande, unlesse it be in his owne defence upon her assalt."

In 1645 Ward completed *The Simple Cobler of Aggawam in America*, published in England in 1647 under the pseudonym of Theodore de la Guard. Professing to be the reflections of a self-exiled cobbler upon the political and religious dissensions that were racking both England and America, it is really a protest against toleration. The author is strongly opposed to "polypiety" in the church, and in the state he would restore the old order with king, lords, and commons. "My heart has naturally detested foure things," he says; "The standing of the Apocrypha in the Bible; Forrainers dwelling in my Countrey, to crowd our native Subjects into the corners of the Earth; Alchymized Coines; Toleration of divers Religions, or of one Religion in Segregant Shapes." The book is amusingly digressive: there are satirical thrusts at women's fashions and some neatly turned couplets. Throughout there is the prophecy of Presbyterianism. It remains a landmark in American letters, for its homely style, interwoven with apt and erudite metaphor, surpasses in vigor anything in Colonial literature written within the author's lifetime. It quickly went into several editions, each carefully edited and supplemented by Ward.

The year of its publication found him again in England, preaching before the House of Commons on a recapitulation of the themes of the Simple Cobbler. In the same year appeared *A Religious Retreat Sounded to a Religious Army*, an appeal to the army to submit to the will of Parliament, which has been attributed to him, as have two other works—a sermon before Parliament published in 1648, and *Discolliminium* (1650). To save church and country from disaster, to observe tradition and eschew the new, was his purpose. Thomas Fuller observed that Ward had "in a jesting way, in some of his books, delivered much smart truth of the present times" (*The History of the Worthies of England*, edition of 1840, III, 187), while Cotton Mather wrote that "He was the author of many composures full of wit and sense" (*post*, I, 522). From 1648 until his death in 1652, Ward was settled in the ministry at Shenfield, England. Although he belonged more to the old than to the new England, the making of New England's heritage belongs in part to him.

[J. W. Dean, *A Memoir of the Rev. Nathaniel Ward* (1868), containing a bibliography; *The Simple Cobler of Aggawam in America* (1843), ed. by David Pulsifer, Preface; J. and J. A. Venn, *Alumni Cantabrigienses*, pt. 1, vol. IV (1927); Cotton Mather, *Magnalia Christi Americana* (1702; ed. cited, that of 1853); *Mass. Hist. Soc. Colls.*, 3 ser. I (1825), VIII (1843), 4 ser. VII (1865), *New Eng. Hist. and Geneal. Reg.*, July 1864; N. B. Shurtleff, *Records of the Gov. and Company of the Mass. Bay*, vol. I (1853); *Essex Inst. Hist. Colls.*, vol. VI (1864); M. C. Tyler, *A Hist. of Am. Lit. during the Colonial Time* (1897), I, 227–41; V. L. Parrington, *Main Currents in Am. Thought*, vol. I (1927); C. A. Harris, in *Dict. Nat. Biog.*]   E.H.D.

WARD, RICHARD (Apr. 15, 1689–Aug. 21, 1763), colonial governor of Rhode Island, was born in Newport, a few months before the death of his father, Thomas Ward, who had settled in Newport in 1671. Richard's mother was his father's second wife, Amy Smith. The boy grew up in his native town, which was already a center for shipping engaged in the West India trade. On Nov. 2, 1709, he married Mary Tillinghast, and fourteen children were born to them. In spite of his large family, Ward became comfortably prosperous; he was not only a successful merchant but owned considerable land in the fertile Narragansett Country.

In 1714 he was elected a member of the Rhode Island Assembly, and thereafter served in various public capacities for many years. On May 7, 1740, he was elected deputy governor, and a few months later became governor on the death of Gov. John Wanton. He continued in office three years, but in 1742 declined to run for a third term. His service as governor came during a period of general unrest in Rhode Island. Not only was the colony feeling the effects of the

War of the Austrian Succession, but it was agitated over three local issues: the paper money question, a controversy with Massachusetts over the common boundary, and, beginning in 1742, a dispute with the mother country over the right of appointment of a judge of the court of admiralty, a question involving the interpretation of the colonial charter. Ward retired from office before the war had fairly begun and before either of the other questions was settled, yet he had much to do with all of them. A council of war, of which he was a member, was created in January 1741; soldiers were recruited in response to his proclamation; Fort George was enlarged, and the colony sloop, *Tartar,* was made ready to go to sea. With regard to the paper-money question, Ward as a merchant belonged to the conservative group, but he was unable to prevent the establishment of another bank of issue. In regard to the Massachusetts boundary he stoutly supported the Rhode Island claims, and as stoutly protested to England in behalf of the charter rights. His refusal to remain in office was due, possibly, to interest in the war, for he was present at the siege of Louisburg in 1745.

During the rest of his life he lived quietly, and died in 1763, probably little suspecting that separation of the colonies from England would soon occur. His children carried on their father's traditions of public service. Samuel, 1725–1776 [*q.v.*], was governor of Rhode Island for three terms. Thomas and Henry each acted as secretary of the colony, and Henry was a delegate to the Stamp Act Congress, while Samuel's son Samuel, 1756–1832 [*q.v.*], served with distinction in the American Revolution.

[References to Richard Ward are found in the biographies of his son and grandson: "Life of Samuel Ward," in Jared Sparks, *Lib. of Am. Biog.,* 2 ser. IX (1846), and John Ward, *A Memoir of Lieut.-Col. Samuel Ward* (1875). See also S. G. Arnold, *The Hist. of the State of R. I. and Providence Plantations,* vol. II (1860); and J. R. Bartlett, *Records of the Colony of R. I.,* vol. V (1860).]   M. A.

WARD, RICHARD HALSTED (June 17, 1837–Oct. 28, 1917), physician and microscopist, was born at Bloomfield, N. J., the son of Israel Currie and Almeda (Hanks) Ward. He was educated at Bloomfield Academy and Williams College, Williamsburg, Mass., and received from the latter institution the degree of A.B. in 1858 and A.M. in 1861. He was graduated in medicine from the College of Physicians and Surgeons in New York in 1862. He was then commissioned an acting assistant-surgeon of volunteers in the Union Army and assigned to duty in a military hospital at Nashville, Tenn., but he was soon compelled to resign on account of

illness. He spent a year in Minnesota regaining his health and in 1863 settled in Troy, N. Y., where he spent the remainder of his busy and useful life. He early associated himself with Dr. Thomas W. Blatchford in the practice of medicine and in the management of the Marshall Infirmary and Sanitarium with its attached hospital for the insane. In this institution he was attending physician, member of the board of governors, and chairman of the medical board. He was appointed instructor in botany at the Rensselaer Polytechnic Institute in 1867 and promoted in 1869 to professor of botany and lecturer in histology and microscopy, continuing these teaching positions until his retirement in 1892. In the midst of a busy career in medical practice and teaching he found opportunity for extensive research in microscopy, with particular reference to its practical application in medicine and natural sciences. He collaborated in experimentation with the early American manufacturers of microscopes and influenced materially the type and mechanism of these instruments. He perfected a number of accessories for the microscope, notably an iris illuminator for the binocular instrument. He was one of the first to demonstrate by the microscope the difference in cellular structure of blood from various animals.

His research in blood structure and in the microscopical study of handwriting caused his services to be widely employed in legal cases involving murder and forgery. He was also a widely known authority upon the question of purity of water supplies and upon adulteration of foods and medicines. From 1871 to 1883 he was in charge of the section on microscopy in *The American Naturalist,* of Salem, Mass., one of the first departments of any American journal to be devoted to this branch of knowledge. He collaborated with the Rev. Alpheus B. Hervey in the American edition of *The Microscope in Botany* (1885), by Wilhelm J. Behrens. In 1889 he published a volume on *Plant Organization,* with a second edition the following year. He contributed numerous articles on topics relating to botany and microscopy to technical journals. In addition to his medical society affiliations he was a member and first president (1879) of the American Society of Microscopists (later the American Microscopical Society), a member of the Boston Society of Natural History, a fellow of the American Association for the Advancement of Science, of the Royal Microscopical Society of London, and of the Belgian Microscopical Society. He was a delegate to the International Medical Congress at Berlin in 1890, and represented the United States at the International Exposition of Microscopy at Antwerp in 1891. He was married, June 10, 1862, to Charlotte Allen Baldwin, of Bloomfield, N. J.; of their four children, a son became a professor of zoölogy at the University of Illinois and later permanent secretary of the American Association for the Advancement of Science. He wrote *Impressions of the Antwerp Microscopical Exposition* (1892), and *Library Expedients in Microscopy* (1900).

[*Who's Who in America,* 1916–17; H. B. Ward, in *Am. Medic. Biog.,* edited by H. A. Kelly, W. L. Burrage; W. B. Atkinson, *Phys. and Surgeons of the U. S.* (1878); *Biog. Record, Officers and Grads., Rensselaer Polytech. Inst.* (1887); *Jour. Am. Medic. Asso.,* Nov. 3, 1917; *N. Y. Times,* Oct. 29, 1917.] J. M. P—n.

WARD, ROBERT DeCOURCY (Nov. 29, 1867–Nov. 12, 1931), climatologist and teacher, was born in Boston, Mass., a descendant of William Ward who was in Cecil County, Md., in the latter part of the seventeenth century. At the age of six months Robert was taken by his parents, Henry Veazey and Anna Saltonstall (Merrill) Ward, to Dresden, Germany, where his father was consul for Chile at the court of Saxony. There he remained four years. He then spent a year in Switzerland, where his father died, and a year in England. In 1874 he returned to Boston and entered Noble and Greenough's School (then Noble's School), from which he graduated in 1885. In 1889 he received the degree of A.B. at Harvard, *summa cum laude,* and that of A.M. in 1893. As a graduate student he made two meteorological investigations, one on the sea breeze of New England and another on the thunderstorms of New England, both published in the *Annals of the Astronomical Observatory of Harvard College* (vols. XXI, pt. 2, 1890; XXXI, pt. 2, 1893).

The year 1889–90 he spent in Europe, returning to Harvard in September 1890 to become assistant to Prof. W. M. Davis in physical geography and meteorology. In 1893 he became assistant in meteorology; instructor in meteorology in 1895; instructor in climatology in 1896; assistant professor in 1900; and professor in 1910 —the first professor of climatology in the United States. In founding and developing his department, from which able teachers went to many institutions, he did a prodigious amount of work in assembling and putting into logical order all he could find on climatology by others. He strove to make simple what others had left involved, and thus became an exceptionally clear and exact writer. His first book, *Practical Exercises in Elementary Meteorology* (1899), was a product of necessity, nothing of the kind being available for his students His next book, which appeared

in 1903, a translation of the first volume of Julius von Hann's *Handbuch der Klimatologie* (1897), served an even greater practical use. His *Climate, Considered Especially in Relation to Man* was published in 1908, and a second edition issued in 1918. His best known book, *The Climates of the United States,* appeared in 1925. It embodies the results of a large amount of personal investigation and of much guided research on the part of his students. His last work, completed just before his death, is an extensive treatment of the climatology of North America for the great Köppen-Geiger *Handbuch der Klimatologie.* He also contributed to scientific journals, and to the eleventh, twelfth, and thirteenth editions of the *Encyclopaedia Britannica.* He was editor of the *American Meteorological Journal,* 1892–96, for many years contributing editor of the *Geographical Review,* and editor of "Current Notes on Meteorology" in *Science,* 1896–1908. He was an extensive traveler, visiting all parts of the United States and much of Europe and South America, and making a trip around the world; wherever he went his observations of weather and climate were keen and abundant, and ready for publication immediately upon his return.

He was president of the Association of American Geographers, 1917, and of the American Meteorological Society, 1920–21, and a member of many other societies at home and abroad. In addition to his other academic duties, he was, from 1900, a member of the administrative board of Harvard College, and for many years chairman of the Board of freshman advisers and a member of the committee on admission. In 1927 he was Harvard exchange professor to the Western colleges. He helped to found the Immigration Restriction League in 1894, and took an active and effective part in all its work. His physique was frail, but the responsibilities he effectively assumed would have been heavy burdens for the most robust, and to him were possible only because he was extremely methodical in all he did. He was a delightful companion, full of information or jovial and witty as occasion required. On Apr. 28, 1897, he married Emma Lane of St. Louis, who survived him but a few weeks; they had two sons and two daughters.

[G. A. Hanson, *Old Kent: the Eastern Shore of Md.* (1876); *Who's Who in America,* 1930–31; *Harvard Alumni Bull.,* Nov. 20, 27, 1931; *Harvard Univ. Gazette,* Dec. 19, 1931; *Harvard Crimson,* Nov. 31, 1931; *Annals of the Asso. of Am. Geographers,* Mar. 1932; *Bull. Am. Meteorological Soc.,* Dec. 1931, May 1932; *Geographical Rev.,* Jan. 1932; *Scientific Mo.,*Feb. 1932; *Science,* Feb. 12, 1932; *Proc. Am. Acad. of Arts and Sciences,* vol. LXIX (1935); *Boston Transcript,* Nov. 12, 1931; personal acquaintance.] W. J. H—s.

WARD, SAMUEL (May 27, 1725–Mar. 26, 1776), colonial governor, member of the Continental Congress, was born in Newport, R. I., one of the fourteen children of Richard Ward [*q.v.*] and Mary (Tillinghast) Ward. Since his father was not only a prosperous merchant, but governor of the colony from 1740 to 1742, the boy grew up in the brilliant society of colonial Newport. He was educated in the grammar school, but was not sent to college because he was destined by his father to be a farmer. In 1745 he married Anne Ray and settled on a farm in Westerly. Five sons and six daughters were born to them.

Ward's election in 1756 as deputy to the Rhode Island Assembly marked the beginning of his public service. For more than a decade thereafter there was a political feud between Ward and Stephen Hopkins [*q.v.*] of Providence, based on personal antipathy, political differences, and, fundamentally, on sectional rivalry. The colony was divided into two hostile camps: the conservative group, the merchants, found a champion in Ward, while the radicals looked to Hopkins. Three times the Ward party triumphed by the election of their leader as governor—in 1762, 1765, and 1766; three times also it met defeat. In 1761 Ward served as chief justice of the colony.

His first term as governor (1762) was uneventful politically, but in his second term (1765), he signed the charter of Rhode Island College (later Brown University), of which he was an original trustee. His second and third terms (1765, 1766) came during the years of agitation over the Stamp Act. His commercial upbringing led him to sympathize with the colonists and, although anxious to maintain law and order, he supported their cause vigorously. He refused to take the oath to submit to, or enforce, the Stamp Act; he denied the request of the collectors of the customs for an extra guard; and he protested to Captain Antrobus of the British vessel *Maidstone* against the impressment of Rhode Islanders into the Royal Navy.

Defeated in 1767 for reëlection, Ward retired to Westerly, but kept in touch with the course of events. He was among the first to hold at his home an indignation meeting over the punishment of Boston after the "Tea Party," and he prepared a series of resolutions which set forth comprehensively the colonial grievances. When the First Continental Congress was called, he and his former adversary Hopkins were chosen delegates. Little is known of the part he played in this assemblage, but he was reëlected to the Second Continental Congress.

In 1776 the sentiment of the Ward family was rapidly crystallizing in favor of independence. Henry Ward, brother of the former governor, was secretary of state of Rhode Island and performed some of the functions of the governor in place of the Loyalist, Joseph Wanton [*q.v.*], and Samuel Ward's son Samuel, 1756–1832 [*q.v.*], with the consent and approbation of his father, received a commission as captain in the 1st Rhode Island Regiment. From the opening of the Second Continental Congress Ward was an active member of the little group of statesmen who were seeking some formula to guide the colonies. Early in the session he was called by Hancock to preside over the Congress when it resolved itself into the Committee of the Whole, and for several months regularly served as chairman at such times. It was his fortune to propose and to help secure the appointment of George Washington as commander-in-chief of the colonial forces. He died of smallpox, contracted in Philadelphia while the Congress was deliberating.

[*"Life of Samuel Ward," in Jared Sparks, Lib. of Am. Biog.*, 2 ser. IX (1846); G. S. Kimball, *The Correspondence of the Colonial Governors of R. I.* (2 vols. 1902–03); E. C. Burnett, *Letters of Members of the Continental Congress*, vol. I (1921); J. R. Bartlett, *Records of the Colony of R. I.*, vol. VI (1861); S. G. Arnold, *Hist. of the State of R. I.*, vol. II (1860); MSS. in the possession of descendants in New York City.]

M. A.

WARD, SAMUEL (Nov. 17, 1756–Aug. 16, 1832), soldier, merchant, the second son of Gov. Samuel Ward, 1725–1776 [*q.v.*], and Anne (Ray) Ward, was born in Westerly, R. I. He was a member of one of the early classes of Rhode Island College (later Brown University), where he graduated with honors in 1771. His father and his uncle were both prominent in colonial affairs, and upon the outbreak of the Revolution he was among the first to answer the call to arms.

Commissioned as captain in the 1st Rhode Island Regiment in 1775, he served with distinction in many campaigns. At the siege of Quebec he was taken prisoner (Dec. 31, 1775), and remained in Canada until his release, in August 1776. Promoted to the rank of major in January 1777, he fought with Washington's army at Morristown and in October was with the forces that defeated Burgoyne. In addition he was one of those who endured the hardships of the winter of 1777–78 at Valley Forge. On Apr. 12, 1779, after his regiment had made an attempt to force the British out of Newport, he received the rank of lieutenant-colonel. Meanwhile, on Mar. 8, 1778, he had married his first cousin, Phebe, daughter of William Greene [*q.v.*] and Catherine (Ray) Greene of Warwick, R. I. They had ten children, of whom seven lived to grow up. One of these, Samuel, 1786–1839 [*q.v.*], was the father of Julia (Ward) Howe [*q.v.*].

In 1781 Ward retired from the military service to begin the life of a merchant. Some time after the conclusion of the war he established himself in New York, in the firm of Samuel Ward & Brother. His business interests required frequent traveling, and he sailed all over the world. Making the arduous voyage to Canton, China, in 1788, he was one of the first Americans to visit the Far East, and he was in Paris when Louis XVI was sentenced to death. Though he had no ambition to play as active a part in public life as had his father and grandfather, the tradition of his family, his commercial wisdom, and his scholarly interests caused him to be highly respected. He became a member of the Society of the Cincinnati in 1784, was elected a delegate to the Annapolis Convention in 1786, was president of the New York Marine Insurance Company from 1806 to 1808, and was one of Rhode Island's representatives at the Hartford Convention in 1814. In 1804 he had moved his residence back to Rhode Island, to East Greenwich, and in 1816 he removed to Jamaica, L. I. In 1828, however, he returned to New York City, where he died.

[John Ward, *A Memoir of Lieut.-Col. Samuel Ward* (privately printed, 1875); *Hist. Cat. Brown Univ.* (1905); *N. Y. American*, Aug. 16, 1832.] M. A.

WARD, SAMUEL (May 1, 1786–Nov. 27, 1839), banker, was born in Warwick, R. I., the fifth son of Samuel Ward, 1756–1832 [*q.v.*], and Phebe (Greene) Ward, the daughter of Gov. William Greene [*q.v.*] of Rhode Island. In 1790, when the boy was four years old, his family moved to New York, where his father engaged in mercantile pursuits with indifferent success. Since the family income was too small to permit of his being sent to college, Ward received only a common-school education and at the age of fourteen began work as a clerk in the prominent banking house of Prime & Sands. In 1808, when he was only twenty-two, he was made a partner and in time he became head of the firm, the name of which was changed to Prime, Ward & King.

Quick to make up his mind and the soul of punctuality, he disliked circumlocution and indecision in others. A believer in the observance of contractual obligations, he was deeply mortified by the suspension of specie payments on May 10, 1837, by the New York banks, an act which he regarded as a blot upon the city's commercial honor. During the ensuing panic several of the American commonwealths repudiated their obligations, and but for the strenuous opposition of Ward the State of New York might have fol-

lowed their example. Repeatedly he called meetings of the leading financiers, and by his persistence induced them to tide the state over the crisis. So great was confidence in the integrity of his firm that he was able in the early part of 1838 to obtain a loan of some five million dollars in gold bars from the Bank of England, which went far towards enabling the New York banks to resume specie payments in May of that year. In 1839 Ward helped found and became president of the Bank of Commerce in New York, the first great financial institution to be incorporated under an act passed by the New York legislature in April 1838 allowing associations of individuals to engage in the banking business. He was recuperating from an attack of gout when during a secondary crisis the Philadelphia banks and those in Southern cities suspended specie payments in October 1839. For a fortnight he fought strenuously and successfully to prevent the New York banks from following suit, but the strain proved too great for his enfeebled constitution and he died towards the close of the following month.

In October 1812 he married Julia Rush Cutler, by whom he had three sons and four daughters. After her death, Nov. 11, 1824, Ward's character underwent a great change. He gave up smoking, became a devout churchgoer, frowned on all fashionable entertainments, and gave freely to good causes. He contributed to the missions and educational institutions of the Protestant Episcopal Church, and in 1830 helped found the University of the City of New York (New York University) of which he was first treasurer. The following year he became the first president of the New York City Temperance Society, and in 1836 he helped finance Stuyvesant Institute, which was intended to be a copy of the Boston Athenæum. A lover of the fine arts, he had a gallery of paintings in his house at the corner of Broadway and Bond Street. His son Samuel, 1814–1884 [*q.v.*], became a well-known figure in political and social circles and demonstrated facility and charm as a writer; of his daughters, Louisa married the sculptor Thomas Crawford [*q.v.*] and became the mother of the novelist Francis Marion Crawford [*q.v.*] while Julia married the humanitarian Samuel Gridley Howe [*q.v.*], had several distinguished children, and as Julia Ward Howe [*q.v.*] became one of the most famous American women of her generation.

[Biog. material appears in John Ward, *Memoir of Lieut.-Col. Samuel Ward* (privately printed, 1875); Charles King, "The Late Samuel Ward," in *The Biog. Annual* (1841); Julia Ward Howe, *Reminiscences 1819–1899* (1899); Laura E. Richards and Maud Howe Elliott, *Julia Ward Howe 1819–1910* (1915); *N. Y Times and Commercial Intelligencer,* Nov. 30, 1839. There are some MSS. in the N. Y. Pub. Lib.] H. G. V.

WARD, SAMUEL (Jan. 25, 1814–May 19, 1884), lobbyist, financier, author, was born in New York City, the son of Samuel Ward, 1786–1839 [*q.v.*] and Julia Rush (Cutler) Ward, and elder brother of Julia Ward Howe [*q.v.*]. He attended Round Hill School, Northampton, Mass., presided over by George Bancroft [*q.v.*], and Columbia College, New York, where he received the degree of B.A. in 1831. He then spent some time in Europe—studying in France, where he purchased the library of Legendre, the mathematician, and in Germany, where he showed equal enthusiasm for student social life and the reigning intellectual fashions. Returning to New York with a reputation for both fashionable and intellectual distinction, he contributed "additions and improvements" to the first American edition (1832) of *An Elementary Treatise on Algebra* by J. R. Young, is credited with reviewing books on Locke and Euler for the *American Quarterly Review* (December 1832, December 1833), and took a prominent part in the social life of the wealthy and leisured class until he entered the banking house of Prime, Ward & King, of which his father was a member. Banking was not to his taste, however, and soon after his father's death in 1839 he withdrew from the firm. Meanwhile, in 1837, he had married Emily, daughter of William B. Astor [*q.v.*]. She died at the birth of their only child, Margaret, and in 1844 Ward married Medora Grymes, daughter of John Randolph Grymes of New Orleans. Two sons, both of whom died young, were born of this marriage, which proved unhappy and resulted in separation.

Lacking the austerity and the financial aptitude of his father, Ward had lost his fortune by 1849 and in that year he joined the gold rush to California. There followed about a decade of adventurous wandering which gave rise to numerous legends. According to his own statements, he mastered every Indian dialect in California in three weeks, conducted a ferry and a billiard parlor. and adapted himself with great success to a rough and primitive environment. In San Francisco he made the acquaintance of young James R. Keene [*q.v.*] and became his confidant; later Keene was able to give his friend invaluable financial advice, which Ward reciprocated by advice and information on social and personal matters. He visited Paraguay and Nicaragua on official or semi-official missions in 1858 and 1862 respectively, and in 1860 published a polemical pamphlet, *Exploits of the Attorney General in California,* "by an early Californian," severely criticizing Jeremiah Sullivan Black

[*q.v.*], attorney general in President Buchanan's cabinet. During the closing years of the Civil War and the administrations of Johnson and Grant he lived in Washington through the sessions of Congress, a lobbyist in the employ of financiers interested in national legislation. His dinners, breakfasts, and other entertainments gained a reputation for elegance, and public officials were eager to be the recipients of his hospitality. He was not only a gourmet, however, but a man of marked social gifts, able to persuade conversationally as well as gastronomically, and was credited with an influence which won him the title "King of the Lobby." In 1865 he published a volume of verse, *Lyrical Recreations,* which he reissued in 1871.

Warm-hearted, charming, generous to the point of prodigality, Ward had an immensely wide acquaintance and was beloved by a considerable circle of intimates. Among these were Seward, Sumner, Garfield, Evarts, Bayard, Ticknor, Thackeray, and William H. Russell, the British war correspondent, whom he accompanied on a tour through the Confederacy in the early weeks of the Civil War. He was a friend and adviser of Longfellow, and in June 1882 contributed a revealing article, "Days with Longfellow," to the *North American Review.* One of his closest friends in New York was William Henry Hurlbert [*q.v.*] of the *World,* who with Ward and the young Earl of Rosebery formed the "Mendacious Club," of three, when Rosebery visited the United States in the early seventies (The Marquess of Crewe, *Lord Rosebery,* 1931, p. 54). These ties of affection were lasting; Ward became "Uncle Sam" to Rosebery, who later characterized him as "the uncle of the human race" (Richards, *post,* p. 115). He was as well known in London as in New York, and was caricatured by "Spy" in *The Vanity Fair Album* (1880). Devoted to all his sisters' children, he was especially close to his brilliant nephew F. Marion Crawford [*q.v.*], and gave much attention during his last years to launching Crawford on his literary career. Death came to him at Pegli, Italy, with nieces and nephews around him, *The Rubaiyat* on the bed beside him, and a copy of Horace under his pillow. Crawford wrote afterward to Julia Ward Howe, "He died as he had lived, full of thought and care for others, combined with a vagueness concerning all points of morality, which would have been terrible in a man less actively good than he was" (Elliott, *My Cousin, post,* p. 18).

[F. Marion Crawford portrayed Ward in the character of Horace Bellingham, in *Dr. Claudius* (1883). Descriptions by his nieces occur in Laura E. Richards, *Stepping Westward* (1931) ; Maud Howe Elliott, *Three*

Generations (1923) and *My Cousin, F. Marion Craw-ford* (1934); and Margaret Terry Chanler, *Roman Spring* (1935). See also Julia Ward Howe, *Reminiscences* (1899); Stephen Fiske, *Off-Hand Portraits of Prominent New Yorkers* (1884); E. D. Keyes, *Fifty Years' Observation of Men and Events* (1884); *Harper's Weekly*, May 31, 1884; *Boston Advertiser, Boston Transcript, Boston Post, Springfield Republican, N. Y. Herald*, May 20, 1884. There are some MSS. in the N. Y. Pub. Lib. A biography by Maud Howe Elliott is in preparation.]
S. G.

WARD, SAMUEL RINGGOLD (Oct. 17, 1817–1866?), negro abolitionist, was born of slave parents on the Eastern Shore of Maryland. His parents ran away to Greenwich, N. J., in 1820. Six years later they removed to New York where the boy received an elementary education and became a teacher in colored schools. He was married in 1838 to a Miss Reynolds. His ability as a public speaker attracted the attention of Lewis Tappan [*q.v.*] and others and led to his appointment in 1839 as an agent of the American Anti-Slavery Society from which he was soon transferred to the service of the New York State Anti-Slavery Society. Licensed to preach by the New York Congregational (General) Association in 1839, he subsequently held two pastorates, at South Butler, Wayne County, N. Y., from 1841 to 1843, where his congregation was entirely white, and at Cortland, N. Y., from 1846 to 1851. He resigned the earlier pastorate because of throat trouble and subsequently studied medicine for a few months. He resumed his anti-slavery labors in 1844 with the Liberty Party and spoke in almost every state of the North. In 1851 he removed to Syracuse where, in October of that year, he took an active part in the rescue of the negro fugitive Jerry. Fearing arrest, he fled to Canada where he became an agent of the Anti-Slavery Society of Canada. He organized branches of the society, lectured, and lent assistance to the numerous fugitives in Canada. In April 1853 he was sent to England to secure financial aid for the Canadian effort and with the help of a committee raised the sum of £1,200 in ten months.

He spoke at both the 1853 and 1854 meetings of the British and Foreign Anti-Slavery Society and delivered numerous other addresses during his stay in Great Britain. He attracted the interest of some of the nobility and met many of the leading philanthropists. His *Autobiography of a Fugitive Negro* (London, 1855), records that John Candler, of Chelmsford, a Quaker, presented him with fifty acres of land in the parish of St. George, Jamaica, and he apparently accepted the gift, for about 1855 he went to Jamaica and in Kingston became the pastor of a small body of Baptists. He continued in this post un-

til early in 1860 when he left Kingston and settled in St. George Parish. The new venture did not prosper and he died in great poverty in or after 1866. During his pastorate in Kingston he is said to have exercised a powerful influence over the colored population and was the head of a political party which controlled local elections. In 1866 he published in Jamaica his *Reflections Upon the Gordon Rebellion.* Ward's extraordinary oratorical ability is mentioned by a number of his contemporaries. He was frequently advertised during his lecture tours as "the black Daniel Webster."

[See Ward's *Autobiography*; W. J. Wilson, "A Leaf from my Scrap Book . . .," *Autographs for Freedom*, vol. II (1854), ed. by Julia Griffiths; *Jour. of Negro Hist.*, Oct. 1925; information from Mr. Frank Cundall, of the Institute of Jamaica, and from Lord Olivier.]
F. L.

WARD, THOMAS (June 8, 1807–Apr. 13, 1873), poet, playwright, and musician, was born in Newark, N. J., the son of Thomas Ward, a well-to-do and prominent citizen of that city, who was a representative in Congress, 1813–17. In 1823 he studied at the College of New Jersey (later Princeton) and, although official record is wanting, is supposed to have taken the degree of M.D. at Rutgers Medical College, New York City, founded in 1825 under the leadership of David Hosack and S. L. Mitchill [*qq.v.*]. He studied and traveled in Europe for a time, then returned to New York City to practise his profession for two or three years. But he had ample private means, and, finding himself more interested in "skirmishing with the muse" than in practising medicine, he was soon giving all his time to the literary and musical occupations of a wealthy amateur. His earliest book, published anonymously, was *A Month of Freedom, an American Poem* (1837), a descriptive-historical-moral effusion in blank verse concerned with a month's vacation spent traveling to Washington, the Catskills, Lake George, Niagara Falls, and elsewhere. It is full of Romantic clichés and drenched in Byronism, but has occasional felicities. Ward published a series of verse tales in the *Knickerbocker Magazine* under the pseudonym of "Flaccus," and in 1842 these and other fugitive verses were collected and published as *Passaic, a Group of Poems Touching That River: with Other Musings*, by Flaccus. The tales deal with legends of the Passaic Valley, and are somewhat less romantic than the earlier book; they are followed by "Musings" (first published in the *New York American*) and by shorter verses under the headings "Humorous," "Serious," "National," and "Satirical." It is thoroughly uninspired verse, but won some attention at the time. At the close of the Civil War Ward published a slender pamphlet called *War Lyrics* (1865), breathing fiery patriotism but a desire for reconciliation after victory.

Meanwhile he had married (evidently some years before the publication of *Passaic*) and had made his house on Forty-seventh Street just west of Fifth Avenue the scene of production for various amateur operettas performed for charity. For at least two of these Ward wrote both words and music. The earlier, *Flora, or the Gipsy's Frolic* (1858), was first produced by a company of wealthy amateurs at "Land's End," Huntington, L. I., on July 30, 1857. The next year it was published, and undoubtedly it was many times performed in the large hall which Ward constructed during the war to house his amateur theatricals in the Forty-seventh Street mansion. In 1869 was published Ward's second operetta, *The Fair Truant,* first produced there on May 2, 1867. In all it is said that forty or fifty of these entertainments were given between 1862 and 1872, producing some $40,000, all of which was devoted to charitable purposes. In 1860 Ward edited a book entitled *The Road Made Plain to Fortune for the Million.* In 1866 he read an original poem at the bi-centennial celebration of the founding of his native Newark (*Collections of the New Jersey Historical Society,* vol. VI, 1866, Supplement, pp. 59–74). His last literary labor was a centennial address, delivered before the New York Society Library in 1872. Ward had at least one child who grew to maturity, a daughter Kate, who married Theodorus Bailey Woolsey of New York City (*The New York Genealogical and Biographical Record,* vol. IV, 1873, p. 201).

[Besides the sources noted above, see R. W. Griswold, *The Poets and Poetry of America* (1874) ; E. A. and G. L. Duyckinck, *Cyc. of Am. Lit.,* vol. II (1875), pp. 294–95 ; C. N. Greenough, ed., *The Works of Edgar Allan Poe,* vol. V, 1914, pp. 242–55 ; and *N. Y. Times,* Apr. 14 (death notice), 17, 1873. The records of Princeton Univ. and Rutgers Medical Coll. have also been consulted.]   E. M. S.

WARD, THOMAS WREN (Nov. 20, 1786– Mar. 4, 1858), merchant, only son of William and Martha (Procter) Ward of Salem, Mass., and a descendant of Miles Ward, who was in Salem as early as 1639, played an important but unobtrusive part in the commercial life of the United States between 1830 and 1853. Born and reared in Salem, he married Lydia Gray on Nov. 13, 1810, of which union were born eight children. For some years he was a partner in the Boston importing and exporting house of Ropes & Ward. During a vacation trip to England in 1828 he visited his intimate friend, Joshua Bates

[*q.v.*], recently admitted to a partnership in Baring Brothers & Company, through which connection, two years later, Ward became the resident American agent of the London house.

As agent (1830–53) for the leading English firm financing the foreign trade of the United States, he held a position of considerable responsibility. The American business of the Barings, almost all of which passed through his hands, annually involved several millions of pounds sterling. He estimated that during his first three years as agent he had granted to American merchants credits, exclusive of bond operations, aggregating $50,000,000. His task was to maintain the personal relationship regarded as significant by English merchant-bankers in all phases of their business with the United States —selecting correspondents, granting credits, arranging for the transfer of shipping documents, collecting debts, negotiating loans, and reporting upon prevailing economic and political conditions. Perhaps Ward's most difficult task was that of attempting to prevent repudiation of bonded indebtedness by the states of Louisiana, Maryland, and Pennsylvania, the securities of which Baring Brothers & Company had sold to English investors.

He exercised a wide range of discretion in managing the affairs of the Barings. It was upon his initiative that Daniel Webster was retained as counsel for the firm, and in an effort to maintain peaceful relations between Great Britain and the United States Ward personally interviewed President Polk in 1845. Although the Barings recognized that his blunt honesty and conservatism caused some more speculative firms, particularly in New York, to regard him with disfavor, they considered him one of the "soundest" men in the United States, and gave him a large share of the credit for the firm's success in weathering the storm of 1837–42. Inasmuch as Baring Brothers & Company was the only one of the seven leading Anglo-American banking houses to pass through the crisis with unimpaired reputation and credit, Ward's accuracy in judging men and conditions must have been extraordinary.

He retired from active business life in 1853. Two of his sons, Samuel G. and John G. Ward, took over the agency, which was managed by the former alone after his brother's death in 1856. From 1828 to 1836 Ward was treasurer of the Boston Athenæum, and from 1830 to 1842 of Harvard. He bequeathed portions of his estate of $650,000 to both institutions as well as to the American Peace Society and the Boston Missionary Society.

[*Essex Inst. Hist. Colls.*, vol. V (1863); *Vital Records of Salem, Mass.* (6 vols., 1916–25); Baring Papers, Pub. Archives, Ottawa, Ont.; *Quinquennial Cat. Harvard Univ.* (1925); Barrett Wendell and others, *The Influence and Hist. of the Boston Athenaeum from 1807 to 1907* (1907); J. E. Semmes, *John H. B. Latrobe and His Times, 1803–1891* (1917); *Boston Daily Journal*, Mar. 5, 10, 1858.]   R. W. H.

WARD, WILLIAM HAYES (June 25, 1835–Aug. 28, 1916), publicist and orientalist, was born in Abington, Mass. A descendant of William Ward who settled in Sudbury, Mass., about 1638, he came of a family of Congregational ministers, his great-grandfather and grandfather having been pastors of the First Church, Plymouth, N. H., while his father, James Wilson Ward, was for twenty-one years pastor of the First Church, Abington. His mother was Hetta Lord Hayes, oldest daughter of Judge William Allen and Susan (Lord) Hayes of South Berwick, Me. When William was seven years old his mother died, and his care and education devolved largely on his father. Under his guidance William began the study of Hebrew at the age of six and was required to read through a Hebrew version of the Bible between the ages of six and nine; at nine he began the study of Greek and during the next three years was required to read the whole Bible through in Greek; at twelve he began the study of Latin and during the next three years read the Scriptures through again in that tongue. His father's library was rich in theological and philosophical works, which in his early teens William was encouraged to peruse.

For brief periods he attended various schools, a year being spent at Phillips Academy, Andover. At seventeen he entered Amherst College, where he was graduated in 1856. After teaching for a short time he studied at Union Theological Seminary, New York, and subsequently at the Yale Divinity School. For a few months he served as tutor at Beloit College, Wisconsin, and then went to Andover Theological Seminary, where he was graduated in 1859. He was licensed to preach in January of that year, and on Aug. 6 married Ellen Maria Dickinson of Sudbury, Mass., whose acquaintance he had made at Beloit. They had one child, Herbert Dickinson Ward [*q.v.*]. He and his wife offered themselves to the American Board of Commissioners for Foreign Missions, but were rejected because of the latter's delicate health. Accepted by the Congregational Home Missionary Society, however, they served two years at Oskaloosa, Kan., enduring many privations and hardships. Ward then resumed teaching, serving on the staff of Williston Academy, Easthampton, Mass., and on that of the Free Academy, Utica,

N. Y., and from 1865 to 1867 as professor of Latin and natural science at Ripon College, Wisconsin. In 1868 Henry C. Bowen [*q.v.*], proprietor of the *New York Independent*, offered him a position on the editorial staff of that paper, which he accepted, remaining associated therewith until his death. He served as associate editor, 1868–70; as superintending editor, 1870–96; as editor, 1896–1913; and as honorary editor, 1913–16. He continued his Biblical and oriental studies, the results of which appeared frequently in articles in his paper, and in learned journals of the day. In 1914 he moved from his Newark, N. J., residence to the ancestral home of the Hayes Family at South Berwick, Me. A carriage accident in 1915 paralyzed his arms, and from that time his strength failed until his death the following year.

The range of Ward's intellectual interest was wide. Throughout his life he read Latin and Greek at sight; he was well versed in astronomy and botany; to the Semitic languages he turned for his recreation. He devoted his days to editorial duties; his evenings to study. He followed the work of Rawlinson and others in deciphering the Assyrian inscriptions, and until the coming of Prof. David Gordon Lyon to Harvard in 1882 he was perhaps the only man in the United States who could read Assyrian. At its fiftieth anniversary, in 1876, he presented Amherst College with a translation of the Assyrian texts in its possession. Ultimately he limited his work in the oriental field to the study of Assyrian and Babylonian seals, regarding which he became the leading authority in the world. In addition to many articles on the subject, he published, *Cylinders and Other Ancient Oriental Seals in the Library of J. Pierpont Morgan* (1909) and *The Seal Cylinders of Western Asia* (1910), which became standard authorities. In 1879 President Charles Eliot offered him the chair of Semitic languages at Harvard, but, believing himself not sufficiently proficient in the grammar of classical Arabic, and regarding the editorial chair as offering a wider scope for his talents, he declined the offer. In the winter of 1884–85 he led the first American exploring expedition to Babylonia and surveyed various sites with a view of determining the best place for a later expedition to excavate. Guided by his results, the University of Pennsylvania uncovered ancient Nippur in 1888–1900. He was twice president of the American Oriental Society.

Great as was his eminence as an orientalist, it was equally great as a publicist. He possessed insight and sound judgment, wielded a facile pen, and wrote in a direct and simple, but flexible style. He discovered and encouraged budding poets, one of whom was Sidney Lanier, for whose *Poems* (1884) he wrote a memorial sketch. He was liberal in theology, irenic in temper, and possessed of a passion for righteousness in civic and national life. He was active in the organization of the Federal Council of Churches, and gave much time and labor to many other organizations. His last book, *What I Believe and Why* (1915), is as remarkable for its insight and constructive thinking as for the simplicity of its style.

[Charles Martyn, *The William Ward Geneal.* (1925); *Amherst Coll.: Biog. Record of Grads. and Non-Grads.* (1927); *Jour. of the Am. Oriental Soc.*, Dec. 1916; autobiog. material in *Independent*, June 28, 1915, June 19, 1916; *Independent*, Oct. 18, 1915, Sept. 11, 1916, Dec. 28, 1918; *Outlook*, Sept. 6, 1916; *Who's Who in America*, 1912–13; *N. Y. Times*, Aug. 29, 1916.]
G. A. B.

WARDEN, DAVID BAILIE (1772–Oct. 9, 1845), diplomat, author, book-collector, of Scottish ancestry, was born at Ballycastle, near Greyabbey, County Down, Ireland, eldest of three sons of Robert and Elizabeth (Bailie or Baillie) Warden. He received the degree of A.M. from the University of Glasgow in 1797, together with prizes for "the best historical and philosophical account of the Application of the Barometer to the mensuration of Heights" and for general proficiency in natural philosophy. In May 1797 he was licensed to preach by the Presbytery of Bangor. Being an ardent patriot, he became associated with the United Irishmen, accepting a colonel's commission in that organization and acting as a confidential agent. Arrested and offered the choice of standing trial or transporting himself forever from His Majesty's dominions, he emigrated to the United States in 1799. Shortly after his arrival he was offered a professorship of natural philosophy at Union College, Schenectady, N. Y., but was prevented from accepting by a previous agreement to act as principal of Columbia Academy at Kinderhook; on Aug. 1, 1801, he became principal tutor of the Kingston Academy, Ulster County, N. Y.

In 1804 he was admitted to citizenship and went to Paris as a private secretary to Gen. John Armstrong [*q.v.*], just appointed minister to France. In accordance with presidential instructions dated July 22, 1808, Armstrong designated him to act as consul *pro tempore*. In 1810, when Armstrong was succeeded by Joel Barlow [*q.v.*], Warden returned to the United States and secured appointment as consul at Paris and agent for prize causes, but he was removed from office June 10, 1814, ostensibly on the ground that during the interim between the death of Barlow and

the arrival of his successor, William H. Crawford [*q.v.*], Warden had assumed the character of consul general, with which he was not officially invested. Meanwhile he had published *An Enquiry Concerning the Intellectual and Moral Faculties and Literature of Negroes* (1810), translated from the French of B. H. Grégoire; and a treatise, *On the Origin, Nature, Progress, and Influence of Consular Establishments* (1813), which was translated into several different languages and freely quoted by the noted British jurist, Joseph Chitty, in his *Treatise on the Laws of Commerce and Manufactures* (1820).

The remainder of Warden's life was spent in France. In his retirement he never ceased to promote the interests of American citizens to the best of his abilities. He had taken with him collections of American plants, animals, and insects; and he now devoted a great part of his energies to attempts to disseminate information concerning America. To this end he published *A Chorographical and Statistical Description of the District of Columbia* (1816); *A Statistical, Political and Historical Account of the United States of North America* (3 vols., 1819), apparently intended as a complete reference work which should defend the democratic experiment by presenting the facts to speak for themselves; *Chronologie Historique de l'Amérique* (10 vols., 1826–44), published also as *L'Art de Vérifier les Dates*, vols. XXXII–XLI; *Bibliotheca Americo-Septentrionalis* (1820), a catalogue of one of his collections of books on America, which collection was purchased by S. A. Eliot and presented to Harvard College in 1823; *Recherches sur les Antiquités de l'Amérique Septentrionale* (1827); and *Bibliotheca Americana* (1831). A second collection which he made of books on America was acquired by the New York State Library in 1845. Both were especially rich in maps and plans of the battles of the American Revolution and in material relating to the Spanish explorations.

Warden was a member of the American Philosophical Society, of the Lyceum of Natural History, New York, and of numerous European societies. Among his correspondents were Thomas Jefferson, John Quincy Adams, Lafayette, Talleyrand, John Howard Payne, Jared Sparks, Nicholas Biddle, John Jacob Astor, Rembrandt Peale, Joseph C. Cabell, Anthony Morris, and Josiah Quincy.

[MSS., Md. Hist. Soc.; *Md. Hist. Mag.*, June–Sept. 1916; *Ulster Jour. of Archæol.*, Feb., Aug. 1907; *Northern Whig* (Belfast), May 12, 1846, Aug. 6, 1906; E. A. Collier, *A Hist. of Old Kinderhook* (1914); *Olde Ulster*, Nov., Dec. 1913; Marius Schoonmaker. *The Hist.*

of Kingston, N. Y. (1888); W. I. Addison, *A Roll of the Graduates of the Univ. of Glasgow* (1898); information as to certain facts from the Misses Alice and Ella Warden of Baltimore, Miss Sophia Warden of Newtownards, County Down, North Ireland, and Dr. W. T. Latimer and Francis Joseph Bigger of the *Ulster Jour. of Archæol.*]   H. H. F.

WARDEN, ROBERT BRUCE (Jan. 18, 1824–Dec. 3, 1888), jurist, author, the son of Robert Bruce Augustine and Catherine E. (Lewis) Warden, was born in Bardstown, Ky. In 1840 he began the study of law in Cincinnati. He served for five years as deputy clerk of the court of common pleas of Hamilton County, and in April 1845 was admitted to the bar. Meanwhile, on Oct. 15, 1843, he had married Catharine Eliza Kerdolff of Cincinnati. They had two sons and a daughter of their own and adopted a daughter of Warden's sister.

In 1851 Warden was elected one of the judges of the county court of common pleas and in 1853–55 was reporter of the state supreme court. A trial for murder by poisoning which he observed intimately during this period determined him to undertake a course of study at the Starling Medical College of Columbus; he later lectured at that college on the forensic doctrines of insanity, elaborating his ideas in a volume entitled *A Familiar Forensic View of Man and Law* (1860). Appointed judge of the supreme court of Ohio by Gov. William Medill to fill the vacancy created by the resignation of Chief Justice John A. Corwin, he took office early in 1855, but served on this bench only a few months before a popular election was held by which Joseph R. Swan was chosen to fill the office. Warden resumed the reportership for a time and then returned to practice, forming a partnership in Columbus with Otto Dresel. Toward the end of the Civil War he removed to Cincinnati and in 1873 to Washington, D. C. Here in 1877 he became a member of the board of health of the District of Columbia, by appointment of President Hayes, serving also as attorney of the board until its expiration. He then practised law in Washington for the rest of his life, in partnership with his son, Charles G. Warden.

In 1874 he published *An Account of the Private Life and Public Services of Salmon Portland Chase.* He was also the author of *A Voter's Version of the Life and Character of Stephen Arnold Douglas* (1860); *A System of American Authorities* (1870); *An Essay on the Law of Art* (1878); and *Law for All* (1878).

[W. A. Warden, *The Ancestors, Kin, and Descendants of John Warden and Narcissa (Davis) Warden* (1901); *The Biog. Annals of Ohio*, vol. II (1905); G. I. Reed, *Bench and Bar of Ohio* (1897), I, 24; C. T. Marshall, *A Hist. of the Courts and Lawyers of Ohio* (1934), I, 303–04; *Weekly Law Bulletin*, Dec. 10,

1888; *Cincinnati Commercial Gazette* and *Washington Post*, Dec. 4, 1888.]   R. C. M.

WARDER, JOHN ASTON (Jan. 19, 1812–July 14, 1883), physician, horticulturist, forester, was the son of Jeremiah and Ann (Aston) Warder, and a descendant of Willoughby Warder who came to Philadelphia in 1699. John's parents were members of the Society of Friends but he was never strictly orthodox in religion. Born in Philadelphia, he spent his boyhood in the suburbs of that city. His bent for nature study was fostered by his association with such men as John James Audubon, François Michaux, and Thomas Nuttall [qq.v.], who visited his father's home. In 1830 he moved with his parents to a farm near Springfield, Ohio, where he gained experience in agriculture and fruit growing. For his further education he returned to Philadelphia and graduated from the Jefferson Medical College in 1836. The following year he established his residence in Cincinnati, where he maintained his medical practice until 1855, when he moved to a farm near North Bend, Ohio. In 1839 he published *A Practical Treatise on Laryngeal Phthisis . . . and Diseases of the Voice,* a translation of the French treatise by Trousseau and Belloc.

His most notable work, however, was done outside the medical profession. He was greatly interested in various branches of science and was a member of the Cincinnati Astronomical Society, the Western Academy of Natural Sciences, and the Cincinnati Society of Natural History. In the fields of horticulture and forestry he was an industrious and practical worker. He was active in the Ohio Wine Growers' Association; was president of the Ohio Horticultural Society for many years; and served as secretary and as vice-president of the American Pomological Society, to the *Proceedings* of which he contributed articles on horticulture. From 1871 to 1876 he was a member of the Ohio State Board of Agriculture. Through his writings and editorial services, also, he made important contributions to horticulture. From 1850 to 1853 he edited the *Western Horticultural Review*, in which he first described the *Catalpa Speciosa*, not previously recognized as a distinct species. For a year (January–December 1854), with James W. Ward [q.v.], he conducted the *Horticultural Review and Botanical Magazine.* In addition to his editorial work, he contributed articles on systematic pomology and fruit culture to these and other publications, including the *American Journal of Horticulture.* He was one of the authors of the "Report of the Flax and Hemp Commission," prepared for the

United States government in 1865; he edited an edition of Du Breuil's *Vineyard Culture* (1867); and wrote *Hedges and Evergreens: A Complete Manual for the Cultivation, Pruning, and Management of All Plants Suitable for American Hedging* (1858) and *American Pomology: Apples* (1867).

Warder gave almost as much attention to forestry as he did to horticulture. In 1873 he was appointed United States commissioner to the International Exhibition in Vienna, and the official report on forests and forestry was prepared by him (*Report of the Commissioners*, 1876, vol. I). From its founding in 1875 he was president of the American Forestry Association until a few months previous to its absorption, in 1882, by the American Forestry Congress, of which he was one of the organizers. Shortly before his death the United States Department of Agriculture commissioned him to report on the forestry of the Northwestern states. He did much to foster landscape gardening and the beautification of parks and cemeteries. He married, in 1836, Elizabeth Bowne Haines of Philadelphia and was survived by four sons.

[L. H. Bailey, *Cyc. of Am. Horticulture* (1902), vol. IV; Henry Howe, *Hist. Colls. of Ohio* (1902, vol. I); *Commercial Gazette* (Cincinnati), July 18, 1883; H. A. Kelly and W. L. Burrage, *Am. Medic. Biogs.* (1920); *Proc. Am. Pomological Soc.*, 1852–83; *Proc. Am. Forestry Cong.*, 1882; *Am. Jour. of Forestry*, Aug. 1883; *Seventeenth Ann. Report of the Ohio State Horticultural Soc.* (1884); *Reports of the Ohio State Board of Agric.*, 1871–76, 1883.]   R. H. A.

WARDMAN, ERVIN (Dec. 25, 1865–Jan. 13, 1923), journalist, was born in Salt Lake City, Utah, but his parents, George and Mary Virginia (Ervin) Wardman, were from New England. He was educated at Phillips Academy, Exeter, N. H., and at Harvard, where he received the degree of A.B. in 1888. Joining the staff of the *New York Tribune*, he made his mark with his reports of the Johnstown flood (1889), and was soon assistant city editor. In 1895 he left the *Tribune* to become managing editor of the *New York Press*, and the next year was made editor-in-chief, a position he held with distinction until 1916, except for a few months spent at the front during the Spanish-American War, in which he served as a member of Troop A, United States Volunteers, as first lieutenant of the 202nd New York Infantry, and as aide-de-camp to Gen. John R. Brooke [*q.v.*] in the Puerto Rico campaign. After the war he resumed his work of making the *Press* an aggressive and effective organ of liberal Republicanism. It was he who, in the late 1890's, coined the term "yellow journalism" (*New York Tribune*, Jan. 14, 1923). His own editorial style was crisp and hard-hitting, though remarkably well informed. In 1905 a series of outspoken editorials concerning an alleged attempt to bribe state legislators resulted in Wardman's being summoned to Albany to explain the sources of his accusations. These he steadfastly refused to divulge on the score of newspaper ethics; his position was later supported by the courts.

During the last four years of Wardman's editorship of the *Press*, Frank A. Munsey [*q.v.*] was the owner. When Munsey bought the *Sun* in 1916 and merged the *Press* with it, E. P. Mitchell [*q.v.*], editor of the *Sun*, assumed editorship of the combined papers, and Wardman became publisher. This position he retained after Munsey bought the *Herald* in 1920 and merged the *Sun* with it. He continued to contribute editorials, however, and after Mitchell's retirement was again in charge of the editorial page. His ability as a business administrator was as marked as his ability as an editor, and Munsey is reported to have called him the best equipped man for his position in New York. He was a clean-cut New England type, "grim jawed" but with a glint of humor in his eye, and with a magnificent physique apparently untouched by the strain of his indefatigable industry. His interests were wide, but as an editorial writer his chief field was labor economics. He was chairman of the labor committee and a member of the arbitration committee of the Publishers' Association. When the United States entered the World War he originated the Sun Tobacco Fund, through which some $500,000 worth of tobacco was distributed among the soldiers. In spite of his vigorous forthrightness in controversy, he was much liked personally and showed his native generosity by many anonymous charities. When he died suddenly of pneumonia early in 1923 the Newspaper Editors' and Publishers' Association held a special memorial meeting and passed resolutions in which he is described as "a shining example of the truth, honor, independence, and integrity that are at the foundation of good journalism" (*New York Times*, Jan. 18, 1923).

Wardman was twice married: first, May 14, 1902, to Caroline Klink Eyre, of Washington, D. C., who died in 1908; second, Feb. 8, 1910, to Violet Boyer of Barrie, Ontario. He was survived by his second wife and by a son. For some years before his death he lived during most of the year at New Rochelle, N. Y., but maintained a country place at Sherbrooke, Canada. He was the author of one novel, *The Princess Olga*, which appeared in 1906.

[*Who's Who in America*, 1922–23; obituaries in *N. Y. Herald*, *N. Y. Tribune*, and *N. Y. Times*, Jan. 14, 1923; editorials in *N. Y. Times* and *N. Y. Herald*,

Jan. 15, 1923; *N. Y. Evening Post*, Jan. 15, 18, 1923; *Editor and Publisher*, Nov. 25, 1916; F. M. O'Brien, *The Story of the Sun* (1928).]   E. M. S.

WARE, ASHUR (Feb. 10, 1782–Sept. 10, 1873), editor, jurist, was born in Sherborn, Mass., the third of the five children of Joseph and Grace (Coolidge) Ware, and a descendant of Robert Ware who was in Dedham, Mass., as early as 1642. His father, a farmer who had lost an arm at the battle of White Plains, was in spite of his lack of a formal education an able surveyor, and was frequently called upon to teach in the town schools. He prepared his son for college with the aid of the local minister, and Ashur was graduated at Harvard in 1804. For a time he was assistant to Dr. Benjamin Abbot [*q.v.*] at Phillips Academy, Exeter, and later tutor in the family of his uncle Henry Ware [*q.v.*], a well-known Unitarian clergyman of Cambridge. At this period he was attracted toward the ministry, but a close study of doctrines led him to a liberal position, and this fact, since he was not a controversialist by nature, caused him to turn to other fields. From 1807 to 1811 he was tutor in Greek at Harvard, and from 1811 to 1815, professor of Greek. He then studied law in the office of Loammi Baldwin [*q.v.*] in Cambridge, and with his classmate, Joseph E. Smith of Boston.

He engaged less in legal practice than in politics, however. With Henry Orne he edited in Boston a Democratic paper called the *Yankee*. In 1817 he moved to Portland, in the District of Maine, partly because of the opportunities there for the practice of law, but mainly to edit the *Eastern Argus*, a paper then engaged in promoting the separation of Maine from Massachusetts. His reputation as a writer and orator continued to grow, and he was an active force both in Maine's "home rule" politics and in the Democratic party. When Maine was made a state in 1820, Ware became secretary of state. On Feb. 15, 1822, President Monroe appointed him judge of the United States district court in Maine. In spite of his lack of judicial experience, he made an exceptional record as a judge, and remained on the bench until 1866. American maritime law was still in its infancy and Ware, by close examination of British precedents and a study of French and Roman law in the original languages, became, in the opinion of Justice Story, perhaps the ablest American authority in this field (*Proceedings of the United States District Court, post*, p. 13). His sympathies were often with the seaman and his decisions, not always welcome to the masters and owners of vessels, did much to raise the standard

of life aboard ship. His opinions were collected and published in 1839 and 1849, and each publication went through a second edition. He contributed several articles to Bouvier's *Law Dictionary*.

From 1811 to 1844 he was a trustee of Bowdoin College. He served, also, as president of the Androscoggin & Kennebec Railroad Company, and was the first president of the Casco Bank (1825). Of the Maine Historical Society he was one of the incorporators. On June 20, 1831, he married, in Portland, Sarah Morgridge, who died June 30, 1870; they had four children.

[G. F. Talbot, in *Colls. and Proc. Me. Hist. Soc.*, 2 ser. VI (1890), and G. F. Emery, in *Ibid.*, 2 ser. VIII (1897); *Proc. of the U. S. District Court for Me. District; Commemorating the Services and Character of Hon. Ashur Ware* (1873); Abner Morse, *A Geneal. Reg. of the Descendants of the Early Planters of Sherborn, Holliston, and Medway, Mass.* (1855); William Willis, *A Hist. of the Law, the Courts, and the Lawyers of Me.* (1863); *Resolutions of the Cumberland Bar, and Address of U. S. District Attorney George F. Talbot on the Retirement of Judge Ware* (1866); E. F. Ware, *Ware Geneal.* (1901); *Eastern Argus* (Portland), Sept. 11, 1873.]   R. E. M.

WARE, EDMUND ASA (Dec. 22, 1837–Sept. 25, 1885), educator, the son of Asa Blake and Catharine (Slocum) Ware, was born in North Wrentham, Mass. He was a descendant of Robert Ware who came to the colony at Massachusetts Bay from England as early as 1642. He attended the Norwich Free Academy and was graduated from Yale College in 1863. He then spent two years teaching at the Norwich Academy and in 1865 went to Nashville to assist in organizing the schools of that city. In 1866 he went to Georgia under the auspices of the American Missionary Association as superintendent of schools for the Atlanta district. In December of this year he was licensed to preach by the Congregational Church, and in August 1867 was appointed superintendent of education for Georgia by Gen. Oliver O. Howard [*q.v.*], of the Freedmen's Bureau. On accepting this position Ware resigned his position with the American Missionary Association, but he retained his interest in its religious and educational work. It was from the Association that he obtained the first $25,000 for Atlanta University which, by resolution of its incorporators, should "never exclude loyal refugees and Freedmen" (Adams, *post*, p. 11). Of this institution Ware was one of the founders and the first president.

The University was chartered in 1867 and opened with a preparatory department in 1869. Normal and college departments were added within the next three years. In 1871 President Ware wrote in his report to the American Missionary Association, "two years ago the corner stone of our first building was laid. During the summer the building was completed. . . . A second building was erected last summer. . . . The whole number of pupils for the year has been 158. . . . Some have come from the Association's schools. Some have had little or no schooling. A large number were brought in by last year's pupils who taught during the summer" (*Twenty-fifth Annual Report*, 1871, pp. 39, 40). Ware was fortunate in beginning his task at a time when the altruistic zeal and moral fervor of the Abolition and missionary movements were at their height, but his own idealism and courage were weighty factors in accounting for the success of the University. He and his associates had profound faith in the mental and spiritual capacities of their students. No small part of President Ware's contribution was communicating that faith to the students themselves, and to the white Southerners who surrounded them. Joseph E. Brown, wartime governor of Georgia, signed a unanimous report of the Board of Visitors which stated in part: "At every step of the way we were impressed with the fallacy of the popular idea (which in common with thousands of others the undersigned have hitherto entertained) that members of the African race are not capable of a high grade of intellectual culture" (*Ibid.*, pp. 44, 45). Ware also understood that the students who flocked to Atlanta, ex-slaves or children of slaves, needed not only a school or college but also a home, and every effort was made to create social intercourse on a high level. In this work, he was associated with his Yale classmate, Horace Bumstead [*q.v.*].

Except for one year when illness necessitated his absence Ware retained the presidency and the active direction of the University until his death from heart disease. He was married, on Nov. 10, 1869, to Sarah Jane Twichell, of Plantsville, Conn. She, with their four children, survived him. A son, Edward Twichell Ware, became the third president of Atlanta University.

[E. F. Ware, *Ware Geneal.* (1901); *Hist. of the Class of 1863, Yale Coll.* (1905); *Obit. Record of Grads. of Yale Coll.*, 1886; M. W. Adams, *A Hist. of Atlanta Univ.* (1930); *Am. Missionary*, Nov. 1885; *Atlanta Constitution*, Sept. 26, 1885.] M. G.

WARE, HENRY (Apr. 1, 1764–July 12, 1845), clergyman, professor of theology, was born in Sherborn, Mass. He was a descendant of Robert Ware who was in Dedham, Mass., as early as 1642, and was the ninth of the ten children of John and Martha (Prentice) Ware. As a boy, he worked on his father's farm and attended the short winter terms of the country school. When he was fifteen his father died and because of the promise Henry had shown, both in mind

and character, his elder brothers decided that he should have the advantages of an education. Accordingly, he was put under the care of the parish minister, the Rev. Elijah Brown, who prepared him for college. In 1781 he entered Harvard, where, four years later, he was graduated, valedictorian of his class. He then took charge of the town school in Cambridge, and at the same time began a course of study with a view to preparing himself for the ministry. On his twenty-third birthday, in the town where he had grown up, he preached his first sermon, and on Oct. 24, 1787, he was ordained pastor of the First Parish Church, Hingham, Mass., succeeding in that office Dr. Ebenezer Gay [*q.v.*].

In this, his first and only pastorate, Ware remained eighteen years. On Mar. 31, 1789, he married Mary, daughter of the Rev. Jonas Clark [*q.v.*] of Lexington. His income of $450 a year proving inadequate for a steadily increasing family, he was "obliged to resort to the only means which seemed to be open to a country clergyman for supplying the deficiency of his salary, that of keeping boarders, and taking the charge of boys to fit for college." It proved, he said, "a very laborious and irksome life, and less profitable than it should have been" (Palfrey, *post*, p. 14). In spite of this handicap, he increased in knowledge and influence and rose to a place of distinction in his profession. Like his predecessor, Dr. Gay, he belonged to the liberal, or Unitarian, branch of the Congregational order, and after the death of Prof. David Tappan, Ware was chosen by the liberals on the board of Fellows of Harvard College as their candidate for the Hollis Professorship of Divinity, the opposing candidate being Dr. Jesse Appleton [*q.v.*]. Ware was nominated by the Fellows and, in spite of strong opposition from some of the Overseers, the nomination was confirmed on Feb. 14, 1805, and he was inaugurated on May 14.

This election, which marked a new era in the history of Congregationalism, gave rise to a memorable controversy between members of the liberal and orthodox parties. In its earlier years, Ware's participation in it was slight, but in 1820 he crossed swords with Dr. Leonard Woods, 1774–1854 [*q.v.*], by publishing that year *Letters Addressed to Trinitarians and Calvinists, Occasioned by Dr. Woods' Letters to Unitarians*. Woods made reply, and in 1822 Ware issued *Answer . . . in a Second Series of Letters Addressed to Trinitarians and Calvinists*, to which, the following year, he added, *A Postscript to the Second Series of Letters. . . .* Some one at the time called the argument the "Wood'n Ware Controversy," by which title it came to be generally known. Ware performed the duties of his office with ability and good judgment. In 1811 he began a course of special instruction for men preparing for the ministry, from which developed the divinity school, organized in 1816, with Ware as professor of systematic theology and evidences of Christianity. Twice, when the college was without a president, he served as administrative officer—in 1810 and in 1828–29. Because of the inconvenience resulting from a cataract on one of his eyes, he resigned the Hollis Professorship in 1840, but continued his work in the divinity school. An unsuccessful operation on his eye seriously weakened him. Before he was entirely incapacitated, however, he was able to arrange and publish some of his lectures under the title *An Inquiry into the Foundation, Evidences, and Truths of Religion* (1842). He died at Cambridge in his eighty-second year.

Ware was respected for his mental attainments and even more for the traits of character he exhibited. He was a man of simple tastes, extreme modesty, gentle disposition, and serenity of mind; yet he was fearless in maintaining his convictions. In the classroom he was noted for his candor, his fairness, and his distrust of ardent partisanship. As a preacher, a contemporary states, "he was too logical, sensible, moderate, and unimaginative," to appeal to all classes (A. B. Livermore, quoted in Eliot, *post*, p. 48). A number of his discourses—chiefly ordination and funeral sermons—were printed, among them one on the death of Washington and one on the death of John Adams. His first wife died July 5, 1805, and on Feb. 9, 1807, he married Mary, daughter of James Otis and widow of Benjamin Lincoln, Jr., who died eight days later; on Sept. 18 of the same year, he married Elizabeth, daughter of Nicholas Bowes of Boston. He was the father of nineteen children, ten by his first wife, and nine by the third. Among them were Henry, John, and William Ware [*qq.v.*]. John Fothergill Waterhouse Ware [*q.v.*] was a grandson.

[E. F. Ware, *Ware Geneal.* (1901); J. G. Palfrey, *A Discourse on the Life and Character of the Reverend Henry Ware, D.D., A.A.S.* (1846); W. B. Sprague, *Annals of the Am. Unitarian Pulpit* (1865); S. A. Eliot, *Heralds of a Liberal Faith* (1910), vol. II; Wm. Ware, *Am. Unitarian Biog.*, vol. I (1850); A. P. Peabody, *Harvard Reminiscences* (1888); *Boston Daily Advertiser*, July 16, 1845.]   H. E. S.

WARE, HENRY (Apr. 21, 1794–Sept. 22, 1843), Unitarian clergyman, son of Henry [*q.v.*] and Mary (Clark) Ware and brother of John and William Ware [*qq.v.*], was born in Hingham, Mass., where his father was pastor, and lived there until 1805, when the elder Henry became professor of divinity at Harvard. The son

received his early education in the schools of his native town and under tutors until 1807, in which year he was sent to Phillips Academy, Andover, Mass. The year following he entered Harvard College, from which he graduated in 1812. He was a somewhat frail, serious-minded youth, religiously inclined from childhood, mingling little in the social life of the college, but taking commendable rank as a scholar. From 1812 to 1814 he taught under Benjamin Abbot [*q.v.*] at Phillips Academy, Exeter, N. H., and then returned to Harvard to complete the preparation for the ministry which he had been carrying on privately. He had written some verse and at a public gathering held in 1815 after the signing of the Treaty of Ghent he delivered a poem, subsequently published under the title *A Poem Pronounced ... at the Celebration of Peace* (1815). On Jan. 1, 1817, he was ordained pastor of the Second Church (Unitarian), Boston, and in October of that year was married to Elizabeth Watson Waterhouse, daughter of Dr. Benjamin Waterhouse [*q.v.*] of Cambridge. John Fothergill Waterhouse Ware [*q.v.*] was his son.

Ware's life was comparatively short and ill health continually interfered with his activities. He was below medium height, thin, and stooping, and was careless as to his dress and personal appearance. His manner did not invite approach and few were on terms of intimacy with him. In spite of these handicaps, however, he became one of the leading ministers of New England, and his writings were widely read both in America and abroad. The whole purpose of his life was usefulness rather than high accomplishment, and into the various fields that he entered he put the full measure of his devotion. He succeeded Noah Worcester [*q.v.*] as editor of the *Christian Disciple* (1819–23), and in 1821 contributed articles, signed Artinius, to the *Christian Register*. In 1822 he projected Sunday evening services for those who had no stated places of worship, a missionary endeavor later carried on by the ministry-at-large. An advocate of preaching without manuscript, he published in 1824 *Hints on Extemporaneous Preaching*. He took a prominent part in the establishment of the American Unitarian Association, and was long a member of its executive committee. At the annual Phi Beta Kappa meeting at Harvard, Aug. 26, 1824, made memorable by the presence of Lafayette, he delivered a poem entitled "The Vision of Liberty." In 1823, one of his three children died, and in less than a year, his wife; on June 11, 1827, he married Mary Lovell Pickard (see E. B. Hall, *Memoir of Mary L. Ware*, 1853). To this marriage were born six children, one of whom was William Robert Ware [q.v.]. The condition of Ware's health led him to resign his pastorate in 1828, but his parishioners would not consent to a separation and the following year gave him a colleague in the person of Ralph Waldo Emerson. Meanwhile, he had been appointed first professor of pulpit eloquence and pastoral care in the Harvard Divinity School. After a seventeen-month sojourn in Europe, during which he visited Wordsworth, Southey, Maria Edgeworth, and other persons of note, he felt unable to carry on both pastoral and professorial duties and, relinquishing his parish, he moved to Cambridge.

During his career at Harvard, though in the latter part of it he took over much of his father's work, he found time for considerable writing. One of his works, *On the Formation of the Christian Character* (1831), went through some fifteen editions and was republished abroad. To provide young people with books suitable for Sunday reading, he projected "The Sunday Library," for which he wrote the first volume, *The Life of the Saviour* (1833). This also had wide circulation. Other publications included sermons, addresses, reviews, and memoirs of Joseph Priestley, Nathan Parker, and Noah Worcester. After his death *The Works of Henry Ware, Jr., D.D.* (4 vols., 1846–47), edited by Chandler Robbins, appeared. He was one of the organizers and the president of the Cambridge Anti-Slavery Society, and was subjected to severe criticism in the University and the papers for publicly espousing the abolitionist movement. Later his ardor cooled, for the impatience and intolerance of the abolitionists were repellent to one of his nature. Forced by failing strength to resign his professorship in 1842, he retired to Framingham, Mass., where he died in his forty-ninth year. His body was taken to Cambridge and was buried in Mount Auburn Cemetery.

[E. F. Ware, *Ware Geneal.* (1901); John Ware, *Memoir of the Life of Henry Ware, Jr.* (1846); W. B. Sprague, *Annals of the Am. Unitarian Pulpit* (1865); S. A. Eliot, *Heralds of a Liberal Faith*, vol. II (1910); *Proc. Mass. Hist. Soc.*, vol. II (1880); *Christian Examiner*, Nov. 1843, Mar. 1846.]   H. E. S.

WARE, JOHN (Dec. 19, 1795–Apr. 29, 1864), physician, editor, and educator, was born in Hingham, Mass. His father, Rev. Henry Ware, 1764–1845 [q.v.], was a minister and Hollis Professor of Theology at Harvard College; his mother was Mary, daughter of Rev. Jonas Clark [q.v.] of Lexington, Mass., and grand-daughter of the Rev. Thomas Hancock, also of Lexington. Two of Ware's brothers became ministers, Henry and William [qq.v.], while another brother, Charles, was a physician.

John entered Harvard College at the age of thirteen and was graduated in 1813. Three years later he received the degree of M.D. from the Harvard Medical School, and in 1814 began practice in Boston. He was poor, patients were few, and he turned his hand to other things besides medicine. For ten years he practised dentistry, kept school, took private scholars into his home, wrote for magazines, published a novel, gave popular lectures, and edited medical publications. The novel, *Charles Ashton* (1823), was issued anonymously; to the *North American Review* he contributed a poem (November 1817), a story (July 1818), and reviews of medical and scientific books. From 1823 to 1826, with John W. Webster and Daniel Treadwell [qq.v.], he issued the short-lived *Boston Journal of Philosophy and the Arts,* and in 1828, with Walter Channing [q.v.], edited the *Boston Medical and Surgical Journal.* During the period before recognition came to him as a teacher of medicine, he edited William Smellie's *Philosophy of Natural History* (1824) and William Paley's *Natural Theology* (1829). His chief medical contribution was an essay, *Remarks on the History and Treatment of Delirium Tremens* (1831), the result of the observations of nearly one hundred cases seen in the course of fourteen years. It was the first important work on the subject in America and ranks with Thomas Sutton's classic account of the same disease published in England in 1813.

James Jackson [q.v.], then Hersey Professor of the Theory and Practice of Physic at the Harvard Medical School, was the first to recognize Ware's worth as a teacher. He was put upon the staff of the school in 1832 as Jackson's associate, and when Jackson resigned in 1836 Ware succeeded him as Hersey Professor. At the school and the Massachusetts General Hospital Ware did his best work, a worthy successor to Jackson although a man of lesser caliber. In 1847 he published *Discourses on Medical Education and on the Medical Profession,* in which he made a strong appeal for the highest standards of medical education in an effort to combat irregular practitioners. He became interested, also, in the campaign for moral improvement and wrote *Hints to Young Men* (1850), which passed through many subsequent editions. His more strictly scientific papers include "Contributions to the History and Diagnosis of Croup" (*New England Quarterly Journal of Medicine and Surgery,* October 1842), and *On Hemoptysis as a Symptom* (1860). The former was based on observation of 131 cases, which he divided into classes, separating membranous croup or diphtheria from the others. He gave an excellent clinical description of this disease, but the paper was most valuable because of his effort to overcome the extreme type of treatment used at the time by other physicians. His work on hemoptysis, based on 386 cases observed over a period of forty years, pointed out the importance of this symptom in the early diagnosis of phthisis.

He was one of the founders of the Boston Society for Medical Improvement in 1839 and served as president of the Massachusetts Medical Society from 1848 to 1852. The lecture hall in the Boston Medical Library serves as a memorial to him. It contains his portrait as well as a bust by Bela Pratt [q.v.]. Ware's chief literary effort was *Memoir of the Life of Henry Ware, Jr.* (1846). His health failed some years before his death, but he lived to complete his *Philosophy of Natural History* (1860). The closing days of his life were saddened by the death of his son, Maj. Robert Ware, killed in battle in 1864. He was married, first, Apr. 22, 1822, to Helen, daughter of Levi and Desire Thaxter Lincoln of Hingham. She died in 1858, having borne him eight children. His second wife, Mary Green Chandler, of Petersham, Mass., whom he married Feb. 25, 1862, was an author. The death of Ware and his son in the same year was gracefully memorialized by Oliver Wendell Holmes in his poem, "In Memory of John and Robert Ware."

[E. F. Ware, *Ware Geneal.* (1901); *Proc. Am. Acad. Arts and Sci.*, May 24, 1864; T. F. Harrington, *The Harvard Medic. School* (1905); N. I. Bowditch, *A Hist. of the Mass. Gen. Hospital* (1872); J. W. Farlow, *The Hist. of the Boston Medic. Library* (1918); W. L. Burrage, *A Hist. of the Mass. Medic. Soc.* (1923); H. A. Kelly and W. L. Burrage, *Am. Medic. Biogs.* (1920); *Boston Daily Advertiser*, Apr. 30, May 2, 1864; *Boston Medic. and Surgic. Jour.*, May 5, 1864; notes from descendants and papers in the Boston Medical Library.]
H. R. V.

WARE, JOHN FOTHERGILL WATERHOUSE (Aug. 31, 1818–Feb. 26, 1881), Unitarian clergyman, was born in Boston, Mass., the son of Henry Ware, 1794–1843 [q.v.] and Elizabeth Watson (Waterhouse) Ware. William Robert Ware [q.v.] was his half-brother. Prepared for college in Cambridge, John graduated from Harvard in 1838, and would have been class poet, it is said, had not James Russell Lowell been in the same class. Entering the Harvard Divinity School, he finished the course there in 1842, and the following year became pastor of the Unitarian church in Fall River, Mass., remaining there until 1846. His next pastorate, which lasted until 1864, was at Cambridgeport, Mass.

During the Civil War, in an independent civil capacity, he rendered much service to the Union cause and especially to the soldiers themselves,

lecturing or giving patriotic talks in various parts of the country, visiting the men in the camps—often in army boots and slouch hat—and preparing tracts, which were published and circulated among the soldiers by the American Unitarian Society. In 1864 he was called to be minister of the First Independent Society of Baltimore. His congregation, made up originally of old Marylanders, was augmented by many new-comers attracted by the quality of his preaching. The two elements did not mix readily, and the more conservative members found Ware's independence and disregard of ministerial conventions not to their liking. Accordingly, after some three years, July 1867, he resigned. Some of his friends then formed a new religious organization, the Church of the Saviour, the services of which were held in the Masonic Temple. So large did the evening attendance become that the use of an opera house was secured, and even this was sometimes over-crowded. In the summer time he held open-air services in Druid Hill Park. He took great interest in the welfare of the freedmen, and had a leading part in establishing schools for colored children, which ultimately were taken over by the city. His activities in this field were carried on in the face of obstacles and at personal risk, necessitating at times his being attended by armed companions. While living in Baltimore he spent his summers at Swampscott, Mass., where he organized a church.

In July 1872 the condition of his health necessitated his returning North, and he became pastor of the Arlington Street Church, Boston, to which he ministered until his death. His preaching was direct and practical, more concerned with the problems of life than with those of theology. His interest was in men rather than in books, and his ruling ambition was to lessen the injustice and unhappiness of the world. A number of his sermons were printed separately and after his death some twenty-seven of them were published in a volume entitled *Wrestling and Waiting* (1882). Two of his books had wide circulation—*The Silent Pastor, or Consolations for the Sick* (1848) and *Home Life: What It Is and What It Needs* (1864). He was married on May 27, 1844, to Caroline Parsons, daughter of Nathan Rice of Cambridge; she died, Sept. 18, 1848, and on Oct. 10 of the following year he married Helen, daughter of Nathan Rice. By his first wife he had two children, and by his second, two. He died in Milton, Mass., after a year of comparative inactivity caused by a coronary affection.

[E. F. Ware, *Ware Geneal.* (1901); *Gen. Cat. of the Divinity School of Harvard Univ.* (1910); S. A. Eliot,

Heralds of a Liberal Faith (1910), vol. III; Boston Transcript, Feb. 28, 1881.] H. E. S.

WARE, NATHANIEL A. (d. 1854), author, public official, was born according to some accounts in Massachusetts and according to others in South Carolina, where as a young man he taught school and practised law. The date of his birth is also variously given as 1780 and 1789. About 1815 he removed to Natchez, Miss., where he married Sarah (Percy) Ellis, daughter of Capt. Charles Percy, of the British navy, an early settler in Louisiana. She lost her mind at the birth of her younger daughter and spent the remaining years of her life in an institution for the insane. Ware was a major of militia and made money in land speculation. He was the last secretary of the Territory of Mississippi, being appointed June 7, 1815, and serving until October 1817, when the first governor of the state took office. From April 1815 to May 1816, in the absence of the territorial governor, Ware was acting governor. He was the first to sign an address to the cotton planters, merchants, and bankers of the South in 1838, proposing a scheme for paper money based upon cotton, the cotton to be marketed through an agreement with English cotton manufacturers and the Bank of England. The banks had suspended specie payments, and the masses of notes in circulation were rapidly depreciating. In response to the address, a convention was held in Macon in 1839, but the scheme of cotton notes, like many other similar ones, came to nothing. Ware lived at different times in Philadelphia, Cincinnati, and Galveston. He was fond of travel and had a variety of intellectual interests, including botany and geology. His two daughters, born in Mississippi, Catherine Ann Warfield [q.v.] and Eleanor Percy Ware Lee, wrote poems and novels.

Ware is best remembered for his *Notes on Political Economy, as Applicable to the United States* (1844), signed "A Southern Planter." The title of the volume suggests the conviction of the nationalist American writers that the dogmas of the classical school of Europe did not suit the economic situation of a new continent with a rapidly increasing population. Ware had doubtless come to know Henry C. Carey [q.v.] in Philadelphia; at any rate the works of this leader of the American optimistic school are often echoed in Ware's work. From residence in the North and from his acquaintance with the natural sciences, Ware was much more alert to opportunities for balanced economic development than were other writers in the South. For him there was no rule except public expediency, and governed by this he moved on to the protectionist position, a course almost unique in a Mississippian of that period. The Malthusian principle of population, he thought, pointed to an undoubted tendency of the birth rate to outrun the means of subsistence, but by no means defined a limit of economic progress. Scientific agriculture, as proved by many instances which he cited, would indefinitely postpone the period of starvation. He grasped, more firmly than some others of his time, the fact that an improved standard of living would in itself lead to a reduced rate of population growth, pride becoming a grateful substitute for poverty in preventing Malthus' forebodings from being realized. The South at the time he wrote was more and more confining itself to staple agriculture, but Ware explained the virtues of a balanced economy, industry and commerce being joined to tillage of the soil.

He is described as "a handsome man . . . his complexion pure and fair as a young girl's, his cheeks freshly colored, his brow white as a lily, —a very venerable-looking man, with long, thin, white locks falling on his neck" (Tardy, *post*, pp. 26–27). He was "full of eccentricities. . . . His domestic trials rendered him bitter and outwardly morose, even to his friends. . . . He was a philosopher of the school of Voltaire, a fine scholar, with a pungent, acrid wit and cold sarcasm . . ." (*Ibid.*). He died near Galveston, Tex., of yellow fever.

[Dunbar Rowland, *Mississippi* (1907), vol. II, and *The Official and Statistical Reg. of the State of Miss.*, *1924–28* (n.d.); sketch of Catherine Ann Warfield, in M. T. Tardy, *Southland Writers* (1870), vol. I.]
B. M.

WARE, WILLIAM (Aug. 3, 1797–Feb. 19, 1852), Unitarian clergyman, writer, was born in Hingham, Mass., the son of Henry Ware, 1764–1845 [q.v.], and Mary (Clark) and a brother of Henry and John Ware [qq.v.]. When William was about eight years old, his father became Hollis Professor of Divinity at Harvard, and the boy was fitted for college, partly in Cambridge by his cousin, Ashur Ware [q.v.], and partly under the Rev. John Allyn of Duxbury. He graduated from Harvard in 1816, and then taught school, first in Hingham and later in Cambridge, at the same time pursuing studies in theology. On Dec. 18, 1821, he was ordained as pastor of the first Unitarian church to be established in New York City. After doing pioneer work there for nearly fifteen years, he resigned in October 1836.

Ware felt, and not without reason, that he was temperamentally unfitted for the work of the ministry. In the latter part of his life, moreover, he was afflicted with epilepsy. Accordingly, after leaving New York he held but two brief pastorates—at Waltham, Mass. (1837–38), and at West Cambridge (1844–45). His principal interests, aside from religion, were in literature and art. In March 1836 he began a series of articles in the *Knickerbocker Magazine,* which he published in 1837 under the title *Letters of Lucius M. Piso from Palmyra, to His Friend Marcus Curtius at Rome.* It portrays with considerable vividness life in the Roman Empire during the later days of Zenobia's reign, and subsequent editions were entitled *Zenobia: or, The Fall of Palmyra: An Historical Romance.* In 1838 he issued a sequel, *Probus: or, Rome in the Third Century,* published afterward under the title *Aurelian: or, Rome in the Third Century.* These works had deserved popularity at home and in England. Becoming proprietor of the *Christian Examiner* in 1839, he edited it from May of that year until January 1844. During this period he wrote *Julian: or, Scenes in Judea* (1841), depicting incidents in the life of Jesus, portions of which had appeared in the *Examiner.* This work, also, went through several editions. In 1848–49 Ware spent more than a year abroad, chiefly in Italy. Upon his return he delivered a course of lectures in several cities, which he published in 1851 under the title, *Sketches of European Capitals.* Another course, which he did not live to deliver, appeared in book form after his death— *Lectures on the Works and Genius of Washington Allston* (1852). He was the author of a memoir of Nathaniel Bacon in Jared Sparks's *Library of American Biography* (2nd ser. vol. III, 1844), and edited *American Unitarian Biography* (2 vols., 1850–51). On June 10, 1823, he was married to Mary, daughter of Dr. Benjamin Waterhouse [*q.v.*] of Cambridge, a sister of the wife of his brother Henry; they had seven children, four of whom survived their father. During the later years of his life he resided in Cambridge, where he died.

[E. F. Ware, *Ware Geneal.* (1901); W. B. Sprague, *Annals of the Am. Unitarian Pulpit* (1865); S. A. Eliot, *Heralds of a Liberal Faith,* vol. II (1910); *Christian Examiner,* May 1852; E. A. and G. L. Duyckinck, *Cyc. of Am. Lit.* (1875); *Boston Transcript,* Feb. 20, 1852.]
H. E. S.

WARE, WILLIAM ROBERT (May 27, 1832–June 9, 1915), architect and educator, the son of Henry Ware, 1794–1843 [*q.v.*], and Mary Lovell (Pickard) Ware, was born in Cambridge, Mass. He was a half-brother of John Fothergill Waterhouse Ware [*q.v.*]. He was educated first in Cambridge, then in Phillips Exeter Academy, and graduated from Harvard College in 1852. From 1852 to 1854 he was a tutor in private families in New York and then returned to Cambridge, where in 1856, after two years in the

Lawrence Scientific School, he received the degree of S.B. He first entered the office of Edward Clarke Cabot [*q.v.*] in Boston and later became one of the first pupils of the atelier which Richard Hunt [*q.v.*] had established in his New York office. In 1860 he began practice with an engineer, E. S. Philbrick. Three years later he formed a partnership with Henry Van Brunt [*q.v.*]. Their office in Boston for many years was among the foremost in the eastern states. Their work includes the First Church, Boston; the former union station, Worcester; the Episcopal Theological School, Cambridge; two dormitories, the alteration of the old university library (in which, for the first time, Henri Labrouste's ideas of stack construction were adapted to American use), and the famous Memorial Hall at Harvard. This work is largely under the influence of Ruskin and his English followers, with much use of picturesque details, horizontal lines, and polychrome masonry. The Memorial Hall has in addition big scale and a commendable simplicity of scheme.

During his early practice Ware had become more and more impressed with the chaotic character of architectural education. The old apprenticeship system had perished, and there was nothing to take its place. Between 1863 and 1865, therefore, he and Van Brunt established an atelier for students in their own office, adding to the customary design and drawing problems a certain amount of systematic instruction in construction, theory, and history. So successful was this experiment that in 1865 Ware was appointed head of a proposed architectural school in the Massachusetts Institute of Technology. In preparation he spent a little over a year in Europe, studying especially the architectural education of France and England. When he returned, he brought with him Eugène Létang to take charge of the work in design in the new school, thus establishing in America for the first time, the École des Beaux Arts system of training in design. In 1881 he was called to New York to found a school of architecture at Columbia University, at first, strangely enough, as a department under the School of Mines. Here he remained until his retirement as professor emeritus in 1903, after a severe breakdown the year before. He made extensive trips to Europe in 1883, and in 1889–90, and in 1903. At Columbia, as at the Massachusetts Institute of Technology, he devised a school which, while borrowing widely from the French system, was in no sense an imitation of it, but a new system, based on American needs and American conditions. The two schools exerted an enormous influence on other and younger schools throughout the country, so that Ware may be called the founder of American architectural education in a very real sense. Meanwhile he had not lost touch with the profession as a whole. Though he dissolved his partnership with Van Brunt when he left Boston, he was a member of the designing board of the Pan-American Exposition of 1900 and designed the buildings for the American School of Classical Studies at Athens. He served as architectural expert and adviser for many important architectural competitions. A member of the American Institute of Architects from 1859 and a fellow from 1864, he was extremely active in Institute matters. He never married. During his last twelve years he lived quietly at Milton, Mass., with his maiden sister Harriet, writing an important series of textbooks.

Ware's importance as an educator lies in his keen appreciation of the special problem of American architectural education. His ideals appear clearly as early as 1865 in a paper read before the Society of Arts of the Massachusetts Institute of Technology, *An Outline of a Course of Architectural Instruction* (1866), and are even clearer in a paper read two years later before the Royal Institute of British Architects, "On the Condition of Architecture and of Architectural Education in the United States" (*Sessional Papers of the Royal Institute of British Architects, 1866–67*). To him the architect was much more than a mere technician; he was also an artist, an exponent of a traditional cultural history, and a member of society as a whole. Thus he felt the French system too limited, too concerned with technique. In his lectures, characterized by a fascinating discursiveness, he emphasized continually the cultural, social, and creative side of architecture. He tried in every way to keep the student's mind broad and curious. For the development of the creative side, he borrowed from France the idea of teaching design by projects to be solved under criticism and by an unusual emphasis on freehand drawing. All of these ideas are still alive, vital parts of the American architectural tradition. To this wise teaching were added the charm and winning simplicity of his own benign personality, so well expressed in his appearance during his later years—his silky white hair and beard, and his gracious and gentle expression. He was the author of many pamphlets and articles in periodicals; *Greek Ornament* (1878); *Modern Perspective* (1883), a classic work; *The American Vignola* (2 vols., 1902–06); and *Shades and Shadows* (1912–13). He was an honorary member of the Royal Institute of British Architects and of the Société Centrale des Architectes Français, and a fellow of the American Academy of Arts and Sciences. There is an excellent portrait of him painted by Brewster Sewall in the Avery Library, Columbia University.

[Emma F. Ware, *The Ware Geneal.* (1901); *Who's Who in America,* 1914–15; Clara T. Evans, biog. in MS. in the Avery Lib., Columbia Univ.; Grace W. Edes, *Annals of the Harvard Class of 1852* (1922); Élie Brault, *Les Architectes par Leurs Oeuvres* (3 vols., 1892–93); *Final Report of the Building Committee . . . Harvard Memorial Fund* (1878); A. D. F. Hamlin, in *Jour. Am. Inst. of Architects,* Sept. 1915; obituary in *N. Y. Herald,* June 10, 1915, *Jour. Am. Inst. of Architects,* July 1915, and *Columbia Univ. Quart.,* Sept. 1915.]   T. F. H.

WARFIELD, BENJAMIN BRECKINRIDGE (Nov. 5, 1851–Feb. 16, 1921), clergyman, was born near Lexington, Ky. His father, William Warfield, a breeder of horses and cattle, was descended from Richard Warfield who settled in Maryland in the seventeenth century. His mother was Mary Cabell (Breckinridge) Warfield, the daughter of Robert J. Breckinridge [*q.v.*]. Prepared for college by private study, he graduated from the College of New Jersey (Princeton) in 1871. After a year of European travel, he became an editor of the *Farmer's Home Journal* of Lexington, attending particularly to matters of livestock. In 1876 he graduated from Princeton Theological Seminary. On May 8, 1875, he was licensed to preach by the Presbytery of Ebenezer, which ordained him on Apr. 26, 1879. On Aug. 3, 1876, he was married in Lexington to Annie Pearce Kinkead, who died on Nov. 19, 1915. In 1876, after graduation from Princeton he studied at the University of Leipzig, and the next winter was assistant minister in the First Presbyterian Church of Baltimore. After a year as instructor in New Testament subjects in Western Theological Seminary at Pittsburgh, he became professor in 1879. In 1887 he was called to be professor of theology in Princeton Seminary, in succession to Archibald A. Hodge [*q.v.*]. There he spent the rest of his life, teaching to the day of his death. He was the chief editor of the *Presbyterian and Reformed Review* from 1890 to 1903 and was a frequent contributor, as he was also to its successor the *Princeton Theological Review*. He published some twenty books on Biblical and theological subjects, besides pamphlets and addresses. This production he maintained by indefatigable intense study in New Testament criticism and interpretation, patristics, theology, especially that of the Reformed churches, and considerable fields of church history. By command of modern languages he kept constantly abreast of theological scholarship.

His work as teacher and writer was governed

by his enthusiastic committal to Calvinism, particularly as stated in the Westminster Confession of Faith, in which he saw "the final crystallization of the very essence of evangelical religion" (*The Significance of the Westminster Standards as a Creed* (1898), p. 36). He held unswervingly to the plenary inspiration of the Bible and was deeply persuaded of the truth of the doctrine of original sin. At Princeton he continued without concessions the theological tradition established by the Hodges. A vivacious teacher, expert in hand-to-hand argument, he moulded many students for a generation and thus influenced the thought of the Presbyterian and other churches. In his writings he was critical or interested in particular subjects rather than constructive or systematic. They contain valuable work in historical theology. His books included *An Introduction to the Textual Criticism of the New Testament* (1886), *The Gospel of the Incarnation* (1893), *The Lord of Glory* (1907), *The Plan of Salvation* (1915), and *Counterfeit Miracles* (1918). Under his will ten volumes composed of his most important articles in periodicals and encyclopedias were published, among them *Revelation and Inspiration* (1927), *Studies in Tertullian and Augustine* (1930), *Calvin and Calvinism* (1931), *The Westminster Assembly and Its Work* (1931), *Perfectionism* (2 vols., 1931–32).

[Necrological Report of Alumni Assoc. of Princeton Seminary, in *Princeton Theol. Seminary Bulletin*, August 1921; *Princeton Theol. Review*, April 1921, May 1921; *Who's Who in America*, 1920–21; Alexander Brown, *The Cabells and their Kin* (1895); J. D. Warfield, *The Warfields in Md.* (1898); p. 40; *N. Y. Times*, Feb. 18, 1921; information from his brother, Ethelbert D. Warfield, Chambersburg, Pa.]   R. H. N.

WARFIELD, CATHERINE ANN WARE (June 6, 1816–May 21, 1877), poet and novelist, was born in Natchez, Miss., the daughter of Nathaniel A. Ware [*q.v.*] and Sarah (Percy) Ellis Ware. Her mother lost her mind at the birth of a second daughter in 1820 and lived for the rest of her life away from home. Her father saw to it that his two daughters, Catherine and Eleanor, should benefit from the best possible tutoring at home. Then, possessed of sufficient means to indulge their desire for further study, he took them to Philadelphia, where they had superior cultural advantages and where they developed into shy and somewhat precocious "blue-stockings." In 1833 Catherine married in Cincinnati Robert Elisha Warfield, the first cousin once removed of Benjamin B. Warfield [*q.v.*] and the son of Elisha Warfield of Lexington, Ky., a physician who had made a fortune as a merchant and who was the owner of the noted horse, Lexington.

The young couple lived in Lexington uneventfully until 1844. In that year she published in collaboration with her sister, Eleanor Percy (Ware) Lee, a volume of verse, *The Wife of Leon, and Other Poems, by Two Sisters of the West*. Since this volume was welcomed with approval, the sisters followed it with *The Indian Chamber, and Other Poems* (1846). Both books were much praised at that time but have for the poetry lover of today no charm whatever, the lines being stilted in style and made colorless by the conventional sentimentalizing of the era. In 1857 the Warfields removed to "Beechmoor," their estate in the Pewee Valley near Louisville. There in comparative retirement she turned with great earnestness to the writing of fiction and produced with some rapidity a series of novels, the first of which was the two-volume *The Household of Bouverie* (1860). It was characteristic of her in its intensity of moral vision and purpose, but also, unfortunately, because of its cheerless pedantic style, its insistence upon rigid principles of conduct, and its quest for sensationalism. Almost unreadable today, this narrative of a hiding criminal who lived upon an elixir of gold won a large public and the approval of various literary critics. Subsequent novels were *The Romance of the Green Seal* (1866); *The Romance of Beauseincourt* (1867) later published as *Miriam's Memoirs* (1876); *Miriam Monfort* (1873); *A Double Wedding* (1875); *Hester Howard's Temptation* (1875); *Lady Ernestine* (1876); *Ferne Fleming* (1877); and *The Cardinal's Daughter* (1877). The struggle between North and South inspired her to return to verse, in which she showed her strong Confederate sympathies; some of this poetry was published in Emily V. Mason's *Southern Poems of the War* (1867). Prejudice against Northerners and their manners is also frankly revealed in her novels that appeared during the period of Reconstruction.

As a novelist her importance lies in her priority in the history of Southern letters rather than in any intrinsic value. She was one of the first woman novelists of consequence in the South. Obviously influenced by the Gothic romancers, by Walter Scott and Charlotte Brontë and Mrs. Henry Wood, she lacked their knowledge of life and their stylistic skill so that her stories sink under an overwrought emotional attitude and a ponderous diction. The best are the first one and those that deal with the life of Miriam Montfort.

[Mary Forrest, *Women of the South Distinguished in Literature* (1861); M. T. Tardy, *Southland Writers* (1870), vol. I; J. W. Townsend, *Ky. in Am. Letters* (1913), vol. I; *Lib. of Southern Literature*, vol. XII (1910), ed. by E. A. Alderman and J. C. Harris; "The

Meadows" in E. M. Simpson, *Bluegrass Houses* (1932); J. D. Warfield, *The Warfields of Md.* (1898), pp. 38, 39; Alexander Brown, *The Cabells and their Kin* (1895).]   G. C. K.

WARFIELD, SOLOMON DAVIES (Sept. 4, 1859–Oct. 24, 1927), financier, was born near Mount Washington, Md., the son of Henry Mactier and Anna (Emory) Warfield, and a descendant of Richard Warfield, who came from Berkshire, England, to Maryland in 1662. His father was prominent in the business and political life of Baltimore. After a common-school education, Solomon obtained a clerkship with George P. Frick & Company and later with D. J. Foley Brothers & Company, both of Baltimore. Forced by ill health to go to his grandmother's country home, he indulged his taste for invention and patented a number of devices, including corn cutters and corn silkers, and soon established in Baltimore the Warfield Manufacturing Company to make them.

Becoming active in politics, he organized a club to support Cleveland in 1888 and afterwards founded and became the president of the Jefferson Democratic Association, the largest independent Democratic organization in Maryland. In 1891 he was nominated by the Independent Democrats for mayor of Baltimore and was indorsed by the Republicans, but he was defeated by Ferdinand Latrobe in a close contest. In 1894 Cleveland appointed him postmaster of Baltimore. He gave the office a progressive business administration, extending the service and for the first time using street cars to transport mail. In spite of being a Democrat, he was reappointed by McKinley and served until 1905. While still postmaster he organized and became president of the Continental Trust Company (1898), which was to be the agency of his later extensive financial operations.

His chief interests were in railroads, public utilities, and cotton manufacturing. Railway consolidation in the South was then in progress, and in 1898 Warfield, with John Skelton Williams [*q.v.*] of Richmond, was a member of the organization committee of the Seaboard Air Line Railway. He became a voting trustee, a director, and a member of the executive committee of the company, but withdrew in 1903. The road having fallen into financial difficulties in the panic of 1907, Warfield was made chairman of the receivers, January 1908, and in two years returned the road to its owners without having assessed the stock or scaled down the bonds, its market value having increased meanwhile over twenty-five million dollars. Warfield became chairman of the executive committee of the reorganized

road and at the time of his death was president of the Seaboard, his management and extension of which were of great importance in the development of Florida. Through participation in the sale of the interest of Baltimore City in the Western Maryland Railway Company to the Gould syndicate, he was made a director of the Missouri Pacific. Fearing that the "duck trust" would move the old-established Maryland cotton duck mills to the South, he formed a local syndicate and became chairman of the board of the International Cotton Mills Corporation (1910), controlling many mills in Maryland and elsewhere. This venture, however, never proved successful; its promotional costs were excessive, and the general drift of the heavy goods industry was toward the cotton fields and the South's cheaper labor supply. Beginning in 1903, he formed a syndicate with a capital of eleven million dollars to purchase the United Electric Light & Power Company of Baltimore. His plans were interrupted by the great Baltimore fire of 1904, which destroyed the large building of the Continental Trust Company. He went to work immediately and secured millions of dollars for the rebuilding of the city. The control of the Consolidated Gas Company having passed to New York interests, he formed a syndicate which brought that control back to Baltimore. Later he joined this company and the only remaining independent electric company of the city with the United Electric Light & Power to form the Consolidated Gas, Electric Light & Power Company. He had long wanted to develop the power resources of the Susquehanna River; unable to do so, after the panic of 1907 he brought the McCall's Ferry current to Baltimore by sale of stock in the Consolidated to the Pennsylvania Water & Power Company. By intensive work he negotiated a contract in 1909 with the Standard Oil Company to bring natural gas to Baltimore from West Virginia. A large proportion of the patrons of the Consolidated thought the terms disadvantageous to them, and the board of estimates of the city would not approve the contract. A bill presented to the legislature to permit a popular referendum on whether the board should negotiate for natural gas was also defeated. The Maryland Public Service Commission was set up in 1910 as a consequence of this fight.

In 1910 Warfield retired from the chairmanship of the Consolidated Gas, Electric Light & Power Company to enter more actively into the development of the Seaboard Air Line, unaware of the tremendous strides which electricity was soon to make. He was director in a number of steamship, railroad, coal, and insurance companies. When the railroads were turned back to their stockholders by the government after the World War, he organized and was president of the National Association of Owners of Railroad Securities, and worked out the plan, incorporated into the Transportation Act of 1920, for equating earnings between strong and weak roads. He was a man of great nervous energy and drove both himself and his associates. Dominating and self-centered, secretive and often indirect in method, he was not lacking in social charm. He was unmarried.

[*Sun* (Baltimore) and *Baltimore American*, Oct. 25, 1927; D. H. Carroll and T. G. Boggs, *Men of Mark in Md.*, vol. III (1911); M. T. Copeland, *The Cotton Manufacturing Industry of the U. S.* (1912); J. J. Esch, *Address . . . on the Occasion of the Dinner . . . Dec. 13, 1920, Given in Honor of S. Davies Warfield* (n.d.); J. D. Warfield, *The Warfields of Md.* (1898); *Who's Who in America*, 1926–27.] B. M.

WARING, GEORGE EDWIN (July 4, 1833–Oct. 29, 1898), agriculturist, sanitary engineer, author, was born at Poundridge, N. Y., the son of George Edwin and Sarah (Burger) Waring and probably a descendant of Jonathan Waring, who came from Tipperary, Ireland, to Huntington, Long Island, in the eighteenth century. George went to school at College Hill, Poughkeepsie, and subsequently studied agricultural chemistry under James J. Mapes [*q.v.*]. The son of a farmer, he first directed his attention to scientific agriculture. In the winter of 1854–55 he gave lectures to farmers in Maine and Vermont, and for the next two years managed Horace Greeley's farm at Chappaqua, N. Y. In 1857 he was appointed drainage engineer of Central Park, New York City, a position he held four years. When the Civil War began, however, he became major of the Garibaldi Guards. He saw service for a short time with the Army of the Potomac and was then sent to St. Louis to recruit troops under Gen. John Charles Frémont. He raised six companies and early in 1862 was made colonel of the 4th Missouri Cavalry, United States Volunteers. He served until 1864, principally in the southwestern part of Missouri.

After the war Waring assumed management of the Ogden Farm near Newport, and remained there ten years. He then engaged in the sanitary drainage of houses and towns as a professional expert, attaining considerable success. The deplorably insanitary condition of Memphis, Tenn., and a series of yellow fever epidemics which culminated in 1878 in a visitation of that disease which cost 5,150 lives in a population of some 40,000, provided Waring with an opportunity to exhibit the ingenuity and daring which char-

acterized him. Following the recommendations of a committee of the National Board of Health, of which he was a member, he installed a system of sewers which was unique in several particulars, not the least of which was cheapness. The pipes were much smaller than customary, were for house sewage only, without manholes, well ventilated, and were flushed every twenty-four hours by means of automatic flush tanks. The Memphis sewers were long a subject of controversy among engineers and Waring was compelled by his experience to modify his opinion with regard to some of their features.

In 1879 he served as special agent for the Tenth Census, in charge of social statistics of cities. His *Report* on that subject appeared in 1886. Appointed street-cleaning commissioner of New York City by Mayor William L. Strong [*q.v.*], he took office Jan. 15, 1895, and continued therein until Jan. 1, 1898. Waring found the department inefficient, badly equipped, and riddled with politics. His efforts to improve it at first met with public ridicule, but in a short time he raised the organization to a high plane of efficiency and was warmly applauded by the whole city. He introduced the three-part separation of refuse at the household—garbage, ashes, and rubbish—to facilitate final disposition; he bought new carts and horses; and he put the sweepers in white uniforms—"not," as he said, "to clean dirty streets but to keep clean streets clean"; he insisted on having "a man instead of a voter at the other end of the broom-handle."

In 1898 Waring went to Havana to collect data for a report to the United States government on the measures it was necessary to employ in order to make that city sanitary and free from yellow fever. He contracted yellow fever and died soon after returning to New York City. His report was completed and submitted to President McKinley by his assistant and executor, G. Everett Hill. A memorial service was held in Cooper Union, at which several distinguished persons made addresses. A permanent memorial to him was created when the Chamber of Commerce of the State of New York raised by public subscription $100,000, the interest on which was to be paid to his widow and daughter during their lifetime. At their death the principal was to be turned over to Columbia University to constitute the Waring Memorial Fund for instruction in municipal affairs. He was married three times: first, Feb. 22, 1855, to Euphemia Johnston Blunt; second, Dec. 27, 1865, to Virginia Clark; and third, July 20, 1898, to Mrs. Louise E. Yates, of New Orleans.

Waring was a prolific writer. Among his best-known books and pamphlets are *The Elements of Agriculture* (1854); *The Handybook of Husbandry: A Guide for Farmers, Young and Old* (1870); *Whip and Spur* (1875); *A Farmer's Vacation* (1876); *The Sanitary Drainage of Houses and Towns* (1876); *The Sewerage of Memphis* (London, 1881); *Report of the Department of Street Cleaning of the City of New York for 1895–'96–'97* (1898); *Street Cleaning and the Disposal of a City's Wastes* (1897); as well as two delightful volumes entitled *The Bride of the Rhine* (1878) and *Tyrol and the Skirt of the Alps* (1880). The sketch entitled "The Garibaldi Guard" in *The First Book of the Author's Club: Liber Scriptorum* (1893) was written by Waring.

[R. N. Waring, *A Short Hist. of the Warings* (1898); Albert Shaw, *Life of Col. Geo. E. Waring, Jr.* (1899); *Charities Rev.*, Dec. 1898; *Rev. of Reviews*, (N. Y.), Dec. 1898; *Nation* (N. Y.), Nov. 3, 1898; *N. Y. Tribune*, Oct. 30, Nov. 7, 23, 1898; *N. Y. Times*, Oct. 30, 1898; *Evening Post* (N. Y.), Oct. 29, editorial, Oct. 31, 1898; information as to certain facts from Waring's son, Guy Waring, and from G. E. Hill.]

G. A. S.

WARMAN, CY (June 22, 1855–Apr. 7, 1914), journalist, author, was born near Greenup, Ill., the son of John and Nancy (Askew) Warman. He was educated in the common schools, and for a time was a farmer and wheat broker at Pocahontas, Ill. In 1880 he went to Colorado, where he worked in the railroad yards at Salida, and was successively locomotive fireman and engineer for the Denver & Rio Grande Railroad. Forced by poor health to give up railroading, he went to Denver to enter journalism and in 1888 became editor of the semi-monthly paper *Western Railway*. In 1892 he started a paper called the *Chronicle* at the new silver mines of Creede, Colo. Meanwhile, both as railway worker and as journalist, he had been writing verses inspired by the grandeur of the Colorado mountains. In 1891 one of these pleasant, facile little poems, "The Canyon of the Grand," won a prize, and in 1892 Warman published a slender volume entitled *Mountain Melodies,* thousands of copies of which were sold on the trains of the Denver & Rio Grande. On Sept. 4 of that year Charles A. Dana [*q.v.*], editor of the New York *Sun,* published a group of Warman's verses in his paper. One of these lyrics, "Sweet Marie," was set to music by Raymond Moore and a million copies were sold in six months. Other popular songs followed, for which Warman sometimes wrote the airs himself.

The silver boom at Creede having collapsed, Warman went to New York City in 1893 to enjoy his celebrity. About this time, seeing in *McClure's Magazine* a railroad story by a man who clearly did not know railroading, he offered to ride a thousand miles in a locomotive cab and give his story to the magazine free if it were not "the best ever." He thereupon rode from New York to Chicago in the engineer's cab of a New York Central flyer and dictated the outline of his tale, "A Thousand-Mile Ride on the Engine of the Swiftest Train in the World" (*McClure's Magazine,* January 1894), immediately upon arrival. The resounding success of this story having opened to him the pages of periodicals both American and English, Warman now produced a long series of short stories and novels depicting the romance and adventure of the frontier and in particular of the spanning of the continent by the trail of the "iron horse." These tales, which have the authenticity of first-hand knowledge and yet belong definitely to the romantic tradition of frontier literature, were collected in a series of volumes: *Tales of an Engineer with Rhymes of the Rail* (1895); *The Express Messenger and Other Tales of the Rail* (1897); *Frontier Stories* (1898); *The White Mail* (1899); *Snow on the Headlight; A Story of the Great Burlington Strike* (1899); *Short Rails* (1900); *The Last Spike and Other Railroad Stories* (1906); *Weiga of Temagami and Other Indian Tales* (1908). He published also a history of American railroad enterprise, *The Story of the Railroad* (1898), and another volume of verse, *Songs of Cy Warman* (1911).

Warman stayed only a few months in New York. For two years he traveled in Europe and the Orient, and for two more he lived in Washington, D. C. He then built a house at London, Ont., which was his home for the rest of his days. He was twice married: first, 1879, to Ida Blanch Hays, of St. Jacobs, Ill., who died in 1887; second, May 17, 1892, to Myrtle Marie Jones, the inspiration of the song "Sweet Marie," whom he met at Salida and married at Denver. Warman died in a Chicago hospital.

[*Who's Who in America,* 1914–15; *N. Y. Times, N. Y. Tribune,* and *Sun* (N. Y.), Apr. 8, 1914; *Literary Digest,* Apr. 25, 1914; Eugene Parsons, "Cy Warman, Bard of the Rockies," in *Interludes,* Summer 1931.]

E. M. S.

WARMOTH, HENRY CLAY (May 9, 1842–Sept. 30, 1931), Union soldier, lawyer, governor of Louisiana, was descended from a family of Dutch extraction which had wandered from Virginia through Kentucky and Tennessee to Illinois. Son of Isaac Sanders and Eleanor (Lane) Warmoth, he first saw the light in a log cabin in MacLeansboro, Ill. His formal education was limited to that received in the village schools and to the training which he was able to pick up as a typesetter in a local printing office. After his father became justice of the peace at Fairfield, the reading of his law books and association with members of the bar inspired the youth with ambition to become a lawyer, and at the age of eighteen he was admitted to the bar at Lebanon, Mo. The outbreak of the Civil War the following year found him established as district attorney of the eighteenth judicial district, which post he relinquished in 1862 to join the Union forces as lieutenant-colonel of the 32nd Missouri Volunteers. After the capture of Arkansas Post he was assigned to the staff of Maj.-Gen. John A. McClernand [*q.v.*] and participated in the battles around Vicksburg, where he was wounded and furloughed. Charged with circulating exaggerations of Union losses, he was dishonorably discharged but was restored through personal appeal to President Lincoln. After the victory of Lookout Mountain and Banks's Texas campaign, he was assigned, in June 1864, as judge of the provost court for the Department of the Gulf, and when this service was ended he found himself, because of consolidations, without a command.

He thereupon opened a law office in New Orleans early in 1865 and soon won a lucrative practice before military commissions and government departments. In November of that year he was elected as "territorial delegate" to Congress by Louisiana Unionists but was denied a seat. In September 1866 he was a delegate to a special convention of Southern loyalists in Philadelphia called to demand protection for the Union men of the South. With a group including former Gov. Andrew J. Hamilton [*q.v.*] of Texas he made a canvas of the Northern states in behalf of the congressional program of reconstruction. In the Republican state convention of 1868 the sentiment in favor of his nomination for the governorship was so strong that the constitutional limitation on age was removed to permit him to become a candidate. The nomination was not without opposition, for he defeated his negro rival by only two votes, and a colored faction withdrew its support in the subsequent election. Warmoth was successful, however, and was reëlected in 1870. His gubernatorial term (1868–72) was characterized by discontent, turbulence, a wild orgy of speculation in state-aided railroads, a depleted treasury, and bitter strife over the question of negro suffrage. Although he signed the bill which opened the restaurants, schools, and railroad coaches to negroes without discrimination, he later vetoed a more radical measure and declared his purpose to harmonize the interests of races and to secure justice for

both. Probably, as he claimed late in life, corruption and extravagance would have been worse except for his opposition. Nevertheless, toward the close of his administration he was under attack from three quarters: from white conservatives, from radical Republican negroes—who denounced him as a traitor—and from the so-called Custom-House faction of the Republican party. By 1872 he had become utterly unavailable for renomination, and in consequence he actively supported the Democratic ticket. In the violent disturbances resulting from an election which culminated in two governors and two legislatures, he became, naturally, deeply involved. He was impeached by the hostile legislature in December 1872 and the trial dragged on until it was dropped some weeks after his term had expired. Many years later he published his own account of this stormy period, *War, Politics, and Reconstrnction* (1930).

Although after 1872 he retired from active party politics, he participated at intervals in political affairs. In 1876–77 he was a member of the Louisiana legislature; in 1879 he served in the state constitutional convention; in 1888 he again headed the Republican state ticket, but, though he made the strongest campaign of his career, was defeated; in 1896 he went to St. Louis to help nominate McKinley for president. He was appointed collector of customs for New Orleans in 1890 by President Harrison and served until 1893, when Cleveland replaced him by a Democrat.

In 1873 Warmoth engaged in sugar planting at "Magnolia Plantation," just below New Orleans. He helped to organize a sugar refining company, and to build a railroad which greatly advanced the development of the west bank of the lower Mississippi. He contributed significantly to the advancement of sugar-refining until it was no longer possible to compete with the foreign product, whereupon he sold his plantation and retired to live quietly in New Orleans. In 1884 he had made a trip to France and Germany to study the sugar industry and upon his return secured the establishment of an experiment station on his plantation. When the Sugar Planters Organization determined to fight for a higher duty and for a bounty, he was selected to conduct what proved a successful struggle. During his long life after the bitter era of Reconstruction he overcame much of the antagonism against him, and hundreds who had earlier opposed him gathered to do him honor at his funeral. He was survived by his wife, Sallie Durand of Newark, N. J., whom he had married May 30, 1877, and by two sons and a daughter.

[In addition to Warmoth's book, mentioned above, see: *Who's Who in America*, 1916–17; Mrs. E. S. du Fossat, *Biog. Sketches of Louisiana's Govs.* (1885); Arthur Meynier, *Meynier's La. Biogs.*, pt. 1 (1882); J. R. Ficklen, *Hist. of Reconstruction in La., through 1868* (1910); Ella Lonn, *Reconstruction in La. after 1868* (1918); *Times-Picayune* (New Orleans), Oct. 1, 1931.]　　　　　　　　　　　　　　E. L.

WARNER, ADONIRAM JUDSON (Jan. 13, 1834–Aug. 12, 1910), soldier, congressman, bimetallist leader, and promoter of industrial enterprises, was a descendant of John Warner, who came to America on board the *Increase* in 1635, soon afterward settled in Hartford, Conn., and later moved to Farmington. Adoniram was born in Wales, Erie County, N. Y., the son of Levi and Hepsibah (Dickinson) Warner. When he was eleven the family went West, settling at Lake Geneva, Wis. Both parents died before he was sixteen. He attended Beloit College for a term, and in 1853 entered New York Central College, at McGrawville. On Apr. 5, 1856, he married a classmate, Susan Elizabeth Butts, by whom he had nine children. After teaching and serving as superintendent of schools in Mifflin County, Pa., he took charge of a school at Mercer.

At the outbreak of the Civil War he was instrumental in organizing the Mercer Rifles, which became Company G of the 10th Pennsylvania Reserves, of which he was made captain. He served in the Army of the Potomac until wounded at Antietam, rising to the rank of colonel. Declared unfit for active service, he was transferred to the Veteran Reserve Corps late in 1863, and stationed at Camp Morton, Indianapolis, being brevetted brigadier-general, Mar. 13, 1865, for gallant and meritorious service during the war. He read law while still in service, and was admitted to the bar of Marion County, Ind., Oct. 2, 1865, but never practised. He resigned from the army Nov. 17, 1865, and soon thereafter went to Marietta, Ohio. He became a member of the firm of Gates, Skinner & Company, operating in the oil fields of southeastern Ohio and West Virginia, and also bought and developed coal lands. To facilitate the marketing of the coal he built two railroads, the Marietta & Cleveland, running from Marietta to Canal Dover, and, some twenty years later, the Walhonding road, serving the district around Cambridge, Ohio. A still later project of his was the U Street trolley line in Washington, D. C.

Soon after the "demonetization" of silver in 1873, convinced of the injustice and folly of the action, Warner placed himself in the forefront of the denunciators. In 1877 he published a tract of ninety-three pages, *The Appreciation of Money: Its Effects on Debts, Industry, and National Wealth.* The following year, after a hotly contested campaign, he won a seat as a Democrat in the Forty-sixth Congress. In each of the three sessions of this Congress he guided a free-coinage bill through the House, but it was as regularly defeated in the Senate. He failed of reëlection to the Forty-seventh Congress, but was elected to the Forty-eighth and the Forty-ninth. The silver agitation had by this time spent its force, and he was not prominent in his second and third terms.

While the silver question was in abeyance, he appears to have carried on correspondence with economists at home and abroad. He attended the First National Silver Convention held in St. Louis in November 1889, and was made its permanent chairman and chairman of a national silver committee. In the latter capacity he called the Second National Silver Convention in 1892, and he became the president of the American Bimetallic League which was there organized. He was now unquestionably the leading figure in the organized silver movement. He supervised the general activity of the League, made speeches, wrote tracts, and conducted three national conventions in 1893 and one in 1894. During the summer of 1895 he made an extended speaking tour with Joseph Sibley [*q.v.*], potential candidate for the presidency of the American Bimetallic Party, which the League was trying to launch. Late in 1895 he acted as the agent for the League in negotiations which led to its consolidation with the National Bimetallic Union and the formation of the American Bimetallic Union, of which he assumed the presidency. Throughout the spring of 1896 the Union, under Warner's supervision, continued its propaganda unabated, and tried to influence the Democrats to nominate Henry Teller [*q.v.*] for the presidency. It gave its full indorsement to Bryan's candidacy, however, and Warner and his associates took an active part in the campaign. In 1899 he delivered an address at a bimetallic conference in Chicago, still maintaining that the only permanent solution to the monetary question lay in bimetalism.

His last years were spent in industrial activities, for the most part in Georgia. He organized the Gainesville Railway Company, which provided the city with a trolley line, and the North Georgia Power Company, which built fifty-three miles of steel towers from Gainesville to Atlanta, the first in the South. The panic of 1907 seriously undermined his companies and he sold out, retiring early in 1910 to Marietta, where he died.

Warner was well over six feet tall and of commanding appearance. As an orator he was not at his best, but he could hold the attention of an audience by his logical, convincing manner. He was essentially a pioneer in spirit, enjoying nothing better than to break ground, but losing interest in a project once it was well launched. His vision was boundless, and he had many ideas which he was unable to carry through. There is no evidence to show that he received any remuneration for his services to the Bimetallic League or Union, other than expenses. He enjoyed an uphill fight, and, convinced of the logic and justice of an enterprise, he was willing to give his whole energy to promoting it.

[C. O. Warner, *Geneal. of the Descendants of Omri Warner and . . . Hist. of Milo Warner and His Family* (1916); *Daily Register-Leader* (Marietta), Apr. 12, 1911; *Daily Times* (Marietta), Aug. 13, 1910; *Cincinnati Enquirer*, Aug. 14, 1910; pamphlets in Wis. Hist. Soc.; Beman Gates, *Letters from Europe, 1868* (1927); J. F. Brennan, *A Biog. Cyc. . . . of Ohio* (1879); *Biog. Dir. Am. Congress* (1928); *Who's Who in America*, 1910–11; MSS. in possession of Warner's daughter.]

M. S.

WARNER, AMOS GRISWOLD (Dec. 21, 1861–Jan. 17, 1900), sociologist, was born at Elkader, Iowa, the posthumous son of Amos Warner, a country physician, who was killed in an accident, and of Esther (Carter) Warner. The latter was a woman of exceptional intelligence and strength of character, actively interested in temperance, woman's suffrage, and other social movements of the day. In 1864 she moved with her four children to Roca, a village near Lincoln, in the Territory of Nebraska. Amos attended country schools until he entered the preparatory department of the University of Nebraska in 1878. Exceptionally well-read, highly intelligent, and full of enthusiasm, he soon became a leader in student affairs. He had an epigrammatic humor which ever afterward gave a pungent flavor to his speaking and writing. He was graduated with the degree of A.B. in 1885.

Entering the Johns Hopkins University for graduate study in economics and the social sciences, he at once attracted attention by his creativeness and his instinct for reality, and was granted a fellowship. Early in 1887 he delivered a speech on social problems at the church attended by John Glenn, the Maryland philanthropist. Through Glenn's influence he was appointed general secretary of the Charity Organization Society of Baltimore, in which position he served while completing his graduate work. In 1888 he received the degree of Ph.D., and that same year, Sept. 5, he married Cora Ellen Fisher, a graduate of the University of Nebraska. In 1889 Warner became associate professor of economics at his alma mater, where his course in the scientific study of industrial corporations was probably the

first in this subject offered in an American university. In February 1891, President Harrison appointed him superintendent of charities for the District of Columbia. The charitable institutions of the District were then in a chaotic condition, but in two years Warner succeeded in organizing an admirable system and in inducing Congress to found a board of children's guardians.

In 1893 he became professor of economics and social science at Leland Stanford Junior University, accepting the position because the institution had just received as a gift the Hopkins Railway Library. He was especially interested in railway problems and visualized a new department which should include not only economic and financial problems but engineering and administrative questions as well. The following year, in addition to a heavy teaching program, he wrote in less than two months *American Charities*, a book of 407 pages, which became a classic in the field of applied sociology, a fourth edition being published in 1930. It was almost the first book of its kind and for many years was accepted as the best.

Warner had inherited enormous vitality and a fairly strong physique, but ten years of research, organizing and administrative labor, and teaching had seriously undermined it. During the Western railway strike of 1893 he was obliged to travel at night on the open deck of a Sacramento River steamer and contracted a violent cold. This developed into tuberculosis, which compelled him to take a leave of absence from Stanford University, in November 1894, and to spend five years in exile in the Southwest. His mental vigor, however, enabled him to continue the social-economic editorials which he had been writing for the *Real Estate Record and Builders Guide* of New York. In 1897, in a brief period of improved health, he returned to Stanford and delivered before the Chapel Union four addresses based on social science, which revealed his broad religious point of view and his spiritual power. These were published after his death under the title *Lay Sermons by Amos Griswold Warner* (1904). Unable to take up teaching again, he returned to the desert and died at Las Cruces, N. Mex., survived by his wife, a son, and a daughter.

In addition to more than a hundred editorials he wrote numerous addresses and articles, many of which are fundamentally valuable in the history of social economics in America. He spoke and wrote clear, vivid, fluent English, enlivened by quaint humor and practical illustrations. He had a pioneering mind, which seized upon essentials. In teaching he was not a drill-master, desiring that his students get ideas and attack practical social problems, rather than depend upon theoretical textbooks. His reputation in the field of applied sociology must rest chiefly on his *American Charities,* which marked the high achievement of his young manhood.

[Biog. prefaces by G. E. Howard to the second (1908) and third (1919) editions of *American Charities,* and to *Lay Sermons*; Edward Ross, in *Charities Rev.,* Mar. 1900; *Who's Who in America,* 1899–1900; family papers in the possession of Warner's daughter, Esther Warner Kellenbarger.]   M. R. C.

WARNER, ANNA BARTLETT (Aug. 31, 1827–Jan. 22, 1915), novelist and author of children's books, was the daughter of Henry Whiting and Anna (Bartlett) Warner, and was descended on both sides from old New England families. Her grandfather, Jason Warner, owned a farm in Canaan, N. Y., and served several terms in the state Assembly. Her father was also a lawyer, and was the author of *The Liberties of America* (1853) and several other books. Anna Warner was born in New York City, where the family for some time maintained a residence. Her mother died soon after she was born, and she and her elder sister, Susan [*q.v.*], were brought up by their aunt, Frances L. Warner. Her early summers were spent in the home of her paternal grandfather in Canaan, but in 1836 her father purchased Constitution Island, in the Hudson River near West Point, intending to use a farmhouse on the island as a summer residence. Severe financial reverses, however, in 1837 forced him to give up his city home, and from that time on, for the most part, the family spent both winters and summers at Constitution Island, though the father was often absent on business, and the two daughters made occasional visits to friends. Constitution Island, which they usually called by the older name of Martelaer's Rock, remained the home of both Susan and Anna Warner as long as they lived.

After 1837 the Warner sisters had to learn to economize, and, as they grew older, they sought to aid with the family expenses. When she was in her early twenties, Anna invented a game called "Robinson Crusoe's Farmyard," and she and her sister earned a little money by coloring cards to accompany the game. Under the name of Amy Lothrop she also began writing stories for children, and, after the success of her sister's first novel, *The Wide, Wide World,* in 1851, she attempted a novel, *Dollars and Cents* (1852). Like her sister's *Queechy,* it made use of both childhood memories of Canaan and more recent experiences with poverty. In 1860 she collaborated with her sister in writing *Say and Seal,*

but in general she devoted herself to books for children. Both with her sister and alone she wrote Bible stories, collections of edifying tales for Sunday school libraries, and Sunday school lessons. Such publications as *Mr. Rutherford's Children* (2 vols., 1853–55) and *Wych Hazel* (1876), which the two sisters wrote together, proved profitable to their authors as well as instructive to their readers. Alone Anna wrote *Stories of Vinegar Hill* (6 vols., 1872), *The Fourth Watch* (copyright 1872), and various works on gardens, such as *Gardening by Myself* (1872). Mr. Warner died in 1875 and Susan Warner in 1885. Anna Warner continued to live on Constitution Island, with a servant, and for a few years more continued to write. In 1909 she published a memoir of her sister. She also carried on the Sunday Bible class which her sister had begun for cadets at the United States Military Academy. The sisters took a strong interest in the Academy, at which their uncle, Thomas Warner, was for ten years chaplain and professor. It was their desire that their island should be attached to the property of the academy, and this was made possible by Mrs. Russell Sage shortly before Anna's death, which occurred in 1915 at Highland Falls, N. Y. Both sisters are buried in the government cemetery at West Point.

Except in minor respects it is difficult to distinguish Anna's work from that of her sister. Though she was somewhat less talented than Susan, her novels and stories have similar virtues and defects. Temperamentally more stable than Susan, she relied less on sentiment, but her work has the same sort of piety, and the blend of realism and romanticism is much the same.

[*Who's Who in America,* 1914–15; Olivia E. P. Stokes, *Letters and Memories of Susan and Anna Bartlett Warner* (1925); Anna B. Warner, *Susan Warner* ("*Elizabeth Wetherell*") (1909); "Bibliog. of the Works of Susan Warner and Anna Bartlett Warner," in *Fourth Ann. Report . . . Martelaer's Rock Asso.* (1923); S. A. Allibone, *A Crit. Dict. of Eng. Lit.* (3 vols., 1858–71); obituary in *N. Y. Times,* Jan. 23, 1915.]   G. H.

WARNER, ANNE RICHMOND (Oct. 14, 1869–Feb. 1, 1913), writer of fiction, was born in St. Paul, Minn., the daughter of William Penn and Anna Elizabeth (Richmond) Warner. Her father, a lawyer of St. Paul, was a descendant of Andrew Warner, yeoman, who had emigrated from England to Massachusetts by 1632 and lived successively in Cambridge, Hartford, and Hadley. Her mother was a descendant of John Richmond, who also emigrated from England to America about 1630. Anne Warner was educated at home by her mother, who was a wit and a lover of Dickens, and by a French tutor. In the quiet which her father's scholarly habits imposed upon his household the child cultivated a love of reading and self-expression, became an accomplished pianist, rode and drove for recreation, and associated almost wholly with adults. The routine of her girlhood was broken only by occasional trips to Nunda, N. Y., to visit her paternal grandmother. When she was eighteen she married (Sept. 12, 1888) Charles Eltinge French (d. 1912), a flour manufacturer of Minneapolis, twenty-five years her senior. After the death of an infant daughter in 1892 she occupied herself by compiling a genealogical tree for her son, *An American Ancestry* (1894).

An eager curiosity to see the scenes she had read about took her to Europe in 1901. She settled in Tours with her two children and in 1902 published a slender volume, *His Story, Their Letters*. After spending two years in France she returned to America and went to live in St. Paul, but she found it distracting to write there. The next year she settled in Munich, and two years later in Hildesheim, Germany. In 1904 she published *A Woman's Will* and *Susan Clegg and Her Friend Mrs. Lathrop*. The instant popularity won by Susan Clegg's homely humor prompted her to write *Susan Clegg and Her Neighbors' Affairs* (1906), *Susan Clegg and a Man in the House* (1907), *Susan Clegg, Her Friend and Her Neighbors* (1910), and *Susan Clegg and Her Love Affairs* (1916). In 1905 she published *The Rejuvenation of Aunt Mary*, which she later dramatized. From 1904 until her death her stories appeared in profusion in the popular magazines, many of the serials being published later as novels. A collection of the short stories, *An Original Gentleman*, appeared in 1908. She wrote easily and rapidly, a simple incident often suggesting an entire story to her. In her lively wit and humor and in her method of writing lay much both of the charm and the impermanence of her stories, which are slight in plot and characterization but fresh, vivacious, and amusing.

As her popularity in America grew it became more difficult for her to write there, her friendly generosity refusing to repel admirers. She returned every year or two, however, for brief visits. From 1906 until 1910 she spent much of her time in Hildesheim. In 1910 she rented a house in Marnhull, Dorset, England, and settled there to give her daughter Anne (b. 1895), who was her constant companion, a less kaleidoscopic home life. When her son, Charles Eltinge French (b. 1889), was ill in America dur-

ing the summer and fall of 1912, she was unable to go to him because of her aged and helpless father, whom she had brought to her English home. She was distracted by anxiety and grief and unable to write. She died suddenly of a cerebral hemorrhage a short time after her son's death.

[L. C. Warner and Josephine G. Nichols, *The Descendants of Andrew Warner* (1919); Anne R. W. French, *An Am. Ancestry* (1894); *Who's Who in America*, 1912–13; "Chronicle and Comment," *Bookman*, Mar. 1908, May 1909, Apr. 1913; obituaries in *N. Y. Times* and *N. Y. Tribune*, Feb. 4, 1913; information from Mrs. French's daughter, Anne French Burnham of New York City.]   V. L. S.

WARNER, CHARLES DUDLEY (Sept. 12, 1829–Oct. 20, 1900), essayist, editor, novelist, was born in Plainfield, Mass., by four years the elder of the two sons of Justus and Sylvia (Hitchcock) Warner. His father was descended from Andrew Warner, who had emigrated from England to Cambridge, Mass., by 1632; and his mother from Francis Cooke, a *Mayflower* Pilgrim. Justus Warner was a farmer of some two hundred acres in western Massachusetts. To his widow and sons this land was virtually all that he left when he died in 1834— this and the injunction, "Charles must go to college." In 1837 Mrs. Warner took her sons to live with their guardian, Jonas Patch, at Charlemont, Mass., and in 1841 removed to her brother's home, Cazenovia, N. Y. At the Oneida Conference Seminary there Charles prepared for Hamilton College, from which he was graduated with the degree of B.A. in 1851, and began the lifelong friendship with Joseph R. Hawley [*q.v.*] which was later instrumental in turning him from the law to writing. Another permanent friend made now was Daniel Willard Fiske [*q.v.*]. As a Hamilton undergraduate Charles contributed articles to the *Knickerbocker Magazine*, and his commencement oration burgeoned forth in 1851 as his first book, *The Book of Eloquence*. Ill health resulting from the strain of earning much of his schooling sent Warner in 1853–54 to Missouri, where he did railroad surveying. He joined a friend in business in Philadelphia in 1855. On Oct. 8, 1856, he married Susan Lee, daughter of William Elliott Lee of New York City. In 1858 he took the degree of LL.B. at the University of Pennsylvania and began practice in Chicago. Hard times and a distaste for the law, however, in 1860 helped decide him upon becoming assistant to his friend Hawley, editor of the *Evening Press* in Hartford, Conn.

Kept at home by near-sightedness, Warner became editor in 1861 when Hawley went to the

Civil War. After the war Hawley entered politics, and the editorial weight of the *Hartford Courant,* with which the *Press* was consolidated in 1867, fell increasingly upon Warner. He found time, however, to write for the *Press* a series of humorous essays about his three-acre farm. Henry Ward Beecher caused these to be published as a book, and himself wrote the introduction for *My Summer in a Garden* (1871). These essays, wrought in the best vein of Warner's urbane humor, brought him instant reputation. There is in them a touch of Lamb, whom Warner avowedly admired, and whose mellow grace lingers in all of Warner's other essays: *Backlog Studies* (1873), *Baddeck* (1874), *Being a Boy* (1878), *On Horseback* (1888), *As We Were Saying* (1891), *As We Go* (copyright 1893), *The Relation of Literature to Life* (copyright 1896), *The People for Whom Shakespeare Wrote* (1897), and *Fashions in Literature* (1902). In May 1868 he went on the first of five trips to Europe, and a series of travel sketches he sent to the *Courant* appeared in book form in 1872 as *Saunterings.* In 1876 and 1877 came *My Winter on the Nile* and *In the Levant,* much the best of his travel-books. Here emerged a distinct vein of Chaucerian humor: Warner likes man, but tolerantly riddles his humbug and foibles. Writing with an informed sense of the places visited, he gave studied impressions, not factual guidebooks merely. Later he added to the literature of travel *In the Wilderness* (1878), *A Roundabout Journey* (copyright 1883), *Their Pilgrimage* (1887), *Studies in the South and West* (1889), and *Our Italy* (1891).

Fiction was not Warner's *métier,* and his four novels constituted his least successful body of work. In 1873 he collaborated with his friend and neighbor Mark Twain on *The Gilded Age,* an uneven book in which Warner's Missouri days loom disproportionately. Sixteen years later he made fiction the Pegasus on which he rode, more hard than skilfully, his ultimate hobby, the social responsibility of wealth. Gone now was the humane and humorous ease of his essays; in its place was the style of a stern moralist. Three novels, *A Little Journey in the World* (1889), *The Golden House* (1895), and *That Fortune* (1899), depict respectively the amassing, misuse, and loss of a great fortune. The weakness of this trilogy was perceived by Warner's friend William Dean Howells, who wrote, "He had not the novelist's habit of using experience imaginatively, structurally." Two biographies dated 1881 virtually complete his writings: a pleasant one of Washington Irving for the American Men of Letters Series, of which Warner was editor, and

a less satisfactory one of Captain John Smith. Warner always remained identified with the *Hartford Courant.* From 1884 to 1898, however, he was a contributing editor of *Harper's New Monthly Magazine,* and with his brother, George H. Warner, and others he edited the *Library of the World's Best Literature* (1896–97), in thirty volumes.

In his maturity Warner was a member of the Hartford park commission and the Connecticut state commissions on sculpture and prisons, vice-president of the National Prison Association, and president of the American Social Science Association and the National Institute of Arts and Letters. Yet it was Warner the essayist who contributed most to American life and letters. He was here an artist of delicate fiber and sure taste. No less was he of notable personality, chiefly marked by urbanity and friendliness. To Howells he wrote, "There is not much good in life except friends," and with friends in many walks of life he was rewarded. He never gained wealth by his writings, though in his lifetime they were popular. His rewards were yet of the sort in which he delighted. Something of a scholar in appearance—straight and slender, with a rugged, aquiline head, deep blue eyes under shaggy brows, and carefully cultivated gray hair and beard—he was in fact a frequent lecturer at the universities, by whom he was abundantly honored. Delicate health marred his late years, and he spent his winters usually in the South. At Norfolk, Va., in April 1900, facial paralysis gave warning of the end, which came suddenly from heart failure in Hartford on Oct. 20. He was survived by his wife. They had no children. In 1904 appeared *The Complete Writings of Charles Dudley Warner* in fifteen volumes, edited by Thomas R. Lounsbury.

[The best biogs. are Annie A. Fields, *Charles Dudley Warner* (1904), and the sketch by T. R. Lounsbury, in *The Complete Writings of Charles Dudley Warner,* vol. XV (1904). See also L. C. Warner and Josephine G. Nichols, *The Descendants of Andrew Warner* (1919); *Report of the Eighty-Ninth Commencement of Hamilton Coll.* (1901); *Mark Twain's Autobiog.* (2 vols., 1924); obituary and letters in *Hartford Daily Courant,* Oct. 22, 1900. Information for this article has been supplied by Miss Mary Barton of Hartford, a close friend of the Warners.]   J. A. P.

WARNER, FRED MALTBY (July 21, 1865– Apr. 17, 1923), governor of Michigan, was born in Hickling, Nottinghamshire, England, the son of Joseph and Eliza (Wooley) Maltby. His parents emigrated to America when he was three months old, and shortly after, upon the death of his mother, he was adopted by Pascal D'Angelus and Rhoda E. (Bosford) Warner, of Farmington, Mich. After graduation from the Farmington High School, he attended the Michigian State College of Agriculture for one term. He then became a clerk in his foster father's general store. A few years later this establishment was turned over to him and he conducted it successfully for twenty years. On Sept. 19, 1888, he married Martha M. Davis of Farmington. Ambitious, resourceful, friendly, Warner engaged with marked success in various lines of business. In 1889 he built a cheese factory in Farmington, and before long established additional plants in eastern Michigan, ultimately becoming a national figure in the cheese-making industry. He was a progressive farmer on a rather large scale, a vigorous promoter of real estate, and an active banker.

His participation in politics began with membership in the municipal council of his home village at the age of twenty-five. In 1894 he was elected to the state Senate, in which he served until 1898. At that time Hazen S. Pingree [*q.v.*] was engaged in his famous struggle with the old Republican party machine. Warner remained friendly with the Pingree faction, though he received the potent machine indorsement as candidate for secretary of state—to which office he was elected in 1900 and 1902—and for governor in 1904. His Democratic opponent for the governorship, Woodbridge N. Ferris [*q.v.*], advocated direct primaries as a means of crushing machine rule. The issue proved popular in a muck-raking era, and Warner, though at first opposed to reform, found it expedient to compromise to the extent of advocating a local option primary law, and won the election. The campaign had converted him, however, to a belief in a general primary law, and he finally forced the legislature to accept such a measure. Once started on a career of reform, he broadened his program, and, accepting the defection of a large number of his followers as a challenge, took the unprecedented step of running for a third successive term. He won the election by the narrowest of margins, and rounded out six years of impressive executive leadership. During his governorship the legislature passed measures for heavier taxation and lower rates on railroads, stricter control of public utilities and insurance companies, conservation of natural resources, encouragement of the dairy industry, food control, factory inspection, and the curbing of stock manipulation.

After his retirement from office at the age of forty-five, he devoted himself to farming and business, retaining, however, a lively interest in politics. From 1920 until the time of his death he was Republican national committeeman from

Michigan. In several respects his career was unique: although he was by background a conservative, experience and power made him more liberal; himself a product of organization politics, he developed into the sturdiest of fighters for reform; ambitious in the field of capitalistic endeavor, he espoused principles designed to curb capitalism. He died in Orlando, Fla., survived by his wife, two sons, and two daughters.

[For sources, reliance must be placed almost entirely upon contemporary newspaper accounts; useful information is to be found in the *Farmington Enterprise*, Apr. 20, 1923, and in the *Detroit News*, Apr. 17, 1923; an impartial estimate of Warner's rôle in Michigan politics may be found in an editorial, *Ibid.*, Apr. 18, 1923; see also, G. N. Fuller, *Messages of the Governors of Mich.* (4 vols., 1925–27); *Mich. Official Directory and Legislative Manual*, 1901–02, 1903–05; and *Who's Who in America*, 1922–23.]　　　　　　　L. G. V–V.

WARNER, HIRAM (Oct. 29, 1802–June 30, 1881), jurist and congressman from Georgia, was born in Williamsburg, Hampshire County, Mass., the descendant of Andrew Warner, an English emigrant who was in Cambridge, then Newtown, Mass., as early as 1632, and the eldest of ten children of Obadiah and Jane (Coffin) Warner. His parents were dependent upon farming for a livelihood and were in moderate circumstances. Their eldest son received, in addition to a common-school training, only one year of high school. This one year was spent under the direction of Mr. Thaxter, who very soon removed to Sparta, Ga., established a school there, and wrote back to young Warner asking him to come to Georgia to help teach in the school. At Sparta and Blountsville, in Georgia, he taught school and read law until he was admitted to the bar in 1824. He began practice in Knoxville, Crawford County, Ga., where he married in 1827 Sarah (Abercrombie) Staples. They had one daughter. From 1828 to 1831 he represented Crawford County in the state legislature. In 1832 he was a delegate to the state's anti-tariff convention, but, becoming dissatisfied with its actions, he withdrew from it. About this time he removed to Talbot County, where he formed a law partnership with George W. B. Towns [*q.v.*]. In 1833 he was elected by the legislature judge of the newly created Coweta circuit of the superior courts, at that time the highest court in the state. His election was unusual not only on account of his youth, but also because he did not live in the circuit. Shortly afterward, however, he removed into the circuit and settled at Greenville, Meriwether County. He was reëlected at the expiration of his term, but in 1840 he was defeated. He then resumed practice, with his brother Obadiah, and devoted considerable time to farming, at which he was very successful. When the supreme court of Georgia was established in 1845, although a Democrat, he was given a position on the court by a Whig legislature. In 1853 he resigned and returned to general practice. Elected to Congress he served from 1855 to 1857.

In 1860 he was a member of the Georgia secession convention, where he opposed secession bitterly but finally signed the ordinance. During the Civil War he lost much of his property as a result of pillage, and, of course, all his slaves. He was also hanged to a tree and left for dead by a band of Wilson's Federal raiders, because he told them he had no gold and could not therefore divulge its place of hiding. Following the war he again became judge of the Coweta circuit, where he served until 1867, when he was appointed chief justice of the supreme court of Georgia. The "Reconstruction" constitution of 1868 brought about a reorganization of the supreme court, and he was reduced to an associate justice. In January 1872, however, he again became chief justice and remained in that position until 1880, when he resigned. He died in Atlanta and was buried in Meriwether County, near his wife. He was widely read in the law and characterized by abundant common sense and rugged convictions. In politics he was first a Jeffersonian Republican and later a Democrat. Throughout his entire career, however, he stood for the Union against state rights, a manifestation, it is thought, of early training. He opposed nullification but favored the extension of slavery. He was reared a Presbyterian and was a constant reader of the Bible, but he never became a communicant of any church.

[W. J. Northen, *Men of Mark in Ga.*, vol. III (1911); memorial in 68 *Ga. Reports*, 845–55; L. L. Knight, *Reminiscences of Famous Georgians*, vol. II (1908); Geo. White, *Hist. Colls. of Ga.* (1854); *Biog. Directory Am. Cong.* (1928); *The Descendants of Andrew Warner* (1919), ed. by L. C. Warner and J. G. Nichols; *Savannah Morning News*, July 1, 1881; information from H. Warner Martin, Washington, D. C.]
                                                                    B. F.

WARNER, JAMES CARTWRIGHT (Aug. 20, 1830–July 21, 1895), Tennessee industrialist, eldest son of Jacob L. Warner, native of Virginia, and Elizabeth (Cartwright) Warner, grand-daughter of Robert Cartwright, pioneer of Middle Tennessee, was born in Gallatin, Tenn. With a common-school education and some training from his father in the tailor's trade, he left home at the age of seventeen to seek his fortune in Nashville. He worked as clerk, first in a wholesale grocery and then in the firm of Kirkman & Ellis, hardware merchants, and on Nov. 3, 1852, he was married to Mary Williams, daughter of a Gallatin neighbor. The young couple moved to Chattanooga, where Warner established a hardware business of his own. He was elected mayor for a term, and was a member of the General Assembly in 1861. Poor health prevented his enlistment in the Confederate army. During the Chattanooga campaign his home was demolished and after the Confederate defeat, Warner and his family as refugees made their way by wagon-train to Nashville.

Like many another Southerner, Warner faced the aftermath of war penniless and in debt. His business ability was recognized, however, and after a brief term as bank cashier he was appointed, in 1868, secretary of the Tennessee Coal & Railroad Company. He now began a significant career of a quarter of a century in developing the mineral resources of the South. The company had been engaged in haphazard coal mining in southeastern Tennessee since the early fifties. Soon promoted to general manger, Warner foresaw coke making as a solution for the company's surplus of slack coal, which in turn might lead to the manufacture of iron with the new fuel. He was not acquainted with the problems of the blast furnace, but after a visit to the iron works near St. Louis, he and his assistant, Col. Alfred M. Shook [q.v.], erected an experimental furnace at Tracy City. The "Fiery Gizzard," as it was called, was too crude to be a commercial success, but the coke experiment led to contracts to supply furnaces in upper Georgia, and to the erection by Warner of the Chattanooga Furnace. In company with ex-Governor Joseph E. Brown [q.v.] of Georgia, he purchased the Rising Fawn iron property in that state in 1874, reorganized the plant on a scientific and paying basis, and sold it in 1882 along with the Chattanooga Furnace for $311,000. This same year Warner was made president of the Tennessee Coal, Iron & Railroad Company, which had recently built its first furnace at Cowan with the most modern equipment. Poor health, which afflicted Warner periodically throughout his life, had forced him to retire from active participation in the company's affairs in 1874, but now, under the new régime of John H. Inman [q.v.] of New York (1882–85), he began a new program of expansion which led to the absorption of a rival English company in the vicinity and eventually to the entry of the Tennessee Company into the Birmingham district.

Warner's most notable achievement was the revival and modernization of the charcoal iron industry in Middle Tennessee. After a thorough investigation of the ore fields of Hickman and neighboring counties, the Warner Iron Company was organized in 1880, composed of Nashville capitalists. Having secured the controlling interest, he had free rein to develop the property along the most improved lines. The fifty-ton hot-blast Warner Furnace, built at a cost of $125,000, set a new precedent in the charcoal iron industry by its efficient operation. Scientific practice was applied all along the line. A charcoal by-product plant was built and three additional furnaces blown in, all of which were sold to the Southern Iron Company in 1889, the Warner Furnace alone being valued at $1,000,000. Warner retained a large interest in the new company, which under A. M. Shook's management experimented successfully in making steel from Tennessee iron, until the panic of 1893 closed the works.

Warner was one of the finer types of the New South's industrial pioneers. Without any formal training, he attacked the varied technical problems of coal and iron with keen perception, and his grasp of financial problems and market trends was perhaps even more remarkable. He accumulated a handsome fortune and his benefactions, performed without publicity, were generous. He had seven sons and one daughter.

[J. B. Killebrew, *Life and Character of James Cart-wright Warner* (1897); *Nashville American,* July 22, 23, 1895; Ethel Armes, *The Story of Coal and Iron in Alabama* (1910); Tenn. Commissioner of Labor, *Second Ann. Report* (1892).]   L. J. C.

WARNER, JONATHAN TRUMBULL (Nov. 20, 1807–Apr. 22, 1895), California pioneer, was born in Hadlyme, Conn., a descendant of Andrew Warner who was in Cambridge, Mass., as early as 1632. Jonathan's parents, who were distantly related, were Selden and Dorothy (Selden) Warner. He appears to have been well educated. In the fall of 1830, in ill health, he reached St. Louis, and in the spring of 1831 was hired by Jedediah Smith [*q.v.*] as the clerk of a trading expedition to New Mexico. The party, with the exception of Smith, who was killed by Comanches, reached Santa Fé early in July. Warner then joined David E. Jackson's trading expedition to California, arriving in Los Angeles on Dec. 5. For two years he trapped and hunted. At the end of 1833 he returned to Los Angeles, where he was employed by Abel Stearns [*q.v.*], and in 1836 he opened a store of his own. In the following year he married, at the mission of San Luis Rey, Anita, daughter of William A. Gale of Boston. About this time he changed his given name to Juan José, chiefly because his middle name was not easily pronounced by those who spoke English, and had no Spanish equivalent. In December 1839, he set out on a visit to the East. While in Rochester, N. Y., in August 1840, he delivered a lecture (later pub-

lished both in England and in America), in which he urged the retention of Oregon, with the acquisition of California, and suggested the practicability of a transcontinental railway.

He was again in California in June 1841. In 1843 he became a Mexican citizen, and on Nov. 28, 1844, received a large grant of land in the Valle de San José, 110 miles southeast of Los Angeles. This was the beginning of what was known as Warner's Ranch, which became famous because of the many notable events occurring on or near it during and immediately after the war with Mexico. Warner was elected to the California Senate from San Diego County in 1850. The following year an Indian uprising drove him and his family from home, but on its suppression they returned. In 1855 he moved to Los Angeles, and in 1858 began publication of a weekly newspaper, the *Southern Vineyard.* In 1860 he was elected to the Assembly. He served for a time as provost marshal of Los Angeles and thereby acquired the courtesy title of colonel. By 1861 all of his ranch property had passed from his hands. He seems, however, to have retained a competency, and his later years were spent in leisurely quiet. He was the joint author (with Benjamin Hayes and J. P. Widney) of *An Historical Sketch of Los Angeles County* (1876). In 1884 he published a pamphlet, *The Warm and the Cold Ages of the Earth in the Northern Latitudes.* He also wrote "Reminiscences of Early California From 1831 to 1846," which was printed in *Annual Publications of the Historical Society of Southern California* (vol. VII, 1909). Toward the end of his life he became totally blind. He died at his home, survived by several children. His wife had died in 1859.

Warner was six feet three in height, a stature that caused him to be familiarly known as Don Juan Largo (Long John). He was dignified, courteous, and friendly. Although essentially a man of peace, he was not without his share in the turbulence of the early days; he seems to have been a member of the vigilance committee of 1836 that put to death a woman and her paramour for an atrocious murder; he had an arm broken in a political row in 1838, and he was twice in serious trouble with the American authorities in the difficult years of 1846–49. Of the American pioneers in the Spanish period he was the most cultivated, and was perhaps the most widely esteemed.

[L. C. Warner and J. G. Nichols, *The Descendants of Andrew Warner* (1919); H. H. Bancroft, *Hist. of Cal.,* vol. V (1886); H. D. Barrows, in *Ann. Pub. of the Hist. Soc. of Southern Cal.,* vol. III (1895); L. A. Williamson, *Ibid.,* vol. XIII (1928); J. J. Hill, *The*

Hist. of Warner's Ranch and Its Environs (1927); An Illustrated Hist. of Los Angeles County, Cal. (1889).]

W. J. G.

WARNER, JUAN JOSÉ [See WARNER, JONATHAN TRUMBULL, 1807–1895].

WARNER, OLIN LEVI (Apr. 9, 1844–Aug. 14, 1896), sculptor, son of Levi and Sarah B. (Warner) Warner, was born in Suffield, Conn., of New England colonial stock. Levi Warner, an itinerant Methodist minister, moved to Amsterdam, N. Y., in 1846. The boy attended district school until his fifteenth year, meanwhile showing talent in drawing faces and carving little figures from chalk. At the outbreak of the Civil War he wished to enlist as a drummer boy, a desire which faded in the bustle of the family's removal to Brandon, Vt. There he went to school until the age of nineteen. He had never seen statues, but he longed to make them, and, knowing no better, he bought plaster, set it, and from the resulting block whittled a bust of his father. This was at least a likeness, and in a spirit of consecration he resolved to become a sculptor. To earn money for his art education he mastered telegraphy, at which he worked six years, in Albion and Rochester, N. Y., and in Augusta, Ga. With money saved from his earnings, he went abroad at twenty-five years of age. He entered the École des Beaux-Arts, studying under Jouffroy, and becoming acquainted with Alexandre Falguière, Antonin Mercié, and Jean Baptiste Carpeaux. His talent, industry, and courage won the regard of Carpeaux, who took him as workman into his private studio and invited him to remain as assistant. Warner declined this opportunity. Times were troublous. The Empire fell, the Republic was declared. In sympathy with the Republic, he joined the Foreign Legion, mounted guard at the fortifications, and did not resume his studies until after the Commune.

In 1872 he returned to the United States, where he suffered tragic disillusionment. He struggled four years in his New York studio and at his father's farm in Westminster, Mass.; he worked for silver manufacturers and designed bronze gas fixtures. At the Centennial Exhibition of 1876 he exhibited a striking medallion of Edwin Forrest. About this time his portrait bust of Daniel Cottier, the art dealer, was hailed by artists and critics as a delightful work, truly classic in feeling, yet far as possible from pseudo-classic taste. Other busts followed, penetrating yet poetic interpretations of character, without recourse to the "painter-like quality" then becoming popular in sculpture. Among the best of these are portraits of J. Alden Weir, the painter (1880), Maud Morgan, the harpist (1881), William C.

Brownell, the critic, and John Insley Blair. The last, a masterpiece of rich modeling, is owned by the Metropolitan Museum.

Warner, born a Connecticut Yankee, has been called a pilgrim strayed from Hellas. Hellenic serenity pervades his standing figure of "Twilight" (1879), his "Dancing Nymph" (1881), his relief of "Cupid and Psyche" (1882), the noble bronze caryatids of his Skidmore fountain at Portland, Ore. (1888), and his reclining "Diana," about to rise at the approach of Actaeon, a figure which expresses the beautiful moment of transition between repose and action. In 1889–91 he was in the Northwest, where he made valuable portrait studies of such notable Indian chiefs as Joseph [q.v.] of the Nez Percés, Vincent and Seltice of the Cœur d'Alenes, Young Chief and Poor Crane of the Cayuses, Lot of the Spokanes, and Moses of the Okinokanes. The Long Island Historical Society owns a number of his Indian heads in terra cotta. His granite drinking fountain (in the manner of the Renaissance and therefore somewhat uncharacteristic of the sculptor) was completed in 1890 and placed in Union Square, New York, but it was later moved to Central Park. Of the two notably fine seated statues by Warner, that of Governor Buckingham, war governor of Connecticut, is in the State Capitol at Hartford, that of William Lloyd Garrison on Commonwealth Avenue, Boston, Mass. In front of the Boston State House is a stately standing figure of Gen. Charles Devens, completed in 1894 and erected in 1898. For the Columbian Exposition of 1893, Warner executed the souvenir half-dollar, colossal heads of famous artists, a statue of Hendrik Hudson, and busts of Governors Clinton and Roswell P. Flower for the New York State building.

He was soon to engage in the more congenial work of designing and modeling two great bronze doors for the Library of Congress, Washington, D. C., the themes being "Oral Tradition" and "Writing." The Tradition door, with its beautiful panels of classically draped figures and its impressive tympanum, had been fully completed before Warner's sudden death as the result of a bicycle accident. For the second door, little that would have satisfied his sensitive spirit had actually been accomplished, and the commission was therefore turned over to Herbert Adams. Warner is well represented in the Metropolitan Museum. He was a member of the National Academy of Design, the Society of American Artists, the National Sculpture Society, and the Architectural League of New York. Because of his high consecration to his art, and his unswerving choice of the monumental rather than the pictorial in sculptural expression at a time when a picturesqueness of sculptural rendering was popularly applauded, his sudden death at the height of his powers was a severe loss to American sculpture. In 1886 he married Sylvia Martinach, daughter of Dr. Eugene Martinach, a New York physician. He was survived by his wife and two daughters.

[W. C. Brownell, in *Scribner's Mag.*, Oct. 1896; "Henry Eckford" (Charles De Kay), in *Century Mag.*, Jan. 1889; C. E. S. Wood, "Famous Indians," *Ibid.*, July 1893; C. H. Caffin, *Am. Masters of Sculpture* (1903); Lorado Taft, *The Hist. of Am. Sculpture* (1903); Suzanne La Follette, *Art in America* (1929); obituaries in *N. Y. Times* and *N. Y. Tribune*, Aug. 15, 1896; private information.]   A. A.

WARNER, SETH (May 6, 1743 o.s.–Dec. 26, 1784), Revolutionary soldier, was born in Roxbury (then Woodbury), Conn., the fourth of ten children of Dr. Benjamin Warner and his wife, Silence Hurd, and a descendant of John Warner, an original settler of Farmington, Conn. He received a common-school education, but as a youth was better known for his skill in woodcraft than his acquaintance with books. In 1763 the family removed to Bennington, and two years later Seth was married to Hester Hurd. Three children were born to them. At that time Vermont was claimed by both New York and New Hampshire. Many of the settlers had received grants of land from Gov. Benning Wentworth of the latter province, but the courts of New York challenged the legality of the grants and sought to oust the occupants. Under the leadership of Warner, Ethan Allen, and others, the people of Vermont resisted, frequently resorting to violence in ejecting surveyors, settlers, and judicial officers representing the authority of New York. On Mar. 9, 1774, Warner was outlawed by the General Assembly of New York and a reward was offered for his apprehension.

These experiences, combined with the atmosphere of frontier life, bred in him a spirit of sturdy independence, and when the Revolution broke out, he ardently espoused the cause of the colonies. He aided Ethan Allen and Benedict Arnold [*qq.v.*] in the surprise of Ticonderoga on May 10, 1775, and himself captured Crown Point on the following day. At a council of officers held there in June, he and Allen were delegated to procure the incorporation of a contingent of the Vermont troops in the Continental service. After appearing in person before the Continental Congress and the legislature of New York, they obtained authorization for the creation of a regiment of Green Mountain Boys, of which Warner was elected lieutenant-colonel commandant on July 26, at a convention of dele-

gates representing the towns in western Vermont. Later in the year he served on the Canadian border under Richard Montgomery [*q.v.*], and, while the latter was besieging St. John's, he defeated (Oct. 31) at Longueuil a relief expedition led by Sir Guy Carleton. After the death of Montgomery and during the retreat of the American forces from Canada in 1776, he was engaged in bringing up the rear and in collecting reënforcements in Vermont. In 1777, when the advance of Burgoyne up Lake Champlain forced the Americans to abandon Ticonderoga, he commanded the rear guard of St. Clair's army and fought a sharp action with the pursuing British at Hubbardton on July 7, as a result of which he retreated to Manchester, where he bent his efforts to rally troops for the defense of Vermont. On Aug. 9, in company with John Stark [*q.v.*], who had come from New Hampshire with a force to aid the Green Mountain Boys, he arrived in Bennington. In the meantime Burgoyne had dispatched an expedition under Colonel Baum to obtain horses and supplies in Vermont. On Aug. 16 the Americans attacked the invaders about five miles northwest of Bennington. Although Warner's movements during the action have been much debated, it is generally agreed that the timely arrival of his regiment in the latter part of the battle turned the tide in favor of the yeomanry of New England. On Mar. 20, 1778, he was appointed brigadier-general by the Vermont Assembly.

While Warner remained in command of his regiment until 1781, he saw little more active service owing to failing health. In the hope of improvement he returned to Roxbury in 1782 where he died. In 1858 his body was transferred from the Old Burying Ground to the Centre Green where a granite shaft commemorates him. He was a man of commanding appearance, more than six feet in height, with kindly though strongly chiseled features. Modest and unassuming, he was not given to advertising his achievements, preferring to let them speak for themselves.

[L. C. Warner and Mrs. J. G. Nichols, *Descendants of Andrew Warner* (1919); Daniel Chipman, *Memoir of Col. Seth Warner* (1848); G. F. Houghton, *Address Delivered before the Legislature of the State of Vermont, Oct. 20, 1848* (1849); E. B. O'Callaghan, *Doc. Hist. of the State of N.-Y.*, vol. IV (1851); Hiland Hall, *Hist. of Vt.* (1868); *Vt. Hist. Soc. Colls.*, vols. I (1870), II (1871); *Records of the Council of Safety and Governor and Council of the State of Vt.*, vols. I–III(1873–75); F. W. Coburn, *Centennial Hist. of the Battle of Bennington* (1877); William Cothren, *Hist. of Ancient Woodbury, Conn.* (3 vols., 1854–79); W. H. Crockett, *Vt., the Green Mountain State*, vols. I–IV (1921); *New-England Hist. and Geneal. Reg.*, Oct. 1880.]   E. E. C.

WARNER, SUSAN BOGERT (July 11, 1819–Mar. 17, 1885), novelist, was born in New York City, the daughter of Henry Whiting and Anna (Bartlett) Warner, and a descendant of William Warner who settled in Ipswich, Mass., in 1637. She was a precocious child, and from an early age she read widely. Both she and her sister Anna Bartlett [q.v.] were devout Presbyterians from their girlhood. Throughout her youth she was subject to periods of extreme melancholy, and all her life she was, like her heroines, given to frequent and copious weeping. In the spring of 1848, when the family's economic situation was far from reassuring, at the suggestion of an aunt she undertook to write a story. The result was *The Wide, Wide World,* on which she worked intermittently until the summer of 1849. During the next few months the novel was rejected by several publishers, but it was finally accepted by George P. Putnam [q.v.] on the recommendation of his mother. It was published at very end of 1850 under the pseudonym of Elizabeth Wetherell and was well received by most of the reviewers. In less than two years there had been thirteen editions in the United States and several editions, both authorized and pirated, in England. It was included in at least one critic's list of the one hundred best novels in English, and it and *Uncle Tom's Cabin* were said to be the two most popular novels written in America in the nineteenth century. Its popularity is all the more striking because there are almost no incidents in the entire novel, which describes the moral and religious development of an orphan in her early teens. A second novel, *Queechy,* begun before the publication of *The Wide, Wide World* and finished in June 1851, was published in 1852, and was almost as popular as its predecessor. This novel also describes the spiritual and intellectual growth of a girl who has to live in comparative poverty on a farm after living in luxury in New York and abroad. In *Queechy,* however, there is a romantic theme, though the hero's romance is subordinated to his religious conversion.

Susan Warner wrote many other books, but none was so popular as her first two. She wrote many stories for children, both with her sister and alone, and a number of novels, among them *Melbourne House* (copyright 1864), *The Old Helmet* (1863), *Daisy* (1868), *Diana* (1877), *My Desire* (1879), *Nobody* (1882), *Stephen, M.D.* (1883), and others. Many of her novels were based on real incidents, and it was her intention to portray real life in her stories. There is a certain amount of realism in all her works, especially in her descriptions of rural customs,

The source of her popularity, however, seems to have been her sensibility, which equaled that of any of the more extravagant English novelists of the later eighteenth century. It was her description of the emotions of her characters— emotions that found expression in tears on almost every page—that compensated in the minds of her readers for the absence of action. To this sensibility was added a strong piety, which was revealed both in the interpretation of character and in direct comments and exhortations. From 1837 to 1885 she spent the greater part of her time on Constitution Island, near West Point. She made occasional visits to New York and Boston, and she was acquainted with some of her literary contemporaries, including Julia Ward Howe and Catharine Maria Sedgwick. She died in Highland Falls, N. Y., in 1885, after an illness of a few days.

[Anna B. Warner, *Susan Warner ("Elizabeth Wetherell")* (1909); Olivia E. P. Stokes, *Letters and Memories of Susan and Anna Bartlett Warner* (1925); "Bibliog. of the Works of Susan Warner and Anna Bartlett Warner," in *Fourth Ann. Report . . . Martelaer's Rock Asso.* (1923); "Religious Fiction," in *Prospective Rev.,* Aug. 1853; Cuyler Reynolds, in *Nat. Mag.,* Oct. 1898; "Tears, Idle Tears," letter to *Critic,* Oct. 29, 1892; S. A. Allibone, *A Crit. Dict. of English Lit.* (3 vols., 1858–71); death notice in *N. Y. Times,* Mar. 19, 1885.]

              G. H.

WARNER, WILLIAM (June 11, 1840–Oct. 4, 1916), lawyer, soldier, congressman and United States senator from Missouri, was born in Shullsburg, Lafayette County, Wis., the son of Joseph and Mary (Dorking) Warner. The youngest of a family of twelve children, he was orphaned at the age of six, and until the age of ten he earned a few dimes occasionally at odd jobs around the lead mines of southern Wisconsin. Thereafter he worked for five years in a country store, saving enough money to pay his way through a two-year academy course. He then taught school for about four years, during which time he studied law at night, and between terms took law courses at Lawrence University, Appleton, Wis., and at the University of Michigan. He did not graduate from either institution, but was admitted to the Wisconsin bar at the age of twenty-one. During the Civil War he became first lieutenant, regimental adjutant, and, in 1863, captain of Company B, 33rd Wisconsin Volunteer Infantry. He served with average merit under Grant in Tennessee and Mississippi, and, because of his fine voice, was chosen to read the Declaration of Independence to both armies in the ceremony of the surrender of Vicksburg July 4, 1863. In 1864 he became major in the 44th Wisconsin Volunteers.

At the close of the war he began a successful

career at the bar in Kansas City. He was city attorney in 1867, circuit attorney in 1868, mayor in 1871, and a leading member of the commission which in 1875 formulated a charter for Kansas City. That instrument, with amendments of 1889 and 1908, was in force until the new manager form of municipal government was adopted in 1925. He was United States district attorney for the western district of Missouri from 1882 to 1884, in 1898, and from 1902 to 1905. In 1884 he was elected to the lower house of Congress, and was reëlected in 1888. His success as a politician is further attested by the fact that he served as a delegate to practically every Republican national convention from 1872 to 1904. Twice he served as commander of the Missouri Department, and in 1888 was chosen national commander of the Grand Army of the Republic. Through his congressional and Grand Army influence, he was largely responsible for the establishment of the Soldiers' Home at Leavenworth, Kan. He was the Republican candidate for governor of Missouri in 1892, but was defeated.

In 1905, for the first time since the Reconstruction era, the Missouri legislature was Republican. After a long and bitter struggle between the two leading candidates, Richard C. Kerens [q.v.] and T. K. Niedringhaus, the choice of the Republican caucus, Warner was put forward as a compromise candidate and elected to the United States Senate. His advocacy of numerous pension bills, and his support of the dependent relative pension bill in the face of the President's veto was highly satisfactory to the old-soldier element. The chief occasion on which he aspired to rise above the level of complacent mediocrity was in connection with the Brownsville, Tex., riot of August 1906. Warner indorsed President Roosevelt's severe discipline of the rioting negro soldiers, making the principal speech in behalf of the administration, and cross-examining the witnesses in the senatorial inquiry into that noted incident. After retiring, he was appointed civilian member of the national board of ordnance and fortifications. Although he held the reputation of being decidedly liberal in his religious convictions, practically his entire legal and political career bore the earmarks of conservatism. He was an unusually able lawyer in jury trials. In August 1866 he married Mrs. Sophia (Bullene) Bromley of Kansas City, by whom he had six children.

[The date of birth is that given in *Who's Who in America*, 1916–17; some other sources give the year as 1839. See also C. W. Whitney, *Kansas City, Mo.* (1908), vol. III; A. J. D. Stewart, *The Hist. of the Bench and Bar of Mo.* (1898); W. L. Webb, *Battles and Biogs. of Missourians* (1900); *Mo. Hist. Rev.*, Jan.

1917; *Biog. Dir. Am. Cong.* (1928); *Kansas City Star*, Oct. 4, 1916; *St. Louis Globe-Democrat*, Oct. 5, 1916.]
H. E. N.

WARNER, WORCESTER REED (May 16, 1846–June 25, 1929), manufacturer, telescope builder, was the son of Franklin J. and Vesta Wales (Reed) Warner, and was born on his father's farm near Cummington, Mass. He was a descendant of Andrew Warner who had settled in Cambridge, Mass., by 1632. Until he was nineteen Warner attended a district school in Cummington and showed a decided preference for mathematics, mechanics, and science, but little love of farming. In 1865 he found work in the drafting room of the American Safety Steam and Engine Company, Boston. When the offices of the company were moved to Exeter, N. H., the following spring, Warner went there to work in the shop as well as the drafting room for three years. There he met Ambrose Swasey, who became his close friend, and in the spring of 1869 the two entered the shops of the Pratt & Whitney Company in Hartford, Conn. Within two years both men were promoted to foremen, Warner having charge of the gear-cutting department and Swasey of a department for building machine tools. They both engaged in "contract work," a system which played a large part in developing individual manufacturing talent, and were so successful that in their eleven years with Pratt & Whitney they jointly accumulated $12,000. In 1880 they undertook to establish their own machine manufacturing business in Chicago, Ill., but the difficulty of obtaining skilled mechanics led them to move in 1881 to Cleveland, Ohio, where they established the Warner and Swasey Company to manufacture turret lathes. This enterprise was wonderfully successful from the start, Warner attending to the administration and Swasey to the manufacturing. They designed and built not only turret lathes but also speed lathes, die-sinking machines, and hand gear-cutters, and such intricate mechanisms as range-finders, gun-sights, and field telescopes for the United States government.

From the days of his youth Warner had been an ardent student of astronomy, and his chief avocation was the engineering of telescopes. The building of astronomical instruments was not included in the original manufacturing scheme of Warner and Swasey, but when the trustees of the Lick Observatory called in 1886 for designs for the great 36-inch telescope, the partners submitted a design incorporating the results of Warner's years of study and work. Their design, which provided much heavier mountings than had ever been used before and heavier construction throughout, won the contract, and the telescope was built and installed under Swasey's personal supervision. Their brilliant success brought the partners world-wide renown. The Lick Observatory telescope was followed by the 40-inch Yerkes telescope, the 72-inch telescope for the Dominion of Canada, and the 60-inch telescope for the Argentine national observatory. For twenty years Warner and Swasey conducted their business without any form of written agreement. In 1900, however, the Warner and Swasey Company was incorporated, with Warner serving successively as president and chairman of the board of directors until he retired in 1911 and removed to his estate, Wilson Park, at Tarrytown, N. Y. He devoted the remaining eighteen years of his life to his astronomical studies and to travel.

During his thirty-years' residence in Cleveland, Warner served as director of several banks, as a trustee of Western Reserve University, the Case School of Applied Science, and the Cleveland School of Art, and as president of the Cleveland Chamber of Commerce. He was active in the founding of the American Society of Mechanical Engineers in 1880, and served as a manager in 1890–93 and president in 1896–97. He was a member of the Royal Astronomical Society, the British Astronomical Association, and the American Association for the Advancement of Science, and received several honorary degrees. In 1916 he endowed the Worcester R. Warner collection of oriental art in the Cleveland Museum of Art. On June 26, 1890, he married Cornelia Fraley Blakemore of Philadelphia, Pa. At the time of his unexpected death in Eisenach, Saxe-Weimar, Germany, he was survived by his widow and one of his three children, a daughter.

[*Who's Who in America*, 1928–29; L. C. Warner and Josephine G. Nichols, *The Descendants of Andrew Warner* (1919); Guy Hubbard, in *Mech. Engineering*, Aug. 1929; J. M. and Jaques Cattell, eds., *Am. Men of Sci.* (4th ed., 1927); J. W. Roe, *English and Am. Tool Builders* (1926); obituary in *N. Y. Times*, June 26, 1929.]
C. W. M.

WARREN, CYRUS MOORS (Jan. 15, 1824–Aug. 13, 1891), chemist, inventor, and manufacturer, was born at Fox Hill, West Dedham, Mass., the eighth of the eleven children of Jesse and Betsey (Jackson) Warren, both parents being of old colonial stock. His father, a descendant of Arthur Warren who emigrated to Massachusetts before 1638, was a blacksmith and the inventor of the swivel or side-hill plough. In 1829 he established a plough factory and foundry at Peru, Vt., and in 1837 moved to Springfield, Vt., where two years later his iron foundry was

wholly destroyed by fire, to the complete impoverishment of the family. Cyrus and his next older brother, Samuel, who obtained their first education in country schools, were ambitious of higher learning and pursued their studies privately, supporting themselves meanwhile by teaching school in winter and by farm work in summer. In 1846 Samuel began the manufacture of tarred roofing in Cincinnati and in the following year asked Cyrus to join him. The business succeeded so well that the two brothers were soon enabled to realize their ambition of securing a college education. In 1852 Cyrus, who had married Lydia Ross on Sept. 12, 1849, moved with his family to Cambridge, Mass., to begin the study of chemistry and zoölogy in the Lawrence Scientific School. He made here the acquaintance of Louis Agassiz [*q.v.*], who became his close friend and adviser. After graduating with the degree of B.S. in 1855, he took his family to Europe, where he studied chemistry first at Paris, then at Heidelberg under Robert Bunsen, at Freiberg in Saxony, at Munich under Justus Liebig, at Berlin under Heinrich Rose, and finally at London.

In 1863 he established in Boston a well-equipped private laboratory where he devoted himself to important researches upon the hydrocarbon constituents of tars. Since the Warren brothers were using various tars in their business, Warren's investigations upon the separation of their components by his improved process of "fractional condensation" (see *American Journal of Science*, May 1865) were of great industrial importance. The process was afterwards applied by Warren to a careful study of the complex mixture of hydrocarbons in Pennsylvania petroleum (*Proceedings of the American Academy of Science*, vol. XXVII, 1893) which may be said to mark the beginning of modern exact research in this field. Later, when the brothers turned to the use of Trinidad asphalt as a roofing and paving material, Warren invented processes of purification. The commercial and industrial development of these enterprises led to the establishment of the Warren Chemical and Manufacturing Company in Boston and the Warren-Scharf Asphalt Paving Company in New York, with Warren as president and treasurer. He took out various patents for processes of fractional distillation, and for improvements in asphalt roofing and paving, and devised an improved apparatus for determining vapor densities and an improved process of organic elementary analysis. In 1866–68 he held the chair of organic chemistry in the Massachusetts Institute of Technology, but the demands of his business enterprises obliged him to resign. The long severe strain to which he was subjected during the business depression of the seventies, and the death of his brother and partner, Herbert M. Warren, in 1880, threw additional burdens upon his shoulders that finally caused a weakening in health. He suffered a paralytic stroke in 1888 and three years later died at Manchester, Vt. He and his wife had four daughters and three sons.

Among self-made successful business men, Warren was an unusual type, his energy, persistence, and administrative ability being coupled with a strong capacity for study and scientific research. He always lamented that the exigencies and entanglements of business prevented him from giving exclusive attention to chemical research. He was the author of thirteen scientific papers, published in Poggendorff's *Annalen der Physik*, the *American Journal of Science*, and the *Proceedings* and *Memoirs of the American Academy of Arts and Sciences*. He left bequests for the promotion of science to Harvard University and to the American Academy of Arts and Sciences. A grant from the C. M. Warren Fund of the American Academy assisted Charles Frederic Mabery [*q.v.*] in his classic researches upon the composition of American petroleums.

[B. W. Davis, *The Warren, Jackson, and Allied Families* (1903) ; *Proc. Am. Acad. of Arts and Sciences . . . May 1891 to May 1892*, vol. XXVII (1893), with bibliog.; Benjamin Silliman, Jr., in *Am. Chemist*, Dec. 1874 ; death notice in *N. Y. Tribune*, Aug. 15, 1891.]

C. A. B.

WARREN, FRANCIS EMROY (June 20, 1844–Nov. 24, 1929), pioneer of Wyoming, United States senator, was born in Hinsdale, Mass., the son of Joseph Spencer and Cynthia Estella (Abbott) Warren. His first American ancestor was Arthur Warren who emigrated from England about 1635 and in 1638 settled in Weymouth. Francis' early schooling was interrupted because of his family's financial condition, but later his own efforts enabled him to attend Hinsdale Academy. His appointment as manager of his employer's farm before he was eighteen years old is evidence of early developing leadership. At the age of eighteen he joined the 49th Massachusetts Regiment to fight for the Union. Near Port Hudson, La., he was one of a group of volunteers to prepare the ground for an artillery charge. Most of his comrades were killed, but Warren escaped with a scalp wound. He was awarded the Congressional Medal of Honor for "courage above and beyond the call of duty."

Soon after the war, he went West and in 1868 settled in Cheyenne, Wyo., becoming manager of a furniture store. Associating himself with the growing cattle and sheep interests of that section, he became one of the great cattle men of the West, and sheep men of a later day referred to him as the patriarch of their industry. In 1883 he formed the Warren Livestock Company. When the National Wool Growers' Association was reorganized in 1901, he became its president.

As soon as he became a resident of Wyoming he began to take a conspicuous part in public affairs. His first election was to the board of town trustees. He served on the Cheyenne city council, as mayor, as a member of the Territorial Senate, and as treasurer of the Territory. In February 1885 President Arthur appointed him governor. He was removed by President Cleveland in November 1886, but was again appointed by President Harrison in March 1889, serving until Wyoming became a state in July 1890. Elected the state's first governor, he resigned in a few days to become United States senator. In this capacity he served until March 1893. He was reëlected two years later, and continued in that office until his death. He was the last Union soldier to serve in Congress. He was a delegate to five Republican national conventions between 1888 and 1912. Before the World War he was chairman of the Senate committee on military affairs, and after the war, of the committee on appropriations.

Characteristics developed in the simplicity of his New England background combined with those of frontier life to give Warren a strong personality. A splendid physique, tireless energy, willingness to work hard, keen judgment, executive ability, and a capacity for friendship made possible his valuable service. Interest in military affairs was natural for one who appreciated the task of settling the Indian country. The problem of reclamation of arid lands commanded his attention always, and he is called the "Father of Reclamation" (Beard, *post*, II, 27). He was actively helpful in securing the establishment of the Petroleum Field Office of the federal Bureau of Mines at the University of Wyoming in July 1924. No problem of the important appropriations committee was too intricate for him to master. Representing as he did the first equal-suffrage state, he supported the equal-suffrage amendment to the Constitution. Concerning the Eighteenth Amendment he said: "I cannot give my support to the joint resolution, because I believe and I think my State believes the same way, that the police power should be provided by State legislation . . . I have believed and I believe now, that progress can be truly made faster where we go just fast enough in these lines of reform so that our laws are obeyed and administered actively and completely" (*Congressional Record,* 65 Cong., 1 Sess., p. 5652).

Warren began his career amid the raw beginnings of the West, stood with it during its formative struggles, and lived to see its dreams turning into realities. He was twice married: first, Jan. 26, 1876, to Helen Smith of Middlefield, Mass., who died Mar. 28, 1902; second, on June 28, 1911, to Clara Le Baron Morgan. By his first wife he had a son and a daughter, the latter becoming the wife of John J. Pershing.

[Sources include I. L. Foster, *Some Descendants of Arthur Warren* (1911); I. S. Bartlett, *Hist. of Wyo.* (1918); F. B. Beard, *Wyo. from Territorial Days to the Present* (1933); *Progressive Men of the State of Wyo.* (1903); *Biog. Dir. Am. Cong.* (1928); *Who's Who in America,* 1926–27; *Nat. Wool Grower,* Dec. 1929; "The Senate's Nestor Views the Scene," *N. Y. Times,* Aug. 18, 1929; *Wyoming State Tribune* and *Cheyenne State Leader,* Nov. 25, 1929. For report (1913) on "unlawful fencing and inclosure" of public lands by the Warren Livestock Company see *House Report 1335,* 62 Cong., 3 Sess.]   H. J. P.

WARREN, GOUVERNEUR KEMBLE

(Jan. 8, 1830–Aug. 8, 1882), soldier, engineer, was born in Cold Spring, N. Y., across the Hudson from West Point, the son of Sylvanus Warren, a close personal friend of Washington Irving and a prominent citizen of Putnam County. Fourth of twelve children, the lad was named for Gouverneur Kemble [*q.v.*], proprietor of a foundry at Cold Spring and sometime member of the House of Representatives. After some instruction in his native town and at Kinsley's School across the Hudson, Warren at sixteen was appointed to the United States Military Academy, with the admonition from Kemble: "We expect you to rank, at graduation, not lower than second." Carrying out instructions literally, he finished number two in his class, July 1, 1850, and was appointed brevet second lieutenant in the restricted Corps of Topographical Engineers. During the next four years he served successively as assistant engineer on the survey of the Delta of the Mississippi River, member of the board for the improvement of the canal around the Falls of the Ohio, head of surveys for the improvement of Rock Island and Des Moines Rapids, and, with Capt. A. A. Humphreys [*q.v.*], as compiler of maps and reports of the Pacific Railroad exploration. Promoted second lieutenant, Sept. 1, 1854, he was chief topographical engineer of the Sioux Expedition of 1855, receiving his baptism of fire on Sept. 3, in the battle of the Blue Water. Promoted first lieutenant, July 1, 1856, he was engaged in making maps and reconnaissances of Dakota Territory and Nebraska Territory until August 1859, when he was detailed as assistant professor of mathematics at the Military Academy.

The opening of the Civil War found him still teaching at West Point, but on May 14, 1861, he became lieutenant-colonel of the 5th New York Volunteers, seeing action at Big Bethel Church, June 10, and subsequently aiding in the construction of defenses around Baltimore and Washington. He was promoted colonel of his regiment Aug. 31, and captain of topographical engineers, United States Army, Sept. 9. In the Peninsular campaign of 1862 he was engaged in the siege of Yorktown and commanded a brigade at Pamunky River and Hanover Court House (May 26, 27). He was wounded at Gaines's Mill, June 27, and brevetted lieutenant-colonel, United States Army, for gallant and meritorious service in that battle. Four days later he commanded the force that repulsed Wise's division at Malvern Hill, and the next day participated in the engagement at Harrison's Landing. He took part in the second battle of Bull Run and the skirmish at Centerville (Aug. 30, Sept. 1, 1862), and commanded a brigade in the Maryland campaign and its sequel, from Antietam to Falmouth, Va. (September–November 1862). Promoted brigadier-general of volunteers, Sept. 26, he served at the battle of Fredericksburg in December. As chief topographical engineer of the Army of the Potomac from Feb. 4, 1863, he saw action in May at Orange Pike, Marye Heights, and Salem. He was promoted major-general of volunteers June 3, 1863, and served as chief engineer, Army of the Potomac, from June 8 to Aug. 12, 1863.

It was at Gettysburg (July 1–3, 1863) that he rendered his most distinguished service. On the second day of that vital struggle, sent at his own suggestion by Meade to examine the Union left, he discovered that Little Round Top, the commanding position, was undefended except for a few signalers. He perceived Longstreet's threat and, intercepting some of Sickles' supports and Sykes's troops on the Peach Orchard road, practically commandeered them for the defense of the hill, just in time to keep Little Round Top from falling into the hands of the Confederates. Had this critical point been taken by Longstreet, it is agreed that the whole Union army would have been forced back in disorder and the day lost. Warren was brevetted colonel, United States Army, for his services in this battle, and in 1888 a bronze statue of him was erected to mark the spot where his alertness and energy came into play. Despite a wound received during the defense of Little Round Top, he continued in action, and was subsequently in temporary command of the II Corps from Aug. 12, 1863, to Mar. 24, 1864, participating in a number of engagements, notably that at Bristoe Station. He was placed regularly in command of the V Corps, Mar. 24, 1864, and with this corps participated in the actions of the Wilderness, Spotsylvania, Cold Harbor, and other engagements, as well as the various assaults on Petersburg. He was promoted major, United States Army, June 25, 1864, and brevetted major-general, United States Army, Mar. 13, 1865.

At Five Forks, Apr. 1, 1865, the last decisive battle of the war, his corps, after conflicting orders, arrived with dispatch on the flank of the Confederates and offered to the cavalry's hard-pressed troops the signal aid that clinched the victory, but to the astonishment of his subordinates and others engaged in that critical action, he was summarily relieved of his command by Sheridan, who had been given authority by General Grant. Transferred to command the defenses of Petersburg and the Southside Railroad, he served here during April and the first half of May, then commanded the Department of Mississippi, May 14–30, 1865. On May 27 he resigned his volunteer commission and reverted to the status of major of engineers, United States Army.

During the later sixties he prepared maps and reports of his campaigns and elaborated for publication the results of some of his early explorations. He served as member of the board of engineers to examine the canal at Washington, D. C., as superintending engineer of surveys and improvements of the upper Mississippi, and as member of the commission to examine the Union Pacific Railroad and telegraph lines. He was also in charge of the survey of the battlefield of Gettysburg. For almost a year, in 1869–70, he supervised the building of the Rock Island bridge across the Mississippi, and there through exposure and over-exertion received the impairment to his health which ultimately caused his death. He continued for twelve years more, however, in the river-and-harbor work of the Corps of Engineers—in the upper Mississippi Valley, along the Atlantic Coast, and in the Great Lakes. On Oct. 10, 1878, he was made a member of the advisory council of the Harbor Commission of Rhode Island, and on Mar. 4, 1879, he was promoted a lieutenant-colonel of engineers. Throughout this period he made repeated requests for a board of inquiry to examine into the causes of his ignominious relief at Five Forks, but since the authorities implicated were then in power, his request was not granted until December 1879. The court then appointed not only fully exonerated and applauded him, but cast reflections upon the manner of his relief. Ironically, however, the findings vindicating him were not published until three months after his death.

Among Warren's published writings were: "Examination of Reports of Various Routes," with Capt. A. A. Humphreys, in *Reports of Explorations and Surveys . . . for a Railroad . . . to the Pacific Ocean,* vol. I (1855) ; *Memoir to Accompany the Map of the Territory of the United States from the Mississippi River to the Pacific Ocean, Giving a Brief Account of Each of the Exploring Expeditions since A.D. 1800* (1859) ; *An Account of the Operations of the Fifth Army Corps* (1866) ; *Report of the Survey of the Upper Mississippi River and Its Tributaries* (1867) ; *An Essay Concerning Important Physical Features Exhibited in the Valley of the Minnesota River* (1874), *Preliminary Report of Explorations in Nebraska and Dakota in the Years 1855–'56–'57* (1875) ; *Report on the Transportation Route along the Wisconsin and Fox Rivers . . . between the Mississippi River and Lake Michigan* (1876) ; *Report on Bridging the Mississippi River between St. Paul, Minn.; and St. Louis, Mo.* (1878). He was a member of a number of scientific organizations, including the American Philosophical Society and the National Academy of Sciences.

Warren was a firm friend, a generous enemy, gentle, sensitive, kind, and stanch. He was passionately fond of flowers. After the death of his father in 1859, he assumed much of the responsibility for the younger members of the family, whose welfare he guarded faithfully and tenderly. On June 17, 1863, he married Emily Forbes Chase of Baltimore, by whom he had a son and a daughter ; two years later his sister Emily married his former aide, Washington A. Roebling [*q.v.*]. Warren died at his home in Newport, R. I., at the age of fifty-two.

[E. G. Taylor, *Gouverneur Kemble Warren* (1932) ; *The Biog. Cyc. of Representative Men of R. I.* (1881) , G. W. Cullum, *Biog. Reg. Officers and Grads. U. S. Mil. Acad.* (3rd ed., 1891), vol. II ; H. L. Abbot, in *Nat. Acad. Sci. Biog. Memoirs,* vol. II (1886) and in *Fourteenth Ann. Reunion, Asso. Grads. U. S. Mil. Acad.* (1883) ; *War of the Rebellion: Official Records (Army)* ; *Proceedings, Findings, and Opinions of the Court of Inquiry . . . in the Case of Gouverneur K. Warren* (1883) ; *Dedication Services at the Unveiling of the Bronze Statue of Maj.-Gen. G. K. Warren at Little Round Top, Gettysburg, Pa.* (1888) ; *Army and Navy Jour.,* Aug. 12, 1882 ; *N. Y. Times,* Aug. 9, 1882.]

W. A. G.

WARREN, HENRY CLARKE (Nov. 18, 1854–Jan. 3, 1899), Orientalist, was born in Cambridge, Mass. His ancestors, who were of English stock, came to New England between 1630 and 1640; his father was Samuel Dennis Warren, and his mother, Susan Cornelia Clarke. In his early infancy a fall from a chaise caused a spinal lesion, as the result of which he grew humpbacked, "and," as he expressed it, "ever since I have been excessively delicate and always ailing" (Harvard Class Reports). Though shut off from most of the activities and pleasures of normal children, youths, and men, he was enabled by his intellectual ability and force of character to rise above physical disabilities and to make important contributions to Oriental scholarship. Most of his work was done while he stood at a high desk with two crutches under his arms to take the weight off his spine; and toward the end of his life he worked while kneeling at a chair, resting the weight of his trunk on his elbows. He made light of his physical suffering, buoyed up always by a sense of humor which never failed him. He was most kind-hearted, generous, and modest, and given to unostentatious deeds of charity.

Prepared for college by private instruction, he took his bachelor's degree at Harvard in 1879, and continued his studies at the Johns Hopkins University (1879–84). His work in college, which centered around Latin, Greek, Sanskrit, and philosophy, was distinguished by his keen interest in the history of philosophy. The natural trend of his mind was toward speculative questions, but he also took an active interest in objective scientific matters. At Johns Hopkins he spent much time in the chemical laboratory, and through all his later years read widely in the natural sciences. He began the study of Sanskrit at Harvard under Prof. James B. Greenough, went to Johns Hopkins in order to study with Prof. Charles R. Lanman [q.v.], and continued with Prof. Maurice Bloomfield after Lanman went to Harvard in 1880. In the summer of 1884 he went to England for a short visit to his brother at Oxford. Contact with the Pali scholar, Prof. Rhys Davids, founder of the Pali Text Society, stimulated his interest in Buddhism and led him to devote all his later scholarly effort to Pali and the sacred books of southern Buddhism. He was the first American scholar to attain distinction in the study of Pali. After his father's death in 1888 he tried the climate of southern California, but soon returned to Boston; his close friendship with Lanman led him to establish himself in Cambridge in 1891. Having inherited substantial means from his father, who was the founder of the Warren Paper Company, he made possible the publication of the Harvard Oriental Series, of which thirty-one volumes were issued between 1891 and 1932.

His most important work, *Buddhism in Translations* (Harvard Oriental Series, vol. III, 1896) has been reissued many times. Nearly half of it

was included by President Eliot in the Harvard Classics. The great skill shown in the selection of the passages and in the order of their presentation, and the vigorous English of the translation, give the book a permanent value. Warren did not live to complete his *magnum opus,* a four-volume edition and translation of Buddhaghosa's *Visuddhimagga* or "Way of Purity," a systematic exposition of the doctrine of Pali Buddhism dating from about 400 A.D. The text was nearly ready for publication at his death, and about one third of the translation had been made. After long delay this work is now in process of being completed and edited for the Harvard Oriental Series.

[C. R. Lanman, "A Brief Memorial," appended to Vol. XXX of the Harvard Oriental Series (1921) and to the seventh and eighth issues of Vol. III, Warren's *Buddhism in Translations*; other sketches by Lanman, in *Jour. Royal Asiatic Soc.,* Apr. 1899, and *Jour. Am. Oriental Soc.,* vol. XX, pt. 2 (1899), the latter repr. from *Harvard Grads. Mag.,* Mar. 1899; Harvard Class Reports, Class of 1879, especially the sixth report (1900); C. W. Huntington, *The Warren-Clarke Geneal.* (1894); *Nation* (N. Y.), Jan. 12, 1899; *Boston Transcript,* Jan. 4, 1899.]   W. E. C.

WARREN, HENRY WHITE (Jan. 4, 1831–July 22, 1912), bishop of the Methodist Episcopal Church, son of Mather and Anne Miller (Fairfield) Warren, was born in Williamsburg, Mass.; William Fairfield Warren [q.v.] was a younger brother. Their father ran a farm, owned a mill, and moved buildings when such service was required. Henry early showed character and ability, and at the age of seventeen was supervisor of the village sawmill. A year later he entered Wilbraham Academy, Wilbraham, Mass., where he prepared for college. In 1853 he graduated from Wesleyan University, Middletown, Conn., having taught science for a time, during his course there, at Amenia Seminary, Amenia, N. Y. After his graduation, he was instructor in ancient languages for two years at Wilbraham Academy.

In 1855 he was admitted on trial to the New England Conference of the Methodist Episcopal Church, was ordained deacon in 1857, and elder in 1859. From 1855 to 1870 he was pastor of churches in Worcester, Mass., Boston, Lynn, Westfield, Cambridgeport, and Charlestown. In 1863 he represented Lynn in the Massachusetts House of Representatives. Transferred to the Philadelphia Conference in 1871, he was stationed at the Arch Street Church, Philadelphia, for three years, at the end of which time he was transferred to the New York Conference and appointed to St. John's Church, Brooklyn. In 1877 he returned to his former charge in Philadelphia, with which he remained until 1879, when he became pastor of the Spring Garden Street Church of the same city. In 1880 he was a delegate to the General Conference, and at that session, such had his reputation become throughout the denomination, he was elected bishop.

His episcopal residence for some four years was at Atlanta, Ga., and while there he took an active interest in the establishment of Gammon Theological Seminary, made possible by gifts of Elijah H. Gammon [q.v.] and designed to prepare men of the African race for the Methodist ministry. Later, he resided at University Park, near Denver, Colo. His duties as bishop took him all over the United States and to Europe, the Far East, Mexico. and South America. He gave many lectures and wrote much for various periodicals. His first book was the result of a visit to Europe—*Sights and Insights; or, Knowledge By Travel* (1874). With Eben Tourjée [q.v.] he prepared *The Lesser Hymnal* (1875). From his college days he was much interested in the natural sciences, a fact which led him to write articles and books of a popular nature on scientific subjects. The latter include *Studies of the Stars* (1878), *Recreations in Astronomy* (1879), and *Among the Forces* (1898). He was also the author of *The Bible in the World's Education* (1892).

He was a man of tall, commanding figure, with a high sense of the dignity of his office, which he never violated, though he is said to have had a rich vein of humor. His contemporaries considered him cold and distant. He had a comprehensive mind and in his preaching dealt with the large and fundamental aspects of the Christian religion. He was married on Apr. 6, 1855, to Diantha Lord Kilgore of Bartlett, N. H., who died on June 21, 1867; and on Dec. 27, 1883, to Mrs. Elizabeth (Fraser) Iliff. He interested himself in the affairs of the University of Denver, especially in the establishment of Iliff School of Theology in 1893—later separated from the University—to the endowment of which his wife gave $100,000. One of his recreations was mountain climbing, and he was president, 1877–78, of the Rocky Mountain Club. He died at University Park, survived by his wife, a son, and two daughters.

[*Alumni Record of Wesleyan Univ.* (4th ed., 1911); *Who's Who in America,* 1912–13; *Christian Advocate,* Aug. 1, 1912; *Zion's Herald,* July 31, 1912; *Rocky Mountain News* (Denver), July 24, 1912.] H. E. S.

WARREN, HOWARD CROSBY (June 12, 1867–Jan. 4, 1934), psychologist, was born at Montclair, N. J., the son of Dorman Theodore and Harriet (Crosby) Warren, and a descendant of Arthur Warren who was resident in Wey-

mouth, Mass., before 1638. At the age of eighteen months he was badly burned and suffered great pain from a succession of operations. The power of endurance which he developed and the emotional restraint which he learned were outstanding traits of his personality. It is not surprising that, under the circumstances, he became introspective at an early age and that, even as a boy, he was interested in religious and psychological problems. Although brought up in a Puritanical household, he was unusually critical of dogmas and taboos, and early developed a dislike for conventional beliefs and explanations, an attitude which marked all of his subsequent thinking. Owing to his bad health, his secondary education was very irregular. He prepared for college under a private tutor and was graduated from the College of New Jersey (later Princeton University) in 1889. A year or two previous to his matriculation, he had become interested in the Darwinian theory, and during his college years he became acquainted with the writings of Spencer, Huxley, Clifford, and Tyndall. It is in this period that we find the source of his unchanging belief in a deterministic interpretation of mental processes and the beginning of his revolt against mysticism. He found the teaching of James McCosh [q.v.] inspiring, but was more attracted by the philosophy of Spencer and the psychology of the British Associationists. An indication of the profound impression made upon him by these British thinkers is the fact that in 1921, after twenty years' work, he published his *History of the Association Psychology.* He also studied the psychology of George T. Ladd and became acquainted with some of the early writings of William James [qq.v.]. In his senior year he was granted the mental science fellowship for graduate work. In 1890 he was appointed instructor in the department of philosophy, and assisted in elementary psychology and logic. After two years of graduate study and teaching at Princeton, where in 1891 he received the degree of M.A., he went to Germany to work in Wilhelm Wundt's laboratory in Leipzig. It was here that he became acquainted with Edward Bradford Titchener [q.v.], with whom he later developed one of the strongest professional intimacies of his life. Later he studied with Hermann Ebbinghaus at Berlin and with Carl Stumpf at Munich. He read Hugo Münsterberg's *Willenshandlung* and was strongly influenced by the psychophysiological aspect of Münsterberg's action theory.

In 1893 he accepted a position as assistant, with the title of demonstrator, in the new psychological laboratory of Princeton. His advance was rapid. In 1896 he became assistant professor, in

1902 professor of experimental psychology, in 1904 director of the psychological laboratory, and in 1914 Stuart Professor of Psychology. On Apr. 5, 1905, he married Catherine Campbell of Attica, Ind. He received the degree of Ph.D. at the Johns Hopkins University in 1917. He worked with courage and persistence toward the formal separation of psychology and philosophy at Princeton, and in 1920 became first chairman of a separate department of psychology. At this time the laboratory was inadequately housed in Nassau Hall. Through his efforts, and in part through his financial support, Eno Hall, a building devoted entirely to psychology, was erected in 1924. In order to have more time for his literary work, he withdrew from the directorship of the laboratory, but remained chairman of the department until 1932.

A few of Warren's numerous papers in scientific journals were on experimental work, but the majority were of a theoretical nature. In 1919 he published his *Human Psychology*. This was followed a few years later by his *Elements of Human Psychology* (1922), which was translated into French in 1923. This textbook was used extensively and made a popular appeal because of its concise description of fundamental facts, its conservatively behavioristic point of view, and the absence of extreme views on the nature of mental processes. Although impressed by John B. Watson's behaviorism, Warren believed strongly in introspection. He admitted the fact of consciousness but was opposed to any form of vitalism. He was a firm believer in a neurological explanation of all mental processes and, in consistency with this view, championed the double aspect of the relation of mind and body in "The Mental and the Physical: the Double-Aspect View" (*Psychological Review,* March 1914), his address as president of the American Psychological Association.

One of Warren's greatest contributions to psychology was the development of the publications of the *Psychological Review*. From 1894 to 1914 he edited or compiled the *Psychological Index,* either alone or in conjunction with other psychologists. In 1901 he was made associate editor and business manager of the publications. He was joint editor of the *Psychological Bulletin* from 1904 to 1934, and editor of the *Psychological Review* from 1916 until his death. He was intensely interested in words and definitions. In 1915 he was appointed chairman of the committee on terminology of the American Psychological Association. When the committee was discharged in 1924 only seventy-nine terms had been defined. Warren therefore determined to

edit a comprehensive dictionary of psychology, and most of his time during his last years was occupied with this task. His *Dictionary of Psychology,* published posthumously in 1934, was practically completed when he died. He was survived by his wife. There were no children.

[Mary P. Warren and Emily W. Leavitt, *A Geneal. of One Branch of the Warren Family* (1890) ; *Who's Who in America,* 1932–33 ; Carl Murchison, ed., *A Hist. of Psych. in Autobiog.,* vol. I (1930) ; H. S. Langfeld, in *Am. Jour. of Psych.,* Apr. 1934 ; S. W. Fernberger, in *Psych. Bull.,* Jan. 1934 ; R. S. Woodworth, in *Psych. Rev.,* Mar. 1934 ; obit. in *N. Y. Times,* Jan. 5, 1934.]
H. S. L.

WARREN, ISRAEL PERKINS (Apr. 8, 1814–Oct. 9, 1892), Congregational clergyman, editor, author, was born in Woodbridge, now Bethany, Conn., of colonial ancestry, son of Isaac and Leonora (Perkins) Warren. His father was a shoemaker, and the son, after receiving a common-school education, was apprenticed to a tailor, but because of a conviction that he ought to enter the ministry he was released from his apprenticeship to prepare for college. Owing to limited resources, he studied mainly without instructors, teaching district schools during two winters. After a short period in the academy at Cheshire, Conn., he entered Yale, where he largely supported himself, chiefly by teaching, and graduated in 1838. After a year in charge of the academy at Cromwell, Conn., he studied at Yale Divinity School, 1839–41. He married, Aug. 25, 1841, Jane Stanley Stow, daughter of Thomas and Phebe (Stanley) Stow of Cromwell, Conn.; she died Feb. 26, 1881. They had three children, of whom one son survived his father. From 1841 to 1845 he served the Congregational Church, Granby, Conn., being ordained pastor Apr. 20, 1842; he was pastor of the Mount Carmel Church in Hamden, Conn., 1846–51, and of the church in Plymouth, Conn., 1851–56.

Early in his ministry Warren began writing for the religious press, especially the *Religious Herald* and the New York *Evangelist*. In 1856 he became associate secretary of the American Seamen's Friend Society in New York and editor of the *Sailor's Magazine*. He was called in 1859 to be secretary and editor of publications of the American Tract Society at Boston, which was under anti-slavery management. During the nearly eleven years of his supervision the Society issued over 300 bound volumes and about 700 minor publications, also four periodicals. He prepared a Sunday School commentary on the Gospels and Acts, and a spelling-book and readers for the freedmen, and edited a large number of small books and tracts for army use. In the fall of 1865 he journeyed through the South, studying the needs of the colored people.

When in 1870 the Boston society was merged with the American Tract Society in New York, Warren undertook some book publishing in Boston and New York. In 1875 the *Christian Mirror,* a long-established weekly journal published at Portland in the interest of the Congregational churches of Maine, came into the hands of Gov. Nelson Dingley [*q.v.*], who transferred it to Lewiston and invited Warren to take editorial charge. He brought to the task a vigorous mind, varied experience in religious editing, indomitable energy, and keen joy in his work. He introduced marked improvements in the paper, and its subscription list rapidly increased. After eighteen months he purchased it and reëstablished it in Portland, where he was its editor and publisher throughout the rest of his life. On Jan. 2, 1882, he married Sarah (Linden) Cushman of Portland, daughter of John Linden and widow of Henry Cushman; she died in 1885 and on Oct. 6, 1886, he married Juliet Marion Stanley of Winthrop, Me.

Warren's published writings, besides numerous pamphlets, include *The Seaman's Cause* (1858); *The Sisters, a Memoir* (1859); *Sadduceeism* (1860, revised edition, 1867); *The Cross Bearer* (1861); *A Chapter from the Book of Nature* (1863); *The Christian Armor* (1864); *The Cup Bearer* (1865); *Jerusalem, Ancient and Modern* (1873); *The Three Judges* (1873), dealing with the Regicides; *Chauncey Judd* (1874); *Parousia, a Critical Study of the Scripture Doctrines of Christ's Second Coming* (1879; enlarged edition, 1884); *Our Father's Book* (1885); *The Book of Revelation* (1886); and *Stanley Families in America* (1887).

[*Biog. Record of the Class of 1838 in Yale Coll.* (1879) and *Supplement* (1889); *Obit. Record Grads. Yale Univ.,* 1893; *The Congreg. Year-Book,* 1893; *Christian Mirror,* Oct. 15, 29, 1892; *Congregationalist,* Oct. 13, 1892; *Daily Eastern Argus* (Portland, Me.), Oct. 10, 1892.]   E. D. E.

WARREN, JAMES (Sept. 28, 1726–Nov. 28, 1808), Massachusetts political leader, was born at Plymouth, the eldest son of James and Penelope (Winslow) Warren, and a descendant of Richard Warren of the *Mayflower.* Graduated from Harvard College in 1745, he settled as merchant and gentleman farmer in his native town, where after his father's death in 1757 he also assumed the office of sheriff for the county. On Nov. 14, 1754, he married Mercy Otis [*q.v.*] and had by her, in the course of time, five sons.

From 1766 until 1778 he held continuously a seat in the lower house of the Massachusetts General Court and Provincial Congress, where he became strongly identified with the left wing of the patriot party, a close friend and trusted adviser of the two Adamses. His activity before 1775 was not so conspicuous as that of James Otis, John Hancock, Joseph Warren, and Samuel Adams, though in his own community he figured prominently as an organizer of the radicals and served on most of the local revolutionary committees. The assertion that he was first to propose the establishment of committees of correspondence is without adequate foundation of evidence. He wrote in 1775 to John Adams: "I am content to move in a small sphere. I expect no distinction but that of an honest man who has exerted every nerve" (*Warren-Adams Letters, post,* I, 78). After the death of Joseph Warren at Bunker Hill, James Warren filled the important position of president of the Provincial Congress of Massachusetts until the dissolution of that body, when he became speaker of the House of Representatives in the new General Court. He was appointed paymaster general for the Continental Army by the Continental Congress and served while the army was at Cambridge and Boston. From 1776 to 1781 he served on the Navy Board for the Eastern Department. In September 1776 the General Court designated him, as one of the three major-generals of the provincial militia, to lead a force into Rhode Island. But, unwilling to be subordinated to a Continental officer of lesser rank, he pled the excuse of recent illness to have himself relieved, and the following year, to avoid the repetition of such embarrassment, he resigned his commission. His conduct in this instance was utilized by his chief political enemy, John Hancock, to undermine his prestige, with the result that he failed of reëlection to the legislature in 1778. Partisan charges against him of irregularity in his Navy Board dealings (*Ibid.,* II, 121–23) were later thoroughly disproved. In 1779 he regained his seat, but in the following year lost it again; and from that time until after Shays's Rebellion he was passed over by the electorate. In 1776 he had declined appointment as justice of the Supreme Judicial Court of Massachusetts, and in 1780 he refused the position of lieutenant-governor.

An ardent exponent of the principles of democracy and simplicity, Warren could not but deplore the wave of reckless extravagance that followed the war. During the rebellion of 1786, while there is no reason to suppose that he ever sanctioned violence, it was plain that his sympathies were largely on the side of the insurgents. Therefore, when in the reaction of 1787 he again entered the House of Representatives, he was at once selected by the popular majority to occupy the speaker's chair. Very soon his unorthodox stand on the question of currency, as well as his wholesale criticism of the way in which the government had handled the insurrection, alienated many of his former friends, who, since the attainment of independence, had become increasingly conservative. Indeed, some suspected that he had been in actual alliance with the rebels (J. Q. Adams, *Life in a New England Town*, 1903, p. 150). Even John Adams seems to have felt that his attitude towards the uprising was somewhat equivocal (*Warren-Adams Letters*, II, 325 n.). Mrs. Warren, however, wrote to Adams that the General had "borne the unprovoked abuse with the Dignity of conscious rectitude and that Philippic calmness which is never the companion of *Insurgency, Anarchy* or *Fraud*" (*Ibid.*, II, 312).

More significant was Warren's able and very emphatic agitation against the ratification of the federal Constitution because of its lack of a bill of rights (*Proceedings of the Massachusetts Historical Society, post*, LXIV, 143–64). On this as on almost every other issue he represented the will of the humbler classes. But once more the trimming tactics of Hancock prevailed, and Warren, defeated as candidate for lieutenant-governor, was obliged to retire from the field of active politics to the less strenuous pursuit of scientific farming. In his later years he was a stanch Jeffersonian Democrat. Twice he tried to re-enter the arena by running for a seat in Congress, but without success. John Quincy Adams commented in his diary during this period: "He was formerly a very popular man, but of late years he has thought himself neglected by the people. His mind has been soured, and he became discontented and querulous" (*Life in a New England Town*, p. 150). Yet in three successive years —1792, 1793, 1794—the legislature selected him for membership in the governor's council, and in 1804, at the age of seventy-eight, he received the honor of being chosen one of the presidential electors for Massachusetts (Massachusetts General Court, Senate Journal, Nov. 20, 1804, MS., vol. XXV, p. 199). He died during the night of Nov. 27–28, 1808.

[The principal source is the *Warren-Adams Letters*, 2 vols., being *Mass. Hist. Soc. Colls.*, vols. LXXII, LXXIII (1917, 1925). See also Emily W. Roebling, *Richard Warren of the Mayflower and . . . His Descendants* (1901) ; Alice Brown, *Mercy Warren* (1896) ; James Thacher, *Hist. of the Town of Plymouth* (1832) ; W. T. Davis, *Ancient Landmarks of Plymouth* (1883), pt. II, and *Hist. of the Town of Plymouth* (1885) ; Charles Warren, "Samuel Adams and the Sans Souci Club in 1785," *Proc. Mass. Hist. Soc.*, vol. LX (1927), and "Elbridge Gerry, James Warren, Mercy Warren and the Ratification of the Federal Constitution in Mass.," *Ibid.*, vol. LXIV (1931) ; *The Writings of Samuel Adams* (4 vols., 1904–08), ed. by H. A. Cushing ; *The Works of John Adams* (10 vols., 1850–56), ed. by C. F. Adams ; J. T. Austin, *The Life of Elbridge Gerry*

(*2 vols., 1828–29*) ; and obituary in *Columbian Centinel*, Nov. 30, 1808.]   G. P. B.

WARREN, JOHN (July 27, 1753–Apr. 4, 1815), surgeon, was born in Roxbury, Mass., the son of Joseph and Mary (Stevens) Warren, and a descendant of John Warren who arrived in Salem on the *Arbella*, June 12, 1630. Joseph Warren was a farmer in easy circumstances who was killed by a fall from a tree in October 1755. Brought up by an intelligent mother, John, the youngest of four brothers, entered Harvard College at the age of fourteen, supported himself by his own exertions, became a good classical scholar, acquired an interest in anatomy and formed a club for its study, and was graduated with high rank in 1771. For the next two years he studied with his brother Joseph [*q.v.*], twelve years his senior, a successful practitioner in Boston. He then went to Salem, where he associated himself with Dr. Edward Augustus Holyoke [*q.v.*]. Here he added to his knowledge of medicine and began to establish himself in practice. The events of 1773, however, caused him to join the patriots as a surgeon in Colonel Pickering's regiment.

According to tradition, Warren took an active part in the Boston "Tea Party," Dec. 18, 1773. When the hostilities of the Revolution actually began, he was with his regiment, although he did not take an active part in the battle of Lexington. He was on his way from Salem to Boston when he learned of the death of his brother Joseph at the battle of Bunker Hill. Giving up his practice, he volunteered at once for service in the ranks. When Washington arrived in Cambridge in July 1775, the medical department of the army was organized and Warren, though only twenty-two, was appointed senior surgeon of the hospital there established. He was one of the first to enter Boston after the evacuation. In 1776 he was transferred to New York and appointed surgeon of the general hospital on Long Island. Later he saw service with the army at Trenton and also at Princeton.

Returning to Boston in April 1777, he began private practice, although he also served as surgeon to the military hospital. Soon he was the leading surgeon of the city. When smallpox was prevalent, Warren, Isaac Rand, and Lemuel Hayward established, in 1778, a hospital for direct inoculation, where many patients were treated. His main interests, however, were in surgery and particularly in anatomy. Since there was no medical school at the time in Boston, he gave a private course of anatomical lectures at the military hospital in the winter of 1780–81, which were attended by men still in the army, other physicians, and a few students. There still existed popular prejudice against dissection, and the demonstrations were carried on with much privacy. The Boston Medical Society, which was organized by Warren and others in 1780, indorsed the course and asked Warren to continue his lectures each winter. A second course, given publicly, attracted many literary and scientific men, including President Willard of Harvard College. The third series of lectures and anatomical demonstrations was equally popular, and was attended by the entire senior class of Harvard College. It was soon clear, however, that a medical department in connection with the college was needed, and on Sept. 19, 1782, Warren was requested to draw up plans for a course of instruction. When the school was established, Nov. 22, 1782, Warren was chosen professor of anatomy and surgery. Shortly after, Benjamin Waterhouse [q.v.] became professor of the theory and practice of physic and Aaron Dexter, professor of chemistry and materia medica. Warren and Waterhouse were inducted into office Oct. 7, 1783, and the first course of lectures was delivered that year.

As a surgeon, Warren was a bold and skilful operator; he performed one of the first abdominal operations recorded in America and was a pioneer in amputation at the shoulder joint. His general practice also was extensive. He played a prominent part in dealing with the epidemic of yellow fever which visited Boston in 1798. Favorably impressed by cowpox vaccination, which was first demonstrated in the United States by Waterhouse in 1800, he did much to promote the adoption of this method of treatment. His most notable contribution to medical literature was a book entitled *A View of the Mercurial Practice in Febrile Diseases* (1813), in which he refers to the treatment of many types of fever which were common in his day. As the leading physician of Boston, he took part in practically all the important medical events of his time. His interests, moreover, reached outside his profession: he was grand master (1783–84) of the Massachusetts Lodges of Free and Accepted Masons, was one of the founders and a president of the Massachusetts Humane Society, and held membership in the Agricultural Society and the American Academy of Arts and Sciences. The honorary degree of M.D. was conferred upon him by Harvard College in 1786. He was married, Nov. 4, 1777, to Abigail, daughter of John Collins [q.v.], and was the father of seventeen children, the oldest of whom was John Collins Warren [q.v.] and the youngest, Edward Warren, his biographer.

[Edward Warren, *The Life of John Warren* (1874); James Jackson, *An Eulogy on the Character of John Warren* (1815); H. A. Kelly and W. L. Burrage, *Am. Medic. Biogs.* (1920); T. F. Harrington, *The Harvard Medic. School* (1905); S. D. Gross, *Lives of Eminent Am. Physicians and Surgeons of the Nineteenth Century* (1861); James Thacher, *Am. Medic. Biog.* (1828); James Thacher, *A Military Journal* (1823); W. L. Burrage, *A Hist. of the Mass. Medic. Soc.* (1923); S. F. Batchelder, *Harvard Hospital Surgeons of 1775* (1920), repr. from *Harvard Alumni Bulletin*; *Repository* (Boston), Apr. 8, 1815; family papers in the Mass. Hist. Soc. and Boston Medic. Lib.]   H. R. V.

WARREN, JOHN COLLINS (Aug. 1, 1778–May 4, 1856), surgeon, the eldest son of John [q.v.] and Abigail (Collins) Warren, was born in Boston. His early education was supervised by his father. Later he went to the Public Latin School, and in 1797 was graduated at Harvard College, valedictorian of his class and president of the Hasty Pudding Club, of which he had been one of the founders. After a year spent with a private tutor in French, he entered his father's office as an apprentice in medicine. In June 1799, however, he went abroad and in London, Edinburgh, and Paris studied under the best teachers of the day, particularly Astley Cooper of Guy's Hospital, London, and Dubois in Paris.

Returning to Boston in December 1802, he at once entered into partnership with his father. He assisted in the anatomical dissections in preparation for his father's lectures at the Harvard Medical School, gave popular lectures to select groups on anatomy and physiology, organized a private medical society, was one of the original members of the Anthology Club, and in 1808, with James Jackson [q.v.], prepared a *Pharmacopeia* for the Massachusetts Medical Society. In 1809 he became adjunct professor of anatomy and surgery at the Harvard Medical School, and in 1815, on the death of his father, he became full professor, a position which he held with great distinction until 1847, when he was made professor emeritus. From 1816 to 1819 he served as dean. With his close associate, Jackson, he practically revolutionized medical education and practice in Boston. The Harvard Medical School was moved from Cambridge to Boston in 1815, funds were raised for the Massachusetts General Hospital and it was opened in 1821 with Warren as surgeon and Jackson as physician, and the *New-England Journal of Medicine and Surgery* was established in 1812. In all three of these important enterprises Warren and Jackson were the prime movers.

Warren was an able surgeon and by no means a timid operator in spite of the painstaking care with which he handled the knife. Before the days of anesthesia he did amputations, removed cataracts, and was the first surgeon in the United

States to operate for strangulated hernia. In 1837, when nearly sixty years of age, he published his most important book, *Surgical Observations on Tumours with Cases and Operations,* with excellent illustrations, a landmark in the history of this subject. A previous publication, *A Comparative View of the Sensorial and Nervous Systems in Men and Animals* (1822), was a fair account of comparative anatomy, but Warren failed to grasp the importance of the work of the Scotch anatomist Sir Charles Bell. In addition to strictly surgical papers, he wrote numerous memoirs and essays. He is remembered especially for his connection with the first public demonstration of ether anesthesia. On Oct. 16, 1846, at the Massachusetts General Hospital, Warren, then in his seventieth year, operated on a patient under ether anesthesia given by W. T. G. Morton [*q.v.*]. To Warren, the outstanding surgeon of his day, belongs the credit for allowing his name and position to be used as a sponsor for this courageous and revolutionary experiment. Warren's account of the operation first appeared in the *Boston Medical and Surgical Journal* for Dec. 9, 1846, and subsequently in *Etherization; with Surgical Remarks* (1848).

Warren had many interests and became a leading figure in New England life. He was active from 1827 to his death in temperance reform, serving for that period as president of the Massachusetts Temperance Society. At the age of seventy-five he gave $10,000 to the temperance cause and made provision in his will for another gift. He was prominently connected with the building of Bunker Hill Monument. At his country estate in Brookline he carried on experiments in farming, and was an active member of the Massachusetts Agricultural Society. He promoted physical education, giving addresses and building a city gymnasium, and published *Physical Education and the Preservation of Health* (1845), and *The Preservation of Health* (1854). Both books went through many editions. Towards the close of his life, he became interested in geology and paleontology, serving as president of the Boston Society of Natural History. The skeleton of a mastodon was procured, set up in a private museum, and described by Warren in a superb volume, *The Mastodon Giganteus of North America* (1852, 1855). His many specimens were left to the Harvard Medical School and form the Warren Museum. He was awarded the honorary degree of M.D. by Harvard in 1819. He married first, Nov. 17, 1803, Susan Powell, daughter of Jonathan Mason [*q.v.*]. She died in 1841 and in October 1843 he married Anne, daughter of Thomas

L. Winthrop. By the first marriage there were six children; John Collins Warren, 1842–1927 [*q.v.*], was his grandson. The elder Warren prepared *Genealogy of Warren* in 1854.

[Edward Warren, *The Life of John Collins Warren* (1860) ; H. P. Arnold, *Memoir of John Collins Warren* (1882) ; *New England Hist. and Geneal. Reg.,* Jan. 1865 ; H. A. Kelly and W. L. Burrage, *Am. Medic. Biogs.* (1920) ; *Surgery, Gynecology and Obstetrics,* Jan. 1926 ; N. I. Bowditch, *A Hist. of the Mass. Gen. Hospital* (2nd ed., 1872) ; Joseph Palmer, *Necrology of Alumni of Harvard Coll.* (1864) ; W. L. Burrage, *A Hist. of the Mass. Medic. Soc.* (1923) ; T. F. Harrington, *The Harvard Medic. School* (1905) ; *Boston Advertiser,* May 5, 6, and 8, 1856 ; *Boston Transcript,* May 5, 7, 8, 1856 ; bibliog. in *Index-Cat. of the Lib. of the Surgeon-General's Office,* vol. XVI (1895) ; family papers in the Mass. Hist. Soc. and the Boston Medic. Lib.]   H. R. V.

WARREN, JOHN COLLINS (May 4, 1842– Nov. 3, 1927), surgeon, the son of Jonathan Mason and Annie (Crowninshield) Warren, was born in Boston. His great-grandfather, John Warren [*q.v.*], his grandfather, John Collins Warren [*q.v.*], and his father were all distinguished surgeons of Boston. Warren prepared for college at the Public Latin School, graduated from Harvard in 1863, and from the Harvard Medical School in 1866. After a course at the Jefferson Medical College in Philadelphia, he spent three years in Europe, principally in London, Edinburgh, Paris, Berlin, and Vienna. Returning to Boston in 1869, he began practice and soon associated himself with the Harvard Medical School and the Massachusetts General Hospital, as his ancestors had done. Passing through all the grades as a teacher of surgery in the Medical School, he became Moseley Professor of Surgery in 1899, and served as such until 1907. In 1908 he was elected an Overseer of Harvard College.

In his profession he was recognized as a surgeon of note and his many published papers were widely read. The first of his publications on surgical pathology was *The Anatomy and Development of Rodent Ulcer* (1872), which won the Boylston Medical Prize. A second book, largely experimental, dealt with *The Healing of Arteries after Ligature in Man and Animals* (1886). His work in this field culminated in a book entitled *Surgical Pathology and Therapeutics* (1895), based on bacteriology, a notable accomplishment. He collaborated with W. W. Keen in the *American Text Book of Surgery* (1892), and edited with A. Pearce Gould, the *International Text-Book of Surgery* (1900). From 1873 to 1880 he was editor of the *Boston Medical and Surgical Journal.* In 1896 he served as president of the American Surgical Association.

Warren's principal interest, however, was in medical progress and medical education. He was largely instrumental in moving the Harvard Medical School to new and larger quarters in 1883 and again in 1906. In raising funds for the buildings taken possession of on the latter occasion, Warren and Henry P. Bowditch [q.v.] took the lead. The money was secured, and a great medical center was established with the School surrounded by hospitals and laboratories. "To Bowditch and Warren belongs the whole credit of the plan, the main credit for its execution" (*Harvard Graduates Magazine, post,* p. 380). For almost a quarter of a century Warren was chairman of the Cancer Commission of Harvard University. The establishment of the Collis P. Huntington Memorial Hospital for Cancer Research, in Boston, stands to Warren's credit alone. He issued a plea for a medical students' dormitory in 1909, and it was added to the medical group before his death. On May 27, 1873, he married Amy, daughter of Gardner Howland and Cora (Lyman) Shaw of Boston. A son, John, became professor of anatomy in the Harvard Medical School and another, Joseph, professor of law in the Harvard Law School.

[*Trans. Am. Surgic. Asso.,* 1928; F. C. Shattuck in *Harvard Grads. Mag.,* Mar. 1928, and in *Proc. Mass. Hist. Soc.,* Nov. 1927; G. H. Monks in *Surgery, Gynecology and Obstetrics,* Oct. 1931; *Reports of the Secretary, Class of 1863, Harvard Coll.,* 1888 and 1913; T. F. Harrington, *The Harvard Medic. School* (1905); *Who's Who in America,* 1926–27; family papers in Mass. Hist. Soc. and Boston Medic. Lib.; *Boston Transcript,* Nov. 4 and 7, 1927.]   H. R. V.

WARREN, JOSEPH (June 11, 1741–June 17, 1775), physician, Revolutionary patriot, born at Roxbury, Mass., was the eldest of the four sons of Joseph and Mary (Stevens) Warren of Roxbury and a brother of John Warren [q.v.]. When the boy was fourteen, his father died. In that year, having been prepared at the school in Roxbury, Joseph entered Harvard College, where he distinguished himself as a student. After graduation in 1759 he was appointed master of the Roxbury Grammar School, where he taught for a year. He became a Free Mason in 1761, and in 1769, when his Lodge, St. Andrew's, united with two others to form a Grand Lodge, he was made provincial Grand Master. Deciding to become a physician, he studied under Dr. James Lloyd. On Sept. 6, 1764, he married Elizabeth, only daughter of Richard Hooton of Boston, who brought him a handsome fortune; by this marriage he had two sons and two daughters.

Warren established himself in Boston, where he formed a friendship with John Adams by the somewhat unusual method of inoculating him for smallpox. He was an excellent physician with a good practice, but soon became deeply inter-

ested in politics, ardently espoused the Whig cause, and rather neglected his own affairs. After the passage of the Stamp Act he was closely associated with Samuel Adams and made a number of speeches at Faneuil Hall. He also became a frequent contributor to the press, and published an article in the *Boston Gazette,* Feb. 29, 1768, which caused Governor Bernard to attempt to prosecute the printers. He was also active in the political clubs of the day, being a member of the North End Caucus, and of a smaller club consisting of lawyers, clergymen, and popular leaders. At the time of the excitement caused by the seizure of Hancock's sloop *Liberty,* Warren played a prominent part as mediator. From this time he was continuously active in town meetings, appearing in concert with Samuel Adams, John Hancock, and James Otis [q.v.]. In 1770 he was one of the committee named by the town meeting after the Boston "Massacre" to inform Governor Hutchinson that the troops must be removed, and on the anniversary of the "Massacre" in 1772 he delivered an impassioned commemorative address. He continued to act on committees and was a member of the group that was practically the executive committee of the popular party from 1772 until it was superseded by the Committee of Safety, of which he was also a member. He was one of the three men chosen to draw up the report, *A State of the Rights of the Colonists* (1772), contributing the second part, "A List of the Infringements of Those Rights." In 1774 he was head of the Boston delegation to the county convention, was a member of the committee charged with receiving the donations of food from other colonies, took the lead in organizing opposition to the Regulating Act, and drafted the "Suffolk Resolves," which he forwarded to the Continental Congress. He also engaged in a multitude of other public duties.

In 1775 he was active on the most important local committees and on Mar. 6 made his celebrated second oration in commemoration of the "Massacre," an address which stirred Boston deeply. As the crisis approached he decided to abandon his profession and enter the army. For the moment he remained in Boston and on Apr. 18 dispatched William Dawes and Paul Revere [qq.v.] to Lexington to notify Hancock and Adams of their danger. When the fighting began there, Warren rode out to join the Patriots and took an active part. On Aug. 23 he was chosen president *pro tempore* of the Provincial Congress, which office he held until his death; on May 12 he was appointed chairman of the committee to apply to the Continental Congress for recommendation to set up a new civil government in Massachusetts; on May 18 he was again chosen a member of the Committee of Safety, of which he had been a member from the beginning; on the 20th he became head of the committee to organize the army in the colony.

Less than a month later, June 14, the Provincial Congress elected him a major-general; he had first been considered for the post of physician-general, but desired more hazardous service. He passed the night of June 16 attending to public business at Watertown, where the Provincial Congress was in session. It is said that, anxious as he was to drive the British out of Boston, he questioned the wisdom of Israel Putnam [q.v.] in projecting a battle at Bunker Hill, since the provincial forces were scantily supplied with ammunition. On the morning of June 17 he met with the Committee of Safety at Cambridge and in the afternoon of that day, on receipt of news from the front, he went to Bunker Hill, where he could look over the situation. Putnam, whom he met there, offered to take orders from him, but Warren replied that he was there as a volunteer only and asked where he could be most useful. Putnam then sent him to the redoubt on Breed's Hill, but on reaching that place he again refused to assume command, stating that he had not yet received his commission and would take part only as a volunteer. In the heavy fighting which followed, while attempting to rally the militia, he was shot dead by a British soldier.

[The best life is Richard Frothingham, *Life and Times of Joseph Warren* (1865), which includes many letters and documents; in the Preface the author reviews the literature on Warren up to the date of publication. A few letters are published in "Warren-Adams Letters," vol. I, being *Mass. Hist. Soc. Colls.,* vol. LXXII (1917). The family history is traced in J. C. Warren, *Geneal. of Warren* (1854). Warren's orations have been several times printed.]　　　J. T. A.

WARREN, JOSIAH (c. 1798–Apr. 14, 1874), reformer, philosophical Anarchist, inventor, was born in Boston and is said to have been distantly related to Gen. Joseph Warren. He appears to have had a fair education, and he early became a musician, playing in local bands. At the age of twenty he married, and soon afterward settled in Cincinnati as an orchestra leader and a teacher of music. On Feb. 28, 1821, he was granted a patent for a lard-burning lamp, and soon afterward established a lamp factory, which proved profitable.

After hearing a lecture by Robert Owen, he became an Owenite, sold his factory, and early in 1825 moved with his family to the colony then forming at New Harmony, Ind. He soon found himself an extreme individualist, opposed not only to community of goods but to all forms of government. Gradually he formulated a theory of society embodying the principle of "sovereignty of the individual," a society wherein interchanges of goods and services should be based solely on cost. In 1827 he returned to Cincinnati, and in May, to test his new views, started what he called an "equity store." Two years later, feeling that he had vindicated his theory, he closed the store, without loss or gain. About 1830 he invented a speed press, which he did not patent. Some two years afterwards one of the Hoe presses was constructed on the same principle. In January 1833 he started a journal, *The Peaceful Revolutionist.* His exceptional inventive talent had enabled him to make his own press, type-moulds, type, and stereotype plates, and he did all the writing, composition, and press-work, but the experiment lasted less than a year. Between 1837 and 1840 he invented the cylinder press, self-inking and fed from a continuous roll of paper, first used in printing the *South-Western Sentinel,* of Evansville, Ind., Feb. 28, 1840; but persistent sabotage by the workmen caused him to destroy it. In 1846 he obtained a patent for a process by which stereotype plates could be made cheaply and easily.

After several experiments with "equity stores" and communities, he moved to New York in 1850. Here he met Stephen Pearl Andrews [q.v.], who became his disciple and chief exponent. Early in the 1850's, at a point on Long Island about forty miles from New York City, he established the town of Modern Times, which became noted as a gathering place for many eccentric characters and lasted until about 1862. His later years were spent mainly in Massachusetts. He died, after a lingering illness, at the home of Edward D. Linton, in Charlestown, and his body was interred at Mount Auburn Cemetery.

Warren is described by Moncure D. Conway (*post,* I, 264–68) as a short, thickset man, with a large forehead, and somewhat restless blue eyes. His industry was tireless, though for a propagandist he wrote and spoke little. His first book, *Equitable Commerce,* appeared in 1846, with later editions in 1849 and 1852. In 1863 he published *True Civilization an Immediate Necessity,* and in 1875 Benjamin R. Tucker brought out another work of his, entitled *True Civilization: a Subject of Vital and Serious Interest to All People.* He also published a number of miscellaneous writings, including *Written Music Remodeled, and Invested with the Simplicity of an Exact Science* (1860). The work of Warren, in music, in mechanics, and in social theory, was notably original. He was the founder in America of philosophical Anarchism.

[Sources include William Bailie, *Josiah Warren, the First Am. Anarchist* (1906); G. B. Lockwood, *The New Harmony Movement* (1905); *Boston Globe*, Apr. 15, 1874; M. D. Conway, *Autobiography* (1904); *Fortnightly Rev.*, July 1, 1865. Warren's theories are developed in S. P. Andrews, *The Science of Society* (1851) and *The Basic Outline of Universology* (1872), and are often expounded in the writings of Benjamin R. Tucker.]   **W. J. G.**

WARREN, MERCY OTIS (Sept. 14, 1728 o.s.–Oct. 19, 1814), historian, poet, dramatist, was born in Barnstable, Mass., the third child of James and Mary (Allyne) Otis, and sister of the more famous James [*q.v.*], who opposed the writs of assistance and the Stamp Act. She was married on Nov. 14, 1754, to James Warren [*q.v.*], by whom she had five sons. They lived for the most part in Plymouth, but in 1781 purchased the Gov. Thomas Hutchinson house in Milton, where they spent ten years. Possessing uncommon talent for literature and politics, and enjoying through both her husband and brother an enviable intimacy with those high in the Revolutionary councils of the province, Mercy Warren became in a manner the poet laureate and later historical apologist for the patriot cause. Her works include several plays, *Poems Dramatic and Miscellaneous* (1790), and a *History of the Rise, Progress, and Termination of the American Revolution* (3 vols., 1805). Two political satires, *The Adulateur,* published in 1773 (reprinted in *Magazine of History,* extra no. 63, pt. 3, 1918), and *The Group* (1775), are deserving of particular mention. Her history is interesting both for the expert knowledge it reveals of public affairs and for its lively and penetrating commentary upon the leading figures of the day, more especially for the caustic analysis of character and motives among the "malignant party" who opposed American freedom. Like her husband, she held strong democratic convictions, and as a consequence dealt severely with men who in her opinion leaned in the "aristocratical" direction.

At a later date she would doubtless have been termed a feminist for her aggressive concern with public affairs and her insistence upon the right of women to have other than domestic interests. To her friend Abigail Adams [*q.v.*] she wrote that while she admitted "the sex" too often gave occasion "by an Eager Pursuit of Trifles" for reflections upon their understanding, yet she believed that if a "discerning & generous Mind should look to the origin of the Error" it would find "that the Deficiency lies not so much in Inferior Contexture of Female Intellects as in the

different Education bestow'd on the Sexes" (Brown, *post,* p. 241). John Adams throughout the Revolutionary period was in frequent correspondence with her, and her other active correspondents on political matters included Samuel Adams, James Winthrop, John Dickinson, Thomas Jefferson, Elbridge Gerry, Henry Knox, and Mrs. Macaulay Graham, the English historian. But the younger generation, on coming into power, showed less respect for her political opinions. When in 1809 she attempted to call her nephew, Harrison Gray Otis, 1765–1848 [*q.v.*], to task for his Federalistic opposition to the Embargo, he affectionately invited her not to meddle in what he conceived to be his personal business (*Warren-Adams Letters, post,* II, 361 ff.).

An amusing though rather pathetic episode in Mercy Warren's later life was her quarrel with John Adams. This was precipitated by the publication of her history, in which Adams felt that he had been done injustice. He objected in a letter dated July 11, 1807, to her statements that "his passions and prejudices were sometimes too strong for his sagacity and judgment" (*History,* III, 392), that since his sojourn in England he had shown a leaning toward monarchy, and that "pride of talents and much ambition, were undoubtedly combined" in his character (*Ibid.,* I, 131–32). Correspondence over this issue was carried on with mounting fury for three months until it was terminated by the unanswerable declaration of Mrs. Warren that Adams' opinions were "so marked with passion, absurdity, and inconsistency as to appear more like the ravings of a maniac than the cool *critique* of genius and science" (*Collections of the Massachusetts Historical Society,* 5 ser., vol. IV, *post,* 489). At length, after almost five years, Elbridge Gerry interceded and managed to effect a reconciliation. Loving letters were exchanged and locks of hair as tokens of a peace which remained unbroken until Mercy's death (*Ibid.,* p. 502 ff.; *Warren-Adams Letters,* II, 382–96). But even in the moment of the revival of their friendship, Adams could not repress the somewhat jaundiced observation to Gerry that "History is not the Province of the Ladies" (*Warren-Adams Letters,* II, 380).

[Sources of chief importance are the *Warren-Adams Letters,* 2 vols., being *Mass. Hist. Soc. Colls.,* vols. LXXII, LXXIII (1917, 1925), and "Corres. between John Adams and Mercy Warren," *Mass. Hist. Soc. Colls.,* 5 ser., vol. IV (1878). See also Emily W. Roebling, *Richard Warren of the Mayflower* (1901); Alice Brown, *Mercy Warren* (1896); Annie R. Marble, in *New England Mag.,* Apr. 1903; Charles Warren, "Elbridge Gerry, James Warren, Mercy Warren," *Proc. Mass. Hist. Soc.,* vol. LXIV (1931); M. C. Tyler, *The Lit. Hist. of the Am. Rev.* (2 vols., 1897); W. C. Ford, "Mrs. Warren's 'The Group'," *Proc. Mass. Hist. Soc.,* vol. LXII (1928) ; and death notice in *Columbian Centinel,* Oct. 22, 1814.]   G. P. B.

WARREN, MINTON (Jan. 29, 1850–Nov. 26, 1907), classical scholar and teacher, was born at Providence, R. I., the son of Samuel Sprague and Ann Elizabeth (Caswel) Warren, a descendant of Richard Warren, a *Mayflower* Pilgrim. He was graduated from the Providence high school in 1866 and from Tufts College in 1870. After a year of teaching at Westport, Mass., he spent the year 1871–72 in graduate study at Yale, under the guidance of William Dwight Whitney, James Hadley, and Thomas R. Lounsbury [*qq.v.*]. He taught then successively at Medford and Waltham (as principal of the high school), and in the autumn of 1876 he went to Germany for further study: first at Leipzig, then at Bonn (under Bücheler), and finally at Strasbourg (under Studemund), where he received the degree of Ph.D. in 1879. His dissertation on the enclitic *ne* in early Latin (presented in part in the *American Journal of Philology,* May 1881) revealed mature scholarship and originality of interpretation; its results have become a part of accepted grammatical doctrine. His acquaintance at Leipzig with two of Ritschl's younger pupils, Georg Götz and Gustav Löwe, bore fruit some years later in the first publication of the St. Gall Glossary. On his return to the United States he was invited to the Johns Hopkins University as associate in Latin. There he inaugurated the Latin Seminary, and in a library well equipped for intensive study in a few chosen fields, in close and personal touch with his students, he worked more in the manner of the director of a laboratory than as an academic teacher of the usual American type. In the conduct of this work he sacrificed, and sacrificed ungrudgingly, his own productivity to his calling as a teacher, not only in time and strength, but also in placing his own ideas and projects at the disposal of his students. During the years 1886–99 twenty-two dissertations are recorded as having been prepared and published under his direction. His own published work is not large in bulk nor does it embrace wide-reaching and novel points of view. But within its range it reveals the orderly erudition and precision which were his characteristics as a scholar, and it won abundant recognition, perhaps more in Europe than at home. His special field of study was early Latin, and he was an acknowledged master in the idiom of Latin comedy. He remained at the Johns Hopkins University as associate professor and professor until 1899, when he accepted a call to Harvard. In 1905 he succeeded George Martin Lane [*q.v.*] as Pope Professor of Latin. He was

active in the founding of the American School of Classical Studies in Rome (later a division of the American Academy in Rome), and was its second director (1896–97) ; he was president of the American Philological Association for the year 1897. He died in Cambridge. He was married on Dec. 29, 1885, to Salomé Machado of Salem, who with a son and a daughter survived him.

Of his publications the more important are: "On Latin Glossaries" (*Transactions of the American Philological Association,* vol. XV, 1885), with complete and first publication of the important glossary in Codex Sangallensis 912; "Epigraphica" (*Harvard Studies in Classical Philology,* vol. XI, 1900) ; "Unpublished Scholia from the Vaticanus (C) of Terence" (*Ibid.,* vol. XII, 1901) ; "On Five New Manuscripts of the Commentary of Donatus on Terence" (*Ibid.,* vol. XVII, 1906) ; "On the *Distinctio Versuum* in the Manuscripts of Terence" (*American Journal of Archaeology,* Jan. 1900) ; "A New Fragment of Apollodorus of Carystus" (*Classical Philology,* Jan. 1906) ; and "The Stele Inscription in the Roman Forum" (*American Journal of Philology,* July, Oct. 1907). Apart from these longer studies almost every number of the *American Journal of Philology* from the beginning in 1880 to 1899 contains some shorter article, note, or book review from his hand.

Warren was a man of vigorous build, and his personality suggested strength. He was a hard-driving, forceful, and incisive teacher, impatient of slowness or ineffectiveness, often sharp in merited criticism, but able to inject enthusiasm and emulation into the tasks he imposed. His nature was open and kindly, and for him his pupils, friends, and colleagues entertained a singular warmth of devotion. He was quick to recognize good work, generous in praise of it, and he seemed to take a peculiar pleasure in contributing from his own store to the work of others. Primarily a teacher of teachers, through his own work and that of his many pupils (who for a generation came to be known as "Warren's men") he earned a conspicuous place among American classical scholars and teachers.

[J. H. Wright, in *Harvard Univ. Gazette,* Jan. 10, 1908; C. R. Lanman, in *Harvard Grads.' Mag.,* Mar. 1908; G. J. Laing, *Ibid.*; S. E. Morison, *The Development of Harvard Univ.* (1930) ; Kirby Smith, in *Am. Jour. Philology,* Oct. 1907, and in *Johns Hopkins Alumni Mag.,* Mar. 1918; *Classical Philology,* Apr. 1908; *Classical Jour.,* Jan. 1908, with portrait; *Tufts Coll. Grad.,* vol. V, p. 196; *Harvard Illus. Mag.,* vol. IX (1908), p. 83; obituary in *Boston Transcript,* Nov. 27, 1907.]   G. L. H.

WARREN, Sir PETER (Mar. 10, 1703–July 29, 1752), British naval officer, son of Michael and Catherine (Aylmer) Warren, was born on the Warren estate at Warrenstown, County Meath, Ireland, where his ancestors had settled in 1282. His mother was the daughter of Sir Christopher Aylmer, first baronet of Balrath, and the sister of Matthew, Lord Aylmer, one of the Lords of the Admiralty and commander-in-chief of the fleet. Peter Warren entered the navy as a midshipman at the age of twelve, remaining in British waters until 1718, when he sailed for the West Indies and the North American coast in the *Rose*. On July 7, 1730, he arrived in New York Harbor as a captain, commander of H.M.S. *Solebay,* a 20-gun frigate, and for the next seventeen years his residence was in New York City.

In June 1731 he acquired title to a number of plots in the city and to "Greenwich House" at the bank of the Hudson, with some twenty acres of ground—the first of six parcels which made up the "Warren Farm" of some three hundred acres, now known as Greenwich Village. The following month he married Susannah De Lancey, elder daughter of Stephen and Anne (Van Cortlandt) De Lancey, sister of James and Oliver De Lancey [*qq.v.*], and grand-daughter of Stephanus Van Cortlandt [*q.v.*]. The wedding reception at the De Lancey home was described in the *New-York Gazette* for July 26, 1731. Five years later Warren purchased a tract of 14,000 acres in the Mohawk Valley, of which his nephew, later Sir William Johnson, became manager, and in 1744 he acquired the famous Warren mansion, demolished in 1865, with forty-six acres, the fifth section of the "Warren Farm," which was completed some time later by a gift of four acres from the city. In 1749 he purchased 100 acres on Turtle Bay. His last city home was 59–65 Broadway (Stokes, *post,* I, 348).

Meanwhile he had commanded successively the *Squirrel,* 20 guns (1735–42); the *Launceton,* 40 guns (1742–45); and the *Superbe,* 60 guns. Early in 1745, when at Antigua, he received orders to cooperate with the expedition projected by Gov. William Shirley [*q.v.*] of Massachusetts against Louisbourg on Cape Breton Island, and on Mar. 13 of that year he set sail in the *Superbe,* with the *Launceton* and *Mermaid,* arriving in time to prevent the French supply ship, *Vigilante,* from entering Louisbourg harbor. This vessel and many other rich prizes were captured. On Saturday afternoon, June 15, just before the capitulation of the fortress, he addressed the army, saying that he would rather leave his body at Louisbourg than not take the city (*Louisbourg Journals, post,* p. 26). His knowledge of American conditions, his sense of strategy, and his ability to work with men of various types all con-

tributed to the success of the expedition. He was promoted to be rear admiral of the Blue Aug. 8, 1745; and with Sir William Pepperrell [*q.v.*], continued in joint supervision of the captured post until, much to his disgust, he was appointed governor of Louisbourg and Cape Breton Island. On Oct. 5 he wrote the Duke of Newcastle asking to be appointed governor of New York, and on June 7, 1746, the day of his final departure from Louisbourg, he asked unsuccessfully for the governorship of New Jersey. As some evidence of his popularity in America, the Admiral Warren, a tavern, was opened at 11–15 Wall Street, and Warren Street, New York City, was named after him. He was also a member of the Governor's Council of New York.

On Nov. 30, 1746, he sailed for Spithead in the *Chester,* arriving Dec. 24, to oppose as impracticable the expedition against Canada projected for the following year. Before he had a chance to return, he was sent on an expedition which culminated in the battle of May 3, 1747, with a French squadron off Cape Finisterre—one of the most important British naval victories since the defeat of the Spanish Armada—in which he was the outstanding hero. On May 29 he was knighted, with the Cross of the Bath; on July 1, he was elected to Parliament; on July 15, he was promoted to be vice-admiral of the White. He then changed his residence from New York City to London and summoned his family to join him.

Sir Peter had command of three later expeditions and retired at the close of the war with £200,000 prize money and a promotion to be vice-admiral of the Red, May 12, 1748. In Parliament he was an outstanding exponent of preparedness (*The Parliamentary History of England,* vol. XIV, 1813, pp. 613, 711). He died in Dublin, and was buried at the church at Knockmark, near Warrenstown; subsequently a monument to him, by Roubiliac, was erected in Westminster Abbey. Of his six children, three reached majority: Anne, who married Charles Fitzroy, created Baron Southampton in 1780; Susannah, who married her cousin, Col. William Skinner of Perth Amboy, N. J.; and Charlotte, who married Lord Abingdon, for whom Abingdon Square, New York City, is named.

[Date of birth from Pedigree of Sir Peter Warren, Office of Arms, Dublin Castle; Thomas Warren, *A Hist. and Geneal. of the Warren Family* (1902); F. J. Aylmer, *The Aylmers of Ireland* (1931); *The Naval Chronicle,* vol. XII (1804); Commission and Warrant Books, Official Correspondence and Logs, Pub. Record Office, London; copies of Admiralty in Letters 480, Colonial Office 5.44 and 5.45 in Lib. of Cong.; I. N. P. Stokes, *The Iconography of Manhattan Island* (6 vols., 1915–28); Warren and DePeyster Papers and Deeds and Misc. MSS. in the library of the N. Y. Hist. Soc.; Gage Papers in William L. Clements Lib.; *Louisbourg Journals, 1745* (1932), ed. by L. E. DeForest; J. S. Mc-

Lennan, *Louisbourg from Its Foundation to Its Fall* (1918); H. W. Richmond, *The Navy in the War of 1739–48* (3 vols., 1920); "The Pepperrell Papers," *Mass. Hist. Soc. Colls.*, 6 ser. X (1898); J. K. Laughton, in *Dict. Nat. Biog.*; bibliography under sketch of Sir William Johnson.]   L. H. R., Jr.

WARREN, RICHARD HENRY (Sept. 17, 1859–Dec. 3, 1933), organist, composer, was born in Albany, N. Y., the son of George William Warren and Mary Elizabeth (Pease) Warren. His father was a self-taught musician who from 1846 to 1858 had been organist of St. Peter's Church, in Albany, and at the time of his son's birth was filling a two years' engagement at St. Paul's in the same city. In 1860, when the boy was one year of age, the family moved to Brooklyn, N. Y., where the senior Warren was organist at Holy Trinity Church for ten years. From 1870 until his death in 1902 he played at St. Thomas' Church in New York City. His father was Richard Warren's first teacher. Following this preliminary instruction the boy studied with Peter A. Schnecker, George Wiegand, and John White, and finally went to Europe where he had lessons with Charles Marie Widor. While abroad he was invited to appear as guest organist in many cathedrals and churches. In 1877 he obtained in New York his first position as organist in America, at the Church of St. John the Evangelist, and remained there for two years. During the season 1879–80 he played at the Madison Avenue Reformed Episcopal Church, and then became organist at All Souls Unitarian Church from 1880 to 1886. For the next nineteen years (1886–1905) he was organist at St. Bartholomew's, and from 1907, at the Church of the Ascension. He was active as a musician until 1921, when he retired to his country home at South Chatham, Mass., where he appeared occasionally as a guest organist at the First Congregational Church. In the years of his retirement he had opportunity to enjoy his hobby, the operation of a small printing press.

From 1886 to 1895 he was conductor of the Church Choral Society, an organization founded by the elder J. P. Morgan. As director of this chorus Warren gave first performances of a number of new works, among them Horatio Parker's "Hora Novissima," produced for the first time by the Society in 1893 at the Church of St. Zion and Timothy. In the summer of 1905 he conducted a series of summer orchestra concerts at St. Nicholas Garden, New York. He also appeared as guest conductor with the New York Philharmonic Society and the Philadelphia Symphony. As a composer he produced a considerable volume of church music—anthems and church services. He also composed several operettas; "Ingala" (1880), "All on a Summer's Day" (1882), "Magnolia" (1886), and "The Rightful Heir" (1899). His opera, "Phyllis" (1897) was produced at the Waldorf-Astoria, New York, in 1900. His most ambitious secular work for chorus was the cantata, "Ticonderoga"; he also composed a number of orchestral works. At the time of his death, at South Chatham, Warren was a widower. His wife, Helen Corbin Hurd, to whom he had been married in 1886, died in New York in 1921. They had no children.

[*Who's Who in America*, 1916–17; Rupert Hughes, *Contemporary Am. Composers* (1900); *Grove's Dict. of Music and Musicians, Am. Supp.* (1930); J. Van Brockhoven, "Richard Henry Warren," *Musical Observer*, Oct. 1910; *Boston Herald, N. Y. Times*, Dec. 4, 1933.]
J. T. H.

WARREN, RUSSELL (Aug. 5, 1783–Nov. 16, 1860), architect and engineer, son of Gamaliel and Ruth (Jenckes) Warren, a descendant of Richard Warren of the *Mayflower,* was born in Tiverton, R. I. One of several brothers who gained success as builders and contractors, he won wide recognition as a conspicuous devotee of the Greek Revival. Removing to Bristol, R. I., at the period of an influx of wealth, he was afforded an outlet for his talents in designing luxurious residences for ship captains and merchants, chief among them the stately DeWolf-Colt mansion (1810). One writer remarks of this house by "the master mind of the Bristol Renaissance" that it is rare to find a design so boldly original in conception transgressing so few architectural tenets (*Architectural Review, post,* Mar. 1901, p. 28.) Warren's first wife was Sarah Gladding, daughter of Capt. John Gladding of Bristol, whom he married on Mar. 10, 1805. After her death in 1817, he married her sister Lydia. He served in the Bristol militia and became major. Later, for a long period, he practised in Providence, R. I. He also was in demand in various other cities, his diversified output including churches, banks, public buildings, and residences. Adaptations of the Greek ideal were always dominant, his structures being distinguished for pillared porticoes and classical colonades, and he developed the cupola motive for dwellings with much success. He passed his winters in the South, chiefly at Charleston, S. C., whose structural beauties he enhanced. Possessed also of engineering skill, he threw a bridge over the Great Pedee River, a feat previously attempted without success. The Warren truss, used the world over in steel bridge construction, is said to have been devised by him. He died in Providence at the age of seventy-seven, survived by his wife. He had no children.

Warren's most notable works in Providence

are the Athenaeum, and the Arcade, housing a nest of small shops under a roof of glass. The Arcade, with its thirteen twelve-ton columns of native granite, was in line with others erected in larger cities about 1828. Philip Hone [*q.v.*], who saw it near completion, described it as of "singular beauty" and added that it would be "much more magnificent than the arcades of New York and Philadelphia" (*The Diary of Philip Hone*, 1927, I, 5). In New Bedford, Mass., the Unitarian Church, the Free Public Library, and a group of patrician residences are among Warren's finest productions. The greatest achievement of his career, however, the stone mansion of John Avery Parker, was lost to New Bedford some years ago. Built in 1834 at a cost of $100,-000, and of more than one hundred feet frontage, it was marked by flanking wings connected with the main pavilion by loggie or peristyles. The interior was remarkable for a magnificent circular staircase, twelve mantels of costly marbles, and great silver-handled doors, each a single panel of solid mahogany. Wonderfully impressive from its great size, it was probably the most successful example in America of the application of the Greek temple type to residential purposes.

[See *Vital Record of R. I.*, vols. IV (1893), VI (1894), ed. by J. N. Arnold; geneal. in article on Theodore Warren in *Representative Men . . . of R. I.* (1908), vol. III; death notice in *Providence Daily Jour.*, Nov. 17, 1860; M. A. De Wolfe Howe, *Bristol, R. I., a Town Biog.* (1930); J. W. Dow, *Am. Renaissance* (1904), *An Architectural Monograph on the Bristol Renaissance* (1917), and articles in *Architectural Rev.*, Mar., July 1901, and *House Beautiful*, Oct. 1901; Howard Major, *The Domestic Architecture of the Early Am. Republic* (1926), which has a picture of the Parker house.]   W. M. E.

WARREN, SAMUEL PROWSE (Feb. 18, 1841–Oct. 7, 1915), organist, composer, was born in Montreal, Canada, the son of Samuel Russell and Harriet Proud (Staynor) Warren. He was eighth in descent from Richard Warren, the London merchant who came to America on the *Mayflower*. His father, a native of Rhode Island, became an organ-builder, worked with Thomas Appleton of Boston, and eventually established his own busines in Montreal. Playing among the awesome rows of organ pipes in his father's shop as a child, Samuel developed an ambition to make those pipes sound. He was given piano lessons and at the age of eleven was deemed sufficiently prepared to study the organ. He proved an apt scholar and at twelve made his first public appearance in recital at St. Stephen's Chapel in Montreal. He became organist at the American Presbyterian Church and officiated regularly for eight years. Upon the completion of his academic studies, he went abroad to continue the study of music. He remained in Berlin four years, 1861–64, studying privately with the celebrated organist, Carl August Haupt. Gustav Schumann was his master in piano; Paul Wieprecht, in theory and instrumentation.

He returned to Montreal but chose New York City as the field of his professional activity. He gave his first public recital there in January 1866 and in April was appointed organist of All Souls Unitarian Church, serving until April 1868. He officiated at Grace Episcopal Church, 1868–74, and at Holy Trinity Episcopal Church, 1874–76. He returned to Grace Church, 1876–94, and from 1895 to 1915, presided over the organ at the First Presbyterian Church, East Orange, N. J. The twenty-four years he served at Grace Church were the most fruitful of his career; his masterly series of more than two hundred and thirty recitals proved him to be one of the great organists of the period. His impeccable musicianship was reflected in the liturgical singing of the splendid chorus choir at Grace Church and in the fine choral work of the New York Vocal Union, which he conducted for eight seasons, 1880–88.

Great personal charm, a self-effacing modesty, great mental capacity, and a truly romantic idealism were Warren's outstanding characteristics. He was a superb teacher and a composer with uncompromising standards. His choral settings for the Episcopal service are of high merit. His ripe scholarship is evidenced in his editions of the organ works of Mendelssohn, Guilmant, and Lemens, no less than in his transcriptions for organ of great symphonic works. Several charming songs reveal his poetic gift. Ever intent upon advancing the cause of true musicianship, he participated in the organization in 1896 of the American Guild of Organists, and in 1902 became honorary president of the Guild. He served as a trustee of the American College of Musicians and was a member of the council of the Boston Conservatory of Music. His scholarly interests were reflected in his valuable library of musical literature, one of the finest of American private collections. With a truly bibliophilic ardor, he gathered original manuscripts, rare books, the published works of the great masters, and the representative extant biographical, historical, and theoretical literature of music.

He was married to Emily Augusta Millard, in Montreal, on Jan. 16, 1867. Mrs. Jeanne Josephine Croker became his wife in 1908. By neither marriage had he any children.

[Personal data from Warren's brother-in-law, Norman Robertson, of Walkerton, Ontario; *Who's Who in America*, 1914–15; *Handbook of Am. Music and Musicians* (1886), ed. by F. O. Jones; *A Hundred Years* of *Music in America* (1889), ed. by W. S. B. Mathews; H. E. Krehbiel, *Review of the N. Y. Musical Season* (5 vols., 1885–90); *Music*, Nov. 1899, and *Musical America*, Jan. 15, 1916; *New Music Rev.*, Dec. 1915; Anderson Galleries, *The Musical Library of the late S. P. Warren* (1916), No. 1240; *Baker's Biog. Dict. of Musicians* (3rd ed., 1919); W. T. Upton, *Art-Song in America* (1930); L. C. Elson, *Hist. of Am. Music* (rev. ed., 1925); *N. Y. Herald*, Oct. 8, 1915.]   E. C. K.

WARREN, WILLIAM (May 10, 1767–Oct. 19, 1832), actor, manager, was a native of Bath, England, the son of Philip Warren, a cabinet-maker. Scorning the efforts of his father to teach him his trade, he made his stage début with a small provincial company at the age of seventeen as Young Norval in *Douglas*. Trained in the rough surroundings of inferior traveling troupes, he finally emerged from a wandering life of hardship and slow advancement. At one time he was in the company of Thomas Jefferson, the founder of a famous stage family. In 1788, when he was under engagement with Tate Wilkinson, one of the leading provincial managers of that day, he had the good fortune to act in support of Mrs. Siddons. In 1796, upon the invitation of Thomas Wignell [*q.v.*], he set out for the United States, arriving in the autumn of that year. He acted in Baltimore, and then in Philadelphia, where he appeared for the first time on Dec. 5 as Friar Lawrence in *Romeo and Juliet* and as Bundle in *The Waterman*. A visit with the Wignell company to New York soon followed, but his associations with the theatre were almost exclusively, both as actor and manager, in Baltimore and Philadelphia. For some time he was in partnership with William Burke Wood [*q.v.*]. At their theatre in Philadelphia, Edwin Forrest [*q.v.*] made his début as Young Norval, with Warren as Old Norval; and both Edmund Kean and Junius Brutus Booth [*q.v.*] acted under their management when they first came to America. Warren was essentially a comedian, especially adept at the acting of old men, but he was equally capable in tragedy. Joseph N. Ireland [*q.v.*] calls him "the most perfect 'old man' of comedy or tragedy then known in America" (*Mrs. Duff*, 1882, p. 19); William Winter [*q.v.*] speaks of "the weight, dignity and rich humor" of his Old Dornton and Sir Robert Bramble, and of his notable Falstaff and Sir Toby Belch (*The Jeffersonians*, 1881, p. 66). Few American managers ever carried for so many years the double burden of management and the acting of important characters.

After a long period of prosperity, Warren's last years were filled with sadness because of his ill health and disappointment because of his business reverses. In December 1829 he retired from management and acted only occasionally

thereafter. Returning to the Chestnut Street Theatre in Philadelphia for a brief engagement, he made his farewell stage appearance on Nov. 25, 1831, as Sir Robert Bramble in *The Poor Gentleman*, being scarcely able to finish the part because of loss of memory. After almost a year of comparative seclusion, he died in Baltimore, where he had made his home during his last months. He was three times married. His first wife, of whom little is known and who was not an actress, accompanied him to America and died not long after. On Aug. 15, 1806, he married Ann Brunton Merry [*q.v.*]. In 1809 he married Esther Fortune, whose elder sister Euphemia was the wife of Joseph Jefferson, 1774–1832 [*q.v.*]. All their six children were connected with the theatre. Hester, the eldest, became the wife of Joseph Proctor [*q.v.*], Anna was the wife of Danford Marble [*q.v.*], the comedian; Emma was first Mrs. J. B. Price and then Mrs. David Hanchett, both of her husbands being actors; Mary Ann married John B. Rice, a theatre manager, later mayor of Chicago and a member of Congress, and retired from the stage in 1856; William [*q.v.*] was the celebrated comedian of the Boston Museum; and Henry, whose daughter, Sarah Isabel, became the second wife of Joseph Jefferson the younger [*q.v.*], was a theatrical manager. Through inherited ability and intermarriage, the Warrens hold a conspicuous place in the annals of the American stage.

[*Life and Memoirs of William Warren* (1889); William Dunlap, *Hist. of the Am. Theatre* (1833); Joe Cowell, *Thirty Years Passed among the Players* (2 pts. 1844–45); F. C. Wemyss, *Twenty-Six Years of the Life of an Actor and Manager* (1847); W. B. Wood, *Personal Recollections of the Stage* (1855); J. N. Ireland, *Records of the N. Y. Stage* (2 vols., 1866–67); William Winter, *The Life and Art of Joseph Jefferson* (1894); biog. of Warren in *Mirror of Taste* (Phila.), Feb.–May, Dec. 1811; *Phila. Dramatic Mirror*, Aug. 21, 1841; *Boston Herald*, Oct. 22, 1882 (valuable article); editorial in *Am. Sentinel* (Phila.) and obituary notice in *Nat. Gazette* (Phila.), Oct. 22, 1832.]   E. F. E.

WARREN, WILLIAM (Nov. 17, 1812–Sept. 21, 1888), actor, was born in Philadelphia, Pa., but after his boyhood and youth in his native city, and after some ten years as a strolling player, he went in 1846 to Boston. He was the son of William [*q.v.*] and Esther (Fortune) Warren. His education in the public and private schools of Philadelphia was brief. He was naturally attracted to the family profession but did not make his first appearance until Oct. 27, 1832, on the occasion of a benefit given in aid of the family at the Arch Street Theatre in Philadelphia, a few days after the elder Warren's death. He then acted Young Norval in *Douglas,* the part and the play in which his father had made his début in England forty-eight years before. James

E. Murdoch [*q.v.*] describes him as "a youth slight in figure, and looking much like a student of divinity at home for a vacation . . . silent and thoughtful in expression, and very formal in manner" (*The Stage,* 1880, p. 414). Thereafter he was associated with and obtained his professional schooling in migratory troupes, and in resident companies at Pittsburgh, Baltimore, Washington, Philadelphia, Buffalo, and other American theatrical centers. One of these engagements was with a company under the direction of the second Joseph Jefferson [*q.v.*], who recalls him as "a tall handsome young man about twenty-five years of age," with "fine expressive eyes, a graceful figure, and a head of black curly hair." He acted in New York very seldom, first in 1841; during a visit to England in 1845, he made his only appearance on the London stage.

The year 1846 marks his arrival in Boston, where he lived and worked for forty-two years. He was first associated with the Howard Athenaeum, where on Oct. 5 he acted Sir Lucius O'Trigger in *The Rivals,* remaining at that theatre only during a part of one season. Joining the stock company at the Boston Museum on Aug. 23, 1847, he acted there for the first time as Billy Lackaday in *Sweethearts and Wives,* and as Gregory Grizzle in *My Young Wife and Old Umbrella.* He soon became one of Boston's leading citizens, not merely in his capacity as an actor but as a gentleman who ranked in social standing with members of every profession and with the foremost men of business. In his *Autobiography,* Joseph Jefferson notes an occasion when with him as guests at Warren's table were Oliver Wendell Holmes, Henry Wadsworth Longfellow, and Mr. and Mrs. James T. Fields [*qq.v.*]. He had begun his stage career by acting a wide range of characters in comedy, melodrama, and tragedy; but, although not lacking in versatility, he eventually made comedy his especial branch of acting, and it is upon his skill as a comedian that his reputation rests. Despite the fact that, with the exception of one season (1864–65) when he went on tour, he remained in one city, in one theatre, and with one stock company, he became one of the most eminent of American actors. Few visitors came to Boston without going to the Museum especially to see the famous actor, and a favorite revival season after season was a comedy, adapted from an old English play, entitled *Seeing Warren.*

His rôles, nearly six hundred in about 14,000 performances, extend from such Shakespearean comedy characters as Touchstone and Polonius through such eighteenth-century comedy rôles as Bob Acres, Sir Peter Teazle, and Tony Lump-kin to leading parts in ephemeral productions of new plays. The demand for his repeated impersonation of Jefferson Scattering Batkins in *The Silver Spoon,* by Joseph Stevens Jones [*q.v.*], is typical of the acclaim he received in popular, though dramatically unimportant plays. If there were no part for him in a play that was put into rehearsal, one was written in so that his absence from the cast might not disappoint his admirers, the most conspicuous example of this being the interpolated character of Penetrate Partyside in *Uncle Tom's Cabin.* One of his associates says of his acting that it "belonged to the best French school. . . . The fine art, the fruition of study, the faithfulness in detail, all were there" (Catherine Reignolds-Winslow, *post,* p. 128), and a well-known critic echoes this judgment, adding: "His acting seems the fine flower of careful culture, as well as the free outcome of large intelligence and native genius. His enunciation and pronunciation of English were beyond criticism" (Clapp, *Reminiscences, post,* p. 56).

To celebrate his fiftieth anniversary on the stage, gala performances were given at the Boston Museum on Saturday afternoon and evening, Oct. 27, 1882, when he played successively Dr. Pangloss in *The Heir-at-Law* and Sir Peter Teazle in *The School for Scandal.* A few months later, on May 12, 1883, he bade farewell to the stage and to the Boston public in the character of Old Eccles in *Caste.* He lived thereafter in retirement, surrounded by his Boston friends and visited by many actors when they came to Boston. He died after a brief illness at the house in Bulfinch Place where he had lived many years. A vast assemblage of friends, acquaintances, and others gathered in Trinity Church to pay tribute to his life and memory, and he was buried in Mount Auburn Cemetery, Cambridge, where also lie Edwin Booth, Charlotte Cushman [*qq.v.*], and other eminent members of his profession. He never married. After his death appeared the *Life and Memoirs of William Warren* (1889).

[*Life and Memoirs of William Warren* (1889); Catherine M. Reignolds-Winslow, *Yesterdays with Actors* (1887); *Autobiog. of Joseph Jefferson* (1889); William Winter, *Life and Art of Joseph Jefferson* (1896) and *Vagrant Memories* (1915); H. A. Clapp, *Reminiscences of a Dramatic Critic* (1902); L. C. Davis, in *Atlantic Monthly,* June 1867; H. A. Clapp, *Ibid.,* Dec. 1888; *Boston Herald,* Oct. 22, 1882; *Boston Transcript,* Nov. 30, 1894, May 27, 1911, and Sept. 20, 1913; obituary in *Boston Transcript,* Sept. 21, 1888.]
E. F. E.

WARREN, WILLIAM FAIRFIELD (Mar. 13, 1833–Dec. 6, 1929), Methodist Episcopal clergyman, educator, first president of Boston University, was born in Williamsburg, Mass., the youngest child of Mather Warren, farmer, sawmill owner, and building mover, and Anne

Miller (Fairfield), woman of remarkable ability and piety. He was a descendant of William Warren who emigrated to Boston from England in 1715 and of John Fairfield, an immigrant to Charlestown in 1635. The boy's religious and reflective temperament was fostered in the family circle and both he and his brother, Henry White Warren [q.v.], became important figures in the Methodist Episcopal Church. He attended the local schools and East Greenwich (R. I.) Academy. Entering Wesleyan University in 1850, he was graduated three years later. He then opened a private classical school in Mobile, Ala. Returning North in July 1854, he was admitted to the New England Conference on trial in 1855 and supplied a church in Ballardvale, Mass., until 1856, meanwhile studying at the Andover Theological Seminary. During 1856–57 he attended the University of Berlin and the University of Halle, spending his vacations traveling in Italy, Greece, Turkey, Palestine, and Egypt. After his return to the United States he preached at Wilbraham, Mass. (1858–59), and at Bromfield Street Church, Boston (1860–61). He was ordained elder in 1861 and returned to Germany to become professor of systematic theology at Missionsanstalt in Bremen, remaining there until 1866. Articles in the *Methodist Review, Bibliotheca Sacra,* and other periodicals, and several books in German, notably *Systematische Theologie einheitlich behandelt* (Bremen, 1865), a volume intended to be an introduction to a larger work, gave him a reputation in theological circles.

When the Methodist Biblical Institute was moved from Concord, N. H., to Boston in 1867 and renamed the Boston Theological School, he became its president, serving as such until 1873. He was closely associated with the three Boston philanthropists, Isaac Rich, Jacob Sleeper [qq.v.], and Lee Claflin in the founding of Boston University and was the guiding spirit in its development. The theological school became its first department. As the university's acting president, 1869–73, and as president, 1873–1903, the work of creating the institution was largely his. His plans, notable in their comprehensiveness, were based upon a fusion of the English emphasis on the humanities grounded in the classics, the German thoroughness in research, and American democracy. Warren maintained that professional and technical schools should exist in comparative independence instead of operating as departments of a single school, and that pure science is better and more economically organized and is kept more vital in connection with schools of applied science. Full three-year

courses in law, in theology, and in medicine were instituted. In 1878 a fourth year was added to the medical course. Advanced schools of oratory and of music were founded, while courses in science and agriculture in cooperation with the Massachusetts Institute of Technology and the Massachusetts Agricultural College took the place of the colleges of science and agriculture of the original plan. The requirements for admission to the college of liberal arts were constantly increased. A college of commerce and navigation was planned but not established until 1913. By 1875 the schools of law, medicine, and theology had a larger enrollment than those of any other American university having these professional departments. Scholarly teachers, most of them with European training, were secured, among them Borden P. Bowne, Henry N. Hudson, and Alexander Graham Bell [qq.v.]. In his zeal for international educational opportunities, Warren completed in 1874 arrangements whereby students of the school of all sciences (the university's graduate school) could study at the National University of Athens and the Royal University at Rome. Warren vigorously opposed attempts to shorten the college course to three years as proposed by his contemporary Charles W. Eliot [q.v.]. His annual reports and his essays contributed to the *Boston University Year Book,* 1874–1904, left few phases of education untouched. He himself was an active teacher, maintaining his position as professor in the theological school from 1867 to 1920. He was dean of the school from 1871 to 1873, and from 1903 to 1911. His course in comparative religions, a subject in which he was an authority, was a famous one. The school under his leadership also offered lectures by representatives of other denominations, and was the first to require sociology and the study of missions in the course leading to a degree.

Warren was actively interested in educational opportunities for women, and Boston University was the first university in America to open the full circle of professional schools to them. It awarded the degree of Ph.D. to a woman for the first time in America when in 1878 it conferred the degree on Helen McGill (Mrs. Andrew D. White). Warren was an original member of the corporation of Wellesley College and president of the Massachusetts Society for the University Education of Women. His arguments for the admission of girls to the Boston Latin School were factors in the establishment of the Girls' Latin School.

His principal publications were concerned with conceptions of the universe held by the ancients. In this field, besides many articles, he published *The True Key to Ancient Cosmology and Mythical Geography* (1882), *Paradise Found* (1885), which went through eleven subsequent editions, and *The Earliest Cosmologies* (1909). His most famous address, a masterpiece of sustained imagery, was published in 1886 under the title *A Quest for a Perfect Religion,* went through five English editions, and was reprinted in Spanish, Japanese, and Chinese. The World Parliament of Religions in Chicago in 1893 was in a remarkable measure a realization of his dream. In his religion, Warren was devout without a trace of fanaticism, tolerant yet sure of his own beliefs, conservative but a believer in the essential soundness of modern approach to Biblical study. Under his educational leadership, insistent on academic freedom and enlightened scholarship, there were trained by his theological faculty the men who, with others like-minded, led the Methodist Episcopal Church, comparatively untroubled, through the storms caused by Darwin's *Origin of Species,* Spencer's *First Principles,* and the Tübingen school of Biblical criticism.

He married, Apr. 14, 1861, Harriet Cornelia Merrick of Wilbraham, Mass., later the first editor of the *Heathen Woman's Friend* and *Der Heidenfrauen Freund.* She was a woman of rare ability and training in languages, being proficient in Latin, German, French, and Italian. They had one son and three daughters. Warren retained his active interest in current affairs until his death at the age of ninety-six in Brookline, Mass. He was buried in Mount Auburn.

[Boston Theological School, *Reports,* 1867–72; Boston University, *Yearbooks,* 1874–1904; Boston University, *President's Reports,* 1874–1903; *Bostonia,* Apr. 1900, July 1903; *Boston Evening Transcript,* Feb. 9, 1924, Dec. 7, 1929; *Zion's Herald,* Dec. 11, 1929; *Meth. Review,* Mar. 1924; G. G. Bush, *Hist. of Higher Education in Mass.* (1891); D. L. Marsh, *William Fairfield Warren* (1930) and *Eliot and Warren* (1932); *Who's Who in America,* 1928–29; partial bibliog. of Warren's writings in *Alumni Record of Wesleyan Univ.* (1883); manuscript autobiog. notes in Boston Univ. Lib.]
R. E. M.

WARRINGTON, LEWIS (Nov. 3, 1782–Oct. 12, 1851), naval officer, was born at Williamsburg, Va., and as a youth attended the College of William and Mary. Little is known of his parents and what is known of his stepfather is discreditable (*William and Mary Quarterly,* October 1929). On Jan. 6, 1800, he was appointed midshipman. Soon thereafter he joined the *Chesapeake* and cruised in the West Indies during the last year of the naval war with France. Retained on the peace establishment of 1801, he participated in the war with the Barbary corsairs, 1802–07, serving on board the *President,*

Vixen, and *Enterprise.* In 1805 he was promoted lieutenant. After commanding a gunboat at Norfolk, he was attached in 1809 to the *Siren,* under orders to proceed to Europe with dispatches. On his return home he was transferred to the *Essex,* which, after cruising off the American coast, also made a voyage to Europe with dispatches.

His first duty in the War of 1812 was performed as first lieutenant of the *Congress,* one of the ships of the squadron of Commodore John Rodgers [*q.v.*]. Soon after his promotion to the rank of master commandant, July 1813, he took command of the sloop of war *Peacock.* Sailing from New York in March 1814, he encountered off Cape Canaveral, Apr. 29, 1814, the British brig *Epervier,* and after a sharp action of three quarters of an hour forced her to surrender, with a loss ten times that of his own ship. In recognition of this notable victory, Congress presented him with a gold medal and the state of Virginia with a sword. He next made an extensive cruise in which he visited the Grand Banks and the coasts of Ireland, the Shetland and Faroe Islands, and Portugal, taking in all fourteen prizes. In his last cruise during the war he rounded the Cape of Good Hope and crossed the Indian Ocean, capturing several large Indiamen, valuable prizes. Entering the Straits of Sunda, on June 30, 1815, he fell in with the East India Company's cruiser *Nautilus,* 14 guns, which he took after inflicting a loss of fifteen men, including the first lieutenant mortally wounded. Warrington's claim that he had not heard of the treaty of peace is disputed by the purser of the British vessel, who said that he spoke to him of the peace before the fight began.

In 1816 Warrington commanded the *Macedonian* during a voyage to Cartagena and conveyed thither Christopher Hughes [*q.v.*], delegated by the American government to effect the release of American citizens imprisoned by the Spanish. He commanded the *Java,* 1819–20, and the *Guerriere,* 1820–21, of the Mediterranean squadron. After a period of duty at the Norfolk navy yard he commanded the West India squadron which was employed in the suppression of piracy. In 1826–30 and again in 1840–42 he was one of the three commissioners of the navy board, an administrative body in Washington, D. C., charged with the administration of the naval matériel. During the intervening decade he was commandant of the Norfolk navy yard. On the reorganization of the Navy Department in 1842 he became the chief of the bureau of yards and docks. In 1844 he was for a time secretary of the navy *ad interim.* In 1846 he was

made chief of the bureau of ordnance, an office
that he held until his death. On Mar. 3, 1817, he
was married to Margaret Cary King of Norfolk,
Va.

[Record of Officers, Bureau of Navigation, 1798–
1858; *Navy Reg.*, 1814–51; *Analectic Mag. and Naval
Chronicle*, Jan. 1816; A. T. Mahan, *Sea Power in Its
Relations to the War of 1812* (1919); Theodore Roosevelt, *Naval War of 1812* (1904); *Daily National Intelligencer* (Washington), Oct. 13, 1851; *Va. Calendar
of State Papers*, vol. X (1892); *Va. Hist. Reg.*, Apr.
1852; *Va. Mag. of Hist. and Biog.*, July 1926.]
                                        C. O. P.

WARTHIN, ALDRED SCOTT (Oct. 21,
1866–May 23, 1931), physician, educator, was
born in Greensburg, Ind. The son of Edward
Mason and Eliza Margaret (Weist) Warthin,
he came of English and Pennsylvania Dutch ancestry. His grandfather was one of the first settlers in Decatur County, Ind., where he set up
a general store; his maternal grandmother, also,
had journeyed to the frontier. With an uncle, a
physician interested in the study of nature, he
went afield collecting specimens; and to please
his invalid mother he took lessons on the piano.
Considered a prodigy by his neighbors, he entered the Cincinnati Conservatory of Music and
in 1887 gained a teacher's diploma. During the
same period he studied at the University of Indiana under David Starr Jordan [*q.v.*], and upon
receiving the degree of A.B. in 1888, he turned
to science. Already he had taught botany. His
decision caused his father to withhold further
aid.

Characteristically undaunted, he enrolled in
the medical department of the University of
Michigan, and, supporting himself by giving
music lessons and serving as church organist,
graduated with the degree of M.D. in 1891. His
potential value to the medical school as a teacher was recognized by the new professor of medicine, George Dock. While assistant (1891)
and demonstrator (1892–95), he learned clinical
medicine, and in 1893 received the degree of
Ph.D. In 1896 he was given charge of the work
in pathology, taking over a department without
material and replacing a teacher who believed
that bacteria had no relation to disease. His intense energy and curiosity, already manifest in
several scientific papers, now found scope. To
procure material he arranged that all specimens
from the clinics be sent to him, and his diagnos-
tic findings soon became a touchstone for the
practitioner, a relationship to clinical medicine
which broadened throughout his life. At first he
did the entire work of the laboratory which he
created, technical and intellectual, teaching large
classes, doing autopsies and research, instructing graduate students, holding seminars, and

even giving a course in medical history. By 1903
he was professor and director. On June 27, 1900,
he married Katharine Angell. They had four
children.

Warthin's summers from 1893 to 1900 were
spent in the pathological laboratories of Freiburg, Dresden, and Vienna. In Vienna he came
upon Dürer's engraving of the knight riding unconcerned past a leering Devil and a bony Death;
and ever after the morbid seemed to him thrice
morbid because expressive of the human predicament. Working and writing on numerous
themes, among them tuberculosis of the placenta,
the hemolymph nodes—which he established as
physiological entities—the cause of Banti's disease, heredity in cancer, traumatic lipæmia, and
mustard gas poisoning, he came to the study of
syphilis, and in some forty papers disclosed its
responsibility for conditions previously unsuspected. His findings were often disputed, yet it
came to be recognized that in general he was but
little more positive than the facts.

Warthin's European experiences made him
keenly conscious that the contribution of medicine to American civilization was barely begun,
and to further it he gave himself to the founding
and support of societies and journals. Possessed
of a terse, vivid style, he wrote extensively and
was in demand as lecturer. He published *Practical Pathology for Students and Physicians*
(1897, 1911) and *General Pathology* (1903,
1908), a translation of the German work of
Ernst Ziegler. He also edited the *Annals of
Clinical Medicine* (1924–31). He became president of several medical organizations, notably
the Association of American Physicians (1928).
Shortly before his death he wrote "Forty Years
as a Clinical Pathologist," which was published
posthumously in the *Journal of Laboratory and
Clinical Medicine* (July 1931).

That concern for his kind which led Warthin
to study syphilis intensively found other expression in *The Creed of a Biologist* (1930). In this
volume he held that man need look no further
for immortality than to his descendants, nor for
a larger task than to better man. Still there
would be old age and death, and to discover a
right attitude toward these he studied the aging
process and collected books and pictures dealing
with the "Dance of Death," a collection which he
bequeathed to the University of Michigan. His
book *Old Age—the Major Involution* (1929) is
unsparingly comprehensive. In *The Physician
of the Dance of Death* (1931) he comments on
pictures which tell of the doctor's surroundings
and behavior when Death lays hands on him.
Its author did not have to gain this knowledge,

for he died of coronary occlusion, deeming it but a trivial asthma.

Warthin was bright-eyed and fresh-colored, quick and strong. He was drastic yet kind, earnest yet cheerful, and most sensitive to beauty. He loved music, gardens, books, and friends. Unpopular in his early years because of a trenchant sincerity, he lived to be widely appreciated without having relinquished it. In 1927 there was published *Contributions to Medical Science Dedicated to Aldred Scott Warthin,* containing scientific papers from members of his thirty-five classes.

[*Jour. of Laboratory and Clinical Medicine,* July 1931; *Annals of Clinical Medicine,* June 1931; *Jour. of Pathology and Bacteriology,* vol. XXXV, no. 1 (1932); *Jour. of Technical Methods and Bull. of the International Asso. of Medical Museums,* no. 13 (1934); *Am. Jour. of Syphilis,* July 1931; *Archives of Pathology,* Aug. 1931; *Am. Jour. of Surgery,* Nov. 1931; *Bolétin de la Asociación Médica de Puerto-Rico,* July 1931; J. McK. and Jaques Cattell, *Am. Men of Sci.* (1927); *Who's Who in America,* 1930–31; *Detroit Free Press,* May 24, 1931.]   P. R.

WASHAKIE (c. 1804–Feb. 15, 1900), a head chief of the eastern Shoshones, who befriended the white settlers and was a stout ally of the United States government, was born probably in Montana; the year of birth inscribed on his tombstone is 1804. He was of mixed Shoshone and Umatilla blood; the statement sometimes made that he was part white was apparently based on his exceptionally light color. In the 1840's he became chief of the Eastern band of Shoshones, often called Washakie's Band, whose general range was the lower Green River Valley. From his youth he was noted for his friendship with the whites. He was well known to the early trappers and at various times was in the employ of the American and Hudson's Bay companies. The overland emigrants found him and his people of great assistance in helping them across dangerous fords and in recovering their strayed animals, and a paper testifying to these acts was signed by more than 9,000 emigrants. Though his name does not appear in the treaty, he is said to have been in the great council of 1851, which met at Fort Laramie and later at the junction of Horse Creek and the North Platte. In the fall of 1862, unable to restrain a considerable part of his band from joining the Bannocks in plundering the emigrant trains and settlements, he took his loyal followers to Fort Bridger; but on the crushing defeat of the hostiles by Gen. Patrick E. Connor [*q.v.*] in the Bear River fight of Jan. 29, 1863, the band was reunited under his leadership.

In the treaty council of 1868 at Fort Bridger, wherein for the sake of the Union Pacific right-of-way the Green River Valley was given up in exchange for the present Shoshone reservation in the Wind River region, Washakie represented both his own people and the Bannocks. In the Sioux War of 1876 he sent from the reservation eighty-six of his warriors, under two of his sons, to join Gen. George Crook [*q.v.*] in time for the disastrous battle of the Rosebud, June 17, and three weeks later himself arrived with 213 more. Leading a scouting party for Crook, he penetrated the country of the hostiles and brought back definite word of their whereabouts. When Crook started northward to join Alfred H. Terry [*q.v.*], Washakie returned home with most of his followers. His declining years were spent on the reservation in the patriarchal rôle of ruler, guide, and counselor of his people. He died at Fort Washakie. A military funeral was accorded him, and a monument was erected over his grave.

Washakie was tall, with a powerful physique capable of great endurance. He has been likened in face and bearing to both Henry Ward Beecher and Robert Collyer [*qq.v.*]. All testimony agrees as to his high character and his kindly disposition. As a chief he was something of an absolutist, brooking little opposition to his policies; and he was also somewhat vain, with a fondness for showy ceremonials. Much of his life was spent in defensive wars against more powerful tribes, and even in old age he ranked high as a warrior. In his later years he renounced many of the customs of the tribe, including polygamy, and joined the Protestant Episcopal Church. It has been said of him (Wheeler, *post,* p. 217) that no Indian of mountain or plain was more widely or favorably known.

[Grace Raymond Hebard, *Washakie* (1930); F. W. Hodge, *Handbook of Am. Indians North of Mexico* (1910); J. G. Bourke, *On the Border with Crook* (1891); H. W. Wheeler, *Buffalo Days* (1925); *Cheyenne Daily Sun-Leader,* Feb. 20, 1900; manuscript notes from Professor Hebard.]   W. J. G.

WASHBURN, ALBERT HENRY (Apr. 11, 1866–Apr. 2, 1930), lawyer and diplomat, was the only child of Edward and Ann Elizabeth (White) Washburn. He was born in Middleboro, Mass., where his father conducted a small manufacturing business, and with the exception of a short period when the family resided in London, Ont., received his early education in the schools of that town. He then attended Cornell University, earning part of his college expenses by serving as secretary to Andrew D. White [*q.v.*], and was graduated in 1889. He entered the consular service and represented the United States at Magdeburg, Germany, from

1890 to 1893. In the latter year, invited to become private secretary to Henry Cabot Lodge [*q.v.*], he returned to America and acted in this capacity until 1896. Meanwhile he studied law at the University of Virginia and at Georgetown University, receiving the degree of LL.B. from the latter institution in 1895. He maintained a close personal and political association with the Massachusetts senator until the latter's death.

From 1897 to 1901 he was assistant United States attorney for the Massachusetts district, the varied business arising in the port of Boston, including the celebrated trials growing out of the murders on the barkentine *Herbert Fuller,* giving him wide experience in federal practice. From 1901 to 1904 he served as counsel for the Treasury in customs cases, becoming a specialist in the intricate problems involved in tariff legislation and the importing business.

In 1904 he resigned his official post and for the next eighteen years engaged in private practice. On Jan. 11, 1906, he married Florence B. Lincoln of Springfield, Mass., by whom he had one son. His professional standing was recognized by his election in 1917 as the first president of the Association of the Customs Bar. His briefs and arguments in *American Express Company et al.* vs. *United States* (4 *Court of Customs Appeals Reports,* 146), the Discount Cases (6 *Ibid.,* 291; 243 *U. S.,* 97), and *G. S. Nicholas and Co.* vs. *United States* (249 *U. S.,* 34) have been considered as of special significance in the field of customs law. The first of these cases attracted international attention, involving as it did interpretation of the "most favored nation clause," and in 1913 Washburn received a decoration from the Norwegian government in recognition of his services. He was a Republican in politics, active in the Massachusetts organization, and in general conservative in his views on political and social problems. His interest in political and international affairs and his inherent scholarly tastes found expression in occasional popular articles in magazines and reviews as well as in more technical contributions to professional journals. From 1919 to 1921 he served as professor of international law and political science in Dartmouth College.

In 1922 he was appointed minister to Austria by President Harding, the first to represent the United States since the collapse of the old empire in the World War. He continued at this post until 1930. He negotiated and signed a treaty of friendship, commerce, and consular rights, June 19, 1928, and an extradition treaty, Jan. 31, 1930. In 1922–23 he was a member of the commission of jurists that considered amendment of the laws of war at The Hague, and he was president of the mixed commission to adjust differences arising out of provisional commercial agreements and other difficulties between Austria and Jugoslavia, 1923–25. Washburn's reports were highly valued by the Department of State for their keen, illuminating, and objective interpretations of events in central and eastern Europe. He was frequently consulted by the officials of the new republic on the problems and difficulties of its formative years. His services in connection with the financial rehabilitation of the country and the extension of credit to the struggling government under the auspices of the League of Nations were regarded as a decisive contribution to its survival. His death in Vienna on Apr. 2, 1930, was followed by a flood of tributes from the leaders of Austria and neighboring countries in recognition of his constant and always unostentatious helpfulness. He had resigned early the preceding January and the submission of his nomination as ambassador to Japan was pending, when he succumbed, after a few days illness, to an infection resulting from a minor injury.

[*Publications of the Dept. of State: Press Releases,* Jan. 11, Apr. 5, May 17, 1930; *Reg. of the Dept. of State, Jan. 1, 1930* (1930); *Who's Who in America,* 1928–29; *N. Y. Times,* Apr. 3, 4, 6, 1930; *N. Y. Herald Tribune,* Apr. 3, 4, 1930; personal acquaintance, information from friends and colleagues, records in possession of Mrs. Washburn.]   W. A. R.

WASHBURN, CADWALLADER COLDEN (Apr. 22, 1818–May 14, 1882), soldier, congressman, governor of Wisconsin, pioneer industrialist, was one of the seven sons (an eighth died in infancy) of Israel and Martha (Benjamin) Washburn. His ancestry on both sides went back to early Massachusetts Puritans —on the paternal side to John Washburn who settled in Duxbury in 1632—and his two grandfathers, Capt. Israel Washburn and Lieut. Samuel Benjamin, served with distinction in the Revolutionary War. In 1809 Washburn's father, who had left the ancestral home in Raynham, Mass., three years before, bought a farm and a store at Livermore, Androscoggin County, Me. Here he married and brought up his numerous brood of children, which included, besides the boys, three girls. Members of so large a family could not stay for long under the parental roof-tree; hence, in 1839, equipped with what education he could get from the town schools, and deeply impressed by the advice of Reuel Washburn, a lawyer uncle, Cadwallader borrowed enough money to pay his way to the West, and was soon in Davenport, Iowa. Here, and across the Mississippi in Illinois, he taught school, worked in a store, did some surveying, and read law. In 1842 he opened a law office at Mineral Point, Wis., a small town not far from Galena, Ill., where his brother Elihu B. Washburne [q.v.] had settled two years before.

The foundation of his great fortune was soon laid. In 1844 he formed a partnership with Cyrus Woodman, an experienced land agent, and gradually abandoned the law for the far more lucrative business of entering public lands for settlers. Before long the partners owned in their own right valuable pine, mineral, and agricultural lands, and for a short time they operated the Mineral Point Bank. After 1855, when the partnership was amicably dissolved, Washburn carried on his now extensive operations alone. Even politics and the Civil War did not interfere seriously with the normal growth of this pioneer fortune. Proud of his honesty, and of the record of his bank, which never suspended specie payments and liquidated by meeting every obligation in full, Washburn rarely won the ill will of his neighbors; but his judgment on business matters was sound, and the opportunities for making money in a rapidly developing country were abundant.

Washburn's excellent reputation, and his early adherence to the principles upon which the Republican party was founded, brought him an unsolicited nomination and election to Congress in 1854. He sat in three successive congresses, in each of which, by an odd coincidence, his brother Israel [q.v.] represented a Maine district, and his brother Elihu an Illinois district. The three brothers, to the satisfaction of their respective constituencies, lent one another much aid, particularly on local matters, but the representative from Wisconsin achieved no very great national prominence. His outstanding act was to oppose vigorously a House plan to pacifiy the South by so amending the Constitution as to continue slavery indefinitely; but his participation in the Washington Peace Convention of 1861 showed his desire to prevent war. When war came nevertheless, his record was admirable. He raised the 2nd Wisconsin Volunteer Cavalry, became its colonel, and by the end of 1862 was a major-general. His command saw hard service in most of the campaigns west of the Mississippi River, and participated in the fighting around Vicksburg. When the war ended, he was in charge of the Department of Western Tennessee, with headquarters at Memphis.

After the war, as a rich man and a former major-general of volunteers, Washburn was clearly marked for a political career if he desired it, but politics never absorbed his chief interest. He served two more terms in Congress, 1867–71, as a thoroughly regular Republican, and one term, Jan. 1, 1872, to Dec. 31, 1873, as governor of Wisconsin. He would probably have welcomed a seat in the United States Senate, or a cabinet appointment, but these honors were denied him, and he was content to devote his later years to the operation and expansion of his vast industrial enterprises. His pine lands brought him into the lumber business and his shrewd acquisition of water-power rights at the Falls of St. Anthony (Minneapolis) on the upper Mississippi enabled him to become one of the nation's foremost manufacturers of flour. In 1856 he helped organize the Minneapolis Mill Company, of which his younger brother, William D. Washburn [q.v.] became secretary. Some fifteen years later C. C. Washburn was one of the first to adopt the "New Process" of milling, which created a demand for the spring wheat of the Northwest and completely revolutionized the flour industry in the United States. Like his great rival, Charles A. Pillsbury [q.v.], he was prompt in substituting rollers for millstones. In 1877 Washburn, Crosby & Company was organized, and two years later reorganized, with Washburn, John Crosby, Charles J. Martin, and William E. Dunwoody [q.v.], as partners. Naturally Washburn's wealth drew him into many other lines of business. He was, for example, one of the projectors and builders of the Minneapolis & St. Louis Railroad.

His private life was saddened, though not embittered, by the insanity of his wife, Jeannette Garr, a visitor to the West from New York City, whom he married Jan. 1, 1849. She became an invalid after the birth of their second child in 1852, and although she survived her husband by many years her mind was never restored. Perhaps as an outlet to his feelings, Washburn took much satisfaction in his philanthropies, among which were the Washburn Observatory of the University of Wisconsin, the Public Library at La Crosse (his residence after 1859), and an orphan asylum in Minneapolis. He suffered a stroke of paralysis in 1881, and died a year later at Eureka Springs, Ark.

[A manuscript sketch of C. C. Washburn's life, prepared by his brother Elihu, together with an extensive collection of Washburn and Woodman papers, is in the possession of the State Hist. Soc. of Wis. See also Gaillard Hunt, *Israel, Elihu and Cadwallader Washburn* (1925); David Atwood and others, "In Memoriam: Hon. Cadwallader C. Washburn," *Wis. Hist. Soc. Colls.*, vol. IX (1882); C. W. Butterfield, "Cadwallader C. Washburn," *Northwest Rev.* (Minneapolis), Mar. 1883; *Biog. Hist. of La Crosse, Trempealeau and Buffalo Counties, Wis.* (1892); C. B. Kuhlmann, *The Development of the Flour-Milling Industry in the U. S.* (1929); W. C. Edgar, *The Medal of Gold* (1925); N. Y. Times, May 15, 1882; *Republican and Leader* (La Crosse), May 20, 27, 1882.]   J. D. H—s.

WASHBURN, CHARLES GRENFILL (Jan. 28, 1857–May 25, 1928), congressman, manufact rer, writer, was born in Worcester, Mass., the eldest son of Charles Francis and Mary Elizabeth (Whiton) Washburn. His grandfather, Charles, twin brother of Ichabod Washburn [q.v.], was a partner of that pioneer in the wire industry. Charles Francis Washburn's entire business life was devoted to it, and his son, after graduation from the Worcester Polytechnic Institute (1875) and Harvard College (1880), at once started a wire-goods business of his own, in which he retained a controlling interest throughout his life. He soon entered the employ of the Washburn & Moen Manufacturing Company. By private study, however, he fitted himself for admission to the bar in 1887, and two years later became general counsel for that corporation. It was then rapidly developing the new wire-fencing branch of its industry, and Washburn was brought into intimate contact with the problems of corporation management and patent litigation. In 1891 he withdrew from the Washburn & Moen Company and began the practice of patent law in Worcester, but soon became president of a newly organized concern, the Washburn Wire Company. Eight years as president of the great textile firm, S. Slater & Sons, brought to him thorough knowledge of another of New England's major industries.

From 1897 to 1901 he was a member of the Massachusetts legislature, serving two years in each branch. His effective work, especially on the committees on taxation, the judiciary, and rules and banking, led to his being called upon repeatedly for tasks requiring hard work and good judgment. By appointment of Gov. Winthrop Murray Crane [q.v.] in 1902 he became a trustee of the Lyman and Industrial schools. He was a member of the committee on revision of the corporation laws (1902), and chairman of a special commission on street railways (1919). In 1917 he was a delegate-at-large to the convention for revision of the constitution of Massachusetts.

He was elected as a Republican in 1906 to fill a vacancy in the national House of Representatives caused by the death of Rockwood Hoar, and he was reëlected for the Sixtieth and Sixty-first congresses. His principal service was on the committees on insular affairs and patents and copyrights. He was mainly responsible for solving in 1909 the most difficult problem which long blocked the codification of copyright laws, namely the problem of "pirated" music for phonographs. On the floor of the House he spoke seldom, but his broad experience in legislation and in practical business lent weight to his discussion of matters relating to corporations and the tariff. After the final hearings upon the Standard Oil and Tobacco Trust cases in 1911, Chief Justice White sought the judgment of Washburn as a business man of broad experience upon the question of the probable effect of construing the first section of the Sherman Law so that it would forbid only contracts in unreasonable restraint of trade. Washburn strongly approved such a construction. (See his *Address on the Government Control of Corporations and Combinations of Capital,* 1911.) In the final decision all but one of the justices followed the Chief Justice in unequivocally reaffirming the application of "the rule of reason" to the Sherman Law, thus reversing the Court's attitude in the Transmissouri case of 1897.

Bad health during the campaign was largely responsible for Washburn's defeat for reëlection in 1910. An intimate friend of both Roosevelt and Taft, he parted company with the former in 1912 because of his advocacy of the recall of judicial opinions. In 1916 he was a delegate to the Republican National Convention. After his retirement from political life he retained the presidency of the Washburn Company, and from its establishment in 1914 until his death he served as a Class B director of the Federal Reserve Bank in Boston; but his energies were mostly devoted to literary and philanthropic activities.

His *Industrial Worcester* (1917) was an important history of the development of a great industrial center by a man who had had close personal associations with most of the leaders in that movement. His *Theodore Roosevelt: The Logic of His Career* (1916) was considered by Roosevelt himself and by his intimates as the most discerning characterization of him that had been written. At Harvard the classmates, Roosevelt and Washburn, had been students under Henry Cabot Lodge, and in 1924, at the request of Lodge, already stricken with fatal illness, Washburn came to his assistance and edited a most important portion of *Selections from the Correspondence of Theodore Roosevelt and Henry Cabot Lodge, 1884–1918* (1925). Only a few months later, before the Massachusetts Historical Society, Washburn presented a discriminating memoir of Henry Cabot Lodge (*Proceedings,* April 1925). His third biography, *The Life of John W. Weeks* (1928), dealt with a former senator from Massachusetts, an intimate personal and political friend. Washburn gave freely of his means and of his counsel as a trustee of the Worcester Polytechnic Institute and of the Groton School, and he was especially devoted to the service of the American Red Cross and of the Episcopal Church. He was married, Apr. 25, 1889, to Caroline Vinton Slater, by whom he had a son and a daughter.

[G. H. Haynes, *Life of Charles G. Washburn* (1931); *Biog. Directory of the Am. Cong.* (1928); *Who's Who in America*, 1926–27; *Boston Transcript*, May 25, 1928.]   G. H. H.

WASHBURN, EDWARD ABIEL (Apr. 16, 1819–Feb. 2, 1881), Protestant Episcopal clergyman, was born in Boston, Mass., the son of Abiel and Paulina (Tucker) Washburn, and a descendant of John Washburn who settled in Duxbury, Mass., in 1632; the missionary educator, George Washburn [q.v.], was a cousin. Edward's father, a merchant of means, was able to give the boy every advantage. He was prepared for college at the Boston Latin School and in 1838 graduated from Harvard with high honors. Reared a Congregationalist, he studied for the ministry at Andover Theological Seminary and at the Yale Divinity School, and was licensed to preach by the Worcester Association of Congregational Ministers in 1842. Reading, reflection, and the influence of friends in the Episcopal Church led him, however, to enter that communion, and on July 12, 1844, he was admitted to the diaconate at Trinity Church, Boston, and on Oct. 9 of the following year, was advanced to the priesthood. After serving as rector of St. Paul's Church, Newburyport, Mass., until 1851, he went abroad for two years, during which time he visited Egypt, Palestine, India, and China. Upon his return he became, in the spring of 1853, rector of St. John's Church, Hartford, Conn., and on June 16 married Frances H. Lindsley of Washington, D. C., by whom he had a daughter. While serving St. John's he also lectured on ecclesiastical polity at the Berkeley Divinity School, Middletown, Conn. In 1862 he was called to St. Mark's, Philadelphia, where he remained three years. From 1865 until his death he was rector of Calvary Church, New York.

Washburn was distinguished by intellectual and moral qualities of a high order. All who knew him paid tribute to his lofty manhood, his spiritual power, and his ministry of honest convictions. He had a rich knowledge of the history, philosophy, and literature of many lands. His mind was predominantly analytical, and he welcomed the modern critical attitude toward the Bible and theology, convinced that it would increase the growth of Christian life. He expressed his beliefs with boldness and in vigorous, eloquent style, though his preaching was of the kind that appeals to the thoughtful rather than to the

masses. Next to Phillips Brooks, perhaps, he was in his day the leading representative of broad churchmanship in the Episcopal communion. He was foremost in the little group which established *The Living Church,* a periodical embodying the point of view and spirit of the more liberal churchmen, and it was edited by his assistant at Calvary Church, William Graham Sumner [q.v.]. The paper was of too intellectual a character to be popular and survived but a year (1869–70). Washburn was also one of the original members of "The Club," a more or less informal association of clergymen, the greatest achievement of which was its successful leadership of the movement which resulted in the establishment of the Church Congress. He was interested in the work of the Evangelical Alliance, attending its meetings in the United States and abroad, and on two occasions, 1873 and 1879, presenting papers at its sessions. His scholarly attainments found employment in his services as a member of the American New Testament company of the revisers of the Bible, and in his labors on "The Two Epistles of Paul to Timothy," 1869, a translation and enlargement of J. J. van Oosterzee's work, which, with Dr. Edwin Harwood, he prepared for Philip Schaff's edition of John P. Lange's *A Commentary on the Holy Scriptures.* He contributed numerous articles to periodicals and in 1875 published *The Social Law of God,* sermons on the Ten Commandments, which went through six or more editions. After his death other writings of his were collected and issued under the following titles: *Sermons* (1882); *Epochs in Church History and Other Essays* (1883), edited by C. C. Tiffany; *Voices from a Busy Life* (copr. 1883), a volume of poems which show some skill in versification, but little originality in thought or form; and *The Beatitudes and Other Sermons* (1884). He died in New York City in his sixty-second year.

["In Memoriam," in *The Social Law of God* (ed. of 1881); C. C. Tiffany, *A Hist. of the Protestant Episcopal Church in the U. S. A.* (1895), in Am. Church Hist. Series; H. E. Starr, *William Graham Sumner* (1925); *New Eng. Hist. and Geneal. Reg.*, Oct. 1866; *Churchman*, Feb. 12, 1881; *N. Y. Tribune*, Feb. 3, 1881.]   H. E. S.

WASHBURN, EDWARD WIGHT (May 10, 1881–Feb. 6, 1934), chemist and educator, was born in Beatrice, Nebr., one of the four children of William Gilmor and Flora Ella (Wight) Washburn. His ancestors, from Little and Great Washburn, England, settled in New England before 1626. His father moved from Houlton, Me., to the frontier town of Beatrice, where he became a successful dealer in building supplies. Although the interests of the family lay chiefly in commerce, civic betterment, and politics, Washburn chose a career in chemistry. An honor student in his high school (which taught no chemistry), he assembled a crude chemical laboratory where he produced explosions which brought parental orders to stop "all this foolishness." At the University of Nebraska (1899–1901) he met his expenses by selling his thoroughbred pony and by tutoring. For a year he taught in the high school at McCook, Nebr., then, because Nebraska could not give him the training he desired, he went to the Massachusetts Institute of Technology. Here he had as teacher A. A. Noyes, and as associates, G. N. Lewis and R. C. Tolman. He was graduated B.S. in 1905 and Ph.D. in 1908, serving meanwhile as research associate. A rare combination of methodical worker and keen and imaginative thinker, he showed in his graduate research work the promise of his later brilliance. His paper, "The Theory and Practice of the Iodometric Determination of Arsenious Acid" (*Journal of the American Chemical Society,* January 1908), was the fruit of a study particularly significant because it prompted the first thermodynamic treatment of "buffer" solutions, so important in later work on indicators. He made the first accurate measurement of true transference numbers and of the relative hydration of aqueous ions.

In 1908 he went to the University of Illinois as associate in chemistry; two years later he was made assistant professor of physical chemistry, and in 1913, full professor. His accomplishments included the development of a " 'simple system of thermodynamic chemistry' bv means of his 'perfect thermodynamic engine,' the measurement of Faraday's constant with the iodine coulometer, and the development of a high precision viscosimeter and of apparatus for the precise measurement of the electrical conductivity of aqueous solutions of electrolytes" (Briggs, *post,* p. 221). In 1915 he published a textbook, *An Introduction to the Principles of Physical Chemistry* (2nd ed., 1921; French translation, 1925). In 1916 he became head of the department of ceramic engineering, and he effectively applied the principles of physical chemistry and thermodynamics to this virgin field until 1922, when he was chosen editor-in-chief of the *International Critical Tables of Numerical Data: Physics, Chemistry and Technology.* For four years he gave himself unsparingly to the exacting labors of preparing the seven volumes of these tables, the first of which appeared in 1926 and the last in 1930, thus making a notable contribution to science and technology.

Assuming the leadership of the division of

chemistry at the National Bureau of Standards in 1926, Washburn infused new life and activity into his department, initiated a program of thermochemical research, instituted and directed an extensive project on petroleum research, was responsible for the isolation of the first crystals of rubber, and found time to make many personal contributions to science. In December 1931 he made his most notable discovery—the fractional electrolysis of water with respect to the isotopes of hydrogen, a discovery which revealed new possibilities in physical, chemical, and biological research. For this achievement he was awarded the Hillebrand prize of the Chemical Society of Washington.

He was the author of approximately a hundred scientific papers; was a member of the National Academy of Sciences, the National Research Council, and numerous professional societies; and carried a tremendous burden of assignments on scientific committees of national and international scope. On June 10, 1910, he married Sophie Wilhelmina de Veer of Boston, by whom he had four children. Washburn's hobbies were the study of world history and genealogy, and his recreations were tennis, bridge, and "twenty questions." He was well informed, and eagerly discussed their own subjects with experts in many fields. Quiet, friendly, yet reserved, by his ability, fairness, and dignity he at once commanded admiration and respect.

[*Am. Men of Science,* 1933; *Who's Who in America,* 1930–31; L. J. Briggs, in *Science,* Mar. 9, 1934; *Bull. Am. Ceramic Soc.,* July 1922; *Industrial and Engineering Chemistry: News Edition,* Feb. 10, 1934; *Nature,* May 12, 1934; *Washington Post,* Feb. 7, 1934; details regarding childhood and ancestry from Washburn's son, William de Veer Washburn; personal acquaintance.]

F. D. R.

WASHBURN, ELIHU BENJAMIN [See WASHBURNE, ELIHU BENJAMIN, 1816–1887].

WASHBURN, EMORY (Feb. 14, 1800–Mar. 18, 1877), governor of Massachusetts, law teacher and writer, was born in Leicester, Mass., son of Joseph and Ruth (Davis) Washburn. He was in the seventh generation from John Washburn who settled in Duxbury in 1632. Emory's father and grandfather were Revolutionary soldiers; the former was deputy sheriff of Worcester County and died in 1807. The boy was educated at Leicester Academy and entered Dartmouth in 1813, where the former pastor of Leicester, Dr. Z. S. Moore [*q.v.*], was professor. In 1815, when Dr. Moore became president of Williams, Washburn transferred to that institution and was graduated in 1817. He studied law with Judge Dewey and then for a year, 1819–20, at the Harvard Law School. He was admitted to the bar in Lenox, Mass., in 1821, and practised in Leicester for seven years, also serving as town clerk. In 1828 he removed to Worcester, where he lived nearly thirty years. He was associated for several years with John Davis [q.v.], afterwards governor and senator. Washburn became the acknowledged leader of the bar of western Massachusetts and won an unusually large proportion of his cases. He was always "ready to plod till midnight" in the services of his clients (*Proceedings of the American Antiquarian Society*, Mar. 20, 1877, p. 11). On Nov. 2, 1830, he married Marianne Cornelia Giles, daughter of Nehemiah and Mary (Cowdin) Giles; they had two sons and a daughter.

Washburn represented Leicester in the Massachusetts House of Representatives from May 1826 to May 1828, and made a report favoring a railroad from Boston to Albany, the first railroad in the state. In 1838 he represented Worcester in the House, and in 1841 and 1842 in the Senate, serving as chairman of the judiciary committee. In 1844 he became judge of the court of common pleas (then the trial court of the state) but resigned in 1847 and returned to practice. In 1853 he was nominated for governor by the Whigs. He was then in Europe and knew nothing about the matter until his return. He was elected and served an uneventful year. The Whig party was rapidly disintegrating and he was defeated for reëlection by the Know-Nothing candidate.

On Mar. 17, 1855, he became lecturer in the Harvard Law School and on Feb. 23, 1856, was appointed to the University Professorship of Law (after 1862 the Bussey Professorship). His subjects were property, criminal law, and domestic relations. He lectured vividly and eloquently, making the dry rules of property live. Undergraduates in the college and professors in other departments used to drop in to his law lectures just to listen to him. In 1860–62 he published *A Treatise on the American Law of Real Property* (2 vols.), which was quickly accepted as the most satisfactory and trustworthy American book on the subject. It was followed by *A Treatise on the American Law of Easements and Servitudes* (1863). Both books went into numerous editions and were greatly valued in their day. When the inauguration of President Eliot was followed by the reorganization of the law school under C. C. Langdell [q.v.], Washburn remained as a loyal though somewhat unsympathetic member of the new régime until his resignation Apr. 3, 1876. He was probably the most beloved instructor who ever taught in Harvard Law School. "Every student seemed the especial

object of his solicitous interest. He not only acted as director, confessor, and inspirer of his pupils during their stay in Cambridge, but somehow found time to correspond with them, often for years, after they had scattered through the length and breadth of the land" (Batchelder, *post*, p. 651). His so-called "private office" at the Law School was "deluged with an unending stream of callers, friends, strangers, students, politicians, and clients" (*Ibid.*). He had an even and sunny temper and was the friendliest of men, "as jolly as a boy" (*Boston Transcript*, Mar. 19, 1877).

On his resignation he opened a law office in Cambridge and was elected in November to represent Cambridge in the House of Representatives, where he was made chairman of the judiciary committee. Though he had never been busier or happier, the strain was too great for him and he died in Cambridge a few months later from the effects of pneumonia. His concerns were extremely varied. He was actively interested in prison reform, industrial education, normal schools, schools for the feeble-minded, education in Liberia, and Massachusetts history. His *Sketches of the Judicial History of Massachusetts from 1630 to 1775* (1840) is still of considerable value. He was vice-president of the Massachusetts Historical Society and long active in the American Antiquarian Society.

[A. P. Peabody, in *Proc. Mass. Hist. Soc.*, vol. XVII (1880), with bibliography; Charles Warren, *Hist. of the Harvard Law School* (1908); *The Centennial Hist. of the Harvard Law School* (1918), with bibliography; S. F. Batchelder, "Old Times at the Law School," *Atlantic Monthly*, Nov. 1902; J. C. Washburn, *Geneal. Notes of the Washburn Family* (1898); *Vital Records of Leicester, Mass., to . . . 1849* (1903); *New England Hist. and Geneal. Reg.*, Oct. 1877; *Central Law Jour.*, Mar. 30, 1877; *Am. Law Rev.*, Apr. 1877; *Albany Law Jour.*, Mar. 24, 1877.]   Z. C., Jr.

WASHBURN, GEORGE (Mar. 1, 1833–Feb. 15, 1915), missionary and educator, was born at Middleboro, Mass., the son of Philander Washburn, a manufacturer, and Elizabeth (Homes), and a cousin of Edward Abiel Washburn [q.v.]. His ancestor, John Washburn, settled in Duxbury, Mass., in 1632. After attending Pierce Academy in Middleboro and Phillips Academy at Andover, he entered Amherst College in 1851. Graduating in 1855, he spent a year in travel through Europe and the Near East, then entered Andover Theological Seminary. After one year there he went to Constantinople as treasurer of the American Board of Commissioners for Foreign Missions. On Apr. 15, 1859, he married Henrietta Loraine, daughter of Cyrus Hamlin [q.v.], president of Robert College. In 1862 he returned to Andover, completed the theological course, and on July 29, 1863, was ordained at Middleboro as a Congregational minister.

Appointed a missionary of the American Board at Constantinople, he also taught at Robert College, which was then located in Bebek, a suburb on the Bosphorus. In the spring of 1868 he left Turkey to devote himself to religious work in New York City but a year later was persuaded by Christopher R. Robert [q.v.] to take charge of the college during President Hamlin's preoccupation with the construction of a building at Rumili Hissar. Organization of a new plan of study, teaching, and administration occupied him until May 1871, when the institution moved to its new quarters, and in June he departed for America. Urged by Hamlin and the trustees, he returned in the autumn to conduct the college while the president was attempting to raise funds in the United States. At first director and professor of philosophy, Washburn became president in 1878. During his twenty-five years in this office the college steadily increased its enrolment, its faculty, its physical plant, its endowment, and its influence among the peoples of the Near East. After 1872 there were many Bulgarian students, a number of whom later became prominent in the political and intellectual life of their country. Both Washburn and Prof. Albert E. Long received immediate information regarding the Bulgarian massacres of 1876 and the first accounts to reach western Europe originated with them. In 1879 both were voted the thanks of the Bulgarian nation by the National Convention. Washburn was later twice decorated by the Bulgarian government and long remained its trusted counselor. During several visits to the United States he secured financial support for the college and was repeatedly consulted on Near Eastern affairs by Secretary Blaine and Secretary Hay and by President Theodore Roosevelt. Using various pseudonyms, he contributed articles on history and current affairs to the *Contemporary Review* and under his own name wrote regularly for American magazines. His valuable study of the geology of the Bosphorus appeared in the *American Journal of Science* (September 1873) and his "Calvert's Supposed Relics of Man in the Miocene of the Dardanelles" was published in the *Proceedings of the American Association for the Advancement of Science* (vol. XXII, pt. 2, 1874).

On Sept. 20, 1903, he resigned the presidency of Robert College, but for another year held his professorship. From 1904 to 1906 he served as treasurer of the college in Boston, then returned for two last years of teaching before settling finally in Boston. Declining appointment as United States ambassador to Turkey because of a conviction that his missionary affiliations made ac-

ceptance unwise, he lectured during 1909 at the Lowell Institute and in the same year published his *Fifty Years in Constantinople,* which is a history of Robert College rather than an autobiography. A man of broad interests and abundant common sense, just and firm in dealing with men, a devout Christian but no proselytizer, Washburn earned the complete confidence of the peoples among whom he worked. As the intimate friend and adviser of Bulgarian, Turkish, British, and American ambassadors and statesmen he exerted an important influence on politics as well as on education in the Near East.

[*Who's Who in America,* 1914–15; *Times* (London), Mar. 18, 1915; F. A. Virkus, *The Abridged Compendium of Am. Geneal.,* I (1925), 644; *Amherst Graduates' Quart.,* June 1915; *Amherst Coll. Biog. Record of Grads. and Non-Grads.* (1927); *Congregational Year-Book* (1915); *Congregationalist,* Feb. 25, 1915; *Boston Transcript,* Feb. 15, 1915; *An Appreciation . . . of the Rev. George Washburn* (1915), printed by the trustees of Robert College; letters and papers in the possession of a grand-daughter, Mrs. Basil D. Hall, Florence, Mass.; information from Dr. C. F. Gates, formerly president of Robert College.]   W. L. W., Jr.

WASHBURN, ICHABOD (Aug. 11, 1798–Dec. 30, 1868) manufacturer, son of Ichabod and Sylvia (Bradford) Washburn, was born at Kingston, Mass. On his father's side he was descended from John Washburn who settled in Duxbury, Mass., in 1632; on his mother's, from Gov. William Bradford. The elder Ichabod, a sea-captain, died when his namesake was an infant, leaving the family in straitened circumstances, and at the age of nine young Washburn was "put out to live" with a chaise and harness maker in Duxbury. He remained with him for five years, learning the trade of harness making, and then returned to his home, where for two years he worked in the cotton mills. He then went to Leicester, Mass., and served a four-year apprenticeship in blacksmithing. Going into business for himself at Millbury, Mass., he began making plows, but soon relinquished this enterprise in order to acquire experience in the more difficult branches of his craft. For a few months he worked in the armory at Millbury, and then found employment with a machinery manufacturer in Worcester, Mass., gaining a knowledge of forging and of finishing all kinds of machinery.

In 1821 he entered into a partnership with W. H. Howard to manufacture lead pipe and machinery used in the production of woolen goods, and the following year he purchased Howard's interest. The demand for the woolen machinery was so great, however, that early in 1823 Washburn gave up making lead pipe and with Benjamin Goddard of Worcester formed the partnership of Washburn & Goddard, manufacturers of machinery for carding and spinning wool. The partners were immediately successful and continued their profitable business for eleven years, eight in Worcester and three in a larger water-power factory in Northville, a suburb. At the end of this period the business had so far outgrown the water-power facilities at Northville that a new site seemed desirable to Washburn; but Goddard preferred to remain where they were, and in 1834 the partnership was amicably dissolved.

Some two years earlier the partners had begun the manufacture of iron wire, of which up to that time little had been made in the United States. The machinery available was crude, capable of drawing but fifty pounds of wire a day, and as a first improvement Washburn devised the wire drawblock. With it the partners increased their production tenfold and were able to build up a substantial branch business of making wire cards. After the partners separated, Washburn continued the manufacture of wire in a new factory in Worcester, directing his whole attention to it until his death and becoming the leader of the industry in the United States. At the suggestion of Jonas Chickering [q.v.] of Boston, he began in 1850 to make steel piano wire and was so successful that thereafter imported wire was discarded. He introduced the galvanized iron telegraph wire so extensively used after 1850, and developed the first continuous method of tempering and hardening wire in 1856. He thus acquired practically the whole of the hoop-skirt wire business, which, at its maximum, amounted to an output of 1,500 tons annually. In operating the many related activities of the business, such as rolling mills, cotton mills to make the cotton for covering crinoline wire, iron and cast-steel furnaces, Washburn at first had the help of his twin brother Charles, but after 1850 his son-in-law, Philip L. Moen was his partner, the main firm being known as I. Washburn & Moen.

Washburn was a devoutly religious man and was deeply interested in the educational facilities of Worcester. Practically the whole of his fortune was bequeathed to religious institutions, to Lincoln (now Washburn) College, Kan., and to the Worcester County Free Institute of Industrial Science (now the Worcester Polytechnic Institute), of which he was an active trustee. He was twice married: first, to Ann Brown of Worcester on Oct. 6, 1823; second, in 1859, to Elizabeth Bancroft Cheever of Hallowell, Me., who survived him. He died in Worcester.

[C. G. Washburn, *Industrial Worcester* (1917); H. T. Cheever, *Autobiog. and Memorials of Ichabod Washburn* (1879); J. W. Roe, *English and American Tool Builders* (1926); *Worcester County Free Institute of Industrial Science: Addresses of Inauguration and*

Dedication . . . Nov. 11, 1868 (1869); *Worcester, Its Past and Present* (1888); *Forty Immortals of Worcester and Its County* (Worcester Bank & Trust Company, 1920); *Worcester Daily Spy*, Dec. 31, 1868.]
C. W. M.

WASHBURN, ISRAEL (June 6, 1813–May 12, 1883), lawyer, congressman, governor of Maine, was a brother of Elihu B. Washburne, Cadwallader C. Washburn, and William D. Washburn [*qq.v.*]. They were born in Livermore, Me., the sons of Israel and Martha (Benjamin) Washburn. Their father sat in the Massachusetts legislature from 1815 to 1819. The failure of his store in 1829 prevented Israel, eldest of eleven children, from attending college, but he studied law with his uncle, Reuel Washburn, and in 1834 was admitted to the bar. He made his home at Orono until 1863, when he moved to Portland. He held several local offices and sat in the Maine legislature in 1842 during the Northeast Boundary dispute. In 1848 he was defeated for Congress but in 1850 was elected, and for the next ten years represented the Penobscot district, first as a Whig and later as a Republican. During part of that time his brothers Cadwallader and Elihu were also in the House, representing Wisconsin and Illinois respectively.

His part in founding the Republican party was his most distinctive work in Washington. On May 9, 1854, the day after the Kansas-Nebraska bill passed the House and ten weeks after the original meeting at Ripon, Wis., he called a meeting of some thirty anti-slavery representatives at the rooms of two Massachusetts congressmen; this group took further steps toward organizing a new party and Washburn is a strong contender for the honor of having been the first to suggest the name "Republican." He used it publicly shortly afterwards in a speech at Bangor. Washburn steadily and strongly opposed the extension of slavery; in 1856 he supported Nathaniel P. Banks [*q.v.*] for the speakership; for a time he was chairman of the committee on ways and means.

On Jan. 1, 1861, he resigned from the House to succeed Lot M. Morrill [*q.v.*] as governor of Maine; later that year he was reëlected. He has been ranked with John A. Andrew and Oliver P. Morton [*qq.v.*] among "the great war governors of the North" (Hamlin, *post*, p. 357), because of his contribution to Maine's excellent war record. Immediately upon the call for volunteers, he summoned the legislature to meet in special session and, though Maine was asked for only two regiments, that body provided for ten, appropriating a million dollars. By 1862, however, recruiting had slackened, and Washburn wrote Lincoln that he would have to resort to drafting to secure "three-year" men. He declined renomination for the governorship and in 1863 was appointed collector of the port of Portland. He was several times disappointed in his cherished ambition of a Senate seat, partly through the opposition of James G. Blaine [q.v.]. In 1878, he lost his collectorship, after planning to buy a newspaper to attack the Blaine group. From Mar. 3 of that year until his death he was president of the Rumford Falls & Buckfield Railroad.

Washburn has been described as a "solid, hard-working man of sound knowledge and of rigid integrity" (Hunt, post, p. 40). Short, serious, and spectacled, he was less impressive than his brothers in appearance. He was quick-tempered, was a good story-teller, and had a strong love of literature. He wrote Notes, Historical, Descriptive, and Personal, of Livermore ... Maine (1874), read papers on the "North-Eastern Boundary" and on Ether Shepley before the Maine Historical Society (Collections, 1 ser., VIII, 1881), and was a frequent contributor to the Universalist Quarterly. He was a trustee of Tufts College from its opening in 1852 until his death, declining an offer of the presidency in 1878. On Oct. 24, 1841, he married Mary Maud Webster of Orono, by whom he had two sons and two daughters. She died in 1873 and he married in January 1876 Rebina Napier Brown of Bangor. He died in Philadelphia, whither he had gone for medical treatment, and was buried in Bangor.

[Gaillard Hunt, Israel, Elihu and Cadwallader Washburn (1925); In Memoriam: Israel Washburn, Jr. (1884); L. C. Hatch, Me., a Hist. (3 vols., 1919); Henry Wilson, Hist. of the Rise and Fall of the Slave Power (3 vols., 1873–77); J. S. Pike, First Blows of the Civil War (1879); C. E. Hamlin, Life and Times of Hannibal Hamlin (1899); Francis Curtis, The Republican Party, a Hist. (2 vols., 1904); F. A. Shannon, Organization and Administration of the Union Army (2 vols., 1928), I, 272; Biog. Dir. Am. Cong. (1928); New Eng. Hist. and Geneal. Reg., Jan. 1884; N. Y. Herald, May 13, 1883; Daily Eastern Argus (Portland), May 14, 1883.]   J.B.P.

WASHBURN, NATHAN (Apr. 22, 1818–Sept. 13, 1903), inventor, manufacturer, was a descendant of John Washburn who settled in Duxbury, Mass., in 1632, and the son of Seth and Catherine (Washburn) Washburn, the latter the daughter of Solomon and Mary Warner Washburn. Nathan was born on his father's farm at Stafford, Tolland County, Conn. In addition to running the farm the elder Washburn owned and operated iron furnaces in Stafford Hollow and Colchester, Conn., and Nathan spent his youth attending school in the winter, and at other seasons working on the farm and puttering around the furnaces. When he was nineteen years old he became a carpenter's apprentice and followed that trade locally for two years.

In 1840 he went to Worcester, Mass., and entered the iron foundry of W. A. Wheeler. After a year there he associated himself with a cousin, Augustus Washburn, and the two engaged in iron foundry work during the succeeding three years in Worcester, Fitchburg, and Ashburnham, Mass., Nathan Washburn showing particular skill in molding, casting, and finishing machine parts. Because of the illness of his partner, he sold out in 1844 and returned to Stafford, where, in association with a friend, he operated a foundry for two years, and then went to Rochester, N. Y. Here he engaged in making castings for cotton and woolen machinery and began supplying the local railroad with iron products. As a result of some investigations which he made relative to the peculiar strains to which pulleys were subjected, he designed an iron pulley so strengthened that it was unaffected by these strains. He next developed an improved railroad car wheel, and on Apr. 3, 1849, patented a cast-iron wheel which in subsequent years came to be known as the "Washburn Chilled Car Wheel." It was much stronger and less likely to break than previous types, for he had discovered a way of cooling cast-iron without cracking it, using in his process charcoal and white sand. As a result, his wheel displaced within a short time every other pattern of wheel.

Selling out his foundry at Rochester in 1849, Washburn returned to Stafford and with E. A. Converse, a woolen manufacturer, organized the partnership of Converse & Washburn for the manufacture of his patented wheel and textile machinery. Converse withdrew in 1854 and Washburn thereafter conducted the business alone. The success of the firm was phenomenal from the start and between 1849 and 1859 mills and foundries were established in Worcester, Mass., in Troy and Schenectady, N. Y., and in Toronto, Canada. The manufacture of iron products for cotton and woolen machinery and the rolling of railroad rails were also undertaken, and by 1857 the concern had an establishment in Worcester covering four acres. During the Civil War it did a large business in the manufacture of gun barrels, Washburn having perfected a new process of puddling pig iron whereby he could produce gun iron superior to that then imported from England. About 1865 he disposed of many of his diversified interests so that he could concentrate his attention in making still further improvements in car wheels. He did, however, become associated with W. C. Barnum and others in the purchase of certain iron ore properties and in operating them. In 1867 he produced a satisfactory steel-tired car wheel at Worcester, and the manufacture and further improvement of this product constituted his major activity for the rest of his life. His wife was Eliza Young of Stafford and at the time of his death, in Stafford Springs, Conn., he was survived by a daughter.

[C. G. Washburn, *Industrial Worcester* (1917); *Commemorative Biog. Record of Tolland and Windham Counties, Conn.* (1903); *Springfield Republican*, Sept. 15, 1903; Patent Office records.]   C. W. M.

WASHBURN, WILLIAM DREW (Jan. 14, 1831–July 29, 1912), representative in Congress, United States senator, mill-owner, son of Israel and Martha (Benjamin) Washburn, was born on a farm in Livermore, Me. Common schools and the academies of Gorham, Paris, and Farmington prepared him for Bowdoin College, where he graduated in 1854. He then studied law with his brother Israel [q.v.] in Orono and with John A. Peters [q.v.] in Bangor and spent a little time in Washington as a clerk in the House of Representatives.

In 1857 he followed his brothers Cadwallader and Elihu [qq.v.] into the West, and settled in Minnesota to practise law. At once he was made secretary and agent of the Minneapolis Mill Company, organized by his brother Cadwallader and others. In 1858 he was elected to the second Minnesota legislature, which never met. From 1861 to 1865 he was federal surveyor-general for Minnesota, living in St. Paul; in 1864 he ran against Ignatius Donnelly [q.v.] for the House of Representatives, but was defeated. Upon retiring from his surveyorship in 1865, he once more became agent of the Minneapolis Mill Company, and took up his residence permanently in Minneapolis. In 1867 he was one of those who launched the *Minneapolis Tribune* and in 1871 he sat in the legislature. Lumbering, with a sawmill at Minneapolis and one at Anoka, development of water power, especially on the west side of the Falls of St. Anthony, real-estate deals, and the manufacture of flour were some of his manifold activities. In 1878, after a brief association with his brother in Washburn, Crosby & Company, he founded the milling firm of W. D. Washburn & Company. Elected to the national House of Representatives, partly as the result of a contest between farmers and millers, he served from 1879 to 1885, working especially for the improvement of the upper Mississippi, for control of its floods, and for the improvement of navigation on the Great Lakes. In 1884 many of his interests were consolidated in the Washburn Mill Company. Railroad build-

ing and management, primarily as a factor in the milling industry, also engaged his attention. He was a leader in organizing and promoting the Minneapolis & St. Louis Railroad, and he was the principal projector of the Minneapolis, St. Paul & Sault Ste. Marie Railway Company, of which he was president until 1889.

His election to the United States Senate in that year was a turning point in his life. Upon taking his seat he dropped most of his active connections with his business enterprises, although he remained a director of the Pillsbury-Washburn Flour Mills Company with which the Washburn Mill Company was merged in 1889. His one term in the Senate, however, scarcely gave him time to make himself a power in that body. Defeated in the legislature by Gov. Knute Nelson [q.v.] in 1895, through what he was inclined to consider political treachery, he made no further attempts at political advancement but busied himself with business, church, social, and philanthropic interests. He had married Elizabeth Muzzy of Bangor, Apr. 19, 1859, and they had eight children. He was one of the founders of the First Universalist Society of Minneapolis. Not a "mixer," living and acting in what many considered an "aristocratic" manner, he was, while not a negligible political factor, more important as a major figure in the business, financial, and social life of his community.

[E. V. Smalley, *A Hist. of the Republican Party* (1896); *Who's Who in America*, 1912–13; Alonzo Phelps, *Biog. Hist. of the Northwest* (1890); E. W. T. Hyde and William Stoddard, *Hist. of the Great Northwest and its Men of Progress* (1901); Isaac Atwater, *Hist. of the City of Minneapolis* (1893); H. P. Hall's *Observations . . . 1849 to 1904* (1904); W. W. Folwell, *A Hist. of Minn.*, esp. vol. III (1926); C. E. Flandrau, *Encyc. of Biog. of Minn.* (1900); C. B. Kuhlmann, *Development of the Flour-Milling Industry in the U. S.* (1929); W. C. Edgar, *The Medal of Gold* (1925); *Northwestern Miller* (Minneapolis), *passim*, and esp., Jan. 25, 1889 and July 31, 1912; *Minneapolis Morning Tribune*, July 30, 1912.]   L. B. S—e.

WASHBURNE, ELIHU BENJAMIN (Sept. 23, 1816–Oct. 23, 1887), congressman, cabinet member, diplomat, historian, was the third of eleven children born to Israel and Martha (Benjamin) Washburn at Livermore, Me. After the failure of the father's country store in 1829 the large family was forced to rely on a small and not-too-fertile farm for subsistence, and as a result several of the brothers, among them Elihu, were early forced to fend for themselves. Leaving home at the age of fourteen, he added an "e" to his name in imitation of his English forebears and embarked on the road of education and hard work which led him to a position not the least prominent among five brothers—Israel, Cadwallader C., William D. [qq.v.], Elihu, and

Charles—notable for their service to state and nation.

A short experience at farm work convinced him that he was not destined for an agricultural career; he disliked his three months of school teaching more than anything he ever turned his hand to; a newspaper publisher to whom he apprenticed himself failed, and while he was working for another printer a hernia incapacitated him for further typesetting. These experiences led him to the decision to study law, and accordingly, after several months in Maine Wesleyan Seminary, Kent's Hill, followed by an apprenticeship in a Boston law office, he entered the Harvard Law School in 1839, where he came under the influence of Joseph Story [q.v.]. Armed with membership in the Massachusetts bar and a few law books, he turned his face westward in 1840, resolved to settle in Iowa Territory.

His brother Cadwallader, who had already settled at Rock Island, Ill., persuaded the newcomer that Illinois was a more favorable location than Iowa, and that the most likely place for a briefless lawyer was the boom town of Galena, where lead mines had recently been opened. Within a month after his arrival Washburne had begun to make a living and some political speeches. He presently formed a connection which was to be of considerable importance, both personally and professionally, with Charles S. Hempstead, the leader of the town's dozen lawyers. The latter, partially paralyzed, needed clerical assistance in his practice and in return threw sundry minor cases to his quasi-partner. This association lasted for a year, after which Washburne practised independently until 1845, when he entered an actual partnership with Hempstead. In this year he married, July 31, one of his benefactor's relatives, Adèle Gratiot, a descendant of the French settlers around St. Louis. Seven children were born to them. Washburne's connection by marriage with Missouri, indirect though it was, commended him to the attention of Thomas Hart Benton [q.v.] on his entry into Congress eight years later, and was of no disadvantage in launching his career.

His moderate earnings from the law were transmuted into a comfortable competence by careful investments in western lands, and he gradually turned his energies into political channels. He became a wheel-horse of the local Whig party, placed Henry Clay in nomination for the presidency at Baltimore in 1844, and ran unsuccessfully for Congress four years later. He was more fortunate in 1852, and in the following year began sixteen years of service in the House which covered the periods of the Civil War and reconstruction. He kept a sharp lookout for the interests of his section (particularly directed toward preventing the misappropriation of public lands to the uses of railroad speculators) and at the same time cast a keen and malevolent eye upon those who would raid the federal treasury. The lobbyist or the known corruptionist fared badly at his hands, and his last long speech in the House (Jan. 6, 1869), on a pension bill, was one of a number of blasts against those who were at the time leading Congress along forbidden paths. For a time he was chairman of the committee on commerce and for two years, chairman of the committee on appropriations, where his efforts to keep down expenses made him the first of a long succession of "watchdogs of the treasury."

Physical disabilities kept him from active military duty during the Civil War but he used his talents in Congress to aid his personal and political friend Lincoln, and to forward the military fortunes of his fellow townsman and protégé, Ulysses S. Grant. He was the sole person to greet Lincoln on his secret arrival in Washington for the inauguration in 1861 (Hunt, *post*, pp. 229–30). He proposed Grant's name as brigadier-general of volunteers and sponsored the bills by which Grant was made successively lieutenant-general and general. When war gave way to reconstruction, Washburne found himself in the forefront of the Radicals and a member of the Joint Committee on Reconstruction. He turned against Lincoln's successor and when members of the vindictive party "competed with one another in phrasing violent abuse of Andrew Johnson . . . Elihu Washburne deserved one of the prizes" (*Ibid.*, p. 238).

His early sponsorship of Grant continued through the campaign of 1868, when Grant heard the news of his election over telegraph wires run to Washburne's library in Galena. His stanch support was rewarded by appointment as secretary of state in Grant's cabinet, a post which he assumed Mar. 5, 1869, resigned Mar. 10, and vacated Mar. 16. It is probable that this was a courtesy appointment preliminary to his designation, Mar. 17, as minister to France, and designed to give him prestige in the French capital. His connection with the Grant administration remained close and he and Grant were friends until the spring of 1880, when an abortive boom for Washburne ran foul of Grant's own futile aspirations for a third term. Washburne himself immediately adhered to Grant's candidacy, though apparently without great enthusiasm, and remained at least outwardly loyal to his former chief. During the convention he himself received as many as forty-four votes, and it was later contended by his friends that with Grant's support he could have received the nomination which went to Garfield. Be that as it may, Grant vented his disappointment on Washburne and the two never met again.

Meantime he had rendered capable service through very trying times in Europe. As minister to France he witnessed the downfall of the empire of the third Napoleon and, remaining until the autumn of 1877, rounded out the longest term of any American minister to France down to that time. He was the only official representative of a foreign government to remain in Paris throughout the siege and the Commune, and his two volumes of memoirs, *Recollections of a Minister to France, 1869–1877* (1887), constitute a valuable account of those exciting days. In addition to his service to his own country, during the war he made himself useful by looking after the interests of German residents of France.

On his retirement from public life he devoted himself to historical and literary activities, serving as president of the Chicago Historical Society from 1884 to 1887 and publishing, in addition to the *Recollections of a Minister*, several works of some historical value, particularly sketches of early Illinois political figures, prepared for the Chicago Historical Society. For the same society he edited "The Edwards Papers" (*Collections*, vol. III, 1884), a selection from the manuscripts of Gov. Ninian Edwards [*q.v.*] of Illinois.

[Gaillard Hunt, *Israel, Elihu, and Cadwallader Washburn* (1925); J. V. Fuller, "Elihu Benjamin Washburne," in S. F. Bemis, *The Am. Secretaries of State*, vol. VII (1928); G. W. Smith, "Elihu B. Washburne," in *Chicago Hist. Soc. Colls.*, vol. IV (1890); *Encyc. of Biog. of Ill.*, vol. II (1894); *Biog. Dir. Am. Cong.* (1928); *General Grant's Letters to a Friend, 1861–1880* (1897), ed. by J. G. Wilson, being letters to Washburne; *Papers Relating to the Foreign Relations of the U. S.*, 1870–77; *Chicago Tribune*, Oct. 24, 1887; Washburne Papers (101 vols.), MSS. Div., Lib. of Cong.]   L. E. E.

WASHINGTON, BOOKER TALIAFERRO (Apr. 5, 1856–Nov. 14, 1915), Negro educational leader, was born on James Burroughs' plantation at Hale's Ford, Franklin County, Va. His father is believed to have been a white man from a neighboring plantation (*Up From Slavery*, p. 2). His mother, Jane Ferguson, was a Negro, a cook in the Burroughs family. He speaks gratefully of her "good, hard, common sense" and "high ambitions for her children" (*Ibid.*, p. 28), and recollects her praying that she and her children might be free. The latter

were an elder brother, John, later director of industries at Tuskegee, and a sister, Amanda. They lived in a one-room cabin with a fire-place and "potato-hole" but without wooden floor or glass windows. He never remembered "having slept in a bed until after our family was declared free by the Emancipation Proclamation" (*Ibid.*, p. 5). He tells us that their food was "a piece of bread here and a scrap of meat there. It was a cup of milk at one time, some potatoes at another" (*Ibid.*, p. 9). On Sundays there were two spoonfuls of molasses from the "big house." Failing other breakfast, he ate of the boiled corn prepared for the cows and pigs. Yet, despite the hard conditions, there was on the plantation considerable mutual affection on the part of slaves and master (*Ibid.*, pp. 20–22).

Soon after emancipation they moved to Malden, near Charleston, W. Va., the children walking most of the way. Here his mother secured Webster's "Blue-back Spelling Book," and Booker soon mastered the alphabet, though, he said, "at that time there was not a single member of my race anywhere near us who could read" (*Ibid.*, p. 27). An elementary school for Negro children was started, but the boy's wages as a worker in the salt-furnace were needed at home, so he had lessons at night with the teacher. Later he attended regular classes, working five hours before school, returning to furnace or mine in the afternoon. Being asked his name by the teacher, he calmly told him "Booker Washington," believing that bearing such a name would make him "equal to the situation" (*Ibid.*, p. 34). Later he found that his mother had named him "Booker Taliaferro." An important incident of these early days was his overhearing two miners talking about a school for Negro people, Hampton Institute. But prior to going there he served a year and a half in the home of Gen. Lewis Ruffner, owner of the salt-furnace and coal mine. Here he soon learned that Mrs. Ruffner "wanted everything kept clean about her, that she wanted things done promptly and systematically" (*Ibid.*, p. 44). Encouraged by her he continued to study evenings and attended school one hour a day. In 1872, at the age of seventeen, he set out for Hampton, about 500 miles distant, with a few dollars and a cheap satchel containing all his belongings. He feared his tramp-like appearance might interfere with his admission to Hampton. But, asked to sweep a room, he found that his lessons in thoroughness at Mrs. Ruffner's stood him in good stead. He swept it three times, dusted it four times. "I guess you will do to enter this institution," was the teacher's verdict (*Ibid.*, p. 53).

He spent three years at Hampton, his tuition being paid by a Northern friend of Gen. Samuel C. Armstrong [*q.v.*], the principal; his board and other expenses he earned as janitor. "Life at Hampton was a constant revelation . . . the matter of having meals at regular hours, of eating on a tablecloth, using a napkin, the use of the bathtub and of the toothbrush, as well as the use of sheets upon the bed" (*Ibid.*, p. 58) were new things in his life, and, above all, his "greatest benefit," was contact with General Armstrong. He learned the trade of brick-mason, graduated in 1875, went as a waiter to a summer hotel in Connecticut, then returned to Malden to teach in a Negro school where he worked fourteen hours a day. The winter of 1878–79 he spent at Wayland Seminary, Washington, D. C., and afterward gave the "post-graduate address" at Hampton, on "The Force that Wins." This created such a favorable impression that he was called in 1879 to take charge of the Indian dormitory and the night school, and also served as secretary to General Armstrong.

In May 1881 General Armstrong received a letter from George W. Campbell, a banker, merchant, and former slave-holder, and Lewis Adams, a mechanic and ex-slave, both of Tuskegee, Ala., asking for some one to start there a Negro normal school, for which they had just secured a charter from the state legislature. Booker Washington was chosen. It is significant that Tuskegee was not established by Northern philanthropy, but was the product of Southern initiative. It opened with forty students "in a dilapidated shanty near the Negro Methodist Church, with the church itself as a sort of assembly-room." Now began incessant labors of thirty-four years. Washington "ate and slept with the people," studying conditions of the Black Belt. Desperately poor and ignorant, they lived mainly on fat pork and cornbread, knew nothing of cleanliness, and raised only cotton. He taught them the dignity of efficient labor, and to "live on the farm off the farm." Teaching, speaking, and traveling in the interest of Tuskegee, he developed his work until when he died the Institute, with its excellent board of trustees on which the white South, the North, and the Negro were almost equally represented, had more than a hundred substantial buildings, owned 2000 acres of local land, and had received from Congress 25,000 acres in northern Alabama; had an endowment of nearly $2,000,000 with an annual budget of $290,000; had 1537 students, 197 faculty members, all Negroes, and taught thirty-eight trades and professions. He

also started many forms of rural extension work; established the National Negro Business League with its many important ramifications, the National Negro Health Week, and various Negro conferences at which the Principal, with his unfailing common sense, resourcefulness, and humor, was at his best. Largely as a result of his labors he could say in 1910, "We have no race problem in Macon County" (*My Larger Education*, p. 308). The high reputation of Tuskegee graduates for character and local leadership became well established.

From 1884, when Washington addressed the National Education Association at Madison, Wis., he was in great demand throughout the country as a public speaker on education and race relations. His addresses were striking for their sincerity, simplicity, and humor; his English was that of the Bible which was his daily study. These addresses, whether before Negro teachers, or members of a Southern legislature, or the Harvard alumni body (after he received an honorary degree in 1891), emphasized much the same points: an education fitted for life, the need of keeping close to Nature, and of cultivating the respect of one's neighbors, white and black. It was his epochal speech at the Cotton States and International Exposition at Atlanta, Ga., Sept. 18, 1893, that brought him national recognition as the leader of the Negro people, succeeding Frederick Douglass who had just died. His desire "to say something that would cement the friendship of the races" resulted in one of his most famous phrases: "In all things that are purely social we can be as separate as the fingers, yet one as the hand in all things essential to mutual progress" (*Up From Slavery*, pp. 221–22). The effect of the speech, with its advice to Southern white men and Negroes alike to "Cast down your buckets where you are," was electric. Clark Howell referred to the address as "one of the most notable speeches, both as to character and as to the warmth of its reception, ever delivered to a Southern audience. The address was a revelation. The whole speech is a platform upon which blacks and whites can stand with full justice to each other" (*Ibid.*, p. 226).

His views were opposed by the Negro "intellectuals" who felt he did not sufficiently emphasize political rights, and that his stress on industrial education might result in keeping the Negro in virtual bondage. He was more interested in making his race worthy of the franchise, which he himself always exercised without difficulty, than in agitating for it in ways which might inflame public opinion. Looking at the controversy after a generation has passed, we can see that there was truth on both sides, but that as far as the welfare of the masses in the South was concerned, and considering the public opinion of his day, which he wished to influence, he adopted the only policy which could be really effective. Two incidents involving race relations attracted almost as much attention as his Atlanta speech. Of his dining with President Theodore Roosevelt at the White House in the autumn of 1901 he said, "Mr. Roosevelt simply found he could spare the time best during and after the dinner hour for the discussion of matters which both of us were interested in" (*My Larger Education*, p. 177). His own custom was consistent. In the North and in Europe he accepted dinner invitations from white people when he thought they would advance the interests of Tuskegee or of the Negro race, but he was extremely modest regarding all the honors shown him by royalty abroad and by leading Americans. The other incident was his call at the apartment of a white family in New York in March 1911, resulting in a misunderstanding which was unfairly played up by some newspapers (see especially the statement of Seth Low, president of the Tuskegee trustees, in *New York Tribune*, Mar. 21, 1911).

He was married three times: first, in 1882, to Fannie N. Smith of Malden, W. Va., a graduate of Hampton, who died in 1884 leaving a daughter; second, in 1885, to Olivia A. Davidson of Ohio, who taught at Tuskegee in the early days and died in 1889 leaving two sons; third, on Oct. 12, 1893, to Margaret James Murray of Mississippi, at the time of their marriage "lady principal" at Tuskegee. He died Nov. 14, 1915, the day after his return home from New York where he had collapsed as a result of over-work. A bronze statue by Charles Keck on the Tuskegee campus shows Washington taking the scales from the eyes of the Negro slave. Below are quotations from his speeches, including his characteristic saying, "No man, black or white, from North or South, shall drag me down so low as to make me hate him." Two tributes, from North and South, are sufficient. Theodore Roosevelt said: "As nearly as any man I have ever met, Booker T. Washington lived up to Micah's verse, 'What more doth the Lord require of thee than to do Justice, and love Mercy and walk humbly with thy God'" (quoted in Scott and Stowe, *post*, p. xi). And Henry Watterson [*q.v.*] wrote: "No man, since the war of sections, has exercised such beneficent influence and done such real good for the country—especially to the South" (Stokes, *post*, Appendix VII, p. 78).

He wrote *The Future of the American Negro*

(1899); *Sowing and Reaping* (1900); *Up From Slavery* (1901), which was translated into at least eighteen languages; *Character Building* (1902); *Working with the Hands* (1904); *Putting the Most into Life* (1906); *Frederick Douglass* (1907); *The Negro in Business* (1907); *The Story of the Negro* (1909); *My Larger Education* (1911); and with R. E. Park, *The Man Farthest Down* (1912). He also edited *Tuskegee and its People* (1905).

[His autobiographical works, *Up From Slavery* and *My Larger Education*; *Booker T. Washington, Builder of a Civilization* (1916), by his secretary, E. J. Scott and Lyman Beecher Stowe; *Selected Speeches of Booker T. Washington* (1932), ed. by his son, E. D. Washington; A. P. Stokes, *Tuskegee Institute: The First Fifty Years* (1931) and "A Brief Biography of Booker Washington Based on Original Sources" (in preparation); obituaries in *N. Y. Times, Montgomery Advertiser*, Nov. 15, 1915, and in other papers.]

A. P. S.

WASHINGTON, BUSHROD (June 5, 1762– Nov. 26, 1829), associate justice of the Supreme Court of the United States, was born in Westmoreland County, Va., the son of John Augustine, brother of Gen. George Washington, and Hannah, daughter of John Bushrod of Bluefield, Va. The Bushrods were one of the first families of Virginia, faithful churchmen, and ardent patriots. After studying under a tutor in the house of Richard Henry Lee, Bushrod entered the College of William and Mary in 1775, graduating therefrom in 1778. Enlisting in the Continental Army as a private, he was present at the surrender of Cornwallis at Yorktown.

After the war he studied law in Philadelphia in the office of James Wilson, whom years later he was to succeed as a member of the Supreme Court of the United States. Admitted to the Virginia bar, he began practice at Alexandria; and in 1787 was elected to the Virginia House of Delegates and a year later to the Virginia State Convention, where he supported Madison and Marshall in their fight for the ratification of the federal Constitution. His growing law practice prompted a removal of his residence from Alexandria to Richmond in 1790, where he received many law students into his office.

To fill the vacancy in the Supreme Court created by the death of James Wilson in 1798, President Adams first turned to John Marshall [*q.v.*], but upon Marshall's declining the honor, tendered the post to Washington, his appointment being confirmed Dec. 20, 1798. At this time the Supreme Court was generally regarded as of little importance in the governmental system. Decisions of consequence had been very few. Declinations of appointments and resignations had been frequent. Joined on the bench within a few years by John Marshall, William Johnson, and other able judges, however, Washington found himself the member of a court whose prestige and power were in the ascendant. To the lot of this group fell the significant rôle of interpreting the Constitution during the critical formative period of the nation's growth, and of formulating the Constitutional theory which was to exert such a vital influence upon future thought and action. Washington's tenure as a justice of the Supreme Court continued until his death, a period of thirty-one years.

He was unacquainted with literature and the arts, but was a devoted and diligent student of the law. By nature mild and conciliatory, yet prompt and firm in decision, he possessed what is generally called a judicial temperament, and as a *nisi prius* judge is said to have been unexcelled. Slow of mind but thorough and clear in reasoning, he rendered a number of opinions influential in the development of American law not only upon Constitutional matters, where he saw eye to eye with Marshall, but also upon admiralty, commercial, and other subjects. Among his notable opinions were those in the following cases: *Marine Insurance Company* vs. *Tucker* (1806), 3 *Cranch,* 357; *Eliason* vs. *Henshaw* (1819), 4 *Wheaton,* 225; *Dartmouth College* vs. *Woodward* (1819), 4 *Wheaton,* 518; *Green* vs. *Biddle* (1823), 8 *Wheaton,* 1; *Thornton* vs. *Wynn* (1827), 12 *Wheaton,* 183; *Ogden* vs. *Saunders* (1827, 12 *Wheaton,* 213; and *Buckner* vs. *Finley* (1829), 2 *Peters,* 586. His courage was such that, sitting as a circuit judge in the case of *United States* vs. *Bright* (24 *Fed. Cas.,* 1232) he did not hesitate to sentence to imprisonment an officer of the state of Pennsylvania for resisting a federal judicial process, though Pennsylvania threatened rebellion if he did.

He was painstaking and methodical in the keeping of his books and accounts and for a period of thirty-five years carefully catalogued and filed away all his letters and papers. To him General Washington devised his library, his public and private papers and letters, as well as the stately "Mount Vernon" with its surrounding 4,000 acres, where, after the death of Martha Washington in 1802, Bushrod made his home. He was also made one of the executors of General Washington's will, and though lacking the business acumen of his distinguished uncle, he was as painstaking in handling the affairs of the estate as he was in respect to his own.

Though Washington favored the abolition of slavery and was in 1816 elected the first president of the American Colonization Society, he was in 1821 made the subject of a bitter attack on humanitarian grounds, for having sold and transported to Louisiana fifty-four "Mount Vernon" slaves, separating many of them from close members of their families. Admitting the substance of the charge, Washington, in a letter published in *Niles' Weekly Register* (Sept. 29, 1821), said: "I do not admit the right of any person to decide for me on this point," and argued that since slaves were property they could legally be made the subject of sale. He contended that insubordination among his slaves and their repeated attempts at escape to the North made their retention unprofitable.

In 1785, Washington married Julia Ann Blackburn, a daughter of Col. Thomas Blackburn of "Rippon Lodge," who had been an aide-de-camp to General Washington during the Revolution. She always accompanied her husband on his rounds as a practitioner and circuit judge. They had no children. In personal appearance Washington was short in stature, sharp-faced, usually negligently dressed, and wore "his dark, unfrosted hair, long and combed back from his forehead" (Warren, *post,* I, 467). He had lost the sight of one eye from over study. An immoderate user of snuff, in later life he frequently had a profusion of the leafy product distributed over his face. He died in Philadelphia and was buried at "Mount Vernon." His wife, prostrated with grief, died while traveling from Philadelphia to "Mount Vernon" to attend his funeral.

[Horace Binney, *Bushrod Washington* (1858); *The Green Bag,* Aug. 1897; *Am. Law Magazine,* July 1845; H. L. Carson, *The Hist. of the Supreme Court of the U. S.* (2 vols., 1902); Charles Warren, *The Supreme Court in U. S. Hist.* (1926), vol. I; E. E. Prussing, *The Estate of George Washington, Deceased* (1927); *Niles' Weekly Reg.,* Sept. 1, 29, 1821; *Tyler's Quart. Hist. and Geneal. Mag.,* July 1922; *Nat. Gazette* (Phila.), Nov. 27, 1829.]   G. W. G.

WASHINGTON, GEORGE (Feb. 11/22, 1732–Dec. 14, 1799), first president of the United States, was born in Westmoreland County, Va., on the estate of his father lying between Bridges Creek and Popes Creek and later known as "Wakefield." The eldest son of Augustine Washington and his second wife, Mary Ball (1708–89), of "Epping Forest," Va., he was descended from Lawrence of Sulgrave, Northampton, England, who was of the fourth generation from John of Whitfield. Four generations later John, son of Lawrence the rector of Purleigh, emigrated to Virginia in 1657–58 and settled in Westmoreland County (Ford, *Writings,* XIV, 331–409; chart opp. p. 319). Augustine Washington was the grandson of John and the son of Lawrence of Bridges Creek, Westmoreland County. He lived in Westmoreland until 1735, when he removed to Little Hunting Creek, on the Potomac. After his homestead there was burned he moved to "Ferry Farm" in King George County, on the Rappahannock nearly opposite Fredericksburg. Augustine died in 1743 and the next half-dozen years of George Washington's life were spent with relatives in Westmoreland and the Chotank region, at "Ferry Farm," and at "Mount Vernon," the home of his elder half-brother Lawrence, who had married Ann Fairfax.

During this period George Washington received the major part of his school training, which totaled seven or eight years. His father and his elder half-brother Lawrence seem to have been his principal, if not his only teachers. The extent of his mother's influence upon Washington cannot be accurately appraised, but from the great respect he accorded her, and the scrupulous manner in which he fulfilled his filial duty, it is justifiable to credit her with a decided influence in the way of discipline and morals. His training in mathematics extended to trigonometry and surveying, which helped develop a natural talent for draftsmanship that found expression in map-making, in designing tabular memoranda, and in giving the pages of his letters an unusual but characteristic pictorial quality. He had a certain appreciation of beauty and a decided appreciation of music and the drama. Early memoranda give an indication of his reading habits and his accounts show purchases of books dealing with military affairs, agriculture, history, and biography, and a fair number of the great novels of the day, such as *Tom Jones, Humphry Clinker,* and *Peregrine Pickle.* He purchased a number of ethical works and ordered and used a bookplate. The quotations that are sprinkled sparingly through his correspondence cover a wide range, and show his familiarity with such authors as Pope and Addison, while his Biblical allusions are varied enough to prove a satisfactory acquaintance with the Book of books. A letter to Lafayette in 1788 (Ford, *Writings,* XI, 265–66) suggests the general outline of his historical and literary knowledge, while his statement to James McHenry in 1797 that he had "not looked into a book" since he came home (*Ibid.,* XIII, 392) adds to the cumulative evidence that he appreciated fully the value of the printed word in his own cultural development. The social intimacy between "Belvoir" and "Mount Vernon," where one of the Fairfax fledglings had nested, brought Washington, at an impressionable age, into contact with the courtly manners and customs of the best English culture. His youthful idealism responded to this stimulus, as it did to the stateliness of the drama,

and the two combined to produce the dignity and poise which were characteristic of his maturity.

Through the Fairfax association developed the first important adventure of his career. When, in 1748, Lord Fairfax sent James Genn, county surveyor of Prince William County, to survey his Shenandoah lands for tenantry, George William Fairfax and George Washington were permitted to go along. The two young men were gone a month, worked hard, and encountered many inconveniences, but gained valuable experience (*Diaries,* I, 3–12). A year later Washington was appointed county surveyor for Culpeper. His duty carried him into wild country where he encountered many hardships, yet his surveys required exactitude and gave him insight into the importance of land ownership. This work was interrupted by the call of duty to accompany Lawrence Washington on his health-seeking voyage to Barbadoes. George was stricken with smallpox on that island and so rendered immune to the disease which raged among the troops he commanded during the Revolutionary War. He returned alone to Virginia to be followed by Lawrence, who died in July 1752, bequeathing the "Mount Vernon" estate in such wise that it shortly became the property of George.

That year he was appointed by Governor Dinwiddie district adjutant for the southern district of Virginia, but was soon transferred to that of the Northern Neck and Eastern Shore. Washington's military ambition, first stimulated by his half-brother's service with Admiral Vernon, was reawakened and increased by his experience in military musters and drills of the Virginia militia. When the French encroached, as was claimed, on the English lands in the Ohio country, he accepted without hesitancy Dinwiddie's appointment (1753) to carry an ultimatum to the trespassers. Though the mission was one of hardship and downright danger, it appealed to Washington as one of honor and possible glory. It certainly was unusual that a colonial governor should appoint a young man of twenty-one to so important a mission, and the exact reasons for the selection are conjectural. Washington was also instructed to strengthen the friendship of the Six Nations with the English. With a party of six frontiersmen, he left Will's Creek in the middle of November 1753 and a week later reached the forks of the Ohio, where he had expected to find the French. But the French had withdrawn for the winter and Washington was faced with a decision between giving up the delivery of the ultimatum, and traveling sixty miles farther into the wintry wilderness to reach the next French post. Before starting on this new journey he endeavored to fulfil the second part of his instructions by holding, at Logstown on the Ohio, a council with such of the chiefs of the Six Nations as he could gather together; but he accomplished little, as the Indians were wary of the English assurances, unbacked by any display of force, when the French were already on the ground with troops and cannon. He found the French at Venango, but the officer there refused to receive his message and directed Washington to the commandant at Fort Le Boeuf. Unwilling to return without accomplishing his main mission, he was forced to proceed one hundred miles farther, through winter-clogged swamp-land, nearly to the shores of Lake Erie. After five days of difficult travel he reached the fort and received in writing a polite refusal to pay any attention to Dinwiddie's ultimatum. On the return journey Washington's horses gave out, and with his guide, Christopher Gist, he undertook to walk back to Will's Creek. He was shot at by a prowling French Indian, nearly drowned in crossing the ice-choked Allegheny on an improvised raft, and nearly frozen from exposure (*Diaries,* I, 40–67). His report to Dinwiddie was printed by the Governor as *The Journal of Major George Washington . . .* (1754) and created a stir in England as well as America.

Washington had described a position at the forks of the Ohio (the present location of Pittsburgh) as the best place for an outpost and Dinwiddie dispatched a small force to forestall the French in building a fort there. He commissioned Washington a lieutenant-colonel and ordered him to reinforce the forks with the militia then assembling at Alexandria. These amounted to 150 men and with them on Apr. 2, 1754, Washington marched. He was met on the way by the news that the French had captured the fort. They named it Fort Duquesne. His force was too small for him to attempt to recapture it but Washington, nevertheless, advanced to Red Stone, the Ohio Company's trading post about forty miles from Fort Duquesne, and began a road for the expedition which Dinwiddie was virtually obligated to undertake. At Great Meadows, Pa., on rumors of a French advance, he built an entrenched camp which he called Fort Necessity, and when informed by friendly Indians of the approach of a French scouting party he marched forward to intercept it. Aided by the Indians, he succeeded in surprising and defeating the French (May 27); their leader, Jumonville, was killed. In reprisal the French advanced in force from Fort Duquesne and Washington fell back to Great Meadows; the retreat would have been

continued to Will's Creek, but he feared being overtaken at some less defensible place than Fort Necessity (*Diaries,* I, 101 n.; *Writings,* Bicentennial ed., I, 87). The attack of the French was sustained for ten hours, then they proposed a parley. The terms offered Washington were generous but contained a bit of clever roguery, unnoticed by his translator, which made the signing of them an admission by Washington that Jumonville had been "assassinated." It was part and parcel of the age-old practice of placing the blame for starting a war; it created a stir at the time, but the truth of the matter has long been understood. The tangled condition into which Virginia's military affairs had been brought by Dinwiddie's management made Washington liable to be commanded by junior and inferior officers and, no relief being granted, he resigned near the end of the year 1754.

In 1755 Great Britain sent an expedition of regulars under General Braddock against Fort Duquesne. For reasons not entirely clear, though Washington's knowledge of the country and the influence of Dinwiddie are the probable explanations, Braddock offered Washington the position of aide on his staff. His military ambitions were still alive and this opportunity to serve under a professional soldier appealed to him. The tradition that his advice was scornfully rejected by Braddock is largely a misapplication of the suggestions Washington made later on the Forbes expedition. On the march toward Duquesne he was taken violently ill and left behind, rejoining Braddock only the day before the action at the Monongahela. In that action, weak and debilitated though he was, he strove to carry out Braddock's orders; he had two horses shot under him and four bullets through his coat before every one, along with the fatally wounded general, was swept from the field by the rush of panic-stricken soldiery. With Braddock's death his appointment as aide ended and he returned to "Mount Vernon." Not having resigned his adjutancy of the Northern Neck he issued a call for the militia of his district to be ready for muster and inspection (*Writings,* Bicentennial ed., I, 158). This was the limit of his authority, but to that extent he prepared Virginia for the expected French and Indian invasion of the frontier.

In the fall of 1755 Dinwiddie appointed him colonel and commander in chief of all Virginia forces, thrusting upon him at the age of twenty-three the responsibility of defending 300 miles of mountainous frontier with about 300 men. It was in this savage, frontier warfare (averaging two engagements a month with raiding Indians), that Washington acquired the habit of thinking and acting for the welfare of a people, and the experience of conducting military operations, however poorly, over an extensive expanse of territory. His letters show the depths to which he was stirred by the plight and suffering of the inhabitants, and his strenuous efforts to protect them from the ravages of the Indians. They also show the causes of his partial failure. With too few troops and inadequate supplies, lacking sufficient authority with which to maintain complete discipline, and hampered by an antagonistic governor, he faced difficulties which closely paralleled those that he met in the Revolution. He encountered in 1756, as he had once before, the supercilious arrogance of the British army officer who called in question his right to command because of a pretended difference between a commission signed by the king and one signed by a colonial governor. Washington rode from Winchester to Boston to obtain a settlement of the difficulty, which otherwise might have disrupted Virginia's frontier defense. The journey had an unexpected but important effect in broadening Washington's viewpoint in respect to the people of the other colonies. It was the longest horseback journey he had made up to that time; but there were few Americans, then and for some years later, who were so continuously in the saddle and few who traveled over so large an expanse of the country as did Washington. With the matter of rank settled to his satisfaction, he returned to Virginia and the disheartening duty of defending the frontier. Lacking pay for his men, lacking clothes, shoes, powder, and even food at times, Washington managed nevertheless to protect the frontier so well that fewer inhabitants fell victims to savage fury in Virginia than in the other colonies (*Writings,* Bicentennial ed., II, 11). He continually urged the capture of Fort Duquesne, but with the governor and legislature at loggerheads, Virginia could not raise a force sufficient to undertake it and Washington's efforts to secure cooperation from Maryland and Pennsylvania in the enterprise were unsuccessful. In 1758, however, Great Britain again sent a force of regulars under General John Forbes [*q.v.*] against the post and Washington, with the title of brigadier (there being then two Virginia regiments) was ordered to cooperate. On this expedition Washington suggested an order of march for the British that was remarkably near the modern open-order method of fighting. It was ignored. The fort was abandoned by the French on the near approach of the British (November 1758) and, the main objective of Virginia's frontier defense being thus

accomplished, Washington resigned shortly thereafter.

He married, on Jan. 6, 1759, Martha (Dandridge) Custis, widow of Daniel Parke Custis, and settled down to the life of a gentleman-farmer at "Mount Vernon." Through Mrs. Custis' offspring by her first husband, Washington's strong, natural love of children, nowhere attested better than in his expense accounts, found ample vent. In the death of young "Patsy" Custis (1773), he experienced one of the great emotional shocks of his life. His troubles with "Jacky" Custis brought home to him the difficult problem of the education of youth, and broadened his viewpoint in educational matters. At various times he contributed generously to educational organizations: to Washington College in Maryland, to Liberty Hall (later Washington and Lee) in Virginia, to the Alexandria Academy, to an academy in Kentucky, and to an academy in the Southwestern Territory. He urged the establishment of a national university in the Federal City and provided an endowment for it in his will. The basis of this idea was largely the "indescribable regret" with which he had "seen the youth of the United States migrating to foreign countries, in order to acquire the higher branches of erudition, and to obtain a knowledge of the sciences." His fear that they would imbibe "maxims not congenial with republicanism" was not based on his doubt of republicanism, but on his perception of the danger of sending youth abroad among other political systems before they had "well learned the value of their own" (Ford, *Writings,* XIII, 52).

He had been elected a burgess from Frederick in 1758, after having been defeated in 1755 and 1757, and took his seat in the session of 1759, when he was thanked by the House for his military services. The succeeding fifteen years of Washington's career were uneventful in a public way but undoubtedly were the most enjoyable of his life. They were spent in developing the farming possibilities of the "Mount Vernon" estate, with the variation of trips to Williamsburg to attend the sessions of the legislature, of neighborly visits to Alexandria, Dumfries, and Fredericksburg, of attendance on the Annapolis races and theatre, of fox-hunts and fishing trips. To his taste for theatricals was added an interest in strange animals which were akin to his interest in unusual plants. In his expense accounts one notes payments for seeing a lioness, a tiger, an elk, a camel, and other animals, and once a reference to a sleight of hand performance. Card-games, billiards, boat-racing, in addition to horse-racing, the theatre, dancing, fishing, gunning, and fox-hunting with horse and hounds—all the usual sports and amusements were enjoyed by Washington. His accounts unintentionally show how often he bore the major part of the necessary expenses and how often he made loans to his friends. From these accounts are to be gleaned much information about Washington's personal tastes and fancies. His snuff-taking and pipe-smoking habits were pre-Revolutionary and temporary; but his liking for oysters, watermelons, Madeira wine, and other delicacies was permanent.

But the pleasant, busy life at "Mount Vernon" was not without its annoyances. Many of these were of such nature as to create and gradually strengthen a conviction of the general unfairness of all things British. It was necessary to purchase practically all the supplies needed for "Mount Vernon": farm-implements, tools of all sorts, paint, hardware, even textiles for clothing, needles, and thread. Washington's yearly invoices of goods purchased from Liverpool and London list great quantities of supplies, for he was buying for the annual consumption of a community of village proportions; when the estates of the Custis children were added to those of "Mount Vernon" the combined needs were enormous. The British commercial restrictions imposed needless hardships upon most business transactions and to these were added the sharp practices of the English factors, who were used by every Virginia planter in transacting his yearly business with the English markets. Complaints were easily passed over as the intervening distance and the time necessary for correspondence gave the Virginian little power to enforce redress. By a process of gradual accretion Washington's disappointing experiences in the Braddock and Forbes campaigns were built upon by these commercial annoyances, and a subconscious antagonism was created which even his strong sense of duty and loyalty could not hold in check.

He was successively reëlected as a burgess from Fairfax, faithfully attended the sessions, and shouldered his share of the legislative duties. From 1760 to 1774 he was also a justice of Fairfax, holding court in Alexandria. His experiences in court and as a burgess did much to clarify his view of the handicapping influences of the British colonial system on America. The Stamp Act brought to a focus the developing colonial antagonism and Washington expressed with the logic of common sense the American attitude towards the claims of Parliament. It "hath no more right to put their hands into my pocket, without my consent, than I have to put my hands into yours for money" (*Writings,* Bi-

centennial ed., III, 233). He pointed out the practical difficulties which lay in the path of the enforcement of the act. "Our Courts of Judicature must inevitably be shut up . . . for . . . we have no Money to pay the Stamps . . . and if a stop be put to our judicial proceedings I fancy the Merchants of G. Britain trading to the Colonies will not be among the last to wish for a Repeal of it" (*Ibid.,* II, 426). The British prohibition of colonial paper money was one of the major grievances; with the balance of trade always against them, paper money was a primal necessity to the colonists. A personal matter was the effort to obtain for the officers and men of the old Virginia regiment the bounty land allotted to them for their services in the French and Indian War. Elected their attorney and agent under a pro-rata agreement as to expenses, Washington pushed the matter to a conclusion, advanced his own funds, some of which he did not get back, and made a hazardous canoe trip with a small party in 1770, down the Ohio and up the Great Kanawha, to locate the land (*Diaries,* I, 401–52). This journey revived his interest in the western territory and increased the knowledge which he had early acquired of its value to the development of the Atlantic seaboard; to an extent, it laid the foundation of his western land policy when president. On this trip Washington killed several buffalo. These animals, it seemed to him, might in the future supply meat for America, so he undertook an experiment with them. At his death, nearly thirty years later, a buffalo cow still remained among the stock animals at "Mount Vernon."

After 1770 the question of British taxes assumed increasing importance in the colonies, and in four short years became the major problem. The device of non-importation was tried, in resistance to British political and economic aggression. Washington strongly supported it, yet prophesied, before 1775, "that more blood will be spilt on this occasion, if the ministry are determined to push matters to extremity, than history has ever yet furnished instances of in the annals of North America" (*Writings,* Bicentennial ed., III, 246). He did not approve of the Boston Tea Party (*Ibid.,* III, 224), while thoroughly in sympathy with the refusal of Massachusetts to submit to the British restrictions. He was one of the burgesses who met in the Raleigh Tavern on May 27, 1774, after the Assembly had been dissolved by the governor, and signed the proceedings of that unauthorized but important meeting, and on July 18 he acted as chairman of a meeting in Alexandria, at which the important Fairfax Resolutions, the work of George Mason [*q.v.*], were adopted. He was next chosen one of Virginia's delegates to the First Continental Congress, 1774, which did little beyond petitioning Great Britain for a redress of grievances. In the interval between that and the Second Congress, Washington was chosen to command the independent militia companies of Frederick, Fairfax, Prince William, Richmond, and Spotsylvania counties and authorized by them to procure equipment, which he did in Philadelphia. The buff and blue uniform chosen by the Fairfax company was the uniform worn by Washington throughout the Revolution, and so has become fixed in the public mind as the Continental Army uniform. At the March session of the Virginia legislature he was elected a delegate to the Second Continental Congress, which convened in Philadelphia May 1775. In that body his most important work was on the committee for drafting the army regulations and planning the defense of New York City. The latter assignment was to exercise a hampering influence upon him later.

His election to command the armies, June 15, 1775, was the result of a compromise between the northern and southern factions which existed, thus early, in Congress. The Massachusetts delegates knew that their only hope was to have the war, which up to then had been centered in the siege of Boston, taken over by the Continental Congress. In bringing about Washington's nomination and unanimous election John and Samuel Adams were the prime movers, and it was natural that Congress should confer the supreme command upon one of its own members when that member was the most prominent southern military character known to it. In his speech of acceptance Washington refused all pay for the arduous employment which he accepted as a duty "at the expense of my domestick ease and happiness" (*Writings*, Bicentennial ed., III, 292). He asked only that he be reimbursed his necessary expenses, of which he kept the account himself with such exactness that after eight years of nerve-wracking warfare his balance was less than a dollar wrong in a total of some £24,700.

When Washington took command of the army at Cambridge on July 3, 1775, he found it little better than a loosely organized mob of raw New England militia whose terms of service were to expire at the end of that year, or sooner. Earlier than most, Washington gave up as hopeless the idea of an accommodation with Great Britain, and the king's speech in October 1775 confirmed him in his belief that no compromise was to be expected (*Writings*, Bicentennial ed., IV, 321).

The belief which persisted in others of the possibility of an accommodation was a hampering influence that prevented the colonies from exerting their full power in opposition to the British; it was, in large measure, the cause not only of lukewarm support of Washington but also of the growth of downright opposition to him, centering in a clique in Congress. The problems of supply and pay for the troops, which Congress had taken over, became a vexation that grew with the months. Efforts to establish discipline encountered bitter hostility; democratic ideas stood in the way and caused to be construed as a snobbish display of fancied superiority the authority necessary to create an efficient military machine. Opposing disciplinary measures, the New Englanders at the same time criticized Washington for the army's lack of it. Fear of a standing army was another difficulty. Obsessed with this fear, in which the phantom of an accommodation with Great Britain played its part, Congress hesitated to decree long-term enlistments for the troops. Washington stood almost alone in his plea for men who could be held in service long enough to make them seasoned soldiers. At the siege of Boston, he was forced to replace one army by another while holding in check twenty seasoned British regiments, and in the New York campaign the main cause of the so-called retreat through the Jerseys was the inability to collect troops to replace the losses caused by expired enlistments and desertions.

At Cambridge scarcity of powder held Washington back from any major operation until 1776; but when a sufficient quantity was accumulated he seized and fortified Dorchester Heights, a position which threatened Boston with bombardment and placed the British fleet in jeopardy. The city was evacuated Mar. 17, 1776, and with his army of newly enlisted troops Washington marched for New York City, which was the next logical base of operations for the enemy. He had already sent Maj.-Gen. Charles Lee to supervise the work of fortification at that place, so that Washington on his arrival found himself partially committed to a plan of defense mapped out by others. He improved the three months before the British arrived by training his army as well as he could, handicapped by an appalling lack of experienced officers, and in preparing against the inevitable consequences of the decree of Congress that New York must be defended. He had sixteen miles of water-front lines to defend with 10,000 men, and when the British had assembled their whole force in New York Bay they numbered 30,000 trained troops, exclusive of a naval force of over 100 vessels. Any defense worthy of the name, under such conditions, was impossible, yet Washington attempted the impossible from his concept of duty to obey the orders of Congress, and from a disinclination to insist upon his own judgment where he believed his military knowledge and experience inadequate. This hesitancy was more evident throughout the New York campaign than at any other period of the Revolution.

The British tactics in that campaign were far from masterly, though ample to insure success. Howe's choice of Long Island as the point of attack was a safe and sure step. Washington was obliged to divide his force as a result. He sent ten regiments to reinforce Brooklyn, a pitiful few to oppose a veteran force of 30,000; but the main body of Americans had to be held on Manhattan to oppose the attack of the British fleet, which only a strong headwind frustrated. Washington himself crossed over to Brooklyn as soon as it was seen that the British ships could not make way against the wind; but the enemy had already outflanked Sullivan and the tragedy was beyond repair. Howe delayed his assault on the Brooklyn fortifications and, on the night of Aug. 29, Washington moved all the troops over to New York. His arrangements were perfect; the British were kept in ignorance and the retreat was rightly considered a military masterpiece. On Sept. 15, the British landed at Kip's Bay and, despite Washington's presence and desperate attempts to rally his men, they fled in panic and a retreat to Harlem Heights became a necessity. British flanking moves pushed Washington, though not without some sharp skirmishing, back to a strong natural position at White Plains. Howe desisted and returned to New York, on the way gathering in Fort Washington, which had been held against Washington's better judgment but not against his orders.

His report to Congress laid down the general principle on which he was waging the war. "We should on all Occasions avoid a general Action, or put anything to the Risque, unless compelled by a necessity, into which we ought never to be drawn" (*Writings*, Bicentennial ed., VI, 28). Inexperienced troops, always inferior in numbers to the British, made this the only possible course of action until Congress was willing to create a permanent army. The odds against him were heavy. His great need was time: time to make a reluctant Congress realize the necessity of his recommendations; time to raise a permanent army after it was finally authorized; and time to train it to fight after it was raised. Dogged perseverance, a straining to the limit of the scant means in his hands, together with British leth-

argy, gained him some of the time he needed. He could complain bitterly to his brother that he was "wearied almost to death with the retrograde Motions of things" (*Ibid.*, VI, 246), and could warn Congress in October 1776 that its army was again "upon the eve of its political dissolution" (*Ibid.*, VI, 152). His belief in the moral righteousness of the American struggle for liberty was based on his sense of the injustice and unfairness of the British course. To him rebellion against the king and change of allegiance were matters demanding scrupulous moral honesty. Not until his concept of honor approved the change did he make it; but the step once taken, turning back was for him unthinkable and impossible. As he wrote to his brother: "Under a full persuasion of the justice of our Cause, I cannot . . . entertain an Idea that it will finally sink tho' it may remain for sometime under a Cloud" (*Ibid.*, VI, 399). The fortitude with which he met overwhelming difficulties was based upon his faith; defeats to him were merely temporary setbacks and victories merely longer or shorter steps toward final success.

The loss of Fort Lee, on the Jersey shore, resulted from the same misplaced confidence in his generals which had lost Fort Washington, yet both disasters were unrecognized blessings. They freed the Continental Army from responsibility for fixed fortifications, in which it had small chance against the trained British forces, and made it a mobile, maneuvering force which could be handled in accordance with Washington's ideas. The Pennsylvania and Jersey militia failed to answer his appeals and, with a steadily dwindling force, he fell back as the British pushed forward. The so-called retreat through New Jersey was a perfect example of Washington's military principle, for it was a retirement before a superior force of the enemy, conducted so slowly and so cleverly that the British expected to encounter strong opposition at almost every point. His grasp of military science, for all his modest disclaimers, was far above that of any of his generals. His plea at this time to Congress for artillery showed a far-sighted comprehension that few could boast (*Writings*, Bicentennial ed., VI, 280–81).

His calls, while retiring through New Jersey, to Maj.-Gen. Charles Lee [q.v.] for reinforcements revealed the first serious military opposition within his own army. Lee delayed marching, apparently with the idea of contesting the supreme command with Washington as soon as the latter's army dissolved or was defeated. The British solved this difficulty by the surprise and capture of Lee, whose troops were promptly marched to Washington's support by the officer next in command. With an army of barely 5,000, Washington reached the Delaware River, swept up all the boats, called in the Princeton rearguard, and crossed into Pennsylvania, where from the west bank he watched the enemy make futile marches up and down the east side, seeking means to cross. The British settled into winter quarters in a series of posts along the Delaware at and near Trenton and in a line across New Jersey to Amboy, confident that the end of the year 1776 would mark the end of the rebel army and of the rebellion. "Short enlistments and a dependence upon militia," Washington felt, would "prove the downfall of our cause" (*Writings,* Bicentennial ed., VI, 347). Yet, under heavy discouragements, he could write to Congress that he conceived "it to be my duty, and it corrisponds [*sic*] with my Inclination, to make head against them [the British] as soon as there shall be the least probability of doing it" (*Ibid.,* VI, 330).

Congress fled to Baltimore, and the protection of Philadelphia forthwith becoming relatively unimportant in Washington's judgment, he fixed his eyes on Morristown, N. J., as the place most threatening to the British arrangements. That place was designated as the rendezvous of the militia and recruits for the army of 1777 and, with the remnant of the army of 1776, on Christmas night Washington crossed the Delaware amid driving ice, crushed the Hessians at Trenton, and dislocated the entire line of British posts along the river. The failure of his two supporting detachments to get across the river postponed the movement to Morristown, of which the Trenton victory was intended to be the first phase. Washington returned to Pennsylvania with nearly a thousand prisoners. A few days sufficed to rest his troops and he again crossed into Jersey, to move northward. Checked by the British reinforcements advancing from New York, he fought the stubborn engagement of the Assunpink, by a forced night march outwitted the enemy, and struck and pierced their line at Princeton. Once he was at Morristown, his position was such a strategic threat to the British that they abandoned their entire New Jersey line and retreated to Brunswick.

Six days before the victory at Trenton he had applied to the Congress, which had fled to Baltimore, for power to handle "every matter that in its nature is self evident," since a necessity of waiting until such things were referred a hundred and thirty or forty miles would in itself defeat the end in view. He had "no lust after power but wish with as much fervency as any Man

upon this wide extended Continent, for an opportunity [*sic*] of turning the Sword into a plow share" (*Writings,* Bicentennial ed., VI, 402). Congress responded with a grant of powers greater than he had asked and for a term of six months; but when Washington used this authority to compel all citizens who had taken out British protection papers to deliver them up and take the oath of allegiance to the United States, or remove at once within the British lines, he was violently criticized in Congress. It took Washington a year and a half to shake himself free from the entanglements which had been created by the interference and mismanagement of Congress; but from 1777 troops could be enlisted for three years or the war, and in January of that year Washington began to build a permanent military machine that could "bid Defiance to Great Britain, and her foreign Auxiliaries" (*Ibid.,* VII, 199). But the exorbitant bounties offered by the states for home-guard and militia service operated to check enlistments for the Continental Army. Washington was still forced to rely upon the militia for swelling his force to a respectable total at times when the British threatened or actually moved against him. He expressed his opinion of the militia to Congress more than once. If 40,000 men had been kept in constant pay since the commencement of hostilities, and the militia never called out, the expense of the war would not have been nearly so great as it was; when the losses sustained for want of good troops were taken into account the certainty of this was placed beyond a doubt. To this he added his pungent and deft characterization of militia which has seldom been bettered. They "come in you cannot tell how, go, you cannot tell when; and act, you cannot tell where; consume your Provisions, exhaust your Stores, and leave you at last in a critical moment" (*Ibid.,* VI, 403). At Morristown the army grew slowly and slowly acquired discipline. Washington's hope was to "be able to rub along till the new army is raised," but how he was to do it he did not know. "Providence has heretofore saved us in a remarkable manner, and on this we must principally rely" (*Ibid.,* VII, 53). His own efforts to "keep the Life and Soul of this Army together" (*Ibid.,* VII, 225) were barely successful and this accomplishment, as much as anything, measures the power of his personality. Congress, he wrote not without satire, thought that when difficulties were distant from them, it had but to say "Presto begone, and everything is done."

Washington's handling of this small, green, poorly equipped army in the spring of 1777 was remarkable. He managed to keep the enemy from plundering New Jersey at will, checking their forays by vigorous skirmishing which proved costly to the enemy and had a valuable seasoning effect on the Continental troops. It also convinced Howe that the risk of marching across New Jersey again to take Philadelphia was too great and, the capture of that town being a major object with him, Howe set about taking it by sea. He succeeded in puzzling Washington completely, for the logical move was up the Hudson River to cooperate with Burgoyne's advance from Canada, and until Howe finally appeared in Chesapeake Bay Washington was kept in a state of wearing suspense. But, with the suspense dissolved, Washington marched south and on Sept. 11, 1777, met Howe at Brandywine Creek. Here his right wing, under Sullivan, was out-flanked by the British and Washington was forced to retreat. Nevertheless, Washington's proximity, for though defeated he refused to withdraw, and the skirmish at Yellow Springs which was interrupted by a cloud-burst, delayed Howe's entry into Philadelphia two weeks.

The Congress adjourned to Lancaster and then to York, Pa., and again intrusted Washington with dictatorial powers for a six-day period, but he used this authority sparingly. Washington's recognition of the necessity of according first place to the civil power made him always willing to exhaust every means before using the military. He admitted to Congress that "a reluctance to give distress may have restrained me too far," and realizing the "prevalent jealousy of military power" among the people, he avoided every act that would increase it (*Writings*, Bicentennial ed., X, 159). Some months later he wisely used justices of the peace to impress provisions, which through them were obtained without causing a murmur. His method of waging the war admitted of attacking the British only when the possible gain was worth the sacrifice involved. He was cautious always, and with reason, for he was unbelievably handicapped by a paucity of information even where he should have been kept informed. "I am as totally unacquainted with the political state of things, and what is going forward in the great national council, as if I was an alien," he wrote somewhat bitterly to Edmund Randolph "when a competent knowledge of the temper and designs of our allies . . . might . . . have a considerable influence on the operations of our army" (Sparks, *Writings*, VI, 314).

There have been few generals who have had to husband their men and supplies so carefully as did Washington and fewer who have been more ready to expend them on a proper occasion. At Germantown (Oct. 3-4, 1777) Washington thought the probable gain outbalanced the probable loss and his surprise attack on the British was less a move to regain Philadelphia than to destroy Howe's army. It failed through no fault of plan, but to some extent it contributed to Howe's later resignation, and both Brandywine and Germantown are to be credited with large influence in the decision of France to aid the United States. Valley Forge and the Conway Cabal were to follow these defeats and, at the time the states should have whole-heartedly supported Washington for their own preservation the intrigue to supplant him in command of the army reached its crisis. The victory of Horatio Gates [*q.v.*] at Saratoga on Oct. 17, 1777, furnished Washington's enemies in Congress the opportunity to draw invidious comparisons. The intrigue was at bottom the culmination of the continuous effort of Massachusetts since 1775 to regain control of the war, which would be an accomplished fact with Gates at the head of the army. Opposition to Washington, engineered by this influence, had been steadily growing, for every criticism was cleverly directed to this end. But James Wilkinson [*q.v.*], a bibulous aide of Gates, babbled of a letter from Maj.-Gen. Thomas Conway [*q.v.*] to Gates; Washington wrote a brief note to Conway with no other purpose than to let that gentleman know that he was not unaware of Conway's intriguing disposition and this note became the bomb that shattered the secrecy of the cabal. Once in the open, the innate character of the cabal and its purposes roused resentments and antagonisms in Congress which compelled its adherents to abandon the move (in some instances even to deny their connection with the plot) and, lacking congressional support, the military part of the scheme collapsed.

But Washington held no resentments; his eyes were fixed upon the purpose of the war, and, since the cause of the nation had not been harmed by the cabal, he did not allow the episode to interfere with more important things. The criticism of contemporaries occasionally wounded his feelings but signally failed to disturb his steady course; it only marked the critics as men of less vision or, as was sometimes the case, of less honesty. For Washington did not doubt "that the candid part of Mankind, if they are convinc'd of my Integrity, will make proper allowance for my inexperience, and Frailities" (*Writings*, Bicentennial ed., VIII, 295). "We have some among Us, and I dare say Generals," he wrote, "who wish to make themselves popular at the expense of others; or, who think the cause is not to be advanc'd otherwise than by fighting; the peculiar circumstances under which it is to be done, and the consequences which may follow, are objects too trivial for their attention, but as I have one great end in view, I shall, maugre all strokes of this kind, steadily pursue the means which in my judgment, leads to the accomplishment of it" (*Ibid.*). His calm self-restraint allowed him to write to Lafayette, who found himself ensnarled in the Conway coil: "I have no doubt but that every thing happens so for the best . . . and that we . . . shall, in the end, be ultimately happy; when, My Dear Marquis, if you will give me your Company in Virginia, we will laugh at our past difficulties and the folly of others" (*Ibid.*, X, 237). Without such self-control it may be doubted if his success would have been so complete.

The Continental Army emerged from the suffering of Valley Forge better trained, as the result of months of steady drill under Baron von Steuben [*q.v.*], and both the army and the country had been heartened by the news of the alliance with France, in March 1778. Here again Washington's value to the Revolution is manifest for, despite every effort of Congress and its commissioners in Paris and regardless of the French secret aid which had been given for nearly two years, France was not ready openly to assist the Americans until convinced that they would not compromise with Great Britain. The battles of Trenton, Brandywine, and Germantown went far toward convincing France, but the main assurance was the character and purpose of George Washington. Gerard, the French minister, who held long interviews with him, became convinced that Washington's attitude was uncompromising and that the army would, to a man, follow him. This confidence Gerard succeeded in instilling in Vergennes, the French minister of foreign affairs and so, in turn, influencing the French king. The Saratoga victory far from being the deciding element, merely contributed to the convincing effect of Washington's indomitable purpose and honesty of character.

Sir Henry Clinton, succeeding Howe in supreme command in America, abandoned Philadelphia as a consequence of the French Alliance and undertook to march across New Jersey to New York. Washington pursued, and the line of march of the two armies converging, he overtook the British at Monmouth. The resulting conflict (June 28, 1778) not only proved that the Continental Army had developed into a fighting machine of considerable efficiency, but also demonstrated anew Washington's ability as a general. He checked the disorderly and unnecessary retreat of General Lee and turned the confusion into an obstinate and successful holding of a

battlefield, from which the British slipped away during the night and made good their retreat to New York City. France's first open aid was D'Estaing's fleet, but his ships, unfortunately, drew too much water to enter New York Bay. The French admiral sailed to attack the British force in Rhode Island, but a storm and the conduct of Maj.-Gen. John Sullivan [*q.v.*] brought this attempt to naught, and created anti-French feeling that required all of Washington's influence and tact to smooth over successfully. D'Estaing sailed for the West Indies and Washington quartered his army for the winter in New Jersey.

Lafayette, who had been with Washington since the summer of 1777, now conceived a plan of returning to France and obtaining a force to conquer Canada. Congress, more attracted by distant glittering schemes than by nearby everyday realities, approved Lafayette's idea, but had the saving sense to send the plan to Washington for an opinion. The calm common sense of his report (*Writings*, Bicentennial ed., XIII, 223-32; see also 254-57) dissolved the dream and showed Congress again that the commander of its armies, despite his keeping his hand scrupulously clear of civil matters, could reason upon them more intelligently than Congress itself. After pointing out the impossibility of collecting the necessary men and supplies, he dwelt upon the consequences of having France and the Indian tribes as neighbors on the north, while Spain would be on the west and south. His analysis was clear even to an obtuse Congress and the plan was laid aside. Lafayette, on his part, met with a refusal from Vergennes to consider the scheme.

The French Alliance, instead of stimulating the Americans to greater effort, operated as a sedative and to Washington's dismay things went from bad to worse. In spite of his urgent pleas to Congress and to the states for supplies and men a disheartening lethargy was displayed everywhere. Unable to move in a major operation, because of lack of troops and supplies (even a lack of powder in August 1779), Washington yet succeeded in sending an expedition into the Indian country under Sullivan, which broke the power of the Six Nations and freed the frontiers from the horrors of Indian warfare. The bright spots in the prevailing gloom were Wayne's victory at Stony Point and "Light-Horse Harry" Lee's capture of Powles Hook. In July 1780 a French army under the Comte de Rochambeau arrived in Rhode Island, the British force there having been withdrawn to New York, but lack of supplies and men prevented real cooperation by

Washington. A conference with Rochambeau at Hartford on Sept. 22, 1780, compelled Washington to lay bare the real situation. The conference could only decide upon a future attack upon New York when the expected second division of the French arrived, or, if this was then impracticable, to transfer the campaign to the South. The situation was described bluntly by Washington: "We have no magazines, nor money to form them; and in a little time we shall have no men. . . . We have lived upon expedients till we can live no longer . . . the history of the war is a history of false hopes and temporary devices, instead of system and œconomy" (Ford, *Writings*, VIII, 468). Another conference with Rochambeau was held in Wethersfield May 21–22, 1781, and the tentative plan of attacking New York without waiting for the expected second French expedition was decided upon. The French marched to the Hudson and joined the American troops; and the combined forces closed in on the British northern defenses of New York City. Then De Grasse arrived with his fleet in the Chesapeake. The siege of the city was abandoned for a move against Cornwallis in Virginia. Leaving a force to threaten New York, Washington, with a detachment of Americans and the whole of the French army, marched southward for a cooperation with De Grasse. The transportation and quartermaster arrangements on this march were all made by Washington. The armies arrived on schedule and the siege of Yorktown progressed steadily to its triumphant conclusion (Oct. 19, 1781) in three short weeks. De Grasse sailed to the West Indies, Rochambeau's army went into winter quarters in Virginia, and Washington led his troops back to the Hudson, making headquarters at Newburgh.

The states now became more supine than before, and Washington's urgent pleas for exertion and his arguments for the necessity of continued effort had small effect. He urged that "unless we strenuously exert ourselves to profit by these successes, we shall not only lose all the solid advantages that might be derived from them, but we shall become contemptible in our own eyes, in the eyes of our enemy, in the opinion of posterity, and even in the estimation of the whole world, which will consider us as a nation unworthy of prosperity, because we know not how to make a right use of it" (Ford, *Writings*, IX, 437). But he was compelled to possess his soul in patience while his countrymen indulged in an orgy of profiteering, even to the extent of carrying on clandestine trade with the British, as they had done at the beginning of the struggle. It was impossible for Washington to stop these things;

they were civil matters to be handled by Congress and the states, but very little was done by either. He was certain the war was not yet over. The king's speech at the opening of Parliament (1782) showed little signs of yielding and the war continued for two dreary years; but no military events of importance took place after Yorktown.

Though the enemy was reduced to inactivity through Washington's efforts, domestic conditions were slowly going from bad to worse. The army, more dissatisfied than ever from neglect and chronic lack of pay, showed an unrest which increased Washington's anxiety daily. The first open display of what was seething underneath came in the shape of a personal letter from Colonel Lewis Nicola [*q.v.*], of the Invalid regiment, who submitted to him a plan for using the army to make Washington a king. The army, at least, would benefit by it and Nicola stated that the idea was prevalent in camp. The proposal shook Washington's soul, for it swept away all that he had so painfully built up during the war, and hinted that the very men on whom he most relied were ready to support him in an apostasy, in a forswearing of honor and principle, for personal power. It was this, more than the idea of a crown, that stunned Washington. He saw his lifework threatened with dissolution through the political and short-sighted muddling of those responsible for the welfare of the army. To find that the men who had followed and trusted him through years of hunger, nakedness, suffering, and bloodshed were now, with victory in sight, ready to fail him, was bitter; and his answer (May 22, 1782) to the proposal was a withering blast which shrivelled the idea of kingship into the ashes of impossibility (Ford, *Writings*, X, 21–24). For a time the dissatisfaction subsided but a few more months saw it rise again in serious form. Anonymous addresses were posted in camp calling on the officers to meet for a discussion of their condition, to address Congress, and to be prepared to take by force, if necessary, what was unjustly denied them. Washington met the situation with a tact, wisdom, and sincerity which neutralized the danger and substituted for overt action further forbearance; and his letter to Congress urging a compliance with the officers' petition put the matter upon personal grounds with unusual emphasis. " 'If, retiring from the field, they [the officers] are to grow old in poverty, wretchedness and contempt; if they are to wade thro' the vile mire of dependency, and owe the miserable remnant of that life to charity, which has hitherto been spent in honor'; then shall I have learned what ingratitude is, then shall I have realized a tale, which will embitter every moment of my future life" (*Ibid.*, X, 181).

Not content with this, he later addressed to the states a circular letter which was largely a plea for justice to the officers and men of the fast-disbanding Continental Army, with which he had ever considered his own military reputation inseparably connected. More than that, it contained some wise advice on civil matters, which ranks it with the Farewell Address, thirteen years later. Now as then he was retiring, as he believed forever, from public service and so felt privileged to speak his mind plainly. In this circular he unconsciously reveals how close to his heart was the national principle for which he had fought, and how earnest his desire that the country prove worthy of the liberty it had gained. Again and again in his letters he showed how important he considered it that the country should take high rank among the nations of the world, and that high rank, he knew, was only to be gained and held by a strong union and by honorable conduct. Four things, he stated, were essential to respectable national existence: (1) "An indissoluble union of the States under one federal head"; (2) "a sacred regard to public justice"; (3) the adoption of a proper national defense; and (4) a spirit of cooperation, and the suppression of local prejudices (Ford, *Writings*, X, 257). He pleaded with the states for the army as he had pleaded with Congress, for the states were really the ultimate powers, and what Congress had promised in the form of half-pay was, he said, the price of the officers' "blood and your independency; it is therefore more than a common debt, it is a debt of honor" (*Ibid.*, X, 262).

There was little of the dramatic in the closing scenes of the war, but Washington intentionally fixed the date for the cessation of hostilities as Apr. 19, 1783, the anniversary of the battle of Lexington. He entered New York, at the head of the troops which still remained in service, as the British evacuated it; he bade farewell to his officers at Fraunces Tavern and set off for Annapolis to resign his commission to Congress. There is some evidence that a slight uneasiness existed in Congress that he might at the last moment decide to become dictator. No such idea could have been entertained by Washington, who resigned "with satisfaction the appointment I accepted with diffidence" (Ford, *Writings*, X, 339). On Christmas eve (1783) he reached "Mount Vernon" and soon afterward could write to a friend: "I feel now, however, as I conceive a wearied traveller must do, who, after treading many a painful step with a heavy burthen on his shoulders, is eased of the latter . . . and from his housetop is looking back, and tracing with an eager eye the meanders by which he escaped the quicksands and mires which lay in his way; and into which none but the all-powerful Guide and Dispenser of human events could have prevented his falling"(*Ibid.*, X, 358). The evidences of Washington's faith in the intervention of Providence in the affairs of man that are scattered through his letters admit of no doubt of his sincerity. Equally apparent are an unusual lack of egoism and a complete absorption in the successful working out of the problem that confronted him.

His financial condition at the close of the war was far from satisfactory. "Mount Vernon," lacking his careful guidance, had deteriorated and now was not even self-supporting. But despite his own financial stringencies, the quiet, unostentatious charity, which is so clearly shown in his accounts, was undiminished; the almost weekly entries of donations to needy applicants continued, and his running accounts were balanced by loss entries in cases of widows and helpless children, and of men who had died in his debt. He had suffered from the depreciation of the Continental currency; amounts owing him from before the war had been liquidated in Continental bills which he had grimly received, because he would not stand accused of repudiating the national money, even though these payments were, on their face, plain subterfuge in debt cancellation. A financial statement of his investments in Continental loan-office certificates, drawn up after the war, shows also that he had loaned every spare dollar to the government in the years of greatest depression and at the times when the outcome of the Revolution was the most doubtful (Washington MSS., 1784, Photostats, Lib. of Cong.).

He had time now (1784) to devote to the idea of opening a route to the western country from tidewater Virginia, by connecting the Potomac and Ohio rivers. This was one of the favorite projects of his life. Before the Revolution, in the Virginia legislature, he was one of the committee appointed to prepare a bill granting authority to form a company for this purpose (J. P. Kennedy, *Journals of the House of Burgesses of Virginia, 1770–1772*, 1906, pp. 292, 297, 304–05). In furtherance of that idea he undertook a horseback journey of observation into the West in the autumn of 1784 (*Diaries*, II, 279–328). He traveled over 650 miles, and returned with knowledge which stood him in good stead later. But his real interest lay in the development of the farms at "Mount Vernon."

His efforts to bring the estate back to a self-supporting condition were discouraging. Slave labor, the only kind available, had proved its inefficiency. No matter how carefully Washington planned, the results went awry because of the clumsy and unintelligent way the work was carried on. Unable either to free his slaves or to develop them into a self-supporting group, he was convinced that the gradual abolition of slavery would prevent much future mischief (P. L. Ford, *The True George Washington*, 1896, p. 154). To gradual abolition, by legislative authority, he pledged his vote. "But," he said, "when slaves, who are happy and contented with their present masters, are tampered with and seduced to leave them; when masters are taken unawares by these practices; when a conduct of this sort begets discontent on one side and resentment on the other; when it happens to fall on a man whose purse will not measure with that of the society [which works to free the slave], and he loses his property for want of means to defend it; it is oppression in such a case, and not humanity in any, because it introduces more evils than it can cure" (Ford, *Writings*, XI, 25–26). Washington had more negroes than he could profitably employ on his farms. "To sell the overplus I cannot, because I am principled against this kind of traffic." Yet he was steadily being pushed toward bankruptcy and may have been saved from it only by his death (*Ibid.*, XIV, 196).

The agreement between Virginia and Maryland in regard to the navigation of the Potomac had led, through meetings at Alexandria and "Mount Vernon," to a call for what is known as the Annapolis Convention, and through this Washington was again to be brought into public life. But at first, in his absorption in the management of "Mount Vernon" and in the affairs of the Potomac Company, this was not clear to him. Life at "Mount Vernon" was pleasantly calm, and his wife's grandchildren filled the measure of his interest. As he wrote to Lafayette: "I have not only retired from all public employments, but I am retiring within myself. . . . Envious of none, I am determined to be pleased with all; and this, my dear friend, being the order for my march, I will move gently down the stream of life, until I sleep with my fathers" (Ford, *Writings*, X, 347). In 1786 this philosophic calm was interrupted by the disturbing news of the rebellion of Daniel Shays [*q.v.*] in Massachusetts, which forced his thoughts again to public affairs. The outbreak added weight to his conviction, which had been steadily growing, that the Articles of Confederation needed revision in the interests of a strong central government. The memories of Valley Forge, of Morristown, of Trenton, of all the instances of needless suffering and difficulty caused by lack of a central power, were vivid, and he wrote vigorously to his friends of the need of strengthening the government and more closely cementing the states. He attended the Federal Convention reluctantly, but as was characteristic when once he decided to do a thing, he gave to the work his full energy and thought. As president of the Convention, possessing the full confidence of every member, he supplied a ground anchor to the proceedings. Much of the confidence afterwards displayed in the Constitution was due to that fact. When its adoption was opposed he admitted that it had imperfections, but maintained that it was the best plan obtainable at that time (*Ibid.*, XI, 205–06; see also a collection of his letters in Max Farrand, ed., *The Records of the Federal Convention*, 1911, vol. III). Since workable machinery was provided for amending the imperfections, his logic was to adopt, and then make the alterations. He saw no choice between this procedure and chaos. In the contest that raged over adoption he expressed two, among many, typically Washingtonian ideas of government. One was that the purpose of the new Constitution was to "establish good order and government and to render the nation happy at home and respected abroad"; and the other, apropos of the theoretical fear of a self-perpetuating president, that "when a people shall have become incapable of governing themselves, and fit for a master, it is of little consequence from what quarter he comes" (Ford, *Writings*, XI, 257). That Washington had completely discarded the idea of monarchy as a just system of government is not open to doubt nor can it be doubted that he was sincere in his belief that the people should govern themselves. He was "sure the mass of citizens in these United States *mean well*, and I firmly believe they will always *act well* whenever they can obtain a right understanding of matters" (*Ibid.*, XIII, 188). Yet it must be admitted that the plan of government which he signed as president of the Federal Convention provided necessary protection for the conservative, property-owning class of citizens and by an elaborate system of counterbalance and check seriously handicapped the common people in exerting much influence upon the course of the government. The explanation of this apparent contradiction lies in the conditions of the time; certainly Washington's justice and honesty are amply proven, and he, less than almost any one else in the Convention, was swayed by considerations of personal property.

Even before the Constitution was adopted, public opinion had fixed on Washington as the first president. He repelled the suggestion when it was made to him and opposed it wherever he decently could. Fame he had never coveted and the purely military ambition of his youth had long since been burned out, as he had gained close acquaintance with the scourge of war. At the age of fifty-six he had no "wish beyond that of living and dying an honest man on my own farm" (Ford, *Writings,* XI, 258). The sense of humor with which he was liberally endowed was usually flavored late in life with a sardonic saltiness, the result of the long, bitter years of the war. "My movements to the chair of government," he wrote, after he had decided to accept and the unanimous election had settled the matter, "will be accompanied by feelings not unlike those of a culprit, who is going to the place of his execution"; for he realized that he was "embarking the voice of the people, and a good name of my own, on this voyage; but what returns will be made for them, Heaven alone can foretell" (*Ibid.,* XI, 379–80). He was sure of his own integrity and firmness, but he could not think with calmness of the possibility of appearing in the light of a bungler and an incompetent. The fortunate outcome of the Revolution, in which he had risked not only his reputation but also his life and fortune, was due, he believed, to the interposition of Providence, and his self-abnegation prevented him from taking credit for the victory. He regarded the Revolution as a great movement of a people and was content with the thought that he had played his part therein with honor. He was as doubtful of his ability to administer the government successfully as he had been of his ability to command the army successfully, and, having already seen the lengths to which partisanship, prejudice, and jealousy could go, he was well aware that this new task would be difficult.

Being unwilling to leave Virginia to become president of the United States with several debts against him, he was compelled to borrow money to clear up local obligations and pay his traveling expenses to the seat of government. He took the oath of office Apr. 30, 1789, on the balcony of the United States Building in New York (the site of the Washington statue, at the old Sub-Treasury building) and delivered his inaugural address in the Senate chamber before both houses of Congress. In it he declined a salary, as he had done when elected commander in chief, but Congress later voted $25,000 annually for the president. Washington accepted this amount for defraying the expenses incident to the office, which in his case exceeded it. The realization that the motive of his every action could be subject to a double interpretation and that by his conduct in any instance he might create a precedent, did not tend to lessen the strain upon his fifty-seven years. In the Revolutionary War he had passed through a long siege of emotional repression, which was part of the price he paid for victory, and he was not quite ready to subject his temper to the same sort of strain, if it could be avoided. He was tired; the tinsel and power of high office did not appeal; and his honesty of thought did not permit him to discount the heavy responsibilities of the presidency. Nothing but that same rigorous sense of duty which had carried him through the Revolution could have drawn him again into public life.

Organizing and coordinating the various parts of the governmental machine and appointing the necessary officials occupied the better part of the year 1789; and in this Washington moved with steady caution. As was natural, he thought first of the men whose measure he had taken during the Revolution. Few offers of high place were made without reasonable confidence, or assurance, that they would be accepted and in these offers Washington's personality counted more heavily with the individuals approached than the power or honor that were involved. Even in the minor appointments, Washington moved cautiously. "A single disgust," he wrote, "excited in a particular State, on this account, might perhaps raise a flame of opposition that could not easily, if ever, be extinguished. . . . Perfectly convinced I am, that if injudicious or unpopular measures should be taken by the executive under the new government, with regard to appointments, the government itself would be in the utmost danger of being utterly subverted by those measures" (Ford, *Writings,* XI, 368). When Congress adjourned in September, Washington toured the New England states in an effort to learn for himself the feeling of the people of that region toward the new government. This tour was productive of little other than a warm welcome from the inhabitants and an unnecessary test of official strength between the President of the United States and Gov. John Hancock [*q.v.*] of Massachusetts, in which the latter came off second best, to the great glee of the citizens of Boston.

The pressing domestic problem was that of attaining financial stability for the nation; this necessarily involved the encouragement of manufacturing and commerce. Besides the existence of commercial restrictions, the retention of the western posts by Great Britain constituted the main foreign problem. Nearly every difficulty which developed bitterness during Washington's two administrations seems to have taken its start from a ramification of one or the other of these problems. Divergent theories of government were the basis of the struggle between Hamilton and Jefferson [*qq.v.*] out of which the well-defined Federalist and Republican groups emerged, but personal factors were evident to Washington. In the Revolution he had wasted no time on anything personal and he could not conceive of anything being more important than the question of national independence; so now as president he could not conceive of a personal quarrel being more important than the task of establishing the government on a firm foundation. To him that task was so formidable as to require the aid of every man, and the only parties he recognized, in his singleness of purpose, were those which supported the government, and the group which, for considerations of private advantage, opposed it. Yet for all his uncompromising attitude toward those things which interfered with the development of nationality, his forbearance toward both Jefferson and Hamilton seems that of a wise parent toward wayward sons. He pleaded with both men to compromise, convinced that the country needed their services, and a fair indication of his estimate of both may be gathered from the character of the plea which he made to each (Ford, *Writings,* XII, 174–79).

Methods and means of strengthening the government were in Washington's view debatable, but not the strengthening itself. All during the Revolution he had labored to dissolve local prejudice of every kind, and to substitute for the provincialism he found in the army a national pride and fellowship in being an American. Despite the acknowledgment that he had failed in this, his efforts had borne some fruit as the soldier returned to civil life at the expiration of his term, carrying with him the somewhat broadened view, which he had acquired almost unconsciously and which leavened, to an extent, the ideas of the people among whom he lived. The first displays of military force by the new government proved disastrous. Both Harmar's and St. Clair's expeditions against the Indians failed; but Washington proudly repelled covert suggestions that Great Britain was willing to cooperate against the savages. His purpose was to "keep the United States free from political connexions with *every* other country, to see them independent of *all* and under the influence of

none. In a word, I want an *American* character that the powers of Europe may be convinced we act for *ourselves,* and not for *others*" (Ford, *Writings,* XIII, 119–20).

The display of political partisanship on the part of the Hamilton-Jefferson factions was an influence in Washington's decision to serve a second term, when his overwhelming desire was to spend the remainder of his life in peace and quiet at "Mount Vernon"; but the foreign situation was undoubtedly the main factor in his decision. France's declaration of war on Great Britain stirred up an emotional enthusiasm that was easily developed into criticism of the President's neutrality, and from criticism to opposition to other acts of his administration. Though sympathizing with the French revolutionists at first, Washington was keenly aware of probable developments. As early as 1789 he saw that the disturbance in France was a "revolution . . . of too great magnitude to be effected in so short a space with the loss of so little blood" (Ford, *Writings,* XI, 435), and when the expected excesses began he speedily sickened of the spectacle. He was unopposed in his reëlection, but during his second term he was subjected to the heaviest strains and to villification and abuse which went beyond the bounds of common decency. Washington believed that twenty years of tranquillity would make the United States strong enough to "bid defiance in a just cause to any power whatever" (*Ibid.,* XIII, 151). He could not comprehend an attitude that could place any other problem ahead of this. In this light must be viewed all his decisions, which were strongly Federalist; they were moves designed to strengthen the national government.

The somewhat hysterical criticism of Washington's official formality and dignified, presidential ceremonial was similar to the democratic opposition he had encountered in establishing discipline in the Continental Army. In 1775 discipline was necessary to make the army efficient, in 1789–90 official ceremony was necessary to insure respect for the new government and clothe it with authoritative dignity. Without precedent to guide him, Washington was feeling his way carefully toward a goal which was as clear to him as was the goal of victory in the Revolutionary War. He defined it in his fifth annual message to Congress. "There is a rank due to the United States among nations, which will be withheld if not absolutely lost, by the reputation of weakness" (Ford, *Writings,* XII, 352). His whole course as president was governed by the purpose of obtaining that rank for the United States. The national bank, the excise tax, and the development of the army and navy into permanent, trained organizations, all common-sense projects of value to the nation, yet gave rise to feelings of uneasiness in many honest but provincial-minded men, who in some instances followed the lead of the unscrupulous. The proclamation of neutrality (1793) and the arrival of Genet [q.v.] furnished an exceptional opportunity to embarrass the administration and to demonstrate sympathy for the French. Genet's recall was finally demanded and all the political frenzy that centered around him subsided with unexpected rapidity. The French danger past, there yet remained the British commercial restrictions, while their retention of the western posts and encouragement of the Indians were also matters demanding prompt and careful attention. Wayne's crushing defeat of the savages at Fallen Timbers eliminated the immediate Indian problem in 1794. To attempt a settlement of the other questions Washington appointed John Jay [q.v.] envoy extraordinary to Great Britain.

Domestic trouble of a serious kind arose in Pennsylvania over resistance to the excise tax. This, the so-called Whiskey Rebellion, was a popular defiance of the tax collectors, accompanied by rioting and violence. It demonstrated that the same state indifference to the national welfare, which had increased Washington's difficulties in the Revolution fourfold, was still to be reckoned with, for, the tax being a federal one and the collection of it a federal matter, Pennsylvania's governor virtually ignored the situation. In the face of growing opposition, which seemed to Washington not a mere natural objection to a tax but a movement sponsored by the democratic societies to overthrow the government (Ford, *Writings*, XII, 451–52, 454–55), he was not at all confident of commanding sufficient support to suppress the outbreak of violence, and when the militia responded to his call with heartening alacrity and spirit his relief was great. The rebellion collapsed and the ringleaders were seized. Again Washington displayed that broad understanding which he had manifested in his attitude toward the Loyalists in the Revolution and toward the malcontents of Shays's Rebellion; he felt that the country could not afford to lose such a number of inhabitants by harsh measures of reprisal. In a short time he granted full pardon to all the insurgents who had signed the oath of submission and allegiance to the United States.

In the year 1795, by the Pinckney Treaty, the southern boundary of the United States was established and the coveted navigation of the Mississippi was secured, with port facilities at New Orleans. Offsetting this came the outburst of criticism over the Jay Treaty. Less than a year after the ratification of the treaty it became plain that none of the dire predictions of its opponents had come true; trade was actually improving and before a year was out the hysterical opposition had subsided. The treaty was no more satisfactory to Washington than to its critics (Ford, *Writings*, XIII, 63–66). Even on some of the points which he considered of prime importance it was not as definite as he desired; but he thought it was the best treaty that could be obtained at the time and it did settle the particular matters in controversy with Great Britain which would have made war probable had they remained in controversy much longer. He withstood this storm of opposition as he had withstood others, confident of his integrity of purpose and sure that the honor and welfare of the nation were served; but he likened the bitter attack to a cry against a mad dog, couched in "such exaggerated and indecent terms as could scarcely be applied to a Nero, a notorious defaulter, or even to a common pickpocket" (*Ibid.*, XIII, 76, 231). To the demand of the House of Representatives for the papers relating to Jay's negotiations he firmly refused to yield, being convinced that what the House really wanted was to establish the precedent that its concurrence was necessary in treaty making. His firmness settled the matter and the question has not been raised since.

In his first administration he had mentioned to Jefferson that he "really felt himself growing old, his bodily health less firm, his memory, always bad, becoming worse, and perhaps the other faculties of his mind showing a decay to others of which he was insensible himself" (P. L. Ford, *The Writings of Thomas Jefferson*, I, 1892, p. 175). In 1796 he set about the preparation of an address that would announce to the people his determination to retire from public life. The increasing weight of years admonished him that retirement was as necessary as it would be welcome. Solicitude for the welfare of the nation to which he had given so much of his thought and strength led him to take advantage of the opportunity to give the disinterested advice "of a parting friend, who can possibly have no personal motive to bias his counsels" (Ford, *Writings*, XIII, 285). He knew, however, that in announcing his retirement he risked being charged with a "conviction of fallen popularity, and despair of being re-elected" (*Ibid.*, XIII, 192).

He had assumed the presidency when the United States was little but a name, without power, prestige, or credit; when he retired from office the country was well on the road to international importance. He had given it dignity, as when he rebuked the French minister for presumption in a diplomatic negotiation (1791) and demanded the recall of Genet; he had demonstrated its power by crushing the Indians and suppressing the Whiskey Rebellion; and he had firmly fixed its credit, through Alexander Hamilton. Treaties with Spain and Great Britain had amicably settled the questions of the navigation of the Mississippi and the Florida and eastern boundaries. For the prosperity of the country he had worked unremittingly, and, though he abhorred war, none knew better than he that unpreparedness added to its horrors. In his first annual message to Congress he enunciated the principle: "To be prepared for war is one of the most effectual means of preserving peace" (Ford, *Writings*, XI, 456). The Farewell Address is partly an explanation of his course as president, with main emphasis upon the necessity of a firm union and a strong central government, for which he had labored incessantly the major part of his public life, and which were not in 1796 so taken for granted as they have finally come to be. Respect for the authority of that government and a solemn warning against the spirit of party he made equally important. The activities of political parties which came under Washington's observation were directed, he thought, solely to the subversion of good government, to a usurpation of power for personal ends, and would logically result in the loss of liberty. Morality and education were urged as necessities for a people's happiness, prosperity, and safety; good faith and justice toward all nations, but favors to none, were enjoined, and a warning was given against the insidious wiles of foreign influence. He hoped that these counsels would "be productive of some partial benefit; some occasional good; that they may now and then recur to moderate the fury of party spirit, to warn against the mischiefs of foreign intrigue, to guard against the impostures of pretended patriotism" (*Ibid.,* XIII, 320).

Washington's steadfast fortitude under the most trying difficulties is to be attributed largely to an unusual knowledge of self. No one would have yielded more quickly, he said, to a standard of infallibility in public matters, had there been such a thing; but lacking that, "upright intentions and close investigation" were his guides (Ford, *Writings,* XIII, 105). Dominated by the single idea and purpose of finding out, if possible, what was of greatest benefit to the nation, and bending all his energies toward accomplish-

ing it, Washington could not comprehend acts of opposition to his carefully considered measures as anything other than so many attempts to destroy the government. Brissot de Warville stated that he never saw Washington "divest himself of that coolness by which he is characterized, and become warm, but when speaking of the present state of America" (*Nouveau Voyage dans les États Unis . . . en 1788,* 1791, Vol. II, 269).

Duty, with Washington, became a moral obligation which was not to be evaded even by honorable means; and the barest outline of his spiritual development reveals the heavy sacrifice of personal inclination to that obligation. Resigning his first military commission in 1754, with no expectation of again entering upon a military career, he was unexpectedly appointed an aide by Braddock, and after Braddock's death he was appointed by Dinwiddie to protect the Virginia frontier; resigning again in 1758 to marry Mrs. Custis, he was appointed to command the American armies at the outbreak of the Revolution; resigning at the end of that war, he confidently expected to live the remainder of his life untroubled by public cares; drafted against his will to be president of the United States, he wished to retire in 1793, but was forced by circumstances to remain; retiring in 1797, as he hoped for good, he was again forced to accept command of the army that was being raised in expectation of war with France in 1798. Half his life was spent fulfilling what he conceived to be his duty at the expense of his domestic ease and happiness. He calmly analyzed the opposition to Adams' administration in 1798–99, as hanging upon and clogging the wheels of government, "Torturing every act, by unnatural construction, into a design to violate the Constitution—Introduce Monarchy—& to establish an aristocracy." Yet he was still able to "Hope well, because I have always believed, and trusted, that that Providence which has carried us through a long and painful War with one of the most powerful nations in Europe, will not suffer the discontented among ourselves to produce more than a temporary interruption to the permanent Peace and happiness of this rising Empire" (Ford, *Writings,* XIV, 142–43). President Adams, following popular will, appointed Washington lieutenant-general and commander in chief of the army it seemed necessary to raise. He accepted, with the understanding that he would not take the field until the troops actually were raised and equipped. He insisted on Hamilton's being second in command, and a heated contest of wills between him and Adams ensued. **In the end**

Adams gave in, but the Provisional Army was not needed and was never personally commanded by Washington. Under pressure of danger to his beloved country the military fire of the Revolution had flamed again, though Washington's steadfast conviction was that war was an unmitigated evil. Changing conditions in France steadily reduced the chance of conflict and Washington once more allotted a greater and greater part of his time to the management of "Mount Vernon." He was not granted opportunity to bring his farms to the point of efficiency he planned, though he had worked out a scheme of rotation of crops in his fields that carried over into the nineteenth century.

His death occurred with startling suddenness. A neglected cold developed into a malignant type of cynache trachealis with which the limited medical knowledge and skill of the time were unable to cope. With his physical strength sapped by mistaken blood-lettings, he fought a losing battle for nearly twenty-four hours. The philosophical calm of his remark that it was "the debt which we all must pay," was only exceeded by the high courage of his declaration, toward the end, "I am not afraid to go" (Ford, *Writings*, XIV, 249). He died at 11:30, Saturday, Dec. 14, 1799. The physical hardships of the Virginia colonial warfare and the later strains of the Revolution had much to do with his final collapse. Though he was a physical giant, over six feet in height and weighing 190 to 200 pounds, with no surplus flesh, he drove himself unsparingly and often beyond his strength; a check-up of the number of letters written daily from headquarters and consideration of the other daily, necessary business justifies the conclusion that, during the Revolutionary War, Washington seldom obtained more than three or four hours of consecutive sleep in any twenty-four.

All contemporaneous descriptions of Washington's appearance agree as to his dignity and impressiveness, many of them enthusiastically so, but Capt. George Mercer, his aide in the Virginia colonial service before Washington obtained world-wide fame, penned a description in 1760 which still remains the best. His frame, Mercer said, gave the impression of great muscular strength. "His bones and joints are large as are his hands and feet . . . rather long arms and legs . . . all the muscles of his face under perfect control, though flexible and expressive of deep feeling when moved by emotion. In conversation he looks you full in the face, is deliberate, deferential and engaging. His voice is agreeable . . . he is a splendid horseman" (P. L.

Ford, *George Washington*, 20 ed., pp. 38–39). An anonymous writer stated that his smile was extraordinarily attractive. His personal charm is attested in many letters of his friends, in the expressed regret of the Virginia colonial officers, on his resignation, at the loss of "such a sincere Friend, and so affable a Companion" (*Writings*, Bicentennial ed., II, 316 n.), in the farewell to his officers, and in the Virginia woman's remark to her friend, that when General Washington becomes "the chatty agreeable Companion, he can be down right impudent sometimes; such impudence, Fanny, as you and I like" (Ford, *George Washington*, 20 ed., p. 110). Add to this the French abbé's note that "The Americans, that cool and sedate people . . . are roused, animated, and inflamed at the very mention of his name" (Abbé C. C. Robin, *New Travels Through North America*, 1783, p. 35), and we have an approximation of the feeling of the people toward him. Leaders of the time, and Washington would have been the last to have denied the value of their assistance, followed and supported him with confidence and enthusiasm: Greene, Sullivan, Wayne in the army; Hamilton, Wolcott, Jay, and Pickering in civil authority. Curiously, the men who opposed him were generally those whose personal ambitions were dependent upon the success of that opposition.

The evolution of Washington's fame until his name was placed high upon the scroll of the world's great, began in 1776–77, when the victories of Trenton and Princeton focused European attention on the hopeless-looking struggle of American backwoodsmen with the most powerful nation in the world. The addition of France to that struggle insured Europe's careful watchfulness of every phase of the conflict and, as Lord John Russell put it, "The success of America was owing, next to the errors of her adversaries, to the conduct and character of General Washington" (*Memorials and Correspondence of Charles James Fox*, Vol. I, 1853, p. 153). Liberty, the basis of the American struggle, was becoming more than an academic definition in European thought and Washington perfectly personified the awakening. As Chateaubriand aptly said (*Travels in America and Italy*, Eng. ed., 1828, vol. I, 106): "He aimed at that which it was his duty to aim at . . . blended his existence with that of his country. . . . The name of Washington will spread with liberty from age to age."

[The miscellaneous Washington MSS. in the Lib. of Cong. are bound in 302 vols., the original letter-books in 35 additional vols., original diaries and account books in over 50 vols., and the contemporaneous Varick

Transcript of Washington's letters during the Revolutionary War in 44 vols. Of Washington letters elsewhere, the Lib. of Cong. possesses 21 boxes and a number of bound volumes of photostats. There are also numerous volumes of copies of miscellaneous Washington records, the originals of some of which cannot now be traced. Numerous letters from and to Washington are in the Continental Congress MSS. in the Lib. of Cong., so that the Washington papers in that library are a more nearly complete collection than that of any other distinguished American. The mass of them is, however, so vast that no comprehensive or complete publication was attempted prior to the Bicentennial. of his *Writings,* begun in 1931 (*post*). J. C. Fitzpatrick, *Calendar of the Correspondence of George Washington . . . with the Continental Congress* (1906), and *Calendar of the Correspondence of George Washington . . . with the Officers* (4 vols., 1915), have been published.

W. C. Ford, *The Writings of George Washington* (14 vols., 1889–93) is the most useful edition, but must be supplemented by that of Jared Sparks (12 vols., 1834–37), which contains some hundreds of letters omitted in the Ford ed., and by J. C. Fitzpatrick, ed., *The Diaries of George Washington* (4 vols., 1925). The Sparks ed. suffers from unjustifiable textual alterations and unnoted omissions. Both the Ford and Sparks eds. are being supplanted by *The Writings of George Washington. . . . Prepared under the Direction of the U. S. George Washington Bicentennial Commission* (1931), ed. by J. C. Fitzpatrick, which will probably extend to 30 vols.; it will be the first complete ed. of Washington's letters. Other valuable sources in print are: S. M. Hamilton, *Letters to Washington, 1752–1775* (4 vols., 1898–1902) ; Jared Sparks, *Correspondence of the Am. Revolution; Being Letters of Eminent Men to George Washington* (4 vols., 1853) ; *George Washington's Accounts of Expenses while Commander-in-Chief* (Facsim., 1917), with annotations by J. C. Fitzpatrick; *Letters from His Excellency George Washington, to Arthur Young . . . and Sir John Sinclair* (1803 and other eds.) ; M. D. Conway, *George Washington and Mount Vernon* (1889), mainly agricultural letters to William Pearce and James Anderson (in vol. IV of the *Memoirs of the Long Island Hist. Soc.*) ; *Letters from George Washington to Tobias Lear . . . from the Collection of Mr. William K. Bixby* (1905). J. D. Richardson, *A Compilation of the Messages and Papers of the Presidents,* vol. I (1896), gives the texts of the important communications to Congress. Washington's travels through the United States are described in J. C. Fitzpatrick, *George Washington, Colonial Traveller, 1732–75* (1927) ; W. S. Baker, *Itinerary of General George Washington . . . 1775 to 1783* (1892), and *Washington after the Revolution, MDCCLXXXIV–MDCCXCIX* (1898).

Nearly every biographer of Washington has fallen under the spell to which Sparks succumbed and has followed, more or less, the example set by the latter in idealizing the man, though some recent biographies have gone to the other extreme. Mention should be made of M. L. Weems, *A History, of the Life and Death, Virtues, and Exploits, of General George Washington* (1800), though no reliance should be placed on this famous work. Washington Irving, *Life of George Washington* (5 vols., 1855–59) is satisfactory from most viewpoints, though its reliance on Sparks lessens the confidence it would otherwise command; John Marshall, *The Life of George Washington* (5 vols., 1804–07) ranks with Irving, but its Federalist bias during the presidential period should be discounted; Vol. I (1837) of Sparks's ed. of the *Writings* is given over to a life of Washington, the interpretations of which must be used with caution. W. R. Thayer, *George Washington* (1922), is an orthodox life; Woodrow Wilson, *George Washington* (1903), is clear and readable but is also an orthodox interpretation ; H. C. Lodge, *George Washington* (2 vols., 1898), is more expansive than Thayer and Wilson, but like them is based upon the partial publications of the *Writings*; Norman Hapgood, *George Washington* (1901), is a modern treatment of merit ; Rupert Hughes, *George Washington* (3 vols., 1926–30) should be used with great caution, but contains bibliographical aids of unusual value; P. L. Ford, *The True George Washington* (1896), republished as *George Washington* (1924), a refreshing study of Washington from various angles, contains a wealth of interesting material which is unnoted as to source and difficult to trace; J. C. Fitzpatrick, *George Washington Himself* (1933), written from his manuscripts, presents many hitherto undeveloped sides of Washington's character. Other recent biographies are S. M. Little, *George Washington* (1929) ; L. M. Sears, *George Washington* (1932).

G. W. P. Custis, *Recollections and Private Memoirs of Washington* (1861) is the source of most of the unprovable traditions about Washington ; B. J. Lossing, *Mount Vernon and Its Associations* (1886), is somewhat more dependable than Custis. The following studies of special phases of Washington's life can be used with confidence: P. L. Haworth, *George Washington, Farmer* (1915), republished as *George Washington, Country Gentleman* (1925) ; T. G. Frothingham, *Washington, Commander in Chief* (1930) ; H. L. Ritter, *Washington as a Business Man* (1931) ; W. C. Ford, *Washington as an Employer and Importer of Labor* (1889) ; J. H. Penniman, *George Washington as Man of Letters* (1918) ; P. L. Ford, *Washington and the Theatre* (1899) ; J. M. Toner, *General Washington as an Inventor* (1892) ; C. H. Ambler, *George Washington and the West* (1936). J. C. Fitzpatrick, *The George Washington Scandals* (1929), among other things, fixes the authorship of the "Spurious Letters." Stephen Decatur, Jr., *Private Affairs of George Washington from the Records and Accounts of Tobias Lear, 1789–92* (1933), is the cash account of the President's expenses and the only financial record (except the *Accounts of Expenses while Commander-in-Chief, ante*) so far published. H. B. Carrington, *Battles of the American Revolution* (1876) supplies collateral background for the military side ; J. C. Fitzpatrick, *The Spirit of the Revolution* (1924) furnishes details of Continental Army headquarters and of Washington's aides ; Paul Wilstach, *Mount Vernon* (1930), is useful to any study of Washington's home life. E. E. Prussing, *The Estate of George Washington* (1927), is an able analysis of Washington's fortune. The best genealogy is in volume XIV of Ford's ed. of the *Writings,* which should be supplemented by the material in *Hist. of the U. S. George Washington Bicentennial Celebration, Literature Series* (1932), vol. III. This series also contains many full texts and extracts, carefully compared in most instances with the manuscripts of Washington's letters and state papers.

The number of portraits of Washington is amazing, yet the really reliable portraits are few. Not all the artists who painted or sketched him from life were competent, and their results are heterogeneous and largely mediocre, while the work of those who never saw him can only be classified as efforts of enthusiastic imagination. The Houdon bust, modeled from life at "Mount Vernon," and Gilbert Stuart's Boston Athæneum portrait are beyond just criticism. Other portraits by Stuart, notably the Channing-Gibbs, and some of Trumbull's work, the St. Memin print, and Sharples' best profile also deserve consideration. See Gustav Eisen, *Portraits of Washington* (3 vols., 1932).]

J. C. F—k.

WASHINGTON, HENRY STEPHENS

(Jan. 15, 1867–Jan. 7, 1934), petrologist, son of George and Eleanor Phoebe (Stephens) Washington, was born in Newark and brought up at Locust, N. J. He attended private schools and prepared for college under tutors. Graduated from Yale in 1886, he was a fellow in physics there for the next two years and then spent six years traveling and studying in the West Indies, Europe, Egypt, Algeria, and Asia Minor, in five of these years being enrolled as a member of the American School of Classical Studies at Athens. His interest in archaeology was permanent, and he repeatedly applied chemical and petrographical methods to the study of its special problems.

During this same period, he studied the volcanic islands scattered through the Grecian and Turkish archipelagoes, developing keen interest in the igneous rocks of the earth's crust. He subsequenly visited many other volcanic islands of the eastern Mediterranean and published a series of petrographic papers on their lavas. Two semesters at the University of Leipzig under the great petrographer Zirkel brought him in 1893 the degree of Ph.D., for his researches on the volcanoes of the Kula Basin in Lydia, near Smyrna. On Oct. 25 of that year he married Martha Rose Beckwith, from whom he was divorced about 1914; there were no children.

In 1895 Washington returned to the United States and after a year as assistant in mineralogy at Yale took possession of the old homestead at Locust, N. J., transforming the smokehouse into a laboratory. For the next ten years there came from this isolated source a constant stream of notable contributions to petrology. In 1899 he became associated with Joseph P. Iddings, Louis V. Pirsson [qq.v.], and Whitman Cross in formulating a systematic classification of igneous rocks based primarily upon chemical composition (Quantitative Classification of Igneous Rocks, 1903). In 1904 he published Manual of the Chemical Analysis of Rocks (4th ed., 1930), which became a standard handbook, used throughout the world. A major and permanent contribution to petrology was his compilation, Chemical Analyses of Igneous Rocks, Published from 1884 to 1913, Inclusive, with a Critical Discussion of the Character and Use of Analyses (1917), a revision and enlargement of an earlier work issued in 1903. The 1917 edition contains 8,600 analyses, all of them rated by Washington as "superior," arranged according to the system of classification of which he was co-author. In 1904 he published The Superior Analyses of Igneous Rocks from Roth's Tabellen, 1869 to 1884, also grouped according to the new system. These great collections are known to every petrologist in the world.

During the years 1906 to 1912 financial reverses made it necessary for Washington to serve as geological consultant in mining and other enterprises, but in 1912 he accepted a position in the Geophysical Laboratory of the Carnegie Institution of Washington, D. C., and in this favorable environment resumed his analytical work with redoubled energy. The list of his publications from the Carnegie Institution, including a number of studies prepared in collaboration with others, embraces one hundred titles. As his interest concentrated upon the distinctive characters of igneous rocks of certain regions, he explored Etna and other Italian volcanoes, the older igneous formations of Sardinia, the Deccan Traps of western and central India, and the Hawaiian Islands. Specimens of igneous rocks from Siberia, Eastern China, Iceland, Greenland, and scattered islets of the Atlantic Ocean, the Pribilof Islands in Bering Sea, the Galapagos group, San Felix and San Ambrosio in the South Pacific all yielded information. His "Petrology of the Hawaiian Islands," an important contribution (published in five parts, 1923–26, in the American Journal of Science), contained sixty-six new complete analyses made by Washington and his assistants.

His great store of information concerning the chemical and mineral composition of igneous rocks of the globe, surpassing that of any other student of the subject, led him inevitably to make generalizations regarding the rocky crust of the earth. His study, "The Chemistry of the Earth's Crust" (Journal of the Franklin Institute, December 1920), republished in the Annual Report of the Smithsonian Institution for 1920, was followed by The Composition of the Earth's Crust (1924), prepared in collaboration with F. W. Clarke. Many honors came to him: he was chairman (1926–29) of the division of volcanology of the American Geophysical Union, 1926–29, and vice-president (1922–23) of the section on volcanology of the International Geophysical Union, a member of the National Academy of Sciences and the American Philosophical Society, vice-president (1922) of the Geological Society of America, president (1924) of the Mineralogical Society of America, and a member of the Archaeological Institute of America. In 1918–19 he was a scientific attaché at the American embassy in Rome. His work in Italy brought him a decoration from the Italian government, and he held memberships in numerous foreign scientific bodies.

[Printed accounts include: Who's Who in America, 1932–33; Am. Men of Science, 1933; Yale Univ. Obit. Record, 1934; J. V. Lewis, in Am. Mineralogist, Mar. 1935; C. N. Fenner, in Science, Jan. 19, 1934; Washington Post, Jan. 8, 1934. A memoir by Whitman Cross, for the National Academy of Sciences, is in preparation.]
W. C.

WASHINGTON, JOHN MACRAE (October 1797–Dec. 24, 1853), soldier, the second son of Baily and Euphan (Wallace) Washington, was born on his father's estate, "Windsor Forest," in Stafford County, Va. His father was a second cousin of George Washington [q.v.]. On Oct. 24, 1814, John became a cadet at the United States Military Academy, where he was graduated July 17, 1817, and appointed third lieutenant of artillery. His first service was in Charleston Harbor, S. C., with the 3rd Artillery, during which he was promoted second lieutenant and appointed battalion quartermaster of artillery, Mar. 20, 1818. In this capacity he served until he was promoted first lieutenant, May 23, 1820, and sent to the Florida frontier.

Under the reorganization of the army, he was transferred to the 4th Artillery, June 1, 1821, and served successively at Savannah Harbor (1821–22), Fort Moultrie (1822–24), and Augusta, Ga. (1824). While at the last station, he was detailed as instructor of mathematics at the artillery school at Fort Monroe, Va., where he remained until 1826. The next year he served at Fort Marion, Fla., and then returned to Fort Monroe as ordnance officer, which post he held until 1833. On May 23, 1830, he was brevetted a captain for ten years' faithful service in one grade (an empty method employed by the government to overcome slow promotion), and on May 30, 1832, was regularly promoted a captain. From 1833 to 1838 he was engaged in the Creek and Florida wars, taking an active part in the battle of Lochahatchee against the Seminoles. During 1838 and 1839, as an assistant quartermaster, he aided Gen. Winfield Scott [q.v.] in the delicate task of transporting the Cherokee nation to Oklahoma, and in the prosecution of the Florida War. After duty at the instruction camp, Trenton, N. J., he was again detailed to assist Scott in the even more delicate undertaking of peacefully quelling the Canadian border disturbances, and was at Dearbornville, Mich., Detroit, and Buffalo, N. Y., until 1842. After the success of Scott's mission, he served successively at Fort McHenry, Md., and Carlisle Barracks, Pa., until 1846.

When the Mexican War began he was placed in command of a light battery of eight guns and joined the forces under Gen. John E. Wool [q.v.] which made the heroic, bloodless, and successful march through unbroken country from San Antonio, Tex., to Saltillo, Mexico. On the first day of the battle of Buena Vista, Feb. 22, 1847, General Wool placed Washington's battery on the right flank of the army, at the critical pass of La Angostura. Washington's deft and determined management of his command was the chief factor in repelling the vigorous attacks of overwhelming numbers of Mexicans. On the second day of the battle, when three regiments of Illinois and Kentucky troops retreated in disorder, he held fast and not only saved the lives of many of the fleeing volunteers, but maintained the key point of the American position by his stanchness and skill. Although six days before this action he had been regularly promoted a major, the news of his commission had not reached him. On Feb. 23, 1847, he was brevetted a lieutenant-colonel for gallant and meritorious conduct in the battle. From June 24 to Dec. 14, 1847, he acted as governor of Saltillo, and during much of the same period was chief of artillery of Wool's division and of the army of occupation. He was then placed in command of the expedition to Santa Fé, and served as civil and military governor of New Mexico from October 1848 until Oct. 23, 1849.

After the cessation of hostilities he served at Fort Constitution, N. H., from 1850 to 1852. In 1853 he embarked with the 3rd Artillery on the steamer *San Francisco,* for transportation to duty on the west coast. In a violent storm off the mouth of the Delaware, he, with three other officers and 178 men, was washed overboard and drowned. In his early career he had married Fanny Macrae, daughter of Dr. Jack Macrae, a nephew of Col. William, brother of Baily Washington. To this union were born three children.

[Sources include F. B. Heitman, *Hist. Reg. and Dict. U. S. Army* (1903); T. H. S. Hamersly, *Complete Regular Army Reg. of the U. S., 1779–1879* (1881); G. W. Cullum, *Biog. Reg. . . . U. S. Mil. Acad.,* vol. I (1879); J. H. Smith, *The War with Mexico* (1919); H. E. Hayden, *Va. Genealogies* (1891); T. A. Washington, *A Geneal. Hist. Beginning with Col. John Washington, the Emigrant . . .* (1891); *Proc. at the Inauguration of the Monument Erected by the Washington Light Infantry to the Memory of Col. William Washington* (1858). The middle name of Washington is that given by the *Va. Mag. of Hist. and Biog.,* Oct. 1914, supported by Heitman; some sources give Marshall.]

W. A. G.

WATERHOUSE, BENJAMIN (Mar. 4, 1754–Oct. 2, 1846), physician and pioneer vaccinator in America, was born at Newport, R. I., one of eleven children of Timothy and Hannah (Proud) Waterhouse. His father, a chair-maker, grandson of Richard Waterhouse who emigrated to Boston in 1669 and later settled in Portsmouth, N. H., is said to have been judge of the court of common pleas and a member of the royal council of the colony. His mother, Quaker-born in Yorkshire, England, was a cousin of Dr. John Fothergill, an eminent practitioner of London. Influenced by a number of learned Scotch physicians practising at Newport and by the reading of medical books in the library of Abraham Redwood [q.v.], Waterhouse was soon drawn to medicine. At the age of sixteen he apprenticed himself to Dr. John Halliburton, a surgeon, but he was also taught by Judge Robert Lightfoot, an Oxford graduate, "remarkably well read in Physic." In the portrait of Waterhouse at the age of twenty-two or three, painted by his school friend, Gilbert Stuart, we see a thoughtful student, "pensive but determined-looking and alert," with the "air of a militant Quaker" (Courtney, *post*, p. 2). Early in 1775 he embarked for London, where he made his home for over three years, while attending lectures in medicine, with his kinsman, John Fothergill. During this time he also spent nine months as a medical student in Edinburgh. In 1778 he went to Leyden to acquire, as he later wrote, "a little of the Dutch phlegm" (Waterhouse, *An Essay on Junius*, 1831, p. vi). There he lived with the American ambassador, John Adams, and his two sons. When he matriculated he placed after his name, *Liberae Reipublicae Americanae Foederatae Civis*, an inscription which caused considerable talk, as Waterhouse was the only American student at Leyden and "the British Ambassador at the Court of The Hague domineered the Dutch as if they were English Colonists" (*Ibid.*, p. vi). The Dutch authorities were so cautious that, before he could obtain the *imprimatur* of the university on his inaugural dissertation, *De Sympathia Partium Corporis Humani* (Apr. 19, 1780), he was constrained to add after his name only the word *Americanus*. Waterhouse was an ardent patriot, although never an active participant in political affairs.

Waterhouse returned to America and settled at Newport in June 1782. Upon the establishment of a medical department at Harvard College in 1783, he, one of the best educated physicians in America, accepted the professorship of the theory and practice of physic, and delivered his *Oratio Inauguralis* (not published until 1829) the same year. He was closely associated at first with John Warren [*q.v.*], the professor of anatomy and surgery, and Aaron Dexter, who held the chair of chemistry and materia medica. In 1786 he published the first part of *A Synopsis of a Course of Lectures, on the Theory and Practice of Medicine*. On July 6, 1791, he delivered a discourse at Concord, Mass., on *The Rise, Progress, and Present State of Medicine* (1792) which, with its emphasis on experimental investigation, reveals Waterhouse as a man far in advance of his time.

In 1799, however, came the most important event in his life. In the beginning of this year he received from John Coakley Lettsom, the London physician, a copy of Edward Jenner's *An In-*

quiry into the Causes and Effects of the Variolae Vaccinae (1798). Waterhouse undoubtedly knew of the previous work of another Boston physician, Zabdiel Boylston [*q.v.*], who in 1721 had used inoculations from smallpox pustules to set up a mild form of the disease in an unprotected patient and thus prevent a more serious attack in the future. Since inoculation smallpox was sometimes fatal, the importance of Jenner's cowpox vaccinations lay in the fact that only a mild disease (vaccinia) resulted, although the degree of protection against smallpox was equally great. Waterhouse published a brief account of Jenner's work in the *Columbian Centinel*, Mar. 16, 1799, with the queer title, "Something Curious in the Medical Line," and a few weeks later at a meeting of the American Academy of Arts and Sciences in Boston showed Jenner's book to the members and told of the probable value of the work. After considerable delay, Waterhouse received from England some vaccine in the form of infected threads, and immediately (July 8, 1800) used it on his son, Daniel Oliver Waterhouse, then five years old. As the vaccine pustule went through the various stages described by Jenner, Waterhouse went on to vaccinate another child, a servant boy. The next step was to see if the children were susceptible to smallpox; at Waterhouse's request William Aspinwall [*q.v.*], head of the smallpox hospital in Brookline, inoculated one of the supposedly protected children with smallpox, choosing the servant boy for the experiment. Although the boy's arm became infected with smallpox, there was not the slightest trace of the general disease. Waterhouse, who had followed his own advice and left "the flowery path of speculation" (*The Rise, Progress,* etc., p. 30), wrote of this: "One fact, in such cases, is worth a thousand arguments" (*A Prospect,* etc., 1800, p. 25).

He continued to vaccinate others with cowpox with equally good results. His first report, *A Prospect of Exterminating the Small Pox,* was published within six weeks, Aug. 18, 1800. It contains a clear account of his work, with the logical conclusion that cowpox protected the body from the infection of smallpox. The news of his work soon spread, but unfortunately vaccination was not taken up exclusively by medical men; impure cowpox matter, sometimes mixed with smallpox, was used by "stage-drivers, pedlars, and in one instance the sexton of a church" (*A Prospect,* pt. II, 1802, p. 8). A serious epidemic occurred, a number of people died, and a feeling of resentment against Waterhouse was soon evident. He finally requested (May 31, 1802) the board of health of Boston to make a complete investigation. An experiment with nineteen persons was successfully carried out by a committee of seven outstanding practitioners, including Waterhouse, and the committee concluded that "the cox-pox is a complete security against the small-pox" (*Ibid.*, p. 64). From 1802 on, with the aid of many physicians and public-minded citizens, Waterhouse made vaccination known throughout the neighboring states. President Thomas Jefferson had about two hundred persons vaccinated with vaccine sent him by Waterhouse (*Ibid.*, p. 33). In November 1802 Waterhouse was able to publish part II of *A Prospect,* giving in orderly arrangement the details of his two-year study, and including letters from Jefferson, Benjamin Rush, Jenner, and others. During the next few years he wrote many articles on vaccination for newspapers, particularly the *Columbian Centinel.* It was through his insistence on maintaining the purity of vaccine virus that vaccination was finally placed upon a secure scientific basis in the United States. In 1810 the main facts of his previous publications were abstracted in a pamphlet, *Information Respecting the Origin, Progress, and Efficacy of the Kine Pock Inoculation.* In honor of his work, Waterhouse was made a member of various scientific societies in the United States, Great Britain, and France.

With his most important contribution to medicine accomplished, Waterhouse turned to his other interests. His lecture of Nov. 20, 1804, to the medical students at Harvard College was printed in 1805, *Cautions to Young Persons Concerning Health . . . Shewing the Evil Tendency of the Use of Tobacco . . . with Observations on the Use of Ardent and Vinous Spirits.* This was Waterhouse's most popular book; five editions were published in America, one in London, one in Geneva (in French), and one in Vienna (in German). He felt that the morals of the students of his time had deteriorated, and that the increase in consumption and nervous disorders was the result of intemperance. It probably was a salutary warning at a time when such a caution was needed. In addition to his position in the Harvard Medical School, Waterhouse gave lectures on natural history in general and on mineralogy and botany in particular, first in Rhode Island College (later Brown University) at Providence, R. I. (1784–86), and from 1788 on at Cambridge. A cabinet of mineralogy was sent to him from London by Lettsom and given to Harvard College. His lectures were first published in the *Monthly Anthology* (1804–08), as a pamphlet in 1810, and finally, in part, as *The Botanist* (1811). As early as 1782 he suggested the formation of a humane society in Rhode

Island similar to those already active in Europe and in 1785 drew up plans, with Dr. Henry Moyes of Edinburgh, for the Humane Society of the Commonwealth of Massachusetts. After some friction with the other founding members, he gave a discourse, June 8, 1790, on *The Principle of Vitality,* showing the importance of long-continued artificial respiration.

By 1810, however, his relations with his colleagues and the governing board of Harvard College had become strained. The Harvard Medical School at Cambridge lacked clinical facilities; the only patients available for demonstration were in the Boston almshouse, then considered a long distance from Cambridge. Waterhouse was eminently satisfied with his course of didactic lectures at Cambridge and bitterly opposed a move to establish the school in Boston near the contemplated Massachusetts General Hospital, a suggestion made by his more energetic colleague, John Warren. The younger men of the time, particularly John Collins Warren [*q.v.*] and James Jackson, 1777–1867 [*q.v.*], sided with Warren. Waterhouse, "little given to the arts of clinical instruction" (Mumford, *post,* p. 247), endeavored to establish a rival school of medicine in Boston, to be known as the College of Physicians; when this failed, he attempted to damage his colleagues by publishing "false, scandalous, and malicious libels upon the other professors" (*Ibid.*). He was forced to resign in 1812. He had been connected with the United States Marine Hospital since 1808, when he wrote the first *Rules and Orders* for the hospital at Charlestown, Mass., and in 1813 Madison appointed him medical superintendent of all the military posts in New England, a position which he held until 1820. The excellent character of his work can be judged by *A Circular Letter, from Dr. Benjamin Waterhouse, to the Surgeons of the Different Posts* (1817), which concerns the diagnosis and treatment of dysentery.

With an assured income for the time being, Waterhouse turned, except for one publication, *An Essay Concerning Tussis Convulsiva* (1822), towards general literature. An anonymous work is attributed to him, unlike any of his other writtings; the book is a romantic narrative, *A Journal of a Young Man of Massachusetts* (1816), the story of a surgeon captured by the British in the War of 1812 and confined to Dartmoor Prison. There is every evidence that the book was a first-hand account, written by the doctor of a small merchant ship, but Waterhouse may have edited or even augmented the manuscript, as he did with another young man's book published some years later. In 1831 he published *An*

Essay on Junius and his Letters, in which he assigned the authorship of the letters to William Pitt, Earl of Chatham. His last literary undertaking was the editorship of John B. Wyeth's *Oregon* (1833), which he published as a deterrent to western emigrations. Issued when he was nearly eighty, the rather senile moralizing of Waterhouse in this book stands out in marked contrast to the fresh, buoyant narrative of the younger author.

Waterhouse lived in his home on Waterhouse Street, Cambridge, until his death at the age of ninety-two. Burial took place at the Mount Auburn Cemetery. His appearance in younger days may be judged by the Stuart portrait; when he was an older man Holmes noted "his powdered hair and queue, his gold-headed cane, his magisterial air and diction" (*post,* p. 421). He married, first, on June 1, 1788, Elizabeth, the daughter of Andrew and Phoebe (Spooner) Oliver. There were four sons and two daughters. One of the daughters married the younger Henry Ware [*q.v.*]; the other, William Ware [*q.v.*]. Elizabeth Oliver Waterhouse died in 1815, and on Sept. 19, 1819, Waterhouse married Louisa, daughter of Thomas and Judith (Colman) Lee. She survived him, without children, and died in 1863.

[See G. H. Waterhouse, "Descendants of Richard Waterhouse of Portsmouth, N. H.," 3 vols., 1934, typescript in Lib. of Cong. and in New England Historic Genealogical Soc., Boston; *Junius and His Letters* (1831) and *A Prospect of Exterminating the Small-Pox* (2 pts., 1800–02), which contain autobiog. material; T. F. Harrington, *The Harvard Medic. School* (1905), vol. I; H. R. Viets, *A Brief Hist. of Medicine in Mass.* (1930); H. A. Martin, in *N. C. Medic. Jour.,* Jan. 1881; J. G. Mumford, *Surgical Memoirs* (1908); T. J. Pettigrew, *Memoirs of the Life . . . of the Late John Coakley Lettsom* (3 vols., 1817); J. J. Abraham, *Lettsom, His Life and Times* (1933); R. H. Fox, *Dr. John Fothergill and His Friends* (1919); O. W. Holmes, in *Medic. News* (Phila.), Oct. 20, 1883; W. R. Thayer, in *Proc. Mass. Hist. Soc.,* vol. L (1917), vol. LV (1922); W. C. Lane, in *Cambridge Hist. Soc. Pubs.,* vol. IV (1909); W. C. Ford, *Statesman and Friend* (1927); letters and notes in Harvard Coll. Lib., Yale Coll. Lib., Boston Pub. Lib., Boston Medic. Lib., and Mass. Hist. Soc.; town records of Newport, R. I.; *Cambridge Vital Records,* vol. II (1915); "Medic. Lit. of R. I.," *Boston Medic. Intelligencer,* Aug. 3, 1824; *Boston Daily Advertiser, Boston Daily Jour.* (death notice), Oct. 3, 1846. The best accounts of Waterhouse's work on vaccination are by W. M. Welch, in *Proc. Phila. County Medic. Soc.,* vol. VII (1885), and J. W. Courtney, *Benjamin Waterhouse, M.D.* (1926), read before the Fifth Internat. Cong. of the Hist. of Medicine, Geneva, 1926. Family papers in the possession of Mrs. W. R. Thayer of Cambridge, Mass., have also been consulted.]   H. R. V.

WATERHOUSE, FRANK (Aug. 8, 1867–Mar. 20, 1930), capitalist, active in shipping enterprises in the Pacific Northwest, was born in Cheshire, England, the son of Joseph and Mary Elizabeth (Horsfield) Waterhouse. He attended private schools, but at fifteen set out for Amer-

ica, landing in Montreal with fifty dollars in his pocket. He earned a living by hard labor during a good part of the next seven years, working in logging camps and as a hod carrier, and later serving as a constable and deputy sheriff. His wanderings took him into Minnesota and Manitoba. After three years in England, he returned to America, settling in Tacoma, Wash., where in 1893–94 he was a stenographer in the offices of the Northern Pacific Railroad. He then spent a few months selling life insurance, did a record business, and removed to Seattle as a general agent.

In January 1895 he became secretary of the Pacific Navigation Company, which operated a fleet of freight and passenger steamers on Puget Sound, and in May of the same year was appointed general manager. When the rush to the Klondike gold fields began he went to England and organized a company to furnish transportation to the northern British Columbia ports and the Yukon; in 1898 this organization established trading posts on the Yukon. He later purchased the interests of his British associates and formed an American concern, Frank Waterhouse & Company. He introduced the fresh meat business into Alaska and placed the first refrigerator boat on the Yukon.

During the Spanish-American War, he chartered a large fleet of ships for transport service, and nearly all livestock supplies from the Pacific Northwest for the army in the Philippines were shipped in his vessels. He established the first line of steamships to give regular service between Puget Sound and European ports through the Suez Canal, and the first line of freighters from the Sound to Hawaii, New Zealand, Australia, North China, and the Malay Peninsula. During the World War, he engaged in the transportation of military supplies from Seattle to Vladivostok.

Waterhouse had many business interests other than shipping. He organized and was president of Waterhouse & Employes, operating farms in eastern Washington, acquired iron and coal mines, the Arlington Dock Company, and other corporations; and was president of the Yellow and the Seattle taxicab companies. His civic interests were fully as numerous. He was president of the Associated Industries of Seattle, 1919–22, and of the Chamber of Commerce, 1921–22, and chairman of the Seattle chapter of the American Red Cross, 1919–26.

Waterhouse died of heart disease at his home in Seattle. In February 1893 he had married Lucy Dyer Hayden of Tacoma, daughter of John C. Hayden, and he was survived by his widow, one son, and three daughters. Another son, deceased, had been a lieutenant in the Royal (British) Flying Corps in the World War.

[H. K. Hines, *An Illustrated Hist. of the State of Wash.* (1893); *Frank Waterhouse & Company's Pacific Ports* (1914); C. B. Bagley, *Hist. of Seattle* (1916), II, 823; Herbert Hunt and F. C. Kaylor, *Wash. West of the Cascades* (1917), III, 128; C. T. Conover, *Mirrors of Seattle* (1923); C. H. Hanford, *Seattle and Environs* (1924); *Who's Who in America,* 1930-31; *Who's Who in Wash. State,* 1927; *Seattle Daily Times,* Mar. 21, 1930; *Seattle Post-Intelligencer,* Mar. 21 and 23, 1930; *N. Y. Times,* Mar. 21, 1930.] G. W. F.

WATERHOUSE, SYLVESTER (Sept. 15, 1830–Feb. 12, 1902), educator, publicist, civic leader, was born in Barrington, N. H., the ninth and last child of Dolla (Kingman) and Samuel Ham Waterhouse, a carpenter whose family entered the colonies in 1669 through Richard Waterhouse, tanner and occupant of Pierce's Island near Portsmouth, N. H. A distinguished member of the family was Benjamin Waterhouse [*q.v.*], Harvard medical professor. When he was nine Waterhouse's right leg was amputated as the result of an accident, and while he was still small another injury cost him his left eye. These misfortunes decided him on a life of scholarship. Preparing himself at Phillips Exeter Academy, he entered Dartmouth in March 1851 and the following autumn enrolled in Harvard College, where he distinguished himself in Greek composition and graduated in 1853 with honors. He spent the next two years in the Harvard Law School, from which he received the degree of LL.B. in 1857. He was acting professor of Latin at Antioch College, Yellow Springs, Ohio (1856–57), and instructor in Greek (1857–64), professor of Greek (1864–68), and Collier Professor of Greek (1868–1901) in Washington University, St. Louis, Mo., holding a chair endowed by four of his former students "in grateful recognition" of his "fidelity, learning and ability." An authority on Greek roots, he held this chair until impaired health forced him to retire in 1901 as professor emeritus.

Waterhouse's interests carried him far from the classical subjects he enthusiastically expounded in the classroom. A firm believer in the future of the Middle West, he was an ardent advocate of improving the Mississippi River, attended numerous conventions on river development, and in 1877 was chosen to write an extended memorial to Congress on the subject. He wrote government pamphlets on the cultivation of ramie and jute, and for twenty years urged Southern farmers to diversify their program with these Asiatic crops. He was United States commissioner to the Paris exposition of 1878, honorary commissioner to the New Orleans world's

fair (1884), and Missouri commissioner to the American exposition in London (1887). He was also greatly interested in the proposed Nicaragua canal. He was a member of the Missouri bureau of geology and mines, secretary of the St. Louis board of trade, and secretary of the American Tariff League for Missouri. Upwards of a hundred of his numerous addresses and newspaper articles were published in pamphlets, many in German, French, and Spanish translations. One called *The Resources of Missouri* (1867) was used widely by the state board of immigration to acquaint prospective residents with Missouri. Other pamphlets discussed iron manufacturing, reforestation, trade with Brazil, city parks, western railroads, removal of the national capital, and a barge system on the inland waterways. Waterhouse also wrote on the early history of St. Louis for J. T. Scharf's *History of St. Louis City and County* (2 vols., 1883), and contributed to Hyde and Conard's *Encyclopedia of the History of St. Louis* (4 vols., 1899).

A third serious injury befell him in 1867 when a fall from a carriage brought on a painful spinal trouble. He died of apoplexy following an operation in a St. Louis hospital in his seventy-second year. His body was cremated and the ashes were laid in Pine Hill Cemetery, Dover, N. H. He had never married. He lived frugally in meager quarters, but he left an estate of approximately $172,000, accumulated through sagacious investments. To Washington University he gave $25,000, to be used only when interest had increased the sum to $1,000,000. He made other grants with time stipulations to educational institutions he had attended in the East. His last weeks he spent among his letters, rereading messages from Emerson, Lowell, Longfellow, Agassiz, Wendell Phillips, and other literary personages who were his friends.

[Sources include G. H. Waterhouse, "Descendants of Richard Waterhouse," 3 vols., 1934, typescript in Lib. of Cong.; William Hyde and H. L. Conard, *Encyc. of the Hist. of St. Louis* (1899), vol. IV; James Cox, *Old and New St. Louis* (1894); J. T. Scharf, *Hist. of St. Louis City and County* (2 vols., 1883); M. T. Runnels, *Memorial Sketches . . . Class of 1853, Dartmouth Coll.* (1895); obituaries in *St. Louis Post-Dispatch* and *St. Louis Republic,* Feb. 13, 1902; information from Waterhouse's niece, Mrs. Lilla K. Durgin of Watertown, Mass., and from Dr. G. R. Throop and Philo Stevenson of Washington Univ., where there is a book of clippings about Waterhouse; records of De Paul Hospital, St. Louis; autobiog. notes in lib. of Dartmouth Coll.] I. D.

WATERMAN, LEWIS EDSON (Nov. 20, 1837–May 1, 1901), inventor, manufacturer, eldest son of Elisha and Amanda Perry (Washburn) Waterman, was born in Decatur, Otsego County, N. Y. He traced his ancestry to Robert Waterman, who emigrated from England to

Plymouth, Mass., about 1636 and later settled in Marshfield. Elisha Waterman was prospering at his trade of wagon-builder when Lewis was born but he died of a fever when the latter was still a small child. The boy obtained no regular schooling until after he was ten years old, but thereafter he devoted as much time as he could to study, even attending the seminary in Charlottesville, N. Y., for a short period when he was fifteen. In 1853 his mother married again, and Waterman accompanied the family to Kankakee County, Ill., where for four years he taught school in the winter and worked as a carpenter in summer. His health would not permit him to continue in manual labor, however, and between 1857 and 1861 he was variously occupied teaching school, selling books, and studying the Pitman system of shorthand. He mastered the subject so thoroughly that during the year before the Civil War he was able to give instruction in it.

Through his experience as a book agent Waterman had discovered that he was an able salesman and in 1862 he gave up teaching to sell life insurance. After some two years he was made the Boston representative of the Aetna Life Insurance Company, in which capacity he continued until 1870, building up a substantial and profitable business. Poor health forced him to give up the Boston agency, and for the next thirteen years he spent much of his time in travel. In 1883 he turned his attention seriously to the perfection of the fountain pen, in which he had been passively interested for several years. A number of fountain pens had been patented previously, but to his mind none of them was satisfactory. He moved to New York City and there began a series of experiments in which he progressed so rapidly that before the year was out he applied for his first patents, which were issued on Feb. 12 and Nov. 4, 1884. His initial improvement was in the ink-feeding device. It consisted mainly of a piece of hard rubber inserted into the open end of the pen barrel and holding the gold pen in position. On the side of this piece of rubber next to the pen was a square groove, in the bottom of which narrow fissures had been made with fine saws; extending from the ink reservoir in the barrel to the nibs of the pen, these fissures automatically controlled the flow of ink. Upon obtaining his patents, Waterman established the Ideal Pen Company in New York to manufacture his pen. Three years later, in 1887, the business had grown to such an extent that it was incorporated as the L. E. Waterman Company, Waterman acting as president and manager until his death. In this capacity he not only successfully directed the manufacturing and selling

branches of his business but also continued to improve the pen, obtaining patents for modifications of his feeding device as well as for improvements of the joints between the nozzle and the barrel and between the cap and the barrel, the most noted being a joint made of disparate cones.

Waterman was twice married: first, June 29, 1858, to Sarah Ann Roberts, in Pittsfield, Ill., and second, Oct. 3, 1872, to Sarah Ellen Varney, in Topsfield, Mass. He died in Brooklyn, N. Y., survived by his widow and by three children of his first marriage, and was buried in Forest Hill Cemetery, Boston, Mass.

[*The Pen Prophet*, Feb. 12, 1905; *Contemporary Am. Biog.*, vol. III (1902); F. D. Waterman, *Waterman Geneal., 1636–1928* (1928); *N. Y. Times*, May 2, 1901; *Brooklyn Eagle*, May 1, 1901; Patent Office records.]

C. W. M.

WATERMAN, ROBERT H. (Mar. 4, 1808– Aug. 9, 1884), sea captain, was born in Hudson, N. Y., a descendant of Robert Waterman who settled in Marshfield, Mass., about 1636, and the son of Thaddeus Waterman, who commanded several New York ships in the early nineteenth century, and of Eliza (Coffin) Waterman. When he was twelve years old, he went to sea as cabin boy on a sailing vessel. In 1829 he was first mate of the crack Black Ball packet ship *Britannia,* sailing between New York and Liverpool under Capt. Charles H. Marshall [*q.v.*]; four years later he was appointed to the command of the *South America,* the finest ship under the Black Ball flag. He retained this command until 1837, when he took over the ship *Natchez,* owned by the New York firm of Howland & Aspinwall, which traded principally with China and the west coast of South America. For several years he continued to command Howland & Aspinwall ships on the run between New York or Boston and Valparaiso and other South American ports.

In 1842 he was sent to China with the *Natchez* and in this trade made a series of remarkable passages. His first two voyages homeward from Canton to New York were made in ninety-two and ninety-four days, respectively, both of which runs were very close to the record, and in 1845 he astounded the maritime world by arriving in New York on Apr. 3, only seventy-eight days from Macao, having established a new world's record. The following year Howland & Aspinwall built the clipper ship *Sea Witch* for him, and in this vessel Waterman established the records which still stand as the best and second best runs between China and any North Atlantic port —seventy-seven days from Macao to New York in 1848, and seventy-four days, fourteen hours from Hong Kong to New York in 1849. In this service, moreover, he had broken every existing record for speed, both in days' runs and over the various sections of the China route. During this period of his life his home was in Fairfield, Conn., where he married, in 1846, Cordelia Sterling, daughter of David Sterling of Bridgeport.

Following his successful voyage of 1849 he made plans to retire from the sea, and after taking the steamship *Northerner* to San Francisco in 1850, bought, in company with Capt. A. A. Ritchie, four leagues of land in Solano County and prepared to settle down. Yielding, however, to the solicitations of the firm of N. L. & G. Griswold of New York, he agreed to take command of their new clipper *Challenge,* then the largest and loftiest clipper ship afloat. Returning to New York, he sailed for San Francisco in the *Challenge* in July 1851. The passage which followed has frequently been cited as the classic instance of a voyage in an American "Hell Ship." It was characterized by numerous acts of insubordination on the part of members of the crew, culminating in an attempt to murder the chief mate and in the deaths, from disease and injury, of nine members of the crew, several of whom were said to have been killed by Waterman himself. On the arrival of the *Challenge* in San Francisco, Oct. 29, 1851, an attempt was made to lynch Waterman, and he was subsequently tried for murder, but was completely exonerated by the testimony of his crew and passengers, who testified that the ship was in deadly peril of seizure by mutineers. Shortly after this incident he was made hull inspector for the government in San Francisco, a position which he held until 1870.

During his life in California, Waterman was regarded as a kindly and sympathetic man and a public benefactor, deeply interested in the welfare of his community. He gave to the city of Fairfield, Cal., the land on which it now stands, naming the place after the town of Fairfield, Conn. About 1859 he built a fine residence a mile from Fairfield, modeling the front of the house to resemble the prow of a ship. He was greatly interested in farming and bred fine strains of poultry and cattle during his later years. He also donated the land for the beautiful Armijo high school and the court house in Fairfield. He died in San Francisco and was buried there, but his body was later removed to Bridgeport, Conn. As a master mariner Waterman made a contribution to the world's sailing records which has probably never been surpassed, and he must be ranked as one of the greatest sea captains of America.

[Unpublished genealogical material relating to the Waterman family collected by Thurston F. Waterman

of Albany, N. Y.; T. G. Cary, "The Vigilance Committee of San Francisco, 1851" (MS., in Lib. of Cong.); *Hist. of Solano County* (1879); C. C. Cutler, *Greyhounds of the Sea* (1930); files of the *Solano Republican,* 1859–84, *passim*; files of the *Commercial Advertiser* (N. Y.), 1833–52, *passim*; official records of the N. Y. Custom House, 1800–52.]   C. C. C.

WATERMAN, THOMAS WHITNEY (June 28, 1821–Dec. 7, 1898), lawyer, was the fourth of eight children. His paternal grandfather, David Waterman, was an ironmaster of Salisbury, Conn.; his father, Thomas Glasby Waterman (1788–1862), graduated from Yale in 1806, studied law, and in 1813 arrived in Binghamton, N. Y., where he married Pamela, daughter of Gen. Joshua Whitney, promoter for William Bingham [*q.v.*] in developing the town site. In 1822 Waterman was made district attorney, and in 1828 published *The Justice's Manual.* He sat in the Assembly in 1824 and in the state Senate, 1827–30, taking part in the preparation of *The Revised Statutes of the State of New York* (3 vols., 1829). After 1831 he turned his attention to lumbering, and amassed a comfortable fortune.

Thomas Whitney Waterman entered Yale in 1838. Three years later he was sent abroad for his health and traveled in England and on the Continent. Returning in 1844, he served an apprenticeship in a law office, was admitted to the bar in 1848, and commenced practice in New York City as an associate of his brother-in-law, Judge James W. White. In the following year he published *A Treatise on the Civil Jurisdiction of Justices of the Peace* (1849), a complete revision, rearrangement, and enlargement of the subject earlier treated by his father, to whom this volume was inscribed. In 1851 he published in three volumes *The American Chancery Digest,* including state and federal equity decisions, with an introductory sketch of equity courts and their jurisdiction. It made a favorable impression on his colleagues, and his professional standing was now deemed a sufficient guarantee of the accuracy of his writings.

During the next nine years he edited an American edition (1851) of Joseph Henry Dart's *Compendium of the Law and Practice of Vendors and Purchasers of Real Estate*; a third edition (2 vols., 1852) of R. H. Eden's *Compendium of the Law and Practice of Injunctions*; two editions (1853, 1860) of J. F. Archbold's *Complete Practical Treatise on Criminal Procedure, Pleading, and Evidence*; a new edition (1853) of *The Wisconsin and Iowa Justice,* originally written by his younger brother, Joshua Waterman; a fourth edition (1854) of John Adams' *Treatise on the Principles and Practice of the Action of*

Ejectment; a second edition (1855) of *A Treatise on the Law of New Trials in Cases Civil and Criminal* by David Graham [*q.v.*], to which Waterman added two volumes; a fourth edition (1856) of William Paley's *Treatise on the Law of Principal and Agent*; and *A Digest of the Reported Decisions of the Superior . . . and of the Supreme Court . . . of Connecticut* (1858). His literary work was interrupted in 1861 by the illness of his father, whose death in January 1862 caused him to return to Binghamton to commence active practice, but the publication in 1865 of his American edition of John Tamlyn's *Reports of Cases Decided in the High Court of Chancery* marked the resumption of his lego-literary activities. This work was followed by *A Treatise on the Law of Set-Off, Recoupment, and Counterclaim* (1869), the success of which led the author to abandon practice once more; a second edition (1873) of 6 and 19 *Wendell's Reports* (two other volumes, 18 and 20, of these reports, containing Waterman's notes, were published in 1901); *A Treatise on the Law of Trespass* (2 vols., 1875), which met hostile criticism from those members of the bar who held the law reports to be the only legitimate fountains of legal wisdom; *A Digest of Decisions in Criminal Cases* (1877); and *A Practical Treatise on the Law Relating to the Specific Performance of Contracts* (1881). His last important work, *A Treatise on the Law of Corporations* (2 vols., 1888), was published just before he suffered a stroke of paralysis from which he never fully recovered. His writings were, for the most part, on phases of law which were rapidly changing, and with the appearance of later volumes of reports his digests were soon out-dated; hence his work has not noticeably affected the thought and development of the law of later generations. In 1850 he married a daughter of the Rev. Edward Andrews, pastor of Christ Church in Binghamton. She died in 1871; two daughters survived their father, who died in Binghamton at the age of seventy-seven.

[J. B. Wilkinson, *The Annals of Binghamton* (2nd ed., 1872); F. C. Pierce, *Whitney* (1895); W. S. Lawyer, *Binghamton* (1900); *Albany Law Journal*, Dec. 31, 1898; book reviews in *U. S. Monthly Law Mag.*, Feb. 1851 and *Am. Law Rev.*, Jan. 1870, Apr. 1873, July, Oct. 1875; *Evening Herald* (Syracuse), Dec. 8, 1898; for T. G. Waterman, F. B. Dexter, *Biog. Sketches Grads. Yale Coll.*, vol. VI (1912) and *Binghamton Standard*, Jan. 15, 1862.]   V. L. W.

WATERS, DANIEL (June 20, 1731–Mar. 26, 1816), naval officer, was born at Charlestown, Mass., the tenth child of Adam and Rachel (Draper) Waters, and the great-grandson of Lawrence Waters who came to Charlestown from Lancaster, England, in 1675. Daniel took up seafaring and became a master mariner, making his home first in Charlestown but after 1771 in the adjoining town of Malden. He was one of the Malden minute-men who were engaged with the British on Apr. 19, 1775, and, as one experienced in ordnance, he was shortly afterward requested by the Malden Committee of Safety to prepare the cannon of the town and "enlist a sufficient number of men to make use of them" (Corey, *post*, p. 754). After the American investment of Boston he had charge of a small gunboat in the Charles River and, on Jan. 20, 1776, he was appointed by General Washington to command the schooner *Lee*, one of six vessels under John Manley [*q.v.*]. In the *Lee* he was active in the ensuing warfare on British communications and captured one enemy vessel in February and another on May 10, the *Elizabeth*, laden with merchandise seized in Boston. In early June, aided by the *Warren*, he took an armed troopship with ninety-four Scotch Highlanders on board, and on June 17 he shared with other vessels in the capture of the transports *Howe* and *Annabella* in Nantasket Road.

Upon the recommendation of Washington and others, he was appointed, Mar. 15, 1777, a captain in the Continental Navy. Serving thereafter as a volunteer under Manley in the *Hancock*, he was given command of the frigate *Fox*, but on July 6 both the *Fox* and the *Hancock* were surrendered to superior forces off Halifax. After he was exchanged in 1778, he made a West Indies cruise in the spring of 1779 in the Continental sloop *General Gates*. He then commanded the Massachusetts ship *General Putnam* in the ill-fated expedition against Castine, Me., in which the American ships were destroyed in the mouth of the Penobscot River to prevent their capture. His most famous exploit came at the close of this year when, in the Boston privateer *Thorn* of eighteen six-pounders, he defeated, in a two-hour action on Dec. 25, two enemy privateers of about equal armament but more heavily manned, the *Governor Tryon* and *Sir William Erskine*. The *Tryon* escaped after her surrender. The *Thorn* suffered eighteen killed and injured, and among the wounded was Captain Waters. John Adams wrote of the engagement, "There has not been a more memorable action this war" (Allen, *A Naval History, post*, II, 417). In January 1780 he also captured the *Sparlin* in a forty-minute battle, and brought both the *Erskine* and the *Sparlin* safely into Nantasket Road in February. His last cruise was in the Massachusetts privateer *Friendship*, to which he was appointed in January 1781. After the war he retired to his farm in Malden, where he died. He was married first, in July 1759, to Agnes Smith, by whom he had a daughter; second, on June 8, 1779, to Mary (Wicox) Mortimer, a widow of Boston; and, third, on July 29, 1802, to Sarah Sigourney, of Boston.

[T. B. Wyman, *Genealogies and Estates of Charlestown* (1879), vol. II; D. P. Corey, *Hist. of Malden* (1899); Thomas Clark, *Naval Hist. of the U. S.* (2 vols., 2nd ed., 1814); *Naval Records of the Am. Rev. 1775–88* (1906); *Mass. Soldiers and Sailors of the Revolutionary War*, vol. XVI (1907); G. W. Allen, *Mass. Privateers of the Rev., Mass. Hist. Soc. Colls.*, vol. LXXVII (1927), and *A Naval Hist. of the Am. Rev.* (2 vols., 1913); *Columbian Centinel* (Boston), Mar. 30, 1816.] A. W—t.

WATERS, WILLIAM EVERETT (Dec. 20, 1856–Aug. 3, 1924), educator, classicist, was born in Winthrop, Me. His father, Jabez Mathews (B.A., Colby, 1843), was a descendant of James Waters who left St. Buttolph, Aldgate, London, in 1630, to settle in Salem, Mass.; his mother, Martha Ellen Webb, traced her lineage to Myles Standish, John and Priscilla Alden, and George Soule, of the *Mayflower* group. Waters attended Woodward High School in Cincinnati, Ohio, and Yale University, where he received the degree of B.A. in 1878. He continued with graduate work at Yale for two years, holding the Clark and the Larned fellowships. After teaching Latin and Greek at Hughes High School in Cincinnati (1880–83), he returned to Yale as tutor in classics. In 1885–86 he engaged in research in classical philology at the University of Berlin under Adolf Kirchoff, Johannes Vahlen, Oldenburg, Albrecht Weber, and Johannes Schmidt, and in 1887 received the degree of Ph.D. at Yale. On June 28, 1888, he married Alma Filia Oyler, daughter of George Washington and Carrie (Pruden) Oyler. He returned to Hughes High School (1887–90), taught Greek at summer sessions of the Chautauqua College of Liberal Arts (1888–90), conducting correspondence courses in Greek under its auspices (1888–95), and served as professor of Greek and comparative philology at the University of Cincinnati (1890–94). After a visit to Greece (1893–94) he accepted the presidency of Wells College, Aurora, N. Y., which he held for six years. In 1900 he joined the group of prominent educators who founded the college entrance examination board and served (1901–02) as assistant secretary. He became associate professor of Greek at New York University in 1901, and from 1902 until his retirement as professor emeritus in 1923 he was professor of Greek there. He made frequent addresses under the free lecture system instituted by the New York board of education, taught Latin at Morris High School, and English, rhetoric, and composition

at the Harlem Evening High School, and was director of a vacation school (1903). After his retirement he was instrumental in raising as a memorial to his predecessor, Dr. Henry Martyn Baird [*q.v.*], an endowment to guarantee to the university permanent membership in the American School of Classical Studies at Athens. He had been elected to the advisory council of this institution in 1904 and remained a member until his death.

Waters was primarily a teacher. Enthusiastic, heedless of the expenditure of time and energy, and responsive always to the interest of his pupils, he was at his best in the classroom. The shyness which he manifested in personal contacts disappeared entirely when he was confronted at one and the same time with a student, a Greek text, and a blackboard. His enthusiasm for literature and philosophy was infectious. He was co-author with William R. Harper of *An Inductive Greek Method* (1888). In 1902 he edited the *Cena Trimalchionis of Petronius Arbiter* and published *Town Life in Ancient Italy*, a translation of Ludwig Friedländer's *Stadtewesen in Italien im Ersten Jahrhundert*. In his latter years he was engaged on a translation of Dio of Prusa for the Loeb Classical Library. He also contributed articles to the *Transactions of the American Philological Association*, the *Pedagogical Journal*, the *Classical Weekly*, and the *New York Evening Post*. He was a member of numerous learned societies. He was a very active member of the West End Presbyterian Church, serving as an elder from 1902 until his death, as superintendent of the Sunday School (1902–05), and as frequent leader of the men's Bible class. He acted as secretary of the class of 1878 at Yale for ten years (1878–88). He took his own life after a year of illness. He was survived by his wife and one son.

[Sources include autobiog. data in *"Vitae"* of the Andiron Club of N. Y. City, vol. I, 1907–23 (unpub. MS.); *Who's Who in America*, 1920–21; *Obit. Record Yale Grads.*, 1925; J. M. Lamberton, *Quarter-Centenary Record, Class of 1878, Yale Univ.* (1905); obit. notices in *Andiron Club Summons*, Mar. 10, 1925; obituary in *N. Y. Herald Tribune*, Aug. 4, 1924; letters from E. O. Waters, Waters' son, E. G. Sihler, and E. D. Perry.] C. J. K., Jr.

WATIE, STAND (Dec. 12, 1806–Sept. 9, 1871), Indian leader and brigadier-general in the Confederate army, was born near the site of Rome, Ga., the son of a full-blood Cherokee, David Oowatie or Uweti, and a half-blood mother whose baptismal name was Susannah. When twelve years old he was sent to a mission school at Brainard near the line between Tennessee and Georgia. There he learned to speak English and received a fair education. Returning to his home he became a planter and at times assisted his elder brother, Elias Boudinot, c. 1803–1839 [q.v.], in the publication of the Cherokee newspaper called the *Cherokee Phoenix*. In 1835 he joined Elias Boudinot, his uncle Major Ridge [q.v.], and John Ridge, in signing the treaty of New Echota. By this treaty the Cherokee in Georgia agreed to surrender their lands, remove west to what is now Oklahoma, and join the Cherokee West, who had migrated to that region some years earlier. The great majority of the tribe bitterly opposed this treaty, but it was ratified by the United States Senate, and the Cherokee were forced to remove in 1838. The feeling of bitterness against the Ridge and Watie group was intense, however, and in 1839 Major Ridge, John Ridge, and Elias Boudinot were all killed on the same day. Stand Watie himself was marked for slaughter but escaped death and became the leader of the minority, or treaty, party. He was married in 1843 to Sarah C. Bell, a woman of intelligence and strength of character. They had three sons and two daughters, but the sons all died before their father, and both daughters died in 1875. Small in stature, he had great physical strength and endurance. He was an able and fearless soldier and was of frank, candid nature.

At the outbreak of the Civil War the Cherokee sought to remain neutral but at last made a treaty of alliance with the Confederacy. Early in 1861 he raised a company of home guards, of which he became captain. Later in the year he raised the first Cherokee regiment of volunteers known as the "Cherokee Mounted Rifles," and he was made its colonel by the Confederate government. In May 1864 he was raised to the rank of brigadier-general. During the entire war he was very active as a raider and cavalry leader and took part in many engagements in Indian Territory and along its border, including the battles of Wilson's Creek and Pea Ridge. He was one of the last Confederate officers to surrender, not yielding up his sword until June 23, 1865. In 1863 the majority party of the Cherokee had repudiated the alliance with the Confederate States, but he remained loyal to the South and was chosen as principal chief by the Southern wing of the tribe.

After the close of the war he went to Washington as a member of the Southern delegation of the Cherokee, but soon he returned home and resumed the life of planter engaging at times in various business enterprises including tobacco manufacturing.

[Letters and papers in Frank Phillips Coll., and Cherokee Archives, Univ. of Okla.; letters in North-

eastern States Teachers' College, Tahlequah, Okla., and in the manuscript colls. of Univ. of Texas; A. H. Abel, *The Slave Holding Indians* (3 vols., 1915–25); M. W. Anderson, *Life of General Stand Watie* (1915); Wiley Britton, *The Civil War on the Border* (2 vols., 1890–99), and *The Union Indian Brigade in the Civil War* (1922); *Nineteenth Ann. Report of the Bureau of Am. Ethnology*, pt. 1 (1900).]   E. E. D.

WATKINS, GEORGE CLAIBORNE (Nov. 25, 1815–Dec. 7, 1872), jurist, son of Maj. Isaac and Marie (Toncre) Watkins, was born at Shelbyville, Ky. He was descended from Thomas Watkins who came from England and settled on Swift Creek in Cumberland (later Powhatan) County, Va., about the middle of the eighteenth century. Following financial reverses, Isaac Watkins moved to Arkansas in 1821, and is said to have built the first tavern and grist mill in Little Rock. After receiving the best educational advantages available in a pioneer settlement, George attended the law school at Litchfield, Conn. Returning to Little Rock in 1837, he formed a law partnership with Chester Ashley, who was the leading lawyer in the state and later United States senator.

On Oct. 16, 1843, Watkins succeeded Robert W. Johnson [q.v.] as attorney general. Becoming chief justice of the state supreme court on Nov. 15, 1852, he soon cleared a crowded docket and won a reputation for the disposal of business in an orderly way. The most important decision rendered while he was on the bench was that in the case of *Merrick* vs. *Avery* (14 *Ark.*, 370), 1854, in which, basing his decision on the reasoning in *The Genesee Chief* vs. *Fitzhugh* (19 *U. S.*, 233), he held that the United States had exclusive admiralty jurisdiction over navigable streams. This decision was made some twelve years before a similar ruling by the Supreme Court (*The Hine* vs. *Trevor*, 71 *U. S.*, 555). Shortly before his elevation to the bench he had formed a law partnership with James M. Curran. Upon the death of his partner he resigned, Dec. 31, 1854, in order to meet the obligations of the firm. By close attention to his practice and by judicious investments he accumulated a competence. On Dec. 20, 1862, he was appointed a member of the military court attending the army of Gen. T. H. Holmes [q.v.]. He was a zealous supporter of the Confederacy and gave three sons to the army, one of whom rose from a private to the rank of colonel and was killed at Atlanta at the age of twenty-two.

He was married twice: first, in 1841, to Mary Crease, who bore him three sons and two daughters; second, to Sophia, widow of his late partner and daughter of Senator W. S. Fulton, who bore him three daughters. He was a man of slender build, being only five feet, five inches in height, and weighing less than one hundred pounds. His last law partner, U. M. Rose [*q.v.*], said of him: "With an extremely delicate and fragile constitution . . . he possessed strong feelings and a nerve of iron. His reverence for the courts and administration of justice amounted to religion" (Hallum, *post*, p. 227). He died in St. Louis, on his way back from Colorado, where he had gone for the benefit of his health.

[F. N. Watkins, *A Cat. of the Descendants of Thomas Watkins* (1852); *War of the Rebellion: Official Records (Army)*; 13–15 *Ark. Reports*; John Hallum, *Biog. and Pictorial Hist. of Ark.* (1887), pp. 275–78; Fay Hempstead, *A Pictorial Hist. of Ark.* (1890), pp. 764–65; J. H. Shinn, *Pioneers and Makers of Ark.* (1908), p. 233; *Biog. and Hist. Memoirs of Pulaski, Jefferson . . . and Hot Spring Counties, Ark.* (1889), p. 516; *Ark. Hist. Asso. Pubs.*, vol. II (1908); *Daily Ark. Gazette* (Little Rock), Dec. 8, 10, 1872; *Green Bag*, Sept. 1892.]   D. Y. T.

WATKINS, JOHN ELFRETH (May 17, 1852–Aug. 11, 1903), engineer, curator, was born in Ben Lomond, Va., the son of Francis B. and Mary (Elfreth) Watkins. His father, a physician, was descended from Thomas Watkins who in the War of the Revolution organized a troop of cavalry; his mother, from Timothy Matlack [*q.v.*] of Philadelphia, the "fighting Quaker," who was a delegate to the Continental Congress from 1780 to 1787. After preparing for college at Treemount Seminary, Norristown, Pa., Watkins entered Lafayette College, Easton, Pa., from which he graduated as a civil engineer in 1871. He then joined the staff of the Delaware & Hudson Canal Company as a mining engineer, but continued his studies as a non-resident student of Lafayette and received the degree of M.S. in 1874.

Meanwhile, after a year with the Canal Company, he had entered the employ of the Pennsylvania Railroad Company as an assistant engineer of construction, with headquarters at the Meadow Shops in New Jersey. In 1873 he was disabled for field work by an accident which resulted in the loss of his right leg, and was later assigned to the Amboy division of the Pennsylvania Railroad. Within a few months he was made chief clerk of the Camden & Atlantic Railroad, but before the year was over he was reassigned to the Amboy division of the Pennsylvania system, which position he held until 1886. In 1884 he became associated with the United States National Museum at Washington, D. C., as honorary curator of transportation, and two years later accepted a salaried position, to which he devoted all of his time for the succeeding six years, building up the technological collections pertaining to the transportation industry. In 1892 he resigned from the National Museum

and returned to the Pennsylvania Railroad to prepare that company's exhibit for the World's Columbian Exposition, held in Chicago in 1893. At its close he took charge of the department of industrial arts (a direct outgrowth of the exposition) in the Field Museum, Chicago, but a year later (1895) he returned to Washington as curator of mechanical technology and superintendent of buildings of the National Museum, which positions he held until his death.

In the course of his twenty years' direct and indirect association with the Museum, Watkins became an authority on the history of engineering and the mechanical arts. Among his best known publications were "The Beginnings of Engineering," read before the American Society of Civil Engineers and published in its *Transactions* (vol. XXIV, 1891), *The Development of the American Rail and Track as Illustrated by the Collection in the U. S. National Museum* (1891), and *The Log of the Savannah* (1891), the last two published originally in the annual reports of the Regents of the Smithsonian Institution for 1889 and 1890. His most extensive literary undertaking was a compilation of the history of the Pennsylvania Railroad, 1845–96, the completion of which was interrupted by his death and which was never published. Aside from his official duties he was very active in 1891 in promoting the Patent Centennial Celebration, held in Washington, and was an active member of a number of patriotic and other societies. He was twice married: first, in 1873, to Helen Bryan of Mount Holly, N. J.; second, Jan. 16, 1886, to Margaret Virginia Gwynn of Philadelphia. At the time of his sudden death in New York City he was survived by his widow and five children, three of whom were of the first marriage.

[F. M. Watkins, *A Catalogue of the Descendants of Thomas Watkins* (1852); *Who's Who in America*, 1901–02; *Ann. Report of the Board of Regents of the Smithsonian Institution . . . 1904: Report of the U. S. Nat. Museum* (1906); *Railroad Gazette*, Aug. 28, 1903; *Stevens Institute Indicator*, July 1900; *Evening Star* (Washington), Aug. 12, 1903.]   C. W. M.

WATSON, ANDREW (Feb. 15, 1834–Dec. 9, 1916), missionary to Egypt, was born in Oliverburn, Perthshire, Scotland, the son of Andrew and Catherine (Roger) Watson. While Andrew was yet a child his father died, and at the age of fourteen he emigrated with his family to the United States. Here, at Lisbon, near Sussex, Wis., he shared in the arduous labor of hewing a farm out of the forest. He had his preparatory education in schools in Wisconsin and graduated from Carroll College in that state in 1857. It was probably while in college that he formed the purpose of becoming a missionary. He attended Princeton Theological Seminary (1858–59) and Allegheny Theological Seminary (1859–60). In preparation for his work as a missionary he took a partial course at Jefferson Medical College (1860–61). On May 15, 1861, he was ordained to the ministry of the United Presbyterian Church and on July 10 was married to Margaret MacVickar of Sussex, Wis. Shortly afterward the newly wedded couple sailed for Egypt as appointees of the foreign mission board of their Church. Here, with the exception of occasional furloughs in America and a few other journeys which took him out of the country, Watson spent more than half a century, sharing in the remarkable development of his Church in the land of his adoption. When he arrived, the Egyptian mission of his board was less than a decade old; at his death there were 13,000 members of his denomination in Egypt.

His first few years were spent at Alexandria; then for several years he resided at Mansûra; from 1873, on, he made his home in Cairo. He shared in many phases of the work of his mission. Acquiring the ability to speak Arabic faultlessly and with great fluency, he came in time to feel that he could express himself more readily in it than in English, and so preferred to preach in it rather than in his mother tongue. He edited a weekly paper in Arabic. For a while he was in charge of a boys' school, and for a brief period he taught in the Assiut Training College. In 1864 he helped found the theological school of his Church which, after several temporary locations, was established at Cairo. From 1869 he taught in it, and from 1892 until his death he was its head. He took a prominent part in obtaining official recognition of the civil and political status of the native Protestant communities in Egypt and for years was his mission's representative in dealing with the Egyptian government. He headed the commission which surveyed the Sudan in preparation for opening of work there. While in the United States, he served in 1890 as the moderator of the United Presbyterian General Assembly, and in 1910 went as a delegate to the World Missionary Conference at Edinburgh. In 1898 he published *The American Mission in Egypt, 1854 to 1896* (2nd ed., 1904). He was widely trusted and loved by the community as a whole, and many of varying social ranks committed to his care the administration of their funds. He was a friend of at least one Coptic Patriarch, of numerous persons connected with the Roman Catholic Church, and of many Moslems. Longing to die in harness,

he was able to keep up his accustomed activities until within a few days of the end of his long life. His death occurred in Cairo, and he was survived by his wife and one son.

[*Necrological Report . . . Princeton Theological Seminary*, 1917; *In Memory of the Rev. Andrew Watson, D.D., LL.D., 1834–1916* (n.d.); *Who's Who in America*, 1916–17; Ann. Reports of the Board of Foreign Missions of the United Presbyterian Church in North America; *Egyptian Gazette* (Alexandria), Dec. 12, 1916; *Missionary Rev. of the World*, Jan. 1917; information from Watson's son, Charles R. Watson.]

K.S.L.

WATSON, DAVID THOMPSON (Jan. 2, 1844–Feb. 24, 1916), lawyer, was born at Washington, Pa., the son of James and Maria (Morgan) Watson. He received his early education in his native town and was graduated at Washington (now Washington and Jefferson) College, with the degree of A.B. in 1864. For a brief period he saw service in the Civil War. Entering the Harvard Law School, he was graduated in 1866 in the same class with Oliver Wendell Holmes, Jr. Two years later he settled at Pittsburgh, where he continued in the active practice of law for nearly a half century, becoming one of Pittsburgh's leading lawyers. For a number of years before his death he was the senior member of the firm of Watson & Freeman. He joined the American Bar Association in 1885 and remained a member for the rest of his life. On June 10, 1889, he married Margaret H. Walker, daughter of William Walker, a Pittsburgh banker.

Watson was retained by the United States Department of Justice as attorney in action brought against the Northern Securities Company in the circuit court, April 1903, to enforce the laws relating to corporate combinations. He was retained, also, by Henry Frick in the litigation between the United States and the Union Pacific Railroad in 1911, and by the Standard Oil Company in several cases. He gained his widest prominence, however, through his connection with the Alaskan Boundary controversy between the United States and Great Britain in 1903. He was the second in rank of the four counsel for the United States, the first being Jacob M. Dickinson [*q.v.*], the third, Hannis Taylor [*q.v.*], and the fourth, Chandler P. Anderson. Watson presented the opening argument in behalf of the United States, following Sir Robert Finlay, who spoke for Great Britain. It was long and able, continuing from Sept. 23 to Sept. 28, inclusive. The report of it fills more than 130 large printed pages. Watson seems never to have held or sought public office. In the multifarious and exacting duties of his profession he found, apparently, all that was needed to engross his attention and satisfy his ambition. He died in Atlantic City, N. J., from heart failure, following an attack of the grippe.

[G. T. Fleming, *Hist. of Pittsburgh and Environs* (1922), vol. III; *Report of the . . . Pa. Bar Asso.*, 1916; *Proc. of the Alaskan Boundary Tribunal* (1904), vol. VI; *Pittsburg Dispatch*, June 11, 1889; *Who's Who in America*, 1914–15; *N. Y. Times*, Feb. 26, 1916.]   C. S. L.

WATSON, ELKANAH (Jan. 22, 1758–Dec. 5, 1842), merchant, canal promoter, and agriculturist, the son of Elkanah and Patience (Marston) Watson, was born at Plymouth, Mass. He was of Pilgrim stock, being sixth in descent, through his mother, from Edward Winslow, third governor of Plymouth Colony; on his father's side he was a descendant of Robert Watson who came to Plymouth about 1632. Young Elkanah received his early education at a grammar school conducted by Alexander Scammell and Peleg Wadsworth [*qq.v.*]. At the age of fifteen he was bound out to John Brown, 1744–1780 [*q.v.*], a prosperous merchant of Providence, R. I. He had already, in 1774, enrolled in a cadet company organized by Colonel Nightingale and in April 1775 asked to be released from his indentures so that he might join the American army besieging Boston. Brown's refusal made him "most melancholy," but Watson was able to serve the patriot cause in other ways, for his employers imported gunpowder for the Continental Army.

In September 1777, when trade in Providence had languished, Watson undertook a dangerous journey to South Carolina to invest funds for the Browns. With more than $50,000 sewed into the linings of his garments he made his adventurous way from Providence to Charleston (some twelve hundred miles) in seventy-seven days. Having safely delivered the funds he, with two companions, set out on a tour of exploration of Georgia and Florida. Dissuaded from entering Florida, they at last turned northward and Watson reached Providence late in April, having visited ten of the original thirteen states.

Watson's apprenticeship was over in January 1779, but a dearth of funds prevented his establishing his own business. He remained in the employ of the Browns and soon embarked for France to carry money and dispatches to Benjamin Franklin [*q.v.*], then one of the American agents in Paris. After a month of Franklin's hospitality he prepared to return to America with valuable papers. Arriving at Nantes he sent his dispatches with the captain of the *Mercury* and opened a mercantile house with a Monsieur Cossoul. The latter took charge of affairs while Watson went to a cler-

ical college at Ancenis to learn French, a study which he continued at Rennes during the winter of 1780–81. He traveled considerably, meeting many interesting characters and greatly enjoying life, while the faithful Cossoul labored at Nantes.

Their business had prospered, the books showing a profit of 40,000 guineas in three years. In 1782 Watson went to England, carrying dispatches from Benjamin Vaughan [*q.v.*] to Lord Shelburne and letters to many influential persons; he opened a London branch of his commercial firm and had his portrait painted by Copley. These glorious days of expansive living were soon curtailed, for the great financial crisis of 1783 threw his several mercantile ventures into the hands of creditors. Liquidation of his affairs required almost a year, after which he embarked upon a tour of the Netherlands (described in *A Tour in Holland in MDCCLXXXIV*, London 1789; Worcester 1790) and of England. Already deeply interested in canals and impressed by their superior convenience and cheapness, he made a special study of the inland waterways of Holland. Upon his return to America late in 1784 he hastened to Mount Vernon to discuss with Washington the feasibility of a system of American canals. He received encouragement, but his early efforts to raise capital were unsuccessful.

In 1785 he laid plans for new commercial enterprises with his old partner Cossoul, who had come to America to join him. Watson was located at Edenton, N. C., and Cossoul established himself in Haiti. Business flourished; Watson's expansive days returned. He purchased a great estate on the Chowan River and became "amply occupied in social convivialities, wandering about the country; in deer hunting and other rural amusements." Again, however, his business collapsed. He sold his plantation, moved north and, after a careful survey of New York state, settled in Albany in 1789. On Mar. 3 of that year he married Rachel Smith, by whom he had three sons and two daughters. Within a comparatively short time he was able to organize the Bank of Albany and was recognized as one of the leading citizens of that community. His enthusiasm for canals had never abated; he incessantly urged his plans upon his influential and wealthy friends. In 1791 three of them, Jeremiah Van Rensselaer, Stephen N. Bayard, and Philip Van Cortlandt, were persuaded to join Watson in a tour of central New York. During this investigation Watson developed a plan for a canal which makes it clear that he was "the first to think his way through New York by water" (Pound, *post*, p. 249). His project was basically sound, but his calculations were extremely faulty. Watson was a prophet whose visions were startlingly accurate, but he often lacked the patience and the talent necessary to their practical achievement. He promoted two canal companies and a stage line from Albany to Schenectady, and in 1798 lobbied successfully for a charter which authorized a company to build a canal around Niagara Falls. He fought for a variety of local improvements, free schools, and turnpike roads. When he fell out with the Dutch directors of the Bank of Albany he was able to secure, through rather dubious means, a charter for the New York State Bank, which he had organized with such success that after four years of operation he was able to retire from active business.

Moving to Pittsfield, Mass., he purchased a large farm and devoted himself to the application of the latest European discoveries in scientific agriculture. He purchased a pair of Merino sheep and imported a special breed of pigs, and, later, an English prize bull, in connection with all of which he carried on energetic publicity campaigns. In 1810, with the enthusiastic aid of some farmer-neighbors, he staged the celebrated "Cattle Show" which preceded the incorporation of the Berkshire Agricultural Society, sponsor of the first county fair in America. It was because of the unflagging efforts of Watson that the county fair early became an American institution. In his later years he corresponded widely upon agricultural subjects, kept in touch with his old friends, traveled extensively, and prepared his autobiography. This volume, left unfinished at his death, was published by his son in 1856 as *Men and Times of the Revolution; or, Memoirs of Elkanah Watson*; a more complete edition appeared the following year. It remains one of the most interesting and intelligent of contemporaneous accounts of the early years of the American Republic. He was the author, also of *History of Agricultural Societies on the Modern Berkshire System* (1820), and *History of the Rise and Progress, and Existing Condition of the Western Canals in the State of New York* (1820). He died in his eighty-fifth year.

[In addition to works cited above, see W. R. Deane, *A Biog. Sketch of Elkanah Watson* (1864); G. A. Worth, *Random Recollections of Albany* (1866); Arthur Pound, *Native Stock* (1931); Robert Troup, *A Vindication of the Claim of Elkanah Watson, Esq., to the Merit of Projecting the Lake Canal Policy* (1821) and *A Letter to the Hon. Brockholst Livingston, Esq., on the Lake Canal Policy of the State of N. Y.* (1822); Jared Van Wagenen, "Elkanah Watson—A Man of Affairs," *New York Hist.*, Oct. 1932; W. C. Neely, *The Agricultural Fair* (1935); *Albany Jour.*, Dec. 12, 1842. Important MSS. are in the Detroit Pub. Lib. and the

N. Y. State Lib. at Albany, where the bulk of Watson's private papers are on deposit.]   F. M.

WATSON, HENRY CLAY (1831–June 24, 1867), newspaper editor, political writer, and author of historical stories for young people, was born in Baltimore, Md. At an early age he went to Philadelphia, and in Philadelphia newspaper offices he received his only education: the printer's trade he learned thoroughly. He was editorially connected with the *North American and United States Gazette* and with the *Philadelphia Evening Journal*. Late in 1861 he went to California, settling in Sacramento, where he became editor of the *Sacramento Daily Union*. In this capacity, he performed successfully duties that today would require the services of several men: he was art critic, book reviewer, news editor and political writer.

Watson's first book, *Camp-Fires of the Revolution; or the War of Independence* (1850), published in Philadelphia when the author was not yet twenty years old, went through several editions. Like most of his many other works, it is a popular treatment of American history. Of his subsequent publications the more important were *The Old Bell of Independence; or Philadelphia in 1776* (1851), *Nights in a Block-House, or Sketches of Border Life* (1852), *The Yankee Tea-Party; or Boston in 1773* (1852), *Lives of the Presidents of the United States* (1853), *Heroic Women of History* (1853), *Thrilling Adventures of Hunters in the Old World and the New* (1853), and *The Camp-Fires of Napoleon* (copr. 1854). The titles indicate the scope of the work Watson attempted, and the form he most frequently used—the narrative sketch, short, vivid, and dramatic. Although his books are no longer read, they were forerunners of the nineteenth-century type of literature that aimed to present the facts of history in interesting form as a means of popularizing knowledge. Watson was also interested in music, which interest found expression in two compilations: *The Ladies' Glee-Book* (1854) and *The Masonic Musical Manual* (1855).

He died at Sacramento, on Monday, June 24, 1867 (not on July 10, 1869, as is usually stated), at the home of a Mrs. Taylor, with whom he resided. He was buried in the City Cemetery. It is clear that he occupied a position of high importance in the newspaper world of his day and that his political writings exerted no inconsiderable influence; yet, only six years after Watson's death, Newton Booth [*q.v.*] was compelled to "wonder how many there are whose hearts used to be daily stirred by the magic eloquence of his pen, who now ever recall his name" (Crane, *post*, p. 497). Ella S. Cummins, in *The Story of the Files* (p. 83), refers to Watson as "a finished scholar and brilliant writer." His editorials written during the conflict between North and South, were, she says, the "greatest glory" of the *Union*. In the judgment of William H. Mills, editor of the *Union* after it merged with the *Sacramento Record,* Watson's style was "finished, distinguished by lucidity, adapted to political, historical, and national themes, with a full appreciation of their bearing on future events and epochs" (Cummins, p. 84). In the short space of six years he made a definite impress on California journalism. Even if some allowance be made for the uncritical enthusiasm of his associates, the fact remains that no student of the California press has been able to discuss California's contribution to early American journalism without mentioning the brilliant work accomplished by Watson.

[*Sacramento Daily Union,* June 25, 1867; *Daily Alta California* (San Francisco), June 26, 1867; Newton Booth, "A Holiday Excursion with H. C. Watson," first pub. in 1873, reprinted in *Themis* (Sacramento), Dec. 31, 1892, and in L. E. Crane, *Newton Booth of Cal.* (1894); E. S. Cummins, *The Story of the Files* (1893).]   H. S. R—n.

WATSON, HENRY COOD (Nov. 4, 1818–Dec. 2, 1875), editor, music critic, was born in London, the son of John Watson, a musician associated with the Covent Garden Theatre. Like his sisters, who were prominent in oratorio, Watson learned to sing as a child, and when he was about nine years of age he made his début as one of the fairies in "Oberon" at the opera. His teachers were his father, William H. Kearns, and Edward J. Loder, a musician who later married Watson's sister. When his voice broke at adolescence he shipped for a voyage of the Mediterranean, but on his return he settled down to the serious study of music. He also wrote poetry, and did some other literary work.

In 1841 he came to New York, carrying with him letters of introduction to William Cullen Bryant, George P. Morris, Park Benjamin, 1809–1864, and Horace Greeley [*qq.v.*]. Benjamin immediately engaged him as music critic for a paper he was then editing, the *New World*. In 1843 Watson founded a magazine of his own, the *Musical Chronicle,* which later became the *American Musical Times.* In 1845 he was associated with Charles F. Briggs and Edgar Allan Poe [*qq.v.*] in establishing the short-lived *Broadway Journal,* and he also contributed to various magazines, among them the *Albion,* and the *New Mirror.* In 1855 he became an editor of *Frank Leslie's Illustrated Newspaper,* and in April 1864 appeared the first issue of his own journal,

Watson's Weekly Art Journal which he edited until 1870. In June 1868 it became the *American Art Journal.* From 1863 to 1867 he acted as music critic for the *New York Tribune.*

In addition to his critical and literary work Watson was active as a musician during his entire New York career. He composed many published songs and pieces, and he delivered a number of lectures at the Vocal Institute. In 1852 he published *A Familiar Chat About Musical Instruments.* He was associated with William Vincent Wallace in organizing the Mendelssohn Concert at Castle Garden, and he wrote the libretto for Wallace's opera, "Lurline." In 1842 he was one of the group that founded the Philharmonic Society of New York. He was also one of the organizers of the American Musical Fund Association, and of the Vocal Society which later became the Mendelssohn Union. He is credited with being the first promoter of music trade-journalism (see Dolge, *post*). John Savage [*q.v.*] is quoted as having said that when Watson "wrote on musical art he wrote with consummate knowledge and with a deep sympathy for all that is most elevating, charming and correct in musical thought. As he was an able critic he was a conscientious one, and strove sometimes to achieve by generosity that which could not be encouraged by severity" (Mathews, *post*, p. 380). Watson died in New York City at the home of his sister.

[There is some confusion regarding the date of Watson's birth. Some sources give 1816, some 1818, and, one, 1815. Consult for information Alfred Dolge, *Pianos and their Makers,* vol. I (1911); W. S. B. Mathews, *A Hundred Years of Music in America* (1889); *Grove's Dict. of Music and Musicians, Am. Supp.* (1930); *N. Y. Tribune,* Dec. 3, 1875.]   J. T. H.

WATSON, JAMES CRAIG (Jan. 28, 1838–Nov. 22, 1880), astronomer, was a descendant of Irish ancestors who came to Pennsylvania before the Revolution. His grandfather, James Watson, pioneered in "Upper Canada," prospered and acquired influence, but his father, William Watson, and his wife, Rebecca Bacon, a native of Nova Scotia, met adversity and removed from the farm near Fingal, Ontario (then Canada West), where James, the oldest of their four children, was born, and settled at Ann Arbor, Mich., in 1850. Father and son found factory work. At the age of thirteen the boy had acquired such mechanical skill that an incompetent engineer was discharged, so that he could take his place. While the engine hummed he studied Latin and Greek. He entered high school but he evidenced greater ability than his teacher and quit. At the age of fifteen he entered the University of Michigan and displayed marked ability in the classics, mathematics and mechanics. Under Francis (Franz F.) Brünnow he mastered theoretical and practical astronomy, completing Laplace's *Mécanique Céleste* at the age of seventeen. While still an undergraduate he ground, polished and mounted a four-inch achromatic objective. After graduation in 1857, he became Brünnow's assistant and contributed fifteen papers to astronomical journals before the age of twenty-one. On Brünnow's resignation in 1859 Watson was made professor of astronomy in charge of the observatory, and when the elder man returned the next year, Watson became professor of physics. His astronomical contributions continued to appear; they chiefly dealt with comets and asteroids. His *Popular Treatise on Comets* (1861) exposed many erroneous ideas. He became interested through Gould in the reduction of the Washington Zones, and devoted much time to that work.

In 1863 Brünnow again resigned and Watson was made professor of astronomy and director of the observatory. Three weeks after appointment he discovered "Eurynome," the first asteroid of his twenty-two discoveries. To aid in asteroid work the production of a series of ecliptic star charts was undertaken, and in 1868 he published his *Theoretical Astronomy,* a complete compilation and digest of the theory and method of orbital determination. It was considered an authoritative work and became a textbook in America, Germany, France, and England. In 1869 he began to work with Benjamin Peirce [*q.v.*] on lunar theory. He participated in three eclipse expeditions, to Iowa in 1869, to Sicily in 1870, and to Wyoming in 1878. He had charge of the expedition to observe the transit of Venus in China in 1874. On his return trip he paused in Egypt long enough to assist Egyptian army engineers in establishing a geodetic survey. In 1878 he became interested in Le Verrier's "Vulcan," and announced the discovery of two intramercurial planets at the eclipse in Wyoming, not subsequently verified.

In 1879 he resigned his position at the University of Michigan and became director of the Washburn Observatory of the University of Wisconsin, at Madison. The building and the construction of instruments were there supervised with scrupulous care. He also began a solar observatory and a student observatory at his own expense. Watson was a vigorous man with robust physique; he weighed 240 pounds. But during the course of this work, he became ill from exposure and died very suddenly. His wife, Annette Waite, to whom he had been married in May 1860, survived him. They had no children.

The National Academy of Sciences was made his residuary legatee with provision to prepare and publish tables of the motion of his asteroids. His extraordinary endowments included quickness of perception, mathematical intuition, an excellent memory, keen analytical power, and mechanical ability. He was an accurate and rapid computer, having once determined the elliptic elements of an orbit at a single sitting. He engaged successfully in many business activities. Though active in community affairs he kept quite aloof from society. Somewhat indifferent to public opinion, he was very sensitive of his scientific reputation.

He was a member of the National Academy of Sciences, 1868; the Royal Academy of Sciences of Italy; and the American Philosophical Society. In 1870 he was awarded the Lalande prize by the French Academy of Sciences, and in 1875 was decorated Knight Commander of the Imperial Order of the Medjidich of Turkey and Egypt, 1875. He received many academic distinctions both in America and abroad. His publications, in addition to the works mentioned, include a work on *Tables for the Calculation of Simple or Compound Interest* (1878), and numerous papers in the *American Journal of Science,* Gould's *Astronomical Journal,* Brünnow's *Astronomical Notices,* and *Astronomische Nachrichten.*

[University of Michigan *Memorial Addresses . . . at the Funeral of . . . James Craig Watson* (1882); biographical sketches by A. Winchell, in *Am. Jour. of Sci.,* Jan. 1881, and G. C. Comstock, *Nat. Acad. of Sci., Biog. Memoirs,* vol. III (1895); *Detroit Free Press,* Nov. 24, 1880.]

W. C. R.

WATSON, JAMES MADISON (Feb. 8, 1827–Sept. 29, 1900), writer of textbooks, was born in Onondaga Hill, Onondaga County, N. Y., the son of Simeon and Sally Ann (Wilber) Watson. His early education in the local district school was supplemented by instruction from his father, a Baptist clergyman. In 1839 his family removed to Oswego County, where his schooling was interrupted by periods of work on farms nearby. At seventeen he had saved enough money to enter Mexico Academy, at Mexico, N. Y., but between July 1844 and June 1848 he had only about twelve months in school, since he was obliged to spend most of each year earning his tuition and living expenses. After teaching school in Oswego (1848–50), he entered Falley Seminary, Fulton, N. Y. During the summer of 1851 he sold textbooks. He was assistant teacher at the Chittenango Seminary for about seven months in 1851–52 and principal of the union school at Howlett Hill, April–July 1852. In 1852–53 he read law in Syracuse and Albany, where he was admitted to the bar, Sept. 7, 1853. A visit to New York the same month resulted in his appointment as general book agent for A. S. Barnes & Company, publishers of textbooks. For some years he traveled throughout the country, introducing the Barnes texts in schools and colleges. Observations in many classrooms led him to the conviction that reforms were needed in the teaching of English. His first textbook, *Word Builder* (1855), which emphasized correct pronunciation and use of words in sentences, was widely adopted soon after its publication. Encouraged by its success, he collaborated with Richard Green Parker [q.v.] in the production of the National Series of readers and spellers (7 vols., 1857–66). Throughout these years, he lectured before teachers' institutes, and taught occasional classes in elocution and gymnastics. A *Handbook of Calisthenics and Gymnastics* (1863), which appeared in various editions, added considerably to his reputation. On Mar. 31, 1871, he married Emma Hopper, daughter of the Rev. Andrew and Margaret (Inslee) Hopper of Newark, N. J. Resigning about this time as agent for the publishing company, he established his residence in Elizabeth, N. J., where he remained until his death. His Independent Series of readers and spellers, begun in 1868, was completed in ten volumes in 1875.

The income from these texts enabled him to devote his time to civic and church affairs. He was deacon of the Central Baptist Church (1877–1900) and a member of the board of managers of the New Jersey Baptist Convention (1884–97). The churches of Elizabeth, at his recommendation, established the "Red Ribbon Club" for the maintenance of law, order, and temperance, and as president, and editor of its journal, the *Red Ribbon Record* (1885–90), he played a prominent part in the temperance movement. He was president of the Elizabeth board of education (1881–82), and president (1882) and corresponding secretary (1883–98) of the New Jersey Sanitary Association.

[J. M. Watson, "Pantography of My Life," 2 vols., and "Jour. of My Travels in the U. S.," manuscript diaries in the possession of his daughter, Mabel M. Watson of Devon, Pa.; *Who's Who in America*, 1899–1900; F. W. Ricord, *Hist. of Union County, N. J.* (1897), pp. 292–96; obituary in *Elizabeth Daily Jour.*, Sept. 29, 1900.]
R. F. S.

WATSON, JOHN CRITTENDEN (Aug. 24, 1842–Dec. 14, 1923), naval officer, was born at Frankfort, Ky., son of Dr. Edward Howe and Sarah Lee (Crittenden) Watson, grandson of John Jordan Crittenden [q.v.], and of ancestry distinguished in both Kentucky and Virginia. After study at Sayre School, Lexington, Ky., he entered the United States Naval Academy at fourteen and graduated in 1860. Promoted to master, Aug. 31, 1861, he saw his first Civil War service in the sail-frigate *Sabine*, in which duty he was commended for his seamanship in the rescue of a disabled transport (*War of the Rebellion, post*, XII, 243). Afterward, as navigating officer in the *Hartford*, flagship of Admiral David Glasgow Farragut [q.v.], he took part in the passing of the forts below New Orleans (Apr. 24, 1862), in the subsequent advance to Vicksburg, and, after promotion to lieutenant (July 16, 1862), in the operations of March 1863 against Port Hudson, Grand Gulf, and Warrington, where he was slightly wounded by a shell fragment. From July 1863 until late in 1864 he was on Farragut's staff as flag lieutenant. Prior to the battle of Mobile Bay he commanded a boat party, July 5, 1864, which destroyed the blockade-runner *Ivanhoe* under the guns of Fort Morgan, and on three nights before the battle he engaged in extremely hazardous boat duty, removing torpedoes from the channel past the fort. Of slight, active build like Farragut, and sharing the latter's fondness for fighting and for reading the Scriptures, he had a devotion for the admiral which was warmly returned. "I am almost as fond of Watson," wrote Farragut to his son, "as yourself" (L. S. Farragut, *The Life of David Glasgow Farragut*, 1879, p. 403). It was Watson who, on the second occasion when this was done in the battle, passed a rope about the admiral to secure him to the mizzen rigging during the fight with the ram *Tennessee*. After the war he went to the European Squadron and was again under Farragut during the latter's European cruise in 1867–68.

Noteworthy in his service prior to the war with Spain were his command of the *Wyoming* (1878–80), which carried the American exhibits to the Paris exposition, his duty as naval representative at the exposition, his command of the new steel cruiser *San Francisco* (1892–94), and his superintendency of the Philadelphia Naval Home (1895–98). He was promoted to captain, Mar. 6, 1887, and to commodore, Nov. 7, 1897. During the Spanish-American War he had command, under W. T. Sampson [q.v.], of the North Cuban Blockading Squadron (May 6–June 21, 1898), and from June 27 to Sept. 20 was in command of the "Eastern Squadron" which was organized, though not actually dispatched, to menace the Spanish coast and force the recall from the East of the Spanish reserve squadron under Camara. He was made rear admiral (Mar. 3, 1899), commanded the Mare Island Navy Yard (October 1898–June 1899), and afterward until

October 1900 was in charge of the Asiatic station, succeeding Admiral George Dewey. From then until his retirement (Aug. 24, 1904), he had duty chiefly on the examining and retiring boards, and was also American naval representative at the coronation of Edward VII. Before and after retirement his home was in Washington, D. C., where for many years he was an elder in the Presbyterian Church. He was married, May 29, 1873, to his cousin, Elizabeth Anderson Thornton, daughter of Judge James Dabney Thornton of San Francisco, Cal., and had five sons and two daughters. His burial was in Arlington.

[*Who's Who in America*, 1922–23; *War of the Rebellion: Official Records (Navy)*, vols. XII, XVIII, XXI; W. H. Powell and Edward Shippen, *Officers of the Army and Navy (Regular) . . . in the Civil War* (1892); L. R. Hamersly, *Records of Living Officers of the U. S. Navy* (7th ed., 1902); J. C. Watson, "Farragut and Mobile Bay—Personal Reminiscences," *War Papers*, no. 98 (1916), pub. by Dist. of Columbia Commandery, Military Order of the Loyal Legion; *Army and Navy Jour.*, Dec. 22, 1923; obituary in *Washington Post*, Dec. 15, 1923.]

A. W—t.

WATSON, JOHN FANNING (June 13, 1779–Dec. 23, 1860), antiquarian, publisher, and financier, was the son of William and Lucy (Fanning) Watson, and was born at Batsto, Burlington County, N. J. His ancestors on both sides had emigrated to America from Dublin, Ireland, his father's ancestors settling in Salem, N. J., in 1667, his mother's in Groton, Conn., in 1641. Watson's father was the owner of several vessels, which he sold at the beginning of the Revolution, when he went to sea as a volunteer. After receiving some education Watson was placed in the counting-house of James Vanuxem in Philadelphia, where he remained until he was nineteen. At that time he offended his employers, who were in the French interest, by joining the Macpherson Blues, a military company organized in 1798 when the French difficulties with the United States were acute. He held a clerkship in the United States War Department until 1804, when he resigned to take charge of some business of Gen. James O'Hara [*q.v.*] of Pittsburgh. This took him to New Orleans, and he was later appointed commissary of provisions for the army posts in Louisiana. The death of his father in 1806 led Watson to return to his mother's home in Philadelphia. He at first engaged in business as a merchant, but in 1809 he opened a book store and, along with others in his trade, entered the publishing business. In 1809 he began to publish *Select Reviews of Literature and Spirit of the Foreign Magazines*, which he sold in 1812 and which in 1813 became the *Analectic Magazine*. He also reprinted Dr. Adam Clarke's *Commen-*

taries on the Old and New Testaments. He married Phebe Barron Crowell of Elizabethtown, N. J., said to be a descendant of Oliver Cromwell, in 1812, and two years later retired from the book business to become cashier of the newly organized Bank of Germantown.

While he was a resident of Germantown he took up seriously the work of authorship, directing his efforts to a study of the pioneer days of Pennsylvania and New York. He began in 1820 to collect in a methodical manner the recollections of the "oldest inhabitants" of Philadelphia. For this purpose he prepared a questionnaire, wrote innumerable letters, and traveled considerably, usually on foot. In 1830 he published in a fat volume of eight hundred pages his *Annals of Philadelphia*, in the back of which were his "Olden Time Researches and Reminiscences, of New York City." The work was illustrated by lithographs, many of them drawn from sketches he made from memory for the artist, W. L. Breton, of buildings which had long ceased to exist. (Joseph Jackson, "Iconography of Philadelphia," *Pennsylvania Magazine of History*, Jan. 1935, pp. 64–65.) He related his curious information in an engaging style, and his thoroughness in procuring documentary evidence at a time when this was not critically regarded soon established his work as a local classic, quoted to the present time (1936) because in many instances it is the only source. The *Annals* were reprinted in 1842 and 1856, and several times after Watson's death. In 1832 came his *Historic Tales of Olden Time, Concerning the Early Settlement and Advancement of New-York City and State*; in 1833, *Historic Tales of Olden Time, Concerning the Early Settlement and Progress of Philadelphia and Pennsylvania*; and in 1846, *Annals and Occurrences of New York City and State*. Even before his *Annals* were published, Watson's antiquarian researches awakened an interest in history of Pennsylvania which culminated in the establishment (1824) of the Historical Society of Pennsylvania. He is said to have persuaded G. W. P. Custis [*q.v.*] to write his *Recollections and Private Memoirs of Washington* (1860), and he was the leader of movements to have the graves of several historical characters properly marked. After serving the Bank of Germantown for thirty-three years, he resigned in 1847 to become treasurer and secretary of the Philadelphia, Germantown & Norristown railroad. In the summer of 1859, upon reaching his eightieth birthday, he retired from business. He died, Dec. 23, 1860, leaving three daughters and two sons, the survivors of seven children.

[See Benjamin Dorr, *A Memoir of John Fanning Watson* (1861); W. P. Hazard, memoir in *Annals of Philadelphia* (1879), which includes some personal researches; B. J. Lossing, in *Harper's Encyc. of U. S. Hist.* (1912), vol. X; obituaries in *Public Ledger* (Phila.), Dec. 25, and *Phila. Daily News*, Dec. 26, 1860. A vol. in MS. of Watson's *Annals* belongs to the Lib. Company of Phila.; another, with a part of his extensive material, is in the Hist. Soc. of Pa.] J.J.

WATSON, JOHN WILLIAM CLARK

(Feb. 27, 1808–Sept. 24, 1890), lawyer, senator in the Confederate Congress, was born in Albemarle County, Va., the son of John and Elizabeth (Finch) Watson. His early education was secured in the schools of his county which, though inadequate, enabled him to equip himself for entrance to the law department of the University of Virginia, where he was graduated with the degree of B.L. in 1830. After practising his profession in Abingdon, Va., from 1831 to 1845, he removed to Holly Springs, Miss., where he formed a partnership with J. W. Clapp, a prominent lawyer of that place.

In Mississippi he continued his alignment with the Whig party and was soon regarded as a trusted adviser in its councils. He was a member of the Mississippi state convention of 1851, and concurred in the action of that body denying the right of secession. During the presidential campaign of 1860, he established a newspaper at Holly Springs and placed it under competent editorial charge with the purpose of attempting to stem the tide of disunion. After the election of Lincoln he was defeated by sixteen votes as an anti-secession candidate for the state convention of 1861. He acquiesced in the withdrawal of Mississippi from the Union, however, and accepted various offices in the Confederate government. From Feb. 17, 1864, until the end of the war, he was a senator in the Confederate Congress. He approved the work of the state convention of 1865, of which he was a member, but he opposed giving any aid or comfort to Jefferson Davis, or doing anything to antagonize the victors. He received thirty-three votes for president of the "Black and Tan" convention of 1868, but when it adopted the proscriptive qualifications he resigned and returned to Holly Springs to lead the canvass in northern Mississippi against the constitution, which was rejected. He took an active part in the overthrow of the Ames régime, and in May 1876, was appointed by Gov. John M. Stone [*q.v.*] a judge of the circuit court. As such he was a "terror to evil doers," but in 1882, at the end of his six-year term, he resumed the practice of law. He reached the peak of his legal career in October 1885, when having been appointed by Gov. Robert Lowry to represent Mississippi before the Supreme Court of the United States in the railroad commission cases, he secured a reversal of the decision of the circuit court of appeals, the Supreme Court ruling that the legislative act, passed in 1884 to regulate rates and to create a railroad commission, was constitutional (116 *U. S., 307*).

Watson was an uncompromising Puritan in character, an elder in the Presbyterian Church at Holly Springs for more than forty years, and one of the pioneer prohibitionists of the state. He invited Frances E. Willard to Mississippi and paid her traveling expenses when she toured the state crusading for prohibition in January 1882. On Sept. 8, 1831, he married Catherine Davis, sister of Prof. J. A. G. Davis, professor of law at the University of Virginia. To this union were born eight children, only two of whom survived the father; two sons were killed in the Civil War. Watson died at Holly Springs.

[*Biog. and Hist. Memoirs of Miss.* (1891), vol. II; Dunbar Rowland, *Mississippi* (1907), vol. II; Reuben Davis, *Recollections of Miss. and Mississippians* (1889); W. B. Hamilton, "Holly Springs, Miss., in the Year 1878," manuscript thesis in Univ. of Miss. Lib.; J. W. Garner, *Reconstruction in Miss.* (1901); *Proc. Miss. Bar Asso.*, 1891; letters of Watson to W. L. Sharkey, Correspondence of the Governors, Series E. No. 65, Dept. Archives and Hist., Jackson, Miss.; *Jour. of the Cong. of the Confederate States*, vols. IV (1904), V (1905).] P.L.R.

WATSON, SERENO

(Dec. 1, 1826–Mar. 9, 1892), botanist, was born at East Windsor Hill, Conn., the tenth of thirteen children of Henry and Julia (Reed) Watson. He was a descendant of Robert Watson who emigrated to America and had settled in Windsor, Conn., by 1639. He was reared on a farm and in 1847 graduated from Yale College, where he displayed an aptitude for the classics. Shy and reticent, he tried teaching, medicine, banking and insurance, editorial work, and farming, with little success. At forty he entered the Sheffield Scientific School to study chemistry and mineralogy, hoping to fit himself for life in California. Reaching San Francisco by the Panama route in April 1867, he soon abandoned hope of farming, and set out to find the exploring expedition led by Clarence King [*q.v.*] and obtain employment in its party, just starting a scientific survey of the Great Basin. King, already annoyed by unpromising applicants for service on this governmental undertaking, was little disposed to favor the middle-aged man, who one July night, dusty and footsore, reached his camp on the Truckee River. However, Watson was permitted to join the party as a volunteer aid, though assigned only menial tasks. Here his varied training, industry, and vigor were much in his favor, and within a month he was receiving a small salary. Soon afterwards, upon the resignation of the botanist of the party, William Whitman Bailey, Watson was commissioned to collect plants and secure data regarding them. Thus, by chance, in his forty-second year he undertook the work in which he was to attain distinction. His collections, which he took to Yale for elaboration, were extensive, well prepared, and accompanied by far more methodical field data than had been taken in earlier governmental surveys. His *Botany* (1871), usually called "Botany of the King Expedition," was the fifth volume in the report of the geological survey, a well-illustrated quarto of five hundred pages. In preparing it, Watson was much aided by Daniel Cady Eaton at Yale, John Torrey at Columbia, and Asa Gray [*qq.v.*] at Harvard. Not only enumerating the plants, it embodied so many keys and group-revisions that it became virtually a flora of the Great Basin and contained phytogeographic matter in advance of its time. Rapidly prepared in finished detail and seen through press by 1871, this impressive work, Watson's maiden effort in scientific publication, gave ample proof that he had found his bent.

Soon afterwards Watson settled in Cambridge, Mass., where in 1873 he became assistant in the Gray Herbarium and the following year its curator, a post he held capably through the rest of his life. Thus settled at Harvard, he undertook the *Botany of California*. Of this great work, the first volume (1876) was collaborative, W. H. Brewer [*q.v.*] of Yale aiding on the *Polypetalae*, and Gray contributing the *Gamopetalae*. The second and even more difficult volume (1880), covering the rest of the flowering plants, ferns, mosses, and hepatics, was prepared chiefly by Watson. This flora, the earliest for its region, greatly influenced subsequent work on the vegetation of the Pacific Slope. In curatorial routine, Watson identified many collections from the western states and Mexico, including the earlier ones of Edward Palmer and C. G. Pringle. Diagnoses of the many new genera and species he encountered were published in eighteen "Contributions to American Botany," appearing chiefly in the *Proceedings of the American Academy of Arts and Sciences,* and including many monographic treatments of difficult groups. To create a guide to the literature of his subject, he spent long evenings compiling his *Bibliographical Index to North American Botany*. The only completed volume was published in 1878 by the Smithsonian Institution. Later he undertook the completion of the *Manual of the Mosses of North America* (1884) begun by Leo Lesquereux and

Thomas Potts James [*qq.v.*], and the continuation of Asa Gray's *Synoptical Flora of North America*. In 1889, aided by John Merle Coulter [*q.v.*], he revised Gray's *Manual of Botany*, extending its range to the one-hundredth meridian. After the King expedition, he did little field work, though for the forestry records of the Tenth Census he made a hurried journey to the Bitter Root Mountains and some other parts of the Northwest. In 1885 he attempted botanical exploration in Guatemala, but was forced by a tropical fever to abandon the undertaking.

Watson was of fine appearance and great dignity, a silent man, who worked steadily, calmly, and with remarkable speed. He remained a bachelor and was something of a recluse; yet to those who ventured to turn to him for aid, he was most kind. He died at Cambridge, of an influenza which caused enlargement of the heart, and was buried by his request in the Harvard Lot at Mount Auburn Cemetery. He was a member of numerous scientific societies both in America and abroad.

[H. R. Stiles, *The Hist. and Genealogies of Ancient Windsor, Conn.* (1891), vol. II; G. L. Goodale, in *Proc. Am. Acad. of Arts and Sciences,* vol. XXVII (1893), with bibliog.; *Obit. Record Grads. Yale Univ.* (1892); *The Jubilee Anniversary Report . . . Class of 1847, Yale Univ.* (1897), ed. by H. B. Chapin; J. M. Coulter, in *Botanical Gazette,* May 1892, with portrait; Walter Deane, in *Bull. Torrey Botanical Club,* Apr. 1892; M. B., in *Scientific American,* Apr. 9, 1892, with portrait; I. Urban, *Berichte der Deutschen Botanischen Gesellschaft,* vol. X (1892); obituary in *Boston Transcript,* Mar. 10, 1892; Yale alumni records; personal recollections.]
                                                        B. L. R.

WATSON, THOMAS AUGUSTUS (Jan. 18, 1854–Dec. 13, 1934), telephone man and shipbuilder, was born in Salem, Mass., the son of Thomas R. Watson, the foreman in a livery stable, and Mary (Phipps), his wife. The boy went to the public schools of Salem until he was fourteen years old and then went to work. In 1872 he got a job in Boston in the electrical shop of Charles Williams, Jr., at 109 Court Street. A number of inventors had their models made at Williams' shop, and in 1874 Watson did some work for Alexander Graham Bell [*q.v.*], with whom he worked thereafter during all the experimental period of the telephone and the years that followed until it was commercially established. When the first telephone organization was formed in 1877, Watson was given an interest in the business and when Bell went to Europe he became the research and technical head of the Bell Telephone Company.

In the spring of 1881 Watson resigned from the Telephone Company and went to Europe for a year. On Sept. 5, 1882, he married Elizabeth Seaver Kimball of Cohasset, Mass.; they had four children. Soon after his marriage Watson settled in East Braintree, Mass., with the idea of becoming a farmer, but his mechanical inclination asserted itself and with Frank O. Wellington as a partner he opened a machine shop and began to build engines and ships. In 1896 they undertook their first contract for the United States government, the destroyers *Lawrence* and *Macdonough*; these were followed by the lightship for Cape Hatteras and the cruiser *Des Moines*. The increasing size of the ships they were building made it necessary, in spite of hard times, to move down to deeper water and to increase the size of their shipyard. An additional consideration influencing Watson's decision to make this move was the large number of unemployed people to whom the new yard would be able to give work. Interest in these people also brought Watson into public education and for a while into politics, in which he worked for better social conditions. In February 1901, the shipyard was incorporated as the Fore River Ship & Engine Company. Among the vessels it produced were the battleships *Rhode Island, New Jersey,* and *Vermont*; two steel schooners, the seven-masted *Thomas W. Lawson* and the six-masted *William L. Douglas*; and two vessels for the Fall River Line, the *Providence* and the *Boston*. The competition of foreign shipbuilding produced a situation which took the control of the company out of Watson's hands, however, and in 1904 he resigned and retired from business. Admiral Frank T. Bowles then took charge of the further development of the concern until the World War, when the plant was sold to the Bethlehem Steel Company.

When Watson was forty, and recognized as a prominent shipbuilder, he and his wife entered the Massachusetts Institute of Technology as students, taking special courses in geology and literature. In geology he became the respected associate of professional scientists, while in literature he became well known as an interpreter of poetry and drama. He was for some time the president of the Boston Browning Society. For a season he was an actor in the company of Sir Frank Benson in England and he had speaking parts in the Shakespeare Festival at Stratford-on-Avon, Apr. 7–May 6, 1911. He became a proficient student of music and painting. No less did he continue to follow the developments of electrical science and the work of the telephone engineers; nor did his inquiry fail to include problems of philosophy and religion. Ever since as a child he first ventured through the alley from the stable yard out into the world, he found the range of his experience immeasurably ex-

hilarating and inspiring; in 1926 he published his autobiography, to which he gave the title *Exploring Life*. He was a fellow of the American Institute of Electrical Engineers, and received three honorary degrees. He died at his winter home at Passagrille Key, Fla.

[Watson's autobiog.; *Who's Who in America,* 1934–35; papers in the Am. Telephone Hist. Lib., 195 Broadway, New York; F. L. Rhodes, *Beginnings of Telephony* (1929); W. C. Langdon, "Thomas A. Watson, 1854–1934," *A. T. & T. Co. Headquarters Bull.,* Dec. 21, 1934, and separately reprinted; *N. Y. Herald Tribune,* Dec. 15, 1934.]   W. C. L.

WATSON, THOMAS EDWARD (Sept. 5, 1856–Sept. 26, 1922), political leader, author, the son of John Smith and Ann Eliza (Maddox) Watson, was born in Columbia County near Thomson, Ga. He was named Edward Thomas, but changed the order in his youth. English Quaker ancestors of his had settled in Georgia by 1768. His grandfather, Thomas M. Watson, a planter, "tall, venerable, imposing" in the eyes of an idolatrous boy, owned forty-five slaves and an estate valued on the tax records at $55,000. With the Civil War, which was associated in the boy's mind with the death of his grandfather and uncle, began the decline of his twice-wounded father to a wretched state of fortune and self-esteem. Romantic and sensitive, yet assertive and ambitious, Thomas confessed much to his diaries and journals, kept a record of his reading, and wrote quantities of verse. He spent two years at Mercer University, a small Baptist college, and two as an impoverished country school teacher. On Oct. 9, 1878, he married Georgia Durham of Thomson, where he now made his home. Two years earlier, having studied law privately, he began his dramatic rise as a criminal lawyer. After eleven years he could estimate his "assets," consisting largely of land, at $30,585. Finding his family in "a miserable shanty skirted by a long marsh," he triumphantly restored them to their old home and administered a public thrashing to the landlord who had mistreated his brother.

In political as in private life Watson assumed the role of agrarian avenger. A rebel and fighter by temperament, he was made by circumstance hostile to the new order and nostalgic for the old. Brought early under the personal influence of Robert Toombs and Alexander H. Stephens [*qq.v.*], he carried over into later movements many of the ideas and something of the spirit of the Confederate agrarians. At twenty-three he directed his first political effort against the state Democratic machine, dominated by capitalist-industrialists, and in his single term (1882) in the state Assembly he maintained this insurgency. As the New South tightened its alliance with the industrial North, and farmers declined in wealth and prestige, Watson's mistrust of Henry W. Grady's message crystallized: such leaders would "betray the South with a Judas kiss." Insisting that the natural ally of the South was the agrarian West, he easily won his race for Congress in 1890 on the Farmers' Alliance platform. Then choosing between fidelity to reform pledges and loyalty to the Democratic party, he boldly announced himself a Populist. His utter fearlessness, his earnestness, and the appealing combination of poet, prophet, and rustic humorist in his nature won a following that was fanatical in its loyalty. Red-headed, scrawny, yet inspiring, Tom Watson became almost the incarnation of the new agrarian revolt in the South.

As the new party's candidate for speaker and its leader in the House, Watson introduced many Alliance reform bills and supported advanced labor legislation. He also introduced the first resolution ever passed providing for free delivery of rural mail (*Congressional Record*, 52 Cong., 2 Sess., pp. 1759–60). In 1891 he founded the *People's Party Paper* and the following year published *The People's Party Campaign Book* (1892), with the subtitle, *Not a Revolt; It Is a Revolution*. Meanwhile, his district had been gerrymandered, and in the bloody and fraudulent election of 1892 his Democratic opponent was declared victor. Undaunted by persecution, he swayed thousands with redoubled denunciations of trusts, capitalist finance, and Democratic policies. The next election, in which he met another defeat, was unquestionably fraudulent and even more bloody, but his fight won praise from radical Populists everywhere. In 1896 he was nominated for the vice-presidency by the national Populist convention before Bryan was chosen to head the ticket. Known as an enemy of fusion with either party, Watson nevertheless accepted the nomination, being assured that only thus could all factions be harmonized, and that the Democrats would withdraw Arthur Sewall [*q.v.*] from their ticket. He campaigned in the West for Bryan, but, contemptuously treated by the Democrats and deserted by Populist fusionists, he admitted that his position was "most humiliating." His small vote was a measure of the demoralization of the Populists that was wrought by fusion.

Embittered by three defeats and what he felt was a betrayal, he retired from public life for eight years and turned to writing. *The Story of France* (1899), a popular history in two large volumes, is a Populist interpretation infused with the author's social philosophy, yet a work of some merit, as is also his *Napoleon: A Sketch of His Life* (1902). His other biographies, *The Life and Times of Thomas Jefferson* (1903) and *The Life and Times of Andrew Jackson* (1912), begun in 1907, are partisan and rambling. *Bethany* (1904) is a sentimental and unorganized novel. Later he published *Life and Speeches of Thos. E. Watson* (1908), *Political and Economic Handbook* (1908), and *Prose Miscellanies* (1912).

As the Populist candidate for president in 1904, Watson polled only 117,183 votes, but gained considerable attention from prominent reformers. In 1905 he founded in New York *Tom Watson's Magazine* (changed to *Watson's Magazine* in 1906), featuring mainly his reform editorials, but also publishing contributions from such authors as Masters, Dreiser, and Gorky. After quarreling with the publishers, he established in Georgia his *Weekly Jeffersonian* and *Watson's Jeffersonian Magazine*. His race for president in 1908 was only a gesture.

New issues now overshadowed the industrialist-agrarian conflict, and Watson, counting forty-four tenants on his broad plantations and estimating his wealth at $258,000, had changed. Old traits of irascibility and vindictiveness gained the upper hand. His politics changed with his character. Shifting his followers from one Democratic faction to the other, he virtually dictated state politics. As bewildered Populists quit his ranks, their places were filled with recruits attracted by his sensational crusades against Catholicism, Socialism, foreign missions, the negro, and Leo M. Frank. Frank, whom Watson had attacked bitterly as an individual and a Jew, was lynched in 1915, after his death sentence for the murder of a girl had been commuted (besides Watson's articles in his magazine and weekly, Sept.–Dec. 1915, see *Augusta Chronicle*, special supplement of Nov. 25, 1915; *New York Times*, Sept. 13, 14, 1915; C. P. Connolly, *The Truth About the Frank Case*, 1915). Then with sudden resurgence of his old spirit Watson arose to denounce American intervention in the World War as "ravenous commercialism," and war-time regimentation as "universal goose-stepping." Until his publications were excluded from the mails and he was temporarily crazed by the death of his two children, he conducted a courageous fight against conscription. Losing his race for Congress in 1918 and the state presidential primary in 1920 by narrow margins, he was overwhelmingly elected to the Senate the latter year on the same platform, the restoration of civil liberties and the defeat of the League of Nations. In the Senate he expressed sympathy for Soviet Russia, organized labor, and oppressed minorities, but his brief senatorial career, ended by his death, while fiery and sensational, was without significant accomplishment.

Some of the pathos and irony of his life may be caught in the "Thomas E. Watson Song," a ballad of "a man of mighty power," who "fought and struggled" and failed. It is still heard in backwoods Georgia.

[Watson MSS., Chapel Hill, N. C., available only by permission of the family; MSS. in possession of family, Thomson, Ga.; J. D. Wade, "Jefferson: New Style," *Am. Mercury*, Nov. 1929; A. M. Arnett, *The Populist Movement in Georgia* (1922); W. W. Brewton, *The Life of Thomas E. Watson* (1926); Daniel De Leon, *Watson on the Gridiron* (1926); obituary in *Atlanta Constitution*, Sept. 22, 1922; "Thomas E. Watson," a Columbia phonograph record.]   V. W.

WATSON, WILLIAM (Jan. 19, 1834–Sept. 30, 1915), engineer, educator, was born at Nantucket, Mass., the son of William and Mary (Macy) Watson. In 1857 he graduated from the Lawrence Scientific School of Harvard University with the degree of S.B. in engineering, having won the Boyden Prize in mathematics, and while serving as instructor in differential and integral calculus, 1857–59, he was awarded a second bachelor's degree, in mathematics, in 1858. Going for graduate study to the University of Jena, he received the degree of Ph.D. there in 1862 and subsequently took a partial course at the École Nationale des Ponts et Chaussées at Paris. While he was in Europe, during the years 1860–63, he collected information on technical instruction which in 1864 was used as a basis in planning the organization of the Massachusetts Institute of Technology. He was appointed to the faculty of the new institution as its first professor of mechanical engineering and descriptive geometry (1865–73) and organized the instruction in these subjects.

In 1867 he visited the Universal Exposition at Paris and took lessons in plaster modeling while there. When he returned to America he brought models illustrating stereotomy, and in his courses introduced for the first time the practice of constructing from the drawings plaster models of the problems which occur in masonry —arches of various kinds, doorways, stairways, domes. While abroad he had also spent some time at Karlsruhe, where he prepared lithographic notes for his lectures on elasticity and resistance of materials. In 1869 he again visited Europe and brought back with him valuable drawings from the Polytechnic School at Karlsruhe as well as a collection of models for instruction in descriptive geometry and mechanism. In

1873 he resigned his professorship in order to devote himself more fully to his studies; in the same year he married Margaret Fiske, daughter of Augustus H. Fiske of Boston, and went as one of the United States commissioners to the Vienna exposition.

He was a member of the American Society of Civil Engineers and of the American Academy of Arts and Sciences (of which he was recording secretary from 1884 until his death). As an active member of the Mathematical and Physical Club, founded in the early eighties, he contributed much in an informal way to further the interests of the instructors in mathematics and physics at Harvard and the Massachusetts Institute of Technology. By his activity in the Society of Arts of the Massachusetts Institute of Technology, which began its work even before the Institute was opened to students and inaugurated the *Technology Quarterly* at a time when technical journals were scarce, he contributed to increase in America the knowledge of recent advances in science and engineering. His published works include: *Papers on Technical Education* (1872); *A Course in Descriptive Geometry* (1873); the chapters on civil engineering and architecture in Vol. III (1876) of the *Reports of the Commissioners of the United States to the International Exhibition Held at Vienna, 1873*, edited by Robert H. Thurston [q.v.]; *On the Protection of Life from Casualties in the Use of Machinery* (1880); *A Course in Shades and Shadows* (1889); *Paris Universal Exposition: Civil Engineering, Public Works and Architecture* (1892); *The International Water Transportation Congress, 1893* (1894), and many technical articles.

[*Trans. Am. Soc. Mech. Eng.*, vol. XXXVII (1916); *Technology Rev.*, Nov. 1915; C. R. Cross, in *Proc. Am. Acad. Arts and Sci.*, vol. LII (1917); *Who's Who in America*, 1914–15; *N. Y. Times*, Oct. 1, 1915.]
                                              T. L. D.

WATTERSON, HARVEY MAGEE (Nov. 23, 1811–Oct. 1, 1891), editor and congressman from Tennessee, was born at Beech Grove, Bedford County, Tenn. His father, William S. Watterson, emigrated from Virginia to Tennessee in 1804, served on Andrew Jackson's staff in the War of 1812, accumulated a fortune as a cotton planter, and was a prominent figure in the Tennessee railroad movement at the time of his death in 1851. Harvey Watterson was educated at Cumberland College, Princeton, Ky. He studied law, was admitted to the bar, and began the practice of his profession at Shelbyville, Tenn., in 1830. The next year he was elected to the lower house of the state legislature and by successive reëlections served until 1839 (*Courier-Journal*, *post*). In that year he was elected to the federal House of Representatives and was reëlected in 1841. According to the testimony of his son, Watterson did not take his duties at Washington seriously, but, provided with an excellent income by his father, directed his energies to revelry and occasional escapades of a graver nature, "his principal yokemate in the pleasures and dissipations of those times being Franklin Pierce" (*Marse Henry, post,* I, 26). At the end of his second term in the house he was sent by President Tyler on a diplomatic mission to Buenos Aires to obtain information on the foreign relations of Argentina, commercial matters, and the war then raging with Uruguay. In February 1844 he was nominated chargé, but the Senate in the following June rejected the nomination (S. F. Bemis, *American Secretaries of State and Their Diplomacy,* vol. V, 1928, p. 216).

Returning to Tennessee in 1845, Watterson was at once elected to the state Senate and was made its presiding officer. In September 1849 he became the proprietor of the *Nashville Daily Union,* whose editorship he took over the following year (S. L. Sioussat, "Tennessee, the Compromise of 1850, and the Nashville Convention," *Mississippi Valley Historical Review,* Dec. 1915, p. 235 n.). He remained as editor of the Nashville paper until 1851, when he went to Washington as editor of the *Washington Union.* Watterson had always been a Democrat, but he was opposed to the extension of slavery and retired from the editorship of the *Union* because he could not support the policy of the administration in regard to the repeal of the Missouri Compromise. He retired to private life in Tennessee, refusing the governorship of Oregon, and, in 1857, a nomination to Congress. He supported Stephen A. Douglas [*q.v.*] in the campaign of 1860. He was a member of the secession convention of Tennessee but opposed secession. He remained a Unionist throughout the war, living in retirement on his plantation at Beech Grove. He supported Andrew Johnson [*q.v.*] during his presidency, and for the ten years after the war lived at Washington engaged in the practice of law. After the death of his wife he divided his time between Washington and Louisville, Ky., where his son, Henry Watterson [*q.v.*], was editor of the *Courier-Journal.* At the time of his death he was on the editorial staff of the *Courier-Journal,* in which his writings were signed "An Old Fogy." He was buried in the Cave Hill Cemetery at Louisville.

Watterson married in 1830 Talitha Black, daughter of James Black of Maury County, Tenn. He was a member of the Presbyterian Church. He was sponsored in his political life by Andrew Jackson [*q.v.*], the close friend of his father. In ante-bellum days he was a man of great influence in Tennessee politics and was the recognized leader of the Union wing of the Democratic party in the last decade before the war. He was a vigorous editor and a writer of merit, but his reputation in that line as in others has been obscured by the fame of his son, and only child.

[See obituary in *Courier-Jour.* (Louisville, Ky.), Oct. 2, 1891; Henry Watterson, "*Marse Henry*"; an *Autobiog.* (2 vols., 1919); *Biog. Dir. Am. Cong.* (1928); and *The South in the Building of the Nation* (1909), vol. XII.]   R. S. C.

WATTERSON, HENRY (Feb. 16, 1840– Dec. 22, 1921), editor and statesman, was born in Washington, D. C., the son of Harvey Magee Watterson [*q.v.*], a member of Congress from Tennessee, and of Talitha Black, also of Tennessee. At that time the "Tennessee dynasty" was in the ascendant. The child, small and sickly, each year made the journey from the capital to the two family homesteads: that of the Wattersons, Beech Grove, in Bedford County, and of the Blacks, Spring Hill, in Maury County, Tenn. A juvenile onlooker in the House, playing at page with the consent of his indulgent father, Watterson was on the floor when John Quincy Adams, then a member, was stricken and carried from his seat to die. He had visited the Hermitage with his father about 1844 and sat on Jackson's knee, and he later met all the other presidents between Jackson and Harding. He died in Harding's time, but he already numbered among his acquaintances Calvin Coolidge, Herbert Hoover, and Franklin D. Roosevelt. His schooling, save for a few terms at the Protestant Episcopal Academy at Philadelphia, was informal; he was the sort of person who readily absorbed education and culture through books and people. The youthful Watterson was for a time looked upon as the possessor of rare talent as a pianist. But a weak left hand and the early failure of sight in his right eye (which later became totally blind) ended his musical studies, although the influence of rhythm upon his journalistic and literary style remained a marked characteristic. As a youth of twelve he played an accompaniment for Adelina Patti, herself aged nine.

By 1856 the family was back in residence in Tennessee, the elder Watterson a strong Union Democrat. The son remained until 1858, when he went East again to engage in newspaper work. After a brief experience working on reportorial assignments for the *New York Times,* Watterson became a reporter for the

Daily States, of Washington—oddly enough holding at the same time "a clerkship, a real 'sinecure' in the Interior Department" (*"Marse Henry,"* I, 59)—and it fell to his lot to report the inauguration of Abraham Lincoln. A Unionist through conviction, although he became a secessionist and Confederate soldier because of sectional sympathies, he was drawn strongly to Lincoln, and some of his best-known writings were devoted to appreciations of the Civil War president. In 1861, for reasons which Watterson thought unsavory (*Ibid.,* p. 81), Secretary of War Simon Cameron [*q.v.*] offered him, through the clerk of the House, J. W. Forney [*q.v.*], a commission as lieutenant-colonel and private secretary. Watterson went home to Tennessee instead, determined to spend his time peacefully in writing until the war cloud was dispelled. He did not think the South could hold out long. But at home he found himself alone. "The boys were all gone to the front, and the girls were . . . all crazy" (*Ibid.,* p. 82). So he joined the Confederate army and, by some loose arrangement not defined, was in and out of it for four years. He was on the staff of Gen. Leonidas Polk [*q.v.*] until he fell ill; then, in his grey jacket, he worked on a Southern propaganda newspaper in Nashville.

After the fall of Nashville he engaged in more desultory soldiering, but he soon found himself appointed editor of the state newspaper at Chattanooga, which he named the *Rebel,* and turned it into the organ of the army. This remarkable journal, copies of which are preserved in Southern archives, was the first medium through which Watterson displayed that color and force of style which were later to make him outstanding among American editors throughout a half-century of active editorship. While editing the *Rebel,* he met his future business partner, Walter N. Haldeman, proprietor of the *Louisville Courier,* who, being a strong Southern sympathizer, had suspended his newspaper and retired behind the Southern lines. Editing the *Rebel,* however, became too precarious as the Union army moved on Atlanta, and, after serving Generals Albert Sidney Johnston and John Bell Hood [*qq.v.*] in various staff capacities, Watterson was offered by the Confederate government an opportunity, if he could reach Liverpool, of selling some cotton to British buyers. The young soldier, after various fantastic adventures with friendly Union officers, found the exits of the country closed, and settled down once more as an editor in Montgomery, Ala.

In 1865 the future "Marse Henry" of editorials and cartoons, the war just over, got an editorial job in Cincinnati on the *Evening Times,* owned by Calvin W. Starbuck. Upon the editor's sudden death Starbuck gave Watterson the place at $75 a week. The *Cincinnati Commercial,* under the inspiration of Murat Halstead [*q.v.*], greeted the young editor's first issue with some telling references to his fresh connection with the Confederate cause. Watterson went to Halstead and asked for quarter, saying that he meant to leave Cincinnati as soon as he could get a grubstake. That visit was the beginning of a friendship and political association which flowered notably through the famous "Quadrilateral" at the Greeley convention in 1872. A brief and successful newspaper venture at Nashville lasted almost through 1866. Watterson married Rebecca Ewing of Nashville on Dec. 20, 1865, and in 1867 took his bride to London. He returned to Nashville to join the staff of the *Republican Banner.* Simultaneously came two offers from Louisville—one from the senescent George Dennison Prentice [*q.v.*] to help edit the *Louisville Daily Journal,* another from Haldeman to become editor of the *Courier,* its publication resumed after the return of its publisher from behind the Southern lines. Watterson proposed consolidation to Haldeman, who declined. He joined the *Journal,* and, after half a year's lively but kindly battle with the *Courier,* the merger was made, and on Nov. 8, 1868, the *Courier-Journal* began its existence.

The *Courier-Journal* was one day old when its young editor began the struggle for the restoration of Southern home rule ("Carpet-Baggery and Peace," *Courier-Journal,* Nov. 9, 1868). Always a foe of slavery, Watterson agitated for the complete bestowal of civil and legal rights upon the negroes in exchange for the return of the South to its homefolk. Carl Schurz and Horace Greeley [*qq.v.*] ranged themselves with the Louisville editor, and, although their cause had a setback in the Greeley-Liberal campaign of 1872, it was won four years later. The Greeley campaign was always held by Watterson to have "shortened the distance across the bloody chasm" (*"Marse Henry,"* I, 266), and it was at the Liberal Republican nominating convention at Cincinnati that he, Schurz, Samuel Bowles, Murat Halstead, and (later) Whitelaw Reid and Horace White [*qq.v.*] formed the Quadrilateral (though they were six, not four), and first met Joseph Pulitzer [*q.v.*], a delegate from Missouri. About 1874 Watterson fixed upon Gov. Samuel Jones Tilden [*q.v.*] as the hope of the party and a reunited country. Carefully and intelligently he began to build up the governor of New York for the presidency, this culminating in the nomination of 1876. To Watterson, Tilden was the "ideal statesman." Except for Lincoln he was the editor's only public hero. During the 1876 campaign Watterson, at Tilden's request, took advantage of a Congressional vacancy through death in the Louisville district and sat, during the summer of 1876 and part of the winter of 1877, in the House as Tilden's floor leader, vociferously watching the contest that ended with the certification of Hayes. It was in this period that the passionate correspondence to the *Courier-Journal* from its Representative-editor in Washington appeared, including the suggestion —so alarming to the Northern press—that "a hundred thousand petitioners . . . ten thousand unarmed Kentuckians" come to the capital to see that justice was done (*Courier-Journal*, Jan. 5, 1877).

After the inauguration of Hayes, the editor returned to his tripod, never again to hold public office, although once he considered being a candidate for the Democratic nomination for governor of Kentucky if that was overwhelmingly desired—which it was not. Never again did he express more than temporary fealty to any Democratic presidential nominee or White House incumbent. He was highly critical of Cleveland and bitterly opposed his third nomination in 1892. The pair never got on, and many were the stories of private reasons for their long estrangement. (See *"Marse Henry,"* II, 116–17, 133–39.) In 1896 the *Courier-Journal* announced it would oppose William Jennings Bryan on the free silver issue. Watterson, on holiday abroad, had no part in the decision. But, learning of it, he cabled back to his partner, Haldeman, the message: "No compromise with dishonor" (*Courier-Journal*, July 13, 1896), and —save for one long editorial, sent from Switzerland—left the conduct of the fight for John B. Palmer and Simon B. Buckner (which meant McKinley) in Kentucky largely to his associate editor, Harrison Robertson. The stand almost destroyed the *Courier-Journal*, so resentful were the Democrats of the state against it, for— chiefly because of its activity—that was the time when, in Robert Ingersoll's phrase, "hell froze over," and Kentucky went Republican. Watterson and Haldeman, working to regain their lost ground, supported William Goebel [*q.v.*] for governor against the Republican nominee in 1898, and by 1900 had managed to figure out a way to support the second nomination of Bryan. In 1908 Watterson allowed Josephus Daniels to use his name as "honorary publicity chairman" in the third Bryan campaign. But he deplored Bryan's appointment as secretary of

state by Woodrow Wilson in 1913 (*Courier-Journal*, Dec. 21, 1912) and assailed him as an impractical dreamer when the Secretary left the cabinet on the war issue.

During the first decade of the twentieth century Watterson's chief national contribution was a series of philippics against "The Man on Horseback," as he called Theodore Roosevelt. Since his editorials were generally carried by telegraph to all newspapers in the country as a matter of news, this crusade became very famous. In the course of it Watterson announced that Roosevelt was unquestionably a paranoiac, determined to assume dictatorship of the country, and urged his family to sequestrate the Colonel. In 1909 he offered to bet the New York *World* a dinner that Roosevelt would quarrel with his chosen successor, Taft, and won the bet easily.

George Harvey [*q.v.*] in 1910 deeply interested Watterson in Woodrow Wilson, behind whom the editor marshaled his forces through the primary contest with Senator James Smith, calling the Governor "the hope of Democracy." But Wilson's blunt admission to Harvey, in answer to a question from the latter, that Harvey's editorial support in *Harper's Weekly* was damaging him with liberals and progressives, offended and alienated the sentimental Watterson, and he attempted to prevent the nomination of Wilson in 1912 (*Courier-Journal*, Feb. 21, 1912). Failing, he became a lukewarm observer and critic, varying from mild to severe, until the issues raised by Charles Evans Hughes and Theodore Roosevelt in 1916 ranged him on Wilson's side. He supported the President enthusiastically that year, and through the war, but he could not accept the idea of the League of Nations, and once more parted company with the President. Charged with being unable to stand by Democratic presidents, he reminded his critics through the *Courier-Journal* that "things have come to a hell of a pass when a man can't wallop his own jackass," an affectedly crude type of retort that, appealing strongly to the humorous sense of the American people, was part of his hold upon his readers.

Many trips abroad and Florida holidays punctuated editorial duties from 1880 on, but invariably Watterson wrote voluminously and frequently from wherever he was. The summer before the World War he was abroad, but he returned after Serajevo to throw himself strongly into an editorial assault against the Central Powers, which he attacked as foes of Christianity. "To hell with the Hohenzollerns and the Hapsburgs," he exclaimed in the *Courier-Jour-*

nal on Sept. 3, 1914, and from then until the armistice, he repeated this stirring objurgation. In 1917 he was awarded the Pulitzer prize for his editorials hailing the declaration of war against the Central Powers by the United States. In August 1918, with two of the three children of his late partner, Haldeman, after litigation with the third growing out of the suppression of a Watterson editorial, the editor sold control of the *Courier-Journal* to Robert W. Bingham, and, after a brief connection as editor emeritus, Watterson, nearly eighty, retired finally to private life, which he spent on his estate, Mansfield, near Louisville, or in Florida and New York City. He showed a mild interest in James M. Cox in the 1920 campaign, but he viewed the triumph of Harding and the anti-Leaguers with serenity. In these years he wrote little, save an occasional letter, with the exception of *"Marse Henry": An Autobiography* (2 vols., 1919), more important for its observations of life and anecdotes of the great than for a real revelation of an astonishing public career. He died at Jacksonville in December 1921, at the age of eighty-one, and was buried in Cave Hill Cemetery in Louisville. During his lifetime he was temporary chairman of several national conventions and author of the resolutions passed by four of these. In these resolutions he put into circulation many resounding phrases which rang from the hustings and were elaborated in his own writings. He was famous and in demand as a public speaker and lecturer. He once in youth wrote a novel, but it is not preserved; for pot-boilers, he collected his lectures as *The Compromises of Life* (1903), and edited a book of *genre* stories by Southern authors, called *Oddities in Southern Life and Character* (1883), a best-seller of its epoch.

His amazing zest for life, his gift for conversation and conviviality, his unusual personal appearance (the fierce blue eye under penthouses of bushy white eyebrows, the flaring mustache and slight goatee, the high, staccato voice combining to make a striking physical type), and his genius for "setting other editors to chattering" about what he wrote—these served to distinguish Watterson among his contemporaries at a time when journalism was personal and editorial writing often had immediate and dynamic effect. Despite the legends, the tipple he liked best was champagne and, after that, wine and beer; although known as "the Colonel," a term he himself abjured, he did not relish whiskey, and the mint-julep yarns and cartoons were imaginative. He was a prodigious worker, a hard and frequent bon-vivant, a gifted idler when occasion permitted, and—in his home circle—a patriarch.

Never were his famous personality and conversational gifts more glamorous than when he sat on the broad verandahs or in his large library at Mansfield, surrounded by his wife, his children, their children, and an assortment of guests and household pets. It was then that he was wont to say, looking back on a life both full and crowded: "I'm a free nigger at last and will never be anything else, hallelujah!" He died convinced that civilization was facing a crisis that might obliterate it "in seventy years," ascribing this largely to godlessness, for he himself was of undoubting Christian faith, though indifferent to the tenets of the sects. But his pessimism about the future was due partly to the triumph of national prohibition and equal suffrage, championed by those whom for many years he had attacked as "red-nosed angels," "Sillysallies," and "Crazyjanes."

[Sources include *Who's Who in America*, 1920–21; files of the *Courier-Jour.* (Louisville), 1868–1921; Watterson's *The Compromises of Life* (1903), and *"Marse Henry": An Autobiog.* (2 vols., 1919); letters to the author from Watterson; long personal and professional association; obituary in *Courier-Jour.*, Dec. 23, 1921. See also *The Editorials of Henry Watterson* (1923), compiled by Arthur Krock; Royal Cortissoz, *The Life of Whitelaw Reid* (1921); R. S. Baker, *Woodrow Wilson: Life and Letters*, vol. III (1931); W. F. Johnson, *George Harvey* (1929); and *Courier-Jour.*, Mar. 2, 1919, Watterson supplement.]

A. K—k.

WATTERSTON, GEORGE (Oct. 23, 1783– Feb. 4, 1854), librarian, was born on shipboard in New York harbor, the son of David Watterston, master-builder, a native of Jedburgh, Scotland. Eight years later his father, attracted by building operations in the federal city, removed to Washington. For several years thereafter David continued to spell the family name "Watterstone." The boy went to Charlotte Hall School in Maryland. Remembered now chiefly as the first librarian of Congress who was not also clerk of the House of Representatives, he spent four fifths of his life otherwise occupied. Beginning to practise law in Hagerstown, Md., he was later in partnership with Thomas Law in Washington. In 1808 his first novel, *The Lawyer, or Man As He Ought Not to Be,* was published. Thereafter he "never missed an opportunity in any of his books to make a derogatory remark about the law and lawyers" (Kennedy, *post,* p. 5). A comedy, another novel, and two poems followed. He was married on Oct. 26, 1811, to Maria Shanley. They had eight children. In 1813 he was engaged as editor of the *Washington City Gazette.* When the British troops approached the capital in 1814, he marched to meet them at Bladensburg and returned soon to find the capitol in ruins, the library burned, and his own house pillaged.

Next year Thomas Jefferson's collection replaced the burned library, and Watterston was made librarian of Congress. With one messenger he did all the work except selecting additions to the collections, a pleasure retained by the congressional committee. Not until 1827 was he given one assistant. His own salary never exceeded $1,500 per year. Starting in 1815 with 6,500 volumes, the library numbered some 15,000 in 1829. He still had time, along with his library work, to write several more books, almost forgotten now (listed in Kennedy, *post*, pp. 55–57). He also edited at different times and for short periods three local newspapers, held several municipal offices, and was actively interested in politics. On May 28, 1829, Jackson summarily displaced him, a stanch Whig and friend of Henry Clay. For the rest of his life he nursed a grievance and, with Scotch persistence, kept up for years his fruitless efforts at reinstatement. A fortnight after his removal he was on the staff of the *National Journal* in Washington and next year became its editor. For fifteen years he continued to publish guide-books, statistical compends, biographical sketches, textbooks, lectures on botany and agriculture. In 1833 he began the movement to build the Washington Monument. He remained as secretary of the Washington National Monument Society from its beginning to his death twenty years later, giving time and energy to every branch of its work. In this closing activity, the longest and most successful of all his efforts, he should have found and doubtless did find the greatest satisfaction of his life. He lived to see the great shaft reach the height of some 150 feet. A few months after his death, construction was entirely stopped and not another stone was laid for nearly a quarter of a century. He died in Washington and is buried in the Congressional Cemetery.

[Papers in the Lib. of Cong.; W. D. Johnston, *Hist. of the Lib. of Cong.* (1904); J. E. Kennedy, *George Watterston, Novelist* (1933); F. L. Harvey, *Hist. of the Washington National Monument* (1903); A. C. Clark, *Greenleaf and Law in the Federal City* (1901); *Daily Union* (Washington, D. C.), Feb. 7, 1854.]

F. W. A.

WATTS, FREDERICK (May 9, 1801–Aug. 17, 1889), commissioner of agriculture, was born in Carlisle, Pa., the son of David and Julian (Miller) Watts and the grandson of Frederick Watts who emigrated from Wales to America in 1760, was an officer in the Revolutionary army, and was afterward brigadier-general of Pennsylvania militia. His father, a graduate of Dick-

inson College, was a successful lawyer in Carlisle. The son also went to Dickinson, where he was a member of the class of 1819, which, however, was never graduated. A few months after he left college in 1819, his father died and during the next two or three years he lived with an uncle, William Miles, on his farm in Erie County. There he acquired a practical knowledge of farming and a taste for farm life that lasted throughout his life. Upon returning to Carlisle he studied law with Andrew Carothers and later formed a partnership with him. In September 1827 he was married to Eliza Cranston, by whom he had three daughters. She died in 1832. In March 1835 he was married to Henrietta Edge, who, with five sons and one daughter, survived him. His ability and character made him a leader in his community for more than fifty years. Active and influential in the affairs of Dickinson College, he was secretary of the board of control from 1824 to 1828 and a member of the board from 1828 to 1833 and again from 1841 to 1844. He was for many years active in the St. John's Episcopal Church. From 1829 to 1845 he reported the cases of the western district of the state supreme court, publishing two volumes of reports with William Rawle, Jr., and Charles B. Penrose a third volume with Penrose only, then ten volumes, for 1832 to 1840, alone, and nine volumes, for 1841 to 1845 with Henry J. Sergeant. From 1845 to 1871 he was president of the Cumberland Valley Railroad Company, in which he had been interested since its organization and remained a director until his death. In 1849 he was appointed judge of the 9th Judicial District. He served until the judiciary of the state was made elective instead of appointive in 1852, when, as a Whig, he was not elected. He formed a partnership with John Brown Parker and enjoyed a successful practice in Carlisle. In 1869 he retired to one of his farms near Carlisle.

For many years he had been a farmer as well as a lawyer and was well known as one who believed in the application of science to farming. He experimented in farm buildings and equipment and in breeds of livestock, and he encouraged agricultural fairs. In 1840 he had been instrumental in bringing about the trial of the McCormick reaper in Pennsylvania. His prominence as a farmer led to his election as president of the Pennsylvania state agricultural society. He was also the organizer and for many years president of the Cumberland county agricultural society. As president of the state society he was successful in putting through the legislature in 1854 a charter for a Farmers' High School, which developed into the Pennsylvania State College. He was the first president of the board of trustees.

In 1871, at seventy years of age, he was appointed federal commissioner of agriculture by Grant. During his term the division of microscopy was established. He was apparently the first commissioner to give much attention to timber interests and obtained an appropriation for a forestry investigation that was the beginning of the forestry division organized several years later. At his suggestion the weather reporting work of the Smithsonian Institution was transferred to the signal service of the war department; and the Congress made an appropriation to collect and publish meteorological information for the benefit of agriculture. After his retirement on June 30, 1877, as commissioner of agriculture, he returned to Carlisle, where he remained till his death. He was buried in Carlisle.

[T. I. Osmond, *Hon. Frederick Watts* (1930); T. I. Mairs, *Some Pa. Pioneers on Agricultural Science* (1928); C. H. Greathouse, "Hist. Sketch of the U. S. Department of Agriculture," 2nd rev., *U. S. Dept. of Agri. Division of Pubs. Bulletin 3* (1907); *Hist. of Cumberland and Adams County, Pa.* (1886); Alfred Nevin, *Centennial Biog. Men of Mark of Cumberland Valley, Pa.* (1876); *Carlisle Herald,* Aug. 19, 1889, *Philadelphia Inquirer,* Aug. 19, 20, 1889; information from Gilbert Malcolm, Carlisle, Pa.]   C.R.B.

WATTS, THOMAS HILL (Jan. 3, 1819–Sept. 16, 1892), governor of Alabama, attorney-general of the Confederate States of America, was born in Alabama Territory not far from the present town of Greenville in that part of the Creek Indian cession which was later organized into Butler County. He was the son of Prudence (Hill) and John Hughes Watts, a prosperous planter, and the great-great-grandson of Francis Watts, possibly of Welsh and English stock, who was in Prince William County, Va., in 1749. The boy received such training as the schools in his section afforded. He then concluded a bargain with his father to accept money for education in lieu of any further claim upon the family estate. With this money he attended the University of Virginia and graduated in 1839. Returning to Alabama just in time to campaign for Harrison, he attracted attention as a stump-speaker. The following year he was admitted to the bar and on Jan. 10, 1842, married Eliza Brown Allen, who died in 1873 leaving ten children. He practised in Greenville, Ala., until 1847, when he moved his law office to the newly established state capital at Montgomery. From the beginning of his career, he combined work in his profession with political activity. He represented Butler County in the state legislature in the sessions of 1842, 1844, and 1845. In 1849 he represented Montgomery County in the lower house of the legislature, and in 1853 he was in the state Senate. As the strength of the Whig party waned in Alabama, he, like many of his contemporaries, found temporary refuge in the Know-Nothing party, and he became its unsuccessful candidate for Congress in 1856. He was a strong supporter of the Union, and in the campaign of 1860 he was the leader of the Union forces in the state, campaigning vigorously for Bell and Everett. The election of Lincoln convinced him that the only safety for state rights lay in secession, and he identified himself with the Yancey faction of the Democratic party. He was a member of the Alabama convention of 1861.

Eager for military glory, he organized the 17th Alabama Regiment of which he became colonel. He saw service at Pensacola, Fla., and at Corinth, Miss., and was honorably discharged Apr. 9, 1862, to become attorney-general of the Confederate States. In 1863 he was elected governor of the state of Alabama. He took office in December 1863. Alabama was hard pressed, and much of the governor's time was given to a hopeless attempt to defend the state against northern invaders. He also made a valiant effort to relieve the distress of the people of the state. Considering the encroachment by the Richmond government just as dangerous as encroachment by the Washington government, he opposed such measures as the conscription of state officials and impressment of private property, as violations of the rights of the states. The collapse of the Confederate government ended his administration and destroyed his fortune in land and some 200 slaves. In 1865 he was sent to a Northern prison. His imprisonment was short, and he received a pardon from President Johnson in 1868. Upon his return to Montgomery, he resumed the practice of his profession and prospered again. He continued to be an active worker for the Democratic party and to be interested in the public welfare and in the affairs of the Baptist Church, of which he was a member. In September 1875 he married his second wife, Ellen (Noyes) Jackson. He died in Montgomery.

[Willis Brewer, *Alabama* (1872); *Confederate Military Hist.* (1899), ed. by C. A. Evans, vol. I; E. B. Culver, "Thomas Hill Watts," *Ala. Hist. Soc. Trans.,* vol. IV (1904); W. L. Fleming, *Civil War and Reconstruction in Ala.* (1905); A. B. Moore, *Conscription and Conflict in the Confederacy* (1924); F. L. Owsley, *State Rights in the Confederacy* (1925); J. B. Little, *The Hist. of Butler County, Ala.* (1885); *Univ. of Va.* (1904), vol. I; typescript in Lib. of Cong. of C. B. Heineman, *Watts Families of the Southern States* (1934); *Daily Register* (Mobile), Sept. 17, 1892.]   H. F.

WAUGH, BEVERLY (Oct. 25, 1789–Feb. 9, 1858), bishop of the Methodist Episcopal Church, son of Capt. James and Henrietta (Turley) Waugh, was born in Fairfax County, Va. His father was a veteran of the American Revolution. Waugh received the typical secondary education of the period and his excellent penmanship aided him when very young in securing a position as copyist in a government office in Washington. He early showed business ability and in 1807 became manager of a store in Middleburg, Va. At the age of fifteen he joined the Methodist Episcopal Church, and while at Middleburg became convinced of a call to preach. Abandoning his business career, he was admitted on trial to the Baltimore Conference in 1809 and was ordained deacon in 1811 and elder in 1813. Until 1828 he served as an itinerant in that conference, eleven years being spent in or near the cities of Washington and Baltimore. On Apr. 21, 1812, he married Catharine B. Bushby of Washington.

Waugh was soon recognized as a preacher of more than ordinary ability, and was sent as a delegate to the General Conferences of 1816 and 1820. The question of reform in Methodist polity was then being agitated and Waugh aligned himself with the group desiring to make the Church more democratic by having the presiding elders elected by the annual Conferences rather than appointed by the bishops, as was then the rule. The Baltimore Conference, however, favored the appointive method, and as a result Waugh was not elected to the General Conference of 1824. Ultimately he lost interest in the movement for reform, chiefly because of what he considered the radical and unfair attitude of some of its leaders, and by 1828 he was championing the *status quo*. At the General Conference of 1828, as a member of the committee on the Book Concern, he showed such a knowledge of business affairs that he was elected assistant book agent of the Church. In 1832 he was made the principal book agent. Under his supervision the Book Concern made progress; the indebtedness was cancelled, the output of literature was increased, and a new building was erected. Waugh was already preparing an optimistic quadrennial report for the General Conference of 1836 when, on Feb. 18 of that year, the headquarters of the Book Concern in New York were destroyed by fire, with a loss of over $200,000. Undaunted by this disaster Waugh and others at once began to raise funds for rebuilding. In this work he was engaged when at the General Conference he was elected bishop on the first ballot.

He began his episcopal labors by presiding over the Troy Conference at Pawlet, Vt., on June 22, 1836, and until his death twenty-two years later he never missed holding a Conference assigned to him. It is estimated that during his episcopacy he made twelve thousand appointments and traveled one hundred thousand miles. After 1852 he was the senior bishop. Having as a young preacher opposed what he thought to be the autocracy of the episcopacy, he took extra precautions to insure justice in making appointments. He refused to be influenced in the conduct of his duties by either the pro-slavery or the anti-slavery groups in the Church. Although he was opposed to slavery, he refused to allow the abolitionist leaders at the New England Conference of 1837 to present anti-slavery petitions. He declared that consideration of the slavery issue was not a part of the business of an annual Conference and held that continued agitation on the subject would only lead to the division of the Church. He was "one of the few Southern men who could oppose New England abolitionists and still command their love, though he could not control their sentiments or action" (quoted by Buckley, *post*, II, 161). At the General Conference of 1844 he endeavored to prevent a division of the Church by proposing with Bishops Soule, Hedding, and Morris the postponement of further consideration of the case of Bishop J. O. Andrew [*q.v.*] until the next General Conference. Although a Southerner by birth, Waugh remained with the Methodist Episcopal Church after the schism. He died in Baltimore as a result of exposure at a revival meeting in Carlisle, Pa., and was buried in Mount Olivet Cemetery.

[T. L. Flood and J. W. Hamilton, *Lives of Methodist Bishops* (1882); W. H. Egle, *Pa. Geneals.* (1896); J. E. Armstrong, *Hist. of the Old Baltimore Conference* (1907); *Minutes of the Ann. Conferences of the Methodist Episcopal Church for the Year 1858* (1858); H. C. Jennings, *The Methodist Book Concern* (1924); J. M. Buckley, *A Hist. of Methodism in the U. S.* (2 vols., 1897); C. B. Swaney, *Episcopal Methodism and Slavery* (1926); *Western Christian Advocate*, Feb. 24, 1858; *Sun* (Baltimore), Feb. 10, 1858.]   P. N. G.

WAYLAND, FRANCIS (Mar. 11, 1796–Sept. 30, 1865), clergyman, educator, fourth president of Brown University, was born in New York City, the eldest son of Francis and Sarah (Moore) Wayland, who emigrated from England in 1793. His father, originally a leather merchant, entered the Baptist ministry in 1807, and held pastorates successively in Poughkeepsie, Albany, Troy, and Saratoga Springs. Francis' mother was a woman of superior mind and rare spirit, and to her early training the son owed many of the salient traits of his own character—abhorrence of meanness and wrong, belief in the divine purpose of life, a stern sense of duty, moral courage, and a passion for the truth. At fifteen he entered the sophomore class of Union College, graduating in 1813. He then studied medicine in Troy and during the winter of 1814–15 attended medical lectures in New York. In 1816, however, obeying an inner urge to the ministry, he went to Andover Theological Seminary, where he came under the quickening influence of Moses Stuart [q.v.], an experience that left an indelible impress upon his whole intellectual life.

Forced by want of means to suspend his theological studies, he returned to Union College as tutor in 1817, remaining until 1821, when he was called to the First Baptist Church in Boston, where he soon acquired recognition as a man of force, originality, and broad vision. His sermon on *The Moral Dignity of the Missionary Enterprise* (1823) became almost a classic in the literature of modern missions and exerted a far-reaching influence upon religious thought both in America and in Europe. His two fast-day sermons, *The Duties of an American Citizen* (1825), further enhanced his reputation.

In 1826 he was recalled to Union College, as professor of mathematics and natural philosophy, but hardly had he entered upon his duties when, in February 1827, he became president of Brown University, an office which for twenty-eight years he conducted with such extraordinary energy and crowned with such high and lasting achievement as to make his administration forever memorable in the history of the institution. His dynamic personality was felt from the first moment: discipline was restored, the standard of conduct and study raised, the whole tone of college life altered. Instruction was vitalized by the banishment of the textbook from the classroom and the substitution of the "analytic method," which kept the student on the alert and developed habits of close reasoning and precise statement. The curriculum was augmented by courses in modern languages, history, economics, and the natural sciences; non-resident professors were dispensed with but the faculty was ultimately enlarged; the library was endowed; facilities for study were greatly improved. The funds of the institution were considerably increased and new buildings were added: Manning Hall, through the munificence of Nicholas Brown [q.v.]; Rhode Island Hall, by means of donations from citizens of the state; and a president's house. The University grew in numbers and reputation, and its president attained general recognition as a preëminent figure in education. Great as an administrator, Wayland was

perhaps even greater as a teacher. Hundreds of his students testified to the intellectual stimulation received in his classroom, to the corrective effect of his personal counsels, to the inspiration caught from his chapel discourses, and above all to the ennobling influence of his lofty character, which produced upon them all an impression of moral grandeur.

His activities were manifold and his influence reached far. His textbooks in moral philosophy, intellectual philosophy, and political economy were widely used, especially the first, which went through many editions and was translated into several languages. He was instrumental in devising a school system for the city of Providence, and was the author of the plan for free public schools in Rhode Island (1828); he was the first president of the American Institute of Instruction (1830), long time a trustee of Butler Hospital, and a member of the state prison board—as such initiating a thorough reform of the institution. In 1838 he outlined a plan for a national university, as the best object to which to devote the Smithsonian bequest. His example in founding a free library in Wayland, Mass., inspired the act of 1851 empowering towns to support public libraries by taxation.

In 1840 he visited France, England, and Scotland. Upon his return, and possibly as a result of certain reflections upon education abroad, he published his *Thoughts on the Present Collegiate System in the United States* (1842), in which he boldly challenged accepted premises and called for a candid reëxamination of the whole problem of higher education. Disappointed in the response to his appeal, and worn by his arduous labors, in 1849 he tendered his resignation as president; but at the earnest solicitation of the corporation was persuaded to remain, upon the condition, however, of support in a project which had long been maturing in his mind, and which he set forth in his famous *Report on the Condition of the University* (1850). In this *Report,* which was impelled by a democratic and generous conception of higher education as a social agency, he advocated a thorough reorganization of the University, with a view to making its services more widely available and more directly contributory to the needs of society. The proposal was adopted; entrance requirements were made more flexible; new subjects were introduced; a limited elective system was inaugurated. The student enrollment increased materially and $125,000 additional endowment was raised, but the resources of the University were insufficient to carry out the plan in its entirety. It pointed the way, however, which higher education was destined to take, and serves as a lasting monument to Wayland's prophetic vision and progressive spirit.

After his retirement, in 1855, Wayland devoted himself to literary, religious, and philanthropic labors, serving for a time as pastor of the First Baptist Church of Providence, and participating actively in the civic life of the community, in which he was revered for the wisdom of his counsels and the nobility of his character. His views on public questions were marked by candor and deep moral earnestness tempered with the tolerance of a great spirit. His utterance was remarkable for its clarity and sincerity; his addresses and sermons abound in passages of great dignity; and an impressive bearing lent added power to the spoken word. He was twice married: first, Nov. 21, 1825, to Lucy Lane Lincoln, who died in 1834; second, Aug. 1, 1838, to Mrs. Hepsy S. Howard Sage. He had three sons, one of whom was Francis [q.v.].

His published works include, *Elements of Moral Science* (1835), *Elements of Political Economy* (1837), *The Moral Law of Accumulation* (1837), *The Limitations of Human Responsibility* (1838); *Domestic Slavery Considered as a Scriptural Institution* (1845), *The Duty of Obedience to the Civil Magistrate* (1847), *University Sermons* (1849), *A Memoir of the Life and Labors of the Rev. Adoniram Judson, D.D.* (1853), *The Elements of Intellectual Philosophy* (1854), *Notes on the Principles and Practices of Baptist Churches* (1857), *Sermons to the Churches* (1858), *Letters on the Ministry of the Gospel* (1863), *A Memoir of the Christian Labors . . . of Thomas Chalmers* (1864), beside some fifty or more sermons and occasional addresses.

[Francis and H. L. Wayland, *A Memoir of the Life and Labors of Francis Wayland, D.D., LL.D.* (2 vols., 1867); J. O. Murray, *Francis Wayland* (1891); G. I. Chace, *The Virtues and Services of Francis Wayland* (1866); Alexis Caswell, *A Sermon on the Christian Work of Francis Wayland* (1867); *Am. Jour. of Educ.*, Dec. 1863; *New Englander*, Jan. 1866; *Atlantic Mo.*, Jan. 1868; W. C. Bronson, *The Hist. of Brown Univ., 1764-1914* (1914), *N. Y. Times*, Oct. 2, 1865.]

T.C.

WAYLAND, FRANCIS (Aug. 23, 1826–Jan. 9, 1904), lawyer, for thirty years dean of the Yale Law School, was born in Boston, Mass., and died in New Haven, Conn. His father, Francis Wayland [q.v.], was long president of Brown University. His mother, Lucy Lane (Lincoln) of Boston, died when he was seven, and he was brought up by his father and his stepmother. In 1846 he graduated from Brown with the degree of A.B., and after studying law at the Har-

vard Law School and in offices in Providence, R. I., and in Springfield, Mass., he was admitted to the Massachusetts bar. In 1850 he went to Worcester, Mass., and practised there for some seven years. On Oct. 6, 1857, he married Martha Read of New Haven, and soon thereafter removed to that city, where he spent the remainder of his life. He served two terms (1864–65) as judge of probate for the New Haven district, and in 1869 was lieutenant-governor of the state.

At this time the financial state of the Yale Law School was such as to threaten its existence. At the instigation of the local bar association and Yale University, three young members of the bar, Simeon E. Baldwin, William C. Robinson [qq.v.], and Johnson T. Platt, took charge of the school in 1869 and endeavored to renew its life. Soon realizing that busy lawyers like themselves could not successfully direct its activities, they sought for a leader, and at Baldwin's suggestion Wayland was chosen. In 1871 he became instructor in law, a year later professor, and in 1873, dean of the school, in which capacity he served until he retired as professor emeritus in 1903. Wayland was worldly wise, urbane, courteous, well-traveled, with independent means and a wide field of acquaintance. At once he identified the school with himself so fully that thereafter each shared the wide and favorable notice accorded the other. Under his direction the school grew and prospered materially. Whereas in 1873 its faculty consisted of four members, its students numbered twenty-one, its course of study was of two years' duration, and its library contained only 2,000 volumes, in 1903 it had fifteen instructors and a like number of special lecturers, a three-year course, 339 students, and a library of 20,000 volumes. In 1876 a graduate course in law, leading to advanced degrees, was established—the first, it is said, in any English or American law school. As a crowning achievement of his life Wayland personally obtained funds to provide a separate building for the law department and this building, named Hendrie Hall in honor of its chief donor, was fully completed and occupied in 1900.

Though Wayland advanced the material prosperity of the school, he was conservative in his views on legal education. His long deanship occurred at a time when C. C. Langdell [q.v.] at Harvard was making those innovations—including the case method of study, the law faculty of full-time teachers, and the requirement of a college degree before admission as a student—which caused the Harvard Law School to be so long preëminent. Against these radical departures Wayland and his faculty stood out, and ultimately the Yale Law School suffered in prestige. Not until some years after his death and during the administration of his successor, Henry Wade Rogers [*q.v.*], were the changes made which restored the reputation of the institution as a leading American law school.

Wayland was not a great legal scholar. For some years he taught the subject of Evidence and lectured upon English constitutional history, but later he limited himself to the latter subject. For the most part, he confined his activities to the public functions of his office and to his relations with his students. The personal qualities which made him so attractive a civic and public figure were such as to win the affection and admiration of young men. He was "of unusual personal charm, eminently companionable, a born story-teller, with a genius for friendship" (*Outlook,* Jan. 16, 1904, p. 149). Of impressive stature, he was a magnificent figure on horseback, his usual means of conveyance.

Wayland was often called upon to serve as a presiding officer. For some years he was president of the American Social Science Association and thereafter was vice-president and chairman of its jurisprudence department (1876–1902). He was president of the board of directors of the Connecticut State Prison for fourteen years, and for a time of the Connecticut Prison Aid Association; he also served as chairman of the executive committee of the National Prison Congress. He was president of the board of visitors to the United States Military Academy in 1874, vice-president of the board of visitors to the United States Naval Academy at Annapolis in 1880, and trustee (1873–88) and thereafter fellow of Brown University. For twenty-five years he was president of the Organized Charities of New Haven. He was interested in criminology and in prison reform and spoke and wrote much on these subjects. In politics he was an active Republican.

His publications include *A Memoir of the Life and Labors of Francis Wayland, DD., LL.D.* (2 vols., 1867), written in collaboration with his brother H. L. Wayland; *On Certain Defects in Our Method of Making Laws,* presidential address at the meeting of the American Social Science Association, Sept. 5, 1881; *Out-door Relief and Tramps* (1877); *The Pardoning Power: Where Should It Be Lodged and How Should It Be Exercised?* (1884); *On Certain Anomalies in Criminal Jurisprudence* (1885); "Some of the Causes Which Tend to Promote the Increase of Crime in the United States," in *Proceedings of the Annual Congress of the National Prison As-*

sociation . . . *Dec. 3–7, 1892* (1893); and other addresses and pamphlets.

[W. C. Robinson, *An Address Commemorative of the Life and Character of Francis Wayland* (1904); L. M. Daggett, "The Yale Law School," *Green Bag,* June 1889; *Report of the President of Yale Univ., 1903–1904* (1904), pp. 150–52; T. S. Woolsey, *Hist. Address in Celebration of the Centennial of the School of Law, Yale Univ., June 16, 1924* (1924); *Yale Alumni Weekly,* Jan. 13, 1904; *Outlook,* Apr. 11, 1903, Jan. 16, 1904; *Who's Who in America,* 1901–02; *New Haven Evening Register,* Jan. 11, 12, 1904.]   C. E. C.

WAYMAN, ALEXANDER WALKER (September 1821–Nov. 30, 1895), bishop of the African Methodist Episcopal Church, was born, a freeman, in Caroline County, Md., the son of Francis and Matilda Wayman. As a boy he worked on a farm with his father, and learned to read by the light of a wood fire. In those days practically his only reading book was the Bible, and his copybooks, the sand and the sides of old buildings. When he was fourteen he was hired out to Benjamin Kerby of Talbot County, whose children taught him all they knew. Returning to Caroline County in 1836, he lived with a James Glanden. Soon afterwards he was converted and joined the Methodist Episcopal Church.

Impelled by the desire to get more education and become a preacher, in 1840 he left home and went to Baltimore, proceeding from there, after a few weeks, to Philadelphia. Here he joined the African Methodist Episcopal Church and was licensed as an exhorter. A Quaker, whose coachman he had become, gave him instruction in English composition. In 1842 he was an assistant on the Princeton, N. J., circuit, taught a small primary school at New Brunswick, and was aided in his efforts to educate himself by students of Rutgers College. The following year he was admitted on trial to the Philadelphia Conference, and after serving two years on the West Chester Circuit was ordained deacon (1845). Subsequent appointments were to Little Wesley Church, Philadelphia, the Salem, N. J., circuit, and Trenton. In 1847 he was ordained elder.

Transferring to the Baltimore Conference in 1848, he became as time went on one of the leaders in his denomination, contributing much to the administration of its affairs and to the extension of its bounds. From 1848 to 1864, with the exception of two years, he was pastor of churches either in Washington or Baltimore. In addition to caring for his own parishes, he organized Ebenezer Church, Georgetown; St. Paul's, South Washington; and Allen Chapel, Good Hope, Md. He was a member of all the General Conferences held during this period and served as assistant secretary. In 1860 he was appointed, with two others, to prepare and publish a new edition of the *Discipline*. At the General Conference of 1864 he was elected bishop. His activities were incessant and his episcopal duties carried him throughout the greater part of the country. At first his labors were largely in the East and South. Soon after the Civil War was over, he inspected the mission work in South Carolina and Georgia, and in 1867 made a tour through these states and Virginia. Subsequently he organized the Virginia, Georgia, and Florida conferences. In 1872 he was assigned supervision of the district that included Indiana, Illinois, Missouri, and California, and thereafter made several journeys to the Pacific Coast. He served as chaplain, Oct. 15, 1874, at the unveiling of the Lincoln Memorial at Springfield, Ill. In the course of his numerous activities he found time to contribute to the historical records of his denomination. His book, entitled *My Recollections of African M. E. Ministers, or Forty Years' Experience in the African Methodist Episcopal Church* (1881), contains much detailed information of value. He also published *Cyclopædia of African Methodism* (1882). He continued his labors well down to the time of his death, which occurred in Baltimore in his seventy-fifth year. He was twice married; his first wife died in 1860; his second, Harriet Ann Elizabeth Wayman, survived him.

[In addition to his *Recollections*, see B. T. Tanner, *An Apology for African Methodism* (1867); R. R. Wright, *Centennial Encyc. of the A. M. E. Ch.* (copr. 1916); *Baltimore American*, Dec. 1, 1895.]

H. E. S.

WAYMOUTH, GEORGE (fl. 1601–1612), navigator, explorer, was a native of Devonshire, England, and had been employed at sea for years, working his way up to a master's rating and attaining some prominence as a navigator. The evidence for the statement that he was sent out in 1593 by the "Russia and Turkey merchants" to discover the Northwest Passage (*Calendar of State Papers, Colonial Series, 1513–1616*, 1862, p. xxxi) is dubious; but he must have been interested in the search, for, on July 24, 1601, the newly formed East India Company discussed a letter received from him "touching his attempte to be made for the discovery of the north west passage to the Est Indies . . ." (Stevens, *post*, p. 182). This company, after long negotiations with the Muscovy Company concerning jurisdiction, decided to ignore the latter and to organize the expedition itself. Waymouth was given £100 "to prepare his instruments and other necessaries" (Stevens, *post*, p. 184), and was promised £500 if he found the passage. He commanded the two ships that sailed, early in

May 1602, from Radcliffe. They passed southern Greenland on June 18 and bore northwestward to Warwicks Foreland and Hudson Strait. There a mutiny, led by John Cartwright, the chaplain, caused the expedition to turn back. The East India Company were naturally disappointed at this early return but the Privy Council cleared the captain of blame. A second expedition was planned but not carried out. Shortly after his return and before his next voyage, Waymouth addressed the king with a manuscript called "The Jewell of Artes" which dealt with navigation, shipbuilding and instruments of war. The treatment of these subjects shows that the author was much better educated than the ordinary sea captain.

On Mar. 5, 1605, he set out as commander of the *Archangel* on a voyage of exploration to Virginia for the Earl of Southampton, the Baron of Wardour, and Sir Ferdinando Gorges. There is reason to believe that this expedition was part of an English Catholic attempt at colonization in America (J. P. Baxter, *Sir Ferdinand Gorges*, 1890, I, 65–67). Sankaty Head, Nantucket, was sighted on May 14, but no landing was made because of the shoals. The *Archangel* stood off to the north and three days later reached Monhegan. For a month the expedition remained near the Georges Islands, trading with the Indians and exploring St. George's River in a shallop that had been brought from England. A cross, which was found by Gilbert in 1607, was set up on one of the islands, now known as Allen Island, and another at the bend of the river near Thomaston, Me. On June 16 Waymouth "waied Anker and quit the Land" (Rosier, *post*, p. 153), carrying with him five captured Indians who later proved useful as pilots to Martin Pring, George Popham [*qq.v.*], and Raleigh Gilbert. In July 1605 the expedition was back in England and the same year appeared an account of it by James Rosier who was employed on the voyage (see Burrage edition, *post*).

In October Waymouth entered into an agreement with Sir John Zouche to assist in planting a colony in Virginia but nothing more was heard of their plans. About that time he prepared a manuscript entitled "Errors and Defects in the usual building of Ships," written, so he asserted, from twenty years' study of mathematics and shipbuilding. In October 1607, James I granted Waymouth a pension of 3s. 4d. *per diem*. In 1609 he engaged in a controversy with Phineas Pett over alleged imperfections in the latter's ships (*Calendar of State Papers, Domestic Series, 1603–1610*, 1857, p. 510). The following year he took part in the siege of Jülich on the Continent, and wrote a manuscript entitled "A Journall Relation of the service at the takeing in of the towne and castle of Gulicke . . ." The last mention of him is the payment of his pension at Easter 1612.

[Henry Stevens, *The Dawn of British Trade to the Eastern Indies, . . . Court Records of the East India Company* (1886); for Waymouth's own account of the voyage of 1602, see Samuel Purchas, *Hakluytus Posthumus or Purchas His Pilgrims* (1906 ed.), vol. XIV, *Hakluyt Society Pubs.,* and Luke Foxe, *North-West Fox* (1635); for the voyage of 1605, *A True Relation of the Most Prosperous Voyage made this present Yeere 1605, by Captaine George Waymouth . . . written by James Rosier* (1605), see edition by H. S. Burrage, *Gorges Soc. Pubs.,* vol. III (1887). See also G. B. Manhart, "The English Search for a Northwest Passage," in *Studies in English Commerce and Exploration in the Reign of Elizabeth* (1924); Thomas Rundall, *Narratives of Voyages Towards the North-West* (1849). "The Jewell of Artes" and "Errors and Defects" have never been printed and are in the British Museum.]　　　　　　　　　　　　R. J. S—y.

WAYNE, ANTHONY (Jan. 1, 1745–Dec. 15, 1796), soldier, was born at Waynesboro, Pa., the only son of Isaac and Elizabeth (Iddings) Wayne. Isaac Wayne with his father Anthony Wayne, of English ancestry, emigrated from Ireland and about 1724 settled in Chester County, Pa., where he acquired some 500 acres of land and a thriving tannery. At the age of sixteen the boy attended a private academy kept by his uncle, Gilbert Wayne, in Philadelphia, where he is said to have been more proficient in feats of mock warfare, suggested no doubt by the Indian wars in progress, than in his classroom subjects. He learned enough mathematics to qualify as a surveyor, with some further application after he left school two years later. In 1765 he was sent by a Philadelphia land company to supervise the surveying and settlement of 100,000 acres of land in Nova Scotia. On Mar. 25, 1766, after the venture had failed, he returned to Pennsylvania and married Mary Penrose, the daughter of Bartholomew Penrose, a Philadelphia merchant. They had two children. He went to live on his father's estate and took charge of the tannery. In 1774 his father died, and Anthony succeeded to the ownership of a profitable establishment that provided him a very comfortable competence. He was of medium height, had a handsome, well-proportioned face with a slightly aquiline nose and high forehead. His hair was dark, his eyes dark brown and penetrating, giving to his face a very animated appearance.

During the early Revolutionary movement he was chairman of the committee appointed in the county on July 13, 1774, to frame the resolutions of protest against the coercive acts of the British government. He was later made chairman of the county committee appointed to supervise the carrying out of the association drawn up by the first Continental Congress. He represented his county in the provincial assembly that met during 1775. On Jan. 3, 1776, he was appointed by Congress to be colonel of a Chester County regiment engaged in continental service, and as a soldier he served through the war. His youth and lack of formal training in the arts of war prevented him from being on friendly terms with many of his colleagues, and he had personal difficulties with St. Clair, Charles Lee, and James Wilkinson. Contemporaries agreed that he was impetuous, yet Alexander Graydon, who called his manner "fervid," admitted that he could "fight as well as brag" (Stillé, *post,* p. 66). Washington admitted his bravery and his self-possession in battle but feared his impetuousness, when, seventeen years later, he chose him to lead the army against the northwestern Indians. In the spring of 1776 he was sent with the Pennsylvania brigade commanded by Gen. William Thompson to reinforce the faltering Canadian expedition. When the Pennsylvanians met the retreating remnants of Montgomery's army at the mouth of the Sorel River, they were sent down the St. Lawrence to attack what was thought to be the advance guard of the British army at Three Rivers. It turned out to be the main army numbering 3,000, and Wayne, whose regiment was in the front of the attack, found himself sustaining a hot exchange with the enemy in order to cover the retreat of his outnumbered countrymen to Fort Ticonderoga. He was placed in command of the garrison of over two thousand men there and had his first taste of wretched provisioning, of sickness, starvation, and mutiny.

On Feb. 21, 1777, he was appointed to the rank of brigadier-general and was called, on Apr. 12, to join Washington at Morristown, N. J., and to take command of the Pennsylvania line. After a season of training and drill his division took an active part in resisting the British in their campaign against Philadelphia. In the battle of Brandywine on Sept. 11, 1777, he occupied the center of the defense opposing the British at their main point of crossing. He was obliged to retreat when the American right was flanked by Cornwallis, who crossed the creek higher up. When Washington then withdrew to the north of the Schuylkill, he sent Wayne to circle around the rear of the British and to surprise and destroy their baggage train. Wayne, however, was himself surprised and, in the battle of Paoli, Sept. 20, received a drubbing. Being accused of negligence in this action, he demanded a court martial and was acquitted.

Rejoining Washington, he played a conspicuous part in the battle of Germantown, on Oct. 4, leading a spirited and almost victorious attack, but was forced back, when difficulties in the rear turned the victory into confusion and defeat. He wintered with Washington at Valley Forge and led the advance attack against the British at the battle of Monmouth on June 28, 1788.

In a reorganization of the army late in 1778, he was transferred to the command of a separate corps of Continental light infantry. This corps, under his leadership, on July 16, 1779, captured by surprise the garrison at Stony Point, the northernmost British post on the Hudson. Over five hundred prisoners, fifteen cannon, and some valuable stores were taken. For his conduct in this affair Congress ordered a medal to be struck and presented to him. Early in 1780 he led some desultory movements against the British on the lower Hudson, aimed to embarrass their collecting of supplies and cattle and to alleviate the attacks being made on Connecticut. When Arnold attempted to deliver West Point to the British on Sept. 25, 1780, Wayne's prompt movement to that post prevented a British occupation. After the Pennsylvania line mutinied in December 1780, Wayne was instrumental in presenting the soldiers' demands for pay and release to Congress and in getting Congress to redress their grievances. In the Yorktown campaign he was ordered south to serve under Lafayette, who was opposing Cornwallis on the lower James River. When Cornwallis withdrew from Williamsburg, Wayne was ordered to attack part of the British army that was mistakenly supposed to be separated from the rest. With some 800 men he attacked the British army of perhaps 5,000 at Green Spring, Va., on July 6, 1781, and, upon discovering the mistake, he led a charge into the British lines that deceived Cornwallis long enough to permit Wayne to extricate himself with only minor losses.

After the British surrender at Yorktown, Wayne, serving under Gen. Nathanael Greene, was sent to oppose the British, Loyalist, and Indian hostiles in Georgia. He had the tact to divide the Indian opposition by spreading news of the American victory so that, when the Creek irreconcilables attacked his small force in May 1782, he was able to rout them. He negotiated treaties of submission with the Creek and Cherokee in the winter of 1782 and 1783. In 1783 he retired from active service as brevet major-general.

From 1783 to 1792 he was engaged in civil pursuits in which he was less fortunate than in military affairs. The state of Georgia conferred upon him an eight-hundred-acre rice plantation, and he borrowed the necessary capital to work it from Dutch creditors, who subsequently foreclosed on the lands. In politics he was a conservative; he had a militarist's contempt for the radicals who took advantage of the revolt against Great Britain to fashion liberal constitutions like that of Pennsylvania, which he considered "not worth Defending" (Stillé, post, p. 71). During the war military affairs were his major consideration; but he said, "let us once be in a Condition to Vanquish these British Rebels and I answer for it that then your present Rulers will give way for better men which will produce better Measures" (Ibid.). Accordingly, as a member of the Pennsylvania council of censors in 1783, he favored the calling of a new constitutional convention. He was a representative of Chester County to the Pennsylvania General Assembly in 1784 and 1785. In 1787 he supported the new federal Constitution in the Pennsylvania ratifying convention. He was elected to Congress as a representative from Georgia and served from Mar. 4, 1791, to Mar. 21, 1792, when his seat was declared vacant because of irregularities in the election and in his residence qualification.

After the failure of Harmar and St. Clair to subdue the Indian tribes of the Wabash and Maumee rivers in 1791, Wayne was named by Washington as major-general in command of the rehabilitated American army. He was strongly opposed to the peace maneuvers of 1792 and 1793 but improved his time constructing a reliable military organization at his training camp at Legionville, Pa., and, later, near Fort Washington and Fort Jefferson in the Northwest Territory. On Aug. 20, 1794, he defeated the Indians at Fallen Timbers on the Maumee River near what is now Toledo, Ohio. This victory was the result of several factors. Wayne had far more resources at his command than had Harmar or St. Clair. He did not hazard an autumn campaign after he received news of the final failure of peace negotiations in August 1793. He was fortunate in that the Indians threw away their opportunity to isolate him, when they made a futile attack on Fort Recovery on June 29 and lost many discouraged tribesmen, who went home. He made every effort to avoid offending the British, thus robbing the Indians of the aid they fully expected in the moment of conflict. Finally, when the Indians had assembled at Fallen Timbers to fight, he delayed battle for three days. Therefore, when he attacked, a large part of the Indians were at a distance breaking their three-day fast, and the rest were in a half-starved condition. The complete submission and surrender at Greenville in August 1795 was made possible by Jay's treaty, the British desertion of the Indians, and Wayne's skill in convincing the tribesmen of the hopelessness of their cause without British support. He died at Presque Isle, now Erie, Pa., on his return from the occupation of the post of Detroit.

[Seventy-three vols. MSS. in possession of Hist. Soc. of Pa.; MSS. in Lib. of Cong.; C. J. Stillé, *Major-General Anthony Wayne* (1893), with many letters; S. W. Pennypacker, *Anthony Wayne* (1908), reprinted from *Pa. Mag. of Hist. and Biog.*, July 1908; J. H. Preston, *A Gentleman Rebel* (1930); T. A. Boyd, *Mad Anthony Wayne* (1929); Thomas Wyatt, *Memoirs* (1848), esp. pp. 17–39; Lieutenant Boyer, *A Jour. of Wayne's Campaign* (1866); *Orderly Book of . . . Wayne . . . 1776* (1859); H. B. Dawson, *Battles of the U. S.* (2 vols., 1858) and *The Assault on Stony Point* (1863); J. G. Leach, *Hist. of the Penrose Family* (1903), pp. 33, 38.] R. C. D.

WAYNE, ARTHUR TREZEVANT (Jan. 1, 1863–May 5, 1930), ornithologist, was a descendant of William Wayne who came to South Carolina about the time of the Revolution. He was born in Blackville, S. C., where his parents, Daniel Gabriel and Harriott Julia (Ward) Wayne, had removed to escape the rigors of the siege of Charleston. Returning home after the war, they sent Arthur at the age of six to Miss Charlotte Smith's school. In 1880 he was graduated with honors from the Charleston High School and completed his formal schooling. A collector of bird eggs from early boyhood, in 1874 he came under the influence of Dr. Gabriel Manigault, who encouraged him to collect for the Charleston Museum, where John Dancer taught him bird-skinning so well that it became with him a fine art. Being under the necessity to earn a living, however, he started life as a clerk in the cotton and naval stores firm of Barden & Murdock Company. This proved an unhappy connection for all concerned; highstrung, nervous, and violently impulsive, he was in taste and temperament wholly unsuited to business life. His next venture was equally unsuccessful. In 1883 an experience so fired the boy's enthusiasm that he abandoned all thought of business, for he accompanied William Brewster, 1851–1919 [q.v.], on several field trips near Charleston in an effort to rediscover Swainson's warbler. The following year on Brewster's return they resumed the quest, successfully; and in 1885 Wayne took the first nest and eggs known to science. In the same year, when returning from a brief trip to New York, he met Robert Ridgway [q.v.] in Washington, and formed another friendship of lifelong influence. On June 6, 1889, Wayne was married to Maria Louisa, the daughter of Philip E. and Elizabeth C. Porcher. They

had no children. She took from his shoulders so many burdens that her unselfish devotion might be said to have made possible his career.

After a few months at McPhersonville, S. C., where he collected for the market, the young couple returned to the home of the bride's parents. In 1892, accompanied by his wife, he began a series of field trips to Florida, taking many specimens of the ivory-billed woodpecker near Oldtown; in 1893 he collected Carolina paroquet near Kissimmee; and in 1894 he made an unsuccessful search for manatee on Indian River. They lived in a cottage near Mt. Pleasant, S. C., until in 1900 they moved into "Wayne's Place," built for them by Wayne's father. Here for thirty years Wayne gave himself to his work with enthusiasm. He was three times interrupted in his work between 1908 and 1928 by periods of nervous breakdown. In spite of these, his continuity of field work was remarkable, and, although he worked in an area already covered by Audubon and Bachman, he added in forty-five years about one bird a year to the fauna of his state. Two sub-species, Wayne's clapper rail and Wayne's warbler, have been named for him. Among his achievements were the re-discovery of Bachman's warbler in 1901, and his discovery of the breeding grounds of the white ibis in South Carolina in 1922. Besides numerous contributions to the *Auk* and other scientific periodicals, his publications include *Birds of South Carolina*, which appeared in 1910 as the first of the *Contributions from the Charleston Museum*, and *A List of Avian Species for which the Type Locality is South Carolina*, which appeared in 1917 as the third volume of Museum series. He contributed in all 190 papers to scientific journals. In 1928 he was elected fellow of the American Ornithologists' Union.

Small, slight, with nervous brown eyes and dark red hair and mustache, his appearance was not easily forgotten. His remarkable memory and rapid abundance of speech were equally impressive. Second to his passion for ornithology were his pleasure in grand opera and in genealogy. His widow survived him.

[Forty years' personal acquaintance; *Who's Who in America*, 1922–23. Alexander Sprunt's "In Memoriam" in the *Auk*, Jan. 1931, is a eulogy. See also *Auk*, July and Oct. 1930. Wayne's manuscript ornithological journal was purchased by the Charleston Museum with his personal collection of 1800 bird skins. Most of his correspondence was destroyed by Mrs. Wayne in 1930, but his letters from William Brewster are in the library of McGill University, Montreal. An obituary is to be found in the Charleston *News and Courier*, May 6, 1930.] A. K. G.

WAYNE, JAMES MOORE (c. 1790–July 5, 1867), associate justice of the United States Su·

preme Court, was a native of Savannah, Ga. His father, Richard Wayne, an officer in the British army, had emigrated to South Carolina, where on Sept. 14, 1769, he married Elizabeth Clifford, and thence moved to Savannah. James was the twelfth of thirteen children. He received his early education under the direction of a Mr. Mackay, an Irishman who had graduated at Trinity College, Dublin, and made such progress that he was ready to enter the College of New Jersey (Princeton) at an early age. Here he read promiscuously, took an active part in his literary society, and was graduated in 1808. Returning to Savannah, he took up the study of law under the tutelage of John Y. Noel. Within a few months thereafter his father died and his brother-in-law became his guardian. He was now sent to New Haven, Conn., to study under Judge Chauncey, who put him through a rigorous and systematic discipline in his chosen field. After twenty months, he returned to Savannah and spent five months more in the office of his guardian. In 1810 he began practice in partnership with Samuel M. Bond, and about this time married Mary Johnston Campbell, daughter to Alexander Campbell of Richmond, Va. They had three children.

At the outbreak of the War of 1812, Wayne became an officer of the Georgia Hussars. Near the end of the war, the Georgia legislature passed an act suspending the collection of debts. Wayne, upholding the view which was popular in the Savannah district, opposed this law and was elected to the Georgia House of Representatives, serving 1815-16. He was then elected mayor of Savannah and served two years. After having reformed the financial administration of the city, he returned to private practice in partnership with Richard R. Cuyler, a leader in the local movement for internal improvements. In this movement Wayne took an important part. Having attended an improvement convention in Knoxville, he found the Georgia route to the West slighted, and later, presiding over a convention in his own state, helped to initiate the development of such a route.

In 1824 he became a judge of the superior court of Georgia, resigning in 1829 to become a member of the federal House of Representatives, where he served for three consecutive terms. During this time he supported the administration of President Jackson in practically all its major measures, including the tariff and internal-improvement legislation as well as the Force Bill and the removal of the deposits from the Bank of the United States. Yet he was not a strict-constructionist, for he held that the federal government had the right to build roads and canals and to charter a bank, although he opposed these measures on grounds of expediency. He took a keen interest in the question of Indian removals and supported Georgia's claim to jurisdiction over the tribes within her borders on the ground that she had acquired this jurisdiction from England and had not surrendered it (*Register of Debates in Congress,* 21 Cong., 1 Sess., p. 1123; May 24, 1830). He served on many important committees and rose to the chairmanship of the Committee on Foreign Relations. Though not an orator, he was a forceful and logical speaker on numerous occasions.

For all these services, President Jackson, on Jan. 9, 1835, appointed him an associate justice of the Supreme Court of the United States. As a member of this tribunal, his opinions in admiralty cases—particularly in that of *Waring* vs. *Clarke* (5 *Howard*, 441)—and in cases involving lands acquired from foreign countries are especially valuable. When the Civil War came on, he took the side of the Union and retained his seat on the bench of the Supreme Court, holding it until his death, from typhoid fever, in Washington, on July 5, 1867. He was the last surviving associate of John Marshall on the bench of the Supreme Court. His remains were taken to Savannah for interment in Laurel Grove Cemetery.

[Wayne's opinions appear in 34–72 *U. S. Reports.* The only good account of his life appeared in John Livingston, *Biog. Sketches of Distinguished Am. Lawyers* (*c.* 1850 ; title page missing) ; this was abridged by George White in *Hist. Colls. of Georgia* (1855). See also "Memoranda," 73 *U. S.,* vii–x ; J. G. Bullock, *A Hist. and Geneal. of the Families of Bellinger and De Veaux* (1895), pp. 85–88; A. G. Feather, *The Supreme Court of the U. S.* (1900); H. L. Carson, *The Supreme Court of the U. S.* (1892) ; Charles Warren, *The Supreme Court in U. S. Hist.* (3 vols., 1922) ; *Biog. Dir. Am. Cong.* (1928); *Daily National Intelligencer* (Washington), July 6, 1867.]   T. P. A.

WEARE, MESHECH (Jan. 16, 1713–Jan. 14, 1786), colonial leader, Revolutionary patriot, and jurist, was born in Hampton Falls, N. H., the son of Nathaniel Weare and his second wife, Mary Waite. He was a descendant of Nathaniel Weare who had settled in Newbury, Mass., as early as 1638. His father was a judge of the superior court, and Meshech, the youngest son in a family of fourteen children, received a good education and was graduated at Harvard in 1735. On July 20, 1738, he was married to Elizabeth Shaw and after her death, to Mehitable Wainwright, on Dec. 11, 1746. He had two children by his first wife, and eight by his second.

He had expected to enter the ministry but abandoned his intention not long after graduation. For some years he devoted himself to the development and management of his extensive farm property. He also studied law and after 1745 gave steadily increasing attention to public affairs. From 1745 to 1755 he represented Hampton in the legislature, and with occasional interruptions this service continued until the overturn of royal government in 1775. This legislative experience was reinforced by a wide variety of committee service, by three years as speaker, eight as clerk, and by attendance at the Albany Congress in 1754. He was also a justice in the superior court from 1747 to 1775 and a colonel of militia.

He was over sixty years of age when the Revolution began, had many associations with the royalist element and was naturally conservative. His contemporary, Paine Wingate [q.v.], declares that he viewed the revolutionary movement "with caution, and certainly with no prepossession in favor of measures the country was adopting" (post, p. 245). His temperate advice at the early provincial congresses aroused some opposition among the more radical leaders, but when the break with the mother country was irreparable his accession to the Revolutionary cause made him the outstanding civilian figure in his state for the ensuing decade. Between 1776 and 1784 he served as president of the Council which was charged with the executive functions of the state, and in addition was chairman of the important committee of safety. He was, as a result, in contact with both continental and other state authorities and much more than a local leader.

In addition to his executive duties he was chief justice from 1776 to 1782, participated in many constitutional discussions, and exercised widespread influence as a leader of public opinion. In 1784 he was elected president of the state (the title of governor did not come into use for several years). A year later he resigned all offices because of failing health. His contemporaries lay great stress on his equable temper, fairness, shrewdness and honesty, qualities of the utmost value in such a formative period. His extensive correspondence and other papers after various vicissitudes passed into the custody of the New Hampshire and Massachusetts Historical Societies and the Library of Congress. They constitute a valuable source of Revolutionary history.

[Weare's official career can be readily traced in the *State Papers of New Hampshire.* See especially vol. XXI (1892), which contains a brief sketch by William Plumer. Consult also W. M. Sargent, *The Weare Family of Hampton, N. H.* (1879); sketch by E. S. Stearns in Warren Brown, *Hist. of the Town of Hampton Falls, N. H.,* vol. I (1900), also privately printed in 1894; Joseph Dow, *Hist. of the Town of Hampton, N. H.* (1893), vol. II; F. B. Sanborn, "Meshech

Weare," *Proc. N. H. Hist. Soc.,* vol. V (1917), pp. 411–13; Paine Wingate, sketch of Weare in *Colls. N. H. Hist. Soc.,* vol. V (1837); C. H. Bell, *The Bench and Bar of N. H.* (1894); F. M. Colby, "The Governor Weare Estate," *Granite Monthly,* July 1881.]

W. A. R.

WEATHERFORD, WILLIAM (c. 1780– Mar. 9, 1824), Indian chief, known also as Red Eagle, was born among the Creek Indians. Most of his life he lived on the right bank of the Alabama River within the present limits of Elmore County, a few miles above the site of Montgomery, Ala., and it is usually said that he was born there. Statements concerning his parentage are contradictory; that his mother was a Seminole and his father a "pedlar" of uncertain character, that he was the son of Charles Weatherford, a prosperous Scotch or English trader, and Sehoy, the half-sister of Alexander McGillivray [q.v.]. He had two Indian wives, Mary Moniac, who died in 1804, and Sapoth Thlanie. Actuated to war against the whites by the visit of Tecumseh [q.v.] in 1811, he, nevertheless, did not take up arms until after the battle of Tippecanoe. Then, ignorant that his cause was already hopeless, he led his followers in a war of destruction and won for himself the hatred and malice of the whites. Although they accused him of the utmost limits of personal degradation, they also described him as able, eloquent, and courageous. At the outbreak of the Creek War he was responsible for the massacre at Fort Mims on Aug. 30, 1813, in which some 500 victims were put to death, men, women, and children with indiscriminate cruelty. He was one of the leaders, apparently with Menewa [q.v.] a principal leader, of the Creeks in the disaster at Horseshoe Bend in 1814, when Andrew Jackson [q.v.] defeated about 1000 Indian warriors barricaded in the great bend of the Tallapoosa River. Shortly after the battle he surrendered to Andrew Jackson (for a discussion of the manner of this surrender and a denial of its dramatic character see *Alabama Historical Society Transactions,* II, 1898).

In the remaining years of his life he seems to have accepted the situation and lived fairly prosperously on a plantation among the white people of Monroe County. His personal reputation improved with that adjustment, and no more was heard of his dissolute habits, whether from a reformation of character or from lack of malice is uncertain. In 1817 he married his third wife, Mary Stiggins, a white woman. He bore no important part in the difficulties and anxieties of his doomed people, and, dying before westward removal was actually accomplished, he was buried in the beloved land of his forefathers.

[G. C. Eggleston, *Red Eagle* (1878) ; J. D. Dreisback, "Weatherford," *Ala. Hist. Reporter*, Mar., Apr. 1884 ; James Mooney, "Myths of the Cherokee," *Nineteenth Ann. Report of the Bureau of Am. Ethnology*, pt. 1 (1900) ; N. H. Claiborne, *Notes on the War in the South* (1819) ; J. F. H. Claiborne, *Life and Times of Gen. Sam. Dale* (1860) ; J. H. Eaton, *The Life of Andrew Jackson* (1817), ch. V ; A. J. Pickett, *Hist. of Ala.* (1851), vol. II, pp. 267–84, 341–53 ; H. S. Halbert and T. H. Ball, *The Creek War* (1895).]   K. E. C.

WEAVER, AARON WARD (July 1, 1832–Oct. 2, 1919), naval officer, son of Lieut. William Augustus Weaver of the United States Navy, and Jane (Van Wyck) Weaver, was born in Washington, D. C. On May 10, 1848, he was appointed a midshipman in the navy and ordered to the coast of Brazil, where he served for four years on the sloop *St. Louis* and the frigate *Congress*. In 1853 he entered the United States Naval Academy, studied there for one year, and was graduated in the class of 1854 and commissioned a passed midshipman. He was given his first assignment in the new steam navy on the *Fulton*. In 1856 he was ordered to Coast Survey duty on the steamer *Walker*, and in 1857 was transferred to the steamer *Arctic*. On this vessel, under Commander O. H. Berryman, he assisted in the survey of Trinity Bay, Newfoundland, for the projected Atlantic telegraph cable, and in deep-sea soundings in the Gulf Stream. Late that year he was ordered to the *Marion* and cruised off the coast of Africa on the lookout for slavers. Off the Congo River the *Marion* captured the bark *Ardennes*, and Weaver, then a lieutenant, brought her to New York, arriving in July 1859.

When the Civil War broke out he was ordered to duty on the steam frigate *Susquehanna*. He participated in the capture of Fort Hatteras and Fort Clarke at Hatteras Inlet, N. C., Aug. 28–29, 1861, and of Fort Beauregard and Fort Walker, Port Royal, S. C., Nov. 7, 1861. The following April, before the fall of Fort Pulaski, he had charge of the *Susquehanna's* armed launches, convoying guns up to the army battery at Venus Point. When in May 1862 the *Susquehanna* cooperated with McClellan's operations in the Peninsular campaign, Weaver participated in the engagement with the Confederate batteries at Sewell's Point. That autumn he was given the command of the steam gunboat *Winona* and joined the Mississippi River Squadron. A period of most arduous service patrolling the lower river followed: on Dec. 14, 1862, he engaged a Confederate battery on Profit Island near Port Hudson, his ship being struck twenty-seven times; the following summer the *Winona* shelled and drove off a troop of Texas cavalry which had attacked the town of Plaquemine, La.;

ten days later Weaver with the assistance of two other gunboats routed a large force of Texas cavalry when they attacked Fort Butler, Donaldsonville, La., over one hundred Confederates being killed or wounded. For this service he was commended by Farragut, and by Maj. H. M. Porter of the army. In January 1864 Weaver was ordered to join the South Atlantic Blockading Squadron and captured the blockade runner *Ada*. In June he was transferred to the steamship *Chippewa* and in her participated in the first attack on Fort Fisher. After the battle Admiral Porter gave him the command of the monitor *Mahopac*, and in this vessel he took part in the second bombardment and the capture of the fort. For his part in the action, he was favorably mentioned by Porter and recommended for promotion, and was also mentioned favorably by Commodore William Radford, commander of the ironclad division. Weaver in the *Mahopac* assisted in the capture of Charleston, and participated in the night bombardment of the works near Richmond just prior to the evacuation of the city.

After the war he rose through the grades to the rank of rear admiral (June 27, 1893), his work being of an uneventful routine nature; on Sept. 26, 1893, he was retired. Thereafter he lived quietly in Washington. On Feb. 13, 1864, he married Ida Hyatt of Baltimore.

[L. R. Hamersly, *The Records of Living Officers of the U. S. Navy and Marine Corps* (4th ed., 1890) ; "Log of the Winona" (MS.), Navy Dept.; U. S. Navy Dept. Office of Naval Records, and Archives; *War of the Rebellion: Official Records (Navy)*, 1 ser., vols. XI, XII, XV, XVI, XIX, XX, and *(Army)*, 1 ser., XXVI (pt. 1), 202–03 ; ann. reports of the U. S. Coast Survey, 1856–57 ; *Who's Who in America*, 1918–19 ; *Army and Navy Reg.*, Oct. 11, 1919 ; *Army and Navy Jour.*, Mar. 5, 1864, p. 477 ; *Evening Star* (Washington), Oct. 3, 1919.]   L. H. B.

WEAVER, JAMES BAIRD (June 12, 1833–Feb. 6, 1912), soldier, congressman, Greenback and Populist candidate for the presidency, was born at Dayton, Ohio, fifth of the thirteen children of Abram and Susan (Imlay) Weaver. His father, a skilled mechanic and millwright, moved in 1835 to a forest-enclosed farm near Cassopolis, Mich., and eight years later to a quarter section of virgin prairie in what soon became Davis County, Iowa. Here on a typical frontier young Weaver grew to manhood. He attended the country schools, and when his father's election to a minor county office took the family to Bloomfield, the county-seat, he had the advantage of the somewhat better schools of that small town. For several years (1847–51) he carried the mail through roadless country and across bridgeless streams, from Bloomfield to Fairfield,

Iowa. In 1853 he accompanied a relative overland to California, and within a few months was cured completely of the gold fever, from which he had suffered since 1848. On his return to Iowa he worked in a store at Bonaparte, and had he consented might have become a partner in the business. By this time, however, he had discovered his aptitude for public speaking, particularly on controversial subjects, and had resolved to become a lawyer. In 1855, after borrowing one hundred dollars at thirty-three and one-third per cent. interest, he entered the Cincinnati Law School. A year later he was graduated and returned to Bloomfield to practise law.

Almost immediately he became absorbed in politics. He had been a Democrat, but, according to his own account, was converted to Free-Soil principles by reading *Uncle Tom's Cabin* and the *New York Tribune*. From 1857 until the outbreak of the Civil War he was active in local Republican circles, and he attended the convention which nominated Lincoln for the presidency, although not as a delegate. When Lincoln called for troops in 1861, Weaver volunteered and was made first lieutenant of the 2nd Iowa Infantry. He was in the thick of the fighting at Fort Donelson, at Shiloh, and at Corinth. On July 25, 1862, probably because his colonel had great confidence in him he was advanced over all the captains of his regiment to the rank of major, and when, during the battle of Corinth, his colonel and lieutenant-colonel were both mortally wounded, he took command. His conduct during this emergency was so gallant that afterwards, with the full approval of the officers who had so recently outranked him, he was commissioned colonel. During the winter of 1863–64, he was stationed at Pulaski, Tenn., where, under orders of a superior officer, he obtained by an assessment upon the inhabitants the means needed to care for some Confederate refugees. Later his political opponents made much more of this incident than the facts warranted. When his term of enlistment expired, in May 1864, he returned to his home in Iowa, and on Mar. 13, 1865, he was brevetted brigadier-general.

Weaver's services to his country and his party launched him upon what would normally have been a successful political career. He failed in 1865 to obtain a nomination for the post of lieutenant-governor, but in 1866 he was elected district attorney of the second Iowa judicial district, and in 1867 he received an appointment as federal assessor of internal revenue for the first district of Iowa, a post which he held until 1873. From this time forward, however, he lost ground with the Republican leaders in his state. He was

a devout Methodist, utterly incorruptible, and an ardent prohibitionist; he denounced the extortions of the politically important railways and other predatory corporations; and he objected strenuously to the stand his party was taking on the currency question. Nevertheless, such was his popularity that only the sharpest political trickery prevented him from obtaining the Republican nomination for Congress in 1874, and for governor in 1875. Undoubtedly these defeats, which he believed wholly unmerited, served to undermine his party loyalty, and to drive him towards the "independents," or "Greenbackers," for whose principles he was developing a great affinity. His views on the money question would not at a later date have been regarded as extreme. He was not an advocate of unlimited inflation, nor of debt repudiation, but he held to the quantity theory of money, and opposed what he deemed the systematic efforts of the creditor class to appreciate the purchasing power of the dollar. As a Greenbacker he won a seat in Congress in 1878, ran for president in 1880, was defeated for Congress in 1882, but won again in 1884 and 1886.

When the Farmers' Alliance succeeded the Greenbackers as the chief exponent of soft-money views, Weaver hastened to identify himself with that organization, and he took a leading part in transforming it into the People's, or Populist, party. With but little opposition he was accorded the Populist nomination for the presidency in 1892. Throughout the campaign the magnetism of his personality, enhanced rather than diminished by his whitened hair and his generally patriarchal appearance, was as effective as on the battlefield of Corinth. His commanding presence coupled with the force and fire of his oratory gave him a bearing where a less able speaker would have been laughed off the stage. Only in the South, where falsified accounts of his Pulaski record were deliberately circulated, was he subjected to the discourtesies so commonly accorded to third-party orators. His defeat was inevitable, but he received a popular vote of over a million, and twenty-two votes in the electoral college. His book, *A Call to Action* (1892), published during the campaign, summarized his own political principles and furnished much of the ammunition used by his supporters during the fray.

Weaver's victories in the eighties had been won by the assistance of the Democrats, and after 1892 he was one of the leading advocates of a fusion of all soft-money forces. When in 1896 Bryan captured the Democratic nomination, Weaver strongly favored his nomination by the

Populists also, and helped to bring it about. Fusion, however, rang the deathknell of Populism, and within a few years Weaver found himself, together with most of the Populist leaders, a Democrat, and without a future in politics. With his political career at an end, his neighbors in the town of Colfax, Iowa, where he spent the later years of his life, showed their good will by choosing him to be their mayor. On July 13, 1858, he married Clara Vinson, a school-teacher who had come to Iowa from St. Mary's, Ohio; they were the parents of five girls and two boys. The year of his death, 1912, there was published *Past and Present of Jasper County, Iowa*, in two volumes, bearing his name as editor-in-chief.

[James B. Weaver, Jr., of Des Moines, Iowa, has in his possession "Memoranda with Respect to the Life of James Baird Weaver" (unpublished), prepared by Weaver himself. Substantial extracts from this document, which gives information only down to 1859, are printed in F. E. Haynes, *James Baird Weaver* (1919), a satisfactory account of Weaver's political career, gleaned largely from the newspapers, and from a scrapbook which Weaver kept. See also E. A. Allen, *The Life and Public Services of James Baird Weaver* (1892); H. C. Evans, *The Pioneers and Politics of Davis County, Iowa* (1929); S. D. Dillaye, "Life of Gen. J. B. Weaver" in *Our Presidential Candidates and Political Compendium* (1880); F. E. Haynes, *Third Party Movements Since the Civil War* (1916); J. D. Hicks, *The Populist Revolt* (1931); *Biog. Dir. Am. Cong.* (1928); F. B. Heitman, *Hist. Reg. and Dict. U. S. Army* (1903); *Who's Who in America, 1910–11*; *Register and Leader* (Des Moines), Feb. 7, 8, 9, 1912.]   J. D. H—s.

WEAVER, PHILIP (b. 1791), cotton manufacturer, was a son of John and Ruth (Wilbur) Weaver of North Scituate, R. I., and a descendant of Clement Weaver who was in Weymouth, Mass., by 1643. As early as 1812 Philip went from his home in Coventry, R. I., to work for the Dudley Cotton Manufacturing Company, Dudley, Mass.; in 1815 he was associated with Weaver, Hutchings & Company, for whom he did work on patterns and rollers. Early in 1816 he moved to Spartanburg District, S. C., accompanied by his brothers, John, Wilbur, and Lindsay, as well as William Sheldon, John Clark, Thomas Slack, William Bates, and Thomas Hutchings. He was unhappy in South Carolina, chiefly because he felt that he and his family— he had married Miriam Keene, by whom he had four daughters—were "looked down upon with contempt" because they were "opposed to the abominable practice of slavery" (Wallace, *post*, II, 411); nevertheless, he remained there for a number of years. Between December 1816 and 1820 he and his associates experienced serious difficulties because of shortage of cash; the Spartanburg Judgment Roll lists several judgments against them for both large and small sums. In 1819 Weaver was arrested for non-payment of

one of these claims, but one Thomas Craven went his bail. The Weaver mill was on land owned by Rev. Benjamin Wofford who was at that early date accumulating the fortune with which he later founded Wofford College. In December 1818 he sold to Nathaniel Gist the tract of sixty acres on the Tiger River containing the mill, but Philip and John Weaver continued to operate the mill after the sale. Philip Weaver owned no land in Spartanburg district until Aug. 14, 1819, when John Withers of Columbia sold Weaver & Company 300 acres on the east side of the Tiger.

Whether or not the Weaver mill was the first cotton mill in Spartanburg District has been a matter of controversy. Kohn (*post*) inclines toward the view that the Weavers were first, while Landrum (*post*) is inclined to accept the claim made for George and Leonard Hill. Wallace (*post*) thinks it reasonably clear that the Weavers a little antedated the Hills as manufacturers in Spartanburg. Certainly both the Weaver and Hill mills provided an energetic element in the cotton manufacturing industry in Spartanburg and Greenville counties which undoubtedly laid the foundation for the extensive textile development before 1860.

Philip Weaver left Spartanburg District before 1826 and subsequently settled in Attica, Ind., where shortly before the Civil War he was killed by a runaway horse. His former associates continued in the manufacturing business: John Weaver built a mill nineteen miles from Greenville, on Thompson's Beaver Dam, and operated it until his death several years after the Civil War; Hutchings built and operated several mills in succession with apparent profit, while in the thirties William Bates established the Batesville Cotton Mill.

[L. E. Weaver, *Hist. and Geneal. of a Branch of the Weaver Family* (1928); Yates Snowden, *Hist. of S. C.* (1920), II, 1167; D. D. Wallace, *The Hist. of S. C.* (1934), II, 411, III, 56; August Kohn, *The Cotton Mills of S. C.* (1907); J. B. O. Landrum, *Hist. of Spartanburg County* (1900), pp. 157–65; Philip Weaver's account book, Wofford College Library; S. C. Judgment Rolls, 532, 593, 595; Spartanburg Mesne Conveyance Office, Q 320, R 9, 10, 12, 79; Greenville Mesne Conveyance Office, T 342.]   R. G. S.

WEAVER, WILLIAM DIXON (Aug. 30, 1857–Nov. 2, 1919), electrical engineer, was born in Greensburg, Pa., the son of Caspar and Maria (Massena) Weaver. After completing his elementary education, in 1875 he entered the department of agriculture and mechanic arts in Kentucky University (later the University of Kentucky). A year later he obtained an appointment to the United States Naval Academy, from which he was graduated in 1880 as a cadet engineer. He accompanied the first Greely relief expedition in 1883 on the *Yantic,* made a cruise of the world as an assistant engineer on the *Omaha* (1885–88), and spent two years in the waters of the Orient. During a leave of absence in 1884 he studied electricity and conducted some investigations in the electrical laboratories of the Sorbonne, Paris, and the School of Electrical Engineering, London. While he was stationed at the Brooklyn navy yard (1890) he designed an electrical recorder, used in speed trials, and an apparatus with electrical adjustments for the calibration of steam-engine indicators. Resigning from the navy in 1892, he joined the firm of E. G. Bernard, manufacturers of electrical apparatus in Troy, N. Y., but after a year he gave this up to engage in editorial work. From 1893 to 1896 he was editor of the *Electrical World.* In 1896 he became associated with James H. McGraw in the founding of the *American Electrician* and was the first editor. Three years later McGraw consolidated the *Electrical World* and *Electrical Engineering* and subsequently absorbed the *American Electrician,* publishing all three as the *Electrical World.* Except for a leave of absence during the Spanish-American War, when he served as volunteer chief engineer on the *Glacier,* Weaver continued as editor until his retirement in May 1912.

He was intensely interested in electrical engineering as a profession and in the organization of professional societies. It was he who in 1895 made the suggestion to Andrew Carnegie which later led to the erection of a building in New York for the engineering societies of the United States. To him is due the plan of organization and development of the Society of Illuminating Engineers. He was a founder of the American Electro-Chemical Society and for six years a manager of the American Institute of Electrical Engineers. He was also active in the development of the electrical engineering library, part of the great Engineering Societies' Library in New York. In 1904 he was made treasurer and business manager of the International Electrical Congress held in St. Louis, Mo., and did much to make it successful. In commemoration of his services in the organization and development of the American Institute of Electrical Engineers, a memorial tablet to him was unveiled at the time of the annual meeting, May 16, 1919. His collection of publications on the French Revolution (now at Princeton University), to which he devoted his leisure, was said to be one of the largest in existence on that subject. After retiring to his home in Charlottesville, Va., he was active in civic affairs. On July 26, 1901, in Bremen, Germany, he married Mildred Niebuhr, by whom

he had seven children. He died in Charlottesville, survived by his wife and six children.

[*Who's Who in America,* 1920–21; *Navy Registers,* 1881–92; *Electrical World,* Oct. 25, Nov. 1, Nov. 8, 1919; *Electrical Rev.* (Chicago), Nov. 15, 1919; *Proc. Am. Institute of Electrical Engineers,* 1919, vol. XXXVIII (n.d.); *Sci.,* June 4, 1920; *Princeton Alumni Weekly,* Oct. 17, 1923; obituary in *N. Y. Times,* Nov. 3, 1919; names of parents, dates of marriage and death, and other information from Mrs. W. D. Weaver of Charlottesville.]   C. W. M.

WEBB, ALEXANDER STEWART (Feb. 15, 1835–Feb. 12, 1911), soldier, college president, was born in New York, the son of James Watson Webb [*q.v.*] and his first wife, Helen Lispenard Stewart. After training in private schools Webb was appointed a cadet in the United States Military Academy, where he was graduated in 1855 and commissioned second lieutenant of artillery. In this same year he married Anna, daughter of Henry Rutgers Remsen. In 1856 he saw dangerous and exacting duty in Florida during the war against the Seminole Indians. After a year of garrison duty at Fort Independence, Mass., and Fort Snelling, Minn., he returned to the Academy, Nov. 10, 1857, as assistant professor of mathematics.

At the beginning of the Civil War he was commissioned first lieutenant, 2nd Artillery, and returned to duty in the field. Having distinguished himself at Fort Pickens and in the first battle of Bull Run, he was appointed assistant to the chief of artillery of the Army of the Potomac. From March to November 1862 he was inspector general on the staff of Gen. William F. Barry [*q.v.*] and served with distinction in the battles of Yorktown, the Seven Days, and Malvern Hill. At the end of the Peninsula campaign, he was sent to Washington as inspector of artillery in the camp of instruction, but in January 1863 was reassigned to duty in the field as assistant inspector general of the V Corps. Relieved of this duty in May, he assumed command of the 2nd (Philadelphia) Brigade, Second Division, II Corps, which he led at Chancellorsville and at Gettysburg. In the latter action Webb's brigade occupied the Bloody Angle, where it bore the brunt of Pickett's charge and had a decisive part in his repulse. For "distinguished personal gallantry in the battle of Gettysburg" Webb was awarded the Congressional Medal of Honor, Sept. 28, 1891.

After Gettysburg he served continuously, commanding the Second Division, II Corps, until the battle of Spotsylvania Court House (May 1864), where he was severely wounded. After his recovery he did court-martial duty in New York until January 1865, when he became chief-of-staff to General Meade. At the end of six months he was appointed assistant inspector general, Division of the Atlantic, which duty he relinquished in February 1866. From June of that year until October 1868 he was principal assistant professor of history, ethics, and constitutional and international law at the Military Academy, then rejoined his regiment for service in Washington. He was unassigned for a year, and honorably discharged from the army at his own request, Dec. 31, 1870, with the rank of lieutenant-colonel. During his career in the service he occupied every rank to that of major-general, either by appointment or by brevet. The honors that came to him in recognition of personal gallantry indicate his importance as a soldier; he had little experience in leading masses of men or in planning large-scale military activities, but he was an inspiring commander under fire and an intrepid fighter. He enjoyed the highest respect and admiration of his men, who, in later years, delighted to honor him by election to high office in veteran organizations, and after his death took a leading part in causing the State of New York to erect a statue of him at the Bloody Angle.

On July 21, 1869, Webb was elected president of the College of the City of New York, in succession to Horace Webster, also a graduate of West Point, and in accordance with the custom then prevailing was appointed also to the chair of political philosophy. He continued in active service until failing powers forced his retirement on Dec. 1, 1902. Though much admired by faculty and students for his personal qualities, he made no original contribution as an educator. He rigidly maintained the fixed curriculum set by his precedessor, and expended a disproportionate amount of his own time and of that of the faculty on routine matters of administration. During his tenure of the presidency, the College maintained the high standards of scholarship set from the beginning, without significant advancement in the scope of its work, but the picturesqueness of his personality and the dignity of his bearing brought to the life of the institution an impressiveness that in some measure made up for his lack of leadership in scholarly attainment. In 1881 he published *The Peninsula: McClellan's Campaign of 1862.*

After his retirement Webb lived quietly at Riverdale, going to the city only occasionally for patriotic celebrations or to fulfill his duties as a member of the New York Monuments Commission (1895–1911) and member of the council of the Military Service Institution. He died at the end of his seventy-sixth year, survived by four daughters and a son.

[*Who's Who in America,* 1910–11; F. B. Heitman, *Hist. Reg. and Dict. U. S. Army* (1903); *The City College: Memories of Sixty Years* (1907), pp. 107–36; *City College Quart.,* Mar. 1910, Mar., June 1911; *In Memoriam, Alexander Stewart Webb, 1835–1911* (Albany, 1916); *Forty-second Ann. Reunion, Asso. Grads. U. S. Mil. Acad.* (1911); *N. Y. Times,* Feb. 12, 13, 14, 1911.]   D. A. R.

WEBB, CHARLES HENRY (Jan. 24, 1834–May 24, 1905), "John Paul," author, was born at Rouse's Point, N. Y., the son of Nathan and Philena King (Paddock) Webb, and was educated in schools at Champlain, N. Y., and Toronto. At seventeen he went to New York City to try newspaper work. As a result of reading the newly published *Moby Dick,* however, he soon shipped on the whaler *Walter Scott* out of Martha's Vineyard, and spent three and a half years in the South Seas and the Arctic. Upon his return in 1855 he rejoined his family, who had moved to Illinois, and for several years engaged in business with an elder brother at Fulton City. Early in 1859 he began contributing poems, usually humorous, to *Harper's Weekly,* and in 1860 obtained a position on the *New York Times,* for which he wrote "Minor Topics," a column of comment. In 1861 he went to the front as a war correspondent, and was present at Bull Run and in some of the early campaigns in the Shenandoah Valley. His articles appeared sometimes over his initials and sometimes, apparently, over the pseudonym, Leo. An association struck up with another correspondent, Edmund Clarence Stedman [*q.v.*], ripened into a lifelong friendship.

From 1863 to 1866 Webb was in California, at first (1863–64) as a member of the staff of the San Francisco *Evening Bulletin.* Although in later years he vigorously and quite properly objected to being classed as a "California humorist," nevertheless these three years were the time of his greatest literary activity and influence. He soon won leadership in the city's literary circle through his facile pen, warm personality, and ready wit, this last only enhanced by a slight impediment to his speech. He became the close friend of Bret Harte, and later of Mark Twain [*qq.v.*]. All three contributed to the *Californian,* which Webb founded as owner and first editor in May 1864. Webb in addition contributed, usually under his pen-name of Inigo, to the *Golden Era,* the *Sacramento Union,* and the *New York Times.* He also wrote two comedies, *Arrah-na-poke* (a parody of Boucicault's *Arrah-na-poque*) and *Our Friend from Victoria,* both produced in San Francisco. Unfortunately the money which he won by writing, he lost by speculation in mines, so that in 1866 he returned to New York City little the richer.

For the next few years he contributed to *Harper's Monthly,* the *Springfield Republican,* and other papers, published *Liffith Lank* (1866), a parody of Charles Reade's *Griffith Gaunt,* and *St. Twel'mo,* a parody of Augusta Jane Evans' *St. Elmo,* and more surely established his name by becoming the sponsor and publisher of Mark Twain's first book, *The Celebrated Jumping Frog of Calaveras County* (1867). On Oct. 11, 1870, he married Elizabeth W. Shipman of Brooklyn, N. Y. In 1872–73 he engaged in business as a broker and banker, but he was caught in the panic of 1873 and returned to journalism. About this time he began the "John Paul" letters for the *New York Tribune,* collected in 1874 as *John Paul's Book.* This became his best-known volume, and resulted in his being known almost as much by the pseudonym as by his own name. For several years after this time he lived abroad with his family. In 1876 he published *Sea-Weed and What We Seed* and *Parodies: Prose and Verse.* After these volumes, however, his interests turned more to *vers de société* (*Vagrom Verses,* 1889; *With Lead and Line,* 1901). His character, always delightful, mellowed still further with age. He frequently spent his summers in Nantucket, but kept his permanent home in New York City, where he died. In his later life he was greatly interested in invention. He patented an adding machine (1868) and a cartridge-loading machine (1874). In 1893, after nearly a decade of preparatory work, manufacture of his "ribbon adder" was begun, but the financial disasters of that year wrecked the enterprise.

In spite of his decided talents, Webb seems unlikely to be long remembered. His parodies could not survive the writings from which they sprang; *John Paul's Book* invites comparison with Mark Twain's work and suffers accordingly; his verses are clever and graceful, but fail to attain a highly poetic level. He will probably be best known as a "western humorist" for his part in the outburst of literary activity which marked San Francisco in the sixties.

[*Who's Who in America,* 1903–05; E. C. Stedman, in *Critic,* Mar. 1902, with portrait; C. W. Stoddard, in *Pacific Monthly,* Mar. 1908; G. R. Stewart, Jr., *Bret Harte* (1931); obituaries in *Publisher's Weekly,* June 3, 1905; and *N. Y. Times,* May 25, 1905; information from Elizabeth Holder Webb, Webb's daughter.]

G. R. S., Jr.

WEBB, DANIEL (*c.* 1700–Nov. 11, 1773), British general, was an Englishman, probably connected with the Wiltshire Webbs. In March 1721, he purchased an ensigncy in the 1st Foot Guards; in April 1722, he became captain-lieutenant, with the rank of captain, in the same corps; and from 1725 to 1732 he led a company in Grove's regiment of foot. In 1732 he became a captain in the 4th Horse, which under Ligonier developed into one of the finest cavalry regiments in the army (Black Horse, 7th Dragoon Guards). He remained with that corps for twenty years. In 1742 he attained the rank of major and led a squadron at Dettingen and at Fontenoy; a few days after the latter battle, in 1745, he was made lieutenant-colonel and commanded the corps for ten years. Such service brought him favorably to the attention of Cumberland, the captain-general, and he was probably the Webb who in 1754 carried out the thankless task of settling the army accounts with Holland for the previous war. In November 1755, he succeeded Dunbar as colonel of the 48th foot, then in America.

On Cumberland's recommendation, who thought him a "sensible, discreet man as well as a good officer," Webb early in 1756 was selected as third in command in North America under Lord Loudoun and James Abercromby [*qq.v.*]; he was given a temporary commission as commander-in-chief, and sent to New York to supervise preparations for the campaign. Reaching New York only nine days before Abercromby, he never took over officially the chief command. The following August, on the news of the fall of Oswego, Loudoun made him a temporary major-general and sent him up the Mohawk River to make a stand against Montcalm's expected attack on the forts there. Panic-stricken by Indian rumors, Webb on his own initiative destroyed the forts and precipitately retreated. The colonists, suspended, as one of them said, in a "spider's web," made him their chief target of scorn. Their outspoken bitterness combined that winter with a severe attack of the palsy to destroy completely his confidence in his own judgment, yet Loudoun had no one else to leave in command in New York in 1757 when the main army was in Nova Scotia. Distrustful of the provincials, fearful that he had been left without sufficient troops, Webb neglected to strengthen the New York posts or to take any of the measures advised by Loudoun. Of Montcalm's designs on Fort William Henry he had sufficient warning, yet for the six days of the siege in August he lay at Fort Edward, fourteen miles to the south, without attempting relief. Pitt recalled him in December 1757. He was, but probably because of his illness, the most incompetent staff officer who served in America during the Seven Years' War. In 1758, as quartermaster-general, he served in Germany, and in 1760 commanded a brigade at Warbourg. He was promoted major-general in 1759, and lieutenant-general in 1761. He became colonel in

1766 of the 8th Foot and in 1772 of the 14th Dragoons.

[Charles Dalton, *George the First's Army*, vol. II (1912); Army Lists; Richard Cannon, *Hist. Records of the British Army: the Eighth or King's Reg. of Foot* (1844), *the Fourteenth, or the King's Light Dragoons* (1847); *Hist. MSS. Commission, Reports on Various Colls.*, vol. VIII (1913); S. M. Pargellis, *Lord Loudoun in North America* (1933); *War in North America, 1748–1765* (1936).]   S. M. P.

WEBB, GEORGE JAMES (June 24, 1803–Oct. 7, 1887), musician, composer, was born at "Rushmore Lodge," Wiltshire, near Salisbury, England. His father, James Millett Webb, was a landowner with large holdings. His wife was Isabel Ann Archer, and George was their eldest child. The environment of the home was musical; the father was an amateur singer, and the mother a talented musician who gave her son music lessons before he was seven years of age. At a boarding school in Salisbury he studied music with Alexander Lucas, and learned to play the violin and piano. He subsequently decided to make music his profession and studied in Falmouth with an organist of that city. Later he determined to emigrate to America and booked passage for New York, but was persuaded to change his destination by the captain of a ship sailing for Boston. He landed in Boston in 1830, and within a few weeks he was appointed organist of the Old South Church. He soon became associated with Lowell Mason [*q.v.*] in his educational projects, and was placed in charge of the secular music of the newly organized Boston Academy of Music. He organized an orchestra at the Academy which gave regular concerts for fourteen years—until 1847. In the same year a Musical Fund Society was organized and Webb became conductor of its orchestra until 1852, when he resigned because of other duties, though he remained president of the society until 1855. He was important in the development of music in Boston because he acted as the link between the pioneer efforts of J. C. Gottlieb Graupner, and the future work of Carl Zerrahn [*qq.v.*] with the orchestra of the Harvard Musical Association.

Meanwhile Webb helped Mason establish a series of Normal Musical Conventions for training teachers in 1836. Attendance at these conventions grew from fourteen in the first year to a thousand in 1849. He collaborated with Mason in compiling song and hymn books—*The Psaltery* (1845); *The National Psalmodist* (1848); and *Cantica Laudis* (1850). Alone he compiled and edited *Scripture Worship* (1834); *The American Glee Book* (1841); and, for the Boston Handel and Haydn Society, of which he was con-

ductor from 1833 to 1836, the *Massachusetts Collection of Psalmody* (1840). He removed to Orange, N. J., about 1870, and lived there for the rest of his life. He occupied himself by giving vocal lessons in New York, and conducting summer normal courses at Binghamton, N. Y. His wife was Caroline Elizabeth Parmella (Haven) Merriam. Of their six children, one daughter became the wife of William Mason, 1829–1908 [*q.v.*].

As a composer, Webb is known principally for the hymn-tune "Webb." This was originally composed for secular words, " 'Tis dawn, the lark is singing." As a hymn-tune it was first used with the text beginning, "The morning light is breaking," but came to be known almost exclusively as the music for "Stand up, stand up for Jesus." Webb composed many songs, choral works, and a few instrumental pieces, but few of them have survived. George F. Root [*q.v.*] termed Webb the "most refined and delightful teacher of the English glee and madrigal" he had ever known (Root, *post*, p. 28). His son-in-law, William Mason (*post*, p. 9), described him as "a gentleman of high culture, thoroughly educated in music."

[W. J. Metcalf, *Am. Writers and Compilers of Sacred Music* (1925); J. T. Howard, *Our Am. Music* (1931); G. F. Root, *The Story of a Musical Life* (1891); William Mason, *Memories of a Musical Life* (1901); typescript book by Mary Sturgis Gray, "Webb Descendants of England" (1930), in the possession of members of the family; *N. Y. Tribune*, Oct. 8, 1887.]   J. T. H.

WEBB, JAMES WATSON (Feb. 8, 1802–June 7, 1884), journalist and diplomat, was born at Claverack, N. Y. Through his mother, Catharine Hogeboom, he came of old New York Dutch stock, and through his father, Gen. Samuel Blachley Webb (1753–1807), an aide of Washington, of old Connecticut stock, his first American ancestor being Richard Webb who was admitted freeman in Boston in 1632 and went to Hartford in 1635. Early orphaned, he was educated at Cooperstown, N. Y., under the guardianship of a brother-in-law, but at seventeen ran away to join the army. Appearing in Washington (1819) armed with a letter of identification from Gov. DeWitt Clinton of New York, he persuaded Secretary of War John C. Calhoun to give him a second lieutenant's commission. He was assigned at first to the artillery at Governor's Island, N. Y., but was transferred in 1821 to the 3rd Infantry at Chicago. There, in 1822, he had a notable frontier adventure, when he volunteered to carry to Fort Armstrong on the Mississippi news of a meditated Indian attack on Fort Snelling, Minn., crossing the forests and prairies of Illinois in the depth of winter while trailed by hostile Indians. As impetuous as he was audacious, Webb fought two duels with fellow-officers, came near fighting many more, and finally (1827) resigned from the army in consequence of one of these embroilments. At this time he was a first lieutenant; his later title of general was conferred at the time of his appointment as minister to Austria (*A Letter . . . to J. Bramley-Moore, post,* p. 5).

On leaving the army young Webb went to New York City and plunged into a journalistic career, eventually to become one of the most influential editors in that age of personal journalism. In 1827 he acquired the *Morning Courier,* and in 1829 acquired and merged with it the *New-York Enquirer,* thereafter continuing as editor and proprietor of the *Morning Courier and New-York Enquirer* until he sold out to the *World* in 1861 and retired from the field. At first stanchly Jacksonian, he deserted Jackson in 1832 on the United States Bank issue, and became a chief prop of the Whig party. He was an anti-abolitionist but a free-soiler, and during the 1850's urged the preservation of the Union even at the cost of war. The *Courier and Enquirer* was one of the old sixpenny "blanket sheets" destined to be starved out by the smaller, cheaper papers, two of which were founded by one-time assistants of Webb's, James Gordon Bennett, the elder, and Henry Jarvis Raymond [*qq.v.*]. With its chief rival, the *Journal of Commerce,* the *Courier and Enquirer* waged a war of size which eventually produced folios containing over two thousand square inches of type. In the 1830's the rivals sent schooners fifty to a hundred miles to sea in a race for incoming news, and established pony expresses to hasten the news from Washington. With the editors of the penny papers Webb later exchanged plentiful invective, until he was called the "best abused" of them all. He was frequently involved in affairs of honor growing out of his editorial activities, on one occasion (1842) escaping prison under the New York anti-dueling law only by the pardon of the governor.

At the outbreak of the Civil War Webb sold his paper and, somewhat to his own surprise, found himself in the diplomatic service. He had journeyed to Vienna in 1849–50 under appointment (Jan. 7, 1850), as chargé d'affaires to Austria, only to be greeted with the news that the Senate had refused to confirm his appointment, perhaps because of a widespread desire to break with Austria in protest against the Hungarian war. He was now (May 31, 1861) made minister to Brazil, and went to his post via France, where he presented the Union cause to Louis

Napoleon, his friend and correspondent since their meeting in 1835 while Napoleon was in exile. Later, through correspondence and another fateful interview (November 1865), Webb was instrumental in securing a promise of French withdrawal from Mexico. The record of his eight strenuous years in Brazil is marked by an alert patriotism and a bold energy verging on rashness. He had the satisfaction of seeing the unfriendly British envoy sent home in disgrace. He fought tirelessly against the aid extended to Confederate privateers, protected the interests of Americans during the Paraguayan War, and secured the settlement of several long-standing maritime claims. Retiring from the service in 1869, he traveled in Europe for two years, and then lived quietly at home, mostly in New York, until his death. His publications include a number of pamphlets: *To the Officers of the Army* (1827) on the occasion of his resignation; *Slavery and Its Tendencies* (n.d.), written in 1856; *A Letter . . . to J. Bramley-Moore, Esq., M.P.* (n.d.), on the affair with the British envoy; and *A National Currency* (1875). He also wrote *Reminiscences of General Samuel B. Webb* (1882).

Webb was twice married: first (July 1, 1823) to Helen Lispenard Stewart, daughter of Alexander L. Stewart, who died in 1848; second (Nov. 9, 1849) to Laura Virginia Cram, daughter of Jacob Cram, millionaire brewer. Of the eight children born of the first union, five grew to maturity, the youngest being Alexander Stewart Webb [*q.v.*], the well-known Civil War general. There were five sons born of the second marriage. Webb's tall figure, massive head, and piercing eyes gave him a dignified, even imposing presence, which he retained until old age, in spite of a half-century's battle with hereditary gout.

[In addition to Webb's pamphlets, see for family data Webb's *Reminiscences of Gen. Samuel B. Webb* (1882); for the Fort Snelling adventure, dedication to *Altowan; or, Incidents of Life and Adventure in the Rocky Mountains* (2 vols., 1846), ed. by Webb; for charges arising out of the *Carolina* claims, *Gen. J. Watson Webb . . . vs. Hamilton Fish* (1875), and J. B. Moore, *A Digest of Internat. Law* (1906), vol. VI, pp. 749–50. See also G. H. Andrews, in *Sketches of Men of Progress* (1870–71), ed. by James Parton; N. A. Cleven, in *Revista do Instituto Historico e Geographico Brasileiro . . . Congreso Internacional de Historia da America* (1925), pp. 293–394; F. E. Stevens, *James Watson Webb's Trip across Ill. in 1822* (1924); Frederic Hudson, *Journalism in the U. S.* (1873); obituary in *N. Y. Times,* June 8, 1884. Webb's dispatches from Brazil were published in *Papers Relating to Foreign Affairs, 1862–69.*]   E. M. S.

WEBB, JOHN BURKITT (Nov. 22, 1841– Feb. 17, 1912), engineer, professor of mathematics, inventor, was born in Philadelphia, Pa., the son of Charles Roe and Eliza Ann (Greaves) Webb. His grandfather, Burkitt Webb, emigrated from England as a young man and settled in Philadelphia. Webb attended the public schools and the drawing school of the Franklin Institute. For several years, while he worked as clerk in a store, he spent his spare time in the study of mathematics and mechanics, and as a pastime designed and built machinery. About 1860 he formed a small company at Bridgeton, N. J., to make electro-magnetic apparatus for playing organs automatically, but the undertaking was abandoned for lack of capital, and for a year or so Webb was a traveling salesman. In 1863, with his former partner, Oberlin Smith, he organized at Bridgeton the Smith and Webb Manufacturing Company to manufacture special machine tools. The business prospered, but poor health compelled Webb to seek some more healthful climate. Going to Ann Arbor, Mich., he entered the University of Michigan to study civil engineering. After receiving the degree of C.E. in 1871, he was called to the chair of civil engineering which had just been established at the University of Illinois at Urbana. During his eight years there he made a study of the scientific schools of Europe, and after his resignation he spent two full years in advanced studies in mathematics and physics at Heidelberg, Göttingen, Berlin, and Paris. Part of this time was spent in experimental work in electricity in Helmholtz's laboratory in Berlin and in the instrument-maker's shop at the University of Berlin. Webb returned to the United States in 1881 to accept the new chair of applied mathematics at Cornell University, Ithaca, N. Y. During the five years that he held this position he delivered lectures on thermodynamics, mechanisms, drawing and drawing instruments; invented a draft gauge and an inertia-less steam-engine indicator; acted as judge at the International Electrical Exhibition, Philadelphia, in 1884; and published an exhaustive study on "Belting to Connect Shafts Which Are Not Parallel and Do Not Intersect" (*Stevens' Indicator, post*, p. 160). In 1886 he was called to the chair of mathematics and mechanics at Stevens Institute of Technology, Hoboken, N. J., where he remained until 1908.

In 1888 he invented and brought out his floating dynamometer, a very simple but effective device for measuring the power delivered by dynamos, motors, and the like. In 1892 he perfected his viscous dynamometer and in 1900 the dynamophone, which by a simple telephonic method measured the twist of a transmission shaft carrying power. In addition he wrote many technical papers on advanced mechanics. His lectures on mechanical paradoxes (such as a man's lifting himself by his own boot straps, rolling a barrel up hill by gravity, etc.) were always well received by enthusiastic audiences. Webb believed strongly in graphical methods, and insisted upon precision and accuracy in the work of his students. He was a member of a number of engineering and mathematical societies both in the United States and Europe, and was a vice-president of the American Association for the Advancement of Science (1885). After his retirement he devoted himself to private consulting practice. He married Mary Emeline Gregory, daughter of John Milton Gregory [*q.v.*], in Urbana, Ill., on Apr. 19, 1876. At the time of his death at his home in Glen Ridge, N. J., he was survived by his widow and six children.

[See Mary E. Cooch, *Ancestry and Descendants of Nancy Allyn (Foote) Webb* (1910); *Who's Who in America*, 1912–13, from which the date of marriage is taken; *The Semi-Centennial Alumni Record . . . Univ. of Ill.* (1918); *Stevens Indicator*, Apr. 1912; *Trans. Am. Soc. Mechanical Engineers*, vol. XXXIV (1913); patent office records; obituaries in *Pub. Ledger* (Phila.) and *N. Y. Times*, Feb. 19, 1912.]   C. W. M.

WEBB, THOMAS (c. 1724–Dec. 10, 1796),

soldier, Methodist preacher, was born in England and became an officer in the British army. He received a quartermaster's commission, Oct. 29, 1754, and was made lieutenant on Nov. 9 of the following year. Sent to America in the campaign against the French, he lost his right eye and was wounded in the right arm on the Plains of Abraham when Wolfe captured Quebec in September 1759. He returned to England and because of his disabilities was retired on a captain's pay. In 1764, under the preaching of John Wesley, he was converted and became a militant Methodist. At a service in Bath, when the appointed preacher failed to appear, Webb was asked to speak in his place and proved so effective a substitute that thereafter he frequently engaged in public exhortation.

About 1766, under appointment as barrack-master at Albany, he came to America. Soon, having heard that there were Methodists there, he visited New York. His appearance at one of their meetings—in striking military garb and with a sword at his side—awakened some consternation, but when he introduced himself as "a soldier of the cross and a spiritual son of John Wesley" he was warmly welcomed. From that time until his final return to England some sixteen years later he was one of the principal agencies in establishing Methodism in America. He assisted Philip Embury [*q.v.*] in preaching to the little congregation that gathered in the "rigging loft" on Horse and Cart (later William) Street; he headed the list of subscribers to the fund raised for the building of Wesley Chapel, completed in 1768, advancing, in addition, three hundred pounds as a loan and securing gifts from friends in Philadelphia. His evangelical zeal took him to Long Island, where he awakened considerable religious interest; to Burlington, N. J., where he preached in the marketplace and in the court house and formed a class; to Philadelphia, where he organized another class of a hundred or more; and to Baltimore. He wrote John Wesley urging that he send preachers to America, and during a visit to England in 1772–73 he made strong appeals in behalf of American Methodism. Upon his return in 1773 he was accompanied by Thomas Rankin and George Shadford, sent by Wesley to labor in the colonies.

Wesley, Asbury, and John Adams all bore testimony to the effectiveness of Webb's preaching. Referring to him in his journal under date of Feb. 2, 1773, Wesley remarked that he admired the wisdom of God in raising up various preachers according to the various needs of men. "The Captain," he says, "is all life and fire: Therefore, although he is not deep or regular, yet many who would not hear a better preacher flock together to hear him" (*The Works of the Rev. John Wesley,* 3rd ed., vol. III, 1829, p. 487). John Adams, less concerned about ecclesiastical regularity, unreservedly commended Webb's preaching after listening to him in Philadelphia, Oct. 23, 1774: "In the evening I went to the Methodist meeting, and heard Mr. Webb, the old soldier, who first came to America in the character of quartermaster under General Braddock. He is one of the most fluent, eloquent men I ever heard; he reaches the imagination and touches the passions very well, and expresses himself with great propriety" (C. F. Adams, *The Works of John Adams,* vol. II, 1850, p. 401). Sometime during the Revolution, apparently, Webb returned to England, for he is known to have been there in 1783. He made his home in Bristol and still continued to engage in evangelistic work. Dying suddenly in that city, he was buried in Portland Street Chapel. He was twice married and had two sons, Gilbert and Charles, both of whom came to America after their father's death and settled in Canterbury, Orange County, N. Y.

[W. C. Ford, *British Officers Serving in America, 1754–1774* (1894); J. B. Wakeley, *Lost Chapters Recovered from the Early Hist. of Am. Methodism* (1858); W. B. Sprague, *Annals of Am. Pulpit,* vol. VII (1859); John Atkinson, *The Beginnings of the Wesleyan Movement in America* (1896); H. E. Luccock and Paul Hutchinson, *The Story of Methodism* (copr. 1926); P. N. Garber, *The Romance of Am. Methodism* (1931); *Gentleman's Magazine* (London), Dec. 1796, p. 1117.]   H. E. S.

WEBB, THOMAS SMITH (Oct. 30, 1771–July 6, 1819), Masonic ritualist, patron of music, was born in Boston, Mass., the son of Samuel and Margaret (Smith) Webb, who had emigrated to America from England shortly before Thomas' birth. In his youth he was apprenticed to a printer in Boston, and later he removed to Keene, N. H., where he worked for a number of years at his trade and first became interested in Freemasonry. The first three degrees of ancient craft Masonry were conferred on him in Keene by the Rising Sun Lodge. In 1793 he moved to Albany, N. Y., where he established a paper-staining factory. In 1797, not yet twenty-six years of age, he published a work which was to establish him as a leading Masonic ritualist, *The Freemason's Monitor, or Illustrations of Masonry.* The book had wide circulation, and its first publication was followed by many successive editions, revised and enlarged long after the author's death. He was known as the founder of the American system of chapter and encampment Masonry. He was the presiding officer of a convention of committees which met in Boston in 1797 to form a general grand chapter of Royal Arch Masons. In January 1799, as chairman of a committee, he presented for this group a constitution which was adopted at a meeting in Providence, R. I. This meeting resulted in the formation of the grand encampment of the United States. The original draft of this constitution, with alterations and additions interlined in Webb's handwriting, was placed on file in the archives of the St. John's Commandery, in Providence.

Late in the same year Webb made his home in Providence, and it was there (and later in Boston) that he became active in musical circles and one of the leading patrons of music. In 1809 he joined a group of music lovers brought together by Oliver Shaw [*q.v.*], the blind organist of the First Congregational Church, to form the Psallonian Society, organized "for the purpose of improving themselves in the knowledge and practice of sacred music and inculcating a more correct taste in the choice and performance of it" (Howard, *post,* p. 141). This society lasted until 1832, and in twenty-three years gave thirty-one concerts.

A few years before his death Webb removed to Boston, where he was a member of a group that founded in 1815 one of the oldest and one of the most important musical organizations in America, the Handel and Haydn Society of Bos-

ton. In March 1815, Webb, J. C. Gottlieb Graupner [*q.v.*] and Asa Peabody signed an invitation
for a meeting to consider "the expediency of
forming a society for cultivating and improving
a correct taste in the performance of sacred music, and also to introduce into more general
practice the works of Handel, Haydn and other
eminent composers" (Howard, *post*, p. 138).
Sixteen answered the invitation and in April the
society was formed. Webb was elected its first
president, and he served more than two years.
The first concert of the Society was held in the
Stone Chapel in Boston, on Christmas night,
1815.

Webb was married to Mrs. Martha Hopkins,
of Boston, in the autumn of 1797. They had five
children of whom only two survived the parents.
After the death of his first wife, he was married,
in 1809, to her sister, who, with their four children, survived him. He was buried with the
Masonic rites in Providence.

[C. C. Perkins, *Hist. of the Handel and Haydn Soc.*,
vol. I (1883–93); J. T. Howard, *Our Am. Music*
(1931); H. W. Rugg, *Hist. of Freemasonry in R. I.*
(1895); *Biog. Encyc. of Representative Men of R. I.*
(1881); *R. I. Am. and Gen. Advertiser* (Providence),
July 20, 1819.]   J. T. H.

WEBB, WILLIAM HENRY (June 19, 1816–
Oct. 30, 1899), shipbuilder, was born in New
York City, a descendant of Richard Webb, a
lowland Scot who settled at Cambridge, Mass.,
by 1632 and later went to Connecticut. His father, Isaac Webb (1794–1840), was a shipwright who, like Jacob Bell [*q.v.*] and Stephen
Smith, moved from Stamford, Conn., to try his
fortune in New York. There the scant mile of
yards along the East River from Grand Street
to Thirteenth Street contributed more than any
other place, except perhaps the Clyde, to the development of shipbuilding between 1807 and
1865. Isaac perfected his art under the able Scot,
Henry Eckford [*q.v.*], and soon developed a
prosperous yard of his own. His chief importance lay in his instructing two youths who became the greatest American shipbuilders of their
time. One was Donald McKay [*q.v.*]; the other
was his own son William. Isaac wanted William
to enter a profession, so he educated him with
tutors and sent him to the Columbia College
Grammar School. The boy, however, stubborn-
ly insisted on following his father's career. At
fifteen he entered upon six years of intensive
study of naval architecture and shipbuilding,
taking only a week's vacation in that time. He
combined in a remarkable way the qualities of
naval architect and shipwright. Like J. W. Griffiths [*q.v.*], he showed bold and successful ingenuity in the designing of vessels. Combined

with this theoretical ability was the practical
sense which enabled him to manage a thousand
workers and make a fortune in turning out more
than a hundred and fifty vessels whose construction was as sound as their design was brilliant.
His unusual versatility adapted itself to both
sail and steam, wood and iron, merchantmen and
warships.

When Webb started building at twenty, New
York's transatlantic sailing packets were the
finest ships afloat. His first product was the
Black Ball packet *Oxford* in 1836, built on a
sub-contract from his father. He had built several other vessels, including the packets *New
York, Pennsylvania, Ville de Lyons,* and *Du-
chesse d'Orleans,* before his father's death in
1840, when he became a partner of his father's assistant, Allen. In 1843 Webb started twenty-five
years of building in his own name. His yard, extending from Fifth to Seventh Streets on East
River, gradually overshadowed the nearby rival
establishments of Brown & Bell, Smith &
Dimon, W. H. Brown, and the Westervelts. The
bald-headed little genius, with his flat nose, close-
cropped whiskers, and bulldog expression, always built on contract, which eliminated much
of the risk. He continued to build such packets
as the *Yorkshire,* the *Guy Mannering,* which
was the first three-decker, the *Ocean Monarch,
Isaac Wright, Ivanhoe, Yorktown,* and *Isaac
Bell.* In 1843 he built the fast pre-clipper *Cohota*
for the China trade, followed by the *Panama* and
Montauk. He ranked high among the builders of regular clippers. His *Celestial,* in 1850,
was the first built expressly for the California
trade, while his *Sword Fish,* in 1851, made the
fourth fastest run to San Francisco. He also
built the *Challenge, Comet, Gazelle,* and *Invin-
cible* (1851); *Australia* and *Flying Dutchman*
(1852); *Flyaway, Snapdragon,* and *Young
America* (1853); *Intrepid,* and *Uncowah* (1856),
and *Black Hawk* (1857). While McKay in his
specialty of clippers, somewhat overshadowed
Webb, eight of the latter's clippers made the San
Francisco run in 110 days or less, against seven
of McKay's.

Clippers, however, were only one of Webb's
varied accomplishments. On a single day, Jan.
21, 1851, he launched a clipper, a Havre packet
and a Pacific Mail steamship. He had already
built the hulls for eight steamships, the machinery being furnished by nearby "iron works."
His only transatlantic liner, apparently, was the
United States in 1848, but that same year he
built for the Pacific Mail Steamship Company
the *California* and *Panama,* followed by the
Golden Gate, San Francisco, and *Yorktown,*

three others being built by his brother Eckford on sub-contract. William also built the *Cherokee, Augusta,* and *Knoxville* for lines to Savannah or New Orleans, as well as a powerful Sandy Hook towboat which bore his name.

During the decline of the merchant marine in the later fifties, Webb turned his attention to warships. In 1857 he built the steam revenue cutter *Harriet Lane.* Conceiving the idea of a powerful steam frigate, he was rebuffed at Washington but visited Russia and persisted until he received a $1,125,000 order for the *General Admiral,* launched in 1858. Adapting his yard to iron, he built for the new Italian navy in 1863 the *Re d'Italia* and *Re di Portogallo.* The former, probably the first ironclad warship to cross the Atlantic, was rammed and sunk by the Austrians at Lissa in 1866. Webb was decorated with the Italian order of Saints Maurice and Lazarus. His masterpiece was the strongest and fastest ironclad of the day, the great ram *Dunderberg,* which was laid down for the Union navy, but, not being launched until July 22, 1865, was sold to the French, who renamed her the *Rochambeau.*

Webb retired from shipbuilding in 1869 after building the Sound steamers *Bristol* and *Providence* and the packet *Charles H. Marshall,* but continued for another four years in less successful efforts to operate steamship lines. He had been an original director of the Pacific Mail and a heavy shareholder in the Panama railroad. Now he started a line to rival the Pacific Mail, as well as lines from San Francisco to Australia and New York to Europe. He had been a pioneer in the guano trade and owned considerable New York real estate. At his death he was a director of several New York traction companies and other corporations. About 1870 he published *Plans of Wooden Vessels,* two volumes of plates showing designs of a hundred and fifty ships he had built. Keenly interested in local welfare, Webb was for fourteen years president of the New York City Council for Civic Reform and led the opposition to the Tammany plans of the Aqueduct Commission. Three times he declined a chance to run for mayor. He established and endowed Webb's Academy and Home for Shipbuilders, opened on May 5, 1894. He died in New York. He had married Henrietta A. Hidden in 1843 and was survived by one son, William E. Webb.

[See J. H. Morrison, *Hist. of N. Y. Shipyards* (1909); *Hist. of Am. Steam Navigation* (1903); G. W. Sheldon, "The Old Shipbuilders of N. Y.," *Harper's Mag.,* July 1882; A. H. Clark, *The Clipper Ship Era* (1910); O. T. Howe and F. C. Matthews, *Am. Clipper Ships* (2 vols., 1926–27); C. C. Cutler, *Greyhounds of the Sea* (1931); R. G. Albion, in *New England Quart.,* Oct. 1932, pp. 690–91; James Parton, ed., *Sketches of Men of Progress* (1870–71), pp. 103–12; Henry Hall, ed., *America's Successful Men of Affairs* (1895), I, 703–09; J. H. Mowbray, ed., *Representative Men of N. Y.* (1898), vol. II, pp. 172–74; *Leslie's Hist. of the Greater N. Y.* (1898), vol. III; *Directory of Directors in the City of N. Y.,* 1899; Henry Hall, "Report on the Ship-Building Industry of the U. S.," *House Miscellaneous Docs.,* 42, 47 Cong., 2 Sess., pt. VIII; *Who's Who in America,* 1899–1900; *N. Y. Herald,* May 6, 1894, and Nov. 1, 1899 (obituary).]

R. G. A.

WEBB, WILLIAM ROBERT (Nov. 11, 1842–Dec. 19, 1926), educator, United States senator, was born near Mount Tirzah, in Person County, N. C., the fifth son of Alexander Smith and Cornelia Adeline (Stanford) Webb, and a grandson of Richard Stanford, congressman from North Carolina (1797–1816). As a child he was given the nickname of "Sawney," which stuck to him through life. His education began in a school conducted by his sixteen-year-old sister, and was continued in the Bingham School at Oaks, N. C. He matriculated at the University of North Carolina in 1860, but he left college in April of the following year to enlist as private in Company H, 15th North Carolina Volunteers. At the battle of Malvern Hill, Va., he was shot three times, receiving a wound in one of his arms that troubled him throughout life. Immediately after the battle he was elected first lieutenant of his company. While recovering from his wounds he reëntered the University of North Carolina but returned to the army early in 1864 as adjutant of Company K, 2nd North Carolina Cavalry. During the Virginia campaign he fought in almost every battle until, three days before Appomattox, he was captured. He was imprisoned first at the Battery, then at Hart's Island, N. Y. On one occasion he escaped, in uniform, and spent a day unmolested sightseeing in New York, but voluntarily returned to prison that night.

After his release he went back to Oaks, N. C. For four years (1866–70) he taught at Horner School, Oxford, N. C., and during that period he completed by correspondence and examination—under the liberal conditions allowed to Confederate soldiers—his work for the degrees of A.B. (1867) and A.M. (1868) at the University of North Carolina. Disgusted with "Carpetbag" and Reconstruction government, he left North Carolina in 1870 for the quieter state of Tennessee, and founded Webb School at Culleoka. Within two weeks the trustees, aghast when he allowed pupils to study out-of-doors, demanded stricter discipline, but Webb refused to "imprison innocent children" and continued his policy of freedom. His, he claimed, was the first "strictly preparatory school" west of the

Alleghanies; all others, he said in a speech delivered at Peabody College, Jan. 29, 1923, regardless of faculty or curriculum, were denominated colleges. He seldom advertised, and printed only a small descriptive circular about the school. He taught only Latin, Greek, mathematics, and English, and used no English grammar. On Apr. 23, 1873, he married Emma Clary of Unionville, Tenn. That year his brother, John M. Webb, whom he later described as "the greatest scholar I have ever seen," joined the faculty. In 1886, when local merchants refused not to sell whiskey to his boys, he moved the school to Bellbuckle, Tenn. The two brothers had $12,000, of which $2,200 went into buildings and $8,000 into books.

Webb was an ardent prohibitionist and a member (1913–26) of the national board of trustees of the Anti-Saloon League of America. In 1896 he campaigned as a Gold Democrat, and served as delegate to the Democratic convention that nominated Palmer and Buckner for president and vice-president respectively. In January 1913 Webb was unanimously elected by the state Senate to fill the unexpired term of the late Senator Robert Love Taylor [q.v.], Newell Sanders, Republican, having previously been appointed by Gov. Ben W. Hooper. As senator he served from Jan. 24 to Mar. 3, 1913, introducing a bill to prohibit desecration of the flag, and making one notable speech in favor of the Webb-Kenyon Bill (named for Representative E. Y. Webb of North Carolina), which prohibited the shipment of liquor into dry states.

He served three times as a lay member of the General Conference of the Methodist Episcopal Church, South. Known as "Old Sawney," the schoolmaster of Tennessee, he was recognized throughout the state as its "first citizen" (*Nashville Banner*, Dec. 20, 1926). He was short and stocky, with gray beard and hair; he wore a black coat that usually had the third button-hole attached to the second button, and a black string tie that was invariably under his left ear. His maxims, like his school, were famous; on his deathbed he sent a characteristic message: "Give the boys my love, and tell them to lead a larger life . . . and dont' forget—never do anything that you have to hide." He died at Bellbuckle, Tenn., survived by his wife, four sons, and four daughters.

[Transcripts of letters, speeches, newspaper articles, and documents in possession of W. R. Webb, Jr., principal of Webb School at Bellbuckle, Tenn.; *Biog. Dir. Am. Cong.* (1928); *Alumni Hist. of the Univ. of N. C.* (1924); Randolph Elliott, "Old Sawney's," in *Atlantic Mo.*, Aug. 1920; *Who's Who in America*, 1926–27; *Nashville Banner* and *Nashville Tennessean*, Dec. 20, 1926; E. W. Parks, "Sawney Webb: Tennessee's Schoolmaster," *N. C. Hist. Rev.*, July 1935.]

E. W. P.

WEBBER, CHARLES WILKINS (May 29, 1819–April 1856), author, journalist, explorer, naturalist, and soldier, was born in Russellville, Ky., the first son and second child of Dr. Augustine Webber (1790–1873), who practised medicine for over half a century in southern Kentucky, and Agnes Maria (Tannehill) Webber, said to be the daughter of John Tannehill, a Revolutionary officer in the Continental Army. Educated at home in an informal way, in 1838 Webber went to Texas, then struggling for independence; there he associated himself with John Coffee Hays [q.v.], and other leading members of the Texas Rangers. Later he studied medicine in Kentucky for a short time, and in 1843 entered the Princeton Theological Seminary to prepare for the Presbyterian ministry. In 1844, however, he went to New York to take up journalism. There he renewed acquaintance with John James Audubon [q.v.], whom he had met during a Rocky Mountain tour. The two men became close friends, and Audubon's influence is to be plainly seen in much of Webber's literary work. Webber began his career with articles on Texas adventure for Winchester's *New World*; when it failed, he wrote for the *Literary World*, the *Democratic Review*, the *Sunday Dispatch*, and *Graham's Magazine*, all in New York City. For two years he is said to have been an editor and joint proprietor of the *American Review* (later the *American Whig Review*). In 1849, the year of his marriage in Boston, he organized an expedition to the Colorado and Gila Rivers, which failed when the horses were stolen by Comanche Indians at Corpus Christi, Tex. About six years later he is reported to have obtained from the New York legislature a charter to form a camel company, a project the necessity of which was apparent to those who knew of the difficulties to be met in crossing Western deserts. In 1855 he went to Central America, still eager for excitement. In the winter of the same year he joined the filibustering party commanded by the military adventurer, William Walker [q.v.], and, according to all accounts, was killed at Nicaragua in the battle of Rivas on Apr. 11, 1856.

Webber's principal works are *Old Hicks the Guide, or Adventures . . . in Search of a Gold Mine* (1848); *The Gold Mines of the Gila* (1849); *The Hunter-Naturalist* (1851), the first volume of a projected series of seven, of which only two were published; *The Texan Virago . . . and Other Tales* (1852); *The Wild*

Girl of Nebraska (1852); *Tales of the Southern Border* (1852); *The Romance of Forest and Prairie Life* (1853); *Spiritual Vampirism* (1853); *Wild Scenes and Song Birds* (1854), volume II of *The Hunter-Naturalist,* illustrated with twenty colored lithographs drawn by Mrs. Webber; *"Sam," or the History of Mystery* (1855), an account of the Jesuits; and *History and Revolutionary Incidents of the Early Settlers of the United States* (1859). A fourteen-page pamphlet, *A Letter to the Country and Whig Party with Regard to the Conduct of the "American Whig Review"* (1847), reveals Webber as no mean master of invective. In it he charges George Hooker Colton (1818–1847) with "falsehood, imbecility, and shameful cowardice," and then dares him to resent his statements.

Webber excelled in descriptions of wild border life; he wrote an easy, rapid, flowing style; his enthusiasm for natural history was real and deep, and his skill in communicating that enthusiasm was his chief strength. His writing reflects a man of strong animal spirits, but one who was able to appreciate the beauty and the poetry, as well as the power and energy, of nature.

[Sources include Webber's own works; E. A. and G. L. Duyckinck, *Cyc. of Am. Lit.* (2 vols., 1855); *New Orleans Medical and Surgical Jour.,* May 1874, for information from Webber's father; private information.]   H. S. R—n.

WEBER, ALBERT (July 8, 1828–June 25, 1879), piano-maker, was born in Bavaria. He was well educated, and became an accomplished musician, particularly as an organist. When he was sixteen years of age he came to America, landing in New York City. He subsequently decided to become a piano manufacturer, and served an apprenticeship with Holden and later with Van Winkle. To earn money for his board he gave music lessons in the evenings, and played the organ in churches on Sundays. Seven years later, when he was twenty-three years of age, he entered business for himself as a piano manufacturer. His first shop was located in the upper stories of a small building at 103 West Broadway, and his complete working force consisted of himself, Edward Stroud, and one case maker. By October 1 the trio completed its first instrument, and by Jan. 1, 1852, five more were ready for sale. In 1857, following a fire which destroyed his shop and equipment, he moved to larger quarters at 155 West Broadway. In 1864 the firm moved again, to the corner of Broome and Crosby Streets, and in 1867 it occupied its own building at 17th Street and 7th Avenue. In 1869 he became a pioneer in the trade by open-ing warerooms on Fifth Avenue, at 16th Street. From that time his pianos became fashionable, and were known for their high quality.

Weber bore most of the burden of running his business himself. He was in charge of all branches, manufacturing and selling, both wholesale and retail. He was of a social disposition, and spent his evenings at the opera, theatre, and concerts. It was generally believed that he overtaxed his strength, and that overwork was the cause of his death at the age of fifty in New York City. After he died, the business of the Weber Piano Company was carried on by Weber's sons. In 1892 it became the Weber-Wheelock Company, and in 1903, through a merger, it was made a division of the Aeolian, Weber Piano & Pianola Company.

Many anecdotes are told of Weber's brilliance. An accomplished pianist, he would often play to prospective customers, and it is said that "seldom would an intending buyer leave his warerooms without having secured a piano" (Dolge, *post,* p. 298). Unlike Chickering and the Steinways, Weber did not invent or create anything new in piano construction, but he was such a thorough craftsman himself, and such a judge of piano tone, that he knew how to employ the most approved methods of piano-making in use during his career. With V. Wilhelm L. Knabe, the Steinways, and Jonas Chickering [*qq.v.*], he was one of those who realized the value to piano manufacturers of concerts by pianists, and he often engaged famous soloists to give concerts in leading cities, thus helping to create "a popularity for the piano in proportion to the growth of wealth in the United States" (Dolge, *post,* p. 175). He is credited with having originated the term "baby grand," to designate the short grand piano.

[The most complete account of Weber's career is found in Alfred Dolge, *Pianos and their Makers,* vol. I (1911). Data on Weber and his firm are contained in a pamphlet issued by the Weber-Wheelock Company, *Greater and Lesser New York* (1897). See also Grove's *Dict. of Music and Musicians, Am. Supp.* (1930), and the *N. Y. Tribune,* June 26, 1879.]
                                    J. T. H.

WEBER, GUSTAV CARL ERICH (May 26, 1828–Mar. 21, 1912), physician, was born in Bonn, Germany. His father, Moritz Ignaz Weber, was an anatomist from the University of Landshut who had been called to the chair of anatomy at Bonn; his mother, a von Podowilz, is reported to have had literary attainments. The boy grew up in a home which was frequented by such intellectual leaders of the day as Jean Paul Richter. While studying at the University of Bonn, young Weber came under the suspicion of having been implicated in the revolution of 1848. He transferred his studies to Munich and spent some time with an uncle, an ophthalmologist. He shortly emigrated to America and went to St. Louis, Mo., where in 1849 he continued his medical studies, interesting himself in particular in original anatomical research. Upon his graduation in 1851 from Beaumont Medical College, St. Louis, he returned to the medical centers of Europe, where his father's reputation opened to him the doors of great clinics and classical teachers. He came to the Vienna of Joseph Skoda, Joseph Hyrtl, Ferdinand Hebra, Karl Rokitansky, and Karl Braun, and continued his studies under the tutelage of the latter. From there he went to Amsterdam and thence to Paris to the clinic of Philibert-Joseph Roux.

Apparently the events following the revolution induced Weber to return to America in 1853. He assumed the position of surgeon at a hospital in New York, which had been left vacant by the death of his brother, Edward Weber, but in 1856, his health having also failed, he left for the West. From 1856 to 1863 he held the chair of surgery in the medical department of Western Reserve College, commonly known as Cleveland Medical College. Under his régime the surgical clinic became very popular, and his reputation grew apace. He was appointed surgeon general of Ohio in 1862 and after his resignation served as surgeon of the 129th Ohio Volunteer Infantry until Nov. 1, 1863. In 1864 he organized the staff of the new St. Vincent Charity Hospital, Cleveland, and in the same year the Charity Hospital Medical College, where he was dean and professor of surgery (1864–70). From 1870 to 1881 he was professor of clinical surgery and dean of the medical department of Wooster University (later the College of Wooster), and in 1881 became the dean of a new school, the medical department of Western Reserve University, which was the result of the fusion of most of the faculty of Wooster with that of the medical department of Western Reserve College. In 1894 he returned to the medical department of Wooster University and remained there until 1896. Toward the end of the century he gradually retired from active academic and professional duties. He was appointed American consul at Nürnberg in 1897 by President McKinley and held the position until 1902. On his return to Cleveland in 1903 he suffered an attack of apoplexy which forced him to spend his later years in his country cottage at Willoughby, Ohio, where he died in 1912.

A general practitioner and surgeon whose field was the entire human body, Weber had acquired a training remarkable for its extent and intensity. In the practice of surgery, which was his passion, he developed both great skill and a deservedly high repute. In his lectures he apparently emphasized general principles rather than factual elements, in the manner of the classical European teachers. His style, as far as one can judge from the few articles he published, was elegant and flowing. He was one of the founders and editors of the *Cleveland Medical Gazette,* which first appeared in 1859. His publications include *Address Introductory to the Opening . . . of the Cleveland Medical College Session, 1856–57* (1856) and "A New Method of Arresting Hemorrhage" (*Medical Record,* N. Y., Apr. 24, 1875). He married Ruth Elizabeth Cheney of New York City in 1854, and had by her two children, a son and a daughter.

[*Who's Who in America,* 1900–01; W. H. Humiston, in *Am. Jour. Obstetrics,* Mar. 1913, with portrait; *Jour. Am. Medic. Asso.,* Apr. 6, 1912; J. H. Lowman, in *Cleveland Medic. Jour.,* Apr. 1912; *Ibid.,* May 1912; Martin Stamm, *Ibid.,* June 1912; H. A. Kelly and W. L. Burrage, *Am. Medic. Biogs.* (1920); obituary in *Cleveland Plain Dealer,* Mar. 22, 1912; information on Weber's work in Cleveland from Dr. F. C. Waite, Western Reserve Univ.]   H. S. R—e.

WEBER, HENRY ADAM (July 12, 1845–June 14, 1912), chemist, pure-food reformer, was born in Clinton Township, Franklin County, Ohio, the son of Frederick and Caroline (Tascher) Weber, both natives of the German Palatinate. During his studies at Otterbein College, Westerville, Ohio, in 1861–63 he became interested in chemistry and went to Germany to perfect himself in this science. After studying at Kaiserslautern (1863–66) and at the University of Munich under Justus von Liebig (1866–68), he returned to the United States. Between 1869 and 1874, as chemist of the geological survey of Ohio, he made comprehensive analyses of the minerals and soils of the state. He was professor of chemistry at the University of Illinois from 1874 to 1882. There he planned a new chemical laboratory for the university which was one of the most complete of its kind, and served as chemist of both the state board of agriculture and the state board of health. In the latter capacity he made an exhaustive sanitary examination of the river waters of the state. During this period he first became interested in pure-food legislation. In 1879 he received the degree of Ph.D. from Ohio State University. About this time, in collaboration with Melville A. Scovell [*q.v.*], he began experiments upon the manufacture of sugar from sorghum, patenting a superheat process of clarification that attracted considerable attention. The work led to the establishment of the Champaign Sugar and Glucose Company for the purpose of manufacturing sucrose from sorghum juice and glucose from the starch of sorghum grain (*Transactions of the Department of Agriculture of Illinois,* vols. XVIII–XIX, 1881–82). Weber devoted his time from 1882 to 1884 to the development of this enterprise, but the natural deficiencies of sorghum as a sugar-producing crop, the reduction of the tariff on sugar, and other economic factors caused the general abandonment of the project. From 1884 until the end of his life Weber was professor of agricultural chemistry at the Ohio State University, Columbus, Ohio. He also served as state chemist of Ohio, and chief chemist of the Ohio state dairy and food commission (1884–97), and became recognized as one of the pioneers in the national pure-food movement initiated by Dr. Harvey W. Wiley [q.v.]. In 1903 he was appointed, with William Frear, Edward Hopkins Jenkins [qq.v.], M. A. Scovell, and H. W. Wiley, a member of the first American committee on food standards, created by Congress. He rendered distinguished service in the movement which led to the passage of the Federal Food and Drugs Act in 1906.

Weber was a member of numerous chemical and scientific societies, and a fellow of the American Association for the Advancement of Science. He was the author of a *Select Course in Qualitative Analysis* (1875) and of numerous bulletins, reports, and articles upon chemical subjects. He died at his home in Columbus, Ohio. He married on Dec. 29, 1870, Rosa Ober of Columbus, Ohio, whom he met in Germany during his student days and who survived him with two daughters.

[*Who's Who in America,* 1910–11; *Semi-Centennial Alumni Record . . . Univ. of Ill.* (1918); obituary in *Ohio State Jour.,* June 15, 1912; information from Weber's nephew, Dr. F. C. Weber.]   C. A. B.

WEBSTER, ALICE JANE CHANDLER (July 24, 1876–June 11, 1916), author, known as Jean Webster, was born in Fredonia, N. Y., the first child of Annie (Moffett) and Charles Luther Webster. Her father, a publisher, was from New England, his wife from the South. Their lineage was British, with a German strain; their American kin included Daniel Boone, Eli Whitney, and Samuel L. Clemens [qq.v.]. Jean Webster attended the public schools of Fredonia, finished preparation for college at Lady Jane Grey School, Binghamton, N. Y. (1896), and received the degree of A.B. from Vassar College (1901). She was an able student but a poor speller. Asked by a horrified teacher, "On what authority do you spell thus?"

she retorted, "Webster." Not to enjoy unearned importance, she tried to conceal the fact that she was Mark Twain's grandniece. While a student she was correspondent for a Poughkeepsie newspaper and contributed several stories to *Vassar Miscellany* (vols. XXVIII, XXIX, 1899–1900). Her major studies were English and economics. Visits to institutions for the destitute and the delinquent impressed her imagination permanently and gave direction to her writing.

After college she became an independent writer for magazines. Her first book, *When Patty Went to College* (1903), originally published serially, she had shaped while a student from her experiences at Vassar. The amusing and enlightening Patty series, including *Just Patty* (1911), lead in their field. In her travels, besides a trip around the world (1906–07), she made long sojourns in Italy, where she found the setting for *Jerry Junior* (1907), and for her favorite, *The Wheat Princess* (1905). Her next books, *The Four Pools Mystery* (1908), published anonymously, and *Much Ado About Peter* (1909), were popular. The attraction of an old house (55 West Tenth Street) brought her near to Greenwich Village. Not in revolt, and coveting a whole view of society, she had the recognition of social workers. The inferential thesis of her novels, *Daddy-Long-Legs* (1912) and its sequel *Dear Enemy* (London, 1914), is that under-privileged children, if given the chance, are capable of succeeding in life and of enjoying its beauty. A moving revelation of child-life in an orphanage, timeless in its humor, justice, and lovable make-believe, *Daddy-Long-Legs* made its creator famous as the spokesman for "the small, blue-ginghamed lonely ones of earth." It was memorable for its long run when dramatized, was translated widely, and was finally universalized on the screen by Mary Pickford, who bought the film rights (1918). In writing it Jean Webster is said to have had in mind her close friend and classmate, Adelaide Crapsey [q.v.], who may also have been the original of Patty (Mary E. Osborn, *Adelaide Crapsey,* 1933, p. 28). In 1915 she wrote a preface for Adelaide Crapsey's *Verse,* which was also published in *Vassar Miscellany,* March 1915. She was a sane and hopeful realist on her way, it was predicted, to leadership, and was already felt indirectly as a humanitarian. Her literary discipline was diligent and practical; she experienced directly, wrote profusely, and cut ruthlessly.

On Sept. 7, 1915, she was married to Glenn Ford McKinney. She died, June 11, 1916, a day after the birth of her daughter. A room at the Girls' Service League, New York City, and a bed at the county branch of the New York Orthopedic Hospital, near White Plains, were endowed in her memory.

[See *Who's Who in America*, 1916–17; *Woman's Who's Who of America*, 1914–15; Alice Sanford in *Vassar Miscellany*, June 1915; Elizabeth Cutting, in *Vassar Quart.*, Nov. 1916; D. Z. D., in *Century Mag.*, Nov. 1916; Ruth C. Mitchell, *Ibid.* (poem); Francis Hackett, in *New Republic*, Mar. 13, 1915; Channing Pollock, in *Green Book Mag.*, Dec. 1914; *N. Y. Times*, Nov. 9, Dec. 13, 1914, and June 12, 1916 (obituary). Information has been supplied by Annie Moffett Webster, Ethelyn McKinney, Prof. H. E. Mills, and other friends of Jean Webster.]   M. M.

WEBSTER, ARTHUR GORDON (Nov. 28, 1863–May 15, 1923), physicist, was born in Brookline, Mass., the only son of William Edward and Mary Shannon (Davis) Webster. He was a descendant of John Webster who settled in Ipswich, Mass., in 1635. He prepared for college at the high school in Newton, Mass. In 1881 he entered Harvard University, from which he graduated with honors in 1885. In college he showed remarkable linguistic talent, but then and later regarded his study of languages as a diversion, demanding little mental exertion, from his favorite studies of mathematics and physics, which upon occasion he would admit make rather severe demands upon the intellect. After serving one year as instructor in mathematics at Harvard, he went abroad in 1886 for advanced study at the University of Berlin. Four years later he received the degree of Ph.D. from this university, his dissertation, *Versuche über eine Methode zur Bestimmung des Verhältnisses der elektromagnetischen zur elektrostatischen Einheit der Elektricität* (1890), presenting the results of an experimental investigation directed by the great experimentalist, Prof. August Kundt. Returning to America in 1890, Webster accepted a position as docent in physics at Clark University, Worcester, Mass., under Prof. Albert Abraham Michelson [*q.v.*], whom he succeeded as head of the department in 1892. His position at Clark University, at that time a strictly graduate school, afforded him the opportunity to develop a systematic and comprehensive course of lectures on mathematical physics which was unsurpassed in scope and thoroughness by any corresponding course offered elsewhere. He soon acquired a mastery of the art of lucid exposition in his lectures which, with an intuitive appreciation of the difficulties of his students, qualified him as an exceptionally good teacher. In effect, he occupied two distinct positions at Clark University—professor of mathematical physics and professor of experimental physics. As a leader in both subjects he was the inspiration of small groups of devoted students who came to him from year to year from America and abroad.

In the period from 1890 to 1917 his own scientific activities in mathematical physics, were, apart from his lectures, chiefly concerned with expository writing on this subject, the major products of which were two excellent treatises: *The Theory of Electricity and Magnetism* (1897), and *The Dynamics of Particles and of Rigid, Elastic and Fluid Bodies* (1904). Many of his scientific colleagues, while fully recognizing the high merits of his expository writings, were prone to regret that his intense devotion to this phase of his activities should effectively preclude the application of his remarkable mental powers toward the solution of the various outstanding problems of theoretical physics. His activities in experimental physics during this period had mainly to do with the development of various gyroscopic instruments, and with sound investigations, one important product of which was a remarkable instrument for the absolute measurement of the intensity of sound. Throughout this period he was a frequent contributor to scientific magazines of articles dealing with topics that interested him in mechanics, sound, and electricity.

In 1917 Webster was appointed a member of the United States Naval Consulting Board. As his contribution to war work he established a school of ballistics at Clark University, and with his assistants undertook the solution of various important ballistic problems. It was a matter of deep regret to him that he was not assigned to war service abroad, as he felt that his extensive knowledge of foreign languages specially qualified him for such service. After the war he continued his work on ballistics and sound, and on a comprehensive treatise entitled *The Partial Differential Equations of Mathematical Physics*. The book was nearly completed at the time of his death in 1923, and was published in 1927 under the editorship of Dr. S. J. Plimpton. Many honors came to Webster in the course of his career. In 1895 (*Science*, Feb. 15, 1895) he received the Elihu Thomson prize for his paper on "An Experimental Determination of the Periods of Electrical Oscillations." In 1903 he was elected the third president of the American Physical Society, which he had been instrumental in founding in 1899. He was the recipient of various honorary degrees, and was a member of many learned societies both in America and abroad.

Webster was distinguished by a singularly imposing personality. His frank expressions of his views, often in satirical or humorous vein, were invariably interesting and pertinent. He wrote numerous articles presenting popular expositions of scientific subjects or setting forth in trenchant style his opinions on matters of general public interest. In speaking or writing, his use of the English language was impeccable. In the latter years of his life he was subject more and more to moods of depression, so intense at times as to be actually pathological. In such a mood, probably, he ended his own life on the morning of May 15, 1923. He was survived by his wife, Elizabeth Munroe (Townsend) Webster of Syracuse, N. Y., whom he married Oct. 8, 1889, and by a son and two daughters.

[See *Who's Who in America, 1922–23*; *Clark Univ. Lib. Pubs.*, Mar. 1924; E. H. Hall, in *Proc. Am. Acad. of Arts and Sciences*, vol. LXII (1928), and in *Sci.*, July 20, 1923; *Class of 1885, Harvard Coll.* (1925); G. S. Fletcher, in *Physical Rev.*, June 1923; *Harvard Grads. Mag.*, Sept. 1923; obituary in *Boston Transcript*, May 15, 1923. Webster's papers are in the Clark Univ. Lib., Worcester, Mass.]   A. P. W—s.

WEBSTER, DANIEL (Jan. 18, 1782–Oct. 24, 1852), statesman, was born in Salisbury, N. H. He was descended from Thomas Webster, who was brought to Ipswich, Mass., *c.* 1635 as an infant and later removed to the southern New Hampshire frontier. His father, Ebenezer Webster, an unlettered but intrepid colonial, took part in Gen. Jeffrey Amherst's invasion of Canada in 1759 and was allotted some 225 acres of land in the upper Merrimack Valley, where he became a founder and local official in the exposed frontier town of Salisbury. Ebenezer was an early and active revolutionary leader and served with distinction as captain in the militia. He also served capably in the state legislature and participated in the ratification of the federal Constitution as a member of the New Hampshire convention. Later in life Captain Webster, who kept this title even after he had been made a colonel in the state militia, was made a lay judge of the county court of common pleas. Webster's mother, Abigail Eastman, of Welsh stock, was a second wife who, like her predecessor, bore Ebenezer five children; of these Daniel was next to the youngest.

A lad of delicate health, Daniel was spared the heavier tasks which his brothers and sisters shared on the rugged New Hampshire farm. He found opportunity instead for the cultivation of his precocious mind and strongly emotional nature. In the random schools of the neighborhood the boy found that in reading he "generally could perform better" than the teachers in charge but his crude achievements in the irk-

some task of writing caused his masters to wonder whether after all his fingers were not "destined for the plough-tail" (*Writings and Speeches*, National ed., XVII, 7). His father, however, not satisfied with his clumsy efforts at certain rural tasks, was determined to save him from a life of arduous toil and shortly announced his intention to give Daniel "the advantage of knowledge" that had been denied to himself. Accordingly, in 1796, Captain Webster enrolled his fourteen-year-old son in the Phillips Exeter Academy. The boy was shy and sensitive about his unfashionable attire and clumsy manners, but he made rapid headway with his studies. Only in declamation was he unable to match his fellows: at the weekly public exhibitions, despite careful preparation, he "could never command sufficient resolution" to leave his seat and present his offerings (*Ibid.*, XVII, 10).

In December 1796 Daniel returned with his father to Salisbury without having completed his course. A brief period of school-teaching ended with an arrangement for him to study under the Rev. Samuel Wood of Boscawen, who had offered to prepare him for Dartmouth College. By August 1797 he had achieved fair success in Latin and Greek and in the meantime had satisfied his omnivorous appetite for reading in the village library. With this uncertain equipment he presented himself for admission to Dartmouth at the opening of the regular fall term. Arriving on horseback with baggage and bedding, Webster began a college course that cost him in four years considerably less than two hundred dollars. The swarthy youngster, who was often taken for an Indian, soon acquired the nickname of "Black Dan." He pursued his studies with energy, yet found time for his two youthful enthusiasms, reading and playing. He graduated not far from the top of his class. He dabbled with enthusiasm in poetry and earned part of his board temporarily by contributing to the village newspaper. In contrast with his failure in Exeter days, he was outstanding in one of the college debating societies and developed a reputation as a speaker that led to his being invited by the citizens of Hanover to deliver, at the age of eighteen, the local Fourth of July oration. In this he revealed a florid style and a tendency toward bombast along with the "vigor and glow" that characterized his early oratorical efforts.

Following graduation Webster began the study of law in the office of Thomas W. Thompson of Salisbury. He had no great enthusiasm for the legal profession and seems to have had doubts as to whether he had the "brilliancy, and at the same time penetration and judgment enough, for a great law character" (*Ibid.,* XVII, 92, 95). But he read "Robertson, Vattel, and three volumes of Blackstone," meantime learning the routine of the law office, and began to "feel more at ease" (*Ibid.,* XVII, 100). After some months, however, he gave up these studies to accept a position as teacher in an academy in the small village of Fryeburg, the salary ($350) making it possible for him to aid his father in keeping his elder brother Ezekiel, in college. Offered reappointment at "five or six hundred dollars a year, a house to live in, a piece of land to cultivate" and the probability of a clerkship of the court of common pleas, he was tempted to settle down to spend his days "in a kind of comfortable privacy" (*Ibid.,* XVII, 110). But father and friends advised him to pursue the study of law and with a careful definition of his ideals he returned, in September 1802, to Thompson's office. The embryo lawyer pondered the limitations of his calling. Conceding the power of the law to help "invigorate and unfold the powers of the mind," he tried to offset the hard didactic style of the legal treatise with excursions into history and the classics and made random attempts of his own at expression in verse and rhyme.

He long expected that only a miracle would make it possible to transfer to "the capital of New England." Now, upon the urgent invitation of Ezekiel, who was teaching school there, he went to Boston and had the rare good fortune to be accepted immediately as a clerk by Christopher Gore [*q.v.*], who had just returned from a diplomatic mission abroad. Influenced by the stimulating scholarship of such an employer and his circle of distinguished associates, Webster's fertile mind developed apace. Upon Gore's advice but to his father's surprise and disappointment he declined the profitable clerkship of the court of common pleas which paternal influence had proudly arranged for him. Admitted to the Boston bar in March 1805, he was recalled to Boscawen by a sense of filial obligation. His intention had been to set up an office in Portsmouth, but his father's illness made it a duty "to drop from the firmament of Boston gayety and pleasure, to the level of a rustic village, of silence and of obscurity" (*Ibid.,* XVII, 200).

In September 1807, some little time after his father's death, he transferred his labors to Portsmouth where he remained for nine "very happy years." To this new home he brought his bride, Grace Fletcher, daughter of a New Hampshire clergyman, whom he married on May 29, 1808

(Fuess, *post,* I, 101n.). In his practice of law, the young attorney promptly won distinction. Following the superior court in most of the counties of the state, he found it possible to achieve a practice worth nearly $2,000 a year. He enjoyed the professional rivalry of Jeremiah Mason [*q.v.*], whom he once rated as the greatest lawyer in the country. From their frequent clashes in court he learned the importance of the most careful preparation of his arguments and of the most effective diction. Webster consciously dropped his earlier florid style and sought to achieve the short incisive sentences with which Mason was so masterful. Meantime, the two rivals at the bar became the best of political friends.

During the Portsmouth period Webster was being drawn more and more into politics. Temperamentally a conservative, he had inherited from his father strong Federalist convictions, which were reinforced by other associations, especially by his contacts with the "bigwigs" of Boston. Satisfied that wealth and intelligence should play a dominant rôle in public life, he early reached the conclusion that the Federalist party combined "more than two thirds of the talent, the character, and the property of the nation" (*Writings and Speeches,* XVII, 115). He grew to maturity amid the fear of French revolutionary ideals of democracy and came to picture them as threatening civil war "when American blood shall be made to flow in rivers, by American swords!" (*Ibid.,* XVII, 79). It was this fear that produced his early devotion to "the bonds of our Federal Union." The Jeffersonian victory of 1800 seemed an "earthquake of popular commotion" under a Constitution which he was free to admit left "a wide field for the exertions of democratic intrigue" (*Ibid.,* XVII, 111–12). He therefore labored in his humble way—in Fourth of July orations and in occasional political pamphleteering—to contribute to the revival of Federalism, to arouse those who were disposed to "sit still and sigh at the depravity of the times," while the "contagion of democracy" threatened to "pervade every place and corrupt every generous and manly sentiment" (*Ibid.,* XVII, 158, 175).

He soon became a champion of the shipping interests of New England and of their protection against the retaliatory measures of Great Britain and France in their war for European supremacy. When Jefferson instituted a policy of economic coercion that struck a ruinous blow at the commercial prosperity of New England, Webster contributed a pamphlet, *Considerations on the Embargo Laws* (1808), which effectively voiced the Federalist opposition. By the time that the controversy over neutral rights had led to the outbreak of hostilities with Great Britain, Webster had achieved a recognized place among the Federalists of Portsmouth. In a Fourth of July oration in 1812 he vigorously condemned the administration for having led the nation into an unjustifiable war (*Ibid.*, XV, 583–98). But, unlike the Federalist die-hards who had been for years at least toying with the idea of separating New England from the Union, Webster renounced the idea of resistance or insurrection and took his stand for full freedom of criticism and "the peaceable remedy of election" (*Ibid.*, XV, 594). A month later in his famous "Rockingham Memorial," presented at a Federalist mass meeting in Rockingham County, N. H., he reiterated his anti-war views even more forcefully (*Ibid.*, XV, 599–610).

The enthusiastic reception of this memorial, both by the convention which proceeded to nominate him for Congress and by Federalists generally, launched Webster, with his election in November, upon a national political career. Made a member of the committee on foreign relations, he presented, on June 10, 1813, a series of resolutions calling upon the government to explain the events immediately preceding the outbreak of hostilities and had the satisfaction of making a powerful impression and of seeing his resolutions adopted eleven days later (*Annals of Congress*, 13 Cong., 1 Sess., cols. 149–51, 302–11). Aiming to embarrass the administration as much as possible, he loosed his eloquence against bounties to encourage enlistments and in favor of the repeal of the Embargo Act; in ringing words he proclaimed the constitutional right of the opposition to voice its protests and to utilize full freedom of inquiry. He himself refused to vote taxes in support of the war and denounced the government's draft bill, not only as an "infamous expedient" but as clearly "unconstitutional and illegal" (*Writings and Speeches*, XIV, 55–69). Webster even suggested the expedient of state nullification of a federal law under "the solemn duty of the State Governments to protect their own authority over their own militia, and to interpose between their citizens and arbitrary power" (*Ibid.*, XIV, 68). Since the conscription bill failed, there was no contemporary test of this doctrine. Webster was careful, however, to repudiate any thought of disunion. During the sessions of the Hartford Convention he was busy at Washington and had in the meantime advised the governor of New Hampshire against appointing delegates to a body that might be unduly influenced by the separatist forces (Curtis, *post*, I, 136).

Reëlected in 1814, Webster became influential in the attempts to make peacetime adjustments to the economic lessons taught in the recent war. Legislation to reëstablish the United States Bank was modified by Calhoun to meet Webster's objections to the lack of adequate safeguards for financial stability and was passed by Congress only to receive a presidential veto. He later voted against the bank bill which did not contain such safeguards but which was signed by the President in April 1816. In the discussions of fiscal policy, including the matter of specie payment for government revenues, Webster revealed an amazing knowledge of and devotion to sound principles of public finance. In the discussion of the tariff he proclaimed himself not an enemy of manufactures, but as opposed to rearing them in hotbeds. His loyalty to the mercantile interests of his section, however, caused him to oppose the high protective duties of the tariff of 1816, especially those originally proposed for cotton, iron, and hemp, which menaced the imports of New England and threatened to add to the cost of ship-building.

In August 1816, midway in his second term in Congress, Webster transferred his residence to Boston, where he sidetracked politics for a law practice that was soon bringing in $15,000 a year. During his last winter at Washington, he had given much of his time to legal work. He was retained before the Supreme Court in three important prize cases and was soon to add to his laurels in the Dartmouth College case. As a result of the complicated operation of party politics in New Hampshire, Webster's alma mater had become a pawn upon the political chess board. A Republican legislature in 1816 enacted a law changing the character of the institution and its governing body, placing it under the thumb of the general court. A suit in which the college trustees sought to defend their rights against the new political forces was carried to the New Hampshire superior court, from which it was appealed to the United States Supreme Court. Webster, after accepting a small fee from the other side, had revealed his sympathies with the college trustees (Fuess, I, 220–21). He had closed the argument for them before the superior court and now for a fee of $1,000, out of which he was to engage an associate, he was placed in charge of the case in the Supreme Court. The notes and briefs of his colleagues furnished most of his materials, but these he carefully overhauled and brilliantly presented (*Writings and Speeches*, X, 194–233). He closed with an appeal in which with consummate pathos he presented the case of the small college which he loved as the case of every college in the land. When on Feb. 2, 1819, the Court in its decision completely upheld the college and its counsel (4 *Wheaton*, 518), Webster became in the opinion of many the foremost lawyer of the time. Three weeks after the Dartmouth College victory he appeared for the Bank of the United States in *McCulloch* vs. *Maryland* (*Writings and Speeches*, XV, 261–67) and received a fee of $2,000 for his services. In three other important cases involving grave constitutional issues that shortly came before the Supreme Court, Webster was to play an important part (*Gibbons* vs. *Ogden, Osborn* vs. *Bank of the United States, Ogden* vs. *Saunders*; Charles Warren, *The Supreme Court in United States History*, 1922, I, 476–88; II, 59, 90, 147–48).

In the midst of a busy law practice Webster could not keep out of the public eye. In December 1819 he opposed the admission of Missouri as a slave state and drafted the memorial of a Boston protest meeting. He made the feature address in favor of free trade at a meeting of New England importers in Faneuil Hall in the autumn of 1820. He was chosen as a presidential elector in the campaign of that year. He played an influential but conservative rôle in the Massachusetts constitutional convention of 1820–21 and helped to hold the democratic forces in check (Fuess, I, 273–80). On Dec. 22, 1820, he delivered at Plymouth a powerful oration in celebration of the two hundredth anniversary of the landing of the Pilgrims. Achieving another great oratorical triumph at the laying of the cornerstone of the Bunker Hill monument on June 17, 1825, he made popular the occasional oratory that was to thrive for decades. He served for a brief period in the Massachusetts House of Representatives in the spring of 1822. In the fall he was drafted to represent Boston in Congress and was promptly made chairman of the judiciary committee when he took his seat in December 1823. A brilliant oration on Greek Independence (Jan. 19, 1824) signalized his return to the national political arena, but he was soon busied with less romantic topics. The tariff question—to him at this time "a tedious, disagreeable subject"—was now to the fore and the financiers, merchants, and ship-builders of Boston expected him to challenge Henry Clay's arguments for protection. Accordingly, on Apr. 1, 2, 1824, Webster attacked the proposed bill and its principles and announced his inability to accord it his vote (*Writings and Speeches,* V, 94–149).

In the preliminaries of the presidential contest of 1824 Webster's private choice was Calhoun; he shared the distrust of New England Federalists for John Quincy Adams. Busied with his own reëlection he avoided any formal commitment, but in the contest in the House he gave his vote to Adams and influenced others in the same direction. Webster had hopes of the mission to Great Britain but Adams showed no inclination to gratify him. Yet, as party lines reshaped themselves under the new administration, Webster became an increasingly loyal supporter. He supported the President's doctrine on internal improvements, pleading for a truly national interest to justify federal aid; he led the futile fight for a revision of the federal judicial system; he made an eloquent appeal for representation in the congress at Panama. Reëlected to Congress almost unanimously, he championed the President in the bitter dispute with Georgia over the Cherokee lands. All the while Webster kept up a busy practice before the Supreme Court and other courts of the country.

In June 1827 he was elected to the United States Senate. The death of Mrs. Webster (Jan. 21, 1828) temporarily destroyed his zest for work and his interest in public affairs. But soon he was in the thick of the fight that accompanied the passage of the tariff act of 1828. The Webster of this period was less satisfied than hitherto with economic theories and more concerned with the realities of life. He had established intimate associations with the Lawrences and Lowells and the mill-owners of his state generally, and had taken a small block of stock when the Merrimack Manufacturing Company was incorporated in 1822 (Fuess, I, 341). The tariff of 1824 had been followed by a vast increase of investment in wool manufacturing and Webster was now (May 9, 1828) frank in stating that nothing was left to New England "but to consider that the government had fixed and determined its own policy; and that policy was *protection*" (*Writings and Speeches,* V, 230). Since the new bill, with all its "abominations," did grant the protection to woolens which the act of 1824 had by implication pledged, he accorded his active support to the measure and helped accomplish its passage. Henceforth, Webster was an aggressive champion of protection.

The months that followed brought bitter disappointments: Adams was defeated for reëlection by Jackson, and Webster's favorite brother, Ezekiel, whom he helped launch a career in New Hampshire politics, died. His energy seemed to ebb and he wondered at times whether he was not growing old. But life took on new meaning following his marriage on Dec. 12, 1829, to Caroline Le Roy, a young and popular representative of New York sophistication, and new and stirring events were ahead. Another month and he was in the thick of the battle against the Calhoun doctrine of nullification. With leonine grace and energy and in the rich tones of his oratory, he met the challenge of Calhoun's mouthpiece, Robert Y. Hayne [q.v.]; rising to the height of his forensic abilities in this famous debate of January 1830 (Ibid., V, 248–69; VI, 3–75), he won what his admirers hailed as a brilliant victory over the cause of state rights and nullification. Praising the Union and what it had accomplished and still promised to achieve for the nation, he declared that in origin it preceded the states and insisted that the Constitution was framed by the people, not as a compact but to create a government sovereign within the range of the powers assigned to it, with the Supreme Court as the only proper arbiter of the extent of these powers. Nullification could result only in violence and civil war, he proclaimed; he was for "Liberty and Union, now and forever, one and inseparable!" No wonder that, with the plaudits of his audience still ringing in his ears, with the nation-wide fame achieved in this great outburst of eloquence, rosy dreams of the White House continued henceforth to play in Webster's mind.

The tariff problem which had aroused Calhoun and the South still remained. Southern efforts to force a reduction of duties led to the measure of July 1832 in which Webster was concerned primarily with maintaining protection upon woolen cloths. But even the lower duties of this act did not satisfy South Carolina which forced the issue of nullification in the ordinance passed by a convention of that state in November. Webster made clear his intention to support the President in his defiance of the nullifiers and crossed lances with Calhoun in an important debate the following February (Ibid., VI, 181–238). Meantime, against his advice, Clay joined with the anti-tariff leaders in pressing legislation agreeable to the latter; finally in March 1833 the "Compromise Tariff" was enacted. Bitterly disappointed, Webster voted with the opposition. The only satisfaction he could find in the outcome was in the thought that "the events of the winter have tended to strengthen the union of the States, and to uphold the government" (Ibid., XVII, 537). To this end and for the honor of being known as the "Defender of the Constitution," Webster had sacrificed for the time even his lucrative Supreme Court practice.

Politics had developed even new intricacies. The opposition forces of varying views but with common interests in vested rights had combined in the Whig party. Naturally, Webster joined the new coalition. Any temptation toward continued cooperation with Jackson was removed by the latter's war on the Bank of the United States, which Webster supported both on principle and as a profitable client. There was the further fact that Webster, who was as careless in handling his own money as he was profound in his mastery of the principles of public finance, was heavily indebted to the bank for loans extended to him. He had actively advocated the recharter bill and had vigorously condemned Jackson's veto, especially the constitutional grounds that it set forth. Reëlected to the Senate in 1833, Webster regarded Jackson's removal of deposits from the bank as presenting an issue that might lead to the presidential office. He distinguished himself, however, by the constructive quality, in contrast to the personal vituperation of his associates, that marked his reply to Jackson's protest against the resolution of censure which the Senate had adopted. As the election of 1836 drew near the Whigs of the Massachusetts legislature nominated him as their candidate. With other Whig nominees in the field, however, he had few enthusiastic supporters outside of New England and Pennsylvania, despite the friendly visit he had paid to the West in the summer of 1833, and he received only the electoral vote of Massachusetts.

Following this defeat, he gave serious consideration to retirement from active politics, either to recoup his fortune, which had suffered with his law practice, or to improve his presidential chances for 1840. Just at this time, one of the worst for profitable investment, he was acquiring with borrowed money extensive land holdings in Ohio, Indiana, Illinois, Michigan, and Wisconsin. His interests were largely speculative, except that he planned a huge country estate near La Salle, Ill., which was for a time operated by his son, Fletcher. His own personal interests continued in his seaside home at Marshfield where, with the continual lure of "the sea, the sea," he lived in almost feudal ease among devoted retainers and entertained with a lavish hand. Unable to realize upon his ill-timed investments, he was increasingly harassed by his creditors and financial embarrassment haunted him to the end. Only the willingness of his wealthy friends to be levied upon in emergency saved him from actual disgrace.

His Massachusetts followers, however, would not consent to his retirement. After another Western tour—which was a veritable series of ovations—during which the panic of 1837 broke, he returned to the special session of Congress and took a brilliant part in the Whig fight against Van Buren's sub-treasury plan, again breaking lances with Calhoun. The question of slavery and the right of petition brought similar clashes and Webster was impressed with the storm clouds so ominous for the future. In the summer of 1839, following reëlection, he and his family visited England where he hoped to find buyers for his western lands and to acquaint himself still further with the details of the menacing boundary dispute between Maine and Canada. He returned to find that the Whigs had nominated General Harrison for the presidency and he participated in the campaign with all the more zest because he expected it to bring to a close his senatorial career, with retirement to the bar in the event of Van Buren's reëlection and the prospect of a cabinet appointment if Harrison should succeed.

The victorious Harrison made Webster secretary of state, after having paid a tribute to his knowledge of public finance by offering the alternative of appointment to the Treasury Department. On Harrison's death a month later, John Tyler, his successor, retained the cabinet in office. Webster had anticipated the enactment of a series of Whig measures such as those for which Henry Clay made himself the spokesman in the ensuing months (*Writings and Speeches,* XVIII, 100). Soon, however, President Tyler, a Southern Whig of the state-rights school, became involved in a dispute with the Clay following when he successively vetoed the two measures by which the Whigs sought to reëstablish a United States bank. In the split that followed all the members of Tyler's cabinet except Webster resigned. The latter, who was extremely unhappy about these conditions and suspicious of the leadership of Clay, tried to play a conciliatory rôle. He regretted "the violence & injustice" which had "characterized the conduct of the Whig leaders"; he was determined, moreover, not to "throw the great foreign concerns of the country into disorder or danger, by any abrupt party proceeding" (*Ibid.,* XVI, 386; XVIII, 110). He was referring to the complicated negotiations over the Maine boundary which, with consummate skill, tact, and dignity and with the cordial cooperation of the President, he carried on and brought to a successful adjustment in the Webster-Ashburton Treaty of 1842. In this agreement was included an arrangement for joint cruising squadrons to operate off the coast of Africa in the suppression of the slave trade, which was expected to terminate a long-standing controversy over the right of search. His emi-

nently satisfactory discharge of his duties in the State Department included successful negotiations with Portugal, important discussions with Mexico, and the preliminaries to the opening of diplomatic relations with China which led to the commercial treaty negotiated by Caleb Cushing in 1844. Meantime, he rejoiced in the enactment of a Whig tariff (1842) which wiped out what seemed to him the iniquities of the measure of 1833 and returned to the principle of protection.

Webster, who had for some time been under strong Whig pressure to resign, at length with some reluctance (May 8, 1843) left the only office which had ever allowed reasonable satisfaction for his ambition and his talents. He had aspired to a diplomatic mission to England and had tried to juggle events to that end but fate dictated his retirement to private life (Fuess, II, 125–28). Burdened with debt, he returned to meet the heavy demands for his legal services that promised to replenish his exchequer. A seat in the Senate was awaiting his convenience and the returned statesman, convinced that the sober business men and conservatives of Massachusetts had never deserted him, took satisfaction in a reconciliation with his old party associates in which he felt no necessity for offering apologies for his recent independent course. He cooperated cheerfully in support of Clay's candidacy for the presidency in the campaign of 1844 and in the following winter allowed himself to be returned to the Senate.

Devoted to the vested interests of his state—indeed, a virtual pensioner dependent upon their bounty—Webster deemed it his "especial business" as a member of Congress "to look to the preservation of the great industrial interests of the country" from Democratic free-trade propensities (*Writings and Speeches,* XVIII, 231; see also *Ibid.,* IV, 47, XVI, 431–32). All the activities of the protectionists, however, did not prevent the reductions under the Walker Tariff of 1846. Meanwhile, as he had feared, the annexation of Texas had been followed by war with Mexico. Webster had opposed the acquisition of Texas and the resulting extension of slavery and now joined in the Whig policy of condemning the war. He held, however, that supplies should be voted as long as the war was not connected with territorial aggrandizement and that the struggle should be brought to a speedy and successful termination. To this end he gave his second son, Maj. Edward Webster, who died of exposure in service near Mexico city.

Though Webster, impervious to the lure of

empire, introduced resolutions repudiating all thought of the dismemberment of Mexico (*Congressional Globe*, 29 Cong., 2 Sess., p. 422), the war ended in a treaty which gave the United States a vast domain carved out of this neighbor republic. Should the new territory be dedicated to freedom or be thrown open to the westward march of negro slavery, was the inevitable question that arose. Webster had been from the start a strong critic of the peculiar institution of the South as "a great moral and political evil," but had conceded that within the Southern states it was a matter of domestic policy, "a subject within the exclusive control of the States themselves" (*Writings and Speeches*, XVIII, 353; XII, 210). He voted consistently for the Wilmot Proviso, but preferred the "no-territory" basis that would prevent a controversy from arising over slavery. With the triumph of the expansionists he saw nothing in the future but "contention, strife, and agitation" (Fuess, II, 171). Dreams of the presidency still haunted him. In the spring of 1847 he had made a Southern tour in which he was dined and wined until his body and spirits drooped. Even after his recuperation at Marshfield and his return to court for many a strenuous session, he took it for granted, at the age of sixty-six, that people were beginning to say, "He is not the man he was" (*Writings and Speeches*, XVIII, 267). The death of his daughter Julia, who had married Samuel Appleton Appleton, and of his son Edward depressed him even more. Of his children only his son Fletcher survived him. When out of sheer expediency his party turned to a military hero, Gen. Zachary Taylor, he acquiesced in his own repudiation with what grace he could.

In the first winter of the new administration Webster beheld with alarm a serious crisis in the sectional controversy. The abolitionist extremists were advocating a dissolution of the Union and the anti-slavery forces in Congress were bent upon pressing their strength to accomplish the exclusion of slavery from the territories, while Southern leaders, increasingly conscious of the seriousness of the minority status of the South, were developing a sense of Southern nationality and preparing, if need be, to launch a movement for a separate Southern confederacy. Like other conservative statesmen, Webster came to feel that the Union was seriously at stake and was determined to do all in his power to avert the danger. It must not be overlooked that Webster, as the champion of protection, was alarmed to find the continued discussion of the slavery question an obstacle to Whig efforts at tariff revision, causing Southern

Whigs whose rights, property, and feeling had been constantly assailed to argue that they would never "give a single vote for the Tariff until this Slavery business is settled," and that Northern men would have to "take care of their own interests" (*Ibid.*, XVI, 541; XVIII, 391). To Webster the more important public question of the tariff was being sacrificed to the slavery controversy (*Ibid.*, XVIII, 370). He had, therefore, become increasingly annoyed at the militant intransigentism of the anti-slavery forces, especially those who would not believe that "I am an anti slavery man unless I repeat the declaration once a week" (*Ibid.*, XVI, 498). While he believed in the power of Congress legally to exclude slavery from the territories, he had stated as early as 1848 that there was "no longer any important practical question" as to slavery extension (*Ibid.*, XVIII, 283). He therefore rose on Mar. 7, 1850, "to beat down the Northern and the Southern follies, now raging in equal extremes" (*Ibid.*, XVI, 534).

In a well-considered speech he declared himself for Clay's compromise measures and poured oil on troubled waters. He spoke "not as a Massachusetts man, nor as a Northern man, but as an American" (*Ibid.*, X, 57). Slavery was an evil but not so great an evil as disunion. There could be no peaceful secession, he informed the South. On the other hand, he condemned the unnecessary severity of the anti-slavery forces and admitted that Northerners had not lived up to their obligations to return fugitive slaves. Congressional prohibition in the territories was useless since a law of nature had settled "beyond all terms of human enactment, that slavery cannot exist in California or New Mexico" (*Ibid.*, X, 82). To the conservative element of the country Webster's performance seemed "Godlike"; but the anti-slavery men, including those of his own party, could see him only as a fallen star. Nor did he recover their good graces. Webster became, after Taylor's death, secretary of state in Fillmore's cabinet (July 22, 1850). He supported the legislation that substantially covered the ground of Clay's compromise measures and followed with concern the storm that still raged. Even as late as the summer of 1851 the question of secession was being discussed in certain Southern states and Webster felt called upon to write a timely letter denying the right of secession and denouncing it as revolution (*Ibid.*, XVI, 622–23). In the State Department Webster conscientiously and creditably performed the duties of his office, writing the famous "Hülsemann letter" in reproof of the attitude of the Austrian chargé toward American policy in the Hungarian revolution and dealing with more than ordinary diplomatic difficulties with Spain, Mexico, Peru, and Great Britain. His presidential aspirations were again revived in 1852, without serious embarrassment to his relations with Fillmore who was also a candidate. But both men were shelved by the Whigs and, sick in mind and body, Webster repudiated General Scott's nomination and prophesied the downfall of his party.

As the summer progressed, serious illness and suffering stared from his dark countenance. Always fond of the good things of life, he had found since his second marriage increasing opportunity for self-indulgence. Lavish hospitalities, with good food and good drink given and received, made him grow portly though rarely sluggish. Only his active life and early rising kept down the inroads of disease. His annual hay fever became increasingly more distressing. Financial worries pressed down upon him and made him wish at times that he "had been born a miser" (*Ibid.*, XVI, 636). By autumn the inroads of a fatal malady, cirrhosis of the liver, had marked his days and he died on Oct. 24, 1852, murmuring, "I still live."

Two score years in the political arena revealed in Daniel Webster two seemingly contrasting but naturally allied forces. Eloquent champion of the American Union, he was also the special advocate of the new industrial interests then so rapidly forging to the fore in the national economy. In their behalf the leonine Daniel, idol of the "best" people of his state and of his section, sacrificed the popular following that would gladly have rallied to the standard of a great democratic chieftain. The penetrating logic and burning eloquence of his oratory, the masterful and magnetic quality of his personality, contributed little toward bringing to him the support of the toiling masses. Life therefore became for Webster a series of great frustrations. A great constitutional lawyer, he found his equals, or betters, among his eminent contemporaries. His victories in statecraft and diplomacy were never on a par with his soaring ambitions. The presidential office seemed to have been reserved for men of less distinction. Even his personal fortunes failed to bring him the sense of security that often assuages frustration. Withal, however, perhaps no Northerner left so strong an impress upon the political life of this great "middle period," or made a more substantial contribution to the preservation of the Union in the supreme test of the sixties.

[The first attempt at general publication of Webster's works resulted in *The Works of Daniel Webster* (6 vols., 1851), ed. by Edward Everett; and in *The Private Correspondence of Daniel Webster* (2 vols., 1857), ed.

by Fletcher Webster, which included his brief autobiography as written in 1829. Collections of his manuscripts were later made, the most complete being that of the N. H. Hist. Soc. at Concord. The Sanborn collection in New York City is less extensive; the Greenough collection in Washington (Lib. of Cong.) is made up largely of letters received from Webster's correspondents; and the Mass. Hist. Soc. collection is very limited. Important additions, largely of unpublished items selected from the New Hampshire collection, were made available in *The Letters of Daniel Webster* (1902), ed. by C. H. Van Tyne; an effort at publishing his complete works was made in the National ed. under the title, *The Writings and Speeches of Daniel Webster* (18 vols., 1903), ed. by J. W. McIntyre. The earliest biography, prepared with Webster's approval, is S. L. Knapp, *A Memoir of the Life of Daniel Webster* (1831). C. W. March, *Reminiscences of Congress* (1850), later published as *Daniel Webster and His Contemporaries* (1852), is a reminiscent account by a wealthy friend. Immediately following Webster's death, a reminiscent biography appeared in the account of his private secretary, Charles Lanman, *The Private Life of Daniel Webster* (1852), which the family made an attempt to suppress. Other gossipy narratives are Peter Harvey, *Reminiscences and Anecdotes of Daniel Webster* (1877); and the brief "Reminiscences of Daniel Webster" by William Plumer, included in the National ed., XVII, 546–67. Personal recollections give value to the work of his literary executor, G. T. Curtis, *Life of Daniel Webster* (2 vols., 1870). H. C. Lodge, *Daniel Webster* (1883), the first brief formal biography, is colored by the abolitionist tradition and influenced by the highly prejudicial chapter on Webster in James Parton, *Famous Americans of Recent Times* (1867). After a number of rather perfunctory lives came the more penetrating work of S. G. Fisher, *The True Daniel Webster* (1911). Recent biographies, including F. A. Ogg, *Daniel Webster* (1914) and S. H. Adams, *The Godlike Daniel* (1930), have been overshadowed by the excellent and more nearly definitive C. M. Fuess, *Daniel Webster* (2 vols., 1930). Among numerous special works and articles particularly worthy of mention are G. T. Curtis, *The Last Years of Daniel Webster* (1878); E. P. Wheeler, *Daniel Webster, The Expounder of the Constitution* (1905); Gamaliel Bradford, "Daniel Webster," in *As God Made Them* (1929); R. L. Carey, *Daniel Webster as an Economist* (1929); H. D. Foster, "Webster's Seventh of March Speech and the Secession Movement, 1850," in *Am. Hist. Rev.*, Jan. 1922; V. L. Parrington, "Daniel Webster, Realist and Constitutionalist," in *The Romantic Revolution in America* (1927); articles by C. A. Duniway in S. F. Bemis, *The Am. Secretaries of State and Their Diplomacy*, vols. V, VI (1928). There is an excellent bibliography in *The Cambridge Hist. of Am. Literature*, vol. II (1918), pp. 480–88. For an obituary, see *Boston Daily Advertiser*, Oct. 25, 1852.]

A. C. C.

WEBSTER, JEAN [See WEBSTER, ALICE JANE CHANDLER, 1876–1916].

WEBSTER, JOHN WHITE (May 20, 1793– Aug. 30, 1850), university professor, owed his painful notoriety to an appalling crime. He was born in Boston, Mass., the son of Redford and Hannah (White) Webster. His father's success as an apothecary ensured young Webster an academic education, foreign travel, and leisure to deliberate upon a profession. He was graduated from Harvard, B.A., 1811, and M.D., 1815. Completing his medical studies in London, he was entered at Guy's Hospital in 1815 as, successively, surgeon's pupil, physician's pupil, and surgeon's dresser. A visit to St. Michael in the

Azores (1817–18) resulted in his first book and in his marriage, May 16, 1818, to Harriet Fredrica Hickling, daughter of the American vice-consul at St. Michael. They had four daughters. From 1824 to 1849 Webster taught chemistry at Harvard, holding from 1827 onward the Erving professorship of chemistry and mineralogy. In Cambridge his scale of living and hospitality exhausted his inheritance and strained his income. His salary was $1,200 a year, while his lectures at the Massachusetts Medical College brought but a few hundreds more.

In 1842 Webster borrowed $400 from Dr. George Parkman, uncle of the historian, Francis Parkman [q.v.]. In 1847, with but little of this repaid, he gave Parkman his note for $2,432, representing the unpaid balance and a further loan. This was secured by a mortgage of Webster's personal property, including a cabinet of minerals. In 1848, still in distress, he borrowed $1,200 from Robert Gould Shaw, Sr., making over to him the minerals already pledged to Parkman. The latter, hearing of this, became furious; he considered Webster fraudulent, and took care to let him know it. Interviews between the two men became acrimonious. Early on Nov. 23, 1849, Webster called at Parkman's house, and arranged a meeting in his own laboratory at 1:30 P.M. Parkman, at about that hour, was seen approaching the Medical College, on Grove Street, Boston. He was not seen again. His disappearance was a mystery for a week, when Littlefield, janitor of the College, who had become suspicious of Webster's conduct, broke into a vault beneath the laboratory and found some human bones. Other human fragments were found in the furnace and in a tea-chest. As a result of this and of Webster's obviously false statements that he had paid Parkman, Webster was arrested. At the police station he attempted suicide by strychnine. His trial (Mar. 19–Apr. 1, 1850) before Chief Justice Lemuel Shaw [q.v.] is famous for the judge's charge and its definitions of circumstantial evidence. Proof that the remains were really Parkman's depended on the testimony of Dr. Nathan C. Keep, who identified Parkman's false teeth, found in Webster's furnace, as teeth made by himself. Webster's conviction was followed by public protests, founded on the usual ill-informed distrust of circumstantial evidence. Webster sent a plea to the governor, asserting his entire innocence, and in the most solemn and affecting language calling upon God as witness to his truthfulness. Later, however, he made a written confession, basing a new plea, for lesser punishment than death, upon his contention that the crime was not premedi-tated, but the governor and council could give no credence to any of his statements, and he was hanged, Aug. 30.

As a teacher, Webster was far from brilliant. He wrote A Description of the Island of St. Michael (1821), was associate editor of the Boston Journal of Philosophy and the Arts (1824–26), compiled A Manual of Chemistry (1826), and brought out editions of Andrew Fyfe's Elements of Chemistry (1827) and Justus Liebig's Animal Chemistry or Organic Chemistry (1841). Indulged as a child and pampered in youth, he developed a petulant and fussy disposition, but his kindly nature was such that for him to commit murder at the age of fifty-six astounded his acquaintances, and gives some weight to his assertion that the act was sudden and unpremeditated. That he had a curiously macabre streak, however, appears from Longfellow's anecdote of a dinner at Webster's home, when the host amazed his guests by lowering the lights, fitting a noose around his own neck, and lolling his head forward, tongue protruding, over a bowl of blazing chemicals, to give a ghastly imitation of a man being hanged (Annie A. Fields, Memories of a Hostess, 1922, p. 153).

[Sources include George Bemis, Report of the Case of John W. Webster (1850), perhaps the best report of any Am. criminal case; colls. of pamphlets on Webster in Lib. of Cong., Boston and N. Y. Pub. Libs., Boston Athenæum, Am. Antiquarian Soc., and Harvard Coll. Lib.; Quinquennial Cat. of Harv. Univ.; A Vol. of Records . . . Containing Boston Marriages from 1752 to 1809 (1903); information from the superintendent of Guy's Hospital; letter of M. A. De Wolfe Howe, in Sat. Rev. of Lit., Dec. 21, 1929; Boston Transcript, Aug. 30, 31, 1850. See also an excellent essay in H. B. Irving, A Book of Remarkable Criminals (1918); E. L. Pearson, Murder at Smutty Nose (1926), which contains (pp. 323–25) a selected bibliog. of the case; and George Dilnot, The Trial of Professor . . . Webster (1928). The date of Webster's marriage and the name of his wife are from Thomas M. Lothrop of Chicago, Ill.; the date of birth is from T. F. Harrington, The Harvard Medic. School (1905), vol. III, p. 1453.]

E. L. P.

WEBSTER, JOSEPH DANA (Aug. 25, 1811–Mar. 12, 1876), soldier and engineer, was born at Hampton, N. H., the son of Josiah Webster, a Congregational minister, and Elizabeth (Wright) Webster. He graduated at Dartmouth College in 1832 and studied law, but in 1835 entered the government service as a civil engineer. He was commissioned in the army, July 7, 1838, as a second lieutenant of topographical engineers and was promoted first lieutenant, July 14, 1849, and captain, Mar. 3, 1853. Resigning, Apr. 7, 1854, he settled in Chicago—where he had connections through his marriage in 1844 to a Miss Wright of that city—and acquired a considerable interest in a company manufacturing agricultural implements. In 1855 he was chosen as one of the three members of the Chicago sewerage commission, which was charged both with the construction of an extensive sewer system and with the raising of the level of a great part of the city.

He was appointed major and paymaster in the volunteer army, July 1, 1861, but never performed duty as a paymaster, for he was sent at once to Cairo, Ill., and employed on fortification and other engineering duties until his appointment, Feb. 1, 1862, as colonel, 1st Illinois Light Artillery. Meanwhile, Grant had selected him as his chief of staff; he served with him at Belmont, Forts Henry and Donelson, and Shiloh. His position was not precisely what the title now suggests. The chief of staff, according to Grant's instructions, was to act as his adviser, and also to look after anything not otherwise attended to. He was a general utility man. On the first day at Shiloh, for example, when the Union troops were being forced back on the river, Grant sent Webster to collect artillery for a last stand, if necessary, on the heights above the landing, and here he assembled one hundred guns. Grant repeatedly recommended his promotion. On Dec. 3, 1862, President Lincoln wrote to the secretary of war: "Let Col. James [*sic*] D. Webster, of Illinois, be appointed a Brigadier General of Volunteers"; but in some way this order was overlooked until Lincoln repeated it. The appointment was not finally made until April 1863, with rank, however, from Nov. 29, 1862. Shortly before, Webster had been put in charge by Grant of all the military railways in the area of his operations. Webster managed them before, during, and after the Vicksburg campaign. He was then designated as Sherman's chief of staff, remaining at the administrative headquarters in Nashville while his commanding general was in the field during the Atlanta campaign and the march to the sea. Thus he was with Thomas at the battle of Nashville. After Sherman reached Savannah the headquarters were transferred, and Webster joined his chief in the Carolinas. He was brevetted major general of volunteers, Mar. 13, 1865, and on Nov. 6 of that year resigned from the army. His entire military service had been passed in close association either with Grant or with Sherman, both of whom had profound confidence in him. Some years after the war, when Gen. William Sooy Smith [*q.v.*], in personal correspondence with Sherman, complained that statements published by the latter had done him injustice, Sherman proposed that the whole case be submitted to Webster as a competent and impartial judge.

After leaving the army Webster returned to Chicago and spent the rest of his life there. He was assessor of internal revenue from 1869 to 1872, assistant United States treasurer from 1872 to 1875, and collector of internal revenue from 1875 until his death. He was survived by his wife and three children.

[*War of the Rebellion: Official Records* (*Army*); F. B. Heitman, *Hist. Reg. and Dict. U. S. Army* (1903); *Biog. Sketches of Ill. Officers* (1862); W. T. Sherman, *Memoirs* (1875); *Chicago Daily Tribune,* Mar. 13, 1876; unpublished records in the War Dept.]

T. M. S.

WEBSTER, NOAH (Oct. 16, 1758–May 28, 1843), lexicographer, was sixth in descent from John Webster (d. Apr. 5, 1661), an emigrant from England to Newtowne (now Cambridge), Mass., c. 1630–33, who became one of the founders of the colony of Connecticut and, in 1656, its governor. John took up land in the township of Hartford, and it was in the village of West Hartford that the lexicographer was born, the fourth of the five children of Noah Webster (Mar. 25, 1722–Nov. 9, 1813) and his wife Mercy (baptized Oct. 8, 1727–died Oct. 5, 1794), daughter of Eliphalet Steele and great-great-grand-daughter of William Bradford [*q.v.*], second governor of the Plymouth colony. The elder Noah owned a farm of ninety acres in West Hartford. He served as justice of the peace, as deacon of the parish church (Congregational), and as captain on the "alarm list" of the local militia. He and his wife were married Jan. 12, 1749. Young Noah early showed a bent for books, and his father after some hesitation decided to send him to college. He got his preparatory training from the local minister, the Rev. Nathan Perkins, and from a Mr. Wales, schoolmaster of Hartford. In September 1774 he was admitted to Yale College, and four years later was duly graduated with the degree of B.A., though the elder Noah had to mortgage his farm to meet his son's modest college bills and the War of the American Revolution interfered markedly with academic studies at Yale as elsewhere.

Webster had settled upon a legal career, but his father was unable to help him further and for several years after his graduation from college he earned his living by teaching and clerical work, reading law with various jurists in his spare time. In 1781 he passed his examinations and was admitted to the bar at Hartford, but he did not begin active practice until 1789, and four years later gave up the law for good. The beginnings of his true career go back to 1782 when, while teaching at Goshen, N. Y., he prepared an elementary spelling book, published at Hartford the next year as the first part of *A Grammatical Institute of the English Language.*

The *Institute* was completed with a grammar (1784) and a reader (1785); all three books were written for the use of school children. In preparing the series Webster was moved by patriotic as well as professional and scholarly considerations. He found the schoolbooks then in use deficient on various counts, not least in their neglect of the American scene. The introduction of his speller includes, among other things, a literary Declaration of Independence by which Webster lived and wrought the rest of his days. Later editions of speller and reader gave expression to Webster's patriotic purposes in their very titles: *The American Spelling Book* and *An American Selection of Lessons in Reading and Speaking*. The speller did not differ radically from previous spellers, and at first did not include the orthographical reforms introduced into later editions and now regularly associated with Webster's name, but it was well arranged, gave convenient rules of thumb, and had the clarity and freshness of presentation characteristic of its author. Above all, it was an American product, nicely calculated to meet the particular needs of the American schools of the day, an outgrowth, indeed, of Webster's own experience as a schoolmaster. In length of vogue and volume of sales, however, it surpassed all expectation. The first edition of 5000 copies was exhausted in little more than a year, and in revised editions, under various titles, the book continued to be issued well into the twentieth century. In 1837 Webster estimated that some 15,000,000 copies of his spelling-books had been printed, and by 1890 the number had risen to more than 60,000,000. The wide and long use of Webster's spellers had much to do with the standardization of spelling and, to a less degree, of pronunciation in the United States along lines differing somewhat from those that prevailed in the mother country. Webster's reader did not have the vogue of the speller, although it went through a number of editions. To the edition of 1787 were added, as Webster explained to Franklin, "some American pieces under the discovery, history, wars, geography, economy, commerce, government, &c. of this country . . . in order to call the minds of our youth from ancient fables & modern foreign events, & fix them upon objects immediately interesting, in this country" (Ford, *post*, II, 454). The reader thus became a book patriotic enough to justify the insertion of the word *American* into its title. Webster's grammar, the second part of his *Institute*, was less successful, commercially, than the other parts. The historian, however, reads it with interest and respect as a forerunner (in

theory, at least) of the scientific English grammars of today, based not on rules taken from Latin grammar or pseudo-logical "principles," but on objective study of the actual phenomena of English speech.

Webster had hardly finished compiling his speller when the problem of the copyright presented itself. At that time the federal government had no authority in such a matter, and none of the newly established states had enacted a copyright law. With characteristic courage and energy Webster began, in 1782, an agitation which cost him more time and money than he had anticipated but led to legislative provision of an American copyright. Webster's initiative and leadership in this agitation not only gave him a place in the annals of the day but also brought him into contact with many of the leaders of the young republic and set going the national reputation which he was to achieve. In particular, the copyright agitation took him into politics, and made him an ardent federalist. Forced as he was to promote copyright legislation in thirteen capitals, he became one of the earliest advocates of a strong federal government, and in 1785 printed his views in a pamphlet called *Sketches of American Policy,* a pamphlet which won the interest of Washington and Madison, and, with an earlier series of articles in the *Connecticut Courant* (from Aug. 26, 1783), gave Webster his start as journalist and pamphleteer. Of his other political writings of the decade ought to be mentioned here, if only for its characteristic timeliness, the pamphlet of October 1787, urging the adoption, by the several states, of the newly submitted federal Constitution.

Webster's activities in favor of copyright legislation took him as far south as Charleston, S. C., and involved much travel and long stays in the chief cities of the country. He earned his living during this period in various ways: by ordinary teaching, by holding singing-schools, and by giving public lectures. While in Baltimore, in the summer and fall of 1785, he wrote five papers on the mother tongue, and read them in public with such success that he was "induced to revise and continue reading them in other towns" (Ford, I, 141). This course of popular lectures, with additions and revisions, was published in 1789 under the title, *Dissertations on the English Language*. The added "Essay on a Reformed Mode of Spelling," included in the volume, is of special interest. Webster's lectures in Philadelphia had led to an acquaintance with Benjamin Franklin, and a subsequent correspondence between the two on spelling reform (a subject in which Franklin had long been interested) brought Webster back to Philadelphia in December 1786 for a visit which turned into a stay of ten months. The essay, and Webster's various experiments with a simplified spelling, grew out of this intercourse with Franklin. The boldness and sweep of Webster's original scheme appear plainly enough in a letter, dated Mar. 31, 1786, which he wrote to George Washington. "I am encouraged," he says, "by the prospect of rendering my country some service, to proceed in my design of refining the language & improving our general system of education. Dr. Franklin has extended my views to a very simple plan of reducing the language to perfect regularity" (Ford, I, 110). Franklin's phonetic alphabet, however, simple though it was, proved too radical for adoption by Webster, who for practical reasons gave up counsels of perfection in favor of a "sufficiently regular" orthography, and with the years yielded ground more and more to the traditional spellers, so that in the end little was left of his reforms. But if Webster proved unable to effect any substantial spelling reforms, his spellers and dictionaries, ironically enough, played a great part in strengthening the grasp of orthographical orthodoxy. The American people, ruthlessly schoolmastered year in year out, became rooted and grounded in the faith, and the reforms brought forward by later generations of scholars, with all the backing of the now full-fledged science of linguistics, failed to shake the hold of that traditional spelling which Webster so reluctantly had made his own.

It was during his second stay in Philadelphia, as supervisor of an Episcopal school, that Webster met Rebecca Greenleaf (May 27, 1766–June 25, 1847), daughter of William Greenleaf, a Boston merchant, and his wife Mary (Brown). Webster and Miss Greenleaf were married in Boston on Oct. 26, 1789. They had two sons, one of whom died in infancy, and six daughters. Toward the end of 1787 Webster had settled in New York, as editor of a new venture called the *American Magazine.* The periodical had proved a commercial failure, and in December 1788 Webster had returned to Hartford, where he began his married life and practised law for several years. In 1793, however, he was induced to settle again in New York and take up once more the work of an editor. With the backing of certain prominent Federalists, he launched a daily newspaper, the *Minerva,* and a semi-weekly, the *Herald,* names which in 1797 were changed to *Commercial Advertiser* and *Spectator* respectively. His journalistic career lasted ten years, though in 1798 he removed to New Haven and thereafter had less and less to do with

the details of management of his newspapers, which, as he tells us, "were established for the purpose of vindicating and supporting the policy of President Washington" (Ford, I, 386) and which became burdensome to him as time elapsed and political conditions changed. In particular, Hamilton's betrayal (as he felt) of President John Adams disheartened Webster and had much to do with his return to his first love, linguistic scholarship. In 1803 he succeeded in disposing of his newspapers and gave up journalism for good. Thenceforth he devoted himself wholeheartedly to what was to prove his chief title to fame, his work as a lexicographer.

A survey of Webster's more important writings up to this turning-point in his life brings out in striking fashion the versatility and productivity of the man. His schoolbooks, such as the three volumes of the *Institute* with their revisions, *The Little Reader's Assistant,* and the series called *Elements of Useful Knowledge,* gave Webster the income which enabled him to retire from journalism and devote himself to study. A popular volume of informal essays was *The Prompter* (1791). The *Dissertations,* mentioned above, were likewise designed for popular reading, but proved a commercial failure. In the economic field, various treatises by Webster moved Lecky to pronounce him "one of the best of the early economists of America" (*A History of England in the Eighteenth Century,* 1882, III, 311). In the medical field Webster wrote, among other things, *A Brief History of Epidemic and Pestilential Diseases* (2 vols., 1799), the standard work on the subject in its day. Of the many political writings, the "Curtius" articles (1795) on the Jay Treaty, the "Aristides" letter to Hamilton (1800), and the *Ten Letters to Dr. Joseph Priestley* (1800) may be mentioned. Webster's edition of John Winthrop's *Journal* (1790) is of special interest as a pioneer work in learned historical publication, while his *Experiments Respecting Dew* (begun in 1790, though not printed until 1809) hold an honorable place among the pioneer American essays in physical science. It has also justly been noted that Webster's activities as statistician and climatologist foreshadowed the work of the census and weather bureaus of later times. These many-sided labors proved an admirable preparation for lexicography, in which the investigator must take all knowledge for his province.

The first fruit of Webster's lexicographical activities was his small work, *A Compendious Dictionary of the English Language* (1806). In its compilation Webster learned the technique of lexicography and tried out ideas of his own, recording, for example, some 5000 words not included in previous dictionaries. Webster however thought of his first dictionary as only preparatory to a larger work, a work upon which he labored steadily for nearly twenty years. Finished in 1825, it came out in two quarto volumes in 1828 under the title, *An American Dictionary of the English Language,* probably the most ambitious publication ever undertaken, up to that time, upon American soil. Financially it proved a disappointment (though not a failure), but its merits at once gave it first place among English dictionaries. It marks, indeed, a definite advance in the science of lexicography. Webster established once for all the practice, already begun in his first dictionary, of freely recording non-literary words, even though he did not push his principles to their logical conclusion and record all words whatsoever, as present practice inclines more and more to do. He justly based his definitions upon the usage of American as well as British writers and speakers, and did not hesitate to record "Americanisms" which he deemed worthy. In defining a word, he proceeded from what he considered its original or primary meaning, and so far as possible derived the other meanings from the primary. In so doing he made many mistakes, because of the deficiencies of current linguistic knowledge, and in some respects he was not abreast with the times, being out of touch, for example, with the comparative and historical linguistic school of his contemporaries Rask, Grimm, and Bopp, but his principles of definition were sound, and the definitions themselves in many cases cannot be bettered today, for Webster was a born definer as well as a man of encyclopedic knowledge. The great weakness of the dictionary lies in its etymologies, which were largely out-of-date before the work came from the press. As a whole, Webster's *American Dictionary* was a scholarly achievement of the first order, richly deserving of its great reputation at home and abroad. His chief contemporary rival in the United States was Joseph Emerson Worcester [*q.v.*], whom he charged with plagiarism, but most of the "War of the Dictionaries" occurred after his own death.

In 1812, Webster removed from New Haven to Amherst, Mass., where he felt he could live more cheaply and with fewer distractions from his scholarly labors. While at Amherst he became interested in local educational needs and helped to found Amherst College. In 1822, however, he returned to New Haven, where he continued to live the rest of his life, except for a year (1824–25) spent in lexicographical work in France and England, and a winter (1830–31) spent in Washington in successful agitation for a revision of the copyright law. His publications during what may be termed his lexicographical period include, besides five dictionaries with abridgments and revisions, a *Philosophical and Practical Grammar of the English Language* (1807), a revision of the Authorized Version of the English Bible (1833), and various essays and addresses. Webster in early life was something of a freethinker, but in 1808 he became a convert to Calvinistic orthodoxy, and thereafter remained a devout Congregationalist.

[H. E. Scudder, *Noah Webster* (1881); Emily E. F. Ford, *Notes on the Life of Noah Webster,* ed. by Emily E. F. Skeel (2 vols., 1912), including list of writings, vol. II, 523–40, and list of "authorities cited"; H. R. Warfel, *Noah Webster: Schoolmaster to America* (1936); C.-E. A. Winslow, "The Epidemiology of Noah Webster," *Trans. Conn. Academy of Arts and Sciences,* Jan. 1934; F. B. Dexter, *Biog. Sketches of the Grads. of Yale College,* vol. IV (1907); W. H. and M. R. Webster, *History and Genealogy of the Governor John Webster Family* (1915); D. S. Durrie, *Steele Family* (1859); J. E. Greenleaf, *Genealogy of the Greenleaf Family* (1896); obituary in *N. Y. Morning Express,* May 31, 1843; public records; family letters.]
K. M.

WEBSTER, PELATIAH (Nov. 24, 1726–Sept. 2, 1795), political economist, was born in Lebanon, Conn., the eldest son of Pelatiah and Joanna (Crowfoot) Smith Webster, and a descendant of John Webster, one of the first settlers of Hartford. After graduation from Yale College in 1746, he studied theology and in June 1749 began to preach in Greenwich, Mass., where on Dec. 20 he was ordained pastor. He married Mrs. Ruth Kellogg of Suffield, Conn., in September 1750 and they had four daughters and a son. His second wife, Rebecca Hunt, whom he married in Boston on Oct. 8, 1785, died in Philadelphia in 1793. In October 1755 Webster left his parish to become a merchant in Philadelphia, and later while maintaining his business, taught for a time in Germantown Academy. In 1765 he visited Charleston, S. C., recording his impressions in a journal (*Publications of the Southern History Association,* vol. II, 1898). On the outbreak of the Revolution his business suffered, and in April 1777, with a cargo of flour and iron bound for Boston, he was seized by the British and held prisoner in Newport for several weeks. The next year he was confined for some time in the Philadelphia jail and much of his property was confiscated, though later all but about £500 was recovered.

Beginning on Oct. 5, 1776, with a letter, in the *Pennsylvania Evening Post* on "the Danger of too much Circulating Cash," he published a succession of studies signed either "A Financier" or "A Citizen of Philadelphia" which were later collected in a volume entitled *Political Essays on the Nature and Operation of Money, Public Finances, and Other Subjects; Published during the American War* (1791). He argued in favor of the support of the war by taxation rather than by loans, a free trade policy, and the curtailment of paper money issues. He has been called "almost the only man of ability and note who held out vigorously against the rag-money party" in Pennsylvania at the time of the issue of bills of credit in 1785 (J. B. McMaster, *A History of the People of the United States,* vol. I, 1883, p. 284). During the struggle in Pennsylvania over the adoption of the Constitution he published *Remarks on the Address of Sixteen Members of the Assembly of Pennsylvania to their Constituents dated September 29, 1787* (1787), in which he cogently demonstrated the specious nature of the objections to the new plan of government, and about the same time he also published *The Weakness of Brutus Exposed: or, Some Remarks in Vindication of the Constitution Proposed by the Late Federal Convention against the Objections and Gloomy Fears of That Writer* (1787), in which he maintained the need for a government with supreme power, "full, definite, established, acknowledged." His faith in a stronger union he had expressed four years before in *A Dissertation on the Political Union and Constitution of the Thirteen United States of North-America* (1783), the pamphlet on which Hannis Taylor [*q.v.*] in the twentieth century rested his claim that Webster was the real author of the Constitution. These exaggerated claims made by Taylor on behalf of Webster have obscured his genuine share in educating the people to the need of a new form of government and his aid in bringing about the adoption of the Constitution, and have also diverted attention from the writings in which he expressed clear and vigorous views on money, credit, taxation, and trade.

[Henry Bronson, "A Historical Account of Connecticut Currency," *New Haven Colony Hist. Soc. Papers,* vol. I (1865); R. R. Hinman, *A Hist. Coll. from Official Records . . . of the Part Sustained by Conn. during the War of the Revolution* (1842); J. B. McMaster and F. D. Stone, *Pa. and the Federal Constitution* (1888); Noah Webster, *A Coll. of Papers on Political, Literary and Moral Subjects* (1843); W. H. and M. R. Webster, *Hist. and Geneal. of the Gov. John Webster Family* (1915); F. B. Dexter, *Biog. Sketches Grads. Yale Coll.,* vol. II (1896); Hannis Taylor, *A Memorial in Behalf of the Architect of Our Federal Constitution* (n.d., c. 1907) and *The Real Authorship of the Constitution of the United States Explained* (1912); E. S. Corwin, "The Pelatiah Webster Myth," in *The Doctrine of Judicial Review* (1914);

Gaillard Hunt, *Pelatiah Webster and the Constitution* (1912), repr. from the *Nation* (N. Y.), Dec. 28, 1911; *Dunlap and Claypoole's Am. Daily Advertiser* (Phila.), Sept. 4, 1795.]   E. D.

WEBSTER–POWELL, ALMA [See Powell, Alma Webster, 1874–1930].

WEED, THURLOW (Nov. 15, 1797–Nov. 22, 1882), politician and journalist, the eldest son of Joel and Mary (Ellis) Weed, was born in Greene County, N. Y., where his grandfather, formerly of Stamford, Conn., had settled with his family after the Revolution. Joel Weed, a hard-working but never prosperous farmer, sometimes in jail for debt, moved in 1799 to Catskill, where his son enjoyed a brief schooling. When he was eight years old Thurlow began to earn what he could by odd jobs at the blacksmith's, the printer's, and on Hudson River boats. In 1808 the family moved to Cortland County, and not long afterward to Onondaga, where young Weed was apprenticed to a printer. Several years in various printers' shops in central New York, broken by a few months' militia service in 1813, brought him little pecuniary gain but gave him an unrivalled education in local affairs. In 1817 he became foreman on the Albany *Register,* and tried his hand at writing news paragraphs and editorials in support of DeWitt Clinton's canal policy. On Apr. 26, 1818, he married Catherine Ostrander of Cooperstown.

During the next four years Weed tried to publish Clintonian papers at Norwich and Manlius, and after both had failed he moved on, almost penniless, to Rochester. There he secured a position on the *Rochester Telegraph,* for which he wrote editorials advocating John Quincy Adams for president. Sent to Albany in 1824 to lobby for a bank charter, he promptly set about uniting the friends of Adams and Clay in a common opposition to William H. Crawford, the candidate of Martin Van Buren. He returned to Rochester with the charter, and also with the knowledge that his time and efforts had become essential to his party (*Life, post,* I, 107). Soon he was campaigning through the western counties in behalf of Adams for president and Clinton for governor of New York. Weed himself was elected to the Assembly. Fortune favored him in business as well as in politics, and in 1825 he was able to buy the *Telegraph.*

Throughout the anti-Masonic excitement that followed the disappearance of William Morgan [*q.v.*] in 1826, Weed was an active member of the local Morgan committee, and gave up the *Telegraph* to publish the *Anti-Masonic Enquirer.* As local political organizations were formed, Weed exerted himself to secure candidates who were "sound" on issues other than the Masonic. He held the "infected district" in line for Adams in 1828 and supported National Republicans locally. Leading Anti-Masons raised a fund to establish a paper at Albany, and employed Weed as editor; he was elected to the Assembly in 1829 to make his presence at the capital possible. On Mar. 22, 1830 the first issue of the *Albany Evening Journal* appeared, Weed being reporter, proof-reader, and often compositor, as well as editor, legislator, and political manager. He remained officially an Anti-Mason through 1832, supporting William Wirt [*q.v.*], the party's presidential candidate, but, as before, saw that the nominees for state offices were National Republicans. Most Anti-Masons, he was convinced, were in sympathy with Clay's "American system," and were inevitably opposed to the dominant "Albany Regency," so closely linked, through Van Buren, to President Jackson. He himself ignored the Bank issue, believing it inexpedient to oppose so popular a movement against "moneyed aristocracy." Drilling his party through the unsuccessful campaigns of 1834 and 1836, he was ready for the opportunity offered by the panic and hard times, and helped create the victories that made William H. Seward [*q.v.*] governor in 1838 and Harrison president in 1840.

Weed was now generally regarded as the dictator of his party, and was charged with dominating Seward, to whom he was bound in closest personal friendship. His great influence, however, was exerted in the field of political management. Others formulated the principles and Weed secured the votes. Patronage he regarded as indispensable; he derived "great satisfaction . . . in bringing capable and good men into public service" (*Life, post,* I, 209), the good men being Whigs. Bribery and legislative favors were in his opinion legitimate party instruments, but he was above taking corrupt profits for himself. His paper was a party organ, providing usable facts and arguments, in terse paragraphs, to gain and hold Whigs to the true faith. He shared Seward's humanitarian views but never to the point of endangering the serious business of elections, and while he recognized Horace Greeley's power, he cast a dubious eye on his "isms," especially in the field of social reform. His own anti-slavery sentiments were sincere, but he was more desirous of getting anti-slavery men to accept Whig candidates than of committing the party openly to their cause; for the abolitionists who clamored for a party of their own he had nothing but scorn.

As the fruits of victory vanished with Tyler's accession to the presidency, followed by Seward's defeat in 1842, Weed lost heart, traveled abroad, and even talked of giving up the *Evening Journal*. The campaign of 1844 was not only unsuccessful but ominous of dissensions to come. Too astute to oppose the government in wartime, he directed his efforts to the future of the territories to be acquired, and supported the Wilmot Proviso. With equal astuteness, early in 1846 he recognized Gen. Zachary Taylor's possibilities as a candidate for the presidency, and advised him not to commit himself on controversial questions. Taylor's election, with Fillmore as vice-president and Seward as senator, promised to establish Weed's power firmly, but with Taylor's death the outlook was changed. Fillmore accepted the compromise measures of 1850; Seward, backed by Weed, was their great opponent; and the Whig division was hopeless. Weed, sure of his party's defeat in 1852, went abroad. Thoroughly anti-Nebraska in sentiment, he was slow to join the new Republican party in 1854 until Seward's reëlection to the Senate was assured. He was opposed to Seward's being put forward by the Republicans as a candidate for the presidency in 1856, believing that his chances of election would be better in 1860. His presidential ambitions for Seward were doomed to disappointment, however; and no little of the feeling against Seward in 1860 was due to his long and close connection with Weed, who was highly unacceptable to former Democrats.

Weed was consulted by Lincoln, during the latter's campaign and after, and had considerable influence on appointments, though he was credited with more than he had. In 1861 he went, with Archbishop Hughes and Bishop McIlvaine [*qq.v.*], on an unofficial mission to conciliate English and French opinion after the *Trent* affair. He was willing to accept the Crittenden compromise in 1861, and, distrustful of "ultra abolitionist" influences on Lincoln, would have preferred an untainted and active War Democrat as the Union candidate in 1864, but McClellan's acceptance of the Democratic platform kept Weed in the Republican lines. His influence in New York, badly shaken by Seward's failure in 1860, declined steadily as the Radicals gained strength after Lincoln's death. He had given up the *Evening Journal* and moved to New York City in 1863, where in 1867 he returned to journalism, becoming editor of the *Commercial Advertiser*. Failing health and sight soon compelled him to abandon editorial work, however. Retaining his deep interest in public affairs, he was a frequent contributor to the press on political subjects and was often consulted by political leaders. For some time he had been writing a desultory autobiography. In 1866 his *Letters from Europe and the West Indies* was published. After his death some of his articles on bimetalism were reprinted in *The Silver Dollar of the United States and Its Relations to Bimetallism* (1889).

He was tall and robust, rather awkward in appearance. His charm of manner, unruffled good-nature, and ready generosity drew into the circle of his friends even those political opponents who had suffered most from his vigorous attacks and rough wit. Seward wrote in early years that he had "had no idea that dictators were such amiable creatures" (*Life*, II, 63), and young Henry Adams, meeting Weed in London, won by "his faculty of irresistibly conquering confidence . . . followed him about . . . much like a little dog." He was, thought Adams, "the model of political management and patient address," "a complete American education in himself" (*The Education of Henry Adams*, 1918, p. 146). He died of old age in his eighty-sixth year and was survived by three daughters, his wife and a son having died many years before.

[Weed's "Autobiography" was published by his daughter, Harriet A. Weed, as vol. I of the *Life of Thurlow Weed* (1884) ; vol. II is a "Memoir" by his grandson, T. W. Barnes. Other sources are: D. S. Alexander, *A Polit. Hist. of the State of N. Y.*, vols. I–III (1906–09) ; S. D. Brummer, *Polit. Hist. of N. Y. State During . . . the Civil War* (1911) ; Frederic Bancroft, *The Life of William H. Seward* (2 vols., 1900) ; F. W. Seward, *Autobiog. of William H. Seward . . .* (1877) and *Seward at Washington* (2 vols., 1891) ; F. H. Severance, "Millard Fillmore Papers," vol. II, being *Buffalo Hist. Soc. Pubs.*, vol. XI (1907) ; Horace Greeley, *Recollections of a Busy Life* (1868) ; Gideon Welles, *Diary* (3 vols., 1911), and *Lincoln and Seward* (1874) ; *Atlantic Mo.*, Sept. 1883, pp. 411–19 ; *Mag. of Am. Hist.*, Jan. 1888 ; *N. Y. Times, N. Y. Tribune,* and *Albany Evening Journal,* Nov. 22, 23, 1882.]

H. C. B.

WEEDEN, WILLIAM BABCOCK (Sept. 1, 1834–Mar. 28. 1912), manufacturer and historian, was descended from James Weeden, who settled in Newport, R. I., in 1638. He was born in Bristol, R. I., the son of John Edward and Eliza (Cross) Weeden. His early education was received in the public schools of Westerly, R. I., and at the Connecticut Literary Institute, Suffield, Conn. He was a student at Brown University with the class of 1852, but left before graduation in order to accept employment with Bradford & Taft, wool merchants of Providence. So successful was he in this capacity that, with the dissolution of the partnership about 1864, he became a member of the new firm of Taft, Weeden & Company. Weeden's business activity was interrupted by his service during the Civil War. He first served as a second lieutenant

in the Rhode Island light artillery, but was advanced to a captaincy after the battle of Bull Run. He continued in active service through the Seven Days' Battle, when he resigned his commission and resumed his business connections in Providence. The important phase of his business life began in 1864, when he organized the Weybosset Mills, control of which he retained until their purchase by the American Woolen Company in 1902. These mills were devoted to the large-scale manufacture of cassimeres and worsteds in the Blackstone Valley and in Providence, and raised Weeden to a position of leadership among men of affairs in southern New England.

While probably best known among his contemporaries as a manufacturer, Weeden will undoubtedly be remembered by posterity chiefly as an historian. As a business man he was content to tread the paths worn by his predecessors. As a writer of history he ranks as a pioneer. It was in the seventies that his interest began to turn to public questions and to history. His first literary effort of importance was *The Morality of Prohibitory Liquor Laws* (1875). This was followed by *The Social Law of Labor* (1882), and *Indian Money as a Factor in New England Civilization* (1884), which appeared in the Johns Hopkins University Studies. In the last-named work he began the cultivation of a field which was to engage his attention for many years. His studies resulted in his most important and widely used work, *Economic and Social History of New England* (2 vols., 1890), covering the period from 1620 to 1789. Despite its undeniable defects of arrangement and organization, this work stamps Weeden as one of the handful of men in America who, when history was still politics, dared to embrace a broader and more all-inclusive view of the subject. Like his contemporary, John Bach McMaster [*q.v.*], Weeden was a social historian who sought faithfully to reproduce the life of the people in different periods. Like McMaster, too, he wrote social history of the static sort, as opposed to the dynamic, interpretative variety associated with Frederick Jackson Turner [*q.v.*] and Charles Beard. He wrote numerous other articles and books, the most important of which were *War Government, Federal and State . . . 1861–1865* (1906), and *Early Rhode Island, a Social History of the People* (1910). His activity as a writer of history earned for him membership in such learned organizations as the American Antiquarian Society, the Massachusetts Historical Society, and the Rhode Island Historical Society.

Weeden was married three times: first, on Oct. 12, 1859, to Amy Dexter Owen; second, on

Dec. 5, 1867, to Hannah Raymer Balch, by whom he had seven children; and third, on Apr. 18, 1893, to Jeanie Lippitt, daughter of Henry Lippitt [*q.v.*]. He died in Providence, survived by his wife and six of his seven children.

[*Who's Who in America*, 1910–11; *Alphabetical Index of the Births, Marriages, and Deaths . . . in Providence*, vols. II (1880), XIII (1910); *Proc. R. I. Hist. Soc., 1911–1913* (1913); *Proc. Am. Antiquarian Soc.*, vol. XXII (1912); T. M. Aldrich, *The Hist. of Battery A, 1st Reg., R. I. Light Artillery* (1904); obituary in *Providence Daily Jour.*, Mar. 29, 1912; information from Weeden's widow and W. W. Weeden, a son.]

J. B. H.

WEEKS, EDWIN LORD (1849–Nov. 17, 1903), painter, born in Boston, Mass., was the son of Stephen and Mary (Lord) Weeks, and a descendant of Leonard Weeks, who emigrated from Somersetshire, England, and settled in Portsmouth, N. H., where he received a grant of land, in 1656. Edwin Weeks studied in the public schools of Boston and Newton, but before finishing his course he had an opportunity to go to Paris, where he began his art education at the École des Beaux-Arts under Léon Bonnat and J. L. Gérôme. While his training was still in progress he journeyed to Tangier, Algiers, and Cairo, where he made a number of striking paintings. Some of these early works were hung in the Paris Salon during his novitiate, and the favorable verdict of the critics, together with the approval of his masters, encouraged him to specialize in Oriental subjects. He traveled to Palestine, and did some work in Jerusalem and Damascus, and then ventured on an expedition to India. There during the eighties and nineties he produced an extensive series of brilliant compositions, many of which were exhibited at the Paris Salon. Notable examples included "Jeypore" and "A Hindu Sanctuary at Bombay" (1884); "The Last Voyage, Souvenir of the Ganges, Benares" (1885) and "The Rajah Starting on a Hunt," both in the Metropolitan Museum of Art, New York; "A Rajah of Jodhpore" (1888); "The Golden Temple of Amritsar" (1890); and "The Barbers of Saharanpore" (1895). His "Departure for the Hunt, India" (1884) is in the permanent collection of the Corcoran Gallery of Art, Washington; "The Porter of Bagdad" was bought by the Cercle Volney, Paris; and the "Three Beggars of Cordova" went to the Pennsylvania Academy of the Fine Arts. At the Paris Exposition of 1900 he was represented by "The Awakening of Nourredin," "On the Road to Ispahan," and "Indian Barber." In these paintings Weeks has given to those who are familiar only with the western world "some idea of the sunlight, the color, and the strange, curiously wrought structures of the East," to quote the words of Samuel Isham [*q.v.*], "and his clear, sure interpretation carries conviction of the accuracy of the reproduction" (*post*, p. 408).

He received many honors in many countries, the crowning one being the coveted ribbon of the chevalier of the Legion of Honor which came to him in 1896. He wrote *From the Black Sea through Persia and India* (1896), *Some Episodes of Mountaineering* (1897), and contributed a number of papers to books and magazines. For many years he made his home in Paris, and it was there that his death occurred in the autumn of 1903, when he was fifty-four. The funeral, which was held at the American Church, was attended by leading French and American artists, and many wreaths were sent by artistic societies in France and the United States. The interment was at Billancourt. A collection of 277 of his paintings and sketches was sold at the American Art Galleries, New York, in March 1905.

[Jacob Chapman, *Leonard Weeks . . . and His Descendants* (1889); *Who's Who in America*, 1901–02; Helen S. Earle, *Biog. Sketches of Am. Artists* (1915); Samuel Isham, *The Hist. of Am. Painting* (1905); *Boston Daily Advertiser*, Jan. 17, 1876, Feb. 16, 1878; *Am. Art Ann.*, 1905; obituaries in *Boston Transcript*, Nov. 17, and *N. Y. Tribune*, Nov. 18, 1903.]

W. H. D.

WEEKS, JOHN WINGATE (Apr. 11, 1860– July 12, 1926), congressman, senator, secretary of war, was born on a farm near Lancaster, N. H., son of William Dennis and Mary Helen (Fowler) Weeks, and a descendant of Leonard Weeks who emigrated from Somersetshire, England, before 1656 and settled in Greenland, originally part of Portsmouth, N. H. As a boy Weeks attended the local school and by doing the chores on his father's farm laid the foundation for the robust health he enjoyed until in his fifties. At sixteen he taught school for a term and then, in 1877, entered the Naval Academy at Annapolis, where he was graduated four years later. He continued in the navy until 1883, when a general curtailment of personnel forced his discharge. For several years thereafter he worked at surveying in Florida, and while so engaged met and married, Oct. 7, 1885, Martha A. Sinclair, by whom he had two children.

Because the climate of Florida did not agree with his wife, Weeks in 1888 accepted an offer to enter the banking and brokerage business in Boston. The firm of which he became a partner, operating under the name of Hornblower & Weeks, was successful from the start and became in time one of the largest and most respected financial houses in America. Weeks himself acquired a fortune and became a business figure of importance. Love for the navy led him to join the Massachusetts naval militia, and during the Spanish-American War he served with this body in its task of patrolling the Massachusetts coast. The social side of this affiliation Weeks prized greatly—conviviality was an outstanding trait in his nature—and he was never so happy as when attending one of the joyous dinners of the "Wardroom Club," an organization of militia members, which were held on the Boston waterfront in a room modeled after the fashion of wardrooms in naval vessels.

Weeks's first political office, that of alderman-at-large of the city of Newton, Mass., where he made his home, came to him in 1900 unsolicited, as did his election as mayor three years later. His experiences in these offices awakened in him a liking for politics with its human contacts, and consequently when in 1904 friends urged him to stand for Congress he consented. He was elected, gave up his business connections, and remained in the House of Representatives until 1913, when the Massachusetts legislature named him to succeed the retiring Winthrop Murray Crane [q.v.] as United States senator. Weeks's stay in the Senate was limited to one term; in 1918 he was defeated for reëlection by David I. Walsh, Democrat. During the Harding-Cox presidential campaign of 1920 Weeks's service as chief of the New York headquarters of the Republican party won him the regard of Harding, who later named him secretary of war. He continued in this office until October 1925, when ill health compelled him to retire.

In Congress, Weeks was hard-working, conscientious, and an able if not an eloquent speaker. He was tall, heavily and powerfully built, a man who without vanity set a correct appraisal on his superior abilities. His demeanor, simple and kindly, caused him to be universally liked and respected—"the smiling statesman" somebody called him. His political views corresponded in the main to orthodox Republicanism. He was for a high tariff and retention of the Philippines. He preferred the Aldrich currency and banking proposals but, in lieu of them, voted for President Wilson's Federal Reserve Act. He was opposed to the prohibition and woman's suffrage amendments, and probably his vote against the latter had something to do with his defeat in the senatorial election of 1918. As secretary of war he brought large business experience to the solution of the many problems left over from the war administration. In February 1925, when sensational controversy arose concerning the adequacy of the nation's air defenses, he appeared before a House investigating committee and contradicted charges made by William Mitchell, the brigadier-general and assistant chief of the army air service. He died in Lancaster, N. H.

[*Who's Who in America,* 1924–25; *N. Y. Times,* July 12, 13, 1926; *Bankers Mag.,* Sept. 1926; *Boston Transcript,* July 12, 1926; C. G. Washburn, *The Life of John W. Weeks* (1928); *Biog. Dir. Am. Cong.* (1928); Jacob Chapman, *Leonard Weeks . . . and His Descendants* (1889).]   W. E. S—a.

WEEKS, JOSEPH DAME (Dec. 3, 1840–Dec. 26, 1896), technical journalist, statistician, was born at Lowell, Mass., the son of Jonathan and Mary (Dame) Weeks. He was a descendant of Leonard Weeks, who settled in Portsmouth, N. H., in 1656, and of Jacob Heard, New Hampshire Revolutionary soldier. After serving with the United States Christian Commission, 1863–65, Weeks entered Wesleyan University, where he prepared for the Methodist ministry, but he was compelled by a throat disorder soon after graduation in 1869 to abandon the idea of a ministerial career. He spent some time in Iowa working on the *Burlington Hawkeye,* moved to Cincinnati, published a *History of the Knights of Pythias* in 1871, and on Feb. 28 of that year married Mattie J. Fowler, daughter of a Pittsburgh industrialist. In 1872 he became editor of the *American Manufacturer,* published in Pittsburgh, which in 1874 was consolidated with the *Iron World.* Two years later he resigned to become associate editor and manager of the Pittsburgh office of the New York *Iron Age,* but in April 1886, he returned to the *Manufacturer,* of which he had secured control, and continued as its editor until his death. His articles in these journals were regarded as authoritative and were widely quoted.

Deeply interested in the problems of industrial relations, Weeks was instrumental, through the Western Iron Association and the Western Pig Iron Association, in fixing iron prices. He was responsible for the first wage scale offered by the manufacturers to the Amalgamated Association of Iron and Steel Workers; and he subsequently presided over a number of wage conferences, enjoying to an unusual degree the confidence of both sides. His studies of labor relations resulted in a number of publications: *Report on the Practical Operation of Arbitration and Conciliation . . . in England* (1879), *Labor Differences and Their Settlement* (1886), *Industrial Conciliation and Arbitration in New York, Ohio and Pennsylvania* (1881). A firm believer in the protective tariff, he testified before congressional fact-finding committees.

As a scientist, Weeks is credited with conducting the experiments that led to the first use of gas in a puddling furnace. The year before his death he investigated the utilization of by-products in coke manufacture in Germany and urged the example on western Pennsylvania. He made a survey of the iron ores of the James River Valley in Virginia. To the *Transactions* of the American Association of Mining Engineers, of which he was president in 1895, he contributed articles on manganese steel, blast furnaces, fuel problems, natural gas, the Bessemer process.

Appointed a special agent for the census of 1880 he prepared reports on the manufacture of coke and glass and an entire volume on wages in manufacturing industries with supplementary reports on trade societies, strikes, and lockouts. For the census of 1890 he prepared the articles on the mining of petroleum, gas, and manganese, and on the manufacture of refined petroleum, coke, and gas. From 1885 to 1895 he was employed by the department of mineral resources of the United States Geological Survey, contributing annually the articles on coke manufacture, crude petroleum, natural gas, and the production of manganese. To the Pennsylvania bureau of industrial statistics he furnished articles on coke. He was judge of awards in the department of mines and mining at the World's Columbian Exposition, 1893. At the time of his death he was assembling statistics for the Pennsylvania Tax Conference Commission, of which he was chairman, and for the national commission appointed to appraise the property of the Monongahela River Navigation Company. An indefatigable worker, he found time to devote to church, civic, and philanthropic affairs in Pittsburgh and to give advice and assistance to young men in science and industry.

[Jacob Chapman, *Leonard Weeks of Greenland, N. H., and His Descendants* (1889); *Iron Age*, Feb. 3, 1876, Apr. 8, 1886, Dec. 31, 1896; *Am. Manufacturer and Iron World*, Jan. 1, 1897; *Trans. Am. Inst. Mining Engineers*, vol. XXVII (1898); *Am. Manufacturer*, Jan. 2, 1873, Mar. 26, 1874, Feb. 17, 1876, Apr. 9, 1886; *Alumni Record of Wesleyan Univ.* (1883); *Pittsburg Post*, Dec. 27, 1896; information from Wesleyan Univ. Alumni Council.] M. S.

WEEKS, STEPHEN BEAUREGARD (Feb. 2, 1865–May 3, 1918), North Carolina historian and bibliographer, was born in Pasquotank County, N. C., of English and Huguenot ancestors resident in the locality since the first half of the eighteenth century. Bereft in infancy of his parents, James Elliott Weeks, a planter, and Mary Louisa (Mullen) Weeks, he was reared in the nearby farmhouse of his father's sister and her husband, Robertson Jackson. After attending neighborhood schools and the noted Horner School at Henderson, where he received his first real intellectual impulse, Weeks entered the University of North Carolina in 1882 and was graduated in 1886 with honors. A year later he received the degree of M.A. and in 1888 that of Ph.D. in English, German, and Latin. His compilation of the *Register of Members of the Philanthropic Society* (Raleigh, 1887) strengthened his interest in North Carolina history, which was fixed as the field of his life's work by study under Herbert Baxter Adams [*q.v.*] at the Johns Hopkins University. There after three years' study he received the degree of Ph.D. in 1891. Weeks was twice married: first, on June 12, 1888, to Mary Lee Martin of Chapel Hill, who died in 1891, and second, on June 28, 1893, to Sallie Mangum Leach of Trinity, grand-daughter of Willie Person Mangum [*q.v.*].

He was professor of history and political science at Trinity College (later Duke University) from 1891 until his resignation in 1893 resulting from a faculty quarrel with the president. In the autumn he returned to the Johns Hopkins University as a fellow by courtesy for a year's study and research. Already his skill and industry in research had produced *The Press of North Carolina in the Eighteenth Century* (1891), "The Lost Colony of Roanoke: Its Fate and Survival" (*Papers of the American Historical Association*, Oct. 1891), "The Religious Development in the Province of North Carolina" (*Johns Hopkins University Studies in Historical and Political Science*, May–June 1892), "Church and State in North Carolina" (*Ibid.*, 1893), "General Joseph Martin and the War of the Revolution in the West" (*Annual Report of the American Historical Association*, 1893), and "The History of Negro Suffrage in the South" (*Political Science Quarterly*, December 1894).

From 1894 to 1899 he held a position in the United States Bureau of Education at Washington, performing editorial work on the annual reports of the commissioner and other bureau publications, and carrying on historical research, the chief results of which were "The Beginnings of the Common School System in the South" (*Report of the Commissioner of Education*, 1896–97) and "Confederate Text-books" (*Ibid.*, 1898–99). Additional publications of this period were *A Bibliography of the Historical Literature of North Carolina* (1895), "Libraries and Literature in North Carolina in the Eighteenth Century" (*Annual Report of the American Historical Association*, 1895), "The University of North Carolina in the Civil War" (*Southern Historical Society Papers*, vol. XXIV, 1896), and his largest and best-known work, *Southern Quakers and Slavery* (1896). Weeks was one of the founders of the Southern History Association at Washington in 1896, a member of its administrative council, and a frequent contributor to its *Publications* (1897–1907).

Compelled by impaired health to change his residence, he entered the United States Indian Service in 1899; and, for eight years as teacher and superintendent in Indian schools at Santa Fé, N. M., and San Carlos, Ariz., he waged a successful struggle with disease, enduring with fortitude the interruption of his work and interests. In 1907 he returned to North Carolina, where he was busy for two years with editorial work on the *Biographical History of North Carolina* (8 vols., 1905–17), edited by S. A. Ashe, to which he contributed many signed sketches. Following a two-year principalship of the high school at Trinity, he again accepted a research position in the Bureau of Education at Washington, for which he studied the history of public school education in a number of states. Over a period of years he compiled an index to the North Carolina census of 1790 (*State Records*, vol. XXVI, 1905) and the monumental *Index to the Colonial and State Records of North Carolina* (4 vols., 1909–14), in the last volume of which is an extensive survey of the colonial and state records of North Carolina.

Coördinate with Weeks's interest in historical research and writing was his life-long zeal in collecting North Carolina books, pamphlets, and manuscripts, and in compiling an exhaustive and critical bibliography of North Carolina. After his death at his home in Washington on May 3, 1918, the Weeks collection of Caroliniana, comprising 10,000 books and pamphlets, and the incomplete bibliography were acquired by the University of North Carolina. Weeks was one of the earliest and most productive of the new school of trained North Carolina historians whose primary concern was the objective presentation of the results of scholarly, painstaking investigation of historical sources.

[Sources include *Who's Who in America*, 1916–17; *Alumni Hist. of the Univ. of N. C.* (1924); T. M. Pittman, in *Biog. Hist. of N. C.*, vol. V (1906), ed. by S. A. Ashe; obituary in *News and Observer* (Raleigh, N. C.), May 4, 1918; S. B. Weeks, *The Weeks Coll. of Caroliniana* (1907); information from Weeks's son, Mangum Weeks, and the U. S. Bureau of Education, which has several of Weeks's unpublished MSS.]

A. R. N.

WEEMS, MASON LOCKE (Oct. 11, 1759–May 23, 1825), Episcopal clergyman, book agent, writer, was born at "Marshes Seat," near Herring Bay, Anne Arundel County, Md., nineteenth child of David Weems, and the youngest by his second wife, Esther (Hill) Weems. His father, reputedly of the noble Scottish family of Wemyss, emigrated before 1722 and, with kins-

folk, founded the Weems family, today spread throughout the South. Of Mason before early manhood nothing is definitely known, though there are picturesque legends of varying credibility. In 1783, when abroad, he was in correspondence with John Adams and Benjamin Franklin, then respectively at The Hague and in Paris, concerning the obstacles to ordination, the British law still requiring the oath of allegiance; this, however, being abrogated in August 1784, by Act of Parliament, Weems and Edward Gantt, Jr., were the first candidates to receive Anglican ordination for service in the United States. Ordained deacon, Sept. 5, 1784, by the bishop of Chester, Weems was admitted to the priesthood a week later by the archbishop of Canterbury. Returning to Maryland, he served from 1784 to 1792 in All Hallows and St. Margaret's parishes. In 1791 he began reprinting a series of improving books by Robert Russel, Hugh Blair, Lewis Cornaro, Capt. Henry Wilson, Hannah More, Mrs. Helme, and Henry Brooke.

On July 2, 1795, he was married to Frances Ewell, daughter of Col. Jesse Ewell, and sister of James Ewell [*q.v.*], and settled her amidst her people in Dumfries, Va., where their ten children were born. He thereafter continued and extended his wanderings, which, as a seller of books, and after 1794 as Mathew Carey's agent, led him for thirty-one years up and down the Eastern seaboard from New York City to Savannah, including the nearer hinterland of Pennsylvania. This agency lapsed only during two intervals—first, when he preached in several Virginia parishes, notably at Pohick Church (thereby laying the only basis for his claim: "Formerly Rector of Mt. Vernon Parish," first printed on a book title in 1809), and again later when he "subscriptioneered" for John Marshall's *Washington*. First and last he step-fathered a goodly number of weighty works by Oliver Goldsmith, William Guthrie, William Burkit, James Hervey, Edward W. Montagu, William Coxe, Henry Hunter, and others, besides Carey's edition of the Bible, first suggested by Weems, who while making very large sales continued to offer ideas for embellishing the successive issues. In these as well as in his editings, compilings, writings, and letters, he showed a knowledge of Biblical and general literature which evinced wide and interested reading. He practised as well as proclaimed a passionate faith in the value of "good books," and from his letters alone no impression is clearer than his own belief that by circulating such he was still doing God's work, having merely transferred his activities from the pulpit to a wider mission field.

By 1799, in his *Philanthropist,* and in 1802, in his *True Patriot,* he was preaching a political doctrine which was twin brother to theological universalism. The bent then discovered toward a solvent of pervasive love as a cure-all and end-all for every ill of human existence grew on him, while in his *Hymen's Recruiting Serjeant* (2 pts., *c.* 1799—of which excerpts are found in almanacs of about 1800—he tinctured his sentimental and vital statistics with magnificent buffoonery. This empirical chemistry makes a masterpiece of what, by a stretch of tolerance, may be called his *magnum opus, The Life and Memorable Actions of George Washington* (*c.* 1800), as also his *Life of General Francis Marion* (1809), both being early examples of the supposedly ultra-modern fictionized biography. The former (in its first version issued anonymously), although inveighed against by many judicial historians or gored to tatters by those of less controlled temperament, was the second best-seller of its day, and held its own through over seventy accredited and varying editions, including five in German (1800–1927). In its fifth edition (1806) the hatchet and cherry-tree story first appeared in book form. Both these books, if taken with an adequate supply of salt, may still delight the palate. The *Life of Doctor Benjamin Franklin* (1815), founded largely on the immortal autobiography, and the *Life of William Penn* (1822) are not such stimulants to historical bile as their precursors, and are of neither interest nor value. Probably the springs of Weems's fancy had been diverted into his moralizing tracts: *God's Revenge Against Murder* (1807), *God's Revenge Against Gambling* (*c.* 1810), *The Drunkard's Looking Glass* (*c.* 1812), *God's Revenge Against Adultery* (1815), *God's Revenge Against Duelling* (1820), and the *Bad Wife's Looking Glass* (1823). His letters (1784–1825) compare more than favorably with any in American annals, in their self-revelation, spontaneity, mother-wit, and racy English, besides, in their book lists, throwing valuable light on the taste of the reading public of his day. In them, as by common report, we learn that he passed his days in a whirl of febrile excitement, whether without or within, never, until toward the end of his laborious life, flagging in energy or zest. He died at Beaufort, S. C., whence his remains were removed for re-interment at his home, Bel Air, near Dumfries, Va.

[Sources include the diary of William E. Duke, MS. in Md. Diocesan Lib., Baltimore; records of Protestant Episcopal Church Conventions in Md., 1783–93 (published *c.* 1788–93); William Meade, *Old Churches, Ministers, and Families of Va.* (2 vols., 1857); obituary in *Reporter* (Warrenton, N. C.), July 8, 1825. See also P. L. Ford and Emily E. F. Skeel, *Mason Locke Weems* (3 vols., 1928–29), with bibliog.; S. G. Fisher, "The Legendary and Myth-Making Process in Histories of the Am. Rev.," *Proc. Am. Philosophical Soc.,* vol. LI (1912); W. G. Simms, *Views and Reviews in Am. Lit.* (1845); L. C. Wroth, *Parson Weems* (1911); W. B. Norris, in *Nat. Mag.,* Feb. 1910.]   E. E. F. S.

WEIDENMANN, JACOB (Aug. 22, 1829– Feb. 6, 1893), landscape architect, was born at Winterthur, Canton Zurich, Switzerland, the son of Jacob and Elise (Gubbler) Weidenmann. After a brief apprenticeship in an architect's office at Geneva, he went to the Akademie der Bildenden Künste, Munich, for his architectural training. After visiting Paris, London, and New York, he found employment as an assistant engineer at Panama, but soon proceeded to Callao, and thence to Lima, Peru, where he worked for about a year as engineer and architect. Having become interested in landscape architecture, about 1861 he returned to America, where the profession was still very young. As superintendent of parks in Hartford, Conn. (1861–68), he designed Bushnell Park, working closely with the Rev. Horace Bushnell [*q.v.*]. He was one of the promoters as well as the designer of the Cedar Hill Cemetery.

In 1870, soon after he had moved his home and his office to New York City, he published his *Beautifying Country Homes; A Handbook of Landscape Gardening.* He spent nearly two years in a visit to Switzerland about this time. In 1874 he entered into a working agreement with Frederick Law Olmsted [*q.v.*]. With Olmsted he was engaged on a number of important works, such as the grounds of the Schuylkill reservoir in Philadelphia, and Congress Spring Park, Saratoga. He was also employed upon the Hot Springs reservation in Arkansas, the grounds of the state capitol at Des Moines, Iowa, and those of the state hospital, St. Lawrence, N. Y., and upon many other public and private works, sometimes alone and sometimes in collaboration with Olmsted. A pioneer in the movement for the cemetery in which enclosures are discarded, monuments restricted, and the whole kept in the nature of a park, in 1881 he wrote a two-part article for the *American Architect and Building News* (Sept. 17, 24) which was a plea for the "modern" cemetery, and in 1888 published *Modern Cemeteries.* It was Weidenmann's intention to compile and publish illustrations of his designs in a volume to be called "American Garden Architecture." He actually prepared for publication many plates, illustrating details, but the work was never completed. Many of the plates are now on file in the New York Public Library. At the time of his death he was laying out Pope Park in Hartford. Of a genial, kindly nature, he kept throughout his life his youthful optimism and his cheerful trust in men. At his death, on Feb. 6, 1893, he was survived by his widow, Anna Marguerite Svàcher, and three daughters.

[Sources include a manuscript biog. by Weidenmann's daughter and other unpublished data in possession of Fine Arts Dept., N. Y. Pub. Lib.; R. F. Wyrick, in *The Cemetery Handbook* (rev. ed., 1932); F. L. Olmsted, Jr., and Theodora Kimball, *Frederick Law Olmsted* (2 vols., 1922–28); G. A. Parker, in *Parks and Recreation*, Oct. 1919, which contains many errors; obituary notice, *Garden and Forest*, Mar. 8, 1893.]

K. McN.

WEIDIG, ADOLF (Nov. 28, 1867–Sept. 23, 1931), composer, teacher, and conductor, was born in Hamburg, Germany, the son of Ferdinand and Hulda (Albrecht) Weidig. His father was a trombonist for thirty-eight years in the City Theatre orchestra at Hamburg. He received his general education in the schools of that city, and began to study violin at the age of twelve with Johannes Jagan, a member of the City Opera orchestra. From 1882 to 1887 he studied in the Hamburg Conservatory with K. L. Bargheer (violin), Hugo Riemann (theory and composition), and J. von Bernuth (piano). When he was sixteen years of age he became a member of the Hamburg Philharmonic Orchestra and played under famous conductors. He entered the Munich Conservatory in 1887 and became a pupil of Rheinberger (harmony, theory, and composition) and Abel (violin), graduating in 1891. In the meantime, 1888, he had composed a string quartet that won for him the Frankfort "Mozart Prize," yielding an annual allowance of 1800 marks for four years. In June 1892, he came to America and settled in Chicago. His abilities as a violinist enabled him at once to enter the Chicago Symphony Orchestra, then the Thomas Orchestra, and he remained a member of the first violin section from 1892 to 1896, when he resigned to devote himself to teaching.

In 1893 he joined the American Conservatory of Music in Chicago, as teacher of violin and theory, and from 1907 till his death he was an associate director of this school. In the course of a few years he became widely known as an original thinker and a distinguished teacher, especially of theory and composition. His scholarly and comprehensive treatise, *Harmonic Material and Its Uses* (1923), was the result of long research and practical experience. His devotion to chamber music led him to become a member (1893–1901) of the string quartet of Theodore Spiering [*q.v.*], in which he played viola. After 1900 he rarely played the violin in public, but he often appeared as an orchestral conductor, especially of his own compositions.

His compositions cover a wide field and show a fine mastery of all the musical means of expression. Though he was sympathetic to the modern musical idioms and encouraged his students to use them, his own style belonged rather to the conservative wing of modernism. He early displayed creative ability and, while a student at Munich, wrote a Symphony in C Minor and an overture, "Sappho," the latter having been performed by the Thomas Orchestra at the Columbian Exposition in Chicago, 1893. He wrote about twenty-five songs and the song-cycle "The Buccaneer" and numerous pieces for piano, for violin and for chorus, three string quartets (in D minor, A, and C minor), a string quintet, a piano trio, a suite for violin and piano, *Opus* 21, Romanza for the cello, *Opus* 14, and Serenade for strings, *Opus* 16. His large orchestral works are: "Semiramis," *Opus* 33 (first performance, 1906), a symphonic fantasy based on a poem by Edwin Markham; "Drei Episoden," *Opus* 38 (1908), based on Clärchen's song from Goethe's *Egmont*; Symphonic Suite in three movements (1914); and "Concert Overture," *Opus* 65 (1919). The Chicago Symphony Orchestra gave first performances of all these except the "Concert Overture" which was played by the Minneapolis Symphony Orchestra with Weidig conducting. In the winter and spring of 1909 Weidig visited Germany and conducted several of his orchestral works, mainly the "Drei Episoden," in Berlin, Hamburg, Frankfort, and Wiesbaden, winning highly favorable criticisms. His compositions are scholarly and brilliantly scored.

On June 29, 1896, he was married to Helen Ridgway, of Hinsdale, Ill., who survived him at the time of his death at Hinsdale. He was a man of genial disposition, of wide information and broad sympathies.

[Information from the family; *Who's Who in America*, 1930–31; *Grove's Dict. of Music and Musicians*, Am. Supp. (1930); *Hugo Riemanns Musik Lexikon* (11th ed., 1929); *Chicago Daily Tribune*, Sept. 24, 1931.]

R. G. C.

WEIDNER, REVERE FRANKLIN (Nov. 22, 1851–Jan. 6, 1915), Lutheran theologian, was born at Center Valley, Pa., the son of William Peter and Eliza Ann (Blank) Weidner. His family was of Pennsylvania German stock, the original American ancestor having been John Weidner, who came to America from the Palatinate in the early part of the eighteenth century. He was graduated from Muhlenberg College, Allentown, Pa., in 1869, and from the Lutheran Theological Seminary, at Mt. Airy, Philadelphia, in 1873. He was ordained the same year. From 1873 to 1878 he was pastor of Grace

Church, Phillipsburg, N. J., and from 1875 to 1877 he spent part of his time teaching in Muhlenberg College. His next pastorate, 1878–82, was at St. Luke's Church, Philadelphia. From 1882 to 1891 he was professor of dogmatics and exegesis in Augustana College and Theological Seminary, Rock Island, Ill. When the Chicago Lutheran Seminary was founded in 1891 in Chicago (now at Maywood, Ill.), he was elected the first president, and acted in this capacity until his death, with the exception of one year as teaching emeritus. Weidner was a great believer in the ecclesiastic future of the West, where he especially learned to know the church life of Lutherans of Swedish antecedents. He believed it his province to train men for the ministry and not to guide the affairs of the organized church. He was rarely found on the general committees or the boards of the church, and found it difficult to sit through the tedious detail of an ecclesiastical assembly.

At the beginning of his teaching career, he leaned heavily on Anglican writers like C. J. Ellicott and J. B. Lightfoot, but later shifted to Lutheran German theologians of the conservative, confessional type. He aimed at bringing the church in America into closer contact with the theological mind of ancient historical seats of Lutheranism. He thought he could reach this goal by writing textbooks on Lutheran theology in English. He became a prodigious compiler. His *Theological Encyclopaedia* (3 vols., 1885–91) is a combination of the work of K. R. Hagenbach and Charles Porterfield Krauth [*q.v.*] on this subject, which he regarded as one of the most important branches taught in a theological seminary. The bibliographies in this work are extended, but scarcely critical. His *Biblical Theology of the New Testament* (2 vols., 1886) works with the findings of B. Weiss. His *A System of Christian Ethics* (1891) is a self-contradictory tome; as all his other works, it is not a logical unity, but an aggregate of notions of various origins.

Weidner visited Europe several times. He observed the curricula of Continental universities, but left no evidence that he understood the prevailing spirit of European university instruction or scholarship, since in his own teaching he stressed textbook, recitation, and bulky assignments. His best effort as a writer of textbooks was *An Introductory New Testament Greek Method* (1889) on which he collaborated with William R. Harper [*q.v.*]. Weidner traveled much in the interests of the Seminary and on lecture tours, working with Dwight L. Moody [*q.v.*], in Northfield, Vt., and with Harper on

Chautauqua programs. He was an excellent preacher, his sermons being of the expository order, rich in applications. He was one of the founders of the *Lutheran Church Review,* but limited his contributions to book reviews. He was high-hearted and straightforward, liked to rule and was at times intolerant. A monument to his executive ability and faith is the Chicago Theological Seminary, the innermost creation of his heart. On July 10, 1873, he was married to Emma Salome Jones of Philadelphia. They had one child. He died in Tangerine, Fla., where he had gone to better his health.

[*Who's Who in America,* 1914–15; H. H. Widener, *The Wideners in America* (1904); *The Luth. World Almanac and Encyc., 1931–33* (1932); biog. sketch by T. E. Schmauk, in *Luth. Ch. Rev.,* Apr. 1915, and by G. P. Lottich, in *Luth. Ch. Work,* Jan. 28, 1915; see also, *Ibid.,* Feb. 11, 1915.]   J.O.E.

WEIGHTMAN, WILLIAM (Sept. 30, 1813–Aug. 25, 1904), chemist, manufacturer, and financier, was born at Waltham, Lincolnshire, England, a son of William Weightman and Anne (Farr) Weightman. When sixteen years of age, he emigrated to America at the suggestion of an uncle, John Farr, who was the founder of the firm of Farr & Kunzi, established at Philadelphia in 1818 to manufacture chemicals. In 1836 the firm became Farr, Powers & Weightman, and after Farr's death in 1847, Powers & Weightman. Under the latter name it attained international recognition among manufacturing chemists. Weightman at first acted as chemist for the firm, but after the death of Powers in 1878 he assumed full charge of the business management as well. He continued in active charge until shortly before his death in 1904. The success of the firm, which was one of the earliest of its kind in America, and the leadership it attained were due largely to the enterprise, ingenuity, and skill of Weightman. The firm early became known for the introduction of new chemicals and the development of processes of manufacture. Weightman was the first to manufacture quinine sulphate, and it was through his efforts that the cheaper alkaloids of cinchona, cinchonidine and cinchonine, became favorably known and widely used as substitutes for quinine at a time when the price of the latter was almost prohibitive. The firm is also credited with having introduced and perfected the manufacture of citric acid in the United States.

As a result of sound management over a period of many years, the business of the firm yielded generous profits, and Weightman amassed a fortune. This was augmented by investments in property so extensive and so profitable that he became the largest real estate owner in Philadelphia and was popularly known as the wealthiest man in Pennsylvania in his time. In addition to being the head of his firm, he was director of the Philadelphia Trust Company, the Northern Trust Company, and the Commercial National Bank. From a professional standpoint, his only interest, other than that manifested in the affairs of his firm, is represented by his connection with the Philadelphia College of Pharmacy, of which he was a member from 1856 until his death. He was a member of the Pennsylvania Historical Society, the Pennsylvania Horticultural Society, and the Franklin Institute. He took no part in social functions or public affairs, but apparently derived his pleasures from his home and his recreation from the cultivation of rare flowering plants at his country home, Ravenhill, in Germantown. On Mar. 17, 1841, he married Louise Stelwagon, by whom he had two sons and a daughter. He died on Aug. 25, 1904, survived by his daughter.

[E. P. Oberholtzer, *Phila., a Hist. of the City and Its People* (1912), vol. III; *Am. Jour. of Pharmacy,* Apr. 1905; *Merck's Report,* July 1927, p. 111; *The First Century of the Am. Coll. of Pharmacy* (1922); obituary in *Pub. Ledger* (Phila.), Aug. 26, 1904.]

A. G. D–M.

WEIL, RICHARD (Oct. 15, 1876–Nov. 19, 1917), physician, medical research worker, was born in New York City, the son of Leopold and Matilda (Tanzer) Weil. His early education was obtained mainly at home and at private schools. Entering Columbia University, where he was graduated A.B. in the class of 1896, he attracted attention by his intellectual versatility, and was offered opportunities for advancement in teaching in several of its departments. He was early attracted to medical research, and with this in mind he devoted much time to biological work. His medical education was obtained at the College of Physicians and Surgeons in New York, where he was graduated in 1900. After a two-year interneship in the German Hospital he went to Europe, where he spent a year and a half in the clinics and laboratories of Vienna and Strassburg. In 1904 he returned to New York to practise and to pursue medical investigation.

In 1905 he was appointed demonstrator in pathology at Cornell Medical College, and in 1908, assistant in experimental pathology. Two years later he was promoted to instructor in experimental therapeutics, and in 1911 assistant professor in the same department. In 1915 he was made assistant professor of experimental pathology, which department was merged the next year with that of experimental medicine with Weil at its head. He held this position until his death. From 1904 to 1910 he was adjunct pa-

thologist to the German Hospital. From 1908 to 1913 he was on the staff of the Mount Sinai hospital, and for about the same period served the Montefiore Home. In 1906 he joined the staff of the Huntington Fund for Cancer Research. Working at the Loomis Laboratory, he devoted himself to the field of the serology of cancer and to the general problems of immunity, a field in which he gained an international reputation. In 1910 he devised an exceptionally delicate clinical test for luetic infection, based upon blood hemolysis by cobra venom. Working upon the subject of anaphylaxis, he promulgated the theory that sensitization is essentially cellular in origin and adduced a wealth of demonstration and argument in its support. His most practical contribution to clinical medicine was the method of transfusing citrated blood, which he perfected and employed.

He was a member of the American Society for the Control of Cancer, the American Society of Clinical Investigation, and the Association of American Physicians. He held the office of vice-president of the American Association for Cancer Research and served as president of the Society of Serology and Hemotology and of the American Association of Immunologists. The council of the American Association of Cancer Research charged him with the duty of establishing the *Journal of Cancer Research* in 1915, of which he was managing editor until his death. He was an associate editor of the *Journal of Immunology* and of the *American Review of Tuberculosis.* Beginning in 1899, he contributed over sixty articles to the journal literature of clinical and experimental medicine.

Shortly after the entrance of the United States into the World War in 1917, he offered his services to the government and was commissioned a captain in the medical reserve corps. After a short service at Fort Benjamin Harrison, Ind., he was promoted to the grade of major and assigned as chief of the medical service at the base hospital at Camp Wheeler, Macon, Ga. He died there of pneumonia after little more than a month of service. He was married in 1905 to Minnie, daughter of Isador Strauss of New York, who, with three children, survived him.

[*Jour. of Cancer Research,* Jan. 1918, with list of Weil's writings; *Jour. of Immunology,* Jan. 1918; *Medic. Record* (N. Y.), Nov. 24, 1917; *N. Y. Medic. Jour.,* Nov. 24, 1917; H. A. Kelly and W. L. Burrage, *Am. Medic. Biogs.* (1920); *Science,* Dec. 7, 1917; *Jour. Am. Medic. Asso.,* Dec. 1, 1917; *N. Y. Times,* Nov. 20, 1917; War Dept. records.] J. M. P—n.

WEIR, JOHN FERGUSON (Aug. 28, 1841–Apr. 8, 1926), artist and teacher, was born at West Point, N. Y., the son of Robert Walter [*q.v.*] and Louisa (Ferguson) Weir. He attended private schools and was tutored by various instructors at the United States Military Academy. He was taught painting by his father and at the National Academy of Design in New York City. Early in the sixties he had a studio of his own in the Tenth Street Studio Building, and was grouped with the "Hudson River School." He married Mary Hannah French, the daughter of the Rev. John W. French, D.D., the chaplain at West Point, on May 17, 1866. His pictures, "The Interior of an Artist's Studio" and "The Gun Foundry," are said to have led to his election as an Associate of the National Academy of Design in 1864 and as an Academician in 1866. During 1868 and 1869 he was in Europe, returning to become the first director of the School of Fine Arts at Yale University, which had been established in 1866. He was professor of painting and design until 1877, and William Leffingwell Professor from 1877 until his retirement in 1913. His masterpiece is probably "Forging the Shaft," owned by the Metropolitan Museum of Art, New York City. He was awarded a bronze medal at the Exposition Universelle in Paris in 1900. Following his retirement Weir and his wife lived in Providence, R. I.

Weir's paintings include *genre*, landscapes, portraits, and flower-pieces. His early studies of industry are the best examples of the first group, "Forging the Shaft" still ranking high among the representations of man in opposition to machinery. "Three Trees," in the Corcoran Gallery in Washington, is a charming landscape, and "East Rock," in the Yale Gallery of Fine Arts, a fine study of rock formation. Many portraits of colleagues are preserved at Yale and the University Club of New York. Admiral Farragut, Elihu Vedder, the painter, and Paul Sabatier, the French savant, likewise sat for portraits. Perhaps the two most notable are those of Weir's cousin, Dr. Robert F. Weir [*q.v.*], at the College of Physicians and Surgeons, New York, and of S. Wells Williams of Yale. "Roses," owned by Nathaniel Vose, Boston, illustrates his flower studies. Always the able craftsman, Weir achieved in his earlier works what a critic of the seventies called "ideal reality." Later his palette took on the lighter tonality of the Impressionist, with a cool green the characteristic note. Weir modelled statues of Benjamin Silliman, the elder (1884), and President Woolsey for sites on the Yale campus, the fountain on the New Haven Green, and the Lafayette plaque on the Pinchot Building, Milford, Pa.

Aside from his art, Weir's activities centered on the development of the Yale School of Fine Arts, where he sought to meet the needs of those who desired both technical and appreciative approaches to the fine arts. The collection of casts, the Alden collection of Belgian woodcarvings, and the Jarves collection of Italian primitives were acquired at his instance, and a chair of architecture was eventually established. A prize scholarship was named in his honor in 1889, and in 1924 the department of architecture was moved into Weir Hall. With a keenly religious nature, Weir sought to clarify spiritual truths in such a manner that they might be discussed as freely as scientific theories; *The Way: the Nature and Means of Revelation* (1889) and *Human Destiny in the Light of Revelation* (1903) were written with this intention. His *John Trumbull* (1901) is still a definitive critique of an early American artist. As a member of the Century Association of New York he delivered an address at the memorial meeting in honor of the artist, Sanford Robinson Gifford [*q.v.*]; he gave the principal address at the fiftieth anniversary of the Yale School of Fine Arts in 1916; and he lectured and wrote extensively on artistic matters throughout his career. Distinguished in his later years by his white hair, moustache, and goatee, his ruddy complexion, and his military step, Weir left a distinct impression on his contemporaries. His appearance is ably suggested in the etching (reproduced in *International Studio,* September 1926) by his brother, J. Alden Weir [*q.v.*]. He was a Scotch mystic, a man of broad culture, and a gracious and charming social being. He and his wife are reported to have lived a romance lasting almost sixty years. He died in Providence, survived by his wife and two daughters, and was buried in New Haven.

[See *Who's Who in America*, 1924–25; *Yale Alumni Weekly*, Apr. 16, 1926, pp. 827, 828; H. T. Tuckerman, *Book of the Artists* (1867); F. J. Mather, *The Am. Spirit in Art* (1927); Samuel Isham, *The Hist. of Am. Painting* (1905); J. L. Chamberlain, ed., *Universities and their Sons* (1899), vol. II, p. 593; obituary in *Providence Jour.,* Apr. 9, 1926. There is a coll. of letters and docs. in the Yale School of Fine Arts, and a coll. of photographs of Weir's works in the N. Y. Pub. Lib. Information has been supplied by Dean E. V. Meeks of the Yale School of Fine Arts, by Mrs. J. D. Perry, Weir's daughter, by W. W. Williams, by A. P. Stokes, and by Irene Weir, Weir's niece, who is preparing a critical biog. of Robert W., John F., and J. Alden Weir. The letters of John F. and J. Alden Weir are being edited by the latter's daughter, Mrs. Mahonri Young.]   W. S. R.

WEIR, JULIAN ALDEN (Aug. 30, 1852–Dec. 8, 1919), painter, was born at West Point, N. Y. His mother was Susan (Bayard); his father, Robert Walter Weir [*q.v.*]. As the youngest of sixteen children he could not have received particular preferment, but he was given every encouragement to further his desire to become an artist. Guided by his father in his early efforts, at eighteen he went to New York to study at the National Academy of Design, and in 1873 he was admitted to the atelier of Gérôme in Paris. In Paris he met Jules Bastien-Lepage, who introduced him to French country life at his home in Damvilliers, journeyed with him to study the Flemish masters in Belgium, and facilitated greatly his *entrée* into the artistic life of Paris. Under Bastien-Lepage's influence Weir began to work directly from nature and to study the great masters of realism, not only in French galleries but in Holland (1874) and Spain (1876), where Velasquez revealed to him a new comprehension of the visible world as manifested in light and values, and furthered his understanding of the work of Manet and Whistler, then being newly acclaimed. His "French Peasant" (1875) shows that at the early age of twenty-three he had an admirable control of his medium and a decided power of visual concentration.

Returning to New York in 1877, he occupied a studio in the Benedict Building, where he painted one of his first pictures to win general recognition—"The Muse of Music" (1882–84), now in the Lotos Club, New York. During trips in Belgium and Holland in 1880–81 with such companions as his brother John [*q.v.*], Bastien-Lepage, and John Twachtman, who was to become a lifelong friend and artistic companion, he purchased for Erwin Davis, the collector, examples of contemporary French masters. It is a tribute to Weir's critical vision and appreciation that he secured the "Woman with a Parrot" and "Boy with a Sword" by Manet and the "Jean d'Arc" by Bastien-Lepage, now in the Metropolitan Museum. At a later time he acquired for Marquand the famous Rembrandt "Portrait of a Man," also in the Metropolitan. About 1883, after nearly ten years of intermittent foreign travel and study, he settled definitely in New York, where he had a studio in the old Tenth Street Building, and became associated with such younger painters as Edwin Abbey, John Twachtman, Theodore Robinson, Albert P. Ryder, William M. Chase [*qq.v.*], and Childe Hassam. His residence abroad had gained him the friendship of J. A. M. Whistler, John Singer Sargent [*qq.v.*], and other painters of international distinction. On Apr. 24, 1883, he married Anna Dwight Baker, daughter of Charles Taintor Baker and Anna Bartlet Dwight, by whom he had three daughters; after his wife's

death he married her sister, Ella Baker, in October 1893.

Spending half the year in the country, alternating between two Connecticut estates, one at Windham, the other at Branchville, Weir passed a tranquil existence in the study of nature, in the companionship of his family and friends, in fishing, hunting, and other rural occupations. Called Julian by his family and intimate friends, but known otherwise as J. Alden Weir, he was universally loved and esteemed. Of impressive appearance, stalwart of build, in feature patterned after the Greek ideal, he was entirely natural, modest, and unaffected in manner. The bust by Olin L. Warner [*q.v.*] is an admirable likeness. In younger life Weir was opposed to the official school of the Academy, and was one of the strong influences in the formation of the Society of American Artists. Later, when the artistic tendency of the two organizations became similar and a consolidation was effected, he resumed exhibiting in the National Academy of Design. He had become a member in 1886, and served as president (1915–17). He was one of the founders in 1898 of Ten American Painters. From 1882 onward he received numerous awards both at home and abroad, one of the latest being the gold medal of the Pennsylvania Academy in 1916 in recognition of his eminent services to American art. He died in New York City of heart failure. A memorial exhibition of his work was held at the Metropolitan Museum of Art in 1924.

In the early period of Weir's painting one sees something of the eclectic. There is little evidence of Gérôme's influence, but "Children Burying a Bird" and other occasional examples show the effect of the naturalistic manner of Bastien-Lepage, not only in a precise realism and a painstaking craftsmanship but also in the predilection for the soft greys and grey-greens which reflect the palette of the French master. Several distinguished portraits, painted in the traditional manner of the studio, exemplify his skilled draftsmanship and highly developed technique, while the studies of his hunting dogs reveal an affectionate understanding and masterful characterization, and the "Still Life with Roses" (illustrated in *Art in America, post*) is set apart by its austere reserve, its imposing design, and the loving and reverential spirit with which it is painted. The French Impressionists and the growing interest in light and color had in the early years of development made a very deep and lasting influence on the style and method of Weir's painting. This became apparent in his show at the American Art Galleries in 1893, where he exhibited in conjunction with Twachtman and the French painters Monet and Besnard. But he was not an Impressionist in the limited sense; his art is more directly related to that of Whistler and to the decorative influence of the Japanese.

His art is decidedly lyrical and intimate. Extremely versatile in the sense that he was a painter of portraits, of *genre,* of still life, and of landscape, using the varied media of oil, water color, pastel, and etching, he nevertheless conceived his pictures within very definite limitations. Never aspiring to the grand manner or the large surface, he was concerned solely with esthetic attributes. His conception was expressed in terms of spatial arrangement, simplification of form, and harmonization of tone, and the very personal way in which he elevated the seemingly commonplace aspect of nature to the realm of highly expressive art. In all his painting there is reflected his own restraint, sincerity, and reasonableness, as well as his subtlety of observation and his delicacy of feeling. He experimented constantly with technique, and his ultimate style is far removed from the early influence of his friend Bastien-Lepage. The color is subdued, marked by neutralized hues of closely related values; the form is manifested by a universal lighting that eliminates strong contrasts; the pigment is applied with short impasto brushwork. The thematic reserve made his style somewhat mannered, but his work has always an unexplainable distinction and charm. Many of his best-known pictures are hung in the Metropolitan Museum, New York, the Art Institute of Chicago, and in the galleries in Washington, D. C.

[See *Who's Who in America,* 1918–19; Weir's semi-autobiog. article on Bastien-Lepage in *Modern French Masters* (1896), ed. by J. C. Van Dyke; Century Asso., *Julian Alden Weir, an Appreciation of His Life and Works* (1921), which contains a list of his works compiled by his daughter; E. H. Blashfield, *Commemorative Tribute to Julian Alden Weir* (1922); Suzanne La Follette, *Art in America* (1929); Samuel Isham, *The Hist. of Am. Painting* (1905); Eliot Clark, in *Art in America,* Aug. 1920; Margery A. Ryerson, *Ibid.,* with list of etchings; H. R. Butler, in *Scribner's Mag.,* Jan. 1916; Duncan Phillips, in *Am. Mag. of Art,* Apr. 1917; Kenyon Cox, in *Burlington Mag.,* May 1909; Frank Weitenkampf, *Am. Graphic Art* (1912); Metropolitan Museum, *Memorial Exhibition of the Works of Julian Alden Weir* (1924); Agnes Zimmerman, *An Essay towards a Catalogue Raisonné of the Etchings . . . of Julian Alden Weir* (1923); obituary in *N. Y. Times,* Dec. 9, 1919, editorial, Dec. 10. Biog. details have been verified by Mrs. Mahonri Young, Weir's daughter.]   E. C.

WEIR, ROBERT FULTON (Feb. 16, 1838– Apr. 6, 1927), surgeon, was the son of James Weir, a prominent pharmacist of New York, and Mary Anne (Shapter) Weir. His grandfather, Robert Walter Weir, was a prosperous merchant, who came to America from Scotland. His mother was of English ancestry. Weir was born in New York City, and his early education was obtained in the public schools. In 1854 he graduated from the College of the City of New York, then the Free Academy, and in 1857 was accorded the M.A. degree from the same institution. During this time he clerked for his father and acquired a considerable knowledge of medicines and their uses, as well as a desire to enter the medical profession. He received the M.D. degree from the College of Physicians and Surgeons, New York, in 1859, having supplemented his courses of study with practical experience in the office of Dr. Gurdon Buck [*q.v.*]. He had also been allowed to make the morning rounds with the house surgeon of the New York Hospital, and for the two years following his graduation, he served as house surgeon there.

In 1861 he entered the United States Army as assistant surgeon and continued in service until the close of the war. His work as the head of one of the largest of the government hospitals, at Frederick, Md., was publicly acknowledged by the surgeon-general. When the war ended, he commenced a general practice in New York City. He was appointed surgeon to St. Luke's Hospital and, from 1873 to 1883, one of the attending surgeons of the new Roosevelt Hospital. From 1876 to 1900 he was attending surgeon to the New York Hospital, but resigned in that year to take charge of the surgical service at the Roosevelt Hospital. From 1870 to 1875 he was professor of surgery at the Woman's Medical College, and in 1883 he became clinical professor of surgery at the College of Physicians and Surgeons and professor from 1892 to 1903. In 1907 he retired completely from public professional life.

Weir was one of the most brilliant surgeons of his time. Dr. W. W. Keen wrote of him: "Weir was a capital operator, careful, judicious and resourceful. I have hardly known a better one. . . . He was indeed a Master Surgeon" (Bradshaw, *post,* p. 508). His operations were often witnessed by many physicians desiring to learn from his technique. Especially notable was his work in connection with surgery of the joints and intestines. He was among the first to recognize duodenal ulcer as an entity. He made an important modification of the Murphy button for its use in gastroenterostomy, and was among the first to adopt Lister's method of antiseptic and aseptic surgery. His contributions to medical literature were many. His thesis at graduation, "Hernia Cerebri," won a prize of $50. In his *Personal Reminiscences* (*post*) are the titles of his papers which describe surgical procedures or operations originated by him. For a list of his many contributions to medical journals, see Shrady (*post*). He served as president of many professional organizations, among them the Practitioners' Society of New York, 1883–84; New York Surgical Society, 1884–85; American Surgical Association, 1899–1900, and the New York Academy of Medicine, 1901–02. He was also a member of the Société de Chirurgie of Paris, and was one of very few to receive an honorary degree from the Royal College of Surgeons in London in 1900.

Forceful, energetic, commanding, Weir gave himself completely to his profession. For hobbies he tried tennis and whist, but felt little enthusiasm for them. His later years were spent for the most part in extensive traveling.

He was twice married: to Maria Washington McPherson of Virginia, on Oct. 2, 1863, and to Mary Badgley Alden of Albany on Nov. 7, 1895. A daughter by his first wife survived him. His portrait by his cousin, John F. Weir [*q.v.*], hangs in the New York Academy of Medicine. Robert Walter Weir [*q.v.*] was his uncle.

[*Who's Who in America*, 1926–27; R. F. Weir, *Pers. Reminiscences of the N. Y. Hospital from 1856 to 1900* (1917); J. J. Walsh, *Hist. of Med. in N. Y.* (1919), vol. V; *Coll. of Physicians and Surgeons, N. Y., A Hist.*, ed. by John Shrady; *Am. Jour. of Surgery*, May 1927; J. H. Bradshaw, article in *Surgery, Gynecology and Obstetrics*, Feb. 1930; *N. Y. Times*, Apr. 7, 1927.]

J. A. H.

WEIR, ROBERT WALTER (June 18, 1803– May 1, 1889), painter and teacher, was born in New Rochelle, N. Y., the son of Mary (Brinkley) and Robert Walter Weir. His father, a native of Paisley, Scotland, settled in New York about 1790, engaged in mercantile and shipping pursuits, and maintained a country-seat in New Rochelle. At ten, as the result of his father's reverses in business, Weir went to work in a cotton factory. He spent the year 1815 in Albany with an uncle, continuing his education there and in New York City, where he made the acquaintance of John Wesley Jarvis [*q.v.*]. In 1817 he entered a mercantile house in the South, and then held a clerical position in New York. For a few months he was instructed by Robert Cook, an English painter in heraldry, between six and eight in the morning, before going to work. In 1821 he turned his entire attention to painting, beginning with a successful copy of a portrait. An early triumph was entitled "Paul Preaching at Athens." He studied anatomy and acquired a knowledge of Italian, and late in 1824, under the patronage of Henry Carey, he

left for Italy, illustrating much of Dante's *Inferno* on the way. In Florence he became a pupil of Pietro Benvenuti, who was frescoing the Pitti Palace, and completed a "Christ and Nicodemus" and an "Angel Relieving Peter" before leaving for Rome a year later. There he lived with Horatio Greenough [*q.v.*], the sculptor, on the Pincian Hill. Returning to America after three years abroad, he opened a studio in New York. He was elected a member of the National Academy of Design in 1829.

In the same year he married Louisa Ferguson. He succeeded Charles Robert Leslie [*q.v.*] in 1834 as instructor in drawing at the United States Military Academy, becoming professor in 1846. Between 1836 and 1840 he was engaged on "The Embarkation of the Pilgrims" for the rotunda of the Capitol, Washington, basing his design on Nathaniel Morton's *New Englands Memoriall* (1669). With the $10,000 he received from this commission he erected a stone church of his own design at Highland Falls, near West Point, the Church of the Holy Innocents, in memory of his two deceased children. Following the death of his wife, Louisa, in 1845 he married Susan Bayard. He had sixteen children, including the two eminent painters, John Ferguson Weir and Julian Alden Weir [*qq.v.*]. He retired after a service of forty-two years in 1876, maintaining a studio in New York until his death. His personality aroused the lasting affection of the generations of students he instructed, among them Grant, Lee, Sherman, and the painter Whistler. His friendliness to his fellow-artists is mentioned a number of times by William Dunlap [*q.v.*], and his ardent churchmanship following his studies for "The Embarkation" by a number of chroniclers. A portrait of Weir by Daniel Huntington [*q.v.*] hangs in the library of the Military Academy.

Weir's works include illustrations, portraits, and "cabinet *genre*." Examples of the latter group are the designs for George P. Morris' *The Deserted Bride* (1853) and "The Drawing Book" in the *American Juvenile Keepsake* for 1835; quaint and sentimental they now appear. His portraits include "Red Jacket," the last chief of the Senecas, "General Winfield Scott," now owned by the Metropolitan Museum of Art, and "Governor Throop" and "Mayor Lee," both of the latter in the New York City Hall. His *genre* studies were literary, historical, scenic, and religious in their subject-matter and largely incidental in their interest. The novels of Scott and Cooper, the country of Italy and the Hudson River, the Bible, the Church, and contemporary political history were explored for subjects. On occasion he painted realistically, as in "The Boat Club," or the "Church of the Holy Innocents, Highland Falls." He designed an altarpiece for the Church of the Holy Cross, Troy, N. Y., the allegorical "War" and "Peace" in the old chapel at West Point, and stained-glass windows for Trinity Chapel and Calvary Church, New York City. Many water-colors came from his studio as well, and he was an assiduous collector of fine prints and engravings.

Criticisms of Weir's work follow in a general way the taste of the critic's own generation. For example, the Rev. S. G. Bulfinch in *A Discourse Suggested by Weir's Picture of the Embarkation of the Pilgrims* (1844) speaks of "The Embarkation" as a "living representation of a most memorable scene," and the sculptor Greenough criticizes chiefly the placing of the highlights. H. T. Tuckerman (1867) praises the composition and historicity of the mural, but notes a dryness of tone. On the other hand, he admires the "Flemish authenticity" of the "Child's Evening Prayer." James Jackson Jarves [*q.v.*] is remarkably anticipatory of later criticisms when he says that Weir showed "considerable skill of manipulation and detail, facility of composition, and those composite qualities which make up an accomplished rather than an original man" (*post*, p. 230).

[See William Dunlap, *A Hist. of the Rise and Progress of the Arts of Design in the U. S.* (3 vols., 1918), ed. by F. W. Bayley and C. E. Goodspeed, which contains autobiog. material; H. T. Tuckerman, *Book of the Artists* (1867); J. J. Jarves, *The Art-Idea* (1864); G. W. Cullum, *Biog. Reg. . . . Officers and Grads. U. S. Mil. Acad.*, vol. I (1891), p. 38; cat. of sale of contents of Weir's studio, N. Y., Feb. 19–21, 1891, in N. Y. Pub. Lib.; obituary and death notice in *N. Y. Times*, May 3, 1889. A crit. study of Weir and his two artist sons is being prepared by Irene Weir.]

W. S. R.

WEISENBURG, THEODORE HERMAN (Apr. 10, 1876–Aug. 3, 1934), neurologist, the son of Herman and Sally (Schwartz) Weisenburg, was born in Budapest, Austro-Hungary, and brought to the United States by his parents who settled first in New York City and later in Bethlehem, Pa. He obtained his preliminary education in the public schools of New York and of Bethlehem, and entered the School of Technology of Lehigh University where he studied chemistry for two years. He then matriculated in the School of Medicine at the University of Pennsylvania, and was graduated in 1899 with the M.D. degree. After a short internship at the Lackawanna Hospital, Scranton, Pa., and a longer one as a resident physician at the Philadelphia Hospital (Blockley), in Philadelphia, Pa., he joined the United States Army in January 1901 and served in the Philippines until No-

vember 1902. He returned to Philadelphia and during the succeeding year and a half worked as a general practitioner in that city. He was registrar to the nervous wards of the Philadelphia General Hospital, 1903–04, and assistant neurologist until 1907 when he was appointed a neurologist and consultant to the department for the insane. He was instructor in neurology and neuropathology in the School of Medicine of the University of Pennsylvania from 1904 until 1907 when he was elected professor of neurology in the Medico-Chirurgical College in Philadelphia. After this institution was absorbed by the University of Pennsylvania he was appointed professor of neurology in the Graduate School of Medicine in July 1917. In much of his work he was associated with his close friend, Charles K. Mills [*q.v.*]. He was president of the Philadelphia Neurologic Society in 1908 and of the American Neurological Association in 1918. He took a large part in making successes of the first Anglo-American Congress of Neurology held in London in 1927 and the International Neurological Congress held in Bern in 1931, and at the time of his death he was president of the Association for Research in Nervous and Mental Diseases. He held membership in many professional societies. In 1926 he was made a corresponding member of the Verein für Psychiatrie und Neurologie in Vienna.

During the World War Weisenburg served as contract surgeon and as an executive officer, first in the Military Neuropsychiatric Training School of the Philadelphia Hospital and later as a major in the Medical Corps; he then rose to be chief of the nervous service in General Hospital No. 1 in New York City. His subsequent work as vice dean and professor of neurology of the Graduate School of Medicine of the University of Pennsylvania stands out sharply. In research and in literature the excellence of his work is amply demonstrated in his work "Comprehensive and Analytic Report on the Epidemic of Poliomyelitis in Philadelphia in 1916," published in the *Transactions of the American Neurological Association*, 1918, and in the paper on "Cerebellar Localization and its Symptomatology," read before the Royal Society of Medicine in London in 1927, and published in *Brain*, October 1927. He was a contributor to neurologic and psychiatric journals, but he was best known as the editor-in-chief of the *Archives of Neurology and Psychiatry*, a position he occupied from August 1920 until his death. His final task was a treatise on *Aphasia, a Clinical and Psychological Study* (1935), published posthumously by his collaborator, K. M. McBride. It furnished deductions as to the unified action of the brain in the formation and use of language in contrast with the extreme ideas of precise, cortical localization for the function of speech. During the period of the World War he was editor-in-chief of the *Manual of Neurosurgery,* issued by the Office of the Surgeon-General, Washington, D. C. He was consulting neuropsychiatrist to many hospitals in and near Philadelphia.

On July 4, 1909, Weisenburg was married to Mrs. Constance Van der Veer Field, the daughter of Dr. G. W. and Ann (Van der Veer) Brown. She, with their daughter, survived him. He was buried at Valley Forge, Pa.

[Personal acquaintance; information from the family; manuscript prepared by Weisenburg; institutional records; *Who's Who in America,* 1932–33; J. W. Croskey, *Hist. of Blockley* (1929); Frederick Tilney, obit. art. in *Arch. of Neurology and Psychiatry,* Oct. 1934; J. W. McConnell, in *Jour. of Nervous and Mental Disease,* Nov. 1934; C. A. Patten, in *Am. Jour. of Psychiatry,* Jan. 1935; *N. Y. Times,* Aug. 4, 1934.]

J. W. M.

WEISER, JOHANN CONRAD (Nov. 2, 1696–July 13, 1760), Indian agent, was born near Herrenberg, in Württemberg, Germany, the son of Anna Magdalena (Uebele) and Johann Conrad Weiser. His father was a magistrate of the village of Gross-Aspach and a man of some means. Following the death of his wife, the elder Weiser and eight of his children emigrated to New York in 1710 and settled at Livingston Manor. In 1714 they removed to Schoharie. Conrad spent the winter of 1713–14 with the Iroquois chief Quagnant, when he learned much of the Maqua (Mohawk) tongue and Indian customs. After his return to his family in July, he quarreled with his new step-mother, ran away the following winter, and set up a farm for himself at an Indian village near Schoharie. He served the white people as an interpreter from 1719 to 1729. On Nov. 22, 1720, he was married to Anna Eve Feck by a German Reformed clergyman. They had fifteen children. He removed his family to Tulpehocken, Pa., in 1729 and cultivated a farm, which in thirty years he increased to about a thousand acres.

When he settled at Tulpehocken, he possessed a knowledge of Indian tongues and an appreciation of Indian affairs rivaled by only a few men in the colonies. He renewed his friendship with Shikellamy [q.v.], the agent of the Iroquois in Pennsylvania, and for many years they worked together. He early saw the significance of the support of the Six Nations in checking French expansion in the West and convinced James Logan of this by 1730. In 1731 and 1736 he arranged for the conferences at Philadelphia, which resulted in winning the Iroquois to the

interests of the Penns. Weiser and **Canasatego,** the Onondaga, firmly cemented the Iroquois alliance by the treaty of 1742, although the Delaware were alienated and the Shawnee became suspicious of the Pennsylvanians (*Minutes, post.,* IV, 577–86. This abandonment of Penn's traditional policy was urged by Weiser as vital to the safety of all the colonies, even at the expense of his own. His view was imperial rather than provincial. In 1743 he averted war between the Iroquois and Virginia, and, through his influence, the Lancaster Treaty of 1744 marked a shifting of the direction of Indian affairs from New York to Pennsylvania (*Minutes, post,* IV, 709–37). In King George's War Weiser and the colony of Pennsylvania supported the Six Nations in their efforts to remain neutral and enabled them to resist the efforts of Sir William Johnson [q.v.], for whom Weiser had little respect. George Croghan [q.v.] and Weiser won over the Western tribes at the treaty of Logstown in 1748, thereby extending Pennsylvania Indian trade to the Mississippi. In 1748 Shikellamy died, and with him went Weiser's commanding position as a backwoods diplomat. He remained one of the best of the interpreters until his death, but Sir William Johnson and George Croghan superseded him in the formulation of policy. He spoke and wrote in German and in English. Several of his hymns, especially "Einweihungs-Lied" (see Weiser, *post,* pp. 401–03), and his Indian reports show literary ability. In his frontier home he maintained a music room furnished with an organ, and in his library, in addition to religious and law books, were the works of Voltaire and Arnholtz. He urged and supported the press of Christopher Sower [q.v.] at Germantown.

For a period of years, from 1735 to 1740 or 1741, most of his energies were absorbed in religious activity. Although born a Lutheran, in Tulpehocken he worshipped at the German Reformed Church led by John Peter Miller [q.v.] and by 1735 was its chief elder. Under the influence of the religious revival of 1735, Miller and Weiser formed a Baptist group and were baptized by Johann Conrad Beissel [q.v.] in May. Following this "religious somersault," Weiser withdrew from the world, grew a beard, and became a "teacher" at Tulpehocken. In August he removed his family to Ephrata and became a member of the cloister under the name of Brother Enoch. His children, Magdalena and Peter, also entered the cloister, but his wife returned to the farm. Weiser now endured fasts and vigils, played the part of evangelist and exhorter, and made at least two proselyting trips to New Jersey.

Beissel and Weiser quarreled, and the latter withdrew from the cloister, being incensed, it is said, among other things at receiving punishment for having four children by his wife during his celibacy. He returned later, however, and was consecrated priest by Beissel in 1740. He was also interested in the Moravian missions to the Indians and made a trip to Onondaga to aid them. In 1742 he was to save Count Zinzendorf's life at one of these missions.

In 1741 he was commissioned justice of the peace for Lancaster County, probably the only German to hold such an office in the colonial period. The following year he was made ranger for northern Lancaster County. At this time he identified himself with the governor's party by exhorting his countrymen to vote against the pacific Quakers in the coming elections. About 1743 he severed his connection with Ephrata, probably with the advice of Henry Melchior Mühlenburg [q.v.], later his son-in-law. He became a naturalized subject of Great Britain in April 1744. His vigorous support of the proprietary party led the Moravians to draw away from him. He joined the Lutheran Church in 1747, and his coreligionists electioneered for him, when he unsuccessfully ran for the Assembly against a Quaker. Upon the erection of Berks County in 1752 he was made a justice of the peace and later served as the first president-judge of the county, from 1752 to 1760. He was also a trustee of the board to educate German youths in Pennsylvania in 1753. He led an expedition on the frontier in the French and Indian War, and he was commissioned colonel in the Berks County regiment. He was one of the commissioners to lay out Reading where he went to live in 1755. There he opened his famous "White Store" and joined the Reformed Church. He lost his health gradually in the last five years of his life. He died on one of his farms, at Womelsdorf.

[Diary and a few papers in Lib. of Cong.; papers in possession of Hist. Soc. of Pa.; J. S. Walton, *Conrad Weiser and the Indian Policy of Pa.* (1900); C. Z. Weiser, *The Life of (John) Conrad Weiser* (1876); J. F. Sachse, *The German Sectarians of Pa.* (2 vols., privately printed, 1899–1900); *Chronicon Ephratense* (1786), tr. by J. M. Hark (1889); H. M. M. Richards, "The Weiser Family," *Pa. German Soc. Proc.*, vol. XXXII (1924); *Minutes of the Provincial Council of Pa.*, vols. IV, V (1851); J. B. Nolan, "Conrad Weiser's Inventory," *Pa. Mag. Hist. and Biog.*, July 1932.]
C. B—h.

WEISS, EHRICH [See HOUDINI, HARRY, 1874–1926].

WEISS, JOHN (June 28, 1818–Mar. 9, 1879), Unitarian minister, author, was born in Boston, the son of John and Mary (Galloupe) Weiss.

His grandfather, also a John Weiss, was a German Jew who had come to the United States as a political refugee and kept a tavern in Germantown, Pa. His father was a barber. Weiss lived his boyhood in Worcester, Mass., attended the public schools and Framingham Academy, and graduated in 1837 from Harvard College. At college he did not stand high in the esteem of the faculty, and was once rusticated, but his temperament—an explosive compound of wit, poetry, and religious idealism—was relished by his classmates. After teaching for a few years, he enrolled in 1840 at the Harvard Divinity School and attended, 1842–43, the University of Heidelberg. He was pastor of the Unitarian Church, Watertown, Mass., where he succeeded Convers Francis, from Oct. 25, 1843, to Oct. 3, 1845, from Mar. 23, 1846, to Dec. 6, 1847, and from June 1862 to June 1869; in the second interval, he was pastor of the First Congregational Society, New Bedford, Dec. 29, 1847, to Jan. 24, 1859. On Apr. 9, 1844, he married Sarah Fiske Jennison of Worcester, who with three sons and two daughters survived him. Impetuous in his enthusiasm, zealous for liberty—which meant open opposition to negro slavery among other things—unpredictably witty, eloquent, and satirical in his sermons, he dazzled, bewildered, and ultimately exasperated his pewholders at Watertown and New Bedford. Unable to find a congenial parish, he was compelled at various times to live on the insecure returns from writing, lecturing, and occasional preaching. He contributed articles, reviews, and poems to several magazines, especially to the *Christian Examiner,* the *Atlantic Monthly, Old and New,* and the *Galaxy,* and was one of the chief supports of Sidney H. Morse's *Radical.* His most substantial achievement was his *Life and Correspondence of Theodore Parker* (1863), which began as a short memoir, undertaken at the suggestion of Joseph Lyman, Parker's literary executor, and grew into a solid, two-volume documentary life of enduring worth. In writing it, however, Weiss incurred the displeasure of Mrs. Parker and of Franklin B. Sanborn, who claimed that Parker had appointed him his biographer. Weiss helped to introduce German literature to New England readers with *The Æsthetic Letters, Essays, and the Philosophical Letters of Schiller, Translated with an Introduction* (1845) and *Goethe's West-Easterly Divan, Translated with Introduction and Notes* (1877). His two original books are *American Religion* (1871) and *Wit, Humor, and Shakespeare: Twelve Essays* (1876), the fullest exhibitions of his high-minded, intensely subjective, somewhat disjointed thought. His conversation, like his sermons and lectures, was a cascade of wit, epigram, and poetic images. He was greatly admired by several of the leaders of his denomination, whose memoirs depict him as a religious genius. He was one of the founders in 1867 of the Free Religious Association. During the last five or six years of his life he lived in Boston, where he died.

[Henry Williams, *Memorials of the Class of 1837 of Harvard Univ.* (1887) ; *Boston Daily Advertiser*, Mar. 10, 1879 ; *Christian Register*, Mar. 29, 1879 ; J. H. Allen, "A Memory of John Weiss," *Unitarian Rev.*, May 1888 ; C. A. Bartol, "John Weiss," *Ibid.*, Apr. 1879, and "The Genius of Weiss," *Principles and Portraits* (1880) ; O. B. Frothingham, "John Weiss," *Unitarian Rev.*, May 1888, reprinted in *Recollections and Impressions* (1891) ; Mrs. J. T. Sargent, *Sketches and Reminiscences of the Radical Club* (1880) ; *Cat. of the Private Library of the Late John Weiss, to be Sold by Auction* (Boston, 1879) ; C. L. F. Gohdes, *The Periodicals of Transcendentalism* (1931) ; M. J. Savage, sketch in S. A. Eliot, ed., *Heralds of a Liberal Faith*, vol. III (1910) ; F. B. Sanborn, *Recollections of Seventy Years* (1909).]   G. H. G.

WEITZEL, GODFREY (Nov. 1, 1835–Mar. 19, 1884), soldier, engineer, was born in Cincinnati, Ohio, the son of Louis and Susan Weitzel, recent arrivals from the Bavarian Palatinate. After preparatory education in the local schools, he entered the United States Military Academy in 1851, graduated July 1, 1855, as second in a class of thirty-four, and was commissioned brevet second lieutenant of engineers. He became second lieutenant July 27, 1856, and first lieutenant, July 1, 1860.

His first duty was on the fortifications of New Orleans, 1855–59. Subsequently, until January 1861, he was assistant professor of engineering at the Military Academy. During this period his wife died as the result of burns sustained when her dress caught fire. Early in 1861 Weitzel was assigned to the engineer company on duty in Washington, and with this company he took part in the expedition to Pensacola, Fla. (Apr. 19–Sept. 17, 1861), which saved Fort Pickens to the Union. In the fall of the same year he was chief engineer of the fortifications of Cincinnati, then returned to Washington in command of an engineer company. On account of his familiarity with the defenses of New Orleans, in the spring of 1862 he was made chief engineer of General Butler's force, which co-operated with Admiral Farragut in the operations against that place. After the surrender, Apr. 30, he served as assistant military commandant of the city. Made brigadier-general of volunteers on Aug. 29, 1862, he was thereafter continuously engaged in field operations in Louisiana until December 1863. He commanded a brigade and provisional division in the siege of Port Hudson, and in the assaults of May 27 and June 14, 1863. During this period he became captain in the regular engineer corps, and received the brevets of major and lieutenant-colonel for gallantry at Thibodeaux and Port Hudson.

In May 1864 he assumed command of the Second Division, XVIII Army Corps, in Butler's Army of the James, but was soon detached to become chief engineer of that army. In this capacity he supervised the construction of the defenses of Bermuda Hundred. In August he became brevet major-general of volunteers, and in September returned to troop duty, commanding first the XVIII and later the XXV Army Corps. He received the brevet rank of colonel in the regular service Sept. 29, 1864, for gallantry at the capture of Fort Harrison, Va., and on Nov. 17, 1864, was promoted major-general of volunteers. In December he was second in command to Butler in the first expedition against Fort Fisher, and exercised the active command of the troops sent ashore. During the final operations against Richmond his command occupied the line between the James and the Appomattox rivers, and took possession of the city upon its evacuation, Apr. 3, 1865. For service in this campaign he received the brevets of brigadier-general and major-general in the regular army. General Butler relied greatly upon him, and General Grant spoke of him as a thoroughly competent corps commander (John Russell Young, *Around the World with General Grant*, 1879, II, 304). He had much experience in command of colored troops. When first assigned to this duty, in 1862, he vigorously opposed the idea of arming slaves, and accepted the command under strong protests; but he was successful with these troops, and in 1864 and 1865 all the infantry regiments of his XXV Corps were colored.

After Lee's surrender, in the concentration of troops in Texas incident to the Maximilian episode, Weitzel commanded the Rio Grande district; but the emergency there having been terminated, he was mustered out of the volunteer service Mar. 1, 1866, and returned to duty with the Corps of Engineers, in which he became a major, Aug. 8, 1866. Thereafter until his death he was engaged in the constructive work of his corps, notably in river and harbor improvement. Of the numerous projects with which he was connected, the most important were the ship canals at the falls of the Ohio and at Sault Sainte Marie, Mich., and the lighthouse at Stannard's Rock in Lake Superior. Taking over the first of these enterprises in 1867 after much work had been done, he carried it to completion in 1873. At Sault Sainte Marie he supervised the building of what was at the time the largest lock in the world—515 feet long and eighty wide, with a lift of eighteen feet. The lighthouse, with a tower rising 101 feet above the water, involved the construction below water level of a solid concrete foundation, sixty-two feet in diameter, on top of a rock situated thirty miles from shore. In connection with his various enterprises, Weitzel made and published translations of several German works dealing with hydraulic engineering and canal construction.

He was made a lieutenant-colonel June 23, 1882, and shortly afterward, because of failing health, was transferred from the Great Lakes to less arduous duty at Philadelphia, where he died in his forty-ninth year. He was married, shortly before the close of the Civil War, to Louisa Bogen of Cincinnati, and was survived by his wife and a daughter.

[G. W. Cullum, *Biog. Reg. Officers and Grads. U. S. Mil. Acad.* (3rd ed., 1891), vol. II; *15th Ann. Reunion, Asso. Grads. U. S. Mil. Acad.* (1884); *War of the Rebellion: Official Records* (Army); J. F. Brennan, *A Biog. Cyc. and Portrait Gallery . . . of Ohio* (1879); *Cincinnati Past and Present* (1872); *The Biog. Encyc. of Ohio of the Nineteenth Century* (1876); *The Biog. Cyc. and Portrait Gallery . . . of Ohio*, vol. III (1884); Charles Moore, *The Saint Marys Falls Canal* (1907); *Army and Navy Jour.*, Mar. 22, 1884; *Phila. Press*, Mar. 20, 1884.]   O. L. S., Jr.

WELBY, AMELIA BALL COPPUCK (Feb. 3, 1819–May 3, 1852), author, was born in Saint Michaels, Md., the daughter of William and Mary (Shield) Coppuck. Her father served in the War of 1812. Soon after her birth her father, a contracting mason engaged in the building of lighthouses for the federal government, removed with his family to Baltimore. She spent her childhood in this city and received there such formal education as she had. When she was about fourteen the family removed to Kentucky, and Louisville became her home for the remainder of her brief life. She early displayed a facility for writing verse, and by 1837 her poems, signed "Amelia," began to appear in George D. Prentice's *Louisville Daily Journal*. Prentice gave her considerable publicity, praising her "artless melodies" and her personal charm. Her fluent verses, pleasantly touched with melancholy, suited the popular taste, and editors of other papers promptly copied her work, giving it wide circulation. In June 1838 she married George Welby, a young Englishman in business in Louisville. Their home soon became a pleasant literary center, where visitors of distinction were to be met.

During the 1840's her popularity grew. A collected edition of the *Poems* by "Amelia" was published in 1845, bound in crimson and gold, and embellished with a romantic frontispiece

illustrating "The Rainbow," one of her most admired poems. Edition after edition followed, until by 1855 fourteen had appeared. Selections from her work were printed in the anthologies made during the decade by Caroline May, T. B. Read, and R. W. Griswold. An engraving of her portrait, painted by Read, was included in his *Female Poets of America* (1848). Edgar Allan Poe (in "Literati") gave her a high place among the poetical ladies to whom he offered gallant if uncritical praise, especially commending her poem "The Bereaved" for its versification and its admirable unity of effect. Echoes of Drake, Willis, Moore, and Mrs. Hemans filled her poems. Byron she admired extravagantly and to him she addressed some lines entitled "I know Thee Not." Her range of subjects was narrow, but she pleased the general reader by the smoothness and simplicity of her verse, her appeal to the heart, and her images from nature. She died two months after the birth of her only child. She is buried in the Cave Hill Cemetery, Louisville, Ky.

[W. T. Coggeshall, *The Poets and Poetry of the West* (1864); (Cincinnati) *Ladies' Repository*, Nov. 1855; *Louisville Daily Jour.*, May 4, 1852; *Sun* (Baltimore), Jan. 22, 1905; information from the family.]

B. M. S.

WELCH, ADONIJAH STRONG (Apr. 12, 1821–Mar. 14, 1889), educator, was born at East Hampton, Conn., the son of Elizabeth (Strong) and Bliss Welch, a bell founder. On his mother's side he was a descendant of Elder John Strong who emigrated from Plymouth to America in 1630; on his father's, of William Welch (or Welsh) who moved from Nova Scotia and settled in East Hampton about the time of the Revolution. About 1839 he went to Michigan, where he prepared for college at an academy at Romeo. He received the degrees of B.A. (1846) and M.A. (1852) from the University of Michigan. In 1846–47 he studied law and was admitted to the bar, but did not practise. After serving as principal of the union school at Jonesville (1847–49), he joined the gold-rush and remained in California something over a year. On his return he became the first principal (1852–65) of the Michigan State Normal School at Ypsilanti, where he was "largely instrumental in giving form and character to the institution and in determining the direction of its early development" (Putnam, *post*, p. 139). He conducted many teachers' institutes (1852–53), aided in organizing the state teachers' association, and became its first president, and served as trustee of the Michigan Agricultural College. In 1865 he went to Florida for his health. He engaged in business at Pensacola and Jacksonville, and was elected to the United States Senate for a short term (1868–69).

Chosen in 1868 first president of the Iowa State Agricultural College, Ames, Iowa, he served in that capacity from 1869 until failing health obliged him to resign in 1883, and later (1884–89) taught history and psychology. As president of a pioneer college with few buildings, poorly equipped, he worked against many physical handicaps; he himself laid out the campus, locating buildings, drives, walks, groups of trees and shrubbery. From the beginning he defended industrial education as a better preparation for life than the long-established classical course, and supported the right of women to a college education. He based the first two courses, in agriculture and in mechanic arts, on fundamental and applied sciences, and for numerous later developments, as originator of plans and policies, he deserves a share of the credit. He is said to have originated the plan of sending college teachers to conduct farmers' institutes about the state (1870–71), a system later followed in almost every state, and he encouraged systematic experimentation in stock raising and in farm products, which the college began in 1880, seven years before the federal act providing for experiment stations. The class instruction in cooking, conducted by Mrs. Welch in her own kitchen, afterwards developed into the large and widely known division of home economics. In 1883 Welch was sent abroad by the United States commissioner of agriculture to report on agricultural schools in Germany, Belgium, and England.

Welch was a man of great charm, well versed in the classics, in philosophy and history, and in psychology. His publications include *Analysis of the English Sentence* (1855), *Report on the Organization and Management of Seven Agricultural Schools in Germany, Belgium, and England* (1885), *Talks on Psychology Applied to Teaching* (1888), and *The Teachers' Psychology* (1889). Having the gift of ready, persuasive, forcible address, he was in great demand as a speaker before educational and industrial organizations. His written addresses are models of clearness, logical order, and style. He expressed frequently his love of beauty and order, and he was deeply religious. He was married first to Eunice P. Buckingham (d. 1866), daughter of Gen. Catharinus P. Buckingham of Ohio, by whom he had a daughter and two sons, and second in 1868 to Mary (Beaumont) Dudley, daughter of Dr. A. L. Beaumont of Jonesville, Mich. He died in Pasadena, Cal., and was buried at Ames.

[B. W. Dwight, *The Hist. of the Descendants of Elder John Strong*, vol. I (1871), p. 201; *Hist. of Middlesex County, Conn.* (1884), p. 215; Daniel Putnam, *A Hist. of the Mich. State Normal School . . . at Ypsilanti* (1899); B. F. Gue, *Hist. of Iowa* (4 vols., 1903); W. O. Payne, *Hist. of Story County, Iowa* (2 vols., 1911); C. E. Bessey, in *Annals of Iowa*, Apr. 1909; *An Hist. Sketch of the Iowa State College of Agriculture* (pamphlet, 1920); *Aurora* (Ames, Iowa), Apr. 1889; *The Bomb* (Ames, 1897); Mrs. A. B. Shaw, in *Alumnus* (Ames), May 1905; obituaries in *Iowa State Register*, Mar. 15, 22, 1889.]   A. B. N.

WELCH, ASHBEL (Dec. 4, 1809–Sept. 25, 1882), civil engineer, son of Ashbel and Margaret (Dorrance) Welch, was born at Nelson, Madison County, N. Y. When Ashbel was seven years old his parents moved to Deerfield, Oneida County, N. Y., and for the next ten years he attended schools in Utica, completing his education in the winter of 1826 at Albany Academy, where he studied under the immediate direction of Joseph Henry [*q.v.*]. In the summer of 1827 Welch began his engineering career as rodman on the staff of the Lehigh Canal, at Mauch Chunk, Pa., where his older brother was resident engineer, and after three years here he became connected with the Delaware & Raritan Canal, in Trenton, N. J., of which he was made chief engineer in 1835.

During the succeeding twenty-five years he engaged in a variety of engineering work in the transportation field. He made the reconnaissances for and subsequently built the Belvidere Delaware Railroad, which followed the banks of the Delaware River from Trenton northward to Manunka Chunk, near the Delaware Water Gap. In addition to looking after all the engineering work of the Delaware & Raritan Canal, he engaged in a consulting engineering practice covering a varied field of activities. He assisted John Ericsson [*q.v.*], for example, in designing the steamship *Princeton*; he made examinations of coal and iron properties in Virginia; he supervised experiments in gunnery initiated by Commodore R. F. Stockton [*q.v.*] of the United States Navy, and made a trip to Europe in 1844 for the special purpose of superintending the construction of a large, wrought-iron gun. In 1847 he designed and built for the Delaware & Raritan Canal at Bordentown, N. J., a wooden lock, the unusual feature of which was that it was constructed upon a quicksand, and in 1852 he accomplished the unusual feat of enlarging the whole of the Delaware & Raritan Canal in three months. The following year he undertook the work of designing and constructing the Chesapeake & Delaware Canal, but in the course of this arduous task, carried on in connection with his many other engineering activities, he broke down physically and was compelled to give up all active work.

After a rest in Europe in 1854, however, he again took up his consulting engineering work, particularly in connection with New Jersey railroads, being engaged in the construction both of the roads themselves and of terminal facilities. In 1862 he was appointed vice-president of the Camden & Amboy Railroad. In this position he worked ceaselessly to bring about the consolidation of the several competing railroad companies in New Jersey, and, largely through his efforts, in January 1867 final arrangements were made uniting the Delaware & Raritan Canal Company, the Camden & Amboy Railroad & Transportation Company, and the New Jersey Railroad & Transportation Company. Welch was immediately made president of the new organization, known as the United Companies of New Jersey, and was in charge of all administrative matters until December 1871, when the properties were leased to the Pennsylvania Railroad Company.

As early as 1845 Welch, with the assistance of Joseph Henry, began a series of experiments in the application of telegraphy to railroad signaling, and in 1865 presented to the Camden & Amboy Railroad Company a plan for telegraphic safety signals. It was immediately accepted and applied on the railroad between Kensington and New Brunswick, and is generally regarded as the earliest installation of the block signaling system which came into general use in the United States. Welch also carried on investigations looking toward the improvement of railroad rolling stock, particularly car trucks and wheels, and made a study of iron and steel rails, publishing many articles on the subject in technical journals. He was an active member of the American Society of Civil Engineers, serving as vice-president in 1880 and being chosen president the year of his death. On Oct. 25, 1834, he married Mary Hannah Seabrook; four children survived him. He died in Lambertville, N. J.

[W. H. Manning, *The Manning Family of New England* (1902); John Bogart and others, *Ashbel Welch* (1883); *Proc. Am. Soc. Civil Engineers*, vol. IX (1883); *Railroad Gazette*, Sept. 29, 1882; *Railway Age*, Oct. 5, 1882; J. E. Watkins, "The Camden and Amboy Railroad," in *Ceremonies Upon the Completion of the Monument Erected by the Pa. Railroad Company at Bordentown, N. J.* (1891); Waldemar Kaempffert, *A Popular Hist. of Am. Invention* (1924); J. B. Snell, *Hist. of Hunterdon and Somerset Counties, N. J.* (1881); *Press* (Phila.), Sept. 27, 1882.]   C. W. M.

WELCH, CHARLES CLARK (June 14, 1830–Feb. 1, 1908), miner, railroad builder, and capitalist, was of English, Scotch, and French descent. Among his ancestors on his father's side were Elder William Brewster of the *Mayflower* and Maj. John Mason of Connecticut. On the maternal side he came of French ancestry, the first American representative being one of the founders of Providence, R. I. His parents, Charles and Pamelia (La Valley or La Valle) Welch, lived on a farm in Jefferson County, N. Y., at the time of their son's birth. On this farm and at the village school young Charles spent his childhood. At the age of fifteen he entered the academy at Watertown, and after receiving some training there he took up teaching. Stories of gold discoveries lured him in 1850 to California, where he engaged for two years in placer and quartz mining in Placer County. Then Australian gold fields beckoned, and he sailed to Sydney. After mining for a year in New South Wales he returned to New York, via Cape Horn.

Presently he moved westward, seeking business opportunities, and settled in Chicago in 1855. The succeeding five years were spent in the real estate and brokerage business. In 1860, iured by mining opportunities, he crossed the plains by stagecoach to Colorado, where he was to make his permanent home. Building on experience, gained in California and Australia, he engaged successfully in gold mining in Gilpin and Boulder counties, operating extensive properties. Then he branched out into other lines. He ran sawmills, operated a tannery and a fire brick plant at Golden, and constructed irrigation ditches. He crossed the plains between Denver and the Missouri River nineteen times during the stagecoach era. Becoming interested in railroads, he was one of the promoters of the Colorado Central Railroad, which was extended west from Golden to the mines and north to a connection with the Union Pacific at Cheyenne. He also built a portion of the Santa Fé line east of Pueblo, Colo. At Louisville, Boulder County, he sank a 200-foot shaft, found a ten-foot vein of coal, and opened and operated the "Welch Mine," which became a large and steady producer. In 1878 he organized an irrigation company and built the Handy Ditch in Larimer County. In the country served by this canal he procured extensive acreage and became a large producer of grain. In 1880 he built the Welch Irrigation Ditch, constructing flumes in Clear Creek Canyon to bring water onto the bench lands northeast of Denver. In 1891 he was one of the promoters of the road that became the electric trolley line between Denver and Golden.

In 1872 Welch was elected to the Colorado territorial legislature from Jefferson County. He introduced the bill for the establishment of the

State School of Mines at Golden and donated the ground for the first building. For many years he served on the board of trustees of the institution. On May 22, 1878, he married Rebecca Jeannette Darrow of Coldwater, Mich., by whom he had two children. He died in Jacksonville, Fla., where he had gone seeking a restoration of health; his body was returned to Colorado for burial.

[*Hist. of Clear Creek and Boulder Valleys, Col.* (1880); W. N. Byers, *Encyc. of Biog. of Col.* (1901); *Sketches of Col.; Being an Analytical Summary and Biog. Hist. of the State of Col.* (1911); W. F. Stone, *Hist. of Col.* (1918), vol. III; *Rocky Mountain News* (Denver), Feb. 2, 1908; E. C. B. Jones, *The Brewster Geneal.* (1908), II, 987.]   L. R. H.

WELCH, JOHN (Oct. 28, 1805–Aug. 5, 1891), congressman, jurist, was born on a farm in Harrison County, Ohio, the son of Thomas and Martha (Daugherty) Welch. His father was of English and his mother of Irish parentage. They were among the early pioneers of Ohio, settling first in Harrison County and moving about 1828 to Athens County. At the age of eighteen, having spent his life until then on the farm, John secured "his time" from his father, and by alternately teaching school to obtain funds and attending classes at Franklin College in New Athens, Ohio, he was able to graduate from that institution in 1828. Traveling some fourteen miles each week to recite, he studied law with Joseph Dana of Athens, but soon broke down physically and for a time ran a sawmill owned by his father. In after years he was fond of telling his grandchildren that he would set the saw and then read Blackstone while it was going through the log. In 1830 he married Martha, daughter of Capt. James Starr; two sons and two daughters were born to this union. In 1833 he was admitted to the bar of Ohio and located for practice at Athens.

Professionally successful from the start, he made a place for himself among such eminent lawyers as Thomas Ewing, Samuel F. Vinton, and Henry Stanbery [*qq.v.*]. After having served from 1841 to 1843 as prosecuting attorney of Athens County, he was elected in 1843 to the Ohio Senate, remaining there for one term of two years. In 1850 he was sent, as a Whig, to the lower house of Congress, where, also, he served but one term, and in 1852 he was a delegate to the national Whig convention that nominated Gen. Winfield Scott for president. From 1862 to 1865 he was a common-pleas judge and while serving as such was appointed by the governor, Feb. 23, 1865, to fill the vacancy on the Ohio supreme court created by the resignation of Judge Rufus P. Ranney [*q.v.*]. In October

1865 he was elected to fill the unexpired term and in October 1867 was elected for a full term. After serving for thirteen years, he returned in 1878 to Athens and resumed the practice of law. In 1887 he published *An Index-Digest to the Reports of Cases Decided in the Courts of Ohio* and later prepared a supplement, which was published after his death. He also wrote a small volume entitled *Mathematical Curiosities* (1883) consisting of new and original rules, puzzles, and an interest table on an entirely new plan— and a number of essays.

His opinions as judge were characterized by their brevity, few being over two or three pages long, and by the almost total absence of any cited cases. They are, however, forcibly stated and clearly reasoned. The positive character of the man is illustrated by the fact that it was his habit, when the court was in consultation, to state his opinion briefly after listening to the other judges, and if they disagreed with him to devote himself to his favorite pastime of solving some mathematical problem while they argued. When the vote was taken his position was already known, for he seldom changed a conclusion he had formed. His mathematical turn of mind made him a particularly valuable member of the court, since much of its time during his presence on the bench was given to the solution of problems of real property, which have in them much that requires the precision of mathematics. Some of his opinions in this field are considered classics, among them that given in the case of *McIntire Administrators et al* vs. *the City of Zanesville* (17 *Ohio State Reports*, 352), wherein he applies the equitable doctrine of "cy-près," holding that where a fund is given by will to the use and support of a "poor school" for the benefit of the poor children of a city in which later a public school system is established, this fund may be used "to buy books and shoes and in rare cases even food" for the poor children attending the public schools. He died in Athens in his eighty-sixth year.

[Welch's opinions are in 16–31 *Ohio State Reports*. Sources include 48 *O. S. R.*, v–vii; *Green Bag*, June 1895; *Proc. Ohio State Bar Asso.*, 1892; *Biog. Cyc. and Portrait Gallery . . . of Ohio*, vol. I (1883); *Biog. Dir. Am. Cong.* (1928); *Athens Jour.*, Aug. 13, 1891.]   A. H. T.

WELCH, PHILIP HENRY (Mar. 1, 1849– Feb. 24, 1889), humorist, journalist, was born at Angelica, N. Y., the son of Joseph B. Welch and his wife, Mary (?) Collins. After passing through the public schools at Angelica, he was employed for twelve years by a New York hardware firm, spending two-thirds of his time on the road. He joined his brother in Oil City,

Pa., and from there sent petroleum reports to *Bradstreet's*. Meanwhile he had been married to Margaret Welles Hamilton, daughter of Theodore and Emily (Welles) Hamilton, of Angelica. There were four children. In 1882 Welch went to Rochester, N. Y., to conduct a column called "The Present Hour" in the *Post-Express*, and thereafter he devoted himself consistently to journalistic humor. In 1883 he left Rochester to spend a few months conducting a column called "Accidentally Overheard" in the Philadelphia *Call*, and then (1884) joined the staff of the New York *Sun*, with which he remained until his death. He had found his own particular vehicle in the short humorous dialogue, usually consisting of a single question and answer; into these tiny paragraphs he packed his dry wit and his easy, good-natured satire on the follies of the day. His jokes in the *Sun* seemed to have been referred to as "Queer Wrinkles," but they appeared anonymously and without a column heading. At the same time that he was grinding out his weekly stint for the *Sun*, Welch was sending similar material to *Puck*, *Life, Judge,* the *Epoch*, the *Times, Drake's Magazine, Harper's Bazaar,* and other periodicals. His jokes were borrowed and stolen all over the country. Week after week the jokes in the San Francisco *Argonaut,* which copied its material from other papers, would be all or nearly all from his pen, though ascribed to many different papers, including some for which Welch had never written in his life. In 1886 Welch was attacked by a cancer in the throat, and was forced to undergo an operation which left his voice impaired. In the summer of 1888 the trouble returned, this time in his chest. A second operation was unsuccessful, and the surgeons did not dare attempt a third. His friends and associates of this time were filled with the deepest admiration of Welch's fortitude and indomitable spirit during these months when he was slowly dying of cancer. He continued to turn off dozens of jokes a week, finally dictating them to his wife when he could no longer write them himself. He died in his fortieth year at his home in Brooklyn and was buried at Angelica.

Through the efforts of Edward Perkins Clark of the *Evening Post* and Alfred Corning Clark, a Welch Memorial Fund was raised to provide for the education of the children. Contributions came from all over the country, ranging in amount from $1 to $10,000; notable contributors were Lowell, Whittier, Mark Twain, and Theodore Roosevelt. During Welch's life he had published only one book, *The Tailor-Made Girl* (1888), a collection of page-length dialogues reprinted from *Puck,* gently satirizing the contemporary well-to-do young lady. As part of the campaign to raise money for the fund, friends now compiled an anthology of his shorter and more characteristic dialogues under the title of *Said in Fun* (1889); illustrations were contributed by most of the well-known humorous illustrators of the day, including W. L. Sheppard, C. D. Gibson, and F. Opper.

[*Journalist,* Jan. 28, 1888; obituaries in *Sun* (N. Y.), *N. Y. Times, N. Y. Tribune,* Feb. 25, 1889; information furnished by Paul H. and Emily H. Welch of New York City, Mary W. Wakely of Angelica, and members of the staff of the *Sun.*]   E. M. S.

WELCH, WILLIAM HENRY (Apr. 8, 1850–Apr. 30, 1934), pathologist, son of William Wickham Welch [*q.v.*] and Emeline (Collin) Welch, was born in Norfolk, Conn., in the house in which both his father and grandfather had lived as physicians for many years. His mother died when he was about six months old, and he was cared for by his grandmother. When he was twelve he was sent to school at the Winchester Institute. There he had as roommate Frederick S. Dennis, also of Norfolk, who became a prominent surgeon in New York and was his lifelong friend. In 1866 he went to Yale, graduating in 1870. After teaching Latin and Greek in a school at Norwich, N. Y., for a year, he entered the College of Physicians and Surgeons of Columbia University but left shortly to spend a year studying chemistry at the Sheffield Scientific School at Yale, where he came under the influence of Oscar H. Allan and George F. Barker [*q.v.*]. In the autumn of 1872 he returned to the College of Physicians and Surgeons to study medicine, and in 1875 was graduated. That spring he went to Europe for several years of study. At Strassburg he had a course in histology with Waldeyer, demonstrations with von Recklinghausen, and some work in chemistry with Hoppe-Seyler. After a summer walking-trip in Switzerland he went to Leipzig, where he worked with Ludwig, and thence, on Ludwig's recommendation, to Breslau to study under Julius Cohnheim, instead of following his original plan of studying under Virchow. There he found himself in a group of men who were later famous —Paul Ehrlich, Carl Weigert, Salomonsen, Albert Neisser, and others. He was there when Robert Koch came to demonstrate to Cohn and Cohnheim his early work on anthrax, which showed the beginning of effective studies of bacteria. After a visit to Vienna, where he was joined by Theophil Mitchell Prudden [*q.v.*], he returned for a time to Strassburg, studying at von Recklinghausen's suggestion inflammation produced in the cornea of the frog. He returned to America by way of Paris and London, hearing Louis-Antoine Ranvier in Paris and Joseph Lister in London.

This first period of study in Germany gave him a clear view of histology, chemistry, physiology, and pathology as they were then being developed there and served as the foundation for his own expanding work in pathology, which he began on his return to New York in the spring of 1878. Dennis, who was beginning his surgical work with Austin Flint and W. T. Lusk [qq.v.], arranged a small laboratory for him at Bellevue Hospital, where he performed the autopsies and taught the students. He lived with Dennis and had some practice in clinical medicine. He refused the invitation of Francis Delafield [q.v.] to teach pathology at the College of Physicians and Surgeons but recommended Prudden, who accepted the place. At the same time he was demonstrator of anatomy, registrar of the Woman's Hospital, and was much occupied in reporting on diagnoses of pathological material.

In 1883 he accepted an invitation to become professor of pathology in the Johns Hopkins University, Baltimore. He spent the year 1884 in Europe studying the new bacteriology under Frobenius and Flugge, pupils of Koch, and then under Koch himself in Berlin. There he found Prudden again and Ehrlich, and the astonishing new horizons suddenly opened before them by the methods and inspiration of Koch stirred his enthusiasm so that from that time on his interest was largely centered in the study of bacteriology. In Baltimore in 1885 he started work with William T. Councilman in rooms in the top of Newell Martin's laboratory of physiology, but a pathological laboratory was soon organized. There a group of men worked under him of whom Welch always spoke with pleasure: Councilman, William S. Halsted [q.v.], G. H. F. Nuttall, Alexander C. Abbott, Franklin P. Mall [q.v.], and B. Meade Bolton. During this time he was especially concerned with the mechanism of the formation of thrombi and with the question of haemorrhagic infarction; the work later led to the publication of his admirable articles on *Thrombosis and Embolism* (1899). He was the inspiration for much brilliant work by the group of his associates. Before the opening of the university hospital, when there was no human material, he found great interest in animal diseases, such as hog cholera and the pleuropneumonia of cattle. Later he devoted himself to the study of diphtheria and pneumonia. He discovered and described in detail the gas-producing bacillus known by his name which was the cause of "gas gangrene" in wounded soldiers

during the World War. With the opening of the hospital in 1889 the selection of men as heads of various departments was greatly influenced by the advice of Welch, who suggested Osler and William Stewart Halsted [qq.v.]. Later, in the same way, for the organization of the school of medicine, which was opened in 1893, he was responsible for the choice of Mall, Abel, and Howell. He himself was the first dean and served in that capacity for several years. In 1896 he established a new type of medical publication, the *Journal of Experimental Medicine*, for the presentation of the results of serious investigation, and was its editor until 1906.

Throughout the earlier years of the Johns Hopkins medical school he was most active in its organization and was perhaps especially influential in determining its character, which was not that familiar at the time in the medical schools of the country. After 1900, though he continued to lecture, his energies were largely devoted to the advance of medical education throughout the country. It was then that the Rockefeller Institute of Medical Research was founded, in a way largely based upon his counsel, and from 1901 to the end of his life he was chairman of the board of scientific directors. From 1906 on, he was associated in a similar advisory capacity with the various activities of the Carnegie Foundation. He was active in many scientific and medical associations. He was president of the Congress of American Physicians and Surgeons (1897), the Association of American Physicians (1901), the American Association for the Advancement of Science (1906), the Association of Pathologists and Bacteriologists (1906), the American Medical Association (1910), and the National Academy of Sciences (1913–16). In addition to his activities in connection with the universities and research foundations in other cities, Welch was deeply interested in those of Baltimore and Maryland, and was long president of the state board of health (1898–1922). In this connection he was frequently consulted by the municipal authorities in matters of public health in the city. He was also a member of the Medico-Chirurgical Faculty of Maryland and its president in 1891. After the entrance of the United States into the World War he served actively with the surgeon-general of the army, visiting many camps and acting as consultant on matters relating to the health of the army; he was made brigadier-general in 1921.

Through all these years his interest in the problems of pathology and bacteriology remained intense. His public addresses, which were many, dealt in general with plans for educational procedures, with broad problems of public health, with the relations of one science to another, and with various periods and personalities in the history of medicine. Some, however, were devoted to topics more closely related to his own field, such as adaptation in pathological processes, morbid conditions caused by the bacillus *aerogenes capsulatus,* and the Huxley lectures on immunity. In 1920 well over three hundred of these were collected in *Papers and Addresses by William Henry Welch,* in three volumes, edited by Walter C. Burket.

Upon the resignation of Ira Remsen [*q.v.*] as president of the Johns Hopkins University in 1912, Welch was appointed chairman of a committee of the faculty and acted virtually as president until President Frank J. Goodnow took office. In 1914 Welch and Wickliffe Rose were asked to advise upon the foundation of a school of hygiene and public health. When the school was opened as part of the Johns Hopkins University in 1918, Welch, who had resigned the Baxley professorship of pathology, was appointed director. The successful development of this school, with its far-reaching influence, through its students, in foreign countries, was brought about by the profound interest of Welch coupled with his skill in the choice of men. In this he was assisted by Dr. W. H. Howell, who later succeeded him as director. In 1925 he published *Public Health in Theory and Practice; an Historical Review.* His work at the school continued until his resignation in 1926. In that year a chair of the history of medicine was endowed by the General Education Board, and Welch entered upon a third career as its occupant. In 1929 the William H. Welch Medical Library, housing the department of the history of medicine, was formally dedicated, with many visitors from abroad taking part in the ceremonies in Welch's honor. Even after his retirement in 1931 Welch continued to work in that department until in the early months of 1933 he became incapacitated by prostatic carcinoma. This confined him to the Johns Hopkins Hospital until his death fourteen months later, on Apr. 30, 1934. He was buried in Norfolk, Conn.

During his later years he made a number of visits to different countries in Europe, among them one in 1905 to sit for the famous Sargent portrait of the "Four Doctors," and another in 1909 to attend university celebrations in Leipzig. His last trip (1927) was for the purpose of purchasing books for the library of the department of the history of medicine. Besides this, at the request of the Rockefeller Foundation, he went in 1915 with Dr. Simon Flexner and Wallace But-

trick [*q.v.*] to China, to study the conditions to be met in the establishment of the Peiping Union Medical College, and later (1921) he went again to Peiping to be present at the formal opening of the school. During his trips to Europe he was always eager to spend some time at a spa such as Carlsbad, and during summers when he did not go abroad he was accustomed to go for a time to Bedford Springs or to Atlantic City, where he could bathe and lie in the sun for long hours. One summer (1931) he spent in Pasadena, where he enjoyed the California climate and saw much of the scientists working there.

Among the numerous portraits of Welch, the best are those of Sargent and Thomas B. Corner. There is also a bronze bust by Konenkov which is an excellent likeness. Further, there exists a moving talking picture in which Welch himself relates the main events of his career. He was short and stout, quite bald in later years, not especially given to niceties in costume. For some years he wore a broad beard, which he later trimmed to a point. He was extremely simple and unaffected in his attitude, and readily approachable. He never married. He lived for all the later years of his life in Baltimore on St. Paul Street, first at 935, then at 807; in each house he occupied the second floor, which was overfilled with books, even the chairs being piled with them. He took his meals at the Maryland Club or at the University Club, of which he was president for many years, and spent a great deal of time in one or the other. On his frequent visits to New York he lived at the University Club, and found it so comfortable that he spent the whole summer of 1932 there, going very often to one of the beaches to swim or lie on the sand, being convinced that long exposure to sunlight maintains health. He was a connoisseur of delicately prepared food and of good cigars, which he smoked constantly, and was a most generous host. He was especially attached to a small group of friends whose conversation in a small room at the club went on for years in a most amusing form. His bodily strength was quite remarkable and his digestive powers extraordinary.

In his relations with the Johns Hopkins University and the medical school there, it was especially his keenness of judgment in any difficult situation and his extraordinary wisdom in organization and in the choice of men that were of great value. His estimate of the results of research was equally penetrating. His interests, however, were by no means confined to medical education. There was no one who seemed so widely read or whose memory could retain in so phenomenal a way every detail of the most miscellaneous reading, in which encyclopedias and the *Dictionary of National Biography* figured largely. All was in order and could be produced at a moment's notice even after many years. His familiarity with the history of music was especially remarkable.

Welch's fame rests upon his service to humanity, and especially to the United States, which such qualities made possible. He grasped at once the significance of the epochal developments in pathology and bacteriology which he witnessed in Europe, and introduced them into America, not only bringing the results of foreign investigations but breathing the whole spirit of this advance into the medicine of America. Later, with great wisdom and foresight, he planned and organized institutions for the promotion of education and investigation throughout the country, an influence felt and treasured in many other countries as well, where aid in these directions was given largely through his advice.

Universities and scientific associations in the United States and abroad conferred a great many honorary degrees and fellowships upon him. He also received a number of medals and decorations, including that of the Legion of Honor. Many banquets were given in his honor: one in 1900 on the twenty-fifth anniversary of his doctorate, when he was presented with a *Festschrift* volume of many papers; another in 1910 on the twenty-fifth anniversary of his professorship; another in 1920 in celebration of his seventieth birthday, with publication of his collected papers and addresses. On his eightieth birthday there were celebrations in many cities, even in Europe and in Asia, and in Washington there was a special meeting at which, among others, President Hoover spoke in his honor.

[See *Who's Who in America*, 1932–33; intro. by Simon Flexner in *Papers and Addresses by William Henry Welch* (3 vols., 1920), ed. by W. C. Burket; *Obit. Record Grads. Yale Univ.*, 1934; *William Henry Welch at Eighty* (1930), ed. by V. O. Freeburg; W. C. Burket, *Bibliog. of William Henry Welch* (1917); Johns Hopkins Univ. Circulars; *Jour. Am. Medic. Asso.*, May 5, 1934; obituaries in *Johns Hopkins Hospital Bull.*, June 1934, and *N. Y. Times*, May 1, 1934; personal letters and notes on conversations with Welch. Dr. Simon Flexner is preparing a biog. of Welch.]

W. G. M.

WELCH, WILLIAM WICKHAM (Dec. 10, 1818–July 30, 1892), physician, was born in Norfolk, Conn. His grandfather, Hopestill Welch, blacksmith in Norfolk, had thirteen children, of whom the third was Benjamin Welch. Benjamin studied medicine under the village doctor, Ephraim Guiteau; married his daughter, Louisa; and practised medicine in Norfolk for sixty years. After the death of his first wife he married Elizabeth Loveland. There were ten children, of whom five sons and three daughters survived. The five sons, all physicians, were Asa G. Welch of Lee, Mass., Benjamin of Litchfield and Salisbury, Conn., James W. of Winsted, Conn., William Wickham of Norfolk, and John Hopestill of New Hartford and Norfolk, Conn. William Wickham Welch, the fourth son, was graduated from the Yale Medical School in 1839 and began the practice of medicine in Norfolk while his father, who died in 1849, was still active. On Nov. 7, 1845, he married Emeline Collin of Hillsdale, N. Y., and by her had a daughter and a son, William Henry [*q.v.*]. His wife died in 1850 when the son was only six months old. On May 2, 1866, he married Emily Sedgwick of Cornwall, Conn., sister of Gen. John Sedgwick [*q.v.*].

His life was devoted to the practice of his profession in Norfolk and the surrounding country. After spending much of the day in his office with patients, he would set out at night in his horse-drawn buggy to visit the sick at whatever distance they lived. He was much in advance of his time in many ways, and very successful in his methods of treatment and the control of nursing. The importance of fresh air impressed him greatly. It is related that when late at night he saw, in passing, the house of one of his patients, windows closed, although he had left orders for abundant fresh air, he would stop his horse, remove the whole window, and carry it home with him. He was especially interested in the treatment of hydrophobia and the bites of venomous reptiles. It does not appear that surgery played any large part in his practice, but he was undoubtedly ready in any emergency. Long after his death his memory continued to be treasured in and about Norfolk. His professional work for fifty years won him the affection of everyone, and he was honored and beloved not only in the sickroom but as a companion and fellow townsman. He was greatly interested in horses and dogs. One or two of his horses were famous, perhaps especially for their endurance throughout his long drives at night. His Dalmatian followed under the buggy until it grew so old that it must be taken on the seat, where it was intolerant of any intrusion.

Welch was a member of the state House of Representatives (1848–50), served in the state Senate in 1851 and 1852, and was elected by the American Party to Congress (1855–57). After that he resumed the practice of medicine but was again a member of the state House of Representatives in 1869 and 1881. He was president of the Norfolk Leather Company, one of the incorporators of the Connecticut-Western Railroad and the Norfolk Savings Bank, and with his brother, John Hopestill, engaged in the knitting business in Norfolk. He died in Norfolk, survived by his wife and children, and was buried in the family plot in the Norfolk cemetery. A drinking fountain for horses was erected in the village in his memory with the inscription, *Fons sum solati talis et ipse fuit.*

[*Obit. Record Yale Grads.,* 1892; Harvey Cushing, in *New England Jour. of Medicine,* May 24, 1934; *Biog. Dir. Am. Cong.* (1928); H. A. Kelly and W. L. Burrage, *Am. Medic. Biogs.* (1920); obituary in *Hartford Courant,* Aug. 2, 1892; information from Dr. W. H. Welch and Senator F. Walcott.]   W. G. M.

WELD, ARTHUR CYRIL GORDON (Mar. 4, 1862–Oct. 11, 1914), musician, composer, was born at Jamaica Plain, Mass., the son of Stephen Minot Weld and his second wife, Georgianna Hallet. He was a descendant of Thomas Weld [*q.v.*]. After attending Harvard University he went abroad in 1879 to study music. He remained in Europe until 1887, studied composition and orchestration with Becker, Foerster, and Von Comiar-Fiedlitz at Dresden, and with Neumann at Berlin. He was graduated with high honors from the Conservatory of Music in Munich where he was a pupil of Rheinberger, Abel and Levi. During the years in Munich he composed a number of works in the larger forms which were publicly performed in that city. These included a string quartet in C (1885), of which one movement was played in America by the Kneisel Quartet in 1890; a "Romanza" for small orchestra (1886), performed in Boston during the following year; an "Andante" and "Scherzo" for septet (1886); and an orchestral suite, "Italia" (1887), which was subsequently presented at the Worcester Festival (1888) and by the Boston Symphony Orchestra (1890). Other works from this period include a composition for soli, double quartet, chorus and orchestra "Benedictus Dominus Israel"; an "Ode in Time of Peace" for double quartet and organ; four madrigals, and many other songs.

After his return to America Weld lived for a time in Milwaukee, Wis., where he was active as a dramatic critic and conductor of an orchestra. Later he came to New York City to work in a field in which he achieved his greatest distinction, as a conductor of musical comedies and composer of incidental music for the theatre. In November 1900 he conducted the first production of "Florodora," and became general musical director for the productions of Henry W. Savage [*q.v.*]. In this capacity he was well known in theatrical circles, and was made a member of the House Committee of the Lambs' Club, in New York. In 1913 he went to London to conduct performances of the musical comedy "Adele," and in the following year he became personal representative for James K. Hackett [*q.v.*]. He arranged the music for Hackett's performance of *Othello,* and took charge of the musical features of all his plays. He met his death this same year. While driving his automobile in the neighborhood of West Point, N. Y., he was stricken with apoplexy, and died almost immediately. His third wife, Claudia Clarke, a musical comedy actress, was with him in the car.

Weld was a colorful person whose presence lent distinction to many gatherings. According to his obituary notice in the *New York Times* (*post*), he was a "striking looking man and was a commanding figure in the orchestra pit." He always wore a monocle. He had three daughters by his first wife.

[C. W. Fowler, *Hist. of the Weld Family* (1879); H. M. Whitcomb, *Annals . . . of Jamaica Plain* (1897); *Grove's Dict. of Music and Musicians, Am. Supp.* (1930); *Hugo Reimanns Musik Lexikon* (11th ed., 1929); *Boston Evening Transcript, N. Y. Times,* Oct. 12, 1914.]   J. T. H.

WELD, THEODORE DWIGHT (Nov. 23, 1803–Feb. 3, 1895), abolitionist, was born in Hampton, Conn., the son of Elizabeth (Clark) Weld and the Rev. Ludovicus Weld, a Congregational minister. He was descended from a line of New England clergymen whose progenitor was the Rev. Thomas Weld [*q.v.*], first minister of Roxbury; his ancestry also included Edwardses, Dwights, and Hutchinsons. In Weld's childhood his family moved to western New York, near Utica, where he passed an active, vigorous youth. Here he met Capt. Charles Stuart [*q.v.*], principal of the Utica Academy, a retired British officer, who was to influence profoundly his character and his career. In 1825, when Charles G. Finney [*q.v.*], the Presbyterian revivalist, invaded Utica, Weld and Stuart joined his "holy band" of evangelists, and for two years they preached throughout western New York. Weld labored chiefly among young men; and when he entered Oneida Institute, Whitesboro, N. Y., to prepare for the ministry, scores of them also enrolled. Here he remained for several terms, his expenses being borne by Charles Stuart, who had long considered him "beloved brother, and son, and friend." During vacations Weld labored for the cause of temperance with such effect that by the end of the decade he was accounted the most powerful temperance advocate in the West. Meantime he had met those philanthropists of New York City, led by Arthur and Lewis Tappan [*qq.v.*], who were financing Finney's revival. Attracted by

Weld's talents, they repeatedly urged him to head various reforms which they were backing; but he steadfastly refused to abandon his preparation for the ministry.

In 1829 Charles Stuart went to England to preach the abolition of West Indian slavery. He soon became noted as a lecturer for the British Anti-Slavery Society, and even more as a pamphleteer; but his most eloquent appeals were addressed to Weld. His persuasions were successful. From 1830 on, Weld was consumed with anti-slavery zeal. His first converts to emancipation were the New York philanthropists. In June 1831 the Tappans called a council in New York City, which proposed the immediate organization of an American anti-slavery society on the British model. After Weld's departure, however, the Tappans decided to postpone organization until emancipation in the British West Indies, which was now assured, had become a published triumph. Previously, Weld had urged the New York philanthropists to found a theological seminary in the West to prepare Finney's converts for the ministry. In the fall of 1831 they acceded, and commissioned Weld to find a site for the seminary. On this journey he advocated the anti-slavery cause at every opportunity. In Huntsville, Ala., in 1831, he converted James G. Birney [q.v.], and at Hudson, Ohio, he abolitionized the faculty of Western Reserve College, Elizur Wright, Beriah Green [qq.v.], and the president, Charles Backus Storrs. For the seminary he selected a project already begun, Lane Seminary at Cincinnati, Ohio. The Tappans secured Lyman Beecher [q.v.], most famous preacher of his time, as president, and a notable faculty. Weld supplied the bulk of the students from the converts of Finney's revivals. Among them he organized in 1834 a "debate" on slavery (Barnes, post, p. 65), which won not only the students, but also Beecher's children, Harriet and Henry Ward, and several Cincinnatians, among them Gamaliel Bailey [q.v.].

Meanwhile, the New York philanthropists had organized the American Anti-Slavery Society. Unfortunately they adopted the British motto of "immediate emancipation"; and though they defined the motto as "immediate emancipation, gradually accomplished," the public interpreted it as a program of immediate freedom for the slaves. The pamphlet propaganda based upon this motto failed disastrously both North and South, and the society's agents, almost without exception, were silenced by mobs. Weld saved the movement from disaster. Forced out of Lane Seminary by its angry trustees in the fall of 1834,

he trained the ablest of his fellow students and sent them out as agents for the American Anti-Slavery Society. Adopting Finney's methods, they preached emancipation as a revival in benevolence, with a fervor which mobs could not silence. Among them, Henry B. Stanton [q.v.] and James Thome became well known; but thirty-two other "Lane rebels" did their parts in establishing the movement in Ohio, western Pennsylvania and New York, Rhode Island and western Massachusetts. Weld, "eloquent as an angel and powerful as thunder," accomplished more than all the rest combined. Indeed, the anti-slavery areas in the West and the field of Weld's labors largely coincide. Among his converts, Joshua R. Giddings, Edwin M. Stanton [qq.v.], and others were later prominent in politics; while the anti-slavery sentiment among New-School Presbyterians was largely due to his agitation among the ministers.

By 1836 the success of Weld's agents was so apparent that the American Anti-Slavery Society decided to abandon the pamphlet campaign, and devote all its resources toward enlarging his heroic band. Weld himself selected the new agents, to the number of seventy, gathered them in New York, and for weeks gave them a pentecostal training in abolitionism. One of the new agents at this conference was Angelina Grimké [q.v.], daughter of a prominent South Carolina family, whom Weld specially trained in the months that followed. During the next few years the "Seventy" consolidated the anti-slavery movement throughout the North. After the agents' conference, Weld, whose voice was permanently injured, continued to work for the cause. He took over the society's publicity, and initiated a new and successful pamphlet campaign among the converts of the "Seventy," in which the most widely distributed tracts, though published anonymously or under the signatures of other authors, were all from his pen. In addition he directed the national campaign for getting anti-slavery petitions to Congress. On May 14, 1838, he married Angelina Grimké, by whom he had three children.

The last phase of Weld's agency was the most significant of all. Certain of his converts in the House of Representatives, having determined to break with the Whig party on the slavery issue, summoned Weld to Washington to act as their adviser. Here he helped secure the adherence of John Quincy Adams; and when Adams opened their campaign against slavery in the House, Weld served as his assistant in the trial for censure which followed (C. F. Adams, ed., *Memoirs of John Quincy Adams*, vol. XI, 1876, pp. 75–79). For two crucial sessions, 1841–43, he directed the insurgents; and then, an anti-slavery bloc within their party being well established, he withdrew from public life. His influence, however, remained paramount. His lobby at Washington was continued by Lewis Tappan; and its organ, the *National Era,* was edited by Weld's convert, Gamaliel Bailey. In its columns was first published *Uncle Tom's Cabin,* which, as Harriet Beecher Stowe herself declared, was crystallized out of Weld's most famous tract, *American Slavery As It Is* (Barnes, p. 231). Moreover, as the movement spread westward, in almost every district it centered about some convert of Weld or his disciples.

Measured by his influence, Weld was not only the greatest of the abolitionists; he was also one of the greatest figures of his time. His anonymity in history was partly due to his almost morbid modesty. He accepted no office, attended no conventions, published nothing under his own name, and would permit neither his speeches nor his letters to be printed. His achievements as evangelist for Western abolitionism were not recorded in the press, largely because he would not speak in the towns, where Eastern papers then had correspondents. Convinced that the towns were subject to the opinion of their countryside, and that "the springs to touch, in order to win them, *lie in the country"* (Weld-Grimké *Letters, post,* I, 287), Weld and his agents spoke only in the villages and the country districts of the West, away from public notice and the press. After the Civil War, Weld took no part in the controversies among the abolitionists as to their precedence in history, and he refused to let friends write of his own achievements. He survived all of his fellow laborers, dying at the age of ninety-one at Hyde Park, Mass., where he had made his home for thirty-two years.

Weld's chief works are: *The Bible Against Slavery* (1 ed., 1837); "Wythe," *The Power of Congress over Slavery in the District of Columbia* (1 ed., 1836); J. A. Thome and J. H. Kimball, *Emancipation in the West Indies* (1 ed., 1837); *American Slavery As It Is* (1 ed., 1839). With J. A. Thome he prepared *Slavery and the Internal Slave Trade in the United States,* published by the British and Foreign Anti-Slavery Society in 1841.

[This account of Weld's life was pieced together from newspapers, letters and pamphlets of the time. It is more fully presented in G. H. Barnes, *The Antislavery Impulse, 1830–1844* (1933); and G. H. Barnes and D. L. Dumond, eds., *Letters of Theodore Dwight Weld, Angelina Grimké Weld, and Sarah Grimké, 1822–* *1844* (2 vols., 1934). See also C. H. Birney, *The Grimké Sisters. Sarah and Angelina Grimké* (1885); obituary in *Boston Evening Transcript,* Feb. 4, 1895.]

G. H. B.

WELD, THOMAS (1595–Mar. 23, 1660/61), Puritan divine, colonial agent, whose surname is also spelled Welde, was born in Sudbury, Suffolk, the fourth son of Edmond Weld, a well-to-do mercer, and Amy his wife. Thomas matriculated at Trinity College, Cambridge, and was graduated B.A., 1613/14 and M.A., 1618. Ordained deacon at Peterborough, Mar. 1, 1617/18, and priest the following day, he was successively vicar at Haverhill, Suffolk, and Terling, Essex. As early as Nov. 25, 1630, his nonconformity attracted Laud's attention and on Nov. 24, 1631, the Court of High Commission deposed him "for his contumacy." On June 5, 1632, he arrived in Boston, and a month later became first pastor of the church at Roxbury. In the following November, John Eliot [*q.v.*] was associated with him as teacher.

Weld was a leading minister in the Bay Colony. When the Antinomian controversy arose, he actively attempted to convince the followers of Mrs. Anne Hutchinson [*q.v.*] of their errors, and participated in the trials of the Antinomian leaders. In 1638 he was chosen overseer of Harvard College. With Eliot and Richard Mather [*q.v.*] he prepared the metrical translation of the Psalms known as the "Bay Psalm Book," the first book printed in English America (*The Whole Booke of Psalmes,* 1640). In 1641, with Hugh Peter [*q.v.*] and William Hibbins, he was sent by the General Court to England to seek financial aid for the colony and to further the work of English church reformation. Within a year the agents collected nearly £2000 in money and supplies, although their subsequent efforts were less fruitful. To advertise their mission, Weld and Peter edited and in part wrote *New England's First Fruits* (London, 1643). Meanwhile, in 1642, Hibbins had returned to Boston, and the other agents' energies were dissipated in pious but ill-managed attempts to send homeless children to New England. Soon Peter embarked in parliamentary service, leaving Weld the only active Bay Colony agent. He secured Harvard's first scholarship fund (Davis, *post*), but failed to forestall Roger Williams' attempt to secure a patent to the Narragansett territory. This failure, the agents' activity in English internal affairs, and their diminished colonial collections led to their curt dismissal, Oct. 1, 1645. Strained relations between the Bay Colony and its erstwhile agents continued. The agents secured for specific colonial purposes funds which the General Court frequently misapplied. English donors, suspecting misappropriations, accused Weld and Peter of embezzlement and refused to donate to the New England Company of 1649. Inadequate bookkeeping beclouded the issues. Weld submitted statements to the General Court and the English corporation (*Publications of the Colonial Society of Massachusetts,* vol. XIV, 1913; *New England Historical and Genealogical Register,* April 1885) and prepared for publication "Innocency Cleared," a defense of himself and Peter (*Ibid.,* January 1882). In 1654 the corporation vindicated them (Massachusetts Archives, X, 202–04).

Like Peter, Weld became enmeshed in English affairs. He plotted the sending of Laud to New England in lieu of execution and in December 1643 heatedly upbraided the aged prelate in the Tower for suspending him (Wharton, *post,* pp. 66, 203, 213–14). In 1644, Weld published *An Answer to W. R. . . . ,* a defense of New England against William Rathband's attacks. Unable readily to accept the tolerating principles of English Independents, he was induced by Presbyterian plotters to edit with additions Governor Winthrop's manuscript account of New England's Antinomian troubles. The resulting book, *A Short Story of the Rise, Reign, and Ruine of the Antinomians* (1644), by emphasizing Congregational intolerance, jeopardized the Independents' political aspirations and placed Weld in an uncomfortable position, but he recovered his standing by publishing *A Brief Narration of the Practices of the Churches in New England* (London, 1645). He served as rector at Wanlip, Leicester, for a time in 1646, and on Feb. 1, 1649/50 was installed at St. Mary's, Gateshead, Durham, where he actively supported the Commonwealth and in various pamphlets denounced Quakerism, uncovered "Jesuit plots," and opposed Anabaptists. Excluding all but the "elect" from the sacraments, he alienated the majority of his people, and shortly before the Restoration he prudently withdrew from Gateshead. Retiring to London, he signed the Congregational ministers' "Renunciation" of Venner's insurrection in January 1661 and died two months later. His first wife, Margaret Deresleye, died at Roxbury after bearing four sons; his second, Judith, whom he married at Roxbury, was buried at Gateshead, May 4, 1656; the third, Margaret, survived him.

[W. G. Weld, "The Family of Weld" (MS.), in New Eng. Hist.-Geneal. Soc.; T. W. Davids, *Annals of Evangelical Non-conformity in . . . Essex* (1863), p. 154; S. R. Gardiner, *Reports of Cases in Courts of Star Chamber and High Commission* (1886), p. 260; Henry Wharton, *The Hist. of the Troubles and Tryals . . . of*

William Laud (1695); *Original Letters . . . to Oliver Cromwell* (1743), ed. by John Nickolls; *The Works of George Fox* (1831), III, 143–49, 369–77; Benjamin Hanbury, *Hist. Memorials Relating to the Independents* (3 vols., 1839); A. G. Matthews, *Calamy Revised* (1934); John Winthrop, *The Hist. of New England* (2 vols., 1825–26), ed. by James Savage; N. B. Shurtleff, *Records of the Gov. and Company of the Mass. Bay* (5 vols., 1853–54); *The Hutchinson Papers* (1865), I, 258; David Pulsifer, *Records of the Colony of New Plymouth,* vol. X (1859); *A Report of the Record Commissioners, Containing Roxbury Land and Church Records* (Boston, 1881); *New Eng. Hist. and Geneal. Reg.,* Jan. 1854, Jan., July 1881, Jan. 1882, Oct. 1895, Apr. 1898; Wilberforce Eames, *The Bay Psalm Book* (1903); A. M. Davis, in *Proc. Am. Antiq. Soc.,* n. s., V (1889) and VIII (1893); *Colonial Soc. of Mass. Pubs.,* vols. XIII (1912), XV (1925); *Mass. Hist. Soc. Colls.,* 4 ser. VI (1863), 5 ser. I (1871); *Proc. Mass. Hist. Soc.,* 1 ser. V (1862), VI (1863), 2 ser. VIII (1894), vol. XLII (1909); C. F. Adams, *Antinomianism in Mass. Bay* (1894).]

R. P. S.

WELLER, JOHN B. (Feb. 22, 1812–Aug. 17, 1875), representative and senator in Congress, governor of California, was born in Montgomery, Hamilton County, Ohio. His parents were of German descent and natives of New York State, whence they migrated to Montgomery about 1810. When John was still a youth they moved to Oxford, Butler County, Ohio. After attending public schools and Miami University at Oxford (1825–29), he studied law in the office of Jesse Corwin, brother of Hon. Thomas Corwin [*q.v.*], and in 1832 was admitted to the bar. For several years he served as prosecuting attorney for Butler County.

In 1838 he was elected to the United States House of Representatives as a Democrat, and served three terms (1839–45). At the outbreak of the Mexican War he enlisted as a private in an Ohio regiment, and rose to the rank of colonel. He was the Democratic candidate for governor of Ohio in 1848, but lost the election by a narrow margin. In January 1849 President Polk appointed him chairman of the commission to run the boundary line between the United States and Mexico under the treaty of Guadalupe Hidalgo. Upon his recall by President Taylor in 1850, he removed to California and opened a law office in San Francisco. The following year the California legislature elected him to the United States Senate as a Union Democrat, to succeed John C. Frémont [*q.v.*]. Early in 1857 he was defeated for reëlection by David C. Broderick [*q.v.*], but was nominated for governor by the Lecompton Democrats and elected. The outstanding political event of his administration (1858–60) was the fatal duel between Senator Broderick and David S. Terry [*q.v.*], which grew out of the bitter Broderick-Gwin feud. In December 1860 Weller was appointed minister to Mexico by President Buchanan, but was recalled the next year by President Lincoln

Shortly after the close of the Civil War, he started on a long prospecting tour through Oregon, Idaho, and Utah to Salt Lake City, eventually returning to the Eastern states and residing for a time in Washington. In 1867 he moved to New Orleans and there practised law until his death from smallpox in 1875. He was married four times: his first wife was a sister of M. C. Ryan of Hamilton, Ohio; his second, the daughter of Hon. John A. Bryan; the third, Susan McDowell Taylor, daughter of Hon. William Taylor, a Virginia congressman, and niece of Senator Thomas H. Benton [q.v.]; the fourth, Lizzie (Brocklebank) Stanton.

When a member of the House of Representatives, Weller served on the committees on commerce, Indian affairs, and ways and means. He favored the independent treasury bill and defended the Van Buren administration. He opposed the Whig tariff bill of 1842 and advocated lowering of duties for the benefit of agriculture. In 1848, in campaigning for the governorship of Ohio, he denounced the Wilmot Proviso. In the Senate he served on the committees on pensions, and on territories, he spoke frequently in support of Pacific Railroad bills and homestead legislation, and warmly espoused the Kansas-Nebraska bill. Later he favored the admission of Kansas under the Lecompton constitution. He was a pro-slavery Democrat, and voted for Breckinridge in 1860. He had considerable talent for debate, an easy command of language, a good presence, and an agreeable voice.

[*Gen. Cat. . . . Miami Univ., 1809–1909* (1909); *Centennial Hist. of Butler County, Ohio* (1905); O. T. Shuck, *Representative and Leading Men of the Pacific* (1870); T. H. Hittell, *Hist. of Cal.*, vol. IV (1897); W. J. Davis, *Hist. of Pol. Conventions in Cal., 1849–1892* (1893); *Biog. Dir. Am. Cong.* (1928); *Daily Alta California* (San Francisco), Aug. 4, 1857; *New Orleans Times*, Aug. 18, 1875.]   P. O. R.

WELLES, GIDEON (July 1, 1802–Feb. 11, 1878), secretary of the navy, son of Samuel and Ann (Hale) Welles, was born in Glastenbury (now Glastonbury), Conn., on land bought from the Indians by his ancestor, Thomas Welles, governor and first treasurer of Connecticut, who had settled in Hartford in 1636. He attended, 1819–21, the Episcopal Academy at Cheshire, Conn., and, 1823–25, the American Literary, Scientific, and Military Academy at Norwich, Vt. (now Norwich University). From his father he received a comfortable living. He studied law, but by January 1826 had become part-owner and editor of the *Hartford Times,* which, under him, was one of the first papers in New England to declare for Jackson. He resigned the editorship in 1836, but continued to be an impor-

tant contributor to the *Times* until he broke with the editor over the slavery question. In 1826 he was elected to the legislature, being its youngest member, and served there from 1827 to 1835. He led fights against imprisonment for debt, property and religious qualifications on voting, religious tests for witnesses in court, and grants of special privilege by the legislature. He disliked banks. He fathered Connecticut's general incorporation law, which became a model for other states. On June 16, 1835, he married Mary Jane Hale of Lewistown, Pa. They had nine children.

A devoted Jeffersonian democrat who believed in freedom for the individual, strict construction, and state rights, Welles helped organize Jacksonian Democracy in Connecticut and was always depended on by Jackson for advice and support. He was elected state comptroller of public accounts in 1835, 1842, and 1843. Jackson appointed him postmaster of Hartford in 1836, and he served until Harrison removed him in 1841. As chief of the Bureau of Provisions and Clothing for the Navy, 1846–49, he made friendships and acquired experience that were later to prove valuable. He was an unsuccessful Democratic candidate for Congress in 1834 and for the Senate in 1850. On frequent trips to Washington during thirty-five years and on at least five journeys to the West, Welles made a host of friends among important leaders. He seldom forgot a face, a name, or a personality. He was an uncanny judge of men.

He left the Democratic party on the slavery question, and helped organize the Republican party when the Democrats supported the Kansas-Nebraska bill. In 1856 he helped establish the Republican organ, the *Hartford Evening Press*, and became one of its chief political writers. He contributed an important series of articles to the *New York Evening Post* and the *National Intelligencer* in the exciting ante-bellum days. In 1855 William Cullen Bryant spoke of him as "long a valued correspondent of the Evening Post" whose "newspaper style is much better than that of almost any correspondent we have" (W. C. Bryant to Welles, July 17, 1855). He was an unsuccessful candidate for the governorship of Connecticut in 1856, Republican national committeeman and member of the national executive committee from 1856 to 1864, and head of Connecticut's delegation to the Chicago convention. Always a moderate, he deprecated extremists of both sections.

Soon after the election of 1860 Lincoln chose him as the New England member of his cabinet (J. G. Nicolay and John Hay, *Abraham Lin-*

coln: A History, 1890, vol. III, 367), but did not offer him the place until Mar. 3, 1861. As secretary of the navy under Lincoln and Johnson, 1861–69, Welles held that office longer than any previous incumbent. More prophetic than others, he foresaw that the war would be long. With similar foresight he told Chase in 1863 that reconciliation would at best require more than a generation (*Diary,* I, 412). He reorganized his department and created overnight a navy where there was none. What ships there were lay scattered over the world. Many officers joined the Confederate navy. In the Ordnance Bureau only two men remained loyal. Two important navy yards fell into Confederate hands. Welles's administration of the Navy Department was much criticized. Some mistakes he did make. The building of light-draft monitors was a costly blunder that arose from failure to supervise Stimers, whose previous record gave the department excessive confidence in him. The Norfolk navy yard need not have been sacrificed. Welles urged its defense, but the inability of the War Department to send protecting troops, the unwillingness of Lincoln to provoke Virginia into secession, and trust of disloyal subordinates by a loyal though hesitant elderly commandant led to its loss. Welles's orders if carried out would have saved at least the ships and armaments. Welles was accused of slowness and undue deliberation; yet he built an adequate navy from nothing with surprising speed. He was charged with extravagance; yet no other war-time business was conducted so economically. He was criticized for allowing his wife's brother-in-law, George D. Morgan, to collect a handsome commission for purchasing ships; yet the commission was normal, and Morgan drove excellent bargains. Several scandals developed in navy yards, but Welles was the first to investigate and punish offenders. No other department more free from political favoritism. Doggedly he withstood demands for favors. He refused to yield to the demands of Hale for a navy yard in his district though that senator headed the naval committee (Welles to J. P. Hale, Jan. 12, 1863). "The pretensions and arrogance of Senators become amazing," he exploded (*Diary,* I, 384). "I will not prostitute my trust to their schemes and selfish personal partisanship," he swore (*Ibid.,* I, 327). He urged a new navy yard at Philadelphia in the face of pressure from his own state to locate it at New London. Welles was convinced that the New York press opposed him because he had offended an influential New Yorker when he refused to buy vessels through his agency (*Ibid.,* II, 259–60). His masterly re-

bukes of naval officers delinquent in duty made him enemies but improved the efficiency of the service. Neither Wilkes's popularity nor Preble's famous name and powerful connections protected them when Welles decided that the good of the service required their removal. He reproved Porter for discourtesy and Phelps for seeking promotion through political pressure. Yet the same vigorous pen defended any officers who deserved it, and his letters of congratulation and praise made the heart glad.

His supervision of naval warfare was creditable. It is hard to determine how much of the credit belonged to him and how much to Gustavus V. Fox [*q.v.*] and to naval officers whom Welles trusted. Welles supervised most matters closely, and intelligently followed experiments in guns, in naval tactics, in new types of ship. He often personally wrote instructions for important engagements. He also knew how to choose reliable advisers and to cooperate with them effectively. Several claim credit for the capture of New Orleans, but Welles certainly contributed greatly to that victory. The failure of Samuel F. du Pont [*q.v.*] at Charleston led to endless disputes and made a bitter enemy of that officer, whom Welles blamed for lack of aggressiveness. "He has a reputation to preserve instead of one to make" (*Diary,* I, 247).

The greatest disputes arose over new ships. The navy had lagged behind France and Great Britain in adopting ironclads, but Welles sponsored their use. Some criticized him for slowness in developing them, others for using them at all. It is significant that in the face of expert and popular skepticism and ridicule Welles studied plans for ironclads as early as March 1861, had Dahlgren report in June on their development in France and Britain, and requested on July 4 and got from Congress a commission to study ironclads and money to build three, if the report was favorable. He conferred in July with the partner of John Ericsson [*q.v.*], saw Ericsson's plans in August, and was so impressed that he rushed Bushnell off to Washington to present them to the Naval Board and curtailed his own vacation in order to speak in their behalf. He signed a contract with Ericsson in September 1861, requested $12,000,000 for ironclads on Dec. 2, and finally got the bill for $10,000,000 passed in the Senate by personal intervention. When, therefore, popular clamor for ironclads burst forth after the battle of the *Monitor* and the *Merrimac (Virginia)* on Mar. 7, he was already using for them $10,000,000 obtained while they were still ridiculed. In a letter of Apr. 25, 1862, Ericsson gave the lie to the attack of the *New*

York Herald on Welles and testified that he had cooperated admirably in building the *Monitor*. Welles also developed heavy ordnance, improved steam machinery, and armored cruisers. The much-criticized steam-engine of Benjamin F. Isherwood [*q.v.*] developed speed not equaled until years later. The exigencies of war made him concentrate on monitors useful against an enemy with no navy. As early as December 1862, however, he warned the naval committees that only fast ironclad cruisers could maintain the position of the Union against other naval powers. After the war, he urged enlargement of inadequate navy yards, their modernization to build, repair, and store ironclads, improvement in the selection of naval cadets, and the establishment of a "steam engineering" department at the Naval Academy. Porter, who disliked him, testified that he had "served his country . . . with fidelity and zeal, if not with conspicuous ability" (D. D. Porter, *Incidents and Anecdotes of the Civil War*, 1885, p. 66). Lincoln wrote on July 25, 1863, "Your department has been conducted with admirable success." The blockade was successful; and naval attacks were often brilliantly executed. Welles's navy was an important factor in the crushing of the Confederacy.

Welles's contribution to the general policies of the government was as important as his departmental administration. He was a close observer and critic of the activities of the War Department and always distrusted Stanton (*Diary*, I, 58–69). In many campaigns he cooperated with the army but found it difficult to do so. Seward's interference in the Navy Department at the time of the Sumter expedition and his tendency to meddle and give orders to Welles and his subordinates annoyed Welles. He suspected Seward's motives (*Ibid.*, I, 12, 36, 204–05, *et passim*). Yet when Seward was attacked by congressional enemies Welles loyally supported him. Welles urged the "closing" of Southern ports instead of permitting other nations to recognize Confederate belligerency by blockading them. When the blockade was established he favored rigid enforcement. On July 22, 1861, long before the army acted, Welles ordered naval commanders to give protection to runaway slaves. On Sept. 25 he issued orders to enlist them in the service. In 1862–63 he protested vigorously against Chase's depreciation of the currency (*Ibid.*, I, 147, 167–69, 232, 494). He opposed the admission of West Virginia as unconstitutional. In 1863 he deplored the suspension of *habeas corpus*, the arrest of Vallandigham, and the suppression of the *Chicago Times* (*Ibid.*, I, 321–22, 432–35). He

disliked the excessive use of power involved in freeing the slaves but favored this as a necessary war measure (*Ibid.*, I, 144). In 1863 he had seen that emancipation involved not only moral and political but also industrial and social relations and wondered whether immediate, universal emancipation might not be injurious to master and slave alike (*Ibid.*, I, 403). While others changed ground he contended to the end that the war was not fought against states but against rebellious individuals and that states could not secede (*Ibid.*, I, 414). He backed Lincoln's moderate program and when Johnson became president supported his efforts to restore Southern states. He early urged Johnson to oust his enemies from office and use the patronage to support his policies (*Ibid.*, II, 398, 556). He helped force James Harlan, James Speed, and William Dennison [*qq.v.*] out of the cabinet and warned Johnson against Stanton's duplicity (*Ibid.*, II, 398, 404). He supported the new conservative party movement of 1866. When the Radicals triumphed in 1866 he continued to urge upon them a program of moderation and to defend Southerners against Radical excesses. During the impeachment he gave Johnson vigorous support.

In 1868 he returned to the Democratic fold, in 1872 became a Liberal Republican, and in 1876 not only supported Tilden but also used his still-effective pen to attack the decision of the Electoral Commission. He convincingly maintained that he had stood consistently upon his principles while parties and politicians shifted ground. Between his retirement in 1869 and his death he published articles in the *Galaxy* (Nov.–Dec. 1871; Apr.–May 1872; Dec. 1872; May 1873; Oct., Nov., Dec. 1873; Sept., Oct. 1876; Jan.–Feb., Oct., Nov., Dec. 1877) which remain important historical documents. One of these was expanded and published as *Lincoln and Seward* (1874). His painstaking diary is a storehouse of historical data, though in its published form (*Diary of Gideon Welles*, 3 vols., 1911) there is no indication of the corrections and revisions made in later years by Welles himself (H. K. Beale, in *American Historical Review*, Apr. 1925, pp. 547–52).

Welles had a commanding figure; yet his bounteous white whiskers and wig gave him benignity. To the navy and to Lincoln he was "Father Welles," to Governor Andrew of Massachusetts "that old Mormon deacon." An Episcopalian by faith, he was deeply religious. A New England conscience, a keen sense of duty, and a methodical mind made him a dependable public servant. An unusual memory, interest in people, and capacity for shrewd analysis of character gave him a wide knowledge of politicians; his letters and diary contain remarkable sketches of his contemporaries. Since he was no orator and his editorials were usually unsigned, others gained greater fame, but a vigorous political style and access to leading newspapers gave him far-reaching influence. Throughout the stormy days of the war he maintained poise and calmness that often encouraged but in crises irritated his associates. Realism and unusual common sense prevented too great disappointment on his part when men fell short of his standards. His severer qualities were softened by marked human kindness, loyalty to friends, and a love of amusing anecdote. Never brilliant, he was competent and, above all, faithful and honest. Pronouncing him "a very wise, strong man," Dana said: "There was nothing decorative about him; there was no noise in the street when he went along; but he understood his duty, and did it efficiently, continually, and unvaryingly" (C. A. Dana, *Recollections of the Civil War*, 1898, p. 170).

[MS. diaries, letters, and articles in Lib. of Cong.; obituary by William Faxon in the *Hartford Daily Courant*, Feb. 12, 1878; C. O. Paullin, "A Half Century of Naval Administration in America, 1861–1911," *U. S. Naval Institute Proc.*, vols. XXXVIII, XXXIX (1912–13); C. B. Boynton, *Hist. of the Navy during the Rebellion* (1876–78); F. M. Bennett, *The Steam Navy of the U. S.* (1896); J. P. Baxter, *The Introduction of the Ironclad Warship* (1933); H. K. Beale, *The Critical Year* (1930), for Welles's course under Johnson; Albert Welles, *Hist. of the Welles Family* (1876); J. H. Trumbull, *The Memorial Hist. of Hartford County, Conn.* (2 vols., 1886); H. R. Stiles, *The Hist. of Ancient Wethersfield* (1904), II, 776–77.]

H. K. B—e.

WELLES, NOAH (Sept. 25, 1718–Dec. 31, 1776), Congregational clergyman, was the son of a farmer of Colchester, Conn., for whom he was named, and of Sarah, daughter of Israel and Sarah Wyatt, also of Colchester. At the age of nineteen he entered Yale College, from which he graduated in 1741, remaining there another year as Dean's Scholar. For the next four years he was engaged in teaching, the study of theology, and occasional preaching. A part of this time he was in charge of the Hopkins Grammar School, Hartford, and from 1745 to 1746, tutor at Yale. After having supplied the Congregational church of Stamford, Conn., for several months, he was invited to become its settled pastor, and was ordained and installed there on Dec. 31, 1746. On Sept. 17, 1751, he was married to Abigail, daughter of Rev. Benjamin Woolsey; they had thirteen children.

His pastorate, terminated by his death, covered thirty years to a day. According to the elder Timothy Dwight [*q.v.*], his talents were distinguished, his learning extensive, and his mind of the imaginative, poetical type. He was "an able preacher; a wise ruler of the church; and an eminently discreet manager of its important concerns" (*Travels in New England and New York,* vol. III, 1822, p. 499). He was prominently mentioned for the presidency of Yale after the resignation of Thomas Clap [*q.v.*] in 1766, and from 1774 till his death he was a fellow of the college. He was a pronounced advocate of resistance to British oppression, setting forth from the pulpit the righteousness and duty of it, both at the time when the Stamp Act was creating excitement and in the opening days of the Revolution. A sermon of his preached before the General Assembly of Connecticut in 1764 and published that year bears the title, *Patriotism Described and Recommended.* He was even more widely known as a defender of the validity of Presbyterian ordination and as an opponent of Episcopacy in the colony. He is now generally credited with being the author of the anonymously published satire, *The Real Advantages Which Ministers and People May Enjoy Especially in the Colonies by Conforming to the Church of England; Truthfully Considered and Impartially Represented in a Letter to a Young Gentleman* (1762). Skillfully and pleasantly written, it was in effect a keen attack upon the English Church and its clergy, and attracted no little attention. In 1763 he published a lengthy address entitled, *The Divine Right of Presbyterian Ordination Asserted, and the Ministerial Authority, Claimed and Exercised in the Established Churches of New England, Vindicated and Proved.* Jeremiah Leaming [*q.v.*], in 1766, published *A Defence of the Episcopal Government . . .,* containing remarks on Welles's address and on one by Charles Chauncy [*q.v.*]. To this Welles replied in *A Vindication of the Validity and Divine Right of Presbyterian Ordination, as Set Forth in Dr. Chauncy's Sermon . . . and Mr. Welle's* [sic] *Discourse, in Answer to the Exceptions of Mr. Jeremiah Leaming* (1767). As a controversialist Welles displayed intellectual vigor, a keen mind, argumentative ability, fairness, and dignity. His death occurred in his fifty-ninth year, and was occasioned by jail fever contracted while he was ministering to British prisoners.

[C. M. Taintor, *Extracts from the Records of Colchester* (1864), p. 106; J. W. Alvord, *Hist. Address Delivered in the First Congregational Church in Stamford, Ct., . . . Dec. 22d, 1841* (1842); E. B. Huntington, *Hist. of Stamford, Conn.* (1868); W. B. Sprague, *Annals Am. Pulpit,* vol. I (1857); F. B. Dexter, *Biog. Sketches Grads. Yale Coll.,* vol. I (1885).]

H. E. S.

WELLES, ROGER (Dec. 7, 1862–Apr. 26, 1932), naval officer and explorer, son of Roger and Mercy Delano (Aiken) Welles, was born in Newington, Conn. He was a direct descendant of Thomas Welles, one of the early governors of Connecticut. In 1880 he was appointed to the United States Naval Academy, graduating in 1884. Three years later he was sent to the North Pacific on the U. S. S. *Thetis,* under Lieut. William H. Emory [*q.v.*], for a cruise in the Arctic and the Bering Sea. On this ship he made three successive voyages into the Polar regions, cruising as far west as Herald Island and Wrangell Land, and as far east as Mackenzie Bay. The last voyage was made under Lieut. Charles H. Stockton [*q.v.*]. During these voyages he acquired considerable knowledge of the Eskimo dialects, and on his return, in collaboration with an interpreter, John W. Kelly, he prepared a pamphlet entitled *English-Eskimo and Eskimo-English Vocabularies* (1890), published by the United States Bureau of Education. In 1891 he was sent as a special representative of the United States for the World's Columbian Exposition to Venezuela and the Guianas, with instructions to explore the Orinoco River. He ascended the river farther than any white man had been before, and brought back an ethnological collection which, with his diary of the journey, is now in the Field Museum, Chicago. For this service he received a certificate and a bronze medal.

During the Spanish-American War Welles acted as executive officer on the converted yacht *Wasp* off the Cuban coast, participating in the battle of Nipe Bay, where the Spanish cruiser *Don Jorge Juan* was sunk. For this service he was given the Atlantic Battle Medal (Nipe Bay). After the war he served on the president's yacht *Mayflower,* attended the Naval War College in 1903–04, and subsequently served three years with the Asiatic Fleet. When the World War broke out, Welles, then a captain, was made director of naval intelligence, a post which he held throughout the war, building up a far-flung censorship personnel. On July 1, 1918, he was given the temporary rank of rear admiral, a promotion made permanent a year later. After the war he commanded successively the first division of the Atlantic Fleet, and the eleventh and fifth naval districts. In September 1925 he was sent abroad as commander of the United States forces in Europe with the *Pittsburgh* as his flagship. He was retired for age on Dec. 7, 1926.

By his own government Welles was awarded the Cuban and Philippine Campaign Medals and the Navy Cross for exceptionally meritorious service in a duty of great responsibility as director of naval intelligence. He was also awarded the Grand Cross of the Order of Naval Merit and Efficiency by the King of Spain, the Second Order of the Rising Sun by the Japanese Government, and was made Grand Officer of the Order of Leopold II by King Albert of Belgium, and Commander of the Legion of Honor by the French Government. He was known in the service as a highly efficient officer and navigator, a strict disciplinarian, but kindly and thoughtful of the welfare of his men, who were devoted to him. On Oct. 17, 1908, he married Harriet Ogden Deen of Staten Island.

[*Am. Ancestry,* vol. IX (1894) ; Albert Welles, *Hist. of the Welles Family* (1876) ; *Army and Navy Reg.,* Apr. 30, 1932; Albert Gleaves, *The Life of an Am. Sailor, Rear-Admr. Wm. H. Emory* (1923) ; *N. Y. Times,* Apr. 27, 1932; *Ann. Report of the Navy Dept. . . . Appendix to the Report of the Chief of the Bureau of Navigation* (1898) ; transcript of Welles's service record in Bureau of Navigation; information from a brother, L. A. Welles, of N. Y. City.]   L. H. B.

WELLING, JAMES CLARKE (July 14, 1825–Sept. 4, 1894), journalist and educator, was born in Trenton, N. J., the only son of William and Jane (Hill) Welling. He received his elementary education at the Trenton Academy and in 1844 graduated from the College of New Jersey (Princeton). After tutoring in Virginia for two years and reading law, he was made associate principal of the New York Collegiate School in 1848. In 1850 he was married to Genevieve H. Garnett, the daughter of Henry T. Garnett of Westmoreland County, Va. She died two years later, leaving a daughter. In 1850 he was appointed literary editor of the *Daily National Intelligencer* in Washington, D. C. Six years later he became associate editor, with actual control of the paper. His learning, legal training, analytical mind, breadth of culture, forceful pen, and wide acquaintance admirably qualified him for the direction of this journal, which was a leading organ of opinion on the eve of the Civil War and continued as such during most of the conflict itself. His articles on constitutional law in its relation to current difficulties stamped the *Intelligencer* as a conservative Unionist organ. He supported the Bell-Everett ticket in 1860. His editorials on the *Trent* affair and the Monroe Doctrine attracted wide attention. He favored the abolition of slavery but questioned the validity of the Emancipation Proclamation, holding that it should be legalized by constitutional amendment. He joined his friend, Edward Bates [*q.v.*], in declaring trials by military commissions to be irregular, a stand later taken by the Supreme Court. His support of McClellan for the presidency in 1864 proved to be a political blunder for both himself and the *Intelligencer.* He resigned in 1865, went to Europe, and then served for a time as clerk of the federal court of claims. He became president of St. John's College, Annapolis, Md., in 1867. After three years at St. John's, he was made professor of rhetoric and English literature at the College of New Jersey.

He resigned to accept the presidency in 1871 of Columbian College, Washington, D. C., now George Washington University. A close friendship with W. W. Corcoran, the institution's chief benefactor, developed. Their aim was to broaden the scope of the institution's activities so as to make Washington the national educational center. By congressional act of Mar. 3, 1873, the college was incorporated as Columbian University, and, in the following year, it was moved from the suburbs to the heart of the city. Its law and medical faculties were enlarged, and scientific and dental schools, as well as a school of graduate studies, were opened. A movement to amalgamate the then defunct University of Chicago with Columbian and to obtain financial support from John D. Rockefeller did not materialize. In addition to his executive duties, he taught the philosophy of history and international law. His interests were multifarious. He was president of the Cosmos Club in Washington in 1880, of the board of trustees of Corcoran Art Gallery from 1881 to his death, of the Washington Philosophical Society in 1884, and the Anthropological Society of Washington in 1891–1892. He was a regent of the Smithsonian Institution from 1884 to his death and chairman of the executive committee during the last eight years of his life. Some of his writings of this period were collected in *Addresses, Lectures, and Other Papers,* published after his death (1903). In the spring of 1894 he resigned the presidency of Columbian to be effective as of the following October, but he died in Hartford, Conn., in September. He was survived by his second wife, Clementine Louise Dixon, to whom he was married in 1882. They had two children.

[George Washington Univ. Records; "Diary of Edward Bates," *Ann. Report Amer. Hist. Asso.* . . . . *1930,* vol. IV (1933), ed. by H. K. Beale; *Evening Star* (Washington), Nov. 6, 7, 1871, Sept. 4, 5, 1894; *Hartford Daily Courant* and *N. Y. Times,* Sept. 5, 1894; private information.]   **L. J. R.**

WELLINGTON, ARTHUR MELLEN (Dec. 20, 1847–May 16, 1895), civil engineer, editor, was born at Waltham, Mass., the son of Oliver Hastings Wellington, a physician, and his wife, Charlotte Kent. Through Benjamin Wellington, who fought at Lexington, Arthur was descended from Roger Wellington, who came to the Massachusetts Bay Colony in 1636. After graduating from the Boston Latin School, Wellington became an articled student of engineering (1863–66) in the office of John B. Henck [*q.v.*], author of the *Field-Book for Railroad Engineers* (1854). He passed the examination for assistant engineer in the United States Navy, but did not accept an appointment. After completing his apprenticeship he became for a time a surveyor in the park department of Brooklyn, N. Y.; next he had two years' experience in railroad surveying in North Carolina and New York, and in 1870 he joined the Buffalo, New York & Philadelphia Railroad, of which he was soon made principal assistant engineer. After two and a half years in this connection he became locating engineer for the Michigan Central, and later was engineer in charge of the Toledo, Canada Southern & Detroit Railroad.

When the depression of 1873 temporarily halted railroad building, he turned to writing and in 1874 published *Methods for the Computation from Diagrams of Preliminary and Final Estimates of Railway Earthwork,* setting forth methods which he had devised. He also published several shorter articles, among them one which in 1876 he expanded into a series of articles ("Justifiable Expenditure for Improving the Alignment of Railways," *Railroad Gazette,* Sept. 1–Dec. 29, 1876), and in 1877 published in book form under the title, *The Economic Theory of the Location of Railways.* This classic treatise went through a half-dozen editions, becoming the standard monograph on railway location.

In 1878 Wellington became principal assistant engineer for the New York, Pennsylvania & Ohio Railroad and in 1881 went to Mexico as engineer in charge of location and surveys of the Mexican National Railway. Later he became its assistant general manager, remaining until 1884, when he was offered an editorial post on the *Railroad Gazette.* In 1887 he became a part owner and one of the editors of *Engineering News.* While serving as editor, he continued in consulting practice, chiefly in connection with public works such as the elimination of grade crossings at Buffalo and the building of terminals at Toronto. He was a member of the board of engineers of the Nicaragua Canal in 1890, and was adviser to the Massachusetts legislature on street railways in Boston. In 1892 he attempted to develop a new type of thermodynamic engine and in 1893 was consultant on railways in Jamaica. In addition he was an active worker in engineering societies. He married Agnes Bates in 1878, and they had one child, a daughter.

[*N. Y. Tribune,* May 19, 1895; *Proc. Am. Soc. Civil Engineers,* vol. XXI (1895); *Appletons' Cyc. for 1895* (1896).]   **T. T. R.**

WELLMAN, SAMUEL THOMAS (Feb. 5, 1847–July 11, 1919), engineer, inventor, was born in Wareham, Mass., the son of Samuel Knowlton and Mary Love (Bessee) Wellman, and a descendant of Thomas Wellman who was in Lynn, Mass., as early as 1640. At the time of Samuel's birth his father was superintendent of the Nashua Iron Company, Nashua, N. H., in which city the boy received his public-school education. Entering Norwich University, Norwich, Vt., he studied engineering for a year and then enlisted in the Union army and served in 1864–65 as a corporal in Company F, 1st New Hampshire Heavy Artillery. On his discharge he returned home and entered the drafting room of the Nashua Iron Company, where his father was still superintendent. Here he worked for two years.

In 1867 his father gave him the task of building, from drawings furnished, a Siemens regenerative gas furnace for the company. Wellman had just completed it when the engineer sent from England by the Siemens Company arrived in Nashua to build the same furnace. The perfection with which the job had been done by young Wellman so amazed the engineer that he forthwith offered Wellman the opportunity of assisting him in erecting other Siemens furnaces. Wellman accepted and during the succeeding six years was engaged in this work in various parts of the country. In Pittsburgh in 1867, at the works of Anderson, Cook & Company, he assisted in starting and operating the first crucible-steel furnace in America. After building two more furnaces for another organization there he spent some time in the offices and steel works of the Siemens agents in Boston, Mass. Then, as a free lance, he constructed for the Bay State Iron Works, South Boston, the first commercially successful open hearth furnace in the United States. Upon the completion of this work he returned to Nashua and built for his father's company an open hearth furnace and rolling mills. In 1873 he went to Cleveland, Ohio, where he designed and built the Otis Steel Works and remained for sixteen years as chief engineer and superintendent.

During this period he began his inventive work in machinery and other equipment for the manufacture of iron and steel, for which he was granted nearly a hundred patents in the course of his life. Two of his inventions brought him worldwide renown. The first, invented in the eighties, was the electric open-hearth charging machine, a device for feeding white-hot steel into open-hearth furnaces; the second, patented Dec. 10, 1895, was an electro-magnet for handling pig iron and scrap steel. In time every open-hearth steel plant of any size throughout the world was equipped with these two devices. In 1890 Wellman with his brother Charles organized the Wellman Steel Company in Cleveland. Six years later they and John W. Seaver formed the Wellman-Seaver Engineering Company, with Wellman as president, and engaged in consulting work, specializing in iron and steel manufacture. Later, this company consolidated with the Webster, Camp & Lane Company of Akron, Ohio, and became the Wellman-Seaver-Morgan Company, of which Wellman was for a time president, and later chairman of the board until his retirement in 1900. He was active in a number of technical and engineering societies both in this country and England, and served as president of the American Society of Mechanical Engineers in 1901. He was married on Sept. 3, 1868, to Julia Almina Ballard of Stoneham, Mass., and at the time of his sudden death at Stratton, Me., he was survived by five children.

[J. W. Wellman, *Descendants of Thomas Wellman* (1918); *Trans. Am. Soc. Mech. Engineers*, vol. XLI (1919); *Iron Age*, July 17, 1919; *The Open Hearth . . . Its Design and Operation* (1920); *Who's Who in America*, 1918–19; *Cleveland Plain Dealer*, July 12, 1919; Patent Office records.] C. W. M.

WELLMAN, WALTER (Nov. 3, 1858–Jan. 31, 1934), journalist, explorer, aeronaut, was born in Mentor, Ohio. He was the son of Alonzo and Minerva (Graves) Wellman and a descendant of Thomas Wellman who was in Lynn, Mass., as early as 1640. Most of Walter's formal schooling was received in a district school in Michigan. At the age of fourteen he started a weekly newspaper at Sutton, Neb.; at twenty-one he founded the evening *Cincinnati Post,* and from 1884 to 1911 he was the Washington correspondent of the *Chicago Herald* and its successor, the *Record-Herald.*

The first enterprise to bring him wide recognition was a trip to the Bahamas in 1891, in the course of which he located, as he claimed, the exact landing spot of Christopher Columbus (*Chicago Herald,* July 4, 1891), and erected a monument to mark the place on Watling Island, or San Salvador. He was fascinated by the unknown lands of the North; in 1894, journeying by boat and sledge over the ice, he reached a latitude of 81° at a point northeast of Spitzbergen and in 1898–99 he led a similar expedition to Franz-Josef Land, reaching a latitude of 82° north. As a consequence of these expeditions he was commissioned in 1906 by Frank B. Noyes, publisher of the *Chicago Record-Herald,* to attempt a trip to the Arctic regions by air. The airship was built in Paris in the spring of that year (see Wellman's article, "The Polar Airship," *National Geographic Magazine,* April 1906) and after some experimental flights was enlarged during the winter of 1906–07. Stormy weather at the base in Spitzbergen delayed trial trips, but on Sept. 2, 1907, Wellman took off for the pole. Continuous and violent squalls nearly wrecked the craft, however, and at last Wellman deflated the ship and returned to Paris, to await a more favorable opportunity. On Aug. 15, 1909, he set out again, with three companions, but after he had covered a distance of only twelve miles the equilibrator broke and he was forced to turn back. He abandoned further attempts to reach the pole by air after the announcement that Robert E. Peary [*q.v.*] had succeeded in doing so on foot.

The most ambitious undertaking of Wellman's career was his attempt to cross the Atlantic by air. The airship *America,* which had been used on previous polar explorations, was rebuilt to a length of 228 feet. It had a lifting capacity of twelve tons and a speed of twenty-five miles an hour. Below the bag of silk and cotton, filled with hydrogen, hung a car of interlaced steel tubing; below the car was a gas tank 150 feet long and two feet in diameter; below the gas tank was a lifeboat with supplies for thirty days, and still lower, an equilibrator which was also a fuel supply, being a string of thirty steel drums filled with gasoline. Prepared for ten days in the air or thirty on the sea, Wellman and five companions took off from Atlantic City, N. J., in a dense fog at eight o'clock in the morning, Oct. 15, 1910. During the flight, for the first time in history wireless messages were sent from land to an airship over water and for several hours messages came back regularly. Trouble was in store, however: one of the motors stalled because of a bad bearing, and the other threatened to set the ship on fire with sparks from the exhaust; the cooling and contraction of the hydrogen at night caused the airship to come to a dangerously low altitude; a northeast wind drove the ship off its course, and it was eventually forced down. The crew was rescued by a steamer some 375 miles off Cape Hatteras, and the *America* drifted away in the wind and was never seen again. Wellman considered the trip a failure, but he had broken the existing world record for time and distance sailing by airship and found himself a hero upon his return to New York. The time in the air was seventy-two hours, and the distance 1,008 miles. In his book *The Aerial Age,* published in 1911, he described the experience fully. It is significant that in all Wellman's dangerous undertakings not a man of his various crews was lost. He was

married twice: first, on Dec. 24, 1878, to Laura McCann of Canton, Ohio, and second, to Belgljat Bergerson of Norway. Four children and his second wife survived him.

[J. W. Wellman, *Descendants of Thomas Wellman* (1918); *Who's Who in America,* 1928–29; *Scientific American,* June 22, 1907, Oct. 1, 29, 1910; *Aeronautics,* Oct., Dec. 1910; *N. Y. Times,* Feb. 1, 1934.]
A. K—n.

WELLONS, WILLIAM BROCK (Nov. 9, 1821–Feb. 16, 1877), clergyman, prominent among the leaders of the Christian Connection in the Southern states, was born near Littleton, Sussex County, Va., the son of Hartwell and Mary W. Wellons. His father was a farmer, and the only formal education William ever received was at winter sessions of country schools. Converted at a camp meeting when he was thirteen years old, he was thereafter governed largely by religious interests. From 1840 to 1845 he taught school, for a part of the time at Airfield, Southampton County, Va. He also conducted religious meetings with such success that in 1845 he was admitted to the Eastern Virginia Conference as a licentiate and in 1846 was ordained a minister of the Christian Connection.

For several years he served as an itinerant, holding revival meetings and organizing churches. While acting as pastor in New Bern, N. C., he married, Apr. 12, 1850, Sarah L. Beasley, a widow. Soon afterward, they removed to Suffolk, Va., which was Wellons' home for the remainder of his life. During these years, he had pastoral oversight of several churches in the vicinity, and was frequently in attendance at conferences and conventions, at which he made his influence strongly felt. In 1854 he was a delegate to the quadrennial Christian Convention held at Cincinnati, and was the Southern member of a committee of three appointed to consider the question of slavery. He was himself a slaveholder and presented a minority report urging that the South be conceded the right to manage its own domestic institutions. The attitude of the majority of the convention was so hostile, however, that finally Wellons announced his withdrawal on behalf of his constituency. Other Southern members followed his example, and in 1856 the General Convention of the Christian Church, South, was organized with Wellons as president. In the meantime, 1855, he had become editor in chief of the *Christian Sun,* the official organ of the Christian Connection in the South, of which he had been an associate editor since 1849, and it was thereafter published in Suffolk. During the Civil War he was forced to discontinue it and remove to Petersburg. At this time he became editor of the *Army and Navy*

Messenger, issued by the Evangelic Tract Society and distributed among Confederate soldiers and sailors. He also did much personal religious work on the field and in hospitals. In 1865 he returned to Suffolk, resumed preaching, labored to reorganize the churches of the neighborhood, and, assuming the financial responsibility himself, began again the publication of the *Christian Sun.* Largely through his influence, the General Convention of the Southern branch of the Christian Connection in 1866 adopted and published a statement of principles and government—an event regarded as significant in the history of the Connection.

Wellons was all his life much interested in education. For some time he conducted a school for young women in his home at Suffolk, and he was instrumental in securing the establishment in 1853 of the Holy Neck Female Seminary in Nansemond County. As a result of a recommendation made by a committee to the Southern Christian Convention in 1870 that normal and theological schools be provided in each of the local Conferences, the Suffolk Collegiate Institute was opened in January 1872 and Wellons was elected principal. As such he served until his death. He took an active part in the temperance movement in Virginia, and during his later years was an advocate of more cooperation on the part of the Christian Connection with other evangelical bodies. He died in his fifty-sixth year of tuberculosis of the lungs.

[E. W. Humphreys, *Memoirs of Deceased Christian Ministers* (1880); P. J. Kernodle, *Lives of Christian Ministers* (copr. 1909); M. T. Morrill, *A Hist. of the Christian Denomination in America* (1912); *Daily Dispatch* (Richmond, Va.), Feb. 17, 1877.]   H. E. S.

WELLS, DAVID AMES (June 17, 1828–Nov. 5, 1898), economist, was born at Springfield, Mass., the son of James and Rebecca (Ames) Wells, and a descendant of Thomas Welles, governor of Connecticut, 1655–59. David graduated from Williams College in 1847, having already become engaged in literary work by assisting in the preparation of *Sketches of Williams College,* published that year. In 1848 he joined the staff of the *Springfield Republican,* in connection with which he displayed mechanical ingenuity by inventing a device for folding paper, to be attached to power presses. He graduated from the Lawrence Scientific School at Cambridge in 1851, where he was a special pupil of Louis Agassiz [*q.v.*]. While at Cambridge he began the publication with George Bliss, in 1850, of *The Annual of Scientific Discovery,* which he continued until 1866. In 1856 he made important improvements in the method of manufacturing textiles. He was a special partner in the publishing firm of G. P. Putnam & Company, 1857–58, and during this period he compiled *The Science of Common Things* (1857) and *Wells's Principles and Applications of Chemistry* (copr. 1858). Later he published *Wells's First Principles of Geology* (1861) and *Wells's Natural Philosophy* (1863), the latter going through fifteen editions.

In 1864 Wells came into wide prominence through the issuance by the Loyalty Publication Company of his first economic work, a pamphlet entitled *Our Burden and Our Strength.* Two hundred thousand copies of this brochure were distributed, and it was translated into French, German, Dutch, and other languages. At that time a lack of confidence in the ability of the United States government ever to discharge its mounting debts had caused the fall of greenbacks and bonds to half their face value. Wells in his pamphlet reassured foreign investors and the people of the North by demonstrating the dynamic character of economic life in the North, with its rapid accumulation of capital and constant introduction of labor-saving devices. Brought by this publication to the attention of Lincoln, Wells was appointed in 1865 chairman of the national revenue commission and in 1866 signed its report making recommendations which became laws. That same year the post of special commissioner of the revenue was created for him, and soon the bureau of statistics was established, of which he put Francis A. Walker [*q.v.*] in charge. The *Reports of the Special Commissioner of the Revenue,* 1866–69, set forth the whole subject of indirect taxes, and recommended the use of stamps in the collection of revenue on liquor and tobacco. In 1867, Wells went to Europe as a member of a commission to investigate costs of industrial production there. As befitted his New England background he was a stanch protectionist, but finding that high wages in America made for efficiency as compared with the backward methods of competing countries, he was converted to free trade, became a member of the Cobden Club, and thereafter for thirty years was a leading advocate of abolition of the tariff. He was a counselor of his close friend, President Garfield, on tariff matters, and later of Grover Cleveland.

The extreme free-trade point of view in Wells's report of 1869 prompted President Grant to abolish the office of special commissioner the following year. Wells, however, was promptly made chairman of the New York state tax commission, and published as one of its reports *Local Taxation* (1871), the earliest really competent study of the subject. His chief problem in New York was to remedy a situation made critical by the increase of the tax burden in that state while contiguous states were attracting capital and enterprise through lenient laws. In 1876 he was named one of the receivers for the Alabama & Chattanooga Railroad, and helped rescue its property. He was one of the trustees of the bondholders who bought in and reorganized the Erie Railway in 1875, and in 1878 he became a member of the board of arbitration of the Associated Railways, deciding on questions of pooling. He took an active interest in politics and was several times a delegate to the Democratic national conventions. He was an unsuccessful candidate for Congress from Connecticut in 1876 and 1890, and he made many speeches in each of Cleveland's campaigns.

Wells wrote a large number of books, pamphlets, and articles, always with a current problem uppermost in his mind. His chief interests were the tariff, the theory of money and the currency question, and taxation. His discussion of all of these took character from his inspection of American economic life, which was marked in his period by progressive lowering of costs of production through the application of science. He, more than others, was the expositor of the nature and consequences of "the machine age." The new economics of production required in his judgment abolition of protective tariffs in order to furnish wide markets, and he was convinced that industrial depressions, with falling prices, were due not to insufficient circulating media, but to sudden and rapid increase in commodities. Some of his most effective writing was in opposition to fiat money or depreciated monetary standards. An excellent example of his work in this field is his *Robinson Crusoe's Money*, issued first in 1876 when resumption was in doubt, and again in 1896 when the "free silver" advocacy was in full swing. Wells was among the earliest to appreciate the importance of what has since been known as "technological unemployment," the displacing of men by machines. He urged the substitution of trained personnel for political hangers-on in tax bodies, sought to bring system into taxation, and was the inveterate foe of the general property tax as applied to intangibles. He accepted the diffusion theory of taxation; his opposition to the faculty theory led him to fight against income taxes. He was an out-and-out apostle of *laissez faire,* and thus missed the later implications of many of the tendencies in American economic life which he discovered and expounded. His writing and speaking was marked by simplicity, candor, and extraordinary facility in the popular adaptation

of statistics. His aptness in illustration was as charming as it was effective; it is evidenced in his *True Story of the Leaden Statuary* (1874). Among his most significant works, beside those mentioned, are *The Relation of the Government to the Telegraph* (1873); *The Cremation Theory of Specie Resumption* (1875); *The Silver Question* (1877); *Why We Trade and How We Trade* (1878); *Our Merchant Marine* (1882); *A Primer of Tariff Reform* (1884); *Practical Economics* (1885); *Recent Economic Changes* (1889); *The Theory and Practice of Taxation* (1900).

Wells died at Norwich, Conn., which had been his residence since 1870. He was married, May 9, 1860, to Mary Sanford Dwight, by whom he had one son; a second wife and a son survived him.

[Albert Welles, *Hist. of the Welles Family* (1876); B. W. Dwight, *The Hist. of the Descendants of John Dwight* (1874); Calvin Durfee, *Williams Biog. Annals* (1871); G. H. Putnam, *Memories of c Publisher* (1915), pp. 35 ff., 357, and *George Palmer Putnam: A Memoir* (1912), pp. 282–8, 346 ff.; *Johns Hopkins Univ. Circulars*, Mar. 1899; *N. Y. Times*, Nov. 6, 8, 1898; E. R. A. Seligman, in *Palgrave's Dict. of Pol. Economy,* vol. III (1926), and in *Encyc. of the Social Sciences,* vol. XV (1935).]
                                                  B. M.

WELLS, ERASTUS (Dec. 2, 1823–Oct. 2, 1893), congressman, street railway builder, was born near Sacketts Harbor, Jefferson County, N. Y., the only son among three children of Otis and Mary (Symonds) Wells. Through his farmer father he was descended from Hugh Welles of Essex County, England, who came to America about 1635, and from James Otis [*q.v.*]. With the death of his father his schooling was stopped when he was fourteen years of age. He clerked in stores in nearby Watertown and Lockport until he was twenty and then he emigrated to St. Louis, Mo. Here in 1844 he induced Calvin Case, a prominent business man, to finance an omnibus, said to be the first conveyance of its kind west of the Mississippi. The youthful driver made most of his first trips alone, but gradually the growing community approved the new mode of transportation and additional vehicles were required. He sold his interest in the omnibus line at a good profit and then managed a lead factory and a sawmill for a time. He returned to street transportation and founded the Missouri Railway Company, in 1859. He headed this enterprise until his retirement at the age of sixty, and also promoted a narrow-gauge railway to Florissant, Mo. He served as an official of two banks, and as a director of the Ohio and Mississippi Railroad. He was also president of the Laclede Gas Light Company in St. Louis.

With his business life Wells coupled an active

political career. He was elected to the St. Louis legislative body in 1848 for a one-year term, and returned in 1855 to serve fifteen years as alderman or councilman. During this time he was instrumental in the enactment of ordinances providing for notable improvements in the police, fire protection and water systems. He resigned in 1869 to take a seat as a Democrat in the Forty-first Congress. After holding office four terms, he was defeated in 1876. Two years later he was reëlected, only to retire voluntarily in 1881 because of ill health. His aptitude for committee work, his devotion to the interests of his section, and his friendship with President Grant, whom he had known in St. Louis, combined to make him a respected member despite the minority status of his party. Wells had two outstanding legislative concerns—the improvement of the Mississippi River and the development of the Southwest. He was ahead of his time in regard to both and a number of his bills died in committee. His unreported bill of 1871, dealing with the opening of Oklahoma, antedated that historic event by more than seventeen years. He also worked for appropriations for various Indian Territory tribes in fulfillment of treaty obligations, and sponsored bills for marine hospitals and other government buildings.

Wells was married twice: in 1850 to Isabella Bowman Henry of Jacksonville, Ill., who died in 1877; in 1879 to Mrs. Daniel W. Bell (Eleanor P. Warfield), of Lexington, Ky. By the former he had five children, two of whom matured, the surviving son being Rolla Wells, who was mayor of St. Louis from 1901 to 1909. Following a long illness he died of locomotor ataxia in his seventieth year at his suburban estate, "Wellston," and was buried in Bellefontaine Cemetery.

[Information from Rolla Wells, L. H. Cannon, and Donald Macleay, of St. Louis; Albert Welles, *Hist. of the Welles Family* (1876); Rolla Wells, *Episodes of My Life* (1933); *Biog. Dir. Am. Cong.* (1928); William Hyde and H. L. Conard, *Encyc. of the Hist. of St. Louis* (1899), vol. IV; J. T. Scharf, *Hist. of St. Louis City and County* (1883), vol. I; L. U. Reavis, *St. Louis: Future Great City of the World* (1875); W. B. Stevens, *Centennial Hist. of Mo.* (1921), vol. II; *St. Louis Post-Dispatch*, Oct. 3, *St. Louis Republic*, Oct. 4, 1893.]　　　　　　　　　　　　　　　I. D.

WELLS, HENRY (Dec. 12, 1805–Dec. 10, 1878), expressman, was born at Thetford, Vt., the son of Shipley Wells, a Presbyterian clergyman who early removed to central New York. The boy worked on a farm and attended school at Fayette. At sixteen he was apprenticed to Jessup & Palmer, tanners and shoemakers at Palmyra. There he met and married Sarah Daggett, who died in Albany on Oct. 13, 1859. In 1861 he married, as his second wife, Mary, the

daughter of Henry Prentice of Boston. About 1841 he became agent at Albany for Harnden's express between New York and Albany. In two years he had established Livingston, Wells & Pomeroy's, operating between Albany and Buffalo, and was himself messenger, making a weekly trip on five or six railroads and two stage lines. The company soon abandoned paying two regular fares for transporting messenger and trunk and arranged a kind of commutation, the forerunner of the present intimate relations between railroads and express companies. He carried mail at six cents for a single letter or one dollar for twenty while the government charged from two to four times as much. With James W. Hale, he offered a through service from New York, Boston, and Bangor, Me., vigorously opposed by the post office. The expressmen had the benefit of popular support, roused by penny postage in England, and the government was forced to pass the five-cent postage act of 1845. In 1844 he opened the line between Buffalo and Detroit, Wells & Company, with William G. Fargo [*q.v.*] as messenger. The service, using lake steamers in summer and wagons and stages in winter, rapidly expanded to Chicago, Cincinnati, and St. Louis. In 1846 he sold his interest in the western service and removed from Buffalo to New York to handle the eastern business, now connected with New York and opening offices in London and Paris. In 1850 competition on the route between Albany and Buffalo led to the merger of the three companies, Wells & Company, Butterfield, Wasson & Company, and Livingston, Fargo & Company, into the American Express Company. Wells was president for eighteen years. About this time he removed to Aurora, N. Y.

In 1852, with associates, he organized in New York, Wells, Fargo & Company for business to California. The president was Edwin B. Morgan [*q.v.*], his fellow citizen of Aurora. The usual route to the Pacific coast was by steamship by way of Panama. Adams & Company were already well entrenched in California. The new company began by buying small, independent express lines, and it found its opportunity in the troubled days of 1885, when Adams & Company failed. In 1857 the California service and the business east of the Missouri were linked by the award of the contract for the overland mail to John Butterfield [*q.v.*], who represented the Wells, Fargo interests. The Wells, Fargo interests also took over the pony express for the last months of its service, which was ended by the completion of the telegraph in October 1861. With its overland connections well established, the company prospered until the completion of the transcontinental railroad changed much of the business. In 1868 the Pacific Union Express Company appeared with an exclusive ten-year contract with the railroad and forced Wells, Fargo to expand its capitalization and absorb this company. Similarly, east of the Missouri River, the Merchants Union Express Company was fighting the American Express Company. In 1868 the American and the Merchants Union companies united under the name of American Merchants Union Express Company, after 1873 the American Express Company. At the time of this consolidation Wells retired as president. For the last ten years of his life he traveled a good deal. At his home in Aurora he was president of the First National Bank and first president of the Cayuga Lake Railroad. In 1868 he founded Wells Seminary, now Wells College. He established schools for stammerers in several cities, presumably because he, himself, suffered from an impediment of speech. He died in Glasgow, Scotland, and was buried in Aurora.

From his thirty-fifth to his sixty-fifth year he saw the country grow rapidly and the carrying trades grow equally. In 1841 carrying the express from Albany to Buffalo was almost within the capacity of one man and in 1870 the great American Express Company operated over railroads as far as the Missouri River. The newly opening far West was a fresh opportunity; and in 1871 the country already supported a regular overland stage and mail route. Though his earlier outlook had anticipated expansion toward Europe, he was able to sense his opportunity in the far West of his own country, and he adapted his business to the spread of population over the continent. Something of his own view of the development of the express business can be found in papers he read before the Buffalo Historical Society in June 1863, *The American Express in its Relation to . . . Buffalo* (1864) and before the American Geographical and Statistical Society of Albany on Feb. 4, 1864, *Sketch of the Rise, Progress, and Present Conduct of the Express System* (1864).

[*Wells Fargo Messenger*, Nov. 1912; Jan., May, Oct. 1913, May 1918; W. I. Lowe, *Wells College and its Founders* (1901); A. L. Stimson, *Hist. of the Express Business* (2nd ed., 1858); E. A. Wiltsee, *The Pioneer Miner and the Pack Mule Express* (1931); *Colls. of the Hist. of Albany*, vol. I (1865), ed. by Joel Munsell; *1844. Walker's Buffalo City Directory* (1844), ed. by H. N. Walker; L. R. Hafen, *The Overland Mail* (1926); *Buffalo Courier*, Jan. 2, 1879; *N. Y. Times*, Dec. 11, 12, 27, 1878, Jan. 3, 1879; "Location of Overland Mail," *Missouri Republican* (St. Louis), June 26, 1857.]
E. H.

WELLS, HORACE (Jan. 21, 1815–Jan. 24, 1848), dentist and anesthetist, a descendant of Joshua Wells who was in Windsor, Conn., as early as 1647, and the eldest child of Horace Wells by his wife Betsy Heath, was born at Hartford, Vt. His parents, who were comfortably situated, gave him a good education in New England church schools and made it possible for him, at the age of nineteen, to go to Boston to study dentistry. In 1836 he moved to Hartford, Conn., where he opened an office, soon acquired a successful dental practice, and in 1838 published a creditable little book entitled *An Essay on Teeth; Comprising a Brief Description of Their Formation, Diseases, and Proper Treatment*. During 1841–42 another young dentist, William T. G. Morton [*q.v.*] of Farmington, Conn., studied dentistry under Wells (J. M. Riggs, in Smith, 1858, *post*, p. 27; also Mrs. Wells, *Ibid.*, p. 29), and they opened a joint office in Boston, but in 1843 the partnership was dissolved and Wells returned to Hartford.

As early as 1840, according to the testimony in 1853 of Dr. Linus P. Brockett [*q.v.*] of Hartford (Smith, 1858, pp. 18–19), Wells was interested in the narcotic effects of nitrous oxide inhalation—which had been known since Humphry Davy's experiments with the gas in 1799—and suggested its use as a means of deadening pain in the extraction of teeth. On Dec. 10, 1844, Gardner Q. Colton [*q.v.*] gave a popular lecture at Hartford to which many were attracted because the lecturer promised to demonstrate the effects of laughing gas. Wells observed that one Samuel A. Cooley, who took the gas, struck his shins and bruised them severely without giving evidence of pain [*cf.* Crawford W. Long]. The day after the lecture, Colton was invited to Wells's office to give him nitrous oxide, and a fellow dentist, John Mankey Riggs [*q.v.*], while Wells was under the influence of the gas, extracted one of his teeth (Dec. 11, 1844) without causing him any pain. Colton taught Wells how to manufacture and to administer the gas and Wells followed up the experiment by extracting teeth from several individuals, none of whom experienced pain. Though familiar with the similar effects of ether, Wells discarded it because he considered nitrous oxide "the least likely to do injury" (Erving, *post*, p. 428). In an interview with Valentine Mott [*q.v.*] of New York, however, he said that he had made use of ether in extractions and voiced his belief that it might be used in major surgical operations (Smith, 1858, p. 81).

Early in 1845 Wells went to Boston with the idea of bringing his use of nitrous oxide before the medical profession. Through his former partner Morton he obtained an opportunity to speak before one of the medical classes of John Collins Warren [*q.v.*]. He told the class of his experiments and offered to give a demonstration if a subject could be found. A patient was secured and the gas administered, but for some unaccountable reason Wells attempted to extract the tooth before the anesthesia was complete. The man cried out, the students jeered, and Wells was humiliated. He returned to Hartford deeply discouraged.

The first printed statement of Wells's claims to the discovery of anesthesia appeared in the *Hartford Courant* on Dec. 7, 1846, nearly two months after Morton had demonstrated the use of ether, and nearly three weeks after Morton's results had been published by Henry J. Bigelow [*q.v.*] in the *Boston Medical and Surgical Journal* (Nov. 18, 1846). Early in 1847 Wells went to Paris and while there published a letter, dated Feb. 17, 1847, in *Galignani's Messenger,* stating his claims to priority and declaring that he had used ether as well as nitrous oxide (reprinted in the *Boston Atlas,* Apr. 2, 1847); on May 12, 1847, he published similar claims in the *Boston Medical and Surgical Journal* of anesthesia and in that same year he brought out a pamphlet of twenty-five pages entitled *A History of the Discovery of the Application of Nitrous Oxide Gas, Ether, and Other Vapors, to Surgical Operations,* in which his early experiments and his claims to the discovery of anesthesia were again described at length.

After ether had become recognized, Wells made two or three abortive attempts to prove nitrous oxide a better anesthetic and induced a number of physicians to carry out major surgical operations with laughing gas. Several of these were comparatively successful, but when on Apr. 27, 1848, Henry J. Bigelow finally yielded to the claims of Wells's supporters and at the Massachusetts General Hospital removed a carcinoma of the breast under nitrous oxide, the state of prolonged asphyxia produced by the gas nearly proved fatal, and Bigelow quickly recognized that for protracted operations of this type nitrous oxide was inferior to ether.

By this time, however, Wells was dead. In the winter of 1847–48 he had opened an office in New York, where he hoped to introduce the use of nitrous oxide. He also began to make experiments with chloroform and frequently inhaled it for its exhilarating effect. While under its influence, on Jan. 21, 1848, he created a disturbance for which he was arrested and locked up in the city prison. Here, suffering from discour-

agement and shame and fearing the loss of his reason, he wrote a long letter to the press (*New York Journal of Commerce,* Jan. 25, 1848) and killed himself by slashing his thigh with a razor. He was just thirty-three years old. In personal appearance Wells was tall, heavy-set, and unusually handsome, with high color, curly hair, and pleasant bearing, but he was exceedingly sensitive and shy. On July 9, 1838, he married Elizabeth Wales, by whom he had one son.

[H. R. Stiles, *The Hist. and Geneals. of Ancient Windsor, Conn.,* vol. II (1892) ; Joseph Wales, *Discovery by the Late Dr. Horace Wells of the Applicability of Nitrous Oxyd Gas, Sulphuric Ether and Other Vapors in Surgical Operations Nearly Two Years Before the Patented Discovery by Drs. Chas. T. Jackson and W. T. G. Morton* (1850 ; 2nd ed., with additions, 1852) ; Truman Smith, *An Examination of the Question of Anæsthesia* (1858) and *An Inquiry into the Origin of Modern Anæsthesia* (1867), the former containing sworn testimony and the latter containing a biog. sketch by P. W. Ellsworth ; R. M. Hodges, *A Narrative of the Events Connected with the Introduction of Sulphuric Ether into Surgical Use* (1891) ; James McManus, "The History of Anæsthesia," *Conn. Quart.,* Jan.–Mar. 1895 ; G. Q. Colton, *A True Hist. of the Discovery of Anæsthesia* (1896) ; E. A. Wells, "Horace Wells," *Boston Medic. and Surgic. Jour.,* Feb. 5, 1925 ; H. W. Erving, "The Discoverer of Anæsthesia: Dr. Horace Wells of Hartford," *Yale Jour. of Biol. and Medicine,* May 1933 ; C. J. Wells, "Horace Wells," *Current Researches in Anesthesia and Analgesia,* July–Aug., Sept.–Oct. 1935, with extensive bibliog.; obituaries in *N. Y. Tribune* and *Boston Transcript,* Jan. 25, 1848, and *Boston Medic. and Surgic. Jour.,* Feb. 2, 1848.]   J.F.F.

WELLS, JAMES MADISON (Jan. 8, 1808–Feb. 28, 1899), governor of Louisiana, seems to have been the grandson of Samuel Levi Wells, a civil engineer who emigrated to America and settled finally about 1760 in Louisiana. His son of the same name and Mary Elizabeth (Calvit) Wells, said to be the grand-daughter of Frederick, sixth Lord Baltimore, became the parents of eight children. The youngest, James, was born at the plantation home, "New Hope," near Alexandria, La. An orphan at the age of eight, he was reared by an aunt until he went away to a Jesuit school at Bardstown, Ky. (St. Joseph's College). He then went to the military school of Alden Partridge [*q.v.*] at Middletown, Conn., and later read law in Cincinnati, part of the time in the office of Charles Hammond [*q.v.*]. About 1829 he decided to devote himself to planting and returned to his native parish, where he was very successful until the outbreak of the Civil War. On May 13, 1833, he married Mary Ann Scott. They had fourteen children. He was one of the largest landed planters of Rapides Parish and created a magnificent summer home, "Jessamine Hill," a few miles south of Lecompte. Educated in the North, he had formed strong convictions against the right of secession, to which he clung tenaciously in spite of his large slave holdings and the condemnation of relatives and friends. Indeed, during the Civil War he was often obliged to seek refuge in "Bear Wallow," the unattractive name of his huge hunting preserve near "Jessamine Hill." When the Federals surrounded Port Hudson, he sought protection from their gunboats. He claimed heavy losses because of his Union sympathies and was pressing his claims for damages at the time of his death.

In February 1864 at a special election ordered by Lincoln, he was chosen lieutenant-governor on the ticket with Michael Hahn, whom he succeeded upon the latter's resignation in March 1865. The following November he was elected governor in his own right on the National Democratic ticket. During his administration the legislature conditionally ratified the Thirteenth Amendment but unanimously rejected his recommendation to approve the Fourteenth Amendment. Furthermore, having become converted to negro suffrage, he was so distasteful to a majority that memorials for his impeachment were presented. When Gen. Philip Sheridan appeared in New Orleans as commander of the district, there arose between him and the governor a quarrel over politics that culminated in Sheridan's removal of Wells from office on June 3, 1867. He continued to be prominent in state politics, however, and was chairman of the Louisiana returning board during the disputed election of 1876. He was such a target of Democratic attack in that controversy that he retired permanently from political life to the quiet of his plantation home. He was a man of good education with an active mind, impressive appearance, and courtly manners.

[MSS. on La. Families by G. M. G. Stafford, Alexandria, La.; papers in possession of grand-daughter, Miss Emily Weems, Washington, D. C.; J. R. Ficklen, "Hist. of Reconstruction in La.," *The Johns Hopkins University Studies,* 28 ser., no. 1 (1910); Alcée Fortier, *Hist. of La.* (1904), vol. IV; *The Amer. Annual Cyc. ... 1864–1867* (1865–1868); *Appletons' Annual Cyc. ... 1899* (1900); *Daily Picayune* and *Times-Democrat* (New Orleans), Mar. 1, 1899.] E. L.

WELLS, JOHN (*c.* 1770–Sept. 7, 1823), lawyer, was born in Cherry Valley, Otsego County, N. Y., and spent his early childhood in that frontier region. His grandfather, John Wells, an emigrant from Ireland, had settled there in 1743. The younger John was the son of Capt. Robert Wells, whose wife was a daughter of the Rev. Samuel Dunlop. In the Cherry Valley massacre of 1778, when a mixed band of Loyalist rangers and Indians devastated the countryside, all of the Wells family were murdered with the exception of John, who was attending the grammar school in Schenectady (Howard Swiggett, *War

out of Niagara, 1933, pp. 152–53). It was many years before Wells recovered from the shock of this tragedy, and when a young man he was dissuaded with difficulty from taking the life of the Indian leader of the raid, who had returned to New York (F. W. Halsey, *The Old New York Frontier,* 1901, p. 323). Until 1783 young Wells remained in Schenectady with an aunt, removing later to New York City and subsequently to the vicinity of Jamaica, Long Island. Having prepared under the Rev. Leonard Cutting and the Rev. Alexander MacWhorter [*q.v.*], he was admitted to the College of New Jersey, where he was graduated in 1788. He then entered upon the study of the law as clerk in a New York law office, and was admitted to the bar as attorney in 1791, and as counselor in 1795.

A Federalist in political sympathies, he revised for publication the collected papers known as *The Federalist,* bringing out the fifth edition in 1802. As editorial associate of William Coleman [*q.v.*] on the Federalist *Evening Post,* he frequently crossed swords with Hamilton's opponent, James Cheetham [*q.v.*] and the opposition sheet known as the *American Citizen.* When William Stephens Smith [*q.v.*], the son-in-law of President John Adams, sued Cheetham for libel in 1805, the defendant, by way of tribute to his opponent's legal talents, employed Wells as counsel. After 1804 he shared with Thomas Addis Emmet [*q.v.*] the bulk of the commercial law practice which had hitherto gone to Hamilton and Burr, and was frequently engaged as special counsel by the city of New York. In the celebrated case of *Gibbons* vs. *Ogden,* involving the right of the state of New York to grant a monopoly of the navigation of its waters by steam, Wells was associated with counsel for Gibbons. He argued unsuccessfully before Kent in 1819 a motion to dissolve the injunction restraining Gibbons from bringing his boat into New York harbor, on the ground that such a grant was unconstitutional since Congress alone had the right to regulate commerce. The court of errors sustained Kent the next year (17 *Johnson,* 488). Wells's death in 1823 prevented his appearing before the Supreme Court when the case was appealed, but in that tribunal, Webster and Wirt, pursuing the same argument, were able to secure a reversal (9 *Wheaton,* 1).

Wells was a man of much ability, and possessed characteristics that made him greatly beloved. Emmet, who had had a wide experience, and was Wells's rival at the bar, said that Wells's argument in *Griswold* vs. *Waddington* was the most able and finished he had ever heard (Johnson, *post,* p. 340). He contracted yellow fever, from which he died, while on a visit of mercy to the poor. In 1796 he married Eliza, daughter of Thomas Lawrence of Newtown, Long Island, and three years after her death in 1812, Sabina Huger of South Carolina. By his first wife he had one son; by the second, two sons and two daughters.

[William Johnson, in 7 *Johnson's Chancery Reports*, 331–43; *Memorial of the Life and Character of John Wells* (1874); *City Hall Reporter and N. Y. General Law Mag.*, Oct. 1833; *N. Y. Evening Post*, Sept. 8, 11, 12, 1823; W. W. Campbell, in *Am. Mo. Mag., Mar. 1838.*]

R. B. M.

WELLS, ROBERT WILLIAM (Nov. 29, 1795–Sept. 22, 1864), jurist, was born at Winchester, Va., the son of Richard Wells. He attended common school in Winchester, and in 1816, upon the recommendation of John George Jackson [q.v.], he became a deputy surveyor and served under William Rector in Missouri for one year. Then he began the study of law under the auspices of Jackson. He studied for perhaps a year under Samuel Finley Vinton [q.v.], at Gallipolis, Ohio. In 1819 he engaged in surveying and in 1820 began the practice of law in St. Charles, the temporary capital of Missouri. He designed the great seal of the state of Missouri, which was adopted on Jan. 11, 1822 (see own letter, King, *post*, pp. 7–11). He took an official part in the St. Charles Agricultural and Manufacturing Society during 1822, and in 1822 and 1824 was elected to the general assembly as representative from St. Charles County. From 1826 until 1836 he was attorney-general of Missouri. He married Harriet Amanda Rector on Jan. 20, 1830, in Jefferson City. She died on Feb. 3, 1834, leaving three children. In 1831 and again in 1832 he was defeated for representative in Congress. On June 27, 1836, he was appointed federal district judge of Missouri, and upon the division of the state into two districts in 1857 he became judge of the western district, a position he held until his death. One of his opinions, an opinion that the retroactive feature of the bankrupt law was unconstitutional, at the September 1842 term of court, was widely criticized and widely approved. Throughout his career he interested himself in the question of legal change and legal reform. In spite of the long tradition in England and America, he opposed the institution of "trial by jury" in civil cases on the ground that a judge trained in legal theory and processes is more competent to attain truth and justice than were any twelve jurors. In 1845 he was a member and presiding officer of the convention that wrote a new constitution, which was, however, disapproved by the voters. In 1847 he published a book on law reform, *Obser-*

vations on the Pleadings and Practice of the Courts of Justice of Missouri, and a Radical Change Therein Recommended, outlining his plans for simplifying pleading, shortening forms of declaring cases, and combining cases in law and equity. In 1849 he appeared before the Senate in behalf of a proposed bill, which was passed that year. His *Law of the State of Missouri Regulating Pleading and Practise of the Courts of Justice* (1849) contains his notations on this law.

He was also interested in various activities in the state. He served as a member of the first board of curators of the University of Missouri. In the 1840's he was a member of the Democratic central committee. He was president of the Osage River improvement convention of 1843, participated in the organization of the Missouri Historical and Philosophical Society in 1845, and served as one of its vice-presidents for several years thereafter. In 1845 he urged the General Assembly to construct the state's first lunatic asylum. During 1850–55 he was active in the promotion of the plank road and railroad movement. He was a charter member of the Missouri fruit growers' association, organized in 1859, and engaged in farming on a fairly large scale. During the Civil War, although owner of a few slaves, he was a stanch Union man and was president of the emancipation convention of 1862 and of the Missouri state Radical emancipation and Union convention of 1863. He died at Bowling Green, Ky., survived by five of his six children and by his second wife, Eliza (Covington) Wells, to whom he had been married in June 1840. He was buried in Jefferson City, Mo.

[R. T. King, "Robert William Wells," *Mo. Hist. Review*, Jan. 1936; W. V. N. Bay, *Reminiscences of the Bench and Bar of Mo.* (1878); *Proc. and Resolutions in the U. S. Circuit Court on the Death of Hon. Robert W. Wells, U. S. District Judge, Mo., Oct. 3, 1864* (1864); *Mo. Republican* (St. Louis), Sept. 23, 1864.]

R. T. K.

WELLS, SAMUEL ROBERTS (Apr. 4, 1820–Apr. 13, 1875), phrenologist, was born in West Hartford, Conn., the son of Russell Wells of Farmington, Conn., and a descendant of Thomas Welles, who emigrated from England, was living in Hartford in 1636, and became governor of Connecticut. Apprenticed in his youth to the trade of tanner, he practised his trade for some years but was ambitious for medical training. The direction of his life was determined, however, by making the acquaintance of the phrenologists, Lorenzo Niles Fowler and Orson Squire Fowler [q.v.], in Boston in 1843. He joined the Fowlers on their lecture tour as an assistant and later accompanied Lorenzo Fowler on lecture tours in the United States, Canada, England, Ireland, and Scotland. On Oct. 13, 1844, he married Charlotte Fowler, the sister of the phrenologists, herself a pioneer phrenologist in America. The same year he became a member of the publishing firm of O. S. & L. N. Fowler, which was then known as Fowlers & Wells. Later the firm became Fowler & Wells. After Lorenzo Fowler removed to England, Wells was the sole proprietor.

Primarily the advocate of phrenology and physiognomy as a means of reading and guiding human character, and as a basis for proper selection in marriage, he also believed in the various other reforms and fads of the period, hydropathy or water cure, temperance, and a vegetarian diet. He taught the utility of shorthand. He advocated improved methods of agriculture, including proper cultivation of the soil, rotation of crops, irrigation, draining, subsoiling, proper fencing, and the proper selection of improved agricultural implements. He was by disposition a business man. Although he undoubtedly believed sincerely in the value of phrenology and its allied methods of character reading, he had an uncritical and unscientific mind. He continued to exploit his beliefs long after they had been discredited. Always ready to listen to new or popular theories, his publishing firm became the voice of much eccentric, trivial, and unsound speculation. He was instrumental, with his wife, in founding and continuing the institute of phrenology. He managed the famous phrenological cabinet in New York City, which for many years drew crowds of curious visitors to have their craniums examined, and to see the remarkable collection of casts. From 1850 to 1862 he edited the old *Water Cure Journal.* He edited the *Illustrated Annual of Phrenology and Physiognomy* from 1865 to 1875. From 1863 to 1875 he edited the more important *American Phrenological Journal and Life Illustrated,* edited earlier by Nelson Sizer [*q.v.*]. The title was changed in 1870 to *Phrenological Journal and Packard's Monthly,* and in 1871 to *Phrenological Journal and Life Illustrated.* He died in New York City.

[Albert Welles, *Hist. of the Welles Family* (1876); *Phrenological Jour.,* Jan. 1885; *N. Y. Tribune,* Apr. 14, 1875.]   E. B. H.

WELLS, WILLIAM CHARLES (May 24, 1757–Sept. 18, 1817), physician and physicist, was born in Charleston, S. C., the second son and fourth child of Robert and Mary Wells. His father was a bookbinder of Dumfries, Scotland, who emigrated to Charleston in 1753 and became a successful printer and bookseller. Wil-

liam grew up near the city waterfront, where he acquired a vocabulary he later regretted, and was sent back to Dumfries to school when ten years of age. Here he remained more than two years, later attended the University of Edinburgh, and finally returned to Charleston in 1771. Displaying an interest in science, he was apprenticed to Alexander Garden, c. 1730–1791 [*q.v.*], and remained with him until 1775. Both he and his father were stanch Loyalists, and upon the outbreak of the Revolution both fled to Great Britain, where Wells attended lectures for three years at the medical school of the University of Edinburgh. He then followed the common procedure of going to London, where he did some work under William Hunter and went the rounds at St. Bartholomew's Hospital. In 1779 he served as a surgeon in a Scottish regiment in Dutch service on the Continent, but soon resigned to study for three months at the University of Leyden. He received the M.D. degree at Edinburgh in 1780. The following year, taking advantage of the British capture of Charleston, he returned to America to look after his father's property; but fled to Florida upon the return of the patriot forces to Charleston. He took a printing press with him and claimed to have founded the first weekly newspaper in that colony.

In 1784, Wells once more established himself in London, and continued to practise medicine there for the rest of his life. In 1788 he was made a licentiate of the Royal College of Physicians. He had the advantage of hospital connections, and the support of such influential friends as David Hume and Matthew Baillie. On the other hand, he was handicapped by a disdain for the practising apothecaries (who might have aided him), and by a temperament which made it difficult for people to approach him. He was also hindered by a debt of £600 incurred in his education. Only after ten years of practice did his income equal his expenditures.

Once he had a living income, he began serious investigations in physics and in medicine. He became a member of the Royal Society in 1793, and several of his more significant experiments in physics were published in the *Philosophical Transactions* of that body. In his studies of vision, he claimed to have been the first to experiment with the use of belladonna in the eyes, and refuted the view that the distance vision of near-sighted persons improved with age (*Transactions,* vol. CI, 1811). Between 1790 and 1810, he wrote about twelve papers of minor importance on various disease conditions, which were published in *The Transactions of a Society for the*

Promotion of Medical and Chirurgical Knowledge. His most significant contribution to science was contained in a paper read before the Royal Society in 1813 and published, along with several other papers, in 1818: *Two Essays: One Upon Single Vision with Two Eyes; The Other on Dew . . . and An Account of a Female of the White Race . . . Part of Whose Skin Resembles That of a Negro . . . By the Late W. C. Wells . . . With a Memoir of His Life, Written by Himself.* In this paper, Wells not only assumed that there had been a biological evolution of human species, but clearly explained the principle of a natural selection in the course of a struggle for existence and a consequent survival of the fittest.

Charles Darwin was not familiar with Wells's essay when he first published his *Origin of Species*; but some time between 1861 and 1866 it was called to his attention by Charles L. Brace [*q.v.*]. In the fourth edition (1866) of his great work Darwin inserted into the historical introduction the statement: "In this paper he [Wells] distinctly recognizes the principle of natural selection, and this is the first recognition which has been indicated . . ." Darwin added that Wells applied the principle only to the races of men and not to the animal world in general. A critical reading of the original paper, however, gives the impression that Wells saw its applicability to zoölogy, but stressed only its ethnological implications because this was the matter in hand. In a word, he understood the principle of natural selection as a mechanism of evolution in animal life, but did not realize the whole significance of the theory.

Wells suffered a stroke of apoplexy in 1800, but continued to work strenuously for some years. He was never married. In the spring of 1817 he began to suffer seriously from a disease of the heart, which caused his death. He appears to have had no active religious connections, but was buried in the parish church of St. Brides' in London beside the graves of his parents.

[*Memoir*, noted above; *Dict. of Nat. Biog.* (London); Elisha Bartlett, *A Brief Sketch of the Life, Character, and Writings of W. C. Wells* (1849); *Morning Chronicle* (London), Sept. 20, 1817.]   R. H. S.

WELLS, WILLIAM HARVEY (Feb. 27, 1812–Jan. 21, 1885), educator, was born in Tolland, Conn., the son of Harvey and Rhoda (Chapman) Wells. He was the descendant of Samuel, the son of Thomas Welles who emigrated from England, settled in Hartford in 1636, and became governor of Connecticut. He worked on his father's farm, attended the district school, spent two terms, 1829–30, at an academy in Vernon, Conn., and then entered an academy at Tolland. He also taught district school at Vernon. Impaired eyesight forced him to abandon going to college, but he began to teach at the grammar school in East Hartford, Conn. In 1834 he spent eight months in the Teachers' Seminary conducted by the Rev. Samuel R. Hall [*q.v.*] at Andover, Mass. In September 1834 he returned to the grammar school in East Hartford and a year later became principal. In 1836 he was recalled to the Teachers' Seminary at Andover as teacher of English and mathematics, where he taught for eleven years. In 1846 he published his school grammar, of which 90 editions were printed, under various titles, by 1859. In 1847 he was elected principal of the Putnam Free School, Newburyport, Mass.; and, until April 1848, when his new duties began, he assisted Henry Barnard [*q.v.*] in conducting teachers' institutes in Rhode Island and Massachusetts. He was an active institute lecturer in the cause of teacher training, president of the Essex County teachers' association, 1848–49, a founder of the Massachusetts teachers' association, its president, 1851–53, and one of the first editors of the *Massachusetts Teacher*. In 1854 he was appointed principal of the state normal school at Westfield, Mass., a position he held until 1856, when he was elected superintendent of public schools in Chicago, Ill. Shortly after his arrival in Chicago, he organized the first high school in the city, for girls as well as boys. Appreciating the need of qualified teachers, he insisted on the establishment of a training department. He succeeded in obtaining a provision in the new city charter to abolish the district organization; and he established a centralized system under the control of a board of education. As early as 1861 he introduced a graded system of schools, and he prepared for it a course of study which was widely used throughout the country. His book on the *Graded Course of Instruction* (1861) was later embodied in *The Graded School* (1862), which went through many editions. In 1857 he became a member of the board of education of the state of Illinois. He was one of the organizers of a state normal school in Illinois in 1857 and was an active member of its board of trustees, 1857–69. In 1860 he was elected president of the Illinois state teachers' association and in 1863 of the national teachers' association.

Resigning from the superintendency in 1864, he spent the rest of his life in business pursuits. He published in 1878 *Historical Authorship of English Grammar*; and, in 1880, *A Shorter Course in English Grammar and Composition.*

He was married three times: first on July 23, 1840, to Hannah Maria Smith, the daughter of Jonathan Smith, of West Springfield, Mass. She died on May 22, 1842. On May 8, 1843, he married Tabitha Sarah Ordway of Andover, Mass., who died on July 8, 1848. On July 30, 1849, he married Lydia Sophronia Graves, the daughter of Cotton Graves of Sunderland, Mass. He had eleven children.

[*William Harvey Wells . . . In Memoriam* (1887); *Am. Jour. of Educ.*, June 1860; *Jour. of the Proc. of Ill. State Teachers' Assoc.* . . . *1868* (1869); A. T. Andreas, *Hist. of Chicago*, vols. II, III (1885–86); H. B. Clark, *The Public Schools of Chicago* (1897); J. W. Cook, *Educational Hist. of Ill.* (1912); John Moses and Joseph Kirkland, *Hist. of Chicago* (1895), vol. II; Albert Welles, *Hist. of the Welles Family* (1876); *Daily Inter Ocean* (Chicago), *Chicago Daily Tribune*, and *Chicago Daily News*, Jan. 22, 1885.]   R. F. S.

WELLS, WILLIAM VINCENT (Jan. 2, 1826–June 1, 1876), writer, was born in Boston, the son of Samuel Adams Wells. He received but slight formal education and at an early age went to sea. For a decade he lived adventurously, visiting many parts of the world, suffering shipwreck five times (see his description, *Pioneer*, July 1855) and rising before the age of twenty to be an officer in the merchant service. He became a member of the Boston and California Joint Stock Mining and Trading Company and in January 1849 sailed as first mate from Boston on the *Edward Everett*. In California he commanded the company's *Pioneer* on what is sometimes erroneously mentioned as the first steamship voyage up the Sacramento River. Upon the break-up of the company soon afterward he mined for two seasons on the Stanislaus and Tuolumne rivers and then spent short periods working as a farmer and as an engineer. Returning to San Francisco, he engaged first in business but about 1853 became a member of the editorial staff of the *Commercial Advertiser*. In the summer of 1854 he sailed as agent of the Honduras Mining and Trading Company to explore the gold-bearing regions in the almost unmapped wilds of eastern Honduras. The record of these seven months of colorful journeying is preserved in his *Explorations and Adventures in Honduras* (1857) and in an article "Adventurers in the Gold Fields of Central America," in *Harper's Magazine* (February 1856). Soon after his return to San Francisco in 1855 he received the appointment as consul for Honduras, an office he held most of the time until 1874. He compiled in about a fortnight, *Walker's Expedition to Nicaragua* (1856), a highly partisan defense of the filibusters' régime. At this time he turned more definitely to journalism, being associated with the *Alta California* and later with the *Daily Times*. He made an expedition to the wilder parts of Oregon which he reported in "Wild Life in Oregon" (*Harper's*, October 1856). In 1858 he joined in the Frazer River gold rush.

By the sixties he had risen to prominence in San Francisco. He had again returned to the editorial staff of the powerful *Alta California*, had gained reputation from his books, and had taken a leading part in the Republican campaign of 1860. In his character he combined love of adventure, conviviality, warmth of friendship, and natural gentility and refinement of manner. He was always a partisan, whether defending his great-grandfather, the Empress Carlotta, the filibusters, or the golden opportunities of Honduras. Although unfortunate in a biographer, these qualities endeared him to his contemporaries. During the Civil War he held the position of cashier and impost clerk in the naval office in San Francisco. During the period of governmental employment he found leisure to work upon his three-volume *Life and Public Services of Samuel Adams* (1865). For this biography of his great-grandfather, he was able to obtain a large number of records preserved in the family, so that his work remains a basic one. In 1865 he accepted an appointment under Emperor Maximilian. He was in Mexico for a short time and conceived a warm-hearted attachment to the imperial régime. He also escaped from official duties long enough to make an "Ascent of Popocatepetl" (*Harper's*, November 1865, and a series of articles in *Overland Monthly*, July–September 1868). He was soon sent to New York City to conduct a bureau aimed to spread throughout the United States propaganda favorable to the empire. He obtained certain concessions in Mexico that promised to make him rich, but the fall of Maximilian put a sudden end to these hopes, and he was forced to return to San Francisco, ill and almost penniless. He was again received upon the staff of the *Daily Times*, but in 1869 he accepted the easier post of clerk for the mayor of the city. With constantly failing strength, he held this appointment until 1874. From this time on, his mind began to be affected, and finally in January 1876 he was admitted to the state asylum for the insane at Napa, where he shortly afterwards died, survived by his widow.

[O. T. Howe, *Argonauts of '49* (1923); Samuel Colville, *Colville's San Francisco Directory, vol. I . . . 1856* (1856); *San Francisco Directory . . . 1868* (1868), comp. by H. G. Langley; *Ibid.* . . . *1871* (1871); *San Francisco Directory . . . 1876* (1876), comp. by D. M. Bishop & Co.; *Alta California* (San Francisco), Aug. 21, 1874, June 3, 1876; *Morning Call* (San Francisco), June 3, 1876, June 24, 1883.]   G. R. S., Jr.

WELSH, JOHN (Nov. 9, 1805–Apr. 10, 1886), philanthropist, was born in Philadelphia, Pa., the son of John and Jemima (Maris) Welsh. His father was a successful merchant who trained his sons to follow in his footsteps. While John's brothers established a firm of their own, he became a partner in Dulles, Wilcox & Welsh, dealing in dry goods. After the death of his father in 1854, Welsh joined his brothers in the family West India trade, which was concerned largely with sugar. He married Rebecca B. Miller on Apr. 30, 1829. She died in 1832. On Feb. 6, 1838, he married Mary Lowber. Absorption in business was not complete, and he became interested in Philadelphia affairs. He was a member of the select council from 1855 to 1857 and member and chairman of the city sinking fund commission from 1857 to 1871. He was much interested in developing the Fairmount Park system, and, after successful leadership in the fight to persuade the city government to take on an enlarged plan, he became a member of the Fairmount Park Commission in 1867 and served until his death. He was a vestryman in St. Peter's Protestant Episcopal Church and was very active in the affairs of the Episcopal hospital. Railroads and banks were also within the scope of his interest, and he was president of the North Pennsylvania Railroad. In 1864 he organized a great sanitary fair for war charities in Philadelphia, but his crowning achievement was his management of the finances of the Centennial Exhibition of 1876. This project started under the handicap of much hostility and the gloom of the panic of 1873; its success made his reputation. When the labor was over, his friends gathered a purse of $50,000 to be presented to him to provide a public memorial of his achievement. He was a trustee of the University of Pennsylvania at this time, and he turned over this gift to establish the John Welsh Centennial Professorship of History and English Literature.

After Hayes was elected president, he and Evarts thought that Pennsylvania was entitled to the British mission and let it be known to Senator J. Donald Cameron that, if the Pennsylvanians in Congress could come to some agreement as to a man, he would be appointed. Cameron thereupon commanded an indorsement of his father, Simon Cameron. The very next day a majority of the delegation came to Hayes and said they had been coerced. Hayes was perplexed, but opportunely there came a committee of Philadelphia business men proposing Welsh for the position. Hayes was delighted to have a blameless Pennsylvanian at his disposal and, without consulting Cameron, sent his name to the Senate. Cameron was nonplussed; but Welsh was above reproach, and Hayes had his way (*Diary and Letters of Rutherford Birchard Hayes,* III, 1924, ed. by C. R. Williams, 514–15; *Times,* Philadelphia, Oct. 31, 1877). Welsh spent a part of two years in London. His tall figure and benign countenance framed in large white whiskers made him resemble English nobility, and he was a social success; but he was old and the English climate brought bronchitis each winter. Also he lost a brother and two sisters while away, and in May 1879 he asked to be recalled. His diplomatic experience was confined to paying the British government the $5,500,000 fisheries award, arranging rather ineptly for an international bimetallic conference, and obtaining the release of an American Fenian from prison.

[*Encyc. of Pa. Biog.,* vol. XII (1919), ed. by J. W. Jordan; J. T. Scharf and Thompson Westcott, *Hist. of Philadelphia* (1884), I; Beckles Willson, *Amer. Ambassadors to England* (1928); *John Welsh Testimonial, Proc. at the Public Celebration of the Endowment of the John Welsh Centennial Professorship of Hist. and English Lit.* (1877); *The Proc. at the Dedication of the John Welsh Memorial . . . 1887* (1887); *Philadelphia Inquirer* and *North American* (Philadelphia), Apr. 12, 1886.]　　　　　　　　　　　　　　　R. F. N.

WEMYSS, FRANCIS COURTNEY (May 13, 1797–Jan. 5, 1859), actor and manager, was born in London, England, son of an officer in the British navy. His mother, Miss Courtney, was born in Boston, Mass. Young Wemyss was put to school in Edinburgh and then went into business with his mother's brother, Thomas Courtney, Jr., in Dundee. He had, as a schoolboy, done some acting, and when he rebelled at his uncle's discipline, he escaped to the stage. After various experiences with provincial companies, he finally reached London, Apr. 2, 1821. There he was seen by the London agent for the Chestnut Street Theatre, Philadelphia, and engaged. He reached New York in November 1822, and on Dec. 11 made his American début at the Chestnut Street as Vapid in *The Dramatist.* The house was poor and his reception not flattering. But he was delighted with the company, which then included William Warren, William Burke Wood, Henry Wallack, the elder Joseph Jefferson [*qq.v.*], and Mrs. Wood. On Apr. 10, 1823, he married a Miss Strembeck. He made his New York début at the Chatham Garden, Sept. 20, 1824, as Marplot, and in succeeding months played a long list of comedy and farcical rôles. Three years later he was back at the Chestnut Street as stage manager, and in January 1829 he became lessee of that house. Unfortunately he took it over at a time of depression. In his autobiography he records that, with others, he started a fund to aid needy actors, that he often acted two or even three new rôles a night for almost no money at all, and that he once even had to sell lottery tickets to keep his family together. But he had the optimism of his profession, for in 1833 he went three hundred miles by stage to open and manage a new theatre in Pittsburgh. In 1834 he was back in Philadelphia as manager of the Walnut Street house, which he renamed the American Theatre. He paid $4150 a year rent, and the theatre bars paid an additional $3000 to the owners. He also tried management at the Arch Street, Philadelphia, and in Baltimore.

His subsequent fortunes are part of the history of the New York stage. In 1841 he became stage manager of the National Theatre, and on Apr. 29 made his appearance as Belmour in *Is He Jealous?* to the Harriet of Charlotte Cushman [*q.v.*]. Most often, for a decade, he was stage manager, or acting manager, of some theatre (as the Bowery in 1846–47). He was the Duncan to Macready's Macbeth, at the Astor Place Opera House, when the famous riots broke out in May 1849. In September 1849, when Barnum made over his famous "lecture room" into a theatre, Wemyss was the manager. There were regular actors, and also a troop of "Druids, just arrived from Stonehenge." There was also vaudeville, with Wemyss taking part. In 1850–51 he was at the National again, with the younger Joseph Jefferson. Since certain young players were announced as his "pupils" in 1853, he must have been giving lessons. From 1855 to 1857 he was with Laura Keene [*q.v.*], but reduced to such minor parts as Sir Charles Marlow in *She Stoops to Conquer.* He was not listed in the casts of the new plays, and evidently had not adapted his style to changing tastes. Almost his last appearance was as stage manager for a huge benefit performance on Dec. 18, 1858, to raise money to buy "Mount Vernon" for a national shrine. He died in New York Jan. 5, 1859, survived by his wife and children.

Wemyss was neither a conspicuously good actor nor a conspicuously successful manager, yet he became a figure in the early American theatre by virtue of good taste, integrity, and conspicuous devotion to his profession, especially exemplified in his lifelong devotion to the theatrical fund, which he helped to found, and which he administered till his death. He also edited sixteen volumes of the *Acting American Theatre*, with portraits by John Neagle [*q.v.*], and wrote an autobiography, *Twenty-Six Years of the Life of an Actor and Manager* (2 vols., 1847), and *Chronology of the American Stage from 1752 to*

1852 (1852). He was a handsome, affable, courteous man. His portrait by Thomas Sully shows a round, pleasant, jovial face, a high, wide forehead, and a mass of very curly hair.

[In addition to Wemyss' *Twenty-Six Years of the Life of an Actor and Manager* (2 vols., 1847), see G. C. D. Odell, *Annals of the N. Y. Stage* (7 vols., 1927–31); and death notice in *N. Y. Times*, Jan. 6, 1859.]
W. P. E.

WENDE, ERNEST (July 23, 1853–Feb. 11, 1910), dermatologist, health official, was born at Millgrove, Erie County, N. Y., the eldest son in a family of ten children born to Bernard Philip and Susan (Kirk) Wende; Grover William Wende [*q.v.*] was a younger brother. His father was an enterprising and successful farmer, and Ernest was able to attend school regularly until he graduated from high school. After teaching for two years at Alden, he began the study of medicine at the University of Buffalo but his course was interrupted when he passed an examination for and entered the United States Military Academy at West Point, July 1, 1875. In a year's time, however, he returned to his medical studies, graduating with the degree of M.D. from the University of Buffalo in 1878. For a thesis on influenza, at graduation, he received honorable mention. He practised at Alden for a short time; then attended Columbia University (1881–82) and later the University of Pennsylvania, from which institution he received the degrees of M.D. in 1884 and B.S. in 1885. The next year and a half he spent in Europe, where he studied skin diseases and microscopy at Berlin and Vienna. Returning to Buffalo in 1886, he established himself in practice there. In 1887 he was appointed to the staff of the University of Buffalo as clinical lecturer in dermatology and the following year was made clinical professor; he was also appointed in 1890 professor of botany and microscopy in the Buffalo College of Pharmacy.

In 1892 he received the appointment of health commissioner, which position he held for thirteen years. In this capacity he became nationally known because of the improvements and reforms which he instituted and which were later copied by many other cities. Soon after taking office he investigated the high death rate in infants and found, from bacteriological studies, that the milk became infected because the imperfect construction of the tubes in the then commonly used long-tube nursing bottles afforded a lodging for bacteria. By city ordinance this type of bottle was abolished, in spite of the opposition of druggists and the indifference of others. He also developed methods for the inspection of the source of the city's milk supply; introduced modern ways of handling contagious diseases; instituted systematic examination, both bacteriological and chemical, of the city's water supply; and brought about periodic inspection of the markets, hotels, and restaurants. The death rate was reduced from twenty-four to fourteen per thousand within one year of his taking office.

Wende was a man of original ideas and had a forceful personality. He wielded a powerful influence for good in his community. His interests and accomplishments were varied; he was an amateur ethnologist, archeologist, and botanist; his hobbies included fishing and hunting. In addition to local and state medical societies, he was a member of the American Dermatological Association, the American Microscopical Society, and the Pan-American Medical Congress. He was at one time vice-president of the American Public Health Association, and was a Fellow of the Royal Microscopical Society and of the American Electro-Therapeutic Association. From 1895 until his death he was associate editor of the *Buffalo Medical Journal*. Civic and other interests claimed his attention and he was the active head of the Municipal League for many years. On Aug. 25, 1881, he married Frances Harriett Cutler of Omaha, by whom he had three children.

[*Jour. of Cutaneous Diseases,* May 1910; J. J. Walsh, *Hist. of Medicine in N. Y.* (1919); *Buffalo Medic. Jour.,* Mar. 1910; *Buffalo Morning Express,* Feb. 12, 1910.]   G. M. L.

WENDE, GROVER WILLIAM (Apr. 6, 1867–Feb. 9, 1926), physician, dermatologist, was born in Millgrove, Erie County, N. Y., the son of Bernard Philip and Susan (Kirk) Wende, and a younger brother of Ernest Wende [*q.v.*]. After receiving his preliminary education in public schools, he entered the University of Buffalo, where he was graduated with the degree of M.D. in 1889. The next few years he spent in graduate study, first at the University of Pennsylvania, and later in Prague, Vienna, and Paris. His training included a thorough grounding in the sciences of bacteriology and pathology in their relation to diseases of the skin.

Returning to Buffalo in 1898, he began the practice of dermatology with his brother Ernest. He was soon appointed to the staff of the University of Buffalo and was professor of dermatology there for twenty-seven years. He found time to write a number of scientific articles in a terse, characteristic style. He described many of the rarer skin diseases and became known as an exceedingly accurate observer. Among the better known of his medical contributions were "Porokeratosis with Report of Case" (*Journal of*

Cutaneous and Genito-Urinary Diseases, November 1898); "A Nodular, Terminating in a Ring Eruption—Granuloma Annulare" (*Ibid.,* September 1909); "Nodular Tuberculosis of the Hypoderm" (*Ibid.,* January 1911); "Pellagra as it Occurs in Buffalo and Vicinity" (*Buffalo Medical Journal,* July 1918); "Keratolysis Exfoliativa" (*Journal of Cutaneous Diseases,* March 1919). Both through his writings and through his scientific discussions at various medical congresses Wende became well known and highly regarded. In 1909 he was elected chairman of the section of dermatology and syphilology of the American Medical Association. He was secretary of the American Dermatological Association from 1905 to 1909 and was elected president of that society in 1911. During the World War he was a member of the surgeon general's committee for supervising the treatment of venereal diseases in the army. His activities were not confined to dermatology. He served as president of the Medical Society of the State of New York, and was a member of the American Association of Pathologists and Bacteriologists, the American Association for Cancer Research, the American Society for the Control of Syphilis, and numerous local medical societies.

His private practice grew to large proportions, necessitating the employment of assistants. He was appointed to the staffs of many hospitals, among which were the Erie County, the Buffalo Sisters of Charity, the German, the Buffalo General, the Children's Municipal, and the United States Marine Hospital, all in Buffalo. One of his hobbies was medical photography. He was solid and vigorous both mentally and physically, quiet-spoken, and scholarly. He reached the pinnacle of his profession because of his ability, his thorough training, his agreeable personality, and his striking physique, and also because he was industrious and eminently honest in all dealings with his fellow men. On his way to attend a dinner of physicians he was struck by a street car and died while being conveyed to the hospital. In 1896 he married Mary Graham, daughter of David and Mary (Graham) Tucker.

[*N. Y. State Jour. of Medicine,* Mar. 1, 1926; *Jour. of the Am. Medic. Asso.,* Feb. 20, 1926; J. E. Lane, in *Archives of Dermatology and Syphilology,* Mar. 1926; J. J. Walsh, *Hist. of Medicine in N. Y.* (1919); *Buffalo Morning Express,* Feb. 10, 1926.]   G. M. L.

WENDELL, BARRETT (Aug. 23, 1855–Feb. 8, 1921), teacher and man of letters, was born in Boston, the son of Jacob Wendell, merchant, and Mary Bertodi (Barrett) Wendell. The founder of his family in America was Evert Janse Wendel, who came from East Friesland to New Netherland in 1640. Evert's grandson, Jacob Wendell, great-grandfather of Wendell Phillips and Oliver Wendell Holmes [*qq.v.*], was the first of the family to move to New England. Successful as a merchant in Boston, he was joined there by his nephew John, who was Barrett Wendell's great-great-grandfather. Wendell was privately prepared for Harvard, from which he graduated in 1877, having more widely read, traveled, and exercised his wit (he was among the early contributors to the *Harvard Lampoon*) than most of his classmates. An unsuccessful attack upon the law, which to him was not a congenial subject, left him uncertain about the future. Just then two most fortunate events happened. The first was his marriage, June 1, 1880, to Edith Greenough of Quincy, Mass. Of this marriage there were four children. How much his family meant to Barrett Wendell is delightfully suggested in his letters. The other happy occurrence was his appointment in 1880 to help Prof. Adams Sherman Hill teach English composition to Harvard undergraduates. How successfully he did so appears from the later eminence of many who took his "English 12" and from such testimony as George Pierce Baker's, who says of Wendell's interest in the early numbers of the *Harvard Monthly* (founded 1885): "Nothing ever did so much to give me a sense that an art is greater than any of its servants as Wendell's praise and blame of those successive numbers" (*Harvard Graduates Magazine, post*, p. 575). Another sort of witness to the same skill and interest is Wendell's *English Composition* (1891), which surpassed any other book on the subject. In the same year appeared *Cotton Mather, the Puritan Priest*, in which, through hard study of manuscripts and rare insight, he humanized a perennially important and puzzling character. His *William Shakespere* (1894) proved his sympathetic understanding of the genius of Elizabethan literature. In 1898 Wendell became the first teacher at Harvard to offer American literature as an object of systematic historical and critical study. From that course there emerged *A Literary History of America* (1900), which helped to bring about a reconsideration of certain literary traditions and greatly increased the active study of American letters, both in and outside of the colleges.

By this time Wendell had become a distinguished figure, and in 1902–03 he gave the Clark lectures at Trinity College, Cambridge, England, and published them in 1904 as *The Temper of the Seventeenth Century in English Literature*. Much more notable was his visit to France in 1904–05, when he inaugurated with great success the exchange of professors between France and Harvard founded by James Hazen Hyde. Rarely have circumstances, combined with great gifts as a lecturer, writer, traveler, and friend, enabled any man to interpret two countries to each other as did Barrett Wendell by his Sorbonne lectures on American literature and traditions, and by his remarkable book, *The France of Today* (1907), the insight of which was verified by the World War. This book, perhaps its author's best work, has been translated into French and German. A permanent memorial of his notable visit to the Sorbonne is the classroom there named "La Salle Barrett-Wendell."

Barrett Wendell's other publications of his later middle age—such as *Liberty, Union, and Democracy, the National Ideals of America* (1906), *The Privileged Classes* (1908), and *The Mystery of Education, and Other Academic Performances* (1909)—testify, as do his letters, to the steady enlargement of his field of thought. He was working toward the conclusion that, as he told the American Academy of Arts and Letters in 1917, he could in his later years of teaching do "no better service than by attempting to show how at least things literary can hardly be understood until we try to think of them together" (Lowell, *post*, p. 183). Such was the purpose of his successful course of elementary lectures on comparative literature and his last book, *The Traditions of European Literature, from Homer to Dante* (1920). The author's ill health did not prevent this, or the classroom lectures out of which it grew, from being an important series of broad and stimulating views.

His teaching was remarkable for a variety of qualities: swift and keen generalization, ready control of the background of events and ideas, profuse and well-chosen illustrations, a humble recognition of the mystery of genius, and unforgettable mannerisms permeated by a spirit of absolute sincerity. Skeptical though he was about the validity of certain phases of scholarship, he cared profoundly for what he called "serious criticism," the object of which he defined (*William Shakespere*, p. 1) as "so to increase our sympathetic knowledge of what we study that we may enjoy it with fresh intelligence and appreciation." He had as an undergraduate been deeply influenced by the teaching of James Russell Lowell and he did much to carry on the tradition established by one whom he himself characterized as "a man who . . . found in literature not something gravely mysterious, but only the best record that human beings have made of human life; . . . Here was a man, you grew to feel, who knew literature, and knew the world, and knew you too; ... There came ... a certain feeling of personal affection for him, very rare in any student's experience of even the most faithful teacher" (*Stelligeri and Other Essays Concerning America*, 1893, pp. 211–12). In Barrett Wendell's case it was always the entire person, never the mere teacher, who spoke. Just before his death, in a letter to H. M. Kallen, an intimate friend whose opinions were generally less conservative than his own, Wendell wrote: "After all, the difference between a reactionary and a radical, at heart, is only that the one longs to retain whatever is good and the other to destroy whatever is evil. Neither can be quite right or all wrong" (Howe, *post*, p. 185).

Wendell was a member of the American Academy of Arts and Letters, the Massachusetts Historical Society, and many other societies. He twice received the honorary degree of Doctor of Letters, and in 1920 he was given "le titre honorifique de Docteur de l'Université de Strasbourg."

[M. A. De W. Howe, *Barrett Wendell and His Letters* (1924); *Proc. Mass. Hist. Soc.*, vol. LIV (1921); A. L. Lowell, *Ibid.*, vol. LV (1922); G. P. Baker, in *Harvard Grads. Mag.*, June 1921; J. R. Stanwood, *The Direct Ancestry of the Late Jacob Wendell of Portsmouth, N. H.* (1882); *Who's Who in America*, 1918–19; *Boston Transcript*, Feb. 9, 1921.]   C. N. G.

WENDTE, CHARLES WILLIAM (June 11, 1844–Sept. 9, 1931), Unitarian minister, author, and hymn-writer, was born in Boston, Mass., the son of Carl and Johanna (Ebeling) Wendte. His father, who emigrated to Boston in 1842 from Hanover, Germany, gained a precarious living by painting frescoes in churches. After his death in 1847 the mother supported her two sons by tutoring in German. Wendte attended the Boston public schools, Chauncy Hall, and the gymnasium at Verden, Hanover, and in 1858 became an apprentice in the wholesale woolen house of Blakes and Kinsley. Threatened with tuberculosis, he went to San Francisco in 1861 and by the friendship of Thomas Starr King [q.v.] secured a custom-house position. After a period of volunteer militia service he entered the Bank of California, which transferred him in 1865 to Virginia City, Nev. Early association with Theodore Parker [q.v.] and his later contact with King turned him to the ministry, and he went East to the Meadville Theological School, Meadville, Pa. (1866–67), then to the Harvard Divinity School (1868–69), from which he was graduated. Wendte became minister successively of the Fourth Unitarian Church in Chicago (1869–75), the Church of the Redeemer (First Unitarian) in Cincinnati, Ohio (1876–82), where his influence upon young Wil-

liam Howard Taft [q.v.] and Alexander Johnson, the sociologist, was decisive, and the Channing Memorial Church in Newport, R. I. (1882–85). In 1886 he became a Unitarian missionary supervisor on the west coast, and also served as minister of the First Unitarian Church, Oakland, Cal. (1886), and of Unity Church, Los Angeles (1898). Resigning to recuperate his health, he became minister of the Theodore Parker Memorial Church in Boston (1901–05).

In 1900 Wendte undertook, till 1920, the general secretaryship of the International Council of Liberal Religious Thinkers and Workers. In this capacity he became secretary of the foreign relations department of the American Unitarian Association (1905–15), meanwhile serving (1905–08) as minister of the First Parish, Brighton, Mass. The first meeting of the Council (later the International Association for Liberal Christianity and Religious Freedom) was held in London (1901) attended by seven hundred delegates from over twenty liberal religious movements of the western hemisphere, and from the Brahmo-Somaj, of India. Succeeding congresses were held in Amsterdam (1903), Geneva (1905), Boston (1907), Berlin (1910), and Paris (1913). For the brilliant success of these cosmopolitan gatherings, Wendte labored indefatigably, traveling throughout Europe, as well as in Egypt, Palestine, and Turkey, meeting and conferring with liberal Protestants, Roman Catholics, Jews, Moslems, and Hindus. His enthusiasm for these ecumenical councils of rational, ethical theism was reinforced by unusual linguistic powers, great personal charm and tact, rich theological scholarship, broad tolerance, and a perfect command of executive detail. Of the proceedings and addresses by leading theological scholars and preachers of the western world, Wendte edited *Freedom and Fellowship in Religion* (1907), the *Proceedings* of the Fifth International Congress (1911), and *New Pilgrimages of the Spirit* (1921). Of a similar American organization, the National Federation of Religious Liberals, Wendte served as secretary from 1908 to 1920. He edited the *Proceedings* of the fifth congress in 1915, *The Unity of the Spirit* (1909), *Freedom and the Churches* (1913), and *Religious Liberals in Council* (1913). He was president (1910–14) of the Free Religious Association, and for it published *The Next Step in Religion* (1911), *The Promotion of Sympathy and Goodwill* (1913), and *World Religion and World Brotherhood* (1914). Wendte died without children, Oct. 9, 1931, in Berkeley, Cal., leaving his widow, Abbie Louise

(Grant) Wendte, whom he married Apr. 28, 1896, in Oakland, Cal.

Wendte regarded his biography, *Thomas Starr King, Patriot and Preacher* (1921), as his most permanent and worthy publication, but all his literary output was of high quality. He published four popular hymnals for liberal church schools and a memoir of Charles T. Brooks [*q.v.*], which appeared in Brooks's *Poems* (1885). His last book, *The Transfiguration of Life* (1930), fitly presents his theological convictions, which formed in general an immanental, ethical theism that he early correlated with the evolutionary hypothesis, as well as with the social progressiveness of the nineties—spiritual in purpose, ethical in method. His autobiography, *The Wider Fellowship* (2 vols., 1927), provides a remarkably vivid and factual synopsis of American social and political history, and of worldwide religious liberalism from 1850 to 1925.

[In addition to Wendte's *The Wider Fellowship* (2 vols., 1927), see *Who's Who in America*, 1930–31; *Gen. Cat. of the Divinity School of Harvard Univ.* (1910); J. T. Sutherland, in *Christian Register*, Oct. 8, 1931; and obituary in *San Francisco Chronicle*, Sept. 10, 1931.]   C. H. L—e.

WENLEY, ROBERT MARK (July 19, 1861– Mar. 29, 1929), philosopher, was born in Edinburgh, Scotland, the son of James Adams and Jemima Isabella (Veitch) Wenley. His father, of Norman-French descent and East Anglian origin, was sometime treasurer of the Bank of England and president of the Institute of Bankers of Scotland; his mother, of Lowland Scotch ancestry, was related to the Sibbald and Romanes families. Wenley's traditions were thus strictly of the upper bourgeoisie. He received his early education at a preparatory school in Edinburgh and later at the Park School and a high school in Glasgow, entering the University of Glasgow at the age of fifteen in November 1876. There, at first, he found his studies too easy to require serious attention, and, being very large and strong, he devoted his energies to athletics, gaining prizes in football, rowing, and swimming, but probably laying the foundation for the heart weakness that was ultimately to cause his death. He also seriously injured his right hand in football, making his handwriting almost illegible. During his second year at the university, his work in philosophy awakened doubts of the strict religious Calvinism in which he had been brought up, and he plunged into a course of intensive study on an attempted schedule of four days a week without sleep. The inevitable nervous breakdown came at last, but not until he had been thrice gold medallist in philosophy and once university medallist, and, what was more impor-

tant, had won the close friendship of the Scottish Hegelian, Edward Caird. During this period of heroic study, he was also influenced by, among his other teachers, Lord Kelvin in physics, Jebb and Sonnenschein in the classics, and John Nichol in English literature. He spent fourteen months in Paris, Rome, and Florence, recuperating from his breakdown, after which he returned to Glasgow, where he received the degree of Master of Arts in 1884, followed by those of Doctor of Philosophy in 1895, and Doctor of Science, from the University of Edinburgh, in 1891. He was married to Catherine Dickson Gibson, the daughter of Archibald Gibson, secretary of the Caledonian Railway Company, in April 1889. From 1886 to 1894 he was assistant professor of logic at the University of Glasgow and also, from 1886 to 1895, was in charge of the philosophy department in Queen Margaret College, as well as being degree examiner in mental philosophy, 1888–1891, and becoming dean of the arts faculty in the latter year. He was at various times president of the University Liberal Club, the Students Representative Council, the Students Union, the Theological Society, the Bothwell Literary Association of Edinburgh, and the Dialectic Society of Glasgow. Invited to the University of Michigan in 1896 to succeed John Dewey, he spent the rest of his life there as head of the department of philosophy, with the exception of the years 1925 to 1927, when he was director of the American University Union in London.

Unusually equipped in both scientific and classical scholarship in addition to his command of his own field, a brilliant and powerful lecturer with a mastery of sarcasm and sardonic wit, he was easily the most influential teacher on the Michigan faculty, attracting the ablest students to his classes. A liberal in religion and a Tory in politics he set forth his particular form of Green-Caird-Bosanquet Hegelianism in a series of volumes: *Socrates and Christ* (1889); *Aspects of Pessimism* (1894); *Contemporary Theology and Theism* (1897); *An Outline Introductory to Kant's "Critique of Pure Reason"* (1897); *The Preparation for Christianity in the Ancient World* (1898); *Modern Thought and the Crisis in Belief* (1909); *Kant and His Philosophical Revolution* (1910); *The Anarchist Ideal* (1913); *The Life and Work of George Sylvester Morris* (1917), probably his most valuable book; *Stoicism and its Influence* (1924). He also contributed numerous articles to J. M. Baldwin's *Dictionary of Philosophy and Psychology* (3 vols. in 4, 1901–05) and to James Hastings' *Encyclopedia of Religion and Ethics* (13 vols.,

1908–26), published a history of *The University Extension Movement in Scotland* (1895), and edited *Poetry by John Davidson* (1924).

[Roy Sellars, in *Michigan Alumnus*, Apr. 6, 1929; De Witt Parker, in *University Council and Senate Records*, 1929–32; *Who's Who in America*, 1928–29; *N. Y. Times*, Mar. 30, 1929; personal recollections.]

E. S. B—s.

WENNER, GEORGE UNANGST (May 17, 1844–Nov. 1, 1934), Lutheran clergyman, was born in Bethlehem, Pa., the son of George and Sarah Ann (Unangst) Wenner. After attending public schools and several private academies he was a student at Pennsylvania College (now Gettysburg), 1860–61, at Yale University, 1861–65, where he received the A.B. degree, and at the Union Theological Seminary 1865–68. He was ordained in 1868 by the Evangelical Lutheran Synod of the State of New York, and the same year he became the pastor of Christ Lutheran Church in New York City, the outgrowth of a small group of Lutherans whom he had addressed in a blacksmith's shop on East Fourteenth Street, while a student in 1866. He remained pastor of this church until his death. It is claimed that this pastorate of sixty-six years is the longest on record in the United States. Though he was active in many fields in the church, he considered preaching and pastoral service his life work. He was a devout, sympathetic, genial, and scholarly leader of his people.

He was a pioneer in weekday religious education. In his German parish paper, *Der Sonntags-gast,* of July 1874, he announced the beginning of regular religious instruction for children. This work was probably largely responsible for his almost unparalleled achievement of maintaining a congregation on the Lower East Side in New York City for two-thirds of a century. In November 1905 he read a paper on weekday religious education before the Interchurch Conference (forerunner of the Federal Council of the Churches of Christ in America), which was highly commended. Since then weekday religious education, in addition to catechization, has been a recognized field of church work. As a young minister in 1870, he planned and organized extensive home missionary programs, especially in Greater New York. He sought to promote Lutheran unity by organizing intersynodical ministerial groups, and was one of the leaders in establishing the deaconess work in the General Synod of the Lutheran Church. From 1904 to 1908 he was president of the Synod of New York and New Jersey; from 1908 to 1910 he was president of the Synod of New York.

He was sensitive to proprieties in the services of the church, and became one of the few liturgical scholars that the Lutheran Church in America has produced. Early in the eighties of the last century, he sought by conference and correspondence to develop a Lutheran liturgical consciousness. There were other leaders of like mind and purpose, among them James W. Richard [*q.v.*]. This growing interest in liturgics resulted in the adoption by the General Synod of the Common Service. A lengthy discussion between him and Professor Richard concerning the Lutheran character of certain features of the Common Service promoted liturgical interest and knowledge throughout the Church. Wenner was chairman of the liturgical committee of the General Synod from 1883 until 1915. Later he doubted the historical justification of the Confiteor and Introit in any Lutheran liturgy, and regretted certain extreme liturgical trends in the Lutheran Church. When he died he left the unfinished manuscript of a volume on liturgics.

Though conservatively Lutheran in his theological opinions and in his attitude toward church usages, Wenner's catholic Christian spirit and church statesmanship made him a recognized leader in interdenominational enterprises. He was secretary of the Evangelical Alliance for forty years, and was one of the founders of the Federal Council of the Churches of Christ in America. He was the author of numerous articles of importance, many of which were published in the *Lutheran Quarterly,* and of three books, *Religious Education and the Public Schools* (1907); *The Lutherans of New York* (1918); and *Sixty Years in One Parish* (1928). In the course of his pastorate Wenner baptized more than 8,000 individuals, confirmed 2,140, performed marriage ceremonies for 4,575, and buried 3,291. On Apr. 14, 1880, he was married to Rebecca Pullman. After her death in 1902, he was married, on Feb. 8, 1915, to Mary Wilson Marshall, who died in 1931. He had no children.

[*Who's Who in America*, 1932–33; G. U. Wenner, *Sixty Years in One Pulpit* (1928); *Alumni Record of Gettysburg Coll.* (1932); *Yale Univ. Obit. Record, Year Ending 1935*; G. L. Kieffer, biographical article in the *Lutheran*, Nov. 15, 1934; *N. Y. Times*, Nov. 2, 1934.]

S. G. H.

WENTWORTH, BENNING (July 24, 1696–Oct. 14, 1770), royal governor of New Hampshire, was a great-grandson of Elder William Wentworth, who came to America from Rigsby, England, in 1636, was closely associated with the Rev. John Wheelwright [*q.v.*], and in 1639 settled at Exeter, N. H. Benning was born in Portsmouth, N. H. The eldest son of Lieutenant-Governor John and Sarah (Hunking) Wentworth, he was listed as fifth in his class at Harvard College, where the order was determined by the social standing of the students' families. After his graduation in 1715, he became associated with his uncle Samuel, a merchant in Boston. On Dec. 31, 1719, he married Abigail Ruck, daughter of John Ruck, a prominent merchant; he had three sons, but none survived him. Wentworth was a member of the New Hampshire Assembly for a short time and became a member of the council in 1734. During the years 1734–39 he made several trips to England and Spain.

With his brother-in-law, Theodore Atkinson, he labored to make New Hampshire independent of Massachusetts, and upon achieving that result Wentworth became the first royal governor of the province, serving for the extraordinary period of twenty-five years. Like other colonial governors, and with no more success, he urged the Assembly to grant him a fixed salary in sterling or proclamation money, since New Hampshire was troubled by a depreciating paper currency. Like most of the royal governors of the century he complained frequently that the Assembly was encroaching upon his powers. The House in appointing chaplains, surgeons, and commissaries, in electing committees to handle supplies for the militia, and in limiting the militia's period of service and field of operations invaded his powers as commander-in-chief. He was not a tactful man and as a result of his determination to uphold the royal prerogative in sending writs of election to new towns became involved in a bitter controversy with the Assembly. A deadlock resulted in 1747, but by 1752 both sides were eager for harmony; the representatives from the new towns were admitted by the Assembly, and Wentworth approved the Assembly's choice, Meshech Weare [q.v.], as speaker.

New Hampshire took a prominent part in military expeditions against the French, furnishing one-eighth of the land forces sent against Louisbourg in 1745 and contributing towards the Louisbourg expedition of 1758 and the various attacks on Crown Point; Wentworth received many thanks from the New Hampshire generals for his attention to the troops. During his administration the province grew in wealth and population. In 1761 the Governor made no less than sixty grants of land west and eighteen east of the Connecticut River. With the conclusion of the French and Indian war many soldiers applied for grants in the Connecticut Valley, in territory claimed by both New Hampshire and New York. The resulting controversy was decided by the British government in favor of New York, but the New Hampshire settlers refused to accept the decision and the matter was not settled finally until the formation of the state of Vermont. Although New Hampshire was represented in the Albany Congress of 1754 it was one of the colonies unrepresented at the Stamp Act Congress of 1765, because Wentworth, by proroguing the Assembly, prevented the election of delegates.

Several attempts were made to remove him from the governorship. Complaints were made that he had too many relatives in office, that he had favored them with grants of land, and that he had grown rich through fees and the practice of reserving for himself 500 acres in each township; other complaints dealt with his exercise of the office of surveyor of the King's Woods. The home government said he neglected his correspondence. After some years of this campaign against him John Wentworth [q.v.] in 1765 presented a defense of his uncle to the Marquis of Rockingham, as a result of which Benning was permitted to resign and his nephew was appointed to succeed him both as governor and surveyor of His Majesty's Woods.

After retiring in June 1767, Benning Wentworth resided at Little Harbor with his second wife, Martha Hilton, whom he had married on Mar. 15, 1760. In his last years he was corpulent and much troubled by gout. He died at Little Harbor and was buried in the Wentworth tomb in the graveyard of Queen's Chapel, St. John's Church, Portsmouth. He provided a handsome fortune for his wife, who was the sole heir to his estate. Wentworth was an aristocrat in bearing and manner and showed that he had the courage of his convictions by the way in which he carried out royal instructions. Probably no colonial governor upheld the royal prerogative with more determination. He was a loyal promoter of the Anglican Church and the leader of a powerful social group; his home at Little Harbor was one of the most spacious country houses of colonial America. He left no issue.

[N. H. Provincial Papers, vols. V–VII (1871–73), X (1877), XVIII (1890); Mass. Hist. Soc. Colls., 6 ser. (1886–99), IV, VI, VII, IX, X; New Eng. Hist. and Geneal. Reg., July 1888; scattered letters (MSS.) in Lib. of Cong., Mass. Hist. Soc., Newberry Lib. (Chicago), New Haven Hist Soc., and British Museum; Nathaniel Adams, Annals of Portsmouth (1825); Jeremy Belknap, The Hist. of N. H., vol. II (1791); C. W. Brewster, Rambles About Portsmouth (1859–69); W. H. Fry, in N. H. as a Royal Province (1908); L. S. Mayo, John Wentworth (1921); J. N. McClintock, Hist. of N. H. (1888); John Wentworth, The Wentworth Geneal. (3 vols., 1878); Boston Gazette, Oct. 22, 1770.]   I. M. S. W.

WENTWORTH, CECILE de (d. Aug. 28, 1933), painter, was born in New York City, probably between 1853 and 1870. Her maiden name was Smith. The names of her parents do not appear in the accounts of her life, but presumably she belonged to a Catholic family, for she attended the Sacred Heart Convent in New York City. While still a young girl Cecilia, as she was then known, went to Paris to study art, and worked there in the studios of Alexandre Cabanel and Edouard Detaille. In the next few years she met and married Josiah Winslow Wentworth. She appears as an exhibitor in the catalogue of the Paris Salon of 1889 as Mme. C.–E. Wentworth, and for the next thirty years she regularly contributed to that annual exhibition portraits and occasional pictures with religious themes. She was made an *officier d'académie* in Paris in 1894. At the Universal Exposition in Paris in 1900 she received a bronze medal for her painting of Pope Leo XIII, who decorated her with the title of grand commander of the Order of the Holy Sepulchre and gave her the papal title of marchesa. In 1901 the French government conferred upon her the title of chevalier of the Légion d'Honneur, and she became an *officier de l'instruction publique*. She was one of the few women painters to have examples of their work purchased for the Musée National du Luxembourg. She received medals at the National Exhibition at Tours, and at other exhibitions at Lyons and Turin, and had the title of *officier* of the order of Nichau Tftikar conferred upon her by Mohammed EuNacer Bacha-Bey (*Who's Who in America, post*). During the greater portion of her active years she maintained a studio at 15 Avenue des Champs Élysées in Paris, returning for occasional visits to the United States, of which she continued to be a citizen despite her many years' residence abroad. In 1931 her husband, who was also a holder of the papal title of marquis, died in Paris. Soon after that the marquise because of a reduced income removed to the Riviera, where she passed the rest of her life. She lived at Nice in very modest circumstances and at the time of her death there in the municipal hospital on Aug. 28, 1933, it was reported that the American embassy in Paris forwarded money to cover her funeral expenses.

Among her sitters were William Howard Taft, Theodore Roosevelt, Archbishop Michael A. Corrigan, John W. Mackay [*qq.v.*], Cardinal Ferrata, and Queen Alexandra of England. The portrait of Pope Leo XIII in the Vatican Museum in Rome, one of her best known, shows him in an attitude of upright alertness that was extremely characteristic. A portrait of Gen. John J. Pershing is in the Invalides Museum in Paris; one of Maj.-Gen. George B. McClellan is in the Metropolitan Museum in New York. She is further represented by "La Foi" in the Lux-embourg in Paris, and by a portrait of a former president of the Senate in the Senate chamber in Paris. Her portraits are noted for their admirable portrayal of character and a certain spontaneity of facial expression. Though she was one of the most prominent women portrait painters of the latter part of the nineteenth century, she was better known in France than in her native America.

[See *Who's Who in America*, 1920–21; Helen Earle, *Biog. Sketches of Am. Artists* (1916); Marchioness of Wentworth, "Souvenirs of Leo XIII," *Independent*, July 23, 1903; *L'Aristocratie Étrangère en France*, 1899–1901, for Cecile de Wentworth's maiden name and the full name of her husband; obituaries in *Am. Art Annual*, 1933, *Art News*, Sept. 16, 1933, *Figaro* (Paris), Aug. 31, *N. Y. Times* and *N. Y. Evening Post*, Aug 30, 1933.]
G. A. C.

WENTWORTH, GEORGE ALBERT (July 31, 1835–May 24, 1906), teacher, author of textbooks in mathematics, was born at Wakefield, N. H., the son of Edmund and Eliza (Lang) Wentworth and a descendant of William Wentworth who emigrated from England in 1636 and signed the "Exeter Combination" three years later. After beginning his education in a district school and the Wakefield Academy, he entered Phillips Exeter Academy in 1852. He remained there for three years, working his way in part but financially assisted by his uncle, Benjamin Lang. In 1855 he entered Harvard College as a sophomore, paying part of his expenses in the next three years by teaching in the neighborhood. Just before graduating in 1858, he was recommended by President James Walker for an instructorship at Phillips Exeter. He was well trained in Latin and Greek, and it was in this field that he began his teaching. In 1859 he was assigned to the department of mathematics, but for some time he continued his teaching of the classics and even gave instruction in other branches. He was married on Aug. 2, 1864, to Emily Johnson Hatch of Covington, Ky., who died on May 1, 1895. For more than thirty years he was at the head of the mathematics department at Exeter, resigning his position in 1891 to devote his full time to the writing of textbooks. For two years, 1883–84 and 1889–90, he was acting principal of the academy and in 1899 was elected a trustee. During his later years he was afflicted with heart trouble and spent considerable time at Bad Nauheim in Germany in search of relief. He died in a heart attack in the railway station at Dover, N. H., survived by two sons and a daughter.

He was an outstanding pupil in his early days at Exeter, being commonly known as "the General," and as a teacher of unusual vigor and dominating power he was a recognized leader, known to the boys as "Bull Wentworth." A multitude of stories and traditions grew up around his name, to be interpreted according to the hearers' own ideals of personality and education. Ignoring all rules of the professional educator, he would often seem to be reading a newspaper while a recitation was in progress but infallibly detected every error in a boy's statement. He coddled no one; he put every boy on his own resources; but his seemingly rough exterior covered a warm heart. His textbooks included his *Elements of Geometry* (1878, with numerous later editions), *Elements of Algebra* (1881), *Practical Arithmetic,* with Thomas Hill (1881), *College Algebra* (1888), and works on trigonometry, surveying, and physics. Not including answer books and teachers' manuals, there were some fifty books copyrighted in his name as sole or joint author, most of them being revisions or elaborations of those mentioned. Of these, the geometry text, which later included both plane and solid geometry, was the most successful. It set a new standard of excellence in the United States and, indeed, abroad. To him, seconded by Edwin Ginn [*q.v.*], his publisher, is largely due the unit page, the condensed step form, and the first notable improvement in America of textbook typography. As a usable geometry it stood supreme for many years. His algebras were noteworthy for the large amount of orderly drill. They were based upon the principles of formal discipline and of learning to do by doing. They furnished the material needed for drill, and they proved of great value to those who were preparing pupils for college entrance examinations. His *Plane Trigonometry* (1882) also marked an advance in scholarship in the secondary school and still more in class-room usability. His *College Algebra,* partly the work of Frank N. Cole, had a great influence for many years on freshman mathematics. Altogether, the schools of the United States owe him much for books that contained a worthy type of mathematics and were at the same time adapted to the needs of the class of schools then dominating the field.

[*Bulletin of The Phillips Exeter Acad.*, Sept. 1906; *Harvard Class of 1858, First Triennial Report* (1861); *Report of the Class of 1858 . . . Fortieth Anniversary* (1898); L. M. Crosbie, *The Phillips Exeter Academy* (1923); F. H. Cunningham, *Familiar Sketches of the Phillips Exeter Academy* (1883); family information and files of his publishers.]   D. E. S.

WENTWORTH, JOHN (Aug. 20, 1737, N.S.–Apr. 8, 1820), last royal governor of New Hampshire, Loyalist, was born in Portsmouth, N. H. His father, Mark Hunking Wentworth, was a wealthy merchant and landowner and his moth-

er, formerly Elizabeth Rindge, belonged to a prominent family of the province. He was descended on his father's side from William Wentworth, who emigrated from England to America some time before 1639; his grandfather, John Wentworth, had served as lieutenant-governor of New Hampshire; his uncle, Benning Wentworth [*q.v.*], held the office of governor for many years following 1741. John was graduated at Harvard College in 1755. He then entered his father's counting-house, and as early as 1759 became one of the proprietors of a township, which was named Wolfeborough, a holding which later absorbed much of his attention.

In 1763 he went to England to represent his father's business interests and his sojourn there profoundly affected his subsequent career. He formed the acquaintance of influential and distinguished Englishmen, among them the Marquis of Rockingham, and he was appointed one of the agents for New Hampshire, serving with Barlow Trecothick, a London merchant. Pursuant to instructions from the provincial Assembly, he used his influence to help secure the repeal of the Stamp Act. Upon the forced resignation of his uncle, Benning Wentworth, he was himself appointed governor of New Hampshire, his commission being dated Aug. 11, 1766. He was also made captain general of the militia and invested with admiralty jurisdiction, and was appointed to the post of surveyor general of His Majesty's Woods in America. He returned to America early in 1767, landing at Charleston, S. C., on Mar. 22. He journeyed northward through the colonies, making certain inspections pertaining to his duties as surveyor, and visiting prominent personages along the way. He took the oath of office as governor at Portsmouth, June 13, 1767.

Wentworth entered upon his new duties possessed of remarkable advantages in the way of family and social prestige, education, knowledge of the world, tact and good sense, and attractive personality. His administration was characterized by energy and a sincere desire to further the welfare of his native province, though it is true that, in accordance with eighteenth-century practice, he saw no impropriety in giving preferment to personal friends and relatives, and appointed to the council several persons related to him by blood or marriage. He displayed great energy in administering the office of surveyor of the King's Woods, making tours of inspection and preventing the private cutting of timber reserved for the Royal Navy. He was especially interested in the development of the interior regions of the province, and was instrumental in securing the division of New Hampshire into five counties

Grants of land and the organization of towns proceeded rapidly under his jurisdiction. He persuaded the Assembly to appropriate money for a survey, on the basis of which an excellent map of New Hampshire was published in 1784. He initiated a policy of road construction as a part of his program for developing the interior. As captain general he devoted attention to re-organizing the militia. A supporter of sound money, he secured the abolition of paper currency in 1771. He was keenly interested in the establishment of Dartmouth College, granting a charter in 1769 and assisting the project by making grants of land, subscribing to the fund, and personally devoting time and attention to the affairs of the college. He was a member of the original board of trustees. As early as 1768 he had begun the development of his estate at Wolfeborough, where he built a large and pretentious house. On Nov. 11, 1769, he was married to his cousin, Frances (Wentworth), widow of Theodore Atkinson, Jr., former secretary of the province, who was also Wentworth's first cousin. In 1771, one Peter Livius, a disgruntled member of the council, drew up a list of charges against Wentworth and his administration, which was later submitted to the home government. After a period of anxiety, in the course of which he formulated a vigorous refutation of the charges and a defense of his conduct, he was vindicated by the Privy Council in 1773.

It was his misfortune that his administration had opened just as relations between the mother country and the colonies were being subjected to severe strain. As the revolutionary disturbances increased, he found himself in a difficult situation. He was unshaken in his loyalty to the Crown, though he disapproved of certain of its policies. He conducted himself with patience and tact, endeavoring to enforce the laws and to check any revolutionary moves. He was particularly anxious to prevent steps toward cooperation between New Hampshire and the other colonies. Events moved rapidly in 1774 and 1775, however, and with the increasing tension, overt acts against his authority were inevitable. At length he and his family took refuge on a British man-of-war at Portsmouth and in August 1775 he sailed for Boston.

When the British evacuated Boston in March 1776, Wentworth proceeded with them to Halifax, later accompanying the military expedition to New York. In 1778 he went to England. During the war he was exiled by the New Hampshire revolutionary government and most of his property was confiscated. Appointed surveyor to what was left of the King's Woods in

North America in 1783, he took up his post at Halifax. He became lieutenant-governor of Nova Scotia (governor, to all intents and purposes) in 1792, an office which he held until 1808. In 1795 he was made a baronet. As in New Hampshire, he performed his duties as governor with success, his policies being concerned with improvement of transportation, education, and the organization of defense measures. He died at Halifax in his eighty-third year. He had been a devoted American until his exile and he never lost his feeling for his native land and province. Of his children only one, a son, survived infancy.

[Nine letter books of Wentworth, covering 1767–1807, are in the archives of the Province of Nova Scotia, at Halifax; transcripts of three of these, 1767–78, are in the state archives of Concord, N. H.; a number of his letters are in the possession of Dartmouth College. In the transcripts of papers of the Commission of Enquiry into the Losses and Services of American Loyalists, N. Y. Pub. Lib., is a statement by Wentworth. Biog. studies include L. S. Mayo, *John Wentworth* (1921); W. C. Abbott, in *Conflicts with Oblivion* (1924); Lorenzo Sabine, in *Biog. Sketches of Loyalists of the Am. Revolution* (1864). See also Jeremy Belknap, *The Hist. of N. H.* (1812); L. B. Richardson, *Hist. of Dartmouth Coll.* (1932); Frederick Chase, *A Hist. of Dartmouth Coll. and the Town of Hanover* (1891), ed. by J. K. Lord; John Wentworth, *The Wentworth Geneal.* (3 vols., 1878); *Mass. Hist. Soc. Colls.*, 6 ser. IV (1891); *Provincial Papers . . . Relating to . . . N. H.*, vol. VII (1873); *The State of N. H.: Miscellaneous Provincial and State Papers*, vol. XVIII (1890); *Two Reports on the Matter of Complaint of Mr. Livius against Gov. Wentworth* (London, 1773), copy in Dartmouth Coll. Lib.; "Case of Councillor Peter Livius *vs.* Governor John Wentworth—testimony for the defense," in *N. H. Hist. Soc. Colls.*, vol. IX (1889); *Boston Daily Advertiser*, Apr. 22, 1820.]
W. E. S—s.

WENTWORTH, JOHN (Mar. 5, 1815–Oct. 16, 1888), editor, congressman, mayor of Chicago, was born at Sandwich, N. H., son of Paul and Lydia (Cogswell) Wentworth, grandson of John Wentworth of the Continental Congress and of Col. Amos Cogswell of the Continental Army. He was descended from William Wentworth who was in Exeter, N. H., in 1639. John attended public schools and various private academies. He taught school one winter, entered Dartmouth College in 1832, and was graduated in 1836. He then went to Michigan and, finding no place as a school teacher in response to his advertisements in the *Detroit Free Press*, he walked to Ann Arbor and Ypsilanti, and still finding no school, walked back to Detroit, sent his trunk to Chicago by the brig *Manhattan*, took a stage to Michigan City, and walked the lake beach to Chicago, arriving with only thirty dollars. He ate his first meal at the boarding-house of Mrs. Harriet Austin Murphy at Lake and Wells streets on Oct. 25, 1836, and thereafter for forty-nine years, unless absent from Chicago, he celebrated his advent into that city by taking dinner with Mrs. Murphy. Within a month he was in editorial charge of the weekly *Chicago Democrat,* denouncing "wildcat" currency, and entering on activities that resulted in a city charter for Chicago, the election of its first mayor, William B. Ogden [*q.v.*], and the designation of Wentworth as its first official printer. Within three years, at a cost of $2,800, he owned the *Chicago Democrat.* In 1840 he started the *Daily Democrat* and made it for years the leading newspaper of the Northwest. During 1841 he spent some six months in Cambridge, Mass., attending law lectures at Harvard, returned to Chicago, and was soon admitted to the bar.

In 1843, when twenty-eight years of age, he was elected to the House of Representatives of the Twenty-eighth Congress, the youngest member of that body. During his congressional service of 1843–51 and 1853–55 he furthered free homestead legislation, helped to initiate and pass bills for Western railway land grants, a national bonded-warehouse system, harbor construction and improvement, and lighthouse erection, and was the unpaid agent of a number of Mexican War veterans claiming bounties, back pay, and pensions. He was an instigator of the notable National River and Harbor Convention of 1847 in Chicago. An original stockholder of the Chicago & Galena Railroad, he headed its committee which arranged consolidation with the Chicago & Northwestern Railroad. On repeal of the Missouri Compromise he left the Democratic party and joined with those of moderate anti-slavery views who founded the Republican party.

He was elected mayor of Chicago in 1857 on a "Republican Fusion" ticket, and announced he would take no salary. He introduced the first steam fire engine and the first paid fire department of the city. He served one year, declined another term, but in 1860 was again elected. During the Civil War he aggressively supported the Lincoln administration, and as police commissioner threw protection around Clement L. Vallandigham [*q.v.*] for an anti-war speech and then replied in a blunt argument hailed as effective; as police commissioner he frustrated a threatened raid aimed at a wholesale release of Confederate prisoners in Camp Douglas. His knowledge of law and politics was in play as a delegate to the 1861 convention to revise the Illinois state constitution, while his long-sustained journalistic advocacy of a well-equipped common-school system made suitable his appointment to the state board of education for the terms of 1861–64 and 1868–72. His final term in Congress in 1865–67 saw him on the ways and

means committee and among the foremost to urge immediate resumption of specie payments.

Year by year he had acquired lots and land in Chicago and Cook County to an extent that brought him the reputation of holding title to more real estate than any other man in Chicago. A stock farm of about five thousand acres at Summit in Cook County was planned by him as a resource and place of heart's ease for his later years, but this vision was never realized: comment ran that during life "he changed his stopping place as often as he did his shirt"; he had the hotel habit, the noise of the city was melodious to him, and the turmoils of politics and affairs more attractive than farming. When asked for his rules of life he said: "I get up in the morning when I'm ready, sometimes at six, sometimes at eight, and sometimes I don't get up at all. . . . Eat when you're hungry, drink when you're thirsty, sleep when you're sleepy, and get up when you're ready." He was active in behalf of state and local historical societies, read reminiscent addresses before them, wrote a three-volume *Wentworth Genealogy* (1878), and grieved over his loss in the Chicago fire of his most cherished manuscripts and papers, including a diary in which nearly every day during many years he had made entries "somewhat in the style of John Quincy Adams." He presented Dartmouth College with $10,000, and served as president of the Dartmouth Alumni Association in 1883. While his discourses at educational institutions were bland and urbane, he was as a stump speaker sarcastic and "blunt as a meat ax" as often as he was argumentative. His quick replies, positive attitudes, and gruff manners had added support from a deep-chested, three-hundred-pound body, a height of six feet six inches, the nickname of "Long John," and a varied anger and drollery. The anecdote was widely told, published, and believed that once when running for mayor he walked out on the courthouse steps and faced a waiting crowd that let out a tumultuous yell of greeting. He gazed in calm scorn at them, not taking his hat off, and then delivered the shortest and most terrifying stump speech ever heard in Illinois: "You damn fools, . . . you can either vote for me for mayor or you can go to hell." He had personal warmth and forthright utterance, once telling a Congressional colleague, Abraham Lincoln, he "needed somebody to run him" as Senator William H. Seward in New York was managed by Thurlow Weed, Lincoln replying that only events could make a President. John Wentworth was married in Troy, N. Y., Nov. 13, 1844, to Roxanna Marie, daughter of Riley Loomis. She was in failing health for many years and died in 1870. Of their five children, only one survived him. His death called forth a remarkable series of commentaries and reminiscences on a figure that had striven with the generations who found Chicago a swamp mudhole and saw it made into an audacious metropolis.

[A. T. Andreas, *Hist. of Chicago* (3 vols., 1884) ; *Biog. Sketches of the Leading Men of Chicago* (1868) ; Joseph Kirkland, *The Story of Chicago* (1892) ; *Encyc. of Biog. of Ill.* (1892) ; *Biog. Dir. Am. Cong.* (1928) ; *Daily Inter Ocean* (Chicago), Oct. 17, 1888 ; "Scrap Book," Chicago Hist. Soc.; files of Chicago newspapers; conversations with persons who knew Wentworth.]   C. S.

WENTWORTH, PAUL (d. December 1793), spy, is assumed, from Gov. John Wentworth's reference to him as "my near relation" (Wentworth, *post,* p. 13) and from his possession of land in New Hampshire, to be a member of the Wentworth family of that colony, but the connection is not traced. A man of apparent education and talents, he lived before the Revolution in many places, the West Indies, New Hampshire, London, Paris, relying for financial support on his abilities as a stock jobber and on the profits of a Surinam plantation. He had one ambition—to obtain from the British government some office that would give him the political prestige he considered commensurate with his dignity and standing as a gentleman. Governor Wentworth, who seems to have thought highly of him, obtained for him, in 1770, an appointment to the council of New Hampshire; but he did not, apparently, care to forsake his financial activities for a minor colonial office. He did, however, serve the colony as its London agent in the early seventies.

With the outbreak of hostilities he, like his kinsman, supported the British side. His travels in America and his wide acquaintance with Americans, both in the colonies and in London, made him valuable to the government, which gave him immediate employment in its spy service, where he hoped the reward of his endeavors would be a baronetcy, a seat in Parliament, and an administrative post. He became one of the important members of the secret service, appointing and directing spies, digesting and interpreting their reports for the ministry, and making frequent trips to the Continent, where,

under assumed names and various disguises, he himself often performed the more dangerous and delicate missions. Through him Edward Bancroft [*q.v.*] was brought into the service, and to him Bancroft's often very valuable reports were made. Wentworth, hating the ungentlemanly nature of his position, was, nevertheless, hardworking, daring, alert, and completely unscrupulous in his methods of obtaining information. His most noteworthy exploit was his attempt to halt the negotiations between France and the United States, which, in December and January 1777–78, he realized were rapidly approaching their culmination. He made frantic efforts to persuade Silas Deane and Benjamin Franklin to consider British terms of reconciliation, going far beyond his instructions in the offers he dangled before them. Franklin finally promised to talk with any regularly appointed peace commissioner, and Wentworth hastened back to London, only to find that George III could not be persuaded of any immediate danger. As a result, Wentworth's activity only served to hasten the French alliance, since Franklin took good care to inform Vergennes that British overtures of peace were being made. By this time Wentworth was aware that his visits to Paris were being closely scrutinized by the police, and thereafter he remained in London. For his services before the French alliance and for the great danger he had run Lord North believed he deserved special recompense; but George III distrusted Wentworth for his stock gambling; and the only return he received, therefore, aside from his salary and expenses was a seat in Parliament in 1780, which lasted six weeks. He stayed on in London after the war, continuing his business activities and making further futile efforts at a political career. In 1790 he retired to his Surinam plantation, where he died.

[B. F. Stevens' *Facsimiles of MSS. in European Archives Relating to America, 1773–1783* in Lib. of Cong.; *Provincial Papers, Docs. and Records . . . New-Hampshire,* vol. VII (1873) ; "The Revolutionary Diplomatic Correspondence of the U. S.," 50 Cong., 1 Sess., *House Miscellaneous Doc., No. 603* (1889), ed. by Francis Wharton, vol. VI, p. 630; S. F. Bemis, "British Secret Service and the French-American Alliance," *Am. Hist. Review,* April 1924; L. D. Einstein, *Divided Loyalties* (1933) ; John Wentworth, *The Wentworth Geneal.* (1878), vol. III, pp. 7–13.]
                                        M. E. L.

VOLUME X, PART 2
WERDEN - ZUNSER

(*VOLUME XX OF THE ORIGINAL EDITION*)

CROSS REFERENCES FROM THIS VOL-
UME ARE MADE TO THE VOLUME
NUMBERS OF THE ORIGINAL EDITION.

CONTRIBUTORS
VOLUME X, PART 2

THOMAS P. ABERNETHY . . . . T. P. A.
CARL WILLIAM ACKERMAN . . . C. W. A.
ADELINE ADAMS . . . . A—e. A.
ARTHUR ADAMS . . . . A—r. A.
JAMES TRUSLOW ADAMS . . . . J. T. A.
NELSON F. ADKINS . . . . . N. F. A.
ROBERT GREENHALGH ALBION . R. G. A.
GUSTAVE G. AMSTERDAM . . . . G. G. A.
GEORGE POMEROY ANDERSON . G. P. A.
RUSSELL H. ANDERSON . . . . R. H. A.
GERTRUDE L. ANNAN . . . . . G. L. A.
KATHARINE ANTHONY . . . . . K. A.
MARGUERITE APPLETON . . . . M. A.
JOHN CLARK ARCHER . . . . . J. C. Ar—r.
RAYMOND CLARE ARCHIBALD . . R. C. A.
JOSEPH CULLEN AYER . . . . . J. C. Ay—r.
JOSEPHINE DASKAM BACON . . J—e. D. B.
HAYES BAKER-CROTHERS . . . H. B-C.
MARSTON BALCH . . . . M. B.
LELAND D. BALDWIN . . . . . L. D. B.
SHEPARD BARCLAY . . . . . . S. B.
GILBERT H. BARNES . . . . . G. H. B.
VIOLA F. BARNES . . . . . . V. F. B.
CLARIBEL R. BARNETT . . . . C. R. B.
JOHN DONALD BARNHART . . . J—n. D. B.
HAROLD K. BARROWS . . . . . H. K. B.
ERNEST SUTHERLAND BATES . E. S. B.
HAROLD H. BENDER . . . . . H. H. B.
JEANNETTE L. BERGER . . . . J. L. B.
THOMAS JEFFRIES BETTS . . . T. J. B.
PERCY W. BIDWELL . . . . . P. W. B.
THEODORE C. BLEGEN . . . . T. C. B.
LOUIS H. BOLANDER . . . . . L. H. B.
CHARLES K. BOLTON . . . . . C. K. B.
WITT BOWDEN . . . . W. B—n.
SARAH G. BOWERMAN . . . . . S. G. B.
JULIAN P. BOYD . . . . . . J. P. B.
FREDERICK EDWARD BRASCH . . F. E. B.
JESSICA HILL BRIDENBAUGH . . J. H. B.
ROBERT BRIDGES . . . . . . R. B—s.
WILLIAM BRIDGWATER . . . W. B—r.
JOHN E. BRIGGS . . . . . . J. E. B.
SAMUEL H. BROCKUNIER . . . S. H. B.
E. FRANCIS BROWN . . . . . E. F. B.
JAMES DOUGLAS BROWN . . . . J—s. D. B.
L. PARMLY BROWN . . . . . . L. P. B.
MARGARET LOUISE BROWN . . M. L. B.
STERLING A. BROWN . . . . . S. A. B.
C. A. BROWNE . . . . C. A. B—e.

ROBERT BRUCE . . . . R. B—e.
G. MacLAREN BRYDON . . . . G. M. B.
OSCAR McMILLAN BUCK . . . O. M. B.
SOLON J. BUCK . . . . S. J. B.
ARTHUR H. BUFFINTON . . . . A. H. B.
C. C. BURLINGAME . . . . . C. C. B.
GEORGE LINCOLN BURR . . . . G. L. B.
CLAUDE A. BURRETT . . . . . C. A. B—t.
HUNTINGTON CAIRNS . . . . H. Ca—s.
ISABEL M. CALDER . . . . . I. M. C.
ORESTES HAMPTON CALDWELL . O. H. C.
AVERY L. CARLSON . . . . . A. L. C.
PATRICK J. CARROLL . . . . P. J. C.
ERMINE COWLES CASE. . . . . E. C. C.
CHARLES LYON CHANDLER . . . C. L. C.
CHARLES E. CLARK . . . . . C. E. C.
ELIOT CLARK . . . . E. C—k.
HUBERT LYMAN CLARK . . . . H. L. C.
ROBERT C. CLARK . . . . . R. C. C.
HARRY CLEMONS . . . . . . H. Cl—s.
KATHERINE W. CLENDINNING . K. W. C.
ORAL SUMNER COAD. . . . . . O. S. C.
FREDERICK W. COBURN . . . . F. W. C.
HOBART COFFEY . . . . H. C—y.
ELBRIDGE COLBY . . . . . . E. C—y.
FANNIE L. GWINNER COLE . F. L. G. C.
ROSSETTER G. COLE . . . . . R. G. C.
CHRISTOPHER B. COLEMAN . . C. B. C.
CHARLES JAY CONNICK . . . . C. J. C.
ROYAL CORTISSOZ . . . . . R. C.
ROBERT SPENCER COTTERILL . R. S. C.
E. MERTON COULTER . . . . . E. M. C.
ISAAC J. COX . . . . I. J. C.
JOHN COX, JR. . . . . J. C., JR.
THEODORE S. COX . . . . . T. S. C.
KATHARINE ELIZABETH CRANE . K. E. C.
VERNER W. CRANE . . . . . V. W. C.
WESLEY FRANK CRAVEN. . . . W. F. C.
CAREY CRONEIS . . . . C. C.
GRACE WICKHAM CURRAN . . . G. W. C.
EDWARD E. CURTIS . . . . . E. E. C.
EDWARD E. DALE . . . . . . E. E. D.
REGINALD ALDWORTH DALY . . R. A. D.
MARJORIE DANIEL . . . . . . M. D.
KENNETH L. DAUGHRITY . . . K. L. D.
WILLIAM H. S. DEMAREST . . W. H. S. D.
JOSEPH V. DE PORTE . . . . J. V. D-P.
BERNARD DeVOTO . . . . . . B. D-V.
EDWARD H. DEWEY . . . . . E. H. D.

Contributors

Everett N. Dick	E. N. D.
Irving Dilliard	I. D.
Frank Haigh Dixon	F. H. D.
Edith Dobie	E. D—e.
John J. Dolan	J. J. D.
Randolph C. Downes . . .	R. C. D.
William Howe Downes . .	W. H. D.
Henry Grattan Doyle . . .	H. G. D—e.
Carl S. Driver	C. S. D.
Raymond S. Dugan.	R. S. D.
Dwight L. Dumond	D. L. D.
Harrison G. Dwight	H. G. D—t.
Arthur Wentworth Hamilton	
Eaton.	A. W. H. E.
Edward Dwight Eaton. . .	E. D. E.
Walter Prichard Eaton . .	W. P. E.
Edwin Francis Edgett . . .	E. F. E.
Milton Ellis	M. E.
Kendall Emerson	K. E.
William M. Emery	W. M. E.
Hallie Farmer	H. F.
Charles Feleky	C. F.
Felix Fellner.	F. F.
Mantle Fielding	M. F.
James Kip Finch	J. K. F.
Charles J. Finger	C. J. F.
Joseph Fulford Folsom . .	J. F. F.
George W. Fuller	G. W. F.
Kemper Fullerton	K. F.
Caroline E. Furness. . . .	C. E. F.
Herbert P. Gambrell . . .	H. P. G.
William A. Ganoe	W. A. G.
Paul N. Garber	P. N. G.
Curtis W. Garrison	C. W. G.
Samuel W. Geiser	S. W. G.
George Harvey Genzmer .	G. H. G.
W. J. Ghent	W. J. G.
George W. Goble	G. W. G.
Harry Gehman Good. . . .	H. G. G.
Dorothy Grafly.	D. G.
Charles Graves	C. G.
Fletcher M. Green	F. M. G.
Anne King Gregorie. . . .	A. K. G.
Martha Gruening	M. G.
Charles Burton Gulick . .	C. B. G.
Sidney Gunn	S. G.
J. G. deR. Hamilton . . .	J. G. deR. H.
Talbot Faulkner Hamlin .	T. F. H.
Miles L. Hanley	M. L. H.
Elizabeth Deering Hanscom .	E. D. H.
Joseph Mills Hanson	J. M. H.
George L. Harding	G. L. H.
Edward Rochie Hardy, Jr. .	E. R. H., Jr.
Alvin F. Harlow	A. F. H.
Brice Harris	B. H.
Gilbert Dennison Harris .	G. D. H.
Freeman H. Hart	F. H. H.
Margaret Harwood	M. H.
George H. Haynes	G. H. H.
Grace Raymond Hebard . .	G. R. H.
Elizabeth Wiltbank Heilman	E. W. H.
Frederick C. Hicks	F. C. H.
Granville Hicks	G. H.
Raymond L. Hightower . .	R. L. H.
Jim Dan Hill	J. D. H.
Edgar L. Hinman	E. L. H.
Mary Frances Holter . . .	M. F. H.
A. Van Doren Honeyman. .	A. V-D. H.
Roland Mather Hooker . .	R. M. H.
John Tasker Howard . . .	J. T. H.
John G. Jack	J. G. J.
Joseph Jackson	J. J.
Edna L. Jacobsen	E. L. J.
William L. Jenks	W. L. J—s.
Willis L. Jepson	W. L. J—n.
Rufus M. Jones	R. M. J.
Philip D. Jordan	P. D. J.
Charles H. Judd.	C. H. J.
Lawrence Kammet	L. K.
Herbert Anthony Kellar .	H. A. K—r.
Katherine Amend Kellock.	K. A. K.
Louise Phelps Kellogg . .	L. P. K.
Howard Atwood Kelly . .	H. A. K—y.
Albert Joseph Kennedy . .	A. J. K.
John D. Kern	J. D. K.
John Kieran	J. K.
David Kinley	D. K.
Richard S. Kirby	R. S. K—y.
Edward Chase Kirkland . .	E. C. K—d.
Alexander Klemin	A. K.
Edgar Wallace Knight . .	E. W. K.
Grant C. Knight	G. C. K.
Rhea Mansfield Knittle . .	R. M. K.
Ernst C. Krohn	E. C. K—n.
Ralph S. Kuykendall . . .	R. S. K—l.
Ernest Preston Lane . . .	E. P. L.
William Chauncy Langdon	W. C. L.
Conrad H. Lanza	C. H. L.
Fred V. Larkin	F. V. L.
Kenneth S. Latourette . .	K. S. L.
Max Lerner	M. L—r.
Charles Lee Lewis	C. L. L.
Frank Rattray Lillie . . .	F. R. L.
Ivan Mortimer Linforth .	I. M. L.
Anna Lane Lingelbach . .	A. L. L.
Mildred E. Lombard . . .	M.E.L—b—d.
Ella Lonn	E. L.
C. W. Lord	C. W. L.
Milton Edward Lord . . .	M. E. L—d.
Alma Lutz	A. L.
Harry M. Lydenberg . . .	H. M. L.
Margaret Lynn	M. L—n.
Howard Lee McBain . . .	H. L. M.
James Dow McCallum . . .	J. D. M.

Contributors

NELSON GLENN MCCREA	N. G. M.
PHILIP B. MCDONALD	P. B. M.
JOSEPH MCFARLAND	J. M.
WALTER M. MCFARLAND	W. M. M.
REGINALD C. MCGRANE	R. C. M.
OLIVER MCKEE, JR.	O. M., Jr.
BLAKE MCKELVEY	B. M—y.
GEORGE MARSHALL	G. M.
ASA EARL MARTIN	A. E. M.
JULIAN R. MEADE	J. R. M.
ROBERT DOUTHAT MEADE	R. D. M.
LEILA MECHLIN	L. M.
NEWTON D. MERENESS	N. D. M.
GEORGE P. MERRILL	G. P. M.
FRANK J. METCALF	F. J. M.
HARVEY C. MINNICH	H. C. M.
BROADUS MITCHELL	B. M—l.
CARL W. MITMAN	C. W. M.
FRANK MONAGHAN	F. M.
ROBERT E. MOODY	R. E. M.
CHARLES MOORE	C. M.
ALBERT MORDELL	A. M.
RICHARD B. MORRIS	R. B. M.
FRANK LUTHER MOTT	F. L. M.
KENNETH B. MURDOCK	K. B. M.
ALLAN NEVINS	A. N.
ROBERT HASTINGS NICHOLS	R. H. N.
ROY F. NICHOLS	R. F. N.
HERMAN C. NIXON	H. C. N.
FREDERIC PERRY NOBLE	F. P. N.
GRACE LEE NUTE	G. L. N.
FRANK LAWRENCE OWSLEY	F. L. O.
FRANCIS R. PACKARD	F. R. P.
STANLEY M. PARGELLIS	S. M. P.
EDD WINFIELD PARKS	E. W. P.
HOWARD M. PARSHLEY	H. M. P.
WILLIAM PATTEN	W. P.
JAMES W. PATTON	J. W. P.
CHARLES O. PAULLIN	C. O. P.
FREDERIC LOGAN PAXSON	F. L. P.
NORMAN HOLMES PEARSON	N. H. P.
JAMES H. PEELING	J. H. P—g.
ERNEST RALPH PERKINS	E. R. P.
EDWARD DELAVAN PERRY	E. D. P.
HOBART S. PERRY	H. S. P.
FREDERICK T. PERSONS	F. T. P.
JAMES M. PHALEN	J. M. P.
DAVID PHILIPSON	D. P.
J. HALL PLEASANTS	J. H. P—s.
JOHN E. POMFRET	J. E. P.
DAVID deSOLA POOL	D. deS. P.
JENNIE BARNES POPE	J. B. P.
CHARLES SHIRLEY POTTS	C. S. P.
RICHARD J. PURCELL	R. J. P.
J. G. RANDALL	J. G. R.
ALBERT G. RAU	A. G. R.
P. O. RAY	P. O. R.

THOMAS T. READ	T. T. R.
WYLLYS REDE	W. R.
AMY LOUISE REED	A. L. R.
CHESTER A. REEDS	C. A. R.
LEON B. RICHARDSON	L. B. R.
DONALD A. ROBERTS	D. A. R.
H. E. ROBERTSON	H. E. R.
BURR ARTHUR ROBINSON	B. A. R.
HERBERT SPENCER ROBINSON	H. S. R.
WILLIAM A. ROBINSON	W. A. R.
WILLIAM M. ROBINSON, JR.	W. M. R., Jr.
DANIEL M. ROBISON	D. M. R.
ANNA ROCHESTER	A. R.
EUGENE H. ROSEBOOM	E. H. R.
MARVIN B. ROSENBERRY	M. B. R.
EARLE DUDLEY ROSS	E. D. R.
GEORGE H. RYDEN	G. H. R.
VERNE LOCKWOOD SAMSON	V. L. S.
CARL SANDBURG	C. S—g.
JOSEPH SCHAFER	J. S.
ISRAEL SCHAPIRO	I. S.
HERBERT S. SCHELL	H. S. S.
LOUIS BERNARD SCHMIDT	L. B. S—t.
M. G. SEELIG	M. G. S.
JOSEPH J. SENTURIA	J. J. S.
ROBERT FRANCIS SEYBOLT	R. F. S.
CHARLES SEYMOUR	C. S—r.
WILLIAM BRISTOL SHAW	W. B. S.
WILLIAM E. SHEA	W. E. S—a.
MARION SHELDON	M. S.
LESTER B. SHIPPEE	L. B. S—e.
CLIFFORD K. SHIPTON	C. K. S.
ELEANOR M. SICKELS	E. M. S.
KENNETH C. M. SILLS	K. C. M. S.
FRANCIS BUTLER SIMKINS	F. B. S.
EDGAR FAHS SMITH	E. F. S.
EDWARD CONRAD SMITH	E. C. S.
WILLIAM E. SMITH	W. E. S—h.
HERBERT SOLOW	H. S.
JAMES P. C. SOUTHALL	J. P. C. S.
E. WILDER SPAULDING	E. W. S.
OLIVER L. SPAULDING, JR.	O. L. S., Jr.
THOMAS M. SPAULDING	T. M. S.
J. E. SPINGARN	J. E. S.
TIMOTHY WILLIAM STANTON	T. W. S.
HARRIS ELWOOD STARR	H. E. S.
J. M. STEADMAN, JR.	J. M. S., Jr.
BERTHA MONICA STEARNS	B. M. S.
RAYMOND P. STEARNS	R. P. S.
WAYNE E. STEVENS	W. E. S—s.
WITMER STONE	W. S.
OLIVER STRUNK	O. S.
CHARLES S. SYDNOR	C. S. S.
THOMAS E. TALLMADGE	T. E. T.
FRANK WILLIAM TAUSSIG	F. W. T.
DAVID Y. THOMAS	D. Y. T.
WILLIAM B. TOWER, JR.	W. B. T., Jr.

Contributors

CHARLES JOSEPH TURCK	C. J. T.	F. ESTELLE WELLS	F. E. W—s.
ALONZO H. TUTTLE	A. H. T.	ALLAN WESTCOTT	A. W.
LENT DAYTON UPSON	L. D. U.	JAMES O. WETTEREAU	J. O. W.
ROLAND GREENE USHER	R. G. U.	JESSIE F. WHEELER	J. F. W—r.
GEORGE B. UTLEY	G. B. U.	GEORGE F. WHICHER	G. F. W.
WILLIAM T. UTTER	W. T. U.	CHARLES E. WILDER	C. E. W.
WILLIAM REYNOLDS VANCE	W. R. V.	JAMES F. WILLARD	J. F. W—d.
LEWIS G. VANDER VELDE	L. G. V-V.	SAMUEL C. WILLIAMS	S. C. W.
CARL VAN DOREN	C. V-D.	SAMUEL WILLISTON	S. W.
MARK VAN DOREN	M. V-D.	JAMES SOUTHALL WILSON	J. S. W.
HENRY R. VIETS	H. R. V.	ROBERT W. WINSTON	R. W. W—n.
HAROLD G. VILLARD	H. G. V.	MAUDE H. WOODFIN	M. H. W.
OSWALD GARRISON VILLARD	O. G. V.	ROBERT H. WOODY	R. H. W.
D. D. WALLACE	D. D. W.	FREDERICK E. WRIGHT	F. E. W—t.
RAYMOND WALTERS	R. W.	WALTER L. WRIGHT, JR.	W. L. W., Jr
RUFUS W. WEAVER	R. W. W—r.	JAMES INGERSOLL WYER	J. I. W.
W. P. WEBB	W. P. W.	KIMBALL YOUNG	K. Y.
HARRY B. WEISS	H. B. W.		

DICTIONARY OF

AMERICAN BIOGRAPHY

—

Werden—Zunser

WERDEN, REED (Feb. 28, 1818–July 11, 1886), naval officer, was born in Delaware County, Pa., the son of Col. William Werden, who served in the Seminole War. He is described as a tall, slim man, with large nose, dark hair and complexion (*Some Records, post,* p. 21). He was appointed a midshipman in the navy on Jan. 9, 1834, and served subsequently in the Brazil and the Mediterranean squadrons and in the *Boston,* 1840–43, on a cruise around the world. Made a lieutenant on Feb. 27, 1847, he was in the sloop *Germantown* during the Mexican War and commanded landing forces at Tuxpan and Tampico. During the next decade his sea assignments included a cruise on the *Vandalia* in the Pacific Squadron, 1849–52, in the *Albany* in home waters and the West Indies, 1853–55, and in the *Cumberland* operating on the African coast against the slave trade, 1857–59. In the Civil War he served in the *Minnesota* at the capture of Hatteras Inlet on Aug. 28, 1861, and in September following took command of the gunboat *Stars and Stripes,* which on Feb. 7, 1862, led the first column of the flotilla in the attack on Roanoke Island. During the next spring he commanded several small vessels in Albemarle Sound and participated in the action of Mar. 13–14 at New Bern. After detachment from this command, Apr. 17, 1862, because of illness, and promotion to commander, July 16, 1862, he was ordered to command the *Conemaugh,* which in July joined the South Atlantic blockading squadron under Admiral Du Pont and operated in the blockade of the Savannah and Stono rivers and other points on the southeast coast. In June 1863 he was again ordered north because of illness and served chiefly at the Philadelphia Navy

Yard until Nov. 28, 1864, when he was selected as fleet captain of the East Gulf Squadron. He was in this duty until the close of the war and had command of the *Powhatan,* which in May 1865 blockaded the Confederate *Stonewall* at Havana until her surrender to the Spanish authorities. Made captain July 25, 1866, commodore Apr. 27, 1871, and rear admiral Feb. 4, 1875, he was stationed at the Mare Island Navy Yard, 1868–71, was head of the New London Naval Station, 1872–74, and commanded the South Pacific Squadron, 1875–76. In 1877 he retired because of failing health. He was married but had no children. He died at Newport, R. I.

[L. H. Hamersly, *The Records of Living Officers of the U. S. Navy and Marine Corps* (4th ed., 1890); *War of the Rebellion: Official Records (Navy); Providence Daily Jour.,* July 15, 1886; *The U. S. Army and Navy Jour.,* July 17, 1886; G. N. Worden, *Some Records of Persons by the Name of Warden, Werden, Worden* (1868); a few letters and papers in Personnel Files, Navy Dept. Lib., esp. letter from T. F. McGrew concerning father.]   A. W.

WERGELAND, AGNES MATHILDE (May 8, 1857–Mar. 6, 1914), historian, educator, was born in Christiania (Oslo), Norway, the daughter of Sverre Nicolai and Anne Margrete (Larsen) Wergeland. The Wergeland family has produced many statesmen, writers, and artists, and the name is one of the greatest in Norway. From childhood Agnes Wergeland nurtured an intense love for the studious life—for science, art, literature, history, and philosophy. She was richly endowed with musical and artistic talent; she studied music with Grieg and won high praise from him; her most casual note-book sketches reveal great natural abilities. She attended a school for young ladies in

I

Christiania in 1879, and then, four years later, she took up the study of old Norse and Icelandic law under the illustrious Germanist and jurist Konrad Mauer, in Munich, Germany. After two years she went to the University of Zürich where she completed her studies in 1890, with the distinction of having been the first woman Norwegian to receive a Ph.D. from that university.

The offer of a fellowship in history at Bryn Mawr College, Bryn Mawr, Pa., brought her to the United States in 1890. She remained at the college for two more years giving lectures in the history of art, and then lectured at the University of Illinois in 1893. From 1896 to 1902 she was a docent in history at the University of Chicago, and acted as a non-resident instructor from 1902 to 1908. The greatest professional opportunity of her life came, however, when she was offered the chairmanship of the department of history in the University of Wyoming in 1902. Here, in the first state to adopt woman's suffrage, she exercised freely her genuine teaching abilities and pursued her scholarly interests unhampered by the prevalent prejudices against women in institutions of higher learning. Here, finally, the bitter memory of her "starvation period" as a student on the Continent and of the years when her divergent intellectual interests stamped her as a "queer foreigner" in the earlier conventional American women's college faded into the background, and her industrious and highly trained mind turned to scholarly production. In 1912 she published *Amerika' og Andre Digte,* and in 1914 *Efterladte Digte.* In 1916, the *History of the Working Classes in France, Leaders in Norway and Other Essays, Slavery in Germanic Society during the Middle Ages,* and *Early Christian Romanesque and Gothic Architecture* were published posthumously. She also contributed to the periodicals: *North American Review, Dial, American Architect,* and *Journal of Political Economy.* Her literary accomplishments in English and German as well as in her native language were remarkable.

In 1904 she became a citizen of the United States. She remained in Wyoming until her death at Laramie, where she is buried. She was never married. As a memorial to her, a $5,000 endowment fund was presented to the Royal Frederik's University at Christiania, to enable Norwegian women students to study history and economics in the United States. A scholarship in history was also given to the University of Wyoming in her honor.

[Personal acquaintance; *Woman's Who's Who of America,* 1914–15; Maren Michelet, *Glimpses from Agnes Mathilde Wergeland's Life* (privately printed,

1916); J. A. Hofstead, *Am. Educators of Norwegian Origin* (1931); *Laramie Daily Boomerang* (Laramie, Wyo.), Mar. 7, 1914.]
G. R. H.

WERNWAG, LEWIS (Dec. 4, 1769–Aug. 12, 1843), pioneer bridge builder, was born in Riedlingen, Württemberg, Germany. It is believed that he came to America in 1786 to evade military service, taking up his residence in Philadelphia. He was connected with various ventures, including the building of machines to make whetstones, the construction of power-mills, experimentation in the use of anthracite coal for fuel, and the invention and improvement of nail-making machinery at the Phoenix Nail Works, Phoenixville, Pa., in which he purchased an interest in 1813; but it is as the designer and builder of wooden bridges that his name will be chiefly remembered.

His first bridge was erected in 1810 across Neshaminy Creek, on the road between Philadelphia and New York. The following year he built a drawbridge across Frankford Creek at Bridgeburg, and named it "Economy." It was of the cantilever type, so designed that the center panel could be tipped up in order to permit masted vessels to pass through. The spans were short, but Wernwag claimed that spans of from 120 to 150 feet could be constructed on the same principle. In the later controversy as to the priority of the use of the cantilever system in the United States, his claims and his work seem to have been totally ignored. His third bridge was built in 1812 across the Schuylkill River at Upper Ferry, later the Fairmount section of Philadelphia. This structure, known as the "Colossus of Fairmount," consisted of a single arch, the span of which was 340 feet, exceeding by nearly 100 feet the greatest existing span in America. This bold design, scientific and architecturally beautiful, probably was never surpassed in America. One Swiss bridge had a span that was fifty feet longer but was comparatively a monstrosity. The Fairmount bridge was completely destroyed by fire on Sept. 1, 1838. In 1813 Wernwag built a bridge across the Delaware River near New Hope., Pa., thirty-two feet in width, divided into two wagon ways and two footways, and consisting of six arch spans of 175 feet. It had trusses with parallel chords, and vertical timber posts and iron rods for diagonals, anticipating in some respects what was later known as the Pratt type. The canal of the Schuylkill Navigation Company, one of the first in the United States, was partially constructed by him in 1817, and the Fairmount water works and dam at Philadelphia were erected in accordance with his plans.

Wernwag removed to Conowingo, Md., in 1819, where he built a bridge over the Susquehanna, and also a sawmill in which he prepared his timber. Moving to Harpers Ferry, Va. (now W. Va.), in 1824, he purchased the Isle of Virginius, and there continued the preparation of his timber. It was his practice to saw all his timbers through the heart to detect unsound wood, and to permit good seasoning. He used no timbers of greater thickness than six inches and separated all the sticks of arches by cast washers, to allow free circulation of the air. If greater strength was needed, he increased the number but not the dimensions of the sticks. In 1830 he constructed a railroad bridge at Manoguay for the Baltimore & Ohio Railroad and contracted for a bridge across the Kentucky River, several smaller ones on the Marysville turnpike, and one in Indiana, which he gave to his sons, Lewis and William. A letter from his son John to Samuel L. Smedley, dated Harpers Ferry, Aug. 27, 1874 (*Engineering News*, Aug. 15, 1885, p. 99), includes a list of twenty-nine bridges built by the father during his active career of twenty-seven years. He died at Harpers Ferry.

[Theodore Cooper, "American R. R. Bridges," *Trans. Am. Soc. Civil Engineers*, July 1889; Robt. Fletcher and J. P. Snow, "A History of the Development of Wooden Bridges," *Proc. Am. Soc. Civil Engineers*, vol. LVIII (1932); J. L. Bishop, *A Hist. of Am. Manufactures*, I (1861), 562 and II (1864), 131; Lewis Wernwag, in *Engineering News*, Aug. 15, 1885.]
B. A. R.

WESBROOK, FRANK FAIRCHILD (July 12, 1868–Oct. 20, 1918), pathologist, educator, was born in Brant County, Ontario, the eldest son of Henry Shaver Wesbrook, formerly mayor of Winnipeg, and Helen Marr (Fairchild) Wesbrook. Both parents were of Loyalist lineage. Most of his youth was spent in the virile atmosphere of a pioneer community, the rapidly growing city of Winnipeg. He received the degrees of B.A., M.A., and M.D.C.M. from the University of Manitoba in 1887, 1888, and 1890, respectively. In 1889 he studied at the McGill University Medical School, Montreal. During 1890 he served as intern in the Winnipeg General Hospital and taught pathology to students of the University of Manitoba. His desire for wider training, however, took him abroad, where he spent a year in the laboratories of King's College, in the wards of St. Bartholomew's Hospital in London, and in the Rotunda Hospital in Dublin. He was then appointed a John Lucas Walker scholar under Roy, professor of pathology at Cambridge, with whom he spent the greater part of three years. Here his work was under inspired leadership and he was surrounded by brilliant companions who made an indelible impression on him. In 1895, the last year of his residence abroad, he spent part of his time at the University of Marburg, Germany, studying pathology under Prof. Karl Fraenkel. He helped investigate an epidemic of cholera at Hamburg and came in contact with the great personalities Virchow and Koch.

In 1895 he accepted an appointment as professor of bacteriology at the University of Minnesota Medical School, and director of the laboratories of the State Board of Health. He also became a member of this board. In 1896 he became professor of pathology and bacteriology, and in 1906 he was appointed dean of the Medical School. Under his vigorous leadership scientific medicine in the University and throughout the State of Minnesota made rapid progress. In 1907 a new building was dedicated to the work in pathology and bacteriology in the Medical School and to the laboratory activities of the State Board of Health. In recognition of his renown as an expert in public health problems, he was appointed in 1904 a member of the Advisory Board of the governmental Hygienic Laboratory, and in 1905 he became president of the American Public Health Association. He became widely known as a leading organizer in medical education and as an authority in problems of public health and sanitation. He was a member of most of the scientific societies in America and of many abroad. In 1912 he was appointed president of the Section on State and Municipal Hygiene at the International Congress of Hygiene and Demography held in Buffalo, N. Y.

In 1913 he was chosen president of the newly established University of British Columbia, where it was apparent that his powers of organization and ability in administration would prove particularly useful. The war soon interrupted his plans for expanding the new university and he threw himself into war work, as chairman of the Provincial Committee on Food Resources, with the same earnestness that marked all of his activities. Scientifically, his world reputation began in 1900 with the publication of a paper, conjointly with L. B. Wilson and O. McDaniel, on the "Varieties of Bacillus diphtherias" in the *Transactions of the Association of American Physicians*. A bibliography of his writings comprises more than fifty titles. On Apr. 8, 1896, he was married to Annie Taylor, the daughter of Sir Thomas W. Taylor, chief justice of Manitoba. She, with their daughter, survived him at the time of his death in Vancouver.

[*Who's Who in America*, 1918–19; *Forty Years of the Univ. of Minn.* (1910); H. W. Hill, obituary article in *Jour. of Bacteriology*, Mar. 1919; P. H. Bryce, "In Memoriam," *Am. Jour. of Pub. Health*, 1918; *Vancouver (B. C.) Daily Sun*, Oct. 21, 1918.]

H. E. R.

WESSELHOEFT, CONRAD (Mar. 23, 1834–Dec. 17, 1904), physician, educator, was born in Weimar, Germany, the son of Robert and Ferdinanda Emilia (Hecker) Wesselhoeft. His father was a medical practitioner who emigrated to the United States with his family in 1840, and established a medical practice in Cambridge, Mass. He later removed to Brattleboro, Vt. At the age of fifteen, Conrad was sent to Germany to attend the Nicolai Gymnasium at Leipzig, from which he was graduated in 1853 at the head of his class. The death of his father caused his return to America, and he completed his studies at the Harvard Medical School in 1856. Through an uncle, Dr. William Wesselhoeft, he became interested in the work of Samuel Hahnemann, and after careful studies of the theories and practice of homeopathy, he became an enthusiastic advocate. After his graduation he settled in Dorchester, Mass., where, on Nov. 18, 1863, he was married to Elizabeth Foster Pope, but several years later he removed to Boston, where he took an active interest in the advancement of homeopathy and became one of the founders of the Boston University School of Medicine. He was associated with that institution from its organization in 1873 until the time of his death, holding the position of professor of materia medica and later that of professor of pathology and therapeutics. He was also a member of the medical staff of the Massachusetts Homeopathic Hospital from the time of its organization in 1855.

In 1876 he published his translation of Hahnemann's *Organon*. Aside from this, most of his work was done for the American Institute of Homeopathy, of which he was elected president in 1879, and to which he contributed a long list of brilliant scientific papers. He was a member of the Massachusetts Homeopathic Medical Society and the Boston Homeopathic Medical Society. Among his most notable papers may be mentioned "The Demands of Modern Science in the Work of Drug Proving," in *Transactions of the American Institute of Homeopathy*, 1891, in which Wesselhoeft reported the results obtained from provers after the administration of saccharum lactis, and thus demonstrated the necessity of control tests in drug proving. Other papers were published in the *Transactions* for 1878, 1880, and 1882. Wesselhoeft was coeditor of the *Homoeopathic Pharmacopoeia of the United States* (1914). It was his constant effort to formulate the principles of homeopathy in accordance with the established principles of modern science.

At his death in Boston he was survived by his wife and a daughter. His brother, Walter Wesselhoeft, also a homeopathic physician, was born in Weimar, Aug. 29, 1838, and died in 1920. He studied in the Universities of Halle and Jena, Germany, and at the Harvard Medical School, from which he was graduated in 1859. He practised for ten years at Halifax, Nova Scotia, after which he had two years of post-graduate study in Germany. He returned to America in 1873 and settled in Cambridge, Mass., where he engaged in general practice. At the Massachusetts Homoeopathic Hospital he held the positions of visiting physician and senior physician to the maternity department. He was professor of obstetrics and clinical medicine at the Boston University School of Medicine. Like his brother, he was a member of city, state and national homeopathic medical societies. He was married twice; first, in December 1868, to Mary S. Fraser, of Halifax, Nova Scotia, and second, on June 7, 1894, to Mary A. Leavitt, of Cambridge. He was the father of seven children.

[*Who's Who in America*, 1903–05; C. H. Pope, *A Hist. of the Dorchester Pope Family* (1888); W. H. King, *Hist. of Homoeopathy* (1905), vol. IV; J. T. Sutherland, biographical article in *Trans. Am. Inst. of Homoeopathy*, 1905; *New Eng. Medic. Gazette*, Jan. 1905; *Hahnemannian Monthly*, Feb. 1905; *Boston Daily Globe*, Dec. 18, 1904.]   C. A. B—t.

WESSELHOEFT, WALTER (1838–1920). [See WESSELHOEFT, CONRAD, 1834–1904].

WESSON, DANIEL BAIRD (May 18, 1825–Aug. 4, 1906), inventor, manufacturer, was born in Worcester, Mass., the fourth of ten children of Rufus and Betsey (Baird) Wesson. His father, a descendant of John Wesson who emigrated from England and settled in Salem in 1644, was engaged in farming and in the manufacture of plows. Wesson grew up at home, worked on the farm, and attended school until he was eighteen years old. He apprenticed himself at that time to his eldest brother, a manufacturer of firearms in Northboro, Mass. Upon completing his apprenticeship in 1846 he worked as a journeyman gunsmith for his brother and for a manufacturer in Hartford, Conn., but on the death of his brother in 1850 he took over the latter's business in partnership with Thomas Warner, an armorer of Worcester. Two years later, however, Warner retired. For a few months Wesson worked to develop the Leonard pistol in Charlestown, Mass., and then entered the employ of Allen, Brown & Luther, gunsmiths in Worcester, Mass., where he met his subsequent partner, Horace Smith [q.v.]. Although his regular work had to do with rifle barrels, in his spare time Wesson tried to perfect a practical cartridge, working particularly on the improvement of a rim-fire metallic cartridge brought to his attention by Cortland Palmer of New York. He was so successful in this that in 1853 he induced Smith to go into partnership with him to manufacture it in Norwich, Conn. In February 1854 the two patented a pistol which was not only a cartridge weapon but had an entirely new and distinct repeating action. Although this repeating action was not entirely successful in pistols, adapted to rifles it became the basic invention incorporated in the world-famous Winchester repeating rifle. When in 1855 the partners sold their rifle patent rights to the Volcanic Arms Company, Smith retired, and Wesson accepted the position of superintendent of the company.

After further experiment on improving the metallic cartridge and on making his repeating action applicable to the revolver, Wesson purchased an open-cylinder revolver invented by Rollin White and induced Smith to reënter a partnership with him in 1857 to manufacture revolvers. The Smith and Wesson revolver was a phenomenal success from the start, for it was the only one made with an open cylinder and using a metallic cartridge. Though it was manufactured at first chiefly for the American market, large contracts were later obtained from most of the countries of Europe, among them one from the Russian government for 200,000 revolvers. Wesson, who looked after the mechanical end of the business, and was always interested in improving the quality of his revolvers and cartridges, in 1869 purchased the shell-extracting device invented by W. C. Dodge (patented Jan. 17, 1865), and about 1887 introduced the "hammerless safety revolver" (patented Apr. 12, 1887), which prevented accidental firing. In 1873 Smith again retired. After carrying on the business for ten years alone, Wesson took his two sons into partnership with him.

Outside of his firm's activities, Wesson was president of the Cheney Bigelow Wire Works, and was a founder and active director of the First National Bank of Springfield. He was of striking and attractive personality, and his philanthropies in Springfield were many. On May 26, 1847, he married Cynthia M. Hawes of Northboro, Mass. At the time of his death, which followed close upon that of his wife, he was survived by two sons and a daughter.

[Who's Who in America, 1906–07; C. B. Norton, Am. Inventions in Breech-Loading Small Arms (1882); J. S. Hatcher, Pistols and Revolvers (1927); S. A. Eliot, Biog. Hist. of Mass. (1909), vol. I; W. R. Cutter and W. F. Adams, Geneal. and Personal Memoirs . . . State of Mass. (1910), vol. IV; obituary in Springfield Sunday Republican, Aug. 5, 1906.]   C. W. M.

WEST, BENJAMIN (March 1730–Aug. 26, 1813), almanac-maker and astronomer, was born at Rehoboth, Mass., where his father, John West, was a farmer, and where his grandfather settled on coming from England. He was entirely self-educated, after his father had settled on a farm in Bristol, R. I., through books lent to him by friends. He moved to Providence, R. I., in 1753, just after his marriage on June 7 to Elizabeth, daughter of Benjamin Smith of Bristol, and opened a private school. He next started a dry-goods store which later included a bookstore, but this venture ended also in the unsettling days preceding the Revolution. Ardently embracing the principles of the Revolution, he was engaged at Providence throughout the war in manufacturing clothes for the use of troops. On the return of peace he again opened a school. In 1786 he was appointed to the professorship of mathematics and astronomy in Rhode Island College (later known as Brown University), a position which in those days was merely a lectureship. But he did not enter upon his duties until the year 1788, after spending a little more than a year of 1787–88 teaching in the Protestant Episcopal Academy, Philadelphia.

At this time West had achieved considerable reputation in New England as an almanac-maker and astronomer. His first scientific publication was An Almanack, for the year of our Lord Christ, 1763 . . ., published by William Goddard [q.v.] on Providence's first printing press, set up in 1762. The first part of the title, after two expansions, became The New-England Almanack, or Lady's and Gentleman's Diary, and it was issued at Providence annually for 1765 through 1781 (except for the year 1769, published in Boston); with John Carter, 1745–1814 [q.v.], the publisher of the last twelve, West had no further connection. By 1767 the almanacs had obtained such an excellent reputation for accuracy that editions were published simultaneously at Boston, Salem, Norwich, and Providence. There was a Boston edition of the New England Almanack . . . for 1767, and a Newport edition (possibly pirated) of the one for 1772. In Boston West revived the name Isaac Bickerstaff, originated in 1707 by Dean Swift, and issued Bickerstaff's Boston Almanac for the Year of our Lord 1768. This was annually continued by West through the issue for 1779 and for 1783-

93 (as published by Benjamin Russell). It was the first illustrated almanac in Massachusetts. There is evidence that West had nothing to do with most other almanacs bearing the name Bickerstaff. He prepared *The North-American Calendar: or Rhode Island Almanac* (published at Providence by B. Wheeler) for the years 1781–87, and *The Rhode Island Almanac* (published at Newport) for the years 1804–06. All these almanacs were for the meridians of Providence and Boston; others were calculated for the meridian of Halifax, Nova Scotia.

West collaborated with some prominent residents of Providence, especially Joseph and Moses Brown [*qq.v.*], in making elaborate preparations for the observation of the transit of Venus in 1769. His 22-page pamphlet, *An Account of the Observation of Venus upon the Sun the Third Day of June 1769,* appeared in Providence the same year and was reprinted (though dated only 1769) between 1800 and Aug. 14, 1814. The greater part of it appeared also in the *Transactions of the American Philosophical Society* (vol. I, 1771). In *Memoirs of the American Academy of Arts and Sciences* (vol. I, 1785) West published an account of an eclipse of the sun observed in Providence, Apr. 23, 1781, and a paper "On the Extraction of Roots." His recommendation of the first edition of Nicolas Pike's *A New and Complete System of Arithmetic* (1788) was printed in this work. The honorary degrees of M.A. were conferred on West by Brown (also LL.D., 1792) and Harvard colleges in 1770, and by Dartmouth in 1782. He was elected a fellow of the American Academy of Arts and Sciences in 1781. Confusion with Benjamin West, the artist, has led standard authorities (*e.g., Harvard Quinquennial Catalogue, post*) to state that he was a member of the American Philosophical Society. For his last year at Brown (1798–99) he was named professor of mathematics and natural philosophy. From 1802 until his death he was postmaster of Providence, and he was succeeded as postmaster by his son-in-law, Gabriel Allen. Four of his eight children were living at the time of his death. A small gouache-drawing, a bust portrait apparently made from life, is preserved at Brown University.

[The date of West's death is often given incorrectly as Aug. 13. See *R. I. Lit. Repository,* Oct. 1814; *Columbian Phenix: or Providence Patriot,* Aug. 28 and Sept. 4, 1813; *The Biog. Cyc. of Representatives of R. I.* (1881); Leonard Bliss, *The Hist. of Rehoboth, Bristol County, Mass.* (1836); J. C. Pease and J. M. Niles, *A Gazetteer of the States of Conn. and R. I.* (1819), pp. 331–33; *Providence Evening Bull.,* Aug. 26, 1913, p. 8, with portrait; S. S. Rider, "Centenary of Isaac Bickerstaff, Esq.," *Providence Daily Jour.,* Jan. 22, 1881; Amos Perry, in *Narragansett Hist. Reg.,* July 1885, pp. 32–34; C. L. Nichols, "Notes on the Almanacs of Mass.," *Proc. Am. Antiq. Soc.,* n.s., vol XXII, pt. 1 (1912); H. M. Chapin, "Check List of R. I. Almanacs," *Ibid.,* n.s., vol. XXV, pt. 1 (1915); *Harvard Univ. Quinquennial Cat.* (1925); *Hist. Cat. Brown Univ.* (1914); Charles Evans, *Am. Bibliog.,* vols. III–XII (1905–34); W. O. Waters, "Am. Imprints . . . Supplementing Evans' *Am. Bibliog.*," *Huntington Lib. Bull.,* Feb. 1933. In Evans, under West's name, there are more than 190 entries (all but one in connection with almanacs); with many of these pubs. West had no connection whatever, and the title of the first entry of an almanac prepared by West, no. 9303, is quite incorrect.]
                   R. C. A.

WEST, BENJAMIN (Oct. 10, 1738–Mar. 11, 1820), historical painter, was born near Springfield, Pa., in a house now on the campus of Swarthmore College. He was the youngest of ten children of John West, member of an English Quaker family, and his second wife, Sarah (Pearson) West, whose father had been a companion of William Penn on his voyage to America. John West, who had been left in England to complete his education when his family emigrated to the new country in 1699 and did not join the others until 1714, was an innkeeper at various times and places (Jordan, *post,* I, 424), and is said also to have been a cooper and a hosier. Though he is often called a Quaker, Benjamin West was not actually a member of the Society of Friends (Hart, *post*). His two sons were brought up in the Anglican communion, and he himself, according to his friend and pupil, William Dunlap (*post,* I, 79), followed no Quaker practices. He was a man of sober cast, however, and undoubtedly his strong Quaker background influenced his behavior.

Many legends surround the early years of his life. Some of these evidently had the sanction of West himself in his interviews with his first biographer, John Galt; but Galt belongs with the romantic biographers, and West, notoriously vain, probably was not averse to his romanticizing. One story tells of his receiving his first colors from the Indians; another, of a creditable sketch he made at the age of six of his little niece. Certain it is that very early his elders recognized his aptitude for art, and began to give him help and encouragement. When he was about eight, a gentleman of Philadelphia named Pennington (or Penington) presented him with his first artist's supplies, to which he added six engravings, the first the boy had ever seen. In Philadelphia, where he went for a short visit about this time, he met William Williams, a painter, who was so struck with his enthusiasm that he supplied him with several books on art. His first commission was one he received at the age of fifteen for a portrait of Mrs. Ross of Lancaster (perhaps the wife of George Ross, *q.v.*). The first public patrons of his immature work were a Mr. Wayne, Dr. Jonathan Morris, and William Henry [*q.v.*], the last of whom advised him to devote himself to historical painting rather than to portraiture and suggested "The Death of Socrates," which West later painted. He also attracted the attention of Dr. William Smith [*q.v.*], provost of the College of Philadelphia, who urged him to come to the city to study. For a time (1756) he was a student at the college with the class of 1757, but he never became a graduate. About this time, by chance, and quite independently, he discovered the principle of the camera obscura. He lived for a while in Strawberry Alley and is said to have painted signs for inns (Watson, *post*, I, 575), as well as portraits, which he supplied for a small fee. Eager to study abroad, he lived frugally and painted assiduously, copying a "St. Ignatius" owned by one of his friends and achieving an ambitious "Trial of Susannah" with about forty figures. About 1759 he went to New York. Offered an opportunity to go to Italy on a ship loaded with wheat and flour, he embarked for Leghorn in 1760, his savings augmented by a generous gift of fifty guineas from a Mr. Kelly whose portrait he had painted.

In Italy, apparently the first American to study art there, he won wide attention. His letters of introduction from friends in America admitted him to the best society, and his charm of manner, good looks, and eager interest brought him popularity. He studied the antique, painted industriously, and followed the fashions of the day in artistic circles. When a serious inflammation of the ankle confined him to bed for a number of months, he devoted himself to making anatomical studies of his own body. In Rome, as in Pennsylvania, his friendships were advantageous. A picture of his, mistaken for one by Anton Rafael Mengs, the celebrated Bohemian artist, was declared to be far superior in mastery of color to those of Mengs, and Mengs himself treated West with kindness and generosity. Fascinated by the paintings of Titian, he sought not only for Titianesque colors, but for delicacy of stroke and subtlety of blended tone. After journeys to Florence, Venice, and Bologna, he returned to Rome to make a study of the work of Raphael, and to paint his "Cimon and Iphigenia" and his "Angelica and Medoro." En route to England, he visited Genoa and Turin, and at Parma was made a member of the Academy, as he had been in Florence and Bologna.

West arrived in England in August 1763, intending to make only a brief visit. He remained for fifty-seven years. At the time, English painting, apart from portraiture, was generally scorned, and artists were somewhat looked down upon, even the great Reynolds being unable to effect any change in the public attitude. Thanks to his important friends in America and Italy, however, West soon gained entrance to the highest circles, where his agreeable manners and his rather romantic history once more ingratiated him. He paid innumerable visits to private and public galleries, and made a lifelong friend of Sir Joshua Reynolds. He first had lodgings in Bedford Street, Covent Garden. About a year after his arrival in England, on Sept. 2, 1764, he was married at St. Martin's-in-the-Fields (Hart, *post*, p. 8) to Elizabeth Shewell, the daughter of a Philadelphia merchant, Stephen Shewell. A story is often told of family opposition to the marriage and of Elizabeth Shewell's midnight flight from her home in order that she might sail to England with West's father and Matthew Pratt [*q.v.*]. West and his wife had two sons, one of whom followed his father in painting, but without very great success.

One of the first pictures West exhibited in England was his "Angelica and Medoro," shown at Spring Gardens in 1764. About this time he met Samuel Johnson, Burke, Dr. Thomas Newton, bishop of Bristol, Dr. James Johnson, bishop of Worcester, and Dr. Robert Hay Drummond, archbishop of York. For Newton, West painted "The Parting of Hector and Andromache" and a portrait; for the bishop of Worcester, "The Return of the Prodigal Son"; and for Dr. Drummond, in whom he found his most powerful patron, "Agrippina Landing with the Ashes of Germanicus." West's paintings, novel in their departure from the robustness of the English school, took the public fancy, and his studio was thronged with visitors. By 1766 he was immensely popular; in certain newspaper notices of the exhibitions he was given more attention than even Reynolds or Gainsborough. Through Drummond, West was presented to George III, who viewed, and approved, his pictures. Thus began a patronage that resulted not only in years of friendship with George III—West came and went freely in the palace—but also in the execution of a great many paintings, among them most of West's finest work. He became a member of the Incorporated Society of Artists, forerunner of the Royal Academy of Arts, in 1765, and by the king's appointment was made a charter member of the Royal Academy, founded in 1768. He received his first royal commission, for "The Departure of Regulus from Rome," in 1769; soon after (1772), he was appointed historical painter to the king.

His time thereafter was almost completely filled in executing the king's orders. In addition to many portraits of members of the royal family, he painted numerous pictures for Buckingham Palace and Windsor Castle. For Windsor a series of pictures was chosen dealing with the victories of Cressy and Poictiers, and for the king's chapel there an ambitious scheme was worked out for a series of thirty-six pictures on the progress of revealed religion. None of these was in any way unconventional, but when West undertook the "Death of Wolfe" (exhibited in the Royal Academy in 1771), he broke away from the custom of depicting heroes in classic togas and represented them in the military costume of the day. The public and the king took exception, and the king refused to buy the picture, which was secured by Lord Grosvenor and in 1918 was presented by its owner to the Dominion of Canada. Reynolds, at first a hostile critic, finally accepted this degree of realism, and the picture at length brought about a kind of revolution in English historical painting, though West had been anticipated in his innovation in other countries and at other times.

During his years as the king's historical painter, at £1,000 a year, West's position was secure. He was accepted everywhere, succeeded Reynolds as president of the Royal Academy (holding the position, with the exception of one year, from 1792 to 1820), and served both English and American art well by his teaching of young artists. In spite of the fact that he lacked true genius, borrowed indiscriminately from other artists, and was complacently blind to his own faults, he had learned much about painting, and to his pupils he never failed to impart lessons in the formation of a good palette, truthfulness of design, and a sound technique. Among his American pupils were Matthew Pratt, Charles Willson Peale, Gilbert Stuart, John Trumbull, Robert Fulton, Rembrandt Peale, Mather Brown, William Dunlap, Washington Allston, Thomas Sully, S. F. B. Morse, Charles Robert Leslie, and Henry Sargent [qq.v.]. West's interest in young artists was unflagging, his generosity unfailing. Apparently quite free from professional jealousy, he aided such a potential rival as Copley in the most friendly way when the latter went to England, and he had a quick eye for the true virtues of the work of beginners. His critical acumen was displayed also in his frequent purchases in the auction rooms, from which he rescued an unrecognized Titian, "The Death of Actaeon," and in such unlikely places as old-iron shops, where he bought Claude's "The Mill" for, it is said, half a guinea. Leigh Hunt, who was connected with West by marriage, has left a charming picture in his *Autobiography* of the

pleasant house at 14 Newman Street, with its gallery hung with West's pictures and enclosing a square of fresh green lawn, of the artist in his white wool gown, working quietly away in his painting-room, and of Mrs. West in her sitting-room, its walls, too, adorned with West's pictures.

For more than twenty years West had received all orders from the king in person, but in 1801 he had word, indirectly, that all work in the chapel at Windsor Castle was to be suspended. By this time George III had begun to show symptoms of the disease of the mind from which he suffered, and though West came back into favor for a short period, he never was restored to the security of his former position. The old painter wrote a dignified remonstrance to the king, set himself to work upon a new series of religious pictures for public sale, and when in the end (1811) his £1,000 was taken away, made no complaint. One of his religious pictures, "Christ Healing the Sick" (1801), was among his most successful, bringing as much as three thousand guineas. Others were his "Christ Rejected" (c. 1815) and "Death on the Pale Horse" (1817). The final break with the king, West's open sympathy with and admiration for Napoleon (which won him public censure, as his sympathies with the colonies in revolution never had), and the death of his wife on Dec. 6, 1814 (*Analectic Magazine,* June 1815, p. 524), marked the beginning of a decline. His last illness, which was slow and languishing, was rather a general natural decay than a specific malady. He enjoyed perfect mental health until his death early in the morning of Mar. 11, 1820. His body lay in state at the Royal Academy, and he was buried with great honor in St. Paul's Cathedral.

As Samuel Isham [q.v.] has pointed out in a sympathetic analysis of West's career, his life was marked by unusual good fortune, not the least of which was the fact that he was "by character, by training, by countless little personal traits, absolutely fitted to the ideals of the time" (*post,* p. 57). Though he spoke with a curious uncouth accent and wrote illiterately, he was a man of handsome and dignified bearing. He was somewhat slow and mild, even-tempered, and thoroughly benevolent. His personal life was above reproach. There are numerous portraits of West, including one by Gilbert Stuart that shows him as a handsome but sober young man; the most pleasing one, perhaps, is that painted in his youth by Matthew Pratt, now in the Pennsylvania Academy of the Fine Arts, where there is also one of Mrs. West. West painted several self-portraits, and a charming group of himself, his wife, and their child. His only serious fault was his complacency, which, as Isham suggests, was almost essential to his success. His discourses to the students of the Royal Academy (in part reprinted in Galt, *post*) had a sincerity and an honest conviction that give weight to his excessively moralistic views on art, whose purpose he believed was to "assist the reason to reveal virtue through beauty." His paintings, so numerous, so large—"ten-acre canvases," Stuart called them—so well-known, and in his own time so much admired, have now little but an historical interest. Few of them are to be seen in England, except in the provincial museums, but a replica of his "Christ Healing the Sick" is in the Pennsylvania Hospital in Philadelphia; his "Death on the Pale Horse" and "Christ Rejected" are in the Pennsylvania Academy of the Fine Arts; "Penn's Treaty with the Indians," one of the best, is in Independence Hall, Philadelphia, and others, among them a self-portrait, are in the Metropolitan Museum, New York, and in the possession of the Historical Society of Pennsylvania. Apart from the fact that West's pictures are thoroughly out of fashion, they exhibit little genuine power; they are formal and uninspired, poor in color, harsh in outline. Yet his position in the history of English and American painting is an important one, and American art in particular owes him a debt of gratitude for his help and encouragement, given so freely, to young American artists.

[There is no adequate biog. of West. The earliest is that written in West's lifetime by John Galt, *The Life and Studies of Benjamin West* (1816), amplified and reprinted as *The Life, Studies, and Works of Benjamin West* (2 vols., 1820). See also William Dunlap, *The Hist. of the Rise and Progress of the Arts of Design in the U. S.* (3 vols., 1918), ed. by F. W. Bayley and C. E. Goodspeed; C. H. Hart, "Benjamin West's Family," *Pa. Mag. of Hist. and Biog.*, Jan. 1908; W. T. Whitley, *Artists and Their Friends in England, 1700–1799* (2 vols., 1928), which contains much interesting material from contemporary sources; *The Farington Diary* (8 vols., 1922–28), ed. by James Greig, also contemporary; Algernon Graves, *The Royal Acad. of Arts . . . Contributors*, vol. VIII (1906); William Sandby, *The Hist. of the Royal Acad. of Arts* (2 vols., 1862); J. W. Jordan, *Colonial Families of Phila.* (1911); J. F. Watson, *Annals of Phila.* (3 vols., 1879–81), ed. by W. P. Hazard; Samuel Isham, *The Hist. of Am. Painting* (1905); obituary and memoir in *Annual Register*, 1820, pts. 1, 2; death notice in *Times* (London), Mar. 13, 1820. An interesting and well-documented short biog. is to be found in Lewis Einstein's *Divided Loyalties* (1933).]   **M. F.**

WEST, FRANCIS (Oct. 28, 1586–1634?), governor of Virginia, was born in England, probably Hampshire, the son of Thomas West, second or eleventh Baron De La Warr, and his wife Anne, the daughter of Sir Francis Knollys. Three of his brothers participated in the establishment of the Virginia colony, Thomas, the third Baron De La Warr [*q.v.*], and his two younger brothers, Nathaniel and John, who became planters, the latter serving as governor, from 1635 to 1637. Francis arrived in Virginia with Newport in 1608 and was a grantee of the second charter in 1609. He was of the group that quarrelled with Captain Smith and in September deposed him in favor of George Percy [*q.v.*] and a council, of which West became a member. His attempt to establish a settlement at the falls of the James River was abandoned with the winter, and his attention was turned to the all-important problem of obtaining supplies. In a small ship he sought trade with the natives, and, failing, sailed for England before the belated arrival of Gates and Somers in May 1610. He evidently returned within the year, succeeded Percy as commander at Jamestown in 1612, was commissioned master of the ordnance in 1617, and became in time one of the most influential of the "ancient planters," with a seat at Westover, near Berkeley Hundred. He quarrelled with Yeardley over the location of the latter plantation, which he claimed infringed upon the lands of the late Lord De La Warr, and when in England the following year joined with other old planters in petitioning for the appointment of a governor of higher birth. He seems to have become infected with the factionalism that rent the company and to have joined with the enemies of Sir Edwin Sandys. He was commissioned in November 1622 admiral of New England, but upon his arrival there the following summer he found "the fisher men to be stuberne fellows" (Bradford, *post*, I, 312) and returned to Virginia. During these last years of the company he joined other older planters in complaints regarding the conditions of the colony, thereby contributing, though probably not intentionally, to the overthrow of the company. With its dissolution, however, he became alarmed lest this step might involve the withdrawal of the political privileges granted in 1618, and signed several protests against any such action.

He continued to hold the confidence of leaders both in England and Virginia, and, succeeding Yeardley as governor in 1627, he held this post until his departure for England in March 1629. He returned by 1631, and is recorded as present at a meeting of the council in February 1633. His will, made while in England in December 1629, was proved on Apr. 28, 1634. It is probable that he died in Virginia early in 1634. His first wife was Margaret, the widow of Edward Blayney. His second wife was Temperance (Flowerdieu), the widow of Gov. George Yeardley [*q.v.*]. Her death occurred shortly after the marriage, and it must have been on his last trip home that he married Jane, the daughter to Sir Henry Davye. A son, Francis, mentioned in the will seems to have been the only surviving child.

[A. F. Pollard in *D. N. B.*; Alexander Brown, *The Genesis of the U. S.* (1890), vol. II; *The Records of the Va. Co.* (4 vols., 1906–35), ed. by S. M. Kingsbury; *Minutes of the Council and General Court of Colonial Virginia, 1622–1632 and 1670–1679* (1924), ed, by H. R. McIlwaine; Great Brit., Public Record Office, *Calendar of State Papers, Col. Series, 1574–1660* (1860); Great Brit., Privy Council, *Acts of the Privy Council, Col. Series . . . 1613–1680* (1908); Wm. Bradford, *Hist. of Plymouth Plantation* (1912), vol. I, pub. by Mass. Hist. Soc.; *Va. Mag. of Hist. and Biog.*, Apr. 1904.]

W. F. C.

WEST, GEORGE (Feb. 17, 1823–Sept. 20, 1901), paper manufacturer, congressman, son of George and Jane West, was born near Bradninch, Devonshire, England. At an early age he went to work in a Bradninch paper factory. After serving a full apprenticeship, in the course of which he was rapidly advanced, he married Louisa Rose, in April 1844, and five years later brought his family to America. In later years, when he had become a millionaire, he made many trips back to Bradninch and gave generously to the support of the village school that others might have educational advantages which his parents had been unable to furnish him. He also bought and operated an idle paper mill there to give employment to the population.

In Massachusetts, where he established himself after arriving in the United States, he was "burned out," and in 1861 removed to Saratoga County, N. Y., where the waterpower on Kayaderosseras Creek had already attracted numerous investors in the paper-making industry. Here West began in a humble way what was to prove a spectacularly successful career in a similar field. He had at his command a thorough practical knowledge of every phase of the industry, executive talent, a genius for organization, and tremendous energy. By 1878 he was sole proprietor of nine busy mills, the total output of which was estimated to exceed that of any other paper manufacturer in the United States and Europe. He made only one kind of paper— manila wrapping—importing the raw materials until the 1880's, when he established a chemical-process (replaced in 1895 by a soda-process) wood-pulp factory, supplied from his own eight-thousand-acre spruce forest near by. In 1875, at Ballston Spa, where he made his home, he began to utilize some of the paper in the making of grocers' bags, and the immediate and increasing demand for this product was the chief basis of his fortune. He maintained in New York City a large store where the bags were sold and where he kept four presses constantly engaged in printing them for his customers. In 1899 he sold his entire mill interests to the Union Bag & Paper Company for $1,500,000.

From the inception of the Republican party he was one of its stanch members. After representing his district for five terms (1872–76) in the New York Assembly, he entered Congress in 1881, where he remained until 1889, except for the term 1883–84. As a legislator his qualities were described as sterling and solid rather than brilliant. Outspoken and firm in his principles, however, he labored to convince his colleagues by personal contact and in committee. He advocated government ownership of telegraph lines and government control of railroads. Entering Congress just when the Democrats were concentrating their efforts on a downward revision of the tariff, he remained a thoroughgoing protectionist, basing his convictions on his actual experience as a manufacturer and an employer of labor both in the United States and in free-trade England. He was willing, however, to afford the producer of raw materials as much protection as the manufacturer. He tried not to merit his own criticism that too much of the personal element entered into legislation, rather than the good of the country as a whole. "I represent my constituents," he said, "not George West." He was survived by his wife, a son and a daughter.

[Files of *Ballston Jour.*, 1860–1901; N. B. Sylvester, *Hist. of Saratoga County, N. Y.* (1878); G. B. Anderson, *A Descriptive and Biog. Record of Saratoga County, N. Y.* (1899); *Biog. Dir. Am. Cong.* (1928); *Who's Who in America*, 1899–1901; *N. Y. Times* and *N. Y. Herald*, Sept. 21, 1901; information from a grandson.]

E. L. J.

WEST, HENRY SERGEANT (Jan. 21, 1827–Apr. 1, 1876), missionary physician, the son of Dr. Silas and Lucy C. (Sergeant) West, was born in Binghamton, N. Y., in the schools of which community he received his early education. In 1844 he entered Yale College but withdrew in his sophomore year because of ill health. Later he studied medicine in the College of Physicians and Surgeons of New York City, where he received the degree of M.D. in 1850. For several years thereafter he practised medicine in Binghamton. On Sept. 20, 1858, he was married in Watertown, Wis., to Charlotte, daughter of Henry and Mary Youts.

The following January, under the auspices of the American Board of Commissioners for Foreign Missions, the Wests sailed from Boston for Turkey to undertake service in the Northern Armenian (later the West Turkey) Mission. Arriving in Smyrna Feb. 22, they proceeded to Sivas, which was their home for the next seventeen years. Once only, in 1868–69, were they again in America. During this furlough West sat as a member of the annual meeting of the American Board, held at Norwich, Conn., in October 1868. He also read a paper before the Medical Society of the State of New York, entitled "Medical and Surgical Experience in Asia Minor," which was published in the Society's *Transactions* (1869). His first letter to the board refers to the extent of his medical service in 1860. It included "thousands of professional calls," one hundred surgical operations, and as many as one hundred "prescriptions" in a single day. During the years that followed he continued to carry this heavy burden of practice. His surgical work involved lithotomy, and ophthalmic and hernia operations. In over one hundred and fifty lithotomic operations there were but six fatalities. In rendering his medical service he traveled widely, often being called to Tokat, Cæsarea, Marsovan, Harput, and Erzerum, the last-named town being 230 miles from Sivas. He also visited Nicomedia and Adrianople, and was everywhere acclaimed for his skill. He gave training in medicine to a number of young Armenian students and doctors, some of whom entered the employ of the Mission or began practice in distant stations. He also conducted Bible classes in Sivas in the language of the region, Armeno-Turkish. Many of his medical fees were devoted to the building of chapels in various stations.

He contracted typhoid pneumonia and died in Sivas, survived by his widow; their children had all died in infancy. According to a minute of the West Turkey Mission, dated April 1877 (*Missionary Herald,* July 1877, p. 227), West was "unassuming, gentle and courteous in manner, firm and resolute in spirit, of integrity never suspected." He had the high respect of officials and natives, and was beloved by his missionary associates in no ordinary degree.

[*Statistics of the Class of Yale, 1848* (1869); *Ibid.* (1898); *Missionary Herald,* July 1876, July 1877; *British Quarterly Rev.,* Jan. 1878; H. A. Kelly and W. L. Burrage, *Am. Medic. Biogs.* (1920); John Shrady, *The Coll. of Phys. and Surgeons* (n.d.), vol. II; *Trans. Medic. Soc. of the State of N. Y.* (1877); records of the Am. Board of Commissioners for Foreign Missions.]
J. C. Ar—r.

WEST, JOSEPH (d. 1692?), colonial governor of South Carolina, was born in England and left his wife there, when he sailed for America. In 1669 he was made agent and storekeeper for the proprietors, deputy for the Duke of Albemarle, and placed in command of three vessels sent to settle Carolina, after the first attempt by John Yeamans [*q.v.*] failed. His selection by the proprietors for the mission shows he was a man of some importance in England. The vessels were ordered to sail by way of Barbados to Port Royal, where the new plantation was to be established. When they arrived at Barbados, Sir John Yeamans, leader of the first expedition and governor in name, joined the fleet and went as far as Bermuda, where he withdrew after appointing William Sayle governor by authority of the proprietors. Sayle, assisted by West, led the settlers to the Ashley River, and a settlement was made at Albemarle Point. When Sayle died in 1671, West was elected governor by the Council and directed the colony through a trying year, in which there was a great scarcity of provisions. Under his wise guidance, the people conserved their supplies. Each man was required to plant crops, and planting and harvesting were emphasized to the exclusion of all other occupations. He pleased the settlers in this way and also gained favor with the proprietors by obtaining the passage of a measure to authorize the payments of debts incurred in the settlement of Carolina. His authority as governor was contested in 1671 by Sir John Yeamans, who had come to the colony the preceding year. Yeamans claimed that the constitution provided that only a proprietor or a landgrave could be governor, and as a landgrave he was the only individual in the colony having the necessary qualifications. West was supported by the Council, who unanimously refused to remove him without an express order from the proprietors. In 1672 such an order was received, and Yeamans became governor. He was not popular and displeased both settlers and proprietors by his reckless exportation of foodstuffs to Barbados for his own advantage, his extravagance, and his apparent subordination of the interests of Carolina to those of Barbados. His acts contrasted unfavorably with those of West, who shone by comparison and was credited with saving the colony in the economic crisis of 1671. When Yeamans died in 1674, West was made a landgrave and returned to the governorship by the proprietors, a position he held until 1682. During his administration laws regulating the status of slaves, servants, and the militia were passed, and the center of settlement was moved in 1679 or 1680 from Albemarle Point to Oyster Point at the junction of the Ashley and Cooper rivers and was known as New Charles Town. In 1682 the name became Charles Town and so continued for one hundred years until in 1783 it was abbreviated to Charleston. West was removed from office in 1682, accused of selling and sending slaves out of Carolina, but was reinstated in 1684. Some time between June

15 and July 12, 1685, he left the province, and there is evidence that he went to New York and died there before 1692.

[Edward McCrady, *The Hist. of S. C. under the Proprietary Government, 1670–1719* (1897); Alexander Hewat, *An Hist. Account of . . . S. C.* (1779), vol. I; W. J. Rivers, *A Sketch of the Hist. of S. C.* (1856); *Great Brit. Calendar of State Papers, Colonial Series, America and West Indies, 1669–1674* (1889); *S. C. Hist. and Geneal. Mag.*, July 1918, Apr. 1919; *D.N.B.*; Correspondence in Public Record Office, London.]

H. B–C.

WEST, SAMUEL (Mar. 3, 1730 o.s.–Sept. 24, 1807), clergyman, author, was born in Yarmouth, Mass., the son of Dr. Sackfield and Ruth (Jenkins) West. He was a descendant of Francis West who settled in Duxbury, Mass., some time before 1639. Soon after Samuel's birth his family moved to Barnstable, and here he received a scanty schooling. He worked on a neighbor's farm to earn enough for a college education and was graduated at Harvard in 1754 after a brilliant academic career. In 1756 he went to Falmouth as schoolmaster, but his interest in theology led him to enter the ministry and on July 3, 1761, he was ordained pastor of the church in what was then a part of Dartmouth, Mass., but in 1787 was incorporated as New Bedford. Here he preached without interim until poor health forced his retirement in 1803. In 1790 a new church was erected in the neighboring town of Fair Haven, and West preached to both churches at the request of the parishioners. He became familiar early with the writings of Calvin, Grotius, Hobbes, and Dupin, and almost from the inception of his ministerial career preached the Arminian doctrine which opened the way for Unitarianism.

During the Revolutionary War he served for a period as chaplain. The service that gained him most renown was that of deciphering for Washington a treasonable code letter sent by Dr. Benjamin Church [*q.v.*] and intended for a British admiral at Newport. After working all night over the code, West found the key, which revealed that the letter contained valuable information concerning the Continental Army's supplies, number of dead and wounded, shipments of gunpowder to Philadelphia, and other matters of importance (Jared Sparks, *The Writings of George Washington*, vol. III, 1834, p. 502). Among his published discourses were *A Sermon Preached before the Honorable Council* (1776), reprinted in J. W. Thornton, *The Pulpit of the American Revolution* (1860), in which he dealt summarily with the tyrannical attitude of England, declaring that "Tyranny and arbitrary power are utterly inconsistent with and subversive of the very end and design of civil govern-

ment" (Thornton, p. 274). Another of his discourses was *An Anniversary Sermon Preached at Plymouth, Dec. 22d, 1777* (1778).

After the war West engaged in the Calvinistic-Arminian controversy, both in the pulpit and through publications. He preached without notes, and, according to Alden Bradford (*post*, p. 426), he "had a good measure of independence in his inquiries." In 1793 he published *Essays on Liberty and Necessity*, an enlarged edition of which appeared in 1795. These essays were a reply to the views of Jonathan Edwards [*q.v.*], and according to West were "penned about twenty years ago." His chief arguments against Edwards were that divine prescience does not imply the necessity of future events; that self-determination is consistent with moral agency; that the Deity's permission of sin is proof for the self-governing power of men; and that volition is an effect which has a cause. Of all the replies to Edwards' *Freedom of the Will*, West's was most thorough and most persuasive. He helped to widen the rift that had already appeared between Calvinist and Arminian. He was much interested in the prophetic portions of the Bible and was convinced that they contained predictions of the course of events in the Revolution (Sprague, *post*, pp. 39, 43). He was also interested in alchemy and was imposed upon by a man who claimed he could turn salt water into fresh (*Ibid.*, 44, 46).

His activities in civil life were extensive. He was one of the committee appointed to frame the Massachusetts constitution, and was a delegate-at-large to the convention that drew up the federal Constitution. He is credited with having persuaded Hancock to vote for the latter instrument (*Ibid.*, pp. 40–41). After his retirement in 1803 he went to live with a son in Tiverton, R. I., where he died. Throughout his life he was noted for his absent-mindedness, and many stories regarding his unconventional appearances have survived. In his later years his memory failed entirely. He was married first, Mar. 7, 1768, to Experience Howland, by whom he had six children; she died in 1789, and in January 1790, he married Lovisa (Hathaway) Jenne.

[Alden Bradford, *Biog. Sketches of Distinguished Men in New England* (1842); W. B. Sprague, *Annals of the Am. Unitarian Pulpit* (1865); S. A. Eliot, *Heralds of a Liberal Faith* (1910), vol. I; Franklyn Howland, *A Hist. of the Town of Acushnet* (1907); Letta B. Stone, *The West Family Register* (1928).]

E. H. D.

WEST, WILLIAM EDWARD (Dec. 10, 1788–Nov. 2, 1857), portrait painter, was born in Lexington, Ky., the son of Edward West, a watchmaker and inventor, a man of uncommon mechanical talents. According to James Reid Lambdin [*q.v.*], young West began by painting miniatures. Several years later he went to Philadelphia to study under Thomas Sully [*q.v.*]. He spent a number of years after that at Natchez, Tenn., where he painted many of the best of his early pictures. In 1822, under the patronage of a resident of Nashville, he went to Europe, and soon won widespread celebrity through his portrait of Lord Byron, painted at Leghorn. (For West's account of the sittings, see Thomas Moore, *Letters and Journals of Lord Byron*, 1885, vol. II, pp. 414–15). During the sittings for a portrait of the Countess Guiccioli, which followed that of Byron, West is said to have met Shelley and Leigh Hunt. In England, where he went next, he painted a number of portraits, including that of Mrs. Hemans. According to the letters of Washington Irving, who visited him there, West was in Paris in the winter of 1824–25. He exhibited at the Royal Academy, chiefly portraits, from 1826 to 1833, and in other London exhibitions until 1837, but by 1840 had returned to America. He appears in New York City directories from 1840 to 1850 and again in 1852. In his later years he went once more to Nashville, where he died.

Almost until the day of his death he was engaged in painting. His first successful pieces were illustrations for Washington Irving's "The Pride of the Village" and "Annette Delarbre," but according to Henry Theodore Tuckerman [*q.v.*] he excelled in "fancy cabinet portraits." Among his more ambitious works were portraits of G. H. Calvert and Thomas Swann. "The Confessional," said to be a favorite of Irving's, is in the collection of the New York Historical Society. West was an intimate friend of Charles Robert Leslie, Washington Irving [*qq.v.*], and Sir David Wilkie.

[William Dunlop, *A Hist. of the Rise and Progress of the Arts of Design in the U. S.* (3 vols., 1918), ed. by F. W. Bayley and C. E. Goodspeed; H. T. Tuckerman, *Book of the Artists* (1867); *The Life and Letters of Washington Irving.* vol. II (1862), p. 228; Algernon Graves, *The Royal Acad. . . . Dict. of Contributors*, vol. VIII (1906) and *A Dict. of Artists . . . London Exhibitions from 1760 to 1893* (1901); *Nashville Union and American*, Nov. 3, 1857.]   W. H. D.

WESTCOTT, EDWARD NOYES (Sept. 27, 1846–Mar. 31, 1898), author and banker, was born in Syracuse, N. Y., the third child of Amos and Clara (Babcock) Westcott (Stephen Babcock, *Babcock Genealogy*, 1903, p. 259). His father was a dentist and the first president of the New York State Dental Society. Edward attended the Syracuse schools until he was sixteen, and then became a junior clerk in the Mechanics' Bank of Syracuse. From 1866 to 1868 he worked in the New York office of the Mutual Life Insurance Company, returning to Syracuse to become discount clerk in the Second National Bank. After its dissolution he was a teller in the First National Bank, and later cashier of Wilkinson & Company, bankers. In 1880 he organized the firm of Westcott & Abbott, bankers and brokers, which flourished until it was involved in the failure of Wilkinson & Company. Westcott then became secretary to the Syracuse Water Commission, serving until June 1895, when failing health compelled him to retire. In 1874 he married Jane Dows of Buffalo, who at her death in 1890 left two sons and a daughter.

The summer of 1895 Westcott spent at Lake Meacham in the Adirondacks, where, suffering from tuberculosis, he began the work by which he is chiefly known—*David Harum, A Story of American Life*. The nucleus of the story—David's cancellation of the Widow Cullom's mortgage (chapters XIX–XXIV)—was completed there. The latter part of the winter of 1895–96 he spent near Naples at Alexander Henry Davis' home overlooking the Bay, the Villa Violante of *David Harum*. Through the following fifteen months of illness and increasing weakness, Westcott continued with genuine delight to recount David's adventures and remarks, and towards the end of 1896 completed them. After thorough revision the manuscript began its now proverbial rounds to New York, Boston, and Chicago, being refused by six well-known publishers. "It's vulgar and smells of the stables," commented one publisher's reader. On Dec. 23, 1897, the manuscript was received by D. Appleton & Company, and was accepted by Ripley Hitchcock on Jan. 17, 1898, in a cordial letter to the author. To abridgment and slight rearrangement the author consented, conscious that publication would probably be posthumous. He died on Mar. 31, not suspecting that appreciation and fame were near.

Six months later, Sept. 23, 1898, *David Harum* was published. Its popularity was immediate and prolonged. By Jan. 1, 1899, the book was in its sixth large printing, and by Feb. 1, 1901, after two years at or near the top of the lists of best sellers, over 400,000 copies had been sold, a record then surpassed only by *In His Steps* and *Trilby*. Thirty-five years after its appearance more than a million copies had been sold, and, for the most of this period, of books published in America it stood second in popularity only to *Quo Vadis*. In 1900 *David Harum* was dramatized, William H. Crane [*q.v.*] playing David for more than two years. Crane also played the leading rôle in a motion-picture version. Westcott's short story, *The Teller*, in which masquerades the John Lenox of *David Harum*, was published, along with a selection from his letters, in 1901. Two poems, "Sonnet" and "Chacun à son bon Goût," appeared in *Harper's Magazine*, January 1900. He wrote occasionally on matters of current political and financial interest, and prepared wholly or in part some of the pamphlets issued by the Reform Club of New York, of which he was a member. Westcott's avocation was music. An excellent singer, he also composed the words and music for several songs.

[The Syracuse Pub. Lib. published in 1918 a pamphlet listing the contents of its unique Westcott collection. The following items in this collection are especially notable: Violet Westcott Morawetz's scrapbook of clippings; Forbes Heermans' scrapbook; typewritten copies of the original MS. of *David Harum*; and *The Teller* . . . *with the Letters of Edward Noyes Westcott* . . . *and an Account of His Life* (1901); also letters, genealogy, portraits, etc. A heated correspondence concerning Westcott ran in the *N. Y. Times: Saturday Rev. of Books and Art*, Oct. 22, 1898–Dec. 23, 1899. Articles about Westcott appeared in *Book News*, May 1899; *Critic*, July 1899, and *Academy*, Sept. 16, 1899. P. M. Paine of Syracuse and others have furnished information.]   B. H.

WESTCOTT, THOMPSON (June 5, 1820–May 8, 1888), historian of Philadelphia, lawyer, journalist, the son of Charles and Hannah (Davis) Westcott, was born in Philadelphia, where his father was a hatter. He received his early education in the English school conducted by the University of Pennsylvania, and when about twelve entered the office of a Philadelphia conveyancer, Charles M. Page. He advanced so rapidly in his employer's service that when he was but seventeen he became a partner. Two years later he began to study law under Henry M. Phillips, and on Nov. 10, 1841, was admitted to the Philadelphia bar. He continued in the conveyancing business for a short period, and then devoted himself to his law practice.

Becoming interested in literary pursuits, he began to write humorous stories for the *St. Louis Reveille*, the *Evening Mirror* of New York, and the *Knickerbocker, or New-York Monthly Magazine*. His stories were signed with the *nom de plume* "Joe Miller, Jr.," and the only remuneration he received for writing them was the joy of seeing them in print. In 1846 he became law reporter for the Philadelphia *Public Ledger* and continued to serve as such until 1851. In May 1848, although he had seen several disastrous attempts at Sunday journalism in his native city, he undertook to edit the *Sunday Dispatch*. Its first number, which appeared May 14, 1848, contained only two advertisements, and the entire proceeds from its sales were twenty-eight cents. Westcott was the entire staff, and continued to do all of the editorial labor for several years. The *Dispatch* provoked earnest and influential opposition from those who objected to a newspaper being published on Sunday, but it was continued with increasing patronage, even though newsboys were arrested for selling it, and at the end of the first year it carried ten columns of advertisements, and was gaining in influence. While its strong, independent policy contributed to its success, Westcott made it of local interest, also, by a feature then new to journalism: he wrote for it several historical series that made it extremely valuable, and engaged other writers to contribute series of a similar nature. Foremost of Westcott's series was his "History of Philadelphia; from the Time of the First Settlements on the Delaware to the Consolidation of the City and Districts in 1854." This series was begun Jan. 6, 1867, and when the editor left the paper, Apr. 26, 1884, he had brought the narrative down only to the year 1829. In addition to editing the *Dispatch*, he became, in 1863, an editorial writer for the *Philadelphia Inquirer*, continuing as such until May 1869, during part of which period he also wrote for the Philadelphia *Commercial List*. He edited the *Old Franklin Almanac* from 1860 to 1872, and the *Public Ledger Almanac* from 1870 until within a year or two of his death.

For a short time after leaving the *Dispatch* he was on the editorial staff of the *Philadelphia Record*. He was the author of several books, but is principally remembered as one of the authors of J. T. Scharf and Thompson Westcott's *History of Philadelphia* (3 vols., 1884), the most comprehensive account of that city that had appeared. Other books published by Westcott were: *Life of John Fitch, Inventor of the Steamboat* (1857); *Chronicles of the Great Rebellion* (1867); *Official Guide Book of Philadelphia* (1875, 1876); *Historic Mansions and Buildings of Philadelphia* (1877). As a student of history Westcott did an enormous amount of independent research work, the bulk of which was reflected in his numerous articles in the *Dispatch*. In the field to which he confined himself he was regarded as authority. He died in Philadelphia.

[*Public Ledger* (Phila.), May 9, 1888; E. H. Munday, "The Press of Phila. in 1870: *Sunday Dispatch*," in *The Proof-Sheet*, Nov. 1870; Joseph Jackson, *Encyc. of Phila.*, vol. IV (1933).]   J. J.

WESTERN, LUCILLE (Jan. 8, 1843–Jan. 11, 1877), actress, was one of two sisters who rose from the most inferior ranks of the stage to astonishing popularity and celebrity. In their earlier days they were billed as "the Star Sisters," the younger, Helen, dying in Washington, D. C.

Dec. 11, 1868 (*New York Clipper, post*). Lucille Western (whose name was originally Pauline Lucille) continued during eight years thereafter to be a conspicuous and in many ways a tempestuous figure on the American stage. She and her sister were born in New Orleans, the daughters of George Western, a comedian, and of an actress who became known after her second marriage to William B. English, an actor and playwright, as Mrs. Jane English. Both Lucille and Helen were on the stage almost from their infancy, being exploited throughout their childhood by their mother and stepfather. As early as 1849, Lucille was dancing at the National Theatre in Boston, and for some seasons both the sisters were acting and dancing in the theatres of the New England circuit, in New York, and elsewhere, in a curious hodgepodge sort of entertainment known as *The Three Fast Men, or, the Female Robinson Crusoes,* its only merit being the opportunity it gave them to show their skill at rapid changes of costume and at the clever and farcical impersonation of mode characters. One of its features was a female minstrel scene.

When Lucille grew to maturity, her forte became the acting of emotional rôles. From season to season she reached New York again and again on her tours throughout the country, and she thus acquired a wide repute at an early age. She was not long past her twentieth year when she made herself famous in a great variety of characters designed especially to reveal a range of feminine emotions and passions, some of the more important being the dual rôles of Lady Isabel and Madame Vine in *East Lynne,* Camille, Lucretia Borgia, Leah the Forsaken, Cynthia in *Flowers of the Forest,* Peg Woffington in *Masks and Faces,* and Mrs. Haller in *The Stranger.* One of her most popular and famous impersonations was of Nancy in *Oliver Twist,* and during two or three seasons she was a leading figure in a triple-star cast that included Edward L. Davenport [*q.v.*] as Bill Sikes, and the younger James W. Wallack [*q.v.*] as Fagin. With Davenport, she also played the Queen in *Hamlet,* and the dual rôles in *East Lynne.* She had been in ill health for some time, but persisted in a continuance of her tours until early in 1877 she reached Brooklyn, where after acting Nancy in *Oliver Twist* through a Wednesday matinée, she was compelled to abandon her engagement at the Park Theatre in that city, dying at her hotel the following evening of pneumonia. She had married James Harrison Meade of St. Louis, Mo., in 1859, and was later separated from him.

Lucille Western was one of the many wayward geniuses of the stage, striking and appealing in everything she did, but impulsive rather than artistic. In her interpretation of character she was emotional on the stage for the simple reason that she was always herself temperamentally emotional. She has been described by one of her fellow actors as having features somewhat of a Jewish cast, with eyes a peculiar gray that seemed at times a bright black and lustrous (Rogers, *post,* p. 537). Had it not been for her spendthrift habits she might have amassed a large fortune as a result of her great popular success on the stage.

[See G. C. D. Odell, *Annals of the New York Stage,* vol. VII (1931) ; H. P. Phelps, *Players of a Century, a Record of the Albany Stage* (1880) ; T. A. Brown, *A Hist. of the N. Y. Stage* (3 vols., 1903) ; J. B. Clapp and E. F. Edgett, *Players of the Present* (3 vols., 1899–1901), *N. Y. Clipper,* Jan. 20, 1877, a valuable source from which the date of birth is taken ; *N. Y. Times,* Feb. 27, 1876, Jan. 12, 1877 (obituary) ; *N. Y. Dramatic Mirror,* Apr. 23, 1898 ; B. G. Rogers, in *Theatre,* Dec. 22, 1888.]
E. F. E.

WESTERVELT, JACOB AARON (Jan. 20, 1800–Feb. 21, 1879), shipbuilder, mayor of New York City, was born in Tenafly, N. J., the son of Aaron Westervelt who had married his cousin, Vroutie Westervelt. He was descended from Lubbert Lubbertson van Westervelt who had come from Meppel on the Zuider Zee with his brother Willem to New Amsterdam in the *Hoop* in 1662. They had settled in Bergen County, N. J., around Hackensack. Aaron, a farmer in comfortable circumstances, removed to New York City in 1805, where Jacob attended the private school of James P. Forrester until his father's death. Attracted to the sea, he took a special course in surveying and navigation, but voyages to Charleston, S. C., and France quickly disillusioned him about the glamor of a sailor's life. He began his long shipbuilding career in 1817 when he became apprenticed to Christian Bergh [*q.v.*], who ranked with Henry Eckford [*q.v.*] at the head of New York's East River shipbuilders. In 1820, Bergh released him to go to Charleston where, with slave labor, he built two schooners. Returning to New York in 1822, Westervelt, together with Robert Carnley, became a silent partner of Bergh until 1835, when Bergh retired. During that time, the yard on Corlear's Hook turned out seventy-one vessels, including several of the transatlantic packets which were the crack ships of the day. Their packets included the *Montano* (1822) ; *Paris* (1823) ; *Edward Bonaffe* (1824) ; *France* (1827) ; *Rhone, Nashville* and *President* (1831) ; *Philadelphia* (1832) ; *Montreal* and *Utica* (1833) ; and *Toronto* (1835).

A year with Carnley in Europe enabled Westervelt to study the most advanced methods of shipbuilding, and when he returned he entered a short-lived partnership with Nathan Roberts, and built two ships across the East River at Williamsburg. In 1841, he entered his third partnership, this time with William Mackey. This lasted about ten years. Westervelt built on his own account for a while and then, in 1859, his son Daniel became the active managing partner for his father until the latter's retirement in 1868. Much of Westervelt's building was done around the old Bergh site on Corlear's Hook. From 1821 to 1868, he is said to have built 247 vessels of all descriptions, including 174 seagoing vessels with a total tonnage of 139,369. These included at least ninety-one ships and thirty-six steamers. Among the East River shipbuilders of the second quarter of the century, he might be ranked second to William H. Webb and just ahead of Jacob Bell [qq.v.].

Continuing at first with packets, Westervelt built the *Baltimore* (1836), *Oneida* (1841), and *Devonshire* (1847). His first important steamships were the 1700-ton *Washington* and *West Point* in 1847. The golden years of clipper construction found Westervelt, like Webb and Bell, working overtime. He produced the *N. B. Palmer, Eureka, Hornet,* and *Golden Gate* in 1851; *Golden City* and *Contest* in 1852; and *Golden State, Resolute,* and *Kathay* in 1853. In 1856, he made a ninety-five-day trip to San Francisco in the *Sweepstakes,* built by his sons in 1853. His son Aaron also built the *Aramingo* in 1851. Except for the *Eureka,* sharp and unpopular, the Westervelt clippers were highly satisfactory, though none attained the perfection of certain McKay and Webb productions. About 1854, he contracted to build the United States steam frigate *Brooklyn* and during the Civil War he built the hulls for several gunboats.

In 1852, during the height of his clipper construction, he was elected mayor of New York City on the Democratic ticket, serving through 1854. In 1870, after his retirement, he became superintendent of docks and from 1873 to his death, he was president of the dock commissioners. He also served many years as president of the Society of Mechanics and Tradesmen. He was a member of the South Reformed Church in New York. On Apr. 25, 1825, he was married to Eliza M. Thompson, who bore him five sons and three daughters.

[W. T. Westervelt, *Geneal. of the Westervelt Family* (1905); J. H. Morrison, *Hist. of N. Y. Shipyards* (1909); "The Old Shipbuilders of New York," *Harper's Mag.,* July 1882; O. T. Howe, F. C. Matthews, *Am. Clipper Ships* (2 vols., 1926–27); C. C. Cutler, *Greyhounds of the Sea* (1930); A. H. Clark, *The Clipper Ship Era* (1910); H. I. Chappelle, *Hist. of Am. Sailing Ships* (1935); N. Y. Herald, Feb. 22, 1879.]
R. G. A.

WESTINGHOUSE, GEORGE (Oct. 6, 1846–Mar. 12, 1914), inventor, manufacturer, was born at Central Bridge, N. Y., the eighth of ten children of George and Emeline (Vedder) Westinghouse. His father, a manufacturer of agricultural implements at Schenectady, N. Y., came of Westphalian stock, settled for three generations in New England; his mother was of Dutch-English ancestry. At the age of fifteen young George ran away to the Civil War, but was brought home by parental authority; at sixteen and a half, however, he was permitted to enlist in the Union army; late in 1864 he was honorably discharged and joined the navy, being mustered out in 1865 with the grade of acting third-assistant engineer. For three months that fall he attended Union College, Schenectady, as a sophomore, but soon returned to his father's shop to resume his contacts with machinery and inventions. On Oct. 31, 1865, he had obtained his first patent, for a rotary steam engine; later, finding it impractical, he made use of the same principle in a water meter. In 1865 he also secured patents on a car-replacer for putting derailed freight cars onto the track, and in 1868 and 1869 he developed a railroad frog. Meanwhile, on Aug. 8, 1867, he married Marguerite Erskine Walker. Their only child was a son, George Westinghouse, third.

It was in the railroad field that Westinghouse made his first major contribution. On Apr. 13, 1869, when he was still under twenty-three, the first air-brake patent was issued to him, and on Sept. 28, 1869, the Westinghouse Air Brake Company was incorporated under the laws of Pennsylvania. Twenty or more air-brake patents were subsequently awarded as the automatic features were developed. This invention was of revolutionary importance; it made high-speed railroad travel safe by replacing the tedious process of tightening down brakes on each car, as had previously been necessary, and enabling the engine driver, from his cab, to slow down and stop the train at will. As the air brake's significance developed, Westinghouse saw the advisability of making all air-brake apparatus standardized and interchangeable, so that apparatus on cars of different roads would work together, and improved brake systems could be used with earlier models. Thus Westinghouse was one of the first industrialists to apply modern standardization of equipment.

As the air-brake system took form, Westinghouse saw the need for adequate railroad signals. In 1880 he began to purchase signal and interlocking switch patents which he combined with his own inventions until a complete signal system had been developed. In 1882 the Union Switch & Signal Company was organized, with headquarters in Pittsburgh. Early in this work, the importance of electrical control of signals came to be recognized, and it was undoubtedly this association with electrical circuits that led Westinghouse to his interest in electrical processes and inventions. During the decade 1880–90 he took out more than 125 patents, in such diverse fields as air-brakes, signals, natural-gas production and control, and electrical power transmission and utilization, and organized, in addition to the two companies already mentioned, the Westinghouse Brake Company, Ltd., in Great Britain, the Philadelphia Company (natural gas), the Westinghouse Machine Company, and the Westinghouse Electric Company, as well as several companies in Europe.

In 1883, when the attention of Westinghouse was attracted to natural gas, this fuel was already being brought into Pittsburgh in a crude manner which led to many dangerous accidents. Applying his special knowledge of compressed-air problems, Westinghouse in two years had applied for some thirty-eight patents on apparatus for the transmission of natural gas. He developed a pressure system of transmission by which the gas was first conducted through eight-inch lines, then the diameter was stepped up to ten inches as the pressure fell, and so on through twelve, twenty, twenty-four, and thirty inches, with successively lower pressure stages. This natural-gas experiment, in which Westinghouse continued during its period of technical development, prepared his active mind for the rapid comprehension of the principles of "high voltage," "step-up" and "step-down" transformers and "low-tension distribution" of electricity which inventors like Gaulard, Gibbs, and Tesla were later to expound to him.

In 1885 ·Westinghouse heard of the inventions of Gaulard and Gibbs, in France, by which single-phase alternating currents could be transmitted at high voltage over very small wires, and then, by "secondary generators" or transformers, stepped down to lower voltages for local distribution. He immediately secured a set of transformers and a Siemens alternating-current generator from Europe, and set up a system in Pittsburgh. At the same time he enlisted the services of three young electrical engineers, William Stanley [q.v.], Albert Schmid, and O. B. Shallenberger, and asked them to build trans-

formers suitable for American conditions. Under his driving energy, the task was completed during the first three weeks of December 1885, and the Stanley "shell-type" transformer was ready for manufacture—in contradistinction to the Gaulard and Gibbs "core-type" transformer. Stanley also introduced the improvement of arranging his transformers in parallel, with constant voltage across the supply circuit, whereas the Gaulard and Gibbs system, as purchased by Westinghouse, contemplated operating the transformers in series. On Jan. 8, 1886, the Westinghouse Electric Company was incorporated, but when the new high-voltage alternating-current single-phase system was ready for the market, it was immediately attacked by many experienced electrical men as being both dangerous and deadly. Ordinances were passed forbidding the high-tension currents to be carried along the streets of cities and towns, and then, as a final brilliant stroke, the opposition succeeded in having a standard Westinghouse alternator purchased as the official means of state execution at Albany, N. Y., thus adding electrocution to the known methods of capital punishment as the outgrowth of a commercial war against the new alternating current. Some fifty years later, however, probably ninety-seven per cent. of all the electricity produced was transmitted as alternating current, fulfilling the Westinghouse vision engendered by the crude iron spools and copper coils imported from the Gaulard and Gibbs laboratories.

In 1886, however, although the new alternating-current system was adapted to light lamps, it was not adapted to run motors, and there were no meters to measure the electricity supplied to customers. Again Westinghouse enlisted his lieutenants, and the meter problem was solved by Shallenberger, who developed an induction meter to operate on alternating current, and even had the nucleus of a motor to exhibit to Westinghouse when the latter called to his aid a young man from Budapest, Nikola Tesla, who had already patented a form of alternating-current motor of the polyphase type. Westinghouse purchased the Tesla patents, and then hired the inventor to improve his system, and after a long period of study, engineering adaptation, and compromise, a two-phase system was developed satisfactory for both lamps and motors. Meanwhile actual experiments in high-tension transmission were carried on. The first, conducted by Stanley at Great Barrington, Mass., in 1886, lighted a number of dwellings and shops. Later, at Lawrenceville, a suburb of Pittsburgh, 400 lamps were supplied with power over a 2,000-

volt transmission line from the center of Pittsburgh.

Shortly afterwards, in 1889, came the removal of the Westinghouse air-brake works from Allegheny to the Turtle Creek Valley at Wilmerding, east of Pittsburgh. Here Westinghouse undertook to build a model factory and model town, patterned after industrial towns abroad. Some time later, the Electric Company was moved from Garrison Alley, Pittsburgh, to the Turtle Creek Valley at East Pittsburgh, where the Machine Company works were also established. Meanwhile other Westinghouse enterprises were being inaugurated all over the world, until the associated companies employed more than 50,000 people.

From 1893, in which year the Westinghouse Electric Company contracted to light the World's Columbian Exposition at Chicago and to develop the power of Niagara Falls, using alternating current, down through 1907, the business of Westinghouse interests flourished, but in 1907, overtaken by the panic of that year, the Electric and Machine companies were thrown into receivership and the founder lost control. In 1908, through a financial plan proposed by him, the former company was restored to its stockholders, Westinghouse continuing as president, but with powers greatly limited. In 1911 he gave up his efforts to resume control, and shortly afterward ceased active connection. It was during this period (1905 to 1910) that Westinghouse rendered great public service as one of the three trustees engaged in the reorganization of the Equitable Life Assurance Society, the other two being Grover Cleveland, former president of the United States, and Morgan J. O'Brien, presiding judge of the New York supreme court. These three, selected for their unquestioned honesty, disinterestedness, and intelligence, were able to bring about the mutualization of the company, preserving the interests of some six million small investors in the $400,000,000 stock of the Equitable.

After relinquishing his connection with the companies he had founded Westinghouse continued his experiments with the steam turbine and reduction gear, and with an air-spring for automobiles, but late in 1913 his health broke and heart disease developed and early in 1914, while in New York City, he died. In his active and many-sided career two accomplishments stand out sharply in their revolutionary influence on civilization: the invention of the air brake and its application to railroading, and the introduction of alternating current for electric power transmission and rotating-field motors.

In the course of forty-eight years he took out some 400 patents. His great imagination continually sought new fields to develop; his characteristic determination and courage invariably carried him through to the final technical triumph. His gifted associate, Nikola Tesla, wrote of him (*Electrical World,* Mar. 21, 1914): "I like to think of George Westinghouse as he appeared to me in 1888, when I saw him for the first time. The tremendous potential energy of the man had only in part taken kinetic form, but even to a superficial observer the latent force was manifest. A powerful frame, well proportioned, with every joint in working order, an eye as clear as crystal, a quick and springy step—he presented a rare example of health and strength. Like a lion in a forest, he breathed deep and with delight the smoky air of his factories. Though past forty then, he still had the enthusiasm of youth. Always smiling, affable and polite, he stood in marked contrast to the rough and ready men I met. . . . And yet no fiercer adversary than Westinghouse could have been found when he was aroused. An athlete in ordinary life, he was transformed into a giant when confronted with difficulties which seemed unsurmountable. He enjoyed the struggle and never lost confidence. When others would give up in despair he triumphed. Had he been transferred to another planet with everything against him he would have worked out his salvation."

[H. G. Prout, *A Life of George Westinghouse* (1921); F. E. Leupp, *George Westinghouse* (1918); S. T. Wellman, *George Westinghouse* (1914); Arthur Warren, *George Westinghouse 1846–1914, A Tribute* (Westinghouse Electric and Manufacturing Company, n.d.); Frank Crane, *George Westinghouse* (booklet, 1925); J. T. Faris, *Men Who Conquered* (1922); F. C. Harper, *Pittsburgh of Today* (1931), vol. II; *Who's Who in America,* 1912–13; *The Alternating System* (1888) and *The Incandescent Lamp as an Article of Manufacture* (1889), both issued by the Westinghouse Electric Company; *The Westinghouse Companies in the Railway and Industrial Fields* (1905); *N. Y. Times,* Mar. 13, 1914; *Electrical World,* Mar. 21, 1914.]

O. H. C.

WESTON, EDWARD PAYSON (Mar. 15, 1839–May 12, 1929), long-distance walker, was born in Providence, R. I., the son of Silas and Maria (Gaines) Weston. His father was a merchant, not too successful, and his mother was a novelist and magazine writer, author of *Kate Felton* (1859) and several other books fairly popular in New England at that time. The family removed to Boston where Edward attended the Adams School and obtained employment in 1853 selling candy, magazines and newspapers on the Boston, Providence & Stonington Railroad. The following year he plied that same trade on the New York-Fall River steamers and in 1855 he was an apprentice to a jeweler for six months.

From that he turned to join a circus as a drummer in the band but was struck by lightning and took it as a warning to quit that mode of life. As a child and youth he was sickly and underweight and took to rambling about Boston and vicinity, doing odd jobs and selling his mother's novels. It was through walking from house to house, and from town to town, that he improved his health and developed himself as a pedestrian.

His first effort at long-distance walking came as a result of a wager with a friend that he could walk from Boston to Washington, D. C., 478 miles by road, in ten consecutive days. He started on Feb. 22, 1861, and planned to be in Washington in time to witness the first inauguration of President Lincoln. He reached the capital on Mar. 4, too late to witness the inaugural ceremony, but the newspapers made much of his performance, especially in view of his youth and rather frail build. He published privately an account of this trip under the title *The Pedestrian* (1862). Newspaper accounts state that he was a Union spy during the Civil War but there appears to be no official evidence to substantiate the report. After the war he became a messenger boy and later a police reporter for the *New York Herald* and, in lieu of telephones, his endurance and speed as a walker gave him the edge on his competitors.

In 1867 he set out definitely to capitalize his ability; he walked from Portland, Me., to Chicago, Ill. (1,326 miles), in twenty-six days. This was his first real professional venture. Forty years later he duplicated this trip and bettered his own record by twenty-nine hours. He walked in races of all kinds, including the six-day go-as-you-please races in the old Madison Square Garden in New York City and the Astley Belt walking race in Agricultural Hall, London, a contest that he won in 1879. In 1883 he toured England on foot, walking fifty miles a day for one hundred days, and in addition delivered temperance lectures at each stopping-place for a church society. He once walked one hundred measured miles in Westchester County, N. Y., in twenty-two hours, nineteen minutes, and ten seconds. In 1909, when he was seventy years of age, he walked from New York to San Francisco (3,895 miles), in 104 days and seven hours. The following year he made the return journey over a shorter route (3,600 miles) in about seventy days. He was a picturesque figure with his white hair, white mustache, velvet tunic, high gaiters, and small cane or "swagger stick." In 1927 he was struck by a taxicab, became partially crippled, and lived for two more years. He was rescued from poverty in his old age by Anne Nichols, the author of "Abie's Irish Rose." He was buried in St. John's Cemetery, Middle Village, New York City, and was survived by his wife, Maria Weston, from whom he had been separated for many years, and two daughters.

[*Who's Who in America*, 1920–21; *Weston and His Walks* (1910); *N. Y. Herald Tribune*, *N. Y. Times*, May 14, 1929; *Brooklyn Daily Eagle*, May 19, 1929; Associated Press Sketch No. 823, in the files of the New York Times, N. Y. City.]   J.K.

WESTON, NATHAN AUSTIN (Apr. 5, 1868–Nov. 29, 1933), economist, was born at Champaign, Ill., the son of Nathan and Jane (Cloyd) Weston. He prepared for college in the local high school and in 1889 received the degree of B.L. from the University of Illinois. The next four years were spent in teaching in the public schools, and he became an instructor in the academy of the University in 1893. On Sept. 4, 1894, he was married to Angelina Gayman of Champaign. They had two children. While teaching he carried on graduate study in economics and history, was awarded a fellowship in the University of Wisconsin, and received the degree of M.L. from the University of Illinois in 1898. He was a fellow at Cornell University and in 1899–1900 an assistant in political economy there. He received the Ph.D. degree from Cornell in 1901. In 1910–11 he studied at the University of Berlin. He was called to the University of Illinois in 1900, where he became professor in 1919. In 1908 he was made assistant director of the courses in business administration and in 1915 acting dean of the College of Commerce. At his own request he was relieved of these administrative duties in 1919 and devoted himself entirely to his teaching, after 1920 to the teaching of graduate students only. He continued, however, to serve on numerous important committees, and his sound judgment and tolerance were highly valued by his colleagues.

His great work was teaching. His students found him a wise counselor and inspiring teacher, who insisted on a broad and rigorous training and stimulated them not only to acquire a wide knowledge of their fields but also to sharpen their ability to analyze data critically and to think logically. His influence on the study of economics was widespread and important, carried by the large number of those who studied under him. He was himself a man of wide reading, professional and cultural, and unusually well acquainted with the literature of economics. His own library was notable for its size and the range of its economic subjects. One of his special interests was the development of the quantity theory of money. His knowledge of the history of economic thought was profound, and he is to be regarded as one of the foremost American students of orthodox classical economic doctrine. He steadfastly refused to write in his field, holding that its existing literature was already unnecessarily voluminous and much of it superficial and repetitious. A follower of the ideas of Alfred Marshall, he thought that little that was new had been added to the field of economic theory in the past forty years, and that much of that was unimportant. His published papers in the field of economics were only three in number: a statistical inquiry into *The Cost of Production of Corn in Illinois in 1896* (1898); "The Study of the National Monetary Commission" in the *Annals of the American Academy of Political and Social Science* of January 1922; and "The Ricardian Epoch in American Economics," a masterly analysis in the *American Economic Review* of March 1933.

[Notes and papers in possession of daughter, Janet Weston, Champaign, Ill.; *Amer. Econ. Rev.,* Mar. 1934; *The Semi-Centennial Alumni Record of the Univ. of Ill.* (1918), ed. by F. W. Scott; *Who's Who in America,* 1932–33; *N. Y. Times,* Nov. 30, 1933.]

D. K.

WESTON, THOMAS (*c.* 1575–*c.* 1644), merchant adventurer and colonist, was largely responsible for financing the first voyage of the *Mayflower.* A successful ironmonger at Aldgate in London, he had joined, by 1617, a group of merchants whose unlicensed shipments of cloth to the Netherlands brought them into conflict with the Merchant Adventurers of London. In 1618 he and his associates were ordered by the Privy Council to give up this trade, and began to seek another market. Having become acquainted with members of the Separatist congregation living in Leyden, Weston learned of their plans for emigration, of their overtures to the Virginia Company, and of the offer made them by Dutch capitalists during the years 1617–20. Securing a patent, Feb. 20, 1620, from the Virginia Company, under the name of John Peirce and his Associates, he went to Leyden and offered to underwrite the Pilgrims' adventure on such generous terms and with such strong, convincing personal assurances of continued and loyal support, that his offer was at once accepted. In the next few months, however, hope that the charter for the Council for New England—with perhaps a monopoly of fishing rights in the northern waters—would soon be issued caused some hesitation on the part of Weston and some of the other merchants as well as those of the Separatists who were especially averse to going to an Anglican colony. Weston's London associates refused assent to the offers he had made at Leyden and the Pilgrim leaders rejected the revised

agreement drawn by Weston and Robert Cushman [*q.v.*], but when summer came, and the Council for New England was still uncharted, the Pilgrims decided to go ahead under the Peirce patent. Weston himself hired the *Mayflower* and organized a group of sixty-seven, including Standish, Alden, and Hopkins, to accompany the thirty-five coming from Leyden, but when the united band met at Southampton and still declined to sign the revised articles, Weston refused to contribute any more money and "deserted" them. They took matters into their own hands, sold part of their goods, and sailed despite him. Some writers (*e.g.,* Azel Ames, *The Mayflower and Her Log,* 1901) have declared that it was Weston's purpose to "steal" the colony, and that he bribed the captain to land in New England instead of in the territory of the Virginia Company, but this view has not been ordinarily accepted and Weston's honesty in the matter has been commonly believed.

After news came of the colonists' safe arrival, Weston relented toward them, fitted out the *Fortune,* and sent thirty-five new colonists but no supplies (July 1621). Meanwhile a patent had been secured from the Council for New England. Cushman sailed on the *Fortune,* and during a three-week stay in New England obtained the requisite signatures to the agreement Weston had desired. In 1622, however, Weston, fired with new ideas, sold his interest to his associates and equipped an expedition of his own, which arrived at Plymouth in June of that year, asking assistance. This they received, although they were distinctly unwelcome, and they presently settled at the site of the later Weymouth. These men were laborers rather than colonists, come to make quick fortunes. They did no steady work, quarreled with the Indians, and in 1623 were rescued by Standish from one of the few dangerous Indian conspiracies of the early years. The remnant, brought back to Plymouth, were soon joined by Weston himself, who had come over alone and without funds on the fishing fleet. He now borrowed from the Pilgrims and began a series of trading voyages along the New England coast. In September 1623, when Robert Gorges came out with a commission from the Council for New England as governor, he carried orders to arrest Weston on the charges that his men had disturbed the peace and that he himself, licensed by Sir Ferdinando Gorges to export ordnance to New England, had sold the pieces abroad for his own profit. The Pilgrims charitably argued his case with Gorges, undertook to oversee his activities, and helped him to sail with his men for Virginia in 1624. Bradford certainly felt that they had borne much from him and had truly returned good for evil.

Weston was a member of the Virginia House of Burgesses in 1628 but subsequently moved to Maryland, where in 1642 he received a grant of 1,200 acres known as "Westbury Manor," was made a freeman of the colony, and became a member of the Assembly. In the next year, probably, he returned to England, and died at Bristol between 1644 and 1647. "His was a strange career of alternate success and failure, touching the history of the colonies at many points yet of significance only in connection with the Pilgrims, whose history would probably have taken a very different turn had he not come to their aid at a critical time. He was typical of one class of men of his age, a roving, resourceful trader, unstable and hot tempered, and in more or less trouble wherever his lot was cast" (Andrews, *post*, p. 331 note). He was survived by one daughter, Elizabeth, who married Roger Conant of Marblehead.

[William Bradford, *Hist. of Plymouth Plantation* (2 vols., 1912), ed. by W. C. Ford; J. A. Goodwin, *The Pilgrim Republic* (1888); C. E. Banks, *The English Ancestry and Homes of the Pilgrim Fathers* (1929); R. G. Usher, *The Pilgrims and Their History* (1918); *New Eng. Hist. and Geneal. Reg.*, Apr. 1896; H. R. McIlwaine, *Jours. House of Burgesses of Va., 1619–1658/59* (1915); W. H. Browne, *Archives of Md.*, vol. I (1883); C. M. Andrews, *The Colonial Period of Am. Hist.: The Settlements*, vol. I (1934); C. F. Adams, *Three Episodes of Mass. Hist.* (1892), I, 45–83.]

R. G. U.

WESTON, WILLIAM (*c.* 1752–Aug. 29, 1833), civil engineer, was born probably in or near Oxford, England, and may have been a youthful pupil of James Brindley (1716–1772), pioneer English canal engineer. Little is known of his professional engagements in his native land except that in 1790 he was engineer of the monumental stone bridge which spans the Trent at Gainsborough, and of a turnpike road there. In 1792 he contracted with the Schuylkill & Susquehanna Navigation Company, of Pennsylvania, to serve for five years as engineer of its canal, already begun, which extended from Philadelphia up the valley of the Schuylkill to Reading and thence to the Susquehanna (years later known as the Union Canal). Arriving in the United States early in 1793, he served this company for about two years, until it became insolvent.

During this period he absented himself, with the company's permission, to engage in surveys and examinations of three other canal projects: in the summer of 1794 the elder Loammi Baldwin [*q.v.*] secured him to plan the Middlesex Canal, connecting Charlestown, Mass., with the Merrimack; George Washington, then president of the "Patowmack" Company, induced him in 1795 to examine and report on the locks under construction at the Great Falls of the Potomac; and he spent parts of 1796 and 1797 as engineer for the Western Inland Lock Navigation Company in New York State. The last-named project, the precursor of the Erie Canal, involved the creation of a water connection between the Hudson, central New York, and Lake Ontario, via the Mohawk River and Oneida Lake. After Weston had, apparently, severed his connection with the Schuylkill & Susquehanna Company he devoted himself for parts of two years to this New York State enterprise.

In 1799 he made for the City of New York an examination of possible sources of future water supply. He recommended damming the Bronx River north of West Farms, and regulating its flow by raising the level of the Rye Ponds (now part of the Kensico Reservoir). He also proposed an interesting dual distribution system, to be put into effect after the water was brought to a reservoir at or near the City Hall Park. Among Weston's last American activities were those in connection with the "Permanent Bridge" crossing the Schuylkill at Market Street, Philadelphia. As designer of the pier foundations, one of which extended to a then unprecedented depth, practically forty-two feet below the water surface, he remained in active communication with the construction company for two years or more after his return to England about 1800. Little information is available regarding Weston's subsequent activities. He seems to have settled in Gainsborough, the home of his wife. In 1813 or 1814 he was offered the position of chief engineer of the projected Erie Canal, but declined it on account of his age and family responsibilities. He died in London.

Weston's standing as an engineer in the United States may be judged by the obvious respect paid to his professional opinions by leading American public men, including George Washington, Robert Morris, Elkanah Watson, Philip Schuyler, Richard Peters [*qq.v.*]; also, by the salary and fees he commanded—certainly large for his day. From the Schuylkill & Susquehanna Company, for example, he received £800 for seven months' service a year, £370 for his examination and report on the Potomac locks; nearly $800 for the New York water supply report; and later an offer of $7,000 to become chief engineer of the Erie Canal. His contributions to American engineering have not been sufficiently appreciated. He showed embryo engineers how to design and build lock canals. He gave advice in connection with the first important American turnpike. In his report on a water supply for New York City he suggested practice far in advance of his day with respect to artificial filters for drinking water and advocated twenty-four inch cast-iron water pipe some years before any cast-iron pipe had been used in the United States. He proposed the first river regulation in the country. His deep coffer dam for the Permanent Bridge was the first in America and probably was not equaled in boldness anywhere for years. His printed reports include, *Schuylkill and Susquehanna Navigation* (1794), and a second report the same year—both are included in *An Historical Account of the Rise, Progress and Present State of the Canal Navigation in Pennsylvania* (1795); *Report ... on the Practicability of Introducing the Water of the River Bronx into the City of New York* (1799); *Western and Northern Inland Lock Navigation Company, Report of Engineer* (1795). The Baldwin collection at the Baker Library, Harvard University, contains manuscript letters and drawings of Weston relating to the Middlesex Canal.

[Richard Peters, *A Statistical Account of the Schuylkill Permanent Bridge* (1807); W. J. Duane, *Letters, Addressed to the People of Pa. Respecting the Internal Improvement of the Commonwealth* (1811); Elkanah Watson, *Hist. of the Rise, Progress and Existing Condition of the Western Canals* (1820); Caleb Eddy, *Hist. Sketch of the Middlesex Canal* (1843); J. V. H. Clark, *Onondaga* (1849); N. E. Whitford, *Hist. of the Canal System of the State of N. Y.* (1906); *Buffalo Hist. Soc. Pubs.*, vols. II (1880), XII (1908); *The Times* (London), Sept. 3, 1833; paper by R. S. Kirby, read before the Newcomen Society, Apr. 22, 1936.] R. S. K—y.

WETHERILL, CHARLES MAYER (Nov. 4, 1825–Mar. 5, 1871), chemist, was born at Philadelphia, the son of Charles and Margaretta Mayer Wetherill, and a first cousin of Samuel Wetherill, 1821–1890 [*q.v.*]. On his mother's side his ancestors were early Pennsylvania settlers of German origin. After instruction in private schools young Wetherill entered the University of Pennsylvania, where he studied chemistry under A. D. Bache and J. F. Frazer [*qq.v.*], and was graduated in 1845. He spent a year studying analytical chemistry in the laboratory of James C. Booth and Martin H. Boyé [*qq.v.*] in Philadelphia, and then continued his chemical work abroad under Pelouze, Fremy, Gay-Lussac, and Dumas in Paris and under Liebig in the University of Giessen, from which he received the degrees of M.A. and Ph.D. in 1848.

On his return to Philadelphia he opened a chemical laboratory for private instruction and analysis, which he conducted until 1853. During this period he made investigations upon minerals, illuminating gas, adipocere, foods, and other products. In 1851 he was elected to the American Philosophical Society and in 1853 was awarded the honorary degree of M.D. by the New York Medical College. In that year he prepared for the New York Crystal Palace Exposition of the Industry of All Nations an exhibit of Pennsylvania minerals and chemical products, for which he published a description. At the conclusion of this exposition Wetherill made a journey through Michigan and other North Central states for the purpose of exploring their mineral resources. On Aug. 12, 1856, he married Mary Benbridge of Lafayette, Ind., to which place he transferred his residence. The next five years he devoted to private research and literary work. He made a chemical analysis of the white sulfur water of Lafayette and published in 1860 his well-known treatise, *The Manufacture of Vinegar.*

In July 1862 he accepted appointment as chemist of the newly created federal Department of Agriculture under Commissioner Isaac Newton [*q.v.*]. He was the first scientist of this department and established a laboratory in the basement of the old Patent Office, where he conducted investigations upon the chemical composition of sugars, sirups, wines, and other agricultural products. His *Report on the Chemical Analysis of Grapes,* which appeared as a separate publication in 1862, was the first scientific bulletin to be issued by the Department of Agriculture. As government chemist Wetherill was detailed by President Lincoln in 1862 and again in 1863 to conduct temporary investigations upon munitions for the War Department. These interruptions in the agricultural work of his new department excited the displeasure of Commissioner Newton, who refused to retain Wetherill longer in his position of department chemist. This event led to a celebrated congressional investigation in which Wetherill was completely exonerated from blame (*Congressional Globe,* Jan. 18, 19, 20, Mar. 21, 1864). From 1863 to 1866 he was chemist of the Smithsonian Institution in Washington, during which period he conducted an important investigation upon the ventilation of the new House and Senate chambers in the United States Capitol extensions. The ninety-page report of his chemical investigation, "Warming and Ventilating the Capitol," was published as *House Executive Document 100* (39 Cong., 1 Sess.).

In 1866 Wetherill accepted the professorship of chemistry in the newly founded Lehigh University of Bethlehem, Pa., a position which he held at the time of his death. During these years he published his *Syllabus of Lectures on Chemical Physics* (1867) and his *Lecture-Notes on Chemistry* (1868). As a professor and organizer he established a brilliant reputation. He furnished plans for the reorganization of the chemical department of the University of Pennsylvania and was offered the directorship of this department. He accepted this position but died at Bethlehem, from heart disease, before he could enter upon his new duties. In the applications of his science to exposition work, ventilation, and agriculture, and in the improvement of college courses in the subject, Wetherill made lasting contributions to American chemistry during the important transition period between 1840 and 1870.

[Sources include: Charles Wetherill, *Tables Which Show in Part the Descendants of Christopher Wetherill* (1882); original letters, papers and documents supplied by Wetherill's son, Richard B. Wetherill, Esq., of Lafayette, Ind.; E. F. Smith, *Charles Mayer Wetherill, 1825–1871* (1929), reprinted from the *Jour. of Chemical Education*; obituary in *Pub. Ledger* (Phila.), Mar. 7, 1871. Wetherill's chemical papers and memorabilia are preserved in the Edgar Fahs Smith Memorial Collection of the Univ. of Pa.]   C. A. B—e.

WETHERILL, SAMUEL (Apr. 12, 1736–Sept. 24, 1816), pioneer manufacturer, founder of the religious society known as the Free Quakers, was born near Burlington, N. J., the son of Christopher and Mary (Stockton) Wetherill. His great-grandfather, Christopher Wetherill, a native of England, emigrated in 1683 to Burlington, where, when on a visit two years before, he had applied for a grant. At the age of fifteen Samuel went to Philadelphia and was apprenticed to a carpenter. On Apr. 5, 1762, he married Sarah Yarnall, his former master's daughter. He carried on business as a master carpenter until the events occurred which led to the Revolution, when he became a manufacturer and a leader in the movement to make the colonies independent of the mother country with respect to manufactured goods. Of the United Company of Pennsylvania for the Establishment of American Manufactures, formed in 1775, he was a prominent promoter. That same year, he established in his own dwelling, and in a building adjoining, a factory for the weaving of "jeans, fustians, everlastings, and coatings." In need of dyestuffs, he became, also, a dyer and chemist. It is said that his timely shipment of supplies to Washington's army at Valley Forge saved it from disbandment (S. P. Wetherill, *post*, p. 6).

Wetherill was one of the little band of Quakers who took the oath of allegiance to the colonies, and expressed his approval of bearing arms for their defense. In consequence of his Whiglike attitude and his militancy he was cut off from fellowship with the Quakers in 1777. With other former members of the Society of Friends he then formed the body called Free, or Fighting, Quakers. He preached regularly for this sect until his death, and since he was regarded as a remarkable speaker, many who were not Quakers came to hear him. S. Weir Mitchell [*q.v.*] gave him a prominent place among the characters in the novel *Hugh Wynne, Free Quaker*. Wetherill sought to make clear the position of his coreligionists in several publications, among which were *A Confutation of the Doctrines of Antinomianism* (1790); *The Grounds and Reason of the Incarnation and Process of Christ Explained* (1791); *The Divinity of Jesus Christ Proved* (1792); and *An Apology for the Religious Society, Called Free Quakers* (n.d.).

Wetherill's adventure in weaving and in the manufacture of dyestuffs decided him to devote himself to the production of chemicals, and in 1785, in company with his son, Samuel Wetherill, Jr., he established a firm for this purpose. About the year 1790 they began the production of white lead—the first to be manufactured in the United States—and in 1804 erected a white lead factory; but it was destroyed by fire, said to have been caused by British business rivals. In 1808, they erected a still larger plant, where they produced white and red lead, litharge, and other products. This factory, also, was consumed by a fire of suspicious origin, but was immediately rebuilt. Wetherill took an active part in civic affairs in Philadelphia, acting as vice-president of the yellow fever committee in 1793, and as a member of the city council 1802–03. In the latter capacity he was one of the watering committee, at that time a position of some importance, since Philadelphia was then installing the first modern water-supply system in the United States.

[Thomas Porter, *Picture of Phila.* (1831); Henry Simpson, *The Lives of Eminent Philadelphians* (1859); S. N. Winslow, *Biogs. of Successful Phila. Merchants* (1864); J. W. Jordan, *Encyc. of Pa. Biog.*, vol. III (1914); Charles Wetherill, *Tables Which Show in Part the Descendants of Christopher Wetherill* (1882); Mrs. S. P. Wetherill, *Samuel Wetherill and the Early Paint Industry of Phila.* (1916).]   J. J.

WETHERILL, SAMUEL (May 27, 1821–June 24, 1890), inventor, soldier, industrialist, was born in Philadelphia, the son of John Price and Maria Kane (Lawrence) Wetherill, and a great-grandson of Samuel Wetherill [*q.v.*]. He received his early education in the schools of Philadelphia and was graduated from the University of Pennsylvania in the class of 1845. He then entered the white lead and chemical works of Wetherill & Brother, an organization which claims to be the oldest business in Philadelphia to continue under one family ownership and name. Here he became a skilful chemist. At the age of twenty-nine he was employed by the New Jersey Zinc Company, and by persistent research invented in 1852 a process for deriving the white oxide of zinc direct from the ore.

To exploit this invention the Lehigh Zinc Company was organized and a manufacturing plant erected in 1853 in what is now a part of Bethlehem but was then named Wetherill in honor of the founder. The production of zinc oxide flourished, and further development by Wetherill resulted in the production, also, of metallic zinc and of rolled zinc sheets (1857). The process employed was later perfected by the importation of Belgian labor—three men in 1859, fifteen in 1860, nine in 1861, six in 1863, and twenty-seven in 1864—and paved the way for the erection of the great pumping engine at Friedensville, Pa. (1872)—the largest in the world (*Scientific American Supplement,* Aug. 5, 1876, pp. 502–04).

In the meantime the Civil War broke out. Wetherill recruited two companies of cavalry in Bethlehem, was commissioned captain of the 11th Pennsylvania Cavalry, Aug. 19, 1861, was promoted to the rank of major, Oct. 1, served throughout a period of three years, and on Oct. 1, 1864, was honorably discharged. The next year, Mar. 13, he was brevetted lieutenant-colonel, United States Volunteers, "for gallant and meritorious services throughout the campaign of 1864, against Richmond, Virginia." Following his military service, Wetherill returned to his manufacturing and commercial interests. On Jan. 1, 1844, he had married Sarah Maria Chattin; she died in 1869, and on Oct. 19, 1870, he married Thyrza A. James. He was the father of ten children, seven by the first marriage, three by the second. He lived to see, in 1881, two of his sons joint purchasers with Richard and August Heckscher of the Lehigh Zinc Works which he had founded in 1853. After the consolidation of this concern with the New Jersey Zinc Company in 1897, the eldest son, John Price Wetherill (1844–1906), invented the Wetherill furnace and the Wetherill magnetic concentrating process for the treatment of refractory ores—developments as notable in metallurgical science as the achievements of his distinguished father. Samuel Wetherill died in Oxford, Md., where he went to reside after retiring from business.

[Charles Wetherill, *Tables Which Show in Part the Descendants of Christopher Wetherill* (1882); J. W. Jordan, *Encyc. of Pa. Biog.,* vol. III (1914); W. C. Reichel, *The Crown Inn, Near Bethlehem, Pa.* (1872); J. M. Levering, *A Hist. of Bethlehem, Pa.* (1903); *Pub. Ledger* (Phila.), June 25, 1890.]   F. V. L.

WETZEL, LEWIS (1764–1808?), Indian fighter, was born probably in Lancaster County, Pa., the son of John and Mary (Bonnett) Wetzel. John Wetzel, originally spelling his name Watzal,

was born probably in the Netherlands and was brought from Switzerland to Pennsylvania in 1747. Of his five sons, Martin, Lewis, Jacob, John, and George, the first four became prominent Indian fighters, and the fifth was killed while scarcely more than a lad. In 1772, with ten other families, the Wetzels removed to Virginia, near Wheeling, now in West Virginia. Four or five years later Lewis and Jacob were captured by Indians but escaped and made their way home with great difficulty. This event was said to have made Lewis a confirmed Indian hater, and thenceforth in conscious preparation for border warfare he devoted himself to woodcraft and athletic pursuits, became an expert marksman, and trained himself to load his rifle while running. He was tall and swarthy, with high cheek bones, scowling, pitted face, piercing black eyes, long black hair, and ears slit and decorated with silk tassels. Though uncouth and silent he was a favorite fiddler at dances. He never learned to read or write. While still a boy he was in the first siege of Wheeling in 1777 and served on several war expeditions, notably the one in 1781 against the Indian village on the site of the present town of Coshocton, Ohio, and he found almost continuous employment as a scout. Though it is probable that he never enlisted in a regularly constituted military force and certainly never held a command, he was one of the best known and most trusted fighters and scouts on the Ohio border by the time he was of age, and, such was his prowess, that his presence in an endangered community was sufficient to revive the most drooping spirits. An implacable enemy of the Indians, he was never known to give quarter. Once, indeed, his conduct was so merciless that he briefly lost caste even among the frontiersmen, because he murdered an old Indian who had secretly released him after his capture by a war party and sentence to the stake. Wetzel's only comment was: "He made me walk, and he was nothing but an Indian" (Allman, *post,* p. 81). In 1789 during the negotiations with the Ohio tribes at Fort Harmar, he waylaid and killed a prominent Indian. The circumstances of his capture by the white soldiers and subsequent escape from trial and punishment for this murder are not certain. One account is that he was sentenced to be hanged, but that outraged border sentiment forced his release.

Soon afterward he went to New Orleans and there was imprisoned for several years, perhaps as a result of innocently having become involved with a counterfeiter. After his release he spent some time on the Missouri but lived mostly near Natchez. According to the account of one branch of the family he married a French woman and lived in Arkansas to old age, but the more probable account is that he died unmarried near Natchez in 1808. Wetzel County, now in West Virginia, was named for him.

[C. B. Allman, *The Life and Times of Lewis Wetzel* (1932); C. B. Hartley, *Life and Adventures of Lewis Wetzel* (1860); R. C. V. Meyers, *Life and Adventures of Lewis Wetzel* (copr. 1883); Draper Coll. in possession of State Hist. Soc. of Wis., Madison, Wis.]

L. D. B.

WHALLEY, EDWARD (d. 1674 or 1675), regicide, was the son of Richard and Frances (Cromwell) Whalley of Kirkton and Screveton, Nottinghamshire, England, and the cousin of Oliver Cromwell. A London business man, probably a woolen-draper by trade, he married, first, Judith, the daughter of John Duffell of Rochester. Their daughter married William Goffe [*q.v.*]. His second wife was Mary Middleton. On the outbreak of the Civil War, Whalley entered the army and was in turn major, 1643, lieutenant-colonel, 1644, and colonel, 1645. He took part in the siege of Gainsborough and the battles of Marston Moor and Naseby. Charles I was entrusted to his care in 1647, and Whalley answered before Parliament for the escape of the King from Hampton Court. He was a member of the High Court of Justice appointed to try the King and signed the death warrant. When Cromwell invaded Scotland in 1650, he appointed Whalley his commissary-general. Whalley took part in the battles of Dunbar and Worcester, and the House of Commons settled on him lands in Scotland to the value of £500 a year. He was one of the officers who presented the petition of the army to Parliament in 1652. He represented Nottinghamshire in the parliaments of the Protector of 1654 and 1656. In 1655 he was appointed major-general over the counties of Nottingham, Lincoln, Derby, Warwick, and Leicester. Although not whole-heartedly in favor of the proposal to revive the title of King in 1657, he was, nevertheless, appointed to Cromwell's House of Lords. He was present when the dying Cromwell named his son Richard as his successor and became a stanch supporter of Richard Cromwell. For this reason the restored Long Parliament negatived his appointment as colonel of a regiment of horse in 1659. He was one of those sent by the army to Monck, but Monck refused to negotiate with him. On Apr. 16, 1660, the Council of State issued a warrant for his arrest, and on May 4, with his son-in-law, William Goffe, he fled from Westminster and took passage for New England in the vessel of Captain Pierce.

Whalley and Goffe arrived at Boston on July 27, 1660, and took up their residence with Daniel Gookin of Cambridge. On receipt of news that they had been excepted from the act of indemnity, they decided to leave Massachusetts. On Feb. 26, 1660/1661, they set out from Boston and on Mar. 7 were at the home of the Rev. John Davenport in New Haven. Pursuants were sent after them from Massachusetts, but they were secreted by friends and managed to elude arrest. They lived in and near New Haven until Aug. 19, 1661, when they removed to the home of Micah Tomkins in Milford. In the fall of 1664, because of the arrival of royal commissioners to investigate and report on the state of New England, they removed to the home of the Rev. John Russell, in Hadley, Mass., where in February 1664/1665, they were visited by their fellow regicide, John Dixwell [*q.v.*]. Letters of Goffe to his wife in England in 1674 indicate that at that time Whalley was rapidly failing in health, and it seems probable that he died at Hadley late in 1674 or early in 1675.

[See bibliog. in sketch of Wm. Goffe; *The Dict. of Nat. Biog.* contains a more detailed account of Whalley's career in England; for evidence of sojourn and death in Maryland see *Pa. Mag. of Hist. and Biog.*, vol. I (1877) and contradiction *Ibid.*, vol. IV (1880).]

I. M. C.

WHARTON, ANNE HOLLINGSWORTH (Dec. 15, 1845–July 29, 1928), writer, was born at Southampton Furnace, Cumberland County, Pa., the daughter of Charles and Mary McLanahan (Boggs) Wharton. She was descended from an old and distinguished family, the founder of which, Thomas Wharton, an Englishman, emigrated to Pennsylvania before 1689 and was an early settler of Philadelphia. He had belonged to the Church of England but became a Friend. One of his sons, Joseph Wharton, from whom also Anne was descended, built at "Walnut Grove" a handsome country house with grounds sloping to the Delaware. There, soon after his death, was held the Mischianza, the famous ball given by the British officers during the occupation of Philadelphia in 1778. For five generations, from the time of their coming to America, the Whartons were successful merchants, importing extensively, and Anne Wharton's father, like his cousin Joseph [*q.v.*], became well known in the iron trade.

She graduated from a private school in Philadelphia and as a young girl began the writing that was to occupy so much of her life. Her work took the form of children's stories, articles for newspapers and magazines, and books. Her field of especial interest was America in colonial and Revolutionary days. Through travel and research, both in Europe and America, she obtained material for her publications and ultimately became an authority on genealogy as well as on colonial life. In 1880 she published the *Genealogy of the Wharton Family of Philadelphia, 1664 to 1880*. Several of her later volumes were based on observations abroad, with more or less of historic interest; these were *Italian Days and Ways* (1906), *An English Honeymoon* (1908), *In Chateau Land* (1911), and *A Rose of Old Quebec* (1913). The field in which she is best known, however, and which she made particularly her own, is that of the manners, customs, and society of America in the seventeenth and eighteenth centuries. The result of her long-continued work in this direction was embodied in several interesting volumes: *Through Colonial Doorways* (1893); *Colonial Days and Dames* (1895); *A Last Century Maid* (1896); *Martha Washington* (1897); *Heirlooms in Miniatures* (1898); *Salons Colonial and Republican* (1900); and *Social Life in the Early Republic* (1902). One of the most interesting of her books, particularly for the account of Sulgrave Manor and the Washington background, is *English Ancestral Homes of Noted Americans* (1915). She was associate editor of *Furnaces and Forges in the Province of Pennsylvania* (1914) and also wrote *In Old Pennsylvania Towns* (1920).

Her varied interest in life led her from history to its kindred subjects, and showed itself not only in the attractive volume on miniatures noted above, but also in articles for periodicals on literary and artistic subjects. In addition to studious habits and a zest for her subject, she brought to her writings clarity of thought, practical common sense, and much personal distinction. She was one of the eminent group of Philadelphia writers of her time, all of distinguished family, that included Dr. S. Weir Mitchell, Horace Howard Furness, Talcott Williams, and Sara Yorke Stevenson [*qq.v.*]. In 1893, she was a judge of the American colonial exhibit at the World's Columbian Exposition at Chicago. She was one of the founders of the Pennsylvania Society of the Colonial Dames of America and was the first historian of the National Society of the Colonial Dames. A member of Old Christ Church, she was fittingly buried from that historic edifice.

[*Who's Who in America*, 1928–29; J. W. Jordan, *Colonial Families of Phila.* (1911), vol. I; Anne H. Wharton, *Geneal. of the Wharton Family of Phila.* (1880); obituary in *Pub. Ledaer* (Phila.), July 30, 1928.]   A. L. L.

WHARTON, CHARLES HENRY (May 25, 1748 o.s.–July 23, 1833), Protestant Episcopal clergyman, was born in St. Mary's County, Md., the son of Jesse and Anne (Bradford) Wharton.

His parents were Roman Catholics, and his early days were spent on the family plantation, "Notley Hall," which Lord Baltimore had presented to Charles's grandfather. A school mistress, and later a master whom he describes as "very competent," gave him his first instruction. In 1760 he was sent to Saint-Omer, France, where he entered the Jesuit college established there in the latter part of the sixteenth century after Catholic education in England was prohibited. It was noted for its excellent teaching of the classics and literature, and for its strict religious discipline. Although Wharton afterwards renounced the doctrines of the Jesuits, he never regretted that at an early period of his life they had planted in his mind many of the great principles of morality and Christian piety. When the Parliament of Paris, in 1762, banished the Jesuits from France, the boys of Saint-Omer's accompanied their masters to Bruges, where Wharton continued his studies. In 1770 he was a student in the English college of the Jesuits at Liège, and by 1773, professor of mathematics there. In the meantime, Sept. 19, 1772, he had been ordained priest.

Sometime between 1773 and 1777 he became chaplain to the Roman Catholics at Worcester, England. He had not lost interest in his native land and doubtless would have returned before he did, had it not been for the outbreak of the Revolution. One of his incidental occupations while at Worcester was the writing of *A Poetical Epistle to His Excellency George Washington, Esq.... from an Inhabitant of the State of Maryland, to Which is Annexed, A Short Sketch of General Washington's Life and Character*. It was printed in Annapolis in 1779, and reprinted in London the following year "for the charitable purpose of raising a few guineas to relieve in a small measure the distresses of some hundreds of American prisoners, now suffering confinement in the gaols of England." The "Short Sketch" annexed was by John Bell and was the first attempt at a life of Washington (Charles Evans, *American Bibliography*, vol. VI, 1910, p. 62). The most significant event of Wharton's residence in Worcester, however, was a change in his religious feelings and views, an experience so painful that it nearly wrecked him physically. A natural disposition to put doctrines to the test of logic and history, and contact with Protestants who displayed the finest fruits of the spirit, led him to make a painstaking study of the Scriptures and the writings of the Fathers. This forced him to the conclusion that the assumed infallibility and authority of the Church and many of its practices were without divine sanction, and that he could not consistently remain in its communion. In the spring of 1783, apparently, he returned to Maryland, for on June 10 of that year he took the oath of allegiance to the government of that state. The following year he published *A Letter to the Roman Catholics of the City of Worcester from the Late Chaplain of that Society . . . Stating the Motives Which Induced Him to Relinquish Their Communion, and Become a Member of the Protestant Church.* A tolerant and able statement, it called forth from Rev. John Carroll [*q.v.*], later archbishop, a distant relative of Wharton, an equally able if somewhat less kindly reply—*An Address to the Roman Catholics of the United States* (1784). This Wharton answered in a vigorous and well-documented pamphlet, *A Reply to an Address . . .* (1785).

After remaining for a time at his ancestral home, Wharton became rector of Immanuel Church, New Castle, Del. From this time on he was one of the leading Episcopal clergymen of the country. A deputy to the first General Convention in 1785, he was appointed one of the committee to prepare a constitution for the Church, and to make the changes in the liturgy needful to bring it into harmony with the American Revolution and the constitutions of the respective states. In 1791–92 he officiated at the Swedish Church, near Wilmington, Del. His health was never the best and for some years he lived on his estate at "Prospect Hill" in the same vicinity. In 1798 he became rector of St. Mary's Church, Burlington, N. J., where he remained for the rest of his life. During this period he was a member of almost all the General Conventions. In 1801 he was elected president of Columbia College, New York, and accepted the office, but for some reason almost immediately resigned. He was one of the founders and principal editors of the *Quarterly Theological Magazine and Religious Repository* (1813–17). On July 21, 1786, the American Philosophical Society elected him a member.

Wharton was one of the best-trained and most learned Episcopal clergymen of his day. He made no parade of his attainments, however, either privately or in his preaching, which emphasized sound doctrine, moral integrity, and Christian charity. Poor health and absence of personal ambition probably account for his not occupying a prominent ecclesiastical or educational position. His mental equipment appears most conspicuously in his controversial writings, which, in addition to those mentioned, included *A Short and Candid Inquiry into the Proofs of Christ's Divinity; in Which Dr. Priestly's* [sic]

History of Opinions Concerning Christ, is Occasionally Considered (1791); *A Short Answer to "A True Exposition of the Doctrine of the Catholic Church Touching the Sacrament of Penance . . ."* (1814); *Some Remarks on Dr. O'Gallagher's "Brief Reply" to Dr. Wharton's "Short Answer . . ."* (1817). The last two and all the letters in the Carroll controversy were reprinted in 1817 under the title *A Concise View of the Principal Points of Controversy between the Protestant and Roman Churches.* They also appear, together with sermons and other writings, in *The Remains of the Rev. Charles Henry Wharton, D.D.*, edited by George W. Doane. For his spiritual no less than for his intellectual qualities, Wharton was held in high esteem. "I do not recollect," wrote Horace Binney [*q.v.*], "a more gentlemanly figure, or a more benevolent or trust-worthy countenance" (Sprague, *post*, pp. 340–41). He was twice married: first, to Mary Weems of Maryland, who died June 2, 1798, and in memory of whom he wrote *An Elegy* (*Remains*, pp. lxxix-lxxxi); second to Ann, daughter of Chief Justice James Kinsey of New Jersey; he had no children.

[Memoir and funeral sermon by G. W. Doane in *Remains*; W. B. Sprague, *Annals of the Am. Pulpit*, vol. V (1859); W. S. Perry, *The Hist. of the Am. Episcopal Church* (1885) and *Jours. of General Conventions of the Protestant Episcopal Church in the U. S.*, vols. I and II (1874); H. W. Smith, *Life and Correspondence of the Rev. William Smith, D.D.* (1880); *Poulson's Am. Daily Advertiser* (Phila.), July 24, 1833.]

H. E. S.

WHARTON, FRANCIS (Mar. 7, 1820–Feb. 21, 1889), lawyer, clergyman, teacher, government official, author and editor, was the son of Thomas Isaac [*q.v.*] and Arabella (Griffith) Wharton of Philadelphia. He was fourth in descent from Thomas Wharton, baptized at Orton, England, 1664, married in Philadelphia, 1689, a successful Quaker merchant whose descendants formed one of the leading families of the city. An uncle of Francis Wharton, Judge William Griffith [*q.v.*] of the United States circuit court, was the author of several law treatises. Francis' father, a prominent lawyer and editor of law reports, is said to have left the Society of Friends to serve as an officer in the War of 1812. He married a member of the Episcopal Church and joined that denomination. Francis' mother was very devout and exercised a profound religious influence over her son.

Wharton graduated from Yale in 1839 and after studying law in his father's office was admitted to the Pennsylvania bar in 1843. He soon won success as a lawyer and for a time served as assistant to the attorney general of Pennsylvania, but he became better known as an authority on criminal law. Among his early works were *A Treatise on the Criminal Law of the United States* (1846), *Precedents of Indictments and Pleas* (1849), *State Trials of the United States during the Administrations of Washington and Adams* (1849), *A Treatise on the Law of Homicide in the United States* (1855), and in collaboration with Moreton Stillé, *Treatise on Medical Jurisprudence* (1855).

On Nov. 4, 1852, Wharton married Sidney Paul, daughter of Comegys and Sarah (Rodman) Paul of Philadelphia. She died in September 1854. From boyhood he had been interested in church work and after the death of his wife he turned to religious activity, becoming a lay preacher and serving as editor of the *Episcopal Recorder*. In 1856 he made a tour of the upper Missouri Valley in a wagon distributing Bibles and tracts and in the fall he accepted appointment as professor of history and literature in Kenyon College, Gambier, Ohio. On Dec. 27, 1860, he married Helen Elizabeth Ashhurst, daughter of Lewis R. and Mary H. Ashhurst of Philadelphia. During his years at Kenyon, Wharton continued his activity as a religious writer, editor, and lay preacher, and on Apr. 11, 1862, was ordained deacon; a month later he was raised to the priesthood. The following year he became rector of St. Paul's Episcopal Church, Brookline, Mass. Resigning his pastorate in 1871, he accepted a professorship in the recently established Episcopal Theological Seminary at Cambridge, where he continued for ten years. In denominational affairs he was a leader of the Evangelical or Low Church school. He was the author of two books on religious themes, *A Treatise on Theism and on the Modern Skeptical Theories* (1859) and *The Silence of Scripture* (1867).

The years which Francis Wharton spent in religious work did not lure him permanently from the field of legal writing. His *Treatise on the Conflict of Laws* (1872), largely written during a six months' stay at Dresden while abroad for his health, in 1870–71, established his reputation as an authority on international law. He lectured on this subject at the law school of Boston University. Other books by Wharton written while at Cambridge bear evidence of his activity during those years: *A Treatise on the Law of Negligence* (1874), *A Commentary on the Law of Evidence in Civil Issues* (1877), *Philosophy of Criminal Law* (1880), *A Commentary on the Law of Contracts* (1882). He resigned his Cambridge professorship in 1881 because of failing health and spent the next two years in Europe. Upon returning to Philadel-

phia, he busied himself revising his books. His early *Treatise on Criminal Law* went through nine editions during his lifetime and a twelfth edition was published in 1932. Some of his other works also appeared in several editions.

At the beginning of the first Cleveland administration Wharton accepted an invitation to become examiner of claims, chief of the legal division in the Department of State, and took office Apr. 15, 1885. In addition to his regular duties he was entrusted by Congress with the compilation of *A Digest of the International Law of the United States* (3 vols., 1886; 2nd ed., 1887). Much of this work was incorporated by John Bassett Moore in *A Digest of International Law* published by the government in 1906. To Wharton was also assigned the task of editing *The Revolutionary Diplomatic Correspondence of the United States* (6 vols., 1889), the manuscript for which he completed shortly before his death. The task was done in a spirit of honesty, discarding the practice by which earlier compilers of American records had deleted passages reflecting on the judgment or motives of the "Founding Fathers." His work as legal adviser to the Department and as a writer on the foreign policy of the United States was notable for the emphasis which he placed on the rights of neutrals. As an officer of the government he insisted upon the neutral rights of American vessels during the insurrection in Colombia (1885). He severely criticized the decision of the Supreme Court in the *Springbok* case (5 *Wallace*, 1), arising from the seizure of a British vessel bound for Nassau during the Civil War, and pointed out the danger of similar infringements of the rights of American commerce by Great Britain when she should become engaged in war with a European power. Wharton died at his home in Washington, and was buried in Rock Creek Cemetery in that city. By his second marriage he had two daughters.

[J. B. Moore, "A Brief Sketch of the Life of Francis Wharton," in *The Revolutionary Diplomatic Correspondence* (1889), vol. I; H. E. Wharton and others, *Francis Wharton: A Memoir* (1891); A. H. Wharton, *Geneal. of the Wharton Family* (1880); *Obit. Record Grads. Yale Univ.* (1890); *Am. Law Rev.*, May–June, 1889; *Evening Star* (Washington), Feb. 22, 1889.]

E. R. P.

WHARTON, GREENE LAWRENCE (July 17, 1847–Nov. 4, 1906), missionary, born on a farm near Bloomington, Ind., was the son of Stanfiel and Ann Esther (Berry) Wharton, and a descendant of Joseph Wharton who emigrated from England and settled in Virginia early in the nineteenth century. Up to the time he was seventeen, young Wharton had received only the most rudimentary education, for his father was constantly on the move. In 1867, for the most part self-prepared, he entered the high school in Terre Haute, Ind., where he remained but a year. Later, he continued his studies in Southern Illinois College, Carbondale, Ill. After teaching for several years, he became pastor of the Church of the Disciples of Christ in Carbondale. Two years thereafter he was ordained and entered Bethany College, where he was graduated in 1876. From 1876 to 1882 he was pastor of the Richmond Avenue Church of the Disciples in Buffalo, N. Y., marrying in the meantime, Aug. 1, 1878, Emma Virginia, daughter of Robert Richardson [q.v.].

On Sept. 16, 1882, he and his wife sailed from New York for India under appointment as missionaries of the newly organized Foreign Christian Missionary Society of Cincinnati, Ohio. Arriving in Bombay, Nov. 7, they proceeded immediately to Ellichpur, Berar, from which they prospected for a suitable location for missionary service. Harda, in the Central Provinces, was finally selected, and became in January 1883 the headquarters of the first India work of the Disciples of Christ. Very early in the history of the enterprise a school for boys was opened. Several native evangelists were engaged from other missions to aid in the Hindi work at Harda and in the surrounding area. During the winter of 1888–89 Wharton undertook additional work among the Gond and Kurku tribesmen of the Satpura mountains. In 1889, accompanied by his family, he made a trip to Australia, partly for the benefit of his wife's health and partly to arouse further interest in the India mission. After spending the following winter in India, they proceeded on furlough to America, where Wharton gave many addresses and enlisted aid for his enterprise. On Oct. 17, 1891, leaving his family behind, he sailed with new recruits again for Harda, journeying by way of England, where he gave missionary addresses among the churches of his denomination. In February 1893, he was commissioned to found a training school for mission workers, which he established at Harda and from which the first class was graduated in 1897. During the great famine of 1897 he temporarily closed the school and rendered conspicuous relief service.

In the spring of 1899, with his family, which had rejoined him, he returned to America. They made their home in the college hamlet of Hiram, Ohio, where Wharton served for several years as pastor of the church. During 1903–04, having resigned this pastorate, he made a tour of the churches of his order in behalf of the India train-

ing school. On Sept. 30, 1904, he sailed for India, arriving in Bombay, Nov. 5. He proceeded to Jabalpur, where, during his furlough, the Bible College, transferred from Harda, had been formally opened under the administration of George William Brown. Until shortly before his death he assisted in the work of education, evangelism, and publication. He was the author of several tracts in Hindi, and of one on the Christian use of the tithe system. He died in a Calcutta hospital and was buried in that city.

[E. R. Wharton, *Life of G. L. Wharton* (1913); *Christian-Evangelist*, Nov. 15, 1906; *Missionary Intelligencer*, Dec. 1906, Jan. 1907.]   J. C. Ar—r.

WHARTON, JOSEPH (Mar. 3, 1826–Jan. 11, 1909), manufacturer, philanthropist, was born in Philadelphia, Pa., fifth of the ten children of William and Deborah (Fisher) Wharton. His father was a cousin of Thomas I. Wharton, a nephew of Samuel Wharton [qq.v.], and a descendant of Thomas Wharton, a native of England, who was in Philadelphia before 1689. Joseph's early education was received in private schools and from a tutor. At the age of sixteen he was sent to the Chester County farm of Joseph S. Walton, where he remained until the age of nineteen, working as an ordinary farm hand in order to regain his health. During the winter months, however, he continued his studies in chemistry at the laboratory of Martin H. Boyé [q.v.] in Philadelphia, and also added to his knowledge of French and German.

His first business experience was secured as clerk in a drygoods establishment during the years 1845–47. In 1847 he cooperated with his brother in establishing a white lead manufactory, which they sold. In 1851 he became a stockholder in the Lehigh Zinc Company, and from 1853 to 1863 was its manager. In this connection he was responsible for the first commercially successful production of spelter—a crude metallic zinc—in America, and built the first spelter works on the Belgian model to be operated profitably in the United States. In the meantime, 1857, he had been one of the founders and become a director of the Saucon Iron Company, the name of which was changed in 1861 to Bethlehem Iron Corporation; ultimately it became a part of the Bethlehem Steel Company. About 1864 Wharton purchased the abandoned Gap Nickel mine in Lancaster County, Pa., and established a plant in Camden, N. J., for the manufacture of metallic nickel and metal copper alloys. For many years he was the only producer of refined nickel in the United States, and in 1875 he succeeded in turning out a pure malleable nickel, which was utilized in the making of many useful articles. In addition to his other interests, he was connected with several railroads, was proprietor of the Andover Iron Company, of Phillipsburg, N. J., and was the owner of large coal tracts and coke works.

Wharton also exerted a strong political influence, particularly with respect to the tariff. He believed in a high protective tariff for all manufacturers as well as for the iron and steel trade, of which he was the leading tariff spokesman for over a quarter of a century. In 1868 he helped organize the Industrial League of Pennsylvania, a protectionist organization. When its work was taken over by the American Iron and Steel Association in 1875, he was elected first vice-president of the Association, and in 1904, its president. Among his published contributions to the discussion of tariff legislation were *International Industrial Competition* (1870, 1872), and *National Self-Protection* (1875), the title of which became one of the chief slogans of the protectionist group.

He took an active interest in educational matters, and was a founder of Swarthmore College, one of the earlier co-educational institutions, established by the Philadelphia and New York Hicksite Friends. He was a member of its board of managers (1870–1909) and was president of the board for nearly twenty-five years (1883–1907). To the support of the institution he gave liberally. He is remembered also for his gift to the University of Pennsylvania in 1881 of $100,000, subsequently increased to about $500,000, for the establishment of a school offering young men an adequate education in the principles underlying successful civil government, and a training suitable for those intending to engage in business or to undertake the management of property. The Wharton School of Finance and Commerce created under the terms of his gift was the first of its kind in the United States and has achieved an international reputation in its field.

Wharton was a man of varied interests. Although he achieved his greatest success as a manufacturer, he was a chemist, geologist, mineralogist, and metallurgist. He was an effective speaker on educational and other questions of public importance. He was interested in art and had some skill in drawing. Among his writings not previously mentioned were: *Is a College Education Advantageous to a Business Man?* (n.d.); *Suggestions Concerning the Small Money of the United States* (1868); *Speeches and Poems* (1926), collected by J. W. Lippincott. On June 15, 1854, he married Anna Corbit Lovering, by whom he had three children.

[A. H. Wharton, *Geneal. of the Wharton Family* (1880); J. W. Lippincott, *Biog. Memoranda Concerning Joseph Wharton* (1909); E. R. Johnson, *The Wharton School—Its First Fifty Years* (1931); *Bull. of the Am. Iron and Steel Asso.*, Feb. 1, 1909; *Iron Age*, Jan. 28, 1909; *Jour. of the Iron and Steel Institute* (London), LXXIX (1909), 482; L. M. Williamson and others, *Prominent and Progressive Pennsylvanians of the Nineteenth Century* (1898), vol. II; *Proc. Am. Philosophical Soc.*, vol. XLVIII (1909); Wilfred Jordan, *Colonial and Revolutionary Families of Pa.*, vol. IV (1932); *Who's Who in America*, 1908–09; *N. Y. Times*, Jan. 12, 1909.]   H. S. P.

WHARTON, RICHARD (d. May 14, 1689), merchant, proprietor, and promoter, was born in England. He was not interested in the religious experiment of the Puritans but emigrated to America early in the Restoration Period to make his fortune. He soon found himself in the center of a rapidly increasing imperialistically inclined group, both transplanted Englishmen and New England Puritans of the second and third generation, who wished to expand commerce, invest capital, and develop the natural resources of the country on a large and monopolistic basis. As an eligible bachelor he had no difficulty in marrying Bethia Tyng from one of the most prosperous New England families. They had three sons. When he lost his first wife he took for his second, Sarah Higginson, the daughter of John and sister of Nathaniel Higginson [*qq.v.*]. They had four daughters. For his third wife he married Martha Winthrop, the spinster grand-daughter of John Winthrop, 1588–1649, the daughter of John Winthrop, 1606–1676, and the sister of Fitz John Winthrop [*qq.v.*]. These marriages were all factors in his success.

Wharton disapproved of New England's commercial relations with the Dutch and favored the navigation laws as a means to shut them out from the colonial trade as well as the carrying trade in general. During the second Dutch War he seized, under letters of marque and reprisal, a Dutch vessel concerned in trade with New England. This act involved New England against its wishes in commercial warfare with the Dutch. Long delay of the trial of the disputed case caused him and his associates to publish a protest, for which affront to the Massachusetts government he lost his privilege as an attorney. After the Dutch recapture of New Netherland he urged attempting to repossess it, not only for the negative reasons of eliminating Dutch commercial competition but more particularly because he saw the tremendous possibilities for developing American commerce on a unified plan with the port of New York as center. The New England theocracy stood as a barrier against development along imperial lines, and it was therefore natural that he should be one of those urging that the government there be remodelled and the power of the church over the state broken. His legal experience showed him the need of an intercolonial court for hearing appeals and sitting on admiralty cases, while his position as a heavily taxed non-freeman made him feel the injustice of a government that taxed wealth but denied its possessor the right to vote, if he happened not to be a Congregationalist. Largely through the influence of men like himself the Dominion of New England was established in 1686, although none of its supporters had desired or expected that the new government would lack a representative legislative assembly.

He was a merchant importer, owning his own wharves and vessels. He sought and received a monopoly of salt production from the General Court of Massachusetts and later applied for a royal monopoly grant. In 1670 he asked of the colonies in the New England Confederation, for himself and associates, exclusive privileges of producing naval stores. Massachusetts and Plymouth granted the petition for a ten year period. His largest scheme was the organization of a company for developing mines in New England, but including the production of salt and naval stores. This plan came to a head during the administration of Sir Edmund Andros [q.v.] and included English as well as colonial investors. The company, through Wharton, petitioned for a royal grant in February 1688, but the overthrow of James prevented the passing of the patent through the seals. Wharton aspired also to be a landed proprietor and was associated with prominent New England men in the Atherton Company and the Million Purchase. His largest venture of this sort was undertaken alone, his Pejebscot Purchase in Maine, a tract of about 500,000 acres. In all these ventures he and his associates had difficulty in acquiring titles to the lands, for such large projects were disapproved of by the Puritan governments of New England, which preferred a more democratic distribution of the land. This objection on the part of the New England authorities furnished one of the main reasons for the impetus given to the Dominion movement. To the surprise and consternation of the various speculators, Andros, governor of the Dominion, was as opposed to the engrossing of large tracts as were the Puritan rulers. This opposition doomed Andros' chances for success, for his chief support had been from the merchants and landed proprietors. Wharton and his associates as well as the Puritans of the old theocracy worked for

a change, although their suggested reforms were along different lines. While in England trying to further his own projects at court and at the same time help the movement against Andros, Wharton died suddenly, leaving his vast estate in a bankrupt condition. By his death the Dominion lost one of its strongest imperialist leaders and the opposition became dominant under the brilliant generalship of Increase Mather [q.v.].

[V. F. Barnes, "Richard Wharton," *Mass. Colonial Soc. Pubs.*, vol. XXVI (1926), with references; Fulmer Mood in *Miss. Valley Hist. Rev.*, Sept. 1934.]

V. F. B.

WHARTON, ROBERT (Jan. 12, 1757–Mar. 7, 1834), mayor of Philadelphia, merchant, sportsman, the second child of Joseph Wharton, by his second wife, Hannah (Owen) Ogden Wharton, was born at his father's country seat, "Walnut Grove," in Southwark, Philadelphia, later the scene of the historic fête, "The Mischianza," given in honor of the British commander, General Howe. A first cousin of Thomas and half-brother of Samuel Wharton [qq.v.], he was a grandson of Thomas Wharton, of Westmorland, England, who emigrated to Philadelphia some time before 1689. As a boy Robert displayed a "decided distaste for learning," and at the age of fourteen was allowed to relinquish his studies and become apprentice to a hatter. After having learned the trade, he did not follow it, but entered the counting house of his half-brother Charles. Subsequently, he engaged in business for himself as a wholesale grocer and as a flour merchant.

In 1792 he was elected a member of the common council of Philadelphia, and in 1796 was appointed alderman. While he was serving in that capacity the sailors on merchantmen then in the harbor went on a strike for higher wages, and being denied, proceeded to terrorize the water front. Armed with clubs and knives, they marched up and down the streets near the river until influential citizens appealed to Wharton to take charge and suppress the rioters, since the mayor of the city was in feeble health and incapacitated. Wharton gathered a force of some sixty police and twenty volunteers, and led them armed with sticks of cordwood against the rioters, who numbered about three hundred. Wharton himself was unarmed, but after being knocked down four times he succeeded in seizing the standard bearer. A hundred men were arrested and the riot was suppressed.

In 1798 Wharton was elected mayor of Philadelphia for the first of fifteen times. Before the election, and while an alderman, he volunteered to take charge of the Walnut Street Jail, since the jailer and several of his deputies had resigned in the face of the yellow-fever epidemic which had broken out in the city. Wharton took up his residence in the prison, and when a mutiny among the convicts broke out he armed himself with a fowling piece, and together with several keepers met the insurgents, whom he called upon to surrender. Since they continued to advance he gave the order to fire, and himself fired immediately. Several of the prisoners fell, two of them mortally wounded. Wharton asked the grand jury to investigate the incident, and they returned a report that he had only performed his duty in upholding the law. His fellow townsmen never forgot these two instances of his courage and devotion. He was reëlected mayor in 1799, and served subsequently in 1806–07, in 1810, from 1814 to 1818, and from 1820 to 1824. In the latter year he resigned, having served as chief executive of Philadelphia more years than any other mayor of that city.

Greatly interested in sports and social activities, Wharton early became a member of the Gloucester (N. J.) Fox Hunting Club, of which he was president from 1812 until it was disbanded in 1818. He was also a member of the Schuylkill Fishing Company from 1790 until 1828, when he resigned, having in the meantime been elected governor sixteen times. His social interests naturally caused him to join, in 1798, the First Troop, Philadelphia City Cavalry, of which body he was elected captain in 1803 without having passed through the intermediate ranks. In 1810, he was elected colonel of the Regiment of Cavalry of Philadelphia, and in 1811 he became brigadier-general of the First Brigade, Pennsylvania Militia. When the First Troop went into active service in 1814, he served as a private under his former lieutenant, resigning to become once more the mayor of Philadelphia. On Dec. 17, 1789, he was married to Salome, daughter of William Chancellor. He had two children, both of whom predeceased him.

[A. H. Wharton, *Geneal. of the Wharton Family* (1880); *A Hist. of the Schuylkill Fishing Company* (1889); Henry Simpson, *The Lives of Eminent Philadelphians Now Deceased* (1859); F. W. Leach, in *North American* (Phila.), Apr. 14, 1907; *Hist. of the First Troop Phila. City Cavalry* (n.d.); *Poulson's Am. Daily Advertiser* (Phila.), Mar. 8, 1834.]   J. J.

WHARTON, SAMUEL (May 3, 1732–1800), merchant and land speculator, was born in Philadelphia, the grandson of Thomas Wharton, a Quaker who emigrated to Philadelphia from Westmorland, England, before 1689, and the son of Hannah (Carpenter) and Joseph Wharton, a prosperous merchant. He was a half-brother of

Robert Wharton [*q.v.*]. He married, before 1755, Sarah Lewis. They had six children. He became a prominent merchant and was associated with John Baynton in the Philadelphia firm of Baynton & Wharton and after 1763 also with George Morgan [*q.v.*] as Baynton, Wharton & Morgan. This concern was engaged in the trade of the newly opened country across the Alleghanies, especially with the Indians. About 1764 the firm launched an ambitious project for exploiting the trade of the Illinois country, later known as the "Grand Illinois Venture"; but a series of reverses obliged the company to go into a voluntary receivership and withdraw completely from the Illinois venture in 1772.

In the meantime, Wharton was becoming deeply interested in land speculation. For several years he seems to have devoted his principal energies to obtaining a large land grant from the Indians by way of restitution for the firm's heavy losses during Pontiac's uprising of 1763. In 1768, at Fort Stanwix, the Six Nations ceded to the "suffering traders" a large tract of land now in West Virginia, which came to be known as the "Indiana grant." Deeming it desirable to have this grant validated by the Crown in 1769, the associates in the project sent Wharton and William Trent [*q.v.*] to England. It is doubtful whether Wharton and Trent ever attempted to obtain the King's sanction for the original Indiana grant. Wharton soon established valuable contacts with prominent English politicians and men of affairs, and with them organized a group styled the Grand Ohio Company, though it was usually referred to as the Walpole Company, from Thomas Walpole, a prominent member. In January 1770 the group petitioned for a grant of some 20,000,000 acres lying between the Alleghanies and the upper Ohio. A scheme had been devised for a new colony, to be called "Vandalia," and a tentative frame of government had even been decided upon. It was rumored in Philadelphia that Wharton was to be the first governor. For years he devoted his very considerable abilities to these plans. He brought influence to bear upon British officialdom, corresponded with his associates in America, and wrote a series of pamphlets in support of the petition of the Walpole group (for list of these pamphlets see *Mississippi Valley, post*, II, 316). Official procrastination and obstruction, however, climaxed by the outbreak of hostilities in America in 1775, caused the complete collapse of the enterprise. Wharton remained in England and in 1779 joined Franklin in France, where the two discussed the possibility of obtaining recognition of the Vandalia claim by Congress.

In 1779 or 1780 Wharton returned to America. He served as a delegate to Congress from Delaware in 1782 and 1783. From 1784 to 1786 he was justice of the peace for the district of Southwark, Pa., and was judge of the court of common pleas in 1790 and 1791. He died at his country home near Philadelphia. His will was probated on Mar. 26, 1800.

[Correspondence and papers of Baynton, Wharton, & Morgan, the Ohio Company manuscripts, and the Wharton manuscripts including the Thomas Wharton Letter Book, 1773–1784, in possession of Hist. Soc. of Pa.; some letters in *Pa. Mag. of Hist. and Biog.*, July 1909 to Jan. 1910; A. H. Wharton, *Geneal. of the Wharton Family* (1880) and in *Ibid.*, vol. I (1877), nos. 3 and 4; *Biog. Directory Am. Cong.* (1928); *Ill. State Hist. Lib. Colls.*, esp. C. W. Alvord and C. E. Carter, "The Critical Period" (1915), "The New Régime" (1916), and "Trade and Politics" (1921); C. W. Alvord, *The Mississippi Valley in British Politics* (2 vols., 1917); C. E. Carter, *Great Britain and the Illinois Country* (1910); A. T. Volwiler, *George Croghan and the Westward Movement* (1926); Max Savelle, *George Morgan* (1932).]   W. E. S—s.

WHARTON, THOMAS (1735–May 22, 1778), merchant, president of Pennsylvania, son of John and Mary (Dobbins) Wharton, was born in Chester County, Pa., the second of five children. First cousin of Robert and Samuel Wharton [qq.v.], he was a grandson of Thomas Wharton of Kellorth, Orton Parish, Westmorland, England, who emigrated to America before 1689. John Wharton was a saddler by trade and coroner of Chester County, 1730–37. His son, Thomas, who was called "Junior" to distinguish him from a cousin by the same name and five years his senior, seems to have had the advantages of a good education. At the age of twenty he was apprenticed to Reese Meredith, a Philadelphia merchant. Later, he established himself in business and for a time, in association with Anthony Stocker under the name of Stocker & Wharton, was one of the principal exporters of Philadelphia. His resolute stand against the Stamp Act (1765), his advocacy of non-importation agreements among American merchants, together with his membership on the committee of correspondence and his avowed sympathy for Boston in 1774, definitely identified him with the Whigs.

Thereafter his energies were devoted less to the business of a merchant and more to Pennsylvania politics. In the summer of 1774 he was on the committee which attempted unsuccessfully to have the Assembly summoned into session and was a delegate to the provincial convention (July 15). In the summer of 1775 the Assembly placed him on the provincial Committee of Safety. In the work of this body he played an active part until it was superseded by the Council of Safety, which the state convention in July 1776 vested with executive authority until the new constitution was put into operation. Of this body, on Aug. 6, Wharton was chosen president. The failure of Philadelphia to elect members to the Assembly and the Council brought unexpected delay in organizing the state government, the resulting confusion being increased by the British invasion of New Jersey. In this emergency Wharton was in constant touch with Washington, and was the principal figure in ordering the Pennsylvania militia to the commander in chief's assistance, and in encouraging enlistments. The danger from without seems to have turned the tide of opinion toward the constitution, and in February 1777, after months of delay, Philadelphia elected a councilor in the person of Wharton. The government was now organized, the Council and the Assembly united in electing Wharton president of the Supreme Executive Council, and on Mar. 5, 1777, the new president was inaugurated with imposing ceremonies.

Commanding the respect of the conservatives, by his energy and patriotism, together with his moderation and tact, he gave dignity to the government and was at the same time acceptable to the back country. Not an ardent constitutionalist, he was desirous of maintaining some semblance of harmony in the state, as his own words show: "if the Government should at this time be overset, it would be attended with the worst consequences not only to this state, but to the whole continent in the opposition we are making to the tyranny of Great Britain. If a better frame of government should be adopted—such a one as would please a much greater majority than the present one, I should be very happy in seeing it brought about" (Armor, *post,* p. 208). The critical times made the task of president a difficult one, especially in a state so hopelessly divided into factions as was Pennsylvania. During his administration bills of credit were issued to carry on the war, laws passed to punish the disloyal, courts organized, and other measures taken to fit the government to the needs of the time. A unique test of Wharton's own loyalty to the cause was afforded in September 1777, when, backed up by the Assembly, he ordered the removal of twenty Quakers from Philadelphia to Virginia, one of them his own cousin, for their suspected British sympathies, going so far as to disregard writs of *habeas corpus* from Chief Justice McKean [q.v.] of the state supreme court. He had much to do in building up Philadelphia's defenses during the summer of 1777 and early in 1778, and, at his suggestion, Washington sent army officers into Pennsylvania to replenish the dwindling regiments. In the fall of 1777, when the British seized Philadelphia, the state government moved to Lancaster. There Wharton succumbed unexpectedly the following spring to an attack of quinsy.

Wharton was married twice. His first marriage, Nov. 4, 1762, to Susannah, daughter of Thomas Lloyd and Susannah Kearney, allied him with a family long prominent in Pennsylvania politics. After her death he married, Dec. 7, 1774, Elizabeth, daughter of William and Mary Tallman Fishbourne. By his first wife he had five children, and by his second, three. Wharton's grandfather was a Quaker, but he, although not a member, was outwardly sympathetic toward the Anglican Church. He was prominent in the social and civic life of Philadelphia and maintained a beautiful country home, "Twickenham," in Cheltenham Township, now Montgomery County.

[A. H. Wharton, *Geneal. of the Wharton Family* (1880); *Pa. Mag. of Hist. and Biog.*, Oct. 1881, Jan. 1882; W. C. Armor, *Lives of the Governors of Pa.* (1872); A. S. Bolles, *Pa. Province and State* (1899); *Pa. Archives*, 1 ser. V–VIII (1853), 2 ser. III (1890), 4 ser. III (1900), 651–72; *Pa. Colonial Records*, vols. X, XI (1852); J. H. Peeling, *The Pub. Life of Thos. McKean, 1734–1817* (1929).]   J. H. P—g.

WHARTON, THOMAS ISAAC (May 17, 1791–Apr. 7, 1856), lawyer, author, was born in Philadelphia, the third child of Isaac and Margaret (Rawle) Wharton. He was a descendant of Thomas Wharton who was in Philadelphia before 1689, and a nephew of Samuel Wharton [q.v.]. Isaac's cousin, Thomas Wharton [q.v.], was the first president of Pennsylvania. After graduating from the University of Pennsylvania in 1807, Thomas Isaac began the study of law in the office of his uncle, William Rawle [q.v.], a leader of the Philadelphia bar. During the War of 1812, he served as a lieutenant in the famous volunteer Washington Guards of Philadelphia. Here his youth and high spirits caused him to quarrel with Capt. John Swift while their respective companies were deploying near Camp Dupont. After some hot words, there was an interchange of sword thrusts in which Wharton was wounded slightly. This incident resulted in his temporary dismissal from the Guards, to which, however, he was soon reëlected. The matter having been referred to a court of honor, Wharton, pursuant to the court's decision, apologized and the matter ended.

At the close of the war he began the active practice of the law and became one of the most learned members of the bar, acquiring, in particular, a mastery over the difficult branches dealing with real property. He found time in his earlier years, however, for diversions of a literary nature. He was one of the brilliant young men who gathered around Joseph Dennie [q.v.], was a member of his Tuesday Club, and a contributor to the *Port Folio*. Wharton also wrote for the *Analectic Magazine* and in 1815 succeeded Washington Irving [q.v.] as editor. So absorbed in the law did he ultimately become, however, that the fine literary career promised by his early writing was never realized. Though he was especially learned in real property law, his knowledge in other legal fields was hardly less profound. Among his early labors was that of compiling *A Digest of Cases Adjudged in the Circuit Court of the United States for the Third Circuit, and in the Courts of Pennsylvania* (1822). In 1830 he was appointed with William Rawle and Joel Jones [q.v.] to codify the civil statute law of Pennsylvania, a task which consumed four years. Legal publications of his include *Reports of Cases . . . in the Supreme Court of Pennsylvania* (1836), and *A Letter to Robert Toland and Isaac Elliot, Esqrs., on the Subject of the Right and Power of the City of Philadelphia to Subscribe for Stock in the Pennsylvania Railroad* (1846), a masterful legal thesis which was instrumental in assuring the formation of the Pennsylvania Railroad. Wharton's success as a lawyer was in no small part due to his scrupulous honesty and exacting ethical standards.

He took a lively interest in various scholarly societies. In 1830 he was elected a member of the American Philosophical Society. He was among the first active members of the Library and Athenaeum companies, and the Historical Society of Pennsylvania was started in Wharton's home by himself and a number of friends with similar interests. He was also a trustee of the University of Pennsylvania from 1837 to his death. Among his non-legal writings are "Notes on the Provincial Literature of Pennsylvania" (*Memoirs of the Historical Society of Pennsylvania*, vol. I, 1826) and *A Memoir of William Rawle* (1840). On Sept. 11, 1817, he married Arabella Griffith, who with four children survived him.

[A. H. Wharton, *Geneal. of the Wharton Family* (1880); H. E. Wharton and others, *Francis Wharton: A Memoir* (1891); Henry Simpson, *The Lives of Eminent Philadelphians Now Deceased* (1859); J. T. Scharf and Thompson Westcott, *Hist. of Phila.* (1884); T. A. Glenn, *Some Colonial Mansions and Those Who Lived in Them* (1900); *Univ. of Pa., Biog. Cat. of the Matriculates of the Coll.* (1894); "Extracts from the Diary of Thomas Franklin Pleasants, 1814," *Pa. Mag of Hist. and Biog.*, Oct. 1915; *North Am. and U. S. Gazette* (Phila.), Apr. 9, 1856; *Legal Intelligencer*, Apr. 18, 1856.]   G. G. A.

WHARTON, WILLIAM H. (1802–Mar. 14, 1839), leader in the Texas revolution, was born in Albemarle County, Va., the descendant of John Wharton who emigrated from Westmorland, England, to Culpeper County, Va., about 1730 and the son of John Austin and Judith (Harris) Wharton. Both his parents died in 1816, leaving five children to the guardianship of an uncle, Jesse Wharton, a lawyer and a representative and senator in Congress from Tennessee. While engaged in the practice of law at Nashville, Tenn., young Wharton met Sarah Ann Groce, who was attending school there. The courtship that followed brought him to Texas and to the home of Jared Ellison Groce, the largest planter and slave owner in all that country. The couple was married at "Bernardo," the home of the bride's father, on Dec. 5, 1827. Jared Groce offered the young people one-third of his vast estate—all the lands he possessed in Brazoria County—and numerous slaves, if they would remain in Texas. With keen intuition, Groce felt that Wharton would be a valuable asset to the new country. The Wharton plantation was situated twelve miles from the Gulf of Mexico on fertile land, with the Brazos River on one side and Oyster Creek on the other. Here a splendid home was built with lumber from Mobile and furniture and interior decoration from Nashville. Here at "Eagle Island"—for such was the plantation called—many important meetings were held that had much to do with shaping the future of Texas. Here John A. Wharton, the first child, who succeeded to the command of the Confederate regiment, "Terry's Texas Rangers," after Terry was killed, grew to manhood.

By the time the Texas Revolution appeared probable, Wharton had become prominent in public affairs. A convention was called at San Felipe for Oct. 1, 1832, with the ostensible purpose of proclaiming loyalty to Santa Anna, but perhaps with the real purpose of petitioning for the repeal of the law of Apr. 6, 1830, which prohibited further colonization in Texas by citizens of foreign countries, including the United States. Wharton was nominated as president, but Stephen F. Austin [q.v.], recognized as the most influential man in Texas, was elected. Wharton wrote the report of the committee asking repeal of the objectionable law of Apr. 6. When a second convention was called, Apr. 1, 1833, Wharton was chosen president. This convention set itself the task of writing a new constitution for Texas, when Texas should be separated from Coahuila. Early in 1835 a large group of Texans, one of whom was Wharton, had given up hope of reform and come to favor complete separation from

Mexico. By July of that year Lorenzo de Zavala and Wharton were openly agitating against Santa Anna. When the Texans organized at Gonzales on Oct. 11, 1835, Austin was elected commander-in-chief, and Wharton was made judge-advocate of the army. He resigned this office on Nov. 8, and four days later was selected by the Consultation to accompany Austin and Branch T. Archer [q.v.] to the United States to solicit aid and support for the Texas revolution. On Apr. 26, 1836, five days after the battle of San Jacinto, he made a stirring *Address* (1836) in the Masonic Hall, New York City, asking for sympathy and pecuniary aid. He did not know that at the time Santa Anna had been captured and the revolution brought near to a close. On May 31, he had a conference lasting several hours with President Jackson, who advised him what Texas should do to prove that the revolution had achieved a *de facto* government. The three commissioners were back in Texas by mid-summer, and on July 20, 1836, they met at Velasco to submit their report. Wharton was chosen a senator from the Brazoria district but resigned in November to accept the appointment from President Sam Houston [q.v.] as minister to the United States. His mission was to negotiate for the recognition of Texas and for its eventual annexation to the United States. While Wharton was in Washington, Jackson urged him to have Texas extend its claims to include California. Wharton wrote: "He is very earnest and anxious on this point of claiming the Californias and says we must not consent to less" (Garrison, *post*, I, 194). Jackson seemed to think that if Texas could be extended to include California, the North would consent to annexation in order to gain a port on the Pacific.

Though Wharton lived to see Texas recognized as an independent republic, he was not permitted to see annexation consummated. In October 1838 he removed his residence from "Eagle Island" to Houston and took a place in the Texas Senate. He died at the home of his wife's brother, Leonard Waller Groce. While preparing to go to "Eagle Island," he drew his pistol to examine it and discharged it accidentally, inflicting a mortal wound. He was buried at "Eagle Island." Wharton County, Tex., was named in his honor.

[E. C. Barker, *The Life of Stephen F. Austin* (1925); J. H. Brown, *Hist. of Texas* (2 vols., 1892–93); "Diplomatic Correspondence of . . . Texas," *Ann. Report Amer. Hist. Assoc.* for 1907 and 1908 (3 pt. in 2 vols., 1908–11), ed. by G. P. Garrison; W. W. Groce, "Major-Gen. John A. Wharton," *Southwestern Hist. Quart.*, Jan. 1916; *Ibid.*, Jan. 1914, Oct. 1928, July 1932, Jan. 1935; names of parents from C. R. Wharton, Houston, Tex.]   W. P. W.

WHATCOAT, RICHARD (Feb. 23, 1736–July 5, 1806), Methodist bishop, son of Charles and Mary Whatcoat, was born in the parish of Quinton, Gloucestershire, England. When he was still young his father died and his mother apprenticed him at the age of thirteen to Joseph Jones of Birmingham. At the conclusion of his apprenticeship of eight years, the greater part of which was spent at Darlaston, Whatcoat located at Wednesbury, where he engaged in business. From youth he was very religious: "I was never heard," he wrote concerning the period of his apprenticeship, "to swear a vain oath, nor was ever given to lying, gaming, drunkenness, or any other presumptuous sin, but was commended for my honesty and sobriety, and from my childhood I had, at times, serious thoughts on death and eternity" (Flood and Hamilton, *post*, p. 107). Although he was reared as an Anglican, in 1758 he became a regular attendant at Methodist meetings and after 1761 began to hold such official positions as class leader, steward, and exhorter. In 1769 he entered the Methodist itinerancy and until 1784 was a preacher under the supervision of John Wesley in England, Ireland, and Wales.

In 1784 Wesley selected him as one of three preachers to go to America to organize the scattered Methodists. He was ordained deacon by Wesley on Sept. 1, 1784, and was made an elder the following day. In company with Thomas Coke [*q.v.*] and Thomas Vasey he arrived at New York on Nov. 3. He aided in the organization of the Methodist Episcopal Church at the Christmas Conference that same year, after which he gave much of his time to the administration of the sacraments to the American Methodists, who until then had had no ordained ministers. From 1785 to 1800 he served as an itinerant preacher and presiding elder, his appointments being to large circuits and districts in the territory between New York and North Carolina. Bishop Asbury [*q.v.*] also employed him as a traveling companion on his long episcopal tours.

In 1786 Wesley asked that Whatcoat be ordained bishop, but the preachers that met in conference in 1787, fearful that Wesley might recall Asbury if Whatcoat was made bishop, refused. Thirteen years later, however, at the General Conference of 1800, he was elected bishop by a close vote over Jesse Lee [*q.v.*]. Whatcoat was sixty-four years old at the time, and during the first year of his episcopacy his travels, made mainly on horseback, took him from New England to Georgia and across the Alleghany Mountains to Kentucky and Tennessee, a distance of 4,184 miles. The hardships of his office proved too much for him and after six years he died at the home of Richard Bassett at Dover, Del.

Whatcoat wielded a great influence on early American Methodism. Although Asbury surpassed him in administrative ability Whatcoat excelled the senior bishop in patience and humility, and won the respect of the preachers and laymen by his kindness, his devotion, and his unique ability in settling ecclesiastical quarrels. He was a strong believer in the Methodist doctrine of sanctification and made holiness the topic for many sermons. Because of his exceptional knowledge of the Bible he was often called a "living concordance." So little thought to secular matters did he give that at his death he did not leave sufficient funds to cover the expenses of his funeral. "A man so uniformly good I have not known in Europe or America" was Bishop Asbury's final tribute to him (*Journal, post*, III, 202).

[Brief autobiog. in P. P. Sandford, *Memoirs of Mr. Wesley's Missionaries to America* (1843); T. L. Flood and J. W. Hamilton, *Lives of Methodist Bishops* (1882); W. B. Sprague, *Annals Am. Pulpit*, vol. VII (1861); P. D. Gorrie, *The Lives of Eminent Methodist Ministers* (1852); Henry Boehm, *Reminiscences, Hist. and Biog. of Sixty-Four Years in the Ministry* (1865), ed. by J. B. Wakeley; Jesse Lee, *A Short Hist. of the Methodists in the U. S. A.* (1810); Nathan Bangs, *A Hist. of the M. E. Church* (4 vols., 1838–41); Abel Stevens, *Hist. of the M. E. Church in the U. S. A.* (4 vols., 1864–67); John Atkinson, *Centennial Hist. of Am. Methodism* (1884); *Jour. of Rev. Francis Asbury* (3 vols., 1821); *Minutes of the Methodist Conferences ... 1773 to 1813* (1813); *Federal Gazette and Baltimore Daily Advertiser*, July 10, 1806.]   P. N. G.

WHEATLEY, PHILLIS (*c.* 1753–Dec. 5, 1784), poet, was born in Africa. When she was about eight years old she was kidnapped and brought in a slave ship to Boston, where she was purchased by John Wheatley, a prosperous tailor of Boston, to be trained as a personal servant for his wife. Phillis, who had been chosen for her appealing charm and sensitive face in spite of physical delicacy, responded at once to her new surroundings. Encouraged by her owners, she made rapid progress. "Without any assistance from School Education," wrote Wheatley, "and by only what she was taught in the Family, she, in sixteen Months Time from her Arrival, attained the English Language, ... to such a Degree as to read any, the most difficult Parts of the Sacred Writings, to the great Astonishment of all who heard her" (*Poems on Various Subjects, post*). She also read extensively in Greek mythology, in Greek and Roman history, and in the contemporary English poets. She early became something of a sensation among the Boston intellectuals, and when she translated a tale from Ovid, it was published by her friends.

Her first verses, written when she was about thirteen years old, were entitled "To the University of Cambridge in New England." They were followed by "To the King's Most Excellent Majesty," written in 1768, "On the Death of Rev. Dr. Sewell," 1769, and other occasional poems. In 1770 *An Elegiac Poem on the Death of the Celebrated Divine . . . George Whitefield,* was published. These are not only remarkable as examples of precocity but, though without originality and revealing the influence of Pope and Gray, are excellent work of their kind. In 1773 her health was failing rapidly and Nathaniel Wheatley, the son of John, took her to England. She had already corresponded with Lady Huntingdon, Lord Dartmouth, and others, who now received her cordially. In addition to her gift for writing she appears to have been an unusual conversationalist and to have had no little personal charm. Her popularity in London was immediate and great. The first bound volume of her poems, published while she was abroad, entitled *Poems on Various Subjects, Religious and Moral* (1773), was dedicated to Lady Huntingdon.

Her visit was cut short by the serious illness of Mrs. Wheatley, who died soon after Phillis' return. Wheatley survived his wife only a short time and their daughter died a little later. By this time Phillis had been freed. In 1778 she was married to John Peters, a free negro. He is said to have been "not only a very remarkable looking man, but a man of talents and information." According to tradition, "he wrote with fluency and propriety, and at one period read law." He was disagreeable in manner, however, and "on account of his improper conduct, Phillis became entirely estranged from the immediate family of her mistress" (*Memoir and Poems, post,* p. 29). He was not able to give her the care her delicate health required, and of her three children, two died in early infancy. Phillis herself, after undergoing hardships, died in Boston, alone and in poverty, when little more than thirty years old; her last child was buried with her in an unmarked grave. In 1834 *Memoir and Poems of Phillis Wheatley* was issued, the memoir being written by Margaretta M. Odell. The *Letters of Phillis Wheatley, the Negro-Slave Poet of Boston* appeared in 1864.

[B. H. Grégoire, *An Enquiry Concerning the Intellectual and Moral Faculties and Literature of Negroes* (1810), translated by D. B. Warden; Jared Sparks, *The Writings of George Washington,* vol. III (1834); R. W. Griswold, *The Female Poets of America* (1849); C. F. Heartman, *Phillis Wheatley: A Critical Attempt and a Bibliog. of Her Writings* (1915); *Phillis Wheatley (Phillis Peters): Poems and Letters* (1915), ed. by C. F. Heartman, with appreciation by Arthur Schomburg; B. G. Brawley, *Early Negro American Writers* (1935).]

WHEATLEY, WILLIAM (Dec. 5, 1816–Nov. 3, 1876), actor, theatrical manager, was born in New York City. His father, Frederick Wheatley (d. 1836), was an Irish entertainer who had strayed from Dublin to America, joining first the famous company of Warren and Wood at Baltimore and Philadelphia (c. 1803), then going to the Park Theatre in New York, where he remained a favorite until his retirement in 1829. Wheatley's mother was the actress, Sarah (Ross) Wheatley (1790–1872), born at St. John, New Brunswick, the daughter of a Scottish officer. She made her American début at the Park on Nov. 12, 1805. The following year she married Frederick Wheatley and left the stage, only to return to it in 1811 upon her husband's failure in a business venture. From this time until her retirement in 1843, she acted with skill, understanding, and conspicuous success in various American theatres, but regularly at the Park Theatre. In the rôles of comic middle-aged and old women (Mrs. Malaprop, Juliet's nurse, etc.), and in the revival of old plays she was, by universal admission, without a rival on the American stage. Of Wheatley's sisters, Julia had some success on the operatic stage as a contralto, married a wealthy New York man, and retired in 1840; Emma married a New York banker's son and retired from the stage, but returned in 1847, acting with great distinction until her death at thirty-two on July 16, 1854, a highly accomplished and beautiful woman.

"Young Wheatley" began his career as Albert in J. S. Knowles's *William Tell* with the visiting actor W. C. Macready, at the Park Theatre, Oct. 13, 1826. The boy's performance won signal public favor and so delighted the English tragedian that he took him on his starring tour through the United States. Returning home to the Park, Wheatley bettered his first success in a magnificent production of *Tom Thumb,* and after its long run found himself established as the chief "juvenile" in the nation's foremost theatre. He underwent a careful and thorough training by his parents before beginning his apprenticeship, in 1833, at the Bowery Theatre as a "walking gentleman." In the summer of 1834 he became the "chief walking gentleman" at the Park, where he continued his rapid advance, winning special recognition as Michael in *Victorine,* Henry Morland in *The Heir-at-Law,* Nicholas Nickleby, Henry in *Speed the Plough,* and Charles in the first American performance of *London Assurance.* He perfected his naturally vivacious and energetic grace, and by painstaking study mastered his dramatic material as few American actors had been known to do. On July 8, 1836, at a benefit for himself at the Park in which he and his sister Emma took the leading parts, he brought out the tragedy, *Sassacus, or the Indian Wife,* generally believed to be his own. He was also for a time manager of the National Theatre, New York.

The Park Theatre declining, Wheatley went to Philadelphia in 1842, where he played with E. A. Marshall's great stock company for one season, ending with a brilliant but premature farewell benefit at the Chestnut Street Theatre on Mar. 24, 1843, in which he acted two of his most characteristic rôles, Doricourt in *The Belle's Stratagem* and Captain Murphy Maguire in *The Serious Family.* Then an unwise venture in Wall Street and an expedition to Nicaragua interrupted his professional career. A year or two later he was back again in the Philadelphia theatres, where, save for another starring engagement at the Park in 1847 with his sister Emma (Mrs. James Mason), he continued to perform until 1852.

In that year he took over for a few months the direction of the Washington (D. C.) Theatre, and thenceforth he divided his efforts between acting and managing. From 1853 to 1856 he shared with John Drew, the elder [*q.v.*], the management of the Arch Street Theatre, Philadelphia, then became sole manager for two years, then co-partner with John Sleeper Clarke [*q.v.*] until the outbreak of the Civil War, when both men withdrew, and Wheatley, in spite of a disastrous fire, revived in a few months the glories of the Continental Theatre in the same city. Early in 1862 Wheatley reappeared in New York at Niblo's Garden and by July had leased that former circus. The following January he also opened the new Chestnut Street in Philadelphia, running the two in conjunction; but after a year's trial he confined himself to the sole management of the better situated theatre in New York. His earliest successes there—*The Duke's Motto, Bel Demonio, The Connie Soogah, Arrah-na-Pogue,* in which he shared the important rôles with the foremost actors of the time—raised Niblo's Garden to a theatre of the first class, celebrated for its star actors and for its sumptuous productions of romantic dramas. In 1866 the unprecedented triumph of *The Black Crook,* in which Wheatley introduced to America for the first time the extravagant ballet spectacle, and committed that playhouse and its metropolitan successors to the new genre, made the fortune of every one concerned in its production and enabled him to retire from the profession, on Aug. 31, 1868, with a handsome competency. The illness and death, however, of his second wife, Elizabeth A. Beckett, on Apr. 1, 1869, soon transformed this elegant old stager into an extremely devout ascetic who dressed like a clergyman and resided, once more remarrying, in quiet seclusion in New York until his death on Nov. 3, 1876. His third wife and one son by his second wife survived him.

Though never permanently identifying his name with any of his rôles, Wheatley stood in the first rank as a general actor, enjoying great popularity as Jaffier, Claude Melnotte, Ranger, Young Rapid, Captain Absolute, and other showy, pictorial characters congenial to him. According to William Winter (*post,* p. 140), Wheatley's bearing was "pompous, yet urbane"; his elocution "stately and sometimes stilted." As manager he succeeded remarkably well in a time when the star system had ruined many of the country's best theatres; but had he cared more for dramatic art than for long runs he would have had a deeper and more lasting influence on the American stage.

[T. A. Brown, *A Hist. of the N. Y. Stage* (3 vols., 1903), and *Hist. of the Am. Stage* (1871); Arthur Hornblow, *A Hist. of the Theatre in America* (1919), II, 99; Laurence Hutton, *Curiosities of the Am. Stage* (1891), p. 17; J. N. Ireland, *Records of the N. Y. Stage* (2 vols., 1866–67); L. E. Shipman, *A Group of Theatrical Caricatures . . . by W. J. Gladding* (1897); William Winter, *Shadows of the Stage* (1893), 2 ser.; death notice in *N. Y. Herald,* Nov. 5, 1876; obituaries in *N. Y. Tribune,* Nov. 4, 1876, *N. Y. Mail, Evening Mirror,* and *N. Y. Clipper,* Nov. 11, 1876; manuscript letters of Wheatley and of Brown in the Theatre Collection, Harvard Coll. Lib.]
M. B.

WHEATON, FRANK (May 8, 1833–June 18, 1903), soldier, was born at Providence, R. I., the son of Dr. Francis Levison Wheaton and Amelia S. (Burrill) Wheaton. On his father's side he was a descendant of Robert Wheaton, who emigrated from Wales to Massachusetts between 1630 and 1636. Young Wheaton attended the public schools, and studied engineering for one year at Brown University, leaving college in 1850 to accept a position with the United States and Mexico Boundary Commission, with which he passed five years in border surveying. In 1855 he accepted an appointment as a first lieutenant, 1st United States Cavalry. He was engaged in Sumner's campaign against Indians in 1857, in the Mormon expedition in 1858, and in fighting in the Indian Territory in 1859.

On Mar. 1, 1861, preceding the outbreak of the Civil War, he became a captain in the 4th Cavalry, and in July the lieutenant-colonel of the 2nd Rhode Island Infantry. This regiment suffered heavily in the battle of Bull Run; its colonel was among the killed and Wheaton was promoted to succeed him. For "admirable conduct" in the battle Wheaton was commended by General Burnside. In 1862 the 2nd Rhode Island joined McClellan's army in the Peninsula campaign, and was reported for efficiency in the battle of Williamsburg (May 5). Late that year, as of Nov. 29, Wheaton was appointed a brigadier-general, United States Volunteers, and assigned to command a brigade in the VI Corps, which he led in December in the attack on Fredericksburg. In May following he again assisted in an attack on that town, incidental to the campaign of Chancellorsville. Wheaton's brigade arrived late at Gettysburg, but participated in the final action on July 3, 1863. Commanding the same brigade of the VI (Sedgwick's) Corps, he had a prominent part in the Wilderness Campaign in the spring of 1864. He had important missions at Spotsylvania and at Cold Harbor, and was one of the first to cross the James River and arrive in front of Petersburg on June 18. He assaulted the outer works of that city, but was unable to seize the main position. Shortly afterward, Wheaton, now commanding a division, was rushed by water to Washington, D. C., to repel a threatened attack by the Confederate Gen. Jubal A. Early. Debarking at noon, July 11, he marched to Fort Stevens, D. C., where an extemporized force of clerks and veterans had been skirmishing with the enemy. By evening Washington was safe, and on the day following, Wheaton definitely repulsed the attackers. He was rewarded by being appointed a brevet major-general. Returning to Petersburg, he had great success in the assault on Apr. 2, 1865, which did much to win the final campaign.

On Apr. 30, 1866, he was mustered out of the volunteer service, and on July 28, 1866, was appointed a lieutenant-colonel of infantry in the Regular Army. He received the honorary degree of A.M. from Brown University in 1865, and was presented with a sword of honor by the state of Rhode Island. In 1872 he successfully commanded the expedition against the Modoc Indians. Appointed a brigadier-general in 1892, he was assigned to command the Department of Texas. In 1897 he was promoted to major-general, and in the same year, May 8, was retired for age. Thereafter, he made his home in Washington. At his death he was survived by his wife and two daughters.

[War of the Rebellion: Official Records (Army); F. B. Heitman, Hist. Reg. and Dict. U. S. Army (1903); J. R. Bartlett, Memoirs of R. I. Officers (1867); The Biog. Cyc. of Representative Men of R. I. (1881); Who's Who in America, 1901–02; Army and Navy Jour., June 20, 1903; Washington Post, June 19, 1903.]
C. H. L.

WHEATON, HENRY (Nov. 27, 1785–Mar. 11, 1848), jurist, diplomat, expounder and historian of international law, was born in Providence, R. I., the son of Seth and Abigail (Wheaton) Wheaton. He was descended through both his parents, who were first cousins, from Robert Wheaton, who emigrated from Wales to Massachusetts between 1630 and 1636, settling first in Salem and later in Rehoboth. Through his mother, Henry was said to be descended also from William Goffe [q.v.], the regicide. Seth Wheaton was a successful merchant and at his death was president of the Rhode Island branch of the Bank of the United States; his wife was a woman of fine intellect and culture, whose influence on her son was exceeded only by that of his maternal uncle, Dr. Levi Wheaton. To him Henry Wheaton wrote in 1843: "I am your debtor in all things, owing you more of what I am than to all others" (Kellen, post, p. 5).

Wheaton was fitted for college at the University Grammar School, Providence, and entered Rhode Island College (now Brown University) at the age of thirteen. When he graduated, in September 1802, he delivered a commencement oration on "Progress of the Mathematical and Physical Sciences during the Eighteenth Century." After reading law in a Providence law office, he went to Europe in the spring of 1805, studied Civil Law at Poitiers, translated into English the new Code Napoléon, and visited Paris. In 1806, after his return from Europe, he began the practice of law in Providence, where in 1811 he married his cousin, Catharine Wheaton, daughter of Dr. Levi Wheaton.

During his college days, Wheaton showed such interest in the public affairs of the French nation that he was known as "Citizen Wheaton" by his fellow students. This interest in government showed itself after his graduation in articles contributed to the *Rhode Island Patriot* and to the *National Intelligencer*; and in a patriotic oration, delivered on July 4, 1810, which was favorably commented upon by Jefferson, to whose school of political thinking all of Wheaton's near relatives belonged. Recognition of his talents came in 1812 when he moved to New York City to become editor of the *National Advocate*, the local organ of the administration party. During the nearly three years of his editorship he wrote intelligently and with learning on the questions of international law and policy growing out of the War of 1812, and was often the mouthpiece of the administration. He served also, from Oct. 26, 1814, as division judge-advocate of the army. In May 1815 he was appointed a justice of the marine court of New York City, an office which he held until July 1819; and for part of this period, beginning in 1816, he held also the office of United States Supreme Court reporter, of which he was the incumbent until 1827. He was a member of the New York State constitutional convention of 1821, in which he stood out for three propositions: incorporation of private corporations only by authority of a general act, local taxation for common schools, and an independent and irremovable judiciary. In November 1823 he was elected to the New York Assembly; and after serving one term was an unsuccessful candidate for a seat in the United States Senate. From April 1825 to March 1827, when he was succeeded by J. C. Spencer [*q.v.*], he served with Benjamin F. Butler and John Duer [*qq.v.*] as a commissioner to revise the laws of New York. While there is no detailed record of his part in this revision (of 1829), there is evidence that he drew up the general plan which was followed by his colleagues. With his pen, he was continuously active. In 1815 he framed a national bankruptcy law and urged its passage by Congress; in the same year he published *A Digest of the Law of Maritime Captures and Prizes*; in 1821 he published *A Digest of the Decisions of the Supreme Court of the United States*; in 1823 he edited William Selwyn's *Abridgment of the Law of Nisi Prius*; and in 1826 he published a meritorious work entitled *Some Account of the Life, Writings and Speeches of William Pinkney*, a second edition of which was included in Jared Sparks's *Library of American Biography* (vol. VI, 1836).

Meanwhile, during twelve of these years, Wheaton published annually a volume of the decisions of the United States Supreme Court. At first he served without salary, depending upon the sale of the *Reports* for his compensation, but beginning in 1817 he received also payment of $1,000 a year. He took his duties seriously and greatly added to the value of the volumes by the extent and excellence of his notes. "No reporter in modern times," said Daniel Webster, "has inserted so much and so valuable matter of his own" (Lawrence, *post*, p. xliv). During this time Wheaton was occasionally associated with Webster and others as counsel in cases heard by the Supreme Court. After his retirement from the reportership, his *Reports* were the subject of a suit (*Wheaton* vs. *Peters*, 8 *Peters*, 591) in which it was decided that "no reporter has or can have any copyright in the written opinions delivered by this court."

The year 1827 marked the beginning of the second phase of Wheaton's career. In that year, President John Quincy Adams appointed him chargé d'affaires to Denmark, and although acceptance of this post meant the renunciation of the benefits to be derived from the professional position that he had reached at home—except

for the profits from the sale of his *Reports*—he sailed for Copenhagen in July, and reached his post in September. His only predecessor here was George W. Erving, who in 1811 had been sent on a special mission in reference to seizures of American vessels. Wheaton's particular duty was to bring these negotiations to a conclusion. He found it a difficult task, for Denmark never admitted violating American neutral rights; nevertheless, Wheaton brought about agreement on a treaty of indemnity, signed Mar. 28, 1830, by the terms of which the sum of $650,000 was paid to the United States for the benefit of American merchants and all Danish claims were renounced. The payment amounted to one-fifth more than the figure Wheaton had been instructed to insist upon. The treaty has a special importance because it was the prototype of treaties of similar purpose later negotiated with France and Naples.

A large part of Wheaton's success in Denmark was due to his interest in the history of Scandinavia and the facility with which he acquired the Danish language. Little more than a year after his arrival in Copenhagen, he published in the *North American Review* (October 1828) an article on Schlegel's study, in Danish, of the public law of Denmark, and he was the familiar associate of the philologist R. C. Rask and the poet A. G. Öhlenschläger. In addition to articles on Scandinavian literature and legal systems, he published *History of the Northmen* (1831). In a revised second edition, which was translated into French in 1844 by Paul Guillot, he definitely committed himself to the view of the pre-Columbian discovery of America by the Northmen. During a visit to England in 1827 he made the acquaintance of Jeremy Bentham and in 1830, while visiting Paris, he was presented to Louis Philippe by Lafayette. In 1833 he returned to the United States on leave of absence, for the purpose of prosecuting his suit against Peters. The outcome of this suit was a considerable financial loss to Wheaton, but his return to Europe was a personal triumph, for, at the request of Prussia, he was appointed chargé d'affaires at Berlin, Mar. 7, 1835.

In June of that year he arrived at his new post, where the United States had not been represented since 1797. The occasion for his appointment was the desire to establish commercial relations with the states of the German *Zollverein* or customs union, which by 1834 had superseded the Confederation set up by the Congress at Vienna. The publication of Wheaton's *Elements of International Law* in 1836 was indirectly the cause of his promotion, Mar. 7, 1837, to be envoy extraordinary and minister plenipotentiary to Prussia, a change which materially aided him in his diplomatic tasks. At the end of six years, on Mar. 24, 1844, he secured signatures to a treaty with Prussia which provided for a reduction of the duty on tobacco and rice and the admission of unmanufactured cotton, duty free. In return, the United States was to reduce the duties on silks, looking-glass plates, toys, linens, and other articles not coming into competition with American products and manufactures. The United States Senate rejected the treaty, however, on the ground that the Constitution gave to Congress the sole power to regulate commerce and pass revenue laws. The Senate disapproved also a treaty providing for the extradition of criminals, which was subsequently revived by President Fillmore and accepted by the Senate. An important series of treaties negotiated by Wheaton and put into effect provided for the abrogation of the *droit d'aubaine* and the *droit de détraction* in Hanover, Württemberg, Hesse-Cassel, Saxony, Nassau, and Bavaria. The first had imposed a tax of ten per centum on all property accruing to emigrants in the United States on the death of relatives at home; and the second had taxed, at the same rate, sales of property by persons about to leave their native country.

It has been the custom to commiserate Wheaton because President Polk, instead of transferring him to Paris or London, saw fit to request his resignation. Having adopted diplomacy as a career, Wheaton took it as a reproof and a disgrace to be involuntarily retired, and many European officials failed to understand the American political exigencies which brought about his recall. According to standards of a later day, however, Wheaton had an extraordinarily long and successful diplomatic career. He served continuously under six successive presidents, J. Q. Adams, Jackson, Van Buren, Harrison, Tyler, and Polk, and he retired at the age of sixty. He presented his letter of recall to the King of Prussia on July 18, 1846, but did not return to the United States until the spring of 1847. Public dinners were given him in New York and Philadelphia, and Harvard College offered him a lectureship in civil and international law. He began the preparation of lectures, but his failing health prevented their completion. He died at Dorchester, Mass., in March 1848, and was buried at Providence, R. I. He was survived by his wife, two daughters, and a son.

Notable as were Wheaton's accomplishments in other fields, his most distinguished achievement was his work as an expounder and historian of international law. All of his training and experience combined to fit him for the writing of his *Elements of International Law,* first published in 1836 while he was accredited to Berlin. The London edition was in two volumes and the Philadelphia edition in one. Prefixed to this treatise was a sketch of the history of international law. The immediate success of the *Elements* encouraged Wheaton to further efforts, by which the prefatory historical sketch was expanded into a separate work of 462 pages entitled *Histoire des progrès du droit des gens en Europe depuis la Paix de Westphalie jusqu'au Congrès de Vienne, avec un précis historique du droit des gens européen avant la Paix de Westphalie.* Written in French for a competition conducted by the French Institute, it won honorable mention. It was published in Leipzig in 1841, and in New York in 1845, with the title, *History of the Law of Nations in Europe and America, from the Earliest Times to the Treaty of Washington, 1842.* He published in Philadelphia in 1842 a study entitled, *Enquiry into the Validity of the British Claim to a Right of Visitation and Search of American Vessels Suspected to be Engaged in the African Slave Trade* (2nd ed., London, 1858).

From a third edition of the *Elements* published in Philadelphia in 1846, Wheaton eliminated the historical sketch and substituted therefor numerous references to the separate *History.* The two are in fact companion volumes, which ought to be read together. One other edition of the *Elements* was prepared by Wheaton—the fourth edition, written in French and published in Leipzig in 1848, and after his death—but it was issued repeatedly in English and in French, and was translated into Italian, Spanish, and Chinese (see Hicks, *post,* pp. 222–23). A two-volume edition, in English, appeared as late as 1929.

According to Professor A. C. McLaughlin, Wheaton's name should be linked with those of the greatest of American legal writers. "In jurisprudence," he says, "Marshall and Kent and Story and Wheaton, by judicial opinion or by written text, laid the foundations of American public and private law, and ably performed a creative task such as rarely, if ever, before fell to the lot of the jurist" (*The Cambridge History of American Literature,* vol. II, 1918, p. 71). Not only on account of his writings and his diplomatic career, but also because of two fortuitous circumstances, will he be remembered. Mention has already been made of the case of *Wheaton* vs. *Peters*; his name is also connected with an even more famous case tried long after his death, *William B. Lawrence* vs. *Richard Henry Dana* (4 *Clifford,* 1). This suit was over the alleged unfair use by Dana, in the eighth edition of the *Elements,* of Lawrence's notes to the sixth and seventh editions (see Charles Francis Adams, *Richard Henry Dana*, 1890, II, 282–327; Hicks, *post*, pp. 223–34). Judged by the honors that he received, Wheaton's place is not insignificant. The doctorate in law was conferred upon him by Brown, Hamilton and Harvard; in 1830, he was elected to membership in both the Scandinavian and Icelandic literary societies; he was a foreign member of the Prussian Royal Academy of Sciences; and in 1842, he was elected to the Academy of Moral and Political Sciences in the French Institute. Some years after his death, a British critic (*Saturday Review*, London, reprint in *Littell's Living Age*, Dec. 5, 1857) commented that "no American ever had about him less of the peculiar stamp which marks the citizen of a new State [than Henry Wheaton]. He was a man of refinement and of great cultivation, and enjoyed public life in the calm and dignified way which is usual with the higher officials of the European nations."

[Sources include: W. G. Hill, *Family Record of . . . James W. Converse . . . Including Some of the Descendants of . . . Robert Wheaton* (1887); letters of Henry Wheaton to his father, 1805–06, in *Proc. Mass. Hist. Soc.*, 1 ser. XIX (1882); W. B. Lawrence, "Introductory Remarks," in Wheaton's *Elements of International Law* (6th ed., 1855); Edward Everett, "Life, Services, and Works of Henry Wheaton," *No. Am. Rev.*, Jan. 1856; Charles Sumner, "The Late Henry Wheaton," *Boston Daily Advertiser*, Mar. 16, 1848; George Shea, "Henry Wheaton and the Epoch to Which He Belonged," *N. Y. State Bar Asso. Reports*, vol. II (1879); W. V. Kellen, *Henry Wheaton—An Appreciation* (1902); F. R. Jones, "Henry Wheaton," *Green Bag*, Dec. 1904; J. B. Scott, "Henry Wheaton," in W. D. Lewis, *Great Am. Lawyers*, vol. III (1907); F. C. Hicks, "Henry Wheaton," in *Men and Books Famous in the Law* (1921); A. B. Benson, "Henry Wheaton's Writings on Scandinavia," *Jour. of English and Germanic Philology*, Oct. 1930; *New Eng. Hist. and Geneal. Reg.*, July 1848; *Boston Daily Advertiser*, Mar. 15, 1848. A doctoral dissertation on Wheaton, by Elizabeth F. Baker, was accepted at the Univ. of Pa. in 1933.]   F. C. H.

WHEATON, NATHANIEL SHELDON (Aug. 20, 1792–Mar. 18, 1862), Protestant Episcopal clergyman, educator, was the eldest son of Sylvester and Mercy (Sperry) Wheaton, of Marbledale, town of Washington, Conn. His grandfather, Joseph Wheaton, born in Seekonk, R. I., was one of the first Episcopalians to settle in that part of Connecticut. Nathaniel was prepared for college at the Episcopal Academy, Cheshire, Conn., and was graduated from Yale College in 1814. After graduation, he taught in Maryland, and studied theology. He was ordained deacon in the Episcopal Church by Bishop James Kemp of Maryland, June 7, 1817, and on May 24, 1818, was advanced to the priesthood. He was rector of Queen Caroline Parish in Anne Arundel County, Md., for some time, but in March 1820 became assistant minister of Christ

Church, Hartford, Conn. He was made rector Apr. 23, 1821, and served for over ten years.

On the incorporation of Washington College (now Trinity) in Hartford in 1823, he was a member of the original board of trustees. Planning to visit England for his health, which was always precarious, he was requested by the trustees to solicit there books and philosophical apparatus. He remained abroad about a year, and secured useful gifts for the infant college. Some of the diaries he kept while in England are preserved in the college library. During his sojourn there he studied architecture, and when a new church for his parish was projected in 1827, he planned it, with the assistance of the architect Ithiel Town [q.v.], and supervised its construction. It is said to be the first truly Gothic church to be built in America. On Oct. 14, 1831, he was elected president of Washington College, in succession to Thomas Church Brownell [q.v.], the founder. Wheaton served till Feb. 28, 1837, with conspicuous success, adding materially to the endowment and the property of the institution.

He resigned the presidency to accept a call to the rectorship of Christ Church, New Orleans. An epidemic of yellow fever devastated the city during his pastorate, and he devoted himself unsparingly to ministering to the stricken people. At one time he was the only Protestant clergyman able to perform his duties. He himself contracted the disease, which permanently impaired his health. In the hope of improving it, he resigned his parish in 1844 and went to Europe. Unhappily his hope was only partially realized, and he was not able to resume the active work of his ministry. He lived in Hartford for a time, but soon removed to Marbledale, where he spent the remainder of his days, living quietly and performing such clerical duties as opportunity and his health permitted. Unmarried, with ample means, he gave a rectory and a tract of ground to St. Andrew's Church, Marbledale, and bequeathed $10,000 to Trinity College, to be the nucleus of a fund for the building of a chapel. As his residuary legatee, the college also received some $10,000 additional.

Among his published writings were an anonymous pamphlet, *Remarks on Washington College, and on the "Considerations" Suggested by Its Establishment*, in reply to a pamphlet published in 1824 and attributed to Roger S. Baldwin [q.v.]. On May 7, 1828, Wheaton preached the Election Sermon in New Haven which was published in 1828 under the title *The Providence of God Displayed in the Rise and Fall of Nations*. His "Address at the Laying of the Corner-Stone of Christ Church, Hartford," and a "Description of Christ Church, Hartford," were printed in the *Episcopal Watchman,* in May 1828 and January 1830, respectively. He contributed to the same periodical (June 1827–August 1829) a number of papers entitled "Notes of a Traveller," which were reprinted with additions under the title *A Journal of a Residence of Several Months in London* (1830). Other publications of his include *An Address Delivered Before the Hartford County Peace Society* (1834); "Happiness or Misery the Result of Choice" (*Protestant Episcopal Pulpit,* December 1834); and *A Discourse on St. Paul's Epistle to Philemon; Exhibiting the Duty of Citizens of the Northern States in Regard to the Institution of Slavery* (1851).

[Records of Trinity College, Hartford; *The Calendar* (Hartford), Mar. 29, Apr. 5, 1862; *American Quart. Church Rev.,* July 1862; E. E. Beardsley, *The Hist. of the Episcopal Church in Conn.,* vol. II (1868); G. W. Russell, *Contributions to the Hist. of Christ Church, Hartford* (1895) and *Additional Contributions . . .* (1908); Samuel Orcutt, *Hist. of the Towns of New Milford and Bridgewater, Conn.* (1882); F. B. Dexter, *Biog. Sketches Grads. Yale Coll.,* vol. VI (1912); *Hartford Daily Courant,* Mar. 22, 1862.]   A—r A.

WHEDON, DANIEL DENISON (Mar. 20, 1808–June 8, 1885), Methodist Episcopal clergyman, editor, and teacher, was born in Onondaga, N. Y., the son of Daniel and Clarissa (Root) Whedon, and a descendant of Thomas Whedon who came to New Haven, Conn., from England in 1657 and later moved to Branford. The younger Daniel was a dreamy, absent-minded boy, more interested in books than in anything else. Hoping that he would become a lawyer, his father had him prepared for college by Oliver C. Grosvenor of Rome, N. Y., and at the age of eighteen he entered the junior class of Hamilton College, where he was graduated in 1828. He then studied law with Judge Chapin of Rochester and with Alanson Bennett of Rome.

In the latter place he was converted under the preaching of Charles G. Finney [*q.v.*], and joined the Methodist Church. In 1830 he was appointed teacher of Greek and mental philosophy in the Oneida Conference Seminary at Cazenovia, N. Y. The following year he returned to Hamilton College as a tutor and in 1833 became professor of ancient languages and literature at Wesleyan College, Middletown, Conn., in which capacity he served for ten years. In 1834 he was admitted on trial to the New York Conference and in due course was ordained deacon and elder. While at Wesleyan, his taste for controversy, manifested throughout his whole career, began to find expression. In articles published in *Zion's Herald* in 1835, in answer to those of Orange Scott [*q.v.*], Whedon opposed the radical abolitionist movement in the Methodist Church, and

in reply to "An Appeal to the Members of the New England and New Hampshire Conferences" issued by the abolitionists, he wrote "A Counter Appeal . . ." (*Zion's Herald,* Apr. 8, 1835), signed by Wilbur Fisk [*q.v.*] and other conservatives. On July 15, 1840, he married Eliza Ann Searles of White Plains, N. Y.

Becoming weary of teaching, he relinquished his professorship in 1843 and became pastor of the Methodist Church in Pittsfield, Mass., and in 1845 of the church in Rensselaerville, N. Y. He was not well fitted for the pastorate, however, for he was not a great preacher nor a man of the people; he lacked voice, training, and emotional quality (*Christian Advocate,* June 18, 1885, p. 392). Accordingly, when, in 1845, he received a call to the chair of logic, rhetoric, and philosophy of history at the University of Michigan, he returned to teaching. He took a prominent part in the affairs of the institution; in the classroom, according to a former pupil, "his commanding presence, imperative logic and *sesquipedalia verba,* always used with mathematical precision, hammered truth into us and clinched it." He was "lank and angular in form and feature with a considerable sprinkling of vinegar at times in his ways of expressing himself" (Shaw, *post,* pp. 95–96). Though willing to apologize for the presence of slavery, he strenuously opposed the extension of it, and because of his utterances and internal dissensions in the college, he was virtually dismissed in December 1851 (*University of Michigan: Regents' Proceedings . . . 1837–1864,* 1915, p. 502).

The following year he opened a school in Ravenswood, Long Island, but increasing deafness soon caused him to abandon the enterprise. After serving churches in New York City and Jamaica, N. Y., in 1856 he was elected editor of the *Methodist Quarterly Review,* which position he held for the next twenty-eight years. In 1852 he had published *Public Addresses Collegiate and Popular.* A vigorous defender of Wesleyan Arminianism, he completed in 1864 a work entitled *The Freedom of the Will as a Basis of Human Responsibility and a Divine Government Elucidated and Maintained in Its Issue with the Necessitarian Theories of Hobbes, Edwards, the Princeton Essayists, and Other Leading Advocates.* While this work had extensive recognition in scholastic circles, Whedon became most widely known through the popular commentaries on the Bible which bear his name. The five volumes on the New Testament appeared between 1860 and 1880. The greater part of them he wrote himself, but his nephew, D. A. Whedon, collaborated in the later ones. Four volumes of those on the Old Testament were issued under Whedon's editorial supervision before his death. Selections from his contributions to the *Methodist Quarterly Review,* and some from other periodicals, appear in *Essays, Reviews, and Discourses* (1887) and *Statements: Theological and Critical* (1887) edited by his son and his nephew, J. S. and D. A. Whedon. He died at the summer home of a son in Atlantic City, N. J., survived by three of his five children.

[Biog. sketch in *Essays, Reviews, and Discourses* (1887); *Minutes of the Annual Conferences of the Methodist Episcopal Church* (1886); Wilfred Shaw, *The Univ. of Mich.* (1920); L. C. Matlack, *The Antislavery Struggle and Triumph in the Methodist Episcopal Church* (1881); *Christian Advocate* (N. Y.), June 11, 18, 1885; *N. Y. Herald,* June 9, 1885.] H. E. S.

WHEELER, ANDREW CARPENTER (June 4, 1835–Mar. 10, 1903), journalist, author, and critic, who wrote under the pseudonyms "Trinculo," "Nym Crinkle," "J. P. M.," and "J. P. Mowbray," was born in New York City, the son of Andrew C. Wheeler, member of the New York state legislature (1835–36). The date of the son's birth is given also as July 4, 1835 (Wheeler, *post*) and as July 4, 1832 (*Sun, post*). He was educated in the New York City schools, and in 1857 entered journalism as a member of the staff of the *New York Times.* The following year, however, in the midst of the Kansas troubles, he was smitten with the Western fever, and for the next year or two lived the life of a pioneer in Kansas and Iowa. During this period he received $100 for a play which toured various western towns. Arriving in Milwaukee in 1859, he became local editor of the *Milwaukee Sentinel,* a position which he retained for three years. There he was in the habit of enlivening things by playing reckless practical jokes, as when on one occasion he so ridiculed a prize poem that the author challenged him, and then he avoided the duel by suggesting absurd weapons ranging from ice-cream freezers to rolling pins. During the Civil War he served as war correspondent, then engaged in newspaper work in Chicago for two years before returning to New York City.

His first engagement after returning to New York was on the *New York Leader,* for which he wrote dramatic criticism under the name "Trinculo." From the *Leader* he went as dramatic and musical critic to the *World,* where his weekly essays signed with his most famous pseudonym, "Nym Crinkle," attracted wide attention for their caustic humor and wide information. When Wheeler passed from the *World* to the *Sun* he continued to use this signature. While still on the *Milwaukee Sentinel,* he had

written a history of the city, *The Chronicles of Milwaukee* (1861), and in 1876 he published *The Iron Trail,* a western travel sketch. He contributed to periodicals, and wrote or collaborated upon several plays and melodramas, from which he derived considerable income. His play, *The Twins,* produced by Lester Wallack, is an adaptation of *A Tale of Two Cities.* Other titles belonging to this period are *The Toltec Cup* (1890) and *The Primrose Path of Dalliance* (1892).

Six or eight years before his death Wheeler withdrew from active journalism and retired to his farm, "Monsey," in Rockland County, N. Y. The break with the urban past was complete. Hiding his identity under the new pseudonym of "J. P. M."—later expanded to "J. P. Mowbray"—he sent to the *Evening Post* a series of vaguely autobiographical letters descriptive of a search for peace and new inspiration in nature, which were later collected and published as *A Journey to Nature* (1901). Other books by "J. P. Mowbray" followed: *The Making of a Country Home* (1901), *Tangled Up in Beulah Land* (1902), and *The Conquering of Kate* (1903). Besides his critical interest in music and the drama, Wheeler was himself an amateur songwriter, painter, and musician, and had made some study of law, medicine, and theology. In his later years he was increasingly prone to reflection on religious themes. He once took to the lecture platform to combat the ideas of Robert Ingersoll, and at the time of his death was working with his friend Edgar M. Bacon on a study of "saddle-bag" Methodist preachers of the Southwest, later published as *Nation Builders* (1905). Wheeler left a widow (his second wife) and three children.

[A. G. Wheeler, *The Geneal. and Encyc. Hist. of the Wheeler Family* (1914); *Who's Who in America,* 1901–02, from which the date of birth is taken; E. M. Bacon, "'J. P. M.,'" *World's Work,* May 1903; obituaries in *N. Y. Herald* and *Sun,* Mar. 11, 1903, *N. Y. Times,* Mar. 11, 14, *Evening Post,* Mar. 10, 14, 1903.]
E. M. S.

WHEELER, BENJAMIN IDE (July 15, 1854–May 2, 1927), university president, was born in Randolph, Mass., the son of Benjamin and Mary Eliza (Ide) Wheeler. He was a descendant of John Wheeler, who is said to have emigrated from England in 1634 and was one of the original proprietors of what is now Salisbury, N. H. The elder Benjamin was a Baptist minister and an austere man. The religious discipline to which the boy was subjected by his father did not, however, breed in him a distaste for religion, and he remained throughout life, at least nominally, a Baptist. To his father, also, he probably owed the beginnings of his intimate knowledge of the Bible, the book which he knew best and which strikingly colored his thought and literary style. From his mother, on the other hand, he obtained the sense of humor and the friendly outlook on life which were no less determining qualities in his character. After attending the Thornton Academy in Saco, Me., Franklin Academy in Franklin, N. H., and Colby Academy in New London, N. H., he entered Brown University, where he was graduated in 1875.

For four years after his graduation he taught in the Providence high school. He then served for two years as instructor in Greek and Latin in Brown University. During these years he left a strong impression on his students by the zest and vigor of his teaching. He also began to display an active interest in politics which continued throughout his life. In 1880–81 he was a member of the school committee of Providence, and he joined a group of young men who formed a Democratic club with the purpose of attempting to overthrow the machine which dominated the government of Rhode Island. Many years later, when he was living in Ithaca, he took an active part in Grover Cleveland's second campaign. Membership in the Democratic party did not prevent him, however, from becoming an ardent friend and supporter of Theodore Roosevelt. In July 1881 he was married to Amey Webb, of Providence. The four years after his marriage he spent in German universities, studying comparative philology and general linguistics, and in 1885 he received the degree of Ph.D., *summa cum laude,* at the University of Heidelberg.

Returning to America, he served for one year as instructor in German at Harvard, and was then called to Cornell as professor of comparative philology and instructor in Latin and Greek, his title being changed in 1888 to that of professor of Greek and comparative philology. He remained at Cornell for thirteen years, during one of which (1895–96) he was absent on leave, serving as professor of Greek literature in the American School of Classical Studies in Athens. He was not only a brilliant and admired teacher, but he took an active interest in his students outside the classroom, guiding them and advising them in their sports and activities. Most of his scholarly work was done while at Cornell. Among his most notable publications were *The Greek Noun-Accent* (1885), his doctoral dissertation; *Analogy and the Scope of Its Application in Language* (1887); *Introduction to the Study of the History of Language* (1891), with H. A.

Strong and W. S. Logeman; *Dionysos and Immortality* (1899), an Ingersoll Lecture at Harvard; and *Alexander the Great: The Merging of East and West in Universal History* (1900).

Wheeler's career at Cornell was brought to a close in 1899 by his acceptance of an invitation to become president of the University of California. When he came to it, the university was not more than forty years old, and under favorable conditions was certain to grow in size and importance with the rapid growth of the state. He had not been in office more than a year when he presented to the regents a list of some fifteen pressing requirements of the university, including new professorships, departments, schools, buildings, and laboratories; and when he came to retire, all these demands either had been fulfilled or were in process of fulfilment. During these twenty years the students and the faculty increased four-fold; twenty new departments were added; new divisions for special scientific research were established in various parts of the state; the summer session and the extension division were expanded; and the material equipment was greatly enlarged. The course of this growth was unquestionably determined principally by President Wheeler. In carrying out his plans his methods were somewhat dictatorial. Indeed, before he accepted the position, he had stipulated with the regents that he should have the sole initiative in the appointment and removal of professors and in matters of salary. Though he held the reins of the institution tightly in his own hand, it cannot be said that he ever restricted the liberty of the faculty in teaching and research. The welfare of the students, furthermore, was always a matter of special concern to him, and he took a direct personal interest in their activities. The system of self-government which he instituted functioned under his guidance with notable success, not only as a means of maintaining public order, but as an effective educational influence. With all his obligations inside the university, Wheeler kept in close touch with the alumni and the people of the state, and the institution was made the object of many benefactions, without which its expansion could not have advanced so rapidly or so successfully.

In 1909–10 Wheeler held the position of Theodore Roosevelt Professor in the University of Berlin, delivering a course of lectures which were later published under the title *Unterricht und Demokratie in Amerika* (1910). His residence in Germany under these favorable conditions renewed and increased his liking for the country, which had begun in his student-days many years before, and when the World War

45

broke out, his sympathies were with the Germans. Consequently, when the United States entered the war his previous well-known friendliness to Germany subjected him to suspicion and embarrassment. It was deemed wise, therefore, in 1918, to appoint three distinguished members of the faculty, who had from the beginning been devoted supporters of the cause of the allies, to act as an unofficial advisory administrative board. To this board he resigned the active conduct of the University, and to all practical purposes it performed the functions of a regent. The existence of such a board was not only desirable on public grounds, but also served to relieve Wheeler of certain duties which, owing to a slight decline in physical vigor, he was already beginning to find unduly heavy. It remained in existence until his retirement—and indeed for six months thereafter, with fuller powers, until his successor assumed office.

He retired in 1919 at the age of sixty-five, after twenty years of service, with the title "Professor of Comparative Philology and President Emeritus." He continued to serve the university in an advisory capacity and for one or two years offered courses in general linguistics. In 1920 he went to Japan as a member of an unofficial commission which was organized and financed by William Alexander of San Francisco, with a view to encouraging friendly relations between Japan and the United States. During the last few years of his life gradually failing health forced him to withdraw from all public activity. In 1926 he went once more to Europe and the following year died in Vienna, survived by his wife and a son.

[A. G. Wheeler, *The Geneal. and Encyc. Hist. of the Wheeler Family in America* (1914); *Hist. Cat. of Brown Univ.* (1914); biog. records, Univ. of Cal.; W. W. Ferrier, *Origin and Development of the Univ. of Cal.* (1930); *Who's Who in America*, 1926–27; *N. Y. Times*, May 4, 1927; personal acquaintance.]
I. M. L.

WHEELER, EVERETT PEPPERRELL (Mar. 10, 1840–Feb. 8, 1925), lawyer, civil service reformer, a first cousin of James Rignall Wheeler [*q.v.*], was a lifelong New Yorker. The son of David Everett and Elizabeth (Jarvis) Wheeler, he was born and bred in Greenwich Village, then a leading suburb of the city. His education was received in Public School 35, the College of the City of New York (then the Free Academy), where he received three degrees, (A.B., 1856; B.S., 1857; M.A., 1859), and Harvard (LL.B., 1859). The story of his early years he himself has told with charming detail (*City College Quarterly, post*). After his

admission to the bar in 1861 Wheeler practised steadily until his death. Eminently fair to opponents and deferential to the bench, he never failed to make the most of his vast legal learning, nor could he be intimidated or imposed on. In admiralty law, a field in which he specialized, some of his cases have become classic (see his *Reminiscences of a Lawyer,* 1927). Not satisfied with mere attainment in the practice of his profession, Wheeler consistently adhered to his belief that a lawyer owes disinterested service to the profession itself. He was one of the founders of the Association of the Bar of the City of New York in 1869, a member of the executive committee (1876–78) and of many important standing committees, and vice-president (1890). He also served on many of the important committees of the New York state and the American bar associations. In 1914–15 he lectured on the preparation and argument of cases before the students of the Yale Law School.

Although he never held elective office Wheeler was a member of the elevated railroad commission of New York (1875) and of the board of education (1877–79), and the candidate of reform Democrats for the governorship of New York in 1894. These official services were less important, however, than his devotion to civil service reform and to societies seeking better government. He assisted in drafting the revised Pendleton Bill which in 1881 established true civil service. Two years later he joined with Edward Morse Shepard [*q.v.*] in writing the bill that applied civil service reform to the state of New York, and in 1884 he drafted the rules for the city of New York. He was a pioneer in the activities of the Civil Service Reform Association, serving as chairman of the executive committee (1880–97), vice-president (1903–13, 1918–25), and president (1913–18). He gave wise and courageous service as chairman of the New York civil service commission (1883–89, 1895–97). In 1894 he worked zealously as one of the "Committee of Seventy" for the election of Mayor William Lafayette Strong [*q.v.*]. His deep passion for good government caused him to sign the "Address to the Citizens" which resulted in the formation of the Citizen's Union in 1899, and he took part in all the activities of the Union, particularly in the campaign of 1901 to elect Seth Low [*q.v.*]. From 1912 to 1918 he worked actively against woman suffrage, serving as president of the Association Opposed to Woman Suffrage and expressing his views with frequency in the letter columns of the *New York Times.* A list of the important committees he headed and of the offices he held is staggering, but to each he gave tireless and intelligent service.

His devotion to honest public service was not without motive in his deeply religious nature. Though forceful in opposition to corruption and unyielding in moral and ethical questions, he was a man of genuine humility and marked sweetness of nature. His deep piety found expression in service to the Protestant Episcopal Church as a vestryman, as deputy to general conventions (1907, 1910, 1913) and as president of the Church Club (1887–90), in work for the Young Men's Christian Association, and in his unflagging labors for the East Side House, a settlement he founded in 1891 and served as president or head worker until his death.

On Nov. 22, 1866, he married Lydia Lorraine Hodges of Rutland, Vt. She died in 1902. His second wife was Alice Gilman, daughter of Daniel Coit Gilman [q.v.], whom he married in Baltimore, Apr. 26, 1904. She and two daughters survived him. His only son, David Everett Wheeler, was killed in the World War.

Wheeler wrote extensively for periodicals in the fields of law, history, and economics. His most important books are *The Modern Law of Carriers* (1890), *Real Bi-Metallism* (1895), *Daniel Webster, the Expounder of the Constitution* (1905), *Sixty Years of American Life* (1916), *A Lawyer's Study of the Bible* (1919). His writing is not distinguished in style, but each of his books and many of his pamphlets made important contributions in their fields.

[Wheeler's *Sixty Years of Am. Life* (1916) deals frankly with his public career and politics of the day; chapters omitted from the book appeared in *City Coll. Quart.*, Mar., Dec. 1917, Oct. 1920. See also *Who's Who in America*, 1924–25; *City Coll. Quart.*, Apr. 1925; *N. Y. County Lawyers' Asso. Year Book, 1925* (n.d.); A. G. Wheeler, *The Geneal. and Encyc. Hist. of the Wheeler Family in America* (1914); obituary in *N. Y. Times*, Feb. 10, 1925.]   D. A. R.

WHEELER, GEORGE MONTAGUE (Oct. 9, 1842–May 3, 1905), topographical engineer, was born at Hopkinton, Mass., a descendant of George Wheeler who was in Concord, Mass., as early as 1638, and the son of John and Miriam P. (Daniels) Wheeler. On July 1, 1862, he was appointed a cadet at the United States Military Academy, nominally from the territory of Colorado, although his family was then residing at Hopkinton. Graduating on June 18, 1866, he was commissioned second lieutenant in the Corps of Engineers, and was employed on surveying duty in California and on the staff of the commanding general, Department of California, until 1871, meanwhile being promoted first lieutenant, Mar. 7, 1867. In 1871 he was selected to take charge of the survey of the territory of the United States west of the 100th meridian, which was to prove the great work of his life, absorbing nearly all his energies until his retirement. The primary object of the survey was the topographic mapping of the country, which was still largely unexplored, but the scope of the work was eventually extended to include exhaustive investigation of geological, zoölogical, and ethnological matters. The field work continued from 1871 to 1879, involving fourteen trips of from three to eight and one half months each. Writing in 1883, Wheeler said: "The field trips were often attended by the greatest hardship, deprivation, exposure and fatigue, in varying and often unhealthy climates at latitudes from 31° N to 47° N and Altitudes from 200 ft. below sea level (in the deserts of Eastern Cal[a]. Death Valley, Amargosa &c) to nearly 15,000 ft. among the mountain peaks of the Sierra Madre (Cal[a]) Sierra Nevada and Cascade Ranges" (manuscript in War Department files). As the work proceeded, partial accounts of one sort or another appeared in some forty volumes. The definitive *Report upon United States Geographical Surveys West of the One Hundredth Meridian* was published between 1875 and 1889 in seven volumes, one supplementary volume, one topographical atlas, and one geological atlas.

Wheeler was promoted to the rank of captain in 1879. The organization of which he was chief lost its identity in that year, being merged in the newly created Geological Survey, but he was occupied most of the time for the next nine years in completing reports and supervising publication. In 1881 he was commissioner of the United States at the third International Geographical Congress and Exhibition at Venice, upon which he published a report in 1885, and then spent some time in investigating governmental survey systems in Europe. Exposure and fatigue during his explorations had broken his health, and a retiring board which examined him in 1883, at his own request, found him permanently incapacitated for active service. No action was taken on its report at the time, however, and he was allowed to continue his work at his own discretion, working as much or as little as he felt able, until 1888. Then the five-year-old report of the board was at last approved, and he was placed on the retired list, June 15, 1888. By an act of Congress approved Sept. 27, 1890, he was given the rank and pay of major from July 23, 1888, the date on which he would have been promoted if he had remained on the active list. He died in New York, where he had spent the last years of his life. His wife was Lucy, daughter of James

Blair and grand-daughter of Francis P. Blair, 1791–1876 [*q.v.*].

[G. W. Cullum, *Biog. Reg. Officers and Grads. U. S. Mil. Acad.* (3rd ed., 1891); F. C. Pierce, *Hist. of Grafton, Worcester County, Mass.* (1879); *Who's Who in America*, 1903–05; *Vital Records of Hopkinton, Mass.* (1911); A. G. Wheeler, *The Geneal. and Encyc. Hist. of the Wheeler Family in America* (1914); *Army and Navy Jour.*, May 6, 1905; *N. Y. Times*, May 5, 1905; unpublished papers in the War Dept.]

T. M. S.

WHEELER, GEORGE WAKEMAN (Dec. 1, 1860–July 27, 1932), jurist, was born in Woodville, Miss., from which place his parents moved to New Jersey not long after the close of the Civil War. His father, for whom he was named, became a judge of the court of common pleas of Bergen County, N. J.; his great-grandfather, Stephen Wheeler, had been a judge of the Fairfield County court in Connecticut. On his maternal side he was of Scotch descent, his mother, Lucy (Dowie), having been born in Edinburgh, though she lived most of her life in Andes, N. Y. After preparation at the Hackensack Military Academy and at Williston Seminary, Easthampton, Mass., Wheeler entered Yale, where he received the degree of A.B. in 1881, and that of LL.B., *cum laude,* in 1883.

After his graduation from the Yale Law School, he and his college classmate, Howard J. Curtis, formed a partnership for the practice of law in Bridgeport, Conn. He at once became active politically, and at the age of twenty-eight was city chairman and a state leader of the Democratic party. From 1890 to 1892 he served as corporation counsel of Bridgeport, and in 1893 was appointed a judge of the superior court, the youngest appointee in the state's history. Here he served as trial judge until 1910, when he was appointed associate justice of the supreme court of errors. In 1920 he became chief justice and served as such until his retirement under the constitutional age limitation in 1930. Twice he declined appointment upon the circuit court of appeals of the United States for the second circuit. In July 1894 he was married to Agnes Leonard Macy, and a son and a daughter survived him.

Active, energetic, generous, and courageous, Wheeler did not limit his activities to the bench but held many positions of trust and honor. He was largely influential in procuring the adoption by the superior court of uniform standards of admission to the bar of the state, and in establishing the state bar examining committee, upon which he served as one of the original members in 1890–92, and again from 1897 to 1919, acting as chairman from 1913 to 1919. He was also a member (1924–32) of the council of the American Law Institute, engaged in restating the common law of the United States. From its inception in 1927 until 1930 he was chairman of the judicial council of Connecticut. In this capacity he was mainly responsible for the rules of summary judgment—an innovation —and the revised rules of discovery of facts before trial; a bill which he prepared and supported to establish a system of district courts to supplant the political justice of the peace and town court system failed of enactment. During the World War he was active as a member of the state council of defense and as chairman of the executive committee of the Bridgeport war bureau. One of his fiery war addresses at a great public meeting is said to have swayed sentiment so that a threatened strike of 5000 operatives in the local munitions factories was called off. For his Americanization work with the Italians in Bridgeport he was decorated by the Italian government as Chevalier of the Order of the Crown of Italy in 1920 and as Grand Officer of the Order in 1928.

Wheeler possessed a gracious and simple personality, which endeared him to many; yet he never hesitated to make enemies, for he supported wholeheartedly whatever he believed was right. In 1925, almost alone, and against opposition which approached abuse, he vigorously but unsuccessfully advocated the enactment of a statute making the buyer of liquor equally amenable to the criminal law with the seller. An example of his power in battle was his impromptu speech which led to the defeat of a resolution for a referendum of the state bar on prohibition (*Connecticut Bar Journal*, July 1929, pp. 188–94). These characteristics of vigor and courage distinguished his judicial career. Although the youngest justice, he was the only one to dissent during his first term, and until he became chief justice his dissents were many and forcefully expressed. As head of the court, he usually carried his associates with him, yet his independence of thought frequently led him where they were unwilling to go. Thus in his last year of service his associates denied recovery for a brutal automobile killing by a hit-and-run driver where there was no one to sustain the plaintiff's burden of proving negligence, and Wheeler reiterated his own stirring dissent of sixteen years earlier, setting forth the view that the common law must grow and expand to prevent injustice. Among the many opinions wherein he spoke for the court, those giving a liberal interpretation to the Connecticut Workmen's Compensation Act passed in 1913 well illustrate his progressive attitude towards the law.

His writings were mainly confined to his judicial opinions (83–172 *Connecticut Reports*). Worthy of mention, however, are the published reports of the Judicial Council of Connecticut for 1928 and 1930, which were prepared by him; his obituary sketch of his associate, Justice Curtis (114 *Conn.*, 739); his address on Daniel Davenport (114 *Conn.*, 743); an article, "Deeds— Inuring of after Acquired Title" (*Central Law Journal*, Dec. 11, 1885), prepared in collaboration with Joseph A. Joyce, and his address to the Judicial Council of Connecticut (*Connecticut Bar Journal*, October 1927). He died in Bridgeport.

[James Byrne, in *Conn. Bar Jour.*, Jan.–Apr. 1933; J. W. Banks, in 115 *Conn. Reports*, 731; *A Hist. of the Class of 'Eighty-One Yale Coll.* (1909); *Ibid.*, vol. II (1930); *Obit. Record Grads. Yale Univ.*, 1932–33; *Who's Who in America*, 1932–33; *N. Y. Times*, July 28, 1932.]   C. E. C.

WHEELER, JAMES RIGNALL (Feb. 15, 1859–Feb. 9, 1918), classicist, archaeologist, a first cousin of Everett P. Wheeler [*q.v.*], was born in Burlington, Vt., the son of the Rev. John Wheeler, president of the University of Vermont from 1833 to 1849, and his second wife, Mary Constance Rignall. He was a descendant of Sergeant Thomas Wheeler who was in Concord, Mass., as early as 1642 and died there in 1704. After he was graduated from the University of Vermont in 1880, James Wheeler went to Harvard University for further study in classical philology. In 1882, when the American School of Classical Studies at Athens was opened under the directorship of William W. Goodwin [*q.v.*], he was one of eight young Americans who formed the student body. In 1883 he resumed his studies at Harvard, and received the Ph.D. degree in 1885. Two years of travel and study in Europe and a thorough training in both the literary and the archaeological branches of classical philology formed the best possible basis for the studies which he thereafter made his life-work.

In 1886 he lectured at Johns Hopkins University, in Baltimore, Md., in 1888–89, at Harvard University, Cambridge, Mass., as instructor in Latin and Greek; from 1889–95 he was professor of Greek at the University of Vermont. He was called to Columbia University in 1895 and he remained there, teaching both Greek literature and Greek archaeology, until his death. When the faculty of fine arts was constituted in 1906 he was made at first acting dean, and later dean, filling this responsible post with distinction until the faculty was dissolved in 1911. His services in non-academic fields were many; he was a member of the Municipal Art Commission of the City of New York from 1916 until his death, and an alumni trustee of the University of Vermont. In 1907 he received, but declined, an urgent call to the directorship of the Boston Museum of Fine Arts.

For the last thirty-six years of his life he was identified more closely with the Athens School than probably any other individual. He was "annual professor" there in 1892–93, taking an active part in the excavations at the Argive Heraeum. In 1894 he was made secretary, and seven years later chairman, of the Managing Committee. For the remainder of his life he carried this heavy burden, with its many and often puzzling problems, without any relief from his academic duties. His grasp of the details of administration was sure, his tactfulness and firmness and patience were endless; and frequent visits to Athens kept him in close touch with the steadily increasing needs of the school. His annual reports as chairman of the Managing Committee from 1901 to 1918 are models of their kind.

His publications, not very extensive, were chiefly of archaeological character, but they included various more strictly literary and philological articles, reviews, and occasional addresses. In joint authorship with Prof. Harold North Fowler, and with the collaboration of Gorham P. Stevens, he published a *Handbook of Greek Archaeology* (1909). A lecture, "Greek Tragedy," published in *Greek Literature: A Series of Lectures Delivered at Columbia University* (1912) is notable for its exact knowledge, its sanity and justness of view, and its beauty of form. Among his more technical articles may be mentioned two published in *Harvard Studies in Classical Philology*: "Coronelli's Maps of Athens" (vol. VII, 1896) and "Notes on the So-Called Capuchin Plans of Athens" (vol. XII, 1901), and his important contribution, in conjunction with Rufus B. Richardson [*q.v.*] to the elaborate work *The Argive Heraeum* (vol. I, 1902), dealing with the inscriptions. From 1906 to 1911, Wheeler was an associate editor of the *American Journal of Archaeology*.

On July 12, 1882, he was married to Jane Hunt Pease, of Burlington; she survived him. There were no children.

[Minute Presented to the Faculty of Philosophy and the Dept. of Classical Philology, Columbia Univ., March 1918 (n.d., privately printed); *Who's Who in America*, 1916–17; A. G. Wheeler, *The Geneal. and Encyc. Hist. of the Wheeler Family in America* (1914); *Bull. Archaeological Institute of America*, Dec. 1918; H. N. Fowler, biog. art. in *Am. Jour. of Archaeology* Jan.–Mar. 1918; N. G. McCrea, biog. art. in *Am. Jour. of Philology*, Jan.–Mar. 1918; *Burlington Daily Free Press*, Feb. 11, 1918.]   E. D. P.

WHEELER, JOHN HILL (Aug. 2, 1806–Dec. 7, 1882), lawyer, diplomat, historical writer, was born in Murfreesboro, N. C., the son of John and Elizabeth (Jordan) Wheeler. His father was a merchant of Murfreesboro and also conducted a profitable shipping business. The younger John prepared for college at Hertford Academy and in 1826 was graduated from Columbian College (now George Washington University). In 1828 he received the degree of A.M. from the University of North Carolina. He studied law under Chief Justice John L. Taylor [q.v.], and was licensed to practice in 1827. That same year he began a service of four terms (1827–30) in the House of Commons from Hertford County. He was defeated for Congress in 1830 and in 1832 was appointed clerk of the commission to adjudicate upon claims of Americans against France for spoliations. He became superintendent of the Charlotte branch of the United States mint in January 1837, and after four years of service was removed to give place to a Whig. In 1842 he changed his residence to Lincoln County, and was elected state treasurer. Defeated for reëlection in 1844, he spent several years in the preparation of his *Historical Sketches of North Carolina* (1851). He was a member of the House of Commons in 1852. Appointed minister to Nicaragua through the influence of James C. Dobbin [q.v.], he assumed office Aug. 2, 1854.

During his incumbency occurred the revolution and the arrival of William Walker's filibustering expedition. Walker [q.v.] captured Granada on Oct. 13, 1855. On Oct. 15, Wheeler visited Corral, the Legitimist president, with peace proposals from Walker, and was imprisoned for two days. Later in the month, the Rivas government was set up with Walker's assistance, and was recognized by Wheeler on Nov. 10. Secretary Marcy refused to receive the Nicaraguan envoy and censured Wheeler for his action. In May 1856, however, the envoy was received, and instructions were sent to Wheeler to recognize the existing government. Before he received them, conditions in Nicaragua had changed and in July Walker was inaugurated president. Although Wheeler knew that such was not the intent of his instructions he recognized the Walker government. His activities had passed all diplomatic bounds of propriety, and Marcy's patience, already sadly tried, now gave out. Wheeler would doubtless have been recalled and dismissed but for the friendly influence of Dobbin. In September Marcy summoned Wheeler to Washington, and, after demanding his resignation several times, finally

secured it two days before the close of the Pierce administration. Thereafter, Wheeler lived in Washington until the outbreak of the Civil War, when he returned to North Carolina. In 1863 he went to Europe to collect historical material and remained there until the close of the war. Returning to Washington, he spent the remainder of his life there, for most of the time engaged in journalistic work. His death came after a long illness.

Wheeler began his historical work in 1843 by compiling for the state *Indexes to Documents Relating to North Carolina*. His *Historical Sketches of North Carolina*, mentioned above, is a badly prepared and ill-assorted collection of documents, state and local history, biographical sketches, and statistics. Like all of his work it abounds in error. Its biographical portions are so partial to members of Wheeler's own party, that it was nicknamed "The Democratic Stud-Book." In 1874 he published *The Legislative Manual and Political Register of the State of North Carolina*. His *Reminiscences and Memoirs of North Carolina*, containing material from his earlier volumes, was published posthumously in 1884. He edited, also, *The Narrative of Colonel David Fanning* (1861). In spite of their defects, his books performed a valuable service in arousing historical interest both in North Carolina and in other Southern states.

Wheeler was twice married: first, Apr. 19, 1830, to Mary Elizabeth, daughter of Rev. O. B. Brown of Washington; she died in 1836, and on Nov. 8, 1838, he married Ellen Oldmixon Sully, daughter of Thomas Sully [q.v.] of Philadelphia, the famous artist. By his first wife he had two sons and a daughter; by the second, two sons.

[S. A. Ashe, *Biog. Hist. of N. C.*, vol. VII (1908); W. O. Scroggs, *Filibusters and Financiers* (1916); a MS. by Wheeler, "Nicaragua," and his scrapbook and papers in Lib. of Cong.; William Walker, *The War in Nicaragua* (1860); J. B. Moore, *A Digest of International Law* (1906); *House Ex. Doc. 103*, 34 Cong., 1 Sess.; manuscript material in Department of State; *Washington Post*, Dec. 9, 1882.]   J. G. deR. H.

WHEELER, JOSEPH (Sept. 10, 1836–Jan. 25, 1906), soldier and congressman, was born near Augusta, Ga., the son of Joseph and Julia Knox (Hull) Wheeler. Both parents were of New England colonial stock; the father, who moved to Augusta in young manhood, was descended from Moses Wheeler, an early settler of New Haven, Conn. After a diffused and unsystematic primary education, the boy was appointed to the United States Military Academy in 1854. Graduating in 1859 with a fine military and a mediocre academic record, he was brevetted a second lieutenant of dragoons and saw two years' service in the Regular Army, some of which was against Indians in New Mexico. Upon secession becoming an accomplished fact, he at once cast his lot with the South and resigned from the army, Apr. 22, 1861.

He was commissioned initially a first lieutenant in the Confederate States Army, but soon was offered the colonelcy of the 19th Alabama Infantry. He fought through the Shiloh campaign with this regiment, gained recognition as a disciplinarian and a leader, succeeded to the command of an infantry brigade, and on July 18, 1862, was placed in command of the cavalry of the Army of Mississippi. He had now definitely assumed the military rôle which was to bring him his greatest distinction. In the next two and a half years he rose successively to brigadier-general, major-general, and lieutenant-general in the Confederate service, but in all this time he held one assignment, the leadership of the cavalry in the western theatre of operations. He covered Bragg's advance into and retreat from Kentucky and took a prominent part in the Murfreesboro and Chickamauga campaigns. After Rosecrans' retirement to Chattanooga, Wheeler executed a masterly raid on the Union communications, which, unlike most Civil War raids, had a material effect on the course of events. His cavalry participated in the siege of Knoxville and then opposed Sherman throughout his long progress through Atlanta to Savannah and finally to Raleigh. In this campaign Wheeler repulsed the attempt of Garrard, Stoneman, and McCook to outflank the Atlanta position, and his were practically the only troops opposed to Sherman in the march to the sea. His forces disintegrated at Joseph E. Johnston's surrender, and Wheeler himself was captured near Atlanta. He was then only twenty-eight years of age. Wheeler was the hero of a spectacular personal encounter with Union cavalry at Duck River, Tenn., June 27, 1863, was three times wounded in the course of the war, and is said to have participated in two hundred engagements and eight hundred skirmishes in that period. His sobriquet of "Fighting Joe" was unquestionably well earned.

Gen. Robert E. Lee bracketed Wheeler with J. E. B. Stuart [q.v.] as one of the two outstanding Confederate cavalry leaders. In breadth of military vision and in delicacy of touch, Stuart was undoubtedly the superior. Nathan Bedford Forrest [q.v.] had a lethal simplicity of action that perhaps surpassed Wheeler at his best, but the latter yielded to none in dogged aggressiveness, in hard hitting, and in reliability. Loyal to the persons and to the conceptions of his many chiefs, he was an ideal and almost invariably appreciated subordinate. Capable opponents, with superior forces of fine cavalry, never succeeded in mastering him. He was beloved and trusted by his men, and despite the fact that excesses were ascribed to his troops in the last days of the Confederacy, he enjoyed general popularity throughout the South.

After the war Wheeler established himself as a commission merchant in New Orleans. On Feb. 8, 1866, he married Daniella (Jones) Sherrod, daughter of Col. Richard Jones of Alabama. Their children were two sons and five daughters. In 1868 Wheeler moved to Wheeler, Ala., named in his honor, and engaged in cotton planting and the practice of law. As the tide of Reconstruction ebbed, he entered politics. In 1881 he was elected to the Forty-seventh Congress, but as the result of a contest was unseated, June 3, 1882, in favor of W. M. Lowe. Upon the death of Lowe soon afterward, however, he was elected to fill the vacancy and served from Jan. 15 to Mar. 3, 1883. He was reëlected to the Forty-ninth Congress and thereafter served continuously from 1885 to 1900.

As a representative he was chiefly active in military and fiscal matters. By virtue of long service he became eventually the ranking Democrat on the Ways and Means Committee, and fought strenuously for the low tariff principle. He pushed various pension bills and was instrumental in the congressional rehabilitation of Fitz-John Porter [q.v.]. On the whole, however, his interests were predominantly local, and he devoted the greater part of his energies to the direct service of his constituency. His chief public contribution was his untiring advocacy of reconciliation between North and South. To a host of people he embodied the reintegration of the Confederacy into the Union. In Alabama there was attached to the glamor of his Civil War record a high degree of personal popularity; and it was in this period that he built up the local esteem which resulted eventually in his choice by that state as one of its two representatives in Statuary Hall in the Capitol at Washington.

Upon the outbreak of the Spanish-American War, Wheeler offered his services to President McKinley and was appointed a major-general of volunteers. The presidential action was recognized and applauded as a significant effort to make the war an instrument to fuse the sections. Wheeler commanded the cavalry division of Shafter's Santiago expedition, landed at Daiquiri, Cuba, precipitated the engagement at Las Guasimas (June 24, 1898), and despite illness was present at the battle of San Juan Hill (July 1).

During the subsequent siege of Santiago, he contributed a disproportionate share of aggressiveness to the American high command. After the surrender of the city and the repatriation of the bulk of the expeditionary force, he commanded the convalescent and demobilization camp at Montauk Point, Long Island. Shortly thereafter he was sent to the Philippines in command of a brigade, but soon returned to the United States. On June 16, 1900, he was commissioned a brigadier-general in the Regular Army; he retired on his sixty-fourth birthday, Sept. 10, 1900. Thereafter he lived uneventfully, dying in his seventieth year, at Brooklyn, N. Y. He was buried in Arlington National Cemetery.

During the Civil War Wheeler wrote *Cavalry Tactics* (1863), a textbook. He was subsequently the author of "Bragg's Invasion of Kentucky" (*Battles and Leaders of the Civil War*, 1887–88, vol. III) and *The Santiago Campaign* (1898), a sketch; and with his wife prepared *American Ancestors of the Children of Joseph and Daniella Wheeler* (n.d.).

[A. G. Wheeler, *The Geneal. and Encyc. Hist. of the Wheeler Family in America* (1914); T. C. DeLeon, *Joseph Wheeler* (1899) and W. C. Dodson, ed., *Campaigns of Wheeler and His Cavalry* (1899), fairly complete but undiscriminating records; J. W. DuBose, *General Joseph Wheeler and the Army of Tennessee* (1912), confined to the Civil War; *War of the Rebellion: Official Records (Army)*; J. P. Dyer, "The Civil War Career of General Joseph Wheeler," *Ga. Hist. Quart.*, Mar. 1935; *Who's Who in America*, 1906–07; *Biog. Dir. Am. Cong.* (1928); G. W. Cullum, *Biog. Reg. Officers and Grads. U. S. Mil. Acad.*, vols. II (3rd ed., 1891), IV (1901), V (1910); *Thirty-seventh Ann. Reunion Asso. Grads. U. S. Mil. Acad.* (1906); *Army and Navy Jour.*, Jan. 27, Feb. 3, 1906; *Brooklyn Daily Eagle*, Jan. 26, 1906.]   T. J. B.

WHEELER, NATHANIEL (Sept. 7, 1820–Dec. 31, 1893), manufacturer, inventor, the son of David and Sarah (De Forest) Wheeler, was born at Watertown, Litchfield County, Conn., of English and Huguenot descent. Moses Wheeler, the first of the family in America, emigrated from England in 1638 and settled in New Haven, Conn., in 1641. After receiving a common-school education Nathaniel learned the trade of carriage-building in his father's shop and specialized in the ornamenting of carriages. In 1841, upon his father's retirement, he took over the business and for five years conducted it successfully. In the meantime he had become interested in manufacturing by hand such metal articles as buckles, buttons, and eyelets, and for a time carried on the two businesses in the same establishment, gradually equipping his metal-ware factory with machinery. In 1848 he formed the partnership of Warren, Wheeler and Woodruff with two men already engaged in the manufacturing of metalware in Watertown, and erected a new factory,

of which he took charge. In New York late in 1850 he saw the newly invented sewing machine of Allen B. Wilson [*q.v.*]. Contracting to supply five hundred machines to the firm controlling Wilson's patent, he engaged Wilson to superintend their manufacture in Watertown. Meanwhile the latter had conceived the idea of a rotary hook as a substitute for his double-pointed shuttle, and was given *carte blanche* by Wheeler to proceed with the perfection of a new rotary-hook machine. Obtaining a patent for this (Aug. 12, 1851), Wheeler and his partners reorganized their company as Wheeler, Wilson and Company, and began to manufacture the machine, Wheeler supervising sales and distribution, and Wilson manufacturing. In less than two years several hundred machines had been sold to the public, and introduced into factories in Troy, N. Y., Boston, Mass., and Philadelphia, Pa. For the better prosecution of the growing business Wheeler reorganized the company in October 1853, under the name of the Wheeler and Wilson Manufacturing Company. Three years later he removed the factory to Bridgeport, Conn., where as president he directed the company's affairs until his death. A four-motion feed which Wilson perfected in 1854 Wheeler immediately incorporated in the company's machine. With these several improvements the Wheeler and Wilson Manufacturing Company quickly became one of the four principal sewing-machine manufacturers of the United States and was one of the four composing the great combination established in 1856 to pool sewing-machine patents. In this Wheeler took an active part.

Besides attending to his growing business he invented and patented a wood-filling compound in 1876 and 1878, a ventilating system for houses and railroad cars in 1883, and a number of minor improvements in the sewing machine. He was a director of the New York, New Haven & Hartford Railroad, and of numerous other organizations, and served in the Connecticut legislature in 1866, 1868, 1870, and from 1872 to 1874. He was twice married: first, on Nov. 7, 1842, to Huldah Bradley of Watertown (d. 1857), and second, on Aug. 3, 1858, to Mary E. Crissey of New Canaan, Conn. He died in Bridgeport, survived by his wife and by two children of each marriage.

[A. G. Wheeler, *The Geneal. . . . Hist. of the Wheeler Family* (1914); Richard Herndon, *Men of Progress . . . Conn.* (1898); W. F. Moore, *Representative Men of Conn.* (1894); F. L. Lewton, "The Servant in the House," *Ann. Report . . . Smithsonian Institution, 1929* (1930); Patent Office records; obituaries in *N. Y. Times* and *New Haven Evening Reg.*, Jan. 1, 1894.]
C. W. M

WHEELER, ROYALL TYLER (1810–April 1864), jurist, was born in Vermont, the son of John and Hannah (Thurston) Wheeler. His father, a native of New Hampshire, moved to Vermont in 1800 and later to Ohio. Royall studied law in Delaware, Ohio, and was admitted to the bar. About 1837 he removed to Fayetteville, Ark., where he became a law partner of Williamson S. Oldham [*q.v.*], afterward a member of the Arkansas supreme court. In 1839 he married Emily Walker of Fayetteville, a native of Lexington, Ky., by whom he had three sons and a daughter.

Removing to Texas in 1839, he settled at Nacogdoches, where he formed a partnership with K. L. Anderson, vice-president of the Republic of Texas. Wheeler rose rapidly in his profession and acquired an extensive practice. He served one term as district attorney, and in 1844 was appointed judge of the court in the old Fifth District, embracing much of the eastern part of the Republic. As district judge he became a member of the supreme court, which was composed of the several district judges sitting *in banc,* and presided over by the chief justice. He was a strong advocate of the annexation of Texas to the Union, and when such union was accomplished, in 1845, he was appointed a member of the supreme court of the state, along with Chief Justice John Hemphill and Associate Justice Abner Smith Lipscomb [*qq.v.*]. After the positions on the court were made elective, in 1851, he was chosen without opposition, and was re-elected in 1856. When Hemphill was sent to the United States Senate in 1858, Wheeler succeeded him as chief justice. The conditions under which he worked during this early period in Texas are shown by the following entry in the diary of Rutherford B. Hayes, who visited Austin in February 1849: "Called at the room of an old law student of Delaware [Ohio], Royal T. Wheeler, now a judge of the Supreme Court. His office as judge, 'den' as he called it, being a log cabin about fourteen feet square, with a bed, table, five chairs, a washstand, and a 'whole raft' of books and papers" (*Diary and Letters,* vol. I, 1922, p. 260).

Although reared a Whig, Wheeler advocated secession with voice and pen. As chief justice, sitting in chambers at Austin, he upheld and enforced the Confederate conscription law, a position in which he was sustained by a majority of the court (26 *Texas,* 387). The turmoil and bloodshed resulting from the great civil strife deranged his mind. One of his biographers, George W. Paschal, a strong Union sympathizer, who later became reporter for the Texas supreme

court, states that Wheeler "fell into the morbid belief that, more than anyone else, he was responsible for the terrible baptism of blood through which our country was passing. Zealous, ardent, and sensitively conscientious, the ordeal was too severe for a man whose temperament always tended to melancholy. His salary became worthless; he was without income; he had saved little of his fortune; there was no probable, and hardly any possible, employment for his children, whom he so much loved. His reason could not stand the severe strain; he perished by his own hands. . . . The distempered and lamented chief justice was as little responsible for the act by which he threw away his life, as he was for the terrible drama in which so many good men perished" (28 *Texas,* viii). His death occurred in Washington County in April 1864.

He was a man of blameless character. While he was not so brilliant of mind as his two great associates on the first supreme court of the state of Texas, his was the genius of hard labor and patient research. His early experience in the criminal practice resulted in his writing the opinion in a large percentage of the criminal cases coming before the court during his twenty years on the bench. His opinions are to be found in the first twenty-six volumes of the *Texas Reports.*

[See 27 *Texas,* v; 28 *Texas,* vi; J. D. Lynch, *The Bench and Bar of Texas* (1885); J. H. Davenport, *The Hist. of the Supreme Court of the State of Texas* (copr. 1917); *Biog. Encyc. of Texas* (1880); Brown Thurston, *Thurston Geneal.* (1892). All the foregoing give year of birth as 1810, but A. G. Wheeler, *The Geneal. and Encyc. Hist. of the Wheeler Family in America,* gives the date as Feb. 2, 1804.]   C. S. P.

WHEELER, SCHUYLER SKAATS (May 17, 1860–Apr. 20, 1923), inventor, engineer, and manufacturer, was born in New York City, the son of James Edwin and Annie (Skaats) Wheeler. He entered Columbia College, but left in 1881 to become assistant electrician in the American branch of the Jablochkoff Electric Light Company. He soon obtained a place on Thomas A. Edison's engineering staff, and was present upon the historic occasion of the opening of the Pearl Street Central Station in New York in 1883, when the incandescent light was introduced. A number of distribution systems were subsequently established under Wheeler's supervision. Among the more notable of these were the underground systems at Fall River, Mass., and Newburgh, N. Y., the latter of which he operated.

Installing and operating plants soon lost their interest for him, while invention and manufacturing claimed his attention. In 1886, after a short period with the Herzog Teleseme Company, he became associated with the C. & C.

Electric Motor Company organized by Charles G. Curtis and Francis B. Crocker [q.v.] for the manufacture of small electric motors. Under Wheeler's direction as designer, electrician, and manager, the business of the concern expanded rapidly. In 1888, however, Crocker and Wheeler severed their connection with the enterprise and founded the Crocker-Wheeler Company, which soon attained a prominent position in the manufacture of motors. Of this concern Wheeler was president from 1889. In addition to his private business he also acted from 1888 to 1895 as electrical expert of the board of electrical control of New York, and upon him devolved the responsibility of seeing that all overhead lines were placed underground. So energetically did he carry out his duty that poles were removed by force when other means failed. In 1895 he resigned this position in order to devote his time exclusively to his manufacturing interests. In that same year the works of the Crocker-Wheeler Company in Ampere, N. J., were completely destroyed by fire. The construction of a modern plant was started immediately, however, and the work of the concern continued meanwhile in tents and sheds.

In 1901 Wheeler presented to the American Institute of Electrical Engineers a remarkable collection of electrical books, the Latimer Clark library, which he purchased in London, including practically every known publication in the English language on the subject of electricity printed prior to 1886. In 1905–06 he served as president of the Institute and at the time of his death was chairman of the committee on a code of principles of professional conduct. He was also a member of the American Society of Mechanical Engineers, and was one of the founders of the United Engineering Society. In 1922 he served as one of the American representatives at the meeting of the International Electrotechnical Commission held at Geneva, Switzerland. He was a contributor to technical journals, and with his partner, Crocker, published *Practical Management of Dynamos and Motors* (copr. 1894), which had many printings and was widely circulated.

Among his more famous inventions were the electric fire-engine system, patented Feb. 24, 1885, the electric elevator, for which he received patents Apr. 21 and Aug. 18, 1885, the series multiple motor control, and parelleling of dynamos, for which he was granted patents over a period of years beginning in 1886. In 1904 he received the John Scott Legacy Premium and Medal of the Franklin Institute for his invention of the electric buzz fan. His death, from angina

pectoris, occurred at his home in New York City. He was twice married: first, in April 1891, to Ella Peterson, by whom he had one son who died in infancy; second, in October 1898, to Amy Sutton of Rye, N. Y., who survived him.

[*Electrical World*, Apr. 28, 1923; *Jour. Am. Inst. Electrical Engineers*, May 1923; *Trans. Am. Soc. Mechanical Engineers*, 1923 (1924); *Power*, May 1, 1923; *Who's Who in America*, 1922–23; *N. Y. Times*, Apr. 21, 1923; material supplied by A. L. Doremus, vice-president of the Crocker-Wheeler Electric Manufacturing Company, Inc., 30 Church St., N. Y. City.]
K. W. C.

WHEELER, WAYNE BIDWELL (Nov. 10, 1869–Sept. 5, 1927), lawyer, prohibitionist, was born on a farm near Brookfield, Trumbull County, Ohio, the son of Joseph and Ursula (Hutchinson) Wheeler. The family was of New England stock, and a great-grandfather of Wayne, Phineas Wheeler of Vermont, was a soldier in the Revolution. The day-time absence from home of Wayne's father, who conducted a stock-buying business in the neighboring village of Brookfield, made it necessary for the boy at an early age to undertake much of the work on the farm. At sixteen, on graduating from the Sharon, Pa., high school, he had his heart set on going to college but met opposition from his parents. Eventually his perseverance won his parents' consent, and to earn his tuition fees he taught school for two years. He then entered the preparatory department of Oberlin College, and received the degree of A.B. from that institution in 1894. In the meantime he worked as janitor, waiter, and financial manager of the *Oberlin Review*, and sold drugs and blackboard desks. He took almost no part in athletics, but was active in other extra-curricular activities, especially public speaking. In his junior year he was the unanimous choice of the faculty for student speaker on prohibition at a Neal Dow celebration. That he spoke eloquently is attested by his own comment, written years later, to the effect that he had poured out his "soul in youthful ardour, anathematizing the saloon and predicting its final overthrow" (Steuart, *post*, p. 39).

In after years Wheeler dated the beginning of his antagonism towards liquor from several terrifying encounters he had had as a child with drunken men. In the atmosphere of Oberlin, which Wheeler later pictured as a "hotbed of temperance people," this early predisposition became hardened into permanent form. In 1893, he met the Rev. Howard Hyde Russell, who had just organized the Anti-Saloon League of Ohio, and on his graduation accepted a place offered him by Russell as manager of the League for the Dayton district. Seeing that the organization had need of some one with legal training, Wheeler resolved to become a lawyer, and for the next year spent all his spare hours studying under the tutelage of a friendly Cleveland attorney. He then enrolled in the law school of Western Reserve University, where for three years, until graduation in 1898, he attended classes and also carried on his work with the League. On receiving the degree of LL.B. he was at once elected attorney for the League's Ohio branch and named "legislative secretary." In 1904, he became superintendent for Ohio, continuing in this post until 1915, when he went to Washington as general counsel (and later legislative superintendent) of the Anti-Saloon League of America. On Mar. 7, 1901, he was married to Ella Belle Candy, daughter of a merchant of Columbus, Ohio. Three sons were born of the union.

From his start as a professional prohibitionist, Wheeler displayed unusual talent for political strategy and campaigning. His first task of importance was to defeat a "wet" candidate for the Ohio State Senate. This he accomplished by getting a prominent Methodist business man to run in opposition, and then by organizing sectarian support for the latter (Steuart, p. 45). During his busy career he prosecuted over 2,000 saloon cases, collaborated in writing state and national prohibition legislation, and defended the constitutionality of prohibition laws before state and federal courts and the Supreme Court of the United States. With others he inspired the promulgation in 1914 of Secretary of the Navy Daniels' order prohibiting beverage liquors on any naval vessel or in any navy yard or station, and he was active also in lobbying the war-time prohibition acts through Congress. After the prohibition Amendment passed Congress, his work with state legislatures helped to bring about ratification in the short period of thirteen months. According to his biographer (Ibid., ch. VIII), Wheeler claimed authorship of the prohibition enforcement measure, the Volstead Act. This claim, however, is disputed.

Measured by any gauge Wheeler was a strong man, though he lacked the qualities of imagination and perspective essential to greatness. He was audacious, tireless, persistent, and imbued with a "passionate sincerity that bordered unscrupulousness" (Steuart, p. 14). Nothing could shake his confidence in the soundness and wisdom of his convictions. He saw little virtue in the policy favored by other prohibitionists of fostering temperance through education. Always he desired "the most severe penalties, the most aggressive policies even to calling out the Army and Navy, the most relentless prosecution. A favorite phrase of his was: 'We'll make them be-

lieve in punishment after death'" (Ibid., p. 14). Wheeler's qualities (including his limitations) might at any other period have carried their possessor no farther than a modest success in business or in the ministry or in politics. In his career he was greatly helped by the circumstances that his work coincided in time with a spontaneous impulse to reform which made its appearance in America shortly after the turn of the century. By 1933, six years after Wheeler's death, the mighty edifice of Prohibition, to the building and shaping of which he had given his life, had been swept out of existence. By some it was believed that had Wheeler lived this result could never have come about. Others held that it was Wheelerism in prohibition which made its ultimate collapse not only possible but inevitable. His death, resulting from a kidney ailment, followed only a few weeks the tragic fate of his wife, burned to death in their country home.

[Who's Who in America, 1826–27; World (N. Y.); N. Y. Times, June 18, 24, 27, 1926, Sept. 6, 1927; Justin Steuart, Wayne Wheeler, Dry Boss (copr. 1928); "Prohibition's Field Marshal," Christian Century, Sept. 15, 1927; Nation, Sept. 14, 1927; Proc. Anti-Saloon League of America, 1927; P. H. Odegard, Pressure Politics: The Story of the Anti-Saloon League (1928); information from Wheeler's associates.]
W. E. S—a.

WHEELER, WILLIAM (Dec. 6, 1851–July 1, 1932), engineer, educator, was born at Concord, Mass., the son of Edwin and Mary (Rice) Wheeler, and a descendant of George Wheeler who came from England to America about 1638. He received his early education in the public schools at Concord, and then entered the Massachusetts Agricultural College at Amherst, where he was a member of the first class (1871) to graduate from that institution. While at college he carried on considerable engineering work besides making an excellent scholastic record. He was first engaged upon railroad work in New York and Massachusetts, becoming resident engineer in charge of the Hardwick division of the Central Massachusetts Railroad in 1872. The following year he opened an office at Boston as a civil engineer and made surveys and plans for the Concord water works, which project was completed under his direction in 1874. During 1874–76, in partnership with his cousin Horace W. Blaisdell, he constructed several stone arch bridges over the Charles River, and reported upon railroad and water-supply projects in Massachusetts.

In 1876 he entered into a contract with the Japanese government to serve for two years as professor of mathematics and civil engineering at the Imperial Agricultural College of Sapporo, Japan, started with the aid of President William

S. Clark [*q.v.*], of the Massachusetts Agricultural College and modeled upon that institution. After Clark's return to America in 1877, Wheeler became president of the college. His work in Japan was fundamentally important. In addition to his teaching duties, he planned and constructed harbor improvements, bridges, highways, and railroads, and founded a weather bureau and an astronomical observatory; he also aided in guiding proper building construction. During his last two years in Japan he was civil engineer of the Imperial Colonial Department. In recognition of his services the Emperor decorated him in 1924 with the Fifth Order of the Rising Sun.

In 1880 he returned to the United States, established an office in Boston, and engaged in engineering. His earlier achievements included water-works projects at Concord, Watertown, and Braintree, Mass., and sewerage and other works at the Massachusetts state prison, Concord. Later, under his supervision water companies were organized and water systems built and operated in municipalities in the other New England states, Florida, Kentucky, Tennessee, and Wisconsin. He developed a wide consulting practice, and became a national authority with respect to water works. He had considerable mechanical ingenuity, and from 1881 to 1883 was granted some fifteen patents, the most of them electric-light reflectors or appliances.

In Concord, Wheeler gave much time to public service, serving on the water and sewer boards, the school committee, the board of health, and the municipal light board. He was a member of the library corporation for thirty-nine years, during twenty-eight of which he was president; for twenty-six years he was trustee of town donations. In 1917–19 he served in the state constitutional convention. For thirty-six years he was a director of the Middlesex Mutual Fire Insurance Company of Concord; he was also a trustee of the Middlesex Institution for Savings —and for a period, its president—and a director of the Concord National Bank. As a trustee of the Massachusetts Agricultural College for many years, he rendered valuable service to that institution. In 1879 he came home from Japan to marry Fannie Eleanor Hubbard of Concord, who returned to Japan with him; they had no children.

[A. G. Wheeler, *The Geneal. and Encyc. Hist. of the Wheeler Family in America* (1914); *Gen. Cat. Mass. Agric. Coll.* (1886); Inazo Nitove, *The Imperial Agric. Coll. of Sapporo, Japan* (1893); *Boston Transcript*, July 2, 1932; information on file with Am. Soc. of Civil Engineers; memoir by Woodward Hudson, prepared for the Social Circle of Concord.]   H. K. B.

WHEELER, WILLIAM ADOLPHUS (Nov. 14, 1833–Oct. 28, 1874), lexicographer, bibliographer, was born in Leicester, Mass., the son of Amos Dean and Louisa (Warren) Wheeler, and a descendant of George Wheeler who emigrated from England to Concord, Mass., about 1638. His father, a graduate of Williams College, was a Unitarian minister. After spending most of his youth at Topsham, Me., Wheeler entered Bowdoin College, from which he received the degrees of A.B. (1853) and A.M. (1856). After teaching in Marlborough and Northfield, he went to Partridge Academy, Duxbury, in 1854. In 1856 he resigned the preceptorship of this school and moved to Cambridge to become the assistant of Joseph Emerson Worcester [*q.v.*] in preparing his quarto *Dictionary of the English Language* (1860). On July 13, 1856, he married Olive Winsor Frazar at Duxbury. In addition to editorial work on the dictionary, he contributed to its appendix a table entitled, "Pronunciation of the Names of Distinguished Men of Modern Times." On the completion of Worcester's dictionary, he accepted from the Merriam Company an editorial position on the Webster dictionary. He supervised the new unabridged quarto edition of Webster and new editions of the National, University, Academic, and smaller editions. To the quarto edition of Webster (1864) he contributed an "Explanatory and Pronouncing Vocabulary of the Names of Noted Fictitious Persons and Places," including also familiar pseudonyms, surnames bestowed upon eminent men, etc. This was enlarged and published separately under the title, *An Explanatory and Pronouncing Dictionary of the Noted Names of Fiction* (Boston and London, 1865). While working on the dictionaries he also prepared, in collaboration with Richard Soule, *A Manual of English Pronunciation and Spelling* (1861). In 1866 he published a revised edition of the Rev. Charles Hole's *Brief Biographical Dictionary*.

In April 1868 he entered the service of the Boston Public Library, and on the death of William E. Jillson in December of the same year he was appointed assistant superintendent. He remained with the library until his early death in 1874. During these years he continued work on the revision of Webster, published an edition of *Mother Goose's Melodies* (1869), with antiquarian and philological notes, and edited a Dickens dictionary. The latter, though almost entirely his own work, was published in 1872 as "By Gilbert A. Pierce, with additions by William A. Wheeler." At the library he undertook to prepare a catalogue for the Ticknor Collection, which the Boston Public Library had taken over in 1871. This catalogue, though a good deal of the work was Wheeler's, was published after his death as by his successor in office, James L. Whitney. He began an encyclopedia of Shakespearian literature, which was never published, and two other reference books, *Who Wrote It?* (1881) and *Familiar Allusions* (1882), both finished by his nephew, Charles G. Wheeler. His critical work at the Boston Public Library appears in the Prince and Ticknor catalogues, in the list of engravings, the bulletins issued from time to time, and in the general card catalogue. Wheeler died at an early age and was never conspicuous, but he found time to do a great deal of useful and practical work. He was always distinguished for accuracy and thoroughness. A characteristic estimate is that of W. D. Whitney in a review of Wheeler and Soule's *Manual of English Pronunciation and Spelling*: "The conscientious and laborious care evidently expended upon the compilation of the work, the general good judgment which it displays . . . are . . . worthy of the fullest recognition" (*post*, pp. 913–14). Wheeler died in Boston, in his forty-first year, leaving a widow and six children.

[Nehemiah Cleaveland, *Hist. of Bowdoin Coll.* (1882); H. G. Wadlin, *The Pub. Lib. of the City of Boston* (1911); A. G. Wheeler, *The Geneal. and Encyc. Hist. of the Wheeler Family in America* (1914); J. L. Whitney, in *Ann. Report . . . Trustees of the Boston Pub. Lib., 1875* (n.d.); S. A. Allibone, *A Critical Dict. of Eng. Lit.*, vol. III (1871); W. D. Whitney, in *New Englander*, Oct. 1861 (review); *Atlantic Monthly*, Aug. 1882 (review); obituary in *Boston Eve. Jour.*, Oct. 29, 1874.]   M. L. H.

WHEELER, WILLIAM ALMON (June 30, 1819–June 4, 1887), vice-president of the United States, was born at Malone, N. Y., the only son and the second child of Almon and Eliza (Woodworth) Wheeler. He came from early Puritan stock, an ancestor, Thomas Wheeler, having been a resident of Concord, Mass., in 1637 and later a founder of Fairfield, Conn. Both his grandfathers were Vermont pioneers and soldiers of the Revolution. In 1827 his father, a promising young lawyer, died leaving no estate, and his mother supported herself and her children by boarding students at Franklin Academy. Young Wheeler worked his way through the academy and in 1838 entered the University of Vermont. During the next two years he led a studious and undernourished existence, once living on bread and water for six weeks.

Leaving college because of financial difficulties and an affection of the eyes, he returned to Malone and studied law under the direction of Asa Hascell. He was admitted to the bar in 1845, and on Sept. 17 of that year married Mary King. After six years, during which he seems to have been unusually successful, he retired from active practice to manage a local bank. In 1853 he was appointed trustee for the mortgage holders of the Northern Railway and in that capacity conducted the business of the company until 1866.

Meanwhile he was active in politics, at first as a Whig, and after 1855 as a Republican. He was district attorney of Franklin County, 1846–49; assemblyman, 1850–51, serving during his second term as chairman of the ways and means committee; state senator and president *pro tempore* of the Senate, 1858–60; member of Congress, 1861–63; and president of the state constitutional convention, 1867–68. His honors in state politics came to him probably because he was capable and independent, yet never openly attacked the Republican state machine. In 1869 he again entered Congress and was at once made chairman of the committee on Pacific railroads. Four years later Senator Roscoe Conkling [*q.v.*], with Grant's tacit approval, intrigued to make him speaker instead of James G. Blaine [*q.v.*]. Wheeler refused to become a party to the plan, partly because Blaine promised to make him chairman of the committee on appropriations—a promise that was never kept—and partly perhaps because of a morbid obsession that his health was precarious which afflicted him in his later years. But for the influence of his wife and his friends he would have resigned his seat and retired to Malone to die. In 1874 he was appointed on a special committee to investigate a disputed election in Louisiana, which had threatened to result in the collapse of civil government in the state. The so-called "Wheeler adjustment" which he proposed proved satisfactory to both parties. With these exceptions his Congressional career was uneventful. He rarely spoke except when he had immediate charge of a bill on the floor. Then he was forceful, persuasive, and adept in parliamentary tactics. In a period when public morals were low he maintained a reputation for scrupulous honesty. Once he indignantly rejected a gift of railroad stock. When the "salary grab" Act of 1873 became law he converted his excess salary into government bonds and had them canceled so that neither he nor his estate could benefit from the measure. He refused to approve a complimentary appropriation for a post-office building at Malone.

When Wheeler was first suggested for the vice-presidency he was practically unknown. Hayes wrote to his wife in January 1876, "I am ashamed to say, Who is *Wheeler?*" (*Diary, post*, III, 301). His nomination that year was the result of an attempt to secure a harmonious balance of sectional elements in the party. During the campaign he spoke logically, though not eloquently, in favor of civil service reform, honesty in administration, and federal assistance in raising educational standards in the South. As vice-president, he was a good presiding officer of the Senate. He cared little for the office, however. His wife had died Mar. 3, 1876, and he found his chief diversion in frequent calls on the Hayes family. Hayes thought him "a noble, honest, patriotic man" (*Ibid.*, IV, 50). If he had succeeded to the presidency, Wheeler would probably have made few changes in policy. In 1881 he became an inactive candidate for one of the senatorial seats made vacant by the resignations of Conkling and Thomas C. Platt [*q.v.*], and the next year declined an appointment to the newly created tariff commission. He had no children. At his death nearly all his estate was bequeathed to missions.

[A. G. Wheeler, *The Geneal. and Encyc. Hist. of the Wheeler Family in America* (1914); F. J. Seaver, *Hist. Sketches of Franklin County* (1918); C. R. Williams, *Diary and Letters of Rutherford Birchard Hayes*, vols. III (1924), IV (1925); W. D. Howells, *Sketch of the Life and Character of Rutherford B. Hayes* (1876); *Biog Dir. Am. Cong.* (1928); D. S. Alexander, *A Pol. Hist. of the State of N. Y.*, vol. III (1909); G. F. Hoar, *Autobiog. of Seventy Years* (1903); *N. Y. Tribune*, June 5, 1887.]
                                                E. C. S.

WHEELOCK, ELEAZAR (Apr. 22, 1711–Apr. 24, 1779), Congregational minister, founder and first president of Dartmouth College, was born in Windham, Conn., the only male child of Ralph and Ruth (Huntington) Wheelock. He was a descendant of Ralph Wheelock who settled in Dedham, Mass., in 1637. In 1729 he entered Yale College, and was graduated in 1733, sharing with his future brother-in-law, Benjamin Pomeroy, the first award of the Dean Berkeley Donation for distinction in classics. During the year following his graduation he continued his studies at Yale, was licensed to preach in 1734, and a year later was installed as pastor of the Second (or North) Society in Lebanon, Conn. Throughout the Great Awakening he was a popular preacher. Participating as fully as he did in the revival, Wheelock was accused by certain of his contemporaries (especially by Charles Chauncy in his *Seasonable Thoughts on the State of Religion in New England,* 1743) of stimulating an excess of fervor and of encouraging the Separatists. To the extent that he was an emotional preacher the charge is substantiated; on the other hand, he was a supporter of the Saybrook Platform and, consequently, a consistent opponent of the church polity of the Separatists.

In addition to his many duties as pastor and itinerant revivalist, and as farmer—by deed of church settlement, by marriage, and by inheritance from his father he was plentifully possessed

of farmland—Wheelock prepared white scholars for college, and in 1743 began to instruct privately the Mohegan, Samson Occom [*q.v.*]. Encouraged by Occom's progress, he envisaged a plan for educating and converting the Indians. In brief, the young Indians were to be removed from their native haunts to Lebanon. The boys were to be drilled in the elements of a secular and religious education, and in "husbandry"; the girls were to substitute "housewifery" for "husbandry" and to be instructed in writing at the school on one day a week. When properly trained the boys were to return as missionaries and teachers to their respective tribes, and the girls were "to go and be with these Youth" (*Narrative, post,* I, 15). To carry out this program Wheelock accepted two Delawares from New Jersey, who arrived at Lebanon, Dec. 18, 1754. Col. Joshua More of Mansfield, Conn., contributed a house and a schoolhouse at Lebanon (hence the name More's or Moor's Charity School). Other pupils were gathered from the New England tribes and from the Six Nations; by the year 1765 Wheelock had received twenty-nine Indian boys, ten Indian girls, and seven white boys, all supported by charity. In that year Wheelock had the pleasure of sending ten "graduates" of the school, including two whites, as missionaries and schoolmasters to the Six Nations; in the same year they reported that one hundred and twenty-seven Indians were attending the various schools in their charge. In 1765, also, Wheelock sent Nathaniel Whitaker [*q.v.*] and Samson Occom to England and Scotland to raise funds; they collected £12,000.

Unfortunately, mission work and recruiting were not progressing to Wheelock's satisfaction. Too many of the Indians sickened and died, turned profligate, and were in various ways inept. Sir William Johnson [*q.v.*] frowned on what seemed to him efforts by Wheelock to acquire territory among the Six Nations; after the Fort Stanwix Congress in 1768, and mainly because of the indiscreet behavior of Wheelock's emissaries to it, Sir William withdrew his favor from the school, and the Indians their children. Wheelock therefore could no longer hope to recruit from the Province of New York. With his parishioners, too, he was having difficulties, mainly concerning his salary, of which he believed he had in no small part been cheated. Furthermore, he desired to enlarge his educational program to include a college as well as a preparatory school. Accordingly he obtained from Gov. John Wentworth of New Hampshire a charter, dated Dec. 13, 1769, for Dartmouth College, to be located in New Hampshire. (The charter was obtained without the consent of the English trustees who supervised the fund collected by Whitaker and Occom in England; the Earl of Dartmouth after whom, but without whose knowledge, the college had been named, was their president.) Against the wishes of Governor Wentworth and of others interested in granting a site in New Hampshire, Wheelock selected Hanover; no adequate reason can be discovered for his choice of this town. Thither, having obtained a dismission from his parish, he removed his family and scholars in the year 1770.

Up to this time his health had been poor; he suffered from "cuticular eruptions," "hypochondriac wind," and asthma. In the new environment his health improved considerably, and he was able to carry an astonishing burden of duties. For the remaining nine years of his life he was president of Dartmouth College and of Moor's Charity School (without salary), supervised building and farming operations and the purchasing of supplies, preached and taught, acted as justice of the peace, arranged for recruiting parties to Canada (for Indian pupils), and begged persistently for money. In 1774 the fund raised in England was exhausted, and for the last five years he was harassed by debt.

He is celebrated in song as a teacher and hospitable entertainer of the Indians, but in the history of education his reputation rests more solidly on his founding of Dartmouth College, and on his maintaining the institution during the turmoil of the Revolution. He was an administrator rather than a scholar or writer; aside from the nine *Narratives* (*post*), in which he recounted the progress of his school, he wrote nothing of any importance. He was married twice: first, on Apr. 29, 1735, to Mrs. Sarah (Davenport) Maltby (d. 1746), by whom he had six children; second, on Nov. 21, 1747, to Mary Brinsmead (d. 1783), by whom he had five children. Of the latter group of children, the eldest son, John [*q.v.*], succeeded his father as second president of Dartmouth College.

[Sources include Wheelock's correspondence, in the possession of Dartmouth Coll.; Eleazar Wheelock, *A Plain and Faithful Narrative of the Original Design, Rise, Progress and Present State of the Indian Charity-School at Lebanon in Conn.* (1763), and the eight continuing narratives (1765–75); David McClure and Elijah Parish, *Memoirs of the Rev. Eleazar Wheelock* (1811); F. B. Dexter, *Biog. Sketches . . . Grads. Yale Coll.*, vol. I (1885), pp. 493–99; Frederick Chase, *A Hist. of Dartmouth Coll.* (1891); L. B. Richardson, *Hist. of Dartmouth Coll.* (2 vols., 1932), and *An Indian Preacher in England* (1933); J. D. McCallum, *The Letters of Eleazar Wheelock's Indians* (1932); *The Papers of Sir William Johnson*, vols. IV–VI (1925–28), VIII (1933); E. B. O'Callaghan, ed., *Doc. Hist. of the State of N. Y.*, vol. IV (1851).]   J. D. M.

WHEELOCK, JOHN (Jan. 28, 1754–Apr. 4, 1817), second president of Dartmouth College, was born in Lebanon, Conn., the eldest son of Eleazar [*q.v.*] and Mary (Brinsmead) Wheelock. Having attended Yale for three years, he transferred to the newly founded Dartmouth College, was graduated in the first class (1771), and appointed tutor. During the Revolution he commanded with some distinction various New Hampshire companies, attaining the rank of lieutenant-colonel. In 1779, on the death of his father, he became president of Dartmouth College, having been nominated in his father's will in lieu of his eldest half-brother, Ralph, an epileptic. His most important problems as president were the financing of Dartmouth College and of Moor's Charity School, the construction of new buildings, the instruction of Indians, and the control of the board of trustees. In 1783 he visited France and Holland to raise funds for the college, but was unsuccessful; fortunately he obtained after persistent efforts certain donations (about £1,300 in all) from a fund raised in Scotland by Nathaniel Whitaker and Samson Occom [*qq.v.*], and controlled by the Society in Scotland for Propagating Christian Knowledge. Other sums were obtained from individuals, from the sale of college lands, from the New Hampshire legislature, and by lottery. Although the income from these various sources was far from adequate, it is to the credit of John Wheelock that he established salaried professorships, built Dartmouth Hall and a chapel, and revived (1800) his father's educational program for the Indians. During his presidency, thanks to the efforts of Nathan Smith, 1762–1829 [*q.v.*], the Dartmouth Medical School was founded (1798).

The first twenty-five years of his presidency were relatively calm, and during them Dartmouth College expanded considerably; the last twelve were embittered by his struggles with the trustees, and the very existence of the college was endangered. The immediate cause of the hostility was the appointment (1804) of Roswell Shurtleff as professor of theology and pastor of the local church, an appointment not approved by the president and symptomatic of a decreasing lack of cooperation between him and the board. Five years later the trustees elected two candidates to fill vacancies on the board, thus aligning the majority of the trustees against the president. It was voted to deprive Wheelock of his professorship, but, because the college was considerably in his debt for his salary as president, the trustees were unable to carry out the vote. In May 1815, wishing to inform the public of the treatment he had received, Wheelock wrote his *Sketches of the History of Dartmouth College and Moor's Charity School, With a Particular Account of Some Late Remarkable Proceedings of the Board of Trustees from the Year 1779 to the Year 1815,* in which (among other matters and writing anonymously) he praised his own work as president and criticized the opposition of the trustees. During the following August the trustees removed Wheelock as president, trustee, and professor, and elected Francis Brown, 1784–1820 [*q.v.*], president.

The problem was now thrown before the public and was taken up by the newspapers of the state, the Democratic siding in general with Wheelock, the Federalist opposing him. In 1816 a Democratic legislature passed a bill changing the name of Dartmouth College to Dartmouth University, and increasing the number of trustees from twelve to twenty-one, the additional nine members to be appointed by the governor (William Plumer) and the members of his council. After some difficulty in securing a quorum the university trustees elected Wheelock president of Dartmouth University; the college trustees refused to accept the bill as passed by the legislature, with the result that both university and college attempted to function at the same time and in the same town. Wheelock was too ill to fulfill the duties of president, and William Allen, his son-in-law, accordingly became acting president. At this stage of the controversy Wheelock died. The case was tried in the New Hampshire courts and ultimately (Mar. 10, 1818) was brought before the Supreme Court of the United States (*Trustees of Dartmouth College* vs. *Woodward,* 4 *Wheaton,* 518) and won for the college by Daniel Webster.

Wheelock was survived by his wife, Maria Suhm, whom he had married in 1786, and by his only child, Maria. He was dictatorial, diffuse in speech and writing, and pedantic. The conflict of his later years, however, has distracted attention from the real services which he performed for Dartmouth College during the period immediately following the Revolution.

[Frederick Chase, *A Hist. of Dartmouth Coll. and the Town of Hanover, N. H., to 1815* (1891), cont. by J. K. Lord (1913); L. B. Richardson, *Hist. of Dartmouth Coll.* (2 vols., 1932); C. M. Fuess, *Daniel Webster* (2 vols., 1930); J. M. Shirley, *The Dartmouth Coll. Causes and the Supreme Court of the U. S.* (1879); obituary in *N. H. Gazette* (Portsmouth), Apr. 15, 1817; Wheelock's correspondence, in the possession of Dartmouth Coll.]   J. D. M.

WHEELOCK, JOSEPH ALBERT (Feb. 8, 1831–May 9, 1906), editor, was the son of Joseph and Mercy (Whitman) Wheelock. He was born in Bridgetown, Nova Scotia, and received his formal schooling at Sackville Academy. At an early age he went to Boston and thence to the newly organized Territory of Minnesota, following the advice of Caleb Cushing, who started Boston investments there. Wheelock reached St. Paul in 1850. After being employed as sutler's clerk at Fort Snelling by Franklin Steele, he began his life work in November 1854 by publishing with Charles H. Parker the *Financial and Real Estate Advertiser,* which was absorbed by the St. Paul *Pioneer and Democrat* in 1858. For a time he was associate editor of the *Pioneer,* but on Jan. 1, 1861, William Rainey Marshall [*q.v.*] made him associate editor of the *St. Paul Daily Press* when it was launched as a Republican organ to oppose the *Pioneer,* a Democratic paper. Marshall's joining the Union army left Wheelock in charge of the new paper. A series of consolidations, ending with the absorption of the *Pioneer* in 1875, made the *St. Paul Daily Pioneer-Press* the most influential newspaper of the northwest. For nearly thirty years the *Pioneer-Press* was Wheelock, and Wheelock was the *Pioneer-Press.*

Wheelock was known almost exclusively through his editorial columns, for he was not a man of easy friendships and "was little known for a man who wielded such a paramount influence over the early destinies of the state. . . . He was polished, reserved, retiring. He cultivated neither the manners of the frontier nor the popular language of the new country" (*Minneapolis Journal, post*). He rarely appeared in print outside his paper, although as commissioner of statistics he brought out in 1860 *Minnesota: Its Place among the States* and in 1862, *Minnesota: Its Progress and Capabilities,* reports which were praised as models of statistical presentation. No office-seeker, his only other public appointment was as postmaster of St. Paul (1871–75), until, in 1893, he was made a member of the city park board. Here he found congenial work, for the activities of this body carried into practice some of the things he had long advocated in the *Pioneer-Press,* and the system of parks and boulevards developed in St. Paul bears witness to the success of his endeavors.

A Republican and editor of the leading Republican paper of the state, Wheelock was no slavish partisan. He disagreed with his party's Reconstruction program and did not hesitate to state his views. For twenty years he fought the faction led by Ignatius Donnelly [*q.v.*], and through his "energy, impetuosity and indomitable will" saved the faction of Alexander Ramsey [*q.v.*] from "utter and ignominious defeat" (*Pioneer-Press, post*). When, in the eighties, the Republicans began to formulate a tariff policy Wheelock was indefatigable in opposing "the general proposition which the practical protectionist of today always tacitly asserts; that if an American citizen chooses to engage in any business under the sun, from the making of ice in Louisiana to the raising of bananas in Maine, he has a right to have a profit secured to him . . . through the medium of a tax on the whole people" (*Ibid.,* May 9, 1883). He would work for freedom of trade "which knows only such duties as may be necessary to equalize the cost of production here and abroad" (*Ibid.,* June 3, 1883). In the eighties he saw the significance of the silver question, and studied and expounded it frequently; in the nineties his editorials were generally acknowledged to have been a most significant factor in keeping Minnesota in the gold ranks, as well as exercising a potent influence over a much wider area. So often did he differ with his party that its leaders more frequently than not looked upon him as a bull in a china shop.

With all his preoccupation with national problems he used his editorials incessantly for what he conceived to be the welfare of St. Paul and Minnesota. When he died, tributes to his influence appeared in papers all over the country. "Joe" Wheelock's demise was a national event. Wheelock married Kate French of Concord, N. H., in May 1861, and at his death was survived by her and three children.

[More is to be learned about Wheelock through his papers than anywhere else. See also C. E. Flandrau, *Encyc. of Biog. of Minn.,* vol. I (1900); H. S. Fairchild, "Sketches of the Early Hist. of Real Estate in St. Paul," *Minn. Hist. Soc. Colls.,* vol. X, pt. I (1905); D. S. B. Johnston, "Minn. Journalism in the Territorial Period," *Ibid.;* "Memorial," *Ibid.,* vol. XII (1908); obituaries and editorials in *Minneapolis Jour.,* May 9, and *Pioneer-Press,* May 10, 1906.]

L. B. S—e.

WHEELWRIGHT, EDMUND MARCH (Sept. 14, 1854–Aug. 14, 1912), architect, was born in Roxbury, Mass., the son of George William and Hannah Giddings (Tyler) Wheelwright, and a direct descendant of John Wheelwright [*q.v.*]. He was educated at the Roxbury Latin School, received the degree of B.A. from Harvard in 1876, and then studied architecture, first at the Massachusetts Institute of Technology, later in Paris; on his return he worked successively in the offices of Peabody and Stearns (Boston), McKim, Mead and Bigelow (later McKim, Mead and White, New York), and E. P. Treadwell (Albany). In 1883 he opened his own office in Boston; in 1888 he formed a partnership with Parkman B. Haven which in 1910 became Wheelwright, Haven and Hoyt. He held

the position of city architect from 1891 to 1895, when, partly at his own suggestion, the office was abolished. He was appointed consulting architect, however, and during much of his remaining life he was intimately associated with a great deal of city building. As city architect his work consisted chiefly of hospitals, schools, and fire engine and police stations. In them all he set a new high level for municipal architecture in the United States. Charles Eliot Norton [*q.v.*] praised him because he "made the beauty of his buildings to reside in their proportions, and in the lines and arrangement of their doors and windows; and he had the strength to discard the superfluous ornament . . . which another man might have been tempted to add" (*Municipal Architecture in Boston,* 1898, preface). Important examples of his work as city architect are Agassiz School, Cudworth School, Bowdoin School, Mechanic Arts High School, Andrews School, the half-timber Long Island Hospital (Boston Harbor), and the charming Georgian Boston City Hospital (South Department). Perhaps his most widely known buildings are the chaste and dignified subway entrances of granite and bronze at the Park Street corner of Boston Common.

In 1900 he was made chief designer of the Cambridge bridge, and undertook a careful study of European bridges as a preliminary to his work. The actual bridge, magnificent when first built, has had its architectural effect spoiled by the later raising of the level of the Charles River by several feet. In 1900 Horticultural Hall was finished, from the designs of Wheelwright and Haven. They were also the architects of the Boston Opera House, completed in 1908. Wheelwright's last work was the $2,000,000 bridge at Hartford, Conn. It was possibly overwork in connection with this that led to his breakdown, and to his death two years later from melancholia in a sanitarium in Thompsonville, Conn. His most important consulting work was on the new building of the Boston Museum of Fine Arts (with R. Clipston Sturgis), of which Guy Lowell [*q.v.*] was architect, and on the Cleveland Museum of Art (with Henry W. Kent), designed by Hubbel and Benes.

Wheelwright's architectural imagination was wide; he sought the monumental, classic solution. Stylistically he was catholic, even erratic. Some of his schools are Italianate, some Georgian, some rather nondescript; the half-timber of the hospitals and the Marine Park Bath House is blatant, and the Boston Opera House and Horticultural Hall have quasi-Georgian red brick and white marble, and terra-cotta detail over-heavy and spectacular. Yet in all the work there is a counter-trend apparent, based on strict practicality and basic simplicity; and some of the municipal work, like the Hook and Ladder House No. 1 and the Eustis School, has a colonial style remarkably pure and charming for its date. In much of the later work, as in his bridges and subway entrances, this trend towards a rational simplicity has led to such delightful results as the brick house for W. S. Patten, South Natick, Mass. (1907), and the rationalized monumentality of the Farragut School in Boston (1904).

Wheelwright married Elizabeth Boott Brooks of Boston on June 18, 1887; his wife, two sons, and a daughter survived him. He was elected a fellow of the American Institute of Architects in 1891, and served two terms as director. He was the author of *School Architecture* (1901) and of many scholarly articles in the architectural press. His work served as the basis for *Municipal Architecture in Boston, from Designs by Edmund M. Wheelwright* (1898), edited by Francis W. Chandler.

[*Who's Who in America*, 1912–13; C. A. Hoppin, *Some Descendants of Col. John Washington . . . and Records of the Allied Family of Wheelwright* (1932); E. M. Wheelwright, "A Frontier Family," in *Colonial Soc. of Mass. Pubs.*, vol I (1895); *Fifty Years of Boston* (1932); I. T. Frary, in *Arch. Record*, Sept. 1916; *Am. Art Ann.*, 1912; Boston city directories; obituaries in *Am. Architect*, Aug. 28, 1912, and *Boston Daily Globe*, Aug. 16, 1912.]   T. F. H.

WHEELWRIGHT, JOHN (*c.* 1592–Nov. 15, 1679), clergyman, was born probably at Saleby, Lincolnshire, England. His father, Robert, and his grandfather, John, were landholders in the Fen district and moderately well to do. Wheelwright was admitted sizar at Sidney College, Cambridge, Apr. 28, 1611, and received the degrees of B.A. in 1614/15 and M.A. in 1618. He was ordered deacon at Peterborough, Dec. 19, 1619, and priested the following day. Through the death of his father and other relatives he early became possessed of landed property, and on Nov. 8, 1621, he married Marie, daughter of Thomas Storre, vicar of Bilsby. After the death of his father-in-law Wheelwright succeeded to the vicarage, Apr. 9, 1623, and retained the position for ten years. In 1633, although apparently he had not resigned, a successor was inducted. In the meantime Wheelwright had become a nonconformist, and had probably come into conflict with his superiors, since he was silenced soon afterward. For three years he lived privately in Lincolnshire. His wife died some time after the birth of their third child, and he married secondly Mary, daughter of Ed-

ward Hutchinson of Alford and sister of William, whose wife was the celebrated Anne.

It is possible that as early as 1629 Wheelwright with four associates had purchased land in New Hampshire from the Indians, though the authenticity of the so-called "Wheelwright deed" remains in question (Bell, *post*, pp. 79–148). At any rate, within some three years of his silencing, Wheelwright emigrated to New England, with his wife and five children, landing May 26, 1636, at Boston, where on June 12 he and his wife were admitted to church membership. It was suggested that Wheelwright become second teacher of the church there, where John Cotton [*q.v.*] was teacher and John Wilson [*q.v.*] pastor, but there was opposition to the proposal, and he became pastor of a new church at Mount Wollaston (now Quincy). Meanwhile the Antinomian controversy, of which his sister-in-law, Anne Hutchinson [*q.v.*], was the storm center, had begun. Wheelwright and Cotton alone among the clergy supported her. On a fast day in January 1637 Wheelwright was asked to speak at the church in Boston and took occasion to denounce the holders of the opposing view, who formed the great majority of clergy and magistrates. Haled before the General Court for this utterance, he was tried and condemned as guilty of "sedition and contempt of the civil authority," but further action was postponed. Much ill feeling had been aroused, however, and in September a synod was convened to review the whole controversy. Wheelwright attended; feeling was heightened; but the only definite result was the defection of John Cotton to the side of the majority. By the General Court meeting in November, however, Wheelwright, still refusing to retract the objectionable passages in his fast-day address, was disfranchised and banished from the colony. He demanded an appeal to the king, but the magistrates answered that the charter gave them final jurisdiction in the matter, and Wheelwright removed from Massachusetts Bay to the Piscataqua region.

After passing the winter probably at Squamscot, in April 1638 he bought land from the Indians at what is now Exeter, N. H. He was joined by his family and a number of friends, and despite the complaints of Massachusetts a community developed, a church was formed, and Wheelwright became its pastor. Shortly, however, Massachusetts extended its jurisdiction to include the new settlement, and some of the inhabitants, with Wheelwright, moved north to what is now Wells, Me. In 1643 he was allowed to visit Boston, and subsequently sent two letters to the authorities—one addressed to the

General Court, the other to Governor Winthrop
—in which he repented of his past conduct and
asked for the release of his banishment; the sentence was reversed in May 1644. Meanwhile
two pamphlets had been issued on the controversy: the first, *A Short Story of the Rise, Reign
and Ruine of the Antinomians* (London, 1644),
the joint work of Governor Winthrop and
Thomas Weld [*q.v.*], attacking Wheelwright;
the second, *Mercurius Americanus* (1645), his
reply. For about two years after his reconciliation with the Massachusetts colony he remained
at Wells, and was then called to the church at
Hampton, N. H., removing to that place in the
spring of 1647. Some eight or nine years later
he went to England, but in 1662 returned to New
Hampshire, becoming pastor of the church at
Salisbury, where he served until his death.

[*Winthrop's Journal* (2 vols., 1908), ed. by J. K.
Hosmer; Nathaniel Bouton, *Provincial Papers . . .
of N. H.*, vol. I (1867); C. F. Adams, *Three Episodes
of Mass. Hist.* (2 vols., 1892) and *Antinomianism in
the Colony of Mass. Bay* (1894); C. H. Bell, memoir,
in *John Wheelwright: His Writings . . .* (1876); John
Heard, Jr., *John Wheelwright* (1930); W. B. Sprague,
Annals Am. Pulpit, vol. I (1857); John and J. A. Venn,
Alumni Cantabrigienses, pt. 1, vol. IV (1927).]
                                          J. T. A.

WHEELWRIGHT, WILLIAM (Mar. 16,
1798–Sept. 26, 1873), promoter of enterprises in
Latin America, the son of Ebenezer and Anna
Coombs Wheelwright and a descendant of the
Rev. John Wheelwright [*q.v.*], was born in
Newburyport, Mass. His father was at first a
sea-captain and then engaged in the West India trade. William attended Phillips Academy,
Andover, with the class of 1814, then at the age
of sixteen shipped as a cabin boy to the West Indies, and after three years of adventure commanded a Newburyport bark to Rio. In 1823,
the *Rising Star,* bound from Newburyport for
Buenos Aires under his command, ran ashore
in the Rio de la Plata. Depressed by the accident, he refused to return home and shipped as
a supercargo on a vessel bound for Valparaiso.
In 1824, he became United States consul at
Guayaquil for five years. There he engaged successfully in trade and observed the many neglected possibilities of the continent which was
just emerging from the wars of liberation. In
1829, he made a hurried trip to Newburyport,
where he married Martha Gerrish Bartlet. Returning to Guayaquil and finding that his $100,-
000 business had been wasted by bad management in his absence, he moved to Valparaiso,
which, with London, was to be his chief scene
of action for many years. He did much to develop the city, building a lighthouse and other

port facilities and providing gas and water
works.

Becoming impressed with the potential advantages of a steamship line along the west coast
of South America, where baffling winds and
calms made the progress of sailing vessels uncertain and the mountainous terrain precluded
a coastal railroad of any length, Wheelwright in
1835 started to seek the permission of the west-
coast nations for such a line. Even the British
minister at Lima called him a "wild visionary,"
while the conservatism, inertia, and instability
of the new republics, often dominated by adventurous despots, led to vexatious delays. By 1838,
however, he had obtained the necessary concessions. Finding that American capital was not
available, he went to England to raise funds.
The propaganda of Junius Smith [*q.v.*] for ocean
steamships had just put London in a receptive
mood, and with the backing of Sir Clements
Markham, P. C. Scarlett, and others, Wheelwright finally secured on Feb. 17, 1840, a British charter for the Pacific Steam Navigation
Company (not to be confused with the American Pacific Mail Steam Ship Company formed
by W. H. Aspinwall [*q.v.*] in 1848 to operate
from Panama to California). Wheelwright became chief superintendent of the company, capitalized at £250,000, and late in 1840 took the
twin 700-ton steamships *Chile* and *Peru* through
the Straits of Magellan to enthusiastic receptions at Valparaiso and Callao, the first termini
of the line. The lack of coal was a handicap in
the beginning, but Wheelwright was constantly
prospecting mineral deposits and developed a
Chilean supply. The company lost £72,000 in
the first five years and for a time the dissatisfied
directors suspended Wheelwright from management, but later prosperity came, and the service
was extended to Panama. Wheelwright in 1844
proclaimed the advantages of a railroad across
the Isthmus.

Soon afterward, railroad development became
his absorbing interest. Between 1849 and 1852
he built the first railroad in South America,
running fifty-one miles from Caldera, the Chilean
port which he developed, into the rich silver and
copper mines at Copiapó. He soon extended
branches to Chañarcillo and to Tres Puntas,
6,600 feet above sea level. In a few years, dividends amounted to double the initial cost of
$3,375,000. In 1850 he gave Chile the first South
American telegraph line. Before the railroad
from Caldera to Copiapó was completed, Wheelwright had conceived his dream of a transandean
railroad, to run southeast diagonally across
South America nearly a thousand miles from

Caldera in Chile to Rosario on the Parana in Argentina, crossing the Andes at San Francisco pass, 16,000 feet above sea level. Finding that Chile regarded the stupendous undertaking as impracticable, Wheelwright decided to begin from the Argentine end and in 1855 secured a concession running from Rosario, 189 miles above Buenos Aires, northwest 246 miles across the pampas to Cordoba in central Argentina. Constant delays resulted from the rival plans of the American railroad builder Henry Meiggs [*q.v.*], from political upheavals, and from the Paraguayan war, but Wheelwright received the political backing of the Argentine presidents Mitre and Sarmiento, and the financial support of Thomas Brassey, the British railroad magnate, for the necessary $8,000,000 capital. The Grand Central Argentine Railway from Rosario to Cordoba was finally opened on May 16, 1870. For the remaining portion of the transandean railway, Wheelwright and Brassey raised $30,000,000 capital, but this was either diverted to naval and military purposes by President Sarmiento of the Argentine or else withheld by Wheelwright and Brassey because they feared such action. International jealousy and other complications delayed the final completion of the transandean railway until 1910.

The creation of the port of La Plata was Wheelwright's final important accomplishment. He noticed that the shallowness of the Plata estuary made it difficult if not impossible for large ships to reach Buenos Aires, and pointed out the advantages of the Bay of Ensenada about thirty miles below, near the spot where he had been wrecked fifty years before. On Dec. 31, 1872, he completed a railroad linking this port of La Plata with Buenos Aires.

By this time the iron constitution of the old man had begun to give way and in 1873 he sailed for England, where he died. His death was sincerely mourned by all Latin America and a bronze statue was erected in his memory at Valparaiso in 1876. It indicates a rather stocky, amiable man of the "John Bull" type; his portrait shows flashing eyes and strong features. His wife and a daughter survived him; another daughter and his only son died earlier. Though he had visited his birthplace rarely—in 1829, 1853, and 1855—he was very generous to his relatives there and left a portion of his ample fortune for the technical education of Protestant youths of Newburyport. His writings included *Statements and Documents Relative to the Establishment of Steam Navigation in the Pacific* (1838); *Report on Steam Navigation in the Pacific, with an Account of the Coal Mines of Chile*

and Panama (1843); *Observations on the Isthmus of Panama* (1844), and "Proposed Railway Route across the Andes," *Journal of the Royal Geographical Society,* vol. XXXI (1861).

[J. B. Alberdi, *Life and Industrial Labors of William Wheelwright in South America* (1877), with introduction by Caleb Cushing; F. M. Noa, "William Wheelwright: The Yankee Pioneer of Modern Industry in South America," *The Arena,* Dec. 1906, Jan. 1907; Leonard Withington, *The Substance of an Address . . . at the Funeral of William Wheelwright* (1873); *Bull. of the Pan-Am. Union,* May 1913, May 1915; Frederick Alcock, *Trade and Travel in South America* (1907); F. G. Carpenter, *The Tail of the Hemisphere* (1923); H. C. Evans, *Chile and Its Relations to the U. S.* (1927); F. N. Otis, *Hist. of the Panama Railroad* (1867); J. J. Currier, *Ould Newbury* (1896); F. W. Goding, *A Brief Hist. of the Am. Consulate General at Guayaquil, Ecuador* (1920); C. M. Fuess, *Men of Andover* (1928); *The Times* (London), Sept. 27, 1873.] R. G. A.

WHELPLEY, HENRY MILTON (May 24, 1861–June 26, 1926), pharmacist, editor, teacher, was born in Battle Creek, Mich., the son of Dr. Jerome Twining Whelpley and Charlotte (Chase) Whelpley. Both his parents were of New England stock, and both came from families of literary and professional activity. His father, paternal grandfather, and brother were physicians; his mother was related to Chief Justice Salmon P. Chase. His maternal grandfather, Warren P. Chase, was senator of Wisconsin and California, and a close personal friend of Abraham Lincoln. Young Whelpley received his grammar school training at Cobden, Ill., and his later education in Otsego, Mich., where he was graduated from the high school in 1880. While attending high school he began the study of pharmacy, working in drug stores in Otsego during vacations and after his graduation from high school. In 1881 he entered the St. Louis College of Pharmacy in St. Louis, Mo., graduating with highest honors in 1883. He managed a drug store in Mine La Motte, Mo., for a year and then returned to St. Louis to work in the editorial department of the *St. Louis Druggist,* which in 1885 became the *National Druggist,* with Whelpley as its editor-in-chief. In 1888 he assumed editorial direction of the *Meyer Brothers Druggist* and continued in this position until his death. In 1884 he began an association of forty-two years with the St. Louis College of Pharmacy, filling the positions of instructor in materia medica and chemistry (1884–86), assistant in microscopy (1884–86), professor of microscopy (1886–1922), professor of pharmacognosy, materia medica, and physiology (1915–26). From 1904 until his death in 1926 he was dean of the institution. During the period 1890–1909 he also served variously as professor of physiology, histology, and microscopy at Missouri Medical College and the St. Louis Post Graduate School, and as professor of materia medica and pharmacy in the Missouri Dental College and the medical department of Washington University. On June 29, 1892, he married Laura Eugenie Spannagel. He died suddenly during an attack of angina pectoris in Argentine, Kan., where he was on a vacation of a few days. He was buried in Bellefontaine Cemetery in St. Louis.

Soft-spoken, Chesterfieldian in manner, always well-poised and self-contained, Whelpley was a keen reader of character who instinctively sifted the good from the bad, but without giving evidence of his appraisal. He was a tireless, intensive worker, yet he did all things with such unhurried ease that even his intimates scarcely realized the variety of his accomplishment. In addition to his school duties and his editorial obligations—either constituting a full task for any man—he was for thirty years probably the most efficient officer in the roster of the Missouri State Pharmaceutical Association. In the American Pharmaceutical Association he held numerous offices, among them those of president (1901) and secretary of the council (1902–08). He became a member of the United States Pharmacopoeial Convention in 1890, served as a member of the board of trustees in 1903, and was secretary from 1910 until his death. He was a collector of material on American Indians, especially those of Illinois and Missouri, a member of the American Institute of Archaeology, and a thorough student of the subject. In addition, he was instrumental in establishing the St. Louis Zoological Garden, and held membership in such diverse organizations as the International Conciliation Association, the Missouri Historical Association, the Mississippi Valley Historical Association, and the St. Louis Society of Pedagogy.

[*Who's Who in America*, 1926–27; J. H. Beal, in *Jour. Am. Pharmaceutical Asso.*, Jan. 1927; C. E. Caspari, *Quart. Bull. St. Louis Coll. of Pharmacy*, Sept. 1926; *Nat. Druggist*, July 1926; *Jour. Am. Medic. Asso.*, July 3, 1926; obituary in *St. Louis Post-Dispatch*, June 26, 1926; autobiog. notes in MS. in the possession of Mrs. Whelpley; personal knowledge.]
M. G. S.

WHERRY, ELWOOD MORRIS (Mar. 26, 1843–Oct. 5, 1927), missionary, the son of James and Sarah (Nesbit) Wherry, was born in South Bend, Pa. Having received his preparation at Eldersridge Academy, he entered Jefferson (later Washington and Jefferson) College, and was graduated with the degree of A.B. in 1862. He then organized a select school at Waynesburg, Pa., and taught there until October 1864. Meanwhile, he united with the Presbyterian church

of the town. Entering Princeton Theological Seminary in the fall of 1864, he was graduated in 1867. On May 8 of that year he was ordained by the Donegal Presbytery, and on July 17 he married Clara Maria Buchanan. The following October he and his wife sailed for India as missionaries of the Presbyterian Church. There he served until 1889, with the usual interruptions of furloughs, and again from 1898 until 1922.

Joining the Panjab Mission, he was first stationed at Rawalpindi and was soon afterward transferred to Ludhiana (Lodiana), where he served until 1883 as writer, editor, and superintendent of the mission press. Thereafter for five years he was professor of Old Testament literature and church history in the resuscitated theological seminary at Saharanpur, U. P., and stated clerk of the Synod of India. From 1889 until 1898 he was stationed in Chicago, Ill., as district secretary of the American Tract Society, having resigned from his mission to educate his two sons and five daughters in America. Reappointed to India in 1898, he resumed service in Ludhiana, where until 1922 he was chiefly occupied with educational and literary work. He was moderator of his Synod in 1900 and labored for the union of the Presbyterian churches in India which was consummated at Allahabad in 1904. He was elected moderator at the General Assembly, Ludhiana, in December 1909. Returning to America in 1922, he took up his residence in Cincinnati. He died of heart failure while visiting in Indiana, Pa., and was buried in Cincinnati.

Wherry's literary work, both as editor and author, was conspicuous and significant. He was the founder of the Urdu periodical *Nur Afshan*, which he edited at Ludhiana, 1872–83 and 1899–1909. He composed many Urdu tracts, including an outline of ancient history and a refutation of Islam, translated into that tongue an adaptation of J. C. Moffat's *Church History in Brief*, and Edward Sell's *Historical Development of the Quran*, and arranged an index of the Roman Urdu Koran. In 1882–84 he published his monumental *Comprehensive Commentary of the Quran*, in four volumes. Among his other works are *Zeinab the Panjabi* (copr. 1895), *Islam; or the Religion of the Turk* (1896), *The Muslim Controversy* (1905), *Islam and Christianity in India and the Far East* (1907), and *Our Missions in India* (1926). In addition, he edited, either independently or jointly, *Missions at Home and Abroad* (1895), *Woman in Missions* (1894), *The Mohammedan World of To-day* (1906), *Methods of Missionary Work among Moslems* (1906), and *Islam and Missions*

(1911). Besides the offices already mentioned, he served as corresponding secretary of the World's Congress of Missions in 1893, as chairman of his mission's publication committee, and as editor of its annual reports. He was an associate member of the Victoria Institute, London. A building of the Ewing Christian High School at Ludhiana bears the name of Wherry Hall in his honor.

[Who's Who in America. 1926–27; E. M. Wherry, Our Missions in India (1926); Indian Standard, Nov. 1927; Missionary Rev. of the World, Feb. 1928; Princeton Theological Sem. Bull., Necrological Report, Aug. 1928; Cincinnati Enquirer, Oct. 6, 1927.]

J. C. Ar—r.

WHIPPLE, ABRAHAM (Sept. 26, 1733–May 27, 1819), naval officer, was born at Providence, R. I., a descendant of John Whipple, one of the original proprietors of the Providence Plantations. He had little formal education. Choosing a seafaring life, he acquired a knowledge of navigation and accounting and engaged in the West India trade in the employ of Nicholas Brown [q.v.]. In 1759–60 he commanded the privateer *Game Cock* and in a six-month cruise captured twenty-three French vessels. On Aug. 2, 1761, he was married to Sarah Hopkins, a sister of Stephen and Esek Hopkins [qq.v.]. In 1772 with a party of fifty men he burned his majesty's schooner *Gaspée*, which had run aground near Pawtucket, a daring exploit, sometimes regarded as the first overt act of the Revolution. When in 1775 the Rhode Island General Assembly ordered two vessels to be fitted out for the defense of trade, it turned to Whipple as the most experienced sea captain in the colony and appointed him commodore of the little fleet. On June 15, the day that he received his commission, he captured the tender of the British frigate *Rose,* the first prize of the patriots taken by an official vessel. After cruising during the summer in Narragansett Bay, he was sent to Bermuda for gunpowder. On his return he transported some naval recruits to Philadelphia, where his ship, the *Katy,* was taken into the Continental Navy, and he was made a captain in the service, the fourth officer in that rank. In the essay that resulted in the capture of New Providence and the inglorious fight with the *Glasgow,* he commanded the *Columbus,* 20 guns. For permitting the enemy to escape he and his superior officers were haled before the Marine Committee at Philadelphia, which, after investigating the charges against him, reported that they amounted to nothing more than a "rough, indelicate" treatment of his marine officers, and ordered him to repair to his ship.

In 1778 he sailed for France in the frigate *Providence* to procure munitions and carry dispatches. After visiting Paris and being presented to the king, he went to sea with a small fleet under his command, and reached home in safety, having taken a few prizes. In 1779 as commodore of several vessels, with the *Providence* as his flagship, he made a cruise and had the good fortune to fall in with a fleet of heavily laden East-Indiamen. He cut out eleven of them, eight of which reached port. The spoils were worth more than a million dollars, one of the richest captures of the war. Later in the year with four Continental vessels he arrived in Charlestown, S. C., where he was entrusted with the naval defense of the city. With one exception, the Continental vessels were dismantled and their guns and crews taken ashore to reinforce the land batteries. On the fall of the city Whipple was made prisoner. Paroled, he was sent to Chester, Pa., where he remained until the end of the war.

For several years the commodore lived on his farm near Cranston, R. I. Responding to a call to the sea, he made a voyage to England as master of the *General Washington.* On the formation of the Ohio Company he emigrated, with his wife, two daughters, and a son, to Marietta, Ohio, where for six years he cultivated a small plot under the protection of the fort. When peace with the Indians was assured, he moved to a farm and supported himself by his own labor until 1811 when Congress granted him a pension. In 1801 his rural pursuits were interrupted while he made a commercial voyage to New Orleans, Havana, and Philadelphia. His ship, the *St. Clair,* is said to have been the first square-rigged vessel built on the Ohio River to make a voyage to the sea. In person Whipple was short, thickset, and muscular, with dark-grey eyes.

[H. E. Whipple, *A Brief Geneal. of the Whipple Family* (1873); S. P. Hildreth, *Biog. and Hist. Memoirs of the Early Pioneer Settlers of Ohio* (1852); G. W. Allen, *A Naval Hist. of the Am. Rev.* (2 vols., 1913); C. O. Paullin, *Navy of the Am. Rev.* (1906); Edward Field, ed., *State of R. I. and Providence Plantations at the End of the Century* (3 vols., 1902); S. G. Arnold, *Hist. of State of R. I. and Providence Plantations* (1860); *Vital Records of R. I.,* vol. XIV (1905); *Congressional Record,* 11 Cong., 2 Sess. (1810), pt. II.]

C. O. P.

WHIPPLE, AMIEL WEEKS (1816–May 7, 1863), soldier and topographical engineer, a descendant of Matthew Whipple, who came from England to Ipswich, Mass., about 1638, was born in Greenwich, Hampshire County, Mass., the son of David and Abigail (Pepper) Whipple. (The year of his birth is usually given as 1818, but his own statements fix the date approximately as October or November 1816.) He applied for appointment to the United States

Military Academy as early as 1834, when he was teaching in a district school in Concord, Mass. Unsuccessful at that time, he entered Amherst College, but finally received a cadetship in 1837, under the name, through a curious clerical error, of Aeriel W. Whipple. He graduated in 1841 and was commissioned second lieutenant of artillery, but was shortly afterward transferred to the topographical engineers, then a separate corps of the army.

His early assignments were at Baltimore, Md., New Orleans, La., and Portsmouth, N. H. On Sept. 12, 1843, he married Eleanor, daughter of John Nathaniel Sherburne of Portsmouth. From 1844 to 1849 he was engaged in the survey of the northeastern boundary of the United States, and from 1849 to 1853 in the survey of the boundary between the United States and Mexico. In commemoration of his services in that part of the country the military post maintained from 1869 to 1884 at Prescott, Ariz., was called Whipple Barracks. From 1853 to 1856 he was employed in locating the route for a railroad to the Pacific, and from then until the beginning of the Civil War, besides supervision of lighthouses, he worked at the channels through the St. Clair flats and the St. Mary's River, opening the Great Lakes to navigation by larger craft. He had been promoted first lieutenant in 1851 and captain in 1855.

As chief topographical engineer he served at the battle of Bull Run, and continued in that capacity on the staff of Gen. Irvin McDowell until the spring of 1862. He was made major in the regular army in September 1861 and brigadier-general of volunteers in April 1862. From April to September he commanded a brigade, and for the following month a division, in the defenses of Washington. His headquarters were near Arlington, and a fort erected in 1863 on the heights there, within the present Fort Myer reservation, was named Fort Whipple. An exceptionally fine example of fortification of its type, it had a perimeter of 659 yards, and provided emplacements for forty-three guns, behind parapets fifteen feet thick on the exposed fronts. In October 1862 Whipple was assigned to command the third division of the III (Stoneman's) Corps. This was used in support of Sumner's "grand division" in its attack on the Confederate left at the battle of Fredericksburg in December, but was not heavily engaged. Both Burnside and Hooker recommended Whipple's promotion to major-general in January 1863. The III Corps, now under Sickles, was on the right on the second day (May 3, 1863) of the battle of Chancellorsville, after Jackson had routed the

XI Corps. The Confederates attacked that flank repeatedly in an effort to roll up the Union line, and here Whipple was mortally wounded. He was removed to Washington, where he died. His appointment as major-general of volunteers was hastily made out just before his death.

[G. W. Cullum, *Biog. Reg. Officers and Grads. U. S. Mil. Acad.* (3rd ed., 1891), vol. II; C. J. Couts, *From San Diego to the Colorado in 1849* (1932), ed. by Wm. McPherson; Balduin Möllhausen, *Diary of a Journey from the Mississippi to the Coasts of the Pacific* (1858), tr. by Mrs. Percy Sinnett; *War of the Rebellion: Official Records (Army)*; T. E. Farish, *Hist. of Ariz.*, vol. I (1915); *Battles and Leaders of the Civil War* (4 vols., 1887–88); *Daily National Intelligencer* (Washington), May 9, 1863; unpublished records in the War Dept.]
T. M. S.

WHIPPLE, EDWIN PERCY (Mar. 8, 1819– June 16, 1886), author, lecturer, was born in Gloucester, Mass., the son of Matthew and Lydia (Gardiner) Whipple. It has been said that Whipple inherited his "chastening, mild blandness" from the paternal side, his wit from the maternal line, but "divested of the envenomed sarcasm so peculiar to the Gardiner family" (Loring, *post*, p. 665). His youth was spent in Salem, where he nourished his love of literature and history. On leaving the high school in 1834 he entered a local bank, writing for the newspapers from the age of fourteen. He passed in 1837 to Dana, Fenno & Henshaw, brokers in Boston. On June 21, 1847, he married Charlotte B. Hastings, a warm friend of Dr. Oliver Wendell Holmes and the circle of his time. They had a son and a daughter.

Whipple became a leader in debate while a member of the Attic Nights Club. In February 1843 an article on T. B. Macaulay in the *Boston Miscellany* opened to him a wider circle and brought commendation from Macaulay himself. In the winter of 1848–49 he issued in two volumes his *Essays and Reviews,* which at once went to a second edition. The next year appeared *Lectures on Subjects Connected with Literature and Life* (1850). He was hailed as a keen, kindly searcher for hidden connections of things. Visitors to Boston were urged to visit the newsroom of the Merchants' Exchange, to which he had gone as superintendent on abandoning brokerage, to see the bent figure of Whipple, with its head of "massive force and breadth of brow," a "capacious dome over a capacious heart" (*Ibid.*, pp. 667–68). In 1860 he resigned his post in the Merchants' Exchange to devote his time to writing and lecturing. During 1872 he was literary editor of the *Boston Daily Globe.*

On the lecture platform, in the heyday of the lyceum movement, he appeared before a thousand audiences. His lectures and essays came forth rapidly in book form: *Character and Characteristic Men* in 1866, *Literature of the Age of Elizabeth,* the Lowell Institute lectures, in 1869, *Success and Its Conditions* in 1871. His *Recollections of Eminent Men* (1887), issued after his death, contained appraisals of Rufus Choate, Agassiz, Emerson, Motley, Ticknor, and others, and a sketch of George Eliot that delighted her husband. The same year appeared *American Literature and Other Papers,* with an introduction by Whittier, his intimate friend. A year later came *Outlooks on Society, Literature, and Politics.*

In these books, and in his papers in *Every Saturday,* he exhibited logical analysis, a playful imagination, discriminating criticism, and a sensitive love of beauty. His heart was free from envy and censure. John Lothrop Motley called him in 1856 "one of the most brilliant writers in the country, as well as one of the most experienced reviewers" (letter quoted in Perry, *post,* pp. 86–87). At his home in Pinckney Street, where "he nestled like a timid bird" (*Ibid.,* p. 123), his "Sunday evenings" attracted those who made a Golden Age in Boston, but the decay of the lyceum system, his own ill health, and the increasing popularity of new authors threw him into retirement. His decline in fame is a case for a literary autopsy. The impatience of audiences tormented him and led to over-dependence on antitheses and anecdotes; where Emerson could survive, he could not. Whipple had a spare figure, rather short, an expressive face, and large lustrous eyes. He was a good talker. His best-remembered saying was that the author of *Leaves of Grass* had every leaf but the fig leaf.

[See J. S. Loring, *The Hundred Boston Orators* (1852) ; Lilian Whiting, in *Springfield Republican,* Feb. 14, 1934; T. W. Higginson, *Short Studies of Am. Authors* (1888 ed.) ; Bliss Perry, in *The Early Years of the Saturday Club* (1918), ed. by E. W. Emerson ; R. H. Stoddard, ed., *Works of Edgar Allan Poe* (1884), vol. VI, pp. 405–15; obituary in *Boston Transcript,* June 18, 1886.]   C. K. B.

WHIPPLE, FRANCES HARRIET [See GREEN, FRANCES HARRIET WHIPPLE, 1805–1878].

WHIPPLE, HENRY BENJAMIN (Feb. 15, 1822–Sept. 16, 1901), Protestant Episcopal bishop, reformer of the United States Indian system, was born in Adams, N. Y., the son of John Hall Whipple, a merchant, and Elizabeth (Wager) Whipple. His first American ancestor was Capt. John Whipple, one of the early settlers of Providence, R. I. After preliminary education at local Presbyterian schools, Henry spent the years 1838 and 1839 at Oberlin Collegiate Institute. Thereafter until he became a clergy-

man he was in business with his father, although in 1843 and 1844 he visited the South and West for the sake of his health. He served one year as inspector of schools, and was appointed major and later division inspector with the rank of colonel on the staff of Major-General Corse. He also served as secretary of the Democratic state convention at Syracuse in 1847.

Although reared a Presbyterian, he was inclined towards the Protestant Episcopal faith, to which his grandparents adhered; this tendency seems to have been strengthened by the influence of his wife, Cornelia (Wright), whom he married Oct. 5, 1842. He was admitted as a candidate for holy orders on Mar. 15, 1848, was ordained to the diaconate Aug. 26, 1849, and, having concluded the necessary studies under the guidance of the Rev. William D. Wilson [*q.v.*] of Christ Church, Sherburne, N. Y., was raised to the priesthood the following year. His first parish was that of Zion Church, Rome, N. Y., where he remained until 1857 with the exception of a year, 1853–54, passed in Florida for the improvement of his wife's health. By special arrangement he served during this period as rector in St. Augustine and missionary to the adjacent region. His rectorship at Rome was so successful that he was called to many other parishes. Accepting the call to organize a new church among the waifs, railroad employees, machinists, and churchless of the south side of Chicago, he spent the years from 1857 to 1859 building up and administering the parish of the Holy Communion.

In 1859 he was elected first bishop of Minnesota and was consecrated on Oct. 13. The following year he established his family at Faribault, which was his residence for the remainder of his life. His new field of activity was one to try the mettle of any man, presenting not only the usual difficult problems of a frontier diocese, but also the problems arising from the United States government's management of the Indians. With respect to the latter he first examined the situation carefully, making extensive tours into the wilderness with great physical inconvenience and danger to himself. His Church already had a mission among the Chippewa; this he strengthened. In 1860 he established a mission among the Sioux. Convinced of the injustice and inhumanity of the government's system, he began to send appeals to local Indian agents, to senators and congressmen, to heads of bureaus and departments in Washington, and, finally, in desperation to the President of the United States. He pointed out in a letter written to President Lincoln on Mar. 6, 1862 (manuscript letter book; abridged in *Lights and Shadows, post,* pp. 510–

14), the fundamental defects of the administration of Indian affairs. His letters were remembered when, in August 1862, the Minnesota Sioux rose and massacred hundreds of whites, inaugurating just what Whipple had predicted—a long series of Indian wars. He went at once to the scene, where he tended the wounded and consoled the bereaved. He then published an appeal (*Saint Paul Pioneer,* Dec. 3, 17, 1862; *Saint Paul Press,* Dec. 4, 1862) to his frenzied fellow Minnesotans to be reasonable, pointing out that the Indians had been goaded to fury by fraud and deceit and that they were using the only weapons left to them. His plea only infuriated the frontier folk, but he stood his ground despite their recriminations and anger. Late in 1862 he went to Washington to make a personal appeal to the President, who forbade the execution of most of the three hundred Sioux condemned to death by a military commission.

Under these emotional distractions, together with the racking experiences of visits to Civil War battlefields, the fatigue of an energetic and successful campaign among Eastern financiers for aid to Minnesota's devastated frontier, and the worry of securing funds for maintaining his diocese, his health failed once more. Suddenly, however, as a result of his heart-moving appeals he found himself the idol of philanthropists in the East. Money came henceforth to him for his work, sometimes in great amounts. Robert Minturn [*q.v.*] of New York made it possible for him to go to Europe in 1864–65 to regain his health, and while in England he won the support of the Established Church. This trip was the first of many which Whipple made to Europe. His simple, moving eloquence appealed to Europeans; his message was a new one; his well-told stories had piquancy; his modesty was disarming.

Upon his return from Europe in 1865 he plunged once more into the campaign for reform of the Indian service. Winning the confidence of the secretary of the interior and that of the commissioner of Indian affairs, he was deluged with requests by government officials for advice and aid and made a member of Indian commissions. In an appeal to Horace Greeley (manuscript, Minnesota Historical Society), Feb. 28, 1867, he made the following concrete suggestions for reform: (1) the perfection of the reservation system; (2) grants of land to individual Indians with inalienable title; (3) an adequate school system; (4) a system of inspection of agencies, schools, and employees. In Grant's administration reform came, for the most part in the ways that Whipple had suggested. For the next two decades he fought valiantly for his "red children,"

exposing fraud, building up mission work in the new Chippewa home in Minnesota—the White Earth Reservation—and making appeals for them by addresses in America and abroad. His work took him on special missions to Puerto Rico and to Cuba. His fame mounted as he grew older, so that he was called to speak or preside at many meetings in America and Europe. In 1871 the Archbishop of Canterbury offered him the bishopric of the Sandwich Islands, but he declined. Queen Victoria commanded an audience in December 1890. In 1897 he attended the fourth Lambeth Conference as presiding bishop of the American Church.

Whipple was an orator of no mean ability, possessing a melodious voice of sufficient compass and power to stir his audiences. In personal appearance he was prepossessing, being six feet two inches in height and weighing about 170 pounds. He had a high forehead, grey eyes, a long face, brown curly hair that turned to snowy whiteness in his later years and was worn long in patriarchal fashion about his shoulders. His Indian name was Straight Tongue. Fishing was a passion with him. He was a famous raconteur. His writings were many, though mostly in pamphlet form or printed in church periodicals. In 1899 appeared his autobiography, *Lights and Shadows of a Long Episcopate,* which was reprinted in 1900 and 1902, and came out in a new edition in 1912. His first wife died in 1890; six children had been born to them, two of whom predeceased their parents. On Oct. 22, 1896, he married Evangeline (Marrs) Simpson of Saxonville, Mass.

[Whipple's diaries, letter books, correspondence, and other papers in possession of the Minn. Hist. Soc., the Protestant Episcopal Diocese of Minn., and descendants; Warren Upham and R. B. Dunlap, "Minn. Biogs.," in *Minn. Hist. Soc. Colls.,* vol. XIV (1912); C. H. Whipple, *A Brief Geneal. of the Whipple-Wright . . . Families* (1917); G. C. Tanner, *Fifty Years of Church Work in the Diocese of Minn.* (1909); *Who's Who in America,* 1901–02; *Minneapolis Jour.,* Sept. 16, 1901.]

                                   G. L. N.

WHIPPLE, SHERMAN LELAND (Mar. 4, 1862–Oct. 20, 1930), lawyer, was born in New London, N. H., youngest of three sons of Solomon Mason Whipple and Henrietta Kimball (Hersey) Whipple. The father—a descendant of Matthew Whipple, who settled at Ipswich Hamlet, Mass., as early as 1638—was a physician, practising over miles of thinly settled rugged country. The pecuniary returns of his practice were small; nevertheless, after preparation at the New London Literary and Scientific Institution (later Colby Academy), Sherman was sent to Yale College. There, by supplementing what he received from home with his earnings as a tutor, he was able to graduate in 1881 with creditable rank. After teaching school for a year, he entered the Yale Law School and graduated with honors in 1884. He was admitted to the Connecticut and New Hampshire bars in the same year, and began practice in Manchester, N. H., but soon moved to Boston. He had few acquaintances and little influence, but through the recommendation of an older brother, already settled there, he obtained bills to collect. His promptness and energy commended him to others, and he was soon engaged in trying personal injury cases. His success was marked, and before he was thirty years old he had acquired the early experience derived from trial of many cases that is almost essential for considerable success as an advocate. Before long he was recognized as perhaps the most successful plaintiff's attorney in Boston. His work ceased to be chiefly devoted to cases of personal injury, but still he generally acted for plaintiffs. He was especially effective in attacking fraud or dishonesty, and in discovering it, however carefully concealed, by cross-examination. He was also frequently engaged in cases of contested wills.

Gifted by nature with extraordinary fitness for advocacy, he enhanced by industry his natural ability. He was a hard fighter, and even in his early practice never afraid to cross swords with leaders of the bar, or to attack for his clients those entrenched behind wealth and high social position. Ready to lead a desperate charge, he could base his case on a forlorn hope, but behind every attack was thorough preparation and shrewd calculation of possible means of attaining success. Although well able to care for his clients under restricted rules of evidence and complex legal procedure, he consistently and vigorously advocated extending the admissibility of evidence and simplifying legal procedure. Among his addresses to bar associations were "The Power of the Courts to Make Law and to Annul Legislation," in which he advocated relieving the courts of "the duty of making decisions on questions involving political, economic and class controversies" (*Proceedings of the . . . West Virginia Bar Association*, 1917, p. 90); "The Legal Privilege of Concealing the Truth" (*Report of the . . . Maryland State Bar Association*, 1922); and "Law and Lawyers in the Twentieth Century" (*Vermont Bar Association, Report of Proceedings*, 1929). During a large part of his career (1899–1919) he practised, in association with others, under the firm name of Whipple, Sears & Ogden; later, merely under his own name. In politics he was a Democrat, but his legal practice precluded devoting much

time to politics. He was, however, in 1911 and again in 1912 the choice of his party for United States senator.

Outside of the court room Whipple was generous and friendly. The wit and humor which he used effectively for the benefit of his clients was not absent from his familiar conversation. During the early years of his success he took many vacations in Europe, but in middle life he acquired a large estate near Plymouth, and spent there what time he could, surrounded by his family and engaged in pursuits appropriate to the country life that he loved, riding horseback and superintending not only the raising of flowers and vegetables but the breeding of Guernsey cattle. In appearance, he was somewhat below middle height, sturdily built, with a large head and firm mouth and chin, clear indications of his courage and tenacity. On Dec. 27, 1893, he married Louise Clough of Manchester, N. H. They had three children, a son and two daughters. He died on Oct. 20, 1930, at his home in Brookline, Mass., without a single day's illness.

[*Who's Who in America*, 1930–31; *A Hist. of the Class of 'Eighty-One, Yale Coll.* (2 vols., 1909–30); memoir in *New England Hist. and Geneal. Reg.*, Jan. 1931; proceedings in the Supreme Judicial Court, Boston, June 3, 1933, on presentation of a memorial to Whipple by the Boston Bar Asso.; obituary in *Boston Transcript*, Oct. 20, 1930; information from Whipple's family.]
S. W.

WHIPPLE, SQUIRE (Sept. 16, 1804–Mar. 15, 1888), civil engineer, author, inventor, was the son of James and Electa (Johnson) Whipple. His father, a farmer and later the owner of a small cotton mill at Hardwick, Mass., where Squire was born, removed with his family to Otsego County, N. Y., in 1817. The boy assisted in farming operations, attended the academy at Fairfield, Herkimer County, taught school for a time, and in 1829 entered the senior class at Union College, Schenectady, where he received the degree of A.B. in 1830. He probably owed his interest in engineering to the construction of the Erie Canal in the region near his home during his boyhood, although he was too young to be a member of the group of engineers who were trained in that great school, and his reputation was achieved not in canal construction but in bridge building. After graduating from college he was engaged in a minor capacity in surveys for the Baltimore & Ohio Railroad and for the Erie Canal. In 1836–37 he was resident engineer of a division of the New York & Erie Railroad; and he was subsequently employed on other surveys for projected railways and canals. In the intervals between his engineering appointments he made surveying instruments, including transits and theodolites, and worked on various inventions. His first original device of note was completed in 1840—a lock for weighing canal boats.

On Apr. 24, 1841, he received his first bridge patent, for a truss of arched upper chord built of cast and wrought iron. Some five years later he devised a truss of trapezoidal form which was frequently used in bridges built during the succeeding generation. This design places him with Ithiel Town, Stephen H. Long, William Howe, and Thomas W. Pratt [qq.v.] among the American pioneers in the development of the pure truss bridge. In 1852–53, on the line of the Rensselaer & Saratoga Railroad near West Troy, N. Y., Whipple employed his truss in the first iron railroad bridge of considerable span (146 feet). This structure contained elements which became typical of American truss-bridge design—the inclined end post and the pin-connection. Whipple described the bridge in detail in a letter published in *Engineering News*, Apr. 7, 1883. In 1872 he built a drawbridge, with a lift span, over the Erie Canal at Utica, and subsequently designed several other short lift spans. Some account of his work, by himself, was published in the *Railroad Gazette*, Apr. 19, 1889.

Whipple's chief contribution to bridge engineering, however, was his publication, in 1847, of *A Work on Bridge Building*, the first notable attempt to reduce the problem to a scientific basis. Previously engineers had built bridges so as to look strong enough to experienced eyes; modern methods of computing stresses and designing the parts of such structures to meet them were unknown; Whipple's book was the first extensive and thorough treatment of the subject. Later, in 1869, he issued a continuation of this treatise, making the woodcuts himself and printing the issue on a hand press in his home. Still later, in 1872, it was published by David Van Nostrand [q.v.], under the title, *An Elementary and Practical Treatise on Bridge Building*; a fourth edition came out in 1883. Whipple died in his home in Albany, widely recognized as a pioneer in his field of engineering. He was an honorary member of the American Society of Civil Engineers and the author of several papers published in the earlier volumes of its *Transactions*. In 1837 he married Anna Case of Utica, N. Y., who survived him; he left no children.

[*Trans. Am. Soc. Civil Engineers*, vols. XXI (1889), XXV (1891), XXXVI (1896); J. A. L. Waddell, *Bridge Engineering* (1916); J. B. Johnson, C. W. Bryan, and F. E. Turneaure, *The Theory and Practice of Modern Framed Structures* (1893); G. R. Howell and Jonathan Tenney, *Hist. of the County of Albany, N. Y.* (1886); *Albany Jour.*, Mar. 16, 1888.]   J.K.F.

WHIPPLE, WILLIAM (Jan. 14, 1730–Nov. 10, 1785), Revolutionary patriot, was the eldest of the five children of William and Mary (Cutt) Whipple, and a descendant of Matthew Whipple who came to America from England before 1638. He was born in Kittery, Me., received a common-school education, and, like many boys of that locality, went to sea at an early age. While still in his early twenties he became master of a vessel, making many deep-water voyages and incidentally engaging in the slave trade, then a legal if not wholly respectable activity, but one which a later generation of New Englanders regarded as anomalous in a signer of the Declaration of Independence. About 1760 he gave up the sea and formed a mercantile partnership with his brother Joseph at Portsmouth.

Revolutionary activity began early in Portsmouth and Whipple was identified with the popular party in many of the disputes which preceded the final break with Great Britain in 1775. In this year he gave up his share in the business and entered public life. He was prominent in the early provincial congresses, a member of the Council in 1776, of the state committee of safety, and closely associated with John Langdon [q.v.] and other patriots in local developments at Portsmouth. In 1776 he was sent to the Continental Congress and shared with Josiah Bartlett and Matthew Thornton [qq.v.] the honor of representing New Hampshire on the Declaration of Independence. He served in Congress until 1779, with the exception of periods of interruption occasioned by short tours of duty in command of militia contingents in the Saratoga and Rhode Island campaigns. He was quite active in committee, and his correspondence expresses exasperation at the inefficient public service, the lack of national spirit and the greed and selfishness of leaders and communities. He had an acute realization of the defects of the commissary and recruiting systems. He emphasized the importance of naval operations, urged the necessity for striking hard blows, taxing heavily, and spreading the burden of the struggle on the entire people. Peace, he repeatedly argued, would be secured by victory in the field and not by diplomatic juggling in Europe. He demanded "spirited measures" against speculators and Loyalists. As to the latter, he wrote Josiah Bartlett in 1779, "I think it high time they were all Hung or Banished" (*Letters of Members, post*, p. 346). He was optimistic as to the outcome of the war, however, even in its most depressing stages and constantly urged his own state to increased efforts in the common cause.

In the last years of the war he continued to be

active in New Hampshire affairs and represented Portsmouth in the legislature for several sessions. From 1782 until his death he was also an associate justice of the superior court. In his later years however, he was badly handicapped by ill health, an autopsy confirming his own belief that for some years he had been performing his duties in imminent danger of the sudden death which finally overtook him while on circuit. His wife was Catharine Moffatt, of Portsmouth. They had no children.

[Arthur Little, "William Whipple, Signer of the Declaration of Independence," *Proc. N. H. Hist. Soc.*, vol. III (1902) ; C. B. Jordan, "Col. Joseph B. Whipple," *Ibid.*, vol. II (1895) ; C. H. Bell, *The Bench and Bar of N. H.* (1894) ; *State Papers of N. H.*, vol. VIII (1874) ; "Records of New Hampshire Committee of Safety," *N. H. Hist. Soc. Cols.*, vol. VIII (1868) ; Nathaniel Adams, *Annals of Portsmouth* (1825) ; *Letters of Members of the Continental Cong.*, vol. IV (1928), ed. by E. C. Burnett.]   W. A. R.

WHISTLER, GEORGE WASHINGTON (May 19, 1800–Apr. 7, 1849), soldier, engineer, son of John and Ann (Bishop) Whistler, was born in the military post at Fort Wayne, Ind. John Whistler, a native of Ireland, served under General Burgoyne in the British army during the American Revolution and after his discharge returned to settle in America; he became an officer in the United States Army and at the time of his son's birth was commandant at Fort Wayne. His wife was a woman of rare charm and force of character. George Whistler was appointed in 1814 to the United States Military Academy, where he distinguished himself as a draftsman. Graduating in 1819, he was commissioned second lieutenant of artillery and assigned to topographical duty. In the winter of 1821–22 he was assistant teacher of drawing at West Point, and then returned to topographical work, surveying the international boundary between Lake Superior and the Lakes of the Woods. In 1828 he was assigned by the government to assist in the location and construction of the Baltimore & Ohio Railroad and was sent by the railroad to England, in company with another West Pointer, William Gibbs McNeill, and a civilian engineer, Jonathan Knight [*qq.v.*], to examine railroads and railroad equipment. After supervising the construction of the first mile of track for the Baltimore & Ohio, he was assigned, with McNeill, to locate the Baltimore & Susquehanna Railroad, and was then engaged in similar work for the Paterson & Hudson Railroad (now part of the Erie system) and for the Providence & Stonington extension of the Boston & Providence Railroad.

In 1833 he resigned from the army, with the rank of first lieutenant, and became engineer to the Proprietors of Locks and Canals at Lowell, Mass., where as director of the machine shop he built a number of railroad locomotives patterned after that of George Stephenson. In 1837 he resumed supervision of the Providence & Stonington Railroad, and in association with McNeill became consulting engineer for the Western Railroad of Massachusetts (now the Boston & Albany). In 1840–42, as chief engineer of this road, he did some of his most noted work, locating the section between Springfield and Pittsfield, through the Berkshires, in a narrow river valley, under especially difficult conditions. His remarkable capacity exhibited in the solution of this problem attracted the attention of Russian officials who were inspecting American railroads, and upon their advice the Czar invited him to become consulting engineer for the projected railroad between St. Petersburg and Moscow.

In 1842 he began his work in Russia, where he displayed great ability and energy. The projected railroad was 420 miles long, with double track, and was to be built in seven years at a cost of $40,000,000. Construction was begun in 1844 and the road was opened for traffic in 1850. Whistler recommended and in the face of some opposition secured the adoption of a narrow gauge track—five feet—instead of the wider gauge later abandoned in America. The rolling stock and other machinery were furnished by an American firm, being manufactured in Russia under Whistler's general direction. Whistler also supervised the construction of fortifications and docks at Cronstadt and the iron bridge over the Neva. He was decorated by the Emperor with the Order of St. Anne in 1847. Before the completion of the railroad he was stricken with Asiatic cholera, and he died in St. Petersburg after a long illness. He was buried at Stonington, Conn., and a monument was erected to him in Greenwood Cemetery, Brooklyn, by his professional associates.

Whistler was twice married. By his first wife, Mary Roberdeau Swift, young sister of his friend Joseph Gardner Swift [*q.v.*], he had a daughter, Deborah Delano ("Dasha"), who married Francis Seymour Haden [see *Dictionary of National Biography,* 2nd Supp.], and two sons, one of whom, George William, was a railroad engineer and continued his father's work in Russia until his death in 1869. His second wife, whom he married Nov. 3, 1831, was Anna Mathilda, daughter of Dr. Charles Donald McNeill of Wilmington, N. C., and sister of his friend William Gibbs McNeill. They had five sons, including James Abbott McNeill Whistler [*q.v.*] and William Gibbs McNeill Whistler, a physician of London.

[G. L. Vose, *A Sketch of the Life and Works of George W. Whistler, Civil Engineer* (1887); G. W. Cullum, *Biog. Reg. Officers and Grads. U. S. Mil. Acad.,* vol. I (3rd ed., 1891); *The Memoirs of Gen. Joseph Gardner Swift* (1890), ed. by Harrison Ellery; information supplied by Wm. Patten, Rhinebeck, N. Y.]

H. K. B.

WHISTLER, JAMES ABBOTT McNEILL (July 10, 1834–July 17, 1903), painter and etcher, was once approached by an American who said: "You know, Mr. Whistler, we were both born at Lowell, and at very much the same time . . . you are 67 and I am 68." To which Whistler promptly replied: "Very charming. And so you are 68 and were born at Lowell, Massachusetts. Most interesting, no doubt, and as you please! But I shall be born when and where I want, and I do not choose to be born at Lowell and I refuse to be 67" (Pennell, *Life, post,* I, 1–2). He chose to be born, instead, at Baltimore or at St. Petersburg, in Russia. As a matter of fact he first saw the light in the house on Worthen Street, at Lowell, which after his death was dedicated to his memory. The family was of old British origin, with an Irish branch from which he was descended. A John Whistler, his grandfather, served with Burgoyne. After Saratoga he returned to England, got his discharge, and once more came to America, enlisting in the American army toward the close of the eighteenth century. Whistler liked to remember him as a soldier of constructive achievement in the West. One of his exploits was the erection of Fort Dearborn in 1803. His son, George Washington Whistler [*q.v.*], born at Fort Wayne on May 19, 1800, following in his footsteps embraced a military career, but ultimately left the army with the rank of first lieutenant and was thenceforth identified with civil engineering. In 1831 he married as his second wife Anna Mathilda McNeill, the sister of a colleague and friend, William G. McNeill [*q.v.*]. He went to Lowell as engineer of locks and canals and there the artist was born. They made more than one move thereafter, first to Stonington, Conn., and then to Springfield, Mass., but there is nothing that calls for comment in this period beyond the fact that "Jimmie" had begun to make pencil drawings at the age of four!

There looms, however, a matter of decisive interest. The Russian commission sent to the United States in 1842 to look into the problems of railroad building and discover an engineer who could preside over the creation of a line from St. Petersburg to Moscow—the famous inflexibly straight line dictated by Czar Nicholas I—of-

fered the post to Lieutenant Whistler. He sailed almost immediately and in 1843 the family followed him. The Pennells, who had access to Mrs. Whistler's journal when they were preparing their official life of the master, say of him at this time: "Whistler as a boy was exactly what those who knew him as a man would expect; gay and bright, absorbed in his work when that work was art, brave and fearless, selfish if selfishness is another name for ambition, considerate and kindly, above all to his mother" (*Ibid.,* I, 12). His health was delicate, involving a heart weakness which in after years to cause him grave trouble, but he had unquenchable energy and spirit, battened upon the picturesqueness of his environment, and devoted himself with something like passion to his lessons at the Academy of Fine Arts. During an illness in 1847 he solaced himself by poring over a volume of Hogarth's engravings, forming then an admiration for the English artist which he never lost. It was in this year that Mrs. Whistler took the children to England and that Deborah, George Whistler's daughter by his first wife, was married to Seymour Haden, destined to win distinction as a surgeon and more durable fame as an etcher. Returning to Russia, the family was again in England in 1848. Sir William Boxall painted at this time the charming portrait of Whistler which is in the Freer collection at Washington. Meanwhile his father was too hard at work in cholera-stricken St. Petersburg and died there from a heart attack on Apr. 7, 1849. The Czar's appreciation of his engineer was so warm that he proposed Mrs. Whistler's settling in Russia, so that her two sons might be entered in the imperial school for pages. She elected to take them back to Stonington and soon afterward to establish herself at Pomfret, Conn., with a view to the continuance of their schooling. Whistler had by this time given evidence of his artistic predilections, but without being unsympathetic to these his mother saw another career for him and in 1851, like his father before him, he was a cadet at West Point.

He stayed there three years, when he earned his dismissal by a misstep in the domain of chemistry. "Had silicon been a gas," he is reported to have said, "I would have been a major general" (*Ibid.,* I, 33). He was very young— barely seventeen when he entered the Academy —and West Point remains but an interlude in his career. He was never meant to be a soldier. Yet those three years left a certain mark upon him. All his life he was inordinately proud of them and they may be said to have placed a kind of cachet upon his natural fighting proclivities, his insistence upon the point of honor, his instinct for ceremonial, and, not least of all, his erect carriage. And if he was deficient in the lore of chemistry, he was, prophetically, at the head of the drawing class at the very moment of his collision with silicon. It was with light-hearted courage that he now faced the world in search of a proper niche for himself. There were ideas in the family of his finding it in the Winans locomotive works at Baltimore. An opening more attractive, momentarily, was found in the Coast Survey at Washington, in which as a draftsman of maps he learned a good deal about the mechanics of etching. The "Coast Survey, No. 1," and the "Coast Survey, No. 2, Anacapa Island," rigidly but ably drawn plates, recall in the body of his *oeuvre* this early, half-unconscious launching of the professional technician.

In 1854 he was in the Coast Survey. In 1855 he was out of it. He was resolved to give himself to art and by this time his mother was willing. With an annual allowance of $350 he sailed for Paris. He was never to come back. Why not? The answer remains a mystery. The writer once asked him to solve the riddle and with a perceptible stiffening of his upright figure, angrily tapping the London pavement with his stick, he replied: "I shall come to America when the duty on works of art is abolished!" But no difference in opinion between himself and his countrymen could cover the case. It is more reasonably to be inferred that he stayed abroad because there his genius naturally flowered, there he found the conditions and friends with whom he was instinctively at home. In Paris, where he was to form his art and win recognition; in London, where his discovery of a beauty ignored by other artists was to lead to the discovery of his highest inspiration, it was but in the nature of things that he should come to regard America as, no doubt, his own land, but somehow, in a way, itself "abroad." In any case it is from 1855, when he reached France, that the life of Whistler begins to cohere, falls "all of a piece," and becomes the true source of the works that we know.

For a primary clue to the steady integration of that life, it is suggestive to revert to the anecdote relating to the place of his birth. The tale embodies a clue in that it points to one dominant fact, a fact that throughout his career it is always Whistler's peculiarly deliberate choice that governs. His was the spirit of a delicately histrionic type that dramatizes its own every movement. He adopted originality as a career, not with the meretricious impulse of the *poseur* but because he could not help himself, because he was invincibly individualized, because in paint-

ing, etching—and in his ordinary walk and demeanor—he was imperiously the artist, inventing and exploiting his own effects. The creative daemon was as urgent in him when he was addressing a postcard, making the ephemeral thing a thing of beauty, as when he was painting a full-dress portrait. Whistler was an exemplar of "self expression" years before the phrase was formulated. Susceptible though he was in his formative period to certain external influences, the expression of his own ideas and not those of any other was with marked rapidity to become as the breath of his nostrils. It is this originality that largely gives him his salience in modern art. It was this originality that made him, even as a young man, seeking his way in Paris, a figure to reckon with and remember.

He was, in some respects, a curious figure, proclaiming himself in dress and manner a Bohemian of the Bohemians, wearing with an air the wide-brimmed, flat hat which appears in the portrait he etched of himself at this time, triumphing merrily over all the vicissitudes of student life, rejoicing his fellows with his high-pitched laugh, and altogether pursuing the fulfillment of his destiny in a spirit of debonair adventure. He had troops of friends, many of them later to become famous. George Du Maurier was among his English comrades, Henri Fantin-Latour and Alphonse Legros were the best beloved of those Frenchmen whom he came to know. For training he entered the atelier of Charles Gleyre, a competent but undistinguished painter in the tradition of Ingres. His attitude toward the latter great Raphaelesque master is a little difficult to define. For a good hour one evening he declaimed to the present writer upon the Frenchman's limitations, stigmatizing him as a bourgeois Greek and asserting that he excelled simply in painting the buttons on a coat. Yet his interlocutor had already seen in New York a copy which Whistler had made of the Frenchman's "Roger et Angelique" and in after years, when he was wont to deplore the incompleteness of his technical education, he once wrote to Fantin that he wished he had been formed as a draftsman under Ingres. The truth probably is that he was, on the whole, not much in sympathy with Ingres, but realized, wistfully, that the master might have taught him how to draw as well with the brush as with the etching needle. Precise information as to just what happened to him under Gleyre is not available but there is no doubt of his readiness to hail the then rising star of Gustave Courbet. All other influences in the melting pot of French art he resisted, not only that of Ingres but that of his rival Eugène Delacroix. The men of Barbizon, the new portents of Impressionism, alike left him cold. Alone the realism of Courbet found him in some measure responsive and the results may be discerned in his earlier paintings, "At the Piano," "The Thames in Ice," "The Coast of Brittany," and "The Blue Wave." But even amidst these a picture like "The Music Room," with its decisively decorative motive, arises to foreshadow the essential Whistler, the artist seeking beauty in truth but subjecting truth to his very personal conception of beauty. He was to feel his way in Paris toward this solution of his artistic problem and he was to have some significant experiences there. In Paris he was to publish, in November 1858, his first group of etchings and in Paris "The White Girl," rejected at the Salon in 1863 as it had been rejected at the Royal Academy, was to make a sensation in the Salon des Refusés which the Emperor had brought into being to honor men like Manet, Fantin, Bracquemond, Jongkind, and Vollon.

From the fifties onward the reader must visualize Whistler as constantly oscillating between Paris and London, with the English capital becoming more and more the field of his labors. The Hadens were there and while there was no love lost between the painter and the surgeon it took some years for an actual break to be developed between them. The figures in "At the Piano" are those of Lady Haden and her daughter. To England also came Whistler's mother to live in 1863, and there he painted the great portrait of her, first shown in 1872 and now in the Louvre. It was in London that he thenceforth painted (1872-77) the long series of portraits which were to do so much to give him his renown, the "Carlyle," the "Miss Alexander," the "Rosa Corder," and that "Peacock Room" which may be seen in the Freer collection, its architectural ugliness redeemed by Whistler's decorations. Indeed, following his itinerary, through the sixties and seventies, despite his frequent visits to France, one almost forgets Paris. Besides the portraits to recall London there are the "Nocturnes," there is the Thames set of etchings, there is the building of his home, the "White House," and there is the suit against Ruskin, to be succeeded by the bankruptcy of the artist.

The trial requires a passage by itself. Ruskin, at the height of his fame, in the fullest pride of his critical authority, had seen eight paintings of Whistler's in the Grosvenor gallery exhibition of 1877. Upon one of these, "Black and Gold—The Falling Rocket," he descended with envenomed words: "For Mr. Whistler's own sake, no less than for the protection of the purchaser, Sir

Coutts Lindsay ought not to have admitted works into the gallery in which the ill-educated conceit of the artist so nearly approached the aspect of wilful imposture. I have seen, and heard, much of Cockney impudence before now; but never expected to hear a coxcomb ask two hundred guineas for flinging a pot of paint in the public's face" (E. T. Cook and Alexander Wedderburn, *The Complete Works of John Ruskin*, 1903-09, vol. XXIX, 160). Whistler brought suit and the case came to trial in November 1878. Details of it fill the first pages of the artist's famous book, *The Gentle Art of Making Enemies* (1890), and the fact that the verdict was for the plaintiff, in the sum of one farthing, is duly recorded. But even without the aid of Whistler's witty marginalia, or the pamphlet on the subject which he printed a month later, the episode demonstrates one transcendent point—that he was in advance of his time, that he had brought into the world something new and strange in creative art, something utterly beyond the comprehension of the British mind, nurtured as it was on the sentimental "subject" picture, the "painted anecdote." Whistler's genius was for a work of art which may perhaps be best exposed, in its quiddity, by some words of his own. "Take the picture of my mother," he said, "exhibited at the Royal Academy as an 'Arrangement in Grey and Black.' Now that is what it is. To me it is interesting as a picture of my mother; but what can or ought the public to care about the identity of the portrait?" (*Gentle Art of Making Enemies*, p. 128). Again, in regard to one of his "Nocturnes," he said: "My picture of a 'Harmony in Grey and Gold' is an illustration of my meaning—a snow scene with a single black figure and a lighted tavern. I care nothing for the past, present, or future of the black figure, placed there because the black was wanted at that spot. All that I know is that my combination of grey and gold is the basis of the picture. Now that is precisely what my friends cannot grasp. They say, 'Why not call it "Trotty Veck," and sell it for a round harmony of golden guineas?'" (*Ibid.*, p. 126). Still another pronouncement of his runs as follows: "As music is the poetry of sound, so is painting the poetry of sight, and the subject-matter has nothing to do with harmony of sound or of color" (*Ibid.*, p. 127). It was a fresh, absolutely new-minted "poetry of sight" that he was born to produce.

It is necessary, in approaching that "poetry of sight," to take note of certain external elements that touched him in the course of its evolution. Courbet counted for much in confirming Whistler's gravitation toward the truthful statement of fact, and as "The Blue Wave" particularly showed, he adopted in a measure Courbet's habit of a robust, almost rude force. He is, like the Frenchman, a naturalistic painter in "The Blue Wave." Then he was sensitive to the appeal of Japanese art, whether in the blue and white of the Orient or in the color print. In the sixties his pictures now and then present figures in Japanese dress, but costume was not, with him, the point. More sympathetically and more durably he took over from Japan a feeling for pattern as pattern. This, indeed, developed into a mode of his own, was to stay with him until he died. There remains the question of Velasquez, whose name has so often arisen in discussion of his art. He knew the examples of the Spaniard in Paris and London. As a young man he saw the considerable group of them in the Manchester Exhibition of 1857. He cherished always a profound admiration for the painter "whose Infantas, clad in inaesthetic hoops," he said, "are, as works of art, of the same quality as the Elgin marbles" (*Mr. Whistler's 10 o'clock*, p. 3). Though he never fulfilled his wish to see the master in his splendor at the Prado, in Madrid, he was somehow enabled to draw near to his secret and he is almost to be counted a disciple. Almost, but not quite. Look at the "Mrs. Louis Huth" or at one or two other low-toned "Arrangements" and in a superficial view of the matter the student might surmise deliberate emulation. But here it is important to observe a distinction. Velasquez, dipping his brush in light and air, as Whistler put it, and causing his people to "live within their frames, and *stand upon* their legs," was first and last constrained to record the fact before him. Whistler, duly regardful of the fact, was constrained to produce a Whistler. Both men seem of the same cult in their painting of black against gray but one is thinking primarily of life and the other of art, of pattern. The distinction is immediately apparent on comparison of one of the Infantas of Velasquez with, say, the "Miss Alexander: Harmony in Gray and Green." If the Whistler, like the Velasquez, is a masterpiece, it is such in a way that is entirely Whistler's. The dress was of his designing. The flowers and the draperies in the background, nay the placing of the Butterfly, his signature, all testify to his vision of his subject as a decorative whole, as a Whistlerian "Harmony." Color was for him a veritable language—a language, by the way, extraordinarily simplified—and he employed it in his "poetry of sight" with amazing felicity and inventiveness. Was something lost in the process? Perhaps. In the "Sarasate," at Pittsburgh, a good deal less than justice is done to the violinist's

ebullient vitality; he is reduced, instead, very nearly to the status of a wraith. But how beautiful the picture is! Moreover, a consideration of Whistler's big portraits, in their length and breadth, must undoubtedly take account of the survival of personality in many of them. The "Mother," the "Carlyle," the "Theodore Duret," the "F. R. Leyland," the "Rosa Corder," the "Lady Meux," and divers others are too subtly expressive for one to do anything else.

They are original, beautiful, altogether distinguished achievements, the portraits. If Whistler had done nothing else his fame would be secure. But he did something else, something that no one had ever done before him. He created the "Nocturne" and thereby added a precious contribution to modern art. He had to break with the Courbet tradition, in obedience to that urge of individuality always active in his bosom. If he had continued in the vein of "The Blue Wave," or "The Thames in Ice" he would have simply ranged himself as one of the better painters of nature in his time. Painting the "Nocturnes" he made the final, most exquisite affirmation of his creative faculty and took a place apart. It is not too much to say that London, and especially the Thames, worked the decisive move. He adored the river and what he felt about it is luminously expressed in the oft-quoted passage in the lecture that he first delivered in London in 1885: "And when the evening mist clothes the riverside with poetry, as with a veil, and the poor buildings lose themselves in the dim sky, and the tall chimneys become campanili, and the warehouses are palaces in the night, and the whole city hangs in the heavens, and fairyland is before us—then the wayfarer hastens home; the working man and the cultured one, the wise man and the one of pleasure, cease to understand, as they have ceased to see, and Nature, who, for once, has sung in tune, sings her exquisite song to the artist alone, her son and her master—her son in that he loves her, her master in that he knows her" (*Mr. Whistler's 10 o'clock*, 1904, pp. 13-14).

It is a paean of faith and that faith energized him to the production of an endless number of "Nocturnes" and "Symphonies" which might not have impressed Ruskin but which have indubitably enriched the art treasure of the world. In color, in pattern, in esthetic feeling, they do more than even the portraits do to bring out Whistler's singularity and creative power. He was not a great designer as Raphael was, nor was his craftsmanship equal to that of Velasquez. He gave us no high imaginative conceptions and in the interpretation of life the human emotion that is in a Rembrandt, for example, leaves him, on comparison, looking poor indeed. But in sheer beauty he is very rich, partly through the simplicity characterizing his design, his arrangement of color, and partly through the play of a feeling far more recondite and mysterious. When he was asked, in the Ruskin trial, if he intended to say that a certain nocturne of his which was produced in court was "a correct representation of Battersea Bridge," he retorted: "I did not intend it to be a 'correct' portrait of the bridge. It is only a moonlight scene and the pier in the center of the picture may not be like the piers at Battersea Bridge as you know them in broad daylight. As to what the picture represents it depends upon who looks at it. To some persons it may represent all that is intended; to others it may represent nothing. . . . My whole scheme was only to bring about a certain harmony in color" (*Gentle Art of Making Enemies*, p. 8). With that "certain harmony of color" he was not only victorious but isolated. It is significant that he has had no followers in the painting of "Nocturnes," as he had had no predecessors. He founded no school in giving to art what was, in fact, an inimitable thing.

His influence upon etching, on the other hand, has been widespread. Perhaps it has been because, with the needle, it was not so much the "poetry of sight" that he sought—though he did not forget it—as just the ponderable truth, defined in bewitching webs of line and subtle nuances of tone. It is one of the paradoxes of his career that the draftsmanship which worried him so much when he was using the brush was ready to his hand when he used the etcher's needle. Already in the French set, which dates from 1858, when he was still in his twenties, he is a master of line and of style. The Thames set, which followed shortly (1860), discloses the same technical authority, the same grasp upon composition, and, by the same token, the personal stroke which was ever after to be his. Upon both these earlier emprises he launched in what might be called the traditional spirit of the art and was closely realistic. But by the time he went to Venice, in the seventies, and in later years, he more and more practised the elimination of intrusive detail and employed a lighter, more stenographic touch, a terser, more broken line. It is this later mode of his that has raised up a horde of clever followers. They sometimes approach his skill but they never match the impalpable quality which places so many of the etchings and dry points beside the "Nocturnes" in paint for beauty and distinction. After all, the Whistlerianism of Whistler is an essence which only "The

Butterfly" could distil. He proved this in many mediums, in oil, in water color, in pastels, and, as regards black and white, not only in the etchings but in the lithographs. He was a constant student of the practical problems involved in the handling of those mediums. There never was a more conscientious craftsman.

Whistler has been described in this narrative as an histrionic type, dramatizing his own life, but there are hardly any dramatic incidents, in the strict sense, to be noted. As is, indeed, the case with so many great artists, his life was in his work a matter of complete absorption. The only episode approaching drama is the rather obscure one of his sudden sailing for Valparaiso in 1866. Then, being at the still impressionable age of thirty-two, he appears to have gone off with others to South America in a warlike frame of mind, on an impulse surging up from his West Point days. He seems to have had some idea of mixing into the trouble going on between the Chileans and the Spaniards and when he reached Valparaiso he at least witnessed a modest bombardment. But beyond the painting of a few harbor pictures his activities were slight and he returned to London before the year was out with no scars to show for his martial excursion. The tale of his having kicked a Haytian across the ship's deck on the way back inspired his friend Dante Rossetti to compose this eloquent limerick (Pennell, *Life*, 1911 ed., p. 100):

> "There's a combative Artist named Whistler
> Who is, like his own hog-hairs, a bristler:
>   A tube of white lead
>   And a punch on the head
> Offer varied attractions to Whistler."

Du Maurier had observed his friend's pugnacious traits long before, when they were young men together in Paris. He recalled them in *Trilby*, portraying Whistler as one Joe Sibley, whose "enmity would take the simple and straight-forward form of trying to punch his ex-friend's head" (Pennell, *Life*, II, 160). When this passage, and others of like nature, appeared in *Harper's Magazine* in 1894, Whistler was so infuriated that he caused them to be suppressed. The truth is that, as a friend who knew him intimately over a long period of years has put it in a private letter: "He could be an Enemy—there is no question of that—but only when provocation he received justified it. He did not mind any one fighting with him in a good square fight, a clashing of honest opinion on either side." The next night after the stormy talk about Ingres, to which reference has been made, the artist and his antagonist were dining in peace and amity together, Whistler the pink of perfec-

tion in his rôle of the enchanting host and talking as only he could talk, wittily and illuminat-
ingly. If the impression exists that his barbs
were envenomed it is due to the devastating wit
with which *The Gentle Art of Making Enemies*
(1890) is filled—to say nothing of the challenge
embodied in the mere title.

That memorable book came into being somewhat fortuitously. Sheridan Ford, an American
journalist, was for compiling and publishing it
in the late eighties. Then Whistler published it
himself, after wrangles and legal contests too
complicated to be summarized here. The main
thing is that it gathered up into a single volume
all the outstanding evidences of Whistler's skill
in attack and riposte, his inexhaustible gaiety—
and his philosophy of art. It opens with his annotated record of the Ruskin affair and the pamphlet on "Whistler v. Ruskin: Art and Art
Critics," which he dedicated to the friend toward
whom he never changed, Albert Moore, the
painter of pictures as exquisite in their way as
Whistler's were in theirs. It preserved the mordant letters which he used to send to the press, to
confound his foes. It contains the deadly notes
which he loved to append to the catalog of an exhibition of his, notes consisting of quotations
from the critics and unerringly calculated to expose the fatuity of those personages. "Mr. Whistler's 'Ten O'clock,' " is reprinted and many more
gems of audacity and literary art—for this ready
scorner of the writing tribe was himself a master of the pen. How fully he knew the secret of
acknowledging a second-class medal with his
second-class thanks! "Pray convey my sentiments of tempered and respectable joy to the
gentlemen of the Committee [one in Munich]
and my complete appreciation of the second hand
compliment paid me" (*Gentle Art of Making
Enemies*, p. 229). Thus he went through life,
airily stinging whoever incurred his displeasure
—critic, artist, author, functionary, and, most
piercingly of all, those who had once been admitted to his friendship only to lapse into the
ranks of "the enemy."

That enemy, to tell the truth, was often characterized by a most exasperating stupidity. Whistler had long to reckon with a public not only
unresponsive but crass and the "cold print" is
there to show how criticism was for many years
unaware of his merit as an artist. He was past
fifty before the honors and the rewards began to
roll in. For decades he was probably as misunderstood an artist as ever lived. His dandiacal
dress, his derisive "Ha! Ha!," his irresistible
impulse to say the witty and often damaging
thing, could not but "put off" many a person

otherwise ready enough to meet him halfway in
the social swirl to which he was addicted. He
was a drawing-room idol and that has its dangers. He amused people perhaps too much, so
that they forgot the unplumbed depths of seriousness in his fundamental purpose. There is
the story of Edgar Degas, overhearing some of
Whistler's sallies and saying: "My friend, you
behave as though you had no talent." And
when his painting of Lady Eden's portrait landed him in a law suit (embalmed in *Eden Versus
Whistler, The Baronet and the Butterfly*, 1899,
an opusculum of dubious value), it led also to a
"row" with George Moore in which Whistler's
challenging of the novelist eventuated in naught.
Some of his vendettas might well have been fore-
gone. On the other hand there can be no question
of his sincerity when on the warpath or of its
close relation to the core of his art. He fought
not for the pleasure of making enemies but out
of loyalty to his esthetic principles. There is a
story of his talking with a friend in a London
hansom on the way to dinner which admirably
conveys what he would himself have called "the
fin mot" of the matter. "Starr," he said, "I have
not dined, as you know, so you need not think I
say this in anything but a cold and careful spirit:
it is better to live on bread and cheese and paint
beautiful things than to live like Dives and paint
potboilers" (Seitz, *Whistler Stories*, p. 33).

The gravity in this dictum was characteristic
of his whole approach to art. He was a prodigious worker. Those who knew him intimately
enough to be about the studio when he was occupied with a canvas report how even when the
light failed he hated to put down the brush, and
conscience was behind every stroke. His career
was one long immersion in the task, and in the
joy of creating beautiful things. He had his reward. The old contumely gave way to applause.
The master was recognized beneath the blithe
flutterings of the Butterfly, and with heightened
appreciation there came a new prosperity. Artists of the rising generation flocked around his
banner and though the Royal Academy never
made him a member of the Society of British Artists, in 1884, elected him to membership and, in
1886, chose him to be president. He served for
two years before the reforms he instituted—all
of them good, and one, the more decorative handling of the exhibitions, especially efficacious—
proved too much for the organization and his
administration came to an end. His followers
withdrew and, as it was like him to say, "The
Artists have come out and the British remain"
(Pennell, *Life*, II, 71). The experience did not
daunt him from again undertaking official re-

sponsibilities. When the International Society of Sculptors, Painters, and Gravers was founded in 1897 he consented to act as president and threw himself with tremendous zeal upon the direction of its affairs. Meanwhile, on Aug. 11, 1888, he was married to Beatrix Godwin, the widow of his old friend, Edward William Godwin, the architect, and his existence had in every way taken on a more stabilized turn.

It was in the early nineties that he went back to Paris and settled in Rue de Bac, where the writer first met him, an engaging apparition in blue jacket and duck trousers, a straw hat in one hand and a little birdcage in the other, every movement graceful and every sentence entertaining. Crushing sorrow was to befall him. Mrs. Whistler died on May 10, 1896, and his world was in ruins. But Whistler was a courageous man. In 1898 he had the energy to ally himself with a school in Paris, the Académie Carmen, established by one of his models, Carmen Rossi. While it lasted, which was not very long, only until 1901, he would visit the atelier and criticize the work of the students. But his methods were too original, too exacting, and, besides, he was unable, ultimately, to give it the necessary attention. His guiding principle seems to have been the virtue of an arduous training, such as he himself had missed in his youth. His health was beginning to go. He sought its betterment in Africa and Corsica. These and other journeys did him no good. In 1902 he was in London again, ailing, and in the summer of the following year the end came. He was buried in Chiswick Cemetery on July 22, 1903.

He died a man of many honors, an officer of the French Legion of Honor, a member of German, French, and Italian bodies of artists. The "Mother" was in Luxembourg, later to be transferred to the Louvre, and paintings and prints of his had been established in collections everywhere, public and private. In the academy at West Point a *stele* designed by Saint-Gaudens was erected. There is a bust of him by MacMonnies in the Hall of Fame of New York University. The Freer Gallery at Washington contains, besides the Peacock Room, an extensive collection of his works, and an invaluable body of Whistleriana has been given to the Library of Congress by the Pennells. A movement was started in London for a monument to him by Rodin but though the commission was in the sculptor's hands for ten years the model he left behind him at his death was so unsatisfactory that the scheme was abandoned. Soon after Whistler's death there was a great memorial exhibition of his works held in London, similar

enterprises were organized in New York and Boston, and in museums and art galleries generally Whistler's art continues to be a living quantity. The numerous memorial episodes testify to what the world has come to think of Whistler. There are certain words of his own, spoken to his friend, the late Edward G. Kennedy, which may also be cited here as pertinent: "When I see the things by these other fellows," he said, "and look at my own, there is something about them that is much better and more dignified." It is a proud judgment but it is a true one and the world must listen willingly enough when he says, as it is easy to imagine him saying: "I shall be born when and where I choose, I shall select what I choose to look at, and I shall paint as I choose." It is, indeed, impossible to deny him. His art speaks with the accent of originality and genius.

[Catalogue of Paintings, Drawings, Etchings, and Lithographs. The International Society of Sculptors, Painters, and Gravers Memorial Exhibition of Works of Late James McNeill Whistler . . . from Feb. 22 to April 15, 1905 (n.d.), the best available list of his works; Frederick Wedmore, Whistler Etchings; A Study and a Catalogue (1886); E. G. Kennedy, comp., The Etched Work of Whistler, with introduction by Royal Cortissoz (6 vols. of plates and 1 vol. of text, 1910); D. C. Seitz, Writings by and about James Abbott McNeill Whistler; A Bibliography (1910); Elizabeth R. and Joseph Pennell, The Life of James McNeill Whistler (2 vols., 1908), the official biography; and The Whistler Journal (1921), very valuable; Elizabeth R. Pennell, The Art of Whistler (1928), available in Modern Library; and Whistler the Friend (1930); Frederick Wedmore, Four Masters of Etching (1883); Mortimer Menpes, Whistler as I Knew Him (1904); O. H. Bacher, With Whistler in Venice (1908); Henry James, "Contemporary Notes on Whistler and Ruskin," in Views and Reviews (1908); T. R. Way, Memories of James McNeill Whistler the Artist (1912), by his lithographer; Royal Cortissoz, Art and Common Sense (1913); D. C. Seitz, Whistler Stories (1913); Theodore Duret, Whistler (1917), trans. by Frank Rutter; A. E. Gallatin, Portraits of Whistler; A Critical Study and an Iconography (1918); James Laver, Whistler (1930); obituary in the Times (London), July 18, 1903; "Whistler Centenary Number," The Index of Twentieth Century Artists, June 1934.]
R. C.

WHITAKER, ALEXANDER (1585–March 1616/17), Anglican clergyman, was born at Cambridge, England. His father was William Whitaker (see *Dictionary of National Biography*), a noted Puritan divine, master of St. John's College and Regius Professor of Divinity at the University of Cambridge; his mother was a daughter of Nicholas Culverwell. Alexander Whitaker received the bachelor's degree at Cambridge in 1604/05 and the master's degree in 1608, and was ordained to the ministry of the Church of England. Appointed to a living in the North of England, he ministered there for a few years, but soon volunteered to go to the newly established colony of Virginia. He arrived at

Jamestown with Sir Thomas Dale [*q.v.*] in the spring of 1611 and within a short while became minister of two new settlements, Henricopolis and Bermuda Hundreds, some fifty miles up the James River. The "Laws Divine, Moral and Martial" brought over by Dale required the minister to preach twice on Sunday and once on Wednesday, with daily morning and evening prayer. His influence was important in cheering and encouraging the scattered little groups of colonists, and in settling their differences. In this work Whitaker continued, living at "Rock Hall," opposite Henricopolis, until his death by drowning in March 1616/17. He was never married.

In the early formative years of the colony, the leaders of the London Company, the ministers who came, and the colonists generally were of the Puritan element in the Church of England. Whitaker, who was of the same school of thought as Sir Edwin Sandys and Rev. Richard Buck of Jamestown, in a letter to his relative, Rev. William Gouge, June 18, 1614, wrote: "I much more muse that so few of our English ministers that were so hot against the surplice and subscription come hither where neither are spoken of" (Goodwin, *post*, pp. 41–42). His words expressed the attitude of welcome toward Puritan ministers and lay people which characterized Virginia until the later part of the reign of King Charles I, when in strong loyalty to the King laws were enacted forbidding Puritan ministers to enter or remain in the Colony. Whitaker undoubtedly helped to form and strengthen this early attitude, and to establish Virginia's characteristic tradition of low churchmanship. In 1613 a sermon written by him, entitled *Good News from Virginia,* was published by the London Company; in it he emphasized the importance of supporting the effort to establish the Colony, urged the conversion of the Indians to the Christian religion, and gave a description of the country. This sermon, with a letter to Rev. William Crashaw dated Aug. 9, 1611, a letter to Sir Thomas Smith, treasurer of the Company dated Henrico, July 28, 1612, and the letter to Rev. William Gouge, mentioned above, are his only known writings. Although his ministry in Virginia was very brief, the expressions of commendation by his associates there and by the officials of the London Company reveal the usefulness of his devoted and unselfish life. Perhaps the best-remembered detail of his pastoral work is that he instructed Pocahontas [*q.v.*] in the principles of the Christian faith when she was held as a hostage at Henricopolis, and baptized her prior to her marriage to John Rolfe.

[Alexander Brown, *The First Republic in America* (1898) and *The Genesis of the U. S.* (1890); William Meade, *Old Churches, Ministers and Families in Va.* (1857); F. L. Hawks, *Contributions to the Ecclesiastical Hist. of the U. S. A.* (1836), vol. I; P. A. Bruce, *Economic Hist. of Va. in the Seventeenth Century* (1895); *Institutional Hist. of Va. in the Seventeenth Century* (1910); John Rolfe, "True Relation of the State of Virginia" (1616), in *Southern Literary Messenger,* June 1839; J. S. M. Anderson, *The Hist. of the Church of England in the Colonies,* vol. I (1845); William Stith, *The Hist. of the First Discovery and Settlement of Va.* (1747); *William and Mary Quart.,* July 1936; E. L. Goodwin, *The Colonial Church in Va.* (copr. 1927).]
G. M. B.

WHITAKER, DANIEL KIMBALL (Apr. 13, 1801–Mar. 24, 1881), editor, was born in Sharon, Mass., the son of the Rev. Jonathan and Mary (Kimball) Whitaker. Preparatory to entering Harvard College, he was educated by his father, a scholar of achievement, and at various small academies. He received the degree of B.A. from Harvard in 1820 and the degree of M.A. in 1823. For his dissertation on "The Literary Character of Dr. Samuel Johnson" he won the Boylston Medal; he also won the Bowdoin Medal for oratory. Upon leaving Harvard he studied privately for the ministry and received a license to preach. When ill health compelled him to try a warmer climate he made a successful preaching tour through several Southern states accompanied by his father. In 1823 his health failed to improve and he abandoned the ministry to live on a farm in South Carolina, and for ten years he devoted himself to the culture of rice and cotton.

When country life became too tranquil for him he moved to Charleston where he studied law and established a practice. He tried several important cases successfully and was known as an orator, but soon he wearied of law and turned to literature. He organized and edited a number of periodicals, including the *Southern Literary Journal and Magazine of Arts,* in Charleston, from 1835 to 1837, the *Southern Quarterly Review,* New Orleans, 1842–47, and the *New Orleans Monthly Review,* New Orleans, 1874–76. Of these the *Southern Quarterly Review* was most successful. It was published in New Orleans instead of Charleston in order to command a more extensive circulation throughout the South and Southwest. Whitaker secured a subscription list of $16,000 and engaged some of the best-known writers of the South as contributors. William Gilmore Simms [*q.v.*] wrote for the magazine frequently although he disliked Whitaker personally. About January 1847 the *Review* was bought by a Charleston gentleman who preferred Southern editorship and secured, first, J. Milton Clapp, and then William Gilmore Simms as editors.

Whitaker returned to Charleston where he remained until 1866 when he took up residence again in New Orleans. During Buchanan's administration he held a government position. After the secession of South Carolina he was employed by the Post Office Department of the Confederate government. His scholarly interests, especially in the classics, were lifelong; he liked to analyze political and historical problems. As a writer he was diffuse but often persuasive. "Whitaker is one of the best essayists in North America," Poe is said to have written, "and stands in the foremost rank of elegant writers" (Jewell, *post*, n. p.). He was a frequent contributor to the *National Intelligencer* (Washington, D. C.), the *Charleston Courier,* and the *New Orleans Times,* but the best of his work appeared in the *Southern Quarterly Review.* As a person he seems to have inspired respect and affection. To the surprise of his friends, familiar with his early prejudice against Catholicism, he was united with St. Patrick's Church of New Orleans in 1878. He died in Houston, Tex., and was buried in New Orleans. Two daughters survived him. Whitaker was twice married: his first wife bore him two sons. After her death he was married to Mrs. Mary Scrimzeour Miller, of South Carolina, the daughter of Samuel Furman.

[Private papers of the family; Harvard Univ. Alumni Records; L. A. Morrison, S. P. Sharples, *Hist. of the Kimball Family in America* (1897), vol. I; E. L. Jewell, *Jewell's Crescent City Illustrated* (1873); W. P. Trent, *William Gilmore Simms* (1892); *New-Orleans Times,* Mar. 26, 1881.]   J. R. M.

WHITAKER, NATHANIEL (November 1730–Jan. 26, 1795), clergyman, was born in Huntington, Long Island, the son of Jonathan and Elizabeth (Jervis) Whitaker. The family soon removed to New Jersey, and Nathaniel was graduated from the College of New Jersey (Princeton) in 1752. He was licensed to preach by the New York Presbytery, and became minister of the Presbyterian Church at Woodbridge, N. J., in 1755. In Woodbridge he married Sarah Smith, by whom he had five children. In 1760 he transferred his activities to the Sixth (Chelsea) Parish of Norwich, Conn.

Here he was a neighbor of the Rev. Eleazar Wheelock [*q.v.*], who in 1754 had established at Lebanon a successful charity school for the education of Indians. At the suggestion of George Whitefield [*q.v.*], Wheelock had determined to send one of his old pupils, the Rev. Samson Occom [*q.v.*], to England to raise funds for this undertaking, and Whitaker was chosen to accompany him as manager of the enterprise. The two envoys, sailing from Boston in December 1765, reached England the following February. Through the influence of Whitefield they were cordially received by such evangelical leaders as William, second Earl of Dartmouth, the Countess of Huntingdon, Sir Charles Hotham, and John Thornton. Two busy years of solicitation, personal interviews, and almost daily preaching were spent in England and Scotland. The gross amount obtained was £12,000, a larger sum than was secured by direct solicitation in England by any other educational institution in America in pre-Revolutionary days. Probably the appeal of Occom was most effective in attaining this result, but the business acumen and industry of Whitaker contributed in no small degree to the success of the mission. Although the fund (placed in the care of a trust headed by the Earl of Dartmouth) for the most part was spent for the purpose for which it was designed, the possession of the endowment was largely responsible for the grant of the charter of Dartmouth College to Wheelock by Gov. John Wentworth [*q.v.*] of New Hampshire in 1769. During his stay Whitaker received the degree of D.D. from St. Andrew's University in 1767. From 1769 to 1784 he was minister of the Third Church at Salem, Mass., and from 1785 to 1790 of the Presbyterian Church at Skowhegan, Me. He died in Hampton, Va.

The insistence of Whitaker upon the Presbyterian form of church government in the hostile soil of New England, resulted in continual friction with his congregations, and, in each case, in his final removal from his position. A number of sermons relating to this issue were published, as well as two upon the doctrine of the regeneration. He was an ardent patriot, and published a sermon upon the Boston massacre, and two vindictive attacks upon the Tories. His activities extended to practical matters: he engaged in trade in Norwich; he attempted to combine the practice of inoculation with the main purpose of his English mission; he established a saltpeter factory in Salem during the Revolution; and he built a new church building in each of his three New England parishes. His fondness for controversy brought him many enemies. The terms "tricky" and "unreliable" are among the mildest which they applied to him. On the other hand, he was singularly handsome, with a good voice and eloquence above the average, he was dignified and positive in manner, and, most of all, possessed a high degree of initiative and driving force.

[The Dartmouth Coll. Lib. has manuscript accounts of Whitaker by his grandson, D. K. Whitaker, and by O. M. Voorhees (from the latter of which the date of birth is taken), as well as the Whitaker collection of

MSS. relating to the English mission. Much of the latter appears in *An Indian Preacher in England* (1933), ed. by L. B. Richardson. See also Frederick Chase, *A Hist. of Dartmouth Coll.* (1891) ; L. B. Richardson, *Hist. of Dartmouth Coll.* (1932) ; Frances M. Caulkins, *Hist. of Norwich* (1866 ed.) ; J. B. Felt, *Annals of Salem,* 2nd ed., vol. II (1849). Scathing references occur in *The Diary of William Bentley, D.D.,* vol. I (1905). For Whitaker's theological writings, see Joseph Haroutunian, *Piety Versus Moralism* (1932). A portrait of Whitaker, painted during his stay in England by Mason Chamberlin, is in the possession of Dartmouth Coll.]

                                    L. B. R.

WHITCHER, FRANCES MIRIAM BERRY (Nov. 1, 1814–Jan. 4, 1852), author, was born in Whitesboro, N. Y., one of the thirteen children of Lewis and Elizabeth (Wells) Berry. Her father, an early settler in Whitesboro, was at the time of her birth owner of "Berry's Tavern," an important hostelry in the county. During her childhood she attended the village school, where she was outstanding because of her unusual memory and her skill in drawing caricatures. Further study at the local academy and French lessons in nearby Utica completed her formal education. She read widely and early tried her hand at prose and verse. Her first work to attract attention was a series of humorous sketches in colloquial dialect called "The Widow Spriggins," which she read to her fellow-members of the Maeonian Circle, a social and literary society in Whitesboro. The admiration these narratives aroused led her to send them to a weekly paper in Rome, N. Y. Encouraged by their publication she began another series in the same vein called "The Widow Bedott's Table-Talk." The first installment of this work, signed with her pen-name "Frank," appeared in Joseph C. Neal's *Saturday Gazette and Lady's Literary Museum* in the autumn of 1846. The immediate popularity of the series brought her an invitation from Louis A. Godey to become a contributor to the *Lady's Book.* On Jan. 6, 1847, she married the Rev. B. W. Whitcher, an Episcopal clergyman, and the following spring accompanied him to his parish in Elmira, N. Y. There she continued to write, supplying Widow Bedott papers to Neal's *Gazette* until 1850. To *Godey's Lady's Book* she contributed a similar series entitled "Aunt Magwire's Experiences," and another in a different style called "Letters from Timberville," incomplete at her death. Some of these sketches were illustrated with her own drawings. Her fame as a humorist did not endear her to her husband's parishioners. Her always strong sense of the ludicrous and the absurd tempted her to satirize much that she found in small-town society. She dealt sharply with the sewing circle, the donation party, and with the pretentiousness of the self-satisfied. As

she was good at portraiture, some of her sketches gave offense to persons who fancied that they recognized the originals. One irate husband threatened legal prosecution for damage done to his wife's character. Besides the humorous works for which she was well known she also wrote a number of hymns and devotional poems. In these her deeply religious nature and her love for the services of the church found expression. Some of them appeared in *Neal's Gazette,* others in the *Gospel Messenger* of Utica. The last two years of her life were spent at her home in Whitesboro. There she worked on a book called "Mary Elmer," which she did not live to finish. After the birth of a daughter in November 1849 she failed rapidly in health. She joined her husband for a brief time in a new parish at Oswego, but illness prevented her remaining. She died at Whitesboro.

After her death her prose writings were collected in two volumes : *The Widow Bedott Papers* (1856), with an introduction by Alice B. Neal, and *Widow Spriggins, Mary Elmer, and Other Sketches* (1867), with a memoir by Mrs. M. L. Ward Whitcher. In 1879 the Widow Bedott was reintroduced to the public in a four-act comedy by Petroleum V. Nasby (D. R. Locke), *Widow Bedott, or a Hunt for a Husband,* which followed the original dialogue closely. The part of the widow was successfully taken by Neil Burgess [*q.v.*], an actor of eccentric female parts.

["Passages in the Life of an Author," *Godey's Lady's Book,* July, Aug. 1853 ; introduction by Alice Neal and Mrs. Ward Whitcher, *ante*; *Some Account of "The Widow Bedott Papers" and the Comedy of that Name* (n.d.) ; information from family ; death date from *Gospel Messenger,* Jan. 9, 1852.]   B. M. S.

WHITCOMB JAMES (Dec. 1, 1795–Oct. 4, 1852), governor of Indiana, United States senator, son of John and Lydia (Parmenter) Whitcomb, was born in Rochester, Windsor County, Vt. His father served as a private in the American Revolution; his first paternal American ancestor, John, emigrated from England and settled in Dorchester, Mass., by 1635. In 1806 the family moved to the neighborhood of Cincinnati, Ohio. James, studious, and a poor farmer, is said to have worked his way through Transylvania University, Lexington, Ky., but there is no record of his attendance. He studied law, and in 1822 was admitted to the bar of Fayette County, Ky. From 1824 to 1836 he practised law at Bloomington, Ind., and from 1826 to 1829 was prosecuting attorney for that judicial district, the fifth. He was elected to the state Senate for the sessions 1830–31 and from 1832 to 1836, standing with the Democratic party as party lines became definitely drawn. In 1836 he was appointed commissioner of the general land office by President Jackson, serving until the end of Van Buren's term, and mastering both French and Spanish for use in his work. In 1841 he established a law office at Terre Haute, Ind., where he soon developed a large and lucrative practice. In the campaign of 1843 he wrote a popular treatise, *Facts for the People,* one of the most effective arguments ever written against a protective tariff. Whitcomb was elected governor over the incumbent, Samuel Bigger—the first Democrat to defeat a Whig for that office—and took office in December 1843. In 1846 he was reëlected over Joseph G. Marshall.

As governor, Whitcomb contributed decisively toward the adjustment of the staggering indebtedness incurred by the state in the building of roads, railroads, and especially canals, under the Mammoth Improvement acts, and in the failure of most of the canal system. Under an arrangement effected by Charles Butler [*q.v.*], attorney for the largest bondholding interests, the bondholders agreed to take as half payment the Wabash and Erie Canal and to accept state "registered" and "deferred" stock for the other half of the bonds, and the state stopped payment of principal and interest on the old bonds. Though there had been default in payment of interest and though investors lost heavily, the state technically avoided repudiation of its debts. Whitcomb vigorously promoted popular education and the development of benevolent institutions. The office of superintendent of common schools was created in 1843; a school for the deaf was developed by the state in 1844; a state hospital for the insane was provided for in 1845 and received patients in 1848; and in 1847 the Indiana Institute for the Education of the Blind was created. He was an ardent supporter of the national administration in the War with Mexico, financed the raising of troops by loans from branches of the State Bank, and personally superintended recruiting in Indianapolis.

On Mar. 24, 1846, he married Martha Ann (Renwick) Hurst, daughter of William Renwick of Pickaway County, Ohio. Mrs. Whitcomb died the following year, shortly after the birth of a daughter who was to become the wife of another governor of the state, Claude Matthews [*q.v.*]. In the election of United States senator by the General Assembly for the term beginning in March 1849, Whitcomb defeated the incumbent, Edward Allen Hannegan [*q.v.*]. In failing health, and suffering severely from gravel, he took little part in the Senate proceedings in the critical years 1849–52, and died in New York City, after a surgical operation. He is buried in Crown Hill Cemetery, Indianapolis. He bequeathed his extensive library to Asbury (De Pauw) University. He was an active member of the Methodist Episcopal Church, and at the time of his death a vice-president of the American Bible Society. He was an accomplished violinist and an eloquent speaker, forceful both in his ideas and in his expression. His personal charm and social grace were strangely crossed with habits of penuriousness in small matters, which, with his elaborate entertainments in the old "Governor's Mansion," were long a tradition throughout the state. He was an inveterate smoker and user of snuff. Somewhat above average height, he was of a compact build, of dark complexion, with a mass of black hair, usually falling in ringlets nearly to his shoulders.

[Charlotte Whitcomb, *The Whitcomb Family in America* (1904); Ind. Senate Jour., 1830–36, 1843–48; Ind. House Jour., 1843–48; Ind. Documentary Jour., 1843–46; J. P. Dunn, *Ind. and Indianans* (1919), vol. I; Logan Esarey, "Internal Improvements in Early Ind.," *Ind. Hist. Soc. Pubs.,* vol. V (1915), and *A Hist. of Ind.* (3rd ed., 2 vols., 1924); Oran Perry, *Ind. in the Mexican War* (1908); O. H. Smith, *Early Ind. Trials; and Sketches* (1858); W. W. Woollen, *Biog. and Hist. Sketches of Early Ind.* (1883); obituary in *N. Y. Daily Times,* Oct. 5, 1852.]   C. B. C.

WHITCOMB, SELDEN LINCOLN (July 19, 1866–Apr. 22, 1930), teacher and writer, was born in Grinnell, Iowa, the son of Abraham Whitcomb and his wife Mary (Fisher) Whitcomb. He was a descendant of John Whitcomb who had settled in Dorchester, Mass., by 1635. His family connection and the pioneer group to which it belonged, were of the type which often came from New England in the period before the Civil War to make settlements in the Middle West, people whose thought and purposes were marked by liberality and integrity. The surroundings of his earlier years contributed to these elements in himself and in his writings. His elementary education was obtained in Grinnell, and he received the degree of A.B. from Iowa College (afterwards Grinnell) in 1887. He later carried on graduate work in Cornell University (1889–91) and in Harvard, Chicago, and Columbia. He received the degree of A.M. in 1893 from Columbia, where in 1893–94 he was a fellow in literature. He also was briefly in the universities of Colorado and Washington. When he began to teach he gave instruction in German and the classics at Stockton Academy, Stockton, Kan. (1887–89), and in civics at the Iowa State Teachers College (1891–92) before he settled to the teaching of English and finally of comparative literature. From 1895 to 1905 he was professor of English in Grinnell College.

In 1905 he removed to the University of Kansas, at Lawrence, where at the time of his death he was professor of comparative literature. From 1912 to 1930 he was editor of the Humanistic Series published by the university.

His written work is of several different types. The result of his study and teaching is found in his *Chronological Outlines of American Literature* (1894) and *The Study of a Novel* (1905), and in various articles and pamphlets. All this work is purposed chiefly to be useful to students of literature. He published also *Lyrical Verse* (1898), *Poems* (1912), *Random Rhymes and the Three Queens* (1913), *Via Crucis* (1915). His poem "The Path-makers," which won a state poetry prize for him, was published in *Poetry* in August 1924. Besides these he issued small collections of his observations of outdoor life: *Autumn Notes in Iowa* (1914), *Nature Notes— Spring* (1907), and papers in different periodicals. He had great curiosity regarding the history of plants and animals, and in his youth and early manhood he made long excursions or undertook outdoor work of some kind. Much later than that he spent whole seasons at some interesting post of observation, as at the Puget Sound marine station, where he several times passed a summer. The records he published have something of a Gilbert White substance and enthusiasm. Another aspect of this interest is found in the faithfulness of the nature element in his poems. The whole body of his poetry could be included in one volume of medium size, but it is of finished quality, fine in feeling and phrase. He was a notable teacher. He provided a lasting stimulus for his students, partly because of an unpredictable personal quality and custom, and partly because of the impressive body of his own knowledge. He was a very modest man, retiring and rather solitary in his habits, not forming wide personal associations. His general social interest is shown, however, in his membership in many organizations, economic, sociological, political, besides the literary and professional societies with which he would naturally be affiliated. He was married twice—first, in 1899, to Dora May Wilbur, who died in 1902; second, in 1919, to Edna Pearle Osborne, who outlived him by a little more than a year.

[Charlotte Whitcomb, *The Whitcomb Family in America* (1904); *Who's Who in America*, 1930–31; *Trans. Kan. Acad. Sci.*, vol. XXXVI (1933), p. 31; funeral address delivered by a friend, Rev. E. M. Vittum of Grinnell; obituary in *Emporia Gazette* (Emporia, Kan.), Apr. 23, 1930.] M. L—n.

WHITE, ALBERT SMITH (Oct. 24, 1803– Sept. 4, 1864), lawyer, representative and senator, jurist, was a descendant of Thomas White,

an early settler of Weymouth, Mass. He was born at the family homestead at Blooming Grove in Orange County, N. Y., the son of Nathan Herrick and Frances (Howell) White. The father was the presiding judge of the Orange County court for twenty years. The son was graduated from Union College in 1822, studied law at Newburgh, was admitted to the bar in 1825, removed to Indiana the same year, and, after brief periods at Rushville and Paoli, in 1829 settled permanently in Tippecanoe County, residing either at Lafayette or on his farm near Stockwell. In 1830–31 he was assistant clerk of the Indiana House of Representatives, and for the four succeeding years was clerk of that body.

In 1836 he was elected to a seat in the national House of Representatives as a Whig, and in March 1839 was elected to the Senate. In the House he served on the committee on roads and canals, and introduced a few resolutions, but refrained from active participation in debates. With Oliver Hampton Smith [q.v.] as his colleague, he took his seat in the Senate, Dec. 2, 1839, at the opening of the Twenty-sixth Congress. A few days later he was appointed a member of the committee on Indian affairs and from the beginning of the third session of the Twenty-seventh Congress until the close of his term, in March 1845, he was chairman of that committee. He became an important member of the committee on roads and canals, and served effectively (1841–45) on the committee to audit and control contingent expenses. When in 1852 the bill for apportioning the membership of the House of Representatives among the several states was before the Senate, he delivered a scholarly and cogent address in favor of "popular" as against "party" representation and advocated measures for the security of the federal government rather than the rights of the states (*Congressional Globe*, 27 Cong., 2 Sess., p. 583).

Between 1845 and 1860 White was engaged in the practice of law and in the building of railroads in the valley of the Wabash. He was the first president of the Lafayette and Indianapolis Railroad, and for three years was manager of the Wabash and Western Railroad. He served once more in the House of Representatives as a Republican from March 1861 to March 1863. His most notable activity was the introduction of a resolution for the appointment of a select committee to propose a plan for the gradual emancipation of slaves in the border states (*Congressional Globe*, 37 Cong., 2 Sess., p. 1563). As chairman of such a committee he reported bills for indemnifying the loyal owners of slaves in Maryland, Missouri, and other states. Although the plan had the warm support of President Lincoln, it was not popular with White's constituents and cost him his renomination. On his leaving the House, Lincoln appointed him (appointment confirmed, Mar. 7, 1863) one of three commissioners to adjust claims of citizens of Minnesota and Dakota on account of depredations committed during the Sioux Indian massacre on the Minnesota frontier in August 1862. A second appointment by Lincoln (confirmed Jan. 18, 1864) made him judge of the United States District Court for Indiana, a position he held until his death at his residence near Stockwell. White was a man of small physique and thin visage, with a large aquiline nose. He was well versed in belles-lettres, and in legal and political lore. He married a member of the Randolph family of Virginia and was survived by his widow, two sons, and two daughters.

[G. W. Chamberlain, *Hist. of Weymouth, Mass.* (1923), vol. IV; B. F. Thompson, *Hist. of Long Island* (1918), vol. II; E. M. Ruttenber and L. H. Clark, *Hist. of Orange County, N. Y.* (1881); W. W. Woollen, *Biog. and Hist. Sketches of Early Ind.* (1883); C. W. Taylor, *Bench and Bar of Ind.* (1895); *Reg. of Debates . . . First Sess., Twenty-fifth Cong.* (1837); *Indianapolis Daily Jour.*, Sept. 6, 9, 1864.]   N. D. M.

WHITE, ALEXANDER (c. 1738–Oct. 9, 1804), lawyer, congressman, commissioner to lay out the city of Washington, D. C., was born in Frederick County, Va., the son of Robert White, a surgeon in the English navy, and his wife, Margaret, a daughter of a Virginia pioneer, William Hoge. He was educated at his father's alma mater, Edinburgh University, and afterward studied law in London at the Inner Temple in 1762 and at Gray's Inn in 1763. On his return to Virginia in 1765 White began to practise law and continued with marked success for nearly forty years. He served almost continuously as king's or state's attorney in several north-valley counties and interspersed his legal work with terms in legislative bodies. His legislative career began with a term in the Virginia House of Burgesses where he represented Hampshire County in 1772. As a burgess he was especially interested in questions of civil and religious liberty. He was not particularly active during the Revolution and was later vigorously attacked because of it. He ably championed the cause of the wealthy Quakers who were exiled to Virginia from Philadelphia because of their alleged Loyalist sympathies. His successful plea for them merited an ample reward but nearly brought disastrous results to his standing with the patriots of the Valley. Following the Revolution White served in the state assembly, 1782–86, and 1788. During this period he played a

dominant part in advancing measures for religious liberty, for reform in the state court system, for the payment of British debts, for taxation reform and for strengthening the central government. He usually voted with Madison and was one of his ablest lieutenants.

When the Virginia Federalists marshalled their forces for the ratification of the new Constitution in 1788 White proved to be their dominant leader in the northwestern part of the state. He wrote continually in the newspapers of that section in defense of the new Constitution and his constituency voted unanimously for ratification. He was chosen as a member of the First Congress in 1789 and was reëlected to the Second Congress. The tide of Jeffersonianism was, however, too strong for his continued conservative federalism and he returned to the practice of law. The two terms in Congress brought his public life to a close except for his service from 1795 to 1802, as one of the commissioners to lay out the new capital at Washington. However, he returned to the state assembly for a brief term (1799–1801) in the vain hope that he might help defeat the famous resolutions aimed at the Alien and Sedition Acts.

As a member of Congress White's chief interests lay in the new capital and in the problems of the tariff. Much of his time was devoted to his rather extensive land holdings in western Virginia and on the "Western Waters." Likewise he was keenly interested in the establishment of several frontier towns and in the development of the navigation of the Potomac River. He was a close personal friend and legal adviser for the three Revolutionary generals, Charles Lee, Horatio Gates [qq.v.], and Adam Stephen. He was twice married but had no children. His first wife was Elizabeth, daughter of Col. James Wood, the founder of Winchester, Va., and his second, Sarah Hite, the widow of John Hite, a grandson of Jost Hite [q.v.]. He is buried at "Woodville," his country estate near Winchester. He was regarded by his contemporaries as the outstanding leader of western Virginia and one of the ablest lawyers in the United States.

[Glass collection of Wood Papers, Winchester, Va.; Adam Stephen Papers, Lib. of Cong., Washington, D. C.; *Biog. Dir. Am. Cong.* (1928); J. H. Tyler, J. F. Hoge, *The Family of Hoge* (1927); E. A. Jones, *Am. Members of the Inns of Court* (London, 1924); W. H. Foote, *Sketches of Va.* (2nd ser., 1856); T. K. Cartmell, *Shenandoah Valley Pioneers* (1909); K. G. Greene, *Winchester, Va. and its Beginnings* (1926); Frederic Morton, *The Story of Winchester in Va.* (1925); *Enquirer* (Richmond, Va.), Oct. 17, 1804.]   F. H. H.

WHITE, ALEXANDER (Mar. 30, 1814–Mar. 18, 1872) pioneer merchant and art collector, son of David and Margaret (Gowe) White, was born at Elgin, Morayshire, Scotland. His father was killed in the battle of Waterloo when Alexander was but a year old. In 1836 White emigrated to America. He unsuccessfully sought a foothold in the South and after various vicissitudes—including shipwreck on the Illinois River, in which several fellow-passengers were drowned—reached Chicago in the spring of 1837. After painting wagons for a time by the day, he established himself independently, building a small frame structure and opening a store with a stock of paints and oils. He prospered, extended his stock to include glass and dyestuffs, and enlarged his plant until it included two retail houses and a large wholesale establishment. In the meantime he steadily invested his surplus accumulations in Chicago real estate. In 1857, after twenty years of prosperous merchandising, he sold that business and confined himself to real-estate investments. Continuing to prosper, he found time to gratify his taste for art. In three trips to Europe (1857, 1866, 1870), he bought many notable paintings, chiefly by European contemporaries, which he supplemented by works of American artists, bought in America. This collection, installed in his residence and opened to the public, was the first private art gallery in Chicago. After his return from Europe in 1867, White and his family resided in New York but returned to Chicago in 1869. Retiring then from active business, White bought an extensive country place in Lake Forest, about twenty-five miles north of Chicago, and opened in his new residence an art gallery containing about a hundred and sixty of the works of the leading contemporary American and foreign artists. Shortly after he returned from his third European art trip, the Chicago fire of October 1871 occurred, and White, holder of much real estate, lost heavily. To provide a rebuilding fund, he sold his art collection at auction in New York (Dec. 12, 13, 1871), critics and connoisseurs pronouncing it the best in America at that time. White entered energetically into ambitious plans for a resuscitation of art in Chicago and for the reëstablishment of other civic enterprises, but his death within six months after the fire transferred that work to other shoulders.

For many years he was closely associated with Chicago improvements and public institutions. He was recognized throughout the country as an art patron and connoisseur, and perhaps did as much to promote American art as any man of his generation. Great weight was attached to his judgment in art matters, and his approval of projects in that field was sought by those promoting them. He was an enthusiastic floriculturist, delighting in the culture of rare plants, and a fine conservatory was a feature of his Lake Forest estate. He was married at Chicago, Dec. 12, 1837, to Ann Reid (1818–1890), daughter of John Keith and Anne (Johnston) Reid of Grange, Banff Parish, Scotland. Eight children were born to them.

[Much information has been furnished by White's daughter, Elsie Keith White. See also A. T. Andreas, *Hist. of Chicago*, vol. III (1886), pp. 758–60; *Art Journal* (London), Feb. 1, 1872, p. 47; *Chicago Tribune*, Mar. 20, 1872 (obituary and editorial).]

G. B. U.

WHITE, ALFRED TREDWAY (May 28, 1846–Jan. 29, 1921), pioneer in housing reform, was born in the old city of Brooklyn, N. Y., the son of Alexander Moss and Elizabeth Hart (Tredway) White. His father, a native of Danbury, Conn., was descended from Thomas White, an early settler of Weymouth, Mass.; his mother's family was of Connecticut origin and had lived in Dutchess County, N. Y., since the first decade of the nineteenth century. Alfred's parents were well-to-do, his father being junior member of the New York importing firm of W. A. & A. M. White.

The boy's secondary schooling was obtained at the Brooklyn Collegiate and Polytechnic Institute and was supplemented by two years at the Rensselaer Polytechnic Institute, Troy, N. Y., where he received the degree of C.E. in 1865. Returning to Brooklyn, he served an apprenticeship in his father's business and was eventually taken into partnership. In the meantime, however, outside interests claimed an increasing share of his attention. As early as 1872 he was giving much thought to the possibility of improved housing for families with small incomes in large cities. Learning that in London, England, model tenements had been built with outside staircases, he could not rest until he had assured himself of the practicability of such a project. In 1876 he built in Brooklyn his first block of small apartments with light rooms. The best features of the London experiment were included, with others applicable to American conditions. Every room had its share of sunlight and air. The old taunt of "philanthropy and 5 per cent" had no sting for White. From the start he disclaimed a philanthropic motive, and with the whole enterprise on a business basis, he was able to show net profits of five per cent year after year, for he was providing his tenants with something that they could not get elsewhere. He was gratified by the fact that the proportion of day laborers and sewing-women in his Brooklyn houses was greater than in the model tenements of London. Well pleased with the outcome of his early effort, he completed in 1890 a large project known as the Riverside Tower and Homes Building. He also erected nearly 300 one- and two-family houses. His buildings sheltered more than 2000 persons. In 1879 he published *Improved Dwellings for the Laboring Classes*; in 1885, *Better Homes for Workingmen;* and in 1912, *Sun-Lighted Tenements: Thirty-five Years Experience as an Owner*. It is not too much to say that the outstanding success of White's operations contributed as much as any one factor to the enactment of New York's tenement-reform legislation of 1895 and later years.

His activities brought him into direct personal relations with various elements in the community and acquainted him with their common needs. He was one of the leading spirits in the Brooklyn Bureau of Charities from its inception in 1878. He was also active in the Children's Aid Society. In politics he was an independent. Mayor Charles A. Schieren [*q.v.*], a Republican, appointed him commissioner of city works in 1893. That office, next to the mayorship the most important in Brooklyn, White administered in such a way as to set new standards of efficiency and economy. In later years his interests broadened to include the educational work for the negro at Hampton and Tuskegee, and a wide range of sociological problems. He gave $300,-000 to the department of social ethics at Harvard. On May 29, 1878, he married Annie Jean Lyman, who died in 1920. Eight months later White himself, skating alone on a small lake in the Harriman State Park, Orange County, N. Y., broke through and was drowned under the ice. A daughter survived him.

[J. M. Bailey, *Hist. of Danbury, Conn.* (1896); W. T. Tredway, *Hist. of the Tredway Family* (1930); H. B. Nason, *Biog. Record Officers and Grads. Rensselaer Polytechnic Inst.* (1887); *Survey* (N. Y.), Feb. 5, 1921; *Who's Who in America*, 1920–21; *Brooklyn Daily Eagle*, Jan. 31, 1921; F. G. Peabody, *Reminiscences of Present-Day Saints* (1927); J. A. Riis, *How the Other Half Lives* (1890) and *Battle with the Slum* (1902); *Harvard Graduates Mag.*, June 1921; *Report of the Tenement House Committee of 1894* (1895).]
W. B. S.

WHITE, ANDREW (1579–Dec. 27, 1656), Jesuit missionary in Maryland, was born in London of gentle parentage. As a proscribed recusant, he was educated in the English refugee colleges on the Continent—at St. Alban's College in Valladolid (1595–), St. Hermenegild's College in Seville, and Douai. After his ordination to the priesthood at Douai (*c.* 1605), he volunteered for the Catholic missions in England, where, with two score of priests, he was apprehended by the authorities and banished on pen-

alty of death if he returned. An exile in the Low Countries, he entered the newly founded Jesuit novitiate at Louvain in 1607 and was received into the Society of Jesus in 1609. Ten years later he was professed with his final vows after having served as a lecturer in theology, sacred scripture, and Hebrew in the various colleges of his society in Spain and Flanders. As a Jesuit of sound learning and linguistic attainments, he continued his teaching in theology at Liège and Louvain until about 1629. Thereafter he took his place on the missions in Hampshire, for which he had experience as a former missionary in Suffolk and Devon (1625–28) in periods of relief from teaching.

As a secret priest living in guarded seclusion, little is known of his career, but he is said to have become interested in Catholic colonization and in the ventures of George Calvert [*q.v.*], first Baron of Baltimore, who corresponded with him from Avalon. He composed the *Declaratio Coloniae Domini Baronis de Baltimore,* which was revised and published by Cecil Calvert as *Conditions of Plantation* with the thought of advertising his projected colony and attracting settlers. While the *Ark* and the *Dove* sailed from Gravesend, White and John Altham [*q.v.*] and Brother Thomas Gervase did not take ship until its departure from the Isle of Wight (Nov. 22, 1633). Baltimore's selection of White as head of the mission met with the approval of the general of the Society of Jesus, Muzio Vitelleschi, and of the provincial, Richard Blount. On landing at St. Clement's (Blackistone) Isle in the lower Chesapeake (Mar. 25, 1634), Father White said mass and commenced his new labors, which included the writing of the *Relatio Itineris in Marilandiam* (a Latin version for his superior; an English account to Sir Thomas Lechford, in the possession of the Maryland Historical Society), described by Leonard Calvert, in May 1634, as the composition of a "most honest and discreet gentleman." The Latin account was discovered in manuscript in the Jesuit archives in Rome by William McSherry, S. J., in 1832 and has appeared in various editions, probably most authentically in Thomas Hughes's *History of the Society of Jesus in North America* (*Documents*, vol. I, pt. I, 1908, pp. 94–107). For ten years White devoted himself to religious work among the white colonists, of whom a number entered the Catholic communion, and to missionary labors among the Patuxent, Piscataway, Potomac, and Anacostan tribesmen. With the Indians he and his associates had reasonable success as soon as he had compiled a grammar, a dictionary, and a catechism in the native tongue.

Despite his religious zeal and militant character, he got along well enough with the Calverts and arranged the scheme of manors for Jesuits as a means of financing the Catholic organization in the palatinate. In the insurrection incited by William Claiborne [q.v.] in 1644, White and two companions were shipped in irons to London by the Puritan victors (1645). Tried for treason, under a statute of 27 Elizabeth, for being a priest in England, White was sentenced merely to banishment on the plea that he was in England through no voluntary action. In vain he sought permission to return to Maryland, and thereupon went in exile to the Low Countries. Despite the imminent danger of death if the law was rigorously enforced, he returned within a few months to England, where under an assumed name he served on the missions and as a chaplain in a noble family of Hampshire. Other than this nothing is known of his career, which is shrouded in doubt, save that in London the "apostle of Maryland" finally passed on to his reward.

[For biog. sketches see *Dict. of Nat. Biog.*; *Cath. Encyc.*; Woodstock Letters, Jan. 1872; R. H. Clarke, in *Metropolitan* (Baltimore), Mar. 1856. See also C. C. Hall, *Narratives of Early Md., 1633–1684* (1910); B. C. Steiner, *Beginnings of Early Md.* (1903); J. C. Pilling, *Proof Sheets of a Bibliog. of the Languages of the N. Am. Indians* (1885); Henry Foley, *Records of the English Province of the Soc. of Jesus* (London, 7 vols., 1875–83); and Coleman Nevils, *Miniatures of Georgetown* (1934). Of White's effects, Georgetown Coll. has a pewter chalice, a missal, and a picture of St. Ignatius which he brought from England. The date of death is sometimes given wrongly as June 6.]

R. J. P.

WHITE, ANDREW DICKSON (Nov. 7, 1832–Nov. 4, 1918), university president, historian, diplomat, came of English stock. A little before 1650 his ancestor, John White, husbandman, with a partner, James Phips, bought a tract in Maine just east of the Kennebec; and after Phips's death White married his widow. Their second son, Philip, saved with the rest in 1676 from the Indians by his shipbuilding half-brother William Phips (the later Sir William), who sailed with them to Boston, was apprenticed to a "housewright" at Beverly, where soon he took to wife a daughter of Andrew Mansfield of Lynn. Their descendants pushed westward, and at Monson their great-grandson Asa White (b. 1750) throve as a builder and owner of mills. (For the whole pedigree see *New England Historical and Genealogical Register*, July 1919, p. 237.) His eldest son, Asa (b. 1774), migrated in 1798 to the rising village of Homer in central New York and prospered as its miller till in 1815 a fire was his ruin. Horace (1802–1860), the elder of his two sons, thus forced to

self-reliance, proved an able man of business, and was already well-to-do when in 1831 he married Clara Dickson (1811–1882), only child of the prosperous Andrew Dickson, the district's assemblyman, who had come from Middlefield, Mass., and of his wife, Ruth Hall, from Guilford, Conn.

Andrew Dickson White, Horace's elder son, born at Homer, was but seven when in 1839 his father moved the family to Syracuse, where he was now a banker and soon a man of wealth. The boy, an eager learner, after training in the schools of Syracuse, private and public, coveted a course at Yale. But his mother had revolted from the New England Calvinism of her village home to become an Episcopalian, and her husband, won by her to religion, was now a zealous churchman. First to a parish school the boy must go, then to the young Geneva College (now Hobart) nearby. He had been from childhood a champion of his mother's church, and always remained so; but the church college he could stand for only a year. When sent back he went into hiding till his father consented to his entering Yale. There he found himself in "the famous class of '53." He was already a wide and thoughtful reader; and, spurning marks, he was by preference a reading man. He was on the "Lit," belonged to Phi Beta Kappa, and took the Clark, Yale Literary, and De Forest prizes. Of his teachers Theodore Dwight Woolsey [q.v.] meant most to him; of his friends none more than Daniel Coit Gilman [q.v.], with whom he now set out for study abroad. A semester at Paris with teachers like Laboulaye, a year as an attaché to the American legation at St. Petersburg (1854–55), a semester at Berlin under Boeckh and Raumer, Ritter and Lepsius—Ranke he could not follow —then a ramble through Italy with Henry Simmons Frieze [q.v.] as a companion, and he was back at Yale for his A.M. There he chanced to hear Francis Wayland [q.v.] urge college men to a career in the West; and after a graduate year at Yale, he became professor of history in the University of Michigan, taking with him as his wife Mary Outwater, a Syracuse neighbor's daughter whom he married on Sept. 24, 1857.

He was only twenty-five. The fraternity boys thought him a freshman and lugged his bags to his hotel. But, says Charles Kendall Adams, then his pupil: "His instruction in history was a genuine revelation to those accustomed to perfunctory text-book work. . . . He not only instructed, . . . he inspired" (H. B. Adams, *The Study of History in American Colleges and Universities*, 1887, p. 98). To the efforts of President Henry Philip Tappan [q.v.] to make the

University of Michigan more like the universities of the European continent he gave hearty support. But in this he was no mere disciple. From his freshman days at Geneva College he had been dreaming of an American university more stately, more scholarly, more free than those he knew. Yale, with its single course, its chairs filled from a single sect, its great scholars wasted in recitation-hearing, did not satisfy him. Abroad with Gilman he had been an eager observer, and European universities had delighted him by their scientific spirit, their freedom of teaching and of study, the breadth of their instruction, the learning and charm of their lectures. He had been at Michigan scarcely a year when to his fellow New Yorker, George William Curtis [q.v.], he unfolded his dream of a state university for New York; and no sooner had the death of his father brought him private wealth than he took steps toward the fulfillment of this dream. From Syracuse, where he was settling his father's estate, he addressed (Sept. 1, 1862) to his friend and fellow liberal, Gerrit Smith [q.v.], an appeal to join him in founding "a new *University,* worthy of our land and time." To this, he wrote, his own earnest thinking and planning had been given for years. It should exclude no sex or color; should battle mercantile morality and temper military passion; should afford "an asylum for *Science*—where truth shall be sought for truth's sake," not stretched or cut "exactly to fit 'Revealed Religion' "; should foster "a new Literature—not graceful . . . but earnest" and "a Moral Philosophy, History, and Political Economy unwarped to suit present abuses in Politics and Religion"; should give "the rudiments, at least, of a Legal training in which Legality shall not crush Humanity"; and should be "a nucleus around which liberal-minded men of learning . . . could cluster" (*Cornell Alumni News,* Aug. 1931, p. 445). His plan for it shows provision not only for languages and mathematics, philosophy and history, law and medicine, but also for agriculture and engineering, and generously for the natural sciences. But Gerrit Smith, stricken in years and in health, could not help; and White himself, worn by teaching and business and by his efforts on behalf of the North in the Civil War, was forced to seek rest abroad.

Returning late in 1863, he found opportunity thrust upon him. His Syracuse townfellows, split between two rivals for a place in the state Senate, named him, though absent, as a compromise; and 1864 found him not only a senator, but chairman of the Senate's committee on education. This gave him large part in codifying

the state's school laws and in creating its new normal schools; and it made him the guardian of that vast landed endowment which by the Morrill Act of 1862 the federal government had given the states for education in "such branches of learning as are related to agriculture and the mechanic arts," but "without excluding other scientific and classical studies." New York's share, the largest, was nearly a million acres and had not been parceled out to her existing colleges. The "People's College," a new enterprise, had indeed a lien upon it all; but its friends had not yet met the conditions of the grant, and Senator Ezra Cornell [q.v.] of Ithaca, who had built up a fortune through the electric telegraph, but at heart was still a farmer, was asking half for a new agricultural college, offering to add a cash endowment. Chairman White would hear of no division and won Cornell to his own plans and to a larger gift. Together they drew the charter of a new university, whose site Cornell made Ithaca, whose name White made Cornell. Its educational clauses, all White's, ensured instruction not only in agriculture and the mechanic arts, but also in "such other branches of science and knowledge as the Trustees may deem useful and proper." "Persons of every religious denomination, or of no religious denomination," were to be "equally eligible to all offices and appointments"; and at no time should "a majority of the board be of any one religious sect, or of no religious sect." The whole land grant was asked; but Cornell in return pledged campus, farm, and a half million dollars. Nay, more; he proposed to locate the lands, as the state could not do, turning over to the university the proceeds of their eventual sale. A sharp struggle with rivals and this charter was granted—in April 1865. Most novel in the new institution were: (1) its democracy of studies, the natural sciences and technical arts not segregated, as elsewhere, but taught with the humanities under one faculty and in common classrooms; (2) its parallel courses, open to free choice and leading to varying but equal degrees; (3) its equal rank for the modern languages and literatures and for history and the political sciences; (4) its large use of eminent scholars as "non-resident professors"; (5) its treatment of university students as men, not boys, their teachers as their friends and companions.

White now thought his task done. His ambitions were a scholar's and writer's. The Michigan chair was still his, and Yale was urging on him the headship of her new school of fine arts. Political office, if he wished it, was within his grasp. But Ezra Cornell would not go on with the university without White as president. White hesitated; but he accepted and set about gathering teachers and equipment. For his non-resident group he won Agassiz and Lowell, George William Curtis, Theodore Dwight, James Hall, Bayard Taylor [*qq.v.*]. Goldwin Smith, whom he had hoped to tempt from England as a non-resident, came, to his joy, as a resident instead; but in the main his resident faculty was of young men.

Despite its heresies the young institution won friends and gifts; and when at its opening, in 1868, six hundred students enrolled, success seemed assured. To the faculty White turned over the care of discipline and of matters curricular. The routine of administration he also gladly devolved on others. His to plan and to create; his to be spokesman to the outer world. His too to teach; and teaching was still his joy. For himself he had reserved the chair of history, though he dealt only with that of Europe. His lectures were always written, and with care; and never was he so busy that some new lecture was not under way. But to his written words he was never a slave. He broke away from them for an anecdote, a personal experience, a direct appeal. He would leave his desk, come to the edge of his platform, and "just talk." But, whether he talked or read, his students were to him live men and women—men and women about to go out to play a part, perhaps a leading part, in the live world of which he spoke. That they might follow his thought, and without waste of attention, he put always into their hands a printed outline; but he had it interleaved for their own notes. It was for them he built up his great library; and not alone with books for research—though fresh research went, if possible, with every lecture—but with books that had themselves made history, first editions, copies that great men themselves had thumbed, the documents, placards, caricatures, left over from the times themselves. These to make his lectures live he showed his students; or, better still, welcomed them to his house for their closer study. His house was a museum of such treasures—the house which from his own purse he built to be Cornell's presidential mansion. But not his classes alone heard White. Whatever one studied at Cornell, one found time for the President's lectures; and, since at Cornell there was no bar to auditors, half his audience was always of faculty and townsfolk.

His pen, always prolific, was busy now in championing his educational theories and in defending the university and its founder against attacks. Fiercest of the critics were those who called the new school "godless" because in the care of no religious group. White showed in answer how almost every step in the advance of education and science had had to meet such charges from the pious, but how religion as well as science had been the gainer by freedom of teaching and research. This reply, at first but a lecture, grew to a magazine article, then in 1876 to a booklet, *The Warfare of Science*; and in the same year his *Paper-Money Inflation in France,* born of his lectures on the French Revolution, took book form for use against the currency juggling then urged on Congress.

Meanwhile, to the University fortune had been harsh. Its working capital had proved inadequate, and its western lands, now subject to state tax, had made it "land-poor." Ezra Cornell, whose purse for a time met every deficit, was all but ruined by the panic of 1873; and White, whose salary and much more had from the first gone to the University or its students, had now to dip more deeply into his own purse and his fellow trustees' to meet debts and finish buildings. The University escaped ruin, but in 1874 Cornell died and White's financial cares grew ever heavier. There had to be respites: in 1871 President Grant made him one of the commission to visit Santo Domingo and report on its fitness for annexation (*Dominican Republic. Report of the Commission of Inquiry to Santo Domingo, 1871*), and in 1872 a trip to the coeducational institutions of the West was needed as a text for his report favoring the admission of women to Cornell. But by 1876 his health was breaking; and the next two years he spent abroad, his pen soon busy on fresh chapters for his *Warfare of Science* and on a series he called "the warfare of humanity," that is, the war against such inhumanities as slavery, torture, witch-persecution. With this new course he came back in 1878 and tried to resume his duties. But his health was still precarious, and in the spring he welcomed the call of President Hayes to the post of minister to Germany. At Berlin his routine duties were heavy, though not uncongenial, and for diplomacy he was fitted, not only by training, but also by his social tastes, his affability, his liking for affairs. But it was as a scholar that best he bore the mantle of Bancroft and of Bayard Taylor. With German men of letters and science his ties grew close, and for Americans studying abroad he could do much. In 1881, when he returned, the University's fortunes seemed of better hope through the great bequest of Mrs. Fiske, but soon the Fiske will suit cast its gloom over all, and White's last years as president were crippled still by Cornell's poverty, though near their close the first great sale of western lands gladdened the outlook. White found time to be a leader in the fight for civil-service reform, and in 1884 helped found the American Historical Association, becoming its first president. Alas, his health grew frailer, he had served Cornell for twenty years, and other tasks were clamoring to be done. In 1885, happy that his old Michigan pupil Charles Kendall Adams [q.v.] was made his successor, he sailed abroad to rest and write.

First came months of recuperation, with Mrs. White, in England and beyond the Channel. They were hardly back, in 1887, when her sudden death left him prostrate. From the blow he rallied but slowly, seeking comfort in penning a memorial. With returning vigor he sought solace in travel, making now a visit to Egypt and to Greece; but first he transferred to Cornell's shelves his rich historical library, while in his honor her departments of history and politics became The President White School of History and Political Science. When he returned late in 1889, his health proved so restored that he not only could resume research, but again become a lecturer; and during the next years he gave courses at many university centers, from Philadelphia to New Orleans. Stanford University, whose first president he could have been, made him a non-resident member of her faculty; and he journeyed thither as the guest of his friend Carnegie, with whom in his private car he visited Mexico and zig-zagged through all the region beyond the Rockies. It was now too that he found (Sept. 10, 1890) a second wife in Helen Magill, a daughter of President Magill of Swarthmore, herself a scholar and teacher.

Late in 1892 President Harrison called him again to the nation's service as minister to Russia. His success there must have satisfied the Washington authorities, for despite the change in 1893 of president and party he was kept there till, in 1894, he insisted on resigning (relieved Nov. 1). But what he could achieve by no means satisfied him. The imperial court, as of old, he found corrupt and fickle, and his best efforts were thwarted by the minor rank of the American legation and its relatively scanty means. Distraction he found in acquaintanceships at court and in society, interested notably by Tolstoi and by the reactionary Pobedonostzeff. Then, too, he found time to work on, and on his return to Ithaca to complete, his *History of the Warfare of Science with Theology in Christendom* (2 vols., 1896). But before this was out of press President Cleveland had named him to the commission charged to find "the true divisional line between Venezuela and British Guiana," then in controversy with Great Britain. His con-

genial associates included his old friend Gilman, and the year was spent pleasantly in research at Washington; but ere its end Great Britain had consented to a judicial arbitration, and the commission published only the reports of its experts. White was still in Washington when the new president, McKinley, made him ambassador to Germany. Since his former service there he had shown himself a friendly interpreter of the "new Germany" and of German thought, and his appointment was welcome to German-Americans and in Berlin. But commercial rivalries had chilled German friendship and the Samoan squabble was at its height. Then came the Spanish-American War and the questions as to the fate of the Spanish colonies. In Foreign Minister Bülow, White had found a temper like his own, and their affable good sense dispelled the clouds. To him, however, the great event of these years was the Hague Conference (1899). He had long urged the folly of war, but did not at first take very seriously the Czar's call "to put an end to the constantly increasing development of armaments." Called to head the American delegation, he awoke to the opportunity. So, too, had President McKinley and Secretary Hay awakened, and their delegates were charged to work not only for the exemption from seizure, during war at sea, of all private property not contraband of war—America's old claim—but also for an international court of arbitration. For the former claim they could gain no hearing; but White submitted for record a memorial and upheld it in a careful speech (F. W. Holls, *The Peace Conference of the Hague*, 1900, pp. 307–20). For the court of arbitration the day was won, and for the international commissions of inquiry urged by White. But not without a struggle. Alfred T. Mahan [q.v.], the naval member of the American delegation, whose able books on the history of sea-power gave his opinions weight, was averse to aught that threatened the efficiency of war; and the German Emperor, who had studied his books, proved so hostile that for long the conference threatened to shatter on the opposition of Germany and her allies. To allay this White did his utmost, and with at least a measure of success. Due wholly to him was the most dramatic event of the conference: the celebration by the Americans of their July 4th by laying a laurel wreath on the tomb of Grotius, the father of international law, with an address in his honor by White.

He returned to Berlin with prestige heightened, and the next years brought him many honors. But death dealt him heavy blows. In July 1901, there died at Syracuse his only son, long a sufferer. September saw the assassination of President McKinley, grown a warm personal friend. But Theodore Roosevelt, who followed, was to White no stranger. Together at the Chicago convention of 1884, as delegates at large from New York, they had fought for the naming of George F. Edmunds, but together had stood by Blaine, the Republican presidential candidate; and their friendship had not lapsed. But the old diplomat had long resolved to leave at seventy the public service; and in November 1902 his resignation took effect.

Even at Berlin he had found time for much else than diplomacy. Andrew Carnegie had invited from him suggestions for the use of his great wealth; and the invitation was not neglected. In 1900 White urged on him the building of a Palace of Justice to house the International Tribunal at The Hague. The idea had come from his colleague of the conference, the great Russian jurist De Martens; but White made it his own, and it was he who eventually won from the generous Scot both the Palace of Peace and its great library of international law. In 1901 he tried to interest him in the project for a national university at Washington, and with such success that in May he could disclose the plan to his friend Gilman and in September spend a week with Carnegie at Skibo. What came of it was the Carnegie Institution of Washington, started early in 1902 with Gilman as president and White as a trustee. He was also an adviser and became a trustee of Carnegie's foundation for international peace.

Nor had his pen been idle at Berlin. His autobiography, long under way, and a biographical volume based on his university lectures were well advanced when he retired; and now, set free from cares official, he took quarters with his family at Alassio on the lovely Riviera, west of Genoa, where by May of 1904 the first task reached completion. Returning then to Ithaca he could send to press the *Autobiography of Andrew Dickson White* (2 vols., 1905) and rest a while among his friends. The lectures, finished at more leisure, appeared in 1910 as *Seven Great Statesmen in the Warfare of Humanity with Unreason.* The seven—Sarpi, Grotius, Thomasius, Turgot, Stein, Cavour, Bismarck—were the heroes about whose deeds, by the biographical method he loved best, he had woven much of his course on the history of modern states; but into their story he had worked also a part of his older lectures on the "warfare of humanity." A later task was unforeseen. In Canada came danger of currency inflation and a public-spirited Toronto business man asked leave to print and circulate his *Fiat*

Money in France (1896), a revision of his earlier work. Once more—in 1912, at eighty—he revised it, but "for private circulation only." Not till 1933 was this edition published in the United States.

At last he welcomed quiet, his routine broken mainly by his winter trip to Washington, for his duties as regent of the Smithsonian Institution and trustee of the Carnegie Institution. In 1914 the great war seemed the defeat of all his efforts for peace; but it could not rob him of his hopefulness or of his fairness, and happily he lived to see it all but ended. In late October of 1918 he gave a dinner to Lord Charnwood, then lecturing at Cornell. His mind was clear, and he as chatty as ever; but he seemed weary and he did not come downstairs again. On Nov. 4 he died. There survived him his second wife and two daughters (one by each marriage), with a daughter of the elder of these and the two sons of his oldest daughter.

In person White was of barely middle stature, slender, brown-haired, bearded; in dress fastidious; in bearing kindly, though not without reserve; in temper active, buoyant, generous. Never robust, he gained great powers of work from a careful regimen; but he was subject to periods of sick headache, and for years his life was threatened by a throat ailment due to exposure in his drives to Ithaca during Cornell's early days. Walking was his exercise and books his only sport; travel and music were his recreation and his medicine. All the fine arts he loved; but architecture gave him greatest joy the world over. The school for it at Cornell was his creation and his pet. An inveterate reader, above all of biography, he was also a charming raconteur and never failed to note down a good story. He was deeply reverent and with a profound faith in God, but never other-worldly. His ambition it was to serve his age and to deserve remembrance. His students he used to urge to give themselves to some great cause, and many were the great causes to which he was himself devoted. Foremost in his youth was doubtless antislavery; in his prime the freeing of inquiry and of teaching; in his old age the abandonment of war and a sterner dealing with high crime. But he was even more a man of action than of speech, and he hoped to be judged, above all, by his work as university founder and moulder.

[For his life the ample source is his *Autobiography* (1905), into which are absorbed all his earlier autobiographic articles. Appended to it is a list of his writings. His correspondence, with diaries and MSS., is still in the keeping of the Cornell Univ. library; but letters and papers subsequent to his retirement, in 1885, from the presidency of Cornell are to be deposited in the Lib. of Congress. Of value for his life are the tributes in the *Cornell Era* for Nov. 1912 at his eightieth birthday, and those at the unveiling of his statue on the Cornell campus, printed in the *Cornell Alumni News*, June 24, 1915. Best informed of the histories of Cornell are E. W. Huffcut, *Cornell University, 1868–1898* (in the U. S. Bureau of Education's "Circulars of Information" for 1900) and the cooperative work bearing the name of W. T. Hewett, *Cornell University: a History* (1905). On these and on the writer's own memories as pupil, librarian, secretary, friend, this sketch is based.]   G. L. B.

WHITE, CANVASS (Sept. 8, 1790–Dec. 18, 1834), was a notable member of the group of pioneer American engineers who received their training on the Erie Canal. His grandfather, Hugh White, a descendant of John White, who came to Boston in 1632, left his home at Middletown, Conn., in 1784 with his wife, five sons, and four daughters, and joined the westward migration which followed the Revolution. He settled in Whitestown, Oneida County, N. Y., and in this township, at Whitesboro, Canvass, second son of Hugh White, Jr., and Tryphena (Lawrence) White, was born. Of slight build and always frail, Canvass White throughout his life constantly struggled against ill health, yet when he died, at the early age of forty-four, he held a place in the first rank of American civil engineers of his day. He was characterized by John B. Jervis [*q.v.*] as having possessed "the most strict engineering mind of any of his time" and having "delighted in plodding over plans and methods of construction" (*post*, p. 42). He attended Fairfield Academy until he was seventeen, then worked in a local store until 1811, when, for the sake of his health, he shipped as supercargo on a merchant vessel bound for Russia. After this adventure he returned to work in the store until 1814, when he enlisted for service in the War of 1812 and was wounded at the capture of Fort Erie.

White became associated with the Erie Canal in 1816 and assisted Benjamin Wright [*q.v.*] in the early surveys. Late in 1817, with the approval of Governor Clinton, he made an extended trip through Great Britain for the purpose of examining canal constructions and bringing back surveying instruments. The acquaintance with British canal practice gained through this trip made him particularly valuable as Wright's principal assistant in the building of the first great American canal, and he became in time its chief expert in designing the locks and their equipment. Up to this time, the only hydraulic cement available in America had been imported at great cost from England. White, while abroad, had investigated cements and upon his return made experiments with limestone found in New York state, demonstrating that a rock found near the

line of the canal in Madison County could be converted into a cement equal to the imported product. He obtained a patent for waterproof cement on Feb. 1, 1820.

He stayed with the Erie Canal for some nine years, holding responsible positions on the Eastern work, including supervision of the important Glens Falls feeder. In 1825 he succeeded Loammi Baldwin, 1780–1838 [*q.v.*], as chief engineer of the Union Canal of Pennsylvania, but was forced by ill health to relinquish the position after about a year. At this time he also made a report on the water supply of New York City. He subsequently became consulting engineer for the Schuylkill Navigation Company, for the locks at Windsor on the Connecticut River, and for the Farmington Canal, and was chief engineer of both the Delaware & Raritan Canal in New Jersey and the Lehigh Canal in Pennsylvania. As the Delaware & Raritan construction was nearing completion, White suffered one of his many breakdowns in health and was advised to go South to recover. He died in St. Augustine, Fla., late in 1834. In 1821 he had married Louisa Loomis, daughter of Charles and Elizabeth (Gay) Loomis, of a Connecticut family. A son and two daughters were born to them.

[Printed accounts appear in C. B. Stuart, *Lives and Works of Civil and Military Engineers* (1871); N. E. Whitford, *Hist. of the Canal System of the State of N. Y.* (1906); J. B. Jervis, "A Memoir of Am. Engineering," *Trans. Am. Soc. Civil Engineers*, vol. VI (1877); John Lawrence, *The Geneal. of the Family of John Lawrence* (1869); Elisha Loomis, *Descendants of Joseph Loomis* (1908); H. J. Cookinham, *Hist. of Oneida County, N. Y.* (1912), vol. II; *Newark Daily Advertiser*, Jan. 10, 1835; *Poulson's Am. Daily Advertiser*, Jan. 8, 1835. The newspapers mentioned give day of death as Dec. 12, but the other sources give Dec. 18.]
                    J. K. F.

WHITE, CHARLES ABIATHAR (Jan. 26, 1826–June 29, 1910), geologist, paleontologist, naturalist, physician, the second son of Abiathar and Nancy (Corey) White, was born in North Dighton, Bristol County, Mass., on a farm which had then been the home of the White family for more than a century. His grandfather and his great-grandfather, both named Cornelius White, were active in the American Revolution; his earliest American ancestor, William, had emigrated from England to Boston about 1640. In 1838 the family left Massachusetts and established a new home on the frontier, near Burlington, in the recently organized Territory of Iowa. Physical conditions were harsh, and opportunities for formal education were almost completely lacking, but the rocks and hills, the forests and streams offered a virgin field for observations in botany, zoölogy, geology, and paleontology. His love for nature in all its aspects thus stimulated,

White became a naturalist of the old school. He made large collections of fossils, including the beautiful crinoids which have made Burlington famous among paleontologists and which furnished the subject of his first scientific paper, "Observations upon the Geology and Paleontology of Burlington, Iowa" (*Boston Journal of Natural History,* Sept. 1860). These collections of fossils served to introduce him to James Hall, Fielding Bradford Meek, Amos Henry Worthen [*qq.v.*], and other geologists of the time, and thus strengthened his desire to become a geologist. In those days, however, it was difficult to earn a livelihood in strictly scientific pursuits, and like many another man of similar tastes he turned to medicine as a profession. In accordance with a common practice of the times, especially on the frontier, he began his studies in the office of a physician; later he studied medicine at the University of Michigan (1863) and at Rush Medical College, from which he was graduated in 1864.

White's work as a physician, begun in Iowa City immediately after graduation, lasted only two years. His self-acquired attainments as a geologist and naturalist were locally so well recognized that when a geological survey was organized in 1866 he was appointed state geologist, and a year later, while still serving in that office (which he held until 1870), he was made professor of geology at Iowa State University. He remained there as professor of natural science until called to the Josiah Little professorship of natural history at Bowdoin College, Brunswick, Me., in 1874. At this time the government surveys of the geology of the western Territories offered opportunities for research in paleontology and stratigraphy and for general exploration that were very attractive to a man of White's training and temperament. He gave up his position at Bowdoin and was employed successively (1875–79) by George Montague Wheeler's survey west of the 100th meridian, by John Wesley Powell's survey of the Rocky Mountain region, and by Ferdinand Vandiveer Hayden's geological survey of the Territories. Through each of these organizations he made important contributions by published reports and descriptive paleontologic studies. When in 1879 the independent government surveys were merged in the newly organized United States Geological Survey, White became curator of invertebrate fossils in the National Museum in Washington, D. C., where until 1882 he rendered invaluable service at a critical time in the organization of the paleontologic collections. As honorary curator of Mesozoic invertebrates, he continued his work in the Museum while he served as a geologist in the Geological Survey (1882–92); in 1892 his resignation from the Survey ended his more active professional duties, though he continued his connection with the National Museum as associate in paleontology.

On Sept. 28, 1848, long prior to the beginning of his professional career, White had married Charlotte R. Pilkington of Dighton, Mass., who shared his life almost fifty-four years. Of their family of eight children, four sons and two daughters survived him. He died in Washington, D. C. He was a member of the National Academy of Science, a founder of the Geological Society of America, vice-president for the section of geology of the American Association for the Advancement of Science (1889), president of the Biological Society of Washington (1883–84), foreign member of the Geological Society of London, and corresponding member of several other European scientific societies. He held several honorary degrees. While White's interests were so broad and varied that he must be classified primarily as a naturalist, his principal scientific contributions were in the field of invertebrate paleontology and stratigraphy, particularly of the Mesozoic. His writings are characterized by a clean simple style which never permits any doubt of his meaning or of his honesty of purpose.

[Sources include autobiog. sketch in MS.; *Who's Who in America*, 1910–11; J. B. Marcou, "Bibliogs. of Am. Naturalists," *Bull. U. S. Museum, no. 30* (1885); T. W. Stanton, in *U. S. Nat. Museum, Report . . . 1910* (1911), p. 71, and bibliog. in *Proc. U. S. Nat. Museum,* vol. XX (1898), supplementing Marcou; W. H. Dall, in *Nat. Acad. of Sci. Biog. Memoirs,* vol. VII (1911); Charles Keyes, in *Annals of Iowa,* Oct. 1914; *Science,* July 29, 1910, pp. 146–49; G. P. Merrill, *The First One Hundred Years of Am. Geol.* (1924); *Biog. Review of Des Moines County, Iowa* (1905); obituary in *Evening Star* (Washington, D. C.), June 29, 1910.] T. W. S.

WHITE, CHARLES IGNATIUS (Feb. 1, 1807–Apr. 1, 1878), Roman Catholic priest and editor, son of John and Nancy (Coombs) White, who were of old Maryland families, was born in Baltimore and educated in the local schools and at Mount St. Mary's College, Emmitsburg. As a seminarian, he studied theology at St. Sulpice in Paris and spent a year in the Sulpician novitiate at Issy prior to his ordination to the secular priesthood in Notre Dame Cathedral by Archbishop Hyacinthe de Quelen (June 5, 1830). On his return to Maryland, Father White served as a curate at Fell's Point (1830–33), as an assistant and as rector of the cathedral in Baltimore (1833–43), as professor of moral theology at St. Mary's Seminary (1843–45), from which he later received the degree of S.T.D. (1848), as pastor of St. Vincent de Paul's Church (1845), as pastor at Pikesville, where he erected a church (1849), and finally as rector of St. Matthew's Church in Washington, D. C. (1857–78), where he became widely known in ecclesiastical and secular circles as a scholarly preacher and as an influential priest. Although a preacher on such important occasions as episcopal consecrations, a second choice for the see of Charleston in 1843, a secretary of the Third Provincial Council of Baltimore (1837) and a theologian at the Fourth Council (1840), and the only priest who had known intimately the nine archbishops of Baltimore, he was never elevated beyond the priesthood. His most severe critic, James Alphonsus McMaster [q.v.] of the *Freeman's Journal,* admitted that he was exemplary in character, pious, severe in temperament, and aristocratic in bearing, but feared that he had not been preserved from the Gallican tendencies of Paris.

While in Washington, White erected a parochial school, St. Matthew's Institute, and St. Stephen's Church; established St. Ann's Infant Asylum, a chapel for colored persons, and a home for aged negroes; introduced the Society of St. Vincent de Paul for social work among the poor; and compiled *St. Vincent's Manual* (2nd ed., 1848). As a musician and artist, he was intelligently interested in hymnology and architecture. Yet his greatest contribution was as an editor and as "one of the outstanding literary figures in the American priesthood" (Peter Guilday, *The Life and Times of John England,* 1927, II, 551). With the Rev. James Dolan, an early social worker in Baltimore, he founded and edited the *Religious Cabinet* (1842), which was continued as the *United States Catholic Magazine* (1843–48). Later he founded and edited the *Metropolitan Magazine* (1853). These magazines compared favorably with contemporary secular publications. Indeed, it was their erudite character that proved their undoing because of a lack of patronage among an uneducated constituency. In 1849 White assisted in founding the archdiocesan weekly paper, the *Catholic Mirror,* which he edited until 1855. In addition, he compiled under varying titles the annual Catholic directory (1834–57), issued a revised edition of J. L. Balmes' *Protestantism and Catholicity Compared in Their Effects on the Civilization of Europe* (1850) and a *Life of Mrs. Eliza A. Seton* (1853) which passed through several editions, published a revised edition of Chateaubriand's *The Genius of Christianity* (1856), translated from the French of Charles Sainte-Foi, *Mission and Duties of Young Women* (1858), and added a chapter on the

Church in the United States to the English translation of Joseph E. Darras' *General History of the Catholic Church* (1866).

[M. J. Riordon, *Cathedral Records* (1906); *Cath. Encyc.;* F. E. Tourscher, *The Kenrick-Frenaye Correspondence* (1920); *N. Y. Freeman's Journal,* Apr. 13, 1878; *Cath. Mirror,* Apr. 6, 1878; *Sadlier's Cath. Directory* (1879), p. 41; address of Archbishop James Gibbons [q.v.] in *In Memoriam; a Record of the Ceremonies in St. Matthew's Church . . . on the Occasion of the Funeral of Its Late Pastor Rev. Charles I. White* (1878); obituary in *Evening Star* (Washington, D. C.), Apr. 1, 1878.]   R. J. P.

WHITE, EDWARD DOUGLASS (March 1795–Apr. 18, 1847), political leader, the son of James and Mary (Willcox) White, was born in Maury County, middle Tennessee. His father was a native of Pennsylvania; his grandfather, of Ireland. In 1799 the family removed to Louisiana, settling in St. Martin Parish. After the transfer of Louisiana to the United States and the organization of the new territorial government, James White was appointed a district judge. His son attended common schools and in 1815 was graduated from the University of Nashville. Returning to Louisiana, he studied law in the office of Alexander Porter [q.v.] and began the practice of law at Donaldsonville. In 1825 he went to New Orleans to accept appointment as associate judge of the city court, but resigned that post in 1828 and removed to Lafourche Parish, where he owned a sugar plantation. He entered the federal House of Representatives in 1829, serving in the Twenty-first, Twenty-second, and Twenty-third congresses. He was opposed to Jackson in politics and is said to have become a personal friend of Henry Clay. In November 1834 he resigned his seat in Congress to seek election as governor of Louisiana; he was successful and served four years, 1835–39. Critical of Congress for seeming to neglect the welfare of his state, especially in matters of tariff protection for sugar planters and certain land claims, he advocated state legislative measures to provoke the attention of Congress. He approved the charter (1835) of the Medical College of Louisiana, the nucleus from which grew the Tulane University of Louisiana. Several bank failures occurred in New Orleans during his administration, and he effectively vetoed a bill to charter the Farmers' Bank in the panic year of 1837. He warned against the activities of the abolitionists.

Before the expiration of his term as governor, he was again elected to Congress, holding the seat for two terms, 1839–43. Giving special attention to local interests, he worked to secure construction funds for the New Orleans mint, the refunding to Louisiana of "moneys paid by her for her militia serving in the Florida war several years ago," relief of private land claimants, and the establishment of new ports of entry and the adoption of regulations to facilitate commerce between the Southwest and Mexico. Upon retiring from Congress, he resumed the career of lawyer-planter, spending the last years of his life at Thibodaux, La. He was a man of good humor, kindly disposition, and unusual common sense, with eccentricities which were the source of numerous anecdotes. He married Catherine S. Ringgold of Washington, D. C., and they had five children, the youngest being Edward Douglass White [*q.v.*], who became chief justice of the United States Supreme Court. The father died in New Orleans about two years after the birth of this son, and was buried in St. Joseph's Catholic Cemetery at Thibodaux, La.

[Alcée Fortier, *Louisiana* (1909), II, 639–42; Charles Gayarré, *Hist. of La.* (1885), IV, 656–58; *Meynier's La. Biogs.* (1882), pt. 1, pp. 20–22; W. H. Sparks, *The Memories of Fifty Years* (1870), pp. 459–61; *Biog. Dir. Am. Cong.* (1928); *Weekly Delta* (New Orleans), Apr. 26, 1847; *Daily Picayune* (New Orleans), Apr. 20, 1847.]   H. C. N.

WHITE, EDWARD DOUGLASS (Nov. 3, 1845–May 19, 1921), chief justice of the United States, was born in Parish Lafourche, La., the son of Edward Douglass White [*q.v.*] and Catherine S. (Ringgold). His paternal great-grandfather emigrated from Ireland to Pennsylvania, where his grandfather, James White, was born. His father was born in Tennessee, but was taken at an early age to Louisiana and there attained considerable prominence in public life. The younger Edward Douglass White received his education at Mount St. Mary's College, Emmitsburg, Md., the Jesuit College in New Orleans, and Georgetown College in the District of Columbia. At the age of sixteen he left college and enlisted as a private in the Confederate army. On the fall of Port Hudson in 1863 he was taken prisoner and shortly thereafter was paroled.

After the war he read law in the office of Edward Bermudez [*q.v.*], was admitted to the Louisiana bar in 1868, and almost immediately went into politics. He was elected to the Louisiana Senate in 1874 and later was appointed to the state supreme court, on which he served from January 1879 to April 1880. His judicial career in the state was cut short because, under a new constitution, the court was reconstituted and his term ended. (For his opinions, see 31, 32 *Louisiana Reports*.) He was early identified with the anti-lottery movement, largely as the result of which he was elected to the United States Senate, where he took his seat on Mar. 4, 1891. Him-

self a successful sugar planter, he fought vigorously for a protective tariff on sugar in the Wilson Bill, continuing his activities in this regard even after he had agreed to accept appointment to the Supreme Court bench.

Before the completion of his term in the Senate, White became the sudden and wholly unexpected beneficiary of the political bad blood that existed between President Cleveland and the Democratic senator from New York, David B. Hill. In 1893 Justice Samuel Blatchford [*q.v.*] of the United States Supreme Court died. He was a resident of New York and it was assumed that his successor would be chosen from that state, more especially since Cleveland himself came from New York. Without consulting Hill, Cleveland nominated first William B. Hornblower and later Wheeler H. Peckham to fill the vacancy on the bench. Under the rule of so-called senatorial courtesy Hill succeeded in defeating both of these nominations, whereupon Cleveland sent in the name of White. Since White was himself a member of the Senate, Hill could not object and the nomination was promptly confirmed. White took the oath of office on Mar. 12, 1894, and remained upon the bench twenty-seven years, being raised to the chief justiceship by President Taft in 1910. In selecting the chief justice from among the associate justices Taft broke with tradition. Furthermore, a more natural choice would have been Charles E. Hughes, who was Taft's own appointee. Taft was probably influenced by his desire to break the "Solid South" politically. This was the second instance of a Southern Democratic Catholic being appointed to preside over the highest court of the land, Roger B. Taney having been chief justice from 1836 to 1864. During his service on the bench White wrote opinions in more than 700 cases.

In 1895 the Supreme Court rendered three decisions that gave rise to widespread criticism and to attacks upon the power of the courts. One of these, in the case of the E. C. Knight Company (156 *United States*, 1), appeared to draw the teeth of the Sherman Anti-Trust Act. Another, in *Pollock* vs. *Farmers' Loan and Trust Company* (158 *United States*, 601), held the federal income tax of 1894 void in part. The third, in the case of Eugene Debs (158 *United States*, 564), growing out of the Pullman strike in Chicago in 1894, upheld the power of the federal government to issue injunctions in labor disputes. White concurred in the first and third of these decisions but dissented in the income-tax case. Agitation for a curb upon judicial review went steadily on, reaching its peak perhaps in the Progressive campaign of 1912 shortly after White became chief justice.

It is difficult to characterize his decisions as a whole. His mind was a middle-of-the-road mind. He was sometimes found with the so-called liberals, as, for example, in 1905 when he dissented in the case of *Lochner* vs. *New York* (198 *United States*, 45), which was made so much of in the campaign of 1912, and when he wrote the majority opinion in *Wilson* vs. *New* (243 *United States*, 332), upholding the famous Adamson Act of 1916 by which a scale of minimum wages for railway employees was fixed. He likewise wrote the opinion of the Court in *Guinn and Beal* vs. *United States* (238 *United States*, 347) in which the grandfather clause of Oklahoma was held void; in the case which upheld the selective draft act (245 *United States*, 366); and in the case which threatened the use of federal power to compel the state of West Virginia to pay her agreed portion of the debt of Virginia (246 *United States*, 565). On the other hand, while he dissented in the Lochner case, which held void the New York law limiting bakery hours to ten a day, he also dissented in *Bunting* vs. *Oregon* (243 *United States*, 426), which upheld an Oregon ten-hour law. Again, while he concurred in the New York Central case (243 *United States*, 188), upholding the New York workmen's compensation act, he dissented in the Mountain Timber Company case (243 *United States*, 219), which upheld the Washington compensation law. He dissented in the Northern Securities case in 1904 (193 *United States*, 197), the first important decision upholding and applying the Sherman Anti-Trust Act. He concurred in the Adair and Coppage cases (208 *United States*, 161; 236 *United States*, 1), both famous in the history of labor, and in the Danbury hatters' case (235 *United States*, 522), holding that the Sherman Act applied to labor unions in their attempt to force unionization by boycott. He dissented in the rent cases, upholding the power both of the states and the national government to prevent profiteering in rents in time of emergency (*Block* vs. *Hirsch*, 256 *United States*, 135; *Brown Holding Co.* vs. *Feldman*, 256 *United States*, 170).

Wilson vs. *New* was probably the most important decision he ever wrote, even though the reasoning he employed left much to be desired, but he is doubtless best known for the "rule of reason" laid down in the Standard Oil and the American Tobacco cases (221 *United States*, 1, 106), interpreting and applying the anti-trust act. He had first announced this rule in 1897 in a dissenting opinion rendered in *United States*

vs. *Trans-Missouri Freight Association* (166 *United States*, 290). It must be said, however, that by applying this rule he wrote into the law something which Congress had not put there and that he did this by a sophistical course of reasoning in which he employed the word "reasonable" first in the sense of moderate or limited, and secondly in the sense of something reached by the process of reasoning. In this way he sought to show that the Court was not overruling itself.

Perhaps without realizing it, he rather accurately described and interpreted his own judicial philosophy in a brief address delivered in 1916 in response to resolutions of the bar upon the death of his colleague, Joseph R. Lamar (*New Republic*, June 1, 1921, pp. 6–8). He said of his late brother on the bench that in the matter of "the relation of the activities of individuals and their results to each other" he keenly appreciated the "duty to adjust between conflicting activities so as to preserve the rights of all by protecting the rights of each." Intensely local as were his affections and his ties, he had a broad conception of his "duty to uphold and sustain the authority of the Union as to the subjects coming within the legitimate scope of its power as conferred by the Constitution." There was a "fixed opinion on his part as to the duty to uphold and perpetuate the great guarantees of individual freedom as declared by the Constitution, to the end that the freedom of all might not pass away forever." In his work on the bench "no thought of expediency, no mere conviction about economic problems, no belief that the guarantees were becoming obsolete or that their enforcement would incur popular odium ever swayed his unalterable conviction and irrevocable purpose to uphold and protect the great guarantees with every faculty which he possessed." At the time of his death in 1921 some one remarked that White's opinions were "models of what judicial opinions ought not to be" (*Nation*, June 1, 1921, p. 781). This is very nearly true. There was no crystal clarity in his reasoning processes and his sentences were long, labored, and involved.

White was an untiring worker, gracious, courteous, modest, genial, with many lovable qualities and a steadfast devotion to the public service. He was full of both dignity and humility. He was especially kind to young and inexperienced practitioners who appeared before the Court. He was extraordinarily popular. A man of enormous bulk, he was nevertheless an inveterate pedestrian and was a well-known figure in Washington because of his striking appearance and the curious little informal hat that he always wore.

He had a remarkable memory. He apparently knew his opinions by heart, including volume and page citations, and seldom referred to the printed page. He was an able presiding officer, speeded up the work of the Court with great energy, and by his engaging manner did much to compromise differences of opinion among his colleagues on the bench. He was married in 1894 to Leita Montgomery Kent.

[Opinions in 152-256, U. S. Supreme Court Reports; New Republic, June 1, 1921, pp. 6–8; Nation, May 3, 1917, pp. 528–29, June 1, 1921, p. 781; Am. Rev. of Reviews, Aug. 1921, pp. 161–70; J. W. Davis, "Edward Douglass White," in Am. Bar Asso. Jour., Aug. 1921; H. L. Carson, in Report of . . . Am. Bar Asso. . . . 1921 (1921), pp. 25–30; Proc. of the Bar and Officers of the Supreme Court of the U. S. in Memory of Edward Douglass White (1921); Loyola Law Jour., "Edward Douglass White Memorial Edition," April 1926; Am. Law Review, July–Aug. 1926, pp. 620–37; Who's Who in America, 1920–21; N. Y. Times, May 19, 20, 1921.]

H. L. M.

WHITE, ELLEN GOULD HARMON (Nov. 26, 1827–July 16, 1915), leader of the Seventh-day Adventist Church, was born at Gorham, Me., the daughter of Robert and Eunice (Gould) Harmon, and a descendant of John Harmon who was in Kittery, Me., in 1667. When she was still a child the family moved to Portland. She was not more than nine years old when a girl playmate in a fit of anger struck her with a stone, knocking her unconscious, a state in which she remained for three weeks. Her face was disfigured and her "nervous system prostrated." Her health was so poor that she had to give up school, and with the exception of a short period of tutoring at home she received no further formal education.

During the stirring evangelistic campaign of William Miller [q.v.] in the forties, she embraced the Advent faith as taught by Miller and looked for the personal return of Christ on Oct. 22, 1844. When this expectation proved baseless, she was deeply disappointed; her health failed rapidly and she seemed sinking into death. In December, however, while she was kneeling in prayer with four other women, a vision came to her in which she seemed to be transported to heaven and shown the experiences that awaited the faithful. Subsequently, she had other visions, accompanied by strange physical phenomena. According to the reports of physicians and others, her eyes remained open during these visions, she ceased to breathe, and she performed miraculous feats. Messages for individuals, churches, and families were imparted to her, occasionally of what would take place in the future, but more often of reproof or encouragement. During a long life span, she exerted the most powerful single influence on Seventh-day Adventist believers. The larger portion of them accepted her visions without question and acted in accordance with her messages.

On Aug. 30, 1846, she married the Rev. James White, born in Palmyra, Me., Aug. 4, 1821, the son of John White. He was ordained a minister of the Christian Connection in 1843, and adhered to the Advent faith. The young couple were penniless, and neither was in good health. After various activities, in 1849 White began to publish a little paper, which soon became the *Advent Review and Sabbath Herald,* the organ of the denomination. It was first issued in various places in New England, then in Rochester, N. Y., and later in Battle Creek, Mich. For years White was in charge of the publishing work of the Adventists. He labored hard for the union of the churches and in 1863 the General Conference was organized. His health broke down about 1864 and his wife nursed him back to health. This experience turned their thoughts to health reform, and in response to a vision which came to the wife, the Western Health Reform Institute was founded in 1866 at Battle Creek. Under the promotion of the Whites, Battle Creek College, the first Seventh-day Adventist school, was founded in 1874. This same year they journeyed to California, where, at Oakland, White established the *Signs of the Times,* the printing establishment of which developed into the Pacific Press Publishing Association. He died at Battle Creek Aug. 6, 1881.

After his death his wife traveled about visiting churches and attending conferences and camp meetings. She labored in Europe from 1885 until 1888, and in 1891 went to Australia, where she remained nine years. In 1901 she turned her attention to Christian work in the Southern states. Largely as a result of her interest the Southern Publishing Association was founded at Nashville, Tenn., in that year. In 1903 she played an important part in moving the denominational headquarters to Washington, D. C., and she also had a very definite part in founding, in 1909, the College of Medical Evangelists at Loma Linda, Cal., which has sent its graduates to many quarters of the world. Her place in the denomination was unique. She never claimed to be a leader, but simply a voice, a messenger bearing communications from God to his people. Her life was marked by deep personal piety and spiritual influence, and her messages were an important factor in unifying the churches. She was a constant contributor to the denominational papers and was the author of about twenty volumes. With her husband she wrote *Life Sketches . . . of Elder James White and His Wife, Mrs. Ellen G. White* (1880) and in 1915 published *Life Sketches of Ellen G. White.* In 1926 *Scriptural and Subject Index to the Writings of Mrs. Ellen G. White* appeared. She died at St. Helena, Cal.

[Autobiog. writings mentioned above; A. C. Harmon, *The Harmon Geneal.* (1920); *Signs of the Times,* Aug. 16, 23, 1881; *Advent Rev. and Sabbath Herald,* July 29, 1915; J. N. Loughborough, *The Great Second Advent Movement* (1905); M. E. Olsen, *A Hist. of the Origin and Progress of Seventh-day Adventists* (1925); D. M. Canright, *Life of Mrs. E. G. White . . . Her False Claims Refuted* (1919); *N. Y. Times,* July 17, 1915.]

E. N. D.

WHITE, EMERSON ELBRIDGE (Jan. 10, 1829–Oct. 21, 1902), educator, author of school texts and books on education, was born in Mantua, Portage County, Ohio, the son of Jonas and Sarah (McGregory) White. He was a descendant of Capt. Thomas White, an early settler of Weymouth, Mass. He was educated in the rural schools of Portage County, in Twinsburg Academy, and in Cleveland University, where he was a student instructor in mathematics. In 1856, after serving as principal of Mount Union Academy, of a Cleveland grammar school, and of the Cleveland Central High School, he was appointed superintendent of the public schools of Portsmouth, Ohio. Failing of reappointment in 1860, he opened in the city a classical school. He moved to Columbus in 1861 to assume the editorship and proprietorship of the *Ohio Educational Monthly,* which he continued until 1875. As editor of this journal, the official organ of the State Teachers' Association, he soon became the leading influence in Ohio schools. Becoming commissioner of common schools (1863–65), he established the state board of school examiners, provided by law financial support for county teachers' institutes, and codified for the first time the school laws of the state. From 1876 to 1883 he served as president of Purdue University, founded in 1874. Under his administration the work of the university was organized and the institution itself permanently established. Upon his resignation in 1883, he moved to Cincinnati to continue his authorship of school texts, and served three years (1886–89) as superintendent of the public schools of the city. He returned to his old home in Columbus in 1891. Possibly no man during these years was more widely in demand in all forms of public school activity than White, and none more regular in his attendance upon the annual meetings of state and national conventions. He was president of the Ohio State Teachers' Association (1863), of the National Association of School Superintendents (1866), of the National Education Association (1872), and of the National Council of Education (1884),

which he had helped to found. He is said to have written the bill establishing a national department of education (see *American Journal of Education,* Mar. 1866, Sept. 1867). He was author of *A Classbook on Geography* (1863), *A New Complete Arithmetic* (1883), *Oral Lessons in Number* (1884), *School Reader* (1886), *The Elements of Pedagogy* (1886), *School Management* (1893), and *Art of Teaching* (1901); *White's New School Register Containing Forms for Daily, Term, and Yearly Records* (1891) was used by teachers in the Middle West almost universally for many years.

White was six feet tall, commanding in figure, dignified in presence, a man of marked fidelity who pursued his work with great earnestness and singleness of purpose. While his reserve and superior scholarship cut him off somewhat from surface popularity, his simplicity and sincerity of mind knit to him in ardent friendship the leading school men of America. A lifelong Presbyterian, he served many years as president of the board of trustees of Lane Seminary, was a frequent delegate to the Presbyterian general assembly, and a delegate to the Pan-Presbyterian Council in Edinburgh in 1877 and in Glasgow in 1896. He was married on July 26, 1853, to Mary Ann Sabin of Huron, Ohio, who died in 1901. There were five children, of whom three survived their father.

[*Who's Who in America,* 1901–02; *The Officers and Alumni of Purdue Univ., 1875–1896* (n.d.); W. M. Hepburn and L. M. Sears, *Purdue Univ., Fifty Years of Progress* (1925); *Ohio Educ. Monthly,* Nov. 1902; W. H. Venable, in *Education,* Jan. 1903, and in *Educ. Hist. of Ohio* (1905), ed. by J. J. Burns; *Proc. Nat. Educ. Asso.* (1903); obituaries in *Cincinnati Enquirer* and *Ohio State Jour.* (Columbus), Oct. 22, 1902.]

H. C. M.

WHITE, GEORGE (Mar. 12, 1802–Apr. 30, 1887), historical writer, teacher, Protestant Episcopal clergyman, was born in Charleston, S. C., the son of poor but industrious parents. His early education seems to have been acquired principally through his own efforts. His parents were Methodists, and at the age of eighteen he was licensed to preach, soon becoming known as the "beardless preacher." In 1823 he moved to Savannah, Ga., where he continued to reside for the next quarter of a century. Here he opened an academy, and with the exception of 1826–27, when he was in charge of the publicly controlled Chatham Academy, he conducted his school, under different names, for some years. He was rigid in his discipline and held his scholars to high requirements; yet he won "the affection of his pupils and the permanent esteem of their parents and guardians" (*Georgian,* May 12, 1843). He long refused to teach girls, because such teaching would necessitate adopting a milder discipline. He established a night school, introduced various apparatus into the classroom, and was in general progressive in his ideas on education. Having come to dislike the Methodist form of government, he joined the Protestant Episcopal Church and in 1833 became a clergyman of that communion. He preached to seamen and during the last five years of his residence in Savannah he engaged in mission work on the islands along the Georgia coast.

White's most valid claim to remembrance rests on his historical work. In 1839 he joined a group of citizens of Savannah in organizing the Georgia Historical Society. His interest led him through long and tedious investigations in Georgia and as far north as New York City, which resulted in the publication ten years later of his *Statistics of the State of Georgia,* a work of great merit. In 1852 he brought out *An Accurate Account of the Yazoo Fraud Compiled from Official Documents,* and two years thereafter, his *Historical Collections of Georgia,* a classic in Georgia bibliography. These last two works were published while White was in Marietta, Ga., whither he had moved in 1849. He remained there until 1854, when he definitely gave up further historical work and entered fully into the service of the Church, first as a missionary to Lagrange and West Point, Ga., and in 1856 as rector of Trinity Church, in Florence, Ala. In 1858 he went to Memphis, Tenn., as assistant rector of Calvary Church, under Bishop James H. Otey [*q.v.*], and the following year became rector, holding this position until two years before his death, when he retired as rector emeritus. During the epidemics of yellow fever and cholera which visited Memphis he rendered heroic service. He married Elizabeth Millen of Savannah and to this union were born eight children, of whom one son and three daughters outlived their father.

[W. J. Northen, *Men of Mark in Ga.,* vol. II (1910); A. D. Candler and C. A. Evans, *Georgia* (1906); C. C. Jones, *Hist. of Savannah* (1890); *Ga. Hist. Soc. Colls.,* vol. II (1842); A. L. Hull, *A Hist. Sketch of the Univ. of Ga.* (1894); H. S. Bowden, *Two Hundred Years of Educ. . . . Savannah, Chatham County, Ga.* (1932); *Jour. . . . the Protestant Episcopal Church in the Diocese of Ga., 1833–1854; Hist. of the Church in the Diocese of Tenn.* (1900); *Memphis Appeal,* 1887; *Public Ledger* (Memphis), May 2, 1887; *Memphis Avalanche,* May 1, 1887.]   E. M. C.

WHITE, GEORGE LEONARD (Sept. 20, 1838–Nov. 8, 1895), conductor of the Jubilee Singers of Fisk University, was born at Cadiz, N. Y., the son of William B. and Nancy (Leonard) White. From his father, a blacksmith who in his spare time played in a local band, he de-

rived a love of music. He attended public school until he was fourteen, when his formal education came to an end. At twenty he was teaching in Ohio and had acquired considerable reputation as a choir leader. With one or two associates he gathered the colored people of the neighborhood and taught them in Sunday schools, the singing in which he led his pupils forming a considerable part of the curriculum. In the early days of the Civil War he joined the "Squirrel Hunters" to defend Cincinnati from the Confederates under Kirby-Smith. Later, as an enlisted man in the 73rd Ohio Regiment, he was at the battles of Chancellorsville and Gettysburg, and served until discharged for illness in 1864. After the war he went to Nashville, Tenn., where he was briefly employed in the quartermaster's department, and then entered the service of the Freedmen's Bureau, under Clinton B. Fisk [*q.v.*]. In 1867 he was appointed instructor of vocal music at Fisk University, Nashville, which had just been founded by the American Missionary Association, and subsequently became a trustee and treasurer of the institution.

In 1870, when it seemed likely that Fisk University must close unless money could be raised, White suggested taking a group of students on a concert tour. He finally won the consent of the trustees and in October 1871, with a band of nine singers, started out. Although they were penniless, only recently emancipated, untutored except for the training White had given them, they repeatedly won hostile crowds and indifferent audiences to enthusiastic admiration, and in March 1872 returned to Nashville with twenty thousand dollars they had earned over and above their expenses. After resting only a week, they started out again with some new recruits, going first to the World Peace Jubilee in Boston. Here their presence was the great feature of the occasion and they received an ovation. In April 1873 they sailed for England and in a tour of Great Britain met with the same astonishing success that had been theirs in America. Subsequently they toured England again and visited the Continent, raising in all more than $90,000 for Fisk University and spreading through the civilized world a new understanding and respect for the character and the capacities of the freedmen. They finally disbanded in Hamburg in 1878. The testimony of all connected with the venture is that without White it could never have taken place. A man of faith, he had great courage and devotion to his work and to the students he had trained. He was extraordinary, too, in his musicianship; although almost entirely self-taught, he maintained standards of performance so high that only his personal influence over the singers kept them from wearying and rebelling. "His ear was exquisite," wrote an associate; "in passages of almost incredible power he would not tolerate anything that was not pure tone" (*Fisk Herald,* October 1911, pp. 5, 6). "He would keep us singing all day until we had every passage . . . to suit his fastidious taste," said one of the singers (*Ibid.,* p. 30).

At Saratoga, Minn., Aug. 11, 1867, White married Laura Amelia Cravath, a missionary of the American Missionary Association and a sister of Erastus Milo Cravath [*q.v.*], first president of Fisk University. She died in Glasgow, Scotland, during the first tour of the singers. On Apr. 12, 1876, during the second European tour, he married Susan Gilbert, a fellow teacher at Fisk, chaperon to the young women among the singers. Forced by an accident in 1885, from which he never fully recovered, to give up his work with the Jubilee Singers, he taught music at the state normal school, Fredonia, N. Y.; in 1886–87 he was at Biddle (later Johnson C. Smith) University in North Carolina; and in later years, with his wife, was connected with Sage College, Cornell University. He died at Ithaca, in his fifty-eighth year, after being stricken with paralysis. His wife, with a son and a daughter of his first marriage, survived him; his eldest son had died in 1890.

[G. D. Pike, *The Jubilee Singers* (1873) and *The Singing Campaign* (1875); *Fisk Herald,* Oct. 1911; annual reports of the Am. Missionary Asso., 1867–76; information as to certain facts from White's daughter, Miss Georgia L. White.]   M.G.

WHITE, HENRY (Mar. 28, 1732–Dec. 23, 1786), Loyalist, was born in Maryland, the son of a British colonel who emigrated to America in 1712. After education in England, he became a merchant in New York City. His position was strengthened by his marriage, on May 13, 1761, with Eva Van Cortlandt, member of one of the colony's wealthy and influential families. By 1769 he removed to one of the largest mercantile establishments in the city. By the time of the Revolution he had extensive holdings in New York City, on Lake Champlain, and south of the Susquehanna. He was appointed to the Council in 1769 and served until the Revolution. He was also a governor of King's College (Columbia University), a founder of the Marine Society of New York, organized mainly for charitable purposes, and one of the incorporators and governors of the New York Hospital.

He joined with the other New York merchants in their objection to the Stamp and Townshend acts and was a member of a committee in 1766 to recommend the erection of a statue to Pitt. He was one of the founders and president, 1772–73, of the Chamber of Commerce, organized in 1768 partially to combat the Townshend acts. After the repeal of the Townshend acts, however, he took no further part in the revolutionary movement. He was one of the three merchants in New York City to whom the East India Company tea was consigned in 1773, but, except to appeal to Governor Tryon for protection for the cargoes, he took no action to make him obnoxious to the radicals who prevented landing the tea. When Tryon went to England in 1774, he made White his agent and attorney, but this fact did not bring White under any direct suspicion from the increasingly powerful radicals. However, a letter of June 1775 from Gov. Josiah Martin of North Carolina, ordering a royal standard and certain other supplies, conceivably for military purposes, was intercepted, but to a committee of the Provincial Congress White explained that he had not sent the standard "lest it might be disagreeable to the people of this place," and that he knew nothing of Martin's actions or plans. The Congress announced itself satisfied (Force, *post,* cols. 1346–47). At the end of 1775 he went to England and returned when the British occupied New York City in 1776. He was one of the signers of the Loyal Address to the Howes and was active in the service of the British, first as a member of a committee to receive donations for equipping provincial regiments and later as an agent for selling prizes. His name was on a list of ten recommended by the Commissioners for Restoring Peace, 1778, for membership on an intercolonial council to govern America.

By the Act of Attainder of 1779, his property was to be confiscated, and he himself was to be executed if found within the state. When the British evacuated New York, he went with his family to live in London. His land in interior New York was sold in small holdings, but the bulk of his city property was, with the exception of one house retained by the state as a residence for the governor, bought in by his son, Henry White, Jr. The terms of his will, drawn in London, May 19, 1786, seem to evidence that he was still a very wealthy man at the time of his death. A copy of a portrait by Copley hangs in the Chamber of Commerce in New York City.

[Lorenzo Sabine, *Biog. Sketches of Loyalists of the Am. Revolution* (1864), vol. II; A. C. Flick, *Loyalism in New York* (1901); Peter Force, *Am. Archives,* 4 ser., vol. II (1839); *Colonial Records of N. Y. Chamber of Commerce, 1768–84* (1867), with hist. and biog. sketches by J. A. Stevens; *Portrait Gallery of the Chamber of Commerce of the State of N. Y.* (1890), comp. by George Wilson; J. A. Stevens, *Henry White* and his Family (1877), reprinted from *Mag. of Am. Hist.*, Dec. 1877; *N. Y. Geneal. and Biog. Record*, Oct. 1905, for will.]   M. E. L—b—d.

WHITE, HENRY (Mar. 29, 1850–July 15, 1927), diplomatist, was born in Baltimore, Md. His father, John Campbell White, of Scotch lineage, was heir to a considerable fortune made in a distillery established in Baltimore by his great-grandfather; his mother, Eliza (Ridgely) White, sprang from one of the oldest Maryland families. The death of his father in 1853 resulted in Henry's spending most of his boyhood at "Hampton," a dozen miles from Baltimore, an estate of the border plantation type where slavery existed. From an early age he was accustomed to travel and to an animated, spacious social life. In 1857–58 he spent more than a year with his mother in Europe. The Civil War made the household unhappy, for his mother and grandparents sympathized warmly with the South. In 1865 Mrs. White married Dr. Thomas Hepburn Buckler [*q.v.*], an eminent Baltimore physician, also a Southern sympathizer, and late that year they took Henry abroad for a protracted residence.

The first five years, 1865–70, were spent chiefly in France, Italy, and Germany. White mastered French and Italian, became familiar with social life in Paris and Rome, and learned much regarding European politics. His mother, while denying him no wholesome pleasures, insisted on strict discipline and hard study, partly under her, partly under tutors, and partly in a French school. She catechized him vigorously upon the Bible; she always spoke and wrote to him in Italian; and she developed in him a natural unselfishness which, with his sunniness of temper, made his personality singularly attractive. In 1870 the Franco-Prussian War drove the household to England. White had hoped to attend Cambridge University, but pulmonary weakness led Dr. Buckler to insist upon an outdoor life for him. In 1871 he took a hunting-box at Market Harborough, and for several years hunted with the principal packs of Leicestershire, Rutlandshire, and Northamptonshire. Throughout life he insisted that the sport afforded a wonderful training in courage, quickness, good temper, good manners, and cool judgment. He frequently visited the Continent and made several visits to the United States, but his best friends were in England, where his social graces gave him ready *entrée* to London society and the country houses.

White's marriage on Dec. 3, 1879, to Margaret Stuyvesant Rutherfurd of New York was a turning-point in his life, for his wife insisted upon his taking up some career. A daughter of the astronomer Lewis Morris Rutherfurd [*q.v.*], she was a woman of exceptional beauty, intellectual tastes, and ambition. Under her prompting White asked a foreign appointment of the Arthur administration; and in July 1883 found himself secretary of legation under Alphonso Taft at Vienna, where he learned diplomatic routine and added German to his languages. A fortunate transfer to the second secretaryship in London at the end of the year then brought him into a legation where his social connections and knowledge of British politics made him particularly valuable. Soon rising to be first secretary, he remained here without interruption until 1893. Successive ministers—Lowell, Edward J. Phelps, and Robert Lincoln—found his tact, skill, and ready access to the best sources of information invaluable. He worked hard over the fishery and sealing disputes, and several times took control of the legation as chargé. Mrs. White was as popular socially as he. In 1893 President Cleveland, despite strong protests from such men as Edwin L. Godkin and Henry Adams, brusquely displaced him for a Democrat.

Four years later, after unofficially acting as Richard Olney's diplomatic agent in clearing up the Venezuelan dispute, White was offered by McKinley the choice between his old London post and the ministership to Spain. His unhesitating acceptance of the former opened eight brilliant years as a subordinate in the foreign service. Ambassadors John Hay and Joseph Choate found him loyal and hardworking. He corresponded with President Roosevelt, Secretary John Hay, and Senator Henry Cabot Lodge on highly confidential terms; he was held in warm regard by Lord Salisbury, Lord Lansdowne, Arthur Balfour, and St. John Brodrick. He thus filled a unique rôle as go-between in numerous unofficial exchanges, an interpreter of both countries, a source of expert information, and an adviser. His letters (Nevins, *post*, pp. 123–242) demonstrate how much he did in these years to smooth the way for the Hay-Pauncefote abrogation of the Clayton-Bulwer treaty, the settlement of the Alaskan boundary, and the termination of the Venezuelan dispute of 1902–03; to advise Hay in handling the Boxer revolt and the Open Door problem; and to further the Anglo-American *rapprochement* which began at the time of the Spanish-American War. It was with these services in mind that Roosevelt later said that he was "the most useful man in the diplomatic service, during my presidency, and for many years before" (Roosevelt, *post*, p. 388).

Appointed ambassador to Italy in March 1905, and ambassador to France in 1907, White found fewer opportunities in these positions than in London. His most important labor during these years was as American representative at the Algeciras Conference (1906). Roosevelt chose White as his agent in his efforts to prevent an immediate conflict, preserve Moroccan integrity, and contribute to a permanent understanding in Europe. Roosevelt cabled asking his opinion of a fair peace plan, and White, after obtaining memoranda from the French and German delegates, submitted a memorandum to Washington. It was on this that Roosevelt primarily based the scheme which he urged upon the Kaiser through Speck von Sternburg. In other ways White aided in preventing a rupture, which would probably have meant war. But he knew that France and Spain had a secret treaty for spheres of influence in Morocco, and realized better than Roosevelt that the latter's intervention had contributed not to the open door in Morocco but to French domination.

President Taft's dismissal of White from the French embassy in 1909 was, as Roosevelt wrote, for personal reasons "unconnected with the good of the service" (Roosevelt, p. 388); and it aroused indignation on the part of Roosevelt, Lodge, and Knox. But White with characteristic generosity cherished no resentment. He lingered in Europe to accompany Roosevelt in 1910 to Berlin and London. Later that year he accepted from Taft an appointment as head of the American delegation to the fourth Pan-American Conference in Buenos Aires. In 1911 he began building a house in Washington. He participated in social life there with great enjoyment, and added a warm friendship with Lord Bryce to his preëxisting intimacy with Lodge, Henry Adams, and Jusserand. The outbreak of war in 1914 found him in Germany, where he had a notable interview with Falkenhayn (Nevins, pp. 323 ff.). Returning to Washington, he kept out of public life, but in 1917–18 acted as regional director of the Red Cross and president of the War Camp Community Service. It was amid such activities that he was surprised by Wilson's appointment of him (November 1918) to the Peace Commission. After talks with Roosevelt, Root, and Lodge on peace terms, he sailed for Paris with Wilson on the *George Washington*.

In Paris, like Lansing and Bliss, White quickly found that he would play a minor rôle in the drafting of the treaty. Yet if minor it was distinctly enlightened and useful. He threw his influence against the excessive demands of Italy,

France, and Poland for territory; a frank talk with Wilson had much to do with the latter's insistence on a plebiscite in Upper Silesia, while White blamed Colonel House severely for improper concessions to Italy at Fiume. He likewise threw his influence against the continuance of the French food-blockade of Germany. He did good service on the Commission of International Régime of Ports, Waterways, and Railways, standing out against French demands for the neutralization of the Kiel Canal. But his most important labors lay in his efforts to enlighten American friends, and particularly Chairman Lodge of the foreign relations committee, about the League of Nations. When appointed by Wilson he had been distinctly hostile to any league, but a brief scrutiny of post-war conditions in Europe converted him into an impassioned advocate of the idea. In his eagerness to bring America into the League he cabled Lodge on Mar. 9, 1919, while Wilson was on the high seas, asking for "exact phraseology of amendments modifying League which Senate considers important" (Nevins, p. 399). Lodge took the absurd view that this message was a trap, possibly instigated by Wilson, and sent a curt refusal (H. C. Lodge, *The Senate and the League of Nations*, 1925, pp. 123–28). The final defeat of the League by the Senate was a heavy blow to White, who had returned to Washington in December 1919 to labor for it.

In the remaining years of his life White devoted much attention to fostering the development of diplomacy as a profession. He himself might be called the first professional American diplomatist. His first wife having died in 1916, on Nov. 3, 1920, he married Mrs. Emily Vanderbilt Sloane. Thereafter he divided his time between Washington, New York, and Lenox. His death on July 15, 1927, at Pittsfield, Mass., followed a brief illness, almost the first of his life. One daughter, married to a member of the German nobility, Count Seherr-Thoss, and one son, John Campbell White, who had also made diplomacy a career, survived him.

[Allan Nevins, *Henry White: Thirty Years of American Diplomacy* (1930); R. B. Mowat, *Americans in England* (1935); Tyler Dennett, *John Hay: From Poetry to Politics* (1933); A. L. P. Dennis, *Adventures in American Diplomacy* (1928); Harold Nicolson, *Sir Arthur Nicolson, Bart., First Lord Carnock* (1930); *Theodore Roosevelt: an Autobiography* (1913); Royal Cortissoz, *The Life of Whitelaw Reid* (2 vols., 1921); Charles Seymour, *The Intimate Papers of Colonel House* (vols. III–IV, 1928); Robert Lansing, *The Peace Negotiations: A Personal Narrative* (1921); obituary in *N. Y. Times*, July 16, 1927.] A. N.

WHITE, HENRY CLAY (Dec. 30, 1848–Dec. 1, 1927), chemist, teacher, and college president, was born at Baltimore, Md., the son of Levi S., and Louisa (Brown) White. After attending the schools of Baltimore, he entered the University of Virginia, where he obtained his chemical training under John W. Mallet [*q.v.*], graduating in 1870. From 1870 to 1872 he taught chemistry successively at the Maryland Institute, the Peabody Institute, Baltimore, and St. John's College, Annapolis. In 1872 he was appointed professor of chemistry at the University of Georgia (which included the Georgia State College of Agriculture and the Mechanic Arts); his connection with this institution continued during the remainder of his life. On Dec. 17, 1872, he married Ella F. Roberts of Chester County, Pa. In 1874 he delivered a "Report on the Complete Analysis of the Cotton Plant," published in the *Proceedings of the Georgia State Agricultural Society . . . February 1874* (1874), which was a notable treatment of the subject.

In addition to his work as university professor he served as state chemist of Georgia from 1880 to 1890. An important duty of this position was the regulatory control of the purity of the fertilizers sold to the planters of Georgia; as a result of this activity he took a prominent part in helping to establish a society of agricultural chemists. After several preliminary meetings of prominent chemists at Washington (1880), Boston (1880), Cincinnati (1881), and Atlanta (1884), the Association of Official Agricultural Chemists was formed at Philadelphia, Sept. 9, 1884; in the early work of this organization White was a leading figure. In 1890 he was appointed president of the Georgia State College of Agriculture and the Mechanic Arts, and from this time on his chief interests were in the field of education. He organized the Farmers' Institutes of Georgia and was unremitting in his efforts to improve conditions in the agricultural population of the state. He resisted successfully, but at great personal sacrifice, the long attempts to separate the College of Agriculture from the University of Georgia. His strenuous efforts in this cause against strong political influences prevented the disruption of the University. He was president of the Association of American Agricultural Colleges and Experiment Stations in 1897–98 and was chairman of its executive committee from 1902 to 1907. In these offices he was instrumental in bringing about a greater degree of cooperation between the state experiment stations and the federal Department of Agriculture. He was chemist of the Georgia Experiment Station from 1888 to 1914 and vice-director from 1890 to 1913. He collaborated with the United States Department of Agriculture in cotton in-

vestigations in 1895–96 and in dietary studies in 1903–05. In 1907 he resigned as president of the Georgia State College but continued in service as professor of chemistry in the University until his death, which occurred at his home in Athens, Ga.

White was the recipient of many honors. He was a member of the American Chemical Society, of the American Association for the Advancement of Science, and of the Georgia Academy of Science; he was also a fellow of the London Chemical Society, a corresponding member of the British Association for the Advancement of Science, and an honorary member of the Belgian Academy of Science. He was president of the Georgia Peace Society in 1911. In addition to his "Analysis of the Cotton Plant" he was the author of *Elementary Geology of Tennessee* (1875), with W. G. McAdoo; *Lectures and Addresses* (2 vols., 1885–91); "Manuring of Cotton," in *The Cotton Plant* (1896); *Abraham Baldwin* (1926); and numerous bulletins, scientific papers, and literary articles.

[*Ga. Alumni Record,* June 1922; *Experiment Station Record,* Apr. 1928; H. W. Wiley, in *Jour. of the Asso. of Official Agric. Chemists,* Nov. 15, 1928; *Who's Who in America,* 1926–27; J. McK. Cattell and D. R. Brimhall, *Am. Men of Sci.* (1921); *Atlanta Jour.,* Dec. 1, 1927.]
C. A. B—e.

WHITE, HORACE (Aug. 10, 1834–Sept. 16, 1916), journalist, economist, was born at Colebrook, N. H., the son of Horace White, a physician, and his wife, Eliza Moore. As agent of the New England Emigration Company, Dr. White founded the town of Beloit, Wis., where his wife and two sons joined him in 1838. Entering Beloit College in 1849, at the age of fifteen, Horace was graduated four years later. He at once entered journalism and in 1854 became city editor of the Chicago *Evening Journal.* The following year he was made Chicago agent of the New York Associated Press. This place, also, he held but a short time for, deeply stirred by the events in "bleeding Kansas," he soon became assistant secretary of the National Kansas Commission. As such it was his duty to receive and forward money, arms, ammunition, and supplies of all kinds to the Free State pioneers—among them John Brown and two of his sons—and to outfit parties of new settlers who passed through Iowa and Nebraska to the scene of the conflict. In 1857 he himself went to Kansas with the expectation of becoming a settler and a leader of the anti-slavery forces.

Returning to Chicago to make final arrangements, he was induced by Dr. C. H. Ray, editor of the *Chicago Tribune,* to accept a position on that paper, of which he was a minority stockholder until his death. In 1858 he reported for it the Lincoln-Douglas debates, thus beginning a warm friendship with Abraham Lincoln and also with Henry Villard [*q.v.*], then correspondent of the New York *Staats-Zeitung*. At the outbreak of the Civil War the *Chicago Tribune* made White its Washington correspondent, permitting him also to hold the important position of clerk of the Senate committee on military affairs, which position gave to him a remarkable insight into the conduct of the war. In 1864 he formed, with Henry Villard and Adams Sherman Hill, in later life the distinguished Boylston Professor of Rhetoric in Harvard University, the first news agency to compete with the Associated Press, serving the *Chicago Tribune, Springfield Republican, Boston Advertiser, Cincinnati Commercial, Rochester Democrat,* and the *Missouri Democrat* of St. Louis. Villard took the field with the Army of the Potomac, and White and Hill covered Washington. With the close of the war this syndicate was dissolved and White became editor-in-chief of the *Chicago Tribune,* remaining as such until his resignation because of ill health in 1874.

In 1877 he joined Villard, then receiver of the Kansas-Pacific Railroad, in the service of that enterprise, subsequently being appointed treasurer of the Oregon Railway & Navigation Company when Villard became president. In 1881 the latter purchased the *New York Evening Post,* and the *Nation,* and placed at their head the distinguished triumvirate, Carl Schurz [*q.v.*], Horace White, and Edwin L. Godkin [*q.v.*], in order to continue the then failing *Nation,* and to establish a politically independent daily newspaper devoted to the highest political and social ideals. The triumvirate lasted, however, only a little more than two years, at the end of which time Schurz retired and Godkin became editor, with White in charge of the financial and economic policies of the two journals. In this field White at once took a position of high authority. His book *Money and Banking, Illustrated by American History,* first published in 1895, was in 1935 still a standard textbook in schools and colleges. When Godkin retired in 1899, White became editor-in-chief of the *Evening Post,* which position he held until his retirement because of failing health in 1903. A profound Greek scholar, he published *The Roman History of Appian of Alexandria, Translated from the Greek* (1899), and, in his retirement, wrote *The Life of Lyman Trumbull* (1913), besides editing various financial textbooks. In 1908 Gov. Charles E. Hughes of New York appointed him chairman of a commission on speculation in securities and commodities, authorized by the legislature of the state. Its report recommended no action by the legislature and placed upon the stock exchange itself "the duty of restraint and reform." Eight of the fourteen recommendations were adopted by the governors of the exchange.

Of exceptionally strong character, White enjoyed the complete respect and the warm regard of friends and associates. He was always more the scholar and the philosopher than the journalist or executive. His modesty was extreme; his repugnance to public appearances, unconquerable. He had an extraordinarily strong grasp of fundamental economic truths which nothing could disturb. A convinced free-trader and an old-fashioned liberal of the Manchester school, he, like Godkin, threw himself passionately into the *Evening Post's* opposition to the annexation of Hawaii, to the American governments' attitude in the Venezuelan imbroglio with England in 1895, and to the war with Spain and the conquest of the Philippines, in all of which opposition he and his associates were actuated by complete devotion to the American ideal as they understood it. Like Godkin, too, he was rigid in upholding the literary and scholarly traditions of the *Evening Post,* the editorial page of which was for thirty-seven years one of the most distinguished in American journalism. White was married first to Martha Root of New Haven, Conn., who died in 1873, and second, in 1875, to Amelia Jane McDougall of Chicago, Ill., who died in 1885. He was survived by three daughters.

[Printed sources include obituary, autobiog. sketch, and editorial in *Evening Post* (N. Y.), Sept. 18, 1916, and One Hundredth Anniversary Ed. of the *Post,* Nov. 16, 1901; Allan Nevins, *The Evening Post; A Century of Journalism* (1922); O. G. Villard, *John Brown* (1910); *Memoirs of Henry Villard* (1904); *Who's Who in America,* 1914–15. Most authorities give the year of White's birth as 1834, but his daughter states that a note in his own handwriting gives the year as 1833.] O.G.V.

WHITE, HUGH LAWSON (Oct. 30, 1773– Apr. 10, 1840), jurist, United States senator, was born in Iredell County, N. C., the eldest son of James White [*q.v.*] and his wife, Mary (Lawson). There can be little doubt but that the influence of his father, a generous and kindly as well as an able man, was the guiding force in Hugh's life. No adequate schools were available, but he became acquainted with the rudiments of classical learning under the direction of the Rev. Samuel Carrick, the local Presbyterian clergyman, and under Judge Archibald Roane [*q.v.*]. When White arrived at his twentieth year, Gov. William Blount [*q.v.*] made him his private secretary. The Indians were giving trouble at this time and Gen. John Sevier [*q.v.*] led an expedition against them. White accompanied him and acquired some notoriety by killing the chief Kingfisher. Shortly afterward he went to Philadelphia to study mathematics under Professor Patterson. Later, he went to Lancaster, Pa., and for a year studied law under James Hopkins.

In 1796 he returned to Knoxville and began the practice of his profession. Two years later he married Elizabeth Moore Carrick, daughter of his old preceptor. In 1801 he was made a judge of the superior court of Tennessee, at that time the highest tribunal of the state judiciary. He resigned this office in 1807 and was elected to the state Senate. The next year he was appointed and confirmed United States attorney for the Eastern District of Tennessee, but soon resigned. In 1809 he was reëlected to the Senate, but the state judiciary was just then reorganized and a supreme court of errors and appeals created, and White was chosen the presiding judge of this tribunal. In 1811 the Bank of the State of Tennessee was chartered and in 1812 began operation in Knoxville with White as president. He continued to act in this capacity until 1827, but accepted no compensation for his services during the periods when he held public office, nor did he receive from the institution any advantage as borrower or indorser. In 1813 Gen. Andrew Jackson was conducting his campaign against the Creek Indians on the Coosa River, and Gen. James White was acting under him. Word reached the younger White that the troops were in great danger and he, with two companions, set out through the wilderness to lend aid. Finding it impossible to accomplish anything material, he returned to Knoxville and persuaded his brother-in-law, Col. John Williams, 1778–1837 [*q.v.*], to go with his regiment—the 39th United States Infantry—to Jackson's aid, and at the battle of Horseshoe Bend, Williams' assistance was invaluable (James Parton, *Life of Andrew Jackson,* 1860, I, pp. 431, 499–500).

In 1815 White retired from the supreme court and in 1817 was again elected to the state Senate. Here he signalized his return by securing the passage of a bill prohibiting duelling in Tennessee. In 1821 he was appointed on the commission to fix claims against Spain under the Florida treaty, and the next year Kentucky made him one of her commissioners to adjust military land claims with Virginia. The first of these appointments occupied much of his time until 1824. The following year Andrew Jack-

son resigned from the United States Senate and White was elected to complete his unexpired term. By repeated subsequent elections he held this seat until his resignation in 1840. As a strict constructionist of the old school, a Jeffersonian and Jacksonian Democrat, he opposed the administration of John Quincy Adams. Becoming chairman of the committee on Indian affairs, he took keen and constructive interest in the concerns of the Indians, and had a large part in the formulation of plans for their removal westward. In 1831 his wife died at Natural Bridge, Va., and he personally drove the conveyance which carried her body back to Knoxville. On Nov. 30 of the following year he married Mrs. Ann E. Peyton of Washington. On Dec. 3, 1832, he was elected president *pro tempore* of the Senate.

As early as 1830 White stated that the Washington *Telegraph* would not do him justice because he refused to support the cause of either Calhoun or Van Buren for the succession. Senator Tazewell also thought he noticed at this time that White was losing ground with the administration. In 1831 President Jackson reorganized his cabinet, which act was looked upon as a move by the administration to further its scheme for promoting the cause of Van Buren. As a part of this reorganization, John H. Eaton [*q.v.*] of Tennessee resigned from the war department and Jackson urged White to accept the vacated post. Had he done so, Eaton was expected to fall heir to his seat in the Senate, but White refused. Jackson had offered him the same place upon his accession to office in 1829, and on that occasion, also, White had refused it (J. S. Bassett, ed., *Correspondence of Andrew Jackson,* IV, 1929, pp. 258–60). Among the reasons that he now gave for his refusal, was that he could not accept office from a friend. He was doubtless sincere in this statement but it is also true that he would have done nothing to aid Van Buren. At any rate, the ways of Jackson and White began to diverge from this point. The candidacy of Van Buren for the succession was unpopular in Tennessee and presently suggestions emanated from this quarter that the Senator himself would become a presidential candidate. In 1834 Jackson threatened that he would ruin White if he did so. White accepted the challenge, and was put in nomination by the legislatures of Alabama (*Address of Gabriel Moore to the Freemen of Alabama,* 1835) and Tennessee, and in the campaign of 1836, with John Tyler as his running mate, received the electoral votes of Tennessee and Georgia. Despite this break with Jackson, White never changed his political principles (T. P. Abernethy, "Origin of the Whig Party in Tennessee," *in Mississippi Valley Historical Review,* March 1926, pp. 507–10). He favored Clay for the presidency in 1840 and promised his support after Clay had given pledges not to push his nationalist program and to oppose the annexation of Texas in order to preserve the balance between North and South (Henry A. Wise, *Seven Decades of the Union,* 1872, pp. 161–70). On Jan. 13, 1840, White resigned from the Senate when instructed by the legislature of Tennessee to vote for the sub-treasury bill (*Letter of the Hon. Hugh L. White to the Legislature of Tennessee,* 1840). He died at his home near Knoxville the following April. By his first wife he had twelve children, but within six years she and eight of the children died of tuberculosis. Two daughters survived him.

Though exposed to all the roughness of the frontier, White was essentially a gentleman; he was mild in all his ways and upright in all his dealings. His intellectual interests were confined strictly to the law, and he was endowed with little sense of humor or imagination. His physical make-up was not unlike that of Andrew Jackson, except that the cast of his lean countenance was contemplative rather than aggressive. He had a conscience as strict as that of any Puritan, but his righteousness took the form of public service rather than mere personal piety; the Republic never had a more disinterested servant.

[N. N. Scott, *A Memoir of Hugh Lawson White* (1856); S. G. Heiskell, *Andrew Jackson and Early Tenn. Hist.* (3 vols., 1920–21); J. W. Caldwell, *Sketches of the Bench and Bar of Tenn.* (1898); H. S. Foote, *The Bench and Bar of the South and Southwest* (1876); *Address of the Honorable Abram P. Maury, on the Life and Character of Hugh Lawson White* (1840); T. P. Abernethy, *From Frontier to Plantation in Tennessee* (1932); *Daily Republican Banner* (Nashville), Apr. 15, 1840; manuscript letters of White in the Calvin Morgan McClung hist. coll. of the Lawson McGhee Lib., Knoxville, Tenn.]

T. P. A.

WHITE, ISRAEL CHARLES (Nov. 1, 1848– Nov. 25, 1927), geologist, son of Michael and Mary (Russell) White, was born in Monongalia County, Va. (later W. Va.). His first paternal American ancestor was one Stephen White who emigrated from England about 1659 and is said to have settled in Baltimore County, Md. White was educated in the public schools of his native town and at West Virginia University, from which he was graduated in 1872. Soon after, he entered upon a graduate course in geology at Columbia University but abandoned it in 1877 on being called to the chair of geology at West Virginia University. He held this position un-

til 1892, devoting his vacations for some years to field work for the state survey in the coal and oil fields of Pennsylvania. In 1892 he entered private business, and in 1897 was appointed superintendent of the newly organized geological survey of West Virginia, for the establishment of which he had been largely responsible. This position he continued to hold during the remaining thirty years of his life, refusing after the first two years to accept a salary. From 1884 to 1888 he served also as assistant geologist on the United States Geological Survey and prepared a report on the "Stratigraphy of the Bituminous Coal Field of Pennsylvania, Ohio, and West Virginia," which was published as *Bulletin 65* (1891) of that organization. This is said to have been the foundation for nearly all subsequent work in the bituminous fields of Pennsylvania and West Virginia. As head of the West Virginia survey, White supervised the preparation of a complete set of topographic maps, covering the entire state, as well as thirty-four geological reports, of which he himself wrote two on oil and three on coal. These reports were largely of an economic nature, but full of detailed stratigraphy.

White's early work in Pennsylvania was accurate and painstaking in the extreme. In doing it he laid, unconsciously perhaps, the foundation for his future discoveries. His most important work, upon which his reputation largely depends and which put him foremost among the petroleum geologists of the world, was his "anticlinal theory" of oil and gas, formulated about 1883. Pointing out that all large gas wells in Pennsylvania and West Virginia were situated either directly on or near the crowns of anticlinal axes, he drew the conclusion that a direct relation existed between gas territory and the disturbance in the rocks caused by their upheaval into arches (*Bulletin of the Geological Society of America,* vol. III, 1892, pp. 204–14). Gifted with shrewd business sense, White made large investments in "wildcat" leases, and thereby not merely proved his theory but gained a substantial competence. In 1904–06 he served as chief geologist of the Brazilian Coal Commission, making a first-hand official report on the coal fields of the southern part of the republic, which was published in both Portuguese and English. At the White House conference in May 1908, he delivered an address on "The Waste of Our Fuel Resources," which had much to do with the subsequent conservation movement.

He was a genial, kindly man, modest and unassuming. His standard of honor was high, and, though he was himself a commercial man, he would never throughout his long career as superintendent of the survey allow himself to be drawn into expert private work within the limits of his own state lest it bring criticism upon his organization. He was president of the West Virginia and Morgantown Board of Trade, director and president of the Farmers' and Merchants' Bank, president of the Morgantown Brick Company, and connected with other business organizations. Public-spirited to an eminent degree and active in civic affairs, he was actively concerned with the Monongalia county hospital and the tuberculosis sanitarium, giving his time as well as funds. One of his largest single contributions was the gift of 1,900 acres of coal lands to the city of Morgantown and West Virginia University. He was one of the founders of the Geological Society of America, its treasurer (1892–1906), and its president in 1920. He was married three times: first on July 27, 1872, to Emily McClane Shane of Morgantown, W. Va., who died in 1874, leaving one child; second on Dec. 4, 1878, to Mary Moorhead, by whom he had five children; third on Feb. 12, 1925, to Mrs. Julia Posten Wildman, who survived him. He died at the Johns Hopkins hospital in Baltimore of a cerebral hemorrhage after an apparently successful operation.

[*Who's Who in America*, 1926–27; D. B. Reger, in *Black Diamond* (Chicago), Dec. 10, 1927; Charles Keyes, in *Pan-Am. Geologist*, Feb. 1928; obituaries in *Wheeling Reg.* and *Sun* (Baltimore), Nov. 26, 1927; personal acquaintance.]   G. P. M.

WHITE, JAMES (1747–Aug. 14, 1821), soldier, pioneer, legislator, was born in Rowan (later Iredell) County, N. C., the son of Irish parents, Moses and Mary (McConnell) White. On Apr. 14, 1770, he married Mary, daughter of Hugh Lawson. They became the parents of seven children, of whom the most noted was Hugh Lawson White [*q.v.*]. During the Revolution James White served as captain of militia, 1779–81. After the passage in 1783 of the act by which the State of North Carolina granted lands to Revolutionary soldiers, White, with Robert Love, Francis Ramsay, and others, began an exploration on the French Broad and Holston rivers, seeking the most advantageous region in which to locate their claims. Upon his return home, he made preparations to remove to the country which he had visited. He first moved to Fort Chiswell, where he remained for a year; in 1785 he went on to the north bank of the French Broad, and in 1786 settled at the present site of Knoxville, Tenn.

White served in the convention (1785) which considered the ratification of the constitution prepared for the abortive State of Franklin and in 1789 was sent by the voters of Hawkins County to the North Carolina House of Commons and also to the convention which ratified the Constitution of the United States. In 1790 William Blount [*q.v.*], governor of the Territory Southwest of the Ohio, appointed him justice of the peace and major of the militia. The following year White's Fort was made the seat of the territorial government, and in 1792, when Knox County was established, White was made lieutenant-colonel of the county militia. In the same year he laid out at White's Fort the town of Knoxville and sold lots for residence. He directed the defense of the town during the Indian troubles of 1793. In 1796 he served in the convention which drew up the constitution for the State of Tennessee and was elected to represent Knox County in the Senate of the new state. The next year that body elevated him to the speakership, but he resigned to permit the election of William Blount after the latter had been expelled from the United States Senate. Blount and John Sevier [*q.v.*] were his intimate friends, and he supported the policies of each of these men in the administration of the affairs of the territory and of the state. In 1798 Sevier appointed him to represent Tennessee in the first treaty of Tellico, with the Indians, and during his public life he played an important part in Indian affairs. He presided over the state Senate in 1801 and again in 1803. In the late nineties he was commissioned brigadier-general of the state militia and participated in the Creek War 1813 with that rank, serving under the command of Gen. John H. Cocke [*q.v.*].

White was a sturdy pioneer, a substantial citizen, and a powerful influence in the councils of the commonwealth, to which he gave a long life of service. He belonged to the Presbyterian Church and donated land for a house of worship in Knoxville. He was also the donor of the site for Blount College, later the University of Tennessee, and was one of the trustees named in its charter (1794). He died at Knoxville and was buried in the yard of the First Presbyterian Church.

[S. C. Williams, *Hist. of the Lost State of Franklin* (1924); J. T. Moore and A. P. Foster, *Tennessee, the Volunteer State* (1923), vols. I, II; J. M. G. Ramsey, *The Annals of Tenn.* (1853); John Haywood, *The Civil and Political Hist. of the State of Tenn.* (1823); F. Mellon, "General James White," in scrapbook of clippings, Tenn. State Lib.; Nancy N. Scott, *A Memoir of Hugh Lawson White* (1856).]   C. S. D.

WHITE, JAMES CLARKE (July 7, 1833–Jan. 5, 1916), dermatologist, was born in Belfast, Me., the fifth of seven children of James Patterson and Mary Ann (Clarke) White. The White family originally emigrated to America from the north of Ireland; one of them, William, with other Ulster folk, founded Londonderry, N. H., in 1725, and another, Robert, Belfast, Me. White's father, a ship-owner, served as mayor of Belfast. White was graduated from Harvard College in 1853 and from the Medical School in 1856. At the suggestion of Calvin Ellis [q.v.], he chose Vienna instead of Paris for his postgraduate work, one of the first American medical students to do so; he was most influenced there by Ferdinand von Hebra, the dermatologist. On returning to Boston, he became an instructor in chemistry in the Harvard Medical School (1858–63) and later adjunct professor of chemistry (1866–71). By 1860, however, he had established, with Benjamin Joy Jeffries [q.v.], the first dermatological clinic in the country. In 1865 he began a long association with the Massachusetts General Hospital, his department of dermatology being ultimately recognized in 1870. In 1871 a chair of dermatology was created for him in the Harvard Medical School, the first of its kind to be established in the United States. This he held until 1902. As a pioneer teacher of dermatology, White was without equal. His fame, at first local, in the end became international. He was one of the founders of the American Dermatological Association in 1876, and served as its first president (1877–87). Dermatological societies throughout the world made him an honorary or a corresponding member. In 1907 he was chosen president of the Sixth International Dermatological Congress, the highest honor that could come to a man in his special field of work. He wrote many valuable scientific papers and one book, *Dermatitis Venenata* (1887), a sound contribution to a then little-known subject.

In addition to his interest in dermatology, White was, from his college days, a student of comparative anatomy and natural history. He became a member of the Boston Society of Natural History in 1856 and served as curator of comparative anatomy for a period of ten years (1859–69). He found much pleasure in mounting skeletons of animals and in collecting an herbarium of wild flowers of New England. He was a member of the American Academy of Arts and Sciences, and president of the Massachusetts Medical Society in 1892. From 1866 on, he was an ardent leader in the reform of medical education. By editorials in the *Boston Medical and Surgical Journal* (of which he was editor, 1867–71) and by public addresses, he spoke plainly in behalf of reform at every opportunity. Many of his ideas, then considered revolutionary, were adopted by the Harvard Medical School

when Charles W. Eliot [q.v.] became president in 1869.

Tall in stature and gracious in appearance, White was an effective speaker and by his presence in various official positions did much to put the subject of dermatology on a sound basis in America. On Nov. 5, 1862, he was married to Martha Anna Ellis, daughter of Jonathan Ellis of Boston. Of three sons, one became a dermatologist in Boston. Towards the close of his life White wrote *Sketches from My Life* (1914), a valuable autobiography.

[The principal source is J. C. White, *Sketches from My Life* (1914), with bibliog. See also *Who's Who in America*, 1916–17; *Report of the Harvard Class of 1853* (1913); T. F. Harrington, *The Harvard Medic. School* (1905), vol. III; *Boston Medic. and Surgical Jour.*, Jan. 20, 1916; Abner Post, *Ibid.*, July 20, 1916; F. C. Shattuck, *Proc. Am. Acad. Arts and Sciences*, vol. LII (1917); Sir Malcolm Morris, in *British Jour. Dermatology*, Jan.–Mar. 1916; *Dermatologische Wochenschrift*, July 8, 1916; *Harvard Grads.' Mag.*, Mar. 1916; obituary in *Boston Transcript*, Jan. 6, 1916.]

H. R. V.

WHITE, JAMES WILLIAM (Nov. 2, 1850– Apr. 24, 1916), surgeon, was born in Philadelphia, Pa., the son of Dr. James William White and Mary Ann (McClaranan) White, and a nephew of Samuel Stockton White [q.v.]. He was descended from the Rev. Henry White who emigrated from England about 1649 and settled in Virginia. White lived and died in Philadelphia, attending first the public schools, then a Quaker private school, from which he entered the medical department of the University of Pennsylvania. He also matriculated in the department auxiliary to medicine, pursuing both courses simultaneously, and in 1871 was graduated with the degrees of M.D. and Ph.D. In the summer of the same year he secured an appointment as analytical chemist with a scientific expedition under the leadership of J. L. R. Agassiz [q.v.], and set out in the *Hassler* for a year's cruise to the West Indies and the east coast of South America, through the Straits of Magellan, and up the west coast of South America and Central America to San Francisco. Years later he visited China and adjacent countries. Upon his return from the South American trip he became a resident physician at the Philadelphia Hospital (1873) and then resident physician at the Eastern State Penitentiary (1874–76), where he interested himself in the study of crime and the mentality of criminals. In 1876 he became attached to the surgical staff of the hospital of the University of Pennsylvania and soon began to lecture on genito-urinary diseases in the medical department of the university. He was professor of clinical surgery (1887–1900) and in

1900 succeeded John Ashhurst [*q.v.*] as John Rhea Barton Professor of Surgery. As a teacher he was clear, concise, and interesting, though rarely inspiring. He resigned the professorship of surgery in 1911, to be made professor emeritus, a trustee of the university, and a manager of the university hospital. He was a president of the University Athletic Association and for a long time dominated it. He was also a commissioner of Fairmount Park, a member of numerous professional associations, and for a quarter of a century an editor of *Annals of Surgery* (1892–1916).

Though he wrote many papers, his most important work was his *Genito-Urinary Surgery and Venereal Diseases* (1897), written in collaboration with Edward Martin. With W. W. Keen he edited *An American Text-Book of Surgery* (1892), and with J. H. C. Simes translated a treatise on syphilis (1882) by A. V. Cornil. He believed that one of his important contributions to surgery was the operation of castration for treatment of hypertrophy of the prostate, but the method is no longer practised. During the World War he wrote *A Primer of the War for Americans* (1914), later called *A Text-Book of the War for Americans,* and *America's Arraignment of Germany* (1915), which set forth arguments for America's entrance into the war on the side of the Allies. In Paris, where he had gone to assist in the organization of the American ambulance unit, he began to notice the first signs of osteitis deformans, from which he suffered until he died of pneumonia in April 1916.

In his early days White was an enthusiastic athlete, a great swimmer, a skilled boxer, a member of Alpine clubs, and a rollicking good fellow known to all his friends and students as "Bill White." He was a gay young surgeon to the 1st City Troop (1878–88), a *bon viveur,* and spent much of his time at social clubs. In the latter third of his life, however, there occurred a sudden change both in his philosophy and in his behavior, said to be the result of a circumstance affecting the private life of a friend, which led him to give up many of his pleasures and take a more responsible attitude toward human affairs. He was married on June 22, 1888, to Letitia (Brown) Disston, daughter of Benjamin H. Brown of Philadelphia (*Philadelphia Press,* June 23, 1888). There were no children.

[W. F. Cregar, *Ancestry of the Children of James William White, M.D.* (1888); *Who's Who in America,* 1916–17; Agnes Repplier, *J. William White, M.D.* (1919); *Alumni Reg. Univ. of Pa.,* June 1918, p. 811; A. C. Wood, in *Surgery, Gynecology and Obstetrics,* Nov. 1922; *Trans. Am. Surgical Asso.,* vol. XXXIV (1916); *Annals of Surgery,* June 1916; Alfred Stengel, in *Am. Medic. Biogs.* (1920), ed. by H. A. Kelly and W. L. Burrage; obituary in *Pub. Ledger* (Phila.), Apr. 25, 1916; personal acquaintance.] J.M.

WHITE, JOHN (fl. 1585–1593), artist, cartographer, and governor of Sir Walter Raleigh's "second colonie" at Roanoke, was probably born in England. Though the written records of his life are limited to fragmentary and frequently uncertain accounts, he left a charming and important series of paintings, done in water colors, which prove him to have been an artist of no mean ability and constitute his chief claim to fame. In the collection are several studies of native life in Florida, Greenland, and the Caucasus, which, if they are his original work rather than copies from other artists, as may be possible, prove that he was already an experienced traveler by 1585. He was commissioned by Raleigh to go with the expedition of that year to Roanoke Island, now in North Carolina, to provide pictures of life in the new world that might stimulate interest in further ventures. Scientific paintings of the flora and fauna of America, as well as of the customs and habits of the native Indians, comprise the major portion of his surviving paintings. At least sixty-three of the paintings were probably done from life in America. They become, therefore, some of the earliest and most valuable of the material for the study of the natural history and aboriginal life of this continent. Twenty-three of his paintings, including two not found among the originals, were engraved by Theodore de Bry for an edition in 1590 of Thomas Hariot's *A Briefe and True Report of . . . Virginia.* He included also adaptations of two maps by White of the Virginia coast, which for half a century thereafter greatly influenced geographers in their delineations of the coastline south of the Chesapeake Bay. White's paintings of natives were used, copied, redrawn, mutilated, and reinterpreted so that for some three centuries they conditioned all pictorial representation of the American Indians.

In 1587 a John White was sent by Raleigh to be governor of his second colony in Virginia. That John White reëstablished the colony of Roanoke. It has been customary to identify the artist as one and the same with this governor, though the identification has lacked satisfactory proof. Strong support for this thesis is provided by the discovery, in the manuscript for Thomas Moffett's *Insectorum* (1634) in the British Museum, that an illustration of White's "Tiger Swallow Tail Butterfly" bore in that manuscript copy the illuminating inscription "*Hanc è Virginiâ Americanâ Candidus ad me Pictor detulit 1587.*" Since the governor was the only known White to have gone out on that expedition, the fact that *"Candidus Pictor"* returned from Virginia in that year with this picture makes possible a reasonably positive identification of the painter and governor as one (for full discussion see Adams, *post*).

He probably went back to England with Grenville in 1585, to return to Virginia as governor in July 1587. Among the settlers of this expedition was his own daughter, Ellinor, who became the mother of Virginia Dare [*q.v.*], the first child of English parentage born in America. The governor's judgment as a leader was apparently not commensurate with his skill as a painter, for he was persuaded late in August to return to England for provisions. The war with Spain interrupted his plans for the colony's relief, and it was August 1590 before he arrived back at Roanoke. The colony had disappeared. Denied time to make a really effective search, he returned home leaving its fate a mystery to this day. From his "house at Newtowne in Kylmore," Ireland, in February 1593 he sent Hakluyt an account of this his "fift & last voiage to Virginia" (Hakluyt, *post*, p. 288).

[Original paintings in British Museum, 75 undoubted originals, also copies in Sloane MSS.; 63 modern hand-tinted photostats of originals in Wm. L. Clements Lib., Ann Arbor, Mich.; excellent reproductions with important essays by Laurence Binyon, "The Drawings of John White," *Thirteenth Vol. of the Walpole Soc.* (1925); Laurence Binyon, *Cat. of Drawings by Brit. Artists ... in the British Museum*, vol. IV (1907); P. L. Phillips, *Va. Cartography* (1896); R. G. Adams, "An Effort to Identify John White," *Am. Hist. Rev.*, Oct. 1935 with bibliography; original narratives in Richard Hakluyt, *The Third and Last Vol. of the Voyages, Navigations ... of the English Nation* (1600); *D. N. B.*]
W.F.C.

WHITE, JOHN BLAKE (Sept. 2, 1781–*c.* Aug. 24, 1859), artist, dramatist, and lawyer, was born near Eutaw Springs, S. C., the son of Blake Leay and Elizabeth (Bourquin) White. He was a descendant of John White who emigrated from Ireland to New England, probably about 1681. White began the study of law in Columbia, S. C., but in 1800 went to London to study painting under Benjamin West [*q.v.*]. On his return to America in November 1803, he made an unsuccessful attempt to establish himself as an artist, first in Charleston, then in Boston (1804). In November 1804 he returned to Charleston, where he resumed his legal studies and in 1808 was admitted to the bar. With the exception of a short period about 1831, when he lived at Columbia, he remained in Charleston for the rest of his life. Continuing his painting in addition to practising law, he produced between 1804 and 1840 a number of historical pictures and portraits. Among the best known of the former are four in the Capitol at Washing-

ton: "Battle of Fort Moultrie," "Mrs. Motte Directing Marion and Lee to Burn Her Mansion to Dislodge the British," "General Marion Inviting a British Officer to Dinner," and "Sargents Jasper and Newton Rescuing American Prisoners from the British." Large steel engravings were made of the last two, which were also engraved respectively for the ten and five dollar banknotes issued by South Carolina in 1861. Other paintings by White of which record is preserved are "Battle of Eutaw Springs," "Battle of New Orleans," "Minister Poinsett Unfurling the United States Flag in the City of Mexico during the Mexican Riots," "The Arrival of the Mail," showing the old post office building, Broad Street, Charleston (now in the City Hall, Charleston). His "Grave Robbers" was exhibited in the Boston Athenaeum in 1833 and described in a catalogue issued at that time. In 1840 he received from the South Carolina Institute a gold medal for the best historical painting. Among his most important portraits are those of John C. Calhoun, still in the possession of the Calhoun family, Charles C. Pinckney, Keating Simons, and Gov. Henry Middleton. He also painted miniatures, one of which is in the possession of descendants living in Charleston. In addition, he wrote a number of plays that were acted in the theatres of Charleston and other cities. Among these were *Foscari, or the Venetian Exile* (1806), *The Mysteries of the Castle* (1807), *Modern Honor* (1812), *The Triumph of Liberty, or Louisiana Preserved* (1819), which is said to have been enacted in the theatre of Petersburg, Va., *Intemperance* (1839), and *The Forgers; A Dramatic Poem* (1899), first printed in the *Southern Literary Journal*, March 1837.

White was married twice. His first wife, whom he met in Boston, was Elizabeth Allston, a relative of Washington Allston [*q.v.*]. They were married in Georgetown, S. C., on Mar. 28, 1805, and had three sons and a daughter. After his first wife's death (1817), he was married on Oct. 2, 1819, to Ann Rachel, daughter of Dr. Matthew O'Driscoll who emigrated from Ireland to South Carolina in 1794. By his second wife (d. 1849) White had five sons and two daughters. One of his sons, Edward Brickell (1806–1882), was a graduate of the United States Military Academy, and a prominent architect and engineer. A portrait bust of White by Clark Mills [*q.v.*] is in the City Hall, Charleston, S. C. An engraved portrait is in the possession of the White family.

[Mabel L. Webber, "Records from Blake and White Bibles," *S. C. Hist. and Geneal. Mag.*, Jan., Apr., July, Oct. 1935, Jan., Apr. 1936; William Dunlap, *A Hist. of the Rise and Progress of the Arts of Design in the*

U. S. (3 vols., 1918), ed. by F. W. Bayley and C. E. Goodspeed, and *Hist. of the Am. Theatre* (2 vols., 1833) ; A. H. Quinn, *A Hist. of the Am. Drama . . . to the Civil War* (1923) ; C. E. Fairman, *Art and Artists of the Capitol of the U. S. A.* (1927) ; *Southern Lit. Jour.,* June, July 1837 ; biog. sketch of Charles Fraser in Fraser Gallery, Charleston ; obituary in *Charleston Daily Courier,* Aug. 25, 1859 ; family records ; information from Anna Wells Rutledge, Charleston, S. C.]

L. M.

WHITE, JOHN DE HAVEN (Aug. 19, 1815–Dec. 25, 1895), dentist, a son of John and Sarah (De Haven) White, was born on a farm near New Holland, Lancaster County, Pa., and received his earliest education in a rural school. When he was seven years old, both of his parents died, and he was bound out to a farmer, a hard taskmaster, from whom he shortly ran away. He served next as a carpenter's apprentice for several years, and at the same time acquired a good preliminary education. In 1836 he began the study of both medicine and dentistry in Philadelphia, the former as a student of James Bryan, M.D., and the latter under the preceptorship of Michael A. Blankman. Shortly thereafter he devoted himself exclusively to dentistry, at first for a few months in Middletown and Bethlehem, Pa. In 1837 he returned to Philadelphia, where he practised as a dentist till a few years before his death. He was graduated from the Jefferson Medical College in 1844.

He was a skilful and successful practitioner, and one of the most enthusiastic leaders of his day in the advancement of dental education. Early in his professional career, Samuel Stockton White and Thomas Wiltberger Evans [*qq.v.*] were among his private students. It is said that Napoleon III invited him in 1865 to join Evans in forming a national dental school in Paris, and that the invitation was declined. Beginning shortly after he entered practice, a few of the progressive dentists of Philadelphia, under his leadership, met on fixed dates for the interchange of professional knowledge and experience. These informal meetings led to the organization, in 1845, of the Pennsylvania Association of Dental Surgeons, in which he took a leading part, serving as its president in 1857. In 1850 he became a member of the American Society of Dental Surgeons and was one of the organizers of the Philadelphia College of Dental Surgery (first session, 1852), in which he was professor of anatomy and physiology (1854–56), and of operative dental surgery and special dental physiology (1854–56). From 1853 to 1859 he was editor-in-chief of the *Dental News Letter,* and from 1859 to 1865 one of the editors of the *Dental Cosmos.* To these and to other dental periodicals he contributed some ninety articles on a wide variety of dental subjects, mostly of a practical character (1845–75). He was vice-president of the American Dental Convention in 1861. Among his later dental students were Charles and Elwood Hopkins and Robert Huey. Theodore F. Chupein was his assistant in practice in 1865 and 1866.

He was a large man of extraordinary physical and mental vigor, constitutionally convivial, fond of literature and music, but bluff and aggressive, with strong prejudices on professional and other subjects. He loved horses and was often in the saddle. One of his chief pleasures from early youth was the writing of verses. Two of his favorite horses are named in the title to a volume of poems which he published in 1870, *Mary Blain and Hazel Dell, and Miscellaneous Poems.* He was prominent in Masonry and spent the last few years of his life in the Masonic Home in Philadelphia, where he died of heart disease in his eighty-first year. In 1836 he married Mary Elizabeth Meredith of Philadelphia (d. July 1895). They had eleven children, of whom two sons, both practising dentists, and a daughter survived them.

[*International Dental Jour.,* Feb. 1896, p. 129 ; *Dental Cosmos,* Apr. 1896, p. 363 ; B. L. Thorpe, in *Hist. of Dental Surgery,* vol. III (1910), ed. by C. R. E. Koch; obituary in *Pub. Ledger* (Phila.), Dec. 26, 1895.]

L. P. B.

WHITE, JOHN WILLIAMS (Mar. 5, 1849– May 9, 1917), Hellenist, was born at Cincinnati, Ohio. His parents were the Rev. John Whitney White, a descendant of John White who settled in Salem in 1638 and Anna Catharine, daughter of Judge Hosea Williams. From New England ancestors, among whom were Governor Carver, Isaac Allerton, Thomas Cushman, and John Webster, he inherited marked energy and independence, combined with a pioneering zeal which inspired him throughout his life to take the initiative in many academic enterprises. He graduated from Ohio Wesleyan University in 1868. On June 20, 1871, he married Mary Alice, daughter of Picton Drayton Hillyer of Delaware, Ohio. After studying in Germany and visiting Greece, he published (1873) an edition of Sophocles' *Oedipus Tyrannus,* which immediately sprang into favor, and led to his appointment as tutor in Greek at Harvard (1874–77). At the same time he continued his studies in the Graduate School, then in its modest beginnings, and received the degree of Ph.D. and A.M. in classical philology (1877) and appointment to an assistant professorship, which he held until his election as professor of Greek in 1884. There followed twenty-five years of vigorous service, in which he rose to prominence as an aid to President Charles W.

Eliot [q.v.] in the expansion of the provincial college into a national university. An article in the *New-England Journal of Education* (Feb. 14, 1878) on "Greek and Latin at Sight" broke completely from older methods of teaching by its insistence on wide and rapid reading. He carried out the principles he had laid down by many courses in Greek authors, of which those in Herodotus and Aristophanes were the most notable. He early interested himself in Greek metres, and in 1878 brought out a translation of J. H. H. Schmidt's *Leitfaden in der Rhythmik und Metrik der classischen Sprachen* (1869). This book, useful at a time when Greek metres were little studied in England and America, was superseded by White's later researches. In 1879 he founded, with Lewis Packard and T. D. Seymour [q.v.] of Yale, the College Series of Greek Authors, with commentary suitable for American students. He was the first to use the stereopticon for the illustration of Greek civilization. He seems also to have been the first to conceive the project of reviving in America Greek plays in Greek, and with his colleagues produced *Oedipus Tyrannus* in Cambridge in 1881. With C. E. Norton and W. W. Goodwin [qq.v.] he organized (1879) the Archaeological Institute of America, and was its president for five years, and later its honorary president. In 1881 he became the first chairman of the managing committee of the American School of Classical Studies at Athens, and served as its professor of Greek literature during the academic year 1893–94. He published many textbooks distinguished for their lucidity and an uncommon sense of the capacities of younger students—among them *First Lessons in Greek* (1876); *Four Books of Xenophon's Anabasis* (1877), with W. W. Goodwin; *Notes on the Birds of Aristophanes* (1888); and *The Beginner's Greek Book* (1891).

Meanwhile his activity as an administrative officer was unceasing. He established for his own department a bureau for teachers, which later became the appointment office for the entire university. An ardent sportsman, horseman, and tennis player, he became in 1882 a member of the first committee appointed to regulate athletic sports and served as its chairman for several years. With J. B. Greenough [q.v.] he founded, and for many years assisted in editing, the *Harvard Studies in Classical Philology*. To it he contributed articles, as also to *Classical Quarterly* (London), *Classical Philology* (Chicago), and 'Εφημερὶς 'Αρχαιολογική (Athens).

In the classroom he was alert and inspiring, exacting rigorous accuracy, but kindly and sympathetic in correction. Many students in financial stress were helped by his unostentatious generosity. Affable and courtly toward all, he maintained close friendships with scholars of other universities, both in America and abroad. His influence on at least one distinguished pupil, James Loeb, may be measured in the Loeb Classical Library, in the establishment of which he took a foremost part. Grieved though he was by the decline of Greek studies in American schools and colleges, he was willing to recognize the trend of the times, and against the opposition even of his friends he introduced a collegiate course for beginners in Greek, and another on the Greek drama in English translations. Frequent visits in Europe made him sensible of the value of older civilizations, while at the same time he never lost contact or sympathy with the liberal and progressive movements in America.

At the age of sixty he resigned his professorship in order to devote himself exclusively to his studies in Greek comedy. He projected, but did not live to make, an edition of Aristophanes in ten volumes. As a preliminary, he published *The Verse of Greek Comedy* (London, 1912) and *The Scholia on the Aves of Aristophanes* (1914). The latter includes a masterly history of Alexandrian scholarship. These two works place him in the front rank of authorities on Aristophanes and, through Aristophanes, Greek life in general. He died at Cambridge, May 9, 1917.

[A. L. White, *Geneal. of the Descendants of John White of Wenham* (4 vols., 1900–09); *Who's Who in America*, 1916–17; *Nation*, May 17, June 21, 1917; *Harvard Alumni Bull.*, vol. XIX (1917), pp. 628–29, with early portrait; G. H. Chase, in *Harvard Grads. Mag.*, Sept. 1917, with later portrait; *Harvard Univ. Gazette*, June 9, 1917, pp. 177–78; S. E. Morison, *The Development of Harvard Univ. . . . 1869–1929* (1930); obituaries in *N. Y. Times* and *Boston Transcript*, May 10, 1917; personal acquaintance.]   C. B. G.

WHITE, RICHARD GRANT (May 23, 1821–Apr. 8, 1885), man of letters, was born in New York, eldest of the five children of Richard Mansfield and Ann Eliza (Tousey) White, and seventh in descent from John White, a follower of Thomas Hooker [q.v.] and one of the founders of Cambridge, Mass., Hartford, Conn., and Hadley, Mass. His father was a prosperous South Street merchant, a prominent Episcopalian of the Low Church party, and an official of the Allaire Iron Works. The boy grew up in Brooklyn, attended the Grammar School of Columbia College, then conducted by Charles Anthon [q.v.], and was admitted to the junior class in the University of the City of New York when but sixteen years old. As a student he was notoriously averse to writing. Music was a passion with him, but his desire to become a professional musician was thwarted by his parents. Upon his graduation in 1839 he began the study of medicine, turned to the law, and was called to the bar in 1845. The next year he helped Cornelius Mathews [q.v.] to edit a short-lived humorous paper, Yanke. Doodle, and made other spare-time ventures into journalism. When his father's fortune collapsed, leaving White to support two unmarried sisters, he turned to writing for a livelihood. As musical critic of James Watson Webb's Morning Courier and New-York Enquirer, then edited by Henry Jarvis Raymond [q.v.], he immediately attained distinction in his new profession. On Oct. 16, 1850, he married Alexina Black Mease, who with two sons, Richard Mansfield and Stanford [q.v.], survived him.

White remained on the Courier staff until 1859, writing musical, art, and literary criticism, and numerous political articles and editorials. During the Civil War he was secretary of the Metropolitan Sanitary Fair and, after a brief connection with the World, was appointed chief clerk of the marine revenue bureau of the New York Custom House (1861–78). Throughout his career he wrote voluminously for periodicals, especially for Putnam's Magazine, the Galaxy, and the Atlantic Monthly. To the London Spectator he contributed useful articles during the Civil War. Among his separate publications were: Handbook of Christian Art (1853); Shakespeare's Scholar (1854); The New Gospel of Peace (4 vols., 1863–66), a mordant, widely circulated satire on "Copperheads"; The Adventures of Sir Lyon Bouse, Bart., in America during the Civil War (1867); Words and Their Uses (1870), witty, influential, and often unsound; Every-day English (1880), a sequel; England Without and Within (1881); The Fate of Mansfield Humphreys (1884), a belated, unsuccessful, but amusing attempt at a novel; and Studies in Shakespeare (1886). He was an acute, learned, and sometimes brilliant student of Shakespeare, one of the first to detect the spuriousness of J. P. Collier's forgeries, and with a little more leisure and a happier geographical situation might have been one of Shakespeare's great editors. His edition, in twelve volumes, of The Works of William Shakespeare (1857–66) was published just as the Cambridge Edition (1863–66) of W. G. Clark, John Glover, and W. A. Wright began a new epoch in the history of the text, and its merits have been consequently obscured. White's text was republished as the Riverside Shakespeare (3 vols., 1883) and was the basis of a revised edition, in eighteen volumes, by W. P. Trent, B. W. Wells, and J. B. Henneman, that was issued in 1912.

White was six feet two inches tall, erect, athletic, and handsome, and until the last years of his life enjoyed robust health. His senses were remarkably acute and his enjoyment of beauty intense. He revered the memory of his forebears, especially of his grandfather, Calvin White, a gentleman of stout Tory principles, on whom, to some extent, he patterned his own character. Francis James Child, James Russell Lowell, and Charles Eliot Norton [qq.v.] were his friends, but he shunned the commonplace literary and journalistic society of New York. The usual representation of him as a disagreeable, humorless snob, coxcomb, and Anglomaniac was a caricature of a high-minded gentleman and an accomplished man of letters. Uncomplainingly he lived his entire life in a city that he detested, earning his living by toilsome, uncongenial occupations. He traveled hardly at all in America, visited England—the land of his admiration—only once, and then when he was past his fifty-fifth birthday, and never saw the continent of Europe. Music, Shakespeare, and the art of violin construction were his three great solaces. He died at his home in New York after a long illness, in his sixty-fourth year.

[Sources include A. S. Kellogg, Memorials of Elder John White, . . . and of His Descendants (1860); A. A. Freeman, "Richard Grant White," New York Univ. Quart., May 1881; E. P. Whipple, "Richard Grant White," Atlantic Monthly, Feb. 1882; "A Shakespearean Scholar," Ibid., Mar. 1886; F. P. Church, "Richard Grant White," Ibid., Mar. 1891; N. Y. Times, Apr. 9, 1885; H. E. Scudder, James Russell Lowell (1901); Laura Stedman and G. M. Gould, Life and Letters of Edmund Clarence Stedman (1910). On his edition of Shakespeare see: J. R. Lowell, in Atlantic Monthly, Jan., Feb. 1859; Jane Sherzer, "Am. Editions of Shakespeare, 1753–1866," Pubs. Modern Language Asso. of America, Dec. 1907; H. R. Steeves, "Am. Editors of Shakspeare," Shaksperian Studies by Members of the Dept. of Eng. and Comp. Lit. in Columbia Univ. (1916).]
G. H. G.

WHITE, SAMUEL (December 1770–Nov. 4, 1809), lawyer, United States senator, was born on a farm in Mispillion Hundred, Kent County, Del., the son of Thomas and Margaret (Nutter) White. His mother was a daughter of David Nutter of Northwest Fork Hundred, Sussex County, Del., his father was possessed of a considerable estate, and from 1777 to 1792 served as one of the justices of the court of common pleas and orphans' court of Kent County. In 1777 he met Francis Asbury [q.v.], who converted him to Methodism. In his journal, Asbury referred to Judge White as his "dearest friend in America." The first conference of Methodist preachers, at which Asbury was appointed first general superintendent of Methodism in America, was held in White's house on Apr. 28, 1779.

Samuel White was sent to the first Methodist

institution of higher learning in America, the recently established Cokesbury College in Harford County, Md., but was not graduated, since the school had no power to confer degrees. About 1790 he began to read law in the office of Richard Bassett [q.v.] at Dover, but since his preceptor was absent much of the time attending sessions of Congress, he transferred to the office of Nicholas Hammond at Easton, Md. He was admitted to the Delaware bar in March 1793 and settled in Dover to practice. Although he gained some reputation as an advocate, he early showed an aversion to routine and when war threatened between France and the United States in 1799, he sought a commission as captain, raised a company, and as a part of Colonel Ogden's regiment, was posted with his command at Scotch Plains, N. J., until disbanded in 1800.

Upon his return to civilian life, White resumed the practice of law at Dover, and in 1800 was chosen a presidential elector. Upon the resignation of Henry Latimer as United States senator, Gov. Richard Bassett in February 1801 appointed White to the vacancy; he was elected by the legislature to serve until the end of the term, and through reëlections retained his seat in the Senate until his death. A Federalist in politics, he often opposed the policies of Jefferson and his party. On Jan. 11, 1802, he spoke against the Apportionment Bill which allowed the state of Delaware only one member in the House of Representatives. On Feb. 22, 1803, he opposed the appropriation for a diplomatic mission to negotiate for the cession of New Orleans and the Floridas, and the next day in a long speech advocated the seizure of New Orleans by force. In November he resisted the appropriation for the purchase of the Louisiana territory, and a month later strenuously opposed the adoption by the Senate of the Twelfth Amendment to the Constitution, relative to the election of the president and vice-president. Although he did not speak often and "in desultory debate was not distinguished" (Bayard, *post*) he prepared his speeches for extraordinary occasions with great care and delivered them effectively. Although "inclined to indolence," he would work hard to make himself master of a subject when stimulated by a "sufficient motive to industry." He was better fitted, however, for the active life of a military man in time of war than for the civil pursuits of peace. His interest in military affairs was rewarded by appointment on Sept. 21, 1807, as adjutant-general of the state militia. He died some two years later in Wilmington, and was buried in "Old Swedes" churchyard. He never married.

[Letter from J. A. Bayard to William Turner, June 27, 1811, in Del. State Archives, Dover; *Governor's Register, State of Delaware*, vol. I (1926); H. C. Conrad, "Samuel White and His Father" (1903), in *Hist. and Biog. Papers, Hist. Soc. of Del.*, vol. IV; *Biog. Dir. Am. Cong.* (1928); H. C. Conrad, *Hist. of the State of Del.* (1908), vol. III; *Poulson's Am. Daily Advertiser* (Phila.), Nov. 8, 1809.]
                         G. H. R.

WHITE, SAMUEL STOCKTON (June 19, 1822–Dec. 30, 1879), manufacturer of dental supplies, was born at Hulmeville, Bucks County, Pa., the eldest child of William Rose and Mary (Stockton) White. His father was a descendant of Henry White who settled in Virginia about 1649; his mother, of Richard Stockton who emigrated from England to Flushing, N. Y., about 1656. His father died when he was eight years old (1830), and shortly afterward his mother removed with her children to her native town, Burlington, N. J. At the age of fourteen he was indentured to his maternal uncle, Samuel W. Stockton of Philadelphia, to learn "the art and mystery of dentistry and the manufacture of incorruptible porcelain teeth." While working with his uncle, he also studied dentistry under John De Haven White [q.v.], not a relative. Upon reaching his majority (1843), he began the practice of dentistry with his uncle Stockton, and superintended the latter's manufacturing business, which had then attained considerable commercial importance.

In 1844 he left his uncle, continued in the practice of dentistry for about a year, and at the same time began the manufacturing of artificial teeth, with a younger brother, James William White, also a dentist, as an assistant. In 1846 he relinquished practice and devoted himself to the manufacture of porcelain teeth, for some years in partnership with Asahel Jones and John R. McCurdy, the firm being successively Jones, White and Company (1847–52), Jones, White and McCurdy (1853–59), Jones and White (1859–61). James W. White was also connected intermittently with the firm. Its business was shortly expanded to include a general line of instruments and supplies for dentists, and flourished from the start. Branch houses, called "dental depots," for the sale of its products were established in New York (1846), Boston (1850), and Chicago (1858). After the withdrawal of McCurdy and Jones, White continued the business in his own name until his death. After his death, the business was conducted under the name of Samuel S. White until 1881, when it was incorporated as the S. S. White Dental Manufacturing Company, of which James W. White was president until his death in 1891. For three-quarters of a century the company was the largest in the world in the production of porcelain teeth, instruments, appliances, and supplies for dentists. The *Dental News Letter,* established by Jones, White and Company in 1847, was succeeded in 1859 by the *Dental Cosmos;* the latter, James W. White personally supervised from its beginning, and served as editor from 1872 until his death.

Samuel White is credited with various important improvements in porcelain teeth, which before his time were deficient in strength and appearance and in other respects. He introduced several new or improved dental chairs and engines, and numerous appliances, instruments, and materials for the dental office and laboratory. He encouraged dental inventors and was always interested in the advancement of the profession. He was a member of the Pennsylvania Association of Dental Surgeons, and served on the executive committee of the American Dental Convention in 1868. In 1872 he accepted the leadership in the legal struggle of the profession against the excessive license fees demanded by the Goodyear Dental Vulcanite Company for the use of vulcanized rubber in artificial dentures, on which they held patents. This involved him in numerous costly personal lawsuits, through which, after seven years of litigation, the Goodyear Company's patents were broken. In November 1879 he was stricken with congestion of the brain, probably as a result of mental strain. His physicians ordered rest in Europe, where he shortly contracted Russian influenza. He died in Paris in his fifty-eighth year, leaving an estate valued at about $1,500,000. He was married on Mar. 31, 1846, to Sarah Jane Carey, by whom he had seven children.

[W. F. Cregar, *Ancestry of Samuel Stockton White* (1888); T. C. Stockton, *Stockton Family of N. J. and Other Stocktons* (1911); *Eighty-two Years of Loyal Service to Dentistry* (1926), pub. by the S. S. White Dental Manufacturing Co.; B. L. Thorpe, in *Hist. of Dental Surgery,* vol. III (1910), ed. by C. R. E. Koch; *Dental Cosmos,* Feb. 1880, pp. 57–63; obituaries in *Press* (Phila.) and *Phila. Times,* Dec. 31, 1879, the latter reprinted *Am. Jour. Dental Sci.,* Jan. 1880, p. 429.]
L. P. B.

WHITE, STANFORD (Nov. 9, 1853–June 25, 1906), architect, was a descendant of John White who came to Cambridge, Mass., in 1632, was one of the early settlers of Hartford, Conn., and later moved to Hadley, Mass. Stanford and his elder brother, Richard Mansfield White, Jr., were born into a New York family in which music and literature were dominant and money a necessary evil. The father, Richard Grant White [*q.v.*], elegant gentleman, recognized Shakespeare scholar, keen and often vituperative critic, composer of music and accomplished 'cellist, made his home the gathering place for authors and musicians. The mother, Alexina

Black (Mease), born in Charleston, S. C., was a sympathetic, pervasive influence in the household. Between her and Stanford the companionship was so close that for twenty years after her husband's death (1885) her son's home was also hers.

The White family spent summers at Fort Hamilton on the Hudson. There Stanford developed such aptitude for drawing and water colors that he seemed destined to become an artist; but John La Farge [*q.v.*] dissuaded him, saying the rewards of an artist were meager and uncertain. So it came about that when nineteen years old, White without systematic training entered the architectural office of Gambrill & Richardson [see H. H. Richardson]. Richardson's slogan, that architecture is one of the fine arts and must be treated as such, especially appealed to White. Like Richardson, White grew into bigness of stature; the two were exuberant, jovial, kindly, discriminately fond of the table, and eminently companionable. For twelve years White served the then master of American architecture, domestic, commercial, and public; he designed details and in part supervised the erection of Trinity Church, Boston, the Albany Capitol, and the Cheney Building, Hartford, among others. He became an adept in Richardson Romanesque.

In 1878, White dropped work to make his first trip to Europe, where he was joined by C. F. McKim [*q.v.*]. During the year previous White had journeyed to New England, with McKim and his partners, W. R. Mead [*q.v.*] and W. B. Bigelow, to study and measure colonial and Bulfinch houses along the Massachusetts coast. Mead regarded this expedition as the turning point of the firm to a style of architecture based on classical precedents (Moore, *post,* p. 41). Augustus Saint-Gaudens was then at work in Paris on his statue of Farragut, for which White was to design the pedestal. The "three red-heads" made a leisurely trip to the South of France. Together they saw and discussed works of beauty and taste as exemplified at Avignon, Arles, St. Gilles, and Nimes. McKim returned to America and White made his headquarters with the Saint-Gaudens family in Paris during thirteen months spent in France, Belgium, Holland, and Northern Italy. White's facile pencil recorded not patterns, but rather the creative spirit of the artist as impressed upon his own curious and youthfully confident mind. Association with Saint-Gaudens tended to stabilize White's judgments and in some degree to moderate his natural exuberance.

In 1879, his money spent, White returned, and, June 21, 1880, took Bigelow's place. So the firm of McKim, Mead & White began. When, in 1881, the Farragut statue was unveiled in Madison Square it struck a new note in American sculpture, and such was the harmony between statute and pedestal that White shared Saint-Gaudens' triumph. On Feb. 7, 1884, White married Bessie Springs Smith, youngest of thirteen children of Judge J. Lawrence Smith, of Smithtown, Long Island. At St. James, on a portion of the ancestral estate of the "Bull Smiths," the Whites developed a summer home which remains as characteristic of White's catholic taste. The made-over farmhouse was furnished with gilded Spanish columns, Renaissance fireplaces, Persian rugs, Roman fragments, Delft tiles—all united according to White's theory that all things intrinsically good can be brought into harmony. Gardens of box, alleys of rhododendrons, broad open spaces of green were surrounded by native forests. On adjoining acres both White and McKim built for members of the Smith family homes of elegance and comfort. In one of those homes McKim died; in the St. James churchyard White is buried. He and his wife made their New York home in Gramercy Park the sumptuous setting for a hospitality representative of the luxurious metropolis of its day.

The transition of McKim, Mead & White from Richardson's exotic Romanesque to a style based on classical precedents as practised in America from its settlement down to Civil War days was by no means abrupt. Circumstances helped them: the rapid increase in wealth and the consequent desire of the traveled wealthy for a share in old-world art and culture paved the way. All three men had training in France and Italy. Moreover, they were imbued with an innate appreciation of beauty, and so were able to give to their buildings that quality of charm which makes architecture alive.

Rapid increase in the work of the office attracted ambitious young men, who, under general direction and supervision, found opportunity for the development of their own talents. Among the youngsters the inspirational White was aptly called Benvenuto Cellini, while the studious McKim was known as Bramante. Saint-Gaudens' caricature of Mead struggling with two kites representing his soaring partners became proverbial. Before the days of architectural schools in universities, this office trained, during the lifetime of the partners, literally hundreds of youths who carried the spirit of their teachers into all parts of the land. Among the draftsmen was Joseph Morrill Wells, who had been in the office a year or more before White came into the firm, and was some months older. Massachu-

setts born, trained in the Boston office of Peabody & Stearns, Wells had a flair for Renaissance architecture, although he never saw Italy until shortly before his early death, Feb. 2, 1890. He designed entirely but one building (the Russell & Irwin building in New Britain, Conn.). "His work was entirely confined to the details of buildings. In that he was simply supreme. Nobody before or since has equalled him in the appropriateness and scale of his ornamentation and this, of course, gave great character to buildings he decorated. The ensemble of these buildings, however, and by implication, the kind of detail, was decided invariably by a member of the firm. . . . In addition to Wells' genius in detail, the important, and perhaps the most important, influence he had upon the firm was his stand for the Classic and particularly the Italian style of architecture. Too much cannot be said with regard to this latter point" (W. M. Kendall, letter to Royal Cortissoz, June 22, 1928, Architectural Record, July 1929, p. 18). Wells arranged programs for Saint-Gaudens' musical Sundays; he was an intimate associate with the three partners, who were drawn to him not more by his high abilities than by caustic wit, intense hatred of shams, and (his shyness overcome) his brilliant conversation. In the Villard houses Wells transformed White's ensemble into the style of the Cancelleria; and he made of the Century Club exterior a thing of rare charm and beauty.

White planned luxurious city and country homes in New York, Newport, and the Berkshires, designed furniture, and ransacked Europe for rugs, pictures, sculptures, and hangings. He fashioned a railroad parlor-car and furnished James Gordon Bennett's yacht. He designed pedestals for Saint-Gaudens and MacMonies, picture frames for Dewing, magazine covers for *The Century* and *Scribner's*, gravestones, book and program covers, and exquisite jewelry. Whatever his prolific hand touched it adorned. He planned a number of churches, among them that Byzantine jewel, the Madison Square Presbyterian Church, the demolition of which in 1919 to make room for business was a cause of regret to those fond of early Christian architecture, as adapted to the distinctly Protestant church service of today. The Judson Memorial in Washington Square remains. Among his clubs are the Century, the Players, and especially the Metropolitan, his supreme achievement in Renaissance architecture. His son has discriminately written of the calm, deliberate, sober perfection of McKim's work in contrast with the restless, sky-rocket vitality of White's creations, "graceful and charming rather than imposing, and often profusely ornamented" in the strife for new effects (L. G. White, *post*, p. 15). The Washington Arch, commemorating the inauguration of George Washington as the first President of the United States, brought to White troubles, expense, and fame. First built of wood in 1889, six years later it was carried out in marble. The Battle Monument at West Point (1896) and the Prison Ship Martyrs Monument in Brooklyn (a modification of his superb but never executed design for Belle Isle Park, Detroit) are among his enduring works. He had the chief part in the restoration of the University of Virginia, originally laid out about 1810 by Thomas Jefferson. In 1895 the Rotunda burned, and the work of rebuilding it and designing several harmonious buildings was intrusted to White, who achieved notable success in carrying out the restoration reverently in the spirit of the original. In general estimation no more charming and dignified group of college buildings exists in America.

Familiar association with the pleasure side of metropolitan life gradually withdrew White from those congenial companionships that marked the first forty years of his life. In 1889, he designed for a group of wealthy New York men (among whom he was a leading spirit) the Madison Square Garden as the center of the city's pleasures. The feature of the building was a tower (an improvement on the Giralda in Seville, Spain) 300 feet in height, surmounted by Saint-Gaudens' statue of Diana. White, who was a stockholder in the Garden corporation and also a leader in the functions it housed, built for himself in the tower an apartment wherein he entertained his fellow artists and visiting celebrities of the opera and stage. His dinners were the talk of the town. On the evening of June 25, 1906, White, after dining with his son Lawrence and another Harvard boy, went late to the summer opening of the Madison Square Garden Roof. He was sitting alone watching the stage performance when Harry Thaw, coming from behind, fired three shots, killing him instantly. The case was tried primarily in the sensational newspapers of the country. The prosecution was persistently conducted by District Attorney William Travers Jerome; the defense, supplied with unlimited money, besmirched White's character. The first trial, long drawn out, ended in a disagreement of the jury; the second, in the commitment of Thaw to the hospital for criminal insane, whence he escaped. As the result of a sanity trial, Thaw was set free. The *New York Times, Sun,* and *Tribune* were in agreement that whatever were the relations of White and Evelyn Nesbit, the chorus girl, he sustained none with

her as the mistress and afterwards the wife of Thaw.

The personality of an artist has historical significance in so far as it affects his work. It is significant that the last two years of White's intense life produced two notable successes, the Gorham and the Tiffany buildings on Fifth Avenue. The latter represents his mastery in using the forms of a Venetian palace in such manner as to keep the spirit of the original architect, while adapting the structure to business uses. John Jay Chapman summed up White's career: "He was a great man in his love for every one; friendship was to him a form of religion. . . . His relation to the merchant class and to the swell mob was of a personal, galvanic kind. He excited them, he buffaloed them, he met them on all sides at once, in sport, in pleasure, antiquities, furniture, decoration, bibelots, office buildings, country houses, and exhibitions. . . . White was the protagonist of popular art in New York City. His was the prevailing influence not only in architecture but in everything connected with decoration" (quoted by L. G. White, pp. 16 f.). No American architect has more fully expressed the spirit of his times. More than this: "Stanford White grasped the spirit of the masters of the Renaissance and brought the living flame of their inspiration across the Atlantic to kindle new fires on these shores" (*Ibid.*, p. 33).

[*The Reminiscences of Augustus Saint-Gaudens* (1913), edited and amplified by Homer Saint-Gaudens, gives the best idea of White's artistic life, as shown in letters. L. G. White, *Sketches and Designs by Stanford White* (1920), with a sketch of his life, gives many designs in fields other than architecture, also a list of works in which White had a leading part. The three volumes of plates, *A Monograph of the Work of McKim, Mead and White* (1915), is an architectural standard in America and England. C. C. Baldwin, *Stanford White* (1931), relates White to his times; Charles Moore, *The Life and Times of Charles Follen McKim* (1929), contains lists of the work of the office and of the men employed therein, and includes many White letters. Janet Scudder, *Modeling My Life* (1925) relates White's helpfulness to young artists. See also Herbert Croly in the *Architectural Record*, May 1902; *Collier's*, Aug. 4, 1906; *N. Y. Times*, June 26, 1906; A. S. Kellogg, *Memorials of Elder John White . . . and of His Descendants* (1860).]   C. M.

WHITE, STEPHEN MALLORY (Jan. 19, 1853–Feb. 21, 1901), senator from California, lawyer, was born in San Francisco, the son of Fannie J. (Russell) and William F. White, both natives of Ireland who had come to America in early childhood. The latter's father, a successful farmer on the banks of the Shannon, became so indignant at the injustice inflicted upon two of his farm laborers by the British authorities that early in the nineteenth century he emigrated with his family to northern Pennsylvania. White's parents arrived in California in January 1849. His father had some ability as a writer, contributing to newspapers and under the name of William Grey publishing a book, *A Picture of Pioneer Times in California* (1881). For twenty years a member of the Democratic state central committee, he left his party to become a leader of the country wing of the Workingmen's party and was their candidate for governor in 1879. White's mother was related to Stephen Russell Mallory [q.v.]. During White's boyhood the family lived on a farm in the Pajaro valley, Santa Cruz County, Cal. At first he was taught at home by his father's sister, and then attended a private school in the vicinity and St. Ignatius College in San Francisco. Later he entered Santa Clara College, and upon his graduation in 1871 began to read law. In 1874 he was admitted to the bar and began practice in Los Angeles, where his success was noteworthy. In 1889, with John Franklin Swift [q.v.], he assisted the United States attorney-general in winning a case in the United States Supreme Court sustaining the constitutionality of the Chinese Exclusion Act (130 *U. S.*, 581). On June 5, 1883, he was married to Hortense Sacriste, by whom he had two sons and two daughters.

White first joined the Independent party, an anti-monopoly and reform group of the seventies. Upon its disappearance in 1877, he became a Democrat. He was elected district attorney of Los Angeles County (1883–84), served one term (1887–91) in the state Senate, and in 1893 attained his real objective—a seat in the United States Senate (March 1893–March 1899). In no case did he seek reëlection. In the Senate he early declared himself in favor of the free coinage of silver, and thus eventually he became associated with the group who controlled the Democratic convention of 1896. A consistent opponent of imperialism, he objected strenuously to the annexation of Hawaii, and to any hasty or unnecessary intervention in Cuba. On Apr. 16, 1898, he made a lengthy and forceful speech opposing a declaration of war against Spain.

Throughout his political life, although he was at times influenced by political exigencies, he continued the warfare begun by the Independent party against "incorporated greed" and "organized corruption." He made no attack upon wealth as such but vigorously resisted attempts to make government the agent of corporations. He was thus the champion of the "country" voters who attributed most of their economic difficulties to the railroad monopoly, and in this rôle he joined combat with many powerful adversaries. Within his own party he was opposed by Stephen Johnson Field [q.v.], whose decisions

in railroad tax cases had been most unpopular, and Senator George Hearst [q.v.], reputedly in alliance with Christopher A. Buckley, Democratic boss and political agent for the Southern Pacific Railroad. In 1890 Leland Stanford [q.v.] was the Republican candidate for the seat White was seeking in the United States Senate; and during the years 1893–96, in the hardest fought battle of his career—a battle waged with such incessant energy that it shortened his life— White defeated the plans of Collis P. Huntington [q.v.] to divert federal funds from San Pedro to a harbor site desired by the Southern Pacific. Though he set himself against corrupt practices in party and in government, he insisted that reform to be permanent must come from the party organization, not from well intentioned people with little or no political experience. When he had secured a commanding position in the party, he helped to eliminate "Boss" Buckley on the ground that he was "useless timber" and a party liability. Both by example and by precept he did much to establish a tradition for honesty in California politics that prepared the way for the reformers of 1910. He died in Los Angeles, survived by his wife and four children. White was a man of marked personal charm, with unusual oratorical powers, a vigorous intellect, and a genuine kindliness and generosity of nature that won him great popularity.

[See *Who's Who in America*, 1899–1900; Edith Dobie, *The Political Career of Stephen Mallory White* (1927); R. W. Gates, *Stephen M. White . . . His Life and Work* (2 vols., 1903); Willoughby Rodman, *Hist. of the Bench and Bar of Southern Cal.* (1909), pp. 257–58; O. T. Shuck, *Hist. of the Bench and Bar of Cal.* (1901); obituary in *Times* (Los Angeles), Feb. 22, 1901. In the lib. of Leland Stanford Univ. is an extensive coll. of the Stephen M. White papers, chiefly letters, with five vols. of newspaper clippings.]
E. D—e.

WHITE, STEPHEN VAN CULEN (Aug. 1, 1831–Jan. 18, 1913), banker, congressman, was born in Chatham County, N. C., the son of Hiram and Julia (Brewer) White. His mother belonged to a Carolina family and his father was descended from a Pennsylvania Quaker who migrated to North Carolina after the close of the Revolutionary War. Hiram White, who hated slavery intensely, refused to do police duty during the wave of dread that swept over the South as a result of Nat Turner's insurrection in 1831, and when Stephen was only six weeks old the family was obliged to leave the state. They settled in a log cabin near Otterville, Jersey County, Ill., not far from the junction of the Illinois and Mississippi rivers. White attended the free school founded by Dr. Silas Hamilton in Otterville, helped about his father's farm and grist mill, and trapped furbearing animals. With the help of an elder brother he prepared for Knox College at Galesburg, Ill., where he received the degree of A.B. in 1854. On leaving college he kept books for a mercantile house in St. Louis for eight months and then entered the law office of B. Gratz Brown and John A. Kasson [*qq.v.*]. An ardent opponent of slavery, White wrote articles for the Republican party during Frémont's presidential campaign. He was admitted to the bar on Nov. 4, 1856, and in the same year moved to Des Moines, Iowa. Here he practised until the end of 1864, during which year he was acting United States district attorney for Iowa.

In the beginning of 1865 he moved to New York state, making his home in Brooklyn. Although he was admitted to the local bar he did not practise, but instead joined the open board of brokers and became a member of the banking and brokerage firm of Marvin & White, with offices in Wall Street. After the failure of this house in 1867, White went into business by himself. In 1869 he became a member of the New York Stock Exchange. He soon became known as a daring, though not always successful, stock manipulator, especially in the shares of the Delaware, Lackawanna & Western Railroad. In 1872 he was obliged to suspend for the second time in consequence of losses sustained through the great fire in Boston. In 1882 he formed the partnership of S. V. White & Company. He was elected as a Republican to the Fiftieth Congress in 1886 and served one term (1887–89), declining a renomination. In 1891 he tried to corner the corn market, but miscalculated the available supply and failed for almost a million dollars instead of making the huge profit he had counted upon. His creditors, however, having faith in his honesty and ability, cancelled their claims against him and returned to him his $200,000 remaining assets. He was readmitted to the stock exchange on Feb. 15, 1892, and by the end of that year had paid off the last of his obligations, with interest.

A warm friend of Henry Ward Beecher [*q.v.*], whose legal expenses in the famous Beecher-Tilton trial he is said to have defrayed, White was a trustee of Plymouth Church from 1866 till 1902 and its treasurer from 1869 till 1902. In that year he retired from much of his business activity to give time to his avocations. Frequently called "Deacon," although he never held the office, he was in his day a well-known and picturesque figure in Wall Street. He was a short, stocky man with a full beard, quick and alert in his movements, cordial in manner, and always attired in a frock coat with a soft, turned-down collar and a black string tie. An astronomer with one of the finest telescopes in America owned by a private individual, he was one of the organizers of the American Astronomical Society, founded in 1884, which subsequently became the department of astronomy of the Brooklyn Institute of Arts and Sciences. In February 1857, at Stanton, Ill., he married Eliza M. Chandler, by whom he had a daughter.

[*Biog. Dir. Am. Cong.* (1928); *Fiftieth Cong.: Official Cong. Dir.* (1888); *Who's Who in America,* 1912–13; *Brooklyn Daily Eagle,* Jan. 18, 1913; *N. Y. Times,* Jan. 19, 1913.]   H.G.V.

WHITE, THOMAS WILLIS (Mar. 28, 1788–Jan. 19, 1843), printer and founder of the *Southern Literary Messenger,* was born in Williamsburg, Va., of English ancestry. His father, Thomas White, was born at York (later Yorktown), Va. A tailor by trade, he married Sarah Davis, the sister of James Davis to whom he was apprenticed. The parents removed to Norfolk for a short time about 1790, and in 1791 to Richmond, where the father had a prosperous tailoring trade until his death from yellow fever in 1796. The widow, left with four children, soon married again. At eleven, Thomas was apprenticed to William A. Rind and John Stuart, printers of the *Virginia Federalist,* and in 1800 removed with them to Washington. Returning to Richmond in 1807, for a short time he managed the mechanical department of the paper owned by his uncle, Augustine Davis, and later that of Samuel Pleasants. Before he had arrived at his twentieth birthday he secured a position as compositor in the office of the *Norfolk Gazette and Publick Ledger.* He was married on Dec. 12, 1809, to a girl of fifteen in Gates County, N. C. Leaving Norfolk in November 1810, he worked at his trade in Philadelphia for two and a half years and in Boston for four. In April 1817 he returned to Richmond, to live there the remainder of his life. He established a successful printing business, and on July 21, 1827, entered into contract to reprint the *Journal* of both houses of the Virginia Assembly from 1777 to 1790 and of the convention of 1778. He stimulated authorship by printing several books by local writers: *Edge-hill, or the Family of the Fitzroyals* (2 vols., 1828) by James Ewell Heath [*q.v.*] and the same author's *Whigs and Democrats* (1839), a comedy in three acts; *The Potomac Muse, by a Lady, a Native of Virginia* (1825); *The Vocal Standard, or Star Spangled Banner* (1824); and *The Pocket Farrier* (1828) by James Ware. One of his most ambitious publications was an edition in two volumes of Eaton Stannard Barrett's burlesque novel, *The Heroine,* from which White's imprint was omitted in order that the book might be praised more successfully in the *Messenger* (December 1836).

The first issue of the *Southern Literary Messenger* came from the press in August 1834 under White's own direction. For the earlier issues he trusted the editorial work to James E. Heath and Conway Robinson [*q.v.*]—Heath wrote the reviews and the articles signed H., and Robinson the articles signed C.—and in November 1834 began a correspondence with Judge Nathaniel Beverley Tucker [*q.v.*] of the College of William and Mary, whose advice thereafter influenced him greatly, as did also that of Lucian Minor [*q.v.*]. Yet he felt that he had the final editorial decision, and wrote proudly to Tucker that he had secured nearly a thousand subscribers. In 1835 Edgar Allan Poe began to contribute to the *Messenger*. He moved to Richmond in the late summer and by the end of the year had assumed the editorship. White was not altogether satisfied with this. It fretted him considerably when Poe "hampered" him in admitting articles to his *Messenger's* pages, and more when he felt that he was making a host of enemies for the magazine. By the beginning of 1837, though the number of subscribers had more than quadrupled, if we may believe Poe's statement, and the *Messenger* had certainly become known throughout the United States, White was still about eighteen hundred dollars in debt for the magazine and had become "as sick of Poe's writings as of himself." Poe's work on the *Messenger* ceased with the January issue of 1837. Congratulating himself on regaining the friendships that he thought the magazine had lost through Poe, White trusted once more to unpaid editorial advice, and sent packages of manuscripts to Tucker and to Minor to be marked for acceptance or rejection. His health, which had been bad as early as 1835, continued to decline until in September 1842 he suffered a stroke of paralysis at the supper-table of the Astor House in New York. He died on Jan. 19, 1843, and was buried from the First Presbyterian Church the next day. Two great sorrows had come to him in the deaths of his nineteen-year-old son on Oct. 7, 1832, and of his wife, Margaret Ann, on Dec. 11, 1837. He was survived by several daughters, among them Mrs. Peter D. Bernard and Poe's friend, Eliza White.

"Little Tom," as Poe once called him in a letter to a friend, was a short stockily-built man of "indomitable energy and perseverance of character." He was somewhat testy at times and given to periods of melancholy, but on the whole was of an open and generous nature. He had only the education that he had picked up in a printer's shop, but he had a shrewd knowledge of the world, wrote a good letter, and was able to hold the respect and confidence of many of the leading men of Virginia.

[The chief source consists of letters in MS. from White to N. B. Tucker, esp. one dated Nov. 17, 1834, in the possession of G. P. Coleman of Williamsburg, Va. See also B. B. Minor, *The Southern Lit. Messenger, 1834–1864* (1905); obituary notices in *Southern Lit. Messenger*, Feb. 1843, and *Richmond Enquirer*, Jan. 21, 1843.]   J. S. W.

WHITE, WILLIAM (Apr. 4, 1748 N.S.–July 17, 1836), first Protestant Episcopal bishop of the diocese of Pennsylvania, was born in Philadelphia, and died in the same city. He was the son of Col. Thomas White, born in London, by his second wife, Esther (Hewlings), widow of John Newman. William's sister, Mary, became the wife of Robert Morris [*q.v.*], financier of the American Revolution. Young White was educated in Philadelphia, graduating in 1765 at the College of Philadelphia, forerunner of the University of Pennsylvania. He was ordained deacon in London, Dec. 23, 1770, and priest, Apr. 25, 1772. On his return to America he was made assistant minister at Christ Church, Philadelphia. In the course of the Revolution the Loyalist rector returned to England and White became rector of the parish, an office which he retained the rest of his life. In February 1773 he married Mary Harrison, who died in 1797, by whom he had eight children.

He was the leader in the organization into a diocese of the parishes of the Church of England remaining in Philadelphia after the war. He was also the foremost advocate of a closer union between the churches of his communion in the various states; and the plan of organization of what became known as the Protestant Episcopal Church in the United States of America which was adopted in 1785 and revised in 1789, was very largely of his devising. He introduced into this plan the fundamentally important principle that the laity should have an equal part with the clergy in all legislation. This principle was a complete novelty in the Anglican communion, though White thought it was to be found in the relation of Parliament to the Church of England. The original constitution of the Church was drafted by him and adopted largely as the result of his efforts. With William Smith [*q.v.*] he was chiefly responsible for the American revision of the Book of Common Prayer, which, with some modern alterations, has remained in use in the Protestant Episcopal Church ever since.

Because of his sagacity, his gifts of leadership,

and his character, he was the naturally designated bishop of the new diocese. Having been
formally elected, Sept. 14, 1786, and provided
with suitable credentials, he was sent to England to receive episcopal consecration. This was
received, Feb. 4, 1787, at the hands of the archbishops of Canterbury and York, and the bishops
of Bath and Wells and of Peterborough, thus
obtaining for the daughter Church in America
English episcopal orders. His consecration had
been made possible by an Act of Parliament dispensing, in such cases as White's, with the customary oaths of allegiance. On his return to
America White at once took up again his pastoral work and at the same time carried on that
of a diocesan. He was not an aggressive Churchman, though he did a surprising amount of controversial writing. He was tactful enough to
recognize the grave limitations under which a
bishop of the Church, once so closely connected
with the English system, must work in order not
to endanger his whole position. Ecclesiastically,
he was conciliatory and inclusive without being
"Latitudinarian," as he has been mistakenly
styled. These characteristics proved invaluable
after White became presiding bishop of the
Church on the death of Samuel Seabury [q.v.]
in 1796, for the era was one of intense party
feeling. His policy of cooperation with men of
other denominations, in which he differed markedly from some of the bishops of his time, brought
him into close touch with much of the benevolent
and religious activity of Philadelphia. In the
administration of his diocese he was hampered
by the heavy duties of his pastoral charge and
he did little to extend the work towards the western part of the state. In this he was markedly
different from his younger contemporary John
Henry Hobart [q.v.] of New York. In Philadelphia and the vicinity, however, White laid
the foundations for a strong Church life which
has remained characteristic of the diocese.

His pastoral work was noted for his active
promotion of the Sunday school, then a new institution and regarded with grave suspicion and
even hostility by the more conservative of the
denominations. His support of it was perhaps
his most important contribution to general religious life. Since his parish had become united
with two other congregations, St. Peter's and
St. James's, he had under him in Philadelphia a
staff of younger clergy whom he trained for
service in the Church. Among such were William A. Muhlenberg, John Henry Hobart, Jackson Kemper [qq.v.]. White's death in 1836 was
universally regarded as a public loss to the community, and not merely to his own Church. He

had become the patriarch of the town. He was
buried at Christ Church, Philadelphia, and his
remains were later placed beneath the chancel of
that church. White could rarely be induced to
preside at public meetings. He appeared to take
little interest in politics and was loth to enter
into public controversy. He at once recognized
the independence of the United States on the
passage of the Declaration of Independence,
however, and altered the liturgy of his Church
accordingly. He was long chaplain of Congress,
was intimate with the early statesmen of the
young nation—several of the more prominent
being in his congregation—and contributed to
their councils in his quiet way.

White was a scholarly man without being a
scholar-bishop of the eighteenth-century type.
His *Comparative Views of the Controversy between the Calvinists and the Arminians* (2 vols.,
1817), is a careful and judicious statement, embodying much original research and patristic
learning. It is probably the best piece of work
of the kind produced in his Church in its first
century. His *Memoirs of the Protestant Episcopal Church in the United States of America*
(1820) is of primary importance to the historian of the Church. A new edition, prepared by
B. F. DeCosta, was issued in 1880. He also published *Christian Baptism* (1808) ; *Lectures on
the Cathechism* (1813) ; and *Commentaries Suited to the Occasions of Ordinations* (1833), as
well as many sermons, charges, pastoral letters,
pamphlets, and addresses. A work against the
Friends he decided finally not to publish.

[Bird Wilson, *Memoir of the Life of the Right Reverend William White, D.D.* (1839) contains a list of
White's minor publications, drawn up by himself, and
a list of unpublished manuscripts. See also W. W.
Bronson, *Account . . . of the Descendants of Col.
Thomas White* (1879) ; J. H. Ward, *The Life and
Times of Bishop White* (1892) ; W. W. Manross, *William White* (1934) ; W. S. Perry, *The Hist. of the Am.
Episcopal Church* (1885), and *Jours. of Gen. Conventions of the Protestant Episcopal Church in the U. S.*
(1874) ; Arthur Lowndes, *Archives of the Gen. Convention: "The Correspondence of John Henry Hobart"*
(6 vols., 1911–12) ; *Poulson's Am. Daily Advertiser*
(Phila.), July 18, 1836. White's library and many of
his unpublished writings are at Christ Church, Phila.,
and at the Divinity School of the Protestant Episcopal
Church, Phila.]   J. C. Ay—r.

WHITE, WILLIAM NATHANIEL (Nov.
28, 1819–July 14, 1867), horticulturist, editor,
was born in Longridge, Conn., a descendant of
Thomas White, an early settler of Weymouth
Mass. His parents, Anson and Anna (Fitch)
White, soon after his birth moved to Walton
N. Y., where he grew up on a farm. He early
became interested in pomology and horticulture,
and was much concerned with the family orchards and garden. After attending the local

school, the Gilbertsville Academy and Collegiate Institute, and the Delaware Literary Institute, he entered Hamilton College as a junior and was graduated in 1847. For the sake of his health, which had never been good, he set out for the South, expecting to find a position as a teacher there. After numerous unsuccessful efforts to find employment in Georgia, he settled at Terminus (later Atlanta), where he secured thirty pupils. He aided in organizing the city government there and in securing a charter. In January 1848 he was induced to move to Athens, Ga., to manage a bookstore owned by W. C. Richards, editor of the *Southern Literary Gazette*. He bought the establishment a year later and continued to run it until his death.

To his deep interest in pomology, horticulture, and the wider field of rural economy he now gave full rein, and soon he came to be a recognized authority in these subjects. He early began to write for the *Atlanta Luminary,* later contributing articles to the *Horticulturalist,* the *Southern Cultivator,* the *Gardener's Monthly,* and the *Southern Field and Fireside*. He made various reports on agricultural subjects to the United States Patent Office and sent weather observations to the United States Observatory and Hydrographical Office. His greatest renown, however, grew first out of his book, *Gardening for the South* (1856), which immediately became the standard work on that subject, and secondly from his connection with the *Southern Cultivator*. He became assistant editor of the *Cultivator* in 1862, and in June 1863 bought a half interest in the enterprise and assumed complete editorial charge. In the midst of the Civil War he announced that, although every other farm paper in the Confederacy had ceased, this publication should continue as long as he had "a country to publish it in" (*Southern Cultivator,* Sept.–Oct. 1863, p. 113). As if to defy Sherman's destructions, in November 1864 he changed the *Cultivator* from a monthly to a weekly. In January 1865 he became sole owner and moved it from Augusta to Athens. With the coming of peace, he soon began to reap considerable profits from his publishing enterprise, but just as his future seemed assured he was stricken with typhoid fever and died.

White married on Aug. 28, 1848, at Walton, N. Y., Rebecca Benedict, his boyhood sweetheart. Nine children were born to them, six of whom died in infancy. He completely identified himself with the South in all his interests and sympathies. In the Civil War he joined the 9th Regiment, Georgia State Guards, but was soon furloughed on account of ill-health. and on Feb.

11, 1864, he was exempted from further service. He was an elder in the Presbyterian Church. He was of a swarthy complexion, with black hair and dark eyes. He was an extremely industrious worker, unassuming, yet sociable.

[See H. K. White, *The White Family* (1906); *Southern Cultivator,* Aug. 1867; A. L. Hull, *Annals of Athens, Ga., 1801–1901* (1906); L. H. Bailey, *Cyc. of Am. Agriculture,* vol. IV (1909); two scrapbooks in the possession of E. S. White, Walton, N. Y.; obituary in *Southern Watchman,* July 17, 1867. The date of birth is from White's daughter.]   E. M. C.

WHITE EYES (d. 1778), Indian chief, was born into the Delaware tribe that lived at what is now Coshocton, Ohio. He became chief counselor and upon the death of Netawatwees, the chief sachem of the Delaware nation, in 1776, succeeded to the station of chief sachem. His leadership coincides with the short period of the attempt of the Delawares to befriend the whites and, by accepting certain of the white man's ways, to create a sound basis for a permanently friendly relation between the two races without the sacrifice of the integrity of either. He was cordial to the efforts of the Moravian missionaries to Christianize and civilize the Delawares but did not himself accept Christianity. He led his people to neutrality in Dunmore's War of 1774, thus incurring the hatred of his victimized neighbors, the Shawnee. In 1775, at the treaty at Fort Pitt, he ostentatiously declared the Delaware nation free of their subservience to the Iroquois and committed the future of his people to the success of the American cause. Assured by the American Indian agent, George Morgan [*q.v.*], of trade with the Americans and of teachers of agriculture, he kept his nation neutral, while practically all the rest of the tribes were joining the British. Morgan's promises, however, were not kept by the Americans; and the nation gradually chose belligerency under the guidance of White Eyes' rivals, Captain Pipe and Bochongahelos. White Eyes was deceived in 1778 into signing a treaty of alliance with the American Confederation. He offered, however, to guide the American troops through the forests in Gen. Lachlin McIntosh's unsuccessful attempt to capture Detroit in 1778. On this expedition, in the moment of his greatest usefulness to the United States, he was murdered by American soldiers, although the authorities were success-ful in making his tribesmen believe he died of smallpox (George Morgan Letters, 1775–1787, Library of Congress, May 12, 1784).

[George Morgan Letter Book, Carnegie Lib. of Pittsburgh; John Heckewelder, "Hist. of Manners and Customs of the Indian Nations," *Pa. Hist. Soc. Memoirs,* vol. XII (1876); G. H. Loskiel, *Hist. of the Mission of the United Brethren among the Indians* (1794); F. W.

Hodge, "Handbook of Am. Indians," *Bureau of Am. Ethnology Bulletin*, 30, pt. II (1910).]   R. C. D.

WHITEFIELD, GEORGE (Dec. 16, 1714 o.s.–Sept. 30, 1770), evangelist, was born in the Bell Inn, Gloucester, England, of which his father, Thomas, was the proprietor. Although a tavern keeper—and none too successful a one—Thomas was descended from a line of clergymen, the earliest of whom was William Whytfeild, who was vicar of Mayfield, Sussex, in 1605. William's son Thomas, and Thomas' son Samuel, grandfather of Thomas who kept the Bell Inn, were also clergymen. Of Samuel's sons, one, his namesake, continued the clerical tradition; another, Andrew, was the father of Thomas. While living in Bristol Thomas married Elizabeth Edwards, and George was the youngest of their seven children. When the boy was two years old his father died. The mother continued to run the inn, deriving therefrom a meager existence. Her financial condition was not bettered when, some eight years after her first husband's death, she married Capel Longden, an ironmonger.

In the not altogether wholesome atmosphere of the Gloucester tavern George Whitefield grew up. The picture of his youthful depravity which he drew during the long days of his first voyage to America is doubtless much over-colored (*A Short Account of God's Dealings with the Reverend Mr. George Whitefield . . . from His Infancy to the Time of His Entering into Holy Orders,* 1740). An impetuous, emotional lad, he was guilty of more or less misconduct, but was probably neither better nor worse than most boys in his circumstances. His mother, a well-meaning but ineffectual woman, seems to have tried conscientiously to direct him aright. Before he was fifteen he persuaded her to let him leave school—where his career had been notable chiefly for the oratorical and histrionic abilities he exhibited—and for over a year he washed mops, cleaned rooms, and served as drawer at the inn. Later, after a sojourn with relatives in Bristol, he reëntered the free grammar school of St. Mary de Crypt, and in 1732, aided by friends, he made successful application for admission as servitor to Pembroke College, Oxford.

Already he had given evidence of being by temperament peculiarly susceptible to religious influences. While at Bristol he passed through a period of "unspeakable raptures," during which he found keen delight in the services of the church and in reading Thomas à Kempis. After his return to Gloucester there was a reaction, and in the early part of his second period at school he became, he confessed, something of a scoffer and a rake; on one or two occasions he got drunk. His religious proclivities conquered in the end, however; he fasted, read pious books, and set out to reform his schoolmates. At the university he faithfully continued his religious practices. After about a year he formed an acquaintance with Charles Wesley, then a tutor at Christ Church, who introduced him later to his brother John and the other members of the Holy Club. Wesley lent Whitefield books, among them Henry Scougal's *The Life of God in the Soul of Man,* from which he got his first idea of religion as a vital union with God. He now began to live by rule, taking the sacrament every Sunday, fasting twice a week, and engaging regularly in charitable ministrations. Failing to find peace through such good works, he increased their number with fanatical zeal until at last he fell ill. During this illness, late in the spring of 1735, he experienced a "new birth," and was filled with a sense of the pardoning love of God and oneness with Him. From this time forth the conviction that such an experience is indispensable to individual and social welfare possessed and governed him completely.

His dynamic career of service began almost immediately. Returning to Gloucester to recuperate from his illness, he converted some of his friends and formed a religious society. A portion of each day he devoted to deeds of mercy, visiting the jail, and ministering to the sick and the poor. It was not till March 1736 that he returned to Oxford. His Gloucester friends had urged him to seek ordination, and some of them had brought him to the attention of Bishop Martin Benson. An interview with Whitefield so impressed the Bishop that although he had announced he would ordain no candidate under twenty-three years of age he offered to make an exception in Whitefield's favor. Accordingly, on June 20, 1736, in the Gloucester Cathedral, he was admitted to deacon's orders, and the following Sunday, in the Church of St. Mary de Crypt, he preached his first sermon. The effect it had upon the curious throng of Whitefield's fellow townsmen was prophetic of the power over audiences he was to exhibit later. In a few days he went back to Oxford and was graduated with the degree of B.A. in July.

For the rest of the year Oxford was his headquarters. The Wesleys were now in Georgia, and Whitefield became the leader of the few "methodists" left at the University. For two months, however, he substituted for his friend, the Rev. Thomas Broughton, as curate of the Tower of London, and for six weeks he officiated at Dummer, Hampshire. Wherever he spoke he captivated his hearers and a most desirable curacy in London was offered him. This he declined, for by the end of the year he, too, had decided to enlist in the Georgia enterprise.

It was to be another twelve months, however, before he could leave for America. Meanwhile, for a youth of twenty-two years, he achieved extraordinary prominence, his name becoming a household word in all parts of England. With fiery zeal, rare dramatic ability, and all the assurance of one who believes himself divinely directed, he set out to preach the "new birth" wherever opportunity offered. In Gloucester, in Bristol, in Bath, and in London thousands flocked to hear him. Incidentally, for charity schools and for the Georgia mission he collected large sums of money. In August 1737 his first published sermon—*The Nature and Necessity of Our New Birth in Christ Jesus, in Order to Salvation*—appeared, and though, like all Whitefield's printed discourses, it had little of the power that made his preaching so effective, it went through three editions within a year. In the meantime seven other sermons of his came from the press. His popularity was not unclouded, however; for the first shadows of the storm of opposition that was to beat upon him all the rest of his life thus early began to gather. Clergymen in whose churches he spoke complained that their regular worshippers were crowded out by the motley throngs that gathered; they also begrudged the money that he took away and called him a "spiritual pickpocket." His habit of mingling freely with Dissenters subjected him to further criticism. The *Weekly Miscellany,* the principal Church of England newspaper, began a series of attacks on enthusiasts, undoubtedly directed principally against Whitefield, in which they were characterized as persons who feel the truth but are unable to defend it, as possessing zeal without knowledge, and as uttering sound without sense (Tyerman, *post,* vol. I, p. 91).

On Dec. 30, 1737, accompanied by several friends, one of whom was James Habersham [*q.v.*], he embarked for Georgia on the *Whitaker,* a transport carrying troops to the colony. With him he took a miscellaneous assortment of pamphlets, books, clothing, tools, hardware, and other supplies. The ship did not leave the English coast until Feb. 2, 1738, and while it was at Deal, John Wesley—Charles had already returned—disembarked, disheartened by his experiences in America. The two did not meet, but Wesley wrote a letter to Whitefield advising him to turn back. Whitefield continued on his way,

however, and on May 7 landed at Savannah. His first stay in America lasted only about four months but was full of activity and plans for the future. He instituted services in Savannah, started several schools, and visited the neighboring settlements. An orphanage conducted by the Salzburgers at Ebenezer interested him greatly, and he determined to establish a similar institution. The idea, he confessed, did not originate with him, but had been suggested to him by Charles Wesley, who had discussed the matter with Oglethorpe (Tyerman, I, 347). In order to raise funds for the project, and also to obtain ordination as priest, he set sail for England by way of Charleston (then Charlestown) on Sept. 9, 1738. He had made a most favorable impression; the supplies he had brought had won him gratitude; he had mingled freely with all classes, including Dissenters; and, unlike John Wesley, had not been zealous for church discipline. Furthermore, he had given support to the numerous freeholders who were petitioning the trustees of the colony to remove certain restrictions they had imposed and to permit the introduction of slave labor.

The period that elapsed before Whitefield's return to America was one of the stormiest in his whole turbulent career. The Georgia trustees appointed him minister of Savannah and on Jan. 14, 1739, Bishop Benson ordained him priest, but from many sides he was subjected to bitter opposition. Practically all the churches of England were closed to him, and he began to preach in the meeting places of the religious societies, in halls, and in the open air. His first out-door sermon was delivered Feb. 17, 1739, to the colliers on Kingswood Hill, near Bristol. Soon he was preaching at Moorfields, Kensington Green, and other resorts of the London populace. A flood of pamphlets of which he was the subject began to come from the press, the most of them hostile. He was attacked from the pulpit and in printed sermons—notably by Dr. Joseph Trapp—and the *Weekly Miscellany* continued its vituperations. Among the charges that were hurled at him were that he was a "raw novice" who assumed the office of an apostle; that he set himself up as a teacher not only of the laity but of the learned clergy, "many of them learned before he was born"; that he was guilty of Pharisaical ostentation, praying on the corners of the street; and that his open-air preaching was a reproach to the Church of which he was a minister. Even leading Dissenters voiced disapproval of him, Dr. Philip Doddridge declaring that "supposing him sincere and in good earnest, I still fancy that he is but a *weak* man,—much too positive, says rash things, and is bold and enthusiastic. . . . I think what Mr. Whitfield [*sic*] says and does comes but little short of an assumption of inspiration or infallibility" (J. D. Humphries, *The Diary and Correspondence of Philip Doddridge, D.D.*, 1829, III, 381). For all these criticisms there was no little justification. Whitefield was not a man of intellectual strength and good judgment, but of impulse and emotion. The journals of his voyage from London to Savannah, published by friends without his knowledge in 1738, were offensively pious and egotistical. His reply to Dr. Trapp's sermons, *A Preservative against Unsettled Notions, and Want of Principles, in Regard to Righteousness and Christian Perfection* (1739), the contents of which he bids that ecclesiastic to receive as "delivered from the mouth of God himself," was inexcusably abusive. He did not conceal the fact that he deemed the clergy in general "earthly minded." Furthermore, his whole course of action as an itinerant preacher was grossly irregular. Such was his zeal, however, and such his ability to present his message with vividness and power, that multitudes which no church could have held gathered about him in the open, and large numbers were soundly converted. While his hearers were chiefly from the common people, there were not lacking members of the aristocracy, notable among them being the Countess of Huntingdon, who was to become one of his stanchest supporters.

On Aug. 14, 1739, he embarked again for America, accompanied by some seventeen men and women who were to assist him in his Georgia enterprise. From the trustees of the colony he had obtained a grant of 500 acres of land and he had collected approximately £1000 for the erection of the orphanage. He reached Philadelphia on Dec. 2, and although he remained in America more than a year, his Savannah parish saw little of him. The major portion of his time was spent in itinerant preaching, which awakened religious excitement all the way from Georgia to Massachusetts. Most of his discourses were delivered in the meeting houses of Presbyterians and Congregationalists or in the open air; the clergy of the Church of England were in general unfriendly. His association with the Presbyterians of the Middle Colonies, especially with the elder William Tennent and his son Gilbert [*qq.v.*], was particularly intimate. In Philadelphia he made a profound impression on the whole city; Benjamin Franklin marveled at the extraordinary effect of his oratory. "It is wonderful," he wrote, "to see the change soon made in the manners of our inhabitants" (John Bigelow, *The Complete Works of Benjamin Franklin*, 1887–88, I, 206). He preached with equal effect in the towns of New Jersey and in New York. On Nov. 29 he left Philadelphia for Georgia, traveling on horseback through Maryland, Virginia, and the Carolinas and preaching all along the way.

Not until January 1739 did he reach Savannah and rejoin the companions who had left England with him. He immediately hired a house and gathered therein all the orphans he could find. In March he began construction of an orphanage on land selected by Habersham some ten miles from Savannah, and gave to the establishment the name Bethesda. His censoriousness and bad judgment soon got him into trouble in various quarters. In several instances his action in taking orphans from those who would have provided for them was inexcusable. He quarrelled with the Rev. Mr. Norris who had been serving as minister at Savannah, charging him with preaching false doctrine, fiddling and card playing. In his preaching he characterized the clergy as "slothful shepherds and dumb dogs." To the inhabitants of Maryland, Virginia, and the Carolinas he addressed a letter officiously condemning them in harsh terms for their treatment of their slaves. This was published in 1740, along with two others attacking the writings of Archbishop Tillotson, in a pamphlet entitled *Three Letters from the Reverend Mr. G. Whitefield*. While Whitefield was on a visit to Charleston, the Rev. Alexander Garden delivered a sermon from the text "Those who have turned the world upside-down have come hither also," and Whitefield retorted with one on the text "Alexander the coppersmith hath done me much evil: the Lord reward him according to his works." Garden also published a reply to Whitefield's letters under the title *Six Letters to the Rev. Mr. George Whitefield* (1740).

On Apr. 2, 1740, he set sail for a second visit to the North. While on shipboard, feeling the need of a wife to help him run the orphanage, he wrote to a "Miss E.," probably Elizabeth Delamotte (Tyerman, I, 368–70), one of the most preposterous proposals of marriage ever made. Eschewing all "passionate expressions" as "to be avoided by those that would marry in the Lord," he pictures the hardships union with him would entail, and asks her if she thinks she is equal to them. Needless to say his suit did not meet with favor. In Philadelphia he preached to thousands from a platform erected for him on "Society Hill." His appeals for the orphanage emptied the pockets of Franklin, who had resolved to give him nothing (*Works*, I, 208). He projected a school for negroes and a refuge for his converts in England who might be persecuted for righteousness' sake. Arrangements were made to secure land at the falls of the Delaware, but the project came to naught. He also visited the Delaware and New Jersey churches again and in New York addressed crowds from an improvised "scaffold."

By June 5, he was once more in Savannah, but late in the month went to Charleston. Here he was summoned by Commissary Garden to appear before an ecclesiastical court—said to have been the first to be convened in the colonies —to answer questions regarding irregularities in his doctrine and practices. His objection to the court as a prejudiced body was overruled and he appealed to the high court of chancery. This appeal halted proceedings in Charleston for a year and a day. Since it did not come to a hearing in England within that time, Whitefield was again summoned before Garden's court. He failed to appear and was suspended from office. Garden's opposition had no effect on Whitefield's activities, however.

From Charleston he set out for New England, where his coming resulted in the same great religious awakening that it had produced in the Middle Colonies. Landing in Newport, R. I., he proceeded to Boston. Here and in the surrounding towns he preached for nearly a month, chiefly in Congregational meeting houses, incidentally collecting some £400 for his orphanage. On his leisurely return southward, he stopped in many places: visited Jonathan Edwards at Northampton, Mass., preached to the Yale students in New Haven on the ill effect of an unconverted ministry, and persuaded Gilbert Tennent of New Brunswick, N. J., to go to Boston and further the revival in progress there. On Dec. 13, he reached Savannah, where he found his orphans installed in their new building. On Jan. 16, 1741, he sailed from Charleston for England, leaving Habersham in charge of the home.

An interval of almost four years elapsed before Whitefield was again in America. He had now become a rigid Calvinist and the first part of this period was marked by an unpleasant controversy with John Wesley, who was preaching free grace and Christian perfection. Whitefield's friends erected a wooden building for him—later replaced by a brick structure—known as the Tabernacle, which became the center of his London activities; he did not, however, abandon his wanderings or his field preaching. In Scotland, because he would not ally himself with the "Associate Presbytery" but insisted on preaching

to any who would hear him, he incurred the bitter enmity of its leaders; in Wales he was made moderator of the first Calvinistic Methodist Conference, and subsequently was elected perpetual moderator. On Nov. 14, 1741, he was married at Caerphilly, Glamorganshire, Wales, to Elizabeth (Burnell) James of Abergavenny, Monmouthshire, England. She was a strong-minded widow about ten years his senior, "neither rich in fortune," he wrote Gilbert Tennent, "nor beautiful as to her person, but, I believe, a true child of God, and one who would not, I think, attempt to hinder me in His work for the world" (Tyerman, I, 531). They had a son, John, born Oct. 4, 1743, who died in February of the following year. There is testimony to the effect that Whitefield and his wife were not happy together, but it is unsupported by facts; it would have been a remarkable woman, however, who could have adapted herself to his views and manner of life.

Accompanied by his wife, he left England for America in August 1744 and on Aug. 26 landed at York, in what is now the state of Maine. For more than a year he tarried in New England, preaching and writing, his only contact with Georgia being through Habersham, who came North to report on conditions in Bethesda. Since Whitefield's first visit to New England the revival he had furthered had awakened distrust and opposition in many of the Congregational leaders. Foremost among them was the Rev. Charles Chauncy, 1705–1787 [q.v.], of Boston, who had published *Seasonable Thoughts on the State of Religion in New England* (1743), in which Whitefield was severely criticized. Other hostile publications followed. To Chauncy and to the faculty of Harvard, which had issued a *Testimony* against him that had received an indorsement from Yale, he wrote replies. He had strong supporters as well as opponents, however, and his preaching continued to draw large audiences. By Jan. 1, 1746, he was in Bethesda. For more than two years he spent part of his time here and the rest in evangelistic journeys, during which he labored in Charleston, S. C., in Virginia, and in Maryland, visited Philadelphia and New York, and made another trip to New England. The people of Charleston gave him £300, with which he bought a plantation and slaves in South Carolina as a source of income for his orphanage. Slavery he defended on Biblical grounds, though he was most solicitous for the welfare of the slaves. In the spring of 1748 he went to the Bermudas, where he spent a number of weeks, and from there returned to England.

The remainder of his career proceeded along much the same lines. In August 1748 the Countess of Huntingdon made him her domestic chaplain. He continued his preaching in England and made journeys to Scotland, Wales, and Ireland. In 1756 he opened a chapel, for the building of which he had raised funds, in Tottenham Court Road, where he subsequently ministered as well as in his Tabernacle. He continued to be the object of attack from various quarters, and in 1760 he was burlesqued as Dr. Squintum, by Samuel Foote in a notorious play, *The Minor*; numerous other publications ridiculing him followed. On Aug. 9, 1768, his wife died.

His activities in Great Britain were broken by four more visits to America. The first of these, beginning in October 1751, was of about seven months' duration, which time he seems to have spent in Georgia and the Carolinas. The second, which extended from May 1754 to March 1755, opened and closed in Bethesda, the intervening period being devoted to a preaching itinerary that included Philadelphia, New York, parts of New England, and Virginia. As was earlier the case, great crowds turned out to hear him. In September he visited Gov. Jonathan Belcher [*q.v.*] at Elizabethtown, N. J., and while there accepted the degree of A.M. from the College of New Jersey. The Seven Years' War prevented him from making his next visit until September 1763. He landed in Virginia and then went to Philadelphia. Because of the condition of his health, he did not visit Georgia until December 1764. Meanwhile, he preached in Philadelphia and New York and visited Boston. While in the last-named city he wrote to a friend in England, asking him to procure books for the Harvard library, which had been burned, and to use his influence in behalf of Wheelock's Indian school. In December 1764 he petitioned the governor of Georgia for a grant of 2,000 acres of land for the establishment of a college at Bethesda. This petition received the support of the Assembly and the governor submitted it to the home government with promise of his support. Later, when back in England, Whitefield sent a memorial to the King asking that a charter, "upon the plan of New Jersey College," be granted. The project seemed likely to succeed, but because the Archbishop of Canterbury and the president of the Privy Council insisted that the charter stipulate that the head of the proposed institution be a member of the Church of England, Whitefield finally let the matter drop.

In September 1769 he left England for the last time. Arriving in Charleston on Nov. 30, he soon proceeded to Bethesda, but on Apr. 24, 1770, sailed for Philadelphia. In this city and in places within a radius of 150 miles he preached almost every day for several weeks. Late in June he moved on to New York. During July he traveled in a hundred-mile circuit which included Albany and towns in western Massachusetts and Connecticut. At the close of the month he went to Newport, R. I., and from there to Providence and northward to Boston. Continuing his travels in this section of New England, he came on Sept. 29 to Newburyport, Mass., and lodged with the Rev. Jonathan Parsons, minister of the First (South) Presbyterian Church, which Whitefield had been instrumental in founding. During the night he had an attack of what was called asthma, and died about six o'clock the following morning. His body was buried beneath the church.

In personal appearance Whitefield was of middle stature, well proportioned and graceful, though somewhat fleshy in his later years. He was of fair complexion and his countenance was enlivened by small, keen, dark blue eyes, in one of which was a noticeable squint caused by an attack of measles in his childhood. He moved with agility and ease and when speaking used many gestures. His manner of life was simple and orderly. He was up at four o'clock in the morning and went to bed at ten, summarily sending any callers home when that hour arrived. With those who consulted him, especially the young, he was inclined to be severe; toward servants he was exacting—no meal was to be a moment late; he was easily irritated but as easily quieted. Both his physical and his mental energy were seemingly inexhaustible; for years he spoke on an average of forty hours a week. No person, perhaps, ever preached to so many and to such varied types of people with so great effect. Scholars, statesmen, actors, members of the nobility, and ordinary laborers all bore testimony to the spell he put upon them. He had a strong, musical voice that could be heard by thousands in the open air and his mastery of it was perfect; "I would give a hundred guineas," said David Garrick, "if I could only say 'Oh!' like Mr. Whitefield" (Tyerman, II, 355). His histrionic gifts would doubtless have made him one of the immortals of the stage. He was a master of pathos and did not hesitate to introduce the element of humor into his sermons.

His influence in America, entirely apart from that which he exerted in Great Britain, was many-sided and far-reaching. With his advent a religious awakening already begun was greatly stimulated and a burst of evangelical activity occurred that had a marked effect not only on the religious and social life but on the political as well. Thousands were added to the churches; doctrinal discussions arose that resulted in a definite American contribution to theology; impetus was given to education, and schools and colleges were established; a social consciousness emerged and philanthropic and missionary work was initiated. The political effects were not so obvious but were equally important. For the first time the American people experienced a common emotion. To a certain extent colonial barriers were broken down and denominations became intercolonial. Whitefield's followers were notorious for ignoring parish and sectional lines, and for disregarding legislation that would restrict their activities. They also sought to limit ecclesiastical and political authority and advocated freedom of conscience and individual liberty. The number of Dissenters in the South was increased and the Established Church correspondingly impoverished, thus weakening one of the links connecting the colonies with England. In these and other respects the Great Awakening prepared the way for subsequent events in American history.

Although others contributed greatly to this movement, Whitefield was its most dynamic representative, its unifying element, and the personification of its tendencies. A flaming apostle, he went up and down the whole Atlantic seaboard, visiting almost all its principal towns; he sent a man of the Middle Colonies to save the sinners of Boston; he cared little for denominational or local distinctions and prejudices; he made his orphans' home an intercolonial charity by persuading people from Georgia to Maine to contribute to its support; he refused to be bound by ecclesiastical rules and conventions and claimed for himself freedom to act according to the dictates of his own conscience; his first coming to America was as a philanthropist and missionary, and to educational institutions he gave hearty and practical support. Of the Great Awakening, he was above all others the Awakener.

During his lifetime Whitefield published a large number of sermons, pamphlets, and letters; also two collections of hymns. The first authorized edition of his journal—*A Journal of a Voyage from London to Savannah in Georgia*—appeared in 1738. Three continuations were published that same year, another in 1740, and two more in 1741. In 1756 he issued *The Two First Parts of His Life, with His Journals Revised, Corrected, and Abridged . . . by George Whitefield*. His *Short Account of God's Dealings With the Reverend Mr. Whitefield*, mentioned above, was followed in 1746 by *A Further Account*, and by *A Full Account . . . to Which is Added a Brief*

Account of the Rise, Progress, and Present Situation of the Orphans-House in Georgia (1747?). The Rev. John Gillies edited *The Works of the Reverend George Whitefield* (6 vols., 1770–72), which does not include all his writings. Gillies also published *Memoirs of the Life of the Reverend George Whitefield*, which appeared in 1772.

[The literature on Whitefield is voluminous; a bibliog. of his publications and of works and articles relating to him appears in F. A. Hyett and Roland Austin, *Supplement to the Bibliographer's Manual of Gloucestershire Lit.*, pt. II (1916); a bibliog. of his publications, in *Proc. of the Wesley Hist. Soc.*, Sept., Dec. 1916. The fullest account of his life and work is Luke Tyerman, *The Life of the Rev. George Whitefield* (2 vols., 1876–77); other lives, in addition to that by Gillies mentioned above, include Robert Philip, *The Life and Times of the Rev. George Whitefield* (1837); Joseph Belcher, *George Whitefield: A Biog. with Special Reference to His Labors in America* (copr. 1857); D. A. Harsha, *Life of the Rev. George Whitefield* (1866); J. P. Gledstone, *The Life and Travels of George Whitefield, M.A.* (1871), and *George Whitefield, M.A., Field-Preacher* (copr. 1901); A. D. Belden, *George Whitefield—The Awakener* (copr. 1930). See also *Edinburgh Rev.*, July 1838; W. B. Sprague, *Annals Am. Pulpit*, vol. V (1859); Joseph Tracy, *The Great Awakening: A Hist. of the Revival of Religion in the Time of Edwards and Whitefield* (1842); *Christian Hist.*, 1743–45; C. H. Maxson, *The Great Awakening in the Middle Colonies* (1920); H. L. Osgood, *The Am. Colonies in the Eighteenth Century*, vol. III (1924); Alexander Gordon, in *Dict. Nat. Biog.*]   H. E. S.

WHITEHEAD, WILBUR CHERRIER

(May 22, 1866–June 27, 1931), bridge expert, was born in Cleveland, Ohio, the son of a Cleveland newspaper man. His general education was obtained in the local schools, but he always considered that the training given by his father, in methods of finding information and then presenting his findings, was the most important in equipping him to teach others how to play bridge successfully. He went into business, was at one time president of the Simplex Automobile Company and was a director in other corporations, went to Europe to represent a number of American companies, and spent the most of a dozen years in Paris. Always having a knack for games, he became a splendid amateur billiardist and golfer while abroad, as well as an expert player of card games. One of the easiest men to know well, he was affectionately called "Whitey" by a legion of friends. Affable, with a ringing laugh, rare sense of humor, and a trustful strain that caused him frequently to sign important contracts without even reading them, he was an intensely human type. He liked to think of himself principally as an investigator, who tried to find out things about the game for others, and as one who taught people how to make their own lives happier.

By the time auction bridge had become a leading game he was one of its ablest players. In 1914 he brought out *Whitehead's Conventions of Auction Bridge,* while engaging in his first professional bridge activities as a side-line to other business interests. In 1921 he published his *Auction Bridge Standards,* which practically revolutionized the entire conception of the game among careful players. It gave a precise valuation of the cards and began the author's contribution to the standardization of the game. His name soon became a household word, wherever the game was played. He was famous for his reiterated statement that "the law of averages is God's Law, and you can't go very far wrong on that." He first popularized the term of "quick tricks" and made clear the reasons why a player should have a certain minimum number of them in a hand before deciding to open the bidding. A complete tabulation of conventions of play and desirable leads came from him shortly in his various succeeding writings, and he developed a complete bidding system, each declaration conveying to a partner a message very specific, within certain definite bounds. Later systems of others have simply carried farther forward the work he started. He was active also in promoting many activities connected with the game. For years he was chairman of the card committee of the Knickerbocker Whist Club in New York, was a founder of the Cavendish Club and its first president. He organized a "bridge cruise," on the *Republic,* taking some 200 players around the West Indies for a series of tournaments on board. Every autumn in his later years he conducted a national convention of bridge teachers. He took part with Milton C. Work [*q.v.*] in the series of bridge games over the radio from 1925 to 1929 and, with Work, was one of the editors of the *Auction Bridge and Mah Jong Magazine,* later the *Auction Bridge Magazine,* during these years. He was the donor in 1930 of the Whitehead trophy for the women's national contract pair championship, still played for annually. At the time of his death, he was chairman of the Vanderbilt Cup committee. His last activity, when his health had begun to fail, was to gather together several other experts in an effort to form a universal system of contract bidding. As that movement was under way, he departed for France on his forty-ninth crossing of the Atlantic to rest and to visit his wife, Parthenia Whitehead, who had continued to make her home in Paris for years. Violating his physician's orders not to work on the way over, he died suddenly on the evening of June 27, 1931, while engaged in a study of bridge problems.

[*Wilbur C. Whitehead—The Man and his Books* (1930); *N. Y. Times,* esp. Jan. 11, June 27, 28, July 11, 25, 1931; a letter of June 24, 1914, from Whitehead to Lib. of Cong.; personal knowledge.]   S. B.

WHITEHEAD, WILLIAM ADEE (Feb. 19, 1810–Aug. 8, 1884), historian, was born at Newark, N. J., the son of William and Abby (Coe) Whitehead. He attended private schools and the Newark Academy until he was twelve, when his parents removed to Perth Amboy, N. J. His father being a banker, the son became a bank messenger and soon made weekly trips to New York City. He spent his leisure hours in reading books, chiefly of a biographical and historical nature, and in studying French and land surveying. In 1828 he went with a brother, John Whitehead, to Key West (where the latter owned a fourth part of the island), and there made a new survey of the division lines of the island. After a year at home (1829) he went to Havana, narrowly escaping shipwreck on the way, visited Key West again, and was appointed collector of the port, entering upon his duties, Jan. 23, 1831. He later became mayor, helped to organize the first Christian congregation (St. Paul's Episcopal Church) and to found a newspaper, and began his meteorological observations, which were continued unremittingly for forty years. A street in Key West perpetuates his name. Except on journeys to the north he remained there until 1838, in the meantime marrying, Aug. 11, 1834, Margaret Elizabeth Parker, sister of John Cortlandt Parker [*q.v.*]. From 1838 to 1848 he was engaged in business in New York City, chiefly as a broker, although he lived in Newark after 1843. On June 1, 1843, he began to make monthly weather reports, which he continued throughout his life. These were made with such "regularity, system, accuracy, and copiousness" that they were reproduced in many newspapers (*Proceedings of the New Jersey Historical Society,* vol. VIII, *post,* p. 188). In 1845 he was a leading organizer of the New Jersey Historical Society and became its first corresponding secretary, holding that position continuously until his death. He was agent of the Astor Insurance Company (1848), secretary of the New Jersey Railroad and Transportation Company (1848, 1859–71), treasurer of the Harlem Railroad (1855–58), and an associate of the American Trust Company of New Jersey (1871–79). After 1879 he gave all his attention to historical and literary pursuits.

His publications were numerous. Most important among them were *East Jersey under the Proprietary Governments* (1846), *The Papers of Lewis Morris, Governor of New Jersey* (1852), *Contributions to the Early History of Perth Am-*

boy and Adjoining Country (1856), *The Records of the Town of Newark, N. J.* (1864), and *Documents Relating to the Colonial History of the State of New Jersey* (8 vols., 1880–85), with others in preparation. A large number of historical addresses appeared in the *Proceedings of the New Jersey Historical Society* between 1848 and 1878, the last being "The Resting Place of the Remains of Christopher Columbus" (2 ser., vol. V, 1878, no. 3, pp. 128–37). Between 1837 and 1882 he published various pamphlets and over six hundred newspaper articles.

He was a member of the Newark board of education (1861–71) and a trustee of the state normal school (1862–84), serving as president of the board during the last thirteen years, and was long active in Trinity Episcopal Church, Newark. Because of ill health, from which he never fully recovered, he went to Europe in 1879. He was a man of unusually fine stature and had great dignity of appearance. He was survived by a daughter and a son.

[S. I. Prime, in *Proc. N. J. Hist. Soc.*, 2 ser., vol. VIII (1885), no. 4; *Ibid.*, 2 ser., vol. XIII (1895), no. 4, p. 237; W. C. Maloney, *A Sketch of the Hist. of Key West, Fla.* (1876); W. H. Shaw, *Hist. of Essex and Hudson Counties, N. J.* (1884), vol. I; obituary in *N. Y. Tribune*, Aug. 9, 1884.]   A. V–D. H.

WHITEHILL, CLARENCE EUGENE (Nov. 5, 1871–Dec. 18, 1932), opera singer, was born in Marengo, Iowa, the son of William Whitehill and Elizabeth Dawson (McLaughlin) Whitehill. As a young man he studied singing in Chicago with L. A. Phelps. During this period he worked as an express clerk, and on Sundays appeared in churches as bass soloist. Urged by Melba and Giuseppe Campanari to prepare for the operatic stage, he finally won financial assistance and went to Paris in 1896 to study for several years with Alfred-Auguste Giraudet and Giovanni Sbriglia. In 1899 he made his operatic début, singing the part of Friar Lawrence in Gounod's *Romeo and Juliet* at the Théâtre de la Monnaie, Brussels. Immediately after this appearance he was engaged to sing at the Opéra Comique, Paris, and the occasion of his performance in *Lakme* marked the first appearance of an American man on the stage of that theatre. In the following season Whitehill returned to America and became the leading baritone of the Savage English Grand Opera Company. Later he went abroad again, to study with Julius Stockhausen at Frankfort and to prepare Wagnerian rôles under the guidance of Frau Cosima Wagner at Bayreuth. From 1903 to 1908 he was the leading baritone at the Cologne Opera House.

In 1909 he made his first appearance in New York in the part of Amfortas in Wagner's *Parsi-*

fal, and from this time his name became closely associated with Wagnerian rôles. From 1909 to 1911 he sang at the Metropolitan Opera House in New York, and from 1911 to 1915 with the Chicago Opera Company. He then returned to the Metropolitan and remained a member of the company until his resignation in May 1932. His resignation aroused a storm of criticism against the management of the opera house, and precipitated a wordy struggle between defenders and critics. In announcing his withdrawal, Whitehill stated that Gatti-Casazza, the general director, entertained a bias against American singers, and that he had wasted the funds of the organization. Gatti-Casazza denied the charge of discrimination or bias, and stated that Whitehill had received the offer of a contract for a shorter season during the coming year, and that the singer had demanded a larger number of performances, a request that could not be granted because of the shorter season (see *New York Times*, May 14, 17, 1932). Seven months later Whitehill died in New York City. He was survived by his widow Isabelle (Rush) Simpson Whitehill to whom he had been married on July 12, 1926.

During his association with American opera companies Whitehill appeared frequently abroad. For five seasons he sang at Covent Garden, London; for three seasons at the Bayreuth festivals; and for two seasons at Munich. On the occasion of the bicentennial celebration of the birth of George Washington, Whitehill portrayed the part of Washington in a sound film which was shown throughout the country. When dressed in the colonial costume, his resemblance to Washington was amazing.

[*Who's Who in America*, 1930–31; *Grove's Dict. of Music and Musicians*, vol. V (3rd ed., 1928), and the *Am. Supp.* (1928) to the same work; *Baker's Biog. Dict. of Musicians* (3rd ed., 1919); W. A. French, "A Bostonian at Bayreuth," *Musician*, Dec. 1909; *Musical Courier*, Mar. 16, 1910; obituary article in *N. Y. Times*, Dec. 20, 1932; tribute by Olin Downes, *Ibid.*, Dec. 25.]
                                        J. T. H.

WHITEHILL, ROBERT (July 21, 1738–Apr. 7, 1813), Pennsylvania official, congressman, son of James and Rachel (Cresswell) Whitehill, was born in the Pequea settlement, Lancaster County, Pa., where his father, a native of the north of Ireland, had settled in 1723. Robert had the advantages of a good elementary education; he studied for a time under the Rev. Francis Alison [*q.v.*], and added further to his knowledge by diligent reading. In 1770 he purchased from the proprietaries of Pennsylvania two tracts of land, comprising 440 acres, in Lauther Manor beyond the Susquehanna (now

Cumberland County). The following spring he erected the first stone house in the manor on a site about two miles from the Susquehanna, near Harrisburg. Here he made his home until his death.

In the pre-Revolutionary period he manifested to a marked degree the democratic sentiments of frontier Pennsylvania. He was a member of his county committee, 1774–75, and as early as the spring of 1776 was outspoken in his advocacy of independence, primarily as a means of overthrowing the control of the eastern counties in provincial politics. In the Pennsylvania convention of 1776 he was the right hand man of George Bryan [q.v.], and played a conspicuous part in drafting the new constitution. With the organization of the state government he began a service which, in various capacities, continued almost uninterrupted until 1805. He was a member of the Assembly, 1776–78; served on the council of safety, October to December 1777, and on the supreme executive council, Dec. 28, 1779, to Nov. 30, 1781; and was again a member of the Assembly, 1784–87, 1797–1801, and of the state Senate, 1801–05. A devout Constitutionalist, he was one of the small group which in this period fanned jealousies and suspicions of the Pennsylvania back country into an opposition which was probably the most vehement experienced by any state and nearly resulted in armed conflict (S. B. Harding, "Party Struggles over the First Pennsylvania Constitution," in *Annual Report of the American Historical Association, 1894,* 1895, p. 393). Robert Morris said of his obstinacy in debate, "Even were an angel from Heaven sent with proper arguments to convince him of his error, it would make no alteration with him" (Mathew Carey, *Debates . . . on . . . Annulling the Charter of the Bank,* 1786, p. 77).

At no period of his official career did Whitehill reflect better his back-country views than as a member of the Pennsylvania convention to ratify the federal Constitution (1787). In the Assembly he sought a delay in the election of delegates in order to allow the inhabitants of the remoter regions of the state to become more familiar with the frame of government. In the convention he resorted to every device to delay or defeat ratification. He insisted that there were inadequate safeguards against a tyranny and on the day of ratification attempted, without avail, to have fifteen articles incorporated as a bill of rights. Three years later, as a further mark of his disapproval of governments with a strong executive and an independent judiciary, he refused to sign Pennsylvania's new constitution on the ground that it was too undemo-

cratic. His suspicions of the judiciary never lessened, and in January 1805, as speaker of the state Senate, he had the satisfaction of presiding at the celebrated impeachment trial of three Pennsylvania supreme court justices.

Whitehill was elected to Congress to fill a vacancy in 1805 and served in that body until his death. A stanch Jeffersonian, he supported the administration regularly, and manifested the same hostility toward the federal judiciary that he had previously shown toward Pennsylvania judges. A proposed amendment introduced by him in 1808 would have limited the tenure of judges to a term of years and would have made them removable by the president on joint address of both houses of Congress. In trials of impeachment he proposed a simple majority only for conviction (*Debates and Proceedings,* 10 Cong., 1 Sess., p. 1680). His wife, whom he married in 1765, was Eleanor, daughter of Adam Reed, western Pennsylvania pioneer. Whitehill died at Lauther Manor.

[W. H. Egle, *Pa. Geneals., Chiefly Scotch-Irish and German* (1896); J. B. McMaster and F. D. Stone, *Pa. and the Federal Constitution, 1787–1788* (1888); Alfred Nevin, *Centennial Biog.: Men of Mark of the Cumberland Valley* (1876); I. D. Rupp, *The Hist. and Topography of Dauphin, Cumberland, Franklin, Bedford, Adams and Perry Counties* (1846); *House and Senate Jours. of Pa., 1790–1805; Minutes of the Supreme Executive Council of Pa.,* vol. XI (1852); *Biog. Dir. Am. Cong.* (1928); *Poulson's Am. Daily Advertiser* (Phila.), Apr. 14, 1813; *Pa. Mag. of Hist. and Biog.,* no. 3, vol. IV (1880), no. 3, vol. XI (1887).]

J. H. P—g.

WHITEHOUSE, FREDERIC COPE (Nov. 9, 1842–Nov. 16, 1911), archeologist, was born in Rochester, N. Y., the son of the Rev. Henry John Whitehouse and his wife, Evelina Harriet Bruen. His grandfather was James Whitehouse, who came to New York City from England in 1801. During his preparation for college he lived for several years in the family of Dr. Henry Drisler, professor of Latin in Columbia College, New York City. In 1861, at the age of eighteen, he was graduated with high honors from Columbia and in 1864 he received the M.A. degree. In 1865 he was graduated from the General Theological Seminary in New York, but he was never ordained as a minister. After this he studied in France, Germany, and Italy, and returned to the United States to be admitted to the bar in New York in 1871. For a great part of his life he lived in Europe, and in 1879 he made his first visit to Egypt, a country which became the scene of his chief interest and activity. His first activities in Egypt concerned the verification of ancient descriptions of the famous "Lake Moeris," described by Herodotus in Book II of his *History.* He made extensive studies of the whole subject, for which his wide reading of ancient and modern authors and a considerable training in science had prepared him, and personally explored this almost forgotten desert region. As a result, in his book, *Lake Moeris: Justification of Herodotus* (1885), he showed Herodotus' account to be in the main not only credible but accurate. The most important fact was the existence of a great valley, the Wadi Raiyan, the floor of which is so far below the level of the Mediterranean that it might well have been used as reservoir, connected with the Nile by a canal represented by the still existing Bahr Yusuf. This theory is now generally regarded as proved.

Whitehouse followed up this discovery (1882) with the bold plan of utilizing the Raiyan Valley for the construction of a reservoir to form an important part of an ambitious project for the better irrigation of Lower Egypt by impounding for later use the surplus of the annual Nile flood. For many years he devoted himself with characteristic energy to the promotion of this plan, producing a steady stream of articles and lectures in support of it. It was received with some favor in official circles in Egypt, and two Turkish orders, the Medjidie and the Osmanie, were conferred upon him in recognition of his labors for the welfare of Egypt. But the plan also met with much opposition on political as well as on economic grounds; and doubtless Whitehouse's unsparing and at times vituperative criticism of the objectors did much to prevent its adoption. The discussion went on for many years, but practically nothing was accomplished by it. The noted engineer Sir William Willcocks, who had been the object of some of Whitehouse's severest criticism, in his *Egyptian Irrigation* (1889) spoke, nevertheless, very favorably of the Moeris-plan, and still more so in *The Assuan Reservoir and Lake Moeris* (1904). In this he was joined by Sir Colin Scott-Moncrieff and Colonel Ross. In 1891 Whitehouse published in England an elaborate *Memorandum on The Raiyan Project and the Action of Her Majesty's Government,* in which he set forth with great bitterness his side of the question.

In connection with this project Whitehouse claimed that a large tract of land in the desert had been promised him by the khedive as a reward for his efforts. This claim he sought to have pressed by the United States diplomatic and consular representatives in Egypt. But he was unsuccessful in this also. Whitehouse was in every way a striking and vivid personality, of fine appearance, with distinctly "the grand manner"; he was an excellent linguist, with a remarkable flow of language, and a well-founded reputation for loquacity. His intense conviction of his own rightness and his vigorous denunciation of his opponents not unnaturally led to the belief that he was an unpractical visionary. Nevertheless, he had a sense of humor that sometimes produced a most unexpected effect when he chose to exercise it.

Whitehouse wrote extensively; a list of his publications on Egyptian subjects to 1884 is to be found in *Senate Document No. 104,* 59 Congress, 1 Session. He contributed many articles to professional periodicals both in America and abroad; among them may be mentioned particularly an important unsigned article in *Engineering* (London), Sept. 11, 1885. The last years of his life were spent chiefly at Newport, R. I.; but he died at the Brevoort House, New York City, after a long illness. He was never married.

[*Who's Who in America,* 1910–11; "The Bruen Family," manuscript genealogy by Whitehouse in the Lib. of Cong., Washington, D. C.; Alfred Milner, *England in Egypt* (11th ed., 1904); *Bull. Am. Geographical Soc.,* Feb. 1912; *N. Y. Herald,* Nov. 17, 1911.]

E. D. P.

WHITFIELD, HENRY (1597–*c.* 1657), clergyman, settler, was born near London, the son of Thomas Whitfield of Mortlake in Surrey, a lawyer, and his wife, Mildred (Manning). Henry was apparently a student at Oxford for a time, was ordained, and became minister of Ockley, in Surrey, where he maintained an assistant out of his earnings. In 1630 he published *Some Helpes to Stirre up to Christian Duties* and in 1631/32 he received the degree of B.D. from the University of Cambridge. At one time or another most of the nonconformists who later came to America lodged with him, notably John Cotton, Thomas Hooker, and John Davenport [*qq.v.*]. With these men he joined in the protest against the prosecution for refusing to read the "Book of Sports," and in the late thirties prepared to leave England. Joining with a group of younger men who were contemplating emigration, he arranged with George Fenwick [*q.v.*] to settle upon the land purchased by Fenwick. In the spring of 1639 he sold his estate, and in July arrived in New Haven. With five associates, one of whom was William Leete [*q.v.*], he purchased land from the Indians and founded a new town at Menunkatuck, later Guilford. In the fall of the same year or the following spring he built a stone house to serve as a fort, which was used as a place of worship until a meeting house could be erected. In the town's constitution, which Whitfield was largely responsible for framing, its policy was declared to be that "wee might settle and uphold all the ordinances of God in an explicit congregational wav wth most purity, peace, and liberty for the benefit both of oʳselves and our posterities after us" (Steiner, *post,* p. 35). His friendship with George Fenwick, agent for the Puritan leaders, greatly assisted him in enlarging the township.

After the incorporation of the Society for the Propagation of the Gospel in New England in 1649, Whitfield became one of its most active members, and continued in this post until his death. As soon as the Guilford settlement was firmly established, he gave a generous portion of his time to the Society's work, preached frequently to the Indians, and materially aided John Eliot [*q.v.*] in the work of conversion. Of his preaching Cotton Mather wrote: "There was a marvelous majesty and sanctity observable in it" (*post,* I, 539).

In 1618 Whitfield had married Dorothy Sheaffe, by whom he had ten children. One of his daughters, Dorothy, married Samuel Desborough, the first magistrate of Guilford. In 1650 Whitfield returned to England where he was pastor of a church in Winchester until his death in 1657. Unable to sell his house at Guilford, he left his wife and a son, Nathaniel, in charge of the property. It is known that he suffered reverses in health and fortune in the later days of his life. His death occurred between Sept. 17, 1657, when he made his will, and Jan. 29, 1657/58, when it was probated.

In 1651 Whitfield published *The Light Appearing More and More towards the Perfect Day,* and in 1652, *Strength out of Weakness;* the latter was reprinted in 1657 under the title, *The Banners of Grace and Love Displayed in the Farther Conversion of the Indians in New England.* Both were collections of "letters" from Whitfield's fellow missionaries, Eliot, John Wilson, William Leverich, Thomas Mayhew, and Thomas Allen. They were reprinted in 1865 in *Sabin's Reprints* (quarto series, no. III and no. V) and are important for the student of early Colonial missionary work.

[Cotton Mather, *Magnalia Christi Americana* (1702), ed. of 1853, I, 592–94; R. D. Smith, *The Hist. of Guilford* (1877); B. C. Steiner, *A Hist. of the Plantation of Menunkatuck* (1897); *New Eng. Hist. and Geneal. Reg.,* July 1897; Joseph Foster, *Alumni Oxonienses ... 1500–1714,* vol. IV (1892); John and J. A. Venn, *Alumni Cantab.,* pt. 1, vol. IV (1927).]   E. H. D.

WHITFIELD, ROBERT PARR (May 27, 1828–Apr. 6, 1910), paleontologist, was the son of English parents, William Fenton and Margaret (Parr) Whitfield. He was born at New Hartford, Oneida County, N. Y., but spent six years (1835–41) in England. He was for the most part self-educated. At thirteen he learned his father's trade of spindle-making in Utica, N. Y.; at twenty he became an assistant in Samuel Chubbuck's instrument-manufacturing shop there, and soon rose to be a partner and manager (1849–56). He was married at twenty to Mary Henry. During these years in Utica he mastered the art of mechanical drafting, was an active member of the Utica Society of Naturalists, and made collections of mollusks and of fossils from Silurian rocks. In 1856 he was engaged by James Hall [*q.v.*], state geologist at Albany, as an assistant in paleontology and geology. In Albany he developed a more profound interest in paleontology. His associations with Hall and such brilliant young assistants as Charles Abiathar White, Fielding Bradford Meek, and William More Gabb [*qq.v.*] added zest to his new work, and he had an opportunity to meet men like Thomas Sterry Hunt, Peter Lesley, James Merrill Safford, J. L. R. Agassiz, Ferdinand V. Hayden [*qq.v.*], and others who came to Albany to confer with Hall. His work during the first year at Albany consisted of preparatory analyses of copious fossil material offered for examination, classification, and description. Then he began to make those beautiful illustrations of graptolites, crinoids, corals, brachiopods, trilobites, cephalopods, and other fossils which gave added distinction to the volumes issued by James Hall on the paleontology of New York, Canada, Ohio, and Iowa. During the twenty years that he remained with the New York state geological survey as its chief illustrator, he made thousands of highly finished drawings of fossils and developed an unusual appreciation of their morphological structure. Little opportunity or permission was granted for the preparation of scientific papers on these objects, but he published two papers under his own name, one with C. A. White, and nine with James Hall.

In 1872 Whitfield was on the staff of the United States geological survey of the Territories. He also was lecturer in geology (1872–75) and later professor of geology (1875–77) at Rensselaer Polytechnic Institute, Troy, N. Y. In 1877 he became curator of geology in the American Museum of Natural History, New York. There he worked on the James Hall collection of fossils, labeling, arranging, and installing the specimens, an undertaking covering many years of effort. During the thirty-two years of his curatorship he identified and classified vast quantities of fossil material from other sources as well. His entries were made in longhand in six large quarto volumes, four of them devoted to American and two to foreign species. Through his efforts, a catalogue of the 8,000 types and figured specimens in the museum collection was prepared and published as Volume XI (1898) of the *Bulletin of the American Museum of Natural History.* The *Bulletin* itself had been established in 1881 largely as a result of Whitfield's urgings, and he was a frequent contributor to it. His carefully prepared scientific papers number more than a hundred. Some of these were short, others monographic. Apart from his work on the New York collections, he found time to study and describe the fossils collected by Clarence King's survey of the fortieth parallel, by Walter B. Jenney's and William Ludlow's expeditions to the Black Hills of South Dakota, and the collection assembled by the geological surveys of New Jersey, Ohio, Indiana, and Wisconsin. He was a fellow of the American Association for the Advancement of Science and of the Geological Society of America, and a member of many other scientific societies.

Although Whitfield was not of robust physique, he was generally in good health, and, being systematic in his habits and punctilious in his attentions to duty, he accomplished an immense amount of work during the eighty-two years of his life. He was quiet, reserved, and unostentatious, and so devoted to his chosen science that he usually spent his short vacations in the field, collecting. His associations with the objects that he loved, and which he conscientiously and unremittingly studied, remained unbroken to the end. The thousands of beautiful drawings and descriptions which he made are indelibly impressed upon the pages of science. In December 1909, after more than thirty-two years in the American Museum, he was made curator emeritus. He died after a lingering illness of several weeks at Troy, N. Y., and was buried in Rural Cemetery at Albany, not far from the graves of Ebenezer Emmons [*q.v.*] and James Hall. He was survived by his son, James Edward Whitfield, a chemist.

[Sources include information from Adam Bruckner, Whitfield's assistant; catalogue records and yearbooks of the Am. Museum, 1875–1909; *Who's Who in America,* 1910–11; L. P. Gratacap, in *Science,* May 20, 1910, and in *Annals N. Y. Acad. of Sciences,* vol. XX, pt. III (1910), with portrait and bibliog. by L. Hussakof; *Am. Jour. Sci.,* June 1910; E. O. Hovey, in *Am. Museum Jour.,* May 1910, with portrait; J. M. Clarke, in *Bull. Geological Soc. of America,* Mar. 1911, with portrait; obituary in *Albany Evening Jour.,* Apr. 7, 1910.]
C. A. R.

WHITING, CHARLES GOODRICH (Jan. 30, 1842–June 20, 1922), journalist, son of Calvin and Mary R. (Goodrich) Whiting, was born in St. Albans, Vt., but spent his boyhood in the neighborhood of Holyoke, Mass., where his father, an expert in paper-making, was long in business. He attended the high school in Chico-

pee Falls, and for a few years in his later teens and early twenties was miscellaneously employed in paper-making, farming, and clerking in country stores. At the age of twenty-six he joined the staff of the *Springfield Republican,* which under the exacting editorship of the second Samuel Bowles [*q.v.*] was already notable as a "school for journalists." Unlike many of his colleagues Whiting did not leave the paper after a period of training; with the exception of an interval of about eighteen months, he remained in Springfield for more than fifty years. As a young reporter Whiting, with his lifelong friend Edward Smith King [*q.v.*], was first assigned to the *Evening News,* a subsidiary of the *Republican* which Bowles discontinued after a short trial. Whiting then left Springfield to become assistant editor of the *Albany Evening Times.* In November 1872 he was recalled to the *Republican,* first as head of the local department, but from 1874 as literary editor. He also served as art critic and general editorial writer. In 1910 he resigned the literary desk to become associate editor of the newspaper, and in that capacity he continued until his retirement in 1919.

Whiting was fortunate in being trained for his work in a discriminating school where his intelligence, wide culture, and gift of style were early recognized. Nevertheless, before he became literary editor he underwent a thorough initiation in general newspaper work. As local editor, with three other members of the overworked staff, he personally covered the Williamsburg flood in May 1874, and secured for his paper in record time a notably complete and vivid story of the disaster (Griffin, *post,* 116 ff.). At the literary desk he brought independent judgment and fine insight to the routine work of book-reviewing. But his most widely appreciated contributions to the *Republican* were his editorial essays on general topics, particularly on country life, the pageant of the seasons, and the charms of the local landscape. Two collections of these pieces were published in book form as *The Saunterer* (1886) and *Walks in New England* (1903).

In the literary life of Springfield and in the promotion of civic aims Whiting took a prominent part. He was a kindly adviser of younger writers and journalists, a chronicler of local history, and a poet on numerous public occasions, notably on the dedication of the Soldiers' Monument (1885), the celebration of the founding of Springfield (1911), the opening of the Auditorium (1913), and the dedication of the Municipal Buildings (1913). His literary distinction was recognized by his election to the

National Institute of Arts and Letters. He was married on June 12, 1869, to Eliza Rose Gray of Adams, Mass. He died at his country home in Otis, Mass., survived by his wife and their two children.

[*Who's Who in America*, 1922–23; G. S. Merriam, *The Life and Times of Samuel Bowles* (2 vols., 1885); S. B. Griffin, *People and Politics* (1923); Richard Hooker, *The Story of an Independent Newspaper* (1924); obituary and editorial in *Springfield Republican*, June 21, 1922.]   G. F. W.

WHITING, GEORGE ELBRIDGE (Sept. 14, 1840–Oct. 14, 1923), organist, composer, was born in Holliston, Mass., the son of Nathan P. and Olive (Chase) Whiting. He early showed his talent for music and when he was five years of age he commenced musical studies with his brother Amos. As a boy he played the piano in a concert at Worcester, Mass., and in 1858 he became the organist of the North Congregational Church in Hartford. By 1862 he was in Boston playing the organ at the Mount Vernon Church, while Edward N. Kirk [*q.v.*] was pastor, and occasionally at the Tremont Temple. During this period he studied the organ with G. W. Morgan, in New York. In 1863 he went to England for study with W. T. Best. Upon his return to America, he was in Albany for three years as organist of St. Joseph's Church, but thereafter returned to Boston and for five years occupied the position of organist and choir director at King's Chapel. For a year he was organist at the Music Hall. In 1867 he was married to Helen Aldrich of Worcester, Mass., and in 1874 went abroad once more for further study. He worked in Berlin with Haupt (harmony) and Radecke (orchestration). From 1876 to 1878 he was in Boston as organist of the Church of the Immaculate Conception, principal instructor of organ at the New England Conservatory of Music, and conductor of the Foster Club. By this time his reputation was well established nationally, and in 1878 Theodore Thomas appointed him head of the organ and composition department of the College of Music in Cincinnati, Ohio. He remained in Cincinnati until 1882, when he returned to Boston to take up once more his duties at the New England Conservatory and to become organist and music director of the Church of the Immaculate Conception. He remained at the Conservatory until 1898, and at the Immaculate Conception until 1910. He died at Cambridge, Mass.

Whiting was a prolific composer and published many works. Among them were a choral march, "Our Country," composed for the inauguration of President Taft in 1909; four concert-études for organ; a "Grand Sonata" for organ; *Twen-*

ty Preludes and Postludes for Organ (two volumes); a cantata, *The Tale of the Viking,* with words taken from Longfellow; five masses on plain-chant melodies, and many smaller works for organ as well as anthems and part-songs for chorus. He was one of the foremost organists of his time, ranking with Clarence Eddy, Harrison M. Wild, Henry M. Dunham [*q.v.*]. Although his compositions are little performed today, he had an important part in developing the art of organ-playing in the United States and in adding his contribution to the American literature of music for that instrument.

[In *Who's Who in America*, 1922–23, Whiting gives 1842 as the year of his birth; however, the *Vital Records of Holliston, Mass.* (1908) provide 1840 as the official date. For other biographical data consult: *Baker's Biog. Dict. of Musicians* (3rd ed., 1919); *Grove's Dict. of Music and Musicians,* vol. V (3rd ed., 1928); J. T. Howard, *Our Am. Music* (1931); *A Hundred Years of Music in America* (1889), ed. by W. S. B. Mathews; E. E. Truette, "Two American Organists and Composers," *Musician,* May 1910; *Choir and Choral Mag.,* Jan. 1903; *Boston Evening Transcript,* Oct. 15, 1923.]   J. T. H.

WHITING, WILLIAM HENRY CHASE (Mar. 22, 1824–Mar. 10, 1865), Confederate soldier, was descended from the Rev. Samuel Whiting who arrived in Boston, Mass., May 26, 1636, and soon settled in Lynn. Although William was born in Biloxi, Miss., his parents, Levi and Mary A. Whiting, were of Massachusetts origin. His father was lieutenant-colonel, 1st Artillery, United States Army. William was prepared for college in Boston and graduated first in his class at Georgetown College, D. C., in 1840. At West Point, in a class (1845) which included Fitz-John Porter, E. Kirby-Smith, and Gordon Granger [*qq.v.*], he established the highest graduate standing that had ever been attained at the Military Academy. Appointed second lieutenant, Corps of Engineers, July 1, 1845, he supervised river and harbor improvements and the construction of fortifications in the South and in California until 1861, working for two years (1856–57) on the Cape Fear River, North Carolina. During this period he married Kate D. Walker, daughter of Maj. John Walker, of Smithville and Wilmington. He was promoted first lieutenant, Mar. 16, 1853, and captain, Dec. 13, 1858, but resigned Feb. 20, 1861, to enter the Confederate service as a major.

After planning new defenses for Charleston harbor and Morris Island, he joined Johnston's Army of the Shenandoah as chief engineer. He arranged the transfer of this army to Manassas, where he was promoted brigadier-general on the field by President Davis (Davis' order, quoted by C. B. Denson, *post,* p. 15). After temporarily commanding Gen. Gustavus W. Smith's division at Seven Pines, May 31, 1862, he received a division permanently. At his suggestion, adopted by General Lee (*Ibid.,* p. 21), early in June his troops reinforced Gen. Thomas J. Jackson [*q.v.*] in the Valley. Returning to Richmond with Jackson, Whiting's division at Gaines's Mill pierced the center of Fitz-John Porter's strong position in a charge characterized by "Stonewall" as an "almost matchless display of daring and valor" (*Official Records, post,* 1 ser., vol. XI, pt. 2, p. 556). After fighting at Malvern Hill, he took command in November 1862 of the military district of Wilmington, N. C. Whiting made the Cape Fear River the best haven in the South for blockade runners, and developed Fort Fisher, at the river's mouth, into the most powerful defensive work of the Confederacy. Appointed a major-general to rank from Feb. 28, 1863, he was suddenly called, in May 1864, to take command at Petersburg, Va. Ill, and unfamiliar with the situation, he failed to execute his part of Beauregard's plan for accomplishing the capture of Butler's army at Drewry's Bluff. Beauregard generously overlooked the error (*Ibid.,* 1 ser., vol. XXXVI, pt. 2, pp. 260–61), and, at his own request, Whiting returned to Wilmington.

Late in December a federal fleet of fifty-five warships bombarded Fort Fisher. Little damage resulted and the fleet departed, only to return on Jan. 13, 1865, and disembark a force of 8,000 troops. General Bragg was ordered to Wilmington, depriving Whiting of the defense of a stronghold which he had safeguarded for nearly three years. Convinced that Fort Fisher would be sacrificed, Whiting repaired thither, refusing command but heroically aiding Colonel Lamb in its defense. After an unprecedented naval bombardment, the Union forces on Jan. 15 assaulted the shattered earthworks. Neither reinforced nor assisted by exterior diversions, the garrison of 1,900 men was overwhelmed and captured. General Whiting, badly wounded, was conveyed to Fort Columbus, Governor's Island, N. Y., where on Mar. 10 he died of his injuries.

Below average height, Whiting was, nevertheless, of martial bearing, handsome, and sinewy. He was idolized by his troops, who affectionately called him "Little Billy." At his best a skilful and dynamic commander, unfortunately, as at Drewry's Bluff, he did not always prove equal to that best; but his contemporaries, Southern and Northern alike, honored him as a brilliant engineer, a dauntless soldier, and a courteous gentleman.

[William Whiting, *Memoir of Rev. Samuel Whiting* (1873); *War of the Rebellion: Official Records (Army)*; C. B. Denson, *An Address . . . Containing a Memoir of the Late Maj.-Gen. William Henry Chase Whiting* (1895); James Sprunt, *Chronicles of the Cape Fear River, 1660–1916* (1916); G. F. R. Henderson, *Stonewall Jackson and the Am. Civil War* (1898); C. A. Evans, *Confederate Mil. Hist.* (1899); *Battles and Leaders of the Civil War* (4 vols., 1887–88); *N. Y. Times,* Mar. 11, 1865.]

J. M. H.

WHITLOCK, BRAND (Mar. 4, 1869–May 24, 1934), writer, mayor, diplomat, was born at Urbana, Ohio (the Macochee of his stories), the son of the Rev. Elias D. and Mallie (Brand) Whitlock. From his maternal grandfather he perhaps inherited more than his name. Maj. Joseph Carter Brand, a Kentuckian with roots in Virginia and Jacobite Scotland, had freed his slaves, moved to Ohio, entered the law, played a part in Abolitionist politics and in the Civil War, served as consul at Nürnberg and mayor four times of Urbana. The grandson's revolt led him at eighteen into free trade and Democracy. He attended high school in Toledo, whither his family had moved, but did not proceed to college. Six years of journalism in Toledo (1887–90) and Chicago (1891–93) were his higher education of experience. He married at twenty-three and lost his wife four months later. He made friendships that shaped the rest of his life. When John Peter Altgeld [*q.v.*] became governor of Illinois, he invited Whitlock to be his secretary. Whitlock declined, in doubt of the destiny of secretaries to the great, preferring a humbler clerkship in the Secretary of State's office at Springfield (1893–97). Thus it befell him in 1893 to make out in secret for Altgeld the pardons of the last three prisoners of the Haymarket riots of 1886, and to share in the ensuing commotion. During this stormy interlude he also read law with Gen. John M. Palmer [*q.v.*], was admitted to the Illinois bar in 1894, and married Ella Brainerd of Springfield on June 8, 1895. In 1897, after passing examinations for the Ohio bar, he opened an office in Toledo.

An ironic experience determined him never again to act for the prosecution. This gave him leisure for his first novel, *The 13th District* (1902), portraying the moral disintegration of a candidate. Meanwhile he became attorney for a humane society, a relation which cemented a friendship with Mayor "Golden Rule" Jones and drew Whitlock into the neo-democratic movement of the town and the day. In the absence of the regular incumbent, Jones often deputed him to sit as city magistrate, thus quickening his sympathy for the thoughtless or unwitting victim of the law and arming him for his long crusade in favor of a humanized legal procedure, for prison reform, against capital punishment. As Jones's most trusted legal adviser he acquired renown by winning a suit, in reversal of a former state supreme court decision, that restored the Toledo police to the mayor's control (*Forty Years of It,* pp. 135–36). In 1904 Jones died. Whitlock was thereupon, in 1905, elected to succeed him, on a home-rule, non-partisan, anti-monopoly platform. He served four two-year terms, announcing after his last election (1911) that he would not run again.

On Dec. 22, 1913, he became American minister to Belgium, retiring to the legation at Brussels for a well-earned repose. He had time to publish *Forty Years of It* (1914), the record of his adventures in liberalism. The outbreak of the World War then drove him into more spectacular adventures. He was fortunate in having for a colleague an old friend and remarkable man, the Spanish Marqués de Villalobar. The two remained in Brussels after the exodus of the government, persuaded the burghers into non-resistance, resisted the invaders on countless occasions themselves, but performed countless services for individuals. Whitlock's reports on Edith Cavell excited intense irritation in Berlin, as did his protests against the deportations, while the troubles of the Commission for Relief in Belgium beset his pillow with thorns. If he was not handed his passports long before he asked for them, it was partly because his had been the official credit of repatriating 91,000 Germans in four August nights of 1914. But his presence in Brussels facilitated, alike for friend and foe, the immense task of organizing the distribution of food among the civil population of Belgium and the occupied zone in France. Although he was offered in 1916 the embassy to Petrograd, he chose to follow the Belgian government into exile near Le Havre. After the war the Belgians overwhelmed him with honors. Raised on Sept. 30, 1919, to the rank of ambassador, he resigned in 1922. His last twelve years of broken health were spent chiefly in Brussels and on the Riviera. It is to be noted that he upon whom the clergy had once looked askance ended his life as a devout Episcopalian. He died under an operation at Cannes, where is his grave.

It would be unjust to say that Whitlock was made by the war. In Toledo he was likewise observed to acquit himself with humanity, dignity, and courage. Not only did he insist upon a fair deal for the working man, liberalize the administration of justice, keep the city government free of graft, and break an ice monopoly that weighed upon the poor, he fought and won a resounding battle against the local power and traction interests. His record as mayor, which attracted nation-wide attention, brought him in 1913 the gold medal of the National Institute of Social Sciences. By that time he had published eight books, including his most considered novel, *The Turn of the Balance* (1907), and an essay, *On the Enforcement of Law in Cities* (1910), which grieved the conventional reformer. His *Belgium: A Personal Record* (2 vols., 1919, issued in various editions and translations), being of the stuff of history, is doubtless his best-known work. He later completed the novel begun in 1914, *J. Hardin & Son* (1923), and brought out seven more books before his death. Of these the most elaborate is *La Fayette* (2 vols., 1929), and the last, *The Stranger on the Island* (1933). His fiction, preoccupied as much of it is with the technique of justice, illustrates what he called his vacillation between letters and politics (*Forty Years of It,* p. 86). He does not belong to the strictest sect of the realists, nor is his style in the astringent taste of the years after the war. Be it recorded of him nevertheless that while practising law, governing a city, coping with invaders, and enduring a painful disease, he had the fortitude to produce eighteen books.

[Whitlock left a fairly complete record of his own life in *Forty Years of It* and *Belgium.* For the Belgian period, see *Correspondence with the United States Ambassador Respecting the Execution of Miss Cavell at Brussels,* Command Paper 8013 (1915); a pamphlet, *The Deportations: Statement by the American Minister to Belgium* (1917); *Papers Relating to the Foreign Relations of the United States, 1918,* supp. 2 (1933), and *1920,* vols. I, II (1935–36), containing a few of his dispatches. See also *Who's Who in America,* 1932–33; obituaries and comments in *Toledo News-Bee,* May 24, 25, 1934; *N. Y. Times,* May 25, 27, 1934; *Publishers' Weekly,* June 2, 1934; *Survey* (N. Y.), June 1934.]
H. G. D—t.

WHITMAN, ALBERY ALLSON (May 30, 1851–June 29, 1901), poet and clergyman of the African Methodist Episcopal Church, was born in slavery in Hart County, Ky., near Mumfordsville. His mother died in 1862, less than a year before he was set free; his father died just after emancipation. After the farm drudgery of his slave boyhood, he became an itinerant manual laborer in shops and on the railroad in Kentucky and southern Ohio. His schooling was brief—probably about seven scattered months. He taught school in Ohio and Kentucky for short periods, and finally entered Wilberforce University, where he remained for six months under the instruction of the Rev. Daniel Alexander Payne [*q.v.*]. After publishing *Essays on the Ten Plagues and Miscellaneous Poems,* he returned to Wilberforce and brought out in 1873 his second work, *Leelah Misled.* He was not a graduate of Wilberforce but was officially connected with the school for a number of years. In 1877, when an elder of the African Methodist

Episcopal Church and financial agent of Wilberforce, he published, in the interests of Wilberforce, *Not a Man and Yet a Man,* with a group of miscellaneous poems. In 1884 appeared *The Rape of Florida,* later issued under the name of *Twasinta's Seminoles.* His duties as pastor carried him from Ohio to Kansas, Texas, and Georgia. He was influential in establishing many churches. His last work was *An Idyl of the South* (1901), comprising two fairly long poems, "The Octoroon" and "The Southland's Charms and Freedom's Magnitude." He died in Atlanta, Ga.

Whitman's poetry is essentially imitative. His *Leelah Misled* is consciously Byronic; *Not a Man and Yet a Man* is a medley of derivations; *Twasinta's Seminoles* recalls Byron and Tennyson. The shorter poems, humorous, sentimental, and topical commentaries, rely frequently on models such as Bryant and Whittier, and strive for "literary" effect. Although he chose subjects of scope and enduring appeal, and was concerned chiefly with tragedies afflicting either characters of mixed blood or the fast-vanishing Indian, his narratives suffer from digressions and incoherence. The incidents are melodramatic, the characters sentimental stereotypes of "blood and tears" romances. "The Freedman's Triumphant Song" and "The Southland's Charm and Freedom's Magnitude" are intellectually unimpressive, phrasing the conventional insistences upon the negro's patriotism, optimism, and deserts. But in spite of lapses of diction, technique, and taste, Whitman's poetry is fluent, and his love for nature seems real and unforced. His reading, which was wide for a man of such scanty educational opportunities, bears witness both to a genuine love for the English poets and to a great aspiration for self-improvement. Any estimate of his work must remain historical. His *Twasinta's Seminoles* was the first poem in Spenserian stanza and his *Not a Man and Yet a Man* one of the longest poems attempted by a man of color. He was the most considerable poet of his race before Paul Lawrence Dunbar [q.v.] in bulk and in familiarity with poetic models, but his distinction is one of ambition rather than achievement.

[The best biog. sources are the prefaces, generally autobiog., of Whitman's publications, especially that of *Leelah Misled.* See also D. W. Culp, *Twentieth Century Negro Lit.* (1902); J. T. Jenifer, *Hist. of the African M. E. Church* (1916); D. A. Payne, *Recollections of Seventy Years* (1888); W. J. Simmons, *Men of Mark* (1887); and Vernon Loggins, *The Negro Author, His Development in America* (1931), which contains the best critical discussion of Whitman's poetry. Other information, including the date of death, has been supplied by Arthur Schomburg and Lawrence Jordan of the N. Y. Pub. Lib.]   S. A. B.

WHITMAN, CHARLES OTIS (Dec. 14, 1842–Dec. 6, 1910), biologist, was born in North Woodstock, Me., the son of Joseph and Marcia (Leonard) Whitman. His ancestry was strictly New England and Puritan. He was a descendant of John Whitman who settled in Weymouth, Mass., about 1638. There is evidence all along the line of his ancestors of great persistence and obstinacy of conviction and belief. His father, a carriage-builder by trade, was a Second Adventist of the hardest kind. His mother was also of New England stock. His early environment was the New England small town and countryside, his grandfather's farm, the open country and the woods; his early education was in the local schools. As a boy he was not interested in usual sports, but was studious, quiet, and rather diffident. His avocations, ornithology and taxidermy, indicated at an early age that zoölogy was to be the ruling interest of his life. He broke with his father's religion and was regarded as an unbeliever. He entered Bowdoin College as a sophomore in 1865, and his commencement address delivered in 1868, "Free Inquiry," was good evidence of an unfettered mind.

From 1868 to 1872 he was principal of Westford Academy, and then taught for two years in the Boston English High School. In the summers of 1873 and 1874, however, he attended Agassiz' summer school of natural history on the Island of Penikese, and then definitely committed himself to scientific pursuits by going to the University of Leipzig to study for three years under the great teacher of zoölogy, Leuckart. He received there the Ph.D. degree. Shortly after his return to America he was appointed to succeed Edward S. Morse [q.v.] in the chair of zoölogy in the Imperial University of Japan at Tokyo, and remained there for a period of two years only. On his way back to America he spent six months in research at the zoölogical station of Naples. From 1883 to 1885 Whitman was assistant in zoölogy at the Museum of Comparative Zoölogy at Harvard University. From 1886 to 1889 he was director of the Allis Lake Laboratory at Milwaukee, Wis., from 1889 to 1892 he taught zoölogy at Clark University, Worcester, Mass., and thereafter until the time of his death was professor and head of the department of zoölogy in the University of Chicago. He was director of the Marine Biological Laboratory at Woods Hole, Mass., from its foundation in 1888 to 1908.

Whitman never indulged in popular teaching; in Japan he had only four students. They, however, became the leaders of zoölogy in their country. In America he would accept only a few research students (see Lillie, in *Journal of Morphology, post*), but he was, nevertheless, a great believer in the vocation of the teacher. As an investigator he was ceaselessly active from 1875 to the time of his death, although he published relatively few technical papers. At his death he left a large accumulation of notes and drawings on evolution in pigeons which were arranged and edited by Oscar Riddle and published under the title *Posthumous Works of C. O. Whitman* by the Carnegie Institution of Washington (No. 257, 3 vols., 1919). His main scientific contributions were in embryology, comparative anatomy, taxonomy, evolution, heredity and animal behavior. His list of more than sixty publications (see Lillie, *Ibid.*) contains a series of delightful essays on theoretical and historical biology, written in a fine, characteristic, polished style. To him belongs the credit for introducing European scientific zoölogy into America, founding, in 1887, the *Journal of Morphology* and establishing a new standard for scientific publication in America. He also edited *Biological Lectures* from 1890 to 1899, and, with M. M. Wheeler, the *Zoölogical Bulletin*, 1897-99. In 1890 he took the leading part in the establishment of the American Morphological Society, which became in 1902 the American Society of Zoölogists. The planning of the Marine Biological Laboratory was done on a national scale and he was successful in securing the cooperation of the leading biologists of the United States. The Laboratory became an ideal station representing all biological interests, available to and governed by all the biologists of the country, and Whitman endowed the institution with original and unique features of organization that have stood the test of time. He was a member of the National Academy of Sciences and a fellow of the American Association for the Advancement of Science.

Whitman's appearance commanded attention for he had many distinctive characteristics. Before forty his hair turned completely white while his beard remained dark. He had blue eyes of startling brilliance and depth, and large, round nostrils. He was quietly courteous in manner and very hospitable to scientific men although he avoided all other society. He never compromised a principle and consequently was frequently involved in controversy. He died in Chicago of pneumonia contracted as a result of exposure, and was buried with simple ceremony at Wood's Hole. He was survived by his wife, Emily Nunn, of Boston, to whom he had been married on Aug. 15, 1884. They had two sons.

[*Who's Who in America*, 1910-11; C. H. Farnam, *Hist. of the Descendants of John Whitman* (1889); C. B. Davenport, "The Personality, Heredity and Work of Charles Otis Whitman," *Am. Naturalist*, Jan. 1917; F. R. Lillie, biographical articles in *Science*, Jan. 13, 1911, *Univ. of Chicago Mag.*, 1911, *Jour. of Morphology*, *Whitman Memorial Vol.*, vol. XXII (1911), No. 4 (containing an account of Whitman's scientific work by E. G. Conklin, A. P. Mathews, T. H. Morgan, J. P. Moore, and Oscar Riddle); A. P. Mathews, biographical article in *Science*, Jan. 13, 1911; E. S. Morse, "Biographical Memoir of Charles Otis Whitman," *Acad. of Sci. Biog. Memoirs*, vol. VII (1913); Tomotaro Iwakawa, Chiyomatsu Ishikawa, Katashi Takahashi, articles in Japanese on Whitman in Japan, *Mag. of Zoölogy* (Tokyo), vol. XXIII (1911); Oscar Riddle, "A Note on Professor Whitman's Unpublished Work," *Univ. of Chicago Mag.*, vol. IV; R. M. Strong, "Some Reminiscences of the Late Professor C. O. Whitman," *Auk*, Jan. 1912; *Chicago Daily News*, Dec. 7, 1910.]

F. R. L.

WHITMAN, EZEKIEL (Mar. 9, 1776–Aug. 1, 1866), representative in Congress, jurist, son of Josiah and Sarah (Sturtevant) Whitman, and descendant of John Whitman who settled in Weymouth, Mass., about 1638, was born in Bridgewater (later East Bridgewater), Mass. His father died when he was two years old. In 1783 his mother married again, and young Ezekiel went to live with his uncle, the Rev. Levi Whitman of Wellfleet, who gave him a rudimentary education. At the age of fourteen he prepared for college under the Rev. Kilborn Whitman of Pembroke, and after fifteen months' study he entered Rhode Island College (later Brown University) in 1791. Desperately poor, he was compelled to leave college in his senior year through lack of funds. He returned just before commencement and, on passing his examinations, received the degree of A.B. in 1795. He disliked Latin and Greek but excelled in other studies. Slow of speech and of motion, he pursued an independent way, and, though he was eccentric and obstinate at times, his honesty and integrity brought him respect. When graduated, Whitman was without funds and considered joining a company of players then performing in Providence, but his friend Peleg Chandler dissuaded him from this as well as from going to sea. He then studied law, first with Benjamin Whitman of Hanover and then with Nahum Mitchell in his native town. In 1796 he spent a year in Kentucky, where he had gone to settle the estate of a deceased Bridgewater citizen. In the spring of 1799, having been admitted to the bar of Plymouth County, he decided to begin the practice of law in Maine, and set out alone on horseback for Turner. In September he removed to New Gloucester, where he remained until January 1807 with steadily increasing success. He then removed to Portland. He was an able jury lawyer, using simple and direct methods, eloquent by reason of clarity and force, and not through rhetorical display. He was a successful advocate for merchants presenting claims under the treaty with Spain in 1819 and later in similar cases under the convention with France of July 1831. Many students studied in his office, among them Simon Greenleaf and Albion K. Parris [*qq.v.*].

Though he preferred the law to politics, he served as representative in Congress from Cumberland County, March 1809 to March 1811. In 1815 and 1816 he was a member of the executive council of Massachusetts. In 1816 he was a member of the Brunswick Convention, which met to consider the separation of Maine from Massachusetts. When members tried by misinterpreting the law to make it seem that the necessary five-ninths of the voters had voted for separation, he vigorously repudiated the action. Again elected to Congress in 1816, he served three continuous terms (March 1817–June 1822). He defended the bill authorizing the apprehension of foreign seamen deserting from merchant ships in the ports of the United States (*Annals of Congress*, 15 Cong., 2 Sess., p. 362). He favored restrictions on slavery in Missouri but opposed the same restrictions in Arkansas (*Ibid.*, p. 1274). He opposed Henry Clay's successful attempts to unite the admission of Missouri with that of Maine (*Ibid.*, 16 Cong., 1 Sess., pp. 836, 1407) and voted against the bill admitting the two states together (for his defense see M. Kingsley and others, *Address to the People of Maine*, 1820). He addressed Congress frequently on the Florida question, strongly condemning Jackson for his action there. In 1819 he was a member of the convention which formed a constitution for Maine. He resigned from Congress, June 1, 1822, in order to take up his duties as judge of the court of common pleas, a position to which Governor Parris had appointed him on Feb. 4. On Dec. 10, 1841, he succeeded Judge Nathan Weston as chief justice of the supreme court of Maine, an office which he filled until Oct. 23, 1848, when, under the provisions of the state constitution, he was compelled to resign. The honesty and integrity for which he was noted in his youth, and later in Congress, enhanced his reputation as a judge. Though ordinarily he was quiet and deliberate, he could act quickly and vigorously in an emergency. His judicial opinions are to be found in *Maine Reports* (vols. XXI–XXIX). In 1832 he published *Memoir of John Whitman and His Descendants.*

His wife, Hannah Mitchell, the sister of his legal instructor, whom he married Oct. 31, 1799, died after a paralytic shock, Mar. 28, 1852. They had a son and two daughters, one of whom mar-

ried William Willis, 1794–1870 [*q.v.*]. Left lonely and desolate by his wife's death, in October 1852 he returned to East Bridgewater, where like many of his family he died at an advanced age. He was buried in Portland.

[See *Biog. Dir. Am. Cong.* (1928); William Willis, *A Hist. of the Law, the Courts, and the Lawyers of Me.* (1863); *Biog. Encyc. of Me. of the Nineteenth Century* (1885); C. H. Farnam, *Hist. of the Descendants of John Whitman of Weymouth, Mass.* (1889); Nahum Mitchell, *Hist. of the Early Settlement of Bridgewater* (1840); Charles Hamlin, in *Green Bag*, Oct. 1895; obituary notices in *New England Hist. and Geneal. Reg.*, Oct. 1866, *Bangor Daily Whig and Courier*, Aug. 4, 1866, and *Daily Portland Press*, Aug. 8, 1866. Comparison should be made between the biog. letter of Peleg Chandler to William Willis, Aug. 23, 1843, and the letter of Ezekiel Whitman to Willis, Apr. 5, 1863 (both in the Willis MSS., colls. of the Me. Hist. Soc.).]   R. E. M.

WHITMAN, MARCUS (Sept. 4, 1802–Nov. 29, 1847), physician, missionary, pioneer, was born at Rushville, N. Y., the third son of Beza and Alice (Green) Whitman, both of colonial New England stock. On his father's side he was descended from John Whitman who settled at Weymouth, Mass., and was made a freeman of the colony in 1638. Marcus was educated partly at Plainfield, Mass., where he lived in his paternal grandfather's family; he studied medicine under Dr. Ira Bryant of Rushville, began practise, and in 1832 was awarded the degree of M.D. by the College of Physicians and Surgeons of the Western District of New York, at Fairfield, Herkimer County. After eight years of practise, four in Canada and four at Wheeler, N. Y., Whitman proffered his services as "physician, teacher, or agriculturist" to the American Board of Commissioners for Foreign Missions. The Board sent him to the West in 1835 with Rev. Samuel Parker [*q.v.*] to make a missionary reconnaissance in Oregon. From Green River, where delegations of western Indians met them sympathetically, Whitman returned to the East and prepared to begin the Oregon mission a year earlier than had been contemplated.

In February 1836, at Angelica, N. Y., he married Narcissa Prentiss, who, like himself, had enlisted under the Board. He secured the Rev. Henry Harmon Spalding and his wife and W. H. Gray, a layman, to assist him. Two Indian boys he had taken East helped to drive the cattle and pack-animals. As far as Green River the mission party traveled under the protection of the American Fur Company. There they fell in with a Hudson's Bay Company caravan which lightened their way to the lower Columbia. Wagons had never passed Fort Hall, but Whitman took a light vehicle, converted into a cart, as far as Fort Boise, thus gaining credit for opening that portion of the wagon road to Oregon. Taking white women across the continent to Oregon was a feat that caught the popular imagination and stimulated emigration thither. The Whitman party reached Fort Walla Walla, at the junction of Walla Walla River with the Columbia, on the first of September. Near that point Parker had selected a situation for a mission to the Cayuses and he had chosen others on the Clearwater among the Nez Percés and on the Spokane among the Flatheads. The party first passed down the river to Fort Vancouver to procure supplies, then founded two stations, Waiilatpu in Walla Walla Valley and Lapwai near the present Lewiston, Idaho. The Whitmans and W. H. Gray remained at Waiilatpu, the Spaldings had charge at Lapwai. The Spokane station was not founded until two years later, after the arrival in 1838 of two more ministers, Cushing Eells and Elkanah Walker, with their wives. The Methodists had begun a mission on the Willamette in 1834; the Catholic missions in Oregon were begun in 1838.

For a time the work among the up-river Indians went forward promisingly. Mrs. Spalding was notably successful as a teacher, while Whitman and Spalding both taught the Indians to farm by means of irrigation, and to appreciate tame cattle, better housing, and some of the other amenities of civilized living. Dissensions in the missionary fraternity, however, engendered complaints to the Board, which, in 1842, ordered one of the stations discontinued and part of the force sent home. Whitman believed this order might be withdrawn if proper representations were made at Boston, and it was for that reason—not, as has been so often asserted, to "save Oregon" politically—that he, with the consent of his co-workers, made the famous "winter ride" east in 1842–43. He left Waiilatpu Oct. 3, 1842, on horseback, with a single companion, A. L. Lovejoy, expecting to cross the mountains during that month and to reach St. Louis by Dec. 1. This he could readily have done under usual conditions, but at Fort Hall he learned that some of the intervening tribes were hostile, and therefore turned south by way of Taos and Bent's Fort. On that long detour winter overtook the travelers, who barely escaped destruction. Nevertheless, Whitman reached Boston early in April, had a successful interview with his Board, and also visited Washington, where he conferred with the secretary of war and perhaps others. He accompanied the great emigration of that year to Oregon, affording the emigrants much aid as physician and, over a portion of the route, as guide, but he did not raise that emigrating company as has been

claimed: the "Oregon fever," the Linn Land Donation Bill, and other agencies were responsible.

Whitman's missionary outlook, roseate for a time, now became discouraging. Contesting the field with the Catholics, whose ceremonialism and pageantry appealed strongly to the natives, was no light task. This was one major difficulty. The presence among the Indians of vicious white men and half breeds was another disturbing factor. With the passing of the years Whitman, who had been a friend of all the Cayuses, came to be regarded by some with coldness and even malice. Their estrangement was so menacing that he partly resolved to remove his family to a place of safety, but unfortunately he delayed too long, and accidental circumstances precipitated a tragedy. The emigrants of 1847 brought the measles in epidemic form. Among the Indian children the disease proved virulent. Whitman's medicine failed to help them, though it kept white children alive. The terrible inference that he was poisoning their children caused the Cayuse outbreak, Nov. 29, 1847, in which Whitman, his wife, and twelve other persons were atrociously murdered. The Whitman massacre led to an Indian war, waged largely by the Oregon settlers, for the punishment of the murderers. The news of the tragedy, carried to Washington during the winter by Joseph L. Meek [q.v.], may have hastened the passage of the Oregon Territory law, and it certainly aroused general sympathy for the isolated community on the Columbia.

In 1843 Whitman was described by Horace Greeley [q.v.] as "a noble pioneer . . . a man fitted to be a chief in rearing a moral empire among the wild men of the wilderness" (New York Tribune, Mar. 29, 1843). His outstanding traits were vigor, resourcefulness, stubborn determination, optimism. Completely dedicated to his cause, he discounted the multiplying evidences of failure; faith, zeal, hopefulness occasionally submerged judgment. No physical portrait of him exists, but from reports, he may be described as an ardent soul in an intensely dynamic body.

[C. W. Smith, A Contribution toward a Bibliog. of Marcus Whitman (1909), repr. from Wash. Hist. Quart., Oct. 1908, lists nearly 200 works; E. G. Bourne, "The Legend of Marcus Whitman," Am. Hist. Rev., Jan. 1901, repr. in Essays in Hist. Criticism (1901), destroys the myth that "Whitman saved Oregon"; Myron Eells, Marcus Whitman (1909), sympathetic, but not wholly sound historically, contains the important letters and journal of Narcissa Whitman, the originals of which, with other Whitman sources, are owned by the Ore. Hist. Soc.; an utterly contrasted work, also valuable for its documentary material, reproduced in part from papers in the Congregational Library, Boston, is W. I. Marshall, The Acquisition of Oregon (2 vols., 1911) ; a concise general history of the Whitman Mission is in Joseph Schafer, *A Hist. of the Pacific Northwest* (2nd ed., 1918) ; see also list of graduates in *Circular and Catalogue of the College of Physicians and Surgeons of the Western District of the State of N. Y. . . . 1839–40* (1839) ; C. H. Farnam, *Hist. of the Descendants of John Whitman of Weymouth, Mass.* (1889) ; C. J. F. Binney, *The Hist. and Geneal. of the Prentice or Prentiss Family* (1883) ; *Trans. . . . Ore. Pioneer Asso., 1891* (1893) and *1893* (1894) ; *Missionary Herald,* 1835–47.]   J. S.

WHITMAN, SARAH HELEN POWER

(Jan. 19, 1803–June 27, 1878), poet, was born in Providence, R. I., second of three children of Nicholas and Anna (Marsh) Power. Her father became a sea-faring man and was absent once for a period of nineteen years, so that the influence of her mother dominated her in practical matters most of her life. She attended private school in Providence and for a time, when she was residing with an aunt, Mrs. Cornelius Bogert, in Jamaica, L. I. In her mature years she read widely in French, German, Spanish, and Italian. After her marriage to John Winslow Whitman, attorney and inventor, at Jamaica, on July 10, 1828, she lived in Boston, but after his death in 1833, she returned to Providence to live with her mother and sister. The house on the corner of Benefit and Church Streets was her home for more than forty years. Her first poem, "Retrospection," was published in Mrs. Sarah J. Hale's *Ladies' Magazine* in 1829, with the signature "Helen." For the remainder of her life she contributed to various magazines verses and articles on religious and literary topics. She was interested especially in mystical discussions and in 1851 published in the *New York Tribune* articles on spiritualism, which were widely reprinted and served to extend her growing correspondence, especially with other writers. Though her first book of verse, *Hours of Life and Other Poems,* did not appear until 1853, she had already been generously represented in R. W. Griswold's *The Female Poets of America* (2nd edition, 1859) and other anthologies, and had frequently been mentioned with praise by critics, especially by Edgar A. Poe [*q.v.*].

Helen Whitman (as she preferred to be named) is remembered chiefly as the woman to whom Poe became engaged after the death of his wife, Virginia, and to whom he wrote the second of his poems entitled "To Helen." He first met Mrs. Whitman in September 1848. The engagement, which followed visits to Providence and a correspondence in a style of heightened romantic passion, was finally broken in December 1848, partly through the poet's instability and partly through the influence of Mrs. Whitman's mother. For Helen Whitman, Poe supplied the chief romantic experience of her life. She always held

that "Annabel Lee" was his message to her, and she cherished his memory faithfully. In 1860 she published her book, *Edgar Poe and His Critics,* in his defense. Of her *Poems,* which she had collected for printing, and which were published by her literary executor, William F. Channing, in 1879, sixteen are associated with Poe and many others echo his cadences and even his words. She generously supplied to a succession of writers biographical material relating to Poe, and in the case of John H. Ingram, the English biographer, she may fairly be considered a collaborator, so copiously did she supply him with aid.

After her mother's death in 1860, the care of her younger sister, Anna, who was eccentric, devolved upon her and conditioned all of her later life. Her verses "In Memoriam," dated April 1878, show that within three months of her own death she wrote with clearness and grace. She thought of herself as frail and her use of ether was supposed to be associated with a weak heart. She died at the home of her friend, Mrs. Albert Dailey, where she lived during the short interval between her sister's death and her own, and was buried in the North Burial Ground in Providence. In 1909, *The Last Letters of Edgar Allan Poe to Sarah Helen Whitman* was published. Two portraits of Mrs. Whitman hang in Providence. The one by Giovanni Thompson in the Athenaeum was painted when she was a widow of thirty-five; the other, in the Hay Library, by John N. Arnold was painted in 1869. She was slight and graceful in figure, quick and vivacious in movement. Her brown hair framed a pale delicately featured face with deep-set eyes. Intellectually she combined with her romantic love of the poetic and the unusual a very sane and realistic sense of the practical. Her letters reveal an honest, generous nature, tolerant and many-sided but cautious and fearful of giving offense. Her poetry compares favorably with that of other popular American women poets of her time; it has grace and sincerity but little originality or vigor. Wide reading is reflected in her lines.

[Caroline Ticknor, *Poe's Helen* (1916) ; *The Last Letters of Edgar Allan Poe to Sarah Helen Whitman* (1909), ed. by J. A. Harrison and Charlotte F. Dailey; letters from Mrs. Whitman to J. H. Ingram, Univ. of Va. ; *Providence Daily Jour.,* July 1, 1878.]   J. S. W.

WHITMAN, WALT

(May 31, 1819–Mar. 26, 1892), poet, was born at West Hills, in the town of Huntington, Long Island, of parents in whom Dutch and English blood predominated. His first known ancestor, Joseph Whitman, seems to have come from England to Stratford, Conn., and thence to Huntington about 1660. The family settled as farmers in the hamlet of West Hills, where Nehemiah Whitman, the poet's great-grandfather, owned several hundred acres, worked by slaves. Nehemiah's widow is said by the poet to have been a great swarthy woman who smoked tobacco and swore at her slaves from the back of a vicious horse which she rode like a man. Their son Jesse married Hannah Brush, a schoolmistress, in 1775, and one of his children was Walter Whitman (1789–1855), the father of the poet. Walter, who added the occupation of carpenter to that of farmer, was a large, silent man; he inherited a leaning toward the Quakers and toward Elias Hicks [q.v.], the famous preacher whom the poet himself was always to remember and revere. The son, given his father's name, signed it to his writings until 1855, when he changed it to Walt, as he had been known at home. His father was married in 1816 to Louisa Van Velsor (1795–1873), of Cold Spring, Huntington. Her father, Maj. Cornelius Van Velsor, a horse-breeder whose joviality and stout red face his grandson liked to celebrate, was pure Dutch, but he had married a woman (Amy Williams) of Welsh descent and Quaker leanings. The poet has had more to say about his mother than about his father; she was not educated, but in sympathy and understanding she was "perfect," and his relations to her were always very close. He was the second of nine children, the eldest and youngest of whom were mentally defective.

In 1823 or shortly thereafter the family moved to Brooklyn, then a town of less than 10,000 inhabitants. Here the poet spent a few years in the public schools, later being remembered by one of his teachers as "a big, good-natured lad, clumsy and slovenly in appearance, but not otherwise remarkable" (Uncollected Poetry and Prose, I, xxvi). In the summers he was taken on visits back to Huntington and to other places on Long Island, and he was subsequently to believe that the early knowledge thus gained of life on farm and seashore, among haymakers, eel-fishers, baymen, and pilots, was one of the few important influences upon his work. The shore, both then and during his young manhood, drew him to it whenever he was free; "I loved, after bathing, to race up and down the hard sand, and declaim Homer or Shakespere to the surf and sea-gulls by the hour" (Autobiographia, pp. 23–24). But he was to be a poet of cities as well as of the sea, and his reminiscences in later life were also of the Brooklyn he had known as a boy, with its old houses and its winding streets, and with its ferries that went across the East River to New York.

His schooling ended in his thirteenth year, or possibly in his eleventh (Uncollected Poetry and Prose, I, xxvii). At eleven he was an office boy first for a lawyer and then for a doctor, the lawyer's son subscribing for him to a circulating library which introduced him to the Arabian Nights and to Sir Walter Scott. In the summer of his thirteenth year he became a printer's devil in the office of the Long Island Patriot, whence he went in the same capacity to the Long Island Star. This was the beginning of his long acquaintance with newspapers, and of a career which during three decades was to identify him with a bewildering number of editorial offices. Between 1833, when his family moved back to Long Island, and 1836, when he joined them there for a brief while, he may have been a journeyman compositor in Brooklyn and New York, making occasional contributions to the papers he worked for and getting his first taste of the theatre and the opera, those mainstays of his education a little later on.

Between 1836 and 1841 he confined his wanderings to Long Island, teaching seven schools in as many towns and editing the Long Islander at Huntington in 1838–39. His contributions to this and other local papers were conventional in their youthful sentiment, the verses dealing generally with the themes of loneliness, unrequited affection, and the grave. In 1839–40, when he alternated between teaching and typesetting at Jamaica, he impressed the wife of his employer, the publisher of the Long Island Democrat, as "a dreamy, impracticable youth," "untidy," "inordinately indolent," "morose," "not at all in tune with his surroundings," and insultingly indifferent to children. "He was a genius who lived, apparently, in a world of his own" (Uncollected Poetry and Prose, I, xxxiii–xxxiv). This world included books among other things, for he was beginning by his own later testimony to read the Bible, Shakespeare, Ossian, the Greek tragic poets, the ancient Hindu poets, the Nibelungenlied, the poems of Scott, and Dante. He was also interested in politics; he electioneered as a Democrat in Queens County in 1840, and in 1841 he was one of several speakers at a Tammany mass meeting in City Hall Park, New York. Yet even this early it would appear that his thoughts turned frequently in upon himself.

From 1841 to 1848 Whitman was associated with at least ten newspapers or magazines in New York and Brooklyn: the Aurora, the Sun, the Tattler, Brother Jonathan, the Statesman, the Democrat, the American Review, the Columbian, the Democratic Review, and the Brooklyn Eagle. The two last were the most important. The Democratic Review was the best literary journal of the day, which meant that Whitman's contributions to it between 1841 and 1845 admitted him to the company of Hawthorne, Poe, Bryant, Longfellow, Lowell, Thoreau, and Whittier. His contributions were not poems but stories—now in the manner of Hawthorne, now in the manner of Poe; sentimental, melancholy, and melodramatic. The few poems he printed elsewhere, while they were competent exercises in conventional verse forms, had nothing either of the method or of the quality which eventually were to distinguish his poetry from that of all others. Their subject matter also was routine, as was that of a temperance novel, *Franklin Evans; or, The Inebriate, a Tale of the Times,* which Whitman wrote for an extra issue of the *New World* in 1842, and which in its bombast and bathos failed to raise itself above the level of rhetoric on which a great deal of reform literature was being written at the moment. All the while Whitman was familiarizing himself with the varied life of the metropolis; he sauntered about the streets, haunted the omnibuses and ferries, became intimate with drivers and pilots, strolled off to the beaches and the bathing crowds, went regularly to the Bowery Theatre to see Fanny Kemble, the younger Kean, the elder Booth, Macready, Edwin Forrest, and Charlotte Cushman, listened to public speeches, and intoxicated himself at the opera with the "vocalism of sun-bright Italy." When in January 1846 he became editor of the Brooklyn *Eagle,* a Democratic newspaper, he was equipped both by his personal and by his professional experience to conduct, as he did for two years, a brisk editorial page which was on the whole enlightened and well written, though naturally it never gave expression to a soul which even in these busy years was possessed with a sense of separateness and bewilderment. Whitman supported most of the contemporary reforms, local and national; he reviewed as many as 200 new books; he celebrated the joys of living in Brooklyn; and on the question of slavery he moved rapidly in the Free-Soil direction—losing his position, indeed, when in January 1848 he protested too vehemently against the failure of the Democratic party to face the issue of slavery in the new states. He was once more without a job.

Within a month, however, he was on his way south, having contracted in a theatre lobby to write for the New Orleans *Crescent.* With his brother Jeff he spent two weeks in February crossing Pennsylvania and Virginia and steaming down the Ohio and Mississippi rivers toward a different sort of city from any that he had known. New Orleans undoubtedly charmed him.

His work was not arduous, so that he had ample leisure for exploring the markets, the levees, the barrooms, the sidewalks, and the cemeteries. Certain of his sketches for the *Crescent* indicate a susceptibility to the women of New Orleans. But it is not necessary to believe the legend that he fell in love with one of these and that the attachment colored all of his later life and work. His statement to John Addington Symonds in 1890 that he was the father of six illegitimate children was not accepted by some of his best friends as true, nor is it more generally credited; and even if it was true there is no evidence that the mother of any of the children had been met in New Orleans. Vague assertions by Whitman in his old age concerning later trips to the South have transferred the scene of his "romance" elsewhere; but it remains doubtful whether he took any such trips. The poem, "Once I Pass'd through a Populous City," has been offered as evidence; but a manuscript version of this poem (*Uncollected Poetry and Prose,* II, 102–03) reveals that it originally referred to an attachment with a man, not a woman. Nor is it possible to say with certainty that Whitman began now, and only now, to write his characteristic poetry; one of his notebooks (*Ibid.,* II, 63 ff.) makes it reasonably clear that he was experimenting introspectively with sexual themes before 1848. The importance of the residence in New Orleans can easily be exaggerated, though it may be significant in that it introduced Whitman to a portion of the country he would never have seen otherwise. As for a romance, it is just as conceivable that he failed to find one there, and that this failure—in a scene so suitable for it—precipitated the lonely *Leaves of Grass.* At any rate, Whitman left New Orleans with his brother after three months, coming home by way of St. Louis, Chicago, the Great Lakes, Niagara Falls, Albany, and the Hudson.

In Brooklyn he returned ostensibly to journalism, writing for the *Freeman,* a Barnburner paper, in 1848–49, for the *Daily Advertiser* in 1850, and for various unknown papers between 1850 and 1854. For two years, 1857–59, he edited the Brooklyn *Times,* and in 1861–62 he published a long series of articles on the early history of Brooklyn in the *Standard.* But he had returned, as only he knew for the time being, to something of much greater importance to himself than journalism. For it was now that he entered definitely upon the seven-year period which came to its end and climax with the publication in 1855 of *Leaves of Grass.*

It has been customary to suppose that Whitman passed through some mystical experience shortly before he wrote the twelve poems which composed the first edition of *Leaves of Grass,* and that this experience consisted in his having a sudden, full apprehension of himself. It is likely that his state of mind throughout the early 1850's was extraordinary, since the book which resulted was extraordinary; but his knowledge of himself was a much older thing. The illumination, if illumination there was, would appear to have been a discovery not of his own nature, which he already knew too well, but of a way in which that nature might be presented to the world and so justified. His existence up to this point must have seemed unsatisfactory to him, not only because in the outward matter of a profession he had managed to be little more than a knockabout journalist, but also, and this is more important, because in inward matters pertaining to his own soul he had been forced to realize how unlike the rest of the world he was. He was to celebrate himself as an "average man," and was always to insist that *Leaves of Grass* had no other value than that; yet he was anything but an average men, and, ignorant though he may have remained concerning his fundamental nature, he must have admitted his uniqueness long before 1850. Early and late his writings bear testimony to the sense of isolation which pursued him. His passion for rubbing through crowds on ferries and buses was not the passion of one whose need for society is normally satisfied. The theme of separation is constant in his work, both prose and verse. He was reserved to the end, so that among his final worshippers there was not one who knew whether he had ever enjoyed his complete confidence.

He was tall and heavy, but he was not the robust individual he claimed to be. Both his body and his mind moved slowly, dreamily. His eyes, as may best be seen in the portraits of 1855, 1863, and 1869, were heavy-lidded and uncommunicative; Emerson spoke of them as "terrible"; John Burroughs called them "dumb, yearning, relentless, immodest, unhuman" (Barrus, *post,* p. 15). Burroughs also is authority for the statement that Whitman's body was "that of a child," and that there was always "something fine, delicate, womanly in him" (*Ibid.,* p. 265). He was more than moderate in his habits, he was fastidious; he never smoked. He was fond of cooking, bathing, and nursing, and he always paid the strictest attention to the dress both of himself and of his acquaintances. As a very young man he was a dandy; after he came back from New Orleans he cultivated the rough garments which in the early photographs made him famous; later on, in Washington, he carefully prescribed the fashion in which his shirts should be made, and invariably wore a gray suit; in his old age his open, lace-edged collar revealed a smooth, delicate neck, he wore in his shirt-bosom a pearl stud approximately an inch in diameter, and he regularly bathed his face and hands with eau de cologne.

Earlier than 1850 he must have recognized that his impulses were extraordinary. He was inordinately excitable by things and persons that touched him, and his notebooks of 1847 (*Uncollected Poetry and Prose,* II, 63) show how painfully conscious of the fact he was. He has been called autoerotic, erethistic, and homosexual; nor is it possible to doubt that some such extremes of nomenclature are necessary to explain certain passages in the "Song of Myself." For in those passages he does not seem to be inventing aptitudes and habits for himself; they could not have been invented, and furthermore, whatever deliberate construction he may have seen fit then or later to place upon them, their treatment retains many a trace of the uneasiness and the terror which a contemplation of them had inspired in him. That he loved men more than women was a fact which he was subsequently to erect into a reason for claiming special insight into the principle upon which democracies would hold together. The fact remains, however, that love for his own sex is the only kind of love about which he is ever personal or convincing, and that in his correspondence he reserves the word "darling" for his mother and for young men alone.

All this has nothing to do with his being a great poet, but it has much to do with the state of mind out of which *Leaves of Grass* grew with such slow and conscious effort. That effort was put forth both by the artist and by the man—was put forth by the man, indeed, in order that he might become an artist and so free himself from the slavery of self-contemplation. *Leaves of Grass* purports to be a poem about "Myself." But in one very important sense it is not personal at all. Or if it is personal, it exploits two selves in Whitman, one natural and one created. The created self is the one which the world has enjoyed, and it is one of the most magnificent fabrications of modern times. Whitman discovered the way to it through a number of channels, the broadest and deepest of these being undoubtedly his reading. Mention has been made of his early acquaintance with Scott and Homer and Shakespeare, the last of whom he knew in the theatre as well as from the printed page and continued throughout his life to discuss with significant eloquence. It is likely, however, that his immediate illumination came through intellectual contact with contemporaries. His review for the *Eagle* in 1846 of Goethe's autobiography shows how excited he was before the spectacle of a man who had explored the universe in terms of himself. Early and late Carlyle stood huge upon his horizon, helping him to find a prose style and convincing him that mystical significances could be discovered in the social behavior of men. Yet it was from Emerson that he caught the final, determining fire. Later on he denied this, attempting, unsuccessfully, to establish that he had never read Emerson before 1855 (*Uncollected Poetry and Prose,* I, 132). It is impossible to read either the early notebooks or the first edition of *Leaves of Grass* without feeling the presence of Emerson everywhere—in the epigrammatic style of the preface and the twelve poems, in the nature of the things said, and in the quality of the egoism. From Emerson he learned his fundamental lesson, that a man could accept and celebrate himself in cosmic language. He could transfer his vision from the eccentric, the unique self to the general, the impersonal one. He could move at once from doubt of Walt Whitman to faith in Man, of whom he might take what he called "Myself" as representative. Bound as he was to brood upon his own nature, he found in Emerson a way to do so which would legitimatize his emotions, liberate himself, and fascinate the world. He seems to have been assisted and supported in this acceptance of himself by the circumstance that in 1849 he had his "bumps" read at the phrenological cabinet of Fowler and Wells in New York and was told that he possessed an unusually high degree of every human quality. From the importance he attached to his own "chart of bumps" and to the claims of phrenology generally it would appear that the experience had convinced him of his signal sanity and his remarkable representativeness; it was thence, perhaps, that he gained the confidence to assert of himself in an anonymous review he wrote of *Leaves of Grass* in 1855 that he was "of pure American breed, large and lusty . . . a naive, masculine, affectionate, contemplative, sensual, imperious person" (*In Re Walt Whitman,* p. 23).

At the same time that he experimented in his notebooks with a new form and mood of poetry he reflected also upon a possible career which he might have as an orator. He never surrendered, indeed, his vision of himself as one who might go forth among the American people and astonish them with fresh and forceful utterances. His notebooks show that he practised even the gestures of the platform, and there is abundant evidence that he devoted a great deal of his time to the planning and writing of lectures. The style of his poetry can best be explained in terms of his apprenticeship in declamation. His temper, however, was not the positive temper of the happy orator, and he seems to have recognized this, as he recognized that the printed broadsides which he also conceived as a medium of expression might not be the most satisfactory medium. At any rate it was to poetry that he applied himself with the greatest zeal in the years after his return from New Orleans, and it was through his poetry, much of which must have been written while he helped his father build houses in Brooklyn (1851–54), that he was to become famous around the world.

Whatever hopes of fame he had, however, were confounded by the reception of his first performance. *Leaves of Grass,* printed in 1855, was a failure with the public. It was a tall, thin volume containing a long preface in prose and twelve poems without titles. The preface rendered an Emersonian account of the relation between the miraculous universe and the no less miraculous soul of man; predicted the future greatness of the American people, who "of all nations at any time upon the earth have probably the fullest poetical nature"; and prescribed the duties of the American poet, as well as suggested the broad rules of his art. The poems included those later to be known as "Song of Myself," "The Sleepers," "I Sing the Body Electric," and "There was a Child Went Forth." The book was incomprehensible to some readers and shocking to others, and it still is one of the most difficult of all books to understand. The man who wrote it never fully understood himself—never, perhaps, understood how excellent he was merely as a poet, occupied as he was both then and later with the thought that he must be first of all a prophet. The complexity of his temperament explains the baffling way he took of gliding back and forth in these poems between his actual and his assumed self; the subtlety and the power of his faculties are evidenced everywhere by images and cadences beyond which no modern poet has gone in the direction either of explicitness or of ellipsis.

The book struck home here and there. A copy sent to Concord elicited the famous letter in which Emerson said: "I am not blind to the worth of the wonderful gift of *Leaves of Grass.* I find it the most extraordinary piece of wit and wisdom that America has yet contributed. I am very happy in reading it, as great power makes us happy. . . . I greet you at the beginning of a great career, which yet must have had a long foreground somewhere, for such a start" (Emory Holloway, *Whitman. An Interpretation in*

Narrative, 1926, p. 118). Emerson was never to publish a word in praise of Whitman, and he is said to have recanted some of this praise in conversation; but he already had done enough. Whitman says he visited him soon in Brooklyn; certainly Thoreau and Bronson Alcott came down to see him, as Bryant came over from Manhattan. There were a few favorable reviews among many that were indignant or bewildered; in *Putnam's Monthly Magazine* for September 1855 Charles Eliot Norton in an unsigned article mingled disapprobation with astonished praise, confining to the secrecy of his desk a poem which he wrote at the same time in imitation of a book that had overwhelmed him against his will; and Edward Everett Hale was complimentary in the *North American Review* for January 1856 (unsigned, in "Critical Notices"). But for the most part the book fell dead from the printer's hands, and even the three rhapsodic reviews of it which Whitman himself wrote for the *Brooklyn Times,* the *American Phrenological Journal,* and the *United States and Democratic Review* failed of any noticeable effect. He could not have known at the moment that a few copies of *Leaves of Grass* had crossed the Atlantic to England, where in time they were to arouse a tempest of admiration.

After a brief retreat to eastern Long Island Whitman returned to the city "with the confirmed resolution, from which I never afterward wavered, to go on with my poetic enterprise in my own way and finish it as well as I could" (*Uncollected Poetry and Prose,* I, liii). By the next year, 1856, he had a second edition ready. This was printed by Fowler and Wells, and it included among twenty-one new poems "Salut au Monde," "Song of the Broad-Axe," "By Blue Ontario's Shore," "Crossing Brooklyn Ferry," and "Song of the Open Road." Stamped on the back in gold letters was the unauthorized legend: "I greet you at the beginning of a great career, R. W. Emerson." An appendix inside reprinted certain press notices and a long letter from the author to Emerson, "dear Friend and Master." This edition was even more unfavorably received, an additional reason for dislike now being the presence of such exploitations of the sexual theme as "Spontaneous Me" and "A Woman Waits for Me." Fowler and Wells, after selling, it is said, a thousand copies, refused to handle the volume any longer, and so it too fell into an apparent oblivion, though certain infatuated readers of it were to be heard from later.

The four years which elapsed before the third edition of 1860 were spent in necessary newspaper work and in writing more than a hundred new poems. It was during this time also that Whitman began to frequent the "Bohemian" society of authors, actors, and artists at Pfaff's restaurant in New York, where he made valuable literary acquaintances. In 1859 he read to some friends a new poem which he called "A Word Out of the Sea" and which was immediately taken for publication by the *Saturday Press,* where the young John Burroughs saw it. Now known as "Out of the Cradle Endlessly Rocking," this poem, upon which Whitman never improved more than perhaps once, gave full and perfect lyric expression to the emotions about death which he had only tentatively touched upon in the first two editions of his book. Henceforth love and death—love as longing and death as the satisfaction of longing—were to be his great themes, though the fact was not so easily apparent to most readers of the edition of 1860–61, which, brought out in Boston by the firm of Thayer and Eldridge, contained two new sections, "Children of Adam" and "Calamus." "Children of Adam" celebrated "amativeness," or the love of men and women; "Calamus" celebrated "adhesiveness," or the love of men for men. The first of these is treated from the greater distance, remaining "athletic" and abstract in Whitman's hands, and in a sense unreal; it is rather in the poems of comradeship or "manly love" that he is intimate and convincing. Only here does he employ the secondary but indispensable themes of bashfulness and jealousy; only here is he tenderly personal, so that one may believe him when he insists over and again that this is his true self speaking. And it is in association with the thought of an unattainable friendship that he utters most touchingly his philosophy of death.

The edition of 1860–61 sold better than either of the others, and Whitman's visit to Boston in connection with its printing brought about his meeting with William Douglas O'Connor [*q.v.*], who was to be his fiercest champion in future years. It also gave him an opportunity, he says, to talk at length with Emerson, who advised him in vain to expurgate his poems. But this edition too was ill-fated. The Civil War reduced Thayer and Eldridge to bankruptcy and the book fell into the hands of pirates; Whitman once more was without a publisher. But the war itself was to engage both his body and his mind during the four years ahead.

The importance of the Civil War in Whitman's life was incalculable. Not only did it determine Washington as his place of residence for eleven years; it influenced and modified every thought he had, and was the occasion of his last great burst of poetry. But he was not drawn into close contact with it until the end of 1862. During 1861 and 1862 he was contributing a series of twenty-five articles called "Brooklyniana" to the Brooklyn *Standard,* and in 1862 he wrote seven articles for the New York *Leader,* four of these dealing with the Broadway Hospital, where he spent some time in attendance upon the sick and wounded, both soldier and civilian. He lived at home with his mother, one of whose sons, George, the poet's junior by ten years, had enlisted in the 51st New York Volunteers, a Brooklyn regiment. He also was writing poems about the war, some of which were to be included in *Drum Taps* three years later. In December 1862 word came that George was wounded in Virginia. Whitman left immediately for Washington, where he happened upon his friend O'Connor and received assistance of a sort which enabled him to find his brother at Falmouth, Va., opposite Fredericksburg. George was recovered by this time, but Whitman saw enough wounded men and heard enough about battles at close range to realize that his life must somehow be involved with the war until it ended. Back in Washington after several days, he accepted Mr. and Mrs. O'Connor's offer of a room in their house; and Major Hapgood, an army paymaster, gave him a desk in his office where he could earn a little money copying documents. Soon he was devoting himself to wounded soldiers, Northern and Southern, in the various huge hospitals about the city. He has left two records of this experience, his letters to his mother, published in 1902, and *Memoranda During the War* (1875). He may not have tended "from eighty thousand to a hundred thousand" soldiers, as he claimed, but there is ample testimony to the faithfulness of his services. He seems not to have been connected, unless for the briefest period, with the Christian Commission; he went entirely on his own, basket on arm, entering the wards in order to talk with the soldiers or read to them, to bring them gifts of oranges, jelly, and horehound candy, to furnish them with paper and envelopes and on occasion to write the letters which they dictated to their families, and even now and then to assist at dressings and operations. His subsequent paralysis he attributed to an infection which he received during these months of exposure to gangrene and fever. Whenever possible he made small gifts of money to the soldiers, out of a fund which he raised in Boston, Salem, Providence, Brooklyn, and New York. He made money for himself by contributions to the New York newspapers, and he attempted to secure a clerkship in some govern-

ment office, but for the present without success.

He saw much of the O'Connors, since he lived with them, and of their friends, among whom was Edmund Clarence Stedman [*q.v.*], a frequent visitor and already an admirer of Whitman. In 1863 he was sought out by John Burroughs [*q.v.*], then living in Washington with his wife, and made to understand how much he had influenced the mind of the younger man; the attachment between the two was strong until the end of Whitman's life. There seem to have been no meetings between Whitman and Lincoln, and if the story (H. B. Rankin, *Personal Recollections of Abraham Lincoln,* 1916, pp. 124–27) that Lincoln had read *Leaves of Grass* before he came to Washington is to be disbelieved (W. E. Barton, *Abraham Lincoln and Walt Whitman,* 1928, pp. 90–94) there is a probability that Lincoln never knew of the poet's existence. But Whitman saw the President a number of times as he rode in the city, and he liked to think that Lincoln was nodding to him from his horse. The death of Lincoln, occurring only a few weeks after Whitman had secured his first clerkship, in the office of the Department of the Interior, was at any rate the occasion for Whitman's masterpiece, "When Lilacs Last in the Dooryard Bloom'd," which was printed as a supplement to *Walt Whitman's Drum Taps,* already in the press (1865). Whitman's letters at the time reveal that he thought *Drum Taps* his best work (Perry, *post,* pp. 150–51), partly because it lacked the "perturbations" of *Leaves of Grass.* The remark is significant of a change which was coming over all his work. Henceforth it is mellower, less egocentric, less nervous, less raw. Henceforth it makes much of religion and the spiritual problems facing society. Henceforth, too, the poems reprinted in successive editions of *Leaves of Grass,* are tempered and shorn of certain excesses. The war, as well as advancing age, had completed the process in Whitman whereby his private nature was lost sight of in the great, gray, kindly figure of the legend.

On June 30, 1865, Whitman was dismissed from his position in the Department of the Interior. He was soon given another in the attorney-general's office, but since the reason for his dismissal had been Secretary Harlan's unwillingness to employ the author of a scandalous book there was occasion now to enlist a wider sympathy for Whitman than the book itself had aroused. O'Connor's pamphlet *The Good Gray Poet,* written in a blue heat of indignation and published in 1866, was the first published volume about Whitman. The second was *Notes on Walt Whitman as Poet and Person* (1867), by John

Burroughs. At least half of this was written by Whitman himself, who desired that the secret be kept until Burroughs' death, as it was. The *Notes* are passionate in their praise and often inaccurate in their information, but they have an interest as showing Whitman's prose style of the period, and as revealing how completely he had made Burroughs his disciple. Burroughs never included the *Notes* in his collected writings, but he wrote more than fifty other books and articles about Whitman before he died. The next year, 1868, O'Connor laid another stone in the foundation of the Whitman legend by contributing his story "The Carpenter," presenting the poet in a disguised and idealized form, to *Putnam's Magazine* for January. Meanwhile Whitman was finding friends and admirers, as well as a number of enemies, abroad; and the next few years saw the beginning of his European vogue. Articles about him appeared in Germany in 1868 and in France, Denmark, and Hungary in 1872. Edward Dowden in Ireland was creating a group of enthusiastic readers, and in England the publication of an expurgated edition of *Leaves of Grass* by W. M. Rossetti (1868) put men like Swinburne, Edward Carpenter, and John Addington Symonds under the spell—Swinburne, however, only temporarily. Mrs. Anne Gilchrist, the widow of Blake's biographer, read Rossetti's edition and wrote an article for the *Boston Radical* (May 1870) which particularly pleased Whitman as being the first tribute to him from a woman. The correspondence between the two which began in 1871 and continued until Mrs. Gilchrist's death in 1885, being interrupted only by her residence in Philadelphia for two years in order that she might be near the poet, is evidence that Mrs. Gilchrist's love was personal as well as literary, though Whitman could only give her friendship and esteem in return. His fame grew steadily, bringing him the first of his English visitors and stimulating a greater and greater amount of discussion in current periodicals.

Whitman's Washington period came to its close when in January 1873 he suffered a stroke of paralysis and was forced to leave for Camden, N. J., where his brother George took him into his house and where he shortly (May 23, 1873) was to witness the death of his mother. His illness and his bereavement were two blows from which he never recovered, and henceforth his life ran gradually downhill. Between 1865 and 1873, however, he had published two new editions of *Leaves of Grass* (1867 and 1871), *Passage to India* (1871), and the prose work *Democratic Vistas* (1871). Both of these latter works reveal again how he had tempered his message with time. "Passage to India," his last great poem, is among other things a recognition of the claims of the past upon our souls, and an admission that America needs all the support she can find in old ideas and religions. *Democratic Vistas,* written more or less in answer to Carlyle's *Shooting Niagara,* is remarkable for the frankness with which it discusses the shortcomings of American democracy so far; the reference of Whitman's idealism is now to the future, in which he still has faith—as, ultimately, he still has faith in the democratic masses of "These States."

Of the nineteen years which remained to him Whitman spent the first eleven in his brother's house in Stevens Street, Camden, and the last eight in a smaller house he had bought for himself at 328 Mickle Street. After eighteen months' absence from his position in the attorney-general's office at Washington he lost it, being henceforth dependent for his living upon his brother, upon friends, and upon the sale of his books, which he conducted partly from his own quarters, receiving orders and filling them with his own hand. His literary income was from time to time augmented through articles for the press, through the sale of new poems, and through the lecture he gave perhaps a dozen times on "The Death of Abraham Lincoln." His illness, from which he never recovered, was less acute during the ten years following 1876, when he formed the habit of going down to Timber Creek, a stream which flows into the Delaware about ten miles below Camden, and enjoying the out-of-doors as a guest of the Stafford family at Laurel Springs. Here he was repaired and refreshed, and here he composed for *Specimen Days* some of the best prose he ever wrote, besides revising his earlier work and preparing new editions for the press.

Before the end came he had issued five new editions of *Leaves of Grass* (1876, 1881–82, 1882, 1888–89, 1891–92); had published three collections containing new poems (*Two Rivulets,* 1876; *November Boughs,* 1888; and *Good-Bye, My Fancy,* 1891); and had published most of the prose which now belongs to his canon. *Memoranda During the War* (1875) was included in *Specimen Days and Collect* (1882–83), which with *Democratic Vistas* came after his death to represent him in prose until the process began a quarter-century later of unearthing his earliest work.

During no portion of this period was he lonely or neglected. His old friends Burroughs and O'Connor were usually within reach, though he was estranged from O'Connor for ten years after 1872. He continued to correspond with Peter

Doyle, a young horse-car conductor whom he had met in Washington in 1866 and with whom he always comported himself half as father and half as lover. More and more visitors arrived for interviews, many of them from England—Edward Carpenter, Oscar Wilde, Lord Houghton, Sir Edwin Arnold, Henry Irving, Bram Stoker, Ernest Rhys, Edmund Gosse. As time went on he found himself surrounded by disciples. Richard Maurice Bucke, a Canadian physician, attached himself to the poet in 1877 and produced the first official biography in 1883, following this pious performance with a number of articles emphasizing the prophetic importance of Whitman, whom he considered one of the first men, along with Bucke himself, to have come under the influence of "cosmic consciousness." Bucke was one of Whitman's three literary executors, and as such was in a position to publish his literary remains. The other two executors were Thomas B. Harned and Horace Traubel [q.v.]—the latter a young man who fell completely under the old poet's influence and took down with a busy pencil almost every remark he let fall.

Two episodes during these years aroused wide discussion and gave new impetus to Whitman's fame. In the *West Jersey Press* of Jan. 26, 1876, appeared an article, apparently by Whitman himself, describing him as "old, poor, and paralyzed," and neglected by his countrymen. A copy of this was sent by Whitman to W. M. Rossetti in England, who had a portion of it reprinted in the *Athenaeum*, where it attracted the fiery eye of Robert Buchanan, the Scotch poet (Blodgett, *post*, pp. 36 ff.). His blast about it in the *Daily News* was the signal for a controversy which ceased neither in England nor in America until relief began pouring in on Whitman in the form of orders for his books. Six years later the action of Osgood & Company, the Boston publishers who had just brought out a new edition of *Leaves of Grass*, in withdrawing the book because of official protests against its indecency, inspired another controversy, O'Connor this time returning to the front rank of the Whitman forces. The result among other things was the sale of 3,000 copies of the Philadelphia edition (1882) in a single day. Meanwhile the fame of Whitman grew steadily in a more normal fashion. Certain "enemies," as he called those who did not think him a great poet, continued to express their doubts—notably Thomas Wentworth Higginson and William Winter [qq.v.] in America and the editors of the *Saturday Review* in England. Swinburne recanted his praise of 1868 and 1872 in a savage article of 1887, and Robert

Louis Stevenson tempered the admiration he had originally felt. But there was at the same time a growing chorus of appreciation. Before the poet died he had been translated into Danish, Dutch, French (by Jules Laforgue and Francis Vielé-Griffin), German, and Italian, and had been the subject of numerous critical studies which ranged all the way from analysis to panegyric.

Whitman's tendency to bask in so much adoration and to surround himself with champions who did his name on the whole more harm than good is pardonable, considering his career, and at the same time pitiable. Of necessity he lived quietly in Camden, though he left it for trips to Colorado in 1879, to Canada in 1880 to visit Dr. Bucke, to Boston (where he saw Emerson for the last time) in 1881, and to his birthplace on Long Island in the same year. In his own mind he mellowed perceptibly, embracing Hegelianism and asserting once more, in "A Backward Glance O'er Travel'd Roads" which prefaced *November Boughs* (1888), the importance to America of religion and of the older literatures. His former impatience with any poetry which was not American had quite disappeared in his old age, as had his tendency to dismiss other American poets than himself as of no account. His mature appraisals of Longfellow, Poe, Whittier, Bryant, and of course Emerson are no less valuable as contributions to criticism than are his meditations on the death of Carlyle.

His death in Camden on Mar. 26, 1892, was the occasion for many attempts to sum up his excellence and his importance. For the most part these were failures, since the shadow of the disciples and the executors still obscured him. During forty years this shadow has gradually been dissipated under the influence of biographical research, a saner criticism, and the passage of time. The claims originally made for him as man and moralist are made less often, and promise to disappear. To the extent that his "teachings" can be proved to have been built upon the unsteady basis of his own unique psychology, proof has been forthcoming—in America, in England, in Germany, and in France. It is now difficult if not impossible to believe that he came into the world to save it, or that he will save it. The world in general pays little attention to his name; he has never been a popular poet, accepted of democracies as he hoped, nor has he been often imitated by other poets, as he also hoped. But as his isolation grows more apparent it grows more impressive, so that his rank among the poets of his country and his century, and indeed of the world, is higher than it has ever been before. His work manages to survive the attacks made either upon its author as a man or upon what George Santayana called before 1900 the "barbarism" of his mind. It survives as certainly the most original work yet done by any American poet, and perhaps as the most passionate and best. It is easier now to comprehend Whitman as the artist that he was, though it is not easy and it never will be. As a maker of phrases, as a master of rhythms, as a weaver of images, as an architect of poems he is often beyond the last reach of analysis. His diaries of the war, his prefaces to *Leaves of Grass,* his *Democratic Vistas,* and his notes on the landscape at Timber Creek are a permanent part of American prose. He himself, looked back at purely as a writer, will always loom a gigantic and beautiful figure in nineteenth-century letters.

[The Harned Collection of Whitman manuscripts in the Lib. of Cong. includes twenty-four notebooks of various dates as well as annotated newspaper clippings, letters, and miscellaneous items. The *Complete Works of Walt Whitman* were published by the literary executors, R. M. Bucke, T. B. Harned, and Horace Traubel, in 10 vols. in 1902. This material has been supplemented by *Walt Whitman's Diary in Canada* (1904), ed. by W. S. Kennedy; *An American Primer* (1904), ed. by Horace Traubel; *Criticism, An Essay, by Walt Whitman* (1913); *The Letters of Anne Gilchrist and Walt Whitman* (1918), ed. by T. B. Harned; *The Gathering of the Forces,* contributions to the Brooklyn *Eagle* (2 vols., 1920), ed. by Cleveland Rodgers and John Black; *The Uncollected Poetry and Prose of Walt Whitman* (2 vols., 1921), ed. by Emory Holloway; *Walt Whitman's Workshop, A Collection of Unpublished Manuscripts* (1928), ed. by C. J. Furness; *I Sit and Look Out; Editorials from the Brooklyn Daily Times by Walt Whitman* (1932), ed. by Emory Holloway and Vernolian Schwarz; *Walt Whitman and the Civil War* (1933), manuscripts and contributions to the New York *Leader,* ed. by C. I. Glicksberg. For bibliographies see the *Complete Works,* vol. VII; *The Cambridge Hist. of Am. Literature,* vol. II (1918), pp. 551–81; *A Concise Bibliography of the Works of Walt Whitman* (1922) by Carolyn Wells and A. F. Goldsmith; and the various annual bibliographies of American literature.

The chief biographies are: R. M. Bucke, *Walt Whitman* (1883); H. B. Binns, *A Life of Walt Whitman* (1905); Bliss Perry, *Walt Whitman: His Life and Work* (1906); Léon Bazalgette, *Walt Whitman; L'Homme et son Œuvre* (1908), published in translation by Ellen FitzGerald (1920); G. R. Carpenter, *Walt Whitman* (1909); Emory Holloway, biographical introduction to *The Uncollected Poetry and Prose of Walt Whitman* (2 vols., 1921); Emory Holloway, *Whitman. An Interpretation in Narrative* (1926); John Bailey, *Walt Whitman* (1926); Jean Catel, *Walt Whitman; La Naissance du Poète* (1929). Reminiscences and miscellaneous biographical material may be found in: John Burroughs, *Notes on Walt Whitman as Poet and Person* (1867, 1871); H. H. Gilchrist, ed., *Anne Gilchrist: Her Life and Writings* (1887); *In Re Walt Whitman* (1893), ed. by his literary executors; T. B. Donaldson, *Walt Whitman: The Man* (1896); W. S. Kennedy, *Reminiscences of Walt Whitman* (1896); I. H. Platt, *Walt Whitman* (1904); Edward Carpenter, *Days with Walt Whitman* (1906); Horace Traubel, *With Walt Whitman in Camden, March 28, 1888–January 20, 1889,* conversations (3 vols., 1906–14); J. Johnston and J. W. Wallace, *Visits to Walt Whitman in 1890–1891* (1917); Elizabeth L. Keller, *Walt Whitman in Mickle Street* (1921). The growth of Whitman's reputation has been studied in W. S. Kennedy, *The*

Fight of a Book for the World (1926); in Clara Barrus, *Whitman and Burroughs Comrades* (1931); and in Harold Blodgett, *Walt Whitman in England* (1934). For psychological analyses of Whitman see: Eduard Bertz, *Der Yankee-Heiland* (Dresden, 1906), and *Whitman-Mysterien. Eine Abrechnung mit Johannes Schlaf* (Berlin, 1907); W. C. Rivers, *Walt Whitman's Anomaly* (1913). For critical studies see: J. A. Symonds, *Walt Whitman: A Study* (1893); Basil de Selincourt, *Walt Whitman: A Critical Study* (1914); Cebria Montoliu, *Walt Whitman: L'home i sa tasca* (Barcelona, 1913); Léon Bazalgette, *Le 'Poème-Evangile' de Walt Whitman* (Paris, 1921). An obituary and a long article were published in *N. Y. Times,* Mar. 27, 1892.]

M. V–D.

WHITMER, DAVID (Jan. 7, 1805–Jan. 25, 1888), early Mormon leader and one of "The Three Witnesses" to the *Book of Mormon,* was born near Harrisburg, Pa., the son of Peter and Mary (Musselman) Whitmer. His father, a hard-working farmer, removed a few years after David's birth to Seneca County, N. Y. The boy received a rudimentary education and grew up to follow the occupation of his father. His family was Presbyterian, but he was affected by the currents of religious unrest of the time and in 1828, while on a trip to Palmyra, N. Y., heard from the village schoolmaster, Oliver Cowdery, about Joseph Smith [*q.v.*] and the "Golden Plates," which the latter had been commissioned by divine messengers to translate. Whitmer's whole family was impressed by the story, and the next year, at the request of Cowdery, David left his spring plowing in order to fetch Smith and Cowdery to the Whitmer homestead. During the month of June the translation of the *Book of Mormon* was completed in his father's house; he was baptized into the newly revealed religion by Smith himself; and shortly thereafter he was one of the three who were privileged by divine oracle to examine the "Golden Plates" and to give witness to their supernatural source yet material character. During the next few months he interlarded proselytizing with farming and on Apr. 6, 1830, he was at Fayette, N. Y., at the formal organization of Smith's new sect. In this year he married Julia A. Jolly.

He followed his leader to Kirtland, Ohio, and when the Mormon Prophet decided to move his rapidly growing flock to the "Promised Land" of Jackson County, Mo., he was among the first to go. He suffered with his fellow-members the intense persecutions of the Missourians and in the fall of 1833 was forced to remove to Clay County to escape the mobs roused against the Mormons. When Smith organized on July 3, 1834, the "High Council of Zion" to manage the Mormon interests in Missouri, Whitmer was made president of the council and for the next year or so was one of the leading men of his denomination there. However, as external pressure from enemies increased and as dissension arose within the ranks of the Mormons themselves, he found himself at odds with the Prophet. Following an attempt in 1836 of one faction to have him replace Smith, there was, at Kirtland, a temporary reconciliation with Smith; but the next year with Martin Harris, Cowdery, and others he was again in conflict with the Prophet. He gave up active participation early in 1838. One of the major charges brought against him was neglect of his moral and religious obligations to his church. He was excommunicated on Apr. 13, 1838. Shortly thereafter he settled in Richmond, Ray County, Mo., where he lived until his death. He became a thoroughly respected citizen and for a number of years sat in the city council and was at one time elected mayor.

After the death of Joseph Smith and the rise of the two chief contending branches of the Mormon Church, he became the object of their special attention. Each faction tried to reconvert him to its own particular creed but failed. In 1847 William E. McClellin, who had been associated with the Whitmer faction in Missouri, tried to reëstablish another Mormon sect under the original name, "Church of Christ," and Whitmer was chosen president; but the attempt was abortive. Nearly twenty years later Whitmer and his own family revived the "Church of Christ" with a simple organization of six officers, two priests, and four elders. A periodical was established and proselytizing, especially among the other Mormons, began. At the time of his death he had about 150 followers.

He made no important contribution to Mormon practices or creed. He found early Mormonism to his liking, because it was marked, he imagined, by the simplicity of primitive Christianity. As the followers of Smith increased, as institutional forms and a priestly hierarchy grew up, he fell into controversy with Smith and with Rigdon—whom he never liked—and before Mormonism really developed many of its most distinctive features, he apostatized. His pamphlet, *An Address to All Believers in Christ by a Witness to the Divine Authenticity to the Book of Mormon* (1887), gives a rather mundane but apparently straightforward account of many events at the beginning of Mormonism. His account of the method of "translating" the "Golden Plates," of the difficulties in getting the *Book of Mormon* printed, his contention that the revelations of Joseph Smith almost always grew out of immediate necessity to answer some practical problem and that they were not to be taken too seriously and certainly that they should never have been published and come to be considered "sacred" documents, his information that in April 1830 when the Mormon church was legally organized there were already seventy baptized followers in the movement and not just six as the official history implies, and his story of the great influence that Rigdon had on Joseph Smith are of great importance to the historian of early Mormonism. Nevertheless in spite of his disaffection he never denied his simple but clearly sincere belief that he saw the "Golden Plates" and that Smith was divinely appointed to reëstablish the true church of Christ.

[*Hist. Record*, May 1887; *Latter-Day Saint Biographical Encyclopedia* (1901), vol. I, ed. by Andrew Jensen; Joseph Smith and H. C. Smith, *History of the Church of Jesus Christ of Latter Day Saints* (4 vols., 1902); Edward Stevenson, "The Three Witnesses to the Book of Mormon," *Latter Day Saints' Millenial Star*, July 12, 1886.]
K. Y.

WHITMORE, WILLIAM HENRY (Sept. 6, 1836–June 14, 1900), antiquarian, was born at Dorchester, Mass., the son of Charles Octavius and Lovice (Ayres) Whitmore, and a descendant of Francis Whitmore who settled in Cambridge before 1648. After studying at the Boston Latin School and English High School he entered the family firm of commission merchants, where he served for nearly twenty-five years, visiting Mauritius, Madagascar, Calcutta, and England. Meanwhile he studied law and painting. In 1874 he was elected to the Boston Common Council as a Republican. He soon became a Democrat, gave up society, and moved to Worcester Street, where he found numerous political friends. With one brief interval, he continued in the Council until 1886, promoting the preservation and printing of records, and the preservation and restoration of the Old State House. His political influence gave him power to advance successfully his antiquarian aims. In 1875 he became a record commissioner, and in 1892 city registrar, taking over the work of the commissioners. Under his supervision twenty-eight volumes of invaluable local records were issued, and manuscript copies of vital records of Boston churches were collected. All this time he wrote frequently for the *New England Historical and Genealogical Register,* the *Nation,* the Prince Society, and the Massachusetts Historical Society. He was also an active trustee of the Boston Public Library (1882–83, 1885–88).

Whitmore's work in its day represented an advance in standards of accuracy, but unfortunately his output was so great that much of his printed work requires careful checking. Much erudition is displayed in his editorial work on *The Andros Tracts* (1868–74), the "Diary of Samuel Sewall" (*Collections of the Massachu-*

setts Historical Society, 5 ser., vols. V–VII, 1878–82), and *The Colonial Laws of Massachusetts* (3 vols., 1887–90). His *The Heraldic Journal, Recording the Armorial Bearings and Genealogies of American Families* (4 vols., 1865–68) and *The Elements of Heraldry* (1866) were pioneer efforts. He also published *A Handbook of American Genealogy* (1862), *The Massachusetts Civil List . . . 1630–1774* (1870), *A Bibliographical Sketch of the Laws of the Massachusetts Colony from 1630 to 1686* (1890), and several reports and pamphlets of a political nature. He printed pedigrees of the families of Whitmore and Hall, Temple, Lane, Reyner, Whipple, Quincy, Norton, Winthrop, Payne, Gore, Vickery, Hutchinson, Oliver, Pelham, Usher, Elliot, Dalton, Batcheller, Wilcox, and others. He was uncompromising in his hostility to false pedigrees. In *The Memorial History of Boston* (4 vols., 1881), edited by Justin Winsor, he wrote on old Boston families. Other interests led him to edit *The Poetical Works of Winthrop Mackworth Praed* (1859), *Abel Bowen, Engraver* (1884), and *The Original Mother Goose's Melody, as First Issued by John Newberry* (1889). Among his fellow workers—but not always harmonious ones—were John W. Thornton, Samuel Gardner and Samuel Adams Drake, Charles Deane [*qq.v.*], W. S. Appleton, J. T. Hassam, A. C. Goodell, and M. P. Wilder. With them he was brilliant in conversation.

He was short, with abundant black hair, dark complexion, keen but imperfect eyes, and resolute expression. One of his friends has said that it was "certainly quite as easy to differ from him as to agree with him" (*Proceedings of the Massachusetts Historical Society, post,* p. 99); another very frank comment was that his "absorption in his chosen interests was of a character bordering on derangement" (*New England Historical and Genealogical Register, post,* p. 68). While kind to the aged and those in misfortune, he was "destitute of clemency" for antiquarians whose efforts distressed him. Toward the end of his life he suffered from disease and could find little relief; his office at the Old Court House was much of the time deserted. Whitmore was married on June 11, 1884, to Fanny Theresa Walling Maynard, daughter of Edward F. Maynard of Boston. He was survived by his wife and a son.

[Sources include *Who's Who in America,* 1899–1900; Jessie W. P. Purdy, *The Whitmore Geneal.* (1907); W. S. Appleton, in *Proc. Mass. Hist. Soc.,* 2 ser., vol. XV (1902), with bibliog.; G. A. Gordon, in *New-England Hist. and Geneal. Reg.,* Jan. 1902; obituary in *Boston Transcript,* June 15, 1900; information from G. K. Clarke, W. P. Greenlaw, Albert Matthews, and W. K. Watkins.]   C. K. B.

WHITNEY, ADELINE DUTTON TRAIN (Sept. 15, 1824–Mar. 20, 1906), author, was born in Boston, Mass., the daughter of Adeline (Dutton) and Enoch Train [*q.v.*] and the descendant of John Traine who emigrated from England in 1635 and settled in Watertown, Mass. Until her marriage in 1843 to Seth D. Whitney of Milton, Mass., she lived in her native city and received her education there, except for a year at a boarding school in Northampton. At the age of thirteen she entered the private school for young ladies kept by George B. Emerson [*q.v.*] in Boston. For the thorough training in Latin and in English composition that she received there, she was always grateful. In a work written after she was seventy, *Friendly Letters to Girl Friends* (1896), appearing first in the *Ladies' Home Journal,* she declared that the methods and ideals of Emerson had been the moulding influences of her life. She was a wide reader of both prose and poetry. What she described as "home and neighborhood books" especially attracted her in her youth, and she found in the works of Miss Edgeworth, Miss Sedgwick, Mrs. Child, and other women writers her first incentive to authorship. She contributed an occasional article to local papers before her marriage, but her regular book-making did not begin until the youngest of her four children was eight years old. Milton became her home after 1843, and there most of her books were written. She won her first success with a little volume called *Boys at Chequasset* (1862), based upon the adventures and interests of her own son. The following year she published *Faith Gartney's Girlhood,* an extremely popular book, which ran to twenty editions. *The Gayworthys* (1865), published both in London and Boston, added to her reputation. After the appearance of two serials in the monthly magazine, *Our Young Folks,* later published in book form—*A Summer in Leslie Goldthwaite's Life* (1866) and *We Girls* (1870)—she wrote two other tales, *Real Folks* (1871) and *The Other Girls* (1873), at the request of her publishers. The four were issued as the Real Folks Series. Over ten thousand copies of this work were sold during the first season.

Her later stories all dealt with some aspects of domestic life, for she believed that the home was the ideal center of a woman's activity. She disapproved of the suffrage movement and took no part in public affairs, except philanthropic enterprises. "My history," she declared in an autobiographical note, "is simply that of my book-writing and the management of my household" (Teele, *post,* p. 553). Elm Corner in Milton and her summer home in Alstead, N. H., formed the background of her life, although travel in Europe and a year's sojourn in the West supplied diversity of scene. She continued to write books and articles for periodicals all her life, her last volume, *Biddy's Episodes* (1904), appearing when she was eighty. Besides her stories for girls she published several collections of verse: *Mother Goose for Grown Folks* (1860); *Pansies* (1872); *Holy-Tides* (1886); *Daffodils* (1887); and *White Memories* (1893), a tribute to three friends, Phillips Brooks, John G. Whittier, and Lucy Larcom. Her books for girls dealt largely with New England scenes and characters. They contained many reflective passages, which gave dignity to the narratives and often lifted the material to a mature level.

[*The Hist. of Milton, Mass.* (1887), ed. by A. K. Teele; R. H. Stoddard and others, *Poets' Homes* (1877); *Who's Who in America*, 1906–07; Henry Bond, *Geneals. . . . of the First Settlers of Watertown* (1855), I, 607; *Boston Evening Transcript*, Mar. 21, 1906; manuscript material from the family.]

B. M. S.

WHITNEY, ANNE (Sept. 2, 1821–Jan. 23, 1915), sculptor, poet, youngest of the seven children of Nathaniel Ruggles and Sally (Stone) Whitney, was born in Watertown, Mass., the town in which John Whitney, her earliest American ancestor, was a leading citizen from 1635 to 1673. She inherited from her parents good looks, perfect health, and liberal ideas. Her father, clerk of the Middlesex Courts, lived ninety-one years, her mother a hundred and one, and she herself ninety-three. Reared with every advantage of the time and place, and educated in private schools, she soon showed a creative mind, eager to express beauty. Yet, though she was nine years older than Harriet Goodhue Hosmer [*q.v.*], her fellow townswoman, she was unknown as a sculptor until long after Harriet Hosmer achieved fame. In 1859, the year when Hawthorne was singing praises of the Hosmer sculptures, her *Poems* were published in New York and won a modest success; a long and highly favorable notice appeared in the *North American Review*, April 1860.

Anne Whitney was in her middle thirties when she began modelling. She had no teacher, but she later attended the anatomy lectures of Dr. William Rimmer [*q.v.*]. In 1860 she opened a studio in Watertown. Her first attempts were portrait busts of relatives and friends; later she turned to ideal figures. Her life-size marble statue of Lady Godiva, exhibited in Boston, was placed in a private collection. Her "Africa," a colossal reclining figure shown in Boston and

New York, her "Toussaint L'Ouverture"—both an outgrowth of her feeling against slavery—and her "Lotus Eater," representing young manhood in a relaxed attitude, had a significance more ethical than artistic. Then came four or five studious years abroad, mainly in Rome, Paris, and Munich. After her return, she established in 1872 a handsome studio on Mount Vernon Street, Boston, and there her important later work was done. She was well past the middle of her long life before her sculpture saw "the light of the public square." It is said that her native state, in awarding her the commission for a heroic marble statue (*c.* 1873) of Samuel Adams, to be placed in Statuary Hall in the Capitol in Washington, stipulated that the carving should be done in Italy, thus necessitating a second stay abroad. The figure stands in a sturdy attitude, arms folded. Of it Lorado Taft wrote: "Although no woman sculptor has succeeded as yet in making a male figure look convincingly like a man, this statue has a certain feminine power, and is among the interesting works of the collection" (*post*, p. 214). In 1880 a bronze replica was erected in Boston. Among her other works were the seated figure of Charles Sumner in Harvard Square, Cambridge, her "Leif Ericsson," on Commonwealth Avenue, Boston, and the seated marble statue of Harriet Martineau at Wellesley College, which was destroyed by fire in 1914. Her many portrait busts include those of Harriet Beecher Stowe, Frances Willard, Lucy Stone, George Herbert Palmer and his wife, President James Walker of Harvard, and President William Augustus Stearns of Amherst. Her "Keats," at Hampstead, England, was modelled from the well-known mask by Hayden. Other works were a statue called "Roma," representing the city as having fallen on evil days, and an unfinished study of Shakespeare in the *Midsummer Night's Dream* mood. Though a reformer and an advanced thinker, Anne Whitney was without self-assertion. A memorable personage in the cultivated circles of Boston, she kept her unaffected dignity and charm until her death. She died in Boston.

[F. C. Pierce, *Whitney: The Descendants of John Whitney* (1895); *Who's Who in America*, 1914–15; F. E. Willard and M. E. Livermore, *A Woman of the Century* (1893); Lorado Taft, *The Hist. of Am. Sculpture* (1903); *Drama*, May 1916, p. 165, pub. by Drama League of America; Harriet P. Spofford, *A Little Book of Friends* (1916); obituary in *Boston Transcript*, Jan. 25, 1915.]

A—e. A.

WHITNEY, ASA (Dec. 1, 1791–June 4, 1874), inventor, manufacturer, was the son of Asa and Mary (Wallis) Whitney, and a descendant of John Whitney, who emigrated from London, England, to Watertown, Mass., in 1635. He was born in Townsend, Mass., where his father was the blacksmith, and at an early age, having obtained a meager education, he went to work in his father's shop. When he became of age, in order to secure a wider mechanical experience he secured employment in various machine shops, wheelwright shops, and machinery manufactories in New Hampshire and New York. About 1820, while working in New Hampshire in a cotton-machinery manufactory, he was delegated by his employer to install the machinery in a new cotton mill in Brownsville, N. Y. Upon completing the work he remained in that town and began in a small way the manufacture of axles for horse-drawn vehicles.

Although successful in this enterprise, about 1827 he gave it up to become a partner in a local cotton-machinery plant and in three years lost what little capital he possessed. He then accepted the opportunity offered him by the Mohawk & Hudson Railroad to take charge of erecting the machinery on the inclined planes at Albany and Schenectady and of the building of railroad cars. While the work was entirely outside the range of his experience, its novelty strongly appealed to him and by earnest application he progressed in three years to the position of superintendent of the railroad. He continued in this capacity until 1839, by which time his reputation had become such that Governor Seward literally drafted him to fill the office of canal commissioner of New York State. While Whitney conducted this office with distinguished ability, railroading continued to interest him deeply and on June 27, 1840, he was granted a patent for a locomotive steam engine. After serving a three-year term as canal commissioner he resigned to enter into partnership with Matthias W. Baldwin [q.v.], pioneer locomotive builder of Philadelphia, Pa., and in 1842 removed with his family to that city from Rotterdam, N. Y. Whitney was the first of Baldwin's partners to possess a railroad experience and this combined with his keen business sense enabled him in the succeeding four years to develop for the company a sound system of management—something it had lacked up to that time. Whitney also applied his talents in other directions, introducing, for example, a locomotive classification, which in 1934 was still used by the Baldwin Locomotive Works.

In his leisure moments he gave serious attention to the improvement of cast-iron car wheels and made such satisfactory progress that in 1846 he decided to devote his whole attention to this work and resigned from the Baldwin organization. On May 27, 1847, he obtained two patents, one for a cast-iron car wheel having a cor-

rugated center web, and another for the method of manufacturing the same. With his three sons he at once organized in Philadelphia the firm of Asa Whitney & Sons. He continued with his metal experiments and on Apr. 25, 1848, obtained a patent for an improved process of annealing and cooling cast iron wheels, which he incorporated in his manufactory. These three patents formed the foundation on which the Whitney car-wheel works soon developed into the largest and most successful establishment of its kind in the United States. At the time of Whitney's death the daily consumption of pig iron was between sixty and seventy tons. With this business well established, Whitney in 1860 permitted himself to be elected president of the Philadelphia & Reading Railroad. The terminus of the road at that time was at Schuylkill Haven, Pa., but it did not reach any of the anthracite coal mines in that vicinity. One of Whitney's first acts was to devise a plan for acquiring the lateral roads by securing a lease of the Schuylkill Valley Railroad. He thus prepared the way for the Philadelphia & Reading to secure all the coal trade of the Schuylkill region. While intensely interested in this new occupation, Whitney was compelled to relinquish it in 1861 because of his poor health and thereafter until his death he lived in retirement in Philadelphia.

He was much interested in technical education and took an active part in the work of technical and engineering societies. His philanthropies were many during his lifetime, and in his will he bequeathed $50,000 to the University of Pennsylvania to establish a chair of dynamic engineering, and $12,500 to the Franklin Institute. He was married in Watertown, N. Y., Aug. 22, 1816, to Clarinda Williams of Groton, Conn., who with three sons and two daughters survived him.

[F. C. Pierce, *Whitney: The Descendants of John Whitney* (1895); *Railroad Gazette*, June 13, 1874; *Manufactories and Manufacturers of Pa. of the 19th Century* (1875); R. H. Sanford, "A Pioneer Locomotive Builder," *Railway and Locomotive Hist. Soc., Bull. No. 8* (1924); *Public Ledger* (Phila.), June 5, 1874; information from family; Patent Office records.]

C. W. M.

WHITNEY, ASA (Mar. 14, 1797–Sept. 17, 1872), merchant, pioneer promoter of a Pacific railroad, was born at North Groton, Conn., the son of Shubael and Sarah (Mitchell) Whitney, and sixth in descent from John Whitney who came from London, England, and settled at Watertown, Mass., in 1635. His father was a fairly successful farmer, whose land was in a particularly stony region. A farmer's life did not attract Asa, however, and sometime before 1817 he went to New York. As buyer for Frederick Sheldon, a New York dry-goods merchant, he traveled extensively abroad (*c.* 1825–36), chiefly in France, where his resemblance to Napoleon Bonaparte often caused comment. There he married Herminie Antoinette Pillet, who died in New York, Apr. 1, 1833. On Nov. 3, 1835, he married Sarah Jay Munro, daughter of Peter Jay Munro and grandniece of John Jay.

Between 1832 and 1836 he purchased a tract of land on Broadway in New York and several parcels in New Rochelle, where he established his father's family in 1832 and provided his younger brothers and sisters with educational advantages that he had missed. In 1836 he became the head of his own firm. Although he was then financially able to meet his obligations, the depression following the panic of 1837 ruined his business and he was compelled to give up all his land. Discouraged by his losses and by the death of his wife, Nov. 12, 1840, he set out for China, where he remained about fifteen months, acting as an agent for several New York firms and on his own account, with such profitable results that he never again engaged in business. He was able, also, to gather sufficient statistical information to show that an American transcontinental railroad would be of great importance in commerce with China, and to formulate a plan for its construction.

Returning to New York in September 1844, he presented his plan to Congress (*House Executive Document, No. 72,* 28 Cong., 2 Sess.). The route which he favored was from Lake Michigan via the South Pass of the Rockies to the Pacific, since it included so much unoccupied but supposedly fertile land which could be sold by government commissioners to provide funds for the railroad. His failure to make demands leading to his own immediate profit was an attitude too altruistic generally to be understood and was responsible for the idea that he contemplated a vast secret speculation. He realized that the public must be educated to the point of demanding such a railroad from Congress. Beginning with his personal reconnaissance of the first eight hundred miles of his route in the summer of 1845, which he reported in a long letter to the press, he carried on for seven years an amazing newspaper publicity campaign; addressed public meetings in all the larger cities and the legislatures of most of the states; tirelessly pursued members of Congress; and wrote articles for periodicals and several pamphlets, chief of which was *A Project for a Railroad to the Pacific* (1849). Opposition to his plan on various grounds convinced him that no further headway could be made with Congress, and

in 1851 he accepted an invitation to present his plan in England as a possibility for Canada. Although he was favorably received, the English were not yet ready to undertake the railroad.

Whitney then dropped the matter, married Catherine (Moore) Campbell, daughter of Maurice Moore of Wilmington, N. C., on Oct. 6, 1852, and retired to an estate in Washington known as "Locust Hill." One who knew him during his later life described him as "a polished gentleman of the old school," whose home contained "many rare and beautiful things he had brought from all over the world and things presented to him by distinguished people"; who "every morning at a stated hour" had a "saddle horse brought to the door and he took his morning ride over his estate" (Brown, *post,* p. 224). He died of typhoid fever, shortly after one transcontinental railroad had been completed and three others begun.

[F. C. Pierce, *Whitney: The Descendants of John Whitney* (1895); G. M. Wright, "Corrections in the Pierce Geneal." (MS.) ; *Atlantic and Pacific Railroad: A. Whitney's Reply to the Hon. S. A. Douglass* (1845) ; N. H. Loomis, "Asa Whitney: Father of Pacific Railroads," *Proc. Miss. Valley Hist. Asso.,* vol. VI (1913); M. L. Brown, "Asa Whitney and His Pacific Railroad Publicity Campaign," *Miss. Valley Hist. Rev.,* Sept. 1933; *Evening Star* (Washington), Sept. 17, 1872; family papers and contemporary newspapers and periodicals.]
M. L. B.

WHITNEY, ELI (Dec. 8, 1765–Jan. 8, 1825), inventor, was born at Westboro, Mass., the son of Eli and Elizabeth (Fay) Whitney and a descendant of John Whitney who emigrated from England to Watertown, Mass., in 1635. On both sides his ancestors were substantial farmers of Worcester County. His father was able to provide well for his growing family and when Eli was twelve years old, proposed that he prepare for college. The boy, however, had shown no particular proficiency in any of the subjects taught in the local school, though he showed a fondness for figures; he helped rather indifferently with the farm work, and evinced special interest only when he was permitted to putter around his father's shop, which was fitted up with a variety of tools and a turning lathe. His mind occupied with all manner of manufacturing schemes, he persuaded his father to let him continue in mechanical work. He made and repaired violins in the neighborhood, worked in iron, and at the age of fifteen began the manufacture of nails in his father's shop. He continued this enterprise for two winters, even hiring a helper to fill his orders. When the demand for nails declined at the close of the Revolutionary War, he turned to making hatpins and almost monopolized that business in his section of the state, although he gave time to the shop only when the farm did not require his attention. By the time he was eighteen his ideas regarding a college education had changed, but when he broached the subject to his father the latter thought him too old to begin the preparatory studies and, furthermore, was not then in a position to provide the necessary funds.

Whitney's mind was made up, however, and to obtain the funds he taught school in Grafton, Northboro, Westboro, and Paxton, and with the money thus earned attended Leicester Academy, Leicester, Mass., during the summer. He entered Yale College in May 1789, at the age of twenty-three. During his three years there he studied diligently, and to augment the funds sent him by his father repaired apparatus and equipment about the college. The story is told that when a carpenter who had reluctantly lent him some tools observed the skill with which he used them, he remarked, "There was one good mechanic spoiled when you went to college" (Olmsted, *post*, p. 11). After his graduation in the autumn of 1792, having decided to become a lawyer, Whitney went South to accept a position as tutor in a gentleman's family, with the understanding that he could devote a portion of his time to reading law. On the boat which he took to Savannah he met the widow of Gen. Nathanael Greene, with her family and Phineas Miller, the manager of her plantation. On his arrival at Savannah, Whitney learned that his prospective employer had hired another tutor, and Mrs. Greene invited him to be her guest. He gratefully accepted and began his law studies, grasping every opportunity to show his appreciation for the kindness of his hostess by making and repairing things about the house and plantation.

During the winter a group of gentlemen who had served under General Greene in the Revolution came to visit Mrs. Greene, and one evening were discussing the deplorable state of agriculture in the South. Large areas of land were unsuitable for the growing of rice or long-staple cotton, although they yielded large crops of green seed cotton. This was an unprofitable crop, however, because the process of separating the cotton from its seed by hand was so tedious that it took a woman one whole day to obtain a pound of staple. One of the gentlemen remarked that the agricultural troubles of the inland portions of the South would be eliminated if some machine could be devised to facilitate the process of cleaning the green seed cotton. Mrs. Greene, thereupon, who had observed Whitney's ingenuity with tools, suggested that he was the per-

son to make such a machine, and forthwith he turned his attention to the problem. Within ten days he had designed a cotton gin and completed an imperfect model in accordance with his plan. He experimented with this model, and by April 1793 had built a larger, improved machine with which one negro could produce fifty pounds of cleaned cotton in a day.

Having indicated the means to the end sought by Mrs. Greene's friends, thus fulfilling in part his many obligations to her, Whitney intended to resume his study of the law, but he was persuaded by Phineas Miller to continue work on the cotton gin with a view to patenting the idea and engaging in the manufacture of the new machine. The two men drew up a partnership agreement on May 27, 1793, to engage in the patenting and manufacturing of cotton gins and to conduct a cotton ginning business. Meanwhile the knowledge that Whitney had built a machine to clean cotton spread like wildfire; and multitudes came from all quarters to see the gin; and before Whitney could secure his patent a number of imitations were in successful operation. Whitney returned to New Haven, however, to perfect, patent, and manufacture his gin as soon as possible. He first made oath to the invention on Oct. 28, 1793, obtained his patent Mar. 14, 1794, and immediately began making cotton gins and shipping them to Miller in Georgia. The partners planned to buy the cotton seed themselves, gin it, and sell the product, because they felt that, protected by a patent, they could maintain a monopoly. This policy proved to be extremely disadvantageous, however, for they could not produce enough machines to gin the rapidly increasing crops nor could they raise sufficient capital to finance the entire cotton crop. Infringing machines were put into operation on every side, and perplexities and discouragements harassed them from the very beginning of the undertaking.

The most formidable rival machine was that of Hodgin Holmes, in which circular saws were used instead of the drum with inserted wires of Whitney's original machine. Whitney later proved that the idea of such teeth had occurred to him, but it was some years before he established his right over the Holmes gin. The partners had difficulty in raising money and had to pay interest rates of from twelve to twenty-five per cent. Furthermore, word came from England that manufacturers were condemning the cotton cleaned by Whitney's gins on the ground that the staple was injured. This news brought their business and the thirty gins operating in Georgia to a standstill until they could prove the fallacy of the opinion, which required nearly two years. In 1797 the first infringement suit was tried unsuccessfully. Many others followed, but it was not until 1807 that Whitney obtained a favorable decision. This was rendered in the United States court, held in Georgia in December 1807 by Justice William Johnson. Whitney, as survivor of Miller & Whitney, had brought suit against a man named Arthur Fort for violation of the patent right and for a perpetual injunction restraining him from use of the gin. After hearing the case, Justice Johnson made a very clear statement covering each of the three main contentions of the defense—that the invention was not original; that it was not useful; and that the machine which the defendant used was materially different from the invention in question. In reference to this last point, the Justice said, "A Mr. Holmes has cut teeth in plates of iron, and passed them over the cylinder. This is certainly a meritorious improvement in the mechanical process of constructing this machine. But at last, what does it amount to, except a more convenient mode of making the same thing? Every characteristic of Mr. Whitney's machine is preserved. . . . Mr. Whitney may not be at liberty to use Mr. Holmes' iron plate, but certainly Mr. Holmes' improvement does not destroy Mr. Whitney's patent-right. Let the decree for a perpetual injunction be entered" (Olmsted, *post*, p. 4). This decision was confirmed by several subsequent decisions, and thenceforth Whitney's patent was not questioned. Meanwhile, however, in 1795 his shops in New Haven had been destroyed by fire; the legislatures of South Carolina and Tennessee which in 1801 and 1802 respectively had voted to purchase patent rights suddenly annulled the contracts; and in 1803 Miller died, disappointed and broken by the struggle.

Whitney continued alone for nine years more, and in 1812 made application to Congress for the renewal of his patent. In spite of the logical arguments which he advanced in his petition, the request was refused. There is probably no other instance in the history of invention of the letting loose of such tremendous industrial forces so suddenly as occurred with the invention of the cotton gin. In 1792 the United States exported 138,328 pounds of cotton; in 1794, the year Whitney patented his gin, 1,601,000 pounds were exported; the following year, 6,276,000 pounds; and by 1800, the production of cotton in the United States had risen to 35,000,000 pounds of which 17,790,000 were exported. Yet Whitney received practically no return for the invention which was due to him alone.

He was a clear-sighted business man as well as an inventor, however, and was quick to realize the mistake he and Miller had made in attempting to monopolize the ginning business. He was so thoroughly convinced that he would never obtain any money from his invention of the cotton gin that as early as 1798 he made up his mind that he had to turn to something else. He chose the manufacture of firearms, and on Jan. 14, 1798, obtained from the federal government a contract for "ten thousand stand of arms" to be delivered in two years. Whitney was not a gunsmith, but he proposed to manufacture guns by a new method, his aim being "to make the same parts of different guns, as the locks, for example, as much like each other as the successive impressions of a copper-plate engraving." This was perhaps the first, certainly one of the first suggestions of the system of interchangeable parts which has been of tremendous significance in industrial development [see sketch of Simeon North].

Whitney's mechanical ingenuity and inventive capacity had been so thoroughly demonstrated, and his reputation for character was so high, that he had no difficulty in finding ten individuals in New Haven to go his bond and furnish the initial capital for the new undertaking. Purchasing a mill site just outside of New Haven, now Whitneyville, he built a factory and began the design and construction of the necessary machinery to carry out his schemes. Because of the extremely low state of the mechanic arts, his difficulties were innumerable. There were no similar establishments upon which branches of his own business might lean; there were no experienced workmen to give him any assistance; and he had to make by himself practically every machine and tool required. The expense incurred and time expended in getting the factory into operation greatly exceeded his expectations, but the confidence of his financial backers and the government seems never to have been impaired. At the end of the first year after the contract was made, instead of 4,000 muskets, only 500 were delivered, and it was eight years instead of two before the contract was completed. So liberal was the government in making advances to Whitney that the final balance due him amounted to little more than $2,400 out of an original sum of $134,000. Whitney, however, had accomplished that which he had set out to do. Workmen with little or no experience could operate his machinery and with it turn out by the hundreds the various parts of a musket with so much precision that "the several parts . . . were as readily adapted to each other, as if each had been made for its respective fellow" (Olmsted, p. 53). Whitney had succeeded in reducing an extremely complex process to what amounted to a succession of simple operations. Besides overcoming a myriad of mechanical difficulties during this eight-year period, he had to work against prejudice and withstand the ridicule which he encountered at every hand; yet by his tenacity he so perfected the manufacture of arms that with the subsequent adoption of his system in the two federal armories, the government saved $25,000 annually. In 1812 he entered into a second contract with the federal government to manufacture 15,000 firearms, and contracted to make a similar quantity for the state of New York, and thereafter his unique manufactory yielded him a just reward. The business which he started employed some sixty men, and at the time the works were built he erected a row of substantial stone houses for his workmen which are said to have been the first workmen's houses erected by an employer in the United States. Of the various machines designed and used by Whitney only one is known to exist. This is a plain milling machine which was built prior to 1818, and is believed to be the first successful machine of its kind ever made.

Whitney enjoyed the refined and cultivated society of his day, but his precarious business life prevented his having a normal domestic life until middle age. On Jan. 6, 1817, in New Haven, he married Henrietta Frances Edwards, who with three children survived him. In person, he "was considerably above the ordinary average, of a dignified carriage, and of an open, manly and agreeable countenance. . . . His sense of honor was high and his feelings of resentment and indignation occasionally strong. . . . The most remarkable trait of his character was his perseverance, very remarkable because it is so common to find men of great powers of mechanical invention deficient in this quality" (Olmsted, post, pp. 61–62). His mind was "independent and original" and he had "nicely balanced judgment" (Ibid., p. 60).

[Denison Olmsted, Memoir of Eli Whitney, Esq. (1846); Papers of the New Haven Colony Hist. Soc., vol. V (1894); J. W. Roe, English and Am. Tool Builders (1926); Henry Howe, Memoirs of the Most Eminent Am. Mechanics (1847); F. C. Pierce, Whitney: The Descendants of John Whitney (1895); F. B. Dexter, Biog. Sketches Grads. Yale Coll., vol. V (1911); D. A. Tompkins, Cotton and Cotton Oil (1901); Conn. Jour. (New Haven), Jan. 11, 1825.]   C. W. M.

WHITNEY, HARRY PAYNE (Apr. 29, 1872–Oct. 26, 1930), financier, sportsman, was born in New York City, the son of William Collins Whitney [q.v.] and Flora (Payne), a nephew of Oliver Hazard Payne [q.v.], and a de-

scendant of John Whitney who emigrated from England to Watertown, Mass., in 1635. He was educated privately and at Yale, graduating from that university in 1894. There he did a bit of writing, even composing poetry, and was editor of the *Yale Daily News*. He next studied law at Columbia University, and read for a time as a student in the office of Elihu Root.

For years he was his father's closest companion and confidant, and was trained to be his business successor. The son's first business venture of consequence took place in 1902, when he acted as guide to Daniel Guggenheim [q.v.] through the silver, lead, and copper districts of the western United States and Mexico. They returned with deeds to nearly $10,000,000 worth of such properties, in which young Whitney had a share. He was made a director of the Guggenheim Exploration Company and other large corporations, such as the Guaranty Trust Company, the Newport Trust Company, the New York Loan Improvement Company, and other banking, as well as mining and railroad concerns. When the elder Whitney died in 1904, half of his fortune, amounting to about $24,000,000, descended to Harry Payne, together with directorships in many corporations.

Whitney was a noted traveler and sportsman; he was keenly interested in yachting and hunted tigers in India, where he was the guest of the Viceroy. He organized and was captain and chief strategist of the "Big Four," most famous of American polo teams, which in 1909 brought the International Cup back from England, where it had remained for many years, and successfully defended it in 1911 and 1913. His polo tactics were later adopted to a considerable degree by the British. He became one of the few "ten-goal" players in the history of the sport, and gave much time to the direction of the game after he retired from active playing. He also devoted much energy to horse racing and to the government of the American turf, being for years an official of the Saratoga and Westchester tracks. His thoroughbreds at one time and another won all the important purses offered on American courses. In 1924, when his racers numbered more than 200, they ran first in 272 races, second in 201, and third in 235. Their winnings, totaling about half a million dollars were the largest among American stables that year.

Whitney held only one public office, that of commissioner of municipal statistics of New York City, which place he resigned after little more than a year's incumbency. In 1921–22 he provided funds for the Whitney South Sea Expedition, sent by the American Museum of Natural History to collect birds of Polynesia. He was a member of more than twenty prominent clubs. On Aug. 25, 1896, he married Gertrude Vanderbilt, whom he had known from childhood. She became a noted sculptor and survived him at his death, together with a son and two daughters.

[F. C. Pierce, *Whitney: The Descendants of John Whitney* (1895); *Yale Univ. Obit. Record,* 1931; *Who's Who in America,* 1930–31; *N. Y. Times, N. Y. Herald Tribune, World* (N. Y.), Oct. 27, 1930; Newell Bent, *Am. Polo* (1929); F. G. Griswold, *The International Polo Cup* (1928); R. V. Hoffman, "Famous Families in Sport," *Country Life,* Apr. 1932; records of Saratoga and Westchester Racing Associations.]

A. F. H.

WHITNEY, JAMES LYMAN (Nov. 28, 1835–Sept. 25, 1910), librarian, was born in Northampton, Mass., the son of Josiah Dwight and Clarissa (James) Whitney. He had for half-brothers such men of letters and science as the distinguished philologist, William Dwight Whitney, and the eminent geologist, Josiah Dwight Whitney [qq.v.]. After early training at home and in boarding school, and preparation for college in the Northampton Collegiate Institute, he entered Yale College in 1852. He was graduated in 1856 with the degree of B.A.; in 1865 he received the degree of M.A. The year following his graduation he remained at Yale as Berkeley Scholar of the House. From New Haven he went in 1857 to New York. There he entered the employ of the publishing house of Wiley and Halsted. A year later he moved to Springfield, Mass., and engaged himself to the book-selling firm of Bridgman & Company. He shortly became a partner, the firm name becoming Bridgman and Whitney. He remained in the book trade until 1868. He then turned to library work, but for many years continued to retain an interest in the Springfield book-selling firm of Whitney and Adams. He had had his first taste of library work at Yale, when during undergraduate years he served as assistant librarian and then as librarian of the Society of Brothers in Unity. Upon electing in 1868 to enter upon an active career in the field, he became assistant librarian in the Cincinnati Public Library. In 1869 he was appointed to the service of the Boston Public Library, a connection that continued for the remaining forty years of his life. In 1874 he was made chief of the catalogue department, a post which he held for the next twenty-five years, and in 1899 he was appointed librarian. Early in 1903 ill health compelled him to resign, but during the next seven years he continued as chief of the department of documents and statistics, a position con-

siderably less onerous and exacting. He died at his home in Cambridge, Mass., in September 1910.

To his chosen field he devoted himself unremittingly. He became known in the world of letters as the compiler and editor of the monumental *Catalogue of the Spanish Library and of the Portuguese Books Bequeathed by George Ticknor to the Boston Public Library,* published in 1879. He also prepared for the library many special catalogues and similar publications. From the point of view of the development of library technique, his great contribution was the building-up of the card-catalogue system of the library.

At the same time he was not forgetful of relations with the outside world. From 1879 to 1887 he served as chairman of the school committee of Concord, Mass., where he was then living. During the same period he was active also in the work of the committee for the Concord Free Library. For a time he was the head of the finance committee, and also treasurer, of the American Library Association, of which he was both a charter and a life member. He was elected to membership in numerous historical and literary societies. By nature companionable and tolerant, he fitted easily into responsibilities and associations with his fellow men. He never married.

[F. C. Pierce, *Whitney: The Descendants of John Whitney* (1895); *Who's Who in America,* 1910–11; *Obit. Record Grads. Yale Univ.* (1911); J. L. Whitney, "Reminiscences of an Old Librarian," *Lib. Jour.,* Nov. 1909; *Ibid.,* Jan. 1900, Oct. 1910, Mar. 1911; H. G. Wadlin, *The Pub. Lib. of the City of Boston* (1911); Boston Pub. Lib., ann. reports, 1897, 1910–11; scrapbook on Whitney in the possession of the Boston Pub. Lib.; obituary and editorial in *Boston Transcript,* Sept. 26, 1910.]

M. E. L—d.

WHITNEY, JOSIAH DWIGHT (Nov. 23, 1819–Aug. 19, 1896), geologist, chemist, was born in Northampton, Mass., the son of Josiah Dwight and Sarah (Williston) Whitney. His father was a thrifty and enterprising banker, descended from John Dwight, who settled at Dedham, Mass., in 1635, and John Whitney, who settled at Watertown the same year; his mother, a daughter of the Rev. Payson Williston of Easthampton, was a teacher at Hopkins Academy, Hadley, and nineteen years old when she married. A few weeks after the birth of her eighth child she died, when Josiah, the eldest, was fourteen. About a year later his father married again, and to this marriage five children were born, one of whom was James Lyman Whitney [q.v.]. Josiah, meanwhile, had been sent to a series of private schools, including the famous Round Hill School founded by George

Bancroft and Joseph Green Cogswell at Northampton, from which he was removed by his conservative father because of its cosmopolitanism. It had been his mother's wish that he enter the ministry, and the tradition of his father's family pointed toward a business career, but while he was attending a school in New Haven, Josiah's interest in science had been excited by Benjamin Silliman's lectures on chemistry. At this time, however, he was as much interested in music, art, and literature. He fitted for college at Phillips Academy, Andover, entered Yale as a sophomore in 1836, and graduated three years later, having acquired an acquaintance with several modern languages and studied chemistry and mineralogy under Silliman and astronomy under Denison Olmsted [q.v.]. He is pictured at this period as a shy youth, distinctly unsocial, though brilliant and fascinating among congenial friends and admired and loved by his family.

For some months after his graduation he studied chemistry with Robert Hare [q.v.] in Philadelphia and in the summer of 1840 joined Charles T. Jackson [q.v.] as an unpaid assistant in the geological survey of New Hampshire, returning to Jackson's Boston laboratory in the winter as assistant geologist to help with the analyses. He began to read law at Northampton in the summer of 1841, planning to enter the Harvard Law School in the fall, but stopped in Boston to hear Charles Lyell lecture on geology and to complete some work in Jackson's laboratory. Realizing at last that science was his field, he now prevailed upon his father to allow him to study in Europe, and sailed in May 1842. Between summers of wandering he spent a winter at the École des Mines in Paris and a winter in Rome, for a short time attended the lectures of the geologist Élie de Beaumont in Paris, and then went to Rammelsberg's laboratory in Berlin to study methods of chemical analysis. Called home by his father for financial reasons, he was able to prolong his stay for a few months by translating from the German of J. J. Berzelius *The Use of the Blowpipe in Chemistry and Mineralogy,* published in 1845 by Ticknor & Fields. He returned to Northampton in January of that year, and in the summer, through Jackson's influence, obtained employment for a few months as mining geologist with the Isle Royale Copper Company, but in December went abroad again to study in the laboratory of Heinrich Rose at Berlin and subsequently with Liebig at Giessen, where his friendship with Wolcott Gibbs [q.v.] began.

His systematic training ended here. No sooner had he returned to Northampton, in May 1847, than he was engaged by Jackson to assist in a survey of the mineral lands of the northern peninsula of Michigan. Matters did not run smoothly and Jackson was compelled to resign at the end of the first year, leaving the completion of the work to the two assistants, Whitney and John Wells Foster. It was a difficult task for men with so little experience behind them, but was completed after a manner (1849), and the two volumes of their report, comprising upwards of 600 pages with forty-five plates and a colored geological map, were issued as Congressional documents in 1850 and 1851. As usual with government publications at that day, they were cheap in style and typography, much to the disgust of Whitney, who had himself drawn many of the illustrations and had made persistent efforts to have them reproduced in a befitting manner.

Establishing himself as a consulting expert in mining after the close of the Lake Superior survey, with headquarters first in Brookline, then in Cambridge, Whitney soon built up a clientage throughout the eastern United States and Canada that gave him opportunity second to none for acquiring information concerning ores, ore deposits, and mining, which he worked up into book form under the title *Metallic Wealth of the United States* (1854). The volume marked an important epoch in the literature of ore deposits and remained the standard work of reference up to the time of Prime's translation (1870) of Bernhard von Cotta's *Die Lehre von den Erzlagerstätten* (1859). In June 1854 he married Louisa (Goddard) Howe, daughter of Samuel Goddard of Brookline; they had one child, a daughter.

During the years 1855–58, with the title of professor in the state university, Whitney served as chemist and mineralogist with James Hall [q.v.] on the geological survey of Iowa, often acting as head of the survey in Hall's absence. He was also member for a time of the Illinois survey under Amos H. Worthen [q.v.], dealing mainly with the deposits of lead and zinc, and for a time was associated with Hall in the geological survey of Wisconsin, investigating the lead regions. In 1860 he was appointed state geologist of California and undertook an elaborate survey. His subordinates and volunteer assistants during the succeeding years included William H. Brewer, James Graham Cooper, William More Gabb, Clarence King [qq.v.], and Baron Friedrich von Richthofen, the geographer, who became his devoted friend. During his years in California Whitney was chairman of a committee to make preliminary plans for a state agricultural and mechanical college, was active in promoting the California Academy of Science, and served as a commissioner of Yosemite Park. At first the survey proceeded well; temporary financial stringencies were tided over by J. D. Whitney, Senior, who was subsequently reimbursed by the state, but scholarly ideals of the geologist and the scope of the enterprise failed to win sympathy from the legislature and in 1868 activities were suspended for lack of appropriations. Three volumes only of the final reports were published by the state. Whitney continued in office until 1874, and later at his own expense and with the aid of the Harvard Museum of Comparative Zoology was able to publish some of the accumulated material. Thus in 1880 the Museum issued *The Auriferous Gravels of the Sierra Nevada of California,* and in 1882 Whitney himself brought out the second of the volumes on general geology. The survey was significant not only for its findings but for the men it trained and the methods it introduced—notably topographical mapping by triangulation (Brewster, *post,* pp. 305–12).

In 1865 Whitney had been appointed to the Harvard faculty to found a school of mines, though he had been given indefinite leave of absence to carry on the work in California. Upon the suspension of the survey in 1868 he had returned to Cambridge and opened the school of mines, and in 1869 took a party of his students to do field work in the mountains of Colorado. In November 1874, when the California work was definitely dropped, he once more took up his residence in Cambridge and in 1875, the short-lived school of mines having been merged with the Lawrence Scientific School, he settled down to teaching at Harvard, being reappointed to the Sturgis-Hooper professorship which had been established for him ten years earlier. This position he continued to hold for the rest of his life. In 1882 he published his last great work, based largely on his western experiences, *Climatic Changes of Later Geological Times.* This volume was a most important contribution to the subject at the time of issue, though the conclusions put forward were not in agreement with those of many of his fellow workers. He also wrote the articles on America for the ninth edition of the *Encyclopædia Britannica,* afterward revising and publishing them in two volumes under the title, *The United States: Facts and Figures Illustrating the Physical Geography of the Country and Its Material Resources* (1889). Another important work of his later years was the preparation for *The Century Dictionary and Cyclopedia,* edited by his brother,

William Dwight Whitney [*q.v.*], of the terms in the fields of mining, metal and metallurgy, geology, lithology, physical geography, and fossil botany. An interesting little volume, *Names and Places* (1888), was a by-product of this activity.

Whitney was independent in thought and action, strong of character and aggressive, wholesomely outspoken in criticism of poor work, and equaled among geologists only by John Peter Lesley [*q.v.*] as a writer of vigorous English. His work in northern Michigan and the lead region of the upper Mississippi Valley, and his *Metallic Wealth of the United States* gave powerful stimulus to the scientific study of ore deposits and raised the calling of the mining geologist to a higher plane. As a teacher of college students he was only moderately successful; it was the work of his colleague N. S. Shaler [*q.v.*] to inspire and discipline the boys; to Whitney came those ready for advanced study, and to these he was an example rather than a schoolmaster. He was primarily "an accurate and painstaking scholar, who set before his pupils an ideal of scholarship and taught them not to make mistakes" (Brewster, *post,* p. 322). Through the few men whom he influenced profoundly he helped to shape the teaching of geology and geography in the schools of America for the succeeding generation. Honors did not come to him as abundantly as to many perhaps less worthy. He was made a member of the American Philosophical Society in 1863 and an original member of the National Academy of Sciences the same year. He was the fourth American (preceded by Dana, Hall, and Newberry) to be elected a foreign member of the Geological Society of London. In 1882, after years of invalidism, his wife died, and within a few days, in Europe, his daughter. Fourteen years later, two years after the death of his brother William, he died, from arteriosclerosis, at Lake Sunapee, N. H.

[F. C. Pierce, *Whitney: The Descendants of John Whitney* (1895); E. T. Brewster, *Life and Letters of Josiah Dwight Whitney* (1909); G. P. Merrill, "Contribution to a History of State Surveys," *U. S. Nat. Museum Bull. 109* (1920) and *The First One Hundred Years of Am. Geol.* (1924); *The Development of Harvard Univ. . . . 1869–1929* (1930), ed. by S. E. Morison; *A Hist. of the First Half-Century of the Nat. Acad. of Sciences* (1913); Max Meisel, *A Bibliog. of Am. Nat. Hist.,* vols. II, III (1926, 1929); *Obit. Record Grads. Yale Univ.* (1900); *Boston Transcript,* Aug. 20, 1896; Clarence King, *Mountaineering in the Sierra Nevada* (1872).]   G. P. M.

WHITNEY, MARY WATSON (Sept. 11, 1847–Jan. 21, 1920), astronomer and teacher, was born in Waltham, Mass., the daughter of Samuel Buttrick and Mary Watson (Crehore) Whitney. Her family was of old New England stock, going back on her father's side directly to

John Whitney who brought his family to the New World in 1635. Her parents, who had intellectual tastes, gave their children a happy home and provided them with excellent educational advantages. Mary attended the public schools of Waltham and early attracted the attention of her teachers by her unusual mental ability and love of study, being especially proficient in mathematics. Unfortunately further training seemed impossible to her since none of the eastern colleges were open to women, but while still in high school she heard of the new college intended especially for women being established in the Hudson Valley by Matthew Vassar [q.v.]. Her earnest desire to go there was gratified by her father, and accompanied by him she presented herself at Vassar College on its opening day in September 1865. She was at once greatly attracted by Prof. Maria Mitchell [q.v.], the distinguished astronomer whose classes she entered. Her superiority and interest endeared her to the older woman and she became one of her most cherished pupils. She graduated in 1868, in the second class. Mary Whitney was much admired by her fellow students and recognized as a leader. Several times she served as president of their newly formed organizations. Her fine presence, good judgment and impartiality made her an excellent presiding officer, while her modesty and kindness of heart won their devoted affection.

After graduation she continued her studies at home, and received the A.M. degree from Vassar in 1872. By personal invitation she attended mathematical lectures given by Prof. Benjamin Peirce [q.v.] at Harvard College, and from 1874 to 1876 she attended lectures in mathematics at Zürich, Switzerland. Occasionally she returned to Vassar to assist Professor Mitchell in some piece of astronomical research, and in 1881 accepted an urgent call to become her permanent assistant. She kept this position until Professor Mitchell resigned in 1888, when she was appointed her successor. She was the director of the Vassar Observatory as well as professor of astronomy. In the former capacity she carried on research work with excellent equipment. She summoned to her assistance one of her own pupils and, working together, they published a long series of positions of comets and asteroids. Later they took up the study of variable stars and the measurement of photographic plates. In all, one hundred publications issued from the Vassar Observatory during her tenure of office which lasted until 1910 when a serious illness forced her retirement. Her research work was marked by accuracy and thoroughness. As a teacher she was noted for her clearness in ex-

plaining difficult mathematical points and for the vividness and elegance with which she presented the more descriptive topics. Many students elected her courses merely to come in contact with her personality. As a member of the faculty, she was highly esteemed for her soundness of judgment and her progressive ideas. As a scholar she was a constant stimulus to her younger colleagues. She read extensively on political and philosophical topics, and had highly developed tastes in literature and music. She was a fellow of the American Academy for the Advancement of Science.

[Personal information; *Who's Who in America*, 1920–21; F. C. Pierce, *Whitney: The Descendants of John Whitney* (1895); C. F. Crehore, *A Geneal. of the Crehore Family* (1887); *Popular Astronomy*, Jan. 1923.]
C. E. F.

WHITNEY, MYRON WILLIAM (Sept. 6, 1836–Sept. 18, 1910), singer, was born in Ashby, Mass., the fourth child of Fanny (Lincoln) and William Whitney (1798–1894). His father, a descendant of John Whitney who settled in Watertown, Mass., in 1635, was a shoemaker and later a farmer, and lived to be the oldest citizen of Ashby. The atmosphere of the Whitney home was musical—the father led the singing at the Ashby Congregational Church and played the bass viol at its services—but Myron found that there was little opportunity in the village for training his talents, and in 1852 went to Boston, where he became a pupil of E. H. Frost. He soon became bass soloist at the Tremont Temple, and on Dec. 25, 1858, made his début as an oratorio singer in a performance of the *Messiah*, given at the Tabernacle. For the next ten years he was active as a singer in the neighborhood of Boston. On Christmas of 1861 he made his first appearance as a soloist with the Boston Handel and Haydn Society, again singing the bass rôle in the *Messiah*. In 1868 he went to Florence to study with Luigi Vannucini. In 1871 he spent a year in England, appearing in London and the provinces, and filling a seven weeks' engagement at Covent Garden. He sang in *Elijah* at the Birmingham festival and had the rôle of Polyphemus in Handel's *Acis and Galatea*. After 1876 he confined his appearance and tours to the United States, where he had already gained distinction. He was a soloist at the Cincinnati festivals of 1873 and 1875, as well as those of 1878 and 1880. In 1876 he was the only soloist at the opening of the Centennial Exhibition in Philadelphia. He was engaged for two tours with the Theodore Thomas Orchestra, and during the season 1886–87 was one of the bassos of the American Opera Company, directed by Thomas. After 1879 he was associated with the

Boston Ideal Opera Company (later the Bostonians), famous for its productions of light operas. He retired from the concert stage in 1890. He died in Sandwich, Mass. On May 4, 1859, he was married to Eleanor Breasha of Boston, by whom he had three children. He was survived by his wife and two sons.

There are many tributes to Whitney's importance as a singer. George Putnam Upton [q.v.] wrote: "He had a smooth, rich, resonant bass, admirably schooled, and delivered with refinement, dignity, and classical repose. As an oratorio singer, indeed, he had no equal in his time, and his superior has not yet been found" (post, pp. 133–34). Elsewhere he has been called "one of the best bass singers ever heard on any stage" (C. E. Russell, The American Orchestra and Theodore Thomas, 1927, p. 165). During the period of his activity on the American stage he is said to have had but one conspicuous rival, Franz Remmertz, the German (Matthews, post). Those who knew Whitney personally invariably spoke of his genial disposition. Upton wrote: "He is the soul of geniality and has a quiet humor that makes him a delightful companion. He has always been universally beloved on and off the stage, and respected and honored as few singers have been" (op. cit.).

[F. C. Pierce, Whitney: The Descendants of John Whitney (1895); Who's Who in America, 1910–11; G. P. Upton, Musical Memories (1908); W. S. B. Matthews and G. L. Howe, A Hundred Years of Music in America (1889); J. C. Macy, in Musician, Dec. 1910; obituary in Boston Transcript, Sept. 19, 1910.]

J. T. H.

WHITNEY, WILLIAM COLLINS (July 5, 1841–Feb. 2, 1904), financier, secretary of the navy, sportsman, was born in Conway, Mass., of Puritan stock; and in spite of great wealth he remained a Democrat through life. He was the son of Brig.-Gen. James Scollay Whitney and Laurinda (Collins) and a descendant of John Whitney who came to Watertown, Mass., from London in 1635. Graduating from Yale in 1863, he attended the Harvard Law School in 1863–64, studied law in the office of Abraham R. Lawrence, and was admitted to the bar in 1865. He made an immediate success at law and politics in New York, gained the confidence of Samuel J. Tilden, took part in the action against the "Tweed ring," and for six years (1875–82) gave effective reorganization to the office of corporation counsel in New York City. He worked through the County Democracy, opposed Irving Hall and Tammany, and became a natural supporter of Grover Cleveland. He went to Washington as Cleveland's secretary of the navy in March 1885.

By his marriage on Oct. 13, 1869, to Flora Payne, sister of a college classmate, Oliver H. Payne, and daughter of Henry B. Payne [qq.v.], Whitney acquired contacts with great wealth and corporate activity. Prior to his appointment to the cabinet he had become identified with the utilities of New York City. In 1883, through the Broadway Railroad Company, he participated in a triangular struggle with Thomas Fortune Ryan [q.v.] and Jacob Sharp for the Broadway street-railway franchise. The fight was won temporarily by Sharp by means of bribery, but in December 1884 Ryan allied Whitney and Peter A. B. Widener [q.v.] with himself. Together they fought Sharp by arousing public opinion, instituting court action, and stimulating legislative investigation. In this connection Whitney's political prominence was a distinct asset (for his methods, see B. J. Hendrick in McClure's Magazine, Nov. 1907, p. 45). The Ryan syndicate finally acquired the franchise. Whitney continued to be active in street-railway affairs until the reorganization of the Metropolitan Street Railway Company in 1902, when he retired from all personal identification with it.

Whitney went to Washington accustomed to the habits of wealthy society; and he and his wife took a lead in the social affairs of the administration. Their remodeled home, with its great ballroom, offered entertainments beyond anything that Cleveland could manage while a bachelor, and the like of which Whitney's colleagues in the cabinet could not afford to undertake. Later, it was from Mrs. Whitney that there came indignant denial of Cleveland's maltreatment of his wife, when opposition canards became too virulent to be ignored. Whitney earned a place in the inner circle of Cleveland's advisers and had more than an ordinary hand in the management of the Navy Department at the moment when transition to a new establishment was under way. "In March, 1885," he declared, "the United States had no vessel of war which could have kept the seas for one week as against any first-rate naval power" (Report of the Secretary of the Navy . . . 1888, p. iii). Congress had in the preceding administration taken the first steps for the creation of a new navy, built, protected, and armed in accordance with modern practice. The earliest of the new units, soon in service, were of greater interest as marking the first steps toward a new craftsmanship than as weapons of naval warfare. Whitney as secretary devoted himself to fighting contractors, particularly John Roach [q.v.], who delivered vessels built according to obsolete specifications, drawn up during the administration of Secretary William E. Chandler [q.v.]; to striking from the navy list the superannuated ships that were not worth repairing; to planning constructive approaches towards an independent establishment; and to the inauguration of the Naval War College at Newport, R. I., where A. T. Mahan [*q.v.*] did his creative work in naval history and theory. Shipyards had to be taught to build vessels of size and soundness, gun foundries large enough to cast the ingots needed by modern guns had to be designed, plants were needed for turning and finishing the great guns and for rolling armor plate. In all of these tasks Whitney showed ingenuity and imagination. He left an effective establishment for his successor when, at the close of the first Cleveland administration, he returned to New York business, society, and sport.

Between the début of his daughter Pauline in 1892, and her marriage in 1895 (New York *World*, Nov. 13, 1895) to Almeric Hugh Paget, the Whitneys were important figures in international society. Whitney played a significant part in connection with the nomination and election of Cleveland in 1892, and he fought Free Silver at the Democratic convention of 1896, but he declined to accept further public office. After the death of Flora Payne Whitney (Feb. 5, 1893) he married Mrs. Edith Sibyl (May) Randolph, commissioning McKim, Mead, and White to build her a house in the style of the Italian Renaissance at Fifth Avenue and 68th Street. Shortly after her early death (May 6, 1899) he withdrew from business and society to devote himself to sport. A lover of horses, he built up a breeding farm near Lexington, Ky., operated a racing stable, begun in 1898, and tried to revive the glories of the race track at Saratoga. On June 5, 1901, a horse, Volodyovski, run but not bred by him, won the English Derby (London *Times*, June 6, 1901). In 1902 he published *The Whitney Stud*. He left at least ten residences at his death. Of his four surviving children, Harry Payne Whitney [*q.v.*] was married to Gertrude Vanderbilt, and Payne Whitney was married to Helen, daughter of John Hay.

[F. C. Pierce, *Whitney: The Descendants of John Whitney, Who Came from London, England, to Watertown, Mass., in 1635* (1895); W. H. Rowe, "The Turf Career of Hon. W. C. Whitney," *Outing*, July 1901; *Obit. Record of Grads. of Yale Univ. Deceased during the Academical Year Ending in June, 1904* (1904); obituaries in *N. Y. Times, N. Y. Tribune,* Feb. 3, 1904; *Who's Who in America*, 1903–05; B. J. Hendrick, "Great American Fortunes and Their Making. Street Railway Financiers," in *McClure's Mag.*, Nov., Dec. 1907; H. J. Carman, *The Street Surface Railway Franchises of New York City* (1919); Allan Nevins, *Grover Cleveland. A Study in Courage* (1932). In some accounts the date of birth is given as July 15.]
F. L. P.

WHITNEY, WILLIAM DWIGHT (Feb. 9, 1827–June 7, 1894), Sanskritist and linguistic scientist, was born at Northampton, Mass., the fourth child of Josiah Dwight Whitney (1786–1869), banker, and Sarah (Williston) Whitney, of old New England stock, strong in body, mind, and character, and in a community where education, religion, thrift, and serious performance were the foundations of society. His grandfather was Abel Whitney (Harvard, 1773), and his paternal grandmother was Clarissa, daughter of Col. Josiah Dwight, of the family that gave three presidents to Yale. His mother was daughter of the Rev. Payson Williston (Yale, 1783) of Easthampton, and sister of Samuel Williston [*q.v.*], founder of Williston Seminary. His eldest brother, Josiah Dwight Whitney [*q.v.*], of Harvard, was an eminent geologist; another brother, James Lyman [*q.v.*], was head of the Boston Public Library; a third, Henry Mitchell, was professor of English at Beloit College; his sister Maria was professor of modern languages in Smith College.

His brothers went to Yale, but William entered, from the public schools of Northampton, the sophomore class at Williams College, where he graduated in 1845 as valedictorian. From boyhood his chief interest had been outdoor life, nature, and natural science, and this interest never left him. In his youth he shot, mounted, and presented to the Peabody Museum at Yale a collection of the birds of New England, including, it is believed, the last wild turkey. In 1849 he spent the summer with his brother Josiah in the United States geological survey of the Lake Superior region, and the report on the botany was published under his name as a chapter of the general report (1851). In 1873, in the middle of his linguistic career, he joined the Hayden expedition in Colorado as assistant in the geographical work of the survey. He was always keen and competent in botany and ornithology.

By all the omens Whitney should have devoted his life to natural science. But a chance occurrence turned him toward linguistics. When he graduated from college, knowledge of Sanskrit in the West, with realization of its significant relationship to the languages of Europe, was scarcely half a century old. Chairs of Sanskrit had been established at Bonn and Oxford little more than a decade before. Early in 1845 William's brother Josiah returned from Europe, bringing with him 341 volumes for his library. Among these was a Sanskrit grammar by Franz Bopp. On Oct. 1, 1845, William began the study of medicine in a physician's office. The next day measles developed. During his convalescence he picked up Bopp's grammar. After his recovery he became a clerk in his father's bank for more than three years, but when he joined the geological survey in 1849 he took the grammar with him. In the fall of 1849 he went to Yale for a year under Edward Elbridge Salisbury [*q.v.*], "the pioneer and patron of Sanskrit studies in America," as Whitney later described him in a dedication. By then, self-taught, he could read simple Sanskrit.

At that time there were no distinctive graduate schools in America, but there was a beginning in the department of philosophy and the arts at Yale, where Salisbury, pupil of Bopp, G. W. F. Freytag, and Christian Lassen, and the only professional Orientalist in the country, had since 1841 been professor of Arabic and Sanskrit. The only class Salisbury ever had in Sanskrit was composed of William Dwight Whitney and James Hadley [*q.v.*]. But what a class! Salisbury himself generously said that it soon became "evident that the teacher and the taught must change places." In 1850 Whitney went to Germany, where he studied three semesters under Bopp, Albrecht Weber, and Karl Lepsius in Berlin, and two under Rudolph Roth in Tübingen.

Meanwhile Salisbury had been making plans at Yale. He created a fund, and on May 10, 1854, the Corporation elected Whitney to a new and separate "Professorship of the Sanskrit and its relations to kindred languages, and Sanskrit literature." Whitney returned to America in August 1853, and a year later went to Yale, where he remained active until his death, despite a call to Harvard in 1869, when Salisbury provided additional endowment for the chair that has since been called the Salisbury professorship of Sanskrit and comparative philology and is now (1936) held by a pupil (Edgerton) of a pupil (Bloomfield) of a pupil (Whitney) of Salisbury. His forty years of labor there, teaching and research, were devoted to four main interests, often overlapping, but still indicative of remarkable versatility, as well as industry: Sanskrit, linguistic science, modern languages, lexicography. His bibliography in the *Whitney Memorial* volume numbers 360 titles.

While a student in Germany he had planned with Roth an edition of the Atharva-Veda, then unpublished, and in Berlin he copied all the manuscripts available, collating them in 1853 with those in Paris, Oxford, and London. The Sanskrit text (alone) was issued at Berlin in 1856 as *Atharva Veda Sanhita,* edited by R. Roth and W. D. Whitney. This was followed by Whitney's "*Alphabetisches Verzeichniss der Versanfänge der Atharva-Saṁhitā*" (*Indische Studien,* vol. IV, 1857); an edition, with text, translation, and notes, of a phonetico-grammatical treatise,

"The Atharva-Veda Prātiçākhya" (*Journal of the American Oriental Society,* vol. VII, 1862); "Index-Verborum to the Published Text of the Atharva-Veda" (*Ibid.,* vol. XII, 1881); *Atharva-Veda Saṁhitā, Translated with a Critical and Exegetical Commentary* (2 vols., 1905), completed and edited by C. R. Lanman. After Roth, Whitney and his American successors have led the world in the study of the Atharva-Veda. In 1871 Whitney published the *Tāittirīya-Prātiçākhya,* with its commentary, edited with text, translation, and notes (*Journal of the American Oriental Society,* vol. IX). One of his hobbies was astronomy, and he spent many leisure hours working on a chart of the heavens as the ancient Orient imagined them (see his *Oriental and Linguistic Studies,* second series). In 1860 he published, with notes, a translation of the *Sūrya-Siddhānta,* a Hindu treatise on astronomy (*Journal of the American Oriental Society,* vol. VI). Mention should be made also of his little classic, "On the Vedic Doctrine of a Future Life" (*Bibliotheca Sacra,* Apr. 1859, republished in *Oriental and Linguistic Studies,* first series).

Whitney's most important work was his *Sanskrit Grammar,* which was issued at Leipzig in 1879, translated into German by Zimmer, and revised by Whitney a decade later. He subordinated to the technique of modern linguistic science the classifications, arrangements, rules, and terms of the ancient and medieval Hindu grammarians, whose traditions had previously prevailed in the West, and he took his material primarily from recorded Sanskrit literature, covering historically both the classical language and the older Vedic. He was too skeptical as to the intrinsic value of Indian linguistic scholarship, but his general emphasis was sound, and his work marks a great transition in the history of Sanskrit study. His method was essentially descriptive and statistical. Regret has been expressed that it was not comparative. But he was limited in time and space, and in the sequel his procedure proved fortunate, for otherwise the advances in Indo-European grammar would long since have outdated his work, whereas in fact it is still indispensable to student and scholar. And it laid the foundations for Wackernagel and other comparative grammarians in the years to come. The *Grammar* was followed by a formal supplement, *The Roots, Verb-forms, and Primary Derivatives of the Sanskrit Language* (Leipzig, 1885).

In linguistics Whitney's work antedated many recent developments, and he held—sometimes unnecessarily, perhaps—theories that have since been overthrown, but he was one of the wisest leaders of his day, entitled to a prominent and permanent place in the history of the study of language, and his books still serve as a valuable introduction to the science. While his writings in this field were general, descriptive, and semi-popular, they discussed, with notable sanity of thought and clarity of expression, fundamental problems of scholarship concerning human speech. Whitney had considerable influence upon the trend of modern linguistic science, especially in his recognition of its distinction from philology, in his opposition to the abstract, figurative, and almost mystic vagueness that still prevailed in certain quarters, and in his conception of linguistics as a historical, and not a physical or natural, science. In 1864 he delivered a series of lectures before the Smithsonian Institution, and later before the Lowell Institute, on the principles of linguistic science. These were published in 1867 under the title *Language and the Study of Language,* and translated into German by Jolly and into Dutch by Vinckers. This was followed, in 1875, by *The Life and Growth of Language,* which was translated into German, French, Italian, Dutch, Swedish, and Russian. Similar discussions are contained also in his two volumes of *Oriental and Linguistic Studies* (collections of previous contributions to various periodicals), which appeared in 1873 and 1874; in his little book, *Max Müller and the Science of Language: a Criticism* (1892); and in many articles.

In his earlier years at Yale Whitney's salary was insufficient for the support of his growing family, and he added to his income by teaching German and French, at first privately and later in college classes. When the Sheffield Scientific School was established he organized its modern language department and became its head. Out of this subsidiary activity grew a list of publications that might well represent the lifework of a prominent professor in modern languages: a series of annotated German texts (1876 ff.); a German reader, with notes and vocabulary (1870); a larger (1869) and a smaller (1885) German grammar; a German dictionary (1877); a French grammar (1886). To these should be added his *Essentials of English Grammar* (1877). These grammars, all for practical use in school or college, show the same clarity, conciseness, and insight that mark his Sanskrit; they anticipated contemporary methods and were widely used and deservedly influential.

A number of the works already mentioned belong to the category of lexicography and works of reference. Under this heading come also his valuable contributions, chiefly from his Atharva-

Veda material, to the great (St. Petersburg) Sanskrit lexicon of Böhtlingk and Roth; his definitions in the 1864 edition of Webster's English dictionary; his articles in Appleton's *New American Cyclopaedia,* Johnson's *New Universal Cyclopaedia,* and the *Encyclopaedia Britannica.* The last decade of his life was largely given to *The Century Dictionary: An Encyclopedic Lexicon of the English Language* (6 vols., 1889–91), of which he was editor-in-chief. His is the only name on the title-page, which says that the work was prepared under his superintendence, and he wrote and signed the preface. He shared responsibility for plan, method, and execution, supervised spelling, pronunciation, etc., and read all the proofs.

Whitney wrote on many subjects, but essentially he was a grammarian. His chief contribution was to the study and teaching of Sanskrit, and there have been few American Sanskritists who were not trained under him or one of his pupils. Neither his writing nor his teaching was fired by any high degree of imagination, enthusiasm, or other emotion. What he wanted was facts, carefully arranged and accurately presented. But he was not cold: his personal sympathy, patience, and kindness were proverbial, as were his natural simplicity and sincerity.

It is almost incredible that any man should have done so much in four decades of productive scholarship—really three, for his last eight years were spent in a state of invalidism. Recognition came to him in abundance from America and abroad. He received honorary degrees from a number of American and foreign universities; he was an honorary member of the Oriental societies of Great Britain and Ireland, Japan, Germany, Bengal, Peking, and Italy, and of the literary societies of Leyden, Upsala, and Helsingfors. He was a foreign or corresponding member of the Institute of France, the royal academies of Ireland, Denmark, Berlin, Turin, the Imperial Academy of St. Petersburg, and the Royal Academy *dei Lincei* of Rome, fellow of the Royal Society of Edinburgh, and Foreign Knight of the Royal Prussian Order *pour le mérite* (succeeding Thomas Carlyle). In 1870 the Berlin Academy awarded him the Bopp prize for his publication of the *Taittirīya-Prātiçākhya.*

An outstanding interest in Whitney's life was the American Oriental Society, which he joined in 1850. He was librarian from 1855 until 1873, corresponding secretary (and editor of publications) from 1857, when he succeeded Salisbury, until 1884, when he was elected president, in which office he served six years. In 1885 he wrote, of himself, "no small part of his work has been done in the service of the Society; from 1857 to the present time, just a half of the contents of its Journal is from his pen" (*Forty Years' Record, post,* p. 178). He was one of the founders and the first president (1869) of the American Philological Association. As chairman of a committee appointed by the Association to study the question of English spelling he prepared the report which was presented in 1876. He was opposed to the principle of "historical" or "etymological" spelling, favored reform, especially the use of the simpler of alternative forms, and held office in the Spelling Reform Association, but he was less active and less radical in the movement than F. A. March [*q.v.*] and others.

On Aug. 27, 1856, Whitney married Elizabeth Wooster Baldwin of New Haven, daughter of Roger Sherman Baldwin [*q.v.*]. Three sons and three daughters were born to them. Whitney was devoted to his family and his home, and in country walks with his children or in conversation with his friends he found his recreation. He was a lover of music and had a good baritone voice. He was of average height and weight, had deep blue eyes, slightly curling reddish hair, and, most of his life, a full beard. He was not orthodox nor a member of any church, but he attended services regularly and knew the Bible thoroughly. In 1886 he learned that he was suffering from a grave affection of the heart (angina pectoris), and that his active life was ended. But so far as his strict regimen permitted he continued his work, serene and objective as ever, although he knew that any day might be his last.

[Whitney wrote his own biog. for *Forty Years' Record of the Class of 1845, Williams Coll.* (1885), which he edited, and his own bibliog. (selected) for *Bibliogs. of the Present Officers of Yale Univ.* (1893), ed. by Irving Fisher. See also *The Whitney Memorial Meeting* (1897), ed. by C. R. Lanman, with photograph and full bibliog.; intro. to Whitney's *Atharva-Veda Saṁhitā* (2 vols., 1905), ed. by C. R. Lanman; T. D. Seymour, in *Am. Jour. Philology,* Oct. 1894; T. R. Lounsbury, in *Proc. Am. Acad. Arts and Sciences,* n.s., vol. XII (1895); Hanns Oertel, in *Beiträge zur Kunde der Indogermanischen Sprachen,* vol. XX (1894), pp. 308–33, ed. by Adalbert Bezzenberger; E. T. Brewster, *Life and Letters of Josiah Dwight Whitney* (1909); and obituary in *New Haven Evening Reg.,* June 7, 1894. The present biog. is indebted to Prof. Marian Parker Whitney for recollections of her father.]   H. H. B.

WHITON, JAMES MORRIS (Apr. 11, 1833–Jan. 25, 1920), Congregational clergyman, educator, author, was born in Boston, Mass., the son of James Morris and Mary Elizabeth (Knowlton) Whiton. He was a descendant of James Whiton of Hingham, England, who emigrated to Plymouth, Mass., in 1635. His first maternal ancestor in America was John Alden of Plymouth Colony. From the Boston Latin

School he entered Yale College, where he won distinction in the classics and English, and was graduated in 1853. After a year of teaching at the high school in Worcester, Mass., he served as rector of the Hopkins Grammar School, New Haven, Conn. (1854–64). In 1861 he received the degree of Ph.D. from Yale, having at the same time pursued theological studies privately under Yale professors. After a year at Andover Seminary (1864–65), he was ordained at Lynn, Mass., on May 10, 1865, and held pastorates there at the First Church (1865–69) and at the newly formed North Church (1869–75). From 1876 to 1878 he was principal of the Williston Seminary, Easthampton, Mass., resigning because of hostility aroused by his book *Is 'Eternal' Punishment Endless?* (1876). His remaining pastorates were at the First Congregational Church, Newark, N. J. (1879–85), and Trinity Congregational Church, New York City (1886–91). During the latter period he was instrumental in forming two other churches of the same denomination in the Bronx. During 1893–94 he was acting professor of ethics and economics in the Meadville Theological School, Meadville, Pa. In 1896 he became a member of the editorial staff of the *Outlook,* engaging also in much miscellaneous literary work. He became one of the promoters of the New York State Conference of Religion in 1899, an organization representing fourteen different denominations. An outgrowth of this movement was a volume of essays, *Getting Together* (1913), which Whiton edited and to which he contributed. His best-known books are *The Gospel of the Resurrection* (1881); *The Evolution of Revelation* (1885); *The Divine Satisfaction; a Critique of Theories of the Atonement* (1886); *Turning Points of Thought and Conduct* (1888); *New Points to Old Texts* (1889); *Gloria Patri* (1892); *Interludes in a Time of Change* (1909); *The Life of God in the Life of His World* (1918). As secretary of his college class he prepared *The Class of 1853, Yale College* (1903). He was also the author of several classical textbooks.

As a preacher Whiton combined thoughtful scholarship with the more popular gifts to a rare degree, and few American clergymen were so gladly heard in English pulpits. He was both broad and progressive. Familiar with all schools of thought, he saw the spiritual truth underlying all forms of faith. He was an able controversialist as well as a writer on spiritual topics, and to timid thinkers was often an object of suspicion. He was married, May 1, 1855, to Mary Eliza Bartlett, who died Sept. 27, 1917. Of their family of two sons and two daughters, the daughters and one son survived their parents.

[A. S. Whiton, *The Whiton Family in America* (1932); *Who's Who in America*, 1918–19; *The Congreg. Year Book . . . 1920* (n.d.); *Congregationalist*, Feb. 12, 1920, pp. 203, 219; *Outlook*, Feb. 4, 1920, p. 186, with portrait; *Obit. Record Yale Grads.* (1921); obituary in *N. Y. Times*, Jan. 28, 1920.]   F. T. P.

WHITSITT, WILLIAM HETH (Nov. 25, 1841–Jan. 20, 1911), Baptist minister, church historian, and theological seminary president, was born near Nashville, Tenn., the son of Reuben Ewing and Dicey (McFarland) Whitsitt. His colonial ancestors were Scotch-Irish Presbyterians who settled in Amherst County, Va., about 1741. His grandfather, James Whitsitt, moved in 1790 to Tennessee, where as the pastor of a group of country churches he effectively aided in the establishment of the Baptist interpretation of Christianity throughout middle Tennessee. William Heth Whitsitt attended Mount Juliet Academy and was graduated from Union University, Jackson, Tenn., in 1861. Enlisting in the Confederate army, he served as a scout under Gen. Nathan Bedford Forrest. Following his ordination as a Baptist minister in 1862, he was appointed chaplain and served throughout the Civil War. He studied at the University of Virginia (1866) and the Southern Baptist Theological Seminary (1866–68), and completed his training with two years of study in the universities of Leipzig and Berlin, where he was under the instruction of Christoph Ernst Luthardt, Ernst Curtius, Richard A. Lipsius, and L. F. K. Tischendorf. After a brief pastorate in Albany, Ga., he accepted (1872) the chair of ecclesiastical history in the Southern Baptist Theological Seminary, Greenville, S. C., where he later taught polemical theology. On Oct. 4, 1881, he married Florence Wallace of Woodford County, Ky. In 1895 he was elected president of the seminary, which in 1877 had been moved to Louisville, Ky. Under his administration the enrollment surpassed that of any other American theological seminary, and his thorough scholarship and courageous devotion to truth commanded the unstinted admiration of his students.

A statement made by Whitsitt in his article upon the Baptists published in *Johnson's Universal Encyclopaedia* (1896) precipitated what was known as "the Whitsitt controversy." He said that "the immersion of adult believers" had been lost in England and that such baptisms were restored by the English Baptists in 1641. A large proportion of Southern Baptists held that a succession of Baptist churches could be traced from New Testament times to the present, though it was admitted that they had not always

borne the name of Baptist; to accept Whitsitt's conclusions made this theory of church succession untenable. When a group of serious scholars in America and Great Britain reviewed the historical material upon which Whitsitt based his conclusions, most of them reached a like conviction as to the origin of the English Baptists, but the controversy lasted for four years, increasing in bitterness as the weakness of the arguments of the church successionists became more evident. Many who recognized the principle of academic freedom became convinced that denominational concord could be gained only through Whitsitt's withdrawal from the institution, and the trustees of the seminary at length accepted his resignation (1899). After a year's rest he accepted the chair of philosophy in Richmond College, Richmond, Va., where he remained until the spring of 1910. He died on Jan. 20, 1911, survived by his wife, a son, and a daughter, and was buried in Richmond. His literary work includes *Position of the Baptists in the History of American Culture* (1872), *The History of the Rise of Infant Baptism* (1878), *The History of Communion among Baptists* (1880), *A Question in Baptist History* (1896), *The Origin of the Disciples of Christ* (1888), *The Life and Times of Judge Caleb Wallace* (1888), *The Genealogy of Jefferson Davis* (1908), "Annals of a Scotch-Irish Family—The Whitsitts of Nashville, Tenn." (*American Historical Magazine and Tennessee Historical Society Quarterly*, Jan., July, Oct. 1904), and numerous articles in reviews and religious newspapers.

[See *Who's Who in America*, 1910–11; E. P. Pollard, in *Rev. and Expositor*, Apr. 1912; J. R. Sampey, *Southern Baptist Theological Seminary, 1859–1889* (1890); W. D. Nowlin, *Ky. Baptist Hist.* (1922); obituary in *Times-Dispatch* (Richmond, Va.), Jan. 21, 1911. For the Whitsitt controversy, see files of *Baptist Argus* and *Western Recorder*, 1896–1900. For James Whitsitt, see W. B. Sprague, *Annals Am. Pulpit*, vol. VI (1860); *Am. Hist. Mag. and Tenn. Hist. Soc. Quart.*, Jan., July, Oct. 1904.]   R. W. W—r.

WHITTELSEY, ABIGAIL GOODRICH (Nov. 29, 1788–July 16, 1858), editor and author, was born in Ridgefield, Conn., the daughter of the Rev. Samuel and Elizabeth (Ely) Goodrich. She was the descendant of William Goodrich who emigrated from England and settled in Wethersfield, Conn., about 1643. She was the grand-daughter of Elizur Goodrich, 1734–1797, niece of Elizur Goodrich, 1761–1849, and of Chauncey Goodrich, 1759–1815, and the sister of Samuel Griswold Goodrich and Charles Augustus Goodrich [*qq.v.*]. Until her marriage to the Rev. Samuel Whittelsey on Nov. 10, 1808, she lived in her native village, where her father served as Congregational minister, farmed forty acres of land, and sometimes took in pupils to be fitted for college. Her brother Samuel Griswold Goodrich (Peter Parley) in his *Recollections (post)* has left an interesting account of rural Connecticut during these years. She grew up in an atmosphere of thrift, energy, and piety, enjoying such educational advantages as her home and the local seminaries afforded. After her marriage she accompanied her husband to his country parish in New Preston, Conn. Ten years later they removed to Hartford, where for six years she served as matron in the American School for the Deaf, of which her husband had been appointed superintendent. In 1824 she and her husband had charge of the Ontario Female Seminary in Canandaigua, N. Y., and from 1827 to 1833 they conducted a similar school in Utica.

While living in Utica she began the work that made her well known to her contemporaries —the editorship of the *Mother's Magazine*. For some years she had been active in promoting maternal organizations in church circles. As the mother of seven children and the wife of a clergyman she was well acquainted with the interests of women in the home; as matron and teacher she had observed a need for domestic and religious instruction. When, therefore, the Maternal Association of Utica noted that "among the multitude of periodicals of the day *not one has been devoted to mothers*" (*Mother's Magazine*, Jan. 1833, p. 3) and promptly established such a publication, she became its editor and contributed regularly to its columns. The purpose of the magazine as set forth in the opening number January 1833, was "to awaken" mothers to "their responsibility"; "to call attention . . . to the importance of having suitable schools and seminaries," emphasize the need for "physical education," and very particularly to stress the domestic education of daughters (*Ibid.*, pp. 4–5). In 1834 she removed to New York City. There the work prospered, attaining a circulation of 10,000 copies by 1837, although a rival publication, the *Mother's Journal and Family Visitant*, appeared in the field in 1836. After the death of her husband in 1842, she carried on the magazine with her brother-in-law, Darius Mead, editor of the *Christian Parlor Magazine*. In 1847 she withdrew from the work for a year but in January 1848 resumed her connection with it under its new proprietor, Myron Finch. The same year Finch purchased the rival *Mother's Journal*, and, contrary to her wishes, decided to unite the two papers. Disagreement followed, and she severed her long connection with

the magazine in 1849. From 1850 to 1852, aided by her son Henry M. Whittelsey, she issued a new periodical of her own, *Mrs. Whittelsey's Magazine for Mothers*, in which she continued to give instruction and advice. She hoped through the influence of mothers to raise the level of social and religious life. She was described by a contemporary editor as queenly in appearance, persuasive in manner, and sensible in judgment (Hale, *post*, p. 872). Her last years were spent in the home of a daughter in Colchester, Conn., where she died. She was buried in Maple Cemetery, Berlin, Conn.

[C. B. Whittelsey, *Geneal. of the Whittelsey-Whittelsey Family* (1898); S. J. Hale, *Woman's Record* (1876); G. L. Rockwell, *The Hist. of Ridgefield, Conn.* (1927); S. G. Goodrich, *Recollections* (2 vols., 1856); pamphlet in N. Y. Pub. Lib., *Mrs. Whittlesey's Reply to . . . Myron Finch*, dated April 1850.]   B. M. S.

WHITTEMORE, AMOS (Apr. 19, 1759– Mar. 27, 1828), inventor, gunsmith, was the son of Thomas and Anna (Cutter) Whittemore, and a descendant of Thomas Whittemore who emigrated from England and settled in Charlestown, Mass., between 1639 and 1645. He was born on his father's farm at Cambridge, Mass. During his boyhood he worked on the farm and in winter attended the district school. Upon completing school he apprenticed himself to a gunsmith and at the end of his apprenticeship set up a shop of his own. The gunsmithing business was poor, however, and for years he was variously and unprofitably employed in and about Boston. About 1795 he entered into a gentleman's agreement with his brother William, Giles Richards, and a number of other producers in the manufacture of brushes for carding cotton and wool. This group, which furnished nearly all the cards then used in the colonies, had three factories in Boston, employed sixty men and two thousand children, and produced about twelve thousand dozen cards a year. Whittemore was in charge of the mechanical equipment which consisted of two types of machines, one for cutting and bending card wire, and one for piercing leather with holes into which the bent wire was placed. Apparently these simple machines did not require much attention, and Whittemore had an opportunity to apply himself to invention, in which he had been interested for years. At all events, in November 1796 he was granted three United States patents, one for a machine for cutting nails, another for a loom for weaving duck, and a third for a "nautical preambulator," which was a form of mechanical ship's log.

Encouraged by the acquisition of these patents, he turned his attention to the problem of devising a machine that would eliminate all hand labor in making cotton and wool cards. A patent was issued to him on June 5, 1797, for a machine which reduced to a series of rapid, precise, and entirely automatic movements all the successive operations of holding and piercing the leather, cutting and binding the wire, and inserting and bending the wire to the proper angle. Early in 1799, after working eighteen months on improving his crude machine, Whittemore went to England to obtain a British patent. His efforts to introduce his machine in England were unsuccessful, and after a year abroad he returned to Boston, where he formed a partnership with his brother William and Robert Williams, under the firm name of William Whittemore and Company, to manufacture both the card-making machine and cotton and wool cards. The partners in the course of the succeeding nine years experienced little success in selling the machines and practically failed. A petition to Congress in 1809, however, yielded an extension of the patent from 1811. Armed with this, they were successful on July 20, 1812, in selling to the newly incorporated New York Manufacturing Company of New York City their patent right and entire stock of machinery for $150,000. Whittemore then retired to his home in West Cambridge (later Arlington), Mass., where he lived until his death. His brother Samuel and his son Timothy purchased the patent and machinery from the New York company in 1818, and Samuel conducted a successful business in West Cambridge for many years. Whittemore married Helen Weston of Cambridge on June 18, 1781. He was survived by twelve children.

[B. B. Whittemore, *A Geneal. of Several Branches of the Whittemore Family* (1893); Benjamin Cutter, *A Hist. of the Cutter Family of New England* (1871); J. L. Bishop, *A Hist. of Am. Manufactures* (2 vols., 1861–62); Henry Howe, *Memoirs of . . . Eminent Am. Mechanics* (1847); Patent Office records; obituary in *Boston Daily Advertiser*, Apr. 1, 1828.]   C. W. M.

WHITTEMORE, THOMAS (Jan. 1, 1800– Mar. 21, 1861), Universalist clergyman, editor, author, financier, was born in Boston, Mass., the fourth child of Joseph and Comfort (Quiner) Whittemore, and a descendant of Thomas Whittemore who emigrated from England to Charlestown before 1645. He attended the public schools of Charlestown, Mass., but the necessitous condition of his family forced him to leave school before reaching his teens. As a boy he seems to have been more than ordinarily self-willed. He was apprenticed to three different trades and twice ran away. In his twentieth year he came under the spell of the popular Universalist preacher, the Rev. Hosea Ballou [*q.v.*]. When in December 1820 he was given a chance to preach before the Universalist congregation in Roxbury, Mass., he acquitted himself very creditably, and at the close of his apprenticeship with a Boston firm of boot and shoe makers in 1821, Ballou invited him to become a member of his family for a year to prepare for the ministry. His studies were frequently interrupted by invitations to preach in Universalist churches. In June 1821 he was asked to become minister of the church in Milford, Mass., and was ordained there on June 13. On Sept. 17, 1821, he was married to Lovice Corbett of Milford, by whom he had a son. A year later he accepted the pastorate of a church in Cambridgeport, Mass. (later part of Cambridge), where he quickly became a conspicuous figure among the group of forceful Universalist preachers and writers of the first half of the nineteenth century. In 1828 he and Russell Streeter purchased the semimonthly *Universalist Magazine* and issued it as a weekly under the title of the *Trumpet and Universalist Magazine*. Streeter shortly sold his share to Whittemore, who became the sole owner and editor. The venture turned out to be extremely profitable, and Whittemore continued as editor of the magazine for thirty-three years. After 1828 books and pamphlets came thick and fast from his pen. Among his publications were *The Modern History of Universalism* (1830), *Notes and Illustrations of the Parables of the New Testament* (1832), a commentary on the *Revelations*, which reveals a curious streak of mysticism in his makeup, and *The Plain Guide to Universalism* (1840). There was a lyrical strain in him which expressed itself in musical compositions and the compilation of a series of hymn books: *Songs of Zion* (1837), containing many tunes from his pen, *The Gospel Harmonist* (1841), two books of *Conference Hymns* (1842–43), and the *Sunday School Choir* (1844). Later in life he turned to biography and produced *The Memoir of Walter Balfour* (1852), *The Life of Rev. Hosea Ballou* (4 vols., 1854–55), and *The Early Days of Thomas Whittemore, an Autobiography* (1859).

He was not less busy in the public life of the town. He was elected in 1830 to the state legislature and was reëlected to that post for several years. There he expressed his unrelenting opposition to compulsory support of religion. He served his town also as selectman for a considerable time. During the years 1833 to 1845 he gave his services as lecturer in the cause of temperance. In 1840 he undertook a radically different line of activity. The bank in Cambridge having fallen into difficulties, he was chosen first as director of the institution and then president, and succeeded in rescuing it from its trouble. Nine years later (1849) he was made president of the Vermont and Massachusetts Railroad, which was involved in deep financial distress. He completed the branch lines, settled the lawsuits pending against the road, and successfully freed it from debt. He died in Cambridge, Mass., while busy revising and enlarging his *Modern History of Universalism.*

[In addition to *The Early Days of Thomas Whittemore* (1859), see J. G. Adams, *Memoir of Thomas Whittemore, D.D.* (1878); B. B. Whittemore, *A Geneal. of Several Branches of the Whittemore Family* (1893); Richard Eddy, *Universalism in America* (2 vols., 1884–86); and obituary in *Boston Transcript,* Mar. 22, 1861.] C. G.

WHITTIER, JOHN GREENLEAF (Dec. 17, 1807–Sept. 7, 1892), poet, abolitionist, was born in Haverhill, Mass., the son of Quaker parents. His father, John Whittier, was a stern, prosaic, but generous man, while his mother, Abigail (Hussey) Whittier, was a kindly soul, who to some extent sympathized with her son's literary leanings. Both parents influenced him considerably by their religious doctrines and tales of local history. On his father's side, he was descended from Thomas Whittier who came to Massachusetts from England in 1638. His youngest son, Joseph, married Mary Peasley, a Quakeress, and their youngest son, also named Joseph, married Sarah Greenleaf, member of a Puritan family believed to be of Huguenot origin. Spending his boyhood and youth on a farm, Whittier came close to nature, and later described the rural scene of his locality more faithfully than had any other writer up to that time. His "Barefoot Boy" has become a classic poem of New England farm life. Overexertion when he was about seventeen resulted in injuries from which he never fully recovered.

His formal education was limited, but what he did not obtain from schools he learned from books. For a brief period he studied under Joshua Coffin, in the unfinished ell of a farmhouse, and at another time, in a school kept by a Newburyport woman. When he was about fourteen he became acquainted with the poems of Burns. He read them studiously and soon began writing poems himself, some of them in Scotch dialect. As time went on his reading came to include books of travel, and history, works on Quaker doctrine and martyrology, Thomas Ellwood's poem *Davideis,* and the writings of Milton, Chatterton, Coleridge, Byron, and others. He also delved into colonial literature, becoming particularly familiar with Cotton Mather's *Magnalia Christi Americana.*

The sending of one of his poems, "The Exile's Departure," by his older sister Mary to the Newburyport *Free Press,* edited by William Lloyd Garrison [*q.v.*], was an important event in young Whittier's life. The poem was published June 8, 1826, and Garrison was sufficiently interested in the unknown author to call upon him. He urged the father to send his son to some school for a further education, but the elder Whittier was averse to such a procedure. Though Garrison continued publishing poems by Whittier, it was Abijah W. Thayer, the editor of the Haverhill *Gazette* (later called the *Essex Gazette*), who made Whittier's work widely known, publishing poems by him weekly. Thayer, also, urged the elder Whittier to send his promising son to an academy and this time the father agreed to do so. At the beginning of May 1827, Whittier entered the newly opened Haverhill Academy, where a poem of his was sung at the inauguration ceremonies. He remained here for about six months, taught school during the winter, and then returned to the academy for another term of six months. During this period he poured forth a steady stream of poems, which appeared not only in the *Free Press* and the *Essex Gazette,* but for a time in the Boston *Statesman,* edited by Nathaniel Greene [*q.v.*]. Thayer proposed the publication of Whittier's poems in book form by subscription, but the project was not carried out.

Through the help of Garrison, Whittier, in January 1829, became editor of *The American Manufacturer* (Boston), serving as such for seven months and resigning in large part because he was needed at home. This was the first of the numerous editorial positions he held during his life. In the early part of 1830 he edited the *Essex Gazette.* After the death of his father in June, he succeeded George D. Prentice [*q.v.*] as editor of the *New England Weekly Review,* published in Hartford, Conn. To this periodical he contributed many poems, stories, and sketches, most of which have remained uncollected. In February 1831 he published his first book, *Legends of New England in Prose and Verse.* Relinquishing the editorship of the *Review* in January 1832 on account of ill health, he issued that same year his *Moll Pitcher,* and edited *The Literary Remains of John G. C. Brainard, With a Sketch of His Life.* During these years he suffered a grievous disappointment because of the marriage to another of Mary Emerson Smith, a relative, for whom he had had a deep affection since boyhood. She is doubtless the heroine of many of his early uncollected love poems and of his famous "Memories" and "My Playmate." His pathetic love letter to her, written May 23,

1829, is the only one of those that passed between them which has been published (L. G. Swett, *John Ruskin's Letters to Francesca and Memoirs of the Alexanders,* 1931, 417–21).

A reading of Garrison's *Thoughts on Colonization* (1832), and a meeting with the author in the spring of 1833 made Whittier an abolitionist. For the next thirty years he devoted himself to the writing of Tyrtaen poems on subjects connected with slavery and its abolition. In December he was a delegate to the anti-slavery convention at Philadelphia, and was one of the signers of its declaration. Prior to the elections of 1834, 1836, and 1838 he secured from Caleb Cushing [*q.v.*] pledges that he would support the demand of the abolitionists, and Cushing attributed his success in the elections largely to the support of his Quaker friend (Pickard, *post,* I, 172). He was practically ostracized socially because of his views and activities, but succeeded in being elected a member of the Massachusetts legislature from Haverhill for the year 1835. On Sept. 4, 1835, he and George Thompson, the English lecturer, were mobbed in Concord, N. H. From May to December 1836 he was again in editorial charge of the *Essex Gazette.* Meanwhile, he sold his farm in Haverhill and moved, in July 1836, to his new home in Amesbury. His activities during the next few years were varied and his labors exacting; he spoke at an anti-slavery convention in Harrisburg, Pa.; he lobbied in Boston in behalf of the abolition of slavery in the District of Columbia; during the summer of 1837 he was employed in New York under the auspices of the American Anti-Slavery Society. From March 1838 to February 1840 he edited the *Pennsylvania Freeman,* to which he contributed daring editorials. The office of the paper was in the new Pennsylvania Hall, Philadelphia, when that building was burned to the ground by a mob in May 17, 1838. In November of that year he published a volume of fifty of his poems. Ill health compelled his resignation from the *Freeman,* and in 1840 he returned to Amesbury.

He was much depressed by the disruption of the American Anti-Slavery Society in that year, but he sympathized with the political-action party, to which Garrison was opposed, and became an aggressive member of the American and Foreign Anti-Slavery Society. In the fall of 1842 he ran for Congress on the Liberty party ticket. The following year he published *Lays of My Home and Other Poems,* which contained some of his best work and placed him among the leading American poets. From July 1844 to March 1845 he edited the *Middlesex Standard,* a Liberty-party paper published in Lowell, Mass., and in his editorials opposed the annexation of Texas. In this paper appeared serially "The Stranger in Lowell," which was published separately in 1845. He also practically edited the *Essex Transcript,* an organ of the Liberty party, published in Amesbury. His anti-slavery poems were collected and published under the title *Voices of Freedom,* in 1846. In January of the following year he became corresponding editor of the *National Era,* published in Washington, and he contributed most of his poems and articles to it for the next thirteen years. In this periodical appeared his only lengthy work in fiction, "Stray Leaves from Margaret Smith's Diary, in the Colony of Massachusetts" (published in book form, under a slightly different title, in 1849) and most of the material in *Old Portraits and Modern Sketches* (1850) and *Literary Recreations and Miscellanies* (1854).

Meanwhile, there was no relaxing of his political activities. He gave John P. Hale [*q.v.*] of New Hampshire much political advice, and thus indirectly helped elect him to the United States Senate; he attacked the administration bitterly for the Mexican War; and in the well known poem, "Ichabod," which appeared in the *National Era,* May 2, 1850, he castigated Webster for the "Seventh of March speech." He was instrumental in inducing Charles Sumner to run for the United States Senate in 1851 on a coalition ticket of Free-Soilers and Democrats, and he urged him to remain a candidate when he wished to retire during the long and bitter fight that ensued in the Massachusetts legislature before he was elected. He was one of the first to suggest the formation of the Republican party and always considered himself one of its founders. In the mid-fifties, though he wrote campaign songs, and poems on the happenings in Kansas, ill health compelled him to abandon some of his activities. His reputation as a poet had meanwhile greatly increased. With the appearance of *Songs of Labor* (1850), *The Chapel of the Hermits* (1853), and *The Panorama and Other Poems* (1856), which contained his "Maud Muller" and the "Barefoot Boy," he took rank with Longfellow and Bryant among the greatest American poets.

During his middle years he had several romances, two of which almost led to marriage. While living in New York, in the summer of 1837, he met Lucy Hooper, a young poetess residing in Brooklyn, and a warm friendship sprang up between them. In 1841 Lucy died of consumption. Whittier never realized to what extent she was attracted to him. When he learned from her surviving sisters the depth of her affection he wrote to them contritely and defensively: "God forgive me, if with no other than kind feelings I have done wrong. My feelings toward her were those of a Brother. I admired and loved her; yet felt myself compelled to crush every warmer feeling—poverty, protracted illness, and our separate faiths—the pledge that I had made of all the hopes and dreams of my younger years to the cause of freedom—compelled me to steel myself against everything which tended to attract me—the blessing of a woman's love and a home" (Albert Mordell, in *New England Quarterly,* June 1934). His most serious affair, however, was with Elizabeth Lloyd, the poetess, with whom he formed a friendship in Philadelphia when he was editing the *Freeman.* In 1853 she married Robert Howell, who died in 1856, and Whittier resumed his friendship with her in 1858. Both were looking forward to marriage when Mrs. Howell irritated the poet by attacking the Quaker creed, of which she herself was an adherent. On Aug. 3, 1859, he wrote her a letter which was tantamount to withdrawing from the semi-engagement that existed between them. Their friendship drifted on for a year or two, and by the end of 1860 it was over.

From the beginning of the Civil War Whittier's life was uneventful. His fame as a poet increased by reason of his many contributions to the *Atlantic Monthly,* in the founding of which he had a part, and to the *Independent.* The summit of his poetic career was reached in the decade of the sixties, during which appeared *Home Ballads* (1860); *In War Time and Other Poems* (1864), containing "Barbara Frietchie"; *Snow-Bound* (1866); *The Tent on the Beach* (1867); and *Among the Hills* (1869). In the summer of 1876 he moved to Danvers, where he lived with his cousins, the three daughters of Col. Edmund Johnson. Here he made his place of abode almost to the time of his death, with occasional visits to Amesbury, which always continued to be his legal residence. He received numerous honors in his later days, was surrounded by friends, and had many visitors. Republican politicians still consulted him. The more important poetical works of his later years were: *Miriam and Other Poems* (1871), *Hazel-Blossoms* (1875); *The Vision of Echard* (1878); *Saint Gregory's Guest* (1886); and *At Sundown* (1890). A complete edition of his works, revised and corrected, in seven volumes, appeared in 1888–89. He died at Hampton Falls and was buried at Amesbury.

Whittier was a tall man with piercing dark eyes and a swarthy complexion, and was somewhat vain with respect to his appearance. Although a genial person, he would occasionally flash out in anger when people did not agree with him. He resented the reputation he had of being a saint. That he was of heroic spirit is beyond question, for he sacrificed much, endured abuse, and faced physical perils in his devotion to the cause which he espoused. He had a fine sense of humor and was adept at telling amusing tales. Toward other people's beliefs he was in general tolerant, and he sympathized keenly with those who were persecuted on account of their race, color, or creed. His religious spirit as expressed in his poems was such that not a few of them have found a permanent place in the hymnals of various denominations. With respect to industrial questions he was always extremely conservative, but he supported the operatives in the Amesbury-Salisbury strike of 1852 (T. F. Currier, in *New England Quarterly,* March 1935). As a means of settling the entire economic problem he recommended obedience to the Golden Rule and the saving of money. He tried to justify the existing system by showing that the laborer derived benefits from his poverty. In his poem, "The Problem," published in 1877, the year of the great railroad strikes, he assailed the labor leaders who sought palliative reforms, as "demagogues" proffering their vain and evil counsels. In the late eighties he refused to aid William Dean Howells in endeavoring to obtain clemency for the convicted Chicago anarchists.

Whittier's standing as a poet has somewhat declined since his day. "Snow-Bound" is still usually considered his masterpiece. A few of his ballads, like "Skipper Iresons's Ride" and "Telling the Bees," and religious poems like "The Eternal Goodness" are still much read and quoted. Critical schools differ as to which of his poems are superior—those treating of rural life or those dealing with colonial history. There is an increasing tendency, however, to regard him as a prophet and to emphasize the value of his abolition poems, in spite of the fact that the occasion that gave rise to them has passed, for the spirit that prompted them was the same spirit that inspired Milton and Shelley to battle against oppression and tyranny. "It is as a poet of human freedom that he must live if he is to hold his own with posterity. . . . He has not a well-defined domain of mastery save perhaps in the verses inspired by the contest over slavery" (W. P. Trent and John Erskine, *Great American Writers,* pp. 144, 147). While some of the abolition poems are still read and admired, notably "Massachusetts to Virginia," there are others which deserve to be revived.

[The largest collection of manuscript material is to be found in the Essex Institute, Salem, Mass., which also has photostats and typewritten copies of letters to be found in libraries elsewhere. Whittier letters are preserved in the Lib. of Cong., the John Pierpont Morgan Lib., N. Y., the Henry E. Huntington Lib., San Marino, Cal., the N. Y. Pub. Lib., the Mass. Hist. Soc., and the libraries of Harvard and Yale. The largest collection of printed material by and about Whittier, and some manuscript material is in the Haverhill Pub. Lib., the N. H. Hist. Soc., Concord, and the Boston Pub. Lib. For other sources, see S. T. Pickard, *Life and Letters of John Greenleaf Whittier* (2 vols., 1894; 1 vol., 1907), and *Whittier-Land* (1904); W. S. Kennedy, *John Greenleaf Whittier—His Life, Genius, and Writings* (1882) and *John G. Whittier, the Poet of Freedom* (1892); F. H. Underwood, *John Greenleaf Whittier: A Biog.* (1884); T. W. Higginson, *John Greenleaf Whittier* (1902); G. R. Carpenter, *John Greenleaf Whittier* (1903); A. J. Woodman, *Reminiscences of John Greenleaf Whittier's Life at Oak Knoll, Danvers* (1908); John Albree, *Whittier Correspondence from Oak Knoll Colls.* (1911); M. V. Denervaud, ed., *Whittier's Unknown Romance: Letters to Elizabeth Lloyd* (1922); F. M. Pray, *A Study of Whittier's Apprenticeship as Poet: Dealing with Poems Written between 1825 and 1835 not available in the Poet's Collected Works* (1930); Albert Mordell, *Quaker Militant, John Greenleaf Whittier* (1933). More complete bibliogs. are in the *Cambridge Hist. of Am. Lit.*, II (1918), 436–51, and in *Quaker Militant*, pp. 333–43. An exhaustive bibliography by T. F. Currier has been announced for publication.]   A. M.

WHITTINGHAM, WILLIAM ROLLINSON (Dec. 2, 1805–Oct. 17, 1879), fourth Protestant Episcopal bishop of Maryland, was born in New York City. His father and grandfather, both named Richard, were brass-founders, who emigrated from Birmingham, England, in 1791 and developed a prosperous industry in New York. His mother, Mary Ann Rollinson, was the daughter of William Rollinson [*q.v.*]. A precocious child, Whittingham learned to read and write in his second year, and at the age when other children were learning the alphabet he could read and write English, Latin, Greek, French, and Hebrew. These he learned chiefly from his parents and not at school. In his nineteenth year he was graduated from the General Theological Seminary, New York City, and became its librarian, collaborating with Prof. Samuel Turner in translating and editing *An Introduction to the Old Testament* (1827), from the German of Johann Jahn. He was ordained deacon (Mar. 11, 1827) by Bishop John H. Hobart in Trinity Church, New York, and advanced to the priesthood (Dec. 17, 1829) by Bishop John Croes in St. Mark's Church, Orange, N. J., where he served as rector (1829–30). On Apr. 15, 1830, he was married to Hannah Harrison, by whom he had a son and two daughters. He was rector of St. Luke's Church, New York (1831–36), and professor of ecclesiastical history at the General Theological Seminary (1836–40).

He was elected bishop of Maryland on May 28, 1840, and consecrated in St. Paul's Church, Baltimore, Sept. 17. During the stormy years from 1857 to 1865 he was sorely tried. He was a man of positive convictions, which had been formed in the North, and, as two-thirds of the laity and three-fifths of the clergy of Maryland were allied with the Confederacy, his position was most difficult and delicate. His ruling that there should be no change in the Prayer-Book services used in public worship aroused violent opposition both during and after the Civil War. He was deeply interested in education and labored tirelessly for the development of church schools. He was also a pioneer in the revival of community life, several brotherhoods and sisterhoods being organized under his auspices. In his early years he was in doctrinal agreement with Keble, Pusey, and the early leaders of the Oxford Movement, but later he became alarmed at its ritual developments. As an ecclesiastical statesman he foresaw the impending growth of the Protestant Episcopal Church in Maryland, and advocated the building of a great national cathedral in Washington and the division of the diocese.

Whittingham was a scholarly ecclesiastic of a kind now well-nigh extinct. His reading and research covered not only classical, critical, and Biblical literature, but every department of sacred and secular learning, and he and his agents ransacked the world for rare and valuable books, both ancient and modern. His choice library of 17,000 volumes, which he bequeathed to the diocese of Maryland, became the nucleus of the Maryland Diocesan Library. The breadth and depth of his learning is evidenced in his published writings, which include *The Pursuit of Knowledge* (1837), *The Voice of the Lord* (1841), *The Godly Quietness of the Church* (1842), *The Priesthood in the Church* (1842), *The Body of Christ* (1843), *The Apostle in His Master's House* (1844), *The Work of the Ministry in a Day of Rebuke* (1846), *Gifts and Their Right Estimate* (1855), *The Work of Christ by His Ministry* (1856), *Conformity in Worship* (1857), and *Fifteen Sermons* (1880). He also translated or edited a number of theological works.

His character and accomplishments were accurately evaluated by Bishop W. C. Doane of Albany, who described him as "full and running over with every kind of learning . . ., a powerful preacher, an able debater, an irresistible controversialist," his word "an authority in the House of Bishops which no one questioned" (Brand, *post*, II, 374–75). There are admirable paintings of Whittingham at the Diocesan House in Baltimore and the General Theological Seminary in New York which reveal a remarkable blend of ascetic self-discipline, intellectual ability, and large-hearted benevolence. He died in Orange, N. J.

[See W. F. Brand, *Life of William Rollinson Whittingham* (2 vols., ed. of 1886), with portrait; W. S. Perry, *The Episcopate in America* (1895); H. C. Potter, *Reminiscences of Bishops and Archbishops* (1906); Hall Harrison, *Life of the Right Rev. John Barrett Kerfoot* (2 vols., 1886); H. G. Batterson, *A Sketch-Book of the Am. Episcopate* (1878); and obituaries in *Churchman,* Oct. 25, and *Sun* (Baltimore), Oct. 18, 1879. In the Md. Diocesan Lib., Baltimore, is a large coll. of Whittingham's papers, including notes, diaries, and correspondence.]   W. R.

WHITTREDGE, WORTHINGTON (May 22, 1820–Feb. 25, 1910), painter, was born in Springfield, Ohio, the son of Joseph Whittredge. He received his first instruction in art in Cincinnati, where even then there were some good pictures and a lively interest in local art. In 1849 he went abroad to study and remained for ten years. He spent half this time in Düsseldorf, where for three years he studied continuously under Andreas Achenbach. During five later winters he lived in Rome, but made visits to London, Antwerp, Paris, and other cities. In Düsseldorf he met Albert Bierstadt and Emanuel Leutze [*qq.v.*], the latter of whom became a life-long friend. Leutze painted his portrait in Düsseldorf, representing him as a young cavalier, wearing a ruff, with sword in one hand and hat in the other, the latter held against his hip (in the Metropolitan Museum of Art, New York). Years later John W. Alexander [*q.v.*] painted his portrait for the National Academy of Design. This too shows him as a picturesque figure, a man of fine presence and physique. When Leutze painted his famous "Washington Crossing the Delaware," it was Whittredge in an old uniform worn by the General who posed for the figure of Washington. Upon his return to the United States in 1859, Whittredge established himself in New York with a studio on Tenth Street in what was then the artists' quarter. He was married on Oct. 16, 1867, at Geneva, N. Y., to Euphemia Foote, by whom he had four children. His first exhibit was a painting, "The Roman Campagna," done in Rome, which he entered in the exhibition of the National Academy of Design in 1859. He was elected an Academician in 1861, and served as president of the Academy in 1865 and from 1874 to 1877. In his connection with the Academy he rendered conscientious service, devoting himself to promoting the interests of his fellow Academicians. He is said, on good authority, to have had "a lifelong habit of kindness and generosity" (Clark, *post,* p. 180).

As a painter Whittredge gave himself to depicting the gentler aspects of nature. In 1866 with Sanford R. Gifford and John F. Kensett [*qq.v.*] he made a trip to the far West and painted a number of pictures of the country between the Mississippi River and the Rocky Mountains, but it was the woods and streams of New York State and New England that he loved best and painted most feelingly. Like all the painters of the Hudson River School, he strove earnestly to represent on canvas exactly what he saw. He was technically well trained and sensitively appreciative of beauty, and his pictures, despite their over-emphasis on detail, possess an individuality and charm that give them lasting value. He was awarded a bronze medal at the Centennial Exhibition in Philadelphia (1876), and silver medals at the Pan-American Exposition in Buffalo (1901) and the Louisiana Purchase Exposition in St. Louis (1904). The Metropolitan Museum of Art owns his "Evening in the Woods," "Camp Meeting" (1874), and, notably, "The Trout Pool." The Corcoran Gallery of Art, Washington, D. C., has "Trout Brook in the Catskills" (1875). He is represented in other well-known museum collections. Among his early works the most famous is "The Poachers," frequently reproduced through the medium of lithography. Whittredge died in Summit, N. J., where he made his home, survived by his wife and three daughters.

[See *Who's Who in America,* 1908–09; A. W. Foote, *Foote Family* (2 vols., 1907–32); Samuel Isham, *The Hist. of Am. Painting* (1905); Edna M. Clark, *Ohio Art and Artists* (1932); *Am. Art Ann.,* 1910–11; death notice in *N. Y. Times,* obituary in *N. Y. Tribune,* Feb. 27, 1910. The name of Whittredge's father is from Cliff Whittredge of Springfield, Ohio.]   L. M.

WHITWORTH, GEORGE FREDERIC (Mar. 15, 1816–Oct. 6, 1907), Presbyterian clergyman and educator, was born in Boston, England. In 1828 his parents settled, according to one authority (Prosser, *post,* II, 574), near Mansfield, Ohio; according to another (Bagley, *post,* I, 141), in Terre Haute, Ind. After serving as an apprentice to a saddler and harness maker, George entered Hanover College, where he was graduated in 1838. On July 17 of that year he married Mary Elizabeth Thomson of Decatur County, Ind., by whom he had seven children. Subsequently, he taught school in Lancaster, Ohio, and Greenburg, Ind., studied law, and in 1843 was admitted to the bar. Soon, however, he determined to enter the ministry, and in 1847 was graduated at New Albany Theological Seminary (later McCormick Theological Seminary).

After serving several Presbyterian churches,

he was invited in 1852 to lead a company of colonists across the continent, and the Presbyterian Board of Home Missions appointed him missionary to Puget Sound. In October 1853 he reached Portland, Ore., where he helped to found the First Presbyterian Church. Proceeding to Olympia, Wash., early in 1854, he organized a church there and in the following year, one in what is now Claquato and another at Grand Mound. He was the first Presbyterian to preach in Seattle (March 1865), and in December 1869 established the First Presbyterian Church there. He served as moderator of the presbytery of Puget Sound, and of the synod; at various times he was also stated clerk of both bodies.

A missionary's wage proving inadequate to support his family, he resigned from the mission about 1856 and turned for some years to secular occupations. From 1856 to 1865 he held many minor government offices and energetically promoted public improvements. He foresaw that Washington coal would prove abundant and good and wrote much upon the subject. In 1866 he became a member of the Lake Washington Coal Company, which soon went out of existence, and in 1868–69, with Daniel Bagley, he operated the Newcastle Coal Mines. He was also a member of the Seattle Coal Company, incorporated in 1870.

Meanwhile, in 1866, he had left Olympia to assume the presidency of the University of Washington. He was an outstanding personage, and the reputation and character he brought to the Seattle institution did much to save it from extinction. He served only until June 28, 1867, but from the spring of 1875 to Christmas of 1876 he again occupied the position. He had charge of the university at difficult times, but under his leadership it made progress. He did much to popularize civil engineering and organized military and engineering departments. In 1883 he established an academy at Sumner, Wash., and in 1890, while president of its trustees, incorporated it as a college. In 1899 the institution was moved to Tacoma and later to Spokane. In his honor it was named by others Whitworth College.

[G. B. Bagley, *Hist. of Seattle* (1916); V. J. Farrar, "Hist. of the Univ.," in *The Washington Alumnus,* Apr. 1921; G. W. Fuller, *Hist. of the Inland Empire* (1928); F. J. Grant, *Hist. of Seattle* (1891); H. K. Hines, *An Illustrated Hist. of the State of Washington* (1898), p. 257; *Morning Oregonian* (Portland), Jan. 18, 19, 1904, Oct. 7, 1907; W. F. Prosser, *Hist. of the Puget Sound Country* (1903); H. W. Scott, *Hist. of the Oregon Country* (1924), ed. by L. M. Scott; C. A. Snowden, *Hist. of Washington* (1909); *Washington Alumnus,* Dec. 17, 1910; *Washington Hist. Quart.,* July 1907, Apr. 1915.]   F. P. N.

WHYTE, WILLIAM PINKNEY (Aug. 9, 1824–Mar. 17, 1908), lawyer, senator from Maryland, was the son of Joseph and Isabella (Pinkney) White. He was the grandson of William Pinkney [q.v.] and of Dr. William Campbell White, an Irish rebel who emigrated to America at the failure of the Irish Rebellion in 1798. William changed his name from White to Whyte to distinguish his family from that of his uncle, with whom his father had quarreled over a matter of business. His early education was under the direction of M. R. McNally, an accomplished scholar who had been secretary to Napoleon Bonaparte. At the age of eighteen, Whyte entered the employ of the banking firm of Peabody, Riggs and Company. When this clerkship proved uncongenial, he resigned to study law in the firm of Brown and Brune. The winter of 1844–45 he studied law at Harvard; he then returned to Baltimore to continue his studies in the law firm of John Glenn. He was admitted to the bar in 1846 and in the same year was elected as a Democrat to the Maryland House of Delegates. In 1851 he entered the Democratic primary as a candidate for Congress but was defeated; two years later he was elected comptroller of the treasury of Maryland. Declining reëlection to this office, he was again a candidate for Congress in 1857, opposing the Know-Nothings, although foredoomed to defeat, in order to expose their corrupt election methods. He contested the election, charging them with the use of fraud and violence. Though he lost by a small vote, the publication of the testimony and the exposure of the proceedings led in the next legislature to the passage of a series of laws effectually ending unfair election practices. At the outbreak of the Civil War, Whyte was drafted by the federal government but was disqualified on physical grounds. His sympathy was for the Confederacy. At the height of the war hysteria he was deprived of his citizenship, but he was later reenfranchised. During this period he traveled abroad. On July 14, 1868, he was appointed to fill, for one year, the vacant seat of Senator Reverdy Johnson [q.v.], who had been sent as minister to Great Britain. In 1871 he was elected Democratic governor of Maryland; he resigned in 1874 to return to the Senate as successor to William T. Hamilton. At this time he was victorious as counsel for Maryland before the arbitration board in the boundary dispute between Virginia and Maryland. During his six years in the Senate (1875–81), the most brilliant of his career, he championed sound currency and helped to devise the form of government for the District of Columbia. He was defeated for reelection by Arthur Pue Gorman [*q.v.*]. Thereafter he was successively mayor of Baltimore (1881–83), attorney general of Maryland (1887–91), and city solicitor of Baltimore (1900–03). In 1906, when his old enemy, Arthur Pue Gorman, died, he was appointed to fill Gorman's vacant senatorial seat.

Whyte died suddenly at his home in Baltimore before the expiration of this last term in office. He had long been known affectionately as the "grand old man of Maryland." He took great interest and pleasure in his horses, which he drove himself every day between luncheon and dinner, and in his collection of the belongings of his grandfather, William Pinkney. He was not a profound student of the law, but he was indefatigable at his work and consistently struggled against class legislation. He was twice married. His first wife, Louisa D. Hollinsworth, to whom he was married on Dec. 7, 1847, died on Oct. 28, 1885. On Apr. 27, 1892, he was married to Mary (McDonald) Thomas, who had been his ward. He had three children by his first wife.

[*Who's Who in America,* 1908–09; *Biog. Dir. Am. Cong.* (1928); W. F. Coyle, *Mayors of Baltimore* (1919); F. A. Richardson and W. A. Bennett, *Baltimore; Past and Present* (1871); *William Pinkney White ... Memorial Addresses* (1909), being *Sen. Doc.* 765, 60 Cong., 2 Sess.; J. J. Chamberlain, *Universities and Their Sons,* vol. V (1900); *Message of William Pinkney Whyte, Mayor, to the City Council of Baltimore* (1882); *Boundary Line Between the States of Va. and Md.* (1876); H. E. Buchholz, *Governors of Md.* (1908); *Independent,* Mar. 21, 1907, p. 667; obituary in *Sun* (Baltimore), Mar. 18, 1908; information from Marjory Whyte.]   H. Ca–s.

WICKERSHAM, JAMES PYLE (Mar. 5, 1825–Mar. 25, 1891), educator, was born in Newlin Township, Chester County, Pa., the son of Caleb and Abigail Swayne (Pyle) Wickersham, and a descendant of Thomas Wickersham who settled in Chester County in 1701. He grew up on his father's farm, attending the local district school and Unionville Academy. To earn the expenses of his tuition at the academy, he taught school in the winter of 1841–42 at Brandywine Manor and in 1843 near Paoli. From 1843 to 1845 he was an assistant teacher at the academy. Abandoning his plan to prepare for the practice of law in deference to the religious views of his parents, who were Friends, he accepted an appointment in 1845 as headmaster of the academy at Marietta, Pa., and within a few years became the principal owner. On Dec. 24, 1847, he was married to Emerine Isaac Taylor, daughter of Dr. Isaac Taylor of Chester, Pa. In 1854 he was elected first county superintendent of schools in Lancaster County. Later in that year he organized the first state convention of county superintendents and presented his plan of

developing a uniform system of school administration. He was chiefly instrumental in the enactment of the school laws of 1854, which provided for the appointment of county superintendents. A county teachers' institute at Millersville Academy, which he established in the spring of 1855, was incorporated in the fall as the Lancaster County Normal School, and in the following year Wickersham resigned the county superintendency to become principal. He urged the establishment of a system of state normal schools and assisted in framing the normal school law of 1857. Under his administration the institution at Millersville became the first state normal school in Pennsylvania (1859) and was a noted center for the training of teachers. During the Civil War Wickersham raised a regiment, which included more than one hundred students and instructors of the Millersville State Normal School. Commissioned colonel of the 47th Regiment, Pennsylvania Volunteer Emergency Militia, July 9, 1863, he served until his command was mustered out, Aug. 14, 1863. He was one of the organizers of the Lancaster County Educational Association (1851), the Pennsylvania State Teachers' Association (1852), and the National Teachers' Association (later the National Education Association), all of which he served as president. In 1870 and 1879 he served as president of the department of school superintendence of the National Education Association.

In 1866 he was appointed state superintendent of common schools. During his administration, he effected a classification of all the educational institutions in the state and a closer union among them, better grading of schools, more complete supervision, and increased provision for improving the qualifications of teachers. By 1874 he had succeeded in having a school established in every district in Pennsylvania. He wrote the educational provisions of the state constitution of 1874, and established the school department as one of the five constitutional departments of the state government. In 1864 he brought about the establishment of the Soldiers' Orphans Schools, which provided homes and education for children orphaned by the Civil War. He was editor and part owner of the *Pennsylvania School Journal* from 1870 to 1881. In 1878, at the request of the governor, he visited various European schools, and was awarded a medal at the Paris Exposition for his exhibit of state school reports, laws, and other documents. On resigning the state superintendency in 1881, he devoted himself to writing, and to the management of the Inquirer Printing and Publishing Company, Lancaster, Pa., of which he had been president since its organization in 1873. His publications include *School Economy* (1864), *Methods of Instruction* (1865), and *A History of Education in Pennsylvania* (1886). He was appointed chargé d'affaires of the United States to Denmark on May 1, 1882, and minister resident and consul general on July 13, 1882. He resigned, Aug. 21, 1882, because of his wife's ill health. He died in Lancaster, survived by one son and three daughters.

[Mary Martin, in *Pa. School Jour.*, Aug. 1891; *Ibid.*, Sept. 1891; J. P. Wickersham, *A Hist. of Educ. in Pa.* (1886); J. S. Futhey and Gilbert Cope, *Hist. of Chester County, Pa.* (1881); Alexander Harris, *A Biog. Hist. of Lancaster County* (1872), pp. 618–20; H. M. J. Klein, *Lancaster County, Pa., a Hist.* (1924), vol. III, pp. 11–12; *Portrait and Biog. Record of Lancaster County, Pa.* (1894); obituary in *Daily New Era* (Lancaster), Mar. 25, 1891; information from Lillian Crawford Schlagle of Phila., Wickersham's grand-daughter.]
R. F. S.

WICKES, LAMBERT (1735?–Oct. 1, 1777), Revolutionary naval officer, the son of Samuel Wickes, was born on Eastern Neck Island, Kent County, Md. His great-grandfather, Joseph Wickes, had settled in Kent County by 1650. In his youth Lambert went to sea, and by 1769 was commanding ships out of Philadelphia and Chesapeake Bay ports. By December 1774 he was part owner of a ship. In the autumn of 1774 he distinguished himself by refusing to ship any tea from London in his vessel, the *Neptune,* and arrived in Annapolis almost simultaneously with the *Peggy Stewart,* which was burned with her cargo of tea by the aroused citizens. His patriotic stand in this instance, together with his acquaintance with Robert Morris [q.v.], probably aided him in securing command of the Continental armed ship *Reprisal* in April 1776. On June 10, 1776, he was ordered by the Committee of Secret Correspondence to carry William Bingham, 1752–1804 [q.v.], to Martinique. Wickes sailed on July 3 from Cape May after a sharp skirmish with the British off that place, where his brother Richard, his third lieutenant, was killed. On the voyage he captured three valuable prizes which he sent back to Philadelphia, and on July 27 appeared off Martinique. As he was about to enter the harbor of Saint-Pierre, he was attacked by H. M. S. *Shark,* Capt. John Chapman, who, after a short engagement, gave up the fight. Captain Wickes won the sympathy of the French governor and populace for his gallantry in the affair. He left Martinique on Aug. 26, with a cargo of powder, 500 muskets and clothing, and arrived in Philadelphia after an uneventful voyage, on Sept. 13. He was commanded immediately upon his return to fit the *Reprisal*

for a two months' voyage, and on Oct. 24 was ordered to carry Benjamin Franklin to France. He sailed with Franklin secretly on Oct. 26, and on Nov. 28 reached the Brittany coast. On his way he took two English prizes. The *Reprisal* was the first American ship of war and Wickes was the first American naval officer to appear in European waters after the Declaration of Independence. He won high praise from Franklin for ability and courage shown on the voyage.

In January 1777 Wickes made a third cruise in the *Reprisal,* this time in the English Channel itself, capturing five British prizes, all of which were taken to the port L'Orient and clandestinely sold. Lord Stormont, the British ambassador, protested bitterly and with much justice at this breach of international law. Stirred to action by his remonstrance the French authorities ordered Wickes to leave port within twenty-four hours but the captain claimed that his ship needed repairs, and thus gained a few weeks' delay. In April 1777, the *Lexington,* Capt. Henry Johnson, and the *Dolphin,* Capt. Samuel Nicholson [q.v.], joined him. These three vessels under the orders of the American commissioners in France, and under the direct command of Wickes, sailed from France on May 28, 1777. They cruised around the west coast of Ireland, thence southward through the Irish Sea, taking eighteen British prizes in all. On the return voyage to France, the *Reprisal* was chased by H. M. S. *Burford,* 74 guns, and escaped only after Wickes threw all his guns overboard. He reached Saint-Malo on June 28. In deference to Stormont's vigorous protests he was detained at Saint-Malo until Sept. 14, when he was allowed to sail for America. On Oct. 1, 1777, his ship foundered in a storm off the Banks of Newfoundland, and all on board perished except the cook. His entire career was distinguished by patriotism and the highest courage. Franklin, who knew him well, spoke of him as "a gallant officer, and a very worthy man."

[Papers relating to Wickes in the Library of Congress, Washington, D. C.; Port records of Annapolis and Philadelphia; letter and will of Wickes, Maryland Historical Society; W. B. Clark, *Lambert Wickes, Sea Raider and Diplomat* (1932); Henry Hardy, *Narrative of Events in the Several Cruises of Captain Lambert Wickes* (Facsimile of copy in U. S. Naval Acad., Annapolis), in Library of Congress; G. A. Hanson, *Old Kent* (1876); G. W. Allen, *A Naval Hist. of the Am. Revolution* (2 vols., 1913); E. E. Hale, *Franklin in France,* vol. I (1887); B. F. Stevens, *Facsimiles of Manuscripts in European Archives Relating to America* (25 vols., 1889–98); *The Revolutionary Diplomatic Correspondence of the U. S.* (1889), vol. II, ed. by Francis Wharton; Peter Force, *Am. Archives,* 5 ser., vols. I–III (1848–53); *Md. Gazette,* Nov. 10, 17, 1774; *Pa. Packet* (Lancaster, Pa.), Feb. 11, 1778.]
L. H. B.

WICKES, STEPHEN (Mar. 17, 1813–July 8, 1889), physician, historical writer, was born at Jamaica, L. I., the son of Van Wyck and Eliza (Herriman) Wickes. He was a descendant of Thomas Weekes who emigrated to Long Island in 1635. He attended the Union Academy in his native town and later entered Union College at Schenectady, N. Y., where he was graduated in 1831. After some work at the Rensselaer Polytechnic Institute at Troy, he began the study of medicine in the office of Dr. Thomas W. Blatchford of that city, and was graduated from the medical department of the University of Pennsylvania in 1834. After a short term of practice in New York City he returned to Troy to associate himself with his former preceptor. Here he lived and carried on a general practice until 1852, when he removed to Orange, N. J., his residence for the remainder of his life. His practice here brought him a reputation for accurate diagnosis, therapeutic skill and an insistence upon the strict regimen of the sick-room. In 1873 he became a member of the medical staff of the Memorial Hospital at Orange. He retired from active practice in 1886, and devoted himself thereafter to his literary work.

Upon his arrival in Orange he joined the Essex District Medical Society and was chosen to represent it in the councils of the New Jersey State Medical Society. His unpaid services as chairman of the standing committee of the state society covered a period of twenty-three years, until his election to the presidency in 1883. From 1861 to 1882 he edited the *Transactions of the Medical Society of New Jersey,* producing an annual volume of original papers to which he added historical items of medical interest from all parts of the state. In addition he edited *The Rise, Minutes and Proceedings of the New Jersey Medical Society, Established July 23, 1766* (1875), which carried the history of the society down to 1800. This work led to the preparation of his most important book, the *History of Medicine in New Jersey, and of its Medical Men, from the Settlement of the Province to A. D. 1880* (1879). The first part consists of historical narrative, while the second part is devoted to medical biography. Other writings include *Medical Topography of Orange, New Jersey* (1859), *Sepulture, its History, Methods and Sanitary Requisites* (1884), the *History of the Newark Mountains* (1888) and *History of the Oranges, in Essex County, N. J.* (1892). His presidential address before the state medical society was a philosophical paper entitled *Living and Dying, their Physics and Psychics* (1884). In addition to his medical and literary inter-

ests he had a part in every local enterprise for the promotion of education and for the moral and intellectual improvement of the community. While a resident of Troy he was a trustee of the Rensselaer Polytechnic Institute. Always interested in historical research, he was a member and corresponding secretary of the Historical Society of New Jersey. He was twice married, on Feb. 24, 1836, to Mary Whitney Heyer, and on Apr. 1, 1841, to Lydia Matilda, the widow of Dr. William H. Van Sinderen, and the daughter of Joseph Howard, of Brooklyn, N. Y. His second wife, two of their daughters, and one daughter of his first wife survived him at his death in Orange.

[*Thomas Weekes Emigrant to America 1635* (privately printed, 1904); *Abraham Howard of Marblehead, Mass., and his Descendants* (privately printed, 1897); H. A. Kelly, W. L. Burrage, *Am. Medic. Biog.* (1920); W. B. Atkinson, *The Physicians and Surgeons of the U. S.* (1878); *Trans. Medic. Soc. of N. J.* (1890); *Medic. News,* Philadelphia, July 13, 1889; *N. Y. Times,* July 9, 1889.] J.M.P.

WICKHAM, JOHN (June 6, 1763–Jan. 22, 1839), lawyer, was born at Southold, Long Island, N. Y., the son of John and Hannah (Fanning) Wickham and a descendant of Thomas Wickham who was made a freeman of Wethersfield, Conn., in 1658. With a view to entering the army, John attended the military school at Arras, France, but preferring the law he went to Williamsburg, Va., during the Revolution to live with an uncle, the Rev. William Fanning, an Episcopal clergyman, and there to prepare himself for the legal profession. Later he practised in Williamsburg until he removed to Richmond in 1790. On Dec. 24, 1791, he married his cousin, Mary Smith Fanning, who died Feb. 1, 1799. As his second wife he married Elizabeth Selden McClurg, the only daughter of Dr. James McClurg [*q.v.*]. Socially prominent, he lived on Clay Street near the home of his friend John Marshall.

The leader of a bar unsurpassed in America, Wickham appeared in many important cases, three of which are unusually noteworthy. In 1793, in the case of *Ware* vs. *Hylton,* he was of counsel for a British creditor who claimed protection of the Treaty of 1783, which provided that the collection of bona fide debts should not be impeded. John Marshall was one of the debtor's attorneys and contended that since Virginia, an independent state, had suspended these debts during the Revolution, they had ceased to be lawful obligations and were not within the terms of the Treaty, an anomalous position in view of his later great decisions. Wickham took the sounder view that by the Constitution treaties were a part of the law of the land and all state legislation inconsistent therewith was invalid. Denied by the lower court, Wickham's contention was sustained on appeal by the Supreme Court (3 *Dallas,* 199). In 1809 Wickham represented the plaintiff in the case of *Hunter* vs. *Fairfax's Devisee* (1 *Munford,* 218; 7 *Cranch,* 603), involving the Fairfax grant, which, although finally decided against him under the title *Martin* vs. *Hunter's Lessee* (1 *Wheaton,* 304) established the doctrine that the Supreme Court has appellate jurisdiction over the decisions of the state courts.

The most spectacular case, however, in which Wickham participated was the trial of Aaron Burr [*q.v.*]. Associated with him were Luther Martin, Edmund Randolph [*qq.v.*], and others, while William Wirt [*q.v.*] assisted the prosecution. An incident occurred which caused popular clamor. Wickham gave a dinner which his friend John Marshall attended—a not unusual event; but Burr also was present! The press denounced the spectacle of the accused in a treason trial dining at the home of one of his chief counsel with the judge who was to try the case. Aware of the obvious implications of such an indiscretion, Marshall probably did not know that Burr had been invited. Early in the trial Wickham pointed out that the Constitution specifically defined treason and for conviction required two witnesses to the overt act. Since the gathering at Blennerhassett's island was alleged in the indictment as the act of treason and since Burr was hundreds of miles away at the time, Wickham contended that Burr had committed no overt act, the constitutional provisions abrogating the common law rule of constructive presence and requiring for conviction physical presence at the commission of the act charged. The Chief Justice adopted Wickham's view and so instructed the jury.

Wickham was one of the greatest pleaders at the bar. His mind was alert yet profound; his wit vivid and brilliant; his style classically pure; and his elocution unusually fine. Extravagantly esteemed by John Randolph of Roanoke, he was even more extravagantly praised by Tom Moore, as the only gentleman the poet found in America (Werner, *post,* p. 46). Wickham had two sons by his first wife, and numerous children by the second.

[A. J. Beveridge, *Life of John Marshall* (1919); C. A. Hoppin, *Wickham* (1899); W. D. Lewis, *Great Am. Lawyers,* vol. II (1907); S. H. Wandell and Meade Minnigerode, *Aaron Burr* (1925); *Reports of the Trials of Col. Aaron Burr* (1808); C. J. Werner, *Geneals. of Long Island Families* (1919); *Va. Mag. of Hist. and Biog.,* Jan. 1922; *Richmond Enquirer,* Jan. 26, 1839.]

T. S. C.

WICKLIFFE, CHARLES ANDERSON (June 8, 1788–Oct. 31, 1869), Kentucky official, congressman, postmaster-general, was the youngest of the nine children of Charles and Lydia (Hardin) Wickliffe, both natives of Virginia. He was born near Springfield, Washington County, Ky., and received his elementary education there. During 1805 he attended Wilson's Academy at Bardstown and then for a year received private instruction under James Blythe, acting president of Transylvania University. Returning to Bardstown, he studied law in the office of his cousin, M. D. Hardin [*q.v.*], and in 1809 was admitted to the bar. He soon became one of the group of Bardstown lawyers which included Ben Hardin, Felix Grundy, John Rowan, and W. P. Duval [*qq.v.*]. This group was as famous for its revelries as for its forensic talent, and Wickliffe early established a reputation as a bacchanalian and a gambler for high stakes.

He was a member of the Kentucky House of Representatives from Nelson County in 1812 and 1813. In the latter year, he married Margaret Cripps and enlisted (Sept. 2) as a private in M. H. Wickliffe's company of Kentucky mounted volunteers, from which station he was shortly promoted to be aide to General Caldwell (*Report of the Adjutant General . . . of Kentucky: Soldiers of the War of 1812,* 1891, p. 147). In 1816 he succeeded his cousin, Ben Hardin, as commonwealth attorney for Nelson County, and in 1820 and 1821 was again a member of the lower house of the Kentucky legislature. In 1823 he was sent to the federal House of Representatives. Here in 1825 he cast his vote for Jackson for president, an action that required a great deal of explaining later, and was perhaps responsible for his lack of committee assignments during the early portion of his congressional service. By successive elections he remained in the House until 1833, and in 1829 became chairman of the committee on public lands. In 1831 he was an unsuccessful candidate for United States senator from Kentucky. Returning to Kentucky in 1833, he was for the third time sent to the legislature by his faithful constituents in Nelson County. Here he served for three years, being speaker of the House in 1835. In 1836 he was elected lieutenant-governor of Kentucky on the Whig ticket and on the death of Gov. James Clark [*q.v.*] in September 1839 Wickliffe succeeded to the office of governor, in which he continued until the following September.

With his appointment by President Tyler as postmaster-general in October 1841 Wickliffe again shifted back to national politics. In this position, which he held until Mar. 6, 1845, he occupied himself with duties of a routine nature, although he is credited with securing a slight reduction in postal rates (L. R. Hafen, *The Overland Mail*, 1926, p. 29). On the issue of the annexation of Texas he was converted to Democracy and so was eligible to receive an appointment from Polk in 1845 as an agent to ferret out and oppose the designs of France and England in Texas (S. F. Bemis, *American Secretaries of State and Their Diplomacy*, vol. V, 1928, p. 185). Returning once more to state politics, in 1849 he was elected as a Democrat to the constitutional convention, in which he was chairman of the committee on the court of appeals, and was vigorous in his opposition to suffrage restrictions (*Report of the Debates and Proceedings*, 1849, p. 36). The next year he was appointed by the legislature on committee to revise the statutes of Kentucky. He opposed the movement for the secession of Kentucky in 1861, and was a member both of the Washington Peace Conference and of the Border State Conference (Lewis and R. H. Collins, *History of Kentucky*, 1882, I, 86, 89). In 1861 he was elected to Congress as a Union Whig and at the close of his term was a candidate of the Peace Democrats for governor, but was defeated (E. M. Coulter, *The Civil War and Readjustment in Kentucky*, 1926, pp. 174–78). He was a delegate to the National Democratic Convention in 1864. His death occurred while he was on a visit to his daughter near Ilchester, Harford County, Md.; and he was buried at Bardstown.

Wickliffe was an able lawyer and acquitted himself creditably in the various positions he held. His continued political success is noteworthy because he was of a haughty and disdainful disposition; among the common people he was commonly referred to as "the Duke." His career was marked by many conflicts both verbal and physical. Like Ben Hardin, he had a talent for vituperation and was not sparing in its use. In his last term in Congress he was thrown from his carriage and was a cripple for the remainder of his life, and for several years before his death he was also blind. He had three sons and five daughters, one of the former being Robert C. Wickliffe [*q.v.*].

[In addition to sources mentioned above, see L. P. Little, *Ben Hardin: His Times and Contemporaries* (1887); J. C. Morton, "Gov. Charles A. Wickliffe," in the *Reg. Ky. State Hist. Soc.*, Sept. 1904; *Biog. Encyc. of Ky.* (1878); *Biog. Dir. Am. Cong.* (1928); *N. Y. Times*, Nov. 3, 1869.]   R. S. C.

WICKLIFFE, ROBERT CHARLES (Jan. 6, 1819–Apr. 18, 1895), governor of Louisiana, was born at Bardstown, Ky. His father was Charles A. Wickliffe [*q.v.*], and his mother, Margaret (Cripps) Wickliffe, was the daughter of Col. Christian Cripps, the hero of many Indian fights. Wealth made possible a liberal education. After a stern discipline in the humanities under Louis Marshall, 1773–1866 [*q.v.*], of "Buckpond," near Versailles, Ky., his training was continued at the Jesuit institution of St. Joseph's College at Bardstown for a year, followed by two years at Augusta College at Augusta, Ky., and was concluded with the last two years at Centre College in Danville, where he graduated in 1840. Removal of the family to Washington, when his father became postmaster-general, afforded him opportunity to study law with Hugh Legaré [*q.v.*], then attorney-general; but he returned to Bardstown for admission to the bar. Failing health interrupted his practice so that he removed to St. Francisville, La., in 1846, where he engaged in cotton planting as well as in the practice of his profession. In 1851 he was sent to the state Senate from West Feliciana Parish, was twice reëlected without opposition, and was chosen president of that body upon the death of the lieutenant-governor, William Farmer. So effective did the Democratic party find him in the campaign against the Know-Nothing party that it made him candidate for governor in 1855, and he carried it to success by a vigorous campaign. Firmly convinced that the South could remain honorably in the Union, he at first disapproved of secession, but, when he saw that the tide could not be stemmed, he endeavored to hasten separation. As a precautionary measure he urged removal of the free negroes from the state to eliminate their influence on the slaves.

At the expiration of his gubernatorial term in 1860, he returned to his planting and legal practice. In 1866 he was elected to Congress but was denied admission, along with all representatives who refused to take the iron-clad oath. In 1876 he was an elector-at-large on the Tilden ticket and served as chairman of the Louisiana delegation at the National Democratic Convention. After a long retirement he last figured in state politics during the campaign of 1891–92, when he was nominated to the lieutenant-governorship on the McEnery ticket. With the defeat of the party he returned to his home and work with all of the energy of his earlier days. He met with great success in his profession. It is recorded that out of fifty men charged with murder he saved all but one from conviction. Hard study, polished manners, and an illustrious name enabled him to render distinguished service to the state of his adoption. He was twice married, in February 1843 to Anna Dawson, of Feliciana, and in 1870 to his cousin, Annie (Davis) Anderson of Brandenburg, Ky.

[Mrs. E. S. du Fossat, *Biog. Sketches of Louisiana's Governors* (1885); Arthur Meynier, *Meynier's La. Biog.,* pt. 1 (1882); Charles Gayarré, *Hist. of La.,* vol. IV (1866); *Daily Picayune* and *Times-Democrat* (New Orleans), Apr. 19, 1895; dates of birth and second marriage from daughter, Mrs. Charles Cotesworth Marshall, Shelbyville, Ky.]   E. L.

WICKSON, EDWARD JAMES (Aug. 3, 1848–July 16, 1923), horticulturist, the son of George Guest and Catherine (Ray) Wickson, was born at Rochester, N. Y. Graduating from Hamilton College in 1869, he went to Utica as a staff-member of the *Utica Morning Herald,* and in 1875 became attached to the *Pacific Rural Press* in San Francisco. It was a period of early experiment on ranch, range, and orchard in California, and Wickson everywhere had a part in organizing new or revivifying old agricultural organizations. He was a founder of the first dairyman's association (1876), and a founder (1879) and long an officer of the California State Horticultural Society, which exerted a strong influence in farming matters and on state legislation. The objectives were always clear to him: to observe method and large-scale production on the great ranches or detailed results on the intensively-worked small place, and deduce therefrom tried knowledge for diffusion to the general public. Under his guidance the *Pacific Rural Press* won a wide reputation for sagacity, reliability, and integrity. From 1879 on, he was also associated with the University of California. At first a lecturer in agriculture, in 1897 he became a full professor in the College of Agriculture. He taught economic entomology, irrigation, dairying, range management, and general farming, as well as his own special subject of horticulture. In 1905 he was appointed dean of the College of Agriculture and professor of horticulture. A few years after he assumed office as director of the agricultural experiment station of the university (1907) there began to stir a movement for more active scientific research in agriculture, coincident with a program of publicity and of rapid expansion in all of the colleges of the university. Wickson distrusted isolated experiment and viewed agricultural research as a luxury that often brought little return for vast expenditure. In 1912 he refused to consider a plan designed to exploit California agriculture and to furnish frequent announcements to the press of insufficiently tried agricultural methods. As a consequence, his resignation as dean and director was demanded by President Benjamin Ide Wheeler, and he retired to the professorship of horticulture with a serenity fortified by the wide-

spread prestige which he enjoyed with rural Californians. His book, *The California Fruits and How to Grow Them,* was the law and the gospel of the little fruitgrower as well as the large one, and went through ten editions from 1889 to 1926; *The California Vegetables in Garden and Field* (1897) reached a fifth edition (1923). Others of his farm books were much used. His *Rural California* (1923) represents his economic views.

Wickson was in great demand as a speaker at conventions, as an officer in societies, as a member of commissions, as a trustee of schools. Wherever he spoke, this tall large-framed man with the prominent features, ruddy countenance, sandy beard, and beneficent manner captured every one within range of his voice. Even his scathing wit was taken in good part, and it seemed difficult for him to make an enemy. On Apr. 27, 1875, he was married to Ednah Newell Harmon of Irvington, Cal., by whom he had six children. In May 1898 he had been advanced to chief of the *Pacific Rural Press* staff and since then had regularly written its editorial page. The issue for July 21, 1923, was still a week ahead when he prepared the editorials for it. At the end of the day, after his habit, he crossed the bay of San Francisco to the family home on the edge of the Berkeley campus, and there within two days he died. He was survived by his wife, two sons, and four daughters.

[*Who's Who in America,* 1922–23; *In Memoriam, Edward James Wickson* (Univ. of Cal., 1924); W. L. Howard, in W. L. Jepson, "Men and Manners," vol. VI, pp. 194–200, in MS.; *Pacific Rural Press,* July 21, 28, 1923; obituary in *San Francisco Chronicle,* July 17, 1923.]   W. L. J—n.

WIDENER, HARRY ELKINS (Jan. 3, 1885–Apr. 15, 1912), collector of rare books, was born in Philadelphia, Pa., of a wealthy, cultivated family. He was a grandson of P. A. B. Widener and William Lukens Elkins [qq.v.]. His father, George Dunton Widener, and his mother, Eleanore Elkins, fostered the boy's love of books. Having prepared for college at the DeLancey School, Philadelphia, and the Hill School at Pottstown, Pa., he entered Harvard College, where he pored over *Book Prices Current* and learned the joy of collecting. Graduating in 1907, he decided to make collecting his life work. He acquired a profound knowledge of bibliography, not only storing up details of rare editions in his retentive memory but seeking out volumes that had human interest. Cowper's *The Task,* a copy once owned by Thackeray, had the novelist's note: "A great point in a great man—a great love for his mother"; Widener's frequent reference to this sentiment bears on the close bond between him and his mother. One of his favorite books was the Countess of Pembroke's own copy of Sir Philip Sidney's *Arcadia* (1613). Stevenson's work made a great appeal to him; *Treasure Island* was always with him on his travels, and in 1912 he printed privately Stevenson's *Memoirs of Himself*. In 1913 Dr. A. S. W. Rosenbach, who started him on his career professionally, printed privately a catalogue of his Stevenson collection.

Widener passed days in the auction room, rummaged through dusty alcoves of book shops and under book-laden tables, and spent happy evenings in conversation with Bernard Quaritch and Rosenbach. Yet he realized clearly that mere gathering of books leaves no permanent profit to mankind. He once told A. Edward Newton that he did not wish to be remembered merely as a collector of a few books, however fine, but in connection with a great library (Newton, *post,* p. 352). With this aspiration, he went to London in March 1912, and spent much time with Quaritch and at Sotheby's. At the Huth sale he obtained Bacon's *Essaies* (1598), saying to Quaritch, "I think I'll take that little Bacon with me in my pocket, and if I am shipwrecked it will go with me" (*Ibid.,* 354). He then set his face homeward. In the early morning of Apr. 15, 1912, he stood on the deck of the stricken *Titanic* while women pushed off in boats, his mother among them, and at 2:20 he went down with the ship. The Harry Elkins Widener Memorial Library at Harvard College was given by his mother and was opened June 24, 1915. A portrait of Widener by Gilbert Farrier is in the library.

[Sources include memoir in A. S. W. Rosenbach, *A Cat. of the Books and MSS. of Robert Louis Stevenson in the Lib. of the Late Harry Elkins Widener* (1913); A. E. Newton, *The Amenities of Book-Collecting* (1918); A. H. Rice, in *Harvard Class of 1907, Twenty-Fifth Anniversary Report* (1932); obituary notices in *Phila. Press,* Apr. 16–20, 1912; information from A. S. W. Rosenbach and A. C. Potter. Cats. of Widener's books and MSS., his Dickens coll., and his Cruikshank coll. were issued in 1918 by A. S. W. Rosenbach.]

C. K. B.

WIDENER, PETER ARRELL BROWN (Nov. 13, 1834–Nov. 6, 1915), financier and philanthropist, was born in Philadelphia, Pa., the son of John and Sarah (Fulmer) Widener, who were of pre-Revolutionary German stock. His early education was good, although his father, who at one time freighted goods between Philadelphia and Pittsburgh and later became a brick-maker, was in very moderate circumstance. He attended the Coates Street Grammar School and attended Central High School for two years. Upon leaving school he became a butcher's boy

in his brother's meatshop. He remained in the meat business for many years, became interested in politics, and was soon an important factor in the local Republican party.

During the Civil War he secured a contract from the Federal government to supply with mutton all its troops that were located within a radius of ten miles of Philadelphia. The contract netted him a profit of $50,000, a very large sum for that time, and he invested this money in certain strategically located street railways and built up a chain of meatstores throughout Philadelphia. His political influence grew rapidly and he was elected to several minor offices. He was a member of the Philadelphia board of education from 1867 to 1870. In 1873 he was appointed to complete the unexpired term of Joseph F. Mercer as city treasurer and the next year was elected to this office, in which he served one term. Philadelphia's political offices at this time carried with them especially large salaries and fees and Widener was able to accumulate a large sum of money.

Meanwhile, he had been buying stock in Philadelphia traction companies. In 1875, he, William L. Elkins [*q.v.*], and several others became definitely interested in street-railway ownership and operation. Eventually they effected a consolidation of all the lines in the city, first as the Philadelphia Traction Company (1883), then as the Union Traction Company, and finally as the Philadelphia Rapid Transit Company. In New York, beginning in December 1884, he was associated with Thomas F. Ryan and William C. Whitney [*q.v.*], supplying large capital to their joint operations and contributing valuable experience in the practical management of street railways. In the development of traction lines in Chicago, he and Elkins were conspicuous. He and his associates also acquired large street-railway holdings in Pittsburgh and Baltimore. Their properties totaled a greater mileage than those of any other similar syndicate. As a street-railway magnate, Widener greatly advanced technical developments. When he first entered the business, horse-cars were used exclusively. He became interested in the use of cable-cars, and then of electric cars, in an endeavor to create the most modern and efficient system of local transportation.

Widener helped to organize the United States Steel Corporation, the International Mercantile Marine Company, and the American Tobacco Company. He had large investments in many other corporations, among them the Pennsylvania Railroad Company, the Standard Oil Company, the United Gas Improvement Company, the Philadelphia Land Title and Trust Company, and the Philadelphia Company for Guaranteeing Mortgages. His directorships were legion and his authority in many cases was complete.

His main interest, outside of business, was in the collection of old and valuable articles. His art collection, which he kept in his beautiful home, "Lynnewood Hall," Elkins Park, a suburb of Philadelphia, contained many of the most valuable paintings, among them the small "Cowper Madonna" by Raphael and "The Mill" by Rembrandt. This collection and that of Chinese porcelains were considered among the finest in the country. He also gathered together rare and valuable bronzes, tapestries, statuary, chinaware, and old furniture. It has been estimated that he gave over eleven millions of dollars in money and property to those institutions and organizations in which he was interested. He built and endowed the Widener Memorial Industrial Training School for Crippled Children (opened in 1906) in memory of his wife and their son Harry K. Widener. He gave his Broad Street residence to the city for the purpose of housing a branch of the Philadelphia Free Library (Josephine Widener Branch), and upon his death he gave the city his valuable art collection. He was then probably the richest man in Philadelphia, his fortune being estimated at from thirty-five to fifty millions of dollars.

Widener traveled extensively and maintained a large library with which he was familiar. He was well informed, an interesting conversationalist and a ready, forceful, and convincing speaker. He was one of the leaders in the consolidation movement which swept the country during the latter part of the nineteenth century and he was among the first wealthy men to share a large part of his accumulations with society. On Aug. 18, 1858, he married Hannah Josephine Dunton. She died in 1905, and two of their three sons predeceased him. Harry Elkins Widener [q.v.] was his grandson.

[B. J. Hendrick, "Great American Fortunes and Their Making. Street Railway Financiers," in *McClure's Mag.*, Nov., Dec. 1907, Jan. 1908; H. J. Carman, *The Street Surface Railway Franchises of New York City* (1919); "The Widener Memorial Industrial Training School for Crippled Children," in F. P. Henry, ed., *Founders' Week Memorial Volume* (1909); "Mr. Widener's Pictures," *Literary Digest*, Mar 16, 1912; "Mr. Widener's Art Collection," *Ibid.*, Nov. 20, 1915; *Who's Who in America*, 1914–15; obituaries in *N. Y. Times*, *Public Ledger* (Philadelphia), Nov. 7, 1915; reproduction of Sargent portrait of Widener, *Current Literature*, Apr. 1903, p. 444; H. H. Widener, *The Wideners in America* (n.d.); fragmentary and inaccurate.]   H. S. P.

WIDFORSS, GUNNAR MAURITZ (Oct. 21, 1879–Nov. 30, 1934), artist, called the "paint-er of the national parks," was born in the Norrmalm section of Stockholm, Sweden, sixth child in a family of thirteen. His father, Laurentius Mauritz Viktor Widforss, was a shopkeeper; his mother, Blenda Carolina (Weidenhayn) Widforss, was the grand-daughter of an engraver at the Swedish mint. The boy cared little for regular school and less for his father's business. Intending to become a muralist, he studied in the Institute of Technology in Stockholm from 1896 to 1900, after which he began the wanderings which took him to Russia, Austria, Switzerland, France, Italy, Africa and finally the United States in search of subjects in nature for his brush and palette. Important recognition first came from the Paris Salon which exhibited two of his paintings in 1912. Among early patrons were Anders Zorn, King Gustav V of Sweden, and Archduke Franz Ferdinand of Austria.

Widforss first came to the United States in 1905. Meeting no encouragement, he returned to Sweden three years later, where his work soon became popular. He came back to the United States again in 1921 on a projected trip to the Orient, but his journey terminated in California whose natural grandeur immediately captivated him. The next year while at work with water colors in Yosemite National Park, he met Stephen T. Mather [q.v.] who, as director of the national parks, was at once enthusiastic about Widforss' handling of the outdoors and urged him to make the national parks his special province. Thereafter until his death the quiet Swede worked zealously under the open sky of the great West—in the canyons of the Colorado and Yellowstone, in Zion and Brice canyons, in the Kaibab forest, at Mesa Verde, Taos, Crater Lake and along the Monterey coast. Whether his subject was drifted mountain snow, the giant cacti of the desert or sunlight filtering through redwoods, he reproduced it with remarkable accuracy and feeling. A careful draftsman, he familiarized himself with geological formations and the architecture of nature generally. His great love was the Grand Canyon and so that its country might become his he became a citizen of the United States, on June 3, 1929. In "hermitlike simplicity" (*The Art Digest*, Jan. 1, 1935), he spent his last years on the rim of that vast chasm, seeking, from many vantage points, to record its many moods in water color and oil. A collection of these studies was exhibited at the National Gallery of Art in Washington, D. C., in December 1924, and was described by the director as the "finest things of the kind that have come out of the west" (*Washington Post*, Dec. 21, 1924).

The artist's work followed devotees of the national parks into all parts of the United States. His paintings illustrated Harold Symmes' *Songs of Yosemite* (1923), and, as interest in these great playgrounds developed, the *Literary Digest* and other magazines reproduced representative studies on their covers. In 1928 Widforss won first prize in the American-Scandinavian exhibition in New York. He also won a first prize of the California Water Color Society, of which he was a member. Soon after a widely viewed exhibit in St. Louis, Mo., in the fall of 1934, he died of a heart attack at the steering wheel of his loaded automobile at Grand Canyon, Ariz., as he prepared to leave the altitude of the rim for a lower elevation as directed by a physician. Friends buried him under the great pines in the little cemetery at Grand Canyon. Widforss had never married. His estate consisted of 150 paintings of the natural wonders which he knew so intimately and loved so deeply.

[Information from Widforss' mother, Mrs. Blenda Widforss, and C. E. Haggart, of Stockholm, Daniel McDade of Grand Canyon, Ariz., and Bishop William Scarlett, of St. Louis; Dagmar F. Knudsen, "A Painter of National Parks," *Sunset*, Jan. 1929, and "A Swedish Water Colorist," *Argus*, Mar. 1929; *Wasp*, Apr. 17, 1926; *Star* (Washington), Dec. 14, 1924, *San Francisco Examiner*, Oct. 25, 1923, Apr. 10, 1927, *Oakland Tribune*, Nov. 8, 1925, *Los Angeles Times*, Jan. 31, 1926, Nov. 18, 1928; *Phoenix Evening Gazette*, Feb. 20, 1929, *San Francisco Chronicle*, Mar. 10, 1929; *St. Louis Post-Dispatch*, Oct. 30, Dec. 2, 1934, and Jan. 28, 29, 1935.]   I. D.

WIECHMANN, FERDINAND GERHARD (Nov. 12, 1858–Apr. 24, 1919), chemist, sugar technologist, and author, was born in Brooklyn, N. Y., the son of Ernst Gustav and Anna Cæcilie (Albers) Wiechmann, both of German ancestry. After attending the Brooklyn schools, he studied chemistry under C. F. Chandler [q.v.] at the Columbia School of Mines, from which he received the degree of Ph.B. (1881) and Ph.D. (1882). The following year he spent in the study of chemistry at the University of Berlin. Upon his return to America he accepted a position as private assistant to Dr. Chandler and instructor in chemistry in the Columbia School of Mines (1884–97). On Mar. 26, 1885, he was married to Marie Helen Damrosch, daughter of Leopold Damrosch [q.v.]. From 1883 to 1885 he acted as chemist for the Brooklyn Sugar Refining Company and then for six months with the Havemeyer Refining Company of Green Point. During the years from 1887 to 1909, as chief chemist for the Havemeyer and Elder Sugar Refining Company of Brooklyn, N. Y. (later the American Sugar Refining Company), he devoted much attention to improving methods of sampling, analyzing, and making sugar. He was among the first in America to propose the use of kieselguhr (patent no. 343,287) as a filter aid in the clarification of sugar solutions. His well-known *Sugar Analysis* (1890) for several decades was the leading treatise upon the subject. He resigned his position with the American Sugar Refining Company in 1909 in order to devote himself to private consulting practice. At this time he took out a series of patents for a vegetable albumin plastic called "protal." In 1911 he was expert and consultant for the Gramercy Refinery of the Colonial Sugars Company in Louisiana. He became interested in the dehydration of sugar-beet cossettes about 1915 and published numerous articles upon the economic advantages of the use of dehydrated cossettes in beet sugar manufacture. From 1918 until his death in 1919 he was chief chemist of the Warner Sugar Refining Company at Edgewater, N. J.

In addition to his *Sugar Analysis*, Wiechmann published *Lecture Notes on Theoretical Chemistry* (1893), *Chemistry—Its Evolution and Achievements* (1899), and *Notes on Electrochemistry* (1906). Under the pen name of Forest Monroe he published a novel, *Maid of Montauk* (1902). He was also a contributor of many articles to chemical and technological journals. He rendered distinguished services for many years as secretary of the International Commission on Uniform Methods of Sugar Analysis at its Vienna, Paris, Berlin, and New York meetings. An accomplished linguist, he officiated as interpreter at international congresses of chemistry, where his kindly, courteous manner won him a host of friends.

[*Who's Who in America*, 1918–19; J. M. Cattell, *Am. Men of Sci.* (1910); *La. Planter and Sugar Manufacturer*, May 10, 1919; *Facts about Sugar*, May 3, 1919; death notices in *N. Y. Times*, Apr. 25, and *N. Y. Tribune*, Apr. 26, 1919.]   C. A. B—e.

WIGFALL, LOUIS TREZEVANT (Apr. 21, 1816–Feb. 18, 1874), senator from Texas, Confederate brigadier-general and senator, was born near Edgefield, S. C., the son of Levi Durand Wigfall, a planter, and Eliza (Thompson) Wigfall. He was the great-grandson of Levi Durand, an Anglican clergyman who emigrated to South Carolina early in the eighteenth century. He attended the University of Virginia the session of 1834–35 and in 1837 graduated from South Carolina College, now the University of South Carolina. Admitted to the bar in 1839, he was soon in bitter political feud, killing young Thomas Bird, and receiving and inflicting a wound in a duel with Preston Smith Brooks [q.v.]. He favored the secession of South Carolina in 1844 in protest against the protective tariff and defeat of the Texas annexation treaty. Meantime he married Charlotte Maria Cross, the daughter of George Warren Cross of Charleston. Three of their five children reached maturity. Removing to Texas Wigfall settled at Marshall in 1848. Early in the crisis of 1849–50 he again declared for separation from the North, hoping that South Carolina would strike the blow necessary to unite the South. As a member of the House of Representatives of Texas in 1850, he led the unsuccessful opposition to the cession of the disputed Santa Fé Territory. In 1857 he was elected to the state Senate, where he became the leader of the "Southern-rights" Democrats and was chosen to the federal Senate in December 1859 over the opposition led by his bitter enemy, Sam Houston.

In the Senate he contended that it was the duty of the federal government to protect slave property in the territories. He supported Breckinridge in 1860, justifying secession upon the compact theory, upon the reservation of this right by three states, and upon international law affecting treaties (*Speech . . . Delivered at Tyler, Smith County, Tex., Sept. 3, 1860,* 1860). He was one of the authors of the Southern address signed Dec. 14, 1860, urging secession and organization of the confederacy (Dunbar Rowland, *Jefferson Davis, Constitutionalist,* 1923, VIII, 460–61). By refraining from voting, Wigfall and five other Southerners enabled the Republicans on Jan. 16, 1861, to deal the death blow to "Crittenden's compromise." As the turbulent session drew to a close he challenged: "We have dissolved the Union; mend it if you can; cement it with blood . . ." (*Congressional Globe,* 36 Cong., 2 Sess., p. 1373, col. 2). The Senate at times went into uproar over his caustic language. He was a ready and commanding speaker, erect and powerful in physique, featured by "a straight, broad brow, . . . a mouth coarse and grim, yet full of power, a square jaw . . . eyes of wonderful depth and light, . . . flashing, fierce, yet calm . . ." (W. H. Russell, *My Diary North and South,* 1863, I, p. 154). On hearing Lincoln's inaugural he predicted war and urged that the Confederacy take the forts, Sumter and Pickens, before reinforcements could reach them. He prolonged his stay in the Senate until Mar. 23, remaining in the counsels of the enemy as a sort of confidential adviser to the Confederacy. Arriving in Charleston, his spectacular visit to Fort Sumter during the bombardment in order to demand its surrender advertised him as a military hero. He became a brigadier-general in the army and was placed in command of the troops in Virginia, known as "The Texas Brigade."

He resigned on Feb. 18, 1862, to accept a seat in the Confederate States Senate.

Advocating strong military measures as necessary to success, he supported conscription and other legislation designed to strengthen the army. He upheld the power of impressment and ably defended the authority of Congress to suspend the writ of *habeas corpus* unimpeded by action of the state governments (*Sentinel,* Richmond, June 14, 1864). Although a latitudinarian with reference to military powers, he adhered strictly to state sovereignty in regard to citizenship and the Confederate judiciary—opposing a Confederate supreme court with appellate jurisdiction over state courts. He early became bitter over President Davis' conduct of the war. He censured him for rejecting Joseph E. Johnston's proposals to concentrate for an offensive in the fall of 1861, and for the defense of Richmond in the spring of 1862. He attributed the loss of Vicksburg to Davis' malignant mismanagement and regretted that Johnston had not been allowed to unite the forces of the West, destroy the enemy, and reclaim the Mississippi Valley. "But the pig-headed perverseness of Davis willed it otherwise" (Wigfall to C. C. Clay, Aug. 13, 1863, Clay Collection). He proposed that the chief executive be deprived of his power as commander-in-chief, and that this power be vested in an officer appointed and removable by the president and Senate (Wigfall to J. H. Hammond, April ?, 1864, Hammond Papers). Bitterly denouncing the removal of Johnston from command, he led the movement that finally made Lee general-in-chief of all the Confederate armies. He was a leader of the Congressional opposition to the president, firing his hearers "with the electrical passion that would blaze in his seamed fierce face . . ." (E. A. Pollard, *Life of Jefferson Davis,* 1869, pp. 419). He entertained an exalted opinion of his own grasp of military science, which made the clash between him and Davis inevitable. After the war he escaped from Galveston to England. He returned to the United States in 1872 and reëstablished residence in Baltimore, Md., with his daughter. Desiring to resume life in Texas, he went to Galveston in January 1874 and died there.

[Dienst Coll., Univ. of Texas, Austin, Tex.; Clay Coll., Duke Univ., Durham, N. C., Johnston Coll., Huntington Lib., San Marino, Cal.; Hammond Papers, Lib. of Cong.; L. W. Wright, *A Southern Girl in '61* (1905); J. T. Trezevant, *The Trezevant Family* (1914); *Ann. Report Am. Hist. Asso. . . . 1929* (1930); *War of the Rebellion: Official Records (Army),* 1 ser., I, V, LIII; *Galveston News,* Sept. 21, 1864, Feb. 19, 1874; *News and Courier* (Charleston, S. C.), Feb. 23, 1874.]   C. W. I.

WIGGER, WINAND MICHAEL (Dec. 9, 1841–Jan. 5, 1901)

WIGGER, WINAND MICHAEL (Dec. 9, 1841–Jan. 5, 1901), third Roman Catholic bishop of Newark, N. J., was born in New York City, the son of John Joseph and Elizabeth (Strucke) Wigger, successful immigrants from Westphalia. He was educated in the parochial school of St. Francis of Assisi, at the College of St. Francis Xavier, and at St. John's College, Fordham (A.B., 1860). Refused admission to the diocesan seminary of New York by Vicar General William Starrs on the score of poor health, Wigger appealed to Bishop James Roosevelt Bayley [q.v.] of Newark, who enrolled him in the Seton Hall Seminary at South Orange and later in the Lazarist's Collegio Brignole-Sale in Genoa, where he was ordained a priest (June 10, 1865). In addition to theological lore, he acquired a fluent knowledge of French and Italian, studied music, and gained considerable physical vigor. After a brief term in the University of the Sapienza, Rome, from which he later received a doctorate in divinity (1869), he returned to America (1866). A curate at St. Patrick's Cathedral in Newark, he profited under the guidance of the learned Msgr. George Doane, and displayed a courageous, straightforward character, a loving interest in the poor, and considerable tact. In 1869 he was appointed to the pastorate of St. Vincent's Church in Madison, N. J.; he later reorganized the finances of St. John's Church in Orange, which struggled with a heavy indebtedness, and then was assigned an easy parish in healthful Summit (1874–76), after which he returned to Madison. In 1880, when Bishop Michael Corrigan [q.v.] was translated to New York, he was named bishop of Newark, though as a German without political finesse his selection had seemed doubtful. Consecrated by Corrigan (Oct. 18, 1881), he soon convinced some of the Irish priests and laity, who resented a German ordinary, that he was honest, affable, and judicious. For the sake of his health, he resided with the faculty of Seton Hall College.

A leader in the Third Plenary Council of Baltimore (1884), he took a decided stand in support of Christian education, parochial schools, and the relief of Catholic immigrants, especially Germans and Italians for whom little had been done. As president of the New York branch of Peter Paul Cahensly's St. Raphael's Society, he established St. Leo's House at the Battery for the care of German arrivals (1889). A participant from 1885 in the annual conventions of the Priester-Verein, he was a friend of Fathers George Bornemann, H. Mühlsiepen, vicar-general of St. Louis, and P. J. Shroeder of the Catholic University in Washington, an intimate friend of Cahensly. Like many other German leaders, these men were vitally interested in national bishops, racial parishes, parochial schools which would preserve both faith and mother tongue, and greater recognition of German numbers and leadership in appointments to positions of consequence in the Church. While Wigger was sympathetic, he did not go the whole distance. Yet he refused to cast aside his German friends when they were misrepresented and attacked by some of the Catholic journals, and when he drew his share of fire his critics learned that the full-bearded German lacked neither courage nor moral stamina. Attached to his diocese, Wigger refused an appointment to the archepiscopal see of Milwaukee (1890), but building churches, organizing parishes, erecting schools, constructing a cathedral, and ministering to the lax Italian immigrants kept him on edge, despite pleasant journeys to the Holy Land and Europe. Subject to pulmonary diseases, he died of a third attack of pneumonia. While not a great figure, he was a courageous prelate whom Bishop James A. McFaul [q.v.] could conscientiously eulogize at his obsequies.

[C. G. Herbermann in U. S. Cath. Hist. Soc., Hist. Records and Studies, Aug. 1901; F. J. Zwierlein, The Life and Letters of Bishop McQuaid, vol. II (1926); "The 'Leo House' for Immigrants," Records Am. Cath. Hist. Soc. of Phila., Dec. 1905; New-Yorker Staats-Zeitung, Jan. 13, 1901; Diocesan Reg. of Newark; and Newark Daily Advertiser, Jan. 4–10, 1901.]

R.J.P.

WIGGIN, JAMES HENRY (May 14, 1836–Nov. 3, 1900)

WIGGIN, JAMES HENRY (May 14, 1836–Nov. 3, 1900), Unitarian clergyman, editor, the son of James Simon Wiggin and Sarah Elizabeth (Robinson) Wiggin, belonged to an old New England family descended from Thomas Wiggin who came to Massachusetts in 1631. James Henry was born in Boston, where the elder James in partnership with his father-in-law, Simon W. Robinson, conducted a prosperous shipping business. The boy attended various schools and in 1850 went on a year's voyage to Malacca Straits and Java in a sailing vessel belonging to his father's firm. After studying for a time in Tufts College at Medford, Mass., at the age of twenty-one he entered the Meadville Theological School. He was graduated in 1861 and was ordained to the Unitarian ministry in the following year. On Nov. 21, 1864, he married Laura Emma Newman of Brattleboro, Vt. He held various Unitarian pastorates in Massachusetts: at Montague, 1861–63; at Lawrence, 1864–65; at Marblehead, 1865–67; at Medfield, 1867–73; at Marlboro, 1873–75. In the latter year he moved to New York City to become editor of a weekly, the Liberal Christian, but he never felt entirely comfortable outside the radius of Boston and in 1876 returned to that city, where for a short period he edited the *Dorchester Beacon,* a suburban newspaper. Until 1881 he occasionally supplied vacant pulpits, but by that date he had become so definitely an agnostic that he felt it his duty to sever all connection with the ministry.

Henceforth he devoted his energy mainly to musical and dramatic criticism, the preparing of indexes, and the revising of books for the press. He translated two volumes in the Little, Brown & Company series of Dumas' works, and he was connected for some years with the Harvard University Press. In 1885 he was asked by Mary Baker Eddy [*q.v.*] to assist in the preparation of the sixteenth edition of *Science and Health,* in the course of which task he revised the entire book, much simplifying Mrs. Eddy's impassioned but obscure style. One chapter wholly written by him, entitled "Wayside Hints," was included in a number of subsequent editions, though ultimately deleted. The great popularity of *Science and Health* dated from his revision. He was also employed by Mrs. Eddy to answer, under the *nom de plume* "Phare Pleigh," a hostile criticism by the Rev. H. B. Heacock of California. From 1887 to 1889 he was an unofficial editor of the *Christian Science Journal.* In 1890 he assisted in the preparation of a new revised edition of *Science and Health,* and in 1891 he revised the first draft of Mrs. Eddy's *Retrospection and Introspection.* His relations with her, however, gradually became more difficult, once the novelty of their strange partnership had worn off, and eventually, during 1891, she accused him of falling under the influence of "Malicious Animal Magnetism," after which they separated. His own account of their relationship was published posthumously in the New York *World,* Nov. 4 and 5, 1906.

He was a devoted theatre-goer and had many friends among the actors, including Sol Smith Russell, Horace Lewis, William Warren, Mrs. John Drew, and Adelaide Phillips. A man of great bulk and much geniality, sybaritic, skeptical, and witty, he was a delightful figure on the streets of Boston in the last days of its cultural glory. Sol Smith Russell is reported to have said that he could as soon think of Boston without the Common as without James Henry Wiggin.

[Information from a son, Albert H. Wiggin, New York City, and from the Am. Unitarian Asso.; E. S. Bates and J. V. Dittemore, *Mary Baker Eddy* (1932); F. C. Springer, *According to the Flesh* (1930); E. F. Dakin, *Mrs. Eddy* (1929); Georgine Milmine, *The Life of Mary Baker G. Eddy* (1909); J. H. Wiggin, *1813–*

Charles E. Wiggin–1888 (n.d.), pp. 135–37; *Christian Reg.,* Nov. 15, 1900; *Boston Transcript,* Nov. 3, 1900.]
                 E. S. B.

WIGGIN, KATE DOUGLAS (Sept. 28, 1856–Aug. 24, 1923), author, pioneer kindergarten worker, was born in Philadelphia, Pa., the daughter of Helen Elizabeth (Dyer) and Robert Noah Smith, both of New England ancestry. Her father, a lawyer, died when she was a child, and a few years later her mother married a physician of Hollis, Me. With her sister and a half-brother, she spent a happy and healthy childhood in Hollis, where she bought in later life the farmhouse, "Quillcote," in which most of her writing was done. She was taught at home by her stepfather for a time, and then attended the district school and a series of private schools. When she was about seventeen the family moved to Santa Barbara, Cal.; there a few years later her stepfather died. In 1877 she went to Los Angeles and entered the first class in kindergarten training conducted by Emma J. C. Marwedel [*q.v.*]. A year later she was selected to organize in San Francisco the Silver Street Kindergarten, the first free kindergarten west of the Rocky Mountains. In connection with this is the California Kindergarten Training School, which she established in 1880 with her sister, Nora Archibald Smith (*c.* 1859–1934), her constant collaborator both in teaching and in the writing of kindergarten literature. Among the fifteen books written or edited by the two sisters were *The Story Hour* (1890), *Children's Rights* (1892), and *The Republic of Childhood* (1895–96). Kate Douglas Smith's marriage in December 1881 to Samuel Bradley Wiggin, a Boston lawyer, ended her daily work at the Silver Street Kindergarten, but her interest in it and in the training school never lapsed; even after moving to New York (1884–85), she visited them regularly, as she did all other important kindergarten centers in the country. Her first mature literary work, *The Story of Patsy* (1883), was written and printed by her only to raise money for kindergarten work, and this and the well-known *Birds' Christmas Carol* (1887) were published in the regular manner only after their success in the first form induced her to enter the field of authorship definitely. Out of the same collection of experiences grew *Timothy's Quest* (1890) and *Polly Oliver's Problem* (1893), a story for girls.

After the sudden death of her husband in 1889, she made her first visit to Europe. This first experience of foreign travel resulted in three popular books—*A Cathedral Courtship* (1893), *Penelope's Progress* (1898), and *Penelope's*

Irish Experiences (1901), all exhibiting the frank and simple biographical method by which the impact of the older civilizations on an attractive, enthusiastic, and witty young American woman was interpreted to her own country and to England by a marked example of this type. On this journey and others she made acquaintances and friends without number in the literary and social world, where she became, as in New York later, and in the Maine village of her adoption, a well-known and well-loved figure. Her charm and social gifts were as marked as her talent, and her keen interest in music and the stage added a long list of artists in these fields to her friends in her own profession. Between 1890 and 1895 she was occupied chiefly with public readings, and with the writing of stories and articles for magazines. She was married on Mar. 30, 1895, to George Christopher Riggs, an American with business connections in Scotland and Ireland, and until her death in 1923 lived in New York City and Hollis, Me., with annual trips of about three months to the British Isles.

In 1903 appeared *Rebecca of Sunnybrook Farm*, one of the most widely sold books of its day. It reveals the autobiographical character of her work as a whole, which never exhibited imaginative flights nor aimed at any constructive picture of life, nor essayed the human comedy, as such, from any broad angle of theory or observation. In it and *Polly Oliver's Problem* there appear the same fresh, natural simplicity of style, the same lack of interest in plot as such, the same faithful transcription of a warmhearted, impulsive nature dramatizing its own objective experiences, with a peculiarly feminine quality of intelligence and wit. It is to be doubted, however, if the history of Rebecca, characterized by Thomas Bailey Aldrich as "the nicest child in American literature," equals *The Birds' Christmas Carol* as an example of the author's best and most characteristic capacities. The brevity of the latter, better suited to her lack of technical structural skill, its wider range of characterization, broader humor, and above all, the touch of pathos which links it to the Dickens tradition that underlies her style, make it the work which Time will most surely spare. In 1917 her collected works were issued in nine volumes; in 1923 *My Garden of Memory: An Autobiography* was published. She died in 1923 at Harrow, England.

[In addition to *My Garden of Memory* (1923), sources include *Who's Who in America*, 1922–23; Nora A. Smith, *Kate Douglas Wiggin As Her Sister Knew Her* (1925), from which the date of birth is taken; Emma S. Echols, in *Polly Oliver's Problem* (1896), Riverside Lit. ed.; *Current Opinion*, Jan. 1924; obituary in *N. Y. Times*, Aug. 25, 1923; correspondence with Nora A. Smith; personal acquaintance. For Nora A. Smith, see *Who's Who in America*, 1932–33, and obituary in *N. Y. Times*, Feb. 2, 1934.]

J—e. D. B.

WIGGINS, CARLETON (Mar. 4, 1848–June 11, 1932), landscape and animal painter, the son of Guy Carleton and Adelaide (Ludlum) Wiggins, was born at Turner, Orange County, N. Y. He was educated in the public schools of Brooklyn, N. Y., and studied art at the National Academy of Design (1870) and under George Inness [*q.v.*]. He exhibited his first picture at the National Academy in 1870. On Oct. 19, 1872, he was married to Mary Clucas of Brooklyn, by whom he had two sons and two daughters. After a year in France (1880–81) he took a studio in New York. His home was in Brooklyn, but he had a summer home at Old Lyme, Conn., where he found many of his best subjects. He was a charter member of the Lyme Art Association. From 1894 onward he was the recipient of many honors and awards; he was elected an Academician in 1906. Among his pictures in public collections and galleries are "A Young Holstein Bull," in the Metropolitan Museum of Art, New York; "The Plow Horse," in the Lotos Club, New York; "The Wanderers," in the Hamilton Club, Brooklyn, N. Y.; and "Evening after a Shower" and "The Pasture Lot," in the National Gallery of Art, Washington, D. C. Other well-known pictures are "On the Road" (1879), "September Day" (1880), "Hillside near Fontainebleau" (1882), "October Morning" (1883), "Gathering Seaweed," "September Harvest" (1884), "Summer Morning" (1885), "Three-year-old Heifer," and "Landscape near Meudon" (1886).

According to Samuel Isham [*q.v.*], Wiggins' work "will stand in any company of his contemporaries"; the same critic alludes to "the gravity of Wiggins, the broad sweeping lines of whose landscapes call up vague memories of men like old Crome or some of their Dutch prototypes" (*post*, pp. 447–48). Wiggins died at Old Lyme, Conn. One of his sons, Guy Carleton Wiggins, also became a painter.

[Sources include *Who's Who in America*, 1930–31; Samuel Isham, *The Hist. of Am. Painting* (1905); J. D. Champlin, Jr., and C. C. Perkins, *Cyc. of Painters and Painting* (4 vols., 1885–87); Helen L. Earle, *Biog. Sketches of Am. Artists* (1915); obituary in *N. Y. Times*, June 13, 1932; information from Guy Carleton Wiggins, Lyme, Conn. Wiggins' full name was John Carleton.]

W. H. D.

WIGGLESWORTH, EDWARD (*c.* 1693–Jan. 16, 1765), educator, theologian, was born in Malden, Mass., son of the poet Michael Wigglesworth [*q.v.*] and his third wife, Sybil (Sparhawk) Avery. Edward attended the Boston

Latin School, where he was an usher, and graduated from Harvard College in 1710. Taking up residence at the College, he continued his studies in divinity. Harvard's first great patron, Thomas Hollis, established a chair of divinity in 1721 and Wigglesworth was made the first Hollis Professor on Jan. 24, 1722. In 1724 he was elected to the Corporation of the college. He married Sarah, daughter of President John Leverett [q.v.], June 15, 1726. The Wigglesworths lived opposite the head of Holyoke Street, on the northerly side of Harvard Street, where Wigglesworth Hall now stands. Sarah died in 1727, and on Sept. 10, 1729, Edward married Rebecca Coolidge, by whom he had three sons and a daughter. In spite of the handicap of increasing deafness, he was constantly active in the pulpit, preaching in a "nervous and sufficiently animated style," and instructing young students in theology. In 1730 he was granted a doctorate in divinity by the University of Edinburgh.

When George Whitefield, the itinerant evangelist, came to Harvard in 1745, to find that "Tutors neglect to pray with and examine the Heart of their Pupils," Wigglesworth was the College's stoutest defender. In *A Letter to the Reverend Mr. George Whitefield* (1745), he openly accused Whitefield of being "an uncharitable, censorious, and slanderous man" (p. 22) and urged him to a public apology. By this defense and his later publication, *Some Distinguishing Characters of the Extraordinary and Ordinary Ministers of the Church of Christ* (1754), he became a leader among the anti-evangelical clergy. Growing reputation brought him in 1761 the offer of the Yale rectorship, which he declined. He died some four years later and was given impressive funeral ceremonies in the College Chapel, with a notable sermon by Nathaniel Appleton and a Latin oration by one of his senior students. His successor in the Hollis Professorship was his son Edward [q.v.].

In addition to the works already mentioned, Wigglesworth published several sermons. In *A Seasonable Caveat against Believing Every Spirit* (1735) and *Some Evidences of the Divine Inspiration of the Scriptures of the Old Testament* (1755), he denied the peculiar gift of God to evangelists in general and Whitefield in particular. A sermon on the death of Hollis, *The Blessedness of the Dead Who Die in the Lord* (1731), and an anti-papal sermon, *Some Thoughts upon the Spirit of Infallibility Claimed by the Church of Rome* (1757) deserve mention because of their cogent style. A last group comprises three sermons in the field of Arminian-Calvinistic controversy: In *A Discourse Concerning the Duration of the Punishment of the Wicked* (1729) Wigglesworth showed himself to be an uncompromising Calvinist. Observable in the second of these three (*An Enquiry into the Truth of the Imputation of the Guilt of Adam's First Sin*, 1738) is the gradual breakdown of unconditional Calvinism and a new emphasis on the independence of the will as opposed to strict accounting to God for the original sin. Here Wigglesworth mirrors the trend of the times. More especially does he show the split between conditional Arminianism, which provides salvation to those men redeemed by faith, and unconditional Calvinism in *The Doctrine of Reprobation Briefly Considered* (1763). He considered the Sub- and Supralapsarian aspects of the older doctrine: the Sublapsarians held that God's decree with respect to original sin was antecedent to His foreknowledge, while the Supralapsarians placed His judgment afterwards. In reply to both points of doctrine Wigglesworth, voicing distinct Arminian sentiments, answered that all election and foreordination are conditional, and that no man is "under irresistible motions, either to good or evil." From the point of view of theological doctrine, Wigglesworth's gradual compromise heralds the advent of Unitarianism.

[Nathaniel Appleton, *A Faithful and Wise Servant Had in Honour . . . A Discourse Occasioned by the . . . Death of the Rev. Edward Wigglesworth* (1765), with a short biog. account appended; Charles Chauncy, "A Sketch of Eminent Men in New England," *Mass. Hist. Soc. Colls.*, 1 ser. X (1809); J. B. Felt, *Ecclesiastical Hist. of New England* (1862); F. H. Foster, *A Genetic Hist. of the New England Theology* (1907); W. B. Sprague, *Annals Am. Pulpit*, vol. I (1857); L. R. Paige, *Hist. of Cambridge, Mass.* (1877), and *Supp. and Index* (1930), by M. I. Gazzaldi; *Col. Soc. of Mass. Pubs.*, vols. XV, XVI (1925), XXXI (1935).]
E. H. D.

WIGGLESWORTH, EDWARD (Feb. 7, 1732–June 17, 1794), educator, theologian, was born in Cambridge, Mass., son of Edward [q.v.] and Rebecca (Coolidge) Wigglesworth and grandson of Michael Wigglesworth [q.v.]. He graduated from Harvard College in 1749 and remained there as resident scholar. In 1756 he became interested in raising funds for the new meeting-house for the First Parish, and was one of its heaviest subscribers. He was made tutor in the College in 1764. The next year, upon the death of his father he was appointed successor to the Hollis Professorship of Divinity. On his induction, June 16, 1765, the Corporation sent for him to make sure of his Divinity principles. He was careful to safeguard his orthodoxy by keeping out of all controversy, except for a single sermon against Popery, and attending exclusively to matters of academic life and instruction.

In October 1765 he married Margaret Hill of Boston, by whom he had three daughters and two sons. She died in 1776; on Jan. 6, 1778, he married Dorothy Sparhawk, who died in 1782; and on Oct. 20, 1785, he married as his third wife Sarah Wigglesworth. He was responsible for the raising of annuities to provide for the widows of ministers and professors, and, although primarily a churchman, he was much interested in civil affairs. His *Calculations on American Population* (1775) discussed the steady increase of the Colonies' population, owing, according to Wigglesworth, to simple living conditions and early marriage. Of the 3,250,000 inhabitants in 1775, he noted, more than 500,000 were slaves—"to the disgrace of America" (p. 12). This pamphlet made some striking prophesies as to the increase of population; he calculated that the "British Americans," as he called them, would double their number every twenty-five years, so that at the end of the twentieth century the population would have mounted to nearly one and a half billion.

During the Revolution, Wigglesworth was among those who held out hopes for reconciliation until the end. In a period of brilliant pulpit patriotism, he was uncommonly silent. Throughout the war, he was closely concerned with College affairs. Appointed a fellow in 1779, he was acting president in 1780, in the interval between the death of Samuel Langdon and the succession of Joseph Willard. Paralysis forced him to resign all public and private offices in 1791. The Overseers of the College granted him a large annuity and he became a professor emeritus. He died after a long illness.

Wigglesworth was a man of many friends. When in 1786 fuel was scarce at the University, he opened his doors to John Quincy Adams as a "free boarder" for the winter. President Quincy later said of him (*post*, II, 261) that he had "an equal reputation for learning, fidelity, and the catholic spirit." With the exception of his pamphlet on population, a Dudleian lecture and a funeral sermon are all that survive of his utterances. The lecture, *The Authority of Tradition Considered* (1778), is vigorously anti-Roman; discussing apostolic succession, he indicates Popery as having for the foundation of all its distinguishing tenets *"tradition, or traditive* interpretations of Scripture." The funeral sermon *The Hope of Immortality* (1779), was delivered on the death of John Winthrop, Hollis Professor of Mathematics, and stressed chiefly

the reward for the good life in the life to come. Wigglesworth lacked the versatility of knowledge that his father and grandfather possessed, but his service as an educator and citizen make him worthy of memory.

[L. R. Paige, *Hist. of Cambridge, Mass.* (1877), with *Supp. and Index* (1930) by M. I. Gazzaldi; Josiah Quincy, *The Hist. of Harvard Univ.* (1860); *Proc. Mass. Hist. Soc.*, 2 ser. XVI (1903); *Col. Soc. of Mass. Pubs.*, vols. XV, XVI (1925), XXXI (1930).]

E. H. D.

WIGGLESWORTH, EDWARD (Dec. 30, 1840–Jan. 23, 1896), dermatologist, was born in Boston, Mass., the son of Edward and Henrietta May (Goddard) Wigglesworth, daughter of Nathaniel Goddard. The family, long prominent in New England, descended from Edward Wigglesworth, who came to America from Yorkshire, England, in 1638. His son, Michael [*q.v.*], was graduated by Harvard College in 1651; subsequently every male Wigglesworth for six generations became an alumnus of Harvard. After a preliminary education in the Boston Latin School, Edward was graduated by Harvard College in the class of 1861. He served for nine months in the Civil War, first with the United States Sanitary Commission, later as a private in the 45th Massachusetts Voluntary Militia and, finally, as a voluntary surgeon with the Army of the Potomac. During the same period he attended the lectures at the Harvard Medical School and was graduated, with the degree of M.D., in 1865. Having independent means, he was able to study dermatology under the best teachers in Europe from 1865 to 1870. Returning home, he began the practice of his specialty, being one of the first physicians in Boston to do so. At his own expense he inaugurated and maintained the Boston Dispensary for Skin Diseases from 1872 to 1877. A group of 179 models of dermatological lesions, duplicates from the Hospital St. Louis collections in Paris, and an extensive library were maintained by Wigglesworth for the use of physicians; the models were ultimately given to the Harvard Medical School and his books to the Boston Medical Library. He served as head of the department of diseases of the skin, Boston City Hospital, for many years and as an instructor in dermatology at the Harvard Medical School.

Although never in very good health, Wigglesworth was an active member of his profession. Many papers on dermatology were contributed by him to local and national societies. He was one of the collaborators of the *Archives of Dermatology*, a quarterly journal of skin and venereal diseases, when it was founded in 1874, and he served as president of the American Dermatological Association in 1885. Other interests centered around the Boston Medical Library, the raising of funds for rebuilding the Harvard Medical School, the health department of the American Social Science Association, and the Colonial Society of Massachusetts. He was active in introducing a law requiring the registration of physicians in Massachusetts (an effort to eliminate quacks), started the Boston *Medical Register,* and attempted, prematurely, to popularize the metric system. So ardent was his desire to see a system of metrics adopted that he spent three years and a small fortune on this project without winning public approval. Although he might have led a life of leisure, he chose one continually devoted to the welfare of others. His charities were wide-spread. Quiet and scholarly, but with a lively wit, Wigglesworth was much beloved by his contemporaries. He was married, on Apr. 4, 1882, to Mrs. Sarah (Willard) Frothingham of New York City. Of three children, a son became director of the Museum of Natural History in Boston.

[H. P. Quincy, memoir in *Colonial Soc. of Mass. Pubs.,* vol. III (1900); *Boston Medic. and Surgical Jour.,* Jan. 30, Apr. 23, 1896; letters and manuscripts in Boston Medical Library; P. A. Morrow, sketch of Wigglesworth in H. A. Kelly and W. L. Burrage, *Am. Medic. Biog.* (1920), *Harvard Coll. Class of 1861, Sixth Report* (1902); bibliography of works, *Ibid., Fifth Report* (1892); *Boston Evening Transcript,* Jan. 23, 1896; information from the Wigglesworth family.]

H. R. V.

WIGGLESWORTH, MICHAEL (Oct. 18, 1631–May 27, 1705), minister, author, was born in England, probably in Yorkshire, the son of Edward and Esther (?) Wigglesworth, and came to Massachusetts Bay with his Puritan parents in 1638. After a few weeks at Charlestown they went to New Haven, where Michael was sent to school with Ezekiel Cheever [q.v.]. His education was interrupted in order that he might help his lame father at home, but he was too frail to be of use, returned to school, and completed his preparation for Harvard. He graduated B.A. in 1651, continued his studies, and was appointed fellow and tutor from 1652 to 1654. On May 18, 1655, he married Mary Reyner of Rowley. He began preaching occasionally at least as early as 1653, and in 1654 or 1655 had an invitation to settle as minister at Malden. After long consideration and a period of preaching in Malden without ordination he was given, in August 1656, a letter of dismission from the Cambridge church and presumably was ordained in Malden soon afterward. Morbidly conscious of his shortcomings, he often thought of giving up his ministry, particularly because from 1657 to 1686 ill health prevented him from performing his full duty in the church. He studied and practised medicine, and also found time to write. His most noted work, *The Day of Doom,* a long poem in ballad meter, was printed in 1662. Almost eighteen hundred copies sold within a year—an extraordinary number in relation to the population at the time. In 1663 Wigglesworth went to Bermuda for about seven months, but gained little in health. By 1686, however, he seems to have been better, and in that year he preached the Election Sermon, and in 1696, the Artillery Election Sermon. It is probable that in 1684 he had been asked to consider taking the presidency at Harvard, and had declined because of his health. He was a fellow of the college from 1697 until his death.

His first wife died in 1659. By her, he had one daughter. In 1679 he married Martha Mudge, in spite of protests from Increase Mather and others on the grounds that she was of lower social rank than he, and was not a church-member. Six children were born of this marriage. Martha Wigglesworth died in 1690 and on June 23, 1691, Michael married Sybil (Sparhawk) Avery, a widow, who outlived him by three years. Their one child, Edward [q.v.], became the first Hollis Professor at Harvard.

Tormented as he was by sickness, Wigglesworth, as physician, minister, and writer, won the love and respect of his contemporaries. Intensely conscientious, ardently religious, and restlessly seeking always to perfect himself in holiness, he wrote verse as a means of serving God, and *The Day of Doom,* like his other works, was designed primarily for edification. Its picture of the judgment day has occasional dramatic flashes and in a few passages hints at a real if undeveloped poetic power. For the most part it is versified theology, obviously calculated to appeal to untutored readers. The ballad meter, which seems inappropriate to the theme, had at least the merit of being familiar to colonists who would have been unlikely to respond to more subtle measures. In a few lines of the poem itself, however, and certainly in bits of his autobiographic writing, Wigglesworth shows imagination and poetic sensitiveness, and it is probable that in a more cultured environment and less obsessed by zeal for pious instruction, he might have achieved some genuine poetry. He had definite artistic desires, but his surroundings and his belief that he must teach as he wrote stifled his powers. Whatever its defects, *The Day of Doom* had great and lasting popularity. The edition of Cambridge, 1701, was labeled as the fifth. Presumably, then, there were four editions in Massachusetts before 1701; certainly there were English editions in 1666 and 1673. It was reissued in 1711, 1715, 1751, 1774, 1777, 1811, 1828, 1867, and 1929, and is said to have been printed and sold as a ballad sheet in colonial New England. Much has been said of the inhumanly cruel theology displayed in the book, but compared with the doctrines held by others, Puritans and non-Puritans, in his time, Wigglesworth's are in no way exceptional; the presentation of them in dramatic form has given them unenviable notoriety. Another example of edificatory verse, *Meat out of the Eater or Meditations Concerning the Necessity, End, and Usefulness of Afflictions Unto Gods Children,* was printed in 1669, had a fourth edition in 1689, and at least two later printings; "God's Controversy with New-England," first printed in *Proceedings of the Massachusetts Historical Society* (1 ser., XII, 1873), is competent versifying about the sins of the colonists. Other bits of his writing have been printed since his death and are listed in Sibley's bibliography.

[The New Eng. Hist. Geneal. Soc. owns sermon notes by Wigglesworth; a book of exercises kept by him in college, containing his Commencement part and two orations on eloquence; as well as two volumes of his manuscript notes, mostly in shorthand. The Mass. Hist. Soc. owns a manuscript book of autobiographic notes and records of religious experiences. The best biography is J. W. Dean, *Memoir of Rev. Michael Wigglesworth* (2nd ed., 1871), which contains Wigglesworth's account of his early years and extracts from his otherwise unpublished work, lists his library, and supplies a documented narrative of his life. J. L. Sibley, *Biog. Sketches of Grads. of Harvard Univ.* (1873), I, 259–86, contains a good brief biography, a bibliography, and a list of authorities on Wigglesworth. These two books supply references to the other sources of information. The best study of Wigglesworth as a writer is F. O. Matthiessen, "Michael Wigglesworth, A Puritan Artist," *New Eng. Quart.* (Oct. 1928). See also K. B. Murdock, "Introduction," in the 1929 edition of *The Day of Doom*; M. C. Tyler, *A Hist. of Am. Lit. during the Colonial Time* (1878), II, 23–35; and D. P. Corey, *The Hist. of Malden* (1899). On the bibliography of *The Day of Doom*, see S. A. Green, in *Proc. Mass. Hist. Soc.*, 2 ser. IX (1895); and M. B. Jones in *Proc. Am. Antiquarian Soc.*, n.s. XXXIX (1930).]   K. B. M.

WIGHT, FREDERICK COIT (Apr. 30, 1859–Dec. 23, 1933), musician, composer, was born in New London, Conn., the son of David and Nancy (Coit) Wight. His grandfather, John Wight, was a Scotch bandmaster of the Coldstream Guards of London who moved to Paris, where he played at the Opéra Comique and married a French opera singer, and then emigrated to America and settled in Providence, R. I. His father was prominent in New London for many years as an orchestra conductor and dancing master. After Wight had received his elementary education at the Coit Street School, his father decided that he would make a musician of him instead of allowing him to attend the

local high school. Accordingly, he laid out a schedule of six hours of music study daily, and in addition to his own teaching procured instruction for his son under such local musicians as Alfred H. Chappell, Frederick Sweetser, and Charles S. Elliott. For five years the boy journeyed once a week to Providence for lessons with David Wallace Reeves, a prominent band leader of the time. From Reeves he learned to compose for band, and received thorough instruction in harmony and composition. In addition to his studies he conducted an orchestra in New London and played the piano for his father's dancing school. In 1876 he enlisted in the 3rd Regiment of the Connecticut National Guard and became a member of its band. The organization attended the Centennial Exhibition at Philadelphia, marched in the Evacuation Parade in New York, and took part in President Harrison's inauguration in Washington. Wight was married on Oct. 29, 1885, to Ora Belle Brown, daughter of Dr. William Leonard Marcy Brown. There was one child, a daughter.

As a composer Wight was distinguished principally for his marches, the first of which was introduced by his teacher, D. W. Reeves, during a concert tour of New England. Many were written in honor of presidents of the United States—McKinley, Wilson, Coolidge, Harding, and others. During McKinley's administration Wight was a guest of honor at a concert of his compositions given in Washington for the benefit of those who had suffered from the loss of the *Maine*. Two of Wight's marches were included on the official program at the inauguration of Theodore Roosevelt. Of his one hundred and fifty compositions, the most ambitious was a comic opera, *A Venetian Romance,* produced at the Knickerbocker Theatre, New York, by the Frank Perley Opera Company in 1903; in revised form it was later presented at the Studebaker Theatre, Chicago, as *The Girl and the Bandit.* Another comic opera was *The Temple of Hymen.* In his last years Wight suffered from reduced finances and was aided by the New London Rotary Club, for whose weekly luncheons he played the piano. He was active until his last years. His last composition, written in 1930, was the "General Payne March," dedicated to Brigadier-General Morris B. Payne of the Connecticut National Guard.

[See W. W. Wight, *The Wights, A Record of Thomas Wight of Dedham* (1890); obituaries in *Day* (New London), Dec. 23, and *N. Y. Times* and *N. Y. Herald Tribune,* Dec. 24, 1933. The date of birth is from New London records.]   J. T. H.

WIGHT, PETER BONNETT (Aug. 1, 1838–Sept. 8, 1925), architect, was born in New York

City, the son of Amherst and Joanna G. (Sanderson) Wight, and a descendant of Thomas Wight who came to Dedham, Mass., in 1635. Peter was educated in the New York public schools and at the Free Academy, now the College of the City of New York, where he was graduated in 1855 with the degree of B.A. During his college course he read works on architecture and the writings of John Ruskin; he also specialized in drawing, in which he was always unusually proficient even for an architect. A postgraduate year spent in drawing and a year as a student draftsman in an architect's office completed his architectural training. In 1858, persuaded by a family friend, Josiah L. James, he went to Chicago and occupied space as an independent architect in the office of Carter & Bauer. He remodeled the Commercial College building, but work became scarce and in 1859 he returned to New York.

During the next three years he studied in the Astor Library, built a bank in Middletown, and a hospital for the insane in Binghamton. At the outbreak of the Civil War he devoted himself for six months to the study of military engineering and drill. In 1862 he was architect for the United States Sanitary Commission and he built the first field hospital for the government, in Washington; but his application for a commission in the army, indorsed by General Burnside, was denied. In 1862 he won his first and most important competition, and as a result, though an unknown youth, had the satisfaction of planning and constructing a building for the National Academy of Design. Its façades, beautifully proportioned and detailed, were in the Italian phase of the Gothic style, so passionately praised by Ruskin. The building stood at Fourth Avenue and Twenty-third Street, New York City. Subsequently, his plans were chosen for the Brooklyn Mercantile Library building and he was commissioned to design the Yale School of Fine Arts. From 1863 to 1868 he was associated in architectural practice with Russell Sturgis [q.v.].

The news of the great fire and an invitation from Asher Carter, his old office companion, led Wight to go to Chicago in December 1871. The firm of Carter, Drake & Wight was formed, which became Drake & Wight on the death, two years later, of Carter (see Wight's article on Asher Carter in the *Western Architect,* January 1925). A great deal of work was done in this office, commercial and domestic rather than monumental, and it became a training ground for many young architects, among them Daniel H. Burnham and John W. Root. Wight centered his activities on fire-proof construction, and

from 1881 to 1891 gave up the practice of architecture to devote himself to the development of terra-cotta structural tile. He claimed to have been the inventor and first user of the "grill foundation," *i.e.,* slabs composed of crossed iron rails imbedded in concrete, although John W. Root [q.v.] is generally regarded as the inventor. He resumed practice and did some not very important work in connection with the World's Columbian Exposition of 1893, but after 1895 devoted himself to the passage of a law in the state of Illinois requiring the examination, licensing, and registration of architects. This law, enacted in 1897, was the first of its kind in America. Wight was elected secretary and treasurer of the board of examiners created by this act, and held this position until he retired from professional activity in 1914. He contributed numerous articles to the *Architectural Record* and the *Inland Architect,* and was active in the work of the American Institute of Architects, serving as secretary in 1869–71, and as president and secretary on several occasions of the Chicago chapter of the Institute. He was married twice: first, Oct. 13, 1864, in New York, to Mary Frances Hoagland; second, Nov. 23, 1882, at Norwich, England, to Marion, daughter of William Olney. By his first wife he had two daughters. On his eightieth birthday he moved to Pasadena, Cal., where he died.

[Sources include, W. W. Wight, *The Wights* (1890); *Am. Architect,* Nov. 5, 1925; *Western Architect,* Oct. 1925; *Jour. Am. Institute of Architecture,* Oct. 1925; *Who's Who in America,* 1918–19; coll. of original drawings in Burnham Lib., Art Institute, Chicago; personal acquaintance. The name of Wight's second wife is spelled "Olney" in *The Wights,* and "Onley" in *Who's Who in America.*]   T. E. T.

WIGNELL, THOMAS (*c.* 1753–Feb. 21, 1803), comedian, theatrical manager, was the son of J. Wignell, an inferior actor in Garrick's company (Wood, *post,* and *The Thespian Dictionary,* London, 1802). He was apprenticed to the business of seal cutting, but abandoned it for his father's vocation. In the fall of 1774 he was sent out to join the American Company by his cousin, the actor Lewis Hallam [q.v.], who was then in England. On the day after his arrival, information was received that the Continental Congress had recommended the cessation of all public amusements. Consequently, without appearing on the American stage, he accompanied his fellow-actors to Jamaica, where he followed his profession for ten years. Apparently his first performance in America occurred on Nov. 21, 1785, when the company resumed its activities in New York.

Wignell was the best comedian seen in Amerisa up to that time, and he quickly became a favorite. Although his powers were limited, he was an actor of intelligence and taste. William Dunlap [*q.v.*], who knew him well, says: "His comedy was luxuriant in humour, but always faithful to his author. He was a comic actor, not a buffoon" (*post,* pp. 81–82). With his short, athletic figure, stooping shoulders, and bow legs, he was well qualified physically for low comedy, but he was also competent in high comedy, Joseph Surface in *The School for Scandal* being one of his most popular characters. He had aspirations toward membership in the firm of Hallam and Henry, the managers of the company, but John Henry [*q.v.*], a rival comedian, vigorously opposed his rise to power. When Wignell discovered that Hallam, though outwardly his friend, was also thwarting his aims, he resigned his position in the spring of 1791 and entered into partnership with Alexander Reinagle [*q.v.*], a prominent musician of Philadelphia, preparatory to forming an organization of his own. Arrangements were made for them to occupy a theatre about to be built in Chestnut Street, Philadelphia, and Wignell went to England to secure players. On his return in 1793, bringing with him the best group of actors America had yet seen, he found awaiting his occupancy the new Chestnut Street Theatre, which far surpassed in size and splendor every other house in the United States. After a delay caused by yellow fever, it was opened on Feb. 17, 1794. The first season was a distinguished one, the acting, music, and scenic effects all being superior to those of the old American Company, which was now centering its efforts on New York. To extend their domain, Wignell and Reinagle built a theatre in Baltimore in 1794, and there a preliminary season was annually conducted. In 1796 Wignell again went to England for reënforcements and engaged, among others, Ann Brunton Merry and Thomas Abthorpe Cooper [*qq.v.*]. The next several seasons at Philadelphia were the most brilliant of their time. In 1797 Wignell and Reinagle conducted a notable summer campaign in New York, but they lost heavily, and the experiment was not repeated. Summer tours, however, were made to other cities, including Washington, where Wignell opened the town's first theatre in 1800. But in spite of the continuous activity of the company, the directors were often in financial difficulties, partly because they heavily stressed the very expensive business of operatic production.

On Jan. 1, 1803, Wignell married Mrs. Merry, who had been a widow for some years. Seven weeks later he died of infection resulting from a blood-letting operation. He is said to have been about fifty years old (Ireland, *post,* I, 70). He was accorded an imposing funeral by his fellow-townsmen, who esteemed him as a generous and honorable man.

[See J. N. Ireland, *Records of the N. Y. Stage,* vol. I (1866); William Dunlap, *A Hist. of the Am. Theatre* (1832); W. B. Wood, *Personal Recollections of the Stage* (1855); Charles Durang, "The Phila. Stage," *Phila. Dispatch,* May 7, 1854–1860, of which there are files at the Univ. of Pa., Hist. Soc. of Pa., and Harvard Univ.; John Bernard, *Retrospections of America* (1887); G. O. Seilhamer, *Hist. of the Am. Theatre,* vols. II–III (1889–91); G. C. D. Odell, *Annals of the N. Y. Stage,* vols. I–II (1927); obituary in *General Advertiser* (Phila.), Feb. 22, 1803.]   O. S. C.

WIKOFF, HENRY (*c.* 1813–May 2, 1884), author and adventurer, was of dubious origins. The date of his birth, as well as his paternity, was carefully and successfully concealed. He was said to be the son of Henry Wikoff, a wealthy physician of Philadelphia, but a manuscript diary preserved in the library of Union College suggests that he was the son of S. P. Wetherill, who was later his guardian. In 1823 he was sent to the academy at Princeton, N. J., kept by Rev. Robert Baird, and in September 1827 entered Yale College. Dismissed near the close of his third year for a student prank, he went to Union College, where he was graduated in 1832. Early in his life he inherited a considerable fortune which maintained him in comfortable circumstances throughout a long and varied career. He became a student in the law office of Joseph R. Ingersoll in Philadelphia in 1831 and despite the fact that he spent most of the next three years in extensive travels in many parts of the Eastern and Middle Western states, he was admitted to the Pennsylvania bar in June 1834.

He at once departed upon a grand tour of Europe and during the six years following visited France, England, Germany, Russia, Greece, and Italy. He was a man of ready wit, deep intelligence, and captivating manners. Armed with the proper introductions, he soon penetrated the most exclusive and interesting circles of European society. It was said that no American of the period knew so many European notables as Wikoff. His interests were many—politics, diplomacy, journalism, the theatre, literature—so that he never found the time to concentrate upon any one of them. His energies were dissipated and he was regarded as an elegant and accomplished dilettante. In 1836 he was made an attaché of the United States legation in London. During the following year he was in Paris and secured many of the personal effects of Napoleon I to take back to Joseph Bonaparte in London. He subsequently received a decoration from the queen of Spain; hence arose the title of "Chevalier" by which he was known to many Americans. When one of his theatrical friends who had contracted to bring the celebrated dancer Fanny Elssler to America died, Wikoff, who had been assisting him in the negotiations, assumed the responsibility and contributed greatly to the success of her American tour in 1840.

During the next decade he became somewhat of a transatlantic commuter, visiting France and England yearly and maintaining his social and political contacts. He was said by persons of discernment to have known more important unwritten political history than any other person of his time. For a short time in 1849 he was editor of the *Democratic Review*; the same year he published *Napoleon Louis Bonaparte, First President of France,* an illuminating book on Louis Napoleon, of whom he was an ardent partisan and a devoted friend. While in England in 1850 he was persuaded by Lord Palmerston to become an agent of the British Foreign Office. During the next year Wikoff was successful in modifying the anti-British tone of two important Parisian newspapers: *La Presse* and *Le Siècle*. Beyond this, he tried to promote a fraternal alliance between the United States and Great Britain. He was zealous and indiscreet, so that after a year Palmerston gave up "the Yankee diplomat."

In 1851 Wikoff was about to marry Jane C. Gamble, an American heiress resident in London. The day before the wedding she left London and went to Genoa, where Wikoff found her. They were reconciled; the lady again changed her mind; and "the Chevalier" attempted a friendly abduction. His fiancée appealed to the British consul, who had Wikoff arrested and thrown into jail. The lady repented and urged clemency, but the consul, probably acting upon instructions from London, pressed the prosecution, which resulted in a sentence of imprisonment. British influence defeated all moves toward a pardon and Wikoff finally spent more than fifteen months in a common jail in Genoa. These experiences produced his best-known book: *My Courtship and Its Consequences* (1855). The same theme was further elaborated in *The Adventures of a Roving Diplomatist* (1857).

He engaged in a pamphlet dispute with Palmerston in 1861, on the question of American slavery, publishing *Secession, and Its Causes, in a Letter to Viscount Palmerston,* and issued *Memoir of Ginevra Guerrabella,* an account of the actress Genevieve Ward [*q.v.*], in 1863. His most important literary production, *The Reminiscences of an Idler* (1880), is filled with charming anecdotes and many profound observations; it covers his career up to 1840. Failing health prevented the completion of his memoirs; he died of paralysis at Brighton, England, in 1884.

[Works cited above; *N. Y. Times,* and *N. Y. Tribune,* May 3, 1884; manuscript records at Yale University and Union College.]   F. M.

WILBUR, CRESSY LIVINGSTON (Mar. 16, 1865–Aug. 9, 1928), vital statistician, was born in Hillsdale, Mich., the son of Rodney G. Wilbur and Frances (Cressy) Wilbur and a descendant of Samuel Wilbur [*q.v.*]. He was educated in the public schools of his native city and at Hillsdale College, where he received the degrees of Ph.B. in 1886, and Ph.M. in 1889. He commenced the study of medicine at the University of Michigan, 1888–89, but completed his training at Bellevue Hospital Medical College (New York University) in 1890. His public health career began in 1893, when he was appointed chief of the Division of Vital Statistics of the Michigan State Department of Health. Although the United States was first among the civilized nations of the world to provide for a periodic enumeration of its population, it lagged shamefully in recognizing the need of recording the births and deaths occurring within its boundaries. In 1880, ninety years after the first federal census was taken, the registration of deaths was reasonably complete in only two states— Massachusetts and New Jersey, and in a number of individual cities in other states. It was fortunate for the cause of public health that, even as a state official, Wilbur considered the national and not merely the local aspects of the problem. Only three years after his Michigan appointment, before the American Public Health Association, he urged the establishment of a permanent census bureau with a division of vital statistics as a means for promoting efficient registration in all the states of the Union.

In 1901 he was appointed expert special agent in charge of extension of the registration area. In 1902 the Census Bureau was made a permanent office, and in 1906 Wilbur became its chief statistician for vital statistics. His persistent, intelligent, and uncompromising efforts toward the upbuilding of a national system of registration were undeterred by the indifference of the general public, the medical profession, and what was even harder to bear—the frequent lack of interest and understanding in official circles. With the appointment of a new director of the census in 1914 Wilbur resigned. He was then invited to take charge of the Division of Vital Statistics of the New York State Department of

Health. In the course of a brief two-year period, he perfected the registration of births and deaths, and laid the foundation for scientifically sound analyses of the vital statistics of the state. In 1916 his health broke down, and he was obliged to retire. After years of invalidism he died in a sanitarium in Utica, N. Y. He knew that he would not live to see the fruition of his labors, but he had given unstintingly to his chosen cause all of his uncommon abilities and, almost literally, his life. His wife, Blanche M. Mead of Hastings, Mich., to whom he had been married on June 30, 1891, one son, and two daughters survived him.

Wilbur's outstanding contribution to American vital statistics was the fostering of a model vital statistics law that led to the establishment of uniform and effective registration in all states. He assisted in the preparation of the second revision of the *Manual of the International List of Causes of Death* (1909), and was responsible for the official English text of this revision (1911). Besides numerous official reports, state and federal, he was the author of two score of published papers, mainly on the subject of registration (see *Annals of the American Academy of Political and Social Science,* March 1911, and *Quarterly Publications of the American Statistical Association,* December 1907). He was a member of the American Public Health Association, the American Medical Association, the American Statistical Association, the International Statistical Institute, and was a Fellow of the Royal Statistical Society of England. He was official delegate of the Census Bureau to the International Congress of Tuberculosis held in Washington in 1908, and served as vice-president at the second decennial meeting of the international commission for the revision of the *Manual of Causes of Death* held in Paris in 1909, at which he was the principal representative of the United States.

[Personal communications from Prof. Walter F. Willcox, Miss Fanny P. Lamson, secretary of Dr. Wilbur in the Census Bureau, and Mr. George H. Van Buren, general supervisor of the Metropolitan Life Insurance Company, and a former associate of Dr. Wilbur in the Census Bureau; J. R. Wilbor, *The Wildbores in America* (1907); *Who's Who in America,* 1918–19; W. H. Guilfoy, "Past and Future Development of Vital Statistics in the United States: III, Cressy L. Wilbur," *Jour. of Am. Statistical Asso.,* Sept. 1926; *Lancet* (London), Sept. 15, 1928; *N. Y. Times,* Aug. 11, 1928.]
J. V. D–P.

WILBUR, HERVEY BACKUS (Aug. 18, 1820–May 1, 1883), pioneer educator of the feeble-minded, was born in Wendell, Franklin County, Mass., the son of Hervey Wilbur, a Congregational clergyman, and Ann (Toppan) Wilbur and a descendant of Samuel Wilbur [*q.v.*]. He was graduated from Newburyport High School, attended Dartmouth College from 1834 to 1836, and then Amherst College, where he received the degree of B.A. in 1838 and that of A.M. in 1841. After a trial of school teaching and civil engineering he took up the study of medicine at the Berkshire Medical Institution, Pittsfield, Mass., where he was graduated in 1843. He began to practise in Lowell, later moving to Dana and thence to Barre. He early became impressed by the reported accounts of the work of Dr. Edouard Seguin [*q.v.*] in the instruction of feeble-minded children. Following the lead of Dr. Seguin he took into his home in Barre in 1848 a group of children of defective mentality, and thus organized the first school for this class of unfortunates in the United States. Except for the published accounts of the Seguin experiment there was no literature in any language dealing with the education of the feeble-minded, and Wilbur was compelled to develop a system of teaching out of his experience with this limited material. In his early work he was at the same time physician, teacher, and gymnastic trainer for his little group. His success was remarkable. He was able to develop marked improvement in intellects so feeble as to seem beyond any aid. The "Institute for Idiots," thus established at Barre, drew the attention of Dr. Frederick F. Backus, of Rochester, N. Y., a member of the state legislature who in 1851 prevailed upon that body to establish an experimental school for the feeble-minded at Albany, N. Y., with Wilbur in charge. This institution was transferred to Syracuse in 1854 and became the New York State Asylum for Idiots.

For the remainder of his life Wilbur devoted himself to the welfare of this institution, and his system of training and instruction became the basis for that adopted by every similar institution not only in the United States but also in Canada and in many European countries. His interest in the feeble-minded led to a similar interest in the insane, in whose behalf he was a constant advocate before the state legislature. He visited various asylums in the United States, studied British asylums and became an authority on the care of the insane. He was a caustic critic of prevailing methods. The greater part of his professional career was marked by controversy over asylum management and the care of inmates. His writings consist mainly of journal articles and pamphlets dealing with the welfare of the feeble-minded and the insane. Notable are a pamphlet on *Aphasia* (1867) and the *Report on the Management of the Insane in Great Britain* (1876). He participated in the founding of Syracuse University, and served as lecturer on mental diseases. He was an active member and one-time president of the National Association for the Protection of the Insane and the Prevention of Insanity.

The qualities which made possible the success of his great work were an indomitable will, unlimited patience, and a genuine pity for his unfortunate charges. In their interest and for a cause that was unpopular he was the best of fighters. He was assisted by an attractive personality and rich social qualities. He was married on May 12, 1847, to Harriet Holden of Barre, Mass., who died in 1870. On Aug. 13, 1874, he was married to Emily Petheram of Skaneateles, N. Y., who, with the two sons of his earlier marriage, and two sons of the later, survived him at the time of his sudden death at Syracuse.

[*Amherst Coll., Biog. Records* (1927) ; H. A. Kelly, W. L. Burrage, *Am. Medic. Biogs.* (1920) ; J. R. Wilbor and B. F. Wilbour, *The Wildbores in America* (1933) ; W. W. Godding, biographical article in *Jour. of Nervous and Mental Disease*, Oct. 1883 ; *Jour. Am. Medic. Asso.*, Sept. 1, 1883 ; *Archives of Med.*, June 1883 ; *Evening Herald* (Syracuse, N. Y.), May 1, 1883.]
J. M. P.

WILBUR, JOHN (June 17, 1774–May 1, 1856), Quaker preacher, leader of the "Wilburites" in New England, was born at Hopkinton, R. I., a descendant of Samuel Wilbur [*q.v.*] and the son of Thomas and Mary (Hoxie) Wilbur. He received a common-school education and for several years taught in the public schools of Rhode Island. On Oct. 17, 1793, he was married to Lydia Collins of Stonington, Conn. Religion of the type in which he was bred by his pious parents soon became the supreme interest of his life. He was recorded a minister of the Society of Friends in 1812, and became an effective preacher of the inspirational or prophetic type. He was known for his rugged moral integrity and for his unswerving convictions.

Wilbur spent the years 1831–33 in an eventful preaching tour in Great Britain and Ireland, where he became the zealous opponent of the evangelical movement, which, under the leadership of Joseph John Gurney (1788–1847), brother of Elizabeth Fry, the famous prison reformer, was invading the Society of Friends. In 1832 Wilbur published in England a series of letters which he had written to George Crosfield, under the title *Letters to a Friend on Some of the Primitive Doctrines of Christianity*. They strongly defended the old-time Quaker position on the Inward Light and emphasized what the writer believed to be dangerous innovations that were threatening to transform the Society of Friends. No mention was made by name of Gurney, but his line of teaching was obviously attacked.

Gurney spent the years 1837 and 1838 on a preaching tour in America, and Wilbur became his settled opponent, challenging the distinguished visitor at many points in his extensive travels. The effect of Gurney's visit in America was quite extraordinary, and in most of the Quaker sections members of the Society of Friends were carried in large numbers over to the evangelical position which Gurney championed. In consequence of this changed attitude, Wilbur's attacks upon Gurney and his movement were resented and produced a serious amount of friction. Disciplinary proceedings were launched against him and as the Monthly Meeting to which he belonged loyally supported him the superior Meetings employed unusual methods to deal with him, which his friends resented. By such proceedings he was finally expelled from membership in 1843. His supporters appealed the case to the New England Yearly Meeting and failing to receive satisfaction, separated in 1845 to the number of five hundred. They were popularly known as "Wilburites" and the larger body, containing 6500, were known as "Gurneyites." Officially the smaller body was called "New England Yearly Meeting of Friends" and the larger body, "The Yearly Meeting of Friends for New England." Separations of larger or smaller groups followed in New York and Ohio, while a large part of Philadelphia Yearly Meeting gave sympathy and support to the "Wilburites." In 1853–54 Wilbur made a second trip to England. He died at Hopkinton, R. I.

[J. R. Wilbor and B. F. Wilbour, *The Wildbores in America* (1933) ; *Jour. of the Life of John Wilbur* (1859) ; William Hodgson, *Selections from the Letters of T. B. Gould* (1860) ; John Wilbur, *A Narrative and Exposition of the Late Proceedings of New England Yearly Meeting* (1845) ; *Narrative of Facts and Circumstances That Have Tended to produce a Secession from the Society of Friends, New England Yearly Meeting* (1845) ; *Report of the Case of Earle et al. vs. Wood et al.* (1855) ; R. M. Jones, *The Later Periods of Quakerism* (London, 1921) ; Edward Grubb, *Separations* (London, 1914) ; *Providence Daily Jour.*, May 6, 1856.]
R. M. J.

WILBUR, SAMUEL (*c.* 1585–July 29, 1656), Rhode Island merchant and colonist, whose name is also spelled Wilbor and Wildbore, was born in England and came to America some time before 1633. The first known fact about him is that with his wife, Anne, he joined the First Church of Boston Oct. 1, 1633. He turned to trade and soon became a person of considerable importance. He owned a parcel of land near the present site of the city of Revere, another near the Roxbury boundary, a house and lot on Essex Street in Boston, and still another house on Milk Street. His interest in public affairs is evinced by the fact that he was one of the small circle of men who bought the Common for Boston from William Blackstone [*q.v.*] in 1634. A year later he contributed £10 for the first Massachusetts free school.

In 1637 he became involved in the Antinomian controversy and was banished for having been "seduced and led into dangerous errors." Accordingly he turned south to the more liberal colony of Rhode Island. He was one of the eighteen purchasers of the island of Aquidneck (now the island of Rhode Island) from the Narragansett Indians, and a few months later established there his wife and four sons. He was one of the signers of the Portsmouth Compact, which organized the infant government; he farmed the lands granted to him; he built and managed the only planing mill in the community. He was chosen clerk of one of the train bands, and subsequently served as sergeant and constable. In 1645 he returned to Massachusetts to find the colony about to declare war on the Narragansetts, whose feud with the Mohegans of Connecticut was endangering the security of New England. Three messengers were therefore appointed to give back to the Indians the presents they had recently offered as promises of peace. Wilbur was one of those chosen for this critical task, which successfully frightened the Indians into submission.

His last years proved to be more tranquil. After the death of his first wife, he married Elizabeth Lechford, widow of Thomas Lechford [*q.v.*], who had been Boston's only trained lawyer. Settling in Taunton, Mass., Wilbur devoted himself to his commercial interests and identified himself with the life of the town. He died in Boston, leaving a comfortable inheritance for his sons. He was one of that courageous early group of settlers who by successfully meeting the many problems of frontier life in the seventeenth century founded American civilization in the wilderness.

[J. R. Wilbor and B. F. Wilbour, *The Wildbores in America* (1933); J. R. Bartlett, *The Records of the Colony of R. I. and Providence Plantations*, vol. I (1856); S. G. Arnold, *The Hist. of the State of R. I.*, vol. I (1859).]   M. A.

WILCOX, CADMUS MARCELLUS (May 29, 1824–Dec. 2, 1890), Confederate soldier, was born in Wayne County, N. C., where his father, Reuben Wilcox, a native of Connecticut, had settled, marrying Sarah Garland, a noted North Carolina beauty. Of this union Cadmus was the second among four children. His parents removing to Tipton County, Tenn., he grew up there, attending the University of Nashville. He entered the United States Military Academy in 1842, at the age of eighteen (*Official Register,*

1843), and was graduated in 1846 in the class with George B. McClellan, Thomas Jonathan Jackson, and George E. Pickett [*qq.v.*]. Apointed brevet second lieutenant, 4th Infantry, he joined General Taylor's forces in Mexico and fought at Monterey, but was promoted second lieutenant, 7th Infantry, Feb. 16, 1847, and transferred to General Scott's army. He was at Vera Cruz, Cerro Gordo, and in the advance on Mexico city, so distinguishing himself that in July General John A. Quitman [*q.v.*] appointed him an aide. Wilcox led the storming party at Chapultepec, and afterward nearly lost his life by mounting an aqueduct under fire to signal the American capture of the Belen gate and entry into the city of Mexico. In 1848, when Lieut. Ulysses S. Grant was married, Wilcox was his groomsman. Three years later he became a first lieutenant, serving in Florida, and then, 1852–57, as assistant instructor of infantry tactics at West Point. Failing health brought him a year's sick leave in Europe. On his return he published *Rifles and Rifle Practice* (1859), the first American textbook on this subject, and in 1860 translated from the French a work on Austrian evolutions of the line.

Having been commissioned captain, Dec. 20, 1860, Wilcox was in New Mexico when Tennessee seceded. Though attached to the Union, he resigned his commission June 8, 1861, and accepted the colonelcy of the 9th Alabama Infantry, Confederate States Army. He was present at First Manassas (Bull Run), and thereafter until Appomattox was with Lee's army in nearly every great battle, establishing a record as one of the best subordinate commanders of the South. He was made a brigadier-general as of Oct. 21, 1861. In the Seven Days' battles his brigade lost 1,055 men out of 1,800. Wilcox himself was never wounded, though he received six bullets through his clothing in ferocious fighting at Frazier's Farm, where he defeated Meade's brigade. At Second Manassas (Aug. 30, 1862), he ably commanded three brigades, and in the Chancellorsville campaign, Sedgwick could hardly have been beaten at Salem Church but for Wilcox's stubborn resistance while awaiting reinforcements (*War of the Rebellion: Official Records, Army*, I ser. XXV, pt. I, pp. 854–61). On July 2, 1863, at Gettysburg, he made a charge which, if supported, might have ruptured the Union center (*Ibid.*, I ser. XXVII, pt. 2, pp. 616–21). The next day, however, with Pickett, he suffered a bloody repulse.

In January 1864 Wilcox was made a major-general, to rank from August 1863. He was given William Dorsey Pender's old division, with which at the Wilderness and Spotsylvania he greatly enhanced his reputation as a skilful tactician. At Petersburg, Apr. 2, 1865, part of his troops held Forts Gregg and Alexander until they were nearly annihilated, enabling Longstreet to cover Lee's retreat westward. Seven days later, at Appomattox Court House, Wilcox's division was ordered to support Gordon's corps in attempting to break through the Union lines, but the Confederate surrender terminated operations. While Grant and Lee negotiated, some of the Union generals, including Sheridan, Ingalls, and Gibbon, rode forward to find their old friend Wilcox, bringing him back to visit Grant.

After the war Wilcox, a bachelor, resided in Washington with the widow and two children of his elder brother. Devoted to their care, he declined leaving them for a commission in the Egyptian army, or in Korea. President Cleveland in 1886 appointed him chief of the railroad division of the General Land Office, a position he retained until his death. In Washington he wrote his *History of the Mexican War*, which was edited by his niece, Mary Rachel Wilcox, and published posthumously (1892). "I know of no man of rank . . . on the Southern side who had more warm friends, *North* and *South*, than Cadmus M. Wilcox," wrote Gen. Henry Heth (Couch, *post*, pp. 34–35). That opinion was justified at his funeral, where Gen. Joseph E. Johnston was chief mourner, while four distinguished Union officers and four Confederates were honorary pallbearers.

[In addition to the volumes of *Official Records* cited above, see 1 ser. II, XI (pt. 2), XII (pt. 2), XIX (pt. 1), XXI, XXXVII (pt. 1), XLVI; C. A. Evans, *Confed. Mil. Hist.* (1890), VII, 342–44; *The Photographic Hist. of the Civil War* (1911), vol. X; *Battles and Leaders of the Civil War* (1887–88), vols. II, III, IV; A. L. Long, *Memoirs of Robert E. Lee* (1886); George Meade, *The Life and Letters of George Gordon Meade* (1913), I, 290–95, II, 75, 89–90; Morris Schaff, *The Battle of the Wilderness* (1910); G. W. Cullum, *Biog. Reg. Officers and Grads. U. S. Mil. Acad.* (3rd ed., 1891), vol. II; D. N. Couch, "Cadmus M. Wilcox," *Twenty-second Ann. Reunion, Asso. Grads. U. S. Mil. Acad.* (1891); *Washington Post*, Dec. 3, 1890.]

J. M. H.

WILCOX, DELOS FRANKLIN (Apr. 22, 1873–Apr. 4, 1928), franchise and public utility expert, was born on a farm near Ida, Mich., the son of Byron M. and Lorain (Jones) Wilcox. He received his elementary education on his father's acres and in the neighborhood schools and entered the University of Michigan, where he was profoundly influenced by John Dewey. When he graduated, in 1894, he had determined to make his life work a definite contribution to the improvement of local government. He presented for the degree of Ph.D. at Columbia in 1896 a thesis entitled *Municipal Government in Michigan and Ohio* (1896), which was followed by *The American City* (1904) and *Great Cities in America* (1910). The first practical application of his purpose was the direction of civic reform agencies in Grand Rapids and Detroit from 1905 to 1907, during which period he edited *Civic News,* the weekly journal of the Detroit Municipal League and the Civic Club of Grand Rapids. He learned much from the struggle for control of public utilities going on in Detroit, particularly with respect to transportation. This insight was most useful when in 1907 he accepted an appointment as chief of the bureau of franchises of the public service commission for the first district of New York (New York City). He resigned in 1913 to become deputy commissioner of the department of water supply, gas and electricity of New York City, a position which he held until 1917. During this period he produced several additional books on city government and published his notable two-volume work, *Municipal Franchises* (1910–11). These volumes on franchises exerted a wide influence and upon them his professional reputation principally rests.

In 1917 Wilcox organized a staff of assistants and established himself as a consultant on utility problems—always on the side of the public. He made an extensive investigation of street railway problems for the Federal Electric Railways Commission in 1919, issuing his conclusions privately as *Analysis of the Electric Railway Problem* (1921). In his Preface he reiterated his opinion that "no permanent solution of the electric railway problem, consistent with the public interest, is possible except in public ownership" (p. xi), a view much more extreme than that of the Commission as a whole. He also participated as an expert in a number of important utility rate cases in which his position regarding several important factors was at distinct variance with that of many other authorities. He was a stanch defender of prudent investment as the basis for rates; objected to the addition of such intangibles as "going value" and "cost of financing"; and insisted that annual charges to operating expenses for depreciation should be consistent with the deduction of accrued depreciation from the rate base, and that both are directly related to the service life of utility property. His depreciation theory was embodied in his monograph, *Depreciation in Public Utilities* (1925).

The technical work underlying his valuations and rate studies was done by his staff, and he correlated the engineering, accounting, economic, and legal phases. He was attacked by utility companies on the score that only engineers and utility builders can make valuations; and finally in the Denver Tramways case, a federal judge granted the company's contention and excluded his testimony. His later activities were directed more particularly toward writing, which included a revision of Robert A. Whitten's two-volume work on *Valuation of Public Service Corporations*. This was completed shortly before his sudden death on Apr. 4, 1928, but a labor still closer to his ideals was left unfinished—a comprehensive work oh the administration of municipally owned and operated utilities. His preliminary outline and partial development of this thesis was published posthumously as a booklet, *The Administration of Municipally Owned Utilities* (1931).

Wilcox spent considerable time, especially in the later years, at his fruit farm, "Wandawood," at Elk Rapids, Mich. He was survived by his wife, Mina M. (Gates), whom he married Feb. 22, 1898, and by four adult children. His technical library, including a file of his writings, was donated to the University of Chicago. A man of great modesty and personal charm, with an effervescent sense of humor, he was an excellent public speaker and an effective writer. Among his publications, besides the more notable works previously mentioned, were: *The Study of City Government* (1897); *City Problems* (1899); *Ethical Marriage* (copr. 1900); *Government by All the People, or the Initiative, the Referendum and the Recall as Instruments of Democracy* (1912); *The Indeterminate Permit in Relation to Home Rule and Public Ownership* (1926); and many reports on special utility problems, as well as pamphlets and magazine articles on local government, franchises, and utilities.

[Wilcox's *Municipal Franchises*, his *Depreciation in Public Utilities*, and a pamphlet, *Why the Utilities Win*; *Who's Who in America*, 1928–29; *N. Y. Times*, Apr. 5, 1928; correspondence with family and associates.]   L. D. U.

WILCOX, ELLA WHEELER (Nov. 5, 1850–Oct. 30, 1919), poet, was the youngest daughter of Marius Hartwell and Sarah (Pratt) Wheeler. She was born in Johnstown Center, Wis., not far from Madison. A few years before her birth, her father, a teacher of the violin, dancing, and deportment in Thetford, Vt., had emigrated to Wisconsin, where after the failure of financial ventures he resumed his teaching of dancing. It was, however, to her mother, also of Vermont stock, that Ella Wheeler Wilcox attributed her literary talents. Interest in writing manifested itself very early. She wrote a novel for the

amusement of her sisters before she was ten, and read eagerly such publications as the *New York Mercury* and the *New York Ledger,* and the books of such authors as Mary Jane Holmes, Mrs. E. D. E. N. Southworth [*qq.v.*], and "Ouida." Having had an essay published in the *New York Mercury* in her early teens, she offered other essays in various competitions, won a number of prizes, and began to send out her poems, the first of which were ridiculed by the editor of the *Mercury.* The first poem published under her name appeared in *Waverly Magazine,* and her first cash payment came from *Leslie's.* Her family, hoping to encourage her in her literary work, sent her for a year (1867–68) to the University of Wisconsin, but she found her work there of little value to her. She continued to write at least two poems a day, many of them being accepted for publication, and by the time she was eighteen she was making a substantial contribution to the family income. For a few months she worked on a trade paper in Milwaukee. Her first book of poems, *Drops of Water* (1872), a collection of temperance verses, was followed by *Shells* (1873), and *Maurine* (1876), a narrative poem. Her first success, however, came with the rejection of *Poems of Passion* by Jansen and McClurg of Chicago on the ground that the volume was immoral. The story appeared in the Milwaukee newspapers, was widely reprinted, and served to insure the book a wide sale when it was published in 1883 by another company. On May 1, 1884, she was married to Robert Marius Wilcox (d. 1916), a manufacturer of works of art in silver, and went to live in Meriden, Conn. A son, born on May 27, 1887, lived only a few hours. Thereafter the Wilcoxes spent their winters in New York, entertaining many writers and artists. In 1891 they built a bungalow at Short Beach, Conn., where they spent their summers. They traveled widely, in the Orient as well as Europe. They both constantly engaged in private charitable enterprises.

Mrs. Wilcox's literary activities did not cease with her marriage. She published some twenty volumes (for the most part, poetry) after 1884, wrote a daily poem for a newspaper syndicate for several years, and contributed frequent essays to the *Cosmopolitan* and other magazines. In 1901 she was commissioned by the New York *American* to go to London and write a poem on the death of Queen Victoria. In 1913 she was presented at the Court of St. James's. During 1918 she toured the army camps in France, reciting her poems and delivering talks on sexual problems. As a result of over-exertion. she fell ill in the spring of 1919. After spending some time in a nursing home in Bath, England, she was brought back to the United States. She died three months later at Short Beach, Conn.

Both she and her husband believed in the possibility of communication with the dead and were frequent attendants at spiritualist séances. After her husband's death she made repeated efforts to communicate with him, and believed that she finally succeeded in doing so by means of the ouija board. She was also interested in theosophy, maintaining that she had learned self-control from an East Indian monk. All her later work, poetry and prose, shows the influence of the teachings of "New Thought." Her autobiographical writings were "Literary Confessions of a Western Poetess" (*Lippincott's Monthly Magazine*, May 1886), "My Autobiography" (*Cosmopolitan*, August 1901), *The Story of a Literary Career* (1905), and *The Worlds and I* (1918). Throughout her life she enjoyed great popularity. She took her work most seriously. Defending herself against critics who spoke of platitudes and sentimentality, she maintained that her poems comforted millions of weary and unhappy persons, and she appears to have been right.

[In addition to Ella Wheeler Wilcox's autobiog. writings, sources include *Who's Who in America*, 1916–17; E. D. Walker, in *Cosmopolitan*, Nov. 1888; *Lit. Digest*, Nov. 22, 1919; Theodosia Garrison, in *Bookman*, Jan. 1920; obituary in *N. Y. Times*, Oct. 31, 1919; information from Ruth Chapin Ritter.]   G. H.

WILCOX, REYNOLD WEBB (Mar. 29, 1856–June 6, 1931), physician, was born in Madison, Conn., the son of Col. Vincent Meigs Wilcox and Catherine Mellicent (Webb) Wilcox. His father's ancestor, William Wilcoxson, one of the original settlers of Stratford, Conn., came to America from England in 1635. His mother was a descendant of Richard Webb who lived in Stamford as early as 1636. Both of his grandmothers claimed as a common ancestor Vincent Meigs, an early settler of Madison. As a young boy, Wilcox showed great aptitude and desire for learning. His early education was acquired at Lee's Academy, a local school. In 1878 he received the degree of A.B. from Yale and in 1881 that of M.D. from Harvard. His desire for further knowledge led him to spend a year in study abroad before entering upon the practice of medicine.

Settling in New York City, he was an active practitioner there for about forty years, finding time, also, to write innumerable articles, to serve on the staff of various hospitals, and to take part in the administration of many medical societies. William Hale-White's textbook, *Ma-*

teria Medica, edited by Wilcox and published in 1892, went through twelve editions; his *Treatment of Disease* (1907), reached four editions; and a second edition of his *Manual of Fever Nursing* (1904) appeared. His hospital connections included St. Mary's and Ossining hospitals, in New York, Eastern Long Island, Greenport, Nassau Hospital, Mineola, and the New Jersey State Hospital at Greystone Park. A charter member of the American College of Physicians, he served as president from 1915 to 1922. He was president also of the American Therapeutic Society, 1901–02; the Medical Association of Greater New York, 1910–13; the Society for Medical Jurisprudence, 1913–14; the Association for Medical Reserve Corps, United States Army, 1914–16; and the American Congress on Internal Medicine, 1915–17. As professor of medicine at the New York Post-Graduate Medical School and Hospital he gave instruction from 1886 to 1908, keeping abreast of the times by making short trips abroad to study during the years 1889–1901 and 1903–1908. He was therapeutic editor of the *American Journal of Medical Sciences* for many years and a member of the revision committee of the *United States Pharmacopoeia*, 1900–10. He served with the army during the World War, reaching the rank of major, and was of the eighth generation in his family to hold a commission since 1636.

A heavily built man, swarthy in complexion, he stood over six feet tall. Strongly inclined to overconfidence, he became unpopular with his colleagues because of his unpleasant, domineering ways, his unwillingness to listen to the opinion of others, and his positive asserting of his own views. In spite of the enemies his personal traits made for him, his investigations in clinical therapeutics and his work in internal medicine won him wide recognition. Outside of his profession his interests seem to have been few. He was a member of several patriotic societies, and was the author of a little book about his ancestors, *The Descendants of William Wilcoxson, Vincent Meigs and Richard Webb* (1893). He was twice married: first, June 5, 1895, to Frances Maud Weeks of New York City; and second, Dec. 12, 1917, to Grace Clarkson, daughter of Col. Floyd Clarkson; no children survived him.

[*Yale Univ., Obit. Record*, 1931; *Quarter-Century Record of the Class of 1878, Yale Univ.* (1905); J. J. Walsh, *Hist. of Medicine in N. Y.* (1919), vol. V; *Annals of Internal Medicine*, Aug. 1931; T. F. Harrington, *Harvard Medic. School* (1905); *Doctor's Who's Who*, 1906; *Trenton State Gazette*, July 8, 1931.]
G. L. A.

WILCOX, STEPHEN (Feb. 12, 1830–Nov. 27, 1893), inventor, engineer, was born in Westerly, R. I., a descendant of Edward Wilcox, who was in Portsmouth, R. I., as early as 1638, and the son of Stephen and Sophia (Vose) Wilcox. His father was a banker and business man, a strong opponent of slavery. Stephen was educated in the common schools of Westerly, and seems to have followed his natural aptitude for mechanics without serving a regular apprenticeship. He was a prolific inventor even as a young man, but when he attempted to patent his devices usually found that he had been anticipated. One of his early inventions was a practical caloric or hot-air engine, which he submitted to the United States Lighthouse Board for operating fog signals. Believing, however, that the field for the hot-air engine was limited, he turned his attention to steam boilers, and, in 1856, invented a safety water-tube boiler with inclined tubes—the germ of the Babcock & Wilcox boiler later well known throughout the world. In partnership with D. M. Stillman of Westerly he was granted Patent No. 14,523 for this boiler, Mar. 25, 1856.

Some ten years later, with his boyhood friend George Herman Babcock [q.v.], he designed a steam generator based on the principal of the earlier boiler, and was granted a patent for it on May 28, 1867. In that year the firm of Babcock, Wilcox & Company was formed to manufacture the boiler; the concern was incorporated in 1881, and Wilcox was vice-president from then until his death. The Babcock & Wilcox boiler and the Babcock & Wilcox stationary steam-engine were used in the first central stations (power plants) in the country and were of considerable significance in the development of electric lighting. Babcock & Wilcox products were used all over the world, and the company opened offices in Cuba and Puerto Rico.

Wilcox was primarily the inventor and mechanic of the combination while Babcock was the executive; the boiler is the Wilcox boiler but is often called the Babcock, because Babcock's name came first in the title of the firm. Wilcox continued his experimentation with engines and boilers till the end of his life, in later years being assisted by his wife's nephew, William D. Hoxie [q.v.]. Much of his work was carried out on his yacht, the *Reverie,* and this circumstance may have been responsible for Hoxie's perfection of the marine form of the Babcock & Wilcox boiler. Wilcox secured, alone or with others, forty-seven patents in forty years. He was married in 1865 to Harriet Hoxie, who survived him. He was handsome and popular, simple and unaffected by his rise to affluence. During the last part of his life he made his home in Brooklyn, N. Y., where he died. Public-spirited and generous, he presented to Westerly, his birthplace, a public library building, which, after his death was enlarged and endowed by his widow, who also carried out their joint plans for many other gifts to the town, including a park and a high-school building.

[*Representative Men and Old Families of R. I.* (1908), vol. I; *Trans. Am. Soc. Mech. Engineers,* vol. XV (1894); *Fifty Years of Steam: A Brief Hist. of the Babcock & Wilcox Company* (1931); J. N. Arnold, *Vital Record of R. I. . . . Washington County* (1894); *Brooklyn Daily Eagle,* Nov. 28, 1893.]   W. M. M.

WILCZYNSKI, ERNEST JULIUS (Nov. 13, 1876–Sept. 14, 1932), mathematician, educator, was born in Hamburg, Germany, the son of Max and Friederike (Hurwitz) Wilczynski. His family emigrated to America while he was still quite young, and settled in Chicago, Ill. He attended elementary school and high school in Chicago and, with the assistance of an uncle, returned to Germany to enter the University of Berlin, where he received the degree of Ph.D. in 1897. He was then in his twenty-first year. After his return to the United States he was a computer in the office of the *Nautical Almanac* in 1898, and then he was appointed instructor in mathematics at the University of California. Here he remained as assistant and associate professor until 1907, with the exception of the period from 1903 to 1905 when he was in Europe as a research associate of the Carnegie Institution of Washington. He was associate professor of mathematics at the University of Illinois from 1907 to 1910 and at the University of Chicago from 1910 to 1914. He was made professor of mathematics at Chicago in 1914 and, after his health failed, professor emeritus in 1926. His death came at Denver, Col., after a lingering illness of about nine years. Most of this time he was confined to his bed, but he never gave up hope of some day returning to his academic duties.

He began his scientific career as a mathematical astronomer and his interest then turned to differential equations, but he attained eminence as a projective differential geometer. This field of geometry was largely created by him. He invented a new method in geometry and established himself as the leader of a new school of geometers. Various scientific honors and recognitions were conferred upon him. He was lecturer at the New Haven Colloquium of the American Mathematical Society in 1906 with E. H. Moore and Max Mason. He was vice-president of the American Mathematical Society, and a member of the council of the Mathematical Association of America. In 1909 he won a prize of the Royal Belgian Academy of Sciences for an original paper in geometry, and he was elected a member of the National Academy of Sciences in 1919. He was also a fellow of the American Association for the Advancement of Science.

One of Wilczynski's primary accomplishments was his mastery of the difficult art of lucid mathematical exposition. He possessed a fine and polished style both in spoken and written English and in German, his native language. He was familiar with French and Italian. His lectures, clear and concise, were greatly admired by his students. His genius and enthusiasm for mathematics attracted many people around him and placed him early in a position of great influence in American mathematical education. His college texts, as well as various labors entirely disconnected with the class room, contributed to this end. A complete bibliography of Wilczynski's publications numbers more than seventy-five (see Lane, in *Bulletin of the American Mathematical Society, post*). He was married to Countess Inez Macola of Verona, Italy, on Aug. 9, 1906. She, with their three daughters, survived him.

[*Who's Who in America*, 1926–27; E. P. Lane, "Ernest Julius Wilczynski—In Memoriam," in *Bull. of the Am. Mathematical Soc.*, Jan. 1933, in *Am. Mathematical Monthly*, Dec. 1932, and a biographical memoir in *Nat. Acad. of Sciences, Biographical Memoirs*, vol. XVI; G. A. Bliss, "Ernest Julius Wilczynski," *Science*, Oct. 7, 1932; *Chicago Daily Tribune*, Sept. 16, 1932.]　　　　　　　　　　E. P. L.

WILDE, GEORGE FRANCIS FAXON (Feb. 23, 1845–Dec. 3, 1911), naval officer, was born at Braintree, Mass., the son of William Read and Mary Elizabeth (Thayer) Wilde and a descendant through his mother of William Thayer who came to New England about 1640. After attending school at Braintree he secured an appointment as midshipman, walked to Boston for his examination, and entered the Naval Academy, then at Newport, R. I., Nov. 30, 1861.

Following his early wartime graduation in the summer of 1864, he served in the *Susquehanna*, which blockaded the *Stonewall* at Havana in the spring of 1865 and later was flagship in the Brazil Squadron. He was made lieutenant Mar. 12, 1868, and lieutenant commander June 26, 1869, continuing in routine sea and shore duty until his promotion to commander Oct. 2, 1885. He then received his first noteworthy independent command, the new steel cruiser *Dolphin*, which in 1886–89 he took on a cruise around the world. After serving in 1889–93 as inspector of the Second Lighthouse District, New England, he was secretary of the lighthouse

board, 1894–98, in which position he was chiefly instrumental in the introduction of gas buoys on the Great Lakes, of telephones from lightships to shore, and of an electric lightship on Diamond Shoal, Cape Hatteras. In the Spanish-American War he commanded the harbor defense ram *Katahdin* on the North Atlantic patrol, April–September 1898. On Nov. 7 following, he took command of the cruiser *Boston*, then stationed at Taku, China, for the protection of American interests at the beginning of the Boxer uprising. The *Boston* during the following winter cooperated with the army in suppressing the Philippine insurrection, and on Feb. 11 landed a marine force which held the town of Iloilo, Panay Island, until the arrival of troops. Later, in command of the battleship *Oregon* from May 1899 to January 1901, Wilde landed marines to occupy the town of Vigan and held it four days, releasing 160 Spanish officers and their families, for which service he received the thanks of the Spanish representative at Manila (see *Report of the Secretary of the Navy*, 1900, p. 503). The *Oregon* on June 28, 1900, struck an uncharted reef in Pechili Gulf, China, but with considerable effort and good seamanship was gotten off and hauled to Kure, Japan, for repairs. He was subsequently at the Portsmouth and (after May 28, 1902) at the Boston navy yard, and from February to May 1904 was commandant of the Philadelphia navy yard; thereafter he was again at the Boston yard as commandant, with promotion to rear admiral Aug. 10, 1904.

He retired at his own request Feb. 10, 1905, and until his death was chairman of the Massachusetts Nautical Training School Commission, making his home at North Easton, Mass., near the scenes of his boyhood. His death from heart trouble followed only a few months that of his wife Emogen B., daughter of Jason Howard of Easton, Mass., whom he married at Braintree Dec. 13, 1868. He had no children.

[L. R. Hamersly, *The Records of Living Officers of the U. S. Navy and Marine Corps* (1902); A. P. Niblack, "Operations of the Navy and Marine Corps in the Philippine Archipelago," in *Proc. U. S. Naval Inst.*, Dec. 1904; *Who's Who in America*, 1910–11; *Boston Transcript*, Dec. 4, 1911; *Army and Navy Journal*, Dec. 9, 1911, Feb. 24, 1912.]　　　　　　A. W.

WILDE, RICHARD HENRY (Sept. 24, 1789–Sept. 10, 1847), poet, congressman, Italian scholar, was born in Dublin, Ireland, the son of Richard and Mary (Newitt) Wilde. Soon after arriving at Baltimore with his family in 1797, the poet's father lost his property because of his partner's participation in the Irish rebellion and in 1802 he died. The next year the mother moved to Augusta, Ga., where her son assisted her in running a store. From her and through his own studies he received most of his education. After studying law privately, he was admitted to the bar in 1809, and in 1811 became attorney-general of Georgia. In 1819 he married Mrs. Caroline Buckle, who died in 1827.

Wilde divided his time between law, politics, and literature. He was elected to Congress for five terms, 1815–17, 1827–35, and was appointed to fill vacancies in 1825 and 1827. His opposition to the Jacksonian Whigs, then dominant in Georgia, his defeat for reëlection in 1834, and his own temperamental dissatisfaction with public life led to his retirement. In June 1835 he went abroad. After extensive travel, he settled in Florence and commenced "The Life and Times of Dante" and "The Italian Lyric Poets." (The unfinished manuscripts are in the Library of Congress.) To Wilde belongs the chief credit for the discovery in the Bargello of Giotto's portrait of the youthful Dante. After his return to America between November 1840 and February 1841, he published his *Conjectures and Researches Concerning the Love, Madness, and Imprisonment of Torquato Tasso* (2 vols., 1842), a well-documented but romantic argument. He moved to New Orleans in 1843 to practise law and in 1847 was appointed professor of constitutional law in the newly organized law department of the University of Louisiana (now Tulane University), where he served until his death.

Wilde's contemporary reputation as a poet rested almost entirely upon "My life is like the summer rose," composed before 1815 as an interpolated lyric in an unfinished epic. In spite of his determination not to publish the poem, it was printed as early as April 1819, in the *Analectic Magazine*, and came to be generally attributed to Wilde. Later its authorship was claimed for the eccentric Irish bard Patrick O'Kelly, and Wilde was charged with plagiarism. As a hoax, Anthony Barclay of Savannah translated the poem into Greek and passed it off as a newly discovered fragment of Alcæus. A lively newspaper controversy over the authorship led Wilde to acknowledge it in a letter to the press dated Dec. 31, 1834 (Davidson, *post*), and to give an account of its origin. During the poet's lifetime it was highly praised and frequently reprinted; it was set to music by Sidney Lanier [*q.v.*] and others. Of Wilde's poems it is the only one to remain generally known. His *Hesperia*, which did not appear until after his death, was intended for anonymous publication as "A Fragment by the Late Fitzhugh de Lancy, Esq." It consists of four cantos addressed to the Mar-

chesa Manfredina di Cosenza (identified by Mr. Aubrey H. Starke as Mrs. Ellen Adair White-Beatty; see *American Book Collector*, May–June 1935). The poem is a series of descriptions of travels in America and Europe, and in diction, meter, stanza form, and sentiment follows the Byron-Thomas Moore tradition. The notes reveal the author's extensive reading, embody some of the results of his studies in Europe, and include original poems, notably the sonnet "To the Mocking-Bird" and "Star of My Love."

Wilde died in New Orleans of yellow fever, and was buried in a vault in that city. In 1854 his remains were reinterred in an unmarked grave in the garden of his home in Augusta. In 1886 he was again reburied, in the "Poet's Corner" of the City Cemetery of Augusta. This reburial was due to the efforts of the Hayne Circle, a literary society, which in 1896 erected a monument to the memory of Wilde and three other Southern poets. Besides a number of separately printed speeches, Wilde's published works consist only of uncollected essays and poems, *Conjectures and Researches Concerning . . . Torquato Tasso*, and *Hesperia: A Poem* (1867), edited by William Cumming Wilde, one of the two sons who survived him.

[A. H. Starke, "Richard Henry Wilde: Some Notes and a Check-List," *Am. Book Collector*, Nov.–Dec. 1933, Jan. 1934; J. W. Davidson, "The Authorship of 'My Life is Like the Summer Rose,'" *Southern Lit. Messenger*, Oct. 1856; S. F. Miller, *The Bench and Bar of Ga.* (1858), vol. II, containing sketch written by Wilde's son correcting account in R. W. Griswold, *The Poets and Poetry of America* (1850); Anthony Barclay, *Wilde's Summer Rose; or The Lament of the Captive; An Authentic Account of the Origin, Mystery and Explanation of Hon. R. H. Wilde's Alleged Plagiarism* (1871); C. C. Jones, *The Life, Literary Labors, and Neglected Grave of Richard Henry Wilde* (1885); T. W. Koch, *Dante in America* (1896); *Biog. Dir. Am. Cong.* (1928); *Daily Picayune* (New Orleans), Sept. 11, 1847; information from Martha Wilde Pournelle, a grand-niece.]   J. M. S., Jr.

WILDER, ALEXANDER (May 14, 1823–Sept. 18, 1908), eccentric philosopher and physician, was born at Verona, Oneida County, N. Y., the son of Abel and Asenath (Smith) Wilder. Both parents were of old American stock, the Wilder ancestry going back to Thomas Wilder who came from England to Massachusetts Bay in 1640 or earlier. Brought up on his father's farm and educated in the common schools, Alexander became a country schoolteacher at the age of fifteen. He is said to have published in 1846, when he was twenty-three, a pamphlet entitled *The Secret of Immortality Revealed,* which showed a strong mystical tendency. For some years he supported himself by teaching, farming, and typesetting. Having taught himself Greek, Latin, and Hebrew, he next took up the study of medicine in order to be independent of doctors in the matter of his own health but became so interested in the subject that he pursued it intensively under the guidance of a local physician and eventually succeeded in obtaining a degree from the Syracuse Medical College in 1850. For the two years following he lectured on chemistry and anatomy in the college. In 1852 he became assistant editor of the Syracuse *Star* but soon went over to the staff of the Syracuse *Journal*; in 1854 he was appointed clerk in the newly created state department of public instruction; for some time he edited the *College Review* and the *New York Teacher*; then in 1857 he moved to the city of New York where for thirteen years he held a position on the editorial staff of the New York *Evening Post*. In 1869 he published *New Platonism and Alchemy*, an enthusiastic biographical and expository study of the Neo-Platonists.

Although a natural heretic and mystic, Wilder possessed a shrewd financial sense, an aptitude for politics, and considerable organizational ability. All his varied talents found expression during the decade of the seventies. Disbelieving in the use of animal matter in medicine, as early as 1848 he had founded a County Botanical Medical Society, and in 1869 he became president of the New York State Eclectic Medical Society, a branch of the National Eclectic Medical Association formed to promote "botanic medicine." From 1867 to 1877 he served as president of the Eclectic Medical College; he was an editor of the *American Eclectic Medical Review*, 1871–72, and of the *Medical Eclectic*, 1873–77. Owing to his reputation as financial expert and political journalist on the *Evening Post,* he was elected an alderman of New York in 1871 on an anti-Tweed ticket. After this experience in politics, he moved to Newark, where he lived until his death. He was professor of physiology in the Eclectic Medical College, 1873–77, and subsequently became professor of psychology in the United States Medical College, serving from 1878 to 1883, when the institution was abolished by court decision. He is said to have published in 1873 *Our Darwinian Cousins*, and he subsequently edited *Ancient Symbol Worship* (1875), by H. M. Westropp and C. S. Wake; *Eleusinian and Bacchic Mysteries* (1875), by Thomas Taylor; *The Symbolic Language* (1876), by R. P. Knight; and *Serpent and Siva Worship and . . . The Origin of Serpent Worship* (1877), by Hyde Clarke and C. S. Wake. In 1875 he brought out *Vaccination a Medical Fallacy,* wherein he declared, "Vaccination is physically and morally wrong, and its advocates are inte-

riorly conscious of it, or else they would trust to argument and conviction," whereas he, in opposing them, professed to base his conclusions on irrefutable evidence. In 1882 he attended Bronson Alcott's School of Philosophy in Concord, and later took part in organizing the "American Akademé" at Jacksonville, Fla. From 1876 to 1895 he was secretary of the National Eclectic Medical Association, editing its annual *Transactions*. In 1901 he published a *History of Medicine,* notable for its discussion of the "new schools" which arose in America in the nineteenth century. His last work, a translation of the *Theurgia* of Iamblichos, was published posthumously in 1911. During his connection with the *Evening Post* he married a cousin, but the marriage was unhappy and a separation ensued.

[Biog. sketch in J. U. Lloyd, "The Eclectic Alkaloids," *Bull. Lloyd Lib. of Botany, Pharmacy, and Materia Medica, No. 12* (1910); *Who's Who in America,* 1906–07; M. H. Wilder, *Book of the Wilders* (1878); R. A. Gunn, "Alexander Wilder," *Am. Medic. Jour.,* Nov. 1908, which makes use of autobiog. material; *Eclectic Medic. Jour.,* Nov. 1908; *Evening Post* (N. Y.), Sept. 21, 1908; *Newark Evening News,* Sept. 19, 1908; *N. Y. Tribune,* Sept. 20, 1908.]   E. S. B.

WILDER, HARRIS HAWTHORNE (Apr. 7, 1864–Feb. 27, 1928), zoölogist, was born in Bangor, Me., the son of Solon Wilder, chorister and teacher of vocal music, and Sarah Watkins (Smith) Wilder, both descendants of old New England stock. The original American ancestor on his father's side was Thomas Wilder, who was settled in Charlestown, Mass., in 1640. He attended various schools in Bangor, and in Cambridge and Princeton, Mass., though most of his early education depended on private instruction, and was graduated from the Worcester Classical High School in 1882. He then entered Amherst College, where he came under the influence of Prof. John M. Tyler, who fostered and strengthened the interest in natural history which he had shown from very early childhood. He was graduated in 1886 and taught biology in a Chicago high school for a time. In 1889 he went to Germany and began graduate work in anatomy and zoölogy under Robert Wiedersheim and Weismann, taking the degree of Ph.D. at the University of Freiburg in 1891. After another year of teaching in Chicago, he became professor of zoölogy at Smith College and remained there in charge of the department of zoölogy until his death. In addition to his earlier work on anatomy, Wilder devoted himself to the study of amphibians, the friction-ridges of the skin (fingerprints), teratology, and anthropology. He was tireless in research as well as in teaching, and published his results in about forty scientific papers and a number of books, among them *History of the Human Body* (1909, revised edition, 1923), *Personal Identification* (1918), written in collaboration with Bert Wentworth, *A Laboratory Manual of Anthropometry* (1920), *Man's Prehistoric Past* (1923), *The Pedigree of the Human Race* (1926). He also wrote *The Early Years of a Zoölogist,* an autobiography published posthumously (1930). His sound classical education, the foundation of his cultured personality, influenced strongly the excellent literary style characteristic of his books.

He had rather short stature, red hair, twinkling blue eyes, an expressive face, and a vivacious, somewhat erratic disposition. In spite of his extraordinary enthusiasm for biological teaching and research, he was always a lively social being, fond of entertaining and full of wit and sparkling conversation. He was talented in many ways, having a pronounced gift for humorous verse, drawing, and wood carving. Rather late in life, on July 26, 1906, he was married to Inez Luanne Whipple, who did graduate work under his direction, and became his colleague at Smith College. They were remarkably compatible and together built up a college department notable for its devotion to the ideals of research. Wilder's personal charm and his continued cheerfulness and industry under the handicap of ill health endeared him to his friends; for scientists, his name will be linked with fundamentally important contributions in the fields of vertebrate anatomy, friction-ridge patterns, and descriptive anthropology. He influenced no small number of students to undertake successfully careers in biological teaching and research. He was a fellow of the American Association for the Advancement of Science.

[*Who's Who in America,* 1928–29; M. H. Wilder, *Book of the Wilders* (1878); Wilder's autobiography, *The Early Years of a Zoölogist* (privately printed 1930), ed. by Inez W. Wilder; *Amherst Coll., Biog. Record* (1927); J. McK. and Jaques Cattell, *Am. Men of Sci.* (1927); H. S. Pratt, obituary notice in *Science,* May 11, 1928; *N. Y. Times,* Feb. 28, 1928.]

H. M. P.

WILDER, JOHN THOMAS (Jan. 31, 1830– Oct. 20, 1917), soldier and industrialist, the son of Reuben and Mary (Merritt) Wilder, was born in Hunter Village, Greene County, N. Y. He was a descendant of Edward Wilder, whose mother Martha Wilder, came to America on the ship *Confidence* in 1638. As a lad John served as apprenticed draftsman in a millwright plant in Columbus, Ohio. Subsequently, he established himself as a foundryman and millwright in Greensburg, Ind., where on May 18, 1858, he was married to Martha Stewart.

He enlisted as a private in the 1st Independent Battery Apr. 21, 1861, and the following day he was elected captain. On June 12 of the same year he was appointed by Gov. Oliver P. Morton lieutenant-colonel of the 17th Indiana Volunteer Infantry, and was advanced to the colonelcy on Mar. 2. His command saw its first field service in West Virginia. It was with Buell's army in the second day's battle at Shiloh, after which Wilder was given command, as senior colonel, of a brigade which served at Munfordville, Ky., and in the Tullahoma campaign in Middle Tennessee. In June 1863, when Hoover's Gap of Cumberland Mountains was held by a strong Confederate force to give time to Bragg's main army to fall back towards Chattanooga, Wilder's brigade by the celerity of its movements forced the Gap open and pursued its defenders on their retreat. This engagement caused the brigade thereafter to be called "Wilder's Lightning Brigade." It was composed of the Indiana and Illinois infantry regiments, but it differed from other infantry commands in that its men were equipped, at the instance of Wilder, with the then new model Spencer repeating rifles, and its troopers were mounted. It led the advance of Rosecrans' army to the environs of Chattanooga and was the first brigade to enter the city. In the major battle of Chickamauga, engaging as a distinct unit, it acquitted itself brilliantly, and Wilder was recommended by Maj.-Gen. George H. Thomas for promotion to the rank of brigadier-general "for his ingenuity and fertility of resource . . . and for his valor and the many qualities of commander displayed by him in the numerous engagements of his brigade with the enemy before and during the battle of Chickamauga." On Aug. 6, 1864, Wilder was brevetted brigadier-general.

Resigning from the army in October 1864, he removed to Chattanooga and took a leading part in the development of the natural resources around that city. In 1867 he founded the Roane Iron Works, and at Rockwood he built one of the first blast furnaces in the South. In 1870 he established a rail mill in Chattanooga. He was also active in the promotion and partial construction (1890–92) of the Charleston, Cincinnati & Chicago Railroad (now the Clinchfield Railroad). For himself and his associates he acquired about half a million acres of iron and coal lands in Kentucky, Virginia, North Carolina, and Tennessee, and built the Carnegie furnace at Johnson City. Tennesseans rank him high among the developers of the state's resources. He served as mayor and postmaster of Chattanooga, as pension agent at Knoxville, and as a commissioner of Chickamauga and Chattanooga

National Park. He was a member of the American Institute of Mining Engineers, and an honorary member of the Iron and Steel Institute of Great Britain.

Tall and well-proportioned, Wilder was a striking figure—capable of the great endurance which his initiative and energy impelled. His first wife died Feb. 29, 1892, and in 1904 he married Dora E. Lee. He died at Jacksonville, Fla., survived by his wife, with five daughters and one son of his first marriage. He was buried in Forest Hills Cemetery, Chattanooga.

[M. H. Wilder, *Book of the Wilders* (1878); W. T. Hale and D. L. Merritt, *A Hist. of Tenn.* (1913); C. D. McGuffey, *Chattanooga and Her Battlefields* (1912); Archibald Gracie, *The Truth About Chickamauga* (1911); H. V. Boynton, *The Nat. Mil. Park, Chickamauga—Chattanooga* (1895) and *Dedication of the Chickamauga and Chattanooga Mil. Park* (1896); John Fitch, *Annals of the Army of the Cumberland* (1863); H. M. Cist, *The Army of the Cumberland* (1882); *Who's Who in America*, 1912–13; *Chattanooga Times* and *Chattanooga News*, Oct. 21, 1917.]   S. C. W.

WILDER, MARSHALL PINCKNEY (Sept. 22, 1798–Dec. 16, 1886), merchant, agriculturist, was born at Rindge, N. H., a descendant of Thomas Wilder, freeman of Charlestown, Mass., in 1640. The eldest son of Samuel Locke and Anna (Sherwin) Wilder, Marshall Pinckney was educated at a district school, at an academy at New Ipswich, and by private tutor. Given choice of occupation at sixteen, he chose farming, a preference which he was forced to yield to the demands of his father's mercantile business. At twenty-one he was given a partnership, a responsibility to which he soon added the duties of postmaster at Rindge and the teaching of vocal music. He moved to Boston in 1825, and was a partner successively in a number of commission firms.

Having acquired a fortune within a reasonable period, he proceeded to exercise his abilities in diverse directions. As representative in the state legislature in 1839, member of the executive council in 1849, president of the state Senate in 1850, an ardent supporter of Webster while he lived, and one of the founders of the Constitutional Union party in 1860, he consistently endeavored to act as a statesman rather than a politician. After the Civil War, during which he strongly supported the government, he took little active part in politics. Shortly after his removal to Boston, he joined the Ancient and Honorable Artillery Company; he was its captain in 1856 and lived to be its oldest past commander. With other public-spirited citizens he founded the Massachusetts Institute of Technology in 1861; he served it as vice-president, 1865–70, and as trustee, 1870–86. He was a

member of the New-England Historic Genealogical Society from 1850 and its president from 1868 to 1886. Through his efforts the Society obtained a new building, created an endowment, enlarged its collections, and encouraged historical research and publication. In the Masonic order Wilder rose to the thirty-third degree and became a member of the Supreme Council.

He gave his first allegiance, however, to agriculture. Changing his residence to Dorchester, a suburb of Boston, in 1832, he planted a nursery and began extensive experiments in horticulture which continued for more than fifty years. He developed many new and important varieties of flowers and fruits, including the famous "Wilder Rose," and at one time had nine hundred varieties of pears growing in his garden. His experiments in hybridization were made possible through regular importations of plants from abroad. The Massachusetts Horticultural Society owed much to his counsel and leadership. It had established Mount Auburn Cemetery, ornamenting it with trees and flowers, and in 1835 Wilder devised a contract whereby, in return for agreeing to the separation of the Horticultural Society from the cemetery project, the Society received a percentage of the sales of cemetery lots, thus accumulating an endowment which by 1878 amounted to more than $150,000. Under Wilder's presidency from 1840 to 1848 the organization built its first hall and otherwise greatly extended its interests. Acting for this Society in 1848 Wilder issued a call for a convention of fruit growers in New York City, which resulted in the formation of the American Pomological Society. Wilder was elected president and served repeatedly for thirty-eight years, during which period the organization molded the whole development of American horticulture. In September 1883 he proposed a reform in the nomenclature of the fruits of America which was later carried out. In his first address before the Norfolk Agricultural Society, which he helped to organize in 1849 and over which he presided for twenty years, he pleaded the great need for agricultural education.

At Wilder's instigation, in September 1851, the several agricultural societies of Massachusetts formed a central board of agriculture. As president of this organization he prevailed upon the legislature to establish a state board of agriculture in 1852. Chosen senior member of this body, he directed its activities until shortly before his death. In 1852 as representative of the new Massachusetts board, he requested other state boards and societies to appoint delegates to a national agricultural meeting in Washington, which resulted in the formation of the United States Agricultural Society. Wilder was made president and held office for six years. This society by its national fairs and exhibitions stimulated agricultural improvement; it was influential in the establishment, in the early sixties, of the office of United States commissioner of agriculture, and supported legislation for the creation of state colleges of agriculture. Wilder was a leader in the formation of the Massachusetts Agricultural College, one of the first to be organized in any state, and was a trustee of this institution to the end of his life. As a member of the United States Commission to the Paris Universal Exposition of 1867 he made a valuable report on the horticultural exhibits there. In 1870 he visited California to survey its horticultural products. The addresses which he delivered as president or other officer of the various societies and institutions with which he was connected would fill volumes. He also contributed numerous articles to agricultural journals such as the *Horticulturist, New England Farmer, Country Gentleman, and Genesee Farmer.*

On Dec. 31, 1820, at Rindge, Wilder married Tryphosa Jewett, daughter of Dr. Stephen Jewett. He had six children by this marriage, two of whom died before their mother, whose death occurred in July 1831. On Aug. 29, 1833, he married Abigail Baker, daughter of Capt. David Baker of Franklin, Mass., by whom he had six children. She died in April 1854, and on Sept. 3, 1855, he married her sister, Julia Baker. By this marriage he had two children. Only six of his fourteen children lived to adult life.

Wilder was a born promoter and leader of men. Original in ideas and practical in developing them, he inspired unusual confidence by his genial character and solid reputation as a man of business. For many years he was known as the chief citizen of Boston; for more than sixty years he devoted his money and his talents to public service, consistently evidencing an intelligence, a whole-hearted enthusiasm, and a lack of self-interest which made him one of the best loved and most influential men of his time. The results of his work are felt today in the various societies and institutions which he founded and developed, and in his valuable contributions to the knowledge and practice of horticulture. He died suddenly, in the midst of his activities, at the age of eighty-eight.

[M. H. Wilder, *Book of the Wilders* (1878); J. H. Sheppard, "Memoir of Hon. Marshall Pinckney Wilder," *New Eng. Hist. and Geneal. Reg.*, Apr. 1867; H. A. Hill, "Marshall Pinckney Wilder," *Ibid.*, July 1888; A. P. Peabody, *A Memorial Address on the Late Marshall Pinckney Wilder* (1888); Robert Manning, *Biog. Sketch of Hon. Marshall P. Wilder* (1887); L. H.

Bailey, *Cyc. of Am. Agriculture* (1909), vol. IV; John Livingston, *Portraits of Eminent Americans Now Living* (1854); Justin Winsor, *The Memorial Hist. of Boston* (1881), III, 596, IV, 274–75, 607–40; *Trans. Mass. Horticultural Soc.*, 1840–48; *Proc. Am. Pomological Soc.*, 1848–86; *Trans. Norfolk (Mass.) Agric. Soc.*, 1849–69; *U. S. Agric. Soc. Jour.*, 1853–58; *Ann. Report of the Sec. of the Mass. Board of Agriculture*, 1853–87; files of the *New England Farmer, Country Gentleman, Horticulturist,* and *Genesee Farmer*; *Boston Transcript*, Dec. 16, 1886.]   H. A. K—r.

WILDMAN, MURRAY SHIPLEY (Feb. 22, 1868–Dec. 24, 1930), economist, was born in the little Quaker town of Selma, Ohio, the eldest child of John and Mary Taylor (Pugh) Wildman. The boy was only eleven when his father died, and during his years of schooling he worked on the farm and at whatever other employment he could find to help support his mother and the three younger children. Deciding that he wanted to be a teacher, he entered Earlham College, a Friends' institution at Richmond, Ind., and in 1893 received the degree of Ph.B. On Aug. 16 of that year he married Olive Stigleman of Richmond. Until 1895 he was teacher of history and science at Spiceland Academy, a Friends' school in Indiana. Here he became interested in banking and in 1895 founded the Henry County Bank, of which he was vice-president and cashier until 1902. For the last three years of this period he was principal of the Spiceland Academy and superintendent of the schools of that town.

In 1902 he went to the University of Chicago to study political economy, where he gave chief attention to the subjects of money and banking, coming especially under the influence of Prof. J. Laurence Laughlin. He received the degree of Ph.D. in 1904, his dissertation being published under the title *Money Inflation in the United States* (1905). Marked by skill in composition as well as by accurate research and judicious selection of material, this study forms a useful chapter in American economic history. Opening the work with a discussion of the contributing psychological forces, he went on to the economic causes and showed how a series of liquidated frontiers set up the cry for easy money. His prejudice against socialist proposals was intensified by his review of the inflationist demands of those without property. In 1905 he became instructor and the following year assistant professor of economics at the University of Missouri. In 1909–10 he was assistant professor of economics in the school of commerce at Northwestern University, in 1910–11, taught economics and commerce, and in 1911–12 was professor of economics and commerce. During his last year at Northwestern he performed effective service as secretary of the National Citizen's League for the Promotion of a Sound Banking System, interviewing business men, writing, and speaking. His teacher, Professor Laughlin, was the League's founder and guiding spirit. It took form in the spring of 1911, when it was apparent that the Aldrich bill, for all of its desirable features, would not be enacted. The League undertook, on behalf of business men, borrowers rather than bankers, to educate the country in the principles of banking reform, including the need of credit reorganization as against mere note issue, and emphasizing the importance of making liquid the sound commercial paper of the banks in the form of credits or bank notes redeemable in gold or lawful money. Regional bankers' control, with government sponsorship, instead of the European system of central banks was favored. This program was thoroughly congenial to Wildman, and his work contributed to the League's influence in bringing about the establishment of the Federal Reserve System.

In 1912 he became head of the department of economics at Leland Stanford Junior University. Here he displayed remarkable aptitude both for administrative and teaching duties, and won the enthusiastic cooperation of his colleagues. From 1925 till his death he was dean of the school of social sciences. He served in the bureau of research of the war trade board and the division of planning and statistics of the war industries board, 1918–19, engaged particularly in making studies of food prices during the war period. His heavy teaching and administrative duties left comparatively little time for writing. He was an active member of the Commonwealth Club of San Francisco, where he had intimate contact with men of affairs, and of other organizations of business men and economists. He was also a member of the committee on statistics and standards of the United States Chamber of Commerce. He died at Stanford University, survived by his wife and a daughter.

[*Who's Who in America*, 1926–27; A. C. Whitaker, in *Stanford Illustrated Rev.*, Feb. 1931; *Ann. Report of the President of Stanford Univ.* (1931); J. L. Laughlin, *The Federal Reserve Act, its Origin and Problems* (1933), especially pp. 56 ff.; *San Francisco Chronicle* and *N. Y. Times*, Dec. 25, 1930.]   B. M—l.

WILDWOOD, WILL [See POND, FREDERICK EUGENE, 1856–1925].

WILEY, ANDREW JACKSON (July 15, 1862–Oct. 8, 1931), irrigation engineer, was born in New Castle County, Del., the son of John and Mary (Hukill) Wiley. He attended Newark Academy, Newark, Del., graduating at the head of his class and winning a scholarship at Delaware College, where he was graduated in engineering in 1882. He then spent a year on surveys and construction for the Baltimore & Ohio Railroad Company in Delaware and Maryland.

In 1883 he entered the field of irrigation work at Boise, Idaho, with the Idaho Mining & Irrigation Company. From 1886 to 1888 he was assistant engineer on construction for the Union Pacific Railway Company in Montana. In the latter year he again became associated with the Idaho Mining & Irrigation Company, in connection with an irrigation project in southern Idaho. From 1892 to 1898 he was chief engineer and manager of the Owyhee Land & Irrigation Company in the construction of a large irrigation project in the same state. Land development and irrigation work was at this time difficult and discouraging in results, and Wiley's financial returns were relatively small, but he became known as a man of the highest integrity "whose word alone was a guarantee of performance" and thus laid a sound foundation for his later accomplishments.

About 1900 conditions became more favorable and during the next thirty years Wiley was busy upon a continuous procession of great irrigation and power projects in Idaho, Oregon, California, and other Western states. In addition to numerous non-federal enterprises, he was also consultant to the United States Bureau of Reclamation from its inception in 1902, and from 1925 he held a similar appointment for the Department of the Interior at large. His assignments included practically all of the major government dams, such as the Belle Fourche, Shoshone, Roosevelt, Pathfinder, Arrowrock, Owyhee, and Hoover (now Boulder). These projects included the ranking high masonry dams of the world, many of them between 300 and 400 feet in height, and the last-named 727 feet. Wiley's work included many detailed studies of design as well as periodical field inspections during construction. He was the first engineer to be named for the Boulder Dam consulting board, where his broad experience and sound judgment were invaluable in the preliminary studies of this great project. He was also consulted about projects of other departments of the federal government, including the design and construction of the Coolidge Dam, the Madden Dam and power plant for the Canal Zone, and the Columbia River Basin power and irrigation project.

Acting as consultant for the British government in 1927–28, he investigated dam sites in the Himalayas, and as a result the Bhakra Dam, about 500 feet high, was designed. His professional engagements also took him to Puerto Rico several times. In 1928, following the great St. Francis dam disaster in California, Wiley was chosen to report upon the safety of the twenty or more bureau of reclamation dams. He also was retained to make a similar investigation for the city of Los Angeles. At the time of his death his consulting engagements included such outstanding works as the $165,000,000 Boulder Canyon project, the $220,000,000 aqueduct of the metropolitan water district of southern California, and the $400,000,000 Columbia River project in Washington.

Wiley was averse to publicity and seldom spoke in public. He greatly enjoyed the companionship of friends and was a genial and entertaining host. His kindness and consideration of others always secured the loyalty and diligence of his associates. His engineering career was exceptionally brilliant and his reputation as a consultant was of the highest, both in the United States and abroad. He made his home in Boise, Idaho, but died in Monrovia, Cal. He never married.

[*Trans. Am. Soc. of Civil Engineers,* vol. XC (1932); *Who's Who in America,* 1928–29; *Engineering News-Record,* Oct. 15, 1931; *N. Y. Times,* Oct. 9, 1931.]

H. K. B.

WILEY, CALVIN HENDERSON (Feb. 3, 1819–Jan. 11, 1887), first superintendent of common schools in North Carolina, was born in Guilford County, N. C., the son of David L. and Anne (Woodburn) Wiley. He was of Scotch-Irish stock, a descendant of William Wiley who in 1754 moved from Pennsylvania to North Carolina. At Caldwell Institute in his native county, one of the foremost preparatory schools of the period, he was prepared for the University of North Carolina, from which he was graduated in 1840. He studied law, was admitted to practice in 1841, and settled in Oxford, S. C., where he also edited (1841–43) the Oxford *Mercury.* In 1847 he published a novel called *Alamance; or, The Great and Final Experiment;* this was followed by another novel, *Roanoke; or, Where Is Utopia?* (1849), which appeared in England as *Adventures of Old Dan Tucker, and His Son Walter* (1851). The backward economic and social conditions of North Carolina in the 1840's aroused Wiley's interest in education. Gaining a seat in the state legislature (1850–52), he secured legal provision for a superintendent of common schools to be chosen by the legislature and to hold office for two years. Though Wiley was a Whig and the legislature Democratic, he was chosen for the position and entered upon its duties, Jan. 1, 1853. He was continuously appointed by a legislature of political opponents until 1865, when all state offices in existence on Apr. 26 of that year were declared vacant. Dur-

ing the thirteen years of his service he labored for a complete reorganization and improvement of education. He visited all parts of the state in his buggy and at his own expense, and through educational speeches, newspaper articles, annual reports, and the *North Carolina Journal of Education* (originally *Common School Journal*) which he established (1856) and edited, and through the Educational Association of North Carolina, which he organized, he aroused wide interest in the cause of popular education. He had previously published at his own expense *The North-Carolina Reader* (1851), which became a standard school text. When he became superintendent he disposed of his copyright, sold all of the copies and the plates at cost, and refused to accept any remuneration. Before the outbreak of the Civil War his services were in demand in states which sought to copy the educational plan of North Carolina, and he was held in high esteem among national educational leaders. In cooperation with Braxton Craven [*q.v.*], he helped to promote the work of Normal College, the first teacher training institution of semi-public character in the state (1852–59). The schools continued to operate even during the war and until 1865; largely through Wiley's efforts the permanent public school endowment was left untouched for military purposes.

Wiley believed in universal free education. At the close of the war he was very decided in his advocacy of the freedmen. A deeply religious man, he sought to apply to education everywhere the ideas of the Christian faith. In his later years he was engaged in patriotic and religious work, principally with the American Bible Society, which he served as general agent in some of the southern states (1869). Settling in Winston, N. C., he assisted in the establishment of a graded school system there. In 1855 he was licensed by the Presbyterian Church to preach; he was ordained in 1866, but he never had a regular charge. On Feb. 25, 1862, he was married to Mittie Towles of Raleigh, by whom he had seven children. He died at his home in Winston.

[S. B. Weeks, in *Report of the U. S. Commissioner of Educ. . . . 1896–97* (1898), vol. II, pp. 1376–1474; E. W. Knight, *Pub. School Educ. in N. C.* (1916), and *Pub. Educ. in the South* (1922); R. D. W. Connor, in *Biog. Hist. of N. C.,* vol. II (1905), ed. by S. A. Ashe, *N. C. Day Program* (1905), and "Ante-Bellum Builders of N. C.," *N. C. State Normal and Industrial Coll. Hist. Pubs.,* no. 3 (1914); A. L. Bramlett, *Popular Educ. in N. C.* (1917); H. C. Renegar, *The Problems, Policies and Achievements of Calvin Henderson Wiley* (1925); C. L. Smith, *The Hist. of Educ. in N. C.* (1888); *Alumni Hist. of the Univ. of N. C.* (1924); obituary in *News and Observer* (Raleigh, N. C.), Jan. 12, 1887.]

E. W. K.

WILEY, DAVID (d. *c.* 1813), Presbyterian minister and pioneer agricultural editor, was probably a native of Pennsylvania. He was graduated from the College of New Jersey (later Princeton) with distinction in 1788 and was a tutor at Hampden Sidney College, Virginia, from November 1788 to April 1790. He studied for the Presbyterian ministry, was a licentiate of the Presbytery of New Castle, and was first called by Cedar Creek and Spring Creek Churches, Huntington Presbytery, in April 1793. He was ordained by the Presbytery of Carlisle, Pa., Apr. 9, 1794. Later he was called for half his time to the Sinking Creek Church, serving as pastor for one year. In October 1797 he resigned this charge, retaining, however, the charge of Spring Creek until June 12, 1799. He continued within the bounds of the Huntington Presbytery about a year longer. It seems probable that he resigned his pastorate to study at Princeton, for he took the degree of M.A. there in 1801. In the same year he moved to Georgetown, D. C., called there by Dr. Stephen Bloomer Balch, a prominent Presbyterian minister and principal of the Columbian Academy, as his successor at the academy. Wiley was a good mathematician, but he was apparently more interested in science itself than in teaching, for it was said of him that "he did not seem to care whether the school kept or not, when he went surveying" (*Records of the Columbia Historical Society, post,* p. 81). For a time he served also as librarian of the Columbian Library, but these duties did not weigh heavily upon him. Under his régime the books were scattered and never regathered, "for the principal and librarian had more than even his mighty mind could manipulate successfully," being at the same time "the superintendent of a turnpike, the editor of an agricultural paper, the postmaster, a merchant, a miller, and a minister" (*Ibid.*). He also served as major of Georgetown from 1811 to 1812. He is said to have died in 1813 in North Carolina, where he had gone on a government survey. He was married and had a large family. The variety and number of his activities may have been due to the fact that he was at times harassed by financial difficulties; it seems clear, however, that he was a man of great public spirit and energy, and of remarkable versatility.

It is in connection with his agricultural activities that he deserves most to be remembered. He was secretary of the Columbian Agricultural Society for the Promotion of Rural and Domestic Economy, organized in 1809 by a number of gentlemen residing in Maryland, Virginia, and the District of Columbia. Embracing as it did several states, it was the germ of a national organization. The *Agricultural Museum,* edited by Wiley in connection with the society, was probably the first agricultural journal published in the United States. The first number appeared from the printing press of W. A. Rind in Georgetown in July 1810, nearly nine years before the first number of the *American Farmer.* The magazine was well edited and contained a considerable amount of original material written especially for it; among its contributors were Joel Barlow, John Taylor (1753–1824), and Benjamin Franklin [*qq.v.*]. It probably never attained a large circulation, and may not have continued after May 1812. A small octavo, it was issued semi-monthly during the first year but later became a monthly.

[T. B. Balch, *Reminiscences of Georgetown, D. C.* (1859); *Records of the Columbia Hist. Soc.,* vol. XV (1912); W. B. Bryan, *A Hist. of the Nat. Capital* (1914), vol. I; S. D. Alexander, *Princeton Coll. during the Eighteenth Century* (1872); W. J. Gibson, *Hist. of the Presbytery of Huntington* (1874); *Hist. Memorial of the Centennial Anniv. of the Presbytery of Huntington* (1896); article on S. B. Balch in *Evening Star* (Washington, D. C.), Apr. 1, 1893.]   C. R. B.

WILEY, EPHRAIM EMERSON (Oct. 6, 1814–Mar. 13, 1893), Methodist clergyman and educator, was born at Malden, Mass., the son of Ephraim Wiley, a Methodist preacher, and Rebecca (Emerson) Wiley. His background was that of New England Puritanism. He was graduated at Wesleyan University in 1837, and upon the recommendation of President Wilbur Fisk [*q.v.*], Emory and Henry College (Emory, Va.), a Methodist institution, elected him in 1838 professor of ancient languages and literature.

At Emory and Henry he served as professor, 1838–52, and as president, 1852–79. In the latter capacity he endeavored to strengthen the struggling school. Through the church press and before Methodist conferences he made pleas for better support. As a result the enrollment for the academic session of 1858–60 reached the highest figure attained during the nineteenth century. By 1861 he had also developed plans for raising an endowment by the sale of scholarships, but during the Civil War the college was forced to cease operations and the buildings were used as a Confederate hospital, of which Wiley was chaplain. After the war he made a desperate effort to recoup the fortunes of the college. In 1879 he resigned as president, although during part of the academic session of 1879–80 he was acting president. From 1881 to 1886 he was president of Martha Washington College at Abingdon, Va., then returned to Emory and Henry as treasurer and financial agent, 1886–93.

During his nearly fifty years at Emory and Henry he wielded a great personal influence. Nearly seven thousand students were enrolled in the institution during that period and the "Wiley imprint" was placed upon the majority of them. Although he was nicknamed "Old Eph," the students always held him in the highest esteem. Through his chapel talks and evangelistic meetings he made Emory and Henry noted for its religious atmosphere. For many years the majority of the trained preachers of the Holston Conference were educated under him. Of this Conference, by which he was admitted to full connection in 1843, Wiley was for many years the acknowledged leader. On nine consecutive occasions he was sent as a delegate to the General Conference of the Church. In 1866 and in 1870 his friends actively supported him for the episcopacy. He was a delegate to the Ecumenical Methodist Conferences in 1881 and 1891.

After removing to Virginia Wiley became a slaveholder and a champion of the rights of the South. He adhered with his Conference to the Methodist Episcopal Church, South, after the schism of 1844 in the Methodist Episcopal Church. During the Civil War and the Reconstruction period certain church property of the Holston Conference was appropriated by Northern Methodists, and beginning in 1867, Wiley kept the question of this property before both sides until a settlement was reached. Between 1866 and 1879 he carried on in various Methodist periodicals debates with Northern leaders over the issues between the Northern and Southern Methodists.

He was twice married; first, Feb. 18, 1839, to Elizabeth H. Hammond of Middletown, Conn.; second, in October 1870, to Elizabeth J. Reeves of Jonesboro, Tenn. There were six children by the first marriage and three by the second. Wiley was buried in the cemetery overlooking Emory and Henry College. "The school is dismissed and the 'Old Master' sleeps," is inscribed on his tombstone.

[Manuscript material concerning Wiley, and some private correspondence are at Emory and Henry College; E. E. Wiley, Abingdon, Va., has a number of his father's MSS. and a three-volume scrapbook containing clippings, sermons, speeches, etc. Other sources of information include the printed journals of the Gen. Conference of the Methodist Episcopal Church, South, 1854–90, and the minutes of the Holston Conference, 1869–93; E. E. Wiley, "The Contributions of Ephraim Emerson Wiley to Holston Methodism" (unpublished thesis for the degree of B.D., Duke Univ., 1934); R. N. Price, Holston Methodism: From Its Origin to the Present Time (5 vols., 1904–14); E. E. Hoss, in Christian Advocate (Nashville), Mar. 23, 1893; B. K. Emerson, The Ipswich Emersons (1900).]   P. N. G.

WILEY, HARVEY WASHINGTON (Oct. 18, 1844–June 30, 1930), pure food reformer, chemist, teacher, author, and lecturer, was born in a log cabin at Kent, Jefferson County, Ind.,

the sixth of the seven children of Preston Pritchard and Lucinda Weir (Maxwell) Wiley, both descendants of Scotch-Irish pioneers who had fought in the Revolution. Young Wiley had his early training in a log schoolhouse, in neighboring district schools, and in his home. In 1863 he entered Hanover College (A.B., 1867). His studies were interrupted in 1864 by the Civil War, in which he served as corporal with the 137th Indiana Volunteers. After teaching for a year (1868), he entered the Medical College of Indiana in Indianapolis, from which he was graduated with the degree of M.D. in 1871. Coincident with his medical studies he taught Greek and Latin at Northwestern Christian University (later Butler College). He received the degree of B.S. at Harvard in 1873, and returned to Indianapolis to assume professorships of chemistry at Butler and the Medical College of Indiana. After a temporary breakdown that obliged him to discontinue all work, he became professor of chemistry at Purdue University, Lafayette, Ind. (1874–83), serving also as state chemist of Indiana. He spent a year in Germany (1878), largely at the University of Berlin in the study of chemistry under A. W. von Hofmann, of physics under Herman L. F. von Helmholtz, and of pathology under Rudolf Virchow. His studies of food adulteration, begun under Sell of the German Imperial Health Office, he energetically continued after his return to Purdue.

In 1883 he accepted an appointment as chief chemist of the United States Department of Agriculture and remained in this position until 1912. This was a period of active productivity along three principal lines. The first was a chemical study of the sugar and sirup crops of the United States, in which he performed technological work upon the application of diffusion to the extraction of sugar from sugar cane and—more important—determined the climatic boundaries within which the sugar beet can be grown successfully in the United States. The second was his work in agricultural chemical analysis, for which he devised many new pieces of apparatus and originated many new methods of procedure. The third, his greatest achievement, was his public service in the campaign against food adulteration. The analyses of American food products, which he began immediately after his appointment as chemist of the Department of Agriculture, revealed a shocking state of adulteration, and Wiley gave the rest of his life to correcting this evil. In the face of prolonged opposition he finally secured in 1906 the passage by Congress of the Food and Drugs Act. Confronted with an even more determined resistance, he then began the administration of this Act under difficulties that would have discouraged a less resolute reformer. When he investigated the effect of benzoate of soda and other food preservatives upon the health of his assistants (his famous "Poison Squad"), his damaging reports aroused so much criticism that President Theodore Roosevelt appointed the Remsen Referee Board to reconsider the question. Although the conclusions of the board differed from Wiley's public sentiment generally was upon his side, and the use of food preservatives has in consequence diminished.

In March 1912, after having completely vindicated himself against unjust charges of maladministration, Wiley resigned his office as chief of the bureau of chemistry. In his twenty-nine years of service he built up an organization from six to more than five hundred employees. During this period he originated many lines of chemical research in such fields as soils, milk products, road construction, and standardization of apparatus that afterwards led to the establishment of separate bureaus. Until 1914 he continued to hold the position of professor of agricultural chemistry at George Washington University which he had assumed in 1899. He devoted the rest of his life to writing and lecturing in the interest of pure food. He accepted a position (1912–30) as director of the bureau of foods, sanitation, and health of the *Good Housekeeping* magazine, for which he wrote monthly articles and conducted a question box. He was very successful on the lyceum and Chatauqua platform, and delivered hundreds of lectures.

Wiley had great natural gifts as a wit, poet, and public speaker. His commanding presence, unfailing humor, and courageous expression of opinion held the attention of every audience. His public services won for him many degrees, medals, decorations, and honorary memberships in societies both at home and abroad. He was a member of the jury of awards at various national and international expositions. In 1907 he was invited to help revise the French pure food law, a service for which he was made a chevalier of the Legion of Honor. He was one of the founders (1884) of the Association of Official Agricultural Chemists, and served as secretary (1889–1912) and president (1886). As president of the American Chemical Society (1893–94), he was successful in doubling the society's membership. He was also president of the Indiana Academy of Science (1901), of the United States Pharmacopoeia Revision Committee (1910–20), and of the American Therapeutic Society (1910–11). In addition to numerous scientific bulletins, he was the author of *Princi-*

ples and Practice of Agricultural Analysis (3 vols., 1894–97), *Foods and Their Adulteration* (1907); *Not by Bread Alone* (1915), *The Lure of the Land* (1915), *Health Reader* (1916), *Beverages and Their Adulteration* (1919), *History of a Crime Against the Food Law* (1929), and *Harvey W. Wiley—An Autobiography* (1930). Although urged to consider nominations as governor and vice-president, Wiley declined all political offices. He was usually a Republican but spoke in the campaign for Wilson in 1912. On Feb. 27, 1911, he married Anna Campbell Kelton, by whom he had two sons. His activity in promoting the cause of pure food continued almost to the day of his death, which occurred in Washington. He was buried in Arlington Cemetery.

[In addition to *Harvey W. Wiley—An Autobiog.* (1930), sources include F. W. Houston, L. C. Blaine, and E. D. Mellette, *Maxwell Hist. and Geneal.* (1916); *Who's Who in America*, 1930–31; *Jour. Asso. Official Agricultural Chemists*, Feb. 15, 1931; obituaries in *Evening Star* (Washington), June 30, and *N. Y. Times*, July 1, 1930; personal acquaintance.]   C. A. B—e.

WILKES, CHARLES (Apr. 3, 1798–Feb. 8, 1877), naval officer, explorer, was born in New York City, the son of John De Ponthieu and Mary (Seton) Wilkes. His grandfather Israel was a brother of John, the English politician (see *The Dictionary of National Biography*), and a son of Israel, a prosperous distiller of London. His father, a successful man of business, was able to give his son a good preliminary education in mathematics, navigation, drawing, and the modern languages. Showing a liking for the sea, Charles in 1815 entered the merchant service, where he remained until he was appointed midshipman (Jan. 1, 1818) partly through the influence of the French minister in Washington. After attending a naval school in Boston, he cruised first in the Mediterranean on board the *Guerriere* and later in the Pacific on board the *Franklin*. During a long period on waiting orders or on leave of absence he found time for study under Ferdinand R. Hassler [*q.v.*], founder of the United States Coast and Geodetic Survey. His marriage to Jane Jeffrey Renwick, sister of the elder James Renwick [*q.v.*], took place on Apr. 26, 1826, two days before his promotion to a lieutenancy. In 1832–33 he was engaged in surveying the Narragansett Bay, and on Feb. 16 of the last-named year his scientific attainments received recognition by his appointment to take charge in Washington of the Depot of Charts and Instruments, out of which grew the Naval Observatory and the Hydrographic Office. In 1836 his work at the depot was interrupted by a trip to Europe to procure astronomical and scientific instruments for a proposed exploring expedition. In 1837–38 he commanded the *Porpoise* and engaged in the survey of St. George's Bank and of the Savannah River.

From early boyhood he had had a desire to make geographical discoveries, and he had been greatly interested in the exploring expedition when it was first proposed in 1828. After several officers had declined to command it, Wilkes, although only a lieutenant, was chosen. A civilian corps of specialists, which included Charles Pickering, James D. Dana, and Horatio E. Hale [*qq.v.*], accompanied the fleet, consisting of the *Vincennes* (flagship) and five other vessels. The expedition was absent from the United States from August 1838 until July 1842. The chief fields of exploration were the coast of the Antarctic continent, the islands of the Pacific Ocean, and the American northwest coast. Some 280 islands in the Pacific and adjacent waters and 800 miles of streams and coasts in the Oregon country were surveyed, and 1600 miles of the coast of Antarctica were laid down. "Wilkes Land" in the last-named region perpetuates the name of the explorer. One of his parties established an observatory on the summit of Mauna Loa, Hawaii, and made valuable observations for a period of several weeks. From 1843 until 1861 Wilkes was on special service, chiefly in Washington, preparing for publication and publishing the information collected by the expedition. In 1844 his *Narrative of the United States Exploring Expedition,* in five volumes, was brought out. There were several later editions and brief popular accounts. The scientific volumes appeared from time to time, the last in 1874. Wilkes contributed *Meteorology* (vol. XI, 1851), *Atlas of Charts* (2 vols., 1858), and *Hydrography* (vol. XXIII, 1861). He also published *Western America* (1849), *Theory of the Zodiacal Light* (1857), and *On the Circulation of Oceans* (1859). In 1847 he was awarded the Founder's medal of the Royal Geographical Society of London for his discoveries and his account of them. Soon after his return in 1842 he was tried by a court martial and sentenced to be publicly reprimanded for illegally punishing some of his men. He was promoted commander from July 13, 1843, and captain from Sept. 14, 1855. On Oct. 3, 1854, he was married to Mary H. (Lynch) Bolton, his first wife having died on Aug. 11, 1843, after bearing him two sons and two daughters.

On Apr. 19, 1861, Wilkes was ordered to the Norfolk navy yard to command the *Merrimac,* but when he arrived there next day he found that she had been scuttled to prevent her capture. He was next ordered to proceed to the coast of Africa and take command of the *San Jacinto.* On Nov. 8 he overhauled the British mail steamer *Trent* in the Bahama Channel and took from her by force the Confederate commissioners, James M. Mason and John Slidell [*qq.v.*], and conveyed them to Boston. News of the exploit had preceded him, and the jubilant North welcomed him as a hero. Secretary Welles sent him a congratulatory letter, and the House of Representatives voted him its thanks, but, as the United States did not have a good case and could not afford to go to war with England, his action was disallowed. On July 6, 1862, he was placed in command of the James River flotilla; a few weeks later he was transferred to the Potomac flotilla.

In September he was made an acting rear admiral, and ordered to take command of a special squadron and operate in the West Indies and Bahamas against Confederate commerce destroyers. He failed to capture the destroyers, offended several foreign governments, who claimed violations of neutrality, and incurred the displeasure of Secretary Welles; consequently, on June 1, 1863, he was recalled. On the discovery that he was three years older than he had been thought to be, his commission of commodore, to which rank he had been promoted from July 16, 1862, was cancelled, and he was placed on the retired list as captain. On Mar. 27, 1863, he was made a commodore on the retired list. These professional discouragements, together with limitations of temperament, brought him into conflict with the Navy Department, and in March-April 1864 he was court-martialed. He was found guilty of disobedience, disrespect, and insubordination, and of conduct unbecoming an officer, and was sentenced to be reprimanded and to be suspended from duty for three years. Later the period of suspension was reduced to one year. On July 25, 1866, he was commissioned rear admiral on the retired list. For a part of 1870–73 he was on special duty. For many years his home was the Dolly Madison house, corner of Madison Place and H Street, Washington, D. C.

[Sources include Wilkes's autobiog. (to about 1845), MS. in Lib. of Cong.; H. H. McIver, *Geneal. of the Renwick Family* (1924); Record of Officers, Bureau of Navigation, 1818–78; *Navy Reg.,* 1819–66; *War of the Rebellion: Official Records (Navy),* 1 ser., vols. I, II, IV, V, VII, XVII; *Diary of Gideon Welles* (3 vols., 1911); *Defence . . . of Lieut. Charles Wilkes* (1842); *Defence of Com. Charles Wilkes* (1864), being House Exec. Doc. 102, 38 Cong., 1 Sess.; obituaries in *Army and Navy Jour.,* Feb. 17, 1877, *Evening Star* (Washington, D. C.), Feb. 8, and *N. Y. Tribune,* Feb. 9, 1877. For the exploring expedition, see, in addition to its publications, J. C. Palmer, *Thulia: A Tale of the Antarctic* (1843), a poem; J. G. Clark, *Lights and Shadows of Sailor Life* (1847); G. M. Colvocoresses, *Four Years*

in a Government Exploring Expedition (1852); L. N.
Feipel, in *Proc. U. S. Naval Inst.*, Sept.–Oct. 1914; J.
E. Pillsbury, *Ibid.*, June 1910; J. D. Hill, *Ibid.*, July
1931; and W. H. Hobbs, in *Geographical Rev.*, Oct.
1932. For the *Trent* affair, see C. F. Adams, in *Proc.
Mass. Hist. Soc.*, vol. XLV (1912); T. L. Harris, *The
Trent Affair* (1896); and *War of the Rebellion: Official
Records* (*Navy*), 2 ser., vol. II. A biog. of Wilkes is
being prepared by Mary E. Cooley, Mt. Holyoke Coll.]

C. O. P.

WILKES, GEORGE (1817–Sept. 23, 1885),
journalist, was a native New Yorker of obscure
origin, possibly the son of George Wilkes, cabinet and frame maker, and his wife Helen. He
became a clerk in the law office of one Enoch E.
Camp and descended thence to journalism as
editor or proprietor of the *Flash, Whip,* and
Subterranean, ephemeral organs of the city's political and sporting underworld. A term in the
Tombs for libel eventuated in a pamphlet, *The
Mysteries of the Tombs: A Journal of Thirty
Days Imprisonment in the N. Y. City Prison*
(1844), which evinced an able pen and sympathy for the exploited and friendless. In 1845 he
and Camp started the *National Police Gazette,*
control of which passed in 1857 to George W.
Matsell, a former police chief, and in 1877 to
Richard Kyle Fox [*q.v.*]. During Wilkes's régime it was a robust, rowdy, scandal sheet, objectionable to vicious and decent men alike.
Gangsters wrecked its office more than once,
but the editors made capital of the attacks.
Wilkes's interest in the West was first manifested in an inaccurate, misleading *History of
Oregon, Geographical and Political* (1845), from
which an excerpt entitled *Project for a National
Railroad from the Atlantic to the Pacific Ocean*
(1845) was issued separately and ran through
four editions by 1847. In 1870, it is said, the
Czar of Russia conferred on him the grand cross
of the Order of St. Stanislas for advocating a
railroad through Russian territory to India and
China. In 1849 he accompanied or followed
his friend David Colbreth Broderick [*q.v.*] to
California, made himself useful to him, and subsequently inherited his fortune. In 1853 he made
his first trip to Europe and published his observations as *Europe in a Hurry.* Ever since his
return from California he had been connected
with the well-known sporting paper, the *Spirit
of the Times,* owned and edited by William Trotter Porter [*q.v.*]. He bought the paper in 1856,
renaming it *Porter's Spirit of the Times* and retaining Porter on the staff until his death, July
19, 1858. From 1859 to 1866 the publication was
known as *Wilkes' Spirit of the Times.*

Wilkes owned it until his own death. Despite
his meager schooling, he was master of a vigorous, vivid, precise style that exactly suited his
hard, truculent disposition, and his signed articles always attracted attention and admiration.
Though the *Spirit* remained primarily a sporting paper, it soon began to reflect its owner's
relish for politics, and its political articles were
influential. Wilkes was on the ground at the battle of Bull Run, was greatly taken with the prowess of the Confederates, and wrote an excellent
account of the action: *The Great Battle Fought
at Manassas . . . Sunday, July 21, 1861* (1861).
Immediately he turned war correspondent and
reported the major engagements for his paper
as if they were a series of sporting events. James
Parton (*General Butler in New Orleans,* 1864,
p. 9) thought Wilkes, Butler, and Lincoln the
three ablest writers developed by the war.
Wilkes despised McClellan and assailed him in
article and pamphlet. During the war he contracted the kidney disease of which ultimately he
died.

After the war he was fairly prominent in Republican politics, ran unsuccessfully for Congress against James Brooks, and hoped for a diplomatic appointment under Grant. With the cooperation of John Chamberlain and his own lieutenant, Marcus Cicero Stanley, he introduced
the American people to the pari mutuel system
of betting. He promoted various famous prize-
fights and often quarreled with the fighters. He
was tall and erect, with dark eyes and a large
moustache, dressed in good taste, and gave generously to charities. He never talked about his
early life. He was married twice. A life-long
reader of Shakespeare, he published as his last
book *Shakespeare from an American Point of
View* (1877, 3rd ed., 1882). A shrewd man of
business, with ample capital in reserve, he grew
increasingly wealthy. In his later years he lived
much in London and Paris, although he died in
his New York house at 352 West Sixty-first St.
On his deathbed the "fighting cock of journalism," a strong Protestant all his life, was converted to Catholicism by a Paulist father, but
his friends scouted the priest's story, and employed the Rev. Dr. R. S. MacArthur [*q.v.*] of
Calvary Baptist Church to bury him.

[*Sun* (N. Y.), Sept. 24, 1885; *N. Y. Herald, N. Y.
Times, World* (N. Y.), Sept. 25, 1885; *N. Y. Tribune,*
Sept. 27, 1885; *Spirit of the Times,* Sept. 26, 1885;
Francis Brinley, *Life of William T. Porter* (1860);
James O'Meara, *Broderick and Gwin* (1881); H. H.
Bancroft, *Hist. of the Pacific States: Cal.,* vols. VI–VII
(1888–90); C. B. Bagley, "George Wilkes," *Wash.
Hist. Quart.,* Oct. 1907–Jan. 1914.]   G. H. G.

WILKESON, SAMUEL (June 1, 1781–July
7, 1848), pioneer, was born in Carlisle, Pa., the
son of John and Mary (Robinson) Wilkeson.
His father emigrated from the north of Ireland

in 1760, settling first in Delaware, then at Carlisle, Pa., and in 1784, having served as lieutenant in the Revolution, took up a soldier's grant in Washington County, near Pittsburgh, with his wife and three young children. Samuel worked on his father's farm and had only a few weeks of schooling. In 1802 he removed to Ohio, near the site of Youngstown. In 1809 he removed to Lake Erie, near the present Westfield, N. Y. There he built keel boats and engaged in the lake and river trade. When, on a trading expedition to Detroit, he found General Harrison's army delayed in the Grand River by lack of transports, he successfully undertook the building of the necessary vessels. With Pennsylvania militia he took part in the unsuccessful defense of Buffalo against the British. Convinced of the commercial possibilities of the ruined village, on his return home in 1814 he loaded a lake boat with the frames and covering for a store and dwelling, embarked his family, and sailed to his new home. As trader, shipowner, contractor, iron founder, and manufacturer he engaged with success in practically all the business enterprises of the frontier community. His uncompromising dealing, as justice of the peace, with unruly disbanded soldiers won him the respect and gratitude of his neighbors; but the accomplishment that marked him as a leader in the community was the construction in 1820, in the face of great odds, of a harbor at the mouth of Buffalo Creek suitable for the western terminus of the Erie Canal. With two others he pledged property to the value of $24,000 to secure a loan of $12,000 from the state of New York. When the superintendent of the work proved incompetent, Wilkeson was asked to take charge. He lacked engineering training and had never seen an artificial harbor of any kind; but the following morning at daylight he was on the job. Neither the plan of the work nor its precise location had been determined. All kinds of makeshift devices were employed. A pile-driver was improvised from a two-thousand-pound mortar. After eight months of unremitting effort a pier eighty rods long was extended, reaching water twelve feet deep. In 1821 he was appointed first judge of common pleas in Erie County, in 1824 was elected state senator, and in 1836 became mayor of Buffalo.

In federal affairs, his chief interest seems to have been the abolition of slavery, which he hoped to bring about gradually with compensation to slaveholders. He was a member of the American Colonization Society, for some time president of its board of directors, and was instrumental in shipping many freed negroes to Liberia. While traveling in Tennessee, he was suddenly taken ill at Kingston and died there. He was married three times, before 1802 to Jane Oram, who bore him six children, and after her death to Sarah St. John, of Buffalo. His third wife was Mary Peters of New Haven, a teacher. A tall man, his appearance was stern and commanding. His fearlessness won him many devoted friends, but his unwillingness to conciliate his opponents, and to explain or justify his actions, involved him in many controversies and provoked bitter enmities. He was an eloquent and convincing speaker. In 1842 and 1843 he published in the *American Pioneer* of Cincinnati a series of articles on his own experiences (reprinted in *Buffalo Historical Society Publications,* vol. V, 1902). These recollections show not only accurate and discriminating observation but also unusual literary powers. Considering his entire lack of formal education, the variety and solidity of his achievements were amazing.

["Recollections," *ante*; Samuel Wilkeson, Jr., "Biog. Sketch," *Buffalo Hist. Soc. Pubs.,* vol. V (1902); *Ibid.,* vol. IV (1896); J. C. Lord, *"The Valiant Man," A Discourse on the Death of the Hon. Samuel Wilkeson* (1848); *African Repository,* Aug. 1848, also May 1838, Jan. 15, 1840.]   P. W. B.

WILKIE, FRANC BANGS (July 2, 1832–Apr. 12, 1892), journalist, was born at West Charlton, Saratoga County, N. Y., the son of John Wilkie and his second wife, Elizabeth (Penny). As a boy of twelve he was placed in service with a neighboring farmer, but, displeasing his employer, he ran away and obtained a position as a driver on the Erie Canal. He was cheated out of his wages at the end of the navigation season, but managed to secure passage down the Hudson to New York City, where for about two years he supported himself by selling newspapers and running errands. Returning home, he worked on the farm and at blacksmithing. In 1855 he entered Union College with the class of 1857, and supported himself by writing and setting type for the *Schenectady Evening Star.* In 1856, leaving college, he followed a friend to Davenport, Iowa, where they began (Sept. 20, 1856) editing and publishing the *Daily Evening News,* an enterprise which collapsed in the financial crisis of 1857. For want of other occupation Wilkie wrote and had published *Davenport, Past and Present* (1858). After various makeshifts and the publication, in Elgin, Ill., of a campaign paper in the interest of Stephen A. Douglas, he became in November 1858 city editor of the *Dubuque Daily Herald.* When war broke out in 1861 he accompanied the 1st Iowa Regiment as army correspondent for the

Herald. His ingenuity in obtaining war news and his clarity in reporting it attracted the attention of Henry J. Raymond [*q.v.*], editor of the *New York Times,* and Wilkie soon became that paper's chief war correspondent in the West, so serving, except for a few months in 1862, until he left the army in 1863. He was with Nathaniel Lyon and John Charles Frémont, and with U. S. Grant [*qq.v.*] from the capture of Fort Henry to the surrender of Vicksburg, witnessing and describing every important battle in the West and Southwest. His accounts, signed "Galway," were crisp and vivid, and he was considered the best correspondent with the western armies. Some of his war sketches were published under the title *Pen and Powder* (1888).

In September 1863 he became assistant editor of the *Chicago Times,* and remained with that paper, chiefly as editorial writer, continuously for twenty-five years, save for the period from 1881 to 1883, when he engaged in independent literary work. He served at two different periods (1877–78 and 1880–81) as European representative of the *Times.* His book, *Sketches beyond the Sea* (1879), deals with his foreign experiences. His *"Walks about Chicago"* (1869) was first printed in the form of articles in the *Times.* His *Personal Reminiscences of Thirty-five Years of Journalism* (1891) deals chiefly with his years with the *Chicago Times* and constitutes not only a partial autobiography, but also practically a biography of Wilbur Fisk Storey [*q.v.*], that newspaper's erratic and irascible editor. After leaving the *Times* in 1888 he wrote for the *Chicago Globe* and later for the *Chicago Herald,* until ill health in 1890 compelled his retirement from active work. He had a fertile imagination and a fund of sarcasm, which he employed effectively in his editorials. His other published writings, generally appearing under the pseudonym "Poliuto," included *The Great Inventions: Their History . . . Their Influence on Civilization* (1883), *The Gambler* (1888), and *A Life of Christopher Columbus* (1892). Wilkie was one of the founders of the Chicago Press Club and its first president (1880). He died at his home in Norwood Park, Ill., and was buried at Elgin, Ill. In 1857 he was married to Ellen Morse, daughter of John Morse of Elgin, who, with one son and an adopted daughter, survived him.

[Two of Wilkie's books, *Pen and Powder* (1888) and *Personal Reminiscences* (1891), are largely autobiog. See also John Moses and Joseph Kirkland, *Aboriginal to Metropolitan Hist. of Chicago, Ill.* (1895), vol. II, p. 56; Newton Bateman and Paul Selby, eds., *Hist. Encyc. of Ill., Cook County Ed.* (1905), vol. I, p. 588; obituaries in *Chicago Times, Chicago Tribune,* and *Daily Inter Ocean* (Chicago), Apr. 13, 1892. The date of birth is sometimes given as 1830.]   G. B. U.

WILKINS, ROSS (Feb. 19, 1799–May 17, 1872), lawyer and jurist, was born in Pittsburgh, Pa., the son of John and Catherine (Stevenson) Wilkins. His father had been a soldier in the Revolution; William Wilkins [*q.v.*] was his uncle. Ross Wilkins was educated at Dickinson College, Carlisle, Pa. Following his graduation in 1816, he studied law in Pittsburgh, and had been admitted to the bar and elected prosecuting attorney by the time he was twenty-one. He practised law in Pittsburgh from 1823 to 1832. On May 13, 1823, he married Maria Duncan, by whom he had seven children. In 1832 he was appointed by President Andrew Jackson, a personal friend, territorial judge of Michigan, an office he held until 1837. In 1835 he served as delegate to the Michigan constitutional convention. In 1836, when the admission of Michigan as a state was being considered, he represented Lenawee County in the "First Convention of Assent" and Wayne County in the "Second Convention of Assent." He was an influential member of both conventions. He was for five years (1837–42) a member of the board of regents of the University of Michigan. He served as recorder of the city of Detroit in 1837 and in the same year was appointed United States district judge of Michigan. When the state was divided into two judicial districts, he became judge of the eastern district, an office which he held continuously from 1837 to 1870, when he resigned. In politics he was a Democrat. He was an ultra-temperance man, a leader in the Washingtonian teetotal movement of the forties. During his late years he was much interested in theology and doctrinal controversy. It is said that he kept his Greek testament constantly at his side. Although he had been a Methodist for many years, he became a Catholic towards the end of his life. He was survived by a son and two daughters.

He was said to resemble Lord Byron and is described by a contemporary as one of the handsomest men of his day. In his later years he was calm and judicial in manner. One of the most important trials at which he presided was that of James Jesse Strang [*q.v.*], head of the Beaver Island Mormon colony (see H. M. Utley, *Michigan as a Province, Territory, and State,* 1906, III, 297–310). As a judge, he is said always to have endeavored to reach the substantial justice of the case, but he was never fond of acute or logical distinctions. His charges to the jury were famous for their classic diction and impressive manner. His published opinions appear in *Federal Cases,* J. S. Newberry's *Reports of Admiralty Cases . . . 1842 to 1857* (1857), *McLean's Circuit Court Reports,* and

H. B. Brown's *United States Admiralty and Revenue Cases* (1876).

[G. W. Jordan, *Colonial and Revolutionary Families of Pa.* (1911), vol. II, pp. 884–86; R. B. Ross, *The Early Bench and Bar of Detroit* (1907), pp. 217–20; G. I. Reed, *Bench and Bar of Mich.* (1897); *Wayne County Hist. and Pioneer Soc. Chronography* (1890), pp. 132–33; *Hist. Colls. . . . Mich. Pioneer and Hist. Soc.*, vol. XXII (1894), pp. 326–28; death notice in *Detroit Free Press*, May 18, 1872; Burton Scrap-Book, vol. II, pp. 9, 95, vol. XVII, p. 47, and Walker Scrap-Book, vol. II, p. 40, in Burton Hist. Coll., Detroit Pub. Lib.; information from Wilkins' grandson, Ross Wilkins of Detroit.]   H. C—y.

WILKINS, WILLIAM (Dec. 20, 1779–June 23, 1865), jurist, senator, diplomat, secretary of war, was born in Carlisle, Pa., the tenth child of John and Catherine (Rowan) Wilkins. He was descended from Robert Wilkins, who emigrated from Wales to Lancaster County, Pa., in 1694. William's father removed from Donegal Township, Lancaster County, to Carlisle in 1763; he was a tavern and storekeeper and during the Revolution served as captain in the Continental Army. In 1783 he removed to Pittsburgh to establish a store, subsequently achieving some prominence and holding various city and county offices. William probably received his early education in Pittsburgh. He attended Dickinson College, Carlisle, in the class of 1802 and, after studying law with David Watts of Carlisle, he returned to Pittsburgh and was admitted to the Allegheny County bar in 1801. In 1806, under censure for serving as a second in a duel, he spent a year in Kentucky with his brother. After his return he became active in city affairs; he was one of the organizers of the Pittsburgh Manufacturing Company, which, largely through his efforts, was chartered in 1814 as the Bank of Pittsburgh, of which he served as president until 1819; he was also president of the Monongahela Bridge Company, of the Greensburg and Pittsburgh Turnpike Company, and from 1816 to 1819 of the Pittsburgh common council.

In 1819 Wilkins was elected as a Federalist to the state legislature, but in December 1820 resigned to accept appointment as president judge of the fifth judicial district of Pennsylvania. In May 1824 he was appointed judge of the United States district court for western Pennsylvania. In 1826 he was an unsuccessful candidate for election to Congress. Elected in 1828 as a Democrat, he resigned before qualifying, principally for financial reasons. He had become an admirer of Andrew Jackson and in 1831 was elected to the United States Senate as a Democrat and Anti-Mason. He gained some prominence during the debates on the nullification question, when he heatedly supported Jackson against Cal-

houn. In 1833 he angered many of his constitu·· ents by his support of the measure removing the deposits from the state banks. On June 30, 1834, he resigned his seat in the Senate to accept appointment as minister to Russia. His negotiations for a treaty of neutral rights and for the renewal of certain trading rights in North America were alike unsuccessful, and he returned in April 1836. In 1840 he again ran for Congress but was defeated. He was elected in 1842, however, but his career in the House was cut short by his appointment in February 1844 as secretary of war in Tyler's cabinet. His main interest seems to have been in territorial expansion, and he suggested means of organizing new territories and spoke in favor of the annexation of Texas. He went out of office in 1845. Ten years later he was elected to the state Senate on the Democratic ticket, where he served one term, during which he sponsored a bill known as the "Wilkins Bill" proposing legislation favorable to the liquor interests.

After the increase in real-estate values in 1855 he found himself in comfortable circumstances, and on an estate of 650 acres in the east end of Pittsburgh he built an elaborate mansion, "Homewood," which became a fashionable social center. He was twice married: first, in 1815, to Catherine Holmes of Baltimore, who died in 1816; and second, Oct. 1, 1818, to Mathilda Dallas, daughter of Alexander J. Dallas [q.v.] of Philadelphia; by his second wife he had three sons and four daughters. Ross Wilkins [q.v.] was his nephew. William Wilkins was known as a man of great amiability and public spirit; he was moderate in his habits, tall and rugged in appearance, and courteous in manner. At the beginning of the Civil War he took an active part in rallying troops and fostering patriotism. He was fond of military display and in 1862 was appointed major-general of the Pennsylvania Home Guard. Wilkins Avenue in Pittsburgh and Wilkins Township and the borough of Wilkinsburg in Allegheny County were named for him.

[The most extensive biog. is S. E. Slick, "The Life of William Wilkins" (unpublished thesis, Univ. of Pittsburgh, 1931). A copy of a manuscript autobiog. of John Wilkins and scattered records of the Wilkins family are in the Hist. Soc. of Western Pa. Consult also L. D. Ingersoll, *A Hist. of the War Dept.* (1879); J. W. F. White, "The Judiciary of Allegheny County," in *Pa. Mag. of Hist. and Biog.*, July 1883; Daniel Agnew, "Address to the Allegheny County Bar Association," in *Ibid.*, 1889; F. M. Eastman, *Courts and Lawyers of Pa.* (1922); *Biog. Dir. Am. Cong.* (1928); B. P. Thomas, "Russo-American Relations, 1815–1867," *Johns Hopkins Univ. Studies in Hist. and Pol. Sci.*, vol. XLVIII (1930); *Hist. of Allegheny County* (1889); *Pittsburgh Gazette Times*, Sept. 21, 1919, July 30, 1922; *Pittsburgh Evening Chronicle*, June 23, 1865;

Pittsburgh Commercial, Daily Pittsburgh Gazette, Daily Post (Pittsburgh), June 24, 1865.]   S. J. B.

WILKINSON, DAVID (Jan. 5, 1771–Feb. 3, 1852), inventor, manufacturer, was born in Smithfield, R. I., the third son of Oziel and Lydia (Smith) Wilkinson. He was a descendant of Lawrance Wilkinson, a prominent Quaker, who came from England about 1645 and settled in Providence, R. I. Oziel, David's father, was the son of John and Ruth (Angell) Wilkinson and was born in Smithfield (now Slatersville), R. I., on Jan. 30, 1744. He was a blacksmith by trade but was an inventive genius as well and at an early period engaged in the manufacture of a variety of iron products. Appreciating the great advantages of water power in the pursuance of his business, he moved with his family to Pawtucket, R. I., about 1783 and established a plant there for the manufacture of farm tools, domestic utensils, and cut nails. The following year he added an anchor-forging shop; still later, a metal rolling and slitting mill; and gradually thereafter with the aid of his sons built up an establishment which by 1800 was recognized as the hub of the iron and machinery manufacturing business of New England. As his sons became active in the concern, Oziel turned to other ventures, and particularly, as a partner with his son-in-law Samuel Slater [*q.v.*], to the manufacture of cotton, in which enterprise he continued active until his death on Oct. 22, 1815.

David Wilkinson entered his father's manufactory in Pawtucket at the age of thirteen, and before reaching his majority had perfected a number of ingenious devices used in the several shops. About 1786 the elder Wilkinson began making iron screws for clothier's and oil presses and the method of cutting and finishing the screw threads was of particular interest to David. He worked on the problem for many years and finally on Dec. 14, 1798, obtained a patent for a machine for cutting screw threads which incorporated the slide rest. This was one of the first, if not the first, invention of this important machine tool in America, but the basic invention must be credited to Henry Maudslay of England (see *Dictionary of National Biography*). In 1788–89 Wilkinson assisted in the development of Slater's cotton machinery through the construction of the iron parts; later he made the patterns and cast the wheels and racks for the locks of the new canal at Charlestown, Mass. About 1800, when the elder Wilkinson became interested in the manufacture of cotton, David and his brother Daniel established an iron manufactory of their own in Pawtucket, known as David Wilkinson & Company. A thriving business was soon built up in the manufacture of textile machinery, the Wilkinson products being sold in practically every state on the Atlantic seaboard. David added a small blast-furnace to the establishment and engaged in the casting of solid cannon. He perfected, also, a mill to bore cannon by water power, the feature of the machine being that the boring tool was stationary and the cannon revolved against it.

After developing a manufacturing business which included the construction of all sorts of textile machinery and other iron products, Wilkinson lost everything in the financial panic of 1829. On the advice of friends and at the instigation of the founders of the town, he moved with his family to Cohoes, N. Y., near Albany, to start a new business. He was unsuccessful in this enterprise, however, and from 1836 until his death he wandered about with his family, getting employment wherever he could, chiefly in canal and bridge construction work in New Jersey, Ohio, and Canada. Busy with other things, Wilkinson never paid much attention to his slide-rest invention of 1798. The tool, however, was widely adopted, particularly in the manufacture of firearms by the United States government. Feeling entitled to remuneration, in 1848 Wilkinson petitioned Congress for some financial reward for his invention. His petition was granted in August of that year and he received the sum of $10,-000. His wife was Martha Sayles, a direct descendant of Roger Williams, by whom he had four children. He died at Caledonia Springs, Ontario, Canada, and was buried at Pawtucket.

[*Trans. of the R. I. Soc. for the Encouragement of Domestic Industry, 1861* (1862); Israel Wilkinson, *Memoirs of the Wilkinson Family in America* (1869); *North Providence Centennial: A Report of the Celebration* (1865); Massena Goodrich, *Hist. Sketch of the Town of Pawtucket* (1876); J. W. Roe, *English and Am. Tool Builders* (1926); A. H. Masten, *The Hist. of Cohoes, N. Y.* (1877); *Providence Daily Jour.*, Feb. 9, 1852; Patent Office records.]   C. W. M.

WILKINSON, JAMES (1757–Dec. 28, 1825), soldier, was born in Calvert County, Md., the grandson of Joseph Wilkinson who emigrated to Maryland from England in 1729. His father, also Joseph Wilkinson, a substantial but not wealthy planter, died when the son was about seven. The boy was taught by a private tutor, began the study of medicine, and continued his studies in Philadelphia. Military life attracted him, even as a medical student, and in 1776 he obtained a captain's commission in the Revolutionary Army, to rank from September 1775. He served in the siege of Boston and then joined Benedict Arnold at Montreal, accompanied him during the retreat to Albany, and in December 1776 became aide-de-camp to Gates. He served at Trenton and Princeton under Washington, who made him lieutenant-colonel in 1777, rejoined Gates, and on May 24, 1777, was appointed deputy adjutant-general for the northern department. Commissioned to report the victory at Saratoga, he proved a tardy messenger; nevertheless Congress brevetted him brigadier-general in November 1777. In the following January he also became secretary of the newly organized board of war. Intrigue was his ruling passion, and hard drinking too often his nemesis. These provocative characteristics brought him into the Conway cabal against Washington and ultimately forced him to resign his multiple honors. Almost immediately he sought the lucrative position of clothier-general; but there were grave irregularities in his accounts, and he was obliged to give it up on Mar. 27, 1781 (*Journals of Continental Congress,* vol. XVII, 1910, ed. by Gaillard Hunt, p. 716; vol. XIX, 1912, pp. 313, 374). Thus was revealed another ruling passion—greed for money—which often led him to overestimate both his ability and integrity. Having in the meantime married Ann, the sister of Clement Biddle [*q.v.*], he took up farming in Bucks County, Pa., became brigadier-general of the state militia, and in 1783 obtained election to the state Assembly.

Seeking a still wider outlet for his restless energy, he undertook a trading venture to the westward and in 1784 entered upon the first major chapter of his devious career, in the rapidly growing district of Kentucky. With his ready tongue and handsome person, his facile but treacherous pen, he supplanted George Rogers Clark [*q.v.*] as leader of the region. His grandiose manner of speaking enabled him to oppose Humphrey Marshall, 1760–1841 [*q.v.*], successfully, but made of the latter an implacable enemy. In August 1785 Wilkinson penned two fervid memorials advocating immediate separation from Virginia. His success evidently convinced him that he might turn prevalent discontent, intensified by Jay's proposed concessions to the Spaniards, to his own financial gain. This, it seems, was the real purpose behind the so-called "Spanish Conspiracy." He first used his distorted charges against Clark to commend himself to nearby Spanish authorities. Then in 1787 he ventured on a trading voyage to New Orleans. By means of personal interviews and specious memorials he made a favorable impression on Gov. Esteban Miró [*q.v.*], disposed of his goods, and petitioned for an exclusive trading monopoly. To strengthen this petition Wilkinson took an oath of allegiance to the Spanish monarch. He so impressed his neighbors on his return to Ken-

tucky that they were willing to entrust him with their produce for the New Orleans market. Availing himself of the local agitation for statehood, he convinced the Spaniards that he was working towards disunion and gained his coveted monopoly for a few years. Ultimately he was granted an annual pension of $2,000. His use of western discontent and the credulity of Spanish officials to build up his personal fortunes was mercenary and despicable, but not necessarily traitorous.

As a member of the Kentucky convention of November 1788, he read an address on separation from Virginia and the navigation of the Mississippi that was comparatively mild in tone, and he linked it with his journey to New Orleans. For this contribution he received the thanks of his fellow members and was empowered to draw up resolutions in keeping with his ostensible views, which merely favored separate statehood (Bodley, *post,* pp. lvii-lxiii). By letter he assured Miró that he had read to the convention the memoir presented at New Orleans during the preceding summer. To strengthen himself with the Spanish executive he reported his efforts to checkmate the influence of a British agent in Kentucky and in the summer of 1789 made another journey to New Orleans. On this occasion he composed a second memorial on disunion and supplemented this with a list of prominent westerners, including himself, to whom the Spanish government might profitably grant pensions (*American Historical Review,* July 1904, pp. 765–66). This list is imposing rather than conclusive, but he induced the impressionable Miró to make him a temporary loan of $7,000 (evidently never repaid) and eventually gained the coveted pension. The Spaniards granted Benjamin Sebastian [*q.v.*] a similar favor, evidently to keep an eye on Wilkinson, but shortly opened the river trade generally and thus rendered Wilkinson's monopoly valueless. That wily agent also endeavored to connect himself with a group of the Yazoo land speculators, only to betray them to the Spaniards. His commercial ventures having proved largely unproductive and his local land speculations, including the founding of Frankfort, disastrous, he betook himself to military service, leaving his tangled business affairs to be settled by Harry Innes [*q.v.*].

In March 1791 he led a force of volunteers against the Indians north of the Ohio. In October he was commissioned lieutenant-colonel in the regular army and in March 1792 brigadier-general under Wayne. During the next five years he quarreled openly with Wayne, whose place he had sought for himself, and secretly plotted to thwart and discredit his superior's plan of campaign (own narrative in *Mississippi Valley Historical Review*, June 1929, pp. 81–90). The Spaniards attempted to send him $16,000 on his pension, but he received barely a third, owing to the death or defalcation of his messengers. In return for such bounty he reported to Carondelet the filibustering activities of George Rogers Clark and urged more vigorous measures against the Kentuckians. Nevertheless in 1795 he refused to meet Carondelet's representative, Gayoso, at New Madrid. In 1796 he took over Detroit from the British and shortly afterward departed for Philadelphia to defend himself and still further to discredit Wayne. The latter's death, rather than his own lobbying, made Wilkinson the ranking officer of the army but did not bring him the coveted rank of major-general. His course at Detroit, after his return there in 1797, made him extremely unpopular. In that same year he resisted a final appeal from Carondelet to make himself the "Washington of the West." Transferred to the southern frontier in 1798, he endeavored to quiet the Indians and to maintain friendly relations with the Spaniards. His convivial visits with Gayoso, who was now governor at New Orleans, gave rise, however, to unfavorable comments about personal land deals and army contracts (Manuscripts of war department, *post*). His schemes to become governor or surveyor-general of Mississippi Territory disturbed the federal authorities. Washington commissioned Andrew Ellicott [*q.v.*] to watch him, and Wilkinson in turn spied on Ellicott. Adams gave Wilkinson his confidence. Hamilton, during threatened hostilities with France, summoned him to confer on western defense and a possible invasion of Spanish territory. Following the party change of 1801 Burr helped him keep his place in the army and Jefferson commissioned him to treat with the various southern tribes (Manuscripts of war department, *post*), a task that kept him traveling a year and a half. Incidentally he obtained commercial privileges for the government on the rivers east of the Mississippi and established a new fort and trading post on the Tombigbee. From these months of wandering he was summoned in 1803 to share with Gov. William C. C. Claiborne [*q.v.*] the honor of taking possession of the Louisiana Purchase. Then craftily arousing Spanish fears with a characteristic memoir, he obtained $12,000 from the Spanish boundary commissioner, invested the major portion of this new retaining fee in sugar, and took sail for New York (*American Historical Review*, July 1914, p. 800). He then began his spectacular but distrustful relations with Aaron Burr [*q.v.*]. The two "conspirators" conferred frequently in Washington, during the winter of 1804–05, and again in the following June at the mouth of the Ohio, where Wilkinson furnished Burr with conveyance to New Orleans and flattering letters of introduction. In September he entertained Burr at St. Louis and commended him to the attention of Governor Harrison of Indiana. Hence public opinion naturally associated the two in some nebulous enterprise—possibly an invasion of Mexico.

Meanwhile in the spring of 1805, the administration enlarged Wilkinson's functions to include the governorship of Louisiana Territory. From his headquarters at St. Louis he might the better feed his own fortune or advance the "conspiracy" with Burr, but at considerable peril to one of his propensity for intrigue. Moreover, his combined military and civilian functions provoked much local controversy and led him to exceed his authority. He was suspected—perhaps unjustly—of profiteering in the site for a cantonment and, more plausibly, in deciding tangled land titles with an eye to his own interests (Louis Houck, *A History of Missouri*, 1908, II, 404). His effort to further the President's plans for exploring the Louisiana Purchase coincided with his presumptive connection with Burr and his intention to engage in the fur trade. This last project led to an ill-concealed alliance with René Auguste Chouteau [*q.v.*] and to three preliminary ventures up the Osage, the Mississippi, and the Missouri. His own son, James B. Wilkinson, directed the last one. A more famous venture, headed by Zebulon M. Pike [*q.v.*], was designed by Wilkinson to open up a feasible military route to New Mexico. This, too, public opinion quickly associated with Burr's mysterious movements, and the disclaimers of the general and of his agent were unable to remove this impression (I. J. Cox, "Opening the Santa Fé Trail," *Missouri Historical Review*, Oct. 1930). After a few months Wilkinson found that his rule was more unpopular in St. Louis than it had been at Detroit. His enemies bestirred themselves to prevent his confirmation as governor but failed by a narrow margin. Jefferson was finally constrained in May 1806 to order him to the southern frontier and ultimately to remove him from the governorship. The President, however, expressed no regret at having bestowed the office on him (*The Writings of Thomas Jefferson*, vol. X, 1905, ed. by P. L. Ford, p. 264).

During the summer of 1806 more serious trouble threatened Wilkinson. Joseph Street [*q.v.*] began to expose his intimacy with Burr and to connect it with the earlier Spanish intrigue. Aroused by this threat, Wilkinson devised desperate measures to save himself. From his headquarters at Natchitoches he warned Jefferson that a plot was on foot to disrupt the Union and to invade Mexico and that he proposed to meet the peril by transferring his troops to New Orleans, the objective point of the conspiracy. This he did during the next few weeks, after arranging with the Spanish frontier authorities to maintain a neutral zone between their respective garrisons. At the same time, he dispatched a messenger to inform the Mexican viceroy of the peril threatening the Spanish dominions and to ask for a sum of money to be expended in his efforts to avert it. His attempt to get money from the Spaniard signally failed; he was far more successful in his approach to Jefferson. Wilkinson, meanwhile, was at New Orleans, making ready to meet the oncoming Burr. With the hesitant support of Governor Claiborne he declared martial law, rebuilt defenses, embargoed vessels, and arrested and imprisoned without regard to law or privilege all whom he regarded as Burr's agents. He overrode the decrees of courts and spirited away those arrested by his arbitrary orders. He even dispatched subordinates up the river to kidnap Burr should the latter be released by the civil authorities. New Orleans, at this period, represented a high point in the domineering procedure previously noted at Detroit and St. Louis. John Adair, a former intimate, was a conspicuous victim, as was Samuel Swartwout [*qq.v.*]. In order to forestall local censure, Wilkinson appealed to Vizente Folch, commandant of West Florida, for help. During this trying period his wife, who never lost faith in him nor failed to share his wandering, died at New Orleans on Feb. 23, 1807.

At the Burr trial in Richmond he assumed the rôle of chief witness but narrowly escaped indictment by the grand jury. Suspected by everyone, except possibly the prejudiced chief executive, he saw Daniel Clark [*q.v.*], his former friend and business associate turn against him, and likewise the Spanish agent, Thomas Power. He was caricatured by Washington Irving, denounced by Andrew Jackson, challenged and publicly insulted by Samuel Swartwout, and even George Hay, Jefferson's mouthpiece, lost confidence in him. The vindictive John Randolph who had headed the grand jury, used the proceedings at this trial to attack the administration and forced Wilkinson to appear before a court of inquiry. The accused outranked all the members of this body which, after six months, acquitted him, but not before he had found it necessary to appeal once more to Folch for vindication.

Availing himself of this dubious decision, Wilkinson requested the administration to give him some proof of confidence that would confound his "dam'd enemies." Jefferson ordered him to New Orleans and, while on the way thither, empowered him to confer with Spanish officials at Havana and Pensacola. Apples and flour were to pave the way for his message, which, it seems, was a proposed alliance between the United States, the Spanish possessions, and Brazil. As a forerunner of Pan Americanism Wilkinson was not a success. His difficulties with the army led to a second congressional inquiry, embracing his whole career. This investigation, hastened by the publication in 1809 of the untrustworthy but damaging *Proofs of the Corruption of General James Wilkinson,* which appeared under the name of Daniel Clark, led to a more thorough inquiry. He again appealed to Spanish officials for vindication but with little success. His defense forced him to sell much of his remaining land in Kentucky. In July 1811 President Madison ordered a court martial to try him. Its verdict, Dec. 25, 1811, of "not guilty" was so worded that the President approved it "with regret." This verdict restored Wilkinson to his command at New Orleans. From that city he was ordered, early in 1813, to occupy Mobile. Later in 1813 he was commissioned major-general and ordered northward to the St. Lawrence frontier. There in the fall of that year his own tardy measures and the failure of Wade Hampton, 1751 or 1752–1835 [*q.v.*] to cooperate with him made a fiasco of the campaign against Montreal. Relieved from regular duty and ordered to Washington, he was an inactive but critical spectator, when the British occupied and burned the public buildings of that city. Attempting to defend his Canadian campaign (*Daily National Intelligencer,* Washington, D. C., July 30, Aug. 3, 4, 1814) he provoked a quarrel with John Armstrong, 1758–1843 [*q.v.*], which led to another military inquiry and acquittal, but he was not reinstated in the service. With the aid of personal friends he published and distributed his *Memoirs of My Own Times,* three turgid and confused volumes of documents, which are as significant for what they omit as for what they contain (3 vols., 1816, "vol. II" of *Memoirs of General Wilkinson* was published in 1810 and in 1811 but was unlike vol. II of the 1816 edition).

On Mar. 5, 1810, he had married as his second wife, Celestine Laveau (Trudeau) Wilkinson. For some years following the publication of his *Memoirs* he lived with her and their young daughters on a plantation below New Orleans. In 1821 Mexico once more claimed his attention, and he betook himself thither in pursuit of a Texas land grant. In Mexico city he bestowed gratuitous advice upon the short-lived Emperor Iturbide, tried to collect claims for Mexico's creditors, and indirectly represented the American Bible Society. Ultimately he obtained an option on lands in Texas, but, before he could fulfill the conditions imposed, he died. He was buried from the house of Joel R. Poinsett [*q.v.*], who obtained for him a Roman Catholic funeral and interment in the Church of the Archangel San Miguel. His remains, along with others, rest unidentified in a common vault under that church.

[Photo-film enlargements of legajos 2373–75 of Papeles de Cuba from Archivo General de Indies at Seville and Papers in Relation to Burr's Conspiracy, both in Lib. of Cong.; the manuscript colls. of war department in the old records division of the adj.-gen. office; the Wilkinson papers (3 vols.) in possession of Chicago Hist. Soc.; the Wayne Papers (esp. vols. XX–XLVI) in possession Pa. Hist. Soc.; Durrett Coll., Harper Lib., Univ. of Chicago, esp. Gardoqui Papers; the Pontalba transcripts of the Louisiana Hist. Soc.; *Memoirs*, *ante*, necessary but unreliable; *Pa. Archives*, 1 ser., vol. X (1854); *Official Letter Books of W. C. C. Claiborne*, 6 vols., 1917, ed. by Dunbar Rowland; *Am. State Papers: Misc.* (2 vols., 1834); *Ibid: Military Affairs*, vol. I (1832), pp. 463–82; *House Report of the Committee to Inquire into the Conduct of General Wilkinson*, 11 Cong., 3 Sess. (1811); *Reports on the Trials of Col. Aaron Burr* (2 vols., 1808), taken in shorthand by David Robertson; *Annals of Cong.*, 10 Cong., 1 Sess., pts. 1, 2 (1852); *Ibid.*, extra Sess. (1853); *Ibid.*, 11 Cong., 2 and 3 Sess. (1853); *Ibid.*, 12 Cong., 1 Sess., pt. 2 (1853); "Reprints of Littell's Political Trans. in Ky. . . . also . . . Wilkinson's Memorial," *Filson Club Pubs.* no. 31 (1926) with intro. by Temple Bodley; "General James Wilkinson's Narrative of the Fallen Timbers Campaign," ed. by M. M. Quaife, *Miss. Valley Hist. Rev.*, June 1929; "James Wilkinson's First Descent to New Orleans in 1787," ed. by A. P. Whitaker, *Hispanic Am. Hist. Rev.*, Feb. 1828; "Papers Bearing on James Wilkinson's Relations with Spain, 1788–1789," ed. by W. R. Shepherd, *Am. Hist. Rev.*, July 1904; "A Faithful Picture of the Political Situation in New Orleans . . . Present Year, 1807," with notes by J. E. Winston, *La. Hist. Quart.*, July 1928; "Gen. James Wilkinson as Adviser to Emperor Iturbide," ed. by H. E. Bolton, *Hispanic Am. Hist. Rev.*, May 1918; James Wilkinson, *Wilkinson* (1935), a family biography; R. O. Shreve, *The Finished Scoundrel* (1933); T. R. Hay, "Some Reflections on . . . Wilkinson," *Miss. Valley Hist. Rev.*, Mar. 1935; E. B. Drewry, *Episodes in Westward Expansion as Reflected in the Writings of . . . Wilkinson* (1933); W. R. Shepherd, "Wilkinson and the Beginning of the Spanish Conspiracy," *Am. Hist. Rev.*, Apr. 1904; I. J. Cox, "Gen. Wilkinson and his Later Intrigues," *Ibid.*, July 1914, and *The West Florida Controversy* (1918); unpub. thesis in lib. of Northwestern Univ., Evanston, Ill., by P. W. Christian, "Gen. James Wilkinson and the Spanish Conspiracy"; W. F. McCaleb, *The Aaron Burr Conspiracy* (1905); Henry Adams, *Hist. of the U. S.*, vol. III (1890); Charles Gayarré, *Hist. of La.*, vol. III (1854); T. M. Green, *Spanish Conspiracy* (1891); J. M. Brown, *Political Beginnings of Ky.* (1889); A. P. Whitaker, *Spanish-Am. Frontier* (1927)

and *Miss. Question* (1934); *National Daily Intelligencer* (Washington, D. C.), Feb. 11, 20, 1826.]

I. J. C.

WILKINSON, JEMIMA (Nov. 29, 1752–July 1, 1819), religious leader, was born in Cumberland, R. I., daughter of Jeremiah and Elizabeth Amey (Whipple) Wilkinson and sister of Jeremiah Wilkinson [*q.v.*]. Her father, a prosperous farmer and a member of the Colony's Council, was almost exclusively interested in profits and politics; her mother, who belonged to the Society of Friends and who might perhaps have exercised more influence on her daughter's development, died, worn out with child-bearing, when Jemima, the eighth of twelve children, was about ten years old. Owing to her prettiness and cleverness, the future prophetess managed to avoid the hard work on the farm and grew up as a self-indulgent girl devoted to the reading of romances and other "frivolous literature," without further discipline than that afforded by irregular attendance in the common schools. Her religious interest was first aroused when she was about sixteen by the sermons of George Whitefield and by the meetings of the "New Light Baptists," an evangelizing sect which just then appeared in Rhode Island. Later, in 1774, the coming of Ann Lee [*q.v.*] aroused a spirit of emulation in her. Soon afterward, during the course of a fever, she fell into a prolonged trance from which she emerged with the conviction that she had died, that her original soul had ascended to heaven, and that her body was now inhabited by the "Spirit of Life" which came from God "to warn a lost and guilty, gossiping, dying World to flee from the wrath . . . to come." Her belief was not shaken by the insistence of Dr. Mann, the physician in charge of the case, that there was no evidence whatever of her having died.

Taking the name of "Public Universal Friend," she began to hold open-air meetings which attracted increasingly large audiences. Her power lay not in the substance of her preaching, which consisted of conventional calls to repentance interlarded with copious scriptural quotations, but in her magnetic personality. Tall and graceful, with beautiful dark hair and hypnotic black eyes, and with better manners than those of the usual "exhorters," she directed her appeal especially to the more educated and wealthy members of the community. Among those interested in her were Gov. Stephen Hopkins [*q.v.*] and Joshua Babcock, a friend of George Washington and one of the incorporators of Brown University. Gathering the most devoted of her followers into a special band of about a score, she led a series of processions on horseback through Rhode Island and Connecticut, she herself, clad in a long flowing robe over otherwise masculine attire, always riding a little in advance of her disciples, who came behind, two by two, in solemn, silent file. She preached with great success in Providence and New Bedford, R. I., and between 1777 and 1782 she established churches at New Milford, Conn., and at East Greenwich and South Kingston, R. I. In the latter town, William Potter, a rich and influential judge, built a special addition to his large mansion for the accommodation of the Universal Friend, who gradually acquired almost complete control over his household and the management of his estate. Meanwhile, in her preaching she began to emphasize the inferiority of marriage to celibacy and also the necessity of subordinating family obligations to the support of her sect, hence she was charged with causing the breakup of numerous families. Furthermore, the claim of her disciples that she was Jesus Christ come again, together with her own discreet reticence as to the exact nature of her relations with the Divine Spirit, thoroughly scandalized the orthodox churches of New England until even the Quakers turned against her. By 1783 the antagonism to her had become so great in New England that she transferred her headquarters to Philadelphia. There, too, however, she encountered much opposition, being actually stoned at one of her meetings, and in 1785 she and her band returned to New England. During the Philadelphia residence her only discourse in print was brought out, *The Universal Friend's Advice, to Those of the Same Religious Society, Recommended to be Read in Their Public Meetings for Divine Worship* (1784).

Finding herself no longer able to obtain a hearing in New England, the Friend in 1788 decided to establish a colony for her group "where no intruding foot could enter." Securing a large tract of land in Yates County, near Seneca Lake in western New York, she sent a part of her band on ahead and in 1790 followed with the rest. Being the first settlers in that region, they encountered many hardships, but their colony, named "Jerusalem," soon began to prosper under the energetic leadership of the Friend. Their land proved fertile, bounty wheat crops were raised, a sawmill and gristmill were built, and a school followed. By 1800 the population of Jerusalem had increased to two hundred and sixty inhabitants. The Friend exhibited great tact and tolerance in her relations with the frontier Indians, by whom she was named "Squaw Shinnewanagistawge" (Great Woman Preacher), and her pioneer venture proved of importance in the pacification of western New York.

Unfortunately, with prosperity there came internal dissensions. Judge Potter and others withdrew after unsuccessful suits against the Friend over the division of property in the colony. She was accused of chicanery and avarice, her habit of demanding personal gifts with her constant phrase, "The Friend hath need of these things," arousing resentment among some of her followers. As she grew older she became more dictatorial in her methods and developed a penchant for degrading forms of punishment for infraction of the society's rules, such as compelling one man to wear a black hood for three months and another to carry a little bell fastened to the skirts of his coat. She had reserved 12,000 acres of the settlement's property for herself, and in the farthest corner of this estate she built an elaborate house, twenty miles from the center of the settlement. There she dwelt in considerable luxury but afflicted with dropsy which destroyed every trace of her early beauty and turned her into a disfigured, embittered old woman, lingering out her days as a spectacle for the curiosity-mongers who visited the neighborhood. The society she had founded disintegrated entirely soon after her death.

[Sources include contemporary accounts in the letters of François, Marquis de Barbé-Mârbois, 1779–85, translated by E. P. Chase under the title *Our Revolutionary Forefathers* (1929) and in the *Travels through the United States* (2 vols., 1799) of François, Duc de la Rochefoucauld-Liancourt; Orsamus Turner, *Hist. of the Pioneer Settlement of Phelps and Gorham's Purchase and Morris' Reserve* (1851), pp. 153–62; Mrs. William Hathaway, *A Narrative of Thos. Hathaway and His Family* (1869); J. Q. Adams, "Jemima Wilkinson, the Universal Friend," in *Jour. of Am. Hist.*, Apr., May, June 1915; R. P. St. John, *Jerusalem the Golden* (1926) and "Jemima Wilkinson," with bibliog., in *Quart. Jour. N. Y. State Hist. Asso.*, Apr. 1930. See also Israel Wilkinson, *Memoirs of the Wilkinson Family* (1869); S. C. Cleveland, *Hist. and Directory of Yates County* (1873); E. W. Vanderhoof, *Hist. Sketches of Western N. Y.* (1907); *The New Yorker*, May 9, 1936. The earliest full biography, David Hudson, *Hist. of Jemima Wilkinson* (1821), was a scurrilous and generally inaccurate work. There is much discrepancy as to dates and minor details among all the biographers.]   E. S. B.

WILKINSON, JEREMIAH (July 6, 1741–Jan. 29, 1831), inventor, farmer, was the son of Jeremiah and Elizabeth Amey (Whipple) Wilkinson and a descendant of Lawrance Wilkinson, a Quaker, who emigrated from England and settled in Providence, R. I., about 1645. Jeremiah was born on his father's farm at Cumberland, R. I., and after obtaining a common-school education went to work on the farm. He was most interested, however, in the forge which had been erected by his grandfather, and he continued the local iron-forging business which his grandfather and father had conducted in connection with their farm activities. In addition, he mastered the gold and silversmith's art, and the wealthier residents of the community were accustomed to furnish him with coins which he would melt and convert into spoons and other articles.

Another successful venture which he undertook at an early period in his life was that of making hand cards for carding wool and for currying horses and cattle. His skill in the production of properly treated iron wire for these cards yielded a superior product which was much in demand, and to supply it Wilkinson perfected a number of inventions to increase his speed of production. One of these was a hand-operated machine for cutting and making the four bends in the wire at one operation and punching the holes in the leather for the whole card at one stroke of the machine. Because of the difficulties of importing wire, after much experimenting he devised his own tools, plates, and dies and drew wire by horsepower—probably the first attempt at wire drawing in the colonies. About 1776, while engaged in the manufacture of his hand cards, Wilkinson ran out of the tacks which he used to secure the leather to the wooden back of the card. Picking up an old iron plate on the floor, he cut it into pointed strips with a pair of tailor's shears and headed the blunt ends in a vise, thus producing crude tacks. This experiment was the first attempted by any one to make nails or tacks from cold iron. Under the development of others the process brought into existence a large and important industry. Aside from these major articles Wilkinson made steel pins and needles, and it is said that his wife purchased a spinning wheel for three darning needles of her husband's manufacture.

Though busy with his iron work, Wilkinson found time to carry on extensive farming and fruit-growing, in connection with which he also employed his inventive skill. For the production of corn syrup he devised a mill to grind the cornstalks, and then pressed them in a common cider mill. He spent the whole of his long life in Cumberland and was twice married: first, to Hopie Mosier (or Mosher), by whom he had five children; second, to Elizabeth Southwick who had six children. Jemima Wilkinson [*q.v.*] was his sister.

[Israel Wilkinson, *Memoirs of the Wilkinson Family in America* (1869); *Trans. of the R. I. Soc. for the Encouragement of Domestic Industry, 1861* (1862); *Pawtucket Chronicle*, Feb. 4, 1831.]   C. W. M.

WILKINSON, JOHN (Nov. 6, 1821–Dec. 29, 1891), Confederate naval officer, was born in Norfolk, Va., the eldest son of Jesse Wilkinson, a commodore in the United States Navy. Through the influence of John Y. Mason, young Wilkinson became a midshipman, Dec. 13, 1837. He was ordered to the South Atlantic aboard the *Independence*. Immediately after his return to the home station in 1840 he was assigned to the sloop *Boston* for a two-year cruise in the East Indies. After a brief assignment to school at Philadelphia he was warranted a passed midshipman, June 29, 1843. A long cruise to the Pacific aboard the *Portsmouth,* followed by a period of illness, deprived him of any active duty on the Gulf during the Mexican War. He was promoted lieutenant, Nov. 5, 1850. Thereafter until the outbreak of the Civil War practically all of his service was ashore or with the home squadron. In the light of his subsequent blockade-running duties for the Confederacy, particularly fortunate was his assignment from June 25, 1859, to Apr. 6, 1861, to command the survey steamer *Corwin,* collecting data for charts of waters on the Florida coast and including the Bahamas. On Apr. 6, he tendered his resignation to enter the Confederacy. In his *Narrative of a Blockade-Runner* (1877, p. 81) he wrote of the United States Navy "that gallant Navy to which it is an honor ever to have belonged. We, who so reluctantly severed our connection with it, still feel a pride in its achievements."

Through the first year of the Civil War he saw shore battery duty in Virginia. He was ordered to the immobile and incomplete ironclad *Louisiana* and, when her capture became certain, Apr. 28, 1862, by virtue of the surrender of the forts, Jackson and St. Philip, and the fall of New Orleans, he, as ranking officer present, ordered her destruction. With the garrisons of these forts he was captured but was exchanged Aug. 5, 1862. Special duty, 1862–63, carried him to England to purchase and command the blockade runner *Giraffe,* which he later rechristened the *Robert E. Lee.* Under his command she was phenomenally successful, over the Nassau to Wilmington, N. C., route, in getting through the blockaders. Indeed, some of Wilkinson's original ruses for baffling the federal cruisers were widely imitated by other blockade runners. On Oct. 16, 1863, he carried a party of daring naval adventurers to Halifax. There he relinquished command of the *Lee* to assume the leadership of these adventurers, whose objective was to capture a northern owned lake steamer, arm her, capture the military prison on Johnson's Island in Lake Erie, and release therefrom into Canada thousands of Confederate prisoners. Federal espionage and Canadian neutrality combined to foil the scheme. Back in the Confederacy he took command of the armed blockade runner *Chickamauga*. She got to sea, Oct. 29, 1864, and within the next week raided to within sight of Montauk Point, scuttling, burning, or bonding seven prizes. He ended his services for the Confederacy as lieutenant in command of the blockade runner *Chameleon*.

He was a sturdily built man, with a full open countenance and a bushy moustache, and hair which was heavy and curly, well down over his ears and to his coat collar. Though an omnivorous reader, Cooper seems to have been the only American author that he considered worth while. Cicero, Virgil, and Cato, from whom he frequently drew many pertinent Latin quotations, were his favorites. For some years after the war he was a business man in Nova Scotia. After the general amnesty he returned to the old family homestead in Amelia County, Va., and died at Annapolis, Md. He never married.

[Personnel records, Naval Records Office, Washington, D. C.; *War of the Rebellion: Official Records (Army)*, esp. 1 ser. vols. III, XI, XVIII, 2 ser., vol. II; own *Narrative, ante*; J. T. Scharf, *Hist. of the Confederate States Navy* (1887); *Army and Navy Journal*, Jan. 2, 1892.]   J. D. H.

WILKINSON, ROBERT SHAW (Feb. 18, 1865–Mar. 13, 1932), negro educator, was born in Charleston, S. C., just before the 54th Massachusetts Regiment entered that city, and was named by his enthusiastic parents for Robert Gould Shaw, the deceased commander of that famous negro organization. His parents, Charles H. and Lavinia (Brown) Wilkinson, were "free persons of color"; at the time of his birth his father kept a butcher shop; later he became janitor of the Porter Military Academy and of the Church of the Holy Communion. Encouraged by his father and the rector of the church, Rev. A. T. Porter, young Wilkinson received his early education at the Shaw Memorial School and Avery Institute, and in 1883 went to Beaufort, S. C., to prepare for entrance into West Point. He was appointed to that institution by Edmund W. M. Mackey, a white Republican congressman, and is said to have passed the entrance examinations but to have been denied admission because of physical disabilities. In 1884 he entered the preparatory department of Oberlin College and graduated from the college with the degree of A.B. in 1891. He had supported himself meanwhile by doing odd jobs in the afternoons and by acting as a writer on a negro newspaper and as a Pullman porter during vacations.

Giving up an ambition to become a lawyer because of pecuniary difficulties, in 1891 he became professor of Greek and Latin in the State Uni-

versity, Louisville, Ky., a negro institution, where he served until 1896. In that year he was called to the professorship of science in the State Agricultural and Mechanical College, a negro institution at Orangeburg, S. C. On June 29 of the following year he acquired an able assistant in his endeavors when he married Marion Raven Birnie, the daughter of Richard Birnie, a Charleston cotton sampler. His success as a teacher was so marked that ambitious white youths came into his laboratory at night to watch his experiments. Having previously taken an active part in the administration of the Orangeburg institution, he was elected to its presidency in 1911 and served brilliantly in that capacity until his death twenty-one years later. When he took office, the school was a neglected academy of 592 students, which received an annual legislative appropriation of only five thousand dollars and in no instance maintained a level of instruction above that of the high school; before his death the institution was a college of 1,691 students which received an annual legislative appropriation of $126,000 and in no instance maintained a level of instruction below that of the high school. Moreover, the morale of the college had been greatly improved by Wilkinson's encouragement of advanced study by members of the faculty and by his emphasis on a balanced compromise between industrial and literary instruction.

He was a patient and urbane little man, always immaculately dressed, whose mind was fertile in practical suggestions for the uplift of his race and keenly alive to all possible sources of revenue for negro education. He won the admiration and support of the white officials and legislators who controlled the educational destinies of South Carolina by eschewing politics and accepting the racial conventions of the state, without, however, groveling before those of whom he asked favors. The intelligent were won with arguments; the indifferent or ignorant by petty gifts. A devout Episcopalian, Wilkinson was a lay reader and the most active colored layman of his Church in South Carolina. In his extensive travels he carried the gospel of social and economic progress into the humblest negro homes. He was active in many negro business and fraternal undertakings, serving as president of the state Business League and as the very efficient treasurer of the state negro organization of the Knights of Pythias. He educated his four children in Northern colleges and left his wife a substantial competence. When he died he enjoyed the esteem of all South Carolinians of both races who were acquainted with his work.

[*Who's Who in America*, 1928–29; *Who's Who in Colored America*, 1927; *The Collegian, State Agricultural and Mechanical Coll., Orangeburg, S. C.*, May 1932; *A Birthday Appreciation: The Class of 1932 Presents Scenes from the Life of Robert Shaw Wilkinson, Feb. 18, 1932* (1932); *News and Courier* (Charleston), Mar. 14, 1932; information from Marion Birnie Wilkinson and Helen Wilkinson Sheffield of Orangeburg, S. C., Wilkinson's wife and daughter.]
F. B. S.

WILL, ALLEN SINCLAIR (July 28, 1868–Mar. 10, 1934), journalist, biographer, and educator, was born at Antioch, Va., the son of William R. and Mildred Florence (Sinclair) Will. He received his early education in Baltimore, attended St. John's College, Annapolis, Md., for several years, and then became principal of a public school in Virginia. Later he taught in a private classical school in Baltimore. He entered newspaper work in 1888 as a reporter for the *Baltimore Morning Herald*. The following year he joined the Baltimore *Sun*, which he served as assistant city editor (1893–96), telegraph editor (1896–1905), and city editor (1905–12). Leaving the *Sun* in 1912, he was successively associate editor and editorial writer of the *Baltimore News* (1912–14) and news editor of the *Philadelphia Public Ledger* (1914–16). From 1917 to 1924 he wrote special articles for the *New York Times* and was assistant editor. From 1923 until the time of his death he wrote book reviews for the *Times* as an authority on American colonial history and historical biography. He returned to teaching in 1920 when he was invited to join the staff of the Pulitzer School of Journalism at Columbia University (associate professor, 1924; professor, 1925). He conducted courses in news writing and book reviewing. In 1925 he joined the staff of Rutgers University in order to organize a department of journalism there. He was made director of the department in 1926 and remained in charge until his death. Realizing that the success of the school depended upon close cooperation with newspapers, he effected an agreement between his department and the New Jersey Press Association whereby many students were absorbed by newspapers soon after their graduation, and he became known as the only man in journalism with a waiting list for young reporters. He described the operation of that agreement and urged its more widespread application in a book which expressed the preoccupation of his later years, *Education for Newspaper Life* (1931).

His most notable literary achievement was his *Life of Cardinal Gibbons, Archbishop of Baltimore* (2 vols., 1922). His friendship with Gibbons (who chose Will, a Protestant, as his biographer) dated back to the time when he was a young reporter on the *Sun*. For more than a year they spent a part of each day in companionable chat together; Will thus obtained a clear insight into the character of the Cardinal as a man, a churchman, and a political power. His other books were *World-Crisis in China* (1900) and *Our City, State and Nation* (1913). He was a contributor to the *Dictionary of American Biography*, and wrote several monographs on civics, American history, biography, and journalism. Those who attacked modern journalism in books and on the public platform had to meet Will's vigorous defense. He said that the articles in one of the New York dailies were the best examples of the world's journalism, "complete, accurate and skillfully expressed, the product of trained observation and orderly thinking" (*Yale Daily News*, Jan. 6, 1926). He was a strict grammarian, however, and deplored widespread imitation of New York slang; crudities of speech annoyed him, and he zealously guarded standards of correct English on many copy desks. He was scholarly and distinguished in appearance, belying the popular picture of a newspaperman. He was tall, with grey hair and twinkling eyes, ruddy-faced and immaculate in appearance. There is a portrait of him at Rutgers. On Feb. 17, 1891, he was married to Allie Stuart Walter of Linden, Va. (d. 1908). He died in New York City, survived by two daughters.

[*Who's Who in America*, 1932–33; Marlen Pew, "Shop Talk at Thirty," *Editor and Publisher*, Mar. 17, 1934; obituary, *Ibid.*, and in *N. Y. Times*, Mar. 11, 1934; newspaper clippings and letters in Columbia School of Journalism; personal reminiscences of Prof. C. P. Cooper; letters and papers in the possession of Mrs. H. S. Willis, Will's daughter, Linden, Va.]
L. K.

WILLARD, DE FOREST (Mar. 23, 1846–Oct. 14, 1910), physician, pioneer in orthopedic surgery, was born at Newington, Conn., the son of Daniel Horatio and Sarah Maria (Deming) Willard, and a descendant of Simon Willard, 1605–1676 [*q.v.*]. In early childhood he had an attack of illness which required tenotomy in later life, leaving him permanently lame. He was graduated from the Hartford High School in 1863 and at once entered Yale College. After a few months he was forced to withdraw because of a defect of his eyes, but in the fall of 1863 he went to Philadelphia and entered the Jefferson Medical College, where he studied under Joseph Pancoast and Samuel D. Gross [*qq.v.*]. In 1864 he matriculated at the University of Pennsylvania, where he was graduated in 1867. His studies were interrupted by service with the United States Sanitary Commission during the last year of the Civil War and by a severe attack of typhoid fever.

After graduation he spent fifteen months in the Philadelphia Hospital as resident physician and then began private practice. He also served on the faculty of the University of Pennsylvania as assistant demonstrator of anatomy (1867–70), assistant demonstrator of surgery (1870–77), lecturer on orthopedic surgery (1877–89), clinical professor of orthopedic surgery (1889–1903), and professor of orthopedic surgery (1903–10). One of the early leaders in the field, Willard organized the department of orthopedic surgery at Pennsylvania and was active in establishing the Agnew ward for crippled children at the university hospital. He advised Peter A. B. Widener [*q.v.*] in planning the Widener Memorial Industrial Training School for Crippled Children and served as surgeon-in-chief of the institution. He also acted as general surgeon at the Presbyterian Hospital for twenty-five years and was consulting surgeon at many hospitals in the vicinity of Philadelphia.

In spite of his many activities, he found time to write extensively and contributed over three hundred articles to professional journals. He was author of one book, *Surgery of Childhood, Including Orthopaedic Surgery* (copyright 1910), and joint author with L. H. Adler of *Artificial Anaesthesia and Anaesthetics* (1891). He was an active member in medical organizations and served as president of the American Surgical Association (1901–02), the Philadelphia Academy of Surgery (1902), the American Orthopaedic Association (1890), the Philadelphia County Medical Association (1892–93), and as chairman of the Surgery Section of the American Medical Association in 1902. He was a delegate to national and international conventions. He gave a great deal of his time to religious and charitable work; he was an elder and trustee of the Second Presbyterian Church in Philadelphia and founded the Midnight Mission for women. His ability and tremendous capacity for hard work were tested in 1877 when the sudden death of a brother left him the additional responsibilities of rearing five small children and managing the Union Steam Forge at Bordentown, N. J. On Sept. 13, 1881, he was married to Elizabeth Michler Porter, the daughter of William A. Porter. They had two children, De Forest Porter Willard, who became a surgeon, and a daughter, who died on the day of her birth. Willard died of multiple neuritis and pneumonia at his home in Lansdowne, Pa. At his death, the list of his activities in connection with various professional, charitable, and educational organizations filled two-thirds of a column in a newspaper.

[*Who's Who in America*, 1910–11; *Willard Geneal.* (1915), ed. by C. H. Pope; *Am. Medic. Biogs.* (1920), ed. by H. A. Kelly and W. L. Burrage; *Encyc. of Pa. Biog.*, vol. IX (1918), ed. by J. W. Jordan; *Jour. Am. Medic. Asso.*, Oct. 22, 1910; *Trans. Am. Surgical Asso.*, vol. XXIX (1911); *Evening Bull.* (Philadelphia), Oct. 15, 1910.]   F. E. W—s.

WILLARD, EMMA HART (Feb. 23, 1787–Apr. 15, 1870), educator, was born in Berlin, Conn., the ninth child of Capt. Samuel and Lydia (Hinsdale) Hart. Her father represented Berlin in the General Assembly and held other civil offices. Brought up in a large family in a rural community, she was trained to do her share of the household tasks. Because the best books available were read aloud at the Hart fireside, and politics, current events, and religious and moral principles were freely discussed, even as a child she took an interest in world affairs and learned to do her own thinking. She attended the district school and Berlin Academy. For several years she taught in Berlin but managed to alternate with this work several months of study at the schools of the Misses Patten and Mrs. Royse at Hartford. Her first teaching experience outside of her native town was at Westfield, Mass. From there in 1807 she went to Middlebury, Vt., to take full charge of the Female Academy, and was unusually successful. She gave up this position in 1809 to become, on Aug. 10, the third wife of John Willard, descendant of Simon Willard [*q.v.*], and one of Middlebury's leading citizens, a physician and politician. Her only child, John Hart Willard, was born in 1810.

Dr. Willard's nephew, a student at Middlebury College, made his home with them. Through him she became familiar with the course of study at men's colleges and realized as never before the educational opportunities of which women were deprived. She studied his textbooks, first geometry, then Paley's *Moral Philosophy* and Locke's *Essay Concerning Moral Understanding*. When in 1814 her husband suffered financial reverses, she opened in her own home a school for young ladies, the Middlebury Female Seminary. At this time there were no high schools for girls, and no college in the world admitted women. Boarding schools, which only daughters of the well-to-do were able to attend, taught the mere rudiments and stressed the accomplishments, such as painting, embroidery, French, singing, playing on the harpsichord, and making wax or shell ornaments. Mrs. Willard proved to her entire satisfaction that young ladies were able to master such subjects as mathematics and philosophy and not lose their health, refinement, or charm. In 1818 she sent to Gov.

DeWitt Clinton of New York *An Address to the Public; Particularly to the Members of the Legislature of New York, Proposing a Plan for Improving Female Education,* published the following year. In this lengthy, well-thought-out document, she appealed for state aid in founding schools for girls, asked that women be given the same educational advantages as men, and showed of what benefit to the state well-educated women would be. She also outlined a course of study, ambitious for that period. As Governor Clinton and several legislators were sympathetic, her plan was presented to the legislature in 1819 and she went to Albany with her husband to plead personally for it. A few recognized the justice and wisdom of her recommendations, but the majority ridiculed and bitterly attacked what they considered interference with God's will for women.

Mrs. Willard then moved to Waterford, N. Y., and established Waterford Academy, chartered by the New York legislature in 1819. She hoped for state aid, but no funds were appropriated. Just as she was in despair over the future of her school, the citizens of Troy, N. Y., offered to provide a building for the Seminary. In 1821, sixteen years before Mary Lyon founded her seminary at Mount Holyoke, Emma Willard's Troy Female Seminary received its first pupils; and it grew in popularity and influence so that she was able to accomplish without state aid what a few years before seemed impossible. She steadily continued her policy of adding higher subjects to the curriculum, placing special emphasis on mathematics, which she felt women needed to train their minds. History, philosophy, and one science after another were introduced, and since she could not at first afford to employ professors to teach these subjects, she studied them and then taught them herself. She evolved new methods of teaching geography and history and published geography and history textbooks which won immediate recognition and were widely used. Among these were "Ancient Geography," published as a section of *A System of Universal Geography* (1824) by William C. Woodbridge [*q.v.*], *History of the United States, or Republic of America* (1828), and *A System of Universal History in Perspective* (1835). She also published a volume of poetry, *The Fulfilment of a Promise* (1831). In general her poems are mediocre, the only one which is well known being "Rocked in the Cradle of the Deep." Hundreds of teachers were trained by her, many of them gratuitously, and sent into the South and West where they carried the message of woman's education. She persuaded her pupils

that they owed it to their country to become teachers for at least a few years. In this way she enabled many poor girls to be self-supporting and led many wealthy girls into a life of usefulness. Outstanding events in her school life were her trip to Europe in 1830, her friendship with Lafayette, her enthusiastic help in founding a training school for teachers in liberated Greece, in connection with which she wrote *Advancement of Female Education; or A Series of Addresses, in Favor of Establishing at Athens, in Greece, a Female Seminary* (1833). That same year she published, also, *Journal and Letters, from France and Great Britain.* She was regal in appearance—a beautiful woman with classic features, gowned always in rich black silk or satin with a white mull turban on her head. Kindly and understanding, she won her pupils' affection at once.

In 1838 she retired from the active management of the Troy Female Seminary, leaving it in charge of her son and his wife. Dr. Willard had died in 1825, and on Sept. 17, 1838, she married Dr. Christopher Yates. The marriage was unhappy from the first, and she left him within a year. In 1843 she was divorced by act of the Connecticut legislature. From 1838 on her interest was primarily in the improvement of the common schools. She worked with Henry Barnard in Connecticut, helping to make the schools there models for other states to follow. She traveled widely through the state of New York, holding teachers' institutes, and in a long tour through the South and West, by stage, canal boat, and packet, did much to arouse interest in education and to impress women with the part they must play in this great movement. Her plea was always for more women as teachers, for higher salaries, and better schoolhouses. Among her later publications were *A Treatise on the Motive Powers which Produce the Circulation of the Blood* (1846), *Guide to the Temple of Time; and Universal History for Schools* (1849); *Last Leaves of American History* (1849); *Astronography; or Astronomical Geography* (1854); and *Late American History* (1856).

Emma Willard was one of the great educators of her day. She was the first woman publicly to take her stand for the higher education of women and the first to make definite experiments to prove that women were capable of comprehending higher subjects. Her Troy Female Seminary was looked upon as a model both in the United States and in Europe. It is now known as the Emma Willard School. Because of the change in public opinion, which her daring, determined stand did much to effect, seminaries and high schools for girls, and later women's colleges and coeducational universities, became a permanent part of American life.

[John Lord, *The Life of Emma Willard* (1873); A. W. Fairbanks, *Emma Willard and Her Pupils* (1898); Alma Lutz, *Emma Willard, Daughter of Democracy* (1929); Thomas Woody, *A Hist. of Women's Education in the U. S.* (1929); Willystine Goodsell, *Pioneers of Woman's Education in the U. S.* (1931); *Troy Daily Times*, Apr. 16, 1870; unpublished letters and catalogues at the Emma Willard School, Troy, N. Y.; unpublished letters in possession of the Conn. Hist. Soc., N. Y. Hist. Soc., Pa. Hist. Soc., and the Lib. of Cong.]

A. L.

WILLARD, FRANCES ELIZABETH CAROLINE (Sept. 28, 1839–Feb. 18, 1898), reformer, known in public life as Frances E. Willard and to her friends as "Frank," was born at Churchville, N. Y., the daughter of Josiah Flint and Mary Thompson (Hill) Willard, and a descendant of Simon Willard [*q.v.*], one of the founders of Concord, Mass. Her parents came from Vermont. They were teachers when they met and married, and they entered college after they were the parents of children. Education, next to religion, played the most important part in their ideals of life. During Frances' childhood they twice journeyed westward. Their first move brought them to Oberlin, Ohio, where they attended college; the second, to Wisconsin, where they built a homestead in the wilderness. Here Frances Willard lived until her eighteenth year.

As a girl she disliked housework and preferred the out-door occupations of her older brother. She liked to hunt and was a good shot. The loneliness of pioneer life was a girlhood grievance and she especially resented the fact that her father would not allow her and her younger sister to ride horseback, thus condemning them all the more to solitude. Frances' mother probably shared her feelings, for when asked years afterwards for a word of advice to pioneer women, she answered without hesitation, "I should say pack up your duds and go where folks live" (Strachey, *post*, p. 8). Frances was taught by her mother and early became an omnivorous reader. The family library consisted of the Bible, *Pilgrim's Progress*, Shakespeare, and odd volumes of travel and biography; but weekly journals, magazines, and paper-bound fiction penetrated by a miraculous mail to the remotest districts, and Frances read this literature also. True to her out-of-doors temperament, she reveled in adventure stories; pirate tales and wild west thrillers formed the chief excitement of her girlhood. In her teens she turned to novel reading, a habit which led in time to a con-

flict between herself and her dogmatic father. The climax came when Frances, on her eighteenth birthday, seated herself with a copy of *Ivanhoe* in her hand and waited for her father's reprimand to follow. When it did, she replied, "You forget what day it is. . . . I am eighteen— I am of age—and I am now to do what *I* think right." Her father found no reply to this declaration and Frances felt that she had won a great victory (*Glimpses of Fifty Years, post*, p. 72).

At seventeen, she was sent to the Milwaukee Female College, founded by Catharine Beecher; the next year she went to the Northwestern Female College in Evanston, Ill., from which she graduated in 1859. She was a good student and valedictorian of her class. Her interest in science was thought to have militated against her religious faith, since she experienced conversion only after an extreme conflict. She fell ill of typhoid fever and in the crisis, fearing that she might die, she made the following pledge to herself: "If God lets me get well I'll try to be a Christian girl" (Gordon, *post*, p. 51). Regarding the pledge as her conversion, she later joined the Methodist Church, and was apparently disturbed by no further religious doubts. After leaving college she continued her education. She set herself a stiff course of reading and study and devoted a strenuous year to self-improvement. When Frances and her younger sister went to Evanston, their mother persuaded her husband to follow them thither, where he found employment in a Chicago bank. By this removal, Evanston became Frances' permanent home.

To an extent difficult to estimate the young women of her generation were influenced by the lives and writings of Charlotte Brontë and Margaret Fuller [*q.v.*], and Frances was one who responded passionately to their ideal of independence for women. A brief engagement to be married distracted her for a time but, her engagement broken, she returned to this ideal with redoubled zeal. In 1860, she took her first position as a teacher in a country school near Evanston. Several other local schools employed her; in 1863–64 she taught at Pittsburgh Female College and in 1866–67 at Genesee Wesleyan Seminary, Lima, N. Y. At a somewhat later period of her life (1871–74) she was president of the Evanston College for Ladies. Spurred on by literary ambitions, she wrote articles for weekly papers and magazines. Her first book, *Nineteen Beautiful Years* (1864)—a life of her younger sister who had died—was published when Frances was twenty-five.

In 1868 she went to Europe with a friend and

traveled for two years. On her return she was asked to talk about her experiences and presently found herself delivering from the pulpit of a large church her first paid public lecture. This venture initiated her career as a public speaker. With her Puritan background, it was natural that she should join the temperance crusade which swept the country in 1874. In that year bands of women appeared everywhere—on the streets and in the saloons—singing and praying against the sin of the liquor traffic. Frances Willard joined one of these bands in Pittsburgh and delivered her first prayer in public kneeling on the sawdust floor of a Market Street saloon. The next week she became president of the Chicago Woman's Christian Temperance Union. From this office she advanced to the secretaryship of the Illinois Woman's Christian Temperance Union and then to the corresponding secretaryship of the National Woman's Temperance Convention. In 1879 she was elected president of the National Woman's Christian Temperance Union and in 1891, president of the World's Woman's Christian Temperance Union. In the meantime she had enlisted her society in the cause of woman's suffrage, had helped to organize the Prohibition Party in 1882, and had been elected president of the National Council of Women.

After her first entrance into the temperance movement, she gave, almost literally, the rest of her life to the cause. For a number of years she received no salary, so anxious was she to give her services to the work to which she felt herself dedicated; but without independent means of support for herself and her mother, she was obliged in the end to accept her living from the organization. Henceforth a salary amounting to what she had received as a college teacher was paid her. Notwithstanding her arduous work and many trials of courage, she found great happiness in promoting the temperance cause. Her liking for politics as well as her talent for oratory found scope for expression therein; her sense of the picturesque was stimulated by the monumental petitions, the spectacular campaigns, and the emblems and slogans it fell to her to invent. Her literary ambitions were turned chiefly into editing the organs of her society and writing its books. In her wildest girlhood dreams of travel and adventure, she could scarcely have imagined that in 1883 she would actually visit and speak in every state and territory of the United States and that, during the latter years of her life, she would have almost a second home in England. Her profoundest faiths and her highest beliefs, her chivalry and her supreme

trust in woman, all bore fruit in the work of the Woman's Christian Temperance Union. She saw temperance as a measure for the protection of the home and the Christian life, and as an ideal involving personal sacrifice. Other leaders have stressed the social and economic aspects of the reform and used more practical methods; but temperance reform has remained for the popular mind very much the reform for which Frances Willard strove, and temperance legislation has risen or fallen according to the strength or weakness of its moral appeal.

After her mother's death in 1892, Frances continued to work as indefatigably as ever but she had lost one of her greatest sources of energy. Her health gave way and many restless journeys failed to restore it; she died from influenza in New York City. So much of a national figure had she become that in 1905 a statue in her honor was placed in the Capitol at Washington by the State of Illinois. Among her publications were *Woman and Temperance* (1883), *Glimpses of Fifty Years* (1889), *A Classic Town; The Story of Evanston* (1892), *A Wheel Within a Wheel; How I Learned to Ride the Bicycle* (1895). She also edited *A Woman of the Century* (1893), in collaboration with Mary A. Livermore [*q.v.*].

[C. H. Pope, *Willard Geneal.* (1915); R. F. Dibble, *Strenuous Americans* (1923); A. A. Gordon, *The Beautiful Life of Frances E. Willard* (1898); Ray Strachey, *Frances Willard: Her Life and Work* (London, 1912); *N. Y. Times*, Feb. 18, 1898.]   K. A.

WILLARD, JOSEPH (Dec. 29, 1738–Sept. 25, 1804), president of Harvard College, was the son of Rev. Samuel and Abigail (Wright) Willard of Biddeford, Me., a great-grandson of Rev. Samuel Willard, 1639/40–1707 [*q.v.*], and a great-great-grandson of Simon Willard [*q.v.*], one of the founders of Concord, Mass. Joseph tried first the sea and then medicine, but his abilities attracted the attention of schoolmaster Samuel Moody of York, who found means to send him to Harvard, where he was graduated in 1765. Because of his progress in the classics he was rewarded with the post of college butler and, in 1766, that of tutor in Greek.

In 1767 he accepted a call to the church in Haverhill, but something prevented his being settled there. He resigned his tutorship to take the pulpit at Beverly, Mass., in 1772, and on Nov. 25 he was ordained despite the objections of a considerable minority. He was married, Mar. 7, 1774, to Mary, daughter of Jacob and Hannah (Seavery) Sheafe of Portsmouth, N. H. During the Revolution he was an active Whig. In 1780 he took part in the formation of the American Academy of Arts and Sciences, and for many years served as corresponding secretary and vice-president, besides being one of the leading contributors to its publications. His position as secretary brought him into correspondence with the leading men of science and letters in Europe and America, and he was soon well known for his work in astronomy and mathematics as well as in the classics. John Adams thought him the equal of David Rittenhouse [*q.v.*] as a scientist.

As early as 1773 Willard's brilliance had caused him to be mentioned for the Harvard presidency, and after the resignation of Samuel Langdon [*q.v.*] in 1780 he was the natural candidate. Such, however, was the condition of the college as a result of the war and the vagaries of the treasurer, John Hancock, that he was not inaugurated until Dec. 19, 1781. Willard was a noted Federalist, which fact probably influenced the General Court to cut off, once and for all, the assistance which the college had received from the government; but the redemption of the Continental certificates of indebtedness, to which Harvard had trustingly clung, made it possible for the new president to repair the ravages of the war. He raised entrance requirements, broadened the field of instruction, founded the medical school, and longed to travel in Europe to learn from the universities there. His correspondence with Richard Price, Joseph Priestley [*q.v.*], and the other European intelligentsia brought the college many valuable gifts. In matters of religion and learning his administration was liberal enough to win their approval. With the teaching staff he was gentle, laconic, and respectful of the opinions of the youngest. The students, awed by his impressive physique and his dignity, did not riot as they did under the presidents before and after him. They failed, however, to see the deep interest which he took in them under his reserve, and thought him stiff and formal. His achievements brought him many honors, including membership in several learned societies, among them the Royal Society of Göttingen and the Medical Society of London. He died at New Bedford Sept. 25, 1804. Of his thirteen children Sidney [*q.v.*] became a professor at Harvard and Joseph [*q.v.*] won distinction in law.

[*Willard Geneal.* (1915), ed. by C. H. Pope; S. B. Willard, *Memories of Youth and Manhood* (1855); W. B. Sprague, *Annals Am. Pulpit*, vol. II (1857); E. M. Stone, *Hist. of Beverly* (1843); *Repertory* (Boston), Sept. 28, 1804.]   C. K. S.

WILLARD, JOSEPH (Mar. 14, 1798–May 12, 1865), lawyer and historian, was born in Cambridge, Mass., the youngest child of Joseph Willard [*q.v.*], president of Harvard College, and Mary (Sheafe) Willard. Sidney Willard [*q.v.*] was his brother. Joseph studied at Phillips Academy, Exeter, N. H., and at a private school in Boston conducted by William Jennison. Entering Harvard, he was graduated with the class of 1816. He then became a student in the law office of Charles H. Atherton of Amherst, N. H., tutoring the Atherton children in return for his own instruction. Later he removed to the office of Judge Samuel P. P. Fay of Cambridge, and finally entered the Harvard Law School, where he received the degree of LL.B. in 1820. He began practice in Waltham, but soon removed to Lancaster, Mass., where he practised for ten years. Here he filled various town offices and was a member of the legislature in 1828 and 1829. His *Sketches of the Town of Lancaster* (1826) led to his election to the American Antiquarian Society and the Massachusetts Historical Society at an unusually early age. He served the latter society as librarian (1833–35), as recording secretary (1835–57), and as corresponding secretary (1857–64).

On Feb. 24, 1830, he married Susanna Hickling Lewis, and shortly thereafter he removed to Boston. He was appointed master in chancery in 1839 and carried on his duties so well that there was hardly an objection to, or an appeal from, his probate decisions. In 1841 he was appointed to one of the clerkships of the Suffolk County courts, and chose to act in the court of common pleas. Here again his decisions were seldom appealed, and those appeals seldom sustained. His extensive knowledge of law and procedure made him of great service to the lawyers practising in the court. When the office was made elective in 1856 he was returned as a matter of course in recognition of the fact that he was a rare type of public servant. He continued in office until his death.

In 1845 he was one of the incorporators of the New-England Historic Genealogical Society, and he was one of the trustees of the old Boston Library. He was a frequent and welcome visitor in the homes of the intellectual leaders who then lived in Concord. In politics he was an ardent Whig. He was a Free-Soiler in 1847 and an abolitionist in 1850; finally, he almost welcomed the Civil War as a surgeon's knife to remove the cancer of slavery. His declining health was shattered by the news of the death of his son, Maj. Sidney Willard, at Fredericksburg, in December 1862. He was a Unitarian by religion and a practising Christian whose contemporaries had only praise for him. In 1858 he published *Willard Memoir, or Life and Times of Major Simon Willard*; a biography of Gen.

Henry Knox he left unfinished at his death, and the manuscript is now in the library of the Massachusetts Historical Society.

[*Willard Geneal.* (1915), ed. by C. H. Pope; *Proc. Mass. Hist. Soc.*, 1 ser. IX (1867), *et passim*; *New-England Hist. and Geneal. Reg.*, Oct. 1865; *Boston Transcript*, May 13, 1865.]   C. K. S.

WILLARD, JOSEPH EDWARD (May 1, 1865–Apr. 4, 1924), diplomat and lawyer, was born in Washington, D. C., the ninth in line of descent from Simon Willard [*q.v.*], one of the founders of Concord, Mass. His father was Joseph Clapp Willard, an officer in the Union Army during the Civil War, and his mother Antonia J. (Ford) Willard, of Fairfax Court House, Va., who was commissioned by Gen. J. E. B. Stuart as honorary aide-de-camp on Oct. 7, 1861, and was captured as a Confederate spy on Mar. 16, 1863. The boy was graduated from the Virginia Military Institute in 1886, studied law for a few weeks at the University of Virginia, and later practised at the Richmond bar with such financial success that he was sometimes spoken of as the richest man in Virginia. He may also have inherited wealth from his father who was at one time owner of the Willard Hotel in Washington. On Sept. 16, 1891, he married Belle Layton Wyatt of Baltimore by whom he had two children. The Spanish-American War gave him a state-wide reputation. Mustered in at Richmond, Va., on May 23, 1898, as captain in the 3rd Virginia Volunteer Infantry, he passed the summer months recruiting a volunteer regiment in Fairfax County. On Nov. 21 of the same year he was commissioned captain and assistant quartermaster in United States Volunteers, and he was discharged on Apr. 2, 1899. From Dec. 7, 1898, to Feb. 11, 1899, he was on duty as acting aide-de-camp to Gen. Fitzhugh Lee, and as assistant quartermaster, VII Army Corps, at Camp Columbia, near Habana, Cuba.

His political career commenced in 1893 with his election, as a Democrat, to the Virginia House of Delegates to represent Fairfax County, which was for many years his home. After eight years in the House he was elected in 1901 lieutenant-governor under Gov. Andrew J. Montague. In 1905 he contested the Democratic nomination for governor with Claude A. Swanson and William H. Mann, and, emerging in third place, obtained appointment as a state corporation commissioner, 1906–1910. Appointed on July 28, 1913, minister to Spain, he was the last of the long line of American ministers to Spain and the first American ambassador to that country, Sept. 10, 1913, to June 28, 1921.

Although he was absent from Madrid during the most trying days of early August 1914 he returned late that month to face the difficult tasks arising from the war. In December he was instructed to reject the Spanish proposal that Spain and the United States cooperate in offering mediation to the belligerents. Again in August 1916 it was necessary for him to inform the Spanish Government of President Wilson's decision not to cooperate with the Spanish King in offering good offices to the belligerents. Somewhat irritated at Wilson's policy of acting without consultation, the Spanish Government in its turn rejected Willard's invitation to lend its support to the President's peace proposals of Dec. 18, 1916. The two governments also failed to cooperate in protesting Germany's submarine policy. After the United States became a belligerent Willard conducted the negotiations that led to the arrangement of Mar. 7, 1918, providing for the exportation from the United States of commodities needed by Spain and the sale by Spain of supplies needed for the American troops in Europe. In 1921 Willard returned to his law practice in the United States. He had business interests in Richmond and Washington, where he was occupied in part with the affairs of his son-in-law, Kermit Roosevelt, and in New York City, where he was living at the time of his death.

[*New York Times*, Apr. 5, 1924; *Willard Genealogy* (1915), ed. by C. H. Pope; *Papers Relating to the Foreign Relations of the U. S.*, 1913–18; E. G. Swem and J. W. Williams, *Register of the General Assembly of Va.* (1918); *Who's Who in America*, 1922–23; F. B. Heitman, *Hist. Register . . . of the U. S. Army* (1903), vol. I; W. A. Christian, *Richmond, her Past and Present* (1912), information from the war department regarding Willard's Spanish War record and his mother's Confederate service.]   E. W. S.

WILLARD, MARY HATCH (Dec. 15, 1856–Mar. 29, 1926), business woman and social worker, was born in Jersey City, N. J., the eldest of the eleven children of Alfrederick S. and Theodosia (Ruggles) Hatch. Her childhood and youth were passed for the most part in comparative affluence, although her father, junior member of the Wall Street banking firm of Fisk & Hatch, met repeated reverses in fortune. The family removed to New York City, where Mary attended private schools. For a number of years their summer home was in Newport, R. I. In 1871 Eastman Johnson [*q.v.*] painted the Hatch "Family Group" (including the parents and grandparents) which now hangs in the Metropolitan Museum of Art as an illuminating and authentic social study of its period. Mary was then fifteen. As she grew older she entered whole-heartedly into the New York society life of that day and attained a place of leadership in it. On June 6, 1882, she married Henry Bradford Willard.

Eight years later, finding herself dependent on her own resources and wholly without training for a business career, she achieved single-handed what might well have seemed an impossibility—the building up, without capital and with only the most meager encouragement at first from any source, of a new business in the heart of New York. While making broth, under the doctor's orders, for a sister-in-law ill with typhoid fever, the thought came to her that many sick persons in need of such aids to recovery were probably unable to obtain them conveniently in New York. She had become an expert in cookery from sheer love of the art and had sought the best available medical advice on dietetics. Accordingly, she established a modest kitchen on Forty-second Street, and since she had no money to spend for advertising or even to advance the first month's rent, she parted with some of her most cherished personal belongings. Practising physicians brought to the Home Bureau, as her enterprise was named, a great part of its early patronage. They quickly learned that her products were dependable and they recommended them to their patients. From broths and jellies the list of prepared foods was extended to include many staples and sick-room delicacies. Then, in response to requests from doctors, other invalids' supplies were added. As a farther emergency service a registry for trained nurses was maintained.

In the Spanish-American War, after the return of the troops to the Montauk Point camp on Long Island, she started diet kitchens to co-operate with the medical corps in restoring hundreds of fever victims to health. Important as that service was, her work in the World War made far greater demands on her energy and organizing ability, for then she was called upon to lead American women in a stupendous effort to supply with surgical dressings—the hospitals of the Allies on the Western Front. In the emergency following the shortage of the manufactured gauze supply, the women of New York made temporary dressings from old linen and cotton. The contribution of 25,000,000 dressings by the national surgical dressings committee headed by Mrs. Willard was recognized by England, France, Belgium, and Italy. She was the recipient of six war-service medals from those governments. For some twenty-five years she served as a member of the board of managers of the State Charities Aid Association of New York, holding from 1901 to 1909 the chairmanship of a committee charged with the placing of dependent orphans in families, for 3500 of whom suitable homes were provided. She died in New York City.

[M. E. Goddard and H. V. Partridge, *A Hist. of Norwich, Vt.* (1905); Elizabeth Jordan, in *Ladies' Home Jour.*, Aug. 1921; *Woman's Who's Who of America*, 1914–15; *N. Y. Times*, Mar. 30, 1926; annual reports of the State Charities Aid Asso. of N. Y., 1901–09; personal information supplied by Mrs. Jane H. Gardiner of New York, a sister of Mrs. Willard.]

W. B. S.

WILLARD, SAMUEL (Jan. 31, 1639/40–Sept. 12, 1707), colonial clergyman and vice-president of Harvard College, was born at Concord, Mass., the son of Simon Willard [*q.v.*], one of the founders of Concord, and his first wife, Mary (Sharpe). He graduated from Harvard in 1659 and received the degree of M.A. in course. In June 1663 he was called to the pulpit of the frontier settlement of Groton, Mass. Despite an unusual degree of resistance by a strong minority he was ordained July 13, 1664. On Aug. 8, he married Abigail, daughter of the Rev. John [*q.v.*] and Mary (Launce) Sherman of Watertown. His parish was early troubled by a case of "diabolical seizure" and in connection with it Willard made one of the best psychic investigations recorded in the witchcraft literature (*Massachusetts Historical Society Collections,* 4 ser. VIII, 1868).

Before the destruction of Groton by the Indians, Willard had become well known in Boston through his printed sermons, and on Mar. 31, 1678, he was installed at the Old South Church as colleague pastor to Thomas Thacher. On July 29, 1679, he married, as his second wife, Eunice, daughter of Edward [*q.v.*] and Mary Tyng; the date of his first wife's death is unknown. Left sole pastor by the death of Thacher, Oct. 15, 1678, Willard acquired distinction as the result of a series of lectures in which he systematically surveyed the entire field of theology. As a master of learning and logic, whose sermons were frequently beyond the comprehension of his simpler hearers, he scorned the "Enthusiasm" of the Baptist preachers and said that such rough things as they were "not to be handled over-tenderly." He pointed out that the Puritans had not intended to establish toleration in New England, and suggested that the Baptists go and hew their own colonies out of the wilderness instead of troubling those established by others (*Ne Sutor ultra Crepidam*, 1681, p. 4). Conservative in theology, he was liberal in the practice of religion, and early relaxed the requirement of a public confession at the time of admission to the church. Edward Randolph [*q.v.*] called him a moderate and reported to the

Bishop of London that he was incurring hatred by baptizing people refused by other churches (R. N. Toppan and A. T. S. Goodrick, *Edward Randolph*, vol. III, 1899, p. 148). When the King demanded the surrender of the colony's charter, Willard opposed Increase Mather [*q.v.*] and advocated submission, but after the experience of having his meeting-house seized by Sir Edmund Andros [*q.v.*], he appeared on the popular side. In a later election sermon he held that "Civil Government is seated in no particular Person or Families by a Natural Right" (*The Character of a Good Ruler*, 1694, p. 20). Although three of the witchcraft judges were Willard's personal friends and parishioners, he was the most outspoken responsible opponent of the methods of the court. Holding that the evidence accepted was but the "Cheats and Delusions of Satan," he advocated (as did the Mathers) a procedure far more enlightened than that provided by English law, and under which no one could have been sent to the gallows. He published an anonymous pamphlet on the subject and is supposed to have aided the accused prisoners. As a result he shared the unpopularity of the Mathers.

Willard was made a fellow of Harvard College in 1692, and on July 12, 1700, he was made vice-president. When President Increase Mather refused to comply with the requirement that the president reside at Cambridge, the administration of the College was turned over to Vice-President Willard (Sept. 6, 1701), and for six years he headed the institution. His succession did not, as has been said, mark a revolution, for he was fully as orthodox as his predecessor, and in 1701 on friendly terms with him. Almost the equal of Mather in intellectual stature, and less prone to quarrels, he would have been the natural candidate of the Mather faction for the presidency, had Increase and Cotton not been in the field. In 1704 he supported the Mather project for a closer association of churches (*Proceedings of the Massachusetts Historical Society*, 1 ser. XVII, 1880, pp. 280–81). He gave the college only a day or two a week, retaining his pulpit and his iron grip on Old South Church affairs. When George Keith [*q.v.*], the Quaker recently converted to Anglicanism, challenged the theology expressed in a commencement thesis, Willard sank him with a broadside of ammunition from Church of England writers (*A Brief Reply to George Keith . . .*, 1703). Failing health caused him to lay down the vice-presidency Aug. 14, 1707, and on Sept. 12 he died. He was one of the most voluminous writers New England ever had; about

twenty years after his death two of his students published his famous lectures under the title *Compleat Body of Divinity* (1726), the largest volume that had ever come from the colonial presses. He had eighteen children.

[*Willard Geneal.* (1915), ed. by C. H. Pope; J. L. Sibley, *Biog. Sketches Grads. of Harvard Univ.*, vol. II (1881), containing complete bibliog. of Willard's works, and C. K. Shipton, *Sibley's Harvard Grads.*, vol. IV (1933); S. A. Green, *Groton during the Indian Wars* (1883), *Early Church Records of Groton, Mass.* (1883), and *Groton Hist. Series* (4 vols., 1887–89); H. A. Hill, *Hist. of the Old South Church* (1890); Sidney Willard, *Memories of Youth and Manhood* (1855); *Mass. Hist. Soc. Colls.*, 5 ser. V–VII (1878–82).]

C. K. S.

WILLARD, SAMUEL (Apr. 18, 1775–Oct. 8, 1859), clergyman, educator, hymn-writer, was born in Petersham, Mass., seventh of the eleven children of William and Katherine (Wilder) Willard and a great-great-grandson of Samuel Willard, 1639/40–1707 [*q.v.*]. Solomon Willard [*q.v.*] was a brother. Samuel did not begin to prepare for college until after he was twenty-one, when an injury to his back made farm work impossible. In 1803 he was graduated at Harvard College. The following year he taught at Phillips Academy, Exeter, N. H., and in 1804–05 was tutor at Bowdoin College. Licensed by the Cambridge Association in 1805, he preached in Cambridge and later lived in Andover for a time, preaching as opportunity offered.

He received a call in 1807 to become pastor of the Congregational church in Deerfield, but his theological views were so broad that the council called to examine him would not ordain him. A month later, however, a second council approved him and proceeded to his ordination. On May 30, 1808, at Hingham, he married Susan Barker. He served the Deerfield church until 1829, when failing sight compelled him to resign. From 1829 to 1836, except for a short time in Concord, he resided in Hingham and for two years taught in a school which his future son-in-law, Luther Barker Lincoln, had opened. He then returned to Deerfield, where he resided until his death, frequently being called upon to preach. The diary which he kept during most of his life records a complete history of the objections made by the council to his religious views. These were repeated in his fiftieth anniversary sermon, preached in Deerfield Sept. 22, 1858 (*History of the Rise, Progress and Consummation of the Rupture, Which now Divides the Congregational Clergy and Churches of Massachusetts*, 1858). They are again stated in an article, "Early Unitarian Movement in Western Massachusetts," written by his daughter and published in the *Unitarian Review* (February

1881). The controversy over his ordination was the first intimation in Western Massachusetts of the liberal theological opinions which finally led to the separation of the Unitarians from the Congregational body. In 1813 several ministers refused to take part in an ordination service with him. Their refusal provoked a pamphlet controversy, in which, also, Willard's views as expressed at his ordination were discussed.

In addition to his pastoral duties Willard gave much time to education and music. He served as superintendent of schools, examined the teachers, and prescribed the textbooks to be used. In order that what he considered proper methods of instruction might be put into effect he published various textbooks, including: *The Franklin Primer* (2nd ed., 1802 and later editions), *Secondary Lessons, or the Improved Reader* (1827), *The General Class-Book* (1828), *Rhetoric, or the Principles of Elocution* (1830), *The Popular Reader* (1834), and *An Introduction to the Latin Language* (1835). Beginning with his first Sunday in Deerfield, he selected all the hymns for his services, and in 1814 published *Deerfield Collection of Sacred Music,* a second edition of which appeared in 1818; this contained both words and music. A book of 158 hymns, words only, entitled *Regular Hymns, on a Great Variety of Evangelical Subjects,* was issued in 1824, containing, as the compiler said, "a greater variety of practical subjects than is to be found in any other, however large, that has ever fallen into his hands." His final work in hymnology was a collection of 518 hymns, original and compiled, adopted while in manuscript by the Third Congregational Society in Hingham, and called *Sacred Music and Poetry Reconciled* (1830). His purpose was to have the emphasis of the words the same in every stanza, and coincide with the emphasis of the tune used. During his eighty-second year he revised his hymns to conform with this plan and called the collection "Family Psalter." It was never published, but the manuscript is in the Library of Harvard University.

[Sources include: *Life of Samuel Willard, D.D.* (1892), ed. by his daughter Mary; W. B. Sprague, *Annals of the Am. Unitarian Pulpit* (1865); Joseph Palmer, *Necrology of the Alumni of Harvard Coll.* (1864); A. P. Putnam, *Singers and Songs of the Liberal Faith* (1875); S. A. Eliot, *Heralds of a Liberal Faith* (1910), vol. II; *Vital Records of Deerfield* (1920); George Sheldon, *A Hist. of Deerfield, Mass.* (2 vols., 1895–96); C. B. Yale, *Story of the Old Willard House in Deerfield* (1887); *Boston Transcript,* Oct. 11, 1859. Authority for year of birth is *Vital Records of Petersham, Mass.* (1904).]   F.J.M.

WILLARD, SIDNEY (Sept. 19, 1780–Dec. 6, 1856), educator, writer, was a son of Joseph Willard, 1738–1804 [*q.v.*], and Mary (Sheafe)

Willard. Joseph Willard, 1798–1865 [*q.v.*] was his brother and Samuel, 1775–1859, and Solomon Willard [*qq.v.*] his first cousins. Sidney was born in Beverly, Mass., when his father, later president of Harvard College, was pastor of the First Congregational Church there. In his seventh year he entered the Hopkins Grammar School, Cambridge, where he remained until 1791; he was then sent, with a younger brother, to the home of his uncle, Rev. John Willard of Stafford, Conn., who prepared him for college. Entering Harvard in 1794, he took high stand as a scholar and graduated in 1798. He remained at the college as a student of theology and, in order to relieve the financial burden of his father, taught a district school in Waltham, Mass., during the winter of 1798–99. In 1800 he was appointed librarian of Harvard. Approved as a preacher the following year, he supplied churches as opportunity offered and in 1802 was called to Wiscasset, Me., but declined. In 1805 he resigned his librarianship. The following year he was engaged in preaching, a part of the time in Burlington, Vt., where he refused an invitation to settle as pastor of the Congregational church. In December 1806 he was appointed Hancock Professor of Hebrew and Oriental Languages at Harvard, which position he held for about twenty-four years. During a part of this time he also gave instruction in English and from 1827 to 1831 performed the duties of professor of Latin. He published in 1817 *A Hebrew Grammar, Compiled from Some of the Best Authorities.*

Willard was connected in one way or another with almost all the Massachusetts magazine ventures of this period. He was one of the committee appointed by the Harvard chapter of Phi Beta Kappa in 1803 to establish and conduct a publication—a project which he himself had proposed. In July 1804 the committee issued the first number of the *Literary Miscellany,* which was continued for two years. In 1807 Willard was made a member of the Anthology Society and thereafter had a hand in editing the *Monthly Anthology.* He became a contributor to the *General Repository and Review,* founded in 1812, and also to the *North American Review and Miscellaneous Journal* after its establishment in 1815. From 1818 to 1831 he occasionally wrote for the *Christian Disciple,* or the *Christian Examiner* as in 1824 it came to be called. In 1831 he established the *American Monthly Review,* the first number of which appeared in January 1832. During its existence of two years under his editorship it attained considerable reputation both in the United States and in England.

Willard was a man of attractive personal qualities and of varied abilities. In a high degree scholarly and literary, he was not without taste and fitness for practical affairs. Before establishing the *American Monthly Review* he had resigned his professorship. The latter years of his life he was much engaged in public services. He was representative in the General Court in 1833, 1837, and 1843; state senator in 1834, 1835, 1839, and 1840; and councillor in 1837 and 1838. He served as selectman of Cambridge, and was one of the committee in 1846 that drafted the petition to the legislature for a city charter. From 1848 to 1850 he was mayor of Cambridge. He was twice married: first, Dec. 28, 1815, at Ipswich, Mass., to Elizabeth Ann, daughter of Asa and Joanna (Heard) Andrews; she died Sept. 17, 1817, and on Jan. 26, 1819, he married Hannah Staniford, daughter of John and Sally (Staniford) Heard of Ipswich. By his first marriage he had a son, and by the second, a son and two daughters. His *Memories of Youth and Manhood* (2 vols., 1855) contains much valuable historical and biographical information.

[In addition to the *Memories* mentioned above, see *Willard Geneal.* (1915), ed. by C. H. Pope; L. R. Page, *Hist. of Cambridge, Mass. 1630–1877* (1877); F. L. Mott, *A Hist. of Am. Mags., 1741–1850* (1930); *Christian Examiner*, Mar. 1857.]   H. E. S.

WILLARD, SIMON (1605–Apr. 24, 1676 o.s.), colonist, fur-trader, the son of Richard and Margery Willard, was baptized at Horsmonden, Kent, England, on Apr. 7, 1605 o.s. Emigrating to Massachusetts in 1634, he settled at Cambridge, where he engaged in the fur trade. In 1635 he joined with Peter Bulkeley [*q.v.*] and others to establish the town of Concord. From this time until his death he was one of the leading men on the Merrimac frontier. At Concord he served as local magistrate and commanded the militia company. He represented Concord in the General Court from 1636 to 1654, except 1643, 1647, 1648, and in 1654 he was chosen assistant and served until his death. In 1653 he was made sergeant-major of the Middlesex regiment. His activities, both public and private, were closely associated with the Indian trade and the affairs of the frontier settlements. In 1641 he was appointed chief of a committee to carry on and regulate the fur trade, and in 1657 he and three associates farmed the trade of the Merrimac for £25. In 1646 and afterward he assisted John Eliot in his work among the Merrimac tribes. He was extensively employed by the General Court in Indian affairs, in locating and laying out land grants, in settling the bounds and regulating the affairs of the frontier towns. In 1659 he sold a large part of his Concord estate and removed to Lancaster, Mass. About

1671 he went to live in the southern part of Groton, now Ayer.

In 1654 he was appointed to command a punitive expedition against the Niantic sachem, Ninigret. On the approach of the English, Ninigret fled into a swamp, and the expedition ended in a parley. Disappointed at this inconclusive outcome, the commissioners of the United Colonies reproved Willard for failure to carry out their instructions. At the outbreak of King Philip's War, in spite of his advanced age, he took charge of the defense of the Merrimac frontier. His most conspicuous service was the relief of Brookfield on Aug. 4, 1675. Ordered thence to the Connecticut Valley, he soon returned to Groton to defend the frontier towns from Chelmsford to Lancaster against the Indians gathered at Mount Wachusett. His duties included the placing of garrisons, the patrolling of the frontier with a party of dragoons, and the relief of threatened settlements. Called away by his duties as magistrate, he was absent when the Indians destroyed Groton in March 1676, but he arrived with a relieving force in time to assist in removing the inhabitants. His own house was destroyed and his family forced to remove to Charlestown. There, after further service on the frontier, he died, "a pious, orthodox man," according to John Hull (diary in *Archaelogia Americana: Trans. and Colls. Am. Antiq. Soc.*, vol. III, 1857, p. 241). He was married three times, first in England to Mary Sharpe, second to Elizabeth, the sister of Henry Dunster [*q.v.*], and third to Mary Dunster, either his second wife's sister or cousin. He had seventeen children, of whom Samuel, 1639/40–1707 [*q.v.*], was the most distinguished.

[Joseph Willard, *Willard Memoir* (1858), with most of the pertinent documents; William Hubbard, *A Narrative of the Troubles with the Indians in New England* (1677); Thomas Wheeler, "Narrative," *N. H. Hist. Soc. Colls.*, vol. II (1827); F. X. Moloney, *The Fur Trade in New England* (1931).]   A. H. B.

WILLARD, SIMON (Apr. 3, 1753–Aug. 30, 1848), clockmaker, was born in Grafton, Mass., the eighth child of Benjamin and Sarah (Brooks) Willard and a descendant of Maj. Simon Willard [*q.v.*], one of the founders of Concord. He had but a limited schooling and when he was twelve years old his father apprenticed him to a clockmaker in Grafton. Within a year (1766) he had made with his own hands and without any assistance a grandfather clock which was pronounced far superior to those produced by his master. For the next nine or ten years little is definitely known of Willard's activities. An older brother was engaged in the clock manufacturing business in Grafton at the time, and Simon may have been employed by him. He may, however, have made clocks for himself, for, clocks marked "Simon Willard, Grafton," are occasionally found. At the time of the Lexington alarm, Apr. 19, 1775, he marched with his brothers in Capt. Aaron Kimball's company of militia to Roxbury, Mass., but he was not war-minded and returned to Grafton after a week. He was drafted into the army later but he paid for a substitute, and presumably remained in Grafton making clocks during the Revolutionary War.

On Nov. 29, 1776, he married Hannah Willard, his first cousin. After her death and that of their child the following August, he apparently determined to leave Grafton, and some time between 1777 and 1780 he went to Roxbury, where he established a combined clock factory and home and occupied it until his retirement in 1839, a period of over fifty-eight years. During his long and active career he manufactured every kind of clock, but specialized in church, hall, and gallery timepieces. He had not been in Roxbury long before his inventive faculties asserted themselves and at the May 1784 session of the General Court of Massachusetts, he was granted the exclusive privilege of making and vending clock jacks for five years. This, his first patent, was for a piece of kitchen furniture used for roasting meat before the open fire. The jack was suspended by a hook from the mantel in front of the fireplace, the meat was hung on a hook on the lower end of the jack, and a clock mechanism within the jack turned the meat before the fire. The invention for which Willard is especially renowned, however, is that for an improved time-piece, which he devised in 1801, and for which a United States patent was granted Feb. 8, 1802. This "Willard Patent Timepiece" at once won popular favor and in the course of time came to be known as a "banjo clock," a name which Willard himself did not use either in his patent specifications or advertisements and sales. How or when the name originated is not known. His third invention was an alarm clock, for which he obtained a patent Dec. 8, 1819, but it was not very successful or popular.

Willard built up an enviable reputation for the quality of the clocks he produced and his clientele was restricted to the wealthier classes. President Jefferson was one of his patrons and as a result, several of Willard's clocks were installed at the University of Virginia. One is today (1936) in the file room of the office of the chief clerk of the United States Supreme Court —still keeping perfect time—and another is contained in the Franzoni case in Statuary Hall in the Capitol at Washington. Willard was an extremely poor business man; he paid no attention to the fact that other clockmakers stole his inventions beyond spurning them personally, and he retired at the age of eighty-six with five hundred dollars. On Jan. 23, 1788, he married as his second wife, Mrs. Mary (Bird) Leeds, and at the time of his death at Roxbury he was survived by several of their eleven children.

[*Willard Geneal.* (1915), ed. by C. H. Pope; J. W. Willard, *A Hist. of Simon Willard, Inventor and Clock-maker* (1911); N. H. Moore, *The Old Clock Book* (1911); W. I. Milham, *Time & Timekeepers* (1923); *Boston Transcript*, Sept. 2, 1848; Patent Office records.]
C. W. M.

WILLARD, SOLOMON (June 26, 1783– Feb. 27, 1861), sculptor and architect, born in Petersham, Mass., was the tenth child of Deacon William and Katherine (Wilder) Willard, a brother of Samuel, 1775–1859, and a nephew of Joseph, 1738–1804 [*qq.v.*]. He was brought up at Petersham and helped his father, a carpenter and cabinet-maker, until October 1804, when he went to Boston to obtain work as a carpenter. In 1808 he built the famous spiral stair in the Exchange Coffee House of Boston. Meanwhile he had studied architectural drawing, possibly at Asher Benjamin's school. In 1809 he began woodcarving, doing all the capitals for the Park Street Church and the Federal Street Church; the same year saw his first sculpture— the colossal eagle on the old Boston Customs House. In 1810 he made the first of several trips south, visiting Virginia, Washington, Baltimore, Philadelphia, and New York. He took up the carving of figureheads for ships about 1813, the most famous being that of the *Washington,* launched in 1816. He also began carving in stone, completing panels for the Sears house and other work for St. Paul's Church, both for his intimate friend Alexander Parris [*q.v.*]. In 1817–18 he made another long trip south to study the Houdon "Washington" in Richmond, as he wished to be the sculptor of the "Washington" lately authorized by the city of Boston. Unfortunately, his elaborate clay models were destroyed during their sea trip back to Boston. During the trip, however, he made the models for the interior plaster work for the Unitarian Church, Baltimore, designed by Maximilian Godefroy [*q.v.*], and later a wooden model of the completed United States Capitol for Charles Bulfinch, to whom he was recommended by Ithiel Town [*qq.v.*]. He refused Bulfinch's request that he take charge of the decorative modeling for the Capitol and, after three months in New York, returned to Boston.

Meanwhile he had been studying architecture,

physics, and chemistry. He now began practising as an architect, besides giving lessons in drawing, sculpture, and the sciences. He made scale models of the Pantheon and the Parthenon for the Boston Athenæum. He invented, though he did not patent, a hot-air heating device used in many churches, and in 1825 was consulted by Bulfinch as to the best way of heating the White House. He was the architect for the Doric United States Branch Bank in Boston (1824) and, with Peter Banner [q.v.], for the new building of the Salem First Church (1826). Among his later architectural works were the Suffolk County Court House, Boston (1825), the Boston Court House (1832), the Norfolk County Court House at Dedham (1826), the Quincy School (1842), and the Quincy Town Hall (1844).

He is famous chiefly as architect of the Bunker Hill Monument, a position to which he was appointed in November 1825. Various others claimed a part in its design, especially Horatio Greenough and Robert Mills [qq.v.], but Willard asserted that he had never seen Greenough's model, and Mills's design only in passing (see Wheildon and Gallagher, post). At any rate, the working drawings were his, and the entire superintendence was in his hands during the long, troubled period of construction (1825–42). In 1843 he published Plans and Section of the Obelisk on Bunker's Hill, with the Details of Experiments Made in Quarrying the Granite. In connection with his work on the monument Willard had discovered the Quincy granite quarries, and with his customary energy he began their exploitation, developing many machines for handling the stone and cutting in the quarries columns and other work for many important buildings, especially the New York Merchants' Exchange. In the forties he retired from the quarry business and became a gentleman farmer in Quincy, characteristically attempting farming in a scientific way. He died in Quincy of apoplexy. Despite his eager restlessness and the insatiable curiosity that made him a student all his life, he was slow of speech, meditative, and basically solitary. He never married, and in his later years became something of an eccentric.

[See C. H. Pope, Willard Geneal. (1915); W. W. Wheildon, Memoir of Solomon Willard (1865); Helen M. P. Gallagher, Robert Mills (1935); Bowen's Boston News-Letter, Nov. 5, 1825, Dec. 2, 1826; Élie Brault, Les Architectes par Leurs Oeuvres (Paris, 3 vols., 1892–93), where the date of death is given incorrectly; notice of death in Proc. Bunker Hill Monument Asso. (1861) and Boston Daily Evening Traveller, Mar. 4, 1861.]

T. F. H.

WILLCOX, LOUISE COLLIER (Apr. 24, 1865–Sept. 13, 1929), essayist, critic, and editor, was born in Chicago, Ill., one of four children of the Rev. Robert Laird and Mary (Price) Collier. Her father, a Unitarian clergyman, was of a Maryland family; her mother's people lived in Iowa. When she was seven her mother died, and soon afterward the father took Louise and her brother, Hiram Price Collier [q.v.], to Europe with him. Louise was taught at first by private tutors. She studied in France, Germany, and England, and then attended the Royal Conservatory of Music in Leipzig (1882–83). Later she lived in England and met some of the eminent men of the period, among them John Bright, Cardinal Newman, and Joseph Chamberlain. In 1887 she joined the faculty of the Leache-Wood Seminary of Norfolk, Va., which at that period was exerting a wide influence upon the cultural development of Tidewater Virginia. Always positive in her tastes and ideas in literature and art, she was one of the most active forces in the school during the three years of her teaching there. She was married on June 25, 1890, to J. Westmore Willcox, attorney of Norfolk, and made Norfolk her home for the remainder of her life. She was a frequent visitor to New York during the years when she was at the same time a publisher's reader and an editorial writer for several periodicals. With her husband and two children, she traveled extensively in Europe. She was at times editorial writer for Harper's Weekly and Harper's Bazar, and a regular writer for the Delineator. From 1906 to 1913 she was a member of the editorial staff of the North American Review, contributing principally critical and review articles. She was also reader and adviser for the Macmillan Company (1903–09) and for E. P. Dutton & Company (1910–17). Her first book, Answers of the Ages (1900), edited in collaboration with Irene K. Leache, was an anthology of quotations from famous people bearing on the nature of God, man, and the soul. Her most original writing appears in The Human Way (1909), a collection of essays on topics ranging from "The Service of Books" to "Friendship," "Out-of-Doors," and "The Hidden Life." Her notable anthology of mystic poetry, A Manual of Spiritual Fortification (1910), was later republished as A Manual of Mystic Verse (1917). Two small books, The Road to Joy (1911), and The House in Order (1917), are collections of essays that show her growing interest in religious and mystical thought. An ably selected anthology of verse for children, The Torch, was issued in two handsome editions, the first in 1924. During the latter part of her life she devoted much of her time to the translation of books by contemporary

French and German authors, among them *My Friend from Limousin* (1923), by Jean Giraudoux; *Gold* (1924), a translation of Jacob Wassermann's *Ulrika Woytich*; *The Sentimental Bestiary* (1924), by Charles Derennes; *The Sardonic Smile* (1926), by Ludwig Diehl; and *The Bewitched* (1928), by J. Barbey d'Aurevilly. Throughout her life she contributed articles to magazines and newspapers, and she lectured frequently on literary and artistic subjects. She was a woman of striking appearance, and an energetic and markedly individual personality. Her power as an intellectual force exerted itself in many ways upon the community in which she lived. She died in Paris, while on a visit to her son, on Friday, Sept. 13, 1929.

[*Who's Who in America*, 1928–29; obituary in *N. Y. Times*, Sept. 14, 1929; information from J. Westmore Willcox.]

J. S. W.

WILLCOX, ORLANDO BOLIVAR (Apr. 16, 1823–May 10, 1907), soldier, was born in Detroit, Mich., the son of Charles and Almira (Rood) Powers Willcox. The family traces its descent from William Wilcoxson, one of the founders of Stratford, Conn. Orlando was appointed a cadet at West Point in 1843, graduated in 1847, ranking eighth in a class of thirty-eight, and was promoted second lieutenant in the 4th Artillery. He joined his regiment in Mexico, and returned home with it in 1848. His next service was on the southern and western frontier, including campaigns against the Seminole Indians in 1856 and 1857; he was promoted first lieutenant Apr. 30, 1850. On Sept. 10, 1857, he resigned his commission, and entered upon the practice of law in Detroit with his brother, Eben N. Willcox.

When the Civil War began he was commissioned colonel of the 1st Michigan Infantry. At Bull Run, where he commanded a brigade, he was wounded and captured, and remained a prisoner for over a year, for several months in close confinement as a hostage for Confederate privateersmen in the hands of the United States, whose status as prisoners of war was under question. Exchanged Aug. 19, 1862, he was made brigadier-general of volunteers, his rank dating from July 21, 1861, the date of the battle of Bull Run. He was assigned to Burnside's IX Corps, with which he served with marked distinction in the Antietam campaign and throughout the rest of the war, commanding a division. While Burnside was in command of the Army of the Potomac, and at various other times, Willcox commanded the corps; he was actively employed at Fredericksburg, Knoxville, and in the final campaigns from the Wilderness to Petersburg. For

distinguished service he received the brevet rank of major-general of volunteers, Aug. 1, 1864, and of brigadier-general and major-general in the regular service, Mar. 2, 1867.

Mustered out of the service, Jan. 15, 1866, he returned to Detroit to resume the practice of law; but on July 28, 1866, he was reappointed in the regular army as colonel, 29th Infantry, and assigned to duty in Virginia. In March 1869 he was transferred to the 12th Infantry, joining it at San Francisco, where he served until February 1878, except for a brief tour as superintendent of recruiting in New York. For over four years (March 1878–September 1882), he commanded the Department of Arizona, and received the thanks of the territorial legislature for his conduct of operations against the Apache Indians. His next station was Madison Barracks, New York, where he was in command until 1886. On Oct. 13 of that year he was promoted brigadier-general, and assumed command of the Department of the Missouri, where he remained until his retirement, Apr. 16, 1887. In 1889 he was made governor of the Soldiers' Home in Washington, and after completing this tour of duty resided for a time in that city. In 1905 he took up his residence in Coburg, Ontario, where he remained until his death.

Willcox was twice married; first, in 1852, to Marie Louise, daughter of Chancellor Elon Farnsworth of Detroit; second, to Julia Elizabeth (McReynolds) Wyeth, widow of Charles J. Wyeth of Detroit. He had six children, five by his first marriage and one by the second. He was the author of an artillery manual, and of two novels dealing with army life and with Detroit. Both of the novels were published under the pen name of "Walter March"—*Shoepac Recollections: A Way-side Glimpse of American Life* in 1856, and *Faca, an Army Memoir*, in 1857.

[G. W. Cullum, *Biog. Reg. Officers and Grads. U. S. Mil. Acad.* (3rd ed., 1891), vol. II; *Thirty-Eighth Ann. Reunion, Asso. Grads. U. S. Mil. Acad.* (1907); *War of the Rebellion: Official Records (Army)*; *Who's Who in America*, 1906–07; *Army and Navy Jour.*, May 18, 1907; *Detroit Free Press*, May 11, 1907.]

O. L. S., Jr.

WILLET, WILLIAM (Nov. 1, 1867–Mar. 29, 1921), artist in stained glass, was born in New York City, the son of George and Catherine (Van Ranst) Willet. His father's occupation as a wood-worker and his mother's musical talent may have been related to young Willet's esthetic enthusiasms. Of his earlier ancestors, Thomas Willet was the first English mayor of New York City; on his mother's side there was the romantic Anneke Jans, wife of Everardus Bogardus [*q.v.*]. Willet never boasted of his ancestors, of his athletic skill, nor of his struggles against poverty after his father's death in 1880. But he did chuckle to recall the hot baked potatoes that kept him warm on windy walks over Brooklyn Bridge before he devoured them. He never mentioned the world-championship medal he won in an English-American Walking Race in 1886, nor his successes in portrait painting in 1885 that, with his mother's position as soloist in prominent churches, kept the Willet home from crumbling. He won a college scholarship in 1884 which he could not afford to accept, but he did study at the Mechanics' and Tradesmen's Institute in 1884–85 and under the artists William Merritt Chase and John La Farge [qq.v.] from 1884 to 1886. His vivid color-sense interested La Farge, and in that master's studio-workshop young Willet learned to make picture windows of the new opalescent glass. Later, when it was exploited by the art-glass industry, Willet rebelled against it and all its works. He appears in Brooklyn city directories from 1887 to 1892 as a designer and as a worker in stained glass. From about 1898 to 1913 he lived in Pittsburgh, where by 1899 he had established the Willet Stained Glass and Decorating Company.

His influence increased after his marriage in 1896 to Anne Lee, daughter of the Rev. Henry Flavel Lee of Philadelphia. Mrs. Willett was herself a trained artist, and through her sympathetic cooperation, he was encouraged in his own efforts and to study old windows in Europe. From his trip in 1902 he returned with renewed convictions. The energy that he had poured into athletics and later into religious work returned to him when in 1902 he first challenged popular taste in Christian art. His tall, slender figure would straighten and his quiet voice would take on power when he talked before interested audiences, large or small. Among the converts to his convictions was the architect of the First Presbyterian Church in Pittsburgh, where minister and congregation preferred picture windows. Willet's "antique" window of 1906 was promptly hidden behind a great organ, but not before it had been observed by Ralph Adams Cram, who gave him a commission for the chancel window in his distinguished Calvary Church of Pittsburgh in 1907. That window was hailed with delight and was followed by many other windows for important buildings. Of these, the best known are the sanctuary window of the chapel at West Point (1910) and the great west window of the Graduate School, Princeton University (1913). The West Point competition was international in scope, and the winning design by Willet has been called the symbol of a regenerated craft in America. Other work by Willet is to be seen in St. John's of Lattington, L. I., Trinity Church in Syracuse, N. Y., Holy Trinity Church in Philadelphia, and Calvary Church in Germantown, Pa. His original designs were exquisite water-color miniatures that seemed almost miraculous as they were developed from a grubby box of water-colors in a dusty shop. His article, "The Art of Stained Glass," appeared in Architecture in April 1918. In 1913 the Willet family moved to Philadelphia, where Willet was president of the Willet Stained Glass and Decorating Company from 1915 until his death in 1921. He was survived by his wife, two daughters, and a son, who also became an artist in stained glass.

[Sources include J. E. Bookstäver, The Willet . . . Geneal. (1914 ed.) ; N. H. Dole, in Internat. Studio, Oct. 1904 ; Am. Mag. of Art, Sept. 1921 ; obituary in Pub. Ledger (Phila.), Mar. 30, 1921 ; information from Willet's son, Henry Lee Willet.]   C.J.C.

WILLETT, MARINUS (July 31, 1740–Aug. 22, 1830), Revolutionary soldier, one of the six sons of Aletta Clowes and Edward Willett, descendant of Thomas Willet (or Willett) of Flushing, was born at Jamaica, L. I. For the greater part of his life he was a resident of New York City, in which place he attended King's College, worked at cabinet making, and thereafter became a merchant of means and the owner of considerable real property. In 1758, he obtained a commission as second lieutenant in Oliver De Lancey's New York regiment; he served with General Abercromby in his unsuccessful expedition against the French at Fort Ticonderoga; and later participated in Col. John Bradstreet's campaign against Fort Frontenac. During the period before the Revolution, he was an outstanding Son of Liberty and a leader of the radical patriots in New York City. He aided in the attack on the arsenal, Apr. 23, 1775, and on June 6, he and his associates seized arms from the British forces which were evacuating the city, an act which was disavowed by the Provincial Congress. From June 28, 1775, to May 9, 1776, he served as a captain in Alexander McDougall's first New York regiment. Participating in 1775 in the invasion of Canada under General Montgomery, he was left in command of Fort St. Johns, captured on Nov. 3.

Returning after a brief period to New York City, he was commissioned lieutenant-colonel, 3rd New York Regiment, on Nov. 21, 1776, and placed in command of Fort Constitution. In May 1777 he was ordered to Fort Stanwix, where he was second in command under Colonel Gansevoort. During an attack on the fort by the British under Col. Barry St. Leger, Willett distinguished himself by leading a successful sortie against the enemy. For his bravery on this occasion, Congress voted, Oct. 4, 1777, to present him with an "elegant sword." In 1778 he joined Washington's army, and fought at Monmouth, under General Scott. The next year he took part in the Sullivan-Clinton expedition against the Indians. On July 1, 1780, he was appointed lieutenant-colonel commandant, 5th Regiment of New York. After the consolidation of the five New York regiments into two, Willett was prevailed upon by Governor Clinton to accept command of a regiment of levies on the Tryon frontier, where, on Oct. 25, 1781, he led the attack in the successful battle of Johnstown.

At the close of the war, Willett was elected to the Assembly, but vacated his seat to accept, in 1784, an appointment as sheriff of the city and county of New York, which office he held until 1788. He failed of election as an anti-Federalist to the New York convention of 1788. In 1790, he was sent by Washington to treat with the Creek Indians, and so successful was his diplomacy that he returned, bringing with him the half-breed chief, Alexander McGillivray [q.v.]. After a succession of festivities, including a reception by President Washington and Governor Clinton, Willett witnessed the conclusion of a treaty with the Creeks, Aug. 7, 1790. Offered an appointment as brigadier-general in the United States Army in April 1792, he declined to serve on the ground that he considered it unwise for the United States to engage at that time in any Indian war (W. M. Willett, *post*, pp. 116–18). He was reappointed sheriff in 1792 for another term of four years. In politics a Republican and long a supporter of Gov. George Clinton, he turned to Burr, was appointed mayor of New York City in 1807 to succeed DeWitt Clinton, and four years later, as candidate for lieutenant-governor in opposition to DeWitt Clinton, he was defeated.

Willett was married on Apr. 2, 1760, in Trinity Church, to Mary Pearsee, who died on July 3, 1793. He next married, on Oct. 3, 1793 (*Weekly Museum*, New York, Oct. 5, 1793), Mrs. Susannah Vardill, the daughter of Edward Nicoll of New York, and the widow of Joseph Jauncey and of Thomas Vardill. This marriage proving an unhappy one, a divorce was obtained by Mrs. Willett (bill filed Nov. 11, 1799; decree filed Apr. 10, 1805). Willett married, for his third wife, probably in 1799 to 1800, Margaret Bancker, daughter of Christopher and Mary Smith Bancker, by whom he had five children. He died at his home at Cedar Grove, New York.

[Sources include H. J. Banker, *A Partial Hist. and Geneal. Record of the Bancker or Banker Families of America* (1909); J. E. Bookstäver, *The Willet . . . Geneal.* (1906); A. C. Flick, *Hist. of the State of N. Y.*, vols. III–V (1933–34); E. H. Hillman, in *N. Y. Geneal. and Biog. Record*, Apr. 1916; *Names of Persons for Whom Marriage Licenses Were Issued by the Secretary of the Province of N. Y., Previous to 1784* (1860); D. T. Valentine, *Manual of the Corporation of the City of N. Y.* (1853); W. M. Willett, *A Narrative of the Mil. Actions of Col. Marinus Willett* (1831); *N. Y. Geneal. and Biog. Record*, Jan. 1888, Oct. 1896, Jan. 1897, Apr. 1919; *N. Y. State Archives: New York in the Revolution*, vol. I (1887); *Public Papers of George Clinton* (10 vols., 1899–1914); D. E. Wager, *Col. Marinus Willett: The Hero of Mohawk* (1891); *N. Y. American*, Aug. 24, 1830; the N. Y. Hist. Soc. has notes prepared by William Kelby regarding Willett's marriages, etc. The journal of Willett's mission to the Creek Indians (76 pp.) is in the N. Y. Pub. Lib.]

E. W. S.

WILLEY, SAMUEL HOPKINS (Mar. 11, 1821–Jan. 21, 1914), pioneer California clergyman and educator, was born in Campton, Grafton County, N. H., the son of Darius and Mary (Pulsifer) Willey. His earliest American ancestor was Isaac Willey who was in Boston, Mass., as early as 1640, soon removed to Charlestown, and later went with John Winthrop, Jr., to what is now New London, Conn. Samuel graduated from Dartmouth College in 1845 and from Union Theological Seminary, New York, in 1848. On Nov. 30 of the same year he was ordained by the Fourth Presbytery of New York. He then went to Medford, Mass., with the expectation of settling there as pastor of the Congregational church.

Circumstances were conspiring to take him to the other side of the continent, however. With the acquisition of California by the United States and the discovery of gold there, the officials of the American Missionary Society felt a duty to the people that were flocking thither. They persuaded Willey to accept a mission to the newly acquired territory, and accordingly, on Dec. 1, 1848, he sailed from New York for the Pacific Coast by way of the Isthmus of Panama. Arriving at Chagres, the ship's company was taken up the Chagres River to Cruces, and then overland to Panama, encountering cholera on the way. After a month's delay, they went up the coast on the *California*, the first steamship to make the trip, and landed at Monterey on Feb. 23, 1849. Two days later Willey conducted his first service there. Monterey was at that time the residence of the governor and army headquarters, and Willey remained until the importance of the place passed with the organization of a state government. The council of administration appointed him chaplain to the post, securing a commission for him from Washington. He opened a school in Colton Hall, where he taught forty or fifty children. Securing subscriptions of some \$1500 from the residents, he sent to New York for books and established what was probably the first public library in California. At the constitutional convention which opened Sept. 1, 1849, he served as chaplain, alternating in the duties of that office with Padre Juan Ramirez. In May 1850 he transferred his activities to San Francisco. Here he labored for twelve years, establishing and becoming pastor of the Howard Presbyterian Church in the section of the city then called "Happy Valley"; taking an active part in the opening of public schools; assisting in editing *The Pacific*, a religious periodical; and serving as representative for the American Missionary Society in the extension of religious work in the state.

Soon after his arrival in California he interested himself actively in a project for founding a college. Although encouraging progress was made, the enterprise met with difficulties which caused its temporary abandonment. When in 1853, however, Henry Durant [*q.v.*] opened an academy at Contra Costa (Berkeley) in the hope that it would develop into a college, Willey became one of his leading advisers and helpers. On Apr. 13, 1855, the legislature incorporated the College of California in Berkeley, with Willey as one of the trustees. The board took over the property and control of the academy, and in 1860 collegiate work was begun. Two years later Willey resigned his pastorate with the idea of continuing his ministry in the East, but was persuaded to remain in California and devote himself to building up the college. Accordingly, he was appointed its vice-president and served as acting president until 1869, when the property and management of the institution were turned over to the board of regents of the University of California, established by legislative enactment in 1868.

For the next ten years (1870–1880) he was pastor of the Congregational church in Santa Cruz, Cal., and from 1880 to 1889, of the Congregational church in Benicia. He then became president of Van Ness Seminary, San Francisco, in which capacity he served until 1896. Thereafter, he made his home in Berkeley, engaged chiefly in writing. He was the author of *Decade Sermons* (1859); *A Historical Paper Relating to Santa Cruz, California* (1876); *Thirty Years in California* (1879); *A History of the College of California* (1887); *The History of the First Pastorate of the Howard Presbyterian Church, San Francisco, California* (1900); *The Transition Period of California From a Province of Mexico in 1846 to a State of the American Union*

in 1850 (1901). He was married, Sept. 19, 1849, to Martha N. Jeffers of Bridgeton, N. J., by whom he had six children.

[In addition to Willey's writings mentioned above, see Henry Willey, *Isaac Willey of New London, Conn., and His Descendants* (1888); *Gen. Cat. Union Theological Seminary* (1919); W. C. Jones, *Illustrated Hist. of the Univ. of Cal.* (1901); *The Congregational Year-Book, 1914*; *Who's Who in America*, 1912–13; *Los Angeles Daily Times*, Jan. 22, 1914.]　　H. E. S.

WILLEY, WAITMAN THOMAS (Oct. 18, 1811–May 2, 1900), senator from West Virginia, was born in a log cabin in Monongalia County, Va., near what is now Farmington, Marion County, W. Va. William, his father, of English descent, had moved west from Delaware about 1782; Waitman's mother, Sarah (Barnes), was born in Maryland of English and Irish stock. As a child, Waitman attended school less than twelve months, most of his youth being spent on his father's farm, first on Buffalo Creek and later on the banks of the Monongahela. He was graduated in 1831 from Madison College, Uniontown, Pa., studied law with Philip Doddridge [*q.v.*] and John C. Campbell, and in Morgantown (then in Virginia) began a practice in which he gained a livelihood and a local reputation. He married Elizabeth E. Ray on Oct. 9, 1834.

A Whig in political faith, Willey served in various minor positions, from 1840 to 1850, and was a delegate to the Virginia constitutional convention of 1850, where he championed western measures, especially white manhood suffrage. He also joined the Methodist Episcopal Church and became active in the Sons of Temperance. He was defeated as a candidate for lieutenant-governor in 1859. The next year, supporting Bell and Everett, he struggled against the tide of disunion, and in the state convention of 1861 voted against the secession of Virginia.

His chief work began with the movement for a new state in western Virginia. Reluctantly he admitted the necessity for dividing the Old Dominion. In the Mass Convention at Wheeling, May 12, 1861, he was one of the conservative leaders who checked the radical movement to create a state government immediately. A new convention, contingent upon the ratification of secession at the polls, met on June 11, and reorganized the government of Virginia in the northwestern counties, under Francis H. Pierpont [*q.v.*] as governor. In addition to consenting to the division of the state, this government later became the reconstruction government of Virginia. By it Willey was elected almost immediately to the United States Senate to fill the vacancy caused by the withdrawal of James M. Mason [*q.v.*].

He presented the constitution of West Virginia and was instrumental in securing its acceptance by Congress and the ratification by the people of the "Willey amendment" providing for the gradual abolition of slavery in the proposed state. He was continued in the Senate by the legislature of West Virginia and was reëlected in 1865. That the West Virginia revolution took the form of law and that the statehood movement was successful were in large measure due to the leadership of Willey and his associates.

In the meantime, he had become a Republican and had campaigned for Lincoln in 1864. He later became a Radical Republican and voted for the impeachment of President Johnson. Usually, but not invariably, he supported party measures. Democratic victory in West Virginia in 1870 resulted in his retirement from office, which he accepted gracefully, closing his work in the state constitutional convention of 1872 by introducing resolutions calling for a cessation of political disabilities. He campaigned for the Republicans in 1868, 1872, and 1876, being a member of the national convention in the last-named year. Local office holding, law, and domestic duties engaged his activities during the remainder of his life. He died in Morgantown, W. Va., in his eighty-ninth year.

[Willey's diary (2 vols., covering 1844–1900 and containing newspaper clippings) and 15 boxes of letters to Willey in W. Va. Univ. Lib.; biog. essay written before Willey's death by his son-in-law, J. M. Hagans, in S. T. Wiley, *Hist. of Monongalia County, W. Va.* (1883), and in abridged form in *Biog. and Portr. Cyc. of Monongalia, Marion and Taylor Counties, W. Va.* (1895); W. P. Willey, *An Inside View of the Formation of the State of W. Va.* (1901); *Biog. Dir. Am. Cong.* (1928); *Wheeling Register*, May 3, 1900.]
J—n D. B.

WILLIAMS, ALPHEUS STARKEY (Sept. 20, 1810–Dec. 21, 1878), soldier, congressman, was born at Saybrook, Conn., the son of Ezra and Hepzibah (Starkey) Williams. His father was a prosperous manufacturer. The son was graduated from Yale College in 1831 and studied for three years in the Yale law school, spending his vacations in travel which took him into every state of the Union and into Texas (then Mexican territory). From 1834 to 1836 he traveled in Europe in company with Nathaniel P. Willis and Edwin Forrest [qq.v.], and after his return to the United States he was admitted to the bar of the state of Michigan and established a practice in Detroit. He was county probate judge from 1840 to 1844. He then bought a controlling interest in the *Detroit Daily Advertiser*, the leading Whig newspaper in Michigan, but he disposed of it when he entered the volunteer army late in 1847 as lieutenant-colonel, 1st Michigan Infantry. The regiment had garri-

son duty in Mexico, experienced some guerrilla warfare, and was mustered out in July 1848. Williams was postmaster of Detroit from 1849 to 1853, then president of the Michigan Oil Company, member of the city council and board of education, and president of the state military board.

In April 1861 he was appointed brigadier-general of state troops and had charge of the camp instruction of Fort Wayne (Detroit) until appointed brigadier-general of volunteers in August. He commanded a division in the Shenandoah Valley campaign of 1862 and a division of the XII Corps at the battle of South Mountain. It was to his headquarters that Lee's famous lost order was brought, giving full information as to the location and plans of the Confederate forces. When Gen. Joseph K. F. Mansfield [q.v.] was killed early in the battle of Antietam, Williams succeeded to the command of the corps. He returned to his division when superseded by Slocum, and led it with conspicuous ability at Chancellorsville and Gettysburg. On the consolidation of the XI and XII Corps, he received the 1st division of the new XX Corps in the Army of the Cumberland, one of Sherman's armies, and served with it through the Atlanta campaign. During the march to the sea and the campaign of the Carolinas he commanded the XX Corps. He was in charge of a military district in Arkansas until his muster out, Jan. 15, 1866. He had proved a competent division and corps commander, large responsibility had been thrown early upon him, and his superiors trusted him. To his men he was always known as "Old Pap" Williams, perhaps because he wore a beard even more luxuriant than was customary in those days.

In 1866 he received a political appointment as minister resident to the republic of Salvador, and served for three years. He was an unsuccessful candidate for governor in 1870, but in 1874 and again in 1876 was elected to congress as a Democrat. He died in Washington during his second term of office. He was, at the time, chairman of the committee on the District of Columbia, a more than ordinarily responsible position at that time, when the government of the District was in the throes of reorganization. He was twice married; first, in January 1838, to Mrs. Jane Hereford (Larned) Pierson of Detroit, and, after her death in 1848, on Sept. 17, 1873, to Martha Ann (Conant) Tillman, the widow of James W. Tillman, of Detroit. He had three children by his first wife and four by his second.

[Joseph Greusel, *Gen. A. S. Williams* (1911); *Memorial Addresses on the Life and Character of A. S. Wil-*

liams (1880); *Representative Men of Mich.* (1878);
Biog. Dir. Am. Cong. (1928); *Obit. Record of Grads.
of Yale Coll. Deceased During Acad. Year Ending June
1879*; *Battles and Leaders of the Civil War* (4 vols.,
1887–88); S. E. Pittman, *Operations of Gen. A. S.
Williams and His Command in the Chancellorsville
Campaign* (1888); F. O. Conant, *A Hist. and Geneal.
of the Conant Family* (1887); W. L. Learned, *The
Learned Family* (2nd ed., 1898); *Evening Star* (Washington, D. C.), Dec. 21, 1878.]   T. M. S.

WILLIAMS, BARNEY (July 20, 1823–Apr.
25, 1876), actor, was born in Cork, Ireland, the
son of Michael Flaherty, who emigrated to
America, and became a grocer and then a boarding-house keeper near the Bowery in New York.
The son, Bernard Flaherty, grew up in that section of Manhattan, and was familiar with the life
of the immigrants who were beginning to stream
in, and with the "fire boys," or volunteer fire
companies, who were so conspicuous and colorful a part of metropolitan existence in those days.
He assumed the name of Williams for the stage.
He is said to have made his début as a super in
New York in 1836 at the Franklin Theatre,
Chatham Square, but his name does not appear
on play bills until June 15, 1840, when he was
playing small parts at the Franklin in a kind of
variety show (Odell, *post*, IV, 397). The top
price for admission was thirty-seven and a half
cents. The next night he was cast in a play called
Gamblers of the Mississippi. In July he danced
a hornpipe, and enacted Pat Rooney in Powers'
farce, *The Omnibus*. But he did not immediately obtain serious recognition, for in June 1843
he was with a circus at Vauxhall Gardens, New
York, enacting Jack in *Jack Robinson and His
Monkey*. He also took part in a blackface act,
for minstrels were just beginning to be the
vogue. In the next half dozen years, however,
he began to find an assured place in the New
York theatre, enacting Irish rôles with a rollicking good nature. To a later age the plays in
which he appeared mean nothing. In June 1848
The Irish Lion and *The Happy Man* were his
vehicles at the Chatham, then managed by Francis S. Chanfrau [*q.v.*]. In that year Chanfrau
was acting his famous Mose the fireman, in *A
Glance at New York*, and it is surprising to find
that on Jan. 26, 1849, Williams enacted the same
rôle in a benefit at the Olympic; he must have
been sure of himself and his public to risk the
comparison.

In 1849 he married Maria Pray, the widow of
Charles Mestayer, and a sister-in-law of William Jermyn Florence [*q.v.*]. She was a popular
actress and singer, and the marriage was fortunate for the happy-go-lucky Barney. Thereafter they always appeared as co-stars, and both
Williams' business and artistic fortunes were

greatly improved by the match. The pair began
almost at once to tour the country in *Born to
Good Luck* and other plays with an Irish male
leading rôle, and were everywhere popular.
Sometimes Barney appeared in the Irish play,
and his wife in a musical afterpiece. Solomon
Franklin Smith [*q.v.*] records that in 1852–53
they made a great hit in New Orleans, and
earned $10,000 on their engagement (*post*, p.
230). They continued their tour to the west
coast, and appeared in San Francisco and the
mountain towns. The following year (1855)
they sailed for England, and made their début
at the Adelphi, London, June 30, 1855, Williams
acting in *Rory O'More*. Williams was so satisfied with his success that he remained abroad
till 1859, when he and his wife returned to America. On Oct. 17, at Niblo's Garden, they reappeared in New York, giving three plays in one
evening. Barney appeared in *Born to Good
Luck*, Mrs. Williams in *An Hour in Seville*, and
both in *The Latest from New York*, by J. S.
Coyne. This bill lasted two weeks, and was then
varied by other plays—*The Irish Lion, O'Flan-
nigan, Shandy Maguire*, etc. The engagement
lasted for thirty-six nights in all, a fairly long
run in those days. From 1867 to 1869 Barney
tried his hand at the management of the old
Wallack's, Theatre (called the Broadway), but
gave it up to resume touring with his wife. He
made his last appearance on Christmas night,
1875, at Booth's Theatre in *The Connie Soogah*
and *The Fairy Circle*. He died Apr. 25, 1876,
at his home on Murray Hill, New York, leaving
a large fortune. He was survived by his wife
and a daughter. In the *New York Tribune* the
following day appeared an appreciative editorial,
saying that he had performed "a very important
work in his little world," and lauding him for
the good cheer he had always brought to audiences.

"Irish Barney" had full cheeks, merrily twinkling blue eyes, a well-shaped mouth wrinkling
with laughter, a compact but graceful figure, and
a rich native brogue. His acting was conspicuous for breadth and florid coloring, and he was
said always to enter the stage with a jovial "who
tread on the tail o' me coat" air. In the parts he
depicted, and in method of depiction, he was
true to the ragged, reckless, drinking Irishman
he had doubtless known in his youth. According to the critics of the sixties and seventies, Dion
Boucicault [*q.v.*] "raised the stage Irishman from
the whiskey still and peat fire to regions of chivalry and poetry." Barney Williams did not follow into those romantic regions. Nor does he
seem, from this distance, to have been a first-

rate actor, in the sense his friend Joseph Jefferson was, or Tyrone Power, the first prominent depictor of Irish characters on the American stage, or even the elder Drew. He was a capital and infectiously humorous entertainer, in broad Irish character, and as such greatly loved and amply rewarded by the public.

[G. C. D. Odell, *Annals of the N. Y. Stage*, vols. IV–VII (1928–31); *The Autobiog. of Joseph Jefferson* (1899); S. F. Smith, *Theatrical Management in the West and South for Thirty Years* (1868); *N. Y. Dramatic Mirror*, Mar. 20, 1898; *N. Y. Clipper*, May 6, 1876; obituary in *N. Y. Tribune*, Apr. 26, 1876.]

W. P. E.

WILLIAMS, BERT (*c.* 1876–Mar. 4, 1922), negro comedian and song writer, was born on the island of New Providence, the Bahamas, the son of Frederick and Sarah Williams. His full name was Egbert Austin Williams. One of his grandfathers was white, but had married an octoroon, and Williams in his subsequent stage career always "blacked up" like a minstrel to appear sufficiently negroid. When he was a child his parents moved to the United States, and he spent his youth in California, where he attended the Riverside High School. Thereafter he joined a small minstrel troupe which toured the mining and lumber camps, and in 1895 he fell in with another of his race, George Walker, with whom he formed a vaudeville team. For a year they drifted about the country, reaching New York in 1896. That year they were put into a musical piece at the Casino, as "filler," and did so well that they were at once engaged at Koster and Bial's, where they performed many weeks, popularizing, among other songs, "Good morning, Carrie." Their vaudeville success continued, till in 1903 they were able to produce a full-fledged musical comedy, *In Dahomey*, with music and words by members of their own race, in which all the players were negroes. This piece, thanks to its novelty, zest, and especially to Williams' fun-making, was a success on Broadway, and was taken to London (May 16, 1903, Shaftsbury Theatre), where its success was repeated; it ran eight months and a "command" performance was ordered at Buckingham Palace. Other similar pieces followed (such as *Abyssinia, The Policy Players*, and *Bandanna Land*) which made the composer, Will Marion Cook, scarcely less well known than the stars.

Walker died in 1909, and thereafter for some years Williams abandoned these all-negro productions and became the leading comedian in the Ziegfeld Follies, where his salary was in four figures, and where, not infrequently, his skits and songs, largely devised and written by himself, were the best part of the entertainment. He was extremely popular with the public everywhere, and such songs as his "Jonah Man" were known far and wide. At this period David Belasco, sensing the potentialities Williams possessed for touching other than the comic stops, offered to star him, but the comedian decided he owed a debt of gratitude to Florenz Ziegfeld [*q.v.*]. He finally left the Follies for two seasons (1919 and 1921) with the Broadway Brevities, and then entered a piece called *Underneath the Bamboo Tree*, with which he was performing when stricken with pneumonia in 1922. He died in New York City, where he made his home.

Williams was over six feet tall, and weighed two hundred pounds. His color was light, and he had no particular negro accent off-stage. By nature he was modest, quiet, genuinely studious, and anything but shiftless. For the stage, he wore the burnt cork traditional with "black face" humor, assumed the most outrageously lazy linguistic peculiarities of his race, and was perpetually a stupid, melancholy victim of hard luck and a world too difficult for comprehension. The formula has been copiously overworked by his imitators (chiefly whites blacked-up). His songs were sung in a rich, lugubrious bass, with a minimum of gesture, but that minimum as wonderfully expressive as Charlie Chaplin's. It was, however, in the telling of certain stories, such as that of the cats who appeared to the preacher in his cabin, each one larger than the one before, and each remarking, after eating a coal from the fire, "We can't do nothin' till Martin comes," that he disclosed an eerie quality of folk imagination which makes it regrettable that he never attempted to fulfil his often declared ambition— "To stop doing piffle, and interpret the *real* negro on the stage." He was, however, a pioneer in winning for talented members of his race an assured place in the American theatre, making possible the many negro plays since the World War, and he accomplished it by tact and character, as well as by comic artistry. He was married in 1900 to Charlotte Williams, a colored player, who survived him.

[Rennold Wolff, in *Green Book Album*, June 1912; G. W. Walker, in *Theatre*, Aug. 1906; *Lit. Digest*, Mar. 25, 1922; Eddie Cantor, in *N. Y. Sun*, Apr. 15, 1922; obituaries in *World* (N. Y.) and *N. Y. Times*, Mar. 6, 1922; Heywood Broun and Ring Lardner, "It Seems to Me," *World* (N. Y.), Mar. 7, 9, 1922.]

W. P. E.

WILLIAMS, CATHARINE READ ARNOLD (Dec. 31, 1787–Oct. 11, 1872), poet, novelist, and biographer, daughter of Capt. Alfred and Amey R. Arnold, was born in Providence, R. I., a descendant of noteworthy stock. Her grandfather, Oliver Arnold, was a distinguished attorney-general of the state. Losing her mother when she was a child, she was entrusted by her father, a sea-captain, to the care of two maiden aunts, under whom her education had a strong religious cast. On Sept. 28, 1824, she was married to Horatio N. Williams in New York City. After a residence of about two years in western New York, Mrs. Williams, with her infant daughter in her arms, left her husband, whom she never saw again. She returned to Providence and subsequently obtained a divorce there. Thrown on her own resources, she opened a school, but abandoned the project with the failure of her health. Eventually she essayed authorship. Her books, covering a considerable range of topics, found great favor in her day. In 1828 she published *Original Poems, on Various Subjects,* the edition being sold by subscription. The poems exhibit a mournful spirit that reflects her early training. Encouraged by a success beyond her expectations, she wrote a story, *Religion at Home* (1829), which passed through several editions. It was followed by *Tales, National and Revolutionary* (1830); *Aristocracy, or the Holbey Family* (1832), a satirical novel; *Fall River, An Authentic Record* (1833), concerned largely with the sensational case of the Rev. Ephraim K. Avery, charged with the murder of a girl; and *Biography of Revolutionary Heroes* (1839), which dealt with the lives of Gen. William Barton and Capt. Stephen Olney. She regarded as her best work *The Neutral French, or the Exiles of Nova Scotia* (1841), which in theme anticipated Longfellow's *Evangeline* (1847); to gather material for it she made a journey through the Canadian provinces. Her last book was a collection of domestic tales, *Annals of the Aristocracy; Being a Series of Anecdotes of Some of the Principal Families of Rhode Island* (2 vols., 1843–45). She left a story in manuscript, "Bertha, a Tale of St. Domingo." Five of her short stories were reprinted by Henrietta R. Palmer in *Rhode Island Tales* (1928). About 1849 she removed to Brooklyn, N. Y., where for three years she cared for an aged aunt. Returning after the death of her aunt to Rhode Island, she built a cottage in Johnston. She died in Providence.

A woman of great energy, she wrote more vigorously than elegantly, and was somewhat didactic, as befitted her tastes and the demands of the times. She shone as a conversationalist and was quick at repartee. In politics she took a deep and, as far as circumstances permitted, an active interest; she had a decided antipathy, as she said, both to kingcraft and to priestcraft. Her carelessness in attire sometimes led to queer situations; calling in calico on a friend at a hotel, she was first escorted into the cellar kitchen. Besides her daughter, Amey R. Arnold, she left an adopted son, Lewis Cass DeWolf, her grandson, whom she termed "my dear son" in her will.

[Sources include S. S. Rider, in *Providence Daily Jour.*, Oct. 14, 1872, and *Bibliog. Memoirs of Three R. I. Authors* (1880), being *R. I. Hist. Tracts*, no. 11, both based on manuscript autobiog. in the lib. of Brown Univ., Providence; registry of vital statistics, Providence; probate records, Providence municipal court; R. I. supreme court records (divorce); Henrietta R. Palmer, *R. I. Tales* (1928), foreword; information from Louis Miller, Manchester, N. H.]   W. M. E.

WILLIAMS, CHANNING MOORE (July 18, 1829–Dec. 2, 1910), Protestant Episcopal bishop, missionary in China and Japan, was born in Richmond, Va., the son of John G. Williams, a farmer, and his wife, whose maiden name was Cringan. He was a descendant of John Williams who emigrated from London to the region of the Rappahannock in 1698. His father died early, and the children knew poverty and hard labor. His mother was deeply religious and gave him a careful training in her faith. Through her care he overcame the ill health that clouded much of his childhood. At about fifteen he went to Henderson, Ky., and there for a number of years was employed by a merchant. There he decided to enter the ministry, and in preparation for that calling attended the College of William and Mary for at least two years, graduating in 1852. In 1855 he completed his work at the Theological Seminary at Alexandria, Va. In 1853 he was ordained deacon and in 1857 priest. While in Alexandria he had been stirred by reports of the work of graduates of the school in Africa and China. In 1859 he and one other were appointed by the board of missions of the Protestant Episcopal Church to initiate the activities of that body in Japan, then recently opened to the residence of foreigners. Landing at Nagasaki, he and his colleague began holding services for English and American merchants, and in 1861 supervised there the erection of what seems to have been the first Protestant church building in the empire. In 1862 ill health compelled his companion to leave the country, and until 1871 Williams was the only representative of his board in Japan. In addition to holding services for foreign residents, he prepared Christian literature in Japanese. He celebrated his first baptism of a Japanese in February 1866. Elected to succeed the first Bishop Boone, he was consecrated in New York in 1866 as bishop of China with jurisdiction in Japan. He returned to the Far East in 1868 and lived for a time in China, but the following year he went once more to the land of his preference, residing first in Osaka and then, beginning with 1873, in Tokyo. In 1874, at his suggestion, his diocese was divided, China being separated from it and he being named bishop of Yedo (Tokyo). For a time, however, he had the oversight of certain districts of the Anglican diocese of Hong Kong.

Under his administration the mission of his church in Japan grew steadily. He himself had direct charge of several congregations, and he established schools, including one for boys in Osaka, another for boys in Tokyo (1874), and the Trinity Divinity School (1878), in which his own board and the two societies of the Church of England united. He translated into Japanese part of the *Book of Common Prayer* and assisted in the formation of a prayer book for the Anglican communion in Japan. He aided the creation of the Seikokwai (1887), in which were united the churches formed under the leadership of the American Episcopalians and of the two societies of the Church of England. In 1889 he resigned his diocese but remained in Japan, serving as bishop until his successor could be appointed, and performing the duties of a parish priest in several congregations. Interested in pioneering, in 1895 he went to Kyoto and helped open new stations in a number of places in that vicinity. Working until the infirmities of age would no longer allow him to go on, he retired to America in 1908 and died in Richmond, Va. Never marrying, he gave himself unstintedly to his calling. Modest almost to a fault, he lived very simply, sought nothing for himself, and disliked praise.

[Louise P. Du Bellet, *Some Prominent Va. Families,* vol. IV (1907); *Who's Who in America,* 1910–11; W. A. R. Goodwin, *Hist. of the Theological Seminary in Va.* (1924), vol. II; *Southern Churchman,* June 27, 1931; *Spirit of Missions,* Jan. 1911; ann. reports of the board of missions of the Prot. Episc. Church, and of the Domestic and Foreign Missionary Soc. of the Prot. Episc. Church; a life in Japanese by K. Orima, ed. by Bishop Motoda; obituary in *Times-Dispatch* (Richmond), Dec. 3, 1910.]   K. S. L.

WILLIAMS, CHARLES DAVID (July 30, 1860–Feb. 14, 1923), bishop of the Protestant Episcopal Church, was born in Bellevue, Ohio, the son of David and Eliza (Dickson) Williams. He graduated from Kenyon College in 1880, was ordained deacon in 1883, and priest the following year. On Sept. 29, 1886, he married Lucy Victoria Benedict of Cincinnati. He served as rector of Fernbank and Riverside, Ohio, from 1884 to 1889, and of Trinity Church, Steubenville, from 1889 to 1893. In the latter year he became dean of Trinity Cathedral, Cleveland, in which capacity he served until consecrated bishop of Michigan, Feb. 7, 1906.

In his religious and social views Bishop Wil-liams belonged to the liberal school of thought. He had strong convictions regarding the proper mission of the Church and was outspoken and fearless in his expression of them. Gratefully acknowledging that the writings of Walter Rauschenbush [*q.v.*] were one of the chief inspirations of his ministry, he became the leading exponent in his own communion of the "social gospel." His activities, addresses, and writings made him widely known in the United States and abroad. In 1910 and 1920 he attended the Lambeth Conference in London; during the World War, he went to France under appointment of the Red Cross; he was a member of the commission connected with the Inter-Church World Movement that investigated the steel industry; in 1921 he visited England with a group of Americans to study the English labor movement in its relations to the Church; he was national president of the Church League for Industrial Democracy. The first of his books, *A Valid Christianity for To-Day,* containing addresses delivered on various occasions, appeared in 1909. His social views are most definitely set forth, however, in the three that followed: *The Christian Ministry and Social Problems* (1917); *The Prophetic Ministry for Today* (1912), consisting of his Lyman Beecher Lectures at the Yale Divinity School; and *The Gospel of Fellowship* (copr. 1923), in which he discusses Christian fellowship as applied to races, nations, industry, and the churches. The last-named volume comprises the Cole Lectures for 1923 at the School of Religion, Vanderbilt University. Bishop Williams died before the date of their delivery and they were read, with some supplementation, by Rev. Samuel S. Marquis. The ideas presented in these volumes were all the outgrowth of Williams' dynamic conviction that the Church should be a potent agency in bringing about a new social order. Although admitting, somewhat reluctantly, that it should minister to the needs of the individual, he insisted that it had long been doing this too exclusively, and that in its philanthropic work it had been taking care of the victims of the economic and industrial system without attempting to remedy the conditions that produced them. Its essential mission, he maintained, is so to transform society that present wrongs, injustices, limitations, and suffering shall no more exist. This end is to be achieved by engendering a world-wide fellowship—a union of intelligences, consciences, and wills in pursuit of the common good. Emphatic was his warning, however, that it is the business of the Church to proclaim principles, and not its business to recommend economic and political programs and methods; it must advocate industrial democracy, but not concern itself with the mechanics of it: ministers are not called to be reformers, but to be prophets. "I am a 'root and branch' Single Taxer . . .," he wrote; "but I have never preached Single Tax from any Christian pulpit and never shall" (*Christian Ministry and Social Problems*, p. 99).

While he enjoyed the affectionate admiration of many, he did not escape harsh criticism from those of more conservative beliefs. At the annual convention of the diocese in 1921 he dramatically offered to resign as bishop, if his personal views were judged an embarrassment to the Church. He died suddenly from a cerebral hemorrhage in his sixty-third year. Four sons and five daughters, with his widow, survived him.

[In addition to Williams' writings, see *Who's Who in America*, 1922–23; *Churchman*, Feb. 24, Mar. 3, 1923; *Detroit Free Press*, Feb. 15, 1923.]   H. E. S.

WILLIAMS, CHARLES RICHARD (Apr. 16, 1853–May 6, 1927), editor, author, was born at Prattsburg, N. Y., son of Ira Cone and Anna Maria (Benedict) Williams, both of New England ancestry. After two years at the University of Rochester, he went to the College of New Jersey (later Princeton), where he received the degree of A.B. in 1875 and won the classical fellowship. After teaching a year in Princeton Preparatory School, he went abroad for two years, studying at Göttingen and Leipzig, and traveling in Italy and Switzerland. He was principal of the high school in Auburn, N. Y., for a year (1878–79), and tutor in Latin at Princeton in 1879 and 1880. He edited *Potter's American Monthly*, Philadelphia, during the first half of 1881, and in the fall went to Lake Forest University, Lake Forest, Ill., as professor of Greek. There he became an intimate friend of the family of William Henry Smith, 1833–1896 [*q.v.*], of the Western Associated Press, a man of large means and varied interests. He was married to Smith's daughter, Emma Almira, on Oct. 2, 1884. In 1883 he became literary editor of the New York *World* and later in the same year was appointed assistant general manager of the Associated Press at New York City. In 1892 he took the position of editor-in-chief of the *Indianapolis News*. Its founder and proprietor, John H. Holliday, retired that year from active management and in 1899 sold his interest to the Smith family; Delavan Smith, Williams' brother-in-law, later became proprietor. In 1911, selling his interest to Smith, Williams retired. As editor, he established and vigorously maintained

such correctness of style and nicety of language that the *News* set a new standard in that respect in its part of the country. The little style book which he drafted for the staff was followed for more than a generation. He gave invaluable training to a group of men who attained prominence in the newspaper and publishing world. Politically, the *News* classed itself as independent; Williams was a Democrat.

Williams' chief interests were literary. While at Lake Forest he edited *Selections from Lucian* (1882). He wrote many occasional poems; a number of them were printed in the *News*, and a volume was privately printed under the title, *In Many Moods* (1910). Later came *Hours in Arcady* (1926) and *The Return of the Prodigal and Other Religious Poems* (1927). His early historical interests were represented by an address on George Croghan (*Ohio Archaeological and Historical Quarterly*, Oct. 1903). At the request of W. H. Smith, who had begun an elaborate life of Rutherford B. Hayes, Williams took up this task and after his retirement devoted much of his time to it, working in the Hayes home at Fremont, Ohio. His *The Life of Rutherford Birchard Hayes* (2 vols., 1914) and his edition of the *Diary and Letters of Rutherford Birchard Hayes* (5 vols., 1922–26) were conscientious and valuable contributions to the history of the United States during the generation centering in the Civil War. After the death of his wife (May 24, 1895), Williams was married on June 23, 1902, to Bertha Rose Knefler, widow of Gen. Frederick Knefler. When he retired from the *Indianapolis News* he made his home at Princeton, N. J., in the former residence of Woodrow Wilson, which he called Benedict House. His interest in the university was indicated, among other ways, by his *The Cliosophic Society, Princeton University* (1916). He died in Princeton, survived by his wife.

[*Who's Who in America*, 1926–27; *Gen. Cat. of Princeton Univ.* (1908); Princeton Univ. records; obituaries in *Indianapolis News* and *Indianapolis Star*, May 7, 1927.]   C. B. C.

WILLIAMS, DANIEL HALE (Jan. 18, 1858–Aug. 4, 1931), negro surgeon, was born at Hollidaysburg, Pa., the son of Daniel and Sarah (Price) Williams. For a time he attended Stanton School at Annapolis, Md., but after the death of his father the family moved first to Rockford, Ill., and later to Janesville, Wis., where he graduated from the high school and from Hare's Classical Academy. He attracted the interest of Dr. Henry Palmer, one of the leading surgeons of that section, and in 1878 began the study of medicine in his office. In 1883 he was graduated with the degree of M.D. at the Chicago Medical College, the medical department of Northwestern University. After an internship in Mercy Hospital he entered practice in Chicago, associating himself with the surgical service of the South Side Dispensary (1884–91). He was appointed demonstrator of anatomy at his alma mater in 1885, holding the position for four years.

Realizing the lack of facilities for the training of colored men as internes and of colored women as nurses, he organized Provident Hospital in 1891, which stands as an enduring monument to him. Its training school for nurses was the first for colored women in the United States. He served on the surgical staff of this hospital from its opening until 1912. This service was interrupted in 1893, when President Cleveland appointed him surgeon-in-chief of Freedmen's Hospital in Washington. During his five-year tenure he reorganized the hospital and established a training school for colored nurses. On Apr. 8, 1898, he married Alice D. Johnson of Washington and later in that year returned to his practice in Chicago. He served on the surgical staff of Cook County Hospital from 1900 to 1906, and from 1907 to the time of his death he was an associate attending surgeon to St. Luke's Hospital. When in 1899 he was appointed professor of clinical surgery at Meharry Medical College at Nashville, Tenn., he inaugurated the first surgical clinics given at that institution. Though careful and methodical in his surgical technique he was a daring operator. He is credited with having performed in 1893 the first successful surgical closure of a wound of the heart and pericardium (*Medical Record,* New York, Mar. 27, 1897). He also perfected a suture for the arrest of hemorrhage from the spleen. The beginning of his surgical career was coincident with the advent of asepsis, which he adopted and followed consistently. When in 1913 the American College of Surgeons was organized he was invited to be a charter member, the only colored man so honored. In addition to being a member of his city and state medical societies and of the American Medical Association, he was one of the founders and first vice-president of the National Medical Association, a society of colored professional men organized in Atlanta, Ga., in 1895. His clinics and didactic instruction at Meharry Medical College were of a high order. Always he was a strong advocate of the negro's right in medical education and of high standards for the special schools of the race. He served the state of Illinois as a member of the board of health (1887–91) and during the

World War he was a medical examiner on the state board of appeals.

Williams was undoubtedly the most gifted surgeon and the most notable medical man that the colored race had produced. Through his connection with Provident Hospital and Meharry Medical College he exerted a profound influence upon the development of surgical thought and practice among numerous negro surgeons, to whom his career was a shining example. His writings were confined to articles on surgical subjects, published in medical journals of the highest class. He was handsome of face and figure, and of attractive personality, and was held in high esteem by his colleagues, regardless of color. His high rating in the surgical world brought him contacts, pleasant and otherwise, unusual to men of his race. Though he experienced them without apparent embarrassment, they left his later life shadowed by over-sensitiveness and bitterness of spirit. These were aggravated by several years of semi-invalidism before his death at his summer home at Idlewild, Mich.

[*Who's Who of the Colored Race,* 1915; *Who's Who in Colored America,* 1927; *Who's Who in America,* 1920–21; J. A. Kenney, *The Negro in Medicine* (1912); *Jour. of the Nat. Medic. Asso.* (Washington, D. C.), Oct.–Dec. 1931; *Jour. Am. Medic. Asso.,* Sept. 5, 1931; *Chicago Tribune,* Aug. 7, 1931.]   J. M. P.

WILLIAMS, DAVID ROGERSON (Mar. 8, 1776–Nov. 17, 1830), pioneer manufacturer, congressman, governor of South Carolina, the son of David and Anne (Rogerson) Williams, was born at Robbin's Neck, near Society Hill in old Cheraws district, South Carolina, where his grandfather, Robert Williams, had been a pioneer pastor of the Welsh Neck Baptist Church. The elder David Williams, a wealthy planter of the Peedee section, died before his son's birth, and his widow afterward removed to Charleston, where the family had previously resided. Under the influence of his mother's pastor, Richard Furman [*q.v.*], David was sent for preparatory training to Wrentham, Mass., and subsequently to Rhode Island College (now Brown University). He withdrew from the college during his junior year, 1795, and returned to South Carolina to redeem his inheritance, which had become heavily involved in debt, thus beginning a career as a planter which remained, in spite of numerous other activities, his basic interest throughout life. From 1801 to 1804 he was in Charleston engaged, first with John E. McIver and later with Peter Freneau, a brother of Philip Freneau [*q.v.*], in the publication of the *City Gazette* and the *Weekly Carolina Gazette.*

Elected as a Democrat, he served in the Ninth

and Tenth congresses (1805–09) and in the Twelfth (1811–13). While he believed that war with Great Britain would benefit only a few merchants at the expense of the general prosperity of the country, he supported the Embargo, although its enforcement bore heavily upon his section. In general, however, he was ill fitted by training and temperament for party regularity. A somewhat theatrical manner and the frequent expression of intense personal feeling won for him the sobriquet "Thunder and Lightning Williams." In the Twelfth Congress, as a member of the distinguished South Carolina delegation that included John C. Calhoun, William Lowndes, and Langdon Cheves [qq.v.], he espoused the cause of the War Hawks and, as chairman of the committee on military affairs, delivered a stinging retort to the attack of Josiah Quincy [q.v.] on a measure for increasing the army which the committee had reported. As one of the brigadier-generals appointed by President Madison in 1813, Williams saw service on the northern frontier during the War of 1812, being associated with Gen. John Parker Boyd [q.v.] at Fort George, but he returned home in disgust before the victory at Lundy's Lane and, after an unsuccessful attempt to secure a command in the campaign against the Creeks in Georgia, resigned from the army early in 1814. Later in the same year, when the South Carolina legislature manifested a tendency to disregard the "avowed candidates" for governor, Williams' name was suggested by John Belton O'Neall [q.v.], and he was overwhelmingly elected although he had not been an aspirant for the office. His administration was a vigorous one, being notable for a spirited controversy with the federal government regarding the equipment of the militia, the settlement of a boundary dispute of long standing with North Carolina, and the purchase of the Cherokee strip in the northwestern portion of the state. At the expiration of his term in 1816, he returned to his plantation, "Centre Hall," near Society Hill, and, with the exception of three years in the state Senate, 1824–27, resolutely resisted all inducements to enter public life again.

Williams was an outspoken enemy of the protective tariff, but he protested vigorously against the nullification movement; indeed opposition to John C. Calhoun was one of the consuming purposes of the last few years of his life. Rather than nullification he advocated the development of domestic manufactures in the South as a means of lessening the dependence of that section upon New England. In this respect he may be regarded as a prototype of the later Southern industrialists. On Cedar Creek near his plantation he erected a mill for the manufacture of cotton yarns. This factory was subsequently enlarged, and in 1829, operating with slave labor, mostly children, under a New England superintendent, Williams was advertising cotton bagging, osnaburgs, and "negro cloth," and was urging the value of his cotton cordage upon John Branch [q.v.], the secretary of the navy. He also operated a hat and shoe factory, and engaged extensively in the manufacture of cottonseed oil. He was interested in scientific farming, was a frequent contributor to agricultural journals, and claimed to have been the first to introduce mules into Southern agriculture (Cook, post, p. 166).

He was killed by a falling timber while supervising the erection of a bridge across Lynch's Creek at Witherspoon's Ferry in Williamsburg district. He was twice married: first, Aug. 14, 1796, to Sarah Power of Providence, R. I.; second, in 1809, to Elizabeth Witherspoon of Williamsburg district, S. C.

[H. T. Cook, *The Life and Legacy of David Rogerson Williams* (1916); J. S. Ames, *The Williams Family of Society Hill* (1910); Henry Adams, *Hist. of the U. S.*, vols. IV and VI (1890); Alexander Gregg, *Hist. of the Old Cheraws* (1867); Robert Mills, *Statistics of S. C.* (1826); C. S. Boucher, *The Nullification Controversy in S. C.* (1916); August Kohn, *Cotton Mills of S. C.* (1907); A. S. Salley, *The Boundary Line between N. C. and S. C.* (1929); *The Diary of Edward Hooker* (1896), ed. by J. F. Jameson; *Biog. Dir. Am. Cong.* (1928); *Centennial Edition of the News and Courier* (1903); *Charleston Courier*, Nov. 19, 1830; David R. Williams Letters, Univ. of S. C. Lib.]

J. W. P.

WILLIAMS, EDWIN (Sept. 25, 1797–Oct. 21, 1854), journalist, author, was born at Norwich, Conn., the fifth son of Joseph and Abigail (Coit) Williams. He was a descendant of John Williams who emigrated to Newbury, Mass., before 1640 from England or Wales. His father was a prosperous merchant of Norwich, a general of the Connecticut militia, a member of the state legislature (1791–98), and one of the organizers of the Western Reserve Land Company (1795). Edwin early went to New York City. For some years he was engaged in trade, but his love for historical and literary work was irresistible, and before long he was exclusively identified with writing, especially in the fields of history, statistics, and geography. He was one of the founders and original members of the American Institute of the City of New York, chartered in 1829, and for a number of years recording secretary (1830–37) and a trustee. He was an active member of the New York Historical Society, the Mechanics' Institute, St. David's Benevolent Society, and other historical and statistical societies. His books show unusual fluency, versatility, and industry, were well regarded by his contemporaries, and are still useful as embodying facts and opinions of that time. At the time of his death he was a contributor to the *New York Herald*.

His publications include *The New York Annual Register*, 1830–45; *The Politician's Manual*, 1832–34; *The Book of the Constitution* (1833); *New York As It Is*, 1833–37; *Narrative of the Recent Voyage of Captain Ross to the Arctic Regions . . . and a Notice of Captain Back's Expedition* (1835), also published as *Arctic Voyages* (1835); *The Statesman's Manual*, 1846–58; *Truths in Relation to the New York and Erie Railroad* (1842); *A Political History of Ireland* (1843); *The Wheat Trade of the United States and Europe* (1846); *The Statistical Companion for 1846* (1846); *The Presidents of the United States* (1849), which also appeared, extended and revised, as volume two of B. J. Lossing and Williams' *National History of the United States* (1855); *The Twelve Stars of the Republic* (1850); *The Napoleon Dynasty* (1852), with C. Edwards Lester; *The New Universal Gazetteer or Geographical Dictionary* (1832), being Part II of the Treasury of Knowledge and Library of Reference (3 vols., 1839); "The Life and Administration of Ex-President Fillmore" (*Statesman's Manual*, 1856).

On Aug. 24, 1834, he was married to Grace Caroline Clarke, who died before him. He died of Asiatic cholera at the Union Place Hotel, New York City, and was survived by a son and a daughter. He was buried at Norwich, Conn.

[See obituary in *N. Y. Herald*, Oct. 23, 1854; *New England Hist. and Geneal. Reg.*, Apr. 1908; *Trans. of the Am. Institute of the City of N. Y.* (1855). The date of birth is sometimes given as Mar. 7, 1797.]

J. I. W.

WILLIAMS, EGBERT AUSTIN [See WILLIAMS, BERT, 1876–1922].

WILLIAMS, ELEAZAR (c. 1789–Aug. 28, 1858), missionary to the Indians, half-breed leader, erroneously called the "Lost Dauphin," was the son of a St. Regis Indian, Thomas Williams, and his wife, Mary Ann Kenewatsenri. Thomas was the grandson of Eunice Williams, daughter of John Williams, 1664–1729 [*q.v.*], minister of Deerfield, Mass., who was captured in 1704 in a French and Indian raid. She married an Indian chief of Caughnawaga and her descendants all bore the name of Williams. Eleazar himself asserted in 1824 (*Wisconsin Historical Society Collections*, vol. VII, 1876, p. 355) that he was born at Sault St. Louis (Caughnawaga, Canada). In 1800 Deacon Nathaniel Ely of Longmeadow, Mass., whose wife

was a Williams, invited Thomas to bring there two of his sons to be educated. John was intractable and was soon sent home, but Eleazar remained with his Puritan relatives for several years. He proved to be an apt scholar, although he never fully mastered the English language.

In the War of 1812 he served as a scout for the Americans on the northern border of New York. After peace was declared he became imbued with a desire to do missionary work among the Oneida, and was appointed lay reader and catechist by Bishop Hobart of the Episcopal Church. He persuaded a number of the New York Indians to embrace the Episcopal faith, a small church was built on the reservation, and the missionary translated the prayer book and hymns into the Iroquois language.

By this success he attracted attention, and he was approached by land agents who were eager to obtain the Oneida reservation. With them he planned to persuade the Oneida to seek a new home in the West, conceiving a grandiose scheme for an Indian empire in the promotion of which he was to play a leading part. In 1821, with the permission of Lewis Cass [*q.v.*], governor of Michigan Territory, he led a party of chiefs to Green Bay, where they negotiated a treaty with the Menominee and Winnebago chiefs by which the Easterners were ceded land on Fox River. (The original parchment copy of this treaty is in the library of the State Historical Society of Wisconsin.) Williams signed the document as an Indian chief; Charles Trowbridge, who signed as Cass's representative, said of him later that he "had all the peculiarities of a half-breed Indian as undoubtedly he was" (*Ibid.*, p. 414).

The next year Williams led a number of his neophytes to their new home in what is now Wisconsin. As their missionary, indorsed by the Episcopal Church, he began at Green Bay a school for Indian and French half-breed children. He did not shine in his role of schoolmaster, however, and ended it by marrying, Mar. 3, 1823, one of his pupils, Madeleine Jourdain, then fourteen years of age, by whom he had a son and two daughters. He took her East, and Bishop Hobart confirmed her and gave her the name of Mary Hobart. Her relatives, the Menominee Indians, gave her a large tract of land on Fox River, and there she and Williams lived, though he was frequently away, persuading new groups of tribesmen to emigrate and pursuing his plans to build an Indian empire. In 1830, however, he visited Washington, where his plans were rejected. Meanwhile, in 1824, he had been superseded as Episcopal missionary at Green

Bay, and while he still preached occasionally to the Oneida at Duck Creek, about 1832 he was repudiated by this group. Thereafter he became impecunious and unsettled, absented himself from his wife and home, mortgaged her land, and lost caste with his former friends.

A handsome man and vain of his personal appearance, Williams as early as 1839 confided to an editor in Buffalo that he believed that he was the real Dauphin of France (*Wisconsin Historical Society Collections*, VIII, 362). In 1841 the Prince de Joinville, son of King Louis Philippe, visited Green Bay, and Williams later claimed that the prince asked him to sign an abdication, which request he refused. Prince de Joinville repudiated this account of his interview with Williams, in whom he said he was interested merely as an Indian missionary. In July 1849 the *United States Magazine and Democratic Review* carried an anonymous article claiming royal birth for Eleazar Williams; his literary executor later asserted (*Putnam's Magazine*, July 1868) that the article was probably by Williams himself. It was not, however, until J. H. Hanson, an Episcopal minister with a romantic turn of mind, published in *Putnam's Magazine* (February 1853) an article entitled "Have We a Bourbon among Us?" that Williams sprang into undeserved fame. Much discussion followed; William Gilmore Simms in the *Southern Quarterly Review* (July 1853) ridiculed Williams' claim, but many others eagerly accepted it. Meanwhile, Williams' fortunes fell lower. About 1850 he accepted a small salary to preach to St. Regis Indians at Hogansburg, N. Y., where he died eight years later in comparative obscurity, still maintaining that he was the Dauphin of France. (See, however, his disclaimer to certain intimates, *Wisconsin Historical Society Collections*, VIII, 367.) His widow lived at her home at Little Rapids on Fox River until her death in 1886. Williams' title to eminence might receive more acceptance had he not been repudiated by the Indians he served and well known at Green Bay for his hypocrisy and deceit, indolence, and desire for notoriety.

Williams' papers and books were presented to the State Historical Society of Wisconsin; they consist of sermons, mostly in the Indian language, of a diary, detailing his interview with Joinville, and of business papers and documents. He published *Prayers for Families and for Particular Persons, Selected from the Book of Common Prayer* (1816); a spelling book (1813) "in the language of the Seven Iroquois Nations"; *Good News to the Iroquois Nation* (1813); and translations of church books. A life of his father which he wrote appeared in 1859. He is credited with simplifying the writing of the Mohawk language by using only eleven letters of the alphabet.

[For material favorable to Williams' claim to be Dauphin of France, see J. H. Hanson, *The Lost Prince* (1854); Francis Vinton, in *Putnam's Mag.*, Sept. 1868; E. E. G. Evans, *The Story of Louis XVII of France* (London, 1893); P. V. Lawson, *Prince or Creole* (1901); D. B. Martin, *Eleazar Williams, 1821–1921* (1921). For criticism of the Dauphin claim, see J. Y. Smith, in *Wis. Hist. Soc. Colls.*, vol. VI (1872); A. G. Ellis and L. C. Draper, *Ibid.*, vol. VIII (1879); W. W. Wight, in *Parkman Club Pubs.*, vol. I, no. 7 (1896). Consult also *Green Bay Hist. Bull.*, vol. I, nos. 5–6 (1925); and S. W. Williams, *The Geneal. and Hist. of the Family of Williams in America* (1847). Mary H. Catherwood's novel *Lazarre* (1901) is founded on Williams' career.]   L. P. K.

WILLIAMS, ELISHA (Aug. 24, 1694–July 24, 1755), Congregational clergyman, rector of Yale College, active in the political and military affairs of Connecticut, was born in Hatfield, Mass., where his father, the Rev. William Williams, was pastor of the Congregational church; Israel Williams [*q.v.*] was Elisha's half-brother. They were descended from Robert Williams who came from England in 1637 and settled in Roxbury, Mass. Elisha's mother, Elizabeth (Cotton), was a grand-daughter of John Cotton [*q.v.*], and also of Gov. Simon Bradstreet [*q.v.*]. At the age of fourteen Williams entered the sophomore class of Harvard College and was graduated with honors in 1711. After studying theology with his father for a time, he went to Wethersfield, Conn., where he later acquired a farm, and on Feb. 23, 1713/14 married Eunice, daughter of Thomas and Mary (Treat) Chester.

A man of great physical and mental energy, wide interests, varied abilities, and roaming disposition, he played a prominent part in several different fields. Soon after his marriage he went to Canso on the coast of Nova Scotia, where he preached to the fishermen. Returning to Wethersfield, he began the study of law. From 1716 to 1719, while the location of the Collegiate School of Connecticut (Yale College) was a subject of heated controversy, he instructed a part of the student body in his home, achieving a high reputation as a teacher; among his pupils was Jonathan Edwards [*q.v.*]. In the meantime, 1717, he was chosen to represent Wethersfield in the General Assembly and was present at five sessions, serving as clerk at four of them and as auditor of public accounts at the other. His experiences during a severe illness that befell him in 1719 apparently awakened him to a more vital interest in religion, and the following year the people of Newington Parish, in the western part of Wethersfield, sought his services as pastor. On Oct. 17, 1722, a formal organization of a church there having been effected two weeks before, he was ordained. Here he served until 1726, when he assumed the duties of rector of Yale College, to which office he had been elected in September of the year preceding.

For some thirteen years he managed the affairs of the institution with dignity and wisdom; its reputation was strengthened, and the number of students steadily increased. When on Oct. 30, 1739, Williams offered his resignation, the trustees accepted it "with great reluctancy" and "with hearty thankfulness for all his past good service" (Dexter, *post*, p. 632). The ostensible reason for his resignation was impaired health, but it was hinted that he aspired to be governor of Connecticut (*Ibid.*). Returning to his farm in Wethersfield, he again became active in public affairs. In 1740 he was sent to the General Assembly, and thereafter served in that body almost continuously up to 1749, at several sessions being chosen speaker. From 1740 to 1743 he was also a judge of the superior court, failing of subsequent appointment, it is said, because of "New Light" sympathies. Generally ascribed to him, though also to Thomas Cushing, speaker of the Massachusetts House of Representatives, 1742–46, is a pamphlet by "Philalethes"—*The Essential Rights and Liberties of Protestants. A Seasonable Plea for the Liberty of Conscience, and the Right of Private Judgment in Matters of Religion, Without Any Controul from Human Authority*... (1744). In it the author criticizes recent restrictive legislation by the Connecticut Assembly. When, during King George's War, the expedition against Cape Breton was under consideration, Williams and Jonathan Trumbull were sent to Massachusetts to confer with Governor Shirley. Later, to his varied experiences Williams added those of an army chaplain, accompanying the Connecticut troops to Louisbourg and being present at the capture of the fortress in June 1745. His aptitude for military duties was such that when the expedition for the conquest of Canada was organized he was made colonel of the Connecticut forces. Since the enterprise was ultimately abandoned, however, he had no opportunity to prove his ability as a commanding officer in the field.

In December 1749 he went to England, primarily to secure payment of money that had been advanced for the Canada expedition and incidentally to solicit funds for the College of New Jersey. He remained abroad for more than two years and came into close association with leaders of the evangelical movement. His wife, who had remained behind, died May 31, 1750, and on Jan. 29, 1751, he married Elizabeth,

daughter of the Rev. Thomas Scott of Norwich, England, the noted Bible commentator. She was a woman of considerable literary attainments and a writer of hymns. After his return to Connecticut, Williams was again sent to the General Assembly, and was one of the Connecticut delegates at the intercolonial congress held in Albany in 1754. He died at Wethersfield in his sixty-first year; of his six children, a son and a daughter survived him.

[C. J. Hoadly, *The Pub. Records of the Colony of Conn.*, vols. VI–X (1872–77); S. W. Adams and H. R. Stiles, *The Hist. of Ancient Wethersfield* (1904); W. B. Sprague, *Annals of the Am. Pulpit*, vol. I (1857); F. B. Dexter, *Biog. Sketches Grads. Yale Coll., with Annals of the Coll. Hist.*, vol. I (1885); Edwin Oviatt, *The Beginnings of Yale* (1916); *New England Hist. and Geneal. Reg.*, Oct. 1858; S. W. Williams, *The Geneal. and Hist. of the Family of Williams* (1847); *New Englander*, Apr. 1876, pp. 303–04; Isaac Backus, *A Hist. of New England, with Particular Reference to the Denomination of Christians Called Baptists* (ed. 1871), II, 60.]

H. E. S.

WILLIAMS, ELISHA (Aug. 29, 1773–June 29, 1833), lawyer, Federalist politician, was born in Pomfret, Conn., one of thirteen children of Ebenezer Williams, a colonel in the Revolutionary militia, and Jerusha (Porter) Williams. He was a descendant in the fifth generation of Robert Williams of Roxbury. As his father died when he was very young, he was brought up under the guardianship of Capt. Seth Grosvenor of Pomfret, Conn., studied law with Judge Tapping Reeve at Litchfield, Conn., and under Chief Justice Ambrose Spencer at Hudson, N. Y., and was admitted to the bar in 1793. In the same year he began the practice of the law at Spencertown, N. Y., moving to Hudson seven years later. He soon forged to the front rank among up-state lawyers and crossed swords on many occasions with the outstanding leaders of the state bar, including Thomas Addis Emmet, Ambrose Spencer, William W. Van Ness, and his political opponent, Martin Van Buren [*qq.v.*], whose solid analytical talents were well matched against the brilliant oratorical gifts of Williams.

Williams was elected a member of the Assembly in 1800 for Columbia County, which he represented at nine other sessions of that body, including the critical war period (1812–15) and extending down to 1828 (S. C. Hutchins, *Civil List and Constitutional History of ... New York*, 1883). Early in his political career he became a recognized leader of the Federalist party in the state. In 1813 he opposed taxation for carrying on an "unjust and unnecessary" war, declaring, "I will not furnish the administration with the means for carrying on this war; I would starve them into peace with all my heart" (*Journal of the Assembly of ... New York* ...

Thirty-Sixth Session, 1813). An associate of rich Federalists of conservative leanings, such as Jacob Rutsen van Rensselaer and others whom he numbered among his clients, he took a strongly anti-democratic stand in the Constitutional Convention of 1821, which he attended as a delegate. He fervently opposed the extension of the franchise to non-freeholders, and, pointing to the French Revolution, warned that political democracy would be followed by an overthrow of the propertied class. Quoting Jefferson to the effect that "great cities were upon the body politic great sores," he concluded that the urban population could not be counted on in times of crisis. Van Buren then retorted that a false construction had been placed upon Jefferson's views (N. H. Carter and W. L. Stone, *Reports of the Proceedings and Debates of the Convention of 1821, passim*).

Williams' devotion to property rights is best evidenced by the large fortune he was able to accumulate in the practice of the law at Hudson and through judicious investments, principally in Seneca County real estate; he left about a quarter of a million dollars at his death. He also served as president of the Bank of Columbia at Hudson for several years. His reputation suffered in 1820, when he testified before a legislative inquiry that he had received payments from the Bank of America for his services in securing its charter in 1812–13 (Ellis, *post,* pp. 177–78; Fox, *post,* pp. 227–28). In 1815 he founded the town of Waterloo, Seneca County, whither he removed with his family fifteen years later on account of poor health. He was tall and dignified in bearing and possessed of brilliant oratorical powers. James Kent [*q.v.*], before whom he had frequently tried cases at the circuit, was impressed with his abilities as a trial lawyer, by what he called his "sagacity and judgment in the examination of witnesses," and "his forcible, pithy, argumentative, and singularly attractive" addresses, which were heightened by his language, voice, and commanding person (Raymond, *post,* p. 13). In *The Poet at the Breakfast Table* (1891 ed., pp. 330–31) Oliver Wendell Holmes relates that he once asked Gulian C. Verplanck: "Who, on the whole, seemed to you the most considerable person you ever met?" and was without hesitation answered: "Elisha Williams." In 1795 Williams married Lucia Grosvenor, a daughter of his former guardian, by whom he had five children.

[Sources include William Raymond, *Biog. Sketches of the Distinguished Men of Columbia County* (1851); S. W. Williams, *The Geneal. and Hist. of the Family of Williams in America* (1847); Alden Chester and E. M. Williams, *Courts and Lawyers of N. Y.* (1925);

Franklin Ellis, *Hist. of Columbia County, N. Y.* (1878), pp. 83–85; P. F. Miller, *A Group of Great Lawyers of Columbia County* (1904), pp. 118–25; obituaries in *N. Y. Evening Post,* July 1, 1833, and *N. Y. Daily Advertiser,* July 2, 3. See also D. T. Lynch, *An Epoch and a Man: Martin Van Buren and His Times* (1929); and D. R. Fox, *The Decline of Aristocracy in the Politics of N. Y.* (1919).]   R. B. M.

WILLIAMS, ELKANAH (Dec. 19, 1822–Oct. 5, 1888), pioneer ophthalmologist, was born on a farm near Bedford, Lawrence County, Ind., the son of Isaac and Amelia (Gibson) Williams, both of Welsh lineage, who had moved westward from North Carolina by way of Tennessee. The father prospered and was able to give the best available educational advantages to the more ambitious of his large family. Elkanah attended the Bedford Academy, and later entered the state university at Bloomington. Transferring to Indiana Asbury (now De Pauw) University, he was graduated there in 1847. After teaching school for a short time he entered the medical department of the University of Louisville, where he received the degree of M.D. in 1850. He began practice in Bedford, but in 1852 moved to Cincinnati, Ohio, and later in the same year left for a prolonged tour of graduate study in the eye clinics of Europe. Influenced by Dr. S. D. Gross [*q.v.*] of Louisville he had set out to be an operating surgeon, later centering his interest upon the surgery of the eye.

Returning to Cincinnati in 1855, he reopened his practice, devoting it exclusively to diseases of the eye and ear and thereby becoming one of the first in the country to limit his practice to this specialty. With surgery of the eye and ear in the hands of the general surgeon and diseases of these organs in the field of the general practitioner, he found opposition and disappointments in his new venture. Soon, however, he achieved a highly lucrative practice and in time became known as the foremost practitioner of his specialty in that section of the country. In 1855 he established a charity eye clinic along the lines of European institutions in connection with the Miami Medical College and became clinical lecturer on diseases of the eye and ear. When the school was reopened in 1865, after having been closed because of the Civil War, Williams joined the faculty as professor of ophthalmology and aural surgery, thus filling the first chair devoted to this specialty in the United States. Throughout his teaching career of over twenty years, he conducted didactic and clinical instruction of the highest order. With a gift for story telling, he made his lectures not only instructive but highly entertaining. He was one of the first in America to make use of the ophthalmoscope. While in Europe in 1854 he had demonstrated its use before an English audience and published an article, "The Ophthalmoscope," in the London *Medical Times and Gazette* (July 1 and 8, 1854), dealing with Dr. André Anagnostakis' modification of Helmholtz' recently devised instrument. He wrote nearly fifty articles on topics relating to his specialty, nearly all of which were published in the Cincinnati *Lancet and Observer,* of which he was co-editor from 1867 to 1873. He also contributed "Injuries and Diseases of the Eyes and Their Appendages" to John Ashhurst's *International Encyclopedia of Surgery* (vol. V, 1884). He was a member and one time president (1876) of the American Ophthalmological Society and a member of the American Otological Society. He was made an honorary member of the Ophthalmological Society of Great Britain in 1884. For twelve years (1862–73) he served on the staff of the Cincinnati Hospital and during the Civil War he was an assistant surgeon in the United States Marine Hospital in Cincinnati.

He was a large man of jovial appearance, with a disposition full of spontaneous generosity and affection. These characteristics, with a ready conversational ability, made him conspicuous and popular in any company of which he was a member. He was compelled to give up his practice and teaching by an organic disease of the brain, which caused his death at the home of a friend in Hazelwood, Pa. He was twice married: first, in December 1847, to Sarah L. Farmer of Bedford, Ind., who died in 1851; second, on Apr. 7, 1857, to Sarah B. McGrew, who survived him.

[*Trans. Am. Ophthalmological Soc.,* vol. V (1890); *Trans. Am. Otological Soc.,* vol. IV (1890); *Hist. of the Miami Medic. Coll.* (1881); H. A. Kelly and W. L. Burrage, *Am. Medic. Biogs.* (1920); *Chicago Medic. Jour. and Examiner,* Nov. 1888; *N. Y. Medic. Jour.,* Oct. 27, 1888; *Cincinnati Lancet and Clinic,* Oct. 13, 1888; *Trans. of the Forty-fourth Ann. Meeting, Ohio State Medic. Soc.* (1889); *Cincinnati Enquirer,* Oct. 6, 1888.]   J. M. P.

WILLIAMS, EPHRAIM (Mar. 7, 1714 N.S.–Sept. 8, 1755), colonial soldier, was born in Newton, Mass., the elder of the two sons of Ephraim Williams by his first wife, Elisabeth Jackson, and a great-grandson of Robert Williams, who settled in Roxbury in 1637. His father, who practised politics, land speculation, frontier warfare, and other crafts, removed to Stockbridge in 1739, where he became the head and forefront of the intrigues against Jonathan Edwards [*q.v.*]. Beaten by Edwards, he retired to Hatfield, where he died in 1754. In his early years, according to tradition, the younger Ephraim followed the sea, visiting England, Spain, and Holland and acquiring the polish and information of a man of the world. With slight formal education, he had a hankering for learning and enjoyed the company of educated men. He was tall, portly, affable, kindly, by nature a soldier and politician. With his father he settled in Stockbridge, which he may have represented, sometime before 1745, in the General Court. In that year, through the influence of his kinsman Israel Williams [*q.v.*], one of the "river gods" who controlled everything worth controlling—civil, military, or ecclesiastical—along the Connecticut, he was commissioned captain and placed in command of the forts and posts extending along the northern boundary of Massachusetts from Northfield to the New York border. He was an efficient, popular commander, taking good care of his men, and a brave but incautious soldier. In time of war he made his headquarters at Fort Shirley (Heath Township) and later at Fort Massachusetts (Adams Township), in time of peace at Hatfield. He was not at Fort Massachusetts, however, when it was surprised and captured by a French and Indian force under Rigaud de Vaudreuil, Aug. 30, 1746.

In 1750 the General Court granted him 190 acres on the great bend of the Hoosac (North Adams) adjacent to Fort Massachusetts, and he also held lots in the West Township (Williamstown). In 1753 he was made a major and in 1755 colonel of a regiment raised to aid William Johnson [*q.v.*] in his projected expedition against Crown Point. At Albany, July 21, 1755, he made his will. Having neither wife nor child, he left a good part of his estate to establish a free school in the West Township, provided that the township fell within the jurisdiction of Massachusetts and was renamed Williamstown. On the morning of Sept. 8 Johnson, then encamped at the southern tip of Lake George, ordered a reconnaissance in force under Williams and the Indian chief Hendrick [*q.v.*], detailing 1000 soldiers and 200 Indians for the mission. Hendrick's comment, "If they are to be killed, too many; if they are to fight, too few" (Perry, *post,* p. 345), went unheeded, and Williams, according to the preponderance of evidence, aggravated the situation by failing to send out scouts. Two hours after starting they walked into an ambush laid by Baron Dieskau. Williams and Hendrick, at the head of the column, were killed by almost the first volley. The approximate site of Williams' death is marked by a monument. The free school established by his liberality was chartered in 1793 as Williams College.

[Ebenezer Fitch, "Hist. Sketch of the Life and Character of Col. Ephraim Williams" (written Jan. 1802), *Colls. Mass. Hist. Soc.,* 1 ser., VIII (1802; repr. 1856); A. L. Perry, *Origins in Williamstown* (3rd ed., 1900);

J. A. Holden, "Col. Ephraim Williams," *Proc. N. Y. State Hist. Asso.*, vol. I (1901) ; L. W. Spring, *A Hist. of Williams Coll.* (1917) ; W. A. Pew, *Col. Ephraim Williams: An Appreciation* (1919) ; A. H. Buffinton, "Did His Foes Catch Col. Ephraim Napping?", *Williams Alumni Rev.*, Mar. 1933 ; S. W. Williams, *The Geneal. and Hist. of the Family of Williams* (1847).]

G. H. G.

WILLIAMS, FRANK MARTIN (Apr. 11, 1873–Feb. 20, 1930), civil engineer, was born in Durhamville, N. Y., the son of William and Ellen L. (Sterling) Williams. He attended the district school at Durhamville, the Oneida High School, and Colgate University, where he received the degree of A.B. with honors in 1895. Upon graduation he engaged for a while in highway and sewer construction in Oneida, during his spare time studying law. He then took a course at the Syracuse University Law School, receiving the degree of LL.B. in 1897, and was admitted to the bar. Thereafter, until April 1898 he was rodman for the New York state engineering department, and in November became resident engineer for the Stanwix Engineering Company of Rome, N. Y., having charge of the construction of the water system and electric-light plant at Charlotte. In April 1900 he reëntered the office of the state engineer, and advanced through the various grades from rodman to resident engineer.

His political career began when he was elected state engineer and surveyor of New York for 1909 and 1910. In this capacity he supervised the preparation of plans and estimates and the awarding of contracts for some $30,000,000 worth of work in the construction of a barge canal to supersede the old Erie Canal. He also served as chairman of the Barge Canal Terminal Commission, making exhaustive studies of waterway terminals in Europe and the United States. In 1911–12 he was chief engineer of the Coleman Du Pont Road, Incorporated, being in charge of the preliminary work—plans, surveys, and estimates—for the proposed Du Pont Boulevard in Delaware; the following year, 1912–13, he became chief engineer of the Portage County Improvement Association, thus assuming the supervision of extensive highway improvement in Eastern Ohio. In 1915, for the second time, he was elected state engineer of New York and retained the office, through reëlections, to the end of 1922. During his administration most of the difficulties involved in the building of the barge canal were overcome, including the problem of railroad crossings and the location and design of terminals. The entire barge canal system was opened for service on May 15, 1918.

After he left the state engineer's office, Williams formed a firm for private engineering practice. His services as consultant were immediately demanded for huge projects, such as the Holland Vehicular Tunnel under the Hudson River, connecting New York City with Jersey City, the Sacandaga Reservoir, and a hydroelectric development in Oswego, N. Y. Shortly before his death he received the high honor of appointment by President Hoover as one of five engineers on the Interoceanic Canal Board, to examine into a waterway across Nicaragua. He was married, June 4, 1907, to Lucy Mary Sterling, and was survived by his wife and one son. He died in Albany.

[*Who's Who in Engineering*, 1925 ; *Who's Who in America*, 1928–29 ; *Trans. Am. Soc. Civ. Engineers*, vol. XCV (1931) ; *Colgate Alumni News*, Apr. 1930 ; N. E. Whitford, *Hist. of the Barge Canal of N. Y. State* (1922) ; *N. Y. Times*, Feb. 21, 1930.] B. A. R.

WILLIAMS, FREDERICK WELLS (Oct. 31, 1857–Jan. 22, 1928), writer and teacher, was born in Macao, China, the son of Samuel Wells Williams [*q.v.*] and Sarah (Walworth) Williams and the descendant of Robert Williams who emigrated to Roxbury, Mass., from Norfolk County, England, in 1637. Most of his boyhood to the age of twelve was spent in China, chiefly in the American legation in Peking; and this fact, together with his father's long life and distinguished service in that country, determined his major interests. For a year he was in the public schools of Utica. Then for four years he prepared for college at the Hopkins Grammar School at New Haven, Conn. He graduated from Yale College in 1879 and spent the two and a half following years in study in Europe, in Göttingen, Berlin, and Paris. Returning to New Haven, he gave most of the succeeding two years to assisting his father in the revision and enlargement of the latter's *Middle Kingdom* (2 vols., 1883), for more than a generation the standard general work in English on China. In 1883–85 he was assistant in the library at Yale. On Nov. 19, 1885, he was married to Fanny Hapgood Wayland and with her he spent a year in Europe. From 1887 to 1893 he was the literary editor of the *National Baptist*, which was directed by his father-in-law, H. L. Wayland.

In 1893 he returned to Yale, this time to teach Oriental history, and he served on the Yale faculty until 1925. In his teaching he covered Central Asia, India, and the Far East and did much to stimulate interest in fields then generally neglected in the curriculums of American colleges and universities. It was to China, however, that he devoted the major part of his attention. Most of his books and numerous articles were on some phase of the history or problems of that country. Of these the chief were *The Life and Letters of*

Samuel Wells Williams (1889) and *Anson Burlingame and the First Chinese Mission to Foreign Powers* (1912). From its inception in 1901 he was associated with Yale-in-China, the Yale foreign missionary society, which developed at Chang-sha a secondary school, a college, a hospital, a school of nursing, and a medical school. As chairman of its executive committee and its board of trustees he gave to it a large share of his time up to the very week of his death. To his wise counsel, his steadfast friendship for all those who served in Chang-sha, and his quiet courage in the recurrent crises that overtook the young enterprise, the undertaking owed much of its success. Aside from his connection with Yale-in-China, his life was that of a member of a university community. As secretary of his college class he devoted much attention to keeping in touch with its members and compiled *A History of the Class of Seventy-Nine, Yale College* (1906). Through his interest in literary matters he held membership in various clubs, which brought him in contact with those of like mind, and he was a member and vestryman of the St. John's Episcopal Church at New Haven. His home was much frequented by those concerned with the Orient and with literature. At the time of his death he had gathered what was one of the best private libraries on China in the United States. Calm and unhurried, he gave the impression on those who knew him of being not so much of a specialist as a cultivated gentleman, widely read and urbane. He died in New Haven.

[Autobiog. sketch in *A Hist. of . . . 1879, ante*; *Who's Who in America*, 1926–27; *Bulletin of Yale Univ.* . . . *Obituary Records . . . 1927–28* (1928); G. H. Williams, *The Williams Family* (1880), reprinted from *New England Hist. and Geneal. Register*, Jan. 1880; *N. Y. Times*, Jan. 23, 25, 28, 1928.]   K. S. L.

WILLIAMS, GARDNER FRED (Mar. 14, 1842–Aug. 22, 1922), mining engineer, was born at Saginaw, Mich., where his father, Alpheus Fuller Williams, operated a sawmill. His mother was Ann Keyes (Simpson) Williams and his grandfather, Oliver Williams, was an early settler of Detroit, having migrated thither from Boston in 1815. Gardner received his preliminary schooling in Michigan and was being fitted for the state university when his father, in 1858, returned from California, where for some years he had been engaged in building flumes and operating placer gold mines, to take the family back with him. Gardner entered the College School at Oakland, Cal., and graduated from the College of California (precursor of the University) in 1865.

After graduation he went to Germany, where he attended the Bergakademie at Freiberg, Sax-

ony, for three years. Returning to America he was appointed assayer of the mint in San Francisco in 1870, but resigned the next year to go to Pioche, Nev., where he was mill superintendent for the Meadow Valley Company for three and a half years. From there he went to Silver Reef, Utah, and between 1875 and 1880, when he became a consultant for a New York exploration company, he was at various places in the West. During the years 1880–83 he visited professionally many western mining regions, especially the hydraulic gold mines at Dutch Flat and Spring Valley, Cal. In connection with these mines he came into contact with Edmund de Crano, subsequently the partner of Hamilton Smith [*q.v.*], and as a result went out to South Africa in 1884 to take charge of a gold mine. It was unsuccessful, however, and the following year he returned to California, but soon afterward was invited by Smith and De Crano to join the staff of their Exploration Company. Various stories are told of his first meeting with Cecil Rhodes, but the only fact that can be definitely established is that Williams met Rhodes on a steamer early in 1887, and in May of that year was appointed manager of the famous De Beers Mining Company (afterward the De Beers Consolidated Mines, Ltd.), a position that he held until 1905, when he returned to the United States. He lived in Washington, D. C., until 1914, then went to San Francisco to spend his remaining years with his youngest daughter.

In 1902 Williams published a 680–page monograph, *The Diamond Mines of South Africa*, telling the whole story of South African diamond mining. There is evidence that Cecil Rhodes chose him as manager for the mines because he was confident that Williams could improve the methods of working. The first production of diamonds had come from a multitude of small square "locations" under many owners, and had resulted in unrestrained competition which threatened to wreck the diamond market. Rhodes and his financial associates undertook to control the market by consolidating control of the deposits, and in consequence it was necessary to devise methods for working the properties as a whole under the conditions created by the previous work. This problem Williams met successfully, and his achievement was an essential factor in making possible worldwide regulation of the price of diamonds.

On Oct. 23, 1872, Williams married Fanny Martin Locke of Oakland, Cal., who was drowned in the shipwreck of the *Spokane* on June 29, 1911. They had three daughters and one son, Alpheus Fuller, who became his father's lieutenant and successor in the management of the South African mines. Characterized by kindliness and sagacity, determination and persistence, Williams was well fitted to cope with pioneer conditions. During the siege of Kimberley, in the Boer War, he was as active in the military operations as his technical responsibilities for the property under his charge permitted.

[Sources include Williams' own monograph, *The Diamond Mines of South Africa* (1902); T. A. Rickard, "Gardner F. Williams—An Appreciation," *Engineering and Mining Journal-Press*, Sept. 23, 1922; *Who's Who in America*, 1920–21; *San Francisco Examiner*, Aug. 23, 1922. The *Directory of Graduates of the Univ. of Cal.* (1916) gives Williams' middle name as Frederick, but it appears as Fred in *Who's Who in America*, 1920–21.]   T. T. R.

WILLIAMS, GEORGE HENRY (Mar. 26, 1820–Apr. 4, 1910), attorney-general, senator from Oregon, was born at New Lebanon, Columbia County, N. Y., the son of Taber and Lydia (Goodrich) Williams. The father was of Welsh, the mother of English descent and both grandfathers were Revolutionary soldiers. During George's childhood his father moved to Onondaga County, N. Y., where the son attended district school and Pompey Hill Academy until he was seventeen. He then read law, was admitted to the Syracuse bar in 1844, and began practice at Fort Madison, Iowa Territory.

After Iowa was admitted to statehood, he was elected a district judge in 1847 and served until 1852. The next year President Pierce appointed him chief justice of the Territory of Oregon. Soon after his arrival at Salem in June 1853 he rendered a decision in favor of a freed negro, Robin Holmes, suing his former owner for the custody of his three minor children (*Quarterly of the Oregon Historical Society*, June 1922). After the call of a convention to meet in August 1857 to form a state constitution, he wrote a letter to the *Oregon Statesman*, July 28, urging the inexpediency of slavery in Oregon (*Ibid.*, September 1908; C. H. Carey, *The Oregon Constitution . . . of 1857*, 1926, pp. 32–33). He was a leading member of the constitutional convention and chairman of the committee on the judicial department. He opposed unsuccessfully the proposal that the property of a married woman should not be subject to the debts of a husband and should be registered separately (Art. XV sect. 5) on the ground that "in this age of woman's rights and insane theories" legislation should "unite the family circle" and make husband and wife one (Carey, p. 368).

Williams retired from the bench in 1857 to take up the practice of law in Portland. He supported Douglas in the campaign of 1860, and as a northern Democrat opposed to slavery in the

call for a Union state convention in 1862. He was a delegate to this body, which met at Eugene in April, and was chairman of the executive committee that carried on the campaign for the Union state ticket, which was entirely successful at the June election. In September 1864 he was elected as a Republican to the United States Senate for the term beginning in March 1865. When Congress met in December of that year he was appointed a member of the Joint Committee on Reconstruction and supported Thaddeus Stevens and the Radicals against President Johnson. He introduced the Tenure of Office bill in the Senate in December 1866, and held at the time that this measure did not take away the power of the President to remove cabinet officers (J. G. Blaine, *Twenty Years of Congress*, vol. II, 1886, p. 270). He claimed authorship for the Military Reconstruction bill, which he introduced in the Senate Feb. 4, 1867, and which was passed by Congress (see his article, "Six Years in the United States Senate," *Sunday Oregonian*, Portland, Dec. 3, 10, 1905). With his Oregon colleague, H. W. Corbett, he voted "guilty" in the impeachment trial of President Johnson. He failed of reëlection to the Senate in 1871, but in February of that year was appointed a member of the Joint High Commission that negotiated the Treaty of Washington with Great Britain, and in May was appointed attorney-general, a position which he held until May 5, 1875. In 1873 Grant nominated him as chief justice to succeed Salmon P. Chase [*q.v.*], but the appointment aroused such criticism and opposition that Williams requested the President to withdraw his name. The Senate judiciary committee refused to recommend him after an inquiry that revealed that Williams had removed from office A. C. Gibbs, United States District Attorney at Portland, Ore., to prevent him from prosecuting election frauds, an action taken at the insistence of Senator John H. Mitchell [*q.v.*], who was said to have been implicated in the use of "bribes and repeaters" (Diary of M. P. Deady, Jan. 7, 1874, and letters of J. W. Nesmith written to Deady from Washington, Dec. 2, 7, 8, 1873, Jan. 10, 1874, in Oregon Historical Society). In 1876 Williams and Gen. Lew Wallace were sent to Florida by the Republican National Committee "to save the state for Hayes" and managed, so Williams wrote afterwards, "to put the returns in such shape that the authorities would know how the people voted."

After returning to Portland he renewed his practice of law and was twice elected mayor of that city, serving 1902–05. In his later years he lent his name in support of the "Oregon System" of popular government and of the woman's suffrage movement.

In 1850 Williams married Kate Van Antwerp of Keokuk, Iowa, who died in 1863; in 1867 he married Kate (Hughes) George. This was the "pushing and ambitious wife" whose "new landau," furnished at public expense and displayed at Washington while the husband was a member of Grant's official family, is said to have helped block the way to her husband's promotion as chief justice (James Schouler, *History of the United States,* vol. VII, copr. 1913, p. 230). He had one daughter by his first marriage and two adopted children. In addition to "Six Years in the Senate," cited above, Williams published *Occasional Addresses* (1895), and "Political History of Oregon from 1853 to 1865" (*Quarterly of the Oregon Historical Society,* March 1901).

[Joseph Gaston, *Portland, Ore.* (1911), vol. II; Charles Warren, *The Supreme Court in U. S. Hist.* (1928), vol. II; *Proc. Ore. State Bar Asso., Eighteenth and Nineteenth Sessions* (n.d.); *Who's Who in America,* 1910–11; *Oregon Native Son,* May 1899; *Ore. Hist. Soc. Quart.,* June 1910; *Morning Oregonian* (Portland), Apr. 5, 1910.]   R. C. C.

WILLIAMS, GEORGE HUNTINGTON (Jan. 28, 1856–July 12, 1894), mineralogist, petrologist, and teacher, was born in Utica, N. Y., the eldest son of Robert Stanton and Abigail (Doolittle) Williams, a grandson of William Williams, 1787–1850 [*q.v.*], and a descendant of Robert Williams who was admitted freeman in Roxbury, Mass., in 1638. The family was well-to-do and influential, and young Williams grew up under conditions of unusual refinement and culture. He was educated in the public schools, at the Utica Free Academy, and at Amherst College, from which he received the degree of A.B. in 1878. There he came under the tutelage of Benjamin Kendall Emerson, one of the most successful teachers of geology in all New England. He returned to Utica and taught at the academy for about a year. In 1879 he went to Germany. After perfecting himself in the language, he studied at Göttingen, where his attention was turned strongly in the direction of mineralogy, and then continued his studies at Heidelberg under the renowned Heinrich Rosenbusch, the first great teacher of microscopic petrography. He remained there for two years, receiving the degree of Ph.D. in 1882. In 1882–83 he was fellow by courtesy at the Johns Hopkins University in Baltimore; he later held there the positions of associate in mineralogy (1883–85), associate professor of mineralogy (1885–89), associate professor of inorganic geology (1889–

91), and professor of inorganic geology (1891–94).

As a teacher, Williams was eminently successful. Young, of pleasing address, companionable, fully informed in all the most recent developments, and particularly enthusiastic over the new departures in microscopic petrography, he attracted students from all parts of the country and soon became one of the leaders in a coterie of fellow workers, among them Joseph Paxon Iddings, James Furman Kemp, Henry Stephens Washington [*qq.v.*], Whitman Cross, and others. Patient with beginners, industrious and far-seeing, he was on his way to building up at Johns Hopkins a department that would vie with the best in European universities. He died at the early age of thirty-eight, of typhoid fever contracted as a result of drinking contaminated water while he was on a field trip in the Piedmont area of Maryland. He was married on Sept. 15, 1886, to Mary Clifton Wood of Syracuse, N. Y., by whom he had three sons.

Williams' enthusiasm was not limited to teaching. Like all good teachers, he was an investigator as well, and in the field of petrology he soon made his presence felt. One of his earlier efforts was *The Gabbros and Associated Hornblende Rocks Occurring in the Neighborhood of Baltimore, Md.* (1886, *Bulletin 28* of the United States Geological Survey), in which he brought out the genetic relationship of the hypersthene-gabbro and the gabbro-diorite, showing for the first time the chemical and physical relationship both of the rocks and of their pyroxenic and amphebolic constituents. A second paper of similar import, perhaps the most valuable of all his publications, was *The Greenstone Schist Areas of the Menominee and Marquette Regions of Michigan* (1890, *Bulletin 62* of the United States Geological Survey). All his publications—reports on research, reviews or articles in dictionaries and encyclopedias—were prepared with great care and fidelity to fact. His only textbook was *Elements of Crystallography* (1890). It is difficult to evaluate the worth of one who died at the height of his effectiveness, but certainly Williams was one of the most brilliant of the younger men in his field, and occupied a position that gave promise of very great usefulness.

[Sources include *George Huntington Williams, a Memorial* (1896, privately printed), with full bibliog.; *George Huntington Williams . . . the Johns Hopkins University,* Oct. 14, 1894; W. B. Clark, in *Bull. Geological Soc. of America,* vol. VI (1895), with bibliog.; obituary in *Sun* (Baltimore), July 13, 1894; personal information.]   G. P. M.

WILLIAMS, GEORGE WASHINGTON (Oct. 16, 1849–Aug. 4, 1891), author, soldier,

Baptist clergyman, was born in Bedford Springs, Pa., the son of Thomas and Nellie (Rouse) Williams, of mixed white and negro blood. His elementary education began in a pay school. During his youth his mind was fired by the arguments of William Lloyd Garrison and Frederick Douglass [qq.v.] and by such literary productions as Mrs. Stowe's *Uncle Tom's Cabin* and *Dred*. In 1862, as soon as his age permitted, he enlisted as a private in the 6th Massachusetts Regiment, rose at once to be an orderly sergeant, and before the war closed was promoted to Gen. N. J. Jackson's staff. In May 1865 he sailed for Texas, where he landed on the Rio Grande and went as colonel at the head of his troops to capture munitions which had been sold to Mexico by the Confederate Gen. Edmund Kirby-Smith. Subsequently he was sent to Carlisle Barracks to drill colored troops. His work was so exemplary that he was recommended by his officers for a commission in the Regular Army, but the Senate refused to confirm his appointment, supposedly because of his color. Upon his retirement from the army he entered Howard University, where, at his own suggestion, he was permitted to organize the institution on a military plan and take charge of the grounds. In 1874 he graduated from Newton Theological Institution, Newton Centre, Mass., and on June 11 of that year was ordained to the Baptist ministry. After supplying the Twelfth Baptist Church, Boston, for a time, he was unanimously elected pastor, but a gunshot wound through the left lung received during the war unfitted him for the rigorous climate of New England, and after about a year he resigned his Boston pastorate and went to Washington, D. C. After an attempt to launch a journal called *The Commoner,* for which he secured such noted contributors as Wendell Phillips and Frederick Douglass but was unable to secure subscribers, he went in 1876 to Cincinnati, where he was chosen pastor of the Union Baptist Church. Here he soon won the respect of Murat Halstead [q.v.], who published his articles signed Aristides in the *Cincinnati Commercial*. Williams' second journalistic venture, the *Southwestern Review,* a weekly newspaper, was more successful than the first, but it failed to absorb all his energy or satisfy his ambition. After attending lectures in the Cincinnati Law School and reading law for two years in the office of Alphonso Taft [q.v.], he was admitted to the Ohio bar. In 1877 he was an unsuccessful candidate for the state legislature, but secured an appointment in the office of the auditor of Hamilton County, whence he entered the federal in-

ternal revenue service as an appointee of President Hayes. In 1879, after a bitter campaign, he was elected to the Ohio legislature for two years. He served as United States minister to Haiti in 1885–86, and in the latter year was a delegate to the World Conference of Foreign Missions at London, where he made a speech on the "Drink Traffic in the Congo." He had become interested in the Congo as early as 1884 and proposed a plan for employing American negroes there in the service of the Belgian government. Visiting the region under Belgian auspices, he published criticisms of the methods of the officials of the Congo Free State (*Report upon the Congo State and Country to the President of the Republic of the United States,* n.d., and *An Open Letter to . . . Leopold II,* 1890). In America he modestly strove for the recognition of his race by writing *History of the Negro Race in America* (1883) and *A History of the Negro Troops in the War of the Rebellion* (1888). He died at Blackpool, England, while an employee of the Belgian government. He was an impassioned orator, a popular speaker, and a clear-thinking writer. Personally, he was somewhat fastidious, kindly and genial in manner. Though a partisan Republican, he was an honest official whose character was above reproach.

[*The Biog. Cyc. and Portrait Gallery of the State of Ohio,* vol. III (1884) ; preface in Williams' *Hist. of the Negro Race in America*; W. J. Simmons, *Men of Mark* (2nd ed., 1891) ; *N. Y. Tribune,* Aug. 5, 1891 ; reminiscences of personal acquaintances.]

W. E. S—h.

WILLIAMS, HENRY SHALER (Mar. 6, 1847–July 31, 1918), paleontologist, was born in Ithaca, N. Y., the son of Mary Huggeford (Hardy) and Josiah Butler Williams, a successful business man and banker. His first American ancestor on his father's side emigrated from Wales to Connecticut sometime before 1656. His great-grandfather, Elias Hardy, born in London in 1746, emigrated early in life to America, living first in Virginia and afterwards in St. John, New Brunswick. Henry was next to the eldest of a large family of brothers and sisters who lived in a spacious, well-ordered home, where questions of the day were vigorously discussed and habits of reading early acquired. He prepared for college in the Ithaca Academy and entered Yale with his brother. Because of his growing interest in science, he transferred to the Sheffield Scientific School, from which he was graduated with the degree of Ph.B. in 1868. As graduate student and assistant in paleontology he remained at Yale two years, receiving the degree of Ph.D. in the field of comparative anatomy in 1871. He was married on Oct. 18,

1871, to Harriet Hart Wilcox of New Haven, Conn. After teaching for a year in Kentucky University, he joined his father and brothers in business, never losing, however, his interest in natural science. In 1879 he was appointed assistant in paleontology at Cornell University. He was made professor of paleontology in 1884, and of paleontology and geology in 1886. In 1892 he resigned to become Silliman Professor at Yale, chosen by James D. Dana [*q.v.*] as his successor. He returned to Cornell in 1904 and in 1912 became professor emeritus.

By his work on the American Devonian, in which he was one of two authorities, Williams made a definite contribution to the development of American paleontology. He was not interested in "species making." His independence of thought was early exhibited in a method of stratigraphical study which he seems to have originated. Collecting faunas along ten or more parallel meridians in southern New York, Pennsylvania, and Ohio across the strike of Devonian rocks, he compared the corresponding zones of various formations. His carefully localized faunules revealed a lateral mutation as well as the recurrence of species and served to hasten the abandonment of the pre-Darwinian idea of the fixity of species, both as biologic entities and as absolute horizon markers. Williams' publications during a period of some forty years show a progression from detailed description of faunas to a steadily deepening "philosophic penetration into the significance of stratigraphy and fossil faunas" (Schuchert, *post*, p. 682). During the close studies of minute varietal characters he also developed the now common photographic method of fossil illustration, treating specimens with ammonium chloride before exposure to the camera. His *Geological Biology* was published in 1895. He was associated with the United States Geological Survey as assistant geologist, geologist, and paleontologist from 1883 until his death, and many of his paleontological studies appeared in its publications.

He was a leader in the founding of the Sigma Xi Society at Cornell (1886) and became its first president; its early policies were largely formulated by him and were reborn in the Yale chapter which he later organized. He also took an active part in the founding of the Geological Society of America (1881), served as treasurer in 1889–91, and exerted his influence to make it a strictly scientific organization of a high type. He was for years associate editor of the *Journal of Geology* (1893–1918) and of the *American Journal of Science* (1894–1918). Though he made no appeal to superficial students, he exer-

cised a lasting influence on his students in research. Considering scientific paleontology an unprofitable field for making a livelihood, he discouraged those he felt unfit for it. But those who worked with him in laboratory and field were fundamentally affected, finding in him an independent thinker, a zealous searcher after the whole truth, and a most sympathetic friend. He died in Havana, Cuba, survived by his wife, two sons, and two daughters.

[See *Who's Who in America*, 1918–19; Charles Schuchert, in *Am. Jour. Sci.*, Nov. 1918; H. F. Cleland, in *Bull. Geological Soc. of America*, vol. XXX (1919), with bibliog.; *Obit. Record Yale Grads.* (1919); H. B. Ward, *Sigma Xi Quarter Century Record* (1913); Stuart Weller, in *Jour. of Geology*, Nov.–Dec. 1918; obituary in *N. Y. Times*, Aug. 1, 1918; personal recollections; information assembled from family records by E. C. Williams, Williams' daughter.]   G. D. H.

WILLIAMS, HENRY WILLARD (Dec. 11, 1821–June 13, 1895), ophthalmologist, was born in Boston, Mass., the son of Willard and Elizabeth (Osgood) Williams, both natives of Salem, Mass. He received his early education at the Boston Latin School and, after the death of his parents, at the Salem Latin School. At first destined for business, he finally entered the Harvard Medical School at the age of twenty-three. Before graduating in 1849, he spent three years in Paris, London, and Vienna, where he became greatly interested in the study of diseases of the eye, then developing as a special field of medicine. Returning to Boston, he organized in 1850 a voluntary class of Harvard students for his lectures in ophthalmology, and began private practice. From 1866 to 1871 he was lecturer in ophthalmology in the Harvard Medical School, and in 1871, when a chair was established, he became the first professor in that subject. He served as ophthalmologic surgeon at the Boston City Hospital from its founding in 1864 to 1891. He was one of the founders of the American Ophthalmological Society (1864) and served as its president (1868–75). He made very valuable contributions to his subject in his writings on the operation for cataract (*Boston Medical and Surgical Journal*, June 26, 1850), the use of a general anesthetic in eye surgery (*Ibid.*, June 18, 1851), and the simplified treatment of iritis with atropine (*Ibid.*, Aug. 21, 28, and Sept. 4, 1856). He published three books: *A Practical Guide to the Study of the Diseases of the Eye* (1862), one of the first American textbooks of ophthalmology; *Our Eyes, and How to Take Care of Them* (1871), first published as a series of papers in the *Atlantic Monthly* (January–May 1871); and *The Diagnosis and Treatment of the Diseases of the Eye* (1881), the best book of its day on the subject. He was one of the first in the

United States to recognize the value of the ophthalmoscope, invented by Hermann von Helmholtz in 1851, for examining the inside of the eye, and should be regarded as one of the founders of ophthalmology in the United States.

He took an active interest in the Massachusetts Medical Society, of which he was president in 1880–82. As a member of the American Academy of Arts and Sciences, he wrote, in the latter years of his life, a few excellent obituary notices of deceased fellows. He was a conspicuous figure at medical meetings, a frequent, vigorous, and persuasive speaker. He was married twice: in 1848 to Elizabeth Dewe of London, and in 1860 to Elizabeth Adeline Low of Boston. Of six sons, three became physicians. Williams died in Boston.

[The chief source is John Green, in *Trans. Am. Ophthalmological Soc.*, vol. VII (1897). See also T. F. Harrington, *The Harvard Medic. School* (1905), vol. II, with bibliog.; H. A. Kelly and W. L. Burrage, *Am. Medic. Biogs.* (1920); *Boston Medic. and Surgical Jour.*, June 27, 1895; *Klinische Monatsblätter für Augenheilkunde*, June 1897; obituary in *Boston Transcript*, June 14, 1895.]   H. R. V.

WILLIAMS, ISRAEL (Nov. 30, 1709–Jan. 10, 1788), Loyalist, was born in Hatfield, Mass., the son of the Rev. William Williams and the great-grandson of Robert Williams who emigrated to Roxbury, Mass., from Norfolk County, England, in 1637. Elisha Williams was a half-brother, Ephraim Williams, a cousin, and William Williams, 1731–1811 [*qq.v.*], a nephew. His mother is said to have been Christian, the daughter of Solomon Stoddard of Northampton and the aunt of Jonathan Edwards and Joseph Hawley [*qq.v.*]. After graduating from Harvard College in the class of 1727, where his father graduated in 1683, he returned to Hatfield. He became a selectman in 1732 and was reëlected annually until 1763. Amassing considerable wealth through trading, farming, and land speculation, he was able by the middle of the century to build a great house at Hatfield and to own one of the few wheeled carriages in that section of the province. About 1731 he married Sarah, the daughter of John Chester of Wethersfield, Conn. They had seven or eight children. His influence in arousing enmity against his cousin, both in Northampton and among the ministry of Hampshire County, was important in Jonathan Edwards' dismissal from the Northampton church in 1750.

In 1744 Williams became second in command of the militia of Hampshire County and four years later was made colonel of the county's regiment. Throughout the French and Indian War he was responsible for the defense of western Massachusetts, a work in which he was distinguished for ability and foresight, although his tactlessness and arrogance made him unpopular with his fellow officers. Meanwhile he was winning recognition in the civil service of the county and province. He was long a justice of the peace and clerk of the county court, while from 1758 to 1774 he was a judge of the Hampshire County court of common pleas. He represented Hatfield in the Massachusetts legislature, with but few interruptions, from 1733 to 1773 and was a member of the governor's council from 1761 to 1767. The years gave him complete political power in his county so that he was called the "monarch of Hampshire"; at Boston he was a supporter of the conservatives and for a decade or more before the Revolution was a close ally of Thomas Hutchinson (*Proceedings of the Massachusetts Historical Society*, 1 ser., vol. XX, 1884, p. 48 n.). But, as in military matters, his autocratic, domineering manner did not make for popularity and, added to his haughtiness and conservatism, caused him to lose political influence in Hampshire County to his more radical cousin, Joseph Hawley. In 1762 he sought to found a college in the Connecticut Valley, but, largely through the opposition of Harvard College, the attempt was frustrated, although Gov. Francis Bernard was at first ready to grant a charter. Later, as executor under the will of Ephraim Williams [*q.v.*], he was instrumental in founding the "free school" that became Williams College.

With the approach of the Revolution Williams was forced into political retirement. In August 1774 he was made a *mandamus* councillor but never took the oath. During the early years of the Revolution he was considered the leading Loyalist in western Massachusetts and frequently was subjected to indignities at the hands of the Hampshire mobs. One of these incidents was celebrated in John Trumbull's *M'Fingal* (1776 with imprint 1775). In 1777 Williams spent several months in jail for his Loyalism and was deprived of his citizenship until 1780. Thereafter he lived quietly in Hatfield until his death.

[Williams Papers in possession of Mass. Hist. Soc.; Massachusetts Archives, vols. XXV, XLIV, Literary, Vol. LVIII, in State House, Boston, Mass.; A. L. Perry, *Origins in Williamstown* (2nd ed., 1896); Lorenzo Sabine, *Biog. Sketches of Loyalists of the Am. Revolution* (1864), vol. II; J. R. Trumbull, *Hist. of Northampton*, vol. II, (1902); D. W. and R. F. Wells, *Hist. of Hatfield* (1910); Harrison Williams, *The Life, Ancestors, and Descendants of Robert Williams of Roxbury* (1934); J. L. Sibley, *Biog. Sketches of Grads. of Harvard Univ.*, vol. III (1885), p. 264, questions the statement that Christian was Israel's mother on the ground that Christian, the child of Solomon Stoddard, was a son; *American Mag.*, Jan. 1788, p. 128, for death notice.]   E. F. B.

WILLIAMS, JAMES (July 1, 1796–Apr. 10, 1869), journalist, diplomat, was born in Grainger County, Tenn., son of Ethelred and Mary (Copeland) Williams and a grandson of James and Elizabeth Williams. Details of his early career are obscure, but he apparently had military experience which brought him the title of captain. In 1841 he founded the *Knoxville Post,* which he edited for some years, developing a facile pen. In 1843 he gained election to the Tennessee House of Representatives. He was evidently a man of great energy and initiative, for after his short career as legislator he and his brother William organized a Navigation Society of which he was president, and he soon became an active promoter of railroads. While engaged in these enterprises he founded the Deaf and Dumb Asylum of Knoxville.

He eventually moved to Nashville, where he continued along with his business interests his interest in public affairs. Here he published numerous essays under the pseudonym of "Old Line Whig." He had been a Whig, but the anti-slavery trend of his party in the North and its final absorption into the Republican party caused him in the late fifties to ally himself with the Democrats. In recognition of his merit as well as of his political importance to the party, President Buchanan appointed him minister to Turkey in 1858. In this capacity he urged upon the state department that consular jurisdiction, which, by agreement with Turkey, was already exercised over criminal cases involving Americans, be extended to include all civil cases as well, and that the right of appeal to the American minister from the consular courts be established in cases involving over fifty dollars or imprisonment. He also traveled through Syria, Egypt, and Palestine in behalf of the American missionaries in these countries and was eventually able to obtain local concessions looking toward their protection.

When Lincoln was elected in 1860 Williams resigned and hastened home in the hope of aiding in some way the settlement of the sectional quarrel so as to prevent war. When war began, nevertheless, he returned to Europe, where he acted as Confederate propagandist and minister at large. In London he gave much aid to Henry Hotze, Confederate propagandist chief and editor of the Confederate organ, *The Index*; indeed, Williams presented the history of the sectional struggle and explained the slavery question better than any other Southern representative abroad. His articles in the *Times,* the *Standard,* and the *Index* had no unimportant part in swinging middle and upper class England to the side of the South. Some of his essays concerning slavery were gathered into a volume published in Nashville in 1861 under the title *Letters on Slavery from the Old World*; after considerable enlargement the book was republished in London as *The South Vindicated.* Under the clever management of Henry Hotze, it was translated into German and circulated among the German people. In 1863 Williams published *The Rise and Fall of the Model Republic.* While laboring in the effort to educate European public opinion, he was in close touch with the Confederate diplomats; and finally, when French intervention in Mexico developed into French conquest with the prospect of Maximilian as puppet emperor, it was Williams who visited Maximilian at Miramar and persuaded him that it would be to his advantage to ally himself with the Confederacy or at least to give it recognition. Williams not only kept John Slidell and James M. Mason [*qq.v.*] posted, but carried on a secret and perhaps more detailed correspondence with President Jefferson Davis concerning the situation. Had not Napoleon III silenced the royal dupe, Maximilian would probably have recognized the independence of the Confederacy.

After the war Williams remained in Germany with his wife, the former Lucy Jane Graham of Tennessee. Like Slidell, he died in Europe (at Gratz, Austria) and was buried there. His two daughters married officers of the Austrian army, both members of noble families; his widow and son later returned to Tennessee.

[*War of the Rebellion: Official Records (Army)*, 2 ser. II, 75; *House Ex. Doc. 68*, 35 Cong., 2 Sess., pp. 69–73; W. T. Hale and D. L. Merritt, *A Hist. of Tenn.*, vol. III (1913); F. L. Owsley, *King Cotton Diplomacy* (1931); *War of the Rebellion: Official Records (Navy)*, 2 ser. III; Pickett Papers, Lib. of Cong.]   F. L. O.

WILLIAMS, JAMES DOUGLAS (Jan. 16, 1808–Nov. 20, 1880), governor of Indiana, eldest of six children of George Williams, of English-Welsh Virginian stock, was born in Pickaway County, Ohio. In 1818 the family moved to a farm near Vincennes in Knox County, Ind. James grew up under pioneer conditions with very little schooling. At his father's death in 1828 he assumed the support of the family. On Feb. 17, 1831, he married Nancy Huffman. Of their seven children three died in infancy. In 1836 he purchased a section of land near Wheatland, and on it made his home for the rest of his life. He acquired a total of some four thousand acres, from which, together with a grist mill, a sawmill, and a pork packing plant, he accumulated "a handsome competence." Of great physical strength, six feet four inches in height and spare of build, he was a hard working as well as an expert and progressive farmer, excelling in raising both grain and stock. He retained pioneer habits, living largely on the products of his farm and wearing, even in Congress, homespun "blue jeans" woven from the fleece of his own flocks.

Williams was active in local, state, and national Democratic organizations. In 1839 he became by election justice of the peace. He served five terms in the Indiana House of Representatives between 1843 and 1869, and three terms in the Senate between 1858 and 1873, sitting altogether in sixteen sessions of the General Assembly. Among the laws he sponsored, one allowed widows to hold small estates of deceased husbands without court action; another distributed a state sinking fund among counties for school funds. He worked for the improvement of the Wabash River to make it navigable, but opposed the retrocession of the Wabash and Erie Canal to the state. He promoted the creation of a state board of agriculture, and was a member of it for sixteen years and president for four. He voted for a contingent war fund of $100,000 for Gov. Oliver Perry Morton [q.v.], but joined in his party's opposition to the administration and was branded a "Copperhead" by Republicans. He was elected to the national House of Representatives in 1874 and in the session of 1875–76 was chairman of the committee on accounts. Both in the state legislature and in Congress he was insistent upon cutting down expenses to the last possible penny. This accorded with his peculiar attire, and the public came to know him as "Blue Jeans Williams."

At the Democratic state convention, Apr. 19, 1876, two factions compromised on him, and he was unanimously nominated for governor against Godlove Stein Orth [q.v.], later replaced by Gen. Benjamin Harrison, as the Republican candidate. Indiana was a pivotal state in the national presidential election, and the campaign was a famous one. Williams made a thorough canvass, especially in the rural districts, taking Daniel W. Voorhees [q.v.] with him as his spokesman at meetings. He was elected by a vote of 213,219 to Harrison's 208,080 and was inaugurated on Jan. 8, 1877. He was a conscientious, painstaking, self-reliant governor. In the labor troubles of 1877 he refused at first to call out the National Guard but finally did so in time to prevent serious outbreaks. The present state capitol was provided for in his administration, begun in 1878, and completed in 1888, well within the amount appropriated ($2,000,000).

Williams died at Indianapolis shortly before the end of his term of office. He was buried in Walnut Grove Cemetery, near his home in Knox County. He was survived by a son and a daughter.

[See *Biog. Dir. Am. Cong.* (1928); Ind. House Jours.; Ind. Sen. Jours.; H. R. Burnett, in *Ind. Mag. of Hist.*, June 1926; W. W. Woollen, *Biog. and Hist. Sketches of Early Ind.* (1883); *A Biog. Hist. of Eminent and Self-Made Men . . . of Ind.* (1880), vol. I; *Proc. in the House of Reps. . . . on the Death of . . . James D. Williams* (Indianapolis, 1881); *Weekly Western Sun* (Vincennes, Ind.), Sept. 10, 1873; obituaries in *Indianapolis Sentinel* and *Indianapolis Jour.*, Nov. 22, 1880. The date of marriage is from a copy of the marriage certificate in the clerk's office, Knox County, Ind.]   C. B. C.

WILLIAMS, JESSE LYNCH (May 6, 1807–Oct. 9, 1886), civil engineer, was born at Westfield, Stokes County, N. C., the youngest son of Jesse and Sarah (Terrell) Williams, members of the Society of Friends. His parents removed to Cincinnati, Ohio, about 1814, then to Warren County, and about 1819 to Wayne County, Ind. For a short period Jesse was a student at Lancasterian Seminary, Cincinnati. Inspired by the great schemes of canal improvement then popular, he selected civil engineering as his life work and secured a minor position on the first survey of the Miami & Erie Canal in Ohio, from Cincinnati to Maumee Bay, the line of which lay for one-half its length through unbroken wilderness. In 1828 he made the final location of the canal from Licking Summit to Chillicothe and constructed one division, including a dam and aqueduct across the Scioto River. He was a member of the board of engineers which decided to use reservoirs rather than long feeders from distant streams for supplying water to the summit level of the canal, as a result of which decision a reservoir covering 15,000 acres was built, the largest anywhere at that time.

In his twenty-fifth year he was appointed chief engineer of the Wabash & Erie Canal and in 1835 the surveys of all other canals in Indiana were placed by the legislature in his hands. In 1836 he was made engineer-in-chief of all canal routes and in the following year the railroads and turnpikes were also placed under his charge; he was thus given supervision of 1,300 miles of public works. In one summer he attended thirteen lettings of contracts, journeying some 3,000 miles mainly on horseback as well as mastering the multitudinous details of construction. When the construction of public works was suspended because of financial stringency, he engaged in mercantile and manufacturing operations at Fort Wayne, 1842–47, and subsequently served the Wabash & Erie Canal as chief engineer, from

1847 to 1876, when it was sold. Meanwhile, he was also chief engineer of the Fort Wayne & Chicago Railroad from 1854 until its consolidation in 1856 with the Pittsburgh, Fort Wayne & Chicago Railway, of which he was a director until 1873.

From 1864 until his resignation in 1869 he was appointed annually by three successive presidents (Lincoln, Johnson, and Grant) a government director of the Union Pacific Railway. He devoted himself to securing the best possible location and the lowest feasible maximum grade through the Rocky Mountains. His report to the secretary of the interior, Nov. 14, 1862 (*House Executive Document No. 15*, 40 Cong., 3 Sess.), showed that the actual cost of constructing and equipping the road was much less than the government subsidy and thus led to the famous Crédit Mobilier investigation. On Jan. 19, 1869, Williams was appointed receiver of the Grand Rapids & Indiana Railroad, with the heavy responsibility of saving a land grant worth seven million dollars by completing twenty additional miles of road through a section remote from settlements within fifty days after the yielding of the frost. He finished this task eight days ahead of the time limit and completed the rest of this 325-mile project in October 1870, performing the duties of both receiver and engineer. In June 1871 he was appointed chief engineer in charge of the completion of the Cincinnati, Richmond & Fort Wayne Railroad, which opened, through the Grand Rapids & Indiana Railroad, a route from Cincinnati to the valuable pineries of northwestern Michigan. He had become an active member of the Presbyterian Church, and was one of the original directors of the Presbyterian Theological Seminary of the Northwest, later McCormick Theological Seminary.

He was married Nov. 15, 1831, to Susan, daughter of William Creighton [*q.v.*] and Elizabeth (Meade) Creighton of Chillicothe, Ohio.

[C. B. Stuart, *Lives and Works of Civil and Military Engineers* (1871); *Biog. Hist. of Eminent and Self-Made Men of . . . Ind.* (1880), vol. II; Hugh McCulloch, *Men and Measures of Half a Century* (1888); *Valley of the Upper Maumee River* (2 vols., 1889); *Railroad Gazette*, Oct. 15, 1886; *Sunday Inter Ocean* (Chicago), Oct. 10, 1886.]   B. A. R.

WILLIAMS, JESSE LYNCH (Aug. 17, 1871–Sept. 14, 1929), author, playwright, editor, was born in Sterling, Ill., the son of Meade Creighton and Elizabeth (Riddle) Williams, and a grandson of Jesse Lynch Williams [*q.v.*]. He prepared for college at the Beloit Academy in Wisconsin, and received the degree of B.A. at Princeton in 1892. As an undergraduate he was one of the editors of the *Nassau Literary Magazine*. He was even then keenly interested in the drama, and with Booth Tarkington and several others founded the Triangle Club, which has ever since been the center of amateur acting at Princeton. In the summer of 1893 he became a reporter on the New York *Sun* under Charles Anderson Dana [*q.v.*]. He did a great deal of newspaper and fiction writing during his years on the *Sun,* and in 1895 published his first volume, *Princeton Stories,* the forerunner of many volumes of college fiction. Years later it was said that in the book Williams had expressed, as no one else could at the time, the spirit of undergraduate life (*Princeton Alumni Weekly, post,* p. 4). For a time (1897–1900) he was connected with *Scribner's Magazine,* but he returned to Princeton as first editor of the *Princeton Alumni Weekly* (1900–03). On June 1, 1898, he was married to Alice Laidlaw of New York, by whom he had three children.

After 1903 he devoted himself to writing. His first play, *The Stolen Story,* produced in 1906, was followed by *Why Marry?* (1917), in which Nat Goodwin was the star; *Why Not?* (1922), a satiric comedy; and *Lovely Lady* (1925). Of these the most popular was *Why Marry?,* based on his book called *"And So They Were Married"* (1914); it ran for a year and was awarded a Pulitzer prize. His books of fiction, in addition to a number of college stories, include *New York Sketches* (1902), *The Married Life of the Frederic Carrolls* (1910), *Not Wanted* (1923), *They Still Fall in Love* (1929), and *She Knew She Was Right* (1930). All his prose fiction was vivid and effective in characterization. He worked over details with unusual care, and he was never satisfied until the last proof was read. The manuscripts of his last novel, *She Knew She Was Right* (1930), which was written four times, are filled with the marks of his intelligent industry. In 1925–26 he held the fellowship in creative art at the University of Michigan. He was elected president of the Authors' League of America in 1921; and in the numerous clubs of which he was a member he had circles of loyal and affectionate friends, many of them outside of his profession. He used to describe himself as "a radical among conservatives, and a conservative among radicals." He had a summer home on an island in Maine, and winter homes in New York and Princeton. He died suddenly of heart disease at the home of Mrs. Douglas Robinson, Herkimer County, N. Y. He was buried in Princeton.

[*Who's Who in America,* 1928–29; records of the class of 1892, Princeton; *Quindecennial Record of the*

Class of Ninety-two of Princeton Univ. (1907);
Princeton Alumni Weekly, Sept. 27, 1929; A. H. Quinn,
A Hist. of the Am. Drama . . . to the present Day
(1927), vol. II; obituary in N. Y. Times, Sept. 15,
1929; long personal acquaintance.]   R. B—s.

WILLIAMS, JOHN (Dec. 10, 1664–June 12,
1729), clergyman and author, was born in Roxbury, Mass., the fifth child and second son of
Deacon Samuel and Theoda (Park) Williams
and a grandson of Robert Williams who was admitted freeman of Roxbury in 1638. John was
prepared in the Roxbury Latin School and graduated B.A. from Harvard College in 1683. For
two years he taught school in Dorchester. He
prophesied as a candidate in the frontier settlement of Deerfield and when some time later a
church was gathered there, he was formally ordained its first pastor, Oct. 17, 1688. In the
meantime, on July 21, 1687, he had married Eunice, daughter of the Rev. Eleazar Mather of
Northampton and grand-daughter of Richard
Mather [q.v.].

Almost from the beginning of Williams' ministry, Deerfield was in peril of French and
Indian attack. Like many of his colleagues, Williams believed the border wars to be occasioned
by God's dissatisfaction with his spiritually apa-
thetic people; nevertheless, he met danger courageously and exhorted his people to stand their
ground. When Queen Anne's War began, he
urged Governor Dudley to strengthen the Deerfield fortifications, but the warning was too late.
Before daybreak, Feb. 29, 1703/04, a party of
French and Indians sacked the town, killed many
inhabitants, including Williams' two youngest
children, and carried the rest into captivity.
Williams' wife, weakened by recent childbirth
and unable to withstand the hardships, was murdered by the savages. Williams was well treated,
although he was separated from his children and
suffered exposure, hunger, and grief. The captives were detained at Fort Chambly, where the
Indians, seconded by Jesuit priests, spared no
effort to convert them to the Catholic faith.
Williams counteracted their exertions among his
fellows so effectively that the priests sent him
to Chateauviche, where he remained more than
two years. Finally, Governor Dudley effected
his release and Williams returned to Boston,
Nov. 21, 1706.

During the following winter he preached in
churches of Boston and vicinity and prepared,
with Cotton Mather's help, The Redeemed Captive Returning to Zion (1707), a book which
won wide approval as a testimony of Congregational fortitude against "Popish Poisons." Despite continued Indian depredations and more
lucrative offers, he returned to his post in Janu-

ary 1707, where "his Presence . . . conduced
much to the rebuilding of the Place" (Sibley,
post, III, 257). On Sept. 16, 1707, he married
Abigail (Allen) Bissell of Windsor, Conn. He
served as chaplain in the expedition of 1711
against Port Royal and, with John Stoddard, as
commissioner to Canada (1713–14) for the return of English prisoners; he regularly attended the yearly meetings of clergymen in Boston
and in 1728 preached the convention sermon.
Deploring the religious indifference of his age,
he strove to restore the pristine spiritual enthusiasm of Massachusetts with sermons devoted to
the principle "That it's a high Privilege to be
descended from godly Ancestors; and 'tis the
important Duty of such . . . to exalt the God of
their Fathers" (A Serious Word To The Posterity of Holy Men, 1729, p. 2). He died at
Deerfield, survived by his second wife, their five
children, and six children of his first marriage.

[The Redeemed Captive Returning to Zion (Springfield, Mass., 1908), in the Indian Captivities Series,
lists the dozen or more earlier editions and includes a
sermon by Williams sometimes entitled Reports of Divine Kindness, or Remarkable Mercies, &c. Letters
by Williams are in Cotton Mather's Good Fetch'd out
of Evil (1706); in the "Winthrop Papers," Mass. Hist.
Soc. Colls., 6 ser. III (1889); and in the Coleman Papers, 1697–1723 (MSS. in the Mass. Hist. Soc. Lib.).
Two funeral sermons were published: Isaac Chauncey,
A Blessed Manumission of Christ's Faithful Ministers
(1729) and Thomas Foxcroft, Eli the Priest Dying
Suddenly (1729). See also "Diary of Samuel Sewall,"
Mass. Hist. Soc. Colls., 5 ser. VI (1879); "Letter Book
of Samuel Sewall," Ibid., 6 ser. I, II (1886–88); "Diary
of Cotton Mather," Ibid., 7 ser. VII, VIII (1911–12);
George Sheldon, Heredity and Early Environment of
John Williams (1905); S. W. Williams, A Biog. Mem-
oir of the Rev. John Williams (1837); Allen Hazen,
"Some Account of John Williams," in Hist. and Proc.
of the Pocumtuck Valley Memorial Asso., vol. II
(1898); New Eng. Hist. and Geneal. Reg., Jan. 1851,
Apr. 1854, Apr. 1856; J. L. Sibley, Biog. Sketches of
Grads. of Harvard Univ. (1885), III, 249–62; W. B.
Sprague, Annals Am. Pulpit, vol. I (1857); S. W.
Williams, The Geneal. and Hist. of the Family of Wil-
liams (1847).]   R. P. S.

WILLIAMS, JOHN (Apr. 28, 1761–Oct. 12,
1818), satirist, critic, miscellaneous writer, better known as Anthony Pasquin, was born in
London. Of exceptional precocity, he was chas-
tised in his teens for a stinging epigram on his
master at the Merchant Taylors' School. In
Dublin he was prosecuted for an attack on the
government. He published books on a variety of
subjects, and as a dramatic critic was the bête
noir of the London theatrical world. (For a bibliography and the details of his colorful European years, see The Dictionary of National Biography.) He emigrated to America, probably in
1797 or 1798, after the loss of a suit for libel
which he had brought against Robert Faulder,
a bookseller. About this time he is said to have
edited a New York democratic newspaper called

the *Federalist,* but no such newspaper is known of that time and place. William Dunlap's diary for 1798 has a number of references to him. On June 29 his "afterpiece 'The federal Oath or (*Columbians*) Americans strike home'" was produced—a piece "of patch'd work," according to Dunlap (*post,* I, 304)—and through one of his friends he applied to Dunlap for "a *situation* in the Theatre . . . next season" (I, 316). Dunlap's impression was far from favorable, however, for he confesses that he "felt an indefinable sort of shrinking from Williams" (I, 342). In 1799 Williams appears as editor and publisher of the *Columbian Gazette,* a New York weekly established on Apr. 6, 1799, and discontinued with the twelfth number, June 22. His editorial announcement was signed John Mason Williams, and in other places he used this middle name or initial, but always with newspapers. He appears again in 1804 as editor of the *Boston Democrat.* He soon fell out with his partners, as is shown in a notice in the *Columbian Centinel and Massachusetts Federalist* for June 27, in which he warned all subscribers and persons indebted to the establishment against making any payment to it until a future legal arrangement was made, a warning emphatically repudiated by his partners, Benjamin True and Benjamin Parks, in the *Democrat* of June 30. Under his pseudonym, Anthony Pasquin, there appeared in Boston (preface dated Sept. 6, 1804) the *Hamiltoniad,* a savage, intemperate, bombastic anti-federalist poem, more important for its extensive notes than for its verse. A *Life of Alexander Hamilton* (1804) is sometimes credited to him. It is possible that he may have spent a year or more in London about 1811–12; his *Dramatic Censor* (London, 1812) issued in twelve monthly parts, is the sole instance of a title published in England during his American years.

Nothing less than mixed metaphors will adequately characterize the deep-rooted, persistent, temperamental infelicities of this man. He was a stormy petrel, and a bull in the literary and political china shops of two continents. His contemporaries dealt even less gently with him, for he was called by Lord Kenyon "a common libeller," by Dr. Robert Watt, "a literary character of the lowest description" (*Bibliotheca Britannica,* 1824, II, 970d) ; and Macaulay's pungent epithets "polecat" (*Edinburgh Review,* Jan. 1843, p. 537) and "malignant and filthy baboon" (*Ibid.,* Oct. 1841, p. 250) may well be regarded as his chief claims to remembrance if not distinction. He was cursed with a sharp tongue, a vitriolic pen, a measure of facility with the then fashionable and seductive Byronic satirical couplet, and withal a nature so devoid of the faintest intimations of tact, moderation, or good taste in the use of such edged tools that he was continually in hot water if not actually in the law's clutches. A typical illustration of his outrageous language and behavior is described in the *Thespian Magazine* (Sept., Oct. 1792, pp. 82–93, 104–09). He was driven in disgrace from his own country to die in America in a destitution traceable to the identical failings which had made him so thoroughly *persona non grata* in England. He died in Brooklyn, N. Y., of typhus fever, on Oct. 12, 1818.

[In addition to *The Dict. of Nat. Biog.,* which has a list of further sources, see P. L. Ford, *Bibliotheca Hamiltoniana* (1886), pp. 79–81, 99; William Gifford, *Works* (1800), vol. II, pp. 41–94, for an account of the libel suit; John Bernard, *Retrospections of the Stage* (1830), vol. II, pp. 215–19; *Diary of William Dunlap* (3 vols., 1930), being *N. Y. Hist. Soc. Colls.,* vols. LXII–LXIV; and obituaries in *N. Y. Evening Post,* Oct. 16, 1818, *N. Y. Columbian,* Oct. 17, and *N. Y. Advertiser,* Oct. 20.]   J.I.W.

WILLIAMS, JOHN (Jan. 29, 1778–Aug. 10, 1837), senator, diplomat, was born in Surry County, N. C., the third son of Joseph and Rebecca (Lanier) Williams. His father, a native of Hanover County, Va., was an active figure in local affairs, and served with the Surry County militia in the Revolution. John received his preparatory education in Surry; later he moved to Knoxville, Tenn., where in 1803 he was admitted to the bar. In 1799–1800, when war with France seemed imminent, he was a captain in the 6th United States Infantry; when the War of 1812 began he raised a force of some two hundred mounted volunteers and as colonel led them to Florida, where they operated against the Seminoles. After successfully devastating Indian territory, they returned to Tennessee in the early part of 1813. Shortly afterward, Williams became colonel of the 39th United States Infantry. He recruited this regiment to a strength of about six hundred, and commanded it under General Jackson in the Creek campaign. In the battle of Horseshoe Bend, it rendered invaluable assistance in bringing about Jackson's victory.

In 1815, he was appointed to fill a vacancy in the United States Senate and in December 1817 took his seat as a regularly elected senator from Tennessee. He acted as the chairman of the committee on military affairs and was a stanch supporter of the administration, voting for the Tariff Bill and for the United States Bank Bill in 1816. In the controversies over the Missouri Compromise and other questions concerning slavery, he usually identified himself with Southern interests. He also supported projects for internal improvements, particularly turnpike development. When his term as senator expired in 1823, he desired reëlection, but during his political life in Washington he had become too closely associated with the Crawford faction of the Democratic party, and Andrew Jackson's managers decided to retire him. This decision precipitated one of the bitterest political fights ever to take place within Tennessee. It became apparent that the Jackson forces could not displace Williams unless their leader himself became a candidate, and it was this factor which brought Jackson into the fight. By a close vote, in which sectional and personal enmities found expression, Jackson was elected; Williams never became reconciled to his defeat. In 1825, President Adams appointed him chargé d'affaires to the Federation of Central America, but after several months in Guatemala he returned, and in 1827 was elected to the state Senate.

Williams married Melinda White, daughter of Gen. James White [q.v.] of Knoxville and sister of Hugh L. White [q.v.]. They had three children: Joseph Lanier Williams, member of Congress from 1837 to 1843; Margaret, first wife of Richmond Mumford Pearson [q.v.] of North Carolina; and Col. John Williams. Williams died in 1837 and was buried in Knoxville. Accounts agree that he was one of the ablest Tennesseans of his time, a brave soldier, and an efficient politician. The rising tide of Jackson's popularity swept him into the obscurity which engulfed many another.

[Military Papers, Old Records Division, Adj.-Gen.'s Office, War Dept.; P. M. Hamer, *Tennessee, A Hist.* (1933), vol. I; S. G. Heiskell, *Andrew Jackson and Early Tenn. Hist.*, vol. I (1920); *Biog. Dir. Am. Cong.* (1928); Zella Armstrong, *Notable Southern Families* (copr. 1918–33), vol. II; *National Banner and Nashville Whig*, Aug. 16, 1837.]   C. S. D.

WILLIAMS, JOHN (Aug. 30, 1817–Feb. 7, 1899), Protestant Episcopal bishop, was born in Old Deerfield, Mass., a son of Ephraim and Emily (Trowbridge) Williams and a descendant of Robert Williams who was admitted freeman of Roxbury, Mass., in 1638. Ephraim Williams was a lawyer of Stockbridge and later of Deerfield, who edited the first volume of *Massachusetts Reports*; he was a son of Dr. Thomas Williams (M.A. Yale 1741) who served as a surgeon under Sir William Johnson in the French and Indian War, a nephew of Col. Ephraim Williams [q.v.], founder of Williams College, and through his mother, Esther Williams, a grand-nephew of Elisha Williams [q.v.], president of Yale College. John entered Harvard College at the age of fourteen in 1831, but at the end of his sophomore year, having become an Episco-

palian through the influence of the Rev. Benjamin Davis Winslow, he transferred to Washington (after 1845 Trinity) College, Hartford, Conn. Here he roomed with James Roosevelt Bayley [q.v.], later Roman Catholic archbishop of Baltimore. After his graduation, in 1835, Williams read for orders in the Episcopal Church under the direction of the Rev. Samuel Farmar Jarvis, rector of Christ Church, Middletown, Conn. On Sept. 2, 1838, he was ordered deacon in Middletown, and on Sept. 26, 1841, was advanced to the priesthood by the Rt. Rev. Thomas Church Brownell [q.v.]. He was a tutor in Washington College from 1837 to 1840, then went abroad, spending almost a year in England and Scotland. He met Pusey, Newman, Keble, and Isaac Williams, later leaders in the Oxford Movement, with most of whom he maintained friendly relations as long as they lived. For a year after his ordination he was an assistant to Dr. Jarvis in Middletown and from 1842 to 1848 he was rector of St. George's Church, Schenectady, N. Y.

On Aug. 3, 1848, just before he was thirty-one, he was elected fourth president of Trinity College, to succeed the Rev. Dr. Silas Totten, resigned, and in 1851 was elected bishop coadjutor of the diocese of Connecticut, being consecrated in St. John's Church, Hartford, Oct. 29, 1851. Increasing episcopal duties led him to resign the presidency of the college in 1853, though his administration had been most successful. During his presidency he had been also Hobart Professor of History and Literature, and after his resignation he was lecturer in history till 1892. He was made vice-chancellor in 1853, and on the death of Bishop Brownell in 1865, became chancellor, serving till his death in 1899. During his presidency of Trinity College, he had gathered a number of students for the ministry about him, and in 1854, after his resignation, a charter for the Berkeley Divinity School in Middletown was granted. He served as dean and as professor of theology and of liturgies in this institution from 1854 until his death. Having succeeded Bishop Brownell as diocesan in 1865, Williams became presiding bishop of the Protestant Episcopal Church, through seniority, in 1887. His diocese prospered under his administration, and his influence in the councils of the general Church was great.

Williams wrote throughout his career. In 1845 he published in Hartford a small volume of translations of Latin hymns, entitled *Ancient Hymns of Holy Church*. In 1848, in New York, he published *Thoughts on the Gospel Miracles*. He edited Edward Harold Browne's *Exposition* of the Thirty-Nine Articles, issuing the first American edition in 1865. Six valuable addresses delivered by him were included in *The Seabury Centenary* (1885). A considerable number of his sermons and addresses were printed, and he contributed many articles to the *Church Review* and to other periodicals. In 1881 he was the first lecturer on the Paddock foundation at the General Theological Seminary (*Studies on the English Reformation*, 1881) and first Bedell Lecturer at Kenyon College, Gambier, Ohio (*The World's Witness to Jesus Christ*, 1882). In 1888 he brought out *Studies on the Book of Acts*. His full lecture notes for the use of his students were printed but not published.

Failing health induced the Bishop to ask for the assistance of a coadjutor, and in 1897 Chauncey Bunce Brewster was elected to that office and consecrated. Williams died at his home in Middletown less than two years later. He was unmarried.

[Records of Trinity College, Hartford; *Churchman*, Feb. 18, 1899; Samuel Hart, *A Humble Master; A Sermon in Memory of the Rt. Rev. John Williams* (1899); *The Am. Church Almanac, 1900* (1899); S. W. Williams, *The Geneal. and Hist. of the Family of Williams* (1847); *Hartford Courant*, Feb. 8, 1899.]

A—r. A.

WILLIAMS, JOHN ELIAS (Oct. 28, 1853–Jan. 2, 1919), industrial mediator, was born in Merthyr-Tydfil, Wales. His parents, John Elias and Elizabeth (Bowen) Williams, brought him to America in 1864 and settled in Streator, Ill., where his father, a coal miner, was killed by a rock fall. Young Williams entered the mines at thirteen and during the next fifteen years became a highly skilled pick miner. He was elected the first secretary and first check weighman of the local miners' union. He had had some public-school training, but his education came chiefly from his daily experiences, study clubs which he organized among his fellow workers, debates with miners in the pits, and considerable reading.

Seizing an opportunity to enter journalism, he was gradually drawn into industrial mediation, helping to settle local disputes between the miners and their bosses. In 1910 he became the official arbitrator for the United Mine Workers of Illinois and the Illinois Coal Operators Association. Two years later his great opportunity came. After the strike of 1910–11 in the Chicago men's clothing industry, Hart, Schaffner & Marx, employing 10,000 workers, signed an agreement with the United Garment Workers of America which provided for an arbitration board for final action on controversies arising under the agreement. Williams was chosen impartial chairman of this board in 1912 and continued as such until his death.

He developed a procedure and philosophy of mediation which created a precedent for later impartial chairmen throughout the country and also profoundly influenced the Amalgamated Clothing Workers and other so-called progressive unions which followed their lead. He became one of the first advocates of union-management cooperation. Considering it his task to help the employer and the union see each other's point of view, then help them find a line of common interest, and finally, through suggestion and invention, assist them in coming to an agreement, he measured his success by the infrequency with which he had to render decisions. He thought that his type of arbitration, which was primarily mediation, could succeed only if it was a continuing procedure and believed that his philosophy of continuous collective bargaining could have meaning only if the workers were represented by a strong, independent, and responsible union. Holding that the men's clothing workers union was of this type, he called it a "school in co-operative management" in which the union had been educated in the rights of both business and labor, and through which the employers had also been educated ("The Church and the Present-Day Labor Struggle," *Biblical World*, March 1914). By way of contrast he criticized the Rockefeller Industrial Relations Plan of 1914, foreseeing that a union instituted by an employer would be "a feeble and spineless thing" (*Survey*, Nov. 6, 1915). He looked for industrial democracy to come, not through revolution but through trades organization, collective bargaining, and industrial partnership between capital and labor.

Williams was largely instrumental in introducing several new devices, including a compromise between the closed and open shop called the preferential shop, which provided that the company should prefer union men in hiring new employees, and, subject to reasonable preference for old employees, dismiss non-union men first when laying off workers. He proposed that his industrial mediation procedure be extended to settling the World War, believing that a common ground for settlement could be found.

Williams was a kindly, genial man who was widely respected for his fair-mindedness. He was a leading spirit in the Illinois Unitarian Conference and became its first president. Most of his theories took a puritanical-ethical turn. He constantly spoke of restraint, responsibility, and the constructive spirit. He saw "the present day labor struggle" as "a struggle for power" (*Biblical World, ante,* p. 155) in which power was being transferred from the employer to the laborer, and believed trade unions inevitable and indispensable because of the "tyrannous pressure" of employers (*Ibid.,* p. 159) ; but he sought "the salvation of society" (*Ibid.,* p. 162) through a renaissance in religion and he called upon his Church to find something beyond the individual good that is worthy of devotion.

In 1877 he married Isabella Dickinson of Morpeth, Northumberland, England. He prided himself upon living simply in the same miner's house for over forty years. In the life of Streator he was a vital force. He successfully managed its opera house for over two decades, organized an orchestra in which he played first violin, composed music for songs, and promoted an open forum. He was also a member of the Society for Psychical Research. In 1917 he was appointed Federal Fuel Administrator for Illinois and administrator for the packing industry. He died in his sixty-sixth year, survived by his widow.

[*John E. Williams* (1929), ed. by J. S. Potofsky; *Who's Who in America,* 1918–19 ; J. A. Fitch, "John Williams—Peacemaker," *Survey,* Jan. 18, 1919 ; *Final Report and Testimony . . . U. S. Commission on Industrial Relations* (11 vols., 1916), I, 697 ; *Chicago Daily Tribune,* Jan. 3, 1919.]   G. M.

WILLIAMS, JOHN ELIAS (June 11, 1871– Mar. 24, 1927), missionary to China, vice-president of the University of Nanking, was born in Coshocton, Ohio, his parents, Elias David and Ann (Edwards) Williams, having migrated from Ponterwyd, a village near Aberystwith, Wales, in 1861. One of his Welsh ancestors was William Williams, author of the hymn, "Guide Me, O Thou Great Jehovah." John's father, Elias David, was a weaver, a coal miner, and a preacher; his mother was a woman of unusual loveliness both of person and of character. From his twelfth until his seventeenth year the boy worked in the mines, until opportunity opened for him to earn his way towards an education. After some months in the high school at Shawnee, Ohio, and two years at Marietta Academy, he entered Marietta College. At his graduation in 1894 he was leading his class. From 1894 to 1896 he was principal of an academy in South Salem, Ohio, and the next three years he spent in the theological seminary at Auburn, N. Y. This cloistered period revealed his need for service in action, and he offered himself to the Presbyterian Board of Foreign Missions as a candidate for a mission field. He was graduated from the seminary in the spring of 1899, on July 24 he was ordained by the Chillicothe Presbytery in Greenfield, Ohio, on Aug.

2 he was married to Lilian Caldwell of South Salem, and on Aug. 14 sailed with his bride for China.

The Boxer outbreak occurred shortly after their arrival and it was necessary for them to take refuge in Kanazawa, Japan, but within a twelvemonth they were again in Nanking. Seven years of language study and of teaching in a Presbyterian boys' school followed. His unusual mastery of the Chinese language led to Williams' appointment in 1906 for special service among the Chinese students in Waseda University, Tokyo. This year in Japan focused his attention on the need of higher education for Christian Chinese, and he began to formulate far-reaching plans for a union missionary university in Nanking.

For such an institution Nanking was an admirable location both because of its reputation as an educational center and because of the notably cooperative spirit among its leading missionaries. By 1910 a union had been effected between the Presbyterian boys' school and a similar school supported by the Disciples of Christ. A year later this was amalgamated with a Methodist college to form the University of Nanking, with Dr. Arthur John Bowen as president and Williams as vice-president—a fortunate combination that proved to be mutually stimulating. Williams had meantime begun an arduous series of journeys to the United States to secure funds. Within a decade the main portion of the university was housed in buildings combining Chinese architecture and western construction, there was an able faculty, and the colleges of arts and science and of agriculture and forestry, combined with a hospital, a language school for missionaries, and a secondary group, were attracting a large enrolment.

In this development "Jack" Williams had proved himself an executive of marked ability— a type of work more suited to his nature than the routine of teaching. His indefatigable labors were brightened by optimism and humor. His home, cheered by the understanding and sympathy of his wife and by the attraction of his three daughters and his son, had become a Christian refuge for Chinese and missionaries alike. This was especially true in the winter of 1926–27 when the revolution started by Dr. Sun Yat-sen in Canton had, under Gen. Chiang Kai-chek, swept rapidly through central China. Apprehensions over the strange alliances within the Kuomintang or Nationalist Party were stifled by the excitement of success.

Nanking was still a stronghold of the northern militarists. But firing began outside its massive walls on Mar. 21, and during the night of the 23rd the city fell. General Chiang had not yet arrived on the scene, and Communist officers issued orders that foreigners be slain and their property looted. The evident intention was to force intervention by the foreign powers, and thereby to create a situation favorable for the spread of Communism. On the morning of the 24th, Williams and a group of his associates, while on their way to the university chapel services, were surrounded and robbed by a motley crowd of soldiers. Williams spoke to them quietly and kindly. For answer, a soldier raised his gun and shot, killing him instantly.

Thus began the so-called "Nanking Incident." The fact that it started with the brutal murder of this friend of China helped to produce three results. The first was the courageous and largely successful attempt of the Nanking Chinese to save the lives of the other missionaries. The second was the loyal effort made by the Chinese faculty and students to carry on the university—an effort that has remarkably fulfilled the hopes of the founders. The third is expressed in words translated from the tribute to his friend which the Hon. Wang Chengting, when minister for foreign affairs, placed on the tombstone over the grave in Nanking: "It was the death of Doctor Williams which awoke the Chinese people to the cold fact that there was no other alternative except to purge the Kuomintang of its Communist members. . . . In the words of an ancient Chinese philosopher, 'One man's death may weigh as heavily as Tai Shan Mountain.' "

[W. R. Wheeler, "John E. Williams of Nanking," in MS.; *N. Y. Times*, Mar. 26, 27, 28, 1927; *Shawnee People's Advocate* (Ohio), Apr. 1, 1927; *Time*, Apr. 4, 1927; *Minutes of the Twenty-second Year of the Kiangan Mission of the Presbyt. Church in the U. S. A.* (1927); *Marietta Coll. Alumni Quart.*, Apr. 1927; *The Ninetieth Ann. Report of the Board of Foreign Missions of the Presbyt. Ch. in the U. S. A.* (1927); *Chinese Recorder*, Sept. 1927; personal recollections.]
H. Cl—s.

WILLIAMS, JOHN FLETCHER (Sept. 25, 1834–Apr. 28, 1895), secretary and librarian of the Minnesota Historical Society, journalist, author, was born at Cincinnati, Ohio, the youngest of eight children. His father was Samuel Williams, a native of Pennsylvania, who had served in the War of 1812 and in the forties helped to found Ohio Wesleyan University; his mother, Samuel's second wife, was Margaret Troutner. He was a descendant of William Williams who emigrated to America in 1784. Williams attended Woodward High School in Cincinnati and Ohio Wesleyan University. He then studied engraving, and not a few examples of his work appeared in magazines of that period.

In 1855 he went to the frontier town of St. Paul, Minn., and for the next fifteen years he was active as a journalist. His interest in the history of the West led him to write many sketches of pioneer days; the experience and reputation that he thus gained won him his election in 1867 as secretary and librarian of the Minnesota Historical Society. The society, though founded as early as 1849, was virtually without means, its membership was small, and its library, stored in what was little more than a closet, was of slight value. Williams promptly took up the task of building up the collections, and his personal acquaintance with prominent men of the state and the vigor of his correspondence led to many valuable accessions of historical material. In 1869 he began to devote his entire time to the work of the society; the same year witnessed the inauguration of regular legislative appropriations for the institution. The society's manuscript possessions expanded slowly during his régime, but the collection of books and pamphlets grew from a total of 2,415 in 1867, when he took office, to 51,740 in 1893, when he resigned. The cramped room that was library, museum, and meeting hall was abandoned in 1868 for more adequate quarters in the state capitol, and by 1893 an agitation had begun for a separate historical building. Five volumes of *Collections* were published by the society during Williams' secretaryship and a sixth, which he edited, was brought out in 1894. These volumes, with two exceptions, were miscellaneous collections of reminiscences and special articles. The exceptions were "A History of the City of St. Paul, and of the County of Ramsey, Minn." (vol. IV, 1876), by Williams himself, and William W. Warren's important "History of the Ojibways" (vol. V, 1885), with a prefatory memoir of the author by Williams. The book on St. Paul contains interesting material, much of which was derived from interviews with pioneers, but it is an antiquarian chronicle, not a history.

In the seventies Williams represented Minnesota as centennial commissioner for the Centennial Exhibition in Philadelphia. He was an active member of the Independent Order of Odd Fellows and for twenty years served it as "Grand Scribe" for Minnesota. In 1889 the historical society authorized a survey of the source of the Mississippi River. Williams supplied considerable material for this investigation, which led ultimately to the establishment of a state park in the Itasca region. A bibliography of some thirty titles of Williams' published works includes biographical sketches, brief historical articles, addresses, a two-volume catalogue of the Minnesota Historical Society library, and a genealogy of the Williams family. A contemporary describes him as "small, polite, obliging, industrious, and . . . a walking encyclopædia of the dead past" (T. M. Newson, *Pen Pictures of St. Paul, Minn.*, 1886, p. 513). He resigned his dual position on the historical society staff in 1893 following a stroke of paralysis; he died two years later in the state asylum at Rochester. He was survived by his wife, Catherine Roberts, whom he married in July 1865, and by several children.

[See J. F. Williams, *The Groves and Lappon . . . Geneal of the Williams Family* (1889); Warren Upham, in *Minn. Hist. Colls.*, vol. VIII (1898); ann. reports, Minn. Hist. Soc., 1867–78, and 1889, pp. 372–74, and biennial reports, 1879–93; obituary in *Daily Pioneer Press* (St. Paul), Apr. 30, 1895. For Williams' connection with the Ind. Order of Odd Fellows, see proc. of *Grand Encampment, I. O. O. F. of Minn.*, 1896, which contains a portrait. A small coll. of Williams papers and much correspondence are in the possession of the Minn. Hist. Soc. The date of death is from records of the Rochester State Hospital.]

T. C. B.

WILLIAMS, JOHN FOSTER (Oct. 12, 1743–June 24, 1814), naval officer, was born in Boston, Mass., where, on Oct. 6, 1774, he was married to Hannah Homer. Little is known of his family and early life, but he seems to have had some connection with the Lane family of Boston (see Fitts, *post*). On May 8, 1776, he was commissioned captain of the Massachusetts state sloop *Republic* and in December was transferred to the *Massachusetts*, another state vessel. In June 1777 he took command of the *Wilkes* and in October of the *Active*, both privateers. In 1778–79 he made two cruises in the state brig *Hazard*, capturing several prizes. On Mar. 16, 1779, off St. Thomas, West Indies, after a sharp action of thirty minutes he forced the British brig *Active*, 18 guns, to surrender. In the unfortunate Penobscot expedition he burnt his vessel to prevent her capture. His next command, the *Protector*, was the largest ship in the Massachusetts navy. On June 9, 1780, southeast of Newfoundland, he engaged the privateer *Admiral Duff* for an hour and a half, until she was destroyed by the explosion of her magazine with a heavy loss of life. In his next cruise he visited the Grand Banks and the West Indies, taking several prizes. Off Nantasket, in the spring of 1781, he was compelled to strike his colors to a superior force consisting of the British vessels *Roebuck*, 44 guns, and *Medea*, 28 guns. After confinement for several months in England, he was exchanged and arrived at Boston in time to take command early in 1783 of the privateer *Alexander*. By his Revolutionary services he

established a reputation as an able seaman and officer.

In 1788 when Boston celebrated the adoption of the federal constitution by Massachusetts he was given a conspicuous place in a procession as the captain of a ship mounted on wheels and is said to have made a striking appearance in his Continental uniform with a speaking trumpet in his hand. From 1790 until his death he commanded the revenue cutter *Massachusetts*, an office to which he was appointed by President Washington. Occasionally, however, he turned his attention to duties outside of those connected with the revenue. In 1792 he communicated to the Boston Marine Society an invention for distilling fresh water from salt water, with appropriate drawings. In 1797, at the request of Jeremy Belknap [*q.v.*], he examined the coast of Maine to determine the various localities visited by George Waymouth [*q.v.*], and made a report of his conclusions (see Belknap, *post*). In 1803 with the assistance of a surveyor he surveyed Nantasket Harbor and reported his results to the federal government. He lived on Round Lane, Boston, which later was renamed Williams Street, supposedly in his honor. He was buried in the Granary Burying Ground.

[J. H. Fitts, *Lane Geneal.*, vol. II (1897); Justin Winsor, *Memorial Hist. of Boston*, vols. III, IV (1881); *New Eng. Hist. and Geneal. Reg.*, Jan. 1848, July 1865, Jan. 1869, July 1887; *Boston Marriages, 1752–1809* (1903); Ebenezer Fox, *Revolutionary Adventures* (1838); Jeremy Belknap, *Am. Biog.*, vol. II (1798); *Mass. Soldiers and Sailors of the Revolutionary War*, vol. XVII (1908); *Acts and Resolves . . . Province of the Mass. Bay*, vols. XX–XXI (1918–22); C. O. Paullin, *Navy of the Am. Revolution* (1906); C. H. Lincoln, *Naval Records of the Am. Revolution* (1906); *Columbian Centinel* (Boston), June 25, 1814.]

C. O. P.

WILLIAMS, JOHN JOSEPH (Apr. 27, 1822–Aug. 30, 1907), Roman Catholic prelate, fourth bishop and first archbishop of Boston, son of Michael and Ann (Egan) Williams, recent immigrants (1818) from King's County and County Tipperary, Ireland, was born in the north end of Boston, Mass., where his father labored at blacksmithing. As a child he attended the Cathedral School, where he profited by the instruction of Father James Fitton [*q.v.*] and attracted the notice of Bishop Benedict J. Fenwick [*q.v.*], who sent him to the Sulpician college in Montreal (1833–41). On graduation from college, he studied theology at St. Sulpice in Paris, where he was ordained a priest (May 27, 1845) by Archbishop Denis Auguste Affre. Appointed a curate at the Cathedral of the Holy Cross in Boston (1845), he became a valued assistant of Bishop John B. Fitzpatrick [*q.v.*], who named him rector of the cathedral in 1855, and selected him as pastor of St. James' Church and vicar-general of the diocese in 1857. In this administrative capacity, he displayed commendable tact in compromising difficulties, and in getting along with priests and people. A man of massive proportions and remarkable vigor, he took an active part in religious and civic affairs during the critical period of the Civil War, and won the respect of the native element in Boston without losing the love of the rapidly increasing Irish population. At the request of Fitzpatrick, he was made titular bishop of Tripoli and coadjutor bishop of Boston with the right of succession; as the bishop died in the meantime, Williams was consecrated bishop of Boston in his own right by Archbishop John McCloskey [q.v.], Mar. 11, 1866. Nine years later Boston was made a metropolitan see with Williams as archbishop, and Cardinal John McCloskey conferred the pallium on him (May 2).

As episcopal ruler of the diocese of Boston for forty years, Williams saw the rise of new sees at Springfield (1870), Providence (1872), Manchester (1884), and Fall River (1905). He witnessed not only a tremendous material growth in churches, institutions, and population, but the social and economic rise of the Irish population as the newer groups of French-Canadians, Poles, Italians, and Portuguese appeared in engulfing waves. While as ordinary of the diocese he does not deserve entire credit for the contributions of his priests and people, yet his leadership actively promoted the construction of the new Holy Cross Cathedral, which was dedicated in 1875, the establishment of St. John's Ecclesiastical Seminary (1884), and the foundation of such charitable institutions as St. Elizabeth's Hospital (1868), the House of the Good Shepherd (1867), the Home of the Aged (1870), St. Mary's Infant Asylum (1872), homes for working boys and girls (1883, 1884), the Free Home for Consumptives (1891), the Holy Ghost Hospital for Incurables (1893), and the Rev. P. J. Daly's Industrial School (1899). Williams had early shown an interest in the poor and afflicted when, as pastor, he founded the first conference of the St. Vincent de Paul Society in New England. In 1868 he established separate parishes for the French-Canadians, and in 1872, for the Italians and Portuguese. The harmonious relations between the various racial elements were due to his compromising tact and catholic devotion to all his people. Interested in education, he ordered the erection of numerous parochial schools, although he once had hopes that the Faribault plan of Archbishop John Ireland [q.v.] might relieve him of this costly program. To staff his schools and charitable foundations, he introduced such additional communities into the diocese as the Sisters of St. Joseph (1873), the Sisters of the Sacred Heart (1880), the Franciscan Sisters (1884), the Carmelite Sisters (1890), and the Marist Fathers (1883). He gave ample support to the Jesuits of Boston College, and to such religious orders as the Augustinian and Redemptorist Fathers. A loyal citizen of blameless life, a pious man, a firm friend of law and order, and a scholar, he was twice offered a doctorate by Harvard University but in humility declined the honor.

One of the founders of the American College in Rome, a member of the Vatican Council, an active participant in the Councils of Baltimore, a connecting link in Boston's Catholic life with the early days of Bishop Cheverus [q.v.], Williams occupied a unique position in the Church when, in 1906, he assigned active control over a well-ordered diocese of six hundred priests and nearly a million communicants to his coadjutor and successor, William H. O'Connell.

[*Who's Who in America*, 1906–07; William Byrne, *Hist. of the Cath. Church in the New England States* (1899), vol. I; *Cath. Encyc.*; *Pilot* (Boston), Mar. 8, 1930; W. H. O'Connell, *Recollections of Seventy Years* (1934); *Boston Transcript*, Aug. 31–Sept. 4, 1907; materials from priests of the diocese.]   R.J.P.

WILLIAMS, JOHN SHARP (July 30, 1854– Sept. 27, 1932), representative and senator from Mississippi, was a grandson of Christopher Harris Williams, a congressman from Tennessee. His forefathers, however, had been more distinguished in military than in civil life, having served as officers in the Revolutionary, Mexican, and Civil wars. His father, Christopher Harris Williams, Jr., a colonel of Tennessee volunteers in the Confederate army, was killed in the battle at Shiloh. Since his mother, Annie Louise (Sharp), had died earlier, the orphaned boy was taken from Memphis, Tenn., his birthplace, to her father's large plantation near Yazoo City, Miss. Here he developed a lasting love for the old plantation way of life. In spite of the general poverty of the Reconstruction period his educational opportunities were excellent. After attending the Kentucky Military Institute, Franklin County, Ky., the University of the South, Sewanee, Tenn., and the University of Virginia, he spent two and a half years in Germany at the University of Heidelberg. Upon his return to America, he studied law at the University of Virginia and later in a law office in Memphis, in which city he was admitted to the bar in March 1877. In December of the following year he returned to Yazoo City, where he devoted the next fifteen years to practising his profession and to raising cotton. He had been married on Oct. 2, 1877, to Elizabeth Dial Webb, of Livingston, Ala.

In 1893 he began a career of sixteen years in the lower house of Congress. During the first ten years he gained a reputation among his colleagues, and to some extent outside of Congress, as a vigorous and skilful debater; he came into more general notice when he was chosen leader of the Democratic minority in the Fifty-eighth Congress. His immediate predecessors had exercised little authority, and the Democrats had become noted for being as unrestrained as a herd of wild steers. With little apparent effort, Williams speedily brought order out of chaos. Capitol correspondents enlivened their accounts of this feat by describing the Democratic floor leader as a "character," remarkable for his fund of good stories, his simple tastes, and his carelessness in dress. His clothes, they wrote, "make no pretense of fitting him. . . . They bag and droop impossibly" (*Bookman, post,* 169); "his black string tie is usually loose and dangling to one side or the other"; his "hair appears never to have been combed" (*Current Literature, post,* p. 160). Since he was partially deaf in his right ear, the side turned toward the Republicans in Congress, he often sat with his head bent forward and to the right, with his hand serving as an impromptu ear-trumpet. He seemed, nevertheless, to hear all that went on, and an alert and well-informed mind was evident when he rose to thrust keenly destructive questions into the heart of an opponent's speech or to ridicule the champions of the protective tariff. No matter how hot the debate, he seemed never to lose his temper and was liked on both sides of the House.

In addition to being a competent and popular field commander of the Democratic forces in Congress, Williams was also influential in determining the objectives of his party. In the Democratic convention of 1904, of which he was temporary chairman, he was the champion of the conservative wing in the struggle over the platform. Although checkmated at this time by Bryan and the radicals, his activities help to explain the moderate platform of his party when it came into power with the election of Woodrow Wilson. His political philosophy was as old-fashioned as his clothes, for he was probably the most consistent Jeffersonian Democrat of his day, constantly striving to apply his fundamental philosophy of government to such current problems as railroads, trusts, tariffs, and the relation between federal and state governments. He contributed to *The Annals of the American Academy of Political and Social Science* two articles, "Federal Usurpations" (July 1908), and "Control of

Corporations, Persons and Firms Engaged in Interstate Commerce" (July 1912), which give a good insight into his mind. In 1912 he gave a series of lectures at Columbia University, which were published the next year under the title *Thomas Jefferson, His Permanent Influence on American Institutions.* In spite of the fact that they were prepared under pressure, they are a thoughtful analysis of Jefferson's views and influence, and are equally good as a statement of Williams' political philosophy.

He was not a candidate for the Sixty-first Congress (1909–11). In August 1907, he had defeated James K. Vardaman [*q.v.*] in the Democratic primary, which in Mississippi insured election, for the senatorial term which was to begin in 1911. The fight was bitter, the more so since it was something of a class struggle. Though Williams was inferior to Vardaman in the power to sway audiences by grandiose oratory and political dramatics, he was much superior in the ability to argue issues on their merits. His career in the lower house gave him immediate recognition in the Senate, where he attained membership on the finance committee and on the foreign relations committee; but since he no longer had to fight against radical leadership in his party or against a dominant opposition party, he appeared less prominent than formerly. He was in close agreement with President Wilson in respect to the entrance of the United States into the World War and its vigorous prosecution, and he also strove to secure the entrance of the United States into the League of Nations. The defeat of the Wilson post-war program and the weakness, as he thought it to be, of Congress in dealing with the bonus question disappointed him. While in this humor he is reported to have remarked: "I'd rather be a hound dog and bay at the moon from my Mississippi plantation than remain in the United States Senate" (Memphis *Commercial Appeal,* Sept. 29, 1932). Realizing that he was growing old and that he could probably do little to change the direction the Senate was going, he retired in 1923 at the end of his second term. The remaining nine years he lived in almost complete political retirement at "Cedar Grove," his old plantation near Yazoo City, "with old books, an old pipe, a dear old wife and very good health and lots of good friends and children and grandchildren" (*Ibid.*). He was survived by six of his eight children, four sons and two daughters.

[*Who's Who in America,* 1932–33; *Biog. Dir. Am. Cong.* (1928); *Official and Statistical Reg. of the State of Miss.,* 1908; *Bookman,* Apr. 1904; *Rev. of Rev.* (N. Y.), Aug. 1904; *Current Literature,* Feb. 1907; *Nation,* May 10, 1917, Oct. 12, 1932; *Evening Appeal* (Memphis), Sept. 28, 1932; *Commercial Appeal* (Memphis), Sept. 29, 30, 1932; Harris Dickson, *An Old-Fashioned Senator* (1925).]

C. S. S.

WILLIAMS, JOHN SKELTON (July 6, 1865–Nov. 4, 1926), financier and public official, was born in Powhatan County, Va., one of several sons of John Langbourne Williams and Maria Ward (Skelton), a grandson of John Williams, born in Ireland, who died in Richmond, Va., in 1860, and a great-great-grandson of Edmund Randolph [*q.v.*]. After attending public school in Richmond, he entered the banking house of J. L. Williams & Sons, founded by his father, which was active in promoting and financing public utilities not only in the Richmond area but throughout the South. In 1895 he married Lila Lefebvre Isaacs, by whom he had two sons. His most important financial task while an investment banker was the formation, beginning in 1895, of the Seaboard Air Line Railway out of an array of shorter railway lines. At thirty-four he became first president of the new railroad. But the venture which was apparently consummated so brilliantly in 1900 soon ran into financial difficulties. After a long struggle with a group of New York financiers headed by Thomas Fortune Ryan [*q.v.*], Williams was forced out of the presidency on Dec. 30, 1903. For a number of years thereafter he and his local banking allies struggled unsuccessfully to regain control of the road. It was a lesson in the power of New York financiers which left him bitterly antagonistic to them.

In March 1913 Williams was appointed assistant secretary of the treasury by President Wilson, at the request of Secretary McAdoo. In January 1914 he was named comptroller of the currency, but his appointment was confirmed by the Senate only after a committee had vindicated him from the charge of using treasury deposits to aid his brother's bank (*New York Times*, Dec. 24, 1913, Feb. 1, 1914). As comptroller of the currency he was *ex officio* a member of the organizing committee which set up the new Federal Reserve system. He served also as a member of the Interstate Commerce Commission's advisory board on valuation. When McAdoo was made director-general of the railroads in December 1917, Williams became his director of finances and purchases, a position which he held until March 1919 along with the comptrollership.

Williams entered upon his duties as comptroller with a vigor that won him many enemies. Three months after assuming the office, in a speech delivered before the North Carolina Bankers' Association (*Democracy in Banking*, 1914), he attacked the concentration of banking control "in

the hands of a dozen men," pointed to the political and economic dangers of huge fortunes, and praised the Federal Reserve system as a means of decentralizing financial control. Later he antagonized the national banks by accusing them of usurious practices. His frequent reiteration of this charge in the course of the next seven years served to reopen old wounds. From April 1915 to June 1916 he was engaged in a series of suits with officials of the Riggs National Bank of Washington, D. C., and although a perjury case against the Bank's directors ended in an acquittal, Williams' charges of irregular practices were sustained and the bank's charter was renewed only after the directors pledged themselves to abide by the law in the future. To his lengthening list of antagonists he added the state banks and state banking officials when in a public statement he contrasted the safety of national and state banks. In his Annual Report for 1917, he advocated the national guaranty of all deposits of $5,000 or less in national banks, to assure depositor confidence in the face of the war situation and to bring money out of hiding. Not until 1933 did the federal government, faced by financial panic, adopt such a policy.

Upon the expiration of Williams' appointment in 1919, bitter opposition was evidenced to his reappointment. He remained in office for two years more, however, although neither the earlier committee recommendation to confirm nor later recommendations to reject the renomination were acted upon by the Senate as a whole. On Mar. 2, 1921, with the accession of a hostile Republican administration two days off, he resigned. Shortly after leaving office, he charged that the Federal Reserve Board, of which he had himself been a member *ex officio*, had by its deflationary policies caused the disastrous decline in agricultural prices which began in 1920; he also attacked certain of the Federal Reserve banks, notably that of New York, for what he termed extravagant expenditures for buildings and salaries. His accusations formed the essential basis for a Congressional investigation, which sustained some of his charges against the Board.

From public life, Williams returned to the Richmond Trust Company, serving as chairman of its board of directors until his sudden death, in 1926, at his home near Richmond, Va. In commenting on his death, the *Bankers' Magazine* (December 1926), which had consistently opposed him during his term of office, characterized him as highly efficient but unnecessarily harsh.

[The Lib. of Cong. has eleven published addresses by Williams. For biog. data, see *Who's Who in America*, 1926–27; *N. Y. Times*, Feb. 1, 5, 1914, Nov. 5, 1926; Carter Glass, "John Skelton Williams," in *Selections* from the Family Hist. of Randolph, Dandridge, Armistead, Langbourne, Carter and Williams Clans in Va. 1650 to 1930 (n.d.). See also Seaboard Air Line Railway circulars, nos. 2, 4, 8, 9, 10, 14 (1903–09) available at Lib. of Cong.; Nomination of John Skelton Williams: Hearing before the Committee on Banking and Currency, U. S. Senate (1919); "The Agricultural Crisis and Its Causes," House Report 408, 67 Cong., 1 Sess.; W. P. G. Harding, The Formative Period of the Federal Reserve System (1925), ch. xvi and passim; Bankers' Magazine, July 1914, Feb. 1915, Jan. 1916, Mar. 1918, Sept. 1920, Dec. 1926; N. Y. Times, Apr. 13, 1915–June 22, 1916 (Riggs case).]   J. J. S.

WILLIAMS, JOHN WHITRIDGE (Jan. 26, 1866–Oct. 21, 1931), physician, obstetrician, was born in Baltimore, Md., the son of Dr. Philip C. and Mary Cushing (Whitridge) Williams. Through his mother he was descended from a family that had practised medicine in America for more than a hundred and sixty years. After three years in the Baltimore City College, he entered the Johns Hopkins University and was graduated in 1886. He took the degree of M.D. at the University of Maryland in 1888, and went at once to Vienna and Berlin for general courses in bacteriology and pathology. Returning, he joined the gynecological-obstetrical staff of the newly opened Johns Hopkins Hospital as associate in obstetrics (1893–96). Although he had planned to devote himself to gynecology, he availed himself of the unusual opportunity in obstetrics afforded by the opening of the Johns Hopkins Medical School and spent the year 1894–95 studying obstetrics in Leipzig, writing a monograph, Contribution to the Histology and Histogenesis of Sarcoma of the Uterus (1894), while in Chiari's laboratory in Prague. He was assistant professor of obstetrics at Johns Hopkins from 1896 until 1899, when the chair was divided, Howard A. Kelly retaining gynecology and Williams becoming professor of obstetrics and obstetrician-in-chief to the hospital. It remained Williams' conviction, however, that these subjects properly and logically should constitute a single department. He undertook the additional responsibilities of dean of the Medical School from 1911 until 1923, when he resigned to devote himself wholly to research and the service of obstetrics in the new woman's clinic building.

Williams' preëminence as a scientist appears in all his writings—some hundred. The earliest deal with bacteriology and pathology under the aegis of Dr. William H. Welch [q.v.]; later his statistical papers became increasingly valuable; others concern rare deformities, the toxemias of pregnancy, syphilis during pregnancy, antenatal care, contracted pelves and general pelvimetry, and the indications for cesarean section. The historical background which prefaced these treatises was of incalculable worth. His Textbook of Obstetrics (1903) was a potent factor in promoting an understanding of the subject, and is still (1936) undoubtedly the best authority in English. Williams was a remarkable teacher, constantly reminding his students that the purpose of their training was to enable them to train others in turn. He was honorary president of the Glasgow Gynecological and Obstetrical Society (1911–12), and president of the American Gynecological Society (1914–15) and of the American Association for the Study and Prevention of Infant Mortality (1914–16). On the day of his funeral one of the first honorary fellowships of the British College of Obstetricians and Gynecologists was conferred upon him. He held several honorary degrees.

His conservative tendencies were revealed not only in his professional life, but in his strong feeling that the simple life of his youth was more abundant than the complexity of later years. He was an ardent exponent of state as against national authority. Under Mayor Preston, with Dr. J. Hall Pleasants he reconstructed along thoroughly scientific lines old Bay View, Baltimore's city hospital, with a full-time staff in pathology, medicine, and surgery. He particularly advocated moderate fees. Early in 1931 he participated in the movement to repeal the Federal law forbidding the dissemination of birth-control literature through the mails.

Williams was broadly educated, a lover of old books, a loyal and devoted friend, honest and straightforward in his thinking. His devotion to science never lessened his consideration for others or his humanity of spirit. On Jan. 14, 1891, he married Margaretta Stewart Brown (d. Feb. 21, 1929), daughter of Gen. Stewart Brown. His second wife, Caroline (Theobald) Pennington, whom he married in April 1930, was the daughter of Dr. Samuel Theobald [q.v.] of the Johns Hopkins faculty. He was survived by his wife and three daughters by his first marriage.

[Who's Who in America, 1930–31; J. M. Slemons, John Whitridge Williams, Academic Aspects and Bibliog. (1935); Jour. Am. Medic. Asso., Oct. 31, 1931; H. J. Stander, Am. Jour. Obstetrics, Nov. 1931; H. M. Little, in Trans. Am. Gynecological Soc., vol. LVII (1933); H. A. Kelly, in Am. Jour. Surgery, Jan. 1932; Bull. Johns Hopkins Hospital, Dec. 1931; Jour. Obstetrics and Gynecology of the British Empire, Spring 1932; Ernst Philipp, in Zentralblatt für Gynäkologie, Nov. 28, 1931; obituary in Sun (Baltimore), Oct. 22, 1931; personal recollections.]   H. A. K—y.

WILLIAMS, JONATHAN (May 26, 1750–May 16, 1815), merchant and soldier, was born in Boston, the son of Jonathan Williams, a prosperous merchant, and Grace (Harris) Williams, daughter of Benjamin Franklin's sister, Anne. Having received their early education in the idence, R. I., son of David and Mary (Atwell) Vinton, and probably a descendant of John Vinton who settled in Lynn, Mass., some time before 1648. Alexander was one of five brothers, three of whom graduated from West Point and entered the army, though later Francis [q.v.] became an Episcopal clergyman. Alexander received a classical education and spent three years in Brown University. He then went to Yale, and graduated from the medical department with the degree of M.D. in 1828. For the next four years he practised his profession in Pomfret, Conn. Although reputed to have been something of a sceptic in his early days, he became convinced of the truth of Christianity and in 1834 turned from medicine to the ministry. After spending a short time in the General Theological Seminary, New York, he was ordained deacon by Bishop Benjamin T. Onderdonk on June 28, 1835, and the following year advanced to the priesthood by Bishop Alexander V. Griswold. In the meantime he had had charge of a church in Portland, Me., for a few months, and then returned to his native city to become rector of Grace Church. Here he remained until 1842, when he was called to St. Paul's Church, Boston. Among his parishioners was young Phillips Brooks, upon whom Vinton made a deep impression. Brooks said of him later, his "vigorous mind and great acquirements and commanding character and earnest eloquence, made him a most influential power and gave a noble dignity to the life of the church in Boston" (Tiffany, post, p. 544). In the contest over the bishopric of Pennsylvania in 1845, which resulted in the election of Alonzo Potter [q.v.], Vinton was one of the candidates put forward for that office. In 1851 he was made a member of the Massachusetts board of education. Leaving St. Paul's in 1858, he was rector of Holy Trinity, Philadelphia, until 1861, of St. Mark's, New York, until 1869, and then, returning to Boston, of Emmanuel Church until 1877. Thereafter, he made his home in Pomfret, Conn., serving, however, as lecturer at the Cambridge Divinity School.

In his day, Vinton ranked among the leading preachers of the Episcopal Church. In appearance and voice he had the physical basis for oratory. "As an imposing and manly representation of the clerical profession, he was imaged in bronze upon the Soldiers Monument on Boston Common, in the act of blessing the troops on their departure for the war" (Allen, post, I, 45). He was a low churchman and was prominent in the evangelical group. He emphasized the need of conversion, was a diligent pastor, and defended the faith with earnestness and logical acumen.

He was one of the signers of the "Muhlenberg Memorial," addressed to the House of Bishops in 1853. When the first American Church Congress was held in 1870, Vinton was chosen to act as president. Collections of his sermons appeared in 1855 and 1867, and many other sermons and addresses were published separately. He was married on Oct. 15, 1835 to Eleanor Stockbridge, daughter of Ebenezer Thompson of Providence, by whom he had six children. His death, from pneumonia, occurred in Philadelphia, where he had gone to take part in the consecration of the Church of the Holy Trinity.

[J. A. Vinton, *The Vinton Memorial* (1858); *Obit. Record Grads. Yale Univ.*, 1881; H. B. Huntington, *A Hist. of Grace Church in Providence, R. I.* (1931); A. V. G. Allen, *Life and Letters of Phillips Brooks* (2 vols., 1900); C. C. Tiffany, *A Hist. of the Protestant Episcopal Church in the U. S. A.* (1895); *Boston Daily Advertiser*, Apr. 27, 1881.]   H. E. S.

VINTON, FRANCIS (Aug. 29, 1809–Sept. 29, 1872), soldier, Protestant Episcopal clergyman, was born in Providence, R. I., the son of David Vinton, a goldsmith and merchant, and Mary (Atwell) Vinton. His first paternal ancestor in America was probably John Vinton who in 1648 was a resident of Lynn, Mass. Two of Francis' brothers, John Rogers and David Hammond, had graduated from the United States Military Academy, and in his seventeenth year, July 1, 1826, Francis entered that institution. In 1830 he graduated, ranking fourth in a class of forty-two, and was commissioned second lieutenant, 3rd Artillery. From 1830 to 1832 he served in garrison at Fort Independence, Mass., and while there began to study law at Harvard. He was on topographical and engineering duty from July 17, 1832, to September 1833, when he was sent to Fort Constitution, N. H. While here, January 1834, he was admitted to the bar. In 1836 he saw active service in the Creek Nation. He was on recruiting duty, when, Aug. 31, 1836, he resigned from the army with the intention of following his brother, Alexander Hamilton Vinton [q.v.], into the ministry.

After studying at the General Theological Seminary, New York, he was ordained to the diaconate by Bishop A. V. Griswold at St. John's Church, Providence, Sept. 30, 1838; the following March he was advanced to the priesthood. On Oct. 8, 1838, he married Maria Bowen, daughter of John Whipple of Providence; she died in childbirth on June 6, 1840, and on Nov. 3 of the following year he married Elizabeth Mason, daughter of Commodore Oliver Hazard Perry [q.v.], by whom he had seven children. For a time he had under his care his nephew, Francis Laurens Vinton [q.v.]. His first parish was at be near the controlling authority, and centralization of control in the hands of the President. Jefferson approved of both recommendations, but neither was heeded by Congress or considered by Madison and Eustis. On July 31, 1812, Williams resigned from the army, embittered because of his failure at West Point and also because at the outbreak of the war he had not been given command of the fortifications at New York. During the war he became brevet brigadier-general of New York militia and was on a committee in Philadelphia for preparing adequate defenses for the Delaware. He was elected to Congress in 1814, but did not live to take his seat.

While in the army, he published *The Elements of Fortification* (1801), a translation from the French made for the war department; *Manœuvres of Horse Artillery* (1808), a translation of the work by Tadeuz Kościuszko. He was instrumental, also, in the founding, during his service at West Point, of the Military Philosophical Society to promote military science and history.

[I. M. Hays, *Calendar of the Papers of Benjamin Franklin in the Lib. of the Am. Philosophical Soc.* (5 vols., 1908); G. W. Cullum, *Campaigns of the War of 1812–15, Against Great Britain* (1879); E. C. Boynton, *Hist. of West Point* (1863); *Am. State Papers. Mil. Affairs*, vol. I (1832); *The Memoirs of Gen. Joseph Gardner Swift* (1890); Arthur Lee, *Observations on Certain Commercial Transactions in France* (1780); J. T. Scharf and Thompson Westcott, *Hist. of Phila.* (1884); *Biog. Dir. Am. Cong.* (1928); *Relfs' Phila. Gazette*, May 17, 1815.]   M. E. L—b—d.

WILLIAMS, LINSLY RUDD (Jan. 28, 1875–Jan. 8, 1934), physician, organizer, son of John Stanton and Mary Maclay (Pentz) Williams, was born in New York City, which was his home throughout his life. He was graduated at the College of New Jersey (Princeton) with the degree of A.B. in 1895, and from the College of Physicians and Surgeons, New York, in 1899. He was then appointed interne at the Presbyterian Hospital, serving from 1900 to 1902, and in the latter year taking further service at Sloane Maternity Hospital. He began the practice of medicine as assistant to Dr. John S. Thatcher, an association which lasted till 1908. At the same time he was successively instructor in histology, assistant in medicine, and chief of the medical clinics at the Presbyterian Hospital, and was visiting physician to the House of Rest for Tuberculosis, to Seton Hospital, and to the City Hospital. On Jan. 18, 1908, he married Grace (Kidder) Ford, widow of Paul Leicester Ford [*q.v.*], by whom he had three children.

In 1914 he was selected for the position of deputy commissioner of health for the state of New York by Dr. Hermann M. Biggs [*q.v.*], newly appointed commissioner under the health law adopted the previous year. In this work Williams was given free scope for the unusual talent for organization which marked his subsequent career. When the United States entered the World War he at once joined the medical corps, with the rank of first lieutenant. He was promoted rapidly and was discharged in 1919 as lieutenant-colonel. In August 1917 his broad experience in public health matters led to his being sent to investigate sanitary conditions in France and England. In October of that year he was made an assistant division surgeon. Later he served as sanitary inspector of the Eightieth Division and was afterwards attached to headquarters as assistant sanitary officer.

As the result, in part, of his war service, he was appointed in 1919 director of the Rockefeller Commission for the Prevention of Tuberculosis in France, succeeding in that office Dr. Livingston Farrand. Appreciation of the success with which he performed the profoundly difficult and delicate duties of this position was shown not only by France, which made him a Commander of the Legion of Honor, but by other governments as well, which studied and put into practice plans for the control of tuberculosis developed by Williams during the three years of his directorship. From 1922 to 1928 as managing director of the National Tuberculosis Association he visited all parts of the United States and won national fame as an organizer of the social and medical forces combating preventable disease and promoting the public health. The later years of his life were devoted, as managing director, to developing the New York Academy of Medicine. To this task he brought the benefit of the broad horizon gained in his world service and through his effort the Academy acquired not only national but also international prestige. The physical plant which houses the Academy is the material monument to his labors, but a more important achievement was the spiritual growth of the institution under the guidance of his wisdom and understanding.

Reserved and distinguished in manner and poise, he gave the impression of judgment, self-control, and resourcefulness which command instant confidence. His counsel was so valued by all who knew him that he was constantly called upon to assume new burdens of responsibility. He was a trustee of Columbia University, a director of the Milbank Memorial Fund, and president of the New York Tuberculosis and Health Association; he served also on countless boards and committees, to all of which he gave unsparingly of his strength and interest. His pleasure appeared to lie in work and in the relaxation afforded by the warm hospitality for which his home was noted. Without doubt such unsparing generosity had made inroads on his physical strength, and when in October 1933 he was seized with a virulent pneumonia, there was not sufficient vitality remaining to fight off the series of complications which ensued.

[Kendall Emerson, in *Jour. of the Outdoor Life,* Feb. 1934; J. A. Hartwell, in *N. Y. State Jour. of Medicine,* Jan. 15, 1934; P. P. Jacobs, in *Bull. of the Nat. Tuberculosis Asso.,* Feb. 1934; *Jour. of the Am. Medic. Asso.,* Jan. 13, 1934; *In Memoriam, Linsly R. Williams* (N. Y. Acad. of Medicine, 1934); J. A. Miller, in *Am. Rev. of Tuberculosis,* Apr. 1934; C. E. A. Winslow, *The Life of Hermann M. Biggs* (1929); *N. Y. Times,* Jan. 8, 1934.]

K. E.

WILLIAMS, MARSHALL JAY (Feb. 22, 1837–July 7, 1902), jurist, son of Dr. Charles M. Williams and Margaret J. Williams, was born on a farm in Fayette County, Ohio. His early education was in the local common schools, in which, by the age of sixteen, he had taught several terms. After spending two years at Ohio Wesleyan University, he began the study of law in 1855 in the office of Nelson Rush at Washington Court-House, Ohio. At the age of twenty, since minors were not admitted to the bar in Ohio, he moved to Iowa where the rules were less stringent, but after practising there for a year, returned to Ohio and settled at Washington Court-House. He soon acquired a large practice which extended into surrounding counties. He was elected prosecuting attorney of Fayette County in 1859 and reëlected in 1861; in 1869 he was elected to the General Assembly and returned in 1871. Upon the establishment of the circuit courts in 1884, he was elected a judge of the court of the second circuit and was chosen by his colleagues as their first chief justice. After but two years' service on this bench he was elected a judge of the supreme court, and assumed office in 1887. Elected for three successive terms, he served for nearly sixteen years, being chief justice by rotation during the last year of each term. In 1891 he became the first dean of the College of Law of Ohio State University, which opened its doors for the first time in October of that year, with thirty-three students in the basement of the Franklin County Court House. He lectured in this school until 1893, when his health began to decline.

Williams' opinions as a supreme court judge are found in 45–66 *Ohio State Reports.* They are not great opinions nor do they show a wide range of scholarship, but they are able—characterized by their brevity, unusual clarity, and reliance upon principles of law rather than decided cases. In accordance with the prevailing spirit of the times, he was conservative in his views of constitutional law, as is evidenced by his concurrence in the decisions declaring unconstitutional the "sub-mechanics lien law" and the progressive inheritance tax law, both later made possible in Ohio by constitutional amendment, but both of which, according to modern legal thinking, were valid without such amendment. In the field of tort law, however, when questions of negligence and liability to injured workmen were involved, he was singularly sympathetic to the claims of the injured party. Infants should be held to the degree of care exercised not by prudent adults but by infants of their own age and experience; railroads cannot by contract relieve themselves of liability for their own negligence; persons having on their premises things which are dangerous and attractive to children are liable for injuries to such children even though they be trespassers; defendants who have the "last clear chance" to avoid an injury either because they saw or ought to have seen the peril of the plaintiff are liable for injury done even though the plaintiff was himself guilty of contributory negligence; a municipality is liable for defects in the streets even though such streets be built with care according to a plan adopted by the city council—these are examples of the liberal doctrines which found expression in his opinions.

While still on the bench and serving as chief justice, he died, in Columbus, leaving a widow, Bertha (Taylor) Williams of Clermont County, whom he had married in May 1860, and one adopted daughter.

[67 *Ohio State Reports,* v–ix; *A Hist. of the Courts and Lawyers of Ohio* (4 vols., 1934), ed. by C. T. Marshall; *Who's Who in America,* 1899–1900; *Green Bag,* June 1895; *Proc. Ohio State Bar Asso. . . . 1903* (n.d.); *Ohio State Jour.* (Columbus), July 7, 1902; *Ohio Legal News,* III, 145, IV, 142.]

A. H. T.

WILLIAMS, NATHANAEL (Aug. 25, 1675–Jan. 10, 1737/38), schoolmaster and physician, was born in Boston, Mass., the son of Deacon Nathanael Williams and his second wife, Mary (Oliver) Shrimpton. He graduated at Harvard in 1693. On Aug. 16, 1698, he "was ordained in the Colledge Hall at Cambridge, to go and preach the gospell and dispense the ordinances to a non-conformist Church at Barbadoes" (Benjamin Wadsworth, manuscript commonplace book, Massachusetts Historical Society, p. 10). In the New England colony in Barbados he married Anne, the daughter of Samuel Bradstreet, and grand-daughter of Gov. Simon Bradstreet [*q.v.*].

After two years the tropical climate drove Williams back to Boston, where he was "employ'd by several Gentlemen to instruct their Sons in

Learning" (Prince, *Funeral Sermon, post.* p. 26). Upon the recommendation of the clergy he was appointed to assist Ezekiel Cheever [*q.v.*] in the Boston Latin School, where he entered upon his duties July 12, 1703. Five years later, upon the death of Cheever, he succeeded to the mastership. There is some evidence that he edited at least one edition of Cheever's famous *Accidence*.

Besides teaching and occasionally preaching— he was a pillar of the Old South Church—Williams "studied Chymistry and Physick, under his Uncle the Learned Dr. James Oliver of Cambridge" (Prince, Preface, *post*). He developed a successful private practice and was at times employed by the colony. He appears, with Zabdiel Boylston and William Douglass [*qq.v.*], in an imaginary debate on inoculation for the smallpox in an anonymous satirical pamphlet by Isaac Greenwood entitled, *A Friendly Debate; or, A Dialogue between Academicus and Sawny and Mundungus* (1722). He was in general an advocate of inoculation. When he entered the chambers of the sick, his "lively Voice and Countenance," said Thomas Prince [*q.v.*], "did good like a Medicine, reviv'd our Spirits, and light-en'd our Maladies" (*Funeral Sermon,* p. 27). He was one of the chief backers of Prince's project for his *Chronological History of New England*.

In April 1723, Williams was offered the rectorship of Yale, but his family, apparently for financial reasons, induced him to decline it. Ten years later he resigned from the Latin School, but after some months succumbed to the call of form and ferule and opened a private school "for the Teaching and Instructing of Children or youth in Reading, Writing or any other Science" ("Records of the Boston Selectmen, 1716–1726," *Reports of the Record Commissioners,* XIII, 282–83). He died, a substantial and heartily respected citizen, at the age of sixty-two. Of his eight children, six died young. His daughter Ann married Belcher Noyes, and his daughter Mary became the wife of the portrait painter, John Smibert [*q.v.*]. Some years after Williams' death, Thomas Prince edited and published *The Method of Practice in the Small Pox . . . Taken from a Manuscript of the Late Dr. Nathanael Williams* (1752).

[*New-England Weekly Journal,* Jan. 17, 1738; Thomas Prince, *Funeral Sermon on the Rev. Mr. Nathanael Williams* (1738), and Preface to *The Method of Practice in the Small-Pox* (1752); *Reports of the Record Commissioners of the City of Boston* (13 vols., 1881–85), *passim*; H. F. Jenks, *Cat. of the Boston Public Latin School . . . with an Historical Sketch* (1886); *Boston Weekly News-Letter,* Jan. 12, 1738.]

C. K. S.

WILLIAMS, OTHO HOLLAND (March 1749–July 15, 1794), Revolutionary soldier, was born in Prince Georges County, Md., the son of Joseph and Prudence (Holland) Williams, who had emigrated from South Wales a few years before. In 1750 the family moved to the mouth of Conococheague Creek, in what was then Frederick County, where many years later (1787) Williams founded the town of Williamsport. His father presently died, leaving only a small estate for the support of his seven children, and the boy at the age of thirteen secured employment in the office of the county clerk at Frederick. In time he became sufficiently qualified to take complete charge of the office. About 1767 he moved to Baltimore, where he remained similarly employed until 1774 when he returned to Frederick and embarked upon a commercial career. On June 22, 1775, he was appointed first lieutenant in a company raised in Maryland under Capt. Thomas Price for service in New England. He participated in the siege of Boston and was promoted to the rank of captain. In 1776 rifle companies from Maryland and Virginia were combined into a regiment of which Williams was appointed major, June 27. At the fall of Fort Washington, Nov. 16, he was wounded in the groin and taken prisoner. At first placed on parole in New York, he was later thrown into the provost's jail, charged with secretly communicating military information to Washington; he shared a cell with Ethan Allen. Insufficient food and unsanitary quarters seriously impaired his health before he was exchanged, Jan. 16, 1778. In the meantime he had been appointed, Dec. 10, 1776, colonel of the 6th Maryland Regiment. Rejoining the army in New Jersey, he took part in the battle of Monmouth, served as deputy adjutant-general under Horatio Gates in 1780, and was present at the battles of Camden and King's Mountain. Gates's successor, Nathanael Greene, appointed him adjutant-general. He commanded the rear-guard during Greene's retreat across North Carolina and took a distinguished part in the subsequent battles of Guilford Court House, Hobkirk Hill, and Eutaw Springs. On May 9, 1782, he was promoted to the rank of brigadier-general.

At the conclusion of the war, he retired from the army. On Jan. 6, 1783, he was elected naval officer of the Baltimore district by the state council of Maryland. After the erection of the federal government under the Constitution of the United States, he was appointed collector of the port by President Washington. In May 1792, on account of ill-health and family responsibilities, he declined a commission as ranking brigadier-general, second in command of the army. In a vain attempt to improve his physical condition, he made a trip to Barbados in 1793. He died at Miller's Town, Va., and was buried in Riverview Cemetery, Williamsport. Over his grave the Mediary Lodge of Masons erected a commemorative shaft. In 1786 he married Mary, a daughter of William Smith, a wealthy merchant of Baltimore. She bore him four sons.

[The Md. Hist. Soc., Baltimore, possesses a large collection of letters and papers relating to Williams. His "Southern Army: A Narrative of the Campaign of 1780" is printed in W. G. Simms, *The Life of Nathanael Greene* (1849), App. Consult also: T. W. Griffith, *Sketches of the Early Hist. of Md.* (1821); William Johnson, *Sketches of the Life and Correspondence of Nathanael Greene* (2 vols., 1822); Osmond Tiffany, *A Sketch of the Life and Services of Gen. Otho Holland Williams* (1851); J. T. Scharf, *The Chronicles of Baltimore* (1874); G. W. Greene, *The Life of Nathanael Greene* (3 vols., 1867–71); J. T. Scharf, *Hist. of Md.* (1879), vol. II; *Hist. of Baltimore City and County* (1881), and *Hist. of Western Md.* (1882), vol. II; E. E. Lantz, in "Maryland Heraldry," *The Sun* (Baltimore), Apr. 2, 1905; James McSherry, *Hist. of Md.* (1849); H. W. Ridgely, *Hist. of Graves of Md. and the D. C.* (1908); S. W. Williams, *The Geneal. and Hist. of the Family of Williams* (1847); *Md. Hist. Mag.*, vols. VII (1912), XXII (1927), *passim*; F. B. Heitman, *Hist. Reg. Officers of the Continental Army* (rev. ed., 1914); M. P. Andrews, *Hist. of Md.* (1929); "Journal and Correspondence of the State Council," *Archives of Md.*, vol. XLVIII (1931).]   E. E. C.

WILLIAMS, REUEL (June 2, 1783–July 25, 1862), senator from Maine, was born in Augusta, then part of Hallowell, Me. Said to have descended from Richard Williams, a Welshman from Glamorganshire who settled at Taunton, Mass., in 1637, he was second of the twelve children of Seth and Zilpha (Ingraham) Williams. His father, tanner and shoemaker, had removed from Stoughton to Hallowell in 1779. In 1798 Reuel went from the Hallowell Academy to read law with Judge James Bridge, and he was admitted to the bar in 1804. By the time he was twenty-four, his ability had attracted attention in Boston, and in 1812, when Bridge retired, Williams received his lucrative practice. This included the important administration of the "Kennebec Purchase" and the Bowdoin College timberlands. He became one of the successful lawyers in Maine. His lack of a formal higher education was compensated by shrewd and lucid thinking, revealed in clear, terse expression. His considerable fortune did not come from the law alone. Even at nineteen, he invested his savings of $1,000 in Augusta real estate. When the old "Kennebec Purchase" came to an end in 1816, he was one of the purchasers of the lands and other interests of the proprietors. He invested in many projects in industry and communication, with very good success until his railroad venture.

A Federalist at first and after 1832 a Democrat, he was active in Maine politics. He sat in the state legislature from 1812 to 1829 and again in 1832 and 1848. Elected to the federal Senate in 1837 to fill an unexpired term, he was reëlected in 1839 but resigned in 1843. He served in 1825 on the commission to divide the public lands between Maine and Massachusetts, in 1832 on the Northeast Boundary Commission, and in 1861 on the commission for defenses in the northern states. He has been awarded the credit, or blame, for removing the state capital in 1827 to Augusta from Portland. His $10,000 contribution ensured the building of the state insane asylum at Augusta, and he worked diligently for the improvement of Kennebec navigation. He helped to give Augusta excellent stage connections with Bangor, railroad connection with Portland, and, through the Augusta Dam, an opportunity for industrial development. From 1832 to 1842, he was a very active supporter of Maine in the boundary dispute with New Brunswick, Canada, not only through his service on the Maine boundary commission but also as a senator. At Washington he proposed frequent measures for defending the frontier and for reopening the question, which led to the so-called Aroostook or Madawaska "War" and the Webster-Ashburton Treaty in 1842. With Thomas Hart Benton, he fought strenuously against ratification of the treaty in the Senate. He was a chief promoter and first president of the seventy-two-mile Kennebec & Portland Railway, running from Portland to Augusta with a branch from Brunswick to Bath, all now part of the Maine Central Railroad. However, he seems to have followed a short-sighted policy during the railroad disputes that stirred the state. The road had constant financial difficulties, and he is said to have lost $200,000.

He had married in November 1807 Sarah Lowell Cony of Augusta. They had one son and eight daughters. He served as trustee of Bowdoin College from 1822 to 1860. In 1853 he was baptized into the Unitarian Church. With all his ability, he was described as coldly reserved toward all but his intimates and "almost too precise and methodical for a man of ordinary impulses" (Poor, *Memoir*, p. 57). He died at Augusta.

[J. A. Poor, *Memoir of Hon. Reuel Williams* (1864), with portrait bust, reprinted from *Me. Hist. Soc. Coll.*, 1 ser., vol. VIII (1881), also pp. 30, 57, 92, 94, 97, 162, 208; *Ibid.*, vol. VI (1859) pp. 59, 358, 3 ser., vol. I (1904), p. 365; *Maine, a Hist.* (3 vols. 1919), ed. by L. C. Hatch, *Gen. Cat. of Bowdoin College* (1912); *Biog. Directory Am. Cong.* (1928); H. V. Poor, *Hist. of the Railroads and Canals of the U. S.*, vol. I (1860); *Portland Daily Advertiser*, July 26, 1862.]   J. B. P.

WILLIAMS, ROBERT (c. 1745–Sept. 26, 1775), pioneer Methodist preacher, was born probably in England and emigrated to America in 1769. He was a member of the Irish Methodist Conference from 1766 to 1769, and was a most energetic preacher. John Wesley, however, objected to Williams' vigorous criticism of the Anglican clergy and also felt that he lacked a teachable spirit. Wesley therefore hesitated to grant Williams' request in 1769 for an appointment as a Methodist missionary to America, but allowed him to go to America on condition that he would work under the supervision of Richard Boardman and Joseph Pilmore [q.v.], the official missionaries whom he was sending. Williams sold his horse and saddlebags in order to pay his debts, and through the kindness of a friend, who paid his passage, he reached America in the autumn of 1769, in advance of Boardman and Pilmore. He began his work in Wesley Chapel in New York City. Between 1769 and 1771 his activities were confined to the region around New York City and to Maryland.

Williams' impetuous spirit caused him soon to seek pioneer fields of labor and early in 1772 he went to Virginia, preaching first in Norfolk. His type of preaching attracted attention, for in his initial sermon, which was delivered in the open air, he used such words as "hell" and "devil" so frequently that many of his listeners thought that he was either swearing or that he was insane. It was with reluctance that hospitality was shown him. He also preached in Portsmouth, and in February 1773 he went to Petersburg, where with the help of Devereux Jarratt [q.v.], the evangelical rector of Bath Parish, he led a great revival of religion. At the Conference of that year he was received into the traveling connection, and appointed to serve in Virginia. In 1774 he organized the Brunswick circuit, which extended south from Petersburg into North Carolina. Soon after this he married, retired from the itinerancy, and established a home on the public road half-way between Portsmouth and Suffolk, where he died.

Upon his arrival in America Williams began to reprint some of Wesley's sermons and pamphlets. These he circulated to such an extent that they "had a very good effect—and withal, they opened the way in many places for our preachers to be invited to preach where they had never been before" (Lee, *post*, p. 48). The other Methodist preachers, however, looked askance at the undertaking. Some feared that Williams was printing the books for his own personal gain; others held that such an enterprise should be under the supervision of all the preachers, and that any profit should be used for religious and charitable causes. As a result, at the Conference of 1773, it was decided that none of them was to print any of Wesley's books without the consent of Wesley and the Methodist preachers in America. Williams had, however, turned the attention of the American Methodists to the value of the religious press.

Williams holds a unique record as a pioneer in American Methodism. He was the first Methodist traveling preacher to come to America, the first that published a book, the first that married, the first that located, and the first that died. He preached the first Methodist sermon and formed the first Methodist circuit in Virginia. He probably organized the first Methodist society in North Carolina. He was the spiritual father of Jesse Lee [q.v.]. Under Williams' guidance William Watters entered the Methodist ministry and became the first native Methodist itinerant.

[John Atkinson, *The Beginnings of the Wesleyan Movement in America* (1896); J. B. Wakeley, *Lost Chapters Recovered from the Early Hist. of Am. Methodism* (1858); Wm. Crook, *Ireland and the Centenary of Am. Methodism* (1866); Wm. B. Sprague, *Annals of the Am. Pulpit*, vol. VII (1859); Jesse Lee, *A Short Hist. of the Methodists in the U. S. A.* (1810); M. H. Moore, *Sketches of the Pioneers of Methodism in N. C. and Va.* (1884); D. A. Watters, *First Am. Itinerant of Methodism, William Watters* (1898); W. W. Bennett, *Memorials of Methodism in Va.* (1871); W. L. Grissom, *Hist. of Methodism in N. C.* (1905); Nathan Bangs, *A Hist. of the M. E. Church* (4 vols., 1838–41); W. H. Meredith, in *Christian Advocate* (N. Y.), Nov. 28, 1907.]   P.N.G.

WILLIAMS, ROGER (c. 1603–1682/83), clergyman, president of Rhode Island, was born in London, England, the son of James and Alice (Pemberton) Williams. His father, "citizen and freeman of London," was of the well-to-do business class, with a shop in Cow Lane and membership in the Merchant Taylor Company. On the maternal side Williams came of a family recently risen into the class of landed gentry. His grandfather was Robert Pemberton of St. Albans and his uncle, Roger, was high sheriff of Hertfordshire. Another maternal relative, Sir James Pemberton, was lord mayor of London. The birth date, 1603, commonly assigned to Williams is merely an approximation. On Feb. 7, 1677/78 he spoke of himself as "aged about seventie five years." By comparing this with several other statements he made, the date may be placed at 1603 or a little earlier.

Williams had a "natural inclination to study," and gave sufficient evidence of it to attract the interest of Sir Edward Coke, who made him his protégé and furthered his education. "This Roger Williams," wrote the daughter of Coke, "when he was a youth would, in a short hand, take sermons and speeches in the Star Chamber and present them to my dear father" (*Narragansett Club Publications,* VI, 239). Coke placed him in the Charterhouse school in 1621 and obtained for him a scholarship. Subsequently he was entered as a pensioner at Pembroke College, Cambridge, matriculating on July 7, 1624. He distinguished himself by winning one of the undergraduate honors and received the degree of B.A. in January 1627. The next two years he continued at Cambridge, preparing himself for the Church; he appears to have taken holy orders before February 1629. Becoming chaplain to Sir William Masham at Otes, in Essex, he enlarged his acquaintance with Puritan families who later played a dominant part in the Civil War.

Near Otes lived Mrs. Masham's mother, Lady Barrington, and her niece Jane Whalley, sister of the regicide. In a short space of time Jane and the young clergyman fell in love, and Williams wrote to Lady Barrington asking the hand of her niece. Lady Barrington had higher aspirations, and her rejection called forth a second letter from Williams in which the ardent young chaplain indignantly accepted her verdict, but declared in his capacity as clergyman that it was doubtful if Lady Barrington were intended for heaven. Williams took his disappointment hard, fell desperately ill, but recovered and found consolation. Mary Barnard, who waited upon Mrs. Masham's daughter at Otes, became his wife on Dec. 15, 1629.

Meanwhile, Williams had already had a call from New England, and during the summer of 1629 had gone with John Cotton and Thomas Hooker [*qq.v.*] to a conference of the founders of the Massachusetts colony at Sempringham. Prospects in the land of Charles and Laud had now become gloomy for men of Puritan belief, and on Dec. 1, 1630, Roger and Mary Williams took ship on the *Lyon.*

Williams was welcomed in Massachusetts as "a godly minister" (*Winthrop's Journal,* I, 57), but he immediately discovered he was once more in a land where the non-conforming were unfree. He received a call from Boston Church but rejected it, because he "durst not officiate to an unseparated people" (*Narragansett Club Publications,* VI, 356). His frank criticism of the Puritan system at once incurred hostility. Going even beyond the principles of the Separatists, he declared that civil governments had no power to enforce the religious injunctions of the Ten Commandments. When he accepted a call as teacher of Salem Church, the civil authorities interfered, and Williams found Plymouth more hospitable. Two years later he returned to Salem

and joined the Rev. Samuel Skelton, to whom he was now assistant, in attacking meetings of the clergy as a menace to the liberties of church congregations. Although Williams was now *persona non grata* with the authorities, Salem accepted his leadership and after Skelton's death in August 1634 took him as minister in defiance of the General Court. An added reason for the hostility of the authorities was his scruple of conscience in regard to imperialistic expropriation of American soil. Williams attacked English claims under the royal charter as a violation of the rights of the Indians. The magistrates, smarting under the charge of imperialism, resented also the appearance of any new affront to the Crown at a time when the rulers of Massachusetts were already under fire. Williams further infuriated the Massachusetts oligarchy by attacking the oath by which they were endeavoring to bind the lower orders to strict submission.

The movement of Salem under Williams in the direction of a more democratic church system eventually roused the fears of the governing class for their own supremacy. Following a series of summonses before ministers and magistrates, the General Court on Oct. 9, 1635, found him guilty of disseminating "newe & dangerous opinions, against the aucthoritie of magistrates" and ordered him banished. (*Records of the Governor and Company of the Massachusetts Bay,* vol. I, 1853, p. 160). Prior to his departure Williams attempted to organize his Salem followers to colonize in Narragansett. The magistrates, fearing the example of a radical community on their southern border, sent to apprehend him. Williams was warned, however, escaped in midwinter, made his way to the friendly Indians at Sowams, and after suffering privations gathered enough followers to found the earliest Rhode Island settlement, Providence, in 1636.

During the Pequot War and subsequent times of trouble, Williams exhibited his characteristic magnanimity and conducted important negotiations with the Indians, rendering signal assistance to the colony which had expelled him. Throughout later years he remained a consistent friend of the Indians, protesting to the Puritan colonies against unfair measures and seeking humane treatment and peaceful relations. Curiously, although he enjoyed the full confidence of the Narragansetts and preached to them, he gave over the attempt at religious conversion. He had himself become skeptical of divine claims of existing churches, and after a few months as a Baptist, in 1639 he became a Seeker, one who accepted no creed although clinging to the fundamental belief of Christianity.

Frontier influences and Williams' liberalism produced local institutions which marked a radical advance over those of the Puritan colonies. The town government became a primitive democracy. All heads of families had an equal voice. Almost the earliest action of the town was to provide for religious liberty and complete separation of church and state. Williams also endeavored at once to provide liberal opportunity for settlers to obtain land. He organized a democratic land association in which the heads of families were to share alike. Other settlers were to be admitted as they came. The land association became more exclusive in after years, but Williams succeeded in keeping it considerably more democratic than was usual in New England.

By 1643 four settlements had sprung up in the Narragansett area. Internal difficulties with individualistic settlers and the external menace of encroachments of ambitious colonies round about had made evident the necessity of a charter. The Puritan colonies were organizing the New England Confederation and were determined to snuff out the independent existence of settlements so likely to infect their own lower orders with notions of religious and political freedom. Massachusetts detached some of the Pawtuxet men from allegiance to Providence, invaded Rhode Island and carried off Samuel Gorton [q.v.] and the Warwick settlers to prison, and at the same time negotiated at London for a Narragansett patent. Meanwhile, to head off the menace to Rhode Island liberties, Williams had already taken ship for England and there, with the powerful aid of Sir Henry Vane [q.v.], managed to circumvent the Bay authorities and secure a patent for the whole area. The charter for the Providence Plantations in the Narragansett Bay was issued Mar. 14, 1644.

While in England Williams threw himself into the liberal cause as a pamphleteer, opposing the Puritan attempt to establish a national church and compulsory uniformity. In his most celebrated work, The Bloudy Tenent of Persecution (1644), he expanded his grounds for believing that "God requireth not an uniformity of Religion," and held that all individuals and religious bodies—pagans, Jews, and Catholics as well as Protestants—were entitled to religious liberty as a natural right. He also attacked the undemocratic character of contemporary governments and declared that "the *Soveraigne, originall,* and *foundation* of *civill power* lies in the *people* . . .''; and that neither *"Kings* or *Parliaments, States, and Governours"* could in justice wield more

power "then what the People give"; "and if so, that a People may erect and establish what *forme* of *Government* seemes to them most meete . . ." (*Narragansett Club Publications,* III, 249–50, 355). English-born and Cambridge-bred, but imbued with the tolerance and democracy of the American frontier, Williams had gone beyond the liberalism even of his friends and compeers, Cromwell and Milton.

Upon Williams' return, William Coddington [q.v.], dominating figure of Newport, who was friendly neither to democracy nor union, delayed organization of the Rhode Island settlements till 1647, and four years later obtained a commission from England splitting the colony and making him governor of Aquidneck for life. Williams then undertook a second voyage overseas, this time accompanied by John Clarke [q.v.]. In 1652 they succeeded in getting Coddington's commission rescinded, and in 1663 Clarke secured a new charter from Charles II. While in England Williams carried on anew his pamphleteering for democratic principles and religious liberty, publishing among other works The Bloody Tenent Yet More Bloody (1652) in reply to John Cotton's The Bloudy Tenent Washed and Made White (1647). On his return he made a celebrated plea for orderly democratic government (*Narragansett Club Publications,* VI, 278–79), reunited the colony, became president and served three terms. During his presidency the Jews first came to Rhode Island. Two years later the Quakers, then hated and hunted throughout New England, found the same safe harbor. Massachusetts sent a protest and a threat. The reply, which Williams appears to have helped frame, was to lecture the Bay on intolerance and make a strong statement of the Rhode Island Way.

The last years of Williams' life were darkened by controversy and Indian war. Although he had welcomed the Quakers as a matter of principle, he disagreed with their views. When George Fox visited Newport, Williams sent a challenge to a debate. Fox departed too soon, but his disciples responded, and in a three-day debate (1672) Williams and his opponents blackened each other with unwonted freedom and added nothing to the reputations of either side (Williams, *George Fox Digg'd out of His Burrowes,* 1676; Fox, *A New England Fire-Brand Quenched,* 1678).

In 1659 Williams had become involved in a bitter controversy with William Harris over Providence boundaries. Had Harris succeeded the town lands would have been extended twenty miles inland and the Narragansetts defrauded of many thousands of acres. Williams never proved himself a more genuine friend of the Indians than in rallying the townsmen to disallow the spurious deeds obtained by Harris. In spite of these and many other efforts in behalf of the natives, the peace for which Williams had labored so long was beyond his power to maintain. In King Philip's War the Narragansetts cast their lot with their brethren, and their old-time friends in the Rhode Island settlements cast theirs with their fellow countrymen. Williams, now a septuagenarian, took part as one of the two captains in command of the Providence forces and had the bitterness in his last years of seeing Providence and Warwick laid in ashes and the once great Narragansett tribe cut to ribbons and enslaved. He lived on a half-dozen years and remained active in town affairs to the last, dying sometime between Jan. 16 and Mar. 15, 1682/83.

Regarded as rash and hasty in judgment by men of rigid and authoritarian temper, Williams was recognized even by these as having the "root of the matter" in him. His influence on later thinkers was inconspicuous, for his writings appealed to the religiously minded men of the seventeenth century rather than to the more secular age which followed. But he was a provocative and significant figure in his own generation, and he left his mark upon the colony which he founded. Colonial thinker, religious liberal, and earliest of the fathers of American democracy, he owes his enduring fame to his humanity and breadth of view, his untiring devotion to the cause of democracy and free opportunity, and his long record of opposition to the privileged and self-seeking.

[*Narragansett Club Pubs.* (6 vols., 1866–74) reprint most of the letters and writings of Williams. Additional letters appear in *Letters and Papers of Roger Williams, 1629–1682* (1924), facsimile repr., Mass. Hist. Soc. Among other fugitive writings are *Christenings make not Christians* (1645); *The Fourth Paper, Presented by Maj. Butler* (1652); *The Hireling Ministry None of Christs* (1652). J. D. Knowles, *Memoir of Roger Williams* (1834), is still useful. The only detailed biography, James Ernst's *Roger Williams* (1932), contains few references to sources and no bibliography. For English background, see *passim*, *New Eng. Hist. and Geneal. Reg.* Materials on Williams' banishment appear in H. M. Dexter, *As to Roger Williams* (1876); and *Proc. Mass. Hist. Soc.*, 1 ser. XII (1873), 337–58. The order of banishment was rescinded by the Massachusetts legislature in January 1936 in compliment to the R. I. tercentenary celebration (*N. Y. Times*, Jan. 22, 26, 1936). For his career in Rhode Island see esp. H. M. Chapin, *Documentary Hist. of R. I.* (2 vols., 1916–19); I. B. Richman, *R. I.: Its Making and Its Meaning* (2nd ed., 1908); *The Early Records of the Town of Providence* (21 vols., 1892–1915); and *R. I. Hist. Soc. Colls.* (1827–). For Williams' influence upon England cf. William Haller, *Tracts on Liberty in the Puritan Revolution* (1934), vol. I, with David Masson, *The Life of John Milton*, vol. III (1873) and James Ernst's article in *R. I. Hist. Soc. Colls.*, vol. XXIV (1931). Excellent appraisals of Williams appear in M. C. Tyler, *A Hist. of Am. Lit. during the Colonial Time*, vol. I (1897), and V. L. Parrington, *The Colonial Mind* (1927). See also H. M. Chapin, *List of Roger Williams' Writings* (1918); James Ernst, *The Political Thought of Roger Williams* (1929); *Winthrop's Jour.* (1908), ed. by J. K. Hosmer; and Cotton Mather, *Magnalia Christi Americana* (1853 ed.), II, 495–99.]

S. H. B.

WILLIAMS, SAMUEL MAY (Oct. 4, 1795–Sept. 13, 1858), Texas pioneer and banker, was born in Providence, R. I., the son of Howell and Dorothea (Wheat) Williams, and a descendant of Robert Williams who was admitted freeman of Roxbury, Mass., in 1638. At the age of thirteen, Samuel went to Baltimore, Md., and became a clerk in the store of his uncle, Nathaniel F. Williams. When he was twenty he was a bookkeeper in New Orleans, where he also served briefly as secretary to Gen. Andrew Jackson [*q.v.*]. The wonderful stories of Texas told him by Stephen F. Austin [*q.v.*] lured him westward, and at the age of twenty-six he wandered to the new settlement of San Felipe de Austin, where in September 1824, he became private secretary to Austin, and also a partner in his great colonization project.

In this capacity he had charge of all drawings, maps, charts, and clerical work in the newly established colony. Largely as a result of his painstaking diligence and excellent handwriting the records of the colony were preserved for future generations. The numerous original letters now in the Rosenberg Library at Galveston bear testimony to his excellent qualifications as an executive secretary and business man. His ability to speak French and Spanish fluently was a valuable aid to him in his work. On one of his journeys to Mexico in the interest of the colony he was imprisoned for eleven months. He finally made his escape on horseback, found his way to San Antonio, and then rejoined the colony. The extensive land speculations in which he engaged after 1834 made him extremely unpopular in Texas. During the troubled days preceding the revolution of 1836, the Mexican authorities proscribed him, put a price on his head, and made several unsuccessful attempts to capture him.

Just before the revolution, Williams resigned his connections with the Austin colony, and organized a mercantile partnership with Thomas F. McKinney at Quintana, Tex., a village at the mouth of the Brazos River. In 1837 the firm opened a similar business at the village of Galveston, and engaged in a number of promotion enterprises. Soon afterwards Williams established his home there. He had married, Mar. 18, 1828, Sarah, daughter of William and Mary Scott, who had come to the Austin colony from Kentucky in 1824; to this union eight children were born. Gradually the firm of McKinney & Williams took on banking functions to supplement its general mercantile business. It planned to open The Commercial & Agricultural Bank at Galveston, for which Williams had secured a charter from the combined Mexican state of Coahuila and Texas on Apr. 30, 1835, but was unable to raise the necessary $100,000 minimum capital. The firm served, however, as the financial backer of the young Republic of Texas. After a delay of twelve years, the bank was finally opened on Dec. 30, 1847. It was the first chartered bank in Texas and carried on an extensive business throughout the state for over ten years. Hundreds of travelers entering Texas by way of Galveston formed banking connections through it with the North and the East. A branch bank was opened at Brownsville on the Mexican border, and carried on a large international as well as local business. The people of Texas, however, as well as those in other parts of the United States were divided on the question of banks. Numerous lawsuits were filed against the Commercial & Agricultural Bank to annul its charter. Finally, with the death of Williams at his Galveston home on Sept. 13, 1858, and the adverse decision of the supreme court of Texas annulling the charter, the bank was closed.

[A. L. Carlson, *A Monetary and Banking Hist. of Tex.* (1930); decisions of the supreme court of Tex., particularly 18 *Tex.*, 811 (1857), 8 *Tex.*, 255 (1852), 23 *Tex.*, 264 (1859); *Hist. of Tex.* (1895); E. C. Barker, *The Life of Stephen F. Austin* (1925); L. J. Wortham, *A Hist. of Tex.* (1924); S. W. Williams, *The Geneal. and Hist. of the Family of Williams* (1847); Samuel May Williams manuscript coll., 1819–58, in Rosenberg Lib., Galveston, Tex.]   A.L.C.

WILLIAMS, SAMUEL WELLS (Sept. 22, 1812–Feb. 16, 1884), missionary, diplomat, and sinologue, was born in Utica, N. Y., the eldest of the fourteen children of William Williams, 1787–1850 [*q.v.*], a printer and bookseller, and Sophia (Wells) Williams. His parents were of old New England stock. Both were deeply religious and active in the work of the church. Because of his mother's ill health, he spent much of his childhood at his grandmother Wells's home at New Hartford, N. Y. As a boy he was studious and somewhat reserved; he early developed the interest in botany which he retained through life. He attended several schools, including one in Paris, Hill, N. Y., and the Utica High School. In 1831–32 he was a student at Rensselaer Polytechnic Institute in Troy. His father, asked to nominate a printer for the Canton press of the American Board of Commissioners for Foreign Missions, suggested him, and he accepted. He spent several months in 1832–33 studying the

printing trade under his father's direction, and in June 1833 sailed for China.

Protestant missions among the Chinese were then twenty-six years old and were carried on by a small group who in China itself could maintain a precarious foothold only at Macao and Canton. Williams spent his first months in Canton, studying Chinese and Portuguese, managing the printing press, and contributing to the *Chinese Repository,* which had been recently initiated by Elijah Coleman Bridgman [*q.v.*]. In 1835 he and the press moved to Macao. Within the next decade, in addition to his direction of the press and his assistance with the *Chinese Repository,* he aided Bridgman in preparing *A Chinese Chrestomathy in the Canton Dialect* (1841) and compiled *Easy Lessons in Chinese* (1842), *An English and Chinese Vocabulary in the Court Dialect* (1844), and a *Chinese Topography* (1844), and edited *A Chinese Commercial Guide* (2nd ed., 1844). From 1845 to 1848 he was in the United States. There (Nov. 25, 1847) he married Sarah Walworth, by whom he had three sons and two daughters. Out of lectures which he gave during this sojourn in the United States grew the first edition of his *The Middle Kingdom* (2 vols., 1848), which for more than a generation was the standard book in English on China. In 1837 he had been a member of the *Morrison* party which attempted, unsuccessfully, to repatriate some shipwrecked Japanese. From one of these he learned enough Japanese to prepare in it a translation of the Gospel of Matthew. Because of this acquaintance with the language he was asked to accompany the Perry expedition as an interpreter, and in that capacity visited Japan in 1853 and in 1854. In 1856 he accepted an invitation to become secretary and interpreter of the American legation to China. At about the same time he completed his *A Tonic Dictionary of the Chinese Language in the Canton Dialect* (1856). His connection with the legation lasted until 1876. He helped negotiate the American treaty of Tientsin (1858), being responsible for the insertion in that document of the clause granting toleration to Christianity; he accompanied the party which went to Peking (1859) for the purpose of exchanging the ratifications of the treaty; he took up his residence in Peking (1863), being several times in charge of the legation in the intervals between ministers; he assisted Sweden (1870) in obtaining a treaty with China; and he compiled his much-used *A Syllabic Dictionary of the Chinese Language* (1874).

On his retirement to America he took up his residence in New Haven, Conn., becoming

(1877) professor of the Chinese language and literature at Yale. The position was largely honorary, as the salary was small and he had no students. In spite of failing strength, however, he used the time to revise and enlarge his *Middle Kingdom* (2 vols., 1883), a task in which he was assisted by his son Frederick Wells [*q.v.*]. He actively opposed the restriction on Chinese immigration, and served as president of the American Bible Society and the American Oriental Society. Earnestly religious, he maintained his active interest in missions to the very last. Although he was a specialist on China and the outstanding American sinologist, his inquiring mind led him to range widely over the field of human knowledge, and he had a vast store of information on a great variety of subjects. Well-built, active, and wiry, but never especially robust, by temperate and regular habits and unremitting diligence he accomplished an enormous amount of work.

[G. H. Williams, "The Geneal. of Thomas Williams," in *New Eng. Hist. and Geneal. Reg.*, Jan. 1880; F. W. Williams, *The Life and Letters of Samuel Wells Williams* (1889); *Biog. Record . . . Rensselaer Polytechnic Inst.* (1887); ann. reports, Am. Board of Commissioners for Foreign Missions; H. Blodget, in *Chinese Recorder*, May–June 1884; Noah Porter, in *Missionary Herald*, Apr. 1884; obituary in *N. Y. Tribune*, Feb. 18, 1884.]   K. S. L.

WILLIAMS, STEPHEN WEST (Mar. 27, 1790–July 6, 1855), medical historian, was born in Deerfield, Mass., the son of William Stoddard and Mary (Hoyt) Williams, and a descendant of Robert Williams who was admitted freeman in Roxbury, Mass., in 1638. Both his father and grandfather were physicians. The Rev. John Williams, 1664–1729 [*q.v.*], was a distant kinsman. After preliminary education at Deerfield Academy, Williams was apprenticed to his father, a man of scholarly taste who maintained an extensive library. Under such excellent conditions he learned the art of medicine, supplementing his studies at home by a winter in New York, attending the medical lectures at Columbia College. Returning to Deerfield, he carried on investigations in botany, chemistry, and local history while waiting for his practice to develop. With Edward Hitchcock [*q.v.*], the geologist, he explored the hills of western Massachusetts, collecting an herbarium of the indigenous medical plants. He published his researches in 1819, *Floral Calendar Kept at Deerfield, Mass.,* accompanied by colored plates painted by his wife. Williams was soon sought out as a teacher, first by Josiah Goodhue, as lecturer on medical jurisprudence in the Berkshire Medical Institution (1823–31), and later by his friend, Westel Willoughby, in the newly founded Willoughby University in Ohio (1838–53). He also lectured at the Dartmouth Medical School in New Hampshire (1838–41). For teaching he added notes to James Bedingfield's *A Compendium of Medical Practice* (1823) and published his own lectures on jurisprudence, *A Catechism of Medical Jurisprudence,* in 1835. He received the honorary degrees of M.D. from Berkshire in 1824, and A.M. (1829) and M.D. (1842) from Williams College. During this period he wrote many papers for the New York Historical Society, the Massachusetts Medical Society, and similar associations.

A number of his writings were medical biographies; these, with others, were put together in one volume, *American Medical Biography* (1845). Not always accurate, the book nevertheless was a worthy successor to, and served to supplement, a previous publication (1828) with the same title, by James Thacher [*q.v.*]. These two books form the basis for all American medical biography up to Williams' time. At the annual meeting of the Massachusetts Medical Society in 1842, Williams gave a paper, "A Medical History of the County of Franklin . . ., Mass." (*Medical Communications of the Massachusetts Medical Society,* vol. VII, 1848), an excellent local history on diseases, climate, and physicians. In addition, he re-issued John Williams' *The Redeemed Captive* (1853), with an accompanying biography of the author, and wrote an authoritative *Genealogy and History of the Family of Williams* (1847).

A man of wide interests, both literary and scientific, he was the most conspicuous medical historian and biographer of his day. He married, Oct. 20, 1818, Harriet T. Goodhue, daughter of Dr. Joseph Goodhue, an army surgeon. Of four children, one son became a physician. Towards the close of his life Williams left Deerfield, the center of all his activities for years, and went to live with his son in Laona, Ill., where he died at the age of sixty-five.

[Presumably the most authentic notice of Williams is that by his daughter, Helen M. Huntington, in *Memorial Biogs. New Eng. Hist. and Geneal. Soc.*, vol. II (1881), which contains an "autobiog.," marred by many errors. See also James Deane, in *Boston Medic. and Surgic. Jour.*, Aug. 9, 1855; *Trans. Amer. Medic. Asso.*, vol. XXIX (1878); and *Boston Evening Transcript,* July 24, 1855.]   H. R. V.

WILLIAMS, TALCOTT (July 20, 1849–Jan. 24, 1928), journalist, was born in Abeih, Turkey, the son of William Frederic and Sarah Amelia (Pond) Williams. His father, a Congregational missionary and a brother of Samuel Wells Williams [*q.v.*], was instrumental in founding Robert College in Constantinople and the American

College at Beirut. The son, brought up in a household where five languages were spoken daily, early acquired the foundation for a knowledge of Eastern languages and culture which was to make him in adult life an authority on the Near East. He was sent to America to be educated, and graduated from Amherst College in 1873. That same year he joined the staff of the New York *World* and became successively Albany correspondent, assistant night editor, and night editor. In 1877 he went to Washington, where, as correspondent first for the *World* and later for the *San Francisco Chronicle* and the New York *Sun,* he emerged as one of the outstanding political reporters of his day. So thorough was his grasp of public affairs that in 1879 the *Springfield Republican,* a newspaper of outstanding national importance, invited him to become one of its editorial writers.

Two years later he left the *Republican* to write editorials for the Philadelphia *Press.* There followed thirty-one years of prodigious activity, during which time he became managing editor and subsequently associate editor of the *Press.* His editorials were brilliant, and in art, literature, and drama his penetrating reviews brought him recognition as Philadelphia's leading critic. He studied finance, and for a number of years wrote a weekly review of business conditions. During this period also he twice collected anthropological material in Morocco for the Smithsonian Institution and the Archaeological Museum of the University of Pennsylvania. His wide interests led him to clip and save news items likely to be of value in his work. In 1880 he began clipping newspapers for items of political or personal interest. As the scope of journalistic interests widened he was soon clipping upon every subject. By 1900 hundreds of boxes were required to hold the accumulated masses of information which became the foundation for the "morgue" of the Columbia School of Journalism, containing more than 1,400,000 clippings.

In 1912 he left the *Press* to become the first director of the Columbia University School of Journalism, which Joseph Pulitzer [*q.v.*] had endowed. He brought to the task of organization the benefit of thirty-nine years of active newspaper life. What was more significant, however, he brought the background and the vision of one who all his life had been noted for a deep scholarliness rare at that time in the development of journalism as a profession. In planning a curriculum for the new school he combined cultural courses with practical training as he had combined them in his own life. The text for his classes in international affairs was the morning's

table copy, which his own experience as a political reporter enabled him to interpret. It is significant of his deep understanding that in 1912 and 1913, he was lecturing to his classes about the coming of the World War, its causes, its participants, and its probable outcome. He proved himself a prophet in more than politics, for in bringing to the school Dr. Edwin E. Slosson [*q.v.*] to teach a general course in science he foresaw and to a great extent originated the reporting of scientific news, which until that time had not been considered of popular interest. He was professor emeritus from 1919 until his death. Talcott Williams' greatest contribution to journalism was his ideal of a journalist as a man of learning, as a man who not only wrote well and accurately, but who understood the meaning of what he wrote.

He married Sophia Wells Royce of Albion, N. Y., on May 28, 1879. In addition to numerous reports, articles, and sections of books, he wrote *Turkey, A World Problem of Today* (1921) and *The Newspaper Man* (1922). He was a trustee of Amherst College (1909–19) and of Constantinople College for Women. He also served on the committee on Babylonian research of the University of Pennsylvania. He was associated with numerous learned societies and charitable organizations.

[See *Who's Who in America,* 1926–27; R. C. E. Brown, *Dr. Talcott Williams,* pamphlet containing address delivered at Columbia Univ., May 16, 1928; "Personalities," *Hampton Mag.,* May 1912; *Rev. of Revs.,* Apr. 1912, Mar. 1928; obituary notices in *N. Y. Times* and *World,* Jan. 25, 1928. A biog. of Williams is being prepared by Elizabeth Dunbar of New York City.]

C. W. A.

WILLIAMS, THOMAS SCOTT (June 26, 1777–Dec. 15, 1861), jurist, was born in Wethersfield, Conn. He was a nephew of William Williams, 1731–1811 [*q.v.*], signer of the Declaration of Independence, and a son of Ezekiel Williams who held many civil and military offices during the period of the American Revolution and was for years sheriff of Hartford County. Thomas' mother, Prudence Stoddard, was a daughter of Col. John Stoddard of Northampton, Mass., chief justice of the court of common pleas, a granddaughter of the Rev. Solomon Stoddard [*q.v.*], and a first cousin of Jonathan Edwards.

Williams was privately tutored by Azel Backus [*q.v.*], and graduated from Yale College in 1794. He studied law at the Litchfield Law School under Judge Tapping Reeve [*q.v.*], who is reported to have said that Williams was the best scholar ever sent from Litchfield. He continued his legal training in the office of Zephaniah Swift [*q.v.*] at Windham, Conn., was admitted to the bar in 1799, and commenced the practice of law at Mansfield, Conn. In 1803 he removed to Hartford, where he soon became prominent in his profession. He held many public offices: he was a representative in the Connecticut General Assembly in the sessions of 1813, 1815, 1816, during the last two years serving as clerk of the House; he was a member of Congress from 1817 to 1819; he was again a member of the Connecticut legislature in 1819, 1825, and from 1827 to 1829; and was mayor of Hartford from 1831 to 1835. In May 1829 he was appointed an associate justice of the supreme court of errors of the state and in 1834 chief justice, which office he held until May 1847 when, about to reach the age of retirement, he resigned.

His career was also distinguished because of his interest in public and charitable affairs. He served from 1840 until his death as president of the American Asylum for the Deaf and Dumb; for a few years he was vice-president of the Connecticut Retreat for the Insane; for a long time he was vice-president of the American Board of Commissioners for Foreign Missions; and from May 1848 until his death he was president of the American Tract Society. He became a member of the First Church of Hartford in 1834 and served as deacon from 1836 until his death, and as a teacher in its Sunday School from 1834 to 1861. He gave liberally to charity and to Yale College during his life and by will at his death. On Jan. 7, 1812, he married Delia, youngest daughter of Oliver Ellsworth [q.v.], Chief Justice of the United States. She died in 1840, and on Nov. 1, 1842, he married Martha Manwaring Coit, daughter of Elisha and Rebecca S. (Manwaring) Coit, who died in 1867. There were no children by either marriage.

Williams' judicial opinions appear in 7–18 *Connecticut Reports*. Outside of these his writings were few. They include a pamphlet, entitled *Chief Justice Williams on the Maine Law, Its Expediency and Constitutionality*, published in Hartford about 1851, being a report of a committee of which he was chairman on the subject of a law for the suppression of intemperance; an address entitled *The Tract Society and Slavery* (1859), defense of the conduct of the American Tract Society in refusing to distribute pamphlets opposed to slavery; and an address as president of the Tract Society at its anniversary in 1852. Both in practice and on the bench Williams was distinguished for his methodical habits, his common sense, his thorough study and mastery of his subject, and the eminent uprightness and purity of his character. A discriminating review of his career by John Hooker (29 *Connecti-*

cut Reports, 611), states that, while other jurists and lawyers may have been more distinguished for their store of legal learning, few have stood higher in professional opinion for the soundness and impartiality of their judgments.

[I. P. Langworthy, "Thomas Scott Williams," first pub. in the *Congregational Quart.*, Jan. 1863, and that same year reprinted as a pamphlet; *Memorial of Hon. Thomas Scott Williams* (n.d.); *Yale Univ.: Obit. Record*, 1859–70; J. H. Trumbull, *The Memorial Hist. of Hartford County, Conn.* (1886); F. B. Dexter, *Biog. Sketches Grads. Yale Coll.*, vol. V (1914); John Hooker, in 29 *Conn.*, 611–14; "Memoranda," in 18 *Conn.*, 254; *Biog. Dir. Am. Cong.* (1928); M. D. McLean, *The Ancestors and Descendants of Ezekiel Williams, 1608 to 1907* (1907); Charles and E. W. Stoddard, *Anthony Stoddard . . . and His Descendants* (1865); *Hartford Courant*, Dec. 16, 1861.]   C. E. C.

WILLIAMS, WILLIAM (Apr. 8, 1731–Aug. 2, 1811), signer of the Declaration of Independence, was born in Lebanon, Conn., the son of Solomon Williams, pastor of the First Congregational Church, and his wife, Mary, the daughter of Samuel Porter, of Hadley, Mass. He was the descendant of Robert Williams who emigrated to Roxbury, Mass., from Norfolk County, England, in 1637. After being graduated at Harvard College in 1751, William began the study of theology under his father's instruction. During the French and Indian War, in 1755, he took part in the operations at Lake George as a member of the staff of Ephraim Williams [q.v.], his father's cousin. At the conclusion of the campaign he returned to Lebanon and shortly thereafter set up in business. On Feb. 14, 1771, he married Mary, the daughter of Jonathan Trumbull, 1710–1785, and the sister of Jonathan Trumbull, 1740–1809 [qq.v.]. They had three children.

He threw himself ardently into the struggle for American independence, employing both his pen and his purse without stint in behalf of the cause (see his "Letter to 'A Landholder,'" *Essays on the Constitution*, 1892, ed. by P. L. Ford). He set forth the claims of the colonists in the press and helped to compose many of the Revolutionary state papers of Governor Trumbull. On his promissory note, in 1775, money was raised to defray the cost of sending Connecticut troops to aid in the capture of Ticonderoga. In 1779, when it was found impossible to purchase much needed supplies for the army owing to the depreciation of the Continental currency, he offered a quantity of specie in his possession, accepting in return paper money that was rapidly becoming worthless. He is said to have remarked that if independence were established he would get his pay; if not, the loss would be of no account to him. In the winter of 1780–81, when a French regiment was quartered at Lebanon, he moved out of his house in order to place it at the disposal of the officers. He was criticized for resigning his commission as colonel of the 12th Regiment at the outbreak of the war in order to accept an election to the Continental Congress, but his personal courage is attested by the fact that in 1781, when word was brought to Lebanon of Benedict Arnold's raid upon New London, he at once mounted his horse and rode twenty-three miles in three hours to offer his services as a volunteer.

He occupied many public offices, often for lengthy periods. He was for twenty-five years, 1760–85, a selectman of Lebanon, for forty-four years, 1752–96, town clerk, for twenty-one years, 1757–76, 1781–84, a member of the lower house of the state legislature, and for nineteen years, 1784–1803, a member of the governor's council. He was repeatedly elected clerk and also speaker of the house and appeared on committees to consider the Stamp Act, the claim of Connecticut to the Susquehanna lands, the case of the Mohegan Indians, and the adjustment of the boundary between Connecticut and Massachusetts. He was appointed to represent Connecticut at various conferences of delegates from the New England states, held to consider matters of common interest. He was a member of the Continental Congress, 1776–78, 1783–84, signing the Declaration of Independence and assisting in framing the Articles of Confederation. In 1777 he was elected to a seat on the board of war. He was a delegate to the convention that met at Hartford in 1788 to consider the adoption by Connecticut of the constitution of the United States, and he voted in favor of it, although objecting to the clause forbidding religious tests (see his "Letter to 'A Landholder,'" *Essays on the Constitution*, 1892, ed. by P. L. Ford). For twenty-nine years, 1776–1805, he was judge of the Windham County Court and for thirty-four years, 1775–1809, judge of probate for the Windham District. He died and was buried at Lebanon.

[Zebulon Ely, *A Ripe Stock Seasonably Gathered, A Discourse occasioned by the Death of the Honourable William Williams* (1812); John Sanderson, *Biog. of the Signers to the Declaration of Independence*, vol. IV (1823); J. W. Barber, *Conn. Hist. Colls.* (1836); G. H. Hollister, *The Hist. of Conn.* (2 vols., 1855); E. D. Larned, *Hist. of Windham County, Conn.* (2 vols., 1874); O. D. Hine, *Early Lebanon* (1880); C. J. Hoadly, *The Public Records of the Colony of Conn.*, vols. XI–XV (1880–90) and *The Public Records of the State of Conn.* (3 vols., 1894–1922); *Roll of State Officers* (1881); H. P. Johnston, *The Record of Conn. Men ... during the Revolution* (1889); *The Lebanon War Office* (1891), ed. by Jonathan Trumbull; *Letters of Members of the Continental Congress*, vols. I–IV (1921–28), ed. by E. C. Burnett; Harrison Williams, *The Life, Ancestors, and Descendants of Robert Williams of Roxbury*

(1934); dates of tenure of office from town and court records.]
           E. E. C.

WILLIAMS, WILLIAM (Oct. 12, 1787–June 10, 1850), printer and publisher, son of Thomas and Susanna (Dana) Williams, was born at Framingham, Mass. He was of the fifth generation in direct descent from Robert Williams, Puritan, who emigrated in 1637 from Norwich, England, to Roxbury, Mass. Here the family lived until 1782, when it moved to Framingham. In 1790 Thomas Williams and his family went from Framingham to New Hartford, near Utica, N. Y. William was an apprentice in the printing shops of William McLean and Asahel Seward in Utica from 1800 to July 1807, when he became partner in the printing firm of Seward & Williams. A man of enterprise, he began at once to make the paper used by his firm, learned wood-engraving—he was perhaps the third such artisan in the country—and in 1814 was taken into the Seward book store as partner. The first Utica directory, issued in 1817, is the first book bearing his name alone as printer. In 1820 he had the largest book store west of Albany. In every year from 1807 to 1838 there appeared with his imprint a half-dozen to twenty titles, chiefly almanacs, collections of music, and devotional, instructional, and anti-Masonic books. Many sold largely for years. At different times he owned or printed, and sometimes edited, various Utica newspapers, notably the *Patriot* and the *Patrol*. He was an ardent Federalist, and in the period from 1821 to 1824 he exerted every effort to have DeWitt Clinton [*q.v.*] elected governor of New York. His editorials on canals, railroads, and negro slavery were influential in central New York. In 1833, with too many irons in the fire, and through indorsing notes for others, he was in financial distress. In 1834 there were two sheriff's sales of his effects, following which his creditors ran the business under his name, retaining him as manager, until 1836; in 1840 all his Utica affairs were finally closed out by creditors. From 1836 to 1846 he lived at Tonawanda, N. Y. In 1841 a fall from the top of a coach progressively affected his mind beyond recovery, and during his last years completely separated him from society. He died in Utica. He was married on Nov. 5, 1811, to Sophia Wells, who died on Nov. 12, 1831, having borne him fourteen children. On Mar. 26, 1833, he was married to Catherine Huntington of Rome, N. Y. He was survived by his wife, one of her sons, and seven children of his first marriage. One of his sons was Samuel Wells Williams [*q.v.*], whose missionary service and notable reputation in China sweetened his father's later years. F. Wells Williams, George Huntington Williams, and Talcott Williams [*qq.v.*] were his grandsons.

Beginning with the War of 1812 Williams also had something of a military career. On Feb. 29, 1812, he was commissioned adjutant of militia by Gov. Daniel Tompkins, and became successively brigade major and colonel on the staff of Gen. Oliver Collins in 1813 during the Sacketts Harbor incident. He was active in raising a Utica company, and was at the front most of the time from February 1813 to July 1814. In 1816 he was commissioned brigade inspector of the 13th New York Infantry, but retained his colonelcy until 1820 or later. In 1832, with entire disregard of comfort and safety, he devoted himself to improving sanitary conditions in Utica during the cholera epidemic, and ministering to the sick and the dead, himself suffering an attack.

As a citizen, he was public-spirited beyond his means. His counsel, his best efforts, and his purse were ever at the service of any enterprise calculated to benefit Utica. He was especially identified with religious activities, and his life was an attractive illustration of his creed. He was one of that group of early New York State small-town printers that included Joel Munsell [*q.v.*] and Webster of Albany, the Phinneys of Cooperstown, Dodd at Salem, and Stoddard at Hudson. While still a village, and solely through the efforts of Williams, Utica was for thirty years an important publishing center, with a production in quality and amount creditable to a great city.

[The chief source is J. C. Williams, *An Oneida County Printer* (1906). See also G. H. Williams, "The Geneal. of Thomas Williams of New Hartford . . . N. Y.," *New Eng. Hist. and Geneal. Reg.*, Jan. 1880; Harrison Williams, *The Life, Ancestors and Descendants of Robert Williams of Roxbury* (1934); F. B. Hough, *Am. Biog. Notes* (1875); M. M. Bagg, *The Pioneers of Utica* (1877); obituary by Thurlow Weed, in *Albany Evening Jour.*, June 12, 1850.]   J. I. W.

WILLIAMS, WILLIAM R. (Oct. 14, 1804–Apr. 1, 1885), Baptist clergyman, author, was born in New York City. His father, Rev. John Williams, a Welsh preacher who came to the United States in 1795, was for twenty-seven years pastor of the Baptist Church in Fayette Street, New York (W. B. Sprague, *Annals of the American Pulpit*, vol. VI, 1860, pp. 358–62). His mother was Gainor Roberts. Williams had no middle name, the initial "R" being added for convenience. A shy, lame boy, he surpassed all his fellow pupils at Wheaton's School and was graduated at Columbia College in 1822 with the highest honors. He studied law and practised for five years with the Hon. Peter A. Jay [*q.v.*], who said of him: "There is not now in the City

of New York a lawyer of profounder talent than this young Williams" (Weston, *post*). Abandoning the law in 1830, he went abroad for study and while in London met Mary S. Bowen, whom he married in April 1847. In 1832 he became pastor of the newly formed Amity Street Baptist Church, which for thirty-five years stood on the street for which it was named and was then moved to Fifty-fourth Street, from which time it was known as Amity Church. Of this church Williams was pastor until his death.

While still a lawyer he first attracted public attention by an address which he delivered at the Hamilton Literary and Theological Institution (now Colgate University), *The Conservative Principles in Our Literature* (1844), which made a profound impression both at home and abroad. This address constitutes the initial essay in his *Miscellanies* (1850). His other books include *Religious Progress* (1850), *Lectures on the Lord's Prayer* (1851), *Lectures on Baptist History* (1877), *Eras and Character of History* (1882). He also published many pamphlets, sermons, and addresses.

He was a man of acute and accurate scholarship and extensive learning, possessing a private library of 25,000 volumes. Because of his quiet and retiring manner he was sometimes regarded as a recluse. He was fully abreast of the times, however, and in important crises exerted a strong influence. His voice was never strong nor his manner commanding; but his weighty thought expressed in glowing periods drew discriminating hearers and he was often rated as a peer of Robert Hall as a rhetorician. While his congregations were never large, they were made up of people of culture, representing various denominations. He was a leader in his own communion and exerted an influence that extended far beyond its borders. Under his presidency of the New York Baptist Union for Ministerial Education, 1850–51, Rochester Theological Seminary was founded. He was a trustee of Columbia College from 1838 to 1848, and was a member of the New York Historical Society, the American Tract Society, and the American Bible Society. He preached his last sermon on Mar. 22, 1885, and was the senior Baptist pastor of New York City at the time of his death. He was survived by his wife and their two sons.

[H. G. Weston, *An Address Delivered in the Madison Ave. Baptist Church, N. Y. City, at the Funeral of the Rev. William R. Williams, D.D., Apr. 4, 1885*; A. C. Kendrick, *The Works of Rev. W. R. Williams, D.D.; a Tribute and a Criticism*; J. L. Chamberlain, *Universities and Their Sons*, vol. IV (1900); J. A. Patton, *Lives of the Clergy of N. Y. and Brooklyn* (1874); William Cathcart, *The Baptist Encyc.* (1881); *N. Y. Observer*, Apr. 9, 1885; *Watchman*, Apr. 9, 1885; *National Bap-*

tist, Apr. 16, 1885; *Examiner*, Apr. 9, 1885; *N. Y. Tribune*, Apr. 2, 1885.]   F. T. P.

WILLIAMS, WILLIAM SHERLEY (d. March 1849), trapper, guide, better known as Bill or Old Bill Williams, was the son of Joseph and Sarah (Musick) Williams and was born probably in Kentucky. After some schooling, he became, according to his own story, an itinerant Methodist preacher in Missouri. In 1825–26 he was a member of Joseph C. Brown's surveying party which marked the greater part of the Santa Fé Trail. In the summer of 1826 he received a new Mexican passport permitting him to trap in the Gila country, and in the following year he visited the Moqui (Hopi) Indians, living among them for a time and explaining to them the Christian religion. In 1832 he was one of a small party of trappers on the Yellowstone, and later in that year he was with a party in northern Texas. In 1833–34 he was a member of the California expedition led by Joseph R. Walker [*q.v.*]. For some years thereafter he trapped the Utah-Colorado country, living at times among the Utes and learning their language. In 1841 he was back in Missouri, but in the following spring left with a party for the mountains. From Bent's Fort, in March 1843, with another party, he set out on a two-year journey which carried him to the Columbia, to the Great Basin, and ultimately to Santa Fé. In November 1848, again at Bent's Fort, he joined the fourth expedition of John Charles Frémont [*q.v.*] as guide. A few weeks later, after struggling through terrible snow-storms and reaching the Continental Divide at the head-waters of the Rio Grande, the expedition came to an end, and after losing eleven men from starvation and cold, the survivors reached Taos. Unjustly, as many think, Frémont blamed Williams for the disaster. A few weeks after the return Williams and another survivor retraced the route from the mountains in the hope of recovering some of the lost property. About the end of March—for the event became known by Apr. 6—both were killed, probably by the Utes.

Of the noted "mountain men" Williams was the most eccentric. He was six feet one in height, gaunt, stooped, red-haired and red-bearded, with a thin, leathery face deeply pitted with smallpox, and small, gray, restless eyes. His voice was shrill, his dress outlandish, his walk a zigzag wabble, and he rode with an indescribable awkwardness. In the settlements he drank inordinately and gambled recklessly, often squandering the proceeds of a season's hunt in a single spree. He spoke a quaint jargon, partly of his own making—a dialect which George F. Ruxton reproduced in his *Life in the Far West* (1849)

and which has become standardized by fiction writers as the normal speech of the trappers. For all his eccentricities, he was notably courageous, as well as shrewd and ingenious in matching wits with the savages, and he had an exceptional sense of the geography of every section he had visited. His name is perpetuated in Bill Williams Mountain, Bill Williams Fork of the Colorado River, and probably the town of Williams, all in Arizona, as well as Williams River, in Middle Park, Colo., and the nearby Williams River Mountains.

[C. L. Camp, "The Chronicles of George C. Yount," *Cal. Hist. Soc. Quart.*, Apr. 1923; J. J. Hill, "Free Trapper," *Touring Topics* (Los Angeles), Mar. 1930; W. T. Hamilton, *My Sixty Years on the Plains* (1905); Albert Pike, *Prose Sketches and Poems* (1834); D. C. Peters, *The Life and Adventures of Kit Carson* (1858); Ruxton, *ante*; Allan Nevins, *Frémont* (1928), II, 397–416; A. H. Favour, *Old Bill Williams, Mountain Man* (1936); C. P. Williams, *Lone Elk: The Life Story of Bill Williams, Trapper and Guide of the Far West* (2 parts, 1935–36).]   W. J. G.

WILLIAMSON, ANDREW (c. 1730–Mar. 21, 1786), "Arnold of Carolina," Revolutionary soldier, is said to have come to America from Scotland as a young child. Reputedly illiterate, but highly intelligent and a skilled woodsman, he probably began his career as a cow driver. On Sept. 22, 1760, he was commissioned lieutenant in the South Carolina regiment which served in James Grant's expedition against the Cherokee. By 1765 he was established as a planter, with several small holdings on Hard Labor Creek of the Savannah, and three years later, with Patrick Calhoun and others, he voiced the needs of the back country in a petition for courts, schools, ministers of the gospel, and public roads. In 1770 he was named to lay out and keep in repair a road to his plantation, "Whitehall," six miles west of Ninety Six. Here he lived with his wife, Eliza Tyler, of Virginia, by whom he had two sons and two daughters.

When the Revolution began, Williamson, a fine-looking major of militia, was so influential in the back country and so sound a Whig, that he was elected to the first provincial congress and was awarded a contract to supply the troops. Appointed to enforce the Association in his district, he was summoned with the militia to support W. H. Drayton against the Loyalists, and for the capture of Robert Cuningham he received the thanks of the provincial congress. Besieged by the Loyalists in Ninety Six, he signed the treaty with them on Nov. 21, 1775, but was in the "Snow Campaign" of December which continued the civil war. In 1776 he led the panic-stricken militia on his second Cherokee expedition, and when he was ambushed at Essenecca his horse was shot under him. Promoted to colonel, he commanded 2,000 South Carolina troops in the devastating campaign which subdued the Cherokee. He received the unanimous thanks of the Assembly and on May 20, 1777, signed the treaty which took from the Indians a large land cession. A popular officer, attentive to the comfort of his men, Williamson was promoted to brigadier-general in 1778 and commanded the South Carolina militia in Robert Howe's Florida expedition, sharing the blame for its failure. In 1779 he was with Lincoln before Savannah; but it was necessary to furlough his deserting militia when the British approached Charleston. He was accused of treason after the fall of that city, when, encamped with 300 men near Augusta, he reputedly concealed the news of Charleston's surrender for a time and avoided action. It is said that he was rewarded with a British commission for advising his officers to return home and take protection, but no documentary evidence of this allegation has been revealed, and his brother-in-law, Col. Samuel Hammond, one of the officers present, affirms that he vainly urged that the struggle be continued from North Carolina (Joseph Johnson, *post*, pp. 149 ff.). After his surrender, he remained at "Whitehall," where he was captured by the Americans in the hope that he might thereby consider himself released from parole. He escaped, however, and went into the British lines at Charleston. So strong was contemporary feeling against him, that when Col. Isaac Hayne captured him, it was supposed that he would be hung in Greene's camp, and his prompt rescue by the British confirmed that supposition. He is credited, however, with having later supplied the Whigs with valuable information through Col. John Laurens, and in 1783 General Greene intervened to save his estates from confiscation. Soon after the war he ended his days in the comfortable seclusion of his home in St. Paul's Parish, near Charleston, leaving a name for honesty and benevolence, and an estate, including ninety-odd slaves, valued at more than £2,600.

[Williamson's will and inventory are in the probate court, Charleston. John Drayton, *Memoirs of the Am. Revolution* (1821) and William Moultrie, *Memoirs of the Am. Revolution* (1802) contain documentary material on his Whig activities. R. W. Gibbes, *Documentary Hist. of the Am. Revolution . . . 1764–1776* (1855) and *1776–1782* (1857) contain many of his letters. See also Henry Lee, *Memoirs of the War in the Southern Department of the U. S.* (1812); Hugh M'Call, *The Hist. of Ga.*, vol. II (1816); William Johnson, *Sketches of the Life and Correspondence of Nathanael Greene* (1822); Lorenzo Sabine, *Biog. Sketches of Loyalists of the Am. Revolution* (1864); Joseph Johnson, *Traditions and Reminiscences* (1851); Andrew Pickens, manuscript letter to Henry Lee, Aug. 28, 1811, Wis. Hist. Soc.; A. S. Salley, *Col. William Hills' Memoirs of the Revolution* (1921); E. A. Jones, *The Jour. of*

Alexander Chesney (1921); Edward McCrady, *The Hist. of S. C. in the Revolution* (1901); *Royal Gazette* (Charleston), July 11, 1781; *Charleston Morning Post*, Mar. 22, 1786.]
                A.K.G.

WILLIAMSON, CHARLES (July 12, 1757– Sept. 4, 1808), British officer, land promoter, and secret agent, the second of three sons of Alexander and Christian (Robertson) Williamson, was born at Balgray, Dumfriesshire, Scotland (*Steuben Farmers' Advocate*, Bath, N. Y., Dec. 1, 1915; Hull, *post*, p. 97). Commissioned as ensign in the 25th Regiment of Foot, Mar. 8, 1775, he had become captain in 1781, when he resigned and as unattached officer started to join Cornwallis in America. He was captured on the high seas and taken prisoner to Boston. Shortly after his release he married Abigail Newell and before the end of 1782 had returned to Scotland with his wife and infant daughter. Early in 1784 he set out on a secret mission to Constantinople. This journey, apparently of a commercial nature, gave him some claim later to speak on Near East affairs.

In 1791 Williamson, as a land promoter in western New York, was appointed to hold in trust a tract of 1,200,000 acres, acquired from Robert Morris [*q.v.*]. His principals were three English speculators headed by Sir William Pulteney (Turner, *Phelps and Gorham's Purchase*, *post*, p. 244). His task was to open up the land to settlers, give titles, and promote local improvements; in order to carry it out he became a naturalized American citizen. As such he held various county offices and was four times (1796–1800) a member of the New York Assembly. To advertise his wilderness domain he issued pamphlets, promoted horse races, patronized a local theatre, and published a local newspaper. To further immigration he built a substantial hotel at Geneva, laid out turnpikes, built bridges, and provided post riders. These manifold activities, prompted both by restless energy and love of display, called for greater expenditures than his principals approved. In consequence he withdrew from his agency in 1802, but not before he, Aaron Burr, and other members of the New York Assembly had secured the passage of a law (Apr. 2, 1798) that permitted aliens for a limited period to give titles to lands within the state (Evans, "Holland Land Company," *post*, pp. 209–13).

Among other influential friends Williamson numbered Alexander Hamilton, who acted as one of his legal advisers (Osgood Papers, *post*). In 1794 he attracted national attention through a controversy with J. G. Simcoe, lieutenant-governor of Upper Canada (Melville Papers, *post*, and *American State Papers, Foreign Affairs*, vol. I, 1832, p. 484). During ten years of colonizing activity he had done much to develop western New York and had acquired a knowledge of American affairs that was to prove useful to him as volunteer adviser to successive British cabinet officers. His services as trustee for the Pulteney estate were rewarded by substantial land grants and £20,000 cash (Williamson Letters, *post*).

Williamson's first assignment after his return to England and to British allegiance in 1803, was to raise a special regiment for service in the West Indies or Spanish America. In this scheme he was only partially successful. He managed, however, to establish covert intimacy with William Armstrong, a later associate of Francisco Miranda, and to renew his friendship with Burr (Melville and Osgood papers). He was empowered to present the latter's Mexican project to the British ministry—a trust that he performed through Henry Dundas, Lord Melville. The impeachment of that nobleman and the military situation in Europe thwarted their joint plan and likewise kept Williamson from joining Miranda (Melville Papers). On revisiting the United States in 1806 he became convinced that Great Britain must pay more attention to transatlantic affairs and advised changing ministries during the next two years to overthrow the "Frenchified" Jeffersonian régime. His numerous memoranda on that subject show a distinct Tory bias, especially when he discussed commercial topics, but he confidently expected to attract British support among eastern merchants and hypothetical western separatists. Despite occasional doubts, he still regarded Burr as a dependable agent in carrying out this policy and was preparing to receive Burr in England when events in Spain called him into service elsewhere. In June 1808 Castlereagh selected him as a messenger to the Spanish West Indies (Williamson Papers, Castlereagh to Williamson, June 4, 1808; C. W. Vane, *Correspondence, Despatches and Other Papers of Viscount Castlereagh*, vol. VI, 1851, p. 369). While pursuing his combined mission of trade and good will he contracted yellow fever in Havana and died on his homeward voyage. He was the father of four children, two of whom, a son and a daughter, survived him. His wife died in Geneva, N. Y., in 1824.

[The chief sources of information concerning Williamson are the unpublished letters to and from him, which are in the Newberry Lib. of Chicago. These are in two general groups: those written by Williamson to his patron, Lord Melville, which were obtained from the Melville Papers, and the family letters, mostly to and from Charles Williamson, obtained from his great-grandson. These groups are supplemented by the Osgood Papers, typed copies of letters to and from Williamson. and other papers, owned by the Rochester Hist. Soc. Among the printed accounts the most important are Orsamus Turner, *Pioneer Hist. of the Holland Purchase* (1849) and *Hist. of the Pioneer Settlement of Phelps and Gorham's Purchase and Morris' Reserve* (1851); P. D. Evans, "The Holland Land Company," in *Buffalo Hist. Soc. Pubs.*, vol. XXVIII (1924), and "The Pulteney Purchase," in *N. Y. State Hist. Asso. Quart. Jour.*, Apr. 1922, pp. 83–104. A suggestive article on Williamson's activities in New York is A. C. Parker, "Charles Williamson, Builder of the Genesee Country," *Rochester Hist. Soc. Pub. Fund Ser.*, vol. VI (1927); one of Williamson's pamphlets is reprinted in E. B. O'Callaghan, *The Documentary Hist. of the State of N. Y.*, vol. II (1850). See also Nora Hull, *The Official Records of the Centennial Celebration, Bath, Steuben County* (1893).]   I.J.C.

WILLIAMSON, HUGH (Dec. 5, 1735–May 22, 1819), statesman and scientist, was born at West Nottingham, Pa. His father, John W. Williamson, was a native of Ireland, of Scotch descent, a clothier, who came to Chester County from Dublin about 1730. He married in 1731 Mary, the daughter of George Davison of Derry, Ireland. She had been brought to America as an infant and had been captured by the pirate Blackbeard. The Williamsons were industrious, thrifty, and religious. Hugh, the eldest of a large family, was designed for the ministry and was prepared for college at New London Cross Roads and at Newark, Del. He was a hard student with a particular bent for mathematics, and was in the first class to graduate from the College of Philadelphia (now the University of Pennsylvania), in 1757. He then spent two years in Shippensburgh settling his father's estate. Subsequently, he studied theology in Connecticut and, while never ordained, was licensed and preached for some time.

Becoming increasingly disgusted with the doctrinal controversies among the Presbyterians, he took up the study of medicine, and at the same time was made professor of mathematics at the College of Philadelphia. In 1764 he went abroad, and at Edinburgh, London, and Utrecht, continued his medical studies, receiving at the University of Utrecht the degree of M.D. Settling in Philadelphia, he began practice, but he was very frail and whenever he had a patient who was in serious danger he developed a fever. Accordingly he began to consider entering upon a business career. He never lost interest in the sciences, however, and to the study of mathematics he was particularly devoted. On Jan. 19, 1768, he was elected to the American Philosophical Society, and in 1769 appointed one of a commission to study the transits of Venus and Mercury. His observations of the comet of that year led him to an original theory regarding comets, which is stated in "An Essay on Comets" (*Transactions of the American Philosophical Society*, vol. I, 1771).

In 1773, after his return from a trip to the West Indies to obtain subscriptions for an academy at Newark, Del., he went to Europe on the same mission. He did not, however, confine his activities to the cause of education. While waiting for his ship to sail he was a witness of the Boston Tea Party, and he carried the first news of it to England. Summoned before the Privy Council for examination, he predicted revolt if the British colonial policy was continued. Just before he left England he obtained by a bold stratagem the Hutchinson-Oliver letters from Massachusetts, which he delivered to Franklin. With Franklin, Williamson established a close friendship, and collaborated with him in numerous experiments in electricity. One of Williamson's papers ("Experiments and Observations on the Gymnotus Electricus, or Electric Eel") was read before the Royal Society and published in its *Transactions* in 1775. He was the author, also, of a letter addressed to Lord Mansfield, called *The Plea of the Colonies,* which appeared anonymously in 1775, answering charges of sedition, turbulence, and disloyalty made against the American colonies and written in the hope of holding the friendship of the British Whigs. In Holland Williamson received news of the Declaration of Independence, and in December 1776 he sailed for home carrying dispatches. The ship was captured off the Delaware capes, but he escaped in a small boat.

He now began his mercantile career, going first to Charleston, S. C., but almost immediately moving to Edenton, N. C., where he eventually built up a large trade with the French West Indies and also resumed the practice of medicine. He offered his services as a physician to Governor Caswell and after a time was sent to New Bern to inoculate troops with smallpox. Soon thereafter he was made surgeon-general of the state troops. He was present at the battle of Camden and subsequently crossed repeatedly into the British lines to care for American prisoners, winning the confidence of the British who also made use of his services. From experience he became an eager advocate of inoculation as an absolutely necessary prerequisite for effective military service. While in camp in the Dismal Swamp he experimented to ascertain if attention to dress, diet, lodging, and drainage would reduce sickness. Only two men, out of a force ranging from five to twelve hundred in number, died in six months, an unheard of record for that day.

Williamson's political life began with his election from the borough of Edenton to the House of Commons in 1782. That same year he was also elected to the Continental Congress, where he served until 1785. He was again a member of the House of Commons, this time from Chowan County, in 1785. Once more elected to the Continental Congress in 1787, he remained a member until it went out of existence. In all his legislative service he was, in the words of Jefferson, "a very useful member, of an acute mind, attentive to business, and of an high degree of erudition" (quoted by Hosack, *post*). He was not an attractive speaker, but was a good debater, with flashes of wit and much force of expression. Williamson's experience in Congress made him favor a stronger form of government, and he accepted appointment to the Annapolis Convention in 1786, but reached there the day of adjournment. Soon afterwards he wrote "Letters of Sylvius" (*American Museum,* August 1787), published anonymously, to show the evils of paper money and to advocate an excise rather than a land or poll tax. He also advocated the promotion of domestic manufactures and the adoption of a national dress. The "Letters" contain an interesting account of commercial and economic conditions in the United States and some valuable information respecting North Carolina. They were also printed in pamphlet form, and appear in *Historical Papers Published by the Trinity College Historical Society* (11 ser., 1915).

Governor Caswell appointed Williamson to succeed Willie Jones [*q.v.*] in the delegation to the Federal Convention of 1787, and he was present during the entire session, much the most active of the North Carolina delegates. He changed his mind rather frequently, eliciting from the French Chargé the remark, "*Il est difficile de bien connoître son caractère; il est même possible qu'l n'en ait pas . . .*" (Farrand, *post*, p. 238). He favored a plural executive, and later, a seven-year term and reëligibility. He wanted legislative election of the executive. In securing the compromise on representation in the two houses, he played a considerable part. He voted for the Constitution, signed it, and worked for its ratification, publishing in a North Carolina newspaper "Remarks on the New Plan of Government" (see P. L. Ford, *Essays on the Constitution,* 1892). He was not a member of the Hillsboro convention of 1788 which refused ratification, but he was elected from Tyrrell County to the Fayetteville convention of 1789, and voted for the ratification ordinance. In 1788 he was elected agent to settle the accounts of the state with the federal government, and in 1789 he was elected to the First Congress and reëlected to the Second.

In January 1789 he married Maria, the daughter of Charles Ward Apthorpe, a wealthy merchant of New York. Upon the expiration of his term as congressman in 1793, he moved to New York, and devoted the rest of his life to literary and scientific pursuits. Among his published works of this period are "Of the Fascination of Serpents" (*Medical Repository*, February, March, April, 1807); "Conjectures Respecting the Native Climate of Pestilence" (*American Medical and Philosophical Register*, July 1810), signed "by an Observer"; "Remarks Upon the Incorrect Manner in Which Iron Rods are Sometimes Set Up for Defending Houses from Lightning" (*Ibid.*); "Observations on Navigable Canals" (*Ibid.*, October 1810); "Observations on the Means of Preserving the Commerce of New York" (*Ibid.*, January 1811); *Observations on the Climate in Different Parts of America* (1811); *The History of North Carolina* (2 vols., 1812); "Observations on the Malignant Pleurisy of the Southern States" (*American Medical and Philosophical Register*, April 1913). Williamson's theory of comets was original, but his work on climate, which showed keen observation and much research, brought him his greatest reputation, securing him membership in the Holland Society of Science, the Society of Arts and Sciences of Utrecht, and an honorary degree from the University of Leyden.

Williamson was one of the original trustees of the University of North Carolina and later a trustee of the College of Physicians and Surgeons, and of the University of the State of New York. He was a founder of the Literary and Philosophical Society of New York and a prominent member of the New York Historical Society. The last years of his life were saddened by the loss of his wife and his two sons. His own health failed slowly and steadily, but his death came suddenly while he was driving in his carriage. His ability is indicated in many varied lines of endeavor. He was an able physician, and as an army surgeon showed himself possessed of initiative, resourcefulness, and constructive ability. In mathematics, astronomy, and general science he took high rank among his contemporaries in America and abroad. He was successful in business and showed originality as an economist. He had advanced ideas on education and was himself a sound scholar. His legislative service, while never brilliant, won him deserved reputation. His historical work was poor. Personally he was pleasant and genial, and was widely popular. He was inclined to be intolerant of those whom he regarded as unsound in religion and on occasion he was a master of "a Johnsonian rudeness" in dealing with those he disliked.

[David Hosack, *A Biog. Memoir of Hugh Williamson* (1820), repr. in *Essays on Various Subjects of Medical Sci.* (1824), vol. I; *Hist. Papers Pub. by the Trinity Coll. Hist. Soc.*, 13 ser. (1919); G. J. McRee, *Life and Correspondence of James Iredell* (1857); Max Farrand, *The Records of the Federal Convention of 1787* (1911); *Biog. Dir. Am. Cong.* (1928); L. I. Trenholme, *The Ratification of the Federal Constitution in N. C.* (1932); *N. Y. Evening Post*, May 24, 1819.]
J. G. deR. H.

WILLIAMSON, ISAAC HALSTED (Sept. 27, 1767–July 10, 1844), governor and chancellor of New Jersey, lawyer, was born in Elizabethtown (later Elizabeth), N. J., which remained his home throughout his life. The youngest son of Gen. Matthias and Susannah (Halsted) Williamson, he was descended from a family which for several generations had been prominent in the town. After attending the common schools, he was admitted to the bar in 1791. He quickly built up a lucrative practice, showing such ability that Aaron Ogden [*q.v.*], the leader of the eastern New Jersey bar, said that he soon found Williamson "pressing on him very hard, and the one whose skill and learning he found the most troublesome as an adversary" (Elmer, *post*, p. 173). His reputation spread to other counties, and for some time he was prosecutor for Morris County, drawing up indictments which long served as models. A Federalist at first, he disagreed with that party about the War of 1812, and in 1815 was elected to the state Assembly on the Democratic ticket. In 1817, when Gov. Mahlon Dickerson [*q.v.*] was chosen United States senator, Williamson was elected by the eastern New Jersey votes in the legislature to succeed him in the dual office of governor and chancellor at $2,000 a year. He continued to be reëlected annually without opposition and served until 1829. The governorship was uneventful during those twelve years of the "era of good feeling."

Williamson's lasting reputation came through his reviving the neglected alternative office of chancellor. New Jersey has followed the old English court system more closely than most of the other states, and until 1844 the governors handled equity and "prerogative" cases as "chancellor and ordinary," though most of them before Williamson had slighted this office. The legislature in 1799 had authorized the chancellor to make, alter, and amend rules of practice "so as to obviate doubts, advance justice, and expedite suits in that court" (Halsted, *post*, p. 10). The first to attempt this seriously, Williamson made an exhaustive study of the English court of chancery and in 1822 drew up a set of fifty-eight rules which at the time of his death had been little altered. The new code was particularly important in its clarification of the situation of mortgages. Enthusiastic about the subject and tireless in research, Williamson presided conscientiously and ably over the court for twelve years, his lack of facility in speech and writing offset by his practical good sense, profundity, and probity. He increased the dignity as well as the effectiveness of the chancery court and laid the foundations for the unique position which it still holds in New Jersey. He was probably instrumental in separating the offices of governor and chancellor in 1844 so that the court would not be dependent upon the fortunes of frequent elections. He also aided the repeal of the statute forbidding the citing of an English precedent made after 1776 in a New Jersey court of law or equity.

His long term as governor-chancellor ended in 1829 when the Jackson element secured the election of G. D. Wall, who yielded to Peter Dumont Vroom [q.v.]. Williamson is said to have declined the opportunity to succeed Charles Ewing [q.v.] as chief justice of the state in 1832. He sat in the state Council, or Senate (1831–32), and was mayor of Elizabeth (1830–33) but thereafter devoted himself to his practice without holding office until the last few weeks of his life, when he was chairman of the state constitutional convention. He seems to have combined successfully geniality with dignity in office. He was married on Aug. 6, 1808, to Anne Crossdale Jouet. They had two sons, of whom one, Benjamin, was graduated from the College of New Jersey (later Princeton) in 1827 and also served as chancellor. Williamson died at his home in Elizabeth.

[See L. Q. C. Elmer, *The Constitution and Government of . . . N. J.* (1872); O. S. Halsted, *Address upon the Character of the Late Hon. Isaac H. Williamson* (1844); John Whitehead, *The Judicial and Civil Hist. of N. J.* (1897); S. G. Potts, *Precedents and Notes of Practice in the Court of Chancery of N. J.* (1841); F. B. Lee, *N. J. as a Colony and as a State* (1902), vol. III, p. 377 and *passim*, with portrait; W. H. Shaw, *Hist. of Essex and Hudson Counties, N. J.* (1884), vol. I, p. 251, vol. II, p. 1057; William Nelson, *Nelson's Biog. Cyc. of N. J.* (1913), vol. I, p. 14; and obituary in *Newark Daily Advertiser*, July 10, 1844. Chancery cases were not reported until 1830. The date of Williamson's birth is sometimes given as 1768.]

R. G. A.

WILLIAMSON, WILLIAM DURKEE (July 31, 1779–May 27, 1846), historian, governor of Maine, was born in Canterbury, Conn., the eldest son of George and Mary (Foster) Williamson, and a descendant of Timothy Williamson who was in Plymouth Colony as early as 1643. His early education was in the common schools of Canterbury and of Amherst, Mass.,

to which the family moved in 1793. He taught for some time in a private school in Pittstown, N. Y., and then in a public school in Amherst, while continuing his studies privately and at Deerfield Academy. In October 1800 he entered Williams College, meanwhile teaching school during the winters. Resenting what he considered a Federalist partisanship that excluded him, a Democrat, from taking part in a Junior exhibition, he transferred in 1804 to Brown, where he graduated in September of the same year. He then took up the study of law in the office of S. F. Dickinson of Amherst, continuing it with Samuel Thatcher of Warren, Me., and Joseph McGaw of Bangor. In the latter place he began the practice of law in 1807. In January 1808 he was commissioned attorney-general for Hancock County. He lost the office in 1809, but, since he was the most active Democratic lawyer in the county, the governor reappointed him in 1811. He occupied the position until 1816, when he was elected to the Massachusetts Senate. For three years he was chairman of the committee on eastern lands. From 1809 to 1820 he was postmaster at Bangor. When the separation of Maine from Massachusetts, of which he was an ardent advocate, took place in 1820, he became the first senator from Penobscot County to the state Senate, and succeeded John Chandler [q.v.] as president of that body when the latter was elected to the national Senate. After Gov. William King [q.v.] resigned, Williamson was acting governor from May 28 to Dec. 5, 1821, when he resigned to take the seat in Congress to which he had been elected the preceding September. He served from Mar. 4, 1821, to Mar. 3, 1823. He was not reëlected. Gov. Albion K. Parris [q.v.] appointed him judge of probate for Penobscot County in 1824. He occupied this position until 1840, when, by an amendment to the state constitution which limited the tenure of judicial offices, he was compelled to retire. In 1834 and 1839 he was commissioner to examine the banks of Maine. In 1840 he was chairman of a commission of the Maine State Prison. He was also president of the Peoples' Bank of Bangor. He was married three times: first, on June 10, 1806, to Jemima Montague Rice of Amherst (d. 1822); second, on June 3, 1823, to Susan Ester White of Putney, Vt. (d. 1824); and third, on Jan. 27, 1825, to Clarissa (Emerson) Wiggin of York (d. 1881). There were five children by the first marriage. Williamson died in Bangor.

The great labor of his life, for which he began gathering materials in 1817, was his *History of the State of Maine,* published in two volumes in 1832 and reissued in 1839. Heavy in style and in need of thorough revision in the light of much material not available to the author, the volumes yet remain an indispensable work in Maine history. Williamson continued to collect materials on history and biography until his death, but, except for a few contributions to the *American Quarterly Register,* 1840–43, and to the *Collections of the Massachusetts Historical Society* (3 ser., vol. IX, 1846), he published little. Some of his manuscripts have been published in the *Bangor Historical Magazine* (July 1885–June 1887, *passim*). All his writings are distinguished for his industry in accumulating facts rather than for style of presentation.

[See Grace W. Edes, in *New Eng. Hist. and Geneal. Reg.,* Jan. 1927–Oct. 1928, esp. Oct. 1927, p. 396; William Cranch, *Ibid.,* Jan. 1847, pp. 90–91; "Extracts from the Diary of the Late Hon. William D. Williamson," *Ibid.,* Apr., Oct. 1876; Joseph Williamson, in *Memorial Biogs. of the New Eng. Hist. Geneal. Soc.,* vol. I (1880); *Me. Hist. and Geneal. Recorder,* vol. V (1888), pp. 73–80; "Hon. William D. Williamson," *Bangor Hist. Mag.,* Feb. 1886; Joseph Williamson, *Ibid.,* May 1868, and article on Williamson MSS. in *Colls. and Proc. Me. Hist. Soc.,* 2 ser., vol. III (1892), pp. 275–79; William Willis, *A Hist. of the Law, the Courts, and the Lawyers of Me.* (1863); death notice in *Kennebec Jour.* (Augusta, Me.), June 5, 1846.]
R. E. M.

WILLIE, ASA HOXIE (Oct. 11, 1829–Mar. 16, 1899), jurist, was born in Washington, Wilkes County, Ga. His father was James Willie, a merchant and farmer of influence, a native of Vermont. His mother, Caroline Emily, daughter of Asa Hoxie, a Quaker, was born in Barnstable County, Mass., but removed to Savannah early in the nineteenth century. Willie was left fatherless at the age of four, his training devolving upon his mother, a woman of culture and determination of character. He attended an academy at Washington, Ga., and later another at Powelton, Ga. In 1846, in company with his older brother, James Willie, he moved to Texas and took up residence with his maternal uncle, Dr. Asa Hoxie, at Independence. A year or so later he began studying law with his brother at Brenham, and in 1849 was admitted to the bar, before he had attained the age of twenty-one, by a special act of the legislature. He began the practice of the law at Brenham in partnership with his brother. In 1852 he was appointed to fill a vacancy in the district attorney's office, and was later elected to that office for a two-year term. In 1857 he removed to Austin to assist his brother in his duties as attorney general, while the latter devoted his energies to indexing and superintending the printing of the criminal and penal codes of the state, which he had compiled and the legislature had adopted in July 1856. A year later Asa removed to Marshall, Tex., and became a partner of his brother-in-law, Col.

Alexander Pope, a partnership that continued, except for the period covered by the Civil War, until 1866. In the latter year he removed to Galveston, where, for the most part, he resided until his death thirty-three years later.

With the outbreak of the Civil War he offered his services to the Confederacy and was placed on the staff of Gen. John Gregg. After the latter's death he saw service under Generals Pemberton, Johnson, Bragg, and Hardee, taking part, among others, in the battles of Chickamauga and Missionary Ridge. During the last year of the war he had charge of the exportation of cotton from San Antonio. Upon the reorganization of the state government in 1866, he was elected to the supreme court for a term of nine years, but fifteen months later he was removed, along with Gov. J. W. Throckmorton and all other members of the state government, by Gen. Charles Griffin, military commander of Texas. In 1872 he was elected congressman-at-large from Texas (Mar. 4, 1873–Mar. 3, 1875), but refused to stand for reëlection. He served as city attorney of Galveston in 1875–76. In 1882 he was elected chief justice of the supreme court of Texas by a very large vote. This position he resigned in 1888 to return to the practice of his profession in Galveston, where he died. He was a conspicuous figure in the history of the jurisprudence of Texas. His opinions, carefully prepared and happily expressed, are to be found in *Texas Reports* (vols. XXVIII–XXX, LVIII–LXX). On Oct. 20, 1859, he was married in Marshall to Bettie Johnson, youngest daughter of Lyttleton and Mary C. Johnson, of Bolivar, Tenn. They had ten children, of whom three sons and two daughters survived their father.

["Proc. Touching the Death . . . of Hon. Asa H. Willie," 92 *Tex. Reports,* xiii; J. D. Lynch, *The Bench and Bar of Tex.* (1885); J. H. Davenport, *The Hist. of the Supreme Court . . . of Tex.* (copyright 1917); *Biog. Encyc. of Tex.* (1880); W. S. Speer, *The Encyc. of the New West* (1881); *Galveston Daily News,* Mar. 16, 17, 1899.]
C. S. P.

WILLING, THOMAS (Dec. 19, 1731, o.s.–Jan. 19, 1821), banker, was born at Philadelphia, the eldest of eleven children of Charles and Anne (Shippen) Willing. His father was a prosperous merchant of English birth who in twenty-six years of business activity in Philadelphia accumulated a fortune of some £20,000 on an initial capital of £1,000. His mother was the granddaughter of Edward Shippen, 1639–1712 [*q.v.*]. In 1740 "Tommy" was sent to England, where, under the supervision of his paternal grandparents, he was educated at schools in Bath and Wells, Somersetshire. In September 1748 he went to London, where he studied for six months at Watt's Academy and also entered the Inner Temple to read law on Oct. 5, 1748. Returning to Philadelphia on May 19, 1749, he entered his father's counting-house and was taken into partnership in 1751. Upon the untimely death of his father in 1754, during a yellow fever epidemic to which he was particularly exposed by his active exertions as mayor of the city, the son assumed control of the business with an inheritance of about £6,000. With Robert Morris [q.v.] he formed the partnership of Willing, Morris & Company, eventually perhaps the leading mercantile firm in Philadelphia.

Willing's diligent application to business did not preclude his engaging in public activities. In 1754 he served as assistant secretary to the Pennsylvania delegation at the Albany Congress; in 1757 he was elected to the common council of Philadelphia; in 1758 he was appointed one of the Pennsylvania commissioners for trade with the western Indians, serving for about seven years; in 1760 he was elected a trustee of the Academy and Charitable School of the Province of Pennsylvania, now the University of Pennsylvania, and served until 1791; he was one of seven commissioners appointed to supervise the surveying of the Pennsylvania-Maryland boundary line; in 1761 he was appointed judge of the orphans' court of Philadelphia; in 1763 he was elected mayor of Philadelphia; a year later he was elected to the provincial Assembly and served until 1767, when he resigned to accept appointment as justice of the supreme court of the province. In 1765 he signed the Philadelphia non-importation agreement directed against the Stamp Act. During the years 1774–76 he firmly championed colonial rights, but he stoutly resisted the "radical" elements that were working for an internal revolution within Pennsylvania as well as a complete break with the mother country. He served as president of the first Provincial Congress of Pennsylvania in 1774, kept in intimate touch with the members of the First Continental Congress, and in 1775 was elected to the Second Continental Congress. He voted against the resolution of Richard Henry Lee [q.v.] for independence in July 1776, "not only because I thought America at that time unequal to such a Conflict . . . but chiefly because the Delegates of Pennsylvania were not then authorized by their instructions from the Assembly or the voice of the People at large, to join in such a vote" (Autobiography, post, p. 126). His English legal training, his extensive mercantile interests, his religious affiliation with the Anglican Church, and his long association with the Penns probably help to explain his stand. When

a new Pennsylvania delegation to Congress was chosen in 1776, he was not reappointed; and in 1777 he ceased to be justice of the supreme court.

Throughout the War for Independence he remained in Philadelphia, but during the British occupation he declined to take the oath of allegiance to the King. He worked unceasingly to maintain the financial standing of his firm in its successive forms of Willing, Morris & Co.; Willing, Morris & Inglis; and Willing, Morris & Swanwick. The credit and prestige of this firm was perhaps the most solid support of Robert Morris in his patriotic financial activities during the war. In 1781 Willing was chosen president of the newly organized Bank of North America. His judgment and diligence were in no small degree responsible for the success of the institution, especially during the economic depression of 1785–86 and the contemporaneous "bank war." He was a cordial supporter of the movement for the new constitution of 1787 and likewise of the fiscal measures of Alexander Hamilton. His daughter, Anne Willing Bingham [q.v.], became the acknowledged leader of Federalist society at Philadelphia. He was appointed by President Washington as one of the commissioners to receive subscriptions to the first Bank of the United States, and he served as its president from 1791 to 1797. Although the board of directors, over which he presided, had final authority over the bank's policy, Willing personally exercised a very solid influence. All during these years he continued in private business, steadily augmenting his fortune until it aggregated about one million dollars. After having enjoyed unusually good health throughout his earlier life, he was suddenly rendered inarticulate by a paralytic stroke on Aug. 10, 1807 (Robert Blackwell to George Willing, Aug. 10, 1807, Wallace Papers, vol. IV, p. 165, Historical Society of Pennsylvania). He resigned the presidency of the Bank on Nov. 10, 1807 (Poulson's American Daily Advertiser, Philadelphia, Nov. 11, 12 and 16, 1807). He subsequently recovered his health but never returned to active banking. He died at his home in Philadelphia.

On June 9, 1763, he married Anne McCall, the eldest daughter of Samuel McCall. They had thirteen children. Willing did not remarry after his wife's death on Feb. 5, 1781. In the course of time he became a veritable patriarch of a numerous and influential family clan in Philadelphia. In his Autobiography (post, p. 128), dated Feb. 4, 1786, he quite correctly says: "My success in life has not been derived from superior abilities, or extensive knowledge, a very small and scanty share of either having fallen to my lot; therefore it can only be ascribed to a steady application to whatever I have undertaken, a civil and respectful deportment to all my fellow Citizens, and an honest and upright conduct in every transaction of life."

[T. W. Balch, *Willing Letters and Papers ed. with a Biog. Sketch of Thomas Willing* (1922), with brief autobiog., will, and scattered letters, and brief biog. *Pa. Mag. of Hist. and Biog.*, Jan. 1922; Letter Book of Charles Willing & Son, June 15–Nov. 30, 1754— Thomas Willing, Nov. 30, 1754–May 1, 1757, Willing & Morris, May 1, 1757–Feb. 6, 1761, and incomplete rough drafts of minutes of board of directors, Bank of the U. S., 1795 and 1800, Hist. Soc. of Pa.; letters in Hamilton Papers, Lib. of Cong.; Oliver Wolcott Papers, Conn. Hist. Soc.; and Gratz Collection, Hist. Soc. of Pa.; Lawrence Lewis, *A Hist. of the Bank of North America* (1882); J. T. Holdsworth, *The First Bank of the U. S.* (1910); C. H. Lincoln, *The Revolutionary Movement in Pa.* (1901); E. A. Jones, *Am. Members of the Inns of Court* (1924).]   J.O.W.

WILLINGHAM, ROBERT JOSIAH (May 15, 1854–Dec. 20, 1914), Baptist clergyman, missionary secretary, born in Beaufort District, S. C., was a descendant of Pierre Robert, the first pastor of the Huguenot Church, Santee, S. C., who emigrated to America after the Revocation of the Edict of Nantes. His paternal great-grandfather, Thomas Henry Willingham, settled upon Sullivan's Island, near Charleston, in 1790, where his son, Thomas Willingham, was born Dec. 23, 1798. The latter became a prosperous merchant and for fifty years was a Baptist deacon. One of his sons, Benjamin Lawton Willingham, moved from the Beaufort District to Macon, Ga., where he amassed a considerable fortune as a cotton factor; his wife was Elizabeth Martha (Baynard). They were the parents of eighteen children, thirteen of whom reached maturity and reared families.

The best known of these was Robert Josiah. Converted when he was thirteen years old, he united with the Concord Baptist Church. He entered the University of Georgia at the early age of fourteen and in 1873 was graduated with high honors. From 1874 to 1877 he was the principal of the high school of Macon, Ga. During this period, he read law, preparatory to taking the bar examination. On Sept. 8, 1874, he married Corneille Bacon. Abandoning his intention of entering the law, he enrolled in the Southern Baptist Theological Seminary and remained there as a student from 1877 to 1879. He was ordained in Macon, Ga., June 2, 1878, and served as pastor of the Baptist Church, Talbottom, Ga., and of two other nearby country churches from 1879 to 1881. During the succeeding five years he was pastor of the Baptist Church at Barnesville, Ga. Accepting the pastorate of the First Baptist Church, Chattanooga, Tenn., in 1887, he led in the erection of a new edifice. In 1891 he

was chosen pastor of the First Baptist Church, Memphis.

Two years later, he accepted the invitation of the Foreign Mission Board of the Southern Baptist Convention to become its secretary. When he took charge, the board not only was without funds but was burdened with a heavy debt. The whole country was suffering from a severe financial depression. So impassioned were his appeals, so arduous were his labors, and so widespread were his activities, however, that within the twenty-one years he served as secretary the annual contributions increased fivefold; the missionaries employed, over threefold; and the number of baptisms reported annually, over twelvefold; while the schools, colleges, and seminaries under the control of the board increased from sixteen to 266. He visited Mexico in 1895 and made a trip around the world in 1907, studying the mission work in Japan, China, Burma, India, and Italy. Upon his return to America, he interpreted foreign missions in a broader way but with no less enthusiasm. One-third of his time was spent traveling over the widely extended territory of the Southern Baptist Convention and under the strain of his unceasing labors his health failed. At his death he was buried in Hollywood, Richmond, Va.

[E. W. Willingham, *Life of Robert Josiah Willingham* (1917); *The Religious Herald*, Dec. 24, 1914; *Who's Who in America*, 1914–15; *Annual of the Southern Baptist Convention*, 1915; *Foreign Mission Jour.*, 1893–1914; *Richmond Times-Dispatch*, Dec. 21, 1914.]
                                                R. W. W—r.

WILLIS, ALBERT SHELBY (Jan. 22, 1843– Jan. 6, 1897), congressman, diplomat, was born in Shelbyville, Shelby County, Ky., a son of Dr. Shelby Willis and Harriet (Button) Willis. At the age of seven he removed to Louisville with his widowed mother, and he made his residence in that city during the remainder of his life. He attended the common schools and graduated from the Male High School in 1860, then taught for two years, studied law, and graduated from Louisville Law School at the age of twenty, too young to be admitted to the bar. After another year of teaching he entered law practice in partnership with his stepfather, J. L. Clemmons, a prominent lawyer of Louisville. In 1872 he was presidential elector (Democratic) from the Louisville district and in 1874 was elected county attorney of Jefferson County, which office he held until 1877. In 1876 he was elected to Congress. He served five terms in the House of Representatives (1877–87), making an excellent though not a distinguished record. During the last two terms he was chairman of the committee on rivers and harbors.

After retiring from Congress, Willis engaged in the practice of law until September 1893, when President Cleveland appointed him envoy extraordinary and minister plenipotentiary to Hawaii. It was a strange and difficult mission to which he was called. In the islands a Provisional Government was in power, following the revolution of January 1893. President Cleveland, on coming into office in March of that year, had withdrawn from the Senate the annexation treaty negotiated by the Harrison administration and had sent J. H. Blount [q.v.] to Hawaii to make an investigation. On the basis of Blount's report, Cleveland adopted the policy of attempting to restore in the islands the status existing before the outbreak of the revolution. Willis was the instrument selected to put this policy into effect. Though he was accredited in the usual diplomatic form to the Provisional Government, it was his business to induce that government to terminate its own existence and submit to the authority of the deposed Queen, from whom a pledge was to be required that she would grant full amnesty to the revolutionists.

Willis arrived in Honolulu Nov. 4, 1893; it was nearly three weeks later before the Hawaiian government received, not from him but through reports from Washington, the first definite indication of the nature of Cleveland's policy. Willis meantime suppressed whatever doubts he may have had as to the wisdom of the policy—there is reason to believe he had some doubts—and went cautiously about his business. With some difficulty the Queen was induced to agree to grant a complete amnesty if President Cleveland succeeded in getting her back on the throne, but the Provisional Government, through its foreign minister, Sanford B. Dole [q.v.], emphatically declined to acquiesce when the restoration plan was presented to it by Willis, and the whole project fell to the ground. The Cleveland policy and its carrying out was a quixotic enterprise and its only important practical result in Hawaii was further to embitter the situation. Willis performed his disagreeable task with perhaps as much tact and consideration as was possible under the circumstances. He continued in office as minister three years longer, until his death, and despite a number of irritating incidents won the respect and friendly regard of all elements in the community. His death in Honolulu was the result of a prolonged illness and shock due to an accident. Willis was married Nov. 20, 1878, to Florence Dulaney of Louisville, and was survived by his wife and one son. He was one of the founders and for some years president of the Sun Life Insurance Company.

[Papers Relating to the Foreign Relations of the U. S., 1894 (App. II), 1895, 1896, 1897; manuscript records of the Provisional Government in Archives of Hawaii; letter by Willis printed in Robert McElroy, Grover Cleveland (1923), II, 63–64; Biog. Dir. Am. Cong. (1928); J. J. McAfee, Ky. Politicians (1886); N. Y. Herald, Sept. 9, 1893; Courier-Journal (Louisville, Ky.), Jan. 16, 1897; Hawaiian Star and Evening Bulletin (both of Honolulu), Jan. 6, 1897; Pacific Commercial Advertiser (Honolulu), Jan. 7, 9, 1897.]
R. S. K—l.

WILLIS, NATHANIEL (June 6, 1780–May 26, 1870), editor, journalist, was born in Boston, Mass., the son of Nathaniel and Lucy (Douglas) Willis, and the sixth in descent from George Willis who emigrated from England to America about 1630. He eventually became well known in Boston as Deacon Willis, the title serving to distinguish him from his more famous son and namesake, and from his father, both of whom were also journalists. His father, Nathaniel Willis (Feb. 7, 1755–Apr. 1, 1831), was part owner of the militant Independent Chronicle of Boston, and served during the Revolution as adjutant of a regiment under the command of Gen. John Sullivan. In 1784 he sold his interest in the Chronicle and pioneered westward, establishing newspapers in Virginia at Winchester, Shepardstown, and Martinsburg. Finally, following closely William Maxwell [q.v.], the earlier publisher in the Northwestern Territory, he founded in Chillicothe, Ohio, the Sciota Gazette.

The son had been left in Boston when his father moved to Virginia, but at the age of seven he was sent for and put to work in the shop at Winchester. He continued in his father's service until he was sixteen, when he returned to Boston to complete his apprenticeship. After serving two additional years as a journeyman, he married and moved to Portland, Me., to enter political journalism. In September 1803 he established there the Eastern Argus in opposition to the Federal party, but his experience was unfortunate. Among other reverses he lost the decision in a suit against him for libel. Unable to pay the judgment, he suffered a prison sentence of ninety days. In 1807, however, under the influence of the Rev. Edward Payson [q.v.] of Portland, he began his lifelong devotion to the letter of the Christian law. After his conversion so many religious expressions continued to appear in the Argus that its political supporters forced him to sell it (1809). He opened a grocery store, but he scrupled at selling rum, and the business failed. In the meantime, a plan came to him for joining his skill as a practical journalist with his increasing interest in religion. He removed to Boston (1812) and after several years of effort began the publication on Jan. 3, 1816, of the Recorder (later the Boston Recorder), which he asserted to be the first religious newspaper in the world. Anent an old controversy as to whether he or Sidney E. Morse [q.v.] founded the *Recorder,* it may be said that only Willis' name, given as the publisher, appears in the first issue. Morse certainly acted as the first editor, but withdrew on Apr. 1, 1817. With the help of subsequent editors Willis was associated with the paper for twenty-eight years. He became identified with the Park Street Church as Deacon Willis, and was known during his long life for his rigid and formal piety. An impression of his formalism, however, should be tempered by a remembrance of his ultimate and finest contribution to journalism, the *Youth's Companion.* Originated in the *Recorder* as a department for children, the feature was produced in separate covers in June 1827, and afforded wholesome, albeit intensely didactic literary adventures for several generations of young people.

Hannah Parker of Holliston, Mass., had become Willis' wife on July 21, 1803. In addition to their eldest son, Nathaniel Parker Willis [q.v.], three others of the nine children showed the influence of their father's profession. It was to their mother, however, that Nathaniel Parker Willis ascribed his "quicksilver spirit." Her personal attractiveness touched by the restraint of her husband's piety, she devoted her life to a Christian training for her children, but to more than one of them she imparted a comeliness and a worldly charm absent in Deacon Willis and his progenitors. Sarah Payson Willis, writing under the pseudonym "Fanny Fern," created a widely popular series of stories for children. Julia Dean Willis wrote many of the unsigned book reviews in the *Home Journal* (New York). Richard Storrs Willis became the editor of *Musical World,* and composed both music and poetry. After the death of his wife (Mar. 21, 1844), Willis married Mrs. Susan (Capen) Douglas. He continued to edit the *Youth's Companion* until 1857, when he sold it to J. W. Olmstead and Daniel Sharp Ford [q.v.], who retained his name as senior editor.

[Nathaniel Willis, "Autobiog. of a Journalist," in Frederic Hudson, *Journalism in the U. S. from 1690 to 1872* (1873); *The Willis Geneal.* (1863), ed. by Abner Morse; F. L. Mott, *A Hist. of Am. Mags., 1741–1850* (1930); H. A. Beers, *Nathaniel Parker Willis* (1885); death notice and editorial in *Boston Transcript,* May 27, 1870.]   K. L. D.

WILLIS, NATHANIEL PARKER (Jan. 20, 1806–Jan. 20, 1867), journalist, poet, editor, dramatist, was born in Portland, Me., the second child of Nathaniel and Hannah (Parker) Willis. Six years later his father, Nathaniel Willis, 1780–1870 [q.v.], removed with his family to

Boston. Young Willis attended the Boston Latin School and prepared for Yale at Andover. In his seventeenth year his first verses appeared in his father's *Boston Recorder,* and while still an undergraduate at Yale, signing usually "Roy" or "Cassius," he became nationally known as a poet. His verse paraphrases of Biblical themes were widely admired in the magazines, and a collection of them chiefly make up *Sketches* (1827), published in the year of his graduation. After earning his degree Willis turned in earnest to journalism. For Samuel G. Goodrich [q.v.] he edited two issues of *The Legendary* (1828) and an annual, *The Token* (1829). Striking out for himself in his twenty-third year, he established in Boston (April 1829) the *American Monthly Magazine.* The venture existed for two and a half years in spite of contrary prophecies from established rivals. Willis soon struck a stylistic pose which greatly offended his sober-minded critics. He pretended to write at a rosewood desk in a crimson-curtained sanctum; he invented a French valet, wrote of his ever-fresh japonica, and invited his readers to imagine themselves on a *dormeuse* with a bottle of Rudesheimer and a plate of olives before them. There is suggestive evidence that Poe's early burlesque, "The Duc de l'Omelette," is aimed good-naturedly at the audacious young editor, but most of his critics were unamused in denouncing his literary and personal affectations. Goodrich alleged that some of these attacks were "dictated by envy, for we have had no other example of literary success so early, so general, and so flattering" (*Recollections of a Lifetime,* 1856, II, 266).

Quitting his magazine and Boston for New York, Willis formed an association with George Pope Morris [q.v.], who was editing the *New-York Mirror.* A plan was soon conceived to send Willis abroad as a foreign correspondent. Five hundred dollars were found for his first expenses, and Morris promised ten dollars for each weekly letter written for the *Mirror.* The twenty-five-year-old Willis of this time was later recalled by Oliver Wendell Holmes [q.v.] as "young . . . and already famous . . . He was tall; his hair, of light brown color, waved in luxuriant abundance . . . He was something between a remembrance of Count D'Orsay and an anticipation of Oscar Wilde" (*The Writings of Oliver Wendell Holmes,* VII, 1891, p. 4, Riverside ed.). Willis had, indeed, increased his fame by publishing two more books, *Fugitive Poetry* (1829) and *Poem Delivered before the Society of United Brothers* (1831), but even though he was conscious of his handsome appearance, his elegant taste in dress, and his ability for meeting and pleasing people of importance, he could scarcely have dreamed of the dazzling adventures which lay before him. The speculative trip extended for nearly five years, and he became for the time, Irving and Cooper excepted, the most famous American man of letters abroad. The details of his travels may be followed in the letters, collected as *Pencillings by the Way* (1844), which appeared irregularly in the *Mirror* from Feb. 13, 1832. Beginning in France, Willis sauntered through Europe, making his way, as he wrote to his sister, "without a sou in the world beyond what my pen brings me." In Paris the American minister made him an attaché. In Florence he was dined by the ex-king of Westphalia, and he became intimate enough with Walter Savage Landor to incur his displeasure, which stands recorded in an addendum to the first edition of *Pericles and Aspasia*. After a six months' cruise on the Mediterranean he made his way to England, arriving at Dover, June 1, 1834. Offers from English periodicals awaited him, and he was soon contributing over the signature "Philip Slingsby" to the *Metropolitan Monthly,* the *Court Magazine,* and the *New Monthly.* Sponsored by Lady Blessington, he was bidden to the drawing-rooms graced by Disraeli, Moore, Bulwer, and their circle. Through another connection there was a breakfast with Charles and Mary Lamb. Barry Cornwall wrote an introduction for his first English publication, *Melanie and Other Poems* (1835). He became fast friends with Joanna Baillie and Jane Porter, and Mary Russell Mitford wrote to a friend that he wa.. "more like one of the best of our peers' sons than a rough republican" (Beers, *post,* p. 142). Through the Skinners of Shirley Park he met Mary Stace, a daughter of Gen. William Stace of Woolwich, whom he married Oct. 1, 1835, after a brief courtship.

Willis' success in England was marred by his indiscretions in too freely reporting his observations to his American readers. J. G. Lockhart began the attack with a scathing review (*London Quarterly,* Sept. 1835) of the original *Mirror* letters. The Tory press followed Lockhart's lead, and, among others, Harriet Martineau and Capt. Frederick Marryat were bitterly censorious. Willis came through the ordeal, losing none of his personal friends or rights of social entry, although only the intervention of seconds kept him from engaging Marryat in combat on the duelling field. With his bride he left England for America in May 1836. Before sailing he had published a collection of the "Slingsby" papers as *Inklings of Adventure* (3 vols., 1836). By

this time he was among the best paid of American writers, but he seems not to have been able to trust journalism to supply a livelihood. He tried in vain for a diplomatic secretaryship and soon turned his talents to a new field. His play, *Bianca Visconti* (1839), a tragedy, was produced with moderate success at the Park Theatre in New York on Aug. 25, 1837. "The Kentucky Heiress" was a stage failure, never published. With *Tortesa, or the Usurer Matched* (1839) he was more fortunate, winning Poe's judgment that it was "by far the best play from the pen of an American author" (*Burton's Gentleman's Magazine,* Aug. 1839). He also continued to travel and write for the *Mirror,* dating his sketches from Washington, where he described Van Buren's inauguration, and from Niagara, where he had gone to prepare the letter-press for *American Scenery* (2 vols., 1840). During these travels he discovered and bought an estate on Owego Creek, and established there a country home, "Glenmary." From this retreat he wrote for the *Mirror* "Letters from under a Bridge," collected as *A l'Abri; or, the Tent Pitch'd* (1839). A difference with Morris, the only obvious rift in their long friendship, now prompted Willis to join Dr. T. O. Porter in establishing the *Corsair,* a short-lived weekly (Mar. 16, 1839–Mar. 7, 1840), significant in the fight for an international law of copyright. The management was left to Porter, Willis sailing for a second visit to England, this time to be gone but a year. His *Pencillings by the Way* had reached a fourth London edition, and *Loiterings of Travel* (3 vols., 1840) was soon on the English market. Perhaps of greatest interest during this visit was his engagement of Thackeray to write for the *Corsair* at "a guinea a close column . . . cheaper than I ever did anything in my life," as Willis wrote to Porter (Beers, *post,* p. 254). His American popularity of this time may be indicated by the anecdote which tells of a commercial gentleman who "guessed Goethe was the N. P. Willis of Germany." Upon his return home in the spring of 1840, rates considered widely munificent were paid him by *Graham's, Godey's,* and other periodicals. He was forced, however, by a press of circumstances to give up his country estate, doing so with a deep regret wistfully expressed in the once-famous "Letter to the Unknown Purchaser and Next Occupant of Glenmary." Removing to New York, he rejoined Morris, and as editors of the *New Mirror,* a weekly, soon changed to the *Evening Mirror,* a daily, they began a partnership lasting until Morris' death. Willis regularly contributed his own poems, stories, and miscellaneous papers. The poems were chiefly *vers de société*, but among them was his effective "Unseen Spirits," praised by Poe. It was for the *Evening Mirror* that Willis employed Poe, marking the beginning of their personal friendship, which was to continue generous and helpful on Willis' part, and to culminate in his refutation (*Home Journal*, Oct. 1849) of Rufus M. Griswold's "Ludwig" article on the death of Poe (*Daily Tribune*, Oct. 9, 1849).

His good fortune was tinged with sorrow by the death of his mother (1844) and of his wife in childbirth (1845). Seeking solace, he embarked with his small daughter, Imogen, for a third and last journey to England and the Continent. His *Dashes at Life with a Free Pencil* (1845) had gone to press before he left America, and his "Invalid Letters from Europe" were collected in *Rural Letters* (1849) and in *Famous Persons and Places* (1854). Morris in the meantime had withdrawn from the *Evening Mirror*, and upon Willis' return in 1846 he joined Morris in his *National Press*, which they renamed the *Home Journal*, their final and most prosperous engagement. Willis married a second time on Oct. 1, 1846, choosing Cornelia Grinnell, nearly twenty years his junior, and acclaimed for her grace, intellect, and energy. Together they began an active life in New York, Willis portraying the news of fashion with Pepysian acumen for the *Home Journal* and becoming himself a colorful part of the daily Broadway scene. Lowell's *A Fable for Critics* records, "He'd have been just the fellow to sup at the Mermaid," and named him "the topmost bright bubble on the wave of the Town." Interpretative of Willis' whole work also is Lowell's " 'Tis not deep as a river, but who'd have it deep?" Not so keen-visioned, however, were some of the critical journalists, Willis' character and his work becoming their target for merciless onslaughts. As all evidence makes of Willis a most urbane gentleman, these personal attacks culminating in *Ruth Hall* (copyright 1854), a mordant satire by his sister, "Fanny Fern," are best explained by a note in his own commonplace book: "A name too soon famous is a heavy weight." In addition to the strain of steeling himself against his persistent critics, he became involved in the notorious divorce trial of Edwin Forrest [*q.v.*]. With Mrs. Willis he joined Bryant, Parke Godwin, and others siding with Mrs. Forrest. As a consequence, he was not only compromised by Forrest but suffered a bodily assault at the hands of the actor.

In 1852 slowly failing health sent him to Bermuda and the West Indies, which brought more travel letters collected as *Health Trip to the Tropics* (1853). With the single exception of his one and unsuccessful novel, *Paul Fane* (1857), his books were almost wholly made up from his magazine pieces, but for most of them there was a demand for simultaneous editions in England and America. More remarkable, he was able to sell reissues of his earlier work in new editions with new titles; practically all his short stories were republished after 1850 in *People I Have Met* (1850), *Life Here and There* (1850), and *Fun Jottings* (1853). In further search of health, in 1853 he again set up a country seat, "Idlewild," not far from Irving's "Sunnyside" on the Hudson. Here in his family circle—which ultimately included two more daughters and two sons, Grinnell and Bailey—there were a few happy years still in store for him. Through his weekly letters to the *Home Journal* "Idlewild" became a celebrated place, and there were famous visits from Bayard Taylor, Charles A. Dana, James T. Fields [*qq.v.*] and others, including his neighbor, Washington Irving [*q.v.*]. The Civil War brought Willis to Washington as the *Home Journal's* correspondent. His name gave him social right of way, and he became a pronounced favorite with Mrs. Lincoln, but his kind of genius found little inspiration in the troubled capital. The death of Morris in 1864 brought added editorial burdens which rapidly drained his failing mind and body. He died at "Idlewild." The funeral was in Boston, and the burial at Mount Auburn. Holmes, Dana, Longfellow, and Lowell were among the bearers of his pall. The legion of readers once eager for the latest from the "Penciller by the Way" has few descendants. The critical rule at first ordered him dismissed as "gigantic in his contemporaneousness" (G. E. Woodberry, *America in Literature*, 1903, p. 63), but revised judgment has accorded him a place of importance in the development of the short story (F. L. Pattee, *The Development of the American Short Story*, 1923, pp. 78–88). Journalism owes him a debt, and greater favor may yet be shown to his epistolary essays, which recreate with quick, bright strokes the famous persons and places of an age now quite of the past.

[See H. A. Beers, *Nathaniel Parker Willis* (1885); *Obit. Record Grads. Yale Univ.*, July 1867; R. E. Spiller, *The American in England* (1926); G. C. D. Odell, *Annals of the N. Y. Stage*, vol. IV (1928); H. T. Peck, in *Bookman*, Sept. 1906; K. L. Daughrity, in *Am. Lit.*, Mar. 1933; *The Works of Edgar Allan Poe*, vol. V (1884), pp. 440–49; and obituary in *N. Y. Times*, Jan. 22, 1867. A biog. of Willis is being prepared by K. L. Daughrity. There are Willis letters in MS. in the Yale Univ. Lib., and a fragmentary diary of Willis' and letters from Jane Porter to Willis in the pub. lib. of Morristown, N. J. Acknowledgment for interest and aid is made to Prof. S. T. Williams of Yale Univ. and to Katherine Cappert Willis, widow of Grinnell Willis.]

K. L. D.

WILLIS, OLYMPIA BROWN [See Brown, Olympia, 1835-1926].

WILLIS, WILLIAM (Aug. 31, 1794–Feb. 17, 1870), historian of Maine, was born in Haverhill, Mass., the second son of Benjamin and Mary (McKinstry) Willis. His father, one of the leading merchant shipowners of the Haverhill-Newburyport district, removed with his family to Portland in 1803. William went first to Phillips Exeter Academy and then was graduated from Harvard College in 1813. He returned to Portland and began reading law in the office of Prentiss Mellen [q.v.]. When the whole Willis family removed to Boston in 1815, he continued his law studies there under Peter O. Thacher and was admitted to the Suffolk bar in 1817. For a year or two he dallied with the idea of a commercial career, but in 1819 he returned to Portland to enter a partnership with Prentiss Mellen, but this relationship was dissolved the next year, when Mellen became chief justice of the new state. In 1835 Willis took, as a younger partner, William Pitt Fessenden [q.v.], and this association lasted for almost twenty years. On Sept. 1, 1823, he had married Julia Whitman, daughter of Ezekiel Whitman [q.v.]. They had eight children. Although allied with distinguished members of the bench and bar in Maine, Willis' interest in the law was secondary to his other concerns. He was an office, not a court, lawyer and always resented the drudgery of the legal profession.

For fifty years he filled the rôle of a "substantial citizen" of Portland. Although he had no desire for political office he was at one time or another senator in the state legislature, mayor of Portland, presidential elector, bank commissioner, and chairman of the state board of railroad commissioners. His considerable business interests included a directorship and vice-presidency in a Portland bank and the presidency of the Maine Central Railroad. He was an early advocate of the advantages of the railroad for Portland and stimulated her efforts to obtain rail connections with Canada and the West. A mainstay of the Unitarian Church, he was still a conservative in religious matters and a humanitarian busy in innumerable causes ranging from the wood fund for poor widows to the recreation of the city library after the great fire of 1866. His avocations were his life. His diaries reveal his love and care for his gardens of fine roses and his cold-house grapery. He found satisfaction for his cultured tastes in the meetings of a

group known as the "Portland Wits," whose interests were literary and historical. For the newspapers he wrote sketches of old houses, articles on the weather, past and present, detailed obituaries of rich and poor, and episodic accounts of Maine history. Successively secretary, treasurer, and finally president of the Maine Historical Society he was also the editor of the first six volumes of its *Collections* (1831-59), and all but the third volume of these contained at least one article from his pen. His chief works were *The History of Portland,* issued in two volumes (1831-33 and 2nd ed. 1865), and *A History of the Law, the Courts, and the Lawyers of Maine* (1863). Only the early adoption of systematic methods of investigation and a retentive memory enabled him to produce this historical flood. He died on a bed that had been set up in his library.

[*The Necrology of Harvard College, 1869-1872* (1872); C. H. Hart, *A Tribute to the Memory of Hon. William Willis. Read before the Numismatic and Antiquarian Society of Phila.... Mar. 3, 1870* (1870); A. W. Packard, "Notice of Hon. William Willis," *Me. Hist. Soc. Colls.,* vol. VII (1876); Pauline Willis, *Willis Records* (1906); *Portland Daily Advertiser,* Feb. 17, 1870; *Daily Portland Press,* Feb. 18, 1870.]

E. C. K—d.

WILLISTON, SAMUEL (June 17, 1795–July 18, 1874), philanthropist, was born at Easthampton, Mass., the son of Sarah (Birdseye) and Payson Williston. His father was a graduate of Yale College, the first pastor of the first church in that town, the descendant of Joseph Williston who was born in Windsor, Conn., before 1667 and cousin of Seth Williston [q.v.]. Samuel obtained his early education in the district school, supplemented by study with his father. He spent a term at the Westfield Academy and a year, 1814-15, at Phillips Academy at Andover but suffered a good deal of difficulty with his eyesight. After several years in farm work and in stores at West Springfield and in New York, where he became a member of the Brick Presbyterian Church under the Rev. Gardiner Spring [q.v.], he returned to Easthampton in 1822. With his father's assistance he bought a farm on which he began to work with energy and enterprise, adding school-teaching during the winter months. On May 27 of that year he married Emily Graves of Williamsburg. They had four children, all of whom died young, and they adopted one son and three daughters. To augment the family income, his wife began covering buttons by hand. He promoted the sale of the product, employed others, and in a few years had the buttons covered in a thousand families in western Massachusetts. He formed a partnership with Joseph and Joel Hayden of Haydenville, Mass. (see sketch of Joseph Shepard Hayden). They manufactured the product, while Williston promoted the enterprise and furnished the capital. On the dissolution of the partnership in 1847, the business was removed to Easthampton, where other factories for the manufacture of suspenders, rubber thread, and cotton were established.

In addition to his business enterprises in Easthampton, he was interested in business corporations, such as banks, railroads, gas and water-power companies in Easthampton, Northampton, Holyoke, and elsewhere, of many of which he was president. He interested himself in politics, but after a term in the lower house of the state legislature in 1841 and two terms in the Senate, 1842 and 1843, he declined further public office. He is best known as a promoter of religious and charitable enterprises, to which he gave over $1,000,000 during his lifetime. In 1841 he founded Williston Seminary at Easthampton and served as president of the board of trustees for thirty-three years. He became a trustee of Amherst College in 1841 and served the rest of his life. Including the endowment of three important professorships there, his benefactions to Amherst during his lifetime amounted to $150,000. He was one of the first trustees of Mount Holyoke Female Seminary and of the Massachusetts State Reform School. He was a builder and promoter of churches and a corporate member of the American Board of Commissioners for Foreign Missions. Handicapped by partial blindness, he absorbed the contents of many books through readers and dictated all his correspondence. He died at Easthampton.

[W. S. Tyler, *A Discourse Commemorative of Hon. Samuel Williston* (1874), with portrait, and *Hist. of Amherst College* (1873); P. W. Lyman, *Hist. of Easthampton* (1866), pp. 54–65, 179–81, and *Hist. Address Delivered at the Centennial Celebration at Easthampton, Mass., July 4, 1876* (1877), pp. 64–69; A. L. Williston, *Williston Genealogy* (1912); *Biog. Cat. . . . Phillips Academy, Andover* (1903); *Springfield Republican*, July 20, 1874.]　　　F. T. P.

WILLISTON, SAMUEL WENDELL (July 10, 1852–Aug. 30, 1918), paleontologist, dipterist, was born in Roxbury, Mass., the son of Samuel and Jane A. (Turner) Williston. On the father's side he was of New England stock, the name having been traced back in Massachusetts as far as 1650. His mother was born in England. His parents removed to Kansas in 1857 under the auspices of the Emigrant Aid Society and settled at Manhattan, where Williston's early education was of the kind available in the pioneer community. In 1866 he entered the Kansas State Agricultural College at Manhattan and in 1872 received the degree of B.S. Though he began the study of medicine under

the preceptorship of a local physician in 1873, he was employed in that year and the following one by Othniel C. Marsh [*q.v.*] of Yale University as a collector in the Cretaceous chalk beds of western Kansas. In 1876 he was called to New Haven by Marsh and remained in his service as collector, preparator, and writer until 1885. During this time he collected in the dinosaur-bearing beds in Colorado and Montana. He also studied medicine and in 1880 received the degree of M.D. from the Yale Medical School. He was married to Annie I. Hathaway on Dec. 20, 1880. Having received the degree of Ph.D. at Yale (1885), in 1886 he was appointed assistant professor of anatomy and in 1888 professor. He served at Yale until 1890, continuing private practice and acting as health officer of New Haven at the same time.

In 1890 he was called to the University of Kansas, where he was professor of geology and paleontology (1890–92) and professor of historical geology, vertebrate anatomy, and physiology (1892–1902). In 1898 he also became dean of the school of medicine, and for some time served on the state board of health and the board of medical examiners. While in Kansas he returned to his interest in paleontology, producing a long series of papers upon the reptiles of the Cretaceous. The most important of these were volumes IV (1898) and VI (1900) of *The University Geological Survey of Kansas,* the first of which contained his classic work on the mosasaurs. Other papers in these volumes were written by the group of students that he had trained in paleontological work. Among his many activities in Kansas was the publication of a large number of papers upon Diptera. He began in this field when there was not a dipterist on the continent. Lacking guidance and sufficient literature, he made slow progress in spite of great effort until he discovered Ignaz R. Schiner's *Fauna Austriaca* (1860), in which he found the Austrian Diptera ably analyzed into their families, genera and species. He was so profoundly impressed with the plan of this work that it largely shaped his later work on the order; he was always trying to analyze and simplify for the help of beginners. The climax of this work was the publication in 1908 of his *Manual of North American Diptera,* a greatly enlarged revision of his two earlier publications on Diptera (1888, 1896), which, besides the analytical matter, contained more than eight hundred figures drawn by his own hand. This volume has been used extensively in the Old World, where there has been nothing similar to it. In a more technical way he monographed the Syrphidae of

North America (*Bulletin of the United States National Museum, No. 31,* 1886) and published extensive contributions to *Biologia Centrali-Americana* (1879–1910), with many shorter papers on Diptera. In the decade 1890–1900 he easily ranked among the three or four world authorities in the order. Several of his students became specialists in Diptera.

In 1902 he was called to be head of the department of vertebrate paleontology at the University of Chicago, and soon entered upon the exploration of the Permian beds of North America, and the description of their amphibian and reptilian fauna. He described a large number of new forms, and made fundamental contributions to the anatomy and classification of these primitive forms. The most important comprehensive works published during this period were his monographs, *American Permian Vertebrates* (1911) and *Water Reptiles of the Past and Present* (1914). His final work, a general description of the osteology of the reptiles, living and extinct, was not completed before his death, but was published posthumously under the editorship of W. K. Gregory as *The Osteology of the Reptiles* (1925). His contributions to paleontology will remain as fundamental for all future work. His vigorous personality made him an inspiring leader in every subject he taught and gathered around him a group of students who carried on the work he had begun. He was a corresponding member of the Geological Society of London (1902) and of the Zoological Society of London, fellow of the American Academy of Arts and Sciences, president of the Sigma Xi Society from 1901 to 1904, and a member of the National Academy of Science (1915). He was survived at the time of his death by his wife, three daughters, and a son.

[See *Who's Who in America,* 1918–19; *Record of the Alumni of the Kan. State Agricultural Coll.* (1914); R. S. Lull, in *Memoirs Nat. Acad. of Sciences,* vol. XVII (1924), with bibliog.; H. F. Osborn, in *Jour. of Geology,* Nov.–Dec. 1918; F. R. Lillie, E. C. Case, and Stuart Weller, in *Univ. Record* (Chicago), Jan. 1919, with portrait; *Samuel Wendell Williston, 1852–1918 . . . Memorial Meeting . . . Univ. of Chicago,* Dec. 9, 1918; obituary in *Chicago Daily Tribune,* Aug. 31, 1918. A *Bibliog. of Samuel Wendell Williston* (1911) and a supplement (1918) were printed in New Haven by J. T. Hathaway; there is also a bibliog. in *Kan. Univ. Quart.,* Oct. 1899. The portion of this article on Williston's work as a dipterist was written by Dr. J. M. Aldrich of the U. S. Nat. Museum.]   E. C. C.

WILLISTON, SETH (Apr. 4, 1770–Mar. 2, 1851), clergyman and home missionary, was born in Suffield, Conn., the great-grandson of Joseph Williston who was born in Windsor, Conn., before 1667, the cousin, once removed, of Samuel Williston [*q.v.*], and the son of Consider and Rhoda (King) Williston. He assisted his father in his trade of saddler and on the farm, and he obtained the elements of an education under teachers near his home. In 1791 he graduated from Dartmouth College. After teaching for three years at Windsor and New London, Conn., and reading a good deal in theology, he was licensed by the Tolland County Association on Oct. 7, 1794. He preached in churches in Connecticut and Vermont, and at Rupert, Vt., was called to be pastor. Hearing of the religious needs of the "Chenango country" in New York, however, in July 1796 he went on his own responsibility to Patterson's Settlement in Broome County. There and for twenty miles south and west, among New England immigrants, he worked with growing success. During a short visit home he was ordained by the North Association of Hartford County on June 7, 1797. In this year and in 1798 he carried his missionary travels northwestward into the Cayuga Lake country. On Dec. 15, 1797, he organized the First Congregational Church of Lisle. Then not more than five churches existed westward in New York. In June 1798 he was appointed to missionary service by the Connecticut General Association (Congregational), which then organized itself as the Connecticut Missionary Society. The next three years he spent in the service of this society. Living at Lisle he worked over the country from the Chenango to the Genesee and northward to Lake Ontario. In his theology he was a follower of Samuel Hopkins, 1721–1803 [*q.v.*], and his preaching, in an important degree, evoked the revival of 1799–1800 in this region. On his tours he preached almost every day, held conferences, visited from house to house in the forests, instructed children, administered the sacraments, organized churches. He records preaching in forty-four settlements, in many the first preacher heard. After riding miles he spent his nights in log cabins, and by firelight did much solid reading.

In May 1801 he became pastor at Lisle, stipulating that he should spend a quarter of his time in missionary work. He spent more, preaching widely in central New York and northern Pennsylvania. He organized nine churches that are recorded, probably more. He was married in May 1804 to Sibyl (Stoddard) Dudley of Stockbridge, Mass., who died in 1849. They had one son. In 1810 he removed to Durham, N. Y., in the Catskills. During his eighteen years' service as pastor there he published several volumes of sermons and religious discussions. In 1828 he received his dismissal at his own request and devoted himself to his missionary travels, honored as one of the principal Christian teachers of the region. In this time he published five more books. His best-known book in its day was *The Harmony of Divine Truth* (1836). He died at Guilford Center, N. Y.

["The Diaries of the Rev. Seth Williston," ed. by J. Q. Adams, *Jour. of the Presbyterian Hist. Soc.*, Dec. 1913–Sept. 1919; letters in *Theological Mag.*, Nov.–Dec. 1796, pp. 159–60, May, June, and July 1797, p. 399; letters and reports of Conn. Missionary Soc., *N. Y. Missionary Mag.*, vols. I–IV (1800–03); W. B. Sprague, *Annals of the Amer. Pulpit*, vol. IV (1858); J. H. Hotchkin, *Hist. of . . . Western N. Y.* (1848); P. H. Fowler, *Hist. Sketch of Presbyterianism within . . . Central N. Y.* (1877).]   R. H. N.

WILLSON, AUGUSTUS EVERETT (Oct. 13, 1846–Aug. 24, 1931), governor of Kentucky, came of a Vermont family. Early in the nineteenth century his forebears removed to Allegany County, N. Y., where Hiram Willson, a lumberman, married Ann Colvin Ennis. In the early 1840's Hiram moved with his family to Maysville, Ky., making the journey down the Allegheny and Ohio rivers on a raft of his own lumber. Here at Maysville his son Augustus Everett Willson was born. In 1847 he was taken by the family to their new home in Covington and in 1852 to New Albany, Ind., opposite Louisville. Following the death of his mother in 1856 and his father three years later, the boy went to live with his grandmother in Allegany County, N. Y. He attended Alfred Academy and in 1865 entered Harvard College. After receiving the degree of A.B. in 1869, he studied for a short time in the Harvard Law School and in the office of Lothrop, Bishop & Lincoln in Boston. In 1870 he entered the law office of John M. Harlan [*q.v.*], in Louisville, Ky., where he was admitted to the bar. He was a junior partner in Harlan's firm from 1874 to 1879, though his law practice was interrupted by a brief service (December 1875–August 1876) as chief clerk of the United States Treasury Department.

Willson's inherited Republicanism was intensified by association with Harlan and it became one of his fixed ambitions to build up the Republican party in Kentucky where, at that time, it was distinctly moribund. With this idea in mind he secured the Republican nomination for the Kentucky Senate in 1879. His defeat for this office was followed by a succession of defeats, 1884–92, for the United States House of Representatives. Such chagrin as he may have felt over these failures was assuaged, at least partially, by his selection as delegate to the Republican National Convention in 1884, 1888, and 1892. Following his unsuccessful campaign for Congress in the last-named year, he retired from politics until 1903, when he was an unsuccessful candidate for the Republican nomination for gov-

ernor. In 1904 he was again a delegate to the Republican National Convention and in 1907 he was elected governor of Kentucky by a small majority. During his entire term he was checkmated by a hostile Democratic legislature, with the result that his administration was barren of constructive acts. He aroused much criticism by pardoning two men convicted of the murder of Gov. William Goebel [*q.v.*] and by declaring martial law in certain sections of western Kentucky where "night-riders" were waging war against the tobacco companies and against planters who refused to join the "pool." Partisan criticisms of his use of the militia alleged that martial law was enforced only in Democratic communities.

After his four years as governor, Willson did not again hold public office, although he was a delegate to the Republican National Convention in 1908 and 1916. He died in Louisville, survived by his wife, Mary Elizabeth (Ekin) Willson, whom he had married July 23, 1877. Their only child had died in infancy. Willson was a member of the board of overseers of Harvard University, 1910–18. Although so long involved in politics, he was at all times more interested in the law. He was amiable in disposition and noted for his courtesy.

[*Reports of the Class of 1869 of Harvard Coll., 1878–1919*; *Who's Who in America*, 1930–31; Charles Kerr, *Hist. of Ky.* (1922); H. Levin, *The Lawyers and Lawmakers of Ky.* (1897); *Louisville Times*, Aug. 24, 1931; *Courier-Journal* (Louisville), Aug. 25, 1931.]   R. S. C.

WILMARTH, LEMUEL EVERETT (Mar. 11, 1835–July 27, 1918), painter and teacher, was born in Attleboro, Mass., of New England Puritan stock. His parents, Benoni and Fanny (Fuller) Wilmarth, were farming people, and each child of the household was expected to take his turn at the daily farm duties. After attending the district school and a school in Boston, he began his art study at the Pennsylvania Academy of the Fine Arts, Philadelphia, in 1854. Varying his studies in Philadelphia with peddling trips in the South and other more or less lucrative jobs, by about 1859 he had accumulated enough to go abroad. He spent three and a half years at the Munich Academy under Wilhelm von Kaulbach, and two and one half years under Jean Léon Gérôme in Paris. Returning to America with his funds exhausted, he was fortunate in securing a commission to paint the decorations in the Park Theatre in Brooklyn. He began in 1866 to exhibit at the National Academy of Design genre paintings, anecdotal and somewhat sentimental in character, but accurate in drawing and pleasing in composition. He was appointed instructor at the Academy art school in 1870, and was elected an associate member of the Academy in 1871. In the spring of 1871 he declined a professorship at Yale because the position at the Academy offered "a larger field of usefulness" (letter to J. F. Weir, May 27, 1871). His election as Academician came in 1873. He continued as the head of the Academy school until 1887, when he requested and was granted a leave of absence for two or three years. Under the influence of younger men who were returning from Europe and bringing with them new methods of painting and teaching, a spirit of change was beginning to be apparent in the small American art world. Wilmarth never resumed an active position and definitely resigned his place in the school in 1889. In his teaching he stood for sound construction, accurate drawing, and a high degree of finish. He was elected in 1892 a member of the Academy council, but resigned in the following year because of ill health. During the years of his teaching he continued to paint and exhibit, with a considerable degree of financial success. In addition to a winter home in Brooklyn, he purchased a farm at Marlboro on the Hudson in 1882, remodeled the house, and built a studio. Not long after this his eyesight began to fail, and in his later life he did very little painting, though he produced some pictures of still life and fruits from his own orchard and vineyard which delighted his patrons with their realism.

The Wilmarth home was always a center of hospitality for friends as well as a gathering place for a group of serious students, who, like Wilmarth himself, became deeply interested in the teachings of Emanuel Swedenborg. Wilmarth had left the stern religious teachings of his childhood behind him and had passed through a period of atheism, but now found great joy and comfort in Swedenborgianism. He was prominent in the Church of the New Jerusalem in Brooklyn, and was one of the founders of the *New Earth,* a Swedenborgian publication, and for several years its editor. He was much interested in the social doctrines of Henry George [*q.v.*], and often wrote articles on religious and social subjects. He was a genial, kindly man, of medium height and rather stocky build, with a full round face. In 1872 he married Emma R. (Barrett) Higginson, who died in 1905. They had no children. Some of his best known pictures are "The Pick of the Orchard," "Ingratitude," "Another Candidate for Adoption," "Sunny Italy," and "Left in Charge"; the last named is in the permanent collection of the National Academy of Design.

[Sources include *Who's Who in America,* 1918–19, corrected and supplemented by information from Wilmarth's family, an intimate friend, and old pupils; records of the Nat. Acad. of Design; letters and records kept by Wilmarth; *Am. Art Ann.,* 1918; *Am. Art News,* Aug. 17, 1918; death notice in *N. Y. Times,* July 29, 1918. The date of birth, from Nat. Acad. records, was supplied by Wilmarth himself. The date of Mrs. Wilmarth's death is from the family.]

G. W. C.

WILMER, JAMES JONES (Jan. 15, 1749/50– Apr. 14, 1814), clergyman, was born on the Eastern Shore of Maryland, the youngest son of Simon and Mary (Price) Wilmer. His father, a planter and presiding justice of the Kent County court, was a grandson of Simon Wilmer who settled in Kent County before 1680. When James was nine years old he was sent to a maternal uncle in England to be educated. He attended St. Paul's School, London, from 1763 to 1768, when he was admitted to Christ Church, Oxford. After eighteen months, however, he returned to America. Recommended by Gov. Robert Eden of Maryland to the Bishop of London, he went back to England for ordination and was licensed, Sept. 25, 1773, for Maryland, but did not obtain a suitable charge at once, and led a rather desultory life for the next few years. The death of his English uncle and Wilmer's mistaken belief that his share of the uncle's estate would make him wealthy seems to have been his undoing; he was unable to settle down seriously and spent most of his time traveling between Maryland and England in search of the fortune which never materialized. Between 1779 and 1789, however, he was rector successively of four Maryland parishes: St. Paul's in Kent County; Shrewsbury, Kent; St. George's, Harford County; and St Stephen's, Kent.

While rector of Shrewsbury, North Sassafras Parish, Kent County, he served as secretary of a convention of the Anglican clergymen of the Eastern Shore, held at Chestertown, Nov. 9, 1780, at which "on motion of the Secretary, it was proposed that the Church known in the province as Protestant, be called the 'Protestant Episcopal Church,' and it was so adopted" (*Journal of the Ninety-fifth Annual Convention of the Protestant Episcopal Church in the Diocese of Maryland,* 1878, Appendix, p. 146). The name was in a short time in general use.

It seems probable that when Wilmer was in England in 1790–91 in pursuit of his inheritance he was attracted to Swedenborgianism, for on his return he became the leader of a group which in Baltimore founded the first New Church Society in America. It was Wilmer's dream at the time that the New Church should become the established church of the United States, and in the

Maryland Gazette (Baltimore) for Oct. 18, 1791, he announced the publication of *A Discourse on a Federal Church as Lately First Commenced in the Town of Baltimore.* The following year he published *A Sermon on the Doctrine of the New Jerusalem Church, being the First Promulgated within the United States of America, Delivered on the First Sunday in April 1792 in the Court House of Baltimore.* Established as a distinct religious society in England in 1788, the Church of the New Jerusalem thus came into existence in America four years later. Wilmer served as minister for a time, but after a year or two of struggle became discouraged and sought to support his family by his pen and by conducting a succession of short-lived schools in Baltimore, Charles Town, and Havre de Grace.

About 1799 he was reinstated as a clergyman of the Episcopal Church and during the next decade held charges in Delaware, Maryland, and Virginia. From 1809 to 1813 he was one of the chaplains of Congress. Appointed in the latter year chaplain in the United States Army, he saw active service in the War of 1812. While attached to the North Western Army he was shipwrecked on the "Chippaway River," and died at Detroit a few weeks later, apparently as the result of exposure. He was married twice: first, May 21, 1783, to Sarah Magee, and second, in 1803, to Letitia, widow of William Fell Day. Several children of his first marriage survived him.

Wilmer was a prolific writer and pamphleteer. His style was lively and readable. His frequent newspaper contributions, usually of a political, religious, or personal character, were often controversial and unrestrained. In 1792 he published *Memoirs, by James Wilmer,* a pamphlet of which the only surviving copy known is that which was presented by the author in 1793 to George Washington, when Wilmer was seeking to have the Swedenborgian church made the national church. Some of his more important books were *Consolation, being a Replication to Thomas Paine* (1794); *Man as He Is and the World as It Goes* (1803); *The American Nepos* (1805), a volume of biographical sketches; and *A Narrative Respecting the Conduct of the British* (1813). In 1796, with William Pechin, he began the publication in Baltimore of a tri-weekly newspaper, *The Eagle of Freedom,* but it lasted only a few months.

[J. H. Pleasants, "Memoirs of the Rev. James Jones Wilmer," *Md. Hist. Mag.,* Sept. 1924; R. B. Gardiner, *The Admission Registers of St. Paul's School* (1884); Joseph Foster, *Alumni Oxonienses ... 1715–1886,* vol. IV (1888); Gerald Fothergill, *A List of Emigrant Ministers to America, 1690–1811* (1904); *Notices and Journals ... of the Protestant Episcopal Church in the Diocese of Maryland ... 1783–89* (n.d.); M. B. Block, *The New Church in the New World* (1932); G. A. Hanson, *Old Kent* (1876); Maryland Parish Registers (MSS.), Md. Hist. Soc.] J. H. P—s.

WILMER, JOSEPH PÈRE BELL (Feb. 11, 1812–Dec. 2, 1878), Episcopal bishop of Louisiana, came of a distinguished family, long active in the Episcopal Church. Son of the Rev. Simon Wilmer and his first wife, Rebecca (Frisby) Wilmer, nephew of Rev. William Holland Wilmer [*q.v.*], and first cousin of Rt. Rev. Richard Hooker Wilmer [*q.v.*], he grew up in Virginia. He was graduated from the Theological Seminary in Virginia, at Alexandria, in 1834, and was ordered deacon in July of that year. From October 1834 to May 1837 he was in charge of St. Anne's Parish, Albemarle County, Va.; in 1837–38 he acted as chaplain at the University of Virginia. In May 1838 he was ordained priest. The following March he was appointed a chaplain in the United States Navy. He resigned his commission in July 1844. For a time, in 1842–43, he had been in charge of Hungar's Parish in Northampton County, Va., and during this time, on Mar. 29, 1842, had married Helen Skipwith of Muhlenburg County. Four sons and two daughters were born to them. After his resignation from the navy, he had charge of St. James-Northam Parish in Goochland County until early in 1849, when he became rector of St. Mark's Church, Philadelphia. He served there until shortly after the outbreak of the Civil War, when, owing to his Southern sympathies, he retired to his summer home, "Plain Dealing," in Albemarle County, Va. The only service he performed for the Confederacy, however, was a journey to England in 1863 to purchase Bibles for the soldiers; on the return voyage he was captured and confined for a short period in the Old Capitol Prison at Washington.

He was consecrated bishop of Louisiana in November 1866, and devoted himself with great energy to the restoration of the Church, which had been left by the war in a sadly disorganized condition. In religious circles he was identified with the high-church party and was noted as an eloquent pulpit orator. In the bitter presidential controversy of 1876, when Louisiana was brought to the verge of revolt, he made a trip to the North despite the protests against his interference in secular affairs in order to lay the situation before President Grant and President-elect Hayes, with the result recorded in history. He died suddenly, as he had always desired, in New Orleans.

Wilmer's writing was confined to occasional

sermons, episcopal addresses, and pastoral letters, and the political pamphlet, *A Defense of Louisiana* (1868). With his amusing absent-mindedness, his keen sense of humor, his wide information, his tenderness, and his deep resentment of injustice, he was one of the most picturesque as well as influential figures of his church in his time.

[H. G. Batterson, *A Sketch-Book of the Am. Episcopate* (1884); W. S. Perry, *The Episcopate in America* (1895); H. C. Potter, *Reminiscences of Bishops and Archbishops* (1906); R. H. Wilmer, *The Recent Past* (1887); *Sun* (Baltimore), Dec. 7, 1878.] E. L.

WILMER, RICHARD HOOKER (Mar. 15, 1816–June 14, 1900), second Episcopal bishop of Alabama, was born at Alexandria, Va., then a part of the District of Columbia, the third child of Rev. William Holland Wilmer [*q.v.*] and his second wife, Marion Hannah Cox. After his father's death in 1827 the boy secured his schooling under straitened circumstances. He graduated from Yale College in 1836 and the Theological Seminary in Virginia three years later, was ordered deacon, Mar. 31, 1839, and priested, Apr. 19, 1840, in the Protestant Episcopal Church, and for the most of twenty-two years ministered in rural parishes in Virginia. In 1843 he had charge for one year of St. James Church, Wilmington, N. C. He grew steadily in power and reputation as a preacher, pastor, and leader. In 1859 his diocese elected him a deputy to the General Convention of the Episcopal Church.

At the beginning of the Civil War Wilmer was ardently active and outspoken in his loyalty to the South. On Nov. 21, 1861, he was elected bishop of the diocese of Alabama. Since the dioceses in the seceded states had withdrawn from the Protestant Episcopal Church in the United States consent was given to his consecration by a majority of dioceses and bishops in the Southern states, acting autonomously, and he was consecrated on Mar. 6, 1862, in St. Paul's Church, Richmond. He took part in the organization of the Protestant Episcopal Church in the Confederate States and returned with his diocese into union with the Episcopal Church in the United States after the collapse of the Confederacy.

Wilmer met the problems of diocesan administration in a war-torn state with an earnestness and power that won for him the loyalty and love of his clergy and people; he ministered to the soldiers in camp and hospital, provided for the care of orphaned children, and gave attention to the religious education of negroes. At the end of the war, when Alabama had become a military district, he came into conflict with the military authority by directing his clergy not to use the prayer for the president and all in civil authority until civil authority should be restored in consequence he and his clergy were suspended from all official duties and their churches closed by order of the commanding general. Strong protest was made, and finally, in January 1866, the military order was rescinded by direction of President Johnson. During the difficult period of reconstruction and the years that followed, facing the widespread poverty of his people and later the problems arising with the development of industry, he labored as a wise and able administrator, endowed with a sense of humor and a wit that could be gentle or caustic as occasion demanded. His reputation as a preacher was nation-wide, and his ability was recognized by the degree of Doctor of Laws conferred upon him by the University of Cambridge when he attended the first Lambeth Conference in 1867.

He published frequent pastoral letters, the most noteworthy being that of June 20, 1865, concerning the prayer for those in civil authority. Others, especially letters on "Efficacy of Prayer" and "Confession of Sin not Profession of Religion," were distributed in large numbers. He published one book, *The Recent Past from a Southern Standpoint* (1887), which went through several editions.

Wilmer married, on Oct. 6, 1840, Margaret, daughter of Alexander and Lucy (Rives) Brown, of Nelson County, Va., who in a long life shared with him contributed greatly to his success. They had three children who grew to adult years. In 1890 the Bishop's increasing infirmities necessitated the election of a coadjutor who relieved him of a part of his burden during the last ten years of his life. He died at the age of eighty-four and was buried in Magnolia Cemetery, Mobile.

[Wilmer's own book, *The Recent Past* (1887); W. C. Whitaker, *Richard Hooker Wilmer* (1907); J. B. Cheshire, *The Church in the Confederate States* (1912); W. S. Perry, *The Hist. of the Am. Episcopal Church* (1885), vol. II, and *The Episcopate in America* (1895); *Obit. Record Grads. Yale Univ.*, 1900; *Churchman*, June 23, 1900; *Daily Register* (Mobile), June 15, 1900.] G. M. B.

WILMER, WILLIAM HOLLAND (Oct. 29, 1782–July 24, 1827), Episcopal clergyman, was born in Kent County, Md., a descendant of Simon Wilmer who settled there before 1680. The fifth son of Simon and Ann (Ringgold) Wilmer, he was one of three brothers to enter the ministry of the Protestant Episcopal Church. He received his collegiate training at Washington College, Kent County, and was ordained in 1808. His first charge was Chester Parish, Chestertown, Md., which he held until he became rector in February 1812 of St. Paul's Church, Alexandria, then in the District of Columbia, but within the diocese of Virginia.

The Episcopal Church in Virginia at that period was so utterly prostrate that a report made to the General Convention of 1811 expressed doubt of the probability of its revival. No diocesan convention had been held for seven years. In March 1812, however, upon the death of the Bishop, James Madison [q.v.], Wilmer united with another young minister, William Meade [q.v.] of Frederick County, in taking steps toward the calling of a convention. When the succeeding convention assembled in 1813 the reins were taken from the hands of the older clergy by four young ministers—Wilmer, Oliver Norris of Christ Church, Alexandria, John Dunn of Shelburne Parish, Loudoun County, and William Meade, the first three being elected members of the standing committee of the diocese. This group entered into correspondence with Rev. Richard Channing Moore [q.v.] of New York, as the result of which Moore was elected bishop of Virginia at the convention of 1814. Wilmer was reëlected president of the standing committee every year, and appointed a deputy from the diocese to every meeting of the General Convention of the Protestant Episcopal Church, from that time until his death. Four times he was elected by the General Convention as president of the House of Clerical and Lay Deputies. One of the leaders of the revival of the Church in Virginia, he was also a notable figure in the life of the Church outside his diocese.

He was profoundly interested in the education of young men for the ministry and a vigorous leader in that field. Beginning in 1815, a rapidly developing interest in this problem was aroused in both Virginia and Maryland. In 1818 the movement took form by the organization in the District of Columbia of the Society for the Education of Pious Young Men for the Ministry of the Protestant Episcopal Church, still in existence as the Protestant Episcopal Education Society. Wilmer became its president and established in Washington in 1819 the *Theological Repertory* as the organ of its cause. He continued as president of the society and editor of the magazine until 1826. In 1821 a theological professorship was established at the College of William and Mary, but it met with much opposition and was unsuccessful. The following year an attempt was made to establish a theological school in Maryland with Wilmer as president, but this also failed of success. In 1823, however, Wilmer, Meade, and others were able to reconcile the divided interests and organized at Alexandria the Theological Seminary in Virginia, with fourteen students and a faculty consisting of Wilmer and Rev. Reuel Keith. Classes were held at first in Wilmer's study and later in his parish house. From this beginning the Theological Seminary in Virginia has had continuous existence.

Wilmer was notably successful in pastoral work. The membership of St. Paul's Church was so greatly increased under his ministry that the church building was enlarged, and in 1818 the present church erected. He was a strong preacher, of deeply spiritual life, and a tireless worker. In addition to his duties in Alexandria he assumed for the period of one year in 1813–14 the rectorship of the newly established St. John's Church in Washington. During his whole ministry he was indefatigable in the effort to resuscitate the Church in dormant parishes, making frequent trips as a volunteer missionary into neighboring counties, holding services, and visiting scattered families. In 1826 he became president of the College of William and Mary and rector of Bruton Parish, Williamsburg, Va. He carried into the administration of College affairs the same spirit of zeal and ability he had shown in his pastoral work, but his labors were cut short by his death in July 1827.

In addition to editing the *Theological Repertory*, Wilmer published a number of sermons and one book, *The Episcopal Manual* (1815), which went through several editions and was held in high esteem for many years after his death as a useful compendium of information and instruction. He entered into a controversy with Roger Baxter, a Jesuit, the substance of which was published as *The Alexandria Controversy* (1817) and, in enlarged form, as *The Controversy between M. B. and Quaero . . . on Some Points of Roman Catholicism* (1818). Wilmer was married three times; first to Harriet Ringgold; second Jan. 23, 1812, to Marion Hannah Cox, who died in 1812; and third, to Anne Brice Fitzhugh. Six children were born of the second union, two of the third. His sons Richard Hooker Wilmer [q.v.] and George T. Wilmer entered the ministry; Joseph P. B. Wilmer [q.v.], bishop of Louisiana, was his nephew.

[Sources include: Va. Diocesan Jours., 1812–28; *Jours. of the General Convention of the Protestant Episcopal Church;* William Meade, *Old Churches, Ministers, and Families of Va.* (1857); R. H. Wilmer, *The Recent Past* (1887); J. P. K. Henshaw, *Memoir of the Life of the Rt. Rev. Richard Channing Moore* (1843); W. A. R. Goodwin, *Hist. of the Theol. Seminary in Va.* (2 vols., 1923–24); W. C. Whitaker, *Richard Hooker Wilmer* (1907); *Richmond Enquirer*, July 31, 1827. The date of birth is sometimes given as Mar. 9, 1784, but R. H. Wilmer, *op. cit.*, and G. A. Hanson,

Old Kent (1876) citing records, support that given above.]

                                         G. M. B.

WILMOT, DAVID (Jan. 20, 1814–Mar. 16, 1868), representative from Pennsylvania, was born at Bethany, Pa., the descendant of Benjamin Wilmot who with his son, William, aged six, emigrated from England to New Haven, Conn., before 1641, and the son of Randall and Mary (Grant) Wilmot. In 1820 his mother died and a step-mother soon took her place. His father, a local merchant, prospered and built a large pillared house in the fashion of the period, where the family lived during David's boyhood. He went to school at the local academy and later at Aurora, N. Y. In 1832 he entered the law office of George W. Woodward at Wilkes Barré, and in 1834 he was admitted to the bar. He settled down in Towanda, Pa., to practise law, and on Nov. 28, 1836, he married Anne Morgan of Bethlehem. For ten years he continued law and politics, with more and more politics and less and less law in the mixture. He was an ardent Jacksonian and an inveterate attendant of political gatherings. He was stout and of average height, rather slovenly in dress, enormous in appetite both in eating and drinking, forceful in speech, and lazy. It was much easier to make extempore political speeches than engage in the drudgery of the law. In 1844 he was active in promoting the indorsement of Van Buren by the Democratic state convention and later in the year was elected to Congress from one of the strongest Democratic districts. He served from 1845 to 1851. The Twenty-ninth Congress contained many Northern Democrats who resented Polk's disregard of Northern interests. Wilmot at first was loyal to the administration, even voting for the tariff of 1846, the only Pennsylvania congressman to do so. He could vote thus with some degree of safety, for his constituents were mostly farmers. However, he, like many others, came to the conclusion that the Southern power was getting too well fortified and that the question was how to stop its further growth (but for a discussion of his motives as more immediately personal and political see R. R. Stenberg, "The Motivation of the Wilmot Proviso," *Mississippi Valley Historical Review*, March 1932). Wilmot and his associates feared the Mexican War meant the annexation of southwestern territory, so when the president on Aug. 8, 1846, asked for $2,000,-000 with which to make peace, Wilmot determined to offer a proviso using the phraseology of the Northwest Ordinance to the effect that slavery should be prohibited in any territory that might be acquired with this money. Jacob Brinkerhoff [*q.v.*] of Ohio had a similar plan. There

was a conference of Northern Democrats, and, after Wilmot had rephrased his proviso, he introduced it the same day, perhaps because he was less identified with the Free-Soil movement. The proviso was adopted in the House but defeated in the Senate.

Wilmot's further service in his two remaining congressional terms was not notable, but his proviso had made him famous and, with his bolt with Van Buren in 1848, placed him among the leaders of Free-Soil men. In 1850 he was so unpopular with the predominant Buchanan wing of the Pennsylvania Democracy that he was beset by a bolting ticket, and in the interests of harmony he withdrew from the campaign for congressman in favor of Galusha A. Grow [*q.v.*], whom he designated. In 1851 he was elected president judge of the 13th judicial district, over which he presided until 1861. He was one of the founders of the Republican party and was its first candidate for governor. In 1860 he supported Lincoln as against Cameron. After the election Lincoln offered him a cabinet position, which Wilmot declined, preferring the Senate. The pretensions of western Pennsylvania politicians prevented his selection for the long term (C. P. Markle to John Covode, Jan. 8, 1861, Historical Society of Western Pennsylvania), but, when Lincoln finally appointed Cameron to his cabinet, Wilmot was chosen to succeed him for the short term, 1861–63. In the Senate, he was a faithful supporter of Lincoln and had the satisfaction of seeing his proviso finally enacted into a law forbidding slavery in the territories, the act approved June 19, 1862. When a Democratic legislature forced him to retire, Lincoln appointed him judge of the reorganized court of claims. His health, however, was failing, and his service, neither continuous nor effective, was terminated by death. He was survived by his wife and one of their three children.

[C. B. Going, *David Wilmot, Free-Soiler* (1924); C. E. Persinger, "The 'Bargain of 1844' as the Origin of the Wilmot Proviso," *Ann. Rept. of the Am. Hist. Asso. . . . 1911*, vol. I (1913); *Press* (Philadelphia), Mar. 19, 1868.]

                                         R. F. N.

WILSON, ALEXANDER (July 6, 1766–Aug. 23, 1813), ornithologist, was born in the Seed Hills of Paisley, in Renfrewshire, Scotland, the son of Alexander Wilson and Mary (McNab). His mother died when he was a child and his father married again. There was a large family and they were often in want, so the boy had little opportunity for more than a rudimentary education. At the age of thirteen he was apprenticed to the weaver's trade, the occupation of most of his relatives and other residents of the neighborhood. The confinement of the loom was irksome to him, for he loved the out-of-doors and even at this time was familiar with the birds and flowers of his native land. Nevertheless, he continued for some ten years as a weaver, and then toured eastern Scotland as a peddler. He was at heart a poet, and was constantly attempting verses, some of which, published anonymously, were attributed to Burns, whom he greatly admired. He realized one of his ambitions in 1790 with the publication of a small volume, *Poems*, but it was an indifferent production and did not bring him the renown he had hoped for.

Discouraged by this failure, by the poverty that surrounded him, and by a brief imprisonment for publishing a bitter personal satire, which was ordered burned by the hangman, he decided to try his fortune in the New World, and with his nephew William Duncan sailed for America on May 23, 1794. Reaching New Castle, Del., in July, he disembarked and proceeded to Philadelphia on foot, rejoicing in the beauty of the country and the new birds which he saw on every side. The opportunities for making a living at his trade proved to be no better than in Scotland, but having spent much spare time in reading and in self education Wilson felt that he was competent to fill the post of schoolmaster. He gave immediate satisfaction to the patrons of his first school and for about ten years followed this calling, teaching in small country schools in various parts of New Jersey and eastern Pennsylvania.

In February 1802 he took over the school at Gray's Ferry on the Schuylkill River just below Philadelphia. This charge made him a neighbor of the naturalist William Bartram [*q.v.*], a man after his own heart, capable of giving him advice and help, with a wide experience as a traveler and with a library to which Wilson was soon made welcome. Association with Bartram proved the turning point in Wilson's life, and the desire for expression for which his meager talent as a poet had proved inadequate found an outlet in the work on the birds of the United States which he was soon planning. Upon perusing the ornithological works in Bartram's library he became fully aware of their shortcomings and felt even then able to supplement them from his own knowledge. Bartram gave him every encouragement, and Wilson began at once to collect specimens and make observations of the birds of the immediate vicinity, meanwhile setting himself to learn to draw and paint them. Failing to master the art of etching which Mark Catesby [*q.v.*] and George Edwards, who were apparently his models, had employed, he engaged his fellow Scot, Alexander Lawson [*q.v.*], to pre-

pare the plates from his drawings, and to the latter almost as much as to Wilson is due the success of the undertaking. In April 1807 Samuel F. Bradford of Philadelphia, then engaged in publishing a new edition of Abraham Rees's *Cyclopaedia*, employed Wilson as assistant editor, and he thus not only escaped from the drudgery of school teaching, of which he had constantly complained, but found opportunity to interest his employer in financing his proposed *American Ornithology*. The preparation of this work now went on apace; the first volume appeared in 1808 and seven had been published by 1813. The eighth was in press, when the author, through overwork in his anxiety to complete his undertaking, so weakened his constitution that he was unable to withstand an attack of dysentery, and died after a few days' illness. George Ord [*q.v.*], Wilson's companion during the last years of his life and his ardent admirer, completed the *American Ornithology* from Wilson's manuscripts and later published two new editions to meet the demand for the book that had developed. While Wilson did not live to enjoy any financial profit from his labors nor much of the praise that they elicited, he was recognized during his lifetime by election to the Columbian Society of Artists, the American Philosophical Society, and the Academy of Natural Sciences of Philadelphia.

Wilson's reputation rests wholly upon his *American Ornithology*, a work of outstanding merit. Nothing like it in any branch of science had appeared in America up to that time and the mere conception of such a work, not to speak of its successful completion, was remarkable. He had access to the writings of Catesby, Latham, Turton, Edwards, and Bartram, but found little in them to help him beyond the names and technical descriptions, so that his book is practically all his own. He wrote well, presenting in a clear style his experiences with the birds and their characteristics as he saw them, with none of the egotism or exaggeration of some writers in their striving for literary effect. From his figures drawn in pencil or in ink, sometimes only an outline, the engraver produced the plate for his criticism. The sample proof was then colored by him as model for the colorist of the other copies, who was apparently an artist, although Wilson did some of this work himself in the first edition and that in the Ord editions was done by Lawson's daughters. Only ten years were devoted to the accumulation of the materials upon which the *Ornithology* is based and to its publication, while J. J. Audubon [*q.v.*], by way of comparison, spent thirty years in field work and painting before he began the publication of his *Birds of America*. Wilson covered only the eastern United States north of Florida, but during the next hundred years ornithologists have been able to add but twenty-three indigenous land birds to his list. Baron Cuvier seems to have expressed the European attitude toward Wilson's volumes when he wrote: "He has treated of American birds better than those of Europe have yet been treated" (quoted by Jordan, *post*, p. 69), and Dr. Elliott Coues has said: "Perhaps no other work on ornithology of equal extent is equally free from error; and its truthfulness is illumined by a spark of the 'fire divine.' . . . Science would lose little, but, on the contrary, would gain much if every scrap of pre-Wilsonian writing about United States birds could be annihilated" (*Birds of the Colorado Valley*, pt. I, 1878, p. 600).

While love of tramping took Wilson over much of the country surrounding Philadelphia, he made comparatively few long journeys. In October 1804, with a companion, he set out to walk from Philadelphia to Niagara Falls and back, publishing after he returned an account of his trip in verse, *The Foresters* (1805), which has been republished several times. In 1808, when the first volume of the *American Ornithology* had appeared, he started on a personal canvass of the country in search of the 250 subscribers at $120 each which were considered necessary before publication could proceed. Traveling partly by stage and partly on foot, he visited the cities and towns from Portland, Me., to Savannah, Ga., making acquaintants and securing valuable correspondents as well as the necessary subscribers and further ornithological information. In 1809 he visited St. Augustine, Fla., and in 1810 he made a journey into the ornithological *terra incognita* which lay west of the Alleghanies in search of additional birds. Going down the Ohio from Pittsburgh in a small boat, he proceeded thence by horseback or on foot to New Orleans, and returned to Philadelphia by sea, but although he secured many interesting specimens there were none that could not have been found east of the mountains. Had he explored Florida, however, instead of rounding it on his voyage, he might have added to his collection many species then quite unknown.

Wilson the man, his friend and biographer George Ord characterized as "possessed of the nicest sense of honor . . . not only scrupulously just, but highly generous . . . social and affectionate," adding, "He was of the *Genus irritabile*, and was obstinate in opinion. It ever gave him pleasure to acknowledge error when the con-

viction resulted from his own judgment alone, but he could not endure to be told of his mistakes" (*post*, pp. xlvi–xlvii). He was of medium height, and thin, with projecting cheek bones and hollow but vivacious eyes. "His complexion was sallow, his mien thoughtful; his features were coarse, and there was a dash of vulgarity which struck the observer at first view, but which failed to impress one on acquaintance" (Jordan, p. 67). Careless but not eccentric in dress, he was very particular about his linen. He was "almost a pure type of the bilious temperament, which is best fitted for constant exertion, and he could bear great fatigue without flinching." His hands were delicate; "he wrote beautifully and played charmingly on the flute." At the time of his death he was engaged to marry Sarah Miller, sister of Hon. Daniel Miller, a member of Congress from Philadelphia, and he was buried in the graveyard of Old Swedes Church, Philadelphia, under a stone erected by his fiancée.

After his death a volume entitled *Poems; Chiefly in the Scottish Dialect, by Alexander Wilson, Author of American Ornithology, with an Account of His Life and Writings* (1816) was printed in Paisley and published in London. Wilson's poems are undistinguished except by their great fidelity to nature; much more felicitous are the charming essays in his *American Ornithology* in which he introduces the reader in an intimate and personal fashion to the birds he loves. He has been called "the pioneer writer of the bird essay" and was certainly one of the pioneers in American nature literature.

[Biog. sketch by George Ord in *Am. Ornithology*, vol. IX (1814); "Life" in *Poems* (1816), mentioned above; William Dunlap, *A Hist. of the Rise and Progress of the Arts of Design in the U. S.* (1834), vol. II; Henry Simpson, *The Lives of Eminent Philadelphians* (1859); A. B. Grosart, *Memoir and Remains of Alexander Wilson* (2 vols., 1876); J. S. Wilson, *Alexander Wilson: Poet-Naturalist* (1906); Witmer Stone, "Alexander Wilson," in D. S. Jordan, *Leading Am. Men of Science* (1910); *Auk*, Apr. 1901, July 1917; studies by F. L. Burns, in *Wilson Bull.* (Oberlin, Ohio), vols. XX–XXII (1908–10), *passim*; *Cassinia*, vol. XVII (1913); Gordon Wilson, *Alexander Wilson* (1930), abstract of thesis, Ind. Univ.; D. C. Peattie, *Green Laurels* (1936).]
          W.S.

WILSON, ALLEN BENJAMIN (Oct. 18, 1824–Apr. 29, 1888), inventor, was the son of Benjamin and Frances Wilson, and was born at Willet, Cortland County, N. Y., where his father was engaged as a millwright. He led a normal boy's life, attending school in the winter and assisting his father, but with the accidental death of the latter in 1835 Wilson was indentured to a neighboring farmer who was also a carpenter. After a year, although but twelve years old, he struck out for himself, working on various farms and picking up a bit of the blacksmith's trade on the side. In 1840 he apprenticed himself to a cabinet-maker at Cincinnatus, Cortland County, N. Y. After learning this trade he again took the road and worked as journeyman cabinet-maker in various parts of the East and Middle West. In 1847, while employed at his trade at Adrian, Mich., he conceived the idea of a sewing machine without having heard of or seen one, but illness and poverty prevented him from converting his idea into a practical form at that time. The following year, however, while employed at Pittsfield, Mass., he progressed to the point of preparing full-sized drawings, and on Feb. 3, 1849, began the construction of his first machine. The machine was very crude, but Wilson could sew with it, and it possessed one very interesting feature, that of a double-pointed shuttle which moved in a curved path and formed a stitch at each forward and backward stroke. In this respect it differed from the invention of Elias Howe [q.v.]. In order to acquire sufficient money to secure a patent, Wilson induced Joseph N. Chapin of North Adams, Mass., to buy a half interest in the invention for $200, and with this he secured a United States patent on Nov. 12, 1850. During the year that this patent was pending Wilson was threatened with a lawsuit by the owners of another patent covering a double-pointed shuttle. In view of the fact that he had no money with which to defend himself, he compromised by conveying half of his patent interest to E. Lee & Company of New York, and agreed to assist in the manufacture and sale of the machines. Shortly after securing his patent he sold all of his interests to the company for $2000, reserving only the rights to manufacture the machine in New Jersey and to use it to sew leather in Massachusetts.

Just before this Wilson had met Nathaniel Wheeler [q.v.], who was so much interested in the invention that he contracted with E. Lee & Company to make five hundred of the machines and persuaded Wilson to remove to Watertown, Conn., to superintend the work. Wilson meanwhile had devised on paper the rotary hook and bobbin as a substitute for the double-pointed shuttle. Devoting his first attention to developing this new contrivance, he obtained a patent on Aug. 12, 1851. Wheeler thereupon took Wilson into partnership with him under the name of Wheeler, Wilson & Company, and began the manufacture of sewing machines with Wilson's new improvement, leaving E. Lee & Company to shift for itself. With Wheeler in charge of the commercial side of the business, which was an immediate success, Wilson contrived a stationary bobbin which became a permanent feature of the Wheeler & Wilson sewing machine. He then turned to the improvement of the feeding mechanism of the sewing machine, and on Dec. 19, 1854, obtained patent No. 12,116 for his four-motion feed, a fundamental invention used on all later sewing machines. Before this patent was issued, however, on account of ill health, and at his own request, he was relieved from active service and responsibility in the company. Thereafter until his death he devoted himself to other inventions, such as cotton-picking machines, and devices for photography and for the manufacture of illuminating gas. Compared with Howe and Isaac M. Singer [q.v.], he did not receive a proper reward for his inventions even though an extension of his patents had been granted by Congress. His revolving-hook system has remained unchanged in principle, and continues in use; a sewing machine embodying the form and principles used in the first type of machine manufactured in 1852 by the Wheeler & Wilson Company is made and used by its successor today (1936). In 1850 Wilson married Harriet Emeline Brooks of Williamstown, Mass., and at the time of his death at Woodmont, Conn., he was survived by his widow and one child. He was buried at Waterbury, Conn.

[E. W. Byrn, *Progress of Invention in the Nineteenth Century* (1900); C. M. Depew, *One Hundred Years of Am. Commerce*, vol. II (1895); F. L. Lewton, "The Servant in the House: a Brief Hist. of the Sewing Machine," *Ann. Report . . . Smithsonian Inst.* (1929); Joseph Anderson, *The Town and City of Waterbury, Conn.* (1896), vol. II; Patent Office records; obituary in *N. Y. Times*, Apr. 30, 1888.]   C. W. M.

WILSON, AUGUSTA JANE EVANS [See EVANS, AUGUSTA JANE, 1835–1909].

WILSON, BIRD (Jan. 8, 1777–Apr. 14, 1859), jurist, Episcopal clergyman and professor of theology, was born at Carlisle, Pa., the son of James Wilson, 1742–1798 [q.v.], and Rachel (Bird) Wilson. In 1789 he entered the College of Philadelphia (united in 1791 with the University of Pennsylvania), graduating in 1792. He studied law under Joseph Thomas of Philadelphia, and was admitted to the bar in 1797. After holding a position under the commissioner of bankrupt law, in 1802 he was appointed president of the court of common pleas in the seventh circuit. Only one of his decisions was ever reversed, and in that case an important new document had been found. He edited his father's writings—*The Works of the Honorable James Wilson* (3 vols., 1804)—and an American edition of Matthew Bacon's *A New Abridgment of the Law* (7 vols., 1811), adding some American and later English decisions. Active in the organization of St. John's Church, Norristown, he served it as warden and as deputy to the diocesan convention.

He was deeply affected when called on to pronounce the death sentence, and late in 1817, partly because of the appearance of another capital case on the docket of his court, he resigned and studied for the ministry. On Mar. 12, 1819, Bishop William White, who had probably directed his studies, ordained him deacon, and about a year later, priest. Soon after, the rector having died, he was called to St. John's, Norristown, and St. Thomas', Whitemarsh. His parish ministry was successful, but short. Elected in 1821 professor of systematic divinity in the General Theological Seminary, in the spring of 1822 he took up his duties in New York. In 1826, at the election of an assistant to Bishop White, Wilson received twenty-six votes out of fifty-four, but withdrew from the contest. He remained canonically resident in the diocese of Pennsylvania, but took no further active part in its affairs. From 1829 to 1841 he was secretary of the House of Bishops. When White died, Wilson, at the request of the family and clergy, wrote the Bishop's biography—*Memoir of the Life of the Rt. Rev. William White* (1839), a readable and accurate account of an important career.

In 1827 the seminary had moved to Twentieth Street, Wilson taking one of the professors' houses. With Prof. S. H. Turner he conducted services for that then suburban neighborhood, and out of them grew St. Peter's Church. His theological position was, like White's, in the moderate Anglican tradition, opposed both to high-church extremes and to Calvinism. As dean of the seminary, an office then held by the resident professors in turn, he presided in 1844–45 over the trial of several tractarian students accused of Roman sympathies, an episode that depressed him greatly. In 1848, feeling himself neither wanted nor useful, he sent his resignation to the trustees, but it was rejected. In 1850 he retired as professor emeritus, and moved to a house near the seminary. The last years of his life he suffered from softening of the brain.

Wilson's learning and teaching ability were held in high esteem. He was gentle but firm, and his theology, like his law, was clear, accurate, and sympathetically interpreted. A good picture of his "old-fashioned Episcopalianism" may be found in his *Address Before the General Theological Seminary* (1823), which is on the study of theology, in a sermon preached in 1826, "The Practical Importance of the Doctrine of the Trinity" (in *A Contribution to the Doctrine of the Atonement*, 1865), and in a *Sermon in the Chapel of the Seminary* (1828), which discusses what to preach.

[W. W. Bronson, *A Memorial of the Rev. Bird Wilson* (1864), with appendix containing lecture notes and two sermons; S. H. Turner, *Sermon in Commemoration of the Late Bird Wilson* (1859); J. H. Hopkins, *The Life of the Late Rt. Rev. J. H. Hopkins* (1873), containing account of the election of White's assistant; death notice in *N. Y. Times*, Apr. 15, 1859.]

E. R. H., Jr.

WILSON, ERNEST HENRY (Feb. 15, 1876–Oct. 15, 1930), plant collector, botanist, was born at Chipping Campden, Gloucestershire, England, the eldest son of Henry and Annie (Curtis) Wilson. At sixteen he entered the Birmingham Botanic Gardens as a gardener, at the same time studying botany at the Birmingham Technical School. Five years later he became a worker and student at the Royal Botanic Gardens at Kew, and in October 1898 entered the Royal College of Science at South Kensington to study botany with the idea of teaching it. He made his first plant-collecting trip in 1899, when he was sent to China by the well-known nursery firm of James Veitch and Sons to collect plants and seeds. After three years, most of which he spent in Hupeh, he returned to England. On June 8, 1902, he was married to Ellen Ganderton of Edgbaston, Warwickshire, by whom he had one daughter. In January 1903 he was again sent by Veitch to China. In these two expeditions he collected two thousand seeds and plants. In 1906 he served as botanical assistant at the Imperial Institute in London. A year later he was engaged by Charles Sprague Sargent [*q.v.*] for a two-year expedition to China (1907–09) as a collector of plants, especially trees and shrubs, for the Arnold Arboretum, Harvard University, and in 1910 made another trip, going to Hupeh and Szechuan. During his previous trips in China he had traveled chiefly by water; the journey of 1910 was a difficult one overland, and Wilson had the misfortune to break his leg, which remained permanently shortened. It was on this expedition that he secured the beautiful Regal Lily, one of his most notable plant introductions. His three other trips for the Arnold Arboretum took him to Japan (1914–15), to Formosa, Korea, and Japan (1917–19), and to India, Australia, New Zealand, and Africa (1920–22), the object of the last trip being to establish closer relations between the Arboretum and other botanical institutions. He introduced to cultivation more than a thousand species of plants (Rehder, *post*, p. 185), many of them widely grown. Among his best known introductions are *Buddleia Davidii magnifica, Kolkwitzia amabilis* or Beauty Bush, and *Malus theifera* or

Tea Crab. He was especially interested in trees and shrubs. He also took a great many valuable photographs and collected thousands of herbarium specimens, which are to be found not only in the Arnold Arboretum but in important herbaria throughout the world (*Ibid.*). In April 1919 he was appointed assistant director of the Arnold Arboretum, and in 1927 he was given the title of keeper. He died at the age of fifty-four, killed with his wife in an automobile accident near Worcester, Mass.

Besides being a remarkably skilful collector, Wilson was a prolific and entertaining writer on horticultural subjects. Among his scientific publications were *The Conifers and Taxads of Japan* (1916), *Plantae Wilsonianae* (3 vols., 1913–17), edited by C. S. Sargent, *A Monograph of Azaleas* (1921), written with Alfred Rehder, and *The Lilies of Eastern Asia* (1925). His more popular books include *Aristocrats of the Garden* (1917), *Plant Hunting* (2 vols., 1927), *China— Mother of Gardens* (1929), and *Aristocrats of the Trees* (1930). Wilson was a member of many botanical and horticultural organizations, and was the recipient of a number of medals and other awards for his work with plants.

[*Who's Who in America*, 1930–31; E. I. Farrington, *Ernest H. Wilson, Plant Hunter* (1931); Alfred Rehder, in *Jour. Arnold Arboretum*, Oct. 1930, with bibliog.; Richardson Wright, in *House and Garden*, Jan. 1931; Leonard Barron, in *Country Life*, Dec. 1930; obituary in *Boston Transcript*, Oct. 16, 1930.]   J. G. J.

WILSON, GEORGE FRANCIS (Dec. 7, 1818–Jan. 19, 1883, manufacturer, inventor, was the eldest son of Benjamin and Mercy Wilson, and was born on his father's farm at Uxbridge, Mass. He was a lineal descendant of Roger Wilson of Scrooby, England, who in 1608 went to Leyden, Holland, with Governor Bradford and other Pilgrims, and whose son, John, emigrated to New England in 1651. Wilson remained at home throughout his early youth, helping his father and attending the district schools, but upon reaching his seventeenth birthday he was apprenticed to Welcome and Darius Farnum at Waterford, Mass., to learn the wool-sorting business. He remained three years and not only mastered the trade but also became thoroughly versed in all the mechanical equipment used. Feeling the need of greater business experience, he spent another year as a bookkeeper in Uxbridge, and in 1840, using his savings, entered the academy in Shelburne Falls, Mass. After his graduation, he spent several years teaching at the academy. In 1844 he took his bride to Chicago, Ill., where he organized the Chicago Academy in the Methodist Episcopal Church at the corner of Clark and Washington Streets. In

four years the enrollment was increased from three to two hundred and twenty-five scholars. For some reason Wilson gave up this work in 1848, returned east to Providence, R. I., and for the next six years was variously employed in manufactures thereabout. In 1855, however, he entered into a partnership for the manufacture of chemicals with Eben N. Horsford [*q.v.*], at that time Rumford Professor of Chemistry at Harvard College, the firm name being George F. Wilson and Company. This undertaking was immediately successful, Horsford determining what products were to be made, and Wilson developing the manufacturing equipment (much of it possessing ingenious mechanical features) for their commercial production. Within two years it became necessary to build a new and larger plant, at East Providence, R. I. At the same time the firm name was changed to the Rumford Chemical Company. Thereafter until his death Wilson continued at its head, building up a prosperous and extensive business.

Aside from the many and varied inventions which he devised for his own establishment, he found time to perfect other inventions, among which were a process of steel manufacture, a revolving paper-pulp boiler, and several improvements in illuminating apparatus for lighthouses. Because of his aptitude for mechanical science and its applications, he was much consulted by others for the solution of mechanical problems. As an avocation he experimented in agriculture and stock breeding, and was actively interested in scientific education. From 1860 to 1862 he represented Providence in the state legislature, and served on the Providence school committee and town council for a number of years. At his death he bequeathed one hundred thousand dollars to Brown University and fifty thousand dollars to Dartmouth College, both for strictly scientific purposes. Wilson was married in 1844 to Clarissa Bartlett of Conway, Mass. (d. 1880). At the time of his death in East Providence, where he resided after 1861, he was survived by five children.

[*Proc. R. I. Hist. Soc.* (1884); graduate records, Brown Univ.; Patent Office records; obituary in *Providence Daily Jour.*, Jan. 22, 1883.]   C. W. M.

WILSON, HENRY (Feb. 16, 1812–Nov. 22, 1875), United States senator, vice-president, born at Farmington, N. H., and named Jeremiah Jones Colbath, was one of the many children of Winthrop and Abigail (Witham) Colbath. The father was a day-laborer in a sawmill. So dire was the family's poverty that soon after the boy's tenth birthday he was bound by indenture to work for a neighboring farmer; he was to have food and clothing, and one month's schooling each winter. For more than ten years he worked at increasingly heavy farm labor. Two neighbors lent him books and directed his reading. By the end of his service he had "inwardly digested" nearly a thousand volumes, including the best in English and American history and biography. At twenty-one he received in quittance "six sheep and a yoke of oxen," which he immediately sold for $85—the first money returns for his years of work. At this period, with the approval of his parents, he had his name changed by act of the legislature to Henry Wilson.

After some weeks of unsuccessful job-hunting in neighboring towns, he walked more than a hundred miles to Natick, Mass., and hired himself to a man who agreed, in return for five months' labor, to teach him to make "brogans." In a few weeks he "bought his time" and began to work for himself. For several years he drove himself hard at the shoemaker's bench, intent upon getting together enough money to begin the study of law. Meanwhile, he was reading incessantly and developing effectiveness in public speaking by taking an active part in the weekly meetings of the Natick Debating Society. To regain his health, broken by overwork, he made a trip to Virginia. In Washington he listened to passionate debates over slavery, and in the nearby slave pen watched negro families separated and fathers, mothers, and children sold at auction as slaves. Many years later he declared: "I left the capital of my country with the unalterable resolution to give all that I had, and all that I hoped to have, of power, to the cause of emancipation in America" (Nason and Russell, *post,* p. 31). With health restored, he turned to study; three brief terms in New Hampshire academies (at Strafford, Wolfborough, and Concord) ended his meager schooling. His savings exhausted, he returned to Natick, paid off his debt by teaching district school in the winter term, and then with a capital of a very few dollars started to manufacture shoes, continuing in this industry for nearly ten years and at times employing over a hundred workers. He dealt with them as man to man, and won their entire confidence and devotion. He was moderately successful in business, but the making of a fortune was not a career that attracted him. On Oct. 28, 1840, he married Harriet Malvina Howe. Their only son, Henry Hamilton Wilson (d. 1866) served with distinction in the Civil War, attaining the rank of lieutenant-colonel of a colored regiment.

In 1840 Wilson supported the Whig candidate, Harrison, for president, believing that the Democrats' financial policy had injured the industrial interests of the North and brought misery to its wage-earners. In that year he was elected to the Massachusetts House of Representatives, and for the next dozen years only twice did he fail to win a seat in one branch or the other of the legislature. In 1845 he was active in the Concord convention in protest against the extension of slavery, and with Whittier was chosen to present to Congress the petition of 65,000 Massachusetts citizens against the annexation of Texas. At the Whig national convention in Philadelphia (June 1848) when General Taylor was nominated for the presidency and no stand taken by the party as to the Wilmot Proviso, Wilson and Charles Allen, another Massachusetts delegate, headed the small group that denounced the Whigs' action, withdrew from the convention hall, and called the convention at Buffalo which launched the Free Soil party. From 1848 to 1851 Wilson edited the *Boston Republican,* the organ of that party. He was mainly instrumental in bringing about in 1851 the coalition—abhorred by all straight party men of that day—which resulted in the election of Charles Sumner to the United States Senate. In 1851 and 1852 Wilson was president of the state Senate. In the latter year he served as chairman of the Free Soil national convention. Believing that the rising American (Know Nothing) party might be liberalized so as to become an important force for the cause of freedom, in 1854, with many other anti-slavery men, he joined that organization. No act of his life drew upon him so much criticism, and he soon came to deplore the step he had taken. He loathed the intolerant nativist spirit of the Know Nothings, and before many months had passed he declared that if the American party should prove "recreant to freedom" he would do his utmost to "shiver it to atoms" (Nason and Russell, p. 121). Over his vehement protest the American National Council at Philadelphia in 1855 adopted a platform as evasive on the slavery issue as had been that of the Whig convention in 1848, and forthwith Wilson again led anti-slavery delegates from the hall in a revolt which dismembered the American party in its first attempt to control national politics.

In January 1855—by a legislature almost entirely "American" in membership—Wilson had already been elected to fill the vacancy in the Senate caused by the resignation of Edward Everett [*q.v.*]. In his very first speech he aligned himself with those who favored the abolition of slavery "wherever we are morally or legally responsible for its existence" (*i.e.* in the District of Columbia and the Territories), and the repeal of the fugitive slave law, declaring his firm belief that, if the federal government were thus relieved from all connection with and responsibility for the existence of slavery, "the men of the South who are opposed to the existence of that institution, would get rid of it in their own States at no distant day" (*Congressional Globe*, 33 Cong., 2 Sess., p. 238). He was outspoken in the debate upon the struggle in Kansas. Following Brooks's assault upon Sumner, Wilson upon the floor of the Senate characterized that act as "brutal, murderous, and cowardly" (*Ibid.*, 34 Cong., 1 Sess., p. 1306). This brought a challenge from Brooks, to which Wilson instantly wrote a reply declining to "make any qualification whatever . . . in regard to those words," and adding: "The law of my country and the matured convictions of my whole life alike forbid me to meet you for the purpose indicated in your letter" (*History of the Rise and Fall of the Slave Power*, II, 487). In many states Wilson took a most active part in the campaign for the election of Lincoln. While peace hung in the balance, he made a powerful speech against the Crittenden compromise (*Congressional Globe*, 36 Cong., 2 Sess., pp. 1088–94).

With the outbreak of the war heavy responsibilities at once devolved upon him. For nine years he had been a member of the Massachusetts state militia, rising to the grade of brigadier-general. In the Senate he had served for several years on the committee on military affairs. To its chairmanship he now brought a combination of long military and legislative experience unequaled by that of any other member of the Senate. With tremendous energy he threw himself into the task of framing, explaining, and defending legislative measures necessary for enlisting, organizing, and provisioning a vast army. Gen. Winfield Scott declared that in that short session of Congress Wilson had done more work "than all the chairmen of the military committees had done for the last twenty years" (Nason and Russell, p. 307). At the end of the session, he returned to Massachusetts and within forty days recruited nearly 2300 men. Simon Cameron, secretary of war, wrote to Wilson, Jan. 27, 1862: "No man, in my opinion, in the whole country, has done more to aid the war department in preparing the mighty army now under arms than yourself" (*Ibid.*, p. 316). He constantly urged Lincoln to proclaim emancipation as a war measure, and he shaped the bills which brought freedom to scores of thousands of slaves in the border states, years before the ratification of the Thirteenth Amendment. In March 1865 he reported from the Senate conference committee the bill for the establishment of the Freedmen's Bureau.

He was a bitter opponent of Johnson's reconstruction policy and attitude toward Congress. In that dark era Wilson was so concerned for the welfare of the freedmen in whose cause he had long been fighting that he could not appreciate the realities of the chaos in which the South had been left by the war, nor the sincerity and self-sacrifice with which many of the Southern leaders were grappling with the problems of reconstruction. He therefore joined with extremists in Congress in imposing tests and restrictions which in the retrospect of seventy years seem unnecessarily harsh and unrelenting. As a result of long tours through the South and West, however, his attitude soon became more conciliatory; he conferred frankly with pre-war Southern leaders, and counseled the freedmen who thronged to hear him to learn something, to get and till a bit of land, and to obey the law. He favored federal legislation in aid of education and homesteading in the impoverished Southern states. In 1872 the nomination of Wilson for vice-president strengthened the Republican ticket. He proved a highly efficient and acceptable presiding officer, though ill health soon made his attendance irregular. In November 1875 he suffered a paralytic stroke in the Capitol and was taken to the Vice-President's Room, where twelve days later he died. He was buried in Old Dell Park Cemetery, Natick.

Through nearly thirty years of public service Wilson did not allow personal ambition to swerve him from the unpopular causes to which he had devoted himself from the beginning—the freeing of the slave, and the gaining for the workingman, white or black, a position of opportunity and of dignity such as befitted the citizen of a republic. To gain these ends he did not hesitate to compromise on what he deemed non-essentials, to cut loose from old party ties, and to manipulate new coalitions to the dismay of party leaders who denounced him as a shifty politician. His sympathies were always with the workers from whose ranks he had sprung, and in his career they found incentive and inspiration. In his own state he was the champion of the free public school, of the free public library, of exemption of workers' tools and household furniture from taxation, and of the removal of property tests from office-holding. In the opinion of Senator G. F. Hoar (*post*, pp. 213, 216–17), Wilson was "a skilful, adroit, practiced and constant political manager"—"the most skilful political organizer in the country" of his day. No other leader of that period could sense as clearly as he what the farmer, the mechanic, and the workingman were thinking about, and he "addressed himself always to their best and highest thought." Wilson brought together much valuable material in the following books: *History of the Antislavery Measures of the Thirty-seventh and Thirty-eighth United States Congresses* (1864); *Military Measures of the United States Congress, 1861–1865* (1866); *History of the Reconstruction Measures of the Thirty-ninth and Fortieth Congresses* (1868); and *History of the Rise and Fall of the Slave Power in America* (3 vols., 1872–77), the last written with the zeal and the bias of a crusader, but without over-emphasis upon his own part in the movement.

[The most detailed account of Wilson is Elias Nason and Thomas Russell, *The Life and Public Services of Henry Wilson* (1876), a laudatory, crudely expanded revision of Nason's campaign biography of 1872. See, also, *Memorial Addresses on the Life and Character of Henry Wilson . . . Delivered in the Senate and House of Representatives Jan. 21, 1876* (1876); *New Eng. Hist. and Geneal. Reg.*, July 1878; G. F. Hoar, *Autobiog. of Seventy Years* (1903); *Biog. Dir. Am. Cong.* (1928); *Evening Star* (Washington) and *Boston Transcript*, Nov. 22, 1875.]   G. H. H.

WILSON, HENRY LANE (Nov. 3, 1857–Dec. 22, 1932), diplomat, was born at Crawfordsville, Ind., the son of James and Emma (Ingersoll) Wilson and the descendant of a well-to-do Scotch-Irish family that emigrated from Londonderry to western Virginia about 1730. His father was a representative in Congress from Indiana, 1857–61, and an officer in the Civil War, and died in 1867 while serving as minister to Venezuela. The boy received a public school education and graduated from Wabash College in Crawfordsville in 1879. He studied law in the office of President Benjamin Harrison at Indianapolis and was from 1882 to 1885 editor and owner of the *Journal* of Lafayette, Ind. He married Alice Vajan of Indiana in October 1884. They had three sons. The next eleven years he spent in Spokane, Wash., practising law and engaging in banking and real estate operations. He lost virtually everything in the panic of 1893.

While in Washington he entered politics, successfully managing the campaign of his brother, John Lockwood Wilson [*q.v.*], for the federal Senate in 1895 and representing the state on the committee that notified William McKinley of his nomination for president. In 1889 President Harrison appropriately offered him the appointment as minister to Venezuela, but he declined it. McKinley appointed him on June 9, 1897, minister to Chile, and he served with ability for seven rather uneventful years, declining the offer of the post of minister to Greece in 1902. He

was considered as having been instrumental in averting differences between Chile and Argentina in 1900 and received a popular demonstration of approval at Santiago. Immediately after the termination of his service in Chile he spent several weeks, at the request of President Theodore Roosevelt, in ascertaining political feeling in several states during the campaign of 1904. In response to his request for a European post, he was appointed minister to Belgium on Mar. 8, 1905. During his four years at Brussels he served as American representative at a conference held in April 1908 "to revise the arms and ammunitions regulations of the General Act of Brussels of 1890," and he represented the President at the coronation of King Albert of Belgium in December 1909. On Dec. 21, 1909, he was appointed ambassador to Mexico, an important and turbulent post. During the period of the overthrow of the Diaz régime and the revolutionary period that followed he was a vigorous defender of American interests. Although his course received the approval of President Taft, he was quite generally believed to have played an improper part in the Huerta-Diaz *coup,* as an aftermath of which President Madero was assassinated. He urged both the Taft and Wilson administrations to recognize the Huerta government, but without success. There was considerable hostility in Mexico towards him, and President Wilson's lack of confidence in the ambassador, whom he had retained in office, was evidenced by his decision to send John Lind [*q.v.*] to Mexico as a special commissioner. In view of the strained situation Wilson tendered his resignation on two occasions, but it was not accepted until the latter part of August 1913, to take effect Oct. 14, 1913.

Although in practical retirement after 1913, he was by no means inactive. During 1915, 1916, and 1917 he served as president of the World Court League, the Security League, and the League to Enforce Peace. In 1923 President Coolidge offered him the appointment as ambassador to Turkey, but there were delays, the appointment was never made, and Wilson applied himself to recouping financial losses suffered over the period of his diplomatic career. His *Diplomatic Episodes in Mexico, Belgium and Chile* appeared in 1927. He died at Indianapolis.

[*Who's Who in America*, 1932–33; *N. Y. Times*, Dec. 23, 1932; *Register of the Department of State*, 1913; R. S. Baker, *Woodrow Wilson: Life and Letters*, vol. IV (1931); dates of birth and appointments from records of state department and his son, Warden McKee Wilson, first secretary of American legation, The Hague.]   E. W. S.

WILSON, HENRY PARKE CUSTIS (Mar. 5, 1827–Dec. 27, 1897), surgeon, pioneer Maryland gynecologist, was born at Workington, Somerset County, Md., the son of Henry Parke Custis and Susan E. (Savage) Wilson. A paternal ancestor, Ephraim Wilson, emigrated to America from Ireland in the early part of the eighteenth century and settled on the Eastern Shore of Maryland, becoming one of the founders of the first Presbyterian Church in America. Wilson was proud of his Parke as well as of his Custis ancestry, the latter connecting him with the Washington and Lee families of Virginia. After taking the degree of B.A. at the College of New Jersey (later Princeton) in 1848, he began to study medicine in Northampton County, Va., under William G. Smith. He attended one course of lectures at the University of Virginia and one course at the University of Maryland, graduating from the latter in 1851 and settling in Baltimore to practise. There he worked with Richard Henry Thomas, whom he accompanied on his daily rounds of visits. For some years he was the only gynecologist in the city. He was the first in the state to remove the uterine appendages by abdominal section and the second in Maryland to perform a successful ovariotomy (1866). He was said to be the second in the world to remove an intra-uterine tumor filling the whole pelvis by cutting it away in pieces (morcellation) after other methods had failed, the patient recovering. In 1880, by abdominal section, he delivered an eight-pound living child from the abdominal cavity, a living child having previously been delivered from the uterus *per vias naturales* (reported in *American Journal of Obstetrics,* Oct. 1880). He also devised sundry instruments for use in gynecological surgery. His writings dealt exclusively with the problems of his specialty.

He served as president of the Medical and Chirurgical Faculty of Maryland in 1880–81 and in his presidential address urged the construction of a fireproof library building (*Transactions,* 1881). That same year he was also president of the Baltimore Academy of Medicine. He was a founder of the Baltimore Obstetrical and Gynecological Society and of the American Gynecological Society, a member of the British Medical Association, and the British Gynecological Association, and an honorary fellow of the Edinburgh Obstetrical Society. His hospital services included those of surgeon in charge to the Baltimore City Almshouse Infirmary (1857–58), and consulting surgeon to St. Agnes Hospital from 1879 and to the Johns Hopkins Hospital from 1889. He was a co-founder with William T. Howard of the Hospital for the Women of Maryland (1882), serving with Howard as visiting gynecologist until his death. This hospital was modeled after the Woman's Hospital of the State of New York founded by James Marion Sims [*q.v.*], and like it made no provision in its early days for private or paying patients.

In 1858 Wilson married Alicia Brewer Griffith, daughter of David Griffith of Baltimore County, who with five children survived him. One son became a physician. A small man, rather stout, alert, careful in dress, Wilson was noted for his courteous manners, personal charm, and open hospitality. He was an elder in the Presbyterian Church until his death, which occurred in Baltimore.

[W. B. Atkinson, *Physicians and Surgeons of America* (1878); I. A. Watson, *Physicians and Surgeons of America* (1896); B. B. Browne, in *Trans. Am. Gynecological Soc.,* vol. XXIII (1898); J. R. Quinan, *Medic. Annals of Baltimore* (1884); E. F. Cordell, *The Medic. Annals of Md.* (1903); H. A. Kelly and W. L. Burrage, *Am. Medic. Biogs.* (1920); obituary in *Sun* (Baltimore), Dec. 28, 1897; personal recollections, and those of old friends.]   H. A. K—y.

WILSON, JAMES (Sept. 14, 1742–Aug. 21, 1798), congressman, jurist, speculator, son of William and Aleson (Landale) Wilson, was born at Carskerdo, near St. Andrews, Scotland. He entered the University of St. Andrews in November 1757, and probably remained there until 1759. He is said to have attended the University of Glasgow some time between 1759 and 1763, going from there to the University of Edinburgh in 1763. In June 1765 he left the University of Edinburgh, probably without a degree. That month he began the study of accounting, but for some reason he abandoned it at once and left for America, arriving in New York in the midst of the Stamp Act disturbances. Equipped with a much better education than most immigrants of the period and having also letters of introduction to prominent persons in Pennsylvania—among them Richard Peters, provincial secretary and trustee of the College of Philadelphia—he secured in February 1766 a position as Latin tutor in this institution. On May 19 his petition for an honorary M.A. degree was granted.

Although he retained his scholarly interests throughout life Wilson saw that advancement in America lay not in some struggling academy, but in the law. He thereupon entered the office of John Dickinson [*q.v.*] and began poring over Coke and the recent lectures of Blackstone. He remained in Dickinson's office about two years, being admitted to the bar in November 1767, but not entering upon practice at that time. With

William White [*q.v.*], one of his earliest friends, he published during his student days a series of Addisonian essays in the *Pennsylvania Chronicle* called "The Visitant." In the summer of 1768 he began practice in Reading, in agreeable proximity to Rachel Bird of "Birdsboro," for whom he had formed an attachment in Philadelphia. His practice among the conservative German farmers was "very far from being contemptible" (Wilson to White, *c.* 1770, Historical Society of Pennsylvania), but increased prospects to the westward, in addition to some obstacles in his suit with Miss Bird, induced him to settle in the Scots-Irish region at Carlisle. Here his practice increased with phenomenal rapidity: by 1774 he was charged with nearly half of the cases tried in the county court and was practising in seven other counties. He purchased a home, livestock, a slave, and, on Nov. 5, 1771, married Rachel Bird. Most of his practice involved land disputes. By 1773 he was borrowing capital to make land purchases and was infected with a virus of speculation that he never shook off. Prospering in law, which occasionally took him into New Jersey and New York, he yet found energy during six years of this early period to lecture on English literature at the College of Philadelphia.

On July 12, 1774, he was made head of a committee of correspondence at Carlisle and elected to the first provincial conference at Philadelphia. There his influence was such that he was nominated, but not elected to the legislature, as a delegate to the First Continental Congress. Immediately he began revising a manuscript entitled *Considerations on the Nature and Extent of the Legislative Authority of the British Parliament.* This he published in time for distribution to members of the Congress. Beginning this study with the "exception of being able to trace some constitutional line between those cases in which we ought, and those in which we ought not, to acknowledge the power of parliament over us" (*Selected Political Essays,* p. 45), Wilson finally reached the conclusion that Parliament had no authority over the colonies in any instance. Only a few had taken this advanced position as early as 1774 yet a careful examination of Wilson's original manuscript (never adequately edited) shows that he had arrived at this conclusion, and defended it with exceptionally able arguments, four years before he revised and published the essay. Ascribed at first to Franklin by *Rivington's New York Gazetteer* and noticed by Tucker and Mansfield as an able statement of the extreme American position, the pamphlet was widely read in America and England. For America its significance became historic with the

Declaration of Independence; but with its prophetic phrase stating for the first time that *"all the different members of the British empire are* DISTINCT STATES, INDEPENDANT OF EACH OTHER, BUT CONNECTED TOGETHER UNDER THE SAME SOVEREIGN" (*Selected Political Essays,* p. 81), it still has meaning as one of the ablest arguments for what the Britannic Commonwealth of Nations has become. It should be noted that in 1774 Wilson was on the extreme Whig left: thenceforward his movement to the right was steady and uninterrupted.

Wilson's notable speech before the provincial conference of January 1775 (*Ibid.,* pp. 85–101) reiterated his position and asserted that there could be such a thing as an unconstitutional act of Parliament. Presaging the distinctive American doctrine of judicial review, he introduced a resolution declaring the Boston Port Act unconstitutional, but it failed of adoption. On May 3, 1775, he was elected colonel of the 4th battalion of Cumberland County associators, though he was never in active service, and three days later he was elected to the Second Continental Congress. He was assigned to various committees, one of which was to secure the friendship of the western Indians. In August and September he attended an unsuccessful meeting with them at Pittsburgh. Early in 1776 he prepared an address to the inhabitants of the colonies (W. C. Ford, *Journals of the Continental Congress,* vol. IV, 1906, pp. 134–46), designed, as he declared to Madison, "to lead the public mind into the idea of Independence" (*Ibid.,* p. 146 n.); but soon popular sentiment had moved beyond Wilson's position and the plan to publish the address was abandoned. On the question of independence he was cautiously attentive to the wishes of his constituents, joining with Dickinson, Rutledge, and Livingston on June 8 in securing a three weeks' delay. This caused a storm of abuse to break about him, and twenty-two of his colleagues in Congress felt it necessary to issue an explanation and defense of his position (manuscript copy in Library of Congress). On July 2 he was one of three out of seven Pennsylvania delegates to vote for independence. During 1776–77 most of his time was occupied with tasks of the board of war and with his quasi-judicial duties as chairman of the standing committee on appeals. His committee assignments, which he discharged industriously, were particularly burdensome. He was one of the first to urge relinquishment of the western claims of the states, to advocate revenue and taxation powers for Congress, to try to strengthen the national government, and to seek representation according to free population, with its corollary of voting by individuals in Congress (E. C. Burnett, *Letters of Members of the Continental Congress*, II, 1923, p. 515 n; Walter Clark, *The State Records of North Carolina*, XI, II, 237).

Despite his espousal of the democratic principle and the sovereignty of the individual, Wilson so bitterly fought the constitution of Pennsylvania of 1776, a product of the democratic forces of the frontier and immigration (J. P. Selsam, *The Pennsylvania Constitution of 1776*, 1936, *passim*), that even his close friend Arthur St. Clair [*q.v.*] thought him "perhaps too warm" (W. B. Reed, *Life and Correspondence of Joseph Reed*, 1847, II, 153). This opposition to George Bryan [*q.v.*] and his party made Wilson's place in Congress increasingly precarious. Early in 1777, sensing his approaching removal, he drew up plans for a congressional legal office similar to that of the British solicitor general or the French *avocat général* (Burnett, II, 215–17). This plan he forwarded to Robert Morris [*q.v.*], hoping that Morris would secure its adoption and urging himself as a candidate for the office. Morris gave his approval, but the plan was not adopted. On Feb. 4, 1777, Wilson's expected removal took place, but the difficulty of finding a successor caused him to be reinstated on Feb. 22. He continued his opposition to the constitution of Pennsylvania, "the most detestable that ever was formed" (letter to Wayne, *c.* 1778, Wayne MSS., Historical Society of Pennsylvania), and his removal from Congress on Sept. 14, 1777, was inevitable. Because of the heat of political feeling in Pennsylvania, Wilson spent the winter of 1777–78 in Annapolis, a move which was subsequently embarrassing to him as an office holder in Pennsylvania (Max Farrand, *The Records of the Federal Convention*, 1911, II, 237).

His taking up residence in Philadelphia in 1778 was indicative of changing viewpoints: once a frontier lawyer dealing in land suits, he now became a corporation counsel; once an extreme Whig, he now became a leader of the Republican Society, an anti-Bryan organization of conservatives; once a Presbyterian, he now became an Episcopalian, the friend of Morris, Duer, Bingham and others of the aristocracy. By acting as counsel for Loyalists and by his interest in privateering, land-jobbing schemes, and various commercial enterprises, he widened the breach between himself and the populace. In 1779, during a period of food shortage and high prices, there was considerable rioting in Philadelphia against profiteers, Loyalists, and their sympa-

thizers. On Oct. 4 a handbill appeared calling upon the militia to "drive off from the city all disaffected persons and those who supported them" (Stan V. Henkels, *Catalogue No. 694: Washington-Madison Papers*, 1892, p. 239). After securing some persons, they sought Wilson "who had always plead for such" (*Ibid.*). Finding civil aid dilatory, Wilson gathered some of his friends, barricaded his home, and defended himself against the attack of the militia. A few persons were killed and wounded, but Wilson was rescued by the timely arrival of the First City Troop and President Reed. He went into hiding for a few days, appearing on Oct. 19 to post a bond of £10,000. The legislature on March 13, 1780, passed an act of oblivion for all concerned in this affair of "Fort Wilson."

With the return of the conservatives to power in Pennsylvania in 1782, Wilson was again elected to Congress, serving also in 1785–87. His principal contributions in Congress at this time were his opposition to a separate peace treaty with England, his proposal to erect states in the western lands (Apr. 9, 1783), and his successful advocacy of the general revenue plan of Apr. 19, 1783 (*The Writings of James Madison*, ed. by Gaillard Hunt, vol. I, 1900, pp. 328–30). On the second of these measures he was charged with being interested in the large land companies (Merrill Jensen, "The Cession of the Old Northwest," *Mississippi Valley Historical Review*, June 1936); and on the third, with being interested in the payment of interest on the loans of the Bank of North America. But he chiefly concerned himself in the decade between 1777 and 1787 with his multiplied business interests, to which he willingly sacrificed his professional practice. In June 1779 he was appointed *avocat général* by the French government for maritime and commercial causes, a post he held until 1783. In 1780 he acted as legal adviser to Robert Morris in the formation of the Bank of Pennsylvania, drawing up plans for this private agency for purchasing army supplies (*Pennsylvania Gazette*, July 5, 1780), and in 1785 he published his *Considerations on the Power to Incorporate the Bank of North America*, an able economic and constitutional argument in which he foreshadowed Marshall's doctrine of inherent sovereignty (*Selected Political Essays*, pp. 17–19). In November and December 1782 Wilson defended Pennsylvania's claims against the charter pretensions of Connecticut before the congressional commissioners at Trenton. His argument, wrote Joseph Reed, was "both laborious and judicious, he has taken much pains, having the success of Pennsylvania much at heart, both on public and private account" (Reed, II, 390). Wilson had invested heavily in lands within the Connecticut claim. The same year he and Mark Bird purchased the Somerset Mills on the Delaware, including a rolling- and slitting-mill, grist-mill, furnace, and sawmill, for which, in 1785, he sought to borrow 500,000 fl. from Dutch capitalists in order to expand the business (Jan. 16, 1785, Wilson MSS., Historical Society of Pennsylvania). Two months later, through Van Berkel, the Dutch minister, he sought to become agent for a gigantic land speculation to the extent of about 2,000,000 fl., offering to subordinate his law practice to this task; this proposal did not materialize. Wilson was also interested at this time in various western land companies, being president of the Illinois and Wabash Company. In the light of these wide-flung interests, Waln's statement that "as an instructor he was almost useless to those who were under his direction" (Sanderson, *post,* VI, 171–72), is plausible.

Wilson's greatest achievement in public life was his part in the establishment of the federal Constitution. With the possible exception of James Madison, with whom he was in agreement on most of the major issues, no member of the convention of 1787 was better versed in the study of political economy, none grasped more firmly the central problem of dual sovereignty, and none was more far-sighted in his vision of the future greatness of the United States. James Bryce thought him "one of the deepest thinkers and most exact reasoners" in the convention, whose works "display an amplitude and profundity of view in matters of constitutional theory which place him in the front rank of the political thinkers of his age" (*The American Commonwealth,* 1888, I, 250 n., 665 n.; see Sanderson, *post,* VI, 154, for a contemporary opinion on this point). Wilson kept constantly in view the idea that sovereignty resided in the people, favoring popular election of the president and of members of both houses. On the fundamental problem of sovereignty he clearly stated that the national government was not "an assemblage of States, but of individuals for certain political purposes" (Farrand, I, 406). He strongly opposed the idea of equal representation in the Senate, and perhaps because of his reserve and inelastic opinions, was not facile at compromise. He was a member of the important committee of detail, charged with preparing the draft of the Constitution (Wilson's draft is in Historical Society of Pennsylvania). Despite his statement that there were "some parts of it, which if my wish had prevailed, would certainly have been altered" (*Selected Political Essays,* p. 159), Wilson signed the Constitution and fought for its adoption.

Wilson was a dominating factor in the Pennsylvania ratifying convention. His speech before that body was widely read in other states, but it brought about renewed attacks upon its author. "James de Caledonia" was burned in effigy at Carlisle (*Independent Gazetteer,* Jan. 9, 1788). The drafting of the constitution of 1790 for Pennsylvania was a part of the reactionary movement following the Revolution, and Wilson was in every sense the author of that document. Modeled precisely on the federal Constituiton (Selsam, p. 259), it represents the climax of his fourteen-year fight against the democratic constitution of 1776. Wilson had sacrificed his private enterprises during the three years that he gave to constitution making, and he seems to have expected some high office in the new federal government. He was prominently mentioned as a candidate for the chief justiceship (*Pennsylvania Gazette,* Mar. 11, 1789), and even went so far as to recommend himself to Washington for that post (Charles Warren, *The Supreme Court in United States History,* 1922, I, 33–34). Washington appointed him associate justice on Sept. 29, 1789.

On Aug. 17, 1789, the trustees of the College of Philadelphia, of whom Wilson was one, acted upon the petition of Charles Smith for permission to give a course in law by appointing Wilson to that early chair. The lectures were opened on Dec. 15 before a distinguished audience including the President and other officers of the federal and state governments. Wilson was keenly aware of his opportunity to lay the foundations of an American system of jurisprudence. In his lectures, therefore, he departed from the Blackstonian definition of law as the rule of a sovereign superior and, discovering the residence of sovereignty in the individual, substituted therefor "the consent of those whose obedience the law requires" (*Selected Political Essays,* p. 251). Upon this foundation he raised his able apologia for the American Revolution, in which he challenged Blackstone's denial of the legal right of revolution. In his lecture, "Of Man as a Member of the Great Commonwealth of Nations," he set forth clearly the implications of the Supreme Court of the United States for judicial settlement of international disputes and for the administration of international law. Wilson's hope of becoming the American Blackstone, however, was doomed to disappointment: except for the first, his lectures were not published until after his death, and have never been cited in courts and law schools with the respect accorded the dicta of the Vinerian lecturer. Lacking the judicial detachment of Kent and Story, he left to them, by his consuming interest in practical concerns, the establishment of the bases of an American jurisprudence.

He made, however, one final effort to establish principles for judicial and legislative interpretation of the federal Constitution. Having been commissioned to make a digest of the laws of Pennsylvania, a task he entered upon with characteristic energy, he recommended himself to Washington in order that "Principles congenial to those of the Constitution . . . be established and ascertained, in complete and correct theory, *before* they are called into practical operation" (Washington Papers, vol. CXVI, Library of Congress). This visionary project to solve for all time the great problems of federal and state relations Washington referred to the attorney general, who pointedly urged the impropriety of "a single person," particularly a judge, determining principles for future guidance (*Ibid.*). When state aid for the Pennsylvania digest was withdrawn, Wilson continued it as a private venture, but did not live to complete it.

Turning from these public interests, he plunged once more into vast land speculations. In 1792 and 1793 he involved the Holland Land Company in unwise purchases of several hundred thousand acres in Pennsylvania and New York. Early in 1795 he bought a large interest in one of the ill-famed Yazoo companies (*University of Pennsylvania Law Review,* January 1908). Aside from these connections, perhaps the nearest approach to a stain on his judicial gown was his effort to influence enactment of land legislation in Pennsylvania favorable to speculators (Wilson MSS., 1793) and his disregard of the terms of a Pennsylvania statute (P. D. Evans, *The Holland Land Company,* 1924, pp. 109–10). Almost at the moment the bubble burst, Wilson conceived one of the most comprehensive schemes for immigration and colonization ever projected in America, involving vast sums of European capital, agencies for gathering settlers on the Continent, chartered vessels of transport, stations for debarkation, and methods of transporting settlers to western lands (MS. draft, Rush Papers, Library Company of Philadelphia). But he was already engulfed in his far-flung projects.

Wilson's judicial determinations were few. He was one of the first to declare an act of Congress unconstitutional and the only justice to decline to serve as a pension commissioner (Max Farrand, "The First Hayburn Case," *American Historical Review,* Jan. 1908). His most noted decision was that in *Chisholm* vs. *Georgia* (2 *Dallas,* 419), in which he answered with positive affirmation the important question whether the people of the United States formed a nation (Warren, I, 95 ff.). It was in his bank opinion of 1784, his law lectures, and his part in the constitutional convention of 1787, that he voiced the theories of national powers to which Marshall gave effective application.

A widower with six children—one of them Bird Wilson [*q.v.*]—after the death of his wife in 1786, Wilson married on Sept. 19, 1793, the nineteen-year-old Hannah Gray of Boston. Their happiness was short-lived. A son by the second marriage died in infancy, and in the summer of 1797 he moved to Burlington, N. J., to avoid arrest for debt. He retained his place on the bench amid criticism and talk of impeachment (G. J. McRee, *Life and Correspondence of James Iredell,* 1857, II, 532). Early in 1798, in acute mental distress, he arrived at Edenton, N. C., where for a time he resided at the home of Judge Iredell. "I have been hunted . . . like a wild beast," he wrote; his powerful faculties bent under the strain, and he had lucid moments only at intervals. He died at Edenton of a "violent nervous fever"; the report of Samuel Wallis that he died by his own hand (J. F. Meginness, *Otzinachson,* 1889, p. 358) is refuted by more valid testimony. In 1906 his remains were reinterred in Christ Church, Philadelphia.

Two outstanding personal characteristics of James Wilson opened the whole corpus of his learned writings to the charge of being special pleading: his ambition for place and power and his avid desire for wealth. His democracy was that of the study, not of the market-place or the hustings. He never captured popular imagination as did Jefferson; he never became a symbol as did Hamilton. Yet he was a prophet of both democracy and nationalism.

[Wilson MSS. (10 vols.), Hist. Soc. of Pa.; R. G. Adams, *Selected Political Essays of James Wilson* (1930), containing bibliography of Wilson's writings and of articles on him; Bird Wilson, *The Works of the Honorable James Wilson* (3 vols., 1804); J. D. Andrews, *The Works of James Wilson* (2 vols., 1896); R. G. Adams' *Political Ideas of the American Revolution* (1922), the best treatment of his political theories; J. B. McMaster and F. D. Stone, eds., *Pennsylvania and the Federal Constitution, 1787–1788* (1888); John Sanderson, *Biography of the Signers to the Declaration of Independence,* vol. VI (1825), by Robert Waln, Jr. The most comprehensive study is Burton Alva Konkle's biography, together with 5 vols. of letters and writings, as yet unpublished. Through Mr. Konkle's kindness the author was permitted to use this extensive manuscript; but in fairness to him it must be stated that he disagrees with this interpretation of Wilson's character and significance.]   J. P. B.

WILSON, JAMES (Aug. 16, 1836–Aug. 26, 1920), agriculturist, secretary of agriculture, was born in Ayrshire, Scotland, the eldest son of John and Jean (McCosh) Wilson, who emigrated to America in 1851. The family first settled in Connecticut, removing in 1855 to a farm in Tama County, Iowa. James attended the common school in the winter and also Iowa (now Grinnell) College. He chose farming as his life work and early became a leader in the community, holding various township offices and membership on the board of county supervisors. He was married May 7, 1863, to Esther Wilbur of Buckingham, Iowa. To this union six sons and two daughters were born.

In 1867 he was elected to the Iowa legislature and, reëlected in 1869 and 1871, was chosen speaker during his third term. In 1872 he was sent to Congress as the Republican representative of the Fifth District and was returned in 1874. After the expiration of his second term he spent five years on his farm. In March 1882 he was appointed a member of the state railroad commission by Governor Sherman, only to resign soon after upon being again elected to Congress. His seat was contested by Benjamin T. Frederick, but the contest was not settled until the last day of the session when Wilson, by a shrewd parliamentary move, gave up his seat in favor of his opponent and secured favorable action by the Democratic House on a bill to place U. S. Grant on the retired list. During his three terms in Congress, Wilson was a member of the committee on agriculture. He was an expert parliamentarian, serving on the rules committee in the Forty-third Congress. During his third term he was given the sobriquet of "Tama Jim" to distinguish him from James Falconer Wilson [q.v.] of Iowa, "Jefferson Jim," who had recently been elected to the United States Senate. He returned home at the close of his congressional career and for the next seven years engaged in farming and in writing for various farm journals, notably the Iowa Homestead. In 1891 he was appointed professor of agriculture and head of the experiment station at Iowa State College, where, with the able assistance of Charles F. Curtiss, who succeeded him as dean of agriculture, he placed agricultural instruction on a scientific and practical basis.

In the presidential campaign of 1896 the first poll indicated that Iowa might be lost to the Republicans; but after a thoroughly organized and intensive campaign it was carried for McKinley by a majority of over 65,000 votes. The Iowa papers now presented strong claims for recognition in the cabinet in return for Iowa's support. Bitter rivalry arose between those who supported A. B. Cummins [q.v.] for attorney-

general, and those who wished J. A. T. Hull to be made secretary of war. Senator Allison requested the chairman of the state Republican committee, H. G. McMillan, to harmonize the factions. He at once interviewed Henry Wallace [q.v.], editor of Wallaces' Farmer, who urged that Wilson be suggested for the post of secretary of agriculture. Cummins and Hull retired from the field in the interest of party harmony and McKinley, who had already come to hold a high opinion of Wilson's character and ability, appointed him to that position. He served as secretary of agriculture in the administrations of McKinley, Roosevelt, and Taft, a period of sixteen years. Under his able direction and personal supervision the department extended its activities into many fields: experiment stations were established in all parts of the United States; farm demonstration work was inaugurated in the South; co-operative extension work in agriculture and home economics was begun; an army of experts and scientists was enlisted to obtain information from all over the world for the promotion of agriculture. The whole country was aroused to the problem of tuberculosis in cattle and the proper care and handling of milk. Legislation dealing with plant and animal diseases, insect pests, forestry, irrigation, conservation, road building, and agricultural education was enacted.

Upon his retirement from the cabinet in 1913, Wilson returned to his home in Tama County. In June of the same year Governor Clarke appointed Wilson and Henry Wallace to investigate and report on agricultural conditions in Great Britain. The last years of his life were spent in retirement. He was a commanding figure, tall, well-proportioned and erect, and was an indefatigable worker. Schooled in the pioneer philosophy and the precepts of the Presbyterian faith, he was a man of high moral principles. Keen preception, great singleness of purpose, and extraordinary patience were his dominant characteristics.

[Who's Who in America, 1920–21; Annals of Iowa, Jan. 1924; Biog. Dir. Am. Cong. (1928); L. H. Pammel, Prominent Men I Have Met (1926); L. S. Ivans and A. E. Winship, Fifty Famous Farmers (1924); Palimpsest, Mar. 1923; E. V. Wilcox, Tama Jim (1920); Ann. Report of the Dept. of Agric., 1912 (1913); Des Moines Register, Aug. 27, 28, 1920, Mar. 5, 1933; N. Y. Times, Aug. 28, 1920; information from a son, James W. Wilson of Brookings, S. D.]
L. B. S—t.

WILSON, JAMES FALCONER (Oct. 19, 1828–Apr. 22, 1895), lawyer, representative in Congress, United States senator, popularly known as "Jefferson Jim" to distinguish him from his fellow Iowan, "Tama Jim" (James

Wilson [q.v.], secretary of agriculture under McKinley, Theodore Roosevelt, and Taft), was born at Newark, Ohio. His father, David S. Wilson, a contractor and builder, was of Scotch ancestry and a native of Morgantown, Va. (now W. Va.); his mother was Kitty Ann (Bramble) of Chillicothe, Ohio. Left fatherless at ten, James aided in the support of the mother and two younger children by serving as apprentice to a harness maker. With brief intervals of school attendance and the personal instruction of sympathetic teachers and ministers he secured what he later termed a "thorough education." While working at his trade he began reading law, and, completing his study under the direction of William Burnham Woods [q.v.], later a justice of the United States Supreme Court, was admitted to the bar in 1851. On May 25, 1852, he married Mary Jewett, and the couple went to Fairfield, Iowa, where they established their home; two sons and a daughter were born to them.

The young lawyer soon took a foremost place on the local circuit but was drawn more and more into politics. Editorials for the local organ gave him standing and offices came in continuous succession. He was one of the most influential delegates in the constitutional convention of 1857, and the same year was appointed to the Des Moines River improvement commission and elected to the state House of Representatives, where he served as chairman of the ways and means committee. Promoted to the state Senate in 1859, he aided in the revision of the state code, published in 1860, and in the special war session of 1861 was named president *pro tempore*.

Elected to the federal House of Representatives to fill a vacancy in December 1861, he was reëlected as a Republican and served until Mar. 3, 1869. In the days of war and reconstruction he had a conspicuous and determining part in the congressional policies. He used fully his strategic position as chairman of the judiciary committee to forward abolition and the Union program. War measures that he fathered included the article prohibiting the use of troops in the return of fugitive slaves, enfranchisement of negroes in the District of Columbia, and the tax on state bank circulation; he introduced the original resolution for an abolition Amendment. During the turmoil of Reconstruction he was one of the ablest leaders among the legalistic Radicals. On every possible occasion he upheld the constitutional prerogatives of Congress. He introduced important amendments to the resolution for repudiation of the Confederate debt, in-

troduced the amendment repealing appellate jurisdiction of the Supreme Court under the Habeas Corpus Act of 1867, gave the final form to the Civil Rights Act, and served on the conference committee on tenure of office. He voted with the minority of his committee against the original impeachment charges in 1867, giving an elaborate argument that was sustained by the House; but in view of a definite case of wilful violation of statutes, as it appeared to his legalistic mind, he became committed to the President's removal. His selection as a member of the committee to formulate the articles and as a trial manager was a recognition of the more moderate element of the Radical wing. His service at the trial consisted in constitutional arguments, most notably on the responsibility of the executive to abide by acts of Congress regardless of his opinion as to their validity.

In 1869 Grant persuaded Wilson to accept the state portfolio. Misunderstandings over the activities of Elihu B. Washburne [q.v.], to whom the office had been granted temporarily to pay another personal debt, caused Wilson to withdraw his acceptance. On two subsequent occasions the invitation to enter the Grant official family was unavailingly renewed. While by no means indifferent to the political scene, he now devoted himself mainly to his profession. A prominent interest of these years and the one that was to bring the main attack upon his record was promotion of the Pacific railroad. In Congress he had been a zealous supporter of this enterprise and in 1868 had shown his confidence in it by profitable though moderate speculation in the stock of the construction company. For six years under Grant and one under Hayes he was a government director of the road. These connections brought him rather prominently into the House investigations of 1873. In the first of these he frankly admitted having secured stock as an investment and regretted that he was unable to secure more. Before the second, he emphatically denied the charge by an ex-official that he had received a check for $19,000 out of a fund for "special legal expenses," and no substantiating proof that he had was offered. The resulting attacks on him by hostile journals apparently did not weaken him in Iowa. Probably the bulk of his constituents agreed with his view that his contribution to this great national enterprise had been praiseworthy and public-spirited.

While mentioned for the Senate from 1866 on his real opportunity did not come until 1882, when all of the other aspirants withdrew; he was reëlected in 1888 without organized opposition. In brilliance and specific achievement his senatorial service fell far below that which he had rendered in the House. He was laborious on committees and helped to frame the original Interstate Commerce Act of 1887 and other measures, but he was clearly in the rank of the "elder statesmen." His health was steadily failing; he was definitely committed to retirement at the close of his second term, and, as it happened, died, at Fairfield, Iowa, within a few weeks of the close of the session. There was lacking, too, a cause to which he could devote himself as he had to anti-slavery. Prohibition was the only substitute. A zealous personal teetotaler, he belonged to the group that sought to commit the Republican party to temperance reform. In 1890 he secured the passage of the Original Package Act, which at the time was regarded as a great triumph for state control of the liquor traffic.

[*Debates, Constitutional Convention of Iowa* (1857); *Trial of Andrew Johnson* (1868); *House Report No. 77* and *No. 78*, 42 Cong., 3 Sess.; Johnson Brigham, *Iowa: Its Hist.* (1915), vol. I; *Protrait and Biog. Album of Jefferson and Van Buren Counties, Iowa* (1890); E. H. Stiles, *Recollections and Sketches of Notable Lawyers and Public Men of Early Iowa* (1916); J. G. Blaine, *Twenty Years of Cong.* (2 vols., 1884–86); *Biog. Dir. Am. Cong.* (1928); *Midland Monthly*, July 1895; *Fairfield Ledger*, Apr. 24, May 1, 8, 1895; *Iowa State Reg.* (Des Moines), Apr. 23, 24, 1895.]

E. D. R.

WILSON, JAMES GRANT (Apr. 28, 1832– Feb. 1, 1914), editor, author, and soldier, was born in Edinburgh, the son of William Wilson [*q.v.*] by his second wife, Jane (Sibbald) Wilson. The father left Scotland in December 1833 and settled in Poughkeepsie, N. Y., as bookseller and publisher. There the son received his education and became his father's partner. After a trip to Europe in 1855, he moved to Chicago, where he edited and published several periodicals. The *Evangel* and the *Chicago Examiner* (1857) seem to have been failures (cf. Fleming, *post*, p. 392); one number of the *Northwestern Quarterly Magazine* appeared in October 1858; the monthly *Chicago Record; a Journal, Devoted to the Church, to Literature, and to the Arts* lived from Apr. 1, 1857, to Mar. 15, 1862, when it passed into other hands and became the *Northwestern Church*.

On Dec. 25, 1862, Wilson was commissioned major in the 15th Illinois Cavalry, and on Sept. 14, 1863, colonel of the 4th United States Colored Cavalry. He took part in various movements in the Mississippi Valley, and in the later years of the war served as military agent for New York state in Louisiana. On Mar. 13, 1865, he was brevetted brigadier-general of volunteers. Resigning on June 16, 1865, he thereafter made New York City his home. On Nov. 3, 1869, he married in New Brunswick, N. J.,

Jane Emily Searle Cogswell. They had one daughter, who married Frank Sylvester Henry, and from whom the father was estranged in later years.

His writings were mainly biographical. Seven volumes of newspaper clippings in the New York Public Library testify to his care in preserving news about those whose careers appealed to him. His most extensive work was *Appletons' Cyclopædia of American Biography* (6 vols., 1886–89; revised, with supplementary volume, 1898–99), which he edited jointly with John Fiske [*q.v.*]. An active churchman throughout his life, he edited *The Centennial History of the Protestant Episcopal Church in the Diocese of New York, 1785–1885* (1886). In 1892–93 appeared *The Memorial History of the City of New York, from Its First Settlement to the Year 1892*, in four volumes. He also edited *The Presidents of the United States*, by John Fiske and others, which was published in 1894, with later issues in 1898, 1902, 1914.

His interest in military affairs is suggested by his *Biographical Sketches of Illinois Officers Engaged in the War against the Rebellion of 1861* (1862). His *Life and Campaigns of Ulysses Simpson Grant* appeared in 1868, and a revision of the same under a slightly different title in 1885. In 1874 he published *Sketches of Illustrious Soldiers*, a second edition of which appeared in 1880. With Titus Munson Coan he edited *Personal Recollections of the War of the Rebellion: Addresses Delivered Before the New York Commandery of the Loyal Legion of the United States, 1883–1891* (1891). In 1897 two studies of Grant by him were published—*General Grant*, in the Great Commanders Series edited by Wilson, and *General Grant's Letters to a Friend*. He also furnished a life of Grant in 1904 for the Makers of American History Series.

From his father, a poet as well as business man, he acquired a fondness for literature. In 1867 he published, under the pseudonym of Allan Grant, *Love in Letters: Illustrated in the Correspondence of Eminent Persons*, which he revised and issued under his own name in 1895; also, in 1867, under the same pseudonym, *Mr. Secretary Pepys; with Extracts from His Diary*. In 1869 appeared his *Life and Letters of Fitz-Greene Halleck* and *The Poetical Writings of Halleck, with Extracts from Those of Drake*. In 1876 he wrote the memoir of the author in Anne Grant's *Memoirs of an American Lady*. He was the author of a two-volume work entitled *The Poets and Poetry of Scotland from the Earliest to the Present Time* (1876). In 1877–78 he addꜩd a sketch of Bryant to an edition of Bryant's *New Library of Poetry and Song* and in 1886 issued *Bryant and His Friends: Some Reminiscences of the Knickerbocker Writers.* His commencement address at St. Stephen's College, Annandale, was published as *The World's Largest Libraries* (1894). In 1902 he provided an introduction to Mrs. Audubon's *Life of John James Audubon, the Naturalist.* His *Thackeray in the United States, 1852–53, 1855–56* appeared in two volumes in 1904. He wrote much for the periodical press, and made many addresses on characters in American history and literature, most of which appeared also as reprints.

Tall, erect, of soldierly bearing, he enjoyed speaking or presiding at public meetings. He was a life member of the New York Genealogical and Biographical Society and its president, 1886–1900; president of the American Ethnological Society, 1900–14; president of the American Authors' Guild (Society of American Authors), 1892–99. After the death of his first wife he married, May 16, 1907, Mary (Heap) Nicholson, widow of James W. A. Nicholson [*q.v.*]. By his will he left to the Metropolitan Museum of Art in New York City his collection of signed photographs of rulers and other notables, sleeve links worn by Washington and by Grant, rings with hair from Washington, and other similar trinkets; the legacy was declined by the Museum, and the collection went to the New York Genealogical and Biographical Society. In 1894 he was knighted by the Queen Regent of Spain for his services in connection with the erection of a statue of Columbus in New York.

[*N. Y. Geneal. and Biog. Record,* July 1914; *Am. Anthropologist,* Jan.–Mar. 1914; *N. Y. Times,* Feb. 2, 1914; *Who's Who in America,* 1912–13; *Who's Who in New York (City and State),* 1914; F. B. Heitman, *Hist. Reg. and Dict. U. S. Army* (1903); H. E. Fleming, *Magazines of a Market-Metropolis* (1906); F. W. Scott, "Newspapers and Periodicals of Ill., 1814–1879," *Ill. State Hist. Lib. Colls.,* vol. VI (1910); Irving Garwood, *Am. Periodicals from 1850 to 1860* (1931).]

H. M. L.

WILSON, JAMES HARRISON (Sept. 2, 1837–Feb. 23, 1925), engineer, cavalryman, author, was born near Shawneetown, Ill., the fifth child of Harrison and Katharine (Schneyder) Wilson. His father, a native of Virginia, was related to the Harrisons of the James River district; his family had emigrated from the Shenandoah Valley to Kentucky, and the Schneyders, from the vicinity of Strasbourg, Alsace, to Indiana, both moving later to southern Illinois. James H. Wilson attended school at Shawneetown, and completed one academic year at McKendree College. He entered the United States Military Academy July 1, 1855, and was no-

tably proficient in horsemanship, rifle practice, and drill. Graduating sixth among forty-one in the class of 1860, he was commissioned second lieutenant of topographical engineers and assigned to duty at Fort Vancouver until ordered East in the summer of 1861. He was chief topographical engineer with Gen. Thomas W. Sherman on the Port Royal expedition and with Gen. David Hunter took part in the reduction of Fort Pulaski. Subsequently, as volunteer aid to McClellan, he served in the battles of South Mountain and Antietam.

A few weeks later Wilson joined Grant's headquarters, and early in 1863 was named inspector-general, Army of the Tennessee, with duties still mainly in the engineers. He was engaged in the action at Port Gibson and the capture of Jackson, Miss., in the battles of Champion's Hill and Big Black Bridge, and in the siege and capture of Vicksburg. Late in September 1863 he carried dispatches to the telegraph at Cairo, and received War Department orders, following the defeat of Rosecrans at Chickamauga, for Grant to proceed to Chattanooga. He was advanced, Oct. 31, to brigadier-general of volunteers—"the only officer ever promoted from Grant's regular staff to command troops" (*Under the Old Flag, post,* I, 267). He participated in the battle of Missionary Ridge, was chief engineer on the expedition for the relief of Knoxville, and in January 1864 was appointed chief of the cavalry bureau at Washington.

By Grant's request at the opening of the spring campaign, Wilson was assigned to command the third division in Sheridan's cavalry corps, Army of the Potomac. He led the advance across the Rapidan, marched through the Wilderness, and during that battle had sharp encounters in the more open country beyond. The division was in the combat of Yellow Tavern, covered Grant's passage to the Chickahominy, formed part of Sheridan's first Richmond expedition, and late in June fought off or eluded greater numbers, mainly of Hampton's cavalry. After a few days in front of Petersburg, Wilson was sent to Sheridan in the Shenandoah Valley, and took part in the battle of the Opequon (Winchester), Sept. 19. In October he was appointed chief of cavalry, Military Division of the Mississippi, with brevet rank of major-general, on a practical equality with Sheridan in the East. The statement, "I believe Wilson will add fifty per cent to the effectiveness of your cavalry" (Grant to Sherman, Oct. 4, 1864), Wilson considered "the greatest compliment of my life" (*Under the Old Flag,* II, 4). He first outfitted Kilpatrick's division for the march to the sea, and then consolidated the remaining cavalry and mounted infantry into a compact corps to operate against Hood's invasion of Tennessee.

Encountering Forrest's cavalry at Franklin, Nov. 30, 1864, Wilson drove it back across the Harpeth River, enabling Schofield to repulse Hood and withdraw to Nashville, where Thomas, greatly assisted by mass formations of the cavalry, defeated Hood on Dec. 15–16. Wilson established winter cantonments north of the Tennessee and had 17,000 men in the saddle for review when Thomas came down from Nashville. With greater numbers present and better equipment, he defeated Forrest at Ebenezer Church, Apr. 1, 1865, and the next day broke through and surmounted the fortifications of Selma, Ala.; in the charge, which he led with the 4th Cavalry, his gelding, "Sheridan," was struck down. Wilson dispersed the defense, demolished or burned the ordnance and ammunition bases, and severed railway communications. He entered Montgomery without resistance, took Columbus, Ga., by assault, destroying its military supplies and shipyard; on Apr. 20 he reached Macon, and there ceased hostilities, but kept military control. Detachments from his command intercepted Jefferson Davis and brought him to Macon.

Gross figures for maximum numbers of cavalry under Sheridan and Wilson in the spring of 1865 are somewhat in Wilson's favor. He was unsurpassed in the cavalry for organizing ability, administration, and steadiness; it is doubtful if Sheridan, Kilpatrick, or Custer ever really excelled his outstanding exploit at Selma. "Of all the Federal expeditions of which I have any knowledge, his was the best conducted," said Richard Taylor (*Destruction and Reconstruction*, 1879, p. 220). His restraint, tact, and good judgment left a favorable impression upon the people of Georgia. In the army reorganization after the war he was appointed lieutenant-colonel of the 35th Infantry, July 28, 1866, but reassigned to the engineers. For four years he superintended navigation improvements, mainly on the Mississippi, resigning from the army Dec. 31, 1870, to engage in railway construction and management. Settling at Wilmington, Del., in 1883, he gave fifteen years to various business enterprises, public affairs, travel, and writing.

As senior major-general in civil life under the retiring age, Wilson volunteered for the Spanish-American War and was designated to command the VI Corps, which, however, was not organized. In July 1898 he conducted part of the I Corps to Puerto Rico, and was appointed military governor of the city and province of Ponce; while marching toward the interior he was ap-

prised of the protocol, and was soon ordered back to the United States. He prepared the I Corps for Cuba, took one division to Matanzas, and in the military occupation was assigned the Matanzas department and later the Santa Clara department and the city of Cienfuegos. Knowing something of China from nearly a year's investigation in 1885–86 of possible railway developments there, he was appointed second in command to Gen. Adna R. Chaffee [*q.v.*] of forces sent to cooperate in suppressing the Boxer uprising; he reached Peking after the allies had rescued the legations, but led the American-British contingent against the Boxers at the Eight Temples. Returning to the United States in December 1900, he was placed by special act of Congress upon the retired list as brigadier-general in the regular service. On Mar. 4, 1915, he was advanced to major-general, a rank he had received twice (1865 and 1898) in the volunteers. By presidential appointment he represented the army at the coronation of King Edward VII in 1902. He never held political or civil office.

Wilson was about five feet, ten inches in height, though his erect, military bearing made him appear a trifle taller; he was somewhat overweight in middle and later life. He stood and walked like a cavalryman who never forgot that he had served with distinction under Grant, Sherman, Sheridan and Thomas, and as an independent commander had led the longest and greatest single cavalry movement in the Civil War. He was a striking personification of the "old army"; the last survivor of his West Point class, he outlived every other member of Grant's military staff and all other Federal corps commanders. Bold initiative, an adventurous and dauntless spirit, aggressive temper, and invariable confidence were his predominant characteristics. He managed widespread and diversified interests with ease, dispatch, and efficiency. Though reserved, often blunt, and sometimes imperious, he was a man of generous nature, on rare occasions sentimental and romantic. Many friendships, notably with John A. Rawlins and Emory Upton [*qq.v.*] were broken only by death. He was a thorough and progressive student of history, with a long, clear view and considerable legal knowledge; an outspoken but fair critic. Among his more significant publications were a number of military biographies, beginning with *The Life of Ulysses S. Grant* (1868), edited somewhat by Charles A. Dana, and including lives of Andrew J. Alexander (1887), William Farrar Smith (1904), his friend John A. Rawlins (1916), and articles, for the Association of

Graduates of the United States Military Academy, on Philip H. Sheridan (1889) and A. McDowell McCook (1904). He contributed "The Union Cavalry in the Hood Campaign" to *Battles and Leaders of the Civil War* (vol. IV, 1888). After his first trip to China he published *China; Travels and Investigations in the "Middle Kingdom"* (1887), of which a third edition was issued in 1901, extended to include an account of the Boxer episode. Long personal acquaintance and war-time association formed the basis for *The Life of Charles A. Dana* (1907), and his own recollections of service in the Civil War, the war with Spain, and the Boxer trouble for the two colorful volumes, *Under the Old Flag* (1912). On Jan. 3, 1866, Wilson married Ella Andrews, who was fatally burned at Matanzas, Cuba, Apr. 28, 1900; three daughters were born to them. He died in Wilmington and his interment was in Old Swedes churchyard there.

[G. W. Cullum, *Biog. Reg. Officers and Grads. U. S. Mil. Acad.* (3rd ed., 1891) and Supplements; *Sixty-second Ann. Report, Asso. Grads. U. S. Mil. Acad.* (1931); *War of the Rebellion: Official Records (Army)*; memoirs of Grant, Sherman, and Sheridan, and histories and narratives of the Army of the Tennessee; John Fiske, *The Mississippi Valley in the Civil War* (1900); J. A. Wyeth, *Life of Gen. Nathan Bedford Forrest* (1899); W. F. Scott, *The Story of a Cavalry Regiment* (1893); E. N. Gilpin, "The Last Campaign," *Jour. U. S. Cavalry Asso.*, Apr. 1908; A. R. Chaffee, "James Harrison Wilson, Cavalryman," *Cavalry Journal*, July 1925; *Official Army Register*, 1925; *N. Y. Times*, Feb. 24, 1925; *Every Evening* (Wilmington), Feb. 23–26, 1925; *Army and Navy Jour.*, Feb. 28, 1925; *Who's Who in America*, 1924–25; correspondence with Wilson's daughter, Mary Wilson Thompson; personal acquaintance.]   R. B—e.

WILSON, JOHN (*c.* 1591–Aug. 7, 1667), minister and writer, was born in Windsor, England. His mother, Isabel Woodhall, was a niece of Archbishop Grindal; his father, William, was for a time Grindal's chaplain and, from 1583 to 1615, canon of Windsor. John Wilson studied at Eton, where in 1601, "though the smallest boy in the school," he won approbation by a Latin speech which he delivered before the Duc de Biron (H. C. M. Lyte, *A History of Eton College*, 1911, p. 186). He went to King's College, Cambridge, as scholar in 1605 and three years later was promoted to a fellowship which would have taken care of him for life; but his conversion to the Puritan point of view by William Ames, and his refusal to conform in chapel, forced him to resign in 1610, just after taking the degree of B. A. The degree of M.A. was awarded him in 1613. He was admitted to the Inner Temple in 1610, but after reading law for a year or two he began preaching, and served as chaplain in several "Honourable and Religious Families," among them that of Henry Leigh. In 1618 Wilson became lecturer at Sudbury in Suffolk, where he

seems to have remained until 1630, despite sundry suspensions for nonconformity. He sailed in that year for Massachusetts, and became teacher of the First Church in Boston, when it was first organized at Charlestown. He went to England in 1631, returning to Boston the next year with his wife, Elizabeth, daughter of John Mansfield, whom he had married probably before May 1615. After another trip to England in 1634 and 1635, he remained in Boston at the First Church until his death, a spokesman of orthodoxy and a constant counsellor of the magistrates. He was one of the first to work for the conversion of the Indians in Massachusetts, and for a while took under his protection a child of Sagamore John, a friendly native who had died of smallpox. In 1637 Wilson went as chaplain in an expedition against the Pequots, and his services were later recognized by a grant of land. With the Rev. John Cotton [*q.v.*] he was at odds occasionally, especially in his unflinching and outspoken hostility to the Antinomians, but in spite of their disagreements the two men shared harmoniously the pulpit of the First Church from 1633 until Cotton's death in 1652.

At Sudbury Wilson wrote a long poem for children, *A Song, or, Story, for the Lasting Remembrance of Divers Famous Works* (London, 1626), reissued in Boston in 1680 as *A Song of Deliverance*. It is said that he wrote enough other verse to fill "a large Folio," but most of this was not printed and is now unknown. His Latin elegy on John Harvard was printed in Cotton Mather's *Magnalia* (1702); his lines on Joseph Brisco were published in a broadside in Boston about 1657, and eight anagrams in verse appeared in Thomas Shepard's *The Church-Membership of Children* (1663) and John Norton's *Three Choice and Profitable Sermons* (1664). In prose he contributed prefatory matter to Samuel Whiting's *A Discourse of the Last Judgement* (1664), Richard Mather's *The Summe of Certain Sermons* (1652), and John Higginson's *The Cause of God* (1663). One of his sermons was printed as *A Seasonable Watchword unto Christians* (1677). Two other publications, *The Day Breaking . . . of the Gospell with the Indians* (1647) and *Some Helps to Faith* (1625), have been ascribed to him. The former may be his (*Proceedings of the Massachusetts Historical Society*, 2 ser., vol. VI, 1891, pp. 392–95); the latter is not.

Wilson was celebrated in his day as one of the most influential of the Massachusetts divines, and was renowned for his skill in making anagrams and writing verse. Today he is less interesting than his contemporaries, John Cotton and Richard Mather [*q.v.*], perhaps because little is left by which to judge his quality. As a poet he has small merit; his work is pious and edificatory rather than artistic. Yet his contemporaries, in spite of his fierce opposition to the Quakers and the unorthodox in general, paint an appealing picture of him as a man famous for his hospitality and loved as well as respected. In Cotton Mather's words, *"great zeal,* with *great love . . .* joined with *orthodoxy,* should make up his pourtraiture" (*Magnalia,* 1853 ed., I, 312). His daughter Elizabeth married the Rev. Ezekiel Rogers; another, Mary, married the Rev. Samuel Danforth; and his son, John Wilson, became in 1651 the first minister of Medfield.

[For biog. sketches see Cotton Mather, *Johannes in Eeremo: Memoirs* (1695), reprinted in *Magnalia Christi Americana* (1702), bk. III, pt. 1; J. G. Bartlett, in *New England Hist. and Geneal. Reg.,* Jan.–Apr. 1907; A. W. M'Clure, *The Lives of John Wilson, John Norton and John Davenport* (1846); W. B. Sprague, *Annals of the Am. Pulpit,* vol. I (1857), pp. 12–15. Some errors and omissions in these are corrected in K. B. Murdock, *Handkerchiefs from Paul* (1927), pp. xli–liii, which has references to other biog. sources and contains all of Wilson's published verse, as well as three previously unprinted poems. The date of birth, sometimes given as *c.* Dec. 1588, is from John and J. A. Venn, *Alumni Cantabrigienses,* pt. I, vol. IV (1927).]   K. B. M.

WILSON, JOHN FLEMING (Feb. 22, 1877–Mar. 5, 1922), author, son of the Rev. Joseph Rogers and Viola Harriet (Eaton) Wilson, was born in Erie, Pa: He was educated at Parsons College, Iowa, and at Princeton University, where he received the degree of A.B. in 1900. He first taught for two years in Oregon at Portland Academy, of which his father was then president. After doing newspaper work in Portland and editing a newspaper at Newport, Ore., he became editor of the weekly San Francisco *Argonaut,* an earthquake edition of which he published at San Jose, Cal., on May 5, 1906, and was associated with the *Oregonian,* the *Pacific Monthly,* and the *Advertiser* of Honolulu. From early boyhood he had spent much time on the water, and in the West, after having qualified as a deck officer, he worked on board seagoing tugs, with pilots in the Columbia River, in dry docks, and for a time on board ship at wireless telegraphy. For nearly two years he lived on light ships and in the Columbia and Tillamook lighthouses. He studied steam engineering and other technical nautical subjects, at one time setting himself to report investigations made by courts having admiralty jurisdiction. Traveling extensively, he lived for a time in Japan. During the World War he served in France (1917–19) in the 7th Battalion, Canadian Infantry.

His first sea story, "When Winds Awake," appeared in *Munsey's Magazine* for August 1900. This was followed by seven stories in the *Over-*

land Monthly during 1902–03. Not a prolific writer, he wrote between 1906 and 1920 about one hundred short stories. These were published in various magazines and collected in *Across the Latitudes* (1911), *Tad Sheldon, Boy Scout* (1913), *Tad Sheldon's Fourth of July* (1913), and *Somewhere at Sea and Other Tales* (1923), the last of which contains his best work. His full-length novels are *The Land Claimers* (1911), *The Man Who Came Back* (1912), which was turned into a play, *The Princess of Sorry Valley* (1913), *The Master Key* (1915), on which a photoplay was based, and *Scouts of the Desert* (1920). His best literary work grew out of a thorough and intimate knowledge of the sea and ships, and of sailors, whose peculiar psychology he presents with remarkable insight and fidelity. His style was influenced by his wide reading of the classics.

Wilson is described as "a short, slight man with keen glance, clean-shaven, weather-beaten face, and muscles of steel" (Blathwayt, *post,* p. xvii). On July 14, 1906, he married Elena Burt of Newport, Ore., from whom he was afterwards divorced. There were no children by her or by his second wife, Alberta Adele Wilson. On Mar. 5, 1922, while he was shaving, his bathrobe caught fire from a gas heater, and he was burned to death. He died in Santa Monica and was buried three days later at Hemet, Cal. He was a member of the Protestant Episcopal Church.

[*Who's Who in America,* 1920–21; R. H. Davis, and Raymond Blathwayt, in Wilson's *Somewhere at Sea and Other Tales* (1923); *Princeton Alumni Weekly,* Mar. 29, 1922; obituary in *Chronicle* (San Francisco), Mar. 6, 1922; death and funeral notices in *Times* (Los Angeles), Mar. 7, 8, 1922.]   C. L. L.

WILSON, JOHN LEIGHTON (Mar. 25, 1809–July 13, 1886), pioneer Presbyterian missionary to western Africa, was the son of William and Jane E. (James) Wilson, descendants of the Scotch-Irish settlers of Williamsburg County, S. C. He was born and died near Salem, S. C., in his father's farmhouse, the first in that region to be glazed and ceiled. Beginning his education in a local log schoolhouse, he continued it at Springville, and in Zion Academy, Winnsboro, S. C., and in 1827 entered the junior class of Union College, Schenectady, N. Y., graduating in 1829. A winter with his uncle, the Rev. Robert W. James, a founder of Columbia (S. C.) Seminary, stimulated his interest in Africa, to which he felt that slave-holding America owed a debt of atonement. His religious life began in a series of meetings at Mount Pleasant, where he taught during the latter half of 1830, and in January 1831 he entered Columbia Seminary and was a member of the first class to be graduated at that institution. After studying Arabic at Andover, he was ordained, in September 1833, by the Presbytery of Harmony, S. C., and soon after, accompanied by a classmate, he sailed for western Africa on an exploring tour of five months.

Upon his return he married, May 21, 1834, Jane Elizabeth Bayard, and, having freed her thirty slaves, took them at their personal expense to Liberia. He did not favor universal or immediate emancipation, and the fact that he retained possession of two negro children who had come to him through entail and refused to leave him, brought such violent assault from abolitionists as to curtail support for his mission at Cape Palmas. After seven years there, he removed the mission to the Gabun. It was in his house that Thomas S. Savage [q.v.], seeing the skull of a gorilla, was prompted to make the investigations that resulted in the publication of his "Notice of External Characters and Habits of Troglodytes Gorilla, a New Species of Orang from the Gaboon River" (*Boston Journal of Natural History*, December 1847). Wilson in his *West Africa* (*post*) records the earliest investigation of this animal in its natural habitat. Hating the slave trade, next to the rum trade, as the bane of Africa, he published a pamphlet, which was widely distributed in England by Lord Palmerston, showing the efficiency of the British fleet in the suppression of that traffic. During nearly twenty years in the field, he gathered much information in thousands of miles of travel, contributed to the *Missionary Herald,* treated the sick, founded schools and churches, and compiled grammars and dictionaries of Grebo and Mpongwee, into which languages he translated certain of the Gospels and tracts.

Returning to America in 1852, he was elected a secretary of the Board of Foreign Missions at the General Assembly of 1853. For the next nine years he lived in New York, where he edited the *Home and Foreign Record* and published his encyclopedic work, *Western Africa, Its History, Conditions, and Prospects* (1856). Upon the outbreak of the Civil War, although he had avoided all part in politics, he resigned his position, and on the day before travel closed returned to the South. He carried on evangelistic work in the Confederate army and served for a time as chaplain. When in December 1861 the Assembly of the Presbyterian Church in the Confederate States of America (later the Presbyterian Church in the United States) was organized, Wilson was placed in charge of its foreign missions and from 1863 to 1872 he also had charge of its home missionary projects. During Recon-

struction he did much to sustain the life of the Southern churches. He wrote for the *Southern Presbyterian Review* and in 1866 founded *The Missionary,* which he edited for nearly twenty years. With the proceeds from the sale of his wife's lands in Georgia, the Wilsons maintained a girls' school in the old homestead at Salem. Here were educated girls from four Southern states who paid tuition only if they were able. He also had a night school for negroes. More than six feet in height, erect and strong, wise and kind, he was further aided in his work by an unusual understanding of the negro and by a marked ability for finance.

[H. C. Du Bose, *Memoirs of Rev. John Leighton Wilson D.D.* (1895); Alfred Nevin, *Encyc. of the Presbyterian Church* (1884); J. DuPlessis, *The Evangelisation of Pagan Africa* (n.d.); W. R. Wheeler, *The Wards of God in an African Forest* (1931); H. A. White, *Southern Presbyterian Leaders* (1911); *Missionary Herald,* Sept. 1886.]   A. K. G.

WILSON, JOHN LOCKWOOD (Aug. 7, 1850–Nov. 6, 1912), lawyer, senator, and publisher, was born in Crawfordsville, Ind., of Scotch-Irish stock, son of Col. James and Emma (Ingersoll) Wilson and brother of Henry Lane Wilson [q.v.]. His father served in the Mexican War, had two terms in Congress, and was a lieutenant-colonel of volunteers in the Civil War. John was his father's messenger during the Civil War and acted in the same capacity in 1866–67 when his father was minister to Venezuela. Before he was seventeen, however, his father died, and thereafter the boy supported himself by odd jobs and by employment as clerk with a surveying crew. He graduated from Wabash College in 1874, studied law in the office of an uncle, was admitted to the bar in 1877. Two years later he was given an appointment in the United States pension bureau, but soon returned to the law. He was elected to the Indiana legislature in 1880.

The West attracted him, and in 1882 President Arthur appointed him receiver of the federal land office at Colfax, Washington Territory. He served four and a half years, during which period the office was moved to Spokane. In 1888 he was a delegate to the Republican National Convention in Chicago, and the following year, at the first state Republican convention of Washington, held in Walla Walla just prior to the admission of the state, he was nominated as representative-at-large in Congress, and in 1889 was elected. He was twice returned as the sole representative from Washington, and in 1895, while serving his third term, was elected United States senator to complete the term left vacant by the failure of the legislature of 1893 to elect a successor to John Beard Allen. Wilson served as senator until the expiration of this term, Mar. 3, 1899.

His activities in Congress resulted in a vast amount of river and harbor development in the Pacific Northwest. The location of the navy yard on Puget Sound was due to his efforts. He is credited with securing the establishment of Fort Lawton at Seattle and the development of Fort George Wright at Spokane. He sponsored a lieu land bill which dissolved the troubles arising from the taking of lieu land by the Northern Pacific Railroad as compensation for losses in the original grant and confirmed the titles of hundreds of farmers who had developed the rich Palouse region and were in danger of being dispossessed. He introduced and secured the passage of a bill, in the Fifty-fifth Congress, creating Rainier National Park. He was interested in the promotion of trade with the Orient and early recognized the needs of Alaska and urged them in Congress.

At the close of his term in the Senate, he returned to his home in Spokane. In 1899, with a loan from James J. Hill [q.v.], he purchased the controlling interest in the *Seattle Post-Intelligencer*. He removed to Seattle in 1903 and devoted his time chiefly to the management of the paper until a few months before his death. He died of heart disease at the New Willard Hotel, Washington, D. C., when he was about to start on a trip around the world with his wife, Edna (Sweet), whom he had married in 1883. He was survived by his wife and a daughter.

[Jonathan Edwards, *An Illus. Hist. of Spokane County, . . . Wash.* (1900); C. A. Snowden, *Hist. of Wash.*, vol. V (1911); Welford Beaton, *The City That Made Itself* (copr. 1914); *Biog. Dir. Am. Cong.* (1928); *Who's Who in America*, 1912–13; *Seattle Post-Intelligencer*, Nov. 7 and 11, 1912, Feb. 4, 1913; *N. Y. Times*, Nov. 7, 1912.]
G. W. F.

WILSON, JOSEPH MILLER (June 20, 1838–Nov. 24, 1902), civil engineer and architect, was born at Phoenixville, Pa., one of three sons of William Hasell Wilson [q.v.], civil engineer, and Jane (Miller) Wilson. He received his education in private schools and in the Rensselaer Polytechnic Institute, where he was graduated with the degree of C.E. in 1858. After a two-year special course in analytical chemistry, he entered the employ of the Pennsylvania Railroad, serving as assistant engineer until 1863, when he became resident engineer of the Middle Division. In 1865 he was made principal assistant engineer in charge of bridges for the entire road, and subsequently, engineer of bridges and buildings, in which capacity he continued until Jan. 1, 1886. He also acted as engineer of bridges and buildings on the Philadelphia, Wilmington

& Baltimore Railroad. In 1869, as a reward for ten years' service, the Pennsylvania Railroad granted him and his assistant, Henry Pettit, six months' leave of absence for travel in Europe.

In 1876, with his elder brother, John Allston Wilson, and Frederick G. Thorn, he organized the firm of Wilson Brothers & Company, civil engineers and architects. John Allston Wilson (Apr. 24, 1837–Jan. 19, 1896), who was senior member of the firm from its formation until his death, had also served the Pennsylvania Railroad and its subsidiaries in various capacities from assistant engineer to chief engineer from 1858 until 1876. He was especially well versed in matters connected with railroad law, a fact which enabled him to serve as an expert advisor or witness in legal cases. In 1886 the other brother, Henry W. Wilson, associated himself with them. The firm members were engineers and architects for the shops of the Northern Central Railway at Baltimore and of the Allegheny Valley Railroad at Verona, Pa.; stations and shops for the Ninth and Third Avenue lines of the New York Elevated and the New York, West Shore & Buffalo Railroad, and stations on the Central Railroad of New Jersey, the Lehigh Valley, and the Philadelphia & Reading. They also served in the same capacity in connection with various buildings in Philadelphia, including the Drexel Institute, the Presbyterian Hospital, and the Holmesburg Prison. Among the structures designed and built by Joseph M. Wilson were the Susquehanna and Schuylkill bridges, the original Broad Street Station, Philadelphia, and the Baltimore & Potomac Station at Washington. For the design and construction of the main exhibition building and machinery hall of the Centennial Exhibition at Philadelphia, 1876, he and Henry Pettit were awarded joint medals and diplomas by the Centennial Commission.

Wilson was chairman of the board of expert engineers on the Washington aqueduct tunnel and reservoir in 1888–89, and in 1888 served on a board to report on terminal problems at Providence, R. I. As one of the expert engineers he examined and reported on the condition of the elevated railroads in New York City; also on the design for the approaches of the New York and Brooklyn suspension bridge. In 1891 he was consultant to the board of rapid transit commissioners for the City of New York. As consulting engineer for the Philadelphia & Reading Railway Company, he had charge of all work on the Pennsylvania Avenue subway in Philadelphia, and the work of improving the water supply of that city was carried out in accordance with his report of 1899.

His writings on scientific and engineering subjects include the "Mechanical," the "Scientific," and the "Historical" chapters for the *Illustrated Catalogue of the International Exhibition of 1876*; historical papers on the International Exhibition of 1876 in *Engineering* (London, 1875–76); "Bridge over the Monongahela River at Port Perry, Pa." (*Minutes of the Proceedings of the Institute of Civil Engineers,* vol. LX, 1880); "On American Permanent Way" (*Report of the British Association for the Advancement of Science, 1884,* 1885); "On Specifications for Strength of Iron Bridges" (*Transactions, American Society of Civil Engineers,* vol. XV, 1886); "The Philadelphia and Reading Terminal Railway and Station in Philadelphia" (*Ibid.,* vol. XXXIV, 1895); "On Schools; With Particular Reference to Trade Schools" (*Journal of the Franklin Institute,* February-October 1890). The Institution of Civil Engineers, London, awarded him the Telford Premium in 1878 for his description of the Port Perry bridge. On May 24, 1869, he married Sarah Dale Pettit, daughter of Judge Thomas McKean Pettit [*q.v.*]; they had two children. In 1874 Wilson was elected to membership in the American Philosophical Society; from 1887 to 1893 he was president of the Franklin Institute.

[*Biog. Record, Officers and Grads. Rensselaer Polytechnic Inst.* (1887); *Trans. Am. Soc. Civil Engineers,* vol. L (1903); *Who's Who in America,* 1901–02; *Minutes of Proc. of the Institute of Civil Engineers* (London), vol. CLIII (1903); *Pub. Ledger* (Phila.), Nov. 25, 1902.]   B. A. R.

WILSON, JOSHUA LACY (Sept. 22, 1774–Aug. 14, 1846), Presbyterian clergyman, was born in Bedford County, Va., the son of Henry Wright Wilson, a physician, grandson of Maj. Josiah Wilson who was in Maryland before 1688. Joshua's mother, Agnes (Lacy) Wilson, was a sister of the Rev. Drury Lacy [*q.v.*] of Virginia. When the boy was about four years old his father died and his mother married John Templin, father of Rev. Terah Templin, a pioneer Presbyterian preacher of Kentucky. In 1781 the family moved to Kentucky, and after the death of his stepfather Joshua bought a farm in Jessamine County, then a part of Fayette County. In his twenty-second year he sold this farm for money to attend an academy at Pisgah. Leaving there in 1796, he next studied under Rev. William Mahon in Mercer County. With less than three years' schooling, he began teaching in Frankfort, but gave it up to "read divinity" under Rev. James Vance, near Louisville. He was licensed to preach by the Presbytery of Transylvania on Oct. 8, 1802. His first charge consisted of the churches of Bardstown and Big

Spring, over which he was installed after his ordination on June 8, 1804. On Oct. 22, 1801, he married Sarah B. Mackay, who became the mother of his eight children, one of whom was Samuel Ramsay Wilson [*q.v.*].

Called to the First Presbyterian Church of Cincinnati on May 28, 1808, Wilson inaugurated a ministry there that continued until his death. Over six feet in height, reserved, and said by some to resemble Andrew Jackson, he exhibited "great energy and decision of character" in promoting the moral and religious welfare of the rising city. An assiduous student himself, he assisted in founding Cincinnati College and was professor of moral philosophy and logic there for several years. He was the first chairman (1828–30) of the board of trustees of Lane Theological Seminary. He fostered Sunday schools, Bible societies, and libraries. With equal conviction he attacked theatres, dancing, and the Masonic order. His theology was that of the Old School, and his defense of Calvinistic doctrines led him into many controversies both within and without his denomination.

His published writings consist of pamphlets and newspaper articles, dealing chiefly with polemical subjects. In 1811 he replied to a Methodist pamphlet by writing *Episcopal Methodism; or Dragonism Exhibited.* His pen was employed against the deists, the New Lights, and Roman Catholicism. After *The Pandect,* which he founded in 1828, passed out of his hands and became the New School *Cincinnati Journal,* he established in 1831 the *Standard,* as an Old School organ. He opposed the "New England theology" and the operation of the "Plan of Union," and published his *Four Propositions against the Claims of the American Home Missionary Society* in 1831. Believing Lyman Beecher [*q.v.*] guilty of propagating heresy, he prosecuted him before Presbytery and Synod. He assisted in the preparation of the "Western Memorial" of 1834 which expressed alarm at "the prevalence of unsound doctrine and laxity in discipline" (quoted by Thompson, *post,* p. 110), and he subsequently signed the "Act and Testimony" of 1835, setting forth the Old School view. A prominent member of the Old School Convention of 1837, he became moderator of the Old School General Assembly in 1839. Though handicapped by bodily disease, he remained in public life until a few weeks before his death, which occurred in Cincinnati.

[The Joshua L. Wilson Papers, Univ. of Chicago; R. L. Hightower, *Joshua L. Wilson, Frontier Controversialist* (1934); *Autobiog., Correspondence, Etc., of Lyman Beecher* (1864), ed. by Charles Beecher; Robert Davidson, *Hist. of the Presbyterian Church in the*

State of Ky. (1847); W. B. Sprague, *Annals of the Am. Pulpit*, vol. IV (1858); R. E. Thompson, *A Hist. of the Presbyt. Churches in the U. S.* (1895); E. D. Mansfield, *Memoirs of the Life and Services of Daniel Drake, M.D.* (1855); G. N. Mackenzie, *Colonial Families of the U. S.*, vol. II (1911); *Cincinnati Morning Herald*, Aug. 15, 1846.]   R. L. H.

WILSON, MORTIMER (Aug. 6, 1876–Jan. 27, 1932), composer, conductor, was born in Chariton, Iowa, the son of Hess John Wilson and his wife, Mary Elizabeth Harper. The elder Wilson was himself a musician, the son of an Iowa farmer of Scotch-English extraction. Mortimer was musically inclined from his earliest years. At the age of five he began to play the organ in a local church. On one occasion he broke open his father's violin and cornet cases, and before the parent returned for supper the lad had taught himself to play all the tunes he knew on both instruments. Then followed a collection of all the instruments of both band and orchestra. He required only one day to learn the intricacies of fingering each. During this period he composed many two-steps and marches for the neighborhood orchestra and some were accepted by a Chicago publisher, but before they were issued Wilson had started the study of composition, realized that his work was immature, and his father was compelled to recover the pieces through a writ of replevin. After preliminary studies in Chariton, Wilson went to Chicago in 1894 for further instruction. He studied violin with S. E. Jacobson, organ with Wilhelm Middleschulte, and theory and composition with Frederic G. Gleason [*q.v.*]. After four years in Chicago he entered the Culver Military Academy as a cadet, and arranged to pay for his board and tuition by organizing and directing a school band. In 1901 he went to Lincoln, Nebr., to head the theoretical courses of the music department of the University of Nebraska, and to revive and conduct the Lincoln Symphony Orchestra. While in Nebraska he wrote two textbooks on composition, *The Rhetoric of Music* (1907), and *Harmonic and Melodic Technical Studies* (1907). In 1908 he went to Leipzig, where for two years he studied composition with Max Reger and conducting with Hans Sitt. In 1912 he accepted an offer to conduct the symphony orchestra of Atlanta, Ga., and from 1913 to 1914 he acted as director of the Atlanta Conservatory of Music. From 1915 to 1916 he was associated with the Brenau Conservatory of Gainesville, Ga., and from 1917 to 1918 with the Walkin Music School in New York City.

Wilson achieved something of a reputation in the field of arranging and writing music to accompany motion pictures, and he was commissioned by Douglas Fairbanks to write original scores to accompany performances of the *Thief of Bagdad* and other films that preceded the day of sound pictures. As a composer Wilson acquired a technique and resourcefulness that had few equals in the country. He was definitely of the Reger tradition, with a fluency and inventiveness in counterpoint that enabled him to develop his musical ideas to the utmost. His dislike for the obvious was the principal obstacle to his success as a composer of pieces that would reach a large sale, and he remained principally a composer for musicians rather than a writer for the general public, or even for a large group of music lovers. He had many pupils in composition, and it was in this field that he was probably most distinguished. His compositions include five symphonies, and "Country-Wedding," a suite for orchestra (manuscript), and many published works: a trio, "From my Youth"; two sonatas for violin and piano; seven organ preludes; three suites for piano, "In Georgia," "Suite Rustica," and "By the Wayside"; a suite for violin and piano, "Suwannee Sketches"; "Overture 1849" (originally composed for the motion picture *The Covered Wagon*); "New Orleans," an overture for orchestra that won in 1920 a $500 prize offered by the Rivoli and the Rialto Theatres, New York; an orchestral fantasy, "My Country"; and numerous short pieces and songs. He died of pneumonia in New York City. On Nov. 23, 1904, he had been married to Hettie Lewis of Chariton, who with a son survived him.

[Most of the material for this article was drawn from information supplied the author by Wilson himself. Consult *Who's Who in America*, 1930–31; *Grove's Dict. of Music and Musicians, Am. Supp.* (1930); J. T. Howard, *Our Am. Music* (1930); M. M. Hansford, tribute in *Am. Organist*, May 1932, *Pacific Coast Musician*, Jan. 30, 1932; *N. Y. Times*, Jan. 28, 1932.]
                                                    J. T. H.

WILSON, PETER (Nov. 23, 1746–Aug. 1, 1825), philologist and administrator, was born in Ordiquhill, Banff, Scotland. He was educated at the University of Aberdeen, where he devoted himself to the humanistic studies, especially Greek and Latin, for which the Scottish universities have long been famous. In 1763 he emigrated to New York City, and presently gained such repute as a teacher that he was appointed principal of the Hackensack Academy in New Jersey. His success in this post was so marked that in 1783 and again in 1786 the trustees of Queen's (afterwards Rutgers) College at New Brunswick tried (but in vain) to add him to their teaching staff, and, still later, in 1792 had his name under serious consideration for the office of president. During the Revolution he represented Bergen County in the New Jersey Assembly from 1777 to 1781, and served with such distinction that at the close of the war in 1783 he was selected to revise and codify the laws of the state. In 1787 he was again a prominent member of the legislature. From 1789 to 1792 he was professor of the Greek and Latin languages in Columbia College, but resigned to accept the position of principal of Erasmus Hall Academy in Flatbush, Long Island. In 1797 he returned to Columbia as professor of the Greek and Latin languages and of Grecian and Roman antiquities, a chair which he held until his retirement with a pension in 1820. Although he had ceased to teach at Erasmus Hall, he continued until 1805 to be titular head of the school, and the trustees, who had come to reply upon his scholarship, deferred to his judgment in all matters of educational policy. In July 1800 Dr. William Samuel Johnson [q.v.] resigned the presidency of Columbia, and his successor was not chosen until a year later. In the interim Wilson and John Kemp [q.v.], professor of mathematics, performed the duties of the office. Wilson survived his retirement five years, dying in New Barbadoes, N. J. He was married twice, his second wife being Catherine Duryea of Bushwick, L. I., by whom he had five daughters and two sons (*New York Genealogical and Biographical Record*, April 1880, p. 69).

Wilson was a sound scholar, and his treatises and editions, though few in number, are interesting monuments of the transit of learning from England to the colonies. In the preface to his *Introduction to Greek Prosody . . . with an Appendix on the Metres of Horace, Adapted to the Use of Beginners* (1811) he laments that, while engaged upon the book, he had not been able to find in America a copy of Thomas Gaisford's brilliant edition of *Hephaestion* (London, 1810). This quest of excellence was characteristic, and is evidenced also in his other works: an edition, with English notes, of Sallust's *Catiline and Jugurtha* (1808) ; *Rules of Latin Prosody for the Use of Schools* (1810) ; the first American edition, with many corrections and additions, of Zacharias Pearce's Greek text of *Longinus on the Sublime, with a Latin Translation and Latin Notes* (1812) ; *Compendium of Greek Prosody* (1817) ; a revision of the treatise of Alexander Adam (of Edinburgh) on *Roman Antiquities* (1819) ; and the Greek text of the *New Testament* (1822).

He was a member of the Dutch Reformed Church and stood high in its counsels ; in fact, he was so eloquent a speaker that he was urged to enter its ministry. His portrait, which hangs in Faculty House, Columbia University (reproduced in *Chronicles of Erasmus Hall, post*, p.

52), shows a man of noble presence, with fine eyes and patrician features, the face of a scholar and a gentleman. Brown University gave him an honorary A.M. in 1786 and Union College an LL.D. in 1798.

[*A Hist. of Columbia Univ., 1754–1904* (1904) ; *Chronicles of Erasmus Hall* (1906) ; W. H. S. Demarest, *A Hist. of Rutgers Coll., 1766–1924* (1924) ; *Mag. of the Reformed Dutch Church*, July 1827 ; *New Brunswick Rev.*, May 1854 ; and death notice in *N. Y. Evening Post*, Aug. 2, 1825.]   N.G.M.

WILSON, ROBERT BURNS (Oct. 30, 1850– Mar. 31, 1916), painter, poet, and novelist, was born at his grandfather's home near Washington, Pa., the son of Thomas M. and Elizabeth (McLean) Wilson. His father was an architect and builder by profession, an inventor by avocation. From both parents the son may have derived some of his artistic and literary abilities. His mother died when he was ten years old. His early education came through the schools of Washington, Pa., and Wheeling. Sometime before he reached his majority he determined to be a painter and, leaving home, attempted to make his living with oils and crayon. For several months he traveled with the Hagenbeck circus in order to study the anatomy of captive lions and tigers. At Pittsburgh in 1871 he met another ambitious young painter, John W. Alexander [q.v.], with whom he traveled to a point near Louisville, Ky. Wilson spent some time in Union County and then moved to Louisville, where a crayon of Henry Watterson [q.v.] brought him local fame. In 1875 he was persuaded to change his residence to Frankfort, Ky. There his facility with colors, his gift for verse, his stalwart physique and handsome face, his buoyant idealism soon made him a social favorite. He painted indefatigably, selling canvases only when necessity prompted him ; he wrote with equal industry ; presently his reputation widened to more than local scope. In 1901 he married in New York City Anne Hendrick, eldest daughter of W. J. Hendrick, a former attorney-general of Kentucky. After the birth of their only child, Anne Elizabeth, in 1902 at Frankfort, the Wilsons made their home in New York, where the painter hoped to increase his income and be at the center of cultural impulses. The last change was not a fortunate one : he disliked the colder climate, he was sensitive to a slackening in appreciation of his work, and he knew the sting of poverty accompanied by deepened responsibilities. Some of his paintings brought good sums ; others almost nothing. In New York his moment of greatest triumph came, perhaps, when his poem, "Remember the *Maine*," in the *New York Herald* of Apr. 17, 1898, supplied the battlecry for the war with Spain. He died in St. John's Hospital, Brooklyn, and is buried in the cemetery at Frankfort. He was survived by his wife and daughter. A portrait of him and three of his best landscapes are in the possession of the Kentucky State Historical Society.

Wilson's work includes portraits, pictures of animals, Scriptural subjects, and landscapes. Although he did not reach the highest eminence in any of these, his landscapes are the best and most characteristic of his productions. They fall somewhere between the work of the Hudson River School and that of George Inness [q.v.], having neither the chromo qualities of the first nor the poetic connotations of the second. Like his writings, they are decidedly sentimental, showing a fondness for blue shadowings and hazes that conceal rugged or unpleasant details. As a poet he belongs to the *fin de siècle* group of Americans that romanticized nature and man in his more genteel affections. His verses, published in the leading magazines, were collected in *Life and Love* (1887), *Chant of a Woodland Spirit* (1894), and *The Shadows of the Trees* (1898). His one novel, *Until the Day Break* (1900), was favorably reviewed for its style and in spite of its narrative defects; it is a Gothic fiction haunted by a sense of doom and made too deliberately sensational. A man of indubitable talent, Wilson suffered through a lack of sound critical advice from his friends.

[Sources include information from Wilson's daughter, Anne Elizabeth Wilson Blochin; *Who's Who in America*, 1901–02; J. W. Townsend, *Ky. in Am. Letters* (2 vols., 1913); C. W. Coleman, in *Harper's New Monthly Mag.*, May 1887; Mildred L. Rutherford, *The South in Hist. and Lit.* (1907); Ida W. Harrison, in *Lib. of Southern Lit.* (1910), vol. XIII, ed. by E. A. Alderman and J. C. Harris; obituaries in *Am. Art Ann.*, 1916, *Am. Art News*, Apr. 15, 1916, and *N. Y. Times*, Apr. 1, 1916.]   **G.C.K.**

WILSON, SAMUEL (Sept. 13, 1766–July 31, 1854), meat-packer, whose appellation, "Uncle Sam," was transferred to the venerable figure personifying the United States government, was born in West Cambridge (now Arlington), Mass., seventh of the thirteen children of Edward and Lucy (Francis) Wilson. The family name was originally spelled Willson. About 1780 the family moved to Mason, N. H., and in 1789 Samuel and his brother Ebenezer set out on foot for Troy, N. Y., where the rest of Samuel Wilson's long life was spent. On Jan. 3, 1797, in Mason, he married Betsey, daughter of Capt. Benjamin Mann. In Troy he engaged in several lines of business—making brick, building houses, running a farm, an orchard, a nursery, a distillery, a sloop line on the Hudson, and a general

store. He was known as a man of the strictest integrity. Genial and friendly, he came to be called "Uncle Sam" Wilson to distinguish him from a younger man of the same name. During the War of 1812, Troy was an important center for assembling munitions and food for the army. At this time, Ebenezer and Samuel Wilson were prosperous meat packers, advertising that they could slaughter and salt more than a thousand head of cattle a week. Among their customers was Elbert Anderson, an army contractor, who required that his purchases must be shipped in oak casks branded E A U S. An ignorant workman asking what the letters stood for got the jesting reply: "Why for Elbert Anderson and Uncle Sam here." Many of the soldiers encamped near Troy who knew the Wilsons personally referred to their beef as "Uncle Sam's"; and eventually in the army and elsewhere the term personified the government itself.

Samuel Wilson was uncle or great-uncle to over a hundred persons, but left few direct descendants. Large, well proportioned, and cleanshaven, in appearance he did not resemble the usual caricatures of "Uncle Sam." Trojans testify that he was fond of a joke and that he quite enjoyed being reminded of his connection with the famous nickname. He died in Troy and was buried in Oakwood Cemetery there.

[This tale does not rest on oral tradition alone. Elbert Anderson died in New York City Apr. 17, 1830, and a few days later the "Uncle Sam" incident was published in a New York paper by one who said he was "an eye witness" and wished to put on record for the benefit of future historians in this personal reminiscence the true origin of the nickname (*N. Y. Gazette*, May 12, 1830). For data concerning Wilson see A. J. Weise, *Hist. of the City of Troy* (1876) and *Troy's One Hundred Years, 1789–1889* (1891); J. B. Hill, *Hist. of the Town of Mason, N. H.* (1858), pp. 167. 209; Freeman Hunt, *Am. Anecdotes* (1830), II, 18–20; *N. Y. State Hist. Asso. Quart. Jour.*, Jan. 1929, pp. 97–98; *Vital Records of Arlington, Mass.* (1904).]
        J.F.W—r.

WILSON, SAMUEL GRAHAM (Feb. 11, 1858–July 2, 1916), missionary and author, was born at Indiana, Pa., the son of Andrew Wilkins and Anna Graham (Dick) Wilson. After attending the public schools of Indiana he entered the College of New Jersey (Princeton) as a sophomore and graduated with honors in 1876, the youngest member of his class. During the next three years he studied theology at Western Theological Seminary, Allegheny, then spent a postgraduate year at Princeton, working in both the Theological Seminary and the College. On July 1, 1880, he was ordained at Indiana, Pa., by the Presbytery of Kittanning. Having been appointed a missionary of the Board of Foreign Missions of the Presbyterian Church in December 1879, he set out for Persia on Sept. 9, 1880.

In November he reached Tabriz and began the study of the Armenian and Azeri Turkish languages with the expectation of specializing in the work of translation. Soon, however, he was preaching and making extensive evangelical tours which kept him on horseback for six weeks each year. In 1882 he was appointed principal of a small boys' school in Tabriz and found his life work in developing it in enrolment, in faculty, and in equipment. After the addition of theological courses in 1892 it became the Memorial Training and Theological School. For many years Wilson was not only head of the school but also treasurer of the Mission. While on furlough in the United States he married, Sept. 16, 1886, Annie Dwight Rhea of Lake Forest, Ill., daughter of Samuel Audley Rhea, pioneer missionary in Persia.

Wilson translated a catechism into Armenian (1885), a church history and an arithmetic text into Azeri Turkish. His valuable *Persian Life and Customs* (1895), based on diaries and numerous contributions to newspapers and magazines, went through several editions and was translated into German and Russian. His *Persia: Western Mission* (1896) is a descriptive and historical sketch. A tale of Armenian life, *Mariam, a Romance of Persia* (1906), was first published serially in the *Presbyterian Banner* and enjoyed a considerable popularity in Sunday school circles. In November 1912, while in the United States, he was seriously injured in a railroad accident, and convalescence detained him until the World War made return to Persia impossible. Devoting himself thenceforth to preaching, lecturing, and writing, he contributed articles to *The Cyclopaedia of Temperance and Prohibition* (1891), the *Missionary Review of the World*, the *Princeton Theological Review*, the *Outlook*, and the *North American Review*. A volume on *Bahaism and Its Claims* (1915) was followed by *Modern Movements among Moslems* (1916), which was based on lectures delivered at Western Theological Seminary on the Severance Foundation. Everything he wrote reflected wide reading and acute observation and was presented in a clear and simple style.

In November 1915 the Mission Board at length permitted him to leave for Persia as chairman of a commission sent by the American Committee for Armenian and Syrian Relief. Traveling via Norway, Archangel, and Petrograd, he was halted at Tiflis and remained in Russian territory until summer, administering relief among Armenian refugees from Turkey. Unremitting labor and exposure to extremes of cold left him so weakened that he fell an easy victim to typhoid

fever shortly after reaching Tabriz early in June 1916. His wife and four children survived him. A man of unusual energy and tact as well as organizing and administrative ability, he was respected by Moslems and revered by Armenian as a martyr to their cause.

[*Record of the Class of '76 of Princeton College*, no. 1–10; *Who's Who in America*, 1916–17; *Princeton Alumni Weekly*, Oct. 11, 1916; *N. Y. Herald*, July 16, 1916; manuscript records of Princeton Univ.]

W. L. W., Jr.

WILSON, SAMUEL MOUNTFORD (*c.* 1823–June 4, 1892), California lawyer, was born at Steubenville, Ohio, to which his father, Peter Wilson, had moved from Philadelphia. His mother's name is said to have been Frances Stokeley. The Wilson family was of English origin and had been established in America since the seventeenth century. Since his father died about 1827, Wilson was compelled to support himself from early youth. He had a limited formal education at the Grove Academy in his native town. At about thirteen he is said to have gone to Wisconsin with an elder brother, a lieutenant in the United States army. At about nineteen he returned to Steubenville to study law in the office of his uncle, Samuel Stokeley, a member of Congress. He was admitted to the bar at twenty-one, and soon moved to Galena, Ill., becoming the law partner of Col. Joseph P. Hoge. In 1853 the partners moved to San Francisco, where the firm continued until 1864. Wilson then formed a brief partnership with his brother, David S. Wilson, which was followed by a partnership with A. P. Crittenden, lasting until the latter's death in 1870. Four years later he formed a partnership with his son Russell, and somewhat later another son was admitted to the firm of Wilson and Wilson.

After serving out an unexpired term as district attorney in Jo Daviess County, Ill., Wilson refused to handle criminal cases, and throughout his life confined himself to civil practice. Only twice did he accept political offices, and both of these were in the line of his professional work: in 1878–79 he was a member of the California constitutional convention where, as chairman of the judiciary committee, he vigorously opposed the radical demands of the followers of Denis Kearney [*q.v.*] and was one of fourteen members who refused to sign the constitution when completed; in 1879 he was a member of the board of freeholders that drafted a new municipal charter for San Francisco, subsequently rejected. He refused appointment by Gov. H. H. Haight to the office of associate justice of the California supreme court; and in 1885 is said to have declined appointment by President Cleveland as minister to China and as minister to Spain. Aside from his strictly legal efforts, his best productions were the orations delivered at the laying of the corner-stone of the state capitol in Sacramento in 1861, and his eulogy of Samuel J. Tilden in 1886.

Perhaps more than any other lawyer of his time, Wilson impressed himself upon the legal history of California, where at the time of his death he was unanimously conceded to be at the head of his profession. For nearly forty years there were few important civil cases in which he did not serve as counsel; and he appeared before the United States Supreme Court more frequently than any other member of the California bar during his lifetime. He bore a leading part in nearly all the noted cases involving California land law, especially as counsel for the hydraulic mining companies in their great contest (1880–86) with the farming interests upon the debris question (*People of California* vs. *Gold Run Ditch and Mining Company*, 66 *California Reports*, 138, 155). He also acquired a great reputation in certain will cases, notably when he successfully defended the will of the late Senator Broderick (21 *Wallace*, 503). So successful was his law practice that he left an estate of over a million dollars, consisting principally of real property in San Francisco. He was equally successful in trying cases before a jury and before a court. As a speaker he was exceedingly fluent, forcibly persuasive, simple and direct, rarely indulging in ornamentation. He depended upon complete mastery of his subject and clarity of exposition rather than upon eloquence. He was of medium stature, slightly built, and of commanding and masterful presence, though simple in his tastes and dress, and free from haughtiness and affectation. On July 5, 1848, he married Emily Josephine Scott, daughter of John Scott, a congressman from Missouri. She and four sons survived him.

[O. T. Shuck, *Bench and Bar in Cal.* (1889), and *Hist. of the Bench and Bar of Cal.* (1901); *Memorial Commemorative of the Life and Services of Samuel M. Wilson . . . Bar Asso. of San Francisco, Aug. 13, 1892*; *Debates and Proc. Constitutional Convention of the State of Cal.* (3 vols., 1880–81); obituaries in *Bull.* (San Francisco), June 4, 1892, and *San Francisco Chronicle*, June 5, 1892.]   P. O. R.

WILSON, SAMUEL RAMSAY (June 4, 1818–Mar. 3, 1886), Presbyterian clergyman, was born at Cincinnati, Ohio, the son of Joshua Lacy Wilson [*q.v.*] and Sarah (Mackay) Wilson. In the spring of 1829 he began preparatory studies at Miami University, Oxford, Ohio, but later transferred to Hanover College, Hanover, Ind., where he received the degree of A.B. in 1836. The next year he entered Princeton Theo-

logical Seminary and graduated in 1840. He was licensed by the Presbytery of New Brunswick on Aug. 5, 1840, and began his ministerial career as a colleague of his father at the First Presbyterian Church, Cincinnati. After his ordination on Apr. 26, 1842, he became co-pastor and upon his father's death in 1846 pastor, remaining as such until his resignation on Mar. 2, 1861.

On the eve of the Civil War he declared his sympathy with the Southern cause, and as a commissioner of the Old School General Assembly of 1861 opposed the resolutions introduced by the Rev. Gardiner Spring [*q.v.*] which acknowledged obligation to promote and perpetuate the integrity of the United States. In the same year he accepted a call to the Grand Street (later Fourth) Presbyterian Church, New York, but resigned because of ill health in January 1863. Later he supplied the Mulberry Presbyterian Church of Shelby County, Ky., for fifteen months, and on Mar. 12, 1865, was installed as pastor of the First Presbyterian Church, Louisville. As a border-state spokesman he opposed the reconstruction policy of the majority of the Old School Presbyterian Church. Before the Assembly of 1865 he pleaded in vain for the "olive branch" instead of the resolutions, later termed the "Pittsburgh Orders," which stigmatized secession as a crime. The following summer he drew up, as the protest of "a little band" against the Assembly's subservience to the federal government's attitude toward the South, the "Declaration and Testimony" which was adopted by the Presbytery of Louisville. One of Wilson's most brilliant speeches was delivered before the Synod of Kentucky in defense of this document and of the Presbytery of Louisville.

Wilson resigned his Louisville church Dec. 9, 1879, and from 1880 to 1883 was pastor of the Second Presbyterian Church of Madison, Ind., but subsequently returned to Louisville, where he died. He was married three times: first, Mar. 25, 1841, to Nancy Campbell Johnston of Cincinnati, who died June 23, 1849; second, Jan. 29, 1852 in Franklin County, Ky., to Mary Catherine Bell, who died Dec. 17, 1874; third, Jan. 11, 1876, in Louisville, to Annie Maria Steele who died Dec. 10, 1920. By his first marriage he had five children; by the second, seven; and by the third, two. Several of Wilson's sermons and addresses were published, among them *Discourses Delivered at the Dedication of the First Presbyterian Church (the Church of the Pioneers) in the City of Cincinnati, Sept. 21, 1851* (1851); *The Causes and Remedies of Impending National Calamities* (1860); *Reply to the Attack of Rev. R. J. Breckinridge upon the Louisville*

Presbytery, and Defence of the "Declaration and Testimony" Made in the Synod of Kentucky (1865); *A Pan-Presbyterian Letter . . . to Presbyterians both North and South* (1875). He also edited *Hymns of the Church* (1872), and was associated with various religious periodicals.

[*Biog. Cat. of the Princeton Theological Sem.* (1933); Joshua L. Wilson Papers, Univ. of Chicago; G. N. Mackenzie, *Colonial Families in the U. S. of America*, vol. II (1911); E. L. Warren, *The Presbyterian Church in Louisville* (1896); E. P. Johnson, *A Hist. of Ky. and Kentuckians* (1912), vol. III; S. M. Wilson, *Hist. of Ky.* (1928), vol. II; *A Memorable Hist. Document; Its Antecedents and Its Outcome: The "Declaration and Testimony" Drawn by Rev. S. R. Wilson* (n.d.); *Herald and Presbyter* (Cincinnati), Mar. 10, 1886; *Courier-Jour.* (Louisville), Mar. 4, 1886; information as to certain facts from Wilson's son, Samuel M. Wilson, Esq., Lexington, Ky.]

R. L. H.

WILSON, SAMUEL THOMAS (1761–May 23, 1824), Roman Catholic priest and provincial of the Order of St. Dominic, was born in London of parents in the merchant class. In 1770 the child, who could not be educated as a Catholic in England because of the penal laws, was sent to the Dominican College, Holy Cross, in ancient Bornhem, Belgium. A pious youth, he conducted himself well. In 1777 he entered the Dominican novitiate, and proceeded to the College of St. Thomas of Aquin in Louvain for his course in theology. Because of an ordinance of Joseph II, the "sacristan emperor" of Austria, Wilson could not take his solemn vows until he was in his twenty-fifth year (Dec. 8, 1785). A year later (June 10), he was ordained a priest of the Order of Friar Preachers (Dominicans) by Bishop Ferdinand M. Lobkowitz of Ghent. Reputed a good scholar, a linguist, and a doctor of sacred theology, Wilson taught at Holy Cross and was vicar-provincial of the community in the years of terror under the French Revolutionists. Finally the blow came, and the faculty of Bornhem, including Wilson, fled in disguise from the Jacobins via Rotterdam to Carshalton in Surrey, England, where the relaxation of the anti-Catholic code permitted the reëstablishment of the refugee college (1794). After teaching there a year, Wilson was ordered back to Bornhem to preserve the property. Courageously he heard confessions and said mass in the homes of friends, conducted the college, bought its buildings at auction on its seizure by agents of the Directory, and held on despite persecution and imprisonment until Napoleon's accession brought partial relief. Discouraged by the secularization of the institution under orders from the papal legate in Paris, the Dominicans turned their attention to America.

Edward D. Fenwick [q.v.] and Robert Angier

emigrated in 1804, and Wilson and William Tuite arrived in Maryland the following year (Sept. 10). By the end of the year, Wilson was in Kentucky as a missionary in the Cartwright's Creek settlement, where he also conducted a grammar school for boys. In 1807 he was named provincial, and in this capacity was responsible for the building of the Church of St. Rose and the College of St. Thomas Aquin near Springfield. As one of the earliest colleges in Kentucky, this school attracted a number of boys, including Jefferson Davis [q.v.], but Wilson found its financial maintenance on the primitive frontier no easy task. Honored as "the shining light of his diocese" by Bishop Benedict J. Flaget [q.v.], he acted as co-consecrator of Bishop John B. David [q.v.] and Bishop Fenwick, thus performing a function quite unusual for a simple priest. In 1822 he founded the first American convent of the now flourishing Sisters of the Third Order of St. Dominic. On his death two years later, Wilson was generally mourned by the Catholics of Kentucky as a priest, educator, and preacher, and by the citizens at large as a pioneer-builder of the state.

[See V. F. O'Daniel, *A Light of the Church in Ky., or the Life of the Vy. Rev. Samuel Thomas Wilson, O.P.* (1932), a detailed study, with a complete bibliog., and *The Rt. Rev. Edward D. Fenwick* (1920); Raymond Palmer, *Obit. Notices of the Friar-Preachers of the English Province* (1884); B. J. Webb, *The Centenary of Catholicity in Ky.* (1884); R. J. Purcell, "Educ. and Irish Teachers in Early Ky.," *Cath. Educ. Rev.,* June 1936; Mary R. Mattingly, *The Cath. Church on the Ky. Frontier* (1936).]

R. J. P.

WILSON, THEODORE DELAVAN (May 11, 1840–June 29, 1896), naval constructor, was born in Brooklyn, N. Y., the son of Charles Wilson, a shipwright, and Ann Elizabeth (Cock) Wilson. After attending the Brooklyn public schools he was employed at the New York Navy Yard, and at the outbreak of the Civil War had served his full term as an apprentice shipwright. He then volunteered for the army and became a non-commissioned officer in the New York state militia, but upon the return of his regiment after three months at the front he joined the navy as a ship's carpenter on Aug. 3, 1861, and served in the *Cambridge,* North Atlantic Squadron, until December 1863. Thereafter until the close of the war he had duty of increasing responsibility in construction and repair work at the New York Navy Yard. He was made assistant naval constructor on May 17, 1866, and was stationed in charge of the construction department at the Pensacola Navy Yard and later at Philadelphia. In 1869 he went to the United States Naval Academy as an instructor in ship construction. Here he remained four years, aside from a tour of European yards in 1870, and published *An Outline of Shipbuilding, Theoretical and Practical* (1873), in part a compilation from various sources. This book was used as a textbook in the Academy. He also published a brief pamphlet, *The Center of Gravity of the U. S. Steamer Shawmut* (1874), and invented in 1870 a new type of air-port and in 1880 a bolt extractor.

On July 11, 1873, he was promoted to the rank of naval constructor. After several years at the Portsmouth Navy Yard he served on the first Naval Advisory Board, created in 1881 to formulate plans for the new steel navy, and on Mar. 1, 1882, he was made chief of the Bureau of Construction and Repair. In this highly responsible post, carrying with it seniority in the Construction Corps and rank equivalent to commodore, he remained during the next eleven years, a period in which the navy in large part was transformed from wood to steel. Innumerable problems were surmounted which arose from the undeveloped state of the American steel industry and the revolutionary changes in design. Under his supervision forty-five ships were built or laid down, including most of the new "White Squadron," at a cost of $52,000,000. In the words of his assistant and successor, Philip Hichborn [*q.v.*], the result of this program was "a monument to the skill, fidelity, and zeal of the late Chief of Bureau . . :" (*Report of the Secretary of the Navy*, 1893, p. 357). He was detached on July 13, 1893, but for some time before had been partly relieved because of ill health. A review of his work in the decade preceding is given in his article, "The Steel Ships of the United States Navy" in the *Transactions of the Society of Naval Architects and Marine Engineers* (vol. I, 1893, p. 116, with an additional reference in vol. II, 1894, p. 22). He was made first vice-president of this society at its organization in 1893, and he was also the first American member (1872) of the British Institution of Naval Architects. After two years' leave of absence he was assigned to the Boston Navy Yard, where he died suddenly from heart failure while supervising the release from drydock of the monitor *Passaic*. He was married prior to 1867 to Sarah E. Stults, and had two daughters and two sons, one of whom became a surgeon in the navy.

[G. W. Cocks, *The Cox Family in America* (1912); *Register of the . . . Navy of the U. S.* (1895); reports of chief of Bureau of Construction and Repair, in *Reports of the Sec. of the Navy*, 1882–93; *New-York Tribune*, June 30, 1896; *Army and Navy Jour.*, July 4, 1896; other information from family sources.]

A. W.

WILSON, THOMAS WOODROW [See WILSON, WOODROW, 1856–1924].

WILSON, WILLIAM (Apr. 27, 1794–Apr. 29, 1857), jurist, was born in Loudoun County, Va. Left fatherless at an early age, he and his only brother worked in a store to help support their mother. William's spare time was spent reading, and at eighteen he began the study of law. Brief military service in the War of 1812 interrupted his preparation for the bar, but in 1817 he felt sufficiently prepared for his chosen profession to seek a location in the West. He began practice in White County, Ill., and in 1818 before he had been in the state a year, received fifteen votes in the legislature for an associate justiceship of the newly organized supreme court. This number was barely short of the majority required for election, but when the first vacancy on the court occurred, in August 1819, the governor appointed Wilson to the place. Upon the expiration of his term as associate justice in 1824, the legislature elected him to the chief justiceship. Thus at the age of thirty he became the third chief justice of the supreme court of Illinois, in which capacity he served until 1848, when after twenty-nine years on the bench he retired, to pass the remainder of his life on his farm in White County, where he died.

His most important decision was probably that given in 1839 in the case of *Field* vs. *The State of Illinois* ex rel *McClernand* (2 *Scammon*, 79), in which the power of the governor to remove a secretary of state appointed by the governor's predecessor was denied, on the ground that the constitution did not expressly place any limitation upon the duration of the term of office. The case was argued by an array of the state's foremost legal talent and attracted wide interest. Wilson's opinion is a forty-four page dissertation on the principles of state constitutional law. His opinions were in general regarded as strong and discriminating, and his style as clear and concise, yet his custom was to jot down his ideas on small pieces of paper and leave it to a clerk to put them into readable form. Wilson would then revise the draft to suit his tastes. A Whig in early life, he became a Democrat upon the organization of the Republican party, but he was never a strong partisan nor did he cultivate the arts of the politician.

Wilson, when young, was described by a contemporary as noble looking; in later years his voice acquired a cracked and unnatural quality, and because of a chronic stomach ailment he became a laudanum addict. Throughout his life he was interested in agriculture and live stock, and upon his estate in White County he bred many horses, cattle, sheep, and swine of a superior type. A noted story teller, amiable and hospitable, he attracted a host of visitors and friends to his country home. He married Mary S. Davidson, a native of Wheeling, Va., in April 1820, and they had ten children, of whom four sons and two daughters survived him.

[Wilson's opinions are found in the first 9 vols. of *Ill. Reports*, being 1 *Breese* through 4 *Gilman*. For biog. data see: *Hist. of White County, Ill.* (1883); Thomas Ford, *A Hist. of Ill.* (1854); *Memoirs of Gustave Koerner* (1909), ed. by T. J. McCormack; *Jour. Ill. State Hist. Soc.*, Oct. 1918; "The Governors' Letter-Books," ed. by E. B. Greene and C. W. Alvord, *Colls. Ill. State Hist. Lib.*, vol. IV (1909); Alexander Davidson and Bernard Stuvé, *A Complete Hist. of Ill.* (1874); Newton Bateman and Paul Selby, *Hist. Encyc. of Ill. and Hist. of Sangamon County* (1912), II, 595; *Memorial Service Feb. 8, 1915, Circuit Court of Lawrence County, Ill.* (1915), on occasion of presentation of portrait to County by Mrs. Alice Stuvé Jerrett, grand-daughter of William Wilson; *Green Bag*, May 1891; *Ill. State Jour.* (Springfield), May 13, 1857.]

G. W. G.

WILSON, WILLIAM (Dec. 25, 1801–Aug. 25, 1860), bookseller, publisher, and verse writer, was born at Crieff, a village in Perthshire, Scotland, of lower middle-class parentage. He had no schooling except from his mother, left a widow in extreme poverty when he was only five. He began to work for a farmer at the age of seven and was apprenticed very young to a cloth dealer in Glasgow. Upright, industrious, and mentally eager, he not only rose in business but educated himself by reading and writing for periodicals, and developed his natural aptitude for music by attending concerts and choral groups. When he emigrated to America (December 1833) he was already known in literary circles in Dundee and Edinburgh as editor of the *Dundee Literary Olio*, as the author of several poems signed "Alpin" or "Allan Grant," which had appeared in Scotch magazines, and as a composer of songs. In the summer of 1834 he moved to Poughkeepsie, where he became a partner of Paraclete Potter, whose bindery and bookstore was already locally famous as a meeting place for leading citizens and writers, and through its circulating library as a center of culture. In 1841 Wilson took over the business, to which he added publishing, and worthily continued the tradition of the place. Several of his poems appeared in the *New York Evening Post*, the *Albion*, the *Knickerbocker Magazine*, and the *Chicago Record*, edited by his youngest son, James Grant Wilson [*q.v.*]. In 1836 he was one of the founders of St. Paul's Church, Poughkeepsie, where he was long a vestryman. His first wife was Jane M'Kenzie, who died in 1826, leaving him with four children. His second wife was Jane Sibbald. The steel engraving prefixed to his *Poems* shows a face smooth-shaven except for close side whiskers, bright-eyed, shrewd yet kind, and with a gleam of quizzical humor.

His poetry, though sincere and technically smooth, is without originality, its language, imagery, and meters recalling Thomson, Young, Burns, Cowper, or Scott. Its themes are the love of simple country life, the nostalgia of the Scotch emigrant, patriotism, freedom, sorrow in bereavement, and the varied experiences of the religious life. The two best known poems are perhaps "The Mitherless Wean" and "Work Is Prayer." The number of famous names on the list of subscribers to the three posthumous editions of his *Poems* (1869, 1875, 1881) is to be accounted for partly by the personal friendship or business relations of himself and his sons with such men as the Chambers brothers of Edinburgh and the popular historian, Benson J. Lossing [*q.v.*], partly by his reputation in the neighborhood as a self-made man who had risen to prosperity and influence by sheer merit. The sale of the volumes as far west as Montana and Colorado, and southward to Arkansas and Texas was an effect of a westward exodus of Poughkeepsie citizens beginning in the 1840's. But the commendations quoted in the advertisement of the third edition must be interpreted as indicating the survival in America as late as 1881 of a highly conservative taste in literature, with standards derived from the eighteenth century.

[In addition to the memoir by B. J. Lossing in Wilson's *Poems* (1869), sources include obituaries in *Telegraph* (Poughkeepsie), Aug. 28, 1860, and *Eagle* (Poughkeepsie), Sept. 1; J. H. Smith, *Hist. of Dutchess County, N. Y.* (1882), p. 383; directories and other local materials.]

A. L. R.

WILSON, WILLIAM BAUCHOP (Apr. 2, 1862–May 25, 1934), labor leader, congressman, first secretary of labor, was born in Blantyre, Scotland, the son of Adam and Helen Nelson (Bauchop) Wilson. In 1870 the family moved to Arnot, near Williamsport, Pa., and Wilson began his career as a miner when he was nine years old. He had little formal schooling but read extensively and at fourteen formed a boys' debating club. On June 7, 1883, he married Agnes Williamson; to them were born eleven children.

Wilson's early activities as a labor leader raised obstacles in the way of his employment as a miner, and his experiences with eviction, blacklisting, injunctions, and even imprisonment caused him to seek temporary employment at farming and other callings, but intensified his devotion to labor unionism and the improvement of working-class conditions (Babson, *post*, pp. 50–55). From 1888 to 1890 he was president of the district miners' union; in the latter year he was a member of the national executive board which organized the United Mine Workers of America, of which he was secretary-treasurer from 1900 to 1908. He was prominently connected with the coal strikes of 1899 and 1902.

In 1891 he was appointed a member of a Pennsylvania commission to revise and codify the state laws relating to the mining of bituminous coal. From 1907 to 1913 he served as member of Congress from Pennsylvania, and during the last two years was chairman of the House committee on labor. In 1911 he was a member of a special congressional committee to investigate the system of "scientific management" of labor developed by Frederick Winslow Taylor [q.v.]. Wilson sponsored an investigation of safety conditions in mines and had much to do with the subsequent organization, in 1910, of the federal Bureau of Mines. In 1912 he secured the passage of the Seamen's Bill for the protection of seamen in the merchant marine. Other measures which he promoted were the eight-hour day for public employees, anti-injunction legislation, protection of the products of free labor from the competition of prison-made goods, the establishment of the Children's Bureau, and the creation of the Department of Labor, of which he was made the first head. His outstanding work as chairman of the committee on labor was formally recognized by his congressional colleagues, Mar. 3, 1913 (*Congressional Record*, 62 Cong., 3 Sess., p. 4804).

As secretary of labor from 1913 to 1921 he organized the new department. The Bureau of Labor, which had been created in 1884, became the Bureau of Labor Statistics. This agency and the Children's Bureau underwent little immediate change. Wilson's main activities were a thorough reorganization of the Bureau of Immigration and Naturalization, which was divided into two agencies; the development of agencies for the mediation and adjustment of industrial disputes; and the formation of the United States Employment Service to handle the problems of war-time employment and transfer of workers. He was also a member and for a time chairman of the federal board for vocational education, and a member of the Council of National Defense. He was president of the International Labor Conference of 1919. In 1926 he was defeated as the Democratic candidate for United States senator from Pennsylvania. He died May 25, 1934, on a train at Savannah, Ga., while on his way to Washington.

In personality, Wilson was somewhat austere but kindly. He was intensely devoted to the welfare of labor but conciliatory, especially in later years, in manner and methods. His most significant work was probably in the promotion of mediation and collective bargaining.

[R. W. Babson, *W. B. Wilson and the Dept. of Labor* (1919); *Biog. Dir. Am. Cong.* (1928); *Who's Who in America*, 1932–33; *N. Y. Times*, May 26, 30, 1934; Chris Evans, *Hist. of the United Mine Workers of America* (2 vols., n.d.); *Minutes of the Ann. Conventions of the United Mine Workers*, 1901–06, and *Proc. of the Ann. Conventions of the United Mine Workers*, 1907, 1908; Annual Reports of the Secretary of Labor, 1913–21; L. L. Lorwin, *The Am. Federation of Labor* (1933).]

W. B—n.

WILSON, WILLIAM DEXTER (Feb. 28, 1816–July 30, 1900), clergyman, educator, the son of William and Rhoda Lane (Gould) Wilson, was born in Stoddard, N. H. He obtained his secondary education in an academy at Walpole, N. H., where he showed such ability in mathematics that on graduation he was appointed a teacher of that subject. Soon deciding, however, to study for the ministry, he entered Harvard Divinity School, from which he was graduated in 1838. After four years as a Unitarian preacher, he became converted to trinitarian principles and joined the Protestant Episcopal Church. From 1842 to 1850 he was rector of a small parish in Sherburne, N. Y. On Nov. 25, 1846, he was married to Susan Whipple Trowbridge. In 1848 he published his first work, *The Church Identified by a Reference to the History of its Origin, Perpetuation, and Extension into the United States* (republished in 1866). In 1850, taking with him a private class of about ten students, he became an instructor in moral and intellectual philosophy in Geneva (later Hobart) Divinity School, where he also acted as treasurer for the associated alumni and, in the last of his eighteen years there, served as acting president. During this period he published *An Explanation of the Rubrics in the Book of Common Prayer* (1854), *An Elementary Treatise on Logic* (1856), and an interesting pamphlet, *Attainder of Treason and Confiscation of the Property of Rebels* (1863), which was an open letter to Judge Samuel A. Foot together with Judge Foot's reply, both writers striving to prove that there were no constitutional restrictions on confiscation in such cases.

In 1868 he was called to the chair of moral and intellectual philosophy in the newly founded Cornell University, where for another eighteen years he was the sole member of his department. He also acted as registrar and had much to do with the organization and administration of the university. This Cornell period was one of great literary productivity, seeing the publication of *The Closing Scenes of the Life of Christ, a Harmonized Combination of the Gospels* (1869); *Lectures on the Psychology of Thought and Ac-*

tion (1871); *Logic, Theoretical and Practical* (1872); *Fancy and Philosophy, an Introduction to the Study of Metaphysics* (1872); *Positive and Negative Terms in Mathematics* (1875); *First Principles of Political Economy* (1875); *The Influence of Language on Thought* (1879); *Order of Instruction in Mathematics* (1876); *Live Questions in Psychology and Metaphysics* (1877); *The Foundations of Religious Belief* (1883). In addition to the diversified interests evidenced by these works Wilson also had a wide command of languages, knowing French, German, Italian, Greek, Latin, Arabic, and Syriac. In 1886 he was made professor emeritus at Cornell, and in the following year he became dean of St. Andrew's Divinity School in Syracuse, N. Y., where he continued to reside until his death. His last works were *The Papal Supremacy and the Provincial System Tested by the Holy Scriptures and the Canon Law of the Ancient Church* (1889), and *Theories of Knowledge Historically Considered with Special Reference to Scepticism and Belief* (1889). He was not an original thinker in any field; his philosophy was merely that of the reigning Scottish school, and his political economy was derived from Mathew Carey [*q.v.*]; but he was, nevertheless, an important cultural influence in American education.

[*Who's Who in America*, 1899–1900; W. T. Hewett, *Cornell Univ.: a Hist.* (3 vols., 1905); *The Ten-Year Book of Cornell Univ.* (1878, 1888); *Hobart Coll. Gen. Cat.* (1897); obituary in *N. Y. Times*, July 31, 1900.]
E. S. B.

WILSON, WILLIAM HASELL (Nov. 5, 1811–Aug. 17, 1902), civil engineer, was born in Charleston, S. C. His grandfather, Lieut. John Wilson, a Scottish military engineer, served in America during the Revolution, married in Charleston, and took his bride back to Scotland. After his death in 1807 his widow took her four children back to Charleston. One of these, John, graduated from the University of Edinburgh and on his return to Charleston married Eliza Gibbes, daughter of William Hasell Gibbes [*q.v.*]. John Wilson had charge of the construction of fortifications near Charleston during the War of 1812. William Hasell, son of John and Eliza, was fourth in line of descent to follow the engineering profession, and his three sons, John A., Joseph Miller [*q.v.*], and Henry W. Wilson, also became engineers.

Educated in the schools of Charleston and Philadelphia, William Hasell Wilson began his career in June 1827 as a volunteer on the engineering corps of the state of Pennsylvania, organized by his father, surveying for a canal or railroad between Philadelphia and the Susque-

hanna River. Until 1834 he was in state employ, serving in various capacities from chainman to principal assistant engineer in location, grading, and bridging for railroad lines west of Philadelphia. As principal assistant engineer of the Philadelphia & Reading Railroad from 1835 to August 1836, he was in charge of construction along the Schuylkill between Pottstown and Bridgeport. This division, nineteen miles long, involved much heavy work, including the Black Rock tunnel and a bridge over the Schuylkill River. The tunnel was driven simultaneously from both ends through solid rock, and so accurate was the instrumental work, to which Wilson gave personal attention, that when it was opened through its entire length of 1,932 feet the variation in alignment and grade did not exceed one-tenth of a foot. From 1838 to 1857 he engaged in general engineering practice and in farming. He made many journeys for the Pennsylvania Railroad in connection with the extension of its line from Philadelphia to Pittsburgh, and his recommendations resulted in the consolidation of several smaller lines to form the Pittsburgh, Fort Wayne & Chicago Railway Company, which provided a direct route between Pittsburgh and Chicago.

Upon the purchase in August 1857 by the Pennsylvania Railroad of the main line of the old "state improvements," Wilson was appointed resident engineer of the Philadelphia & Columbia Railroad, running over that route. The road had deteriorated under the uncertainty of state control and required rehabilitation as well as enlargement of facilities. In the following year, the line from Columbia to Mifflin, fifty miles west of Harrisburg, was added to Wilson's division, and in 1859 he was given charge of maintenance of way as well as new construction over the entire main line of the Pennsylvania and its branches, between Philadelphia and Pittsburgh. After 1862 he held the title of chief engineer. He also constructed the works of the Altoona Gas Company and served as its president from 1859 to 1871. In January 1868, since the trackage under his supervision had increased to 1152 miles, he was relieved of the duties of maintenance of way by his son, John A. Wilson, and during the next six years gave his attention exclusively to construction. For the Pennsylvania Railroad, in 1869, he laid out, developed, and assumed the general management of Bryn Mawr, nine miles from Philadelphia—a project to stimulate suburban travel; he continued this connection until 1886. In 1874, relinquishing his position of chief engineer, he organized the real-estate department of the Pennsylvania Railroad

Company, which he headed for ten years. From 1884 until his death he was president and director of several roads leased by the Pennsylvania.

On Apr. 26, 1836, Wilson married Jane Miller of Delaware County, Pa., who died May 11, 1898, Besides the three sons already mentioned they had four daughters. Wilson wrote *Notes on the Internal Improvements of Pennsylvania* (1879), *A Brief Review of Railroad History from the Earliest Period to the Year 1894* (1895), and *Reminiscences of a Railroad Engineer* (1896), as well as various professional reports.

[*Who's Who in America*, 1901–02; Wilson's *Reminiscences*, mentioned above; *Public Ledger* (Phila.), Aug. 18, 1902.]   B. A. R.

WILSON, WILLIAM LYNE (May 3, 1843–Oct. 17, 1900), educator, cabinet officer, representative in Congress, was born at Middleway, Jefferson County, Va. (now West Va.), the son of Benjamin Wilson, a native Virginian of Scotch-Irish ancestry, and Mary Whiting (Lyne) Wilson, also of old Virginia family. His father died before William was four years old, but the family was left with moderate means. Wilson's early life was spent in Charles Town, the county seat, where he attended the Charles Town Academy. He showed much precocity, especially in public speaking, and when in 1858 home study enabled him to enter the junior year of Columbian College in Washington, D. C., attracted attention by his brilliancy. Upon graduation in 1860 he was offered a teaching position in the college, but preferred continuing his studies at the University of Virginia. Here the Civil War overtook him, and, enlisting in 1861 in the 12th Virginia Cavalry, he served throughout the conflict. Until the spring of 1863 he fought entirely in the Shenandoah Valley, but later was under J. E. B. Stuart [*q.v.*] in the Army of Northern Virginia, and in the last days of hostilities was with Lee at Appomattox. In December 1862 he was captured in a skirmish near Harper's Ferry, but immediately exchanged. A diary kept intermittently during his service shows that he was a brave soldier, devoted to his officers and especially to Turner Ashby [*q.v.*], but too much a student to enjoy warfare.

After the war the offer of an assistant professorship of ancient languages at the struggling Columbian College was renewed, and he entered upon his duties in September 1865. At the same time he enrolled in the law department. He graduated LL.B. in 1867 and was admitted to the bar in 1869, but the test oath in West Virginia and the general poverty of the South deterred him from practice, and he remained a teacher until 1871. Towards the end his small

salary ceased. He had married Nannine Huntington, daughter of a fellow professor, on Aug. 6, 1868, and the first of his six children had arrived. In 1871 he returned to Charles Town and, since the test oath had been abolished, formed a law partnership with his cousin, George W. Baylor. In the next dozen years of practice he not only made a modest living in an overcrowded field but laid the foundations of his political career. Great sociability, geniality, and sympathy made him popular, while the community felt pride in his learning and his unimpeachable honesty. He spoke frequently and wrote on political topics for the local press. In September 1882 the regents of West Virginia University unanimously elected him president of that weak and faction-torn institution, and in the same fall he was chosen to Congress.

He was able to begin the reorganization of West Virginia University before resigning in June 1883, but he greatly preferred his work in Congress, where for twelve years he served with enjoyment and growing usefulness. From beginning to end his most important labors were bent toward tariff reform. Representing a state which desired protection for coal, he was originally expected to side with the high-tariff minority in the Democratic party, but when the Morrison Bill was introduced in 1884 he stood resolutely by his reform convictions. To him the tariff was pernicious in building up an excessive Treasury surplus, laying heavy burdens on the farmer and workman, breeding monopolies and trusts, and fettering normal commercial processes and commercial growth. In the next Congress he supported the second Morrison Bill, in 1887 he was delighted by Cleveland's tariff-reduction message, and in 1888, as a member of the ways and means committee, he helped frame the Mills Bill. In debate on this measure he first reached national prominence by a masterly speech, May 3, 1888, that the New York *World* characterized as an "oasis in the dreary waste of the tariff discussion"; while in floor exchanges his repartee was equal to Tom Reed's. He was one of the principal opponents of the McKinley Bill in 1890. Meanwhile, his pen helped him become more prominent. In July and August 1889 he wrote a series of articles for the Baltimore *Sun* on "Trusts and Monopolies," and two years later took charge of a tariff reform department in the *St. Louis Republic*. He became head of the executive committee of the National Association of Democratic Clubs, and in 1892 was permanent chairman of the Democratic National Convention. He was too amiable to make an effective presiding officer, but his opening speech was a brilliant effort (*Letters of Richard Watson Gilder*, 1916, p. 230).

Wilson was the logical chieftain to lead the tariff reform battle in Congress when Cleveland came to power in 1893. Made chairman of the ways and means committee on Aug. 23, he led that body in framing the so-called Wilson Bill, and wrote the elaborate report with which it was introduced on Dec. 19. Its chief features—the free admission of raw materials like coal, iron ore, lumber, and wool, a conservative reduction on manufactured articles, and the substitution of *ad valorem* for specific duties—represented his idea of practicable reform and disappointed radicals like Mills and Watterson. Like Cleveland, he acquiesced in rather than earnestly supported the two percent. income tax, believing it just but fearing it inexpedient. He delivered carefully prepared speeches on almost every important schedule, with special attention to the free list. In closing the debate, on Feb. 1, 1894, he made the greatest speech of his career. For two hours he held a jaded audience enthralled; he ended amid riotous enthusiasm, and was hoisted in triumph to the shoulders of Henry St. George Tucker and William Jennings Bryan as the bill passed, 204 to 140. It was his last victory, however; the protectionist Senate so mutilated the bill that few reform elements were left; when it was returned with some six hundred amendments Wilson was unable to rally his following, and the House, after balking for nearly a month, ignobly accepted them.

In the Republican landslide of 1894 Wilson lost his congressional district; it had always been closely divided, the exploitation of lumber, coal, and oil resources had built up many small industrial towns with Northern and negro workmen, and its political complexion had changed. President Cleveland at once offered him the postmaster-generalship in succession to Wilson S. Bissell. His two years in this office (Mar. 3, 1895–Mar. 5, 1897) were marked by vigilant and progressive management of a department usually associated with political spoils. He inaugurated the rural free delivery, made numerous minor improvements in the postal system, effected economies, and enlarged the classified civil service (see *New York Times*, May 11, 1896, editorial). He was unable, however, to obtain congressional support for his excellent plan of districting and consolidating post offices where they were too numerous. A stanch believer in the gold standard, he gave much time during 1895–96 to efforts to prevent a Democratic stampede to the free coinage of silver. Just before the Chicago convention he wrote an article for the *World*, wide-

ly reprinted, on the "fatality" of making silver the issue and thus dividing the party. After the convention he condemned Bryan as head of the forces of "repudiation, socialism, anarchy, etc., temporarily miscalled by the grand old name Democracy" (Diary, July 10, 1896). For a time he was discussed as nominee of the Gold Democrats, but he advised the selection of John M. Palmer. In a campaign speech for Palmer in his home, Charles Town, he was roundly hissed; his diary shows deep and at times almost hysterical feeling on the issue.

The close of Cleveland's administration found Wilson rusty in law and financially embarrassed. He therefore gratefully accepted the presidency of Washington and Lee University at Lexington, Va., which offered a small salary, and, as he put it, "a dignified post of retirement." In the four years left him he did much to strengthen the institution; he occasionally lectured outside, and his weekly talks to students were often quoted in the press. Always a small, frail man, with the appearance of a poet or scholar, he contracted typhoid, and tuberculosis followed. Cleveland and several other friends proposed to raise money to send him to Arizona to write a history of the second Cleveland administration, but his disease progressed too fast, and death came suddenly. In his honor Cleveland and others raised $100,000 to endow a chair of political economy at Washington and Lee. A rare spirit, scholarly, brilliant, and devoted to duty, he had ill fitted the rough hurly-burly of politics, but had nevertheless made his mark in parliamentary history.

[J. A. Quarles, "William Lyne Wilson," *Sewanee Rev.*, Jan. 1901; W. H. Wilson, "William Lyne Wilson," *Pubs. Southern Hist. Asso.*, July 1901; *Times* (Richmond, Va.), Oct. 18, 1900; *Appletons' Ann. Cyc. . . . 1900* (1901); *Biog. Dir. Am. Cong.* (1928); J. A. Barnes, *John G. Carlisle, Financial Statesman* (1931); Allan Nevins, *Grover Cleveland, A Study in Courage* (1932) and *Letters of Grover Cleveland* (1933); O. S. Straus, *Under Four Administrations* (1932); diaries of William L. Wilson, and account of his personality written by Newton D. Baker, his secretary while postmaster-general in the possession of the undersigned.]
A. N.

WILSON, WOODROW (Dec. 28, 1856– Feb. 3, 1924), christened Thomas Woodrow, twenty-eighth president of the United States, was born in Staunton, Va. The Scotch strain was predominant in his ancestry. His mother, Janet (called Jessie) Woodrow, was born in Carlisle, England, close to the Scotch border, the daughter of a Scotch minister, descended from a long line of Presbyterians. His paternal grandfather, James Wilson, a genial, vigorous man of affairs, emigrated from Ulster. Grandparents on both sides came to the United States in the early nineteenth century. Joseph Ruggles Wilson, his father, himself a Presbyterian minister, was brought up in Ohio. Woodrow Wilson's immediate background in a family sense was that of the Middle West; in a literary sense, through his father's interests, it was English. Three years before his birth the family moved to Virginia, and in his second year to Augusta, Ga. His boyhood was thus of the South. In 1870 his father became professor in the theological seminary at Columbia, S. C., and pastor of the First Presbyterian Church. Four years later he moved to a pastorate in Wilmington, N. C. Woodrow Wilson's early years were thus colored by an atmosphere of academic interest and intense piety. The impressions of horror produced upon him by the Civil War were indelible. With an early-maturing mind and a keen delight in the personal and intellectual companionship of his father, he lived a youth largely separated from those of his own age and imbibed his learning at home. He spent a year (1873–74) at Davidson College, in North Carolina, and in the autumn of 1875 entered the College of New Jersey (Princeton).

As an undergraduate he was a leader in debating, studied the art of public speaking, spent long hours over the lives of British statesmen. During his senior year he wrote an outstanding essay, published in the *International Review* in August 1879, entitled "Cabinet Government in the United States." His serious intellectual interests did not lead him to seek high marks in his classes. At graduation, in June 1879, his aspirations turned definitely to a career in public life. The natural path to it seemed to be the law, and he entered the school of the University of Virginia, where he was less interested in formal law courses than in British and American political history. In poor health he returned to Wilmington, N. C., in December 1880, and in 1882 set up in law practice with Edward Ireland Renick in Atlanta, Ga. The venture did not prosper. Wilson's intensity of intellectual interest in large political problems, his unwillingness to yield political convictions, his repugnance to the purely commercial practice of law, all unfitted him for success in the Atlanta courts. In the autumn of 1883 he gave up his almost clientless practice and entered the graduate school of the Johns Hopkins University.

He thus embarked upon a career for which he was ideally equipped and which in turn was to prepare him for public life. At Johns Hopkins under the training of Herbert Baxter Adams [*q.v.*] he found his creative literary powers actively stimulated. He rebelled against the German methods of post-graduate work and was disinclined to enter upon specialized research. A brilliant development of his favorite theme entitled "Committee or Cabinet Government" (published in *Overland Monthly,* Jan. 1884) secured for him a fellowship in the history department, and in January 1885 he published his first, perhaps his most important, book, *Congressional Government,* a clear, beautifully written analysis of American legislative practice with emphasis upon the evils that resulted from the separation of the legislative and executive branches of government and from the consequent power of congressional committees. With this as his thesis in June 1886 he was awarded the Ph.D. degree by Johns Hopkins.

In the meantime he had married and secured a job. His marriage to Ellen Louise Axson took place on June 24, 1885. There thus came into his life its most important single influence, a woman capable of enduring the economic hardships that go with the life of a young teacher, appreciative of his capacity, and profoundly sympathetic with his ideals. Three daughters were born of this happy marriage: Margaret Wilson; Jessie Woodrow Wilson who later married Francis B. Sayre; Eleanor Randolph Wilson who married William Gibbs McAdoo. In the autumn of 1885 Wilson began to teach history at Bryn Mawr College. He thus secured a living, although a bare one, and an opportunity to write. In 1888 he was called to Wesleyan University as professor of history and political economy, and for two years threw himself actively into faculty and undergraduate interests, wrote essays and book reviews, and published a comprehensive textbook in political science, *The State.* In 1890 his alma mater called him to her faculty as professor of jurisprudence and political economy.

Wilson came to the Princeton faculty as a young man not yet thirty-four, only eleven years out of college. He cared little for the scholarly distinction that comes from intensive research; but the breadth of his reading and the verve of his intellectual curiosity guaranteed his influence among faculty and undergraduates. Concerned not merely with the idea but with its effective expression, he labored incessantly over the art of literary expression, including that of epigrammatic phrase. By rigid self-criticism he learned to eschew the florid and unnecessary. "A man who wishes to make himself *by utterance* a force in the world," he wrote to a friend in 1897, "must—with as little love as possible, apply critical tests to himself" (Reid, *post,* p. 69). Twenty years later, as president of the United States, he was enabled, by this devotion to the art of expression, in his own phrase, to "wield the sword of penetrating speech." Distinguished and popular in the lecture hall, a leader of the younger liberals on the faculty, he was chosen in 1896 to make the principal address at the sesquicentennial celebration of the founding of the College. His experience broadened as he came into contact with literary circles and as he traveled through the West on lecture tours. His confidence increased as he perceived that he could interest and dominate audiences of a more general sort than those of the classroom. With delight he discovered that his professional field permitted him to develop in popular terms a philosophy of public life. On June 9, 1902, following the resignation of Francis Landey Patton [q.v.], he was unanimously elected president of Princeton.

As professor, Wilson had already crystallized his ideas of necessary academic reform and he welcomed the presidency for the chance it gave to put them into effect. He was dissatisfied with the Princeton collegiate routine. His conviction that "the object of a University is simply and entirely intellectual" (Reid, p. 78) found little support in an undergraduate body dominated at the time by social and athletic ideals. Nor did Wilson believe that the Princeton course of study, chiefly characterized by the lecture system in which he himself so greatly excelled, provided adequate intellectual incentive. "From childhood up," his eldest daughter wrote (to E. M. House, Aug. 19, 1934, Yale House Collection), "I have heard him talk about the importance of developing the mind by using it rather than stuffing it, that the only value of books was their stimulating power—otherwise they were worse than useless." He meditated a thorough revolution in Princeton's attitude toward college life that would give to the serious scholar the prestige he had rightly earned and reduce the social and athletic "side shows" to a subordinate place (R. S. Baker, *Life*, II, 218).

Structural reorganization he believed to be essential. The principles of his plan were embodied in a double and interlocking scheme: the Preceptorial System and the Quad Plan. The first would provide opportunity for individual instruction; the second would coordinate the social and intellectual life of the college. Strongly impressed by his visits to Oxford and Cambridge he realized the educational value of small groups, where the mind of the instructor could touch directly that of the student, and where he could help the student to correlate and assimilate the scattered information picked up in formal courses or reading. "He said," wrote his daughter, "that there ought to be in every university a professor to teach the relation of things. . . . The essence of the cultured mind was its capacity for relating knowledge" (to E. M. House, Aug. 19, 1934, Yale House Collection). In 1905 he called to the faculty a group of forty-seven young scholars whose first duty should be individual supervision of the students and the development of small discussion groups for the interchange of ideas. The principle of the plan was sound—it has since been adopted in the honors courses and tutorial work of leading colleges—and it was successfully applied.

Wilson was equally insistent that if the scholarly aspects of college were to dominate life in Princeton, they could not be divided from the social. The existing undergraduate organization of clubs was of a purely social character and because of their exclusive character brought no benefit to those very undergraduates who most needed it. In 1907 a committee of the trustees reported that the tendencies of the clubs were such that "the vital life of the place will be outside the University and in large part independent of it" (Reid, p. 103). Wilson's plan, again modeled upon English university organization, was to divide the university into colleges, developing the upper-class clubs themselves into colleges. "By a college I mean not merely a group of dormitories, but an eating hall as well with all its necessary appointments where all the residents of the college shall take their meals together. I would have over each college a master and two or three resident preceptors, and I would have these resident members of the faculty take their meals in hall with the undergraduates. . . . Each college would thus form a unit in itself, and largely a self-governing unit" (R. S. Baker, *Life*, II, 221).

The Quad Plan, so-called because each college was planned as a quadrangle around a central court, embodied Wilson's dislike of traditional privilege, his love of free opportunity, his hope of giving to the preceptorial system a social environment and thus facilitating contacts between cultured and immature minds. The Western alumni and a majority of the faculty, especially the younger members, approved it. But unlike the preceptorial system it touched vested interests. Clubmen of the alumni, especially in the East, protested and some of the older members of the faculty wished to go slowly. The board of trustees, realizing the intensity of feeling in the opposing groups, voted to request the President to withdraw his proposal. The power of the clubs, Wilson bitterly remarked, proved to be greater than the interest of the University. This was merely another indication of his earlier conviction that "the side shows were swallowing up the circus" (R. S. Baker, *Life*, II, 218).

Ironically enough this academic defeat brought Wilson before the American public and helped to open his path to politics. He was presented to the country as the champion of the underprivileged, as the supporter of democratic principles "so hateful to the old order at Princeton, to the bosses and politicians in state and nation" (Reid, p. 113). Nor has that defeat dimmed his academic prestige in the light of history. Twenty years later, Yale and Harvard in their College and House plans brought to realization the vision which he had opened up to the Princeton trustees. In this, as in his preceptorial system, Wilson proved himself the educational prophet, ahead of his time.

Another setback came to Wilson in the development of plans for the Graduate College. This he had conceived as the center of the intellectual life of the University, to be placed in the physical center. Dean West, of the Graduate College, preferred a more distant site and with the Wyman bequest for its building, he himself being an executor, persuaded the trustees to adopt his policy. Such defeats are the lot of a college president, but Wilson saw in them a blockade to the development of his ideal of a democratic coordinated university. His disappointment was intensified by the growth of bitter personal feeling between his opponents and his supporters. He considered the possibility of resignation and a return to the literary life.

At this juncture fate opened to him an opportunity to carry on the struggle for democracy in a wider field. The tide of political discontent against Republican "standpatters" was running strong, and in 1910 the Democrats were seeking available candidates for the elections. In New Jersey Col. George B. M. Harvey [*q.v.*], who in 1906 had spoken of Wilson for president, urged him upon the state organization as an ideal candidate for governor. Here was a man who "by utterance" could win popular support; a man, furthermore, who because of his fight against privilege in a university could be dramatized as the champion of the masses. Doubtful and puzzled, the machine leaders of New Jersey allowed themselves to be persuaded to nominate the Princeton President. Wilson himself hesitated as this vision of his early life again took form. Finally he agreed, stipulating that he be bound by no pledges of patronage. On Oct. 20, 1910, he resigned the presidency of Princeton and on Nov. 8 was elected governor of New Jersey.

The New Jersey governorship proved to be but a brief interlude in Wilson's career, as he himself had regarded it, a training school for a larger arena. But at no time did his qualities of leadership find clearer expression. Regarded by the machine politicians as a naïve theorist and suspected by the reformers as the tool of the machine, he speedily disillusioned both groups. The power and eloquence of his acceptance address and his campaign speeches provoked the enthusiasm of the mass of voters. The first trial of strength with the machine left him triumphant. He dared to fight James Smith, Democratic organization leader, in his contest for the Senate, and in the words of a political reporter "licked the gang to a frazzle" (R. S. Baker, *Life*, III, 127). Driving forward reform measures with vigor, by the end of the first session he secured the enactment of the most important proposals of his campaign: a primary election law, an invigorated public utilities act, a corrupt practices act, an employers' liability act.

Within a brief ten months New Jersey was studied by reformers as a practical example of the possibilities of reform, and Wilson himself began to attract the attention of national political leaders. Of these none was more sagacious than Col. E. M. House, the friend and adviser of successive governors of Texas. Wilson and House first met in the autumn of 1911, became friends immediately, and entered upon a relationship described by Sir Horace Plunkett as "the strangest and most fruitful personal alliance in human history" (*House Papers, post,* I, 44). House's liberal humanitarianism and his insistence upon a government responding to the needs of all classes were unshakable; he and Wilson never differed in principle. But his attitude was always tempered by his sense of what was immediately attainable. From the moment he met Wilson, House was convinced that here was the ideal president of the United States—a man of courage and imagination, a Democrat untouched by "Bryanesque heresies," an Eastern reformer of unmatched eloquence who would sacrifice personal success to principle. He set himself to work for the nomination of the New Jersey Governor, whose formal campaign was managed by William F. McCombs. House exercised his influence in Texas to win the forty votes of that state in the nominating convention. Bryan, who suspected Wilson of being the tool of Harvey and the New York interests, was next brought through House into a less distrustful attitude. In the meantime Wilson's reputation as a forceful and eloquent speaker was steadily developed through a series of widely delivered addresses.

At the Baltimore convention in June 1912, Bryan's influence was dominant. Of the four leading candidates, Champ Clark, Oscar W. Underwood, Judson Harmon [*qq.v.*], and Wilson, he favored the first. But he was primarily interested in pledging the convention to a repudiation of Tammany Hall as offensive to all liberals. Voting reached a deadlock. The issue was decided by Bryan who declared that he would support no one who was supported by Tammany. Clark equivocated. Disregarding the advice of McCombs, Wilson stated flatly that he would not accept the nomination if it depended upon the Tammany vote. Bryan, already half won to Wilson, released the Nebraska delegates from their pledges and cast his own vote for him. From that moment the tide turned in Wilson's favor. On the forty-sixth ballot he was nominated by the necessary two-thirds majority.

In 1912, because of the personal quarrel between Roosevelt and Taft and the political split between Republican progressives and conservatives, the Democratic nomination was tantamount to election. On Nov. 5 Wilson was elected president with 435 electoral votes as against 88 for Roosevelt and 8 for Taft. It was the largest electoral majority in the history of the American presidency up to that time, although it represented a popular minority. Wilson entered the White House the champion of what he called the "New Freedom," a conservative reformer, eager to return to the common people equality of privilege threatened by the "interests" of industry, finance, and commerce. Distrustful of radical remedies such as the recall of judicial decisions, he had profound confidence in the Gladstonian philosophy of live and let live, and believed that the first essential to government at Washington was to render it sensitively responsive to public opinion. Such principles he expounded in general terms in his campaign speeches, a series of magnificent manifestoes which in a few months established him as the unquestioned leader of American liberalism.

The most serious difficulty faced by the President resulted from the inexperience of Democratic leaders in the conduct of government, for sixteen years had passed since the last Democratic administration. The cabinet as finally selected proved to be of more than adequate administrative ability. Bryan, who was appointed secretary of state, was a necessity in the cabinet. For sixteen years he had been party leader and still wielded tremendous influence in the country and in Congress. If Wilson was to lead the enormous Democratic majority successfully through the mazes of tariff and currency reform, he needed Bryan's political influence behind him. The new President was determined at the outset to

rectify what he regarded as the great flaw in the American form of government by establishing a close working connection between the executive and the legislature. On Apr. 8, 1913, he appeared before the two houses of Congress to deliver his first message, thus reviving a custom that had lapsed since Jefferson discontinued it and one that gave him opportunity to exercise his persuasive rhetorical powers. Resolved to push through fundamental reforms in the tariff and in banking, he utilized the large Democratic majority to achieve extraordinary legislative triumphs. Of these, the most important were the Underwood Tariff and the Federal Reserve Act. The first, providing for notably lowered tariff schedules and a federal income tax, was passed in October. The second, designed to facilitate the flow of capital through twelve reserve banks, under the direction of a federal board, met strong objections from conservative bankers and radical currency reformers. It was nevertheless passed in December. The third major aspect of Wilson's program took form in the creation of the Federal Trade Commission and in the Clayton Anti-Trust Act designed to prevent interlocking directorates and declaring that labor organizations should not "be held or construed to be illegal combinations in restraint of trade." These bills were passed in the early autumn of 1914.

The principle of this legislation, in Wilson's mind, was to liberalize the industrial system, to eliminate special privilege, "to make men in a small way of business as free to succeed as men in a big way . . . to destroy monopoly and maintain competition as the only effectual instrument of business liberty" (R. S. Baker, *Life*, IV, 374). He had to meet the opposition of influential industrialists and to control the wilder reformers in his own party. Much of his success was due to the fact that Congress itself was young, political patronage only partly distributed, and as a consequence the Democratic majority, after many years in the wilderness, obedient to party discipline. It was due also to the readiness of public opinion to respond to reform measures, for the spirit of progressiveness was still alive. The chief factor in Wilson's early legislative success was his own genius for leading public opinion, for clarifying the larger political aspects of the issues involved, and his capacity for building in the country a fire behind opposition. For a year and a half he was irresistible. By the middle of 1914, however, he began to encounter the criticism that harassed him at Princeton and in the second year of his New Jersey governorship: that he was too restless and wanted to go too fast. The feeling was intensified by the industrial depression of 1913–14.

Fate was in an ironical mood in decreeing that Wilson, primarily interested in the domestic problems that touched the freedom of the individual, should be forced to give his major attention to international affairs just as he, the determined pacifist, was later compelled to lead his country in the greatest war of history. Philosophically his conception of foreign policy was akin to that of Gladstone. He was opposed intellectually and temperamentally to an imperialism fostered by private commercial interests, and believed intensely in the political wisdom and moral necessity of utilizing the national strength in foreign affairs with careful restraint. "It is a very perilous thing," he said in his most important early speech on foreign affairs, at Mobile, Oct. 27, 1913, "to determine the foreign policy of a nation in the terms of material interest." And he added: "I want to take this occasion to say that the United States will never again seek one additional foot of territory by conquest" (Baker and Dodd, *Public Papers, The New Democracy, post,* I, 67).

Upon such a policy of restraint Wilson hoped to base relations with Latin-America, which for the first sixteen months of his administration formed the most important aspect of American diplomacy. He set for himself the task of creating an atmosphere of good will and of eliminating traditional jealousy of the North American Republic. The problem was made more difficult by conditions in Haiti, Central America, and especially in Mexico, where revolution produced political chaos and threatened American investments. The Mexican imbroglio with its irritating and almost explosive consequences harassed Wilson for three years. How could he help to restore order and promote justice? The simple method of supporting General Huerta, who had seized power through the assassination of his predecessor, he discarded immediately. "We have no sympathy with those who seek to seize the power of government to advance their own personal interests" (Mar. 12, 1913, *American Journal of International Law,* Apr. 1913, p. 331). He steadily resisted pressure based upon the doctrine that Huerta's régime promised at least the restoration of order. A moral issue was involved in non-recognition. In the meantime he would take no action beyond lifting, in February 1914, the arms embargo put on in 1913. "We can afford to exercise the self-restraint of a really great nation which realizes its own strength and scorns to misuse it" (*New Democracy,* I, 49).

Events soon tested the spirit of patience inherent in this policy of "watchful waiting." In April 1914, following the arrest of American sailors at Tampico, Admiral Mayo demanded an apology and salute which Huerta refused. On Apr. 21, American marines and blue-jackets seized the terminal facilities at Vera Cruz in order to prevent the landing of munitions from a German ship. American lives were lost. Wilson himself, the determined pacifist, almost despaired. "I do not see what other course was open to us or how we could have avoided taking such steps as we have taken. The next move is for Huerta. It depends upon him how far this thing shall go. I sincerely pray God it may not have to go to the length of definite war" (R. S. Baker, *Life,* IV, 332). Fortunately at the moment of deepest gloom, on Apr. 25, the three chief states of South America, Argentina, Brazil, and Chile, offered mediation. The proposal was immediately accepted. As Wilson wrote privately, it presented an exit from a blind alley.

The results of the mediation conference by no means cleared the Mexican situation. War was averted and Huerta's resignation was hastened. Disorder continued, however, and the raids of the guerrilla leader Villa even threatened the American border. In the spring of 1916 Wilson was forced to dispatch a small force under General Pershing across the border in pursuit of Villa. A clash with Carranza's troops at Carrizal in June resulted in the capture of American cavalrymen. The national guard had to be mobilized for the protection of the border. To the end of his administration the President was plagued by Mexican anarchy.

Wilson's cooperation with the A. B. C. Powers had the advantage of creating confidence in him among the South American countries, thus enabling him to undertake a comprehensive Pan-American policy of understanding and peace. In the autumn of 1914, at the suggestion of House, he sketched the essential articles of an agreement to provide for international security in the Western Hemisphere. The first article carried the essence of the plan and forecasted clearly the later Covenant of the League of Nations: "Mutual guaranties of political independence under republican form of government and mutual guaranties of territorial integrity" (*House Papers,* I, 209–10). The agreement was actively discussed with the ambassadors of the A. B. C. Powers, who at first hailed it with enthusiasm. It was destined, however, after the entrance of the United States into the World War, to be merged in Wilson's more comprehensive plan for a world organization built upon a similar model.

The Mexican problem and its attendant negotiations had the effect of bringing Wilson into
close diplomatic relations with Great Britain.
British interests tended to support Huerta and
a direct clash with the British Foreign Office
was avoided chiefly because of the restraint displayed by the foreign secretary, Sir Edward
Grey. His confidence in Wilson, whose Mexican
policy was well represented at St. James's by
Ambassador Page, was strengthened by the
President's successful determination to secure
repeal of the Panama Tolls Act. It was deepened,
in December 1913, by the visit of Grey's secretary, Sir William Tyrrell, which led to a return
visit to England by Colonel House in the spring
of 1914. Their conversations raised the possibility of a close Anglo-American understanding
which, in the mind of House, could be developed
by the inclusion of Germany to end the mutual
distrust of Triple Alliance and Triple Entente
and assure world peace. In May 1914, Wilson
sent House to Berlin where the latter laid the
suggestion before the Kaiser in a private interview. The British, hoping to discover a method
of ending the naval race with Germany, expressed
cordial but cautious interest. Events moved too
fast, and the outbreak of the World War put an
end to the plan.

American intervention in the European war
was dreamed of by very few persons during the
first nine months of the struggle. From Wilson's
private papers we can discover that he shared
the general prepossession in favor of the Allies
that characterized the Eastern states and equally
that he was determined that this should in no
way affect a policy of complete neutrality. At
the very beginning of the war he warned the nation against entertaining any feeling of partisanship; he was himself so far successful that he
was brutally abused by each side as being favorable to the other. But the problem of neutrality
involved a good deal more than simply minding
one's own business. Both the Allied regulation
of neutral maritime trade and the German submarine campaign infringed American rights and
interests. Could the neutral position of America
be adequately protected from the one side or the
other without endangering the principle of peaceable negotiation to which, on both philosophical
and emotional grounds, he had dedicated his
policy?

During the first six months of the war the
issue lay almost entirely with the Allies, who refused to accept the Declaration of London as a
code of maritime operations without modifications that denatured it. They extended the contraband lists, brought neutral ships into harbor

for search, detained cargoes, applied the doctrine
of continuous voyage to conditional contraband.
On Dec. 26, 1914, the United States issued a formal and comprehensive protest against Allied
methods of maritime control. But the sharpness
of this diplomatic conflict was at once alleviated
by the German decree of Feb. 4, 1915, declaring
the waters around the British Isles a war zone,
threatening to sink all belligerent merchant ships
met within that zone, and giving warning that
neutral ships might also be sunk.

The German declaration changed the whole
character of relations between the United States
and Germany, and at once threw the quarrel
with the Allies into the background. Wilson
stressed the fact that the submarine warfare, necessarily based upon the method of sinking without warning, involved the blind destruction of
neutral property, whether contraband or not, and
perhaps of the lives of non-combatants. Without
hesitation he drew a distinction between property and lives, between interference with material rights for which later compensation could
be made, and destruction of American lives for
which no adequate compensation could be made.
On Feb. 10, he sent to Germany a warning that
laid the basis of his whole policy toward submarine warfare. Destruction of an American
vessel or American lives, would, he stated, be
regarded as "an indefensible violation of neutral
rights" and the United States would be constrained to hold the German Government "to a
strict accountability for such acts" (*Foreign Relations 1915 Supplement*, pp. 98–100).

The German submarine commanders were instructed to avoid sinking neutral ships, so far
as possible. But the series of dreaded "accidents"
began to appear. On May 7 the *Lusitania* was
sunk and over a thousand persons drowned,
among them 128 Americans. From this moment
the issue was finally clarified in Wilson's mind.
The Germans must not use the submarine against
merchant ships except according to recognized
rules of warning, with due provisions for the
safety of passengers and crew. The firmness
with which he demanded that Germany give up
the "ruthless" submarine campaign led in June
to the resignation of Bryan, who saw in Wilson's
insistence upon the preservation of traditional
neutral rights the danger of war with Germany.
The patience which the President displayed
aroused bitter resentment on the American seaboard, where, as the submarine campaign continued, popular feeling demanded a diplomatic
rupture with Germany. But the combination of
Wilson's patience and firmness finally triumphed,
at least temporarily. Following the sinking of

the *Arabic* in August 1915, the German ambassador, Bernstorff, announced the promise of his Government that "liners" would not be attacked without warning. In the spring of 1916 Wilson finally drew from Berlin, following the sinking of the *Sussex,* the more comprehensive agreement to abandon the ruthless submarine warfare altogether.

This promise was extracted by the definite threat of a diplomatic rupture. Unless Germany should "effect an abandonment of its present methods of submarine warfare against passenger and freight-carrying vessels, The Government of the United States can have no choice but to sever diplomatic relations with the German Empire altogether" (*Foreign Relations 1916 Supplement,* p. 234). Such a rupture, in Bernstorff's opinion, would lead inevitably to active American intervention. There was no longer any doubt in Berlin, Bernstorff records, "that persistence . . . would bring about a break with the United States" (Bernstorff, *post*, p. 213).

In meeting what he regarded as a series of outrageous affronts by Germany, Wilson never permitted his sense of responsibility to be overclouded by natural emotion. "The country is undoubtedly back of me," he wrote privately on Sept. 20, 1915, "and I feel myself under bonds to it to show patience to the utmost. My chief puzzle is to determine where patience ceases to be a virtue" (to House, Yale House Collection). Always he held to the double principle he formulated at the moment he was smarting under the news of the sinking of the *Arabic:* "1. The people of this country count on me to keep them out of the war; 2. It would be a calamity to the world at large if we should be actively drawn into the conflict and so deprived of all disinterested influence over the settlement" (to House, Aug. 21, 1915, Yale House Collection).

On the other hand, Wilson made it clear that whereas the trade dispute with the Allies could form a subject of negotiation, there could be no compromise with Germany over the unrestricted submarine campaign. He yielded no legal right to the Allies and by his protests built up a case for damages; in the meantime immediate commercial interests were largely protected by private arrangements between American shippers and the British government. But the unrestricted use of the submarine, he insisted, struck directly at basic American rights in a way that precluded later compensation, rights which if once surrendered could not be regained. The sinking of American ships and the drowning of American citizens, whether passengers or sailors, he regarded as an attack upon national sovereignty.

The right of Americans to travel freely on the high seas he would not yield. "For my own part," he wrote to Senator Stone, who advocated an evasion of the issue, "I cannot consent to any abridgement of the rights of American citizens in any respect. . . . We covet peace and shall preserve it at any cost but the loss of honor. . . . What we are contending for in this matter is of the very essence of the things which have made America a sovereign nation" (*Foreign Relations 1916 Supplement,* p. 177).

There was thus a limit to Wilson's patience. He publicly set it at the line where admitted neutral rights were infringed after protracted warning, and he made it a point of national self-respect and honor to defend those rights. "I know that you are depending upon me to keep this Nation out of the war," he said in January 1916. "So far I have done so and I pledge you my word that, God helping me, I will if it is possible. But you have laid another duty upon me. You have bidden me see to it that nothing stains or impairs the honor of the United States, and that is a matter not within my control; that depends upon what others do, not upon what the Government of the United States does. Therefore there may at any moment come a time when I cannot preserve both the honor and the peace of the United States. Do not exact of me an impossible and contradictory thing" (Speech of Jan. 31, 1916, *New Democracy,* II, 48).

Wilson's policy toward Germany received striking confirmation from Congress, which voted in March 1916 to table the Gore-McLemore resolutions designed to warn American citizens not to travel on belligerent ships. He received equal support for his ultimatum to Germany following the sinking of the *Sussex.* Still further confirmation came in the national election of 1916. During the summer and early autumn it was clear that in the Northeast the Democrats must expect decided defeats at the polls, partly because of dislike of Wilson's reform legislation, largely because after Roosevelt's desertion of the Progressives normal Republican majorities would control the election in those regions. In the Middle West Wilson was strong, chiefly because of his progressive leadership. German-Americans were on the whole opposed to him, but he could count on the pacifist vote. "He has kept us out of war," was the most powerful argument west of the Mississippi. The result of the election was so close that for twelve hours it was generally conceded that the Republican candidate, Charles E. Hughes, had been elected. Wilson himself went to bed believing that his term of office was ended. He had decided to resign immediately, after appointing Hughes secretary of state, so that, following the vice-president's resignation, Hughes would automatically take up the presidential office without having to wait until the following March. Only when the returns from the West came in, was it seen that the Republican majorities in the East had been wiped out and that Wilson was reëlected by 277 votes to 254 for Hughes.

Wilson's victory was generally ascribed to the pacifists. He lost no time in preparing to justify their confidence by a determined move for peace. Since the early autumn of 1914 he had never ceased to explore possible avenues of mediation but had met constant rebuffs. Each side counted on peace terms that precluded negotiation. In the autumn of 1915 the President approved a plan suggested by House, whereby mediation might be enforced through a threat to join the side which refused it. Another trip to Berlin convinced House that the Germans expected impossible terms. In London he received more encouragement and was able to draft with Grey a memorandum promising that Wilson would call a peace conference, setting forth certain terms, and indicating that if Germany refused either the conference or the terms the United States would enter the war to stop it. Wilson approved the memorandum. But all through the spring and summer the Allies refused any sign of willingness to enter a conference.

After the election, Wilson decided to issue a public call to the belligerents. He had received clear intimation from Germany that unless peace negotiations were started the submarine war would be resumed. The Germans without waiting for Wilson issued on Dec. 12 a statement of their willingness to enter a conference but in such a tone as to discourage any hope of terms that the Allies would consider. On Dec. 18 Wilson published his own note, requesting the belligerents to state their war aims: "an interchange of views would clear the way at least for conference" (*Foreign Relations 1916 Supplement*, pp. 98–99). Neither the German nor the Wilson suggestion produced any effect upon the Allies. The Germans immediately began to plan resumption of unrestricted submarine warfare, even though realizing that it would array the United States against them.

Conscious of the danger, Wilson worked desperately to stave it off by pushing forward his plans for a peace conference. On Jan. 4, 1917, in reply to House's suggestion of the need of military preparation "in the event of war," he insisted: "There will be no war. This country does not intend to become involved in this war.

We are the only one of the great white nations that is free from war today, and it would be a crime against civilization for us to go in" (*House Papers*, II, 412). Anxiously he urged on Bernstorff the need of securing from Germany specific conditions of peace, armed with which he might go to the Allies. On Jan. 22, 1917, he delivered before the Senate a speech designed to serve as the basis for a negotiated peace, a settlement that would leave neither the one side nor the other crushed and revengeful, "a peace without victory."

Had Germany then held her hand it is possible that Wilson might have been able to start negotiations. The Allies were nearing the end of their financial resources. Given a little time the President might have exercised strong pressure upon them. The warning given to American investors by the Federal Reserve Board against Allied short-term credits, in the preceding November, indicated clearly the method by which pressure could be applied. But whatever chance of negotiations existed was spoiled by Germany. On Jan. 9 the decision approving the resumption of unrestricted submarine warfare was taken. On Jan. 31 it was announced to the United States that the pledges given after the *Sussex* ultimatum would no longer be observed. Wilson did not hesitate. His hopes of peace negotiations suddenly dashed, he decided immediately to give the German Ambassador his passports. "From that time henceforward," writes Bernstorff, "—there can be no question of any earlier period, because up to that moment he had been in constant negotiation with us—he regarded the Imperial Government as morally condemned. . . . After the 31st January, 1917, Wilson himself was a different man. Our rejection of his proposal to mediate, by our announcement of the unrestricted U-boat war, which was to him utterly incomprehensible, turned him into an embittered enemy of the Imperial Government" (Bernstorff, p. 385).

Wilson still refused to believe that the diplomatic rupture meant war. "Only actual overt acts" would persuade him that the Germans would carry their threats into effect. He was willing to negotiate everything except the right to sink passenger and merchant ships without warning. But the Germans showed no sign of weakening. "If Wilson wants war," wrote the Kaiser, "let him make it, and let him then have it" (*Official German Documents, post*, II, 1336). Given such determination on each side, American participation became merely a matter of time. Opinion in the United States was infuriated by the virtual blockade of cargoes in American ports; yet more by the publication of the Zimmermann note suggesting a German-Mexican-Japanese alliance and the Mexican reconquest of Texas, New Mexico, and Arizona. Still the President waited. He was not going to be forced into war by any material interest or emotional wave.

Finally, on Mar. 27, following the sinking of four American ships, he made the decision. On the eve of his war message he pondered the misery that would come. "For nights, he said, he'd been lying awake going over the whole situation. . . . He said he couldn't see any alternative, that he had tried every way he knew to avoid war . . . had considered every loophole of escape and as fast as they were discovered Germany deliberately blocked them with some new outrage . . . it was just a choice of evils" (J. L. Heaton, comp., *Cobb of "the World,"* 1924, pp. 268–70). On Apr. 2, 1917, he appeared before Congress to ask a declaration that a state of war existed with Germany. On Apr. 6, the resolution was voted by overwhelming majorities.

The declaration of war represented the all but unanimous sentiment of the American people. The anti-German feeling, at first characteristic of only the Atlantic seaboard, had spread westward, and with it the feeling that the Allies represented the cause of democracy and justice. The intimate financial and economic relations of the United States with Great Britain and France combined with an intellectual sympathy to foster a tendency to condone Allied infractions of neutral rights and to condemn as barbarism every German infraction. Pro-Ally feeling would not have been sufficient of itself to bring the United States into the war. But it created a state of mind which made the German declaration of the submarine war zone, followed by the Zimmermann telegram and the sinking of American ships, appear to Americans as a direct attack. Wilson was certainly never touched by any commercial or financial interest. Much more than the average American he was determined to avoid war. But he was not immune from the general pressure of opinion created by a variety of factors, and when he finally asked for the declaration of war he shared the conviction that imperial Germany was an international criminal.

Once in the war, Wilson was determined that the full strength of the nation should be concentrated on victory. The task of transforming a non-military industrial population of one hundred million souls into a belligerent machine involved one of the most wholesale transformations of history. There had been little preparation. For this the President must bear his share

of responsibility, for he had been slow to admit the possibility of armed intervention by the United States. By the end of 1915 he came to the belief that steps should be taken to improve the efficiency and size of the military establishment and navy. In August 1916 he approved the creation of the Council of National Defense, charged with the "coordination of industries and resources for the national security and welfare." Preparation for war, however, had not gone very far. Wilson perceived the possibility of American participation, as his speeches and private papers of 1916 indicate; but at no time until the final break did he grasp emotionally its imminence.

But with the declaration of war, Wilson recognized that every interest must be subordinated to the attainment of victory. His leadership was distinguished in two respects. First, he created a national consciousness of common effort, made the people feel that this was a people's war and one in which every citizen must be glad to make his individual sacrifice. In the second place, the President, having selected for the vital military and administrative posts the men to carry through the technical details of organization and operation, never interfered with them and supported them unreservedly. These two aspects of Wilson's leadership made it possible for the nation to accept the emergency measures, very distasteful to American instincts but essential to victory: the army draft, the supervision and control exercised by the War Industries Board, the food and fuel control, the national administration of railways. They facilitated the national response to the appeal for a popular financing of the war effort through the Liberty Loans. They guaranteed to the military and administrative leaders an authority which, despite many mistakes, finally built up a fighting machine capable of coordinating the efforts of the home front with those of the fighting front in France. The steady support he gave to the secretary of war, Newton D. Baker, enabled him, in the face of sniping criticism, to proceed methodically and with ultimate success to the organization of a national service of supply that met the needs of an overseas force which finally numbered two million men. In France, General Pershing was guaranteed the full authority necessary to develop this force into a unified army. In no other war ever waged by the United States was the opportunity for dishonest profit so largely eliminated and partisan political influence so thoroughly eradicated.

Wilson expressed a willingness to go to all lengths to achieve effective coordination with the Allies without surrendering the independence of American policy. He insisted that the United States was not an allied but an "associated" power, and never admitted the right of the European associates to speak for America in matters of policy. But he demanded the creation of machinery that would enable the United States to supply the necessities of those associates as rapidly and effectively as possible. This demand resulted in the American war mission of November 1917 which gave strong support to the plan for a Supreme War Council, and in combination with the British and French, successfully organized the various boards of interallied coordination.

The President's supreme contribution to victory lay in his formulation of war aims. He gave to the American and Allied peoples a consciousness that they were fighting for a peace worthy of the effort and sacrifice; and he doubtless weakened the enemy's "will to victory" by unfolding the vision of a new world organization that offered a better chance of ultimate happiness than any German triumph. The basis of permanent peace, he believed, must consist in the confidence of each nation that it would not be attacked, a confidence which could be achieved only through a system of international cooperation for security. This had been the principle of his Mobile speech and his Pan-American policy, and it underlay the House mission of 1914. Stimulated by the suggestions of Sir Edward Grey, as early as Dec. 24, 1915, he set down as an essential guarantee "a league of nations to secure each nation against aggression and maintain the absolute freedom of the seas" (Yale House Collection). Public expression of such a program formed the culmination of the speech of May 27, 1916, his very words suggesting at once an extension of the projected Pan-American Pact to the entire world and forecasting Article X of the League of Nations Convenant: "a virtual guarantee of territorial integrity and political independence" (New Democracy, II, 188).

Thus almost a year before American participation in the war, Wilson outlined certain principles which would justify American cooperation in world affairs. He elaborated them in his address to the Senate of Jan. 22, 1917, when he set forth the terms of a desirable peace upon which the belligerents might agree, insisting upon the principle of the Monroe Doctrine for the entire world, and demanding a concert of Powers capable of maintaining international tranquillity and the right of small nations. These principles he took for his text on Apr. 2, 1917, when he asked Congress to declare that a state of war

existed with Germany. It is true that he now insisted upon the absolute defeat of the Imperial Government. It was no longer to be a "peace without victory." But the elevated purpose of the war and the final utilization of victory must not be forgotten in the heat of the struggle, and the ideals of peace time must be kept alive.

There was implicit in this program a conflict with the several war aims of the Allies, at least as set forth in the various secret treaties of 1915 and 1916. Wilson came to realize the fact. Later he testified before a Senate committee that "the whole series of understandings among the Allies was first disclosed" to him at the Peace Conference. But he had been informed of the most important of them by Mr. Balfour in April 1917, in some detail (House Papers, III, 61). This he may have later forgotten. He certainly recognized their general tenor. Writing to House on July 21, 1917, he said: "England and France have not the same views with regard to peace that we have by any means. When the war is over we can force them to our way of thinking, because by that time they will among other things be financially in our hands" (Yale House Collection).

Avoidance of acute difference with the Allies was achieved during the summer and autumn of 1917 by stressing the attack upon German autocracy and not pressing for any general agreement upon ultimate war aims. Wilson's hand, however, was forced by the Russian Revolution and the insistent public demand for a restatement of war aims. Allied leaders found it impossible to agree upon any general formula, far less upon any concrete statement of terms. House returned to the United States to tell Wilson that in order to maintain the morale of liberal and labor forces in the Allied countries he must make a comprehensive statement himself. On Jan. 8, 1918, the President delivered before the Congress the speech of the Fourteen Points. This was not designated as a public international charter but as a diplomatic weapon, to meet the Bolshevik drive for peace and to strengthen the morale of the Allied liberals. The six general points repeated ideals already enunciated by Wilson: open diplomacy, freedom of the seas, removal of trade barriers, reduction of armaments, impartial adjustment of colonial claims, a league of nations. The eight special points, dealing with immediate political and territorial problems, were not so far apart from the purposes declared by Lloyd George three days previously. The address was of particular significance in American policy for the reason that for the first time Wilson regarded territorial terms as America's business and laid down territorial conditions as a prerequisite of American cooperation. By the speech Wilson committed himself not merely to full participation in the general world problem of preserving the peace, but to an interest in the local problems peculiar to Europe that might disturb the peace.

The ultimate significance of the speech of the Fourteen Points lay in the fact that when the Germans in the early autumn of 1918 recognized the inevitability of defeat, they seized upon it as a general basis of peace negotiations. In the spring of that year after the imposition of the peace of Brest-Litovsk upon Russia and with the peril of German victory in France imminent, the President refused any suggestion of compromise. But as the German armies, facing disaster, began their retreat, Wilson hoped to hasten their surrender by promising Germany protection against political or economic annihilation and the just treatment to which every nation has a claim. To him, therefore, the Germans turned in early October as to a savior from the destructiveness of Allied wrath.

Public sentiment in the United States was strongly against any negotiation with the Germans. Among the Allied leaders there was irritation that the appeal had been made to Wilson. It is reasonably clear that if it had been made to the Allies as a whole it would have been refused forthwith. The Germans would then have girded themselves for the last-ditch defense planned by Ludendorff and Prince Max; the fighting would have continued, in the words of Marshal Foch, "maybe three, maybe four or five months. Who knows?" (*House Papers,* IV, 91). By his interchange of notes with the Germans, Wilson gave the demand for peace in Germany an opportunity to gain force; once started the peace flood could not be stemmed. Thus on Oct. 23, he was able to hand to the Allies Germany's acceptance of an armistice ensuring to them "the unrestricted power to safeguard and enforce the details of the peace to which the German Government has agreed" (*Foreign Relations 1918 Supplement,* no. 1, vol. I, p. 382).

There were complaints at the time that Wilson, by his handling of the negotiations, saved Germany from invasion and an unconditional surrender. Actually what Wilson offered the Allies was not peace but merely the opportunity to make it. They were still free to refuse if they chose. Naturally they accepted the opportunity. Wilson's diplomacy resulted in complete victory and also saved several months' fighting. More serious is the criticism that Wilson lured the Germans into peace and the overthrow of the imperial régime by the promise of conditions which he did not intend or was unable to make good. It is a favorite German theme. It will not withstand critical analysis. When the German government proposed the Fourteen Points as the basis of peace, they might have insisted upon a clarification, reserving specific rights. Prince Max knew and stated that the Fourteen Points meant that Germany would doubtless lose important territory, Alsace-Lorraine, the Polish corridor, the colonies. He wished to send to Wilson a memorandum asking for definite guarantees. But he was not allowed to make any reservations lest the negotiations be broken off. The representative of the Supreme Command, Haeften, declared that "the definition of the Fourteen Points would endanger the whole armistice action" (*The Memoirs of Prince Max of Baden,* 1928, II, 39). Germany, with her armies still in the field, preferred to take her chance on the Fourteen Points undefined, rather than lose the chance of peace. There is in all this no question of being "lured into a trap."

Wilson had also to carry on a diplomatic contest with the Allies. Until the armistice negotiations they had not taken the Fourteen Points seriously. Clemenceau had not even read them. The general disposition in the Supreme War Council was to assume that their acceptance or refusal should be left to the Peace Conference. Colonel House, acting as Wilson's representative on the Council, insisted that Allied approval of the Fourteen Points must be a condition precedent to any armistice. Otherwise there would be no guarantee whatever against terms totally inconsonant with the whole Wilsonian program. The Allied leaders for a time refused to give formal or informal approval to the Fourteen Points. House responded with the threat that lacking such approval Wilson would be forced to tell Germany that the Allies refused the basic conditions, and would then ask the American Congress whether the war should continue in order to enforce European terms, although the American terms had been accepted by Germany. The threat proved sufficient. The Allies accepted the Fourteen Points and later speeches of Wilson as the basis of the peace, with one elucidation defining the meaning of "restoration," and one reservation providing for later discussion of "freedom of the seas." Wilson accepted both, and by his note of Nov. 5 transmitted to Germany the qualified acceptance by the Allies of the basic conditions of peace. Thus was completed the so-called Pre-armistice Agreement. On Nov. 11, the German and Allied delegates signed the armistice.

Wilson was at the height of his influence. The

quondam college professor had become the greatest single personal force in the world. He had led the United States to victory in the greatest war of history. He had imposed his will upon defeated and triumphant Europeans. He was hailed as savior by the populations of Central Europe, freed from Hapsburg and Hohenzollern rule; he was the apostle of British liberals, French artisans, and Italian peasants. Allied leaders confessed their recognition of his power by their anxiety as to how he might use it. But the difficulties of capitalizing victory were far greater than those involved in winning it. During four years the mind of the world had been turned to war, and it was impossible to create an atmosphere favorable to permanent peace. The sense of common interest forced by the danger of a German victory evaporated when the danger disappeared. The political ideals of Wilson could not easily be transplanted to Europe; when applied to specific problems they might or might not prove practicable; and they involved principles which were bound to contradict each other.

At this critical moment Wilson made three mistakes, the bearing of which was only later perceived. He was regarded by Europe as politically supreme in the United States, and the belief accounted for much of his influence abroad. But in the November elections he publicly made of Democratic success at the polls a question of personal confidence, asking the voters to choose Democrats as an indication of personal trust. He thus abdicated his national leadership to assume the rôle of party leader. Democratic defeats in that election gave the appearance of a national repudiation, and threw control of the Senate foreign relations committee into the hands of his personal enemies. A second mistake lay in his choice of a peace commission. No member of the Commission really represented either the Republican party or the Senate. Wilson lost thereby the chance of winning support from his domestic opponents and stimulated partisan opposition. His supreme mistake lay in his decision to go to the Peace Conference in person. "He was the *God on the Mountain*," writes Colonel House, "and his decisions regarding international matters were practically final. When he came to Europe and sat in conference with the Prime Ministers and representatives of other states, he gradually lost his place as first citizen of the world" (Seymour, *American Diplomacy, post,* p. 399). Apart from these mistakes Wilson faced detailed difficulties. Delays in the calling of the Conference, resulting from domestic political problems in Europe, permitted the cooling of idealistic aspirations and the development of national particularism. The political leaders, himself included, failed to realize the vital importance of a definite program and a carefully studied organization of the Conference. The American commission was ill-organized, American delegates on the various commissions received no regular instructions, and the American program was never considered and developed comprehensively.

In spite of errors and difficulties Wilson achieved his main triumph at the very beginning of the Conference by forcing acceptance of the League of Nations Covenant as an integral part of the treaty of peace. He was equally successful in leading the commission chosen to draft the Covenant through a series of meetings which culminated in unanimous approval of a version, which on Feb. 14, 1919, he read to a plenary session of the Conference. When he sailed for the United States on the 15th he felt that his main work had been accomplished.

He returned a month later to find in Paris a definitely unfavorable atmosphere. When general principles were applied to specific questions it became clear that many of the Wilsonian ideals were impracticable. It was not so much a conflict between obvious right and wrong as between contradictory rights. Above all the discussion hung the cloud of industrial unrest and social revolution, making it vitally important that decisions should be rapidly reached and uncertainty dispelled. Was it not better to make an inconsistent decision, trusting to the League of Nations to rectify it, rather than to leave the world in chaos?

To discover that in their application his principles were at variance with each other, to adjust himself to the necessity of compromise, produced in Wilson a violent nervous shock. It was the worse because of a severe attack of influenza that struck him during the most important of the April negotiations. For a moment he considered the advisability of deserting the Conference and leaving Europe to settle her own problems. He ordered the *George Washington* to be in readiness to take him home. But such a desertion would do nothing to improve the state of Europe, quite the contrary, and would mean the end of the League. If he stayed on and refused to accept compromise, even though he might compel Clemenceau, Orlando, and Lloyd George to accept his own detailed solutions, it would mean the overthrow of their governments and the appearance at the Conference of more bitter reactionaries. When he tried an appeal to the people, over the heads of the delegates, as in his Fiume appeal to Italy, he was openly rebuffed by

Italian public opinion and the unity of the Conference shaken. A firm stand against the Japanese meant their departure from the Conference; and who was to enforce the decisions of the Conference against them in the Far East?

Thus Wilson was forced to agree to a series of compromises which left liberals disappointed and Germans bitter. Yet the necessity of the compromises is apparent from the fact that the nationalists in both France and Italy were equally disappointed. The Fourteen Points were certainly disfigured, but without them and Wilson the treaties would have been far less liberal. Wilson agreed that Germans must pay in addition to direct damages the cost of pensions, but he saved them from total war costs. At the price of promising American aid to France in case of German aggression, in conjunction with Great Britain, he prevented the separation of the Rhine lands from Germany. He prevented the annexation of the Saar by France and made possible its ultimate return to Germany. He forced the system of mandates for the German colonies. He extracted from Japan the informal promise to return Shantung to China (*House Papers*, IV, 453, 455). Above all he secured the adoption of the League of Nations Covenant, with its provisions for open diplomacy through the registration of treaties, progressive limitation of armament, an international court, and the avoidance of war. Wilson's failures did not lie in the terms of the Versailles Treaty, which was destined never to be applied as designed. His failure came later in America when his defeat by the Senate removed the essential basis of that treaty.

Neither Wilson himself nor those Americans who accompanied him, as they returned after the signing of the Versailles Treaty, felt that he had been defeated. They believed, rather, that in view of the difficulties of the situation he had accomplished a larger part of his program than might have been expected. There remained only the problem of winning the approval of the United States Senate. Properly handled that problem was far less difficult than many solved by Wilson in Europe. Public opinion generally favored the League and cared little about the details of the treaties. The League was supported by outstanding public figures such as Taft and Root. In the Senate itself Wilson could count on the support of all but a few Democrats and on the majority of the Republicans. His chief opponent, Senator Lodge, hoped to add some amendments or reservations, but not to defeat the Treaty and the Covenant. The balance of power was held by a group of moderates, led by Kellogg and McCumber, who desired "mild" reserva-

tions that would not touch the significance of the Covenant. A few conciliatory gestures by the President would have sufficed to win the two-thirds vote necessary to ratification.

Wilson's attitude was not conciliatory. He intimated to the Senate committee on foreign relations that he would permit no changes in Covenant or Treaty. As opposition developed, his tone became more unyielding. The issue shifted from the merits of the Covenant to the question of authority between President and Senate, even to a personal quarrel between Wilson and Lodge, chairman of the committee. In the hope of winning popular support Wilson set forth on Sept. 3, on a country-wide tour in the course of which he made some thirty speeches. It ended suddenly. On Sept. 25, at Pueblo, physically and emotionally exhausted, he was threatened with a complete nervous collapse, and he was hastily brought back to Washington. For three days he seemed not so ill, but on the morning of Oct. 2 Dr. Grayson, hurriedly called to the White House, found Wilson physically helpless. "The President is paralyzed" (Hoover, *post*, p. 101). His life was saved, but for weeks that followed he was incapable of transacting official business. Nor for months could he undertake any effort, physical or mental, that required initiative.

Wilson's illness was a hammer-blow of fate. Had he died, it seems certain that his successor would have made the compromises with the Senate necessary to ratification of the Covenant. Had he recovered sufficiently to receive the advice of those in touch with political realities, it is possible that he might himself have perceived the necessity of compromise. But completely isolated from the political situation he could do no more than maintain his earlier position: the Covenant must be ratified without essential changes; the reservations introduced by Senator Lodge, in his opinion, would nullify it. The supporters of the Covenant were divided between those who stood behind Wilson and the "mild reservationists." It was impossible to find a two-thirds majority for any resolution of ratification.

In the winter, hope for the Covenant again appeared. Viscount Grey, whose eloquent letters in 1915 had seriously influenced Wilson in favor of a League, was sent to the United States as special ambassador. For weeks he waited, hoping for an interview with the sick President. This was denied him. But on his return to England, he published a letter in which he stated that the success of the League demanded the adherence of the United States; if such adherence depended upon the inclusion of the Lodge reservations in the act of ratification, they ought to be accepted by Europe. It was a suggestion to Wilson that, in the circumstances, compromise with Lodge was wise. The suggestion was not followed. When the Treaty and Covenant were once more introduced into the Senate, Wilson maintained his objections to the Lodge reservations. He advised his supporters to vote against the resolution of ratification in company with the bitter-end opponents of any league whatsoever. Even so, the two-thirds necessary to ratification lacked only seven votes. So close was the United States to entering the League. Thus ironically did fate ordain that the nation should be kept out of the League at the orders of the man who had done more than any other to create it.

Wilson's statesmanship cannot be fairly adjudged on the basis of the handling of the Treaty in the Senate. His nervous and physical collapse was complete. From the time of his April illness in Paris there were many indications of a progressive breakdown certain to affect his political judgment and his personal dealings with men. After October, he lived in a sick-room, emerging merely for simple recreation or purely formal tasks which taxed his strength to a point that left no opportunity for reasoned consideration of difficult questions. The President was thus divorced from political realities. Even Colonel House was excluded, though there was no personal quarrel. Wilson may have known nothing of House's letters to him; they remained unanswered. "I feel that had not illness overtaken the President, all would have been well," wrote Ike Hoover, who had watched closely the relations between the two men since Wilson entered the White House. "He needed Colonel House, and in a way, fully realized the fact. But this illness changed the entire aspect of things" (Hoover, p. 95). The political effects of the separation were tremendous.

For three years after the end of his term of office, Wilson led a retired life in Washington. He formed a law partnership with Bainbridge Colby, but his physical condition permitted no active work. He was seen in public on few occasions. The reaction against the idealism of his own administration which followed the Republican victory of 1920, left him wrapped in dignified silence. His mind was clear and reasonably active but the physical machine was broken. Tired out, no longer able to influence opinion as prophet of higher political aspirations, he confessed that he was "tired of swimming upstream" (*Ibid.*, p. 108). On Sunday, Feb. 3, 1924, he died in his sleep.

Wilson was propelled into public affairs by his natural qualities and his sense of responsibility for their use. By taste and inheritance he was designed for a circumscribed, quiet life, and he was probably happiest while still a college professor. His personal feelings lay close under the skin. He was always dependent upon the help and encouragement he received from his domestic circle; his craving for feminine sympathy is revealed in his correspondence with Mrs. Reid and Mrs. Peck, friends from whom he constantly sought a purely intellectual understanding. His first wife died in the midst of the European War crisis of August 1914. He was married for a second time, on Dec. 18, 1915, to Edith Bolling Galt who survived him.

Qualified by personal and intellectual gifts for the public life, he never capitalized them fully. Of rather more than middle height, carefully dressed, erect, with square features and powerful jaw, eyes that shifted suddenly from merriment to severity, in appearance he was impressive and attractive. To those who worked closely with him he displayed a magnetism of personality—genial, humorous, considerate—and an expansive wealth of mental quality; and from them he evoked admiration and affection. But in dealing with men whom he did not like or did not trust Wilson would not call such advantages to his service. He was equipped by intellectual stature, by oratorical capacity, and by sincerity of emotion to lead a nation or the world; but he was handicapped in meeting the simplest problem of political tactics because he carried into public life the attitude of a private citizen. Simple in his pleasures, naturally averse to heterogeneous gatherings, interested in people because of what they were rather than because of what they could do to help or hinder, he refused many of the sacrifices of exacting taste demanded by the rough game of politics.

Wilson's prejudices were strong, often ill-founded, and he would not yield them to political exigencies. Because of them he alienated important leaders in the world of business and of journalism. At the close of his public career he was generally pictured in the public mind as a self-willed and arbitrary egoist, and the picture doubtless accounts for his personal unpopularity after the Peace Conference. Most of the bitter criticism was entirely undeserved. In the sense that he was always acutely interested in his own reactions to life, he might be termed an egoist, although the term would be entirely misleading if it implied selfishness, for no one was more considerate of the feelings and interests of those around him. But he matched himself constantly against his duties and his opportunities, and was unsparing in self-criticism. Sharply sensitive to the sympathies and advice of those for whom he cared, he had little respect for the arguments of personal or political enemies.

As lecturer and writer Wilson had a genius for simplification, for the clarification of the complex and the explanation of the relation of things. These qualities he carried into his political speeches and they account in part, at least, for the effect he exercised upon men's minds through his oratory; as he would say, "by utterance." He never sought the favor either of undergraduates or the public by condescending to cheapness of tone. But he labored incessantly to manufacture the phrase that would make the idea appealing. Popular approval he regarded as the ultimate test. Without it lectures, articles, or speeches were in vain, and policies, however justifiable, futile. By personal taste an aristocrat, he put his faith in the common man and accepted the democratic verdict as final.

The public force of Wilson's speeches resulted only in part from clarity of expression and piquancy of phrase; they were equally characterized by strong and effective moral fervor. His religious feeling was never separated from any aspect of his life; he strove consciously to measure everything by spiritual rather than material values. Publicly as well as privately he was not afraid to make an absolute distinction between right and wrong. Many of his speeches are political sermons. Not a few of his listeners and readers were irritated by the apparent dogmatism with which he laid down judgments, and contended that, like his favorite Gladstone, he claimed an intimacy with the designs of Providence that could scarcely be justified. But for the masses there was a strong appeal in the obvious sincerity of his conviction that a policy should be adjudged according to its morality, that the more power an individual or a nation possessed the greater was the obligation to avoid wrongdoing.

Wilson's political philosophy was simple. He was a liberal individualist, insistent upon the right of unprivileged persons and small nations to be freed from the control of more powerful groups. The principles of the New Freedom as applied to tariff and currency reform or labor legislation, and the doctrine of self-determination for oppressed nationalities spring from the same source. He looked upon his policies as primarily policies of emancipation. He had a good deal of eighteenth-century confidence in the virtues of the natural man; a feeling that if the latter-day abuses of privilege and despotism

could be wiped out, both domestic and international problems could be set on the road to solution. Nor did he admit any real contradiction between the idea of freedom and the restraint of law, between national self-determination and international control. Just as the liberty of the individual is assured by the Constitution, so the independence of nations can be guaranteed by a "concert of free peoples." Thus he was able to speak of the League of Nations as "a disentangling alliance."

The extraordinary success of his program up to a certain point, whether domestic or international, was facilitated by the threatened bankruptcy of the industrial system and the completed bankruptcy of the diplomatic system. His legislation of 1913–14 rode on the wave of the 1912 reform movement. His plea for international security, reflecting plans already sponsored by Roosevelt, Taft, Root, and Grey, was driven home to the hearts of the people by the tragic lessons of the World War. It was Wilson, however, who by his qualities and not merely because of his office, capitalized the opportunity and wakened the world to a great vision. He was not able to transform the dream into fact. But just as it is certain that the nations will pursue the hope of establishing an international organization for the guarantee of peace, so it is certain that Wilson will remain historically the eminent prophet of that better world.

[No general manuscript collection of Wilson papers has as yet been made available to the student. The unpublished correspondence of Wilson and House in the Sterling Library at Yale Univ. is open to qualified scholars. The most important edition of published papers is R. S. Baker and W. E. Dodd, The Public Papers of Woodrow Wilson (6 vols., 1925–27) : College and State (2 vols.) ; The New Democracy (2 vols.) ; War and Peace (2 vols.). For Wilson's writings, see Harry Clemons, An Essay towards a Bibliography of the Published Writings and Addresses of Woodrow Wilson, 1875–1910 (1913), continued to cover later writings by G. D. Brown (1917) and H. S. Leach (1922). The most important of Wilson's literary works are: Congressional Government, A Study in American Politics (1885) ; The State: Elements of Historical and Practical Politics (1889) ; Division and Reunion, 1829–1889 (1893) ; An Old Master and Other Political Essays (1893) ; Mere Literature and Other Essays (1896) ; George Washington (1896) ; A Hist. of the American People (5 vols., 1902) ; Constitutional Government in the U. S. (1908). His campaign speeches of 1912 are included in The New Freedom (1913). A convenient edition of his general papers is Selected Literary and Political Papers and Addresses of Woodrow Wilson (3 vols., 1925–27). The most important general biography thus far undertaken and based upon original sources is R. S. Baker, Woodrow Wilson: Life and Letters (5 vols., 1927–35). It covers Wilson's career through 1915. Other volumes are in preparation. It is distinctly favorable in tone and includes many personal letters. Memoirs and correspondence of those close to Wilson are: I. H. Hoover, Forty-two Years in the White House (1934) ; D. F. Houston, Eight Years with Wilson's Cabinet (2 vols., 1926) ; Mary A. Hulbert, The Story of Mrs. Peck: An Autobiography (1933) ; E. G. Reid, Woodrow Wilson:

The Caricature, The Myth, and the Man (1934); Charles Seymour, ed., The Intimate Papers of Colonel House (4 vols., 1926–28); J. P. Tumulty, Woodrow Wilson as I Know Him (1921). Brief personal appreciations are: E. A. Alderman, Woodrow Wilson: Memorial Address Delivered before the Two Houses of Congress (1924); Robert Bridges, Woodrow Wilson: A Personal Tribute (1924). General brief biographical studies are: J. R. Bolling, Chronology of Woodrow Wilson (1927); George Creel, The War, The World and Wilson (1920); Josephus Daniels, The Life of Woodrow Wilson (1924); W. E. Dodd, Woodrow Wilson and His Work (1920); W. B. Hale, Woodrow Wilson: The Story of a Style (1920); David Lawrence, The True Story of Woodrow Wilson (1924); Charles Seymour, Woodrow Wilson and the World War (1921); Wells Wells, Wilson the Unknown (1931); W. A. White, Woodrow Wilson; The Man, His Times, and His Task (1924). No seriously critical study of Wilson has been published; for unfriendly contemporary interpretation see J. M. Beck, The Passing of the New Freedom (1920); Theodore Roosevelt, The Foes of Our Own Household (1917). Contemporary foreign estimates are found in British Government, Peace Handbooks, Issued by the Historical Section of the Foreign Office, vol. XXV (1920), "President Wilson's Policy"; William Archer, The Peace President (1919); H. W. Harris, President Wilson: His Problems and His Policy (1917); A. M. Low, Woodrow Wilson, An Interpretation (1918); Daniel Halévy, Le Président Wilson (1918).

Memoirs and biographies covering the general political problems of the Wilson administration are: Frederick Palmer, Newton D. Baker (2 vols., 1931); J. H. Bernstorff, My Three Years in America (1920); W. J. and M. B. Bryan, The Memoirs of William Jennings Bryan (1925); Constantin Dumba, Memoirs of a Diplomat (1932); J. W. Gerard, My Four Years in Germany (1917); Samuel Gompers, Seventy Years of Life and Labor (2 vols., 1925); J. J. Jusserand, Le sentiment américain pendant la guerre (1931); H. H. Kohlsaat, From McKinley to Harding (1923); A. W. Lane, ed., The Letters of Franklin K. Lane, Personal and Political (1922); War Memoirs of Robert Lansing (1935); T. R. Marshall, Recollections (1925); W. G. McAdoo, Crowded Years (1913); Henry Morgenthau, Ambassador Morgenthau's Story (1918); B. J. Hendrick, The Life and Letters of Walter H. Page (3 vols., 1922–25); T. N. Page, Italy and the World War (1920); W. C. Redfield, With Congress and Cabinet (1924); Stephen Gwynn, ed., The Letters and Friendships of Sir Cecil Spring Rice (2 vols., 1929); Hermann Hagedorn, Leonard Wood, a Biography (2 vols., 1931).

Contrasting estimates of Wilson's administration at Princeton are given in H. J. Ford, Woodrow Wilson, the Man and His Work (1916), favorable; and R. E. Annin, Woodrow Wilson, a Character Study (1924), critical; see also Bliss Perry, And Gladly Teach (1935). The Princeton phase has yet to be studied adequately. For Wilson's early years in politics, see James Kerney, The Political Education of Woodrow Wilson (1926), a critical but friendly appreciation. W. F. McCombs, Making Woodrow Wilson President (1921) is marred by the author's egotistic bitterness and should be read in conjunction with M. F. Lyons, William F. McCombs, the President Maker (1922). On the handling of social and economic reform see N. D. Baker, How Woodrow Wilson Met Domestic Questions (1926?); The Democratic Text-Book, 1912; Herbert Croly, Progressive Democracy (1914); P. M. Warburg, The Federal Reserve System (2 vols., 1930); Carter Glass, An Adventure in Constructive Finance (1927).

For Wilson's foreign policy the official sources are numerous. The correspondence with the belligerent governments is found in U. S. Dept. of State, Papers Relating to the Foreign Relations of the United States, Supplement, The World War, 1914 (1928)—1918 (1933); Supplement, Russia, 1918 (3 vols., 1931–32). A convenient edition is that published by the Dept. of State, Diplomatic Correspondence between the United States and Belligerent Governments Relating to Neutral Rights and Duties (1916). See also Carlton Savage, Policy of the U. S. toward Maritime Commerce and War, vol. II (1936), a State Dept. publication containing many documents; 74 Cong., 2 Sess., Hearings of the Special Committee to Investigate the Munitions Industry. The most important details of Wilson's policy can only be studied from his private letters, of which those to Colonel House are the most important. For the German attitude see Carnegie Endowment for International Peace, Official German Documents Relating to the World War (2 vols., 1923); for Wilson's policy on the peace settlement, J. B. Scott, ed., Official Statements of War Aims and Peace Proposals (1921). A general study of Wilson's foreign policy, not covering the Peace Conference, is Charles Seymour, American Diplomacy during the World War (1934); see also his American Neutrality, 1914–1917 (1935). Walter Millis, Road to War: America, 1914–1917 (1935), is a journalistic treatment, appreciative of Wilson's difficulties and critical of his advisers. A brief contemporary survey for the years of neutrality with conveniently arranged documents is E. E. Robinson and V. J. West, The Foreign Policy of Woodrow Wilson (1917).

The most important survey of Wilson at the Peace Conference is R. S. Baker, Woodrow Wilson and World Settlement (3 vols., 1922), marred by its eulogistic tone and lack of appreciation of European conditions but containing many documents. The most comprehensive collection of documents is included in D. H. Miller, My Diary at the Conference of Paris (21 vols., n.d.). Important memoirs and studies on American policy at Paris are: B. M. Baruch, The Making of the Reparation and Economic Sections of the Treaty (1920); Georges Clemenceau, Grandeur and Misery of Victory (1930); E. M. House and Charles Seymour, eds., What Really Happened at Paris (1921); Sisley Huddleston, Peace-Making at Paris (1919); J. M. Keynes, The Economic Consequences of the Peace (1920), brilliantly and unreliably critical of Wilson; Robert Lansing, The Big Four and Others of the Peace Conference (1921), and The Peace Negotiations, a Personal Narrative (1921); Harold Nicolson, Peacemaking, 1919 (1933); G. B. Noble, Policies and Opinions at Paris, 1919 (1935); André Tardieu, The Truth About the Treaty (1921); H. W. V. Temperley, ed., A Hist. of the Peace Conference of Paris (6 vols., 1920–24); Gabriel Terrail, Le Combat des Trois (1932); C. T. Thompson, The Peace Conference Day by Day (1920). For the origins of the League of Nations see D. H. Miller, The Drafting of the Covenant (2 vols., 1928). Wilson's speeches on the League are collected in Woodrow Wilson's Case for the League of Nations (1923). For the conflict with the Senate see C. A. Berdahl, The Policy of the United States with Respect to the League of Nations (1932); H. C. Lodge, The Senate and the League of Nations (1925); Charles Seymour, La Politique de Wilson et le Sénat (1925). For the closing months of the Wilson administration, aside from I. H. Hoover, ante, see G. S. Viereck, The Strangest Friendship in History, Woodrow Wilson and Colonel House (1932); Bainbridge Colby, The Close of Woodrow Wilson's Administration (1930).]   C. S—r.

WILTZ, LOUIS ALFRED (Oct. 22, 1843– Oct. 16, 1881), governor of Louisiana, was born at New Orleans, the son of J. B. Theophile and Louise Irene (Villaneuva) Wiltz. He attended public school until the age of fifteen, when he began work for a commercial establishment. At the age of eighteen he joined a New Orleans artillery company, and he saw active service in the Confederate army, becoming a captain, a prisoner of war, and, after being exchanged, a provost marshal. In 1862 he married Michael, the daughter of Charles G. Bienvenu, a planter of St. Martinville. They had seven children. After the war he became an accountant in his uncle's commission house, a partner in 1871, and, with the failure of the house in 1873, a banker. His activities were not limited to commercial pursuits, however, as he became a Democratic political factor in stormy days, when Democratic leadership required both alertness and even physical boldness. He was a member of both the parish and the state central committees of his party and was elected to the state legislature in 1868. At the same time he was made a member of the New Orleans common council and a school director. He became president of the city board of aldermen. He was defeated in the election for mayor of New Orleans in 1870, elected in 1872, and defeated for reëlection in 1874. As mayor he endeavored in vain to straighten out the city financial chaos, particularly the policy of issuing temporary obligations or certificates against anticipated tax receipts. He was interested in giving effect to the will of John McDonogh [*q.v.*], who had willed property to the city for schools. In 1874 he issued from New Orleans *The Great Mississippi Flood of 1874 ... A Circular ... to the Mayors of American Cities and Towns and to the Philanthropic throughout the Republic. ...*

He was returned to the legislature in 1874 and was the successful candidate for speaker in 1875, supported by the Democrats who acted with surprising speed and unity against the "Radical" Republican group that had the support of Gov. William Pitt Kellogg [*q.v.*]. He was a man of force, a good speaker, and able to preside in spite of the presence of police, military men, pistols, and gubernatorial displeasure. He was elected lieutenant-governor in 1876 on the ticket with Gov. Francis T. Nicholls [*q.v.*] and with him took office, when President Hayes withdrew federal troops from Louisiana. In 1879 he served as president of the state constitutional convention, and in the same year he was elected governor. He died in office, of tuberculosis, and was buried with the rites of the Roman Catholic Church.

[Alcée Fortier, *Louisiana* (1909), vol. II; J. S. Kendall, *Hist. of New Orleans* (1922), vol. I; *Constitution of the State of Louisiana ... 1879* (1879); J. H. Kennard, *Argument, with Statement of Facts ... to Show that ... L. A. Wiltz ... Was Lawfully Elected ... Speaker* (1875); *Daily Picayune* (New Orleans), Oct. 16–18, 1881; date of birth from statement concerning record of the board of health in *New-Orleans Times*, Oct 18, 1881, p. 8, col. 4.]

H. C. N.

WIMAR, CARL (Feb. 19, 1828–Nov. 28, 1862), frontier painter, baptized Karl Ferdinand, was born in Siegburg, near Bonn, Germany, the son of Ludwig Gottfried and Elizabete (Schmitz) Wimar. At the age of fifteen he emigrated with his mother, then Mrs. Mathias Becker, to St. Louis, Mo., where his stepfather had gone in 1839. The shy boy was fascinated by the western life and soon became attached to the Indians who visited the bustling trading post. His artistic talent, manifested at school in Germany, began to develop when he was apprenticed to an ornamental artist, and his imaginative decorations crossed the plains on covered wagons, on the carriages of medicine peddlers, and went up and down the Mississippi on steamboats. In 1849 he received word that he had been bequeathed a sizeable sum by a cultured Pole, who had been impressed by the boy's ambition when as a stricken traveler the foreigner was cared for in the Becker home in St. Louis. This enabled Wimar to go in 1852 to Düsseldorf where he studied five years, first under Joseph Fay and then with Emanuel Leutze [*q.v.*]. To this sojourn abroad belong some of his best-known paintings, including "The Capture of Daniel Boone's Daughter," one of a series; "Attack on an Emigrant Train," awarded first prize at the St. Louis fair in 1869 and shown in the retrospective exhibit of the World's Columbian Exposition in 1893; and "The Captive Charger," which, after many years in private hands in London, was presented in 1925 to the City Art Museum, St. Louis. This museum possesses also four other paintings by Wimar. His "Buffalo Hunt by Indians," painted the next year for Henry T. Blow, won praise from William F. Cody [*qq.v.*] as a faithful picturization of the hunts held by certain tribes. This work, probably Wimar's best, hangs in the Jefferson Memorial, Forest Park, St. Louis.

On returning from Germany, Wimar found that the Indians had virtually stopped visiting St. Louis. More anxious than ever to paint them, he made at least three trips on steamboats of the American Fur Company to trading posts on the upper Missouri and Yellowstone Rivers. These expeditions brought him into contact with Crows, Yanktons, Brulés, Poncas, and Mandans, and yielded sketches and rude photographs from which he painted in winter. Friendly ways won him the esteem of his red-skinned subjects, who showered him with costumes, weapons, implements, and trinkets which he studied minutely in order to have his detail exact. He painted fellow-townsmen for a livelihood, but every possible free moment he gave to depicting the life of the Indians and the West.

Wimar's last work was to decorate the St. Louis courthouse with four historical panels. For this work, long since ruined by inexpert renovation, he and his half-brother, August H.

Becker, employed at the instance of William Taussig [*q.v.*], received $1000. Stricken with "cons..mption," Wimar had to be lifted to the scaffold as the project neared the end, and upon its completion he died. He was thirty-five years of age. His widow, previously Anna von Senden of St. Louis, to whom he had been married on Mar. 7, 1861, later became the wife of Charles Schleiffarth. An only child, named Winona, died two years after her father. His high cheek bones, tanned skin, pigeon-toed, shambling gait, trapper clothes, and long black hair led many to believe the artist himself an Indian. Wimar was a good draughtsman and vivid colorist, but his paintings, like those of George Catlin [*q.v.*], are valuable chiefly as historical and ethnological records. "It is Wimar's distinction as an artist," said the *Review of Reviews* a half century after his death (Feb. 1909, p. 262), "that he early appreciated and made pictorial use of materials that his contemporary artists practically ignored."

[Parents and date of birth from baptismal records in Siegburg; information from Chas. Reymershoffer and L. H. Cannon of St. Louis, Mo.; W. R. Hodges, *Carl Wimar* (1908), and an article by same author, *Am. Art Rev.*, Mar. 1881; *Arts in St. Louis* (1864), ed. by W. T. Helmuth; F. C. Shoemaker, *Missouri's Hall of Fame* (1918); Wm. Hyde, H. L. Conard, *Encyc. Hist. of St. Louis* (1899); Herman ten Kate, "On Paintings of North American Indians . . .," *Anthropos, Revue Internationale* (Vienna), May–Aug. 1911; L. M. C. Kinealy, biog. article in *Mirror* (St. Louis), Feb. 18, 1909; *Mo. Republican*, Sept. 20, 1860, July 4, Dec. 1, 1862; *Daily Mo. Democrat, St. Louis Daily Union*, Dec. 1, 1862; *Westliche Post* (St. Louis), Sept. 29, 1886; *St. Louis Globe-Democrat*, Nov. 20, 1887, Mar. 5, 1889; *St. Louis Republic*, Nov. 18, 1894, Feb. 5, 1905; *St. Louis Post-Dispatch*, Feb. 22, 1903.]   I. D.

WIMMER, BONIFACE (Jan. 14, 1809–Dec. 8, 1887), Roman Catholic archabbot, was born at Thalmassing, Bavaria, where his parents, Peter Wimmer and Elizabeth Lang, kept a tavern and tilled a small farm. The boy, who was christened Sebastian, at fourteen entered the Latin school at Regensburg, and at seventeen the seminary there to study for the priesthood. In 1827 he matriculated at the University of Munich. After two years he decided to study law and even thought of enlisting in the Bavarian army of volunteers in the war for Greek independence, when he received a scholarship at the Georgianum, a boarding-school for divinity students. Resuming his theological studies, he was ordained priest at Regensburg on Aug. 1, 1831. On Dec. 29, 1833, he made his solemn vows as a Benedictine at the monastery of Metten, taking the name of Boniface. For the next twelve years he held various positions as pastor of Stephansposching, procurator of Scheyern, and professor in Metten, Augsburg, and Munich.

As early as 1843 he asked permission to go to the United States to minister to the emigrant Catholic Germans. Among other things, a conference in Munich with Peter Henry Lemke [*q.v.*], pastor of Carrolltown, Pa., ripened his plan of founding a Benedictine monastery for that purpose, and on July 25, 1846, he left Munich with four ecclesiastical students and fourteen young laymen. Landing in New York, Sept. 16, he went first to Carrolltown, where he had bought a farm before leaving home. When he found this ill-suited, he accepted the offer of Bishop Michael O'Connor of Pittsburgh to settle on the church-lands of St. Vincent in Westmoreland County, Pa. On Oct. 24, 1846, he invested his eighteen companions with the religious habit, a ceremony which marked the beginning of the Benedictine Order in the United States. During the following winter the community suffered much in the scattered little buildings, but in 1847 new arrivals and fresh supplies from home increased the hope for success, and the Superior petitioned Rome to approve the foundation as a Benedictine monastery. In 1848 he started a college and seminary, and a year later began to build a more spacious cloister. From that time to the end of his life, building operations rarely ceased at St. Vincent. He also took over the parish at St. Vincent and whenever possible made missionary tours through western Pennsylvania. In a trip abroad he succeeded in procuring the first Benedictine nuns from the convent of Eichstaett (1852). Three years later he applied to Rome to raise his foundation to the rank of an abbey; on Aug. 24, 1855, Pope Pius IX granted his petition and appointed him the first abbot. At that time the monastery had almost one hundred and fifty members.

The new abbot sent men to Minnesota (1856) to found a priory (now St. John Abbey and University), to Kansas (1857), where they began St. Benedict Abbey and College at Atchison, and to San José, Tex., where they established a foundation given up during the Civil War. At about the same time other houses were established at Carrolltown (1848), St. Marys (1851), and Johnstown, Pa. (1852), Covington, Ky. (1858), Erie, Pa. (1859), Chicago, Ill. (1861), Richmond, Va. (1867), and Pittsburgh, Pa. (1868). In 1870, as president of the American-Cassinese Congregation, which he had founded (1866), Wimmer attended the Vatican Council in Rome. During the next ten years he began a monastery in North Carolina (later Belmont Abbey and College), sent missionaries to Alabama who paved the way for St. Bernard Abbey and College, Cullman, and founded an agricultural school for negroes on Skidaway Island, near Savannah, Ga. This last, which was especially dear to him, did not prosper. In 1883, when Wimmer celebrated the golden jubilee of profession, Pope Leo XIII conferred on him the title of archabbot and the privilege of wearing the *cappa magna* for pontifical functions. At that time his missionaries were in twenty-five states of the Union, ministering to over 100,000 souls, especially among Germans, Irish, Italians, Indians, and negroes. During the last period of his life Wimmer also educated boys from Bohemia to become missionaries among their countrymen, and in 1885 founded a priory in Chicago (later St. Procopius Abbey, Lisle, Ill.). In 1886 he sent Fathers to Colorado who established a priory which became Holy Cross Abbey, Canon City. On his deathbed he gave consent to a foundation in Ecuador, South America, which was later discontinued. Of middle stature and robust exterior, Wimmer was a man of a very practical mind and marked determination. In the beginning of his career he had to oppose an exaggerated asceticism on the part of some of his followers and the attempt of the Ordinary of the diocese to limit his activities. In 1858 a religious charlatan who succeeded in entering the ranks of his monks and who used the tendency of the prelate towards mysticism for his personal advantage almost disrupted his work and had to be expelled (1862). In general, the abbot believed that missionary activity would revive the former glory of his order. He himself never considered earthly gain, and the poorer the petitioners, the surer they were of obtaining help.

[Oswald Moosmüller, *St. Vincenz in Pennsylvanien* (1873), and *Bonifaz Wimmer* (1891); *St. Vincenz Gemeinde and Erzabtei* (1905) and *St. Vincent's* (1905), pamphlets published by the Archabbey Press; *Wissenschaftliche Studien und Mittheilungen aus dem Benedictiner-Orden* (1881), vol. I, pp. v–xiv, vol. II, pp. 351–61; Gerard Bridge, *Early St. Vincent* (1920); S. J. Wimmer, in *Records Am. Cath. Hist. Soc.*, vol. III (1891); Felix Fellner, *Ibid.*, Dec. 1926, pp. 299–301; obituary in *Studien und Mittheilungen aus dem Benedictiner—und dem Cistercienser-Orden*, vol. IX (1888); letters of Wimmer in St. Vincent archives.]
F.F.

WINANS, ROSS (Oct. 17, 1796–Apr. 11, 1877), inventor and mechanic, was sixth in descent from Jan Wynants, who came to America from the Netherlands about 1662. The seventh child of William and Mary Winans, first cousins, Ross was born on a farm in Sussex County, N. J. He received a good common-school education and while on a journey to New York City picked up a book which led him to a study of mechanical principles. In Baltimore in 1828 to sell horses to the new Baltimore & Ohio Railroad (Hungerford, *post*, I, 77), he became interested in the

problems of the new system of transportation, and devised a model "rail wagon," having the "friction wheel" with outside bearings, thus setting, for at least a century, the distinctive pattern for railroad wheels. In Winans' model car in one of the upper rooms of the Exchange, the venerable Charles Carroll [*q.v.*] of Carrollton, in the presence of most of the prominent men of Baltimore, was drawn along a track on the floor by a ridiculously small weight suspended over a pulley by twine. Shortly afterward, when George W. Whistler, Jonathan Knight, and William G. McNeill [*qq.v.*] were sent abroad by the railroad company to study the railroad system of England, Winans went also. While abroad he allowed his patent wheel to be used for experimentation, with the result that he was ruthlessly plundered of its most valuable feature.

Upon his return he entered the service of the Baltimore & Ohio as engineer (1829–30), assisting Peter Cooper [*q.v.*] with his famous *Tom Thumb* engine. As a member of the firm of Gillingham & Winans, about 1834 he took charge of the Mount Clare shops of the railroad company, devoting the next twenty-five years to the improvement of railroad machinery. He planned the first eight-wheel car ever built for passenger purposes and is credited with the innovation of mounting a car on two four-wheeled trucks. In 1842 he constructed a locomotive known as the *Mud-Digger,* with horizontal boiler; it was put into service in 1844. In 1848 he produced the heavy and powerful "camelback" locomotive, noted for power on steep grades. Unlike most inventors, Winans was eminently practical; at his shop more than one hundred locomotives were constructed for the Baltimore & Ohio company during the period when the "camelback" was in favor. In time, however, the company decided that locomotives of less weight were more economical on the rails. Numerous pamphlets and bitter newspaper communications to prove the superiority of his "camelback" proved unavailing in the face of experience, and about 1860 Winans retired from locomotive building. Meanwhile, in 1843 he had been invited, doubtless through Whistler's influence, to go to Russia to furnish rolling stock for the railroad between Moscow and St. Petersburg. He declined, but sent his sons Thomas De Kay Winans [*q.v.*] and William in his stead.

During the Civil War his sympathies were with the Confederacy. He experimented with a steam gun, which was seized by the Union troops on the suspicion that it was intended for the South. As a member of the Maryland legislature which met in Frederick in 1861, he shared in the misfortunes of that body. He was twice arrested, in May and September 1861, and twice released on parole.

In his later years Winans and his family spent an immense sum on the development of the "cigar-steamer," a long, narrow vessel which left the shape of its hull as a heritage to the modern ocean liner. He was much interested in projects for improving Baltimore, and published numerous pamphlets on problems of local hygiene and water supply. He also wrote several unorthodox works on religious subjects, the most significant of which was *One Religion: Many Creeds* (1870). He erected, as a philanthropy, more than a hundred houses for rental at moderate rates to working people, but his investment of over $400,000 proved ultimately a failure. He married twice: first, Jan. 22, 1820, Julia De Kay of New Jersey, who died in 1850; second, in 1854, Elizabeth K. West of Baltimore. He had four sons and a daughter, Julia, who became the wife of George W. Whistler, Jr., half-brother of the artist James McNeill Whistler [*q.v.*].

[*Baltimore American and Commercial Advertiser,* and *Sun* (Baltimore), Apr. 12, 1877; *Baltimore News,* Apr. 12, 18, 1911; J. T. Scharf, *Hist. of Baltimore City and County* (1881); J. E. Semmes, *John H. B. Latrobe and His Times* (1917); Edward Hungerford, *The Story of the Baltimore and Ohio Railroad* (1928); manuscript geneal. in the possession of the Md. Hist. Soc., which has also a volume of Winans pamphlets thought to be complete; Winans MSS. in the possession of Reginald Hutton, Esq., a descendant, in Baltimore, consisting of letters, diaries, account-books, and miscellaneous papers bearing on numerous patents; *Annual Reports of the Baltimore & Ohio Railroad.*]   E. L.

WINANS, THOMAS DE KAY (Dec. 6, 1820–June 10, 1878), engineer and inventor, eldest son of Ross Winans [*q.v.*] and Julia (De Kay) Winans, was born at Vernon, N. J., but was taken to Baltimore when but ten years old. Inheriting his father's mechanical tastes, he was apprenticed, after a common-school education, to a machinist, under whom he displayed such skill that before he attained his majority he was intrusted with the headship of a department in his father's establishment. Indeed, when he was scarcely eighteen years old, he had been charged with the delivery of some engines for the Boston & Albany Railroad, and while executing this commission is said to have first met George W. Whistler [*q.v.*], who was afterwards called to Russia as consulting engineer of the projected railroad from St. Petersburg to Moscow. In 1843 Ross Winans declined Whistler's invitation to take charge of the mechanical department of the Russian railroad, but sent his sons, Thomas and William, to St. Petersburg in his place, commissioning them with the delivery of a locomotive built for the Russian road.

With Joseph Harrison [*q.v.*], a member of the Philadelphia firm of Eastwick & Harrison, locomotive builders, Thomas Winans, against the competition of all foreign bidders, secured the contract to equip the Russian railroad in five years with locomotives and other rolling stock. The firm of Harrison, Winans & Eastwick, organized for the Russian enterprise, established shops at Alexandrovsky, near St. Petersburg, and completed their contract more than a year before the time agreed upon. One contract led to another, so that orders, approximating nearly $2,000,000, which included all the cast iron for the first permanent bridge over the Neva River at St. Petersburg, were added to the original award of $5,000,000, and the contemplated visit of a few months was prolonged to a residence of five years. In Russia, on Aug. 23, 1847, Winans married Céleste Revillon, a Russian of French and Italian descent. They had four children, of whom only two survived their father. In 1851 he returned to America, leaving his brother to fulfill the remaining contracts, which were completed by 1862. In 1866 the firm, including George W. Whistler, Jr., now Winans' brother-in-law, was recalled to Russia under a new contract of eight years' duration, but in 1868 the government took over their interests by the payment of a large bonus.

With the exception of visits to Europe, Winans thenceforth resided in Baltimore at "Alexandroffsky," the house he had begun to construct in 1853, named in memory of his Russian experience. To a country residence near Baltimore he gave the name "Crimea." On but two occasions did he emerge from his retirement: upon the completion of the Baltimore & Ohio Railroad he consented to serve as a director in order to lend it the benefit of his skill and experience; and at the outbreak of the Civil War in 1861 he established a soup station opposite his home, where four thousand persons were fed daily. Invention remained his favorite pastime, and for many years he conducted elaborate, costly, and generally successful experiments of the most diverse kinds. Particularly noteworthy was the cigar-shaped hull which he and his father devised in 1859, designed for high-speed steamers in trans-Atlantic service. Among other products of his mechanical genius were a device which made the organ as easy of touch as the piano, a mode of increasing the strength and volume of sound on the piano, an improvement in ventilation which he applied at "Alexandroffsky," glass feeding vessels for fish, adopted by the Maryland Fish Commission, and an ingenious use of the undulation of the waves to pump the water of a spring to the reservoir at the top of his villa at Newport, R. I. Compared with his father's practical inventions, these might be termed the *divertissements* of a gentleman of leisure. In addition to his mechanical gifts, he had a natural skill in clay-modeling. He died at Newport, in his fifty-eighth year.

[*Baltimore American and Commercial Advertiser*, and *Sun* (Baltimore), June 11, 1878; J. E. Semmes, *John H. B. Latrobe and His Times* (1917); Joseph Harrison, *The Iron Worker and King Solomon* (1869), with memoir and appendix.]

E.L.

WINANS, WILLIAM (Nov. 3, 1788–Aug. 31, 1857), Methodist clergyman, was born on Chestnut Ridge in the Allegheny Mountains of western Pennsylvania. When he was two years old his father died, leaving his widow with five children to rear. William was taught to read and write by his mother and an older brother, and as soon as he was strong enough began to work in the iron foundries near his home. When he was sixteen he moved with his mother to Clermont County, Ohio. She was a devout Methodist, and after they moved to Ohio Winans' interest in religion was awakened; in 1807 he became a Methodist class-leader and exhorter. Feeling called to preach, he was admitted on trial into the Western Conference of the Methodist Episcopal Church, Oct. 1, 1808. For two years he served circuits in Kentucky and Indiana but in 1810 volunteered for pioneer work in the Mississippi territory. In 1812 he was ordained deacon. The following year he was assigned to New Orleans, but his labors there were hindered by the military operations, and in 1814 he returned to Mississippi. He was ordained elder in that year and became a member of the Tennessee Conference. In order to recoup his physical and financial resources he settled, after his marriage in 1815 to Martha DuBose, and for five years taught school in Mississippi.

Returning to the itinerancy in 1820, he was thereafter the outstanding figure in Mississippi Methodism until his death. He served as trustee of Elizabeth Female Academy and Centenary College and in 1845 and 1849 acted as traveling agent for the latter institution. Under his leadership the first Methodist Church in New Orleans was erected. In 1824 he was the superintendent of the Choctaw Mission of the Mississippi Conference. Although he had no formal education, he endeavored after he entered the itinerancy to read daily fifty pages, in addition to portions of the Bible, and by this private study became comparatively learned, and an able debater. In 1855 he published a volume of sermons entitled *A Series of Discourses on Fundamental Religious Subjects*. He was also an occasional contributor to secular and religious periodicals. Taking an active part in the discussion of national political issues, he was an ardent Whig and was once a candidate for Congress. During the presidential campaign of 1844 he opened Clay meetings in Mississippi with prayer, for which he was severely criticized by the Democratic newspapers. He was also much interested in the work of the American Colonization Society.

In every General Conference of the Methodist Episcopal Church from 1824 to 1844, inclusive, Winans championed the *status quo* of Methodist polity and doctrine. He fought attempts to weaken the power of the episcopacy and was active in opposing abolitionist tendencies. With other Southern delegates he sponsored the resolution adopted by the General Conference of 1836 which condemned abolitionism, and he even contended that the Methodist officials should be slaveholders in order to overcome the opposition of the slaveholding class to Methodism and thereby give the Church access to the slaves. At the General Conference of 1844 he delivered the first speech in defense of Bishop J. O. Andrew [*q.v.*] and was a member of the committee that drafted the famous "Plan of Separation" for the division of the Church. He was subsequently a delegate to the convention held at Louisville, Ky., in May 1845 that organized the Methodist Episcopal Church, South, and was elected to the General Conference of the new body in 1846, 1850, and 1854. He died in Amite County, Miss.

[Winans' diary, his unpublished autobiography, and much of his correspondence are in the possession of his grandson, Hon. William A. Dickson, Centreville, Miss. Rev. M. L. Burton, Gulfport, Miss., also has some of Winans' unpublished correspondence. Brief biog. sketches are in J. G. Jones, *A Complete Hist. of Methodism as Connected with the Miss. Conference of the M. E. Ch. South* (2 vols., 1908); C. F. Deems, *Annals of Southern Methodism for 1855* (1856); *Minutes of the Ann. Conferences of the M. E. Ch. South, 1845–57* (1859); Abel Stevens, *Hist. of the M. E. Ch. in the U. S. A.* (4 vols., 1864–67). See also J. J. Tigert, *A Constitutional Hist. of Am. Episcopal Methodism* (1904); L. C. Matlack, *The Hist. of Am. Slavery and Methodism from 1780 to 1849* (1849); *Daily Picayune* (New Orleans), Sept. 5, 1857.]

P. N. G.

WINCHELL, ALEXANDER (Dec. 31, 1824–Feb. 19, 1891), author, teacher, and geologist, son of Horace and Caroline (McAllister) Winchell, and a brother of Newton Horace Winchell [*q.v.*], was born in the town of Northeast, Dutchess County, N. Y. He was a descendant in the seventh generation of Robert Winchell, an Englishman who settled first in Dorchester in 1634 and removed to Windsor, Conn., in 1635; on his mother's side he was of Scotch-Irish ancestry. His first inclinations seem to have been toward mathematics and astronomy, but he decided to study medicine and was sent to the

Stockbridge Academy at South Lee, Mass., for two years. Being then but sixteen and too young to begin his medical studies, he taught school during 1841 and 1842. He found the profession agreeable, abandoned his earlier intentions, and in the fall of 1842 entered Amenia Seminary, Dutchess County, N. Y. He matriculated at Wesleyan University, Middletown, Conn., in 1844, to graduate in 1847, entering almost at once upon a remarkably diversified career of teaching, lecturing, and writing. He first essayed teaching in the Pennington Male Seminary of New Jersey, where he showed his fondness for natural history by studying the local flora; he also studied languages and made amateur experiments in electricity. Returning to accept the chair of natural history at the Amenia Seminary, he gave his first public geological lectures in 1849. In 1850 he assumed charge of an academy at Newbern, Ala., but resigned the following year to open the Mesopotamia Female Seminary at Eutaw. In 1853 he accepted the presidency of the Masonic University at Selma, Ala. Meanwhile, he made extensive natural history collections, which were forwarded in part to the Smithsonian Institution at Washington and brought him in touch with Prof. Spencer Fullerton Baird [q.v.] and other naturalists of his day. An outbreak of yellow fever at Selma and the offer of the chair of physics and civil engineering at the University of Michigan took him in the fall of 1853 to Ann Arbor. In 1855 he was given the new chair of geology, zoölogy, and botany at Michigan, a position he continued to hold until 1873. During this time he wrote profusely for the public press, lectured, and organized and directed a short-lived state geological survey (1859–61) that came to an end through the failure of the legislature to make the necessary appropriations. In 1869 a reorganization took place and Winchell was again made director, but he resigned in 1871, owing, it is said, to the hostility of personal enemies. Disappointed by his failure, he resigned his university position and accepted the chancellorship of Syracuse University (1872–74), but, finding conditions less favorable than he had been led to expect, he resigned there as well. After an unsuccessful attempt at a school of geology in Syracuse, and a professorship of geology and zoölogy at Vanderbilt University (1875–78), he returned to his old home at Ann Arbor and in 1879 was unanimously recalled to the chair of geology and paleontology at the university, where he remained until his death. He was chairman of the committee to organize the Geological Society of America, and served as president in 1891.

With the exception of the brief periods with the Michigan survey, and two years in a study of the Archaean problem in Minnesota, Winchell's geological work was of an intermittent nature. The most important result of his Michigan survey, from an economic standpoint, was the localization of the salt beds of the Saginaw valley. His reputation rests rather on his success as a teacher, public lecturer, and writer of popular treatises than on his work as a geologist. He took an advanced stand on the subject of evolution and perhaps on the whole did as much as any one man in America to reconcile the supposed conflict between science and religion. He was a good speaker and a skilful teacher, though he had little interest in any but the ablest of his students. The books for which he was best known are his *Sketches of Creation* (1870), *The Doctrine of Evolution* (1874), *Preadamites* (1880), *Sparks from a Geologist's Hammer* (1881), *World Life* (1883), and his textbook, *Geological Studies* (1886). Of these his *World Life,* which covered systematically the entire field of world history, shows the most careful research and the deepest thought. The extreme diversity and profuseness of his writings is indicated by his published bibliography, which consists of over two hundred and fifty titles. Winchell was married on Dec. 5, 1849, to Julia F. Lines of Utica, N. Y. He died from aortic stenosis, a disease from which he had long suffered. He was survived by his wife and two of their six children.

[See N. H. and A. N. Winchell, *The Winchell Geneal.* (1917) ; N. H. Winchell, in *Am. Geologist,* Feb. 1892, with bibliog., a somewhat eulogistic account; H. L. Fairchild, *The Geological Soc. of America* (1932) ; *List of Books and Papers Published by Prof. Alexander Winchell* (1886) ; *Am. Jour. of Sci.,* Apr. 1891 ; obituary in *Detroit Free Press,* Feb. 20, 1891. There is a large coll. of Winchell MSS., including many letters, in the possession of the Minn. Hist. Soc.]   G. P. M.

WINCHELL, HORACE VAUGHN (Nov. 1, 1865–July 28, 1923), geologist, mining engineer, came of a family conspicuous for its work in geology. He was born at Galesburg, Mich., the son of Newton Horace [q.v.] and Charlotte Sophia (Imus) Winchell, both of old New England stock. He studied at the University of Minnesota and the University of Michigan, and was graduated from the latter in 1889. Interested in the practical application of economic geology and attracted by his father and his uncle, Alexander Winchell [q.v.], to a study of the iron-ore deposits of Minnesota, he worked first as assistant state geologist of Minnesota and then for the Minnesota Mining Company. His book, *The Iron Ores of Minnesota* (1891), which he wrote with his father, became a standard work of reference.

Before the first production of ore was made from the great Mesabi range in 1892, young Winchell had prepared reports and maps of it, predicting its coming importance and explaining correctly the origin of the ores, but those interested financially refused to consider his predictions, and geologists disregarded or adopted without credit to him the early theories which he advanced. The panic and depression of 1893 ended his explorations for the Minnesota Iron Company, and he established a laboratory and office in Minneapolis with F. F. Sharpless, but his professional engagements turned him toward the West. In 1898, at the suggestion of David W. Brunton [q.v.], he went to Butte, Mont., in connection with litigation between W. A. Clark and the Anaconda Copper Mining Company. This was the beginning of a long and mutually profitable engagement of his services by the Anaconda interests. As head of the geological department of this company, he served in the famous "apex law" suits against Frederick Augustus Heinze [q.v.]. His systematic organization of geological data and close studies of the occurrence of the ore set a mark for others to strive for, and encouraged mining companies to establish geological departments. Some of the results of his researches could not be published at that time because of lawsuits and commercial rivalry, but later geologists recognized his pioneer work in the explanation of the origin of ore deposits. For two years (1906–08) he was chief geologist for the Great Northern Railway, with headquarters in St. Paul, and his recommendations led to its purchase of extensive iron and coal lands. Still retaining a connection with the Anaconda company, he broadened his general consulting practice in 1908 and made examinations in many parts of the world. In particular, he testified as an expert in cases of mining law involving application of the puzzling "apex law," on which he was a leading authority. While reporting in 1917 on mineral properties in the Caucasus and elsewhere in Russia, he witnessed the Kerensky revolution. He was elected president of the American Institute of Mining and Metallurgical Engineers in 1919. As one of the founders of the periodical, *Economic Geology,* he turned over to it the good-will and following of the old *American Geologist.* In 1921 he removed from Minneapolis to Los Angeles. A generous interest in public service was shown by his earnest attempts to improve the tangled laws governing prospecting and mining; in the controversy over the Cunningham coal claims in Alaska he protested vigorously against the government's arbitrary cancellation of them.

Winchell had a ready ability in expressing opinions both orally and in print, although in personality he was modest and generous. His wide interests included music, natural history, literature, and art. After his death his valuable library was given to the Engineering Societies Library of New York by his wife and the Anaconda company. On Jan. 15, 1890, he was married to his cousin, Ida Belle Winchell of Ann Arbor, daughter of Prof. Alexander Winchell; his wife survived him.

[The best source is T. A. Rickard, *Interviews with Mining Engineers* (1922). See also *Who's Who in America,* 1922–23; *Engineering and Mining Jour.-Press,* May 27, 1922, Aug. 4, 1923; *Mining and Metallurgy,* Sept. 1923; death notices in *Los Angeles Sunday Times* and *Minneapolis Sunday Tribune,* July 29, 1923.]

P. B. M.

WINCHELL, NEWTON HORACE (Dec. 17, 1839–May 2, 1914), geologist, archaeologist, was born in Northeast, Dutchess County, N. Y., the son of Horace and Caroline (McAllister) Winchell. He was educated in the public schools of his native town and the academy of Salisbury, Conn., and at the age of sixteen began teaching in a district school in Northeast. In 1858 he entered the University of Michigan, where his brother Alexander [q.v.] was professor of geology, remaining for eight years, alternately studying and teaching in the schools of the vicinity. Two years previous to his graduation in 1866 he was superintendent of public schools in St. Clair, Mich., and for the first three years after graduation, in the schools of Adrian, Mich. It is not strange, considering the influence of his brother, that his interest and studies were mainly geological, though he was also devoted to botany and archaeology. He served as assistant to his brother on the Michigan state geological survey (1869–70) and in 1870–72 likewise assisted John Strong Newberry [q.v.] on the survey of Ohio. In 1872 he became state geologist on the newly organized survey of Minnesota, holding the position until the completion of the work in 1900. From 1874 to 1900 he performed also the duties of professor of geology in the University of Minnesota. In addition to serving as geologist of a military exploring expedition to the Black Hills under William Ludlow [q.v.] in 1874, he spent some time in Paris (1895–96, 1898) in special work in petrology.

As state geologist, Winchell published annual reports for each year from 1872 to 1894 inclusive, and one for 1895–98. These reports, ranging from pamphlets to volumes of five hundred pages or more, treated many important features of the state and included notes on ornithology, entomology, and botany. In addition, there were ten bulletins on special subjects and six quarto volumes forming the final reports. These covered the general geology of the state, with monographic treatises on the great iron-ore deposits of the Vermilion and Mesabi ranges and an investigation of the building-stone resources of the state. Winchell's most valuable geological studies were probably those on the recession of the falls of St. Anthony at Minneapolis, which had occupied, it was estimated, a period of some eight thousand years. His glacial and archaeological studies led him to the conclusion that man existed on the American continent during the latter part of the Ice Age, and possibly much earlier. His last paper, "The Antiquity of Man in America Compared with Europe," was delivered as a lecture before the Iowa Academy of Sciences on Apr. 24, 1914, but a week before his death. This and *The Aborigines of Minnesota* (1911) constituted the most important of his archaeological work.

Winchell was one of the founders of the Minnesota Academy of Sciences and of the Geological Society of America, which he served as president in 1902, and a member of numerous other scientific organizations, some of them foreign. He was a founder of the first American geological periodical, the *American Geologist,* which was published under his direction and editorship at Minneapolis for a number of years (1888–1905). His work throughout was characterized by great diligence and honesty of purpose, if not brilliance of accomplishment. He died in Minneapolis, Minn. He was married on Aug. 24, 1864, to Charlotte Sophia Imus of Galesburg, Mich., by whom he had five children. His two sons, Horace Vaughn [*q.v.*] and Alexander Newton, also became geologists.

[The chief source is the memoir, with bibliog., by Warren Upham in *Bull. Geological Soc. of America,* Mar. 1915. See also *Who's Who in America,* 1914–15; H. F. Bain, in *Economic Geology,* Jan. 1916; Warren Upham, *Ibid.*; and obituary in *Minneapolis Sunday Tribune,* May 3, 1914. There are Winchell MSS. in the colls. of the Minn. Hist. Soc.]   G. P. M.

WINCHESTER, CALEB THOMAS (Jan. 18, 1847–Mar. 24, 1920), teacher and editor, was born in Montville, Conn., son of the Rev. George H. and Lucy (Thomas) Winchester, and a descendant of John Winchester who came to Hingham, Mass., in 1635. Caleb's father and grandfather were both Methodist ministers. He prepared for college at Wilbraham Academy, Wilbraham, Mass., and in 1865 entered Wesleyan University, Middletown, Conn., where he edited the *College Argus,* and with three classmates formed a quartet which developed into the University glee club. Graduating with the degree of A.B. in 1869, he was appointed librarian and served in that capacity until 1885. On Dec. 25, 1872, he married Julia Stackpole Smith of Middletown, who died June 25, 1877, and on Apr. 2, 1880, Alice Goodwin Smith.

From his arrival at Wesleyan as a freshman, he knew no other home. In 1873 he was made professor of rhetoric and English literature, and in 1890 Olin Professor of English Literature, which position he held until his death. A scholar and a student of distinction, he gained world-wide recognition as an authority in his chosen field. A gifted writer, he devoted his talents to his classroom and public lectures rather than to the reading public. A man of catholic tastes and varied interests, he was an inspirational force to his pupils. If he destroyed his scholars' respect for certain inferior forms of writing, he substituted the enjoyment to be derived from appreciation of the truly great.

He made many appearances upon public lecture platforms and in the classrooms of other universities. His most enduring book is *Some Principles of Literary Criticism* (1899), which was reprinted several times and remains a standard university textbook. Upon its publication a reviewer remarked: "It is seldom that a book on the method of an art is anything more than a collection of dry formulae, lacking in the sap of life." This author, however, "distinctly adds to the books which promote the enjoyment of good literature. The secret of it all is, of course, that Professor Winchester is first a lover of literature for its own sake, and afterwards a critical analyzer of its methods" (*Life,* Feb. 1, 1900, p. 86). Other books of which he was the author include *The Life of John Wesley* (1906), *A Group of English Essayists of the Early Nineteenth Century* (1910), and *William Wordsworth: How to Know Him* (1916). His editorial work, which was extensive, is represented in such publications as *Selected Essays of Joseph Addison* (1886, 1890), *Five Short Courses of Reading in English Literature* (1891, 1900, 1911), *The Sir Roger de Coverley Papers* (1904), and *A Book of English Essays* (1914). He was also one of the editors of *The Methodist Hymnal* (1905), in which a hymn by him—"The Lord Our God Alone is Strong"—appears. He was the author of numerous prayers in *The Chapel Service Book for Schools and Colleges* (1920), contributed many articles, chiefly on literary subjects, to the *Methodist Review* and *Zion's Herald,* and did much editing of material published by Wesleyan University. At his death he was survived by his wife and one son.

[*A Memorial to Caleb Thomas Winchester* (1921), ed. by G. M. Dutcher; F. W. Hotchkiss, *Winchester*

Notes (1912); Who's Who in America, 1918–19; Wesleyan Alumnus, Apr. 1920; N. Y. Times, Mar. 25, 1920; Wesleyan Argus (editorial), Mar. 25, 1920; Evening Post (N. Y.), editorial, Mar. 26, 1920; Christian Advocate (N. Y.), editorial, Apr. 1, 1920; Hartford Courant, Mar. 25, 1920.]
W. B. T., Jr.

WINCHESTER, ELHANAN (Sept. 30, 1751–Apr. 18, 1797), clergyman, one of the early exponents of Universalism, was a native of Brookline, Mass., the son of Elhanan and Sarah Winchester. His father had three wives and fifteen children, Elhanan being the first born. He was a descendant of John Winchester who emigrated to Massachusetts in 1635, settling in Hingham, but later moving to Muddy River (Brookline), where he died in 1694. The elder Elhanan was a farmer and mechanic, and the boy's schooling was limited. He had an unusual mind, however. One Sunday his father asked him to note from what passage in the Bible the minister took his text. After the service Elhanan not only gave the desired information, but repeated large portions of the sermon and told how many persons were present and the number of beams, posts, braces, rafters, and panes of glass in the meeting house. Endowed with the type of mind that made this feat possible, he found learning easy, and to knowledge of English subjects he added, as time went on, a working acquaintance with Hebrew, Greek, and French.

In 1769 he was. converted and joined a local church; on Jan. 18 of the next year he contracted his first marriage—four more were to follow; soon he began to preach. A little later he went to Canterbury, Conn., was immersed, and associated himself with an open-communion Baptist church. He had characteristics as a speaker which, from the beginning to the end of his ministry, drew large audiences, and about 1771 his preaching in Rehoboth, Mass., started a revival that resulted in the establishment of a Baptist church, of which he was ordained pastor. Within a year, however, he had become a close-communion Baptist and a strict Calvinist, a change in attitude that caused dissension in the church and his withdrawal from it. In 1774, having in the meantime preached in several Massachusetts towns, he went to South Carolina and took charge of a Baptist church at Welch Neck, on the Great Peedee River, where he remained until 1780, when he became pastor of the Baptist church of Philadelphia. His ministry in Philadelphia lasted seven years; the largest church building in the city was crowded by those who came to hear him preach; and he won the regard and friendship of such notable men as Benjamin Rush and John Redman [qq.v.]. Meanwhile, his reading and study had led him to accept the doctrine of universal restoration, which fact disrupted his church. Though the majority of the members sided with him, both pastor and adherents were driven out by the orthodox remnant. Thereafter, Winchester held services in the hall of the University of Pennsylvania.

Feeling called to proclaim the gospel in England he left Philadelphia in 1787 for London. Here, too, his preaching attracted many, and he gathered a congregation to which he ministered in the chapel in Parliament Court. Among those to whom he became warmly attached were Thomas Belsham, Joseph Priestley, and John Wesley. During this period, also, he published a number of works setting forth his theological views, which were widely read both in England and America. Among them were *The Universal Restoration: Exhibited in a Series of Dialogues Between a Minister and His Friend* (1788); *The Restitution of All Things . . . Being an Attempt to Answer the Rev. Dan Taylor's Assertion and Re-Assertions in Favour of Endless Misery* (1790); *The Three Woe Trumpets* (1793), the substance of two discourses delivered in Parliament, Feb. 3 and 24, 1783; *The Face of Moses Unveiled by the Gospel, or, Evangelical Truths, Discovered in the Law* (1787); *A Course of Lectures on the Prophecies That Remain to be Fulfilled* (3 vols., 1789–90); *The Process and Empire of Christ, from His Birth to the End of the Mediatorial Kingdom; a Poem in Twelve Books* (1793). For two years, also, he conducted in London a periodical called *The Philadelphian Magazine*.

In May 1794, when at the height of his influence, Winchester suddenly left England for America. His family life had been fraught with trouble. His first wife, Alice Rogers, died in April 1776. That same year he married Sarah Peck of Rehoboth, who lived only a few months thereafter. His third wife, Sarah Luke, of South Carolina, whom he married in 1778, died in 1779. Two years later he married Mary Morgan of Philadelphia, a widow, whose career was cut short a year and nine months later. Seven children were stillborn and one other lived but seventeen months. After the death of his fourth wife, his friends advised him to desist from further matrimonial ventures, but believing that a minister, in order to avoid reproach, should not remain single, he married another widow, Maria Knowles. She proved subject to fits of temper in which she committed violent assaults upon her husband. It was after one of these that Winchester left England, planning to make provision for her support in America and then return. She followed him, however, and prevailed upon him to live with her again; but his days were now numbered and within two years he died of tuberculosis at Hartford, Conn., at the age of forty-five. Meanwhile, he had preached in various places and added to his numerous publications *Ten Letters Addressed to Mr. Paine; Being an Answer to His First Part of the Age of Reason* (1795) and *A Plain Political Catechism* (1796), the latter, an exposition of the evil effects of infidelity and the French influence, written, it is said, at the suggestion of Timothy Pickering. He compiled two hymnals and in 1773 he published *A New Book of Poems on Several Occasions*. Intellectually he was probably the ablest of the early American Universalists; he introduced Scriptural interpretation among them; and his influence both in America and England was extensive.

[F. W. Hotchkiss, *Winchester Notes* (1912); William Vidler, *A Sketch of the Life of Elhanan Winchester* (London, 1797); E. M. Stone, *Biog. of Rev. Elhanan Winchester* (1836); J. E. Hoar, "Elhanan Winchester, Preacher and Traveler," in *Pubs. of the Brookline Hist. Soc.*, no. 2 (1903); Hosea Ballou, "Dogmatic and Religious Hist. of Universalism in America," in *Universalist Quart.*, Jan. 1849; Richard Eddy, *Universalism in America* (2 vols., 1886) and "Hist. of Universalism," in *A Hist. of the Unitarians and the Universalists in the U. S.* (1894), being Vol. X of the Am. Ch. Hist. Ser.; F. B. Dexter, *The Literary Diary of Ezra Stiles* (1901), II, 547, III, 389.]　H. E. S.

WINCHESTER, JAMES (Feb. 6, 1752–July 26, 1826), soldier, was born in Carroll County, Md., near the present Westminster, the third child of William Winchester, who came from England to Maryland about 1730, and of Lydia (Richards) Winchester, daughter of Edward Richards of Baltimore County, Md. James and his younger brother George were educated by tutors and in local schools; in 1776 they enlisted in the Maryland Battalion of the Flying Camp, for service in the Revolution, and both were promoted for bravery on the battlefield. At Staten Island, Aug. 22, 1777, James was wounded and taken prisoner, being held for a year before he was exchanged. He was captured again at Charleston, S. C., in 1780, but was soon released. James as captain and George as lieutenant fought through the southern campaign under General Greene, were present at Yorktown in 1781, and then returned to Maryland.

Together they moved in 1785 to Middle Tennessee (then the Mero District of North Carolina) and settled on a large tract of land. George held several local offices and ran a mill before he was shot and scalped by Indians near the town of Gallatin, July 9, 1794. James Winchester served in the North Carolina convention in 1788, and successively as captain, colonel, and brigadier-general of Mero District, becoming famous for his Indian campaigns. When Tennessee was admitted to statehood in 1796, he was elected state senator, and speaker of the Senate. In the years that followed he held numerous other local offices. Meanwhile, through farming, milling, and commercial transactions he grew wealthy, and built an imposing stone house on his plantation, "Cragfont." Probably in 1803 he married Susan Black, for in November of that year he had the state legislature legitimatize the four living children of their common-law union, which had begun in 1792 (*Acts of the Tennessee Legislature*, 1803, Act XXXVI, pp. 82–83). Fourteen children were born to them.

When war with England began in 1812, Winchester was appointed a brigadier-general in the United States Army, and placed in command of the Army of the Northwest, succeeding William Henry Harrison [q.v.], but after some dispute as to seniority, Harrison was commissioned major-general and given the complete command. In an effort to protect the frontier, Winchester moved with the left wing from Fort Wayne to Fort Defiance, defeated one body of British and Indians, and constructed Fort Winchester. Moving on to Frenchtown, on the River Raisin in southeastern Michigan, he defeated another British force, but on Jan. 22, 1813, was surprised by a force of some 2,000 men, and almost his entire army was killed or captured. Winchester himself was imprisoned in Canada for over a year. After exchange, he was placed in command of the Mobile District. Following the defeat of the British at New Orleans, their fleet stopped off Mobile Harbor and on Feb. 12, 1815, captured Fort Bowyer, but sailed away without attempting to take Mobile. When news of peace arrived, Winchester resigned and returned home.

In 1816 Robert B. McAfee [q.v.], in his *History of the Late War in the Western Country*, accused Winchester of gross negligence and military incapacity in the River Raisin campaign. Winchester unsuccessfully demanded an official inquiry, and wrote a defense of his conduct in which he attacked General Harrison for failing to send promised reinforcements (*Historical Details, Having Relation to the Campaign of the North-Western Army, under Generals Harrison and Winchester, during the Winter of 1812–13; together with Some Particulars Relating to the Surrender of Fort Bowyer*, 1818; unique copy in Hayes Memorial Library, Fremont, Ohio). The quarrel was bitter, but it seems that loose organization and impassable frontier roads, combined with negligence by both men, caused the defeat and massacre. In 1819 Winchester was appointed commissioner to run the Chickasaw

Boundary Line between Tennessee and Mississippi. It was his last official position. Through his remaining years he was active, intermittently, in business ventures and in the founding of Memphis, Tenn., but mainly he lived in ease until he died and was buried at "Cragfont." His son Marcus was first mayor of Memphis; his nephew, James (1772–1806), with whom the General has sometimes been confused, was a federal circuit court judge for the Maryland district.

[Sources include: J. H. DeWitt, "General James Winchester," *Tenn. Hist. Mag.*, June, Sept. 1915; Winchester Papers in Tenn. Hist. Soc. Lib., Nashville; F. W. Hotchkiss, *Winchester Notes* (1912). See also C. E. Slocum, "The Origin, Description, and Service of Fort Winchester," *Ohio Archaeol. and Hist. Quart.*, Jan. 1901; F. B. Heitman, *Hist. Reg. of Officers of the Continental Army* (1914); B. J. Lossing, *The Pictorial Field-Book of the War of 1812* (1868).]   E. W. P.

WINCHESTER, OLIVER FISHER (Nov. 30, 1810–Dec. 11, 1880), manufacturer, was born in Boston, Mass., the son of Samuel and Hannah (Bates) Winchester. He was a descendant in the fifth generation of John Winchester who was admitted freeman in Brookline in 1637. His boyhood was a difficult one, for the early death of his father threw Winchester on his own resources when he was very young, and by the time he was twenty years old he had worked on farms in various parts of New England, learned the carpenter's and joiner's trades, and clerked in stores. Between 1830 and 1837 he was employed in construction work in Baltimore, Md., and then opened a men's clothing store there, a feature of which was the manufacture and sale of shirts. In 1847 he sold this business to engage in the jobbing and importing business with John M. Davies in New York City. The partners also began the manufacture of shirts by a new method invented and patented by Winchester on Feb. 1, 1848, and were so successful that about 1850 they established a new factory in New Haven, Conn. Winchester took entire charge and in five years accumulated an appreciable fortune. Meanwhile, he had become a heavy stockholder in the Volcanic Repeating Arms Company of New Haven and through his stock purchases became by 1856 the principal owner. In 1857 he brought about its reorganization as the New Haven Arms Company, with himself as president. The company had inherited the repeating-rifle inventions of Jennings, Tyler Henry, and Horace Smith and D. B. Wesson, as well as the services of Henry as superintendent of the factory. For the first few years Winchester manufactured repeating rifles and pistols, and gave Henry every opportunity to experiment on the improvement of both products, as well as of ammunition. The result was that in 1860 he began the production of a new repeating rifle, using a new rim-fire copper cartridge, which came to be known as the Henry rifle. Although it was primarily a sporting gun, it was privately purchased and used considerably during the Civil War by entire companies and regiments of state troops. It was by far the best military rifle of the time but was not adopted by the federal government. In 1866 Winchester purchased the patent of Nelson King for loading the magazine through the gate in the frame. When this invention was incorporated in the Henry rifle, a new firearm, the Winchester rifle, came into existence. Winchester then reorganized the New Haven Arms Company as the Winchester Repeating Arms Company, and established a factory at Bridgeport, Conn. In 1870 he erected a permanent plant in New Haven. From its first appearance the Winchester rifle was very popular, and Winchester built up an extremely successful business, augmenting it through the purchase of the patents and property of the American Repeating Rifle Company in 1869 and of the Spencer Repeating Rifle Company in 1870. In 1876 he purchased the invention of Benjamin B. Hotchkiss [q.v.] of the bolt-action repeating rifle, and after making necessary improvements added this to the products of his company. Finally, in 1879, he purchased the mechanism invented by John M. Browning [q.v.], but the resulting Winchester single-shot rifle incorporating this invention was not produced until several years after Winchester's death.

Winchester served as councilman in New Haven in 1863, and the following year was presidential elector at large for Lincoln. In 1866 he was elected lieutenant governor of Connecticut on the ticket with Gov. Joseph R. Hawley. His philanthropies were many; in particular, he made generous gifts to Yale University. He married Jane Ellen Hope of Boston on Feb. 20, 1834, and at the time of his death in New Haven was survived by his widow and two children.

[*Biog. Encyc. of Conn. and R. I.* (1881); F. W. Hotchkiss, *Winchester Notes* (1912); C. W. Sawyer, *Firearms in Am. Hist.*, vol. III (1920); Patent Office records; obituary in *New Haven Evening Reg.*, Dec. 11, 1880.]   C. W. M.

WINCHEVSKY, MORRIS (Aug. 9, 1856–Mar. 18, 1932), poet, essayist, editor, was born in Yanovo, Lithuania, son of Sissel Novachovitch, his original name being Lippe Benzion Novachovitch. In later years he adopted the name Leopold Benedict in private life, but was always known to Yiddish readers as Morris Winchevsky. As a child he moved with his family to Kovno, where he received a thorough Hebrew education and also attended the Russian government school. In 1870 he went to Wilna ostensibly to prepare himself for entrance into the rabbinical seminary, but instead improved his secular education, acquiring also a good knowledge of German. At this period he was already composing poems in Russian and Hebrew. Instead of entering the seminary he accepted a position in a commercial firm in Kovno. Sent by his firm to the city of Oryol (Central Russia) in 1875, he became acquainted with the Russian radical and socialist literature of the time. When in 1877 his firm transferred him to Königsberg, Prussia, he began to take an active part in socialist propaganda, the Russian-Jewish student colony and the growth of the Socialist party there providing a fertile field. He founded a Hebrew monthly, *Asefath hakhamim,* as a supplement to M. L. Rodkinson's *Ha-kol* for the dissemination of views on social questions. His Hebrew writings were mostly signed even in later years under the pen-name Ben-Nez. Upon the promulgation by the Prussian government in 1879 of the *Sozialistengesetz* he was arrested and spent several months in prison. Expelled from Prussia, he went to Denmark but was again arrested in Copenhagen and released only if he would leave the country. After a brief period in Paris, he went to London.

Joining the Communist Workers' Educational Society in London which had been founded by Karl Marx and Friedrich Engels, Winchevsky began his propagandist work among the immigrant Jewish masses of the laboring classes, employing Yiddish, their mother-tongue, as his medium. Due recognition has been accorded him as the pioneer of the Yiddish socialist press and literature. In 1884 he founded the first Yiddish socialist periodical, *Der Polischer Yidel,* and was also the author of the first brochure on socialism in Yiddish, entitled *Yehi or* (1884). He was one of the founders and the chief contributor to the *Arbeiter-Freund.* In 1894 he emigrated to America to take over the editorship of *Emeth,* a weekly family paper devoted to literature and culture. With the founding of the Yiddish daily, *Forward,* in 1897, he became its most representative contributor. He was also associated with many other periodicals in the rapidly growing Yiddish socialist press in the United States, and was at one time editor of the Yiddish monthly, *Zukunft.*

He also occupies a high place in Yiddish literature as poet and writer. Although he frequently depicts Jewish life in his writings, it is characteristic of him that the Jew is but an accident of his theme. The language is Yiddish; everything else is universal. The freeing of society from the yoke of oppression is the burden of his songs.

His poems, heartfelt, touching, with a true lyric quality, present the dark and sordid aspects of the life of the laborer. His socialistic bias is pronounced, but the pictures he portrays are true to life, though somewhat cold in coloring. As a man of high culture, conversant with the literatures of Russia, France, Germany, England, and America, he followed closely all the rules of prosody and poetic composition. Many of his poems of labor and struggle have been sung and recited not only in England and America but later also in Soviet Russia, because of the deep love and sympathy they display for the worker and the exploited. When in 1924 he traveled throughout Russia as a guest of the Soviet government he was everywhere acclaimed, and a collection of his proletarian poems, *Kamps-Gesangen,* was published in Minsk in his honor. He was equally effective in his prose. He wrote dramas, fables, novels, and feuilletons. His Yiddish style is smooth, idiomatic, and carefully balanced. Particularly fascinating were his epigrams, his philosophical reflections, and the satirical sketches which he ascribes to the *Meshugener philosoph* (crazy philosopher). He also translated into Yiddish a number of works from European authors, including Ibsen, Korolenko, and Victor Hugo. A revised edition of his collected works in ten volumes was published in New York, 1927–28, under the editorship of Kalman Marmor.

[Leo Wiener, *The Hist. of Yiddish Lit.* (1899); *Evreyskaya Encyc.* (Russian); Zalman Reisen, *Lexicon fun der Yiddisher Literatur,* vol. I (Wilna, 1926); Salomon Wininger, *Grosse Jüdische National-Biographie,* vol. I (1925); Kalman Marmor, biog. in vol. I of Winchevsky's *Gesamlte Werk* (1927–28); obituary in *N. Y. Times,* Mar. 20, 1932.]   I. S.

WINDER, JOHN HENRY (Feb. 21, 1800–Feb. 8, 1865), Confederate soldier, the son of William H. Winder [*q.v.*] and his wife, Gertrude (Polk) Winder, was born in Rewston, Somerset County, Md. He was the grand-nephew of Levin Winder [*q.v.*], sometime governor of Maryland and a descendant of John Winder of Cumberland, England, who emigrated to America about 1665. He was graduated from the United States Military Academy at West Point in 1820, assigned to service with the artillery, and later served as instructor of tactics at the Academy while Jefferson Davis was a cadet. He resigned in 1823 for a period of four years but was then assigned to duty in Maine, Florida, and elsewhere, and was brevetted major and later lieutenant-colonel for his conduct in the Mexican War. On Nov. 22, 1860, he attained the regular rank of major of artillery but resigned on Apr. 27, 1861 because of Southern sympathies.

On July 8, John Beauchamp Jones [*q.v.*] wrote from Richmond, "there is a stout gray-haired old man here from Maryland applying to be made a general" (*Diary, post,* I, 59). He was appointed brigadier-general and made provost-marshal and commander of the Northern prisons in Richmond. In this thankless position he soon received severe criticism. During the next few months he was upbraided for issuing passports through the lines too freely, but the mistake here lay largely with Secretary of War Benjamin. He was repeatedly criticized for the conduct of Baltimore "rowdies" whom he employed as detectives and assistants. Among the distasteful tasks to which he was assigned were the returning of stragglers, absentees, and deserters to their commands, the guarding of prisoners and assisting with their exchange, and the maintenance of order among the unruly element in the war-swollen population of the Confederate capital. During April 1862 he fixed prices in Richmond and secured some little temporary relief. In April 1864 he was reported as being also in charge of the prison at Danville, Va., and a few months later, most of the enlisted men having been removed to Andersonville and many officers to Macon, he was put in command of all the prisons in Alabama and Georgia. On Nov. 21, 1864, he was appointed commissary-general of prisoners east of the Mississippi. Not long afterwards he died in Florence, S. C., of disease brought on by the fatigue and anxiety occasioned by his duties. Winder was twice married: first, in 1823, to Elizabeth, the daughter of Andrew Shepherd of Georgia; and second, to Mrs. Catherine A. (Cox) Eagle, the widow of Joseph Eagle, a planter on the Cape Fear River.

The extent of Winder's blame for the suffering and death in the Southern prisons is still in dispute. He was described by one escaped Northern prisoner as a "regular brute" (*War of the Rebellion: Official Records,* XXXV, pt. 2, p. 220), and was accused by a citizen of Greensboro, N. C., of venality and of insulting and profanely abusing private citizens brought before him (*Ibid.,* LI, pt. 2, pp. 815–16). On the other hand, instances were cited of his kindness to individual prisoners, and he made efforts to ameliorate conditions within the prisons, coming into conflict with the commissiary-general, Lucius B. Northrop [*q.v.*]. Winder was vigorously defended by Samuel Cooper, Jefferson Davis, and James A. Seddon [*qq.v.*]. Davis probably explained much when he wrote that Winder was "no respecter of persons" (Rowland, *post,* p. 495), Seddon, when he wrote that his "manners and mode of speech were perhaps naturally some-

what abrupt and sharp," that "his military bearing may have added more of sternness and imperiousness" (*Ibid.,* p. 475). His task was rendered impossible by the refusal of the Northern government to continue exchanges, by the inadequacy of men, clothing, food, and medicines.

[Information from the Newberry Library, Chicago, Ill.; R. W. Johnson, *Winders of America* (privately printed, 1902); W. H. Polk, *Polk Family and Kinsmen* (1912); J. T. Scharf, *The Chronicles of Baltimore* (1874); G. W. Cullum, *Biog. Reg. . . . Officers and Grads. . . . U. S. Mil. Acad.* (1891); W. B. Hesseltine, *Civil War Prisons* (1930); *War of the Rebellion:Official Records* (*Army*), see index; *Report on Treatment of Prisoners,* 40 Cong., 1 Sess., 1868–69; J. B. Jones, *A Rebell War Clerk's Diary* (new ed., 1935, 2 vols.); *Photographic Hist. of the Civil War* (1911), vol. VII; Dunbar Rowland, *Jefferson Davis Constitutionalist* (1923), vol. VII.]

R. D. M.

WINDER, LEVIN (Sept. 4, 1757–July 1, 1819), soldier and governor of Maryland, was a great-grandson of John Winder, who emigrated from Cumberland, England, to Virginia in or before the year 1665, soon removed to the Eastern Shore of Maryland, became an influential landholder, held minor civil offices in Somerset County, and rose to the military rank of lieutenant-colonel. His son John was married to Jean Dashiel. Their son William was married to Esther Gillis and Levin Winder was born to them in Somerset County. With limited educational equipment young Winder was preparing for the practice of law when the outbreak of the Revolutionary War interfered with his plans. The Maryland Convention made him, Jan. 2, 1776, a first lieutenant under Nathaniel Ramsay [*q.v.*]. Before the year was out he was a captain in the 4th Regiment of the Maryland line. He was promoted to the rank of major, Apr. 17, 1777, and to that of lieutenant-colonel, June 3, 1781. Retiring from the service, Nov. 15, 1783, he became engaged in agricultural pursuits near Princess Anne in his native county.

He returned to public life as a representative of Somerset County in the Maryland House of Delegates in November 1806, and served three successive terms of one year each. For the last term he was chosen speaker of the Federalist majority while the governor and the Senate were democratic. As a Federalist, he was opposed to the declaration of war against Great Britain in 1812, and when the violence of the democratic mob in Baltimore against the *Federal Republican and Commercial Gazette,* a vitriolic Federalist newspaper, published by Alexander Contee Hanson [*q.v.*] and Jacob Wagner, had reacted in favor of the Federalists, he was elected governor by the General Assembly, in November 1812, by a majority of fifty-two to twenty-nine. He was reëlected in 1813 and 1814. As an anti-war governor Winder was concerned chiefly with the protection of the shores of Chesapeake Bay from the enemy. The prizes taken by the fast sailing "clipper" ships of Baltimore, serving as privateers, caused that city to be a particular object for attack. The federal government was more disposed to use its scant resources for the protection of Virginia and other Democratic states than for that of Federalist Maryland. On the approach of a British fleet in March 1813, Winder appealed to the secretary of war for aid. The response was evasive. The following month, while the enemy was plundering citizens of the state, he appealed directly to President Madison, but the response was no more favorable. Convinced that the state must rely almost wholly on its own resources, he called a special session of the General Assembly in May, laid before it his correspondence with the federal authorities, and asked for such action as the exigencies of the situation demanded. The Assembly responded with an appropriation of one hundred thousand dollars for the payment of militia, an appropriation of $180,000 for the purchase of arms, ordnance, and military stores, and a resolution authorizing a loan of $450,000. With these resources Winder rallied the patriotic fervor of the citizens of Baltimore and so directed military operations that the attacks of the British at North Point and Fort McHenry were frustrated. Until the close of the war only small losses of life and property were sustained elsewhere in the state. The year following the expiration of his third term as governor, he was elected to a seat in the state Senate. He served until his death in Baltimore, leaving a widow, formerly Mary Sloss, and three children.

[R. W. Johnson, *Winders of America* (privately printed, 1902); *Archives of Md.*, vol. XVIII (1900); *Votes and Proc. of the Senate and House of Delegates of the State of Md.*, 1806–19; *Niles' Weekly Register*, July 11, Nov. 14, 1812; J. T. Scharf, *Hist. of Md.* (1879), vol. III; H. T. Powell, *Tercentenary Hist. of Md.* (1925), vol. IV; H. E. Buchholz, *Governors of Md.* (1908); *Baltimore Patriot and Mercantile Advertiser*, July 3, 1819.]   N. D. M.

WINDER, WILLIAM HENRY (Feb. 18, 1775–May 24, 1824), lawyer and soldier, was the son of John Winder of Somerset County, Md., and a descendant of another John Winder who settled in that county about 1665. He was educated in his native county and then studied law. In 1799 he was married to his cousin Gertrude, the daughter of William Polk of Somerset County. John Henry Winder [*q.v.*] was his son. In 1802 he moved to Baltimore where he built up an extensive law practice. In March 1812 he was appointed lieutenant-colonel of infantry, was promoted to the rank of colonel in July, served

on the northern frontier, was appointed brigadier-general, Mar. 12, 1813. In June he was captured at the Stony Creek affair and released on parole, so that he was not again available for field service for a year. In August 1814 he commanded at the battle of Bladensburg. Here the militia stood their ground while the British were crossing the river and all the casualties were at first on the British side; but when the enemy deployed and attacked, the Americans—except a small naval contingent under Joshua Barney [*q.v.*]—scattered over the countryside. The British spent the next day destroying the public buildings in Washington, and some private ones as well, and withdrew to the coast unmolested. Winder was discharged from the army on June 15, 1815, and resumed the practice of law in Baltimore, where he died nine years later. One of the most eminent lawyers of his time, universally respected in his own community, he came to be remembered only for his brief and disastrous military career.

As to the responsibility for the Bladensburg disgrace there has been endless dispute. Henry Adams (*post*) is scathing in his denunciation of Winder's incompetency. On the other hand, a court of inquiry presided over by Winfield Scott spoke favorably of him. Certainly the administration was grossly negligent in providing for the defense of the city, and the militia were nearly useless for fighting purposes; a British officer who fought against them (Gleig, *post*, p. 121), declared that "no troops could behave worse than they did." Nevertheless, some of them were active and enterprising young men, and although they could not have stood up and fought against the veteran British on the march, they could have made the march so laborious that perhaps the expedition would have been abandoned. All this would have been a lark for the militiamen, but Winder gave them no opportunity to enjoy it. Again, when battle was joined at Bladensburg, it seems that the troops were capable of a better fight if they had been properly handled. Thus, although Winder was not primarily at fault for the disaster, he must take some part of the blame.

[Henry Adams, *Hist. of the U. S.* (Scribners ed., 1921, vol. VIII); J. T. Scharf, *Chronicles of Baltimore*, (1874); J. S. Williams, *Hist. of the Invasion and Capture of Washington* (1857); G. R. Gleig, *A Narrative of the Campaigns of the British Army at Washington and New Orleans* (1818); Spectator (John Armstrong?), *An Enquiry Respecting the Capture of Washington* (1816); R. H. Winder, *Remarks* [on Spectator's pamphlet] (1816); *Report of the Committee Appointed ... to Inquire Into the Causes ... of the Invasion of the City of Washington* (1814); E. D. Ingraham, *Sketch of the Events which Preceded the Capture of Washington* (1849); *Niles' Weekly Register*, May 29, 1824; *Baltimore Patriot and Mercantile Advertiser*, May 25,

1824; collection of about 500 letters dealing with Winder's military career, Johns Hopkins University.] T. M. S.

WINDOM, WILLIAM (May 10, 1827–Jan. 29, 1891), representative and senator from Minnesota, secretary of the treasury, was the son of Hezekiah and Mercy (Spencer) Windom, Quaker offspring of pioneer settlers in Ohio. Born in Belmont County, in that state, he moved with his family in 1837 to Knox County, a still newer frontier. The boy made up his mind to become a lawyer, to the distress of his parents, who, however, aided him as he worked his way through Martinsburg Academy and then read law with Judge R. C. Hurd of Mount Vernon. There, admitted to the bar at the age of twenty-three, he began practice, entered politics, and was elected public prosecutor as a Whig.

After a few years he determined to try his fortune in Minnesota Territory, and in 1855 settled in Winona. Becoming a member of the firm of Sargent, Wilson & Windom, he practised law, dabbled in real estate, and was elected to Congress as a Republican, when the state was admitted in 1858. His service in the House lasted until 1869. He was a member of the Committee of Thirty-Three, a supporter and friend of Lincoln, and in the contest between Johnson and the Radicals, allied himself with the latter. For two terms he was chairman of the committee on Indian affairs; he headed a special committee to visit the Indian tribes in 1865 and also a committee to investigate the conduct of the Indian commissioner in 1867. After the Sioux outbreak he was one of the signers of the memorial urging the President to have all the captured Indians hanged. While generally fair in his attitude towards Indians, he always considered the Sioux beyond the pale.

Windom sought a senatorial position in 1865, but it was not until 1870 that he reached the Senate, being appointed to fill the vacancy caused by the death of D. S. Norton. In the following session the legislature elected another for the remaining weeks of Norton's term, but chose Windom for the full term from 1871 to 1877. He was reëlected in 1877, resigned in 1881 to become secretary of the treasury (Mar. 8–Nov. 14), and then, after Garfield's death, was again selected to complete his own term. His most notable service in the Senate was probably his chairmanship of the special committee on transportation routes to the seaboard, which submitted a two-volume report (*Senate Report, 307, 43* Cong., 1 Sess.) advocating competitive routes under governmental control, development of waterways, and the establishment of a bureau to collect and publish facts. Both in the House and in the Senate

he urged a liberal policy towards railroads, and he was a supporter of homestead legislation. A strong nationalist, he declared, Feb. 28, 1881, when the Panama canal project was being pushed by a French company, that "under no circumstances [should] a foreign government, or a company chartered by a foreign government, have control over an isthmian highway" (*Congressional Record, 46* Cong., 3 Sess., p. 2212). From 1876 to 1881 he was chairman of the committee on appropriations, and after 1881 chairman of the committee on foreign relations.

In the Republican National Convention of 1880 Windom's name was brought forward by the Minnesota delegation, which supported him faithfully until the stampede to Garfield. As Garfield's second choice for secretary of the treasury, opposed vigorously by James G. Blaine for the place, Windom obtained high commendation for his successful refunding of over $600,000,000 in bonds at a lower interest rate and without specific legal authorization. The secretaryship made no real break in his senatorial career and he confidently expected to be reëlected in 1883, but a combination of circumstances—notably his mistake in opposing the renomination of Mark Hill Dunnell for Congress, since he feared Dunnell had an eye on his own seat, dashed his hopes ("Benjamin Backnumber," in the *Daily News,* St. Paul, Jan. 23, 1921). His chagrin was such that after a year's vacation in Europe he took up his residence in the East and never returned to Minnesota.

For six years Windom was out of office, devoting himself to the law and his considerable holdings in real estate and railroad securities. In 1889 he was again called to the treasury department and held the secretaryship until his death, which occurred suddenly at Delmonico's, New York, after he had delivered an address to the New York Board of Trade and Transportation. His tenure was marked by no especially significant features, although an unstable economic situation, aggravated by monetary disturbance, made his position both important and delicate.

A high-tariff man and generally an advocate of sound money, although he was a believer in international bimetalism and had voted for the Bland-Allison Act of 1878, Windom stood out from the rank and file of his Western contemporaries and hence, for the most part, was looked upon as safe by conservative Eastern Republicans. No scandal ever attached to his name in a period when too many of his contemporaries had to defend reputations not altogether invulnerable (C. T. Murray in Philadelphia *Times,* reprinted in *Daily Pioneer Press,* June 2, 1880). On Aug. 20, 1856, Windom married Ellen Towne Hatch of Warwick, Mass., who survived him, with a son and two daughters.

[W. W. Folwell, *A Hist. of Minn.,* vols. II, III (1924–26); G. A. Wright, "William Windom, 1827–1890" (MS.), Univ. of Wis. thesis in Minn. Hist. Soc.; *Memorial Tributes to the Character and Public Services of William Windom, Together with His Last Address* (1891); C. E. Flandrau, *Encyc. of Biog. of Minn.* (1900); W. H. C. Folsom, *Fifty Years in the Northwest* (1888); T. C. Smith, *The Life and Letters of James Abram Garfield* (1925), vol. II; R. P. Herrick, *Windom the Man and the School* (1903); *Biog. Dir. Am. Cong.* (1928); *N. Y. Times,* Jan. 30, 1891; *Daily Pioneer Press* (St. Paul), Jan. 30–Feb. 1, 1891; *Washington Post,* Jan. 30–Feb. 3, 1891.]   L. B. S—e.

WINEBRENNER, JOHN (Mar. 25, 1797– Sept. 12, 1860), clergyman, founder of the General Eldership of the Churches of God in North America, was born on a farm near Walkersville, Frederick County, Md., the third son of Philip and Eve (Barrick) Winebrenner, and a grandson of Johann Christian Weinbrenner, who emigrated from the Rhenish Palatinate to Pennsylvania in 1753 and settled ultimately at Hagerstown, Md. From his mother he inherited a strain of Scottish blood, and in temper and appearance he was more Scotch than German. Although he dated his conversion from Easter Sunday, Apr. 6, 1817, his ambition, even in early boyhood, was set on the ministry. He attended an academy at Frederick; entered Dickinson College, at Carlisle, Pa., shortly before it closed its doors in 1816 for a few years; studied theology for three years in Philadelphia under Samuel Helffenstein, son of J. C. A. Helffenstein [*q.v.*]; and, having been elected pastor of the German Reformed congregation at Harrisburg, was ordained at Hagerstown on Sept. 28, 1820, by the General Synod of the German Reformed Church. His charge included four rural filials: Middletown, Schupps, and Wenrichs in Dauphin County, and Schneblys (Salem) in Cumberland.

His work began auspiciously, for he was a man of real ability, but within two years the extravagance of his revivalistic methods had split his congregations into irreconcilable factions. His conservative, better educated parishioners would not tolerate a minister who demanded total abstinence from them, fraternized with Methodists, held prayer meetings on four evenings of the week, and conducted a "protracted meeting" until four o'clock in the morning, but he won followers, and many of them, among the lowly. Excluded from his Harrisburg church, he preached in the market place or wherever he could gather a crowd. For several years he lived as an itinerant evangelist, conducting camp-meetings at various places in central and west-

ern Pennsylvania and in western Maryland. He preached with terrific effect; when he leaned out over the pulpit and shook his long forefinger at his hearers, the more impressionable among them would have fainting fits. In 1828 the German Reformed Synod dropped his name from its roster. On July 4, 1830, Winebrenner had himself rebaptized; the rite was performed in the Susquehanna River at Harrisburg by a young disciple, Jacob Erb. That summer he and his helpers organized themselves as the General Eldership of the Church of God. The sect grew and extended its activities into Ohio, Indiana, and the Middle West. In 1845 the general organization changed its name to that of the General Eldership of the Churches of God in North America. In 1926 it claimed 428 churches and 31,596 members.

Its founder was for thirty years its leader and theologian, but his leadership was often disputed, and even as a theologian he did not always have his own way. He disliked the idea of footwashing as an "ordinance," but many of his followers came from the foot-washing sects and, arguing from his own principles of Biblical exegesis, compelled him to accept it. His other teachings were a medley of primitive Methodist and Baptist doctrines. He continued to live in Harrisburg until his death and devoted most of his time to the general work of the sect. He edited and published two church papers, the *Gospel Publisher,* 1835–40, and the *Church Advocate,* 1846–57; compiled English and German hymn books; and issued several volumes of sermons and doctrinal disquisitions. For a time, in his efforts to support his family, he was proprietor of a drug store. He also sold thousands of Chinese mulberry trees to his followers on the theory that they would then grow rich by raising silkworms, but the scheme failed, and the resulting scandal died hard. Throughout his sphere of influence *Morus multicaulis* became a fighting word. He was married twice: on Oct. 10, 1822, to Charlotte M. Reutter of Harrisburg, who bore him several children and died in 1834; and on Nov. 2, 1837, to Mary Hamilton Mitchell of Harrisburg, who, with their four children, survived him for many years. He died at Harrisburg after an illness of two years. In 1868 the Churches of God raised a monument to his memory in the Harrisburg Cemetery.

[George Ross, *Biog. of Elder John Winebrenner* (1880); C. H. Forney, *Hist. of the Churches of God in the U. S. A.* (1914); article by Winebrenner in I. D. Rupp, *He Pasa Ekklesia: An Original Hist. of the Religious Denominations at Present Existing in the U. S* (1844); T. J. C. Williams and Folger McKinsey, *Hist. of Frederick County, Md.* (1910), II, 708–09, 1341–42; *Reg. of the Members of the Union Philosophical Soc. of Dickinson Coll.* (1850); *Verhandlungen der General*

Synode der Hochdeutschen Reformirten Kirche in den Vereinigten Staaten, 1820–28.]   G. H. G.

WINES, ENOCH COBB (Feb. 17, 1806–Dec. 10, 1879), prison reformer, educator, minister, was born in Hanover, N. J., the son of William Wines and his first wife, Eleanor Baldwin. The family shortly moved to a farm at Shoreham, Vt. There Enoch prepared himself for Middlebury College, from which he was graduated in 1827. He abandoned a brief experiment with a classical school in Washington, D. C., in 1829 to become schoolmaster of midshipmen on the United States frigate *Constellation,* an experience that provided material for his *Two Years and a Half in the Navy* (2 vols., 1832). On June 14, 1832, he was married to Emma Stansbury, who in time bore him seven sons. Purchasing the Edgehill Seminary at Princeton, N. J., in the same year, he conducted a boys' school on the pattern of the German gymnasia. Declining fortunes at the school led him in 1839 to try an instructorship at the People's College in Philadelphia, but within a few years he purchased another classical school in Burlington, N. J., which likewise failed to flourish. During this period he published several tracts and for a short time edited a monthly magazine, the *American Journal of Education,* agitating for the establishment of normal schools, and describing educational developments in Prussia and elsewhere. In the late forties he turned to the study of theology and produced a fat volume of *Commentaries on the Laws of the Ancient Hebrews* (1853), in which he attempted to demonstrate the Biblical origin of the essential principles of civil liberty and popular government. In 1849 he was licensed to preach by the Congregationalists and filled successive pulpits at Cornwall, Vt., East Hampton on Long Island, and Washington, Pa. During the six years of his last pastorate (1853–59) he likewise filled the chair of ancient languages at Washington College. A call to the presidency of the newly founded City University of St. Louis took him west in 1859, but the outbreak of the Civil War closed its doors in 1861.

Returning east, he accepted the secretaryship of the reviving Prison Association of New York and thus at the age of fifty-six entered upon his major life work. His energetic appeals to local churches and to the city and state authorities increased the revenues of the society from an average of $2,349 during its first thirteen years to $12,768 in 1863 and made possible a greatly expanded program. When his inspection of the state prisons revealed desperate overcrowding and other unsatisfactory results of a politically unstable administration, Wines proposed that the society undertake a comprehensive study of the problem in order to prepare a reasoned program for presentation at the forthcoming state constitutional convention. Accordingly in 1865, with Theodore William Dwight [*q.v.*], he visited all the prisons of the northern states and prepared a monumental *Report on the Prisons and Reformatories of the United States and Canada* (1867). In conclusion the authors recommended the creation of a nonpartisan board of commissioners whose terms should be staggered over a period of years in order to secure a permanent program of prison development. Although the state failed to adopt the necessary constitutional changes, this document and succeeding annual reports by Wines greatly stimulated a widespread movement towards prison reform and encouraged such experimenters as Zebulon Reed Brockway [*q.v.*] at Detroit. Simultaneously in 1866 Wines and Franklin Benjamin Sanborn [*q.v.*] gave wide publicity in America to the Irish-Crofton system of graded prisons and ticket-of-leave discharge, ideas which shortly germinated into the American systems of parole and indeterminate sentence and the young men's reformatories. Meanwhile Wines undertook to organize the agitation for reform by calling a national convention in 1870. The "Declaration of Principles" adopted by the Cincinnati Congress provided a sufficient program for prison reformers for the remainder of the century. Wines was chosen secretary of the National Prison Association which resulted from this first gathering and remained its guiding spirit until 1877, when it was temporarily disbanded.

Following one of his own recommendations approved at Cincinnati, he secured a joint resolution from Congress creating a special United States commissioner empowered to invite the countries of the world to an international congress on prison reform. When in 1871 he was appointed to the position he visited most of the countries of Europe, studying their prison methods and inviting their cooperation. Largely as a result of his efforts twenty-two nations were represented at the first International Penitentiary Congress at London in 1872, from which sprang an international and several national organizations. Wines was chosen honorary president of the second international congress when it convened at Stockholm in 1878. Already his labors, characterized by sentiment, optimism, and a rare ability for organization, had coupled his name with that of John Howard. Fortunately, before his death in the following year he had completed his final work, *The State of Prisons and of Child-Saving Institutions in the Civilized*

World (1880). He died in Cambridge, Mass. One of his sons was Frederick Howard Wines [*q.v.*].

[The chief sources are *Penal and Reformatory Institutions* (4 vols., 1910), pub. by the Russell Sage Foundation, and letters in MS. in the possession of William St. John Wines of Springfield, Ill. See also *Am. Jour. of Educ.*, Sept. 1860; *Cat. of the Officers and Students of Middlebury Coll.* (1917); Blake McKelvey, "A Hist. of Am. Prisons from 1865 to 1910," thesis in Harvard Univ. Lib.; obituary in *N. Y. Tribune*, Dec. 12, 1879.]

B. M—y.

WINES, FREDERICK HOWARD (Apr. 9, 1838–Jan. 31, 1912), social reformer, was born in Philadelphia, Pa., the son of Enoch Cobb Wines [*q.v.*] and Emma (Stansbury) Wines. He was a descendant of Barnabas Wines who emigrated from Wales and was a freeman in Watertown, Mass., in 1635. Graduating at the head of his class from Washington College (later Washington and Jefferson) in 1857, he entered Princeton Theological Seminary but was forced by an infection of the eyes to discontinue his studies. In 1860 in St. Louis, Mo., he secured a license to preach and an appointment from the American Sunday School Union to missionary labors, with his headquarters in the frontier town of Springfield, Mo. In 1862 he was commissioned hospital chaplain in charge of refugees at Springfield. In 1864 he returned to Princeton, where he was graduated from the theological school (1865). He was ordained by the presbytery of Sangamon on Oct. 29, 1865. He shortly received a call to the First Presbyterian Church of Springfield, Ill., where he remained until 1869. On Mar. 21, 1865, he was married to Mary Frances Hackney of Springfield, Mo., by whom he had eight children.

The organization of the Illinois state board of public charities in 1869 and the appointment of Wines as its secretary enrolled him in the work to which he was to devote the rest of his life. Among the early secretaries of such boards he enjoyed the longest term (1869–92, 1896–98) and was able to exert an influence on the early development of eleemosynary institutions that was rivalled only by that of Franklin Benjamin Sanborn, William Pryor Letchworth [*qq.v.*], and H. H. Hart of Minnesota. He attended most of the early meetings of the National Prison Association and eagerly cooperated in its revival in 1884, serving as secretary from 1887 to 1890. In 1878 he was the Illinois delegate to the International Penitentiary Congress at Stockholm and took advantage of the opportunity to visit charitable institutions in Europe, establishing connections that enabled him to serve as an importer of new ideas for the rest of his life. Thus from his observations in England he brought back the

germ of the plan for the Kankakee State Hospital, the first institution in America to apply the detached ward, or cottage system, to the housing of insane; he cited English experience when urging the elimination of chains and other physical restraints in the care of defectives, and in the early eighties he was among the first to urge the development in America of "pathological research" and hydrotherapy. He was one of the leading spirits in the move to separate administrators from theorists in the annual Social Science Congresses, establishing in 1878 the National Conference of Charities and Corrections, over whose deliberations he presided in 1883. In 1886 he began the *International Record of Charities and Correction,* a monthly which continued until it was absorbed (1888) into the *Charities Review.* During the administration of J. P. Altgeld [*q.v.*] he was relieved from responsibility in Illinois and found time to deliver numerous addresses, including a series on the history and philosophy of prison reform before the Lowell Institute of Boston. Later he expanded this material into his volume, *Punishment and Reformation* (1895), which remained for many years the most satisfactory treatment of the subject in English.

Wines early gave attention in his state reports to the statistical analysis of sociological data, and during the Tenth Census he was named special adviser in the preparation of the report on *The Defective, Dependent and Delinquent Classes of the Population of the United States* (1881). In 1897 he was appointed assistant director of the Twelfth Census and was given major responsibility for the preparation of the *Report on Crime, Pauperism and Benevolence in the United States* (2 vols., 1895–96). Having moved to Washington in 1898, he continued to make his home there and in Beaufort, N. C., until called back to Illinois to fill the post of statistician under the newly established board of control in 1909. There he started the *Institution Quarterly* and otherwise maintained his active services until the end. He died in Springfield, Ill.

[F. H. Wines, *The Descendants of John Stansbury of Leominster* (1895); E. W. Willcox, *Geneal. Outline of the Wines Family* (1908); *Who's Who in America,* 1910–11; *Biog. and Hist. Cat. of Washington and Jefferson Coll.* (1902); *Biog. Cat. of the Princeton Theological Seminary* (1933); A. S. Bowen, in *Institution Quart.,* Mar. 31, 1912; H. H. Hart, *Ibid.,* Dec. 31, 1912; obituary in *Ill. State Reg.* (Springfield), Feb. 1, 1912.]

B. M—y.

WING, JOSEPH ELWYN (Sept. 14, 1861–Sept. 10, 1915), farmer, agricultural journalist, and lecturer, was the son of William Harrington and Jane (Bullard) Wing. He was a descendant of Daniel Wing who emigrated to Boston in

1632. In 1637 the family settled near Sandwich on Cape Cod. Wing was born at Hinsdale, N. Y., and at the age of six went to Mechanicsburg, Champaign County, Ohio, where his father bought a small, infertile farm. He was educated in the district school, the village high school, and Elmira Academy in New York. Except for a year in northern Florida, he worked on his father's farm until March 1886, when he went west. Not liking mining, his first work there, he became a cowboy on the Range Valley Ranch on the Green River in Utah, and had become foreman and part owner before he returned to Ohio in 1889 to manage the home farm in cooperation with his two brothers. His plan for making Woodland Farm profitable included the raising of sheep and of alfalfa, a crop then little known east of the Mississippi. Both sheep and alfalfa proved successful, and "Joe" Wing, or "Alfalfa Joe," as he was often called, began to advocate the improvement of farm lands by the use of lime and phosphates, and the growing of sweet clover, soy beans, and other legumes. He became the first strong propagandist for alfalfa in the central and eastern states, was largely responsible for its prominence there, and came to be recognized as an authority on the type of soil suitable for its culture, and on methods of seeding and handling the crop. His *Alfalfa Farming in America* (1909) became the standard work on the subject.

He lectured widely on subjects connected with farming at institutes and colleges, and soon after returning to the home farm began to write for agricultural papers, including the *Country Gentleman* and the *Ohio Cultivator*. In 1896 he was invited by Alvin H. Sanders to write for the *Breeder's Gazette*. Two years later he joined the *Gazette* as staff correspondent and became a national figure in agricultural journalism. Taking advantage of Wing's love of the road, Sanders sent him throughout the United States and over much of Europe to secure material for his articles. In time he became a very proficient photographer and furnished his own excellent illustrations. During the Taft administration he was sent to South America and Europe by the tariff commission to study methods and costs of wool production. His books include *Sheep Farming in America* (1905), *Meadows and Pastures* (1911), and *In Foreign Fields* (1913). While successfully practical, he was at the same time a dreamer, something of a poet at heart, and a lover of natural beauty. He was a member of the Protestant Episcopal Church. On Sept. 19, 1890, he was married to Florence Staley, by whom he had three sons. He died in his fifty-fourth year at Marion, Ohio, after a lingering illness of pellagra.

[W. E. Ogilvie, *Pioneer Agricultural Journalists* (1927); L. S. Ivins, and A. E. Winship, *Fifty Famous Farmers* (1924); *Owl* (Wing geneal. mag.), Sept. 1902, Sept. 1907, June 1908, Sept. 1909, Mar. 1913, and Dec. 1915; A. H. Sanders, *Live Stock Markets*, Aug. 24, 1933, and in conversation; *Breeder's Gazette*, Sept. 23, 1915; obituary in *Ohio State Jour.* (Columbus), Sept. 11, 1915; correspondence with Mrs. Wing and Andrew S. Wing.]   R. H. A.

WINGATE, PAINE (May 14, 1739–Mar. 7, 1838), Congregational clergyman, legislator, and jurist, was born at Amesbury, Mass. He was the sixth of the twelve children of the Rev. Paine and Mary (Balch) Wingate, and a descendant of John Wingate, who came to America as early as 1658 and settled at Dover, N. H. The elder Paine Wingate was graduated at Harvard in 1723 and spent a long life as pastor at Amesbury. His son was graduated at Harvard in 1759, studied theology, and on Dec. 14, 1763, was ordained pastor of the Congregational Church at Hampton Falls, N. H. On May 23, 1765, he married Eunice Pickering of Salem, Mass., a sister of Timothy Pickering [*q.v.*]. Their married life of more than seventy years, and the great age attained by both, Mrs. Wingate passing the century mark, have often been cited as examples of family longevity.

The Hampton Falls congregation was a contentious body and after a series of disagreements with it involving matters of church policy and theology, Wingate in 1771 offered his resignation, which was to take effect in 1776; he did not, however, perform ministerial duties to any considerable extent during the intervening years. In 1776 he moved to Stratham, N. H., and took possession of a farm purchased some years before. Here he maintained a residence for the rest of his life. His correspondence with his brother-in-law, Timothy Pickering, shows that he shared the latter's interest in agricultural improvements and was able to make a comfortable living from his farm. He was not in sympathy with the radical party in the early years of the Revolution. Nevertheless, his frequently expressed desire for reconciliation, his moderate attitude at the provincial congresses, and his refusal to sign the "Association Test" of 1776, while producing charges of "lukewarmness" and "Toryism," do not appear to have destroyed public confidence in his essential integrity and patriotism. In 1781 he was a delegate to the state constitutional convention. Two years later he served in the state legislature and in 1787 was elected to the last Congress under the Confederation. He supported the proposed Constitution and after its ratification was chosen senator from

New Hampshire, drawing a four-year term in the subsequent allotment. On conclusion of this service he was elected for a single term to the federal House (Mar. 4, 1793–Mar. 3, 1795). He was active in committee work rather than in debate, but his correspondence throws considerable light on the processes of inaugurating the new government, and on the personalities and issues involved. For the most part he supported Federalist principles, but probably reflected the dominant sentiment of New Hampshire when he opposed Hamilton's funding scheme. In later years he acquired a profound distrust for "French principles" which would have qualified him for membership in the Essex Junto, but with the Federalist tide running strong in 1794 he was defeated, apparently as less dependable than party needs required.

He served another term (1795) in the state legislature, and in 1798 became judge of the superior court, retiring on reaching the age of seventy in 1809. The courts had not yet experienced the salutary influence of Jeremiah Smith [q.v.] and other jurists learned in the law, and according to William Plumer (post), who practised before them, the judges were too often unacquainted with legal principles and inclined to decide individual cases on the basis of abstract ideas of justice. Wingate, he declares, was "predisposed to sacrifice law to equity," but his ideas of equity were uncertain. "Of the technicalities of the law, its form and modes of procedure and the principles of special pleading he was profoundly ignorant." He may be considered, however, to have performed important services on the bench in a formative period when popular confidence in the courts was an essential barrier to general confusion. After his retirement he spent his remaining years on his Stratham farm, where, as the "last survivor" of the many groups and activities with which he had been associated, he was often consulted by historians and antiquarians. He had five children—two sons and three daughters.

[C. E. L. Wingate, *Life and Letters of Paine Wingate* (2 vols., 1930) and *Paine Wingate's Letters to His Children* (copr. 1934); C. H. Bell, *The Bench and Bar of N. H.* (1894); William Plumer, in *N. H. State Papers*, vol. XXI (1892); *Biog. Dir. Am. Cong.* (1928); Warren Brown, *Hist. of the Town of Hampton Falls, N. H.* (1900); *Boston Daily Advertiser*, Mar. 12, 1838.]
W. A. R.

WINGFIELD, EDWARD MARIA (fl. 1586–1613), adventurer and first president of the Virginia colony, stemmed from a family long noted for distinguished public service. His grandfather was Sir Richard Wingfield, Lord Deputy of Calais and trusted ambassador of Henry VIII.

Thomas, Sir Richard's second son, was sponsored by Queen Mary and acquired consequently the name of Maria, which survived in the family for several generations. Following the death in 1546 of his first wife, Thomas married a member of the Kerrye or Kaye family of Yorkshire, and of this union Edward Maria, of Stoneley in Huntingdonshire, was the eldest son and heir. There seems to be no record of the exact date of his birth, but the known facts regarding his parentage prove that he was past middle age when he sailed for Virginia in 1606.

He was at that time an experienced soldier, having served with others of his family in Ireland and the Netherlands under Queen Elizabeth. As early as 1586 he sought in return for this service a grant of 3,000 acres in Limerick and 4,000 in Munster. He was one of the first to become interested in the establishment of the Virginia colony, and together with Sir Thomas Gates [q.v.], George Somers, and Richard Hakluyt headed the list of those to whom the Virginia charter was granted on Apr. 10, 1606. Alone of this group he sailed with the first settlers. On the night of their arrival within the Virginia capes, Apr. 26, 1607, the box containing their sealed orders was opened, and soon thereafter the council, of which Wingfield was a member, selected him as president.

The infant colony was from the first torn by faction and strife, and Wingfield was naturally the chief sufferer. Ere the summer was out supplies had run short and the little community was wracked by severe epidemics. The colonists, disillusioned, gnawed by fear, and seized with suspicion and hatred, filled the air with recriminations. Wingfield was removed from office on Sept. 10, 1607, and sent home the following spring after several months of imprisonment. He arrived May 21, 1608.

He drafted then a spirited defense of himself entitled "A Discourse of Virginia." While there is no question that he failed to rise to the emergency in Virginia, this document discloses, in conjunction with other contemporary accounts, the pettiness and contradictory nature of the charges brought against him. Most revealing of all were the repeated accusations of plans to desert the colonists, of favoritism in the distribution of supplies, and of having lived in great plenty and style while the settlers were dying of starvation. His task was well-nigh an impossible one, and others essaying the same rôle fared little better. Wingfield offered several suggestions for changes in the management of the colony's affairs, and probably exercised considerable influence in the reorganization which ac companied the granting of the second charter in 1609. In this instrument he was named as a grantee, and with an adventure of £88 he was one of the larger individual investors in the London Company. He is known to have been living at Stoneley in 1613, but his death probably occurred shortly thereafter.

Wingfield's "Discourse of Virginia," presenting an account of the colony from June 1607 to his departure and a rather able refutation of the charges against him, was discovered in the Lambeth Library by Rev. James Anderson and first published by Charles Deane in 1860 (*Transactions and Collections of the American Antiquarian Society,* vol. IV). Its chief influence, in addition to partially redeeming Wingfield's reputation, was to excite a prolonged and heated dispute regarding the trustworthiness of John Smith's accounts of early American history.

[J. A. Doyle, in *Dict. Nat. Biog.*; Alexander Brown, *The Genesis of the U. S.* (2 vols., 1890); Lord Powerscourt, *Muniments of the Ancient Saxon Family of Wingfield* (1894); Edward Arber, *Travels and Works of Captain John Smith* (2 vols., 1910); George Percy [q.v.], *Percy's Discourse of Virginia* (Am. Hist. Leaflets, no. 36, 1913), also pub. in Samuel Purchas, *Hakluytus Posthumus, or, Purchas His Pilgrimes,* vol. XVIII (1906); *Calendar of State Papers, Col. Ser., 1574–1660* (1860); Susan M. Kingsbury, *The Records of the Va. Company of London,* vol. III (1933).]
W. F. C.

WINKLER, EDWIN THEODORE (Nov. 13, 1823–Nov. 10, 1883), Baptist clergyman, editor, and writer, was born in Savannah, Ga., the second child of Shadrach and Jane Wetzer Winkler. He was prepared for college at Chatham Academy, and graduated from Brown University in the class of 1843. For the next two years he was a student in the Newton Theological Institution. He then returned South and for a brief period supplied the Baptist church in Columbus, Ga. In 1846 he was ordained and for a year edited the *Christian Index,* the Baptist paper of Georgia. From 1847 to 1849 he was pastor of the church in Albany, Ga., and from 1849 to 1852 of one in Gillisonville, S. C.

The separation of the Southern from the Northern Baptists in 1845 had led to the organization of the Southern Baptist Convention and the establishment of new missionary agencies. A group of leading ministers and laymen, feeling that the Southern Baptists should have their own publishing agency, formed and located in Charleston, S. C., the Southern Baptist Publishing Society, and in 1852 Winkler became its executive secretary, serving for two years, in the second of which he edited the *Southern Baptist.* In 1854 he became pastor of the First Baptist Church of Charleston. During the Civil War he served as chaplain in the Confederate army. Returning to

Charleston, he took charge of Citadel Square Baptist Church, and continued his connection with it until 1872. For the next two years he was pastor of the Baptist church in Marion, Ala., at the end of which time he became editor of the *Alabama Baptist;* in this position he served until his death.

For ten years he was president of the Home Missionary Board of the Southern Baptist Convention. Reared in the South and educated in the North, deeply interested in the moral and spiritual welfare of the negroes, he was diligent in promoting good feeling between the two sections of the country and between the white and colored races. He was often invited North to deliver addresses upon important occasions. In 1857 he prepared a catechism, *Notes and Questions for Oral Instruction of Colored People,* that was widely circulated and extensively used, and in 1871 he delivered a sermon before the American Baptist Home Mission Society, the missionary agency of Northern Baptists, upon the education of the colored ministry. As corresponding editor, he served upon the staff of Baptist papers, North and South. Twice he was invited to accept a professorship in the Southern Baptist Theological Seminary, but declined. His scholarly attainments are displayed in his *Commentary on the Epistle of James* (1888) in the American Commentary Series edited by Alvah Hovey [q.v.]. His other published works include *The Spirit of Missions* (1853); *The Sacred Lute* (1855), a collection of popular hymns; *Rome, Past, Present and Future* (1877). His writings are distinguished by scholarly accuracy and a clear and forcible style. He was married and had children.

[*Hist. Cat. Brown Univ.* (1905); William Cathcart, *The Baptist Encyc.* (1881); *Ala. Baptist,* 1874–83; B. F. Riley, *A Memorial Hist. of the Baptists of Ala.* (1923); *Daily Register* (Mobile), Nov. 11, 1883; *Standard* (Chicago), Nov. 22, 1883.]   R. W. W—r.

WINLOCK, JOSEPH (Feb. 6, 1826–June 11, 1875), astronomer and mathematician, was born in Shelby County, Ky., the son of Fielding and Nancy (Peyton) Winlock. He came of a notable Virginian family. His grandfather, Joseph Winlock, was an officer in the American Revolution who settled in Kentucky before it became a state and later served in the War of 1812, becoming a brigadier-general. Fielding Winlock was a lawyer who received a part of his training in the office of Henry Clay. He served with his father in the War of 1812 and later held various positions of honor. Joseph Winlock was graduated from Shelby College, Shelbyville, Ky., in 1845, and was immediately appointed professor of mathematics and astronomy in that institution. As a result of meeting Benjamin Peirce [q.v.] in May 1851 at the meeting of the American Association for the Advancement of Science in Cincinnati, he went to Cambridge, Mass., in 1852 to take part in the work of the office of the *American Ephemeris and Nautical Almanac*. Among the computers for the *Almanac* at the time were Simon Newcomb, Truman H. Safford, and Maria Mitchell [qq.v.]. In 1857 Winlock was called to Washington, D. C., as professor of mathematics in the United States Naval Observatory, but he soon resigned to return to Cambridge as superintendent of the *American Ephemeris*. In 1859 he was chosen head of the department of mathematics of the United States Naval Academy. During the Civil War, however, he returned to Cambridge a second time as superintendent of the *American Ephemeris*. In February 1866 he became the third director of the Harvard College observatory and Phillips Professor of Astronomy. Later he was given the additional title of professor of geodesy. He held these positions until his death, which came suddenly and unexpectedly at Cambridge in June 1875.

With a rare talent in mechanical construction and invention, Winlock directed his energies at the Harvard observatory both to the improvement of existing equipment and to the acquisition of new instruments. Before buying a new meridian circle, for which he raised the funds among the friends of the observatory, he spent four months in Europe, visiting the principal observatories and making himself familiar with the best instruments for obtaining accurate positions of stars. Although his interests lay especially in the astronomy of position, he championed also some of the earliest spectroscopic studies of stars, nebulae, comets, the aurora, and especially of the sun at the total eclipses of 1869 and 1870. During his administration, the time service was perfected which furnished accurate time to the people of Boston and its vicinity. He has been described as a man "of few words but of much thought, of no pretensions but of great performance," who revealed to those who worked with him "unusual disinterestedness, keen appreciation, and a delightfully serene nature" (Bailey, *post*, p. 242). On Dec. 10, 1856, he was married at Shelbyville, Ky., to Mary Isabella Lane of Palmyra, Mo. (d. Feb. 19, 1912). They had two sons and four daughters.

[Arthur Searle, "Hist. Account," in *Annals of the Astronomical Observatory of Harvard Coll.*, vol. VIII, pt. I (1876); D. W. Baker, *The Hist. of the Harvard Coll. Observatory* (1890); S. I. Bailey, *Hist. and Work of Harvard Observatory* (1931); *Proc. Am. Acad. of Arts and Sciences*, vol. XI (1876); obituary in *Boston Evening Transcript*, June 11, 1875.]   M. H.

WINN, RICHARD (1750–Dec. 19, 1818), Revolutionary soldier, congressman, although he was born in Fauquier County, Va., and died at Duck River, Tenn., is identified primarily with South Carolina, where he spent his best years and made his reputation. He was probably a younger son of Minor and Margaret (O'Conner) Winn of Fauquier; his father was doubtless the Minor Winn, who in 1774 obtained a grant for 800 acres on Wateree Creek, near the present town of Winnsboro, S. C. Richard, however, as a deputy surveyor, had purchased lands in that neighborhood as early as 1771. At the opening of the Revolution, he was commissioned, June 17, 1775, first lieutenant in the 3rd South Carolina Regiment, the regiment of rangers commanded by William Thomson [q.v.]; four months later he was commissioned a justice of the peace. In 1776, he took part in the battle of Fort Moultrie, and the following year, as captain in command, he made a spectacular defense of Fort McIntosh, Ga. He helped defend Charleston in 1780, and after the capitulation, having joined the guerrillas of Thomas Sumter [q.v.] as major, he was wounded at Hanging Rock. He also took a distinguished part in the skirmish at Fishdam Ford and in the battle of Blackstock. In 1782 he represented the district between Broad and Catawba in the Jacksonborough Assembly. Upon the resignation of Richard Henderson [q.v.] in 1783, he was made a brigadier-general, and in 1800 was promoted to be major-general of militia.

After the war, in 1783 he was named a commissioner to lay off Camden District into counties, and two years later he deeded 100 acres on the boundary of Winnsboro to the Mount Zion Society for the education of youth, an organization of which he had been a member since 1777. Elected to the South Carolina legislature, he was named in 1786 a commissioner to buy lands for the new state capital, Columbia, and later to sell lots therein. In 1788 he became superintendent of Indian affairs for the southern district and was associated with Andrew Pickens [q.v.]. As lieutenant-governor of the state, he served with John Drayton [q.v.] from 1800 to 1802. His longest public service, however, was in Congress. Elected as a Republican (Democrat) to the Third Congress, defeating Sumter, he was reëlected to the Fourth, and, upon the resignation of Sumter, he won a seat in the Seventh Congress, serving 1793–97 and 1803–13. In 1813 he removed to Duck River, Tenn., and became a planter, with mercantile interests in addition. He died five years later and was probably buried at Duck

River. By his wife, Priscilla McKinley, he had several children.

[D. W. and E. J. Winn, *Ancestors and Descendants of John Quarles Winn* . . . (1932) ; Joseph Johnson, *Traditions and Reminiscences Chiefly of the Am. Rev. in the South* (1851) ; Edward McCrady, *The Hist. of S. C. in the Revolution* (2 vols., 1901–02) ; F. B. Heitman, *Hist. Reg. of Officers of the Continental Army* (1914) ; J. L. M. Curry, "Richard Winn," *Southern Hist. Asso. Pubs.*, July 1898 ; *Biog. Dir. Am. Cong.* (1928), erroneous in certain particulars ; *The Papers of John Steele* (1924), ed. by H. M. Wagstaff ; *The State Records of N. C.* (1895–96), vol. XXI.]

A. K. G.

WINNEMUCCA, SARAH (*c.* 1844–Oct. 16, 1891), a woman of the Shoshonean tribe of Paviotsos, commonly called Paiutes, was born near Humboldt Lake, Nev. Her father was Winnemucca, a chief. She was named Tocmetone or Thocmetony, but it was by her father's name that she was generally known among the whites, even after her marriage, when she became Sarah Winnemucca Hopkins. Her grandfather, also Winnemucca, called by Frémont "Captain Truekee," was a devoted friend of the whites and is said to have served with the Pathfinder during the California campaign of 1846. Sarah, with her mother and other members of the band, was taken by him to California, probably about 1848, for several years, and in 1860 was again in the state, where for a short time she attended a convent school in San José. She learned to speak and write English readily and with a fair degree of correctness. In the frequent clashes between her people and the whites she essayed the rôle of peacemaker, though not always successfully. In 1868 she began to act as an interpreter on the reservation. In 1876 she taught an Indian school on the Malheur reservation in Oregon. She came to the attention of Gen. O. O. Howard during the ferment preceding the Bannock War of 1878, and, with a sister-in-law, served as his "guide, messenger and interpreter" till the close of the conflict, performing many acts of conspicuous daring. In the winter of 1879–80 with her father she went to Washington to intercede for her people, who had been arbitrarily removed to the Yakima reservation. In January 1880 she was appointed interpreter at the Malheur agency, and during a part of 1881 she taught an Indian school at Vancouver Barracks, Wash. Later in the year she went east and lectured in Boston and elsewhere. At some time before Jan. 9, 1882, she was married to Lieutenant Hopkins. In 1883 she published *Life Among the Piutes: Their Wrongs and Claims*, edited by Mary Tyler Peabody Mann [*q.v.*]. Its pointed charges of corruption in the Indian service created a storm, and she became the target for a great deal of personal abuse. With money obtained on her lecture tours and

from her writings a tract was bought near Lovelock, Nev., where she conducted a school for three years. On the death of her husband, probably about 1886, she abandoned the school and went to live with a sister at Monida, Mont., where she died.

"The Princess," as she was sometimes called, is said by Howard to have been "sweet and handsome" as well as "very quick and able" (*post*, p. 234). She conversed well, carefully selecting her language, but her writing seems to have required considerable emendation. She was shrewd, intelligent, and notably courageous. In habits and customs she conformed to the standards of white civilization.

[*Life, ante ; Handbook of Am. Indians*, pt. 2 (1910) ed. by F. W. Hodge ; O. O. Howard, *Famous Indian Chiefs I Have Known* (1908) ; *The Hist. of Nevada* (2 vols., 1913), ed. by S. P. Davis ; E. P. Peabody, *Sarah Winnemucca's Practical Solution of the Indian Problem* (1886).]

W. J. G.

WINSHIP, ALBERT EDWARD (Feb. 24, 1845–Feb. 17, 1933), editor, educational lecturer, teacher, clergyman, was born in West Bridgewater, Mass., the son of Isaac and Drusilla (Lothrop) Winship. He was a descendant of Lieut. Edward Winship who settled in Cambridge in 1637. Winship's first teacher was a young girl who taught a class of children in her mother's kitchen in his native village. Later he attended the East Greenwich Academy, East Greenwich, R. I. After a brief service with the 60th Massachusetts Volunteers in the Civil War, he taught a country school at Gorham, Me. (1864–65), served as principal of an elementary school in Newton, Mass. (1865–68), and was a student and instructor in the State Normal School at Bridgewater, Mass. (1868–71). He then established himself in the book business in Boston, just in time to be burned out by the Boston fire of Nov. 9, 1872. Although he had been married on Aug. 24, 1870, to Ella Rebecca Parker of Reading, Mass., and the first of their six children had been born, he now entered the Andover Theological Seminary (1872–75). As minister of the Prospect Hill Congregational Church, Somerville, Mass. (1876–83), he organized and taught evening classes for workers in the packing-house district, which were among the earliest community classes in adult education in America (G. F. James, *Handbook of University Extension*, 1893, pp. 241–44). During this period Winship also established himself as a popular lecturer and contributor to the press.

The national educational phase of Winship's work began with his appointment in 1883 as district secretary of the New West Education Commission, one of the national societies of the

Congregationalist denomination, which had established scores of schools in Utah, Idaho, Colorado, and New Mexico. Though his work had to do largely with finances, he also interested himself in educational progress. In March 1886 he resigned to assume the editorship of the *Journal of Education* (Boston). For the next forty-seven years he conducted the *Journal*, contributing editorials, articles, news-notes, book-reviews, and regular departments, at the same time carrying on the unceasing activity as educational lecturer throughout the United States that led to his being described as "the circuit rider of American education." For many years he also edited the *American Teacher*, which became in 1896 the *American Primary Teacher*. During the year 1891, in addition to his work on the *Journal of Education*, he served as editor-in-chief of the *Boston Traveller*. He found time as well to produce a number of books, among them *The Shop* (1889), *Horace Mann: the Educator* (1896), *Great American Educators* (1900), *Jukes-Edwards: a Study in Education and Heredity* (1900), *Danger Signals for Teachers* (1919), *Educational Preparedness* (1919), *Fifty Famous Farmers* (1924), written with L. S. Ivins, and *Educational History* (1929).

During all these years he was observing new movements and new personalities in education, catching their significance and spreading their educational gospel through the *Journal*. Thousands of struggling teachers got their first encouragement from him, and hundreds became state or national figures in education through his publicizing of their achievements, which otherwise might have gone unnoticed. He was the first to give national prominence to the work of Edward J. Tobin, of Cook County, Ill., in rural education, of Cora Wilson Stewart in combatting illiteracy, of Josephine Corliss Preston, and of many other educational pioneers. A man who never lost touch with the soil, he was enthusiastic about rural education, about the teaching of agriculture in rural schools, and about boys and girls who, as part of their school work, raised the biggest squashes or the plumpest chickens. Active in the life of Boston and New England, a New Englander in every fibre, he nevertheless was devoid of any trace of provincialism. He was a thorough believer in free, public, democratic education, and the growing influence of the great educational foundations caused him real concern (see "Standardization—Wise and Otherwise," *National Education Association, Journal of Proceedings*, 1915). He was a consistent advocate of the school as a community center, of the teaching of music and art in the schools, and of health work and physical education.

He received several honorary degrees, served as a member of the Massachusetts State Board of Education (1903–09), as president of the National Educational Press Association (1895) and the American Institute of Instruction (1896), and was a member of President Hoover's Advisory Commission on Illiteracy. The National Education Association, in whose upbuilding he had an important part, paid him repeated tributes, and in 1932 elected him honorary president for life. At the time of his death he had attended every convention but one of the Association since the beginning of his educational work. His portrait in oils, by Donna Wilson Crabtree, hangs in the Washington headquarters building of the Association.

[*Who's Who in America*, 1932–33; *Who's Who in Am. Educ.*, 1929–30; J. M. Cattell, *Leaders in Educ.* (1932); A. E. Winship, in *Jour. of Educ.*, Sept. 13, 1926; *Ibid.*, Jan. 3, 31, 1918; *Ninth Yearbook Educ. Press Asso. of America*, 1933; J. W. Crabtree, in *Nat. Educ. Asso. . . . Proc.* vol. LXXI (1933), and *What Counted Most* (1935); W. J. Cooper, in *School Life*, Mar. 1933; editorial in *N. Y. Times*, Feb. 18, 1933; obituary in *Boston Transcript*, Feb. 17, 1933; letters from Laurence L. Winship.]   H. G. D—e.

WINSLOW, CAMERON McRAE (July 29, 1854–Jan. 2, 1932), naval officer, was born in Washington, D. C., the son of Francis and Mary Sophia (Nelson) Winslow, and a descendant of John Winslow, who was a brother of Edward Winslow, 1595–1655 [*q.v.*]. He was also a descendant of Edward Winslow, 1669–1753 [*q.v.*]. His father, a naval commander, was a cousin of John A. Winslow [*q.v.*]. After attending school in Roxbury, Mass., his home after his father's death, he entered the United States Naval Academy on a presidential appointment, Sept. 20, 1870, and was graduated, June 21, 1875. His early service included duty in the *Tennessee* on the Asiatic and North Atlantic stations, in the coast survey, and in the *Kearsarge* of the European Squadron, 1885–87. He was made full lieutenant in 1888, and after two years at the torpedo station at Newport, R. I., he commanded the torpedo boat *Cushing*, 1890–93. During the Spanish-American War he was in the cruiser *Nashville*, and, May 11, 1898, commanded four ship's launches in a cable-cutting operation at Cienfuegos, Cuba. Sections were cut from two cables, despite a heavy rifle fire from the shore in which two men were killed and eleven wounded. Winslow, who received a wound in the hand, was commended by the executive officer of the *Nashville* for "excellent judgment and consummate coolness," and was advanced five numbers (reports of Winslow and others, appendix to *Report of the Chief of the Bureau of Navigation,* 1898, p. 195 ff.). In an article which he wrote for the *Century Magazine,* March 1899, Winslow somewhat piously ascribed his remarkable success in this highly dangerous undertaking to "the protection which God gives to those who fight in a righteous cause" (p. 717).

He served in 1899 on Rear Admiral W. T. Sampson's staff in the cruiser *New York,* and in 1900–01 in charge of the New York branch of the Hydrographic Office. He was then for a year flag lieutenant of Rear Admiral F. J. Higginson in the North Atlantic Squadron and in 1902–05 at the Bureau of Navigation and an aide to President Roosevelt. During the Russo-Japanese peace negotiations of 1905 he commanded the yacht *Mayflower* when the president received the peace commissioners on board, Aug. 5, at Oyster Bay, and was senior officer of the vessels which conveyed them thence to Portsmouth, N. H. After commanding the *Charleston* in 1905–07, and the battleship *New Hampshire* in 1908–09, and serving as naval supervisor of New York harbor, he was promoted to the rank of rear admiral, Sept. 14, 1911, and in 1911–13 he commanded successively the 2nd, 3rd, and 1st divisions of the Atlantic Fleet. Three months at the Naval War College, Newport, were followed by command of the Special Service Squadron, April–September 1914, during friction with Mexico. His flagship, the *New York,* was stationed with the main fleet at Vera Cruz. After a year at the War College he commanded the Pacific Fleet from September 1915 to July 1916. Though then of age for retirement, he was retained in active duty during the World War period, and served from September 1917 to October 1919 as inspector of naval districts on the Atlantic coast. After his final retirement he lived chiefly in Newport.

As indicated by his frequent selection for staff duty, he was of strong personality and outstanding ability, particularly in the field of navigation and ship handling. His death occurred in Boston, and his burial was in the Winslow family plot at Dunbarton, N. H. He was married, Sept. 18, 1899, to Theodora, daughter of Theodore Havemeyer, of Mahwah, N. J., and had three daughters and three sons, the eldest of whom became a naval officer.

[Information from family sources; *Who's Who in America,* 1930–31; Service Record, Bureau of Navigation, Navy Dept.; Arthur Winslow, *Francis Winslow, His Forebears and Life* (1935); E. S. Maclay, *A Hist. of the U. S. Navy* (new ed., 1901), vol. III; *Army and Navy Jour.,* Jan. 16, 1932; *N. Y. Times,* Jan. 3, 1932.]   A. W.

WINSLOW, EDWARD (Oct. 18, 1595–May 8, 1655), Pilgrim father, author, was born at Droitwich, Worcestershire, England, the son of Edward and Magdalene (Ollyver or Oliver) Winslow, people of some property and education. He himself received an excellent education (though not at a university) and had early social advantages enjoyed by none of the other Pilgrims. Apparently while traveling on the Continent in 1617 he came to know of John Robinson's Separatist congregation at Leyden and joined them, marrying Elizabeth Barker there on May 16, 1618. He earned his living as a printer, perhaps employed by William Brewster [*q.v.*], and despite his youth became an active member of the community. He sailed on the *Speedwell* in 1620, trans-shipping to the *Mayflower* when the former turned back. With him he took two servants, George Soule and Elias Story, and he purchased £60 stock in the venture. Three of his brothers later reached Plymouth.

Winslow aided in the first explorations and was one of the small band who landed at the site of Plymouth on Dec. 11/21, 1620. He was chosen envoy to greet Massasoit [*q.v.*] when that chief appeared at the settlement in the spring of 1621, and made the colonists' first treaty with the Indian. In July he was principal envoy to visit Massasoit at his home and in a later visit probably saved Massasoit's life. Next to Myles Standish Winslow was the Pilgrims' most important man in dealing with the Indians throughout his career in America. On May 12, 1621, his first wife having died in March, he married Susanna (Fuller) White, a widow—the first marriage at Plymouth. In 1622 he sent back to England by the *Fortune* four narratives of explorations and dealings with the Indians, and Gov. William Bradford [*q.v.*] sent a narrative of the voyage and the first year of the colony. The latter was retained by the captain of a French privateer which captured the *Fortune,* but Winslow's narratives reached London and were printed by George Morton [*q.v.*] in *A Relation or Iournall of the beginning and proceedings of the English Plantation setled at Plimoth in New England* (1622). They were thus the first accounts of these happenings to be published which had been written in America.

In the fall of 1623 he went to England, returning to Plymouth in March following, bringing "3. heifers and a bull, the first beginning of any catle of that kind in ye land" (Bradford, *post,* I, 353). Later in 1624 he became one of the five assistants, now appointed for the first time, and returned to England to negotiate with the merchants with whom the colonists had quarreled before sailing in 1620. Here he published a narrative of the years 1621–23, *Good News from New England or a True Relation of Things Very Remarkable at the Plantation of Plymouth in New England . . . Written by E. W.* (1624). This, with the narratives previously mentioned, completes the only contemporary record of the first years, for Bradford's *History* seems not to have been begun before 1630. While in London, in a dramatic scene before the Merchant Adventurers, Winslow defended the Pilgrims with such success from accusations sent back to England by John Oldham [*q.v.*] and John Lyford that he was able to establish better relations, to borrow money, and to purchase supplies. His arrival at Plymouth in 1625 at the moment when Oldham was being beaten out of the colony is one of the dramatic scenes in Pilgrim history.

Winslow was one of the "undertakers" who in 1627 assumed the colony's debts in return for its trading privileges and he became the most active of their explorers and traders, setting up posts in Maine, on Cape Ann, on Buzzard's Bay, and later on the Connecticut River. This trade was in large measure the secret of Plymouth's commercial success. In 1629 Winslow superseded Isaac Allerton [*q.v.*] as the colony's agent, and in its interest made several further trips to England. He was largely instrumental in securing a grant of land in 1630 from the Council for New England and defended the colonists before the Privy Council in 1633 against the charges of Christopher Gardiner [*q.v.*], Ferdinando Gorges, and others. While he was attempting a similar mission for the Massachusetts colony in 1634, however, Archbishop Laud accused him of "teaching" in the Pilgrim church and of celebrating marriages, though a layman. These charges Winslow admitted, and he was in consequence thrown into prison for four months.

Always active in the administrative and judicial work of the colony, he was assistant nearly every year from 1624 to 1646, was governor in 1633, 1636, and 1644; aided in organizing the New England Confederation, and was Plymouth's representative. He played an important part in reorganizing colonial and local government in 1636 and in drafting the new code of laws, and resisted valiantly the encroachments of Massachusetts, Rhode Island, and Connecticut upon Plymouth's trading posts. In 1646 he was induced by Winthrop, much against the wishes of the Pilgrims, to return to England to defend the Massachusetts Bay Company against the charges of Samuel Gorton [*q.v.*]. When the latter published a tract stating his case (*Simplicities Defence against Seven-Headed Policy*,

1646) Winslow replied with *Hypocrisie Unmasked by the True Relation of the Proceedings of the Governour and Company of the Massachusetts against Samuel Gorton . . .* (1646). To a tract written by John Child—*New-Englands Jonas* [Winslow?] *Cast up at London* (1647)— he retorted with *New Englands Salamander Discovered by an Irreligious and Scornfull Pamphlet* (1647). In 1649 he published *The Glorious Progress of the Gospel among the Indians in New England*, which led to the founding that year of the Society for the Propagation of the Gospel in New England, of which he was one of the incorporators.

These and other activities kept him occupied in England, and he never returned to Plymouth. In 1654 Cromwell appointed him chairman of a joint English and Dutch commission to assess damages for English vessels destroyed by the Dutch in neutral Denmark. At the end of that same year he was appointed chief of three commissioners, with Admirals Venables and Penn, to capture the Spanish West India colonies. Failing in this purpose, the fleet seized Jamaica, thus beginning the British possession of that island. On the return voyage Winslow died of fever, May 8, 1655, and was buried at sea with high honors. He was the first man to achieve success in England after receiving his training in affairs in America. He is the only Pilgrim of whom a portrait is known; his was painted in London in 1651.

[Winslow's own writings and William Bradford, *Hist. of Plymouth Plantation* (2 vols., 1912), ed. by W. C. Ford, are the chief authorities; Nathaniel Morton, *New-Englands Memoriall* (1669), was partly based on Winslow's papers, now lost; the best edition of Winslow's first narratives appears in *Mourt's Relation* (1865), ed. by H. M. Dexter; his *Good News from New England* is repr. in Alexander Young, *Chronicles of the Pilgrim Fathers* (1841), and with notes in Edward Arber, *The Story of the Pilgrim Fathers* (1897); *Hypocrisie Unmasked* was reprinted by the Club for Colonial Reprints, Providence, in 1916. Some letters of Winslow's are in Bradford's Letter Book, in *Mass. Hist. Soc. Colls.*, I ser. III (1794). See also R. G. Usher, *The Pilgrims and Their Hist.* (1918); J. A. Goodwin, *The Pilgrim Republic* (1888); D. P. and F. K. Holton, *Winslow Memorial* (2 vols., 1877–88); Thomas Birch, *A Coll. of the State Papers of John Thurloe* (1742), III, 249–52, 325; C. H. Firth and R. S. Rait, *Acts and Ordinances of the Interregnum* (3 vols., 1911); *Cal. of State Papers, Col. Ser., 1574–1600* (1860).]   R. G. U.

WINSLOW, EDWARD (Nov. 1, 1669–Dec. 1, 1753), silversmith, was born in Boston, Mass., the son of Edward and Elizabeth (Hutchinson) Winslow. His mother was the daughter of Capt. Edward Hutchinson, killed in King Philip's War, and the grand-daughter of Mistress Anne Hutchinson [*q.v.*]. On his paternal side he was the grandson of John Winslow of the *Fortune* and Mary Chilton of the *Mayflower* company, and the grandnephew of Gov. Edward Winslow [q.v.]. By marriage, also, he was allied with prominent families. His first wife was Hannah, the daughter of the Rev. Joshua Moody; the second was Elizabeth Pemberton; and the third was Susanna (Furman) Lyman. Winslow had a long record of public service in Boston. He was appointed constable in 1699, a tithing-man in 1703, a surveyor in 1705, overseer of the poor, 1711–12, and selectman in 1714. In 1714 he was also appointed captain of the artillery company. His death notice in the *Boston Evening Post,* Dec. 3, 1753, under events of Dec. 1, says: "about 9 o'clock, after a long Indisposition, died Edward Winslow, Esq., who had just entered the 85th year of his Age. This Gentleman had formerly, for many Years, been High Sheriff of the County of Suffolk, and Colonel of the Regiment of Militia in this Town; but by Reason of Age and Infirmities of Body, laid down those Posts, and has for several Years past, till his Death, been a Justice of the Peace and of the Quorum, and one of the Justices of the Inferior Court of Common Pleas for the County of Suffolk, and also Treasurer of the said County."

With all these public services he was yet able to produce a quantity of fine silverwork, which for historical as well as esthetic reasons is among the silver most valued by American collectors. There are some examples in the Metropolitan Museum, New York. There were other silversmiths in Winslow's family. His cousin, Samuel Vernon [q.v.], his sister's nephew, William Pollard, and his own nephew, William Moody, were members of his trade, and the last was one of his apprentices. That his business was lucrative is evidenced by the estate he left, which was valued at £1,083. His marks are described as "shaded Roman capitals, fleur de lis below, in a shaped shield, or shaded Roman capitals in a rectangle," or in double circles (French, *post,* p. 127).

[See Arthur Winslow, *Francis Winslow, His Forebears and His Life* (1935), from which the names of Winslow's wives are taken; *Report of the Record Commissioners of the City of Boston* (1908), p. 112, for date of birth; S. G. Drake, *Hist. and Antiquities of Boston* (1856); F. H. Bigelow, *Hist. Silver of the Colonies and Its Makers* (1917); C. L. Avery, *Early Am. Silver* (1930); Hollis French, *A List of Early Am. Silversmiths and Their Marks* (1917); E. A. Jones, *The Old Silver of Am. Churches* (1913); *Metropolitan Museum,* cat. of the Clearwater Coll.]   K. A. K.

WINSLOW, EDWARD FRANCIS (Sept. 28, 1837–Oct. 22, 1914), soldier, railroad builder, was born in Augusta, Me., the son of Stephen and Elizabeth (Bass) Winslow, and a descendant of Kenelm Winslow who came to Plymouth, Mass., from Droitwich, England, about 1629.

When Edward was about nineteen he left his native place and made his way to Mount Pleasant, Iowa, with the expectation of entering the banking business. Becoming interested in railroad construction, however, he associated himself with the builders of the St. Louis, Vandalia, & Terre Haute Railroad.

When the Civil War interrupted this enterprise, Winslow, in August 1861, recruited at Ottumwa, Iowa, Company F, 4th Iowa Cavalry, of which he became captain. The regiment was mustered into the service Nov. 3, 1861, and, after being equipped in St. Louis, was sent to join the Army of the Southwest, commanded by Gen. Samuel R. Curtis [q.v.]. Winslow's first engagement was at Little Rock. At Helena he acted as assistant provost marshal of the district of eastern Arkansas, and received his majority Jan. 3, 1863. In April his regiment was attached to General Sherman's XV Army Corps, and from then until after the investment of Vicksburg was the only cavalry regiment in Grant's army. On May 12, 1863, Winslow was wounded at Fourteen-mile Creek. He was appointed colonel, July 4, 1863, and given command of the cavalry forces of the XV Corps, with the rank of chief of cavalry. His command was always on the outer lines of the army at Vicksburg. In February 1864 it repulsed General Polk, advancing from Jackson, destroyed the Mobile & Ohio Railroad, and took the city of Jackson, Miss. In April 1864 Winslow was given command of a brigade, consisting of the 3rd and 4th Iowa and the 10th Missouri cavalry regiments, together with a battery of four guns. This brigade conducted itself with distinction at the battle of Brice's Cross Roads, June 10, 1864. Winslow was then given command of the Second Division of the Cavalry Corps of the district of West Tennessee. He took part in all the operations against General Price and was brevetted brigadier-general of volunteers, Dec. 12, 1864, for gallantry in action. His brigade took active part in the expedition against Selma, Montgomery, Columbus, and Macon in the spring of 1865, and alone took the city of Columbus by assault against a superior force. After hostilities ceased he was in command of the Atlanta military district. He was honorably discharged on Aug. 10, 1865.

Returning to civil life, Winslow resumed construction work on the St. Louis, Vandalia & Terre Haute Railroad, and built fifty miles of it. In 1870, with Gen. James H. Wilson [q.v.], he constructed the St. Louis & South-Eastern Railway. Under appointment from President Grant he served as expert inspector of the Union Pacific Railroad upon its completion and acceptance by the government. From July 1874 to March 1880 he was vice-president and general manager of the Burlington, Cedar Rapids, & Northern. He then became president of the New York, Ontario & Western and formed an association to build the West Shore Railroad. On Nov. 1, 1879, he became vice-president and general manager of the Manhattan Elevated Railway in New York City. Subsequently, he served as president of the St. Louis & San Francisco Railway Company, and vice-president of the Atlantic & Pacific Railroad Company. Under this double responsibility his health failed and he was compelled to retire. Later he made his home in Paris. On Sept. 24, 1860, he married Laura-Laseur Berry, daughter of Rev. Lucien Berry of Greensburg, Ind.; they had no children. Winslow died from heart disease at Canandaigua, N. Y.

[D. P. and F. K. Holton: *Winslow Memorial* (2 vols., 1877–88); J. H. Wilson, *Under the Old Flag* (1912); W. F. Scott; *The Story of a Cavalry Regiment* (1893); *Annals of Iowa*, Apr. 1915; F. B. Heitman, *Hist. Reg. and Dict. U. S. Army* (1903); *N. Y. Times*, Oct. 24, 1914.]   P. D. J.

WINSLOW, HUBBARD (Oct. 30, 1799– Aug. 13, 1864), Congregational clergyman, teacher, and writer, was born in Williston, Vt., the son of Nathaniel Winslow by his first wife, Joanna (Kellogg). His father had moved to Vermont from Salisbury, Conn., soon after the Revolution. All three of his sons entered the ministry, one of them being Miron [*q.v.*], a noted missionary. Their first American ancestor was Kenelm Winslow, a native of Droitwich, Worcestershire, England, who was admitted freeman of Plymouth on Jan. 1, 1632/3. Hubbard Winslow was brought up on his father's farm, became a school teacher when he was seventeen, and at the age of twenty went to Phillips Academy, Andover, Mass., to prepare for college. In 1821 he entered Middlebury College, but the next year transferred to Yale, where he was graduated in 1825. Up to this time he had been known as Asher H. Winslow, but he now discarded his first name. He began his theological studies in the Yale Divinity School, spent the year 1826–27 at Andover Theological Seminary, and, returning to Yale, completed his course there in 1828.

On Dec. 4 of that year he was ordained pastor of the First Congregational Church of Dover, N. H., in which capacity he served until 1832. In the meantime, he was married, May 21, 1829, to Susan Ward Cutler, daughter of Joseph and Phebe (Ward) Cutler of Boston. Called to succeed Lyman Beecher [*q.v.*] as pastor of the Bowdoin Street Church, Boston, in 1832, he became one of the popular preachers of that city, his

church being crowded on all occasions. A high-strung, nervous person, he was never in the best of health and in 1840 visited Europe for recuperation. Resigning his pastorate in 1844, he bought an estate on Beacon Hill and established the Mount Vernon School for Young Ladies, which he conducted until 1853. The next nine years of his life were taken up with travel, writing, and some teaching and pastoral work. He was in charge of the First Presbyterian Church, Geneva, N. Y., from 1857 to 1859, and of the Fiftieth Street Presbyterian Church of Brooklyn from 1859 to 1861, during which time he also taught in a school for young ladies in New York, conducted by his son-in-law. Broken in health, he retired to Williston, Vt., in 1861, where he died some three years later.

Winslow became widely known through his writings. He was a frequent contributor to periodicals and while in Boston edited, 1837–40, with Jacob Abbott and Nehemiah Adams [*qq.v.*], the *Religious Magazine*. He had a lucid style and the ability to make dry subjects interesting. Some of his publications had extensive circulation both in the United States and abroad. Two of his books, *The Young Man's Aid to Knowledge, Virtue, and Happiness* (1837) and *Are You a Christian?* (2nd edition, copr. 1839), were extraordinarily popular, many thousands of copies being printed. Two more substantial works which he prepared later, *Elements of Intellectual Philosophy* (1850) and *Elements of Moral Philosophy* (1858), also went through a number of editions. Among his other publications were *Discourses on the Nature, Evidence, and Moral Value of the Doctrine of the Trinity* (1834), *Christianity Applied to Our Civil and Social Relations* (1835), *The Appropriate Sphere of Woman* (1837), and *The Christian Doctrine* (1844). He had a daughter and three sons, one of whom was William Copley Winslow [*q.v.*].

[D. P. and F. K. Holton, *Winslow Memorial*, vol. II (1888); *Gen. Cat. Yale Divinity School* (1922); *Gen. Cat. of the Theological Sem., Andover, Mass., 1808–1908* (1908); *Boston Recorder*, Aug. 26, 1864.]
H. E. S.

WINSLOW, JOHN (May 10, 1703–Apr. 17, 1774), colonial soldier, was a great-grandson of Gov. Edward Winslow [*q.v.*] of the Plymouth colony, a grandson of Gov. Josiah Winslow [*q.v.*], and the second son of Isaac and Sarah (Wensley) Winslow. He was born in Marshfield, Mass. Both his brothers attained some fame: Capt. Josiah fell fighting Indians in Maine in 1724, and Edward died a Loyalist in Halifax. John got a poor education and could never write a literate letter without a scribe's aid. By his thirty-eighth year he had held a few local posts in Plymouth, including a captaincy of militia.

His military career began in 1740, when the Massachusetts council appointed him captain of a company in the West Indian expedition, led by Edward Vernon [q.v.], and he was subsequently taken into British pay with Gooch's American regiment. He served at Cartagena and in 1741, for he was an excellent recruiting officer, returned to Massachusetts for reinforcements. After Gooch's was reduced he was given, in 1744, a company in Handasyd's regiment, from which he immediately exchanged into Phillips's regiment in Nova Scotia. There he served without distinction until 1751, when he exchanged with George Scott, a half-pay captain in Shirley's reduced regiment, and returned home to look after his estates. For two years he represented Marshfield in the General Court. In 1754 Governor Shirley sent him, as major-general, to take a regiment of 800 men up the Kennebec River, with the double object of maintaining the Indian alliance and of building forts. Winslow had an interest of his own in the region, for the long dormant Plymouth colony patent there, in which he had connections, had lately been revived. He built Fort Western (now Augusta) as a trading-post for the proprietors, and Fort Halifax (named Winslow in 1771). His men penetrated far enough northwest to make the route seem feasible for some future attack on Quebec.

The next year Shirley appointed him lieutenant-colonel of one and commandant of both the New England battalions raised under British pay for the reduction of French forts on Chignecto Isthmus in conjunction with regulars. The whole force was under Robert Monckton [q.v.]. The vexed question of rank so embittered relations between the two that Monckton failed to give Winslow sufficient credit for his part in the capture of Forts Beauséjour and Gaspereau. When Gov. Charles Lawrence of Nova Scotia decided upon the expulsion of the French inhabitants, the brunt of carrying out the task fell upon Winslow's shoulders. In 1756 Shirley brought him back to command the provincial army raised in New England and New York for the reduction of Crown Point, but his best efforts and his most sentimental hopes could not fit that ungainly force for action before Aug. 22, and then Lord Loudoun [q.v.], commander-in-chief, refused to hazard its destruction. Winslow remained at Lake George throughout the autumn, cooperating wholeheartedly with the British troops. Except for a brief command of militia in 1757, it was his last military service. He never received adequate remuneration, and to the end of his life put in fruitless claims to the colonies and to Great Britain for pay or preferment. Nevertheless, after his death, his name remained on the half-pay lists, presumably for his widow's benefit, until 1787.

Winslow represented Marshfield again in the General Court in 1757–58, and 1761–65. He found a place on a few minor committees, but was instrumental in surveying and supervising the Kennebec River development and was a commissioner on the St. Croix boundary in 1762. By his first marriage, in 1725, to Mary Little, who died in 1744, daughter of Isaac Little of Pembroke, he had two sons, Pelham, fort major of Castle William and a Loyalist, and Isaac, who became a physician. After his marriage to Bethiah (Barker) Johnson of Hingham, he moved about 1766 to that town, where he died.

[See *Hist. of the Town of Hingham, Mass.* (1893), III, 331; M. W. Bryant, *Geneal. of Edward Winslow of the Mayflower . . .* (1915); E. F. Barker, *Barker Geneal.* (1927); *Records of the Town of Plymouth*, vol. II (1892); *Acts and Resolves . . . of the Province of the Mass. Bay* (17 vols., 1869–1910); *Me. Hist. Soc. Colls.*, 1 ser. IV (1856), VIII (1881), 2 ser. XII (1908), XIII (1909). Winslow's journal in Nova Scotia, belonging to the Mass. Hist. Soc., is printed in *Nova Scotia Hist. Soc. Colls.*, vols. III, IV (1883–85). His account of the Kennebec expedition is in *Military Affairs in North America, 1748–1765* (in press, 1936), ed. by S. M. Pargellis; his memorial for preferment to Pitt is in the Chatham Papers, 73, Pub. Record Office, London; see also Lorenzo Sabine, *Biog. Sketches of Loyalists of the Am. Rev.* (1864), II, 439–44; C. H. Lincoln, *Corres. of Wm. Shirley* (1912); and S. M. Pargellis, *Lord Loudoun in North America* (1933).]

S. M. P.

WINSLOW, JOHN ANCRUM (Nov. 19, 1811–Sept. 29, 1873), naval officer, was born at Wilmington, N. C. Though his mother, Sara E. (Ancrum) Berry Winslow, was related to the South Carolina Rhetts, his father, Edward, a descendant of John Winslow, brother of the colonial governor, was but recently from New England. At the age of fourteen the son was sent to Dorchester, and later to Dedham, Mass., for his preparatory education. His liking for the sea caused Daniel Webster to procure Winslow a midshipman's warrant before he had passed his sixteenth year.

In the junior grades his service was varied but typical. He had his share of shore duty between long cruises to distant stations, one on the Pacific, one to Brazil, and one to the Mediterranean. Prompt action in Boston harbor, Oct. 27, 1841, in connection with a fire in the hold of a Cunard steamer, brought him a sword-knot and a pair of epaulettes—the gift of Queen Victoria; he lost them however, when the *Missouri* burned at Gibraltar, Aug. 26, 1843. He also lost, Dec. 16, 1846, the schooner *Morris*, his first command, in a gale while blockading Tampico, Mexico. This event was more than counterbalanced by the reputation for gallantry he had acquired the previous October as commander of one wing of a landing party in the expedition against Tabasco. On Sept. 14, 1855, he was promoted to the rank of commander. Notwithstanding his successes, his marriage to his cousin, Catherine Amelia Winslow of Boston, Oct. 18, 1837, and the rapid development of an innate Episcopalian piety combined to generate in him a loathing of the sea and the sinful ways of those who followed it.

At the outbreak of the Civil War he was on shore duty at Boston. Having become a rabid abolitionist, he had for once the satisfaction of applying for and receiving service afloat from a stern sense of duty. He was invalided home, December 1861, from command of the riverboat *Benton,* when the link of a breaking tow chain slashed deep into his forearm. By June 1862 he was back on the Mississippi, but he had missed the joint offensive with Grant that had won Tennessee for the Union. An attack of malaria, the promotion over his head to flotilla commander of D. D. Porter [*q.v.*], a battle-tested officer, his extreme abolitionism, and the humiliating Federal reverses of that summer made Winslow vociferously critical of a war with the mere political objective of saving the Union. "Until the slaves are manumitted we shall do nothing, then we shall go onward to fight God's battles and relieve thousands of His praying Christians" (letter to his wife, Sept. 4, 1862, Ellicott, *post,* p. 88). Notwithstanding his promotion to captain by seniority in July 1862, Winslow soon found himself back in Massachusetts "awaiting orders." He was finally sent to the *Kearsarge,* a third-class man-of-war that ordinarily would not have rated a skipper of such high rank and service.

Through 1863–64 he patrolled from the Azores to the English Channel. So zealously did he pursue his duties that he permanently lost the sight of a long-inflamed eye because he would not put into port long enough for a specialist to treat it. Even so he missed the C.S.S. *Florida* at Brest. While watching the C.S.S. *Rappahannock,* at Calais, he received word that Raphael Semmes [*q.v.*], with whom he had shared a stateroom aboard the old *Raritan,* was at Cherbourg with his notorious *Alabama.* In hopes of restoring the sagging prestige of the South by a victory in European waters, Semmes offered battle on Sunday, June 19, 1864. It was characteristic of Winslow that he was holding a religious service for the men off duty when the lookout reported the *Alabama's* approach. Nominally the opposing sloops-of-war were equal, with the odds slightly against Winslow because all his officers, but one, were volunteers from the merchant marine. Actually the long-undocked *Alabama* was slower and her ammunition badly deteriorated by her long tropical cruises. Her destructive force was further minimized by spare chains that Winslow had draped (an arrangement Farragut had popularized with his wooden ships at New Orleans) abeam of the vital parts of his ship. Winslow's victory was complete and all the more glorious by virtue of its European setting. All the high ranking Confederates, it is true, escaped capture by being picked up by the English yacht *Deerhound,* but there is reason to believe that Winslow at the moment desired it so, for they would have certainly been unjustly tried for piracy. Semmes's subsequent vindictive statements to the British public concerning the battle, however, led Winslow to regret their freedom.

Amid wild acclaim in the United States, Winslow was promoted to commodore, effective the date of the battle. Until the end of the war the North used him at civic functions to stimulate the fervor of the public. Through 1866–67 he commanded the Gulf squadron. Promoted to rear admiral, Mar. 2, 1870, he took command of the Pacific fleet. Because of ill health he was ordered home to be retired, Nov. 19, 1872, but by a special act of Congress he was continued on the active list. He died at Boston Highlands, Mass., survived by his wife, two sons, and a daughter.

[D. P. and F. K. Holton, *Winslow Memorial,* vol. I (1877); *War of the Rebellion: Official Records (Navy)*; Personnel Records, Naval Records Office, Washington, D. C.; J. M. Ellicott, *The Life of John Ancrum Winslow* (1902); *Battles and Leaders of the Civil War* (4 vols., 1887–88); Raphael Semmes, *Service Afloat* (1869, 1903); W. M. Robinson, *The Alabama-Kearsarge Battle* (1924), reprinted from *Essex Institute Hist. Colls.,* vol. LX (1924); *A Record of the Dedication of the Statue of Rear Admiral John Ancrum Winslow, May 8, 1909* (1909); J. D. Hill, *Sea Dogs of the Sixties* (1935); *Army and Navy Jour.* Oct. 4, 1873; *Boston Transcript,* Sept. 30, 1873.]   J. D. H.

WINSLOW, JOHN BRADLEY (Oct. 4, 1851–July 13, 1920), jurist, was born at Nunda, Livingston County, N. Y., son of Horatio Gates Winslow, principal of Nunda Academy, and Emily (Bradley) Winslow. Both the father and mother were of Puritan stock. When John was two years old, ill health compelled his father to give up teaching and lead a more out-of-door life. As a consequence he removed first to the state of Ohio, where he remained for two years, then to Racine, Wis., where he purchased a bookstore business and a small tract of land. John attended the common schools and was graduated at Racine College in 1871. He became an instructor in Greek at that institution, subsequently studied in the law office of E. O. Hand, and in 1874 entered the law school of the University of Wisconsin, from which he received the degree of LL.B. in 1875.

He practised law in Racine successfully and in April 1883 was elected circuit judge of the first judicial circuit. On May 4, 1891, he was appointed a justice of the supreme court to succeed David Taylor, deceased. Although a member of the Democratic party, which was decidedly in the minority, he was elected a member of the supreme court against determined opposition from the opposing party. He was thereafter reëlected three times without opposition. In December 1907 he became chief justice by virtue of seniority. He was married, Jan. 19, 1881, to Agnes Clancy, and was survived at his death by his wife, two sons, and four daughters.

Winslow was six feet one inch in height and though of slight build had a commanding presence. He was a devout member of the Episcopal Church and for many years a lay reader. As a judge, both at the circuit and on the supreme bench, he proved an excellent administrator as well as a profound student of jurisprudence. His opinions as a member of the supreme court won him a national reputation and on more than one occasion he was seriously considered for appointment to the Supreme Court of the United States. He combined in an unusual degree analytical power with ability to express himself in clear, forceful language. His insight into the social implications of the functions discharged by the judicial department of the government was unusual. The spirit as well as the letter of the law was constantly before him. The character of his work is disclosed in such opinions as those rendered in *Nunnemacher* vs. *State* (129 *Wis.*, 190) and *Income Tax Cases* (148 *Wis.*, 456). His political philosophy regarding the importance of parties in a republican government is embodied in a dissenting opinion in *State ex rel. McGrael* vs. *Phelps* (144 *Wis.*, 1, at p. 51). His greatest opinion, *Borgnis* vs. *Falk Co.* (147 *Wis.*, 327), dealt with the constitutionality of the workmen's compensation law and laid the foundation for much of the so-called progressive legislation in Wisconsin and the nation. It has been cited many times and in practically every jurisdiction in the country. It not only embodies his social and legal ideals but from a literary standpoint is probably his most finished opinion.

Winslow won and held not only the confidence and respect of the people of his state but their affection as well. He made many public addresses and was often called upon to preside at important public meetings. He wrote numerous articles for law magazines and was the author of two well-known books—*The Story of a Great Court* (1912), a history of the supreme court of Wisconsin from 1848 to 1880, and *Winslow's Forms of Pleading and Practice Under the Code* (1906, 1915), partially annotated, which found a place in the leading law offices of all the code states.

["In Memoriam," 174 *Wis. Reports*, xxxiii; *The Wis. Blue Book*, 1919; *Proc. State Bar Asso. of Wis.*, vol. XIII (1921); *Jour. Am. Inst. of Criminal Law and Criminology*, Nov. 1920; *Jour. Am. Bar Asso.*, Sept. 1920; *Who's Who in America*, 1920–21; *Milwaukee Sentinel*, July 14, 1920; personal acquaintance.]

M. B. R.

WINSLOW, JOHN FLACK (Nov. 10, 1810–Mar. 10, 1892), industrialist, was born in Bennington, Vt., the fourth child of Richard and Mary Corning (Seymour) Winslow. His father had come to Vermont from Lyme, Conn., and was a descendant of Kenelm Winslow, who emigrated to America about 1629. When John was five years old his parents moved to Albany, N. Y., where the boy was educated at select schools until he was seventeen. He then entered a commercial house in Albany as a clerk, and after several years there secured a position in a commission house in New York, where he remained until he was twenty-one. For a year he was agent for his company in New Orleans, and in 1832 returned North and secured the management of the Boston agency of the New Jersey Iron Company.

In the two years that he held this position he is said to have worked diligently and mastered its details. At all events, late in 1833 he went into the iron industry on his own account and for four years engaged successfully in the production of pig iron in Bergen and Sussex counties, N. J. In 1837 Erastus Corning [*q.v.*], head of an extensive hardware enterprise in Albany, undertook to add to his business the production of iron. Winslow, upon invitation, joined Corning in this venture, and the ensuing partnership of Corning & Winslow continued under various firm names for upwards of thirty years. They controlled both the Albany and the Rensselaer iron works, which under their direction became the largest producers of railroad and other iron in the United States. Winslow made Troy, N. Y., his residence during this thirty years' period. In conducting the business he was most progressive and showed an almost uncanny sense of what would prove successful in his adoption of new processes. It was Corning and Winslow, for example, who delegated Alexander L. Holley [*q.v.*] in 1863 to purchase in England the American rights to the Bessemer steel process, and subsequently to design and build at Troy a Bessemer steel plant, which, put into operation in 1865, was the first plant of its kind in America. Again it was Winslow who, seeing the merits of John Ericsson's design of iron-clad war vessels, appeared in 1861, in company with John A. Griswold [q.v.] of Troy and C. S. Bushnell of New Haven, Conn., before President Lincoln and the naval board and secured a contract for the construction of one vessel. Winslow risked both reputation and money in manufacturing the machinery and iron plating for the vessel and in financing the whole undertaking, but the brilliant success of the *Monitor* in its engagement with the *Merrimac,* Mar. 9, 1862, fully vindicated his faith.

Throughout his residence in Troy he was much interested in local politics and in social and benevolent enterprises. From 1865 to 1868 he was president of Rensselaer Polytechnic Institute. In 1867 he retired from active business and removed from Troy to Poughkeepsie, where he resided until his death. He continued his interest in public affairs and in addition served as a director of several banks, as president of the Poughkeepsie & Eastern Railroad, and as president of the company constructing the bridge over the Hudson River. He was twice married: first, Sept. 12, 1832, to Nancy Beach Jackson of Rockaway, N. J.; second, Sept. 5, 1867, to Harriet Wickes of Poughkeepsie, by whom he had two children.

[D. P. and F. K. Holton, *Winslow Memorial* (2 vols., 1877–88); H. B. Nason, *Biog. Record, Officers and Grads. of the Rensselaer Polytechnic Inst.* (1887); F. B. Wheeler, *John F. Winslow, LL.D., and the "Monitor"* (1893); *Troy Daily Times,* Mar. 10, 1892; *Poughkeepsie Eagle,* Mar. 11, 1892.]   C. W. M.

WINSLOW, JOSIAH (*c.* 1629–Dec. 18, 1680), governor of Plymouth Colony from 1673 to 1680, was the first native-born governor in America. The son of Edward Winslow, 1595–1655 [q.v.], and Susanna (Fuller) White Winslow, he grew up in the homes of the Pilgrim leaders, who gave him an excellent education. His father soon moved from Plymouth, Josiah's birthplace, to Marshfield. Josiah studied at Harvard College, but left without taking a degree (J. L. Sibley, *Biographical Sketches of Graduates of Harvard University,* vol. I, 1873, p. 16). In Boston he met and courted Penelope Pelham, daughter of Herbert Pelham, treasurer of the college and assistant governor of Massachusetts Bay, and married her, probably in 1657; this was an unusual step, for the Pilgrims seldom married outside the Pilgrim church. In 1651 Josiah Winslow seems to have been in London with his father and to have had painted the portrait which

now hangs in Pilgrim Hall. His wife's portrait, also preserved, can hardly have been painted at the same time and it may be that hers is among the first portraits painted in America. Winslow's poem on the death of Governor William Bradford, printed in Morton's *Memoriall* (*post*) in 1669, is one of the earliest written in America.

Winslow soon became known as a military man and in 1652 commanded the militia at Marshfield. In 1657 he was chosen assistant, serving continuously until 1673; in 1658 he became Plymouth commissioner for the United Colonies, in which capacity he served until 1672; and in 1659 he was made commander-in-chief of the Colony, succeeding Myles Standish, whose office had been vacant since his death in 1656. He captured Alexander, son and successor of Massasoit [q.v.], in 1662, thus ending for years any danger from an Indian uprising. On Sept. 5, 1672, he was one of the six signers of the new Articles of Confederation of the New England Colonies, which he had probably helped to frame.

The following year he became governor of New Plymouth. One of his earliest measures was the establishment in 1674 of the first public school at Plymouth. When the Indian uprisings began in 1675, he signed the declaration of war and issued a famous statement denying any legitimate grievance to the Indians because the Pilgrims had honestly bought their land. He was immediately elected commander-in-chief of the forces of the United Colonies and so became the first native-born commander of an American army. Taking the field against the Narragansetts, he burned many villages and won a decisive battle on Dec. 19, 1675, though at the cost of many lives. The colonial losses were increased by exposure during the return march, undertaken in spite of advice from Capt. Benjamin Church [q.v.] that the troops be permitted to recuperate in the captured Narragansett stronghold. Illness compelled Winslow to retire from active command in February 1676, at which time he put Church, the real hero of the war, into control of the armies.

There is reason to believe that Josiah Winslow was more liberal and tolerant than the earlier Pilgrims. His statecraft was conspicuously shown by his handling of Edward Randolph [q.v.], the English investigator, who arrived at Plymouth in 1677 to search out the shortcomings of the colonists and departed well pleased, even promising to secure for the Pilgrims the charter from the Crown which their fathers had sought so long. Winslow was negotiating with the authorities in London to this end when he died. Reputed the greatest gentleman and most accomplished citizen of Plymouth, he kept a much greater state at his house, "Careswell," in Marshfield than was then common in New England, and succeeded, ably aided by his wife, whose charm, beauty, and social graces were widely admired, in establishing a new social life in the Old Colony.

[*Records of the Colony of New Plymouth* (12 vols., 1855–61), including the records of the Commissioners of the United Colonies; G. M. Bodge, *Soldiers in King Philip's War* (3rd ed., 1906); Nathaniel Morton, *New-England's Memoriall* (1669; 6th ed., 1855); M. A. Thomas, *Memorials of Marshfield* (1854); D. P. and F. K. Holton, *Winslow Memorial,* vol. I (1877); R. N. Toppan, *Edward Randolph,* vols. II–III (1898–99); *Cal. of State Papers, Col. Ser., America and West Indies, 1675–1676* (1893) and *1677–1680* (1896).]

R. G. U.

WINSLOW, MIRON (Dec. 11, 1789–Oct. 22, 1864), missionary, was born in Williston, Vt., the son of Nathaniel and Joanna (Kellogg) Winslow, a brother of Hubbard Winslow [*q.v.*], and a descendant of Kenelm Winslow who came to the Plymouth Colony about 1629. From the age of fourteen until he was twenty-one Miron served as clerk in a village store and then was in business for himself for two years in Norwich, Conn. In 1811 he united with the Congregational Church of Norwich, and began to consider the possibility of becoming a missionary. He had continued his studies while in business and was able to enter Middlebury College in 1813 with advanced standing. Graduating in 1815, he proceeded to Andover Theological Seminary in January of the following year, and in 1818 received the degree of B.D., and an honorary degree of A.M. from Yale. While engaged in his professional studies he traveled during vacations collecting funds for foreign missions, and wrote *A Sketch of Missions* (1819). In June 1818 he was licensed to preach by the Londonderry Presbytery, East Bradford, Mass., and on Nov. 4, in Salem, Mass., he and Pliny Fisk, Levi Spaulding [*q.v.*], and Henry Woodward, were ordained as missionaries. On Jan. 11, 1819, in Norwich, Conn., he married Harriet Wadsworth Lathrop, daughter of Charles Lathrop. Six children were born of this union.

On June 8, 1819, Winslow and his wife sailed from Boston for India with Spaulding, Woodward, and John Scudder [*q.v.*] and their wives, arriving at Calcutta on Oct. 19, and at Jaffna, Ceylon, Feb. 18, 1820. He was stationed at Oodooville, Ceylon, from July 1819 to 1833, working among the Tamils of that region as preacher, educator, and translator. In the latter year his wife died and he spent the next two years in America, writing during the time *A Memoir of Mrs. Harriet Wadsworth Winslow, Combining a Sketch of the Ceylon Mission* (1835). Returning to the East in 1835, accom-

panied by his second wife, whom he married Apr. 23, 1835, Catherine (Waterbury), widow of Ezekiel Carman, he arrived at Madras on Mar. 22, 1836, visited Madura, and continued on to Ceylon. Instructed to open in Madras a new station, especially for printing and publication, he removed thither in August 1836 and made this city his residence for the remainder of his life, visiting America again but once (1856–57). He was chosen by the Madras Bible Society to serve on its committee for revising the Tamil Bible, an undertaking upon which he was engaged for many years. At the same time he worked on the *Comprehensive Tamil and English Dictionary of High and Low Tamil,* which was published in 1862. This monumental work had been begun in 1833 by a Jaffna missionary of the Church Missionary Society and had been continued by Levi Spaulding (Tamil) and Samuel Hutchings (English-Tamil). The final comprehensive edition by Winslow, containing 67,450 words with definitions, was heralded as "a noble contribution to Oriental Literature" (*Missionary Herald,* May 1863, p. 132). Winslow's health was poor at times, and he had at last to withdraw from service, leaving India Aug. 29, 1864, bound for home. His journey, however, ended at Capetown, South Africa, where he died and was buried. His second wife died in 1837, and on Sept. 2, 1838, he married Anna Spiers, who died in 1843. On Mar. 12, 1845, he married Mrs. Mary W. (Billings) Dwight, who died Apr. 20, 1852, and on May 20, 1857, he married Ellen Augusta Reed. By his second wife he had one daughter, and by his third, three sons.

[Elias Loomis, *Memoirs of Am. Missionaries* (1833); *Missionary Herald,* May 1863, Feb., Mar. 1865; *The Encyc. of Missions* (2nd ed., 1904), which is in error as to date of death; *Cat. of Officers and Students of Middlebury Coll.* (1917); *Gen. Cat. of the Theological Sem., Andover, Mass.* (1909); D. P. and F. K. Holton, *Winslow Memorial* (2 vols., 1877–88).]

J. C. Ar—r.

WINSLOW, SIDNEY WILMOT (Sept. 20, 1854–June 18, 1917), manufacturer, capitalist, was born in Brewster, Mass., the son of Freeman and Lucy (Rogers) Winslow, and a descendant of Kenelm Winslow, who came to Plymouth, Mass., about 1629. The family moved to Salem, and there, after completing his education in the city high school, Sidney went to work in a small shoe factory that his father had established. About 1883 he and some associates started the Naumkeag Buffing Machine Company to manufacture machines for buffing leather used in the making of shoes. Soon they secured control of the Beverly Gas & Electric Company and consolidated it with other companies in adjacent towns. In these enterprises Winslow was the moving spirit.

The capital and credit that he derived from them he used in the development of machinery for the manufacture of shoes, and in 1899, with Gordon McKay [*q.v.*] and the Goodyear Company, formed the United Shoe Machinery Company, of which he became the president. It manufactured nearly all the shoe machinery used in the United States. Some of its machines were leased, and in the lease was a clause forbidding the lessor to use any other make of machine. Competition was thus rendered extremely difficult, and accordingly the United States government brought suit against the company in 1911, but the Supreme Court in repeated decisions up to 1918 declared in the company's favor. Congress then enacted legislation making it illegal to engage in interstate commerce if machinery was leased on condition that the lessor should not use machinery of a competitor, and in 1922 the Supreme Court ruled the so-called "tying clause" of the United States Shoe Machinery Company illegal.

Winslow was dead before this litigation was over, but it was his methods that were on trial. Whatever may be said against his methods of dealing with competition, he made valuable contributions to the development of American industry. The plant of the United Shoe Machinery Company in Beverly, Mass., became a model one, providing in manifold ways for the health, comfort, education, and security of its employees. Winslow recognized the rights of workers and furthered harmonious relations between them and their employers. He reduced the cost of manufacture by eliminating unnecessary management, and constantly added features making for efficiency, at the same time dispensing with others that caused delay or waste. His activities were not restricted to manufacturing, for he took a prominent part in the financial affairs of New England, and he was one of the principal owners of the *Boston Herald* and *Boston Traveller,* important morning and evening newspapers. By investing capital and participating in the management of numerous other business enterprises he became a conspicuous figure in the economic affairs of the nation. On Nov. 28, 1877, he married in Peabody, Mass., Georgiana Buxton, who died in 1908; four children survived him. He died in Beverly after a short illness.

[*Who's Who in America,* 1916–17; *Times* (Beverly), *Evening News* (Salem), *Boston Transcript,* and *Boston Herald,* June 19, 1917; S. A. Eliot, *Biog. Hist. of Mass.,* vol. X (1918); J. C. Welliver, "Sidney W. Winslow, Czar of Footwear," *Hampton's Mag.,* Sept. 1910; Thomas Dreier, *The Story of Three Partners* (n.d.),

pub. by the United Shoe Machinery Company; D. P. and F. K. Holton, *Winslow Memorial,* vol. I (1877).]
S. G.

WINSLOW, WILLIAM COPLEY (Jan. 13, 1840–Feb. 2, 1925), clergyman of the Protestant Episcopal Church, archaeologist, was born in Boston, the son of the Rev. Hubbard Winslow [*q.v.*], a Congregationalist clergyman, and Susan Ward (Cutler). After preparation at the Boston Latin School, he entered Hamilton College, Clinton, N. Y., and was graduated in 1862. His theological education he obtained at the General Seminary in New York between 1862 and 1865. On July 2 of the latter year he was ordained deacon and on May 3, 1867, priest, by Bishop Horatio Potter of New York. Shortly after his ordination he spent several months in Italy studying archaeology and ancient sculpture. Upon his return he assumed the rectorship of St. George's Church, Lee, Mass. This position, which was his only full rectorship, he filled from 1867 to 1870. From 1877 to 1882 he was chaplain of St. Luke's Home in Boston.

Winslow's literary work began while he was a student in college. In 1860 he was associated with two prominent students of Yale University in founding the *University Quarterly Review,* which was published for one year; while a senior he was co-editor of the *Hamiltonian.* After his graduation he was for a short time on the staff of the New York *World* and later (1864–65), with the Rev. Stephen H. Tyng [*q.v.*] of St. George's Church, New York, was associate editor of *Christian Times.* Winslow's deepest interest, however, was in archaeological research. In 1880 his studies led him to visit the monuments and sites of Egypt and when the discovery of Pithom (Exodus 1:11) was announced, he began a correspondence with Sir Erasmus Wilson and Amelia B. Edwards, noted English Egyptian scholars, which led to his founding the American Branch of the Egypt Exploration Fund. In 1883 he became honorary treasurer of this Fund for America; in 1885, its vice-president; and in 1889, honorary secretary. For probably a dozen years after he founded the American Branch he devoted nearly all his time to its interests and to making Egypt known to the American people. During the years 1886–89, as a result of Winslow's enthusiasm, the Boston Museum was enriched with a notable collection of Egyptian monuments, which included the statue of Rameses II, the gigantic column from Bubastis, the head of Hathor, the Hyksos sphinx, the statue of a son of Rameses II, the processional from Bubastis, and the palm-leaf column from Ahnas; besides these, among the precious relics obtained from

Abydos, was the sard and gold sceptre of King Khasekhemui of the second dynasty, oldest known sceptre in the world, which was placed in the Museum in 1902. Winslow raised a great amount of money for Egyptian exploration and also persuaded Amelia B. Edwards to make her brilliant American lecture tour.

Winslow was honorary fellow of the Royal Archaeological Institute, corresponding member of the British Archaeological Association, honorary correspondent of the Victoria Institute, honorary fellow of the Royal Society of Arts and Sciences, and fellow of the Antiquarians of Scotland. He was on the honorary rolls of numerous state historical societies and also on those of the Nova Scotia and Quebec societies, and the Montreal Society of Natural History. His last important recognition was an election as honorary fellow of the Society of Oriental Research at Chicago in 1917. He received doctorates from many universities both in America and in Europe. He married twice: first, June 20, 1867, Harriet Stillman Hayward, who died in September 1915; second, May 24, 1917, Elizabeth Bruce Roelofson, who died Jan. 12, 1923. One daughter by his first wife survived him. He died at his home on Beacon Street in Boston.

[D. P. and F. K. Holton, *Winslow Memorial* (2 vols., 1877–88); A. E. George, *William Copley Winslow, D.D., A Sketch of His Life and Labors in Archaeology* (1903); *Who's Who in America*, 1924–25; *Americana*, Oct. 1918; *Boston Transcript*, Feb. 2, 1925.]

A. W. H. E.

WINSOR, JUSTIN (Jan. 2, 1831–Oct. 22, 1897), historian, librarian, born in Boston, Mass., was a descendant of Samuel Winsor who was born in Duxbury, Mass., in 1725. Of five children of Nathaniel Winsor, Jr., a prosperous merchant, and Ann Thomas (Howland) Winsor, only Justin and one sister lived to maturity. After a short term at a boarding school in Sandwich, Justin was sent to the Boston Latin School where he prepared for Harvard College. His interest in history developed early; even as a boy he attended meetings of the New-England Historic Genealogical Society and began to collect material for his first book, *A History of the Town of Duxbury*, which was published in 1849 during his freshman year at Harvard. Greatly attracted by letters, he had visions of becoming a poet. He studied hard and read widely but cared little for his routine college work and finally abandoned it in his senior year without remaining to take his degree, which was given to him fifteen years later as of the class of 1853. In October 1852 he went to Europe and spent two years, mainly in Paris and Heidelberg, studying French and German. Subsequently he also mastered

Dutch, Spanish, Portuguese, and Italian. **Before** his return to Boston in 1854 he had determined to become a man of letters. On Dec. 18, 1855, he married Caroline T. Barker, taking her to his father's home in Blackstone Square where they lived for many years as part of a united family.

From 1854 to 1868 Winsor wrote steadily for periodicals, turning out a constant stream of criticism, poetry, comment, and fiction, although he produced no book. Late in 1866 he was appointed a trustee of the Boston Public Library and the next year he wrote a masterly report upon it. In 1868, when the superintendent had died and the assistant was dying, Winsor was asked to take charge temporarily, but he proved so able that after a few weeks he was urged to remain permanently, and continued as librarian for some nine years. His administration was notably successful, but occasional conflicts with the city authorities and an intense dislike of municipal politics made him glad to resign his position in September 1877 to become librarian at Harvard College in succession to John L. Sibley [*q.v.*]. Before assuming his new and very congenial duties, he went to London to attend the first International Conference of Librarians.

Winsor's most important service in his library posts was probably his work toward liberalizing the relations between libraries and their users. In spite of his intense interest in his own particular institutions and his bibliographical and historical activities, he found time for aiding greatly in promoting the library movement throughout the country. He was one of the founders of the *Library Journal* and of the American Library Association, of which body he was first president, 1876–85, and president again in 1897, elected especially to represent the Association at the international meeting in England.

It is likely that his contacts at Harvard greatly stimulated his interest in historical research. In 1880, the year he moved to Cambridge, he published *The Reader's Handbook of the American Revolution* (copr. 1879), which after a half century is still an indispensable bibliographical manual. In the same year he was asked to edit a history of Boston on a very large scale. In this undertaking he displayed not only his extraordinary learning but an exceptional executive ability. The plan of the work was mainly his own, but he had seventy contributing authors. Agreeing to finish the task in two years, he brought it to completion in twenty-three months —*The Memorial History of Boston* (4 vols., 1880–81)—characterized in 1897 by Professor Edward Channing (*post*, p. 198) as the best work of its class produced up to that time in any country. The success thus achieved led him to undertake a yet longer work, on somewhat similar lines, for the whole country. This was the *Narrative and Critical History of America* (8 vols., 1884–89). The work was made up of narrative chapters, largely by other contributors, and of critical bibliographical essays mainly by himself. The emphasis depended on the available cartographical and bibliographical material to be described and consequently, for the general reader, the work offers a disappointing lack of proportion, but for the scholar it remains one of the important compilations, especially of information concerning continental North America up to the ratification of the Constitution of the United States. The *Narrative and Critical History* was followed by four volumes from his own pen: *Christopher Columbus* (1891), *Cartier to Frontenac* (1894), *The Mississippi Basin* (1895), *The Westward Movement* (1897). In all of these works Winsor's interest in cartography played a promient part. Using maps at first merely as an aid to his historical studies, he rapidly became the leading cartographer in the United States, and through his study of maps solved a number of historical problems which had previously been insoluble. In addition to his books, he published an enormous number of articles and notes, besides official reports. He died at the age of sixty-six. His only child, a daughter, had died two years earlier, leaving him one grand-daughter.

[H. E. Scudder, in *Proc. Mass. Hist. Soc.*, 2 ser. XII (1899); Edward Channing, in *Am. Hist. Rev.*, Jan. 1898; W. C. Lane, in *Harvard Graduates' Mag.*, Dec. 1897; W. C. Lane and W. H. Tillinghast, in *Library Journal*, Jan. 1898; C. R. Markham, in *Geog. Jour.*, Jan. 1898; C. K. Bolton, in *New Eng. Hist. and Geneal. Reg.*, July 1898; *Report of the Harvard Class of 1853* (1913); *Boston Daily Advertiser*, Oct. 23, 1897.]
J. T. A.

WINSTON, JOHN ANTHONY (Sept. 4, 1812–Dec. 21, 1871), planter, governor of Alabama, Confederate soldier, was born in Madison County, in what is now Alabama, the son of William and Mary (Baker) Winston. His grandfather was said to be Anthony Winston who was born in Hanover County, Va., served as an officer in the Revolutionary Army, and removed to Madison County in 1810. The boy received such education as private schools afforded and spent some time in Cumberland College, now the University of Nashville, at Nashville, Tenn. In 1832 he married Mary Agnes Walker. In 1834 or 1835, he bought a large plantation in Sumter County, Ala., and became a planter. He followed this occupation successfully for ten years and then opened a cotton commission house in Mobile. He remained in this business until his death,

although he never surrendered his interest in planting and owned large plantations in Alabama, Mississippi, Arkansas, and Texas. After his first wife's death in 1842, he married a second wife, Mary W. Logwood, from whom he was divorced by act of the legislature in 1850.

He was a member of the state House of Representatives in 1840 and again in 1842. In 1843 he was elected to the state Senate and served until 1853, as president of that body for two terms, 1845 to 1849. He was a leader of the Southern-Rights Democrats in the state. He became governor of Alabama in 1853 and, reëlected, served until 1857, the first person born in the state to hold that office. He earned the title of the "veto governor" by vetoing some thirty bills passed by legislature, most of them to grant state aid to railroads, since he regarded this as a business for private capital. He saved the state of Alabama from the burden of debt with which other states were loaded during the period. He had a ready tongue and a keen sarcastic wit. He was an opponent dreaded in debate, and he often was able to drive colleagues into support of his position because they lacked courage to defend their own. He was not always consistent in his position. In 1848 at the Baltimore convention of the Democratic party he led his colleagues to indorse Cass and to accept the doctrine of popular sovereignty in defiance of instructions given the delegation at the time of its election. He broke with Yancey at this time, and much of his later political action seems to have been determined by his hostility to that leader. In 1860 he was a delegate to the Charleston convention. He now insisted that the delegation must obey its instructions and withdraw from the convention, when the platform adopted failed to give adequate protection to Southern rights. He took this position, although he himself did not approve of the instructions and although Yancey was willing to disregard them and reach some sort of a compromise with the Northern Democrats. Upon Winston, therefore, must rest responsibility for the disruption of the Democratic party in the Union and in the state of Alabama. During the campaign, he supported Douglas as the only candidate who could possibly save the Union; and he denounced the withdrawal of the Alabama delegation from the Charleston convention as a deliberate plot on the part of Yancey to wreck the Union.

At the election of Lincoln he threw himself with ardor into the building of the Confederacy. He served as Alabama commissioner to the state of Louisiana and was colonel of the 8th Alabama Infantry. He was a strict disciplinarian and not popular with his men. He served in the Penin sular campaign, but he resigned after that campaign. He was a delegate to the state constitutional convention of 1865, and he was elected to the United States Senate for the term 1867 to 1873, but he refused to take the oath of allegiance and was denied a seat.

[Willis Brewer, *Alabama* (1872); Wm. Garrett, *Reminiscences of Public Men in Ala.* (1872); *Trans. Ala. Hist. Soc.*, vol. IV (1904); J. W. DuBose, *The Life and Times of Wm. Lowndes Yancey* (1892); Richard Taylor, *Destruction and Reconstruction* (1879); D. L. Dumond, *The Secession Movement* (1931); *Mobile Daily Register*, Dec. 22, 1871.]   H. F.

WINSTON, JOSEPH (June 17, 1746–Apr. 21, 1815), Revolutionary soldier, public official, was born in Louisa County, Va., the son of Samuel Winston and a descendant of William Winston, who emigrated to America about the middle of the seventeenth century. Joseph was a cousin of Patrick Henry, his grandfather, James Winston, being a brother of the Virginia orator's grandfather, Isaac Winston (Valentine Records, Virginia State Library; Genealogy of the Winston Family, Virginia Historical Society). At seventeen, young Winston volunteered under Captain Philips as a ranger to fight the Indians. Captain Philips and Capt. George Moffitt united forces, but on Sept. 30, 1763, were ambushed and defeated between Fort Young and Fort Dinwiddie. Winston's horse was shot under him and he received two wounds. Concealing himself in the underbrush, while the Indians were off in pursuit of fugitives he escaped on a comrade's back and after three days, during which the two subsisted upon wild roseberries, managed to reach a place of safety.

About 1769 he moved to Surry County, N. C., where his career was an uninterrupted success. A devoted patriot, he was a member of the Hillsboro Convention, Aug. 20, 1775, which took steps to organize a provincial government. In February 1776 he went on an expedition against the Scotch Loyalists assembled at Cross Creek. Appointed major of militia, Sept. 9, 1775, he served under Rutherford against the Cherokees, July–September 1776, and also as the ranger of Surry County. The year following, he was a member of the House of Commons and a commissioner to treat with the Cherokees. In 1780 he marched under Col. W. L. Davidson [*q.v.*] in pursuit of Bryan's Loyalists, and participated in the skirmish on New River and at Alamance. At the battle of King's Mountain, Oct. 7, 1780, Winston commanded a portion of the right wing of the patriot army. The legislature of 1781 voted him "an elegant mounted sword" for defeating Major Ferguson (Walter Clark, *The State Records of North Carolina*, vol. XVII, 1899, p. 697). In

1800 he was a presidential elector, voting for Jefferson and Burr; twice he served in the North Carolina House and five times in the Senate; in 1793–95 and 1803–07 he was a member of Congress. From 1807 to 1813 he was a trustee of the University of North Carolina. On the formation of Stokes County he became a lieutenant-colonel. His home up in the Blue Ridge, "within a squirrel's jump of heaven," was the center of hospitality in his community. He was survived by three sons born at a single birth. An imposing statue was erected on the Guilford battle ground to mark his final resting place, his body having recently been reinterred there by the Guilford Battle Ground Association. Winston (now Winston-Salem), N. C., was named for him.

[L. C. Draper, *King's Mountain and Its Heroes* (1881); W. K. Boyd, "The Battle of King's Mountain," *The N. C. Booklet*, Apr. 1909; J. H. Wheeler, *Hist. Sketches of N. C.* (1851); David Schenck, *N. C. 1780–81* (1889); *Biog. Dir. Am. Cong.* (1928); letters and other material in Lib. of Univ. of N. C.] R. W. W—n.

WINTER, WILLIAM (July 15, 1836–June 30, 1917), dramatic critic and historian, poet, essayist, was born in Gloucester, Mass., son of Capt. Charles and Louisa (Wharf) Winter. His boyhood was chiefly spent in Boston, however, where he attended school. He was graduated from the Harvard Law School in 1857 and was admitted to the Suffolk bar, but he later recorded that he "declined his first case" and never practised this profession. His heart was set on a literary career. In 1854, when only eighteen, he had published a volume of poems (*Old Friends*, p. 133), and had secured sporadic employment as a reviewer on the *Boston Transcript*. That same year he reviewed a volume of poems by Thomas Bailey Aldrich [*q.v.*], and the two precocious youths thus became acquainted and remained close friends all their lives. About this time young Winter met Longfellow, who encouraged him in his literary ambitions, and set a strong stamp on his mind and style. For a brief time Winter took the stump around New England in the anti-slavery cause. In the winter of 1856–60 he left Boston to try his fortunes in New York. Of the conditions of "the 'Modern Athens'" of that time he wrote late in life, "I found them oppressive, and I was eager to make my escape from them" (*Old Friends*, p. 56). How they were oppressive he does not record, but at that time literature in Boston was chiefly produced by "the best families," and a young writer without social prestige may have lacked congenial society.

In New York Winter found precarious employment as assistant to the famous "Bohemian,"

Henry Clapp, Jr., in editing the *Saturday Press,* a satirical publication rather too pungent for popular success in those days. He also found congenial society among the "Bohemians," a group which met in the cellar of Pfaff's café on Broadway near Bleecker Street, and numbered, among others, Walt Whitman, T. B. Aldrich, Fitz-James O'Brien, and occasionally Artemus Ward [*qq.v.*]. For Whitman, Winter had little sympathy. He has described him with tart sarcasm in *Old Friends,* recording as well that Whitman characterized him as "a young Longfellow"—a phrase "that, doubtless, he intended as the perfection of contemptuous indifference" (*Ibid.,* p. 140). The group was, mostly, impecunious, but full of talent and high spirits, and Winter's later records of it are perhaps the most accurate that exist. Clapp's paper lasted but a year or two, and from 1861 to 1867 Winter served as dramatic and literary critic of the *Albion.* In 1865, however, he secured a much more solid position as dramatic critic of Horace Greeley's *Tribune.* He continued to hold this post for forty-four years, finally resigning in 1909. During the first twenty-five years he built up a nation-wide reputation both as dramatic reviewer and stage historian, at the same time writing much poetry and several books of essays. But from the nineties on, his reputation as critic declined; with modern realism, a new style of drama came to the stage with which Winter was out of sympathy, and the new generation of theatre-goers turned away from him.

Meanwhile he had begun a series of dramatic biographies, histories, and critical studies which had the merit, too rare in such books, of factual accuracy. In 1881 he published *The Jeffersons,* a study of four generations of the theatrical family, ending with his friend, the younger Joseph Jefferson [*q.v.*]. It was followed by books on two of his other intimate friends among actors, *Henry Irving* (1885) and *Life and Art of Edwin Booth* (1893), and by *Ada Rehan: a Study* (1891), and a series called *Shadows of the Stage* (3 vols., 1892–95). Early in the twentieth century appeared *Other Days* (1908), a book of theatrical reminiscences, *Old Friends* (1909), literary reminiscences, *The Life and Art of Richard Mansfield* (2 vols., 1910), and *Shakespeare on the Stage* (2 vols., 1911–15), an invaluable depository of the "traditional" interpretations employed by actors in Shakespearian rôles, a number of whom Winter had himself observed. His *The Wallet of Time* (2 vols., 1913), in part made up of his more recent reviews of contemporary plays, illustrates the kind of opposition realistic drama had to meet at his hands; his attacks on

Ibsen were particularly vitriolic. His final work, *The Life of David Belasco* (2 vols., 1918), was completed by his son and issued posthumously. Taken as a whole, these books are a mine of accurate information concerning the American stage and give vivid pictures of past performances.

Two of Winter's books which were widely read in the nineties were *Gray Days and Gold* (1891) and *Old Shrines and Ivy* (1892), essays chiefly about England and the homes and haunts of its great literary figures. The *Poems of William Winter,* a definitive edition, was issued in 1909, but he continued to write verse all his life, much of it of "occasional" or elegiac nature. In 1876 he read the poem, "The Voice of Silence," at the centennial gathering of the Army of the Potomac at Philadelphia; he read a poem in Boston at the dinner given for Oliver Wendell Holmes on his seventieth birthday; and he mourned the passing of player after player in appropriate stanzas, so that he was sometimes jocularly referred to by his colleagues as "weeping Willie." He was also, in his middle years, often called on as a speaker. His address, *The Press and the Stage,* delivered in New York, Jan. 28, 1889, in reply to attacks on newspaper criticism by Dion Boucicault [*q.v.*], is interesting and valuable. Unfortunately, the printed edition was limited to two hundred and fifty copies. In 1903 he made the English adaptation of Paul Heyse's *Mary of Magdala* for Mrs. Fiske, and had earlier made stage adaptations of Shakespeare's plays for Booth and Augustin Daly. In the latter years of his service on the *Tribune* his reviews of contemporary plays were so contrary to current taste that they ceased to be useful to the paper, the public, or the theatre. After his retirement from daily journalism in 1909, he wrote reviews for *Harper's Weekly* for a season or two, and worked on his historical and reminiscent books. He died on June 30, 1917.

Both Winter's style and critical attitude were paradoxical. He was a sentimentalist, and a stanch defender of art for morality's sake; Victoria herself could not have been more rigid in restricting the dramatist's choice of subject. When he praised, it was in eighteenth-century periodic sentences, rich with sentimental appeal. In style and attitude could be felt the influence of his early adoration of Longfellow and an education in Old World models. But when he attacked, the sentimentalist turned satirist, and his style became the sardonic weapon of Henry Clapp. Realities he denied the dramatist often furnished his vocabulary of invective. Perhaps his most famous, as well as his most cruel, phrase was that describing two popular but incompetent players in *Romeo and Juliet,* who, he said, "resembled nothing so much as a pair of amorous grasshoppers pursuing their stridulous loves in the hollow of a cabbage leaf." His attacks on Sir Arthur Pinero, Henry Arthur Jones, and especially Ibsen in the nineties were full of pungent wit and lively phrase. But he could not grasp what these men were really after; he could not adjust himself to the change from romanticism to realism in art. That was his tragedy, and, as his influence declined, it clouded and embittered his later years. He never lost, however, his power to analyse acting, and he was probably the best judge of the actor's art to occupy a critic's seat in America. Neither did he lose a certain delight in combat and a proud faith in the dignity of the stage. For many years he made a collection of clippings detailing the moral lapses of clergymen, and when some minister attacked the theatre or its people, it was Winter's delight to get out his clippings and compile a column or more of ministerial crimes by way of retort. And he was never intimidated to cease his attacks on the so-called "Theatrical Syndicate," which he termed an organization of vulgar and ignorant shopkeepers.

On Dec. 8, 1860, Winter married Elizabeth Campbell, a novelist of Scotch origin, by whom he had five children. Most of his life in New York he lived on Staten Island, a neighbor to his friend George William Curtis [q.v.], with summers spent in England or California. He was somewhat short in stature, had finely chiselled features, and wore always a moustache. Hair and moustache grew snow-white with the turn of the century, and his body seemed frail as he came down the aisle on the arm of his son Jefferson. To his younger confrères he was almost a ghost from a different age of art. His handwriting was famous for its illegibility—on a paper, too, edited by Horace Greeley. And as he either feared or despised elevators, he wrote his copy after the theatre standing at a ledge of the ground floor counting-room, and sent it upstairs by an office boy.

[In addition to Winter's books, especially *Other Days* (1908), *Old Friends* (1909), and *The Wallet of Time* (2 vols., 1913), see *Who's Who in America*, 1916–17; and obituary in *N. Y. Tribune*, July 1, 1917.]

W. P. E.

WINTHROP, FITZ–JOHN [See WINTHROP, JOHN, 1639–1707].

WINTHROP, JAMES (Mar. 28, 1752–Sept. 26, 1821), librarian and jurist, was a son of Prof. John Winthrop [q.v.] of Harvard and Rebecca (Townsend) Winthrop. He was graduated from Harvard in 1769 and a year later took over the work of the librarian, to whose post he was formally appointed in 1772. On the day of Bunker Hill he left to others the packing of the college books for removal to safety, and went into the battle, where he was slightly wounded. For a time that year he was postmaster of Cambridge, but he laid down that and took the office of register of probate for Middlesex. When Professor Winthrop died in 1779, James was considered for his chair of mathematics and natural philosophy, but his intemperate manner and his eccentricities militated against him. The next year he encouraged the students in the revolution which deposed President Samuel Langdon [q.v.], being motivated, contemporaries said, by spite. In 1787 the Corporation of the College forced him to choose between the library and the probate office, and he left the former.

Winthrop was one of the first members of the American Academy of Arts and Sciences, and in its *Memoirs* (vol. II, pt. I, 1793, pp. 9–17) he published fallacious solutions of the problems of trisecting the angle and duplicating the cube, to the great mortification of the other members (Florian Cajori, *The Early Mathematical Sciences in North and South America*, 1928, pp. 21–22). After serving as a volunteer against Shays's rebels he was considered for his father's professorship when it again fell vacant, but encountered public opposition (*Herald of Freedom,* Boston, Jan. 6, 1789). In 1791 he was appointed judge of common pleas for Middlesex, and in the same year surveyed for a proposed Cape Cod canal. He was a promoter of the West Boston Bridge and the Middlesex Canal, and a founder of the Massachusetts Historical Society. In the *Literary Miscellany* he published some articles on ancient history containing many statements "which seem to have been familiarly known to him, but which were not known before, and have not been confirmed since" (Sidney Willard *Memories of Youth and Manhood*, 1855, II, 140–41). His chief literary efforts, however, were directed toward the interpretation of the Biblical prophecies, which led him to believe that the European confederation of 1810 marked the beginning of a world union to be under a Guardian of the Law residing at Jerusalem. Although his learning was not deep, it was broad, and in his old age, having mastered all of the common languages, he took up Russian and Chinese. In politics he was a rabid Republican, which, in conjunction with his past experiences, turned him from Federalist Harvard to Allegheny College, which was being founded by his friend Timothy Alden [q.v.]. He became an overseer of the new institution, and bequeathed to it his large and valuable library. He died in Cambridge, unmarried, Sept. 26, 1821.

[A. C. Potter and C. K. Bolton, "The Librarians of Harvard Coll.," *Lib. of Harvard Univ., Bibliog. Contributions*, no. 52 (1897), pp. 30–31; E. A. Smith, *Allegheny—A Century of Educ.* (1916), pp. 43–49; Alden Bradford, in *Colls. Mass. Hist. Soc.*, 2 ser., vol. X (1823); E. B. Delabarre, "Middle Period of Dighton Rock Hist.," *Pubs. Colonial Soc. of Mass.*, vol. XIX (1918), and "Recent Hist. of Dighton Rock," *Ibid.*, vol. XX (1920); *Proc. Mass. Hist. Soc.*, 1 ser., vol. I (1879), p. 338, vol. XII (1873), p. 69, vol. XIII (1875), p. 229; obituary in *Columbian Centinel*, Oct. 3, 1821.]
C. K. S.

WINTHROP, JOHN (Jan. 12, 1587/88 o.s.–Mar. 26, 1649), first governor of Massachusetts Bay, came of a Suffolk family of good social position. His father, Adam Winthrop, was lord of the manor of Groton; he was a lawyer by profession and for some years auditor of St. John's and Trinity colleges, Cambridge. His first wife, by whom he had four daughters, was Alice, sister of Dr. John Still, master of Trinity College and bishop of Bath and Wells; his second wife, Anne Browne, was the daughter of a well-to-do tradesman. John, the third child of the second marriage, was born at Edwardstone, a village immediately adjoining Groton, in Suffolk. On Dec. 8, 1602, he was admitted to Trinity College, Cambridge, where he matriculated at Easter, 1603. Although throughout his life he was characterized by charm and a cheerful disposition, he began when quite young to discipline himself to Puritan habits of living, a discipline intensified after a severe illness in early adolescence. When he was only seventeen he left Cambridge, without taking a degree, to marry, Apr. 16, 1605, Mary Forth, some five years his senior, daughter and heiress of John Forth of Great Stanbridge, Essex.

Adopting his father's profession to augment the income from his lands, Winthrop was admitted at Gray's Inn, Oct. 25, 1613, and eventually established a legal practice in London. His wife died June 26, 1615, having borne six children, when the eldest, John [*q.v.*], later governor of Connecticut, was only nine years old. In December the father married Thomasine Clopton, daughter of William Clopton of Castleins, near Groton; she died, with her infant, a year later. In April 1618 Winthrop married Margaret, daughter of Sir John Tyndal of Great Maplestead, Essex, a woman remarkable alike for mind and character. This marriage, which lasted until the death of Margaret Winthrop in 1647, was distinguished by exceptional sympathy and understanding.

Since 1609 Winthrop had been a justice of the peace at Groton; about 1619 his father relinquished to him the lordship of the manor. His legal practice in London was extensive and fairly lucrative; in 1626 he was appointed one of the limited number of attorneys for the court of wards and liveries; he frequently drafted petitions to be presented in Parliament; in 1628 he was admitted to the Inner Temple. For some reason, however, by 1629 his practice seems to have waned and from that time his financial affairs troubled him deeply. He was a man of high reputation and somewhat expensive connections, of good blood, accustomed to liberal hospitality and an ample scale of living, fond of books and quiet rather than of the conflicts of the market place; he had a position in the county to maintain, and a growing family. Of gentle disposition and deeply religious, he watched with anxiety the increasing economic, political, and religious confusion of the times. A Puritan of the type of Milton, he was much concerned for the future of both religion and morals. All these elements in a complex national and personal situation were factors influencing his decision to emigrate to the New World.

In 1628 a group of Puritans had obtained from the Council for New England a grant of land in eastern Massachusetts, and John Endecott [*q.v.*], with some fifty settlers, had been dispatched to join a smaller number already there. Meanwhile, the number of those interested in such an enterprise increased, and in March 1629 Charles I issued a charter incorporating the Governor and Company of the Massachusetts Bay in New England, with a grant of territory of approximately the same geographical limits as the earlier grant from the Council for New England. Plans for emigration on an extensive scale were then begun. Winthrop became interested in this company and after carefully writing down and weighing the arguments on both sides of the proposition, in general and as they concerned him individually, resolved in spite of opposition from friends and relatives to take his family to New England. The document recording his "Reasons to be considered for iustifienge the undertakers of the intended Plantation in New England" (*Life and Letters, post*, I, 309–37) has been preserved.

As soon as his interest was seriously manifested, he was rapidly drawn into the executive work of the new corporation. It was decided that the colony should not be a mere plantation, operated on the ground by settlers working for the profit of a mercantile company in England, but a settlement of permanent dwellers in America working for themselves, and for this reason the momentous decision was made to transfer the legal company with its General Court and the actual charter itself to America. The effect of the move, the full significance of which may not have been foreseen, was to make an ordinary mercantile charter the assumed constitution of a self-governing community. The plan necessitated the choice of a new set of officers from among those who were planning to emigrate, and at the meeting of Oct. 20, 1629, Winthrop was chosen governor in place of Matthew Cradock, who remained behind. There is ample testimony regarding the importance attached to Winthrop's joining the company, and to his acceptance of the responsible leadership of the group in America.

On Mar. 22, 1630, Winthrop embarked at Southampton in the *Arbella* with three of his sons, leaving the rest of his family to follow later. The ship did not get under way until Apr. 8, and reached Endecott's settlement at Salem on June 12. At Yarmouth, before the voyage began, a paper was drawn up and signed by Winthrop and other leaders disclaiming any intention of withdrawing from the Church of England (*The Humble Request of His Majesties Loyall Subjects the Governour and the Company Late Gone for New England*, 1630). During the voyage Winthrop wrote out a description of what he thought the colony ought to be and of the means to be used in securing the desired end ("A Modell of Christian Charity," *Winthrop Papers, post,* II, 282–95). About six or seven hundred persons took passage in the *Arbella* and other vessels of the little fleet; two or three hundred more arrived almost simultaneously, and another thousand soon afterward. These numbers and the fact that, owing to the transfer of the charter and company organization to America, the entire management was local, gave Winthrop a position very different from that held by the governors of any of the other early plantations.

He first planned to settle at Charlestown and built the frame of his house there, but soon removed to Boston, which seemed to offer a better site for the center of government and the town which would grow up about it. A little later he built a summer home at Mystic. His wife, his son John, who had remained in England to sell the estate there, and all but one of the other children—Deane, who was at school—sailed from England in the *Lion,* in August 1631, and reached Boston Nov. 4. An infant daughter, whom Winthrop had never seen, died on the voyage. A son had died in England after the departure of his father, and another in New England.

The term of governor was one year, and Winthrop was elected in 1631, 1632, and 1633. The office was not an easy one and the earliest years of the colony were full of anxiety and hard work, but there was no untoward incident except a brief but warm quarrel with the touchy and overbearing deputy governor, Thomas Dudley [*q.v.*]. The freemen were beginning to be restive, however, and in April 1634, at the spring meeting of the General Court, requested to be shown the charter, which apparently they had never seen. They then found that under its provisions the General Court was the only body entitled to legislate, and they inquired why some of its powers had been usurped by the magistrates. Winthrop answered that the General Court had become unwieldy and suggested that it permanently abrogate some of its powers. The freemen, however, in spite of the Governor's popularity, refused to invalidate their charter privileges; and to concentrate authority in the hands of the leaders. In September 1633 the Rev. John Cotton [*q.v.*] had arrived at Boston and he at once became the leading clergyman in the colony. Politics and religion were inextricably mixed in the commonwealth, and Cotton aspired to be a leader in both. At the meeting of the General Court, May 14, 1634, he preached the sermon and propounded the doctrine that a magistrate ought to be reëlected continually unless there were sufficient reason that he should not, and that officials had a vested interest in their offices similar to a freehold. The answer of the freemen (*i.e.,* members of the company, who alone exercised the franchise) to this extraordinary doctrine came immediately: Winthrop was turned out of office and Dudley elected in his stead. At this time, in response to a request, Winthrop submitted his accounts since his first election, and they showed that he had personally advanced considerable sums for the commonweal. In December 1634 another dispute occurred: seven men were to be chosen to divide the town lands of Boston; the freemen refused to elect a certain magistrate to the committee, feeling that the richer men would hold back lands and not divide them among the poorer, and Winthrop refused to serve under the circumstances. At a new election he and all the other magistrates were chosen. As one of the results of the work of this committee Boston Common was forever reserved for the use of the town.

In October 1635 Hugh Peter and Henry (afterward Sir Henry) Vane [*qq.v.*] arrived in the colony, and at once began to trouble the political waters. As one result of their investigation into the causes of dissension in Massachusetts, Winthrop and Dudley were asked to appear, Jan. 18

1636, before a meeting of a group of self-appointed investigators, including John Cotton, Gov. John Haynes, and others. Both Winthrop and Dudley denied that there was now any trouble between them, but Winthrop's general policy came under discussion and he was accused of having been too lenient in discipline and judicial decisions. The ministers were asked to consider the matter and when they reported next morning that the charge was just, Winthrop, who had not the strength to stand against the united clergy, agreed to adopt a stricter course in future. Thus another step was taken toward the theocracy of later days. In accordance with the aristocratic tendencies of the leaders, especially the clergy, a plan nowhere provided for in the charter was adopted by the General Court in 1636 whereby certain magistrates should be chosen for life or good behavior. Winthrop and Dudley unfortunately allowed themselves to be chosen the first two members of this unconstitutional life council, which was opposed to the trend of public opinion, was always unpopular, and lasted only a few years.

About this time the Antinomian controversy over the teachings of Mistress Anne Hutchinson [q.v.] began to rock the colony, and in this struggle Winthrop, then deputy governor, took a part. At the May election in 1637 passion ran so high that the court was held at Newton instead of in Boston. Vane, who had been governor, was defeated, and Winthrop was once more elected to the office. The General Court had passed an act prohibiting the harboring in the colony of any person for more than three weeks without permission of a member of the life council or of two magistrates. Designed especially to prevent increase by immigration in the number of followers of Mrs. Hutchinson, this measure encountered vigorous opposition which called forth from Winthrop "A Defence of an Order of Court Made in the Year 1637" in which he presented the best arguments in favor of the exclusive policy so long pursued by Massachusetts. Vane replied, in "A Briefe Answer . . .," on the side of freedom, and Winthrop wrote a rejoinder (*The Hutchinson Papers*, vol. I, 1865, pp. 79–113). The law was enforced almost at once, however, and a number of newcomers allied to the cause of Mrs. Hutchinson were forced to leave the colony soon after arrival. The Antinomian controversy had now come to a head. Winthrop, who had received the rebuke of the clergy for his leniency, had gradually grown more narrow and severe. When Mrs. Hutchinson, sentenced to banishment, asked the reason for her sentence, he replied: "Say no more; the Court knows wherefore and is satisfied" (Thomas Hutchinson, *History of the Province of Massachusetts-Bay*, vol. II, 1767, p. 520). Winthrop wrote an account of the whole controversy which was incorporated by Thomas Welde [q.v.] in *A Short Story of the Rise, Reign, and Ruine of the Antinomians* (1644).

The following year, governor again, Winthrop had to protect the charter from the most serious attack yet made upon it in England, which he did in an able letter to the Lords Commissioners for Plantations. In 1639 he was again chosen governor, though there was some murmuring that there was danger of the office becoming his for life. Toward the end of the year he learned of serious financial losses in England, resulting from the dishonesty of his agent there, and for the rest of his life, despite generous aid from his son John, he was heavily handicapped by lack of money. Owing partly to his own desire to retire and partly to the fear of a life tenure already noted, he was not elected governor in 1640, although he still held office as a member of the Court of Assistants.

He was again elected to the chief magistracy in 1642, however. During this term there occurred the famous controversy over the negative voice. In a lawsuit between one Mistress Sherman and Capt. Robert Keayne over the ownership of a sow, the magistrates and the deputies, always up till then sitting as one house, had been unable to agree, the deputies being on the side of the poor woman and the magistrates—who perceived the legal aspects of the case—on that of the rich man. The more democratic element in the colony objected strenuously to what they considered the blocking of justice when the small number of magistrates vetoed the action of the much larger number of deputies. Winthrop wrote a treatise appealing to English precedents and the Old Testament, to show that if the magistrates could not veto the actions of the deputies the colony would be a democracy and that "there was no such Governm^t. in Israel" (*Life and Letters*, II, 430). As a result of this controversy, in 1644 the negative voice of the magistrates was insured by the permanent separation of magistrates and deputies, who afterward sat as two houses.

The following year Winthrop, still governor, saw realized the plan which he had advocated as early as 1637 of a confederation of the several New England colonies for certain purposes, mainly military. He was at the head of the Massachusetts commissioners for framing the articles for the United Colonies and was the first president of the confederation after it was formed. A less happy feature of that year's term of office was the D'Aulnay-La Tour affair, which brought upon Winthrop more, and more merited, criticism than any other episode of his public life. Two French officials in Acadia, La Tour and D'Aulnay, had been engaged in an armed controversy with which Massachusetts was not concerned. La Tour turned up at Boston and received from the Governor official permission to hire ships and men, although Winthrop had not obtained the opinion of the General Court but had consulted only a few of the magistrates and deputies. Since the matter involved the questions of neutrality and war, it should also have been referred to the newly created confederation. The commissioners of that body condemned the act of Massachusetts in the next year, and the colony gave D'Aulnay compensation—in the form of "a very fair new sedan, (worth forty or fifty pounds where it was made, but of no use to us), sent by the Viceroy of Mexico to a lady, his sister, and taken in the West Indies by Captain Cromwell, and by him given to our governor" (*Winthrop's Journal*, II, 285).

In 1644 Endecott was elected governor and Winthrop deputy governor. It was a year of much earnest discussion in the colony over the principles of government, and Winthrop wrote a discourse called "Arbitrary Government Described and the Governm^t^. of the Massachusetts Vindicated from that Aspersion" (*Life and Letters*, II, 440–54), which was circulated in manuscript. It created a stir among the more radical members of the House of Deputies and was even termed a seditious libel. In spite of all repression, the frontier was exerting its influence in creating a democratic atmosphere, and Winthrop was losing touch with his people. An episode in 1645 did much to restore his popularity, however. Trouble had arisen in Hingham over the election of a militia officer; it was claimed that the magistrates had exceeded their powers, and Winthrop was singled out for impeachment, but at the trial he was wholly vindicated and the complainants were fined. After the verdict he made a short but famous speech on liberty, defining the two kinds, natural and civil, and the nature of the office of the people's elected representatives (*Ibid.*, II, 339 ff.). From that year he was elected governor annually until his death, although the contentions over Robert Childe and Samuel Gorton [*qq.v.*], in 1646 and 1647, and the severe measures taken by Winthrop with respect to both persons, brought about an active opposition. On June 14, 1647, Margaret Winthrop, the mother of eight of his children, died, and in December he married a fourth wife, Martha, daugh-

ter of Capt. William Rainsborough, R.N., and widow of Thomas Coytmore of Boston. One son, who died in early childhood, was born of this marriage. Winthrop survived his third wife less than two years, however, dying when he was only sixty-one years old, aged by hard work, anxiety, and sorrow.

Winthrop's portrait depicts a man of refinement and sensitiveness rather than of aggressive strength of character. His letters reveal an extremely tender and affectionate nature. In writing he had an excellent, grave and measured style of English prose, and although it was hastily jotted down as affairs permitted, his journal, frequently called his "History of New England," is a source book of the greatest importance. In government he had no faith in democracy, believing that, once chosen, representatives should govern according to their own best judgment. He was modest and self-sacrificing, and his integrity was always beyond question.

[The first two volumes of Winthrop's manuscript journal were published in 1790 under the title *A Journal of the Transactions and Occurrences in the Settlement of Massachusetts and the Other New England Colonies from the Year 1630 to 1644*; later the third manuscript volume was discovered, and was published with the others as *The History of New England* (2 vols., 1825–26; rev. ed., 1853), edited by James Savage. The most useful edition is *Winthrop's Journal* (2 vols., 1908), edited by J. K. Hosmer. Winthrop correspondence is found in *Mass. Hist. Soc. Colls.*, 3 ser. IX–X (1846–49), 4 ser. VI–VII (1863–65), 5 ser. I, IV, VIII (1871–82), 6 ser. III, V (1889–92); *Winthrop Papers*, a new and complete collection, pub. by the Mass. Hist. Soc., of which vols. I and II (1929–31) have appeared. The standard biography is R. C. Winthrop, *Life and Letters of John Winthrop* (2 vols., 1864–67). See also J. H. Twichell, *John Winthrop* (1891) in Makers of America Series, and *Some Old Puritan Love-Letters—John and Margaret Winthrop* (1893); G. W. Robinson, *John Winthrop as Attorney: Extracts from the Order Books of the Court of Wards and Liveries, 1627–1629* (1930); E. A. J. Johnson, "Economic Ideas of John Winthrop," *New Eng. Quart.*, Apr. 1930; Stanley Gray, "The Political Thought of John Winthrop," *Ibid.*, Oct. 1930; "Evidences of the Winthrops of Groton" (4 pts., 1894–96), being 4 parts of J. J. Muskett, *Suffolk Manorial Families*, vol. I (1900); R. C. Winthrop, *A Pedigree of the Family of Winthrop* (1874); John and J. A. Venn, *Alumni Cantabrigienses*, pt. 1, vol. IV (1927); S. E. Morison, *Builders of the Bay Colony* (1930). Sources for political history are *Records of the Gov. and Company of the Mass. Bay*, vols. I–III (1853–54), ed. by N. B. Shurtleff; and "Acts of the Commissioners of the United Colonies of New England," in *Records of the Colony of New Plymouth*, vol. IX (1859), ed. by David Pulsifer. C. M. Andrews, *The Colonial Period of Am. Hist.: The Settlements*, vol. I (1934), is especially good for the English background.]   J. T. A.

WINTHROP, JOHN (Feb. 12, 1605/06 o.s.– Apr. 5, 1676), colonial governor of Connecticut, was the eldest son of John Winthrop [*q.v.*], first governor of Massachusetts Bay, by his first wife, Mary Forth. Eldest of the six children of the marriage, he was born at the manor house in

Groton, Suffolk, England, when his father was eighteen years old. Before the boy was ten, his mother died. He was sent to the celebrated Free Grammar School of Bury St. Edmunds, and at sixteen entered Trinity College, Dublin, living somewhat under the supervision of his uncle by marriage, Emanuel Downing, then resident in Ireland. Subsequently he studied law in London and was admitted a barrister at the Inner Temple, Feb. 28, 1624/5. He soon gave up the law, however, and through the influence of Joshua Downing, then one of the commissioners of the Royal Navy, secured an appointment in May 1627 as secretary to Captain Best, and served with the fleet which was dispatched to the relief of La Rochelle. Because of the complete failure of the expedition he had no hope of promotion, and thought for a time of going to New England with the settlers who sailed in 1628 under John Endecott [*q.v.*], but instead started on an extensive tour of Europe. After fourteen or fifteen months—three spent at Constantinople, two at Venice and Padua—and visits to Leghorn and Amsterdam among other places, he returned to London and found that his father had resolved to emigrate to New England. This decision met the young traveler's favor: all countries, he said, had come to seem to him like so many inns, "and I shall call that my country, where I may most glorify God, and enjoy the presence of my dearest friends" (*Life and Letters of John Winthrop,* I, 307).

When the father sailed for America in 1630, the son remained behind in England to settle many business affairs, to sell the family's landed property, and to look after his stepmother and several of his brothers and sisters. On Feb. 8, 1631, he married his cousin, Martha Fones, and in the following August embarked for America with all the other members of the family, save one younger brother. After ten weeks at sea, they landed at Boston on Nov. 4. In March following he was elected an Assistant, and just a year later was the leader of a group of twelve men who founded Ipswich. He remained there until after the death of his wife and an infant daughter in the autumn of 1634. In October of that year he sailed for England. His vessel was driven ashore on the coast of Ireland by a storm and he landed at Galway, stopped at Dublin on the way to Scotland, and then drove to London, visiting influential Puritans on the way. While he was in England, his father's friends Lord Say and Sele and Lord Brooke undertook to start a plantation in Connecticut, making young Winthrop governor and agreeing to supply him with men, money, and supplies. His commission,

issued in July 1635, appointed him governor for one year after arrival at his post. He set sail with his second wife, Elizabeth, daughter of Edmund Reade of Wickford, Essex, and stepdaughter of the Rev. Hugh Peter [*q.v.*], who, with Henry Vane [*q.v.*], took passage in the same vessel, reaching Boston on Oct. 6, 1635.

An advance party was at once sent out to prepare for the Connecticut settlement by building a fort at Saybrook, the defense of which was soon entrusted to Lion Gardiner [*q.v.*]. Winthrop followed the pioneers in March 1636. In the autumn he hastened back to Boston, after the birth of his daughter, Elizabeth, and it is doubtful that he visited Connecticut again during his year as governor. He once more settled at Ipswich, where he was chosen lieutenant-colonel of the Essex militia and one of the prudential men of the town. By the autumn of 1639 he appears to have moved to Salem, much to the regret of the inhabitants of Ipswich, of whom a considerable number claimed in a petition that they had been induced to settle there only on condition that Winthrop would remain with them for life.

About this time, the elder Winthrop lost a considerable part of his property and the son came to his assistance. He had given up his right of entail to the family estates in England in order to arrange for his father's emigration, but he had a moderate fortune of his own, inherited from his mother. His father's financial difficulties, however, put a burden upon him and he thereafter sought to give more time to his personal affairs. He sold some of his landed property, the General Court made him a grant of money, and he also obtained a grant of Fisher's Island in Long Island Sound. He began the manufacture of salt and tried to interest English capital in the erection of iron works. In order to promote his various industrial schemes, he sailed again for England, Aug. 3, 1641, and was gone over two years. With a group of skilled workmen he had gathered together he embarked for the return voyage in May 1643 but did not reach Massachusetts until autumn, after an extraordinarily long trip.

After examining favorable sites for iron works in Maine, New Hampshire, and Massachusetts, he set up a furnace at Lynn and another at Braintree, where in 1644 the General Court granted him 3,000 acres for the encouragement of iron making. In the same year he was given leave to found a settlement in the Pequot country of Connecticut for a similar purpose. He had built a house on Fisher's Island, to which place he took his family, and at the same time was building a more permanent home at what was to become New London. He was made a magistrate for

Pequot (New London) in 1648 but also retained his public offices in Massachusetts, and made frequent journeys between the two colonies. After the death of his father in 1649, he decided to remain permanently in Connecticut, declining re-election as an Assistant in Massachusetts after having served continuously for eighteen years. In 1650 he was admitted a freeman of Connecticut and in May 1651 was elected an Assistant. A few years later he moved to New Haven, where he again undertook to develop iron works and would probably soon have been chosen governor of the New Haven Colony had not Connecticut acted first, electing him chief executive in 1657. His consequent removal to Hartford marked the permanent attachment of his interest to the Connecticut Colony.

Since the Connecticut laws did not permit two successive gubernatorial terms, he was elected lieutenant-governor in 1658, but after that the law was altered and from 1659 until his death in 1676, he was annually elected governor. The most important among his many services to the colony during his eighteen years as its head was his mission to England in 1661–63 to obtain a charter. Possessed of many influential friends and a winning personality, he gained the favor of the king, and returned to New England with the most liberal charter that had yet been granted to any colony, making Connecticut almost an independent state and including within its new boundaries the former colony of New Haven. This provision aroused intense opposition in New Haven, but in the long run proved advantageous. In 1664 Winthrop was present by request of the British commander at the surrender of New Netherland.

Winthrop had always possessed a strongly scientific mind and had been particularly interested in chemistry. While in England in 1663 he was elected a member of the Royal Society—the first member resident in America—and in New England his knowledge of medicine was much in demand. He was ahead of his period in that his varied interests were scientific rather than theological, and also in that he believed that New England's future lay in manufacturing and commerce rather than in agriculture. The papers which he contributed to the Royal Society and his letters to scientific friends abroad deal with a range of subjects including trade, banking, new methods in manufacture, and astronomy. He predicted the discovery of a fifth satellite to Jupiter, although the instruments of his time were not powerful enough to confirm his theory. In his commercial undertakings he was not successful. Neither his iron, lead, nor salt works prospered, and a number of his mercantile ventures brought him heavy losses because of the hazards of the Dutch War. Though at his death he left an unusually large estate in land in Connecticut, Massachusetts, and New York, his old age was harassed by continual anxiety over his business affairs. He twice requested to be relieved of the office of governor, but each time the colony refused, increasing his salary from time to time and making him occasional grants of land. In 1675, at the outbreak of King Philip's War, he asked for a third time to be relieved of the responsibility of office, but again the colony declined. In September he went to Boston to attend a meeting of the Commissioners of the United Colonies; he spent the winter there, and in March took a cold, which led to his death in April.

Winthrop was undoubtedly one of the most engaging New Englanders of his day, and probably the most versatile. Wherever he settled and to whatever he turned his hand, it was with the greatest reluctance that his temporary associates would let him go. He was tolerant and kindly toward some of the same persons who were treated harshly in Massachusetts, such as Samuel Gorton, John Underhill, the Quakers, and Roger Williams. The last named, with whom Winthrop formed a lasting friendship, once wrote to him: "You have always been noted for tendernes toward mens soules. . . . You have been noted for tendernes toward the bodies & infirmities of poor mortalls" (*Massachusetts Historical Society Collections*, 4 ser. VI, 305). Though probably a lesser character than his father, he was certainly one of the ablest and most interesting of his own generation.

[T. F. Waters, *A Sketch of the Life of John Winthrop the Younger* (1899), being *Ipswich Hist. Soc. Pubs.*, vol. VII; F. J. Kingsbury, "John Winthrop, Jr.," *Proc. Am. Antiq. Soc.*, n.s. XII (1899), 295–306; S. E. Morison, *Builders of the Bay Colony* (1930); R. C. Winthrop, *Life and Letters of John Winthrop* (2 vols., 1864–67); *Records of the Gov. and Company of the Mass. Bay* (5 vols., in 6, 1853–54), ed. by N. B. Shurtleff; *The Public Records of the Colony of Conn.*, vols. I–II (1850–52), ed. by J. H. Trumbull; "Acts of the Commissioners of the United Colonies," *Records of the Colony of New Plymouth*, vols. IX–X (1859), ed. by David Pulsifer; *Winthrop Papers*, vols. I, II (Mass. Hist. Soc., 1929–31); correspondence and other papers in *Mass. Hist. Soc. Colls.* (see bibliog. of John Winthrop, Sr.); correspondence with founders of Royal Soc., *Proc. Mass. Hist. Soc.*, 1 ser. XVI (1879); Thomas Birch, *The Hist. of the Royal Soc.* (4 vols., 1756–57); *Jour. Chem. Educ.*, Mar. 1926, Dec. 1928.]

J. T. A.

WINTHROP, JOHN (Mar. 14, 1638–Nov. 27, 1707), soldier, governor of Connecticut, third of the name in America and usually known as Fitz-John Winthrop to distinguish him from his father and grandfather, was born at Ipswich,

Mass., the son of the second John Winthrop [*q.v.*] and Elizabeth (Reade) Winthrop, daughter of Edmund Reade of Wickford, County Essex, England. After the death of his grandfather, the first governor of the Massachusetts Bay Colony, when the boy was ten years old, his father removed permanently to Connecticut, where he held various lesser offices and was governor continuously for eighteen years before his death. Fitz-John Winthrop entered Harvard College but discontinued his studies before obtaining his degree in order to accept a commission in the Parliamentary Army in England. He engaged in military campaigns in Scotland and entered London with General Monk at the time of the restoration of Charles II in 1660. While in London after the Restoration, he was elected a member of the Royal Society. In 1663 he returned to Connecticut and made his home in New London. In 1671 and 1678 he was sent as deputy from that town to the Connecticut General Assembly. He was always keenly interested in military affairs and in June 1672 was appointed chief military officer for New London County. The next year, when the Dutch attacked Southold, Long Island, Winthrop was sent as commander of the Connecticut troops to protect the town and forced the Dutch to retreat to New Amsterdam. He served also, with distinction, in the Indian wars of 1675–76.

After his father's death in 1676 Winthrop spent a large part of his time in Boston. He was appointed to the governor's council by Joseph Dudley [*q.v.*] in 1686, and he served on the council of Sir Edmund Andros [*q.v.*] at the close of the latter's administration. He was accused of plotting to overthrow Andros, but the charge cannot be proved. After Andros' defeat Winthrop returned to Connecticut and helped to reëstablish the government under the Connecticut charter, which Andros had suspended. For this service he was elected one of the Assistants of the governor of Connecticut in 1689.

In the following year, war having been declared between England and France, he was appointed major-general and commander of a united force of approximately 850 men from New York and Connecticut who were expected to invade Canada and capture Montreal. When Winthrop arrived at a point 150 miles north of Albany, however, he found that his Indian allies were afraid to advance and that Gov. Jacob Leisler [*q.v.*] of New York had not supplied the provisions and munitions promised; he therefore returned to Albany and abandoned the invasion. Leisler, hoping to place the blame for the failure on Winthrop, arrested him after his army was

on the far side of the Hudson River and threatened to court-martial and execute him, but he was rescued by some of the Mohawk Indians who had made up a part of his army. He returned to Connecticut, where an investigation of his conduct by the Connecticut General Assembly freed him of all blame, and severely condemned Governor Leisler. Winthrop was granted forty pounds by the Assembly for his services.

In 1693 the legality of the Connecticut charter was questioned and Winthrop was sent to London to plead for confirmation of the charter by King William. He was successful in his mission, and upon his return to Connecticut was rewarded by a grant of £300 by the General Assembly. Five years later, when Gov. Robert Treat [*q.v.*], because of his great age, refused to continue as governor of Connecticut, Winthrop was elected in his stead, and was reëlected annually until his death, in Boston, in 1707. By his wife, Elizabeth, daughter of George Tongue, he had one child, a daughter, who married Col. John Livingston of Albany but left no descendants. Fitz-John Winthrop, while not as great a figure as either his father or grandfather, was like them an able administrator and a man of impeccable integrity in public and private life. He was greatly beloved by the people of Connecticut.

[R. C. Winthrop, *A Short Account of the Winthrop Family* (1887) ; J. C. Frost, *Ancestors of Henry Rogers Winthrop and His Wife Alice Woodward Babcock* (1927) ; F. C. Norton, *The Govs. of Conn.* (1905) ; F. M. Caulkins, *Hist. of New London, Conn.* (1852) ; J. H. Trumbull and C. J. Hoadly, *The Public Records of the Colony of Conn.*, vols. II–V (1852–70), see Index ; Benjamin Trumbull, *A Complete Hist. of Conn.* (1818) ; E. B. O'Callaghan, *Docs. Rel. to the Col. Hist. of the State of N. Y.*, vols. II (1858), III (1853), IV (1854), and vol. XIV (1883), ed. by Berthold Fernow.]

R. M. H.

WINTHROP, JOHN (Dec. 19, 1714–May 3, 1779), astronomer, physicist, and mathematician, was born in Boston, one of the sixteen children of Adam and Anne (Wainwright) Winthrop, and a descendant of John Winthrop, 1587/88–1649 [*q.v.*]. Several of his forefathers had already distinguished themselves in the affairs of the colony, particularly in science. His great-granduncle, John Winthrop, 1606–1676 [*q.v.*], known as the first industrial chemist in America, became the first fellow of the Royal Society of London (1663) in the American colonies. A distant cousin, John Winthrop, a fellow of the Royal Society in 1734, became well known as a collector of minerals, fossils, and other geological specimens. In 1728, at the age of fourteen, John Winthrop was graduated from the Boston Latin School and entered Harvard College, from which he was graduated in 1732. The following six years he spent in his father's home, where he became absorbed in private studies and laid the foundation for his future scientific career. In 1738, at the age of twenty-four, he was elected second Hollis professor of mathematics and natural philosophy at Harvard College, succeeding Isaac Greenwood [*q.v.*]. When he was examined for the professorship by the Overseers of the College the question of his theological adherence was not raised for fear it would prove too broad for Harvard at that time. He not only carried on instructions but also gave public lectures and demonstrations in physical science. His research work, mainly in the field of astronomy, was carried out over a period of forty years, during which he came to be considered one of the outstanding scholars in the country. His results were all published in the *Philosophical Transactions of the Royal Society,* and brought him considerable recognition in England.

His first work was a series of sun-spot observations, made on Apr. 19, 20, 21, 22, 1739. These seem to be the first set of observations on sunspots in the colony, and records are still preserved at the Harvard Library. Fully aware of the importance of various astronomical problems, Winthrop was kept well informed by the authorities at the Royal Observatory at Greenwich and the Royal Society of London, and pursued his studies with the aid of his own splendid library. His next undertaking was a study of the transit of Mercury over the sun, on Apr. 21, 1740 (see *Transactions,* vol. XLII, 1742–43). The next two communications to the Society were observations on the transits of Mercury on Oct. 25, 1743, and Nov. 9, 1769 (*Ibid.,* vols. LIX, 1769, LXI, 1771, pt. 1). The problem of these transits was the question of exact determination of longitude between Cambridge and London, as well as the equation of time and the study of the Newtonian laws of gravitation. Winthrop established at Harvard, in 1746, the first laboratory of experimental physics in America and demonstrated with a series of lectures the laws of mechanics, light, heat, and the movements of celestial bodies according to the Newtonian doctrines. Count Rumford as a young man attended those lectures, and they doubtless contributed to his own distinguished career as a scientist and inventor. Winthrop's other publications include scientific papers published in the *Philosophical Transactions,* volumes LII, LIV, LVII, LXIV, 1761–74, *Relation of a Voyage from Boston to Newfoundland, for the Observation of the Transit of Venus* (1761), and *Two Lectures on the Parallax and Distance of the Sun* (1769).

In 1751 Winthrop's next progressive step as a scholar was to introduce to the mathematical curriculum at Harvard College the elements of fluxions, now known as differential and integral calculus. This marked a definite beginning of an epoch in mathematical study in the United States. In 1755 a severe earthquake shook New England, and a study of this phenomenon was made by Winthrop. His conclusions proved that he was a scientist with theories more modern than those for which he was given credit (*Transactions,* vol. L, 1757, pt. 1). In April 1759, he delivered a lecture on the return of Halley's comet of 1682, which was the first predicted return of a comet. In a second discourse during the same month, he discussed the true theory of comets according to the work of Newton's *Principia,* and also according to the laws formulated by Kepler, with the predictions of Halley (*Two Lectures on Comets, Read in the Chapel of Harvard-College,* 1759). In 1761, with great foresight and diligence, he made preparations to observe two events of great astronomical importance, the transits of Venus in 1761 and 1769 (see *Transactions,* vols. LIV, 1764, LIX, 1769). During the transit of Venus of 1761, under the direction of Winthrop, Harvard College sent the first astronomical expedition to St. John's, Newfoundland. The principal problem of this transit was the study of the parallax of the sun. Winthrop was the main support of Franklin in his theories and conclusions relative to his experiments in electricity. He also carried on magnetic and meteorological observations for over twenty years, records and computations of which are still preserved. In addition to these observations, studies were made of the physical appearance of Venus (*Ibid.,* vol. LX, 1770), eclipses of Jupiter's satellites, partial solar eclipses, and aberration of light.

During the Revolution Winthrop was an ardent patriot and espoused the cause of the colonies. He was a counselor and friend of Washington, Franklin, and of others who stood high in the founding of the new republic. In his own field he was honored as few others of his period. He was America's first astronomer and Newtonian disciple. The Royal Society elected him as a fellow in 1766 and the American Philosophical Society enrolled him as a member in 1769. From the University of Edinburgh he received the honorary degree of LL.D. in 1771, and his alma mater conferred the same degree upon him in 1773, the first honorary degree of doctor of laws conferred by Harvard University. Though he had no active part in the undertaking, the founding of the American Academy of Arts and Sciences in Boston may be attributed directly to

Winthrop's interest and influence (Brasch, in *Sir Isaac Newton, post,* p. 334). He died in Cambridge at the age of sixty-five, honored as a scholar, scientist, and astronomer who passed away in the fulness of his fame. He lies buried with his ancestors in the old King's Chapel burying-ground, Boston. His first wife was Rebecca Townsend, the daughter of James Townsend of Boston, and the step-daughter of Charles Chauncy, 1705–1787 [*q.v.*]. Their intention to marry was recorded on July 1, 1746. After her death in 1753, he was married to Hannah Fayerweather, the widow of Farr Tolman (marriage intention date, Mar. 24, 1756). She survived him, with several children by his first wife. James Winthrop [*q.v.*] was his son.

[R. C. Winthrop, Jr., *A Pedigree of the Family of Winthrop* (privately printed, 1874) ; *Boston Marriage Records from 1700 to 1751* (1898) ; *Boston Marriages from 1752 to 1809* (1903) ; "Correspondence Between John Adams and Prof. John Winthrop," *Mass. Hist. Soc. Colls.,* 5 ser., vol. IV (1878) ; F. E. Brasch, articles on Winthrop in *Pubs. of the Astronomical Soc. of the Pacific,* Aug.–Oct. 1916, and in *Sir Isaac Newton . . . A Bicentenary Evaluation of His Work* (1928) ; Edward Wigglesworth, *The Hope of Immortality: A Discourse Occasioned by the Death of . . . John Winthrop* (1779) ; *Boston Gazette and Country Jour.,* May 10, 1779.]   F. E. B.

WINTHROP, ROBERT CHARLES (May 12, 1809–Nov. 16, 1894), representative and senator from Massachusetts, was born on Milk Street, Boston, in the house of his great-uncle, James Bowdoin, 1752–1811 [*q.v.*], the son of Lieut.-Gov. Thomas Lindall and Elizabeth (Temple) Winthrop and the descendant of John Winthrop, 1587–1649 [*q.v.*]. After an active three years at Harvard College he was graduated in 1828, studied law in Daniel Webster's office, and was admitted to the bar in 1831. Somewhat of a dandy, he led subscription balls and used unspent energy in the state militia. He married on Mar. 12, 1832, Eliza, the daughter of Francis Blanchard of Boston. They had three sons and a daughter. Elected to the General Court in 1834, he served as speaker for three out of his six years there. He was handsome and eloquent, with the prestige of a famous family to aid him. Elected to Congress, he served from Nov. 9, 1840, to May 25, 1842, when he resigned to be with his wife until she died on June 14. Reëlected he served from Nov. 29, 1842, to July 30, 1850, as speaker in the Thirtieth Congress, 1847–49. As speaker he antagonized the more ardent anti-slavery men and in 1849 was defeated for a second term by Free-Soilers. In the Senate, to which he was appointed on the resignation of Webster in 1850, he faced immediately the Fugitive Slave Bill, which was passed over his rather reluctant opposition. He had promised to vote for "a just, practicable and constitutional mode of diminishing or mitigating so great an evil as slavery." At home he was defeated in 1851 for the Senate by Charles Sumner, an advocate of no quarter with the slavery interests. Whittier claimed that Winthrop held "in his hands the destiny of the North" (S. T. Pickard, *Life and Letters of John Greenleaf Whittier,* 1894, I, 374), but he was forced into the background by men better fitted for the rough politics that must precede a civil war.

Defeated, he turned to history and education. On Oct. 15, 1859, he married, as his second wife, Laura (Derby) Welles, who died Apr. 26, 1861. He held aloof from the newly formed Republican party, an outgrowth of the dying Whig party, but took a hand in the Kansas controversy in 1856, suggesting that General Scott be sent there. His plan was killed by the Democrats. In the Frémont-Buchanan-Fillmore fight for the presidency he opposed Frémont and agreed with Fillmore that the candidate would be elected by the "suffrages of one part of the Union only to rule over the whole United States" (Rhodes, *post,* II, 204, 206). In the McClellan-Lincoln campaign of 1864 he opposed Lincoln's reëlection, contending that McClellan had made his own platform and did not stand on the declaration that the war was a failure. He devoted fully half of his long life to the activities of a scholarly gentleman of leisure. His addresses on great occasions—especially the *Oration on the Hundredth Anniversary of the Surrender of Lord Cornwallis* (1881), by invitation of both houses of Congress—continue to be important in the history of American oratory. He served on the vestry of Trinity Church in Boston for sixty years. In old age, wearing a broadcloth overcoat with velvet collar and a cape, tall, bent but impressive, he went regularly to St. Paul's in Brookline. The Peabody Education Fund gave him, as chairman of the board, an opportunity to improve education in the South. A member of the Massachusetts Historical Society from 1839 to 1894 he served for thirty years as president. He wrote incessantly for its publications and lent hospitality to its many gatherings. He married on Nov. 15, 1865, Adele, the widow of John Eliot Thayer and the daughter of his friend, Francis Granger [*q.v.*]. She died in 1892. He survived, quoting the words of Keble, "Content to live, but not afraid to die" (*Memoir, post,* p. 345).

[R. C. Winthrop, *A Memoir of Robert C. Winthrop* (1897) ; *Proc. Mass. Hist. Soc.,* 2 ser. vol. IX (1895), esp. the remarks of C. F. Adams, pp. 234–41 ; J. F. Rhodes, *Hist. of the U. S. from the Compromise of 1850,* vols. I, II (1893), vol. IV (1899) ; *Index to Proc.*

Mass. Hist. Soc., 1884–1907, for glimpse of his amazing activity; N. Y. Tribune, Nov. 17, 20, 1894.]
C. K. B.

WINTHROP, THEODORE (Sept. 28, 1828–June 10, 1861), author, was born in New Haven, Conn., the third son of Francis Bayard Winthrop by his second wife, Elizabeth Woolsey, sister to President Theodore Dwight Woolsey [q.v.] of Yale and niece to the elder Timothy Dwight [q.v.]. His father, merchant of New York and lawyer of New Haven, was descended from John Winthrop, 1587–1649 [q.v.]; his mother, related to six presidents of colleges, was great-granddaughter of Jonathan Edwards [q.v.]. Winthrop grew up in New Haven, perusing many books in his father's large personal library, roaming through the surrounding country, and listening to sea tales at thriving city wharves. Educated at an old-fashioned dame-school and specially prepared by Silas French, he entered Yale in 1843. Dismissed in November 1844, "for breaking Freshmen's windows," he loitered through a winter with a half-brother in Marietta, Ohio, reëntered Yale, and graduated with the class of 1848, having divided his time between spasmodically serious study, debating, occasional writing for the Yale Literary Magazine, and pulling an oar in the college boat. Next year he studied "Logic and Language" and then planned to study law at Harvard, but in 1849 ill health frustrated the project. For relaxation and physical recuperation, he traveled in Europe for a year and a half.

Thereafter for a dozen years his occupations were intermittent and his journeyings many, while, in prose and verse, in extended letters home, and in extensive entries in his "journal," both indited in a manner far from informal, he acquired the facility at writing that led him to literature. In 1851 he began "a new life" in the New York office of the Pacific Mail Steamship Company, visited Europe again, served as ticket seller on the Panama Railroad (1853), traveled to San Francisco and Oregon, mounted a fresh horse and started home across the plains. He went to Darien with Lieut. Isaac G. Strain [q.v.] late in 1853, studied law in a New York office, vacationed at Mount Desert, was admitted to the bar (1855), traveled the Adirondack and Maine woods with Frederick E. Church [q.v.], the painter, "stumped" part of the state of Maine for Frémont in 1856, started a law partnership in St. Louis, fell ill, and returned to New York (1857) to let law give way permanently to literature. His initial effort, a novel called Mr. Waddy's Return, written in 1855, lay unpublished until 1904. The first of his work to be print-

ed was a detailed and ornate description of a picture by his friend Church, A Companion to the Heart of the Andes (1859). On Staten Island, he spent part of his time in writing and part, says George William Curtis, "in walking and riding, in skating and running," leaping fences, even turning somersaults on the grass. In 1861, full of high ideas, he enlisted in the 7th New York Regiment which, after guarding Washington, came home when its month was up. But not Winthrop. He accompanied "Ben" Butler to Fortress Monroe as "military secretary," participated in the confused engagement at Great Bethel on June 10, 1861, and there, leading the advance, was struck by a bullet and fell dead. His life, as Curtis said, "suddenly blazed up into a clear, bright flame, and vanished" (Cecil Dreeme, post, p. 5).

To James Russell Lowell he had sent wartime anecdotes and descriptions which appeared that summer in the Atlantic Monthly (June, July 1861). Winthrop's family offered his unpublished manuscripts to Ticknor & Fields, who promptly issued three novels: Cecil Dreeme (1861), John Brent (1862), Edwin Brothertoft (1862). Their early success was phenomenal. Two volumes of personal narratives followed: The Canoe and the Saddle (1863) and Life in the Open Air (1863). Repeated editions by successive publishers testified to the quality of Winthrop's writing and to his popularity for forty years. However, though partly a pioneer in contemporaneous "novels of locality," describing the open West in John Brent and Washington Square in Cecil Dreeme, he was distinctively of his own time and generation. His conspicuous death brought his name to prominence, and for a half century his writings maintained his fame, but when Mr. Waddy's Return (1904) appeared, its editor felt that it needed "thorough revision and intelligent condensation," and in one critic it aroused nothing more than "the Pandora-like feeling that used to accompany the opening of old trunks in the twilight garret" (J. B. Kerfoot, Life, Feb. 23, 1905, p. 222).

[See biog. sketch by G. W. Curtis in Cecil Dreeme (1861); Laura W. Johnson, The Life and Poems of Theodore Winthrop (1884); Elbridge Colby, Bibliog. Notes on Theodore Winthrop (1917), The Plates of the Winthrop Books (1918), and articles in Nation, June 29, 1916, and Yale Alumni Weekly, Jan. 23, 1920; N. Y. Times, June 13, 1861; obituary in Appleton's Ann. Cyc., 1861. Winthrop's MSS. are in the N. Y. Pub. Lib.]
E. C—y.

WINTON, ALEXANDER (June 20, 1860–June 21, 1932), pioneer automobile manufacturer, was the son of Alexander and Helen (Fea) Winton, and was born in Grangemouth, Scotland. At twenty, after obtaining a common-school education in his native town, he emigrated to the United States and found work in the marine engine department of the Delamater Iron Works, New York City. After a short stay there he obtained a position as an assistant engineer of an ocean steamship and continued in this work for more than three years. In 1884, having married meanwhile, he gave up the sea and removed to Cleveland, Ohio, where he began a bicycle-repair business. In the succeeding six years he built up a reputation, and at the same time perfected and patented a number of improvements in bicycle mechanisms. These included a ball-bearing device that made balls run on flat surfaces, an invisible crank-shaft fastening, and an invisible handle-bar clamp. Rather than sell these inventions to manufacturers, in 1890 Winton established the Winton Bicycle Company and successfully pursued the business of manufacturing bicycles for more than ten years. While thus engaged, the talk of "horseless carriages" reached him, and as early as 1893 he began giving attention to gasoline engine design for automotive use. In 1895 he built a gasoline motor bicycle and in September 1896 completed his first gasoline motor car. This had a two-cyclinder vertical engine with friction clutch, electric ignition, carburetor, regulator to control the engine speed, engine starter, and pneumatic tires. In spite of the ridicule of his banker and his friends, Winton proceeded immediately with the building of a second and improved automobile. In March 1897 he formed the Winton Motor Carriage Company, and in July of that year made with his new car the first reliability run in the history of the American automobile—a nine-day trip from Cleveland to New York by a circuitous route, totalling 800 miles in 78 hours and 43 minutes actual running time. Winton's hopes of interesting capital in his machine by this test of endurance were not immediately realized, but before the year was out he had sold sufficient stock in his company to proceed with the construction of four cars. The first of these was completed and sold, Mar. 24, 1898, for a thousand dollars—the first sale in America of a gasoline automobile made according to set manufacturing schedules. Winton repurchased this car several years later, and it is now in the National Museum at Washington. He sold the other three machines soon after the first and had sold twenty-five more by the end of the year. All these cars were constructed in accordance with his general motor vehicle patent, No. 610,466, granted to him on Sept. 6, 1898, one of the early American patents in the automotive field.

Winton was one of the most energetic, skilful, and progressive automobile pioneers in the United States. He designed, built, and raced automobiles both in the United States and abroad, his racer, "Bullet No. 1," establishing a record of a mile in 52.2 seconds in 1902 at Daytona Beach, Fla. This was the first time the beach at Daytona was used for automobile racing. All Winton's automobiles after 1904 were equipped with four-cylinder engines and all after 1907 with six-cylinder engines. He was the first in America to experiment with straight eight-cylinder engines (1906), and as early as 1902 had designed external and internal brakes on the same brake-drum, the latter but one of the many innovations introduced by him which have become common. With his automobile company a success, Winton, whose greatest interest lay in engine design and experiment, about 1912 turned his attention to the Diesel engine. That year he organized the Winton Gas Engine and Manufacturing Company, and began the manufacture of improved Diesel engines for marine, industrial, municipal, and railroad power plants. He also organized and was president of the Electric Welding Products Company and of the Lindsay Wire Weaving Company, both in Cleveland. With all these activities, he continued to act as president of the automobile company, maintaining the Winton car in the front rank of American automobiles until Feb. 11, 1924, when this business was completely liquidated in favor of the Diesel engine business. Several years before his death he disposed of this and retired from all active industrial connections. Winton was an active member of a number of technical and business associations, and was greatly interested in yachting, being at the time of his death ex-commodore of the Interlake Yachting Association. He was married four times: first, on Jan. 18, 1883, to Jeanie Muir MacGlashan of Scotland (d. 1903); second, in 1906, to La Belle MacGlashan of Scotland (d. 1924); third, in 1927, to Marion Campbell at Covington, Ky., from whom he was divorced in 1930; and fourth, on Sept. 2, 1930, to Mrs. Mary Ellen Avery. He was survived by his widow and seven children of his earlier marriages.

[Who's Who in America, 1930–31; J. R. Doolittle, The Romance of the Automobile Industry (1916); Alexander Winton, "Get a Horse," Sat. Evening Post, Feb. 8, 1930; E. O. Randall and D. J. Ryan, Hist. of Ohio (1912), vol. V; E. M. Avery, A Hist. of Cleveland and Its Environs (1918), vol. III; Trans. Am. Soc. of Mechanical Engineers, vol. LIV (1932); obituaries in Cleveland Plain Dealer and N. Y. Times, June 23, 1932; records of U. S. Nat. Museum.]   C. W. M.

WIRT, WILLIAM (Nov. 8, 1772–Feb. 18, 1834), attorney general of the United States, was the youngest son of Jacob and Henrietta

Wirt. Jacob was a native of Switzerland, his wife of German origin. They supported themselves in a simple manner as tavern keepers in the quiet village of Bladensburg, Md. Here William, a curly-haired, blue-eyed boy with a ready smile and a vivid imagination, was born and spent his early childhood. When the rattle of stagecoach wheels gave way to the tread of marching men of the Revolution, he learned to beat the time of the martial airs, and when a French dancing master came to town, he learned the minuet and performed for the amusement of the villagers. But life was not all play for William. His father died when he was two years of age, and his mother when he was eight. A small patrimony, the guardianship of his uncle Jasper, and the interest of Peter Carnes, a lawyer and friend of the family, made it possible for the child to receive the rudiments of an education. He first attended school in his native village. At seven years of age he was sent to Georgetown, and then to a school in Charles County, Md. In 1783 he was entered in the grammar school of the Rev. James Hunt of Montgomery County, whose influence and whose library were important factors in shaping the mind of the child. In 1787 the school was discontinued and William, now in his fifteenth year, was faced with the necessity of finding means of self-support. One of his fellow students in Hunt's school was Ninian Edwards [q.v.], later an important figure in the history of Illinois. His father, Benjamin Edwards, now invited Wirt to become a private tutor in his home. Wirt accepted the offer, remained for twenty pleasant months, and turned his mind to the study of law. Being now in his seventeenth year and in poor health, he decided to take a horseback trip to Georgia to visit his old benefactor Mr. Carnes, who, meanwhile, had married his sister Elizabeth. By spring his health was restored and he returned to Maryland, remaining for a short while at Montgomery Court House. Here he entered upon the study of law with William P. Hunt, son of his former teacher. After about a year spent in this manner, he heard that there was an opening for a young lawyer in Culpeper County, Va. Disposing of what was left of his small inheritance in Maryland, he hastened to Virginia where, after five months, he was admitted to the bar.

His original equipment consisted of a rapid and indistinct enunciation, a considerable degree of shyness, a copy of Blackstone, two volumes of *Don Quixote,* and a copy of *Tristram Shandy.* His reading was not confined to law, and his genial disposition tempted him to devote more time to social recreation than was good for his work. Nevertheless, he continued for one or two years to practise in Culpeper with increasing success. He made many friends both in his own county and in neighboring Albemarle. Among the latter was Dr. George Gilmer of "Pen Park," whose eldest daughter Mildred was married to Wirt on May 28, 1795. The young couple took up their residence at Dr. Gilmer's estate. Among the charming circle which centered in this cultured home, Wirt became especially attached to Francis Walker Gilmer [q.v.], youngest son of the family, and to the junior Dabney Carr [q.v.] of the neighboring estate of "Dunlora." Carr and Wirt rode the Virginia circuit together, and they remained throughout life the most intimate of friends. Wirt was fond of pleasure and companionship and the revelries of Virginia society sometimes encouraged him to a degree of excess. Dr. Gilmer died a year or two after the marriage of his daughter, and on Sept. 17, 1799, she followed him to the grave. Thus ended the happiest period of Wirt's life, but the friends of these years were never supplanted in his affections.

He now transferred his residence to Richmond to pursue the practice of his profession in a larger field. He was immediately elected clerk of the House of Delegates and served in this capacity during three sessions of the Assembly. In May 1800, he served with George Hay and Philip Norborne Nicholas [qq.v.] as counsel for James Thomson Callender [q.v.] in his famous trial before Judge Samuel Chase under the Alien and Sedition Acts. Thus was Wirt's name first brought conspicuously to the attention of the public. In 1802 the clerk of the House was elected by the legislature to preside over one of the three chancery districts into which the state had just been divided. Acceptance of this post made it necessary that Wirt transfer his residence to Williamsburg, and on Sept. 7 of the same year he was married to Elizabeth Washington, second daughter of Col. Robert Gamble of Richmond. This event proved to be a major turning point in his life. Henceforth he devoted more time to work and less to pleasure, and within a few months he decided, for financial reasons, to give up the chancellorship and devote himself once more to the practice of law. At first he thought of going to Kentucky for this purpose, but his friend Littleton W. Tazewell [q.v.] persuaded him to come to Norfolk. He did not, however, remove his residence to that city until the beginning of 1804.

It was in 1803 that Wirt began his literary career by publishing the first of "The Letters of the British Spy" in the Richmond *Argus.* They came out anonymously and were supposed to be the contemporary observations of an English traveler upon Virginian society and other miscellaneous topics. The authorship was at once recognized, and the letters had an enormous popularity, going through numerous editions within a few years. The work was the product of a keen and restless mind wearied of the constraints of its professional activity and wishing to roam at leisure and further afield. Wirt was, in fact, a scholar by avocation. With little formal education, he mastered the Latin classics and read much of theological and other lore. *The Letters of the British Spy* (1803) was followed by an inconspicuous series of essays entitled *The Rainbow* (1804).

In 1806 Wirt removed his residence back to Richmond. His legal reputation had been growing rapidly, and during the next year was given a sensational stimulus by his appearance in the prosecution of the case against Aaron Burr (E. B. Williston, *Eloquence of the United States,* 1827, IV, 394–417). The increased prestige which the Burr trial brought Wirt prompted Jefferson to propose that he seek a seat in Congress (*The Writings of Thomas Jefferson,* vol. XI, 1904, p. 423), but he declined the suggestion. He did, however, take an active part in supporting Madison's campaign for the presidency and published several letters in his behalf in the Richmond *Enquirer.* The unexpected sequel to this series of events of 1808 was his election to the House of Delegates. This was the only post to which he was ever elected by the people, and he retired from it at the end of one term. He did not care for the life of a politician He was ambitious, however, for literary fame, and in 1810 started the publication of another series of essays which he called "The Old Bachelor." Thirty-three numbers were published, the last appearing in 1813, but, though they had a degree of success and went through several editions in book form, they did not acquire the popularity attained by *The Letters of the British Spy.* In 1814, Washington having been captured by the British, Wirt took the field as captain of artillery, but this was only a measure of home defense. His earlier dreams of military glory had vanished. His one ambition was to acquire a competency and retire to the country to live a life of literary ease. This dream, however, was never to be realized. In 1816 he argued his first case before the Supreme Court of the United States, and shortly thereafter was appointed by President Madison as United States attorney for the district of Richmond.

The autumn of 1817 saw the consummation of the two major phases of Wirt's career. After twelve years of laborious and oft-interrupted effort, he now published his *Sketches of the Life and Character of Patrick Henry* (1817). This was the first work which came out under his own name, and was his most serious literary effort. His material was acquired largely from men who had known Henry and it was presented in a laudatory and ornate manner. The biography did not exhibit Wirt's talents at their best. The other consummation was his appointment by President Monroe to the attorney-generalship of the United States, which post he held for twelve consecutive years. He was the first attorney general to organize the work of the office and to make a systematic practice of preserving his official opinions so that they might serve as precedents for his successors ("Opinions of the Attorneys General of the United States from the Commencement of the Government . . . to the 1st March, 1841," 26 Cong., 2 Sess., *House Exec. Doc. No. 123*). As was the custom, he continued his private practice and was much engaged in the Baltimore courts. In 1819 he took part before the Supreme Court in the cases of *McCulloch* vs. *Maryland* (4 *Wheaton*, 316) and the Dartmouth College case (4 *Wheaton*, 518). In 1824 he was associated with Webster in the case of *Gibbons* vs. *Ogden* (9 *Wheaton*, 1). In 1826 he was appointed president of the University of Virginia and professor in the School of Law (*The Writings of Thomas Jefferson,* Vol. XIX, 1903, p. 492), but declined the honor. In the autumn of this year a service in memory of Thomas Jefferson and John Adams was held in the hall of the House of Representatives, and Wirt delivered the principal address (E. B. Williston, *Eloquence of the United States,* 1827, V, 454–503).

While the election of 1824 was in progress, Wirt took no part in the contest. When John Quincy Adams became president, he urged the attorney general to retain his post, and this Wirt did. When Andrew Jackson succeeded Adams in 1829, Wirt returned to private life and removed his residence to Baltimore where he continued his professional activities to the end of his life. Having cast his lot with the opposition to Jackson, Wirt favored Henry Clay for the succession in 1831 and was chosen to sit for Baltimore in the national Whig convention. Shortly afterward the Anti-Masons held a convention in that city and named Wirt as their candidate for the presidency. Strangely enough he accepted the candidacy in the belief that, since Anti-Masons would not support Clay, he might be nominated by the Whigs and thus unite both groups against Jackson. But the Whigs refused to desert Clay, whereupon Wirt wished to withdraw his candidacy but could not do so without seeming to desert those who had nominated him. Thus he was an unwilling candidate for the presidency in 1832. As far as Masonry was concerned, he joined the order in his youth, had had little contact with it in later years, and was apparently not greatly concerned over this issue in the election, his principal object being to unite all forces against the administration.

Shortly after his retirement from office, Wirt attempted to establish a colony of German immigrants on a tract of land which he owned in Florida, but the immigrants decamped and the experiment failed. He had hoped that this settlement would serve as a retreat for himself and his family during his declining years, but this was not to be. After a brief illness he died in Washington of erysipelas on Feb. 18, 1834. The Supreme Court and both houses of Congress adjourned to do him honor, and the President of the United States and the highest officers of the government accompanied his body to its tomb in the National Cemetery. He had twelve children by his second marriage, of whom seven or eight lived to maturity (Perry, *post*, p. 530).

William Wirt was an unusual figure in the annals of America. His generous features bore some resemblance to those of the poet Goethe—ample brow, large whimsical mouth, kindly twinkling eyes, and a shock of curly hair. He was by nature endowed with a vivid imagination, a keen love of music and of life, and an ingenuous, playful disposition. He was never fond of work, and his personal charm and oratorical gifts were always his major weapons. His early style of speaking and of writing was ornate, but, later realizing the necessity for rigid, logical thinking, he tried to correct this fault. The fact that his reputation rests largely upon his opinions as attorney general shows that he succeeded.

[The first account of the life of Wirt was written by P. H. Cruse and published with the tenth edition of *The Letters of the British Spy* (1832). Making use of this work and of a large collection of correspondence, J. P. Kennedy published his well-known *Memoirs of the Life of William Wirt* (2 vols., 1849; new and revised ed., 2 vols., 1850). Though many other briefer notices have appeared, practically nothing of importance has been added. F. W. Gilmer, *Sketches, Essays and Translations* (1828) gives a florid description of Wirt's eloquence. The account in F. W. Thomas, *John Randolph of Roanoke and Other Sketches* (1853), was written before the appearance of Kennedy's biography. Among more recent notices are H. H. Hagan, in *Eight Great American Lawyers* (1923); H. W. Scott, in *Distinguished American Lawyers* (1891); J. H. Hall, in W. D. Lewis, ed., *Great American Lawyers*, vol. II (1907); and B. F. Perry, in *Biographical Sketches of Eminent American Statesmen* (1887). Selections from Wirt's writings have appeared in E. C. Stedman and E. M. Hutchinson, eds., *A Library of American Literature* (11 vols., 1888–89); E. A. and G. L. Duyckinck, eds., *Cyclopaedia of American Literature* (2 vols., 1855); and elsewhere. In addition to the correspondence pub-

lished in Kennedy's work, there are letters in N. W. Edwards, *A History of Illinois from 1778 to 1833 and Life and Times of Ninian Edwards* (1870); *Reminiscences of Patrick Henry in the Letters of Thomas Jefferson to William Wirt* (1911); and in other collections of the correspondence of Jefferson. For obituary see *Daily National Intelligencer*, Feb. 19–21, 1834.]

T. P. A.

WISE, AARON (May 2, 1844–Mar. 30, 1896), rabbi, was born at Erlau, Hungary, the son of Rabbi Joseph Hirsch Weisz and Rachel Theresa (Rosenfeld) Weisz. His family had been represented in the rabbinate for over two hundred years, Wise being the sixth in direct succession to hold rabbinical office. His earliest Hebrew education was directed by his father. Later he studied in Talmudical schools of Hungary, and especially under Israel Hildesheimer at the Jewish Seminary of Eisenstadt, where he received the degree of rabbi (1867). He then attended the universities of Berlin, Leipzig, and Halle, and received from the latter the degree of Ph.D., his thesis dealing with angelology and demonology in rabbinic writing. For several years he served as superintendent of schools in his native town. In 1870 he married Sabine de Fischer Farkashazy, daughter of Moritz de Fischer Farkashazy, the industrialist. He was for a time identified with the extreme orthodox party in Hungary, acting as secretary of the organization Shomre Ha-Dath (Observers of the Law), and editing a Judeo-German weekly in its support. In 1874 he emigrated to the United States, and became rabbi of congregation Beth Elohim in Brooklyn. In March 1875 he was called to the pulpit of Temple Rodeph Sholom of New York, and served it for the rest of his life. When he came to the pulpit of Rodeph Sholom, the younger members of this orthodox congregation showed a decided leaning towards reform. The older members, on the other hand, were averse to changes. Wise steered a middle course, modernizing the temple services in some ways while retaining many of the old time-honored customs and ritual practices. He gave a prominent place to the study of Hebrew in the religious school of the congregation, and made it the cornerstone of the curriculum at a time when many were relegating Hebrew to the background or omitting it altogether. He edited a new prayer-book, *The Temple Service* (1891), for the congregation, and instituted Sabbath eve services at eight o'clock instead of at sundown. Under his ministry, his congregation became conservatively reformed in character and grew to be one of the influential Jewish congregations in New York City.

A profound Hebrew scholar and a man of wide culture, he assisted Bernard Fischer in his revision of Johann Buxtorf's Hebrew lexicon. He was a member of the Society of German Oriental Scholars (*Deutsche Morgenländische Gelehrten-Gesellschaft*). He contributed to the yearbook of the Jewish Ministers' Association of America and to other periodicals, and was for some time editor of the *Jewish Herald* of New York and of the *Boston Hebrew Observer*. Besides his revision of the prayer-book he also wrote *Beth Aharon*, a handbook for religious schools. He was closely identified with the charitable organizations and activities of his community. In 1891 he founded the sisterhood of his temple, which subsequently established the Aaron Wise Industrial School in his memory. He gave liberally of his time and energy to the Hebrew free schools maintained by his congregation as an offset to Christian missionary activities which were then actively directed towards the proselytizing of the Jewish youth. He was well known for his personal charities. He was one of the founders of the Jewish Theological Seminary of New York in 1886. He was a preacher of eloquence, forcefulness, and sincerity. His humanity, good nature, ready wit, and engaging personality made him especially beloved in his congregation and popular in the community at large. He died in New York. He was survived by his widow, three sons, and three daughters, one of his sons, Stephen Samuel Wise (b. 1872) following the rabbinical traditions of the family.

[Sources include Isaac Markens, *The Hebrews in America* (1888); *Hist. of the Congregation Rodeph Sholom of N. Y., 1842–1892* (1892); *Jewish Encyc.*; *Am. Hebrew* (N. Y.) and *Jewish Messenger* (N. Y.), Apr. 3, 1896; *N. Y. Herald*, Mar. 31, 1896; *World* (N. Y.) and *N. Y. Daily Tribune*, Mar. 31, Apr. 3, 1896; information from Dr. Stephen S. Wise.]

D. deS. P.

WISE, DANIEL (Jan. 10, 1813–Dec. 19, 1898), Methodist Episcopal clergyman, editor, writer, was born in Portsmouth, Hampshire, England, the son of Daniel and Mary Wise. His formal education was received in the grammar school of Portsmouth, and in a classical school of which officials of Christ Church, Oxford, were the patrons. After leaving school he was apprenticed to a grocer, but soon opened an academy in Portsmouth.

In 1833 he emigrated to the United States and went to Grafton County, N. H., where he taught school. Having been converted under Methodist influences in England, in 1834, at Lisbon, N. H., he was made a local preacher by the quarterly conference of the Landaff Circuit. His gifts as a writer and speaker were at once recognized and in addition to preaching he lectured frequently, especially in behalf of the anti-slavery cause. Removing to Massachusetts in 1837, he supplied churches at Hingham and Quincy and was employed by anti-slavery societies. Always literary in his tastes, he also edited the *Sunday School Messenger* (1838–44), said to have been the first Methodist publication of its kind, and the *Ladies' Pearl* (1840–43), a monthly magazine for the edification of women. In 1840 he was received into the New England Conference of the Methodist Episcopal Church on trial, but was not ordained elder until 1843. Meanwhile, he served churches in Ipswich, Lowell, and Springfield. When in 1843 a considerable number of Methodists withdrew from the Church and formed the Wesleyan Connection, a non-episcopal and anti-slavery denomination, Wise was inclined to join them, and in 1844 was without pastoral charge. Finally deciding to remain in the Methodist Episcopal fold, he became, in 1845, a member of the Providence Conference. During the next twelve years he was pastor at Nantucket, Mass., Hope Street Church, Providence, R. I., and Fall River and New Bedford, Mass.

His literary abilities and his reputation as a keen controversialist led to his appointment in 1852 as editor of *Zion's Herald*. Through this publication he gave strong support to those who favored the exclusion of all slaveholders from the Methodist Church. In 1856 the General Conference elected him corresponding secretary of the Sunday School Union and editor of its publications. This position he occupied for sixteen years, after 1860 also serving the Tract Society in the same capacities. A partial failure of voice compelled him to curtail public speaking and after 1872 he made his home in Englewood, N. J., and devoted himself principally to writing. For a few months in 1887–88 he was editor of the *Methodist Review*.

His books, published over a long period, were numerous and included religious works, biographies, and stories for young people, many of the last named appearing under the pseudonyms Lawrence Lancewood and Francis Forrester. Among his earlier productions were *The Path of Life: or, Sketches of the Way to Glory and Immortality* (1848); *The Young Lady's Counsellor* (1852), outlining the sphere and duties of young women and the dangers that beset them; and *Popular Objections to Methodism, Considered and Answered* (1856). His biographical writings include *Uncrowned Kings* (1875), stories of men who rose from obscurity to renown; *Heroic Methodists of the Olden Times* (1882); and a series of brief sketches of English and American literary figures, including among others, Spenser, Shakespeare, Milton, Addison, Carlyle, Wordsworth, Longfellow, and Irving.

These sketches all appeared in 1883. Wise was most widely known perhaps for his tales for young people, written with a moral and religious purpose. Their character is suggested by such titles as *Dick Duncan: The Story of a Boy Who Loved Mischief* (1860); *Jessie Carlton: The Story of a Girl Who Fought with Little Impulse the Wizard* (1861); and *Stephen and His Tempter* (1873). Many of these tales appeared under the serial titles "Glen Morris Stories," "The Lindendale Stories," and "The Windwood Cliff Series." In August 1836 Wise was married in New York to Sarah Ann Hill. He died in Englewood, survived by two daughters.

[*Year Book of the New England Southern Annual Conference,* 1899; *Zion's Herald,* Dec. 28, 1898; *Christian Advocate* (N. Y.), Dec. 29, 1898; *Sun* (N. Y.), Dec. 20, 1898.]   H. E. S.

WISE, HENRY ALEXANDER (Dec. 3, 1806–Sept. 12, 1876), congressman, governor of Virginia, Confederate general, was born at Drummondtown (Accomac Court House), Va. He was of mixed English and Scotch descent, and his paternal ancestors had been prominent citizens of the Eastern Shore of Virginia since the first John Wise arrived from Devonshire, England, in 1635. Henry's father was Maj. John Wise, a Washingtonian Federalist who served in the Virginia House of Delegates from 1791 to 1802 and was speaker from 1794 to 1799. Major Wise was married twice, the second time to Sarah Corbin Cropper, daughter of Gen. John Cropper of Accomac County, an ardent Revolutionary patriot. Sarah was "a handsome blonde of a highstrung nervous temperament, and a temper of her own" (Barton Wise, *post,* p. 8)—characteristics that reappeared in her son, Henry.

Left an orphan at an early age, Henry lived a free country life. After preparation by private tutors and at a classical school in Accomac County he was sent to Washington College, Washington, Pa., and was graduated with honors in 1825. Later he attended for two years the law school of Judge Henry St. George Tucker [*q.v.*] of Winchester, Va., an expounder of the old Virginia doctrine of state rights. In 1828 Wise opened a law office in Nashville, Tenn., and on Oct. 8 married Ann Eliza Jennings, daughter of a Presbyterian minister. Two years later he returned to Accomac County and resumed there his legal practice.

In 1833 he ran for Congress as a Jackson Democrat and, although his district was largely Nullificationist, made a vigorous speaking tour and won a notable personal triumph. Strong words used in the campaign, however, led to a duel with his opponent, Richard Coke [*q.v.*] and Coke was slightly wounded. Wise was continued in Congress until his resignation in 1844. Despite his youth, he soon made a reputation as a debater and speaker of the "old-fashioned florid, denunciatory type." A tactless and unduly aggressive defender of Southern rights, he became the chief antagonist of John Quincy Adams [*q.v.*] in his effort to repeal the "Gag Law" against anti-slavery petitions. Breaking with Jackson on the bank question, with sixteen other members of Congress, the "Awkward Squad," he went over to the heterogeneous Whig party. He later vigorously opposed Van Buren, ran in 1840 as a Whig elector, and made a strenuous canvass for the successful Harrison-Tyler ticket.

In 1837 the house occupied by his family in Drummondtown was set on fire by an incendiary, and his wife's consequent dread and anxiety caused her to give birth prematurely to a child and brought on the illness from which she died. The next year he became involved as a second in a duel between two congressmen, W. J. Graves and Jonathan Cilley, but the opprobrium he received was partly undeserved. In November 1840 he was married to Sarah Sergeant of Philadelphia, daughter of John Sergeant, 1779–1852 [*q.v.*].

Wise had been partly responsible for the nomination of Tyler as vice-president in 1840, and after the death of Harrison became President Tyler's close friend and the leader of the Tyler adherents in Congress. He declined the navy portfolio in Tyler's cabinet and his appointment as minister to France (1843) was rejected by the Senate. Grateful to George McDuffie and John C. Calhoun [*qq.v.*] for their friendship in the latter connection and anxious to obtain as successor to A. P. Upshur [*q.v.*] a secretary of state in favor of the annexation of Texas, Wise, in a typical "spirit of rashness," exceeded his authority from Tyler by offering Calhoun, through McDuffie, the appointment to the office. Tyler was pained and indignant but promptly ratified Wise's offer (Tyler, *post,* II, 293–94) and thus alienated the Benton faction. Shortly before, Jan. 19, 1844, Tyler had appointed Wise minister to Brazil. Here he manifested active opposition to the slave trade. In 1847 he returned to Accomac County and resumed his legal practice.

Though an outspoken defender of slavery, Wise was in many respects liberal and progressive. This attitude was now shown successively in his connection with the Virginia constitutional convention of 1850–51, in his opposition to the Know-Nothing movement, and in some of his actions as governor of Virginia. For many decades the western part of the state had complained of unfair domination by the eastern part, and before 1850 there had even been threats of separation. At the same time Wise was characterizing his own eastern district as "old, moss-grown, and slip-shod" and in speeches to the people was pleading with them to awaken. Moreover, as early as 1837, while praising the many fine qualities of the Southern people, he had condemned their undue admiration for "old things and ways" and declared many were "too metaphysical and likely, as Mr. Letcher used to say of old Virginia, to die of an abstraction" (Barton Wise, *post,* p. 142).

Seeking election as a delegate to the constitutional convention, Wise spoke courageously in favor of the white basis of representation. He was the only white-basis delegate elected east of the Blue Ridge; he won great popularity in the western counties, but an eastern organ, the *Richmond Whig* (June 4, 1850), branded him as a modern Jack Cade. On the convention floor he was one of the most important figures and played a prominent part in securing the compromise suffrage and taxation reforms. During the conventions he lost his second wife, a pious Northern lady never wholly reconciled to slavery even in the benevolent form displayed on her husband's plantation. In November 1853 he married Mary Elizabeth Lyons, sister of James Lyons, a prominent Richmond lawyer.

Wise was a delegate to the Democratic convention of 1852 and played an important part in transferring the support of the Virginia delegation to Franklin Pierce, thus helping to secure his nomination. In 1854 he was nominated by a combination of Tidewater and Trans-Allegheny delegates as Democratic candidate for governor of Virginia. The ensuing campaign against the Know-Nothing candidate was one of the most exciting in the history of the state. Wise stumped the state to the Ohio border; a person present when one of his speeches was delivered wrote that it required about three hours and a half and "for argument, wit, satire, and lofty eloquence" he never heard it surpassed (Goode, *post,* p. 34). He not only condemned the Know-Nothings for their secrecy and intolerance but declared they bore an Abolitionist taint. He also dwelt on his favorite topics of public improvements and industrial development of the state. He was elected governor by a majority of 10,180 and broke the force of the Know-Nothing wave in the South. It must be remembered, however, that the Catholic issue was unimportant. Wise was governor from 1856 to 1860. He continued to advocate internal improvements, advanced a scheme for state insurance of life and property, and en-

deavored to reorganize and improve the armament of the state militia; but as governor he is best known for his very active if somewhat excited rôle in quelling the John Brown raid. It has been argued that he should have given more heed to the evidence of John Brown's insanity, but this view fails to appreciate sufficiently the prevailing state of mind.

Following his triumph over the Know-Nothings, Wise was considered as a possible candidate for the presidency. His influence did much to hold the Virginia delegation to Buchanan in the Democratic convention of 1856, and he doubtless hoped to be the second choice in case of Buchanan's defeat. He thus became largely responsible for Buchanan's nomination and was hailed by Robert Tyler [*q.v.*], then of Pennsylvania, a Buchanan manager, as "the Warwick of the hour" (Auchampaugh manuscript, *post,* quoting Tyler letter). Wise was disappointed, however, in the amount of influence he obtained over Buchanan.

A delegate to the Virginia convention of 1861, Wise favored "fighting in the union"—upholding Southern rights, by force if necessary, without secession—but yielded to the demand for secession and became a fiery advocate of the Southern Confederacy. Although past middle age and without military training, he volunteered for service and in May 1861 was made brigadier-general. This appointment was largely political but added strength in the western part of Virginia. Wise raised a legion in that section; served there and at Roanoke Island, N. C., where his son, Capt. O. Jennings Wise, formerly editor of the *Richmond Enquirer,* was mortally wounded; and later served on the South Carolina coast, in the defense of Richmond and Petersburg, and in the retreat to Appomattox. As a general he was too independent and outspoken to fit well into the Davis military administration, but displayed his usual aggressive courage. On the day following the battle of Sailor's Creek, Apr. 6, 1865, Gen. Robert E. Lee promoted Wise to the rank of major-general. Gen. Fitzhugh Lee, in his final report, declared that "the disheartening surrounding influences" during the retreat to Appomattox had no effect upon Wise, and that his spirit was as unconquerable as four years before.

After the war he practised law in Richmond, most of the time with his son John S. Wise [*q.v.*]. Though without sympathy for the Radical party in the state, he opposed the method of rehabilitation devised by the Conservative organization. He would never ask for amnesty for himself, but urged the young Virginians to make the best of the new conditions. A man of tall, very lean appearance and piercing eyes, an inveterate chewer and swearer, rough but warm-hearted, of great ability, though lacking in moderation and judgment, he was one of the last of the great individualists in Virginia history. He wrote *Seven Decades of the Union* (1872), mostly a review and eulogy of the life of President Tyler. He died in Richmond, survived by his wife, two sons, and three daughters.

[J. C. Wise, *Col. John Wise of England and Va.* (1918); Barton Wise, *The Life of Henry A. Wise* (1899); J. S. Wise, *The End of an Era* (1899); L. G. Tyler, *The Letters and Times of the Tylers* (2 vols., 1884–85); *War of the Rebellion: Official Records (Army)*; State Executive Documents, Va. State Lib.; J. P. Hambleton, *A Biog. Sketch of Henry A. Wise* (1856); *Biog. Dir. Am. Cong.* (1928); John Goode, *Recollections of a Lifetime* (1906); C. H. Ambler, *Sectionalism in Va.* (1910); J. C. McGregor, *The Disruption of Va.* (1922); Mrs. A. G. Beach, in *Ohio Archaeological and Hist. Quart.*, Oct. 1930; H. T. Shanks, *The Secession Movement in Va.* (1934); P. G. Auchampaugh, *Robert Tyler: Southern Rights Champion* (1934); Clement Eaton, in *Miss. Valley Hist. Rev.*, Mar. 1935; MSS. of C. L. Eaton and P. G. Auchampaugh, containing copies of Wise's letters; *Dispatch* (Richmond), Sept. 13, 1876; information from L. G. Tyler and other Virginians.]   R. D. M.

WISE, HENRY AUGUSTUS (May 24, 1819– Apr. 2, 1869), naval officer, author, was born at the navy yard in Brooklyn, N. Y., the second son of Capt. George Stewart Wise of the United States Navy and Catherine (Stansberry) Wise, member of a prominent Delaware family. He was a descendant of John Wise who settled in Virginia in the first half of the seventeenth century. After his father's death about 1824, Wise was taken to Craney Island near Norfolk, Va., where he was reared in the home of his grandfather, George Douglas Wise. In 1834, at fifteen, he was appointed midshipman by his kinsman and guardian, Henry Alexander Wise [*q.v.*], receiving his training, as was customary at the time, on shipboard. During the Mexican War he served on the razee *Independent* and participated in naval operations in the Gulf of California. He once carried important dispatches through the hostile lines from Mazatlán to Mexico City, a feat which he was able to perform because of his somewhat dark coloring and his familiarity with the language of the country. His experiences during the war are described in *Los Gringos, or an Inside View of Mexico and California, with Wanderings in Peru, Chili, and Polynesia* (1849). A later book, *Tales for the Marines* (1855), tells much of his early life in the navy. In 1849 Wise was stationed in California at what later became the San Francisco navy yard. Meantime he had been promoted through the grades; in 1840 he was made a passed midshipman, in 1846 a master, and in 1847 a lieutenant. During the next two decades he continued to find some time for his writing and published *Scampavias from Gibel-Tarek to Stamboul* (1857), *The Story of the Gray African Parrot* (1860), which was a book for children, and *Captain Brand, of the "Centipede"* (1864), besides making regular contributions to scientific journals. His books, which were all written in a popular manner, were published under the pseudonym of Harry Gringo. Wise also became recognized as an authority on ordnance. While in France recuperating from a serious injury, he was ordered to investigate secretly the new Krupp discoveries. In 1860 he was sent to Japan as a member of the United States Japanese Commission.

Upon the outbreak of the Civil War, he was subjected to a severe mental ordeal. He had a strong traditional attachment to Virginia, but he had spent most of his life in the navy, and his mother and his wife were Northern women. He decided it was his duty to remain in the Union navy and, by a cruel order, was soon sent to Portsmouth, near his early home, Craney Island, to burn the Gosport navy yard. He carried out the order and later burned the *Cumberland*. On July 16, 1862, he was promoted commander and on July 26 was made assistant in the bureau of ordnance, "abandoned" by its chief and principal clerks at the outbreak of the war. In the responsible work of its administration Wise's ability as a writer and his knowledge of ordnance problems proved almost invaluable, and his unceasing labor during these difficult times was thought to have brought on the disease of which he died (*Army and Navy Journal*, May 1, 1869). On June 25, 1863, he was appointed acting chief of bureau; on Aug. 25, 1864, chief of bureau, and on Dec. 29, 1866, captain. In 1868 he resigned the bureau position and was given a leave of absence. He died the following year in Naples, Italy. On Aug. 20, 1850, he had been married to Charlotte Brooks Everett, daughter of Edward Everett [*q.v.*], who with their four children survived him.

His service record shows numerous leaves of absence, the result in most cases of delicate health. During these periods he traveled and collected material for his writing. Secretary Gideon Welles [*q.v.*], no gentle critic, described him as "pretty sagacious, but mentally timid, though not, I apprehend, wanting in physical courage" (*Diary, post,* III, 123), and Admiral David Dixon Porter [*q.v.*] praised his "indomitable energy" as chief of the bureau of ordnance.

[Sources include J. C. Wise, *Col. John Wise . . . His Ancestors and Descendants* (1918); *War of the Rebellion: Official Records (Navy)*; E. W. Callahan,

List of Officers of the Navy of the U. S. . . . . 1775–1900 (1901); Diary of Gideon Welles (3 vols., 1911); Army and Navy Jour., May 1, July 3, 1869; N. Y. Daily Tribune, Apr. 12, 1869, containing extracts from Wise's testimony before the Joint Cong. Committee on ordnance, with the partisan criticism of the Tribune's correspondent; information from Navy Dept.; N. Y. Times, June 23, 1869. The dates of birth and marriage are from Wise's daughter. There is correspondence in MS. with Henry Alexander Wise in the Lib. of Cong.]
R. D. M.

WISE, ISAAC MAYER (Mar. 29, 1819–Mar. 26, 1900), rabbi, was born in Steingrub, Bohemia, the son of Leo and Regina (Weis) Weis. Until he was nine the boy attended his father's private Hebrew day school. He then went to live with his grandfather, Dr. Isaiah Weis, a physician in the town of Durmaul. He became a pupil in the Jewish day school there and also received private instruction from his grandfather, a man learned in Hebrew lore. At twelve, when his grandfather died, he was thrown upon his own resources, the father's limited means making it impossible for him to do anything for the boy. Though so young, he had already decided upon the rabbinate as his career. He therefore journeyed to Prague, one of the chief centers of Jewish learning in Europe, where he attended several rabbinical schools, notably that conducted by Rabbi Samuel Freund, a great Talmudist. In 1835 he entered the most famous rabbinical school in Bohemia, that of Rabbi Aaron Kornfeld in Jenikau. Two years later the government issued a decree to the effect that any candidate for the rabbinate must pursue certain studies at the gymnasium and the university before he would be permitted to enter the active ministry. Young Weis therefore returned to Prague, where he attended the gymnasium and studied at the university for two years, and later went to the University of Vienna for one year. When he was twenty-three he appeared before a rabbinical court, or Beth Din, composed of three famous rabbis, Solomon Judah Rappaport, Samuel Freund, and Ephraim Loeb Teweles, who conferred on him the title of rabbi. On Oct. 26, 1843, he was elected rabbi of the congregation in the town of Radnitz, Bohemia. He was married on May 26, 1844, to Therese Bloch (d. 1874), daughter of a Jewish merchant in the neighboring town of Grafenried, by whom he had ten children. The restrictions and inhibitions then still in force against the Jews in Bohemia and in the conduct of the rabbinical office fretted him, and he had several unpleasant encounters with governmental functionaries. Becoming infected with the American fever, as he expressed it many years later, he departed from Radnitz in May 1846 and arrived in New York, July 23. It was probably about this time that he changed the spelling of his name. Through the aid of Max Lilienthal [q.v.], to whom he had a letter of introduction, he was enabled to gain a foothold in his profession. In September 1846 he was elected rabbi of the Jewish congregation of Albany, N. Y. He espoused the cause of liberal Judaism from the start. He remained in Albany until 1854, when he was elected rabbi of the Bene Yeshurun congregation of Cincinnati. He officiated there until the time of his death in 1900.

After a few months in Cincinnati he began publishing a weekly newspaper, the Israelite (later the American Israelite). Appalled by the religious disorganization among the Jews in the United States, he devoted his unusual talent for organization first towards urging a union of the congregations of the country, second towards establishing a theological seminary, and third towards founding a rabbinical conference. As early as 1848 he had issued an appeal for a union of the congregations, the first document of the kind to appear in the United States. This document, entitled "To the Ministers and Other Israelites," is remarkable in that the young enthusiast laid down in it the program which guided his activity for the next quarter century. In July 1873 the Union of American Hebrew Congregations was organized, which from very small beginnings attained country-wide proportions. The second of his great projects was realized with the founding on Oct. 3, 1875, of the Hebrew Union College, an institution for the education of rabbis. At this time all the rabbis in the country were foreign-born and had been educated in European schools. Wise felt that Israel in the United States was orphaned so long as the congregations were not shepherded by men of American training and filled with the American spirit. He served as president of the Hebrew Union College until his death twenty-five years later. When on July 11, 1883, he conferred the degree of rabbi on the four young men who constituted the first class of rabbis to be ordained in the United States, one of the dreams of his life was fulfilled. He now applied himself with fervor to the consummation of the third article in his program—the founding of a rabbinical organization. This was achieved when in July 1889, in Detroit, the Central Conference of American Rabbis, at present (1936) the largest rabbinical organization in the world, was organized. Wise served as president of this organization during the remaining eleven years of his life.

There can be little doubt that Wise was in his day the foremost figure in Jewish religious life in the United States. His life work consisted in the welding of the spirit of Judaism with the free spirit of America, and he was one of the latter-day prophets of the universalistic interpretation of Judaism. During his lifetime, reactionary forces seemed now and then to gain the upper hand, but Wise never lost faith in the ultimate triumph of the liberal religious principle, and his elasticity and youthfulness of spirit never forsook him. When at the age of eighty-one the end came, the visions of his youth had been realized, and great institutions in American Judaism had arisen as he had planned them. The Union of American Hebrew Congregations, the Hebrew Union College, and the Central Conference of American Rabbis constitute his triple memorial. A very prolific writer, besides his editorial writings in the *Israelite* Wise published many books and pamphlets. Chief among these may be mentioned *History of the Israelitish Nation from Abraham to the Present Time* (1854), *The Cosmic God* (1876), *History of the Hebrews' Second Commonwealth* (1880), and *Pronaos to Holy Writ* (1891). His *Reminiscences* were published in 1901. After the death of his first wife he was married on Apr. 25, 1876, to Selma Boudi of New York, by whom he had four children. At the time of his death in Cincinnati he was survived by his wife, five daughters, and six sons.

[In addition to Wise's *Reminiscences* (1901), translated from the German by David Philipson, see the biog. by David Philipson and Louis Grossman in *Selected Writings of Isaac M. Wise* (1900); David Philipson, *Isaac M. Wise* (1933), being Jewish Tract, No. 22; M. B. May, *Isaac Mayer Wise* (1916); J. R. Marcus, *The Americanization of Isaac Mayer Wise* (privately printed, 1931); A. S. Oko, *A Tentative Bibliog. of Dr. Isaac Wise* (1917); *Cincinnati Enquirer*, Mar. 26, 27, 1900.]
D. P.

WISE, JOHN (August 1652–Apr. 8, 1725), Congregational clergyman, born at Roxbury, Mass., and baptized Aug. 15, 1652, was the fifth son of Joseph and Mary (Thompson) Wise. He attended the free school at Roxbury and graduated from Harvard in 1673. Having studied theology, he preached at Branford, Conn., 1675/76, declining, however, a call to that parish. While at Branford he served as chaplain of forces acting against the Narragansett Indians. In 1677/78 he preached at Hatfield, Mass., and in 1680 was called to Chebacco, a newly organized parish of Ipswich. He was the minister of that church until his death, although for some reason his ordination was delayed until Aug. 12, 1683. Throughout his life he was active and influential in both civil and ecclesiastical affairs. When Gov. Edmund Andros [*q.v.*] attempted to raise money by a province tax, Wise led his townsmen to resist—one of the notable cases of resistance in colonial times—and in consequence

in October 1687 was seized and tried by a court presided over by Joseph Dudley [*q.v.*]. Wise was found guilty, find £50 and costs, deprived of his ministerial function, and put under bonds of £1,000 to keep the peace (*The Andros Tracts*, edited by W. H. Whitmore, vol. I, 1868, pp. 82, 85–86; *Edward Randolph*, edited by R. N. Toppan, vol. IV, 1899, pp. 171–82). On Nov. 24, Andros reversed the judgment in so far as to allow Wise to resume his functions as minister to his church (*Proceedings of the Massachusetts Historical Society*, vol. XII, 1873, p. 109). After Andros was deposed, Wise was chosen by his town one of the two representatives to go to Boston and help reorganize the former legislature. He also brought suit against Dudley for refusing him the privilege of *habeas corpus* and is said to have recovered damages. In 1690 he was appointed by the General Court chaplain of the expedition against Quebec and wrote an account of it, which was published in 1902 in the *Proceedings of the Massachusetts Historical Society* (2 ser. vol. XV).

Partly as a result of the Brattle Street Church episode in 1699–1700, when despite the opposition of most of the clergy an independent congregation chose and installed Benjamin Colman [*q.v.*] as its pastor, the Mathers and others initiated a movement to establish associations of clergy that were intended to exercise functions hitherto exercised by the individual churches. In November 1705 Increase Mather published a pamphlet, *Questions and Proposals,* in which the plan was set forth. Wise saw in the new movement the beginning of a reactionary revolution. He allowed it to run its course for a while but in 1710 published *The Churches Quarrel Espoused,* an extremely able pamphlet which gave the death blow to the movement. He followed this in 1717 with *A Vindication of the Government of New-England Churches,* in which he considered the fundamental ideas of civil as well as religious government. Wise had been called "the first great American democrat" (Tyler, *post,* p. 115). He was an extremely forceful and brilliant writer, perhaps the most so of any American in the colonial period. No one else equaled him in "the union of great breadth and power of thought with great splendor of style; and he stands almost alone among our early writers for the blending of a racy and dainty humor with impassioned earnestness" (*Ibid.,* p. 114). In 1772 his two pamphlets were reprinted as sources for language and arguments in the controversy then raging. They were reprinted again in 1860. His writings were remarkable expositions of the foundations of government from the democratic point of view, written so attractively and powerfully as to be veritable trumpet blasts of liberty. In 1721 he published *A Word of Comfort to a Melancholy Country,* a pamphlet in support of paper money, a favorite project of the democratic movement. With others he presented a remonstrance against the sentence of one of the witchcraft victims, and was a signer of the petition in 1703 to the General Court asking it to reverse the convictions. He is said to have been "of towering height, of great muscular power, stately and graceful in shape and movement; in his advancing years of an aspect most venerable" (*Ibid.,* p. 104). He married on or before Dec. 5, 1678, Abigail, daughter of Thomas Gardner of Roxbury or Brookline, who survived him and by whom he had seven children.

[John White, *The Gospel Treasure in Earthen Vessels, A Funeral Sermon on . . . the Death of . . . John Wise* (1725); J. L. Sibley, *Biog. Sketches of Grads. of Harvard Univ.,* vol. II (1881); W. B. Sprague, *Annals of the Am. Pulpit,* vol. I (1857); *The Cambridge Hist. of Am. Lit.,* vol. I (1917), which contains bibliog.; M. C. Tyler, *A Hist. of Am. Lit. During the Colonial Time* (1897), vol. II; H. M. Dexter, *The Congregationalism of the Last Three Hundred Years* (1880); A. McF. Davis, *Colonial Currency Reprints,* vols. I (1910), II (1911); V. L. Parrington, *The Colonial Mind* (1927).]   J. T. A.

WISE, JOHN (Feb. 24, 1808–Sept. 29, 1879), balloonist, was born in Lancaster, Pa., the birthplace of his father and mother, of German and English descent. He was educated in the local schools and graduated from the Lancaster high school. At fourteen he read a German newspaper account of a balloon voyage to Italy and developed a definite desire to study aerostatics in practical fashion. He began his experiments with paper parachutes. Later, with a parachute made of four ox-bladders, he dropped a cat thirty feet from a housetop without injury to the animal. He then experimented with hot-air paper balloons of the Montgolfier type. Watching the ascension of one of these balloons, he was seized with the desire to experience "the sublime feeling of sailing in air," as he put it. Before this desire was satisfied, however, he served an apprenticeship of four and a half years as cabinetmaker and then worked until 1835 as a pianoforte maker. All this experience was to serve him in good stead when he met with mechanical difficulties in the making of his balloons.

Wise's first ascent was made in Philadelphia in 1835 in a balloon of his own design, which he built before he had ever seen a balloon or an ascension. From then on he devoted his life entirely to aerostatics, not as an adventurer but as a scientific pioneer in ballooning. He developed a balloon varnish superior to those in use at the time and attempted to simplify the construction of balloons by cementing the seams, an idea which did not prove practicable. He constantly studied meteorological conditions and the effects of storms. As a result of these studies, he came to believe that a steady wind blew from west to east at an altitude of two to three miles which could be used to advantage by balloonists. During one of his ascents in a thunder-storm, the balloon rose so rapidly as a result of dropping ballast that the gas expanded faster than it could escape through the neck of the balloon and the balloon burst. The bag flared out, however, and acted as a parachute, permitting a safe descent. As a result of this accident, Wise developed a rip panel, and demonstrated several times that a forced descent might be made quickly by pulling the rip cord and using the balloon as a parachute. He also had to his credit one of the first definite proposals in aeronautical tactics, which was a plan to capture the city of Vera Cruz by dropping bombs from a balloon attached to a warship by a five-mile cable.

He believed that a trip to Europe could be made by a balloon if it could stay in the air for fifty hours, utilizing the supposedly steady wind from west to east. To test this idea a voyage from St. Louis to New York was projected. The balloon ascended on July 1, 1859, with Wise, three passengers, and a bag of mail, but it was caught in a storm over Lake Ontario, the heavy mail bag had to be thrown overboard, and the balloon finally came to earth near Henderson, N. Y. In this trip Wise set a distance record of 804 miles which was not surpassed until the year 1900. When two petitions to Congress (1843, 1851) for a grant of money to construct a balloon and make a trip to Europe were rejected, he finally came to an agreement with the *Daily Illustrated Graphic* of New York for the construction of a balloon to make the voyage. The balloon, completed in 1873, was 160 feet high, including the car and lifeboat slung underneath, and had a total lift of 14,000 pounds. Wise quarreled with his backers, however, and the balloon started on its flight to Europe with only Washington H. Donaldson, aeronaut, George A. Lunt, navigator, and Alfred Ford, newspaper correspondent. It crashed at New Canaan, Conn. On Sept. 29, 1879, while attempting another long voyage in a balloon called the "Pathfinder," Wise and his companion were drowned in Lake Michigan. Wise had a son, Charles E. Wise, of Philadelphia, also an aeronaut.

Wise's demonstrations regarding the safety of balloons, his invention of the rip panel, and his long-distance record of 804 miles definitely establish his right to being considered the first American aeronaut of any consequence. His writings, *A System of Aeronautics* (1850) and *Through the Air* (1873), give evidence of an original, searching, and impartial mind.

[See "The Longest Voyage," *Aeronautics,* Jan. 1894; "Wise upon Henson," *Aeronautical Ann.* (1895); F. S. Lahm, in *Flying,* Jan. 1913; *St. Louis Globe-Democrat,* Sept. 29–Oct. 7, and Oct. 15, 19, 25, and 26, 1879.]   A. K.

WISE, JOHN SERGEANT (Dec. 27, 1846– May 12, 1913), lawyer, politician, author, was born in Rio de Janeiro, Brazil, the son of Henry Alexander Wise [*q.v.*] and Sarah (Sergeant), the daughter of John Sergeant, 1779–1852 [*q.v.*], and sister-in-law of Gen. George Gordon Meade [*q.v.*]. The elder Wise returned in 1847 to his home on the Eastern Shore of Virginia, and John lived with him here and in the gubernatorial mansion in Richmond. After preparation in private schools, he entered the Virginia Military Institute in 1862 and remained two years. On May 15, 1864, he fought bravely with the cadets at New Market, Va., receiving a slight wound (see his *Memorial Address . . . at New Market, Va.,* 1898), and shortly afterwards was commissioned drill master with the rank of second lieutenant in the Confederate army. He served in Virginia until the end of the war and was the bearer of the first news that reached Jefferson Davis at Danville, Va., of the impending surrender of Lee's army, experiences he described in *The End of the Era* (1899).

In 1865 he entered the University of Virginia, where he was awarded a debater's medal and was graduated in law in 1867. In his novel *The Lion's Skin* (1905) he gives a valuable picture of life at the University in the Reconstruction period. Before he was twenty-one, he had begun the practice of law in Richmond, Va., and on Nov. 3, 1869, he married Evelyn Beverly Douglas of Nashville, Tenn., daughter of Hugh Douglas, a Tennessee Unionist. Continuing his interest in military affairs, he was captain of the Richmond Blues from 1878 to 1882 and restored its old, distinctive uniform; he also served on the board of visitors of the Virginia Military Institute.

In 1873 he began the political career which won him such unenviable notoriety. He accused the state Conservative party of corruption and became a leader of a so-called reform group in Richmond politics. After declining in 1878 a nomination for Congress in favor of Gen. Joseph E. Johnston [*q.v.*], he ran unsuccessfully in 1880 as a Readjuster, but in 1882, as the Republican

and Coalition candidate, defeated the formidable "Parson" John E. Massey for congressman-at-large. His affiliation with the Republican party and his tactless political utterances won him the hatred of many Virginians, and he received several challenges to duels. Undoubtedly he was more liberal than many of his opponents and more willing to adjust himself to new political conditions, but the impression remains that he was a political opportunist. He became a leader in the political machine of William Mahone [*q.v.*]. In 1882 he had been appointed federal district attorney but resigned after his election to Congress. The Republican candidate for governor in 1885, he was defeated by Fitzhugh Lee [*q.v.*], but contended that the Democrats won by improper methods. At that period even respectable people in the South were willing to employ or condone methods, ordinarily questionable, in order to control the ignorant negro vote.

In 1888, seeking better business opportunity and a more friendly scene, he removed from Virginia to New York City. Early in his professional career he had been appointed counsel for the company which built the first electric street railway in Richmond and had thus come into contact with Northern capitalists who were developing the infant electrical industry. He now became leading counsel in important litigation between street railway and other companies, and an international authority on law as applied to problems in the field of electricity. About six years before his death he became practically an invalid and returned to Northampton County, Va., where he lived "surrounded by his books, his dogs, and his memories."

Wise was a man of unusual abilities. He was a most attractive speaker and raconteur, an excellent sportsman, and a gifted writer. In view of his extreme frankness, his political vagaries, and his real charm and power as a writer, it is a misfortune that he could not afford to devote more time to literature. Besides the books mentioned above, he wrote *Diomed; The Life, Travels, and Observations of a Dog* (1897), and *Recollections of Thirteen Presidents* (1906). He died at the summer residence of Henry A. Wise, near Princess Anne, Md., survived by his wife and seven children, and was buried in Richmond.

[Information from Wise's family and contemporaries; *Times-Dispatch* (Richmond, May 13, 1913); *Biog. Dir. Am. Cong.* (1928); C. C. Pearson, *The Readjustor Movement in Va.* (1917); Wm. Couper, *The V. M. I. New Market Cadets* (1933); N. M. Blake, *William Mahone of Va.* (1935); J. C. Wise, *Col. John Wise of England and Va.; His Ancestors and Descendants* (1918); *Who's Who in America,* 1912–13.]

R. D. M.

WISE, THOMAS ALFRED (Mar. 23, 1865–Mar. 21, 1928), actor, known as Tom Wise, was born in Faversham, England, son of Daniel and Harriet (Potts) Wise. His father was a sea captain, who died before Tom's birth. His widow emigrated to America three years later, and Tom was reared in California, earning his own living, he later declared, from the time he was nine. He began to act at eighteen, picking up what jobs he could on the coast, in variety shows. On Aug. 27, 1883, while he was traveling with "Ingham's Combination Troupe" (seven people), the coach which carried them rolled down an embankment in the mountains. In 1885 William Gillette saw him act in San Francisco, and brought him east in *The Private Secretary,* but he got no nearer Broadway than the Grand Opera House on Eighth Avenue. He did not reach Broadway till 1888, when he appeared there in *Lost in New York.* From that time, he was a familiar figure in the New York theatre, filling a niche of his own, in farce-comedy especially. During the nineties he was often seen in the farces of George Broadhurst, and in 1899 appeared in *The Wrong Mr. Wright* in London. Among the plays he acted in during this decade were *Gloriana* (1892), *On the Mississippi* (1894), *The War of Wealth, The House That Jack Built,* and *Are You a Mason?* In 1901 he acted with Arnold Daly at Wallack's Theatre. The appearances with Daly were followed by *Vivian's Papas* (1903), *Mrs. Temple's Telegram* and *The Prince Chap* (1905), and *The Little Cherub* (1906), with Hattie Williams. In 1907 he was in a musical comedy called *The Lady from Lane's,* and the following season in *Miss Hook of Holland.* In 1908 he appeared as co-star with Douglas Fairbanks in a play written by himself and Harrison Rhodes, *A Gentleman from Mississippi,* a political comedy. He then wrote, again with Rhodes, and acted in a play called *An Old New Yorker* (1911). In the same year he and Rhodes wrote and produced a play called *The Greatest Show on Earth,* which was followed by a revival of *Lights o' London.* In the autumn of 1911 he acted with John Barrymore in *Uncle Sam,* in 1912 in *Captain Whittaker's Place,* by Joseph Lincoln, in 1913 in *The Silver Wedding,* and in 1914 in Edward Sheldon's dramatization of *The Song of Songs.* In 1916 he was back in a more congenial play, taking the place of James K. Hackett [*q.v.*] as Falstaff in *The Merry Wives of Windsor,* when Hackett, who had produced the play with elaborate sets by Joseph Urban [*q.v.*], fell ill. After co-starring with William Courtenay in 1917 in Lee Dodd's Comedy, *Pals First,* in September 1918 he realized an ambition to impersonate P. T. Barnum, in a play called *Mr. Barnum,* written by himself and Harrison Rhodes. Later appearances were in *Cappy Ricks* (1919), as Sir Oliver in the Players' Club revival of *The School for Scandal* (June 1923), as Sir Anthony in *The Rivals,* with Mrs. Fiske (1924–25), in *The Adorable Liar* (1926), and with Eleanor Painter in *The Nightingale* (1927). His later years were made difficult by illness. He made his last appearance in Chicago, in *Behold This Dreamer,* on Oct. 31, 1927. He died in New York, Mar. 21, 1928. Wise was one of the players most energetic in organizing the Actors' Society, for mutual protection, and was its president in 1908–10; the society later became the Actors' Equity Association and won a famous strike for better conditions. He was at all times devoted to the betterment of his profession and the welfare of his fellow players, with whom he was a great favorite. He married Gertrude Whitty, an English-born actress, on Nov. 11, 1895.

Wise was a fat man, with a fat man's voice and the traditional fat man's amiability. It doomed him, of course, to "character" rôles, and more or less to rôles expressive of unctuous good nature. "It's a Tom Wise part" became a common saying on Broadway when a play was being cast which contained such a rôle. Such parts, of course, occurred frequently in farcical comedies, but Wise was a thoroughly competent character actor, and his own attempts at dramatic authorship were prompted by a desire to create rôles for himself of higher caliber. He chose P. T. Barnum, no doubt, because of his close physical resemblance to the great showman, and he created the resemblance with the very minimum of facial make-up. But he was not so skilful a dramatist as he was actor, and his own plays never quite realized his ambitions, though *A Gentleman from Mississippi,* in which Wise enacted a genial but shrewd politician, was a considerable popular success. His Falstaff was richly comic and unctuous; could he have played it in *Henry IV* instead of *The Merry Wives,* it might have been his best memorial.

[*Who's Who in America,* 1926–27; Burns Mantle and G. P. Sherwood, *The Best Plays of 1909–1919* (1933); Harvard Coll. Lib., Theatre Coll.; obituaries in *N. Y. Times* and *N. Y. Herald Tribune,* Mar. 22, 1928.]

W. P. E.

WISLIZENUS, FREDERICK ADOLPH (May 21, 1810–Sept. 22, 1889), traveler, author, physician, was born at Königsee, Schwarzburg-Rudolstadt, Germany. Both his father, a pastor in the evangelical state church, and his mother, whose maiden name was Hoffmann, died during an epidemic following the retreat of Napoleon's army from Moscow. The three children of the union were adopted by the mother's brother and his wife, who reared them with devoted care. Adolph attended the gymnasium of Rudolstadt, the capital, later studying the natural sciences at the University of Jena and at Göttingen and Tübingen. He became deeply stirred by the political unrest of the time, and after taking part in an abortive uprising of students at Frankfurt-am-Main, Apr. 3, 1833, he fled to Switzerland. At Zürich he continued his studies, later spending some time in the Paris hospitals. In 1835 he arrived in New York, and in the following year he began practice as a country physician at Mascoutah, St. Clair County, Ill. A yearning to see the Far West prompted him, in April 1839, to ascend the Missouri to Westport, where he joined a fur-trading party for the mountains. From the trappers' rendezvous on Green River he went on to Fort Hall, in the present Idaho, intending to reach the Pacific Coast. He altered his course, however, and with a few companions returned by way of Brown's Hole, the Laramie plains, the Arkansas River, and the Santa Fé Trail to St. Louis. In the following year he published in that city *Ein Ausflug nach den Felsen-Gebirgen im Jahre 1839*, afterwards translated by his son and issued as *A Journey to the Rocky Mountains in the Year 1839* (1912). For the six years following his return he practised medicine in St. Louis in partnership with Dr. George Engelmann [*q.v.*].

In the spring of 1846, resolved on another adventure, he provided himself with a scientific outfit and joined the trading caravan of Albert Speyer for Santa Fé and Chihuahua. The caravan, supposed to be carrying arms for the Mexican government, was pursued by a detachment of Stephen Watts Kearny's army, but was not overtaken. From Santa Fé it moved on southward, Wislizenus closely observing the fauna, flora, and geology of the region, and collecting specimens. At Chihuahua he had a perilous experience with an anti-American mob, and with some companions was sent under guard into the mountains. The arrival of Alexander W. Doniphan's regiment in March 1847 restored the prisoners to freedom, and Wislizenus, joining the command as a surgeon, returned by way of the Rio Grande, the Gulf, and the Mississippi to his home. His account of the journey was submitted to the Senate by Thomas H. Benton, and appeared in 1848 as *Memoir of a Tour to Northern Mexico* (being *Senate Miscellaneous Document 26*, 30 Cong., 1 Sess.). The earlier narrative, despite some amusing slips in the use of proper names and in references to the various

Indian bands encountered, remains a classic of the late trapper period; and the later one, which was praised by Alexander von Humboldt, gives for most of the region traversed the earliest record of scientific observation. A German translation of the later narrative was published in 1850 in Brunswick.

Wislizenus did heroic duty throughout the cholera epidemic of 1848–49 in St. Louis. In 1850 he sailed for Europe, and at Constantinople, on July 23, he was married to Lucy Crane, sister of the wife of George P. Marsh, then the American minister to Turkey. On again reaching the United States, he voyaged to California to choose a home. Dissatisfied, he returned, and with his wife and infant son, whom he had left in New England, settled in St. Louis in 1852. He was one of the founders of the Missouri Historical Society and also of the Academy of Science of St. Louis, to the *Transactions* of which he was a frequent contributor. He became deeply interested in atmospheric electricity and recorded many observations of his experiments. Failing eyesight resulted, some years before his death, in total blindness. He died at his home.

[Wislizenus' given name often appears simply as Adolphus or Adolph. In addition to his son's memoir in *A Jour. to the Rocky Mountains . . . 1839* (1912), see death notice and obituary in *St. Louis Republic*, Sept. 24, 25, 1889, from which the date of death is taken; and *Down the Sante Fé Trail . . . the Diary of Susan Shelby Magoffin* (1926), ed. by Stella M. Drumm.]

W. J. G.

WISNER, HENRY (1720–Mar. 4, 1790), member of the Continental Congress, powder manufacturer, was the eldest son of Hendrick Wisner, who came to America with his father, Johannes in 1714, from Switzerland, settled on Long Island, and later with his wife, Mary Shaw of New England, moved to Goshen, Orange County, N. Y., where Henry was born. Like his father, Henry engaged in farming in Goshen, which always remained his home. Although he received but little formal schooling, he early rose to leadership in his local community and from 1759 to 1769 represented Orange County in the New York Colonial Assembly. In 1774 he was chosen to represent it in the First Continental Congress, where he signed the non-importation agreement. He was a member of the New York Provincial Congress (1775–77), and in April 1775 was selected by that body one of the colony's delegates to the Second Continental Congress, of which he was a member from May 1775 to May 1777. He strongly favored the Declaration of Independence and was present when it was adopted, but together with the other members of the New York delegation he was under instructions not to vote. He was one of the committee of the New York Provincial Congress which drafted the first constitution for the state, and after its adoption he sat in the first five sessions of the Senate, from 1777 to 1782.

Early in the Revolutionary War on the urgent request of Washington and the Continental Congress, New York took measures to encourage through the promise of loans and bounties the manufacture of powder and firearms for the Continental Army. Wisner was then operating in Ulster County one of the two powdermills in the colony. With the zeal that marked all his undertakings he immediately increased its output and erected two more mills in Orange County, meanwhile conducting experiments to improve the quality of the powder and teaching others his methods. He served on committees to determine means for securing saltpeter, sulphur lead, and gunflints; to keep open and in repair the roads leading through the Highland passes to the Hudson so that supplies might reach the army; and to establish military post offices for the conveyance of intelligence between Albany and headquarters at Fishkill. He often advanced money of his own to purchase needed supplies. He enjoyed the confidence of Gen. George Clinton, and though he sometimes acted contrary to orders, he not only was upheld by the officers and by the Provincial Congress, but was commended for his foresight, good judgment, and quick action.

Wisner rendered valuable service in 1776 in expediting the laying of the first chain designed to obstruct the passage of the British up the Hudson River. After the taking of Forts Montgomery, Clinton, and Constitution by Sir Henry Clinton in October 1777, new defenses had to be planned, and in January 1778 Wisner was appointed by the New York Provincial Convention one of a committee of eight to confer with General Putnam, with the result that a second chain was thrown across the Hudson, this time at West Point, and new fortifications were erected which proved effectual. At the close of the war, Wisner probably returned to his farm, but in 1788 he was a member of the New York convention called to act on the federal Constitution. He cast his vote against it because he feared the delegation of so much power to the central government. He was twice married: first, about 1739, to Sarah (or Mary) Norton, and second, in April 1769, to Sarah (Cornell) Waters; he had five children.

[G. F. Wisner, *The Wisners in America* (copr. 1918); *Public Papers of George Clinton*, vols. I–VII (1899–1904); *Jours. of the N. Y. Provincial Cong.* (1842); *Calendar of Hist. Manuscripts Relating to the War of the Revolution in the Office of the Secretary of State, Albany, N. Y.* (1868); E. M. Ruttenber, *Obstructions to the Navigation of Hudson's River . . . Original Documents Relating to the Subject* (1860); E. C. Burnett, *Letters of Members of the Continental Cong.*, vols. I, II (1921, 1923); Franklin Burdge, *A Memorial of Henry Wisner* (1878) and *A Second Memorial of Henry Wisner* (1898).]   E. L. J.

WISTAR, CASPAR (Feb. 3, 1696–Mar. 21, 1752), manufacturer of glass, was born in Wald-Hilsbach, Baden, near Heidelberg, the son of Johannes Caspar and Anna Catharina Wüster. His father was huntsman to Carl Theodore of Bavaria. Coming of age, Caspar emigrated to America, his ship reaching port at Philadelphia, Sept. 16, 1717. Though he lacked capital, he saved enough to undertake successfully the manufacture of brass buttons, advertised as "warranted to last seven years." In 1725 he joined the Society of Friends, and on May 25, 1726, he married Catharine Jansen, daughter of a prominent Quaker family. They had three sons and four daughters.

Some years later Wistar began the making of window and bottle glass. In 1738 he purchased for this purpose large pine-wooded tracts of land in Salem County, West Jersey, a location that offered abundant fuelage, an ample supply of silica, and adequate water transport facilities. He had sent across the sea for four experienced Belgian glass-blowers, and on July 30, 1740, the glass-house was "brought to perfection so as to make glass." This proved to be one of the earliest successful cooperative undertakings in the country. Wistar furnished all the materials for glass-making, and the workmen received one-third of the profits. Other glass workers, natives of Belgium, Germany, and Portugal, sailed from Holland for "Wistarberg" in 1748. Though it is credited with being the first flint-glass works in America, no advertisements are known which indicate that flint glass was manufactured at Wistarberg either during these earlier periods or later. When Wistar died, he stipulated by will that his son Richard should supervise the glass factory. Although Richard used every resource to avert catastrophe, the American Revolution and the economic depression that preceded it caused the failure of the Wistar works. Richard died in 1791; the furnace fires were soon drawn, and an industry whose influence was to extend through the years was no more.

The Wistarberg output is controversial; the volume is controversial; the quality of the glass manufactured is controversial. The factory began with the making of coarse green bottle-glass; it may have ended with flint glass. The thing that counts, however, is what came to be known as "the Wistar technique and tradition," one of the two most vital influences in early American glass production. A highway "with stage" was constructed from Philadelphia "to the doors of the Glass House" at Allowaystown. Fashion flocked. Fashion carried away splendid off-hand blown pitchers, vases, bowls—mementos of the occasion. The foreign-born blowers also fashioned fanciful wares for their brides, for neighbors, for a "personage." In so doing they created Hispano-Germanic-American forms and ornamentations which speak of Cadalso and Thuringia, of Spanish frivolity, Dutch sturdiness. Wistar glass is a satisfying utilitarian ware, decoratively pleasing, free in line, bold in execution, yet marked by a delicacy of wave and curve, of finial and handle. Despite its expansive, bulbous forms, the Wistar technique as manifest in pitchers is neither unbalanced nor incongruous. The uneven crimped foot remains sturdy, the mouth is ample and pours without dripping, the handles are made for human hands. Even with super-imposed decoration about the body, plastically applied threads encircling the neck, crimpings at the base of the handle, there is no appearance of over-elaboration. After the Revolution, Wistar's workmen established other glass industries, both locally and at distant points in New York State and the Middle West, and there carried on the tradition in isolated places, creating new manifestations of beauty and bequeathing to America fundamental designs in glassmaking.

[R. W. Davids, *The Wistar Family* (1896) ; *A Sketch of the Life of Caspar Wister, M.D.* (1891) ; F. W. Hunter, *Stiegel Glass* (1914) ; Rhea M. Knittle, *Early Am. Glass* (1927) ; J. D. Weeks, *Report on the Manufacture of Glass* (1883) ; Thomas Cushing and C. E. Sheppard, *Hist. of the Counties of Gloucester, Salem, and Cumberland, N. J.* (1883) ; records in MS. in colls. of the Hist. Soc. of Pa. ; R. M. Reifstahl, in *Internat. Studio*, Apr. 1923 ; Esther Singleton, in *Antiquarian*, Feb. 1924 ; G. S. McKearin, in *Country Life*, Sept. 1924, and in *Antiques*, Oct. 1926 ; Malcolm Vaughn, in *Internat. Studio*, July 1926 ; Hazel E. Cummin, in *House Beautiful*, Oct. 1929.] R.M.K.

WISTAR, CASPAR (Sept. 13, 1761–Jan. 22, 1818), physician, was born in Philadelphia, Pa., the son of Richard and Sarah (Wyatt) Wistar, and a grandson of Caspar Wistar [*q.v.*], glass manufacturer. He attended the Penn Charter School and began his medical studies under Dr. John Redman [*q.v.*]. He attended the courses at the medical school at the time of the separation of the College of Philadelphia and the newly created University of the State of Pennsylvania, receiving the degree of B.M. from the latter in 1782. The following year he went abroad and, after studying for a year in London went to Edinburgh University, where he received the degree of M.D. in 1786. In Edinburgh he served

two terms as president of the Royal Medical Society, a student organization, and assisted in founding a natural history society. His graduating thesis, *De Animo Demisso,* was dedicated to Benjamin Franklin and Dr. William Cullen. After a tour of the Continent he returned to Philadelphia in 1787. The College of Physicians of Philadelphia had been organized in January 1787, and it is a token of the esteem in which young Wistar was held that he was elected a junior Fellow in April, only a few months after his return. In 1789 he succeeded Benjamin Rush [*q.v.*] as professor of chemistry in the medical school of the College of Philadelphia. When the University of the State of Pennsylvania and the College of Philadelphia were united in 1792 as the University of Pennsylvania, he was made adjunct professor to William Shippen [*q.v.*], professor of anatomy, surgery, and midwifery. Separate chairs of surgery and midwifery were later given to Philip Syng Physick and Thomas Chalkley James [*qq.v.*]. On Shippen's death in 1808, Wistar succeeded him as full professor of anatomy and midwifery, and from 1810 until his death continued as professor of anatomy. In 1811 he published his *System of Anatomy,* the first American textbook on that subject. His chief achievement as a practical anatomist was the elucidation of the correct anatomical relations between the ethmoid and sphenoid bones. Wistar's other writings are all comprised in his *Eulogium on Doctor William Shippen* (1818) and a half-dozen communications to the American Philosophical Society (*Transactions*, III, 1793 ; IV, 1799, n.s., I, 1818).

His other activities were varied. He was one of the physicians to the Philadelphia Dispensary and a member of the staff of the Pennsylvania Hospital (1793–1810), served valiantly during the yellow fever epidemic of 1793, and in 1809 founded a society for the promotion of vaccination. In 1787 he was elected a member of the American Philosophical Society, and throughout his life it was a predominating interest with him. He was elected curator in 1793 and vice-president in 1795, and from 1815 to 1818, succeeding Thomas Jefferson, he served as president of the Society. On Sunday evenings (later on Saturday) Wistar kept open house for the members of the Society and visiting scientists in his large mansion at the corner of Fourth and Prune (now De Lancey) Streets. The house is still standing (1936) and is lived in by some of Wistar's collateral descendants. After his death a group was organized to perpetuate these "Wistar Parties," and from 1818 until 1864 the "Wistar Association," composed of from eight to twenty-four members chosen from the membership of the American Philosophical Society, entertained in succession at their homes during the months from December to May. In 1886 the Wistar Association was reorganized, and its parties have continued a feature of social life in Philadelphia. Wistar had an extensive correspondence with foreign scientific men, including Humboldt, Cuvier, and Sömmering. The Abbé Correa da Serra, Portuguese minister to the United States, was a frequent visitor at his house. In 1818 Thomas Nuttall [q.v.] named for him the beautiful plant Wistaria.

Wistar was married twice. By his first wife, Isabella Marshall, daughter of Christopher Marshall, whom he married on May 15, 1788, he had no issue. By his second wife, Elizabeth Mifflin, whom he married on Nov. 28, 1798, he had two sons and a daughter. His children left no descendants. For some years before his death he suffered from heart disease, with severe attacks of angina pectoris. He died on Jan. 22, 1818. Even the ill-natured and caustic Charles Caldwell [q.v.] writes of Wistar's genial and generous disposition. Though he criticizes him for unpunctuality in keeping professional engagements and speaks disparagingly of his ability as a lecturer in his early years, he regarded Wistar as infinitely superior in scholarship to any of his professional colleagues and says that in his later life he excelled in lecturing. After his death Wistar's family presented his large anatomical collection to the University of Pennsylvania for an anatomical museum. This was added to very materially by William Edmonds Horner [q.v.] and other successors of Wistar, and for many years was known as the Wistar and Horner Museum. In 1892 it was taken over by the Wistar Institute of Anatomy and Biology, which was founded and generously endowed by Wistar's great-nephew, Isaac Jones Wistar (1827–1905).

[See William Tilghman, *An Eulogium in Commemoration of Dr. Caspar Wistar* (1818), with notes in MS. in the lib. of the Coll. of Physicians of Phila.; Charles Caldwell, *An Eulogium on Caspar Wistar, M.D.* (1818); David Hosack, *Tribute to the Memory of the Late Caspar Wistar, M.D.* (1818); Joseph Carson, *Hist. of the Medic. Dept. of the Univ. of Pa.* (1869); W. S. W. Ruschenberger, *An Account of . . . the Coll. of Physicians of Phila.* (1887); *Autobiog. of Isaac Jones Wistar* (2 vols., 1914); H. A. Kelly, *Some Am. Medic. Botanists* (1914), which contains material supplied by Dr. T. J. Wistar, Wistar's grand-nephew; W. S. Middleton, in *Annals of Medic. Hist.* (1922), vol. IV; death notice and obituary in *Poulson's Am. Daily Advertiser*, Jan. 23, 24, 1818. See also R. W. Davids, *The Wistar Family* (1896); J. R. Tyson, *Sketch of the Wistar Party of Phila.* (1898); and H. L. Carson, *The Centenary of the Wistar Party* (1918). The Coll. of Physicians of Phila. has a number of Wistar's lecture note-books in MS., as well as a copy by S. B. Waugh of the portrait of Wistar by Bass Otis.]   F.R.P.

WISTER, SARAH (July 20, 1761–Apr. 21, 1804), diarist, was descended from pure German stock on her father's side and from pure Welsh on her mother's. The family name, originally Wüster, took the Anglicized forms of Wister and Wistar in the two branches of the family. John Wüster, born near Heidelberg, had joined his brother, Caspar Wistar [q.v.], in Philadelphia, Pa., in 1727 and made a considerable fortune as a wine merchant, much of which was invested in real estate. His son, Daniel Wister, was the father of Sally. Her mother was Lowry Jones, whose great-grandfather, Dr. Edward Jones, had been a founder of the Welsh colony in Merion and Haverford townships and had married a daughter of Dr. Thomas Wynne, speaker of the first Pennsylvania Assembly.

The birthplace of Sally Wister was the fine residence built by her grandfather Wister on High Street. She attended the school kept by the well-known Quaker, Anthony Benezet [q.v.]. There among her intimate friends were Deborah Norris, Anna and Peggy Rawle, Sally Burge, and other girls from the best families, who were later to be notable women of the city. After she completed her elementary studies she must have had some training in literature and the classics, for her writing shows acquaintance with Latin and French and a cultivated taste for reading. She frequently quotes poetry and was happy to receive a "charming collection" of books that included Fielding's *Joseph Andrews*. It is possible that she also learned needlework at school, for Capt. Alexander S. Dandridge complimented her on her skill in making a sampler. After the outbreak of the Revolution, when the British were threatening Philadelphia, Daniel Wister moved his family to the Foulke farm, on the Wissahickon, some fifteen miles away. There Sally kept up a correspondence with Deborah Norris until the British entered Germantown. On that day, Sept. 25, 1777, she began "a sort of journal of the time," as she says, a record of everyday events and experiences, intended as communications to her "saucy Debbie," though they never reached the latter until many years later. After Sally's death her brother, Charles J. Wister, lent the manuscript to the distinguished mistress of Stenton. The journal is one of the most interesting of its kind. Its author was a vivacious girl of sixteen, with a sense of humor and an eye for the dramatic, who gives a naïve yet faithful account of her impressions. It is thus valuable not only as a commentary on the history and the social conditions of the time but as a human document. The journal was continued until June 20,

1778, shortly before the family returned to Philadelphia.

Sally Wister developed into a fine type of woman. Occasionally she wrote verse, some of which was published in the *Port Folio*. After the death of her grandfather the family moved to Grumblethorpe, his country house in Germantown, where she spent the remainder of her life. As the years passed she became deeply religious and devotedly attached to her charming mother, whom she survived only a few months.

[The biog. sketch in *Sally Wister's Jour., A True Narrative, Being a Quaker Maiden's Account of Her Experiences with Officers of the Continental Army, 1777–1778* (1902), ed. by A. C. Myers, is the best account of Sally Wister's life. See also J. W. Jordan, *Colonial Families of Phila.* (1911), vol. I; *A Memoir of Charles J. Wister* (1866); H. M. Jenkins, *Hist. Colls. Relating to Gwynedd* (1897); J. T. Scharf and Thompson Westcott, *Hist. of Phila.* (1884), vol. II; and W. S. W. Ruschenberger, *A Sketch of the Life of Caspar Wister, M.D.* (1891).]   A. L. L.

WITHERS, FREDERICK CLARKE (Feb. 4, 1828–Jan. 7, 1901), architect, was born in Shepton Mallet, Somersetshire, England, the son of John Alexander and Maria (Jewell) Withers. After completing his school education at King Edward's School, Sherborne, he entered the London office of Thomas Henry Wyatt, where he received his architectural training, in company with his brother, Robert J. Withers, who, staying in England, later became a Fellow of the Royal Institute of British Architects. In 1853 Frederick emigrated to America, one of a number of young English architects attracted about the same time by the opportunities offered in an expanding young country. In America he seems to have been in close touch at an early period with his compatriots, Calvert Vaux [*q.v.*] and Jacob Wray Mould. After practising for some time in Newburgh, N. Y., where Vaux was living and working as a partner of Andrew Jackson Downing [*q.v.*], he followed Vaux to New York and eventually became (1864) a partner of Vaux and Olmsted, working with them especially on the architectural treatment of Central Park. (Drawings in the New York Park Department show Vaux and Withers associated as early as 1860.) Mould was also working with them, Withers and Vaux on the larger elements, and Mould on details and decoration. Soon after the Civil War began, Withers enlisted and served with a volunteer engineer regiment. In 1862 he was invalided home and resumed practice, with Vaux until 1871, later alone. In 1856 he married Emily A. deWint (d. 1863), a relative of Downing's wife, and on Aug. 4, 1864, Beulah Alice Higbee (d. 1888). He had eleven children, three by his first wife; eight by his second.

During Withers' later life he resided at Yonkers, where he died.

Withers enjoyed a high reputation during his lifetime and had a wide practice, chiefly in the designing of institutions and churches. For some time he was architect of the Department of Charities and the Department of Correction in New York City, for which he designed the Jefferson Market Police Court and Prison and the Chapel of the Good Shepherd on Welfare Island. He was also the architect of the Hudson River Asylum, Poughkeepsie, and the Columbia Institute for the Deaf and Dumb, Washington, D. C. (1867). He is, however, best known as a church architect. Among his churches important examples are the First Presbyterian Church, Newburgh, N. Y. (1857), St. Michael's, Germantown, Pa. (1858), the Dutch Reformed Church, Fishkill-on-Hudson (1859), St. Paul's, Newburgh, N. Y. (1864), the First Presbyterian, Highland Falls, N. Y. (1868), the Episcopal Church, Matteawan, N. Y. (1869), Calvary Episcopal Church, Summit, N. J. (1872), and St. Thomas', Hanover, N. Y. (1874). He was also the architect of the Astor memorial reredos and chancel fittings of Trinity Church, New York. In 1866 Vaux, Olmsted, and Withers won the competition for a proposed memorial chapel at Yale, but the building was never erected. Withers was the author of *Church Architecture: Plans, Elevations, and Views of Twenty-One Churches and Two School Houses* (1873).

Withers' work stands half-way between the archaeological Gothic Revival of the elder Richard Upjohn [*q.v.*] and the mannerisms of the developed Victorian Gothic of such men as Russell Sturgis [*q.v.*]. He used the horizontal banding and polychrome masonry of the latter style with discretion and restraint, but always seemed to be searching for a new, modern, and personal, rather than a merely archaeological expression of generally Gothic ideals. His work was especially valuable in keeping up the standard of church architecture during a period when American taste was in a woefully chaotic state.

[Sources include *Who's Who in America*, 1899–1900; C. D. Higby, *Edward Higby and His Descendants* (1897); N. Y. city directories; *Biog. Dir. of the State of N. Y.* (1900); Élie Brault, *Les Architectes par leurs Œuvres* (Paris, 3 vols., 1892–93); *Am. Art Ann.*, 1903; *Papers Read at the Royal Inst. of British Architects . . . 1866–67* (1867); *Am. Architect and Building News*, Jan. 19, 1901; obituary in *N. Y. Times*, Jan. 8, 1901; information from Margaret Withers of Washington, D. C., Withers' daughter.]   T. F. H.

WITHERSPOON, JOHN (Feb. 5, 1723–Nov. 15, 1794), Presbyterian clergyman, signer of the Declaration of Independence, president of the College of New Jersey, was the son of the

Rev. James and Anne (Walker) Witherspoon. He was born at Yester, near Edinburgh, Scotland. Though he was not a direct descendant of John Knox, as alleged, the family tree is sprinkled with Calvinist dominies. He attended the ancient Haddington Grammar School and at the age of thirteen matriculated at the University of Edinburgh, where he remained for seven years, taking the degree of master of arts in 1739 and the divinity degree in 1743. He was licensed to preach by the Haddington Presbytery, Sept. 6, 1743, and in January 1745 received a call to Beith in Ayrshire, where he was ordained Apr. 11. On Sept. 2, 1748, he married Elizabeth Montgomery, by whom he had ten children, five of whom died in childhood. In 1757 he became pastor of the congregation in the flourishing town of Paisley.

His Scottish ministry lasted until 1768. Early allying himself with the Popular Party, he became one of its leaders. This faction was conservative, striving to maintain a purity of doctrine that was distasteful to many of the clergy. For twenty years Witherspoon attacked the Moderates for their apparent willingness to sacrifice the great dogmas of the Church for a dubious humanism in science and letters. It was his conviction that sermons should be more than expositions of morality, and in his diatribe *Ecclesiastical Characteristics* (1753), which quickly ran through seven editions, he excoriated the spiritual vacillation of the "paganized Christian divines" of his day. In 1757, enraged by the appearance of a play written by a churchman, he published *A Serious Enquiry into the Nature and Effects of the Stage,* in which he declared the drama to be an unlawful recreation because it agitates the passions too violently and therefore is not recreative in effect. In brief, he was reenacting the old story of a sterner generation waging a losing fight against the more comfortable philosophy of a more cultured age (Collins, *post,* I, 29). In one respect, however, the Popular Party was completely identified with the people, namely, in its solicitude for "the right of personal conscience." The General Assembly in the interest of more efficient church organization insisted upon obedience to the ecclesiastical authorities in the appointment of ministers. Witherspoon, in defending the traditional rights of the people in choosing their own ministers, emerged as the champion of popular rights.

The fight between the factions was long and bitter. Witherspoon was ever on the offensive, confounding his enemies in a stream of published satires and invectives. These were read eagerly both at home and abroad by those of the Calvinist persuasion. In 1759 as moderator of the Synod of Glasgow and Ayr he delivered the last of his great doctrinal sermons, *The Trial of Religious Truth by Its Moral Influence,* in which he stoutly maintained all the orthodox points, painted a gloomy picture of the religious decadence of the country, and condemned in no uncertain terms the weakness and intellectual dishonesty of the ministry whereby "an unsubstantial theory of virtue" was being preached instead of "the great and operative views of the Gospel" (Collins, I, 55). In 1768, after having refused calls to Rotterdam and Dublin, he left Paisley to assume the presidency of the College of New Jersey. He had originally been elected in November 1766, but had declined at that time out of deference to the wishes of his wife. He had fought a gallant fight, and though retreating he was in reality leaving a stage which he had outgrown. In 1764 the University of St. Andrews had conferred upon him the degree of D.D. in recognition of his signal abilities and leadership.

Witherspoon's American career reveals many activities, political, religious, and educational. In accepting the call to New Jersey he undertook considerably more than an educational mission. The Presbyterian Church in America at that time was divided in counsel. Happily, Witherspoon, the choice of the New Side school, held views that were welcome to those of the Old Side. His leadership, apparent from the start, gave the church the necessary drive it needed to extend itself in a new country. The factional schism was healed, the organization was strengthened, a close association was established with the Congregationalists, and the Presbyterian Church, revitalized by the Scotch-Irish influx, grew rapidly. By 1776 it was strongly entrenched in the Middle Colonies and on the frontier where it enjoyed for a brief span almost a monopoly of the religious activity. With this growth Witherspoon was intimately identified. His unrivaled position in American ecclesiastical circles was based upon a perfect familiarity with the historic principles, discipline, and forms of Presbyterianism. During the closing years of his life he could boast that a decided majority of the members of the General Assembly had been his own students.

Though not a profound scholar, Witherspoon was an able college president. During the period 1768–76 the College of New Jersey took on a new lease of life. The endowment, the faculty, and the student body steadily increased. The Revolution, however, precluded a continuance of growth for many years. The student body was dispersed, the college could not be used for educational purposes, and its President was less and less in residence. Witherspoon introduced into

Princeton the study of philosophy, French, history, and oratory, and he insisted upon a mastery of the English language. It was his conviction that an education should fit a man for public usefulness. Book learning for its own sake did not greatly appeal to him, for were there not many learned in various subjects "whom yet we reckon greatly inferior to more ignorant persons in clear, sound common sense?" (*Works, post,* IV, 17). Nor did he place a high value upon acquisitive scholarship. "The person who addicts himself to any one of these studies . . . cannot be a man of extensive knowledge; and it is but seldom that he can be a man of a liberal or noble turn of mind, because his time is consumed by the particularities, and his mind narrowed by attending to one particular art" (*Ibid.,* p. 18). As in Scotland, Witherspoon had little patience with any credo that smacked of intellectual imagery or subtlety. He decried Berkeleyanism, so popular in many American circles, and exterminated it at Princeton. He stood four-square upon doctrines empirical and to him America owes, for what it is worth, the philosophy of "common sense" that permeated its thinking for so long.

Witherspoon had disapproved of ministers participating in politics, and this fact, possibly, delayed his appearance upon the political stage. It was not until 1774 that he manifested more than a casual interest in the controversy with the mother country. His opening activities were unheralded; he was merely making common cause with his neighbors. He was a county delegate, acting upon committees of correspondence and serving at provincial conventions. During the winter of 1775–76, as chairman of his county delegation, he was concerned principally in bringing New Jersey into line with the other colonies. He was conspicuous only in the movement leading to the imprisonment of the royalist governor, William Franklin [*q.v.*]. On June 22, 1776, he was chosen as a delegate to the Continental Congress. This appointment prevented him, though the contrary is alleged, from sitting on the committee that drafted and secured the adoption of the state constitution (Collins, I, 215). He arrived in Philadelphia at the time when Congress was on the point of adopting a resolution of independence and drafting the Declaration. Though he did not carry the Declaration by a dramatic "nick of time" speech on July 4, as extravagant admirers have claimed, it is known that he performed on July 2 the equally valuable service of urging advance where others would delay, assuring Congress that the country "had been for some time past loud in its demand for the proposed declaration" and stating that in his judgment "it

was not only ripe for the measure but in danger of rotting for the want of it" (*Ibid.,* I, 217–21).

Witherspoon had a clearer comprehension of the controversy between the colonies and the mother country than most. In the summer of 1774, in an essay, unpublished at the time, he laid out a course of action that was identical with the one followed by Congress: "To profess loyalty to the King and our 'backwardness' to break connection with Great Britain unless forced thereto; To declare the firm resolve never to submit to the claims of Great Britain, but deliberately to prefer war with all its horrors, and even extermination, to slavery; To resolve union and to pursue the same measures until American liberty is settled on a solid basis . . ." (*Works,* IV, 214–15). Witherspoon's writings had a wide influence in Great Britain as well as at home. A sermon delivered at Princeton in May 1776, *Dominion of Providence over the Passions of Men,* was the first of a steady stream of opinions and arguments that came from his pen. In resolving in terse phrases the controversy with Great Britain he was unexcelled. "It is proper to observe that the British settlements," he wrote, "have been improved in a proportion far beyond the settlements of other European nations. To what can this be ascribed? Not to the climate; not to the people, for they are a mixture of all nations. It must, therefore, be resolved singly into the degree of British liberty which they brought from home, and which pervaded more or less their several constitutions" (*Ibid.,* II, 441). "Is there a probable prospect of reconciliation on constitutional principles? Will anybody show that Great Britain can be sufficiently sure of our dependence, and yet be sure of our liberties?" (*Ibid.,* IV, 320).

Witherspoon served in Congress with some intermissions from June 1776 until November 1782. He was appointed to more than one hundred committees and was a member of two standing committees of supreme importance—the board of war and the committee on secret correspondence or foreign affairs. He took an active part in the debates on the Articles of Confederation; assisted in organizing the executive departments; shared in the formation of the new government's foreign alliances; and played a leading part in drawing up the instructions of the American peace commissioners. He fought against the flood of paper money, and opposed the issuance of bonds without provision for their amortization. "No business can be done, some say, because money is scarce," he wrote. "It may be said, with more truth, money is scarce, because little business is done" (*Essay on Money,*

1786, p. 58). Witherspoon's ability to execute the manifold tasks set before him, and his all-enduring patience and high courage in the face of recklessness and despair are the qualities that give him rank among the leaders of the American Revolution.

He spent his last years, from 1782 to 1794, in endeavoring to rebuild the college. During his lifetime, however, the institution at Princeton never fully recovered from the effects of the Revolution. He did not as he wished spend his remaining days *in otio cum dignitate,* for he could never refuse a call to service. In 1783 he returned to the state legislature, and again in 1789. In 1787 he was a member of the New Jersey ratifying convention. From 1785 to 1789 he was engaged in the plan of organizing the Presbyterian Church along national lines. The catechisms, confessions of faith, directory of worship, and the form of government and discipline were largely his work. He was moderator of the first General Assembly, meeting in May 1789. His last years were sad and difficult, owing to the forlorn condition of the college exchequer, the depleted state of his purse, and the death of his wife. On May 30, 1791, he married Ann Dill, widow of Dr. Armstrong Dill. He was at that time sixty-eight and his bride twenty-four, and the marriage caused considerable comment; two daughters were born of the union, one of whom died in infancy. Blind the last two years of his life, Witherspoon died on his farm, at "Tusculum," at the age of seventy-one, and was buried in the President's Lot at Princeton. In 1800–01 *The Works of John Witherspoon,* in four volumes, appeared, and a nine-volume edition of his works was published in Edinburgh in 1815. In an article in the *Pennsylvania Journal* in 1781 he pointed out the divergence of the language spoken in America from that in England, and coined the term "Americanism."

[The most scholarly biography and one containing a complete bibliog. is V. L. Collins, *President Witherspoon* (2 vols., 1925). For a shorter, less critical account see W. B. Sprague, *Annals of the Am. Pulpit,* vol. III (1858). For his administration of Princeton, John Maclean's *Hist. of the Coll. of N. J.* (1877) is authoritative. The principal manuscript source is Ashbel Green's sketch of Witherspoon's life, preserved in the N. J. Hist. Soc. Lib., Newark. See also D. W. Woods, *John Witherspoon* (1906) and I. W. Riley, *Am. Philosophy: The Early Schools* (1907).]
J. E. P.

WITHERSPOON, JOHN ALEXANDER (Sept. 13, 1864—Apr. 26, 1929), physician and medical educator, was born at Columbia, Maury County, Tenn., the son of John McDowell and Mary (Hanks) Witherspoon. His father was a farmer, lawyer, and judge of the county court. His great-grandfather, in the paternal line, was an officer in the Revolutionary army and a nephew of John Witherspoon [*q.v.*], a signer of the Declaration of Independence and early president of the College of New Jersey. John Alexander received his academic education in the schools of Maury County and at Austin College, Sherman, Tex. He studied medicine for two years in the office of a physician at Columbia, Tenn., before entering the University of Pennsylvania school of medicine, where he received the degree of M.D. in 1887. In later years he carried on further study in New York, as well as in Germany, France, England, and Scotland. Upon graduation he began the practice of medicine in his home town. On Nov. 8, 1888, he was married to Cornelia Dixon of Ashwood, Tenn. In 1889 he joined the faculty of the medical department of the University of Tennessee, Nashville, as professor of physiology, and two years later became professor of medicine. He acted also, for a brief period (1892–93), as professor of obstetrics and gynecology in the University of the South at Sewanee, Tenn. In 1895 he assisted in the reorganization of the medical department of Vanderbilt University, Nashville, Tenn., going abroad to study the medical schools of Europe and to buy supplies for the new department. Upon his return he became professor of medicine and clinical medicine, in which capacity he served until his death.

Witherspoon's greatest contribution to medical science in the South was made through his work at Vanderbilt. In addition to his classroom lectures, he worked untiringly to raise the standards of medical education. He served on the council on medical education of the American Medical Association (1904–13) and was active in the Association of American Medical Colleges, of which he was president in 1909. He assisted in the founding of the *Southern Medical Journal* (1908), was editor-in-chief during the first two years of its existence, and was an associate editor from 1911 to 1915. Over a period of thirty-two years, beginning in 1894, he contributed articles to various professional publications, including not only the *Journal of the American Medical Association,* the *Southern Medical Journal,* and the *Southern Practitioner,* but journals of the state associations of Tennessee, Texas, Illinois, and Wisconsin, as well as those of Louisville, Cincinnati, and Detroit. These articles dealt not only with the subject of medical education and its standards but with a variety of diseases and their treatment.

Throughout the period of his connection with Vanderbilt University, Witherspoon engaged in private practice in Nashville. He was also active in city, state, regional, and national medical associations. In addition to being a member of the American College of Physicians, he was at various times president of the Nashville Academy of Medicine, the Tennessee State Medical Association, the Southern Medical Association, and the Mississippi Valley Medical Association. In 1912 he became president of the American Medical Association, which he represented at the International Medical Congress in London, and subsequently served as a member of the House of Delegates of that body for eight years. His personality and his ability as a speaker won him prominence outside his profession as well: in 1909 he represented the American government at the dedication of the statue of George Washington in Budapest.

[*Who's Who in America*, 1928–29; *Jour. Am. Medic. Asso.*, June 15, 1912, May 4, 1929; *Southern Practitioner*, July 1912; P. M. Hamer, *The Centennial Hist. of the Tenn. State Medic. Asso.* (1930); J. T. Moore and A. P. Foster, *Tenn., the Volunteer State* (1923), vol. II; obituaries in *Nashville Tennessean*, Apr. 26, 1929.]
                                   D. M. R.

WITTHAUS, RUDOLPH AUGUST (Aug. 30, 1846–Dec. 19, 1915), chemist and toxicologist, was born in New York City, the son of Rudolph A. Witthaus and Marie Antoinette (Dunbar) Witthaus. He was brought up in New York and attended the schools there, and in 1867 received the degree of A.B. from Columbia University. The following two years he spent abroad, studying at the Sorbonne and the Collège de France. On his return to America he entered the College of Medicine of the University of the City of New York and was graduated M.D. in 1875. While in college, he had been allowed to convert a stable of his father's into a laboratory where he amused himself with chemical experiments, and when financial reverses forced him to earn his living, he turned to the subject which had always fascinated him. He was associate professor of chemistry and physiology at the University of the City of New York (1876–78), where he was later professor of physiological chemistry (1882–86), and professor of chemistry and physics (1886–98). Other appointments included the positions of professor of chemistry and toxicology, University of Vermont (1878–1900), and professor of chemistry and toxicology, University of Buffalo (1882–88). In 1898 he became professor of chemistry and physics at Cornell University, where he retired in 1911 as professor emeritus.

Witthaus won world-wide eminence in the field of legal medicine, and testified in some of the most notable murder trials in the United States. He found time to write many articles on toxicol-

ogy and chemistry, and was the author of a number of important books. Among his books, most of which went through a number of editions, are *Essentials of Chemistry, Inorganic and Organic* (1879), *General Medical Chemistry for the Use of Practitioners of Medicine* (1881), *Medical Students' Manual of Chemistry* (1883), and *A Laboratory Guide in Urinalysis and Toxicology* (1886). What may be regarded as his greatest achievement was *Medical Jurisprudence, Forensic Medicine and Toxicology* (4 vols., 1894–96), which he edited with T. C. Becker. The fourth volume, on toxicology, was the work of Witthaus alone. A second edition was printed in 1906–11. Valuable articles by Witthaus on different types of poisoning appeared in A. H. Buck's *A Reference Handbook of the Medical Sciences* (9 vols., 1885–93). He belonged to chemical societies in Berlin and Paris, and was fellow of the American Academy of Arts and Sciences and of the New York Academy of Medicine.

A man of broad culture and wide learning, quiet and uncommunicative, Witthaus devoted his entire life to his work and his books. Much of his time in later years was spent poring over his own books and cataloguing them, and few days went by in which he missed his hours of study at the library of the New York Academy of Medicine, where his own fine library was deposited at his death. His friends were few. He was extremely cynical and so often irascible that it was difficult to get along with him. He was a man of small stature, lean as well as short, of sandy complexion. His portrait, painted by Fagnani, was left to Jennie Cowan of New York. He was married, Feb. 23, 1882, in the Church of the Transfiguration, New York, to Bly-Ella Faustina (Coles) Ranney, daughter of Edward O. Coles of New York, from whom he was later separated. His death in 1915 followed a long illness.

[*Who's Who in America*, 1914–15; *Medic. Record*, Dec. 25, 1915; *Jour. Am. Medic. Asso.*, Jan. 8, 1916; *Science*, Apr. 14, 1916; H. A. Kelly and W. L. Burrage, *Am. Medic. Biogs.* (1920); obituary in *N. Y. Times*, Dec. 21, 1915; account of will in *N. Y. Herald*, Dec. 23, 1915.]
                                   G. L. A.

WOERNER, JOHN GABRIEL (Apr. 28, 1826–Jan. 20, 1900), probate judge, author, was born in Möhringen, Württemberg, Germany, the youngest of fourteen children of Elizabeth (Ulmer) and Christian Woerner, a poor but well-born carpenter. When he was seven, his parents emigrated to Philadelphia, where the boy worked in a bakery. In 1837 the family removed to St. Louis. There he added two years at a German school to his scant education. After three years, 1841–44, in country stores in the Missouri Ozarks, where he came in contact with the self-reliance of the frontier, he became printer's devil on the St. Louis *Tribune,* an influential German daily, which he served successively as pressman, shop foreman, and editor. Although he had become an American citizen on July 12, 1847, his sympathy with the revolutionists took him to Germany in 1848. He did not participate but reported the insurrection for several American newspapers, including the *New York Herald* and his own. Returning to St. Louis after two years, he purchased the *Tribune* and, changing its politics from Whig to Democratic, threw it behind Thomas H. Benton [*q.v.*]. In 1852 he sold the newspaper, began to study law, and, on Nov. 16, married Emilie, the daughter of Friedrich Plass, and a native of East Friesland, Hanover, Germany. The next year he became court clerk. Successively he was clerk for the St. Louis aldermen, 1856, city attorney, 1857–58, and councilman, 1861–64. Denied a seat in the Missouri Senate in 1863 following a contest in that body, he was reëlected in 1866, allowed to take his seat, and became an outstanding legislator in spite of belonging to a negligible Democratic minority. Missouri's railroad policy for many years was influenced by a committee report that he prepared (Scharf, *post,* I, 695). An uncompromising supporter of Lincoln and a lieutenant-colonel in the state militia during the Civil War, he opposed what he regarded as unjust Reconstruction measures; in the legislature he worked against ratification of the Fifteenth Amendment.

As probate judge of St. Louis for six terms, 1870–94 inclusive, he accomplished his most important work. Scrupulously honest and constantly seeking to improve estate laws, he became widely known as an authority on probate judicature (*Missouri Historical Review,* July 1921, pp. 601–2, 610). His two-volume *Treatise on the American Law of Administration* (1889) was a pioneer work, as was its complement, *A Treatise on the American Law of Guardianship* (1897). Reforms he proposed to conserve estates against numerous fees and expenses, brought him national notice. Chief among his non-legal writings was *Die Sclavin* (1891), an abolitionist drama, which began a popular career on the German stage of the Middle West in 1874 in St. Louis. In his last year he published a novel of Missouri before the Civil War, with characters from life and a philosophical tone, *The Rebel's Daughter: a Story of Love, Politics and War* (1899). Associated with Carl Schurz, Henry C. Brokmeyer, William T. Harris, Joseph Keppler, Emil Preetorius and George Engelmann [*qq.v.*], he was a participant coworker in the St. Louis Movement in philosophy and education. He was also

a founder of the St. Louis Philosophical Society. He played several musical instruments, composed for the piano, studied languages, read voluminously, and devised chess problems. His wife died in 1898 survived by four of their five children. He died at home of paralysis.

[W. F. Woerner, *J. Gabriel Woerner* (1912); A. J. D. Stewart, *The Hist. of the Bench and Bar of Mo.* (1898); W. B. Stevens, *Centennial Hist. of Mo.* (1921), vol. IV; J. T. Scharf, *Hist. of St. Louis City and County* (1883), vol. I; H. L. Conard, *Encyc. of the Hist. of Mo.* (1901), vol. VI; *Mo. Hist. Rev.,* Oct. 1920, p. 116, Jan. 1931, p. 213, July 1931, pp. 613–15; *Mo. Hist. Soc. Colls.,* vol. V (1928), pp. 265–66; *St. Louis Post-Dispatch,* Jan. 21, 1900.]   I. D.

WOFFORD, WILLIAM TATUM (June 28, 1823–May 22, 1884), planter, legislator, soldier, son of William Hollingsworth and Nancy M. (Tatum) Wofford, was born in Habersham County, Ga. His ancestors, coming from Cumberland, England, settled first in Pennsylvania, but soon removed to Spartanburg, S. C.; his grandfather established iron works near that place and served as a colonel in the American Revolution. William H. Wofford, who settled in Georgia in 1789, died shortly after his son's birth, and the boy was reared by his mother, a native of Virginia. He attended a local school and the Gwinnett County Manual Labor School, studied law in Athens, Ga., and in 1846 began practice in Cassville. During the Mexican War he served as a captain of volunteer cavalry under General Scott.

During the decade of the fifties Wofford attained distinction at the bar, developed a prosperous plantation, served in the legislature, 1849–53, and as clerk of the lower house, 1853–54. In 1852, with the assistance of John W. Burke, editor of the *Athens Banner,* he established the *Cassville Standard,* a Democratic weekly. He was a delegate to the Southern Commercial Convention of 1857 at Knoxville, Tenn., and to that of 1858 at Montgomery, Ala. A firm anti-secessionist, he carried his county with him and, as a member of the state convention of 1861, voted against the secession resolution.

After Georgia had withdrawn from the union, however, Wofford loyally offered his services to his state, and was commissioned colonel of the 18th Georgia Regiment. After brief service in North Carolina, he was attached to Hood's brigade and took part in the campaigns around Richmond in 1862. After Hood's promotion Wofford commanded the brigade at Second Manassas (Bull Run), South Mountain, and Sharpsburg, and was commended by Hood for "gallant conduct" and "conspicuous bravery." He served under Brig.-Gen. Thomas R. R. Cobb and, after Cobb's death at Fredericksburg, was promoted, Jan. 19, 1863, to the rank of brigadier-general. He led the brigade at Chancellorsville and rendered valuable service under Longstreet at Gettysburg. Against the wishes of Lee, who considered him one of the best brigadier-generals in the division, Wofford was sent with Longstreet to East Tennessee, where he led the unsuccessful assault on Knoxville. He was then attached to Kershaw's division, and saw service in the desperate campaigns of 1864 around Richmond and Petersburg, and in the Shenandoah Valley. Twice, at Spotsylvania and in the Wilderness, he was wounded. Placed in command of the Department of Northern Georgia, Jan. 20, 1865, at the request of Governor Brown, he raised some 7,000 troops and defended that region against the turbulent and lawless element which infested it. He surrendered to Gen. H. M. Judah at Resaca, Ga., on May 2, 1865.

The war being over, Wofford devoted his energy and means to the care of the starving and the economic, industrial, and educational rehabilitation of his devastated section of the state. Elected to Congress in 1865, he was refused his seat by the Radical Republicans, but through the aid of Judge Kelly of Pennsylvania obtained much-needed food and supplies for his district. He was instrumental in organizing the Cartersville & Van Wert and the Atlanta & Blue Ridge railroads, served as a trustee of the Cherokee Baptist College at Cassville and the Cassville Female College, and gave land and money with which to establish the Wofford Academy. In 1877 he was an influential member of the state constitutional convention. He worked effectively for the payment of the state debt, the broadening of the suffrage, the development of an educational program, and the maintenance of a state penitentiary instead of the leasing of convicts.

Wofford married Julia A. Dwight of Spring Place, Ga., in 1859 and to this union were born six children, three of whom died in infancy. After the death of his wife in 1878, he married, in 1880, Margaret Langdon of Atlanta. Gentle, yet firm in all his convictions, he was beloved by his people and idolized by his soldiers. He died at his home near Cass Station, and was buried in the Cassville Cemetery.

[I. W. Avery, *The Hist. of the State of Ga.* (1881); A. D. Candler, *The Confed. Records of . . . Ga.*, vols. III, IV (1910); A. D. Candler and C. A. Evans, *Georgia* (1906), vol. III; *Convention Sketches: Brief Biogs.* (1877); C. A. Evans, *Confed. Mil. Hist.* (1899), vol. VI; *Jour. of the Constitutional Convention of . . . Ga.* (1877); *Jour. . . . of the Convention of the People of Ga.* (1861); W. J. Northen, *Men of Mark in Ga.*, vol. III (1911); C. E. Jones, *Ga. in the War* (1909); *War of the Rebellion: Official Records* (Army); *Atlanta Constitution*, May 24, 1884.]
                                   F. M. G.

WOLCOTT, EDWARD OLIVER (Mar. 26, 1848–Mar. 1, 1905), United States senator and politician, was born in Longmeadow, Mass., the third son of the eleven children of Samuel and Harriet A. (Pope) Wolcott, and a descendant of Henry Wolcott who settled in Windsor, Conn., in 1636. His father was a Congregational minister. The family moved to Chicago (1859) and then to Cleveland (1862), where Edward attended the Central High School. He served as a very youthful private during the final months of the Civil War. In 1866 he entered Yale College but left to enter business and then to study (1870–71) in the Harvard Law School, from which he received the degree of LL.B. in 1875. His brother, Henry, had moved to Colorado, and in September 1871 Edward joined him in Blackhawk. He taught school there for a short time and then went to the thriving town of Georgetown, where he began the practice of law. He remained more or less active in his profession during the remainder of his life. Joel F. Vaile (1888) and Charles W. Waterman (1902) became his partners, and the firm prospered in the service of the Denver and Rio Grande Railroad and of other corporations.

Though a successful lawyer, Wolcott owes his place in Colorado's history to his ability as a conservative leader of the local Republican party. His political career opened in Georgetown. In 1876 he was elected district attorney and town attorney, and promptly made a name for himself as an energetic and eloquent public prosecutor. Two years later he was elected to the Colorado Senate, where he served from 1879 to 1882. He moved to Denver in 1879. His rise to eminence was rapid. At first a supporter of Nathaniel P. Hill [q.v.] in his struggle with Henry M. Teller [q.v.] and others for the control of the party and its patronage, he later joined the ranks of the Teller faction. Recognized as a party leader, he "forced his own election to the United States Senate" in 1889 (Dawson, *post*, I, 147); he was reëlected in 1895, but failed in 1901 and again in 1902–03. His activities were normally along party lines. He worked with Matthew S. Quay and other Republican leaders for the furtherance of party measures. On the other hand, since he came from a metal mining state, he was in his earlier years an ardent advocate of the free coinage of silver. As such, he opposed the repeal of the Sherman Act in 1893. After the repeal he modified his ideas about silver and thought to gain relief for the mining states through international bi-metallism. He proposed (1895) and was later (1897) made chairman of the unsuccessful commission which sought to interest

France and Great Britain in the matter. In 1896, when Bryan and the Democrats espoused the cause of free silver, he refused to desert his party as Teller had done. By this refusal he alienated many of his friends and lost any chance of reëlection to the Senate. His most notable activities in that body, aside from his advocacy of silver, were his opposition to the Federal Election Bill in 1890 and to President Cleveland's Venezuelan message.

Wolcott was a large man, always very carefully dressed. His manner towards strangers and enemies was often arrogant, towards friends often free. He was a "high liver," lavish in the expenditure of money, thoughtless in giving. His marriage to Frances (Metcalfe) Bass on May 14, 1891, ended in divorce in 1900. He died in Monte Carlo while in search of health and diversion. His body lies in Woodlawn Cemetery, New York.

[T. F. Dawson, *Life and Character of Edward Oliver Wolcott* (2 vols., 1911, privately printed) is an authorized biog., subject to the defects of such biogs. See also *Who's Who in America*, 1903–05 ; *The Biog. Record of the Class of 1870, Yale Coll. 1870–1911* (n.d.) ; *Biog. Dir. of the Am. Cong.* (1928) ; Samuel Wolcott, *Memorial of Henry Wolcott* (1881) ; obituary in *Rocky Mountain News* (Denver), Mar. 2, 1905.]

J. F. W—d.

WOLCOTT, OLIVER (Nov. 20, 1726–Dec. 1, 1797), signer of the Declaration of Independence, governor of Connecticut, was born in Windsor, Conn., the youngest son of Roger [*q.v.*] and Sarah (Drake) Wolcott. He was graduated at Yale in 1747, having led his class for four years. Before he left college, Governor Clinton of New York commissioned him (Jan. 21, 1747) to raise and serve as captain of a company in connection with the ill-fated expedition to Canada. Subsequently he studied medicine with his brother, intending to practise in Goshen ; but when the county was organized in 1751, he moved to Litchfield, where his father owned property, and became its first sheriff, an office he held for twenty years. Henceforth he devoted himself to a legal and public career. Four times chosen as deputy for Litchfield (1764, 1767, 1768, and 1770), he was elected assistant in 1771 and reëlected annually until 1786; he was judge of the court of probate for Litchfield (1772–81) and judge of the county courts in and for Litchfield (1774–78). He became a major in the militia in 1771, a colonel in 1774. On Jan. 21, 1755, he married Laura, daughter of Capt. Daniel and Lois (Cornwall) Collins of Guilford, by whom he had five children, among whom was Oliver [*q.v.*].

Throughout the Revolution Wolcott played a varied part. In April 1775 the Assembly sent him to Boston to interview General Gage (C. E. Carter, *The Correspondence of General Thomas Gage*, vol. I, 1931, p. 398), and appointed him a commissary to supply stores and provisions for the troops. In July the Continental Congress named him one of the commissioners of Indian affairs for the northern department. He met representatives of the Six Nations at Albany that year, and helped settle the Wyoming Valley and the New York-Vermont boundary questions. To judge from later remarks, he supported the war in order to ensure the continuance of the Connecticut brand of civil and religious liberty. As a "Republican of the Old School," whose "ideas of government . . . were derived from the purest sources" (Oliver Wolcott, Jr., *post*, p. 76), he abhorred the appearance of fanatic democracy among a people whose morals and virtues he believed to be rapidly declining.

Wolcott was first elected a delegate to the Continental Congress in October 1775, and except in 1779, when he was not chosen, attended from three to six months every winter or spring until 1783. He participated in the early agitation over the Declaration of Independence, but left Philadelphia because of illness the end of June, and his substitute, William Williams, signed in his stead. After he returned, Oct. 1, 1776, he was permitted to sign also. On his journey north in July he carried off from New York to Litchfield the leaden equestrian statue of George III for the ladies to melt into bullets (Oliver Wolcott Papers, Connecticut Historical Society). His committee service in Congress was comparatively unimportant, but he gained some reputation as a man who spoke his mind. He was, for instance, one of a minority of four against inflicting the death penalty on Americans who, in the vicinity of American headquarters, aided the enemy (*Journals of the Continental Congress*, X, 205). The caustic Thomas Rodney characterized him thus : "a man of Integrity, is very candid in Debate and open to Conviction and does not want abilities; but does not appear to be possessed of much political knowledge" (Burnett, *post*, VI, 19).

During the summers Wolcott's time was occupied with active military affairs. In August 1776 he commanded as brigadier-general the fourteen militia regiments sent to New York to reinforce General Putnam on the Hudson River. In December he was put in command of the 6th Militia Brigade in northwestern Connecticut. On his own responsibility, in September 1777, he led a force of three or four hundred volunteers from his brigade to join Gates's army against Burgoyne. As a major-general in 1779, he had the task of defending the Connecticut seacoast against Tryon's raids. In May 1780 he was added to the council of safety, the state executive committee for the prosecution of the war.

After the treaty of peace was signed, Wolcott resigned from the Congress to devote himself to domestic affairs, and though he served as commissioner at the Treaty of Fort Stanwix in 1784 to make peace with the Six Nations, he resigned from that post too in 1785. Without a popular majority in the state elections of 1787, he was chosen lieutenant-governor by the legislature. A member of the state convention which accepted the Constitution, he admired in it the safeguards against faction. In 1789 he helped conclude a treaty with the Wyandottes, extinguishing their title to the Western Reserve. He was president of the Connecticut Society of Arts and Sciences, and the recipient of an honorary degree from Yale. On Samuel Huntington's death in January 1796, he succeeded to the governorship, and was elected to that office in May. A presidential elector in 1797, he cast his vote for Adams and Pinckney. He died in office after two uneventful years as governor, and was buried in Litchfield.

In person Wolcott was tall, erect, dark-complexioned, dignified, with urbane manners. The eulogies stress his strength of will coupled with toleration and moderation, his integrity and deep Puritan faith, his incessant activity, and his unwavering opposition to the "specious sophistry of new political theories."

[Oliver Wolcott, Jr., in John Sanderson, *Biog. of the Signers to the Declaration of Independence,* vol. III (1823) ; Samuel Wolcott, *Memorial of Henry Wolcott* (1881) ; F. B. Dexter, *Biog. Sketches Grads. Yale Coll.,* vol. II (1896) ; A. C. White, *The Hist. of the Town of Litchfield* (1920) ; F. B. Dexter, *The Literary Diary of Ezra Stiles* (1901) ; Azel Backus, *A Sermon Delivered at the Funeral of . . . Oliver Wolcott* (n.d.) ; H. P. Johnston, *The Record of Conn. Men in the . . . Revolution* (1889) ; E. C. Burnett, *Letters of Members of the Continental Cong.* (7 vols., 1921–34) ; Oliver Wolcott Papers, in the Conn. Hist. Soc., Hartford ; George Gibbs, *Memoirs of the Administrations of Washington and John Adams . . . from the Papers of Oliver Wolcott* (2 vols., 1846) ; *Conn. Jour.* (New Haven), Dec. 7, 1797.]   S. M. P.

WOLCOTT, OLIVER (Jan. 11, 1760–June 1, 1833), secretary of the treasury, governor of Connecticut, was born at Litchfield, Conn., the eldest son of Oliver Wolcott, 1726–1797 [*q.v.*] and Laura (Collins) Wolcott of that place. After being tutored by his mother he entered the town grammar school to prepare for Yale College, and immediately after his graduation in 1778 commenced the study of law under Tapping Reeve [*q.v.*]. His participation in the military events of the Revolution was limited to volunteer

service during two minor campaigns in 1777 and 1779. Declining a commission as ensign, he accepted an appointment in the quartermaster's department and supervised the safekeeping and conveyance of army stores and ordnance at Litchfield. When he came of age he was at once admitted to the bar, and shortly thereafter removed to Hartford, where diligence as a clerk in the office of the committee of the pay-table, coupled perhaps with his family's influence, led to his appointment in January 1782 to the committee itself. In May 1784 he was appointed a commissioner, in concert with Oliver Ellsworth [*q.v.*], to adjust and settle the accounts and claims of Connecticut against the United States. In May 1788 he was selected to fill the new office of comptroller of public accounts, and reorganized the financial affairs of the state in a manner which met with the approval of the Assembly. During this period of his career he acquired self-confidence and formed practical habits of intense and persevering application to business which served him well in later life. On June 1, 1785, he married Elizabeth Stoughton; they had five sons—three of whom died in infancy—and two daughters.

In September 1789, with the strong support of the Connecticut delegation, Wolcott was appointed auditor of the new federal Treasury, assuming his post early in November. Secretary Hamilton left most of the routine elaboration of departmental forms and methods to his subordinates, and Wolcott was incessantly and laboriously employed. His "rare merit" and distinguished conduct induced President Washington, upon Hamilton's recommendation, to appoint him comptroller in June 1791. When the Bank of the United States was organized in the autumn of that year he was instrumental in devising a plan for the establishment of branches, which the stockholders adopted. It would appear that the presidency of the bank was offered to him, but was declined. Wolcott served quietly and efficiently as comptroller. He never wavered in his loyalty to Hamilton, and their close official contact was supplemented by a lasting private friendship. When Hamilton resigned Wolcott was appointed by President Washington to succeed him (Feb. 2, 1795).

Though he brought little political strength to the cabinet, Wolcott impressed Washington with his ability and integrity and won the President's unfeigned esteem and affection. On larger questions of fiscal policy he constantly sought and received Hamilton's advice. The mounting expenditures of the federal government, the extreme fluctuations and wild speculations in American foreign commerce, and the increasing demoralization of the European money-markets, especially that of Amsterdam, created grave problems for the Treasury. To add to Wolcott's difficulties the Republican majority in the House of Representatives during the Fourth Congress (1795–97), under the leadership of Albert Gallatin [q.v.], sought to wrest the initiative in financial matters from the department. Congressional disinclination to levy adequate additional taxes or to confer satisfactory borrowing power obliged Wolcott and the other commissioners of the sinking fund in 1796–97 to sell a considerable portion of the government's stock in the Bank of the United States in order to reimburse some of the overdue temporary loans by which that institution had crippled itself. Under Gallatin's relentless pressure the House of Representatives veered steadily in the direction of specific rather than blanket appropriations, thereby curtailing the quasi-independence in apportioning governmental funds which Hamilton had so cavalierly employed. Pressure upon the Treasury was eased when the French crisis induced Congress to impose direct taxes along lines mapped out by Wolcott and in 1798 a five million dollar loan at eight percent. interest was floated.

In the meantime, Wolcott was becoming involved in a labyrinth of political intrigue which left a lasting shadow upon his reputation. Throughout the years 1797–1800 he enjoyed the confidence of President John Adams [q.v.], but his deeper loyalty, not to say subservience, to Alexander Hamilton, led him to cooperate with Pickering and McHenry in promoting Hamilton's wishes rather than those of the chief executive. When Adams finally reconstructed his cabinet, in 1800, Wolcott escaped the purge; Adams liked and trusted him. Wolcott, however, most reprehensibly collaborated in the preparation of Hamilton's indiscreet circular letter attacking the political character of the President. When the Hamiltonian effort to elect Thomas Pinckney over the head of Adams collapsed, Wolcott finally proffered his resignation (Nov. 8, 1800, effective Dec. 31). Adams accepted it with "reluctance and regret." Upon Wolcott's invitation the House of Representatives appointed a committee to investigate the treasury department, which reported (Jan. 28, 1801) that "the financial concerns of the country have been left by the late Secretary in a state of good order and prosperity" (Gibbs, post, II, 476). Republican newspapers, however, were raising a storm of malicious criticism regarding his alleged countenancing of defalcations in the public accounts and his alleged incendiary responsibility for fires in the war office (Nov. 8, 1800) and the treasury building (Jan. 20, 1801).

When Wolcott left Washington early in February 1801, his whole property consisted of a small farm in Connecticut and a few hundred dollars in cash. Quite unexpectedly President Adams appointed him judge for the second circuit—Vermont, Connecticut, and New York—under the new Circuit Court Act of Feb. 13, 1801, but he had barely accustomed himself to his new duties when the Republican Congress, by repealing the Circuit Court Act (Mar. 8, 1802) swept away his office. Simultaneously with this blow, he suffered the indignity of having the rectitude and efficiency of his late treasury administration impugned by a House committee report (Apr. 29, 1802). To these charges he replied convincingly in a strong pamphlet entitled *An Address to the People of the United States* (1802).

Burdened with the support of a family, "satiated" with public employment, unwilling to confine himself to a small farm in Litchfield, Wolcott was urged by Hamilton to remove to New York and establish himself in business. Through Hamilton's intervention he entered (Feb. 3, 1803) into an extremely liberal agreement with James Watson, Moses Rogers, Archibald Gracie, and William Woolsey of New York City for the formation of a commission and agency firm to be known as Oliver Wolcott & Company. His four partners each advanced $15,000 capital, Wolcott none at all; but he was to be the managing partner at a salary of $3,000 a year and one-fifth of the profits. In 1804 the company made its first venture in the China trade and after the partnership was amicably dissolved at Wolcott's suggestion in April 1805, he concentrated his main energies in that field.

In 1810–11 he was elected to the main board of directors of the Bank of the United States and after the charter lapsed (Mar. 4, 1811) he played a prominent rôle in the launching of the Bank of America chartered by the New York legislature in 1812, serving as president until he was ousted in April 1814 by a "secret cabal" for political reasons (Wolcott to Tobias Lear, May 11, 1814; Wolcott Papers, post). This event proved to be a turning point in his career. Although he had been a firm Federalist, bitterly resentful of "perfidious Virginians" when he first moved to New York, his political principles underwent a steady modification, leading some of his erstwhile friends to suspect his sanity (Timothy Pickering to James McHenry, Mar. 17, 1810, B. C. Steiner, *The Life and Correspondence of James McHenry*, 1907, p. 556). During the closing years of the War of 1812 he became a "War Federalist," and his outspoken defense of the war during the critcial year 1814 attracted the favorable attention of Connecticut Republicans, who had so long and so unsuccessfully striven to subvert the Federalist oligarchy which ruled "the land of steady habits."

Winding up his business in New York during the summer of 1815, Wolcott returned to Litchfield, Conn., and set himself up as a gentleman farmer. For several years he assisted in promoting manufacturing enterprises in his home state. When a coalition of opposition elements in Connecticut formed the Toleration Party, Feb. 21, 1816, he was chosen as candidate for governor in competition with the Federalist incumbent, John Cotton Smith [q.v.]. Defeated in April 1816, he was elected by a narrow margin in 1817 and the political revolution in the state got under way. As governor Wolcott pursued a tactful policy of moderation, cooperation, and compromise. Charged with political apostasy, he nevertheless proved "an ideal man to work out the state's transition" (Purcell, post, p. 334). After Federalist control of the aristocratic council was finally overthrown and Wolcott was reëlected virtually without opposition (April 1818), a constitutional convention was held (Aug. 26–Sept. 16, 1818), over which he presided. The new constitution which he was influential in drafting separated church and state, guaranteed complete freedom of conscience, separated the powers of government, and established a somewhat more influential executive and an independent judiciary. Proving himself both able and popular, Wolcott was reëlected governor year after year. His social and economic views were, nevertheless, too progressive for the period. His expert views on taxation were reflected in comprehensive and constructive readjustments in 1819, but his efforts to promote state aid for agriculture and industry, to maintain an efficient public-school system, to secure a mechanics' lien law, to foster internal improvements, and to regulate the banking system more rigidly came to naught. Finally the aging executive was eliminated from the ticket by the Republican caucus in 1826 and though he ran as an independent in the election of April 1827, he was defeated by a small margin by the machine candidate, Gideon Tomlinson. This final repudiation of Wolcott by the state he had served so well was doubtless influential in his subsequent removal to New York City, where he remained until his death.

[Oliver Wolcott Papers in the Conn. Hist. Soc.; Letter Book of Oliver Wolcott & Company, 1803–05, and of Oliver Wolcott, 1805–08, N. Y. Pub. Lib.; Account Books, 1803–15, N. Y. Hist. Soc.; scattered important original letters in Hamilton Papers, Lib. of Cong., in Rufus King Papers, N. Y. Hist. Soc., and in Jeremiah Wadsworth Papers, Conn. Hist. Soc. Consult also George Gibbs, Memoirs of the Administrations of Washington and John Adams, Edited from the Papers of Oliver Wolcott (2 vols., 1846); C. G. Bowers, Jefferson and Hamilton (1925); and the published writings of Hamilton, Washington, Adams, Rufus King, George Cabot, and James McHenry. For Connecticut politics see R. J. Purcell, Connecticut in Transition, 1775–1818 (1918) and J. M. Morse, A Neglected Period of Connecticut's History, 1818–1850 (1933). Other sources include, F. B. Dexter, Biog. Sketches Grads. Yale Coll., vol. IV (1907); Samuel Wolcott, Memorial of Henry Wolcott (1881); New-York American, June 3, 1833.]   J. O. W.

WOLCOTT, ROGER (Jan. 4, 1679–May 17, 1767), colonial governor, was the son of Simon and Martha (Pitkin) Wolcott of Windsor, Conn., and a grandson of Henry Wolcott who settled in Windsor in 1636. Roger never attended school and was eleven years old before his mother, who had been educated in London, taught him to read and write. Four years later he was apprenticed to a clothier, whom he left in 1699 to set up a successful business of his own. On Dec. 3, 1702, he married Sarah Drake—who was to bear him fifteen children before her death in January 1748—and with her moved across the river to South Windsor. "In a few years my buildings were up and my farm made profitable," he wrote later (Autobiography in Memorial, post, p. 85). Through the aid of borrowed books, a retentive memory, and clear judgment, he also laid the foundations of an extensive knowledge of literature, history, and even the Newtonian philosophy.

As a selectman for Windsor in 1707, Wolcott modestly began his long public career. Two years later he was admitted to the bar and elected a deputy to the Assembly. He was clerk of the lower house in 1710 and 1711, named a justice of the peace in 1710, and in 1711 served as commissary of Connecticut stores in Hovenden Walker's abortive expedition against Quebec. In May 1714 the freemen elected him assistant, and barring two years, 1718 and 1719, re-chose him annually until he became deputy-governor in 1741. He filled that post until 1750, when he was elected governor. During these years he served on numerous and important committees, including those which considered boundary questions, the revision of laws, Indian affairs, bills of credit, and the Mohegan Indian and Lechmere cases. He became judge of the Hartford County court in 1721, of the superior court in 1732, and in 1741, chief justice. In the military organization of the colony he steadily advanced from a captaincy in 1722 to be colonel of the 1st Regiment in 1739. Both Governor Shirley of Massachusetts and Governor Law of Connecticut commissioned him, a man of sixty-seven, as major-general in 1745, second in command on the expedition which took Louisbourg. His journal on the siege gives six reasons why that victory was gained through God's providence; "but humanly speaking," he says, "it was because our soldiers were freeholders and freeholders' sons, while the men within the walls were mercenary troops."

Wolcott served ably as governor until 1754. In the May election that year Thomas Fitch [q.v.] overwhelmingly defeated him. The report spread that as governor he had been negligent in guarding the treasure of a disabled Spanish snow and that the colony would have to stand the loss. The old man felt his defeat keenly as, "a discarded favorite," of whom no one "took any more notice than of a common porter" (Autobiography, p. 88). By 1755 he was exonerated and lost the election by only 200 votes. The rest of his life he spent on his farm, in his spare time reading church history, for all his life he had "made the Bible his test."

To Wolcott belongs the honor of writing the first volume of verse published in Connecticut, *Poetical Meditations, Being the Improvement of Some Vacant Hours* (1725), in which the longest poem, a heroic narrative of the Pequot War, is "A Brief Account of the Agency of the Hon. John Winthrop in the Court of King Charles the Second." His prose was far better. In a pamphlet, *A Letter to the Reverend Mr. Noah Hobart: The New English Congregational Churches Are, and Always Have Been, Consociated Churches* (1761), and again in "A Letter to the Freemen of Connecticut" (*Connecticut Gazette*, Mar. 28, 1761), he wrote with a directness and idiom rare in his day, and with a sturdy natural wisdom that explains the veneration in which he was held. He could see the universal history of Christianity in the church controversy at Wallingford, Conn., over the installation of the Rev. James Dana [q.v.] in 1758, maintained that a mixed church government of laity and clergy was healthiest, and discerned the connection between religious and political self-government. He believed that only through the virtues of industry, frugality, and temperance could the distress of Connecticut, and of America in general, be relieved. Oliver Wolcott, 1726–1797 [q.v.], was his son.

[The best account of Wolcott's life is the sketch in "The Wolcott Papers," *Conn. Hist. Soc. Colls.*, vol. XVI (1916), ed. by A. C. Bates. Additional papers, including Wolcott's autobiography, are in Samuel Wolcott, *Memorial of Henry Wolcott* (1881). Wolcott's "Memoir for the History of Connecticut," written in 1759 to President Clap of Yale, is in *Conn. Hist. Soc. Colls.*, vol. III (1895), and the "Journal of Roger Wolcott at the Siege of Louisbourg," in vol. I (1860). See also Joseph Perry, *The Character of Moses Illustrated*

and Improved (n.d.), and *Conn. Courant* (Hartford) July 27, 1767.]
S. M. P.

WOLF, GEORGE (Aug. 12, 1777–Mar. 11, 1840), congressman from Pennsylvania, governor, was born in Northampton County, Pa., the son of George and Mary Margaret Wolf. His father emigrated in 1751 from Alsace, Germany, to Northampton County, where he established himself on a farm in Allen Township. The boy obtained his education in a classical school near home. After completing his course he worked for a time on his father's farm and later acted as principal of the local academy. He was clerk in the prothonotary's office in Easton, and, with his regular duties, he read law in the office of John Ross, a lawyer of that county and later a judge of the state supreme court. At the age of twenty-one, he was admitted to the bar, and, opening an office in Easton, he soon built up a lucrative legal practice. On June 5, 1798, he married Mary Erb. They had nine children. The following year he entered politics as an adherent of the Republican-Democratic party in the state and was appointed postmaster of Easton in 1801. Later he served for a time as clerk of the orphans' court of Northampton County. He was a member of the lower house of the state legislature in 1814. After his defeat for the state Senate in the next election, he devoted his time to his legal practice. Elected to the federal House of Representatives and reëlected three times, he served from Dec. 9, 1824, until he resigned in 1829, before the Twenty-first Congress convened. In Congress he was an ardent supporter of the protective tariff and other measures designed to foster American industry. In 1829 he was elected governor on the Democratic ticket and resigned his seat in Congress. To this office he was reëlected in 1832. The period of his governorship of six years was one of great activity and intensity of feeling in Pennsylvania, as in the nation as a whole. At the outset, party organizations were being disrupted by the anti-masonic movement, and the state was in the midst of its elaborate and expensive program of internal improvements, which through mismanagement had brought it to the verge of bankruptcy. He soon reëstablished the credit of the state through the practice of economy, the reorganization of the financial system of the state, and the institution of new taxes. Acting on his recommendation, the legislature in 1830 appointed a commission to revise the statute law of the state, a revision that was badly needed, since no revision of any consequence had been made for more than a century. The most enduring achievement of his administration was the passage of the free public school act in 1834.

This, the main objective of his policy, he advocated in public addresses and in messages to the legislature with such fervor and logic that the public gradually came to its support. Although an admirer of President Jackson and a stanch upholder of his policy with reference to the nullification proceedings of South Carolina in 1832, he disapproved of the President's attitude toward the Second United States Bank, and he signed a resolution of the legislature instructing the congressmen from Pennsylvania to labor for the renewal of the bank charter. This action was partly responsible for the disruption of the Democratic party in the state and Wolf's defeat for a third term in 1835. In 1836 President Jackson appointed him to the newly created post of comptroller of the treasury. Two years later he resigned from this office to accept the collectorship of customs at the port of Philadelphia, a position he held until his death.

[C. A. Beck, *Kith and Kin of George Wolf* (1930); *Pa. Archives,* 4 ser., vol. V (1900); W. C. Armor, *Lives of the Governors of Pa.* (1872); H. J. Steele, "The Life and Public Service of Governor George Wolf," *Proc. Pa. German Soc.,* vol. XXXIX (1930).]

                                                A. E. M.

WOLF, HENRY (Aug. 3, 1852–Mar. 18, 1916), wood engraver, was born in Eckwersheim, Alsace, the son of Simon and Pauline (Ettinger) Wolf. At fifteen he left home and obtained employment in a machine shop in Strasbourg. There a wood engraver, Jacques Lévy, encouraged his artistic efforts and later took him into his shop. In November 1871 Wolf arrived in America and almost immediately found work in Albany. Two years later he went to New York, to remain there until the end of his life. In 1873 he entered the evening art school of Cooper Union and worked in the life class for two years. At the same time he worked at wood engraving in the art department of Harper Brothers under Frederick Juengling [q.v.]. In a note book, neatly and accurately kept, he recorded all the blocks he cut (789) between 1877 and the year of his death. The earliest of these were for *Scribner's Monthly* and *St. Nicholas.* At first and for some years young Wolf from time to time produced blocks for other engravers, notably Smithwick and French, and Juengling. Among these were illustrations for Appleton's school readers. But it also happily fell to his lot to engrave the works of some of the leading illustrators of the day, such as Howard Pyle, Edwin A. Abbey, Joseph Pennell, A. B. Frost [qq.v.], Mary Hallock Foote, Reginald Birch, and others. A commission received in 1879 to engrave the illustrations for William Mackay Laffan's articles on the Tile Club, for *Scribner's,* brought

him into close association with some of the foremost painters, and the following year he engraved his first reproductions of paintings—works by Walter Shirlaw, George Inness, John Singer Sargent [qq.v.], and others—as illustrations for William C. Brownell's "The Younger Painters of America" (*Scribner's Monthly,* May, July 1880). Similar commissions followed, and Wolf's skill increased until he became preëminent in the reproduction of paintings by contemporary American artists through the medium of wood engraving. Before half-tone photo-engraving came into use about 1880, wood engraving was chiefly a black line process, but through this invention the white line became supreme, and the rendition of tones and textures possible. Wolf was quick to master the new medium and to realize its adaptability. Only one other—Timothy Cole—ever carried it to such perfection as he, and thereby Wolf made a unique and distinguished contribution to the art of the world.

He began doing book illustrations in 1882, engraving blocks for J. B. Lippincott and other publishers. In a portfolio issued by the Society of American Wood Engravers in 1887 he was represented by cuts of a landscape painted by Robert S. Gifford and "New England Peddler" by Jonathan Eastman Johnson. A decade later he made, by way of experiment, a number of original blocks—landscapes of subtle and sensitive character but without significant merit. About this time he also began publishing some of his blocks himself, issuing them in limited editions as collectors' items. This led to orders for blocks from collectors. George A. Hearn, William T. Evans, Richard Canfield, Charles L. Freer, and others commissioned him to engrave for them portraits of themselves by distinguished painters or other canvases in their collections. Among the blocks that he published privately are Whistler's portraits of his mother and of Thomas Carlyle, which are by some considered his masterpieces. Of equal merit, however, is his engraving of his own portrait painted by Irving R. Wiles, published in *Harper's Monthly Magazine,* January 1906. For the *Century Magazine* (beginning April 1898) he engraved a series of portraits of women painted by Gilbert Stuart. His work covered, in fact, a broad field, including fashion books and illustrations for juvenile books, magazines, novels, and art publications. In 1908 he was elected a full member of the National Academy of Design. He was also a member of the International Society of Sculptors, Painters, and Gravers, London, and the Union Internationale des Beaux Arts et des Lettres, Paris. He received honorable mention at the Paris Salon (1888) and at the Exposition Universelle, Paris (1889), silver medals at Paris (1900) and Rouen (1903), and a grand medal of honor at the Louisiana Purchase Exposition, St. Louis (1904). His engravings are to be found in the permanent collections of the Metropolitan Museum; the New York Public Library; the Library of Congress; the Carnegie Institute, Pittsburgh; the Albright Gallery, Buffalo; the municipal gallery, Strasbourg; and the Victoria and Albert Museum, London.

He was married on Sept. 25, 1875, to Rose Massée, daughter of Hermann Massée, merchant of Hamburg, Germany. Of their two sons, one became an artist. Throughout his life Wolf enjoyed robust health. His chief recreation was walking. He had an exceedingly courteous, genial manner, and his life throughout was uncommonly successful and happy. He died in New York City, survived by his wife and sons.

[*Who's Who in America*, 1914–15; R. C. Smith, *Life and Works of Henry Wolf* (1927), with cat. and bibliog.; C. H. Caffin, in *Harper's Mag.*, June 1916; Frank Weitenkampf, *Am. Graphic Art* (1924); *Academy Notes* (Buffalo), Apr. 1906; obituary in *N. Y. Times*, Mar. 20, 1916; personal acquaintance.]
L. M.

WOLF, INNOCENT WILLIAM (Apr. 13, 1843–Oct. 14, 1922), Roman Catholic abbot, was born at Schmidheim, Rhenish Prussia. His parents, John Wolf, a school teacher, and Gertrude (Molitor) Wolf, had nine children, of whom William was the youngest. In 1851 the family emigrated to Brighton, Wis., where the father bought a farm and also instructed the children of the parish. Three years later, following two of his brothers, William went to St. Vincent College, Latrobe, Pa., where he took an academic course. In 1860 he decided to enter the Benedictine Order at St. Vincent Abbey, and on July 11, 1861, he pronounced his religious vows and took Saint Innocent as his patron saint. After his philosophical and theological studies he was ordained priest, May 26, 1866. Because of his extraordinary talents, Abbot Boniface Wimmer [*q.v.*] sent him to Rome in 1867 to take a postgraduate course in the sacred sciences. He studied at the Sapienza, where he received the degree of doctor of divinity, and in 1870 returned to St. Vincent College to teach theology. During the next years he held also the office of master of novices, treasurer of the abbey, and finally prior of the monastery.

While traveling in the West for his health, Father Innocent was elected first abbot of St. Benedict, Atchison, Kan. (Sept. 29, 1876), a monastery which had been founded from St. Vincent in 1857. At that time the monastery had only eleven priests, who conducted a college of fifty-three students and administered a parish with several missions. The institution was heavily in debt, especially on account of the large church which had been built there. Abbot Innocent at once took a very active part in reducing the financial burden and shared in all the work of his subjects, performing manual labor in the fields, teaching in the classroom, and serving on the altar and in the pulpit as a churchman. Gradually a group of stately buildings arose around the large church and indicated in some measure the interior growth of the institution. Later (1910) even these became inadequate to the needs of the community and college, and it was decided to build an entirely new group of buildings on a neighboring hill overlooking the Missouri valley. In 1918 the college was accredited by the Catholic Educational Association, and in the following year it became affiliated with the University of Kansas. In 1919 a preparatory department, Maur Hill Preparatory School, was established. After carrying the burden of his office forty-four years, the Abbot was granted a coadjutor (1921) and gradually retired from the government of the monastery. He died a year later. At that time St. Benedict Abbey had grown to ninety-seven members, its college and seminary were equal to the best in the Middle West, and its missionary activities extended to seventeen parishes in three states.

During all this time Abbot Innocent continued his favorite studies in the liturgy of the Church. He often assisted writers on this subject and became the chief contributor to the *Ceremoniale Monasticum* which was published by the abbey student press in 1907. His administrative qualities were of such a high order that at the death of Archabbot Wimmer in 1887 he was chosen as his successor, but he declined the honor. He served as president of the American Cassinese Congregation (1890–93, 1899–1902), and in 1916, on the occasion of his golden sacerdotal jubilee, Pope Benedict XV honored him by granting him the *cappa magna* for pontifical functions. On that occasion the whole town also fêted its illustrious churchman. Abbot Innocent was of small stature, with a long, flowing reddish beard. At first sight he seemed severe and taciturn; he knew this only too well and referred to himself at times as "an innocent wolf." He was always kind toward those who were in difficulties or in need, and he became a counsellor for many priests and prelates in the Middle West. His aim of bringing about a greater centralization of power in the Benedictine Order was not shared by the majority of his confrères.

["St. Benedict's from 1856 to 1932," MS. in St. Benedict's archives; letters of Abbot Innocent in St. Vincent archives; *Abbey Student*, Oct. 1916, Nov. 1922; and obituary in *Kansas City Star*, Oct. 15, 1922.]
                                                        F. F.

WOLF, SIMON (Oct. 28, 1836–June 4, 1923), lawyer, publicist, communal worker, was born in Bavaria, the son of Levi Wolf and Amalia Ulman. As a lad of twelve he migrated in 1848 to the United States, where several uncles had already settled. He entered his uncle's business at Uhrichsville, Ohio, but a commercial career did not attract him and he took up the study of law, graduating with honors from Ohio Law College in Cleveland, 1861. He was admitted to the bar at Mt. Vernon, Ohio, the same year. After practising law for a year at New Philadelphia, Ohio, he moved to Washington, D. C., where he lived until his death. On Aug. 2, 1857, he was married to Caroline Hahn. They had six children. After her death, he was married, on Nov. 3, 1892, to Amy Lichtenstein. In 1869 he was appointed recorder for the District of Columbia, and from 1878 to 1881 he was civil judge. In 1881 President Garfield appointed him United States consul general in Egypt, but after a year he resigned because of illness in his family.

In addition to his official duties, he gave his time freely to many local philanthropic and cultural institutions, regardless of their sectarian character. An able lecturer, an eloquent speaker, and a lover of his fellowmen, he was always at the front of any fight which involved issues where human or civic rights were at stake. As an orator he was in demand for national political campaigns for many years. His reputation, however, rested largely upon his vigorous championship of the civic and religious rights of his persecuted coreligionists, the Jews of eastern Europe, and the influence which he wielded with the administration in Washington on their behalf. For more than half a century he was in close contact with the most influential men in political life and enjoyed the personal acquaintance of every president beginning with Abraham Lincoln. When persecution of the Jews of Rumania became acute during Grant's administration he was the leading advocate of the appointment of Benjamin F. Peixotto [q.v.] as consul to Bucharest, with a view to devising plans for ameliorating their condition. He was one of the leading factors in inducing President Roosevelt to forward a petition to Russia after the Kishineff massacre in 1903. His advice was sought during President Taft's administration in connection with the abrogation of the Russian treaty, and he interested President Wilson in plans for the protection of the Jewish religious minorities in the peace treaties at the close of the World War. He was active within the Independent Order B'nai B'rith, which he joined in 1865. For many years he served this organization as a member of the executive committee, and was president in 1904–05. He was the founder of the Hebrew Orphan's Home in Atlanta, Ga., and its lifelong president. Upon his motion the Board of Delegates of American Israelites was merged in 1878 with the Union of American Hebrew Congregations, and he was for many years the chairman of the Board of Delegates on Civil Rights of that body. Through his inspiration the B'nai B'rith raised funds for the presentation of the statue "Religious Liberty," by Moses J. Ezekiel [q.v.], to Fairmount Park, Philadelphia. His services were also given to the Masons of the United States, to the Order Kesher shel Barzel, and to the Red Cross Association.

In the midst of an active life, Wolf found time for literary work. In addition to numerous papers and articles for the periodical press, he was the author of *The Influence of the Jews on the Progress of the World* (1888); *The American Jew as Patriot, Soldier and Citizen* (1895); *Mordecai Manuel Noah* (1897); an autobiography, *Presidents I Have Known from 1860 to 1918* (1918); and, in conjunction with Max J. Kohler, *Jewish Disabilities in the Balkan States* (1916). After his death the Council of the Union of American Hebrew Congregations published as a memorial volume *Selected Addresses and Papers of Simon Wolf* (1926).

[*Who's Who in America*, 1922–23; *Jewish Encyc.* (new ed., 1925), vol. XII; *Am. Hebrew*, Oct. 20, 27, 1916; June 8, 1923; The *Jewish Tribune and the Hebrew Standard*, June 8, 1923; *Jahrbuch der deutschamerikanischen historischen Gesellschaft von Illinois* (*Deutsch-Am. Geschichtsblätter*), vol. XIV (1915), p. 386; biographical sketch by Max J. Kohler in *Am. Jewish Year Book for 5685*, 1924–25; *Evening Star* (Washington, D. C.), June 5, 1923.]   I. S.

WOLFE, CATHARINE LORILLARD (March 1828–Apr. 4, 1887), philanthropist, art patron, was a daughter of John David [q.v.] and Dorothea Ann (Lorillard) Wolfe of New York City. From childhood her environment was such as ample wealth provided for a nineteenth-century American home. She became a leader in New York society and enjoyed the advantages of travel. As she grew older she took part in some of her father's philanthropic activities, chiefly under church auspices. When she had reached middle age the death of her father made her heiress of both the Wolfe and the Lorillard millions, and it was then estimated that she was the richest unmarried woman in the world, although it is doubtful whether her entire estate ever greatly exceeded $12,000,000. Continuing her father's gifts to various causes and adding projects of her own, she dispensed at first $100,-000 a year, but later more than doubled that average. In the fifteen years 1872–87 she gave away more than $4,000,000. For the building of schools and churches, especially in the West and South and in some instances in foreign lands, she gave hundreds of thousands of dollars. Grace Church in New York received from her large building funds, besides an endowment of $350,000, and for the diocese of New York she provided a central building. St. Luke's Hospital, the Italian mission in Mulberry Street, and the newsboys' lodging-house at East Broadway and Gouverneur Street were also among the recipients of her bounty. At the time of her death she was called the "most munificent benefactor of the Protestant Episcopal Church" (*Churchman,* N. Y., Apr. 9, 1887, p. 398).

Her gifts for secular objects, less numerous than those for religion, were still significant. Her contribution to the Union College endowment of $50,000 and her outfitting of the Babylonian archaeological expedition of 1884 under Dr. William Hayes Ward [*q.v.*] both indicated a broadening of interest. About 1873 she had commissioned a cousin, John Wolfe, who was an art connoisseur, to collect a gallery of paintings for her Madison Avenue house in New York. This collection, one of the most noteworthy in America, was many years in forming. It consisted chiefly of the works of nineteenth-century European artists, and comprised a hundred and twenty oils and twenty-two water colors. In 1887 it was valued at $500,000. In her will she bequeathed the entire collection with an endowment of $200,000, to the Metropolitan Museum of Art. A contemporary art critic characterized this gift as "probably the largest bequest ever made to Art by a woman" (Walter Rowlands, in *Art Journal,* London, 1889, p. 12). The donor died of Bright's disease in her New York home, leaving no relatives nearer than cousins.

[W. W. Spooner, *Hist. Families of America* (1907), pp. 282–83, with portrait; Frances E. Willard and Mary A. Livermore, *A Woman of the Century* (1893); W. R. Huntington, in *Churchman* (N. Y.), Apr. 16, 1887; obituary, *Ibid.,* Apr. 9, 1887; *N. Y. Tribune,* Apr. 5, 1887, Apr. 7 (editorial), Apr. 9 (editorial and will), Apr. 17.]   W. B. S.

WOLFE, HARRY KIRKE (Nov. 10, 1858–July 30, 1918), psychologist. educator, was born in Bloomington, Ill., of ancestors prominent in Virginia and Kentucky. His parents were Jacob Vance and Ellen B. Wolfe. His father, a graduate of Indiana University, served for fifteen years as high school principal, lawyer, and legislator in Indiana, and then in 1871 settled on a farm in Nebraska, near Lincoln. There the parents maintained a cultured home, reared and educated a large family, and supported educational and political institutions. Harry Kirke, the eldest son, took the degree of A.B. at the University of Nebraska in 1880. He then went in 1883 to the University of Berlin to win a doctorate in the classics. The next year, however, he transferred to the University of Leipzig, and became one of the early American students in psychology with Wilhelm Wundt. In 1886 he received the degree of Ph.D. at Leipzig and returned to Nebraska as a high school teacher. In 1888 he went to a school position in San Luis Obispo, Cal. There he married (Dec. 19, 1888) Katherine H. Brandt of Philadelphia, Pa. Wolfe returned to the University of Nebraska in 1889, commissioned to organize work in philosophy and psychology. At first designated lecturer, he became in 1890 associate professor and in 1891 professor and head of department. He at once began to prepare a laboratory for experimental psychology, one of the earliest to be established in America. The work was immediately successful. In a half dozen years he had sent forward into eastern graduate schools such men as Walter B. Pillsbury, Madison Bentley, Hartley Alexander, and several others of professional note, while students were crowding his classrooms and laboratories.

In the spring of 1897 certain administrative problems hung over the University of Nebraska. The effort of Wolfe to bear some hand in their solution proved unfortunate, and resulted in action by the Board of Regents (Mar. 29, 1897) to discontinue his services. It seems clear that both sides to that controversy used less than sound judgment. But its effects upon the professional career of Wolfe were disastrous. He was indeed offered other posts in psychology. But hoping still and always to serve the people of the West, he rejected offers from distant universities and threw himself rather into the work of modernizing the secondary schools. From 1897 to 1901 he was superintendent of schools in South Omaha, and from 1902 to 1905 principal of the Lincoln High School. In 1905 he went to the University of Montana as professor of philosophy and education, but returned to the University of Nebraska in 1906 as professor of educational psychology. Three years later he was shifted back to his old position and became professor of philosophy, his own portion of the work lying then, however, entirely in psychology. But his sudden death from angina pectoris came too soon to permit his new career in pure science to attain its full fruition. His publications are to be found in Wundt's *Philosophische Studien,* Bd.

III (1886); *University Studies* (Nebraska), July 1890; *Psychological Review*, July 1895, January 1898; *North-Western Journal of Education*, July 1896; *American Journal of Psychology*, January 1898; *Nebraska Teacher*, 1912–14; *Mid-West Quarterly*, July 1918. Much assembled psychological material remained unpublished at his death.

Wolfe possessed a personality of rare attractiveness and had a peculiar genius for teaching. Under his inspiration the new psychology, with the educational and social program suggested by it, carried a marked stimulation. Yet his dominant interest was essentially ethical—a passion for human welfare, to be advanced by sound and educated thinking and acting. This also fostered his lifelong interest in philosophy, in which he resembled his own teacher, Wundt.

[Sources include *Who's Who in America*, 1916–17; *Portrait and Biog. Album of Lancaster County, Neb.* (1888); J. M. Cattell, *Am. Men of Sci.* (1910 ed.); *Univ. Jour.* (Lincoln, Neb.), Oct. 1918; obituary article in *Science*, Sept. 27, 1918; official records of the University of Nebraska.]   E. L. H.

WOLFE, JOHN DAVID (July 24, 1792–May 17, 1872), merchant and philanthropist, was born in New York City, a son of David and Catherine (Forbes) Wolfe. His grandfather, John David Wolfe, had emigrated from Saxony early in the eighteenth century. David Wolfe and a brother were partners in a hardware business at the corner of Maiden Lane and Gold Street. In 1816 the boy succeeded to his father's half-interest in the hardware store, his partner at first being a cousin, who later withdrew from the firm, which was thereafter styled Wolfe & Bishop. The business prospered, and long before he was fifty Wolfe was rated among New York's wealthy merchants. To add to his resources he made fortunate investments in city real estate. Weathering the financial panic and depression of 1837, he found himself five years later in so secure a position that he thought he might safely retire from business. That, however, did not mean for him a cessation of activity. The thirty years of life that remained were crowded with varied forms of effort.

For two decades before the Civil War and for seven years after its close he ranked among those laymen of the Protestant Episcopal Church in America who were distinguished for faith and works as well as for gifts to the church treasury. Beginning as a vestryman of Trinity Church, in his later years, to the day of his death, he served as senior warden of Grace Church. With few exceptions, his most important benefactions were for distinctively religious objects. In a time

when frontier conditions generally prevailed west of the Missouri River he was one of a small group of wealthy Eastern men interested in church institutions in that new country. He founded, under church auspices, a High School for Girls and Wolfe Hall at Denver, before Colorado had been admitted to statehood, and generously supported a diocesan school for girls at Topeka, Kan. He provided a building for the theological seminary connected with Kenyon College, Gambier, Ohio. The dioceses of Kansas, Nebraska, Colorado, Iowa, Utah, Nevada, and Oregon all received liberal grants from him, especially for educational uses. He prepared and circulated at his own expense a "Mission Service," containing excerpts from the Book of Common Prayer. This was translated into four languages. He carried forward the work begun by William Augustus Muhlenberg [q.v.] at St. Johnsland on Long Island, including a home for crippled and destitute children and a home for aged and destitute men. He also built a cottage for the Sheltering Arms charity in New York City. He took an important part in promoting the Home for Incurables at Fordham, St. Luke's Hospital, and other metropolitan institutions. He was president of the American Museum of Natural History and of the Working Women's Protective Union. His time was chiefly spent in mastering the details of every cause to which he gave support and in seeking to make his aid and that of others more effective. He married Dorothea Ann, the daughter of Peter Lorillard and the aunt of Pierre Lorillard [q.v.]. She died in 1866. A daughter, Catharine Lorillard Wolfe [q.v.] survived him and carried forward many of his philanthropic activities.

[E. A. Duyckinck, *Memorial of John David Wolfe . . . Read before the N. Y. Hist. Soc., June 4, 1872* (1872); H. C. Potter, *A Good Man's Burial. Sermon . . . May 26, 1872* (1872); *Jour. Proc. 14th Ann. Convention of the Protestant Episcopal Church in . . . Kan.* (1873), pp. 41–43; *National Mag.: A Monthly Jour. of Am. Hist.*, July–Aug. 1893; *N. Y. Geneal. and Biog. Record*, Apr. 1877, p. 89.]   W. B. S

WOLFSKILL, WILLIAM (Mar. 20, 1798–Oct. 3, 1866), trapper, California pioneer, of German-Irish ancestry, was born near Richmond, Madison County, Ky. In 1809 the family moved to the Missouri frontier, settling in the future Howard County. Six years later the boy went back to Kentucky to attend school. Returning to Missouri, he left Franklin in May 1822, with the second Santa Fé expedition of William Becknell [q.v.]. In 1823 he trapped the Rio Grande, and in 1824 was with the first party of American whites known to have entered southern Utah. He went home in 1825, but in the following spring, with Ewing Young [*q.v.*], returned to the Southwest, trapping the Gila country and engaging in several fights with the Indians. He was again in Missouri at the end of 1827, and in the spring of 1828 left for New Mexico with a trading caravan. He became a Catholic and a Mexican citizen in 1830.

From Taos, at the end of September 1830, he set out as the leader of a trapping party, which included George Yount [*q.v.*], and which opened a new route, approximating what became known as the western part of the Spanish Trail, to California. Arriving at Los Angeles in February 1831, the company dissolved. Wolfskill for a time engaged in hunting the sea-otter, and at San Pedro put together the schooner *Refugio,* one of the first vessels constructed on the coast. In 1832 he settled in Los Angeles as a carpenter. Four years later he acquired some land east of the village, and in 1838 began to develop it as a vineyard. In January 1841 he married Magdalena Lugo of Santa Barbara. In the same year he planted an orange grove, the first in the region except that belonging to the San Gabriel Mission. He also obtained a large grant in the Sacramento Valley, on which he established John Reid Wolfskill, one of his four brothers, all of whom settled in California.

Wolfskill became wealthy and influential. In 1844 he was chosen a *regidor* (councilman) of the village. Abstaining from politics, he devoted himself to his fields. He introduced the persimmon and the Italian chestnut, brought in improved machinery, and was the first to ship oranges commercially. Just before his death he began the erection of a substantial business building in Los Angeles. He died at his ranch, survived by four children. He remained a Catholic to the end, and left, says Bancroft (*post,* V, 779) "an enviable reputation as an honest, enterprising generous, unassuming, intelligent man." He was essentially a pioneer, breaking new ground in each of the several activities in which he engaged.

[H. D. Barrows, "William Wolfskill, The Pioneer," in *Ann. Pub. of the Hist. Soc. of So. Cal.,* vol. V, pt. 3 (1903); H. H. Bancroft, *Hist of Cal.,* vols. III–V (1885–86); C. L. Camp, "The Chronicles of George C. Yount," *Cal. Hist. Soc. Quart.,* Apr. 1923; J. J. Hill, "Ewing Young in the Fur Trade of the Far Southwest, 1822–1834," *Quart. of the Ore. Hist. Soc.,* Mar. 1923.]

W. J. G.

WOLFSOHN, CARL (Dec. 14, 1834–July 30, 1907), musician, was born in Alzey, Hesse, Germany, the son of Benjamin and Sara (Belmont) Wolfsohn. His father was a physician who was fond of music, his mother a pianist. Carl showed musical talent very early. He began to take piano lessons at the age of seven and was soon placed under the guidance of Aloys Schmitt at Frankfort, with whom he studied two years. Here he made his début as a pianist in December 1848 in the Beethoven piano quintet. He then studied two years with Vincenz Lachner, made successful concert tours through Rhenish Bavaria, and went to London, where he lived two years before coming to America in 1854. He settled in Philadelphia, and for nearly twenty years wielded a wide influence through his varied activities as pianist, teacher, and conductor. During this period he gave annual series of chamber-music concerts and for two seasons gave symphony concerts with a Philadelphia orchestra.

In 1863 he attracted nation-wide attention by presenting all of the Beethoven piano sonatas in a series of recitals, first in Philadelphia, then in Steinway Hall, New York City. The series was repeated the following year in both cities with notable success. Soon after this he gave the entire piano works of Schumann, then of Chopin, in a similar series of concerts. In 1869 he founded the Beethoven Society, and four years later was induced to remove to Chicago to conduct there a similar society organized especially for him. Its first concert took place on Jan. 15, 1874, and the society soon attained an active membership of about two hundred. This was the first important choral organization for mixed voices in Chicago. Its semi-social character made it a strong cultural influence. Wolfsohn directed its activities until 1884, when, because of other enterprises, interest waned and it was disbanded. In the three annual concerts of the society he introduced to Chicago such works as Beethoven's Mass in C and Choral Fantasia, Bruch's *Odysseus,* and Gade's *Crusaders.* In addition he gave monthly chamber-music and piano recitals. In the spring of 1874 he repeated the series of ten Beethoven sonata recitals, in the next spring the piano works of Schumann, and in 1876 those of Chopin. He was a prodigious worker, and his untiring energy and enthusiasm led him in 1877 to plan a series of historical recitals covering the whole literature of the piano. The public, however, became rather surfeited with piano music, interest lagged, and after the fifteenth recital the project was abandoned.

Wolfsohn wrought valiantly in the army of devoted pioneers who laid the foundations of musical life in America. Beethoven was his musical idol, yet after the age of sixty he took up the study of Brahms, who was then just beginning to be known in America, and played publicly nearly all of his piano works. He was also one of the earliest in America to espouse the cause of Wagner's music. From 1856 on he was closely associated with Theodore Thomas [*q.v.*] in chamber-music in Philadelphia and Chicago and on tour. The trio evenings of Wolfsohn, Thomas, and Kammerer ('cellist) were notable events in Chicago. He was essentially a pianist, but, while he possessed an adequate technique, he played from the standpoint of the musical scholar rather than the virtuoso. He had singularly broad musical sympathies. Through his performances and his unflagging zeal he did much to raise the standards of chamber-music and piano-playing both in Philadelphia and Chicago. He had a wide and influential following as a teacher of piano, but for conscientious reasons never gave more than four lessons a day. His most famous pupil was undoubtedly Fannie Bloomfield Zeisler [*q.v.*]. Wolfsohn was thin and wiry in appearance, high-strung, wholly uncommercial in all his artistic ventures, the soul of honesty, intolerant of pretense and sham. He was never married. He died at Deal Beach, N. J., following a surgical operation, and his ashes repose in the French Pond Crematory.

[Personal data from Mrs. Theodora Sturkow-Ryder, Chicago, and his niece, Miss Amelia Meyenberg, New York City ; *Grove's Dict. of Music and Musicians, Am. Supp.* (1930) ; W. S. B. Mathews, *A Hundred Years of Music in America* (1889) ; G. P. Upton, *Musical Memories* (1908) ; Florence French, *Music and Musicians in Chicago* (1899) ; F. C. Bennett, *Hist. of Music and Art in Ill.* (1904) ; *Music*, June 1897 ; *Chicago Daily Tribune,* Aug. 1, 1907.]   F. L. G. C.

WOLLE, JOHN FREDERICK (Apr. 4, 1863–Jan. 12, 1933), organist, composer, and conductor of the Bach Choir, was born in Bethlehem, Pa., which has been, since its founding in 1742, the headquarters of the Moravian Church in North America and a center of musical and educational activities. His ancestry was German and Swiss, and included numerous musicians. His father, the Rev. Francis Wolle (1817–1893), clergyman, educator and naturalist, served for twenty years as principal of the Moravian Seminary in Bethlehem, one of the earliest boarding schools for girls in the United States. His mother was Elizabeth (Weiss) Wolle. Wolle was educated in the Moravian Parochial School, where for a time after graduation (1879–80) he taught mathematics. Without any special instruction he learned to play the organ as a boy. His first formal lessons were taken when he was twenty, under David Duffle Wood [*q.v.*]. Going to Germany in 1884, he studied for a year under the celebrated Josef Rheinberger at Munich. Wolle's career as an organist included twenty years (1885–1905) as organist of the Moravian

Church, Bethlehem, and eighteen years (1887–1905) as organist of Lehigh University. He gave recitals at the Chicago world's fair in 1893, at the Louisiana Purchase Exposition in St. Louis in 1904, and later in many churches throughout the East. He was one of the founders of the American Guild of Organists. On July 21, 1886, he married Jennie C. Stryker. In his earlier years he wrote hymn tunes, songs, pieces for piano and organ, chorus and orchestral selections, and he also made transcriptions for organ of Wagner and of Bach compositions.

The work that brought Wolle fame was his founding and conducting of the Bethlehem Bach Choir, which Henry T. Finck [*q.v.*] termed "the best choir in the United States" (*Evening Post,* New York, May 29, 1916). His inspiration for it came, as he used to relate, one spring day in 1885 when, in Munich, he heard a large chorus sing the St. John Passion. To him the singing was a summons to devote his life to interpreting the music of Bach. Returning to Bethlehem, Wolle won over the 115 singers of the Choral Union so that they followed him in rendering the St. John Passion for the first time in the United States. His singers did not follow him in his project of producing Bach's Mass in B-minor. It was not until 1898 that, upon the initiative of Ruth Porter Doster, a body of singers presented themselves for Wolle's direction and the Bach Choir was organized. They gave the first complete American rendition of the B-minor mass on Mar. 27, 1900. It was so successful that a more ambitious festival was planned for 1901. Of this second festival H. E. Krehbiel wrote that Wolle's singers "accomplished miracles" (*New York Tribune,* May 25, 1901, p. 9), and W. J. Henderson reported that the performance was one in which "the sublimity of the music was perfectly disclosed" (*New York Times,* May 25, 1901). Six Bach festivals were held in the Moravian Church in the years 1900, 1901, 1903, and 1905. Then Wolle was called to the chair of music in the University of California and there served six years (1905–11). At Berkeley he conducted a chorus of citizens and students who in 1909 and 1910 sang the B-minor mass and the St. Matthew Passion. After the reorganization of the Bach Choir in Bethlehem in 1911, Wolle conducted Bach festivals at Lehigh University from 1912 to 1932. The choir of from 250 to 300 voices sang occasionally in New York, Philadelphia, Washington, and other Eastern cities, but there were no extended concert tours. Instead, music lovers from all parts of the United States and from foreign countries made pilgrimages to Bethlehem each May for the two-day program of Bach's music, in which the B-minor mass was the second-day fixture and magnet. In the ivy-clad stone church on the university campus they heard the singing of Bach's oratorios and cantatas not as a concert but as a religious service with no applause, the congregation joining in the chorales. The accompaniment was given by players of the Philadelphia Symphony Orchestra and by T. Edger Shields, organist.

The slender, vibrant Wolle who, without baton, conducted these festivals in fulfillment of his youthful dreams is credited with these, among other, achievements: he established a record for first productions of Bach's compositions in America; he devised a unique system of instruction by which the singers began their study of a difficult Bach chorus by learning the final measures first of all; he developed an interpretation of Bach which emphasized the religious spirit, the emotionalism, the humanity of Bach; he demonstrated the possibilities of community singing by building his choir, year after year, from men and women of a relatively local area and, by his leadership, arousing a devotion of which it was said: "These singers, forgetful of self, sing out of worshipping hearts to the glory of God." Wolle died in Bethlehem, survived by his wife and a daughter. Following his funeral in January 1933, the members of the Bach Choir gathered about his grave and hummed the chorale, "World Farewell." In May 1933 they sang the B-minor mass as a memorial service.

[Raymond Walters, *The Bethlehem Bach Choir* (1923); *Who's Who in America*, 1932–33; obituary in *N. Y. Times*, Jan. 13, 1933.]   R. W.

WOOD, ABRAHAM (fl. 1638–1680), soldier, explorer, landowner, was one of the most interesting and important figures in the history of early colonial Virginia. His early life is obscure. It is possible that he was the Abraham Wood who came to Virginia in 1620 as an indentured servant in the *Margaret and John* and who as late as 1625 was in the service of Capt. Samuel Mathews on his plantation near Jamestown. In May 1638 Wood is found patenting four hundred acres in Charles City County, and the following year two hundred acres in Henrico County. By successive patents he became one of the great landowners of the colony. In 1644 he became a member of the House of Burgesses for Henrico County and served in that capacity for two years. He sat for Charles City County in 1654 and 1656. He became a member of the Council in the spring of 1658 during the period of the provisional government and served on it for at least twenty-two years. In 1676 he was appointed a member of the special commission of oyer and terminer for Virginia to settle the affairs of the colony after Bacon's Rebellion.

He began his military career in 1646 as a captain of militia at Fort Henry. In 1656 he became colonel of the Charles City and Henrico regiment, the group of the militia most actively engaged in Indian fighting. He was later made a major-general and for a decade ranked with the governor as one of the chief military figures of the colony. In 1646 he undertook to maintain a fort and garrison at Fort Henry (now Petersburg) and in return was granted the fort with its buildings, six hundred acres of land, and other privileges. This became both the residence and the business headquarters from which he traded and sent his agents on expeditions into the western country. He himself accompanied Edward Bland on his expedition to Occoneechee Island in 1650. The story that Wood or his agents during the following decade reached the Mississippi River is unproved and improbable (Alvord and Bidgood, *post*, pp. 52–55). In September 1671 Wood sent out a small party under Capt. Thomas Batts with a commission "for the finding out of the ebbing and flowing of the Waters on the other side of the Mountains in order to the discovery of the South Sea." This expedition achieved the first recorded passage of the Appalachian mountains. The next party sent out by Wood in April 1673 under James Needham [*q.v.*] traced the trail to the present site of Tennessee and opened the trade with the distant Cherokee Indians. Because of the opposition of the Occaneechi Indians they were forced to return to Fort Henry; they again started out on May 17. Having successfully reached the Cherokees, Needham came back to Fort Henry in September 1673. He was murdered the following year while making a second journey to the Cherokees. Bacon's Rebellion temporarily interrupted the explorations of the western country. So active had Wood been in this movement that prior to 1676 "the history of westward expansion during the period is almost a biography of this remarkable man" (*Ibid.*, p. 34). His last recorded public service was in March 1680 when he was conducting negotiations with the threatening confederacy of hostile Indians. It is thought that he died shortly after this time.

[W. N. Sainsbury, *Calendar of State Papers, Colonial Ser., America and West Indies, 1669–1674* (1889), and *Calendar . . . 1675–1676* (1893); W. H. Hening, *Statutes at Large . . . of Va. . . . from 1619* (Richmond, 1819–23); C. W. Alvord and Lee Bidgood, *The First Explorations of the Trans-Allegheny Region by the Virginians, 1650–1674* (1912).]   F. M.

WOOD, DAVID DUFFLE (Mar. 2, 1838– Mar. 27, 1910), organist, was born in Pittsburgh,

Pa. His father was Jonathan Humphrey Wood, the eldest son of Abinah Wood, a shipbuilder of Pittsburgh, and his mother was Wilhelmina I. Jones. David, the third son of their marriage, was born in a log cabin on the outskirts of the city. When but a few months of age he lost the sight of one eye through an inflammation caused by a cold. Two years later his other eye was injured during a romp with his sister, and a subsequent attack of scarlet fever so aggravated the injury that he became permanently blind. When he was not yet five years of age his parents entered him as a pupil in the Pennsylvania Institution for the Instruction of the Blind at Philadelphia, where he remained until he was graduated in 1856. He studied music under Wilhelm Schnabel and Ernst Pfeiffer, a German who had come to America as a member of the Germania Orchestra. Aside from the elementary instruction he gained from these teachers during his boyhood, he was self-taught in the art he later followed as a profession.

In the years 1854 and 1855 Wood was a "pupil teacher" in music at the school, and following his graduation filled positions as organist in small churches for about six years. In 1862 he returned to the Institution as an assistant teacher of music, and three years later became one of the two principal assistants to the instructor of music. In 1887 he was made the principal instructor, and he held that position until his death. He was appointed organist of St. Stephen's Church, Philadelphia, in 1864, and in 1870 the duties of choir-master were added to his post. He served St. Stephen's for the rest of his life, and from the years 1884 to 1909 he also played the organ at the evening services at the Baptist Temple. In addition to his teaching at the Institution he was for thirty years instructor of organ at the Philadelphia Musical Academy, and had many private pupils. He was a founder of the American Guild of Organists.

In learning new music Wood engaged a private secretary to describe the pieces from the printed page. She would read first the notes for the right hand, and then for the left. This was all that was necessary for memorizing an entire piece. It is said that his sense of sound was so remarkably acute that he would frequently call his pupils to task for wrong fingering. Wood particularly esteemed as an interpreter of the works of Bach, and he was the owner of the first complete set of Bach's organ works brought to Philadelphia (1884). His *A Dictionary of Musical Terms, for the Use of the Blind* was published in 1869. As a composer Wood wrote a number of anthems which were published post-humously. One of his songs, "I've Brought Thee an Ivy Leaf," achieved popularity in the United States and in England. He was twice married: first to Rachel Laird, a fellow pupil at the Institution, on Oct. 16, 1856; and then to Alice Burdette, of Philadelphia, on July 14, 1898. When he died in Philadelphia at the age of seventy-two, he was survived by his second wife and a young daughter.

[*Who's Who in America*, 1908–09; *David D. Wood*, pamphlet, issued by the Pennsylvania Institution for the Instruction of the Blind; *Grove's Dict. of Music and Musicians, Am. Supp.* (1930); *New Music Rev.*, Aug. 1910; *Musical America*, Apr. 2, 1910; *Foyer*, Apr. 1914; *Diapason*, Mar. 1, 1935; *Public Ledger* (Philadelphia), Mar. 28, 1910.]   J.T.H.

WOOD, EDWARD STICKNEY (Apr. 28, 1846–July 11, 1905), physician and chemist, was born in Cambridge, Mass., the son of Alfred and Laura (Stickney) Wood. Both the Wood and the Stickney families were among the first settlers of Essex County, Mass., in the early seventeenth century. Son of a local grocer, Wood prepared for college in the Cambridge schools and was graduated from Harvard College in the class of 1867. During the course he decided on medicine as a profession and showed a particular preference for chemistry. After serving as a house pupil at both the United States Marine Hospital in Chelsea and the Massachusetts General Hospital in Boston, he received the degree of M.D. from the Harvard Medical School in 1871. His appointment to fill a vacancy in the department of chemistry at the Medical School, created by the resignation of James Clarke White [*q.v.*], turned Wood toward biological chemistry. He first spent six months in study in Berlin and Vienna. Upon his return he began to lecture to the students at the Harvard Medical School, being one of the first in the United States to offer a systematic course in medical chemistry. Appointed to a full professorship in 1876, he continued as such until his death in Pocasset, Mass., in 1905. During this time he acted also as chemist to the Massachusetts General Hospital, Boston.

Besides his teaching and hospital work, Wood was active in many allied branches of his subject. He served on sanitary commissions for both the city of Boston and the state of Massachusetts, reporting on the local water supply and the facilities for gas lighting in Boston. For a number of years he was a member of the commission which revised the 1880 issue of the United States Pharmacopoeia. His articles on arsenical poisoning and blood stains were notable contributions to those subjects. He revised K. T. L. Neubauer and Julius Vogel's *A Guide to the Qualitative and Quantitative Analysis of the Urine* (1879), and contributed a number of articles to Francis Wharton and C. J. Stille's *Medical Jurisprudence* (4 vols., 1882–84), and to R. A. Witthaus and T. C. Becker's *Medical Jurisprudence* (4 vols., 1894–96). As a legal expert in chemistry, he was considered without a peer in the United States, and it was in the capacity of an expert witness in murder trials that he was best known to the public of his time. He was just and fair, unshaken by the art or skill of cross-examination. He has been described as "calm, unruffled, unconcerned as to the effect his testimony might have upon the jury" (Lincoln, *post*, p. 26). A man of the highest character, he was often willing to help the opposing counsel, so confident was he of the finality of his results. His most notable case was the Higgins-Marston murder trial in Denver, Colo., in 1878. Wood was a member of the Massachusetts Medical Society, the American Pharmaceutical Association, the American Academy of Arts and Sciences, and other scientific bodies. He married, first, Irene Eldridge Hills (Dec. 26, 1872), who died in 1881, leaving a daughter; and, second, Elizabeth A. Richardson (Dec. 24, 1883), who survived him without children.

[F. H. Lincoln, *Harvard Grads'. Mag.*, Sept. 1905; *Harvard Coll. Class of 1867, Secretary's Report* (1907); *Boston Transcript*, July 12 and 15, 1905; J. C. Warren, *Proc. Am. Acad. of Arts and Sci.*, Dec. 1916; *Boston Medic. and Surgical Jour.*, July 20, 1905, and Feb. 8, 1906.]   H. R. V.

WOOD, FERNANDO (June 14, 1812–Feb. 14, 1881), congressman, mayor of New York, son of Benjamin and Rebecca (Lehman) Wood, was born in Philadelphia, Pa. He traced his descent from Henry Wood, a Quaker, of Newport, R. I., who in 1682 bought a large farm near the site of Camden, N. J. His father failed in business, spent several years in the West, and about 1822 became a tobacconist in New York City. Young Fernando attended a private school until he was thirteen, when he became a broker's messenger. In his early manhood he was a dealer in wine and cigars, clerk, auctioneer, ship chandler and grocer; and twice after business failures he worked as a cigarmaker. Entering politics in 1834, he became chairman of the young men's committee of Tammany Hall (1839–40) and member of Congress (1841–43), where he urged the adoption of the floating drydock and helped Morse get an appropriation for his telegraph. He was dispatch agent for the state department (1844–47), meanwhile engaging in business as a ship chandler and merchant. At the beginning of the gold rush he sent a ship to Cali-

fornia, making large profits which he invested in New York and San Francisco real estate.

He had meanwhile become one of the three or four leaders of Tammany Hall. In 1850 he was defeated for the mayoralty through allegations of fraud made in a lawsuit by his partner in the California enterprise. He was elected mayor in 1854 and reëlected in 1856 with the support of many reputable bankers and merchants. He was influential in creating Central Park (*Sixteenth Annual Report, 1911, of the American Scenic and Historic Preservation Society*), recommended the establishment of a municipal university and a free academy for young women, and received the thanks of temperance societies for enforcing the liquor laws. But graft permeated many departments of the city government. The Republican legislature shortened his second term by half, created the metropolitan police force under a state board, and transferred numerous municipal functions to other authorities, thus, by confusion and conflict of jurisdictions, making possible the progressively greater corruption which reached its culmination under William Marcy Tweed [*q.v.*]. Believing the acts to be unconstitutional, Wood resisted their enforcement. When fifty metropolitan policemen attempted to arrest him at City Hall the municipal police clubbed them off until a regiment of militia intervened. In dispensing patronage he neglected other Democratic leaders, and they ousted him from Tammany Hall and defeated his reëlection.

Already widely known, Wood was on friendly terms with President Buchanan and several Southern Democrats. He made a large loan to Stephen A. Douglas in 1858 to finance his senatorial campaign against Lincoln. Failing to regain control of Tammany Hall, Wood organized his personal following—business men, mechanics, immigrants, and stevedores—as Mozart Hall. In obedience to a single will it surpassed any previous political organization in the city. It secured his third election as mayor in 1859 and enabled him to appear at the National Democratic Convention of 1860 at the head of a contesting delegation with pro-Southern leanings. His power was further increased when his younger brother, Benjamin (1820–1900), who had benefited from municipal contracts, purchased the *Daily News* in 1860 and became a Congressman (1861–65). In his annual message, Jan. 7, 1861, after expressing the opinion that the Union would shortly be dissolved, Wood proposed that New York should "disrupt the bands" which subjected it to up-state tyranny and become a free city with a nominal duty on imports. After the outbreak of war he recommended to the council the appropriation of $1,000,000 to equip Union regiments. He was defeated for reëlection by a Republican with reform support. As the war dragged on he reversed his attitude, denouncing the war in bitter terms and advocating peace by conciliation. Early in 1863 he joined with Clement L. Vallandigham [q.v.] in organizing the peace Democrats.

Wood was a member of the House of Representatives, 1863–65, and 1867–81. In 1864 he urged that the additional taxes on whiskey should be collected from speculators who had engrossed the existing supply as well as from distillers. Reflecting faithfully the dominant banking and mercantile interests of New York, he insisted, often in opposition to his own party, upon a sound currency and a tariff for revenue only. He spoke often, denouncing Republican reconstruction measures, and exposing graft and administrative incompetence. Bold and outspoken, though always courteous, he early won recognition as a minority spokesman. The Democrats gave him their complimentary votes for speaker in 1873, but when they controlled the House two years later they passed him by. After 1877 he was majority floor leader and chairman of the ways and means committee. He presented a comprehensive tariff bill in 1878 which would have reduced the duties and corrected many anomalies in the hodgepodge of tariff acts of the Civil War period (*Congressional Record*, 45 Cong., 2 Sess., pp. 2035, 2393–2402). It failed of enactment because of defections from his own party. In 1880 he introduced a bill for the refunding of the national debt, which was modified in committee and passed the House in January 1881 (*Ibid.*, 46 Cong., 2 Sess., pp. 281, 989, 3 Sess., pp. 772–73).

Wood had an almost uncanny aptitude for estimating the course of public opinion and a genius for political organization. In gaining and keeping power he was audacious, ruthless, and resourceful. His engaging manners won friends easily, but he also made bitter enemies who took pains to present his character unfavorably. He was married three times: to a Miss Taylor in 1832; to Ann Dole Richardson on Apr. 23, 1841, who died Dec. 9, 1859; and to Alice Fenner Mills on Dec. 2, 1860. He died at Hot Springs, Ark., survived by his widow and eleven of his sixteen children.

[Sources include *A Model Mayor* (1855); X. D. MacLeod, *Biog. of Hon. Fernando Wood, Mayor of the City of N. Y.* (1856), eulogistic in tone; Abijah Ingraham, *A Biog. of Fernando Wood, a Hist. of the Forgeries, Perjuries and Other Crimes of Our "Model" Mayor* (1856); *A Condensed Biog. of Fernando Wood* (1866), bitterly hostile; S. D. Brummer, *Political Hist. of N. Y. State during the Period of the Civil War* (1911); I. N. P. Stokes, *The Iconography of Manhattan Island, 1498–1909*, vol. III (1918); J. A. Scoville, *The Old Merchants of N. Y. City*, vol. II (1863); Gustavus Myers, *The Hist. of Tammany Hall* (1901); M. R. Werner, *Tammany Hall* (1928); D. T. Lynch, "*Boss" Tweed* (1927); E. C. Kirkland, *The Peacemakers of 1864* (1927); *Docs. of the Board of Aldermen of the City of N. Y.*, 1855–63; *Biog. Dir. Am. Cong., 1774–1927* (1928); *Memorial Addresses on the Life and Character of Fernando Wood* (1882); 46 Cong., 3 Sess.; obituary sketches in *N. Y. Times, N. Y. Herald, World* (N. Y.), and *N. Y. Tribune*, Feb. 15, 1881; information from Wood's son, Henry A. Wise Wood. A biog. by Don Seitz, "Fernando Wood, Democrat," exists in MS.]
E. C. S.

WOOD, GEORGE (January 1789–Mar. 17, 1860), lawyer, was regarded by contemporaries as the leader of the New York bar and the greatest lawyer New Jersey had produced. Surprisingly little is known of his early life. He was born of Quaker parents at Chesterfield, Burlington County, N. J. In 1805 he entered the College of New Jersey (later Princeton) with a year's advanced standing and was graduated in 1808. He then studied law under Richard Stockton, 1764–1828 [q.v.], was admitted to the bar in 1812, and began his practice at New Brunswick. Within a few years his reputation surpassed that of his tutor. He appeared more frequently than any other New Jersey lawyer before the Supreme Court of the United States. The law of New Jersey owes to his practice many important principles, particularly on the subject of charitable devises, which had been practically undeveloped. A leading case in *Hendrickson* vs. *Shotwell* (reported in full with arguments of counsel as *The Society of Friends Vindicated*, 1832), in which he represented the Orthodox Friends in their controversy over property with the "Hicksites."

In 1831 he moved to New York City, where his earlier successes were continued. He represented the Presbyterian, Dutch, and Methodist Episcopal churches in cases involving property, was counsel for the city in boundary cases, and appeared in the Lorillard will case involving the disposition of $3,000,000. Perhaps his most important case in this period was *Martin* vs. *Waddell* (16 *Peters*, 367, or 41 *United States*, 367), in which he gave a clear exposition of the law concerning the right of the sovereign to lands under water. His practice indicates that other lawyers were in the habit of bringing their desperate cases to him. He was accustomed to leave the search for prior decisions to junior counsel while he concentrated on the principles involved. His preparation was always thorough, his knowledge profound, and his memory accurate. Often he went from court to court carrying the most intricate details of cases in his mind, with only a few penciled notes to guide him. He is described as having "the art of thinking while he spoke, and thinking as he would were he writing" (William M. Evarts, in *New York Times*, Mar. 22, 1860, p. 2). When he finished the preliminary statement of a case he had already by implication argued it fully. He was not an orator, but relied upon his power of clear, direct, and comprehensive statement.

He took little part in politics. His preferences were known to be with the Federalists, then with the Whigs, and toward the close of his life with those who wished at all costs to preserve the Union. He once declined to become a candidate for governor of New Jersey. In Tyler's administration his friends strongly urged his appointment to a vacant justiceship of the Supreme Court of the United States. In 1850 he presided over a Union-saving meeting at Castle Garden which approved the passage of the slavery compromise, and in 1852 he urged the nomination of Webster for the presidency. Personally he was dignified, unostentatious, and modest to the point of self-effacement. He was survived by his widow, two sons, and several daughters.

[L. Q. C. Elmer, *The Constitution . . . of N. J.* (1872); L. O. Hall, in *Green Bag*, July 1899, with portrait; Charles Edwards, *Pleasantries about Courts and Lawyers* (1867); *Hist. of the Bench and Bar of N. Y.*, vol. I (1897), ed. by David McAdam; *The Diary of Philip Hone* (2 vols., 1927), ed. by Allan Nevins; obituaries in *N. Y. Tribune* and *N. Y. Herald*, Mar. 20, 1860.]
E. C. S.

WOOD, GEORGE BACON (Mar. 12, 1797–Mar. 30, 1879), physician, was born at Greenwich, N. J., the son of Richard and Elizabeth (Bacon) Wood. His father was a prosperous Quaker farmer, a descendant of Richard Wood who emigrated from England to Philadelphia in 1682. Wood was graduated from the University of Pennsylvania with the degree of A.B. in 1815. Shortly thereafter he began to "read medicine" with Dr. Joseph Parrish [*q.v.*], and then entered the medical department of the University of Pennsylvania, from which he received the degree of M.D. in 1818. Almost at once he entered upon a remarkable career as practitioner, educator, and author in which he became a leader of the medical profession not only in the city of Philadelphia, where he made his home, but throughout America. In 1822 he was made professor of chemistry in the Philadelphia College of Pharmacy, and in 1831 professor of materia medica. Resigning from the College of Pharmacy in 1835, he became professor of materia medica and pharmacy in the University of Pennsylvania, and in 1850 professor of the theory and practice of medicine. He retired in 1860 as professor emeritus. From 1835 to 1859 he was an attending physician to the Pennsylvania Hospital. He

was elected president of the College of Physicians of Philadelphia in 1848 and continued in that position until his death in 1879, his administration the longest in the history of the organization. He also served one year (1855–56) as president of the American Medical Association. For ten years (1850–60) he was chairman of the national committee for the revision of the United States pharmacopeia, and for twenty years (1859–79) he was president of the American Philosophical Society. From 1863 until his death he was a trustee of the University of Pennsylvania, and from 1874 the first and only president of the board of managers of the university hospital.

On Apr. 2, 1823, he married Caroline Hahn, who died during the sixties, only daughter of Peter Hahn. As she was not a Quaker, he married "out of meeting," which resulted in separating him from the Society of Friends. They had no children. Wood died, as he had lived, in Philadelphia, Mar. 30, 1879, aged eighty-two years.

In addition to his collections of specimens, charts, and models (on which he had spent some $20,000), and all his medicinal plants, with $5,000 for the establishment of a botanical garden and conservatory, Wood left to the University of Pennsylvania $50,000 to maintain a department auxiliary to medicine which he had founded and himself maintained at a personal expenditure of $2,500 annually from 1865 to 1879. To the university hospital he left $75,000 to establish the Peter Hahn ward. From 1866 until his death he had made an annual contribution of $500 to the College of Physicians, on condition that the library should be open daily; his bequest of $10,000 was designed to constitute a permanent fund for this purpose. At the time of his death he also cancelled a mortgage of $5,000 which he held on the building of the College of Physicians, and gave to it all the medical books in his library, copies of which were not already in its possession. He was a man of great personal charm and power, vigorous, dominating, quick-tempered. He was an indefatigable student and a voluminous writer, frequently working until four o'clock in the morning. Together with his intimate friend, Dr. Franklin Bache [*q.v.*], he compiled a monumental work, *The Dispensatory of the United States* (1833), which went through many editions, greatly supplemented and enlarged. He also wrote a *Treatise on the Practice of Medicine* (1847), which ran through a number of editions; a *Treatise on Therapeutics and Pharmacology, or Materia Medica* (1856); a long list of papers, lectures, addresses, and syllabi; and *The History of the University of Pennsyl-*

vania (1834). Although he probably made no discoveries and added nothing to the general sum of medical lore, his life and work had great usefulness. His aristocratic disposition may be judged from his remark to his nephew, Horatio Charles Wood [*q.v.*], "Horatio, I would have thee know that I never have and never will demean myself by riding in a street car; when I ride, I ride in my carriage" (*Transactions of the Philadelphia College of Physicians*, 1920, *post*, p. 202).

[*Univ. of Pa. Biog. Cat. Matriculates of the Coll.* (1894); Joseph Carson, *A Hist. of the Medic. Dept. of the Univ. of Pa* (1869); *Universities and Their Sons: Univ. of Pa.* (1901), ed. by J. L. Chamberlain; *Boston Medic. and Surgical Jour.*, Oct. 24, 1849, p. 236; W. S. W. Ruschenberger, in *Am. Jour. Medic. Sci.*, Oct. 1879; *Medic. Record*, Apr. 5, 1879, p. 335; William Hunt, in *Phila. Medic. Times*, Apr. 26, 1879; Henry Hartshorne, in *Proc. Am. Philos. Soc.*, vol. XIX (1881); S. Littell, in *Trans. Coll. Physicians of Phila.*, 3 ser. vol. V (1881); H. C. Wood, *Ibid.*, 3 ser. vol. XLII (1920); obituary in *Pub. Ledger* (Phila.), Mar. 31, 1879; Wood family records.]   J. M.

WOOD, HORATIO CHARLES (Jan. 13, 1841–Jan. 3, 1920), physician, teacher, was born in Philadelphia, Pa., the son of Horatio Curtis and Elizabeth Head (Bacon) Wood, and a descendant in the sixth generation of Richard Wood, Quaker, who emigrated from England to Philadelphia in 1682 and later settled in New Jersey. His education was begun when he was three years old; at four he was sent to boarding school at Westtown, where he was the smallest boy among two hundred pupils, and where he said he received "valuable lessons in physical tenacity and endurance of punishment without flinching" (De Schweinitz, *Transactions of the College of Physicians, pos⁺*, p. 156). From there he went to the Friends' Select School in Philadelphia. At an early age he developed a passion for natural science and haunted the Academy of Natural Sciences, where Joseph Leidy [*q.v.*] took an interest in him. In 1861, when he was but twenty years old, the Academy published the first of his papers, "Contributions to the Carboniferous Flora of the United States," and a "Catalogue of Carboniferous Plants in the Museum of the Academy" (*Proceedings . . . 1860*, vol. XII, 1861). In 1862 he was graduated from the medical department of the University of Pennsylvania with the degree of M.D., continuing his studies as resident physician at Blockley and the Pennsylvania Hospitals. From the latter he entered the United States army in the midst of the Civil War. He returned to Philadelphia at the close of the war. On May 10, 1866, he married Elizabeth, daughter of James Longacre. A daughter and three sons, two of whom became physicians, were the offspring of this marriage.

Wood began his teaching career as a "quiz-master" in the practice of medicine, therapeutics, and chemistry at the University of Pennsylvania. From 1866 to 1876 he was professor of botany. Soon he became devoted to the study of nervous diseases, and by 1873 had earned a lectureship on nervous diseases and by 1876 a clinical professorship, which he held until 1901. From 1876 to 1906 he was also professor of materia medica, pharmacy, and general therapeutics.

Wood was a man of great physical and mental activity, and of unusual industry. His work embraces four separate fields: natural science (botany and entomology); experimental pharmacology, physiology, and pathology; medical jurisprudence; and nervous diseases and related subjects. His scientific bibliography includes almost three hundred papers, and six books: *Thermic Fever and Sun-stroke* (1872), *A Treatise on Therapeutics* (1874), *Brainwork and Overwork* (1880), *Nervous Diseases and Their Diagnosis* (1887), *Syphilis of the Nervous System* (1889), and *The Practice of Medicine* (1897), written with R. H. Fitz. In addition, with J. P. Remington and S. P. Sadtler, he revised *The Dispensatory of the United States*, written by his uncle, George Bacon Wood [*q.v.*], from the fifteenth to the eighteenth edition. He was at one time a collector for the Smithsonian Institution, and was a member of its expeditions to the Bahama Islands and into the Mexican Desert. His reputation as an entomologist may be judged by the fact that J. L. R. Agassiz [*q.v.*] entrusted to him the specimens of *Myriapoda* that he had collected on his expedition to Brazil in 1866. His publications brought him the Boylston prize, the Warren prize, and the special prize awarded by the Philosophical Society of Philadelphia. Wood served on the medical staff of the Philadelphia Hospital (Blockley) from 1870 to 1883, and on the neurological staff from 1883 to 1888. He was president of the College of Physicians of Philadelphia (1902–04) and of the Neurological Society (1883), and editor of *New Remedies* (1870–73), the *Medical Times* (1873–80), and the *Therapeutic Gazette* (1884–1900). Though Alfred Stillé [*q.v.*] preceded him as the author of a work on therapeutics, Wood's writing took and kept the field. Stillé's therapeutics was based upon experience, Wood's upon experiment, and the latter ushered in a new era. Wood died in Philadelphia.

[*Who's Who in America*, 1918–19; Guy Hinsdale, in *International Clinics*, 12 ser. vol. IV (1903); Henry Beates, Jr., in *Am. Jour. of Pharmacy*, Aug. 1905; George de Schweinitz, in *Alumni Reg. of the Univ. of Pa.*, vol. XI, 1906–07, p. 196; H. A. Hare, in *Therapeutic Gazette*, May 15, 1920; H. C. Wood, "Reminiscences," *Trans. Coll. of Physicians of Phila.*, 3 ser.

vol. XLII (1920); G. E. de Schweinitz, H. A. Hare, C. K. Mills, and F. X. Dercum, *Ibid.*; obituary in *Pub. Ledger* (Phila.), Jan. 5, 1920.]   J. M.

WOOD, JAMES (July 12, 1799–Apr. 7, 1867), Presbyterian clergyman and educator, the son of Jonathan and Susanna (Kellogg) Wood, was born at Greenfield, N. Y., near Saratoga. Having studied at three academies, earning his expenses meanwhile by teaching district school, he graduated from Union College, Schenectady, N. Y., in 1822. For a year he taught in Lawrenceville, N. J., and then took the last two years of the course in Princeton Theological Seminary, graduating in 1825. After a year in charge of churches at Wilkes-Barre and Kingston, Pa., he was ordained by the Presbytery of Albany on Sept. 5, 1826. During the next eight years he was pastor of the churches at Amsterdam and Veddersburg, N. Y. From 1834 to 1839 he was an agent of the Presbyterian board of education for Virginia and North Carolina, and then for the West and Southwest.

In the controversy which caused the division of the Presbyterian Church in 1837 he was a strong adherent of the conservative or Old School party. He published in 1837 a pamphlet, *Facts and Observations Concerning the Organization and State of the Churches in the Three Synods of Western New-York and the Synod of Western Reserve*. These synods were exscinded from the Church by the General Assembly of 1837, and became the nucleus of the New School Church. Wood's pamphlet upheld the charges of irregularity in organization and unsoundness in doctrine which were thought to justify the General Assembly's action. He continued the controversy in 1838 in *Old and New Theology: or, An Exhibition of Those Differences with Regard to Scripture Doctrines Which Have Recently Agitated and Now Divided the Presbyterian Church*. This book, of which enlarged editions were published in 1845, 1853, and 1855, reveals a keen disputant and a rigid conservative.

In 1839 Wood was appointed professor in the theological department of Hanover College, a young institution at Hanover, Ind. A year later this department was moved to New Albany, Ind., and named New Albany Theological Seminary (later McCormick Theological Seminary and now the Presbyterian Theological Seminary, Chicago). Wood served the seminary until 1851, being one of two professors, and for part of this time sole professor. By indefatigable activity he secured considerable increase in the seminary's funds. In his relations with the students he showed the friendliness and practical helpfulness which always characterized him. He left New

Albany to work again for the board of education, as general agent for the West and Southwest from 1851 to 1854, and as associate corresponding secretary, living in Philadelphia, for the following five years. In 1859 he became president of Hanover College and was soon facing the grave difficulties caused by the Civil War. The college's large constituency in Kentucky and Tennessee was cut off, many students entered the armies, and serious indebtedness was incurred. As to the strength and wisdom of Wood's administration there was controversy both in the college and in the synod, but it was realized later that he had averted temporary if not permanent discontinuance of the institution. Besides teaching a variety of subjects, he maintained and even increased the college's property. He kept the faculty together in spite of heavy burdens, and held the loyalty of the students. During his presidency, in 1864, he was moderator of the General Assembly of the Old School Presbyterian Church. In 1866 he became the first president of Van Rensselaer Institute, at Hightstown, N. J., where he died in his first year of service. He was married on Oct. 3, 1826, to Janetta Pruyn of Milton, N. Y. He wrote many tracts and articles in religious periodicals and a *Memoir of Sylvester Scovel, D.D., Late President of Hanover College*, which appeared in 1851.

[*Biog. Cat. of the Princeton Theological Sem., 1815–1932* (1933); reports of the board of education in *Minutes of the Gen. Assembly of the Presbyterian Church in the U. S. A.*, 1851–52, 1855–59; L. J. Halsey, *A Hist. of McCormick Theological Sem.* (1893); W. A. Millis, *The Hist. of Hanover Coll.* (1927); Alfred Nevin, *Encyc. of the Presbyterian Church in the U. S. A.* (1884); biog. material by his son, Rev. E. P. Wood (1877), in Princeton Theological Sem. Lib.]
R. H. N.

WOOD, JAMES (Nov. 12, 1839–Dec. 19, 1925), Quaker leader, farmer, was born at Mount Kisco, N. Y., the son of Stephen and Phoebe (Underhill) Wood. After attending Reynolds Academy at Bedford, N. Y., and Westtown School at Westtown, Pa., he entered Haverford College, where he studied for three years (1854–57), leaving at the end of his junior year. He continued to be a student throughout his life, with wide interests in many fields, especially in all branches of agriculture, and in history and anthropology. He was married on June 6, 1866, to Emily Hollingsworth Morris of Philadelphia (d. 1916). They had three children. Wood became widely known as an expert farmer, horticulturist, and sheep-raiser on his extensive farm near Mount Kisco, and he was the author of many papers on agriculture and kindred subjects. He was president of the Bedford Farmers' Club and was sought for throughout the state as a lecturer on agricultural subjects. He traveled extensively in Europe and on the American continent. He lectured frequently on historical and archeological subjects, wrote many historical brochures on local historical topics, and was president of the Westchester County Historical Society from 1885 to 1896. He took an important part in the founding of the New York State Reformatory for Women at Bedford, and was president of its board of managers from 1900 to 1916, during which period he was recognized as a leader on prison reform and on methods of correction.

He was descended from a long line of Quaker ancestors in both branches of his family, and his major life-interest was in the spiritual concerns and the public work of the Society of Friends. He was a student of Quaker history, and a recognized interpreter of Quaker ideals and polity. He was presiding clerk of the New York Yearly Meeting of Friends for more than a generation (1885–1925). He presided over the general conference of Friends held in Richmond, Ind., in 1887, and he was clerk of the Five Years Meeting in 1907. He was chairman of the committee which drafted the uniform discipline now in use (1936) in most of the American meetings. In 1893 he was chosen to present the views and ideals of the Society of Friends at the parliament of religions held at the time of the Columbian Exposition in Chicago. His address was published under the title, "Our Church and Its Mission" (*World's Congress of Religions*, 1894). In 1898 he wrote a pamphlet on *The Distinguishing Doctrines of the Religious Society of Friends*, which had a wide circulation. On the two-hundredth anniversary of the New York Yearly Meeting of Friends he prepared an historical review of the two centuries of Quakerism in that state. He was one of the founders of the *American Friend*.

His services to higher education in America were extensive and important. He was an influential manager of Haverford College from 1885 until his death. He was elected a trustee of Bryn Mawr College in 1887 and served several terms as president of the board before his resignation in 1918. He also gave much time and thought to the promotion of the circulation and study of the Bible. He was chairman of the Westchester County Bible Society from 1893 until his death, and president of the American Bible Society from 1911 to 1919. He died at Mount Kisco, survived by a son and a daughter.

[*Who's Who in America*, 1924–25; *Biog. Cat. Matriculates of Haverford Coll.* (1922); J. T. Scharf, *Hist. of Westchester County, N. Y.* (1886), vol. I; *Proc.... Gen. Conference of Friends, ... Richmond, Ind.* (1887); *Proc. of the Five Years Meeting*, 1902, 1907; R. M. Jones, in *Am. Friend*, Dec. 31, 1925; obituary in *N. Y. Times*, Dec. 20, 1925.]
R. M. J.

WOOD, JAMES FREDERICK (Apr. 27, 1813–June 20, 1883), Roman Catholic prelate, was born in the old Mifflin house in Philadelphia, Pa., in which his father, James Wood, an English immigrant, conducted business as an auctioneer and importer. James attended the school of St. Mary de Crypt, Mr. Sanderson's private school, and probably some English academy, for the family appears to have sojourned in England for some time. At all events, the Wood family settled in Cincinnati, Ohio, in 1827, and the youth became a clerk in the local branch of the Second National Bank. In 1833 he was paying teller and in 1836 cashier of the Franklin Bank of Cincinnati. Received into the Catholic Church in 1836 by Bishop John B. Purcell [*q.v.*], Wood was sent in 1837 to the Irish College in Rome. He then continued in the College of the Propaganda, specializing in higher theological studies and canon law while serving as a prefect of discipline. After his ordination to the priesthood by Cardinal Fransoni (Mar. 25, 1844), Father Wood returned to his diocese and became an assistant at the cathedral (1844) and later rector of St. Patrick's Church, Cincinnati (1854). As early as 1848, he was third on the list of nominees for the vacant see of Louisville. Appointed titular bishop of Antigonia and coadjutor to Bishop J. N. Neumann [*q.v.*] of Philadelphia, Wood was consecrated by Bishop Purcell, Apr. 26, 1857.

Bishop Wood was unusually active, for he took over the financial administration of the diocese and the management of the "Bishop's Bank," which had been under the care of M. A. Frenaye. Obliged to carry the burdens of the office without the authority, the coadjutor was not happy until he succeeded to the diocese in 1860. As a convert, he was rather rigorous, over-zealous, and probably unsympathetic to the Irish. A bitter foe of secret societies, he condemned the Fenians, excommunicated Catholics who belonged to the criminal Mollie Maguires, and reprobated all Irish political movements in the United States, although he dispatched at least $60,000 for Irish famine relief in 1880–83. During the Civil War he responded wholeheartedly to Gov. Andrew G. Curtin's request for nursing nuns and military chaplains. By 1864 he had completed the cathedral. A year later he purchased a site in Overbrook for the Seminary of St. Charles Borromeo, which was removed from the city in 1871 (A. J. Schulte, *Historical Sketch of the Philadelphia Theological Seminary of St. Charles Borromeo*, 1905). An accessible, democratic, charitable man, Wood founded the Catholic Home for Destitute Girls and a house of the Good Shepherd, and introduced the Little Sisters of the Poor into the diocese. As a stout exponent of Catholic education, he brought in the Sisters of the Holy Child, of Third Order of St. Francis, and of Mercy, established the Sister Servants of the Immaculate Heart, and trebled the number of parochial schools. An ardent patron of the American College in Rome, he served as treasurer of its board and in this capacity insisted that its funds be kept in America.

In 1867 he petitioned successfully to have the diocese of Harrisburg and Scranton carved out of the diocese of Philadelphia, and saw two of his priests, Jeremiah Shanahan and William O'Hara, appointed to the new sees. An assistant at the pontifical throne (1862), he sent large donations to Rome, attended the ceremonies commemorative of the martyrdom of SS. Peter and Paul (1867), voted for the promulgation of the doctrine of papal infallibility (although because of ill health he left the Vatican Council before the final vote), called a meeting of protest against the spoliation of the Papal States, and attended the golden anniversary services of Pius IX as a bishop. On Feb. 12, 1875, Philadelphia was made a metropolitan see with Wood as its first archbishop. In the local controversy over the opening of the Centennial Exhibition on Sundays, he took the liberal view that the Sabbath should be a day of recreation for working classes. Active almost to the end of his life in provincial councils and diocesan visitations, he always abstained from politics. Respected by Protestants, he won the good will of his people and the respect of the two hundred and fifty priests who labored under his strict rule.

[R. H. Clarke, *Lives of the Deceased Bishops of the Cath. Ch. in the U. S.,* vol. III (1888), pp. 533–47; *Cath. Encyc.*; J. L. J. Kirlin, *Catholicity in Phila.* (1909); Wood's pastoral letters, esp. those of 1865, 1867, 1875; F. E. Tourscher, *The Kenrick-Frenaye Correspondence* (1920); *Records Am. Cath. Hist. Soc.* (1884), *passim*; *Am. Cath. Hist. Researches* (1884), *passim*; *N. Y. Freeman's Journal*, June 30, July 7, 1883; obituary in *Press* (Phila.), June 21, 1883.]

R. J. P.

WOOD, JAMES J. (Mar. 25, 1856–Apr. 19, 1928), engineer, inventor, son of Paul H. and Elizabeth (Shine) Wood, was born at Kinsale, County Cork, Ireland. In 1864, when he was eight years old, he came to America with his parents and settled in Connecticut, where he began his schooling. At eleven years of age, however, he went to work for the Branford (Conn.) Lock Company. He continued his schooling as best he could and when the family moved to Brooklyn, N. Y., he was able to enter the Brook-

lyn evening high school, from which he graduated in 1876. During the day he worked for the Brady Manufacturing Company, and the mechanical experience he gained, coupled with that which he had received earlier in Connecticut, enabled him to complete in two years with only night attendance the course in mechanical engineering and drafting at the Collegiate and Polytechnic Institute, Brooklyn.

By this time Wood was superintendent of the Brady Company, which organization was engaged at the time in making castings and parts for the electric dynamo machines invented by James B. Fuller of the Fuller Electric Company and by Hiram S. Maxim [q.v.] of the United States Electric Lighting Company. This work aroused in Wood a keen interest in electric lighting and in 1879, after much study and experiment, he designed and built an arc-light dynamo of his own, patented Oct. 19, 1880. This machine was so efficient that the Fuller Electric Company in 1880 gave up the manufacture of Fuller's dynamo in favor of Wood's, taking Wood into partnership and reorganizing the company as the Fuller-Wood Company. This dynamo was the first of a long series of inventions made by Wood in the succeeding forty-eight years which brought him about 240 patents, chiefly in the electrical field. After five years with the Fuller-Wood Company he became a consulting engineer, his chief client being the Thomson-Houston Company, and when this concern, in the early 1890's, joined the group of organizations which together became the General Electric Company, Wood was retained as factory manager and chief engineer, later becoming consulting engineer of the Fort Wayne Works, Fort Wayne, Ind., where he continued until his death.

While the major portion of his inventions were devised after his removal to Fort Wayne, he had made a number in the five-year period (1885–90) during which he was a resident of New York. One of the most notable of these was a dynamo and arc-lighting system for flood lighting, which was first successfully used to light the Statue of Liberty in New York Harbor in 1885. He also manufactured a Brayton type of internal combustion engine, which was installed in the first Holland submarine, and designed the machines for constructing the main cables used on the original Brooklyn Bridge. When he went to Fort Wayne, his dynamo and arc lamp were already in extensive use under the name of the Wood arc-lighting system, but in the course of the succeeding years he added accessory equipment to the system, inventing meters, switches, coils, and other devices. Between 1900 and 1918 his inventions centered about alternating current generators, motors, transformers, enclosed alternating current arc lamps, circuit breakers, and numerous small motor applications such as vibrators and fans.

Wood had few outside interests and was little known except in the electrical industry. In recognition of his valuable contributions in his chosen field he was made a Fellow of the American Institute of Electrical Engineers. On Jan. 20, 1916, he married Nellie B. Scott of New Hampshire, Ohio, and at the time of his death, in Asheville, N. C., where he had gone for his health, he was survived by his widow and three children.

[*Who's Who in America*, 1928–29; *Jour. Am. Institute Electrical Engineers*, May 1928; *Electrical World*, Apr. 28, 1928; *N. Y. Times*, Apr. 21, 1928; Patent Office records.]   C. W. M.

WOOD, JAMES RUSHMORE (Sept. 14, 1813–May 4, 1882), surgeon, was born to a Quaker couple, Elkanah and Mary (Rushmore) Wood, at Mamaroneck, N. Y. His father, a miller, moved to New York City to conduct a leather shop, and here the son received a meager elementary education in a Quaker school. He began his medical studies in the private classes of Dr. David L. Rogers, then took courses at the College of Physicians and Surgeons of New York and at the Vermont Academy of Medicine at Castleton, where he was graduated in 1834. After a period of service as demonstrator of anatomy at the latter school he returned to New York in 1837 to practise medicine on the Bowery, later moving over to Broadway.

He early centered his interest on operative surgery and secured a place upon the staff of the city almshouse, out of which he and two associates created Bellevue Hospital in 1847, becoming its medical board. From that time to his death he was a moving spirit in the institution, with its growth becoming known as the master surgeon of the greatest hospital in the United States. He did much for the improvement of the hospital service, introducing in 1869 the first hospital ambulance service in any city (*Surgery, Gynecology, and Obstetrics, post,* p. 443). Through his efforts Bellevue opened on May 1, 1873, the first training school for nurses in the United States. In 1856, with other members of the hospital staff, he organized the Bellevue Hospital Medical College, in which he was at once appointed professor of operative surgery and surgical pathology.

As an operating surgeon his speed and dexterity were the marvel of a time when these were the prime requisites of surgery, since the use of anesthetics was then but beginning. These, together with sound after-treatment by rest, cleanliness, and free drainage of operative wounds gave him unusually good results. He was a bold and radical operator. He treated by ligation aneurism of practically all of the larger arteries, including the common carotid and the external iliac, with great success. He is credited with being one of the first to cure aneurism by pressure. He did notable work in the surgery of nerves. He removed Meckel's ganglion successfully four successive times, an operation seldom performed. He achieved an international reputation for bone surgery, particularly for the periosteal reproduction of bone. He produced the practical regeneration of the lower jaw after its entire removal for phosphorous necrosis. He had notably successful results in the resection of the knee joint. He perfected an instrument, called a bisector, for rapid operation for vesical calculus. In the rôle of instructor, whether in classroom or clinic, he was inclined to the theatrical. His entries into the amphitheatre were timed for effect, and he was wont to make his appearance in a black gown with a red rose or carnation pinned over his heart. Applause was expected. While he was an able teacher, the handicap of his poor early education was always apparent, particularly in his frequent misapplication of Latin phrases. From the beginning of his connection with Bellevue he collected post-mortem material, which grew into the Wood Museum, one of the richest collections of pathological material in the world. He was chiefly instrumental in the passage of the act by the state legislature granting for anatomical dissection the unclaimed bodies of all vagrants.

His writings were mainly case reports in journal articles, his most notable paper being "Early History of the Operation of Ligature of the Primitive Carotid Artery" (*New York Journal of Medicine,* July 1857), with a wealth of detailed case reports. He was a member of the New York Academy of Medicine and of the New York and Massachusetts state medical societies, and was twice president of the New York Pathological Society. He was still at the height of his professional career when he died in New York. He was married in 1853 to Emma Rowe, daughter of James Rowe, a New York merchant.

[See *Boston Medic. and Surgic. Jour.,* May 11, 1882; *Medico-Legal Jour.,* Sept. 1883; *Medic. Record,* May 13, 1882; *Medic. and Surgic. Reporter,* Jan. 7, 1865, pp. 197–200; *N. Y. Medic. Jour.,* Jan. 12, 1884; *Trans. Medic. Soc. of the State of N. Y.* (1885); *Surgery, Gynecology, and Obstetrics,* Mar. 1929, which is authority for date of birth given above; H. A. Kelly and W. L. Burrage, *Am. Medic. Biogs.* (1920); *N. Y. Tribune,* May 5, 1882. Year of birth is frequently given as 1816.]   J. M. P.

WOOD, JETHRO (Mar. 16, 1774–Sept. 18, 1834), inventor, was the son of John and Dinah (Hussey or Starbuck) Wood. His birthplace may have been Dartmouth, Bristol County, Mass., the early home of the family, though the vital records of that town contain no mention of his birth. At an unknown date, sometime before 1783, the family, which was in moderate circumstances, moved to White Creek, Washington County, N. Y., where it is possible Jethro was born. Here, Jan. 1, 1793, he married Sylvia Howland. Some seven years later he moved with his family to Cayuga County, New York, establishing his residence on a farm near Poplar Ridge, where he lived until his death. He was a member of the Society of Friends but did not have the usual sober mien of this sect.

Wood's claim to fame rests upon his invention of improvements on the plow. His first patent on a cast-iron plow was issued on July 1, 1814. Detailed information regarding it has disappeared, but it seems not to have been highly regarded by others or satisfactory to the inventor. He had difficulty in manufacturing and in inducing his neighbors to use a cast-iron plow, which they thought would poison their land. He continued to improve his original invention and on Sept. 1, 1819, received a patent for the plow for which he is so well known. It was made by others without Wood's leave and he and his heirs waged a continual fight against infringers. His patent was extended for an additional period of fourteen years and near the close of this term the infringement fight was finally won but to little avail. A congressional committee which investigated the question of a further extension of the patent found that Wood and his family had received $8,595 from his plow but had expended most of it in costs and charges. A bill for a further extension of the patent was passed by the Senate but was defeated in the House of Representatives. Later the state of New York appropriated $2,000 for his heirs.

Wood has frequently been referred to as the inventor of the cast-iron plow, but cast-iron had been used in the Norfolk plow in 1721 and by 1791 plows with interchangeable moldboards, landsides, and shares of cast-iron were known and in use in Great Britain. In the United States cast-iron shares were made as early as 1794 and Newbold's patent for a cast-iron plow made in one piece was issued in 1797. Peacock's plow of 1807 was made in three pieces, with the moldboard and landside of cast iron. That of Stephen McCormick [q.v.], 1819, with its cast-iron moldboard antedated Wood's second invention. Wood's improvement over the existing

models lay largely in the shape of the parts, particularly the moldboard. He vaguely described this as a kind of "plano-curvilinear figure" of peculiar shape in which diverging lines from front to rear and at least one transverse line were straight. The importance of longitudinal and transverse straight lines had been emphasized by Small, Pickering, and Thomas Jefferson. The peculiar virtue of Wood's plow lay in the shape resulting from the extended use of longitudinal straight lines and the combination of good balance, strength, light draft, interchangeability of parts, the use of cast-iron, and the cheapness of manufacture. His design and principles of construction were copied throughout the North, as were those of Stephen McCormick in the South. For what he did to perfect the cast-iron plow and to bring it into extended use, he deserves much credit.

[Frank Gilbert, *Jethro Wood, Inventor of the Modern Plow* (1882); *A List of Patents Granted by the U. S. for Inventions and Designs from Apr. 10, 1790 to Dec. 31, 1836* (1872); *Plough Boy* (Albany), Sept. 16, 1820; *Am. Agriculturist*, Apr. 1848; *Scientific American*, Mar. 17, 1877; E. H. Knight, *Am. Mechanical Dict.*, vol. II (1877); J. R. Passmore, *The English Plough* (1930); E. G. Storke, *Hist. of Cayuga County, N. Y.* (1879); *Cong. Globe*, 29 Cong., 1 Sess., pp. 291, 1028; 30 Cong., 1 Sess., pp. 248–49, 264, 271; 31 Cong., 1 Sess., pp. 1504–05, 1711–14, and App., pp. 1208–09; *N. Y. Session Laws*, 1868, II, 1618; Cyrenus Wheeler, "The Inventors and Inventions of Cayuga County, N. Y.," *Cayuga County Hist. Soc. Colls.*, no. 2 (1882); Emily Howland, "Early Hist. of Friends in Cayuga County, N. Y.," *Ibid.*; William and Solomon Drown, *Compendium of Agriculture* (1824).]   R. H. A.

WOOD, JOHN (c. 1775–May 15, 1822), political pamphleteer and map-maker, was born in Scotland, had educational connections in Edinburgh, lived in Switzerland at the time of the French invasion in 1798, and on his return to Scotland published in 1799 *A General View of the History of Switzerland*. He emigrated to the United States about 1800 and was recommended to Aaron Burr [q.v.] as a teacher of languages and mathematics. He was for a time a tutor of Burr's precocious daughter, Theodosia [q.v.], and became useful to Burr as a facile writer willing to support his political program. Wood published in Philadelphia in 1801 *A Letter to Alexander Addison, Esq. . . . in Answer to His Rise and Progress of Revolution*. With the tone of bitter invective and personal abuse characteristic of many of the impassioned journalists of the period, he prepared *The History of the Administration of John Adams* for publication in 1802. It contained an ill-digested assortment of party diatribes from the partisan press and party hack writers, and some compositions from Wood's pen. Burr decided it would be more dangerous than helpful to his party and undertook to suppress it by buying up the edition. After much altercation Burr failed to pay the sum agreed upon, and the volume was published with the added zest given in the title, *The Suppressed History* (1802). This incident gave birth to a succession of charges and countercharges between the Burr and Clinton factions in New York, articulate through the pamphlets of their respective spokesmen, John Wood and James Cheetham [*q.v.*].

In the winter of 1805–06 Wood went to Kentucky, "an elderly looking man, of middle size, and ordinary dress, with a Godfrey's quadrant stringed to his shoulder, a knapsack on his back" (Marshall, *post*, II, 375). He began with associates the publication in Frankfort of the *Western World,* a weekly of Republican faith that in July started a series of tales of the plans of James Wilkinson, Harry Innes [*qq.v.*], and others with the agents of Spain. Wood later asserted that only the first of these was published with his approval and that, when he failed to prevent the publication of the others, he withdrew from the paper (Temple Bodley, *Reprints of Littell's Political Transactions in and Concerning Kentucky,* 1926, pp. xcvi–xcvii, being Filson Club Publications, no. 31). He seems to have returned to the East after a brief season in Kentucky and published in 1807 at Alexandria, Va., *A Full Statement of the Trial and Acquittal of Aaron Burr.* He settled in Richmond, where he eschewed politics for his mathematical and scientific interests, winning a certain esteem in that city while he acquired the reputation of being an eccentric person. He published in Richmond in 1809 *A New Theory of the Diurnal Rotation of the Earth.* When the Virginia legislature in 1816–17 provided for an accurate chart of each county of the state and a general map of the state, Thomas Jefferson recommended Wood to Gov. W. C. Nicholas [*q.v.*] as a man fit and ready to undertake the survey and map-making, speaking in high praise of his mathematical abilities (A. A. Lipscomb and A. E. Bergh, *The Writings of Thomas Jefferson,* vol. XIV, 1904, pp. 455–56.). In 1819 Wood signed a contract with the state to execute and deliver in five years a map of each county and a general map of the state. By February 1822 he had returned maps of all the counties except six, and at his death in May 1822 it was believed that he had completed a fifth part of the general map. While Wood had received $33,000 on this project, which he had expected to finish in a few months, on his death the completion of the work was turned over to Herman Boye, who constructed the so-called nine-sheet map of Virginia, published in 1827. The verdict of a careful student of Virginia car-

tography on Wood's map-making is that "the county charts which he constructed . . . probably indicate as careful execution and fidelity to facts, as was possible, under the difficult circumstances attending such a large survey at that time" (Swem, *post*, pp. 102–03).

[See E. G. Swem, "Maps Relating to Va.," *Bull. Va. State Lib.,* vol. VII (1914); Humphrey Marshall, *The Hist. of Ky.* (2 vols., 1824); A. J. Beveridge, *The Life of John Marshall* (4 vols., 1916–19); Justin Winsor, *Narrative and Crit. Hist. of America,* vol. VII (1888), pp. 334–45; letters of James Cheetham to Thomas Jefferson, *Proc. Mass. Hist. Soc.,* 3 ser., vol. I (1908), pp. 51–58; obit. notices in *Richmond Enquirer,* May 17, 21, 1822. Thirty-two of the county maps executed by Wood are in the Va. State Lib.] M. H. W.

WOOD, JOHN TAYLOR (Aug. 13, 1830–July 19, 1904), naval officer, was born at Fort Snelling, Minn., then in Iowa Territory. His father, Robert Crooke Wood was an army surgeon and from 1862 to 1865 assistant surgeon-general. His mother was Anne Mackall (Taylor), daughter of Gen. Zachary Taylor and a sister of Jefferson Davis' first wife. Wood entered the Naval School at Annapolis in June 1847 for a brief preparatory course. After serving on the frigate *Brandywine* (Brazil station) and the ship of the line *Ohio* in the Pacific Ocean during the Mexican War, he was warranted a midshipman to rank from Apr. 7, 1847. He reentered the school, July 1, 1850, for five months' instruction and then, ordered to the sloop-of-war *Germantown,* saw service on the African coast. He returnd to the renamed Naval Academy Oct. 1, 1852, and was graduated June 10, 1853, ranking second in his class. He served successively on the sloop-of-war *Cumberland* in the Mediterranean, as assistant commandant at the Academy, on the frigate *Wabash,* the flagship of the Mediterranean Squadron, and as assistant instructor of naval tactics and nautical gunnery at the Academy. He was warranted a master on Sept. 15, 1855, and was later promoted lieutenant to date from Sept. 16, 1855. He tendered his resignation on Apr. 21, 1861, but was dismissed as of Apr. 2, 1861, though he was actually on duty at the Academy for several days after Apr. 21. The date of his dismissal was not corrected in the printed records of the Navy Department until 1931 (*Register of Officers of the Confederate States Navy,* Government Printing Office, 1931). After residing on his farm in Maryland for a time he was commissioned, as of Oct. 4, 1861, a lieutenant in the Confederate navy from Louisiana.

Following a tour of duty in the naval shore batteries at Evansport, Potomac River, he served on the ironclad *Virginia (Merrimack),* participating in the victory at Hampton Roads, Mar.

8–9, 1862, in the rout of the *Monitor* and consorts on Apr. 11 and May 8, 1862, and in the repulse of the enemy at Drewry's Bluff, Va., May 15, 1862. In October 1862 he conducted the first of his famous midnight expeditions, capturing and burning the schooner *Frances Elmor* off Bluff Point on the Potomac River, and the ship *Alleghanian* in Chesapeake Bay. He was appointed naval aide-de-camp to President Davis Jan. 26, 1863—appointment confirmed Feb. 9—with the statutory rank and pay of colonel of cavalry. In this capacity he made frequent inspections of naval defenses and ship constructions, and served as liaison officer between the army and the navy. His adventurous spirit was not content with staff duty, however, and in August 1863 he organized another expedition in the Chesapeake, which resulted in the capture of the United States war schooners *Satellite* and *Reliance* (after severe hand-to-hand fighting) and the transport schooners *Golden Rod, Coquette* and *Two Brothers*. For this exploit he received the thanks of Congress and promotion to commander. In a third boat expedition in February 1864 he captured and destroyed the Federal gunboat *Underwriter* at New Bern, N. C. In April 1864 he participated in the successful siege of Plymouth, N. C., and in August commanded the steam sloop *Tallahassee* on a raid extending from Wilmington to Halifax, Nova Scotia, and back, during which he captured thirty-three vessels, destroyed twenty-six vessels and released five on ransom bond and two without bond. For this exploit he was given a captaincy (Feb. 10, 1865). He was with President Davis in the retreat from Richmond, April–May 1865, but managed to escape through Florida to Cuba. He enjoyed the special confidence of General Lee and of the entire navy, and his brilliant accomplishments compelled the praise of the enemy (see *Official Records, post,* 1 ser. IX, 589). He was modest in deportment but executed his boldly conceived plans with skill and daring.

After the war he settled in Halifax, where he engaged in shipping and marine insurance, and there died. On Nov. 26, 1856, he married Lola Mackubin, daughter of George and Eleanor Mackubin of Annapolis, Md.; eleven children were born of this union.

[Unpublished archives, Naval Records and Library, Washington; *War of the Rebellion: Official Records (Army),* 1, 2, 3 ser.; *(Navy),* 1, 2 ser.; R. U. Johnson and C. C. Buell, *Battles and Leaders of the Civil War* (4 vols., 1887–88); *Century Magazine,* Mar. 1885, Nov. 1893, July 1898; W. D. Harville, "The Confederate Service of John Taylor Wood" (unpub. thesis, Southern Methodist Univ., Dallas, Tex., 1935); *Jour. of the Cong. of the Confederate States* (1904–05); private papers of Miss Lola M. Wood, Maddox (St. Mary's County), Md.; *U. S. Naval Academy Graduates' Association,* 1925, pp. 18–19; *Morning Chronicle* (Halifax, N. S.), July 20, 1904.]
                                        W. M. R., Jr.

WOOD, JOSEPH (c. 1778–c. 1832), miniaturist, portrait painter, was born in Clarkstown, Orange County, N. Y., the son of a respectable farmer who was also sheriff of the county. Wishing his son to follow his own calling, the father frowned upon his artistic tendencies. Finally, at the age of fifteen, Joseph ran away to New York, hoping to become a landscape painter and to find a position that would help him improve his drawing. In both objectives he was bitterly disappointed, and spent several friendless years variously working and playing the violin for a livelihood. One day he saw some miniatures in a silversmith's window on Broadway and, persuading the proprietor to accept him as apprentice, was finally allowed to examine and copy one of the miniatures. For several years he worked as a silversmith, but about 1804, having made the acquaintance of another young artist, John Wesley Jarvis [q.v.], Wood went into partnership with him. The two young men started a flourishing business in *eglomisé* silhouettes, sometimes taking in as much as a hundred dollars a day. William Dunlap [q.v.], who visited the two young men, describes them as artists who "indulged in the excitements, and experienced the perplexities of *mysterious marriages*; and it is probable that these perplexities kept both poor, and confined them to the society of young men, instead of that respectable communion with ladies, and the refined circles of the city, which Malbone enjoyed" (*post,* II, 214). These "mysteries and perplexities" are also cited as possible causes of the none-too-friendly dissolution of the Wood-Jarvis partnership about 1809. Through Jarvis, Wood met Edward Greene Malbone [q.v.], one of the foremost American miniaturists of the day, and received instruction from him in the art of the miniature from the preparation of the ivory to the finishing of the picture. Malbone also rendered Wood considerable assistance and was his friend so long as he lived.

Wood maintained a studio in New York until 1812 or 1813, having set up for himself after the break with Jarvis, but moved to Philadelphia and exhibited regularly at the Pennsylvania Academy of the Fine Arts until 1817. By 1827 he was established in Washington, and it is possible that he painted also in Baltimore. He was a prolific worker, turning out innumerable portraits and miniatures as well as pencil sketches and silhouettes. Among his oils are a cabinet-size painting of Andrew Jackson and a portrait of Henry Clay. A miniature of Jackson by Wood was engraved in 1824 by James B. Longacre, while his portrait of Clay was lithographed in 1825 by Albert Newsam. He also painted a miniature of John Greene Proud. A watercolor portrait of an unknown man is inscribed on the reverse, "presented to Edith McPherson by Mrs. Abby Wood, 1839." Whether or not the Mrs. Wood thus mentioned was his widow is unknown. In his later years, whether through dissipation or other adversity, Wood slipped into a state of poverty, in which he died in Washington about 1832 at the age of fifty-four (*Ibid.*, II, 230). Nathaniel Rogers, who became his pupil in 1811 and was his paid helper for several years, is said to have befriended him and his children in their adversity (*Ibid.*, III, 17).

[See "Sketch of the Life of Mr. Joseph Wood,"*Port-Folio* (Phila.), Jan. 1811; William Dunlap, *A Hist. of the Rise and Progress of the Arts of Design in the U. S.* (3 vols., 1918), ed. by F. W. Bayley and C. E. Goodspeed; Theodore Bolton, *Early Am. Portrait Draughtsmen in Crayons* (1923), and *Early Am. Portrait Painters in Miniature* (1921), both of which give an incorrect date of death; H. B. Wehle and Theodore Bolton, *Am. Miniatures, 1730–1850* (1927).]   D. G.

WOOD, LEONARD (Oct. 9, 1860–Aug. 7, 1927), soldier, pro-consul, was born at Winchester, N. H. He was the first of three children of Charles Jewett and Caroline (Hagar) Wood, both of whom came from deep-rooted New England stock. Wood spent his youth at the seashore village of Pocasset, Mass., where his father had sought surroundings favorable to the cure of an illness (malaria) contracted during Civil War service. The boy led a frugal, outdoor life, going to the district school, being tutored for two years by Miss Jessie Haskell, who greatly influenced his character, and attending Pierce Academy, Middleboro. In 1880 his father died; and Leonard, who had decided to adopt his profession, entered Harvard Medical School. Despite financial handicaps, he completed the course creditably, and after a short and stormy internship at Boston City Hospital received his M.D. in 1884. He tried private practice in Boston, found it unattractive and unremunerative, and decided to seek commission in the Army Medical Corps. No immediate vacancies existed, but he was offered an interim appointment as contract surgeon and was ordered to report to Arizona. There he was instantly plunged into the operations against the Apaches of Geronimo [*q.v.*], culminating, after long marches, indescribable hardships, and occasional small engagements, in the chief's surrender. Wood had done duty as physician, commander of troops, and hostage. His courage, endurance, and leadership won enthusiastic official commendation.

There ensued for Wood a period of routine military duty in California and the East, where he soon acquired a reputation as a capable physician and as an athlete. He had been regularly commissioned in 1886 and in 1891 he was promoted captain, assistant surgeon. On Nov. 18, 1890, he had married Louisa A. Condit Smith of Washington, D. C. To them came in time three children, two sons and a daughter. In 1895 he was transferred to Washington. Soon President and Mrs. McKinley became his patients. In June 1897 he met Theodore Roosevelt and the two men were instantly drawn together. The necessity and morality of war with Spain stood high among the convictions which united them. When war was precipitated they combined forces to organize the 1st United States Volunteer Cavalry, better known as the "Rough Riders," of whom Wood, by virtue of his practical experience, took command as colonel. The regiment was recruited at San Antonio, Tex., trained and disciplined a few weeks, and slightly more than half of it was forced through the confusion at Tampa into the Cuban expedition. Wood led the regiment in the first clash, Las Guasimas, June 24, 1898. He succeeded to the command of a cavalry brigade for the fighting around San Juan Hill a week later. After the surrender of Santiago he was appointed military governor of that city. The town was notoriously filthy and disease-ridden. In addition he found it starving from the siege. The Cubans were hostile toward their late enemies, the Spaniards, and suspicious of American intentions. Wood brought them food, order, justice, sanitation, and public works. So markedly successful was he that, in October 1898, he was given charge of the entire province of Santiago. He applied the policies developed in the city to the larger area with such success that, in December 1899, he was appointed military governor of Cuba, in succession to Maj.-Gen. John R. Brooke [*q.v.*].

At this juncture, when Leonard Wood was about to become a national and international figure, his traits and character were fully developed. Physically he was a giant, enduring and of relentless energy. Mentally he was equally energetic and his capacity for work seemed endless. He was shrewd, with a keen insight into human nature. His patriotism was strongly nationalistic. He felt that, for both Cuba and the Philippines, the happiest destiny would be permanent inclusion in the United States; but his honesty demanded that this come about through their own volition. He appreciated wealth, but did not regard it as important. He was exceedingly ambitious. His singleness of purpose and sheer joy in conflict gave him great powers of accomplishment and assured him enemies and endless conroversy. His ability, sincerity, and charm of manner bound men as individuals to him. He was never a felicitous speaker, but these same qualities enabled him to appear before gatherings with great effect.

As military governor of Cuba his term lasted until May 20, 1902. In this period the affairs of the island were thoroughly stabilized and organized. Educational, police, and fiscal systems were established. The administration of justice was modernized and made effective. The relations of church and state were composed. Railroads were chartered and regulated. Great advances were made in sanitation, and it was during Wood's administration that Walter Reed [q.v.] made his epochal investigations into the transmission of yellow fever. Agriculture and Commerce made encouraging progress. An electoral system was set up; and finally the transmission of the government to duly chosen Cuban officials was smoothly effected. The integrity of Wood's administration was as high as its efficiency. This task was his most complete and clean-cut achievement. A generation after his departure, his was probably the American name most honored and respected by the Cubans. Upon his death Cuba voted his widow a pension in advance of similar action by the United States Congress.

For Wood a short stay in the United States and a visit to Europe followed. He attended the German grand maneuvers, first sensed the international tensions that preceded the World War, and had his attention directed to the problems of citizen armies and compulsory military service. In 1903 he was sent to the Philippines as governor of the Moro Province, consisting of Mindanao and adjacent islands. Though on a smaller scale, his problems were similar in scope to those in Cuba; but here he dealt with a semi-savage people and a primitive civilization. By reason, persuasion, and fighting he pacified the province, inaugurated reforms, and brought about a relatively high degree of prosperity, though he has been criticized for his ruthlessness in stamping out Moro institutions (Buell, *post*, p. 112).

On Aug. 8, 1903, he was promoted major-general in the regular army. His responsibilities in Cuba and the vicissitudes of army reorganization had brought him already two temporary appointments as brigadier-general and two more as major-general, all of volunteers. On Feb. 4, 1901, he had been promoted brigadier-general in the regular army. This advancement, involving his elevation from a captaincy in a staff corps had aroused serious resentment in the service. When, as senior brigadier-general, his name

came up for promotion to major-general, this personal opposition was reënforced by enemies of his Cuban days acting through "Mark" Hanna (58 Cong., 2 Sess., *Senate Executive Document C. Nomination of Leonard Wood to be Major-General. Hearings Before the Committee on Military Affairs*, 1904). On Hanna's death the fight collapsed, and feeling in the army against Wood on this account diminished rapidly thereafter.

From Mindanao Wood went in 1906 to command the Philippine division of the army for two years and then returned to the United States. In 1910 he served as special ambassador to the Argentine Republic at its independence centennial. In the spring of 1910 he was appointed chief of staff of the army for a four year term, which began July 16. His first problem was the subordination of the various bureaus of the War Department to the military hierarchy developed by the creation of a General Staff in 1903. Out of this grew an epic internecine and personal feud in the War Department between the Chief of Staff and the Adjutant General. It resulted in the retirement of the latter and the substantial achievement of Wood's aims. He sought also to organize the far-scattered regular army into a coherent force. In this, though aided by the necessity of concentrating troops on the Mexican border, he was only partially successful. He gave close attention to the provision of war material. He saw the necessity of building up reserves of trained man-power and, as a step in this direction, initiated civilian training camps in 1913.

In 1914 he was reassigned to the Department of the East and engaged in the preparedness movement, with the Plattsburg training camps as its focus and some form of universal military service as his own ideal. His activities frequently contravened the desires of the Wilson administration, brought him censure, and built up in Washington a distrust of his subordination. This situation was aggravated by his close association with Theodore Roosevelt. When the United States entered the World War, although senior officer of the army, he was passed over as the commander of the expeditionary force in favor of Maj.-Gen. John J. Pershing. This decision on the part of the administration was obviously legitimate, and there flowed from it almost necessarily the implication that there was no appropriate subordinate position for Wood in France. Unfortunately, after training the 89th Division at Camp Funston, Kansas, Wood was summarily and spectacularly relieved from its command on the eve of embarkation. The treatment accorded him became automatically one of the rallying points of critics of the conduct of the war; and the net cumulative effect was to confirm his exclusion from any outstanding participation in the war effort at home. He had made major contributions to American military success, but they were those of the peace years: the popularization of conscription and the successful demonstrations of officers' training camps.

In 1916 Wood had been a receptive candidate for the Republican nomination for the presidency, and following the war he openly sought his party's indorsement for the office. His activity in the preparedness agitation had made him widely known. His nationalism struck a popular chord; and many regarded him as Woodrow Wilson's victim and Theodore Roosevelt's heir. On the other hand, his strenuousness and his loose affiliation with the Republican organization were repugnant to the party hierarchy; and on the first count there was reflected accurately the sentiment of a country drifting in the backwash of the war. He came to the Chicago convention of 1920 with the largest single following of delegates, and developed a balloting strength in excess of 300; but his supporters were outmaneuvered on and off the convention floor. Following the inauguration, President Harding appointed Wood, with W. Cameron Forbes, a member of a special mission to the Philippine Islands. Almost simultaneously Wood was offered and accepted the provostship of the University of Pennsylvania, subject to the demands of his Philippine mission.

This academic post he was destined never to fill; upon the conclusion of the commission's investigations, Wood remained in the Far East as governor general of the Philippines. His primary objectives were three: to restore the economic stability of the Islands, to inaugurate administrative reforms, and to reinvest the governor general and his administration with a fuller measure of executive power. In all these undertakings he was successful, despite strenuous and vociferous local opposition. Numerous complaints were lodged against him in Washington by the parliamentary and independence groups of Filipinos, but he was sustained by the President and the Secretary of War. In 1924 he helped to block American legislation for Philippine independence.

By 1927 Wood's health had deteriorated seriously in the tropics. He had been troubled in particular by the recurrence of a tumor in his skull, the result of an accident at Santiago, Cuba, which pressed on his brain, inducing paralysis of the left side of his body. He returned to the United States for a third surgical treatment of this affliction, and on Aug. 7, 1927, died as a result of the operation. Wood was awarded the Congressional Medal of Honor for his services in the Apache campaign and received the Distinguished Service Medal after the World War. He was decorated by four foreign governments and held numerous honorary degrees. He was the author of *Our Military History. Its Facts and Fallacies* (1916), of numerous articles, bearing chiefly on preparedness, and, with W. Cameron Forbes, of the *Report of the Special Mission to the Philippines* (1921).

[Hermann Hagedorn, *Leonard Wood* (2 vols., 1931) is the authorized biography and lists most of the important articles about him. During his presidential candidacy four uncritical biographies appeared: J. H. Sears, *The Career of Leonard Wood* (1919); E. F. Wood, *Leonard Wood, Conservator of Americanism* (1920); W. H. Hobbs, *Leonard Wood, Administrator, Soldier and Citizen* (1920); and J. G. Holme, *The Life of Leonard Wood* (1920). More critical comments, along with some praise, are in R. L. Buell, "The Last Proconsul," *New Republic*, Dec. 9, 1931; M. L. Quezon and Camilo Osias, *Governor-General Wood and the Filipino Cause* (1924); C. A. Thompson, *Conditions in the Philippine Islands* (1926); Carleton Beals, *The Crime of Cuba* (1933). See also *N. Y. Times*, Aug. 7, 1927; *Army and Navy Journal*, Aug. 13, 1927; Johnson Hagood, "General Wood as I Knew Him," *Saturday Evening Post*, Oct. 22, Dec. 17, 1932. The Wood Papers are deposited in the Lib. of Cong.]   T.J.B.

WOOD, MARY ELIZABETH (Aug. 22, 1861–May 1, 1931), librarian in China, was of English ancestry, and both of her parents, Edward Farmer and Mary Jane (Humphrey) Wood, came of New England stock. She was born near Batavia in the township of Elba, N. Y., where she attended private and public schools. From childhood she had a sympathetic interest in people, and in later years her recollections of Batavia neighbors were as illuminating as pages of *David Harum*. Starting with the old-fashioned qualification of being "a great reader," she grew up to become librarian of the Batavia library. Later she took library courses at Pratt Institute and at Simmons College. That, however, was after her first journey to China. This journey, in 1899, was planned as a visit to her brother, a missionary. But the need for teachers at Boone College in Wuchang induced her to prolong her visit and, in 1904, to accept appointment under the American Church Mission. The library at Boone was a tiny affair, little used. Elizabeth Wood, well-nigh single-handed, undertook an arduous campaign for a building and an adequate supply of books. The building—her "Ebenezer"—was erected in 1910. Then, as she said, she moved on "to Ur of the Chaldees." Traveling libraries were organized. Young Chinese were sent to the United States for library training. Lecture tours were arranged for them on their return. To meet the need for less expensive training, a library school was started in 1920. China was ripe for modern library development, and the Chinese response was enthusiastic.

Acting on the suggestion of an influential graduate of Boone, in 1923 Elizabeth Wood journeyed to Peking (later Peiping) to propose a nationwide movement. Chinese leaders united in a petition to the United States that an unassigned portion (about $6,000,000) of the Boxer indemnity be remitted for public-library development. She followed the petition to Washington (1924), and personally interviewed in its behalf over five hundred senators and congressmen. Old-fashioned in dress but of impressive personality, she became one of the notable figures at the Capitol. Her understanding of people, her tireless persistence, and her obvious unselfishness made her the most potent influence in the passage of the bill. In one respect the bill fell short of complete success; "educational and other cultural activities" were named, not libraries. The administration of the fund was entrusted to the China Foundation, a Sino-American board. To secure expert testimony, Elizabeth Wood persuaded the American Library Association to send Dr. A. E. Bostwick of St. Louis as its representative to China. His tour, arranged by the Chinese Association for the Advancement of Education, achieved official and popular prominence. Coincident with the tour came the organization of the Library Association of China. As a result, a portion of the fund was allotted to establish the Metropolitan Library in Peking, and a modest grant was made to the Boone Library School.

Elizabeth Wood's remaining days were devoted to raising an endowment for the school. In 1927 she spent several months in Washington working towards the cancellation of China's "unequal treaties." Her efforts in behalf of the Chinese people, which had ranged from securing shelters for 'rikisha coolies and books for soldiers to cooperation with educational leaders and progressive officials, were bringing to her unusual expressions of Chinese approval in a period of anti-foreign feeling; and an elaborate triple anniversary in honor of her coming to China, of the building of the Boone Library, and of the founding of the library school was about to be celebrated when she died in Wuchang on May 1, 1931.

[In addition to *The Boxer Indemnity and the Lib. Movement in China* (n.d.) and *China's First Lib. School: The Boone Lib.* (n.d.), pamphlets compiled by Mary E. Wood with the collaboration of Samuel Tsu-Yung Seng and Thomas Chin-Sen Hu, sources include *Hankow Herald*, May 2, 1931; *Hankow Newsletter*,

May–June 1931, with an art. by the Rt. Rev. L. H. Root, Bishop of Hankow; A. E. Bostwick, in *Libraries*, June 1931; *Libraries in China* (1929); Marion D. Wood, in *Lib. Jour.*, June 1, 1931; *Boone Lib. Central China Coll.... Triple Anniversary Celebration, May 16, 1930*; obituary in *N. Y. Times*, May 2, 1931; unpub. material supplied by the Am. Church Mission, several friends, and Mary E. Wood's brother, the Rev. Robert E. Wood of St. Michael's Church, Wuchang.]   H. Cl—s.

WOOD, REUBEN (*c.* 1792–Oct. 1, 1864), jurist, governor of Ohio, was born in Middletown, Rutland County, Vt., the eldest son of the Rev. Nathaniel Wood, formerly a chaplain in the Continental Army. Reuben received his early education at home but at the age of fifteen went across the Canadian border to reside with an uncle. He studied the classics with a Catholic priest and began to read law with an attorney, but was forced to flee from Canada at the outbreak of the War of 1812 to escape forced military service, and landed at Sacketts Harbor, N. Y., after a hazardous crossing of Lake Ontario in a small boat. For a brief period he did military service and then studied law with Gen. Jonas Clark of Middletown, Vt.

Wood moved to Cleveland, Ohio, in 1818, the third lawyer to appear in that village of six hundred inhabitants. He was successful as a jury lawyer, but was soon drawn into politics, being elected to the state Senate in 1825, and serving three terms (1825–30). In January 1830 the legislature elected him president judge of the third common pleas circuit, a position he held until February 1833, when, chosen by the Assembly, he began a service of fourteen years on the Ohio supreme court. A Whig majority refused him a third term in 1847, but his services were recognized by the Democratic party in 1850, when it made him its candidate for governor. He was elected by a plurality over William Johnston, Whig, and Edward Smith, Free Soiler. In his inaugural he showed his anti-slavery leanings by criticizing the newly enacted federal Fugitive Slave Law, though he did not countenance nullification or violence. His first term was reduced to one year by the state constitution of 1851, which changed gubernatorial elections to odd-numbered years. He was easily reëlected over Samuel F. Vinton, Whig, and Samuel Lewis, Free Soiler. In this campaign, Salmon P. Chase [*q.v.*], then United States senator, left the Free Soil party and supported Wood.

His second term was marked by much significant legislation to carry out provisions of the new constitution, but the lack of a veto power limited the governor's influence over the legislature. The general anti-bank, hard money position of his party had his approval, though he was not regarded as an extremist. At the National

Democratic Convention of 1852, he was a possibility for the presidential nomination, but the presence of factions in the Ohio delegation destroyed whatever chances he had. In July 1853 Wood resigned as governor to become American consul at Valparaiso, Chile, a minor but supposedly lucrative post. Though he was soon acting American minister, he was dissatisfied and returned to Ohio in 1855 to resume his law practice in Cleveland, and presently to retire to his farm, "Evergreen Place," Rockport. In the party split of 1860, Wood, a supporter of the Buchanan administration, presided over a bolting state convention to name a Breckinridge electoral ticket in opposition to the regular Douglas ticket. He became a Union man at the outbreak of the Civil War, however, and had been chosen to preside over a great Union mass meeting in the campaign for the reëlection of Lincoln when his death occurred.

Wood's tall, lean frame gained him the sobriquet, "the old Cuyahoga chief." His love of fun and practical jokes and his Yankee wit added to his popularity, though he was rather blunt of speech and at times somewhat tactless. He was married in 1816 to Mary Rice, daughter of Truman Rice of Clarendon, Vt., and was survived by his wife and two daughters.

[Wood's judicial opinions are in 6–15 *Ohio Reports*; his papers as governor, in the Ohio Archæological and Hist. Soc. Lib. The events of his administration are covered in C. B. Galbreath, *Hist. of Ohio* (1925), II, 542–50. His part in the politics of the 1850's may be found in E. H. Roseboom, "Ohio in the 1850's," unpublished doctoral dissertation, Harvard, 1932. A biog. sketch by his grandson, N. H. Merwin, is in manuscript in the Western Reserve Hist. Soc. Lib., Cleveland. Brief accounts of his life are in Harvey Rice, *Pioneers of the Western Reserve* (1883), and "Western Reserve Jurists," *Mag. of Western Hist.*, June 1885; S. P. Orth, *A Hist. of Cleveland, Ohio* (1910), vol. I; J. F. Brennan, *A Biog. Cyc. and Portrait Gallery of . . . Ohio* (1879); *Cleveland Herald*, Oct. 3, 1864; *Daily Ohio State Jour.* (Columbus), Oct. 5, 1864. See also E. B. Kinkead, "A Sketch of the Supreme Court of Ohio," *Green Bag*, May 1895.]
E. H. R.

WOOD, SAMUEL (July 17, 1760–May 5, 1844), book publisher, was born on his father's five-acre farm in the town of Oyster Bay, Long Island, the only child of Samuel and Freelove (Wright) Wood, and a descendant in the fifth generation of John Wood who emigrated to Pennsylvania in 1678 from England. After his father's untimely death at twenty-seven, the boy's name was changed from William to Samuel, and his baptism is so recorded in St. George's Church, Hempstead, Dec. 25, 1762. He grew up in poor circumstances, but he early developed a thirst for knowledge and a love of reading. He joined the Society of Friends in early life, and became an active and influential member. He

married, Aug. 8, 1782, in Westbury Meeting, Mary Searing of Searingtown, L. I., by whom he had thirteen children. From 1787 to 1803 he taught in schools in Manhasset, L. I., Clinton, Hibernia Mills, and New Rochelle, all in New York State. In 1804 he opened a small store in New York City for the sale of stationery and books, mostly second-hand. Concerned about the lack of attractive books for children, he soon began a remarkable series of little books, mostly unbound, of sixteen to twenty-eight pages, not over four inches high. His earliest known imprint is on *The Young Child's A B C, or First Book, printed by J. C. Totten, for Samuel Wood* (1806), illustrated with woodcuts by Alexander Anderson [*q.v.*]. All later books were printed on his own press. By 1815 Wood had produced a large number, among them *Devout Meditations* (1807), *The Animal Economy* (1808), and *Poetic Tales for Children* (1814). Besides selling all he could, it was his habit to carry his pockets filled with books to give out to children who might otherwise not get them. He wrote a few of the early books he published, and amended some English ones to suit American conditions.

In 1815 he took into partnership two of his sons, Samuel S. and John, under the firm name of Samuel Wood and Sons. Samuel S. Wood went to Baltimore and maintained a branch house there for several years. The business developed into a large house of general publishing and sale, wholesale and retail, of books and stationery. In 1817 Samuel Wood and Sons occupied a new building, and another son, William Wood (1797–1877), was admitted to the firm. Thus was founded the publishing house of Samuel Wood and Sons, which, with the single exception of the Methodist Book Concern, was the oldest publishing house in New York City and existed 128 years. William Wood had become especially interested in medicine and medical books, probably from association with his brother Isaac (1793–1868), a prominent New York physician, and eventually the firm became the largest publishers of medical books in America. It was William who posted on the bulletin board of the *Commercial Advertiser*, Nov. 3, 1820, a notice to merchants' clerks and apprentices, "disposed to form a Mercantile Library." Out of this effort grew the library of 50,000 volumes which served a great need for nearly a century, until the establishment of the New York Public Library rendered it no longer necessary. After Samuel Wood's retirement in 1836, the business was continued as Samuel S. and William Wood until 1861, under William Wood's name until 1863, and from that time until 1932 as William Wood & Company.

Immersed in business, Samuel Wood still found time for the relief and betterment of the poor, the sick, the unfortunate, and after his retirement he gave all his time to charitable work. He was one of the founders of the Society for the Prevention of Pauperism (1817), out of which grew the House of Refuge, the first state aid for unfortunate children, and was one of the prime movers in the establishment of the New York Institution for the Blind (1831), the first institution of its kind in America. He was also a member of the Manumission Society, the Society of the New York Hospital, and the Public School Society, the last of which he served as trustee for twenty years. Stricken with paralysis, he lingered on a few years, dying in his eighty-fourth year. He was buried in the quiet cemetery of the Quakers in Prospect Park, Brooklyn.

[Sources include Arnold Wood, *John Wood of Attercliffe, Yorkshire . . . and His Descendants* (1903); W. C. Wood, *One Hundred Years of Publishing, 1804–1904* (1904); W. H. S. Wood, *Friends of the City of N. Y.* (1904); W. O. Bourne, *Hist. of the Pub. School Soc. of the City of N. Y.* (1870); J. H. Manning, *Century of Am. Savings Banks* (1917); records of N. Y. Monthly Meeting and of Westbury Monthly Meeting of the Religious Soc. of Friends, MSS. in Friends' Record Room, N. Y. City; minutes of the N. Y. Asso. for the Educ. of Colored Male Adults, MSS.; minutes of the Manumission Soc., MSS.]   J. C., Jr.

WOOD, SARAH SAYWARD BARRELL KEATING (Oct. 1, 1759–Jan. 6, 1855), earliest fiction writer of the state of Maine, was born in York, Me., at the home of her grandfather, Judge Jonathan Sayward, wealthy Loyalist trader and representative of York County in the Massachusetts General Court. His daughter Sarah married Nathaniel Barrell of Portsmouth, N. H., member of a prominent Boston mercantile family, who was serving as lieutenant in Wolfe's army at Quebec when his daughter was born. Sarah Barrell was brought up in her grandfather's home, in the society of influential and cultivated relatives and friends. On Nov. 23, 1778, she married Richard Keating, a clerk of Judge Sayward's, described as "easy in manners, well informed, of excellent good sense, a social good neighbor" (sketch in MS. by Mrs. Wood). The young couple lived happily together, in the house given them as Judge Sayward's wedding present. Here their three children were born, the last of them four months after the untimely death of Mr. Keating, June 23, 1783. During the twenty-one years of her widowhood at York, Mrs. Keating wrote and published four novels, besides probably contributing anonymously to the *Massachusetts Magazine* and other periodicals. Her first novel, *Julia and the Illu-*

minated Baron (Portsmouth, 1800), has reference to the supposed subversive activities of the secret society, the Illuminati, in France. It has the distinction of being perhaps the most thoroughgoing example in American literature of the Gothic romance of the Radcliffe type. Her second book, *Dorval: or the Speculator,* is disappointing because the promised "wholly American" work, satirizing the contemporary furor over land speculation, is weakened by the pointless, rambling, and improbable narrative. These were followed by *Amelia, or the Influence of Virtue, an Old Man's Story* (1802), which appeared, like the others, anonymously at Portsmouth, and by *Ferdinand and Elmira: a Russian Story* (Baltimore, 1804), a highly fanciful tale of tangled loves, mistaken identity, and overworked coincidence.

On Oct. 28, 1804, Mrs. Keating married Gen. Abiel Wood, a wealthy widower of Wiscasset, where she lived in considerable style until some years after his death in 1811. Thereafter until 1830 she lived near her son, Capt. Richard Keating, in Portland. There she published the first volume of *Tales of the Night* (1827), containing two long narratives, "Storms and Sunshine; or the House on the Hill," a story of domestic misfortunes succeeded by returning prosperity, and "The Hermitage," in which faithful love is rewarded by union after an intervening marriage. No second volume appeared, and Mrs. Wood is said, after the appearance of Scott's novels, to have destroyed much of her own manuscript in self-disparagement. At Portland Madam Wood, as she was usually called, was somewhat of a celebrity because of her literary reputation, her keen mind, and her distinctive costume. She is described as wearing customarily a "high turban or cap . . . and when she went out . . . a plain black bonnet so far forward as to nearly hide her features" (Goold, *post,* p. 406). For three years after 1830 she lived in New York City with her son, Captain Keating. In the summer after his tragic death in January 1833, when his ship was crushed in the night by floating ice in New York Harbor, she returned to Maine to live with a granddaughter at Kennebunk. In her last years she wrote several interesting reminiscent sketches for friends and descendants. She died at Kennebunk.

[The fullest biog. account is that of William Goold in *Colls. and Proc. Me. Hist. Soc.,* 2 ser., vol. I (1890). See also H. E. Dunnack, *The Me. Book* (1920); C. E. Banks, *Hist. of York, Me.* (1931), vol. I, pp. 375, 389–401; C. A. Sayward, *The Sayward Family* (1890); W. D. Spencer, *Me. Immortals* (1932), pp. 313–16; the Abiel Wood coll. of MSS. in the possession of Mrs. Richmond White, at Wiscasset; and death notice in *Eastern Argus* (Portland, Me.), Jan. 9, 1855. The Me. State Lib. has the most nearly complete coll. of

WOOD, THOMAS (Aug. 22, 1813–Nov. 21, 1880), surgeon, was born in Smithfield, Jefferson County, Ohio, the son of Nathan and Margaret Wood, members of Quaker families long resident in West Chester, Pa. Since his father, a poor farmer, could give him few advantages, he was largely self-educated. He began the study of medicine with Dr. W. S. Bates of Smithfield, entered the medical department of the University of Pennsylvania in 1838, and received his medical degree the following year, with a graduation thesis entitled "Hydrated Peroxide of Iron." Following graduation he received an appointment to the Friends' Asylum for the Insane near Philadelphia. In 1842 he returned to Smithfield and established himself for practice. After a year of study abroad (1844) he settled in Cincinnati, Ohio, where he spent the rest of his life in highly successful practice. The year following his arrival he was appointed professor of anatomy and physiology in the Ohio College of Dental Surgery, a position that he held for a number of years. In 1853 he was appointed demonstrator of anatomy at the Medical College of Ohio, later becoming in turn professor of anatomy and professor of surgical anatomy. Though a thorough master of his subjects, he had but mediocre success as an instructor. He was an exceedingly modest and unassuming man, with a mild, gentle manner and soft low voice which further impaired his usefulness as a teacher. He was nevertheless highly regarded for his undoubted ability. As an aid in his school work he wrote *A Compendium of Anatomy, Designed to Accompany the Anatomical Chart* (n.d.). This and a few case reports in journal articles constituted his entire literary output. He was owner and co-editor of the *Western Lancet* of Cincinnati from 1853 to 1857.

Though he practised general medicine and was an accomplished internist, it is for his surgical abilities that he deserves remembrance. He was a highly successful and daring operator, particularly skilful in diseases of women, with a record of having performed all the major operations of the surgery of his day. Had he been a less modest man, and had he given to the medical profession a worthy current account of his work, he undoubtedly would have attained a reputation as one of the country's greatest surgeons. For years he headed the surgical staff of the Commercial (later the Cincinnati) Hospital. After the battle of Shiloh he rendered surgical service to the wounded upon the field and in the Cincinnati hospitals to which they were transferred. He

was a member of the American Medical Association and of the Cincinnati Academy of Medicine. In addition to his strictly professional interests, he was well informed in the natural sciences, taking a special interest in the study of geology and entomology, in both of which he made extensive collections. He was an able microscopist, though it is not recorded that he made any use of the microscope in his medical work. Of an inventive turn of mind, he devised several instruments to aid in geometrical calculations. He is also credited with the authorship of much unpublished poetry.

He was chief surgeon for the Cincinnati, Hamilton and Dayton railroad, and it was in the service of this road that he met his death. While dressing the infected wounds of victims of a railroad accident, he contracted a septicæmia that resulted fatally. On Mar. 14, 1843, he married Emily A. Miller at Mount Pleasant, Ohio. In 1855 he married Elizabeth J. Reiff of Philadelphia, and following her death in 1871 he married, on July 27, 1876, Carrie C. Fels of Cincinnati. Two sons followed him in the choice of medicine as a career.

[*Cincinnati Lancet and Clinic*, Nov. 27, 1880; *Cincinnati Medic. News*, Dec. 1880; H. A. Kelly and W. L. Burrage, *Am. Medic. Biogs.* (1920); obituaries in *Cincinnati Enquirer* and *Cincinnati Commerical*, Nov. 22, 1880.]   J.M.P.

WOOD, THOMAS BOND (Mar. 17, 1844–Dec. 18, 1922), missionary and educator, was born at Lafayette, Ind., the son of the Rev. Aaron Wood, an eminent clergyman of the Methodist Episcopal Church, and Maria (Hitt) Wood, daughter of a rich land- and slave-owner. He received the degree of A.B. from Indiana Asbury University (later De Pauw) in 1863 and from Wesleyan University, Middletown, Conn., in 1864. From 1864 to 1867 he taught German and natural science in Wesleyan Academy, Wilbraham, Mass., where he met and married (July 23, 1867) the teacher of music, Ellen Dow of Westfield, Mass. He entered the New England Conference of the Methodist Episcopal Church (1865), was ordained deacon (1867) and elder (1868), and was transferred to the North-West Indiana Conference (1868). After serving two years as president of Valparaiso College, Valparaiso, Ind. (1867–69), he was appointed by the missionary society of his church to work in Argentina.

For more than forty years he devoted himself to the work in South America. From 1870 to 1877 he was at Rosario de Santa Fé, where he preached in English and Spanish, German and Portuguese, and established a Protestant school for boys and the first work of the Women's Foreign Missionary Society of the Methodist Episcopal Church. He also served as chairman of the board of examiners of city schools, as member for a time of the city government, as professor of physics and astronomy in the national college (1875–77), as president of the national educational commission of Argentina, and as United States consul (1873–78). He was admitted to the practice of law in the Argentine federal court in 1875. From 1877 to 1881 he was at Montevideo, Uruguay, where he started and edited *El Evangelista,* the first Spanish evangelical weekly in the world, wrote *Breves Informaciones* (1881), a handbook of Methodism, and was joint editor of the first Spanish hymn and tune book used in Protestant services (1881).

He was superintendent of the missions of the Methodist Episcopal Church in South America for eight years (1879–87) and in 1881 was a delegate to the first Methodist Ecumenical Conference in London. From London he was sent to Mexico and then returned to the United States (1882–84). On returning to Uruguay he contracted a fever which necessitated a removal into the country district occupied by Waldensians, where he established and had charge of the first Protestant school south of the United States legalized to grant the degree of A.B. (1887–89). In 1889 he founded the Methodist Theological Seminary in Buenos Aires and continued as its president until 1891. During these years he labored incessantly to remove the ban on religious liberty at that time written into every constitution south of the Rio Grande, and in 1891 he removed to Peru, the center of the struggle. There for twenty-two years (1891–1913), with indomitable courage and masterful will, in the face of persecution, reviling, and personal danger, he championed religious liberty (including civil marriage), the spread of popular education, and social reform.

He was not only superintendent of all Methodist work in Peru, Ecuador, and Bolivia (1891–1905), establishing the South America Conference (1893), the Western South America Conference (1898), the Andes Conference (1905), and the North Andes Mission (1910), but he also took on numerous other responsibilities. He was founder and president of the Technical School of Commerce in Lima (1899); he established normal schools in Ecuador for the government, and was sent by the president to the United States to secure teachers for them (1900); and he became president of the theological seminary in Lima. Between 1903 and 1906 he founded the Methodist Episcopal Church in Panama in English and Spanish, started the

Young Men's Christian Association and the University Club for Americans and school work for the natives in the Canal Zone, and acted as United States chaplain there (1905–06). From 1907 to 1913 he was again superintendent of the North Andes Mission; president of the theological seminary in Lima; founder, with his daughter, of the Lima High School for girls; and superintendent of public schools in the city of Callao. It was overwork in translating the Gospel of St. John into the language of the Quichua Indians that resulted in the complete nervous breakdown from which he never recovered. He returned to the United States in 1913, and was retired in 1915.

Wood had numerous avocations. An amateur astronomer, he made charts of the southern constellations and cooperated with astronomers at the Cordoba (Argentina) observatory in important astronomical work and discoveries; he was a singer of unusual range, power, and training; he played several musical instruments, and drew and lettered with artistic talent. He never asked or took a vacation in forty-two years, but found recreation in his tasks and in pacing the wide flat roofs and studying the skies. He has been well called a "Pan-American Christian." His last years were spent in Tacoma, Wash., where he died, survived by his wife and four children.

[*Alumni Record of Wesleyan Univ., Middletown, Conn.* (1883); *Alumnal Record De Pauw Univ.* (1915); H. C. Stuntz, *South Am. Neighbors* (1916); W. S. Robertson, *Hispanic-American Relations with the U. S.* (1923); *Christian Advocate* (N. Y.), Dec. 28, 1922; *Pacific Christian Advocate,* Feb. 27, 1930; obituary in *Tacoma Daily Ledger,* Dec. 19, 1922; files and reports of the Bd. of Foreign Missions, M. E. Church; family records.]
          O. M. B.

WOOD, THOMAS JOHN (Sept. 25, 1823–Feb. 25, 1906), soldier, was born in Munfordville, Ky., the son of Col. George T. and Elizabeth (Helm) Wood. After a country schooling, he entered the United States Military Academy at West Point in 1841. His first roommate was Ulysses S. Grant. Following his graduation in 1845 he gave up his graduation leave to join General Taylor's staff at Palo Alto. During this campaign he brought Taylor's guns opportunely into action with ox-teams, and distinguished himself at Buena Vista by penetrating the Mexican lines in a brilliant reconnaissance. Though commissioned in the engineers, Wood, craving activity, transferred on Oct. 19, 1846, into the 2nd Dragoons. In that regiment and with the 1st, 4th, and 2nd Cavalry he rose through grades to colonel on Nov. 12, 1861. Almost continuously on the frontier, he participated in Indian campaigns, the Kansas border troubles, and Colonel Johnston's expedition to Utah. Enjoying a well-earned leave, he toured Europe in 1859–60, and news of secession reached him in Egypt in January 1861.

He returned home and within six months had mustered 40,000 Indiana troops into Federal service at Indianapolis. Here he met, and on Nov. 29, 1861, was married to Caroline E. Greer, daughter of James A. and Caroline (King) Greer of Dayton, Ohio. Appointed brigadier-general of volunteers on Oct. 11, he was given an Indiana brigade, and, in the spring of 1862, a division. At Stone's River his brigades alone retained their position throughout the battle, and on Dec. 31, 1862, although he was wounded, he refused to quit the field until night ended the fighting. The next year at Chickamauga, the removal of his division from the line on Sept. 20 permitted the Confederates to break through and demoralized the Union right. A bitter controversy concerning responsibility for this disaster ensued between Rosecrans and Wood (*War of the Rebellion: Official Records, Army,* 1 ser., vol. XXX, part 1, 1902), but the latter retained his command and the implicit confidence of Rosecrans' successor, General Thomas.

On Nov. 25, in the brilliant capture of Missionary Ridge, his troops were the first to overrun the main Confederate defenses. The Atlanta campaign afforded him play for his tactical as well as his fighting abilities. At Lovejoy's Station, Sept. 2, 1864, he was again badly hurt, but declined a sick leave. His shattered leg wrapped in a buffalo robe, he continued commanding his troops, and General Sherman declared that his example of fortitude was worth 20,000 men to the army (*Annual Reunion, post,* p. 119). Thus he endured the last Tennessee campaign, and taking command of the IV Corps in December he conducted the infantry pursuit of Hood's broken army after Nashville. Tardily appointed major-general of volunteers on Jan. 27, 1865, immediately after the war, he won the gratitude of Mississippians by his humane military administration of their state. Owing to his injuries, he was retired as major-general, United States Army, June 9, 1868. He passed his later years at Dayton, Ohio, where he was conspicuously active in veteran organizations. He assisted in marking the battle lines at Chickamauga. He was appointed to the Board of Visitors at West Point in 1895 and lived to become the last survivor of the class of 1845.

[*Who's Who in America,* 1906–07; G. W. Cullum, *Biog. Reg. . . . U. S. Mil. Acad.* (1891); *Ann. Reunion, Asso. of Grads. U. S. Mil. Acad.,* 1906; *War of the Rebellion: Official Records* (Army), see index volume; *Battles and Leaders of the Civil War* (1887–88), vols. I, III, IV; M. F. Steele, *Am. Campaigns,* vol. I (1909); T. B. Van Horne, *Hist. of the Army of the*

Cumberland (2 vols., 1875), and *The Life of Maj.-Gen. G. H. Thomas* (1882); *Memoirs of Gen. W. T. Sherman* (2nd ed., 1886), vol. I; *Personal Memoirs of U. S. Grant,* vol. II (1886); *Ohio State Jour.* (Columbus), Feb. 26, 1906.]

J. M. H.

WOOD, WALTER ABBOTT (Oct. 23, 1815– Jan. 15, 1892), manufacturer of agricultural implements, inventor, was born in Mason, Hillsboro County, N. H., the second son of Aaron and Rebecca (Wright) Wood, and a descendant of Jeremiah Wood who was in America by 1709. In 1816 Aaron Wood moved to Rensselaerville, near Albany, N. Y., and engaged in the construction of plows and wagons. There Walter attended public school and assisted his father in the shop, acquiring great skill in the handling of tools. About 1835 he went to Hoosick Falls, N. Y., and for four years worked as a blacksmith for Parsons & Wilder, where he was considered the best workman in the establishment. About 1840 he went to Nashville, Tenn., to work in a carriage factory. Returning to Hoosick Falls in the late forties, he formed a partnership with John White for the manufacture of plows, but in the fall of 1852 he severed this connection and, with J. Russell Parsons, founded the firm of Wood & Parsons, to build mowing and reaping machines under the John H. Manny patents. This partnership was dissolved a year later, and Wood continued in the business alone. In 1855 he purchased the Tremont Cotton Mills, converting it into a mower and reaper factory. Throughout the fifties he introduced numerous changes and improvements in the Manny machines, some of which were patented, so that by 1860 the Wood mowers and reapers had become markedly different from the original machines. Only two machines were sold in 1852, but thereafter the business grew rapidly. It was incorporated in 1865 under the title of the Walter A. Wood Mowing and Reaping Machine Company, with Wood as president. By 1865 sales had increased to 8,500 annually; in 1891 they reached 90,000. Fire destroyed the factory in 1860 and again in 1870, but each time Wood ordered it rebuilt on a larger scale. The chief machines made by Wood were a mower, a combined mower and hand-rake reaper, self-rake reapers of the chain-rake and reel-rake types, the Sylvanus D. Locke wire binder, and the H. A. and W. M. Holmes twine binder. Of these implements the mower and the two binders were perhaps the most famous.

In the course of his career Wood took out some forty patents for various improvements in mowing and reaping machines. He introduced his machines into Europe in 1856 and in time built up an extensive foreign business. He won more

than 1,200 prizes in agricultural society exhibitions in the United States, in foreign countries, and at world's fairs between 1855 and 1892.
In connection with the Paris Universal Exposition of 1867 he was made a chevalier of the
Legion of Honor, and in 1878 an officer in the
order; at Vienna in 1873 he was decorated with
the Imperial Order of Franz Josef. He served
as Republican representative in Congress from
March 1879 to March 1883. A member of St.
Mark's Episcopal Church, he gave liberally to
charities and was a generous patron of Hoosick
Falls, which owed much of its prosperity to his
factory. He was noted for his democratic relations with his employees. He was married twice:
in 1842 to Bessie A. Parsons (d. 1866), and on
Sept. 2, 1868, to Elizabeth Warren Nichols (or
Nicholls). There were two children by each
marriage. Wood died at Hoosick Falls.

[See G. B. Anderson, *Landmarks of Rensselaer
County, N. Y.* (1897); W. S. Wood, *Descendants of
the Brothers Jeremiah and John Wood* (1885), which
gives the name of Wood's first wife as Betsey; cata-
logues of the Walter A. Wood Mowing and Reaping
Machine Co., 1867–1900; *In Memoriam—Walter A.
Wood* (privately printed, 1893); *Farm Implement News*
(Chicago), Jan. 21, 1892, July 20, 1893; obit. note in
Albany Evening Jour., Jan. 16, 1892.]   H. A. K—r.

WOOD, WILLIAM (fl. 1629–1635), author,
emigrated from England to Massachusetts in
1629, and probably settled in Lynn, where one
of his name was made a freeman in 1631. The
dedication of his one book to Sir William Ar-
myne of Lincolnshire suggests that he came
from that county, as did so many other early
New Englanders. Possibly he had been at Cambridge University, where several William Woods
are recorded at dates which would have been
possible for him (J. G. Bartlett, "University
Alumni Founders of New England," *Publications of the Colonial Society of Massachusetts,*
vol. XXV, 1924, pp. 20–21). He left the colony
on Aug. 15, 1633, and on July 7, 1634, his book,
New Englands Prospect, was entered in the Sta-
tioners' Register in London. On Sept. 3, the
General Court of Massachusetts Bay voted to
send letters of thanks to various benefactors
to "this plantacon"—among them "Mr. Wood"
(N. B. Shurtleff, *Records of the Governor and
Company of the Massachusetts Bay,* vol. I, 1853,
p. 128). Presumably this was in recognition of
Wood's book, the best description of Massachusetts Bay which had appeared. In it the author
speaks of his intention to return to New England. Possibly he did. A William Wood came
over in September 1635, and is described as a
husbandman, twenty-seven years old. Whether
this was the author is doubtful, and even if it
was, his later career is uncertain. One William

Wood was chosen representative from Lynn in
1636, and in the next year went to Sandwich
(Frederick Freeman, *The History of Cape Cod,*
vol. I, 1858, pp. 127–28). This may have been
the writer of *New Englands Prospect,* but there
is no secure evidence, since another William
Wood was granted land in Salem in 1638 (*Essex
Institute Historical Collections,* vol. IX, 1869,
p. 70). Still another appeared in Concord in
1638 and died in that town in 1671 (C. W.
Holmes, *A Genealogy of the Lineal Descendants
of William Wood,* 1901, pp. 9, 259). The William Wood who went to Sandwich was there in
1643, and town clerk in 1649, but the case is
complicated by the fact that in 1639 another William Wood seems to have died in Sandwich
(Freeman, *op. cit.,* vol. II, 1862, pp. 44, 169).

Wood's *New Englands Prospect* is an account
of New England as its author saw it from 1629
to 1633. The first part is given to a description
of the country and its settlements; the second, to
Wood's observations on the Indians. The book
is clearly the work of a man with some literary
training, and some background of reading. It
offers rich material for the historian, and is
unusual among books of its type for real vigor
of style and relatively polished form. It was
sufficiently popular to have London editions in
1634, 1635, and 1639. In 1764 it was reprinted
in Boston with a preface, ascribed either to
James Otis, or, more probably, to Nathaniel
Rogers (*Proceedings of the Massachusetts Historical Society,* 1 ser., vol. VI, 1863, pp. 250,
334–37). Alexander Young's *Chronicles of the
First Planters of the Colony of Massachusetts
Bay* (1846) contains a partial reprint; complete
editions were issued in 1865 (edited by Charles
Deane for the Prince Society) and in 1898 (edited by E. M. Boynton).

[See also J. B. Felt, *Annals of Salem,* I (1845), 516;
Alonzo Lewis and J. R. Newhall, *Hist. of Lynn* (1865),
pp. 113, 165, 169; Lemuel Shattuck, *A Hist. of the
Town of Concord* (1835), pp. 371, 388; C. H. Walcott,
Concord in the Colonial Period (1884), pp. 37, 72, 73.
For criticism of Wood's book, see M. C. Tyler, *A Hist.
of Am. Lit., 1607–1765* (1878), I, 170–79.]   K. B. M.

WOOD, WILLIAM BURKE (May 26, 1779–
Sept. 23, 1861), actor, theatrical manager, was
born in Montreal, the son of a New York goldsmith who had gone to Canada before the British occupation of New York and returned about
1784. His mother was Thomizen English. After a brief private schooling liberally supplemented from his earliest years by frequent visits
to the theatres, he was apprenticed clerk in a
counting-house at twelve, passed a year in the
West Indies for his health, returned and was
jailed for debt in Philadelphia, and in 1798, poor,

emaciated, ill-equipped for serious dramatic work but inspired with vague notions of his talent, journeyed alone to Annapolis, Md., and obtained a place in the company of Thomas Wignell [*q.v.*], an old family friend, making his début there on June 26 as George Barnwell. It was a bad start, as Wood himself relates; nor was the sickly youth successful in his other tragic rôles that season. Not until a second sojourn in Jamaica had restored his powers and he came back to play Dick Dowlas in *The Heir-at-Law* did he find his true dramatic forte, genteel comedy. Henceforth, acting at Washington, Baltimore, Philadelphia, and in summer at Alexandria, where Wignell's famous company filled regular engagements, Wood grew steadily in skill and public favor. Before his twenty-third year he was treasurer of the company's Chestnut Street Theatre in Philadelphia, its headquarters; and when Wignell died in February 1803, leaving the control and the property to his widow and Alexander Reinagle, the musician, Wood became assistant to the acting manager, William Warren [*q.v.*], and was dispatched to England in search of new actors. Returning from this profitable tour of the British theatres, Wood married on Jan. 30, 1804, Juliana Westray, a favorite actress of the company, and began his long collaboration with Warren which made their fame. The company prospered, and Wood, upon whom fell the actual duties of managing, was not reluctant when in 1809, Reinagle dying, one or two Philadelphia friends furnished him the means to buy from Warren an equal share in the company's property and management. Following a début at the Park Theatre in New York, Sept. 12, 1810, as De Valmont in *The Foundling of the Forest,* then his best rôle, Wood joined his former chief in the autumn of 1810.

The new partnership endured for sixteen years, raising the theatres under its control, particularly the Chestnut Street (the "Old Drury" of Philadelphia), to international eminence, despite the gravest obstacles. With numerous English players in the company and still more English plays in the repertory, it managed to steer a safe path through the dangerous years of the War of 1812 and the subsequent economic depression. When in April 1820, while the troupe was away at Baltimore, its splendid gas-lit Chestnut Street Theatre burned to the ground uninsured, carrying with it the precious scenery, machinery, wardrobe, library, music, lights, and all, the partners leased the Olympic in Walnut Street and went on playing until a second "Old Drury" could be reared and opened in 1822. By a judicious management it preserved the organization amid the hazards of the costly starring system, yet brought nearly every actor of note to its boards, including, for his first American appearance, the youthful Edwin Forrest [*q.v.*]. The permanent company, which, besides Warren and the Woods, included Joseph Jefferson, Blissett, Bernard, Harwood, Francis, Bray, Burke, the Barretts, the Duffs, and others, introduced also, in the face of growing rivalry in New York, a very large proportion of new plays, some of them composed at Wood's suggestion and for particular members, while still keeping fresh a popular taste for the European dramas of tradition. Such systematic success could only result from a remarkable discipline of all the actors and a rare coördination in the management. "Warren and I," says Wood, "seemed to be very happily adapted as counterparts or correlatives of one another; for while he had great abilities and judgment in laying out a campaign and viewing the season in a sort of abstract way, I found myself always able to execute, which he was never inclined to do, the details incident to his general scheme" (*Personal Recollections,* p. 326). They had, however, never been very warm friends; and when in 1825 Wood saw their unanimity waning, he offered to buy out his partner, who was surprised, incredulous, unwilling. At length, friction increasing, they signed separation papers, leaving the sole management to the tired and corpulent Warren.

For two dull seasons Wood went on acting at the Chestnut, then in the autumn of 1828 undertook the management of the new Arch Street Theatre. Despite good houses, difficulties with the trustees and the inefficient company caused his resignation within three months; and early in 1829 he and his wife joined the forces at the Walnut Street. There Wood remained to enjoy a ripening prosperity and renown until Nov. 18, 1846, when, the only survivor of the original Philadelphia company, he took a final benefit before a most distinguished audience as Sergeant Austerlitz in the appropriate drama, *The Maid of Croissy, or The Last of the Old Guard.* In 1855 Wood published his *Personal Recollections of the Stage,* a full and indispensable if slightly egoistic account of his associations over forty years. He died, Sept. 23, 1861.

[In addition to Wood's *Personal Recollections* (1855), see T. A. Brown, *Hist. of the Am. Stage, 1733–1870* (1870); hist. of the Phila. stage, in *Phila. Sunday Despatch,* beginning May 7, 1854, collected in bound vols. in the Univ. of Pa. lib.; R. D. James, *Old Drury of Phila.* (1932), which contains the text of Wood's manuscript diary or daily account book; Arthur Hornblow, *A Hist. of the Theatre in America* (2 vols., 1919); William Dunlap, *A Hist. of the Am. Theatre* (1832); *The Warren Family* (privately printed, 1893); F. C. Wemyss, *Twenty-Six Years of the Life of an Actor and Manager* (2 vols., 1847); notice of Wood's farewell in *Sat. Courier* (Phila.), Nov. 28, 1846; death notice in *Phila. Inquirer*, Sept. 25, 1861; and Wood's original costume designer's notes (autograph) and autograph letters in Theatre Coll., Harvard College lib.]

M. B.

WOOD, WILLIAM ROBERT (Jan. 5, 1861–Mar. 7, 1933), congressman, was born at Oxford, Ind., the son of Robert and Matilda (Hickman) Wood. He received his early education in the local public schools and after learning the trade of harness maker decided to study law. In 1882 he obtained the degree of LL.B. from the University of Michigan and began the practice of law at Lafayette, Ind. He was a partner successively of Judge W. DeWitt Wallace (1882–84), of Capt. W. H. Bryan (1884–91), and of J. Frank Hanly (1897–1904), thereafter practising alone. On May 16, 1883, he married Mary Elizabeth Geiger, who died in 1924. In 1890 he entered public life as prosecuting attorney for Tippecanoe County, being returned to office in 1892. Elected state senator in 1896, he served in the Indiana legislature for eighteen years; he was twice president *pro tempore* of the Senate and Republican floor leader for four sessions. In 1915 he took his seat in the national House of Representatives as a member of the Sixty-fourth Congress.

Entering the House with a long legislative experience behind him, he advanced rapidly and quickly attracted attention, becoming known as one of the most active Republican critics of the Wilson administration. On Dec. 22, 1916, he presented the resolution which resulted in the long and much-publicized investigation of the alleged leak in the news concerning Wilson's peace note to Germany. As chairman of the Republican national congressional committee, from 1920 until his retirement from public life, he played an important part in framing Republican policies and mapping party strategy. He was a loyal party man, but on occasion independent, both of thought and action. He was a delegate to the Republican National Convention in 1912, 1916, 1920, and 1924, and at the convention of 1916 placed Charles W. Fairbanks in nomination for the presidency. In the campaign of 1928, he was in charge of the Western speakers bureau at Chicago.

Though the House had abler orators, Wood could speak effectively from the floor and was usually in the thick of the battle. As chairman of the powerful appropriations committee in the Seventy-first Congress he was among the most influential of the House leaders. His political philosophy, essentially rural, included suspicion of the "money power." Economy and retrench-

ment had few more aggressive champions during a period of steady expansion in the size and cost of the federal government, though he was active in building up the merchant marine, strongly urging federal loans to shipbuilders. Wood was a lawmaker of the old school, one who had reached the top by hard work and conscientious application to his duties rather than by intellectual brilliancy and the conception of new legislative ideas. His background linked him to the earlier period of American life, when business was individual and when money was made not so much by speculation and by combining corporations and selling stock to the public as by a careful accumulation of the pennies. This explains perhaps his assaults on Wall Street. He had little use for the direct primary, which he predicted would eventually lead to the destruction of representative government. The social life of the capital had no amenities for him, and golf, the pastime of so many of his colleagues, he regarded as an "old man's game"; his favorite diversion was fishing.

Wood was defeated for reëlection in 1932 and died in New York City, as he was preparing to embark on a Mediterranean cruise, four days after his retirement from public office.

[*Who's Who in America*, 1932–33; *Biog. Dir. Am. Cong.* (1928); "The Perfect Congressman," by "the Gentleman at the Keyhole," *Colliers*, Oct. 31, 1931; R. P. DeHart, *Past and Present of Tippecanoe County, Ind.* (1909), vol. II; *N. Y. Times*, Mar. 8, 1933; *Evening Star* (Washington), Mar. 7, 1933.]   O. M., Jr.

WOODBERRY, GEORGE EDWARD (May 12, 1855–Jan. 2, 1930), poet, critic, and teacher, was born in Beverly, Mass., the son of Henry Elliott and Sarah Dane (Tuck) Woodberry. He was descended from colonial New England stock on both sides; his first American ancestor, John Woodberry, settled in Salem in 1626 and was one of the founders of the settlement at Beverly. Many of his forebears were sea-captains and sailors, and his own poetic preoccupation with the sea and his taste for wandering in strange places show that he was of their blood. He was educated at Phillips Exeter Academy, Exeter, N. H., to which he remained deeply attached all his life, and at Harvard College, which he entered with the class of 1876, though on account of illness and poverty he was unable to graduate until 1877. There, he tells us, Henry Adams formed his mind on the intellectual and Charles Eliot Norton on the esthetic side (*Selected Letters*, p. 207). From Adams he acquired a certain individual attitude toward history, and from Norton a lifelong devotion to the culture of the Mediterranean world, but many other influences played upon him at the time. We catch a glimpse of him cataloguing the library of

James Russell Lowell (C. E. Norton, ed., *Letters of James Russell Lowell*, 1894, II, 180), and he was present at Emerson's last lecture. He was even then somewhat of a "character" in the New England sense; the college authorities refused to permit him to deliver his class oration on "The Relation of Pallas Athene to Athens," and it was printed privately; and President Eliot, in a letter of the period, while strongly commending his high moral character, deprecated the altogether too vigorous manner in which the young Woodberry expressed his personal opinions. He was, and remained, a representative of New England Transcendentalism on its more or less rebellious side, and Emerson, Wendell Phillips, and the drum-beats of the Civil War reverberate throughout his life.

From 1877 to 1878 and again from 1880 to 1882 he was professor of English in the University of Nebraska; and this brief experience of western life left a deep impression on him, in the way peculiar to his genius (see especially "The Ride," in *Heart of Man*). He had begun his literary career in his undergraduate days as an editor of the *Harvard Advocate*; he had been contributing to the *Atlantic Monthly* since 1876 and to the *Nation* since 1878, and he now became a constant contributor to both until 1891. For a year, in 1888, he was literary editor of the *Boston Post*. His first book, *A History of Wood-En-graving* (1883), was hardly more than a higher form of hack-work. It was followed two years later by his life of *Edgar Allan Poe*, which attracted attention and dissent because of the cold impartiality with which the defects of Poe were analyzed in all their detail. Woodberry did not like Poe, but he endeavored to be scrupulously fair; and certainly no lover of Poe has brought to light more material for the study of Poe's life and genius, both in this work and elsewhere, culminating in the two-volume *Life of Edgar Allan Poe* twenty-four years later. In 1890 he published *The North Shore Watch and Other Poems* and *Studies in Letters and Life,* and these established his reputation as a poet and as a critic. The title-poem of the former was an elegy on the death of a friend, sincerely and even passionately felt, though full of echoes of Shelley and other masters of the elegiac form; and throughout the volume, which contained the fine philosophic poem "Agathon" and the well-known sonnets "At Gibraltar," the Platonic tradition of European poetry mingles with a deep American patriotism. The *Studies in Letters and Life,* largely made up of his *Atlantic* and *Nation* articles, emphasized the relation between literature and the imaginative and other experience that had

produced it, and exhibited his characteristic combination of a virile idealism with a certain feminine sensibility.

In 1891, upon the recommendation of Lowell and Norton, he was appointed professor of literature in Columbia University, a title that was changed to professor of comparative literature in 1900. The thirteen years at Columbia were the fullest and richest in his life. He was brilliantly successful as a teacher. He attracted around him all the most alert elements in undergraduate life, athletes as well as scholars, and not only aroused in them a new interest in literature, but gave them a new point of view with which to interpret it and the life of which it was an expression. He had a special gift of friendship with the young, and a quietly persuasive way of encouraging their youthful idealisms. The boyish aggressiveness to which President Eliot had referred had long been superseded by a gentleness of demeanor almost wistful, but his students recognized the core of obstinacy and strength beneath it, and "manly" and "manliness" were words that often appeared in their tributes to him. Under his guidance the undergraduate society of King's Crown was formed; a new undergraduate periodical, the *Morningside,* was founded, and a volume of *Columbia Verse* published. Later he built up a graduate department which transformed the methods of higher instruction in literature and left a deep mark on university teaching in this field throughout the country; the series of Columbia University Studies in Comparative Literature in which his students' work appeared represented an important academic departure in that the studies were not the dry bones usually associated with doctoral dissertations but, at least in intention, real books both in form and in content.

During this period Woodberry published two volumes of verse (*Wild Eden,* 1899; *Poems,* 1903), two volumes of essays (*Heart of Man,* 1899; *Makers of Literature,* 1900), a biography (*Nathaniel Hawthorne,* 1902), and a brief history of American literature (*America in Literature,* 1903, translated into French in 1909). In *Wild Eden* is some of his most charming verse, with a new note of lyric intensity; much of it is reminiscent of Shelley, but with Woodberry's own New England overtones. His *America in Literature* is characterized by a certain detached insight, but it exhibits a narrowness of sympathy which brushes aside the racier writers like Walt Whitman, Thoreau, Mark Twain, and Herman Melville; and this is equally true of his later article on "American Literature" in the eleventh edition of the *Encyclopaedia Britannica.* The biography of Hawthorne is written with a subtle perception of the character of that shy genius, and represents Woodberry's high-water mark as a biographer. His *Heart of Man* contains striking essays on "Democracy" and "A New Defence of Poetry," and is perhaps his most characteristic book. It is an interpretation of the imaginative elements common to poetry, religion, and politics; and the impression it made on William James (*Letters,* 1920, II, 89) represents in a measure a final judgment on Woodberry's literary work: "The essays are grave and noble in the extreme. I hail another American author. They can't be popular," because they lack "that which our generation seems to need, the sudden word, the unmediated transition, the flash of perception that makes reasonings unnecessary. Poor Woodberry, so high, so true, so good, so original in his total make-up, and yet so unoriginal if you take him spotwise—and therefore so ineffective."

Woodberry's very success as a teacher, as well as his informal and somewhat unacademic mode of life, the reticences of a New England "character," and other causes, led to jealousy and controversy; and suddenly, for reasons still obscure, he resigned his chair early in 1904 while on a year's leave of absence. The rest of his life was of a wholly different pattern. Part of it was spent as a sort of itinerant teacher, lecturing for longer or shorter periods at various colleges and universities—at Amherst during the spring term of 1905, at Cornell for one month in 1907 and three months in 1908, at Wisconsin during the second semester of 1913-14, at California during the summer session of 1918—and at all these institutions he left behind him friends and disciples. Part of the time was spent in lonely wandering in his favorite Mediterranean world, where he made friends with one or two writers like the Neapolitan dialect poet Salvatore di Giacomo but mostly with peasants and all sorts of simple folk; out of this came the book on *North Africa and the Desert* (1914) as well as a number of poems. But most of the time was spent in Beverly, writing or dreaming in the house occupied for generations by his ancestors; and his later years were lightened by the friendship and help of a few friends and former students. The Woodberry Society was organized in 1911, and printed several of his writings privately. He received various academic distinctions, and he was a member of the American Academy of Arts and Letters, Fellow of the American Academy of Arts and Sciences, and Honorary Fellow of the Royal Society of Literature of England.

His retirement from Columbia was immediately followed by the publication of a number of works largely based on his academic and other lectures (*The Torch,* 1905; *The Appreciation of Literature,* 1907; *Great Writers,* lectures delivered at the Johns Hopkins University, 1907; *The Inspiration of Poetry,* 1910), as well as one of his most important biographies (*Ralph Waldo Emerson,* in English Men of Letters Series, 1907) and several volumes of verse. A series of lectures on Race Power in Literature delivered before the Lowell Institute of Boston in 1903, *The Torch* is probably the fullest expression of his philosophy of literature, and exhibits the deep sense of race and tradition which was fundamental in his thought; but it should be borne in mind that for Woodberry "race" represented not so much an ethnic entity as a spiritual quality of mind made up of imaginative memories and experiences. During the last fifteen years of his life he added little of importance except a series of sonnets, *Ideal Passion* (1917), steeped in the atmosphere of the Mediterranean and containing some of his finest and most mature verse, and *The Roamer and Other Poems* (1920), in which most of his poetry is collected. Besides the work already enumerated, he edited a considerable number of books, including *The Complete Poetical Works of Percy Bysshe Shelley* (1892) and, with E. C. Stedman, *The Works of Edgar Allan Poe* (10 vols., 1894-95).

Woodberry began as a "character" and ended as one, but the nature of the character changed under the stress of life. The desire for privacy, always strong in him, in his last years became a passion. The realities of American life clashed with his democratic dreams, but the old toughness that had enabled him to cope with the clash or to rise above it had dwindled away. The feeling that he was out of touch with life, that he had been passed by, and perhaps some tormenting inner problem, produced in him an increasing but quite unjustified sense of failure. His lecture on *Wendell Phillips* (1912) had been a noble protest against all the injustices and deteriorations of American life; and in the previous year (*A Scholar's Testament, post,* pp. 7-11) he had expressed, without a trace of his usual reserve, some of his most militant doubts and convictions. But after the World War he became more and more melancholy and resigned, and the rebellious side of the old Transcendentalism faded away. He died in the Beverly Hospital on Jan. 2, 1930.

Woodberry thought of himself essentially as a poet, and his verse is often pure and delicate, but echoes of the great literature of England, Italy, and Greece form the undertone of all his music. If he lacked what he liked to call "poetic energy" and belonged, as he said of Poe, "to the men of culture instead of those of originally perfect power," it should be remembered that his self-selected models were the great "literary" poets such as Spenser, Milton, Shelley, and Tennyson, or the poets of Italy, where all poets are in a sense "literary"; and his special note of subdued lyrical eloquence, though alien to the conversational standard imposed on American poetry by the generation that followed him, is not without its own individual flavor. As a critic he occupies a position of no mean importance. Some of his essays (like that on Virgil and others) are literary masterpieces; the first two lectures of *The Torch* hold their place side by side with the best that has been written of man's imaginative life by any American. In his best critical work there is a subtle intuition of the emotional experience that produced the work of literature and a deep sense of its relation to the spiritual background of western man. His prose style at its best is, as William James said, "grave and noble in the extreme," but at its worst, as in the study of Swinburne, sinks into a wordy grandiloquence. As a teacher he deserves to rank with the most inspiring that the country has produced. His intellectual life might be summed up by saying that it was a frustrated effort to effect a marriage of New England individualism with the Platonic and Catholic tradition of Europe.

[There is no adequate account of Woodberry's life. Bibliogs. of his writings are included in L. V. Ledoux, *George Edward Woodberry: A Study of His Poetry* (1917) and in *George Edward Woodberry . . . An Appreciation by John Erskine* (1930). His coll. essays were published in six vols. in 1920–21, and a vol. of *Selected Poems,* ed. by three of his former students, in 1933. He was a charming and indefatigable letter-writer, and information in regard to his later life can be gleaned from his *Selected Letters* (1933), with an introduction by Walter de la Mare, and *A Scholar's Testament: Two Letters from George Edward Woodberry to J. E. Spingarn* (Amenia, N. Y., 1931), the latter containing one of the really notable letters of Am. lit. See also *Who's Who in America,* 1928–29; and obituary in *N. Y. Times,* Jan. 3, 1930. The Poetry Room endowed in his honor in the Harvard Univ. Lib. contains about 1,500 letters written to him and about 30 written by him, as well as other interesting memorials; numerous presentation copies of books received by him are contained in the lib. of Phillips Exeter Acad.]
J. E. S.

WOODBRIDGE, JOHN (1613–Mar. 17, 1695), colonial magistrate, clergyman, and author, was the eldest son of John Woodbridge, minister at Stanton, Wiltshire, England, and Sarah (Parker) Woodbridge, the grandson of Robert Parker, the famous Puritan divine. He was trained for the ministry at Oxford, whence the oath of conformity drove him without a degree, and in the spring of 1634 he emigrated to New England with his uncle, Thomas Parker [q.v.], settling at Newbury, Mass., where

Parker was ordained pastor. Woodbridge was chosen by the Newbury settlers as their first town clerk (1636–38), as selectman (1636), as deputy to the General Court (1637–38, 1640–41), and in 1638 and 1641 by appointment of the General Court he was commissioner for small causes at Newbury. About 1639 he married Mercy, daughter of Gov. Thomas Dudley [q.v.], and in 1640–41, with his brother-in-law, Simon Bradstreet [q.v.], was a leading spirit in the settlement of Andover, securing a patent from the Indians and helping to extinguish conflicting claims to the site.

Gradually, however, he inclined to the ministry and in 1643, upon the advice of Parker and Dudley, he deserted civil and agrarian pursuits to serve for two years as schoolmaster in Boston. On Oct. 24, 1645, he was ordained first pastor of the church at Andover, where he remained until 1647, when friends persuaded him to return to England. There he served as minister of Andover, Hampshire, 1648–50, and of Barford St. Martin, Wiltshire, 1652–62. Well known to Independent leaders, he was chaplain to the parliamentary commissioners who treated with the King at the Isle of Wight in 1648 and assistant to the Wiltshire Committee in 1657. Ejected from his parish in 1662, he taught school at Newbury, Berks, until the Bartholomew Act necessitated his departure. He returned to Massachusetts in the following year, and soon was settled as assistant to his aged uncle, still pastor at Newbury.

Within two years dissensions arose which eventually forced Woodbridge to retire from the ministry. One Edward Woodman created factions at Newbury by alleging that Parker abused his pastoral authority to "sett up a Prelacy & have more power than the Pope" and that Woodbridge was an "Intruder, brought in by Craft & subtilty & so kept in" (quoted by Coffin, *post,* p. 74). Although the Woodman party were repeatedly censured by civil and ecclesiastical authorities, they persisted in irregular proceedings. Through their machinations Woodbridge was dismissed from his ministry, May 21, 1670, but he stayed to support Parker until an investigating committee of the General Court, on May 15, 1672, requested him "not to impose himselfe or his ministry (however otherwise desirable) vpon" the Newbury church.

From "*Cœlestial Dealings,*" he thereupon turned to "*Mundane affairs,*" in which his exertions were more acceptable. In England he had become a friend of William Potter, with whom he had discussed plans to expand credit and facilitate commerce by establishing a "Bank of

Money." Seeing the financial straits of New England when he returned in 1663, he revived the schemes, interested merchants, and in 1667–68 presented to the Council a concrete proposal (Davis, *post*, pp. 112–14, 116–18) to erect a bank of deposit and issue with land and commodities as collateral. He experimented with the plan in March 1671 and later with such success that a decade afterwards (September 1681) a group of merchants joined the enterprise, issued bills, "and had rational Grounds to conclude, that it would work it self up into Credit, with discreet men." To advertise the scheme and to silence objectors Woodbridge published in March 1681/82 *Severals Relating to the Fund . . .,* the first American tract on currency and banking extant (A. M. Davis, *Colonial Currency Reprints 1682–1754*, 4 vols., 1910, I, 3–8, 109–18). The outcome of the plan is not recorded, but it did not impoverish its author, for Woodbridge reaped "remarkable blessings of God upon his own *private estate*" (Mather, *post*, I, 543).

In his later years, he was again appointed Newbury's commissioner for small causes (1677–79, 1681, 1690), and elected assistant in 1683–84. His contemporaries generally revered him as an honorable and judicious magistrate, a great scholar, and a pattern of goodness. Yearning constantly after spiritual affairs, he devoted more than half of his long life to material matters. His advanced monetary theories illustrate the rapid transfer of ideas from Old England to New in the seventeenth century; his experimentation foreshadowed the Massachusetts land banks. His wife preceded him to the grave, July 1, 1691, leaving him, besides one who had died in infancy, eleven children.

[Louis Mitchell, *The Woodbridge Record* (1883); *Col. Soc. of Mass. Pubs.*, vol. VIII (1906); Joshua Coffin, *A Sketch of the Hist. of Newbury* (1845); J. J. Currier, *Hist. of Newbury* (1902); *Mass. Hist. Soc. Colls.*, 5 ser. I (1871), 317–19, V (1878), 400; *Proc. Am. Antiq. Soc.*, n.s., III (1885), XV (1904); A. M. Davis, *Currency and Banking in . . . Mass. Bay* (2 vols., 1901); W. B. Weeden, *Econ. and Social Hist. of New England* (2 vols., 1890); *Records of the Gov. and Company of the Mass. Bay* (5 vols., 1853–54); Cotton Mather, *Magnalia Christi Americana* (1702; ed. of 1820); W. B. Sprague, *Annals Am. Pulpit*, vol. I (1857); Edmund Calamy, *The Nonconformist's Memorial* (1775), ed. by Samuel Palmer; A. G. Matthews, *Calamy Revised* (1934).]   R.P.S.

WOODBRIDGE, SAMUEL MERRILL (Apr. 5, 1819–June 24, 1905), clergyman of the Reformed Church in America, professor, theologian, was born at Greenfield, Mass. For many generations in America and in England there had been at least one ordained minister in his family: John Woodbridge, born in 1493, was a follower of Wycliffe; in the fifth generation from him, John Woodbridge [*q.v.*], student at Oxford until he refused to take the oath of conformity, was the first of the name to hold a pastoral charge in New England. In the fifth generation from this divine was Rev. Sylvester Woodbridge, who married Elizabeth Gould. Samuel Merrill Woodbridge was their son. He graduated from the University of the City of New York in 1838 and from the New Brunswick Theological Seminary in 1841, having meanwhile joined the Dutch Reformed Church (Reformed Church in America). Licensed by the Classis of New York and ordained by the Classis of Long Island, he became pastor of the church of South Brooklyn, which he served from 1841 to 1850. Subsequently he was pastor of the Second Church of Coxsackie, N. Y., 1850–53, and the Second Church of New Brunswick, N. J., from 1853 to 1857, when he was appointed by the General Synod of the Reformed Church to the professorship of ecclesiastical history and church government in the Theological Seminary at New Brunswick. In this office he remained for forty-four years, resigning in 1901; he was then made professor emeritus.

For the first eight years of his professorship he taught pastoral theology in addition to church history, and also served at Rutgers College on the adjoining campus as professor of metaphysics and mental philosophy, 1857–64. At times during his long service, when occasion arose, he was professor of theology *pro tem*. From 1883 to 1888 he was dean of the seminary, and from 1888 to 1901, president of the faculty. In his earlier ministry Woodbridge was an eloquent and powerful preacher; congregations crowded to hear him. To the last he was impressive in thought and in all public address; his venerable appearance and solemn voice made him seem in the pulpit and in the class room a very prophet of God. He was firmly devoted to the traditional Reformed theology, a champion of its great points of doctrine and of the authority of the Scriptures. Though uncompromising as to principles, he was kindly and generous and not without a sense of humor. He published an *Analysis of Theology* (1872–73; 2nd ed., 1882), a *Manual of Church History* (1895), and an *Outline of Church Government* (1896), as well as occasional sermons, articles, and addresses. By his first wife, Caroline Bergen, whom he married in February 1845, he had one daughter; the mother died in 1861, and on Dec. 20, 1866, he married Anna Whittaker Dayton, by whom he had two daughters. He died in New Brunswick, N. J., at the age of eighty-six.

[Louis Mitchell, *The Woodbridge Record* (1883); E. T. Corwin, *A Manual of the Reformed Church in America* (1902); *Minutes of the General Synod, R.C.A.,*

1905; S. D. Clark, *The New England Ministry Sixty Years Ago: The Memoir of Rev. John Woodbridge* (1877); *Fortieth Anniversary of Samuel M. Woodbridge* (New Brunswick Seminary, 1897); *Biog. Record Theol. Sem. New Brunswick, 1884–1911* (1912); *Newark Evening News*, June 24, 1905.] W. H. S. D.

WOODBRIDGE, WILLIAM (Aug. 20, 1780–Oct. 20, 1861), governor of Michigan, United States senator, was born in Norwich, Conn., the son of Dudley Woodbridge, a minuteman, and Lucy (Backus) Woodbridge. He was a descendant in the sixth generation of John Woodbridge [q.v.] who settled in Newbury, Mass., in 1634. When the family in 1789 moved to Marietta, in the Northwest Territory, William and a brother were left behind to complete their schooling. In 1797 William chose instead of his father's alma mater, Yale College, the famous law school of Tapping Reeve [q.v.] at Litchfield, Conn. After about three years there he rejoined his father's family. His educational training also included about a year's study of French among the settlers at Gallipolis and several years in a Marietta law office. In this law office he met Lewis Cass [q.v.], whose friendship played an important part in determining his career. In 1806 he was admitted to the bar in Ohio, and on June 29 of that year he married Juliana, daughter of John Trumbull [q.v.], the poet. His long career of office-holding began with eight years of service in Ohio as assemblyman, county prosecuting attorney, and state senator. No doubt influenced by his vigorous advocacy of the War of 1812 and by the strong recommendation of Cass, President Madison in 1814 appointed Woodbridge secretary of the Michigan Territory and collector of customs at Detroit (confirmed, Oct. 5, 1814). Woodbridge was an energetic official: largely because of his initiative, Congress in 1819 granted Michigan the right to representation by delegate even though it continued in the first stage of organization prescribed by the Ordinance of 1787. Chosen Michigan's first territorial delegate, Woodbridge was an ardent and effective advocate of the confirmation of old land titles, of government roads and exploratory expeditions, of Michigan's claims in the boundary dispute with Ohio. He declined to serve a second term as delegate, but continued in the secretaryship until Michigan entered the second stage of territorial government in 1824. Except for a four-year term as territorial judge (1828–32), he held no office during the next ten years. The movement for statehood prompted his return to the public scene. He was a delegate to the constitutional convention of 1835 and a state senator in 1838–39. The exuberance of the first state administration and the effects of the panic of 1837 brought a widespread demand for a change from Democratic control; in 1839 Woodbridge, now the recognized Whig leader of the state, received his party's nomination for governor on a platform of "Woodbridge and Reform," and won the election. The new governor's messages to the legislature reveal a comprehensive program of rehabilitation of the state, including revision of taxes, stricter banking and currency regulation, drastic retrenchment in plans for internal improvements. He pushed vigorously the claims of the young state against the federal government in matters of public domain, land grants, appropriations for internal improvements. Expressing his program in terms of general policy rather than in a prescription of specific remedies, Woodbridge appears more the special advocate pleading constitutional principles than the practical administrator; yet during his fourteen months as governor, appreciable progress was made in his program. In February 1841 a faction of Whigs in the legislature, dissatisfied with the caucus nominee for United States senator, enlisted the aid of the Democrats and elected Woodbridge. Woodbridge's career in the Senate (March 1841–March 1847) was not undistinguished. His reports as chairman of the committee on public lands were praised by leading statesmen of both parties; he sponsored several successful measures for internal improvements; and, according to Webster, he suggested an important provision in the Webster-Ashburton treaty (*Congressional Globe*, 29 Cong., 1 Sess., App. p. 536). He chose not to stand for reëlection. The remaining years of his life were spent in retirement on his farm on the outskirts of Detroit. He died in Detroit, survived by a daughter and three sons.

Woodbridge's career exemplifies admirably the mutually contradictory characteristics so often developed when a natural conservative comes to spend a lifetime in a frontier community. Aristocratic in temperament, versatile in interests, cultivated in tastes, happiest when enjoying his large library and conversation with his more learned friends, his intimate knowledge of frontier conditions and needs made him a determined fighter for the rights of the people and for the advancement of the adolescent state. He was enthusiastic in the cause of public schools, and one of the most valuable friends of the youthful University of Michigan. Although he lacked the arts of the successful politician, he won the confidence of the people as a man of integrity and abundant common sense.

[In addition to *Messages of the Governors of Mich.*, vol. I (1925), ed. by G. N. Fuller, an important source, see *The Woodbridge Record* (1883); M. K. Talcott,

Woodbridge

Geneal. of the Woodbridge Family (n.d.), reprinted from *New Eng. Hist. and Geneal. Reg.*, July 1878; Charles Lanman, *The Life of William Woodbridge* (1867), brief and uncritical; F. B. Streeter, *Political Parties in Mich., 1837–1860* (1918); J. V. Campbell, *Outlines of the Political Hist. of Mich.* (1876); Silas Farmer, *Hist. of Detroit and Wayne County* (1890), vol. II; *Biog. Dir. Am. Cong.* (1928); and obituary in *Detroit Free Press*, Oct. 22, 1861. Most of Woodbridge's papers are in the Burton Hist. Coll. of the Detroit Pub. Lib. A few have been published in *Mich. Pioneer and Hist. Colls.*, vols. XXXIII (1902) and XXXVII (1909–10). The Woodbridge-Gallaher Coll. of the Ohio State Archaeologicai and Hist. Soc. is of some importance for the earlier years. The Woodbridge materials are being edited by Dr. M. M. Quaife.]

L. G. V.–V.

WOODBRIDGE, WILLIAM CHANNING (Dec. 18, 1794–Nov. 9, 1845), educator, son of the Rev. William Woodbridge by his second wife Ann (or Nancy) Channing, was born in Medford, Mass. He was a descendant of the Rev. Timothy Woodbridge of Hartford, Conn., who was born in England and came to America with his father, the Rev. John Woodbridge [*q.v.*], when the latter returned to Massachusetts in 1663 after an absence of sixteen years. On the Channing side, he was a grandson of John, and a cousin of William Ellery Channing, 1780–1842 [*q.v.*]. The elder William Woodbridge (1755–1836) was a clergyman and teacher of note: he was the first preceptor of Phillips Academy, Exeter, later conducted several other schools, being especially interested in the education of young women, and published two or three textbooks. Apparently he paid more attention to his son's mind than he did to his physical condition, for under his father's preparation the boy was able to enter Yale College in his fourteenth year, the youngest in his class, but for much of his life was a semi-invalid. After graduating in 1811, he spent nearly a year in further study at Philadelphia, where his father then resided.

He began his teaching career in 1812 as principal of the academy in Burlington, N. J., but in 1814 returned to New Haven, where he attended lectures in the sciences and studied theology under the elder Timothy Dwight [*q.v.*]. When Dwight died in 1817, Woodbridge entered Princeton Theological Seminary. Shortly, however, he was asked to become an instructor in the asylum for the deaf and dumb recently established in Hartford, Conn., by Thomas H. Gallaudet [*q.v.*]. Relinquishing an early formed purpose to become a foreign missionary, he accepted this call to serve the unfortunate at home and became connected with the asylum in December 1817. He was licensed to preach, however, by the Congregational ministers of Hartford North Association, Feb. 3, 1819, and from time to time supplied Connecticut churches. The preceding year he had declined a financially attractive call to the College of William and Mary as professor of chemistry. By 1820 the condition of his health was such that he relinquished his position at Hartford and in October went to southern Europe.

One of his duties had been the teaching of geography, a subject which then received but little attention in the public schools. He had devised a system of instruction, and while abroad he gathered geographical information for textbooks he was preparing. After his return to Hartford, in July 1821, he spent the next three years chiefly on work connected with their completion and publication. In 1821 he issued *Rudiments of Geography, on a New Plan, Designed to Assist the Memory by Comparison and Classification*; this went through many editions. In 1824 appeared his *Universal Geography, Ancient and Modern*, to which Emma Willard [*q.v.*], who had originated a similar method of teaching the subject in her Troy (N. Y.) Female Seminary, contributed the section on ancient geography. These textbooks produced a revolution in the method of presenting geographical facts in the schools.

The condition of his health caused Woodbridge to go to Europe again in 1824. He remained abroad five years, during which time he studied the educational systems of Switzerland and Germany, spending some time at Hofwyl, on invitation of Philipp von Fellenberg, the great educational reformer. Returning to the United States in 1829, he was physically unable to undertake teaching duties but in 1831 purchased the *American Journal of Education*, first edited by William Russell [*q.v.*], the title of which he changed to *American Annals of Education and Instruction*. Settling in Boston, he devoted his time and no little money to this publication for several years. On Nov. 27, 1832, he married Lucy Ann Reed of Marblehead, Mass., who had been a teacher in the school of Catharine Beecher [*q.v.*] in Hartford. The scope of the *Annals* under Woodbridge's management was broad. It gave much attention to the education of teachers, agriculturists and mechanics, and defectives, and made a specialty of information regarding foreign educators and their methods. Woodbridge himself contributed "Sketches of the Fellenberg Institution at Hofwyl, in a Series of Letters to a Friend" (January 1831–December 1832). His name appears as editor through 1837, but in October of the preceding year his health again compelled him to go to Europe. His wife died in Frankfort, Germany, in 1840, and in October 1841 he returned. He lived but four years longer, spending three winters in Santa Cruz, West Indies, and dying in Boston in his fifty-first year.

Although physically handicapped, he did much for the advancement of education in a comparatively short lifetime. To this cause he contributed a large share of his income. He helped awaken the public to a recognition of the importance of normal schools; he was a pioneer in advocating the teaching of physiology and music in the common schools; he recommended the use of the Bible as a literary classic; and he was one of the early American expounders of the Pestalozzian system.

[Louis Mitchell, *The Woodbridge Record* (1883); F. B. Dexter, *Biog. Sketches Grads. Yale Coll.*, vol. VI (1912); W. A. Alcott, in *Am. Jour. of Educ.*, June 1858, and in Henry Barnard, *Educ. Biog.: Memoirs of Teachers, Educators, and Promoters and Benefactors of Educ.* (1859); F. L. Mott, *A Hist. of Am. Mags., 1741–1850* (1930); *Boston Daily Advertiser*, Nov. 11, 1845.]

H. E. S.

WOODBURY, CHARLES JEPTHA HILL (May 4, 185:–Mar. 20, 1916), industrial engineer, expert on fire prevention, was born in Lynn, Mass., the son of Jeptha Porter Woodbury and Mary Adams (Hill) and eighth in direct descent from John Woodbury of Somersetshire, England, who came to Gloucester, Mass., in 1623. He was a lifelong resident of Lynn. He married there, Nov. 26, 1878, Maria H. Brown, daughter of Joseph G. Brown, and there he died. His wife and three daughters survived him.

Woodbury prepared at the Lynn High School for the regular course at Harvard, but family circumstances compelled him to seek a practical rather than a cultural training, and accordingly he entered the Massachusetts Institute of Technology, graduating with the degree of C.E. in 1873. He never, however, lost his predilection for history, literature, and art. By nature a serious worker, he spent his vacations in the City Engineer's Office of Lynn and thus made an early start in his professional career. Soon after graduation he took a position as superintendent of a mill at Rockport on Cape Ann. In 1878 he became engineer and later vice-president of the Boston Manufacturers Mutual Fire Insurance Company. While in this position he conducted investigations into lubricating oils, the principles of mill construction, and automatic sprinklers. He also devised improved methods of inspection and reporting and invented many improvements in electric lighting and wiring for the purpose of fire prevention. From 1894 to 1907 he was assistant engineer of the American Telephone & Telegraph Company with supervision of fire prevention and insurance for their properties throughout the country. From 1894 until his death in 1916 he was also secretary of the National Association of Cotton Manufacturers, with whom the fire hazard was a specially serious matter. After 1907 he engaged in private practice as a consulting engineer, and during his entire career wrote and lectured extensively on technical, commercial, and insurance subjects.

Woodbury was an active member of many scientific organizations, including the American Society for the Advancement of Science, the American Society of Civil Engineers, the American Society of Mechanical Engineers, and the American Institute of Electrical Engineers. From 1913 until his death he was president of the Lynn Historical Society. He received numerous honors: several honorary degrees, the Alsatian Medal of the Société Industrielle de Mulhouse (1893) for his work on mill construction—the first instance of its award to an American, the John Scott Medal of the Franklin Institute (1885) for his formulation of the insurance rules of electric lighting, and the medal of the National Association of Cotton Manufacturers (1910) for his *Bibliography of the Cotton Manufacture* (2 vols., 1909–10).

Woodbury was a man of rugged frame and robust physique, capable of long-sustained effort and daily accomplishing an extraordinary amount of work. He was of commanding presence, authoritative in his knowledge of the subjects in which he specialized and in his manner toward those with whom he worked, yet genial and cooperative and invariably winning their loyalty. He left his mark as an avid seeker for facts and as a forceful executive in securing the adoption of improved methods; industry is indebted to him for the greater safety and efficiency in working conditions that resulted from his labors.

[Pamphlets and papers in the Engineering Societies Library, N. Y. City; papers in the American Telephone Historical Library, N. Y. City; papers in possession of the Woodbury family; *Register of the Lynn Hist. Soc.*, no. 20 (1916); *Jour. Am. Soc. Mech. Engineers*, Apr. 1916; *Who's Who in America*, 1916–17; *Lynn Item* and *Lynn News*, Mar. 20, 1916; *Boston Transcript*, Mar. 20, 1916; *Boston Herald*, Mar. 21, 1916.]

W. C. L.

WOODBURY, DANIEL PHINEAS (Dec. 16, 1812–Aug. 15, 1864), soldier and engineer, the son of Daniel and Rhapsima (Messenger) Woodbury, was born in New London, Merrimack County, N. H., and received his early education at Hopkinton Academy, in the same county. He then entered Dartmouth College, but left in 1832 upon his appointment as a cadet at the United States Military Academy. He was graduated in 1836 and commissioned second lieutenant in the 3rd Artillery, but was transferred soon afterwards to the engineers. For some years he was employed on the construction of the Cumberland road in Ohio, then in the construction and repair of fortifications in Boston and Portsmouth harbors, and in the War Department in Washington. From 1847 to 1850 he was engaged in building Fort Kearny, on the Missouri River, and Fort Laramie, which later developed into the city of Laramie, Wyo. These were two of the military posts established to guard the route to Oregon. Later he served in North Carolina and Florida, where among other duties he supervised the construction of Fort Jefferson in the Tortugas and Fort Taylor at Key West. Both of these fortifications were regarded as of immense importance for the maintenance of naval control of the Gulf of Mexico, and they afterwards came within Woodbury's command during the Civil War. He was promoted first lieutenant in 1838 and captain in 1853.

At the outbreak of the Civil War he was stationed in Washington, D. C., the early defenses of which he had a share in planning. He helped to make the reconnaissance on which McDowell's orders for the battle of Bull Run were based, and personally conducted Hunter's and Heintzelman's troops on their march to turn the Confederate left flank. Commenting on the causes of the defeat, in his official report, he remarked: "An old soldier feels safe in the ranks, unsafe out of the ranks, and the greater the danger the more pertinaciously he clings to his place. The volunteer of three months never attains this instinct of discipline. Under danger, and even under mere excitement, he flies away from his ranks, and looks for safety in dispersion" (*Official Records, post,* II, Part I, 344). Woodbury was promoted major of engineers in August 1861, appointed lieutenant-colonel in the volunteer army in September, and on Mar. 19, 1862, was commissioned brigadier-general of volunteers. In the Peninsular Campaign he commanded the engineer brigade of the Army of the Potomac, constructing the siege works before Yorktown and the immense system of roads and bridges necessary for the army's passage over the Chickahominy River and through the White Oak Swamp. He was in the defenses of Washington through the autumn of 1862, returning to the field before the battle of Fredericksburg, where he was responsible for the throwing of the pontoon bridges over the Rappahannock by which the army crossed to the attack and retreated after the battle. In March 1863 he was assigned to command the district including Tortugas and Key West. He died at the latter place of yellow fever.

Woodbury was the author of two engineering treatises: *Sustaining Walls* (1845; 2nd ed., 1854), and *Elements of Stability in the Well-*

Proportioned Arch (1858). On Dec. 12, 1845, he was married, at Southville, N. C., to Catharine Rachel Childs, the daughter of Thomas Childs [*q.v.*]. She and their four children survived him.

[Elias Child, *Geneal. of the Child, Childs and Childe Families* (1881); M. B. Lord, *Hist. of the Town of New London, N. H.* (1899); G. W. Cullum, *Biog. Reg.* . . . *U. S. Mil. Acad.* (1891); *War of the Rebellion: Official Records (Army),* see index volume; *Army and Navy Jour.,* Sept. 3, 1864.]   T. M. S.

WOODBURY, HELEN LAURA SUMNER (Mar. 12, 1876–Mar. 10, 1933), social economist, author, was born in Sheboygan, Wis., a descendant of William Sumner, who came to America in 1636 and settled in Dorchester, Mass. Her father was George True Sumner, later a district judge in Colorado; her mother, Katharine Eudora (Marsh) Sumner, granddaughter of Jerome Luther Marsh, pioneer editor of newspapers in Wisconsin and in Colorado. When Helen was five years old, the family moved to Durango, Colo., where, except for six months' homesteading on a ranch in the Montezuma Valley, they lived for eight years, and then settled in Denver. From the East Denver High School she went to Wellesley College where she received the degree of bachelor of arts in 1898. Her college life was interrupted by a year at home, but she completed the four years' work in three.

As an undergraduate she exhibited a lively interest in political and economic questions and a vigorous reaction against injustice and special privilege. During the McKinley-Bryan campaign (1896) she tried her hand at a novelette upholding free silver, which was published under the title *The White Slave: or the Cross of Gold* (copyrighted 1896). The strikes in Colorado led by the Western Federation of Miners made a deep impression on her and when she went to the University of Wisconsin in 1902 for graduate study she was a strong believer in the rights of labor. She was secretary to Prof. Richard T. Ely for a time and then became an honorary fellow in political economy and an active collaborator in John R. Commons' American Bureau of Industrial Research.

Her name first appeared as an author on labor subjects with the publication in 1905 of the widely known college textbook, *Labor Problems,* on which she collaborated with Prof. Thomas S. Adams. In 1906 she returned to Denver for a year to make a special study of equal suffrage in Colorado for the Collegiate Equal Suffrage League of New York State. The results were published in *Equal Suffrage* (1909). Her next work, based on exhaustive study of widely scattered original sources, was an authoritative history of American labor in the late 1820's and the years immediately following. It was accepted as a dissertation for the degree of Ph.D. at Wisconsin in 1908 and became generally available under the title, "Citizenship, 1827–1833," as a section of the *History of Labour in the United States* (1918) by John R. Commons and others. She was also an associate editor of *A Documentary History of American Industrial Society,* edited by Commons and published in 1910–11. A second original historical contribution, a pioneer in its field, was her "History of Women in Industry in the United States," published in 1910 by the United States Bureau of Labor Statistics as volume IX of its *Report on Condition of Woman and Child Wage-earners in the United States.*

In Colorado she had joined the Socialist party, and she was one of several who organized a Socialist group at the University of Wisconsin. She was an early member of the Intercollegiate Socialist Society and for many years before her death, a member of the national council of its successor, the League for Industrial Democracy. In 1910, when abroad studying the industrial courts in Germany, France, and Switzerland, she was a listener at the Copenhagen Congress of the Socialist International. She always believed in the ideal of production for use and not for profit, but she abandoned Marxism as inapplicable to the American economy and turned instead to James MacKaye's socialist theories.

Appointed in 1913 as industrial expert in the newly organized United States Children's Bureau, she directed a series of studies on the administration of child labor (employment certificate) laws, prepared by the bureau staff. The painstaking factual reports, to which she gave detailed oversight, were the basis for an analytical study by her, *Standards Applicable to the Administration of Employment Certificate Systems,* published by the bureau in 1924. After two years as industrial expert, she was appointed assistant chief of the Children's Bureau. Heavy administrative work was interfering with the research work in which she was most interested and in June 1918 she became director of investigations, a position which she held until her marriage, Nov. 25, 1918, to Robert Morse Woodbury. Although she then resigned from the regular staff, she continued to work with the bureau until 1924. From 1924 to 1926 she was on the staff of the Institute of Economics, engaged in formulating a program for adequate statistics in the field of labor. Subsequently, until December 1928, she was associated with the *Encyclo-*

pedia of the Social Sciences, to which she was a contributor. She also contributed to the *Dictionary of American Biography.*

Simple, without conceit, she did not permit her serious scholarly interests to chill her warm human interest nor her quick liveliness. She was one of the first in the American academic world to study and analyze labor problems. She always questioned the possibility of solving them in a capitalist world, but she turned more and more to social legislation and did pioneering work in the technique of its administration. She died at her home in New York City.

[W. S. Appleton, *Record of the Descendants of William Sumner of Dorchester, Mass.* (1879); *Who's Who in America,* 1932–33; S. S. E. Gilson, in *Wellesley Mag.,* June 1933; *N. Y. Times* and *N. Y. Herald-Tribune,* Mar. 12, 1933; information furnished by her family; personal acquaintance.]
                                       A. R.

WOODBURY, ISAAC BAKER (Oct. 23, 1819–Oct. 26, 1858), composer, was born in Beverly, Mass., the son of Isaac Woodberry (spelled thus in *Vital Records, post*) and his wife, Nancy (Baker). As a youth he was apprenticed to a blacksmith and spent his spare time in music study. At the age of thirteen he went to Boston, where he continued his studies in music and learned to play the violin. Six years later he went abroad for study in London and Paris. He returned in 1839 to Boston, where he taught music for six years. Later he joined the Bay State Glee Club, an organization which gave concerts in various parts of New England. On reaching Bellows Falls, Vt., he was persuaded to live there for a time to organize and conduct the New Hampshire and Vermont Musical Association. He went to New York, where for a few years prior to 1851 he directed the music at the Rutgers Street Church. He also became editor of the *American Monthly Musical Review.* Ill health made it necessary for him to leave New York in 1851, and he again went to Europe. While abroad he purchased new music by foreign composers for the *Review* and for the music books he compiled and edited. Upon his return to the United States he determined to spend his winters in the South for the sake of his health. He started from New York in the fall of 1858. On reaching Charleston, S. C., he fell ill and, three days after his arrival, died. He left a widow and six children.

It was principally as an editor that Woodbury was important, although many of his original compositions were published. One of his early songs, "He Doeth All Things Well, or My Sister," was published in Boston in 1844. A song that had considerable vogue for a number of years was "The Indian's Lament" (1846), with the much-quoted first line: "Let me go to my home in the far distant West." Among the music books he compiled and edited were the *Boston Musical Education Society's Collections* (1842) and the *Choral* (1845), both in collaboration with Benjamin F. Baker [*q.v.*]; the *Dulcimer* (1850); the *Lute of Zion* (1853); and the *Cythara* (1854). These works proved highly popular, and on one occasion the publishers advertised that *Dulcimer,* a "live music book," had sold "125,000 Copies in Two Seasons" (*Dwight's Journal of Music,* Jan. 22, 1853). For use in the South, Woodbury compiled the *Casket* (1855), published by the Southern Baptist Society, as well as the *Harp of the South* (1853). He also wrote several educational treatises, principally the *Self-Instructor in Musical Composition and Thorough Bass, ... with a Translation of Schneider's ... Arranging for the Work on Full Orchestra and Military Band,* originally issued in 1844. Woodbury's music, at the time of his death, is said to have been "sung by more worshippers in the sanctuary than the music of any other man" (Metcalf, *post,* pp. 282–83). Woodbury was of gentle disposition, and "had a beautiful voice and sang in various styles, but excelled in the ballad and descriptive music" (*Ibid.*).

[*Vital Records of Beverly, Mass.,* vol. I (1906); F. J. Metcalf, *Am. Writers and Compilers of Sacred Music* (1925); J. T. Howard, *Our Am. Music* (1930); W. S. B. Mathews, *One Hundred Years of Music in America* (1889); Nathan Crosby, *Ann. Obit. Notices* (1859).]   J. T. H.

WOODBURY, LEVI (Dec. 22, 1789–Sept. 4, 1851), senator, cabinet officer, associate justice of the Supreme Court, was born in Francestown, N. H., the second of ten children of Peter and Mary (Woodbury) Woodbury. He was a descendant of John Woodbury, who emigrated from Somersetshire, England, to Massachusetts in 1623. Levi attended the village school, Atkinson Academy, and Dartmouth College, where he graduated with honors in 1809. He studied law with Judge Jeremiah Smith, 1759–1842 [*q.v.*], also in the Litchfield (Conn.) Law School, and in Boston. After his admittance to the bar in 1812, he practised in Francestown and Portsmouth, popularized himself as a logical speaker in defense of President Madison in the War of 1812, wrote the Hillsborough resolves, and was clerk of the state Senate in 1816. In June 1819 he married Elizabeth Williams Clapp, the daughter of Asa Clapp and Elizabeth Wendell Quincy, and removed to Portsmouth, where their home was a popular meeting-place for his political friends. There were four daughters and a son. In 1817 his erstwhile boarding-house friend, Gov. William Plumer [*q.v.*], appointed him associate jus-

tice of the state superior court, a position which he held until he was elected governor in 1823 by the "Young America" faction of the Democracy and the Federalists. He recommended in his message as governor more education for females, soil surveys, diversified crops scientifically selected, wool production, exhibits of useful inventions, county lectures on agriculture and mechanics, which were advanced projects for his day (*Writings, post,* I, 464 ff.). Because of party factions, he was defeated for a second term, but was elected to the legislature (1825), where, as speaker of the House, he was chosen United States senator (1825–31). A representative of the commercial interests of New England, and often known as the "Rock of New England Democracy," he served on such important committees as commerce, navy, and agriculture, where he used his influence as an isolationist and as a supporter of a mildly protective tariff. He advocated the annexation of Texas, even at the expense of war (June 4, 1844, *Writings,* I, 355), and the occupation of Oregon. He declined reelection, but his friends in Portsmouth chose him without his consent for the state Senate in 1831. In May, however, he was appointed secretary of the navy. In this office he reformed rules of conduct and procedure, and left an expanded navy when he retired in June 1834.

As early as 1829, he was an opponent of the policy of the Bank of the United States. He charged its officers with political favoritism, but was willing to continue its existence if its board of directors were equally divided between the two major political parties. Failing in effecting such a plan, he, as secretary of the navy, finally agreed with President Jackson that the deposits of the government in the Bank should be removed to certain selected banks. When the Senate refused to confirm the recess appointment of Roger B. Taney [*q.v.*] as secretary of the treasury, Jackson appointed and the senate accepted Woodbury in his stead (June 27, 1834). His calm determination, scholarship, and logic were what Jackson needed to substantiate the attacks of F. P. Blair and Amos Kendall [*qq.v.*] on the Bank in the *Globe.* Beginning in January 1835, he refused to receive the Bank's drafts in payment of debts owed to the United States, censured it for retaining the dividends of the United States in the French indemnity case, and assumed a rather harsh attitude in disposing of the stock owned by the United States (Catterall, *post,* pp. 299–301, 372–75). He favored the independent treasury, maintaining that the government needed no banks to care for its funds, and that Congress had no constitutional power to recharter the Bank. He warned the country against inflation (1836), attempted to popularize the use of hard money, begged his friends in Congress to use the government's unprecedented surplus in the treasury for public works (1835–36), especially the construction of fortresses and roads on the frontiers, and the purchase of sound state bonds to form a provident fund looking toward the reduction of the tariff and a probable early decrease in the federal revenues. He stanchly opposed the division of the surplus among the states and predicted that through unbridled use of those funds undue inflation would result. When the deposit banks began to suspend specie payments because of the severe panic of 1837, he perfected a scheme by which public holders of federal warrants and drafts drawn on federal deposits did not lose because of depreciated paper money. Federal contracts and sound state banks were benefited greatly by his policy. In the midst of his troubles with the currency he was offered but declined the office of chief justice of New Hampshire. Retiring from office with Van Buren, Woodbury was elected to the United States Senate (1841), where he defended his fiscal policies and supported Democratic measures. He spoke at length for the veto power of the president, claiming that without it the executive would be a "mere pageant" (1842). He loyally supported Polk in 1844, though he had little faith in Polk and his Southern friends.

In 1845 he declined an appointment as minister to Great Britain, but President Polk nominated him an associate justice of the Supreme Court on Sept. 20, 1845, during a recess of the Senate; he was confirmed on Jan. 3, 1846. The docket was crowded with cases after 1846. He concurred in a decision upholding the constitutionality of state prohibitionist legislation (5 *Howard*, 617); in *Jones* vs. *Van Zandt* (5 *Howard*, 215) he gave the opinion of the Court that slavery was "a political question, settled by each state for itself." He dissented in *Luther* vs. *Borden* (7 *Howard*, 1, 47), and in the Passenger Cases (7 *Howard*, 283, 518), involving the constitutionality of the passenger tax statutes of New York and Massachusetts. His dissenting opinion in the case of *Waring* vs. *Clarke* (5 *Howard*, 441), denying that admiralty jurisdiction extended within the body of a country, even on tidal waters, is also noteworthy. His reasoning was "cogent and accurate, but not concise" (quoted in Warren, *Supreme Court, post*, II, 203). Because of his record as statesman and jurist he was considered as a Democratic presidential nominee in 1848, and, had he lived, he might have been a strong candidate in 1852, al-

though the Free-Soil wing would have accepted him reluctantly. In 1851 he died in Portsmouth, N. H.

As a man Woodbury was calm, self-possessed, and courageous, temperate in habits, a puritan in morals, an indefatigable worker. He was a conservative in politics—a party man and a strict-constructionist; slavery, for instance, he thought was wrong, but the laws upholding it must be obeyed until duly repealed. In other ways he was more progressive; he believed in systematic physical education as a supplement to mental training; he advocated free public schools and normal training for teachers, the establishment of lyceums, institutes, and museums for adult education, and the production of simplified literature on science, philosophy, and history for popular use. Confident of the intelligence and enterprise of his countrymen, he looked forward to free lecture halls, Sunday libraries, cheaper newspapers, prison reform and poor relief, and above all, democratic government run by an educated people.

[Sources include Woodbury MSS., Blair MSS., Van Buren MSS., in MSS. Div., and "Scrapbook of Newspapers . . . on the Life of Judge Woodbury" in Rare Book Room, Lib. of Cong.; Treat MSS., in Lib. of Mo. Hist. Soc., St. Louis; and *Writings of Levi Woodbury, LL.D.* (3 vols., 1852). Woodbury's opinions in the state court appear in 1–2 *N. H. Reports*; his reports as sec. of the navy in *Am. State Papers . . . Naval Affairs*, vol. IV (1861); opinions in U. S. circuit court, in C. L. Woodbury and George Minot, *Reports of Cases . . . First Circuit* (3 vols., 1847–52); and in Supreme Court, in 4–11 *Howard*. For biography see: C. L. Woodbury, *Geneal. Sketches of the Woodbury Family* (1904), "Levi Woodbury," in *Memorial Biogs. of the New Eng. Hist. Geneal. Soc.*, vol. I (1880), "Memoir of Hon. Levi Woodbury," in *New Eng. Hist. and Geneal. Reg.*, Jan. 1894; William Cranch, "Sketches of Alumni . . .," *Ibid.*, Jan. 1847; Robert Rantoul, *Eulogy on the Hon. Levi Woodbury* (1852); "Proc. in Relation to the death of Judge Woodbury," 12 *Howard*, iii; *U. S. Mag. and Dem. Rev.*, July 1838, Mar. 1843; D. H. Hurd, *Hist. of Rockingham and Strafford Counties, N. H.* (1882); C. H. Bell, *The Bench and Bar of N. H.* (1894). See also Charles Warren, *A Hist. of the Am. Bar* (1911) and *The Supreme Court in U. S. Hist.* (2 vols., 1928); R. C. H. Catterall, *The Second Bank of the U. S.* (1903); W. E. Smith, *The Francis Preston Blair Family in Politics* (1933); *N. H. Patriot and State Gazette* (Concord, N. H.), Sept. 10, 1851.]   W. E. S—h.

WOODFORD, STEWART LYNDON

(Sept. 3, 1835–Feb. 14, 1913), soldier, diplomat, was born in New York City, the son of Josiah Curtis and Susan (Terry) Woodford and the descendant of Thomas Woodford, a native of Lincolnshire, England, who emigrated to America in 1690. The boy went to Columbia College, now Columbia University, a year, then transferred to Yale College for a year, and returned to Columbia and was graduated in 1854. He studied law in the offices of Brown, Hall & Vanderpoel and in 1857 was admitted to the bar and began practice in New York City. On Oct

15, 1857, he was married to Julia Evelyn Capen of New York, who died in 1899. He was a delegate to the convention that nominated Lincoln and, following Lincoln's election, was given the honor of carrying to Washington the electoral vote of his state. In 1861 he was made assistant federal district attorney for New York but soon resigned to enlist as a private in Company H of the 127th New York Volunteers. His company elected him captain, and, when the regiment was ordered to the front, he was commissioned lieutenant-colonel. He took part in the defense of Washington and was at Suffolk, Va., when it was besieged by Longstreet. On the surrender of Charleston, he became the first military governor of that city. In May 1865 he was brevetted brigadier-general of volunteers, and he resigned in August.

A man of distinguished and ingratiating appearance, he continued to take an active part in politics. From 1867 to 1869 he was lieutenant-governor of New York and in 1870 ran for the governorship on the Republican ticket but lost. Elected to Congress, he served from Mar. 4, 1873, until he resigned on July 1, 1874. He participated in the important debates on the resumption of specie payments. In October 1875 he took part in *Joint Discussions between Gen. Thomas Ewing of Ohio and Gov. Stewart L. Woodford . . . on the Finance Question . . . at Circleville, Wilmington, Tiffin, and Columbus, Ohio* (1876). At the Republican National Convention of 1876 he nominated Roscoe Conkling for the presidency and was himself put in nomination for the vice-presidency. In January 1877 he was appointed federal district attorney for the southern district of New York, an office he held until 1883. In 1896 he became a member of a committee that drafted the charter for Greater New York and in that year was permanent chairman of the Republican state convention. The next year McKinley named him minister to Spain. As minister at Madrid, he pursued a course designed at once to bring about betterment in conditions in Cuba, then in revolt against Spain, and also to prevent war between the United States and Spain over Cuba. Through the exercise of patience and an unsuspected skill in negotiation he was successful in bringing the Spanish government to acceptance of the demands of President McKinley. However, owing to no fault of his own, his work was unsuccessful. In 1898 he returned to the practice of law in New York City, where he was also a director and general counsel for the Metropolitan Life Insurance Company, trustee of the Franklin Trust Company, and of the City Savings Bank of Brooklyn, as well as of numerous other organizations. In 1909 he was president of the Hudson-Fulton Celebration Commission and afterwards made a tour of courtesy to the European countries that had been represented at the celebration. He died in New York, survived by a daughter and by his widow, Isabel (Hanson) Woodford, whom he married on Sept. 26, 1900.

[Some papers and "Recortes Periodisticos de los Diarios de Madrid," 10 vols. of clippings from Madrid newspapers during Woodford's ministry, 1897–98, in Lib. of Cong.; *Bulletin of Yale Univ.: Obituary Record of Yale Grads., 1912–13* (1913); Walter Millis, *The Martial Spirit* (1931); *Who's Who in America, 1903–05; N. Y. Times* and *Sun* (N. Y.), Feb. 15, 1913.]
W. E. S—a.

WOODFORD, WILLIAM (Oct. 6, 1734–Nov. 13, 1780), Revolutionary soldier, was born in Caroline County, Va. His father, Maj. William Woodford, was an Englishman who emigrated to Virginia in the latter part of the seventeenth century; his mother, Anne Cocke, daughter of Dr. William Cocke, secretary of the colony. William enjoyed the educational advantages customary among young men of his class in Virginia. He served as a commissioned officer of the provincial forces during the French and Indian War and as justice of the peace of Caroline County. On June 26, 1762, he married Mary, daughter of Col. John Thornton; two children were born to them.

On Jan. 1, 1774, he was elected a member of the committee of correspondence of Caroline County, and on Dec. 8, a member of the committee to enforce the "Association." From July 17 to Aug. 9, 1775, he sat as alternate to Edmund Pendleton [*q.v.*] in the Virginia Convention. On Aug. 5 he was appointed colonel of the 3rd Regiment, and on Oct. 25 his troops repulsed an attempt on the part of Governor Dunmore's men to burn Hampton. Shortly thereafter he was directed by the Virginia committee of safety to proceed with his regiment and the Culpeper militia to the vicinity of Norfolk for the purpose of keeping Dunmore's movements under observation. The order meant "the passing over in favor of a subordinate commander of Patrick Henry, colonel of the 1st Regiment and ranking officer of the Virginia forces" (H. J. Eckenrode, *The Revolution in Virginia*, 1916, p. 75). As a consequence, a warm dispute arose between Henry and Woodford regarding the scope of their respective commands. On Dec. 9 Woodford defeated more than three hundred Loyalists, convicts, and negro slaves, and two hundred British regulars at Great Bridge, thereby compelling Dunmore to evacuate Norfolk and take refuge on board ship. In the meantime two hundred North Carolina troops under Col. Robert Howe [*q.v.*] had arrived. Although Howe outranked Woodford, the two officers exercised joint command over their combined forces during the subsequent operations about Norfolk.

Upon the recommendation of the Virginia Convention, the Continental Congress on Feb. 13, 1776, appointed Woodford colonel of the 2nd Virginia Regiment. On Feb. 21, 1777, he was promoted to the rank of brigadier-general. He fought at Brandywine (where he was wounded), at Germantown, and at Monmouth, and shared the sufferings of the patriots at Valley Forge. In 1778 and 1779 he was with the Continental army in New Jersey. On Dec. 13, 1779, Washington ordered him to proceed with a detachment of seven hundred men to the aid of Charleston, S. C., then besieged by the British. Going from Morristown, N. J., to the Elk River, Woodford journeyed by water to Williamsburg, Va., and thence overland to Charleston, where he arrived on Apr. 17, 1780, having made a march of five hundred miles in twenty-eight days. Upon the capture of the town by Sir Henry Clinton on May 12, 1780, Woodford was made prisoner. He was taken to New York, where he died and was buried in Old Trinity Church Yard. In 1789 Woodford County, Ky., was named in his honor.

[Valuable data from public and private archives supplied by Miss Catesby Woodford Willis of Fredericksburg, Va., a descendant of Gen. Woodford, who is preparing a biog. Published sources include *Royal Gazette* (N. Y.), Nov. 15, 1780; Peter Force, *Am. Archives*, 4 ser. III (1840), IV (1843), VI (1846); R. R. Howison, *A Hist. of Va.*, vol. II (1848); W. C. Ford, *The Writings of George Washington*, vols. III (1889), V, VI (1890), and *Jours. of the Continental Congress*; F. B. Heitman, *Hist. Reg. of Officers of the Continental Army* (1914); "The Letters of Col. William Woodford to Edmund Pendleton," *Richmond College Papers*, vol. I (1915); E. C. Burnett, *Letters of Members of the Continental Congress*, vols. I–III (1921–26), V (1931); H. R. McIlwaine, *Justices of the Peace of Colonial Virginia* (1922); B. P. Willis, *Daily Star* (Fredericksburg), Apr. 11, 1922; Marshall Wingfield, *A Hist. of Caroline County, Va.* (1924); L. G. Tyler, in *Tyler's Quart. Hist. and Geneal. Mag.*, July, Oct. 1930, Jan., Apr. 1931; J. C. Fitzpatrick, *The Writings of George Washington*, vols. I–XI (1931–34); J. W. Jordan in *Pa. Mag. of Hist. and Biog.*, Jan. 1900.] E. E. C.

WOODHOUSE, JAMES (Nov. 17, 1770– June 4, 1809), chemist, physician, was born in Philadelphia, Pa., the second son of William Woodhouse, an officer in the army of the Young Pretender, and his wife, Anne Martin, daughter of Dr. William Martin of Edinburgh. Immediately after their marriage (1766) the parents went from Alnwick, England, to Philadelphia, where the father began business as a bookseller and stationer. No records in regard to other children of this worthy couple have been discovered. James Woodhouse began his academic life in the University of the State of Pennsylvania (later the University of Pennsylvania) in his fourteenth

year (1784), receiving the degree of B.A. in 1787, and that of M.A. in 1790. Placing himself under the supervision and preceptorship of Benjamin Rush [*q.v.*], he became a student of medicine and in 1792 received the degree of M.D. upon the presentation of an inaugural dissertation, "On the Chemical and Medicinal Properties of the Persimmon Tree and the Analysis of Astringent Vegetables." This contribution met with general acclaim and very probably caused Woodhouse to abandon medicine for chemistry, for in the same year he founded the Chemical Society of Philadelphia, one of the earliest chemical societies in the world. It was an international organization, of which for seventeen years Woodhouse was senior president. On his assumption of the chair of chemistry in the University of Pennsylvania in 1795, Woodhouse entered upon a career of research which continued through a period of fourteen years with remarkable consequences. It was there, by devotion and unusual skill, accompanied with inexhaustible patience, that he gave the most convincing arguments against the doctrine of phlogiston; frequently his demonstrations were made in the presence of Joseph Priestley [*q.v.*], believer in the phlogiston theory, who was a regular visitor to Woodhouse's small but famous laboratory. There, too, he liberated by original methods the metal potassium (1808) and performed elaborate experiments on nitrous oxide gas, confirming its anaesthetic properties (1806). He executed all the chemical analytical work (1798) necessary to establish the basaltic nature of certain important rock formations, and exhibited attractive experiments on the conduct of metals toward nitric acid. Besides these results he engaged in profound studies on the chemistry and production of white starch, superior to Polish starch; the industrial purification of camphor (1804); the demonstration of the superiority of anthracite coal over bituminous coal for industrial purposes (1808); and conducted an extended series of trials on bread-making.

Woodhouse's contributions to American chemistry were noteworthy in several ways. He was a pioneer in plant chemistry, in the development of chemical analysis, in the elaboration of industrial processes, and in the use of laboratory methods of instruction in chemistry. His *The Young Chemist's Pocket Companion* (1797) was probably the first published guide in chemical experiment for students, and able students of the science, among them Robert Hare and the elder Benjamin Silliman [*qq.v.*], were attracted to his laboratory. He issued an attractive edition of James Parkinson's *The Chemical Pocket-book* (1802), and revised Samuel Parkes's *A Chymi-*

cal Catechism (1807) and J. A. C. Chaptal de Chanteloup's celebrated Elements of Chemistry (2 vols., 1807), all of which he annotated copiously. He died of apoplexy at the early age of thirty-eight. He was unmarried.

[See E. F. Smith, James Woodhouse, a Pioneer in Chemistry (1918); Joseph Carson, A Hist. of the Medic. Dept. of the Univ. of Pa. (1869); J. L. Chamberlain, Universities and Their Sons: Univ. of Pa., vol. I (1901), p. 302, which gives the names of Woodhouse's parents as John and Sarah (Robinson) Woodhouse; death notice in Poulson's Am. Daily Advertiser (Phila.), June 6, 1809.]   E. F. S.

WOODHULL, ALFRED ALEXANDER (Apr. 13, 1837–Oct. 18, 1921), military surgeon, was born at Princeton, N. J., the son of Dr. Alfred Alexander and Anna Maria (Salomons) Woodhull. He was a descendant of Richard Woodhull, who emigrated from Northampton, England, to Long Island, probably in 1648, and also of John Witherspoon [q.v.], signer of the Declaration of Independence. Woodhull prepared at Lawrenceville School for the College of New Jersey, where he received the degree of A.B. in 1856 and that of A.M. in 1859, the latter coincident with his graduation from the medical department of the University of Pennsylvania. During the two years following his graduation he practised medicine, first at Leavenworth and later at Eudora, Kan.

With the outbreak of the Civil War he was active in the recruitment of a troop of mounted rifles for the Kansas militia, in which he was commissioned a lieutenant. Before the unit was mustered into the Federal service, he received, Sept. 19, 1861, an appointment to the medical corps of the regular army. He served throughout the war on various field and hospital duties. His most important assignment was to the Army of the James as medical inspector (1864–65). He received the brevet of lieutenant-colonel for faithful and meritorious service in March 1865. At the close of the war he was assigned to the Army Medical Museum in Washington, where he prepared the "Surgical Section" of the Catalogue of the United States Army Medical Museum (1866), an important volume supplementary to the Medical and Surgical History of the War of the Rebellion. Important details, following a long tour of duty in the office of the surgeon-general, included the position of instructor in military hygiene at the Infantry and Cavalry School at Fort Leavenworth, Kan. (1886–90) and command of the Army and Navy Hospital at Hot Springs, Ark. (1892–95). In 1895 he was detailed as medical inspector of the department of the Colorado, and in 1899 he became chief surgeon of the department of the Pacific at Manila. He was retired in 1901 and in 1904 he was ad-

vanced to the grade of brigadier-general on the retired list. After his retirement he returned to Princeton, where for five years (1902–07) he was lecturer on personal hygiene and general sanitation at the university. He continued his residence in Princeton to the time of his death.

For fifty years Woodhull was an industrious contributor to medical literature. In 1868 he published A Medical Report upon the Uniform and Clothing of the Soldiers of the United States Army. He contributed several papers on the pharmacology and clinical use of ipecacuanha (1875–76), advocating the use of the drug in the treatment of dysentery, a practice since generally accepted. He was awarded the gold medal of the Military Service Institution for his paper on "The Enlisted Soldier," which was published in its Journal for March 1887; in 1907 he received the Seaman prize for an article on the scope of instruction in hygiene and sanitation for military and naval service schools, published in the same Journal, March–April 1908. In 1891 he was sent to England to make a study of the medical service of the British Army, upon which he published a report in 1894. He wrote Provisional Manual for Exercise of Company Bearers and Hospital Corps (1889), and Notes on Military Hygiene for Officers of the Line, which went through four editions (1898–1909). He supplemented his lectures at Princeton by writing Personal Hygiene: Designed for Undergraduates (1906). His non-medical writings included a Quarter Century Report of the Class of 1856 of the College of New Jersey (1881) and The Battle of Princeton (1913), a tactical study of that engagement. He was one of the early members (1894) of the Association of Military Surgeons. He had a strong sense of personal dignity, which somewhat masked a disposition essentially kind. His mind was a storehouse of the most accurate medico-military knowledge, especially in regard to the Civil War. He was married on Dec. 15, 1868, to Margaret, daughter of Elias Ellicott of Baltimore, Md., who survived him.

[M. G. Woodhull and F. B. Stevens, Woodhull Geneal. (1904); Who's Who in America, 1920–21; Military Surgeon, Dec. 1921; I. A. Watson, Physicians and Surgeons of America (1896); Jour. Am. Medic. Asso., Nov. 5, 1921; State Gazette (Trenton, N. J.), Oct. 19, 1921.]   J. M. P.

WOODHULL, NATHANIEL (Dec. 30, 1722–Sept. 20, 1776), president of the New York Provincial Congress and brigadier-general in the Revolution, was the son of Nathaniel Woodhull and Sarah (Smith), daughter of the second Richard Smith of the "Bull" Smith family of Smithtown. The Woodhulls had been identified with Long Island ever since the earliest of them, Richard Woodhull, emigrated to America from England about 1648. Nathaniel's parents occupied the ancestral estate at St. George's Manor, Mastic. Here he was born, and, as the eldest son, was prepared in the English fashion to succeed his father. He early entered military service, however, and by 1758 had the rank of major. He served under General Abercromby in the campaign against Crown Point and Ticonderoga, and under General Bradstreet at the reduction of Fort Frontenac (Kingston). In 1760, as colonel of the 3rd Regiment of New York Provincials, he took part in the invasion of Canada directed by General Amherst. His journal of this expedition was published in the *Historical Magazine* (New York) for September 1861.

During the period of peace that followed, Woodhull had time for farming and for participation in the affairs of his local community. He married in 1761 Ruth Floyd, sister of William Floyd [*q.v.*], signer of the Declaration of Independence. Objections to England's mode of taxing the colonies was voiced formally in the New York Assembly in 1768, and in the election following its dissolution, Suffolk County showed its approval of such objection by choosing Woodhull one of its two representatives in the new Assembly. For six years, 1769–75, he continued there, protesting against what he believed was arbitrary interference by the Crown in colonial affairs. He represented Suffolk also in the convention which chose delegates to the First Continental Congress, and in the New York Provincial Congress which in May 1775 assumed control of the colony and reorganized the militia, putting Suffolk and Queens counties under Woodhull's charge. In October 1775 he was made brigadier-general. When word came in August 1776 that the British had landed on Long Island and were threatening New York from Brooklyn, he was not in attendance at the Provincial Congress, of which he had been elected president the year before, but was absent on leave at Mastic. He was ordered to Jamaica to command his militia in the removal of stock and other supplies that might be useful to the enemy to the eastern end of the island and in furnishing protection to the inhabitants. With scarcely a hundred militiamen—two regiments ordered to reinforce him failed to arrive—he succeeded in driving a large quantity of stock out of the enemy's reach. The disastrous outcome of the battle of Long Island on Aug. 27, however, cut him off entirely from the rest of the army, and in this desperate situation, he retired to his headquarters at Jamaica to await fresh orders, which he confidently expected. Repeated appeals to the Provincial Congress and to Washington in his behalf met with no practical response. Committees were dispatched to aid him with "advice"; Connecticut was asked to send troops, but none came. There are various versions of his capture near Jamaica by a detachment of British dragoons, but it seems in keeping with his soldierly character to suppose that he did not yield his sword without a fight and that he was wounded in his attempt to escape from his captors. His subsequent ill treatment which resulted in his death within a few weeks raised him to the rank of hero and martyr. He was buried at Mastic. He was survived by his wife and a daughter.

[M. G. Woodhull and F. B. Stevens, *Woodhull Geneal.* (1904); *Jour. of the Votes and Proc. of the Gen. Assembly of the Colony of N. Y., from 1766 to 1776 Inclusive* (1820); *Jours. of the Provincial Cong. . . . of the State of N. Y.* (1842); L. R. Marsh, *An Oration on the Life, Character, and Pub. Services of Gen. Nathaniel Woodhull* (1848); Thomas Jones, *Hist. of N. Y. during the Revolutionary War* (1879), ed. by E. F. de Lancey; *Calendar of Hist. MSS. Relating to the Revolutionary War in the Office of the Secretary of State, Albany, N. Y.* (1868), I, 134.]   E. L. J.

WOODHULL, VICTORIA CLAFLIN (Sept. 23, 1838–June 10, 1927), reformer, was born in Homer, Ohio, the daughter of Reuben Buckman and Roxanna (Hummel) Claflin. She was one of ten children, of whom another daughter, Tennessee Celeste (1846–1923), also became well known. Their parents were poor and eccentric. The father was compelled to leave Homer under suspicion of arson while Victoria was yet a child, and the citizens gave a benefit to help the rest of the family out of town. The mother became a fanatic on the subjects of spiritualism and mesmerism. Victoria asserted in after years that she herself had begun to have visions at the age of three, and that Demosthenes, whom she claimed as a familiar spirit, had first appeared to her when she was ten. The family moved about from town to town in Ohio, and presently Victoria and Tennessee began giving spiritualistic exhibitions. In 1853, before she was sixteen, Victoria married Dr. Canning Woodhull (by whom she had two children), but did not cease her career as a charlatan. The Claflin family traveled for a time as a medicine and fortune-telling show, selling an Elixir of Life, with Tennessee's portrait on the bottle, while her brother Hebern posed as a cancer doctor. Victoria and Tennessee thereafter worked together as clairvoyants, making long stays in Cincinnati, Chicago, and elsewhere. In 1864 Victoria divorced Woodhull and began traveling with a Col. James H. Blood, whom she was supposed to have married in 1866.

In 1868 the two sisters went to New York,

taking several members of the Claflin family with them. Tennessee had married one John Bartels, but never used his name, preferring to sign herself as "Tennie C. Claflin." The two reached the ear of the elder Cornelius Vanderbilt [q.v.] through his interest in spiritualism; they opened a stock brokerage office in the financial district, and through Vanderbilt's advice made considerable profits in the stock market. Victoria became interested in a socialistic cult, the Pantarchy, one of whose tenets was free love, which was headed by Stephen Pearl Andrews [q.v.]. In 1870 the sisters launched *Woodhull and Claflin's Weekly*, which advocated equal rights for women, a single standard of morality and free love, and campaigned against prostitution and abortion. Blood and Andrews wrote most of the material, though a great deal of it voiced Mrs. Woodhull's own views. The *Weekly* also proposed her as president of the United States. In January 1871 she appeared before the judiciary committee of the national House of Representatives and pleaded for woman's suffrage. She began giving lectures on that and other subjects, and proved to be a magnetic and compelling speaker. The Equal Rights party nominated her for the presidency in 1872, and she went to the polls and made a futile attempt to vote. Among her published lectures and pamphlets are *Origin, Tendencies and Principles of Government* (1871), *Stirpiculture, or the Scientific Propagation of the Human Race* (1888), *Humanitarian Money* (1892), and, with her sister, *The Human Body the Temple of God* (1890). Theodore Tilton [q.v.], a young reporter on the *Independent*, became interested in Mrs. Woodhull, and she later described publicly a liaison with him lasting, as she said, six months. Angered by the attacks of the sisters of Henry Ward Beecher [q.v.] upon them, the Claflin sisters precipitated the greatest sensation of the period by publishing in the *Weekly*, Nov. 2, 1872, the story of the alleged intimacy of the eminent clergyman with the wife of Tilton. They were arrested for uttering an obscene publication and spent two periods in jail, but were acquitted. In 1876 Victoria obtained a divorce from Blood. When in January 1877 Cornelius Vanderbilt died, some of his children brought suit to annul his will; during the trial the sisters sailed for England, and it was whispered that Vanderbilt money had paid them to go.

In the following December, after a lecture by Mrs. Woodhull at St. James's Hall, London, one of her hearers, John Biddulph Martin, one of a wealthy English banking family, offered her marriage and was accepted, but his family objected so strongly that it was six years before the wedding took place (Oct. 31, 1883). In 1885 Tennessee married Francis Cook, later a baronet and also owner of a Portuguese estate which brought him the title of Viscount de Montserrat. Both sisters became noted for charitable works, and in their latter years were received by not a few of the socially elect in England. Victoria continued lecturing and writing. In July 1892 she began issuing a magazine, the *Humanitarian,* with her daughter, Zulu Maud Woodhull, as associate editor. She and her sister made several trips to America, stirring up a sensation on almost every occasion. Lady Cook died in 1923, and Mrs. Martin four years later.

[Sources include *Who's Who in America, 1926–27* (see Victoria Martin); Emanie N. Sachs, *"The Terrible Siren"* (1928); Leon Oliver, *The Great Sensation —Hist. of the Beecher-Tilton-Woodhull Scandal* (1873); G. S. Darewin, *Synopsis of the Lives of Victoria C. Woodhull and Tennessee Claflin* (London, 1891); M. F. Darwin, *One Moral Standard for All: Extracts from the Lives of Victoria Woodhull . . . and Tennessee Claflin* (1895); Madeleine Legge, *Two Noble Women* (1893); Henry Clews, *Fifty Years in Wall Street* (1908); records of Tilton-Beecher trial, City Court, Brooklyn, Jan.–June 1875; H. G. Clark, *The Thunderbolt* (1873); Theodore Tilton, *Golden Age Tracts, No. 3, Victoria C. Woodhull* (1871); obituary of Tennessee Claflin in *N. Y. Times,* Jan. 20, 1923; obituary of Victoria Woodhull, *Ibid.,* June 11, 1927.]
A.F.H.

WOODIN, WILLIAM HARTMAN (May 27, 1868–May 3, 1934), secretary of the treasury, was born at Berwick, Pa., the son of Clemuel Ricketts and Mary Louise (Dickerman) Woodin. Since 1835, when his grandfather established a foundry at Berwick, the family had been engaged in the production of iron. William was educated at the Woodbridge School in New York City and the School of Mines of Columbia University, where he was a member of the class of 1890 but did not graduate. He entered his father's plant as a molder and cleaner of castings, became general superintendent in 1892, and in 1899 president of the Jackson & Woodin Manufacturing Company at Berwick. Resigning that post within the year to enter the employ of the American Car & Foundry Company as district manager, he was made a director in 1902 and president in 1916. For many years he was chairman of the board of the American Locomotive Company, and he served as an officer or director of a number of other enterprises.

A fellow trustee of the Warm Springs Foundation, he was a close personal friend of Franklin Delano Roosevelt, and though previously a Republican, he gave Roosevelt his active support in the presidential campaign of 1932, after the election becoming one of the inner circle of Roosevelt's advisers. He served as treasurer of a special finance committee which raised $1,000,000 to pay off the $793,000 debt and the obligations of the Democratic National Committee, and on Feb. 21, 1933, his selection as secretary of the treasury in Roosevelt's cabinet was announced.

Woodin entered upon his duties as secretary of the treasury at one of the most critical moments in the nation's history. The financial system of the country, weakened by huge withdrawals of deposits, increasing lack of confidence, and the effect of the depression which began in 1929, was perilously near collapse. Woodin's task was both to restore confidence and to carry out Roosevelt's financial and monetary policies, which involved a sharp break, at many points, from those of his predecessors. To this double assignment he addressed himself with great energy and unbounded devotion to his chief. Though he belonged to the conservative school that viewed with mistrust some of the financial policies of the Roosevelt Administration, his personal relations with the President remained as warm as ever. Throughout the financial crisis Woodin supervised most efficiently the promulgation of the new banking regulations and the final warnings to the hoarders of gold. In November 1933 he issued a statement affirming his faith in the "New Deal" and his loyalty to his chief. Roosevelt, on his part, stood by Woodin when demands for his resignation were made by members of Congress after his name had appeared on a list of preferred customers of J. P. Morgan & Company, made public as a result of an investigation by the Senate Banking Committee. Under the strain of his responsibilities, however, Woodin's health gave way; on Oct. 31 he tendered his resignation, which was not accepted, but shortly afterward, at the insistence of the President, he took an indefinite leave of absence, going to Arizona in the hope of conquering a throat infection by a change of climate. On Dec. 13, 1933, he again tendered his resignation, which the President finally accepted on Dec. 20, making public its acceptance on Jan. 1, 1934. Woodin died in New York in the following May.

An unusual combination of business man and artist, Woodin was exceedingly fond of music and although he had little theoretical knowledge became an amateur composer of some note. His favorite instrument was the guitar and his compositions included suites, songs, and waltzes. Some of his children's pieces were published as *Raggedy Ann's Sunny Songs,* in December 1930; other works were "A Norwegian Rhapsody" (*Étude,* August 1934), "The Fire Chief" (copr. 1933), and the "Franklin Delano Roosevelt March," played at his friend's inauguration.

Woodin was also a numismatist and a collector of Cruikshank's drawings. He married Annie Jessup of Montrose, Pa., on Oct. 9, 1889, and was survived by his wife, three daughters, and a son.

[Charles Miller and John Chapman, "Woodin Notes: Avocations of a Financier," *Saturday Evening Post,* Oct. 14, 1933; "Composer Enters the Roosevelt Cabinet," *Musician,* Mar. 1933; Clinton Gilbert, "Lucky Woodin," *Collier's,* Apr. 29, 1933; *Who's Who in America,* 1932–33; *Étude,* Aug. 1934; *N. Y. Times,* Feb. 22, 1933, May 4, 1934.]
O. M., Jr.

WOODROW, JAMES (May 30, 1828–Jan. 17, 1907), Presbyterian clergyman, uncle of Woodrow Wilson [*q.v.*], was born in Carlisle, England, son of the Rev. Thomas and Marion (Williamson) Woodrow. In 1837 his family settled in Chillicothe, Ohio, and in 1849 James was graduated with highest honors from Jefferson College, Canonsburg, Pa. In 1853, after several years of teaching in Alabama academies he became professor of natural science at Oglethorpe University, Milledgeville, Ga. He was granted an immediate leave of absence for graduate study at Harvard under Louis Agassiz [*q.v.*] and at Heidelberg, where in 1856 he took the degree of Ph.D., *summa cum laude*. Rejecting an offer to lecture at Heidelberg he returned to Oglethorpe, where he taught until 1861. On Aug. 4, 1857, he married Felie S. Baker, daughter of a clergyman, and on Apr. 8, 1860, he was ordained to the Presbyterian ministry.

In 1859 there was created at the Presbyterian Seminary, Columbia, S. C., a "Professorship of Natural Science in Connexion with Revelation" whose purpose was "to evince the harmony of science with the records of our faith, and to refute the objections of infidel scientists" (quoted in *Dr. James Woodrow, post,* p. 13). Somewhat "oppressed with a sense of responsibility and self-distrust" (*Ibid.*), Woodrow accepted the chair in 1861 at the behest of the Synods of South Carolina, Georgia, and Alabama. He rose rapidly to a position of distinction in the service of his church and his community. During the Civil War he was chief of the Confederate chemical laboratory at Columbia; from 1861 to 1872 he was treasurer of foreign missions of the Southern General Assembly; from 1861 to 1885 he was editor of the *Southern Presbyterian Review,* a quarterly; and from 1865 to 1893 he was the publisher of the weekly *Southern Presbyterian.* Although he continued to hold his professorship in the theological seminary until 1886, he became associated with the University of South Carolina as professor of science in 1869, subsequently becoming dean of the school of liberal arts and sciences and finally president, 1891–97.

He succeeded in maintaining the reputation of the college during the agrarian ascendency of Benjamin R. Tillman [*q.v.*].

Woodrow became a figure of nation-wide interest in 1884 upon the publication of his address, *Evolution,* delivered before the Alumni Association of the Columbia Theological Seminary on May 7 of that year. Denying that there is any essential conflict between the Bible and science, he maintained that an understanding of the theory of evolution would lead not to doubt but to a more profound reverence for God's plan of creation (*Evolution,* pp. 29, 30), and insisted that "The Bible does not teach science; and to take its language in a scientific sense is grossly to pervert its meaning" (*Ibid.,* p. 6). These utterances made him the storm center of a controversy in the Southern church that lasted until 1888. He was charged with teaching and promulgating opinions of a dangerous tendency, calculated to unsettle the mind of the Church respecting the accuracy and authority of the Holy Scriptures as an infallible rule of faith (*Record and Evidence, post,* p. 1). His assertion that the body of Adam was probably the product of evolution from the body of some lower animal was the specific tenet that aroused most ire among his opponents (*Ibid.*). What Woodrow had argued was that the verse: "The Lord God formed man of the dust of the ground . . ." was not inconsistent with the belief that man was the descendant of other "organised" beings. "The narrative," he wrote, "does not intend to distinguish in accordance with chemical notions different kinds of matter, . . . but merely to refer in a general incidental way to previously existing matter, without intending or attempting to describe its exact nature" (*Evolution,* pp. 16, 17).

Woodrow courageously defended his views before the several synods responsible for the welfare of the Seminary and, on appeal, before several meetings of the General Assembly. His speech before the Synod of South Carolina in 1884 is one of the most enlightened expositions in the ecclesiastical history of the South (*Southern Presbyterian Review,* January 1885, pp. 1–65). In the end, however, he was removed from his chair, and the General Assembly sustained the admonition of the responsible synods. Although his fight did not, unfortunately, settle the conflict of religion and science in the South, the cause of truth was greatly advanced. Woodrow's dismissal was not held to affect his good standing in the church, and thereafter on several occasions he served as commissioner to the General Assembly and in 1901 was moderator of the Synod of South Carolina. He received honorary degrees from three Southern colleges as well as from his alma mater and was a member of many scientific societies at home and abroad. He died in his seventy-ninth year and was buried in Elmwood Cemetery, Columbia. His wife and three daughters survived him.

[*Dr. James Woodrow as Seen by His Friends* (1909), ed. by Marion W. Woodrow, contains a good brief biography by Dr. J. W. Flynn. This large volume contains *inter alia* many of the sermons and the writings of Dr. Woodrow. Official sources are *Record and Evidence in the Case of the Presbyterian Church in the U. S. versus James Woodrow* (1888), which includes the essay *Evolution* and Woodrow's speech before the Synod of S. C.; *Complaint of James Woodrow versus The Synod of Ga.* (1888) ; and *The Minutes of the General Assembly* (Southern), 1884–88. See also E. L. Green, *A Hist. of the Univ. of S. C.* (1916) ; *Who's Who in America,* 1906–07 ; *The State* (Columbia, S. C.), Jan. 18, 1907. The *Central Presbyterian,* the *Southwestern Presbyterian,* and similar periodicals reflect varying opinions concerning the evolution controversy.]

J. E. P.

WOODRUFF, CHARLES EDWARD (Oct. 2, 1860–June 13, 1915), ethnologist, army medical officer, was born in Philadelphia, Pa., the son of David Stratton and Mary Jane (Remster) Woodruff. After graduation from the Central High School, Philadelphia, in 1879, he attended the United States Naval Academy for three years but did not graduate. He taught mathematics in the high school at Reading, Pa., for one year and then entered Jefferson Medical College, where he was given his medical degree in 1886. He immediately entered the medical corps of the United States navy as an assistant surgeon, but after one year he transferred to the army, with the grade of first lieutenant and assistant surgeon. Routine post duty occupied his time until the Spanish-American War, when he went to the Philippine Islands as brigade surgeon under Major-General Wesley Merritt [*q.v.*] in the first expeditionary force. In 1902 the Philippine insurrection took him back to the Islands, where he served as brigade surgeon of the 4th Brigade. It was during this tour of duty that he collected the material for his first book, *The Effects of Tropical Light on White Men* (1905), in which he held that the deleterious effects of tropical residence upon white men were due to the influence of the actinic or chemical rays of the sun. He believed in the greater resistance of the brunette type to these rays and in their better adaptability to tropical life, and advocated the wearing of clothing containing orange or red color for protection. Though his views were supported by a wealth of practical experience and by ingenious argumentation, they have been largely exploded by research showing sunlight to be relatively less important than the combination of heat and humidity in the physiological changes caused by a hot climate. The theme of the first book was expanded in *Medical Ethnology* (1915). His most important book is *The Expansion of Races* (1909), called by enthusiastic admirers the most outstanding contribution to the literature of anthropology since Darwin's *Origin of Species*. It is an absorbingly interesting collection of anthropological and ethnological material, to which he endeavored to give interpretation. He was the author of over seventy journal articles, mainly on military medicine, but embracing a wide variety of other topics. Noteworthy among these are "An Anthropological Study of the Small Brain of Civilized Man and Its Evolution" (*American Journal of Insanity*, July 1901) and "Evolution of Modern Numerals from Ancient Tally Marks" (*American Mathematical Quarterly*, Aug.–Sept. 1909). He contributed the article on medical ethnology to the third edition of *A Reference Handbook of the Medical Sciences* (1914), edited by T. L. Stedman. His writings have the quality of holding the interest. They are clear and simple in style, and lucid in argument. They show, however, the lack of that judicial attitude of mind necessary to the research worker in any field.

Woodruff was of distinguished appearance and manner. He was an excellent public speaker and conversationalist, and he had the gift of binding his associates to him with affectionate regard. Despite impaired health he went again to duty in the Philippine Islands in 1910. Though himself of a pronounced brunette type, he returned in such physical condition that he was retired from active service in 1913 with the grade of lieutenant-colonel. In 1914 he became associate editor of *American Medicine,* to which he had for years been a regular contributor. A long period of semi-invalidism from arteriosclerosis ended with his death at his home in New Rochelle, N. Y. He was married at Washington, D. C., on Dec. 22, 1886, to Stella M. Caulfield of that city, who, with two sons, survived him.

[*Who's Who in America*, 1914–15; *Am. Medicine,* June 1915; *Trans. Am. Therapeutic Soc.* (1917), with portrait; *Lancet Clinic*, June 26, 1915; *N. Y. Medic. Jour.*, June 19, 1915; *Medic. Record* (N. Y.), June 19, 1915; H. A. Kelly and W. L. Burrage, *Am. Medic. Biogs.* (1920); obituary and editorial in *N. Y. Times,* June 15, 1915.]

J. M. P.

WOODRUFF, THEODORE TUTTLE (Apr. 8, 1811–May 2, 1892), inventor, manufacturer, is believed to have been the son of Simeon and Roxanna (Tuttle) Woodruff, who in 1800 had moved from Litchfield, Conn., to Burrville, a hamlet outside of Watertown, N. Y. There young Woodruff was born. Until he was

sixteen years old he worked on his father's farm and attended the district schools. He was then apprenticed to a wagon-maker in Watertown, and three years later entered a local foundry and machine works as a pattern-maker. He remained there for many years, becoming an expert craftsman and something of an inventor. He is said to have been ridiculed by older craftsmen for his schemes, among them one advanced shortly after the coming of the railroad in the 1830's for the construction of sleeping-cars for trains. Though he had no opportunity at the time to develop the idea, in the course of subsequent years as a journeyman he gained experience in the building of railroad cars in various places and eventually became master car-builder for the Terre Haute and Alton Railroad at Alton, Ill. On Dec. 2, 1856, he received two patents (No. 16,159 and No. 16,160) for a railway-car seat and couch. With capital furnished by three friends a sleeping-car was built in 1857 under Woodruff's direction by T. W. Watson and Company of Springfield, Mass. It contained twelve sleeping sections, six on each side of the car. With some difficulty Woodruff secured the consent of the New York Central Railroad to demonstrate his car on the night express between New York and Buffalo. Obliged to pay full fare for himself, he personally managed it, charging fifty cents a passenger. After some months he transferred it to Pittsburgh, Pa., where he successfully demonstrated it to the Pennsylvania Railroad.

Assured of the purchase of additional cars by this company, Woodruff was joined late in 1858 by his brother, Col. Jonah Woodruff, and the two began on a small scale the manufacture of sleeping cars in Philadelphia, Pa., under the firm name of T. T. Woodruff and Company. On May 31, 1859, and Jan. 24, 1860, Woodruff obtained two additional patents for improvements of his car seat and couch. About 1862, with the reorganization of the business as a stock company under the title of the Central Transportation Company, he sold out his interest and retired to Mansfield, Ohio, where he engaged in banking for eight years. Returning to Philadelphia, he established a general foundry business known as the Norris Iron Company at Norristown, Pa., and resumed his inventive work, patenting on May 14, 1872, a process and the apparatus for the manufacture of indigo and on Nov. 5, 1872, a coffee hulling machine. The cost of exploiting these devices, however, coupled with the financial depression of the period, brought Woodruff's business career to an end in bankruptcy in 1875. Thereafter, until his death when he was struck by an express train at Gloucester, N. J., he continued with invention on a small scale in the hope of recouping his losses. Among his later patents were those for a steam plow, an improved surveyor's compass, and a method of ship propulsion by the use of screw propellers at the sides of the vessel. He was survived by a daughter and was buried in Watertown.

[J. A. Haddock, *The Growth of a Century . . . Hist. of Jefferson County, N. Y.* (1895) ; *The Manufactories and Manufacturers of Pa. of the Nineteenth Century* (1875) ; Joseph Husband, *The Story of the Pullman Car* (1917) ; accounts of death in *Phila. Record* and *Pub. Ledger* (Phila.), May 3, 4, 5, 1892 ; Patent Office records ; information on the Woodruff family from the Roswell P. Flower Memorial Lib., Watertown, N. Y.]
C. W. M.

WOODRUFF, TIMOTHY LESTER (Aug. 4, 1858–Oct. 12, 1913), merchant, lieutenant-governor of New York, was born in New Haven, Conn., the son of John and Jane (Lester) Woodruff. His father was a clockmaker with little education but with considerable ability for practical politics and was a member of Congress, 1855–57 and 1859–61. Timothy was orphaned by the death of his mother, when he was two years old and of his father eight years later. The family estate was sufficient to provide a good education for him. He was prepared for college at Phillips Exeter Academy and entered Yale College in 1875. He was obliged to repeat his junior year and left college in 1879. In 1889 he received the M.A. degree and was enrolled as a graduate with his class. Subsequently he took a commercial course at Eastman's National Business College in Poughkeepsie. On Apr. 13, 1880, he married Cora, the daughter of Harvey G. Eastman [*q.v.*]. She died on Mar. 28, 1904. In 1881 he removed to Brooklyn and obtained employment as a clerk in the warehousing division of Nash & Whiton, salt and provision merchants. He advanced rapidly to a leading position in the firm, which he reorganized as the Worcester Salt Company. Meanwhile he had developed a warehousing and wharfage business of his own. At a favorable opportunity he sold it and invested the proceeds in a diversified group of companies, the most important being the Smith-Premier Typewriting Company, in which he had a controlling interest. Before the close of the century he was also president of the Provident Life Assurance Co., of the Maltine Manufacturing Company, and a director of the Pneumo-Electric Company at Syracuse, of a paper mill on the upper Hudson, and of two banks. With few exceptions the distribution of his investments remained unchanged at his death.

His political career began when he joined a Republican club on first moving to Brooklyn. His work in the organization attracted the attention of Thomas C. Platt [*q.v.*] who made him a member of his board of strategy. As park commissioner of Brooklyn in 1895, he gained great popularity by advocating the construction of good roads and bicycle paths. The next year he was elected lieutenant-governor for the first of three successive terms. He acquired control of the Kings County organization by 1897, healed factional rifts, and made it the chief stronghold of the Republican party in the metropolitan area. His rule over it, maintained chiefly by his personal popularity, was benevolently autocratic. In 1900 he was a candidate for the vice-presidential nomination, which was given to Roosevelt. His ambition to be governor was disappointed in 1904, when Platt lost control of the organization to Benjamin B. Odell [*q.v.*]. When Roosevelt's friends defeated Odell two years later, Woodruff became chairman of the state executive committee. He conducted the gubernatorial campaign for Charles E. Hughes acceptably, but opposed him after the election on many matters of policy. He was ousted from the chairmanship after considerable difficulty and delay. In 1912 he joined the Progressive party. While speaking at a fusion rally in the interest of John Purroy Mitchell's candidacy for mayor he was stricken with apoplexy and died a few days later. Though not of the first rank, he had uncommon gifts for political leadership and organization, and in more fortunate circumstances he might have had an opportunity to demonstrate his capacity for public administration. He was survived by his son by his first wife and by his second wife, Isabel (Morrison) Woodruff, to whom he was married on Apr. 24, 1905.

[*Obituary Record of Yale Graduates, 1913–14* (1914) ; *Who's Who in America*, 1912–13 ; *Autobiog. of Thomas Collier Platt* (1910) ; C. W. Thompson, *Party Leaders of the Time* (1906) ; *Current Literature*, Sept. 1912 ; *N. Y. Tribune* and *N. Y. Times*, Oct. 13, 1913.]
E. C. S.

WOODRUFF, WILFORD (Mar. 1, 1807–Sept. 2, 1898), fourth president of the Utah branch of the Mormon Church, was born in Farmington, now Avon, Hartford County, Conn., the son of Aphek and Beulah (Thompson) Woodruff. His mother died in 1808, and he and his two brothers were brought up by their stepmother. He had little schooling, and as he grew to manhood he combined farming with learning the trade of miller from his father. Although of a mystical religious nature and in spite of rather frequent exposure to religious revivals, he did not join any denomination until in December 1833, a year after he and his brother Azmon had settled in Richland, Oswego County, N. Y. Then he was converted to Mormonism. On hearing of the new gospel of Joseph Smith [*q.v.*], so the account runs, he "immediately received a testimony of the genuineness" of the "message" (Jenson, *post,* p. 20). He was baptized two days later, ordained a teacher, and was soon active converting others in the community. In April 1834, under the stimulation of Parley P. Pratt [*q.v.*], he removed to Kirtland, Ohio, where he first met the Prophet Smith himself. Shortly thereafter Smith dispatched him and others to succor the distressed Mormons in Missouri, and, from this time till his death over sixty years later, he dedicated his life to his new-found faith. He rose rapidly in official favor and on Apr. 26, 1839, under the shadow of the enforced exodus of the Mormons from Missouri, he was ordained an apostle by Brigham Young [*q.v.*] and thus took his place in the highest counsels of his church.

During the period of Mormon residence in Nauvoo, Ill., he served as member of the city council, was a chaplain in the Nauvoo Legion (the Mormon military organization), and business manager of the official Mormon periodical, the *Times and Seasons.* Early in the summer of 1844, with others he left Illinois to combine proselyting with the curious and somewhat preposterous political campaign in support of the candidacy of Joseph Smith for the presidency of the United States. Upon hearing of Smith's assassination, he returned to Nauvoo, where he strongly supported Brigham Young and the "Twelve Apostles" as the proper successors to Smith. In 1846 he assisted in the removal of the Saints from Illinois and was in the first coi pany of pioneers to enter the valley of the Grea Salt Lake on July 24, 1847. Aside from his missionary travels, the rest of his life was spent in building up the Mormon communities in Utah. For twenty-one years he served in the territorial legislature. He helped to stimulate scientific horticulture and irrigation, for, when not occupied with his official duties, he gave his active attention to well-planned farming. In 1880, when John Taylor [*q.v.*] became president of the Mormon Church, Woodruff replaced him as president of the quorum of the "Twelve Apostles," thus becoming second in command, and on Apr. 7, 1889, he succeeded to the presidency. At the elaborate celebration in July 1897 to commemorate the half-century of Mormon settlement in Utah he took an active part, though advanced in years. The next year his health failed rapidly, and he removed to California in the hope of improving his condition. He died in San Francisco and was buried in Salt Lake City.

He was one of the most effective proselyters of his faith. In the years 1834 to 1836 he had his first missionary experience in Arkansas and Tennessee. In 1837 he assisted in opening up Mormon activities in Maine and elsewhere in New England. While the main body of the church was establishing itself in western Illinois, he and several of his fellow apostles were having signal success in converting thousands of persons in Great Britain to Mormonism. Again in 1844, after his friend Brigham Young was in the saddle in Nauvoo as Smith's successor, Woodruff and other apostles were sent to Great Britain to make sure that the large body of British converts should follow Young and the apostles rather than James J. Strang and Sidney Rigdon [*qq.v.*], the other chief contenders for Smith's prophetic rôle. So, too, when the exodus from Illinois was imperative, he traveled throughout the Atlantic seaboard states to strengthen the Mormon missionary work there. For years he kept a detailed journal of his life, and he delighted in a quantitative rehearsal of his accomplishments. Thus he naïvely records that "from the beginning of my ministry in 1834 until the close of 1895 I have traveled in all 172,369 miles; held 7,655 meetings; preached 3,526 discourses; organized 51 branches of the Church and 77 preaching places; my journeys cover England, Scotland, Wales, and 23 states and 5 territories of the Union" (Cowley, *post,* p. vi). His interest in chronicling the events of his time led to his being made assistant church historian in 1856, and in 1875 he became official historian and recorder of his denomination. His journals, in fact, have proved invaluable to all interpreters of Mormonism.

He was married to Phebe Carter on Apr. 13, 1837, but like most other leaders of Mormonism he was converted to plural marriage by the Prophet Smith, and he took four additional wives. His five wives bore him a total of thirty-three children, twenty of whom survived him. Following the enactment of the Edmunds-Tucker law against polygamy in 1882, like other prominent Mormons he was forced into voluntary exile to avoid arrest. In September 1890, finding that the prosecution of other Mormons for infraction of the anti-polygamy statute had become more and more effective and was disintegrating the morale of his followers, he issued his famous "Manifesto" in which, speaking for his church, the practice of plural wifery was officially abandoned. He was essentially a mystic, completely earnest and sincere in his religion. He firmly believed in the divine guidance of his life. He states in his journals that "my life abounds in incidents which to me surely indicate the direct interposition of God whom I firmly believe has guided my every step. On 27 distinct occasions I have been saved from dangers which threatened my life" (Cowley, *post*, p. vi).

[M. F. Cowley, *Wilford Woodruff . . . History of His Life and Labors as Recorded in His Daily Journals*, 2nd ed., (1916); Andrew Jenson, *Latter-day Saint Biographical Encyc.*, vol. I (1901); *Deseret Evening News* (Salt Lake City), Sept. 2, 1898; *Salt Lake Tribune*, Sept. 3, 1898.]   K. Y.

WOODRUFF, WILLIAM EDWARD (Dec. 24, 1795–June 19, 1885), newspaper publisher, editor, was born at Fireplace, Long Island, the son of Nathaniel and Hannah (Clark) Woodruff. After the death of his father, he served an apprenticeship as printer on the *Long Island Star* (1808–15). He enlisted for the War of 1812 but saw no active service. Deciding to go west, but with no particular goal in view, he went to Louisville, Ky., then to St. Louis, and Memphis. Buying a small printing-press, he loaded it on a couple of pirogues that he lashed together, and, with a man to help, poled or punted his way to the mouth of the Arkansas River, and on Oct. 30, 1819, landed at Arkansas Post. Twenty days later, on Nov. 20, the first number of the *Arkansas Gazette* appeared. The staff was himself, the office and shop his one-room log cabin; subscriptions paid in advance there were none. The sheet, which was eighteen inches square, was neat in typographical arrangement, well-written, and carefully punctuated. Such was the beginning of the newspaper that has run without intermission, except during the Civil War and while the office was being removed to Little Rock in 1821, to the present day (1936), first as a weekly, afterwards as a daily and weekly. Until 1830 it was the only newspaper published in the Territory of Arkansas. Its policy was always strongly Democratic. In 1838 Woodruff sold his newspaper property, but in 1841 it fell into his hands, and he took up his old task until 1843, when he again sold out. Three years later he established the *Arkansas Democrat*, and in 1860 he combined the two papers, using the title *Arkansas Gazette and Democrat*, though the latter name was soon dropped. The last issue under his management appeared in March 1853, when he sold his interest and retired to private life. He died in Little Rock, leaving three sons and five daughters. He had been married on Nov. 14, 1827, to Jane Eliza Mills.

Editorials from Woodruff's pen, the record of his life, and the testimony of those who knew him show him to have been a man of the highest kind of honesty, and downright and thorough sincerity. Somewhat slightly built, he did not give the impression of one likely to adventure into frontier life. Yet he did not lack spirit and courage. On one occasion, in territorial times when organized law was weak, a border braggadocio took exception to something Woodruff had published and entered his office, threatening alarming things. One course only was left to the editor, and, taking that course, repugnant though it was to him, in self-defence, he shot and killed the man. Both public and legal opinion found Woodruff well justified. As commentator on public affairs he judged calmly, reasoned pertinently, saw clearly, and pronounced seasonably. He wrote gracefully and eloquently, avoided personalities, and was generally regarded as one whose intellectual cultivation gave him superiority over other men.

[Fay Hempstead, *Hist. Rev. of Ark.*, vol. I (1911); *Ark. and Its People, A Hist.*, vol. III (1930), ed. by D. Y. Thomas; obituary in *Daily Ark. Gazette*, June 20, 1885; information from Jane Georgeine Woodruff, Woodruff's daughter.]   C. J. F.

WOODS, ALVA (Aug. 13, 1794–Sept. 6, 1887), college president, Baptist minister, was born in Shoreham, Vt., and was the eldest of six children of Abel and Mary (Smith) Woods. His father was a Baptist clergyman, a half-brother of Leonard Woods, 1774–1854 [*q.v.*]. Abel Woods's father was one of the early settlers of Princeton, Mass., and taught the first public school in that town. Alva Woods received his early education in the public schools of Shoreham and at Phillips Academy, Andover, Mass., where he was fitted for college. He entered Harvard College in the fall of 1813 and was graduated with honors four years later. He followed this with a course in the Andover Theological Seminary (1817–21). Ordained a minister of the Baptist Church on Oct. 28, 1821, he accepted a position as professor of mathematics, natural philosophy, and ecclesiastical history at Columbian College (later George Washington University), Washington, D. C., but before beginning his teaching duties he was sent as an agent to the Atlantic states and Great Britain to collect funds, books, and apparatus for the college. While abroad he spent some time attending lectures at Oxford, Cambridge, Edinburgh, and Glasgow, returning to his college duties in November 1823. After a year's teaching at Columbian College he was chosen professor of mathematics and natural philosophy in Brown University. In February 1828 he became president of Transylvania University at Lexington, Ky. He remained in this position until March 1831, and there is some indication that his tenure was not altogether comfortable either to himself or to the trustees of the university (*Letters of Rebecca Gratz*, 1929, p. 215, ed. by David Philipson). The destruction of the main building of Transylvania by fire in May 1829 so crippled the usefulness of that institution for the time being that Woods felt free to accept the offer of the presidency of the newly established University of Alabama. He moved his family to Tuscaloosa in March 1831 and on Apr. 12, 1831, was inaugurated as president (T. M. Owens, *History of Alabama and Dictionary of Alabama Biography*, 1921, vol. II, p. 1358). He remained president of the university until December 1837. William Russell Smith [*q.v.*], fourth president of the university, says in his *Reminiscences of a Long Life* (1889) that Woods was not a success as president and that his life in that position was a life of storms. It may be assumed that much of Woods's unpopularity in Alabama was due to his dislike of slavery; he had been chosen president on the recommendation of James G. Birney [*q.v.*], the noted abolitionist (Jesse Macy, *The Anti-Slavery Crusade*, 1929, p. 35). In July 1837, in the midst of student rioting and rebellion, he tendered his resignation for the ostensible reason that his health was impaired and that he wished to educate his son in the free states.

Refusing the presidency of three western colleges and a professorship in a theological institution, Woods removed to Providence, R. I., where he gave his attention to preparing his son for Brown University. He was financially independent, and gave his services gratuitously for a number of years as chaplain for the prisoners in the various state institutions. He was a trustee of Brown University (1843–59) and of Newton Theological Institution, Newton Center, Mass., after 1853. In 1868 his *Literary and Theological Addresses* was printed in Providence in an edition of fifty copies. Woods was married, Dec. 10, 1823, to Almira Marshall (d. 1863), eldest daughter of Josiah and Priscilla Marshall of Boston, Mass. He had two children, of whom the elder survived him. He died in Providence.

[The chief source is the biog. sketch in *Woods's Literary and Theological Addresses* (1868), of which there are copies in the libraries of Transylvania Coll. and the Univ. of Ala. See also *Harvard Univ., Quinquennial Cat.* (1925); F. E. Blake, *Hist. of the Town of Princeton . . . Mass.* (1915), vol. II; *Biog. Cat. . . . Phillips Acad., Andover* (1903); *Gen. Cat. Theological Seminary, Andover, Mass., 1808–1908* (n.d.); Robert and Johanna Peter, *Transylvania Univ.* (1896), being Filson Club Pub., no. 11; A. F. Lewis, *Hist. of Higher Educ. in Ky.* (1899); obituary in *Providence Daily Jour.*, Sept. 7, 1887. Information has been supplied by Mrs. C. F. Norton, librarian of Transylvania Coll., and by Alice S. Wyman, librarian of the Univ. of Ala.]

R. S. C.

WOODS, CHARLES ROBERT (Feb. 19, 1827–Feb. 26, 1885), soldier, was born at Newark, Ohio. He was a descendant of a family that originated in Ulster and settled successively in Virginia and Kentucky. His father, Ezekiel S. Woods, moved in 1818 from Kentucky to Ohio,

where he engaged in farming and in general merchandising. His mother was Sarah Judith (Burnham) Woods of Zanesville, Ohio. He spent his boyhood on the farm, for a time was apprenticed to a cooper, and received only a common education from a tutor. In 1848 he was appointed a cadet at the United States Military Academy at West Point, and he was graduated in 1852 as a second lieutenant, 1st Infantry. He then served three years in Texas, four more in Washington, and was engaged in minor Indian warfare. In 1860 he returned to his home and was married to Cecilia Impey. He commanded the expedition of 200 men on the *Star of the West*, in a futile attempt to relieve Fort Sumter at the beginning of the Civil War. He served in the Shenandoah Valley and in West Virginia during the early part of the war, and in November 1861 was appointed colonel of the 76th Ohio Infantry, organized in his home town. This regiment he led at the capture of Fort Donelson in February 1862, and later at Shiloh. Assigned to command a brigade, he participated in the advance on Corinth, and in expeditions along the Mississippi River. His attacks at Milliken's Bend and at Island No. 65 resulted in the destruction of much enemy property. For serving gallantly in the subsequent Vicksburg campaign, he was appointed a brigadier-general of volunteers in August 1863.

Renewing his expeditions in the Mississippi Valley, he destroyed the Confederate transport *Fairplay*, and large stocks of stores, and in the autumn marched east to take part in the Chattanooga campaign. His brigade constructed a bridge over Lookout Creek, and led the assault that captured Lookout Mountain. He served throughout the Atlanta campaign in 1864 and played a prominent part at Resaca and at Atlanta, where after his flank had been turned he faced about, rolled back the enemy, and retook guns previously lost. He participated in Sherman's march to the sea and the subsequent advance north through the Carolinas. For these services he was brevetted major-general. He was then employed in reconstruction duty in the South until he was mustered out of the volunteer service in September 1866. He rejoined the regular army as a colonel of infantry and served mostly in the West. He led an expedition against Indians in Kansas in 1870, and in the Kit Carson fight. In 1871 his health declined, and he was retired for disability three years later. He returned to Ohio to engage in farming and gardening on his estate, "Woodside," until his death. He was of great physical strength, and was widely esteemed both as a soldier and as a citizen. He was a brother of William Burnham Woods [*q.v.*].

[R. H. Burnham, *The Burnham Family* (1869); G. W. Cullum, *Biog. Reg. . . . U. S. Mil. Acad.* (1891); *War of the Rebellion: Official Records* (Army), see index volume; *Battles and Leaders of the Civil War* (1887–88), vols. I, III, IV; *Weekly Advocate* (Newark, Ohio), Mar. 5, 9, 1885.]   C. H. L.

WOODS, LEONARD (June 19, 1774–Aug. 24, 1854), Congregational clergyman, professor of theology, was born in Princeton, Mass., a son of Samuel and Abigail (Whitney) Underwood Woods. He was a descendant of Samuel Woods who came to New England soon after 1700 and settled in Chelmsford, Mass. Leonard displayed mental precocity at an early age and developed a great fondness for reading. Overcoming the opposition of his father, who wished him to become a farmer, he began preparation for college and with only three months' systematic instruction, at Leicester Academy, matriculated at Harvard, where he was graduated with first honors in 1796. Deciding to enter the ministry, he pursued a course of theological study, in part privately and in part with Dr. Charles Backus of Somers, Conn. Late in 1798 he was ordained pastor of the church at Newbury (now West Newbury, Mass.), his only charge.

At that time a schism seemed imminent in the orthodox Congregationalism of Massachusetts, with the Hopkinsians, or extreme Calvinists, on the one side, and the Old Calvinists of more moderate views on the other. Between these parties Woods was destined to play the part of mediator. He became a contributor to the Hopkinsian *Massachusetts Missionary Magazine* in 1803 and also to the Old Calvinist *Panoplist* in 1805, and his irenic efforts led to the consolidation of the two publications in 1808. In like manner the Hopkinsian Massachusetts Missionary Society of 1799 and the Old Calvinist Massachusetts General Association of 1803 owed their union to his conciliatory spirit. The Hopkinsians had projected a theological seminary at Newbury, and the Old Calvinists, one at Andover, and each party had settled on Woods as its professor of theology. His wise measures contributed largely to the consolidation of the two foundations at Andover, where, at the opening of the Seminary in 1808, he became the first professor of theology, and so continued for thirty-eight years.

In his theological opinions Woods never swerved from the moderate Calvinism of his earlier maturity. While not brilliant, his teaching was thoughtful and solid; he was courteous and patient and had a genuine interest in his students. While not by nature a controversialist, he nevertheless participated in the famous "Wood'n Ware Controversy" (1820–22) with Prof. Henry Ware, 1764–1845 [*q.v.*], of Cambridge, a pamphlet war over certain doctrines of Calvinism. Of a polemic character, also, are his *Letters to Nathaniel W. Taylor* (1830) and *An Examination of the Doctrine of Perfection as Held by Rev. Asa Mahan . . . and Others* (1841).

In addition to numerous pamphlets, he was the author of the following books: *Lectures on Infant Baptism* (1828); *Lectures on the Inspiration of the Scriptures* (1829); "Letters to Young Ministers" in *The Spirit of the Pilgrims*, February–July 1832; *An Essay on Native Depravity* (1835); *Lectures on Church Government* (1844); *Lectures on Swedenborgianism* (1846); *Theology of the Puritans* (1851). Some of the foregoing material is also included in *The Works of Leonard Woods, D.D.* (5 vols., 1850–51). His last years were devoted to the writing of his *History of the Andover Theological Seminary*, which was first published by his grandson in 1885.

Woods was one of the founders of the American Board of Commissioners for Foreign Missions in 1810, and was a member of its prudential committee from 1819 to 1844. He was a founder of the American Tract Society in 1814, the Education Society in 1815, and the American Temperance Society in 1826. His first wife was Abigail Wheeler, whom he married Oct. 8, 1799, and by whom he had four sons, one of whom was Leonard [*q.v.*], and six daughters. After her death in 1846 he married the widow of Dr. Ansel Ives of New York, who survived him. He died in Andover.

[E. A. Lawrence, *A Discourse Delivered at the Funeral of Rev. Leonard Woods* (1854), and "Leonard Woods," *Congregational Quart.*, Apr. 1859; W. B. Sprague, *Annals of the Am. Pulpit*, vol. II (1857); Williston Walker, *Ten New England Leaders* (1901); F. E. Blake, *Hist. of the Town of Princeton . . . Mass.* (1915), vol. II; H. K. Rowe, *Hist. of Andover Theological Sem.* (1933); *Congregationalist*, Sept. 8, 1854; *Boston Transcript*, Aug. 25, 1854.]   F. T. P.

WOODS, LEONARD (Nov. 24, 1807–Dec. 24, 1878), college president and clergyman, was born in Newbury, Mass. His father, Leonard [*q.v.*], was an influential member of the early faculty of Andover Theological Seminary; his mother, Abigail Wheeler, was a woman of marked character and ability. Upon graduating from Phillips Academy, Andover, Leonard entered Dartmouth, but after less than one term removed to Union College, Schenectady, N. Y., where he was graduated with the degree of bachelor of arts at the head of his class in 1827. His feats in the composition of Greek iambics and hexameters were regarded as remarkable. Prof. Charles Carroll Everett [*q.v.*] pictures him in college (*post*, p. 7) as of light, spare form, of almost feminine softness of feature allied with manly firmness, resolution and capacity for rather uncommon muscular performances. Upon his graduation President Eliphalet Nott [*q.v.*] predicted that he might become a distinguished linguist or mathematician or a man of general literature (Everett, p. 9).

He chose to enter the ministry, however, going to Andover Theological Seminary, where he completed his course in 1830. The next two years he spent as Abbot Resident at Andover, living the life of a scholarly recluse and devoting ten hours a day to his books. In addition to giving some instruction, he prepared *Lectures on Christian Theology* (2 vols., 1831–33), a translation of the work of G. C. Knapp. This achievement gave him a considerable reputation as a scholar and as a theologian. In 1830 he was licensed to preach by the Londonderry Presbytery, and in 1833 was ordained by the Third Presbytery of New York, having preached acceptably at the Laight Street Church. For the next three years he was editor of the *Literary and Theological Review* in New York City, but was called in 1836 to the chair of Biblical literature at the Bangor (Me.) Theological Seminary.

In 1839, before he reached the age of thirty-two, he was chosen the fourth president of Bowdoin College, in which position he remained for twenty-seven years—the longest administration in the history of Bowdoin, except that of William De Witt Hyde [*q.v.*]. He brought to the office an excellent theological training, sound if not brilliant scholarship, an impressive reputation as a university preacher, and a character that soon inspired affection and respect. During the long term of his presidency he strove to substitute personal influence for the more formal college discipline of the day. He relied very largely on the honor of the young men under his charge and often made a deep impression upon the students by his own attitude and character. At one time, for example, he had certain intemperate students join with him in a pledge of total abstinence for the remainder of their course. He was an excellent teacher, employing the recitation and not the lecture method. He was largely responsible for the planning and erection of King Chapel. He was likewise instrumental in winning for the college the reversionary interest in the estate of James Bowdoin, displaying in the long drawn out litigation remarkable legal learning and acumen. In 1840 he traveled abroad, receiving impressions that much influenced his administration. At Oxford he met Stanley and Newman and other leaders of the Oxford movement, writing "Dr. Pusey has treated me as a

brother" (Park, *post*, p. 44). In Paris he dined with Louis Philippe, where it is recorded "he interested the king, and charmed the queen, and captivated the princesses" (*Ibid.*, p. 45). He spent some hours at the Vatican with Pope Gregory XVI, conversing in Latin and winning the Pope's admiration both for his scholarship and his charm.

Toward the close of his administration his popularity suffered from the fact that, an extreme pacifist, he was not in sympathy during the Civil War with the cause of the North. In 1865, however, he presided with his usual grace at Commencement, when he conferred the degree of doctor of laws upon General Grant. The next year he resigned, partly because both his attitude toward the war and his stand against sectarian influences in education were unpopular, and partly because of impairment of health. In 1867 he went abroad and engaged in historical studies on the early history of Maine. Returning to Brunswick, he continued his researches until on Aug. 8, 1873, his library, the apple of his eye, was destroyed by a disastrous fire with the loss not only of books but of precious manuscripts. This experience broke his health and spirit, and for the rest of his life he was an invalid. He died in Boston and was buried in Andover.

Woods never married. His life was that of the scholar and divine who, though he was called to an administrative post, seemed to have been an idealist and to have preserved the independence of one who always lived somewhat apart from the world. His personality was more potent than his written words. His mind has well been described as that of the best type of English churchman. He was catholic in his tastes and studies, but the center of all his hopes and interests was in religion. His motto was "First, that what is true is useful, and, secondly, that it ought to be uttered whether it is useful or not."

[Nehemiah Cleaveland and A. S. Packard, *Hist. of Bowdoin College* (1882); L. C. Hatch, *The Hist. of Bowdoin College* (1927); E. A. Park, *The Life and Character of Leonard Woods, D.D., LL.D.* (1880); C. C. Everett, *Leonard Woods, A Discourse* (1879); *Union Alumni Mo.*, Jan. 1916; *Gen. Cat. of the Theological Sem., Andover, Mass., 1808–1908* (n.d.); *Boston Transcript*, Dec. 26, 1878.] K. C. M. S.

WOODS, ROBERT ARCHEY (Dec. 9, 1865–Feb. 18, 1925), settlement worker, sociologist, and reformer, was born in the East Liberty section of Pittsburgh, Pa. He was of Scotch-Irish stock, the fourth of five children of Robert Woods, an emigrant from Londonderry, Ireland, and Mary Ann (Hall) Woods, whose parents had emigrated from Belfast. Prepared in the public schools of Pittsburgh, Woods entered Amherst

College, where he came under the influence of Charles E. Garman [*q.v.*], professor of philosophy. He was graduated in 1886, and then went to Andover Theological Seminary. Uncomfortable about Scotch Presbyterian dogma, here he flung himself wholeheartedly into Dr. William Jewett Tucker's courses in social economics, the first to be offered in a theological seminary. He read voluminously on social questions, visited New York and Boston to meet leaders of labor unions and to study reform movements, and wrote on social topics for religious and secular papers. He spent part of one summer assisting the chaplain of Concord Reformatory. In 1890 Dr. Tucker [*q.v.*] sent him to England to study reform movements. He resided in Toynbee Hall during part of 1890–91, and was deeply influenced by the founder of settlement work, the Rev. Samuel A. Barnett.

During the latter half of 1891 Woods lectured at Andover, published his book, *English Social Movements* (1891), and in December was placed by Dr. Tucker in charge of opening Andover House in Boston, the first "settlement" in that city and the fifth in the United States. Under Woods, who was its head until his death, Andover House (renamed South End House in 1895) became one of the most important laboratories in social science in the United States. His book, *The City Wilderness,* published in 1898, was the first thorough-going study of a depressed area in an American city, based on the method of Charles Booth's monumental *Life and Labour of the People of London* (9 vols., 1892–97). It was followed by a companion study of the north and west ends of Boston, *Americans in Process* (1902). These studies laid the foundation of Woods's outstanding contribution to sociology and social work—the concept that the neighborhood or village is the primary community unit, and that towns, cities, metropolitan areas, the nation itself, are "federations" of neighborhoods. He called his collected essays and papers, published in 1923, *Neighborhood in Nation-Building.*

Woods located the buildings of South End House in three highly individualized neighborhoods. He set up fellowships for study and social research at Amherst and Dartmouth colleges, Harvard and Brown universities, to attract and prepare men for service in the field of social work. He lectured on social ethics at Andover Theological Seminary, 1890–95, and at the Episcopal Theological School, Cambridge, 1896–1914. Though he distrusted private ease, he toiled in season and out to secure public advantages such as parks, playgrounds, gymnasiums, schools, libraries, museums, and concerts. He believed in and strove for public licensing of occupations with physical or moral hazards, was a leader in the state and national prohibition movement, urged public supervision and discipline of all forms of individual indulgence and excess, and ceaselessly advocated governmental commissions to supervise and review the activities of public service corporations. His influence was most important in maintaining the intellectual integrity of the settlement movement against its besetting sin of sentimentality. He spared neither himself nor anyone else in the search for realities. He organized the settlements of Boston into a federation and brought about the organization of the National Federation of Settlements in 1911, serving as its secretary until 1923 and then as president until his death. The recreation and the neighborhood planning movements had the way prepared for them by Woods's ideas. With Albert J. Kennedy he wrote *Handbook of Settlements* (1911), *Young Working Girls* (1913), and the authoritative text on the history and accomplishment of settlements in the United States, *The Settlement Horizon* (1922). His last publication of any consequence was in different vein: a campaign biography, *The Preparation of Calvin Coolidge* (1924).

Woods married Eleanor Howard Bush in Cambridge, Mass., Sept. 18, 1902. In person he was a little over six feet tall, massive in build, with finely modeled aquiline features. Calm, affable, soft-spoken, kindly, reserved to the point of diffidence, there was that about him which made the tough-minded hesitate to stir him. His deep-seated mysticism was held in check by loyalty to objective facts. He had a sensory equipment of unusual delicacy which he distrusted more than he enjoyed. Seeking a fine result, he stripped off all that was extraneous: alcohol, tea and coffee, tobacco, sexual passion, luxuries of any kind, he looked upon as hindrances to self-fulfillment, hence fundamentally anti-social. The aspect of beauty which stirred him most was the generous and heroic movement of the soul.

[Eleanor H. Woods, *Robert A. Woods* (1929); *Amherst Coll. Biog. Record* (1927); *Who's Who in America,* 1924–25; *Boston Transcript,* Feb. 19, 1925; personal acquaintance.] A.J.K.

WOODS, WILLIAM ALLEN (May 16, 1837–June 29, 1901), jurist, was born in Marshall County, near Farmington, Tenn., the youngest of three children of Allen Newton Woods and his wife, who was a daughter of William D. Ewing. His father, a theological student, died at the age of twenty-six, when young Woods was but a month old. Both of his grandfathers were well-to-do slave-owning farmers of Scotch-Irish descent, but his father was a strong abolitionist. When he was seven years old, his mother married Capt. John Miller, also an abolitionist, who in 1847 moved to Davis County, Iowa, with his wife and her children. The death of his stepfather shortly thereafter put Woods to work on his mother's farm at the age of ten. During the next few years his desire to earn money for an education carried him through a gamut of occupations from field and forest to brick yard, sawmill, grist mill, and finally to a clerkship in the village store. Meanwhile he attended the local school for several months each year, in his sixteenth year becoming a student in the Troy Academy and a year later a teacher in the same school. In the fall of 1855 he was sufficiently prepared to enter Wabash College at Crawfordsville, Ind. Graduating from the classical department in 1859, he immediately became a tutor in the college, and in the fall of 1860 became a teacher at Marion, Ind. The attention of his students was diverted by the opening events of the Civil War, however, and his school completely dissolved after the first battle of Bull Run.

An ardent believer in the Union cause, Woods immediately enlisted, but an injured foot disabled him for service. After his graduation from college he had privately studied law. A military career now being denied him, he definitely chose the law as his profession and in 1861 was admitted to the bar at Marion, Ind. One year later he removed to Goshen and opened an office. Following two years in the state legislature (1867–69), where he served on the judiciary committee, he was elected, in 1873 and again in 1878, judge of the thirty-fourth judicial circuit of Indiana. In 1880 he was elected to the supreme court of the state, but had served only two years when, upon the appointment of President Arthur, he became judge of the United States district court for Indiana. After serving in this capacity until Mar. 17, 1892, he was appointed by President Harrison as judge of the seventh United States circuit court, a position he held until his death, rounding out a judicial career of twenty-eight years in four different courts. After he became a federal judge he made his home in Indianapolis.

The most widely known case in which Woods served as judge was *United States* vs. *Debs* (64 *Federal Reporter,* 724), in which he granted an injunction against strikers interfering with trains carrying the United States mails, and then for violation of the injunction ordered the imprisonment of Eugene Debs [*q.v.*] for a term of six months. In this action Woods was sustained by the Supreme Court of the United States (158 *United States,* 564). Criticism of the opinion ran so high that Woods felt called upon to write an article in defense of the power of the federal courts to imprison for a contempt of the kind committed by Debs ("Injunction in the Federal Courts," *Yale Law Journal,* April 1897).

Woods was of large frame and of impressive appearance, and was fearless in the expression of his opinions. Inclined somewhat to combativeness, he was ever ready to meet an opponent in debate. His judicial opinions, though not weighted with citations of authorities, were clear and forceful. In political faith he was a Republican and in religion a Presbyterian. On Dec. 6, 1870, he was married to Mata A. Newton of Des Moines, Iowa, by whom he had a son and a daughter. He died at Indianapolis.

[*Who's Who in America,* 1899–1900; G. I. Reed, *Encyc. of Biog. of Ind.,* vol. I (1895); C. W. Taylor, *Biog. Sketches . . . of the Bench and Bar of Ind.* (1895); Will Cumbach and J. B. Maynard, *Men of Progress, Ind.* (1899); *Commemorative Biog. Record of Prominent . . . Men of Indianapolis* (1908); *Chicago Legal News,* July 6, 1901; W. W. Thornton, "The Supreme Court of Ind.," *Green Bag,* June 1892; *Report of the Sixth Ann. Meeting State Bar Asso. of Ind.* (1902); obituaries in *Indianapolis News* and *Indianapolis Jour.,* June 29, 1901.]   G. W. G.

WOODS, WILLIAM BURNHAM (Aug. 3, 1824–May 14, 1887), jurist, brother of Charles Robert Woods [*q.v.*], was born in Newark, Licking County, Ohio. His father, Ezekiel S. Woods, a native of Kentucky, was a farmer and merchant of Scotch-Irish extraction; his mother, Sarah Judith (Burnham) Woods, was of New England stock. After three years at Western Reserve College, Hudson, Ohio, Woods transferred to Yale, where he graduated with honor in 1845. Returning to Newark, he began the study of law in the office of S. D. King, an able attorney with a large practice. After admission to the bar in 1847, he formed a partnership with his preceptor which continued until the outbreak of the Civil War. In 1856 he was elected mayor of Newark and in 1857, being elected as a Democrat to the General Assembly of Ohio, was chosen speaker of the House. Two years later he was returned and became the leader of his party, now the minority. He was bitterly opposed to President Lincoln and his policies and even after the firing upon Fort Sumter counseled delay in passing the "million dollar loan" bill designed to put the state in position to defend itself and to carry out the requests of the President. Very soon, however, he committed himself completely to the cause of the Union and his eloquent speech declaring his intention to stand by the government and urging the unanimous passage of the bill marks the change in the policy of the Democratic party in Ohio. He also successfully urged the passage of a bill exempting the property of volunteers from execution for debt during their service at the front.

In February 1862 he entered military service as lieutenant-colonel of the 76th Ohio Infantry, and during the war, except for three months, was constantly in the field, taking part in the battles of Shiloh, Chickasaw, Bayou Ridge, Arkansas Post (where he was slightly wounded), Jonesville, Lovejoy Station, and Danville. He was also at the sieges of Vicksburg and Jackson and participated in Sherman's march to the sea. When he was mustered out, Feb. 17, 1866, he was a brigadier-general and a brevet major-general.

After the war he settled in Alabama, taking up the practice of law first in Mobile and then in Montgomery, where he also engaged in cotton planting near by. He was now an ardent Republican and as such was active in the reconstruction program of the government, being elected in 1868 as chancellor of the middle chancery division of Alabama. Appointed by President Grant, in 1869, a judge of the United States circuit court for the fifth circuit, which included Georgia and the Gulf states, he moved to Atlanta, where he lived for eleven years. Because of the disorganization of the state courts in these states the work of the federal courts was unusually heavy and difficult. Woods's opinions as circuit judge were reported by himself in the four volumes (1875–83) of *Woods's Reports* of the fifth circuit.

In 1880, upon the resignation of William Strong [*q.v.*] from the Supreme Court of the United States, it seemed generally agreed that his successor should come from the South. "The proper South is now without any representative on the bench," said the *Albany Law Journal*; "She certainly ought to have one, if not two" (Dec. 11, 1880). Accordingly, Woods was appointed by President Hayes and in Dec. 21, 1880, was commissioned as an associate justice of the United States Supreme Court. His service on this bench was only a little over six years but during that time he wrote 218 opinions. During his tenure of office the Supreme Court was determining the question of the civil rights of the negro under the new amendments to the Constitution. Woods wrote the opinion in *U. S.* vs. *Harris* (106 *U. S.*, 629) which finally determined that the protection of these rights was not to be found in federal statutes or by indictments in the federal courts. He also wrote the opinion in *Presser* vs. *Illinois* (116 *U. S.*, 252) which definitely decided that the Bill of Rights to the federal Constitution including the second amendment in regard to the right to keep and bear arms, was a limitation on the power of the federal government only and in no way applied to the states. Many of his opinions were in patent and equity cases involving intricate details and a mass of testimony, and in these cases he showed an unusual ability in analyzing the complicated record. His opinions, never lengthy, were cogent and free from all display of rhetoric.

Woods died in Washington, D. C., survived by his wife, Anne E. Warner of Newark, Ohio, whom he had married June 21, 1855, and by a son and a daughter.

[Woods's opinions appear in 103–119 *U. S. Reports.* For biog. data see: "In Memoriam," 123 *U. S. Reports,* 761; *Am. Law Rev.,* Feb. 1881; II. L. Carson, *The Hist. of the Supreme Court of the U. S.* (1902), II, 480; N. N. Hill, *Hist. of Licking County, Ohio* (1881); *Obit. Record Grads. Yale Univ., 1880–90* (1890); R. H. Burnham, *The Burnham Family* (1869); F. B. Heitman, *Hist. Reg. and Dict. U. S. Army* (1903), vol. I; *Washington Law Reporter,* June 8, 1887; *Washington Post,* May 15, 1887.]

A. H. T.

WOODWARD, AUGUSTUS BREVOORT (1774–June 12, 1827), jurist, political philosopher, the son of John Woodward, a shopkeeper, and his wife, Ann Silvester, was born in New York City and christened Nov. 6, 1774. He was named Elias Brevoort for his mother's uncle by marriage, but he later exchanged Elias for Augustus, occasionally using both names. At fifteen he entered Columbia College, graduating in the class of 1793. His family had moved to Philadelphia, and he spent a short time there as an employee in the Treasury Department. In 1795, while living in Rockbridge County, Va., he met Thomas Jefferson, whose admirer and friend he became. After a short residence in Greenbrier County, now in West Virginia, he received a legacy of £150 under the will of Elias Brevoort, and in 1797 went to Georgetown, D. C., where he engaged in the practice of law and speculated in real estate.

In addition to conducting a satisfactory law practice, he gave considerable time to scientific conjecture and civic affairs. In 1801 he published his first book, *Considerations on the Substance of the Sun,* and in that and the following year took an active part in obtaining the incorporation of the City of Washington, being elected a member of its first council. During the years 1801–03 he published under the pseudonym Epaminondas a series of eight pamphlets with the title *Considerations on the Government of the Territory of Columbia.* He was employed by Oliver Pollock [*q.v.*] to present his claim to Congress, and published his argument, *A Representation of the Case of Oliver Pollock,* in 1803, with a *Supplement to the Representation* in the same year; they were reprinted together in 1806.

In February 1805 President Jefferson appointed Woodward one of the three judges of the new Territory of Michigan and he removed to Detroit in June. For that city, which had recently been destroyed by fire, he prepared a new plan based upon the plan of the city of Washington; this plan was adopted, though later greatly modified, and the main street at right angles to the Detroit River was named Woodward Avenue. The governor and the three judges formed the legislature of the territory, but it was Woodward who compiled its early laws, *The Laws of Michigan* (1806), known as "The Woodward Code." At the request of citizens of Detroit he passed the winter of 1805–06 in Washington, obtaining needed legislation regarding the title of lands in Michigan. In 1809 he published *Considerations on the Executive Government of the United States of America* and in 1811, in the Philadelphia *Aurora,* a series of articles relating to the establishment of a department of domestic affairs in the national government.

Woodward was the dominant figure in the court and legislative body of Michigan and was often in opposition to the governor, William Hull [*q.v.*]. After the surrender of Detroit in 1812 he was the only federal official who stayed in the city, but in February 1813 he went to Washington, where he remained until the fall of 1814. While there he completed a book which had been in preparation for several years, *A System of Universal Science,* published in 1816. An elaborate attempt at a classification of knowledge and the nomenclature of its divisions, it contained the idea which was expanded in 1817 in an act drawn by Woodward and passed by the governor and judges creating the "Catholepistemiad, or University, of Michigania." To this institution which began at once to function in a small way upon the appointment of its faculty—the Rev. John Monteith and the Rev. Gabriel Richard [*q.v.*], the corporate existence of the University of Michigan has been traced by judicial decision.

A law passed by Congress in 1823 provided that the terms of the judges of Michigan should expire Feb. 1, 1824. President Monroe expected to reappoint Woodward, but at the last moment was dissuaded by false testimony relating to his character and habits and did not make the appointment; Monroe soon became satisfied that he had been misled, however, and when a vacancy occurred in a federal court in Florida, appointed Woodward to that position in August 1824. Here he served until his death, at Tallahassee, less than three years later.

In 1825 he collected and published under the title *The Presidency of the United States* a series of articles criticizing the Cabinet system which had appeared in the *National Journal* of Washington. In Florida as well as in Detroit he was active in encouraging movements for intellectual and social improvement. He was interested in real estate in Washington, in Detroit, and in Tallahassee; as part owner of the land covered by the present city of Ypsilanti, Mich., he was responsible for its name.

Woodward never married. He was a man of strong character, interested in many things, a thorough lawyer, positive and independent in his views, regardless of popularity, somewhat eccentric, and occasionally arbitrary. His philosophic and political ideas were at times visionary, but his plan for the "University of Michigania," though ridiculously pedantic in some respects, indicates an advanced notion of the duty of the state toward education.

[Woodward MSS. in Burton Hist. Coll., Detroit Pub. Lib.; *Mich. Pioneer and Hist. Colls.,* vols. VIII (1886), XII (1887), XXIX (1901); *Mich. Hist. Mag.,* Oct. 1925; Charles Moore, *Governor, Judge, and Priest; Detroit 1805–1815* (1891), and "Augustus Brevoort Woodward," in *Records of the Columbia Hist. Soc.,* vol. IV (1901); B. A. Hinsdale, *Hist. of the Univ. of Mich.* (1906); *Daily Nat. Intelligencer* (Washington, D. C.,), July 7, 1827.]　　　　　　W. L. J—s.

WOODWARD, CALVIN MILTON (Aug. 25, 1837–Jan. 12, 1914), educator, was born near Fitchburg, Mass. Great-great-grandson of John Woodward who settled at Westminster, Mass., in 1751, he was sixth among eleven children of Isaac Burnapp Woodward, Unitarian farmer and bricklayer, and Eliza Wetherbee, his wife. The boy attended the common schools and supported himself in Harvard College, where he was graduated in 1860 with distinction. In 1862–63 he was a captain in the 48th Massachusetts Volunteers, but except for this period spent the Civil War years as principal of the Brown High School in Newburyport, Mass., where he married Fanny Stone Balch, Sept. 30, 1863. In 1865 he became vice-principal and teacher of mathematics in the academy of the newly organized Washington University, St. Louis, Mo. In 1869 he was made professor of geometry in the university and the next year dean of the polytechnic school and Thayer Professor of Mathematics and Applied Mechanics. He served as dean until 1896, and when the school of engineering and architecture was reorganized in 1901, he returned to the dean's office. This post he distinguished until his retirement in 1910.

As originator and director from its organization of the St. Louis Manual Training School, opened in 1880 under the auspices of Washington University, he accomplished his most important work. A large institution for general education on a new and definite plan, admitting boys as young as fourteen, this school became a leading educational experiment of the time and was the model for similar schools quickly established in other cities. Woodward declared the essential feature of manual training to be "systematic study of tools, processes and materials" (*Report of the Commissioner of Education, . . . 1903*, 1905, I, 1019), and urged its adoption not only to aid those inclined to industrial life, but as a means of assisting all boys to discover their "inborn capacities and aptitudes whether in the direction of literature, science, engineering or the practical arts" (*Ibid.*, pp. 1019–20). For girls he advocated domestic science as manual training's counterpart.

Woodward's community was large. In 1886 on invitation from the Royal Commissioner of Education for the United Kingdom he delivered a series of lectures on manual education in Manchester. He was a member of the St. Louis board of education from 1877 to 1879 and from 1897 to his death (president, 1899–1900 and 1903–04), and of the board of curators of the University of Missouri from 1891 to 1897 (president, 1894–97). He was president of the American Association for the Advancement of Science, 1905–06, of the St. Louis Academy of Science, 1907–08, and of the North Central Association of Colleges and Secondary Schools, 1909–10. His publications include: *A History of the St. Louis Bridge* (1881), *The Manual Training School* (1887), *Manual Training in Education* (1890), *What Shall We Do With Our Boys?* (1898), *Rational and Applied Mechanics* (1912), "The Change of Front in Education" (*Proceedings of the American Association for the Advancement of Science,* vol. L, 1901), "Lines of Progress in Engineering" (*Ibid.,* vol. LIV, 1904), "The Science of Education" (*Ibid.,* vol. LVII, 1907), "The Rise and Progress of Manual Training" (*Report of the Commissioner of Education, 1893–94,* 1896, vol. I), "At What Age Do Pupils Withdraw from the Public Schools?" (*Ibid., 1894–95,* 1896, vol. II), "Manual, Industrial and Technical Education in the United States" (*Ibid., 1903,* vol. I) and numerous articles in periodicals.

Survived by his widow and three daughters from among their nine children, Woodward died at his home, two days after being seized by paralysis. He was buried in Oak Hill Cemetery, Kirkwood, Mo. The day he was stricken he had spent soliciting funds for a manual training school for negro boys. In equipment, love for his work, and kindling enthusiasm he approximated the ideal teacher.

[W. S. Heywood, *Hist. of Westminster, Mass.* (1893); *Who's Who in America,* 1914–15; Wm. Hyde and H. L. Conard, *Encyc. of the Hist. of St. Louis* (1899), vol. IV; *Jour. of the Asso. of Engineering Societies,* Mar. 1914; L. F. Anderson, *Hist. of Manual and Indus. School Educ.* (1926); C. P. Coates, *Hist. of the Manual Training School of Washington Univ.* (U. S. Bureau of Educ., 1923), "The Veering Winds," *Industrial Arts Mag.,* Sept. 1926, and "A Semi-Centennial Tribute to the Memory of Calvin Woodward," *Industrial Education,* Oct. 1926; C. A. Bennett, "Fifty Years Ago," *Ibid.,* June 1929; *St. Louis Post-Dispatch,* Jan. 12, 1914, and *St. Louis Republic,* Mar. 10, 1910, Jan. 12, 13, 1914; information from Woodward's daughter, Mrs. Fanny Woodward Mabiey, of Webster Groves, Mo.]

I. D.

WOODWARD, HENRY (c. 1646–c. 1686), surgeon, first English settler in South Carolina and pioneer of English expansion in the lower South, was perhaps a native of Barbados; he may have been related to Thomas Woodward, surveyor of Albemarle County, N. C., in 1665. As a youth he joined the Carolina settlement begun in 1664 near Cape Fear. In 1666 he accompanied Robert Sandford, secretary of Clarendon County, on his voyage of exploration to Port Royal. There he volunteered to remain among the Indians to learn their language, and was given "formall possession of the whole Country to hold as Tennant att Will" of the Lords Proprietors of Carolina (*Collections, post,* p. 79), but the Spaniards shortly appeared and carried him off to Florida. He lived for a time with the parish priest of St. Augustine, professed Catholicism, was made official surgeon, and acquired important information concerning the affairs of the Spaniards, as he had earlier of the Indians on the northern Florida border. In 1668 he escaped with the buccaneer Robert Searles when the latter raided St. Augustine. For a time he sailed the Caribbean as surgeon of a privateer, hoping to return to England with his report. Shipwrecked at Nevis in August 1669, he took passage with the Carolina fleet of 1669–70, to become, as interpreter and Indian agent, the most useful servant of the Proprietors in South Carolina.

Woodward's unique services in exploration and Indian diplomacy began in 1670 with his journey inland to "Chufytachyqj" (Cofitachique?) on the Santee. He was early instructed by Lord Ashley, later Earl of Shaftesbury, to make private searches for gold and silver; and in 1671 he undertook a secret mission by land to Virginia. In 1674 Shaftesbury made him his agent in opening the interior Indian trade, and in 1677 his deputy. In the fall of 1674 Woodward traveled alone to the town of the warlike Westo on the Savannah River, subsequently describing his journey in "A Faithful Relation of My Westoe Voiage" (Salley, *post*). The alliance he then formed was for several years the cornerstone of Carolina Indian relations; with arms supplied by Woodward the Westo began their destructive raids against the Spanish missions in Guale (coastal Georgia). In 1680–81, however, the South Carolina planters, jealous of the monopoly established by the Proprietors in 1677 over the inland trade, attacked the Westo and expelled the remnant of the tribe from the province, and Woodward was in disgrace. In 1682 he went to England and secured pardon and reinstatement. There he also obtained from the Proprietors an extraordinary commission to explore the interior beyond the Savannah River.

It would seem that Woodward had already established some sort of relations with the Lower Creeks, perhaps as early as 1675. He now pressed the trading frontier of Carolina rapidly westward to their towns on the middle Chattahoochee. Lord Cardross at Stuart's Town (Port Royal) had hoped to engross the Creek trade, and he arrested Woodward at Yamacraw in the spring of 1685; but by summer Woodward had led a dozen Charles Town traders to the Kasihta and Coweta towns. There he precipitated a sharp conflict with Franciscan missionaries and Spanish soldiers from Apalache. The issue was at first doubtful; but by 1686, when Woodward, ill, made the dangerous journey back to Charles Town in a litter, followed by 150 Indian burdeners laden with peltry, he had laid a firm foundation for the English alliance with the Lower Creeks. Woodward apparently never returned to the West, and probably died shortly after his greatest adventure.

After the death of his wife, Margaret, he married a widow, Mrs. Mary Browne, daughter of a leading Carolina planter, Col. John Godfrey. Among his numerous distinguished descendants were Robert Y. Hayne and the poet Paul Hamilton Hayne [*qq.v.*].

[J. W. Barnwell, "Dr. Henry Woodward, the First English Settler in S. C., and Some of His Descendants," *S. C. Hist. and Geneal. Mag.*, Jan., July 1907; *S. C. Hist. Soc. Colls.*, vol. V (1897); Woodward's "Faithfull Relation" in *Narratives of Early Carolina* (1911), ed. by A. S. Salley, Jr.; *Cal. of State Papers, Colonial Ser., America and West Indies*, 1669–88 (1889–99); H. E. Bolton and Mary Ross, *The Debatable Land* (1925); V. W. Crane, *The Southern Frontier, 1670–1732* (1928), with references therein.]   V. W. C.

WOODWARD, JOSEPH JANVIER (Oct. 30, 1833–Aug. 17, 1884), army medical officer, was born in Philadelphia, Pa., the son of Joseph Janiver and Elizabeth Graham (Cox) Woodward. He was a brother of Annie Aubertine Woodward Moore [*q.v.*]. After graduation from the Central High School, Philadelphia, he entered the University of Pennsylvania, where he received the degree of M.D. in 1853. He began practice in Philadelphia, and associated himself with the University of Pennsylvania as demonstrator in operative surgery and clinical surgical assistant. Later he was placed in charge of the surgical clinic of the school dispensary. With the onset of the Civil War he entered the medical corps of the army as an assistant surgeon in June 1861. He participated in the first battle of Bull Run as surgeon of an artillery regiment and took part in all the engagements of the Army of the Potomac until May 1862, when he was assigned to the office of the surgeon general in Washington. Here, in addition to the duty of planning hospital construction, he was surgical operator for major cases in the Judiciary Square and Church military hospitals, and had charge of medical records. When the Army Medical Museum was established, he became assistant to John Hill Brinton [*q.v.*], the curator. In 1869 he was put in charge of the preparation of the medical section of the *Medical and Surgical History of the War of the Rebellion,* for which George Alexander Otis [*q.v.*] prepared the surgical section. This monumental work appeared in six volumes (1870–88), the first two under Woodward's name. For careful and painstaking research in the literature of the subjects covered they are unsurpassed. On June 26, 1876, he became a major.

While practising in Philadelphia Woodward had developed an interest in pathological histology and microscopy, and in the museum he was assigned to work of a similar character. He soon began experimentation with the new science of photo-micrography, which he was one of the first to apply to the uses of pathology and in which he attained an international reputation. The results of his earlier experiments are recorded in a paper "On Photomicrography with the Highest Powers, as Practiced in the Army Medical Museum" (*American Journal of Science and Arts,* Sept. 1866). He was instrumental in developing many improvements in the photomicrographic camera and its lighting. The results of his later observations are covered by numerous journal articles and a series of letters to the surgeon general, notable among the latter the *Report on the Magnesium and Electric Lights as Applied to Photo-micrography* (1870) and the *Report on the Oxy-Calcium Light as Applied to Photo-micrography* (1870). Other writings include *The Hospital Steward's Manual* (1862) and the medical section of the *Catalogue of the United States Army Medical Museum* (1866–67). He is credited with the authorship of *Ada, a Tale,* published in 1852 under the pseudonym of Janvier. He was a member of the National Academy of Sciences, the Association for the Advancement of Science, and the Washington Philosophic Society, and the first army officer to hold the presidency of the American Medical Association (1881). He was in constant attendance upon President Garfield during the long weeks that intervened between the shooting and his death in September 1881. Woodward was of a sensitive, highstrung organization, and the confinement, anxiety, and labor incident to this duty proved too much for a mind and body already overstrained by incessant work. His *Official Record of the Post-Mortem Examination of the Body of Pres. James A. Garfield* (1881) is practically his last writing. The last several years of his life were spent on sick leave, the earlier part in Switzerland. An ever-deepening melancholia was terminated by his death in a sanitarium at Wawa, Pa., from injury due to a fall.

Woodward was twice married. A son of the first marriage, Janvier Woodward, became an officer in the navy. His second wife, who survived him, was Blanche Wendell of Washington, D. C.

[J. M. Toner, *Jour. Am. Medic. Asso.*, Aug. 1884; J. S. Billings, in *Nat. Acad. of Sci., Biog. Memoirs*, vol. II (1886); G. V. Henry, *Military Record of Civilian Appointments in the U. S. Army*; J. C. Hemmeter, in *Military Surgeon*, June 1923; *Medic. News*, Aug. 30, 1884; D. S. Lamb, *A Hist. of the Army Medic. Museum, 1862–1917* (n.d.); F. B. Heitman, *Hist. Reg. ... U. S. Army* (1903); obituary, War Dept., Surgeon General's Office, 1884; obituary in *Press* (Phila.), Aug. 19, 1844; War Dept. records.]　　J. M. P.

WOODWARD, ROBERT SIMPSON (July 21, 1849–June 29, 1924), engineer, mathematical physicist, administrator, was born at Rochester, Mich., the son of Lysander Woodward, an enterprising, public-spirited, and progressive farmer, and of Peninah A. (Simpson) Woodward, of New England stock. He graduated with the degree of C.E. from the University of Michigan in 1872 and immediately entered the United States Lake Survey to spend some ten years in triangulation along the Great Lakes; the two years following this period, 1882–84, he spent with the federal commission appointed to observe the transit of Venus.

In 1884 he was appointed astronomer on the United States Geological Survey and, shortly thereafter, its chief geographer. At that time the Geological Survey was comparatively new, but its members—including G. K. Gilbert, Clarence King, and Thomas C. Chamberlin [qq.v.]—were enthusiastic and eager for accomplishment. The atmosphere stimulated original work and during the next decade Woodward wrote his most important scientific papers. These contributions were of a geophysical nature, having in part to do with the deformation of the earth's surface as the result of the removal or addition of load over a large area and in part with the secular cooling of the earth. He also studied the field methods for topographic mapping and for primary and secondary triangulation and put them on a practical engineering basis. The years 1890–93 he spent with the Coast and Geodetic Survey, working on the problem of base-line measurement in primary triangulation. He developed the iced-bar apparatus for measuring base-lines and for calibrating steel tapes and was the first to prove that base-lines could be measured with sufficient accuracy by means of long steel tapes. This work was of fundamental importance to geodesy and resulted in the saving of much expense and time in field work; also it placed the primary triangulation work of the Coast and Geodetic Survey on a higher plane than had previously been possible. In 1893 Woodward was appointed professor of mechanics and mathematical physics at Columbia University; shortly thereafter he became dean of its College of Pure Science. Here he spent twelve years as teacher and administrator and was remarkably successful in both fields. In 1904 he was chosen president of the Carnegie Institution of Washington, in which post he served through 1920. The earlier years were a critical period for the Institution, which needed his mature judgment and experience to discriminate between worth-while projects and the far greater number of suggested projects of doubtful promise. His common sense and sense of humor, however, enabled him to meet the problems that confronted him and his sane and kindly attitude bred confidence that he would handle fairly each proposal submitted.

Woodward was awarded many honors; he was a member of the National Academy of Sciences and served as president of the American Association for the Advancement of Science (1900), the American Mathematical Society (1898–1900), the New York Academy of Sciences (1900–01), the Washington Academy of Sciences (1915). From 1884 to 1924 he was one of the editors of *Science*, and in 1888–89, of the *Annals of Mathematics*. With Mansfield Merriman, he edited *Higher Mathematics* (1896), a college textbook, to which he himself contributed the chapter on probability and the theory of errors. He was the author of more than a hundred papers, published in various scientific journals.

Woodward married, in 1876, Martha Gretton Bond, who with three sons survived him. Simple and friendly in manner, he won and kept the affection of those who knew him and his home was a center of hospitality. He died in Washington, D. C., in his seventy-fifth year.

[F. E. Wright, memoir with full list of writings, in *Bull. Geol. Soc. of America*, vol. XXXVII (1926); *Who's Who in America*, 1924–25; *Science*, July 11, 1924; *Evening Star* (Washington), June 30, 1924.]

F. E. W—t.

WOODWARD, SAMUEL BAYARD (Jan. 10, 1787–Jan. 3, 1850), pioneer expert on mental diseases, was born in Torrington, Conn., the son of Polly (Griswold) and Dr. Samuel Woodward, and a descendant of Dr. Henry Woodward who eimgrated from England in 1635 and settled in Dorchester and later in Northampton, Mass. The boy received his early education in the district school of Torrington and in his father's office. He began the practice of medicine at twenty-one under a license from the medical board of his county. Later he received an honorary degree of M.D. from Yale. In 1810 he went to Wethersfield, Conn., where he established a practice that made him the sole physician of 3,000 persons for twenty years. In 1815 he married Maria Porter of Hadley. They had eleven children, eight of whom survived their father.

Instrumental in founding the Connecticut Retreat for the Insane in Hartford (1824), Woodward traveled all over the state collecting funds for its establishment and was offered the position of superintendent, but urged instead the appointment of his friend, Dr. Eli Todd [*q.v.*], whose ideals of love and kindness in the treatment of the insane were similar to his own. He refused the position again in 1834, although he was one of the medical visitors of the institution as long as he remained in the vicinity. From 1827 until 1832 he was resident physician at the state prison, and instituted many humane methods in the treatment of prisoners. He was one of the medical examiners of the Yale medical school for several years and was offered a position on the faculty, which he declined. It was his hope to establish an asylum for inebriates, but that dream was never realized. He was elected to the Connecticut Senate on the Democratic ticket in 1830, but refused all later offers of political office. In 1832 the first board of trustees of the Massachusetts State Lunatic Asylum at Worcester appointed him superintendent, and he remained there until 1846, winning a notable reputation. Before his time there had been no adequate accommodations for the relief or custodial care of the insane, and his success in meeting the problem, like that of Todd in Hartford, caused nation-wide comment. His publications were con-

fined chiefly to his reports, of which the Massachusetts legislature alone ordered 3,000 each year, but he also wrote several books, essays, and lyceum lectures. He was the founder and first president of the Association of Medical Superintendents of American Institutions for the Insane (later the American Psychiatric Association), and urged the establishment by Dr. Samuel Gridley Howe [*q.v.*] of what later became the Massachusetts School for Idiotic and Feeble-minded Youth. He was of great aid to other states in passing laws for the feeble-minded, and his services were always in demand as an expert court witness in cases involving mental disorders.

Woodward was six feet, two and one-half inches tall, weighed 260 pounds in his prime, and possessed great physical and mental energy and forcefulness. One of his contemporaries wrote of him that though he was "very civil and accessible to all, he seemed born to command" (Chandler, *post*, p. 133). In 1846, in broken health, he retired to Northampton, where he died, Jan. 3, 1850.

[Sources include S. A. Fisk, in *Boston Medic. and Surgical Jour.*, Jan. 16, 1850; George Chandler, in *Am. Jour. of Insanity*, Oct. 1851; H. A. Kelly and W. L. Burrage, *Am. Medic. Biogs.* (1920), which gives the place of birth as Torringford; unpub. notes of Dr. Henry Barnard in the archives of the Neuro-Psychiatric Institute, Hartford, Conn.; Woodward's reports on the Mass. State Lunatic Asylum, Worcester; obituary in *Worcester Palladium*, Jan. 9, 1850.]

C. C. B.

WOODWORTH, JAY BACKUS (Jan. 2, 1865–Aug. 4, 1925), geologist, born at Newfield, N. Y., was the only child of the Rev. Allen Beach Woodworth and Amanda (Smith) Woodworth. The son inherited a special love for nature, but his concentration on the earth sciences was delayed until his twenty-fifth year. After attending various grammar schools he graduated from the high school at Newark, N. J., and then went into the service of the New York Life Insurance Company and later became an assistant manager in the Edison Illuminating Company of Boston, Mass. In 1890 he entered the Lawrence Scientific School of Harvard University, and, under the inspiration of Nathaniel S. Shaler [*q.v.*], began technical training for his life work. At Harvard in 1894 he won the degree of B.A. with honors. In 1893 he was appointed instructor in geology. In 1901 he became assistant professor and in 1912 associate professor of geology, a position he held until his death. On Sept. 21, 1891, he was married to Genevieve Downs, who died in 1911.

Woodworth was steadily active in advancing geological science. His first publications were concerned with the glaciology of New England, a subject which he studied intensively and fruitfully throughout his professional life. For many years he cooperated with his senior colleague, Shaler, and in 1896 they published "The Glacial Brick Clays of Rhode Island and Southeastern Massachusetts" under the United States Geological Survey (*Seventeenth Annual Report,* 1896), in which Woodworth was listed as assistant geologist for fifteen years. Three years later they published joint memoirs on "The Geology of the Narragansett Basin" (*United States Geological Survey, Monograph No. 33,* 1899), and a report on "The Geology of the Richmond Basin, Virginia" (*United States Geological Survey, Nineteenth Annual Report,* 1899). In 1902 Woodworth independently published a Survey report on the Atlantic coast Triassic coal field. Among the many other products of his researches were important papers on the Pleistocene geology of parts of New York State (*New York State Museum, Bulletin 48,* 1901, and *Bulletin 83,* 1905), and a report on a Shaler Memorial expedition to Brazil and Chile (*Bulletin of the Museum of Comparative Zoology,* vol. LVI, 1912). Woodworth was alive to the value of seismological studies in relation to geology and was a pioneer in this vast field of research. In 1908 he established at Harvard one of the first seismological stations in America, and from that time until the end of his life was the unsalaried director and observer of this station. His records of the passage of earthquake waves of local and distant origin through his station were sent for comparative study to seismological stations elsewhere. The record of his efficient work was a leading reason for the improvement in 1933 of the Harvard station, which is now (1936) one of the best equipped in the world.

During the thirty-two years thousands of Harvard students were taught by Woodworth the principles of geology. By both temperament and scholarship he was equipped to cover the broad subject. In addition, he had much to do with the training of professional geologists at his university. When the United States entered the World War, Woodworth took service as instructor in the Reserve Officers Training Corps and also acted as chairman of a committee of the National Research Council on the use of seismographs in war. He was a member of many scientific societies. He died in Cambridge, survived by his one child, a daughter.

[*Who's Who in America,* 1924–25; W. A. Woodworth, *Descendants of Walter Woodworth of Scituate, Mass.* (1898); Arthur Keith, in *Bull. Geol. Soc. of America,* vol. XXXVII (1926), with bibliog.; W. M. Davis and R. A. Daly, "Geology and Geography," in *The Development of Harvard Univ.* (1930), ed. by S. E. Morison; R. W. Sayles, in *Harvard Grads.' Mag.,* Mar. 1926; J. M. Cattell and D. R. Brimhall, *Am. Men of Sci.* (3rd ed., 1921); obituary in *Boston Transcript,* Aug. 5, 1925.]
          R. A. D.

WOODWORTH, SAMUEL (Jan. 13, 1784–Dec. 9, 1842), playwright, poet, and journalist, was born in Scituate, Mass., the son of Benjamin Woodworth, a Revolutionary soldier, and Abigail (Bryant) Woodworth, and a descendant of Walter Woodworth, freeman of Scituate in 1640. Because his family was poor and the educational advantages of Scituate were meager, young Woodworth had but a desultory schooling. About 1800, determining to learn the printer's trade, he went to Boston, where he served with Benjamin Russell [*q.v.*] an apprenticeship that lasted until 1806. During this time he frequently published verses in the newspapers, and in 1805–06 edited a juvenile paper called the *Fly,* in which John Howard Payne [*q.v.*] seems to have had a part. Because of financial difficulties he was obliged, probably in 1807, to leave his native state. He settled in New Haven, Conn., where he started in 1808 the *Belles-Lettres Repository,* a weekly periodical which lasted less than two months. Expressing his bitterness towards Connecticut in a satirical poem called *New-Haven,* he set forth for Baltimore, where he also stayed but a brief time. He proceeded in 1809 to New York, which now became his permanent home. He at once entered the printing business, and on Sept. 23, 1810, married Lydia Reeder (*New-York Evening Post,* Sept. 24, 1810), by whom he had a large family.

Nominally a printer, Woodworth engaged in countless journalistic and literary pursuits as a means of adding to his slender income. His long journalistic career started with the publication of the *War* (1812–14), a weekly chronicle of America's struggle with Great Britain. In 1817 he became the editor of a newspaper called the *Republican Chronicle,* but the following year he retired from the editorship. The next year (1819) he established the *Ladies' Literary Cabinet,* but in 1820 withdrew as editor for "want of patronage." For a few months in 1821, he published a magazine in miniature form entitled *Woodworth's Literary Casket.* But this failing, he became editor in 1823 of the *New York Mirror,* which his friend, George P. Morris [*q.v.*], had just founded. Though this periodical continued for many years, Woodworth himself, for some unknown reason, severed his connection with it at the close of the first year. Three years later (1827) he made one further journalistic venture in the *Parthenon,* which had but a brief run. During these years of experimentation he also published two Swedenborgian magazines, the

Halcyon Luminary (1812–13) and the *New-Jerusalem Missionary* (1823–24).

To these periodicals and to the press at large Woodworth was a frequent contributor of poetry over the signature "Selim." Three early poems—*New-Haven* (1809), *Beasts at Law* (1811), *Quarter-Day* (1812)—were bitter social satires. His later work, collected by his son in 1861, reveals great productivity, but little artistic merit. He could write with equal ease a patriotic ode, a religious effusion, a sentimental ballad, or a bit of *vers de société*. Yet little has survived save "The Bucket" ("The Old Oaken Bucket") and "The Hunters of Kentucky." In 1816 he also published a novel, *The Champions of Freedom,* the scenes of which were drawn from the War of 1812. In the field of the drama, however, he made a slightly greater contribution to American literature. Although his first play, *The Deed of Gift* (1822), was a somewhat feeble comic opera on a domestic theme, and his second, *La Fayette* (1824), was of no lasting importance, his third attempt, *The Forest Rose* (1825), was "one of the longest-lived American plays before the Civil War" (Coad, *post*, p. 166). The success of this play was due chiefly to his creation of the Yankee character, Jonathan Ploughboy. His *The Widow's Son* (1825), a significant though somewhat less popular drama, was a domestic tragedy laid in New York during the Revolutionary period. "The Cannibals," "Blue Laws," and "The Foundling of the Sea" were plays produced in 1833, but never published. Another drama, *King's Bridge Cottage* (1826), "written by a Gentleman of N. York," has sometimes been attributed to him.

In spite of every effort to eke out an existence, he was repeatedly reduced to poverty. In 1828 and 1829 special theatrical benefits were given to relieve his "pecuniary misfortunes." Finally in February 1837 an attack of apoplexy, resulting in paralysis, incapacitated him for further work. Friends again came forward; benefit performances were given; and he lingered on in his crippled state until 1842. Though his works sometimes reveal a certain asperity of character, the result, in part, of his failures fully to adjust himself to the world of action, yet he was in the main amiable, and had a reputation for great honesty. In religion he was an ardent Swedenborgian.

[Sources include preface to *The Poems, Odes, Songs . . . of Samuel Woodworth* (1818); memoir by G. P. Morris, in *The Poetical Works of Samuel Woodworth* (2 vols., 1861); E. A. and G. L. Duyckinck, *Cyc. of Am. Lit.* (1855), II, 70–71; *Critic*, Jan. 24, Mar. 7, 1829; *N. Y. Mirror*, Mar. 1, 1828, July 29, Oct. 28, Nov. 11, and Dec. 2, 1837, and Dec. 17, 1842 (obituary); *Evening Post* (N. Y.), Nov. 2, 1837; *Autograph Album* (N. Y.), Apr. 1934; A. H. Quinn, *A Hist. of the Am. Drama from the Beginning to the Civil War* (1923); O. S. Coad, in *Sewanee Rev.*, Apr. 1919; information furnished by Kendall B. Taft, who is preparing a biog. of Woodworth. For family hist., see Samuel Deane, *Hist. of Scituate, Mass.* (1831), and *Vital Records of Scituate, Mass.* (1909), I, 418, II, 335. For a fairly complete bibliog., see P. K. Foley, *Am. Authors* (1897). Important Woodworth MSS. are in the N. Y. Pub. Lib. and the colls. of the Hist. Soc. of Pa.]   N. F. A.

WOOL, JOHN ELLIS (Feb. 29, 1784–Nov. 10, 1869), soldier, was born in Newburgh, N. Y. He was only four years old at the death of his father, who had been a soldier under General Wayne in the storming of Stony Point. The mother may have died also about this time, for the child was removed to Troy to live with his grandfather, James Wool, of Schaghticoke, N. Y. His formal education was limited to that of a country school, and at the age of twelve he entered the store of a Troy merchant and remained with him six years. During the next decade he worked at various places and was largely his own schoolmaster; he spent one year reading law in the office of John Russell, an eminent lawyer. When the War of 1812 broke out, he raised and headed a company of volunteers in Troy, and on Apr. 14, 1812, he was commissioned a captain in the 13th Infantry. He was severely wounded at the battle of Queenstown, and was promoted a major in the 29th Infantry on Apr. 13, 1813. For gallant conduct in the battle of Plattsburg he was brevetted a lieutenant-colonel on Sept. 11, 1814. He was made colonel and inspector-general of the army on Apr. 29, 1816, and maintained this grade for more than a quarter of a century. Concurrently he nominally had the grade for several years of lieutenant-colonel of the 6th Infantry, and from Apr. 29, 1826, the brevet rank of brigadier-general for ten years of faithful service in one grade.

In 1832 he was sent by the government to visit the military establishments of Europe for the benefit of the army, and in 1836 he personally aided Winfield Scott [*q.v.*] in the delicate mission of transferring the Cherokee nation westward. On June 25, 1841, he was made a full-fledged brigadier-general, his rank at the opening of the Mexican War. On May 15, 1846, he was ordered to Washington, D. C., whence he was sent to Cincinnati to receive the disorganized volunteers of Kentucky, Tennessee, Ohio, Indiana, Illinois, and Mississippi. Working and traveling incessantly, without a proper staff, he prepared and mustered-in 12,000 volunteers in six weeks. On Aug. 14 he arrived in San Antonio to take over his new command for the intended march through Chihuahua. Immediately he set about obtaining information on the surrounding country, disciplining and training his dispirited and unsoldierly force of 1,400 men, and collecting supplies, so that he was able to start on Sept. 26. After traversing 900 miles of thick, unbroken, hostile country, he arrived in Saltillo on Dec. 22, even though his command had been rendered immobile for twenty-seven days by Taylor's unfortunate armistice. But Wool took advantage of this delay to drill and discipline his men in the wilderness. When orders were received to proceed, he was on his way in two hours. Throughout the march, the men had been forced to level hills, fill ravines, construct bridges, scale mountains, and make roads, but because of Wool's watchfulness and preparedness there was little ill-health and no bloodshed. For sheer audacity and control, his march ranks with that of Xenophon. His celerity and efficiency were largely responsible for the victory of Buena Vista. It was he who selected the fine position at La Angostura and who held the Mexicans while Taylor went back to Saltillo. He was voted a sword and thanks by the Congress "for his distinguished services in the War with Mexico and especially for the skill, enterprise and courage" at Buena Vista. He was also brevetted a major-general, and was presented with a sword by the State of New York.

From 1848 to 1853 he commanded the Eastern Military Division, and from 1854 to 1857 the Department of the Pacific, where in 1856, by active campaign, he suppressed Indian disturbances in Washington and Oregon. From then on he commanded the Department of the East. At the opening of the Civil War he saved Fortress Monroe by timely reënforcements and was afterwards in command of the Department of Virginia. On May 16, 1862, he was regularly made a major-general, and was successively in command of the Middle Military Department and the Department of the East until July 1863. Because of age and infirmity he was retired from active service on Aug. 1, 1863. He died at the age of eighty-five in Troy, N. Y., was given a large military funeral, and was buried in Oakwood Cemetery. Although Wool was a rigid disciplinarian and was superior in organizing ability, he had great personal benignity. He left a bequest of $15,000 to Rensselaer Polytechnic Institute. In Troy a seventy-five-foot monument on which is an inscription by William Cullen Bryant, was erected to his memory and that of his wife, Sarah Moulton, to whom he had been married on Sept. 27, 1810. She survived him only four years.

[H. W. Moulton, *Moulton Annals* (1906); A. J. Weise, *Troy's One Hundred Years* (1891); Francis Baylies, *A Narrative of Maj. Gen. Wool's Campaign in Mexico* (1851); J. H. Smith, *The War with Mexico* (2

vols., 1919); W. H. Powell, *List of Officers of the Army of the U. S., 1779 to 1900* (1900); *U. S. Mag. and Democratic Rev.,* Nov. 1851; F. B. Heitman, *Hist. Reg. U. S. Army* (1903); John Frost, *Am. Generals* (1848); L. B. Cannon, *Personal Reminiscences of the Rebellion* (1895); *Troy Daily Times,* Nov. 10, 1869.]

W. A. G.

WOOLF, BENJAMIN EDWARD (Feb. 16, 1836–Feb. 7, 1901), composer and music critic, was born in London, where his father, Edward Woolf, was a musician, painter, and literary man. His mother was Sarah (Michaels) Woolf. In 1839 the family emigrated to New York, where Edward Woolf conducted orchestras and aided in founding *Judy,* a comic periodical for which he drew many sketches. There were four boys in the family, of whom M. A. Woolf became a well-known caricaturist; Solomon W. Woolf, a mathematician; Albert E. Woolf, an artist, inventor, and chemist. Benjamin was trained in music and drawing by his father, and in academic subjects in the New York public schools. In 1859 he joined the orchestra of the Boston Museum, then conducted by Julius Eichberg [*q.v.*], for whose operetta, *The Doctor of Alcantara,* he wrote the libretto. The success of this piece led Woolf to turn to writing plays and light operas, among which were *The Mighty Dollar, Off to the War,* and more than sixty other pieces, most of them now forgotten but very popular in their day. The operetta, *Pounce & Co., or Capital vs. Labor* (1882), for which Woolf wrote both the words and the music, was an especially effective hit. During his years of intensive composing Woolf lived mostly in Boston, though for two seasons (1864–66) he conducted the orchestra of the Chestnut Street Theatre, Philadelphia. For a short time he was similarly engaged at New Orleans. He was married on Apr. 15, 1867, to Josephine Orton, actress, of the Boston Museum Stock Company.

In 1870 he became a member of the staff of the *Boston Globe.* A year later he had an invitation from Col. Henry J. Parker, Boston publisher, to join the editorial staff of the *Saturday Evening Gazette,* then a prosperous and influential publication. Although the *Gazette* articles were unsigned, Woolf's hand is easily recognized in the reviews of music and the drama during many years. On Parker's death in 1892 he became publisher and editor, but the fortunes of this weekly journal were waning. Leaving the *Gazette,* he became music critic of the *Boston Herald,* and for it he wrote reviews notable for their clarity and severity. Henry M. Dunham [*q.v.*] says of him in recalling the reactions of the younger musicians of the eighties and nineties toward criticism: "We disliked him extremely because of his rough and uncompromising style. He had almost no concession to offer for anyone's shortcomings, and on that very account what he had to say carried additional weight with the artist he was criticising" (*The Life of a Musician*, 1931, p. 220). Philip Hale, on the contrary, long a distinguished music critic, praised Woolf's causticity as employed solely against "incompetence, shams, humbugs, snobs and snobbery in art," and stated that when Woolf began to write for the *Gazette* music criticism in Boston was mere "honey daubing" of local favorites (*Musical Courier, post,* p. 29). This critic, according to Hale's recollection, was never severe towards really promising beginners, to whom he gave personal advice and often financial aid. Woolf continued to do creative as well as critical writing. His last important piece was *Westward Ho,* produced at the Boston Museum in 1894. Essentially a hard-working journalist, living unobtrusively at Brookline, he died suddenly, to be almost as quickly forgotten.

[Sources include *The Am. Hist. and Encyc. of Music,* vol. II (1908), ed. by W. L. Hubbard; Philip Hale, in *Musical Courier,* Feb. 13, 1901, and in *Boston Morning Jour.,* Feb. 8, 1901; *Boston Daily Globe,* Feb. 8, 1901; information from Woolf's nephew, S. J. Woolf of New York City. There is a nearly complete file of the *Sat. Evening Gazette* in the Boston Pub. Lib.]   F. W. C.

WOOLLEY, CELIA PARKER (June 14, 1848–Mar. 9, 1918), settlement worker, clergyman, author, was born at Toledo, Ohio, the daughter of Marcellus Harris and Harriet Maria (Sage) Parker. The family moved to Coldwater, Mich., and Celia spent her girlhood there, graduating from its "female" seminary. On Dec. 29, 1868, she married Jefferson H. Woolley, a young dentist. In 1876 the couple removed to Chicago, and Celia Woolley at once became interested and active in the literary and civic life of the city. She had already begun to write, and for some years her intellectual life expressed itself chiefly through poems, hymns, and stories. Being the child of religious liberals and concerned from early years with religion, she at length decided to study for the ministry, and at forty-six was ordained into the Unitarian fellowship (Oct. 21, 1894) in Geneva, Ill. She served as pastor of the Unitarian Church at Geneva from 1893 to 1896. She then accepted the pastorate of the Independent Liberal Church in Chicago but resigned two years later to spend in lecturing and writing the time she could spare from wifely duties. Moreover, she apparently felt that she had not yet found the vehicle of expression that would enable her to make her most effective contribution to society. She now more and more became interested in social service work, and in 1904

established Frederick Douglass Center, a settlement on the south side of Chicago, for work among negroes. Accompanied by her husband, she took up residence there and, surrounded by the colored people, to whom she unselfishly gave her time and energy, lived there the remaining fourteen years of her life, earnestly trying by this sincere gesture to improve relations between the races. Instead of ostracism, this altruistic expression brought forth sympathy and respect as well as gratifying cooperation from many quarters. Her position of influence in Chicago's cultural and social service circles was enhanced rather than lessened. She was active in woman's club work, being for years a member of the Fortnightly Club (Chicago) and of the Chicago Woman's Club (president, 1888–90), and she was one of the founders of the Religious Fellowship League and of the Chicago Political Equality League. Her books include *Love and Theology* (1887), *A Girl Graduate* (1889), *Roger Hunt* (1892), and *The Western Slope* (1903). In 1884 she became a member of the editorial staff of *Unity,* a religious weekly of Chicago, edited by Jenkin Lloyd Jones [*q.v.*], maintaining connection with the magazine in one capacity or another to the end of her life.

Mrs. Woolley was a reformer who won by clear intellect and fine womanly qualities rather than by aggressiveness. She possessed high organizing ability and brought to her negro settlement help from many influential people of Chicago. A friend has remarked that the negroes never thoroughly understood her, or she them, but mutual respect developed. Under the name of the Urban League, the settlement still functions (1936). Mrs. Woolley was tall, slender, graceful, with the clear English type of face, and not without a certain beauty. She died at Frederick Douglass Center, survived by her husband, and was buried in Oakwoods Cemetery, Chicago. She had no children. A memorial service was held at Abraham Lincoln Center (Chicago) on Apr. 7, 1918.

[*Who's Who in America,* 1916–17; *Unity,* Apr. 18, 1918 (memorial number); *Christian Register,* May 2, 1918; *Unitarian Yearbook,* 1918–19; obituaries in *Chicago Tribune,* Mar. 10, and *Chicago Herald,* Mar. 11, 1918; information from the Rev. Dr. Rowena Morse Mann, Chicago, and Mrs. Frances B. Wheeler, Geneva, Ill.]   G. B. U.

WOOLLEY, JOHN GRANVILLE (Feb. 15, 1850–Aug. 13, 1922), prohibitionist, was born at Collinsville, Ohio, the son of Edwin C. and Elizabeth (Hunter) Woolley. He attended small-town schools and Ohio Wesleyan University, where he graduated in 1871, then enrolled in the law school of the University of Michigan and graduated in 1873. On July 26, 1873, he married Mary Veronica Gerhardt of Delaware, Ohio. By her he had three sons.

In 1875, Woolley was elected city attorney of Paris, Ill., but finding the town too small for his ambitions he removed to Minneapolis, Minn., where he practised law with great success and in 1881 was elected prosecuting attorney. He had become addicted to alcohol, however, and, hoping that by making a fresh start elsewhere he could master his appetite for drink, he resigned his office and moved to New York. About the same time, 1885–86, he was admitted to practice before the United States Supreme Court. In New York his hopes for self-reform came to naught, and he continued in his old ways, to the great damage of his health and his work. He was "on the verge of suicide" (W. E. Johnson) in 1888 when, in his own words, he "became a Chrisitan and a party Prohibitionist at the same instant" (*Standard Encyclopedia of the Alcohol Problem*, p. 2909).

This was a turning point in his life. Thereafter he eschewed drink and dedicated himself to driving it from the lives of others. He gave himself without stint to the cause of prohibition and before long attained a position of world leadership in the movement. In 1892–93, under the patronage of Lady Somerset, English prohibitionist, he traveled up and down the British Isles, speaking almost every day for seven months to audiences which crowded the biggest halls. In 1901 and again in 1905, he made tours abroad. In New Zealand he gave vigor to the local prohibition movement through more than thirty (Johnson) lectures delivered before great audiences. In Hawaii he established a branch of the Anti-Saloon League, of which he was made superintendent in 1907.

In 1898, at Chicago, Woolley and an associate began the publication of a prohibition periodical called the *Lever*. Its modest success led him the following year to purchase the *New York Voice,* which he combined with the *Lever* under the name *New Voice,* with headquarters in New York. This periodical he edited until the end of 1906. In 1900 he was nominated for the presidency of the United States by the Prohibition party and in the election received 209,936 votes. He continued his prohibition activities until 1921, when failing health caused his retirement, but the death of his wife shortly thereafter left him so lonely that when the World League against Alcohol asked him to survey the drink problem in Europe, he accepted. While in Spain on this assignment he died. His body was returned to Paris, Ill., for burial.

Woolley's literary works were ephemeral and superficial but were admired and widely read by prohibitionists. The most important of his books, all of them dealing with prohibition and consisting for the most part of reprints of his editorials and speeches, are: *Seed* (1893); *The Christian Citizen* (1900); *A Lion Hunter* (1900); *Temperance Progress of the Century* (1903), with W. E. Johnson; *South Sea Letters* (1906), with his wife; and *Civic Sermons* (8 vols., 1911). He projected the *Standard Encyclopedia of the Alcohol Problem* (6 vols., 1925–30), later completed by the American Issue Publishing Company of Westerville, Ohio.

Woolley's appearance suggested a personality genial and tolerant, pleasing and sympathetic—in harmony with the kindliness and gentleness which infused his writings and lectures. By his friend W. E. Johnson he was compared to Wendell Phillips in his power over his audiences.

[*Who's Who in America,* 1922–23; *N. Y. Times,* Aug. 14, 1922; *Standard Encyc. of the Alcohol Problem,* vol. VI (1930); letters from William E. ("Pussyfoot") Johnson.]   W. E. S—a.

WOOLMAN, JOHN (Oct. 19, 1720–Oct. 7, 1772), Quaker leader and advocate of the abolition of slavery, was born at Ancocas (later Rancocas) in the province of West Jersey. He was one of thirteen children of Samuel and Elizabeth (Burr) Woolman. Contrary to legend, Woolman's forbears were men of substance; his grandfather, who had emigrated to Burlington from Gloucestershire in 1678, was a Proprietor of West Jersey, and his father in 1739 was a candidate for the provincial assembly. John Woolman's formal education ended with that afforded by the neighborhood Quaker school, but he improved his mind by wide reading. After serving a tailor's apprenticeship he set up shop in Mount Holly, and on Oct. 18, 1749, he married Sarah Ellis of Chesterfield. His worldly affairs prospered to such an extent that he felt constrained to curtail them. "I saw that a humble man," he wrote, "with the Blessing of the Lord, might live on a little, and that where the heart was set on greatness, success in business did not satisfie the craving; but that comonly with an increase of wealth, the desire for wealth increased" (*Journal, post,* 164). In addition to his trade he was much employed with such matters as surveying, conveyancing, executing bills of sale, and drawing wills. From time to time he taught school, publishing a primer that ran through sveral editions. At the time of his death he was the owner of several hundred acres, including a fine orchard.

As a youth he was profoundly religious, with

leanings toward mysticism, and it was his other-worldliness in thought and deed that was to distinguish him. At the age of twenty-three he felt himself called to the Quaker ministry, and forthwith embarked upon a series of journeys that extended through thirty years and led him from North Carolina to New Hampshire and from the northern frontier of Pennsylvania to Yorkshire, in England. Though he was active with other leading Quakers in opposing conscription and taxation for military supplies, and in Indian conversion, his ministry revolved principally about the question of slavery. His experience in executing bills of sale for slaves early convinced him that slave-keeping was inconsistent with Christianity (*Ibid.*, 161). In 1746 he visited Virginia to view with his own eyes the consequences of "holding fellow men in property." "I saw in these Southern Provinces," he wrote, "so many Vices and Corruptions increased by this trade and this way of life, that it appeared to me as a dark gloominess hanging over the Land, and though now many willingly run into it, yet in future the Consequence will be grievous to posterity. I express it as it hath appeared to me, not at once, nor twice, but as a matter fixed on my mind" (*Ibid.*, 167). Year in and year out Woolman, traveling on foot, went from place to place arousing sleepy consciences against "reaping the unrighteous profits of that iniquitous practice of dealing in Negroes." He visited especially the slave-trade centers, such as Perth Amboy and Newport. From his hatred of slavery rose many of the singularities that colored the last years of his life. Sugar, for example, was objectionable to him because it was the product of slave labor.

Little was achieved by Woolman during the years of his ministry. New Jersey did, however, in 1769 impose a high duty upon imported slaves, and in 1776 the Philadelphia Yearly Meeting disowned those members who refused to manumit their slaves. Yet Woolman's teachings left a permanent imprint upon all thinking opponents of slavery, both in America and in Great Britain. His writings upon the subject, especially his *Journal* (1774) and his essay, *Some Considerations on the Keeping of Negroes* (1754), served to perpetuate his views. He was interested, too, in the social amelioration of the poor, the landless, and those who were compelled to labor under unjust conditions. Indeed, his essay, *A Plea for the Poor* (1763), was republished as a Fabian Society tract in 1897. Woolman died of the smallpox at York, England, while laboring among the poor.

Woolman's fame is greater in England than in America. His *Journal*, acclaimed by Ellery Channing as "the sweetest and purest autobiography in the language" (quoted by Whittier, *post*, p. 2), has gone through more than forty editions. It enjoys a high esteem—among literary men because of the simplicity of its style, and among a wider audience for the revelation of the *schöne Seele* that it embodies. "If the world could take John Woolman for an example in religion and politics . . .," wrote G. M. Trevelyan, "we should be doing better than we are in the solution of the problems of our own day. Our modern conscience-prickers often are either too 'clever' or too violent . . . 'Get the writings of John Woolman by heart,' said Charles Lamb—sound advice not only for lovers of good books but for would-be reformers . . . Woolman was not a bigwig in his own day, and he will never be a bigwig in history. But if there be a 'perfect witness of all-judging Jove,' he may expect his meed of much fame in heaven. And if there be no such witness, we need not concern ourselves. He was not working for 'fame' either here or there" (*post*, 139, 142). Few will quarrel with the dictum that the honor of making the first modern formulation of an explicit purpose to procure the abolition of slavery "belongs to the Quakers, and in particular to that Apostle of Human Freedom, John Woolman" (A. N. Whitehead, *Adventures of Ideas*, 1933, p. 29).

[The definitive edition of Woolman's writings is *The Jour. and Essays of John Woolman* (1922), ed. by A. M. Gunmere, which contains an admirable biog. and a complete bibliog. See also *The Dict. of Nat. Biog.*, which contains some errors; J. G. Whittier, intro. to the 1871 ed. of the *Jour.*; and G. M. Trevelyan, *Clio, a Muse, and Other Essays* (1913).]   J. E. P.

WOOLSEY, MELANCTHON TAYLOR (June 5, 1780–May 19, 1838), naval officer, was born in New York State, the son of Col. Melancthon Lloyd Woolsey, an army officer in the Revolution and subsequently for many years collector of revenue at Plattsburg, N. Y. His mother, Alida (Livingston) Woolsey, was the daughter of a clergyman and a sister of John Henry Livingston [*q.v.*]. After beginning the study of law young Woolsey, desirous of a more active life, entered the navy as a midshipman on Apr. 9, 1800. His first sea duty was in the West Indies on board the *Adams* during the last year of the naval war with France, an active service that proved a good school for the young midshipman. He participated in the war with the Barbary corsairs in the squadron of Commodores Dale and Morris (1802–03) and the squadron of Commodore Barron and Rodgers (1804–07), returning home as a lieutenant of the *Constitution*, a grade to which he was promoted in 1804, although his permanent rank dated from 1807. In

1808 he began a service on the Great Lakes that was to last more than seventeen years. Delegating his duties on Lake Champlain to a subordinate officer, he established his headquarters at Oswego on Lake Ontario and constructed there the *Oneida,* with the aid of Henry Eckford [*q.v.*].

On July 19, 1812, the British squadron made its appearance off Sacketts Harbor, whither Woolsey had moved his headquarters. Failing to reach the open lake with the *Oneida,* he anchored her near the shore, unloaded all her guns on her shore side, and placed them in a battery on the bank. Declining the British summons to surrender, he fought a superior force for two hours until it withdrew, leaving him victorious. In November, now next in command under Isaac Chauncey [*q.v.*], he participated with his ship in the attack on Kingston, and in May and July 1813 in the joint army and naval operation against York. Commissioned master commandant on July 1813, he was placed in command of the *Sylph,* a larger and swifter ship, and took part in the subsequent operations of Chauncey. In May 1814 the important duty of convoying some heavy guns from Oswego to Sacketts Harbor fell to him. He ran his vessels up a creek and, reënforced by some Indians, militia, and light artillery, by a successful ambush he captured or destroyed the whole of a British force sent to intercept him.

He was promoted captain from Apr. 27, 1816. In time the Sacketts Harbor naval station decreased in importance and was no longer worthy of an officer of high rank. In 1825 he was placed in command of the *Constellation* and until the following year was employed in the suppression of piracy in the West Indies. He then received the command of the Pensacola navy yard, where he remained until 1830. In 1832–34 he commanded the Brazil Squadron, hoisting the flag of a commodore. This was his last service afloat or ashore. He died at Utica, N. Y., while on waiting orders. His wife, Susan Cornelia (Tredwell) Woolsey, to whom he had been married at Poughkeepsie, N. Y., on Nov. 3, 1817, and their seven children survived him. A son, Melancthon Brooks Woolsey, 1817–74, entered the navy and rose to the rank of commodore.

[Records of Officers, Bureau of Navigation, 1798–1840; Veterans Administration, War of 1812 Records; *U. S. Navy Reg.,* 1814–38; M. L. Woolsey, *Letters of Melancthon Taylor Woolsey* (1927), and *Melancthon Lloyd Woolsey* (1929); C. J. Peterson, *Hist. of the U. S. Navy* (1852); R. W. Heeser, *Statistical and Chron. Hist. of U. S. Navy,* vol. II (1909); *Niles' Nat. Reg.,* June 2, 1838; Theodore Roosevelt, *Naval War of 1812* (Putnam, 1910); J. F. Cooper, in *Graham's Mag.,* Jan. 1845; *Morning Herald* (New York), May 22, 1838.]
C. O. P.

WOOLSEY, SARAH CHAUNCY (Jan. 29, 1835–Apr. 9, 1905), author, was born in Cleveland, Ohio, the eldest child of John Mumford and Jane (Andrews) Woolsey. Her father was a brother of the tenth president of Yale College, Theodore Dwight Woolsey [*q.v.*], a nephew of the eighth, Timothy Dwight, 1752–1817 [*q.v.*] and the uncle of the twelfth, Timothy Dwight, 1828–1916 [*q.v.*]. She grew up in an attractive home on Euclid Avenue in Cleveland, surrounded by an atmosphere of modest wealth and leisure. Always vigorous, with a great gusto for life, she enjoyed almost equally the many books the house afforded and the acres of garden and woodland that enclosed it. As a student, first in private schools in Cleveland, later in Mrs. Hubbard's Boarding School in Hanover, N. H., she was outstanding in her classes, delighting especially in history and literature. About 1855 the family removed to New Haven, Conn., and this city became her home for almost twenty years. During the Civil War she devoted herself with characteristic energy to hospital work and helped to organize the nursing service. After her father's death in 1870, she spent two years abroad, chiefly in Italy, with her mother and sisters. Upon their return they built a charming house in Newport, R. I. There she lived for the rest of her life, except for summers spent at Northeast Harbor, Me., at Onteora Park in the Catskills, and occasional visits to Europe.

Although she had amused herself from childhood by writing little tales and poems, she published nothing until after the Civil War. Then books, poems, and magazine articles, signed "Susan Coolidge," rapidly made her well known. She contributed to many of the best known periodicals in America from 1870 to 1900. She was the author of three volumes of poetry: *Verses* (1880); *A Few More Verses* (1889); and *Last Verses* (1906), printed after her death with a memoir by her sister. She edited the *Autobiography and Correspondence of Mrs. Delany* (2 vols., 1879), *The Diary and Letters of Frances Burney, Madame d'Arblay* (2 vols., 1880), and *Letters of Jane Austen* (1892), wrote a *Short History of the City of Philadelphia* (1887), made occasional translations from the French, and acted as consulting reader for her publishers, Roberts Brothers. But she was known chiefly as a popular writer of stories for young people. Her first book for girls, *The New-Year's Bargain,* appeared in 1871, and from then until 1890 she produced a new volume almost yearly. Her tales were lively in tone, sensible, wholesome, and pleasingly moral. Among the best known were: *What Katy Did* (1872), *What Katy Did*

At School (1873), Mischief's Thanksgiving (1874), Nine Little Goslings (1875), For Summer Afternoons (1876), Eyebright (1879), A Guernsey Lily (1880), Cross Patch (1881), A Round Dozen (1883), A Little Country Girl (1885), What Katy Did Next (1886), Clover (1888), Just Sixteen (1889), In the High Valley (1891), The Barberry Bush (1893), Not Quite Eighteen (1894), An Old Convent School in Paris and Other Papers (1895). Her vivid personality and many-sided interests endeared her to friends and relatives. She wrote easily, talked well, was fond of games of all sorts, sketched, painted, and took an active part in the religious and social life about her. She was a notable addition to any group because of her stimulating wit, her wide knowledge of books, and her ability to share with others her abounding zest for living.

[Intro. to Last Verses, ante, G. Van R. Wickham, The Pioneer Families of Cleveland (1914); Outlook, Apr. 15, 1905; clippings and list of books from Little, Brown & Co.; information from the family.]

B. M. S.

WOOLSEY, THEODORE DWIGHT (Oct. 31, 1801–July 1, 1889), scholar, educator, president of Yale College, was born in New York City, where his father, William Walton Woolsey, was a prosperous hardware merchant. He was a descendant of George Woolsey who came to New England by the way of Holland about 1623, went to New Amsterdam, and finally settled on Long Island. Theodore's mother, Elizabeth, was a sister of the elder Timothy Dwight [q.v.], and a grand-daughter of Jonathan Edwards [q.v.]. The Woolsey family moved to New Haven in 1808 for the education of two older sons, and Theodore attended the Hopkins Grammar School there, and, after the family's return to New York, a school in Hartford, where he lived with his uncle Theodore Dwight, 1764–1846 [q.v.]. Finishing his preparation for college in Greenfield Hill, Conn., Woolsey entered Yale toward the close of his fifteenth year and graduated as valedictorian of his class in 1820. After studying law for a brief period in the office of Charles Chauncey of Philadelphia, his step-mother's brother—Woolsey's mother died in 1813—he entered Princeton Theological Seminary, where he remained until 1823, when he returned to Yale as tutor and there completed his theological studies.

He was licensed to preach, but being extremely conscientious and subject to periods of acute consciousness of sin and moral responsibility that depressed him at intervals all his life, he seriously doubted his fitness to undertake the work of the ministry; furthermore, his tastes were pre-eminently those of the scholar. Accordingly, in May 1827 he went abroad for further study. The first winter he spent in Paris, where he did work in Arabic; he then moved on to Germany, where he attended lectures at Leipzig, Bonn, and Berlin, devoting himself principally to the Greek language and literature; he visited England, and spent some months in Rome. His social advantages were numerous, and travel and personal contacts made him, he confessed, more and more a cosmopolite. "One thing, however," he wrote his father, "remains in my mind unchanged, and that is an utter repugnance and a fixed decision not to engage in the work of the ministry. . . . I have endeavored to gain a minute and thorough knowledge of the Greek language, and to lay a foundation for an acquaintance such as few in America possess with classical literature, in order to teach it" (T. S. Woolsey, post, p. 636).

With this ambition possessing him, he accepted in 1831 the professorship of the Greek language and literature in Yale College. His career was to be a much broader and more varied one than he planned, for his interests and intellectual resources were too many and diverse to permit of his being confined within the comparatively narrow limits he had set. For the next fifteen years, however, he devoted himself chiefly to the Greek classics. To many whom he taught he became their ideal of the scholar, while to the teaching equipment in his field he contributed a number of textbooks, whose thoroughness, accuracy, and literary appreciation brought them into extensive use. They included The Alcestis of Euripides (1834), The Antigone of Sophocles (1835), The Prometheus of Æschylus (1837), The Electra of Sophocles (1837), and The Gorgias of Plato, Chiefly According to Stallbaum's Text with Notes (1842). "As a disciplinarian he was strict, but yet always just. He was quick in temper, in decision, and in action, and was ready to sustain the authority of the College government at all times" (Dwight, Memorial Address, post, p. 14). In 1846 he was called to the presidency of the college. At first he declined, doubtful of his fitness and still hesitating to be ordained to the ministry, but was finally persuaded to accept, and on Oct. 21, 1846, was both inducted into office and ordained. During the twenty-five years of his incumbency the college made greater progress than in any similar period of time theretofore: improvements were effected in the method of education; the faculty was enlarged and strengthened; the curriculum was enriched; the requirements for promotion and for degrees were made more exacting; new buildings were erected; the endowment was increased; and in 1871, by act of the Connecticut General Assembly, alumni representation in the corporation was made possible.

When he reached the age of seventy he resigned the presidency but until 1885 served as a member of the corporation. At the beginning of his administration he had relinquished the teaching of Greek and commenced giving instruction in history, political science, and international law. In the last two subjects he became a recognized authority at home and abroad. His *Introduction to the Study of International Law, Designed as an Aid in Teaching and in Historical Studies*, which first appeared in 1860, went through several subsequent editions both in the United States and in England. Another major work was his *Political Science: or, The State Theoretically and Practically Considered* (1878), which, while severely criticized as unscientific in treatment and based upon theological assumptions, was commended for its historical information and practical discussion of political questions (see *North American Review*, January–February, 1878). Two less ambitious treatises were his *Essay on Divorce and Divorce Legislation* (1869), much of which had appeared in articles published in the *New Englander*, and *Communism and Socialism* (1880), a reprint of articles contributed to the *Independent*, New York, of which Woolsey was one of the founders. Both works are largely historical but contain many practical observations and implications. Among his other publications were *The Religion of the Present and of the Future* (1871), a collection of sermons, and *Helpful Thoughts for Young Men* (1874); he edited, also, the third edition of *On Civil Liberty and Self-Government* (1874) by Francis Lieber [*q.v.*], and the second edition of Lieber's *Manual of Political Ethics* (2 vols., 1875). In his later years he again made valuable use of his classical knowledge as chairman of the New Testament company of the American committee for revision of the English version of the Bible.

Woolsey was tall but somewhat bent, and of slender, wiry frame. His scholarly countenance was enlivened by eyes of remarkable brightness and penetration. The surroundings and experiences of his youth had made him in many ways a man of the world and freed him from certain Puritan inhibitions; he had, however, a strong sense of moral and religious responsibility. His knowledge was extensive and accurate and he set high standards of scholarship, but as a teacher he had little personal magnetism. His dignity and reserve tended to keep people at a distance. Honest and thorough himself, he despised super-

ficiality and pretense. As an administrator he displayed strong convictions and will, but was clear-visioned and of sound judgment. Woolsey Hall at Yale was named in his honor, and numerous other memorials to his character and services have been established there. He was twice married: first, Sept. 5, 1833, to Elizabeth Martha Salisbury, who died Nov. 3, 1852; second, Sept. 6, 1854, to Sarah Sears Prichard. By his first wife he had nine children, one of whom was Theodore Salisbury Woolsey [*q.v.*]: and by the second, four.

[*Family Records . . . of the Ancestry of My Father and Mother, Charles William Woolsey and Jane Eliza Woolsey* (copr. 1900); B. W. Dwight, *The Hist. of the Descendants of John Dwight of Dedham, Mass.* (1874); T. S. Woolsey, "Theodore Dwight Woolsey," *Yale Rev.*, Jan., Apr., July 1912; F. B. Dexter, *Sketch of the Hist. of Yale Univ.* (1887); G. P. Fisher, "The Academic Career of Ex-President Woolsey," *Century Mag.*, Sept. 1882; Timothy Dwight, *Theodore Dwight Woolsey, D.D., LL.D., Memorial Address* (1890), and *Memories of Yale Life and Men* (1903); A. P. Stokes, *Memorials of Eminent Yale Men*, vol. I (1914); *Morning Journal and Courier* (New Haven), July 2, 1889.]
H. E. S.

WOOLSEY, THEODORE SALISBURY (Oct. 22, 1852–Apr. 24, 1929), jurist, educator, and publicist, was born in New Haven, Conn., the son of Theodore Dwight Woolsey [*q.v.*], then president of Yale College, and Elizabeth Martha (Salisbury) Woolsey. He entered Yale College at the age of fifteen. As a youth he was frail; perhaps it was this that caused him during his student days to live in the relative seclusion of his father's home rather than in the college dormitory, and it may have confirmed his disposition, so noticeable throughout life, to keep himself in the background, though his ability and personality peculiarly fitted him to occupy positions of prominence. Upon graduation in 1872, he immediately entered the Yale Law School, where he studied without interruption, save for the grand tour of Europe during the years 1873–75, until he received the degree of LL.B. in 1876, having won a prize for a dissertation on the civil law. He was married on Dec. 22, 1877, to Annie Gardner Salisbury of Boston, by whom he had two sons. In the same year he was appointed instructor in public law in Yale College, and in 1878, despite his extreme youth, he was called to be professor of international law in the Yale Law School. This position he occupied until his retirement in 1911, save for a four-year period (1886–90) of residence in California in the hope of bettering his wife's health. He served as acting dean of the Yale Law School from 1901 to 1903.

Beginning his career at a time when in the United States international law had little inter·

est even for lawyers, he worked persistently and effectively to bring the American public to an awareness of the deep significance of international relationships and the importance of international law. He prepared for publication J. N. Pomeroy's *Lectures on International Law in Time of Peace* (1886), published a much enlarged edition of his father's famous *Introduction to the Study of International Law* (6th ed., 1891), and prepared a series of articles relating to international law for *Johnson's Universal Cyclopedia* (8 vols., 1893–97). In 1912 he published in the *Yale Review* (Jan., Apr., July) the first two chapters of a life of his father, written with a vivid charm that fills the reader with regret that the biography was never completed. Other articles of general appeal appeared in popular magazines, but his chief activity lay in discussing in public addresses, and in articles published in professional and scientific journals, problems arising in connection with current events in international relations. In 1898 seventeen of these essays and addresses were collected in book form as *America's Foreign Policy*. These essays, while often sharply critical of the foreign policies adopted by the American government, were yet characterized by ripe learning, and a rare breadth and sanity of vision. Woolsey's views now stand, almost without exception, justified by the events of the intervening forty years. In 1910, as a member of the American Bar Association's committee on international law, he prepared a luminous report on pending international questions. He was early associated with the activities of the American Society of International Law, made contributions to the pages of its *Journal*, and for many years served upon its editorial board. In 1921 he was elected an associate of the Institut de Droit International at Paris.

Conquering the frailty of his youth, Woolsey became a keen sportsman and hunter of big game, and was an extensive traveler. He became much interested in old silver and the iron work of colonial American smiths, and wrote charmingly of his collections (see *Harper's New Monthly Magazine*, Sept. 1896). He served on the New Haven board of common council (1880–81), and on the board of park commissioners (1914–28), securing legislation that provided for New Haven a system of public parks administration that is admirable for its efficiency and freedom from political interference. He was an active member of the board of directors of the New Haven Bank from 1899 to the time of his death. In his will he left to Yale University his books on international law, and also a handsome bequest to be used in maintaining and enlarging the collection

of works on international law, diplomatic history, and kindred printed and written materials. He died in New Haven.

[*Who's Who in America*, 1928–29; C. C. Hyde, in *Am. Jour. Internat. Law*, July 1929; *Obit. Record Grads. Yale Univ.*, 1928–29; *Grads. Yale Law School* (1911); N. G. Osborn, *Men of Mark in Conn.*, vol. II (1906), pp. 279–80; *Am. Law School Rev.*, Mar. 1930; obituary in *N. Y. Times*, Apr. 25, 1929.]   W. R. V.

WOOLSON, ABBA LOUISA GOOLD (Apr. 30, 1838–Feb. 6, 1921), author, lecturer, teacher, was born in Windham, Me., the second child of William and Nabby Tukey (Clark) Goold. She was educated at the Portland High School for Girls. In the year of her graduation (1856) she married the principal of the school, Moses Woolson, a native of Concord, N. H., seventeen years her senior. They lived in Portland until 1862, when they moved to Concord. In 1868 they went to live in Boston. Mrs. Woolson's married life was spent in travel, lecturing, teaching, and literary and social activity. She was at one time professor of belles-lettres at the Mount Auburn Ladies' Institute in Cincinnati, Ohio, "lady-principal" of the high school in Haverhill, Mass., and an assistant in the high school in Concord, N. H. She lectured on English literature in important eastern cities, as well as on the Pacific coast during a visit to California. She visited Europe in 1883–84 and in 1891–92, and lectured upon her return on "Historic Cities of Spain." She was a frequent contributor to Boston periodicals, where she employed the technique of the informal essay with considerable skill and charm, and published two volumes of collected sketches, *Browsing among Books* (1881), and *George Eliot and Her Heroines* (1886). She served in 1886 as official poetess at the centennial celebration in Portland, Me., and again in 1888 at the dedication of the Fowler Library in Concord, N. H.

She contributed to the *Boston Journal* a series of essays which in 1873 she collected into one volume, *Woman in American Society*. John Greenleaf Whittier, a personal friend, wrote the foreword, referring to the articles as "gracefully written, yet with a certain robust strength,—wise, timely, and suggestive, . . . the well-considered words of a clear-sighted, healthful-minded woman." The book has real charm, and intrinsic as well as historical interest; it is the mild and humorous protest of an intelligent woman against the social, economic, and intellectual bondage of her sex. In the essays on physical education for women and dress reform she is slightly radical but not militantly feministic. Not in sympathy with the eccentricities of the Bloomer movement, she proposed a costume that should not sacrifice

521

its femininity, but should be both more beautiful and more practical than the heavy, awkward, confining fashions of her day. Her interest in this subject led to her association with a group of four women physicians in a series of lectures given at Boston and surrounding towns; these she later edited as *Dress-Reform: a Series of Lectures Delivered in Boston, on Dress As It Affects the Health of Women* (1874). She was founder and first president of the Castilian Club of Boston, and a member of the Massachusetts Society for the University Education of Women, and of the Moral Education Society of Massachusetts, serving terms as president of each. After the death of her husband in 1896 she engaged much less in public activity. In summer she lived on the family farm at Windham, Me., and in winter at a Boston hotel. Her last publication was a small volume of verse, *With Garlands Green* (1915), privately printed at Cambridge, Mass. She died in Maine.

[The most important source is a Goold family MS. by Nathan Goold in the Colls. of the Me. Hist. Soc. See also *Who's Who in America*, 1906-07; Frances E. Willard and Mary A. Livermore, *A Woman of the Century* (1893); obituary in *Boston Transcript*, Feb. 7, 1921.]　　　　　　　　　　　　　J. H. B.

WOOLSON, CONSTANCE FENIMORE (March 1840–Jan. 24, 1894), author, was born at Claremont, N. H., the youngest of the six daughters of Charles Jarvis and Hannah Cooper (Pomeroy) Woolson. Her father was a descendant of Thomas Woolson who settled in Cambridge, Mass., before 1660; her mother was a niece of James Fenimore Cooper [*q.v.*]. Soon after Constance's birth the Woolsons removed from Claremont to Cleveland, Ohio, where the father established himself successfully in business. There Constance attended Miss Hayden's School and the Cleveland Seminary. As a young girl she accompanied her father on long drives through Ohio and Wisconsin, and on trips to the family cottage at Mackinac Island, and in this way acquired a thorough knowledge of the lake region. At eighteen she was graduated from Madame Chegary's School in New York City at the head of her class. Except for a time during the Civil War when she was in charge of a post office in one of the sanitary fairs, she lived a life of leisure in Cleveland until 1869, the year of her father's death. She had already published *Two Women* (1862), a poem, and now financial considerations led her to turn to writing as a profession. The work of her first five years of authorship, at a time when interest in regional literature had been aroused by the work of Bret Harte, was concerned very largely with her experiences in the lake region. She contributed stories, poems, and travel sketches to *Harper's*, the *Galaxy, Lippincott's,* the *Atlantic Monthly*, and other leading magazines. In 1873 she published, under the name of Anne March, a reminiscence of her early life in Cleveland called *The Old Stone House*. But the nine tales in the collection *Castle Nowhere: Lake Country Sketches* (1875) easily constitute the choicest products of these first years. During the early seventies, with her mother and widowed sister, she traveled extensively up and down the Atlantic seaboard between Cooperstown, N. Y., and St. Augustine, Fla. From 1873 until the death of her mother in 1879 she lived chiefly in the Carolinas and in Florida. St. Augustine became the focal point of her writings on the South and the chief rival of Mackinac Island in her affections. There she wrote for the magazines many stories and sketches of southern life during the reconstruction period, the best of which were reprinted in *Rodman the Keeper: Southern Sketches* (1880). Between 1877 and 1879 she wrote a number of able critical articles for the "Contributors' Club" of the *Atlantic Monthly*. In 1879 she sailed for Europe, where she spent the remaining fourteen years of her life. She made a tour of England and France, and then settled, so far as she can be said to have settled anywhere, in Florence, but during the intervals of her arduous literary work she traveled extensively. After a visit to Egypt in 1890, she lived in England, principally at Oxford, until the spring of 1893, when she returned to Italy. She spent the last months of her life in several of the old palaces that line the Grand Canal in Venice. Her death occurred on Jan. 24, 1894, after a serious illness, and was reported at the time as suicide. She was buried in the Protestant Cemetery at Rome.

During the sojourn in Europe she published all five of her novels, two collections of short stories, a travel volume, and a considerable number of stories, poems, and sketches that appeared only in American periodicals. Her first novel, *Anne* (1883), completed before she left America, is in its best portions a tale of Mackinac Island. With one exception her other novels are likewise narratives in which the regional setting is important: *East Angels* (1886) is laid in St. Augustine, *Jupiter Lights* (1889) in southern Georgia and the northern lake region, and *Horace Chase* (1894) in North Carolina and Florida. Her shortest and in many respects her best novel, *For the Major* (1883), is a comparatively unlocalized account of village life in the eastern Appalachians. The posthumous collections of European stories, *The Front Yard* (1895) and *Dorothy* (1896), are accounts of Americans projected, in the manner of her friend Henry James [*q.v.*], against the background of an older civilization. Though he suggests a certain weakness in her "predilection for cases of heroic sacrifice" and her "delicate manipulation of the real" for the sake of glamor, James himself offers her praise for her minutely careful observation, her skill in "evoking a local tone" (especially in *East Angels*) and her "general attitude of watching life, waiting upon it and trying to catch it in the fact" (*post*). Her work is frequently overlooked by contemporary American readers, but there is an unobtrusive artistry about many of her novels and short stories, and a desire to present life in certain restricted circles with verisimilitude, that should insure her a lasting audience among the discriminating.

[The date of birth is frequently given wrongly as Mar. 5, 1848. The chief biog. sources are three books by Constance Woolson's niece, Clare Benedict: *Voices out of the Past* (1929), from which the date of birth is deduced (p. 164), *Constance Fenimore Woolson* (1930), and *The Benedicts Abroad* (1930), all privately printed. See also J. D. Kern, *Constance Fenimore Woolson* (1934), with bibliog.; Henry James, *Partial Portraits* (1888); F. L. Pattee, *The Development of the Am. Short Story* (1923); *Harper's Weekly*, Feb. 3, 10, 1894; *N. Y. Times*, Jan. 25, 1894 (death notice) and Jan. 26 (denial of suicide).]   J. D. K.

WOOLWORTH, FRANK WINFIELD (Apr. 13, 1852–Aug. 8, 1919), merchant, son of John Hubbell and Fanny (McBrier) Woolworth, was born on a farm at Rodman, Jefferson County, N. Y. In boyhood he attended country schools at Greatbend, N. Y., did farm work, and in his teens had two brief terms in a business college at Watertown, the county seat. There was in his youth no augury of his future great success. In fact, although his favorite boyhood game was "playing store," although a mercantile career was the only course he craved, yet he seemed deplorably inept at it and was a long time in finding himself. At nineteen, for the sake of experience, he took a place as clerk in a village grocery store, receiving no wages for two years. At twenty-one he was taken on six-months' trial at a store in Watertown, receiving no salary for the first three months, and after that $3.50 a week, which was just what he paid for board and lodging. In the course of two years his pay advanced to $6 weekly, out of which he supported himself and saved a little money. In 1875 a "ninety-nine cent store" appeared in Watertown and did a large business. Here Woolworth got his first inkling of the notion of selling a large array of articles at one fixed price. A Watertown man decided to try the ninety-nine cent plan in Port Huron, Mich., and took Woolworth along as clerk at $10 a week; but he was such a poor salesman that his salary was soon cut to $8.50. Discouraged, he

fell ill and went back to his father's farm to recuperate. He married Jennie Creighton of Watertown on June 11, 1876. A year later his old firm, Moore & Smith, took him back again as clerk. In 1878 he heard for the first time of a store's having a counter on which nothing but five-cent goods was sold. He induced his own employers to try the scheme, and it proved a startling success.

Woolworth now persuaded W. H. Moore to back him to the extent of three hundred dollars in a five-cent store in Utica, but the venture was a failure and was closed in three months. He came to the conclusion that the variety of goods had not been large enough and—again with Moore's help—opened a store in Lancaster, Pa. (June 1879), which was a paying venture. The addition of a line of ten-cent goods was the final move that insured success. Calling his brother, C. S. Woolworth, and his cousin, Seymour H. Knox, into service with him, he presently began launching other stores, as funds permitted. Those in Philadelphia, Harrisburg, and York, Pa., and Newark, N. J., were at first unproductive because Woolworth had not studied the locations for them with sufficient care. But others in Buffalo, Erie, Scranton, and elsewhere were successful. Two other men, F. M. Kirby and Earl P. Charlton, also became partners. After a few years Woolworth sold his interest in the Buffalo and Erie stores to Knox, and thus began the S. H. Knox & Company chain of five- and ten-cent stores. The other partners, including C. S. Woolworth, also started chains of their own, but all remained friendly and in general avoided trespassing on each other's territory. In 1912 the four chains—Knox, Kirby, Charlton, and C. S. Woolworth—were all absorbed by the F. W. Woolworth Company, as were two stores belonging to W. H. Moore, Woolworth's early employer. More and more the Woolworth stores began having goods manufactured especially for them, sometimes taking the entire output of a factory on a year's contract. To add more articles to his line, to sell things at five and ten cents which had never sold for so little before, was Woolworth's constant aim, and a key to his success. In fulfilment of a boyhood dream, he erected the Woolworth Building, 792 feet high, in New York City (completed in 1913), which was for some years the world's tallest building and a wonder to tourists. At his death in 1919 his company owned more than a thousand stores in the United States and Canada; its volume of business in 1918 was $107,000,000. Woolworth's own fortune was estimated at $65,000,000. He was survived by his wife and two daughters.

[C. R. Woolworth, *The Descendants of Richard and Hannah Higgins Woolworth* (1893); R. A. Oakes, *Geneal. and Family Hist. of the County of Jefferson, N. Y.* (1905), vol. I; *Who's Who in America*, 1918–19; *Fortieth Anniversary Souvenir, F. W. Woolworth Co., 1879–1919*; *The Master Builders* (1913); G. A. Nichols, *Printers' Ink*, Apr. 17, 1919; *McBride's Mag.*, Dec. 1915; *Everybody's Mag.*, Oct. 1917; *Outlook*, Apr. 30, 1919; *Bankers' Mag.*, May 1919; *Lit. Digest*, May 3, 1919, and Jan. 8, 1921; obituary in *N. Y. Times*, Apr. 9, 1919.]   A. F. H.

WOOSTER, CHARLES WHITING (1780–1848), commander in chief of the Chilean navy, was born in New Haven, Conn., the son of Thomas and Lydia (Sheldon) Wooster, and the grandson of David Wooster [q.v.] who was one of the eight brigadier-generals named by the Continental Congress in 1776. Charles Wooster was also a descendant of President Thomas Clap [q.v.] of Yale College. At the age of eleven he went to sea, and at twenty-one he commanded the ship *Fair American*. He married Frances Stebbins, who died in 1816; their son was born in 1810. During the War of 1812 Wooster commanded the privateer *Saratoga* and captured twenty-two British vessels—including the letter-of-marque *Rachel,* after a celebrated naval action off La Guayra, Venezuela (*Niles' Weekly Register,* Jan. 13, 1813). In 1814 a battalion of Sea Fencibles was raised for the defense of New York Harbor and Wooster was made captain and then major in this force.

After the war he returned to service in the United States merchant marine until José Miguel Carrera and Manuel Hermenegildo de Aguirre interested him in the Chilean struggle for independence from Spain. On Oct. 8, 1817, he was commissioned captain in the Chilean navy by the dictator, Bernardo O'Higgins, and soon afterward sailed from New York in command of the armed bark *Columbus,* which he stated that he had bought and outfitted personally. On Feb. 4, 1818, he reached Buenos Aires, and on Apr. 25 arrived at his destination, Valparaiso, with his cargo of munitions of war. Here the *Columbus* was formally transferred to the Chilean government, being renamed *Araucano.* On Oct. 28, 1818, Wooster commanded the Chilean man-of-war *Lautaro* which bottled up the Spanish warship *Maria Isabel* in Talcahuano harbor, and he was himself the first to board her. Exactly a month later Lord Cochrane arrived in Chile as commander in chief of the Chilean navy. As a result of differences between them, Wooster retired from the navy in January 1819, devoting himself to whaling thereafter until he reëntered the service in March 1822 as chief of the Chilean naval forces. On Nov. 27, 1825, he sailed from Valparaiso to attack the last stronghold of the Spaniards in Chile—the Island of Chiloé, which he successfully assaulted in cooperation with the land forces under General Freire on Jan. 11, 1826. "Wooster, like an aroused lion, rose above the fire and death which were on all sides of him and concentrated all the enemy's fire on one place," wrote President Vicuna of Chile (Chandler, *post,* p. 127), who commissioned Wooster rear admiral in the Chilean navy on Nov. 4, 1829. Toward the end of 1835, after numerous differences with the government, Wooster left Chile, with a pension, and returned to the United States after eighteen years' absence. He died at San Francisco, Cal., in 1848, in great poverty.

[David Wooster, *Geneal. of the Woosters in America* (1885); George Coggeshall, *Hist. of the Am. Privateers* (1856); *Pub. Papers of Daniel D. Tompkins* (3 vols., 1898–1902); C. L. Chandler, *Inter-American Acquaintances* (2nd ed., 1917), with bibliog., and "Admiral Charles Whiting Wooster in Chile," *Ann. Report Am. Hist. Asso. . . . 1916*, vol. I (1919); Narciso Demadryl, *Galeria Nacional . . . de Chile* (1854); Luis Uribe Orrego, *Nuestra Marina Militar* (1910); *Manifesto que da en su despedida de Chile el Contra-Almirante D. C. W. Wooster* (1836).]   C. L. C.

WOOSTER, DAVID (Mar. 2, 1711–May 2, 1777), Revolutionary brigadier-general, was born in the part of Stratford, Conn., that became Huntington, the seventh child of Mary (Walker) and Abraham Wooster, by trade a mason. He graduated from Yale College in 1738, a classmate of Phineas Lyman [q.v.]. Three years later the colony appointed him lieutenant, and the next year captain, of the sloop *Defence,* an armed vessel for the protection of the coast. He was at Louisburg in 1745 as a captain of Connecticut troops, and on July 4 he sailed for France with prisoners of war for exchange. Capitalizing the excitement in London over Louisburg's surrender, he returned a captain in Sir William Pepperrell's new British regiment of foot. In March 1746 he married Mary, the daughter of Thomas Clap [q.v.], the president of Yale College. They had four children. He served with Pepperrell's regiment till its reduction on half-pay and returned to New Haven, bought the old Wooster place, and set up as merchant. There also, in 1750, he organized Hiram Lodge, one of the first lodges of Free Masons in the colony, of which he was first master. During the Seven Years' War he acted as colonel of a Connecticut regiment in all campaigns but those of 1755 and 1757. He was at Ticonderoga in 1758 and with Amherst in later campaigns. In 1757 he represented New Haven in the Assembly. At the end of the war he went back to his business and in 1763 became collector of customs in New Haven.

In April 1775 the Connecticut Assembly appointed him major-general of six regiments, and colonel of the 1st Regiment. The next month, on the request of the New York council, he was ordered to New York, where throughout the summer he commanded Connecticut troops at Harlem and on Long Island. The Continental Congress named him in June on its list of brigadier-generals, the only general officer in the colonies not raised to full continental rank. Piqued that his long military record should not raise him above younger men, he quarrelled with Philip Schuyler in northern New York, where he was ordered in September, and later with Arnold at Quebec. He was present with Connecticut troops at Montgomery's siege and capture of St. Johns, and at Montreal. He was left in command there, when Montgomery went on to attack Quebec, and on the latter's death he became the ranking officer in Canada. He was not a success; he was tactless, hearty rather than firm with his undisciplined troops who adored him, at times brutal towards the civilian population of Montreal. "A general . . . of a hayfield" (Smith, *post,* II, 230), dull and uninspired, garrulous about his thirty years of service, he showed incapacities that Silas Deane (*Connecticut Historical Society Collections,* II, 1870, 288) had suspected two years before, and with which Washington was in guarded agreement. In April he assumed command of the forlorn American army before Quebec until superseded by Thomas. The next month the congressional commissioners reported him totally unfit to command. Congress recalled him, but subsequently acquitted him of incapacity and permitted him to continue as brigadier-general without employment. Reappointed major-general of Connecticut militia in the autumn of 1776, he served on the borders, mostly at Westchester, during the winter. During Tryon's raid on Danbury in April 1777, with troops from New Haven, he stationed himself in the British rear at Ridgefield, while Arnold and Silliman attempted to intercept the enemy in front. In a brief action on April 27, as he was rallying his men, he received a mortal wound. He left two children. Congress voted him a monument in June, as a defender of American liberties, but it was never erected. The present monument at Danbury was set up in 1854 by the Masons.

[H. C. Deming, *An Oration upon the Life and Services of Gen. David Wooster* (1854); F. B. Dexter, *Biog. Sketches of the Grads. of Yale College,* vol. I (1885); J. R. Case, *An Account of Tryon's Raid on Danbury in April 1777* (1927); A. P. Stokes, *Memorials of Eminent Yale Men* (2 vols., 1914); J. H. Smith, *Our Struggle for the Fourteenth Colony* (2 vols., 1907), unsparing in criticism; some letters and papers in Lib. of Cong.]

S. M. P.

WOOTASSITE [See OUTACITY, fl. 1756–1777].

WOOTTON, RICHENS LACY (May 6, 1816–Aug. 21, 1893), trapper, pioneer settler, was born in Mecklenburg County, Va. In 1823 his father, David C. Wootton, moved with his family to Christian County, Ky. In the summer of 1836 young Wootton journeyed to Independence, Mo., and thence by wagon-train to Bent's Fort. For the next four years his trading and trapping journeys carried him to almost every section of the Western fur country. In 1840 he was for a time a hunter for the fort, and in the following year, on the site of the present Pueblo, Colo., started a ranch for the rearing of buffalo calves. Three years later he was actively engaged in trading among the Indians. In February 1847 he took part in suppressing the insurrection in Taos. He next joined Col. A. W. Doniphan [*q.v.*], at El Paso del Norte, to serve as a scout on the Chihuahua expedition. He was in the battle of Sacramento (Feb. 28, 1847), and immediately thereafter returned with dispatches to Santa Fé. At Taos he established himself in business, but in the following year guided Col. Edward Newby in his Navajo campaign. About 1850 he married Dolores, the daughter of Manuel Le Fevre, a French-Canadian pioneer; she died in 1856 and some years later he remarried.

In 1852, with twenty-two helpers, Wootton drove a flock of nearly 9,000 sheep to California, a feat antedating by a year the famous Carson-Maxwell drive. He next engaged in freighting. Chance brought him to the new settlement of Denver in the winter of 1858–59. In 1862 he moved south to a point near Pueblo, where he started farming, only to be washed out by the great floods of 1864. In the following year, in partnership with George C. McBride, he began the enterprise for which he is perhaps best known. Over the roughest portion of the mountain division of the Santa Fé Trail, a stretch of twenty-seven miles from Trinidad, Colo., across Raton Pass and down to the Canadian River, he built a substantial road, and near the crest erected a residence and an inn and set up a tollgate. The road was opened in 1866 and proved highly profitable, but in 1879 it was paralleled by the Atchison, Topeka & Santa Fé Railroad, and the collection of tolls was discontinued. Wootton remained there, however, until 1891, when his residence was destroyed by fire. He then settled near Trinidad, where two years later he died, survived by his second wife and three children.

Wootton, known familiarly as "Uncle Dick," was above medium height and strongly built, with a large, roundish head and a jovial face which he shaved smooth, though he wore his hair somewhat long. His manner was kindly and genial, and he was notably generous and helpful. Few, if any, of the frontiersmen had so varied a career. He had many combats with the savages, and as an Indian fighter he was, according to Inman (*post*), second only to Carson.

[H. L. Conard, *"Uncle Dick" Wootton* (1890), largely an autobiog.; *Hist. of N. Mex.* (1907), I, 102–08; Bess McKinnan, "The Toll Road over Raton Pass," *N. Mex. Hist. Rev.*, Jan. 1927; *Portr. and Biog. Record of the State of Col.* (1899); Henry Inman, *The Old Santa Fé Trail* (1897); G. D. Bradley, *Winning the Southwest* (1912); *Denver Republican*, Aug. 23, 1893.]
W. J. G.

WORCESTER, EDWIN DEAN (Nov. 19, 1828–June 13, 1904), railroad official, born in Albany, N. Y., was the son of Eldad and Sarah (Chickering) Worcester and a descendant of William Worcester who had emigrated from England and settled in Salisbury, Mass., by 1640. Eldad Worcester was a lawyer and Edwin as a boy spent much time in his father's office copying law papers. When he was fifteen his formal schooling was ended by the death of his father. His early business activities included a clerkship in his uncle's grocery store and later in the law office of Rufus W. Peckham [*q.v.*]. He engaged in trading of various kinds, including the handling of country produce over the newly opened railroad to Boston, and for a time in 1848 was connected with the Ransom Stove Works. In 1852 he entered his brother's law office in Albany, but was also employed occasionally in the Albany City Bank, of which Erastus Corning [*q.v.*] was president, and in the Commercial Bank of Albany. Deeply interested in law and in accounting, he spent much time in private study and lost no opportunity to enlarge his information and experience.

In 1853 the ten railroad companies whose lines extended from Albany to Buffalo were consolidated into the New York Central Railroad, and Worcester was called in by Corning to assist in solving the many problems of accounting and procedure that arose in connection with the project. He was made chief accountant but soon became treasurer and held this position through the troublous times occasioned by the panic of 1857 and the Civil War. In 1867 Cornelius Vanderbilt, 1794–1877 [*q.v.*], took active control of the company, and thereafter Worcester was closely associated with him. He played an important part in effecting the consolidation of the New York Central and the Hudson River railroads in 1869 and shortly afterward became secretary of the enlarged system with wide and undefined powers. This position he retained until his death. Because he had been on the ground from the beginning, his experience, combined with his trained competence, made his services in constant demand in the development of a great system. In the lease of the Harlem Railroad and in the reorganization of the Lake Shore he was an active participant and he became treasurer of the Lake Shore in 1873. In that year he appeared before the Senate Committee on Transportation Routes to the Seaboard, which was the first important federal investigation of the railroad industry. His intimate knowledge of railroad development made him an ideal witness for the roads and he discussed the various railroad problems, such as rate practices, competition, finance, capitalization and consolidation, with expert familiarity. He negotiated the terms under which the first exclusive "fast mail" train was operated between New York and Chicago. After the death of Commodore Vanderbilt, Worcester maintained the same close relations with his son, William H. [*q.v.*], and when the latter took over the Michigan Central Railroad in 1878 Worcester was made secretary of that company. In 1883 he added the vice-presidency of the Lake Shore and of the Michigan Central to his other functions. He was also in demand as a director of subsidiary lines. When he died, in New York City, he had been an important official of the New York Central system for more than fifty years.

On Apr. 30, 1855, Worcester married Mary Abigail Low of Albany, who survived him, with their daughter and four of their six sons.

[*Railroad Gazette*, June 17, 1904, general news section; *Thirty-fifth Ann. Report of the . . . N. Y. Central and Hudson River Railroad Company* (1904); "Report of the Select Committee on Transportation Routes to the Seaboard," *Senate Report 307*, pt. 2, 43 Cong., 1 Sess. (1874); S. A. Worcester, *The Descendants of Rev. William Worcester* (1914); *Who's Who in America*, 1903–05; *N. Y. Times*, June 14, 1904.]
F. H. D.

WORCESTER, JOSEPH EMERSON (Aug. 24, 1784–Oct. 27, 1865), lexicographer, geographer, historian, was born in Bedford, N. H., a nephew of Noah and Samuel Worcester [*qq.v.*] and the second son of Jesse and Sarah (Parker) Worcester. He was one of fifteen children, fourteen of whom, like their father, taught at one time or another in the public schools. Joseph spent his youth on the family farm in Hollis, N. H. The local public schools offered meager opportunities for education, but, according to his brother Samuel, Joseph studied at home "with that quiet and unwearied perseverance and resolute energy, which were marked traits of his character through his whole life" (*Granite Monthly, post*, p. 247). At the age of twenty-one he entered Phillips Academy, Andover, Mass., and at twenty-five, the sophomore class at Yale College, graduating in 1811.

For five years following his graduation he taught in Salem, Mass., where Nathaniel Hawthorne was one of his students. In 1819, after two years spent in Andover, he settled permanently in Cambridge. While teaching at Salem, Worcester prepared his first work, *A Geographical Dictionary, or Universal Gazetteer, Ancient and Modern,* published in 1817. It was followed in 1818 by *A Gazetteer of the United States,* in 1819 by *Elements of Geography,* in 1823 by *Sketches of the Earth and Its Inhabitants,* and in 1826 by *Elements of History, Ancient and Modern.* All of these works were extensively used as textbooks.

In 1828 appeared the first of his long series of dictionaries, an edition of *Johnson's English Dictionary, . . . with Walker's Pronouncing Dictionary, Combined.* The following year he prepared an abridgment of Webster's large dictionary of 1828, and in 1830 his own *Comprehensive Pronouncing and Explanatory Dictionary of the English Language* appeared. This volume contained what may be called Worcester's one permanent contribution to lexicography and the English language in America, the idea of a sound intermediate between the *a* of *hat* and that of *father.* This sound, which has since come to be known as the "compromise vowel," offered an escape to those who were too timid to use, in such words as *fast, grass,* and *dance,* the then fashionable vowel of *hat,* and were ashamed of the vowel of *father,* which, as Worcester said, seemed "to border on vulgarism."

Worcester's 1830 dictionary evoked from Noah Webster [*q.v.*] a rather ill-natured charge of plagiarism. This attack was the first move in a half-century long battle for supremacy between the two great rival series of dictionaries, a battle which degenerated later into the graceless and petty commercial strife between the rival publishers known as the "War of the Dictionaries." This was at its height in 1860, when the publication of the Worcester Quarto had followed close on the 1859 Webster, though there was an active exchange of hostilities earlier when the 1846 Worcester and the Goodrich Webster had almost coincided. Worcester's main personal contribution to the fight, after his refutation of Webster's charges in 1830, was the publication in 1853 of a pamphlet entitled *A Gross Literary Fraud Exposed,* a bitter and indignant denial of the statement on the title page of the London edition of his *Universal Dictionary* that it was "compiled from the materials of Noah Webster."

After the publication of his *Comprehensive . . . Dictionary* in 1830 Worcester spent seven or eight months in Europe, where he collected books on philology and lexicography. A manuscript journal of this trip was preserved among his papers. On his return in 1831 he assumed his eleven-year editorship of *The American Almanac and Repository of Useful Knowledge.* When he was fifty-seven years old, he married, June 29, 1841, Amy Elizabeth McKean, who at that time was forty. The daughter of Prof. Joseph McKean of Harvard, she proved a "ready and helpful assistant" in her husband's labors.

While *A Universal and Critical Dictionary of the English Language* (1846)—next to the 1860 Quarto, Worcester's most important work—was passing through the press, he suffered from cataract. After a series of operations his left eye was saved, but the right became entirely blind. In spite of this handicap, the work on the dictionaries went on. Enlarged and improved editions of the *Comprehensive* appeared in 1847 and 1849. In 1855 it appeared with the title *A Pronouncing, Explanatory, and Synonymous Dictionary of the English Language,* with the discrimination of synonyms made an important and distinguishing feature. It also listed, for the first time in an English dictionary, Christian names of men and women with their etymological significations. In 1860, when Worcester was seventy-six, appeared the most elaborate and important of all his works, the illustrated Quarto, *A Dictionary of the English Language.* Among its new features were a historical sketch of dictionaries and an improved treatment of synonyms. The illustrations were hailed by many critics as an original feature, but the idea had been used before him in Bailey's Dictionary and Blount's *Glossographia.* Worcester's work did not end with the publication of his Quarto. For the remaining five years of his life, he made daily annotations for a future revision. He died in Cambridge, Oct. 27, 1865.

Lacking the fiery and at times evangelical zeal of his great and successful rival, Noah Webster, Worcester was distinguished for practical common sense, sound judgment, and enormous industry. Both men were diligent, but in temperament and attitude contrasted sharply. Worcester, a conservative, held more closely to British usage, especially that of Johnson and Walker, while Webster, in the words of H. E. Scudder, "walked about the Jericho of English lexicography, blowing his trumpet of destruction" (*Noah Webster,* 1881, p. 290). Webster's preference for a local and somewhat provincial usage, and especially his innovations in spelling, aroused violent opposition, most of all in the literary circles of Boston, where, as Oliver Wendell Holmes genially reported, "literary men . . . are by special statute allowed to be sworn [on Worcester's Dictionary] in place of the Bible" (*Works,* vol. III, 1892, p. 8). Reviewing the 1860 edition, Edward Everett Hale stated that only two books would be necessary in establishing a new civilization, "Shakespeare and this dictionary" (*Christian Examiner,* May 1860, p. 365). Though Webster had a much wider circulation, Worcester was in general preferred by the fastidious, and, in 1860, there was much justification for such a preference (*Atlantic Monthly,* May 1860). The supremacy of Webster was not established until after 1864, when *Webster's . . . Unabridged,* the work of many competent hands, appeared. Although Worcester has long been forgotten by the general public, he continued to have some devoted followers well into the twentieth century. During his lifetime his achievements were recognized by election to the Massachusetts Historical Society, the American Academy, the Oriental Society, and the Royal Geographical Societ yof London.

[Sarah A. Worcester, *The Descendants of Rev. William Worcester* (1914); Ezra Abbott, in *Proc. Am. Acad. of Arts and Sciences,* vol. VII (1868); S. A. Allibone, *A Critical Dict. of English Lit. and British and Am. Authors* (1871), vol. III; F. B. Dexter, *Biog. Sketches Grads. Yale Coll.,* vol. VI (1912); G. S. Hillard, biog. sketch in Worcester's *A Dict. of the English Language* (Phila., 1878, and other editions); William Newell, memoir, in *Proc. Mass. Hist. Soc.,* vol. XVIII (1881); A. P. Stokes, *Memorials of Eminent Yale Men* (2 vols., 1914); S. T. Worcester, "Joseph E. Worcester, LL.D.," in *Granite Monthly,* Apr. 1880, and *Hist. of the Town of Hollis, N. H.* (1879); G. P. Krapp, *The English Language in America* (2 vols., 1925); M. M. Mathews, *A Survey of English Dictionaries* (1933); S. A. Steger, *Am. Dictionaries* (1913); pamphlets and advertisements of the rival publishers, G. & C. Merriam (Webster) and Jenks, Hickling, & Swan and successors (Worcester), particularly in the years 1854 and 1860; contemporary reviews of Worcester's and Webster's dictionaries as listed in A. G. Kennedy, *A Bibliog. of Writings on the English Language* (1927); *Boston Transcript,* Oct. 27, 1865.]   M. L. H.

WORCESTER, NOAH (Nov. 25, 1758–Oct. 31, 1837), clergyman, editor, "Friend of Peace," was born in Hollis, N. H., and was the eldest of five brothers, four of whom, Noah, Leonard, Thomas, and Samuel [*q.v.*], entered the ministry. They were the sons of Noah Worcester by his first wife, Lydia (Taylor), grandsons of Francis Worcester, a Congregational clergyman, and descendants of Rev. William Worcester, who emigrated from England and was the first pastor of the church at Salisbury, Mass., established in 1638. The elder Noah commanded a company at the beginning of the Revolution, was a justice of the peace for forty years, and a member of the convention that framed the constitution of New Hampshire. Young Noah received a little schooling each winter until he was sixteen, when he became a fifer in the Revolutionary War, serv-

ing for eleven months and barely escaping capture at the battle of Bunker Hill. Again, in 1777, he was a fifer for two months, taking part in the battle of Bennington. Meanwhile, he had become a teacher—at the Plymouth, N. H., village school —and for some years united teaching with farming. In Plymouth he met Hannah Brown, born in Newburyport, Mass., whom he married on his twenty-first birthday. In 1782 they removed to Thornton, N. H.

During the first five years of his residence there he served as selectman, town clerk, justice of the peace, and representative in the state legislature. He was also a farmer, teacher, and shoemaker. All the while he was educating himself, and had become interested in religious subjects. In 1816, at the suggestion of the minister in a neighboring town, he applied successfully for a license to preach. Late that same year his own pastor recommended him as his successor, and on Oct. 18, 1787, he was ordained minister of the Congregational church at Thornton, a position which he held for some twenty-two years. In November 1797 his wife died, leaving him with eight children, and in May 1798 he married Hannah Huntington, a native of Norwich, Conn. When the New Hampshire Missionary Society was formed in 1802, he became its first missionary and traveled the northern part of the state in its interests as well as ministering to his own parish. Because of the illness of his brother Thomas, pastor at Salisbury, N. H., he left Thornton in February 1810 and for the next three years was associated with him in caring for the Salisbury church.

For some time he had been making a thorough study of the doctrine of the Trinity and in 1810 he published *Bible News of the Father, Son, and Holy Spirit, in a Series of Letters,* setting forth conclusions which were essentially Unitarian. The Hopkinton Association of Ministers, to which he belonged, passed a vote condemning the book. This action caused him to write *A Respectful Address to the Trinitarian Clergy Relating to Their Manner of Treating Opponents* (1812) and several other pamphlets. The book found favor with theological liberals, however, and in 1813 Worcester was asked to become the first editor of the *Christian Disciple* (later the *Christian Examiner*), a monthly periodical projected by a group of Unitarians which included Channing and Lowell. He accepted the position, removing to Brighton, Mass., and for five years conducted the paper successfully, writing much of its contents himself.

By nature he was gentle and irenic; controversy was repugnant to him; and in time he came to regard war, whether offensive or defensive, as unjustifiable, accepting the doctrine of non-resistance as applied both to individuals and nations, and believing that love is the surest weapon for subduing all foes. The last part of his life was devoted to the promotion of peace, and to this cause he made his most important and lasting contribution. In 1814 he published *A Solemn Review of the Custom of War*, which, translated into various languages, was circulated throughout the world. It gave impetus to the founding of peace societies, among them the Massachusetts Peace Society, formed in 1815, of which he became secretary. At the close of 1818 he turned over the editorship of the *Christian Disciple* to the younger Henry Ware [*q.v.*], and the following year established *The Friend of Peace*, which he conducted until 1828.

At the age of seventy he severed his official connections and spent his last years in study and writing, publishing *The Atoning Sacrifice, a Display of Love—Not of Wrath* (1829), which went through several editions; *Causes and Evils of Contentions Unveiled in Letters to Christians* (1831); and *Last Thoughts on Important Subjects* (1833). In addition to the works already mentioned he published a number of sermons and pamphlets. He died and was buried at Brighton, Mass., but his body was later removed to Mount Auburn Cemetery, Cambridge.

[S. A. Worcester, *The Descendants of Rev. William Worcester* (1914); Henry Ware, Jr., *Memoirs of the Rev. Noah Worcester, D.D.* (1844); W. E. Channing, *A Tribute to the Memory of the Rev. Noah Worcester, D.D.* (1837); W. B. Sprague, *Annals of the Am. Unitarian Pulpit* (1865); William Ware, *Am. Unitarian Biog.*, vol. I (1850); S. A. Eliot, *Heralds of a Liberal Faith*, vol. II (1910); *Christian Examiner*, Jan. 1838.]
H. E. S.

WORCESTER, SAMUEL (Nov. 1, 1770–June 7, 1821), Congregational clergyman, was born in Hollis, N. H., the son of Noah and Lydia (Taylor) Worcester, and a younger brother of Noah Worcester [*q.v.*]. As a boy he worked on his father's farm, attending school winters, and at the age of seventeen became himself a teacher of district schools. He felt that he was not "made for a farmer," and in spite of violent opposition from his father, he determined to fit himself for a profession. Accordingly, in his twenty-first year, giving his father a promissory note for the value of his services during the remainder of his minority, he went to the New Ipswich Academy for further preparation and in the spring of 1792 entered Dartmouth College. Here, although compelled to absent himself winters to earn money by teaching, he distinguished himself as a scholar, graduating as valedictorian in 1795. He then pursued studies in theology, first, under

Rev. Samuel Austin [*q.v.*] of Worcester, Mass.; and later, while teaching in Hollis and at the New Ipswich Academy. On Sept. 27, 1797, he was ordained pastor of the Congregational Church of Fitchburg, Mass., and on Oct. 20, he married Zervia, daughter of Dr. Jonathan Fox of Hollis, by whom he had eleven children.

His first pastorate lasted but five years and gave rise to serious dissensions. Worcester was an inflexible Hopkinsian Calvinist. This fact brought him into conflict with Universalists and other liberals in his parish, and prompted him in 1800 to deliver and publish a series of six sermons on eternal judgment. Although his church supported him loyally, disaffected members of the parish employed all possible measures to force his resignation, and finally on Aug. 29, 1802, an ecclesiastical council dissolved the pastoral relation. Receiving a call from the Tabernacle Church, Salem, in November of the same year, he accepted it after some months of hesitation and was installed as its pastor on Apr. 20, 1803. His ministry here was successful and happy. In 1804 he was chosen professor of theology in Dartmouth College, but, on the advice of an ecclesiastical council, he declined the office. He became involved in 1815 in a famous controversy with William Ellery Channing, 1780–1842 [*q.v.*]. In June of that year the *Panoplist* published a review attributed to Jeremiah Evarts [*q.v.*], of *American Unitarianism; or a Brief History of the Progress and Present State of the Unitarian Churches in America*, a pamphlet containing portions of Thomas Belsham's biography of Rev. Theophilus Lindsley, a leader of English Unitarians. Channing in a published letter addressed to Rev. Samuel C. Thacher [*q.v.*] took emphatic exception to the characterization of American Unitarians in this review. Worcester replied in *A Letter to the Rev. William E. Channing . . .* (1815), and an exchange of pamphlets followed during which Worcester wrote a second and a third letter, both published in 1815. The controversy contributed no little to the growing separation in name and in fact of the liberal and orthodox factions in the Congregational body.

Worcester was active in the inauguration and forwarding of missionary activities. In 1799, while still in Fitchburg, he had been associated with the forming of the Massachusetts Missionary Society. In 1803 he became one of a group of clergyman which began the publication of the *Massachusetts Missionary Magazine*, to which he contributed, as he did also to the *Panoplist*, with which the *Magazine* was merged in 1808. He was one of the founders of the American

Board of Commissioners for Foreign Missions, in 1810, and became its first corresponding secretary. To the furthering of its expanding enterprises he devoted much time and energy. He was also prominent in organized efforts to combat intemperance. His duties as corresponding secretary for the American Board became so heavy that in 1819 Rev. Elias Cornelius was made associate pastor of the Tabernacle Church. In January 1821 Worcester went South for the benefit of his health and to visit missionary stations. His health did not improve, however, and he died at Brainerd, Tenn., in June. In 1844 his body was removed to Harmony Grove Cemetery, Salem, Mass. More than thirty of his sermons and addresses were published; a collection of these, *Sermons on Various Subjects,* appeared in 1823. To provide orthodox churches with a suitable hymnal, he also issued in 1815 *Christian Psalmody,* an abridgment of Watts's psalms and hymns, with select hymns from other authors and select harmony.

[S. A. Worcester, *The Descendants of Rev. William Worcester* (1914); S. M. Worcester, *The Life and Labors of Rev. Samuel Worcester, D.D.* (2 vols., 1852); W. B. Sprague, *Annals of the Am. Pulpit,* vol. II (1857); *Missionary Herald,* successor to the *Panoplist,* July, Aug. 1821.]   H. E. S.

WORCESTER, SAMUEL AUSTIN (Jan. 19, 1798–Apr. 20, 1859), missionary and translator, was born at Worcester, Mass., the descendant of William Worcester who emigrated from England to Salisbury, Mass., before 1640, the cousin of Joseph Emerson Worcester [*q.v.*], and the nephew of Noah and Samuel Worcester [*q.v.*]. The son of the Rev. Leonard and Elizabeth (Hopkins) Worcester, he was reared at Peacham, Vt., where his father taught him to farm and to set type. In 1819 he graduated from the University of Vermont, of which his uncle, Samuel Austin [*q.v.*], was president. He graduated from the Theological Seminary at Andover in 1823. On July 19, 1825, he married Ann Orr of Bedford, N. H., who died on May 23, 1840. Their daughter Ann Eliza married William Schenck Robertson [*q.v.*] and became the mother of Alice Mary Roberston [*q.v.*]. He was ordained a minister in Park Street Congregational Church at Boston, on Aug. 25, 1825, and departed almost immediately for Brainard Mission in the Cherokee Country of eastern Tennessee, where he remained as supervising missionary for two years. Under his supervision in 1827 types were made in Boston for the Cherokee alphabet, invented by Sequoyah [*q.v.*]. He soon afterward went to New Echota, Ga., where he served as missionary, translating portions of the Bible from Greek to Cherokee. These together

with many tracts and other religious works he printed on the press of the *Cherokee Phoenix,* the Cherokee newspaper which he had helped establish, and to which he was a frequent contributor. In 1831 he was arrested by officers of the state of Georgia and in September 1831 was sentenced to four years imprisonment for violation of a Georgia statute forbidding white persons to live in the Indian country without taking an oath of allegiance to the state and obtaining a license to reside among the Indians. His case was appealed to the Supreme Court of the United States, which decided in 1832 that the act of the Georgia legislature was unconstitutional (6 *Peters,* 597), but Worcester was not released from prison until Jan. 14, 1833.

Soon after his release from prison he transferred his activities to the Cherokee living west of the Mississippi River in what is now Oklahoma. He reached their country in May 1835 and after a short stay at Dwight Mission removed to Park Hill and began the work of establishing the Park Hill Mission. His task of erecting and equipping the new buildings was no doubt made easier by the fact that he had learned carpentry and the cabinet maker's trade, while in the Georgia penitentiary. In time the mission grew to be the largest and most important institution of its kind in the Indian Territory. The buildings included not only the church and school but also a boarding hall, gristmill, homes for the teachers and missionaries, and a book bindery and printing office, where he set up what was, doubtless, the first printing press in the Indian Territory. On this he printed in the Cherokee language thousands of copies of portions of the Bible, together with hymn books, tracts, a primer, and the Cherokee Almanac that was issued annually from 1838 to 1861. Religious material was printed not only for the Cherokee but also at times for the Creeks and Choctaw. He was for many years secretary of the Cherokee temperance society, which numbered more than fifteen hundred Cherokee among its members. He also organized in 1841 the Cherokee Bible society, which before his death had distributed among these Indians more than five thousand copies of the portions of the Bible he had translated and printed in the Cherokee language. Unlike many of the earlier missionaries he was quick to see the possibilities of the Cherokee written language invented by Sequoyah and earnestly urged the Cherokee to learn and to use it. On Apr. 3, 1841, he married, as his second wife, Erminia Nash, who had been born at Cummington, Mass. She died at Fort Gibson, Indian Territory, on May 5, 1872. He was buried beside the body of his first wife in the little Worcester Cemetery a short distance southwest of Park Hill.

[Letters among missionary letters, Andover-Harvard Theological Lib., Cambridge, Mass., in Alice Robertson Coll., Tulsa Univ., Tulsa, Okla.; letters and copies in possession of Okla. Hist. Soc.; Althea Bass, *Cherokee Messenger* (1936); R. S. Walker, *Torchlights to the Cherokees* (1931); S. A. Worcester, *The Descendants of Rev. Wm. Worcester* (1914).]   E. E. D.

WORDEN, JOHN LORIMER (Mar. 12, 1818–Oct. 18, 1897), naval officer, was born at Westchester County, N. Y. He was the son of Ananias and Harriet (Graham) Worden and the great-grandson of Surgeon Andrew Graham, who was on the Connecticut Committee of Public Safety in the Revolution. He was appointed midshipman on Jan. 10, 1834, and after three years in the Brazil Squadron and seven months at the Philadelphia Naval School was made passed midshipman, July 16, 1840. In 1840–42 he was in the Pacific Squadron, and in 1844–46 at the Naval Observatory. During and after the Mexican War he served in the storeship *Southampton* and other vessels on the west coast. Duty at the Naval Observatory (1850–52) and cruises in the Mediterranean and Home Squadrons occupied most of the next decade. Stationed in Washington just before the Civil War, he was sent south, on Apr. 7, 1861, with secret orders to the squadron at Pensacola for the reinforcement of Fort Pickens. After delivering his message he was arrested on his return journey near Montgomery, Ala., and held prisoner until his exchange seven months later.

Though hardly recovered from illness due to his confinement, he reported, Jan. 16, 1862, to command Ericsson's new ironclad *Monitor,* then building at Greenpoint, L. I. After supervising her completion he commanded her on her rough passage down the coast. Disaster was constantly threatened by leaks, foul air, defective steering gear, and other faults of experimental construction. Worden later declared that the difficulties then overcome were as great as those of the subsequent battle (see Schley, *post,* p. 106). Reaching Hampton Roads about 9 P.M. Mar. 8, all hands spent a disturbed night in preparation for meeting the *Merrimac* next day. In the battle, vital for the maintenance of the Northern blockade and revolutionary in its influence on naval design, Worden had his station in the pilot house, forward of the turret. After three hours of fighting he was wounded in the face and nearly blinded by a shell exploding just outside. The command was taken over by his first officer, Samuel D. Greene [*q.v.*], but when the *Monitor* returned after temporary withdrawal the *Merri-*

mac had also withdrawn. For his resolute conduct of the action, and in the general relief at its outcome, Worden at once gained national renown. The devotion of his ship's company is demonstrated in the exclamation, "How I love and venerate that man," used by his young lieutenant, Greene, in a letter to the latter's mother (*Proceedings of the United States Naval Institute,* November 1923, p. 1845). Congress gave him a special vote of thanks and advanced him from commander to captain on Feb. 3, 1863. From October 1862 to April 1863 he commanded the monitor *Montauk* in the South Atlantic Blockading Squadron, engaging on Jan. 27 in a four-hour action with Fort McAllister which served chiefly as a favorable test of the monitor type, and a month later destroying, by five well-placed shots, the Confederate cruiser *Nashville* under the guns of this fort. His vessel was struck fourteen times on Apr. 7 in the general monitor attack on Charleston.

Detached shortly afterwards, he was subsequently engaged in ironclad construction work at New York till after the close of the war. He was made commodore, May 26, 1868; rear admiral, Nov. 20, 1872; and was superintendent of the Naval Academy (1869–74). From 1875 to 1877 he commanded the European Squadron, which visited many ports of northern Europe and was in the eastern Mediterranean during the Russo-Turkish War. Thereafter he was a member of the Examining Board and President of the Retiring Board until his voluntary retirement on Dec. 23, 1886, when Congress awarded him for life the full sea pay of his grade. His home continued to be in Washington, D. C., where he died of pneumonia. His funeral was at St. John's Episcopal Church, Washington, and his interment at Pawling, N. Y. He was married to Olivia Taffey, and she and their four children survived him.

[Two letter-books (Personnel Files) and official reports (Captains' Letters), Navy Dept. Library; J. T. Headley, *Farragut and Our Naval Commanders* (1867); *War of the Rebellion: Official Records* (Navy), see index volume; L. H. Cornish, *Nat. Reg. of the Soc. of the Sons of the Am. Revolution* (1902); W. S. Schley, *Forty-Five Years under the Flag* (1904); *Army and Navy Jour.,* Oct. 23, 1897; *Washington Post,* Oct. 19, 1897.]   A. W.

WORK, HENRY CLAY (Oct. 1, 1832–June 8, 1884), song-writer, was born in Middletown, Conn., the son of Alanson and Aurelia Work, and a descendant of Joseph Work who emigrated to Connecticut from Ireland in 1720. His father was a militant abolitionist, who, in order to help in the cause of freeing runaway slaves, moved his family to Quincy, Ill., when Henry was three years of age. In Illinois and Missouri he aided about four thousand slaves to escape by maintaining his home as one of the "stations" of the Underground Railroad. His efforts were rewarded with imprisonment, and upon his release in 1845 the family returned to Middletown. Henry Work received a common-school education in Middletown and later in Hartford, where he became an apprentice in the printing shop of Elihu Greer. In a room above the print shop Work found an old melodeon; he practiced on it, studied harmony, and began writing a few songs to sing to his friends. In 1854 he went to Chicago to ply his trade as printer, but he continued to write songs. His success was at first indifferent, but when "We're Coming, Sister Mary" (composed for the Christy Minstrels) was published, it achieved wide circulation and brought the author a substantial return. In 1864 he wrote his famous temperance song, "Come Home, Father." This was tremendously successful, and, as a "story-song," was thoroughly in keeping with the taste of the period. For years it was sung in the play, "Ten Nights in a Barroom." The opening lines of Work's long "serio-comic" poem, *The Upshot Family* (1868), are typical of his other efforts in rhyme:

> "Far up in Vermont,
>   Where the hills are so steep
> That the farmers use ladders
>   To pasture their sheep . . ."

Work's publisher, George F. Root [q.v.], of the firm of Root & Cady, persuaded him to try his hand at writing Civil War songs. Because of his abolitionist background Work willingly lent his talents to the Northern cause and contributed "Kingdom Coming" (1861), "Babylon is Fallen!" (1863), "Wake Nicodemus" (1864), "Marching through Georgia" (1865), and a number of other highly partisan songs. Following the success of "Kingdom Coming," Root & Cady offered Work a contract as a song-writer for the firm, and he was able to abandon his work as a printer. He maintained his headquarters in Chicago until the great fire of 1871, when the firm of Root & Cady was ruined financially and the plates of all his songs were destroyed. For a time he lived in Philadelphia and then moved to Vineland, N. J., where he had joined his brother and an uncle in purchasing one hundred and fifty acres of land for speculative purposes. The venture was not succesful. By 1875 Root & Cady was reëstablished, and Work returned to Chicago, where he resumed his career as songwriter, with even more financial success than before. The song "Grandfather's Clock," published after the Civil War, is said to have sold over 800,000 copies, and to have brought the composer $4,000 in royalties. The exact number of Work's published songs is not known, although the records of his family show a list of seventy-three (Work, *post*). He died in Hartford, Conn., while visiting his mother, and was buried in the Spring Grove Cemetery beside his wife, who had preceded him in death about a year. They had been married in Chicago between 1860 and 1864. Her mental illness in her last years was the burden of Work's sorrow before his death. Two of their three children had died in Chicago.

[B. Q. Work, *Songs of Henry Clay Work* (privately printed, n.d.) ; George Birdseye, "America's Song Composers," *Potter's Am. Monthly*, Apr. 1879; W. S. B. Mathews, *One Hundred Years of Music in America* (1889) ; J. T. Howard, *Our Am. Music* (1930) ; Henry Asbury, *Reminiscences of Quincy, Ill.* (1882) ; *Hartford Courant*, June 9, 1884 ; information from Mrs. B. H. Work of Glastonbury, Conn.]   J.T.H.

WORK, MILTON COOPER (Sept. 15, 1864–June 27, 1934), auction and contract bridge expert, lawyer, was born in Philadelphia, Pa., the son of Robert D. and Anna K. (Whiteman) Work. His parents were both enthusiastic players of whist, the popular card game of that day, and he himself was quite skilful before he became a student at the University of Pennsylvania. While still in college, he arranged what was probably the first duplicate contest held in the United States. He was catcher on his college nine, manager of the football team, and a player of cricket, then very popular. Upon his graduation from the University of Pennsylvania (B.A., 1884; LL.B., 1887), he set out upon a career which brought him note as a lawyer in Philadelphia. After an injury at golf he gave more and more attention to the study of cards as an avocation. As early as 1895 he brought out a short book called *Whist of To-day*; his first book on bridge, *Auction Developments,* was published in 1913. When the United States entered the World War, he abandoned his law practice and spent his time giving lectures and bridge demonstrations throughout the country in behalf of the Red Cross. After that his popularity as a bridge expert was assured. His advice was so clear that his books and articles, of which he published many, won a larger number of readers during the ensuing years than those of any other expert. Soon bridge teachers in every part of the country looked to him for tutelage. His activity in the famous radio bridge games of 1925 to 1930, during most of the time in conjunction with Wilbur C. Whitehead [q.v.], and his work with Whitehead as an editor of the *Auction Bridge Magazine* had a tremendous influence in increasing the number of bridge players.

Many of the phases through which the game passed, from whist to contract, were influenced profoundly by Work's clear-thinking, orderly, legal mind. A member of practically every important committee, he drafted many rules and frequently served as chairman of the committee in charge. After the advent of contract, he was in the forefront of those with bidding systems to offer to the rank and file of players. His own system underwent many changes until he became a participant in the movement of 1931–32 to bring about a universal system of bidding. Later he carried forward with successive revisions of his own method, which was always distinguished by the "artificial two-club game-demand" bid he had developed. Always a member of many bridge clubs, he did not sponsor one of his own until after the advent of contract, when he built the Barclay Club of Philadelphia to a position of prominence both socially and in the world of bridge. He was president of the United States Bridge Association, formed a few years before his death, and during his last few years he returned successfully to tournament competition.

A man of great height, dominant bearing, and patrician appearance, he was impressive on a speaker's platform. His voice, with an unusual measured emphasis, was known to millions who had heard him in person or "on the air." He was the most tireless worker of his time in bridge. Though he was reputed to have made a fortune out of bridge, he left no great amount of money at his death, and he preferred to think of himself as a popularizer of the game who brought its pleasures to more people than anyone else. Work was married twice: first to Millicent Dreka, from whom he was divorced; second, to Margaret (Hazelhurst) Patton, who survived him.

[*Who's Who in America*, 1932–33; *Univ. of Pa., Biog. Cat. of Matriculates* (1894); *N. Y. Times*, June 27, 1934 (obituary), June 28, July 13 (will); obituary in *Evening Bull.* (Phila.), June 27, 1934; long personal acquaintance.]   S. B.

WORKMAN, FANNY BULLOCK (Jan. 8, 1859–Jan. 22, 1925), explorer and writer, was born in Worcester, Mass., the daughter of Alexander Hamilton Bullock, a governor of Massachusetts, and Elvira (Hazard) Bullock. She was a grand-daughter of Augustus George Hazard [*q.v.*]. She was educated at Miss Graham's Finishing School in New York City and was taken abroad, where she attended schools in Paris and Dresden. She returned to Worcester in the spring of 1879 and two years later (June 16, 1881) married Dr. William Hunter Workman, a prominent physician. There was one daughter, who later became a geologist. In 1886 Mrs.

Workman and her husband visited Norway, Sweden, and Germany. Three years later ill health forced Dr. Workman to resign his practice. The following nine years the Workmans spent largely in Germany, with visits to southern Europe, northern Africa, Egypt, Palestine, and Greece. Subsequent travels carried them—frequently on bicycles—through India, Ceylon, Java, Sumatra, and Cochin-China. Mrs. Workman's career as an explorer began in 1899, when, with her husband, she made her first trip to the Himalayas. On subsequent expeditions to the Himalayas and to the Karakoram (or Mustagh) Range, she achieved the world mountaineering record for women (1906). She made numerous first ascents, climbed a number of peaks with elevations of over 20,000 feet, crossed and explored glaciers, discovered watersheds, and mapped previously unsurveyed territory. The titles of the books in which she and her husband collaborated give a roughly chronological account of their expeditions: *Algerian Memories* (1895), *Sketches Awheel in Modern Iberia* (1897), *In the Ice World of Himálaya* (1900), *Through Town and Jungle* (1904), which dealt with India, *Ice-Bound Heights of the Mustagh* (1908), *Peaks and Glaciers of Nun Kun* (1909), *The Call of the Snowy Hispar* (1910), *Two Summers in the Ice Wilds of Eastern Karakoram* (1917). These books are of permanent value to geographers studying the regions which they explored. The unsettled nomenclature of the Himalayas and Karakorams, however, necessitates some care in the use of the names given by the Workmans. The scholarly background of the writers enabled them to treat with historical perspective the inhabited countries they studied, but their comments on the inhabitants and their art forms do not show the sociological understanding for which later writers have striven. In addition to these books, Mrs. Workman wrote a number of articles for such magazines as *Harper's*, *Putnam's*, and the *Independent*. Both books and articles are illustrated with excellent photographs.

An accomplished linguist, Mrs. Workman lectured before learned societies both in Europe and in America, and was the first American woman to lecture before the Sorbonne of Paris. Her accomplishments were recognized by many honors. She was an *officier de l'instruction publique* of France (1904), the recipient of the highest medals of ten European geographic societies, a fellow both of the Royal Geographical and the Royal Scottish Geographical societies, and a member of the Royal Asiatic Society. She was a student of literature and art, and an ardent

Wagnerite, attending the Wagner festivals at Bayreuth for five seasons. During the World War she lived in France. She died at Cannes. After cremation at Marseilles, her ashes were brought to the Rural Cemetery at Worcester.

[Sources include *Who's Who in America*, 1918–19; A. W. Tarbell, in *New England Mag.*, Dec. 1905, with photograph; Fanny B. Workman, in *Nat. Geographic Mag.*, Nov. 1902; correspondence with Dr. W. H. Workman, who supplied the date of death and other information, Chandler Bullock (a nephew), G. T. Richardson of the *Worcester Evening Post*, G. F. Booth of the *Worcester Telegram and Gazette*, and Dr. C. S. Brigham of the Am. Antiquarian Soc.; obituary in *N. Y. Times*, Jan. 27, 1925. The date of birth is from Worcester records.] E. W. H.

WORMELEY, KATHARINE PRESCOTT (Jan. 14, 1830–Aug. 4, 1908), author, philanthropist, was born in Ipswich, England, the second of three daughters of Ralph Randolph and Caroline (Preble) Wormeley, and sister of Mary Elizabeth Wormeley Latimer [*q.v.*]. Her father was a rear-admiral in the British navy. When Katharine was about eighteen, the family settled in the United States, where she spent the remainder of her life. Before leaving Europe she saw much of the best English and French society, and met Thackeray when he was awaiting the verdict of the reading public on *Vanity Fair*. She was in Paris at the time of the second funeral of Napoleon, and describes it vividly in "Napoleon's Return from St. Helena" (*Putnam's Monthly*, July 1908). During the Civil War she participated in relief measures for Union soldiers, and later was superintendent of a hospital for convalescent soldiers at Portsmouth Grove, R. I. She wrote a sketch of the purposes and work of the United States Sanitary Commission, compiled from documents and private papers (1863). Her *The Other Side of War* (1889) consists of letters from the headquarters of the United States Sanitary Commission during the Peninsular campaign in Virginia in 1862. She lived many years in Newport, R. I., where she took an active part in public affairs, especially those relating to sanitation, charitable organizations, work of women and girls and their instruction in domestic science. She founded the Girls' Industrial School at Newport and carried its expense for three years, after which it was taken over by the public school system.

She is best known for her translations of the works of noted French writers, particularly Balzac, to which she devoted herself from the early eighties to the end of her life. She also wrote *A Memoir of Honoré de Balzac* (1892). Some of her chief translations are *The Works of Balzac* (1899–), Paul Bourget's *Pastels of Men* (1891, 1892), several works of Alexandre Dumas (1894–

1902), a number of the plays of Molière (1894–97), *The Works of Alphonse Daudet* (1898–1900); *Memoirs of the Duc de Saint-Simon* (1899); *Letters of Mlle. de Lespinasse* (1901); *Diary and Correspondence of Count Axel Fersen* (1902); and Sainte-Beuve's *Portraits of the Eighteenth Century* (1905). It is said that she "had so wrapped herself up in the work of translating the *Comédie Humaine* that she apparently came to look upon its author as a personal charge" (*Bookman, post*, p. 479), and rose vehemently to his defense when someone expressed an opinion which she considered derogatory. The same sympathy and understanding which prompted her philanthropic work aided her success in the literary field. She was an accomplished French scholar and understood French culture, so that in her translations she was never enslaved to her text, but conveyed spirit as well as actual meaning.

She spent the last years of her life in Jackson, N. H., where she died after a short illness resulting from a fall on the steps of her house. Her remains, after cremation, were buried in Newport, R. I., beside the grave of her father.

[*Who's Who in America*, 1908–09; Frances E. Willard and Mary A. Livermore, *A Woman of the Century* (1893); Sara A. Shafer, in *Dial*, Feb. 1, 1904; *Bookman*, Jan. 1908; obituaries in *Dial*, Aug. 16, 1908, and *Newport Mercury* (Newport, R. I.), Aug. 8, 1908; private information.] S. G. B.

WORMELEY, MARY ELIZABETH [See LATIMER, MARY ELIZABETH WORMELEY, 1822–1904].

WORMLEY, JAMES (Jan. 16, 1819–Oct. 18, 1884), steward, caterer, and hotel keeper, was born in Washington, D. C., of negro parentage. Until his parents settled in Washington in 1814 they had lived with a wealthy family of Virginia but had never been held as slaves. The father, Pere Leigh Wormley, had straight black hair, and the children in the family were said to have grown up thinking they were of Indian blood. The mother was fair-skinned and was known locally for her beauty and kindly character. At an early age James Wormley became a hack-driver for his father, who kept a livery stable in the hotel section of Washington. Later he drove his own hack. His integrity, industry, and straightforward manner won the interest and confidence of his patrons, and he soon secured most of the trade of the two chief hotels, the National and Willard's. These early patrons included many of the leading public men of the day, not a few of whom remained his lifelong friends and benefactors. About 1841 he married Anna Thompson of Norfolk, Va., by whom he had three sons and a daughter. While still a young man he went West, visiting California during the gold rush of 1849 and for a time working as a steward on a Mississippi River steamboat. He also served in a similar capacity on naval vessels at sea, returning to Washington to become steward for the Metropolitan Club when its first clubhouse was opened.

His success in this venture encouraged him to undertake an independent business, and shortly before the outbreak of the Civil War he opened a hotel and catering establishment on I Street near Fifteenth, while his wife ran a thriving confectionery store next door. Wormley's business prospered, and in 1871 he moved into larger and improved quarters at the corner of H and Fifteenth streets, the property on I Street becoming an annex to the new hotel. His establishment maintained a high standard of service and its cuisine had a national reputation. For more than two decades Wormley's Hotel, as it was known, was the temporary home of nationally and internationally famous men, and its parlors were the scene of many distinguished social gatherings. Wormley was equally successful as a caterer. In 1868 he accompanied Reverdy Johnson [q.v.] to London to act as steward at the American legation and assure the successful entertainment of the British statesmen. While abroad he visited Paris.

His industry, ability, and business acumen brought him a considerable fortune and at the time of his death, which occurred in Boston, he was said to have been worth a hundred thousand dollars. Throughout his life he maintained the strictest business integrity. In his later years he enjoyed the friendship and patronage of many distinguished and influential men, but he never made political use of the confidence placed in him nor allowed others to do so. He spent his life in serving others, but he was never servile in manner and exacted the same respect which he accorded. He was intensely interested in the problems and welfare of the negro and was in correspondence with Charles Sumner [q.v.] and other friends and benefactors of his race. His three sons aided him in his business, but his grandchildren were educated and trained to serve their people.

[*Evening Star* (Washington), Oct. 17, 18, 20, 25 (editorial), 1884; *Washington Post*, Oct. 18, 20, 1884; *Jour. of Negro Hist.*, Apr. 1935, Jan. 1936; *Boyd's Directory of the District of Columbia*, 1871, 1872; information from two granddaughters, the Misses Josephine and Imogene Wormley.] V. L. S.

WORMLEY, THEODORE GEORGE (Apr. 1, 1826–Jan. 3, 1897), physician, toxicologist, was born at Wormleysburg, Pa., the son of David

and Isabella Wormley. The family was of Dutch origin, the original immigrants having come to America about the middle of the eighteenth century. His father died when Wormley was an infant, and he was reared by his mother, to whom he may have been chiefly indebted for his love of nature and delight in music. After three years (1842–45) at Dickinson College, Carlisle, Pa., he began to study medicine, in the old-fashioned way, under a "preceptor," Dr. John J. Meyers, with whom he spent two years. He then entered the Philadelphia College of Medicine, from which he was graduated with the degree of M.D. in 1849. He began the practice of medicine in Carlisle, Pa., but soon moved to Chillicothe, Ohio, and then to Columbus, where he remained twenty-seven years. In Columbus he met and married Ann Eliza Gill, daughter of John Loriman and Mary Waters Gill. For many years he served as professor of toxicology at Capitol University, Columbus (1852–63), and at Starling Medical College (1852–77). In 1867 he published *The Micro-chemistry of Poisons*, a work of such merit that it immediately became the classic writing upon the subject. The beautiful illustrations for the first edition were drawn by Mrs. Wormley. When it was found that the cost of engraving them on steel would be such as to prohibit publication, she actually learned the art of steel-engraving so as to reproduce them. The added illustrations for editions that appeared after Mrs. Wormley's death were drawn by one of her daughters. In Ohio Wormley was state gas commissioner (1867–75), chemist to the state geological survey (1869–74), and editor of the *Ohio Medical and Surgical Journal* (1862–64). During the Civil War he served on a relief commission to provide stores and surgical assistance for the armies in the field. In 1874 he was one of the vice-presidents of the centennial of chemistry, and in 1876 he delivered an address on medical chemistry and toxicology before the international medical congress held in Philadelphia. In 1877 he accepted the chair of chemistry and toxicology in the medical department of the University of Pennsylvania. This he held until his death, which was caused by Bright's disease.

Wormley was a most punctilious man and a true scientist, with whom, "in searching for the truth, time and labor ceased . . . to be factors" (Smith, *post*, p. 278). He was always at work before nine and continued after five, longer hours than most of his colleagues. His lectures, delivered from carefully prepared notes, were without ornament or embellishment, and would have been dull had it not been for the numerous, well-conducted experiments by which they were illustrated. Wormley knew and loved flowers, and was expert in his knowledge of fishes—a new and brilliantly colored one, *Etheostoma iris,* he named. He also played well upon the flute, bugle, and French horn, and transcribed concerted pieces that he and a group of music-loving friends played. He had many acquaintances but few intimate friends, being too reserved, self-contained, and preoccupied.

[John Ashhurst, *Trans. College of Physicians of Phila.,* vol. XIX (1897) ; E. F. Smith, in *Jour. Am. Chemical Soc.,* Apr. 1897 ; J. L. Chamberlain, ed., *Universities and Their Sons: Univ. of Pa.,* vol. I (1901) ; H. A. Kelly and W. L. Burrage, *Am. Medic. Biogs.* (1920) ; obituary in *Pub. Ledger* (Phila.), Jan. 4, 1897 ; personal recollections.]   J. M.

WORTH, JONATHAN (Nov. 18, 1802–Sept. 5, 1869), governor of North Carolina, was a native of Guilford County, N. C. He was the eldest son of Dr. David and Eunice (Gardner) Worth, and through his father traced his ancestry back to early settlers of Massachusetts ; one branch of the family, many of them Quakers, moved to North Carolina from Nantucket before the Revolution. Worth went to the neighborhood oldfield schools and to Caldwell Institute in Greensboro, and then studied law under Archibald D. Murphey [*q.v.*], whose niece and ward, Martitia Daniel, he married on Oct. 20, 1824. In the same year he began practice at Asheboro. He was shy and retiring and made slow progress, but in 1830 he was elected to the House of Commons and, reëlected for a second term, gained a confidence in himself that ended his difficulties. In addition to his practice he engaged in numerous business enterprises, operating several plantations and a turpentine tract and furthering the building of railroads and plank roads.

In the legislature of 1831 he took the lead in formulating the protest of the House of Commons against nullification, but he was a bitter opponent of the Jackson administration, and became an enthusiastic and partisan Whig. He was an unsuccessful candidate for Congress in 1841 and again in 1845. For a number of years he was clerk and master in equity in Randolph County, but in 1858 he returned to the legislature, where he served two terms in the Senate and one in the Commons. In 1860 he actively opposed the secession movement in the legislature, voting against the bill to submit the question of a convention to the voters, against all the bills for military preparation, and, after the call for troops, against the call of a convention. Resolved to have no part in secession, he refused to be a candidate for the convention, but his mind was definitely made up to support the South and he did so in all sincerity. In 1862 he was elected state treas-

urer, and in handling an almost impossible task displayed financial capacity of a high order. Though he hated the war, he took no part in the peace movement, but, foreseeing the outcome, was happy when peace finally came. The provisional governor, W. W. Holden [*q.v.*], continued him as treasurer, but he resigned in the autumn of 1865 to accept nomination for governor from a group of old Union men who distrusted Holden. Worth was elected, and was reëlected in 1866, serving until 1868 when, congressional reconstruction having taken place, he was removed by order of General Canby, commanding the second military district.

Throughout his term of office he gave President Johnson and his policy whole-hearted support. His position was one requiring the soundest judgment and the greatest care and tact. Unfriendly elements had to be reconciled, a faction bitterly hostile to the Governor—and to every one opposed to their ideas—had to be watched, a suspicious administration in Washington had to be reassured, and a watchful and hostile North had to be satisfied. All of these ends but the last he accomplished, and that was beyond the power of any Southern man mindful of the people he represented. Worth, unlike most of his supporters, favored the ratification of the new constitution submitted in 1866, but he strongly opposed the ratification of the Fourteenth Amendment. Though bitter in his hatred of congressional reconstruction, he established friendly relations with Gen. Daniel E. Sickles, who first commanded the second district, and was thus able in many respects to mitigate the harshness of military rule. After his removal from the governorship in 1868 his health failed rapidly, and he died in Raleigh the following year.

Worth possessed no touch of brilliance, but was heavily endowed with practical sense and acquired from study, reflection, and experience unusually sound judgment and a genius for taking good advice, which, combined with integrity, won him widespread confidence. Given to seriousness, he was, nevertheless, a very human person. He was the father of eight children.

[*The Correspondence of Jonathan Worth* (2 vols., 1909), ed. by J. G. deR. Hamilton ; S. A. Ashe, *Biog. Hist. of N. C.,* vol. III (1905) ; J. G. deR. Hamilton, *Reconstruction in N. C.* (1914) ; *Daily Standard* (Raleigh, N. C.), Sept. 7, 1869, which gives day of death as Sept. 6.]   J. G. deR. H.

WORTH, WILLIAM JENKINS (Mar. 1, 1794–May 7, 1849), soldier, was born in Hudson, Columbia County, N. Y., of Quaker parents. His father was Thomas Worth, a seaman, one of the original proprietors of Hudson, and his mother was a daughter of Marshall Jenkins. He was related to John Worth Edmonds [*q.v.*]. After a common school education, he entered a store in Hudson, but removed shortly to Albany, where he continued his mercantile pursuits until the opening of the War of 1812, when he applied for a commission in the army. He was appointed first lieutenant, 23d Infantry, Mar. 19, 1813. After he had served as private secretary in the official family of Gen. Morgan Lewis, he was selected by Gen. Winfield Scott [*qq.v.*] as aide-de-camp. At Chippewa and Lundy's Lane his zeal and intrepidity were eulogized by Scott in his report of the battles. At Lundy's Lane he was so severely wounded that for a time it was felt he would die. As it was, he was confined to his bed for a year and lamed for life. He was brevetted a captain for his work at Chippewa and a major for Niagara. Though somewhat crippled, he remained in the army after the war, serving both in the 1st Artillery and in the Ordnance Department. From 1820 to 1828 he was commandant of cadets at the United States Military Academy, although he was not a graduate of the Academy. On July 25, 1824, he was brevetted a lieutenant-colonel for ten years of faithful service in one grade. He became colonel of the 8th Infantry, July 7, 1838, and as such commanded in Florida at the battle of Palaklaklaha, where the Seminoles were disastrously defeated. For "gallantry and highly distinguished services" in that engagement he was brevetted a brigadier-general by President Polk.

When the war with Mexico was brewing Worth was ordered to join Zachary Taylor in the Army of Occupation. Here he was second in command until David E. Twiggs [*q.v.*] appeared. With Twiggs he took part in an acrimonious and unfortunate controversy over rank. He fought well in the battles of Palo Alto and Resaca de la Palma, and was the first to plant the flag on the Rio Grande. At Monterey, where the weather buffeted him and he was left to his fate by Taylor on Independence Hill, he so successfully stormed the heights and the town that a large part of the victory should be credited to him. He was rewarded, Sept. 23, 1846, by a brevet of major-general and by a resolution of Congress, Mar. 2, 1847, presenting him with a sword. Shortly after that battle he was transferred south with Scott's victorious army, where he took part in all the engagements from Vera Cruz to Mexico City. At Cerro Gordo he showed energy and efficiency, and diligently pursued the flying Mexicans after the battle. At Churubusco, Chapultepec, and Mexico City, he again showed himself to be an indomitable force upon the field.

A certain deficiency in temperament and char-acter which displayed itself most noticeably off the battlefield caused Worth's reputation to suffer. He was narrow and self-centered; at Vera Cruz the suggestion that he might be president was his undoing. His governorship of Puebla was fraught with unsound decisions, harassment of the soldiers, and a disregard of the native population. When mildly called to account, his ambition took refuge in hostility to Scott. Toward the end of the expedition, he found opportunity to enter into a cabal with Pillow and Duncan against Scott, who had given him his start and treated him with every consideration. His letters caused articles to be written in the newspapers in the states; the purport untruthfully credited the triumvirate and discredited Scott with ridicule and contempt (W. R. Benjamin's and Mrs. K. S. Hubbell's collections of Worth's letters). When called upon for an explanation, he became truculent, defiant and insulting, so that Scott had to place him in arrest. Worth's failings robbed him of the full glory of his attainments in campaign, but as a leader in battle few have surpassed him. His proud, resolute, commanding mien under fire and his promptness and decision in giving orders inspired his subordinates with confidence. After the war he was placed by Scott in command of the Department of Texas, where he was seized by cholera and prematurely died. He had been married, on Sept. 18, 1818, to Margaret Stafford of Albany, N. Y., who, with their three daughters and a son, survived him.

[H. M. Benedict, *A Contribution to the Geneal. of the Stafford Family* (1870); W. F. Scarborough, "William Jenkins Worth—Soldier," *Americana*, July 1929; A. R. Bradbury, *Hist. of the City of Hudson, N. Y.* (1908); Fernando Wood, *Address . . . at the Funeral Ceremonies . . . of Maj.-Gen. Worth* (1857); W. H. Powell, *List of Officers of the Army . . . 1779 to 1900* (1900); W. A. Ganoe, *Hist. of the U. S. Army* (1924); J. H. Smith, *War With Mexico* (2 vols., 1919); *New Orleans Weekly Delta*, Sept. 10, 1847, May 21, 1849.]
W. A. G.

WORTHEN, AMOS HENRY (Oct. 31, 1813–May 6, 1888), geologist, was born at Bradford, Vt., the son of Thomas Worthen, an enterprising farmer, and Susannah (Adams) Worthen, who is said to have been a direct descendant of Henry Adams, the founder of the distinguished Adams family in America. He was educated at Bradford Academy. On Jan. 14, 1834, he was married to Sarah B. Kimball of Warren, N. H., by whom he had seven children. Of these, the sole daughter died in infancy, but the six sons all reached manhood. In August 1834 Worthen moved to Kentucky, but before the year was out he was teaching school in Cumminsville, Ohio. In June 1836 he moved to Warsaw, Ill., and there, with his wife's brothers, he entered the dry-goods business. In 1842 he moved to Boston, probably because of the business depression in Warsaw engendered by Mormon difficulties in the county.

In Illinois he had been greatly attracted by the geode beds and other geological features in the Warsaw area. When he went east, he took with him several barrels of the geodes; but instead of selling them at the fancy prices they then commanded, he traded them for a cabinet of sea-shells that he realized at once were related to forms preserved in the shales and limestones of his adopted state. In attempting to learn more about these fossils, he stumbled onto Dr. Gideon Mantell's *The Medals of Creation* and *The Wonders of Geology,* and his study of these books crystallized in him the desire to become a scientist. When he returned to Warsaw in July 1844, he became more and more engrossed in geology, and at last he retired from business, though with financial loss. In the meantime, his collections had grown apace, and he was becoming well known to eastern scientists. Many of his specimens were borrowed by James Hall [*q.v.*] of Albany and were described in the latter's account of the paleontology of Iowa.

After the establishment of a geological survey of Illinois, Worthen found sporadic employment under the direction of J. G. Norwood, but it was not until 1855 that he began his first active geological duties, under Hall on the Iowa survey. Meanwhile the Illinois survey work had languished. When in 1858 Worthen was appointed state geologist, there were turned over to him a single report on the lead mines of Hardin County and a few field notes. With his own great energy and a great deal of enthusiasm on the part of some of the ablest specialists of his day, whom he was sagacious enough to hire, he soon turned a moribund bureau into an organization seething with activity. During his term of office he published seven large volumes of the *Geological Survey of Illinois* (8 vols., 1866–90), and had the material for the eighth ready for the press at the time of his death. Considering that the geological work of the state was completed, he intended to resign when the last volume was printed. Judged by later standards the work had scarcely begun, but every county in the state had been considered in the reports, and the state's major mineral resources had been outlined. A much more lasting contribution to science made in Worthen's publications was the description of 1626 species of fossils, comprising 1073 invertebrate animals, 297 vertebrates, and 256 plants. Nearly 1500 of these were described for the first time in these volumes, and all were beauti-fully illustrated. Although Worthen's hand is seen in every page of these publications, his numerous able assistants also contributed heavily to the scientific papers. Worthen himself was chiefly interested in the classification of the Lower Carboniferous strata, and he is still regarded by many as the pioneer in this important stratigraphic work. Worthen was always affable, but even up to the last he had an unceasing ambition to carve out a real scientific career for himself; thus he had little time for the less serious things in life. Although he set no great store by such honors, he was elected to a number of European as well as American honorary societies, among them the American Philosophical Society and the National Academy of Sciences.

[N. W. Bliss, in *Geological Survey of Ill.,* vol. VIII (1890); C. A. White, *Ibid.,* with full bibliog., and memoir in *Nat. Acad. of Sci. Biog. Memoirs,* vol. III (1895); E. O. Ulrich, in *Am. Geologist,* Aug. 1888.]

C. C.

WORTHEN, WILLIAM EZRA (Mar. 14, 1819–Apr. 2, 1897), civil engineer, son of Ezra and Mary (Currier) Worthen, was born at Amesbury, Mass. His father was one of the projectors of the city of Lowell, Mass., and was made the first superintendent of the Merrimack Mills there in 1822. William was prepared for college in Boston, and graduated at Harvard in 1838. He began his professional career as an assistant in the office of the younger Loammi Baldwin [*q.v.*] upon water-supply and hydraulic work in Lowell and Boston, then in similar capacity was associated with James B. Francis [*q.v.*], another well-known engineer. In 1840–42, he was engaged under George W. Whistler [*q.v.*] upon the Albany & West Stockbridge Railroad, with seven miles of road in his charge. Returning to Lowell with Francis, he designed and built many dams and mills and carried on other hydraulic work in eastern Massachusetts and southern New Hampshire.

After a visit to Europe, he settled in New York in 1849, engaging in building and mill construction. He also built the dam across the Mohawk River at Cohoes, N. Y., and the floating docks for the Jersey City depots of the Erie Railway. He was widely known as an expert upon pumping machinery, and was called upon both to design and to test such machinery in New York, Cincinnati, and St. Louis. He also selected pumping engines for Boston and tested large pumping units at Brooklyn, Lawrence, Philadelphia, Milwaukee, and other cities. He had much practice in the measurement of flow of water in canals, reporting upon this subject for Paterson, Trenton, Passaic, Indianapolis, and other places. In addition to his consulting practice, he served for a time as engineer of the New York & New Haven Railroad, of which he was made vice-president in 1854. From 1866 to 1869 he was sanitary engineer to the New York Metropolitan Board of Health, and served on a number of engineering boards in connection with various municipal projects. In Brooklyn he reported upon an extensive addition to the sewer system. With James B. Francis and Theodore S. Ellis, in 1874 he served upon a committee to report upon the failure of Mill River dam, at Williamsburg, Mass. (*Transactions of the American Society of Civil Engineers,* vol. III, 1874, pp. 118–22). In 1890–91 he was chief engineer of the Chicago Main Drainage Canal.

Worthen was the editor of *Appleton's Cyclopedia of Drawing* (1857, many later editions), and the author of *First Lessons in Mechanics* (1862) and *Rudimentary Drawing, for the use of Schools* (1864), as well as a number of professional papers read before the American Society of Civil Engineers and published in its *Transactions.* He was president of that society in 1887 and was made an honorary member in 1893. He married Margaret Hobbs of Boston, who survived him, but they left no children.

[*Trans. Am. Soc. Civil Engineers,* vol. XL (1898); G. P. Brown, *Drainage Channel and Waterway* (1894), for Worthen's connection with the Chicago Drainage Canal; *N. Y. Times,* Apr. 3, 1897.]   H. K. B.

WORTHINGTON, HENRY ROSSITER (Dec. 17, 1817–Dec. 17, 1880), engineer, inventor, was the eldest child of Asa and Frances (Meadowcraft) Worthington, and was born in New York City. He was a descendant in the sixth generation of Nicholas Worthington who emigrated from England about 1650 and settled in Connecticut. After being educated in the public schools of his native city, Worthington, who had shown early a decided bent for things mechanical, sought employment that enabled him to become a hydraulic engineer while still a very young man. He concentrated his attention on the problems of city water supply, became thoroughly familiar with steam engines and mechanical pumps, and engaged in experiments intended to improve these machines. Canal navigation interested him, too, and it was in this connection that he made his first invention. As early as 1840 he had an experimental steam canal-boat in operation which was fairly successful except that when the boat was stopped it became necessary to resort to a hand pump to keep the steam boiler supplied with water. To overcome this deficiency he invented an independent feeding pump which was automatic in its action and was controlled by the water level within the steam boiler (patent, Sept. 7, 1840).

After pursuing his canal navigation experiments for four or five more years and obtaining a patent on Feb. 2, 1844, for an improvement in the mode of propelling canal boats, he turned his attention again to pumping machinery and perfected a series of inventions between 1845 and 1855 which made him the first proposer and constructor of the direct steam pump (patent No. 13,370). In 1859, after establishing a pump-manufacturing plant in New York, he perfected his duplex steam feed pump (patent No. 24,838) and in the following year built the first waterworks engine of this kind. In the duplex system one engine actuated the steam valves of the other, and a pause of the pistons at the end of the stroke permitted the water-valves to seat themselves quietly and preserve a uniform water pressure. A distinct improvement on the Cornish engines used at the time, Worthington's pump embodied one of the most ingenious advances in engineering in the nineteenth century and its principle was widely applied. Because of their reliability and low operating cost, these pumps were greatly used thereafter in America for waterworks and for pumping oil through long pipe lines in the oil fields; they are still used (1936) for boiler feeding, tank and ballast pumping, and for hydraulic-press work. Worthington also originated a pumping engine that used no flywheel to carry the piston past the dead point at the end of the stroke. He devised, too, a number of instruments of precision, as well as machine tools which in themselves entitled him to a high place in his profession. In addition to directing his pump-manufacturing plant, which employed over two hundred men, he was president of the Nason Manufacturing Company in New York. He was a founder of the American Society of Mechanical Engineers and a member of other technical societies. On Sept. 24, 1839, he married Laura I. Newton of Alexandria, Va., and at the time of his death he was survived by his widow, two sons, and two daughters (*New York Times, post*).

[George Worthington, *Geneal. of the Worthington Family* (1894); *Trans. Am. Soc. Mech. Engineers,* vol. II (1881); *Am. Machinist,* Jan. 8, 1881; *Sci. American,* June 26, 1923; G. F. Westcott, *Sci. Museum, South Kensington, Handbook of the Colls. Illustrating Pumping Machinery* (2 pts., 1932–33); obituary in *N. Y. Times,* Dec. 18, 1880; Patent Office records.]
C. W. M.

WORTHINGTON, JOHN (Nov. 24, 1719–Apr. 25, 1800), lawyer, was born in Springfield, Mass., the son of John and Mary (Pratt) Worthington and the grandson of Nicholas Worthington who emigrated from England to Saybrook, Conn., about 1650. He was graduated from Yale College in 1740 and remained to study theology. From 1742 to 1743 he was a tutor at Yale, leaving to study law under Phineas Lyman [*q.v.*] of Suffield, Conn., then part of Massachusetts. He began to practise law at Springfield in 1744, where with Joseph Hawley [*q.v.*] of Northampton he did much to raise the standing of the bar in that part of the province. For many years he was the king's attorney, or public prosecutor, in western Massachusetts. When the French and Indian War broke out he took an active part in the raising and provisioning of troops. He was colonel of one of the Hampshire regiments, a post he held until the outbreak of the Revolution. On Jan. 10, 1759, he married Hannah, the daughter of the Rev. Samuel Hopkins of West Springfield. She died on Nov. 25, 1766, leaving four daughters, one of whom married Jonathan Bliss and another Fisher Ames [*qq.v.*]. On Dec. 7, 1768, he married Mary Stoddard, the daughter of Col. John Stoddard of Northampton. Gradually he became a man of considerable wealth, to a large extent through land speculation. One of his ventures resulted in the settlement in 1768 of the town of Worthington, Mass., which was named for him.

Meanwhile he had become the political dictator of Springfield; he was regularly a member of the board of selectmen and moderator of the town meetings. For many years high sheriff of Hampshire County, he had great influence in the county's affairs. He represented Springfield at the Massachusetts General Court almost continuously from 1747 to 1774, an able legislator who grew steadily more conservative as the province moved towards revolution. He attended the Albany Congress in 1754 and a decade later favored the calling of the Stamp Act Congress, although he declined to be a delegate to its meetings at New York in October 1765. From 1767 to 1769 he was a member of the governor's council but was not reëlected in 1769, apparently because he supported the governor in the quarrel with the House of Representatives. In 1774 he was appointed a *mandamus* councillor, but a mob forced him to recant his Loyalism. His political influence at an end, he planned to emigrate to Nova Scotia, but friends prevailed upon him to remain in Massachusetts. Gradually he became reconciled to the separation from Great Britain, contributed funds for the army and by 1778 was again active in Springfield politics. He served on the commission that settled the Massachusetts-Connecticut boundary in 1791. Throughout his declining years he was interested in local affairs and was one of the incorporators of the company that began the building of canals around the falls of the Connecticut River in the last decade of the century.

[George Bliss, *An Address . . . at Springfield . . . 1828* (1828); F. B. Dexter, *Biog. Sketches of the Grads. of Yale College*, vol. I (1885); M. A. Green, *Springfield, 1636–1886* (1888); J. G. Holland, *Hist. of Western Mass.* (1855), vol. I; Lorenzo Sabine, *Biog. Sketches of Loyalists of the Am. Rev.* (1864), vol. II; Emory Washburn, *Judicial Hist. of Mass.* (1840); George Worthington, *The Geneal. of the Worthington Family* (1894).]

E. F. B.

WORTHINGTON, THOMAS (July 16, 1773–June 20, 1827), governor of Ohio, senator, was born near Charleston, Va. (now in W. Va.), the son of Robert and Margaret (Matthews) Worthington and the descendant of Robert Worthington, an English emigrant who settled in Maryland about the middle of the seventeenth century. Upon the death of his father, he was cared for by his elder brothers and by William Darke [*q.v.*], a friend of his father. His education was not systematic, but his writings indicate better training than was usual on the frontier. He went to sea on a Scotch merchantman in 1791 and spent two years in travel. Upon his return to the Virginia frontier he studied surveying, and in 1796 his calling took him to Chillicothe, Ohio. In association with Duncan McArthur [*q.v.*] he engaged in the purchase of Virginia military land warrants, locating his holdings largely in the neighborhood of Chillicothe. On Dec. 13, 1796, he married Eleanor Van Swearingen, and in the spring of 1798 he removed, together with his brother-in-law, Edward Tiffin [*q.v.*], to Chillicothe. Worthington was well-to-do, partly through his wife's inheritance, and was able to set up the establishment of a country gentleman after the Virginia fashion. His whole life was marked by his piety. Although an active Methodist, he exemplified Quaker humanitarianism. The portrait by Rembrandt Peale in the state capitol at Columbus shows him as distinguished in appearance, six feet in height, with ruddy complexion, dark eyes, and sandy hair. Throughout his life he interested himself in the management of his large farm and his mills.

He and Tiffin, working in complete harmony, soon became dominant figures in Ohio politics. Worthington was a member of the territorial House of Representatives from 1799 to 1803. In 1800 he was appointed register of public lands, in charge of sales, at Chillicothe. He was one of the leaders of the "Chillicothe Junto," which accomplished the triumph of Jeffersonianism in Ohio and the admission of the state to the Union. In the interest of statehood he made a trip to Washington in 1801, where he gained the esteem of the new administration. He was an influential member of the convention that drafted the first state constitution in 1802. He was a representative to the first General Assembly in 1803 and again sat in that body the session of 1807–08. Tiffin became the first governor of the state, and Worthington one of the first federal senators. He served from 1803 to 1807, was reelected in 1810, and resigned December 1814 to become governor of Ohio. As senator, his counsel had considerable weight, especially in matters concerning the public lands and the Indian frontier. He voted against the declaration of war with Great Britain, because he felt the country was unprepared and because he had conscientious scruples against war. This vote did not prevent his election as governor in 1814. He was reelected in 1816. As state executive he was able to accomplish little, because the governors were almost powerless under the first state constitution, but his messages to the legislature were remarkable for suggested social reforms, such as the regulation of saloons, better treatment of paupers and convicts, and the regulation of the sale of lands for taxes. He was responsible for the founding of the state library. During his incumbency he was instrumental in the establishment of a branch of the Bank of the United States at Chillicothe, which affected his later political career adversely. Upon his retirement from the governorship he became active in the promotion of better agricultural methods, in a state-supported school system, and in the Ohio canal system. He served in the state House of Representatives in 1821–23 and again for the session of 1824–25. He was distressed in his latter years by business reverses suffered in the depression of 1819. He died in New York City after a lingering illness, survived by his widow and a large family. Sarah Worthington King Peter [q.v.] was his daughter.

[Worthington papers in State Lib., Columbus, Ohio, and Lib. of Cong.; McArthur Papers, Lib. of Cong.; A. B. Sears, "The Public Career of Thomas Worthington," unpublished doctoral dissertation, Ohio State University, Columbus, 1932; Sarah W. K. Peter, *Private Memoir of Thomas Worthington* (1882); F. T. Cole, "Thomas Worthington," *Ohio Arch. and Hist. Pubs.*, vol. XII (1903); *Scioto Gazette* (Chillicothe), July 5, 1827.]   W. T. U.

WOVOKA (c. 1856–October 1932), Indian mystic and originator of the Ghost Dance religion, was born near Walker Lake in what is now Esmeralda County, Nev. He was a full-blood Indian, said to be the son of Tavibo, a religious leader, either a preacher or a dreamer, and a member of the Paviotso or Paiute tribe living in an isolated valley of sage prairie, bounded by vast, ice-crowned sierras, the breeder of a long line of religious teachers and prophets. Like most of his tribe, Wovoka made a satisfactory

adjustment to the white settlers and earned a good living on the ranch of a white man, David Wilson, from whom he received the nickname by which he was usually known among the whites, Jack Wilson. He also acquired an inadequate knowledge of the English language and some notion of the white man's theology. Until he was about thirty he lived obscurely in his valley, industrious and dependable. Then he had some kind of a spiritual experience, possibly a trance associated with illness and the primitive excitement of the tribe during an eclipse of the sun on Jan. 1, 1889, or possibly one of the many varieties of mystic contemplation that baffle the explanations of a workaday world. Out of this he evolved a philosophy and the Ghost Dance that swept the Indian country and became important in the white man's political economy in the Messiah agitation of 1890. The Ghost Dance was an indefinable and varying mixture of mysticism, hypnotism, primitive superstition and a lost people's yearning after happiness. The teaching of Wovoka was simple, with the same simplicity that is noticeable in great religions; and it was founded on the doctrine, common among many peoples in the grip of adversity, that the time was now at hand for a renewal of an old worn-out world. He taught that from Heaven he had a direct message to his people, to do right, to love one another and all men, to live at peace with the world, and to pray and hope for a day of reunion, in a state of everlasting happiness, for all Indians, the quick and the dead.

At first he assigned a definite time for translation into a state of bliss, most particularly in the year 1891; but, as the changing seasons of that designated year lengthened past the appointed time, he was forced to shift his teaching to a vague belief in some future better life, to be awaited with pious hope and to be anticipated and perhaps hastened by participation in the mysteries of the dance. After the excitement of the Ghost Dance had passed, he gradually sank back to the obscurity from which he had come and died all but unnoticed by his white brethren.

[Files of the Adj.-Gen. Office, War Dept., and of the Office of Indian Affairs, Department of the Interior; James Mooney, "The Ghost-Dance Religion," *Fourteenth Annual Report of the Bureau of Ethnology*, pt. 2 (1896); *Evening Star* (Washington, D. C.), Oct. 5, 1932.]   K. E. C.

WRAGG, WILLIAM (1714–Sept. 2, 1777), colonial official, Loyalist leader, the eldest child and only son of Samuel and Marie (DuBose) Wragg, was born in South Carolina, probably in Charlestown. His father, a wealthy Charlestown merchant, who served in the provincial Assembly after 1712 and in the Council from 1717 until his death, was given a barony, variously known as the "Signiory of St. Giles," the Ashley Barony, and the Wragg Barony, for his services in bringing emigrants to the colony.

When William was four years old his father sailed with him for England. Just outside Charlestown harbor they were captured by Blackbeard, the pirate, who held them until he was furnished with a store of drugs from Charlestown. Released, they continued the voyage, and Wragg remained in England until he was grown. According to tradition, he was educated at one of the older public schools and at one of the universities, and finally at the Middle Temple, to which he was admitted in 1725. He was called to the bar Nov. 23, 1733.

Returning to South Carolina he lived the life of a country gentleman. He inherited the barony from his father and also acquired a great property by the will of John Skene, who died in 1768. He owned more than two hundred negroes and at the opening of the Revolution was one of the richest men in the province. His wealth, his education, his social position, his strong character, and his unfailing courage, all contributed to make him a notable figure. A contemporary said of him, "he would have been a real ornament to Sparta or Rome in their most virtuous days" (quoted in Jones, *post*, p. 221). He was made a member of the council in 1753 and a justice of the peace in 1756, and was a member of the Assembly from 1763 to 1768 when, although he was re-elected, he refused to qualify. On Aug. 10, 1769, he was again placed on the council.

In his public career he was consistently a supporter of the governor and the Crown. Alone in the Assembly in 1766 he voted against approving the action of the Stamp Act Congress, and when in 1769 he was published as a non-subscriber to the non-importation agreement, he defended his action in a powerful protest entitled, "Reasons for not Concurring in the Non-Importation Resolution" (*South Carolina Gazette*, Sept. 4, 1769, quoted by McCrady, *post*, 655-56). When a resolution to erect a statue to William Pitt was under discussion, he suggested that one of George III be substituted.

As a result of his loyalty, soon after this episode he was appointed chief justice, though he had never practised law. He returned the commission, however, in order that no man might say that "the hope of preferment had influenced his preceding conduct," a "proof of his disinterestedness and delicacy" that his people admired (Ramsay, *post*). With the approach of the Revolution, Wragg never wavered in his loyalty to Great Britain. When he refused to sign the non-

importation agreement and frankly expressed his belief that the work of the Continental Congress constituted rebellion, he was ordered not to leave his barony. Continuing his refusal to conform, and claiming his right to liberty of speech and belief, he was banished in 1777, and sailed in the *Commerce* for Amsterdam. On Sept. 2, his vessel was wrecked off the coast of Holland and he lost his life—according to one account, in saving the life of his infant son; according to another, in giving aid to the crew. A tablet to his memory, the first to be erected to an American, was later placed in Westminster Abbey.

Wragg was twice married; first, in England, to Mary Wood, who died Dec. 22, 1767, and second, on Feb. 5, 1769, to his cousin, Henrietta Wragg of Charlestown, who survived him. A daughter of the first marriage married John Mathews [q.v.]; a daughter of the second, William Loughton Smith [q.v.].

[E. A. Jones, *Am. Members of the Inns of Court* (1924); Edward McCrady, *The Hist. of S. C. under the Royal Govt., 1719-1776* (1899); *S. C. Gazette*, Dec. 6, 1780; *S. C. Hist. and Geneal. Mag.*, Apr. 1910, Oct. 1916, July 1918; David Ramsay, *The Hist. of S. C.* (1809), II, 532-38.]   J. G. deR. H.

WRAXALL, PETER (d. July 10, 1759), soldier and secretary for Indian affairs in the province of New York, was the son of John Wraxall, a resident of Bristol in England, and belonged to a family which appears to have enjoyed good social and political connections. From scattered allusions it may be inferred that Peter Wraxall, having been born in England, probably spent some time in Holland and before coming to America had been in Jamaica. A residence in Holland would help to account for the familiarity with the Dutch language which was a valuable asset to him in connection with his activities in New York.

Wraxall's name appears upon the muster rolls of New York in 1746—the first reliable evidence of his presence in the province. He apparently commanded a company of Long Island militia raised for an expedition against Canada, but did not get beyond Albany. In 1747 he went to England on personal business and did not return to New York until May 1752. While in England he secured the King's appointment to the offices of secretary and agent for Indian affairs in New York, and town clerk, clerk of the peace, and clerk of the common pleas in the county and city of Albany, the commissions being dated Nov. 15, 1750. Shortly after returning to New York, he entered upon his duties as secretary for Indian affairs, but in the meantime, Governor Clinton had appointed another person to the offices of town clerk, etc., and he never assumed the duties of this position. As secretary for Indian affairs, Wraxall attended councils and kept a record of proceedings. In 1754 he was chosen secretary to the Albany Congress, which probably brought him prominently to the attention of William Johnson [q.v.]. Shortly before the Congress, he had forwarded to Lord Halifax "An Abridgment of the Records of Indian Affairs . . . transacted in the Colony of New York from the year 1678 to the year 1751" (see McIlwain, post). This compilation, including his own comments, was an arraignment of the Albany fur traders and of the Albany commissioners in charge of Indian affairs, whom he accused of playing into the hands of the French. There is reason to think that this document was influential in helping to secure for Johnson his subsequent appointment as superintendent of Indian affairs.

Early in 1755, Johnson secured permission from General Braddock to attach Wraxall to himself in his capacity as secretary for Indian affairs. Wraxall accompanied Johnson on his Crown Point expedition and was present at the battle of Lake George, Sept. 8, 1755. Wraxall had in the meantime been commissioned captain in the New York forces and on this expedition served Johnson not only as secretary but also as aide-de-camp and judge advocate, being entrusted by his superior with various important administrative and political matters. He subsequently saw little active military service, but he continued to serve Johnson as secretary until his own death. Johnson valued his services in the field of Indian affairs very highly, observing that he had "a peculiar Turn that way." In the winter of 1755–56, he prepared a memorandum entitled "Some Thoughts upon the British Indian Interest in North America, more particularly as it relates to the Northern Confederacy commonly called the Six Nations" (Documents, post, VII, 15–31), which has been characterized as "unquestionably the ablest and best paper on the Indian question written during this earlier period" (C. W. Alvord, in Historical Collections . . . Michigan Pioneer and Historical Society, vol. XXXVI, 1908, p. 26).

Wraxall was married on Dec. 9, 1756, to Elizabeth Stillwell. He resided during the last year or two of his life in New York City, where he died. His great service to the colonies consisted in helping to check the French power among the Indians during the period from 1752 to 1759. Had he survived the French and Indian War he would unquestionably have found wider fields of usefulness in the realm of Indian affairs as subsequently administered by his friend and patron, Sir William Johnson.

[By far the best account of Wraxall appears in C. H. McIlwain's editorial introduction to An Abridgment of the Indian Affairs . . . Transacted in the Colony of N. Y. (1915); see also D. J. Pratt, "Biographical Notice of Peter Wraxall," in Proc. Albany Inst., vol. I (1873); E. B. O'Callaghan, Docs. Rel. to the Colonial Hist. of the State of N. Y., vols. VI, VII (1855, 1856), and The Doc. Hist. of the State of N. Y., vol. II (1850); James Sullivan, The Papers of Sir William Johnson, vols. I–III (1921–22); Joel Munsell, The Annals of Albany, vol. X (1859); Wraxall's will and notice of his death in N. Y. Hist. Soc. Colls., Pub. Fund Ser., vol. XXIX (1897); J. E. Stillwell, The Hist. of Capt. Richard Stillwell (1930). The date of Wraxall's death is given as July 11 by two contemporaries (Docs., ante, VII, 433, and Stillwell, ante, p. 57, but the N. Y. Mercury of July 23, 1759, states that he died July 10 and was buried July 11.]   W. E. S—s.

WRIGHT, BENJAMIN (Oct. 10, 1770–Aug. 24, 1842), senior engineer of the Erie Canal, was born in Wethersfield, Conn., the son of Ebenezer and Grace (Butler) Wright and a descendant of Thomas Wright, an early settler of Wethersfield. Having a talent for mathematics, he studied surveying, and knowing that there was opportunity for those "capable of surveying and preparing title deeds" in the new settlements of the Mohawk Valley in New York, he persuaded his father, a small farmer, to move with his family to Fort Stanwix, now Rome, N. Y., in 1789. From this new home, then a frontier settlement, he carried out land surveys (1792–96) said to have totaled more than 500,000 acres in Oneida and Oswego counties.

As this area developed into one of the important agricultural sections of the state, Wright became interested in the problem of transporting surplus products to a market. Since roads were then little better than trails and there seemed to be little hope of permanently improving them, he turned his attention to canals. In 1792 the Western Inland Lock Navigation Company had been formed and had completed some pioneer construction, near Little Falls on the Mohawk, under an English engineer, William Weston [q.v.]. After Weston's return to England, Wright became interested in the further projects of this company and made surveys for them in accordance with ambitious plans which for financial reasons could not be carried out. During this same period, Wright acted as agent of the proprietors of the newly opened lands, for whom many of his earlier surveys had been made. He thus became a leading member of the community, was repeatedly elected to the state legislature, and in 1813 was appointed a county judge.

In 1811 he made an examination of a canal route from Rome on the Mohawk to Waterford on the Hudson, for the state canal commissioners. In 1816, upon the more effective organization of the Canal Board, the work of construction was entrusted to Wright and to James Geddes [*q.v.*], another local surveyor-judge-engineer. Finally, following a law enacted in 1816, the Erie project was actually launched; Geddes was appointed to have charge of the western section, Wright of the middle, and Charles C. Broadhead of the eastern. The first ground was broken July 4, 1817, at Rome. As the construction of the canal progressed, another capable engineer, David Thomas, took over the work on the western section, Geddes turned to the problems of the Champlain Canal, and Wright, having completed the middle section, became responsible for the difficult eastern division. A part of the canal was opened for service in 1820, and the great work was completed in 1825.

In addition to his abilities as a surveyor, and his practical knowledge of construction, Wright appears to have been a most able executive. He gathered around him a remarkable group of young men, all of whom afterwards occupied important positions in the engineering field. Canvass White [*q.v.*], who died early, was his chief dependence for the design of locks and also contributed the important discovery that hydraulic cement could be produced from a deposit near the line of the canal. John B. Jervis [*q.v.*], another assistant, lived to become the foremost American civil engineer of pre-Civil War days. David Stanhope Bates had charge of the difficult crossing at the Irondequoit Valley and also of the Rochester aqueduct. Nathan S. Roberts [*q.v.*] was in charge from Lockport to Lake Erie. The Erie Canal was thus the great American engineering school of the early nineteenth century, and Wright, as the presiding genius of the undertaking, has fairly been called the "Father of American Engineering."

The success of the Erie Canal awakened a spirit of internal improvement in all the states of the then small Union. Wright acted as consulting engineer on a number of canal projects during the last years of the Erie work—the Farmington Canal in Connecticut, the Blackstone Canal in Rhode Island, and the Chesapeake & Delaware Canal. In 1825 he became consulting engineer for the Delaware & Hudson Canal, which bold undertaking was completed by his associate Jervis. Resigning as chief engineer of the Erie in 1827, Wright was chief engineer of the Chesapeake & Ohio Canal from 1828 to 1831 and of the St. Lawrence Canal in 1833. He was also consulting engineer for the Welland Canal, for surveys for the New York & Erie Railroad, for the Harlem Railroad in New York, and for railroads in Virginia, Illinois, and even Cuba.

On Sept. 27, 1798, Wright married Philomela Waterman, daughter of Simeon Waterman of Plymouth, Conn. They had nine children, eight of whom survived their parents; one son, Ben H. Wright, was also a civil engineer and carried out some of the later projects on which his distinguished father had made reports. Wright died in New York City in his seventy-second year. Jervis (*post,* p. 42), writing many years later, remarked that while Wright probably drew no plans for the Erie Canal he was a "sagacious critic" of plans drawn by others and excelled them all in the vital element of practical judgment.

[C. B. Stuart, *Lives and Works of Civil and Military Engineers of America* (1871) ; J. B. Jervis, "Memoir of Am. Engineering," *Trans. Am. Soc. Civil Engineers,* vol. VI (1878) ; *New Eng. Hist. and Geneal. Reg.,* July 1866 ; Curtis Wright, *Geneal. and Biog. Notices of Descendants of Sir John Wright* (1915) ; N. E. Whitford, *Hist. of the Canal System of the State of N. Y.* (2 vols., 1906) ; *Buffalo Hist. Soc. Pubs.,* vol. II (1880) ; *N. Y. Tribune,* Aug. 25, 1842.]   J.K.F.

WRIGHT, CARROLL DAVIDSON (July 25, 1840–Feb. 20, 1909), statistician, social economist, public official, was born at Dunbarton, N. H., the third of seven children of Nathan R. and Eliza (Clark) Wright. His father was a Universalist minister, and moved frequently from one charge to another. The boy grew up principally in Washington, N. H., attending the public schools and academy of that place and working on his father's farm. After further study in academies at Reading, Mass., Alstead, N. H., and Chester, Vt., he began reading law in 1860 with William P. Wheeler, of Keene, N. H., at the same time teaching in country schools. He continued his law study in Dedham and Boston until September 1862, when he enlisted as a private in the 14th New Hampshire Volunteers. He was rapidly promoted, had responsible assignments in and near Washington, D. C., was later given staff duty under Sheridan in the Shenandoah campaign, and eventually became colonel of his regiment. Returning to the law, he was admitted to the bar of New Hampshire in October 1865, and to that of Massachusetts two years later. He settled in Reading, Mass., and married, Jan. 1, 1867, Caroline E. Harnden, daughter of Sylvester Harnden of that town. Two daughters were born to them. Wright had an excellent practice in Boston in patent cases. He was twice elected to the Massachusetts Senate from the Reading district (1871, 1872), in his second term greatly improving the militia system of the state.

The turning point in his career was his appointment by Gov. William B. Washburn as chief of the Massachusetts Bureau of Statistics of Labor in 1873. This bureau, established four years earlier, was the first in the United States, but had been involved in controversy and came near being abolished. Wright remained at its head from 1873 to 1888, fifteen years of critical economic development of Massachusetts and the United States. His work of gathering labor statistics in the chief industrial state provoked criticism from all sides. The mere fact of official inquiry was resented by bumptious employers, and they feared that the Bureau was set up to further the aims of labor; the workers, on the other hand, found fault because Wright did not make himself their inveterate partisan. From the beginning, encouraged by Gen. Francis A. Walker [q.v.], he resolved that his official statistics should be gathered and published with an eye solely to full and frank exposition. He held to this policy throughout his long career, and especially by means of the National Convention of Chiefs and Commissioners of Bureaus of Statistics of Labor, which he organized in 1883 and of which he was president for practically twenty years, he impressed this purpose upon the rapidly increasing number of officials who were coming into the field. Without his example in precept and practice many of his colleagues—poorly trained political appointees—would have brought the new state bureaus into prompt discredit.

The variety of Wright's investigations, made as often as possible upon the ground, was great, ranging through rates of wages, cost of living, strikes, and lockouts, to pauperism, crime, divorce, illiteracy, housing, and labor legislation. Soon he had won the confidence of those who were suspicious or acrimonious at the start, being reappointed by succeeding governors without question. In lectures in Boston and elsewhere, and in an essay on *The Relation of Political Economy to the Labor Question* (1882), he revealed a social philosophy from which he did not depart. Despite his occupation of fact-finding, his thinking owed much more to ethics than to economic analysis. Noted for his tact, cordiality, and kindness, he was passionately devoted to harmony and constantly exerted himself for reconciliation between capital and labor. He desired concessions by both sides, cooperation to be maintained through sincere industry of the workers, and abundant tolerance and welfare facilities extended by employers conscious of their social responsibility. The notion of abiding class cleavage was anathema to him.

The establishment of the United States Bureau of Labor in the Interior Department was due not a little to Wright's influence; he became the first commissioner by appointment of President Arthur in 1885, relinquishing his Massa-

chusetts post three years later. During the twenty years of his commissionership his good influence upon labor bureaus of the states and of foreign governments was broadened and confirmed. He was chairman of the commission which investigated the causes of the Pullman strike of 1894, was recorder of the commission which inquired into the anthracite strike of 1902, and probably determined the findings and recommendations of both reports. He was called upon to complete the Eleventh Census. He was honorary professor of social economics in the Catholic University at Washington, 1895–1904, professor of statistics and social economics at Columbian (later George Washington) University after 1900, and planned and supervised the first volumes of the series of studies on the economic history of the United States financed by the Carnegie Institution. Among his publications may be mentioned particularly *The Industrial Evolution of the United States* (1895); *Outline of Practical Sociology* (1899); and his presidential address in *Quarterly Publications of the American Statistical Association,* March 1908. He was president of the American Statistical Association from 1897 to his death, and received honors from foreign governments, among others the Cross of the French Legion of Honor. In 1902 he was chosen the first president of Clark College, Worcester, Mass., and in 1905 he resigned from the Bureau of Labor. He died four years later in Worcester, after a lingering illness, and was buried at Reading.

[H. G. Wadlin, "Carroll Davidson Wright, a Memorial," in *Commonwealth of Mass., Fortieth Ann. Report on the Statistics of Labor, 1909* (1911), S. N. D. North, "The Life and Work of Carroll Davidson Wright," with full bibliog., *Quart. Pubs. Am. Statistical Asso.,* June 1909; R. H. I. Palgrave, *Palgrave's Dict. of Political Economy,* ed. by Henry Higgs, III (1926), 809–11; *Who's Who in America,* 1908–09; *A Memorial of the Great Rebellion; Being a Hist. of the Fourteenth Regt. of N. H. Vols.* (1882); *Springfield Daily Republican,* Feb. 21, 1909.]   B. M—l.

WRIGHT, CHARLES (Oct. 29, 1811–Aug. 11, 1885), botanical explorer, born in Wethersfield, Conn., was the son of James and Mary (Goodrich) Wright, and a descendant of Thomas Wright who emigrated from England in 1635 and later settled in Wethersfield. After attending the Wethersfield grammar school, he entered Yale College, from which he graduated, with Phi Beta Kappa honors, in 1835. Interested in botany from early youth, he cultivated his favorite science during his college days; he seems never to have had a teacher in the subject. Almost immediately after his graduation from Yale, he accepted a position as tutor to the children of a wealthy planter at Natchez, Miss., a position lost a year later as the result of the ruin of his employer in the financial stringencies of 1836–37. Like many others Wright fled to Texas from the panic of 1837. From 1837 to 1845 he followed the practice of surveying and of teaching school at various places in eastern Texas, and explored the hitherto unknown botany of that region. A collection of dried plants he sent to Prof. Asa Gray [q.v.] of Harvard College in the spring of 1844 opened a correspondence destined to have important results for American botany. He moved in 1845 from eastern to central Texas, and taught school for a number of years there, for one year at the short-lived Rutersville College, and for longer periods as private tutor or schoolmaster. He continued, meanwhile, his botanical study and correspondence with Gray. In the summer of 1849, he accompanied a battalion of United States troops from San Antonio to El Paso, collecting plants all the way. The collections proved to be rich in new species; many of these were published in Part I of Gray's *"Plantæ Wrightianæ"* (*Smithsonian Contributions to Knowledge,* vol. III, 1852). After another year of teaching in central Texas, Wright was associated, from the spring of 1851 to the summer of 1852, with the United States and Mexican boundary survey as botanist. His extensive collections, made this time largely in New Mexico and Arizona, were studied by Gray, and the new species described in Part II of the *"Plantæ Wrightianæ"* (*Ibid.,* vol. V, 1853), and in the *Botany of the Mexican Boundary Survey* (1859). In the summer of 1852 Wright left Texas never to return.

He received appointment, shortly, as botanist to the North Pacific Exploring and Surveying Expedition under John Rodgers (1812–1882) and Cadwalader Ringgold [qq.v.], and accompanied the expedition from June 1853 to the spring of 1856. He made notable collections of plants at the Cape of Good Hope, Hongkong, the Loo Choo Islands, and in Japan. Returning to America in the fall of 1856, he began the botanical exploration of the isle of Cuba, a task that continued, with interruptions, until July 1867. His Cuban collections, with their numerous new species in all classes of plants, were described in various works by A. H. R. Grisebach, W. S. Sullivant, D. C. Eaton, P. F. Müller, M. J. Berkeley, and M. A. Curtis. With the completion of this notable work Wright's active career as an explorer may be said to have come to an end. During Gray's absence in Europe in 1868, Wright acted as curator of the herbarium at Cambridge, and for six months during the winter of 1875–76 he was librarian of the Bussey Institution. The last ten years of Wright's life were spent in quiet retirement at Wethersfield. In this locality he collected so assiduously that it is now extremely difficult for botanists to collect plant species not previously reported by him. He died of heart failure at Wethersfield. He never married.

Daniel Cady Eaton [q.v.] described Wright as "almost without an equal" as a collector and observer of plants (Thatcher, *post,* pp. 180–81), and Gray considered that his services to botany and the botanists of his generation could not be overestimated. Wright was a "person of low stature and well-knit frame, hardy rather than strong, scrupulously temperate, a man of simple ways, always modest and unpretending, but direct and downright in expression, most amiable, trusty and religious" (Gray, *post,* p. 17).

[J. B. Standish, "Wright Family in Wethersfield, Conn.," MS. in the possession of the author; Curtis Wright, *Geneal. and Biog. Notices of Descendants of Sir John Wright* (1915); T. A. Thatcher, *Biog. and Hist. Record of the Class of 1835 in Yale Coll.* (1881); *Obit. Record Grads. Yale Coll.* (1886); S. W. Geiser, in *Southwest Review,* Spring 1930, with portrait, and in *Field & Laboratory,* Nov. 1935; Asa Gray, in *Am. Jour. Sci.,* 3 ser., vol. XXXI (1886); E. O. Wooton, in *Bull. Torrey Botanical Club,* vol. XXXIII (1906); Gray-Wright corres., MSS. in lib. of the Gray Herbarium, Cambridge, Mass.; Wright-Engelmann corres., MSS. in lib. of the Mo. Botanical Garden; obituary in *Hartford Courant,* Aug. 13, 1885.]   S. W. G.

WRIGHT, CHARLES BARSTOW (Jan. 8, 1822–Mar. 24, 1898), financier and railroad president, was born in Wysox, Bradford County, Pa., the son of Rufus Wright. His father, a currier by trade, had moved from the Connecticut Valley in 1814 and erected in his new home on the upper Susquehanna the first tannery in that region. In 1830 he settled in Athens, Pa., where Charles attended the Athens Academy until he was fifteen. Taking a job as clerk in a general store at Leraysville, he was in four years a partner in the enterprise. In 1843 he was commissioned to investigate the land holdings of a group of eastern capitalists in the neighborhood of Chicago, and his three-year sojourn in that section, during which he acquired the interests of his principals and engaged extensively in transactions in land, laid the foundation of a considerable fortune. Returning to Erie, Pa., he entered a banking co-partnership which founded a branch house in Philadelphia in 1855. He became interested in the financing and construction of railroads, and took an active part in the building of the Philadelphia and Erie railroad. Upon the discovery of petroleum in western Pennsylvania, he formed a syndicate to construct a railroad to Oil City, Pa., which with its later additions proved very profitable. Meanwhile he had removed to Philadelphia and had come into close business relations with Jay Cooke [*q.v.*].

In 1870 he entered the directorate of the Northern Pacific Railroad to represent Cooke's $5,000,000 syndicate, the first money raised for the construction of the road, and from this time for nearly a decade he devoted his attention almost exclusively to this enterprise. More than once, in the financial crisis that followed, Wright used his individual credit to rescue the road from its difficulties. In 1872 he visited the west coast as a member of a committee to choose a terminal point on Puget Sound. On his return he was made chairman of the finance committee and early in 1873 was prevailed upon to accept a vice-presidency with headquarters in New York. At this time the road was in a desperate condition. Five hundred miles had been constructed, and the Missouri River had been reached at Bismarck, N. D., but the railroad's bonded debt was over thirty millions, and there was a floating debt of five and a half millions. In 1874 Wright was made president, and in April 1875 the entire property was placed in the receiver's hands. A reorganization was effected in six months by the conversion of the bonds into preferred stock. In the accomplishment of this remarkably speedy and adequate reconstruction Wright played a dominating part. But the road had no funds with which to continue building, and its floating debt was pressing. Wright had to quiet creditors and secure a breathing spell, use the assets that the company possessed for its best interests, and operate the five hundred miles of road through a country just being opened to settlement. At the close of 1876 the road had paid expenses and showed a small surplus. Further aid from Congress was sought. When that failed, construction had to depend upon the road's own credit. A short line to Puget Sound was built, and in 1877 the problem of direct connection with St. Paul was solved by securing an expiring charter and raising the money for construction. Early in 1879 work was renewed through the road's own resources on the main line west of Bismarck. In May 1879 Wright resigned the presidency on account of his health. Although the financial difficulties of the road were not over, much had been done to put it on a sound basis, and further building seemed assured. After a short stay in Europe Wright again accepted the chairmanship of the finance committee and became responsible for securing the necessary funds to complete the gap between the eastern and western sections. He severed his connection with the railroad in 1893, and for the rest of his life confined himself to his banking interests in Philadelphia. He had an abiding faith in the Northwest and its development, and had many investments in the territory that the Northern Pacific was opening. His benefactions in Tacoma included the founding of the Annie Wright Seminary for Young Ladies.

He was twice married. His second wife, by whom he had two sons and two daughters, was Susan Townsend of Sandusky, Ohio. He died in Philadelphia.

[*Railroad Gazette*, April 1, 1898; Henry Hall, ed., *America's Successful Men of Affairs*, vol. II (1896); E. V. Smalley, *Hist. of the Northern Pacific Railroad* (1883); obituary in *Pub. Ledger* (Phila.), Mar. 25, 1898; information from W. T. Wright, Wright's son.]
F.H.D.

WRIGHT, CHAUNCEY (Sept. 20, 1830–Sept. 12, 1875), philosopher, one of nine children of Ansel and Elizabeth Boleyn (or Bullen) Wright, was born in Northampton, Mass., where his family had lived ever since the first American ancestor had settled there in 1654, Samuel Wright, who had come to Boston from England in 1630. Chauncey Wright's grandfather had been a Revolutionary soldier; his father was a deputy sheriff and successful dealer in "West India Goods and Groceries." As a boy, Chauncey was reserved, much given to solitude, and inclined to melancholy. In 1848 he entered Harvard College, where he was a laborious rather than brilliant student. Little interested in literature or languages, he concentrated his attention on mathematics, natural science, and philosophy.

Immediately upon graduation in 1852 he became one of the computers for the newly established *American Ephemeris and Nautical Almanac,* for which he devised new methods of calculation. From 1863 to 1870 he was recording secretary of the American Academy of Arts and Sciences, editing the annual volume of proceedings. He lived quietly as a bachelor in Cambridge, lodging in the house known as "The Village Blacksmith's," contributing occasionally to the *Mathematical Monthly,* and in 1864 beginning the publication of a notable series of philosophical essays in the *North American Review,* then edited by Charles Eliot Norton. In 1870 he delivered a course of University Lectures in Harvard College on the principles of psychology. After this, he produced a number of important philosophical essays during the brief span of years that remained to him. His article on "The Uses and Origin of the Arrangements of Leaves in Plants" (*Memoirs of the American Academy of Arts and Sciences,* n.s., vol. IX, pt. II, 1873), advancing an evolutionary explanation, received the especial commendation of Darwin, and his reply, entitled "The Genesis of Species" (*North American Review,* July 1871), to St. George

Mivart's attack on Darwinism was republished in England at Darwin's instance. A thoroughgoing naturalist, in his most valuable article, "Evolution of Self-Consciousness," he anticipated philosophic trends of a quarter-century later in his instrumentalist conception of mental activities. Deeply influenced by Hamilton, Mill, and Herbert Spencer, though keenly critical of the latter's metaphysics, he was one of the first to introduce to America the methods of British empiricism. In 1874 he became a regular member of the Harvard faculty as instructor in mathematical physics but had taught for only a year when his untimely death occurred. Almost utterly devoid of personal ambition, he wrote too little to secure any popular recognition, and as a forerunner of William James he was quickly forgotten, his work being completely overshadowed by the enormous productivity of his successor in the same school of thought. He was ranked, however, by Charles Eliot Norton "among the as yet few great thinkers of America," and he certainly brought to philosophy one of the most trenchant and creative minds that America had yet produced.

[The best of Wright's essays were collected in *Philosophical Discussions* (1877), containing a long biog. sketch by Charles Eliot Norton. See also *Letters of Chauncey Wright* (Cambridge, 1878), ed. by J. B. Thayer with running biog. comments; John Fiske, *Darwinism and Other Essays* (1879); and death notice in *Boston Transcript*, Sept. 14, 1875.]   E. S. B.

WRIGHT, ELIZUR (Feb. 12, 1804–Nov. 21, 1885), reformer, actuary, was born at South Canaan, Conn., probably a descendant of Thomas Wright, an early settler of Wethersfield. His father, also Elizur Wright, mathematician of parts and graduate of Yale, was, like his forebears, a farmer and teacher; and his mother, Clarissa Richards, came from a long line of New England sea-captains. In 1810 the family moved to Tallmadge, Ohio, in the Western Reserve, where the father cleared a farm and founded an academy. Here young Elizur prepared for college. He worked his way through Yale, graduating with distinction in mathematics in 1826. During the following year, as master of Groton Academy, he fell in love with one of his pupils, Susan Clark, whom he married Sept. 13, 1829. A professorship in the newly founded Western Reserve College, then located at Hudson, called him back to Ohio.

In 1832, the genius of anti-slavery evangelism, Theodore Weld [*q.v.*], visited Hudson and moved not only Wright but also his colleague, Beriah Green [*q.v.*], and the president, George Storrs, to agitate immediate abolition in the Western Reserve. Amid rising hostility, Storrs was struck down with tuberculosis, Green accepted the presidency of Oneida Institute, and Wright resigned. Through Weld, he was appointed secretary to the New York Anti-Slavery Society, and, after its organization in December 1833, corresponding secretary of the American Anti-Slavery Society. In this capacity he edited the *Quarterly Anti-Slavery Magazine* (1835–37) and the society's tracts, wrote its reports, and supervised the agents in the field. While his powers were exceeded by others in the movement, his devotion was unsurpassed; and during the crucial years of the agitation, 1834–38, he was indispensable. In 1839, when various controversies began to divide the movement, Wright resigned to become editor of the *Massachusetts Abolitionist*, organ of the conservative opponents of William Lloyd Garrison [*q.v.*]. Here he advocated third-party action by abolitionists so vigorously that he was dropped at the end of the year.

For a time, Wright and his growing family approached actual want. With characteristic courage, he published *Fables of La Fontaine* (2 vols., 1841), a translation made for his children, and sold the books from door to door at home and then in England. Upon his return in 1846 he started a newspaper in Boston, the *Weekly Chronotype*, in which he tilted against the protective tariff, slavery, and life insurance companies. Like its editor, the paper was too individualistic to represent organized reform, but its success was such that in 1850 it was purchased by the *Weekly Commonwealth*, organ of the Free Soil party, with Wright as editor. Unable to conform to party discipline, he was dismissed in 1852, though at the time he was defendant in the Shadrach case, one of the most famous of the fugitive-slave trials.

Meanwhile, several life insurance companies, stirred to self-examination by Wright's strictures upon their methods, employed him to prepare tables which would show total reserves required for safety. These tables enabled life insurance companies for the first time to formulate reserve policies which were exactly adapted to their obligations. Aware, however, that many companies were interested primarily in profits and salaries, in 1853 Wright began lobbying in the Massachusetts legislature for a law to force all companies doing business in the state to maintain adequate reserves. His lobby was a one-man affair, and it was not until 1858 that his effort was rewarded by legislation (*Acts and Resolves ... of Massachusetts*, 1858, ch. 177). Its passage forced large companies everywhere to conform their reserve policies to the law in order to do business in Massachusetts and to compete with Massachusetts companies outside the state. Wright, being the only one who understood the intricacies of the new statute, was appointed commissioner of insurance to see to its enforcement. Through his annual reports, in which unsound companies and dishonest practices were pilloried, he secured an extraordinary degree of conformity to sound insurance practice throughout the nation. Though the title often applied to him, "father of life insurance," misstates his censor's function, his efforts probably had more to do with the development of sound standards for life insurance than those of any other man in its history.

In his annual reports, Wright maintained that the reserves of life insurance companies belonged in justice to their policy holders, and in 1861, against the united opposition of the insurance companies, he secured the passage of the famous non-forfeiture law (*Acts and Resolves*, 1861, ch. 186), by which companies were forbidden to appropriate reserves to their own use. This triumph roused such hostility that Wright was ousted in 1866 by legislation abolishing his office. He was immediately retained as actuary by several companies, at a high salary for his day, and continued his "lobby for the widow and orphan." After thirteen years more of unremitting effort, in 1880 he secured legislation which compelled insurance companies to pay policy holders in cash the full value of lapsed policies (*Ibid.*, 1880, ch. 232). In order to retain their business, companies outside the state promptly conformed their practice to the Massachusetts law. Meanwhile, as a private citizen Wright continued to publish his findings of fraud, theft, perjury, and bribery in insurance company practice, especially in New York; though it was not until 1905, a generation later, that the state of New York was moved to action against these practices. In his last years he worked successfully for a great park for Boston on Middlesex Fells, for conservation in the West, and for other reforms. In the midst of these activities, he died.

Elizur and Susan Wright had eighteen children, of whom six died in infancy. Of their descendants, many have achieved high distinction in various forms of public service.

[P. G. Wright, "Life of Elizur Wright" (MS.), in the possession of Prof. Quincy Wright, Univ. of Chicago; F. P. Stearns, *Cambridge Sketches* (1905); *Letters of Theodore Dwight Weld, Angelina Grimké Weld, and Sarah Grimké* (2 vols., 1934), ed. by G. H. Barnes and D. L. Dumond; H. R. Stiles, *The Hist of Ancient Wethersfield* (1904), vol. II; Curtis Wright, *Geneal. . . . of Descendants of Sir John Wright* (1915); F. B. Dexter, *Biog. Sketches Grads. Yale Coll.*, vol. IV (1907); *Ohio Observer*, 1832–34; Minutes of the Executive Committee, American Anti-Slavery Society, 1835–40 (MS.), Boston Pub. Lib.; *Mass. Abolitionist*, 1839–40; *Weekly Chronotype*, 1846–50; B. J. Hendrick, "The Story of Life Insurance," *McClure's Mag.*, June 1906; *The "Bible of Life Insurance"* (1932), reprinting *Mass. Reports on Life Insurance 1859–1865* (1865), together with biog. sketch of Wright; Ellen Wright, *Elizur Wright's Appeals for the Middlesex Fells* (1893); *Boston Transcript*, Nov. 23, 24, 1885; Wright's many pamphlets and books.]   G. H. B.

WRIGHT, FRANCES (Sept. 6, 1795–Dec. 13, 1852), reformer, free thinker, was born in Dundee, Scotland, the daughter of James Wright, a man of means and radical opinions who promoted the circulation of Thomas Paine's *Rights of Man* in his environment. Her mother, who was part English, was a daughter of Duncan Campbell, an army officer. Both parents died when Frances was barely two and a half years old, leaving to the child the heritage of an inquiring mind and a large fortune. She was brought up and educated by conventional relatives of her mother in London, but was a difficult and rebellious child and as soon as her legal status permitted turned her back on London and returned to Scotland. She had had good masters, however, and she now directed her fine abilities toward liberal studies. At eighteen she wrote a sketch purporting to be the story of a young disciple of Epicurus (published in 1822 under the title, *A Few Days in Athens*), which contained the well-worked-out materialistic philosophy that she followed throughout life. When her guardians suggested that to complete her education she should make the grand tour of Europe, she declared that rather than gaze on the political oppressions of the post-Napoleonic era she would prefer to travel in free America.

Accordingly Frances Wright and her younger sister, Camilla, arrived in New York for the first time in 1818. The next two years were for her years of cultivation and adventure. She frequented the intellectual society of New York, had a play produced anonymously—*Altorf*, a story of the Swiss struggle for independence, produced at the Park Theatre in 1819 and published the same year—and made a thorough tour of the Northern and Eastern states. With materials for a book on her travels, she returned to England in 1820 and the following year published *Views of Society and Manners in America* (1821).

It was this book, written in a tone of appreciation unusual among European authors, that led to her friendship with General Lafayette. Her next visit to the United States was timed to coincide with his. She arrived in New York in September 1824 and with her sister accompanied Lafayette during most of his triumphal tour through the states, sharing in the vast celebrations prepared to receive him. With Lafayette, she visited Thomas Jefferson and James Madison and discussed with them the problem of negro slavery. The plan of emancipation which she evolved, influenced somewhat by the ideas of Robert Owen, was presented to them and had their approval. Investing a large part of her fortune in land in western Tennessee—a tract which she called Nashoba—she there launched her experiment in emancipation. She calculated that slaves working on the land would earn their freedom in about five years, and she proposed then to colonize them. Her plan, though attended by incidental troubles and disasters, was actually carried out. She purchased slaves in the fall of 1825 and colonized them in Haiti in the summer of 1830. Meanwhile, socialist recruits within the colony had introduced the idea of free unions as opposed to marriage, an innovation which had threatened to wreck the experiment soon after its beginning. Frances Wright, who had visited Europe to restore her health, defended her colleagues in principle at least, and this attitude of hers made the name "Fanny Wright" anathema to the public.

Between 1828, when she joined Robert Dale Owen [q.v.] in editing the *New Harmony Gazette,* and 1830, Frances Wright caused a further shock to public sensibilities by appearing on the platform as a lecturer. She attacked religion, the influence of the churches in politics, and the existing system of education based on authority; and defended equal rights for women and the replacement of the legal obligation of marriage by a union based on moral obligation only. This last doctrine, of course, aroused the most opposition. The rationalistic reforms she proposed, however, anti-conventional as they were, were considered less of a reproach to her than her "unfeminine" action in appearing as a public speaker. The daily newspapers were immoderate in their condemnation, and she was several times nearly mobbed.

She published *Course of Popular Lectures* in 1829 (2nd ed., 1931; vol. II, 1836). In 1829 she settled in New York and began, Jan. 28, to publish the *Free Enquirer,* virtually the *New Harmony Gazette* under a new name. Robert Dale Owen soon relieved her of most of the editorial work, enabling her to extend her lecture tours. Occupying, with her sister, an estate on the East River near the farm later owned by Horace Greeley, she became the leader of the free-thinking movement in New York, which, after a period of inactivity following the French Revolution, had reawakened. This group advocated as a fundamental reform free education maintained and controlled by the state and urged the working class to organize politically; they formed an Association for the Protection of Industry and for the Promotion of National Education and joined the Workingmen's Party, which, however, shortly disintegrated because the working men were indifferent to the educational aims and hostile to the "infidelity" of their *Free Enquirer* allies

A trip abroad followed this episode, during which Camilla died, Feb. 8, 1831, and on July 22 Frances Wright married William Phiquepal D'Arusmont, a Frenchman who had been one of her co-workers at New Harmony and in New York. The marriage, of which one daughter was born, was terminated by divorce.

Returning to the United States with her husband in 1835, she continued writing and lecturing, taking up for public discussion such modern causes as birth control, the emancipation of woman, and the more equal distribution of property. Though she had no sympathy with Garrisonian abolitionism she urged gradual emancipation of the slaves and colonization of the freedmen outside the United States. In 1836 she supported Andrew Jackson's attack on the Bank of the United States and advocated the independent treasury. In her last years she gave a great deal of time to propaganda for the abolition of the banking system, maintaining that capital of all kinds should be held by the state, by which all citizens should be employed. In the winter of 1851–52, while living in Cincinnati, she broke her hip in a fall and never fully recovered. A year later she died.

Frances Wright was a woman of extraordinary physical and moral courage, unusual intellect, and considerable imagination. Her fearlessness and initiative contributed definitely to the emancipation of women, though her influence was exerted more by her example than by her doctrines.

[W. R. Waterman, *Frances Wright* (1924), based in part on MSS. in the possession of Frances Wright's grandson, the Rev. William Norman Guthrie, New York; *Biog., Notes, and Political Letters of Frances Wright D'Arusmont* (1844), which contains some autobiog. material; Amos Gilbert, *Memoir of Frances Wright* (1855); Charles Bradlaugh, *Biogs. of Ancient and Modern Celebrated Free Thinkers* (1858); G. B. Lockwood, *The New Harmony Movement* (1905); R. D. Owen, *Threading My Way* (1874); S. B. Anthony and others, *Hist. of Woman Suffrage* (3 vols., 1881–87); *Cincinnati Daily Gazette,* Dec. 15, 1852.]

K. A.

WRIGHT, GEORGE FREDERICK (Jan. 22, 1838–Apr. 20, 1921), geologist, clergyman, was born at Whitehall, N. Y., of sturdy, New England pioneering stock, the son of Walter and Mary Peabody (Colburn) Wright. His was the best type of Puritan home, and his early training gave him the deep interest in religion and the joy in simple things that he ever afterwards retained. After attending country schools and an academy at Castleton, Vt., he entered Oberlin College (A.B. 1859), and was graduated from the Oberlin Theological Seminary in 1862. He was married on Aug. 28, 1862, to Huldah Maria Day. His first pastoral charge was in the small village of Bakersfield, Vt., and it was there that he developed his interest in geology (1862–72). From 1872 to 1881 he was pastor of the Free (Congregational) Church of Andover, Mass. Behind the parsonage in Andover ran a gravel ridge supposed by geologists to be of marine origin, but Wright's study of it convinced him that it was due to glacial action. His theory of the glacial origin of such ridges in New England, presented before the Essex Institute of Salem in 1875 and before the Boston Society of Natural History in 1876, was indorsed by Clarence King [q.v.] and brought by him to the attention of geologists the world over (*Proceedings of the Boston Society of Natural History,* vol. XIX, 1878, p. 47). In 1880 Wright was asked to serve on a distinguished commission selected to investigate the discoveries made by Charles Conrad Abbott [q.v.] of what were reputed to be the remains of paleolithic man in the Trenton, N. J., glacial deposits. Wright's interest in the Ice Age now became intertwined with his interest in the antiquity of man, and this, in turn, with his theological interest in the Biblical account of man's origin.

These three interests furnished the pattern for his subsequent life. He became the stoutest champion of the late close of the Ice Age, not more than 7,000 years ago; of the relatively limited time of its duration, not more than 30,000–90,000 years; and of the origin of man within the glacial period. In the course of his geological investigations he became associated with Peter Lesley [q.v.] as assistant geologist of the Pennsylvania survey (1881–82) in tracing the southern edge of the great terminal moraine running through New York, Pennsylvania, Ohio, Kentucky, Indiana, and Illinois. The study of the more western part seems to have been done by Wright alone, under the auspices of the Western Reserve Historical Society (*United States Geological Survey, Bulletin 58,* 1890). This work has been of fundamental importance for all subsequent study of the glacial epoch. In 1886 Wright made the first scientific study of the Muir Glacier in Alaska, which added greatly to his fame as an expert in glacial geology. He was chosen three times to give the Lowell Lectures (1887–88, 1891–92, and 1896–97); the first he finally embodied in his best known book, *The Ice Age in North America* (1889). Meanwhile he had been teaching at Oberlin, where he was professor of

New Testament language and literature (1881–92) and of the harmony of science and religion, a chair especially endowed for him (1892–1907). His most significant service along theological lines was as editor of *Bibliotheca Sacra* (1883–1921). Under Wright the journal was for nearly forty years one of the most respected mediums of expression for the more scholarly conservative thought of the Church. He also assisted his son in the later years of his life in editing the twelve volumes of *Records of the Past* (later absorbed by *Art and Archaeology*). On Sept. 22, 1904, five years after the death of his first wife, he married Florence Eleanor Bedford. Emeritus professor from 1907 until his death, he gave himself unremittingly to literary work, leading at the same time a life of singular dignity, simplicity, and sincerity.

Two of Wright's geological trips deserve special mention—the first, a journey to Greenland in the summer of 1894, when he was shipwrecked; and the second, the truly remarkable journey across Asia and through Turkestan, which he undertook in his sixty-third year, before the completion of the Trans-Siberian Railway. As a souvenir of the latter trip he brought back the liturgy of St. John Chrysostom, set to music by Tchaikovsky. He translated this and adjusted the English form to the music (published by P. Jurgenson, Moscow and Leipzig). Among his books are *Asiatic Russia* (2 vols., 1902), *Scientific Confirmations of the Old Testament* (1906), *Origin and Antiquity of Man* (1912), and *Story of My Life and Work* (1916), a charmingly written sketch.

[In addition to Wright's *Story of My Life and Work,* which contains a full bibliog., see *Who's Who in America,* 1920–21; and obituary in *Cleveland Plain Dealer,* Apr. 22, 1921.]　　　　　　　　　　K. F.

WRIGHT, GEORGE GROVER (Mar. 24, 1820–Jan. 11, 1896), jurist, United States senator, the fifth son of John and Rachel (Seaman) Wright, was born at Bloomington, Ind. Though left fatherless at an early age, he was able to enter the state college (later Indiana University) in his native town at fifteen. After graduating in 1839 he studied law in the office of his brother, Joseph Albert Wright [q.v.]. In September 1840, having been admitted to the bar, he began practice at Keosauqua in Iowa Territory. There, on Oct. 19, 1843, he was married to Hannah Mary Dibble, by whom he had seven children, and there they lived until 1865, when they moved to Des Moines. Wright soon became active in politics. He was prosecuting attorney for Van Buren County (1846–48), served as state senator in the second and third General Assemblies, and on Jan. 5, 1855, was elected by the General Assembly chief justice of the state supreme court. He was not a candidate for reëlection in 1859, when judges were chosen by popular election, but in 1860 he was appointed by the governor to fill a vacancy, and his selection was later confirmed by election. He was reëlected in 1865 and served until August 1870, after he had been elected United States senator.

Almost continuously for fifteen years during the formative period of Iowa government and jurisprudence, Wright exercised a dominant influence upon the attitude of the supreme court. Rigorous in basing decisions upon principles rather than political expediency, he helped to establish precedents on many vital questions. Though he favored temperance and a majority of the voters had supported a statute prohibiting liquor traffic in 1855, he argued in a dissenting opinion that the whole act was unconstitutional because it had been referred to the electorate, which was contrary to the regular legislative process (*Santo et al.* vs. *State of Iowa,* 2 Clarke, 165, *post*). On another occasion the supreme court decided that the Iowa General Assembly had given counties authority to borrow money to aid railroads. Wright contended that the state legislature could confer such power specifically, but had not done so; later cases sustained his view (*Clapp* vs. *County of Cedar,* 5 Clarke, 15, *post*). He was not, however, a chronic dissenter. He wrote many important opinions and formulated the Iowa interpretation of legal rules pertaining to domestic relations, libel, contracts, and technicalities of procedure. One who knew all the judges of the Iowa supreme court during the first seventy years considered Wright "entitled to rank first in the importance and value of his services to the jurisprudence of Iowa" (Cole, *post,* I, 100–101).

As a United States senator from 1871 to 1877, Wright succeeded in representing the interests of his constituents without sacrificing his judicial attitude to partisan exigencies. He opposed resumption of specie payments and favored expansion of paper currency based entirely upon the credit of the government because the growing West needed more money. He voted against the salary grab act, worked futilely for prohibition of the liquor traffic in territories, tried to reform senatorial procedure, and proposed judicial settlement of presidential election contests. He was not a candidate for reëlection. He returned to the practice of law in Des Moines with two of his sons, but devoted his attention chiefly to his business interests. Though no longer engaged in active practice, he served as president of

the American Bar Association in 1887 and 1888. Lecturing on professional ethics and other subjects in the law school of the state university (1881–96), which he had helped to found in 1865, was among the most pleasant experiences of his later years. Because of his rich experience, high character, quick wit, and genial disposition the students idolized him; indeed, his popularity was as wide as his acquaintance.

[J. L. Pickard, in *Iowa Hist. Record,* Apr. 1896; E. W. Stiles, *Recollections and Sketches of Notable Lawyers . . . of Early Iowa* (1916), pp. 417–22; C. C. Cole, *The Courts and Legal Profession of Iowa* (1907), vol. I, p. 101; short autobiog. in *Annals of Iowa,* Jan. 1915; W. P. Clarke, *Reports of Cases . . . in the Supreme Court . . . of Iowa,* vols. I–XXIX (1855–70); obituary in *Iowa State Reg.,* Jan. 12, 1896.] J. E. B.

WRIGHT, HAMILTON KEMP (Aug. 2, 1867–Jan. 9, 1917), medical scientist, was born at Cleveland, Ohio, the son of Robert and Elizabeth (Wyse) Wright of English and Canadian ancestry. He received his early education in Boston, Mass., and graduated in medicine from McGill University in Montreal in 1895. After a short term as medical registrar and neuropathologist in the Royal Victoria Hospital in Montreal, he accepted the offer from Sir Michael Foster of the John Lucas Walker scholarship at Cambridge University, where he worked in neuropathology. In 1897 he become assistant director of the London County Laboratories, where he made a special study of the pathology of *tabes dorsalis.* He studied at Heidelberg and other continental universities in 1897–98. In 1899 he was sent by the British Colonial Office to make a study of beriberi in the Straits Settlements. During the four years that he spent in this work he induced the authorities to build under his supervision an admirably equipped laboratory for medical research at Kuala Lumpur, of which he become director. He advanced materially the knowledge of beriberi. He combatted the theory that it was due to a specific organism growing on rice, but concluded that food was an agent in its transmission. The years from 1903 to 1908 were occupied with medical research, first at the Johns Hopkins University in Baltimore, later at various places in the United States and Europe. In 1908 he was appointed by President Theodore Roosevelt to the International Opium Commission and attended the Shanghai meeting of the Commission in 1909. He was retained by the State Department to make the preparations for American participation in the International Opium Conference of 1911 at The Hague. He attended this conference and the second one at the same place in 1913 as delegate and chairman of the American delegation. He was instrumental in the preparation of the Harrison Narcotic Law and other federal legislation for the regulation of the sale of habit-forming drugs which was passed by Congress soon after the second Hague conference. During the early part of the World War he was engaged in civilian relief work in France; there, in 1915, he sustained a fracture of the ribs and a severe nervous shock from an automobile accident. He never fully recovered. He died from pneumonia at his home in Washington, D. C.

To his gifts as a medical investigator he added unusual organizing ability, together with courage and common sense. With a fine presence and a cultured voice, he was an excellent public speaker and an efficient advocate for medical science. An ambitious man, he would have reached still greater public prominence but for his comparatively early death. Incident to his work in the Straits Settlements he published *The Malarial Fevers of British Malaya* (1901), *An Inquiry into the Etiology and Pathology of Beri-beri* (1902), and *On the Classification and Pathology of Beri-beri* (1903). His reports on the opium problem (1909) and on the second international opium conference (1913) were issued by the United States government as presidential messages. Wright was a member of the British Medical Association, the American Association for the Advancement of Science, the American Asiatic Society, the American Society of International Law, and the Washington Academy of Sciences. He was married on Nov. 22, 1899, to Elizabeth Washburn, daughter of William Drew Washburn [q.v.], by whom he had five children. Mrs. Wright carried to completion certain scientific work upon which he was engaged at the time of his death.

[Sources include *Who's Who in America*, 1916–17; *British Medic. Jour.*, Apr. 7, 1917; *Jour. Am. Medic. Asso.*, Jan. 20, 1917; H. A. Kelly and W. L. Burrage, *Am. Medic. Biogs.* (1920); obituary in *Evening Star* (Washington), Jan. 11, 1917, with portrait; McGill Univ. records. Wright usually omitted his middle name.]   J. M. P.

WRIGHT, HENDRICK BRADLEY (Apr. 24, 1808–Sept. 2, 1881), congressman, was born at Plymouth, Luzerne County, Pa., the first child of Joseph and Ellen (Hendrick) Wadhams Wright. His father, descended from John Wright who emigrated from England in 1681 with William Penn, was a farmer and merchant, was widely read and, despite a profession of the principles of the Society of Friends, inordinately fond of poetry and the theatre. His mother came from Connecticut. According to one of her sons, she had "some sort of Yankee talent, though there are none of her family that I know of, who have

done anything marvellous, excepting by way of fattening oxen, etc." (C. E. Wright to H. B. Wright, Oct. 13, 1834, Wright MSS., *post*). Hendrick helped on the farm, attended the public schools, and in 1824 entered the Wilkes-Barre Academy, where he excelled in scholarship, public speaking, and theatricals. In May 1829 he entered Dickinson College but never secured a degree. Early in 1831 he returned to Wilkes-Barre, entered the law office of John N. Conyngham, and on Nov. 8 was admitted to the bar.

His success was astonishingly rapid, for within a few months he had clients throughout northeastern Pennsylvania; they "believed and said that no jury could resist him" (Kulp, *post*, p. 3). As an ardent Jacksonian Democrat he became a colonel of militia and in 1834 was appointed district attorney for Luzerne County by George M. Dallas [q.v.]. He was soon the leader of the faction opposed to the leadership of Andrew Beaumont. He was elected to the lower house of the state legislature in 1841, 1842, and 1843, and in the last year served as speaker. His legislative service was characterized by aid to new railroad corporations, internal improvements, and such social reforms as the repeal of the law for imprisonment of debtors. He was elected chairman of the Democratic convention of 1844 in Baltimore by the opponents of Van Buren. Wright's prominence on this occasion led him to secure the secret support of Henry A. P. Muhlenberg [q.v.] for a seat in the United States Senate, but Muhlenberg's untimely death and Wright's failure to secure a complimentary nomination for Congress sent these hopes glimmering. He then looked to Polk for some office, preferably that of collector of the port of Philadelphia, but Polk ignored him. Wright blamed James Buchanan for this, perhaps rightly, but his open break with Buchanan did not come until 1857, when Buchanan failed to reward him for his part in the campaign of 1856. Defeated in 1850 and 1854, he was elected to the national House of Representatives in 1852, and again, as a War Democrat, in 1860, having been nominated by both the Democratic and Republican parties. He made a speech in reply to Clement L. Vallandigham [q.v.] on Jan. 14, 1863, that was quoted enthusiastically by Northern papers, but in 1864, dissatisfied with the changed objects of the war, he supported George Brinton McClellan [q.v.] for president. On his return to private life in 1863 he began to publish in the *Anthracite Monitor*, a labor organ, a series of articles which were subsequently published in book form as *A Practical Treatise on Labor* (1871). This was an obvious bid for labor support and marked the beginning of his progressive abandonment of the old Democratic party. He was nominated by the Democrats for Congress in 1876, and 1878, but it was largely due to the labor and Greenback element that he was elected. At last, in 1880, he forsook the Democratic party for the support of these factions and was defeated. His last years in Congress were devoted to an unsuccessful effort to secure loans for homesteaders on public lands. Wright was widely read but unscholarly. His oratory and facile pen won him a deserved but unenviable title: "Old-Man-Not-Afraid-to-be-Called-Demagogue." He was wealthy, but his philanthropy, illustrated in the annual distribution of thousands of loaves of bread, was inevitably associated with his political aspirations. He was married on Aug. 21, 1835, to Mary Ann Bradley Robinson and had ten children, of whom five survived him.

[Though Wright's *Hist. Sketches of Plymouth* (1873) contains some biog. data, the foregoing is based upon his MSS. including diaries, newspaper clippings, and political corres., which belong to the Wyoming Hist. and Geological Soc., Wilkes-Barre. See also G. B. Kulp, *Families of the Wyoming Valley*, vol. I (1885), pp. 2-14; *Biog. Dir. Am. Cong.* (1928); *Nat. View* (Washington, D. C.), May 22, 1880; *Wilkes-Barre Daily Union-Leader*, Sept. 2, 1881; *Wilkes-Barre Daily Record*, Sept. 3, 1881; *Phila. Press*, Sept. 3, 1881.]
J. P. B.

WRIGHT, HENRY (Jan. 10, 1835–Oct. 3, 1895), professional baseball player, known as Harry Wright, was born in Sheffield, England, the eldest of five children of Samuel and Ann (Tone) Wright. He was taken to the United States about 1836 and was educated in the grade schools of New York City. Leaving school, he was employed for a time by a jewelry manufacturing firm and, as a youngster, became prominent in athletics, particularly cricket and the growing game of baseball. In 1856 he became the professional bowler for the St. George Cricket Club on Staten Island, N. Y., where his father was cricket instructor; at about the same time he also began to play baseball with the team of the Knickerbocker Club, a celebrated amateur organization. Though a professional at cricket, he was still an amateur at baseball, there being no professionals in those days. In 1866 he went to Cincinnati as instructor and bowler for the Union Cricket Club of that city. In July of the same year he organized and captained the Cincinnati Baseball Club. For two seasons he was the pitcher of the baseball team, and thereafter, through his active playing career, he always played center field. At that time some skilled players were paid for their services, but the Cincinnati Red Stockings, organized, managed, and captained by Harry Wright, became in 1869 the first full professional team in baseball history. On that same team was George Wright, Harry's younger brother, who also rose to fame as a ball player. In 1869 and 1870 the Cincinnati Red Stockings toured the country, winning eighty-seven games before losing one. When the Cincinnati team was disbanded in 1871, Wright went to Boston to play for and manage a team newly organized there. At the end of the season of 1874 he toured England with a baseball team. The baseball party also played cricket games with some of the best of the English teams and fared very well in such contests, although the Wright brothers were the only real cricketers in the group. In 1876 the National League of Professional Baseball Clubs was organized, and Wright became the manager of the Boston team. His active playing days were over, but as a manager and leader of players he was prominent in helping to put professional baseball on a respectable, sober, and sportsmanlike basis. He managed the Boston team until the end of 1881, the club winning two championships under his leadership. He managed Providence in 1882 and 1883, another club in the National League, and in 1884 went to Philadelphia to manage the National League club there until the close of the 1893 season. He was then appointed chief of umpires of the National League and held that office until the time of his death.

He was fairly tall, well built, and a very graceful athlete in his playing days. He was a striking figure on the field with his "sideburns," his long moustache, and his tuft of beard. By his skill as a player, his example as a sportsman, and his deportment as a gentleman, he did much to improve the standard of baseball in his day and was a noted figure in American sport for some thirty years. He was married three times: first, on Sept. 10, 1868, to Mary Fraser of New York City, by whom he had four children; then to a Miss Mulford, by whom he also had four children; and then to his first wife's sister, by whom he had no children. He died of pneumonia in a sanatarium in Atlantic City, N. J., and is buried in Brooklyn, N. Y. He was survived by his third wife and seven of his children.

[Harry Ellard, *Base Ball in Cincinnati* (1907); A. G. Spalding, *America's National Game* (1911); George Morland, *Balldom* (1926); obituary in *N. Y. Times*, Oct. 4, 1895; information from George Wright.]
J. K.

WRIGHT, HORATIO GOUVERNEUR (Mar. 6, 1820–July 2, 1899), soldier and engineer, was a native of Clinton, Conn., his parents being Edward and Nancy Wright. He entered the United States Military Academy, graduated second in his class, and was appointed second lieutenant, Engineer Corps, July 1, 1841. Before 1846 he had served as assistant to the board of engineers and as instructor at the military academy, and had accompanied the secretary of war on a military inspection tour. The following ten years he spent in Florida, superintending river and harbor improvements at St. Augustine and on the St. John's River, and constructing fortifications at Tortugas and Key West. Having become a captain, July 1, 1855, he was assistant to the chief engineer at Washington when the Civil War began.

In a daring attempt to destroy the Norfolk navy yard dry dock on the night of Apr. 20, 1861, Wright was captured but was soon released. Late in May he began building Fort Ellsworth and other defenses of the capital, and at Bull Run was chief engineer of the division under Samuel Peter Heintzelman [q.v.]. Shortly after that disastrous battle he became chief engineer for the brilliantly successful Port Royal expedition, and commanded the 3rd Brigade, which occupied Fort Walker on Nov. 7. Promoted brigadier-general of volunteers on Sept. 14, 1861, in the following February he headed the expedition which seized Jacksonville, St. Augustine, and other points in Florida, going thence to Morris Island, S. C., and leading a division in the attack on Secessionville, June 16, 1862. The Department of the Ohio was now (Aug. 19) entrusted to him, and he cooperated efficiently with Generals D. C. Buell and W. S. Rosecrans [qq.v.] in their Kentucky and Tennessee campaigns until again ordered east, May 18, 1863. Here he took the 1st Division of Gen. John Sedgwick's VI Corps. His brigades saw little fighting at Gettysburg, but on Nov. 7 following, they carried the Confederate redoubts at Rappahannock Bridge in a dashing assault, and forced the river crossings, subsequently taking an important share in the Mine Run campaign. Beginning May 4, 1864, Wright participated in every battle of the Wilderness campaign. After the death of General Sedgwick at Spotsylvania, May 9, he took the VI Corps, which he commanded thereafter, and his troops bore the brunt of the terrible fighting in the Bloody Angle on May 12. Commissioned major-general of volunteers from this date, in July with his corps he was hurriedly sent to save Washington from Early's raid, and repelled the enemy, July 12, at the very edge of the capital. He fought under Sheridan in the autumn campaign in the Shenandoah Valley, and on Oct. 19 at Cedar Creek, where he was wounded, he commanded the army until Sheridan's arrival. Returning to Petersburg, his troops were the first to penetrate the

Confederate works on Apr. 2, 1865, and were chiefly instrumental in capturing Ewell's corps at Sailors' Creek on Apr. 6. From July 20, 1865, to Aug. 28, 1866, Wright commanded the Department of Texas.

Thenceforward he became engaged on such important engineering projects as the East River bridge, New York; the Sutro tunnel, Nevada; Delaware Breakwater Harbor of Refuge; the South Pass jetties on the Mississippi, and the completion of the Washington Monument. He was also active in the improvement of heavy ordnance and gun carriages. Meantime promoted through grades to brigadier-general in the regular army, and chief of engineers on June 30, 1879, he was retired on Mar. 6, 1884. On Aug. 11, 1842, Wright married Louisa M., daughter of Sam and Emily (Slaughter) Bradford, of Culpeper, Va., whose remains rest beside his in the Arlington National Cemetery. He died in Washington, D. C., survived by his wife and two daughters. Paradoxically, his very excellences have minimized Wright's reputation. A man of superb physique and commanding presence, as engineer and soldier he always did well, exciting neither criticism nor controversy, which frequently bring men to public notice.

[In addition to *War of the Rebellion: Official Records* (*Army*), sources include *Who's Who in America, 1899–1900*; F. B. Heitman, *Hist. Reg. . . . U. S. Army* (1903), vol. I; G. W. Cullum, *Biog. Reg. . . . U. S. Mil. Acad.*, vol. II (1891); *Battles and Leaders of the Civil War* (4 vols., 1887–88), ed. by R. U. Johnson and C. C. Buel; obituaries in *Washington Post*, July 3, and in *Army and Navy Jour.*, July 8, 1899; geneal. data from Conn. Hist. Soc. and Miss Katie Winfrey, Culpeper, Va. There are refs. to Wright in M. F. Steele, *Am. Campaigns* (1909); *Personal Memoirs of U. S. Grant*, vol. II (1886); *The Life and Letters of George Gordon Meade* (1913), vol. II; and *Personal Memoirs of P. H. Sheridan* (2 vols., 1888). See also Wright's ann. reports as chief of engineers, 1879–84, and *Report on the Fabrication of Iron for Defensive Purposes* (1871), written with I. G. Barnard and P. S. Michie.]

J. M. H.

WRIGHT, JAMES LENDREW (Apr. 6, 1816–Aug. 3, 1893), pioneer labor leader, was born in County Tyrone, Ireland, of Scotch-Irish parentage. After a brief residence in Saint John, New Brunswick, the Wright family settled in Philadelphia in 1827. Wright was educated at the Mount Vernon Grammar School and at Charles Mead's private academy, a circumstance which seems to indicate that his family was for a time well-to-do. He was later apprenticed to George W. Farr, a tailor, whom he served six years. Thereafter he continued in tailoring and opened his own shop in Frankfort, Pa., in 1847. Seven years later he became the manager of a large Philadelphia clothing store. In his late years, along with Terence V. Powderly [q.v.]

and John W. Hayes, Wright engaged in several commercial ventures, including the soliciting of advertising from Armour and other employers whom, as labor leader, he had previously fought.

As early as 1837 Wright joined the Tailors' Benevolent Society of Philadelphia, but his career as a labor leader was delayed by the middle-class interludes. In 1862 he and Uriah Smith Stephens [q.v.] helped organize the Garment Cutters' Association, a benevolent organization, whose president he was for a number of years. In 1863 he helped establish the Philadelphia Trades' Assembly and was elected its treasurer. In 1869 Stephens, Wright, and five others founded the Noble Order of the Knights of Labor, whose name Wright devised, and of which he was a leading functionary for more than two decades. He served as temporary chairman of the Pittsburgh convention in 1876 which endeavored to set up a national labor organization. As a member of the Knights' delegation he helped determine the convention's final decision for Greenbackism and against socialism and a political labor party.

The countrywide flare-up of labor militancy which resulted from the use of federal and state troops in suppressing the great strike of July 1877 took in part political form, and Wright entered politics. The Harrisburg convention of the United Workingmen in that year nominated him for Pennsylvania state treasurer; he polled more than 52,000 votes, or some ten per cent. of the total cast. As Greenback-Labor candidate for state secretary of internal affairs in 1878, he got about 82,000 votes. The economic revival of 1879 swept aside the political labor movement, and Wright thereafter was active chiefly as a leader of the Knights of Labor, the most important labor organization of the period. He contributed much to building and extending its influence and to shaping its policies. He died in 1893 at his home in Germantown.

[There is no biog. of Wright. Consult J. R. Commons and others, *Hist. of Labour in the U. S.* (2 vols., 1918); N. J. Ware, *The Labor Movement in the U. S., 1860–95* (1929); G. E. McNeill, ed., *The Labor Movement* (1887); death notice in *North Am.* (Phila.), Aug. 7, 1893; obituary in *N. Y. Tribune*, Aug. 6, 1893, which gives Aug. 4 as the date of death.] H. S.

WRIGHT, JOHN HENRY (Feb. 4, 1852–Nov. 25, 1908), Hellenist, was born at Urmia (later Rezaieh), Persia, where his parents, the Rev. Austin Hazen and Catherine (Myers) Wright, were missionaries. At the age of eight he was sent home to be educated, and studied at College Hill (Poughkeepsie) and Dartmouth College (A.B., 1873). After serving at Ohio Agricultural and Mechanical College (later Ohio

State University) as assistant professor of ancient languages and literature, he spent two years in Leipzig, where he devoted himself chiefly to Sanskrit and classical philology, and returned to become associate professor of Greek at Dartmouth (1878–86). On Apr. 2, 1879, he married Mary Tappan, daughter of Eli Todd Tappan [q.v.], president of Kenyon College. From Dartmouth he was called to the Johns Hopkins University as professor of classical philology; he served also as dean of the collegiate board. In 1887 he accepted a professorship of Greek at Harvard, where he remained until his death.

His wide experience with students from different parts of the country fitted him eminently for the post of dean of the Harvard Graduate School, which he filled from 1895 until his death. His range in teaching was encyclopaedic, and a keen critical sense, fortified by wide reading, gave him what seemed like the power of divination in interpreting difficult texts. At Harvard he originated and conducted courses in classical archaeology and in Greek history, until the establishment of separate chairs in those subjects. Sophocles was his favorite author, but he also treated writers as far apart as the philosopher Plato and the traveler Pausanias. A witty speaker, a writer possessing charm, he addressed the National Education Association in 1882 on "The Place of Original Research in College Education" and the New Hampshire Teachers' Association in 1884 on "The Greek Question." At Baltimore in 1886 he spoke on "The College in the University and Classical Philology in the College." In 1886 he published a translation of Maxime Collignon's *Manuel d'Archéologie Grecque.* His researches in Greek history led him to a correct chronology of the political and economic disturbances in Athens at the close of the seventh century B.C. before the discovery of Aristotle's *Constitution of the Athenians* confirmed his results; unfortunately these were delayed in print until 1892, when his article on "The Date of Cylon" was published. On the publication of the recently discovered *Mimes* of Herodas, Wright made important contributions to the understanding of the text in his *Herondaea* (1893). In 1894 he was president of the American Philological Association. Versed in epigraphy as well as in paleography, he issued in 1896 a monograph on *The Origin of Sigma Lunatum.* He was coeditor of the *Classical Review* (1889–1906), the *Classical Quarterly* (1907), Twentieth Century Textbooks (1900), and editor-in-chief of the *American Journal of Archaeology* (1897–1906). In 1902 he assumed supervision of *A History of All Nations,* in twenty-four volumes. He also edited *Masterpieces of Greek Literature* (1902), and in 1904 addressed the Congress of Arts and Sciences at the Louisiana Purchase Exposition in St. Louis on *Present Problems of the History of Classical Literature* (1906). He went to Athens in 1906 as professor of Greek literature at the American School of Classical Studies. The recent exploration by the School of the Cave of Vari, on Mount Hymettus, inspired him to write a remarkable monograph on *The Origin of Plato's Cave* (1906).

Holding firm and reasoned convictions, he was gentle and patient in defending them. His wife, a woman of rare charm and culture, a novelist and writer of short stories, aided him in simple and gracious hospitality. He died at Cambridge, Mass.

[*Who's Who in America,* 1908–09; S. E. Morison, *The Development of Harvard Univ.* (1930); H. W. Smyth, in *Harvard Grads.' Mag.,* Mar. 1909; *Harvard Univ. Gazette,* Dec. 18, 1908; *Nation,* Dec. 3, 1908; obituary in *Boston Herald,* Nov. 26, 1908; personal acquaintance.]   C. B. G.

WRIGHT, JOHN STEPHEN (July 16, 1815– Sept. 26, 1874), editor, promoter, publicist, real-estate operator, and manufacturer, was born at Sheffield, Mass., the eldest son of John and Huldah (Dewey) Wright, both of New England ancestry. On the paternal side he was a descendant of Thomas Wright who emigrated to America in 1635 and later settled in Wethersfield, Conn. As a boy he was instructed by his mother's brother, Chester Dewey [*q.v.*]. About 1832 he set out for the West with his father, a merchant, with a stock of goods, intending to settle at Galena, Ill. Arriving at Chicago on Oct. 29, 1832, they decided to remain there and built a hewn log building at Lake and Clark Streets, which was then so far from the business center that their store was called "the Prairie Store." Young Wright took a census of Chicago in 1833 and published one of the first lithographed maps of the town in 1834. In the latter year he began his real-estate business, and in about two years he held property worth $200,000. At one time he bought 7,000 acres of canal land, and in 1836 he purchased a warehouse and dock preparatory to entering the shipping business. In the panic of 1837 this fortune was entirely lost. After the crash he served as secretary and general manager of the Union Agricultural Society and issued for it the *Union Agriculturist,* beginning in 1839. In 1841 this paper was combined with the *Western Prairie Farmer* under the double name and was thus continued until the close of the following year. In January 1843 Wright became the owner of the publication and

changed its name to the *Prairie Farmer.* J. Ambrose Wright took over the active editorship of the paper, while Wright directed its business affairs and contributed an occasional article to the educational department. He continued his connection with the *Prairie Farmer* until 1857.

In his trips through the Middle West in a buggy, soliciting subscriptions and contributions for his paper, he learned much of the agriculture and the resources of the country, and grew more and more enthusiastic over its prospects. In 1845 he wrote for the New York *Commercial Advertiser* a series of articles about the products of the West and the advantages of Illinois and Chicago. Other articles of a similar kind were written for the New York *Evening Post,* the *American Railroad Journal,* and other papers. In 1847 he wrote another series advocating the construction of railroads in the West. In 1848, when he worked for a land grant to build a railroad from Chicago to the Gulf of Mexico, he printed and distributed to postmasters along the proposed route six thousand copies of petitions to Congress urging that the road be built, lobbied for the bill in Washington, and urged that the state make provision for building the road and paying the state debt through the land grant.

After his marriage on Sept. 1, 1846, to Catherine B. Turner of Virginia he again entered the real-estate business and was so successful that by 1857 he had acquired a second fortune. In the meantime he had become interested in a self-raking reaper invented by Jearum Atkins [*q.v.*] and in 1852 had begun the manufacture of the Atkins Automaton. In 1856 he made 2,800 of these machines and was proving himself a real factor in this growing business. A circumstance of his manufacturing operations of that year led to his undoing. Because of a shortage of seasoned timber he had been forced to make the reapers from unseasoned wood, which warped in the harvest heat. Had it not been for the expenditure of $200,000 to make good his guarantee on these machines, Wright might have maintained himself through the panic, but this loss and the collapse of other business swept away his fortune a second time. Even after this reverse he continued his promotional work. In 1859 he formed a land company, sought to interest eastern capitalists, and continued to promote it for several years. After the Chicago fire he characteristically renewed his expression of faith in the city.

Wright was one of the conspicuous leaders in the educational life of the state. In 1835 he built, at his own expense, the first public school building erected in Chicago. He labored with Jonathan Baldwin Turner [*q.v.*] in the interests of a state school system and assisted in promoting organizations to further it. His paper, the *Prairie Farmer,* was a strong and consistent supporter of public education. He advocated and predicted the formation of a park system connected by boulevards in Chicago. In addition to articles and numerous pamphlets, he compiled a rambling, bombastic volume, *Chicago, Past, Present and Future* (1868), and wrote *Citizenship Sovereignty* (1863), *Illinois to Massachusetts, Greeting!* (1866), and a *Reply to Hon. Charles G. Loring upon "Reconstruction"* (1867). His writings of this period were rambling and verbose, and gave evidence of the weakening of his mind. His reason finally gave way, and he was committed to an asylum in Philadelphia, where he died.

[Curtis Wright, *Geneal. and Biog. Notices of Descendants of Sir John Wright* (1915); A. W. Wright, *In Memoriam, John S. Wright* (1885); E. O. Gale, *Reminiscences of Early Chicago and Vicinity* (1902); A. T. Andreas, *Hist. of Chicago*, vol. II (1885); H. H. Hurlbut, *Chicago Antiquities* (1881); J. S. Wright, *Chicago, Past, Present and Future* (1868); obituary in *Chicago Daily Tribune*, Sept. 30, 1874.]   R. H. A.

WRIGHT, JONATHAN JASPER (Feb. 11, 1840–Feb. 18, 1885), negro educator and associate justice of the supreme court of South Carolina, was born in Luzerne County, Pa., presumably of free parents. His father seems to have been a farmer. After attending Lancasterian University at Ithaca, N. Y., Wright began the study of law in a private office at Montrose, Pa., at the same time teaching school. In 1865 the American Missionary Society sent him to South Carolina to organize schools for colored people; after one year he returned to Pennsylvania, where he achieved the distinction of being the first negro admitted to the bar in that state. He soon returned to South Carolina as a legal advisor of refugees and freedmen, a position he resigned in 1868. He was a member of the state constitutional convention of 1868, and in the same year he was elected state senator from Beaufort, S. C. On Feb. 1, 1870, while a senator, he was elected by the legislature to fill an unexpired term on the bench of the state supreme court, at that time probably the only man of his race ever to hold such a judicial position in the United States. He was subsequently elected (1870) for the full term of six years. The white public did not object strongly to Wright's election, for it was known that the Republican legislature was determined to elect a negro and Wright was preferred to any other. His career on the bench gave evidence of considerable ability; though he left the more important decisions to his two white colleagues, his opinions were clearly expressed and judicious in tone.

During the contested election of 1876, Wright became the center of a heated controversy between Daniel H. Chamberlain and Wade Hampton [*qq.v.*], rival claimants for the governorship. When the contest was carried to the supreme court, the chief justice was mortally ill and could not attend. Thus it became imperative that Wright and his associate, A. J. Willard, known to be friendly toward Hampton, should be of the same opinion if a conclusion was to be reached. On Feb. 27, 1877, Willard and Wright signed an order which said, in effect, that Hampton was the legal governor. Two days later, however, Wright reversed his opinion and asked that his signature to the original order be revoked. Nevertheless, the order was executed and Hampton was declared governor (*Ex parte Norris, 8 South Carolina,* 408 ff.). The explanation of Wright's action probably lies in the fact that this was a time of tremendous excitement, when bloodshed seemed imminent and when a presidential as well as a state election might hinge upon the decision; undoubtedly great pressure was brought upon him by Republicans and Democrats alike. Following the overthrow of the Republican government, he resigned, effective Dec. 1, 1877. Corruption charges brought against him through the Democratic investigating committee were unsubstantiated and never pressed. There seems to be no doubt that he was personally honest.

He was a striking full-blooded negro, nearly six feet tall, described as having "a finely chiseled face and handsomely developed head." He was a good speaker, confident and clear-headed, but inclined to lisp. Throughout his career he was a moderate in politics, seeking to conciliate rather than to antagonize the races. He was definitely interested in the advancement and improvement of his race, but he was keenly aware of the negro's lack of education and experience in government, and he lamented the fact that able white men were seldom found in the Republican party of South Carolina. Following his resignation, he sank into comparative poverty and obscurity; there is no record that he practised his profession. He was never married. After a lingering illness of tuberculosis, he died at his rooming place in Charleston.

[See *Proc. Constitutional Convention of S. C.* (1868); J. S. Reynolds, *Reconstruction in S. C.* (1905); A. A. Taylor, *The Negro in S. C. during the Reconstruction* (1924); F. B. Simkins and R. H. Woody, *S. C. during Reconstruction* (1932); *Report of the Joint Investigating Committee on Public Frauds* (Columbia, 1878); Edward McCrady, *A Rev. of the Resolutions of the Press Conference* (Charleston, 1870), which contains a denunciation of Wright; R. H. Woody, in *Jour.*

of Negro Hist., Apr. 1933; obituary in News and Courier (Charleston), Feb. 20, 1885.] R. H. W.

WRIGHT, JOSEPH (July 16, 1756–1793), portrait-painter, die-sinker, was born in Bordentown, N. J., one of three children and only son of Joseph Wright and Patience (Lovell) Wright [q.v.], noted modeler in wax and secret American agent in Europe during the Revolution. After the death of her husband, Mrs. Wright about 1772 settled in London with her children. She was in comparatively affluent circumstances through the success of her work, and gave Joseph a good education and a thorough grounding in clay and wax modeling. In London he also studied painting with John Trumbull (1756–1843) under Benjamin West [qq.v.]. By 1780 he was exhibiting at the Royal Academy, where he showed a portrait of his mother. Before 1782 he painted a portrait of the Prince of Wales, later George IV. Skilled as modeler and portraitist, and with knowledge of die-sinking, he went to Paris in 1782 and there painted portraits of fashionable ladies under the patronage of his mother's intimate friend, Benjamin Franklin.

Later in the same year he sailed from Nantes for America, but suffered shipwreck and was forced into a Spanish port, finally reaching Boston penniless after a ten weeks' voyage. With him he brought letters to influential persons in Boston and Rhode Island, as well as a letter from Franklin to Washington which, in October 1783, enabled him to paint the General and Mrs. Washington at headquarters in Rocky Hill near Princeton. There he met William Dunlap [q.v.]. In 1784 he painted another Washington portrait in military uniform to be presented through Robert Morris to Count de Solms for his collection of military portraits. After Washington became president Wright wished to paint him again, but was refused because of stress of duties. A crayon drawing from life, however, was made in 1790 without Washington's knowledge while he sat in his pew in St. Paul's Chapel, New York. This portrait Wright later etched and published on small cards. It is the only etching known to have been executed by Wright himself. While Congress was sitting at Princeton, Patience Wright was agitating in Europe for a portrait of Washington by some European sculptor, and Wright was commissioned to make a plaster cast of Washington's features. Dunlap records, however, that the cast was dropped and broken as Wright removed it from the face. Washington refused to repeat the ordeal.

In 1783–84 Wright was in Philadelphia, but by 1787 he had established himself in New York, where he married a Miss Vandervoort, niece of the Revolutionary patriot, Col. William Ledyard [q.v.]. In 1790 he followed Congress to Philadelphia, and shortly afterwards executed a family group showing himself, his wife, and their three children (in the Pennsylvania Academy of the Fine Arts). That same year J. Manly published the "Manly Medal" by Samuel Brooks of Philadelphia, which bore a portrait of Washington attributed to Wright, and is said to have been the first Washington medal produced in the United States. In Philadelphia Wright practised as portraitist, modeler, and die-sinker, his skill in the last profession gaining him in 1792 appointment by Washington as first draftsman and die-sinker of the newly established United States mint. Dunlap mentions a design for a cent made by Wright in 1792, although there is no trace of ultimate execution. The first official coins and medals of the United States, however, were probably Wright's work. He made dies for a Washington medal after the Houdon bust, and for a medal voted by Congress to Maj. Henry Lee. Among his paintings are portraits of Madison and his family, and one of John Jay executed in 1786 (in the collections of the New York Historical Society). His portraits of Washington, especially the miniature portrait made in St. Paul's Chapel, were copied by English engravers and appear in work by such men as Joseph Collyer, John Gadsby Chapman, and Thomas and George Wyon. Wright also made a chalk drawing of his own head; a bust of him by William Rush [q.v.] is in the Pennsylvania Academy of the Fine Arts. Wright and his wife died in Philadelphia during the yellow fever epidemic of 1793 sometime before Oct. 11.

[W. S. Baker, The Engraved Portraits of Washington (1880), and Medallic Portraits of Washington (1885); J. T. Scharf and Thompson Westcott, Hist. of Phila., 1609–1884, vol. II (1884); D. M. Stauffer, Am. Engravers upon Copper and Steel (1907); C. H. Hart, in Pa. Mag. of Hist., July 1908; William Dunlap, A Hist. . . . of the Arts of Design in the U. S. (3 vols., 1918), ed. by F. W. Bayley and C. E. Goodspeed; G. G. Evans, Hist. of the U. S. Mint at Phila. (1885); F. H. Stewart, Hist. of the First U. S. Mint (1924).]
D. G.

WRIGHT, JOSEPH ALBERT (Apr. 17, 1810–May 11, 1867), governor of Indiana, congressman, and diplomat, was born at Washington, Pa., of English-Welsh descent. He was the son of John and Rachel (Seaman) Wright, and a brother of George Grover Wright [q.v.]. He removed with his parents to Bloomington, Ind., about 1819, and there assisted his father in a brick yard until the latter's death in 1823. After two years at the state seminary (later Indiana University), he began the study of law in Bloomington in 1825, was admitted to the bar in 1829, and the same year removed to Rockville, Parke

County, to begin practice. After two terms in the Indiana House of Representatives (1833, 1836) and one in the state Senate (1839), he served one term (1843–45) in the national House of Representatives. His principal speeches were on the subject of the tariff, in which he made a forceful plea in behalf of the consumer (*Congressional Globe*, 28 Cong., 1 Sess., pp. 545–46, 548–50), in behalf of the right of petition (*Ibid.*, p. 197) and in favor of the construction of a canal across Central America to connect the Atlantic with the Pacific (*Ibid.*, 28 Cong., 2 Sess., pp. 308–09). Defeated for reëlection to Congress, in 1849 he was elected governor of Indiana and in 1852 was reëlected. He served from December 1849 to January 1857. As governor, Wright's most determined efforts were directed toward raising the standard of living of the farmers. The State Agricultural Society and the State Board of Agriculture were organized, and he recommended the organization of county agriculture societies and legislation to promote the diffusion of popular and scientific knowledge among the farmers. He also recommended legislation for the regulation of the liquor traffic, urged the improvement of wagon roads by grading and drainage, and proposed the appointment of a commission to regulate the promoting, building, and operation of railroads.

Wright was appointed by President Buchanan (June 1, 1857) minister of the United States to Prussia. At this post he was persistent in activities for the protection of naturalized citizens of the United States, of German origin, especially from the operation of Prussian laws relative to military service. He was more successful in procuring German agricultural publications for distribution in the United States, and arranged for the exchange of German and American seeds. Before his departure from Berlin when recalled in May 1861 he sought a proclamation by the Prussian government disapproving the course taken by the Confederate States. In February 1862 he was appointed to fill a vacancy in the United States Senate caused by the expulsion of Jesse D. Bright [*q.v.*] and served until January 1863. He was re-appointed minister to Germany, June 30, 1865, and served until his death in Berlin. Wright was a tall man with agreeable features, strong clear voice, and fluent tongue. He married Louisa Cook, a farmer's daughter, in 1831.

[W. W. Woollen, *Biog. and Hist. Sketches of Early Ind.* (1883); J. P. Dunn, *Ind. and Indianans* (1919); Logan Esarey, *A Hist. of Ind.* (2 vols., 1915–18); *Papers Relating to Foreign Affairs*, 1861–67; instructions and dispatches, Prussia, MSS. in Dept. of State; *Indianapolis Daily Jour.*, May 13, 14, 1867.]   N. D. M.

WRIGHT, JOSEPH JEFFERSON BURR (Apr. 27, 1801–May 14, 1878), army medical officer, was born at Wilkes-Barre, Pa., to a family of English descent, long resident in that community. He received the degree of A.B. from Washington College, Washington, Pa., in 1821 and in 1825–26 was a student in the School of Medicine of the University of Pennsylvania. He took up a rural practice in Luzerne County near his native town but on Oct. 25, 1833, was appointed an assistant surgeon in the United States army. Joining at Fort Gibson, Indian Territory, he served for the next seven years at various posts in the Middle West. He took part in the Seminole War (1840–41, 1843) and was with the 8th Infantry in the occupation of Texas in 1846. With Gen. Zachary Taylor's army in the invasion of Mexico, he took part in the battles of Palo Alto and Resaca de la Palma, and had charge of a hospital at Matamoras. In the following spring he was medical purveyor of the army that left Vera Cruz for the capture of Mexico City, participating in the battles of Cerro Gordo, Contreras, Churubusco, and Molino del Rey. He treated successfully the grape-shot perforation of the chest of Gen. James Shields, received at Cerro Gordo, and reported this remarkable case in F. H. Hamilton's *Practical Treatise on Military Surgery* (1861). At San Antonio, Tex., on the staff of William Jenkins Worth [*q.v.*] when a highly fatal epidemic of cholera occurred (1849), Wright furnished a detailed account to *Southern Medical Reports* (vol. I, 1850). He was on field duty with troops quelling disturbances in Kansas in 1857 and in the Utah expedition of 1858. He entered the Civil War as medical director of the Department of Ohio on the staff of Gen. George B. McClellan. He was present at the battles of Rich Mountain and Carrick's Ford in West Virginia, for which engagements he organized the field medical service and general hospitals. On account of advancing age he declined the detail to accompany McClellan to the Army of the Potomac, and joined the staff of Gen. Henry W. Halleck at St. Louis, Mo. In April 1862 he went to the cavalry recruiting depot at Carlisle, Pa., as surgeon, where he remained until he was retired from active service with the grade of colonel on Dec. 31, 1876. He died of a stroke of apoplexy shortly over a year later at his home in Carlisle. He had been brevetted colonel on Nov. 29, 1864, and brigadier-general on Mar. 13, 1865. He contributed case reports to the surgical volume of the *Medical and Surgical History of the War of the Rebellion* (6 vols., 1870–88), and in a special report on malaria made to the surgeon-general in 1843 he reported the successful use of quinine sulphate in dosage considered excessive up to that time. All his writings are in the florid style much employed in his time, but since entirely outmoded in medical writing.

He was a man of conspicuous tact and courtesy, with a high sense of justice and honor, and a high conception of the obligations of the soldier. He was married to Eliza Jones, daughter of Amasa and Elizabeth (Huntington) Jones, and was survived by a son, Joseph P. Wright, who followed his father in the career of army surgeon, and two daughters, wives of army officers.

[*The Huntington Family* (1915); *Cat. of Grads. of Jefferson Medic. Coll.* (1869); G. M. Kober, in *Mil. Surgeon*, Nov. 1927; *Medic. Record*, June 15, 1878; H. A. Kelly and W. Y. Burrage, *Am. Medic. Biogs.* (1920); obituaries in *Carlisle Herald* and *Press* (Phila.), May 16, 1878.]   J. M. P.

WRIGHT, LUKE EDWARD (Aug. 29, 1846–Nov. 17, 1922), governor-general of the Philippines, secretary of war, was born in Giles County, Tenn., the son of Archibald and Mary Elizabeth (Eldridge) Wright and the great-grandson of Duncan Wright, an emigrant from Scotland. His father was chief justice of the supreme court of Tennessee. The family removed to Memphis in 1850, where Luke attended the public schools. When the Civil War broke out, a tall rangy boy looking older than his fifteen years, he enlisted in the Confederate army and was assigned to Company G, 154th Senior Tennessee Regiment. Later he became a second lieutenant. For bravery under fire at Murfreesboro in 1863 he was cited for gallantry. After the war he was a student, 1867–68, at the University of Mississippi but did not graduate. On Dec. 15, 1868, he married Katherine Middleton Semmes, the daughter of Raphael Semmes [q.v.]. They had five children. He read law in his father's office, was admitted to the bar, and settled down to practice in Memphis. In 1878, during a severe epidemic of yellow fever at Memphis, with other public-spirited and courageous citizens he formed a relief committee that put down panic, provided medical and nursing care for the sick, distributed food, and buried the dead. The nomination of Bryan by the Democrats in 1896 caused him, a life-long Democrat but a conservative by temperament, to bolt the party. In 1900 McKinley appointed him a member of the second Philippine commission. In 1901 he became vice-governor of the Philippines, and a little later, in 1904, governor, succeeding William H. Taft. On Feb. 6, 1905, his title was changed to governor-general. Obstructionism by Filipino politicians made his labor as administrator both difficult and dis-

agreeable. Strong, competent, perhaps a little too unbending, he defied opposition, charted his own course and kept to it. Late in 1905 Roosevelt asked him to become the first ambassador of the United States to Japan. He accepted, regretfully. An associate to the Philippine administration, Dean C. Worcester, characterized Wright's withdrawal as a grave mistake, by which "the islands were deprived of the services of a very able and distinguished man, . . . who had the courage of his convictions, and whose convictions were thoroughly sound" (*The Philippines Past and Present*, 1914, I, 352).

After a year at Tokio he returned to Memphis. In June 1908 Roosevelt called him again to public office, once more to succeed William H. Taft, now Republican nominee for president, this time as secretary of war. His acceptance, on the assumption that he would be retained in the post if Taft should be elected, is said to have led to a misunderstanding that became one of the larger causes for the quarrel between Taft and Roosevelt (Mark Sullivan, *Our Times*, IV, 1932, 320–25). An English visitor to the Philippines at the time Wright was governor-general wrote of him: "He is a strong character, as generous and courteous as he is personally courageous" (John Foreman, *The Philippine Islands*, 3rd ed. 1906, p. 564). To this it may be added that his outer person was a mirror of his inner traits. Tall, broad-shouldered, with snow-white hair, eyes a steely gray but with a kindly twinkle in them, he inspired respect in his adversaries, warm affection in his friends.

[*Tenn., the Volunteer State* (1923), vol. II, ed. by J. T. Moore; J. M. Keating, *Hist. of . . . Memphis* (1888), vol. II; J. P. Young, *Standard Hist. of Memphis* (1912); *U. S. Army Recruiting News*, May 1, 1933; *N. Y. Times*, Nov. 18, 1922; information from family; letter from Alfred Hume, chancellor of the Univ. of Miss.]   W. E. S—a.

WRIGHT, MARCUS JOSEPH (June 5, 1831–Dec. 27, 1922), soldier, editor of Confederate records, author, was born in Purdy, Tenn., the son of Benjamin and Martha Ann (Hicks) Harwell Wright. His grandfather, John Wright, a native of Savannah, Ga., served as a captain in the Revolutionary War. His father, also of Savannah, fought as an officer of the 39th United States Infantry in the Creek War and later in the War with Mexico. Wright was educated in the academy at Purdy. After studying law, he moved to Memphis, where he became clerk of the common law and chancery court. He served as lieutenant-colonel of the 154th Infantry, Tennessee militia, which was armed and equipped several years before the Civil War, and entered the Confederate service with this regiment in

April 1861. In 1862 he acted as military governor of Columbus, Ky. In 1862 he received promotion to the rank of brigadier-general (confirmed, Apr. 22, 1863). He commanded his regiment in the battles of Belmont and at Shiloh, where he was wounded. Recovered, he led a brigade in the campaign around Chattanooga, November 1863. He was also active in the defense of Atlanta until the Confederate evacuation of that city, when he assumed command of Macon, Ga. In December 1864 he was appointed to organize forces in west Tennessee, and in the early part of 1865 he was assigned to the command of the district of north Mississippi and west Tennessee. He surrendered at Granada, Miss., and retired to law practice in Memphis, where for some time he also acted as assistant purser of the United States navy yard. On July 1, 1878, he was appointed by the United States government as agent for the collection of Confederate archives, in which service he continued until his retirement in June 1917. It was largely as a result of his tactful efforts that the attitude of Southerners toward the compiling and editing of the Civil War papers became more cordial, and he succeeded in obtaining many records that had been concealed. This work very materially aided in the publication of the extremely valuable collection, *War of the Rebellion: Official Records of the Union and Confederate Armies.* Wright contributed articles to the publications of the Southern History Association and the American Historical Association. He was also the author of a number of books, among them *Reminiscences of the Early Settlement and Early Settlers of McNairy County, Tenn.* (1882), *Some Account of the Life and Services of William Blount* (1884), *Great Commanders: General Scott* (1894), *The Official and Pictorial Record of . . . American Expansion* (1904), *Tennessee in the War, 1861–1865* (1908), *General Officers of the Confederate Army* (1911), and *Memorandum of Field Officers in the Confederate Service* (n.d.).

Wright was twice married: first to Martha Spencer Elcan of Memphis; second, to Pauline Womack of Alabama. He died at his home in Washington, D. C., survived by his second wife and four of his five children. He showed little outstanding brilliance as a general officer in the Confederate army. His services as an organizer of troops were evidently regarded highly by the commanders under whom he acted, however, for they frequently assigned him to command important posts. His greatest claim to attention lies in his ability as a compiler, editor, and collector of records concerning the Civil War. Certainly no Southerner contributed more to the collection and preservation of the records of that conflict.

[See *Who's Who in America,* 1922–23; *Diary of Brigadier-Gen. Marcus J. Wright* (n.d.), which contains a biog. sketch; W. R. Cox, *Address on the Life . . . of Gen. Marcus J. Wright* (1915); *War of the Rebellion: Official Records* (*Army*); C. A. Evans, ed., *Confederate Mil. Hist.* (1899), vol. VIII; records in the office of the adjutant-gen., War Dept.; obituary in *Washington Post,* Dec. 28, 1922.]   C. S. D.

WRIGHT, PATIENCE LOVELL (1725– Mar. 23, 1786), modeler in wax, Revolutionary spy, was born in Bordentown, N. J., of Quaker parents named Lovell. From childhood she was apt in modeling from dough, putty, and wax. On Mar. 20, 1748, she was married to a man much older than herself, Joseph Wright of Bordentown, who died in 1769, leaving her with three children. Already well known in the colonies for her wax portraits, about 1772 (see Walpole, *post,* VIII, 237) she went with her children to London, where she opened an exhibition room in Cockspur Street. There she displayed historical groups, and busts and life-size figures of notable people of the day, and for the rest of her life she had a remarkable vogue. She was tall, vigorous, outspoken; her intelligence was keen, her talk entertaining. The king and queen, whom (so she said) she often addressed familiarly as "George" and "Charlotte," came to her "repository" and watched her at work. The nobility and gentry did likewise. Later she is said to have lost the king's favor by scolding him for the American war. Within three years after her arrival she had modeled a bas-relief of Benjamin Franklin and had made busts of the king and queen, of Lord Chatham, of Thomas Penn and his wife, Lady Juliana, and many other notables. In 1775 the *London Magazine* had a full-page drawing of her at work and a laudatory article styling her "the Promethean modeller." The critical Abigail Adams, writing from London in 1784, described her as "quite the slattern," and later in the letter, as "the queen of sluts," but Mrs. Adams, repelled as she was by the "hearty buss" bestowed alike on the gentlemen and ladies of her party, was much impressed by the waxworks (*Letters, post,* 177–78). After the death of Chatham, Mrs. Wright's lifelike wax portrait was placed among the waxworks in Westminster Abbey, where it may still be seen.

Though details are lacking, it is generally conceded that Patience Wright played well the part of patriot spy. The rude simplicity of her manner veiled an astute mind, and she was able to glean tidings of English military plans, information later to be sent off to Franklin at Passy. In

1777 she wrote to him, "I meet with the greatest politeness and civility from the people of England... I now believe that all my romantick education, joynd with my father's, old Lovell's courage, can be serviceable yet further to bring on the glorious cause of civil and religious liberty" (*Connoisseur, post,* p. 20). In 1781 she made a visit to Paris, where she met prankish Elkanah Watson, who ordered from her a wax bust of Franklin and incidentally was sufficiently impressed by her extraordinary qualities to give in his memoirs a vivid sketch of her personality. She wrote to George Washington in 1783 about a copy of a bust her son Joseph [*q.v.*] was reported to have made of him, saying that she hoped to have the honor of making from it a model in waxwork. Washington's highly complimentary reply is among the manuscripts in the British Museum. Her hope to make portraits from life of the other great American leaders, expressed in a letter to Thomas Jefferson in 1785, was not fulfilled. She died in London a few months later, leaving her son and two married daughters, one of whom, Phoebe, was the wife of John Hoppner, the artist.

[Sources include William Dunlap, *A Hist. of the Rise and Progress of the Arts of Design in the U. S.* (1918), vol. I, pp. 151–56, ed. by F. W. Bayley and C. E. Goodspeed; *The Letters of Horace Walpole,* vol. VIII (1904), No. 1448, and vol. XI (1904), No. 2047, ed. by Mrs. Paget Toynbee; *London Mag.,* Nov. 1775, pp. 555–57; *Letters of Mrs. Adams, the Wife of John Adams* (1848); *Men and Times of the Revolution; or Memoirs of Elkanah Watson* (1856); C. H. Hart, *Browere's Life Masks of Great Americans* (1899), and article in *Connoisseur,* Sept. 1907; Ethel S. Bolton, *Wax Portraits and Silhouettes* (1914); F. E. Waska, in *Brush & Pencil,* Sept. 1898; Lewis Einstein, *Divided Loyalties* (1933); W. T. Whitley, *Artists and Their Friends in England, 1700 to 1799* (1928), vol. II; obituary in *Gentleman's Mag.,* Apr. 1786. There is a short biog. in *The Dict. of Nat. Biog.*]   A–e A.

WRIGHT, PHILIP GREEN (Oct. 3, 1861– Sept. 4, 1934), teacher, economist, poet, craftsman, was born in Boston, Mass., the son of a musician of distinction, John Seward Wright, and of Mary Clark (Green) Wright. His grandfathers were Elizur Wright and Beriah Green [*qq.v.*]. His boyhood and youth were spent in Boston. He earned his way through Tufts College by teaching at Goddard Seminary and serving in the summers as postmaster, ticket agent, and printer at the Maplewood Hotel in the White Mountains. He graduated at the head of his class in civil engineering in 1884, taught mathematics at Buchtel College, Akron, Ohio, for two years, took the degree of M.A. at Harvard in 1887, and worked as a civil engineer and a life-insurance actuary a few years. In 1892 he went to Lombard College, Galesburg, Ill., and for twenty years at this small school he held the chair of mathematics, so to speak, nominally. His courses in astronomy, in financial history of the United States, in English theme writing were a delight and a lasting memory to his students. He had married in 1888 Elizabeth Quincy Sewall of St. Paul, Minn., also a grandchild of Elizur Wright, by whom he had three sons. For many years the Wrights kept open house on winter Sunday evenings to students interested in books and reading. From this stemmed the Poor Writers' Club. The libretto of a musical farce-comedy, "The Cannibal Converts," publicly produced by college students, came from Wright's facile pen at this time. In the basement of the Wright house was installed the Asgard Press, Wright and his wife bringing a book through all processes. Among its publications were three books of verse by Wright—*The Dial of the Heart* (1904), *The Dreamer* (1906), *A Baker's Dozen for a Few Score Friends* (n.d)—and a prose fantasy, *The Plaint of a Rose,* and a sheaf of juvenilia called *In Reckless Ecstasy* (1904) by Charles A. Sandburg.

After teaching economics at Williams College (1912–13), and at Harvard (1913–17), Wright went in 1917 to Washington with his old friend and teacher, Frank W. Taussig, to serve as assistant to David J. Lewis, a member of the United States Tariff Commission. In 1922 he joined the original staff of the Institute of Economics, later part of the Brookings Institution. Before his retirement from the Brookings Institution in 1931 he had completed three volumes in the field of commercial policy—*Sugar in Relation to the Tariff* (1924), *The Tariff on Animal and Vegetable Oils* (1928), *The Cuban Situation and Our Treaty Relations* (1931)—and was joint author of another volume, *The Tariff on Iron and Steel* (1929). By 1933 he had produced two more formidable volumes of tariff studies, bearing on Pacific relations and Oriental trade. Before the American Economic Association in 1932 he presented the thesis that "if nations desire to maintain permanent peace, tariff making must be made subject to international law" (*American Economic Review,* Mar. 1933, p. 26), receiving a spontaneous ovation. He printed privately in 1933, under the title *Outcasts of Efficiency,* a plan "to put the unemployed at work with the existing idle plant and machinery in supplying their own needs." He held that the federal government was the only agency "powerful enough to ... lift the pall of depression from the whole country," and, though he constantly reiterated his view that Americans prize an economic order based on free enterprise, individual initiative, and private property, he argued that conditions were so desperate that in-action was hazardous, and that a new social mechanism to create a better adjustment between production and demand would save the existing economic system from collapse. In his long poems, "The Captain of Industry" and "The Socialist," he set forth the American business man, and the opposed revolutionary; in "The Cry of the Underlings" he achieved an authen-tic proletarian poem of bitter wrath and of a reck-oning to come. In reprints of the latter in the labor press it has gone to millions of readers. In 1934 he and his wife completed a biography of their grandfather, Elizur Wright.

The tributes paid him after death by friends and associates were remarkably lavish and affec-tionate. To one he was "the only man I have ever known who, by the many facets of his gen-ius, lent credibility to the many-sided personali-ties of the Renaissance" (*Philip Green Wright, post*, p. 16). On his studies in economics, their conscientious accuracy of detail, their severely precise reasoning, an eminent economist com-ments, "Nothing better has been done by any economist of our generation" (F. W. Taussig, *Ibid.*, p. 23), and one of his younger associates in the Poor Writers' Club attests of him as a teach-er, "I had four years of almost daily contact with him at college, for many years visited him as often as possible, and there never was a time when he did not deepen whatever of reverence I had for the human mind" (*Ibid.*, p. 15).

[Memorial brochure, *Philip Green Wright* (privately printed, n.d.) ; information from family and friends ; personal recollections ; obituary in *Evening Star* (Washington), Sept. 5, 1934.] C. S—g.

WRIGHT, ROBERT (Nov. 20, 1752–Sept. 7, 1826), United States senator, representative, governor of Maryland, the son of Solomon and Mary (Tidmarsh) Wright, was born in Queen Annes County, Md. His father was a member of the Maryland House of Delegates, 1771–74, and of the Maryland Convention of 1775, signed the Association of the Freemen of Maryland on July 26 of that year, served as chairman of the committee of correspondence for Queen Annes County, and for fourteen years was a judge of the Maryland court of appeals. At home and at such schools as Queen Annes and Kent counties afforded, Robert Wright obtained an elementary education sufficient to enable him to study law; he was admitted to the bar in 1773 and practised at Chestertown until the outbreak of the Revolu-tionary War. In February 1776 he marched from Queen Annes County with a company of minute men against the Loyalists on the Eastern Shore of Virginia, and from July 7, 1777, he served as captain of a company in Col. William Richard-son's battalion of the Maryland line. In 1784, after the conclusion of peace, he was elected a member of the Maryland House of Delegates for Queen Annes County. He was not returned by that county a year later, but in 1786 was a mem-ber for Kent County. His next appearance in the General Assembly was in the Senate, in 1801, and the same year he was elected to a seat in the United States Senate.

In the federal Senate Wright was a stanch supporter of the administration of Thomas Jef-ferson. His first speech, delivered Jan. 15, 1802, was in support of a motion for the repeal of the act passed late in the Federalist administration of John Adams by which the judiciary system was reorganized and sixteen new circuit judge-ships created. On Jan. 20, 1806, he introduced a bill for the protection and indemnification of American seamen. Resigning later that year to become governor of Maryland, he was twice re-elected by the Assembly, serving until May 1809. Steadfast in his loyalty to Jefferson, when the President's commercial policy had become un-popular from its ruinous effect on Maryland ex-ports Wright called a meeting in Annapolis and procured from it not merely an indorsement of the administration but resolutions urging Jeffer-son to withdraw his refusal to be a candidate for a third term. On May 6, 1809, Wright resigned the office of governor to become a candidate for appointment as a judge of the Maryland court of appeals. This candidacy was unsuccessful but in 1810 he was elected to fill a vacancy in the fed-eral House of Representatives. He took his seat in that body Dec. 3, 1810, and served through re-elections until Mar. 4, 1817. He was defeated at the polls in November 1816, but was successful in 1820 and served from March 1821 to March 1823. He was a member of the House Commit-tee on the Judiciary in the Fourteenth Congress and a member of the Committee on Foreign Af-fairs in the Seventeenth. As a party leader he participated freely in the debates on the floor of the House, opposing the rechartering of the Bank of the United States in 1811 but supporting meas-ures for the protection of American commerce and for the prosecution of the War of 1812. In 1822 he was appointed judge of the district court for the lower Eastern Shore of Maryland and on that bench he administered justice until his death at "Blakeford," Queen Annes County. Just before or shortly after the close of the Revo-lution Wright married Sarah DeCourcy, daugh-ter of Col. William DeCourcy; his second wife was a Miss Ringgold of Kent County. A son was born of each marriage.

[*Archives of Md.*, vols. XI (1892), XVI (1897), and XVIII (1900); H. F. Powell, *Tercentenary Hist. of Md.* (1925), vol. IV; H. E. Buchholz, *Govs. of Md.* (1908); R. H. Spencer, *Geneal. and Memorial Encyc. of the State of Md.* (1919), vol. II; *Biog. Dir. Am. Cong.* (1928); *Daily Nat. Intelligencer*, Sept. 14, 1826.]
N. D. M.

WRIGHT, ROBERT WILLIAM (Feb. 22, 1816–Jan. 9, 1885), satirist, lawyer, newspaper editor, amateur scientist, was born in Ludlow, Vt., the third son of Stephen and Zibiah (Richardson) Wright. His father, a cooper, was fifth in descent from Edward Wright, who emigrated from Bromwick, Warwickshire, England, and settled in Concord, Mass., about 1650. Having been graduated in the class of 1842 from Yale, Wright taught for three years in the public schools of Boston while he studied in a law office. He was admitted to the Suffolk bar, in Boston, in 1845 and almost immediately moved westward to the territory of Wisconsin, where he practised law for ten years, most of the time at Waukesha. During this period he edited *Practical Legal Forms* (1852). In 1856 he quitted the West and settled in Waterbury, Conn., where, though he still practised law for a time, he entered upon the journalistic career which was to occupy him chiefly for the rest of his life. Until he retired in 1877 he was successively editor of the Waterbury *Journal*, the Hartford *Daily Post*, the New Haven *Daily News*, the New York *Daily News*, the New Haven *Daily Lever*, the *Daily State Journal* of Richmond, Va., and the New Haven *Daily Register*. From the time he lived in Wisconsin he was an ardent Whig, and when this party broke up he transferred his uncompromising partisanship to the Democrats. Not only did his sharp pen write for his party, but he worked actively in political affairs. For three years he was secretary to James E. English [*q.v.*]. For the presidential election of 1880, he wrote a series of acidulous lyrics to popular music, known as *The Hancock and English Campaign Song Book for 1880*.

From his youth he dabbled in literature. In 1864 he published, under the name "Horatius Flaccus," *The Church Knaviad, or Horace in West Haven*, and in 1867, under the name "Quevedo Redivivus, Jr.," *The Vision of Judgment, or The South Church: Ecclesiastical Councils Viewed from Celestial and Satanic Stand-points*, two biting satires based on a local clerical dispute arising over loyalty to the Union cause. In 1871, in imitation of Bret Harte's poem on the "Heathen Chinee," he published under the name "U. Bet," *The Pious Tchi-Neh*, a pasquinade on the Connecticut gubernatorial election of that year. Though Wright's poetry was often brilliant in its imitation of satiric verse forms, his reputation as an American satirist has suffered from the parochialism of his subjects. Had he turned to national events, he might well have gained a national reputation. He was probably best known, nationally, for his anti-Darwinian study, *Life; Its True Genesis* (1880), in which he developed a variation of the vitalistic explanation. The book appeared late in the controversy and, though widely reviewed by the religious and secular press, was ignored by the leading controversialists, and can be said to have had no real influence. At the time of his death, Wright was engaged in writing a continuation of this work, which he called *Biodynamics*. He was also deeply interested in astronomy, and asserted that he had been the first to record the comet of 1861.

Wright was twice married: on Aug. 13, 1844, to Laurine Louise Luke, by whom he had five children, and on Oct. 14, 1852, to Sarah Louise Martyn, by whom he had three. He died in Cleveland, Ohio.

[Sources include an autobiog. sketch in *Biog. Record Class of 1842 of Yale Coll.* (1878), which Wright edited; *Obit. Record Grads. Yale Coll. . . . 1885*; secretary's records, class of 1842, in Yale lib.; J. S. Hart, *A Manual of Am. Lit.* (1873); obituary in *Cleveland Herald*, Jan. 10, 1885.]
N. H. P.

WRIGHT, SILAS (May 24, 1795–Aug. 27, 1847), United States senator, governor of New York, was a descendant of Deacon Samuel Wright, an early settler of Springfield and Northampton, Mass. The fifth child of Silas and Eleanor (Goodale) Wright, he was born in Amherst, Mass., but grew up in Weybridge, Vt., where he worked on his father's farm and attended district school. At fourteen he entered Addison County Grammar School and at sixteen Middlebury College. After graduation in 1815 he studied law at Sandy Hill, N. Y., with Roger Skinner, was admitted to the bar in 1819, and began practice in Canton, N. Y., boarding with his father's friend, Medad Moody, whose daughter Clarissa he married on Sept. 11, 1833. They had no children.

In 1821 Wright became county surrogate, and within the next decade held a number of local offices and attained the rank of brigadier-general in the militia. An ardent Madisonian in college, Wright was throughout his life a stanch nationalist and Democrat. He led northern New York from the fold of the Clintonians to the "Bucktails," to the "Republicans," thence to the Jacksonian Democrats, and to the left wing of that party. In 1823 he was elected to the state Senate, where he served from Jan. 1, 1824, until December 1827. His firm belief that the yeomanry were usually right made him vote for manhood suffrage and direct election of justices of the peace, yet he held that the people needed the leadership of bosses and honest use of the spoils system to attain the party unity in which lay their hope in the battle against special privilege. He voted against a law providing for the direct election of presidential electors because its adoption would be disadvantageous to the party's candidate, William H. Crawford [q.v.], and voted for the removal of DeWitt Clinton [q.v.] as canal commissioner. He consistently opposed the granting of bank charters by the legislature. In 1827, as chairman of the committee on canals he made a report opposing the extension of the canal system except when the expected revenues promised to reimburse the treasury. By this time he had become a member of the directing group known as the "Albany Regency."

In 1827 Wright took his seat in Congress. At this time he favored a tariff designed for the protection of agriculture as well as manufactures. As a member of the House committee on manufactures he helped frame the "tariff of abominations" of 1828 and took a leading part in defending it; but later, in 1842, he characterized his action as a great error, made through lack of understanding of the subject (Gillet, post, II, 1422). He was reëlected in 1828, but resigned in the next year to become comptroller of New York (1829–33). During his years in this office he continued to oppose the building of canals except such as would pay for themselves, and he advocated a tax to replenish the General Fund.

Resigning the comptrollership in January 1833, he became United States senator to complete the unexpired term of William L. Marcy [q.v.], who had been chosen governor. Reëlected in 1837 and 1843, Wright was appointed successively to the committees on agriculture, commerce, finance, and post offices and post roads. Master of his subject, cool, and deliberative, logical and powerful in reasoning, he came to hold a high rank "for solid judgment and unselfish service" (Turner, post, p. 114). Benton called him the "Cato of the Senate." Taking his seat when his friend Van Buren was vice-president and the personal choice of President Jackson as his successor, Wright was soon recognized as manager of Van Buren's political interests and with his uncannily accurate sense of public opinion became Van Buren's "most effective lieutenant" (Ibid., p. 118)—a lieutenancy that was almost a partnership. Wright voted for the "Force Bill" and the compromise tariff of 1833; Van Buren consulted him before answering Jackson with regard to the removal of the federal deposits from the Bank of the United States, and, at the President's request, entrusted him with the presentation of resolutions favoring removal (Jan. 30, 1834; Van Buren, "Autobiography," post, pp. 729–30). Subsequently Wright with Benton procured the expunging of the resolution censuring Jackson.

Following Van Buren's election to the presidency Wright became chairman of the Senate finance committee (Dec. 21, 1836–March 1841). All measures for rechartering the Bank of the United States he firmly opposed. He opposed the distribution of the ever-mounting surplus among the states, advocating instead its use for defense, investment in easily convertible stocks of states or the United States, or use for general government expenses to permit the reduction of the tariff. The panic of 1837 and suspension of specie payment by the state banks made his position one of great importance. In preparation for the special session of Congress called for September, he contributed to the St. Lawrence Republican seven articles, beginning June 20, 1837, urging the complete divorce of federal finance from the banks and stricter regulation of banking by the states. At the special session he introduced the administration's relief bills, which were adopted, and a bill for the establishment of an independent treasury system, the plan for which he elaborated Jan. 31, 1838. He continued to head the fight for the independent treasury until the bill was passed in 1840.

After Tyler's accession in 1841, relegated to the committees on commerce and claims, Wright urged a tax-and-pay policy; he continued to oppose distribution of the proceeds of the sale of public lands and increase in the tariff. Yet seeing no chance of any other revenue bill passing Congress he reluctantly voted for the high-tariff act of 1842, which automatically ended distribution while raising duties. Declining Tyler's offer of appointment to the Supreme Court in 1844, he campaigned for Van Buren's nomination, refusing to be considered himself for the presidential nomination and declining, when nominated, to be a candidate for the vice-presidency. Reluctant to leave the Senate, he nevertheless resigned through party loyalty, entered the contest for the governorship of New York, and carried the state for Polk. He was offered the secretaryship of the treasury as a reward, but declined.

During his governorship his sturdy support of the policy incorporated in the "stop and tax" law of 1842 led him to veto a bill for canal extension, thus alienating the conservatives. His suppression of violence during the anti-rent disturbances—when, though he sympathized with the tenants' grievances and advocated their redress by law, he called out the militia and prosecuted the ring-leaders—caused bitter feeling in the anti-rent districts; his advocacy in 1846 of a tax on income from rents, short-term leases, and no distress for rent, alienated the landlords; his banking policies lost him the banking interests. Thus, although in 1846 he was renominated for the governorship, he failed of reëlection. His followers ascribed his defeat to the influence of the "Hunkers" or conservatives within the party, coupled with the coolness of the national administration.

Before his retirement to private life, however, Wright had the satisfaction of seeing the fight against privilege in New York reach lasting success when the reforms he had advocated in the rent system and a provision for a popular check on appropriations for public works were put into effect through the new constitution of 1846. In that same year his tariff policy triumphed, when the revenue tariff enacted by Congress followed closely outlines drawn by him in two speeches of 1844 (Senate, Apr. 19 and 23; Watertown, N. Y., Aug. 20), and the independent treasury became permanent. Successful with these old issues, he returned to friendly Canton where he attended the Presbyterian church, cultivated his thirty acres, died, and was buried. Many found honesty his outstanding characteristic; Benton simplicity; Van Buren, "perfect disinterestedness." His death precipitated the "Barnburner" revolt just when a growing community of interest between the northern radicals and the "free, grain-growing states" of the Northwest pointed to a new party on the issue of slavery in the territories, and Wright, who though not an abolitionist had opposed Calhoun's treaty for the annexation of Texas because it insisted upon the protection of slavery there and had upheld the Wilmot Proviso, was being talked of for the presidency.

[Manuscript sources include personal letters in the possession of St. Lawrence Univ., Canton, N. Y., and H. F. Landon, Esq., Watertown, N. Y.; correspondence with Flagg, Hoffman, and Tilden in N. Y. Pub. Lib., Ransom Cooke and Erastus Corning in N. Y. Stat Lib.; Van Buren, Marcy, and Polk papers, Lib. of Cong. Printed sources include "Calhoun Correspondence," *Ann. Report Am. Hist. Asso. . . . 1899,* vol. II (1900) and *1929* (1930); "The Autobiography of Martin Van Buren," *Ibid., 1918,* vol. II (1920); Thomas Hart Benton, *Thirty Years' View* (1854); C. Z. Lincoln, *State of N. Y.: Messages from the Govs.* (1909), vol. IV; letters and speeches in R. H. Gillet, *The Life and Times of Silas Wright* (2 vols., 1874). Other important biographies are J. D. Hammond, *Life and Times of Silas Wright* (1848), repr. as vol. III of his *Hist. of Pol. Parties in the State of N. Y.* (3 vols., 1852); and J. S. Jenkins, *The Life of Silas Wright* (1847). W. E. Chancellor, *A Life of Silas Wright* (1913) was a campaign document for Governor Sulzer. For genealogy see Curtis Wright, *Geneal. and Biog. Notices of the Descendants of Sir John Wright* (1915). See also David Murray, "The Antirent Episode in the State of N. Y.," *Ann. Report Am. Hist. Asso. . . . 1896,* vol. I (1897); E. I. McCormac, *James K. Polk* (1922); W E. Smith, *The Francis Preston Blair Family in Politics* (2 vols., 1933); D. R. Fox, *The Decline of Aristocracy in the Politics of N. Y.* (1919); H. D. A. Donovan, *The Barnburners . . . 1830–1852* (1925), which has a critical bibliog.; Gates Curtis, *Our Country and Its People: A Memorial Record of St. Lawrence County, N. Y.* (1894); H. F. Landon, *The North Country: A Hist.* (1932), vol. I; D. S. Alexander, *A Pol. Hist. of the State of N. Y.,* vols. I, II (1906); F. J. Turner, *The U. S.: 1830–50* (1935); *Albany Evening Atlas,* Aug. 28, 1847. Wright figures in a novel, *The Light in the Clearing* (1917), by Irving Bacheller, a fellow countryman of the "North Border."]

M. S.

WRIGHT, THEODORE LYMAN (Sept. 13, 1858–Oct. 4, 1926), teacher of Greek, was born in Beloit, Wis., the son of Theodore Lyman and Jane (Newcomb) Wright, and was in the seventh generation of descent from Samuel Wright, one of the early settlers of Springfield (then Agawam), Mass. Samuel Wright was the son of a London merchant, Nathaniel Wright, who had an interest in the *Arbella,* which brought John Winthrop to Salem in 1630. Samuel was deacon in the First Church of Springfield, and when the first minister returned to England, Wright was chosen "to dispense the word of God" and allowed fifty shillings per month while thus serving. He became one of the original settlers of Northampton, where he died in 1665. The elder Theodore Lyman Wright entered Yale in 1825, but ill health cut short his college course. After teaching some years in Hartford, Conn., he removed to Beloit in the Wisconsin Territory, where he engaged in business and manufacturing. He was a man of dignified bearing, high character, and civic influence. His son Theodore graduated with distinction at Beloit College (1880), taught the classics in Beloit Academy (1881–83), took the degree of M.A. in Greek at Harvard (1884), and studied at the American School of Classical Studies in Athens (1887). In 1888 he was called to Beloit College as assistant professor, and in 1892 became full professor of Greek literature and art. He was already recognized as a teacher of originality and charm, and throughout nearly forty years of continuous service he was held by his students in ever-deepening admiration and devotion. He was for years summer lecturer for the Bureau of University Travel (1904–26). He married, Mar. 29, 1909, Jean V. Ingham of Buffalo, N. Y., who died July 28, 1910. In addition to instructing in Greek, he organized courses in Greek literature and Greek art in English, which were largely elected. A noteworthy feature of his work was the presentation of Greek dramas in English, translated by his classes. In this his stimulating thought and dramatic talent had full scope. During a period of twenty-five years more Greek plays were seen in Beloit than in any other American community.

Wright's verses for special occasions were felicitous and of penetrating characterization. His most important production of this sort was "The Four Horizons," in commemoration of the fiftieth anniversary in 1897 of the founding of the college. The *Beloit Pageant, from the Turtle to the Flaming Wheel* (1916), written mainly by him, was given by some two thousand performers of various nationalities on the eightieth anniversary of the founding of the city. Translations by him of a few Greek dramas have been printed. He was a member of the Beloit school board (1898–1902, 1917–20) and of the park board from its organization in 1915.

He was of medium stature, alert, responsive, his vivid dark eyes gleaming under heavy brows. He was exacting, yet considerate, of illuminating insight and whimsical humor, a great-hearted friend. Probably no student ever came under his influence without feeling throughout life the touch of his quickening personality. The colony of Greeks in Beloit idolized him; they presented his portrait bust to the Theodore Lyman Wright Art Hall of the college on its dedication in 1930.

[Curtis Wright, *Geneal. and Biog. Notices of Descendants of Sir John Wright of Kelvedon Hall* (1915); M. A. Green, *Springfield, 1636–1886* (1888); *Who's Who in America*, 1926–27; *In Memoriam, Theodore Lyman Wright* (1926), pamphlet; E. D. Eaton, *Hist. Sketches of Beloit Coll.* (1928).]   E. D. E.

WRIGHT, WILBUR (Apr. 16, 1867–May 30, 1912), pioneer in aviation, was born at Millville, near New Castle, Ind., third of five surviving children of Milton and Susan Catharine (Koerner) Wright. His father, descended from Samuel Wright, an early settler of Springfield, Mass., was of good English and Dutch stock, a bishop of the United Brethren in Christ, and editor of the *Religious Telescope*; the mother, of German-Swiss extraction, had an ingenious mind and was constantly contriving household appliances and toys. Wilbur and his brother Orville, born Aug. 19, 1871, at Dayton, Ohio, grew up in Dayton, where manufacturing on a limited scale stimulated ingenuity. To earn pocket money they sold home-made mechanical toys and Orville started a printing business, building his own press. Later they launched a weekly, the *West Side News*, with Wilbur as editor. Wilbur read much and made a good record in high school; he helped his father sometimes by writing for the church magazine, and in articles in the *West Side News* gave early evidence of an incisive style. Partly by virtue of his age he was more mature in judgment and more likely than his brother to carry through an undertaking once

begun. Orville was a dreamer; he read less, disliked writing, was the more prolific in suggestion, and more impetuous. In all their enterprises the brothers were inseparable partners. About the time Orville reached his majority they formed the Wright Cycle Company and began to build the "Van Cleve" bicycle, which soon established a reputation. Their shop was poorly equipped and they learned to achieve much with small means.

In 1896, while Orville Wright was recovering from typhoid fever, news of the death of the German aeronaut Gustav Lilienthal stimulated hours of discussion between the brothers concerning the possibility of flying and gave an impetus toward serious experimental work in that direction. From Octave Chanute's *Progress in Flying Machines* (1891), S. P. Langley's *Experiments in Aerodynamics* (1891), the *Aeronautical Annual*, L. P. Mouillard's *L'Empire de l'Air* (1881), E. J. Marey's *Animal Mechanism* (1874), and articles by Lilienthal they obtained all the scientific knowledge of aeronautics then available.

Planning to experiment with a captive, man-carrying glider, they first experimented with kites, and in 1899 Wilbur Wright built a model biplane with a wing spread of five feet which he flew as a kite. From this and other experiments and their studies of all accepted tables of air pressure, they concluded that a machine of 200 square feet of supporting area would be adequate. The brothers were in communication with Octave Chanute [*q.v.*] during this time, and improved on his trussed biplane construction. They also hit upon the idea of reducing air resistance by placing the body of the operator in a horizontal position. Furthermore, their first glider had a front surface for longitudinal stability and control and also as an innovation, a method devised by Wilbur Wright for obtaining lateral balance by warping the extremities of the wing to decrease the lift on either side, thus supplying a rolling moment at the will of the pilot. Vertical steering was not provided in the first captive glider, but the Wright brothers understood its functions and incorporated it a few years later in their second glider. Their discovery of a control system about all three axes of the airplane was a major contribution to the progress of aviation.

With the advice of the Weather Bureau, the inventors selected for their experiments a narrow strip of sand termed Kill Devil Hill, dividing Albemarle Sound from the Atlantic near the little settlement of Kitty Hawk, N. C. Near the end of September 1900 they were in camp at

Kitty Hawk. The principal sandhill, slightly over a hundred feet in height and with a slope of ten degrees, was ideal for their purpose. They attempted to fly the glider as a kite, but found the lifting capacity less than they had expected, whereupon they turned to free gliding, and were soon making glides of more than three hundred feet and operating safely under perfect control in winds of twenty-seven miles an hour. Their work was painstaking, thoroughly scientific, with a careful tabulation of data and critical examination of all conclusions. The glides indicated that a vertical steering rudder was essential, that the warping could be relied upon for lateral control, that the movement of the center of pressure on a curved wing produced instability, and that calculations based on existing data were in error.

Compelled thenceforth to find their own basic data, they returned to Dayton, where Orville Wright devised a wind tunnel sixteen inches square and some eight feet long, with a gasoline engine turning a metal fan to supply the necessary wind. Using a simple but ingenious weighing apparatus, they tested over two hundred wing and biplane combinations in this tunnel, determining accurate values for lift, drag, and center of pressure. They had already found a method of experimentation greatly superior to Langley's whirling arm.

Utilizing the figures thus secured they built a new glider, and in September and October 1902 were again making flights at Kill Devil Hill. During this season a vertical steering rudder fully counteracted the turning moments introduced by the warping of the wings. The glider was well balanced, it could be controlled with ease, and the flights confirmed their wind-tunnel data. Nearly a thousand glides were made, some of them covering distances of more than six hundred feet. Early in 1903, in strong winds, they made a number of such flights in which they remained in the air for over a minute, often soaring for many seconds over one spot.

The time had now come for constructing a powered machine. With their new pressure tables, the question of wing design was comparatively easy. The problems of stability and control they now understood. The curved wings were carefully braced with wooden struts and wires. They built their own motor, which had four horizontal cylinders of four-inch bore and four-inch stroke and developed some twelve horse-power. The warping device was included; the elevator or horizontal rudder was placed ahead of the machine, the vertical rudder far behind. The pilot was to lie flat on his stomach beside the motor. Two airscrews were used, chain driven from the motor, turning in opposite directions to avoid gyroscopic effects. To keep the machine from toppling forward in landing, long skids extended out in front of the main wings. There were no wheels; launching was accomplished by a catapult, comprising a monorail, a towline, and a falling weight to give the initial momentum. The total weight of the machine was 750 pounds, fully loaded, and it subsequently proved capable of a speed of thirty-one miles per hour.

With their new machine the Wrights arrived at their camp at Kill Devil Hill on Sept. 25, 1903. A succession of bad storms delayed the flights until Dec. 17, when, in spite of a general invitation to the public, only five persons were present to witness the experiment. About 10:30 in the morning Orville Wright made the first successful powered flight. After running the motor a few minutes he released the wire that held the machine to the track and it started slowly forward into a twenty-seven mile wind, with Wilbur Wright running at the side holding the wing to balance the machine on the track, until after a forty-foot run it lifted. Its course in the air was erratic, partly because of lack of experience on the part of the operator and partly because the front elevator was overbalanced. After twelve seconds a sudden descent, when the plane was 120 feet from the point at which it had soared into the air, ended the flight. At noon the same day, the fourth flight was made by Wilbur Wright, who covered 852 feet and remained in the air fifty-nine seconds. After this flight, a sudden gust of wind turned the airplane over and one of the spectators was thrown head over heels inside it. He was not seriously injured, but airplane and power plant were so damaged that for the time all possibility of further flight was ended.

The Wrights had received no popular encouragement; even their father laughed at them; their friends thought them near lunacy. Nevertheless, although the destruction of their first powered machine was a severe loss, they found the resources to build a stronger machine and continued their experiments with systematic improvements. On Oct. 5, 1905, at Huffman Field, Dayton, during a circular flight of twenty-four miles, they solved the problem of equilibrium in turning. They now abandoned other business and devoted all their energies to the construction of a practicable machine and to business negotiations. Not yet protected by patents, at first they withheld details of their powered machine so as not to stimulate rivals, but on May 22,

1906, they received Patent No. 821,393, for a flying machine.

Neither the publication in January 1906 in *L'Aerophile,* of an enthusiastic account of the Wrights' flights from 1903 to 1905, nor an enthusiastic announcement by the Aero Club of America, inspired any action by the American government; but in 1907 after the Wrights had made successful negotiations with foreign governments, the interest of the War Department was awakened. In earlier proposals the brothers had offered to give all their inventions to the world for the sum of $100,000, but the indifference they had encountered in the meantime led them to withdraw this offer. At the very end of the year 1907, after an interview between Wilbur Wright and the chief signal officer, Gen. James Allen, specifications were issued and bids asked for a "gasless flying machine" to carry two men weighing 350 pounds, with sufficient fuel for 125 miles. Twenty-two bids were received, but only three were accepted. The Wrights offered to build a biplane and instruct two operators for $25,000, and they alone completed the contract. Meanwhile, resuming their experiments at Kitty Hawk, they made flights which were reported at great length by newspapers.

Immediately after these successful trials, Wilbur went to France, leaving Orville to demonstrate their contract machine at Fort Myer, Va. On the morning of Sept. 9, 1908, the latter made fifty-seven complete circles over the drill field at an altitude of 120 feet, remaining aloft one hour and two minutes and thus establishing several records on the same day. On Sept. 17, however, while he was flying at a height of about seventy-five feet, a blade of the right-hand propeller struck and loosened a stay wire of the rear rudder. Instantly the wire coiled about the blade, snapping it across the middle. The machine became difficult to manage and plunged to the earth; the inventor suffered a fracture of the thigh and two ribs and his passenger, Lieut. Thomas E. Selfridge, died within three hours of a fractured skull. This accident was the most serious in the joint career of the brothers. That they had so few is a tribute to their skill and coolness in emergency and to their sensitiveness to every air disturbance. In June 1909 Orville Wright reappeared at Fort Myer fully recovered, accompanied by Wilbur and his two mechanics, and completed the official tests with no evidence of nervousness.

Meanwhile, Wilbur, in France, had been flying at the race course at Hunandrières near Le Mans, arousing the admiration and enthusiasm of thousands. The French regarded the quiet and taciturn aeronaut, with his gaunt form, his weather-beaten face, and piercing, hawk-like eyes, with reverence and awe. He made flights to altitudes of 300 feet and more, and concluded a satisfactory arrangement with a French syndicate for the construction of his machine in France. After his return, during the Hudson-Fulton celebration in the fall of 1909, he made demonstration flights from Governors Island, N. Y., around the Statue of Liberty, up to Grant's Tomb, and back, which resulted in the formation of the American Wright Company.

In their subsequent business dealings Wilbur Wright took the lead. Negotiations were concluded in England, France, Germany, Italy, and America, but while the brothers received material rewards for their efforts, they did not attain anything like the wealth which more avaricious men might have secured. Wilbur Wright lived to gain wide fame and recognition, but died of typhoid fever, May 30, 1912, just as the airplane was approaching its more modern development. He had never married.

Throughout the period of their experimentation both Wrights published accounts of their work and expositions of their theories. Notable articles by the elder brother were "Some Aeronautical Experiments" (*Journal of the Western Society of Engineers,* December 1901) and "Experiments and Observations in Soaring Flight" (*Ibid.,* August 1903); the two collaborated in writing "The Wright Brothers' Aeroplane" (*Century Magazine,* September 1908) and "The Relation of Weight, Speed, and Power of Flyers" (Appendix IV to A. F. Zahm's *Aerial Navigation,* 1911); while "How We Made the First Flight" (*Flying,* December 1913), was written by Orville Wright alone after the death of his brother.

[François Peyrey, *Les Premiers Hommes-Oiseaux* (Paris, 1909); Griffith Brewer, "The Life and Work of Wilbur Wright," being the fourth Wilbur Wright Memorial Lecture, *Aeronautical Journal,* July–Sept. 1916; J. R.. McMahon, *The Wright Brothers: Fathers of Flight* (1930); C. G. Abbot, "The Relations between the Smithsonian Institution and the Wright Brothers," *Smithsonian Misc. Colls.,* Sept. 29, 1928; Curtis Wright, *Geneal. and Biog. Notices of Descendants of Sir John Wright* (1915); *Who's Who in America,* 1912–13; *N. Y. Times,* May 31, 1912.]   A. K.

WRIGHT, WILLIAM (Nov. 13, 1794–Nov. 1, 1866), manufacturer, United States senator, was born near Nyack in Rockland County, N. Y., the son of Dr. William Wright. His father, a descendant of old Connecticut stock, came from Saybrook, Conn., was graduated from Yale in 1774, studied and practised medicine at New Haven, and moved across the Hudson about 1785. His death upon a southern trip in 1808 made it necessary for the son to earn a living, and abandon his college preparatory studies at Poughkeepsie Academy. At fourteen Wright began his long career as a manufacturer of harness and saddlery, being apprenticed to Anson Greene Phelps [*q.v.*], who was at that time engaged in that business in Hartford. Wright took part in the defense of Stonington in 1814 and the next year, when Phelps went to New York to make a fortune in metals, Wright, with savings of three hundred dollars, moved to Bridgeport. There he married Minerva, daughter of William Peet, who apparently financed Wright's partnership with Sheldon Smith in the saddlery business.

In 1822 the firm of Smith & Wright moved from Bridgeport to Newark, N. J., which was just then becoming a very active center of the leather industry; with Edwin Van Antwerp and William Faitoute later as silent partners, they developed an extensive factory. It is said to have become one of the largest establishments of its kind in the country, to have contributed much to the industrial development of Newark, and to have attained a commanding position in the southern trade. The improvement of roads and opening up of new agricultural lands stimulated the demand for harness and saddlery, and the European importations were poorly suited to the needs of the West and South. The West began its own saddlery but the South did little. Starting with a branch at Charleston, S. C., Smith & Wright soon had agents in all the principal southern cities. Wright seems to have become the dominant member of the firm and had built up a considerable fortune by the time he retired from active business in 1854.

His wealth and position in the industrial world seemed to have been the chief reasons for his political prominence. From 1840 to 1843 he was the fifth mayor of Newark. In 1843 he began two terms in the national House of Representatives. He was a candidate for the New Jersey governorship in 1847 but was defeated by Daniel Haines [*q.v.*]. Never a strong partisan, he shifted about 1850 from Whig to Democrat. He was elected to the United States Senate in 1853, was defeated for reëlection in 1858, but returned again to serve from 1863 until his death. He is said never to have debated in either house, and his chairmanship of the Senate committee on manufactures alone saves him from virtual oblivion in the records. The congressional eulogists stressed his urbanity, integrity, toleration, and spotless life. His portrait indicates a man erect, dark, and smooth-shaven, with an expression of marked strength and determina-

tion. An Episcopalian, he was the chief benefactor of the House of Prayer at Newark. He died at his home in Newark after a painful illness, survived by his wife, a son, and a daughter.

[W. H. Shaw, *Hist. of Essex and Hudson Counties* (1884), vol. I, p. 582; *Biog. and Geneal. Hist. of the City of Newark* (1898), vol. II, p. 16, with portrait; William Nelson, *Biog. Cyc. of N. J.* (1913), vol. I, p. 126; F. J. Urquhart, *Hist. of the City of Newark* (3 vols., 1913); *Biog. Dir. Am. Cong., 1774–1927* (1928); F. B. Dexter, *Biog. Sketches Grads. Yale Coll.*, vol. III (1903), p. 544; *Cong. Globe*, 39th Cong., 2 Sess., pp. 147–50, 180; obituaries in *N. Y. Herald* and *N. Y. Tribune*, Nov. 2, 1866.]   J. B. P.

WROSETASATOW [See OUTACITY, fl. 1756–1777].

WU P'AN-CHAO [See NG, POON CHEW, 1866–1931].

WURTZ, HENRY (*c.* 1828–Nov. 8, 1910), chemist and editor, was born in Easton, Pa., the son of John J. and Ann (Novus) Wurts. The founder of his family in America is said to have been the Rev. Johannes Conrad Wirtz (or Wurts) who emigrated from Switzerland to America about 1727. After the customary school education young Wurtz entered the College of New Jersey (later Princeton), where his interest in scientific pursuits was awakened by studies under Joseph Henry and John Torrey [*qq.v.*]. After his graduation in 1848, he studied chemistry at the Lawrence Scientific School of Harvard under Eben Norton Horsford [*q.v.*]; conducted in the laboratory of Dr. Oliver Wolcott Gibbs [*q.v.*] in New York a series of mineral analyses, in which he called attention to a supposed new mineral, "melanolite," and to the availability of the greensand of New Jersey as a source of potash (*American Journal of Science*, July, Nov. 1850); and worked as assistant (1851) at Yale under Prof. Benjamin Silliman, the younger [*q.v.*], with whom he was associated in various researches. For two years (1854–56) he was state chemist and geologist of the New Jersey geological survey, conducting an important research upon the composition of the water of the Delaware River (*Ibid.*, July 1856). In the summer of 1857 he made geological explorations in Gaston and Lincoln counties, N. C., in which he discovered cobalt and nickel ores (*Ibid.*, Jan. 1859). In 1858 he was appointed professor of chemistry and pharmacy in the National Medical College of Washington, D. C. (later George Washington University). During this connection he published a research on blowpipe manipulations (*Ibid.*, Mar. 1859) and served as chemical examiner in the United States Patent Office. In 1861 he removed to New York City, where he opened a private laboratory for general consulting work. Among other studies he conducted a research upon sodium amalgams for extracting precious metals from their ores (*Ibid.*, Mar. 1866), for which he secured a patent in 1865, and investigated an asphaltum albertite-like mineral of Virginia for which he proposed the name "grahamite," making also various suggestions as to its utilization (*Ibid.*, Nov. 1866).

From 1868 to 1871 he edited the *American Gas Light Journal*, continuing at the same time his chemical practice in a private laboratory at Hoboken. He devised a new method (1869) of manufacturing fuel gas by the alternating action of air and steam upon cheap coal (patent No. 99,738); published chemical and sanitary reports upon the Passaic River (*American Chemist,* Sept., Oct. 1873) and upon the water supply of Newark and Jersey City (*Ibid.*, Mar. 1874); and prepared an important paper on "New Processes in Proximate Gas Analysis" (*Ibid.*, Mar. 1875). In 1876 he was appointed a judge of exhibits and a special examiner of ceramic materials at the Philadelphia Centennial Exhibition. In connection with this he published an important research upon the chemistry and composition of the porcelains and porcelain rocks of Japan and China (*Ibid.*, Dec. 1876), for which he received a medal from the Centennial Commission. In the same year he published a long speculative paper upon geometrical chemistry (*Ibid.*, Mar. 1876), in which he anticipated some of the work of later investigators.

His numerous contributions to the theory and practice of chemistry led to his being awarded the honorary degree of Ph.D. in 1877 by the Stevens Institute of Technology. During the next ten years he was busily engaged in developing processes for increasing the yields of paraffin oils and other by-products by the distillation of coal. He devoted the remaining years of his life to his private consulting practice as chemical expert, during the course of which he took out numerous patents relating to the distillation of paraffin hydrocarbons and other chemical products. He died at his home in Brooklyn, N. Y., survived by four sons and a daughter. In mineralogy his name is perpetuated by the mineral wurtzilite.

[Sources include Princeton alumni records; bibliog. by Benjamin Silliman, Jr., in *Am. Chemist,* Aug.–Sept. 1874, pp. 109–10; and obituary notices in *Nature,* Dec. 1, 1910, *Brooklyn Daily Eagle,* Nov. 10, 1910, and *N. Y. Times,* Nov. 11, 1910.]   C. A.B—e.

WYANT, ALEXANDER HELWIG (Jan. 11, 1836–Nov. 29, 1892), landscape painter, son of Daniel and Hannah (Shanks) Wyant, was born at Evans Creek, Tuscarawas County, Ohio. Shortly after his birth his parents moved to De-

fiance, Ohio, where Alexander attended the village school and was later apprenticed to a harness maker. As a child he showed an aptitude for drawing, but his interest in art found little encouragement. In 1857 he had the good fortune to see some pictures by George Inness [*q.v.*], and he made the long trip to New York to seek the artist's advice. Encouraged by Inness, he succeeded in securing material assistance from Nicholas Longworth of Cincinnati and was enabled to study in New York, where he was represented in the exhibition of the National Academy of Design in 1864. A year later he sailed for Germany to study under Hans Gude at Karlsruhe. But his independent nature was not happy under direct tutelage, and his study under the Düsseldorf master was not long continued. Before returning to America he traveled in England and Ireland. Several of the Irish studies, and pictures which he made from them, reveal his direct interest in nature, rather than the art of the galleries. In 1869 he was elected a full member of the National Academy for his picture "The Upper Susquehanna." Interested in the scenic beauty of the newly discovered West, he joined a government expedition bound for Arizona in 1873. But the exposure and lack of proper food proved too much of a strain for one unaccustomed to physical hardship. Paralysis of the right side was followed by a long illness, after which Wyant was obliged to learn to paint with his left hand.

His later life was uneventful. His physical infirmity restricted his activities and colored to an apparent degree his outward character. Introspective and solitary, nervous and irritable, he was not given to social amenities. The winter months were passed in his studio in New York but each year the season in the country was extended. Several dated pictures indicate that he painted in the country overlooking Lake Champlain, and later he built a house at Keene Valley, N. Y., where Inness, Roswell M. Shurtleff [*q.v.*], Walter Clark, and others painted during the warm season. In 1880 he married Arabella Locke, daughter of John Bell Locke and Mary Ann (Brereton), by whom he had a son. The summer studio was changed to Arkville in the Catskill Mountains in 1889. The position of the house on a mountain slope commanding a view of the Delaware Valley allowed the artist to study the varying conditions of light and the fleeting aspects of nature which inspired the dominant mood of his pictures. Apart from occasional drives he seldom ventured far from this immediate vicinity. In the closing years of his life he suffered greatly from bodily pain, and physical activity became more and more difficult. He died at his studio, 52 East Twenty-third St., New York, on Nov. 29, 1892, survived by his wife and son.

The style of Wyant's early painting (before 1873) was influenced by the Düsseldorf masters then in vogue and is associated with the so-called "Hudson River School." It is characterized by a photographic fidelity to nature. The angle of vision is wide and extended, the subject panoramic in effect, the sentiment imbued with the romanticism of the time. The color is conventional, the technique thin and precise, the drawing keenly sensitive to naturalistic detail. The masterpiece of the early style is "The Mohawk Valley" (1866), in the Metropolitan Museum, but some of the smaller and less known pictures exemplify the more objective interest of the painter. As a pure naturalist he is unsurpassed. In Wyant's middle period the mountain environment determined the subject matter of his pictures. The interest centers on the more intimate charm of woods and fields, revealed by the momentary changes of light or deepening shadow, and he becomes the painter of sylvan woods, of mossy rocks, and mountain brooks or, following in the path of the axe, he sees his picture in the clearing, the mountain valley, and the clouds. Typical are "In the Still Forest," in the Worcester Museum, originally designed as an over-mantle decoration, "An Old Clearing" (1881), in the Metropolitan Museum, and "In the Adirondacks." In his ultimate expression Wyant is far more than a painter of local landscape. His pictures have a thematic conception, an organized unity, and a universal appeal. He did not paint directly from nature. Mood is transcendent. Simple in composition, the rhythmic action of his pictures is rendered by the movement of light and dark sequences related to a fixed point of focal concentration. Naturalistic form is simplified and subordinated to the major motive. Among the most impressive examples of his mature style are "Passing Clouds," "Early Morning," "A Sunlit Vale," "End of Summer," "Driving Mists," "Moonlight and Frost," in the Brooklyn Museum, "Landscape in the Adirondacks," in the Metropolitan Museum, "The Connecticut Valley," and "Landscape," in the Corcoran Gallery of Art.

Wyant used a simple palette. Black and white, permanent blue, yellow ochre, burnt sienna, raw sienna, and light red were in constant use; occasionally a touch of emeraude with blue, or of cadmium to intensify a green. He often remarked that the key to a landscape was in the sky, and in his most impressive pictures the sky is of dominant interest, the landscape serving as a foil or frame to bring out its subtle and elusive gradations. He was a master of aerial perspective and atmospheric envelopment.

A poetic tonalist, Wyant remains one of the outstanding masters of American landscape painting during the later half of the nineteenth century. His art is associated with the general tendency the return to nature inaugurated in painting by the English master Constable and continued by the masters of Barbizon. Not so emotional as Inness, he does not attain the same dramatic effect. His work is more limited and his expression more reserved, but in consequence his pictures are more even. He had not the austere solidity, the fullness of form, or the perfect relation of method to style, which characterizes his prototype, Théodore Rousseau, but he had a more subtle sense of tonal relation and atmospheric envelopment. This brought to his technique a greater freedom of brushwork and the suggestion rather than the precise definition of form. In this respect he is more truly related to Corot, and his art is a transition from the earlier school to the later impressionists.

[Eliot Clark, *Alexander Wyant* (1916) and *Sixty Paintings by Alexander H. Wyant* (1920); Eleanor R. Gage, in *Arts and Decorations,* Aug. 1912; E. V. Brewster, *Ibid.,* Feb. 1919; J. C. Van Dyke, *Am. Painting* (1919); Samuel Isham, *The Hist. of Am. Painting* (1905); C. H. Caffin, *Am. Masters of Painting* (1902); obituary in *N. Y. Tribune,* Nov. 30, 1892; information from members of Wyant's family.]   E. C—k.

WYATT, Sir FRANCIS (1588–August 1644), colonial governor of Virginia, was of a Kentish family closely identified with the growth of Protestantism in sixteenth-century England. His great-grandfather, Sir Thomas Wyatt, poet and courtier of Henry VIII's time, was granted in 1540 the possessions of the Cistercian monastery at Boxley. His grandfather, Sir Thomas Wyatt the younger, was executed in 1554 for his leadership of an abortive rebellion upon the occasion of Queen Mary's marriage to Philip II. His father, George, was married to Jane, daughter of Sir Thomas Finch of Eastwell, Kent, and as the eldest son by this union Francis became heir to the family seat at Boxley Abbey. He was knighted in 1603, and married in 1618 to Margaret, daughter of Sir Samuel Sandys, eldest son and heir to Archbishop Edwin Sandys.

It is to this connection with the Sandys family that his interest in Virginia was in all probability due. Sir Edwin Sandys, his wife's uncle, gained control of the London Company in 1619, and for two years thereafter pressed forward with unusual energy plans formed in the preceding year for the regeneration of the colony. Unfortunately, these plans miscarried, and by 1621 the company's resources and the adventurers' enthusiasm were well nigh exhausted. With the expiration of the term of Gov. George Yeardley [*q.v.*] in that year, Sandys drew upon his own family for a new group of officers to be entrusted with a final attempt to retrieve the company's fortunes. Wyatt, whose first investment in the company apparently is represented by the transfer of four shares to his name in November 1620, was designated governor. With him as minister to the governor's tenants went his brother, the Rev. Hawte Wyatt. George Sandys [*q.v.*], brother to Sir Edwin, assumed the duties of the new and important post of treasurer. By no means the least important part of their baggage as they arrived in October 1621 were duplicate copies of all instructions sent out with Yeardley in 1618 (see Kingsbury, *post*, III, 98–109, 468–82), to which fact we are indebted for much of our knowledge of the company's program at that significant turning-point in the colony's history. The plan embodied in these famous documents could now, it was hoped be put into effect.

Before he had been in office six months the Indian massacre of 1622 forced Wyatt to turn from the prospect of building Virginia into a prosperous community serving the ends of mercantilist policy to face the stern realities of a situation which threatened the very destruction of the colony. Relying heavily upon the experience of older settlers, especially Yeardley, he acquitted himself well. The difficulties of his position were increased by the inability of the company to provide adequate succor from home, and by the fact that this revelation of the company's weakness led directly to its dissolution in 1624. In the actions leading to the recall of the company's privileges he sensed a threat to the colony's privileges, and rallied the planters to demand the preservation of their liberties. At a time when the discredited leaders of the Sandys faction were excluded from all direction of the colony's affairs, he was asked to continue in office as the first royal governor of Virginia. In this capacity he summoned the famous "convention" assembly of 1625 which pressed neglected petitions made in 1623 and 1624 regarding the colony's needs, asking especially the continuation of the "liberty of . . . generall Assemblie." The news of his father's death in 1623 had made him long anxious to return home to take possession of his estates, but he remained at his post until 1626, when it was possible to report a hopeful prospect for continued peace and for prosperity.

In 1639 Wyatt returned to Virginia to succeed Sir John Harvey as governor. The status of the Virginia assembly had remained in doubt since the dissolution of the company. By what seems a happy coincidence Wyatt was enabled through his official instructions to carry the news to the planters that their "liberty of generall Assemblie" had been finally confirmed by the royal government. In 1641, after a none too happy term, he was replaced by Sir William Berkeley [*q.v.*]. He was buried at Boxley Abbey on Aug. 24, 1644. A capable and respected leader in the experimental period of English colonization, Wyatt's greatest claim to fame probably lies in his efforts to make secure the practice of representative government in the Virginia colony.

[There is a brief life of Wyatt in *The Dict. of Nat. Biog.* See also C. M. Andrews, *Our Earliest Colonial Settlements* (1933) and *The Colonial Period of Am. Hist.: The Settlements*, vol. I (1934); W. F. Craven, *Dissolution of the Va. Company* (1932); T. J. Wertenbaker, *Va. under the Stuarts* (1914); *The Victoria Hist. of the County of Kent*, vol. II (1926); "The Visitation of Kent . . . 1619–1621," *Harleian Soc. Pubs.*, vol. XLII (1898); Susan M. Kingsbury, ed., *The Records of the Va. Company* (4 vols., 1906–35); H. R. McIlwaine, ed., *Jours. of the House of Burgesses of Va., 1619–1658/59* (1915), and *Minutes of the Council and Gen. Court of Colonial Va., 1622–1632, 1670–1676* (1924); W. L. Grant, James Munro, and A. W. Fitzroy, *Acts of the Privy Council . . . Colonial Ser., 1613–1680*, vol. I (1908); W. N. Sainsbury, *Calendar of State Papers, Colonial Ser., 1574–1660* (1860); Alexander Brown, *The First Republic in America* (1898).]
W.F.C.

WYCKOFF, WALTER AUGUSTUS (Apr. 12, 1865–May 15, 1908), author, sociologist, was born in Mainpuri, India, the son of the Rev. Benjamin DuBois Wyckoff, a Presbyterian missionary, and Melissa Wyckoff. On his father's side he was a descendant of Pieter Claesen who emigrated from Holland to New Netherland in 1637. While still a small boy, he was sent to America to prepare for college at the Hudson Academy and later at the Freehold Institute. On graduation from the College of New Jersey (later Princeton) with the degree of B.A. in 1888, he entered the Princeton Theological Seminary. After a year, however, he interrupted his theological course for a period of study and travel in Europe. He had returned to America and was planning to resume his preparation for the ministry when he became convinced that his knowledge of social problems was bookish and inadequate. To learn at first hand more concerning the character and life of the unskilled worker, he set out in July 1891 to work his way on foot from Connecticut to California. Despite hardships which were accentuated by limited physical strength and unusually sensitive tastes, he persisted in his purpose and reached San Francisco early in 1893. His next ventures were abroad. Engaged as a private tutor, during the next two years he traveled twice around the world.

He returned to Princeton in 1894 for further graduate study as fellow in social science. The following year he was appointed lecturer in sociology. While holding this post, he wrote an account of his earlier trip across the continent as an unskilled laborer. Appearing first serially in *Scribner's Magazine,* the simple realism of his story attracted widespread attention. Published in two volumes, *The Workers; an Experiment in Reality—The East* (1897) and *The West* (1898), the account was heralded as an outstanding contribution to sociological literature. In 1898 Wyckoff was appointed assistant professor of political economy in Princeton University, a post which he filled until his death. As a teacher, he attracted large classes of students through his stimulating treatment of social theories and problems. More an observer and critic of social conditions than a systematic sociologist or economist, he drew largely on his own experience and wide general reading. In 1901 he published a third volume, *A Day with a Tramp and Other Days,* based on experiences during the transcontinental journey. His other writings, which included a number of magazine articles, were largely popular in nature. On June 25, 1903, he married Leah Lucille Ehrich, a gifted musician. A chronic ailment grew worse not long after his marriage and brought on his death in 1908 when he was but forty-three years of age. He was survived by his wife and a daughter. Modest, keenly sympathetic, and warm-hearted, he attracted many loyal friends.

Wyckoff's contributions to sociology were limited by his lack of systematic grounding in social sciences. Yet, though *The Workers* is almost devoid of conclusions or constructive proposals, his realistic reports of the conditions surrounding the lives of unskilled laborers aroused in students and the public a keener appreciation of social problems and contributed to the growing movement for more adequate welfare programs.

[See W. F. Wyckoff, in *Somerset County Hist. Quart.,* July 1913, Oct. 1916, Jan. 1917, and *The Wyckoff Family in America* (1934), ed. by M. B. Streeter; *Who's Who in America,* 1908–09; *Gen. Cat. Princeton Univ.* (1908); *Princeton Seminary Necrological Report* (1909); cats. and academic records, Princeton Univ.; *Biog. Cat. Princeton Theological Seminary* (1933); obituary in *N. Y. Daily Tribune,* May 16, 1908; corres. and interviews with friends and colleagues of Wyckoff. The maiden name of Wyckoff's mother is given by some sources as Johnson, by others as Fielder.]

J—s. D. B.

WYETH, JOHN (Mar. 31, 1770–Jan. 23, 1858), editor, publisher, the son of Mary (Winship) and Ebenezer Wyeth, was born in Cambridge, Mass. He was a descendant in the fourth generation of Nicholas Wyeth who emigrated from England before 1645 and settled in Cam-

bridge. His father, a farmer, is said to have been one of the minute-men called to serve at Bunker Hill. At a very early age John became a printer's apprentice. On attaining years of majority he went to Santo Domingo, where he became superintendent of a large printing establishment. Soon, however, during an insurrection of the blacks, he lost all he had built up, and escaped from the island only with the aid of a friend. Finally he arrived in Philadelphia on board ship, disguised and working as a sailor. For a while he worked there in different printing establishments. In 1792, with John W. Allen, he purchased the *Harrisburg Advertiser* in Harrisburg, Pa., the first newspaper of the city, which had been started about 1791 by Maj. Eli Lewis of Lewisberry. With this they began the career of the *Oracle of Dauphin County & Harrisburg Advertiser,* which was successfully carried on until November 1827, a four-page paper with bold, clear type. The policy of the paper was to support Federalist views, although its columns were held open to the expression of views of all parties. In October 1793 Wyeth was appointed first postmaster of Harrisburg under Washington, of whom he had always been a great admirer and supporter. During the Adams campaign he gave consistent and strong editorial support to Adams. Yet he was removed from the postmastership in July 1798 by the postmaster-general of Adams' administration on the grounds of incompatibility between that office and the editing of a paper. During the period of editing the *Oracle of Dauphin* Wyeth established a bookstore and general publishing house. There were many imprints of value, some of them quite extensive. Probably the best known was Alexander Graydon's *Memoirs* (1811). A music book of Wyeth's own compositions had a circulation up to 120,000 in several editions, and a supplement of the second part a circulation of about 25,000. Wyeth was a stanch and early friend of the Harrisburg Academy for Boys and in 1809, upon its incorporation, was elected one of the original trustees for a term of three years. He resigned, however, after little more than a year's service.

He was a man of cheer, practical philosophy, industry, and thrift. He sent all his thirteen children to college and left them what was considered, in those days, a sizable fortune. This fortune had its foundation in real estate speculation, both in Harrisburg and in Philadelphia. He was keenly interested in many public improvements in Harrisburg. Shakespeare House, built by him in 1822, having a good-sized ballroom and theatre, was a lyceum and social center until well toward the twentieth century (*Harrisburg Tele-*

graph, Mar. 30, 1931). Buildings of today (1936) bear his name because they were constructed on the sites of those owned by him. He maintained an active interest in reading and in social activities up to within a short time preceding his death. He was a stanch Unitarian and worked unsuccessfully for several years to establish a church of his faith in Harrisburg.

Wyeth's first wife, Louisa Weiss, the daughter of Lewis and Mary Weiss of Philadelphia, whom he married on June 6, 1793, was the mother of all his children. She died in 1822. On May 2, 1826, he married Lydia Allen of Philadelphia, and lived in that city until the time of his death. One of his grandsons was John Allan Wyeth [*q.v.*].

[W. H. Egle, *Hist. of the Counties of Dauphin and Lebanon* (1883), and *Pa. Geneals.* (1896); Marian Inglewood, *Then and Now in Harrisburg* (1925), p. 144; G. H. Morgan, *Annals ... of Harrisburg* (1858); G. P. Donehoo, *Harrisburg and Dauphin County* (1925); obituary in *Pub. Ledger* (Phila.), Jan. 25, 1858; minutes of the board of trustees, MS. in Harrisburg Acad.; certified copy of Wyeth's will, Bk. P, vol. I, p. 445, Dauphin County Court House; records of real estate transactions in deed books (see indices); copy of entries in family Bible, made by Wyeth, in the poss. of Eleanor Shunk of Harrisburg, Wyeth's great-granddaughter.]   C. W. G.

WYETH, JOHN ALLAN (May 26, 1845–May 28, 1922), surgeon, medical educator, was born in Missionary Station, Marshall County, Ala., the son of Judge Louis Weiss and Euphemia (Allan) Wyeth, and a grandson of John Wyeth [*q.v.*]. He was educated in the common school at Guntersville, a town founded by his father. In 1861 he entered La Grange Military Academy in Alabama, but spent only a year under its rigid discipline, for at seventeen he joined the Confederate army. After playing an active part in many skirmishes and engagements, he was taken prisoner in October 1863 and held until April 1865. For years he suffered from the effects of unhealthful living conditions in prison. He became a superintendent of a large cotton plantation in Franklin (later Colbert) County, Ala., after the war, but soon gave up this position because of his ill health. In 1867 he began the study of medicine, graduating from the medical department of the University of Louisville in 1869. He had practised for only two months, when, feeling that his medical education had been insufficient, particularly in its lack of laboratory and clinical training, he decided to give the next few years to earning money for postgraduate study. Going to New York in 1872, he discovered that there were no special courses for graduate students in medicine. He attended lectures at Bellevue Medical School, however, and devoted much of his time to clinics in surgery and dissection. He re-

ceived his *ad eundem* degree in 1873. At this time he taught himself to be ambidextrous, a valuable accomplishment for a surgeon. From 1874 to 1877 he was prosector to the chair of anatomy at Bellevue Hospital. When ill health forced him to retire, he studied abroad for two years. There he met Dr. J. Marion Sims [*q.v.*], whose daughter, Florence Nightingale Sims, he married on Apr. 10, 1886. On his return to New York he submitted to a number of eminent New York physicians his plans for a postgraduate school of medicine, which he had long dreamed of establishing. As a result, the New York Polyclinic Hospital and Medical School was organized in 1881. Wyeth devoted the remainder of his life to it, serving first as surgeon-in-chief and later as president. He ultimately gave up a large private practice in surgery to confine his energies exclusively to the Polyclinic Hospital.

Wyeth devised a number of new surgical procedures. In 1876 he won a prize offered by the Bellevue Hospital Medical College Alumni Association for his essay on the surgical anatomy of the tibio-tarsal articulation (*American Journal of the Medical Sciences,* Apr. 1876). After the appearance in his *The Surgical Anatomy of the Carotid Arteries* (1876) his ligation of the external carotid artery became an accepted procedure, and his bloodless amputation at shoulder and hip joints (see *Medical Record,* Jan. 13, 1894), first performed in 1889 and 1890, is known as Wyeth's operation. He reported on his new method for treating inoperable tumors by injection of boiling water in 1903. His most important work in his own field was *A Textbook on Surgery* (1887). A prolific writer, he contributed largely to non-medical literature as well. He served as president of the New York Pathological Society (1885–86), the New York State Medical Association (1901), the American Medical Association (1901–02), and the New York Academy of Medicine (1907–10). In 1914 his autobiography, *With Sabre and Scalpel,* was published. His first wife died in 1915, leaving two sons and a daughter. In 1918 he was married to Marguerite Chalifoux, dietitian at the Polyclinic Hospital. He died suddenly of heart trouble.

[In addition to Wyeth's *With Sabre and Scalpel* (1914), see *Boston Medic. and Surgical Jour.,* June 8, 1922; *Internat. Jour. of Surgery,* June 1922, and Feb. 1923, pp. 77–79; *Jour. Am. Medic. Asso.,* June 3, 1922; *N. Y. Medic. Jour.,* June 21, 1922; J. J. Walsh, *Hist. of Medicine in N. Y.* (1919), vol. V; L. R. Paige, *Hist. of Cambridge, Mass.* (1877); *N. Y. Times,* May 29, and June 4, 1922.]   G. L. A.

WYETH, NATHANIEL JARVIS (Jan. 29, 1802–Aug. 31, 1856), trader, explorer, was the son of Jacob and Elizabeth (Jarvis) Wyeth of

Cambridge, Mass., and a nephew of John Wyeth [q.v.]. His father, a descendant of Nicholas Wyeth who settled in Cambridge in 1645, represented a prominent colonial family, was a graduate of Harvard and owner of Fresh Pond Hotel. On Jan. 29, 1824, Nathaniel married his cousin, Elizabeth Jarvis Stone, and in the same year became manager of an ice company owned by Frederic Tudor [q.v.] which reaped the annual winter crop of Fresh Pond. It was said at his death that practically every implement and device used in the ice business had been invented by Nat Wyeth. He also was successful in establishing with Tudor an important trade in ice to the West Indies. His larger fame, however, rests on an adventurous project undertaken during a five-year interlude in his regular occupation. This was an attempt to exploit the Columbia River and regions adjoining it for fish, furs, timber, and agricultural resources. If he had been successful, he would have planted in Oregon an American commercial and agricultural colony.

Wyeth was one of the ardent souls stirred up over Oregon by that inveterate propagandist, the Boston pedagogue, Hall Jackson Kelley [q.v.]. Unlike Kelley, however, he was a man of action, gifted with tremendous energy, determination, and leadership. When Kelley's plan to lead a colony to Oregon in the spring of 1832 evaporated, Wyeth fitted out a cargo which he sent around the Horn and himself enrolled a very small company for an overland expedition. The ship never reached the Columbia, and when Wyeth himself arrived with a remnant of his party there was nothing he could do except make his way back home, which he did toward the end of 1833. A young cousin, John B. Wyeth, who accompanied the party as far as the Rocky Mountains, later published an account of the trip, *Oregon, or a Short History of a Long Journey* (1833), which was prepared under the editorship of Benjamin Waterhouse [q.v.] with the intention of discouraging westward adventurers and was characterized by Nathaniel Wyeth as a book "of *little lies* told for gain."

On his return to Boston Wyeth was able to organize a company to back a project for salmon packing on the lower Columbia, fur trading south of the river, and growing tobacco for the Indian trade. The company fitted out a ship, the *May Dacre*, scheduled to reach the Columbia in the early summer of 1834 to begin fishing and packing salmon. That plan failed, for the ship, damaged by lightning, was laid up for repairs three months at Valparaiso and actually entered the Columbia the day after Wyeth's party, in September 1834. Consequently, she was loaded with timber for Hawaii. Wyeth was accompanied on this trip by Thomas Nuttall and John Kirk Townsend [qq.v.], the latter of whom in 1839 published his *Narrative of a Journey across the Rocky Mountains to the Columbia River*. He spent the winter in Oregon, part of the time as an honored guest of John McLoughlin [q.v.], chief factor of the Hudson's Bay Company at Vancouver, who effectually prevented his would-be rival's success as a fur trader but accorded him every social hospitality. Wyeth built a small fort called William at the mouth of the Willamette, on Wappato or Sauvies Island, where he had hoped also to begin farming operations. On his way west he had brought into the Rocky Mountains a bill of trade goods which had been ordered by the Rocky Mountain Fur Trading Company of St. Louis, whose leaders had facilitated his first expedition. When they refused to fulfil their contract to take the goods, he built Fort Hall as a rival trading house, and this he afterwards sold to the Hudson's Bay Company. It became a famous station on the Oregon and California overland trail.

With more courageous and financially able support, Wyeth would probably have succeeded in his venture. As it was, he went back to his ice business. Yet in some respects his western adventure proved a success. Through it he familiarized important sections of the eastern population with the facts about Oregon, physically and politically, and thus made it easier for Congress and the administration to maintain American interests there; on his second expedition he convoyed the party of Jason Lee [q.v.], who established the first mission, resulting in the first American settlement in Oregon; and he left in that country, as settlers, a number of his men. Wyeth, in short, was one of "the pioneers of the pioneers" of Oregon.

[In addition to the chief source, *The Corres. and Jours. of Capt. Nathaniel J. Wyeth* (1899), ed. by F. G. Young, see L. R. Paige, *Hist. of Cambridge, Mass.* (1877), p. 705; S. P. Sharples, in *Cambridge Hist. Soc. Pubs.*, No. 2 (1907), pp. 33–38; R. G. Thwaites, *Early Western Travels*, vol. XXI (1905), which reprints the accounts of J. B. Wyeth and, more important, J. K. Townsend; C. H. Carey, *Hist. of Ore.* (1922), a detailed general account; A. B. Hulbert, *The Call of the Columbia* (1934); Joseph Schafer, *A Hist. of the Pacific Northwest* (1918 ed.); obituary in *Boston Transcript*, Sept. 2, 1856.]
J.S.

WYLIE, ANDREW (Apr. 12, 1789–Nov. 11, 1851), educator, first president of Indiana University, was born at Washington, Pa., the son of Adam Wylie who emigrated from Antrim, Ireland, about 1776 and became a farmer in Fayette County, Pa. He was educated at home and in local schools until the age of fifteen, when he entered Jefferson College, Canonsburg, Pa., supporting himself by tutoring and odd jobs until his graduation, with first honors, in 1810. For the next two years he was a tutor and at twenty-three succeeded to the principalship of the college. This office he ably administered for four years, resigning only as the result of dissatisfaction over his approval of plans for the consolidation of Jefferson College with Washington College, Washington, Pa. Soon after his resignation, April 1816, he was named president of Washington College. He resigned, Dec. 9, 1828, to become the first president of Indiana College, which had been established by act of legislature, Jan. 24, 1828, as successor to the Indiana Seminary at Bloomington. He held this office until his death. When Wylie assumed office the faculty consisted of himself (as professor of moral and mental philosophy, political economy, and polite literature), two instructors, and sixty students. In 1838 the college became Indiana University and in 1842 a school of law was opened. Wylie's work as an educator was distinguished by the introduction of a system of study called "specialization by rotation," in which the student devoted himself to one subject at a time, mastering it before going to the next. His administration was marked by a slow but steady growth.

In early life Wylie embraced the tenets of Presbyterianism, was licensed to preach by the presbytery of Ohio, Oct. 12, 1812, and was pastor of a church at·Millers Run, Pa., for several years after 1813. But the Presbyterian doctrine became unsatisfactory to him because of its extreme "sectarianism," and in 1841 he united with the Protestant Episcopal Church. In December he was ordained deacon and in May 1842 priest. He was described as "tolerant and patient to a fault of everything but meanness and duplicity," for the most part affable but occasionally brusque in manner (Harding, *post*, pp. 10–11). His literary style is said to have possessed "humor and spirit." He was the author of *English Grammar* (1822), *The Uses of History* (1831), *Eulogy of General Lafayette* (1834), *Latin and Roman Classics* (1838), and *Sectarianism Is Heresy* (1840). He was married in May 1813 to Margaret Ritchie, who survived him.

[T. A. Wylie, *Indiana Univ.* (1890), pp. 47–57; S. B. Harding, *Indiana Univ., 1820–1904* (1904), with photograph; Kate M. Rabb, *A Tour through Ind. in 1840* (1920); Theophilus Parvin, *Address on the Life and Character of Andrew Wylie, D.D.* (1858); *Indianapolis Sunday Star*, Sept. 21, 1931.]   P. D. J.

WYLIE, ELINOR MORTON HOYT (Sept. 7, 1885–Dec. 16, 1928), poet and novelist, was born at Somerville, N. J., the daughter of Henry Martyn and Anne (McMichael) Hoyt. On her father's side she was descended from

Simon Hoyt who settled in Massachusetts before 1630. Although her branch of the family had lived in Pennsylvania since the end of the eighteenth century, where her grandfather, Henry Martyn Hoyt [*q.v.*], had been governor, there was in her nature a "Puritan marrow" of which she was conscious and proud. Her great-grandfather, Morton McMichael [*q.v.*], had been owner of the Philadelphia *North American* and mayor of the city, and her grandfather, Morton McMichael, was a Philadelphia banker whose cultivated interest in her she later said had been a large part of her education.

Her parents took her to Rosemont, a suburb of Philadelphia, when she was two years old, and lived there for ten years. In 1897 her father, having become assistant attorney-general of the United States, moved his family to Washington, where he became solicitor-general in 1903. Elinor Hoyt led, till she was twenty-five, the customary existence of formal Philadelphia and official Washington. She attended Miss Baldwin's school in Bryn Mawr and Mrs. Flint's (later Holton Arms) in Washington, and studied drawing in a class at the Corcoran Gallery of Art. Her summers were spent with her family—she was the eldest of five children—at North-East Harbor, Mount Desert, Me. In 1903 she and her sister Constance went to Paris and London for the season with their grandfather McMichael. He introduced them to his friends Sir Henry Irving and Ellen Terry, and Bram Stoker, who was charmed by the two girls, afterwards dedicated *The Jewel of Seven Stars* (1904) to them. In 1905 Elinor Hoyt was married to Philip Hichborn, son of Admiral Philip Hichborn [*q.v.*], and in 1907 had a son also named Philip. Her outward life seemed uneventful and fashionable till December 1910, when she suddenly eloped with Horace Wylie of Washington.

The Hoyts, the McMichaels, the Hichborns, and the Wylies were all so conspicuous in Philadelphia and Washington that the episode raised an enormous scandal which affected her whole subsequent life. Philadelphia and Washington never forgave her, and the newspapers never forgot. The actual circumstances were obscure, perhaps even to her. But it must be remembered that she had been very close to her erudite grandfather McMichael, who had died in 1904, and to her brilliant father, who died in 1910. Philip Hichborn, nearly her own age, was interested in sport and wrote stories about horses (collected and published as *Hoof Beats* the year of his suicide, 1912). She found life with him increasingly uncongenial and fell in love with Horace Wylie, some fifteen years her senior, an erudite and brilliant man who had qualities which she could not do without. Although she was still far from being the poet she was to become, she had a restless intellect which could not be bound in a situation which cramped and threatened to destroy her.

As Horace Wylie's wife refused to divorce him, Elinor Hichborn and he went early in 1911 to England. There they lived, as Mr. and Mrs. Horace Waring, first at Burley in the New Forest, then at Merrow Down, and from 1914 to 1915 at Witley, near Godalming. In 1912 her mother had printed for her in London, as a gift, a small volume of her verse, *Incidental Numbers*, in which there are only hints of the felicity which marks all her mature poems. In a sense she was still at school, with Horace Wylie and rural England for her teachers. Burley and Witley were quiet harbors from the storm of scandal in America, which invented all sorts of wild, untrue things about her, such as a romantic residence in Corsica, which she never saw. She left England only for occasional holidays in France. The World War having made England a distressing place to live in, she and Horace Wylie returned in July 1915 to Boston, where, his divorce having been granted, they were married the following year. During the next three years they passed two summers in a cottage in Somesville, Mount Desert, and a winter in Augusta, Ga., and in December 1919 went back to Washington. He obtained a minor post with a government bureau, and she wrote more and more poetry, but they had few friends outside the members of her family. Now, however, she had her first acquaintance with men of letters, with Sinclair Lewis, who wrote his *Main Street* in Washington, and William Rose Benét, who had been a friend of her brother Henry at Yale. Her poems began to be mature and to be accepted for publication. In 1921 she left Washington for New York, her home for the short remainder of her life.

She made a swift and shining entrance into the literary society of Manhattan. Nobody there held her history against her. Fastidious and magical, snow-white except for her rich bronze-colored hair and her short-sighted, observant, lustrous eyes, she was a scholar and a lady among the general run of authors. At the same time, she had what she called her "johnny-cake side," a charming, gay informality when she chose. Men and women admired and adored her, and spoiled her with the praise for which she had an insatiable yet humorous appetite. Her poems appeared in many magazines, and a volume, *Nets to Catch the Wind*, was published in 1921 with immediate applause. She was invited to the MacDowell colony at Peterborough, N. H., for the summer of 1922, and again in 1923, 1924, 1925. For a time *Vanity Fair* paid her a weekly salary to select its poetry. In 1923 she collected another volume of poems, *Black Armour*, and published her first novel, *Jennifer Lorn: a Sedate Extravaganza*. The same year she was divorced from Horace Wylie and married to William Rose Benét. The long chapter of her elopment and education was closed, and, with whatever pain and confusion, she put it behind her.

After this marriage she spent the winter of 1924–25 with her husband and his three children in New Canaan, Conn., but for the most part she lived in various apartments in New York—her last three years in Ninth Street—and went in the summer either to the MacDowell colony or to England, with possible excursions to Paris (1925, 1926, 1927, 1928). When the Literary Guild was organized at the end of 1926 she became one of the editors. Though she had many claims, professional and personal, upon her time, she wrote steadily. Her second novel, *The Venetian Glass Nephew* (1925), ran as a serial in the *Century Magazine*. Her third, *The Orphan Angel* (1926), called *Mortal Image* in England, was selected for distribution by the Book-of-the-Month Club, and brought her unexpected money and fame.

The Orphan Angel is a strange but characteristic record of Elinor Wylie's lifelong worship of Shelley. Without too much exaggeration she may be said to have been in love with him from childhood, and she liked to be assured that he would have been in love with her if he had had a chance. She could smile at the idea, but she cherished the emotion. In *The Orphan Angel* she imagined that Shelley, not really drowned in the Gulf of Spezia, had been picked up by a Yankee ship and brought to America. Her imagination could show him her native country, to which she was deeply attached, and could accompany him on his adventures across the shaggy continent of 1822. Her passion drove her to laborious researches into the conditions of pioneer America. And it may have been her jealousy which saw to it that Shiloh (as Shelley), while much courted by women, was won by none of them. Sometimes Elinor Wylie seemed not so much to love Shelley as to identify herself with him. That her voice was shrill in moments of excitement disturbed her less than it would have done if Shelley's had not been shrill too. In *Mr. Hodge and Mr. Hazard* (1928), her last novel, she presented in Mr. Hazard a character who was not quite Shelley and not quite herself but was in various respects like them both. In all literature there is hardly another instance of a spiritual affection so intense as Elinor Wylie's for Shelley. He was the chief master of her heart and mind.

Yet in the writings devoted more or less to him she was often indirect and comic, teasing him as she teased herself. Her intellect was too bright and free not to make use of comedy, as in all her novels. *Jennifer Lorn* she called an extravaganza, *The Venetian Glass Nephew* a philosophical fairy tale. Her prose style had an amused formality which resembled her own manners and conversation. She was not downright enough to write realistic fiction, preferring to tell fantastic stories in a sharp, undeluded idiom. Her novels belong to high comedy, and the passage of time, while it may reduce their audience, has not yet touched their lively colors.

In her poetry she was more direct than in her prose, terse, proud, light, strong, surprising, and memorable. A dozen or so of her poems are established for good in the national anthology, and she must be ranked with the distinctive lyric poets of the English language. This rank she owes especially to the sonnets called *One Person*, first printed privately in England in 1928 and included in the volume *Angels and Earthly Creatures* published the next year in New York. *Trivial Breath* (1928), the poems since *Black Armour* which she wished to preserve, showed no great advance upon her two earlier books. But in May and June of 1928 she wrote, in England, nineteen sonnets in which all the passion and tenderness of young love are uttered with the splendor and accuracy of a subtly accomplished mature poet. About the "One Person" to whom they were addressed she was publicly reticent, and her life was not disrupted by the profound experience.

In October, still in England, she had a stroke which slightly paralyzed one side of her face. She came back to New York in December. Her beauty had been a part of her career, and she felt that she could not bear to be disfigured, however slightly. A few days later, having prepared her last volume of poems for the printers, she had another stroke and died.

[Elinor Wylie's *Collected Poems* (1932) and *Collected Prose* (1933) contain all her lasting work, and the *Prose* has biog. and critical notices of her by Carl Van Vechten, Carl Van Doren, Stephen Vincent Benét, Isabel Paterson, and William Rose Benét. See also *Who's Who in America*, 1928–29; *Elinor Wylie: the Portrait of an Unknown Lady* (1935), by her sister, Nancy Hoyt, which brings together much intimate material but is unsystematic and wanting in detail; W. R. Benét, *The Prose and Poetry of Elinor Wylie* (1934); Elizabeth Sergeant, *Fire under the Andes* (1927); Emily Clark, *Innocence Abroad* (1931); Rebecca West, *Ending in Earnest* (1931); Carl Van Doren, in *Harper's Mag.*, Sept. 1936 and obituary in *N. Y. Times*, Dec.

17, 1928. The present account is based upon personal knowledge and upon information furnished by Horace Wylie and W. R. Benét.]
C. V–D.

WYLIE, ROBERT (1839–February 1877), landscape and genre painter, was born at Douglas, in the Isle of Man, and was taken to the United States by his parents when a child. The family settled in Philadelphia, Pa., where Wylie began his art studies as a pupil of the Pennsylvania Academy, and worked for a time as an ivory carver. His work attracted the attention of the directors of the institution, and about 1864 they sent him to France to continue his training. In Paris he entered the École des Beaux-Arts and worked under Jean-Léon Gérôme. He also became a pupil of Antoine-Louis Barye, the famous sculptor of animals. At the Paris Salon of 1869 he exhibited his "Reading the Letter from the Bridegroom," and at the Salon of 1872 he received a second-class medal for his "Breton Fortune-Teller." Other Salon exhibits were "Baz-Walen, demandeur en mariage dans la Basse-Bretagne" (1870), "L'Accueil de l'Orphelin, Bretagne" (1873), and "Le Conteur de Légendes" (1878). According to the Salon catalogue of 1878 he was a pupil of Thomas Couture.

Wylie was one of the first of the large American colony to discover the attractions of Brittany. About 1865 he established himself at the little fishing village of Pont-Aven, where he lived and worked until the time of his death in 1877. Among his American colleagues there were Frederick A. Bridgman, William L. Picknell [qq.v.], and Clement Swift. The pictures Wylie sent to the Salon made a profound impression on French painters and led several of them to join the artist colony at Pont-Aven. In that place he was well known not only to the artists but also to the peasantry; at the sale of his studio effects after his death, his humble neighbors vied with each other to obtain souvenirs. His more important works are "Death of a Vendean Chief," in the Metropolitan Museum, New York; "Mendicants" and "Card Players," privately owned in Baltimore; "Breton Group," privately owned in Philadelphia; and "A Fortune-Teller of Brittany" (1872), in the Corcoran Gallery of Art, Washington. His paintings are few in number, for he was not prolific. His drawing was especially good; he had an admirable sense of composition; his color was sober; and his artistic sentiment and sympathy for humanity were pronounced. He died in France as the result of an aneurism. He was unmarried.

[See Clara E. Clement and Laurence Hutton, *Artists of the Nineteenth Century* (2 vols., 1879); cats. of the Paris Salon, 1870, 1872, 1873, 1878; cat. of the Metropolitan Museum, 1926; cat. of the Thomas B. Clarke coll., 1899; obituary in *Art Jour.* Apr. 1877. The date of death is given variously as Feb. 4, 13, and 14.]

W. H. D.

WYLIE, SAMUEL BROWN (May 21, 1773–Oct. 13, 1852), clergyman of the Reformed Presbyterian Church, educator, was born in Moylarg, County Antrim, Ireland, the son of Adam and Margaret (Brown) Wylie. His father was a farmer of some means, and the boy was given the rudiments of a sound classical education. Thus equipped, he entered the University of Glasgow, where he distinguished himself as a student and in 1797 was awarded the degree of master of arts. He then secured a teaching position in Ballymena, Ireland, but in a few months his connection with efforts in behalf of Irish independence made it expedient for him, in company with others, to leave the country.

In the latter part of 1797 he arrived in Philadelphia, where the most of his remaining life was spent and where he rose to prominence in educational and religious circles. His first teaching was in a school at Cheltenham, a nearby town. In 1798 he was appointed instructor in the grammar school of the University of Pennsylvania. Meanwhile, he studied theology under the Rev. William Gibson and was licensed to preach by the Reformed Presbytery on June 24, 1799. The following year, June 25, he was ordained at Ryegate, Vt., being, it is said, the first Covenanter to receive ordination in America (Glasgow, *post*, p. 741). He immediately made a tour of the South as one of a commission appointed to see that the edict of the Reformed Presbyterian Church forbidding its members to hold slaves was obeyed. In 1802 he was sent by his denomination as a delegate to the sister churches in Scotland and Ireland.

He and his companions had formed a congregation soon after their arrival in Philadelphia, and on Nov. 20, 1803, he was installed as its pastor. Under his leadership, which terminated only with his death, this body developed into a large church. His educational work went on with little interruption, however. When the Presbytery established a theological seminary in Philadelphia in 1810, he was appointed professor and served until 1817; he was reëlected in 1823 and resigned in 1828. In that year he became professor of Latin and Greek in the University of Pennsylvania and held that position until 1845, when he was made professor emeritus; from 1836 to 1845 he was also vice-provost. On Jan. 17, 1806, he was elected a member of the American Philosophical Society. He was married, Apr. 5, 1802, to Margaret Watson of Pittsburgh, by

whom he had seven children, four of whom survived him.

According to a contemporary he exhibited all the best traits of the Irish—"a genial temper, an open hand, and a heart full of . . . human kindness" (John Forsyth, in Sprague, *post*, p. 38). Along with them, however, went an "indomitable patience, a persistent energy, which no difficulties could affright . . ." (*Ibid.*). He was a laborious student, was thoroughly versed in the classics, and was familiar, it is said, with some fourteen languages. He was a strict disciplinarian, and in school and home held those associated with him to a rigorous routine. His large frame and stately bearing commanded respect. His best-known writings were *The Two Sons of Oil; or, The Faithful Witness for Magistracy & Ministry upon a Scriptural Basis* (1803), an able presentation of the position of the Covenanter Church, and *Memoir of Alexander McLeod, D.D.* (1855), which appeared after Wylie's death. He also published several sermons and a Greek grammar.

[W. I. Addison, *A Roll of the Grads. of the Univ. of Glasgow* (1898); W. B. Sprague, *Annals of the Am. Pulpit*, vol. IX (1869), "Reformed Presbyterian," pp. 34–39; W. M. Glasgow, *Hist. of the Reformed Presbyterian Church in America* (1888); *Fiftieth Anniversary of the Ordination of the Rev. T. W. J. Wylie, D.D., and of His Installation as Pastor of the Wylie Memorial Presbyterian Church* (1893); J. N. McLeod, *Preparation for Death the Business of Life: A Discourse on the Death of the Rev. Samuel Brown Wylie* (1852); *North American and U. S. Gazette* (Phila.), Oct. 15, 1852.]

H. E. S.

WYLLYS, GEORGE (Oct. 6, 1710–Apr. 24, 1796), Connecticut official, was born in Hartford, Conn., the eldest surviving son of Hezekiah and Elizabeth (Hobart) Wyllys. His father and grandfather both held office in the colonial government; his great-grandfather, George Wyllys, emigrated from Warwickshire, England, to Connecticut in 1638—having sent his steward over two years before to make ready for him—and some time later served as governor of the colony. The younger George was born in the Wyllys mansion, built by his great-grandfather, on the grounds of which grew the tree known in history as the "Charter Oak," in which the Connecticut charter was hidden when Governor Andros attempted to seize it.

Wyllys attended Yale College, graduating with honors in the class of 1729. The year following, because of the illness of his father who had held the office since 1712, he was chosen secretary of the colony of Connecticut, *pro tempore*. After four years, his father's health not having improved, he was inducted into the office of secretary and continued to serve in this position until his death. His record of continuous service in the same office for sixty-six years is without equal in the history of Connecticut, for during this time he was never absent from a session of the General Assembly. He also succeeded his father as town clerk of Hartford, in December 1732, and held that office until his death sixty-four years later. In 1738 he became captain of the militia, and in 1757 served as lieutenant-colonel in the war against the French. At the time of the Revolution he was thought by many to sympathize with the British, but three of his sons served with distinction on the American side, and while their father may not have felt the separation from Great Britain to have been necessary, he quickly became reconciled to the new order when the fact was accomplished. He continued in office throughout the war and for many years thereafter. His portrait was painted about 1790, by Ralph Earle [q.v.], and is in the possession of the Connecticut Historical Society.

Wyllys married Mary Woodbridge, daughter of his cousin, Rev. Timothy Woodbridge of Simsbury, Conn. They had four sons and two daughters. He died in Hartford in his eighty-sixth year, considered the most eminent man of his generation in Connecticut by many of his contemporaries.

[G. D. Seymour, *Capt. Nathan Hale . . . Maj. John Palsgrave Wyllys* (1933); F. B. Dexter, *Biog. Sketches Grads. Yale Coll.*, vol. I (1885); A. B. Chapin, *Glastenbury for Two Hundred Years* (1853), p. 162; Louis Mitchell, *The Woodbridge Record* (1883); Abner Morse, *A Geneal. Reg. of the Descendants of Several Ancient Puritans*, vol. II (1859); *New Eng. Hist. and Geneal. Reg.*, July, Oct. 1859, Jan. 1883; *The Pub. Records of the Colony of Conn.*, vols. VII–XV (1873–90); "The Wyllys Papers, 1590–1796," *Conn. Hist. Colls.*, vol. XXI (1924); *Conn. Courant* (Hartford), May 2, 1796.]   R. M. H.

WYMAN, HORACE (Nov. 27, 1827–May 8, 1915), inventor, was born in Woburn, Middlesex County, Mass., where his father manufactured boots and shoes. The son of Abel and Maria (Wade) Wyman, he was descended from John Wyman, one of the pioneer settlers of Woburn, who emigrated from West Mill, Hertfordshire, England, in 1640. Horace Wyman obtained a sound early schooling in the public schools and subsequently attended the Warren Academy, Woburn, and the Francestown (N.H.) Academy. In 1846 he entered the employ of the Amoskeag Manufacturing Company, Manchester, N. H., to learn the trade of machinist, and for the next fourteen years he was variously employed in manufacturing establishments in New England. These included the Lowell Machine Company's Works, at Lowell, the Hinckley Locomotive Works at Boston, and the shops of the Holyoke Water Power Company at Holyoke, where he became a draftsman in 1854.

About 1860 Wyman met George Crompton [q.v.], a manufacturer of looms at Worcester, Mass., and shortly thereafter moved to that city to become associated with Crompton as superintendent of his establishment. He now began to show his inventive talent, which brought him over two hundred patents during his life, all pertaining to the improvement of looms and other textile machinery. Upon the death of Crompton in 1886 and the reorganization of the Crompton Loom Works, Wyman was made manager, holding that position until 1897 when, upon the consolidation of the Crompton Works and those of Lucius J. Knowles [q.v.] as the Crompton & Knowles Loom Works, he became vice-president and consulting engineer for the new enterprise. He retained these positions thereafter until his death.

One of Wyman's first patents, issued to him on Oct. 29, 1867, was for a loom. This was followed by a loom-box operating mechanism patented Jan. 31, 1871; a pile-fabric loom, patented July 2, 1872; and an improved shedding mechanism, patented Jan. 5, 1875. Following these came a group of inventions, some patented jointly with Crompton, involving improvements which permitted certain fabrics to be woven in more than one color and in larger pieces than before. Wyman also developed processes by which rugs and carpets could be woven in larger sizes. His patent of July 15, 1879, was for the first American "dobby" loom and one of his last but very important inventions was the weft replenishing loom having drop shuttle boxes; this was patented Jan. 8, 1901. Textile mills throughout the world are still using machines of which the basic invention was Wyman's, and at the time of his death he was regarded as having done more for the loom industry than any other single individual. His improvements in process and mechanism were in great part responsible for the success of the Crompton & Knowles Loom Works. Wyman served at one time on the board of aldermen of Worcester. He had few outside business interests but was active in several local technical societies and a member of the American Society of Mechanical Engineers. He found time, too, to publish two books on family history: *The Wyman Families in Great and Little Hormead, Herts County, England* (1895) and *Some Account of the Wyman Genealogy* (1897). He was married at Woburn, in 1860, to Louise B. Horton, and at the time of his death at his country home in Princeton, Mass., was survived by two daughters. He was buried in Worcester.

[Horace Wyman, *Some Account of the Wyman Geneal.* (1897); *Trans. Am. Soc. Mech. Engineers*, vol. XXXVII (1915); E. B. Crane, *Geneal. and Personal*

Memoirs of Worcester County, Mass. (1907), vol. III; Worcester Gazette, May 8, 1915; Patent Office records.]
C. W. M.

WYMAN, JEFFRIES (Aug. 11, 1814–Sept. 4, 1874), anatomist and ethnologist, brother of Morrill Wyman [q.v.], was born at Chelmsford, Mass., the third son of Dr. Rufus and Ann (Morrill) Wyman. He was named in honor of a famous Boston doctor, John Jeffries [q.v.], of whom Rufus Wyman had been a pupil. Jeffries Wyman attended private schools in Charlestown and Chelmsford until he was ready to enter Phillips Exeter Academy, where he prepared for college. He was not a brilliant student and spent much time in the woods and fields. Nevertheless he was ready for Harvard at the age of fifteen and entered in the fall of 1829. He graduated with his class in 1833; during his senior year, a severe attack of pneumonia left him with impaired lungs and a weakened constitution and for the rest of his life he avoided New England winters as far as possible, seeking the milder climate of the Southern states. In the summer of 1834 he began to study medicine under the guidance of his father and of Dr. John C. Dalton [q.v.]; at the end of two years he became an assistant in the Massachusetts General Hospital, and in 1837 he received the degree of M.D. During these years he cultivated two gifts which were invaluable to him in his subsequent career. He had been noted even in his college days for his skill in preparing objects of natural history, and a skeleton of a bullfrog which he prepared when an undergraduate was exhibited for many years as a model of its kind. His ability as an artist was a natural accompaniment of his skill as a preparator and added much to the instructiveness and charm of his lectures in later years.

Wyman found his first years of practice financially difficult, despite aid in the form of an appointment as demonstrator in anatomy under John C. Warren [q.v.], but the turn in his fortunes came in 1840, when John Amory Lowell, trustee of the recently established Lowell Institute, made him curator and one of the first lecturers. Wyman was regarded by the critics as too quiet, but by those who knew anything of the field, his lectures on comparative anatomy and physiology were recognized as notable not only for their content but for the skill and charm of their illustration and delivery. To Wyman, however, the important thing was the generous compensation for the lectures, which enabled him to make a visit to Europe and carry on his studies in Paris and London. Called home by the death of his father, he resumed his practice, but he never earned much as a physician and was glad to accept, in 1843, a professorship of anatomy and physiology in the medical school of Hampden-Sidney College, Richmond, Va. Aside from the remuneration and the privilege of teaching, this position enabled Wyman to spend the winter and spring months in a climate milder than that of Boston, but he nevertheless relinquished it in 1847 to accept appointment to the Hersey Professorship of Anatomy at Harvard, which promised fuller scope for his talents. From 1857 to 1866 he was associated with his brother, Morrill Wyman, and others, in a private medical school in Cambridge. He was much interested in the development of an anatomical museum at Harvard and during the remainder of his life he gave a large amount of his time and efforts to building up such a museum as an aid to his teaching.

In 1848–49, another course of Lowell Institute lectures improved his financial situation so much that he spent the summer in an expedition to Labrador on a fishing schooner. On Dec. 19, 1850, he married Adeline Wheelwright, who became the mother of two daughters. The winter of 1851–52 he spent in Florida, where his collecting instinct had full play and the out-of-door life in the mild climate brought improvement to his health. In 1854, accompanied by his wife, he again visited Europe, giving special attention to the museums in the various capitals. Greatly depressed by the death of Mrs. Wyman the following year, he made an excursion to Surinam in 1856 with two of his students, penetrating with canoes the interior of the country and returning with extensive collections for his cherished museum. On the expedition he suffered from tropical fever, however, and his slow recovery left him in no better health. Accordingly, in 1858, he accepted an invitation from Capt. J. M. Forbes to visit South America in company with his friend George Augustus Peabody. This journey took him to La Plata and thence across South America to Valparaiso, whence he came home by way of Peru and Panama, bringing a vast amount of material for the Harvard museums. In 1861 he married Annie Williams Whitney, who died in February 1864, shortly after the birth of their only child, a son who was named for his father.

In 1866, through the munificence of George Peabody [q.v.], a department and museum of archeology and ethnology was established at Harvard, with Wyman as curator, and to this new task he devoted much of his time and energy for the remainder of his life. He never lost his interest in comparative anatomy, however, and at the time of his death the museum, to which he was devoted, occupied generous space in Boylston Hall—the main floor and first gallery filled with specimens of zoology and anatomy, the second gallery occupied with archeological objects, the nucleus of the present Peabody Museum. During the summer of 1874 Wyman was particularly busy with curatorial duties owing to alterations in Boylston Hall. He probably overtaxed his strength, for when he went as usual to the White Mountains late in August he failed to recuperate, and at Bethlehem, on Sept. 4, a severe pulmonary hemorrhage abruptly terminated his life.

Wyman was not a voluminous writer. Although he published more than 175 scientific papers, a large proportion of them were a page or less in length and very few contained more than a dozen pages. His most important papers were those dealing with the structure of the gorilla, first scientifically described by him, from a skeleton sent to Boston through the instrumentality of Thomas S. Savage and John Leighton Wilson [qq.v.]. The accuracy and clarity of these notices gave him an international reputation. His monograph on the nervous system of the frog, published by the Smithsonian Institution in 1852–53, and papers on the anatomy of the blind fish of Mammoth Cave, published in the *American Journal of Science* between 1843 and 1854, are also noteworthy. From 1862 to 1867 he made a series of experiments and careful observations on the appearance of organisms in boiled water which convinced him that spontaneous generation was highly improbable. In the closing years of his life he became greatly interested in the "shell heaps" of Maine, Massachusetts, and Florida and in the information they might yield regarding the character and customs of their builders. His chief work in this field, a monograph of ninety-four pages dealing with the fresh water mounds of the St. John's River, Florida, was published in 1868, after his death.

It is obvious that Wyman's widespread reputation as the leading anatomist of America did not rest primarily on his publications. It was the result, rather, of the personality and high character which made him admired and in many instances deeply loved by his students, who found in him as unselfish a man as he was an extraordinary teacher. He abhorred self-advertising and was frequently rebuked by his colleagues and friends for his excessive modesty and aversion to publicity. He shrank from controversy and would never make any effort to claim priority for his work, saying that the truth was bound to triumph in the end. Like his intimate friend Asa Gray [q.v.], he was devoutly re-

ligious, but he accepted the doctrine of evolution in the days of the great controversy without hesitation or the least shaking of his faith. He made friends everywhere, in all circles, and his death called forth expressions of loss from an unusual variety of men; tributes in prose from Oliver Wendell Holmes and in verse from James Russell Lowell are chief among these. Wyman was chosen president of the American Association for the Advancement of Science in 1857, but never assumed the duties of the office. To Harvard University and to the Boston Society of Natural History he gave unstinted service throughout his life; of the Boston Society he was president from 1856 until his resignation on account of his health in 1870.

[Asa Gray, in *Proc. Boston Soc. of Nat. Hist.*, vol. XVII (1875); O. W. Holmes, in *Atlantic Monthly*, Nov. 1874; B. G. Wilder, in *Pop. Sci. Monthly*, Jan. 1875, repr. in *Leading Am. Men of Science* (1910). ed. by D. S. Jordan; A. S. Packard, *Memoir of Jeffries Wyman* (1878), also in *Biog. Memoirs Nat. Acad. Sci.*, vol. II (1886); Morrill Wyman, "List of Scientific Papers and Works by Jeffries Wyman," in *Animal Mechanics* (1902); *Boston Medic. and Surgic. Jour.*, Sept. 17, 1874; T. F. Harrington, *The Harvard Medic. School* (1905), vol. II; *Memorials of the Class of 1833 of Harvard College* (1883); *Boston Transcript*, Sept. 7, 1874.]   H. L. C.

WYMAN, MORRILL (July 25, 1812–Jan. 30, 1903), physician, a descendant of Francis Wyman who had settled in Woburn, Mass., by 1640, was born in Chelmsford, Mass., the second son of Rufus and Ann (Morrill) Wyman. His father (July 16, 1778–June 22, 1842), a graduate of Harvard College in 1799 and of the Harvard Medical School in 1804, was a noted physician, one of the early psychiatrists of America, who established a high standard for the humane treatment of the insane at the McLean Asylum in Boston as early as 1818. Wyman's brother Jeffries [q.v.] was for years professor of anatomy at the Harvard Medical School. Prepared at Phillips Exeter Academy, Morrill Wyman graduated from Harvard College in 1833 and from the Harvard Medical School in 1837, serving his last year as a house pupil at the Massachusetts General Hospital under James Jackson [q.v.] and others. He began practice in Cambridge, where he continued for more than sixty years as a physician much beloved in his community.

During this period he found time to devote to the more scientific aspects of medicine. In 1846 he published *A Practical Treatise on Ventilation*, dealing particularly with the ventilation of public buildings and hospitals. This work, which was an authority for many years, was followed in 1848 by a report for the American Academy of Arts and Sciences on ventilators and chimney-tops (*Proceedings,* I, 307 ff.), an important contribution. His most effective service to American medical science, however, was rendered in 1850. For some years before that time he had been considering the possibility of improving the operation of thoracentesis, or surgical drainage of the pleural cavity, a procedure not known in America but used in London as early as 1840. On Feb. 23, 1850, by means of a very small hollow exploring needle and trocar, he removed twenty ounces of fluid from the chest of a patient. This operation was repeated two days later with great success. In April 1850, in association with Henry Ingersoll Bowditch [*q.v.*], he operated upon a second patient, this time with the aid of a suction pump. These cases and others were reported by Wyman and Bowditch at a meeting of the Massachusetts Medical Society in May 1851, and by Bowditch in the *American Journal of Medical Sciences* for April 1852. The substitution of the small hollow needle in the place of the large cannula formerly used made the procedure safe and simple, and the discovery is an important landmark in the history of the treatment of pleurisy. Wyman's third contribution to medicine was a practical book, *Autumnal Catarrh (Hay Fever)*, published in 1872 and reprinted with additions in 1876. Wyman, long a sufferer himself, clearly described this form of allergy for the first time, and mapped out certain regions, particularly the White Mountains, where the disease was not prevalent.

In 1853 he was appointed adjunct Hersey Professor of the theory and practice of medicine in the Harvard Medical School, as an associate of John Ware [*q.v.*]. He resigned in 1856, and early in 1857, with Ware, Jeffries Wyman, and J. P. Cooke, formed a private medical school in Cambridge. He was a strong supporter of President Lincoln and during the Civil War served as an inspector of hospitals. From 1875 to 1887 he was an overseer of Harvard College. He was the founder, in 1886, of the Cambridge Hospital, one of the buildings of which bears his name, and for many years served as consulting physician to the Massachusetts General Hospital. On Aug. 14, 1839, he married Elizabeth Aspinwall Pulsifer, daughter of Capt. Robert Starkey Pulsifer, a Boston shipmaster. A son and a daughter survived him.

[Morrill Wyman, Jr., *A Brief Record of the Lives and Writings of Dr. Rufus Wyman . . . and His Son Dr. Morrill Wyman* (1913), with bibliography; H. P. Walcott, in *Harvard Grads. Mag.*, June 1903; *Memorials of the Class of 1833 of Harvard College* (1883); T. F. Harrington, *The Harvard Medic. School* (1905), vol. II; *Boston Medic. and Surgical Journal*, Feb. 5, 1903; *Boston Transcript*, Jan. 31, 1903.]   H. R. V.

WYMAN, ROBERT HARRIS (July 12, 1822–Dec. 2, 1882), naval officer, the son of Thomas White Wyman, of the United States Navy, and Sarah S. L. (Harris) Wyman, was born in Portsmouth, N. H. On Mar. 11, 1837, he was appointed a midshipman in the Navy. He was assigned to the *Independence* in the Brazil Squadron, was transferred to the *Fairfield,* and in 1838 joined the sloop *John Adams,* commanded by his father, and sailed to the East Indies on a voyage lasting two years. The journal kept by him on these three ships is preserved at the library of the United States Naval Academy. On his return he entered the Philadelphia Naval School, where he studied one year, and in 1843 he was promoted to passed midshipman. In the Mexican War he served in the Home Squadron under Commodore Conner, took part in the expedition against Tampico in November 1846, and participated in the bombardment and capture of Vera Cruz and the Castle of San Juan d'Ulloa in March 1847.

When the Civil War broke out he was in command of the steamer *Richmond,* but in July 1861 was transferred to the *Yankee* and in September to the *Pocahontas,* in the Potomac Flotilla, a squadron of small fast steamers organized to keep open communications on the Potomac River, and to cut off rebel intercourse with Maryland. A month later he was transferred to the steamer *Pawnee,* joined Admiral Du Pont's squadron, and participated in the capture of Port Royal, S. C., with its protecting forts. After the battle he was sent back to the Potomac and given command of the flotilla. In April 1862 he made an expedition up the Rappahannock River as far as Fredericksburg, capturing nine vessels, burning forty small schooners, and destroying bridges. In July 1862 he was made commander and ordered to the gunboat *Sonoma* for duty on the James River, but was soon transferred to the West India Squadron. Here in 1863 he captured two blockade runners, the *Britannia* and the *Lizzie.* The last two years of the war he served in the Navy Department on special duty.

After the war he commanded successively the *Colorado* and the *Ticonderoga* in the European Squadron. He was detailed in 1871 to the Hydrographic Office, at Washington, D. C., was given charge of that office, and during a period of eight years did notably constructive work. His writings include: *Coasts of Chile, Bolivia, and Peru* (1876); *The Marshall Group* (1870); *Winds, Currents, and Navigation of the Gulf of Cadiz* (1870); *Sailing Directions, English Channel* (1872); *Navigation of Coasts and Islands in the Mediterranean Sea* (1872); and *Revised Instructions for Keeping Ship's Log-book* (1877).

His translations include: *General Examination of the Atlantic Ocean . . .*, from the French of Capt. Philippe de Kerhallet, of the French Navy (1870, *Hydrographic Office Publication,* 22); *General Examination of the Indian Ocean . . .*, also from Kerhallet (1870, *Hydrographic Office Publication,* 24); *General Examination of the Mediterranean Sea . . .*, from the French of Capt. A. Le Gras, of the French Navy (1870, *Hydrographic Office Publication,* 25); and *Hurricanes . . .*, from the French of Captain de Kerhallet and M. Keller (1872).

Wyman was commissioned rear-admiral on Apr. 26, 1878, and given command of the North Atlantic Squadron. At the time of his death he was chairman of the Lighthouse Board with offices in Washington. He was married to Emily Madeline Dallas, the daughter of Alexander J. Dallas [*q.v.*], on Sept. 27, 1847. They had a daughter and two sons, one of whom died in infancy. His wife and two children survived him.

[Information from the family; U. S. Navy Dept. Archives (Naval Records); *Papers of Francis G. Dallas, Naval Hist. Soc. Pubs.*, vol. VIII (1917), ed. by G. W. Allen; L. R. Hamersly, *Records of Living Officers, U. S. Navy and Marine Corps* (4th ed., 1895); *Reg. . . . of the U. S. Navy, 1837–82; War of the Rebellion: Official Records (Navy),* see index; U. S. Treasury Dept., *In Memoriam: Rear Admiral R. H. Wyman* (1882); Lucien Young, *Cat. of Works by Am. Naval Authors* (1888); *Army and Navy Jour.,* Dec. 9, 1882, Jan. 27, 1883; *N. H. Gazette* (Portsmouth), July 17, 1821; *Daily Evening Times* (Portsmouth), Dec. 4, 1882; *Portsmouth Jour.,* Dec. 9, 1882.]

L. H. B.

WYMAN, SETH (Mar. 4, 1784–Apr. 2, 1843), burglar, was born in Goffstown, N. H., and was the son of Seth and Sarah (Atwood) Wyman. His father had been a soldier in the Revolution, and his great-grandfather was the only surviving officer of the force led by Capt. John Lovewell in the famous fight with Indians near Fryeburg, Me., in 1725. According to his own account, Wyman was a thief almost from infancy, stealing a silver dollar from a house to which his mother took him, and accounting for his possession of it by pretending to find it on the way home. While still a child he stole tobacco for the use of his mother, who "chewed, smoked, and snuffed," and a sister who "helped her in the smoking department" (*The Life and Adventurers of Seth Wyman,* p. 9). Continuous thieving and malicious mischief caused him to be suspected and accused of many crimes, but he was nearly twenty before he was forced to confess his guilt and pay for what he had stolen. After this his house was frequently searched unsuccessfully for stolen goods, but he was twice committed to the county jail in Amherst to await trial. He claims to have made daring attempts to escape

that required great strength and fortitude, and to have brutally beaten a fellow prisoner much larger than himself, but as he calls himself tall though his recorded height is five feet eight inches, this may be exaggeration. He tells also of intermittent vagabondage, incessant thieving, occasional amatory escapades, burglaries alone or in association with others, passing counterfeit money, and of sometimes deviating into honest or semi-honest employment by farming or manufacturing sleighs with stolen tools and from stolen material. In June 1817 he was convicted of larceny in Augusta, Me. (then Augusta, Mass.), and committed to the state prison in Charlestown for three years, but he was pardoned in August 1818. There was no belief in his reformation by the pardoning authorities, for the statement that he was "duly sensible of the moral evil and fatal tendency of his past faults" was crossed out on the official document, and his release was recommended in order to shift to his native New Hampshire the cost of maintaining his wife and six children, then inmates of the Boston almshouse. On Apr. 20, 1820, he was committed to the New Hampshire State Prison in Concord for stealing cloth, and he served every day of his three years' sentence. He returned to Goffstown, where he died, his last years being rendered inactive by the approach of age and a fall from a building on which he was working that seriously injured his back.

Wyman was an audacious and incorrigible thief and swindler, but his prominence was more literary than criminal, as his autobiography, *The Life and Adventures of Seth Wyman, Embodying the Principal Events of a Life Spent in Robbery, Theft, Gambling . . .* (1843), received more notice than most accounts of criminal careers. In its subject matter it seems to imitate the exploits of Henry Tufts, and is less varied and vigorous than its model; but it is also less stilted and pedantic in style, and some of this may be due to the personality of its subject. On Dec. 18, 1808, Wyman married in Boston Welthy (Loomis) Chandler, divorced wife of Nathaniel Chandler, who had already lived with him for several years and borne him two children, four others being born later.

[In addition to *The Life and Adventures of Seth Wyman* (1843), sources include G. P. Hadley, *Hist. of the Town of Goffstown, 1733–1920* (2 vols., 1922); T. B. Wyman, geneal. of the Wyman family, MS. in lib. of the New England Hist. Geneal. Soc.; information on Wyman's prison sentences from the Mass. State Prison, the office of the secretary of state of Mass., and the N. H. State Prison.]

S. G.

WYTHE, GEORGE (1726–June 8, 1806), signer of the Declaration of Independence, statesman, professor of law, and chancellor of Virginia, was born on his father's plantation on Back River, Elizabeth City County, Va. He was the second of three children of Thomas and Margaret (Walker) Wythe. His brother Thomas died in 1755. His sister Ann married Charles Sweeney; her grandson was to play a sinister and tragic rôle in Wythe's life. Wythe's father, a member of the House of Burgesses, was the grandson of Thomas Wythe, gentleman, who emigrated from England to Virginia about 1680. His mother was the daughter of George Walker, a Quaker of "good fortune" and learning, and the grand-daughter of George Keith [q.v.], a well-known scholar and divine. Wythe's father died in 1729, and, the elder son being heir at law, his mother found herself in moderate circumstances. Possessing an unusually good education for that period, she taught her younger son Latin and the fundamentals of Greek. She died while he was still a youth, and he received little formal education. After a brief attendance at the College of William and Mary, probably in the grammar school, he studied law in Prince George County under Stephen Dewey, a family connection, who apparently neglected him. At the age of twenty he was admitted to the bar and became associated in practice with John Lewis, a prominent attorney in Spotsylvania County. The association soon became more personal, for in December 1747 Wythe married Lewis' sister, Ann, the daughter of Zachary Lewis; she died the next year. Wythe remained at Spotsylvania for about eight more years, indulging, it is said, in "the amusements and dissipations of society" (Tyler, post, p. 55).

In 1754, while Peyton Randolph [q.v.], attorney-general of the colony, was in England on a mission, Wythe held this office, but resigned when his friend returned a few months later. The next year his brother died, and Wythe succeeded to the large estate. Having represented Williamsburg in the House of Burgesses (1754–55), he now made it his home. About 1755 he married Elizabeth Taliaferro, daughter of Col. Richard and Eliza Taliaferro of "Powhatan," James City County; Wythe survived his second wife by nineteen years, while their only child died in infancy. He practised diligently, began to study the law in earnest, delving also into the classics and the liberal sciences, and was admitted to the bar of the General Court. His brilliant career really began in 1758 with the advent of Gov. Francis Fauquier [q.v.], a learned, cultured gentleman and a Fellow of the Royal Society. Wythe became his intimate friend, together with William Small, professor of mathe-

matics and natural philosophy at William and Mary, and, later, the youthful Jefferson. These friendships were important factors in his life. Wythe again went to the House of Burgesses, representing the College of William and Mary (1758–61) and Elizabeth City County (1761–68); he was mayor of Williamsburg (1768), a member of the William and Mary board of visitors (1769), and clerk of the House of Burgesses (1769–75). Meanwhile trouble with England was brewing.

By Virginia law, approved by the Crown, the salary for ministers was set at sixteen thousand pounds of tobacco; in 1758, however, without royal consent, Virginia commuted these salaries at a fixed monetary rate. When in 1763 the Rev. Thomas Warrington sought damages in the Elizabeth City County court over which Wythe presided, the court upheld Virginia's action. A similar claim by the Rev. James Maury in the Hanover County court resulted in the famous Parson's Case whereby Patrick Henry won acclaim and the parson one penny's damages. When the British Parliament, in 1764, announced the Stamp Tax, Wythe with other Virginians maintained that England and Virginia were coordinate nations united by the Crown alone, a concept later ably expounded by Richard Bland [q.v.]. The Virginia resolutions of remonstrance were drafted by Wythe, but, too bold for most of his colleagues, were modified before adoption. In 1765, however, when Patrick Henry introduced his famous resolutions (the occasion of his Cæsar-Brutus speech), Wythe, Bland, and others opposed adoption, urging that no further action be taken until the earlier resolutions, analogous in principle, had been answered.

When war threatened in 1775 Wythe wisely recommended a regular army instead of militia; when hostilities began he volunteered. Almost immediately, however, he was sent to Congress, where he served until the close of 1776. He ably supported Richard Henry Lee's resolution for independence and signed the Declaration of Independence. A member of the committee to prepare a seal for Virginia (adopted in 1776), he probably designed it. Classic in concept, it is strongly republican—the shield noticeable by its absence—with the ominous motto, *Sic Semper Tyrannis*. With Jefferson and Edmund Pendleton [q.v.] he was assigned the tremendous task of revising the laws of Virginia, his portion covering the period from the revolution in England to American independence. The committee's report, embracing one hundred and twenty-six bills, was made to the General Assembly in 1779, most of the bills being adopted in 1785 under Madison's leadership, a few being passed earlier. The revision was thorough, intelligent, and consistent with the American political upheaval. Meanwhile, Wythe was speaker of the House of Delegates (1777) and in 1778 became one of the three judges of the new Virginia high court of chancery. Henceforth he was Chancellor Wythe.

The following year he began that part of his career which, perhaps, constitutes his greatest service to America. On Dec. 4, 1779, the board of visitors of the College of William and Mary, led by Jefferson, then governor of Virginia and a member of the board, established the "Professorship of Law and Police," the first chair of law in an American college and but twenty-one years junior to the Vinerian professorship of English law at Oxford. Wythe, Jefferson's own mentor in the law, became its incumbent. His lectures, following Blackstone, contrasted English and Virginia law, and were supplemented with moot courts and legislatures. Regarded as the pride of the college, Wythe literally charted the way in American jurisprudence.

Although he participated in the organization of the Constitutional Convention, Wythe apparently did not stay long, owing to other duties. But in 1788 he represented Williamsburg at the Virginia convention which ratified the Constitution, engaging little in debate but presiding over the committee of the whole and offering the resolution for ratification. In his supporting speech he emphasized the derivative character of federal power. During the same year, the state judicial system was reorganized, and Wythe became sole chancellor, holding this office until 1801, when three chancery districts were created; he continued, however, to preside over the Richmond district. Removing to Richmond, he resigned his professorship in 1790 but formed a small law school of his own. Among his students was Henry Clay [q.v.], who also was clerk of the court.

Scrupulously impartial, erudite and logical in his opinions, Wythe was compared by classically minded Virginians to Aristides "the Just." One of his opinions demands special consideration. As chancellor he was *ex officio* member of the supreme court of appeals. In the case of *Commonwealth* vs. *Caton* (4 *Call*, 5) in 1782 he delivered a peculiarly significant opinion. By Virginia's constitution the pardoning power in cases of treason resided in the General Assembly. Three convicted prisoners pleaded a resolution by the House of Delegates as a pardon. On review Edmund Pendleton, president of the supreme court of appeals, held that the lower house did not intend to violate the constitution, since

it had sent the resolution to the Senate, which failed to assent; hence there was no pardon and no constitutional question before the court. In his concurring opinion, however, Wythe declared *obiter dictum*, "Nay, more, if the whole legislature, an event to be deprecated, should attempt to overleap the bounds, prescribed to them by the people, I in administering the public justice of the country, will meet the united powers at my seat in this tribunal; and pointing to the Constitution, will say to them, 'here is the limit of your authority; and hither shall you go but no further'" (4 *Call*, 8). This is among the earliest enunciations of the doctrine of judicial review, America's unique contribution to juridical theory, and at the time it was the most complete. Some of Wythe's decisions were condemned at first but later were admired for their independent and disinterested justice. The supreme court of appeals generally affirmed Wythe's decisions, but sometimes reversed them. A tinge of personal feeling and restraint marred his relations with Edmund Pendleton, his greatest rival of both bench and bar. In 1795 Wythe published *Decisions of Cases in Virginia by the High Court of Chancery, with Remarks upon Decrees by the Court of Appeals Reversing Some of Those Decisions*. Convinced of the justice of his decrees, he undoubtedly desired vindication.

Magnificently ethical as an attorney, Wythe refused unjust causes and abandoned cases regarding which he had been misled, returning the fee. While he was industrious and faithful to his clients' interests, he viewed the lawyer as an instrumentality of justice. His mind was methodical rather than facile, but it penetrated deeply. Possessed of broad education and culture, he was probably the foremost classical scholar in Virginia, and was widely read in Roman and English law. He was of middle height and well proportioned, unostentatious in appearance and habits, polite and courteous in address. He was a vestryman in the Episcopal Church, but deemed forms and modes of faith unimportant. Agreeing substantially with Jefferson and Madison in political theory, he favored representative republicanism rather than undiluted democracy. With other eminent Virginians of the period he was opposed to slavery and by his will emancipated his servants. This will led to Wythe's tragic death. His grand-nephew, George Wythe Sweeney, was named principal beneficiary, while a legacy to a servant was to come to him if the servant died. To secure this legacy, or perhaps the inheritance, Sweeney, who was apparently in financial difficulties, poisoned some coffee with arsenic. The servant drank some;

Wythe also drank some, perhaps fortuitously. The servant died first, but Wythe lingered long enough to disinherit Sweeney, who, tried for murder, was acquitted for lack of evidence, since the testimony of the colored cook, the principal witness, was not admissible in Virginia courts at that time. The venerable chancellor's last thoughts were of the suitors in his court, and of the delay and expense which his death would entail. He was buried in Richmond, where he died, in the churchyard of historic St. John's Church.

[No biog. of Wythe has been written. The best short sketches are those of L. G. Tyler, in *Great Am. Lawyers*, vol. I (1907), ed. by W. D. Lewis, and of John Sanderson, in *Biog. of the Signers to the Declaration of Independence*, vol. II (1822). Wythe's decisions are in *Va. Reports*. See E. G. Swem, *Va. Hist. Index*, vol. II (1936), and, for valuable but scattered material, Wythe's *Decisions of Cases in Va. by the High Court of Chancery* (1852, 1903), which contains a memoir; biog. sketch in Daniel Call, *Report of Cases in the Court of Appeals of Va.*, vol. IV (1833), pp. x–xv; W. G. and M. N. Stanard, *The Colonial Va. Reg.* (1902); W. W. Hening, *The Statutes at Large . . . of Va.*, vol. IX (1821), pp. 175–76; H. B. Grigsby, "The Hist. of the Va. Federal Convention of 1788," *Colls. Va. Hist. Soc.*, n.s., vols. IX–X (1890–91); *Official Letters of the Governors . . . of Va.* (3 vols., 1926–29), ed. by H. R. McIlwaine; *Letters of Members of the Continental Cong.* (7 vols., 1921–34), ed. by E. C. Burnett; *The Writings of Thomas Jefferson* (9 vols., 1853–54), ed. by H. A. Washington; William Wirt, *Sketches of the Life and Character of Patrick Henry* (1817); J. P. Kennedy, *Memoirs of the Life of William Wirt* (1856), vol. II; William Meade, *Old Churches, Ministers, and Families of Va.* (2 vols., 1857); *William and Mary Coll. Quart.*, Jan. 1895, p. 180, July 1901, p. 34; R. M. Hughes, *Ibid.*, Jan. 1922, pp. 40–47; "Early Spotsylvania Marriage Licenses," *Va. Mag. of Hist.*, Oct. 1896, p. 99; *Ibid.*, July 1898, pp. 102–03 (Wythe's views on religion); *Tyler's Quart. Hist. and Geneal. Mag.*, Jan. 1928, p. 212; obituary in *Enquirer* (Richmond), June 10, 1806; funeral oration by William Munford, *Ibid.*, June 13, 17, 1806.]   T. S. C.

XÁNTUS, JÁNOS (Oct. 5, 1825–Dec. 13, 1894), ornithologist, was born at Csokonya, county of Somogy, Hungary, the son of Ignácznak Xántus. His ancestors were Greeks who had emigrated to Transylvania in the fifteenth century, receiving there the rank of Hungarian noblemen. Xántus bore the title, de Csik Tapolcza. He passed the bar examination at Pest (1847), entered the Hungarian national army at the outbreak of the war of independence in 1848, and was first lieutenant of infantry when captured by the Austrians in February 1849. After his release he was again arrested, this time for patriotic utterances at Prague, and forced to serve in the Austrian army. He escaped in 1850 and after many vicissitudes went to the United States at the end of 1851. He worked first as a laborer, but on Dec. 1, 1852, was engaged as topographer of the Pacific Railroad expedition. For a while he taught Latin, Spanish, and German at New Orleans. He served as a member of the United States survey expedition to ascertain the most practicable route for a railroad from the Mississippi River to the Pacific Ocean (1855–57) and then as member of the United States Coast Survey stationed at Fort Tejon and Cape St. Lucas, Cal. In California he made valuable collections of birds for the Smithsonian Institution, discovering many new species, which were named after him. At the conclusion of his work he was attached to the United States navy and entrusted with the command of another expedition which had as its object the meteorological observation of certain parts of the Pacific Ocean. He finished this in August 1861, having discovered eighty-nine islands and sand banks. After a short visit in Hungary he was appointed United States consul at Manzanillo, Mexico, and led a scientific research party into the Sierra Madre. In 1864 he took up permanent residence in Hungary. He traveled in eastern Asia on a mission for the Hungarian government in 1869–71 and returned with extensive collections. He was the keeper of the ethnographical division of the National Museum, Budapest, until his death, which occurred in Hungary.

His descriptions and catalogues of new species of birds appear in *Proceedings of the Academy of Natural Sciences of Philadelphia* (vols. X–XII, 1859–61). His account of his travels in the United States he published in two Hungarian volumes, *Levelei Ejszakamerikából* (Pest, 1858), which consisted of letters, and *Utazás Kalifornia déli Részeiben* (Pest, 1860), which dealt with Southern California. Copies of these are eagerly sought by collectors of California items, but are exceedingly difficult to find. Accounts of his later travels appear in Hungarian periodicals.

[The chief biog. sources are the obituary in Magyar *Földrajzi Társaság, Földrajzi Közlemények*, vol. XXII (1894), pp. 377–81, which also appears under the title, *Bulletin de la Société Hongroise de Geographie*; commemorative paper by Jenö Cholnoky, *Ibid.*, vol. LIII (1925); and Sándor Mocsáry, in *Emlékbeszédek A Magyar Tudományos Akadémia Tagjairól*, vol. IX, pt. IX (1899), with a good bibliog. of Xántus' writings. References to Xántus and descriptions of the birds named for him appear in *Ibis*, vol. V (1863); ann. reports, Smithsonian Inst., 1858–64; U. S. War Dept., *Reports of Explorations and Surveys . . . from the Miss. River to the Pacific Ocean*, vols. VIII–IX (1857–58), being *House Exec. Doc. 91*, 33 Cong., 2 Sess.; Eugene Pivány, *Hungarian-Am. Hist. Connections* (1927); G. N. Lawrence, in *Memoirs Boston Soc. Nat. Hist.*, vol. II, pt. 3, no. 2 (1874), and *Annals Lyceum Nat. Hist. of N. Y.*, vols. V (1860), VII (1862); S. F. Baird, T. M. Brewer, and Robert Ridgway, *A Hist. of N. Am. Birds: Land Birds* (3 vols., 1874); and *The Water Birds of N. America* (1884); Elliott Coues, *Key to N. Am. Birds* (1872); D. G. Elliot, *The New . . . Species of the Birds of N. America* (1869); Robert Ridgway, *The Birds of North and Middle America* (8 vols., 1901–19), being *U. S. Nat. Museum Bull. No. 50*; S. F. Baird and J. G. Cooper, *Ornithology . . . Land Birds* (1870), in *Geo-*

logical *Survey of Cal.*; autograph letters from Xántus to G. N. Lawrence, in the possession of the writer.]

C. F.

YALE, CAROLINE ARDELIA (Sept. 29, 1848–July 2, 1933), educator, was born on her father's farm in Charlotte, Vt., the daughter of William Lyman and Ardelia (Strong) Yale and the descendant of Thomas Yale, the stepson of Theophilus Eaton and uncle of Elihu Yale [*qq.v.*], who emigrated from England in 1637 and settled in New Haven, Conn. Her father was earnestly religious, interested in education, politics, and social movements. Her mother was to her children the "ideal of all that was worthy of admiration and emulation" (*Years, post,* p. 226). Religion was woven into every fibre of the family life. After some years with tutors at home, the family removed to Williston, Vt., in order that the children might have more advantages. Especially strong there was the influence of the Congregational Church, which the little girl soon joined. She was a delicate child, restricted in activity. Characteristically, she and her mother decided that her life must be planned in spite of her limitations. In 1866 she went to Mount Holyoke Female Seminary, now Mount Holyoke College, and spent two years in eager study. Almost inevitably she entered the teaching profession, first at Brandon, Vt., and then at Williston, Vt.

In 1870 came an invitation to join the staff of the recently established Clarke Institution for Deaf Mutes, now the Clarke School for the Deaf, in Northampton, Mass. There she was associated with Harriet B. Rogers [*q.v.*] in the use of the oral method—to teach the deaf to read the lips and to speak. She began her work in September 1870, and for the next sixty-three years her story and that of the school are one. With a singleness of purpose rarely shown in human life, she lived in and for the school, bringing to it a personality richly endowed, an unswerving fidelity, a mind open to every suggestion of progress. Always the individual child was the center of her attention, and her object was the "restoration to the greatest extent possible of the deaf child to a place in the society of normal people" (*Years, post,* p. x); and for this end spiritual and moral education was as necessary as intellectual. A loyal friend herself, she was loyally supported by a friendly staff; but all who worked with her knew that she was the animating force of the school. Her appearance was distinguished. Tall and spare, with cameo-like features, lambent eyes, and firm but mobile mouth, she moved a queen; and, far more than she realized, she taught by living. When she entered

the school there were five teachers and forty pupils, and the oral method of instruction was still experimental; when she died there were thirty-two teachers and one hundred and forty-five pupils, and of the approximately two hundred schools for the deaf in this country all but two use the oral method. Graduates of the normal classes of the school were teaching in thirty-one states and in nine foreign countries. This development was largely her work. In 1886, on the resignation of Harriet B. Rogers, she became principal. In 1889 she opened normal classes for the training of teachers of the deaf and retained the direction of these classes after her retirement to the position of principal emeritus in 1922.

She was trustee of several state institutions and held high office in teachers' associations. One of her most valued services was as a member of the school board of Northampton for twenty-five years. In addition to many articles in educational journals she published *Years of Building: Memories of a Pioneer in a Special Field of Education* (1931), an account of her life and of the Clarke School that is perhaps too objective and gives too little credit to her own unique personality. An occasional trip to Europe and many journeys to educational conferences varied her life without diminishing her concentration on her work. In her last years she suffered from disabling and painful infirmities without loss of cheer and courage. Her death closed a career unique in education.

[*Years of Building, ante*; annual reports of the Clarke School for the Deaf, esp. that of 1933; Elihu Yale, *The Yale Family* (1850), p. 170; *Hampshire Gazette* (Northampton, Mass.), July 3, 1933.]

E. D. H.

YALE, ELIHU (Apr. 5, 1649–July 8, 1721), official of the East India Company, for whom Yale College was named, was the son of David (b. 1613) and Ursula Yale, and the grandson of Thomas and Ann (Lloyd) Yale of Plas-Grono, near Wrexham, Denbighshire, Wales. After her husband's death Mrs. Ann Yale married Theophilus Eaton [*q.v.*]. In 1637, with him and her children David, Ann, and Thomas Yale, she went to New Haven. Four years later David Yale, a merchant credited with a £300 estate, sold out to his brother Thomas and moved to Boston, where Elihu was born. Not a church member himself David joined those who objected to the theocratic government of Massachusetts. He returned to England in 1652, and when Elihu was thirteen entered him in William Dugard's private school in London.

In 1671 Elihu Yale was appointed a writer in the East India Company at £10 a year; he arrived at Fort Saint George (Madras) on June

23, 1672. Five years more found him a factor with doubled salary, his only civil function the judging of native cases at the Choultry. He was married on Nov. 4, 1680, to Catherine, the six-month widow of Joseph Hynmers, long a wealthy factor and councilor of Madras. He became a member of the council, successfully negotiated a deal with the Marathas, and passed through the grades of mintmaster, customer, and bookkeeper to rank as the governor's valued second in command. On July 25, 1687, he became president and governor of Fort Saint George. The Company found him a stanch support in its new policy of founding civil and military power in India. He ruthlessly suppressed piracy. He built Fort Saint David at Cuddalore, named for his son who died in 1687, but in the native wars had to acknowledge the supremacy of the Great Mogul. In 1690 friction developed in the council between the governor and the new municipality of Madras. Bitter personal recriminations led to an administrative deadlock. Yale applied home for an arbiter, and found himself superseded when one appeared on Oct. 23, 1692. He was charged, among many violent counts, with having favored the private trading ventures of his brother Thomas and himself at the Company's expense, and admitted that he had amassed a fortune of 500,000 pagodas (£175,000). Before his accounts were cleared he was compelled to disgorge at least £3,000, for which he later petitioned the Company, and he was not permitted to sail for England until 1699. He settled in the old family estate of Plas-Grono, and was named high sheriff of Denbighshire in 1704. But he built also a mansion in Queen's Square, London, and carried on a diamond merchant's trade, corresponding with Gov. Thomas Pitt of Madras (Narcissus Luttrell, *A Brief Historical Relation of State Affairs*, 1857, VI, 324; British Museum, Add. MSS. 22,842–50). Two of his three daughters married into the aristocracy.

Through gifts to schools, churches, and missionary societies Yale acquired some reputation as a philanthropist. Learning of such propensities, Jeremiah Dummer [*q.v.*], Connecticut's agent in London, suggested that the struggling Collegiate School at Saybrook might well reap the benefit, and of the books collected for the school in 1714 some forty volumes came from Yale. When a new building was begun at New Haven, the trustees appealed to Cotton Mather, who wrote Yale in January 1718 intimating that the name of Yale College might easily adorn his munificence with a fame more enduring than the pyramids. In June Yale sent over for the school three bales of goods, some books, and a

portrait of George I by Kneller. The total gift was worth about £800; the goods were sold for £562 12s., the largest private contribution made the college for over a century. At the September commencement both the building and the school received their new name.

In that same September a goldsmith for whom Yale had stood surety absconded with nearly £14,000 of government funds. The Exchequer sued Yale and recovered; the House of Lords upheld the judgment (*Yale* vs. *Rex, 2 Brown, 375, post*). In 1720 he moved to the country, leasing from a son-in-law the manor of Latimers, Buckinghamshire, where his wife is buried (*Records of Buckinghamshire,* vol. VI, No. 1, 1887, p. 42). After his death most of his goods were sold at auction; a few, including two tapestries and a portrait by Enoch Zeeman (1717), have since come into the possession of Yale College. On his tomb in Wrexham churchyard are the lines:

Born in America, in Europe bred,
In Africa travell'd, and in Asia wed,
Where long he liv'd and thriv'd; in London dead.

[For a discussion of the place and date (sometimes given as 1648) of Yale's birth, see F. B. Dexter, in *A Selection from the Miscellaneous Hist. Papers of Fifty Years* (1918). See also R. H. Yale, *Yale Geneal.* (1908); F. B. Dexter, *Doc. Hist. of Yale Univ.* (1916); Josiah Brown, *Reports of Cases . . . in the High Court of Parliament* (2 vols., 1779). For Yale's career in India, see H. D. Lane, *Vestiges of Old Madras* (4 vols., 1913); A. T. Pringle, *The Diary and Consultation Book of the Agent Governor and Council of Fort St. George, 1682–1685* (4 vols., 1894–95), *Press List of Ancient Records in Fort St. George, No. 1–6, 1670–1699* (Madras, 1891–97); *The Diary of William Hedges* (3 vols., 1887–89), ed. by Henry Yule; *The Diaries of Streynsham Master* (2 vols., 1911), ed. by R. C. Temple; Shafaat Ahmad Khan, *Sources for the Hist. of British India in the Seventeenth Century* (1926); E. J. Thompson and G. T. Garratt, *Rise and Fulfilment of British Rule in India* (1934). Mrs. F. E. Penny's novel, *Diamonds* (1920), deals with Yale's Indian activities.]

S. M. P.

YALE, LINUS (Apr. 4, 1821–Dec. 25, 1868), inventor, manufacturer, was the son of Linus and Chlotilda (Hopson) Yale, and was born at Salisbury, Herkimer County, N. Y. He was a descendant of Thomas Yale, an uncle of Elihu Yale [*q.v.*], who emigrated from England in 1637 and settled in New Haven. From his father, who was an inventor of ability, having to his credit a threshing machine, a process for pressing millstones, and a sawmill head block dog, Yale inherited a mechanical temperament; he was, in addition, somewhat artistic. He was well educated and for a number of years devoted himself to portrait painting. About 1840 his father invented a bank lock, which he began to manufacture in Newport, N. Y., and shortly afterwards Yale undertook, independently, the same sort of business. Bank locks in those days were of very intricate construction and high in cost, and there was great rivalry among the manufacturers, all of which was a great stimulus to the industry. Yale brought out one of the first of his locks—it was the reputation of his father's locks which first caused the association of the name with the product—about 1851. This was made in the shop which he had established at Shelburne Falls, Mass., and was called the "Yale Infallible Bank Lock." It was known as the "changeable type"; that is, the key was made up of component parts which could be separated and reassembled to change the combination. His next lock, the "Yale Magic Bank Lock," was an improved modification of his first product. It was followed by the "Yale Double Treasury Bank Lock," a masterpiece of ingenious design and skilful workmanship, the most notable of the bank locks operated by keys. About 1862 Yale began marketing his "Monitor Bank Lock," the first of the dial or combination bank locks, and the following year brought out the "Yale Double Dial Bank Lock." The principles of construction used in the latter have since come into general use in the United States.

By this time Yale's reputation was well established. Between 1860 and 1865 he undertook the improvement of small key locks, devising the "Cylinder Lock," which was based on the pin-tumbler mechanism of the Egyptians. Patents covering this separate cylinder, pin-tumbler lock, using a small flat key, were issued to him on Jan. 29, 1861, and June 27, 1865. Since Yale's business as a consultant on bank locks left him little time and he lacked the necessary financial resources to equip his plant for the manufacture of the small locks, he went to Philadelphia in the hope of interesting others in the new venture. Through William Sellers [q.v.] he met John Henry Towne [q.v.] who brought about the establishment in October 1868 of the Yale Lock Manufacturing Company, with his son, Henry Robinson Towne [q.v.], and Yale as partners. The partners immediately began the construction of a plant at Stamford, Conn., Yale leaving most of this activity to Towne and continuing his consulting work on bank locks. Three months later, however, while he was in New York on this business, he died suddenly of heart failure. He was married to Catherine Brooks at Shelburne Falls on Sept. 14, 1844, and was survived by his wife and three children.

[See R. H. Yale, *Yale Geneal.* (1908); A. A. Hopkins, *The Lure of the Lock* (1928); obit. notice in *N. Y. Daily Tribune*, Dec. 28, 1868, which contains several errors; and Patent Office records.]   C. W. M.

YANCEY, WILLIAM LOWNDES (Aug. 10, 1814–July 27, 1863), secessionist, the son of Benjamin Cudworth and Caroline (Bird) Yancey, was born at his grandfather's home "The Aviary," Warren County, Ga. His mother was a daughter of William Bird of Pennsylvania, who had removed to Georgia in 1796. His father began the practice of law at Abbeville, S. C., as a contemporary and friend of John C. Calhoun, but died in August 1817, leaving his widow with two young sons, William Lowndes, aged three, and a baby, Benjamin Cudworth. The widow returned to her father's home in Warren County, but a few years later went to live in Hancock County, Ga., near Mount Zion Academy, taught by Nathan Sidney Smith Beman [q.v.]. He married Mrs. Yancey in 1822 and took her and the two children to Troy, N. Y., where he became pastor of the First Presbyterian Church. It was in Beman's church, in 1826, that Charles Grandison Finney [q.v.] preached at the beginning of his great revival. Beman became the recognized leader of the liberal New School Presbyterians. He was actively identified with the anti-slavery movement, a close friend of Theodore D. Weld, Lewis Tappan, and Joshua Leavitt. One may only speculate on the course of history, had Yancey remained in Beman's home until the beginning of active anti-slavery agitation in the mid-thirties or under the influence of his later benefactor and teacher, the Unionist, Benjamin F. Perry [q.v.], instead of becoming a slaveholding planter and lawyer of the Southwestern Black Belt.

Young Yancey meanwhile, however, was educated in the schools of Troy and at Williams College, 1830 to 1833. He left college before graduation and entered the law office of an old friend of his father's, Benjamin F. Perry at Greenville, S. C., in 1833. The nullification controversy was at its height; Greenville was on the border line between the plantation district and the up-country; and Yancey plunged into the debate. as the stanch Unionist editor of the *Greenville Mountaineer.* On Aug. 13, 1835, he married Sarah Caroline Earle, the daughter of a wealthy Greenville planter. They lived for a time on a farm near Greenville but removed to Dallas County, Ala., in the winter of 1836–37. Two years later, while visiting at Greenville, he killed his wife's uncle, Robinson M. Earle, in self-defense. He was sentenced to a fine of $1,500 and a year's imprisonment, which was commuted to $500 fine by Gov. Patrick Noble. In Alabama he rented a plantation near Cahawba. He and his brother, Benjamin Cudworth Yancey, bought the Wetumpka *Commercial Advertiser* and the

Wetumpka *Argus* in the spring oɪ 1839. He also bought a farm near Wetumpka but was forced to resume the practice of law, when his stock of slaves was almost wiped out by poison. He rose rapidly in the profession, and was soon regarded as the leading advocate in the state. He was elected to the lower house of the state legislature in 1841, and to the upper house in 1843, attaining wide renown as the stanch supporter of representation apportioned on the basis of white population only, the legal rights of married women, a free public school system, and a sound, nonpolitical state banking system. Elected to Congress in 1844, and reëlected, he served from Dec. 2, 1844, until his resignation on Sept. 1, 1846. His first debate in Congress, on Jan. 7, 1845, was with Thomas L. Clingman [*q.v.*]. Thomas Ritchie's *Richmond Enquirer* said it was the first step to "a very high distinction in the councils of the nation" (*Life, post,* p. 141). Its immediate result, however, was a duel with Clingman in which neither duellist was injured (*Memoranda of the Late Affair ... between ... Clingman ... and Yancey,* 1845, ed. by J. M. Huger). Yancey was relieved of all political disabilities arising from fighting a duel by special act of the Alabama legislature, passed over Gov. Joshua L. Martin's veto. He held no public office after resigning from the Senate until elected to the state secession convention.

William L. Yancey and the movement for Southern independence are inseparable in history. It would seem presumptuous to say that without him there would have been no Confederate States of America, but it is probably so. The secession movement did not receive its impulse from politicians any more than did the anti-slavery movement. Both were of the people, and they carried along the politicians who were willing to go, brushing the others aside. Each was, in short, a repudiation of parties, of the machinations of politicians, and an appeal to fundamental principles rather than political expediency. From 1847 to 1861, the Wilmot Proviso to the inauguration of Lincoln, the leaders of both the old parties trimmed their principles and compromised their differences for the sake of party continuity—but not Yancey. He resigned from Congress in 1846, because the whole process was to him inadequate and superficial; but he wielded, during the next fifteen years, a powerful leadership, unobserved by most men, unrealized by himself. He was not a party man. There was nothing cunning, cautious, or even skilful about his mental processes. The qualities essential to the politician were entirely foreign to his constitution. He was, in fact, an annoyance to party men all his life, and they variously considered him everything from an unwelcome pest to an insufferable fire-brand. The key to his career is to be found in his own words, spoken in 1847: "If this foul spell of party which binds and divides and distracts the South can be broken, hail to him who shall break it" (*Life, post,* p. 206). The "spell" was broken in the winter of 1860–61, and the accomplished fact was a monument to the unwavering courage, the intellectual honesty, and the indefatigable labors of Yancey.

The Alabama Platform, written by him in 1848 in answer to the Wilmot Proviso, was his own confession of faith (*Ibid.,* pp. 212–13). He never deviated from it, even when the allurements of the vice-presidency were dangled before him in 1860, and he presented it to the people of the South on every occasion with an oratorical excellence seldom equalled. It was a simple statement of abstract principles: a constitution designed to curb the will of the majority and preserve to the states all powers not expressly granted to the federal government, equal rights of citizens and states in the territories, and the duty of Congress to protect property rights therein so long as they remained in the territorial status. This platform of principles was indorsed by the legislatures of Alabama and Georgia and by Democratic conventions in other states; it contains every cogent item in the many restatements of Southern rights, particularly the Davis resolutions, the Dred Scott decision, and the majority platform of the Charleston convention. Yet, at the time, it was revolutionary, so much so that the disaffection aroused in Democratic ranks within the state caused Yancey to remark: "Except for my courage to dare to do no wrong in this great matter, I should ... seek peace by yielding the principles ... as a sacrifice to the angry passions of my assailants" (*Ibid.,* p. 216). He carried the platform to the National Democratic Convention at Baltimore, where it was rejected by a vote of 216 to 36. In an eloquent *Address to the People of Alabama by W. L. Yancey, Late a Delegate ... to the National Democratic Convention ... 1848* (1848), he appealed to the South from this decision. During the next twelve years, he made it the creed of the South, not of the Southern Democrats alone.

This phase of his work remains obscure, because his private correspondence is no longer available; but, in its main outlines, it is fairly definite. It was no mean task to arouse a people to a realization of prospective dangers, remote as they were from the immediate effects of abolition agitation, and divided, as they were, by the bitter rivalry of partisan politics. The union of all Southern men in a sectional party could come only with disintegration of the existing parties and the submergence of partisan hatreds by some impending threat to common institutions. Seeing clearly the requirements of the situation, he cautioned the supporters of Troup and Quitman in 1852 "to avoid all efforts to irritate the feelings and excite the opposition of the two great national parties in the South," because they were *the ranks from which we expect to draw recruits,* hereafter, to the standard of the South, when occasion shall arise for rearing it" (*Life, post,* p. 270).

Meanwhile, the work of arousing the South went forward along three lines. Southern rights associations were formed everywhere. They were non-partisan, designed to bring prominent men of all parties together and promote active discussion of the interests of the South. In practice they served a dual rôle of fostering pressure politics in elections and promoting the choice of stanch state-rights men for nominations to public office within each party. The idea probably originated with Edmund Ruffin [*q.v.*] of Virginia, but Yancey was actively identified with the movement and, in 1858, sought to perfect the system by organizing the League of United Southerners. The specific object, stated by Yancey in a public address at Benton, Ala., and repeated at the state convention in 1860, was "to elevate and purify" political parties by forcing them "to abandon the law of compromise and to adopt the law of the constitution"; to counteract the bitterness of partisan rivalry; and to promote by consultation the best means of advancing the interests of the South, unity in its counsels and "its rights in the Union" (*Speech . . . Delivered in the Democratic State Convention . . . 1860,* 1860, p. 8). The second approach was through the hustings. The prevailing practice of engaging leading men of both parties to meet in public debate was an ideal arrangement. Such occasions were invariably local holidays and brought thousands of both parties together for great barbecues. Yancey was always in demand. Holding no public office, being a partner in the distinguished law firm of Elmore & Yancey, and being the most brilliant orator in the Southwest, he was in a good situation to reach men of all political faiths. He delivered hundreds of addresses, and there is no record of his ever having failed to hold his audience for as many hours as he cared to speak. Thus was the ground work laid for the "occasion" of which he spoke in 1852. When the campaign of 1860 approached, he dominated the Democratic party in Alabama.

The party was virtually united and controlled the state. The old Whig party had disintegrated after the election of 1852, long enough for its adherents to have lost some of their partisan bias; and old line Whigs as well as old line Democrats stood by the principles expressed in the Alabama Platform, however much they might disagree as to whether the election of a Republican president would constitute a legitimate cause for secession. He outlined the third course that should be pursued in a speech at Columbia, S. C., in 1859. "Can we have any hope of righting ourselves and doing justice to ourselves in the Union? If there is such hope, it would be our duty to make the attempt. For one, I have no such hope, but I am determined to act with those who have such hope, as long, and only as long, as it may be reasonably indulged; not so much with any expectation that the South will obtain justice in the Union, as with the hope that by thus acting, within a reasonable time, there will be obtained unity amongst our people in going out of the Union" (*Ibid.,* pp. 10–11). A contest was certain to arise in the Charleston convention between Southern rights and "squatter sovereignty." It should be pressed to a conclusion. If the Southern demands were rejected, a grand constitutional Democratic party should be organized, candidates presented to the people in the presidential election; and, if a Republican president should be elected, secession carried through before his inauguration.

That was the situation, when he went into the state Democratic convention at Montgomery, on Jan. 11, 1860. The state legislature had already anticipated the probable election of a Republican president, to be followed by a test of sectional strength, by appropriating $200,000 to arm the state and by making it mandatory for Gov. Andrew B. Moore to call a state convention in that event. Yancey again prepared the Alabama platform of principles, a restatement of the platform of 1848 in line with all that had transpired meantime: (1) that the constitution is a compact between sovereign states; (2) that citizens of every state were entitled to entry into the territories with their property of every description, and to protection by the federal government; (3) that neither Congress nor its creature, a territorial legislature, could abolish slavery in a territory; (4) that the people of a territory held no constitutional power to do so until they framed a state constitution preparatory to entry into the Union. The platform also instructed the state delegation to the federal convention at Charleston to present this platform for adoption and to withdraw if it were rejected. It set up a committee to call a state convention for the purpose of determining upon a line of action consistent with such exigencies as might arise. In this state convention, he gave the clearest answer we have to the charge made then and ofttimes repeated that he was a secessionist *per se:* "It is charged against me that I have no hope of obtaining justice to the South in the Union. If this is an error, I cannot help it. Hope comes not to one's bosom at the mere bidding. The events of the last quarter of a century are enough to blast the hopes of every well-wisher of his country. . . . My only hope is that when the hour of trial comes, as come it must, all—all without distinction of party —who claim this as the land of their nativity or adoption will be found with locked shields, ready to defend our rights on every field where they are assailed" (*Ibid.,* p. 14).

The issue was not pressed to a conclusion in the Charleston convention, but to a qualified rejection of the Southern platform. It came after a brilliant and final statement of the conflicting principles by Yancey for the Southern Democrats and George E. Pugh [*q.v.*] for the Northern Democrats. It was the greatest forensic effort of Yancey's career (*Speech . . . Delivered in the National Democratic Convention . . . 1860,* 1860) ; and it was followed by the withdrawal of a majority of the Southern delegates. His known preference for the organization of a sectional party and his suspected disunion leanings were a hindrance to reunion. The Southern Democracy, however, reluctant to take the final step, returned delegations to the adjourned convention at Baltimore. The Douglas adherents completed the destruction begun at Charleston by refusing to seat the Yancey delegation from Alabama. There was a further exodus of delegates, who organized, under Yancey's guiding genius, the Constitutional Democratic party and nominated Breckinridge for the presidency. It was regarded as Yancey's party. He was the most prominent man in the campaign and delivered more than a hundred speeches from Boston to New Orleans. Following Lincoln's election, he dominated the proceedings of the Alabama convention and penned the ordinance of secession. In March 1861 he was sent to England and France as a commissioner from the Confederate States of America. Returning in 1862, he was elected to the Senate of the Confederacy and served until his death. He died in Montgomery, survived by his widow and five children.

He left no record of disillusionment, if such resulted, from his mission to England and France, other than to say in a personal letter from London, "the anti-slavery sentiment is universal. 'Uncle Tom's Cabin' has been read and believed" (Yancey to Reid, July 3, 1861, Yancey Papers). He returned to Alabama to battle as valiantly against centralization at the expense of personal liberty in the Confederacy, as ever he had battled in the Union, but with little success and, apparently, with little hope. He was a fine combination of independent spirit and fiery energy. He made no obeisance to power or position, scorned patronizing acclaim, and recognized only the dictates of his own judgment. In his oratory as in his public career, he adhered inflexibly to truth as he saw it, without reference to side influences however legitimate. This quality frequently gave to his position a degree of impracticality and to his oratory a singular individuality. He never altered his style or the level of his remarks to conform to the nature of his audience, utterly disregarding their prejudices. He possessed an enchanting voice, an inexhaustible supply of facts and words—words, too, which were unmusical and offensive at times, but very expressive of his scorn for opponents' errors. His oratory was animated conversation, with little of the artfulness, adroitness, or brilliantly turned phrasing so common to refined public speakers, but freighted with passionate conviction and simple flowing eloquence.

[The state archives, Montgomery, Ala., for letters, copies of letters from newspapers, newspaper clippings, and the files of Yancey's newspapers as well as those of his opponents ; J. W. DuBose, *The Life and Times of William Lowndes Yancey* (1892) and "Yancey: A Study" in *Gulf States Hist. Mag.,* Jan. 1903 ; *Southern Editorials on Secession* (1931), ed. by D. L. Dumond.]

D. L. D.

YANDELL, DAVID WENDEL (Sept. 4, 1826–May 2, 1898), physician, was born at "Craggy Bluff," his father's country home near Murfreesboro, Tenn., the son of Lunsford Pitts Yandell [*q.v.*] and Susan Juliet Wendel. When he was five years of age the family moved to Lexington, Ky., and six years later to Louisville. His early training was under private instructors, after which he attended Centre College, at Danville, Ky., for several years with little distinction and without graduating. Nor was he credited with much diligence at the University of Louisville, where he studied medicine under his father and was graduated in 1846. He did, however, develop a talent for writing and when, following graduation, he spent two years in the hospitals of London, Dublin, and Paris, he sent back two series of letters for publication, one on his general observations to the *Louisville Journal,* 1846–47, and another on medical topics to the *Western Medical Journal.* Thus early he was developing the style and command of language which so strongly marked his later writings. Returning to Louisville in 1848 he began to practise his profession and was appointed demonstrator of anatomy in the University of Louisville. Of fine appearance and manner, and with the prestige of his European studies, he quickly established a busy general practice, with a rapidly growing reputation as an operating surgeon.

This auspicious beginning was interrupted in 1851 by ill health which compelled him to retire to a farm near Nashville, Tenn. Two years of farm life not only materially improved his health but awakened latent tastes for the country and for wild life that marked the remainder of his career. Returning to Louisville he was soon one of the foremost practitioners of the city. He founded the Stokes Dispensary and pioneered in medical education by establishing classes in clinical medicine. This work was soon transferred to the University of Louisville, where he was appointed to the chair of clinical medicine. Shortly thereafter, with the onset of the Civil War, he joined the Confederate army under General Buckner at Bowling Green, Ky. After a short service here and with the command of General Hardee he was assigned to the staff of Gen. Albert Sidney Johnston as medical director of the Department of the West. He served in this capacity throughout the war, participating in the battles of Shiloh, Murfreesboro, and Chickamauga. After the death of General Johnston at Shiloh he served successively on the staffs of Generals Beauregard, Hardee, Joseph E. Johnston, and Edmund Kirby-Smith [qq.v.].

At the close of the war he returned to Louisville and attended the meeting of the American Medical Association at Cincinnati in 1865. In nominating Samuel D. Gross [q.v.] for the presidency, he made a speech which went far in healing the breach in the profession caused by the Civil War. He was himself elected a vice-president of the association. In 1867 he returned to the University of Louisville as professor of the science and practice of medicine, and in 1869 he was made professor of clinical surgery, a post he held for the rest of his life. His vivid personality, rich voice, and his command of language made him a teacher of clinical surgery unequaled in his time. His work as an operating surgeon, though based on sound diagnoses, showed no special originality. It was, however, marked by mechanical deftness and a degree of surgical cleanliness unusual at a time before surgical asepsis was known. In 1870 he and Theophilus Parvin [q.v.] established the *American Practitioner*, which after sixteen years was merged with the *Medical News* to form *The American*

Practitioner and News. He edited this journal from its founding until shortly before his death. To it he contributed the greater part of his literary work in the form of editorials and articles dealing with surgical subjects. He was elected president of the American Medical Association in 1871 and president of the American Surgical Association in 1889. Noteworthy are his presidential addresses to these bodies, the later one on "Pioneer Surgery in Kentucky" delivered in 1890. He was also a fellow of the Philadelphia College of Medicine. In 1887 he was surgeon-general of the Kentucky militia. Progressive arterio-sclerosis reduced him to invalidism during the last five years of his life and to a state of dementia during his last months. He died at his home in Louisville. Beyond the practice of medicine his chief interest was in hunting, which he pursued from one end of the country to the other. His home was a museum of hunting trophies. He was a royal host and a lover of good living. He was married to Francis Jane Crutcher of Nashville, Tenn., in 1851. Of four children, his only son was drowned in the Cumberland River in 1866 at the age of twelve years.

[*Trans. Southern Surgical and Gynecological Asso.*, 1902; *Trans. Am. Surg. Asso.*, 1899; *Am. Practitioner and News*, May 15, 1898, Apr. 15, 1899; *Philadelphia Medic. Jour.*, May 14, 1898; *Ky. Medic. Jour.*, Nov. 1917; *Am. Medic. Jour.*, Nov. 1917; *Am. Medic. Biogs.* (1920), ed. by H. A. Kelly and W. L. Burrage; *Courier-Jour.* (Louisville, Ky.), May 3, 4, 1898.] J. M. P.

YANDELL, LUNSFORD PITTS (July 4, 1805–Feb. 4, 1878), paleontologist, physician, pioneer in medical education in the Ohio Valley, was born on a farm near Hartsville, Sumner County, Tenn., the son of Dr. Wilson Yandell of North Carolina and Elizabeth (Pitts) Yandell. In his early years he attended the Bradley Academy, Murfreesboro, Tenn., and began the study of medicine in his father's office. He attended medical courses at the Transylvania University, Lexington, Ky., in 1822–23, and at the University of Maryland at Baltimore, where he was graduated in 1825. Returning to Tennessee, he settled for practice at Murfreesboro in 1826. He removed to Nashville in 1830 and in the following year to Lexington, Ky., to accept the professorship of chemistry and pharmacy in Transylvania University. Following six years in this position, he went to Louisville, where he participated in the establishment of the Louisville Medical Institute in 1837, a school that became the medical department of the University of Louisville in 1846. In the faculty of the new school he held the chair of chemistry and materia medica, and after 1849 that of physiology as well. He taught until 1859, when he accepted a position in a medical school in Memphis, Tenn. With the onset of the Civil War he joined the Confederate service as a hospital surgeon, but in 1862 he was persuaded to enter the ministry of the Presbyterian Church by the Memphis Presbytery. He was ordained as pastor of a church at Dancyville, Tenn., in 1864, but he resigned three years later, and returned to Louisville and to the practice of medicine. Though filling thereafter no office in the school which he helped to found, he was until his death active in its affairs and a continuing factor in its growth and success. He continued in a prosperous practice of internal medicine, with occasional exercise of his ministerial vocation, until his death from pneumonia at his home in Louisville.

Early in his career Yandell developed a decided bent toward scientific inquiry. He saw in the recently settled country of the Ohio River Valley a most fruitful field for exploration of natural phenomena, animal and vegetable life, rocks and waters, together with the prevailing diseases with their causes, prevention, and cure. While at Lexington he sought to infuse his love of science into his classes, but it was not until his removal to Louisville that he entered seriously into the work for which he is best known. In the vicinity of Louisville were the coral reefs of the falls of the Ohio, the fossiliferous beds of Beargrass Creek, and numerous quarries in near-by Kentucky and Indiana. It was with this material that he achieved an international reputation as an explorer and student in the field of geology and paleontology. In 1847 he published with Dr. B. F. Shumard *Contributions to the Geology of Kentucky.* In the following years he wrote a number of journal articles in relation to fossils which he had uncovered and studied. Notable among these papers is "On the Distribution of the Crinoidea in the Western States," published in the *Proceedings of the American Association for the Advancement of Science,* vol. V (1851). He also memorialized the name of his scientific associate, Dr. Shumard, in an article, "Description of a New Genius of Crinoidea," published in the *American Journal of Science and Arts,* November 1855. His own name has been perpetuated by masters in paleontology in the naming of a number of fossils which he brought to light. Through his active years he gathered together a veritable museum of specimens relating to natural history, which he bequeathed to his son and namesake, who aided him in their collection and preservation.

Yandell is credited with the authorship of a hundred articles in various periodicals dealing with medical themes, geology, local history, biography, education, and religion. Beginning with an article, "What Fossils Teach," in September 1873, he contributed to *Home and School,* a Louisville journal, a noteworthy series of scientific articles in a popular vein. He left uncompleted a biographic work upon the medical men of Kentucky. From 1832 to 1836 he was editor of the *Transylvania Journal of Medicine and the Associated Sciences* (Lexington), and from 1840 to 1855 co-editor of the *Western Journal of Medicine and Surgery.*

He was a member of many medical and scientific societies. In April of the year preceding his death he was elected to the presidency of the Kentucky State Medical Society. He was twice married: first, in October 1825, to Susan Juliet Wendel, and second, in August 1861, to Eliza Bland. By his first wife he had three sons and a daughter. Of the sons, David W. Yandell [*q.v.*] and Lunsford Pitts, Jr., followed their father in the choice of a medical career.

[Several Yandell letters published in *Filson Club Hist. Quart.* July 1933; T. S. Bell, "Memorial Address upon the Life and Services of Lunsford P. Yandell, *Am. Practitioner* (Appendix), 1878; *Nashville Jour. of Med. and Surgery,* Feb. 1878; *Trans. Am. Medic. Asso.,* 1878; *Trans. Ky. Medic. Soc.,* 1878; *Ky. Medic. Jour.,* Nov. 1917; *Am. Med. Biogs.* (1920), ed. by H. A. Kelly and W. L. Burrage; Robert Peter, *Hist. of the Medic. Dept. of Transylvania Univ.* (1905), Filson Club Pub. No. 20; *Courier-Jour.* (Louisville, Ky.), Feb. 5, 1878.]
J.M.P.

YATES, ABRAHAM (1724–June 30, 1796), Revolutionary patriot, Antifederalist pamphleteer, congressman, also known as Abraham Yates, Jun., was born in Albany, N. Y., and baptized on Aug. 23, 1724. He was a grandson of Joseph Yates the immigrant, and the ninth son of Christoffel Yates and Catelyntje (Winne). He married Antje De Ridder, who like himself attended the Dutch Reformed Church of Albany, and to them were born four children. A surveyor, lawyer, and land speculator, he has sometimes been called a financier. He served as sheriff of Albany from 1754 to 1759 and many terms on the Albany Common Council, 1754–73. A radical Whig by conviction during the pre-revolutionary and war periods, he was an associator and an active member and chairman of the Albany committee of correspondence from 1774 to 1776. The county of Albany elected him to every one of the New York provincial congresses and conventions of 1775–77; he was chairman of the committee of the convention (1776–77) which drafted the first constitution of the state of New York, and of the committee of six for putting the new government into operation. His other services during the Revolution included membership in the committee on arrangements for the Continental regiments of New York, service as a state senator, 1777–90, and service as one of the commissioners for loans authorized by Congress, 1777–82.

Like other members of the Yates family, particularly Robert Yates [*q.v.*], Abraham was an ardent Antifederalist during the 1780's. An able pamphleteer, he wrote frequently and eloquently, sometimes under the pen names "Rough Hewer" and "Rough Hewer, Jr.," in defense of the sovereignty of his state and in opposition to Congressional aggrandizement. His printed letters and pamphlets are perhaps the ablest exposition of the point of view of the agrarian democrats and Anti-federalist followers of Gov. George Clinton [*q.v.*]. Although he voted in 1781 for granting the impost to Congress, he fought it consistently in subsequent years, stressing the potential tyranny of federal tax collectors. (See *Political Papers Addressed to the Advocates for the Congressional Revenue*, 1786.) He played the rôle of an Antifederalist in the Continental Congress, 1787–88, and fought the proposed Federal Constitution from the state Senate. In 1792, however, he was chosen a presidential elector on a ticket pledged to Washington and Adams. From Oct. 19, 1790, to his death in 1796, he was mayor of Albany, in which office he seems to have been capable and energetic.

[The Abraham Yates, Jun., papers in the New York Public Library, which have been consulted, include numerous "Rough Hewer" papers and correspondence as well as chapters on phases of New York history. See also *Biog. Dir. Am. Cong.* (1928) ; A. C. Flick, ed., *Hist. of the State of N. Y.*, vols. III, IV (1933) ; Joel Munsell, *Colls. on the Hist. of Albany*, vol. I (1865) ; *Calendar of Hist. MSS. Relating to the War of the Revolution in the Office of the Secretary of State, Albany, N. Y.* (2 vols., 1868) ; E. B. O'Callaghan, *Calendar of Hist. MSS. in the Office of the Secretary of State, Albany, N. Y.*, pt. 2 (1866) ; Jonathan Pearson, *Contributions for the Geneals. of the First Settlers of the Ancient County of Albany* (1872) ; Cuyler Reynolds, *Albany Chronicles* (1906) and *Hudson-Mohawk Geneal. and Family Memoirs* (1911), I, 294; E. W. Spaulding, *N. Y. in the Critical Period* (1932).]   E. W. S.

YATES, JOHN VAN NESS (Dec. 18, 1779– Jan. 10, 1839), lawyer and secretary of state of New York, was the son of Robert Yates [*q.v.*] and Jannetje Van Ness. He was born in Albany and was a resident of that city throughout his life. Well educated in the classics and in the law, he was known for his versatility and brilliance of mind. His edition of the *History of New York* by William Smith, 1728–1793 [*q.v.*], with a continuation to 1747 by the editor, appeared in 1814 and his *Collection of Pleadings and Practical Precedents with Notes Thereon* in 1837. He was the author of several other legal works. His failure to collaborate with J. W. Moulton in a *History of the State of New York*

(1824–26), the first volume of which bears his name, is one evidence of his erratic nature. Critics commented on his instability of character, his laxness and his plebeian associations. His principles were democratic and his policies Democratic-Republican.

Yates was a member of the committee appointed by the Albany Common Council to petition the legislature to provide for the construction of the first state capitol. On Apr. 2, 1806, he was appointed captain of a company of light infantry in an Albany regiment which a year later offered its services to the president in case of war with England. In 1808 he became involved in a controversy with Chancellor John Lansing [*q.v.*] which brought the court of chancery into conflict with the supreme court of the state. Yates, a master in chancery that year, commenced a suit in the name of P. W. Yates without the latter's knowledge and was imprisoned by the Chancellor on the ground that attorneys and solicitors in chancery were required by law, before bringing suit in the name of another attorney, to obtain the latter's consent. Yates's counsel, Thomas Addis Emmet [*q.v.*], obtained his client's release on a writ of *habeas corpus* issued by the supreme court. Recommitted by the Chancellor (4 *Johnson*, 318), Yates appealed to the court of errors, where his arrest was declared illegal (6 *Johnson*, 337). He failed, however, in a subsequent suit against the Chancellor for false imprisonment (5 *Johnson*, 282; 9 *Johnson*, 395).

Most of Yates's appointments to public office he received as a partisan of the Clintons. He served twice as recorder of Albany (1808–09; 1811–16), one term in the Assembly (1819), and eight years as secretary of state of New York (appointed 1818–26). A Presbyterian, he was married in the First Presbyterian Church at Albany on June 7, 1806, to Eliza Ross Cunningham. He died at Albany, survived by his wife and several children.

["Records of the First Presbyterian Church in the City of Albany," ed. by R. W. Vosburgh (typewritten MS., transcribed 1917) ; *Case of J. V. N. Yates . . . Decided in the Supreme Court of N. Y., in August Term, 1809* (1809) ; J. D. Hammond, *The Hist. of Political Parties in the State of N. Y.* (2 vols., 1842) ; G. R. Howell and Jonathan Tenney, *Hist. of the County of Albany* (1886) ; Joel Munsell, *Annals of Albany* (10 vols., 1850–59) ; A. J. Parker, *Landmarks of Albany County* (1897) ; G. A. Worth, *Random Recollections of Albany* (1866) ; David McAdam and others, *Hist. of the Bench and Bar of N. Y.*, I (1897), 523 ; *Albany Evening Journal*, Jan. 10, 14, 1839.]   E. W. S.

YATES, MATTHEW TYSON (Jan. 8, 1819– Mar. 17, 1888), missionary to China, was born in Wake County, N. C., about eighteen miles west of Raleigh, the son of William and Delilah Yates. His father was a farmer, none too prosperous, and Matthew, the second of ten children, spent the first nineteen years of his life in the paternal home, helping from the time he was old enough to do so in the varied manual labor of the farm. The home was a devout one, and his father, a deacon in a Baptist church, kept open house to the traveling preachers of that fellowship. From his boyhood Yates was religious. At about the age of seventeen, in a camp meeting, he passed through the experience of conversion and soon came to believe that he must obtain an education and probably enter the ministry. He had read with deep emotion the life of an early American Baptist missionary, Ann Hasseltine Judson [q.v.], and by it had been moved to consider spending his life in that calling. Prepared at Wake Forest Hill Academy, he entered Wake Forest College and graduated in 1846. He was not brilliant as a student and was forced to devote much of his time to earning a livelihood, but he was a conscientious and persistent worker.

Before graduation he had finally determined to be a missionary. Accordingly he applied to the Foreign Mission Board of the Southern Baptist Convention and was appointed to China. On Sept. 27, 1846, he married Eliza E. Moring, on Oct. 18 following he was ordained, and soon thereafter he sailed with his bride for China, arriving in Shanghai in 1847. Here he was the pioneer of his society, although within a few weeks he and his wife were joined by two other couples. The future commercial metropolis of China had only recently been opened to foreign residents, thus during most of his career Yates was laying foundations. The task was not easy. He found his eyes unequal to the strain of reading the written Chinese characters, but he became a master of the Shanghai colloquial dialect and greatly enjoyed preaching in it. In the decade after his arrival a band of rebels captured the native city and the property and work of the mission suffered; then came the American Civil War and for years, during the conflict and much of the Reconstruction period, he received no assistance from home. For twenty years or so he was without a foreign colleague; from 1869 to 1876 his voice failed and he was unable to preach. Yet during the years of adversity he supported himself and his family by acting as interpreter to the municipal council of the foreign community and to the American consulate, by serving as vice consul for the United States, and by judicious investments in Shanghai real estate. Yates was so successful financially that he was able to support a Chinese preacher from his own funds, to build a substantial church, and to take

his family to Europe when health made that advisable. He never ceased to be a missionary, and later, when assistance from the United States was resumed, he gave up his business enterprises and devoted his full time to the Church. Not only in Shanghai but in other cities in Kiangsu province he initiated centers of his denomination, and opened a number of out-stations. He was active, too, in literary work, although his writing in Chinese was done through an amanuensis. He prepared tracts, including *Ancestral Worship and Fung Shuy* (1867) ; *The Tai-Ping Rebellion* (1876) ; a series of lessons for those beginning the study of the spoken language; and a translation into the Shanghai vernacular of all of the New Testament except the book of Revelation. He was still at work on the New Testament when death overtook him, in Shanghai.

In appearance Yates was tall, erect, and dignified. In manner he had the courtliness and courtesy of the Southern gentleman. His converts were not numerous; at the time of his death the churches under his care had only about one hundred members, but he had a wide acquaintance among the Chinese and had won the esteem of many.

[C. E. Taylor, *The Story of Yates, the Missionary, as Told in His Letters and Reminiscences* (1898) ; *Chinese Recorder*, Apr., Nov., 1888; G. W. Paschal, *Hist. of Wake Forest Coll.* vol. I (1935) ; annual *Proceedings* of the Southern Baptist Convention.]   K. S. L.

YATES, RICHARD (Jan. 18, 1815–Nov. 27, 1873), Civil War governor of Illinois, was born in Warsaw, Ky., the son of Henry and Millicent (Yates) Yates, whose common grandfather, Michael Yates, hailed from Caroline County, Va. In 1831 the family moved to Sangamon County, Ill., and Richard was sent to Illinois College at Jacksonville, where in 1835 he received the first graduating diploma issued by that institution (C. H. Rammelkamp, *Illinois College: A Centennial History*, 1928, p. 69). Already known as a boy orator, he spoke at graduation on "The Influence of Free Institutions in Moulding National Character" (*Ibid.*, pp. 69–70). After studying law at Transylvania University he was admitted to the bar (1837) and began practice at Jacksonville, which remained his home during his whole public career. For three terms (1842–46, 1848–50) he was a member of the state legislature. Elected to Congress in 1850 and again in 1852 he had during one of his terms the distinction of being the only Whig member from Illinois. In this period he favored the homestead act, opposed the Kansas-Nebraska bill, supported the movement to establish colleges with federal land grants, and spoke vigorously for extending an official welcome to the Hungarian patriot Kossuth. Having taken an antislavery stand he joined the Republican party and was a member of the national conventions which nominated Lincoln in 1860 and Grant in 1868. As contrasted with that of radical abolitionists, however, his attitude was conservative, resembling Lincoln's. In party conferences looking to the governorship in 1860 N. B. Judd and Leonard Swett were more prominently mentioned than Yates; but his popularity in doubtful counties turned the balance and he became the party choice. He was elected over James C. Allen, Democrat, by a vote of 172,000 to 159,000; and served as governor from January 1861 to January 1865.

During the war he was widely known as a vigorous state executive, upholding Lincoln's hand and showing great ardor in the raising of troops and in other complex matters of war administration. At times his zeal outran the efforts of the government at Washington so that he was advised to reduce the number of regiments and discharge excessive recruits (*Annual Report of the Adjutant General of the State of Illinois,* 1863, pp. 18–19). He gave U. S. Grant his first Civil War commission and assignments, putting him in charge of camps for organizing volunteers, giving him staff duty at Springfield, and tendering him the colonelcy of the 21st Regiment of Illinois Volunteers (June 1861). War duties pressed heavily upon him as he attended to military appointments, approved a variety of new army units, called special legislative sessions, recommended emergency laws, visited "the boys" in camp and hospital, reviewed Illinois troops in battle areas, attended to voluminous complaints by soldiers' parents, promoted the raising of bounties, conferred with other governors and with Lincoln, and made hot speeches playing upon war emotions and searing the Democrats. When the Democratic majority in the legislature of 1863 opposed the existing conduct of the war and embarrassed the governor by passing (in the lower house) a resolution urging an armistice and recommending a national convention to restore peace (while at the same time opposing secession and disunion), Yates seized upon a disagreement in the matter of adjournment as the opportunity for exercising his constitutional prerogative of proroguing the Assembly. Overlooking the fact that the Democrats supplied their share of enlistments and otherwise supported the Union, the Republicans stigmatized their opponents as traitors; and the war years became a period of wretched party bitterness in the state. Through all this the governor was personally popular, and his prestige was increased by the success of the war in which Illinois reported over 250,000 enlistments.

After the war Yates served one term (1865–71) in the United States Senate. Party regularity marked his course: he favored vindictive measures against the South, voted for President Johnson's conviction in the impeachment proceeding, and supported the prevailing radical Republican program, which he justified with convincing patriotic unction and oratorical flourish. He died suddenly at St. Louis while returning from Arkansas, whither he had gone as federl commissioner to inspect a land-subsidy railroad. He was buried with full honors at Jacksonville.

Yates was married on July 11, 1839, to a "dark eyed little beauty," Catharine Geers, a native of Lexington, Ky. She outlived him by thirty-five years, dying in 1908. They had two daughters and three sons, one of whom, Richard, was governor of the state, 1901–04, and congressman during several terms. Oratorical skill and a strikingly handsome appearance were among the rich personal endowments that contributed to Yates's career. His use of liquor sometimes led to over indulgence, and there is record of his lack of sobriety when inaugurated as governor (*Memoirs of Henry Villard,* 1904, I, 148). When criticized on this score in 1868 he admitted the fault, apologized "without reserve or defense," and explained that his use of stimulants after exhaustive labor had not interfered with the performance of public duty ("Address to the People of Illinois," *Chicago Tribune,* Apr. 25, 1868, p. 2). It has been said that "no governor of any State [was] more watchful of the State's interests . . . or more loved by [his] people . . ., including the troops in the field" (Shelby M. Cullom, *Fifty Years of Public Service,* 1911, p. 45). "His success in political life," writes another, "was largely due to his personality; he was endowed with a manly carriage, fine presence, cordial manner and happy speech" (Jayne, *post,* p. 144). He is honored above other Illinois governors in a beautiful bronze statue at Springfield.

[There is no biography of Yates, and this sketch has been based upon scattered sources, including newspapers, minor essays and obituaries, manuscript collections, state archives, and information generously supplied by Catharine Yates Pickering, daughter of Richard Yates the younger. The date of birth, usually given (even by Yates himself) as 1818, has been verified as 1815 by reference to the family Bible. The voluminous Yates papers, though preserved by his son Richard, have not been open to historical use. In the archives at Springfield the governor's letterbooks and incoming correspondence for the Yates administration are missing. Yates's messages and speeches are conveniently available at the Ill. State Hist. Lib. See also: *Richard Yates, War Governor of Ill.* (1924), address by Richard Yates the younger at the dedication of the statue of Yates in Springfield, Oct. 16, 1923; C. M. Eames, *Historic Morgan and Classic Jacksonville* (1885); L. U. Reavis, *The Life and Public Services of Richard Yates* (1881); *The Diary of Orville Hickman Browning*, vols. I and II (1927–33), being *Ill. Hist. Colls.*, vols. XX, XXII; A. C. Cole, *The Era of the Civil War* (1919); *Biog. Dir. Am. Cong.* (1928); speech by Richard Yates the younger, Feb. 12, 1921, containing letters from Lincoln to Yates, in *Cong. Record*, 66 Cong., 3 Sess., pp. 3074–79; *Report of the Adj. Gen. of Ill.* 1861–65; I. O. Foster, "The Relation of . . . Illinois to the Federal Government during the Civil War" (MS.), doctoral dissertation, Univ. of Ill., 1925; Richard Yates the younger, *Descendants of Michael Yates* (1906); William Jayne "Richard Yates' Services . . . as War Governor," *Trans. Ill. State Hist. Soc.*, 1902; E. L. Kimball, "Richard Yates: His Record as Civil War Governor of Illinois," *Jour. Ill. State Hist. Soc.*, Apr. 1930; *Chicago Tribune*, Nov. 28, 29, 1873; *Jacksonville Daily Journal*, Nov. 29, 1873.]   J.G.R.

YATES, ROBERT (Jan. 27, 1738–Sept. 9, 1801), Revolutionary patriot, jurist, was born in Schenectady, N. Y., the son of Joseph and Maria (Dunbar) Yates of that place. His great-grandfather, Joseph Yates, had migrated as a young man from England and settled in Albany, where he died May 20, 1730. Robert's grandfather, also named Robert, moved to Schenectady in 1711. After receiving a good classical education in New York City and reading law with William Livingston [q.v.], later governor of New Jersey, Yates was admitted to the bar May 9, 1760, at Albany, which remained his residence for the rest of his life. He served for four years, 1771–75, on the board of aldermen. A radical Whig during the period of controversy before the Revolution, he was a member of the Albany committee of safety and represented the county of Albany in the four provincial congresses and the convention during the years 1775–77. The provincial congress in 1776 appointed him to the committee of safety and the convention of 1776–77 assigned him to membership on the secret committee to obstruct the channel of the Hudson, the committee on arrangements for the Continental regiments, the committee to cooperate with General Schuyler (of which he was chairman), and the important committee of thirteen which drafted the first constitution of the state.

Before the new state government was established Yates was appointed, May 8, 1777, a justice of the supreme court, in which capacity he served with integrity and impartiality. On the bench, as well as during his service on the committee of safety, he incurred some criticism from Whigs for his fairness toward Loyalists. As justice and later as chief justice (1790–98), he was *ex officio* a member of the council of revision, but he seems to have written very few of the veto messages of the council. He was appointed, Apr. 28, 1786, to fill a vacancy on the commission which disposed of the controversy with Massachusetts over New York's western boundary and in March 1780 he was named one of the commissioners to settle the perennial dispute with Vermont. Five years later he sat on the commission which apportioned to New York claimants the $30,000 which Vermont paid to satisfy New York land titles.

During the middle 1780's Robert Yates became a recognized leader of the Antifederalists. He was a supporter of Gov. George Clinton and with Clinton opposed such concessions to the federal Congress as the right to collect impost duties. (Some of his papers appear in *Political Papers Addressed to the Advocates for a Congressional Revenue*, 1786.) In 1787 he was appointed with the Antifederalist John Lansing and the Federalist Alexander Hamilton to represent New York in the Convention at Philadelphia. A member of the compromise committee, Yates, with his colleague Lansing, left the Convention on the day the committee reported, July 5, on the ground that the Convention, which had been called to revise the Articles of Confederation, was exceeding its powers in attempting to write a new instrument of government and that the consolidation of the states into a national state would impair the sovereignty of New York. After the publication of the Federal Constitution Yates attacked it during the winter in a series of letters signed Brutus (answered by Pelatiah Webster [q.v.] in *The Weakness of Brutus Exposed*, 1787), and in June 1788, in letters signed Sydney, which appeared in the *New York Journal*. Some of the Antifederalist papers signed "Rough Hewer" have been attributed to him. In the Poughkeepsie convention which ratified the Constitution on behalf of New York he was one of the three or four outstanding Antifederalist leaders and voted against ratification. He seems, however, to have accepted the result so completely that he was willing in 1789 to run for governor with Federalist support against his old friend Clinton. In spite of Hamilton's active support Yates received only 5,962 votes to 6,391 for Clinton. A logical candidate for governor in 1792, he declined to run. In 1795 when Clinton was no longer a candidate Yates was the Antifederalist candidate for governor but ran second in the election to the Federalist John Jay. Having reached the constitutional age of sixty Yates resigned as chief justice in 1798. In 1800 he was one of the commissioners for settling the title to the lands in Onondaga County. A man of modest means, he is said to have died comparatively poor. By his wife, Jannetje Van Ness, whom he married Mar. 5, 1765, he had six children, four of whom, including John Van Ness Yates [*q.v.*], survived him. Twenty years after Yates's death, his notes on the debates and proceedings of the Federal Convention were published by his widow under the title, *Secret Proceedings and Debates of the Convention Assembled . . . for the Purpose of Forming the Constitution of the United States* (1821).

[Yates's notes on the Federal Convention were reprinted in Jonathan Eliot, *Debates . . . on the Adoption of the Federal Constitution*, vol. IV (1830); in *Sen. Doc. 728*, 60 Cong., 2 Sess. (1909), together with his letter to Gov. Clinton on leaving the Convention, and a short biog.; and in *The Records of the Federal Convention* (1911), ed. by Max Farrand. Some of his Antifederalist writings appear in P. L. Ford, *Essays on the Constitution* (1892). See also J. D. Hammond, *The Hist. of Political Parties in . . . N. Y.* (2 vols., 1842); Joel Munsell, *Colls. on the Hist. of Albany*, vol. I (1865); Jonathan Pearson, *Contributions for the Geneals. of the First Settlers . . . of Albany* (1872); John Sanders, *Centennial Address Relating to the Early Hist. of Schenectady* (1879); A. B. Street, *The Council of Revision of the State of N. Y.* (1859); G. A. Worth, *Random Recollections of Albany* (1866); *Calendar of Hist. MSS. Relating to the War of the Revolution* (2 vols., 1868); *Names of Persons for Whom Marriage Licenses were Issued . . . Province of N. Y., Previous to 1784* (1860).]

E. W. S.

YEADON, RICHARD (Oct. 23, 1802–Apr. 25, 1870), lawyer, editor, was born in Charleston, S. C., the only son of Richard and Mary (You) Adams Yeadon and grandson of the English immigrant Richard Yeadon and his wife Mary Lining. Graduating from South Carolina College in 1820, Yeadon was admitted to the bar in 1824. In 1831, during the nullification controversy, he became a constant contributor to the *City Gazette* in support of its Unionist policy. On July 1, 1832, without giving up his law practice, he became editor of the *Charleston Daily Courier,* the leading Unionist journal of the state, and six months later he became a part owner. Ill health forced him to retire from the editorship Nov. 4, 1844, though he long continued to contribute editorials.

An ardent Whig, he opposed John C. Calhoun [*q.v.*] but praised his wisdom in crushing the Bluffton movement of R. B. Rhett [*q.v.*] in 1844 for re-asserting nullification. When Rhett in 1856 offered for governor and sought to rouse secession sentiment, Yeadon declared him unfit for leadership and denounced his effort to undo the Union-preserving influence of Buchanan's election. Taunted as a "traitor" for his Unionism, he protested that none would sacrifice himself for his state more willingly than he. Secession once ordained, he bought Confederate bonds generously and gave largely for equipping Confederate soldiers and building a navy. He offered a reward of $10,000 for the capture dead or alive of Benjamin F. Butler [*q.v.*] after President

Davis declared that Federal officer an outlaw. Throughout the war, with men like R. W. Barnwell and James Chesnut [*q.v.*], Yeadon supported President Davis against radicals led by Rhett. Yeadon's election to the legislature in 1862 by a vote overtopping that given to extremists expressed the conservatism always strong in Charleston. Insistent on the supremacy of law, he was determined in defense of legal rights. He supported the Citadel authorities in the student rebellion of 1858, and when Dr. R. W. Gibbes [*q.v.*] was ejected from the council chamber which he had entered to report proceedings for the *South Carolinian,* Yeadon prosecuted Gibbes's suit for damages and won a small award.

Yeadon had many non-professional interests. He operated a peach farm at his country place near Aiken and fancied fine horses. On Dec. 23, 1829, he married Mary Videau Marion, great-grand-niece of Gen. Francis Marion [*q.v.*], and subsequently compiled a genealogy of his wife's family. He was chiefly responsible for removing the body of Hugh S. Legaré [*q.v.*] from Massachusetts to Charleston. He served at least three terms (1856–60; 1862–64) in the state House of Representatives, where he contributed to strengthening financial and simplifying testamentary and land-title law and opposed the re-opening of the African slave trade. He originated the ordinance establishing the Charleston High School, secured the Council's donation of $1,000 a year for a century to the College of Charleston, and gave liberally for establishing a chair of political economy in the latter institution. He was industrious, hospitable, witty. Ill health intensified his sudden changes from exultation to depression. Childless, he adopted a nephew—killed in the war—and two of his wife's nieces. Though a believer in Christianity, he joined no church. He began life poor, but through his practice accumulated about $400,000, two thirds of which disappeared through the war. His wife survived him.

[W. L. T. Crocker, "Richard Yeadon" (MS.), master's thesis, Univ. of S. C., 1927; W. L. King, *The Newspaper Press of Charleston, S. C.* (1882); A. S. Salley, Jr., "Century of the Courier," in *Centennial Edition of the News and Courier* (1903); B. F. Perry, *Reminiscences of Public Men* (1883); B. F. Butler, *Autobiog.* (1892); Laura A. White, *Robert Barnwell Rhett* (1931); D. D. Wallace, *The Hist. of S. C.* (1934), vols. II, III; A. C. Cole, *The Whig Party in the South* (1913); *Charleston Daily Courier*, Apr. 26–28, 1870.]

D. D. W.

YEAGER, JOSEPH (*c.* 1792–June 9, 1859), engraver, publisher of children's books, and railroad president, was one of a family of five boys and three girls. The family probably lived in Philadelphia, Pa. Joseph early occupied himself with engraving; a line engraving by him, entitled "Symptoms of Restiveness," is dated 1809. From this date until about 1845 he was active in Philadelphia as a general engraver in line and etcher of portraits. Some of his signed plates appear in the children's books published by William Charles [*q.v.*] of Philadelphia in 1814 and 1815, and no doubt he did unsigned work for other publishers. Of his thirty-five or forty known engravings about half consist of etchings of portraits and half of line engravings of scenery and views of buildings. Among his engravings are "The Great Bend of the Susquehanna River in Susquehanna County, Pennsylvania," in the *Portfolio* (1811); "The Death of Addison" in *Fears of Death* (1819); the atlas and title page of John Marshall's *Life of Washington* (Philadelphia, *c.* 1822); plates for *Life in China* (Philadelphia, 1842); a number of plates in the *New Edinburgh Encyclopedia*; a title-page vignette in *Confessions of Harry Lorrequer* (Philadelphia, 1842); two plates after Cruikshank in *Sketches by Boz* (Philadelphia, 1838); and illustrations by Phiz in *Nicholas Nickleby* (Philadelphia, 1839). In 1830 and later his work appeared in the *Casket* and its successor, *Atkinson's Casket*. From 1819 until 1836 he lived at 37 Chester St., where he published and sold prints, including his own. In 1837 his address was 30 Washington Row. From 1839 to 1847 it was 30 Palmyra Square. From all such locations he conducted his engraving business, which in addition to the titles enumerated included many others, such as the "Battle of New Orleans," "The Exchange, New York," "United States Branch Bank, New York," "Interior of an Indian Lodge," book illustrations, and engravings of a commercial nature. In 1824 he was in partnership with William H. Morgan, carver and gilder of 114 Chestnut St., Philadelphia, who also published "National Prints" and toy books for children. Morgan and Yeager sold their toy books at both wholesale and retail. Their stock included approximately sixty titles, many of them being well-known nursery and folk tales. The exact dates of this partnership are not known.

In 1848 Yeager became president of the Harrisburg and Lancaster Railroad Company, with an office in 16 Merchants Exchange. The railroad, more correctly known as the Harrisburg, Portsmouth, Mount Joy and Lancaster Railroad, extended only thirty-seven miles and was later absorbed by the Pennsylvania Railroad. Yeager was also a member of the board of controllers of the fourth school section of Philadelphia (1841–45). He died at his home in Philadelphia and

was buried in Laurel Hill Cemetery. His estate amounted to at least $55,000, and included railroad bonds and real estate in both city and country.

[I. B. Weiss, *Joseph Yeager* (1932), reprinted from *Bull. N. Y. Pub. Lib.*, Sept. 1932; D. M. Stauffer, *Am. Engravers upon Copper and Steel* (1907), and Supplement (1917), ed. by Mantle Fielding; Phila. city directories; obituary in *Phila. Daily News*, June 11, 1859.]
H. B. W.

YEAMAN, WILLIAM POPE (May 28, 1832–Feb. 19, 1904), Baptist minister, was born in Hardin County, Ky. His great-grandfather, Moses Yeaman, about the middle of the eighteenth century moved with his family from New Jersey to the "Red Stone" country of southwestern Pennsylvania." A few years later he removed to Kentucky, and finally settled in Ohio. Moses' grandson, Stephen Minor Yeaman, born on a farm near Lebanon, Ohio, married Lucretia Helm, sister of John L. Helm who became governor of Kentucky. Six sons of this marriage chose the profession of law, though two subsequently entered the Baptist ministry. George Helm Yeaman, the second son, served two terms in Congress, was minister resident at Copenhagen for five years, and in 1872–76 was lecturer in the law school of Columbia College, now Columbia University, New York City.

William Pope Yeaman, the third son, studied law in the office of his uncle, Gov. John L. Helm, and at the age of nineteen was admitted to the Kentucky bar. For nine years, first in Elizabethtown and later in Calhoun, he devoted himself to the practice of the law. He was an elector on the Bell and Everett presidential ticket in 1860. Reared in the Methodist Episcopal communion, he severed his relation with that body to become a Baptist. In 1860 he was ordained and assumed the pastorate of the Baptist Church of Nicholasville, Ky. Two years later, he became pastor of the First Baptist Church, Covington, Ky., and subsequently served the Central Baptist Church, New York City (December 1867–1870) and the Third Baptist Church, St. Louis, Mo. (1870–76). In 1877 he led in the organization of the Garrison Avenue Baptist Church (later the Delmar Avenue Baptist Church), St. Louis, and for two years was its pastor. In St. Louis he was for a time one of the editors of the *Central Baptist*, the denominational organ for Missouri. From 1884 to 1886 he was secretary of the Board of State Missions for the General Association of Missouri Baptists, and it has been said that "the tremendous amount of labor which he performed in this field, his convincing arguments and his stirring appeals did more to arouse Missouri Baptists to the great cause of missions than anything else in our history" (Douglass, *post*, p. 282). For twenty years, from 1877 to 1897, he was the moderator of the General Association of Missouri Baptists and for a number of years held also the extremely important office of corresponding secretary. In 1875–76 he served as chancellor of William Jewell College, Liberty, Mo., and from 1893 to 1897 he was president of Grand River College, Gallatin, Mo. He was president of the board of curators of Stevens College and of the board of curators of the state university. In 1880 he was chosen a vice-president of the Southern Baptist Convention. He wrote *A History of the Missouri Baptist General Association* which was published by authority of the Association in 1899. His friends twice proposed him for the Democratic nomination for political office—once as congressman, once as governor—but neither time was he nominated. He spent his declining years on a farm near Columbia, Mo., serving the Baptist Church at Walnut Grove in Boone County. He had married before reaching his majority Eliza Shackelford of Hardin County, Ky., and three sons and five daughters were born of the union. He died in his seventy-second year, three weeks after the death of his wife.

Yeaman was the product of an age and an environment in which the Christian minister was the recognized leader in all realms of social life. Of commanding presence, eloquent in the pulpit and on the platform, independent in thought and utterance, he was probably the ablest leader of Missouri Baptists during the most critical period of their history.

[J. C. Maple, *Life and Writings of Rev. William Pope Yeaman* (1906); J. C. Maple and R. P. Rider, *Mo. Baptist Biog.*, vol. I (1914); R. S. Douglass, *Hist. of Mo. Baptists* (1934); R. S. Duncan, *A Hist. of the Baptists in Mo.* (1882); William Cathcart, *The Baptist Encyc.* (1881); E. L. Starling, *Hist. of Henderson County, Ky.* (1887), pp. 644–45; *Am. Baptist Yearbook*, 1868–1904; *Kansas City Journal*, Feb. 20 1904.]
R. W. W—r.

YEAMANS, Sir JOHN (1610/11–August 1674), colonial governor, was baptized in Bristol, England, Feb. 28, 1610/11. He was probably the son of John Yeamans, a brewer, of Bristol. A stanch royalist, he entered military service and rose to the rank of colonel in the royalist army. In 1650, when the Commonwealth was in the ascendancy, he emigrated to Barbados. His first wife, daughter of a Mr. Limp, had presumably died, for he married the widow of Lieutenant-Colonel Berringer of Barbados, a daughter of Rev. John Foster.

When the Lords Proprietors were granted Carolina in 1663, Yeamans, seeing an opportunity for himself and other ambitious Barbadians, negotiated through his son, Maj. William Yea-

mans, for the right to establish a colony there with himself as governor. Successful in his negotiations, he was made a baronet Jan. 12, 1664/65, on the recommendation of the proprietors, for his expected services in promoting settlement. Commissioned governor, Jan. 11, 1665, he sailed from Barbados in October to choose a suitable location. A site on the Cape Fear River was selected, but after remaining with the settlers only a short time Yeamans returned to Barbados. The settlement languished and was abandoned in 1667. Later the proprietors sent out a second expedition under Joseph West [*q.v.*] which reached Barbados in 1669. Yeamans still held the title of governor of Carolina and had also been appointed a landgrave. He decided to accompany the expedition, but went only as far as Bermuda, and returned home after appointing William Sayle governor by authority of the proprietors.

In 1670 he demonstrated his continued interest in the colony by offering inducements for settlement, and in 1671 he was there in person, built a home, and introduced the first negro slaves. He claimed the governorship on the ground that a provision in the charter stipulated that a proprietor or a landgrave must be governor, and he alone met the requirement. West, who had been elected by the Council to succeed Sayle on the latter's death in 1671 but had never been commissioned, was so popular that the Council refused to replace him until commanded to do so. The necessary command was received in 1672, and Yeamans became governor. He was instructed to establish another port town on the Ashley River, and accordingly laid out the site of Charles Town. He was unpopular with both people and proprietors. Objections were made to his reckless exportation of food to Barbados for his own profit at a time when there was a scarcity of provisions, to his extravagance, and to his attempt to subordinate Carolina to Barbados. His lack of genuine interest in the colony was apparent from his conduct. Twice he took a leading part in expeditions to Carolina only to abandon them, and when he finally settled there, his chief concern was to have himself appointed governor. His commission was revoked by the proprietors on Apr. 25, 1674, and West was commissioned in his stead, but word of the change had not yet reached Carolina when Yeamans died. His will, proved in December 1674, shows that he had eight children.

[Edward McCrady, *The Hist. of S. C. under the Proprietary Govt.* (1897); B. R. Carroll, *Hist. Colls. of S. C.* (2 vols., 1836); W. J. Rivers, *A Sketch of the Hist. of S. C.* (1856); Alexander Hewat, *An Hist. Account of the Rise and Progress of the Colonies of S. C.*

and Ga. (2 vols., 1779) ; *S. C. Hist. and Geneal. Mag.*, Jan. 1908, Apr. 1910, July 1918, Apr. 1919—articles which correct many errors in earlier accounts ; *Cal. of State Papers, Colonial Ser., America and West Indies*, 1661–80 (1880–96) ; J. A. Doyle, in *Dict. Nat. Biog.*]

H. B—C.

YEARDLEY, Sir GEORGE (*c.* 1587–November 1627), adventurer, planter, and twice governor of colonial Virginia, was a distinguished representative of that group of London citizenry which contributed so substantially to American colonization. His father, Ralph, was a member of the Guild of Merchant Taylors. His mother, Rhoda Marston, was of another city family. George, a second son, as a youth entered service in the Netherlands, where he established connections with Sir Thomas Gates [*q.v.*] which shaped the course of his later life.

Sailing for Virginia with Somers and Gates in 1609, he served with credit in a military capacity for several years thereafter. From the departure of Sir Thomas Dale [*q.v.*] in April 1616, he was acting governor until May 15, 1617. Though it is likely that his rule was characterized by a laxity diminishing to some extent its efficiency, his long experience in the colony and the reaction against the use of martial law which accompanied the reforms of 1618 made him a strong candidate for governor in that year of revived hope and revised plans.

Consequently, he was commissioned governor on Nov. 18, 1618. King James added to his rank the distinction of knighthood, and Sir George sailed for Virginia the following January. His instructions, among the most important documents in the history of English colonization, called for the abolition of martial law, directed the summoning of the first representative assembly in an English colony—over which Yeardley had the distinction of presiding—and provided for important changes in the terms and conditions of land tenure. In addition, he was charged to reduce the production of tobacco, to superintend experiments with many new commodities such as silk, wine, and iron, to prepare for the reception of hundreds of new settlers who presently were to follow, and to make all arrangements necessary to the settlement of those private plantations, commonly called hundreds, financed by voluntary associations of adventurers under patents from the company, by which it was hoped to speed the advent of Virginia's prosperity.

For the failure of this new program, which was ultimately responsible for the bankruptcy and dissolution of the London Company, Yeardley bears only a small portion of the blame. The many errors of judgment in the leadership of Sir Edwin Sandys, whose followers gained control of the company in the spring of 1619, made the Governor's position well nigh hopeless. Denied time for adequate preparation and forced to receive without previous warning hundreds of ill-equipped colonists, he protested strongly to Sandys and wisely counseled against overhasty action, but with little effect. His own failing was an inability to arouse the colonists to a wholehearted cooperation with the company's purposes. In this, however, he was only partially at fault. His instructions directed proceedings against several of the more influential planters, and since he was of necessity identified with the Sandys party at a time when the venom of factionalism was penetrating deep into the vitals of the company, it was impossible for him to escape its dire effect in the colony. Sorely tried and beset through three years, he retired at his own request, but without protest from the company's leaders, in 1621.

He was then able to devote more attention to his private investment in Southampton Hundred, a plantation of 80,000 acres in which the leading members of the Sandys party were the chief investors and of which he was governor and captain. He continued as a member of the colonial council, rendered valiant service in the emergency created by the Indian massacre of 1622, and at the time of the proceedings against the company joined with other leading planters in protesting against any action likely to involve a recall of the colonists' liberties. In the unsettled state of affairs which followed the dissolution of the company Yeardley carried to England in 1625 important petitions from the "convention" assembly of that spring presenting the needs of the colonists and requesting the continuation of their general assembly. Although he failed to secure a definite commitment on the latter point, the reaction of the Privy Council was reassuring and indicates that Yeardley made a tactful and able representative of the settlers. The favorable impression made upon the king's officers led to his being commissioned as governor again, on Mar. 14, 1626, a post which he held until his death. He was buried Nov. 13, 1627; his will (see *New England Historical and Genealogical Register*, January 1884, pp. 69–70) left a not inconsiderable estate to his wife, Temperance (Flowerdieu) and their children, Argall, Francis, and Elizabeth.

[J. A. Doyle, in *Dict. Nat. Biog.* ; Alexander Brown, *The Genesis of the U. S.* (1890), vol. II ; P. A. Bruce, *The Va. Plutarch* (1929), vol. I ; *Am. Hist. Mag.*, Oct. 1896 ; J. H. R. Yardley, *Before the Mayflower* (1931), to be used with caution ; *Records of the Va. Company* (4 vols., 1906–35), ed. by S. M. Kingsbury ; *Journals of the House of Burgesses of Virginia*, 1619–1658/9.

(1915), ed. by H. R. McIlwaine; *Minutes of the Council and General Court of Colonial Va., 1622–1632, 1670–1676* (1924); *Cal. of State Papers, Colonial Ser., 1574–1660* (1860); *Acts of the Privy Council of England, Colonial Ser.,* vol. I, *1613–80* (1908); some of Yeardley's correspondence, in the Ferrar Papers, Magdalene College, Cambridge; C. M. Andrews, *The Colonial Period of Am. Hist.,* vol. I (1934); W. F. Craven, *Dissolution of the Va. Company* (1932).]   W. F. C.

YEATES, JASPER (Apr. 17, 1745–Mar. 14, 1817), lawyer, jurist, son of John and Elizabeth (Sidebottom) Yeates, was born at Philadelphia. His grandfather, Jasper, a native of Yorkshire, came to Philadelphia soon after William Penn, and acquired extensive business interests in Pennsylvania and Delaware. John Yeates was a merchant engaged in foreign trade. After receiving a common-school education Yeates attended the College of Philadelphia, where he received the degree of B.A. in 1761, studied law under Edward Shippen, 1728/29–1806 [q.v.], and was admitted to the bar on May 8, 1765. Shortly thereafter he moved to Lancaster and established a successful practice. On Dec. 30, 1767, he married Sarah, daughter of Col. James and Sarah (Shippen) Burd, this union allying him with two of the oldest and most influential families in the province. There were at least four children.

From the beginning of his career as a lawyer Yeates was active in local politics. Throughout the controversy with the mother country he was a Whig of moderate tendencies and until the last persisted in his hopes for reconciliation. He was chairman of the Lancaster County committee of correspondence in 1775 and a captain of associators in 1776, but saw no active military service because of an appointment by Congress to a commission to negotiate a treaty with the Indians at Fort Pitt shortly before his battalion joined Washington's army. Although ready to acquiesce in separation from Great Britain when it became a fact, he was opposed to any change in the provincial government. "*Absolute necessity* alone should . . . justify an innovation in the constitution," he maintained, and such justification he could not find (Balch, *post,* p. 248). With the Pennsylvania constitution of 1776 he was manifestly dissatisfied: "The Clamors of the Red-Hot Patriots Have subsided Into Easy Places And Offices of Profit! The posts of mere Trust go a begging! No one can be found to accept *them!* Whenever I reflect on the times I am seized with the blue devils. I walk about the room in a sweat, look at my family, and wish them and myself out of the way of vexation" (to Col. James Burd, Mar. 29, 1777; Balch, p. 259). His opposition soon became more open and he worked tirelessly to bring about the election of an Assembly controlled by the opponents of the state constitution. Needless to say he viewed with deep satisfaction the revision of that instrument in 1789–90 and the adoption of the Federal Constitution in 1787, the ratification of which he helped to bring about in the Pennsylvania convention.

On Mar. 21, 1791, Gov. Thomas Mifflin [q.v.] appointed Yeates an associate justice of the Pennsylvania supreme court, a post he held until his death. Four volumes of cases, covering the years 1791–1808, were reported by him (*Yeates' Reports*) and his opinions appear also in the six volumes of *Binney's Reports* and 1–2 *Sergeant and Rawle.* During his justiceship he was a member of the commission appointed by President Washington to treat with the inhabitants of western Pennsylvania in the Whiskey Insurrection. His conciliatory disposition was a prominent factor in bringing about an agreement and the restoration of order. He was one of the three judges against whom the Pennsylvania legislature brought unsuccessful impeachment proceedings in 1805 because they had imposed a fine and prison term on one Thomas Passmore for contempt of court. Yeates was a prudent business man and left a considerable fortune for his day, $240,000. Throughout his life he displayed a keen interest in civic improvements and in new methods of farming. He loved literature and had a large library. He died at Lancaster and was interred in the churchyard of St. James' Episcopal Church, of which he was a member.

[C. I. Landis, "Jasper Yeates and His Times," *Pa. Mag. of Hist. and Biog.,* July 1922; *Biog. and Geneal. Hist. of the State of Del.* (2 vols., 1899); *Letters and Papers Relating Chiefly to the Provincial Hist. of Pa.* (1855), ed. by Thomas Balch; William Hamilton, *Report of the Trial and Acquittal of Edward Shippen, . . . Jasper Yeates and Thomas Smith . . . on an Impeachment . . . 1805* (n.d.); B. C. Atlee, "Jasper Yeates," *Green Bag,* Sept. 1893; *Poulson's Am. Daily Advertiser* (Phila.), Mar. 18, 1817.]   J. H. P—g.

YEATMAN, JAMES ERWIN (Aug. 27, 1818–July 7, 1901), banker, civic leader, philanthropist, was born at "Beechwood," near Wartrace, Tenn., five generations removed from John Yeatman of Virginia, whose paternal line went back to Dorsetshire, England. He was second among six children of Thomas Yeatman, a prosperous banker and manufacturer of iron materials, and Jane Patton (Erwin), of Buncombe County, N. C., who as a wealthy widow later married John Bell [q.v.], presidential candidate in 1860. Educated privately and at the New Haven Commercial School, Yeatman enjoyed a sojourn abroad and in 1842, after an apprenticeship in his father's extensive business at Cumberland, Tenn., became its representative in St. Louis, Mo.

Here scrupulous honesty soon won him a leading place among businessmen. In 1847 he joined in erecting "Yeatman's row," an imposing housing project for the times, and in 1850 was one of the founders of the Merchants' Bank. Ten years later he gave up a flourishing commission business to become president of this institution, reorganized as the Merchants' National Bank; thereafter for thirty-five years he was largely responsible for the important place it occupied in the Mississippi Valley's financial life. In 1850 he asked Congress for a right of way through Missouri for the Missouri Pacific Railroad, of which he was an incorporator. He was the first president of the St. Louis Mercantile Library Association (1846), first head of the board of trustees of the St. Louis Asylum for the Blind, and a generous benefactor of Washington University. In 1889 he was named one of the original trustees of the Missouri Botanical Garden in the will of Henry Shaw [q.v.]. He was also secretary and trustee of the St. Louis Medical College.

Yeatman's most important work was performed as president of the Western Sanitary Commission, created by order of Maj.-Gen. John C. Frémont [q.v.] at St. Louis, Sept. 5, 1861. Cooperating with Dorothea L. Dix [q.v.], then in St. Louis, Yeatman gave virtually the whole of his time to organizing hospitals, recruiting nurses, improving prison conditions, establishing soldiers' and orphans' homes and schools for refugee children, and distributing sanitary supplies. Under his direction what were probably the first railroad hospital cars were outfitted on the Pacific Railroad and early in 1862 the commission placed on the Mississippi a hospital boat, the first of many such craft. Yeatman spent much time in the field and the soldiers knew him affectionately as "Old Sanitary" (Stevens, post, I, 297). In 1863 he made a trip along the lower Mississippi inspecting the plight of freedmen; President Lincoln asked him to head the Freedmen's Bureau when it organized, but Yeatman declined. The final report of the Western Sanitary Commission showed that it had received $770,998 in cash and stores valued at $3,500,000. Unquestionably Yeatman's genius for organization, tireless energy, and integrity were leading factors in the success of this pioneering effort at mitigating the misery of war.

Yeatman was married, Sept. 11, 1838, to Angelica Charlotte Thompson of Alexandria, Va., great-grand-daughter of Charles Willson Peale [q.v.]; she died May 7, 1849, and on May 5, 1851, he married Cynthia Ann Pope of Kaskaskia, Ill., daughter of Nathaniel Pope [q.v.]. His second wife died July 3, 1854. More than six feet tall, courtly and genial, Yeatman had an impressive presence. His great brick residence, "Belmont," was a center of St. Louis' gay and leisurely antebellum society. Two of his five children were living when he died of the infirmities of age in his eighty-third year in a St. Louis hospital. He was buried in Bellefontaine Cemetery. In his last years his charitable gifts were so numerous that he left little besides his extensive library (Eliot, post, p. 10). His city mourned him as its first citizen. Winston Churchill, who had Yeatman "very definitely in mind" when he drew the character of Calvin Brinsmade for The Crisis (1901), regarded him as "the flower of the American tradition."

[Who's Who in America, 1901–02; W. C. Hall, Descendants of Alexander Robinson and Angelica Peale (1896); E. C. Eliot, An Address Upon the Laying of the Corner Stone of the James E. Yeatman High School (1903); James Cox, Old and New St. Louis (1894); William Hyde and H. L. Conard, Encyc. of the Hist. of St. Louis (1899); L. U. Reavis, St. Louis the Future Great City of the World (1875); J. T. Scharf, Hist. of St. Louis City and County (1883); W. B. Stevens, Missouri, the Center State (1915); J. G. Forman, The Western Sanitary Commission (1864); W. R. Hodges, The Western Sanitary Commission (1906); Rev. of Revs. (N. Y.), Aug. 1901; St. Louis Post-Dispatch, July 7, 8, 9, 1901, and St. Louis Daily Globe-Democrat, Dec. 27, 1901; certain information from Mrs. Sara Yeatman Graham, Lakeland, Fla., Yeatman's granddaughter, Alfred C. Carr, St. Louis, his grandson, and Winston Churchill, Maitland, Fla.]   I. D.

YELL, ARCHIBALD (August 1797–Feb. 23, 1847), soldier, congressman, governor of Arkansas, was born in North Carolina; practically nothing is known of his ancestors except that they came to America before the Revolution. He migrated to Tennessee and served with Andrew Jackson against the Indians and against the British at New Orleans. After reading law and being admitted to the bar, he served under Jackson against the Seminoles in Florida. His courage won the admiration of "Old Hickory," who as president rewarded him by a succession of federal appointments. After a term in the Tennessee legislature as representative of Bedford County, Yell moved to Little Rock, Ark., to take charge of the federal land office under an appointment confirmed Dec. 21, 1831. In a few months he resigned to resume the practice of law, but in January 1835 was appointed territorial judge in Arkansas. He is reputed to have been as fearless on the bench as on the field of battle. According to one story, when no one dared serve on a posse to arrest a desperado known to be in a local saloon, the Judge entered the saloon, grabbed the criminal by the throat, and ordered him into court (Herndon, post, I, 247).

When Arkansas was admitted to statehood in

1836, Yell was elected the first representative in Congress and served until 1839. He was elected governor in 1840 but resigned in 1844, at the request of the Democratic convention, to run again for Congress in opposition to David Walker [q.v.]. In this campaign Yell demonstrated that he could be all things to all men. At a shooting match he won the beef, donated it to the poorest widow in the neighborhood, and ordered a jug of whiskey for the crowd; while at the next place, where a camp meeting was in progress, he was soon in the "Amen corner" leading the singing (Hallum, post, p. 117). He was elected, and took his seat in 1845, but at the outbreak of the Mexican War left Congress without resigning and was commissioned colonel of the 1st Arkansas Volunteer Cavalry. In the fall of 1846 —still without resigning—he chose to remain in the field. Treating his seat as vacant, Governor Drew ordered an election, and Thomas W. Newton presented his certificate of election to the House on Feb. 6, 1847. The committee on elections reported favorably to Newton, but the House refused (Mar. 3, the last day of the session) to take up the report (*Congressional Globe*, 29 Cong., 2 Sess., pp. 339 ff., 527, 573); nine days earlier Yell had been killed at the battle of Buena Vista while leading a charge of his troops.

As a member of Congress Yell supported the annexation of Texas and Polk's Oregon policy and was interested in strengthening the army and in public lands. As governor he demanded strong measures for the control of the State Bank and the Real Estate Bank, which had been created in the previous administration, and had already suspended specie payments. He recommended a board of internal improvements, made appeals for education, and recommended agricultural schools, based upon the liberal donations of the national government, as the type best suited to the needs of an agricultural society (*Journal of the House of Representatives . . . of the State of Arkansas*, 4 Sess., 1843, App., pp. 2–12). He was attached to the common law and vetoed a bill giving married women control of their own property, among othe. reasons because the bill as drawr left the husband liable for his wife's debts. Yell was five feet ten inches high, had auburn hair and piercing eyes, and was considered a handsome man. He married three times and was the father of five children. His first wife died in Tennessee; the second, Nancy, died Oct. 3, 1835; the third, Marie, Oct. 14, 1838. Yell was a Mason and founded the first lodge in Arkansas, at Fayetteville.

[*Biog. Dir. Am. Cong.* (1928), inaccurate in many respects; *Ark. Hist. Asso. Pubs.*, vol. II (1908); court records, Washington County Court House; *Jour. Exec. Proc. of the Senate of the U. S.*, vol. IV (1887), for federal appointments; J. H. Smith, *The War with Mexico* (2 vols., 1919); John Hallum, *Biog. and Pictorial Hist. of Ark.* (1887); D. T. Herndon, *Centennial Hist. of Ark.* (1922), I, 246–51.]   D. Y. T.

YEOMANS, JOHN WILLIAM (Jan. 7, 1800–June 22, 1863), Congregational and Presbyterian clergyman and educator, was born at Hinsdale, Berkshire County, Mass. His great-grandfather Yeomans had come from England to that state. Because of his mother's death in his childhood he was brought up by her parents. They were poor people and apprenticed him to a blacksmith, but he was determined to get an education, and before the end of his term bought from his master the remainder of his time. In Troy, N. Y., and Albany he studied, supporting himself by teaching. After a year and a half he entered the junior class of Williams College, where he graduated in 1824, second in rank to Mark Hopkins [q.v.]. The next two years he spent in Andover Theological Seminary. During the year 1826–27, while he was a tutor at Williams, he gathered a congregation in the neighboring town of North Adams which became its First Congregational Church, and raised money for a church building. On Nov. 12, 1828, he was ordained and installed as pastor, at the dedication of the church. After a ministry of four years he was called to the First Congregational Church of Pittsfield, Mass., whence in 1834 he went to the First Presbyterian Church of Trenton, N. J. A pastorate of seven years there ended with his election to the presidency of Lafayette College, Easton, Pa. That institution was then going through a period of radical change, abandoning some experimental features of its early years—particularly dependence of the students on manual labor and assuming a more conventional character. Yeomans consequently encountered difficulties and dissension and could not achieve progress. After three years he resigned, leaving a name as an able teacher and strict disciplinarian. In 1845 he became pastor of the Mahoning Presbyterian Church of Danville, Pa., which he served until shortly before his death.

He was chosen moderator of the General Assembly of the Old School Presbyterian Church in 1860. His year of office saw sharp division in the church, for some Southern leaders were already advocating secession. Responding to a strong desire of Northern Presbyterians, Yeomans in December 1860 issued a circular letter urging the observance of a national day of prayer on Jan. 4, 1861. In the General Assembly of that year he opposed the resolutions introduced by the Rev. Gardiner Spring [*q.v.*], by adopting which the Assembly pledged support to the Federal government. In an eloquent speech he deprecated sectional cleavages in the church, and pleaded vainly that the Assembly should act conservatively, lest a schism occur and the Northern part become an anti-slavery body. From the beginning of the war, however, he strongly upheld the Federal cause; his last act before weakness overcame him was to go with difficulty to his door and wave a salute to a body of returning soldiers. He died at Danville at the age of sixty-three.

Yeoman's toilsome early life and struggle for education rendered him industrious, energetic, and enduring. His learning was broad, but his chief and lifelong interest was in metaphysics. He contributed articles on philosophical and theological subjects to the *Biblical Repertory and Princeton Review*. As a preacher he was studious and thoughtful, with much oratorical grace and fire. He was married in 1828 at North Adams to Lætitia Snyder of Albany, N. Y., who with three sons and two daughters survived him. Two of his sons were Presbyterian ministers.

[*Gen. Cat. of Officers, Grads. and Non-Grads. of Williams Coll.* (1930); *Gen. Cat. of the Theol. Sem., Andover, Mass., 1808–1908* (n.d.); *Proc. in Commemoration of the Organization in Pittsfield, Feb. 1764, of the First Church of Christ* (1889), containing information about Yeomans from his son, Rev. A. Yeomans; W. B. Owen, *Hist. Sketches of Lafayette Coll.* (1876); J. M. Wilson, *The Presby. Hist. Almanac*, 1864; L. G. VanderVelde, *The Presbyterian Churches and the Federal Union, 1861–1869* (1932).]   R. H. N.

YERGER, WILLIAM (Nov. 22, 1816–June 7, 1872), lawyer, judge was born in Lebanon, Tenn., the eighth of the eleven children of Edwin Michael and Margaret (Shall) Yerger, who had removed from Westmoreland County, Pa., in the same year in which he was born. Several of his nine brothers, especially George Shall and Jacob Shall Yerger, subsequently became prominent as lawyers in Tennessee and Mississippi. In 1833 he graduated from the University of Nashville, and he was admitted to the bar before reaching his majority. On May 23, 1837, he was married to Malvina Hogan Rucks. They had twelve children. Within the year of his marriage, the young lawyer removed to Jackson, Miss., where he soon made a favorable impression. His dominant traits were diligence, mental strength, and courtesy. His professional success was so great that he attained a practice reputed for some years to be the largest and most lucrative in the state. His political success would doubtless have been greater had not his convictions frequently led him to run counter to public opinion. He was a stanch member of the minority

Whig party. Although he was an associate justice of the supreme court of Mississippi from 1851 to 1853, he failed to be reëlected because he delivered an opinion, which he knew would be most unpopular, fixing on the state full responsibility for the payment of the Mississippi Union Bank bonds (*The State of Mississippi* vs. *Hezron Johnson, 25 Miss.*, 625). Also, he opposed the secession movement in a notable speech before the legislature in 1861, and in 1863 he and William L. Sharkey [*q.v.*] sought to bring Mississippi back to the Union, believing that the fall of Vicksburg had determined the course of the war. Yet in spite of the divergence between his views and those of the masses, the latter showed their confidence in him by keeping him in the state legislature during the Civil War; before its end he had been elevated to the presidency of the Senate.

Immediately after the war Charles Clark, the Confederate governor, sent Yerger and Sharkey to inquire from President Johnson the terms on which Mississippi could reënter the Union. Although they were not received as official commissioners from Mississippi, they had a satisfactory conference as private citizens. Upon returning, Yerger made a report of his mission to the Mississippi constitutional convention of 1865, of which he was a member. This report, well salted with conservative advice, has been judged as the ablest speech before that body. Immediately after he delivered it an ordinance was adopted declaring slavery destroyed in Mississippi (Garner, *post*, pp. 88–90). A few months later Gov. Benjamin G. Humphreys sent him on another mission to the President, and in July 1866 he was selected as a delegate to represent Mississippi in the Philadelphia convention of supporters of Andrew Johnson. During the period of congressional Reconstruction his advice was of course not sought by those in power in Mississippi. Before the supremacy of the native whites was reëstablished he was dead.

[J. D. Lynch, *Bench and Bar of Miss.* (1881); J. W. Garner, *Reconstruction in Miss.* (1901); H. S. Foote, *The Bench and Bar of the South and Southwest* (1876); Reuben Davis, *Recollections of Miss. and Mississippians* (1889); Dunbar Rowland, *Mississippi* (1907), vol. II; *Biog. and Hist. Memoirs of Miss.* (1891), vol. I; *Pubs. Miss. Hist. Soc.*, vols. III (1900), V (1902), VIII (1904), and centenary series vol. I (1916); *Cat. of the Officers and Grads. of the Univ. of Nashville* (1850); geneal. data from Mrs. Florence Yerger Guilbert, Jackson, Miss., a daughter.]   C. S. S.

YERKES, CHARLES TYSON (June 25, 1837–Dec. 29, 1905), financier, traction magnate, the son of Charles Tyson and Elizabeth Link (Broom) Yerkes, Quakers, was born in Philadelphia. His father was president of the

Kensington National Bank; one of his ancestors, Anthony Yerkes, was settled in Germantown as early as 1702. At seventeen, leaving Central High School, Yerkes began his business career as clerk with James P. Perot & Brother, commission brokers. He opened his own brokerage office in 1859 and joined the stock exchange. On Dec. 22 he married Susanna Guttridge Gamble. Three years later he had made enough money to start his own banking house, and in 1866 his feat in disposing of a Philadelphia bond issue at par when the city bonds had been selling at 65 established his reputation as a brilliant dealer in municipal securities. During these years he mastered the secrets of the connection between politics and finance. By 1871, the financial dictatorship of Philadelphia was practically within his grasp, but the Chicago fire of that year brought panic on the Philadelphia stock exchange which caught him over expanded. Called upon to deliver up money he had received as the city's agent in the sale of municipal bonds, he was unable to do so, and after trial was sentenced to two years and nine months in the penitentiary for technical embezzlement. He served seven months of his term before he was pardoned.

Coming out of prison to face a hostile and gossipy world, he managed somehow to reëstablish himself financially and, when the failure of Jay Cooke & Company precipitated the panic of 1873, Yerkes made a bold plunge and recouped his former losses. He expanded his railway investments and in 1875 helped organize the Continental Passenger Railway Company, of which he was the largest stockholder until it was absorbed in the Union Railroad system in 1880. But in spite of his financial success his position in Philadelphia society was uncomfortable. His marriage—to which six children had been born—was proving unhappy and gossip linked his name with that of the daughter of a prominent Philadelphia politician. Having obtained a divorce from his first wife and married (Sept. 23, 1881) Mary Adelaide Moore, a well-known beauty, he moved with her in 1882 to Chicago.

Here he started a brokerage firm, but his eye was on bigger game. With the help of a loan from Peter A. B. Widener and William L. Elkins [qq.v.], the Philadelphia traction kings, he got an option on a North Chicago street-railway line, and with further borrowings on the stock as collateral he found himself, in 1886, in majority control of all the major North Chicago and West Division street-car companies. For some fifteen years after that he extended and entrenched his hold upon the Chicago transit system. He replaced forty-eight horse-car lines

with cable traction, increased the surface lines by five hundred miles, applied electricity to 240 miles, and built the ingenious Downtown Union Loop. These physical improvements, however, were only by-products of his financial activity. His methods were so devious that his empire of street-railway enterprises became known as the "Chicago traction tangle." It was a network of construction companies, operating companies, and holding companies, of interlocking directorates and friendly contracts, of financial manipulation and political corruption. The record of his corporate activity was a palimpsest on which was written reorganization after reorganization, with a heavy admixture of stock watering in each. He himself, in summing up his formula for success in the street-railway business, said one had only to "buy old junk, fix it up a little, and unload it upon other fellows" (Russell, post, p. 355). The Chicago newspapers during the 1890's were filled with reports of protest. Overcrowding of cars, defective motors, double fares, long intervals between cars, blockades of cars—these were the common complaints. When asked why he did not provide enough cars to handle the passenger load, Yerkes made his famous reply, "It is the strap-hangers that pay the dividends" (Ibid., p. 358).

Rival lines sprang up, but Yerkes' tactics against them were singularly effective. When the prospective competitor had invested heavily and was borrowing money to complete his line, Yerkes would start juggling the competitor's stock, spreading damaging rumors on the stock exchange, and instigating troublesome lawsuits (Chicago Tribune, Oct. 6 and 23, 1893; Chicago Evening Post, Oct. 6, 12, and 18, 1893; Chicago Times, Oct. 7 and 19, 1893; Chicago Herald, Oct. 8, 1893). One of his principal weapons was the court injunction. His primary concern, however, was with politicians; his whole fortune depended upon getting and extending public franchises for the use of the city streets and he became a master of the arts of political bribery and legislative manipulation. In the early nineties, maneuvering himself into control of the state nominating conventions, he saw to it that a safe legislature was elected and in 1895 secured the passage of the Humphrey bills, renewing his franchises for a century without any payment to the city. Gov. John P. Altgeld [q.v.] refused to be bribed, however, and vetoed the bills, and subsequently the legislature reversed itself by a large majority. In revenge Yerkes saw to it that Altgeld's radicalism was so publicized as to prevent his reëlection. Gov. John R. Tanner, who succeeded him, was more pliant and in 1897 the

Allen bills became law, authorizing the Chicago City Council to do what the Humphrey laws would have done directly. The immediate effect of the new legislation was to send the Yerkes stocks soaring on the exchange (*Chicago Tribune,* June 10, 1897).

This was the moment of Yerkes' triumph, but it marked also the beginning of his loss of control over the city and state legislative bodies. His methods had become too blatant to be suffered any longer. "Revolutions," said one Chicago paper, "are caused by just such rapacity" (quoted in the *New York Times,* Apr. 24, 1897). The city legislators who had helped Yerkes were dubbed the "Boodle" aldermen. Indignation mass meetings were held and there was marching in the streets. On the night when the aldermen were to vote on putting the Allen law into effect for Chicago, the City Hall was surrounded by a crowd armed with guns and nooses. The vote went against Yerkes. In the fall elections every one who had voted for the Allen law in the state legislature was defeated and in the winter of 1899 the law was almost unanimously repealed. Yerkes' attempt to extend his franchises had cost him a round million in bribes and had proved unsuccessful. By 1901, largely because of this episode, bills were being introduced into the state legislature calling for municipal ownership and control of the street railways.

Yerkes found himself not only politically blockaded but socially ostracized as well. Opposed by powerful financiers who considered his business methods dangerous and regarded him as a menace to stable finance, he sold his holdings to his friends Widener and Elkins in 1899 for something less than $20,000,000. Before he left Chicago he made public his business accounts, in which students have since found amazing revelations of buccaneering methods. Returning first to his Fifth Avenue mansion in New York City with $15,000,000 in cash, he went in 1900 to England, where he became head of the syndicate which built the London subways. Things did not go entirely well, however, and although he was still planning to build the greatest system of urban transportation in the world, he was a broken old man, sailing close to bankruptcy, when he died in 1905.

During the last years of his life Yerkes was estranged from his wife and at his death it became known that he was about to divorce her to remarry (*Chicago Tribune,* Dec. 30, 31, 1905). He loved to surround himself with beautiful and expensive things, ranging from a gold bedstead, formerly belonging to the King of the Belgians, to a magnificent conservatory. His New York mansion had two immense art galleries where he hung the paintings gathered in his European travels—collections which were sold after his death—and he had medieval stained glass in his office windows. His name will be perpetuated by the Yerkes Observatory, at Lake Geneva, Wis., given by him to the University of Chicago in 1892 and dedicated in 1897.

[For Yerkes' street-railway activities consult B. J. Hendrick, *The Age of Big Business* (1919), in the Chronicles of America Series; "Street Railways of Chicago," in *Municipal Affairs,* June 1901; J. A. Fairlie, "The Street Railway Question in Chicago," *Quart. Jour. of Economics,* May 1907; C. E. Russell, "Where Did You Get It, Gentlemen?" *Everybody's Mag.,* Sept. 1907; Edwin Lefèvre, "What Availeth It?" *Ibid.,* June 1911. See also J. S. Currey, *Chicago, Its Hist. and Its Builders* (1912); *The Biog. Dict. and Portrait Gallery of Representative Men of Chicago* (1892); *A Hist. of the City of Chicago* (1900); T. W. Goodspeed, *A Hist. of the Univ. of Chicago* (1916); J. G. Leach, *Chronicle of the Yerkes Family* (1904); *N. Y. Times,* Dec. 30, 1905, and *Chicago Tribune,* Dec. 30, 31, 1905; Theodore Dreiser, *The Financier* (rev. ed., 1927) and *The Titan* (1914), novels based on the life of Yerkes; George Marshall, in *Encyc. of the Social Sciences,* vol. XV (1935). For public opinion of Yerkes see *Chicago Daily Tribune, Chicago Record, Chicago Times, Chicago Evening Post, Daily Interocean* (owned by Yerkes), and *N. Y. Times* from 1890 on.]   M. L—r.

         M. F. H.

YOAKUM, BENJAMIN FRANKLIN (Aug. 20, 1859–Nov. 28, 1929), railroad executive, was born near Tehuacana, Tex. His father, Franklin Yoakum, was a country physician and later a minister of the Cumberland Presbyterian Church. His mother was Narcissa (Teague) Yoakum. When about twenty, he became a rod man and chain bearer in a railroad surveying gang. He was promoted to boss of a gang and surveyed new railroad routes in many parts of the West. He became a land boomer and immigration agent for Gould's lines. Later he applied his experience to his own railroads by drilling artesian wells and by bringing European peasants from New York to cultivate the Trans-Mississippi and Rio Grande valleys. At the age of twenty-five, he became traffic manager of the San Antonio & Aransas Pass Railway. During the next twenty years, he became general manager, vice-president, and president of a number of other railroads. The most important of these was the St. Louis & San Francisco Railroad (the "Frisco"), which became allied with the Rock Island Company in 1903. He became chairman of the executive committees and was a dominant figure of both companies. He brought under his control some 17,000 miles of old and newly constructed railroad into the "Yoakum Lines" (*New York Times,* Nov. 28, 1929, p. 27).

In December 1909, however, the Rock Island sold its interests in the "Frisco" to a group headed by Yoakum and Edwin Hawley. They were also said to control the Chesapeake & Ohio Railway and four minor lines, while Yoakum was also a director of the Seaboard Air Line Railway. The "Frisco" and affiliated lines went into the hands of receivers during the financial stringency of 1913 and were broken down into their component lines. The Interstate Commerce Commission attributed the failure to the purchase of unprofitable mileage in the Southwest, the payment of extravagant commissions to banks and bankers, and to the unjustified payment of dividends upon preferred stock issues at a time when standards of maintenance of the road and of equipment were being reduced (Interstate Commerce Commission, *Reports and Decisions,* vol. XXIX, 1914, 139–211). Investigation showed, among other things, that most of the new mileage of the "Frisco" was built by construction companies in which the directors and prominent officials of the "Frisco"—especially Yoakum—were heavily interested. After these new lines were built, they were sold to the "Frisco" at greatly enhanced values. Nine of these roads were sold to the "Frisco" for over $26,500,000 at a profit of almost $8,500,000. In the construction of one of these lines, in which he was particularly interested, a profit of 75% on investment was obtained. He justified these transactions on the grounds that it was difficult to finance pioneering enterprises, and that public opinion had changed concerning what are proper corporate acts (see his statement in *Railway Age Gazette,* Dec. 19, 1913, pp. 1197–98). Writing in 1915, W. Z. Ripley called the "Frisco's" failure the "most shameful case" of "grave abuse in connection with finances of construction" (*post,* p. 42) in recent years.

While carrying on these manipulations, Yoakum set himself up as an authority on railway problems. He wrote articles for popular magazines and lectured about railways before clubs and labor unions. He thought the Hepburn Act of 1906 was not burdensome, but he wanted a fixed government policy—and no further railway regulation. He protested that the agitation against railways and capital in general, in addition to the threat of new legislation, made investors hesitant. He called upon the nation to "stand shoulder to shoulder for the rights of both the public and the law-abiding corporations," and insisted that "not one in a hundred of the corporations of this country has gone wrong." He asserted that "war against capital means war against labor," the farmer, the merchant, and the manufacturer ("What the Railroads Need," *Harper's Weekly,* Nov. 28, 1908, p. 25). He spoke of the supreme importance of Wall Street

to the country especially for the building and extension of railroads ("The People, the Railroads, and the Government," *World's Work,* July 1907, p. 9152).

He continued as a director of several of the "Frisco" lines even after the receivership, and apparently his enthusiasm for making profits from building new lines was not greatly dampened. His great ambition was to extend his lines through Mexico, connecting the Mississippi Valley with the Panama Canal. He was therefore greatly disturbed by the practical cessation of railway building following the depression of 1913 and 1914. He rationalized his desire for credit for additional construction into a theory for bringing the country out of a depression, by building more railroads, settling part of the unemployed on the public domain, increasing the food supply, and stimulating manufacturing for railways. In his later years, he became greatly interested in the farm problem. He had long realized that the earnings of his railroads were largely dependent upon the crops and incomes of farmers. However, he first became interested in the farm debt situation after a chance conversation with a mortgage-ridden onion farmer. He thought the solution lay in cutting the interest burden through the organization of agricultural cooperative banking, and by reducing the spread between farmer and consumer and stabilizing farm prices through farm marketing cooperatives. He wanted farmers to strengthen themselves financially by operating their own "trusts"; but not through fighting railways and other "trusts" ("The High Cost of Farming," *World's Work,* September 1912, p. 533). He married Elizabeth Bennett, the daughter of a pioneer Southwestern banker. They removed to New York City in 1907. They also had an excellent farm at Farmingdale, Long Island, which Yoakum liked so well that he became an advocate of the commuter's life.

[W. Z. Ripley, *Railroads, Finance, and Reorganization* (1915); *Poor's Manual of Railroads,* 1905, 1910; "Investigation of Railroads," *U. S. Senate Doc. No. 373,* 63 Cong., 2 Sess. (1914); *Who's Who in America,* 1928–29; *System,* Aug. 1916, p. 181; *Railway Age,* Dec. 7, 1929; *N. Y. Times,* Nov. 28–30, Dec. 1, 14, 1929; *World* (N. Y.), Nov. 28, 1929.]   G. M.

YOAKUM, HENDERSON (Sept. 6, 1810–Nov. 30, 1856), Texas historian, was born in Powell's Valley, Claiborne County, Tenn., a son of George and Colly (Maddy) Yoakum. He was of Welsh descent, and his American forbears had lived successively in New York, Pennsylvania, Virginia, and Tennessee. Until Yoakum entered the United States Military Academy in 1828, he lived on his father's farm and at intervals attended country schools. In 1832 he was graduated from the Academy and became a brevet second lieutenant in the 3rd Artillery. He was married to Eveline Connor of Roane County, Tenn., on Feb. 13, 1833, resigned from the army six weeks later, and settled at Murphreesboro to study, and later to practise, law. As captain of the Murphreesboro Sentinels, a company of Tennessee mounted militia, he served during the last half of 1836 under Gen. John Pollard Gaines [q.v.] on the Sabine frontier; and in 1838 he was colonel of a regiment of Tennessee infantry in the Cherokee war. The next year he was elected to the Tennessee Senate, and until 1845 took an active interest in politics. He was a partisan of James K. Polk, favored the annexation of Texas, and late in 1845 moved to Huntsville, Tex., where, on Dec. 2, he was admitted to the bar of the Republic of Texas. On the declaration of war with Mexico, Yoakum enrolled in Col. J. C. Hays's regiment of Texas mounted rifles, and was a first lieutenant at the battle of Monterey. When his enlistment expired, Oct. 2, 1846, he returned to Huntsville to devote himself to his law practice.

In July 1853 he removed to his country home, Shepherd's Valley, near Huntsville, and there completed his *History of Texas from Its First Settlement in 1685 to Its Annexation to the United States in 1846* (2 vols., 1855), for half a century the standard history of the region. It was republished, with additional notes by Dudley G. Wooten and a series of new chapters covering the years 1820 to 1845, in Wooten's *A Comprehensive History of Texas, 1685 to 1897* (2 vols., 1898). Yoakum was aware of certain imperfections in his work, principally those common to pioneer explorations of historical fields. He knew of important materials for the Spanish and Mexican periods which were inaccessible to him (*History*, I, 3–4); and in dealing with the period of the Republic of Texas he did not avoid partisanship. A contemporary reviewer noted that the author was evidently an enthusiastic admirer of Gen. Samuel Houston (*De Bow's Review*, Sept. 1857; C. W. Raines, *A Bibliography of Texas*, 1896, p. 223). Judge P. W. Gray, to whom the *History* was dedicated, regretted that it had not been more carefully revised and considered that Yoakum had been at times "rather too unpretending" for his theme (Gray to Yoakum, Feb. 18, 1856, in Yoakum Papers, *post*). Although Yoakum's partisanship for Houston is unmistakable, he acknowledges no assistance from him in the preparation of the work. According to family tradition, however, Houston accompanied Yoakum to the battlefield of San Jacinto and there related the story of the campaign, while Yoakum took notes. Of the 1040 pages of the *History*, 214 are given over to documents of considerable importance.

The *History* was Yoakum's only published work. A year after its publication he died suddenly in the old Capitol Hotel in Houston. He was survived by his wife. He was a man of wide intellectual interests, an able lawyer, and an effective, although not a rousing, speaker. One of the fifty-four counties in west Texas, created in 1876, was named in his honor.

[In his early military records, Yoakum appears as Henderson K. Yoakum. Sources include A. T. McKinney, in *A Comprehensive Hist. of Tex., 1685 to 1897* (2 vols., 1898), ed. by D. G. Wooten; Z. T. Fulmore, *The Hist. and Geography of Tex. as Told in County Names* (1915); *Biog. Souvenir of the State of Tex.* (1889); F. B. Heitman, *Hist. Reg. . . . U. S. Army* (1903), vol. I; G. W. Cullum, *Biog. Reg. . . . Grads. U. S. Mil. Acad.*, vol. I (1891); Evelyn M. Carrington, in *Dallas Morning News*, Aug. 21, 1932; H. S. Thrall, *A Pictorial Hist. of Tex.* (1879); H. H. Bancroft, *Hist. of the Pacific States of N. America*, vol. XI (1889); Yoakum Papers in Tex. State Lib., from which the date of death is taken, and Dallas Hist. Soc.; information from Thomas Yoakum of San Marcos, Tex., the adjutant-gen. of the U. S. A., the asst. adjutant of the U. S. Mil. Acad., and the records of the adjutant-gen. of Tex.]

H. P. G.

YOHN, FREDERICK COFFAY (Feb. 8, 1875–June 5, 1933), illustrator, painter, was born in Indianapolis, Ind., the son of Albert Brown and Adelaide (Ferguson) Yohn. His father was a scholarly man, a partner in Yohn Brothers, booksellers of Indianapolis. The family is believed to have been of Danish origin, the original settler having emigrated to Maryland toward the end of the eighteenth century. Encouraged by his artistically inclined parents, Yohn was early trained to observe, and as a child drawing was his favorite occupation. While still at high school he drew sixteen portraits at a Republican state convention for an Indianapolis newspaper. After one year in the Indianapolis Art School he studied for three years at the Art Students' League in New York under Henry Siddons Mowbray [q.v.]. In 1895 he opened a studio in Twenty-third Street. "A lot of composition and plenty of action are what I care most about," he once said (*New York Times Saturday Review, post*, p. 94), and Adolphe Menzel, Daniel Vierge, Alphonse de Neuville, Edwin Abbey [q.v.], and Howard Pyle [q.v.] were the favorites he studied. His first illustrations were made for James Barnes's story, *For King or Country* (1896). He was given one drawing to do for Henry Cabot Lodge's "The Story of the Revolution" (*Scribner's Magazine*, Jan.–Dec. 1898); it resulted in his doing about thirty-five. At twenty-four he was sent by *Scribner's Magazine* to England to make seventeen illustrations for Theodore Roosevelt's "Oliver Cromwell" (*Scribner's Magazine*, Jan.–June 1900). Serious, reticent, a tireless worker, he spent half his time in research. In addition to sound draftsmanship and dramatic action, accuracy of racial physiognomy and expression became a passion with him. He had a special knowledge of costume and arms that often surprised and confounded would-be critics. Though a specialist in battle scenes, which he painted with knowledged fidelity to spirit and detail, he never witnessed a battle. Authors whose books he illustrated said that he realized imaginatively and with poignant directness the creative intention of the writer. On Jan. 11, 1908, he married Gertrude Klamroth, a talented musician, daughter of Albert Klamroth of New York, and moved to Westport, Conn. In 1910 he moved to Silvermine. He died at Norwalk, survived by his wife and two sons.

Among the many stories he illustrated are John William Fox's *The Little Shepherd of Kingdom Come* (1903), *The Trail of the Lonesome Pine* (1908), *The Heart of the Hills* (1913), and *Erskine Dale, Pioneer* (1920); Mary Johnston's *Audrey* (1902), *Sir Mortimer* (1904), and *Lewis Rand* (1908); K. D. Wiggins' *Rebecca of Sunnybrook Farm* (1903); F. H. Burnett's "The Head of the House of Coombe" (*Good Housekeeping*, Apr. 1921–Jan. 1922); Irving Bacheller's *Dri and I* (1901); Maurice Thompson's *Alice of Old Vincennes* (1900); and others by Frederick Palmer, Jack London, G. W. Cable, T. N. Page, F. Hopkinson Smith, Meredith Nicholson, E. W. Hornung, and C. T. Brady. He also illustrated Frederick Funston's *Memories of Two Wars* (1911). He painted Spanish-American War scenes for *Collier's Weekly* and many historical scenes for the Continental Fire Insurance Company, the Glens Falls Fire Insurance Company, and Ginn & Company. During the World War he painted "America's Answer," the second official war picture; a series of important paintings for *Scribner's Magazine* depicting all branches of the service; many posters; and for the marines, "Crossing the Meuse," which is in the Navy Department. In 1930 he painted five canvases depicting the history of the Massachusetts Bay Colony which were reproduced by the *Boston Herald*. Numerous historical subjects were duplicated for private collections. Over a hundred of his drawings are in the Library of Congress.

[*Who's Who in America*, 1932–33; *Indianapolis News*, July 1, 1899; Otis Notman, in *N. Y. Times Sat. Rev.*, Feb. 16, 1907; W. D. Howie, in *Boston Transcript*, Dec. 17, 1927; *Boston Herald*, Apr. 5, 1930; A. B. Paine, in *Brush & Pencil*, July 1898; obituary in *N. Y. Times*, June 6, 1933; information from **Yohn's** wife and sons.]

W. P.

YORKE, PETER CHRISTOPHER (Aug. 15, 1864–Apr. 5, 1925), Roman Catholic priest and controversialist, son of Capt. Gregory and Brigid (Kelly) Yorke, was born in Galway, Ireland. As a lad he attended the local St. Ignatius College and was graduated from St. Jarlath's College in Tuam (1882). Thereupon he studied theology in Maynooth Seminary until 1886, when he was adopted for the diocese of San Francisco and was transferred to St. Mary's Seminary in Baltimore, Md. He was ordained a priest by Cardinal Gibbons in December 1887. As an assistant at St. Mary's Cathedral, San Francisco (1888–94), he was granted a leave of absence to study at the Catholic University of America, Washington, where he received advanced degrees in theology (S.T.B., 1890; S.T.L., 1891). In 1906 the Roman Congregation of Studies by special decree awarded him a doctorate in sacred theology. As chancellor of the diocese of San Francisco from 1894, editor of the diocesan journal, the *Monitor*, from 1895, assistant at St. Peter's Church (1899–1903), permanent rector of St. Anthony's Church in Oakland (1903–13), and rector of St. Peter's Church (1913–25), Yorke had a distinguished career as a pastor and as a preacher whose impressive appearance and theological learning challenged attention.

His interest in education resulted in a series of popular texts in religion for parochial and Sunday schools (1900–04) and in his selection as vice-president of the National Catholic Educational Association (1918, 1921–23). In 1899 he published a criticism of the sectarianism of the state university and of Leland Stanford University, which he regarded as unduly favored by the state (*Letters on Education in California*), with the result that three years later he was appointed a regent of the university by Gov. H. T. Gage, for whose election he had worked. As founder of the Catholic Truth Society of San Francisco (1897), he compiled several religious tracts. A prolific writer, he published *Lectures on Ghosts* (1897), reprinted as *The Ghosts of Bigotry* in 1913; *Note-Book of French Literature* (1901); *The Roman Liturgy* (1903); *Altar and Priest* (1913); and *The Mass* (1921). Two volumes of *Sermons* (1931), edited by Ralph Hunt, and *Educational Lectures* (1933) were published after his death.

Yet it was as a hard-hitting controversialist who was a master of argument and bitter, but quotable, invective that he was most famous. He fought a successful, fiery campaign against the forces of bigotry on the west coast which were inspired by the American Protective Association (*Yorke-Wendte Controversy,* 1896). He was an active laborite, and organized labor constantly turned to him as a speaker, as an advocate in its difficulties, and as a mediator in such controversies as the teamsters' strike and the street railway strike of 1906–07 (see I. B. Cross, *Frank Roney . . . an Autobiography,* 1931). Among some employers, indeed, he was regarded as a radical if not something of a demagogue. An ardent Irishman whose interest in Irish nationalism had merely increased with distance from the old land, he preached in Maynooth (1899), lectured brilliantly on Irish historical and literary subjects, organized an Irish fair in San Francisco in 1902, established the California branch of the Gaelic League, collected $20,000 for Dr. Douglas Hyde's Gaelic language revival in Ireland (1905), established an Irish weekly, the *Leader* (1902), which gave him an uncensored organ for his views, and battled for the establishment of an Irish republic as vice-president of the Sein Fein organization in the United States and as state president of the Association for the Recognition of the Irish Republic (1921). A factor in municipal affairs, a leader in civic betterment, the founder of a working-girls' home called Innesfael, a campaigner for total abstinence from liquor, and an active relief worker in the days of the earthquake and fire, Father Yorke's life was intense. And at the end, his friends were numerous, and his enemies respected him as a fighting man of honest and decided intentions.

[See *Who's Who in America,* 1924–25; *Am. Cath. Who's Who* (1911), which gives the father's name as George; *Monitor* (San Francisco), Apr. 1925; *San Francisco Chronicle,* Apr. 6–9, 1925.]   R. J. P.

YOU, DOMINIQUE (*c.* 1772–Nov. 14, 1830), buccaneer (lieutenant of Jean Laffite [*q.v.*], was born, according to tradition, at Port-au-Prince in the present Haiti, but the record of his burial gives his birthplace as Saint Jean d'Angély, France. Tradition also says that for a time he served in the French navy and that he was a member of Leclerc's ill-fated expedition against Haiti in 1802. It seems probable that he was connected with Haiti; many of the men who fled from Haiti at the time came to Louisiana. At any rate, by about 1810 "Captain Dominique" had joined the group of smugglers lodged at Barataria under the leadership of the Laffites. Dominique became one of the most prominent of the outlaws; he seems to have displayed courage and skill in forays on Spanish vessels in the Gulf. He claimed that he had letters of marque from Cartagena, but the Cartagenan flag was a

poor blind for lawlessness; the position of the ephemeral republic of Cartagena among nations was, at best, insecure, and there seems to have been no thought of admiralty ruling on prizes. Dominique captured many Spanish vessels.

After the destruction of the establishment at Barataria, Dominique, like Laffite and many other Baratarians, joined the American forces protecting New Orleans against the British. He and Beluche, another notable buccaneer, were given commands in Andrew Jackson's artillery. Dominique served well in the battles of Jan. 1 and Jan. 8, and was specifically praised in Jackson's general order of Jan. 21, 1815. With the other Baratarians he was pardoned for his former crimes by President Madison. He seems to have accompanied Laffite for a time, but by 1817 was permanently settled in New Orleans. He seems to have dabbled in politics as a Jackson man, but apparently he had no great political power. With Nicholas Girod, a former mayor of New Orleans, he is said to have concocted a plan to rescue Napoleon from Saint Helena and bring him to New Orleans, to live in a house prepared for him there. To Dominique was assigned the difficult task of delivering the former emperor from his jailers and bringing him to the United States in the *Seraphine,* but before the vessel could leave New Orleans word came of Napoleon's death.

Dominique lived on until 1830, when he died in want, too proud to ask aid of his friends. He was buried with some pomp, and upon his tombstone, beneath the symbol of Free Masonry, were graven words of praise that proclaim him *"intrépide guerrier sur la terre et sur l'onde"* and call him a *"nouveau Bayard."* By the time of his death he was already a figure of legend, and today many tales of his heroism and of his piratic adventures are told in Louisiana.

[See H. C. Costellanos, *New Orleans As It Was* (1895); Lyle Saxon, *Lafitte, the Pirate* (1930); A. L. Latour, *Hist. Memoir of the War in West Fla. and La. in 1814–15* (1816); Vincent Nolte, *Fifty Years in Both Hemispheres* (1854), p. 208; G. W. Cable, in *Century Illus. Monthly Mag.,* Apr. 1883; Alexander Walker, *Jackson and New Orleans* (1856); Charles Gayarré, *Hist. of La.,* vol. IV (4th ed., 1903); death notice in *Le Courrier* (New Orleans), Nov. 16, 1830; Lafitte Coll. in Rosenberg Lib., Galveston; burial record in Saint Louis Cathedral, New Orleans, from which the date of death and the approximate date of birth are taken.   W. B—r.

YOUMANS, EDWARD LIVINGSTON (June 3, 1821–Jan. 18, 1887), writer, editor, and promoter of scientific education, was the eldest son of Vincent and Catherine (Scofield) Youmans, and was born at Coeymans, in Albany County, N. Y. Two faiths, Quaker and Puritan, and two strains, Dutch and English, were intermingled in his ancestry. His father was a mechanic and farmer, and his mother had been a teacher. Sent to school at three years of age, Edward soon became an eager reader. Work on the farm developed an interest in labor-saving appliances; and a few scientific books fixed his interests for life. Beyond the elementary school he was practically self-educated. His first occupation, teaching a country school, and a projected college course had to be given up when ophthalmia, aggravated by the treatment of an ignorant quack, almost destroyed his sight. Going to New York City for medical aid, he came in contact with Horace Greeley, Walt Whitman, and more particularly with William Henry Appleton [q.v.], the publisher. More than half-blind, he was aided by his sister, Eliza Ann Youmans (b. 1826), who read to him and carried on chemical experiments for him. He constructed a frame which enabled him to write unaided. Undertaking to write a history of scientific discovery and then to compile a practical arithmetic, he was anticipated in both efforts. A third project was completed, and in 1851 he published *A Class-Book of Chemistry,* which became a standard text and remained in use long enough to require two revisions from his pen.

Medical treatment and the improvement of his general health had now so far restored his eyes that he was able to read and to go about alone. At thirty his most active period was just beginning. He was for the next two decades a popular lecturer on science (1851–68). Making use of the lyceum system then in its heyday, he annually traversed the midwest states, speaking on chemistry and its applications, on "ancient philosophy and modern science," on evolution, and on other scientific and educational subjects. He was attracted in 1856 by Herbert Spencer's *Principles of Psychology* and formed a connection with the author. As a result he became a disciple of Spencer and the chief promoter in the United States of his publications. He continued writing on his own account and issued a *Chemical Atlas: or the Chemistry of Familiar Objects* (1854), and a *Hand-Book of Household Science* (1857), a text in domestic science. He also edited a collection of papers on scientific education under the title, *The Culture Demanded by Modern Life* (1867), and a series of papers by well-known scientists which he called *Correlation and Conservation of Forces* (1864). He was married in 1861 to Catherine E. (Newton) Lee, the widow of William Little Lee [q.v.]. His wife's literary abilities were of great service to his editorial and promotional work. They had no children.

The International Scientific Series, initiated by Youmans in 1871, provided a vehicle for publishing scientific books which were at once authoritative and of popular interest. Among the distinguished scientists who contributed to the series were Darwin, Liebig, Helmholtz, and Huxley. The first volume to be issued was Tyndall's *Forms of Water* (1872). In the absence of international copyright, arrangements were made to publish the volumes simultaneously in Europe and America. The series was well received, and more than fifty volumes were issued during Youman's lifetime. In the same period he secured the establishment (1872) of the *Popular Science Monthly* (later the *Scientific Monthly*). In the conduct of this journal he was greatly aided by his brother, William Jay Youmans [q.v.]. To the International Scientific Series and the *Monthly* he devoted the last fifteen years of his life, in his editorials in the *Monthly* stressing especially the need for scientific education. It was in persuading original investigators to write for the educated non-scientific public, and in providing texts and reference books for teaching science in schools that this "apostle of evolution" and national teacher of science did his best work.

[See John Fiske, *Edward Livingston Youmans* (1894), which contains selections from Youmans' writings and corres.; Eliza Youmans, in *Pop. Sci. Monthly,* Mar. 1887; H. G. Good, in *Sci. Monthly,* Mar. 1924; obituary in *N. Y. Tribune,* Jan. 19, 1887.]

H. G. G.

YOUMANS, WILLIAM JAY (Oct. 14, 1838– Apr. 10, 1901), scientific writer and editor, was the youngest son of Vincent and Catherine (Scofield) Youmans, and was born at Milton, near Saratoga, N. Y. During his youth his brother, Edward Livingston Youmans [q.v.], was winning success as a textbook writer and lecturer on science. A result of this achievement was to draw William into similar lines of study and to carry him forward under Edward's direction. He worked on his father's farm and attended district schools until 1855, and made final preparation for college at Fort Edward Academy. He studied first under Charles A. Joy at Columbia, then at Yale (1860–61), where the first American doctorates in philosophy were conferred that year by the Sheffield Scientific School, and took a degree in medicine at the University of the City of New York (later New York University) in 1865. Physiology and chemistry were his chief interests. The year after receiving his degree he went abroad, chiefly to study in London with Thomas Huxley. Immediately upon his return he prepared for publication *The Elements of Physiology and Hygiene: a Text-Book for Edu-*

cational Institutions (1868) by Huxley, which had been entrusted to him by the author for adaptation "to the circumstances and requirements of American education" (preface, p. iii). Besides some teaching aids he added seven chapters on hygiene. When this task was completed, he began the practice of medicine at Winona, Minn.

He returned to New York about three years later when his brother projected the *Popular Science Monthly*. He was actively engaged on that journal from the first number in May 1872 and was sole editor after his brother's death (1887) until it was sold in 1900, when he retired. His chief literary work was done upon this magazine. Every month for many years, under the heading, "Editor's Table," he wrote two or more articles on scientific progress, scientific education, and the application of science to practical, intellectual, and moral advance. He was, like his brother, an "exponent of the evolution philosophy of Herbert Spencer," and both Spencer and Huxley wrote for him. A special feature of his editorship was the publication each month of the biography of a leading American or European scientist or teacher of science. The sketches, which are of permanent value, were nearly all from his pen. About fifty of them were republished under the title, *Pioneers of Science in America* (1896). Beyond the covers of the *Monthly* he also for twenty years (1880–1900) contributed to *Appletons' Annual Cyclopaedia,* preparing for each issue four major articles on the year's advances in chemistry, metallurgy, meteorology, and physiology, besides occasional miscellaneous articles. His editorial successor on the *Popular Science Monthly* said of his life that it was "devoted with rare singleness of purpose to the diffusion of science" and described him as "gentle, kind and noble" (*Popular Science Monthly, post,* p. 112). As an editorial writer he was vigorous, outspoken, not afraid of controversy and frequently involved in it, for his ideas were often not the accepted ones.

Throughout his life he was devoted to outdoor activities and sports. In the hills near Mount Vernon, N. Y., he had a farm from which he expected to derive a great deal of pleasure in his retirement; but within a year an attack of typhoid fever ended his life. Youmans was married to Celia Greene of Galway, N. Y., on Aug. 2, 1866. To them were born two sons and two daughters.

[*Who's Who in America,* 1899–1900; *Appletons' Ann. Cyc.,* 1901, with portrait; *Popular Sci. Monthly,* May 1901; *N. Y. Times, N. Y. Tribune, Sun* (N. Y.), Apr. 11, 1901.]   H.G.G.

YOUNG, AARON (Dec. 19, 1819–Jan. 13, 1898), physician and botanist, was born at Wiscasset, Me., the son of Aaron and Mary (Colburn) Young. His father was for many years a surveyor of lumber and justice of the peace in Bangor. Young, always in delicate health as a child, became stone deaf as the result of an illness at about ten years of age. In spite of his handicap the boy went to Gorham Academy and attended Bowdoin College. An early interest in botany and natural history was further stimulated by Prof. Parker Cleaveland [*q.v.*] of Bowdoin, and Young served as an assistant in Cleaveland's department during 1840 and 1841. During this period he also was secretary of the Bangor Natural History Society. Leaving college after two years, without a degree, Young went to Philadelphia, where he sought the advice of many aurists regarding his deafness. He "was by them in turn puked and bled and bistered and setoned, and scraped in his pharynx, but to no avail, for he remained perpetually deaf" (Spalding, *post,* p. 1280). With courage undaunted, however, he went to the Jefferson Medical College for one session (1842–43) but did not graduate.

Returning to Maine, Young tried to practise as an aurist; he gave up at the end of a year and became an apothecary in a drugstore in Bangor owned by Daniel McRuer, a prominent surgeon. While thus occupied for the next four years he kept up his studies in botany. In 1847 he was appointed state botanist of Maine, a position which he held for two years. With George Thurber [*q.v.*], J. K. Laski, and others, Young explored Mount Katahdin and the Castine Bay region. Reports were published by Thurber and Laski in local newspapers (reprinted in the *Maine Naturalist,* Dec. 1926, June 1927). Young's account, one of the first surveys of Mount Katahdin, was printed in eight instalments in the *Maine Farmer* from Mar. 16 to May 25, 1848. At the same time a *flora exsiccata,* in twenty volumes, was projected; only the first volume of *A Flora of Maine* (1848) was issued, parts of which have survived in the Gray Herbarium of Harvard College. It consists of dried plants attached to each sheet, with their identifications. The plan was given up after two years, and, when further funds were not granted by the state legislature, Young lost his position. His botanical work was sound, although his scheme of publication was visionary and expensive. A pioneer in afforestation and with a wide interest in seaweeds, fungi, mineralogy, and mining, Young corresponded widely, particularly with the English botanists, M. J. Berkeley and W. H. Harvey.

From 1850 on, he led a roving, desultory life. He practised in Auburn, Lewiston, and Portland as an ear surgeon; peddled a panacea called "Dr. Young's Catholicon"; wrote, set up, and printed three small weekly newspapers between 1852 and 1854, the *Farmer and Mechanic,* the *Pansophist,* and the *Touchstone*; published the *Franklin Journal of Aural Surgery and Rational Medicine* in Farmington, Me. (1859), chiefly important for its eulogy of Young's teacher, Parker Cleaveland; and contributed a few case reports to general medical literature. During the Civil War, a "copperhead" in politics, he used both his tongue and his pen with great freedom. With public opinion in Bangor against him, he was forced to flee for his own safety to New Brunswick. He remained out of the United States until he was rescued by Hannibal Hamlin [*q.v.*], then senator from Maine, and sent as American consul to Rio Grande do Sul, Brazil, in 1863. There he remained quietly until 1873. Some of his annual reports are of considerable value, especially that for the year 1864 (*Letter of the Secretary of State . . . Commercial Relations of the United States,* 1865, pp. 798–818, being *House Exec. Doc. 60,* 38 Cong., 2 Sess.). The last years of his life are obscure. He returned to Boston in 1875 to practise and became a member of the Massachusetts Medical Society. He died in Belmont, Mass., in 1898. He never married. His brother, the Rev. Joshua Young, a graduate of Bowdoin College (1845), became a famous abolitionist and was driven from his church in Burlington, Vt., after preaching the funeral sermon for John Brown, 1800–1859 [*q.v.*].

[The chief sources are J. A. Spalding, in *Am. Medic. Biogs.* (1920), ed. by H. A. Kelly and W. L. Burrage; and A. H. Norton, in *Rhodora,* Jan. 1935, with portrait. See also notes in the Gray Herbarium, Harvard Coll.; review by Asa Gray of *A Flora of Me.,* in *Am. Jour. Sci. and Arts,* May 1848; cats. of Bowdoin Coll., 1840, 1841; *Index Cat.,* Surgeon-General's Lib., Washington, D. C.; *Boston Medic. and Surgical Jour.,* Feb. 10, 1898. For a note on Joshua Young, see Mary C. Crawford, *The Romance of Old New England Churches* (1904).]

H. R. V.

YOUNG, ALEXANDER (Sept. 22, 1800–Mar. 16, 1854), Unitarian minister and antiquarian, was born in Boston, Mass., the son of Alexander and Mary (Loring) Young. His father was a well-known printer. The son's salutatory oration in Latin at his graduation from Harvard College in 1820 was highly commended, and his valedictory several years later was called "amusing," foreshadowing his gift as a story teller. On finishing his brilliant career at the Harvard Divinity School in 1824, he entered at once on his pastorate at the New South Church on Church Green in Boston (ordained, Jan. 9, 1825), where he remained for nearly thirty years, vindicating the confidence reposed in so young and inexperienced a clergyman. He was a typical Unitarian of that period, neither radical nor reactionary, gifted as a preacher, kindly, grave, and rather stern in his bearing. Those who heard him in the pulpit commended his sound thinking, his scorn of theatrical methods, and his power of voice, as well as energy of manner. He soon came to hold positions of honor in the community, serving as an overseer of Harvard College (1837–53) and as corresponding secretary of the Massachusetts Historical Society. During his pastorate he printed a dozen eulogies on eminent and wealthy Bostonians, and from time to time contended in print that "evangelical Unitarianism" would benefit also the "poor and unlearned."

In 1831–34 he issued *The Library of the Old English Prose Writers,* in nine volumes, witnesses to his own great library and his profound learning. But his tastes were antiquarian, and the fruits of his study can still be seen in his *Chronicles of the Pilgrim Fathers of the Colony of Plymouth from 1602 to 1625* (1841), and his *Chronicles of the First Planters of the Colony of Massachusetts Bay from 1623 to 1636* (1846). These works still hold their own as reprints of source material, with many critical comments. He planned a similar work on Virginia. A reviewer of the first work, "C. D.," proved to be Charles Deane [*q.v.*], with whom he contracted a life-long intimacy. They came together daily at the Old Corner Book Store of the publishers Little & Brown, meeting there George Livermore, Jared Sparks, Charles Sumner, Edward A. Crowninshield, James Savage, George Ticknor, and occasionally Longfellow. They discussed rare books like the Dibdins' and those printed at Walpole's Strawberry Hill Press, and indeed the whole range of literature, as well as current events. Of Young it was said that "few were more fond of anecdote, or could tell a better story . . . His wit and humor had the true flavor, like the *bouquet* of choice wine" (Deane, *post,* p. 433). He was devoted to James Savage [*q.v.*], then issuing notes to Winthrop's *History of New England* and a *Genealogical Dictionary of the First Settlers of New England,* and read often Savage's quaint footnotes in the Winthrop. He loved also Boswell's *Johnson* and contended that it should be read every year. Izaak Walton's philosophy he made his own. He was short and stocky, with broad face and up-standing hair. He was married on Nov. 1, 1826, to Caroline James and had twelve children. He died in Boston, survived by his wife and eight of their children.

[See W. B. Sprague, *Annals Am. Pulpit*, vol. VIII (1865); Charles Deane, "Memoir of George Livermore," *Proc. Mass. Hist. Soc.*, vol. X (1869), which has three delightful pages about Young; obituary in *Boston Transcript*, Mar. 16, 1854; portrait in *New England Mag.*, Nov. 1898, p. 341. A memoir by Chandler Robbins, in *Colls. Mass. Hist. Soc.*, 4 ser. vol. II (1854), is singularly uninforming.]   C. K. B.

YOUNG, ALFRED (Jan. 21, 1831–Apr. 4, 1900), Roman Catholic priest and musician, son of Thomas and Sarah Agnes (Stubbs) Young, was born in Bristol, England, from which as an infant he emigrated with his parents to Philadelphia, Pa., and finally to Princeton, N. J. A precocious lad, he was graduated from the College of New Jersey (later Princeton) in 1848 and from the medical school of the University of the City of New York (later New York University) in 1852. In the meantime, he transferred his allegiance from the Protestant Episcopal to the Roman Catholic Church (Nov. 27, 1850) in conformity with the step taken by his brother in 1843. Experiencing a call to the ministry, he studied theology at St. Sulpice in Paris and was ordained a priest at St. Patrick's Cathedral in Newark, Aug. 24, 1856. Appointed an instructor in the classics and an assistant to Bernard McQuaid [*q.v.*], the rector of Seton Hall College, he found time to act as pastor in Princeton village, where as an alumnus of the college he found friendly associations (1857–61). After a temporary assignment as pastor at St. John's Church, Trenton, he joined the recently established Society of St. Paul (1862).

Young fitted well with the group of convert priests led by Isaac Hecker [*q.v.*], and he became a zealous missionary whose eloquent sermons were heard from pulpits in all parts of the United States. He was an early leader in the movement of laymen's retreats and in missions for non-Catholics, as well as an indefatigable controversialist in disputes with Dr. J. M. King, John Jay, 1817–1894 [*q.v.*], and Robert G. Ingersoll [*q.v.*]. A skilled musician, he was one of the first American enthusiasts for a restoration of the Gregorian chant and congregational singing, establishing a Gregorian society to explain the chant, founding the famous Paulist Choir (1873), lecturing on music, and writing a number of articles on Gregorian music which appeared in the *Catholic World*. In addition to writing some poetry and composing devotional hymns, he compiled several hymnals in the hope of fostering congregational singing as an auxiliary to the priest at the altar: *The Complete Sodality Manual and Hymn Book* (1863), which

was reprinted as *Catholic Hymns and Canticles* (1888), *The Office of Vespers* (1869), *The Catholic Hymnal* (1884), and *Carols for a Merry Christmas and a Joyous Easter* (1885). Aside from several essays in the *Catholic World* and in the *American Catholic Quarterly Review*, he published a long book, *Catholic and Protestant Countries Compared* (1895), to which is appended a list of American converts of some distinction. Long a delicate man, Young spent the last three years of his life in a wheelchair, becoming a familiar figure, with his long white beard, to the children of the West Fifty-Ninth Street section of New York.

[W. T. Leahy, *The Cath. Church of the Diocese of Trenton* (1907); J. M. Flynn, *The Cath. Church in N. J.* (1904); *Cath. World*, May 1900; *Am. Cath. Quart. Rev.*, Apr. 1895, pp. 421–24; *Sun* (N. Y.), Apr. 5, 1900.]   R. J. P.

YOUNG, ALLYN ABBOTT (Sept. 19, 1876–Mar. 7, 1929), economist, was born at Kenton, Ohio, the son of Sutton Erastus and Emma Matilda (Stickney) Young. Both his parents were teachers, his father, superintendent of the public schools and later a lawyer, and his mother, a teacher in the high school until her marriage. His undergraduate work was done at Hiram College in Ohio, where he graduated in 1894, and he received the Ph.D. degree at the University of Wisconsin in 1902. He married on Aug. 10, 1904, Jessie Bernice Westlake of Madison, Wis., by whom he had one son. He entered on a remarkably varied academic career, going to teach at Western Reserve University in 1902, to Dartmouth College in 1904, to the University of Wisconsin in 1905, to Leland Stanford Junior University in 1906, to Washington University at St. Louis in 1911, to Cornell University in 1913, to Harvard University in 1920, and to the London School of Economics and Political Science of the University of London in 1927. He was secretary of the American Economic Association from 1913 to 1919, and its president 1925; president of the American Statistical Association in 1917; and in 1928 president of Section F, on economic science and statistics, of the British Association for the Advancement of Science. During the World War, he was one of the group of scholars gathered by Col. E. M. House for the study of international problems preparatory to the expected peace settlement, and he went to Paris with that group in 1918–19. He remained there for several months and was consulted more particularly on the reparations question and on post-war international trade policies. In 1927, being then professor in Harvard University, he accepted an appointment for three years as professor at the London School of Economics. He died in London.

He was a scholar of signal ability and of wide range. He combined a firm grasp of economic theory with an understanding of the realities of life, and was a mathematician and statistician as well as an economist; and also—a further indication of wide range—a competent musician. In his main field, economics, his position was eclectic yet forward-moving. He was steeped in the classic economics of the nineteenth century and appreciated its achievements; understood the developments in the early twentieth century and was proficient in the use of the mathematical tools for the more precise formation of theory; and sympathized with the so-called institutionalists in the demand for a closer interrelation between economic study and general social analysis. Universally admired, he was prevented only by an untimely death from exercising a far-reaching influence on the thought of his generation.

His published work is meager. Some elaborate papers and articles, and a great number of reviews and notes, were printed in periodicals and the publications of societies. The more important of these were gathered in a volume, *Economic Problems New and Old* (1927). Others of note were an article on "Pigou's Wealth and Welfare" in the *Quarterly Journal and Economics* (August 1913); addresses on "Increasing Returns and Economic Progress," before Section F of the British Association for the Advancement of Science in the *Economic Journal* (December 1928) and on "English Political Economy," his inaugural address at the London School in *Economica* (March 1928); a number of papers and articles on vital statistics, among them his presidential address "National Statistics in War and Peace," in the *Publications of the American Statistical Association* (new series, vol. XVI, 1918); and a series of statistical papers in the *Review of Economic Statistics* (October 1924, January 1925, April 1925, and July 1927) on bank statistics in the United States.

[*Economica*, April 1929; *Economic Journ.*, June 1929; *Bulletin de l'institut international de statistique*, vol. XXIV, pt. 1 (1930), pp. 371–72, with a list of publications in the field of statistics; *Harvard University Gazette*, April 1929; *American Economic Review*, June 1929; *Times* (London), Mar. 8, 1929.] F. W. T.

YOUNG, BRIGHAM (June 1, 1801–Aug. 29, 1877), second president of the Mormon Church and colonizer of Utah, was born in Whitingham, Windham County, Vt., the ninth of the eleven children of John and Abigail (Howe) Young. His father, a farmer from Hopkinton, Mass., had been a Revolutionary soldier. Whitingham is some seventy-five miles southwest of Sharon, Vt., where Joseph Smith, 1805–1844 [*q.v.*] was born, and the Young family belonged to the class of restless, poverty-stricken frontier-drifters from which the Prophet came. John Young moved to western New York state when Brigham was three, settling in several places, all near the scenes of the Smith wanderings. In his early manhood Brigham also drifted widely over this, the "burnt-over" country, where revivals had charged the atmosphere with evangelical and millennial fervor. He was a journeyman house painter and glazier as well as a competent Yankee farmer and handyman when, on Oct. 8, 1824, he married Miriam Angeline Works of Aurelius, Cayuga County. They settled in Mendon, Monroe County, in 1829—some forty miles from Palmyra and Fayette where, in 1830, Smith published *The Book of Mormon* and established the Church of Jesus Christ of Latter-Day Saints.

Young had shown a strong but entirely intellectual interest in religion and, after inquiring into a dozen frontier sects, had joined the Methodists at twenty-two. In common with many of the "burnt-over" district, he desired a practical religion based on literal interpretation of the Bible, capable of application to daily life, and offering a millennial future to those who were willing to work for it. Mormonism exactly filled those specifications. *The Book of Mormon* reached him within a few weeks of publication. He studied it carefully for two years, sought further instruction, and was finally baptized at Mendon on Apr. 14, 1832. He accepted the divine inspiration of Joseph Smith, and the doctrines and destiny of the church, with a faith which thereafter was never assailed by doubt. His conversion integrated his energies; the rest of his life was devoted to building up the church in highly practical ways.

His wife, who had borne him two daughters, died in September 1832. In July 1833, having converted all of his family who had not preceded him into Mormonism, he led a band of converts to Kirtland, Ohio, where he began his rise in the church, and, on Feb. 18, 1834, married Mary Ann Angell. He traveled throughout the eastern United States as the most successful of the Mormon missionaries; accompanied Zion's Army, the grotesque expedition which Smith led to Missouri to oppose the persecutions in Jackson County; and in February 1835 was made third in seniority of the newly organized Quorum of the Twelve Apostles, the administration body which was to rank just below the Prophet in the government of the church. By 1838, when the Mormons were expelled from Missouri, he had become the senior member of that body and consequently, during the imprisonment of Smith, directed the removal to Nauvoo, Ill. Dispatched to England with his friend Heber C. Kimball [q.v.] toward the end of 1839, he headed there the most successful of all the Mormon missions. It is significant that, returning to Nauvoo in 1841, he became the leading fiscal officer of the church, at a time when administrative control was essential to compensate Smith's rapidly intensifying aberrations. He had made at least three polygamous marriages by May 1844, when he was sent on a stumping tour in behalf of Smith's campaign for the presidency of the United States. In July he was in Boston where he learned of the murder of the Prophet, two weeks after its occurrence. Hurrying back, he reached Nauvoo on Aug. 6, finding the church in panic and imminent danger of dissolution. His genius for leadership asserted itself and he at once proved himself the strongest personality among the Mormons. In a series of dramatic moves, which have always had the flavor of miracle for his followers, he rallied the church, gave its fervent sentiments direction, and, with only unimportant defections, welded its fanatical loyalty in support of the Twelve Apostles, of whom he was the head.

Young was at that time forty-three. The rest of his life is the story of a unique experimental society, one of the most successful colonizing endeavors in the history of the United States. He took command of a church already habituated and responsive to despotic control and shaped to cooperative effort by poverty, persecution, singularity of dogma, and millennial visions. The expulsions from Ohio and Missouri, now reënforced by expulsion from Illinois, had demonstrated its inability to survive in the American social system; and Smith, although he taught that the church must eventually return to Jackson County, had contemplated moving it to the western wilderness. Young carried out this removal and so saved Israel. The energies of the society were concentrated on preparations for the exodus which, with assistance from the foreign missions and the United States Government (the Mormon Battalion being enlisted for a march to California), was completed in 1846 and 1847. Young had himself elected president of the church at Winter Quarters, Nebr., Dec. 5, 1847, thus settling the technical question of succession. The mass migration was conducted with great but by no means unprecedented success—considering the movement to Oregon, the Mormon problems were those of psychology rather than of organization or supply. What determined his selection of the valley of Great Salt Lake as the site of Zion is not certainly known. Young and his counselors had studied the government publications and other literature on the entire Far West and had had excellent opportunities to discuss it with explorers, military men, and the fur traders who knew it best. The Salt Lake valley had occasionally been pronounced the most promising part of the intermountain region but it looked barren and forbidding, and its very unattractiveness must have had a heavy influence on his decision, since it would protect the church against Gentile aggression during the vital first years. Unquestionably he hoped for a long period of isolation (the valley was Mexican soil when he settled there and he was thus outside American jurisdiction), but that dream was broken by the rush to California in 1849 and ended by the completion of the Union Pacific Railroad twenty years later.

Arrived in Deseret (the Mormon name, changed to Utah by Congress), he at once displayed colonizing genius of the greatest brilliance. For his scientific city planning there was precedent in the preaching of Smith and the earlier practice of the Saints and other societies. For the immediate adoption of irrigation, which was indispensable to agricultural success, there was ancient precedent in the Southwest and California, across both of which the Mormon Battalion had marched. But the tactics of occupying the desert seem to have come solely from Young's understanding of immediate necessities and future possibilities. Maneuvering his people with the authority of an army commander, he detached groups to occupy fertile, well-watered valleys throughout the intermountain country, each group supplied with a proper quota of mechanics and other specialists. This policy gave the Mormons a chain of outposts against the Indians, set the form for the irrigation system of the West, and tremendously increased the cooperative strength of the church; what was even more important, it gave the Mormons the best real estate of the region. From the first Young also pursued a vigorous immigration policy. His missionaries covered the civilized world, bringing a steady stream of immigrants to increase the wealth of Zion. He devised the Perpetual Emigration Fund to assist them on a loan basis and conducted a series of public works to occupy them while places were being found for them in the system. The greatest headway was made among tenant farmers and the city unemployed, to whom the promise of land was even more seductive than that of celestial glory; these classes also had the docility and malleability which were essential to his success.

Isolation in a desert environment was as effective a stimulus to cooperation as the opposition of the Gentiles had been. The production of food and shelter and the immigration, the creation of communities a thousand miles west of the frontier, above all the development of the irrigation system, were possible only to an autocratically directed cooperation. If Young was soon nationally infamous as a despot who brooked no inquiry within his church and used its full power against those outside who interfered with his purposes, it was because nothing less than a united effort could preserve the group. He saw that the first essential was agricultural development and so forbade the opening of mines. This costly surrender of most of Utah's mineral wealth to Gentiles gave the church a landed base which has remained impregnable. The high freight rates of ox-team transport from the East and a clear realization of the debtor status of frontier communities led him to develop home industries, which increased amazingly during the first thirty years. He supported them with a curious system, a blend of the Rochdale Plan and the joint-stock company, and, when necessary, with the tithing fund of the church (*Quarterly Journal of Economics,* May 1917, pp. 474, 479). His policy utilized the cooperative experience of the Mormons, but also it gave to the church organization financial and industrial interests separate from the people and began a change from cooperation to mere corporate control which accelerated after Young's death. He met the threat of Gentile commercial competition by organizing Zion's Cooperative Mercantile Institution and similar businesses which kept Mormon money at home. Belief in cooperative self-sufficiency grew on him (he was really thinking in terms of a religious totalitarian state) and toward the end of his life he revived the United Order of Enoch, a mystical communism revealed by Smith and discarded long before. All but one of its branches perished within a year and Young's successor was forced to terminate the one that survived (*Quarterly Journal of Economics,* Nov. 1922, pp. 159–65).

Young's greatest achievement was his transformation of a loose sacerdotal hierarchy, consecrated by Smith's revelations to apocalyptic duties, into a magnificent fiscal organization for the social and economic management of the church. He had little interest in the supernatural, announced only one revelation (devoted to the organization of the westward march), and promulgated few doctrines. Accepting Smith's priestly system, he made it a social instrument and to this realistic revision the survival, the

prosperity, and the social achievements of Mormonism are due. His genius for using the sentiments for purposes of group development is shown in his cherishing the persecution-neurosis of the Mormons—by a skilful manipulation of Gentile hostility to unify the efforts of the church. Even polygamy served him in that endeavor. He also moderated the millennial and evangelical fervor of the Mormons, confining the power of revelation securely to the ruling oligarchy, and ruthlessly cutting off those who reverted to the earlier habits. He discountenanced prophecy, the interpretation of dreams, speaking in tongues, and similar evangelical gifts, asserting his fundamental tenet: that the Kingdom must be built upon earth before it could aspire to its celestial inheritance. When, following the famine and economic and financial stress of 1854 and 1855, the church reverted to evangelical frenzy and conducted a blood-purge in 1856 and 1857, however, he was forced to bow to it. The notorious Mountain Meadows Massacre occurred at this time (September 1857); Young, though not directly responsible for it, may be charged with the constructive responsibility of all dictators. Yet even here he was able to utilize the aroused sentiments to recover what control he had lost under the stress of famine and of his greatest blunder, the handcart emigration of 1855.

Young's twenty-year embroilment with the national government and the occasional local terrorism were the political expression of a social and economic fact (see De Voto, *post*). He was dictator of a society whose methods, institutions, and ideals were radically different from those of nineteenth-century American society. He was not a brilliant politician outside his own group but, even if he had been, hostility would still have been inevitable. He tried to make the theocracy co-extensive with the political state. That end he achieved for some twenty years, but was forced, after the organization of Utah Territory by act of Congress in 1850, to permit the exterior form of government to come increasingly into accord with the American system. Although political strife reached the brink of war in 1857, when President Buchanan sent an expeditionary force under Albert Sidney Johnston to Utah, he preserved his system intact for another twelve years. It was then sufficiently strong to adjust without loss in essentials to the inevitable formal compromise. Appointed the first governor of the Territory, he refused to vacate the office when displaced; though he yielded on the approach of Johnston's army, his successors were mere figureheads and Young governed as effectively as before. Neither the displacement of the Mormon legal machinery nor the prosecution of Young and other leaders by Gentile judges, spurred on by a national agitation, in any way impaired the structure of Mormon society. That he brought his religious, social, and economic system, the Mormon Church, to successful operation and preserved its identity against a hostile nation and against the main currents of American social evolution in the nineteenth century is the measure of Young's greatness. In such men as George Q. Cannon, Wilford Woodruff, Heber C. Kimball [qq.v.], and Jedediah M. Grant he had invaluable assistants, but they were only assistants, instrumentalities of his will.

He was perhaps the foremost social pragmatist of his time. He had no interest in systematic thought and was impatient of theory. His genius lay in his ability to use the group sentiments of Mormonism for group ends. It was, besides, an executive and administrative genius of the highest order. His mind worked rapidly and carried a myriad relevant details about every activity and personality of his church. At least three-quarters of his sermons are devoted to practical management, and they instruct his followers in the minutest details of daily life from dish-washing and community slaughter houses to freight schedules and the strategy of empire building. His formal schooling amounted to only two months, and though a patient reader he learned best from specialists. He built up a splendid educational system but held it to severely practical ends, not least among them the conditioning of the young in Mormon sentiments. He wrote with difficulty and not well, but the language of his sermons, which were extemporaneous, is vivid, clear, idiomatic, and exquisitely appropriate to his audience.

Ruthless and domineering as a leader, he was in private life a genial and benevolent man, who had strong family affections and loved dancing, singing, music, and the theatre, and loved most of all the sight of his people enjoying themselves and improving themselves while they built up the kingdom. He had just enough kinship with Joseph Smith to develop a mild interest in such harmless reforms as dietary systems, uniforms for women, and Dio Lewis's exercises, but never permitted such experiments to encroach on his or his church's interests. He had a few residual Puritan traits: he opposed liquor (but put the church into the liquor business) ; he had a fanatical belief in salvation by labor and abhorred waste; he hated gambling and card-playing and, granted the terms of polygamy, sexual misbehavior. He stood about five feet ten and was strongly and compactly built, but grew stout at middle age. The number of his wives is variously given from nineteen to twenty-seven. An indeterminate number of them never shared his bed, having been married as honorable pensioners or for doctrinal purposes. He had fifty-six children. His household bore a curious resemblance to the "consociate families" of earlier experimental societies, and his personal wealth enabled him to give polygamy a grace it had nowhere else.

[The best source is Young's sermons in *Journal of Discourses* (26 vols., 1854–86). The best biography is M. R. Werner, *Brigham Young* (1925) but its failure to project the Mormon sentiments must be repaired with F. J. Cannon and G. L. Knapp, *Brigham Young and His Mormon Empire* (1913), which, though hostile, has an indispensable point of view. Susa Young Gates and Leah D. Widtsoe, *The Life Story of Brigham Young* (1930) has valuable intimate detail. For economic and sociological analysis see: E. E. Ericksen, *The Psychological and Ethical Aspects of Mormon Group Life* (1922) ; Hamilton Gardner, "Coöperation among the Mormons," *Quarterly Journal of Economics*, May 1917; Hamilton Gardner, "Communism among the Mormons," *Ibid.*, Nov. 1922; Bernard De Voto, "The Centennial of Mormonism," *Forays and Rebuttals* (in press, 1936). See also W. A. Linn, *The Story of the Mormons* (1902) ; obituary in *Deseret Evening News*, Aug. 29, 31, 1877.]   B. D—V.

YOUNG, CHARLES AUGUSTUS (Dec. 15, 1834–Jan. 3, 1908), astronomer, was born at Hanover, N. H., the son of Ira and Eliza M. (Adams) Young. The Young and Adams families, coming originally from England, had lived in New Hampshire for several generations, and for two generations had been intimately connected with Dartmouth College. Ebenezer Adams [q.v.], the father of Eliza, occupied the chair of mathematics and philosophy there from 1810 to 1833. He was succeeded in the professorship by his son-in-law, Ira Young, who held the chair (changed in 1838 to that of natural philosophy and astronomy) until his death in 1858. Both are remembered as born teachers, rich in knowledge, patient and skilful in imparting it. The carrying on of this family succession—for Charles Young was appointed to the same chair in 1866—is one of the most striking facts of Young's life. Another is that he entered Dartmouth in 1849, at fourteen, and graduated in 1853, at eighteen, at the head of his class of fifty.

Having completed his work in advance, he accompanied his father in the spring and summer of 1853 on a trip to Europe looking for instruments with which to equip the Shattuck Observatory, then being built at Dartmouth. His first position, however, was in the classics, which he taught at Phillips Academy at Andover, Mass., from 1853 to 1855. The following year, still cherishing the plan which he had long had of becoming a missionary, he attended the Andover Theological Seminary, continuing for a part of the year his teaching at the academy. In January 1857, however, he started on the scientific career to which heredity and training called him as professor of mathematics, natural philosophy, and astronomy in Western Reserve College at Hudson, Ohio. In the following summer (Aug. 26) he married Augusta S. Mixer, by whom he had three children. During the Civil War the students' military company, with Young as captain, responded to the call of the governor of Ohio in 1862, and served for four months as Company B of the 85th Ohio Volunteer Infantry.

Back at Dartmouth in 1866 as professor of natural philosophy and astronomy, Young took up more actively his pioneering studies in solar physics with a spectroscope of his own design. He sketched the changing forms of the prominences, and later photographed them; he found and listed bright lines in the spectrum of the chromosphere; he studied the spectra of sunspots, often detecting line reversals. These important observations, together with details of the construction of spectroscopes, he published in a series of "Spectroscopic Notes" in the *Journal of the Franklin Institute,* the first one appearing in August 1869. Observing the total eclipse of the sun on Aug. 7, 1869, at Burlington, Iowa, he determined the time of contact by watching one of the spectral lines as it shortened; examined the spectra of prominences and independently discovered the bright line in the corona which was long wrongly identified with the 1474 iron line; and detected the faint continuous spectrum of the corona. At the eclipse of Dec. 22, 1870, in Spain, he saw the lines of the solar spectrum all become bright for perhaps a second and a half (the "flash spectrum") and announced the "reversing layer." On an expedition to the high altitude of Sherman, Wyo., in 1872 he more than doubled the number of bright lines he had observed in the chromosphere, and, by a comparison of observations, concluded that magnetic conditions on the earth respond to solar disturbances. In 1873 he went to Peking (later Peiping) to observe the transit of Venus and while there made his first studies on the "flexure" of the broken transit. He organized expeditions to observe the eclipses of 1878 in Denver, of 1886 in Russia, and of 1900 in Wadesboro, N. C. In 1882 he mounted apparatus on the lawn of the Princeton Observatory to observe the transit of Venus. In 1876, using a grating, he made the first good quantitative determination of the rate of rotation of the sun. In 1877 he accepted the call to the College of New Jersey (later Prince-

ton) as professor of astronomy. There he soon had a well-equipped observatory of instruction, and in 1882 the 23-inch telescope was mounted in the Halsted Observatory. He made a series of measures of double stars, determined the polar flattening of Mars, and observed the spectra of comets.

He also lectured for many years at Mount Holyoke College and at Bradford Academy. Two series of lectures were given at Williams College, and he was in great demand for occasional lectures. His book, *The Sun* (1881), went into numerous editions and was translated into several languages. His exceptional ability as a teacher has had its influence on many students of astronomy through his textbooks: *A Textbook of General Astronomy for Colleges and Scientific Schools* (1888), *The Elements of Astronomy* (1890), *Lessons in Astronomy* (1891), and the *Manual of Astronomy* (1902). There would be almost unanimous agreement that Young's books were among the best textbooks in astronomy ever written; his pupils as nearly unanimously considered him the best of teachers. He was an associate of the American Academy of Arts and Sciences, of the Royal Astronomical Society, of the philosophical societies of Manchester and of Cambridge, and of the Società degli Spettroscopisti Italiani. He held numerous honorary degrees, among them that of LL.D. granted him by Princeton at his retirement in 1905, when the student body rose and gave a triple cheer for "Twinkle." He died in Hanover, survived by two sons.

[See *Who's Who in America,* 1906–07; *Gen. Cat. Dartmouth Coll.* (1925); *Gen. Cat. Theological Seminary, Andover, Mass., 1808–1908* (n.d.); E. B. Frost, in *Astrophysical Jour.,* Dec. 1909, and *Sci.,* Jan. 24, 1908; *Am. Jour. Sci.,* Feb. 1908; Hector MacPherson, in *Observatory,* Mar. 1908; *Monthly Notices Royal Astronomical Soc.,* Feb. 1909; *Pubs. Astronomical Soc. of the Pacific,* Feb. 10, 1908; J. M. Poor, in *Pop. Astronomy,* Apr. 1908; *Pop. Sci. Monthly,* July 1905; obituary in *N. Y. Times,* Jan. 5, 1908, which gives the date of death as Jan. 4.]   R. S. D.

YOUNG, CLARK MONTGOMERY (Sept. 3, 1856–Feb. 28, 1908), South Dakota educator, was born at Hiram, Ohio. His father, Erastus Montgomery Young, a carpenter and cabinetmaker, had moved to Ohio from Connecticut as a youth. His mother, Chestina Allyn, had been born in Ohio but was also a member of a Connecticut family, the daughter of Pelatiah Allyn, who assisted materially in 1850 in the founding of Western Reserve Eclectic Institute (later Hiram College). After attending the school near his farm home, Young was enrolled in the preparatory department of Hiram College (1875–78) and then for two years taught in the public schools of Kenton, Ohio. He returned to Hiram College in 1880 and received the degree of Ph.B. in 1883.

Through the influence of a brother, Sutton E. Young, who had settled in Dakota Territory, he secured the principalship of the public schools at Scotland, Dakota Territory. In 1884 he was superintendent of schools at Mitchell, and in 1885 he accepted the superintendency of the schools at Tyndall, assuming at the same time proprietorship of a weekly newspaper, the Tyndall *Tribune*. He continued the dual rôle of educator and newspaper publisher and editor until 1892. He was appointed in 1889 a member of the territorial board of education on which he served until 1890. In 1892 he became professor of history and political science at the state university at Vermillion. The university during this period was considerably weakened by the economic ills with which the western states were harassed, as well as by frequent bickerings of factionalism within the faculty. Through his dignified attitude, practical counsel, and keen sense of perspective, Young contributed largely to the academic prestige attained by the institution. When in 1901 the university became definitely organized into colleges, he was appointed the first dean of the college of arts and sciences. He held this position from 1902 until his death.

Young rendered notable services to the cause of education in South Dakota. He served as president of the South Dakota Educational Association (1892–93), became the editor of the *South Dakota Educator* in 1900, and contributed materially to the drafting of school laws for the state, particularly in 1901. When the courses of study for the public schools were revised in 1905 and 1906, he played a prominent part, serving as chairman of the committee that effected a reorganization of the high school system. His effective work at teachers' institutes made him one of the most widely known institute instructors in the state. He was the author, with G. M. Smith, of *The State and Nation* (1895), *The Elements of Pedagogy* (1898), and *History and Government of South Dakota* (1898). He was married on Aug. 1, 1883, to Loretta F. Murray, by whom he had three sons and one daughter.

[*Who's Who in America*, 1908–09; *S. Dak. Alumni Quart.*, Apr. 1908; *Volante* (Univ. of S. Dak.), Mar. 10, 1908; *Dakota Republican* (Vermillion), Mar. 5, 12, 1908; information from Young's wife and a son, and from M. S. Baker, Hiram Coll., Hiram, Ohio.]

H. S. S.

YOUNG, DAVID (Jan. 27, 1781–Feb. 13, 1852), astronomer, poet, teacher, and almanacmaker, was born at Pine Brook, Morris County, N. J., a son of Sarah (Mott) and Amos Young,

a farmer. He was a great-grandson of Robert Young of Scotland who settled at Perth Amboy, N. J., in 1685. Young's writings give evidence of a trained mind, but no record has been found of his attendance at college. His contemporaries called him "a natural astronomer." Wherever acquired, his was a liberal education. His religious poem, *The Contrast,* published at the age of twenty-three, evinces wide reading and matured thinking, and a brilliant and correct technique; his later effort, *The Perusal,* is cosmic and Miltonian. He had a school at Elizabeth-Town for some time, and had just passed the age of twenty when he terminated the connection, May 1801. He had applied the preceding March for a school at Turkey (later New Providence), N. J., with characteristic humor asking the trustees to show a good recommendation from their former master. Apparently he was engaged. At least he found there a wife, for on May 28, 1808, he married at Newark, where he then perhaps lived, Mary Atkins of Turkey. They had no children. He seems to have taught school, perhaps intermittently, during these early years, and also later in life, the latter period in and about Hanover Neck, Morris County. Tradition holds that he was a poor disciplinarian, and found it hard to accommodate his teaching to the younger mind.

As "David Young, Philom" he first appears as almanac-maker in 1814, the publication being the *Citizens' & Farmers' Almanac,* published by Jacob Mann of Morristown, N. J. From then until his death perhaps no year passed without his name on one or more almanacs, among them the *Farmers' Almanac, Hutchins' Improved Almanac,* the *Family Christian Almanac,* and the *Methodist Almanac.* His longest services were with Mann's publication and with the *Farmer's Almanac,* published by Benjamin Olds of Newark. His quaint interpolated forecasts, "Now plant corn," "Hereabouts expect snow," and others, were somewhat humorous accommodations to the popular mind. Tradition relates that he satisfied a group of French scientists in New York with his calculation showing that no eclipse could have been the cause of the recorded phenomenon of darkness at the crucifixion of Jesus. His intellectual superiority, however, depends not on tradition but on his published works: *The Contrast* (Elizabeth-Town, 1804), a poem in two parts done in blank verse; *The Perusal, or the Book of Nature Unfolded* (Newark, 1818), to which is added a reprint of *The Contrast*; *Lectures on the Science of Astronomy* (Morristown, 1821), delivered during 1820 at various places; *A Lecture on the Laws of Motion* (Caldwell,

N. J., 1825); *The Wonderful History of the Morristown Ghost* (Newark, 1826), "thoroughly and carefully revised" from a former anonymous narrative written in 1792 by Ransford Rogers, schoolmaster, and perpetrator of the gold-finding hoax; and *The Astonishing Visit* (Newark, 1836), a sermonic address based on the VIII Psalm, in the light of astronomy. While basically in harmony with the theology of his generation he abhorred superstition and appealed to a day when "science and truth will finally prevail." A substantial marble stone marked his grave in Hanover Churchyard until 1900, when a more imposing monument of granite was substituted, the old stone being whimsically removed to the Pine Brook cemetery near his birthplace.

[See *Around the Block* (1900), a booklet by Mrs. A. E. Kitchell, a pupil of Young's; E. A. Aggar, "How Time's Flight Was Noted," *Newark Sunday News*, Dec. 27, 1903; and J. F. Folsom, in *Proc. N. J. Hist. Soc.*, Oct. 1927. There is a very inclusive coll. of Young's almanacs and astronomical and poetic works in the N. J. Hist. Soc., as well as an astronomical dial plate of metal he had made for his own use. The name of Young's mother is from MS. B. 1402 in the N. J. Hist. Soc.]

J.F.F.

YOUNG, ELLA FLAGG (Jan. 15, 1845–Oct. 26, 1918), educator, was born in Buffalo, N. Y., the daughter of Theodore and Jane (Reed) Flagg, both of Scotch Presbyterian descent. Because of frail health in childhood, she did not attend the early grades of the elementary school but spent much of her time in watching her father at his forge, or in cultivating a garden. After a short period in grammar school she was admitted at the age of fourteen to the high school of Chicago, to which city her parents had moved; at seventeen she began to teach in the public schools. In 1868 she married William Young, a merchant, who died the following year.

After some years as teacher she became a principal, and from 1887 to 1899 was a district superintendent, in the Chicago schools. During the last four years of this period she was a member of a seminar of John Dewey's at the University of Chicago, receiving the degree of Ph.D. in 1900. From 1899 to 1904 she was professor of education at the University; from 1905 to 1909, principal of the Chicago Normal School; and from 1909 to 1915, superintendent of the public school system of the city. In 1917, two years after she withdrew from the school system, she became a member of the Woman's Liberty Loan Committee; she died while in this service.

The period of her public career, which extended from 1862 to 1918, was one of rapid change in the educational system of the country and in the social and professional status of women. She was a member of the Equal Suffrage Association and an ardent leader in the movement to secure a place for women in public life. She helped to organize the women teachers of Chicago and of the country. In 1910 she was elected the first woman president of the National Education Association, after a bitter struggle. She was active in the movement to introduce art, commercial subjects, home economics, and manual training into the public schools. She resisted political interference with the schools and in 1913, by resigning from the office of superintendent, compelled the reorganization of the Chicago Board of Education, which had planned to depose her; she was reappointed by the reorganized board.

She was associated in social work with Jane Addams. While teaching at the University of Chicago she published a number of monographs and articles setting forth educational principles developed in cooperation with John Dewey. Among these were her doctoral dissertation, *Isolation in the School* (1900), and two later monographs, *Ethics in the School* (1902) and *Some Types of Modern Educational Theory* (1902). Later she prepared notable reports as superintendent of the Chicago schools. She contributed to educational journals and was a frequent speaker at meetings of educational associations. In all her utterances she emphasized the importance of providing pupils with concrete, interesting experiences. She favored methods of teaching which give pupils the largest personal liberty and cultivate in them a sense of responsibility, maintained that methods of teaching should be based on psychological studies of the natural tendencies of children's minds, and also agreed with Dewey in favoring the organization of schools in such a way as to bring them into harmony with social conditions.

Her administrative career was characterized by vigor. She coördinated the activities of the school system and brought it to a high degree of efficiency. Involved in controversy, she was charged with inflexibility, dictatorial methods, a persistent tendency to choose women for important positions, and improper cooperation with teachers' organizations bent upon securing increases in salary and permanent tenure. Nevertheless, she gained the devotion of her associates by her willingness to delegate responsibility and to support loyally those whom she intrusted with appointments. Throughout her career as an administrator she was active in improving the training of teachers. She was a sharp critic of inefficiency and a stimulating supervisor. Her hold on the teaching force of the city of Chicago is attested by the existence among the women teachers of the Ella Flagg Young Club.

[J. T. McManis, *Ella Flagg Young and a Half-Century of the Chicago Public Schools* (1916); *Who's Who in America*, 1918–19; *Public Schools of the City of Chicago . . . Ann. Report*, 1910–15; *Chicago Daily News*, Oct. 26, 1918; *Chicago Sunday Tribune*, Oct. 27, 1918.]

C. H. J.

YOUNG, EWING (d. Feb. 15, 1841), trapper, Oregon pioneer, was born and reared in Eastern Tennessee. He was probably with the expedition under William Becknell [*q.v.*] which in the fall of 1821 opened the Santa Fé Trail, and thereafter for a number of years he operated as a trapper from Taos. In August 1826 he appears in the New Mexican records as "Joaquin Joon," the leader of a company which visited the Gila and incidentally were victors in a spirited battle with a band of Pima and Maricopa Indians. Three years later he led a party which included young Kit Carson [*q.v.*] across the Mohave Desert into California, where he trapped the San Joaquin River. He returned to Taos in April 1831, and in the fall united with David Waldo [*q.v.*] and David E. Jackson in organizing two expeditions for California. Young arrived in Los Angeles in March 1832, but the plans of the company failed, and he decided to remain on the coast. In October he set out on an expedition that carried him over a great part of California and to the Colorado River at Yuma, returning to Los Angeles in the early summer of 1834.

Near San Diego, in May, Young met Hall Jackson Kelley [*q.v.*], promoter of the Oregon colonization movement, and became deeply interested in that project. He joined Kelley at Monterey, Cal., and the two, with twelve others and a cavalcade of horses and mules, arrived at Fort Vancouver on Oct. 27. Dr. John McLoughlin [*q.v.*], local head of the Hudson's Bay Company, had received word from Governor Figueroa to look out for a party of horse-thieves, and though showing kindness to Kelley would accept no explanations from Young. The trapper resolved, however, to remain, and settled on the Chehalem, where he developed a farm. For two and a half years he was virtually ostracized. Early in 1837, however, he was enabled to join with his neighbors in a project for bringing in cattle. With ten others he went to California, where he soon cleared himself of the charge against him and purchased some 800 head of cattle, more than 600 of which he succeeded in taking to the Willamette. Exonerated of blame, he at once became a leader in the Oregon community and remained so till his death. In 1838 he erected a sawmill which enabled the settlers to build frame houses; he extended the cultivation of his lands, producing large crops of grain, and zealously cooperated with the other pioneers for the development of the community. In 1840 his health failed and he died at his home the next year. The problem of administering his estate prompted the first exercise of civil government in Oregon, the election of a probate judge by a meeting of the settlers. As Young was supposed to have no heirs, the proceeds of the sale of his estate were turned over to the provisional government. Early in 1855 a young man calling himself Joaquin Young and asserting himself to be the natural son of the trapper, born of a Mexican woman in Taos after his departure, made claim as his heir. On Dec. 3 the territorial supreme court awarded the claimant judgment in the sum of $4,994.64.

Young was a man of great natural abilities. As a trapper and explorer he was, almost from the beginning, a leader, and as a pioneer settler he attained a position of first importance in his community. He was active, enterprising, fearless, and scrupulously honest. It is said of him that he was the first exponent of democratic organization and procedure in Oregon, and that largely through him the first effective steps were taken toward freeing the settlement from the tyranny of the Hudson's Bay Company. Probably he had little schooling; he had, however, a keen intelligence, and he wrote well. Among his effects was a two-volume edition of Shakespeare, which he is supposed to have carried with him in all his many wanderings.

[F. G. Young, "Ewing Young and His Estate," *Ore. Hist. Soc. Quart.*, Sept. 1920; J. J. Hill, "Ewing Young in the Fur Trade of the Far Southwest," *Ibid.*, Mar. 1923; E. L. Sabin, *Kit Carson Days* (2 vols., 1935); F. W. Powell, *Hall Jackson Kelley, Prophet of Oregon* (1917); *Narratives of the Trans-Mississippi Frontier: Hall J. Kelley on Oregon* (1932), ed. by F. W. Powell; C. M. Walker, in *Tran. . . . Ore. Pioneer Asso.; for 1880* (1881).]

W. J. G.

YOUNG, JESSE BOWMAN (July 5, 1844–July 30, 1914), Methodist Episcopal clergyman, editor, and writer, son of the Rev. Jared H. Young, a Methodist minister, and Sarah (Bowman) Young, was born in Berwick, Pa. A pale, delicate-looking boy, fond of books and averse to outdoor activities, he was sent to Dickinson Seminary, Williamsport, Pa., to prepare for college. The outbreak of the Civil War awakened soldierly inclinations in him, however, and though restrained by his mother from enlisting until December 1861, he then joined the 4th Illinois Cavalry, in which his uncle, Samuel M. Bowman, was a major. At that time Jesse was in his eighteenth year. In 1862 he joined the 84th

Pennsylvania Volunteers, of which his uncle had been made colonel, remaining with it until he was mustered out, Dec. 4, 1864, and rising to the rank of captain. He was present at a number of important engagements, including the battle of Gettysburg. In later years he recorded his experiences in *What a Boy Saw in the Army* (1894), a well written book designed especially for young people and illustrated with pen drawings by Thomas Francis Beard [*q.v.*].

After the war he returned to Dickinson Seminary, where he was graduated in 1866; two years later he received the degree of A.B. from Dickinson College. He then joined the Central Pennsylvania Conference of the Methodist Episcopal Church, was ordained deacon in 1870, and elder in 1872. He was pastor of churches in Pennsylvania until 1888, in which year he transferred to the St. Louis Conference and was appointed to the Grand Avenue Church, Kansas City, Mo., of which he was in charge until 1892. By this time he had become well known in the Church, not only as an effective preacher and Sunday School worker, but also as a writer, and the General Conference of that year elected him editor of the *Central Christian Advocate*, St. Louis. In this capacity he served until 1900. Subsequently, he held pastorates at the Walnut Hills Church, Cincinnati (1900–08), at Snyder Memorial Church, Jacksonville, Fla. (1908–12), and at Bluffton, Ind. (1912–13). He was a member of the General Conferences of 1896 and 1900, and a delegate to the Ecumenical Conference of Methodism held in London, England, in 1901. On Dec. 22, 1870, he married Lucy Minshall Spottswood of Williamsport, Pa. He died of nephritis in Wesley Hospital, Chicago, survived by his wife and five children.

A facile writer, Young contributed frequently to religious periodicals and wrote several books in addition to that which recounts his war experiences. Among them were *Days and Nights on the Sea* (1888), *Helps for the Quiet Hour* (1900), *Our Lord and Master* (1903), *The Hungry Christ and Other Sermons* (1904), and *Today: An Age of Opportunity* (1909). His most ambitious literary undertaking, perhaps, was *The Battle of Gettysburg* (1913), an extensive treatment of that engagement, illustrated by maps and pictures, which his connection with the battle, his long residence near the scene of the conflict, and much investigation particularly fitted him to make.

[*Ann. Report of the Adj.-Gen. of Pa.* (1867); *Year Book of the North Ind. Ann. Conference,* 1915; *Who's Who in America,* 1914–15; *Central Christian Advocate,* Aug. 5, 1914; *Christian Advocate* (N. Y.), Aug. 6, 1914; *Chicago Tribune,* July 31, 1914.]   H. E. S.

YOUNG, JOHN (June 12, 1802–Apr. 23, 1852), congressman, governor of New York, was born in Chelsea, Vt., but moved a few years later to Freeport, now Conesus, Livingston County, N. Y. His father, Thomas Young, an eccentric but persevering farmer, and his wife Mary Gale could give their only child nothing beyond the ordinary district schooling, but through his own efforts the youth acquired a knowledge of the classics, and after a period of teaching entered upon a law clerkship which led to his admission to the bar of the supreme court of the state in 1829. He began to practise in Geneseo, and continued to maintain an office there and to pursue his profession in the interims between his periods of public service. In 1833 he married Ellen Harris of York, who with several children survived him.

Young early inclined to politics. Beginning as an ardent Jacksonian Democrat he ran unsuccessfully in 1828 for the office of county clerk. He entered the Assembly in 1832 under the Anti-Masonic banner, and in 1836–37 and 1841–43 represented his district in Congress as a Whig. He sought constantly to serve his constituents. He supported the bill providing for the distribution of the proceeds from the sales of public lands, the tariff bill of 1842, and other regular Whig measures—all of which President Tyler vetoed—and at the end of the Twenty-seventh Congress signed the Whig justificatory manifesto. When in 1845 he again represented Livingston County in the Assembly, he had become adept at taking advantage of tactical opportunities offered by factional divisions within parties. Against a Democratic majority led by Horatio Seymour [*q.v.*], he pushed through to a successful vote the Whig measure providing for the calling of a convention to revise the constitution, bringing to its support all but two of the Whig votes and the "Hunker" wing of the Democratic party. This was undoubtedly his most outstanding achievement, and made him his party's leader in the state.

Before his nomination for governor in 1846 he intimated in writing that he favored pardoning those Antirent rioters who had been imprisoned during the term of Gov. Silas Wright [*q.v.*]. As the candidate of both Whigs and Antirenters he overwhelmingly defeated Wright for reëlection, and almost immediately on taking office in January 1847 granted such a pardon, thereby alienating the conservatives of his own party. Practically stripped of appointive power by the new constitution, which he himself had favored, he filled such offices as were still at his disposal without consulting Thurlow Weed [*q.v.*] and others who had aided in his election. He incurred unpopularity also by reiterating a statement made in 1846 to the effect that he believed in sustaining the United States and its citizens "against a foreign enemy, at all times, and under all circumstances, right or wrong" (Lincoln, *post*, IV, 416), but his positive efforts in helping prosecute the war with Mexico once it was declared won much popular approval. His governorship was not particularly noteworthy, and he did not seek reëlection.

Although a firm friend of Clay, he supported Taylor for president in 1848 because he felt that after Clay's crushing defeat in 1844 Taylor was the most available Whig. As a reward he was appointed assistant treasurer of the United States in New York City, which position he occupied until his death. Young was "a man of decided ability, quick in apprehension, and energetic in action," who, though "strong in his feelings, and clear in his plans . . . lacked discretion and overrated the means at his disposal" (*New York Times*, Apr. 24, 1852). He died in New York City of pulmonary tuberculosis, from which he had suffered for a number of years.

[Letters in N. Y. State Lib., Albany; L. L. Doty, *A Hist. of Livingston County* (1876); W. P. Boyd, *Hist. of the Town of Conesus, Livingston County, N. Y.* (1887); J. S. Jenkins, *Lives of the Govs. of the State of N. Y.* (1851); *Third Ann. Meeting of the Livingston County Hist. Soc.* (1879); *Biog. Dir. Am. Cong.* (1928); C. Z. Lincoln, *State of N. Y.: Messages from the Governors* (1909), vol. IV; D. S. Alexander, *A Pol. Hist. of the State of N. Y.*, vol. II (1906); files of the *N. Y. Herald*, 1846–52.]   E. L. J.

YOUNG, JOHN CLARKE (Aug. 12, 1803– June 23, 1857), educator and Presbyterian minister, was born in Greencastle, Pa., the posthumous son of Rev. John Young. Both father and mother, Mary (Clarke) Young, were of Scotch-Irish descent. Having studied under John Borland in New York City, Young attended Columbia College there for three years, but completed his college work in Dickinson College, graduating in 1823. He became a tutor in the College of New Jersey and graduated from Princeton Theological Seminary in 1827. One year later he accepted the pastorate of the McChord (now Second) Presbyterian Church, Lexington, Ky. When the presidency of Centre College, Danville, became vacant in 1830, upon the resignation of Dr. Gideon Blackburn [*q.v.*], Young was elected to the place. The institution had graduated only twenty-five young men during the eleven years of its existence, and had a student body of thirty-three. At the time of Young's death in 1857, the college had more than 250 students and an endowment in excess of $100,000; it had attained a secure place among the strong liberal-arts colleges of the South and Middle West, and had just graduated a class of forty-seven.

Young was a notable figure in the development of Presbyterian policies throughout his life. In 1834, in addition to his duties as college president, he accepted the pastorate of the Presbyterian Church of Danville, and so successful was his ministry that in 1852 he organized the Second Presbyterian Church to care for the students of the college without overcrowding the parent church. Twice moderator of the Synod of Kentucky, he became in 1853 the moderator of the General Assembly. Being specially gifted as an extemporaneous speaker, he was frequently heard in the church courts as the spokesman for moderate and practicable measures. In the New-School controversy, he deplored the violent measures that led to the division but remained loyal to the Old-School Assembly. In relation to the slavery issue, he twice freed groups of his own slaves and publicly debated in favor of including in the proposed Kentucky constitution of 1849–50 a clause providing for the gradual emancipation of the slaves; but he opposed the radical demands of the abolitionists. The habits of his mind were quiet, peaceful, and practicable, and his great success as educator and preacher was due to the happy combination of high principle and common sense. Several of his sermons and addresses were published, among them *An Address to the Presbyterians of Kentucky, Proposing a Plan for the Instruction and Emancipation of Their Slaves* (1836), written for a committee of the Synod; *Scriptural Duties of Masters* (n.d.), a sermon preached in 1846; and *The Efficacy of Prayer* (1858).

Young was twice married: first, Nov. 3, 1829, to Frances Breckinridge, who died in 1837, and second, in 1839, to Cornelia Crittenden, daughter of John J. Crittenden [*q.v.*]. He was thus connected with two of the most prominent Kentucky families of the period. Of his ten children, one son, Dr. William C. Young, also a Presbyterian minister, was president of Centre College from 1888 till his death in 1896, and two daughters, Sarah Lee and Eugenia, made generous gifts to the college in memory of their father and brother.

[R. J. Breckinridge, in *Danville Quart. Rev.*, Mar. 1864; Lewis and R. H. Collins, *Hist. of Ky.* (1874), I, 475; Z. F. Smith, *The Hist. of Ky.* (1886); S. M. Wilson, *Hist. of Ky.* (1928), III, 16–17; *Gen. Alumni Cat. of Centre Coll.* (1890); inaugural address of Dr. Wm. C. Young, in *The Centre Coll. of Ky., Inaugural Ceremonies, Oct. 9, 1889* (1889); E. H. Roberts, *Biog. Cat. Princeton Theol. Sem.* (1933); interviews with Miss Eugenia Young.]   C. J. T.

YOUNG, JOHN RICHARDSON (1782–June 8, 1804), physician, was born at Elizabethtown, near Hagerstown, Md., the son of Dr. Samuel and Ann Richardson Young. He was graduated from the College of New Jersey (later Princeton) in 1799. Taking up medicine as a vocation, he began his studies under the preceptorship of his father and continued them at the University of Pennsylvania, from which he was graduated with the degree of M.D. in 1803. He returned to enter practice with his father. One year later he died at his home in Hagerstown of pulmonary tuberculosis. As most of that brief period was one of invalidism, Young's name would by now have been forgotten, had it not been for his original work of investigation done as a student and published in his inaugural thesis for the degree of M.D. The thesis bears two dedications, one to his father, the other to Dr. Benjamin Smith Barton [q.v.], distinguished and versatile professor of materia medica, botany, and natural history in the University of Pennsylvania. The latter dedication is said to be "in respect to his talents, and gratitude for many favors received," and as Barton's name is several times mentioned in the thesis, it may be presumed that Young received inspiration and suggestion from him in the prosecution of his experiments.

The thesis, entitled *An Experimental Inquiry into the Principles of Nutrition and the Digestive Process* (1803), was republished in Charles Caldwell's *Medical Theses* (vol. I, 1805). It begins with some general facts relating to the digestibility and digestion of "nutrientia," and then describes Young's experiments. The most important of these were made upon large frogs, into whose stomachs smaller frogs, living and dead, and various materials were introduced for varying lengths of time, to be removed as desired for later examination, or from whose stomachs gastric juice was removed with a teaspoon for chemical examination. His discoveries showed that gastric juice is itself acid and that its acidity is not the result of fermentation, as had been previously thought; that it is on account of its acidity that it dissolves the bones of such animals as are swallowed whole and sometimes alive by snakes, frogs, toads, etc.; that no digestion can take place so long as the tissues swallowed are alive, even if they be paralyzed, but that it begins the moment they die; that swallowed live creatures do not begin to digest until they have died of asphyxiation in the stomachs of those that swallowed them, and that the stomach does not digest itself because it is alive. These experiments, it should be remarked, pre-

ceded by twenty years the famous studies of digestion made by William Beaumont [q.v.] in the traumatically fistulated stomach of Alexis St. Martin, but for a long time, as a result of Young's early death, no attention was given to his work, so original, so ingenious, and of such far-reaching importance.

[H. A. Kelly, in *Johns Hopkins Hospital Bull.,* Aug. 1918; H. A. Kelly and W. L. Burrage, *Am. Medic. Biogs.* (1920); obituary in *Maryland Herald,* June 13, 1804.]

J. M.

YOUNG, JOHN RUSSELL (Nov. 20, 1840–Jan. 17, 1899), journalist, was born in Tyrone County, Ireland, the eldest child of Scottish parents, George Young, a weaver, and Rebecca (Rankin) Young. He had two sisters and a brother, James Rankin Young, who later became a congressman. His father emigrated to the United States, when the boy was less than a year old, and settled first in Downington, Pa., and later in Philadelphia. His elementary education was begun at the Harrison Grammar School in Philadelphia, but he graduated from a New Orleans high school, having gone to that city after the death of his mother in 1851 to live as the ward of an uncle. At the age of fifteen he returned to Philadelphia and became assistant proof reader for a relative, William Young, a publisher and printer. In August 1857 he obtained a position as copy boy for the Philadelphia *Press,* of which John W. Forney [q.v.] was editor. Forney became interested in him, and invited him to his home, where many important men of the day gathered. He soon became a reporter for the *Press* and in 1861, while in Washington with Forney, was sent to the front as a war correspondent. He was, perhaps, the first to report the facts of defeat and retreat from the battle of Bull Run, an account that brought him fame and led to his being made managing editor of Forney's two daily newspapers in 1862. He was one of the founders of the Union League of Philadelphia in 1862.

In 1865 he went to New York at the request of Jay Cooke to help with the publicity for the federal loan. He also wrote articles for the *New York Tribune,* which won the approval of the editor, Horace Greeley. He became a column writer and at the age of twenty-six was made managing editor of the *Tribune.* In 1870 he was sent abroad by George S. Boutwell, the secretary of the treasury. Again, in 1871 he visited Europe on a confidential mission at the request of Hamilton Fish, the secretary of state. To conceal the true nature of his errand it was given out that he went to see about the sale of government bonds. This brought him to Paris during the exciting last days of the commune, of which he wrote a vivid report. In 1872 he accepted an editorial position on the *New York Herald* and spent the next few years in London and Paris, where he did some notable work for his paper. He met many distinguished men, sketches of whom were included in his *Men and Memories* (2 vols., 1901) posthumously edited by his widow. When Grant visited London in 1877 on his tour around the world he invited Young to accompany him. The story of this is interestingly told in *Around the World with General Grant* (2 vols., 1879). This trip was the beginning of an interest in the Far East and of a friendship with Li Hung Chang, one of the greatest of recent Chinese statesmen. It also resulted in a friendship between Young and Grant, who was so much impressed by Young's ability that he persuaded Arthur to appoint him minister to China in 1882. He won the confidence of the Chinese to an extent seldom achieved by Western representatives. He settled many of the outstanding claims of the United States against China, in itself a real accomplishment. His most important efforts were made in an attempt to mediate between France and China in the dispute over Annam and Tong King; and, while not entirely successful, he was nevertheless instrumental in the final peace arrangement. In 1885 he resumed his editorial work on the *Herald,* still most of the time in London and Paris. In 1890 he returned to Philadelphia. In 1897 McKinley appointed him Librarian of Congress. It was during his period of office that the books were moved from the Capitol to the new Library of Congress, a work not quite completed at his death.

In appearance he was rather short and stout. His fine head was sculptured by Frederick Mac-Monnies and displayed as a perfect example of the head of an intellectual man. He was very quiet but nevertheless possessed great charm and the ability to make friends easily. He understood human nature, and this gift enabled him to bring people of opposed views together for amicable discussion. Among his friends he numbered statesmen, journalists, actors, writers, men and women of all countries. His greatest work was in journalism, and Alexander K. McClure has said of him that "no man in the list of our illustrious editors has reared a grander monument to the progress of American journalism" (Foreword, *Men and Memories, ante,* p. ix). He was married three times; first to Rose Fitzpatrick, second to Julia Coleman, an adopted daughter of Marshall Jewell [*q.v.*], and third to May (Dow) Davids. Survived by his third wife and by two

sons, he was buried from St. John's Episcopal Church in Washington.

[John Russell Young Papers in Lib. of Cong.; official correspondence in archives of the state department; *Men and Memories, ante*; information from members of the family; *Washington Post,* Jan. 18, 1899.]

J. L. B.

YOUNG, JOHN WESLEY (Nov. 17, 1879– Feb. 17, 1932), mathematician, was born in Columbus, Ohio. His father, William Henry Young, a native of West Virginia, served in succession as colonel in the Civil War, as United States consul in Karlsruhe, Germany, and as professor at Ohio University, Athens, Ohio, and finally retired to devote himself to business. While on the Continent he married Marie Louise Widenhorn, born in Paris of a German father and a French mother. The son's early schooling in Columbus was followed by six years in the Gymnasium at Baden-Baden. Graduating from Ohio State University in 1899, he remained for a year of graduate work in mathematics and philosophy. His frequent contacts with his talented brother-in-law, E. H. Moore, helped to concentrate his interest on mathematics. He received the degrees of A.M. (1901) and Ph.D. (1904) at Cornell University. He began his teaching as instructor at Northwestern University in 1903, and became preceptor at Princeton in 1905, assistant professor at the University of Illinois in 1908, and head of the department of mathematics at the University of Kansas in 1910. The following summer he taught at the University of Chicago, and in the fall went to Dartmouth College, where the remaining years of his life were spent. On July 20, 1907, he married Mary Louise Aston, a former school mate, by whom he had one daughter. He died in Hanover, N. H., of heart disease. He was survived by his wife and daughter.

It is not surprising that the product of an international marriage and an international education should develop to an unusual degree those characteristics of tolerance, open-mindedness, and sympathy which mark the successful teacher. Highly imaginative and philosophical, patient and thorough, he not only contributed to the growth of mathematics through his own researches, but by suggestion and helpful criticism encouraged others in their work. His contact with colleges and universities of varied types and in different parts of the country brought to him a comprehensive view of higher education in America, as well as a wide friendship among American mathematicians. His life spanned the years in which America was "coming of age" in science as well as in other ways. This process in mathematics was furthered by the growth of the American Mathematical Society, and Young as editor of its *Bulletin* and member of its council for eighteen years (1907–25) helped to guide this growth. His deep interest in the improvement of mathematical education led him to take an active part in the formation of the Mathematical Association of America. This organization made him chairman of a committee on college entrance requirements in mathematics, which was soon enlarged to make it nationally representative and received generous financial assistance from the General Education Board. The final report of this committee, *The Reorganization of Mathematics in Secondary Education* (1923), had far-reaching influence on mathematical instruction in the United States.

Young was a member of most of the well-known mathematical societies of Europe and America, and a regular attendant at the international congresses of mathematics. He served in an editorial capacity for the *Mathematics Teacher,* the Colloquium Publications of the American Mathematical Society, and the Carus Mathematical Monographs, of which he wrote one, *Projective Geometry* (1930). With Oswald Veblen, he published *Projective Geometry* (2 vols., 1910–18), based on a set of postulates created by the authors which permitted the postponement of the difficult topics of linear order and continuity, and thus greatly simplified the logical treatment of a considerable body of geometry. His *Lectures on Fundamental Concepts of Algebra and Geometry* (1911) aroused widespread interest and was translated into Italian.

[*Who's Who in America,* 1930–31; R. D. Beetle and C. E. Wilder, in *Bull. Am. Math. Soc.,* Sept. 1932, with bibliog.; *Am. Math. Monthly,* June–July 1932; obituary in *Manchester Union* (Manchester, N. H.), Feb. 18, 1932.]
C. E. W.

YOUNG, JOSUE MARIA (Oct. 29, 1808– Sept. 18, 1866), Roman Catholic prelate, was born in Shapleigh, Me., to Jonathan Young, a graduate of Harvard, a Universalist, a farmer, and son of an English immigrant, and his wife, Mehetable Moody, daughter of William Pepperell Moody of Saco, Me., who boasted of descent from an ancestor who came from England in 1634 and founded a family prolific in teachers, Congregational ministers, and hardy tillers of a rugged soil. His name seems originally to have been Joshua Moody Young. He was trained in a country school and in Saco, Me., where he lived with his uncle, Sam Moody, a sturdy Congregationalist and small banker. Apprenticed in the shop of the *Eastern Argus* of Portland, he learned printing and soon undertook the publication of the *Maine Democrat* at Saco. There he developed a passion for reading and for re-

ligious argumentation with a Catholic co-worker and lifelong friend, John Crease, through whom he met Bishop Benedict J. Fenwick [*q.v.*] and the scholarly Father Charles D. French [*q.v.*] of Portland. In 1828 he joined the Catholic Church, into which eight brothers and sisters later followed him (William Byrne, *History of the Catholic Church in the New England States,* 1899, II, 495). At the time he changed his name to Josue Maria. In 1830 he went west for his health. As a wandering journeyman printer, he worked in Kentucky and in Ohio before settling down in Cincinnati, where he found employment on the *Catholic Telegraph* and spent his idle hours teaching Sunday school and in relief work among the poor. Urged by Bishop J. B. Purcell [*q.v.*], he studied for the priesthood at Mount St. Mary's Seminary, Emmitsburg, Md.

Ordained in 1838 (Lamott, *post,* p. 354) Father Young acted as a diocesan missionary, taught at St. Xavier's Academy in Cincinnati, and served zealously as pastor of St. Mary's Church in Lancaster, Ohio. Purcell admired this rigid, determined, energetic New Englander who was still a Puritan in character and outlook on life and apparently had Pope Pius IX name him for the diocese of Pittsburgh when Bishop Michael O'Connor [*q.v.*] selected the poorer see of Erie. He refused to accept, but when O'Connor was transferred back to Pittsburgh, he accepted the see of Erie and was consecrated on Apr. 23, 1854, at St. Peter's Cathedral, Cincinnati. During a tenure of a dozen years Young created a well-organized diocese, won the love of the Irish, who ordinarily resented a "foreign" bishop, built over a score of churches despite the unfavorable financial conditions of the Civil War period, increased his priesthood from fourteen to over fifty, gave St. Mary's Church in Erie to the Benedictines, promoted an academy and hospital of the St. Joseph nuns in Erie, and promoted academies at Corsica and Meadville.

[See R. H. Clarke, *Lives of the Deceased Bishops of the Cath. Church in the U. S.,* vol. II (1888); *Sadleir's Cath. Dir. Almanac,* 1867, p. 46; J. G. Shea, *Hist. of the Cath. Church in the U. S.,* vol. IV (1892); J. H. Lamott, *Hist. of the Archdiocese of Cincinnati* (1921); *N. Y. Freeman's Jour.,* Sept. 29, 1866.]
R. J. P.

YOUNG, LAFAYETTE (May 10, 1848–Nov. 15, 1926), newspaper editor and publisher, was born on a farm in Monroe County, Iowa, near Eddyville, one of the seven children of John and Rachel (Titus) Young. During the fifties his father operated a horse-power woolen mill at Albia, Iowa, and Lafayette worked in this mill as a small boy. When the mill burned, about 1861, he learned the printer's trade in the office of the *Albia Sentinel,* which was published by an older brother. By 1866 he was working for Mills & Company, largest Des Moines printers, for ten dollars a week. Thus he had little opportunity to attend school as a boy, but while working at the printer's trade in St. Louis in 1868–69 he attended night school. In 1870 he returned to Des Moines to become city editor of the *State Register,* and on Mar. 20 of that year married Josephine Bolton. The next year he established at Atlantic, Iowa, the *Atlantic Telegraph,* a weekly paper which he made a daily in December 1879. In 1873 he was elected to the state Senate, where he served by successive reëlections through 1880, and again from 1886 through 1888. As state senator he took a prominent part in the legislation fixing railroad freight and passenger rates. In March 1890 he purchased the *Des Moines Capital,* which he edited and published during the remainder of his life. He was an unsuccessful candidate for the Republican nomination for governor in 1893. In the next year he was elected state binder and held that office from 1895 to 1900. During the Spanish-American War he was with the army of William Rufus Shafter [*q.v.*] in Florida and in Cuba, as a newspaper correspondent, making the acquaintance of Theodore Roosevelt, which continued as a warm personal attachment, with frequent exchange of letters, to the end of Roosevelt's life. In 1900 he was delegate-at-large from Iowa to the Republican National Convention, and made the speech placing Roosevelt's name before the convention for vice-president. He was a guest of the Taft party on its trip of inspection of the Philippines in 1905, continuing his journey around the world. He had by this time gained a wide reputation as a public speaker and newspaper correspondent, and following this tour he delivered many lectures on Chautauqua and lyceum platforms. On the death of Senator Jonathan P. Dolliver [*q.v.*] in 1910, he was appointed to the vacancy, holding office until the election of W. S. Kenyon by the Iowa General Assembly, Apr. 12, 1911. In 1913 he served as newspaper correspondent in the Balkan states and for several months in 1915 was a war correspondent in Europe. For a short time he was held as a spy by the Austrian government. From May 1917 until the end of the war he served as chairman of the Iowa State Council of Defense.

In the later years of his life he was in great demand as a public speaker. His homely philosophy, sparkling epigrams, and ready humor made him one of the best of after-dinner speakers; and his wide acquaintance and extensive travel furnished materials both for speaking and for his editorials in the *Capital,* which were widely quoted. He had a good platform presence and a genial, friendly nature. He died in Des Moines, survived by his wife and two sons.

[The best short biog. is that in *Annals of Iowa,* Apr. 1927. See also *Who's Who in America,* 1926–27; *Biog. Dir. Am. Cong.* (1928); B. F. Gue, *Hist. of Iowa,* vol. IV (1903); Johnson Brigham, *Des Moines,* vol. II (1911); *Des Moines Capital,* Nov. 16–19, 1926; *Des Moines Reg.,* Nov. 16, 1926.]   F. L. M.

YOUNG, PIERCE MANNING BUTLER (Nov. 15, 1836–July 6, 1896), soldier, congressman from Georgia, was born in Spartanburg, S. C., the son of Robert Maxwell and Elizabeth Caroline (Jones) Young. His father practised medicine in Spartanburg and in 1839 removed to Cartersville, Ga. A delicate child, Young was tutored by his father and, then attending the Georgia Military Academy at Marietta, graduated in 1856. He began the study of law but in 1857 was appointed to the Military Academy at West Point, from which he resigned, with considerable misgivings, in March 1861 to enter the Confederate army. Commissioned second-lieutenant of artillery in April 1861, he was stationed at Pensacola. He was soon made first lieutenant and aide-de-camp to Gen. W. H. T. Walker, then was appointed adjutant of T. R. R. Cobb's legion, and, sent to Virginia, was promoted major in 1862 for gallantry in action. As lieutenant-colonel he commanded the cavalry of the legion under Wade Hampton in August 1862 and was wounded slightly at Burkittsville. He was again wounded at South Mountain and was promoted colonel. His gallantry under fire at Fleetwood, or Brandy Station, and Gettysburg won the commendation of his superiors. Wounded at the second engagement at Brandy Station, he was promoted brigadier-general in 1863, was given command of Hampton's brigade, and won the praise of Stuart. After recuperating from another wound received at Ashland, he was, in 1864, temporarily placed in command of Hampton's division, but later was sent to Georgia to raise reënforcements and to defend Augusta against Sherman. He was, in spite of General Wheeler's opposition, made major-general in December 1864 and served in Georgia and South Carolina to the end of the war.

After the war, he retired to his plantation, "Walnut Grove," near Cartersville, Ga. With courtly manners and great personal magnetism, an effective speaker, and almost universally beloved, he soon entered political life as a representative in Congress, from July 25, 1868, to Mar. 3, 1869. In the next Congress the House decided he had not been elected; but, elected to fill the vacancy thus caused, he took his seat and served from Dec. 22, 1870, to Mar. 3, 1871. Reelected twice he served until Mar. 3, 1875. He opposed the Radical measures, supported internal improvements, and was a member of the military affairs committee and the board of visitors of West Point. He was appointed a commissioner to the Paris Exposition in 1878. He was consul general to St. Petersburg, now Leningrad, from 1885 to 1887, when he resigned because of lack of health. He was appointed minister to Guatemala and Honduras in 1893, when he obtained an apology from both Honduras and Costa Rica for interfering with the rights of United States citizens. On the whole he developed friendly feelings and commercial relations with the Central American States. Because of failing health he left his post in 1896 to return home, but he died in New York at the Presbyterian Hospital. Commander of the Georgia division of United Confederate Veterans, his funeral was conducted at Cartersville, Ga., by that and the Masonic order. He was buried in Oak Hill cemetery there. He never married.

[Files of the Joint Committee on Printing, Washington, D. C., esp. nephew's statement of birthdate from family Bible; scrapbook in possession of family; *Confederate Military Hist.* (1899), vol. VI, ed. by C. A. Evans; C. E. Jones, *Ga. in the War* (copr. 1909); W. J. Northen, *Men of Mark in Ga.*, vol. III (1911); *War of the Rebellion: Official Records* (Army); *Southern Hist. Soc. Papers*, vol. XXV (1897); *Courant Am.* (Cartersville, Ga.), July 9, 16, 23, 1896.]   F. M. G.

YOUNG, SAMUEL HALL (Sept. 12, 1847–Sept. 2, 1927), missionary to Alaska, was born at Butler, Pa. His father, Loyal Young, a Presbyterian minister, was of Massachusetts ancestry while his mother, Margaret (Johnston) Young, was of Scotch-Irish stock. After a schooling irregular because of physical weakness and the necessity of teaching from time to time for his support, Young graduated in 1875 from the College of Wooster, Ohio. He studied for one year in Princeton Theological Seminary and for two years in Western Seminary, Allegheny, Pa., where he graduated in 1878. The appeal of Sheldon Jackson [q.v.] moved him to offer himself to the Presbyterian Board of Home Missions for service in Alaska, when only one American missionary was there. Ordained by the Presbytery of West Virginia in June 1878, he reached Fort Wrangell in July and began work among the Stickeen Indians. On Dec. 15, at Sitka, he married Fannie E. Kellogg, who had gone there as a missionary shortly before his arrival. In August 1879 he organized at Fort Wrangell the first Protestant and first American church in Alaska. With John Muir [q.v.], who in this year came to Alaska for the first time, he explored Glacier Bay and discovered the Muir Glacier. The next year they traveled and mapped an in-

side route to Sitka. Muir gave to a glacier in Endicott Arm the name "Young." As organizer and secretary of the first territorial convention in 1881 Young drafted a memorial to Congress asking for better government. During 1882–83 he spoke extensively in the United States for Alaskan missions and also followed up the memorial, which resulted in the act of Congress of 1884 establishing the district of Alaska and providing civil officers and schools. By 1888, when Young resigned his place at Fort Wrangell, Christian missionary work was proceeding in all the principal tribes of southern Alaska, largely because of his initiative.

During 1889–92 Young served churches in Long Beach and Wilmington, Cal., and in and near Chicago. From 1892 to 1895 he was pastor of the Presbyterian Church of Cedar Falls, Iowa, and then became instructor in Biblical history and pastor of the college church at Wooster. Called back to Alaska by the Klondike gold rush, he spent the winter of 1897–98 at Dawson, gaining strong influence among the miners and organizing a church. In the spring of 1899 he settled at Nome, where he devoted himself chiefly to caring for typhoid sufferers, almost died himself of the fever, and finally established a church. In 1901, after a winter at Ithaca, N. Y., he returned to Alaska as general missionary of his board. Another winter at home was followed by eight years in Alaska—four passed at Fairbanks (1904–08) and two at Cordova. In 1910 he was recalled to the New York office of the board, but the next year, then sixty-four, he went to isolated mining camps beyond the Yukon, staying until 1913. From that year to 1921 he was on the staff of the board as special representative for Alaska. As secretary for Alaska of the Home Missions Council he assigned fields to the denominations, envisaging a "United Evangelical Church of Alaska." Thither he went again in 1921, as general missionary to reorganize all the Presbyterian work. Retiring in 1924, he lived at Bellevue, Wash. During a visit in West Virginia he was killed by a trolley-car near Clarksburg. His wife had died in 1915; they left three daughters.

Young published some verse and four volumes of prose—*Alaska Days with John Muir* (1915), *The Klondike Clan* (copr. 1916), *Adventures in Alaska* (1919), and (posthumously) *Hall Young of Alaska* (copr. 1927), an autobiography. He was a man of inexhaustible energy, vitality, humor, and devotion.

[Young's writings; *Gen. Biog. Cat. Western Theol. Sem. of the Presbyt. Ch., 1827–1927*; *Who's Who in America*, 1926–27; *N. Y. Times*, Sept. 4, 1927; manuscript records Presbyt. Board National Missions.]   R. H. N.

YOUNG, THOMAS (Feb. 19, 1731/32–June 24, 1777), patriot, physician, was born in New Windsor, Ulster County, N. Y., the son of John and Mary (Crawford) Young. His father came to New York in 1729 with his kinsman, Charles Clinton, father of James Clinton [q.v.]. Thomas Young attended a local school, borrowed books from Colonel Clinton, and acquired an understanding of French, Latin, and Greek, with a speaking knowledge of German and Dutch. In 1753 he began the practice of medicine in Amenia, Dutchess County, N. Y., and his fame spread during the next decade through eleven counties. He advocated the use of calomel in certain cases when other members of his profession did not dare use it (Benjamin Rush, *Medical Inquiries and Observations,* 2nd ed., 1805, III, 230, 252) and was especially successful in treating smallpox. He married Mary, daughter of Capt. Garret Winegar, and they had two sons and four daughters. Young, who was a deist, is said to have collaborated with Ethan Allen [q.v.] in writing *Reason the Only Oracle of Man, or a Compendious System of Natural Religion* (1784); the text is certainly not like any of Allen's other writings. Young was also the author of an epic poem of 608 lines—*A Poem Sacred to the Memory of James Wolfe ... Who Was Slain upon the Plains of Abraham ... September 13, 1759*—vividly describing Wolfe's siege of Quebec. Copies of this rare pamphlet, which was published anonymously in 1761, are owned by the New York Historical Society, Yale University, and Brown University.

About 1760 Young purchased of a Dutch trader, John Henry Lydius, a tract of land in what is now Vermont. The title, which rested on Indian deeds, proved to be tainted with fraud and after prolonged litigation Young was left almost penniless. In 1764, over the signature "Philodicaius," he published *Some Reflections on the Disputes between New-York, New-Hampshire, and Col. John Henry Lydius,* a small pamphlet in defense of the Lydius claims. In the same year he moved to Albany and two years later, to Boston, where he was a neighbor and friend of Dr. Joseph Warren [q.v.]. In 1774–75 he contributed articles on medical topics to the *Royal American Magazine.*

In Albany he had actively opposed the operation of the Stamp Act. In Boston for seven years he was known as one of the "lesser incendiaries." Once he was nearly assassinated by his political enemies. He had a large personal following at town meetings and was the first president of the North End Caucus. On Mar. 5, 1771, he delivered the first of the annual orations commemo-

rative of the Boston Massacre. Next to Samuel Adams, he was the most active member of the Boston Committee of Correspondence. He spoke at Old South Meeting House, Dec. 16, 1773, a few hours before the tea was thrown overboard into Boston Harbor, and then without disguise helped to destroy the tea.

The British having closed the port of Boston to commerce, in September 1774 Young took his wife and children to Newport, R. I. There he labored in the patriot group until April 1775, when friends detected a plot to kidnap him and take him to England to be tried for treason. He escaped to Philadelphia; his family rejoined him, and he practised in that city. He soon became secretary of the Whig Society and associated with the small group of radical leaders who with the counsel of Benjamin Franklin framed the constitution of Pennsylvania. When in the spring of 1777 delegates from the New Hampshire Grants appeared in Philadelphia and sought to persuade Congress to recognize that district as a state, Young was a helpful adviser to the visitors. He suggested for the new state the name "Vermont," making the first known use of the title in a public letter dated Apr. 17, 1777 (*Records ... of Vermont, post,* I, 394–95). The Pennsylvania constitution, a copy of which Young supplied to the petitioners, became the basis of the constitution of Vermont. Congress, influenced by its New York members, in the week after he died passed a vote of censure on him for his diligence in behalf of the independence of Vermont.

Under the direction of Dr. Benjamin Rush, Young was a senior surgeon in one of the Continental hospitals in Philadelphia, and while caring for wounded and sick soldiers contracted a virulent type of fever, of which, after only a day's illness, he died. He left almost no property and his wife had to be aided by Philadelphia friends, and later by his brother, Dr. Joseph Young, a noteworthy New York patriot. In 1785 and 1786 Ethan Allen and Gov. Thomas Chittenden made a futile effort to persuade the Vermont Assembly to make a land grant to Young's widow, then in great need, in recognition of his services to the state.

[A biography of Young is in preparation by the writer of this sketch. See J. S. Loring, *The Hundred Boston Orators* (1852); *Records of the Council of Safety and Gov. and Council of the State of Vt.,* vol. I (1873); *Pa. Mag. of Hist. and Biog.,* Oct. 1898; Hiland Hall, *The Hist. of Vt.* (1868); Zadock Thompson, *Hist. of Vt.* (1853), pt. 2, pp. 51, 106; A. M. Hemenway, *The Vt. Hist. Gazetteer,* I (1868), 568; I. Q. Leake, *Memoir of the Life and Times of Gen. John Lamb* (1850); F. S. Drake, *Tea Leaves* (1884); John Pell, *Ethan Allen* (1929). The longest account, H. H. Edes, "Memoir of Dr. Thomas Young," in *Colonial Soc. of Mass. Pubs.* vol. XI (1910), although it uses a sketch of Young by

his brother, Dr. Joseph Young, contains a number of errors.]
            G. P. A.

YOUNGER, THOMAS COLEMAN (Jan. 15, 1844–Mar. 21, 1916), desperado, better known as "Cole" Younger, was born near Lee's Summit, Jackson County, Mo., the son of Col. Henry Washington and Busheba (Fristoe) Younger. He seems to have had some education, since in his later years he was an avid reader of history and theology and he spoke and wrote with grammatical correctness. Though his father was a Unionist, his own sympathies were Southern, and at seventeen he became a Confederate guerrilla, serving under Quantrill and Anderson. Later he joined Gen. Joseph O. Shelby's "Iron Brigade," and became a captain. His service with the Confederates brought suspicion upon his family, who were often harassed by militia and irregulars, and on July 20, 1862, his father was robbed and murdered by a company of "Jayhawkers." After the war he declined to settle down but chose instead the career of a freebooter. It is probable that with Frank James he organized the group that became, under the reputed leadership of Jesse James [q.v.], the most noted band of brigands in American history. Tall, powerful, and of commanding appearance, of great native intelligence, and of imperturbable coolness and presence of mind, he may well have been quite as influential in the counsels of the company as was its ostensible leader. Informed opinion connects him with virtually all the spectacular bank robberies and train holdups of the first ten years of the band's history. One brother, James, was usually with him; another, Robert, on at least two occasions, and a third, John, was but beginning his apprenticeship when he was shot to death, Mar. 16, 1874.

With his remaining brothers, the Jameses, and three others, Younger participated in the disastrous attempt to rob the bank at Northfield, Minn., Sept. 7, 1876, in which two citizens were murdered. Three of the brigands were killed, the James brothers escaped, and the three Youngers were shot down and captured. At their trial, in November, they pleaded guilty and were sentenced to life imprisonment. Six years later a Confederate veteran of Missouri, Capt. W. C. Bronaugh, began a campaign for their release on the alleged ground that they were not criminals at heart but victims of the Civil War who had been driven into crime by persecution. Their good conduct as prisoners helped their case, and the movement gained many adherents. On July 10, 1901, the two surviving brothers (Robert had died in 1889), were paroled by the Minnesota Board of Pardons, on condition they would not leave the state. A year later James committed suicide because of a love affair. Early in 1903 Cole Younger was pardoned, and he at once returned to Missouri. For a time he lectured, at another time was with Frank James in a Wild West exhibition, and later employed himself in various ways. His conduct as a citizen won the commendation of all who knew him. He died near his birthplace, after a year's illness.

[The most reliable material appears in Robertus Love, *The Rise and Fall of Jesse James* (1926) and W. C. Bronaugh, *The Youngers' Fight for Freedom* (1906). See also A. C. Appler, *The Guerrillas of the West, or the Life, Character, and Daring Exploits of the Younger Brothers* (1876); *The Story of Cole Younger, by Himself* (1903); W. C. Heilbron, *Convict Life at the Minn. State Prison* (1909), containing a sketch of the Northfield robbery by Cole Younger; *St. Louis Globe Democrat,* Mar. 22, 1916.] W. J. G.

YOUNGS, JOHN (April 1623–Apr. 12, 1698), Colonial soldier and official, was born in Southwold, England, and baptized Apr. 10, 1623. The eldest son of the Rev. John and Joan (Herrington) Youngs, he came to Salem, Mass., with his parents, May 11, 1637, and removed with them about three years later to Long Island. The father was leader of the group that settled Southold and built there the first Christian church in Long Island. The son is first heard of as master of a bark operating between the colonies on the mainland and the island. In 1653 he visited several Connecticut towns seeking aid in raising a force to drive the Dutch from New Amsterdam. His mission unsuccessful, he came into conflict with the authorities as a result of his criticism of affairs in Southold and New Haven. The matter was soon adjusted, and from 1654 to 1656, under orders of the colonies, he commanded a patrol in the Sound to prevent the operations of hostile Indians. About 1653 he married Mary Gardner, daughter of his father's third wife; she bore him five children and died in 1689. Some two years later he married Mrs. Hannah Tooker, the thrice-widowed daughter of Barnabas Wines.

In 1660 he was appointed deputy from Southold to New Haven, and magistrate. He strongly favored the union of Long Island with Connecticut, and on Oct. 19, 1662, appeared at Hartford to urge the inclusion of this union in the new charter of Connecticut. Eight days later, at Hempstead, he proclaimed the complete jurisdiction of Connecticut in the towns of Long Island. This action was protested by Petrus Stuyvesant [q.v.] in letters to Gov. John Winthrop, Jr. (*Documents, post,* XIV, 518), but during the following year Youngs commanded the Southold militia and a troop of horse in an attack on

Flushing, and on May 12, 1664, he became a member of Winthrop's council. During the summer he resumed command of the militia and aided in the capture of New Amsterdam, a service that received special recognition from Gov. Richard Nicolls [q.v.]. On Mar. 1, 1665, he represented Southold at an assembly in Hempstead where Long Island, Staten Island, and Westchester were combined to form Yorkshire, and the laws of the Duke of York were promulgated.

Although Youngs was a strong partisan of the English against the Dutch, he preferred the Puritan rule of Connecticut to that of York's agents, and he led a protest against the Duke's laws. When, in 1673, the Dutch retook New York, Southold and neighboring towns, under Youngs's leadership, rejoined Connecticut. They continued this union after the English regained control; in a letter to Gov. Edmund Andros [q.v.], Youngs and two others justified the action on the ground that during the Dutch attack they had received help only from Connecticut. Youngs finally gave way, however, and on Oct. 31, 1676, Southold accepted a patent from the Duke of York with Youngs and six others as patentees. He served as high sheriff of Yorkshire from 1680 to 1683. On June 29, 1681, he was designated to draw a petition to the Duke of York for a representative assembly in the Colony. The petition was granted and the Assembly held its first meeting in New York on Oct. 17, 1683. Later in the year Youngs was one of the commissioners to determine the boundary between New York and Connecticut. His military record was recognized in his appointment as lieutenant-colonel of horse of Suffolk in 1686, and as colonel of Suffolk County militia in 1689. Named a member of the council to Governor Dongan in 1686, he began twelve years of service in this high office, being appointed to the councils to Governors Sloughter, Fletcher, and Bellomont. In 1691 he was one of the judges who convicted Jacob Leisler [q.v.] of treason for usurpation of the governorship. At his death Youngs was a leading citizen and official of the New York colony. His independence and courage had brought to a larger field the qualities of a father who braved the wilderness rather than submit to the tyranny of conscience imposed by Laud.

[Selah Youngs, Jr., Youngs Family (1907); Berthold Fernow, Docs. Rel. to the Colonial Hist. of the State of N. Y., vol. XIV (1883); Martha B. Flint, Early Long Island (1896); Benjamin Trumbull, A Complete Hist. of Conn. (1818); J. H. Trumbull, The Pub. Records of the Colony of Conn., vols. I, II (1850–52); Epher Whitaker, Hist. of Southold, L. I. (1881).]
D. A. R.

YOUNT, GEORGE CONCEPCÍON (May 4, 1794–Oct. 5, 1865), trapper, California pioneer, was born on Dowden Creek, Burke County, N. C., one of eleven children. His father, Jacob Yount, had served under Gen. Nathanael Greene [q.v.] at the siege of Charles Town, S. C. In 1804 the family moved to Cape Girardeau, Mo. The father and five sons, including George, took part in guarding the settlements against Indians during the War of 1812. In 1818 George married Eliza Cambridge Wilds, daughter of a well-to-do settler from Kentucky, began the development of a farm in Howard County, Mo., and set himself up as a cattleman. For a time he prospered, but the embezzlement of his savings by a trusted neighbor left him impoverished. In the fall of 1825, making what provision he could for his wife and two children, he joined an expedition to Santa Fé. He soon became a trapper, and under Ewing Young [q.v.] took part in several expeditions. In 1827 he organized a party to trap the Arizona rivers, but at the mouth of the Gila, Sylvester Pattie, James Ohio Pattie [q.v.], and six followers seceded, and Yount and the others returned. With another company, in the winter of 1828–29, he journeyed northward to the trapper rendezvous at Bear Lake and for the next two years trapped the northern country. The name Yount's Peak, given to the mountain at the source of the Yellowstone, commemorates his activities in that region.

About this time he met Jedediah Strong Smith [q.v.], just returned from a tragic adventure in California, and what he heard Smith tell of that strange land determined him to see it for himself. Returning to New Mexico, he joined the Pacific-bound expedition of William Wolfskill [q.v.], which left Taos at the end of September 1830 and arrived in Los Angeles in the following February. Up and down the coast he worked at various tasks, after a time finding a measure of success as a carpenter and shingle maker. In 1834 he journeyed farther north, and at the missions of San Rafael and Sonoma found employment. In the following year he joined the Roman Catholic Church at the time adding Concepcíon to his name—and became a Mexican citizen. He then selected a broad and beautiful tract in the still unsettled Napa Valley and applied for a grant. Gen. M. G. Vallejo [q.v.] befriended him, and in the spring of 1836, three years before John A. Sutter [q.v.] settled at Sacramento, he established himself as the lord of Caymus Rancho and the guardian of the northern frontier against the wild Indians. Employing Christianized Indians as laborers, he built a fort and began the cultivation of his grounds. After the arrival of the first American emigrant company in 1841, he sent for his family. His wife, supposing him dead, had remarried, but his two daughters, one of whom had been born after his departure, joined him early in 1844. After the conquest the influx of settlers caused him heavy losses, but by 1855 he had recovered much of his property. In the same year he married a Mrs. Gashwiler, a woman of cultivation and charm. At his hospitable residence many visitors were entertained, and his later days were passed in serene contentment. He died at his home. Nominally a Catholic, he was also a Mason; he was buried with full Masonic honors; an Episcopalian minister preached his funeral sermon, and his will provided for the erection of a church to be used by all denominations.

[C. L. Camp, "The Chronicles of George C. Yount," *Cal. Hist. Soc. Quart.*, Apr. 1923, with bibliog.; J. L. Ver Mehr, *Checkered Life in the Old and New World* (1877); Elizabeth A. Watson, *Sketch of the Life of George C. Yount* (privately printed, 1915?); information from F. P. Farquhar, Esq., San Francisco.]

W. J. G.

YULEE, DAVID LEVY (June 12, 1810–Oct. 10, 1886), railroad promoter, senator from Florida, was born in St. Thomas, West Indies. His grandfather, of Portuguese extraction, was an official in Morocco, to whom the name Yulee is said to have been given as a Moorish title. Fleeing from Morocco as the result of a revolution, with his wife, an English Jewess whose maiden name was Levy, he took refuge in England, where his son took the name of Moses Elias Levy, received a university education, went into trade, and ultimately removed to Puerto Rico. Later he became a lumberman in St. Thomas, made a fortune, and obtained from the Spanish large tracts of land in central and east Florida. At nine years of age David Levy was sent to Norfolk, Va., to a preparatory school, where he remained for six years until compelled to leave by the refusal of his father, who had become a religious socialist, to contribute further to his support. He then went to live with an overseer on one of his father's plantations in Florida at Micanopy. He later studied law in St. Augustine in the office of Robert R. Reid, later territorial governor of Florida. He was admitted to the bar in 1836.

He was a delegate to the Florida constitutional convention at St. Joseph in 1838, in 1841 was chosen as a Republican for territorial delegate to Congress, and was senator for the newly admitted state of Florida from July 1, 1845, to Mar. 3, 1851. It was at this time, on Jan. 12, 1846, that by special act of the Florida legislature his name was changed to David Levy Yulee. In 1846 he married a daughter of Charles A. Wick-

liffe [*q.v.*] of Kentucky, who died in 1884. He was defeated for reëlection, but in 1855 he was again elected senator, and served from Mar. 4, 1855, until his resignation, on Jan. 21, 1861, following the secession of Florida. His most important work in the Senate was done as chairman of the committee on naval affairs and on post offices and post roads. He advocated the building of iron ships and the adoption of cheap ocean postal rates. In his first term he was one of the leaders of the Southern movement of 1848–50 and was a member of the caucus committee to draw up the Address to the Southern People. He opposed the admission of California as a free state and was an advocate of secession in 1850. It was his prominence in the Southern movement that brought about his defeat for reëlection. However, he was much more conservative in 1860, the change being due, perhaps, to his increasing railroad holdings. He had been one of the earliest railroad promoters in the South and while territorial delegate had obtained an appropriation for a railroad survey of Florida. In 1853 he had incorporated the Atlantic & Gulf Railroad, which, after many difficulties, he brought to completion in 1860, connecting Fernandina on the Atlantic with Cedar Keys on the Gulf. He supported Douglas for the Democratic nomination in 1860 but broke with him over the question of secession. Upon the secession of Florida he actively urged the immediate seizure of United States forts within the state. During the war he devoted his energies to his plantation and to the running of his railroad, engaging in a spirited, and successful, altercation with the Confederate authorities who wished to use its material for the repair of more vital lines. At the close of the war he was imprisoned at Fort Pulaski until released on the intervention of Grant. The following years he devoted to his railroad, then in ruins, finally sold it to English capitalists, and in 1880 went to live in Washington where a married daughter was living. He died in New York, survived by a son and by several daughters. He was buried from the New York Avenue Presbyterian Church in Washington of whose congregation he was a member.

[Information, esp. date of birth from statement of daughter, Mrs. Wm. Belden Noble, Washington, D. C., in files of Joint Committee on Printing, Washington, D. C.; C. W. Yulee, "Senator Yulee of Florida," *Fla. Hist. Soc. Pubs.*, Apr.–July 1909, a filial biog.; H. G. Cutler, *A Hist. of Fla.* (1923), vols. I, II; *War of the Rebellion: Official Records* (*Army*), 1 ser., vol. I; *National Republican* (Washington, D. C., Oct. 11, 1886.]

R. S. C.

YUNG WING (Nov. 17, 1828–Apr. 21, 1912), educator, diplomat, Chinese official, promoter, reformer, was born in the village of Nam Ping, on Pedro Island, about four miles southwest of Macao, in South China, the son of Yung Ming-kun and Lin Lien-tai. At the age of seven his parents placed him in a school which had recently been opened in Macao by Mrs. Karl Gütz-laff, the aunt of Sir Harry Parkes and the wife of one of the earliest Protestant missionaries to China. The school broke up before he had acquired more than a smattering of English, and, after various vicissitudes, at the age of thirteen he entered a school at Hongkong maintained by the Morrison Education Society and taught by Samuel Robbins Brown [q.v.]. When in 1847 Brown returned to the United States, he was able, through the generosity of friends, to take Yung Wing and two other Chinese with him. Yung was placed in Monson Academy, in Massachusetts. Upon finishing there, he entered Yale in 1850 and graduated in 1854, the first Chinese alumnus of an American college. In the course of his contact with missionaries, he had espoused the Christian faith, and while in America he had become a naturalized citizen of the United States. He had, moreover, forgotten most of his mother tongue. However, he had formed the purpose of making possible for Chinese youth the kind of Western education which had been his. He wished in this and in other ways to assist China, then only slowly and reluctantly opening its doors to the Western world, to make the adjustment to the Occident which he saw to be inevitable. He therefore returned to China very soon after graduation. It was long before he could gain the ear of Chinese officialdom, and for several years he engaged in a variety of pursuits which seemed to bring him no nearer his goal. In 1863, however, he entered the service of Tsêng Kuo-fan, the most prominent Chinese of the day. Sent to the United States by his patron, he purchased machinery for making modern arms, and had it installed in Shanghai, the inception of the Kiangnan Arsenal; later he persuaded his patron to start a school of mechanical engineering. Through official contacts thus begun, he was able to realize his long-cherished dream of placing Chinese youths in the United States for education. At his suggestion the Chinese government in 1870 created the Chinese Educational Commission. He was placed in charge as one of the two commissioners, and between 1872 and 1875 one hundred and twenty Chinese boys were sent to the United States. In 1881, because of the fears of some of the conservatives that they were becoming denationalized, the students were recalled and the Commission came to an end.

During his years in America with the Commission, Yung married (Feb. 24, 1875) Mary Louise Kellogg, served as assistant to the Chinese minister (1878–81), and went on an official mission to report on the condition of Chinese coolies in Peru. From 1881 to 1883 he was in China. He then returned to the United States and did not again go to China until 1895, when the defeat of China by Japan once more made reform possible. He was summoned to China at the instance of the progressive viceroy, Chang Chih-tung, and for a few months he was in his service. In 1897 and 1898 he obtained a concession for a railway from Tientsin to Chinkiang, and contracted with an American firm for a loan to build it. The object failed, however—in part because of German opposition. With the coming into power of the reactionaries, he fled (1899) to Hongkong and was there most of the time until 1902. He then returned to the United States and resided in Hartford until his death. He was survived by his two sons. His autobiography, *My Life in China and America*, was published in New York in 1909.

[In addition to Yung's *My Life in China and America* (1909), see *Who's Who in America*, 1912–13; *Obit. Record Yale Grads.*, 1911–12; H. B. Morse, *The Internat. Relations of the Chinese Empire* (3 vols., 1918), for background; *Yale Alumni Weekly*, May 3, 1912; A. G. Robinson, in *Peking and Tientsin Sunday Times*, July 23, 1933; obituary in *Hartford Courant*, Apr. 22, 1912.]

K. S. L.

ZACH, MAX WILHELM (Aug. 31, 1864–Feb. 3, 1921), orchestral conductor, composer, was born in Lemberg, Galicia, the son of Heinrich and Julia (Deim) Zach. He received his education in the lower and middle schools of Lemberg and Vienna. His early music instructors were Czerwinski in piano and Bruckmann in violin. At the age of sixteen, he entered the Vienna Conservatory of Music, and studied piano under Joseph Edler, violin under Siegmund Bachrich and Jakob M. Grün, harmony under Robert Fuchs, and counterpoint and composition under Franz Krenn. Compulsory military service claimed him at nineteen. He entered the Austrian army as a musician, and served three years in the band of the 31st Regiment. He attained the rank of sergeant, was solo violinist in the regimental orchestra, and on occasion acted as conductor. Through routine scoring of music for military band, he acquired a wide knowledge of instrumentation and an astonishing facility in score reading.

In the summer of 1886 Wilhelm Gericke [q.v.] visited Vienna in search of new talent for the Boston Symphony Orchestra. His attention was directed to the gifted young Galician violinist, and he promptly engaged him. For twenty-one seasons (1886–1907) Zach played viola in the Boston Symphony, serving under Wilhelm Gericke, Arthur Nikisch, Emil Paur, and Karl Muck. He became a member of the Adamowski String Quartette in 1890 and served as violist of that notable organization until it disbanded in 1906. He had from time to time composed marches and waltzes in the "Viennese" style: "Harlequin en Voyage"; "Waldgeist"; "Oriental March"; "Austria March"; "Military March"; and "Hussar Drill March." These were performed by the Boston orchestra under his baton so successfully that he was placed on the staff of "Pop" conductors and served (often in alternation with others) during the seasons 1895–1902 and 1905–07. He organized a miniature symphony orchestra and for several summers conducted series of concerts at Keith's Theatre in Boston. During the summer of 1904 he conducted the Boston Band at the Louisiana Purchase Exposition in St. Louis.

In 1907 the St. Louis Choral-Symphony Society engaged him to conduct the St. Louis Symphony Orchestra, then about to begin its twenty-eighth season. He found in St. Louis an orchestra capable enough but absolutely lacking in discipline. Zach's apprenticeship under Gericke stood him in good stead. He was a leader with dignity and restraint, and he subjected each section of the orchestra to a tremendous amount of strenuous training, and ultimately developed a perfection of ensemble and a flexibility of interpretive power that made the St. Louis Symphony Orchestra one of the half-dozen great American orchestras. Through annual tours of the Southwest, the influence of the orchestra was markedly increased. Zach was a skilful program builder. While presenting the classical masters most effectively (he gave St. Louis its first "Beethoven Cycle" in 1910), he enlarged the repertoire of the orchestra by the performance of modern works of all schools. His persistent advocacy of the American composer constitutes his most significant contribution to American musical progress. During the fourteen seasons of his leadership, he produced forty-five symphonic compositions of major importance by twenty-six American composers. The very last concert that he conducted, featured the works of Leo Sowerby, the young Chicago composer. Twelve days later, septic pneumonia terminated his career. He was buried at Forest Hills, Mass. Zach's cultural interests were broad, and he was an able linguist and a brilliant conversationalist. He was married to Blanche Going of Boston, Mass., July 4, 1891. They had four children.

[Personal data from Leon Henry Zach of Boston and Eleanor Zach Webster of Palmyra, N. Y.; *Who's Who in America*, 1920–21; M. A. DeWolfe Howe, *Boston Symphony Orchestra* (rev. ed. 1931); E. C. Krohn, "The Development of the Symphony Orchestra in St. Louis," in *Papers and Proc. of the Music Teachers' Nat. Asso.*, 1924; *Internat. Who's Who in Music*, 1918; Carl Engel, "Max Zach As He Worked and Lived," *Boston Evening Transcript*, Feb. 5, 1921; death notice, *Ibid.*, Feb. 3, 4, 1921; *St. Louis Post-Dispatch*, Feb. 3, 1921.]   E. C. K—n.

ZACHOS, JOHN CELIVERGOS (Dec. 20, 1820–Mar. 20, 1898), educator, Unitarian clergyman, author, and inventor, was born in Constantinople, the son of Nicholas and Euphrosyne Zachos, natives of Athens. The father, a general in the Greek army during the Grecian Revolution, died in 1824 in battle. In 1830, Zachos was brought to America by Dr. Samuel Gridley Howe [q.v.]. He attended preparatory school at Amherst, Mass., and in 1836 entered Kenyon College, Gambier, Ohio, where he was graduated B.A. with honors in June 1840 and delivered the Greek oration for his class. From 1842 to 1845 he studied at the Medical School of Miami University, in Oxford, Ohio, but did not take a degree. On July 26, 1849, he married Harriet Tomkins Canfield, by whom he had six children. He was associate principal (1851–54) of the Cooper Female Seminary, at Dayton, Ohio, one of the editors (1852–53) of the *Ohio Journal of Education*, and principal (1854–57) of the Grammar School of Antioch College, Yellow Springs, Ohio. In this latter position, which also involved the teaching of literature, he was associated with Horace Mann [q.v.].

At the outbreak of the Civil War, Zachos joined the Union army as assistant surgeon, enlisting under Gen. Rufus Saxton, and was stationed at Parris Island, Port Royal, S. C., being practically governor of the island. He had studied theology privately for some time, and when the war ended he was ordained pastor of the Unitarian church in West Newton, Mass. In 1866–67 he was pastor of the Unitarian church at Meadville, Pa., and professor of rhetoric at the Meadville Theological School. From 1871 until his death he made his home in New York City. There he taught literature and oratory at Cooper Union, which he also served as curator.

Especially interested in spoken English, Zachos produced several textbooks in elocution and oratory, including *The New American Speaker* (1851), *Analytic Elocution* (1861), *A New System of Phonic Reading without Changing the Orthography* (1863), *The Phonic Primer and Reader* (1864), and *The Phonic Text* (1865), "A Method of Teaching Reading by the Signs of Sound without Altering the Orthography of the

Language or Introducing any New Letters." In 1876, he patented a machine for printing a legible English text at a high reporting speed, having the types fixed in eighteen shuttle bars of which two or more might be placed in position simultaneously, the impression being given by a common plunger. He patented improvements on this device in 1883 and 1886.

In 1876 Zachos published *A Sketch of the Life and Opinions of Mr. Peter Cooper,* which is still an important source, and in the following year edited *The Political and Financial Opinions of Peter Cooper, with an Autobiography of his Early Life.* Under the name "Cadmus," he wrote *Our Financial Revolution: An Address to the Merchants and Professional Men of the Country, without Respect to Parties* (1878), which Peter Cooper [q.v.] commended to the "careful perusal of every lover of his country," and *The Fiscal Problem of All Civilized Nations* (1881). With firm faith in democracy and education, he ardently believed that the privileges of both should be extended to all, regardless of color, race, or creed. This spirit is evident in his *Phonic Primer and Reader* of 1864, "Designed Chiefly for the Use of Night-Schools Where Adults are Taught, and for the Myriads of Freed Men and Women, Whose First Rush from the Prison-House of Slavery is to the Gates of the Temple of Knowledge." At the time of its publication there was considerable discussion throughout the country concerning the educability of the negro. With a series of tests drawn up by an organization in Boston to determine the question experimentally, Zachos demonstrated that negroes were capable of benefiting by instruction. In the early sixties this was more than an academic question, and Zachos' stand is a tribute to his courage. He died at his home in New York City and was buried in Boston; three of his children survived him.

[Private sources; records of institutions with which Zachos was connected; *The Antiochian,* July 1874, July 1879; F. A. Canfield, *A Hist. of Thomas Canfield . . . with a Geneal.* (1897); *Cooper Union . . . Thirty-ninth Ann. Report . . . 1898* (n.d.); *Appletons' Ann. Cyc. . . . 1898* (1899), p. 581; *N. Y. Daily Tribune, Sun* (N. Y.), and *N. Y. Times,* Mar. 21, 1898.] H.S.R.

ZAHM, JOHN AUGUSTINE (Sept. 14, 1851–Nov. 10, 1921), Roman Catholic priest, provincial of the Congregation of the Holy Cross, Notre Dame, Ind., was born at New Lexington, Ohio, the son of Jacob Michael Zahm, a native of Alsace, and of Mary Ellen Braddock of Loretto, Pa. He attended the primary school at New Lexington, but in 1863 the family moved to Huntington, Ind., and from 1863 to 1867 John Augustine studied in public and parochial schools of that place. He entered the University of Notre Dame on Dec. 3, 1867, where he won distinction for scholarship and received the degree of bachelor of science in 1871—one of a class of three. After his graduation he entered the Congregation of the Holy Cross on Sept. 17, 1871. During the years following, up to 1875, he pursued ecclesiastical studies in the seminary at Notre Dame besides teaching in the University. He was ordained a priest at the completion of his studies on June 4, 1875.

His activities for the next thirty years included educational service as a teacher, a lecturer, and an organizer of the Western Catholic Summer School, and administrative service as procurator general of the Congregation of the Holy Cross at Rome, 1896–98, and as provincial, 1898–1905. From 1905 until his death he was occupied chiefly as a writer on scientific subjects and on lands and peoples. He was a contributor to the *American Ecclesiastical Review,* the *Dublin Review,* the *Outlook,* and other periodicals. Among his scientific and theological books may be mentioned: *Sound and Music* (1892), *Catholic Science and Catholic Scientists* (1893), *Bible, Science and Faith* (1894), *Evolution and Dogma* (1896), *Science and the Church* (1896). As a result of two journeys to South America he produced in succession four volumes which are authoritative texts on the history and progress of the South American republics. The first of these, *Up the Orinoco and down the Magdalena* (1910), was followed shortly by *Along the Andes and down the Amazon* (1911), published under the pseudonym J. H. Mozans, with an introduction by Theodore Roosevelt. In 1916, *Through South America's Southland* appeared, as a result of the expedition of former President Roosevelt into South America. This expedition was made at the suggestion of Zahm and he was a member of it. The fourth South American volume, *The Quest of El Dorado,* appeared in 1917. Two other books, *Woman in Science* (1913), published under the pseudonym J. H. Mozans, and *Great Inspirers* (1917), are concerned, the first with the achievements of women in the physical sciences, the second with Paula and her companions as the inspiration of St. Jerome and Beatrice as the inspiration of Dante. In 1921 Zahm set out on what he announced would be his last journey, planning to recheck a completed manuscript which was published posthumously as *From Berlin to Bagdad to Babylon* (1922). He got no farther than Munich, where he was stricken with pneumonia and died. He was buried at Notre Dame, Ind.

Zahm was a prodigious worker. In person he

was of medium height, well fleshed, his face normally serious; to all but those who knew him well he seemed remote and cold. Among his friends he counted Pope Leo XIII, the Cardinals Vannutelli, Archbishop Ireland, Cardinal Gibbons, Former President Theodore Roosevelt, and Former President Taft. He planned and directed the erection of Science Hall at the University of Notre Dame, and left his famous Dante library to the University.

[K. M. Healy, in *America*, Dec. 3, 1921; John Cavanaugh, in *Catholic World*, Feb. 1922; *Who's Who in America*, 1920–21; *N. Y. Times*, Nov. 12, 1921; *Evening Star* (Washington, D. C.), Nov. 12, 1921; private correspondence of Father Zahm in the archives of the Congregation of the Holy Cross.]   P. J. C.

ZAKRZEWSKA, MARIE ELIZABETH (Sept. 6, 1829–May 12, 1902), physician and pioneer in the movement for the emancipation of women, was born in Berlin, Germany. The Zakrzewski family, formerly extensive landowners in Poland, were dispersed in 1793. Marie's father, Ludwig Martin Zakrzewski, went to Berlin, where he served as an army officer and later as a governmental official, but his liberal tendencies lost him his position, and his wife, descended from the gypsy tribe of the Lombardi, became a midwife in order to support her family of seven children. Marie, the eldest, left school at the age of thirteen. A studious, unattractive child, she took a great interest in nursing and ultimately decided to become an *accoucheuse*. She became a special student at the great Charité Hospital in Berlin, graduated, and began practice within its walls, but friction soon developed between her and the authorities. Thwarted in her desire to become a physician, she emigrated with one of her sisters to America, arriving in New York in May 1853. There she remained in poverty for a year, earning, by sewing, a meager living for herself, her sister, and two more of the children who had joined her. Not unmindful of her original idea in coming to America, she turned to Elizabeth Blackwell [*q.v.*], already qualified as a physician, for help in obtaining a medical education. In spite of the fact that she could hardly say a word in English, she was sent to Cleveland Medical College, a department of Western Reserve College, which had opened its doors to women in 1847. Helped by friends and encouraged by the dean, John J. Delamater, she received her degree of M.D. in 1856.

She returned to New York, helped Elizabeth Blackwell and her sister to raise funds both there and in Boston, and served as resident surgeon in the newly founded New York Infirmary (1857), staffed entirely by women. The next year she accepted the chair of obstetrics in the New

England Female Medical College, Boston. After three years, dissatisfied because of the lax standards of the college and the failure of the trustees to build her a hospital for clinical work, she resigned. Willing friends assisted her in starting a little ten-bed hospital of her own, the nucleus of the large New England Hospital for Women and Children. For some years she acted as resident physician, matron, head nurse, and general manager. She was virtually head of the hospital from its founding (1862) for a period of forty years. Here she carried on her duties as a physician and taught two generations of women to become nurses or doctors. At the same time her private practice increased rapidly, and she became the outstanding woman physician in New England. In addition, she gave many lectures on a wide variety of subjects, and became an outspoken and radical abolitionist, closely associated with William Lloyd Garrison, Wendell Phillips [*qq.v.*], and others. Retiring in 1899, she died a few years later after a period of invalidism. She never married. A pioneer in rights for women, she opened the way, with the Blackwells, for the entrance of women into medicine. With a sound intellect and a large and sympathetic heart, she unselfishly devoted herself to the service of humanity.

[See autobiog. notes in Caroline H. Dall, *A Practical Illus. of "Woman's Right to Labor"* (1860); *Marie Elizabeth Zakrzewska: a Memoir* (1903); Agnes C. Vietor, *A Woman's Quest* (1924), which is partly autobiographical; *Boston Evening Transcript*, May 13 and Oct. 30, 1902.]   H. R. V.

ZAMORANO, AGUSTIN JUAN VICENTE (May 5, 1798–Sept. 16, 1842), pioneer printer, executive secretary of California under the Mexican régime, was born at St. Augustine, Fla., the son of Gonzalo Zamorano y Gonzalez, a native of Muriel, Old Castile, Spain, and Francisca Sales del Corral, of Havana, Cuba. The father, who was treasurer, auditor, and quartermaster of the Spanish province of East Florida, was appointed in March 1811 treasurer of the province of Guanajuato, in Mexico, and there Agustin received his schooling and grew to manhood.

During the final phases of the Mexican war for independence he became a cadet in the army (May 1, 1821) and took part in the campaign that ended in national freedom. The next few years he spent at the city of Mexico, receiving the training of a military engineer. When José M. Echeandia was made governor of California in February 1825, Zamorano was appointed executive secretary and reached San Diego in October. On Feb. 15, 1827, he married María Luisa Argüello, by whom he had seven children. Shortly after Manuel Victoria assumed the governorship, in January 1831, Zamorano, still secretary, became also commandant of the *presidio* at the capital, Monterey, with the rank of captain. Victoria's rule proved unpopular and revolt broke out in December 1831 at San Diego. The governor was seriously wounded and was captured by the revolutionists. Zamorano, as the senior loyal officer, assumed the military command and maintained the established government in three of the four presidial districts until the arrival in January 1833 of a new governor from Mexico.

Zamorano is remembered chiefly as the first printer in California. His first imprints were letterheads produced from woodblocks; these are known to have been in use during the years 1826–29. In 1830, the official letterheads were printed from type and in the following year, 1831, habilitated stamped paper (*papel sellado*) was printed from the same type; all the existing imprints of this period give evidence of being pounded proofs. In June 1834, the ship *Lagoda*, out of Boston, delivered to Zamorano at Monterey a wooden-framed Ramage printing press, type, and other equipment. Soon afterward, Zamorano issued his *Aviso al Publico* (1834), a broadside announcing the establishment of a printing office and quoting prices. He is known to have produced twenty-one imprints, in addition to letterheads and stamped paper headings. Of these, eleven were broadsides or folders of an official character, six were of a miscellaneous nature, and four were books: *Reglamento Provincial para el Gobierno Interior* (1834), sixteen pages, containing the rules adopted by the territorial legislature to govern its organization and deliberations; José Figueroa's *Manifiesto a la Republica Mejicana* (1835), 188 pages, by far the most important work printed in California before the American occupation; *Catecismo de Ortologia* (1836) and *Tablas para los Niños que Empiezan a Contar* (1836), school books.

Zamorano served as territorial secretary and as commandant at Monterey until November 1836, when a revolution led by Juan Bautista Alvarado [*q.v.*], deposed acting governor Nicolás Gutiérrez. Zamorano then removed to San Diego, where he played a leading part in the fruitless resistance to Alvarado's government offered by the inhabitants of the southern part of the territory. In the spring of 1838, leaving his family in California, he returned to Mexico. From some time in 1839 until late in 1840, he was military commander of Lower California, with headquarters at La Paz, and was then called to Mexico for staff duty. On the appointment of Manuel Micheltorena as governor of California,

early in 1842, Zamorano was named as adjutant inspector of the territory and sailed with the new governor from Mazatlan. He was desperately ill when the expedition reached San Diego, Aug. 25, 1842, and a few weeks later he died.

[Sources include: G. L. Harding, *Don Agustin V. Zamorano, Statesman, Soldier, Craftsman, and California's First Printer* (1934), and "A Census of California Spanish Imprints, 1833–1845," in *Cal. Hist. Soc. Quart.*, June 1933; R. E. Cowan, *A Bibliog. of the Spanish Press of Cal.* (1919); George Tays, "Revolutionary Cal." (1932), doctoral thesis (MS.), Univ. of Cal.; H. H. Bancroft, "California," *Hist. of the Pacific States,* vols. XIII–XIX (1884–90); and transcripts of documents in Mexican archives in Bancroft Lib., Univ. of Cal. The largest collections of imprints produced by Zamorano are at the Bancroft Lib. and the Henry E. Huntington Lib., San Marino, Cal.]   G.L.H.

ZANE, CHARLES SHUSTER (Mar. 3, 1831–Mar. 29, 1915), judge, was born at Tuckahoe, Cape May County, N. J., one of ten children of Andrew and Mary (Franklin) Zane and a descendant in the sixth generation from Robert Zane, an English serge-maker, who was a member of the Quaker colony founded in 1676 at Salem, N. J. His mother, said to have been a relative of Benjamin Franklin, died when he was nine. He grew to possess the simple purity of Quaker character without Quaker religious convictions. Indeed, he was to be a life-long agnostic. At sixteen or seventeen, equipped with a rural schooling, he left his father's farm to spend several years as grocery clerk and livery-stable owner in Philadelphia before joining his eldest brother in Sangamon County, Ill. From 1852 until 1855 he was a student at McKendree College, Lebanon, Ill., and for some months thereafter taught school. Then he studied law under James C. Conkling, in Springfield, and was admitted to the bar in 1857. He opened a law office above that of Abraham Lincoln, whom he idolized; later, when Lincoln became president, Zane followed him as the law partner of William H. Herndon [*q.v.*], whose niece, Margaret Drusilla Maxcy, he had married at Springfield, on Apr. 6, 1859. Eight years later, when Herndon retired, Zane became the partner of Shelby M. Cullom [*q.v.*], continuing as such until 1873 and serving, meanwhile, first as city attorney of Springfield, then as county attorney of Sangamon. In 1873 he was elected an Illinois circuit judge and for eleven years, through successive reëlections, he traveled dusty roads, delivering oral opinions. Up to this time Zane had been a plain, honest, common-sense family man, undistinguished by any work he had the opportunity to perform.

In 1884, on recommendation of Cullom, President Arthur appointed him chief justice of Utah Territory to enforce the drastic Edmunds Law against polygamy and related offenses. During his incumbency, from September 1884 to January 1894 with a year interregnum (1888–89), this practice, regarded by Mormons as a sacred duty, was crushed by legal machinery in a manner that left no legacy of resentment. For this astonishing achievement Zane, through his judicial statesmanship, was more responsible than any other person. At first, his rigorous rulings and severe sentences as a nisi prius judge caused the Mormons to call his régime "a judicial reign of terror." But his enforcement of the laws of a Mormon legislature with equal rigor, courtesy, and impartiality gradually compelled their respect, the more quickly, no doubt, because of the fact that his known agnosticism acquitted him of any charge of religious bias. Finally, after years of suffering on the part of the Mormons, came the Woodruff Manifesto of Sept. 25, 1890, abandoning polygamy as an article of faith and ordering Mormons to conform to the law. Zane had repeatedly urged such a pronouncement, and when it came, unlike most others, he accepted it as utterly sincere. Now he praised the character of the Mormons, attacked proposed legislation to disfranchise them, helped to gain amnesty for those convicted and to secure the return of church property forfeited under the Edmunds-Tucker Law. It was not remarkable that, when Utah was admitted to the Union, Mormon joined Gentile to elect him first chief justice of the state. On Jan. 4, 1896, he took the oath of office.

Failing reëlection with the rest of his ticket, Zane remained among these people to practise law from Jan. 1, 1899, until his death of apoplexy at Salt Lake City. His opinions (collected in *Utah State Reports*, vols. 4–9, 13–18) are marked by lucid statement, simplicity of language, and infrequent citation of precedents. They are not otherwise extraordinary. Moreover, they indicate that the epithet "government judge" was not entirely undeserved. He was the author of "The Death of Polygamy in Utah," *Forum*, Nov. 1891; "The Constitution" [of Utah], in *Report of the Second Annual Meeting of the Territorial Bar Association of Utah* (1895); "Lincoln as I Knew Him," *Sunset. The Pacific Monthly*, Oct. 1912. Zane was erect, active, blue-eyed, lean-faced. In maturity he wore a clipped beard. He was survived by six of nine children, and is buried in Oak Ridge Cemetery, Springfield, Ill.

[The best obituary sketch is in *Deseret Evening News* (Salt Lake City, Utah), Mar. 29, 1915; see also editorial, Mar. 30, 1915. Genealogy based on records of N. J. Hist. Soc. Often Zane's birthdate occurs as Mar. 2, 1831, and birthplace as Marsh River Township, Cumberland County, N. J. The statements here are based on information from the family. For Zane's rôle in Mormon trials see: J. M. Zane, "A Rare Judicial Serv-ice," *Jour. Ill. State Hist. Soc.*, Apr.–July 1926; O. F Whitney, *Popular History of Utah* (1916); B. H. Roberts, "The History of the Mormon Church," in *Americana Mag.*, especially issues for May and June 1915 (adverse criticism). For miscellaneous information see: Paul and Chester Farthing, eds., *Philo History: Chronicles and Biographies of the Philosophian Literary Society of McKendree College* (1911); J. C. Alter, *Utah, the Storied Domain*, vol. I (1932), pp. 465–66; S. M. Cullom, *Fifty Years of Public Service* (1911).]

J.J.D.

ZANE, EBENEZER (Oct. 7, 1747–Nov. 19, 1812), pioneer, was born at a farm on the South Branch of the Potomac near what is now Moorefield, Hardy County, W. Va. Little is known of his parents except that his father migrated to the Potomac Valley after he was expelled from a Quaker meeting in eastern Pennsylvania because he married outside the Society of Friends. Ebenezer came of age in the year that the frontier to the Ohio River was officially opened by the Iroquois cession at the treaty of Fort Stanwix. Since he and his brothers, Silas and Jonathan, had already explored in those lands, in 1769 they led the frontier advance by establishing their claims under Virginia law to the lands at the mouth of Wheeling Creek, to which place they brought their families in 1770.

The Wheeling settlement became the important Ohio River terminus of the road from Cumberland, Md., over which emigrants were moving westward in increasing numbers. Ebenezer Zane was active in the land speculation that was one of the causes of Dunmore's War, although he refused to countenance the violence against the Indians that preceded it. During the war he was a colonel and disbursing agent of the Virginia militia at Fort Fincastle, Wheeling. He supported the Patriot cause during the Revolution, taking a prominent part in repelling the British-Indian besiegers of Fort Fincastle, rechristened Fort Henry, in 1777 and 1782. His sister was the famous Betty Zane who successfully braved the Indian gunfire in the siege of 1782 to bring an apron-load of gunpowder from a nearby storehouse to the fort. His brother Jonathan learned much of Ohio lands as a soldier under Crawford in the Sandusky expedition of 1782.

Zane's speculative activity in land continued after the Revolution. In 1785–87 he was often the host for the United States surveyors of the Seven Ranges and he and Jonathan were active in making salt at the Muskingum River Salt Licks ten miles below what is now Zanesville, Ohio. After the treaty of Greenville in 1795, by which the south Ohio lands were given up by the Indians, Zane petitioned Congress in March 1796 for permission to open a road from Wheeling to Limestone, Ky., and by an act approved

May 17, 1796, Congress granted him three lots, each a mile square, to be located respectively where the road crossed the Muskingum, the Hockhocking and the Scioto, on condition that Zane blaze the road himself before Jan. 1, 1797, that he pay to the United States federal bounty warrants to the amount of the acreage granted, that he provide ferries across the three rivers, and that he survey his three tracts at his own expense. On two of these tracts the towns of Zanesville and Lancaster were laid out in 1799 and 1800 respectively. The third tract lay across the Scioto River from Chillicothe.

Zane married Elizabeth McCulloch before he left the South Branch of the Potomac, and was the father of thirteen children. He was buried in the Zane family plot near Martin's Ferry, Belmont County, Ohio, not far from Wheeling.

[J. A. Caldwell, *Hist. of Belmont and Jefferson Counties, Ohio* (1880); A. B. Hulbert, *Hist. Highways of America*, vol. XI (1904); C. L. Martzolff, "Zane's Trace," *Ohio Archaeol. and Hist. Quart.*, July 1904; A. S. Withers, *Chronicles of Border Warfare* (1895), ed. by R. G. Thwaites; C. E. Sherman, *Original Ohio Land Subdivisions, being Vol. III, Final Report (in Four Volumes) Ohio Cooperative Topographic Survey* (1925).]   R. C. D.

ZEILIN, JACOB (July 16, 1806–Nov. 18, 1880), marine corps officer, was born in Philadelphia, Pa., the son of Jacob Zeilin, a tavern keeper. Nothing is known of his youth previous to his admission to the United States Military Academy at West Point as a cadet on July 1, 1822. He remained here several years, but was not graduated. On Oct. 1, 1831, he entered the marine corps as a second lieutenant. After a preliminary training at the marine barracks in Philadelphia and Charlestown, Mass., he joined the sloop *Erie,* stationed on the coast of Brazil, 1835–37. He was promoted to the rank of first lieutenant, from Sept. 12, 1836. From 1838 to 1842 he was again at the marine barracks in Charlestown. From 1843 to 1845 he was with the frigate *Columbia,* at first on the coast of Brazil and later in the Mediterranean. During the Mexican War he was attached to the frigate *Congress* of the Pacific Squadron and participated in several landing expeditions in California and Mexico. For gallantry in action at the San Gabriel River in California, he was brevetted major from Jan. 9, 1847. He was promoted captain from Sept. 14 of that year. After the *Congress* returned home by way of the East Indies he remained on shore for four years. In 1853–54 he served as fleet marine officer of the East India Squadron under Matthew C. Perry [*q.v.*], first on board the *Mississippi* and later on board the *Susquehanna.* The marines of the squadron were

organized into a battalion with Zeilin in command, and they participated in the memorable events leading to the opening of Japan. In 1859 Zeilin was in the Mediterranean with the *Wabash,* and was later stationed at the marine barracks at Norfolk, Philadelphia, and Washington, D. C.

In the first battle of Bull Run he commanded one of the four companies of marines that cooperated with the army and was wounded in the battle. In August 1863, with a company of marines, he joined Admiral John A. B. Dahlgren [*q.v.*], off Charleston, S. C., and participated in the engagements against the defenses of that city. Returning to the North on sick leave, he was stationed at the marine barracks at New York until ordered to Washington as commandant of the marine corps, with the rank of colonel from June 10, 1864. On Mar. 2, 1867, he was given the rank of brigadier-general, the first officer to attain that grade. He served as commandant until he was retired on Nov. 1, 1876.

After a long period of ill health, he died of cirrhosis of the liver contracted in the East Indies. He was survived by a wife, Virginia (Freeman) Zeilin, to whom he was married at Norfolk, Va., on Oct. 23, 1845, and two daughters. Shortly before his death his only son, Lieut. William F. Zeilin of the Marine Corps, was accidentally killed. Both father and son were buried in the Laurel Hill Cemetery at Philadelphia.

[*Navy Register*, 1832–81; *Reg. of the Officers and Cadets of the U. S. Mil. Acad.*, 1823–25; *Army and Navy Jour.*, June 12, Nov. 20, 27, 1880; R. S. Collum, *Hist. of U. S. Marine Corps* (1903); *War of the Rebellion: Official Records* (Navy), 1 ser. vols. IV, XI, XIV (1896–1902); pension records, Veterans Administration; *Washington Post*, Nov. 19, 1880.]
                                        C. O. P.

ZEISBERGER, DAVID (Apr. 11, 1721–Nov. 17, 1808), Moravian missionary to the Indians, was the son of David and Rosina Zeisberger of Zauchtenthal, Moravia. His family migrated to Herrnhut, Saxony, in 1727, and when his parents went to Georgia in 1736, the boy remained in school at Herrnhut. Later he was indentured to an importer in Herrndyk, Holland, whence he ran away to London because he resented an unjust punishment. Here Count Zinzendorf [*q.v.*] took him in hand and persuaded Governor Oglethorpe [*q.v.*] to send him to Savannah to join the Moravian colony. With this group he left Georgia in 1739 for Pennsylvania and was present on Christmas Eve in 1741 when Zinzendorf christened Bethlehem.

In 1745 Zeisberger and Christian Frederick Post [*q.v.*] were invited to live in the lodge of Chief Hendrick [*q.v.*] of the Iroquois that they might learn the Maqua (Onondaga) dialect, but the agitation against Germans in New York resulted in their arrest and imprisonment. Through the influence of Governor Thomas of Pennsylvania and of Conrad Weiser [q.v.], they were released in order to take part in Indian negotiations then pending. At once Zeisberger, Weiser, and Bishop A. G. Spangenberg [q.v.] hastened to Onondaga to attend a Long House, at which, on June 20, they assisted in arranging the treaty that allied the Six Nations with the English.

From this time until his death over sixty years later Zeisberger was constantly involved in the complicated politics of the frontier resulting from the long-continued struggle between France and Great Britain. While his knowledge of Indian habits and tongues made him invaluable in conferences, his mind and heart were centered upon the lives of the red men and the process of making them useful members of society. Between 1745 and 1763 he spent a total of more than ten years in the lodges of the Six Nations, loved and admired by their leaders, and, like Sir William Johnson [q.v.], initiated into some of their tribes. His intimate contact with these confederated friends of the English convinced him that the best means of assuring the safety of the whites lay in ameliorating the savagery of the Delawares and cognate tribes, who for years had been sullenly resentful of their conquest by the Iroquois and as a consequence were prone to yield to the seductive influence of the French. In 1763 he lived with the Delawares in the Wyoming Valley, assisting them in the building of the village of Friedenshütten. When colonial policies gradually pushed them westward, he followed them in their trek through the wilds of upper Pennsylvania. So effective was his contact with them that when in 1771 they entered the Ohio area he was able to establish a self-supporting Christian Indian settlement at Schoenbrunn in the Tuscarawas Valley.

Here Zeisberger erected the first church building and schoolhouse west of the Ohio River, surrounding it with the log-cabins and cornfields of the converts. Within three years Gnadenhütten, Salem, and Lichtenau near by were centers of similar life, and it seemed that the process of making the Indian a useful member of colonial society had well begun. The tide of settlement toward the West, however, resisted by the new policy of the council for the colonies in London, together with the further threat of savage red men in the territory beyond, boded storm for both white settlers and Indian converts. During the Revolution the whites were inclined to view all Indians as potential allies of the British and in consequence the position of the Moravian villages became increasingly difficult. In 1781 Zeisberger and his assistant J. G. E. Heckewelder [q.v.] were taken as prisoners to Detroit and the Schoenbrunn colony was scattered along the shores of Lake Erie. After a searching examination by the British governor the missionaries were acquitted as neutrals, but, dreading the hatred and fear of the whites, the Christian Indians gradually abandoned their old villages and settled in small groups near Detroit and on the Thames in Canada. This change of base was not accomplished without stain of blood, however. In March 1782 Simon Girty [q.v.] and a band of white settlers led by Captain Williamson inveigled the unsuspecting inhabitants of Gnadenhütten into their cabins and massacred them all. From 1782 to 1786 Zeisberger lived with a group of the converts at (New) Gnadenhütten, in what is now Michigan; from 1786 to 1798 he helped establish settlements at New Salem, Ohio, and Fairfield, Canada. In 1798 he settled with a remnant of his "brown brethren" at Goshen, Ohio, whence, after his death in 1808, they once more took up the long trek, this time to Kansas.

At the age of sixty, June 4, 1781, Zeisberger married Susan Lecron of Lititz, Pa., who became his sturdy support in the dwindling work. They had no children. When he died he had lived among the red men for sixty-two years, and he is said to have acquired not only their speech, but also their taciturnity and their habits of thought and action. In the course of his career he published *Essay of a Delaware-Indian and English Spelling-Book* (1776), *A Collection of Hymns for the Use of the Christian Indians of the Missions of the United Brethren in North America* (1803); *Sermons to Children* (1803), in the Delaware tongue, containing also "Something of Bodily Care for Children" translated into Delaware by Zeisberger from the German of A. G. Spangenberg; *The History of Our Lord and Saviour Jesus Christ* (1821), in Delaware, edited by Samuel Lieberkuhn; "*Verbal Biegungen der Chippewayer (Delawaren)*," in J. L. Vater's *Analekten der Sprechenkunde* (pt. 3, 1821). Several valuable unpublished manuscripts of his are in the library of the American Philosophical Society, Philadelphia: "*Deutsch und Onondagisches Woerterbuch*" (7 volumes); Onondaga and English Vocabulary (shorter form); and "*Onondagische Grammatica.*" His *Grammar of the Language of the Lenni Lenape or Delaware Indians,* translated from the German manuscript by P. S. Du Ponceau, was published in 1827; *Zeisberger's Indian Dictionary* (1887), was printed from the manuscript in the Harvard College Library; and a "History of the Indians," evidently written for Bishop Loskiel, was published in the *Ohio Archæological and Historical Quarterly,* January–April 1910.

[E. A. de Schweinitz, *The Life and Times of David Zeisberger* (1870); *Diary of David Zeisberger* (2 vols., 1885), ed. by E. F. Bliss; G. H. Loskiel, *Geschicte der Mission der Evangelischen Brüder unter den Indianern* (1789), translated by C. I. LaTrobe as *Hist. of the Mission of the United Brethren among the Indians in North America* (1794); J. G. E. Heckewelder, *A Narrative of the Mission of the United Brethren among the Delaware and Mohegan Indians* (1820); *Ohio Archæol. and Hist. Quart.,* Apr. 1909, Jan. 1912; diaries and correspondence, as well as duplicate MSS. of all works, in archives of the Moravian Church, Bethlehem, Pa.]

A. G. R.

ZEISLER, FANNIE BLOOMFIELD (July 16, 1863–Aug. 20, 1927), pianist, was born in Bielitz, Austrian Silesia, the daughter of Salomon and Bertha (Jaeger) Blumenfeld. Her father emigrated to America in 1866, settling in Appleton, Wis., where he was joined the following year by his wife and three children, Fannie being the youngest. In 1869 the family removed permanently to Chicago. Fannie received her first instruction on the piano from her brother, Maurice Bloomfield [*q.v.*], but her first systematic training came from Bernhard Ziehn [*q.v.*], with whom she studied several years. In 1873 she became a pupil of Carl Wolfsohn [*q.v.*] and made her first public appearance at a concert given Feb. 26, 1875, by the Beethoven Society with Wolfsohn conducting. On the advice of Madame Essipoff, who heard her play during her American tour of 1877, the young pianist in June 1878 went to Vienna, where she spent five years of intensive study with Leschetizky. She returned to America in the summer of 1883 and in the fall gave her first full concert in the old Hershey Hall, Chicago, with great success. Her first appearance with orchestra was in New York with Frank B. Van der Stucken [*q.v.*], in one of his "novelty concerts." She soon became recognized as one of the foremost pianists in America.

In the fall of 1888 she went to Leschetizky again and coached with him till March 1889. Then, with a few intervening years of maturing experience, she made her first European tour in the fall of 1893, appearing with the great orchestras of Berlin, Leipzig, Dresden, and Vienna. In the latter city, after a performance which evoked unusual enthusiasm, a severe illness interrupted the tour, and she returned home. In the fall of 1894 she went back for a second tour, confined largely to Germany and Austria, and won significant triumphs wherever she played. The young stranger from America was lauded by the German critics for her "faultless technique," her energy, and the depth and fullness of her poetic feeling. A third European tour, made in 1898, was confined largely to England, but it included a notable performance at the Lower Rhine Music Festival at Cologne under Franz Wüllner. A fourth tour was made in 1902 in Germany, Austria, Switzerland, Denmark, and Paris, and a fifth in 1911–12, covering all of western Europe. At her first Paris appearance with the Lamoureux Orchestra in 1902, a famous incident occurred. A violently hostile anti-foreign gallery claque attempted to prevent her from playing, but with characteristic courage and tenacity she held her ground, and, by her impassioned and masterly performance of the Saint-Saens C-Minor concerto, turned the noisy tumult into an overwhelming triumph.

The wide range of her available repertoire was remarkable. During a tour in California in March 1912 she played eight recitals in San Francisco, with no repetitions, within the space of eighteen days. Among her public appearances in her later years two were of quite extraordinary interest. After an absence of two years from the concert stage and following a long illness, she gave a concert in Chicago in Orchestra Hall, Feb. 3, 1920, at which she played with the Chicago Symphony Orchestra three concertos in succession—the Mozart C-Minor, the Chopin F-Minor, and the Tchaikovsky B-flat Minor. Five years later the Chicago Symphony Orchestra gave a special concert, on Feb. 25, 1925, to celebrate her golden jubilee as an artist. On this occasion, which proved to be her last public appearance, she played the same piece, the Beethoven "Andante Favori," with which she had begun her public career just fifty years before, and then two concertos—the Schumann and the Chopin F-Minor. She received a thrilling ovation, not merely as a personal tribute, but because of the remarkable fact that there was in the performance no suggestion of declining powers. Her death came two years later after a protracted illness. On Oct. 18, 1885, she was married to Sigmund Zeisler [*q.v.*], who throughout their married life maintained a rare sympathy with and appreciation of her art. He and their three sons survived her. As an interpreter she had full mastery of a wide range of styles, yet possibly excelled in moods demanding virile incisiveness, technical brilliance, and dramatic intensity. She was a woman of wide intellectual and cultural sympathies, democratic in her personal intercourse, frank and outspoken in her convictions, simple and unostentatious in her life. She wielded a large influence as a teacher, was devoted to the welfare of her students, and was as exacting a task-master with them as she had always been with herself. Lofty idealism, unremitting industry, indomitable energy, and absolute sincerity were the foundations on which her whole life and art were built.

[*Who's Who in America,* 1926–27; *Internat. Who's Who in Music,* 1918; *Grove's Dict. of Music and Musicians* (3rd. ed.), vol. V (1928); R. G. Cole, article in *Papers and Proc. Music Teachers Nat. Asso.,* 1927; W. S. B. Mathews, in *Music,* Nov. 1895; *Musical Observer,* Apr. 1908; *Chicago Sunday Tribune,* Aug. 21, 1927.]   R. G. C.

ZEISLER, SIGMUND (Apr. 11, 1860–June 4, 1931), lawyer, was born in Bielitz, Silesia, Austria (later Poland), the son of Isaac L. and Anna (Kanner) Zeisler. Graduating in 1878 from the Imperial College in Bielitz, he began the study of law and political science at the University of Vienna, receiving the degree of J.D. in 1883. He then emigrated to America and in 1884, after a year's study at Northwestern University, was granted the degree of LL.B. and also was awarded a prize for the best essay on an original thesis, "Rights and Liabilities of the Finder of Chattels Casually Lost on Land" (*Chicago Legal News,* July 5, 1884). The essay, written in English, was the more remarkable because the author had begun the study of English only the year before. Very shortly after entering upon the practice of law in Chicago in 1884, he became associate counsel in a *cause célèbre,* the Chicago Anarchists Case. His efforts on behalf of the defendants in that case, though unsuccessful in acquitting them of the charge of murder, identified him as a political liberal and as one with the courage to espouse unpopular causes which he thought to be just. Writing of the Anarchists Case forty years after the event, he concluded that the verdict of history will be that the defendants were "convicted not because they had been proved guilty of murder, but because they were anarchists" (*Illinois Law Review,* Nov. 1926, p. 250).

During the years that Zeisler was engaged in the general practice of law in Chicago, he was assistant corporation counsel for Chicago (1893–94), master in chancery for the circuit court of Cook County (1904–20), lecturer on Roman law at Northwestern University (1884–86 and 1892–93) and on constitutional law at John Marshall Law School (1901–04). A Democrat in politics, he bolted Bryan in 1896 on the money issue, but rejoined him four years later on the anti-imperialist policy, and campaigned throughout the country in support of the Democratic ticket. For

many years he was active in the Municipal Voters League and from 1925 until his death was its president. He was also a member of the executive committee of the Civil Service Reform Association and of the advisory committee of the American Judicature Society.

A man of wide culture, Zeisler wrote or lectured frequently in the fields of art, music, literature, and science. He paid his way through Northwestern University in part by writing music criticisms for a German newspaper in Chicago. He was an earnest advocate of the abolition of the requirement of unanimity in the verdict of a jury (*Proceedings of the Illinois State Bar Association,* 1890, pp. 54–56), of a non-partisan system for the selection of judges (*Chicago Legal News,* Nov. 16, 1912, pp. 117–19), and of other reforms in the judicial system ("Defects of the Jury System," *Ibid.,* Oct. 13, 1900). His criticisms in these matters, written in a clear and forceful style, were always scholarly and constructive. Possessed of a deep, resonant voice, and of the ability to speak extemporaneously, in accurate English and with perfect diction, he became an eloquent platform orator and a powerful advocate before courts and juries. In some of his more important cases his argument extended over a number of days. He had marked dramatic ability, which he often used in his speeches with telling effect. Though noticeably proud, at times hot-tempered, occasionally tactless and over-resentful of criticism, he was unusually free from prejudice, and had the courage at all times to express his convictions even at the price of expediency. He was erect in posture and carried himself with rare dignity.

Zeisler's first wife, whom he married on Oct. 18, 1885, was Fannie (Bloomfield) Zeisler [*q.v.*], internationally famous concert pianist. They had three sons, all of whom survived their parents. After Mrs. Zeisler's death he married Amelia Spielman, Jan. 23, 1930. He died in Chicago.

[*Who's Who in America,* 1930–31; F. B. Crossley, *Courts and Lawyers of Ill.* (1916), vol. II, pp. 468–69; *Ann. Report Ill. State Bar Asso.* (1932), pp. 397–98; obituary in *Chicago Tribune,* June 5, 1931; information from Paul Zeisler, Zeisler's son.]   G. W. G.

ZENGER, JOHN PETER (1697–July 28, 1746), printer and journalist, was born in Germany and at the age of thirteen emigrated with his family to New York with the large company of Palatines sent to America by Queen Anne in 1710. His father died on shipboard, leaving to his widow, Johanna, the care of John Peter and a younger brother and sister (I. D. Rupp, *A Collection of Thirty Thousand Names of . . . Immigrants,* 1876, p. 444). Zenger was one of the large number of immigrant children apprenticed by Governor Hunter, his mother in 1711 ratifying his articles of indenture for a term of eight years to William Bradford [*q.v.*], "the pioneer printer of the middle colonies." At the expiration of his indentures he contracted a short-lived marriage with Mary White in Philadelphia, July 28, 1719 (*Pennsylvania Archives,* 2 ser. IX, 1896, p. 78) and settled at Chestertown, Kent County, Md., where in 1720 he petitioned the Assembly to be allowed to print the session laws. The petition was granted, but no trace of these session laws can be found. Shortly thereafter he made a successful application to the same body for naturalization, but soon returned to New York, this time as a widower, and on Sept. 11, 1722, married Anna Catherina Maulin. A year later he was made a freeman of the city.

In 1725 he formed a partnership with Bradford; the one book extant bearing their joint imprint is *Klagte van Eenige Leeden der Nederduytse Hervormde Kerk* (1725). In the following year Zenger set up for himself on Smith Street, removing to Broad Street in 1734. During this period he printed a few polemical tracts and a number of unimportant works, principally theological in character and in the Dutch language. In 1730 he brought out Peter Venema's *Arithmetica,* the first arithmetic text printed in the colony.

In the early thirties, the erection of a court of exchequer and the summary removal of Lewis Morris [*q.v.*] from the chief justiceship by Gov. William Cosby [*q.v.*] brought about a powerful revolt by lawyers, merchants, and people of all classes. Morris, James Alexander, and William Smith, 1697–1769 [*qq.v.*] set up Zenger as editor of an anti-administration paper, the *New-York Weekly Journal,* which was opposed by Bradford's *New York Gazette,* organ of the government. From the very first number of Zenger's paper, Nov. 5, 1733, an independent and truculent spirit was infused into New York journalism. The major articles, which bear a legalistic stamp, were undoubtedly contributed by his more highly-educated backers (E. B. O'Callaghan, *Documents Relative to the Colonial History of . . . New York,* vol. VI, 1855, pp. 6, 21; William Smith, *The History of the Late Province of New York,* 1830, II, 9), but as publisher, Zenger was legally responsible. He was an indifferent printer, with a poor knowledge of English, but the articles from his own pen show a courageous and polemical spirit.

In the fall of 1734 steps were taken for his punishment. The Council ordered numbers 7, 47, 48, and 49 of the *Journal,* containing certain doggerel rhymes, to be burned, but the court of quarter sessions would not suffer the order to be entered and the aldermen forbade the whipper to obey it. It was finally done by a negro slave of the sheriff. A few days later Zenger was arrested; his bail was fixed at £400 for himself and £200 for his sureties, and, since this was more than he could furnish, he was remanded to prison. For several days he was held incommunicado, and in all he was confined for nearly ten months, during which period his paper continued to appear every Monday, the business being managed by his wife, who received her instructions from her husband "through the Hole of the Door of the Prison" (*Journal,* Nov. 25, 1734).

In April term, 1735, he was brought to trial for criminal libel. When his counsel, Smith and Alexander, attacked the validity of the appointment of De Lancey and Philipse as judges, they were promptly disbarred. But when the case came up again in August, Zenger was represented by Andrew Hamilton [d. 1741, *q.v.*] of Philadelphia, who, despite the strict construction of the common law of criminal libel which then prevailed, pleaded for the right of the jury to inquire into the truth or falsity of the libel, and when his course was blocked by the court, appealed to the jury, who responded with a verdict of not guilty, to the acclaim of spectators and populace. In his newspaper Zenger printed a complete verbatim account of the trial, the first major victory for the freedom of the press in the American colonies. His report, printed separately as *A Brief Narrative of the Case and Tryal of John Peter Zenger* (1736), aroused great interest both in the Colonies and in Great Britain, and went through numerous editions.

As a reward for his services, Zenger was made public printer in 1737 for the colony of New York and was appointed to the same office in New Jersey the following year. Despite these appointments, however, he and his family always seem to have been in financial straits. On his death in 1746 he was survived by his wife and six children. The *Journal* was published by his widow until December 1748, when it was taken over by John Zenger, a son of his first marriage, who continued it until 1751, when the publication ceased entirely.

[For the life of Zenger see Livingston Rutherfurd, *John Peter Zenger: His Press, His Trial, and a Bibliog. of Zenger Imprints. . . . Also a Reprint of the First Edition of the Trial* (1904); Isaiah Thomas, *The Hist. of Printing in America* (2nd ed., 2 vols., 1874); C. R. Hildeburn, *Sketches of Printers and Printing in Colonial N. Y.* (1895); *N. Y. Evening Post,* Aug. 4, 1746. The N. Y. Pub. Lib. possesses a good, though not complete, file of the *New-York Weekly Journal* (for other files in New York, see E. B. Greene and R. B. Morris, *A Guide to the Principal Sources for Early Am. Hist.*

(*1600–1800*) *in the City of N. Y.* (1929, p. 71), together with photostats of all known issues, a considerable number of imprints, and other relevant material. See *N. Y. Pub. Lib. Bull.*, July 1898; C. F. McCombs, "John Peter Zenger, printer," *Ibid.* (1933), pp. 1031–34. For a list of Zenger's imprints, see C. R. Hildeburn, *A List of the Issues of the Press in N. Y.* (1889). Accounts of the trial appear in H. L. Osgood, *The Am. Colonies in the Eighteenth Century* (1924), II, 458–62; J. B. McMaster, "A Free Press in the Middle Colonies," *Princeton Review*, Jan. 1886; L. R. Schuyler, *The Liberty of the Press in the Am. Colonies before the Revolutionary War* (1905); *Minutes of the Common Council of the City of New York, 1675–1776* (1905), vols. II, III; and Cadwallader Colden, "Narrative of Cosby's Administration, 1732–37," MS. in N. Y. Hist. Soc.]

                                         R. B. M.

ZENTMAYER, JOSEPH (Mar. 27, 1826–Mar. 28, 1888), inventor and manufacturer of scientific instruments, was born at Mannheim in southern Germany. After finishing school he learned the trade of a skilled mechanic and scientific instrument-maker in some of the best establishments in his native land. He was an ardent lover of liberty and republican institutions, and took an active part in the political struggles that culminated in the revolution of 1848. Forced to leave Germany, he emigrated in 1848 to the United States, where a year later he married Catherine Bluim in Cleveland, Ohio. He secured employment first in Baltimore and afterwards in Washington, and finally in 1853 he set up for himself as an instrument-maker in Philadelphia, where he lived the rest of his life. His shop at the corner of Eighth and Chestnut Streets, though it had only the most modest equipment in the beginning, came to be a landmark in Philadelphia and was for many years the rendezvous of a group of notable scientific and professional men in the city. His ingenuity and superior workmanship, above all the boldness of his scientific conceptions, attracted the attention and won the admiration of leaders of science of that day not only in Philadelphia but in other parts of the country as well. The microscopes he made were found to be in many respects so superior to the instruments imported from abroad that they were soon in great demand all over the United States, and during the Civil War Zentmayer supplied most of those used in government hospitals. Once fully embarked on this enterprise, Zentmayer applied himself to it with an industry and a zeal that never flagged. He made a number of improvements both in the objective and in the stand of the microscope (see *Appletons' Annual Cyclopædia*, 1884, and *Journal of the Franklin Institute*, July 1877), and nearly all the microscopes in use today embody some of his inventions. In 1865 he invented his famous photographic lens (patent No. 55,195). This was a hemisymmetrical doublet composed of two single meniscus lenses made of the same crown glass, in which the rear lens was simply a copy of the front lens on a reduced scale. The center of the interior stop was at the common center of curvature of the two concave surfaces of the doublet. The combination was free from distortion and was practically achromatic with respect to both the visual and the actinic focus. One of its chief advantages was that the focal length of the lens, and consequently the size of the image on the sensitive plate, could be readily changed simply by substituting one of a set of several similar lenses in place of the rear meniscus. Owing to its efficiency and at the same time to its simplicity of construction and cheapness of manufacture, Zentmayer's photographic lens, which was a subject of much discussion and controversy in the optical journals of that day, enjoyed a deserved popularity.

In 1874 the Elliott Cresson gold medal was awarded Zentmayer by the Franklin Institute for his scientific inventions. For his improvements of the microscope he likewise received gold medals at the Centennial Exhibition in Philadelphia in 1876 and at the Paris Exposition in 1878. He was a member of many scientific organizations, and published a number of papers in the *Journal of the Franklin Institute* (May 1870, June 1872, May 1876, July 1877). He was a man of affable and engaging manners, and of great open-mindedness, sincerity, and integrity. Devoted as he was to science, he was also a lover of literature and music. He died in Philadelphia.

[Biog. sources include Henry Morton and Coleman Sellers, in *Jour. Franklin Inst.*, Dec. 1888; C. A. Oliver, in *Proc. Am. Philos. Soc.*, vol. XXXI (1893); unpub. paper by H. V. Hetzel, 1888, in the possession of Dr. William Zentmayer of Phila.; death notice in *Pub. Ledger* (Phila.), Mar. 29, 1888. For Zentmayer's photographic lens and the controversy over it, see Moritz von Rohr, *Theorie und Geschichte des photograph. Objektivs* (Berlin, 1899), p. 123; *Jour. Optical Soc. of America*, vol. XXIV (1934), p. 77; *Jour. Franklin Inst.*, July 1866, May 1867, Sept. 1868. For a description of "*das Sang-Zentmayersche Umkehrprisma*," see Siegfried Czapski and Otto Eppenstein, *Grundzuege der Theorie der optischen Instrumente* (Leipsig, 1924), p. 593.]

                                       J. P. C. S.

ZERRAHN, CARL (July 28, 1826–Dec. 29, 1909), musician, conductor, was born in Malchow, Mecklenburg-Schwerin, Germany. Little is known of his childhood, but it is said that he had his first music lessons at the age of twelve from Friedrich Weber in Rostock. Later he studied in Hanover and in Berlin. Political events in Central Europe in 1848 forced Zerrahn, like hundreds of other musicians, to emigrate to America. He accordingly joined the ranks of the Germania Society, a little orchestra whose members were largely recruited from Gungl's orchestra in Berlin. Zerrahn was the flute player of the Germanians, and he was with the group from the time of its first concert in New York, Oct. 5, 1848. After it disbanded in September 1854, he settled in Boston, where he was elected conductor of the Handel and Haydn Society in 1854, a post he held for forty-two years. He was also active as conductor of a number of other organizations. From 1855 to 1863 he conducted one of the several orchestras in Boston known by the name of "Philharmonic." From 1865 to 1882 he directed the concerts of the Harvard Musical Association, and from 1866 to 1897 he was conductor of the Worcester (Mass.) festivals. Until his retirement in 1898 he was a teacher of singing, harmony, and composition at the New England Conservatory of Music in Boston. Because of his association with practically all the important musical events that occurred in Boston and New England during his residence there, Zerrahn was extremely influential, particularly in the development of choral singing.

In 1869, and again in 1872, Zerrahn was prominently identified with the "Peace Jubilees" organized and carried out by Patrick S. Gilmore [q.v.], the bandmaster. Zerrahn was chorus director for both of these festivals. At the first "jubilee" in Boston, he had under his direction a chorus of ten thousand voices. It was an epoch-making affair, and aside from such feats of showmanship as the introduction of real anvils hammered by real fireman for the "Anvil Chorus," and the booming of cannon (fired by electricity) to mark the rhythm of national airs, genuine artistic achievements were reached in the orchestral and choral numbers presented. Three years later (1872) at Gilmore's second "jubilee," the size of the chorus was doubled, but the results were not so happy as at the first concerts; it was impossible for even so experienced a conductor as Zerrahn to keep such a vast body of singers together.

Zerrahn lived for over ten years after his retirement, and died in Milton, Mass., at the home of one of his two sons. His name is inseparably connected with an important period of American musical history, the last half of the nineteenth century, and through his varied activities his impress on choral music will long be felt.

[W. S. B. Mathews, *A Hundred Years of Music in America* (1889); C. C. Perkins and J. S. Dwight, *Hist. of the Handel & Haydn Soc.,* vol. I (1883); L. C. Elson, *The Hist. of Am. Music* (rev. ed., 1925); J. T. Howard, *Our Am. Music* (1930); P. S. Gilmore, *Hist. of the Nat. Peace Jubilee and Great Musical Festival* (1871); W. R. Spalding, *Music at Harvard* (1935); *Musical Courier,* Jan. 5, 1910; *Boston Evening Transcript,* Dec. 29, 1909.]   J. T. H.

ZEUNER, CHARLES (Sept. 20, 1795–Nov. 7, 1857), composer and organist, properly Heinrich Christoph Zeuner, was born at Eisleben (near Halle) in Saxony, and was educated in Germany. An unsupported contemporary tradition that makes him a pupil of Johann Nepomuk Hummel, the pianist, may have basis in fact. It is also probable that as a young man he lived for some time in Erfurt and studied with Michael G. Fischer. Several of his early works are dedicated to residents of Erfurt, and it was there, and in Frankfurt-am-Main, that compositions and arrangements of his were first published. The date of his emigration to the United States is usually given as 1824. But as late as 1826 an advertisement in the *Allgemeine musikalische Zeitung* (Leipzig) invites subscriptions to an edition of one of his masses, to be published in Frankfurt, and there is no reason to believe that he left Germany much before 1830. On reaching the United States, he adopted the Christian name of Charles and settled in Boston, where, on Sept. 24, 1830, he was elected organist to the Handel and Haydn Society. With this association began the productive and eventful part of his career. Most of his published and unpublished works date from this period. A number were heard for the first time at the society's concerts; some, indeed, were written expressly for them. Zeuner appeared as soloist at these concerts with organ concertos of his own composition in 1830 and again in 1834, and he provided orchestral accompaniments for numerous choral works in the society's repertory. At the same time he served also as a church organist and as president of the Musical Professional Society. Chosen president of the Handel and Haydn Society in 1838, he promptly became involved in a quarrel with the members of his board of trustees, resigned at their request in February of the following year, and, refusing reelection as organist, left Boston for Philadelphia. There he held various positions as organist, notably at St. Andrew's and at the Arch Street Presbyterian Church. But a growing eccentricity, variously described as peculiarity of demeanor, temporary derangement, and even as harmless lunacy, led him to retire, before long, from the musical scene. Moving to Camden, N. J., he lived, during his last years, in relative obscurity and isolation until pronounced melancholia, coupled with a morbid interest in spiritualism, drove him to suicide. He was unmarried. His musical library is now in the Library of Congress.

Zeuner's chief publications are *Church Music, Consisting of New and Original Anthems, Motets, and Chants* (1831); *The American Harp* (1832), also a collection of church music; *The*

Ancient Lyre (1833), a volume of hymn tunes; and *Organ Voluntaries* (1840). He published many popular songs and piano pieces, and contributed to Lowell Mason's *Lyra Sacra* (1832) and other similar collections. A large number of compositions, including a mass and three cantatas, remain in manuscript. His most ambitious composition, *The Feast of Tabernacles,* an oratorio in two parts, the words by the Rev. Henry Ware, Jr., of Cambridge, was the first American work of its kind. Written about 1832, it was presented for the first time in full at the Odeon, May 3, 1837, by the Boston Academy of Music. Although it was repeated several times, it seems to have had but slight success. Choruses from it were published in Boston in 1837.

Twenty years ahead of the "foreign invasion," 1848, Zeuner was one of the first thoroughly grounded musicians to settle in the United States. Employing the conventional German style of the 1820's, his more serious compositions are at least fluent and pleasing, show real skill in handling orchestral and choral masses, and have occasional moments of genuine dignity.

[*N. Y. Musical Rev. and Gazette,* Nov. 14, 28, Dec. 12, 1857; *Western Musical World,* Feb. 1868; S. P. Cheney, *The Am. Singing Book* (1879), p. 195; C. C. Perkins and J. S. Dwight, *Hist. of the Handel and Haydn Soc.,* vol. I (1883–93); F. J. Metcalf, *Am. Writers and Compilers of Sacred Music* (1925); *Report of the Librarian of Cong. for . . . 1930,* pp. 200–05; report of death (giving Zeuner's name as Gunner) in *Daily News* (Phila.), Nov. 9, 1857.]   O. S.

ZEVIN, ISRAEL JOSEPH (Jan. 31, 1872–Oct. 6, 1926), story-writer, humorist, editor, best known under his pseudonym, Tashrak, son of Judah Leib and Feige (Muravin) Zevin, was born in Horki, Mohilev (White Russia). He was educated in the Cheder (Jewish elementary school) and privately, acquiring a comprehensive knowledge of the traditional Hebrew studies and Talmudic lore. In 1889, at the age of seventeen, he emigrated to New York City. He started as peddler and newsboy in Park Row, satisfying his hunger for learning by studying evenings. He even attempted the study of medicine. While selling candy from a stand in the Bowery, however, he composed a few Yiddish stories which were published in the *Jewish Daily News* (*Jüdisches Tageblatt*). They attracted so much attention that he was invited to join the staff. With the interval of a short time as editor of the *Yiddishe Presse* in Philadelphia, he was associated with the *Jewish Daily News* until his death as one of its chief contributors, also serving for some time after the death of John Paley [*q.v.*] as its editor-in-chief. In 1908 he married Sophia Berman, by whom he had two daughters.

As a journalist endowed with a clear and popular style Zevin played his part in the development of Yiddish journalism in America. His reputation in Yiddish literature, however, was won as a writer of humorous stories, and here he gained his huge following, often being called the Yiddish Mark Twain. His keen powers of observation and intimate knowledge of Jewish-American life enabled him to penetrate the foibles of the immigrant Jewish masses and depict in humorous vein the pathetic vicissitudes of their lives as they adjusted themselves to their new environment. Ghetto scenes, the daily incidents of congregational and fraternal activity, the conflict of Orthodox parents with their American-born children, the manifold commercial and occupational kaleidoscope of New York's East Side —such is the backgronnd against which moves a variegated assortment of Jewish types. In such characters as Chayyim the Custom-Peddler, Joe the Waiter, Simche the *Shadchen* (marriage-broker), Berl the Butcher-Boy, Zevin presented to his readers an unforgettable gallery of portraits, easily recognizable, which they greeted with laughter and delight. Zevin, however, did not laugh at his characters; he laughed with them. He had shared their joys and sorrows, their hopes and disappointments.

Zevin was bodily deformed, being a hunchback, the result of a fall when he was a two-year-old child, but nature had amply compensated him by endowing him with a sound mind and a charming personality. An excellent conversationalist, romantically inclined, affable and bubbling with wit and humor, he was always the center of attraction. Overflowing with life and energy, he maintained his literary production at full pitch. In addition to his regular weekly feuilleton for the *Jewish Daily News* he contributed to the leading Yiddish journals in the United States and abroad. He also wrote in Hebrew and in English. During the years 1914–17 some eighty of his humorous stories appeared in the Sunday magazine section of the *New York Herald.* Of his selected Yiddish writings issued in book form worthy of note are *Tashrak's beste Erzeilungen* (New York, 1910), *Maaselech far Kinder* (New York, 1919), *Fun Achzen dis Dreisig* (New York, 1929), a novel of American-Jewish life. In the last years of his life he began collecting and rendering into popular Yiddish the ancient Jewish folklore, his mastery of the original rabbinical sources being here of great avail. The fruits of these studies were *Ale Agodos fun Talmud* (3 vols., New York, 1922), a collection of legends, fables, allegories, anecdotes, historic and biographic stories contained in the Babylonian and Jerusalem Talmud, and a similar work drawn from the Midrash entitled *Der Ozer fun ale Midroshim* (4 vols., New York, 1926). He also published *Ale Mesholim fun Dubner Maggid* (2 vols., New York, 1925), a collection of the parables of Jacob Kranz, the the famous preacher of Dubno (Poland) in the eighteenth century.

[Zalmen Reisen, *Lexicon fun der Yiddisher Literatur*, vol. IV (Wilna, 1929); Salomon Wininger, *Grosse jüdische National-Biographie*, vol. V (1935), p. 505; Ba'al Machshovos (I. Eljaschew), *Schriften*, vol. IV (1913); *Der Americaner*, Oct. 15, 1926; obituary in *N. Y. Times*, Oct. 7, 1926; family data and personal acquaintance.]   I. S.

ZIEGEMEIER, HENRY JOSEPH (Mar. 27, 1869–Oct. 15, 1930), naval officer, was born in Allegheny, Pa., the son of Joseph and Regina (Meyer) Ziegemeier. His parents subsequently moved to Canton, Ohio, where he spent most of his childhood. He entered the United States Naval Academy on May 21, 1886, and was graduated in 1890. He then served in several ships chiefly in the Pacific. He was made an ensign, July 1, 1892, and was at the torpedo station, Newport, R. I., from October 1895 to July 1897. He then joined the gunboat *Annapolis* and served in her on blockade and convoy duty during the Spanish-American War, commanding the first and second division guns in the actions at Baracoa and Port Nipe Bay, Cuba, on July 15 and July 21, 1898 (see *Appendix to the Report of the Chief of the Bureau of Navigation, Annual Report of the Navy Department*, 1898), and participating also in the occupation of Ponce, Puerto Rico, on July 28. He was made lieutenant, Mar. 3, 1899. After a year in the battleship *Indiana*, he was at the Naval Academy from 1900 to 1902 as an instructor in modern languages, and again from 1905 to 1908 as an instructor in seamanship. In the intervening period he was navigator in the *Hartford,* and from 1908 to 1911 navigator and subsequently executive in the *West Virginia.*

Upon his promotion to the rank of commander, Mar. 3, 1911, he was assigned to duty with the General Board of the navy, and was its secretary from February 1912 to July 1913. He then commanded successively the *Annapolis* and the *Denver,* and was in charge of the torpedo flotilla of the Pacific Fleet from June to September 1915. After another two years as secretary of the General Board, with promotion to the rank of captain on Aug. 29, 1916, he commanded the battleship *Virginia* during the World War from June 1917 to July 18, 1919. In the *Virginia* he operated with the Atlantic Fleet until the summer of 1918, and thereafter had command of convoys taking American troops to France and returning

with them after the armistice. His services won him the award of the Navy Cross. Following the war he had charge in 1919–21 of the organization and training of the Naval Reserve Force. He commanded the new battleship *California* in 1921–22, and, after promotion to the rank of rear admiral in June 1922, was director of naval communications until May 1923. He was then commandant of the Norfolk navy yard until January 1925; commander of Battleship Division 3, Battle Fleet, until June 1927; and after five months in charge of the Division of Fleet Training at Washington, was, from November 1927 to June 1928, commandant of the 9th Naval District and the Great Lakes Training Station. Thereafter he was commandant of the 13th Naval District and the Puget Sound navy yard. His death was the result of a sudden heart attack during a golf game. His funeral was at the navy yard in Bremerton, Wash., and his burial in Forest Lawn Cemetery, Los Angeles, Cal. He was married first, on Sept. 18, 1895, to Ida Wernet of Canton, Ohio, who died in 1915, and second, on Nov. 16, 1921, to Jewel Ridings of Los Angeles, by whom he had one daughter. His second wife survived him.

[*Who's Who in America*, 1930–31; L. R. Hamersly, *Records of Living Officers of the U. S. Navy and Marine Corps* (7th ed., 1902); Service Record, from the Bureau of Navigation, Navy Dept.; *N. Y. Times*, Oct. 16, 1930; *Army and Navy Jour.*, Oct. 18, Oct. 25, 1930; information from family sources.]   A. W.

ZIEGFELD, FLORENZ (Mar. 21, 1869–July 22, 1932), theatrical producer, was born in Chicago, Ill., son of Florenz Ziegfeld, founder of the Chicago Musical College, and Rosalie (De Hez) Ziegfeld. The parents were German Catholics. The son was educated in the Chicago public schools, and began active association with amusement enterprises by importing bands and other musical features for the World's Fair of 1893. He then became manager for Eugene Sandow, the strong man, exhibiting him at the fair, and later around the country. The first play he managed was *A Parlor Match* (1896), in which he introduced a young player he had seen in Paris, Anna Held. He advertised her by methods which Barnum might have envied, including a tale about her milk baths, and she appeared successively in *Papa's Wife, The Little Duchess, The Parisian Model,* and *Mlle. Napoleon.* All these were plays with songs, and in mounting them Ziegfeld exhibited a *flair* for costumes and pretty girls and stage pictures which led him, in 1907, to experiment with a type of production rather new to America, the so-called "review." He called it *The Follies of 1907,* and it was so favorably received that it was followed by a successor each season for more than twenty years. The *Ziegfeld Follies* became noted all over the country for the lavish beauty of costumes, scenery, and stage tableaux, for the pulchritude of the chorus girls, and also for the liberal display of their charms. It became more than a jest that Ziegfeld set the style in feminine form. (He called it, for his trade mark, "Glorifying the American Girl.") The desire for slenderness was undoubtedly increased by the popularity of his chorus types. At the same time, the production standards of musical comedy were raised by the real beauty of his settings and ensemble effects. The humor of the librettos was generally turned over to such comedians as Will Rogers, Bert Williams [*q.v.*], Eddie Cantor, and Leon Errol, who sometimes improvised their own skits. Ziegfeld's contribution was the selection of the music and of beautiful girls, in sets by Joseph Urban [*q.v.*] or tableaux by Ben Ali Haggin, lavishly produced but controlled by an instinctive taste. In 1914 Ziegfeld produced *The Midnight Frolic* on top of the New Amsterdam Theatre, which continued until the advent of prohibition. In 1916, with Charles Dillingham, he took over for a time the ill-fated Century Theatre, for the production of spectacular musical plays. Among his most successful productions, in addition to the *Follies*, were *Sally*, with Marilyn Miller (1920), *Show Boat* (1927), *Bitter Sweet* (1929), and *Rio Rita*, with which he opened the Ziegfeld Theatre, Feb. 2, 1927. This theatre, on Sixth Avenue near Central Park, was designed for him by Joseph Urban especially to house his type of spectacular musical comedy. It was modernistic in plan and decorative scheme, and was a departure in American theatre design. Two years later, however, came the depression. Ziegfeld's productions, mounted at great cost, and necessarily exacting a high tariff of the public, were not calculated to survive lean purses. His fortunes ebbed, and when he died in Hollywood in 1932, he left little of the great sums he had once taken in. His theatre became a movie house. Ziegfeld married Anna Held in Paris in 1897, separated from her in 1908, and was divorced from her in 1913. On Apr. 11, 1914, he married the actress, Billie Burke, who with a daughter survived him.

Gene Buck, who wrote many of the *Follies* for Ziegfeld, once described him as a "quiet, lanky, long-faced dreamer" (*New York Times*, IX, p. 1, July 31, 1932). In youth he was lanky, and also swanky, with a dark, rather saturnine countenance. In later life he put on weight and grew a dapper little moustache, which contrasted oddly with his somewhat Mephistophelian cast of features. Like most great showmen, he probably was in truth a dreamer, seeing resplendent visions of great stage effects, and gambling vast sums of money on attaining them. (Some of his productions cost over $200,000.) He had the showman's love of sending long telegrams when a letter would have served, of possessing five expensive motor cars when one was all he could ride in, and he was extremely jealous of his leadership in musical comedy production. That leadership, however, was based on real ability, and he was fully aware of what he was doing. In his line, he was an artist. He brought the musical review to America, and developed it in visual artistry to a point it had never attained elsewhere. The effects of his taste and standards continue to be felt on the American lyric stage.

[*Who's Who in America*, 1932–33; Eddie Cantor and David Freedman in *Collier's*, Jan. 13–Feb. 17, 1934; J. P. McEvoy, in *Sat. Eve. Post*, Sept. 10, 1932; *N. Y. Times*, July 23–25, 31, 1932; *N. Y. Tribune*, July 24, 1932; Theatre Coll., N. Y. Pub. Lib.; Theatre Coll., Harvard College Lib.]
                          W. P. E.

ZIEGLER, DAVID (1748–Sept. 24, 1811), soldier, pioneer, was born in Heidelberg on the Neckar, then in the Palatinate. According to one biographer he was born on Aug. 16 (Rattermann, *post*, p. 269), but he may have been the Johann David Ziegler listed in a register in the Lutheran *Providenz Kirche* as born on July 13, 1748, to Johann Heinrich Ziegler, hatmaker, and his wife, Louise Fredericka Kern (Katzenberger, *post*, p. 128). Enlisting under Weisman in 1768, he served in the Russian army against the Turks on the lower Danube and in the Crimea, and was wounded and promoted to commissioned officer. At the end of the war in 1774 he emigrated to Pennsylvania and settled in Carlisle. At the news of the battle of Lexington he joined as third lieutenant the battalion of riflemen led by William Thompson [*q.v.*], which took part in the siege of Boston. He fought at Long Island, Brandywine, Germantown, Paoli, and Monmouth, being wounded in the first battle. He was commissioned captain on Dec. 8, 1778. He was commissary general of the Department of Pennsylvania, with headquarters at Waynesboro (1779–80) and served with his regiment around New York for a year. In June 1781 his regiment joined Lafayette in Virginia, serving there until after the siege of Yorktown. In January 1782 his unit was attached to Greene's army in South Carolina, with which he remained until mustered out, Jan. 1, 1783.

He returned to Carlisle and opened a grocery store, but left it to accept a captain's commission under Josiah Harmar [*q.v.*] about the middle of 1784. During the next six years he was stationed at Forts Mackintosh (Beaver, Pa.), Harmar

(Marietta, Ohio), Finney (at the mouth of the Miami River), and Washington (Cincinnati), and at the Falls of the Ohio. On Feb. 22, 1789, at Marietta he married Lucy Anne Sheffield, a native of Jamestown, R. I. In 1790 he was with Harmar on his indecisive expedition against the Indians. In the crisis that followed, Ziegler, since Oct. 22 a major of the 1st Infantry, was sent to Marietta and succeeded in averting the Indian menace from that district. He was with Arthur St. Clair [q.v.] in the fall of 1791 on his disastrous campaign and covered the retreat of the army after the defeat. When St. Clair departed for the East he left Ziegler in command of the army, but the intrigues of James Wilkinson [q.v.] and others who were his seniors in the services so disgusted him that on Mar. 5, 1792, he resigned from his command and from the army. He bought a farm about four miles from Cincinnati but sold it in 1797 and opened a store in the town. During the first two years after the incorporation of Cincinnati in 1802 he was president of the council, an office which carried with it the duties of chief magistrate. He served as the first marshal of the Ohio district (appointment confirmed, Mar. 3, 1803) and as adjutant-general of Ohio (1807), and at the time of his death was surveyor of the port of Cincinnati (appointment confirmed, Dec. 9, 1807). In politics he was an ardent Democratic-Republican.

He was of medium height, with dark complexion and round, good-natured face. His carriage was erect and martial, and he was always affable and polite. He was an able administrator and disciplinarian, thoroughly honest and straightforward in his dealings with others, noted for his deliberation, care, and precision in business and military affairs. While he was in the army his company was "always considered the first in point of discipline and appearance" (Denny, *post*, p. 123). He seems never to have learned to speak English well. He left no children.

[Ziegler's name occurs repeatedly in *Pa. Archives*, 2 ser., vols. X–XI (1880), 5 ser., vol. II (1906), and in *Military Jour. of Maj. Ebenezer Denny* (1859). See also Emil Klauprecht, *Deutsche Chronik in der Geschichte des Ohio-Thales* (1864); H. A. Rattermann, in *Hist. Reg. . . . Relating to Interior Pa.*, Dec. 1883; Mary D. Steele, in *Mag. of Western Hist.*, May 1885; Henry Howe, *Hist. Colls. of Ohio* (1908 ed.), vol. I, p. 853; G. A. Katzenberger, in *Ohio Archaeological and Hist. Quart.*, Apr.–July 1912, which contains a portrait and reprints an obituary from the *Western Spy* (Cincinnati), Sept. 28, 1811.]   L. D. B.

ZIEGLER, WILLIAM (Sept. 1, 1843–May 24, 1905), manufacturer, patron of polar exploration, son of Francis and Ernestina Ziegler, was born in Beaver County, Pa. His parents removed to Iowa when he was still an infant. In Muscatine, Iowa, after some rudimentary schooling, he

first worked at the printer's trade and then, at eighteen, served briefly as a pharmacist's apprentice. After graduating in 1863 from a business college at Poughkeepsie, N. Y., he sought and found work in a wholesale drug house in New York City. Later he studied for a time at the College of Pharmacy of the City of New York and in 1868 began business for himself in a small way, dealing in extracts and other supplies for bakers and confectioners. Baking powder was a comparatively new product, and in 1870, with two other men, Ziegler organized the Royal Chemical Company and began the manufacture of Royal Baking Powder, long the most popular brand in America. Incorporated in 1873, the Royal Baking Powder Company became enormously prosperous. In 1880 it was paying seventy percent. dividends on 1600 shares of stock at $100 par value each. The success of the company was largely due to Ziegler's energy and knowledge of the business; but he could not agree with his partners, and after a long legal struggle, culminating in 1888, he sold his interest in the company for $3,000,000. He then bought the Price Baking Powder Company of Chicago and the Tartar Chemical Company of Jersey City. In 1899 these companies, together with two others, were united with the Royal in what was popularly known as the Baking Powder Trust, with a capital of $20,000,000 (*New York Times*, Mar. 2, 1899). Ziegler was believed to be the moving spirit in this consolidation, though he denied it. He was indicted in Missouri in 1903 for bribery of members of the legislature, but the governor of New York refused to extradite him, and he was never tried (see *New York Tribune*, Nov. 16–17, 1903, and Jan. 2, Feb. 2, 1904).

In 1890 he undertook to prevent the acquisition by the city of Brooklyn, where he lived, of the Long Island Water Company, which certain aldermen had bought for $500,000 and which they proposed to sell to the city for $3,500,000. He bought stock in the company, brought suit as a stockholder to block the deal, and finally succeeded in having the purchase price reduced to $2,000,000. He refused nomination for the mayorship of Brooklyn in 1893. In 1901 he financed an unsuccessful expedition in search of the North Pole, headed by Evelyn B. Baldwin. The party returned to Norway on Aug. 1, 1902, sixteen days after a relief ship had sailed in search of it. Baldwin and Ziegler now parted company, and the latter sent another polar ship out from Trondhjem, Norway, in June 1903, under Anthony Fiala, who had been a photographer with the first expedition. This party was not heard from for more than two years, and its patron died without knowing its fate. Just before his death, however, he had sent out two relief ships, which rescued the men in August 1905. Caches of supplies left by the first expedition had kept them alive, and, though they had not reached the Pole, they had made valuable scientific studies. In his later years, Ziegler dealt in realty on a large scale. The value of his estate at death was estimated at $30,000,000. On July 22, 1886, he married Electa Matilda (Curtis) Gamble. He had no children of his own but adopted two.

[Who's Who in America, 1903–05; N. Y. Times, N. Y. Tribune, World (N. Y.), Sun (N. Y.), May 25 (obituaries), Aug. 11, 12, 1905; The Ziegler Polar Expedition, 1903–1905 . . . Scientific Results (1907), ed. by J. A. Fleming; Harper's Weekly, June 22, 1901; Anthony Fiala, Fighting the Polar Ice (1906) and articles in McClure's Mag., Feb., Mar. 1906.]   A. F. H.

ZIEHN, BERNHARD (Jan. 20, 1845–Sept. 8, 1912), musical theorist and teacher, was born at Erfurt in Prussian Saxony, Germany. His father, a shoemaker by trade, gave him a good education. After graduating from a seminary for teachers, young Ziehn received an appointment as teacher at Mühlhausen, where he remained for three years. He then emigrated to America to teach at a German Lutheran school in Chicago and arrived upon the scene of his future labors in November 1868. For two years he taught German, history, higher mathematics, and musical theory. School teaching irked him, and at the end of this period he abandoned the profession of schoolmaster and devoted himself completely to the study and teaching of musical theory. He had not made an intensive study of music at Erfurt, but he was a born scholar and his increasing preoccupation with music soon became the dominating passion of his life. Whatever musical literature he possessed was destroyed in the Chicago fire of 1871, save his collection of Beethoven sonatas. With these as a cornerstone, he resumed his researches into the nature of musical grammar and syntax. He became one of the greatest of autodidacts. Gifted with an unusual memory, he had at his fingertips the harmonic devices of all masters. His penetration of harmonic and contrapuntal structure was systematic and daringly logical.

By 1886 the manuscript of Ziehn's great treatise on harmony was completed. It was published at Berlin in 1888 as *Harmonie—und Modulationslehre*. It was less a textbook on harmony and modulation than an epoch-making work on harmonic analysis, with hundreds of examples from musical literature. By deriving his classification of chords directly from the practice of the great masters and not from some pseudo-scientific theory of overtones, he placed his harmonic analyses on a solid basis. Such was the logic of his harmonic derivation that he forecast the entire modern impressionistic harmonic technique. In 1907 he published the first volume of a completely recast English version of this work as *Manual of Harmony*. The second volume was never published, but presumably is preserved in manuscript. In the year 1911 he brought out his treatise on *Five- and Six-Point Harmonies,* with eight hundred examples and five masterly harmonizations of German chorales. His noteworthy contribution to contrapuntal technique, published as *Canonical Studies—A New Technic in Composition* (1912), went to press as he lay on his deathbed. The development of the idea of symmetrical inversion of melodic phrases constitutes one of his most brilliant achievements. In his earliest publications, *System der Uebungen für Clavierspieler* and *Ein Lehrgang für den ersten Unterricht,* published at Hamburg in 1881, he invented finger exercises in contrary motion so as to insure the symmetrical development of both hands.

Ziehn was a solitary figure. He held aloof from contemporary opportunism, and labored to solve the problems of his beloved art. An outstanding achievement was his solution of the unfinished final fugue in Sebastian Bach's *Art of the Fugue,* a problem that had baffled the best minds for over a century. Gustav Nottebohm arrived independently at practically the same solution, but to Ziehn belongs the priority. This scholarly feat inspired the pianist Ferruccio Busoni to write his monumental *Fantasia Contrappuntistica* in 1910. Ziehn's greatest contribution to the history of music was his monographic demonstration of the spuriousness of the *St. Lucas Passion,* a choral work traditionally attributed to Bach. He was a constant contributor to the German music journal, *Die Allgemeine Musik-zeitung,* and startled conservative Germany with his fierce attacks on Hugo Riemann, a scholar whose truly encyclopedic knowledge covered too much ground to be always solid. Most of Ziehn's musicological writings were reprinted in 1927 by the German-American Historical Society of Illinois in a volume of "Gesammelte Aufsätze zur Geschichte und Theorie der Musik," *Jahrbuch der Deutsch-Amerikanischen Historischen Gesellschaft von Illinois,* vois. XXVI–XXVII (1927). He wielded a trenchant pen and was as much feared for his caustic wit as he was admired for his profound erudition. His critical essays deal with subjects as remote as the old church modes and as recent as the latest harmony texts. He made propaganda for Anton Bruckner when that great symphonist was practically unknown in America. His conception of musical ornamentation was accepted by Theodore Thomas [*q.v.*], his intimate friend and admirer, as authoritative. A modern German critic, Bruno Weigl, designates him the most original theorist of the nineteenth century (Weigl, *Harmonielehre*, 2 vols., 1925).

Ziehn had a powerful physique that promised long usefulness, but a cancer of the larynx put a period to that. He was married to Emma Trabing, of Chicago, who, with a son, survived him. A daughter died in infancy.

[Valuable data from Julius Gold of San Francisco, and Wilhelm Middelschulte, of Chicago ; F. C. Bennett, *Hist. of Music and Art in Ill.* (1904) ; Winthrop Sargeant, "Bernhard Ziehn, Precursor," *Musical Quart.*, Apr. 1933 ; Ferruccio Busoni, "Die Gotiker von Chicago," *Signale für die Musikalische Welt* (Berlin), Feb. 2, 1910 ; Julius Gold, "Bernhard Ziehn's Contributions to the Science of Music," *Musical Courier*, July 1, 1914 ; C. E. R. Mueller, article in *Allgemeine Musik-zeitung*, Oct. 4, 1912 ; *Musical Courier*, Sept. 18, 1912 ; obituary by G. D. Gunn, *Chicago Daily Tribune*, Sept. 9, 1912 ; articles by Julius Goebel and Th. Otterstrom, in "Gesammelte Aufsatze," *Jahrbuch, supra* ; *Hugo Riemanns Musiklexikon* (11th ed., 1929), vol. II ; E. J. Dent, *Ferruccio Busoni* (1933).]   E. C. K—n.

ZIMMERMAN, EUGENE (Dec. 17, 1845– Dec. 20, 1914), capitalist and railroad official, the son of Solomon and Hannah J. (Briggs) Zimmerman, was born at Vicksburg, Miss. In 1856 he removed with his parents to Clifton, a suburb of Cincinnati, Ohio. In 1858 his father, a native of Ohio, died, and two years later his mother died. Although his father had owned some property in Vicksburg, consisting of slaves and a foundry, and retained his business relations with that city after removing to Cincinnati, all of the property was lost during the Civil War. Zimmerman was educated at Farmers' College at College Hill, Ohio, and at Gambier, Ohio, where he prepared to enter Kenyon College. At the outbreak of the Civil War, he left school and joined the Federal forces. He served with the navy and at the end of the war was acting-master of the *Ouachita*, in the Mississippi squadron. After the war he acquired an interest in a planing mill and a lumber yard at Hamilton, Ohio, which he sold after two years and invested in petroleum. In 1874 he sold his interest in this business to the Standard Oil Company. In 1878 he married Marietta A. Evans, the daughter of Abraham Evans of Urbana, Ohio, who died in 1881, leaving one daughter, Helena, who, in 1900, married the ninth Duke of Manchester.

He entered the railroad business first as engineer in the construction of railroads out of Cincinnati and then helped build the Chesapeake &

Ohio bridge at Cincinnati. As a member of the board of directors, vice-president, and president of the Cincinnati, Hamilton & Dayton Railroad, he was active in the reorganization and enlarging of the system. In July 1904 he obtained control of the Pere Marquette Railroad Company and, with it, the Chicago, Cincinnati & Louisville Railroad. In 1905 the Erie Railroad, which wanted the Cincinnati, Hamilton & Dayton as a feeder, contracted with John Pierpont Morgan for the purchase of the stock of the latter road on a commission basis. On Dec. 4, 1905, Judson Harmon [*q.v.*] was appointed receiver of the roads. Later, on Dec. 19, 1914, Frederick W. Stevens in testifying before the Interstate Commerce Commission claimed that Zimmerman and his associates loaded $24,000,000 worth of obligations on the railroad and doubled that property's annual interest payments in the first year after acquiring control; and that the Cincinnati, Hamilton & Dayton road then entered into a 999 year lease of the Pere Marquette system and guaranteed that road's bonds. Subsequently Morgan volunteered to take the stock himself from the Erie, thereby incurring a loss, it is claimed, of more than $12,000,000 (see *New York Times*, Dec. 20, 1914). The sudden death of Zimmerman did not give him an opportunity to give his own explanation of this transaction. In 1910 Zimmerman sold the Ann Arbor Railroad Company, one of his properties in Michigan, and retired from active business, although he still retained control of his extensive coal and iron lands in the middle west and his large holdings of stock in the Standard Oil Company.

[*Hist. of Cincinnati and Hamilton County* (1894) ; *Who's Who in America*, 1912–13 ; *War of Rebellion : Official Records (Navy)*, 1 ser. vol. XXVI, for naval rank on Aug. 4, 1865 ; W. Z. Ripley, *Railroads, Finance, and Organization* (1915) ; *Poor's Manual of Railroads*, 1904, 1905, 1906 ; *Cincinnati Enquirer*, Dec. 20, 1914 ; *Cincinnati Commercial Tribune, Cincinnati Post*, and *N. Y. Times*, Dec. 21, 1914.]   R. C. M.

ZINZENDORF, NICOLAUS LUDWIG, Count von (May 26, 1700–May 9, 1760), leader of the Unitas Fratrum or Moravian Church, was born in Dresden and died at Herrnhut on his Saxon estate near Bertelsdorf. The second son of Georg Ludwig, Count von Zinzendorf und Pottendorf, a Saxon cabinet minister, by his wife, Carlotta Justina von Gersdorf, he was a scion of an ancient, wealthy noble family originally domiciled in Lower Austria. His career as a whole belongs to German biography, but for thirteen months he played a decisive personal part in American ecclesiastical affairs.

The letters of Augustus Gottlieb Spangenberg and George Whitefield [*qq.v.*] induced him to visit Pennsylvania. With his daughter Benigna and a retinue of five he landed at New York Dec. 2, 1741, and proceeded to Philadelphia, where he was entertained by John Stephen Benezet. He lost no time in seeking out Henry Antes [*q.v.*], leader of the Associated Brethren of the Skippack, for the Count's chief purpose was to unite all the Pennsylvania German Protestants in an association to be known as the Congregation of God in the Spirit. Although he did not attempt to obliterate sectarian differences immediately, aiming only at mutual understanding and sympathy, he probably hoped that the Moravians would exercise a commanding influence over the other groups and ultimately absorb them. Meanwhile, the better to carry out his purpose, he had divested himself temporarily of his office of bishop in the Moravian Church and desired to be known as Ludwig von Thürnstein, a plain Lutheran clergyman. Through Antes he issued a call for a "union synod" or free conference to be held Jan. 1, 1742, at Germantown. During the next six months six similar conferences were convened at various places — Falkner Swamp, Oley, Germantown, Philadelphia—but the Count's noble dream of Christian union could not be realized among a people incurably addicted to separatism and controversy. Instead, he was assailed unmercifully by Samuel Blair, John Philip Boehm, Christopher Sower, Gilbert Tennent [*qq.v.*], and everyone else who could afford to print a pamphlet, and in June he abandoned his plan. The movement that he had started did not, however, die out at once. Its best consequence was that it stimulated the Lutherans and the Reformed to organize congregations and call pastors from Germany. During the latter half of 1742 Zinzendorf made three journeys in the interest of Moravian missions among the Indians: June 24–Aug. 2 to the Minnisinks, the Blue Mountains, the Aquanshicola, and the Upper Schuylkill, holding a successful parley with chiefs of the Six Nations at the house of Johann Conrad Weiser [*q.v.*] near Womelsdorf, Berks County; Aug. 10–Aug. 31 to Shekomeko, Dutchess County, N. Y., where he organized an Indian congregation; and Sept. 24–Nov. 9 to Shamokin. He also ministered to Lutherans and Reformed at Philadelphia, Germantown, and elsewhere, not always with happy results, and aided in establishing Moravian congregations at Bethlehem (which owes its name to him), Nazareth, Philadelphia, Hebron, Heidelberg, Lancaster, and York, Pa., as well as at New York and on Staten Island; in connection with a few congregations schools were started. He sailed for England from New York Jan. 9, 1743.

[The bibliog. appended to J. J. Sessler, *Communal Pietism among Early Am. Moravians* (1933), is the best guide to the study of Zinzendorf's Am. career. The most useful works are: A. G. Spangenberg, *Leben des Herrn Nicolaus Ludwig Grafen und Herrn von Zinzendorf und Pottendorf* (8 pts., Barby, 1772–75); an abridged version of the same, tr. by Samuel Jackson, *The Life of Nicholas Lewis, Count Zinzendorf* (1838); L. T. Reichel, *The Early Hist. of the Church of the United Brethren (Unitas Fratrum), Commonly Called Moravians, in North America* (1888); J. M. Levering, *A Hist. of Bethlehem, Pa.* (1903); J. T. Hamilton, "A Hist. of the Unitas Fratrum," in Am. Church Hist. Ser., vol. VIII (1894); W. C. Reichel, *Memorials of the Renewed Church* (1870); W. J. Hinke, *Life and Letters of the Rev. John Philip Boehm* (1916); *Nachrichten von den vereinigten Ev.-Luth. Gemeinen in Nord-America*, vol. I (1886), ed. by W. J. Mann and B. M. Schmucker.]

G. H. G.

ZOGBAUM, RUFUS FAIRCHILD (Aug. 28, 1849–Oct. 22, 1925), illustrator, was the son of Ferdinand and Mary B. (Fairchild) Zogbaum. He was born in Charleston, S. C., but moved to New York just before or just after the outbreak of the Civil War. His father and uncle were partners in the New York firm of Zogbaum & Fairchild, manufacturers of musical instruments.

Zogbaum studied at the University of Heidelberg, at the Art Students' League of New York (1878–79), and in Paris under Léon J. F. Bonnat (1880–82). On his return to America, he settled in New York and devoted himself to the delineation of army and navy life. In pursuit of material of this nature he traveled widely by sea and land, observing the actual operations of the naval and military forces, which he pictured with spirit and vivid realism. In his historic essays he dealt with such themes as "Old Ironsides," with her crew clearing ship for action, the *Vandalia* during the terrific hurricane in Samoa, the attack of the *Merrimac* on the Cumberland in Hampton Roads, and the surrender of Lee at Appomattox. From his own observation on the scene of action, he delineated the stirring episodes of the Spanish-American War in Puerto Rico, in the Caribbean, and along the Cuban coast. Many of these subjects were used for illustrations in books and magazines. Over forty of his pictures were shown in an exhibition at the Avery Galleries, New York, in the winter of 1899. In addition to his oil paintings, water colors, and illustrations, he produced a number of mural decorations of a historic and patriotic character, among them the "First Minnesota Regiment at the Battle of Gettysburg," in the state capitol, St. Paul, Minn.; the "Battle of Lake Erie," in the Federal Building, Cleveland, Ohio; and "Hail and Farewell," in the Woolworth Building, New York. He also painted a few portraits, including those of Rear Admiral William Rogers Taylor, in the Naval War

College at Newport, R. I., Dr. Henry Loomis Nelson, which belongs to Williams College, and Dr. St. Clair Smith, painted for the Flower Hospital, New York. The historic value of his work is notable, and his expression of strenuous action and the spirit of combat is not the least of his merits as an artist.

Zogbaum was the author of three books: *Horse, Foot, and Dragoons* (1888), a series of sketches of army life; *"All Hands"* (1897); and *The Junior Officer of the Watch* (1908). He contributed to *Scribner's Magazine* (Jan. 1915) a copiously illustrated article, "War and the Artist," in which, however, he made only incidental allusions to his own work. In September 1878 he married Mary F. Lockwood. He died in New York at the age of seventy-six, survived by his widow, three sons, and a daughter.

[*Who's Who in America,* 1912–13; *Am. Art Ann.,* 1925; Charleston city dir., 1852; inscriptions from Unitarian churchyard, Charleston; cat. of exhibition, *Times,* Oct. 24, 1925; information as to certain facts from a son, R. F. Zogbaum, Esq.]   W. H. D.

ZOLLARS, ELY VAUGHAN (Sept. 19, 1847–Feb. 10, 1916), minister of the Disciples of Christ, educator, was born near Lower Salem, Ohio. His father, Abram, a blacksmith and farmer, was of German descent, his first American ancestor having been brought to Pennsylvania as a child sometime between 1730 and 1740; Ely's mother, however, Caroline (Vaughan), was of old New England stock. Work in the blacksmith's shop and on the farm hardened the boy physically, and the discipline of a religious home gave him character. His parents were among the early Disciples in Ohio. At the age of twelve he was sent to a private school in Marietta and later to the preparatory department of Marietta College; but when only eighteen, Oct. 22, 1865, he married Hulda Louisa McAtee of Washington County, Ohio, and for some years thereafter worked on a farm and taught school winters. In 1871 he entered Bethany College, where he was graduated in 1875.

He was immediately appointed adjunct professor of ancient languages, beginning an educational career which with little interruption was to continue throughout his life. After a year's teaching, he was made financial agent of the college and raised some $27,000 to tide it over a financial crisis. Toward the close of 1876 he was called to the presidency of the Kentucky Classical and Business College at North Middletown, and for seven years directed its affairs with notable success. He resigned with the intention of entering the ministry, but consented to act for a year as president of Garrard Female College, Lancaster, Ky. He then served as pastor of the

Christian Church, Springfield, Ill., until 1888, when he was called to the presidency of Hiram College. During the fourteen years he held this position the number of students increased and the resources and equipment of the institution were largely augmented. In 1902 he assumed the presidency of another denominational college— Texas Christian University, then located at Waco—where his business ability and success in raising money were again utilized to good advantage. His last contribution to the educational enterprises of the Disciples was in Oklahoma, where, in October 1906, he went to establish Oklahoma Christian University (later Phillips University), chartered Oct. 7, 1907. Of this institution he served as president and president emeritus until his death, at which time it had five buildings and some 400 students.

Zollars was a man of restless temperament, great energy, good judgment, and no little administrative ability. He was a firm believer in higher education under Christian auspices, and held that its chief function was to make the individual socially efficient. Together with his other work he did much teaching of the Bible, and wrote several books of an expository nature. Among them were *The Great Salvation* (copr. 1895), *Hebrew Prophecy* (copr. 1907), *The King of Kings* (1911), *The Commission Executed* (1912), and *The Abrahamic Promises Fulfilled* (1913). In 1912 he published *Baccalaureate and Convocation Sermons.* He died at the home of his daughter in Warren, Ohio.

[F. M. Green, *Hiram College* (1901); J. T. Brown, *Churches of Christ . . . in the U. S., Australasia, England, and Canada* (1904); *Who's Who in America,* 1914–15; *Christian Standard,* Feb. 19, Mar. 11, 1916.]   H. E. S.

ZOLLICOFFER, FELIX KIRK (May 19, 1812–Jan. 19, 1862), journalist, congressman, and soldier, was born in Maury County, Tenn., the son of John Jacob and Martha (Kirk) Zollicoffer. Of Swiss descent, he was the great-grandson of Jacob Christopher Zollicoffer, who came to America in the early eighteenth century with Baron de Graffenreid [*q.v.*] and was associated with the settlement at New Bern, N. C. His grandfather, Capt. George Zollicoffer, a Revolutionary soldier, received a land grant in Tennessee. Although Felix's father owned a thousand acres, the boy was taken out of the old-field school to work one year on the plantation; for one year he attended Jackson College at Columbia, Tenn. At sixteen, he entered newspaper work in Paris, Tenn., but after two years his paper failed and he became a journeyman printer in Knoxville until he worked off his indebtedness. In 1834 he became editor and part owner of the Columbia *Observer*, and in addition helped to edit in these years the *Southern Agriculturist* and the Huntsville (Ala.) *Mercury*. Also he dabbled in literature: one essay, "Hours," printed in *The Literary and Miscellaneous Scrap Book* (1837) of William Fields (later *The Scrap Book*), was often declaimed by schoolboys. In 1835 he was appointed state printer of Tennessee; the following year he abandoned journalism to serve one year as lieutenant in the Seminole War. On Sept. 24, 1835, he was married to Louisa Pocahontas Gordon, daughter of Capt. John Gordon of the "Border Spies." Of their eleven children, the five boys died in infancy.

Gradually Zollicoffer became a political power in the state. In 1842 he was appointed associate editor of the Nashville *Republican Banner*, to aid the Whig James C. Jones [*q.v.*] in his approaching gubernatorial campaign against James K. Polk. Never strong, Zollicoffer conducted the campaign successfully while suffering from aneurism of the aorta. As soon as he had recovered, he was appointed adjutant-general and state comptroller (1845–49), and then served as state senator from 1849 to 1852. But these minor offices were small indication of his political power, for he was Tennessee's "Warwick and king-maker" beyond any question, as was proved in 1850 when he returned to the *Banner* as editor and forced the nomination by the Whigs and the eventual election of William Bate Campbell as governor. Two years later he ran for congressman, but neglected his own campaign to work for Gen. Winfield Scott, whose nomination he had opposed in the Whig convention. So bitter was this campaign that John Leake Marling [*q.v.*], editor of the Democratic Nashville *Union*, in an editorial on Aug. 20, 1852, charged Zollicoffer with misrepresenting Franklin Pierce's views on slavery and the South, and virtually termed him a liar. In the duel which followed, both men were wounded: Zollicoffer slightly in his pistol hand, Marling seriously in the head. It was generally thought that the quarrel was political rather than personal, and the two men later became reconciled. Chiefly through Zollicoffer's efforts, Scott carried Tennessee; Zollicoffer was elected to Congress, and resigned from the *Banner*. He served until 1859, but declined to run for a fourth term.

As a state-rights Whig he worked steadily for peace and understanding between the sections, supported the American or Know-Nothing party in 1856, and toured New York in 1860 in support of John Bell's candidacy for the presidency. In 1861 he was a member of the peace conference at Washington; he was speaking at a rally against secession when news of war reached Nashville. Immediately Gov. Isham G. Harris [*q.v.*] offered him a major-generalship and the command of the Tennessee troops, which he declined on account of lack of experience, but he did accept a commission as brigadier-general in the Confederate Army. He was put in command of East Tennessee, to try to check the strong Unionist tendencies there. Late in 1861 he was ordered to move with his army to Mill Springs, Ky. At the battle of Fishing Creek, Zollicoffer went past his own lines; meeting with the Federal troops under Col. Speed S. Fry, he requested them not to fire. But his aide-de-camp fired at Fry, and when the Federal troops retaliated Zollicoffer was killed. His body was returned to Nashville for burial. Although he was not the first Confederate general killed in action, his death shocked the entire South, and brought forth universal and deserved tribute to his bravery and ability.

[Octavia Zollicoffer Bond, "General Felix Kirk Zollicoffer, C. S. A.," unpublished, dated 1924, in Tenn. State Library, and *The Family Chronicle and Kinship Book of Maclin, Clack, . . . and other Related American Lineages* (1928), for the American family; Ernst Götzinger, *Die Familie Zollikofer* (1887), for the Swiss connections; eulogistic sketch by M. J. Wright, in *Southern Bivouac*, July 1884, pp. 485–99; Nashville *Republican Banner*, 1852; Nashville *Union*, Aug. 20–22, 1852.]   E. W. P.

ZUBLY, JOHN JOACHIM (Aug. 27, 1724– July 23, 1781), Presbyterian clergyman, member of the Continental Congress, pamphleteer, was born in St. Gall, Switzerland, and received his schooling at the Gymnasium at that place. On Aug. 19, 1744, he was ordained at the German Church in London and the same year went to Purrysburg, S. C., following his father, David ("Direktor des Berichthauses"), who had emigrated to America in 1736. Two years after his arrival, Zubly married Ann Tobler, Nov. 12, 1746. Of this union two daughters survived the father. In answer to a call from the Independent Presbyterian Church at Savannah he removed to Georgia, entering upon his duties in 1760. Able and energetic, "a learned man," and a person of a "warm and zealous spirit" (*The Works of John Adams*, vol. II, 1850, pp. 421–22), he spoke English, Dutch, French, Latin, and German, and his writings indicate acquaintance with Coke, Blackstone, Rapin, and Montesquieu. Several of his sermons were published. In September 1770 the College of New Jersey gave him the honorary degree of A.M. and four years later, that of D.D.

He participated in many phases of Georgia's religious and civil life. Occasionally he preached to congregations other than his own, to the German Lutherans especially. He became the chief spokesman and defender of the dissenting groups against "Episcopal oppression," particularly respecting oaths, burials, fees for tolling the bell, and marriage licenses (*Proceedings of the Massachusetts Historical Society*, 1 ser. VIII, 1866, pp. 214–19). He gradually accumulated a large amount of property in land and slaves, and he held minor civil offices from time to time, such as clerk of Christ Church parish. In July 1775, when the provincial congress of Georgia met in Savannah, he was chosen a delegate from that town. As a member of the congress he served on the committees which prepared an address to Gov. James Wright, a petition to the King, a letter to the Continental Congress, and a message to the inhabitants of the province. He was one of those chosen by this congress to represent Georgia in the Continental Congress at Philadelphia.

Zubly at first cooperated heartily with the Congress. He participated in the debates on fortifying the Hudson River and on the state of trade, and served as a member of the standing committee on accounts or claims. Opposed to a complete break with Great Britain because he dreaded the establishment of a republic, which to him was "little better than government of devils" (*Journals of the Continental Congress*, Ford ed., III, 491), he was unwilling to support the demand of the radical members for independence. When in October 1775 Samuel Chase publicly accused him of disloyalty to the cause of America, he suddenly departed for Georgia, leaving for his fellow delegates a message that he was "greatly indisposed." Soon after his return to Savannah the council of safety of Georgia took him into custody. Late in 1777 he was banished from the province and half of his estate was confiscated. He lived in South Carolina for two years, but when the royal government was restored in Georgia in 1779, he returned and again took up his pastoral work. He lived in Savannah until his death, "after a long and painful illness," two years later.

Zubly wrote and preached where Loyalist sentiment was strong, where opportunities for familiarity or even acquaintance with the arguments and activities of the foremost colonial leaders were comparatively few. His conception of the fundamental differences between Great Britain and America was clear, even if his observations on them were not profound or original. He published a number of pamphlets and articles, *The Stamp-Act Repealed* (1766); "An Apology for a Law Suit" (*Georgia Gazette*, June 3, 1767– Apr. 6, 1768, never reprinted); *An Humble In-*

quiry (1769), reprinted under the title, *Great Britain's Right to Tax Her Colonies* (1774); *Calm and Respectful Thoughts on the Negative of the Crown* (1772); a sermon, *The Law of Liberty* (1775), in which he described the British constitution and proposed methods of opposition to oppressive acts which might lead to war; and an appeal to Lord Dartmouth on behalf of the colonies published in the *London Magazine*, January 1776. He also discussed the relations of Parliament and the colonial assemblies, the nature of government, law, and liberty. He thus acquainted the inhabitants of the most southern and isolated colony with many of the ideas which were current in the more populous regions further north.

[*The Literary Diary of Ezra Stiles* (1901), ed. by F. B. Dexter; *Extracts from the Itineraires and Other Miscellanies of Ezra Stiles* (1916), ed. by F. B. Dexter; A. D. Candler, *The Colonial Records of the State of Ga.*, vols. IX, XI (1907), and *The Revolutionary Records of the State of Ga.*, vol. I (1908); *Journals of the Continental Congress* (W. C. Ford, ed.), vol. III (1905); *The Royal Georgia Gazette*, 1781; C. C. Jones, Jr., *Biog. Sketches of the Delegates from Ga. to the Continental Cong.* (1891); E. C. Burnett, *Letters of Members of the Continental Cong.*, vol. I (1921); W. B. Sprague, *Annals Am. Pulpit*, vol. III (1858); M. L. Daniel, "John Joachim Zubly—Georgia Pamphleteer of the Revolution," *Ga. Hist. Quart.*, Mar. 1935; information from the records of St. Gall, Switzerland.]

M. D.

ZUNSER, ELIAKUM (Oct. 28, 1836–Sept. 22, 1913), Yiddish bard and poet, was born in Wilna (formerly Russia). His father, Feive Zunser, a poor carpenter, died when Eliakum was barely seven years old, leaving the family in direst straits. After a few years of study in the Yeshivah (Talmudical school) under the most miserable conditions, young Zunser was apprenticed to an embroiderer of military uniforms, meanwhile studying modern Hebrew writers and acquiring the elements of a secular education in his spare hours. As a boy of fourteen he was impressed in the military barracks at Bobruisk, along with some eighty other youngsters who had been snatched away from their homes under the recruiting system then prevailing under Nicholas I. In the barracks he composed his first songs, reciting the woes of the unfortunate *Poimaniks* (impressed recruits), and even trained a choir of the boys to sing them. His song, *"Di Yeshuah,"* written upon the occasion of their deliverance five weeks later, won acclaim. His facility in creating popular songs was already beginning to be known, and he now commenced earning a livelihood as *Badchen* (bard) a familiar figure in Jewish ghetto life, whose calling was to amuse the guests at weddings and festivities with impromptu doggerel. In 1862 he married his first wife, by whom he had four children. Nine years later he lost all four children in a cholera epidemic, and shortly thereafter his wife. This tragic misfortune elicited his well-known poem, *"Der Potshtover Glekl"* (The Postilion). Upon settling in the city of Minsk, however, he later found happiness in a second marriage, and his fame as *Badchen* grew steadily. Wherever he appeared he drew large crowds of listeners, until eventually his influence over the masses attracted the suspicion of the Russian police. In 1889 he emigrated with his family to the United States. Shortly after his arrival he made a tour of the country, reciting his poems and meeting everywhere with great success. Later he settled in New York City and opened a small printing establishment on the East Side, but continued to write and compose.

As author and composer of Yiddish folksongs he was the most prominent figure of his day; no other has held the masses so completely under his sway. He dignified the function of the *Badchen,* which had hitherto been the by-name of a coarse, uncultured jester. He himself liked the cognomen of "Eliakum *Badchen*" by which he was known, and would use it as his signature even after he had gained fame as a poet. In fact he lacked the lyric touch of the true poet, his verse being chiefly intellectual, moral, didactic, allegoric, and national in tendency. Yet because of their apposite content and the pleasing melodies to which he set them, his songs spread over the length and breadth of Russia, Poland, Galicia, and Rumania, wherever Yiddish-speaking people lived. Many of his songs became household tunes long before they were ever in print. He became the articulate voice of the Jewish Ghetto, for he touched in his rhymes upon events affecting the welfare of his co-religionists. It was his endeavor to give a true picture of the period in which he lived. He scourges the hypocrite, the usurer, the oppressor, and bewails the plight of suffering Jews in the Diaspora. Joyous as was his nature, he had suffered deeply both the misfortunes of ordinary humankind and the sorrows of Israel. He was one of the first to encourage Jewish colonization in the Holy Land. His stirring song, *"Shivath Zion,"* dedicated to the first pioneer settlers in Palestine after the violent pogroms in Russia following the accession of Alexander III to the throne, had a magical effect upon vast audiences. This and other songs were powerful in spreading the Palestinian ideal. In another famous song, *"Di Soche"* (The Plough), he idealizes the farmer's life in contrast with that of the city dweller. In America Zunser became an ardent admirer of American institutions and the spirit of liberty. His muse gave ample expression to his patriotic feelings for the land of his adoption, often comparing conditions in the United States with those in Czarist Russia. To his popular American songs belong "Columbus and Washington," "The Peddler," "The Immigrant," "Slaves Were We."

After the publication of his *Shirim hadashim* (Wilna, 1861) he composed over six hundred songs, some of which were translated into other languages. For the Jewish stage he wrote a version of the sale of Joseph (*Mekhirath Joseph*). Many of his poems, some with accompanying music, have appeared in selected editions. Of editions published in the United States mention may be made of *Ale Werk* (3 vols., 1920) and *Selected Songs* (1928), arranged for voice with piano accompaniment. He was survived at the time of his death by his wife and seven children.

[*A Jewish Bard; Being the Biog. of Eliakum Zunser* (1905); *Jewish Encyc.* (1925 ed.), vol. XII; Leo Wiener, *The Hist. of Yiddish Lit. in the Nineteenth Century* (1899); J. H. Bondi, *Aus dem jüdischen Russland vor vierzig Jahren* (1927); Hutchins Hapgood, *The Spirit of the Ghetto* (1902), pp. 91–98; M. Pines, *Geshichte fun der Yiddisher Literatur,* vol. I (Warsaw, 1911); S. L. Citron, *Drei literarishe Doros,* vol. I (Wilna, 1920); Zalmen Reisen, *Lexicon fun der Yiddisher Literatur,* vol. III (Wilna, 1929); obituary in *N. Y. Times,* Sept. 23, 1913.]   I. S.